THE GREAT PICTORIAL HISTORY OF

WORLD CRIME

MADERE
VERMOU

VOLUME II

THE GREAT PICTORIAL HISTORY OF

WORLD CRIME

Jay Robert Nash

Published By HISTORY, INC.

Distributed By Scarecrow Press Inc.

Published by History, Inc., Wilmette, IL

Distributed By Scarecrow Press, Inc., 4501 Forbes Blvd., Suite 200, Lanham, MD 20706

Library of Congress Catalog Card Number: 2004100992

THE GREAT PICTORIAL HISTORY OF WORLD CRIME: a narrative, illustrated history of worldwide crimes and criminals from ancient times to the present. Includes bibliographic references and index.

ISBN: 1-928831-20-6 (hardbound; 2 vols. $249.50
ISBN (Volume II): 1-928831-22-2
1. Crime—Criminals—World—History—Bibliography

Design by Cathy Anetsberger-Edens

Manufactured in the United States of America

9 8 7 6 5 4 3 2 1

TABLE OF CONTENTS

CHAPTER NINE:
MURDER/CELEBRITY SLAYINGS

The act of murder, man's most heinous crime, has been practiced throughout history by all manner of celebrities in the highest social stratas. These headline-capturing killers—members of the aristocracy and the wealthy class, bankers, physicians, attorneys, politicians and modern-day media creatures—have riveted the attention of the public, turning their bright fame to dark infamy. Such slayers loomed large in the collective imagination of their times, their lethal acts expanding their images and enhancing their legends through the ploys of publicity, which even the stark reality of homicide could not easily destroy. These uncommon humans all committed the common crime of murder and yet, for many, their fame ironically increased through such reprehensible acts.

In many such murders, the celebrity was the victim, the killer often seeking the fame held by his prey, as if to make it his own, as if to don his victim's mantle of fame by taking that life. Such was the traditional reason for many murders in the Old West, where the novice gunfighter aspired to attain the notoriety of his victim, the established gunslinger, by killing him with a faster draw and thus earn himself a niche, no matter how infamous, in the annals of history. Jack McCall, a cowardly roustabout in Deadwood, had no thought of slapping leather with the "Prince of Pistoleers," James Butler "Wild Bill" Hickok. He simply shot his victim in the back, while the famed gunfighter sat in a saloon playing poker. After shooting "Wild Bill," McCall was no longer a seedy drunk, but the famed killer of a famous gunman.

In more modern days, killers like David Mark Chapman, the slayer of Beatle John Lennon, became so attached to his singing idol that he assumed his victim's personality, this mentally disturbed but ardent fan imitating his victim in almost every physical detail, even marrying a woman of Japanese extraction, as had Lennon. Only days before murdering Lennon, Chapman took his victim's name to add to his adopted personality. Such personality envy had long been translated into a murderous mania. It took the life of 51-year-old political activist Allard Lowenstein on March 14, 1980, when his protégé, Dennis Sweeney, lethally shot the political activist five times in his Rockefeller Plaza offices in New York. Sweeney, later sent to an insane asylum, stated that Lowenstein had "been controlling my life for years. I've put an end to it." A similar identity problem existed in the troubled mind of 22-year-old Paul DeWitt, who, on September 9, 1980, stabbed to death Everett Clarke, his drama coach and the voice of "The Whistler," of radio fame, in Clarke's offices at Chicago's Fine Arts Building.

The motives had sharper definitions in many other celebrity slayings. Even among the rich, money was often a prime motive, as was the case of Dr. Bennett Clarke Hyde, who, in

New York political activist Allard Lowenstein, killed in 1980 by a deranged man, who once followed his radical chic cause.

Dennis Sweeney murdered Allard Lowenstein because "he was controlling my life"; Sweeney was sent to an asylum.

Chicago's Everett Clarke, the radio voice of "The Whistler," who was murdered by one of his own drama students.

1909, embarked upon the wholesale murders of his in-laws, so that his wife and he could inherit a fortune. The same ambition motivated Dr. Arthur Warren Waite, who also attempted to eliminate his in-laws in 1916. The fiery Candace "Candy" Mossler, stood trial with her 24-year-old nephew, Melvin Lane Powers, for the June 30, 1964 murder of her tycoon husband, Jacques Mossler, in their lavish home in Key Biscayne, Florida. Again, prosecutors insisted, the motive was money—Candy wanted to obtain Mossler's $7 million fortune and, to achieve this end, she sent her burly nephew to fatally stab her oil-rich husband thirty-nine times. Such classic murder-for-profit cases was epitomized by the icy entrepreneur Claus von Bulow, who reportedly overdosed his wealthy wife with insulin injections in 1979-1980 to obtain the millions she had left him in her will. Obsessed in obtaining wealth at any cost, rich socialite, Patrizia Reggiani Martinelli—called Italy's "Black Widow"—simply hired a hit man to murder her ex-spouse and fashion tycoon, Maurizio Gucci, in 1995.

In some instances, murder by a celebrity was due to overwhelming debt, as was the case of Charles Chapin, the famed editor of the New York *Evening World*. While drowning in debt from his wild stock speculations, and unable to bear the thought that his beloved wife of thirty years would go through life as a pauper, Chapin shot Nellie Chapin to death on the night of September 16, 1918, while both were in bed in their suite at New York's Hotel Cumberland. Chapin went to prison for life, allowed to cultivate the prison's gardens and gleaning

Actor Paul Kelly, who shot a man to death in a Hollywood triangle; he served a short prison term before returning to the cameras and the crime he committed was almost forgotten by Hollywood producers and the public alike.

One-time child actor Robert Blake (right), with Scott Wilson, appearing in the 1967 film, *In Cold Blood*, a movie that reportedly proved prophetic in that Blake was charged with murdering his wife in 2001 (tried in February 2004).

another type of fame as the "Rose Man of Sing Sing," until his death in 1930.

Money brought about the killing of actor Sal Mineo in 1976, and money stimulated the gruesome, homosexual murders of silent screen star Ramon Novarro in 1968 and media tycoon John S. Knight III in 1975. Burglars in search of money brought about the deaths of scores of distinguished citizens. Typical was the case of Henry C. Heinz, the leading banker in Atlanta, Georgia, who interrupted burglar Horace Blalock as the intruder was rummaging through Mrs. Heinz's sewing bag, thinking it to be a purse, while in the darkened library of the Heinz mansion on the night of September 29, 1943. Heinz, in a wild struggle that overturned furniture and lamps, was shot to death by Blalock, before the burglar fled. He was later identified, convicted and sent to prison, being paroled on May 18, 1955. An almost identical crime occurred when millionaire burglar Bernard C. Welch, Jr., invaded the posh home of Michael J. Halberstam, one of the most distinguished physicians in Washington, D.C., and fatally shot Halberstam during a burglary on the night of December 5, 1980 (see chapter on Burglary).

Some celebrities not only committed murder, but received little or no punishment for their crimes. Sherman Billingsley, the famed owner of New York's Stork Club, reportedly shot and killed a bootlegger in the early 1920s, but was never brought to trial. Paul Kelly, the taciturn tough-sounding actor of the 1920s-1940s, shot and killed a man in a love triangle and did only a brief prison stint before returning to the cameras. The same fate befell football star and movie actor O. J. Simpson, who narrowly escaped conviction in his wife's 1994 murder, although his guilt was so blatantly evident that he was not again invited to go before the cameras.

Oddly, Simpson came to the defense of fellow actor and aging child star Robert Blake, after Blake was charged with the shooting murder of his wife Bonny Lee Bakley, outside an Italian restaurant in Studio City, California, on May 4, 2001 (he awaits trial at this writing). Irrespective of Blake's possible guilt in this homicide, his money, influence and image, as has been the case in too many celebrity killings, may assure his acquittal, typically and unequally tipping the scales of justice in favor of the powerful. Such inequitable results were prosaically summed up by none other than William Barclay "Bat" Masterson (1853-1921), the intrepid peace officer of the frontier, who became a celebrated sports writer for the New York Morning *Telegraph*. He was found dead at his desk in the city room, his head resting on an open-carriage cast-iron Underwood typewriter. Found rolled into the typewriter was a sheet of copy paper on which Masterson had written his last words: "I have found that things break about even in this old world of ours. For instance, ice—the poor get it in the winter and the rich in the summer."

Opposite page at left: A policeman itemizes the debris in the ransacked Philadelphia home of media tycoon John S. Knight III, who was murdered by three homosexual hustlers in 1975.

A CUCKOLDING KILLER/February 15, 1551

Though born into British bluebloods, Alice Arden (1516-1551) conducted her private life like a common street-walker. Arden was the stepdaughter of Sir Edward North whose father had won world renown as the translator of Plutarch. Her husband, Thomas Arden was wealthy and of the gentleman class who gave his wife every comfort, moving her into a large mansion in Faversham, England, in 1544. Alice, however, betrayed his trust at every opportunity to see her lover, Richard Mosby (or Mosbie), a rakish tailor who had once been a servant in the North household and who had maintained a sexual liaison with Alice since seducing her when she was but a teenager. Arden, on the other hand, was a man twice her age, one who was retiring and considerably less passionate than the interloper, Mosby. Tiring of her pretended marriage, Alice, a practical schemer, made plans to kill her husband so that she could spend the rest of her days with the ardent Mosby.

Unlike most wives with murder on their minds, Alice Arden made no secret of her desire to get rid of her husband. She solicited ideas from known enemies of Thomas Arden. There were many. One such was a painter named Clark who proposed that he paint Alice on a large canvas, this portrait to hang in Arden's bedroom. He would temper the oil with poison and when Arden retired he would breath in the poison fumes emanating from the canvas and die in his sleep. The fumes would be gone by morning, Clark promised, and thus the murder weapon would vanish along with the unwanted spouse.

Alice told Clark that such a plan was too risky. A servant might enter the room and breathe the fumes or she herself might die of the deadly oils while sitting for the portrait. No, Clark's plan would not do. She preferred a more direct approach. Alice went to a man named Green who hated Thomas Arden since having been bested by Arden in a land dispute. Alice offered him £10 if he would provide two men, who would kill her husband. Green, in turn, hired two local Faversham ruffians named Shakebag and Black Will to perform the deed.

On February 15, 1551, Mosby invited Thomas Arden to a game of backgammon, making sure that the victim's back was to a large closet. (Shakebag and Black Will had been hiding in Arden's huge mansion for some time with Alice providing them with food and drink until the opportunity to kill her husband presented itself.) As Arden and Mosby began playing, Mosby suddenly shouted, "And now, sir, I may take you if I will!"

"Take me which way?" replied Arden, puzzled at the sudden outburst, not realizing that this was the signal to the assassins to strike. Black Will leaped from the closet and began to strangle Arden with a towel. Mosby grabbed a heavy pressing iron and brought this down upon Arden's head several times. He fell apparently dead to the floor and the killers, aided by a servant named Michael, dragged the body into the counting room. The resilient Arden, however, came to life again and Black Will smashed him on the head, a killing blow.

Alice Arden wanted to make sure. She rushed into the room with a long knife and plunged this several times into her husband's chest. The body was then taken to a nearby field and left there. Alice then sent out word by some servants to the local townspeople that her husband had not returned to dinner and that she was worried that he might have been attacked by highwaymen, who were then plagu-

A contemporary print shows the murder of Thomas Arden in 1551 by his wife Alice, her lover and several servants.

ing the area. Villagers carrying torches conducted a search of the fields and Arden's body was discovered hacked to pieces.

Alice was confident that the local authorities would conclude that Arden had been the victim of highwaymen. She neglected to see, however, that her plan was impossible from the beginning due to its inept execution. Bloody carpet hairs covered the shoes of the victim and a trail of blood led from the mansion to the garden. It was obvious to the local mayor that Arden had not been killed on a lonely road, but inside his own house and his body then dragged outside. A search of the grounds around the mansion unearthed the bloody towel and knife used to murder Arden. The Mayor bluntly told Alice that he suspected her of having a hand in her husband's demise. Alice became indignant, replying archly, "I would you should know that I am no such woman!"

The Mayor showed her the bloody towel and the gore-coated knife. Alice Arden trembled for a moment in silence, then confessed to the murder, dramatically taking the bloody towel and pressing it to her face, moaning, "Oh, the blood of God, help for this blood that I shed!" Mosby was found in his room, pretending to be asleep. He was awakened and accused of the killing. Boldly he denied committing the crime which was equally stupid in that his hose and purse were still covered with his victim's blood. Green, the man who had supplied the killers, fled with Black Will and Shakebag. Black Will was captured near Flushing and hanged. Shakebag, who had only stood by as a lookout during the murder, was hunted down near Southwark and run through by swords in the hands of his pursuers.

The killing of any high born person in England at that time unleashed savage retribution on the part of the authorities, who ordered wholesale arrests and executions, a sweeping revenge that encompassed the innocent as well as the guilty. One of Alice Arden's maidservants, who knew nothing of the murder, was burned at the stake. George Bradshaw, who had carried messages between Alice and Mosby, unaware of their contents, was seized and instantly hanged. Adam Fowl, who ran a local inn, the Fleur de Lys, was strapped to the underside of a horse and taken to London where he was thrown into the darkest dungeon of Marshalsea Prison. His crime had been serving two tankards of ale to Alice and Mosby when they stopped at his inn during one of their clandestine meetings.

The servant Michael was hanged in chains at Faversham, while Mosby and his sister Susan, who had helped in the murder plot, were taken to Smithfield, where they were hanged at the same time. Alice Arden found no quick relief at the end of a rope. She was made into a public spectacle and served as a warning to any other rebellious wives, who thought to murder their husbands. She was taken to Canterbury and, after thousands of spectators had been assembled, rode to the stake in an open cart on March 14, 1551. She was tied to a stake and then slowly burned to death while the great throng dinned catcalls and insults into her ears throughout her prolonged and torturous death.

THE MURDER OF SIR THOMAS OVERBURY/ September 15, 1613

Lady Frances Howard (1593-1632) was at the center of one of England's most famous Royalist intrigues of the Seventeenth Century. Jealousy, passion, and greed were at the heart of the matter, and, in the end, one of the court's most learned men paid with his life.

Frances Howard, at the time she joined the royal court of James I.

Frances Howard was only fifteen when she was introduced to Robert Carr, the homosexual lover of King James I. By currying the favor of the king, Carr had become the second-most powerful figure in the land. His sexual favors were rewarded with a peerage. James, a bloated and petulant monarch, had made his dandy the Viscount Rochester.

Carr had made the acquaintance of Sir Thomas Overbury, a knight of high intellectual capacities, but one who showed slavish devotion to those considered favorites of the King. It was Overbury who introduced Carr to Frances Howard, the daughter of the Earl of Suffolk. The 15-year-old charmer turned the head of Viscount Carr. He temporarily forgot about his royal obligations in his obsessive pursuit of the teenager. Carr, who was unable to read or write, engaged Overbury to write his love letters. At first Overbury was a willing participant to the intrigue and eager to please Carr. When Frances Howard's husband, the 14-year-old Earl of Essex, returned from his travels, Overbury condemned the relationship as immoral.

Angered with Overbury and fearing that he might make her reckless sexual liaisons public, Howard enlisted Anne Turner, a reputed witch and alchemist, to help her prepare a poison to be administered to the truculent Overbury. Meanwhile, Carr inveigled the King to imprison Overbury in the Tower of London on a petty charge. The guards who stood

Frances Howard, at the time she became Countess of Somerset.

watch over Sir Thomas were replaced with men sympathetic to the scheming Carr and his mistress.

Anne Turner then went about her lethal chores, securing poison from a physician named James Franklin. Tarts and various candied jellies were laced with rose algar, sublimate of mercury, arsenic, and diamond powder, before being fed to Overbury by Sir Gervase Helwys and his assistant Richard Weston. There was enough poison in the delicacies to kill twenty people. Not surprisingly, Overbury died on September 15, 1613. Three days later, Frances' marriage to the Earl of Essex was annulled and King James bestowed on Carr the title of Earl of Somerset. Carr married Frances in a great ceremony, and soon they became the favorites of the court, commanding enormous power and prestige.

Their crime might have been covered up if not for the deathbed confession of Paul de Lobel, an apothecary's assistant who had participated in the poisoning plot. De Lobel named the conspirators, and on October 23, 1615, Richard Weston was hanged at Tyburn. He was followed in death on November 9, 1615 by Mrs. Turner. Sir Gervase Helwys and James Franklin marched to the gallows on Nov. 20, 1615 and Dec. 9, 1615. A great public outcry led to the arrest and conviction of Carr and his wife on May 24, 1616. Lady Somerset was prosecuted by Sir Francis Bacon, who treated her, at the king's behest, with only the greatest respect.

Both were convicted and ordered to hang, but through King James' intervention Carr and his wife were spared the death penalty. The king no doubt feared that he might also be named as a co-conspirator by the vengeful Carr, so he was anxious to placate the culprits. Though they escaped the gallows, it can be said that Carr and Lady Somerset endured a fate perhaps worse than death. They retired to their country estate, where they soon grew tired of each other. The rancor Lady Somerset felt for her husband was such that she did not speak to him for five years. She died in 1632 from a painful uterine disorder.

"I HAVE SPARED HIS LIFE"/January 18, 1760

Lawrence Shirley Ferrers (Fourth Earl Ferrers, 1720-1760), a descendent of England's royal Plantagenet family, possessed great wealth and he enjoyed a high social standing. He was also a short-tempered, volatile man, who, through arrogance and pride, put himself above the law. In 1752, Ferrers married the daughter of Sir William Meridith, a union that quickly soured. His cruel treatment caused his wife to petition Parliament for a legal separation, which was granted in 1758, along with an official order that Ferrers pay his aggrieved ex-spouse considerable and protracted payments.

This governmental degree only served to bring Ferrers' lethal personality to the surface. Anyone who offended him, or he thought offended him, became the target of his murderous wrath. On one occasion, armed with a gun, Ferrers threatened his servant and ordered him to kill his own brother. The servant, however, fled and told Ferrers' brother what had happened. The brother and his wife left the estate immediately. Not so lucky was a man named John Johnson, who was named by the courts to act as the receiver of the rents on behalf of Ferrers' estranged wife. Johnson had first refused to accept the task, but Ferrers himself persuaded him to do so.

The relationship between the two men grew strained. Ferrers suspected Johnson and the trustees of his estate of

The titled Lawrence Ferrers is shown fatally shooting his steward, John Johnson, in 1760.

The public hanging of Lawrence Ferrers drew a large crowd of spectators to Tyburn.

cheating him out of a contract for some coal mines. The charge was unfounded, but Ferrers nevertheless resolved to kill Johnson. At the time, Ferrers was living in the village of Stanton-Harold in Leicestershire, and Johnson was his tenant. On January 18, 1760, Johnson arrived at Ferrers' door as ordered. Ferrers produced a written "confession" of Johnson's imagined villainy and ordered him to sign it. When Johnson refused, Ferrers ordered him to drop to his knees. He shot Johnson in the chest, then summoned a surgeon to attend to his victim's wounds.

By the time the surgeon arrived, Ferrers had consumed a large quantity of port wine. He told the doctor, "Now I have spared his life, I desire you would do what you can for him." The physician could do nothing for Johnson, who died the next morning. The physician reported the blatant killing to authorities, who ordered Ferrers arrested. Ferrers, however, locked himself in his house and refused to surrender to officials. Meanwhile, a mob gathered outside his home. A collier named Curtis finally helped take Ferrers into custody and accompanied him to the local jail. A charge of willful murder was returned and Ferrers was bound over for trial, arriving in London on February 14, 1760.

Ferrers' body, on public display at Surgeons' Hall, before it was dissected.

After two months' confinement in the Tower of London, Ferrers was brought before the House of Lords on April 16, 1760. There was no question about his guilt, so the issue of his sanity occupied much of the deliberations. Ferrers defended himself, claiming that he had not been in his right mind when he fatally shot Johnson, but his defense arguments failed to persuade his peers. A verdict of guilty was returned, and on May 5, 1760, Ferrers was taken to Tyburn to be executed. After the hanging, the body was removed to Surgeon's Hall for dissection and public display, according to the sentence of the court.

WAS MOZART MURDERED?/December 5, 1791

Almost from the moment of Wolfgang Amadeus Mozart's untimely demise on December 5, 1791, his death in rumor, gossip, song, poetry, and literature has been attributed to his arch rival, Italian composer Antonio Salieri (1750-1825). Mozart (Johannes Chyrsostomus Wolfgangus Theophilus Mozart, 1756-1791) was a boy prodigy who startled the world with his virtuoso playing of the harpsichord, violin, and organ from age four, composing small musical pieces before his fifth birthday. His father, court composer and violinist Johann Georg Leopold Mozart, took his son and daughter, Maria, from their native Salzburg on several tours which saw the children enthrall the crown heads of Europe. When at home, little "Wolferl" mesmerized Austrian emperor Francis I, who would sit at the boy's side while he played, calling him "my little magician."

Mozart as a child, 1763; painting by Pietro Antonio Lorenzoni.

A precocious and outgoing child (he would never lose his mirthful childishness as an adult), Mozart captivated queens and future queens of Europe with his charming personality. As a child, he once slipped on the marbled floor of the Austrian palace housing archduchess Marie Antoinette, later to become the hapless queen of France. She picked up the little boy who abruptly kissed her cheek and said: "You are very kind. When I grow up I will marry you."

At age nine, Mozart astonished the king of England by playing every piece of music put before him, compositions he had never seen until that moment. Later that year, he composed his first symphony (he had already published several sonatas at age seven). In 1769, Mozart was given the honorary title of concertmaster to the Archbishop of Salzburg, a demanding prelate who paid the gifted child very little money.

In 1767, at the age of eleven, Mozart responded to the suggestion of Austrian emperor Joseph II by composing an opera *buffa La Finta Semplice*, which was then acknowledged to be an "incomparable work," yet it was at this early age that Mozart felt for the first time the seething envy of his musical elders whose deep resentment of his outstanding genius caused his work to be suppressed. When the Archbishop of Salzburg heard of the rejected work, he ordered that it be performed at his palace and was so overwhelmed by the compositions that he made Mozart his maestro di capella, a position that was unfortunately honorary and paid next to nothing.

Seeking funds, Mozart, accompanied by his father, went to Milan, Italy, in 1770, where the boy genius composed his second operatic masterpiece, *Mitridate, r di Ponto*, which was produced at Teatro Reggio Ducal and won for Mozart instant acknowledgment as one of the great composers of that day or any other. This work was performed on December 26, 1770, and the greatest musical professors of the day earlier scoffed at the idea of a 14-year-old boy orchestrating a full opera for the largest orchestra then in the world at Teatro Reggio Ducal. Further, this boy led that orchestra by playing the harpsichord throughout its twenty performances. Again, jealous and viciously envious competitors denounced the boy, but even their shrieks were drowned out in the overwhelming praise he received. Reportedly, one of those who witnessed the explosive success of Mozart was a 20-year-old impoverished, but musically gifted youth, Antonio Salieri, and, from that moment on, he hated this genius with an insidious and lifelong passion that, some would later claim, evidenced itself in Mozart's murder.

Mozart went on creating at a furious pace, producing masterpiece operas including *Idomeneo, r e di Creta* (1781), *Die Entfhurung aus dem Serail* (1782), Le nozze di Figaro (1786; English title: *The Marriage of Figaro*), Don Giovanni (1787), *Cosi fan tutte* (1790), and *Die Zauberflote* (1791; English title: (*The Magic Flute*). He married a beautiful, but capricious soprano, Constanze Weber (1763-1842), who was as financially irresponsible as her inspired husband. Though Mozart received many commissions, he was denied a high musical office in his native Austria. Oddly, this was due to the mortal enemy his music had made, Salieri, who had traveled to Austria with F.L. Gassmann, and who convinced Emperor Joseph to sponsor him. Salieri's own operas, *Le Donne Letterate* (1770) and *Armida* (1771), were great successes in Vienna, at the same time that Mozart was taking Italy's musical world by storm.

Child prodigy Mozart playing at the piano, November 1763, accompanied by his father, Leopold Mozart, and his sister Nanneri; watercolor by Louis Carrogis de Carmontelle.

When Mozart returned to Vienna, he supported himself by teaching and taking occasional commissions, but he was denied any significant court-appointed positions, thanks to Salieri's venomous intrigues. Although highly respected for his own fine work, Salieri saw in Mozart a posthumous threat to that work, one that would overshadow and eclipse almost all the composers of that great musical day so that posterity would remember Mozart and ignore Salieri. This was undoubtedly Salieri's gnawing fear, one that reportedly led to murderous loathing.

There was much in Mozart's background to point to Salieri's bone-marrow resentment of his rival. The Austrian genius had been raised in comfort, encouraged from the cradle to perform and excel, pampered and cuddled in his infant creativity by the kings and queens of Europe. Mozart had been given every opportunity and had taken rich advantage of the stage opened to him. His father had long been recognized as a respected composer. From childhood, the world and the future belonged to Wolfgang Amadeus Mozart. To Salieri the world had offered little hope of success or recognition. Born in Legnano, Italy, Salieri's merchant father died bankrupt and the youth had to beg the support of the rich Mocenigo family, who grudgingly secured for the boy a berth in the choir school of St. Mark's in Venice. Here he diligently studied music and inched his way toward musical composition. He did not possess the

Mozart (lower left-hand corner at piano) is shown as a child playing for guests at a tea in the residence of Prince Louis-Francois de Conti, in 1766; painting by Michel Barthelemy Olivier.

lightning burst of imagination and dynamic composition of Mozart. He was a meticulous creator of impressive church music. Where the unpredictable Mozart arrested, disturbed, and inspired the spirit, Salieri soothed it.

Salieri worked with and showed respect for Haydn, Beethoven, Gluck, and all the other composers of that illustrious musical era. To only one did he display a fist of malice, a mask of hate—Mozart. This cancerous loathing for Mozart is quite clear to anyone comparing the works of both composers; they both sought to dominate Italian opera. Mozart succeeded and was Salieri's only rival, one he could never dominate. It was easy for Salieri to be on affable terms with all other composers; none but Mozart competed with him for the high honors that Italian opera could bestow. The honors and the kudos went to Mozart. He was the light, Salieri only an interesting reflection.

It was written by the Russian poet Alexander Pushkin that Salieri attended the premiere of Don Giovanni, but so consumed by envy was he that he could not restrain himself from hissing during the performance, causing the startled audience to look in shock to his box. Realizing that he had dropped his guard, Salieri rose and left the opera, his secret hatred for one greater than himself momentarily, blatantly exposed. Pushkin's chilling portrait of Salieri's grotesque envy ends with the poet's conclusion: "The envious man who was capable of hissing at Don Giovanni was capable of poisoning its creator."

Was Pushkin accusing Salieri of murder? When the poet wrote his drama masterpiece *Mozart and Salieri* in 1826 (adapted as an opera by Nikolai Rimsky-Korsakov in 1898), Salieri had been dead less than a year and it was much rumored then, as it had been immediately after Mozart's death in 1791, that, indeed, Salieri had poisoned the Austrian genius to finally rid himself of his tormentor. Pushkin's intent, however, was not to accuse Salieri of actual physical murder, but a murder of spirit, a murder of the soul, since it was Salieri who intrigued against Mozart in his last years, plotting to keep the composer penniless, whispering calumnies about the composer into the ears of patrons and aristocrats, who subsequently declined to sponsor Mozart, and forming a critical cabal that negated and rejected all the work Mozart produced.

The composer's production in his last years was stupendous. (Mozart would die leaving more than 600 musical compositions completed.) To support himself he wrote operettas, arias, duets, tercets, and quartets with orchestral accompaniment. He traveled about Europe writing almost to order as each commission appeared. This furious work exhausted the composer and he soon fell ill, but his impoverished condition demanded that he take on one more work, a commission offered

Mozart at Verona, 1770; oil painting by Saverio della Rosa.

from a mysterious stranger demanding that Mozart hurriedly complete a *Requiem*. Mozart accepted the commission (some time in July 1791) but he expressed his superstitious fears that this stranger, who would not identify his master, represented not an admiring aristocrat, but death itself, and was a harbinger of his own demise. Mixed with this foreboding was Mozart's illness, diagnosed by some as a form of typhus or "high military fever," a euphemism of the day for a fever accompanied by a rash. Yet this was no more than a misleading rumor. Actually, no real diagnosis was ever made by Mozart's attending physicians.

Mozart had just returned from Prague when he began to feel ill. His feet and hands began to swell and he vomited his food. He grew weaker and weaker, but continued to work on the Requiem for the mysterious stranger who made two more furtive visits to the composer with payments. This stranger has been assumed to be, by some, a cloak-wrapped, hat-shrouding figure who was none other than Salieri in disguise, his sinister aim being to drive Mozart to his death, knowing he was ill, but also knowing that the composer would complete his musical task though it meant his death, such was his dedication to his art.

It was later learned that the messenger was a representative of Count Franz von Walsegg, who later stated that he had commissioned the Requiem to honor his late wife and that he

Mozart with his sister and father (and portrait of his mother), winter, 1780-1781; painting by Johann Nepomuk della Croce.

had operated so secretly because he intended to pass off Mozart's work as his own. This story in itself is strange in that von Walsegg brands himself a thief after Mozart's death when there is no motivation for such a self-destructive admission. But it is not so strange to consider the commission coming from von Walsegg, friend of Antonio Salieri, if the Salieri murder conspiracy theory is to be accepted.

Salieri was much on Mozart's fever-wracked brain toward the end of his days. He spoke of this powerful enemy, illustrating how Salieri had purposely failed to intervene with the emperor on his behalf and plotting against his receiving commissions and recognition for his work, intriguing with Austrian aristocrats to keep Mozart from being named to any significant musical post that would afford him a reasonable income and some relief against the exhausting, killing routine of his work. Mozart complained that he had "the taste of death" on his tongue and that he sincerely believed he was slowly being murdered. "I shall not last much longer," he told his wife. "I am sure that I have been poisoned. I cannot rid myself of this thought." Constanze related this to Mozart's first biographer, Franz Niemetschek, and repeatedly quoted his remarks to her second husband, Georg Nikolaus von Nissen, who also wrote a biography of the composer. It was this statement, coupled with remarks that implied that Salieri was behind the poisoning, that identified, without direct accusation, charge or trial, Antonio Salieri as the killer of Wolfgang Amadeus Mozart.

Mozart about a year before his mysterious death, 1789-1790; painting by Joseph Lange.

The room at the Villa Bertramka, in Prague, where Mozart composed most of one of his masterworks, *Don Giovanni*.

Just how the poisoning was accomplished, if in fact such poison was administered to Mozart, has never been satisfactorily explained, yet the symptoms of Mozart's illness, the swelling of the limbs, the "taste of death" in his mouth, the vomiting, all of this could easily be attributable to arsenic, then the most popular method of murder. The Borgias had used arsenic with great effect during the Renaissance. The French had used arsenic with such regularity to rid themselves of unwanted relatives that it became known as poudre de succession ("inheritance powder"). A clever crone living in Naples, Italy, known as La Toffana or Toffania (1653-1723), sold arsenic wholesale to women wanting to get rid of truculent husbands, disguising the lethal grams by mixing them with the herb Cymbalaria, which gave the powder properties which prevented identification of the usual symptoms of arsenic poisoning, or so it was claimed.

In Mozart's day, such murder methods were still very much in vogue, guns and knives too uncivilized to be employed by any intellectual murderer. Poison was the method of the secret killer. Since arsenic had a distinct taste, it was best administered with strong wine. Some later claimed that Salieri, always mindful that he had enough enemies to fear, protected himself against just such a demise by never drinking anything but water so that his taste buds could detect the presence of arsenic at a sip.

A great deal of this kind of speculation regarding Mozart's death was encouraged by the odd fact that no death certificate was made out which specified the composer's illness. He was casually attended by Dr. Nicholas Closset who thought so little of his distinguished patient that even when he was contacted at the theater and told that Mozart was dying, Closset refused to leave until the drama ended. When he did arrive at Mozart's home, he applied cold compresses to the composer's fever-wracked head, which apparently sent Mozart into shock and caused his death two hours later. He was in a coma for the last few hours of his life and did not speak, according to one account. Yet his wife insisted later that he talked intelligently about the completion of his Requiem with others right up to his last moments, telling several composers gathered at his bedside how he wanted the kettle drums to be used in the Requiem, making the sound of these kettle drums, this being his last utterance.

Following Mozart's painful death on the morning of December 5, 1791, a great deal of speculation ensued. Some claimed the composer died of typhus, tuberculosis, grippe, meningitis, heart failure, dropsy, or rheumatic fever. The arsenic theory blossomed, as did a similar theory about mercury poisoning, but nothing could be proved. The body was never examined, no autopsy was ever performed. And, because of the manner in which Mozart found his lowly grave, no autopsy could ever be made, let alone exhumation made, since the body of this greatest of operatic composers could not be found. He was buried the following afternoon with only five friends to see him interred. One of these faithful mourners was none other than Antonio Salieri.

Mozart's wife, Constanze, having been overcome with grief, was not present to oversee what became a shameless display of disaffection and disregard for the dead genius. Salieri and four others followed the body to a pauper's grave. It was sewn into a sack and thrown into a hole, covered with earth, no gravestone nor marker to signify the resting place of the great composer. This brutal treatment was later explained as merely the practice of a new austere burial system ordered by the practical Emperor Joseph who hated burial pomp and had outlawed for a short time the use of coffins. Moreover, it was later reported that a violent rainstorm drove off the five mourners so that they never even accompanied the body to its final resting place and that two itinerant grave-diggers, unaware of the prestigious corpse they were burying, flung the body into its pit and neglected to erect a marker so that the identification of this lonely grave and its occupier was forever lost to history.

Examining records for the weather of that day, it appears that there was no storm and that the mourners had no reason to abandon Mozart to his oblivion. There was also no earthly reason for Salieri's presence, although his defenders later claimed that because he accompanied his rival to the grave was proof enough that he had nothing to do with Mozart's death and, in fact, made a purposeful display of grief as a sign of regret at having mistreated the genius when he was alive. Yet it could be as easily said that Salieri, if guilty of poisoning his hated superior in art, followed the body to its last resting place to make sure that there would be no marker, no gravestone to which generations of admirers could later come. He, Salieri, would deprive Mozart of this signal honor as he had deprived him of the court honors and positions in life; Salieri's vengeance thus reached beyond death and into posterity.

The presence of Salieri at Mozart's nameless grave, if he indeed had been the instrument of the composer's death, would have been in keeping with a long-standing tradition in which the killer visits the grave of his victim. Dozens of subtle murderers have attended the funerals of their victims, either to allay suspicion their absence would otherwise create or even to gloat over their lethal achievement. In Salieri's instance this would no doubt have been felt a triumph over his artistic foe, one he had never enjoyed in life. If he did attend this miserable funeral out of belated regret or in merely observing the proper decorum, it would stand to reason that Salieri would also never have permitted the disgraceful act of burying Mozart in an unmarked grave. His defenders have never addressed that question. Moreover, if Salieri had had Mozart poisoned with arsenic, he would have known that the body would best be buried in a plot never to be located, that the corpse, if later exhumed and carefully examined, even in that early day, would certainly have revealed the presence of arsenic.

A sensational case, that of Mary Blandy in 1752, almost four decades before Mozart's strange death, involved an exhumed body that had clearly shown evidence of arsenic. Miss Blandy's sensational trial in England featured a crude, but dramatic display by a physician, Dr. Addington, wherein he was able to prove that Miss Blandy's father had been poisoned with arsenic. This poison was long in evidence after death, as anyone employing it in Mozart's day would have known. No, it would have served Antonio Salieri's end to make sure that Mozart's grave was never found and that his body was never exhumed and examined. Salieri, it was also later claimed, after dominating the court and church music of Austria for fifty years, attempted to commit suicide and, failing, lingered long enough to confess his murder of Mozart. No proof exists that such a confession was ever made. Salieri did portray the image of the understanding artist following Mozart's death, befriending the dead composer's wife and securing a music position for his arch rival's son, Wolfgang Xavier. But then such a show of consideration would further remove suspicion from him, it could also be claimed. Years later Constanze wrote a letter to a friend in Germany in which she stated that her son "would not, like his father, have to fear envious men who had designs on his life."

Composer Antonio Salieri, Mozart's bitter rival, whose jealousy many claimed caused him to murder the great composer, a claim dismissed by other historians.

According to another theory, subscribed to by many who have long chronicled the strange rites and customs of secret societies, Mozart was murdered by Salieri and others for violating the secret rites of the Masons. The Masons had had a long and strange history of taking revenge on one of their own, especially any sworn member, who ever dared to reveal the secret rituals of this ancient brotherhood. Not only was Mozart a Mason, as many were later to ruefully point out, but he had blatantly violated the masonic rituals by exposing these cabalistic rites in one of his last works, *The Magic Flute*. Mozart, like most of his musical contemporaries, including Salieri, was a high-ranking Mason and it was thought that he had betrayed the brotherhood when composing The Magic Flute, which, on the surface, appeared to be pro-Mason but was, in reality, a subtle mockery of its sacred customs and misapplication of The Queen of the Night, the Men of Armor, and other Masonic figures proscribed from public display. There was even one claim that this opera was Mozart's subtle signal to the world that he intended to establish his own version of a Masonic order, a lodge which he intended to call "The Grotto."

Salieri, therefore, according to this theory, easily coupled his personal hatred for Mozart with his Masonic obligation to rid the brotherhood of a mocking violator of all the society held dear and sacred. In the light of Masonic victims of the past and that day and days to come, if one subscribes to this conspiratorial theory, Mozart was not an exceptional victim of the brotherhood's wrath, but a typical choice for elimination. The sect of Masons to which he belonged stemmed from the Knights of Malta, established during the Crusades, a militant, bloody organization that especially selected governmental and social leaders to assassinate. These killings did not constitute random bloodletting, but were carefully selected as a way of controlling the destiny of western civilization. Since most of the original founders of this Masonic sect were noblemen, they sought to protect the aristocracy at all costs, and any king who either diminished their power through liberal concessions to the masses or oppressed them in any way to increase the power of the monarchy became likely candidates for assassination.

Initiates into the brotherhood, upon reaching certain degrees of status, were shown by senior Masons the ritual of murder enacted upon any who betrayed the brotherhood. In Mozart's day, this rite was not figurative, but utterly literal and remained so for some time to come. Among the listed royal victims murdered by the most virulent Masonic sect, those thought to be powerful enemies of Freemasonry, were Leopold II of Austria and Gustavus III, king of Sweden, both dying a year after Mozart, the Swedish sovereign dying of a gunshot wound received at a masked ball in a bizarre plot. It was claimed with some logic that the horrendous 1888 slashing deaths by the anonymous Jack the Ripper in London involved the Masons, and the Masonic presence in the assassination of Abraham Lincoln was real. Those in the performing arts who had demonstrated their hostility towards the Masons, it was said, were murdered by the sect to prevent these influential artists from molding public opinion against the brotherhood. Gotthold Lessing, the renowned German drama critic, and the poet Schiller were claimed to be in this number, as was Mozart, undoubtedly the most influential composer of his era.

Such killings enacted against fellow masons who showed themselves turncoats to the society were reportedly long in evidence after Mozart's death. In the U.S., a Mason named William Morgan, to earn much-needed funds, wrote a pamphlet revealing the secret rituals of his Masonic lodge. Morgan, a Royal Arch Mason, before printing the booklet, sent off a copy of his manuscript to have it copyrighted and it was detected by

England's Mary Blandy (1719-1752), who poisoned her father to death with arsenic, the same method some claim that was employed in the murder of Mozart; Blandy, with a leg iron on her left foot, was hanged at Oxford.

another Mason who, according to the story, promptly took action. Morgan was abducted and taken to Fort Niagara, New York, sometime in 1826 where he was bound and gagged and thrown into the Niagara River to meet a watery death.

This river murder was much in keeping with Mozart's shabby and anonymous burial. It was part of the Masonic blood ritual to make sure a condemned member went to rest in "no decent burial ground." This, of course, would explain why Salieri and his fellow Masons, irrespective of their contempt for their fallen brother, accompanied Mozart to his obscure plot of earth, to make sure that the corpse would be interred in a place of unhallowed ground, unmarked, lost forever, finding "no decent burial ground." This conspiracy is a tale unproven, but one that is strung together with the threads of enough historical consistency to warrant attention, if not concern. Mozart's tragic, premature end and the shameful way in which his remains were treated, his own deathbed words of being poisoned, the near-sinister posture of Antonio Salieri, all of this points to no clear indication of murder, but the question of murder is undeniably present, chillingly real. It will be asked again and again, from this century to the next. The evasive answer, sadly, resides within a lost grave under obscure earth.

"TO KILL WITHOUT REMORSE"/ December 14, 1834

Pierre Francois Gaillard Lacenaire (AKA: Mohossier, 1800-1836) was destined to remain a minor literary figure in France's illustrious history of belles lettres. His ruthless dedication to add murder to his criminal pursuits, however, brought him to national attention. Lacenaire had a dark, brooding philosophy that was early on expressed in pamphlet form, these meager writings later transforming this petty swindler and murderer into a kind of anti-hero. "To kill without remorse is the highest of pleasures," Lacenaire wrote in one of his essays. "It is impossible to destroy in me my hatred of mankind. This hatred is the product of a lifetime, the outcome of my every thought. I never pitied any one who suffered, and I don't want to be pitied myself." The famed author Victor Hugo was one who did take pity. So, too, did the Russian novelist Fyodor Dostoyevsky, whose inspiration to write *Crime and Punishment*, stemmed partly from his deep familiarity with the Lacenaire case.

This literary oddity was born in Francheville, France, the son of a wealthy merchant in the iron trade. According to Lacenaire's memoirs, he was a neglected child who took a

France's Pierre Lacenaire, an embittered writer, who was also a thief, forger and cold-blooded killer, was beheaded by the guillotine in 1836.

back seat to his pampered older brother, a situation that profoundly influenced his thinking. He was a docile but petulant student at the Alix Seminary, where an instructor would later recall that he was "remarkable for his love of work." Upon completion of his studies, Lacenaire—a name he added to the family name of Gaillard—went to Paris to study law, but economic misfortunes made it no longer possible for him to pay for his continuing education. Lacenaire worked at a number of unproductive jobs as a merchant and bank solicitor until, with no other recourse, he decided to join the army. He fought on the side of the rebels in Morea, on the Greek Peloponnesus, then returned to France in 1829 to face yet another family setback. He discovered that his father was bankrupt and his own financial resources were depleted.

Russian novelist Fyodor Dostoyevsky, who used Lacenaire as a role model for his book, *Crime and Punishment*.

During this period, Lacenaire fought a duel with the nephew of the celebrated novelist, orator, and statesman Benjamin Constant. He emerged the victor, but he came away from the experience with an entirely different view of life and death. For the first time he realized that it was possible to kill without feeling any personal remorse.

In 1829 Lacenaire received his first prison sentence on a charge of swindling. Following his release from jail in 1830, he embarked upon his short-lived literary career. In the next three years, he wrote numerous lyric poems, songs, and essays, none of which earned him a living wage. Not satisfied with the artist's life, he once again resorted to fraud, which got him a thirteen-month sentence in the jail at Poissy in 1833. While he was incarcerated awaiting trial, Lacenaire met a man named Vigouroux, the editor of *Bon Sens*, a radical political journal that attacked the structure of government and the French monarchy. Vigouroux found a willing advocate in Lacenaire, an early-day existentialist bored with the normal values of that day. He agreed to write an essay, *On the Prisons and the Penitentiary System in France*, for the news supplement.

Lacenaire's riveting article described the horrors of the French penal system. "In this atmosphere of licentiousness, of cynicism in act and speech, of hideous and revolting stories of crime, for the first time the wretched youth finds himself blushing at the last remnant of innocence and decency, which he had still preserved when he entered the prison; he begins to feel ashamed that he is less of a scoundrel than those about him, he dreads their mockery and their contempt; for, make no mistake, there are such things as respect and contempt even in the galleys, a fact that explains why certain convicts are better off in jail than in a society, which has nothing for them but contempt ..."

Author Victor Hugo visited the condemned Lacenaire in his cell to listen to the killer recite his scathing verses.

Despite his new fame as an essayist, Lacenaire was resigned to being a professional cheat and thief. Following his release from prison in 1834, Lacenaire took on a partner, Pierre Victor Avril, a former carpenter, who had also turned to crime. "I was the intelligence, Avril the arm," Lacenaire would say. They contrived a plot to decoy a bank messenger to their lodging on the pretense of cashing a forged bill and killing him, as bank messengers in those days carried large amounts of cash to complete their transactions.

Lacenaire selected a man familiar to him. The bank messenger Chardon had served time in the same jail as Lacenaire five years earlier, where the two men developed a mutual dislike for each other. Lacenaire explained later, "I have overcome all my passions, save one, revenge." On the morning of December 14, 1834, the two thieves called on Chardon at his residence on the Rue Martin. Chardon invited them to an outer room, where the two men attacked him. As Chardon struggled to free himself from Avril's vise-like grip, Lacenaire stabbed him with a dagger, then Avril used a hatchet to kill him. Hearing Chardon's infirm mother stirring in a bedroom, Lacenaire entered the room and struck her with a file, then removed the bed mattress and used it to suffocate her. Avril then looted the place, taking several dish covers, a soup ladle, and a black silk cap. The value of the items the thieves took barely exceeded 500 francs, far less than what they had intended when they planned the robbery. Still, Lacenaire and Avril appeared satisfied. They celebrated "the perfect crime" over cognac at the Reaped Ear pub, and then went to the theater.

The commissary of police found the bodies two days later. Two weeks after the murders, Lacenaire, posing as "Monsieur Mahossier," appeared before a teller at a bank on the Rue Montorgueil. He said he wanted to negotiate a bill drawn by one of his debtors and that he wanted the matter settled by December 31, 1834. When Lacenaire left, the teller instructed a messenger to take 3,000 francs to the address Lacenaire had given him after the messenger completed his appointed rounds. The 18-year-old messenger, whose name was Genevay, complied. He appeared at Lacenaire's residence late in the day on December 31. Upon being admitted, the messenger placed the money on the table and was about to leave when he was struck from behind by a Lacenaire henchman named Francois

A page from Lacenaire's memoirs which depicts the author as being controlled by the Devil.

(also known as "Red Whiskers"), an ex-soldier Lacenaire had hired for the job. Genevay, his shoulder ripped open by the same bloody file used on Chardon, cried out in pain. His screams could be heard on the street, and Francois, an amateur criminal, fled in panic.

Genevay survived to report the matter to the police. Inspector Canler of the Surete believed the attack was nothing more than a simple case of robbery and assault. He diligently traced the gang's movements to the Faubourg du Temple, an inn in the country where Francois was hiding out. A check of the registry showed the name of "Mahossier." The landlady recalled this person also went by the name of "Monsieur Bton." Francois was brought before Genevay, who had accompanied investigating officers and he promptly identified Francois as the assailant. Then a hunt for Bton or Mahossier ensued.

Inspector Canler interviewed 500 suspects before locating Bton in a Paris jail. The inspector loosened Bton's tongue by plying him with wine and promising him his freedom if he cooperated. Bton told Canler that an associate named Gaillard, which literally means the "gay one," was the man police sought, admitting that he had introduced Francois to Gaillard (Lacenaire). But Canler had little success finding the "gay one." Lacenaire was by then covering his tracks. He had betrayed his partner, Avril, who had been imprisoned, along with Francois, in the Poissy jail, after authorities received a tip from Lacenaire that Avril had committed a forgery.

Reflecting on their partner's betrayal, the prisoners decided to inform on Lacenaire, identifying him to Chief Inspector Pierre Allard of the Surete. When police officers arrived at his residence, Lacenaire merely shrugged at their accusations and confessed to the Chardon murders, the Genevay assault, and a dozen lesser crimes. "You realize, of course, that it will finish you," Canler interjected. "I know that. It doesn't matter so long as it finishes them too," Lacenaire smirked, intending to have his associates march to the guillotine with him.

During his incarceration Lacenaire was visited often by Victor Hugo and Theophile Gautier, France's most celebrated writers, who listened attentively as the killer recited passages of original verse. From an adjacent cell Francois roared his disapproval. "Here's a pretty orator! Gabbler! Gabbler! How they all listen to Lacenaire. They'll be applauding him soon!" The trial of the three felons began at the Court d'Assizes of the Seine Department on November 12, 1835. Lacenaire was defended by a former schoolmate, who had attended the Alix Seminary with him, but the lawyer died in the middle of the trial. "I wash my hands of it," Lacenaire said, quoting the words of Pontius Pilate. He was reconciled to his fate.

A four-day trial ended in conviction. Francois received a life sentence. Avril and Lacenaire were condemned to death. On January 9, 1836, the two men walked to the guillotine at the St. Jacques barrier on the south side of Paris. Lacenaire looked his executioner square in the eye and said: "Nothing simpler. I am not afraid!" The blade was dropped at 8:33 a.m. This would-be literary lion of France went to his death gripping hatred for society. He had longed for death, his self-pitying memoirs showed, at one point writing: "All night I strode along the quay. I lived ten years in an hour. I wanted to kill myself and I sat on the parapet at the Pont des Arts, opposite the graves of those stupid heroes of July [the French Revolution] ... Henceforth my life was a drawn-out suicide; I belonged no longer to myself, but to cold steel [the guillotine] ... Society will have my blood, but I, in my turn, shall have the blood of Society." Only seconds after his decapitation by the guillotine's rushing blade, the executioner held high the severed head of Lacenaire, a grisly gesture greeted by roaring cheers and applause from blood-lusting spectators, a crowd of thousands, numbering far in excess the few readers who had purchased the scant writings of this lonely, lethal essayist.

A MURDEROUS FRENCH DUKE/ August 18, 1847

The Duke de Praslin (Theobald Charles Laure Hugues, Duc de Choiseul-Praslin, 1810-1848) was the scion of a distinguished noble French family that was directly related to the line of the reigning King Louis Philippe. In 1829, at the age of nineteen, Duke de Praslin married Fanny Sebastiani, who also came from a noble line and was the niece of the Duke of Coigny.

Petite and pretty, de Praslin's bride brought with her a huge dowry, which enriched the dwindling de Praslin coffers. The union produced ten children and the couple seemed relatively happy, spending their days in a comfortable Paris house on the Rue St. Honor, which belonged to the Sebastiani family. They also spent time in a gloomy, dank castle in Melun, the ancestral de Praslin estate.

The many de Praslin children needed considerable supervision and, in 1841, an attractive, intelligent, and utterly desirable housekeeper and governess arrived. Her name was Henriette Deluzy-Desportes, but the de Praslin family referred to her as Mademoiselle Deluzy. The duke, by then tired of his wife, who had worn herself out in twenty years of childbirth and maintaining a staggering household, slowly attached his affections to the reliant, strong-willed governess.

For six years, de Praslin carried on a cautious affair with Deluzy, who actually became the female head of the house and the woman the de Praslin children turned to for emotional support. The duchess was all but ignored in this strange atmosphere. Finally, unable to endure the impossible situation anymore, she asked the duke to break off the affair and send Deluzy away. He refused, curtly informing his wife, "My dear, if she goes, so do I."

The duchess then played her last card, threatening to divorce her husband unless he gave up his mistress. Fearing the loss of his wife's considerable income, de Praslin promised that he would set matters straight and call a halt to his unfaithful practices. He suggested that his wife take the children to the Melun estate, while he made final arrangements to send Deluzy away.

In July 1847, the duchess and the children went to the country but de Praslin, instead of dismissing the voluptuous governess, rented a luxurious apartment for her in Paris and spent almost a whole month in Deluzy's bed. The duchess returned to her Paris house to find her husband absent. Fanny de Praslin went to bed with nervous apprehension. She noticed that the hinges of the door leading to her bedroom had been removed. She consoled herself that she was safe, nevertheless, since the house was full of servants and her husband's bed chambers were close by. A cord was close to the duchess' bed which, when pulled, would ring bells in the servants' quarters, summoning them.

About 4 a.m., on August 18, 1847, the still house was suddenly filled with the piercing shrieks of a woman, screams so loud that they could be heard in the street outside by passersby. This was followed by choking and coughing sounds and then ominous silence. Responding to these cries inside the house were two servants, August Charpentier, de Praslin's

The Duke de Praslin, one of France's wealthiest men, who murdered his wife in 1847 for the love of another woman.

Fanny Sebastiani, the goddaughter of Emperor Napoleon I, married the Duke de Praslin and suffered death at his hands.

The magnificent chateau, where the de Praslins dwelled and where Fanny was murdered.

valet, and Emma Leclerc, the personal maid to the duchess. The doors to the duchess' bedroom were bolted and the entrance to her bathroom was jammed shut with a wedge. The valet found that the exit from the bedroom to the garden was also locked and he broke a panel of glass, getting inside a passageway that connected the bedrooms of the duke and duchess. The door between the bedrooms was unlocked.

Inside the dark bedroom of the duchess, the valet could smell gunsmoke and blood. He was joined by another servant and the two of them investigated the bedroom, finding Fanny de Praslin lying on the floor, her head against a sofa. Her nightgown was covered with blood and more than forty savage wounds had pierced her flesh.

Charpentier looked through the window of the bedroom and saw for a fleeting moment a tall, gaunt figure wearing a red brocaded nightgown, a vision he later described, "like a red devil!" Charpentier turned to another servant named Merville and gasped, "The duke."

"Then why doesn't he give the alarm?" asked Emma Leclerc, who stood now holding a guttering candle over the grisly scene. Examining the duchess, the servants grimaced in horror as they discovered sword cuts slashed across the small woman's breasts. Furniture was toppled everywhere and a trail of blood indicated that the duchess had tried to escape by running madly about the room, chased by a monster, who savagely slashed at her. There was a discernible trail of blood leading from the bedroom to the door that led to the duke's bedroom. Suddenly, the duke strode into the room, standing before his slain wife and servants and then exclaimed in a calm voice, "Oh, my God in Heaven! Some monster has murdered Fanny! Get a doctor!"

August Charpentier knew it was too late to call a doctor. He went into the street and stopped a policeman. Chief Inspector Pierre Allard of the Surete, the very man who had supervised the investigation in the notorious Lacenaire case thirteen years earlier, arrived a short time later. He examined the bedroom and found a pistol under a divan. He sniffed its muzzle but realized it had not been fired. The duchess' head had been crushed with a heavy instrument and Allard believed that the pistol had been the murder weapon. Allard asked the duke if he knew the owner of the pistol. "Yes," replied the duke in a

Servants are shown entering the duchess' bedroom to find Fanny de Praslin dead, stabbed more than forty times.

The many murder weapons used by de Praslin to rid himself of an unwanted wife.

King Louis-Philippe of France was reluctant to sign the order for de Praslin's execution; he sent the duke a bottle of poison, with a note telling him to commit suicide to preserve the image of the French aristocracy.

rather off-handed way, "It is mine." He then said he had grabbed the pistol in his bedroom when he heard his wife's screams and had run into her bedroom, where he found her lying on the floor. When he lifted her, he said, his clothes became coated with blood. He did not want to frighten the children, he said, so he went to his bedroom to change, then returned to his wife's bedroom to find the servants bending over his wife's body.

Allard checked all of the duke's swords and knives and found them to be spotless and in their wall mounts. The duke sat in a chair implacably staring back at his inquisitor. Allard pointed out the trail of blood that led from the duchess' bedroom to that of the duke's. De Praslin reminded the inspector that he had already admitted lifting his wife's bleeding body and that her blood had soaked his clothes and caused the trail when he went to his room to change. Allard then pointed out that the butt of the Duke's pistol was coated with blood and that hairs obviously from his wife's head still clung to it. The gun, Allard pointed out, had not been seized to ward off a murderous home invader, but had been employed as a murder weapon.

The Luxembourg jail, where de Praslin swallowed poison and broken glass, suffering a painful death.

Moreover, Allard had noticed that the duke was limping and he asked de Praslin to explain this injury. The aloof De Praslin assumed an injured and offended air. He finally responded airily, "I have no further explanations to make. I am a peer of France. I do not account for myself to police officers." With that, he dismissed Allard, but the inspector had already decided that the duke was, indeed, the murderer. He concluded that it would be dangerous to place such a distinguished personage in custody, that to do so was to risk his career, but he believed he had no choice. Armed with considerable evidence, Allard went to ministers of the king some days later and accused the duke of murdering his wife. He had obtained the diary kept by the duchess, along with her letters, all of which were filled with descriptions of her husband's infidelities with Deluzy. Here, of course, was the motive for the murder. De Praslim killed his wife so that he could be with his sensual

The de Praslin murder case was profiled in the moody 1940 film, *All This, and Heaven Too*, with Charles Boyer (shown in bed at left) as the duke and Bette Davis, right, portraying the governess (Henriette Deluzy-Desportes).

mistress. King Louis Philippe reluctantly signed the order for de Praslin's arrest.

Inspector Allard first came under heavy criticism for arresting a nobleman. But the intrepid Allard prepared a meticulous report, describing in detail how he had inspected the butt of the pistol with a magnifying glass and found the hairs affixed to it, mingled with blood. Moreover, he had taken some hairs from the murder victim's head and matched these to those on the gun. This proof, coupled with the duchess' letters and diary, convinced the king that de Praslin would have to face a trial that would certainly prove sensational and embarrassing to the crown. To avoid a scandal that might also taint the aristocracy, the king reportedly sent de Praslin a small bottle of poison and a message that he should do the honorable thing and preserve the good image of his peers by committing suicide. De Praslin not only drank the poison, but broke up the bottle and swallowed the small shards of glass in an attempt to hide the evidence causing his demise.

There were some bizarre sequels to this murder. Before her death, the duchess had had a recurring nightmare, one which she had described to friends and servants. She had dreamed of awakening to see the Devil standing over her, dressed in a shiny bright red costume, moving ominously toward her and then retreating until disappearing into a wall. Years after the duke and duchess were dead, one of their children found a bright red brocaded bal-masque costume of Mephistopheles. The duke had apparently worn this on several occasions, appearing before his wife at night in an attempt to drive her insane, a condition which would have allowed him to divorce her.

Henriette Deluzy was also arrested and jailed for three months while Allard and other officers incessantly interviewed her. She repeatedly stated that she had had nothing to do with the murder of her employer the duchess, and Allard was finally convinced of her innocence and released her. Deluzy migrated to the U.S., settling in New York, where she later became the principal of the Female Art School. She married the Reverend Henry M. Field in 1851 and moved in high literary circles, becoming one of the most distinguished women in New York, although her past, on rare occasions, emerged to haunt her. At one high-society gathering at the Century Club, a Count Goureski, familiar with the de Praslin scandal, hissed repeatedly through his false teeth at Henriette Field, "Mur-der-ess! Mur-der-ess!" The elderly count was finally asked to leave or be thrown through a window.

Nathaniel Hawthorne, who lived near the Fields, learned of Deluzy's scarlet past and, used her as the role model for his mysterious character Miriam in *The Marble Faun*. When Henriette Field died in 1875, her funeral was attended by all the literary and high society lights of the city and her casket was borne to its grave by such luminaries as William Cullen Bryant and Peter Cooper. The famous diarist George Templeton Strong marked her passing: "Died. Mrs. Henry Field ... I knew her at one time quite well and she was universally liked, being uncommonly clever and cultivated. Her plainness made it incredible that the Duke de Praslin should have been in love with her."

THE PARKMAN MURDER/November 23, 1849

Dr. John White Webster, who earned his medical degree from Harvard and was a professor of chemistry and mineralogy at the Massachusetts Medical College in the 1840s, stepped beyond the halls of the academy to become one of America's most notorious killers. His office was directly below that of Oliver Wendell Holmes, Sr., who would later offer testimony in Webster's sensational murder case, one involving the killing of Dr. George Parkman, a savage crime that shocked that gentler age and providing a grim story that filled the pages of the national press for months.

Dr. John White Webster, an esteemed medical teacher, who murdered his creditor, Dr. George Parkman.

Webster apparently was forced to borrow money from various sources to cover the debts he had incurred from his high living. Far from a reclusive bookworm, the Cambridge physician enjoyed entertaining the cream of the literary set. Henry Wadsworth Longfellow was a frequent guest at Webster's table. To remain in good standing with the scions of Boston society, Webster was required to spend money he did not have. With an annual salary of $1,200, Webster could ill afford extravagant parties. He soon found himself borrowing large sums of money from his closest friends.

Dr. George Parkman, a money-lending skinflint, who dunned Webster for the return of his $400 loan.

Parkman, a colleague of Webster's who donated the land upon which the Massachusetts Medical School nia, but the telling blow had smashed Parkman's skull and killed him. Reflecting on Parkman's angry denunciations months later, Webster wrote: "I was excited by them to the highest degree of passion." Fearful of the consequences, Webster decided to use his medical skills to dispose of the body. After locking the office doors, he hauled the body into his washroom and cut it into pieces. The college janitor, Ephraim Littlefield, had witnessed an earlier argument between the two men and had seen Parkman arrive earlier that afternoon, obviously angry. The door to Webster's office and the door to an adjoining office were locked. Littlefield touched the wall that backed Webster's assay furnace and found it hot. Even as Littlefield stood wondering what Webster was doing, the doctor was busy burning Parkman's severed head.

The Massachusetts Medical College at Harvard University, where Dr. Webster taught and where, in his laboratory, he murdered Dr. Parkman.

Dr. Webster shown beating Dr. Parkman to death with a piece of kindling in his medical laboratory on November 23, 1849; he then dissected the body and attempted to burn the remains in his furnace.

Webster disposed of most of the body parts, but, ever the academic, kept a few bones as specimens for teaching and research, grim artifacts later used in securing his conviction. Three days after Parkman's murder, a $3,000 reward was offered for the safe return of the missing Parkman, the reward posted by Parkman's brother-in-law, Robert Gould Shaw. Rumors to the effect that the good doctor had been abducted by a kidnapping gang and was to be held for ransom circulated through town. Spurred on by the promise of a sizeable reward, most of Boston's inhabitants turned out to search for the missing man. The tenement districts were invaded by search parties, and every suspicious character and drunkard was taken in for questioning.

An Irish immigrant who was found with $20 in his pocket became a suspect, but he was released after some questioning. Littlefield, the snooping janitor, however, conducted his own investigation. He tried to gain access to Webster's dissection vault, but found that the chamber was securely locked. The janitor spent the next two days tearing apart the wall that covered up Webster's bloody deed. Finally, Littlefield broke into the locked vault. He found a bloody pelvis and parts of a leg, and immediately contacted the police.

A diligent police investigation uncovered more of Parkman's body parts and Webster was arrested and charged with the murder. When en route to jail he tried to commit suicide by taking strychnine, but vomited the poison before it had any effect. His trial received tremendous public attention. By not allowing any of the spectators to sit in the gallery longer than five minutes, more than 60,000 spectators witnessed the trial. Many of them had come from as far as New Orleans. Webster, who pleaded that he had not intended to commit the murder, but was only acting from uncontrolled anger, was convicted and sentenced to death. The jury was convinced of his guilt, believing he had committed premeditated murder because he had dissected the body, and then tried to conceal it from view.

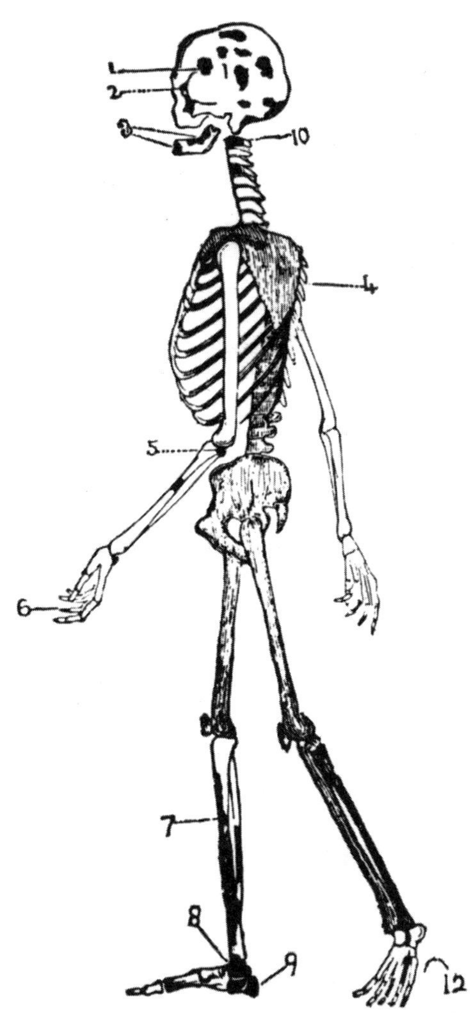

A reconstructed skeleton of Parkman's body; numbered bones were retrieved from Webster's furnace.

British author Charles Dickens, who, upon his arrival at Boston, asked to see "the room where Dr. Parkman was murdered."

Webster was hanged in August 1850. A letter written shortly after Webster's execution reveals the extent of the horror that was felt by the residents of this genteel New England community. It read in part: " ... the terrible Cambridge tragedy still seems to darken our sky though it is a great comfort to know the poor doctor seemed to die penitent. He wrote a letter to Dr. Parkhurst (the Reverend) entreating that some softer feelings might at least be recovered towards his family, that his wife and children were wholly innocent, and that she had often expressed her gratitude to him for his (the Reverend's) help in her spiritual culture. I hear she is tranquil, but what their plans are I know not."

The Parkman murder remained a lively topic of discussion for years, much to the embarrassment and chagrin of his socially connected family. Twenty years after the murder the celebrated British novelist Charles Dickens visited the city. When asked which tourist attraction he most wanted to see, Dickens replied: "The room where Dr. Parkman was murdered."

THE MURDERING "COUNT" PRADO/ January 15, 1886

An articulate Frenchman and self-styled nobleman of questionable origins, "Count" Louis Prado (AKA: Linska de Castillon, Pranzini, the American) was known for attracting wildly different types of women. He never divulged his familial background in any detail, though he reportedly was the son of the president of a South American country. Prado's luck as a criminal wore out at the same time as his skills with women. He would have gotten away with murder if he had not offended two mistresses who were arrested in connection with a robbery he committed.

Paris police were unable to catch the killer of Marie Agaetan, found with her head almost severed by a razor in her apartment in the Rue Caumartin on January 15, 1886. Many people were arrested for the murder, but all were released due to lack of evidence. The Agaetan case might have been placed on the permanently unsolved list if not for a robbery committed by Prado on November 28, 1887, one in which he tried to steal diamonds from a room at the Hotel du Palais in Paris, but was thwarted by a hotel employee. He fired two bullets at police chasing him, gravely wounding one, and was arrested for attempted murder.

Murderer Louis Prado was captured by Paris police during a robbery; he was executed in 1888.

Several weeks later, Prado's two mistresses, Eugenie Forestier, twenty-seven, and Mauricette Couronneau, the mother of his child, were arrested for holding some jewelry stolen from a shop at Royan, these jewels having been bestowed upon the unwitting females as gifts from Prado, who had served four months' imprisonment for theft in 1883. The humiliation of her arrest so angered Forestier that she turned state's evidence against her former paramour in connection with the murder of Agaetan.

"Dr." Karl Pranzini, who murdered a woman and her daughter in Paris during an 1887 robbery (he was guillotined that year); Prado often used Pranzini's name as an alias.

Like the murderer Dr. Karl Pranzini, with whom he is often compared, and whose last name he even used as an alias, Prado all but confessed his guilt to his mistress the night he committed the murder. Prosecuted from November 5 to November 14, 1888 at the Paris Assizes, Prado's eloquence was ineffective against his mistress' testimony. Forestier recalled how he repeatedly got up to wash his hands during the night of January 14, 1888—the night of the Agaetan murder—to destroy his bloodstained clothing, throw out a razor, and give her a 100-franc note apparently cut with a razor.

Other witnesses confirmed that Prado, tried under what he said was his real name, Linska de Castillon, was the man seen with Agaetan the night she was slain. Prado's faithful Spanish wife, herself in possession of jewels stolen in Royan, supported her husband even after meeting his mistresses. Her one-sided fidelity was not enough, however, and Prado, thirty-four, was found guilty of murder and executed December 28, 1888. The mistresses were acquitted.

THE KNICKERBOCKER CLUB MURDERS/ 1898

Handsome, debonair playboy Roland Burnham Molineux (1868-1917) was a Yankee blueblood whose father, General Edward Leslie Molineux, distinguished himself in the Civil War. The son frequented the prestigious Knickerbocker Athletic Club on East Forty-Fifth Street, New York City, and was well known to its board of directors as a gadfly. Molineux continually harassed the club managers to cancel memberships of people he didn't like or those he thought to be his social inferiors.

In matters of the heart, Molineux was also persistent. In the fall of 1898, Henry C. Barnet, a wealthy produce broker who was also a member of the Knickerbocker Club, was courting Blanche Cheeseborough, an attractive young woman who had also attracted Molineux's covetous eye. Barnet received a box of Kutnow's Stomach Powder, a popular patent medicine, through the mail. Although he had not ordered it and did not know who the sender was, Barnet ingested the contents of the package and became deathly ill. His physician was of the opinion that something other than the powder had brought on the illness. But before he died, Henry Barnet blamed the powder and called himself a "damned fool" for accepting medicines sent through the postal system. The cause of death was

The handsome New York playboy-killer, Roland Burnham Molineux (shown in work-out clothes), who poisoned rivals and those he thought unfit to be members of his Knickerbocker Athletic Club.

New York's prestigious Knickerbocker Athletic Club, which became the center of a number of poisonings in 1898.

Harry Cornish, the club's athletic director, angered Molineux, who sent him a bottle of "patent medicine," laced with cyanide, but Cornish's aunt took the medicine instead and died.

listed as the aftereffects of diphtheria. Eleven days later Blanche Cheeseborough married Molineux.

On December 23, 1898, Knickerbocker Club athletic director Harry Cornish received in his mail a small box containing a bottle of headache remedy and a silver toothpick holder. Cornish took it as a practical joke. The bottle was obviously a humorous warning not to overdrink on the holidays. Cornish gave the bottle to his aunt, Katharine Adams, saying he had no use for it. On December 28, 1898, the woman complained of a severe headache. Cornish suggested she try a teaspoon of the remedy mixed with water. Mrs. Adams complained of the medicine's bitterness and within moments fell to the floor in convulsions and died. Cornish, who had sampled the potion, also became sick.

An autopsy report showed that Adams died from cyanide poisoning. The Knickerbocker Club's doctor, having remembered Cornish's story about the gift bottle, went to Cornish's home and analyzed the bottle's contents. It contained a lethal amount of cyanide of mercury. The police were immediately called. The toothpick holder, it was determined, came from Hartdegen's jewelry store in Newark, New Jersey, and had been sold on December 21, 1898 to a man asking for a suitable bottle to add to a lady's dressing table. A wigmaker told police he had sold a red wig on December 21, 1898 to a man bearing a striking resemblance to Molineux. Next, the police found out that the killer had rented two postal boxes, one to receive mail for "H. Cornish," and one for "H.C. Barnet." The press checked the mailing lists of several patent medicine companies. A Cincinnati firm reported that they had sold two boxes of Kutnow's Powder to an "H.C. Barnet" and "H. Cornish" on December 21, 1898. The handwriting was nearly identical to the lettering on the package sent to Cornish. Subsequently, Molineux was identified as the individual who had rented the postal boxes.

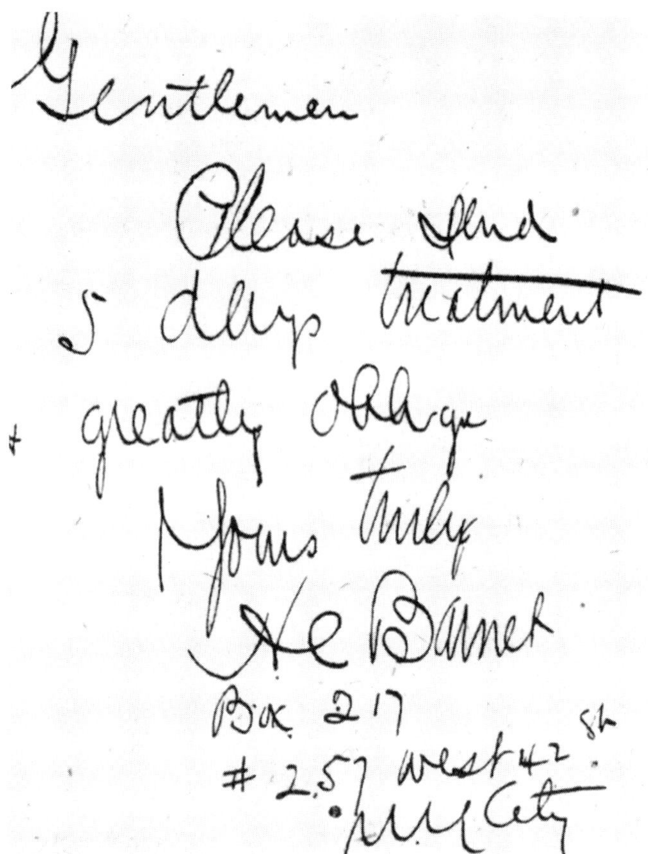

Gentlemen
Please send
5 days treatment
+ greatly oblige
Yours truly
H C Barnet
Box 217
257 west 42 St.
N.Y. City

A forged letter written by Molineux (he used the name of one of his victims, Henry C. Barnet), requesting patent medicine, which the killer dosed with cyanide; this letter and others were later used in court to convict Molineux of the Knickerbocker Club murders.

Molineux was arrested and charged with poisoning Mrs. Adams. His trial lasted from November 14, 1899, to February 11, 1900. The murder motive, Assistant District Attorney James W. Osborne explained, came from the personal enmity Molineux harbored against Cornish. On more than one occasion he threatened to quit the club unless Cornish was fired as athletic director. The details of Molineux's profligate life-style made sensational reading. A New Jersey woman named Mary Melando told the court that the defendant had seduced her at the age of thirteen, and then shared living quarters with her. Though she did not wish to testify against Molineux in court, Melando admitted that some stationary submitted in evidence against him was the same type she had found in the drawer of his desk.

The jury considered all the evidence and, after an eight-hour deliberation, Molineux was found guilty. Three weeks later, he was sentenced to death and was sent to Sing Sing to await execution. For the next eight months he remained on death row, while his attorneys argued for a new trial. During this time, he wrote a memoir of prison life titled The Room with the Little Door, which became a critical success in the literary world. On October 15, 1901, the higher court set aside the judgment and ordered a new trial on the grounds that the testimony concerning Barnet was inadmissible.

The second trial commenced in 1902, and this time Molineux returned to court with a new lawyer and public opinion decidedly in his favor. The long months of incarceration won him much sympathy, and attorney Frank C. Black, a former governor of New York, succeeded in producing handwriting experts who refuted the testimony given in the first trial. Black also contended that Cornish had murdered Mrs. Adams in order to court her daughter. The jury returned a verdict of not guilty. Molineux's celebrity status landed him a job with several newspapers, and theatrical impresario David Belasco produced one of his plays. In 1913, following his divorce from Blanche and subsequent remarriage, Roland Molineux was committed to an insane asylum for what was ostensibly called a "nervous breakdown." He died in the King's Park State Hospital on November 2, 1917. "Couldn't make much sense of him," commented an attendant at the hospital. "He raved a lot about poisons and a 'better class of people.'"

"HE DIED OF BAKED BANANAS"/ September 23, 1900

William Marsh Rice was an enterprising New Englander who left his home in Springfield, Massachusetts in the 1830s to seek his fortune in Houston, Texas, then a raw frontier town, which held great promise for men of vision and destiny. Rice quickly proved that he was such a man. He made a fortune in land speculation, retail merchandising, and oil. He developed large portions of the Southwest, owning entire blocks of real estate in Texas, Georgia, Louisiana, and Oklahoma.

Though he was enormously wealthy, Rice had no children to inherit his great fortune. He lived with his second wife Elizabeth in a pretentious mansion in Dunellen, New Jersey. After she passed away in July 1896, the aging widower moved to New York City, where he took up residence in the Berkshire Apartments, a radical departure from the ostentatious lifestyle he had led in New Jersey. Rice' constant companion during these years was his 23-year-old secretary Charles F. Jones, whom he met at the Capital Hotel in Houston, one of the many properties he owned in the Lone Star state.

Jones, who had worked as a clerk at the hotel store, accompanied Rice to New York in May 1897, serving as secretary, valet, and devoted servant. They lived a simple life, receiving few callers, while going about their business quietly. Seemingly content in old age, Rice was tormented by one major problem. His late wife had left behind a will bequeathing a large chunk of the Rice fortune to her relatives, under the terms of the Texas community law, which stated that the husband and wife were equal partners even though the assets were in the name of the husband. Rice maintained that he had been a resident of New York since 1865, though business concerns drew him back to Texas in 1893.

Shortly before his wife's death, Rice brought a suit against O.T. Holt, executor of the estate in an effort to have the will declared null and void. He was adamant in this matter, for the old man desired to leave behind a legacy "for the good of mankind." In 1891, he incorporated under Texas law the not-for-profit "Rice Institute," which was designed to advance the arts, science, and literature. In 1893 and again in 1896 he drafted wills naming the Rice Institute as residuary legatee, which accounted for about fifteen-sixteenths of his entire estate.

In 1899, with matters at an impasse, Holt enlisted the aid of Albert T. Patrick, a 34-year-old Texas lawyer whose shady dealings nearly resulted in disbarment proceedings brought against him. Patrick moved to New York to avoid any unpleasantness, but in the process he created some of his own. The lawyer interviewed a score of acquaintances in a vain attempt to prove that Rice was actually a New York resident. In the process he hit upon a novel scheme. In November 1899, Patrick dropped by the Berkshire apartments to pay a social call on the impressionable Jones.

Patrick introduced himself as Mr. Smith, a cotton buyer from Texas who was eager to transact some business with Rice. Since it was late at night, Jones informed the stranger that his employer could not be disturbed. Patrick nodded. He wasn't really interested in meeting William Marsh Rice, but was more interested in cultivating Jones, the one man who could help him realize a fortune.

Texas tycoon William Marsh Rice, murdered for his millions in 1900.

Patrick returned later to confess his true identity. He explained that he had been acting on the behest of Elizabeth's heirs. What he proposed, at least on the surface, appeared to be a foolish plan. If the $55-dollar-a-week secretary could draft a letter on Rice's personal stationery admitting his Texas residency, Patrick would then have the old man sign it himself. In return, the gullible Jones was promised a $250 honorarium. Jones agreed and prepared the document to Patrick's specifications. But when the lawyer was slow in handing over the money, Jones slipped it into the drawer. "No money, no letter," Jones told Patrick.

Patrick's greatest skill was persuading people to his way of thinking. He was an effusive, self-assured man who inspired confidence in others. It wasn't long before he had convinced Jones to show him a copy of the 1896 will with the promise of more money yet to come. Patrick then drafted a will suitable to the interests of his clients. By the terms of the new will, Rice would leave half of his estate to Albert Patrick, named as sole executor. The remainder would go to the relatives with only a small portion earmarked for the Rice Institute. "I want you to type this on Mr. Rice's typewriter and using his stationery," Patrick told Jones. "I'll make sure it's witnessed and signed." In return for his agreement to appear on the witness stand and testify to the legitimacy of the will, Jones was promised that he would receive a handsome sum of money. One lingering problem which Patrick was unable to address concerned Rice himself. Why would he sign a document so detrimental to his own interests? Patrick had already answered that question in his own mind; he would murder the millionaire.

Patrick diligently drafted a will that bequeathed $10,000 a year to Rice Institute for as long as the old man should live, and as an added gesture of "good will" it was decided to set aside $5,000 for the construction of a monument to tower above the old man's grave. Albert Patrick used a bottle of ink from Rice's own desk to replicate Rice's signature on several bank drafts, which were then cashed. The new will was completed on June 30, 1900. It was witnessed by two of Patrick's office employees: David L. Short and Morris Meyers. Short was introduced to Rice as the commissioner of deeds for the State of Texas, and very sympathetic to the old man's plight. These two men functioned as "plants" whose sole purpose was to establish Patrick's close ties to Rice.

In August, Patrick dropped by to see Jones. He inquired about the old man's health, adding: "Don't you think Rice is living too long for our interest?"

Charles F. Jones, the gullible young assistant to Rice, who was manipulated into murder.

"It does seem that way," Jones replied, suggesting that Dr. Walter Curry, Patrick's long-time friend might be enlisted to the cause. "He wouldn't do a thing of that kind!" Patrick intoned. "There must be some simple measure we can take." Jones suggested chloroform. He had read in a magazine that it was virtually impossible to detect the drug in an autopsy. Jones agreed to procure the substance. He sent $5 to his brother in Texas for a bottle containing four ounces of chloroform. Patrick instructed his young friend to start administering mercury tablets to Rice in order "to break him down." On Sept. 1, 1900, the trusted valet started giving Rice two mercury tablets a day until he began suffering the ravages of diarrhea. Patrick stepped up the dosage until Rice's condition began to worsen.

About two weeks later a lady friend of Rice's, Mrs. Van Alstyne visited her ailing friend and advised him to eat nine bananas to unclog his stomach. Jones then gave him some more mercury. Albert Patrick would ruefully recall: "It was silly to have given him the mercury pills. If he had been left alone he might have died from eating the bananas."

On September 23, 1900, Jones supplied the coup-de-grace. Slipping into Rice's bedroom late that night, Jones constructed a "cone," which he fashioned from some towels and placed this over the sleeping man's face. He dropped a sponge soaked with chloroform into it, gradually increasing the quantity. A half-hour later he conveyed the news to Patrick by telephone: "Mr. Rice is very ill," meaning that Rice was dead. Dr. Curry was summoned and he signed the death certificate in the following manner: "Cause of death: old age and weak heart; immediate causes indigestion, followed by diarrhea and mental worry." Patrick issued instructions that Rice be cremated right away. A forged cremation letter was handed to John S. Potter, the embalmer.

The letter might have served its purpose if Patrick had shown some discretion. But the next morning he sent David L. Short to the bank to cash a $25,000 check "endorsed" by Rice. The clerk at the banking house of S.M. Swenson and Sons examined the signature on the check and grew suspicious. He couldn't help but noticing that the name of the payee on the face of the check was "Abert T. Patrick." But the endorsement was signed "Albert T. Patrick." A second bank clerk named Walter O. Weatherbee said that the check required a proper endorsement in order to be cashed. Bank Manager Eric T. Swenson attempted to phone Mr. Rice, but Jones explained that the check was good, and was consistent with the old man's instructions. Swenson was still suspicious. Pressed for a further explanation, Jones admitted that his employer had died.

Albert T. Patrick (right), the scheming attorney, who arranged through Charles Jones to kill Rice and acquire his millions through a forged will.

Patrick appeared at the bank to inform Swenson that he held a $65,000 check that had been signed by Rice, and all of his securities and bonds. He curtly informed the bank proprietor that the body was being cremated the next day.

Swenson then asked: "What did Mr. Rice die of?"

Without a moment of hesitation, Patrick replied: "He died of baked bananas."

"What? Bananas? Patrick explained that Rice's friend, Mrs. Van Alstyne had suggested that Rice eat baked bananas to relieve his diarrhea. "He got nine of them and ate them, and I believe that is what killed him."

By now Swenson suspected treachery. He contacted the New York District Attorney and the city Detective Bureau, which launched an immediate investigation. It was only then that the relatives learned about Rice's untimely death. An autopsy revealed that Mr. Rice had expired from congestion, caused by a "gas or vapor." On October 4, 1900, Jones and Patrick were arrested on forgery charges and were incarcerated in the Tombs. Turning to his young henchman Patrick said: "it's over boy."

"What can we do?" Jones asked.

"I suggest that *you* commit suicide," Patrick replied. Patrick was bailed out three months later, but was rearrested and charged with murder after Jones confessed the plot to the District Attorney.

Charles Jones was offered a deal. In return for his cooperation the prosecution agreed to drop all pending charges against him. Jones readily agreed, supplying all the damaging evidence when the trial convened on January 22, 1902. Patrick entered a not guilty plea, accusing his one-time partner of being "an incredible liar." The balding lawyer conducted his own defense, but he was unable to shake the testimony of the experts, who stated that the signatures on the Rice bank checks were definite forgeries, shown by the "breaks in continuity and pen lifts." The jury retired on March 26, 1902. After a brief deliberation Patrick was convicted of murder and sentenced to death in the electric chair by Judge John William Goff, who later went on to become a justice of the Supreme Court. Jones, the actual killer, was freed. He returned to Texas and dropped out of sight. Patrick however, continued to fight to have his conviction overturned.

Using money supplied by his millionaire brother-in-law John T. Milliken, Patrick succeeded in winning a new trial from members of the state legislature. However the governor vetoed the idea. The matter was taken before the U.S. Supreme Court which denied Patrick's appeal. Before the sentence of death could be carried out, however, Governor Frank Higgins commuted the sentence to life imprisonment. The decision was roundly criticized by the media. Edmund Pearson commented in the New York *Tribune* that: "if he got out, he would be invaluable as a counselor to tell murderers how to escape." Patrick's legal wranglings continued until November 28, 1912, when Governor John Dix granted him an unconditional pardon on the grounds that "the hostile atmosphere which surrounded the defendant when he was tried precluded a fair trial."

Dix cited a 1910 report issued by the Medico-Legal Society of New York, which concluded that Rice could not have died from chloroform poisoning judging by the condition of the lungs at the time of the autopsy. It was alleged at the time that Milliken offered to deposit $100,000 in any financial institution the governor so desired. He vowed to forfeit the money to charity if his brother-in-law failed to prove his innocence within a year of release. Patrick walked out of Sing Sing a free man about the same time that the Rice Institute opened its doors to its first students. He retired to the Southwest to practice law. Patrick died some years later without making good on his brother-in-law's boastful claim.

The legacy of William Marsh Rice endures on the campus of the liberal arts university in Houston bearing his name. If Albert Patrick's scheme had been carried out to the fullest extent, it is unlikely that the school would have become a reality. Instead, a $5,000 marker would be the only testament to the vision of this great philanthropist, who is remembered in a bronze statue of his likeness that towers in the center of the Academic Court of the Rice Institute.

THE ERRANT COLONEL GRIFFITH/1903

Like William Marsh Rice, Colonel Griffith J. Griffith (1852-1919) was a most generous philanthropist. During his lifetime, he gave Los Angeles, California, two of its greatest landmarks, the 4,100-acre Griffith Park, complete with the copper-roofed Griffith Park Observatory, and the Greek Theater, still one of the most exceptional outdoor amphitheaters in the U.S. But there was a darker side to Griffith, as well, a side shaded by his excessive abuse of alcohol.

His chronic drinking caused Griffith to have delusions, the most prominent of which was that his wife, Christina Griffith, was trying to poison him. This hallucination grew, in part, out of Griffith's hatred for the Roman Catholic Church. Christina Griffith was involved in several community activities associated with the church and in his liquor-damaged mind, Griffith thought that after his wife killed him, the Catholic Church would attempt to take the fortune he had built in real estate. In his mind, Griffith plotted ways to head off this imagined intention.

Griffith's "counter-scheme" was carried out one summer day in 1903 while he and Christina were vacationing at the Arcadia Hotel in Santa Monica, California. In their suite, he handed his wife a prayer book, ordered her to kneel and pray, and took out a pistol. As she pleaded for mercy, he began to read a series of questions regarding her loyalty to him and her alleged plot to poison him.

"Oh Papa, you know I have always been true to you!" she tearfully insisted.

Griffith ignored her pleadings. He placed the gun to his wife's temple, but as he pulled the trigger, she jerked her head away. The bullet destroyed her left eye.

Wounded and fearing for her life, Christina jumped out of the hotel room window and fell two stories onto a veranda,

Colonel Griffith J. Griffith (who donated Griffith Park to Los Angeles), shot out his wife's left eye in an attempt to kill her in 1903.

breaking her leg. She limped away and found help. When Griffith was located, he insisted that she had shot herself with his pistol.

The city of Los Angeles, acknowledging Griffith's high standing and valuable patronage, was prepared to ignore what they determined was simply a "domestic squabble," but Mrs. Griffith's family was bent on pressing charges. These relatives hired a team of accomplished prosecutors, led by former California Governor Henry T. Gage. Griffith's counsel was the famous, highly successful defense attorney, Earl Rogers. Rogers was well-versed in an emerging field called "psychiatry," and his plan was to call for a defense of insanity due to alcohol abuse.

Early in the proceedings, Rogers created an uproar by demanding a continuance to give him time to effectively defend his client. He then suddenly withdrew the continuance on the first day of the trial. The prosecutors were caught off guard; they had devoted all their time to gathering evidence to reject Rogers' continuance plea and had not further organized their strategy.

The jury eventually found Griffith guilty of assault with intent to murder. He was sentenced to two years in prison and released on good behavior after serving one. He died in 1919. Although his defense probably eased Griffith's sentence, Rogers took the loss hard, and was rumored to have flirted with suicide for some time after the trial. He died, destitute and alone, in a Southern California rooming house in 1922.

PERILS OF A FLORADORA GIRL/June 4, 1904

On June 4, 1904, New Yorkers out for a morning stroll on West Broadway near Franklin Street were jarred by the sharp sound of a gunshot coming from a passing hansom cab. Without so much as looking through the trap in the top of the cab to check on his passengers, the driver drove swiftly to the nearest pharmacy. Passersby who rushed to the aid of the cab's occupants found a dying man and a grieving woman inside. Recognizing the gravity of the victim's wound, the driver proceeded to the Hudson Street Hospital, where Francis Thomas "Caesar" Young was declared dead on arrival, the result of a bullet wound in his chest.

As the facts of the shooting were revealed, the public learned that Young, a well-known gambler and man about town, had been conducting a secret affair with attractive Nan Randolph Patterson, the cab's other occupant. The 22-year-old Patterson, was a member of the road company of the popular Floradora review. She came from a well-respected family, her father being the supervising architect at the U.S. Treasury. Following a disastrous marriage to a teenaged beau that ended in divorce, Patterson became a Broadway showgirl, joining the Floradora troupe.

It was not uncommon for the "Floradora Girls" to find wealthy husbands from among the fawning admirers along the "Great White Way" of Broadway. The New York theatre world was a happy escape for many young dandies and rich society gentlemen, who were locked in troubled or mundane

Nan Patterson (second from right) when she appeared with the famous Floradora Sextette in New York; these chorus girls were much-sought by social lions and millionaires.

An artist's rendering of how Nan Patterson shot and killed her lover, Caesar Young, a married gambler who jilted her, while the couple rode in a hansom cab on June 4, 1904.

"With his left shoulder pressing me and his cheek almost touching mine he fumbled about for a minute. Suddenly his right hand came around with a jerk and touched my breast sharply. At that very instant the cab jolted and I heard a little muffled noise—nothing the least resembling the sharp crack of a pistol; I never dreamed of such a thing. The next instant he began to lean more heavily against me, and then—his head rolled into my lap. I put my hand on his cheek--IT WAS GROWING COLD!"

Another artist's rendering shows how Caesar Young awkwardly and improbably shot himself to death (according to the path of the lethal bullet), while Nan Patterson sat next to him.

marriages. Men of financial means often sought an after hours tete-a-tete with winsome chorines, and this was Caesar Young's intention when meeting the fetching Nan Patterson in 1902.

Young was an amateur athlete in his early days in England. After settling in America, he became a racetrack gambler. He had an uncanny ability to pick winning horses, and developed a reputation of being a fair judge of talent in breeding race ponies. Young had been married for ten years when he met Patterson on board a train bound for California. The two carried on their affair publicly, with little regard for the rigid social proprieties of the day.

Caesar Young attempted to placate both his mistress and his wife, sometimes keeping them in separate hotels in New York City. He juggled his social calendar precariously, spending days with his wife and nights with Patterson. Patterson reportedly campaigned hard and long to have Young divorce his wife and marry her, once even feigning pregnancy. Young, however, was unwilling or unable to leave his wife. When the pressure got to be too great for him, he offered to pay Patterson's passage to Europe. She refused, and Young and his wife booked passage instead. The voyage was apparently intended to break Patterson's hold on Young and renew the bonds of his marriage.

On June 3, 1904, the night before the Youngs were to sail to Europe on board the *Germanic*, Young and Patterson spent the evening together. They drank and argued into the early hours of the morning. Patterson pressed Young to leave his wife. Witnesses to their conversation that evening claimed that Young had called Patterson insulting names and had thrown $100 at her. "I never want to see you again," he was heard to shout in a Manhattan restaurant. Patterson, in turn, warned that Young would not be able to escape her fury.

Despite this threatening encounter, Young met Patterson early the next morning. He left the hotel room he was sharing with his wife around 7 a.m., telling her he was going out to buy a new hat and get a shave, and promising to meet her at the dock before the ship's 9:30 a.m. departure time. He met his estranged lover near Columbus Circle, where they repaired to a tavern for a brandy and whiskey breakfast, then rode together in the hansom cab.

When the hansom arrived at the hospital after the shooting, a gun, still warm from being fired, was found in Young's coat pocket. Patterson claimed that he had shot himself in the

Nan Patterson, shown passively responding to a harassing Assistant District Attorney, William Rand, in one of her three grueling trials, emerged victorious, finally being set free in 1905.

chest because he was despondent about leaving her. "Caesar, Caesar, why did you do this?" Nan sobbed. It seemed unlikely to the police that if Young had shot himself, he would have carefully placed the gun back in his pocket. Despite her protestations of innocence, Patterson was formally charged with Young's murder and put on trial in November 1904 at the old Felony Court on Lower Broadway.

Patterson was defended by the pugnacious Abraham Levy, a veteran of more than 300 homicide cases. He was opposed by Assistant District Attorney William Rand, who hammered away at the defense's contention that Young was a suicide victim. The direction of the bullet's entry and the powder burns made it impossible for Caesar Young to have fired the shot, Rand insisted. The canny Levy appealed to the sympathy of the jury, making exaggerated references to Nan's brokenhearted father (who looked and played the part well) throughout the weeks of testimony.

Nan stuck to her story throughout the trial. Attorney Levy implored the jury to believe that Caesar Young had met her in Columbus Circle to beg her forgiveness and shot himself in desperation when she refused to give it. "Do you believe that this empty, frivolous, if you like, pleasure-loving girl could conceive the plot that would permit her at one second to kill and in the next cover this act by a subtle invention?" Levy said to the jury. Rand found it difficult to win a conviction from an all-male jury against so charming a defendant.

When a juror became seriously ill during the deliberations, a mistrial was declared. Undaunted, Rand pursued the matter further. The second trial, which began in December, ended with a hung jury. When the third trial ended on May 3, 1905 with yet another deadlocked jury, the judge ordered all charges against Nan Patterson dropped. The outcome of the case pleased her many admirers, who cheered her as she left the courtroom.

Patterson celebrated her freedom by getting drunk. Her liberation was such a popular cause that a children's ditty grew out of it: "Nan is free, Nan is free,/She escaped the electric chair,/Now she's out in the open air." Nan Patterson was unable to capitalize on her new-found notoriety. She was given star billing in several popular musicals, including a Pennsylvania production of the Lulu Girls, but theatrical offers diminished after it was quickly learned that she had little or no talent for the stage. After remarrying (and later divorcing) her first husband, Nan Patterson faded from public view, remembered as a titillating curiosity of that much-gilded Edwardian era.

Heir to a Pittsburgh coke fortune, playboy Harry K. Thaw was kicked out of Harvard for gambling, then took a suite of rooms in a New York whorehouse.

Evelyn Nesbit in the days when she was a model for artists and photographers.

"THIS MAN RUINED MY WIFE!"/June 25, 1906

Few murders among America's social elite and super rich rivaled the sensational 1906 murder of architect Stanford White by the demented millionaire Harry Kendall Thaw (AKA: John Smith, 1872-1947). The slaying of White was a public affair, committed in front of hundreds of horrified spectators. Thaw performed this deed with arrogance and disdain, as if dismissing an annoying servant or an unwanted party guest. Thaw was used to having his own way since childhood, and as far as he was concerned, his killing of Stanford White, ostensibly over an affair with Thaw's beautiful wife, Evelyn, was merely a nasty chore he was compelled to perform. Ironically, his wife, the former Evelyn Nesbit, had been, like Nan Patterson, a member of the Floradora Sextette.

The pampered Thaw was the son of a Pittsburgh magnate who had cornered the coke market in a short time and had accumulated a then staggering fortune of $40 million. Harry Thaw was the profligate heir to this fortune. Terribly spoiled by an overindulgent mother, Thaw's education was a shambles, although he was sent to the finest schools, including Harvard, where he ignored his studies and spent most of his time conducting high-stake poker games in his suite of rooms off campus. He was finally dismissed for gambling activities. Thaw's father was so vexed at his son's wastrel ways he reduced his allowance to $2,000 a year. Thaw whined and carped until his mother awarded him an additional $8,000 a year. Still the headstrong Thaw complained that this was only pin money for a man of his esteem and standing.

Taking a lavish suite of rooms in Manhattan, Thaw attempted to buy his way into several prominent men's clubs, but he was barred because of his eccentricities. Incensed, Thaw rented a horse and tried to ride it into these clubs, knocking down doormen and porters. He was arrested and escorted home. His mother paid his fine. A short time later, Thaw participated in a marathon poker game with New York sharpers and lost $40,000. His mother paid the gambling debt.

To vent his wild rages and satiate his sexual perversions, Thaw took another apartment inside one of New York's fanciest bordellos. There he brought young, gullible women, promising them careers on Broadway or, at least, in the chorus lines of important musicals. After Thaw inveigled the women to his brothel apartment, he fiendishly attacked them, raping them and beating them with sticks and whips.

The bordello madam, Susan Merrill, later stated that she heard a woman screaming in Thaw's apartment and when she could bear it no longer, forced her way inside. She later testified: "I rushed into his rooms. He had tied the girl to the bed,

Evelyn Nesbit as a chorus girl, playing the role of a singing peasant; White spotted her in the chorus and began dating her, making her his mistress and lavishing riches upon her while he kept her in luxurious style.

Famous and wealthy, architect Stanford White was noted for designing many New York monuments and mansions; at night he lived the life of a rajah, taking his pick of Broadway beauties, including the ravishing Evelyn Nesbit.

naked, and was whipping her. She was covered with welts. Thaw's eyes protruded and he looked mad."

Merrill ordered Thaw out of the house, and when he refused, she called the police. The millionaire playboy was escorted from the brothel despite his protests that he had paid rent a year in advance. He was barred from the brothel and Madam Merrill was happy to repay him his advance rent. A short time later, Thaw was ejected from one of the finer Fifth Avenue shops.

The sales manager refused to have his models show the latest gowns to a bevy of Broadway tarts Thaw paraded into the emporium. At this point Thaw had what was later described as a "sort of fit. His eyes bulged and rolled, and he screamed like a child having a tantrum." Police escorted the playboy outside and sent him home; the whores were locked up. In retaliation, Thaw rented a car the next day and drove it through the shop's display window, almost running over the gaping manager. Thaw was again arrested and fined.

Mrs. Thaw advised her son to leave Manhattan and take a European vacation. Thaw sailed for Paris where he scandalized a city that was weaned on scandal. He rented an entire floor of the Georges V Hotel and invited the city's leading prostitutes to a party that lasted several days and cost him $50,000. He was finally asked to leave the hotel after he was discovered whipping naked women down the hotel corridors.

Another product of Pittsburgh at that time was a 16-year-old sultry brunette, Evelyn Nesbit. She came from poverty and had little formal education, but she had singing and dancing talent and, after being a photographer's model for a short period of time, soon won a spot in the prestigious Floradora Sextette. While performing in the Floradora chorus, she caught the lecherous eye of Stanford White, the most distinguished architect in New York. White, who was tall and heavyset, weighing some 250 pounds, wore a sweeping handlebar mustache and was always sartorially dressed, glittering with a diamond stickpin, gold watch chain, an expensive jewel-encrusted watch fob, and rings.

White was many times a millionaire, having made a fortune designing the resplendent Fifth Avenue mansions of New York's wealthiest movers and shakers. He was a high society

Evelyn Nesbit wearing her "gorgeous Japanese kimono," posing in this photo for Stanford White in his posh New York studio in 1902, and where, she later told her husband, Thaw, White seduced her in a mirror-covered room.

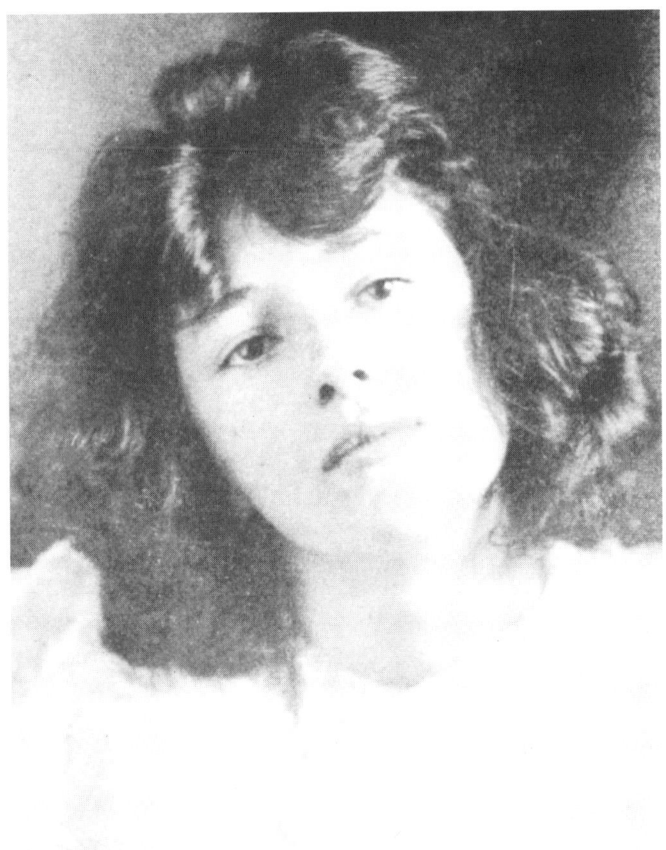

Evelyn Nesbit in 1905, when she met and married millionaire Harry K. Thaw, and became his sadomasochistic slave, forced to relate to her husband real and imagined sexual transgressions by her former lover, Stanford White.

architect, who catered exclusively to the super rich, although he was known widely for having designed the elegant Washington Square Arch and the Hall of Fame at New York University. He had also designed Madison Square Garden, including its restaurant, arcade, fashionable shops, the amphitheater, where prizefights and horse shows were held, and the magnificent roof garden, where resplendent musicals were performed for open-air audiences, who dined while watching the shows.

The tower of Madison Square Garden was reserved by White for himself. There he maintained a lavish home-away-from-home (he was married but seldom saw his wife). This apartment featured a red velvet swing which hung from the ceiling of the tower. According to Evelyn Nesbit's later statements, White was in the habit of bringing his mistresses and one-night stand show girls to the tower where he would swing them high so that he could lasciviously look beneath their billowing skirts. (The portrait of White as a lewd and lustful old man was painted by Nesbit at her husband's trial, certainly a colored, prejudiced view which was designed to vindicate Thaw's murderous actions, although White's skirt-chasing habits were certainly well known long before he ever met Nesbit.)

For three years, Nesbit carried on a relationship with White. He lavished gowns and jewels on her, paid for her stylish apartment and chauffeured limousine, and took endless photos of her in seductive poses. When he tired of her, he sent her away to a finishing school.

Harry Thaw had also seen Evelyn Nesbit on the stage briefly and knew that she was White's pampered mistress. While she was in boarding school, he contrived to meet her and then pursued her slavishly until she accepted his marriage proposal. Thaw, however, after the nuptials on April 4, 1905, was more concerned with White than he was with his own wife, persecuting Nesbit for her former relationship with the architect. He insisted that she refer to White as "The Beast" or "The Bastard." When she refused, he told her that she must, at least employ the letter "B" whenever she mentioned White. This Nesbit did.

Thaw took his 19-year-old bride to Europe, but it turned out to be a nightmarish honeymoon. Aboard the luxury liner carrying the couple to France, Nesbit later claimed, Thaw tied her to a bed and whipped and beat her until her body was coated with red welts. She finally told her unhinged husband what he wanted to hear or all she could imagine that was vile and rotten about Stanford White.

Nesbit told Thaw that White had tricked her into going to the Madison Square Tower apartment on the promise of marriage, but once there, he stripped and raped her, and then forced her to mount the red velvet swing naked while he took obscene photos of her. This story, following the perverted design of both Thaw and his wife, drove Thaw into blind rages and he forced his wife to repeat this story often so that he could work himself into a frenzy about White, vowing terrible revenge against "The Beast."

The popular rooftop open-air theater of the Madison Square Garden, which White had designed and where, in front of hundreds of horrified spectators, Harry Thaw shot and killed Stanford White on June 25, 1906; while panicking spectators raced for elevators and stairways, Thaw held the murder weapon above his head to indicate that he did not intend to murder anyone else that sultry night.

On the warm night of June 25, 1906, Harry Thaw took his berserk revenge on Stanford White. Harry and Evelyn Thaw were dining in Rector's with two of Thaw's friends, when White and a party of people left one of the private dining areas. Thaw stiffened as Evelyn passed him a handwritten note which read "The B. is here." She had followed his instructions of informing Thaw any time she saw White in public. Thaw crumpled the note and pocketed it, then patted his wife's hand and said: "Yes dear, I know he's here. I saw him. Thank you for telling me."

A few hours later White was sitting at the best table on the Madison Square Garden rooftop to witness a new, frothy musical, "Mamzelle Champagne." White was interested in one of the chorus girls and had arranged for an introduction to the girl through the stage manager following the performance. Harry and Evelyn Thaw, and two of their friends also arrived at the Madison Square Garden rooftop.

When Evelyn saw White sitting alone and watching the show, she asked Thaw to take her home, particularly after noticing her husband's agitated state. She told Thaw that the show bored her and he got up and began to escort her and their friends to the elevator. Suddenly, he was gone. Minutes later he stood glaring down at Stanford White. The architect looked up at Thaw, whom he knew and disliked. "Yes, Thaw, what is it?" White reportedly asked the staring young man. Without a word, Thaw reached into his pocket and withdrew a revolver, pointing it only a few feet from White's head. He fired one shot and then two more. White, his face a mass of blood, collapsed on the table, then fell sideways, taking the table with him. He sprawled dead on the floor with a bullet in his head and two more in his shoulder.

A terrible silence engulfed the crowd. The show stopped, performers frozen on the stage. The band did not play a note. Hundreds of customers present gaped at the bizarre scene of Thaw standing over the fallen White and then piercing screams came from some women and everyone made a mad dash for the exits, knocking over tables and chairs in a panic to escape what they thought was a madman on the loose. Thaw, to signal no further murderous intent, raised the revolver over his head and emptied the remaining three live cartridges from the weapon, which fell to the floor. He said something that was later interpreted to mean: "I did it because this man ruined my wife!" Some claimed that Thaw said: "This man ruined my life."

Within seconds, Thaw, still holding the weapon above his head, made his way to the elevator, where his wife and his friends waited in shock. "My God, Harry," Evelyn said. "What have you done?"

The roof garden was by then in pandemonium with women screaming and men shouting for police officers. The manager leaped upon a table and shouted to the band: "Go on playing!" To the stage manager he cried: "Bring on the chorus!" At this

Millionaire murderer Harry K. Thaw in his cell in the Tombs, dining on a catered meal from Delmonico's; his meals were brought to him from the finest restaurants throughout his imprisonment during his trial.

Thaw is shown with his protective and over-indulgent mother, Mrs. William Thaw, who vowed that she was "prepared to spend $1 million to save my son's life"; she spent twice that amount, even, reportedly, bribing jurors.

moment, a doctor was leaning over White and saw part of White's face blown away, his entire head was blackened by powder burns from bullets fired at close range. The physician pronounced White dead.

In the elevator lobby, Thaw, still clutching the weapon, was confronted by an off-duty fireman who said: "You'd better let me have that gun." Thaw meekly turned it over. A policeman then arrived and Thaw submitted to arrest. He was marched to the Center Street Station, where he said his name was John Smith, adding that he was a student living at 18 Lafayette Place, New York City. He was searched and his own identification papers quickly revealed his true identity.

"Why did you do this?" a sergeant asked Thaw.

Thaw stared blankly at the policeman for some moments, then replied: "I can't say." He refused to make any more statements until his lawyer arrived. Thaw was charged with murder and placed in a cell in the New York Tombs to await trial. Fifteen months passed before Thaw was brought into court, a stalling tactic designed by Thaw's brilliant defense attorney, California criminal lawyer, Delphin Delmas, who had defended hundreds of clients in murder trials and claimed never to have lost a case.

Delmas was called "the little Napoleon of the West Coast bar." Hired for an estimated $100,000 by Thaw's mother (the figure was never substantiated and it may have been twice that amount), Delmas told the elderly Mrs. Thaw that because her son chose to execute his victim in public, the best they could hope for would be to keep him out of the electric chair. To that end, Delmas mounted a crusade to blacken the name of the victim, a shameless and brazen technique to win Thaw any kind of sympathy.

Press agent Ben Atwell was hired by Mrs. Thaw to destroy the image of Stanford White and stories soon began to appear in New York newspapers, which detailed White's profligate ways. One story dealt with 15-year-old model, Susan Johnson, who had been inveigled to White's Madison Square Tower apartment, which the *Evening Journal* described as being "furnished in Oriental splendor." The tale was told how Susan Johnson was plied with liquor, seduced, and soon afterward abandoned by the heartless White to make her way penniless through life. The vilification campaign against White went on day after day, month after month, until, it seemed that Stanford White had seduced half the female population in New York City.

Mrs. Thaw made no excuses for unleashing the dogs of slander and libel against the dead Stanford White. "I am prepared to spend $1 million to save my son's life," she had announced. The publicity campaign and legal fees for her son's

This photo of a sultry Evelyn Nesbit Thaw was released at the time of her husband's trial, ostensibly by the defense, to show that she had driven her husband to commit murder.

Evelyn Thaw is shown whispering her testimony during her husband's murder trial to District Attorney William Travers Jerome, her testimony too shocking for an open court.

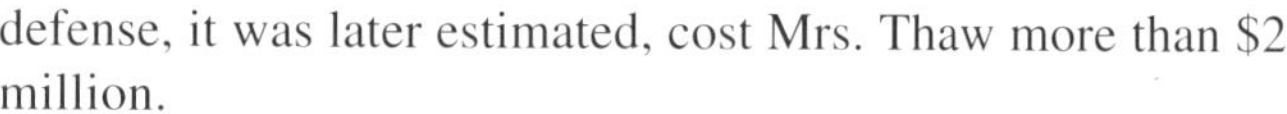

defense, it was later estimated, cost Mrs. Thaw more than $2 million.

Thaw himself was not spared negative publicity. His sordid exploits with prostitutes and his wife were leaked to the press by the prosecution, which was headed by the famous William Travers Jerome, New York's district attorney. Said Jerome before the trial: "With all his millions, Thaw is a fiend! No matter how rich a man is, he cannot get away with murder, not in New York!" Jerome's aides unearthed a lawsuit filed against Thaw in 1902 that had been brought by Ethel Thomas. Her story was almost identical to the one later told by Evelyn Nesbit. After meeting Thaw, Thomas had been swept off her feet by Thaw who oozed affection and respect. He had given her flowers, jewels, and clothes.

"One day," Thomas stated in her deposition, "I met him by appointment and we were walking toward his apartment at the Bedford, and he stopped at a store and bought a dog whip. I asked him what that was for and he replied laughingly: 'That's for you, dear.' I thought he was joking, but no sooner were we in his apartment and the door locked than his entire demeanor changed. A wild expression came into his eyes and he seized me and with his whip beat me until my clothes hung in tatters."

The most bizarre ploys were used by the defense to create hatred for White and glean sympathy for the "befuddled" Thaw. One story related how a medium had conducted a seance on July 5, 1906, and that a "spirit from beyond appeared to insist that he, a long-departed soul named Johnson, had guided Harry Thaw's hand" and the spirit was the true killer of Stanford White, not Thaw!

Famed Los Angeles criminal defense attorney Delphin M. Delmas, called the "Napoleon of the West," was hired for a fortune by Mrs. William Thaw to save her son's life.

Finally, on January 21, 1907, Thaw was brought to trial. Thaw himself took the stand to appear penitent and remorseful, saying: "I never wanted to shoot that man. I never wanted to kill him ... Providence took charge of the situation." Apparently Thaw had read the account of the seance and was now pinning the blame on the spirits. Delmas and his battery of lawyers insisted Thaw was not in his right mind when he killed White, that he suffered from "dementia Americana," a neurosis coined by Thaw's attorneys who explained that such a mental malady was singularly American, one wherein American males believed that every man's wife was sacred and if she were violated, he would become unbalanced, striking out in a murderous rage.

District Attorney Jerome fought back against this psychological gobbledygook, cross-examining Evelyn Nesbit

Harry Thaw, right, in 1908, after a jury found him not guilty by reason of insanity; he was sent to the New York State Asylum for the Criminally Insane at Matteawan.

Evelyn Nesbit with second husband, dancer Jack Clifford in 1915; she attempted to revive her theatrical career, but her star had faded and she was later reduced to sideshow attractions.

with dogmatic persistence. He asked about the character of her husband and her replies were so explicit that she insisted on whispering her answers to him. Her responses were later whispered for the court reporter recording the trial transcript and then her sordid stories were shown in printed form to the jury members. By then, however, the jury believed that Stanford White was a beast in human form and deserved to die, that he had ruined the lives of dozens of young women and that Thaw, who was unhinged at the time of the shooting, was merely doing what any noble-minded American male would do, taking vengeance for wronged women all over the U.S.

By April 11, 1907, the jury was deadlocked. Its members could not agree, seven holding for conviction, five others insisting on a not guilty vote. Thaw was tried again, and, on February 1, 1908, he was found not guilty "by reason of insanity." This was the verdict Delmas had sought. His client would not face the electric chair. Thaw was sent to the New York State Asylum for the Criminally Insane at Matteawan, New York, ordered to remain there for life.

When Mrs. Thaw's millions could not move the courts to release her son, she reportedly financed Thaw's escape on August 17, 1913. Thaw was escorted through unlocked doors to freedom, where a limousine was waiting for him. He was driven to Canada and a luxury apartment. The U.S. State Department brought heavy pressure against Canadian officials to have Thaw returned to the U.S. and he was finally turned over, but he was placed in a Concord, New Hampshire, jail where, as had been the case in the New York Tombs while he awaited his trials, Thaw dined on catered meals and was offered every convenience and comfort. His lawyers battled extradition to New York until December 1914 when they secured another trial for the murderer.

Harry Thaw, shown upon his release from an asylum for the criminally insane, sailing for Europe on the *Aquatania*; he had escaped in 1913 from Matteawan, and was shielded by his mother until he was recaptured.

Thaw and Nesbit are shown at a brief re-union in 1925, but their conversation was strained; Thaw died in 1947 and Nesbit, after struggling with alcohol and drugs and performing small parts in B-movies, died in a Hollywood nursing home in 1967.

Farley Granger, playing Thaw, holds a revolver high above his head after shooting Stanford White (played by Ray Milland, slumped at table) at Madison Square Garden in the 1955 film, *The Girl in the Red Velvet Swing*.

In the third trial, the same evidence and testimony was examined, but the jury, on July 16, 1915, returned a verdict of not guilty and also stated that Thaw was no longer insane and urged his release. He was set free. In 1916, Thaw was back in the news, accused of kidnapping, beating, and sexually molesting 19-year-old Frederick B. Gump. He was arrested, jailed, and went through another trial, where he was declared insane. Another hearing was held and Thaw was declared sane and the charges were dropped. It was reported that Thaw's mother had bestowed more than $500,000 on the Gump family to convince them to drop the charges. Thaw then resumed his eccentric lifestyle, buying his way through life. He died in February 1947 of a heart attack, a wizened, shrunken creature of seventy-six.

Evelyn Nesbit Thaw had her moment of glory and infamy during the Thaw trial and for some years afterward. She was abandoned by the Thaw family, who reportedly bought her off. She later appeared as a vaudeville attraction, billed as "the girl in the red velvet swing." In 1915, though she had long been divorced by the irresponsible Thaw, Nesbit insisted that her newly born son was Thaw's child, that she had bribed guards at Matteawan to allow her into Thaw's rooms for a night of bliss. Thaw angrily denied this and his parentage. His lawyers reportedly paid her off and she, like Nan Patterson before her, faded from the limelight.

THE MURDERING FORTUNE-HUNTER/1909

Dr. Bennett Clarke Hyde (b.1869) was an opportunistic physician who reportedly tried to wipe out an entire family through systematic poisoning. At age forty, the tall, good-looking Hyde was married to the niece of Thomas Swope, the richest man in Kansas City, Missouri. Hyde was the medical adviser to the Swope family and lived in Swope's huge mansion. Swope, in 1909, was eighty-two and in ill health. He appointed James Hunton, an old family friend, as executor of his will and estate.

Hyde realized that to control the Swope millions, he would have to position himself in Hunton's role. When Hunton fell ill in September 1909, Hyde treated him, or, more specifically, mistreated him by using an ancient cure-all advocated by doctors. He bled Hunton to "purify" his blood. In truth, Hyde simply bled the old man to death and then attributed the cause of his death to apoplexy, signing Hunton's death certificate himself.

Swope was so overwhelmed by the death of his good friend that he himself grew ill and Dr. Hyde tended to him. A nurse attending to Swope later reported that Dr. Hyde took her aside one day and said to her: "Now that Hunton is dead, Mr. Swope will require a new administrator for his estate. I think it would be a good idea if you suggested to Mr. Swope that I take over those duties." The nurse refused, telling Hyde that it was not her place to make such suggestions. Hyde then went into Swope's bedroom and gave him a number of pills. In a few minutes, Swope's pallor turned a marked blue and his skin was cold to the touch, according to the nurse.

"I wish I hadn't taken those pills!" Swope cried out to the nurse.

Hyde told the nurse to leave the millionaire's room, ordering her to boil some water. When she returned with the water about ten minutes later, she saw Hyde covering Swope's face with a bed sheet. "He's gone, poor soul," the doctor told her.

"What? Already?" The nurse checked Swope's pulse. There was none. He was dead and the nurse found it hard to believe that the patient could have died in such a short amount of time, especially from the symptoms he had manifested.

"At that age, they can go quickly," Dr. Hyde told her. He then added that the cause of death was apoplexy, the same malady that had also ended Hunton's life. Swope's millions were then distributed to several nephews and nieces. Mrs. Frances Hyde received more than $250,000, of which her husband immediately took control. Though that was a great fortune for the day, Dr. Hyde meant to obtain the rest of the Swope millions.

Four of the five nephews and nieces were quickly stricken by what their doctor diagnosed as attacks of typhoid. Christian Swope, one of the nephews, died in November 1909, while being tended by Hyde in the old Swope mansion, but the others recovered. Hyde reported the death as a result of typhoid. The family nurse, who had held deep suspicions about Dr. Hyde, went to Frances Hyde and told her: "People are being murdered in this house."

Instead of becoming alarmed, the devoted spouse angrily fired the nurse and then reported the nurse's statements to the

Dr. Bennett Clarke Hyde, who thought to systematically kill all the wealthy Swope family members of Kansas City, Missouri, to gain a huge inheritance; he was charged with murder in 1910.

Frances Swope Hyde was the only member of the Swope family who believed in her husband's innocence and remained at his side through four long trials.

family lawyer, which brought suspicion upon Hyde himself. The lawyer cautioned Mrs. Hyde to employ another doctor to tend to the still-living nieces and nephews. Another doctor was brought in and he consulted with a bacteriologist, who reported that there were no typhoid germs in the family's water supply system. Hyde no longer tended to the sick Swope relatives and they quickly recovered.

While under suspicion, Hyde began taking long walks at night and was followed on one of these nocturnal sojourns. He was seen taking something from his pocket, which he crushed into a mound of snow. The object, a capsule, was retrieved by the person following the doctor; it proved to contain grains of potassium cyanide, a deadly poison. Family members went to the police and a full-scale investigation ensued. The bodies of Hunton and Swope were exhumed and were found to contain strychnine and cyanide. Hyde had cleverly poisoned both men with the two poisons, knowing that each poison would disguise the symptoms of the other.

The physician was charged with murdering Swope and Hunton on February 9, 1910. The resulting trial made headlines coast to coast. Shocked readers learned how Hyde intended to murder off the entire Swope family to gain the family millions. Only Frances Hyde believed her husband innocent and she put up the money to cover the $100,000 bond to free her husband until the conclusion of his trial.

During the trial, a pharmacist testified that Hyde had purchased both strychnine and cyanide from him. At the time, said the pharmacist, Hyde said he needed these deadly poisons to get rid of wild dogs that had been "howling near my house and causing me no end of sleepless nights." Then Dr. L. Stewart, a bacteriologist, testified that Hyde had come to him, stating that he intended to take up the study of bacteriology and, for that purpose, he needed typhoid germs.

Stewart gave these cultures to Hyde but, a short time later, he grew nervous about releasing such dangerous germs to Hyde and went to Hyde's home, asking that the cultures be returned. Hyde told him that, unfortunately, he had dropped the glass slides containing these cultures and that he had thrown them out for fear of contamination. This was only a few days before Christian Swope died of typhoid.

Such damning testimony brought a verdict of guilty after a month-long trial. Dr. Hyde was given a life term but, before leaving for prison, the physician turned to reporters and used his greatest weapon, his wife, who was convinced of his innocence. "This case is not closed," Hyde told members of the press with a smug smile. "My wife Frances will not forsake me. She knows that this is a plot by certain members of the Swope family to get rid of me. They have hated me from the start, thought of me as an interloper. Yes, Frances will know what to do."

Frances Swope Hyde remained loyal to her murderous husband, as he knew she would. She hired the most expensive and talented lawyers available and they bombarded the courts with every known appeal. Mrs. Hyde went so far as to hire a publicist, who spread the news that the Swope family had formed a conspiracy to defame her husband. By that time, Mrs. Hyde had denounced her entire family and had vowed her undying loyalty to her imprisoned husband.

Mrs. Hyde's lawyers found some technical errors in her husband's trial and convinced the Supreme Court of Kansas to order a new trial in 1911. At the end of this trial, one juror grew ill and the proceedings were declared a mistrial. This juror's ailments were never disclosed and it was claimed that he was bribed to feign sickness. A third trial ended in a hung jury. It was again claimed that Mrs. Hyde's money was used to bribe several members of this jury to bring about a hung jury.

Hyde was sent to trial a fourth time in 1917, and this trial, like the two before it, had been the systematic plan of Hyde's clever lawyers. As soon as this trial commenced they moved to have their client released, pointing out a rule of law that stated that their client had gone to trial three times and, according to existing laws, could not be tried a fourth time.

Dr. Bennett Clarke Hyde was released and went to live with his wife. He no longer practiced medicine. Almost a decade later, Mrs. Hyde separated from her husband. She had complained to him one day of a stomach ache and he told her that he would prepare a special medicine for her. At that juncture, Mrs. Hyde thought it was time she left her husband, preferring the treatment of another doctor and, apparently, the preservation of her own life.

THE MURDER OF A CHAMPION/ October 15, 1910

Acting out of jealousy over a woman's affections, Walter Kurtz shot and killed possibly the greatest middleweight boxer in history. Stanley Ketchel, born Stanislaus Kaicel on Sept. 14, 1886, in Grand Rapids, Michigan, earned the nickname of the "Michigan Assassin" early in his career. After running away from home at the age of sixteen, Ketchel worked his way west doing menial labor on the railroad and in mining camps. Before he could accomplish his dream of becoming a cowboy, he discovered a talent for fighting. Ketchel's temper frequently got him into fights which he invariably won.

In Butte, Mont., in 1903, Ketchel got his big chance. The Big Casino saloon management offered a $50 purse to anyone who could defeat the local champion, Kid Tracey. Tracey's reputation was such that Ketchel was the only opponent. Although Tracey and everyone else discounted the slightly built, teenaged opponent, Ketchel knocked Tracey out in the first round.

After this first formal victory, Ketchel traveled throughout Montana racking up victory after victory. He had a particularly vicious style in the ring, which he achieved by imagining that his opponent had insulted his mother, for whom Ketchel bore a deep affection. His "maniacal" style, however, gained him fifty-nine wins in sixty-three fights in his professional career, forty-nine by knockouts. He won the middleweight championship in 1908, by beating Jack Sullivan. He lost this crown in the same year to Billy Papke on a foul, but reclaimed the title in the same year by beating Papke to a pulp.

Within a year, Ketchel fought what many thought was the greatest fight of his career, one arranged by his manager, Wilson Mizner. The only prizefighter of note that Ketchel had not yet fought and beaten was heavyweight champion

Tenacious prizefighter Stanley Ketchel became middleweight champion in 1908.

Jack Johnson. Ketchel agreed to fight Johnson even though Johnson outweighed Ketchel by forty pounds. Johnson scoffed at the smaller man and refused to train for the fight, expecting to win easily.

To his surprise, the fight went into the twelfth round before Ketchel finally succumbed to one of Johnson's powerful punches. During that fierce battle, Ketchel's savage onslaught all but devastated the black champion. At one point, Ketchel landed a right cross that rocked Johnson and sent him crashing to the canvas. (Johnson later stated that Ketchel's punch was the hardest he ever received.) He barely managed to evade a ten-count. Johnson stood up and furiously attacked Ketchel, almost cartwheeling (as motion pictures of this classic fight show) across the ring to land his own knockout blow on Ketchel's chin.

Although Ketchel went on to win a few more fights, the Johnson fight had ruined his health. In the fall of 1910, he traveled to Conway, Missouri, to stay at a ranch owned by R. P. Dickerson, a close friend. Once there, Ketchel became involved with Goldie Smith, the buxom, blonde ranch cook. Smith was also involved with one of the ranch hands, Walter Kurtz, actually a Navy deserter whose real name was Walter Dipley. Smith told Ketchel that Kurtz had been her lover before Ketchel had arrived at the ranch and that she was worried he might become violent over their affair.

"I'm not worrying about that stiff," Ketchel said.

Kurtz, however, planned lethal revenge and, on the morning of October 15, 1910, entered the ranch's dining room, where Ketchel was having his breakfast. He pointed a rifle at the champion and shouted: "Throw up your hands!"

Ketchel glared at the ranch hand and then waved him off, saying: "Beat it, you bum!"

"You may be a prizefighter," replied Kurtz, "but you can't come down here and insult my woman without paying for it!"

Ketchel started to rise from his chair when Kurtz fired a single shot from the rifle, the bullet striking the fighter in the back, mortally wounding him. Ketchel fell to the floor and Kurtz went to him, rifling the victim's pockets and taking $2,000 in cash he knew Ketchel always carried. He slipped Ketchel's diamond ring from his finger and then fled. Ketchel was taken to a hospital in Springfield, Missouri, where he died that night.

Kurtz, who had fled on foot to a nearby farmhouse, was captured by a farmer who held a shotgun on him until police arrived. He mounted a weak defense at his trial, saying to a jury: "Well, I told Ketchel to throw up his hands and I had to shoot him when he did not obey." He was convicted and sentenced to prison for life, but was paroled in 1934.

The death of Stanley Ketchel was widely mourned; many thought him to be the greatest fighter who ever entered a boxing ring. His body was taken home to his mother and buried in the family plot outside of Grand Rapids, Michigan. His manager and friend, Wilson Mizner, learned of Ketchel's murder with shock and disbelief. Mizner wept, then said: "That darling kid can't be dead. Start counting over him—he'll get up!"

Ketchel, left, is shown meeting heavyweight champion Jack Johnson, center, before a classic fight in Coloma, California on October 16, 1909; Ketchel was murdered by a jealous ranch hand the following year.

"HERE YOU GO! HERE I GO!"/ JANUARY 23, 1911

Fitzhugh Coyle Goldsborough (1880-1911) was born into a wealthy Philadelphia family and had two interests in life: reading popular sentimental novels and doting on his socially ambitious sister. If Goldsborough ever heard his father chastise his sister for some slight offense, Fitzhugh would rush to her defense, threatening his father with physical harm if he so much as laid a hand on the girl. His father and mother excused these outbursts, believing their high-strung son was simply overprotective of his sister and they interpreted his pathological obsession with his sister's welfare as deep affection. But there was a strain of madness in their volatile son.

In 1911, a novel by David Graham Phillips, *The Fashionable Adventures of Joshua Craig*, captured Goldsborough's overactive imagination. The story concerned a selfish, egocentric young woman of the leisure class, a character with whom Goldsborough and his sister both believed to be the sister, though they had no reason to believe that Phillips knew her.

Phillips was a rising star in the New York literary world. Born in Indiana, he had attended Princeton before becoming a reporter for the New York *World*. Phillips once said that, given the choice, he would "rather be a reporter than president." He attained success with such best-sellers as *The Great God Success*, and had, at age forty-three, just finished another book, *Susan Lenox: Her Fall and Rise* (published posthumously in 1917 and thought by critics to be a minor masterpiece, which was brought to the screen in a fine 1931 film starring Greta Garbo and Clark Gable) when he encountered Goldsborough in New York's Gramercy Park on January 23, 1911.

Before that fatal moment, Goldsborough had concluded from the Phillips' novel he had been reading that the writer had purposely wronged his sister. He never bothered to learn whether or not Phillips even knew the girl (he had never met her) before he set out to murder the novelist.

Phillips had stepped out of his Gramercy Park apartment to mail a new short story to the *Saturday Evening Post* when Goldsborough approached him. The withered, poorly-dressed young Goldsborough could have been mistaken for a tramp, and Phillips reached into his pocket for a few pennies to give to Goldsborough.

Goldsborough took a few steps backward, refusing the handout and startling the writer, who noticed a wild look in his blinking eyes. The young man suddenly produced a pistol and shouted: "Here you go!" He moved his arm in an arc, describing a purposefully-made circle in the air, firing a pattern of shots designed to hit the victim in several fatal areas of his body, striking Phillips from the chest to the knees.

Seconds later, without looking at Phillips, who had fallen

Fitzhugh Coyle Goldsborough, the pampered, unbalanced son of a wealthy Philadelphia family, who murdered a man he never knew in 1911 over an insult that he imagined.

Novelist David Graham Phillips, who was fatally shot by Goldsborough in New York's Gramercy Park over an imagined insult he had written in one of his books.

Opposite page left: Greta Garbo and Clark Gable in the 1932 film, *Susan Lenox—Her Fall and Rise*, based upon the Phillips' novel, which was published six years after he was murdered by Goldsborough.

to the ground and was writhing in pain, Goldsborough turned the gun on himself. To startled passersby, he shouted: "Here I go!" and placed the pistol to his temple, firing a single shot that blew away part of his head.

Phillips was carried to the Princeton Club, where he lay on a sofa only a few feet from where Stanford White's coffin had been placed in an elaborate funeral following White's murder by another social elitist and madman, Harry Thaw. Removed to Bellevue Hospital, doctors at first believed that Phillips would survive his wounds. He could not explain the reason why Goldsborough had shot him, but told police from his sickbed that on the morning of the shooting he had received a strange telegram signed with his own name, one that made no sense to him, but he presumed that it had been sent by the deranged Goldsborough.

Police later learned the real motive for the murder when Goldsborough's parents came forward to explain their son's peculiar obsession with *The Fashionable Adventures of Joshua Craig*. By then it mattered little, since Phillips was dead, having taken a turn for the worse the day after the shooting. Before he died, the promising and robust author told physicians: "I can fight two wounds, but not six."

THE DENTIST AND THE PECK MILLIONS/ 1916

Like the methodical Dr. Bennett Clarke Hyde before him, Dr. Warren Waite, a practicing dentist, was a patient slayer in eliminating his in-laws in order to obtain their fortune. Born in Grand Rapids, Michigan to struggling farmers, Waite looked covetously upon the richest family in town as his exclusive prey. He dated Clara Louisa Peck through high school and continued his relationship while he was a student at the University of Michigan, where he studied dental surgery. After going to Europe to continue his studies, Waite maintained a prolonged and passionate correspondence with Clara Peck, whose father was John E. Peck, a lumber king and worth millions.

The local papers in Michigan, as was the editorial custom of small-town papers, dutifully reported Waite's progress, noting that he had graduated from the University of Glasgow with honors and had gone on to practice his dentistry on the mouths of the mighty, until he was appointed the chief dentist to the most powerful mining corporation in South Africa. Clara Peck had remained faithful throughout the travels and travails of the wandering dentist and was overjoyed at the news that he would soon be returning home to Grand Rapids.

Waite appeared in town on Christmas Day, 1914. He promptly resumed his love affair with Clara Peck, despite the objections of her wealthy father, who thought the prospective

Michigan heiress Clara Louisa Peck, who married the handsome Arthur Warren Waite in 1915, little knowing that her husband intended to murder her parents in order to gain their fortune.

Tall and charming, Dr. Arthur Warren Waite had schemed to marry Clara Peck before embarking on his insidious plan of murder, creating a fake past as a successful dentist in Europe.

Mrs. John E. Peck, Waite's mother-in-law, visited her daughter and son-in-law; Waite administered lethal bacterial doses to the elderly woman, while he sang her favorite tunes at her deathbed.

Lumber tycoon John E. Peck, who also visited his daughter and solicitous son-in-law, and met the same fate as his wife on March 12, 1916, also dosed to death with deadly bacteria.

son-in-law too ambitious. Nevertheless, the couple married on September 9, 1915. Peck gave the newlyweds a lavishly appointed, rent-free apartment on Manhattan's Riverside Drive and an allowance of three hundred dollars a month. Waite appeared to set up his dental practice, but he spent most of his time playing tennis and having little time for his wife. Clara Peck Waite was more than patient. When her parents objected to Waite's time-wasting, Clara sprang to her husband's defense, writing to her father: "But he has his profession and his tennis. He's Metropolitan Amateur champion. Isn't that wonderful?"

The enterprising Waite, however, was not playing that much tennis. He spent most of his time carrying on a torrid affair with Margaret Weaver Horton, the wife of Henry Mack Horton, a distinguished aeronautical engineer. To keep the beauteous, raven-haired Mrs. Horton in style (their trysting was elitist, confined to the uppercrust Plaza Hotel), Waite needed money, much more than his in-laws had bestowed upon him. He had carped about money even on his wedding night, shouting at Clara that the apartment and monthly allowance amounted to a pittance. "I expected fifty thousand dollars outright!" he had roared.

There were other ways than working to obtain the necessary funds to finance his affair with Mrs. Horton, the dentist reasoned. He would murder the Pecks and the inheritance of their fortune would fall to his wife and subsequently come under his control. (In this regard, Waite almost duplicated the modus operandi of Dr. Bennett Clarke Hyde. In fact their cases are so similar as to suggest that Waite had studied the Hyde case in detail and decided to employ Hyde's murder methods, but avoiding the pitfalls that ensnared that 1909 killer.)

Waite suddenly missed the company of his in-laws, and invited Mrs. Peck to visit him and her daughter in New York, staying in their apartment. She arrived on January 10, 1916. Ten days later she was dead. Her sudden death shocked the family, but it was fondly remembered how Waite had shown his mother-in-law every kindness during her brief and fatal illness. He had brought the sick woman flowers every day, and provided footwarmers. He played her favorite tunes on a record machine and crooned to her in his fine tenor voice. His consideration extended to detailed funeral preparations, which included a prompt cremation, in order, Waite compassionately explained, to avoid a drawn-out funeral that might vex grieving family members.

John Peck was appreciative of his son-in-law's kind treatment of his ailing wife and began to tell his associates how considerate his son-in-law had become. So impressed with Waite was the lumber tycoon that he agreed to stay in New York with his daughter and her husband. In less than a month, on March 12, 1916, he, too, was dead. Again, Waite urged cremation, but this time Clara and her brother, Percy Peck, objected, saying that their father's body had to be shipped back to Grand Rapids, where he would be given a funeral befitting one of the state's leaders of industry. The Waites accompanied the body to Michigan, but Waite was too busy to remain long, returning to New York to attend to his burgeoning dental business, which really amounted to no more than a few disgruntled patients.

In Waite's absence, Percy Peck received a telegram from someone named "K. Adams," which read: "Suspicions aroused. Demand autopsy. Examine body." Peck was already suspicious and had for some time believed his brother-in-law was less than an honorable man. He had his father's body examined, doctors discovering that the old man's intestines were loaded with arsenic and chloroform had been found in the dead man's brain tissue. Percy Peck tried in vain to convince his sister that her husband was a plotting murderer whose only aim was to acquire the Peck fortune through eliminating its family members.

"I won't think of it," Mrs. Waite stated emphatically.

"Clara," her brother said, "don't you honestly think Warren killed Mama and Papa?"

"Nonsense," replied Clara. "He wouldn't have poisoned them. He loved them too much."

At this family gathering, Clara's maiden aunt, Mrs. Catherine Peck, rushed to Waite's defense, pointing out that her wonderful nephew-in-law "neither drinks or swears. I like him so well I gave him a three thousand dollar wedding present." She added that she also gave Waite thirty thousand dollars to invest in the stock market. Clara Peck Waite, however, was in for a shock when learning that New York police

Mrs. Elizabeth Hardwicke (left, shown with Clara Peck), a distant Peck relative, sent a telegram under the alias of "K. Adams," urging authorities to examine John Peck's body.

New York police experts are shown examining Waite's test tubes and microscopic slides in the dentist's apartment; they found the deadly typhoid and anthrax germs Waite had used to murder his in-laws.

Embalmer Eugene Oliver Kane (his bowler hat tilted to hide his face from news photographers) is shown with his wife after being arrested for putting arsenic into the veins of John Peck, in order to disguise Waite's lethal germ doses.

examiners had discovered an atomizer used by Dr. Waite, one that was filled with typhoid and anthrax germs. Mrs. Elizbeth Hardwicke, a distant Peck relative, then told NYPD detectives that she had seen Waite on several times in the company of the attractive Mrs. Horton. Mrs. Hardwicke had come to believe that Waite intended to murder the entire Peck family in order to gain the Peck fortune so that he could then live in luxury with the beguiling Mrs. Horton. It was Mrs. Hardwicke who had sent the mysterious telegram to Percy Peck. She also detailed her murder theory to the police, who embraced her story and arrested Waite for murder.

Waite laughed uproariously when handcuffed and taken to a police lockup, saying to detectives: "Why, the thing is too absurdly amusing to even discuss it."

It was not amusing to investigators, who then learned that Waite had tried to use his germ-laden atomizer on Clara Peck. She had refused to inhale the atomizer several times at Waite's urging after she contracted a slight cold. Before that time, Waite had convinced her to revise her will, one in which she left her entire estate of a half million dollars "to my beloved Warren." Investigators learning of this quickly concluded that although she never made any statements to the effect, Mrs. Waite had grown suspicious of her overly solicitous husband.

Detectives then detained Oliver Eugene Kane, the timid and frightened embalmer, who had prepared John Peck's body. He broke down immediately, blurting: "Waite told me that the D. A. was going to ask me for a specimen of my embalming fluid. He asked me if I could put some arsenic in it. I said I couldn't because it's against the law to put arsenic in embalming fluid." The quivering and quaking little embalmer then told detectives that Waite had thrust nine thousand dollars into his hand. "I-I—kept the money," Kane said. "I was so scared I buried it out in the sand at Orient Point on the tip of Long Island. But I didn't put any arsenic in the fluid."

Confronted with Kane's statements, Waite confessed, but not before swallowing a handful of sleeping pills in a frantic suicide attempt. A detective stuck his fingers down the dentist's throat, causing him to vomit, then go into a dead faint. When revived, Warren Waite took another tack, claiming insanity. He screamed: "A bad man from Egypt dwells in my body! He makes me do bad things! He struggles for possession of my soul!"

Waite then abandoned this position and gave the police a long and coherent confession. His life had been nothing more than a sham, he said. He had graduated from the University of Michigan by using another student's work. He had forged his postgraduate certificate at Glasgow and had secretly written and mailed reports of his sterling career in Europe, which the local papers printed without challenge. He had done all of this, he said, as part of an elaborate plan to obtain the Peck fortune, one which he coveted since his impoverished boyhood. That plan, Waite admitted, involved the murder of each and every Peck relative.

While working at New York's Flower Hospital, Waite explained, he stole drugs, and collected deadly bacterial slides. He droned in chilling detail: "In November 1915, to test my knowledge and to test the effect of germs, I inoculated myself with cultures of anthrax, typhoid, and pneumonia. By the time

Dr. Arthur Warren Waite (center) is shown under arrest, charged with the murders of his in-laws.

Defiant and smug, Waite, center, stands outside the courtroom where he had been convicted and sentenced to death; he went to the electric chair on May 1, 1917.

Mrs. Peck arrived in January 1916, I was ready for her." He went on to say that he sprayed Mrs. Peck's food with anthrax and typhus germs, and, when she fell ill, pretended to administer curative drugs by spraying her throat with deadly germs—typhoid, influenza, anthrax, diphtheria, and tuberculosis, plus giving her powdered sleeping tablets each night. "It took just ten days," the killer gloated.

The same routine was practiced on John Peck, but he proved too tough. To hurry the old man's demise, Waite put damp sheets on Peck's bed and let him lie in drafts. He burned flypaper and left open containers of chlorine gas in Peck's bedroom. Still, the tycoon did not die. "Finally, I resorted to arsenic," Waite said. "Even that didn't kill the old fellow. On the last night, I tied a rag soaked with chloroform over my father-in-law's face and I held it in place with a pillow until he was dead."

Waite was not finished, adding as if an afterthought: "Oh, yes, Aunt Catherine. I tried to kill her, too." He grinned at the grim-faced detectives—in fact he had been grinning throughout his entire confession—then stated: "I kept her car windows open when I took her riding. I put ground glass in her marmalade, but she thought it was sand and returned it to the grocer."

"Are you crazy?" one of the detectives asked Waite.

"I think not," Waite replied calmly, "unless it is crazy to want money."

Tried and convicted, Waite was sentenced to death. Upon hearing this sentence in court, he sighed, then exclaimed: "What a relief!"

Warren Waite, poor boy gone wrong from the start, sauntered to the electric chair on May 1, 1917. He sat down calmly in the death seat. As electrodes were affixed to the shaved areas of his body, he looked about and with his last words commented: "Is this all there is to it?"

MURDER AT THE SAVOY/July 19, 1923

Frenchwoman Marie-Marguerite Laurient (b. 1891) began her affair with Egyptian Prince Ali Kamel Fahmy Bey in May 1922 in Paris, following her divorce from her first husband. The 23-year-old Prince Ali, attached to the French legation in Cairo, was extravagant and allegedly had a sadistic bent. It was rumored in Egypt that Ali was homosexual, but this was not in evidence when he passionately pursued Laurient, who had years before her marriage called herself Maggie Mellor. He was captivated by the elegant brunette divorcee, who was ten years his senior, and took her back to Cairo where he suggested they live together.

When Laurient balked, the prince proposed marriage, and Laurient accepted, but with conditions. A contract was drawn up that permitted her to wear western-style clothing and to divorce the prince at any time. In return, she would convert to the Muslim faith, thereby ensuring Ali's inheritance. But when the religious ceremony took place, Fahmy ordered the divorcee clause removed, allowing him to take three wives if he pleased.

Marguerite found Fahmy to be an abusive husband. He frequently beat her and assigned a houseboy to follow her throughout her day, even when she undressed. The couple traveled to London on July 10, 1923, and registered at the elegant Savoy Hotel. That night they quarreled bitterly about an operation Marguerite was scheduled to undergo. Prince Ali wanted it performed in London, but Marguerite insisted on travelling to Paris to have it done. While they ate supper in the hotel dining room, a band leader strolled by the table to take requests. "I don't want music," Marguerite told the band leader in French—she did not speak a word of English. "My husband has threatened to kill me tonight!"

The band leader thought the elegant-attired woman was making an amusing remark and suavely replied: "I hope you will still be here tomorrow, madame."

The couple retired to their suite at 1:30 a.m. A luggage porter passing their door a short time later saw Fahmy burst from the room in agitation, his face scratched. "Look at my face!" he shouted to the porter. "Look at what she has done!" But the porter only reminded him to keep quiet. Seconds later three shots rang out. The porter rushed to the room to find the prince lying on the floor of his suite.

The hotel manager was summoned. Princess Fahmy, tears running down her cheeks, had thoughts only for herself. As she stood next to her fallen husband, she said: "Oh, sir, I have been married six months, which has been torture for me. I have suffered terribly."

Wounded, Fahmy was taken to a hospital where he died a short time later. Princess Fahmy was charged with his murder. The lurid trial of Marguérite Fahmy opened in London's Central Criminal Court on September 10, 1923, before 49-year-old Mr. Justice Rigby Swift. The prosecution was headed by the redoubtable Percival Clarke. It was thought that the Fahmy case was open and shut, and that Princess Fahmy would soon be behind bars for life or, worse, go to the hangman. She was, however, represented by two of England's most able lawyers, Sir Edward Marshall Hall and Sir Henry Curtis-Bennett. Hall's defense was brilliant if unorthodox.

Hall portrayed the prince as a stalking brute whose entourage of perverts and degenerates had made Marguérite's life miserable, and who, on the night in question, tried to kill her. Hall had obtained a telling piece of evidence from the prison medical officer at Holloway Prison, where Princess Fahmy had been jailed, following her arrest. The physician stated that he examined the woman at that time and found three abrasions on the back of her neck, apparently caused by a man's hand. Fahmy had tried to strangle his wife on the night of the shooting, Hall said, and she had simply defended her life when her lethal husband advanced toward her with gun in hand, wrestling the gun away from him and then pulling the trigger of the Browning .32-caliber pistol.

In a chilling recreation, Hall took the actual murder weapon and demonstrated the shooting for the benefit of the jury. For an instant he pointed the weapon at the jury, acting out the role of Prince Ali, who had reportedly advanced on his wife in a threatening manner. Hall crouched and snarled and hissed in a convincing imitation of the murderous Fahmy. The hushed courtroom then watched Hall drop the gun to the floor. The lawyer later insisted that that part was an accident, but it had a powerful effect on the jury, which returned a verdict of not guilty after only an hour's deliberation. The jurors all but ignored the fact that Princess Fahmy had shot her husband at point-blank range.

Prince Fahmy Bey, shown in his Rolls Royce outside London's posh Savoy Hotel, where he was shot to death by his attractive wife in 1923.

Princess Marguerite Fahmy, reportedly an abused wife, who stood accused of murdering her sadistic husband in a sensational trial.

The brilliant Sir Edward Marshall Hall, who won an acquittal for Princess Fahmy, a victory that added greatly to his illustrious legal career.

The acquittal of Princess Fahmy created a sensation in England and on throughout Europe. Hall's defense had been laced with prejudice in depicting Egyptian culture as uncivilized and catering to myriad perversions and that the murder victim was a millionaire "Oriental" who preyed upon Western women to degrade them and destroy their values of decency. Criticized for such conduct, Hall defended himself, saying: "The only thing that I remember saying that might be misunderstood was that it was a mistake for Western woman to marry Eastern man, and his idea of his rights toward a wife were those of possession instead of mutual alliance."

Princess Fahmy enjoyed the limelight for the next few years, even appearing in some minor French films. Oddly, the sloe-eyed, sultry woman enacted in one movie the role of an Egyptian wife, the very role model she had resisted in real life to the point of homicide.

"THE CRIME OF THE CENTURY"/ May 21, 1924

Although the calculating and coldblooded murder committed by Nathan F. Leopold, Jr. (1906-1971) and Richard A. Loeb (1907-1936) was labeled a kidnapping, it had little or nothing to do with abducting anyone for ransom or sexual satisfaction. It was merely a devise, a clever ruse to shroud the real but murky intent of the killers, which was murder in its most fiendish conception. Their unconscionable act was heralded by a sensation-hungry press as "the crime of the century," but that grim appellative would later be applied to the 1932 Lindbergh kidnapping (see chapter on Kidnapping), and the perplexing assassination of U.S. President John F. Kennedy in 1963 (see chapter on Assassination). In 1924, however, the crime committed by Leopold and Loeb stunned the nation, shocked the world and resulted in one of the most dramatic criminal trials on record in the worldwide community of man.

Richard Loeb as a boy in his cowboy costume, brandishing a six-shooter, and a fierce image that latter-day psychiatrists interpreted as inherent aggression.

Nathan Leopold and Richard Loeb were the products of great wealth, two brilliant students, who had been allowed to expand their personalities and intelligence at will without having to work or worry about money. They had, since early childhood, been given everything, and as a result, they indulged their fantasies as their millionaire parents had satisfied their childish cravings. These two University of Chicago students, brilliant by comparison to other youths their age, had proven themselves superior in all their pursuits.

The resplendent Loeb mansion in Chicago's Hyde Park, where Richard Loeb was spoiled by his millionaire parents, who ignored his odd behavior.

Leopold, with an estimated I.Q. of 200, had graduated from the University of Chicago at age eighteen, the youngest ever to do so. He spoke nine languages fluently and was an expert botanist and ornithologist. There was, however, little warmth in his home. Leopold lived in a loveless household. Money replaced affection. His father, Nathan Leopold, Sr., was a millionaire transport tycoon who assigned a governess to his son at an early age. Babe, as Leopold had been nicknamed, came under the supervision of a sexually disturbed woman who had the boy practice all sorts of sexual perversions with her, distorting his young mind.

Early on, the Leopolds noticed their son's reluctance to associate with girls and they unreasonably placed him in an all-girl's school to correct his attitude. The governess went with the boy, continuing to warp his sexual growth. Moreover, this strange situation caused Leopold to reject female companionship altogether. By the time Leopold graduated from college, his mother was dead and his father, as usual, compensated for the loss by showering his son with money. He gave his son $3,000 and sent him on a European tour.

When Leopold returned, he was given a new car and a $125-a-week allowance and then ignored. Leopold immersed himself in the works of Friedrich Nietzsche, advocate of the superman concept. But the youth was anything but the physical ideal. He was stoop-shouldered and undersized. He had an overactive thyroid gland and he was physically unattractive with huge, bulging eyes and a weak chin. He was a sexual deviate at age fourteen, when he met Richard Loeb, another early-aged homosexual.

Loeb was later to fulfill Leopold's concept of the superman. He was also the son of a millionaire, and like Leopold,

The Leopold mansion in Hyde Park, where Nathan Leopold's millionaire parents indulged his whims and left him to his own strange pursuits.

The mansion in Hyde Park, which was the home of Bobby Franks, the randomly selected murder victim of Richard Loeb and Nathan Leopold.

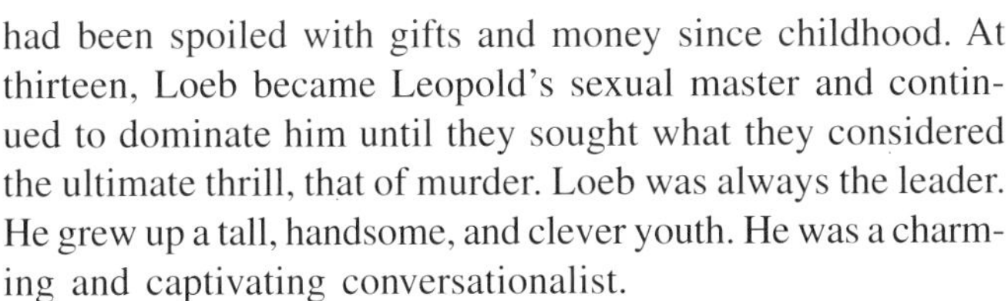

had been spoiled with gifts and money since childhood. At thirteen, Loeb became Leopold's sexual master and continued to dominate him until they sought what they considered the ultimate thrill, that of murder. Loeb was always the leader. He grew up a tall, handsome, and clever youth. He was a charming and captivating conversationalist.

Loeb's father was a senior executive for Sears, Roebuck, and Co., and he bestowed a $250-a-week allowance on his son, a sum that amounted to twice that earned by most men during the early 1920s. Loeb also suffered from physical defects. He had a nervous tic, stuttered at times when nervous, and suffered fainting spells, which had been interpreted as petit mal epilepsy. He often talked of suicide with Leopold, and his character, beneath the glossy charm he showed to others, was decidedly morose and fatalistic.

A graduate of the University of Michigan at age seventeen, Loeb believed himself to be an excellent detective, and his most passionate daydream was to commit the perfect crime. He often talked of this with Leopold, who encouraged his superman theories with such a crime. The two not only satisfied each other in their sexual liaison, but they fed upon each other's egos and together believed themselves to be perfect human beings. The youths had two driving obsessions. With Leopold it was abnormal sex, and with Loeb, crime.

Leopold and Loeb were later termed by their own defense attorneys as "moral imbeciles." It was Loeb who led the pair into active crime. At first Leopold resisted the idea, but Loeb perversely withheld his sexual participation until Leopold agreed to commit crimes with him. They signed a mutual pact in which both agreed that they would support the other's needs, no matter how perverse, degenerate or amoral.

This agreement had been signed when Leopold was fourteen and Loeb was thirteen and the youths embarked on setting fires, touching off false fire alarms, committing petty thefts, and vandalizing the homes of their wealthy neighbors. They spent months creating an elaborate system in which they could expertly cheat while playing bridge, the game of the rich and socially esteemed, the very caste to which Leopold and Loeb belonged and which they held in high contempt, the same contempt they extended to the ignorant and uneducated. They constantly argued with each other, but neither formed friendships with other children. The arguments grew violent and Loeb beat up Leopold on several occasions. Both boys threatened to murder each other some day. Loeb laughed at this idea, saying he would kill himself before Leopold could murder him.

When Leopold told Loeb that he would be going on an extended tour of Europe, Loeb proposed that they commit a spectacular crime before Leopold's ship sailed. Leopold was reluctant, but Loeb appealed to his lover by cleverly positing the idea as worthy of Friedrich Nietzsche, Leopold's intellectual idol. Loeb wrote Leopold a note which read: "The superman is not liable for anything he may do, except for the one crime that it is possible for him to commit—to make a mistake." This prompted Leopold to reconsider Loeb's proposition. The most dangerous crime, the most serious crime, was the only type of crime that Loeb would consider and that, of course, was murder.

They would kidnap and kill someone, and then send a ransom note and collect money for a victim who was already dead, mocking the awful crime they meticulously planned to commit. They were utterly unconcerned with the identity of the victim, as long as that person came from wealthy parents, who could afford to pay the ransom.

Loeb took Leopold to his room and showed him a typewriter that he had stolen in November 1923 from the University of Michigan, when he graduated. Since this typewriter could not be traced to them, Loeb reasoned, the ransom note could be typed on it. The next step was to obtain a car that could be used for the kidnapping. Both boys knew, of course,

The contract for the rental of the murder car which Leopold signed, using the alias of Morton D. Ballard, a document later used against him.

Richard Loeb's name appears on a library card that he mistakenly left at the Morrison Hotel, when he and Leopold checked in under assumed names, one of the many mistakes made by the killers.

that their own cars might be identified, so they established fake identities which would enable them to rent a car. This element of their plan was elaborate, but it provided the youths with some dramatic play-acting.

One spring morning in 1924, Leopold, using the alias of Morton D. Ballard, checked into Chicago's Morrison Hotel. He registered as a salesman from Peoria. He then went to the nearby Rent-A-Car agency and selected a sedan. The salesman asked for a reference and Leopold gave him the name of Louis Mason, along with a phone number. The salesman called Mason (who was really Loeb) who gave "Ballard" an excellent recommendation. Leopold then took the car around for about two hours and returned it to the agency, telling the salesman that he would pick it up later when he needed it. Loeb and Leopold had already used their aliases to open up bank accounts. They intended to deposit the ransom money in these accounts.

Several weeks before the crime, Leopold and Loeb had boarded the 3 p.m. train for Michigan City, Indiana, which was just outside Chicago. Loeb brought along some small parcels to simulate the size of those in which the ransom money would be paid and threw these parcels from the rear platform of the observation car at points selected by Leopold, open fields where Leopold had, months before, spent time studying birds.

Returning to the car rental agency, Leopold obtained a car on May 20, 1924, and he and Loeb then drove to a hardware store on 43rd and Cottage Grove Avenue. Here they purchased a chisel, a rope, and hydrochloric acid. All these were tools of murder. The rope was to be used to garrote their victim, the chisel to stab him in case he struggled too much, and the acid to obliterate their victim's identity. The murderous pair debated the use of sulfuric acid before opting to use hydrochloric.

On the morning of May 21, 1924, Loeb wrapped adhesive tape about the handle of the chisel to allow a firmer grip. This, along with the rope and acid, were placed in the rented car, along with strips of cloth to be used to bind their victim, and a lap robe to cover the body. A pair of hip boots were also put into the car to be used in burying the body in a swamp the killers had previously selected. Both Leopold and Loeb each pocketed a loaded revolver, and Loeb carried the ransom note typed the day before. This note demanded $10,000 for the return of the victim, who they had no intention of returning.

Neither boy needed the ransom money, but they had to make it appear that the kidnappers were lowly, money-craving underworld types, motivated by cash, not the "supreme thrill" they both sought. This element of the plan Loeb thought to be the most ingenious. Police, he told Leopold, always pinned their investigations on motive and worked backward; with the false clue of cash-hungry kidnappers planted, the police would never look for two respectable, well-to-do students. Never, he said.

The most bizarre aspect of these dark procedures was the fact that on the very day they planned to commit the crime, May 21, 1924, the boys had not yet picked out a victim. This cold indifference was the root of their inhumanity, their utter lack of moral code. They did not care about the human life they were about to take. The identity of their victim was of total unconcern to their clinical minds. The person to be killed was merely another element of their test to prove their own superiority. The victim was a number, an object, a thing. Leopold and Loeb sat down and wrote out a list of possible kidnap victims. First they thought to kidnap and murder Loeb's younger brother, Tommy, but they dismissed the idea, only because both felt that it would be difficult to collect the ransom from Loeb's father and that Loeb might arouse suspicion.

Little William Deutsch was then discussed. He was the grandson of multimillionaire philanthropist Julius Rosenwald. He, too, was eliminated since Rosenwald was the president of Sears, Roebuck and Co., and thus, Loeb's superior. The Deutsch boy was simply "too close to home" for the murderous youths. Richard Rubel, one of their few friends, was also considered as a candidate for the kidnapping-murder. Rubel often had lunch with Leopold and Loeb, but he was dismissed after the killers concluded that his father was a tightwad and would probably refuse to pay a ransom for his son.

What to do? The boys finally decided to pick a random victim in the neighborhood. They got into the rented car and cruised around a few blocks near Leopold's home, focusing upon the young boys coming and going from the Harvard Preparatory School. This was an exclusive school which was attended by children of wealthy parents.

As they drove about, the killers casually discussed their problem. They agreed that they should select a small child since neither of them was strong enough to subdue a child with any strength. They stopped next to the Harvard School yard, spotted little John Levinson, and decided then and there that he would be their victim. But since neither knew the address of the Levinson family, they drove to a nearby drugstore and looked it up in the phone directory. They wanted to make sure that they would have the correct address in order to send the ransom note. By the time the pair drove back to the schoolyard, the Levinson boy was leaving. Leopold, who had brought along binoculars for the purpose of selecting a victim at some distance, spotted Levinson across the field.

Loeb drove at considerable speed around the block in order to catch up with their prey, but the Levinson child went up an alley and vanished. Frustrated, the pair drove about aimlessly, searching for a victim. As they drove down Ellis Avenue, they spotted some boys playing. One of them was

Right: Heir to millions, 14-year-old Bobby Franks was selected by Loeb and Leopold at the last minute as their murder victim.

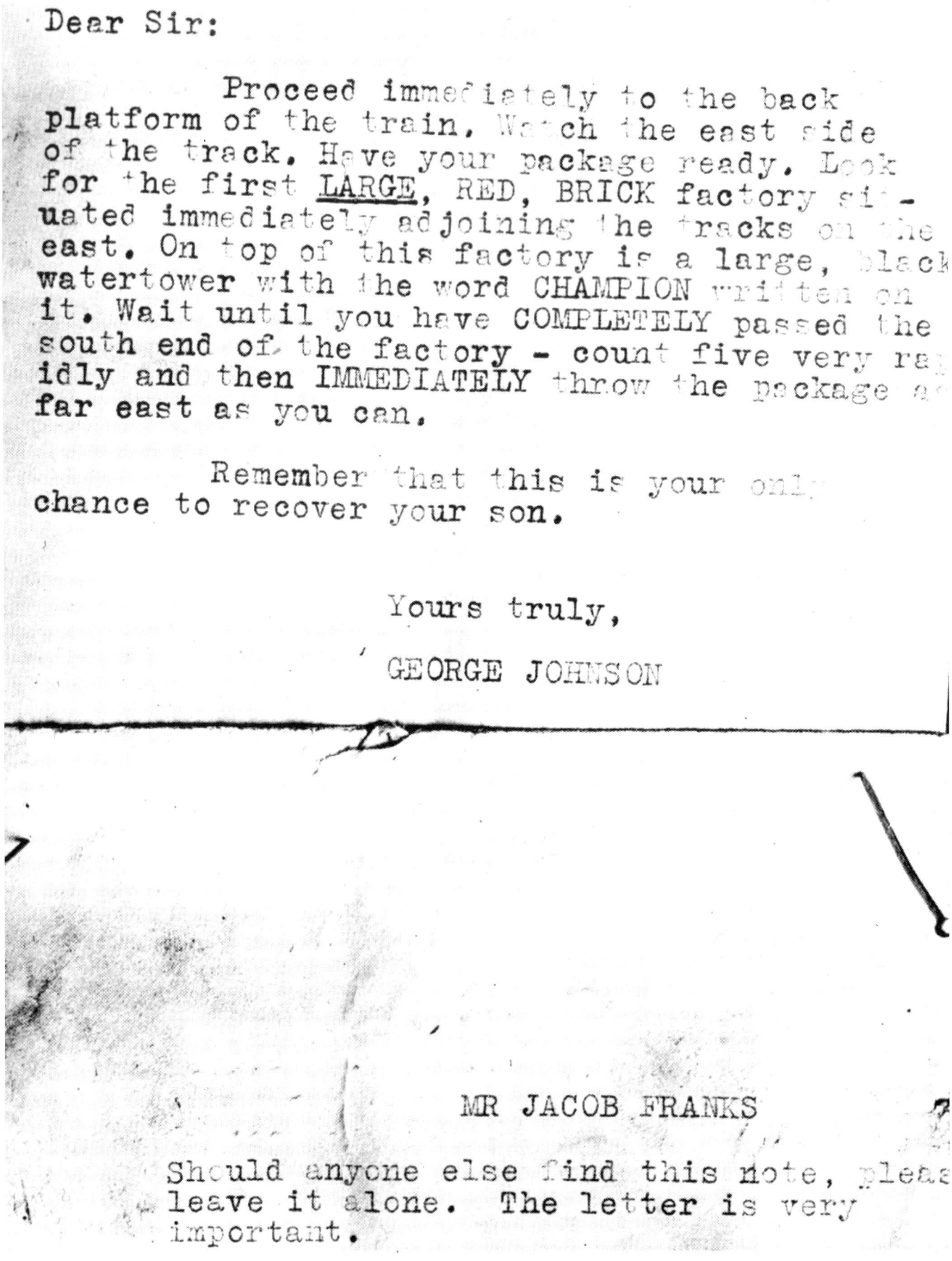

Dear Sir:

Proceed immediately to the back platform of the train. Watch the east side of the track. Have your package ready. Look for the first LARGE, RED, BRICK factory situated immediately adjoining the tracks on the east. On top of this factory is a large, black watertower with the word CHAMPION written on it. Wait until you have COMPLETELY passed the south end of the factory - count five very rapidly and then IMMEDIATELY throw the package as far east as you can.

Remember that this is your only chance to recover your son.

Yours truly,

GEORGE JOHNSON

MR JACOB FRANKS

Should anyone else find this note, pleas leave it alone. The letter is very important.

The ransom note sent by Leopold and Loeb to Jacob Franks, which promised the return of Bobby Franks if they received

Bobby (or Bobbie) Franks, a distant relative of Loeb's. "He's perfect," Loeb stated, telling Leopold that the Franks child came from great wealth, that the boy's father, Jacob Franks, was a multimillionaire box manufacturer, and could certainly afford to pay the ransom for his child, one he doted upon. After parking the car at a curb, Loeb called 14-year-old Bobby Franks to the car. Loeb asked Bobby if he wanted to go for a ride.

"No thanks," Bobby said. He looked at Leopold who gave him a long, hard stare. "I don't know this man," Franks said, pointing to Leopold. There was some apprehension in his voice. "Besides, I have to go home," he said. Loeb persisted, telling Bobby that they would drive him home. He recalled playing tennis with the Franks boy and knew the child had an avid interest in the sport. Loeb then told Bobby that he had a new tennis racket he wanted to show him.

The Franks boy got in the back seat of the car. Leopold remained in the front seat behind the wheel, driving and Loeb got into the back seat with Bobby Franks. Leopold drove northward as Loeb fondled the rope he intended to use to strangle Franks. He quickly discarded this idea as being too clumsy. He grabbed the chisel and with four lightning moves, stabbed the startled child four times. The helpless child fell to the floor, gushing blood from savage wounds to the head.

Leopold turned briefly while driving to look in the back seat to see the dying boy. He saw the contemptuous sneer on Richard Loeb's face. Loeb had enjoyed killing the child and said so. Leopold winced at the sight of the blood and groaned: "Oh, God, I didn't know it would be like this!" Leopold continued driving through heavy traffic. Meanwhile, Loeb ruthlessly tied up the child, stuffed strips of cloth in his mouth, and then threw the lap robe over him.

Bobby Franks lay on the floor of the back seat of the sedan slowly bleeding to death. Leopold kept driving about aimlessly until dusk. He then parked the car and the boys went to a restaurant to get sandwiches. They were waiting for the cover of darkness before hiding the body at a site selected earlier. Leopold called his father and told him he would not be home until late that night.

The boys then got back into the car and began driving south. They stopped at another restaurant and ate a heavy meal, finding themselves famished, even though they had just eaten sandwiches. Outside, parked at the curb, the windows of the car open, the lap robe and the body of the Franks boy beneath it was open to the view of all passersby. This was another element of the contempt the killers displayed for the ability of anyone to detect their crime.

It was Loeb's belief that no one in the world cared about anyone else. He joked with the somber Leopold about the fact that anyone passing the car outside could lean through the windows and pick up the robe and discover the body. "But nobody will," he said in a low voice. Both were wholly insensitive to the murder they had committed. They ate their way through a five-course meal, concerned only with completing the routines they had established for themselves.

At nightfall, the killers got back into the car and drove to an area called Panhandle Tracks at 118th Street. Here a swamp drained into an open culvert and this was the spot they had selected as the burial site for their victim. Loeb got into the back seat of the car and checked the Franks boy. "He's dead," he announced proudly. He then stripped the boy of his clothes and poured the acid over the child's face to mar his features and prevent identification. While Loeb was performing this monstrous task, Leopold was slipping into his pair of hip boots. He then took the child, walked to the culvert, and stuffed the body into the pipe.

Jacob Franks (shown in court), never paid the ransom for his abducted son Bobby, learning that the boy was dead before he could make payment.

It was difficult work and Leopold removed his coat. As he did so, he made the one mistake that would spoil the so-called "perfect crime" he and Richard Loeb had so carefully planned. His glasses fell from the pocket of his coat. Moreover, he believed that he had thoroughly hidden the body of their victim, but in the darkness he failed to notice that a small, naked foot protruded from the drainpipe. He grabbed his coat and went back to the car.

The boys then parked the car near a large apartment building. They noted that the back seat and the lap robe were stained with Bobby's blood. They abandoned the car and then burned the robe in a vacant lot. They went to Leopold's house and there burned all of Bobby's clothes, except the metal he had been wearing, his belt buckle and class pin. They typed the Franks' address on the envelope of the ransom note and then left, driving to Indiana where they mailed the note and buried the class pin, belt buckle, and shoes of Bobby Franks.

The killers then drove back to Chicago and Leopold called

In an incredible photo, Richard Loeb (wearing light coat at extreme right) is shown helping detectives search for the missing Bobby Franks; Loeb's ego compelled him to subtly challenge the police by appearing to help them in their quest for the boy he had murdered.

Jacob Franks, who had been worried ever since his child failed to come home that afternoon. Leopold told Franks: "Your boy has been kidnapped. He is safe and unharmed. Tell the police and he will be killed at once. You will receive a ransom note with instructions tomorrow." Without allowing Franks to respond, Leopold hung up. The boys then made themselves drinks and played cards until past midnight in Leopold's room, working out the final details of their "perfect crime."

A ransom note signed "George Johnson" was delivered to Franks the next day. It demanded that Franks pay $10,000 for the return of his child, the payment to be made in twenty- and fifty-dollar bills. The bills were to be placed in a cigar box and this box was to be wrapped in white paper and then sealed with wax. Franks would receive more instructions at 1 p.m. that day, the note stated. Franks had by then notified the police of his son's kidnapping through his lawyer. The police were told that the Franks wanted no publicity in fear that the kidnappers would murder their child, as the anonymous caller had threatened.

Meanwhile Leopold and Loeb had second thoughts about the bloodstains in the rented car. They retrieved it, drove to the Leopold house, and parked it in the family garage. Sven Englund, the Leopold family chauffeur, noticed the boys scrubbing down the back seat of this car. When he asked them about it, they told him that they had been drinking

Chicago police detectives are shown inspecting the culvert, where a railroad worker found the body of Bobby Franks; he had been stabbed, strangled and beaten to death.

The glasses that were found near the culvert, where the killers buried their victim at night; they proved to be unique prescription glasses that belonged to Nathan Leopold, Jr.

The typewriter, which the killers used to write the ransom note—its keys ripped out by Loeb—was recovered from the Jackson Park lagoon, where the boys had tossed it, and later traced to the killers, another mistake made in the so-called "perfect crime."

An apprehensive Richard Loeb, sits uncomfortably at the wheel of the Willys-Knight car that had been rented on the day of the murder, while State's Attorney Robert E. Crowe interrogates him; by this time Crowe was convinced he had nabbed the killers.

Classmates of the slain Bobby Franks carry his coffin-encased body, en route to a funeral home; at that moment Leopold and Loeb were held in hotel suites, where detectives played a cat and mouse game with the two murderers, trying to "break" them.

State's Attorney Robert Crowe, center, and his staff pose with Loeb, left, and Leopold, right of Crowe, following the confessions of both youths; they blamed each other for the actual killing but most assumed Loeb had murdered Bobby Franks.

Clarence Darrow, America's most celebrated criminal defense attorney, center, is shown with Nathan Leopold, Sr., and Jacob Loeb, who reportedly paid him fabulous retainers to save the lives of their murderous sons. (Another report had it that Darrow received only $30,000 from the elder Leopold, and that the senior Loeb paid nothing, reneging on his promise to pay an estimated $1 million.)

Darrow, center, with his clients, Leopold, left, and Loeb, right, before the bench at their arraignment for murder; Darrow's clients proved to be arrogant and often uncooperative, while he attempted to mount what all believed to be a hopeless defense.

wine in the back seat of the car, borrowed from a friend, and had spilled wine on the seat. They were merely trying to remove the stain before returning the car to their friend.

Englund, who had been berated and humiliated by both Leopold and Loeb over the years, would later prove his lack of affection for Leopold by staunchly maintaining that Leopold's own car never left the family garage on the night of the Franks murder, rebuffing Leopold's claim that he and Loeb had been using Leopold's car that night, cruising for girls.

Upon reflection, Loeb concluded that the murder plan was not perfect after all. The typewriter on which the boys wrote the ransom note bothered Loeb. Even though it was an item stolen the previous year, he feared its discovery. Leopold drove through Jackson Park slowly while Loeb tore the keys from the typewriter and threw them into a lagoon. He threw the dismantled typewriter into another lagoon. By then it was time to contact Jacob Franks once more. Loeb boarded a train en route to Michigan City. He went to the observation car and, at the writing desk of this car, left a note addressed to Jacob Franks in the telegram slot of the desk, behind many forms.

This move would present yet another wrinkle in the "perfect murder" plan. Loeb wrote on the envelope: "Should anyone else find this note, please leave it alone. The letter is very important." Loeb got off the train at 63rd Street to be met by the waiting Leopold. Apparently, the boys intended to inform Franks that the note was on the train and have the victim's father personally retrieve it. However, Andy Russo, a train worker, rummaged through the forms in the telegram slot looking for a piece of paper to write on and found the letter addressed to Franks. Russo personally delivered the letter to Franks the next morning.

By this time, however, Jacob Franks knew that his little boy was dead. A member of a train crew working alongside the culvert, where the body had been hidden spotted the boy's foot sticking from the drainpipe and the corpse was quickly removed and identified by a member of the Franks family. The newspapers were given the full story and huge headlines announced the brutal murder.

A massive, widely publicized manhunt for the ruthless killer ensued. Scores of suspects were picked up, hustled into police headquarters, and grilled. Leopold and Loeb quickly realized that no ransom would ever be paid and that their perfect crime had serious flaws. Leopold grew silent and morose. He kept to his room, staying out of the limelight. Richard Loeb, however, reveled in the manhunt and played amateur detective. He boldly approached police officials searching through his neighborhood for clues and arrogantly offered his sleuthing services.

Loeb babbled his crime theories into the ears of detectives and followed them about during their investigations. To one he remarked: "If I were going to pick out a boy to kidnap or murder, that's just the kind of cocky little son-of-a-bitch I would pick." The detective took a long look at Richard Loeb and then encouraged him to talk further, inviting the self-appointed sleuth to accompany officers on their quest for the killer. Such conduct on the part of killers was not uncommon. In this instance, Loeb's voluntary aid to the police was spawned by his desire to present himself as a suspect and still outwit them. It was all a game, a challenge to Loeb, who felt himself superior to the "dumb coppers" who bumbled about looking for a killer, who was right beneath their noses and secretly jeering at them.

Then the "bumbling" police began to make discoveries that unnerved Loeb. Loeb's stolen typewriter was found in the shallow waters of the Jackson Park lagoon and the keys to it were found in another lagoon. Then the bloody, tape-wrapped chisel was found. The most startling discovery was that of Leopold's glasses. The police traced the horn-rimmed glasses to the manufacturer, Albert Coe and Co. Officials at the firm reported that the glasses were unusual, the frames being specially made for only three people. One pair belonged to a lawyer, who had been visiting Europe for some time. The second pair was owned by a woman and she was wearing them when police arrived to interview her. The third pair had been sold to Nathan Leopold, Jr., dear friend of Richard Loeb, the boy who had been dogging the footsteps of investigating detectives, the self-appointed Sherlock Holmes of Chicago.

Robert E. Crowe, the shrewd, tough state's attorney for Cook County, had Leopold brought into his office for questioning. He showed him the glasses and asked him if they were his. Leopold said no, his glasses were at home. Crowe sent Leopold back home with two detectives, but thorough searching of the Leopold home failed to produce the glasses. Then Leopold was told that the glasses had been found near a culvert at 118th Street, and Leopold, thinking fast, told Crowe that he often went to that area for his bird-watching studies.

Crowe was hesitant to charge Leopold, initially believing that he was a victim of circumstance. He came from incredible wealth and his social position was lofty. There was no

Chicago newsmen are shown in the press room of the courthouse where the Leopold-Loeb trial occurred, these scribes drinking coffee spiked with bootleg booze; Jake Lingle, of the Chicago *Tribune* (third from left in hat, holding a sandwich) was murdered seven years later on orders of crime czar Al Capone—see Gangs, Gangsters and Organized Crime); Hilding Johnson (in foreground at right, wearing cap), a star reporter for the Chicago *Daily News*, became the role model for the colorful "Hildy Johnson" in the celebrated play (and later film), *The Front Page*, by Ben Hecht and Charles MacArthur.

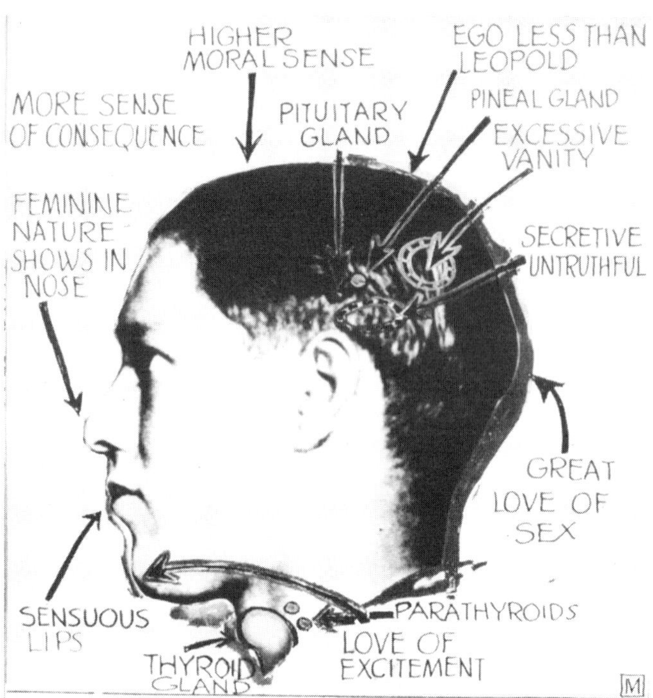

This annotated illustration of Richard Loeb, created by phrenologist James N. Fitzgerald, purports to pinpoint the criminal nature of Loeb through an examination of his physiological characteristics.

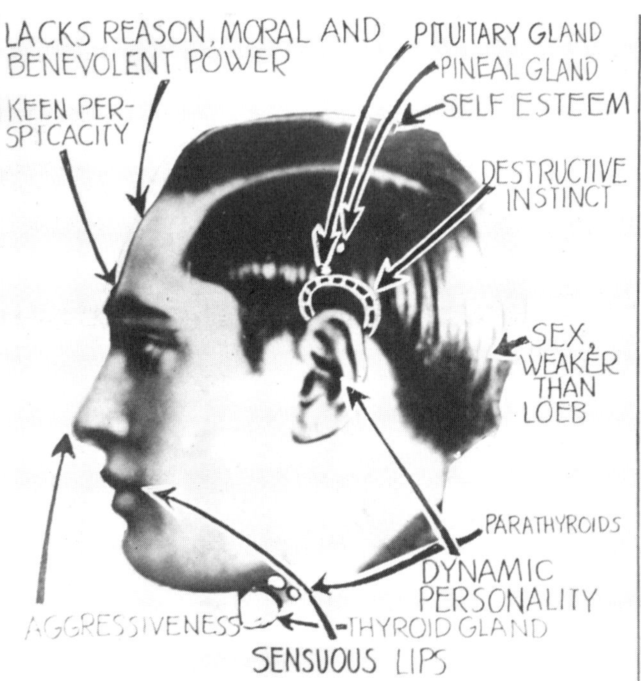

Fitzgerald also created a "criminal profile" of Nathan Leopold, Jr., again pinpointing the degenerative nature of the murderer, employing the methods of phrenology, which has long since become a discarded science.

reason for Crowe to believe that Leopold had anything to do with the killing of Bobby Franks. Yet he had Leopold interrogated by two detectives who kept questioning him about his glasses and his whereabouts on the night of the murder.

Leopold first stated that he could not recollect what he was doing on the night of May 21, 1924, but he later said that he and his friend Richard Loeb had been driving around looking for girls and picked up two attractive girls named Edna and Mae. He could not remember their last names. The four of them, Leopold insisted, had gone to a Chinese restaurant on the South Side and had dinner on the murder night. Leopold then said that he and Loeb had been drinking gin out of a flask and that he did not want to talk about his outing with Loeb and the girls because Loeb's father strongly disapproved of drinking and he did not want his friend Loeb to get into trouble.

Leopold truthfully said he did not know the murdered boy, but was acquainted with his family. He admitted to reading "everything I could find" about the murder in the local papers. He also said that he had seen photos of the glasses found at the murder site, but he never believed them to be his own, which he had lost near the spot some time earlier. Leopold stressed his ability to buy anything he wanted, implying he had no need to kidnap anyone to obtain ransom money. "My father is rich," he said. "Whenever I want money, all I have to do is ask for it. And I earn money myself teaching ornithology."

Crowe realized that, despite Leopold's high social position, he was a primary suspect in the killing of Bobby Franks. He ordered Leopold taken to a comfortable room in the LaSalle Hotel and questioned further. Crowe also ordered Richard Loeb picked up and taken to another room in the same hotel. He was also to be questioned to see if his statements contradicted Leopold's. They did.

Loeb insisted that on the murder night he was at home. He had not gone anywhere with Leopold. He said nothing of the two girls. No one but Crowe and a few high-ranking police officials really believed that either boy was guilty of the Franks murder. Newspaper reporters who knew the boys were allowed to interview them and felt they were innocent, caught in a web of circumstantial evidence.

Both boys remained calm and freely talked to reporters and the police. They were officially under arrest, but they were not formally charged. They were held as "guests" of the city while the lengthy interrogations went on. Their families did nothing to free them, believing that the youths would soon be released and that the questioning was merely a matter of routine.

Crowe continued to play the fatherly host to the boys. He even took them to the posh Drake Hotel where they leisurely ate an expensive dinner for which the city paid $102, a lavish sum for those days. For Crowe it was money well spent. One reporter later claimed that he interviewed Leopold who modestly displayed "his superior education." The reporter was so impressed with the calm demeanor of Leopold that he asked a psychiatrist friend to interview Leopold, which he did. The psychiatrist later stated that "this boy certainly had no part in the murder." The psychiatrist later denied having made any such statement.

Leopold appeared to be cooperative at every turn. He

Clarence Darrow, right, in a masterful summary, is shown addressing Judge John Caverly, extreme left, in August 1924, one that moved the juror to tears and undoubtedly brought about Caverly's decision to imprison the youths for life.

Darrow, center, at the defense table, his youthful clients sitting behind him; he was exhausted by the trial, later stating: "From that day, I have never gone through so protracted a strain, and could never do it again, even if I should try."

Their lives saved, Nathan Leopold, Jr., left, and Richard Loeb, center, still smug and contemptuous of the law, are escorted into Illinois State Prison at Joliet to serve out life terms.

Height	74.7	L. Foot	27.0	Col. of Eyes	Age. 19	Beard. Ch Dk
Eng. H'ght	5.8 3/4	L. M. Fin.	11.6		Apparent Age. Illinois	Hair. Ch Dk
Hd. Length	19.6+	L. L. Fin.	8.9	Sl. blue		Comp. Med
Hd. Width	15.2	L. Fore A.	47.8+		Student	Weight. 160

Remarks Incident to Measurement

9305

Build Med. Chin

Teeth Good

Remarks

Measured at Joliet, Illinois, State Penitentiary. Sept 12, 1924

The prison photos and record of Richard Loeb; he was an incorrigible homosexual at Joliet, sexually preying upon any prisoner he coveted and paying off guards to look the other way during his attacks; he was stabbed to death in 1936 by a prisoner he attempted to rape.

said to one reporter: "I don't blame the police for holding me. I was at the culvert the Saturday and Sunday before the glasses were found and it is quite possible that I lost my glasses there. I'm sorry this happened only because it will worry my family. But I'll certainly be glad to do what I can to help the police."

It was apparent that Leopold was enjoying the limelight shed upon him by the press. He pontificated on art, literature, politics, sports, and especially philosophy, as if giving lectures, pointing out that he favored such writers as Oscar Wilde and Friedrich Nietzsche, but he added: "I won't add Socrates, for I never thought such a lot of him." Loeb adopted the same kind of superior air. For sheer arrogance and bluff, their equal had never been seen.

Leopold and Loeb family members believed that the police were merely using the boys to see if they had information that might lead to the identification of the real killer. Nathan Leopold, Sr., said: "While it is a terrible ordeal both to my boy and myself to have him under suspicion our attitude will be one of helping the investigation, rather than retarding it ...The suggestion that he had anything to do with this case is too absurd to merit comment." Loeb's father had been ill for several weeks and made no comment from his sickbed, but Mrs. Loeb coolly told a reporter: "The affair will so easily straighten itself out."

While the police were politely interrogating the boys, two newspaper reporters, Al Goldstein and Jim Mulroy, of the Chicago Daily *News*, conducted their own dogged investigation. They interviewed dozens of persons, chiefly the friends of Leopold and Loeb. One of them, Arnold Maremont, told Goldstein that he was a member of a legal study group to which Leopold belonged. The group met once a week to write "dope sheets" to prepare for examinations. Maremont stated that several of these meetings were held in the library of the Leopold mansion. He recalled that Leopold usually had a large Hammond typewriter, which the group used to prepare the "dope sheets." But in one meeting Leopold produced a small portable typewriter that was used to type some "dope sheets."

Maremont had some of these sheets typed on the portable typewriter, which Loeb had stolen in 1923. Goldstein and Mulroy took these pages to H.P. Sutton, an expert working for the Royal Typewriter Company. Sutton compared the "dope sheets" and the ransom letter and pronounced that they were one and the same. When confronted with this, Leopold still held onto his nerve, saying that the typewriter belonged to Maurice Shanberg, who had brought the typewriter to the study group.

Shanberg angrily denied this allegation and then Leopold, thinking quickly, stated that another student friend, Leon Mandel, owned the typewriter. Mandel was in Europe. Then Leopold said that the typewriter was still somewhere in his house. Another thorough search in the Leopold home failed to unearth the typewriter. Of course, the typewriter was the one found in the Jackson Park lagoon.

More and more evidence mounted against the boys. Sven Englund, the Leopold chauffeur, was brought in for questioning. Englund told Crowe that Leopold, contrary to Leopold's claim, had not used his red Willys-Knight car on the night of the murder. Leopold had insisted that he had been driving this car around that night with Loeb and two girls in it. Crowe turned to one of his aides and exclaimed: "God damn it! I think we got them!"

Crowe then ordered Richard Loeb into his office and Loeb was confronted with this new evidence. When he heard that Englund had insisted that he had been working on Leopold's car on the murder night, trying to fix its noisy brakes, and that it never left the garage, Loeb's face went ashen. He slumped in his chair and found it difficult to speak. Finally, he said: "My God! He told you that?" He asked for a cigarette and then let out a brief, low-voiced curse.

Leopold, in another room, was faced with the same evidence given by Englund. He remained passive and silent. "There were no two girls in that car, were there, Nathan?" one of his interrogators said, "Just one little boy, Bobby Franks. Why don't you come clean and get it off your conscience? Your alibi about driving around with Dickie Loeb and those girls is exposed as a lie by your family chauffeur." Leopold merely smiled, proving his superiority to such police tactics.

Loeb, on the other hand, had lost his composure as the questioning went on into the early morning hours of the day after the boys had been picked up. He trembled and was visibly shaken with each new question that pointed to his guilt. Crowe studied him for some time, realizing that though he was the leader of the pair, he was the weaker of the two and his veneer of bravado and haughty airs had evaporated. He showed all the signs of a trapped animal. Crowe then decided to bluff with the more stoic Leopold. At 4 a.m., he walked into the room, where Leopold sat calmly puffing on a cigarette and said: "Well, your pal has just confessed, told us the whole story."

A sneer passed Leopold's face: "Do you think I'm stupid. I'm not going to believe that. Anyhow, it's impossible. There's nothing to confess!"

Crowe had all the evidence and more. His men had tracked down the rented car used in the murder and then traced its user to the Morrison Hotel. The car rental agent and employees at the hotel identified a photo shown to them by detectives as that of Morton D. Ballard, the young man who had rented the car and had checked into the hotel. Crowe walked back and forth in front of Leopold, saying nothing. He then stopped and slowly removed his glasses, wiping the lenses meticulously as he stared down at Leopold, who stared back at him.

Crowe then slipped the glasses into the breast pocket of his coat, much in the manner Leopold claimed he had done before losing his glasses at the culvert area. Leopold smiled slightly at the ploy, but his smile faded when Crowe began to talk quietly. Said Crowe: "What about your getting the other automobile at the Rent-A-Car Company because your car was red and too conspicuously? What about the false identity at the Morrison Hotel? What about waiting in hiding on Ingleside Avenue for Johnny Levinson to appear? Your friend says you planned the kidnapping. He says you were the one who killed Bobby Franks."

Leopold crushed a cigarette angrily into an ashtray and then nervously lit another. He realized that only Richard Loeb could have provided the information Crowe had re-

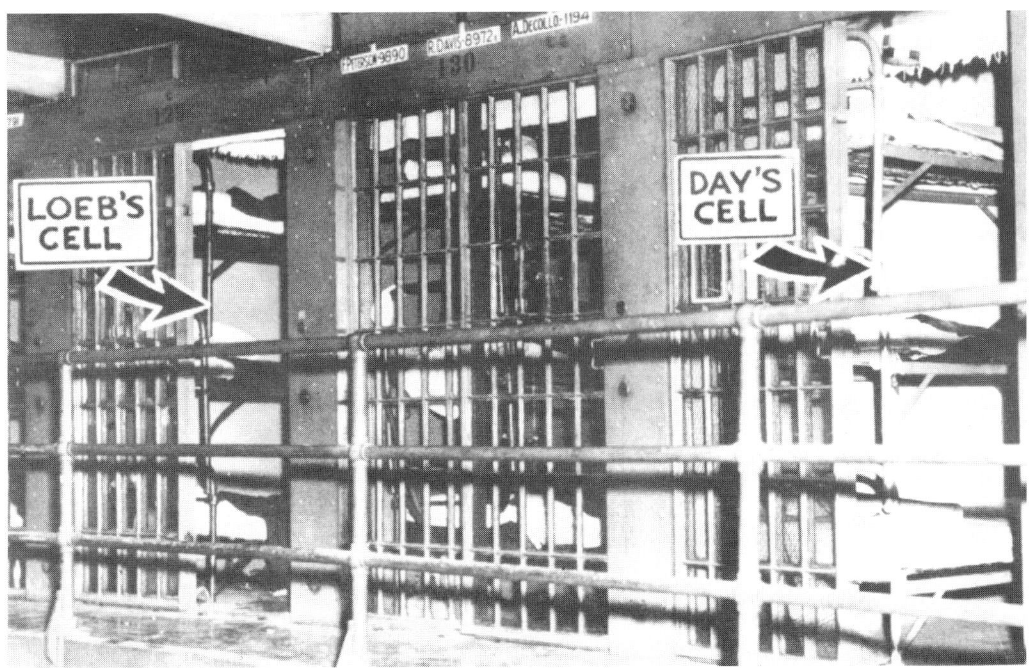

The cells occupied by Loeb and James Day, the man who killed Loeb; guards were reportedly bribed by Loeb to put Day close to him.

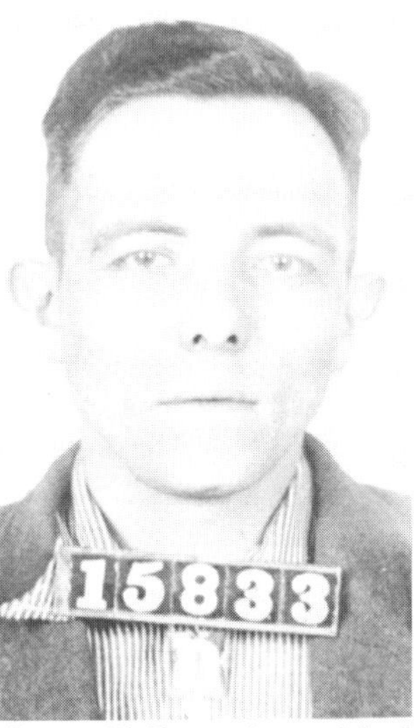

James E. Day, who stabbed Loeb to death, was later acquitted, the killing termed "justifiable homicide," in that he was defending himself against a predator.

Nathan Leopold's cell at Joliet, where he was allowed to keep birds and pursue his ornithology studies.

lated. He had not, but Crowe had pieced this information together from various statements the boys had made to their interrogators.

Leopold concluded that his alibis and excuses were useless. He began to confess and Crowe had a court stenographer take down his statements. He then marched into the hotel room where Loeb sat and played the same game. Loeb nodded slowly and then he began to confess, detailing the murder of Bobby Franks. Their stories matched in every detail except one. Each said that they were driving the car when Bobby Franks was killed and that the other did the actual murder.

Most authorities later determined that Loeb was the actual killer. Their conclusion was based upon Loeb's statements; he described in exact detail how Leopold killed the Franks child, while Leopold could only offer slight information on how many times the boy was stabbed and how the rags had been stuffed down his throat to prevent his crying out. Both were nevertheless charged with murder.

When the boys were first brought together after their confessions, Loeb said to Leopold: "We're both in for the same ride, Babe, so we might as well ride together." Leopold turned to a detective and repeated his claim that Loeb was the killer. Loeb, hearing himself denounced by his best friend, sneered and turned to Crowe, saying: "He's only a weakling after all."

The fathers of these merciless killers realized that their sons were headed straight for the electric chair. They also knew that one man might save them from that fate, Clarence Darrow, the greatest criminal attorney of the day. Darrow was hired to defend the boys, but he knew that he had no hope of freeing the boys. Their guilt was completely established. They were also so unsavory that he could not make appeals on behalf of their inhuman characters. He took on their defense for only one reason.

The case offered an opportunity for him to attack the concept of government-sanctioned execution. "While the State is trying Loeb and Leopold, I will try capital punishment," he declared. He wisely chose to abandon a jury trial and pleaded his clients guilty before Judge John R. Caverly. Darrow knew Judge Caverly to be a fair-minded and exceptionally conscientious jurist, and he played to Caverly's sensitivities regarding the taking of human life.

For thirty-three grueling days, Clarence Darrow put on one of the greatest and most dramatic performances ever seen in a U.S. courtroom. His tireless assault on capital punishment remains a classic argument to this day. He fought with all his strength and intellectual powers. He also exhausted every ounce of his emotion to save two boys he himself had branded as guilty.

Darrow's summation was stunning. He ended with: "I am pleading for the future ... I am pleading for a time when hatred and cruelty will not control the hearts of men, when we can learn by reason and judgment and understanding and faith that all life is worth living and that mercy is the highest attribute of man ... If I can succeed ... I have done something for the tens of thousands of other boys, for the countless unfortunates who must tread the same road in blind childhood ..."

Judge Caverly was deeply moved by Darrow's appeal. He also stated that Illinois had never executed boys of the age of Leopold and Loeb, and having that precedent, sentenced both youths to life imprisonment for the murder of Bobby Franks and ninety-nine years each on the charge of kidnapping. Clarence Darrow had achieved the impossible. He had saved the lives of two youths who had, in everyone's mind, been destined for the electric chair.

Darrow's fee was reported to have been $1 million but he had difficulty in obtaining the one and only payment he did receive, $30,000 paid by Nathan Leopold, Sr. Loeb's father reportedly paid not a red cent. Jacob Loeb disowned his son, Richard, after the sentence and died a few months later. When Leopold finally paid Darrow, he handed him his check and then said to Darrow with the same kind of arrogance displayed by his son: "The world is full of eminent lawyers, who would have paid a fortune for a chance to distinguish themselves in this case." With that he walked wordlessly from the offices of the man who had saved his son's decidedly worthless life.

Leopold and Loeb were sent to the Northern Illinois Penitentiary at Stateville, outside Joliet. Though Judge Caverly had stated in his deliberation that both boys were to be kept separate for the rest of their lives, this order was immediately ignored once the boys were put behind bars. They were placed

Nathan Leopold, Jr., shown overjoyed at the time of his prison release in 1958; he moved to Puerto Rico, where he married in 1961, working as a technician and dying in 1971.

in cells separated only by one other cell. The "Fun Killers," as the press had dubbed them, were allowed desks, filing cabinets, and their own private libraries. Their cells, which were in a special wing, were left open at night so they could visit each other.

Leopold and Loeb were separated from the rest of the prisoners and given special meals, often catered from restaurants, in the officers' mess. Both youths were permitted to walk freely outside the prison, where Leopold kept a garden. They washed in the officers' shower and they were provided with bootleg liquor and even narcotics for which they were charged $1 a shot. Visitors were allowed to see the boys at all hours and at any time, in total disregard of prison rules. Leopold and Loeb could make phone calls at any time from a phone in the prison storeroom. They had all the money they could use to bribe the guards and officials to continue living lives of relative comfort.

Richard Loeb was the worse offender of the two. While Leopold retreated into books and his garden, Loeb sauntered about the prison, selecting any young prisoner he admired and then foisting his homosexual attentions on his victim, while guards ignored his vile sexual assaults. In 1936, Loeb was attracted to a young prisoner, James E. Day. Loeb accosted Day in the library on one occasion and said that he loved him and that Day should "be broad-minded and be nice to me." Day, disgusted at such behavior, pushed Loeb away. But Loeb insisted that Day respond to his affection. Day later stated: "I never had a peaceful day. He was always after me. I became desperate. I had to get him off my back. I was looking for the right day."

The day occurred on January 28, 1936. Day was in the shower alone and Loeb entered, stripping and then trying to assault Day. Loeb brandished a razor and barked at Day: "Do as you're told! Keep your mouth shut and get your clothes off!" Day pretended to go along with the idea but then, when Loeb was off guard, Day kicked him in the groin and the two men struggled for the razor. In the fight Loeb slashed Day several times, until Day wrenched the razor away from him and used it to fatally slash Loeb. Loeb staggered naked from the shower, walking down a corridor before falling into the arms of another convict.

Loeb had been slashed fifty-six times. He was rushed to the prison hospital where his mother visited him within hours. Leopold was brought to his bedside and held his hand. Loeb said to his partner in murder: "I think I'm going to make it." He died a few minutes later. When Clarence Darrow was informed of Loeb's passing, he remarked: "He is better off dead. For him death is an easier sentence."

Nathan Leopold continued to be the star boarder at the penitentiary until his parole on March 13, 1958. He said at a press conference: "I am a broken old man. I want a chance to find redemption for myself and to help others." To that end, he traveled to Puerto Rico, where he worked as a laboratory technician in a small church. He later met Trudi Feldman Garcia de Quevedo, a widow who owned a flower shop. They married in 1961.

Leopold then wrote a book, *Life Plus 99 Years*. At a press conference connected with the book's release, Leopold was asked about the murder of Bobby Franks. He replied: "The crime is definitely still the central part of my consciousness. Very often it occupies the forefront of my attention, and I can think of nothing else. More often, it is not the center of my attention, but it always is present in the background." It was the same kind of mannered, cautious statement that Leopold had made when he was first confronted with his awful guilt by police in 1924.

A year after Leopold's release, the 1959 film, *Compulsion*, was released, starring (left to right) Bradford Dillman (in a Loeb role model), Dean Stockwell (in a Leopold role model) and Orson Welles (in a jarring role model of Clarence Darrow).

Bobby Franks, three decades after his death, was a memory in the mind of Nathan Leopold, where the victim had been an idea in Nathan Leopold's mind in 1924. Nothing really had changed. For all the posturing of remorse and rehabilitation, Leopold still observed his crime and his long-dead victim as a distant intellectual entity, not as a flesh-and-blood young boy whose life he and the equally perverted Richard Loeb had snuffed out in the exercise of their "perfect crime." Nathan Leopold, Jr. had gone on to live out a life. Bobby Franks had perished at age fourteen, slaughtered by two bestial killers who feared only the failure of their own mad schemes.

"THE REAL McCOY"/August 24, 1924

Norman Selby (AKA: Kid McCoy, The Real McCoy, 1873-1940), was a rough and tumble prizefighter from the bare-knuckle era, who left behind an enduring cliche in American slang: "the real McCoy." Although during Prohibition the phrase meant pure unadulterated alcohol, it originated before the turn of the century when Selby was in his heyday. "I'm in a saloon with a charming lady as usual," the fighter recalled. "A drunk is making passes at her. I try to brush him off without too much fuss. 'Beat it,' I says. 'I'm Kid McCoy.' He laughs and says: 'Yeah? We'll I'm George Washington.' I have to clip him a short one and down he goes. He wakes up ten minutes later, rubs his jaw, and says, 'Jeez, it was the real Mc-Coy!'" That oft-told tale was recounted by Damon Runyon and other literary lions, who wrote of Selby's checkered career in and out of the prize ring.

Selby, calling himself Kid McCoy, won the middleweight and welterweight championships in 1895 and 1897. He flattened the reigning champion, Tommy Ryan, in a grueling fifteen-round affair after bluffing his opponent into thinking he was something less than advertised. Selby had sent a letter to Ryan before the bout begging him to "go easy," and carry him for a few rounds. Ryan eased up on his calisthenics and was wholly unprepared for what was to follow in the ring. "The bastard played possum!" cried Ryan after losing the decision.

Selby retired in 1897 at the age of twenty-four. He was worth half-a-million dollars, part of which was invested in a Broadway cabaret that became the favorite watering hole for celebrities of show business and the sporting world. In 1900 Selby was lured out of retirement for a bout with "Gentleman" Jim Corbett who beat him easily. Within the next two decades Selby married nine different women each one of whom took a sizeable chunk of his assets in divorce settlements. In 1924, his fortune all but gone, the out-of-shape ex-fighter moved to Los Angeles to work as a Hollywood movie extra. He accepted employment as a security guard in an aircraft factory and became friends with Hub Kittle, a celebrated flyer and a likely suspect in a number of holdups.

About this time, Selby began a dangerous affair with Theresa Mors, the wife of Albert Mors, one of Los Angeles' leading art and antique dealers. Mors did not appreciate it when the boozing fighter fell in love with his wife. His rancor only increased, when his wife filed for divorce and went to live with the "real McCoy" in an apartment at Hoover and Seventh streets. Happily in love, Selby proposed marriage and Mors readily accepted. Meanwhile, Mors filed a countersuit against his estranged wife naming Selby as corespondent. He advised the U.S. Treasury Department that Theresa Mors was involved in smuggling diamonds. By this time Selby had had enough. He warned Mors to leave his lover alone. Mors then had the police remove Selby from his home.

Norman "Kid McCoy" Selby, a boozing, brawling prizefighter who won the middleweight and welterweight titles in 1895 and 1897, married ten times and by 1924 was penniless when he was convicted of manslaughter and assault.

The press by now had gotten hold of this scandal and everybody had an opinion to offer to these snooping scribes. Sam Schapp, who owned a millinery store next to the antique dealer, described Selby as a dangerous opportunist bent on securing a $125,000 property settlement bound to come Mrs. Mors' way after her divorce went through.

By this time, Theresa Mors began to hedge in her relationship with Selby, but not enough to suit her estranged husband. Albert Mors began acting crazy. He stole from his wife, and then on the night of August 12, 1924, moved out of the

General Douglas MacArthur, among a bevy of famous people—including New York Governor Al Smith, entertainer Sophie Tucker and actor Lionel Barrymore—asked that Selby be paroled; the fighter was released in 1932, dying eight years later.

family home in the Hollywood Hills to take up residence at the Westgate Hotel. He signed an alias on the guest register.

The room overlooked an alley only a few doors away from the flat Selby and Mrs. Mors had rented. Around midnight the tenant who lived one floor below heard a dull thud coming from Selby's apartment. She then looked out her window and saw a man racing down the stairwell; the fleeing man, she later claimed, was Albert Mors. Two hours later a drunken Selby appeared in a Hollywood police station asking to see the officer, who had forcibly removed him from Mors' home some days earlier. "It's lucky for him he's not here," Selby stammered. "And why was that?" asked one police officer. "Hell, I'll be in the can tomorrow," Selby replied cryptically.

The police drove Selby home and told him to sleep it off. At 3 a.m. the following morning Selby appeared at the bedroom window of Jennie Thomas, his sister. Looking haggard and drunk, Selby explained that he had just killed Theresa Mors. He then stumbled from the house and headed toward Mors' antique store, where he waited patiently for the owner to arrive. Armed with a .32-caliber pistol, he captured a janitor, Mors, and a clerk, ordering them all to sit quietly on one side of the room as the first customers entered. Selby then forced the customers to surrender their cash and valuables and freed only those who appealed to him. Later that morning, Selby shot and wounded a customer, who tried to escape. Fleeing from the store, he ran into Sam Schapp and his wife. "My God! What are you doing?" Schapp asked. Before they could make any sense of the situation, Selby turned his gun on them and shot them down.

Selby commandeered a passing car and tried to escape on foot, but was brought down by a passing policeman. Investigators later found Theresa Mors lying dead on the floor of her apartment, neatly covered by a bed sheet and a picture of Selby perched at her side. Questioned by Captain Herman Cline of the Los Angeles police, Selby, after he had sobered up, explained that Theresa Mors had committed suicide because of her despondency over her husband's attempt to frame her on smuggling charges. He went on to say that he had struggled with her, but the gun had gone off accidentally. Then, believing that he had killed the woman, Selby tried to drink himself to death, but had only succeeded in passing out. He recalled little or nothing about his armed invasion of Mors' shop.

Selby was arraigned on murder, armed robbery, and assault charges. The prosecution charged that the defendant had murdered his lover because she had decided not to marry him and planned to return to New York. Defense attorney Jerry Giesler represented Selby. Under cross-examination, he demanded an answer from Mors as to why he had checked into the Westgate Hotel on the night of the murder, a perplexing question that went unanswered. Giesler, whose client list would one day be studded with the names of some of Hollywood's biggest celebrities, tried to convince the jury that Theresa Mors stabbed herself with a butcher knife and then inflicted a gunshot wound. However, even he was forced to admit that such a maneuver would be difficult if she had in fact used her left thumb to pull the trigger.

The murder charge was reduced to manslaughter and Selby was found guilty after ninety-nine hours of deliberation. He was sentenced to one to ten years for manslaughter and one to fourteen years on each of the assault charges. He served eight years at San Quentin, during which time Governor Al Smith, Sophie Tucker, Douglas MacArthur, and Lionel Barrymore petitioned for his early release. Selby emerged as a tragic, but sympathetic figure who had won himself many friends during his incarceration. He was released in 1932 and married for the tenth and last time. In 1940, the year he died, Selby reflected on his times. "It's no fun telling people you're Kid McCoy if they've heard of you before." They hadn't. He died a forgotten man.

THE SUN-WORSHIPPER AND HIS "FIRE PRINCESS"/December 10, 1929

Following WWI, wealthy Americans, many of them young and purposeless, went to Europe, specifically Paris, where they embraced the expatriate life. Their lifestyle, though labeled as vice-ridden at home, was an expression of art in Europe. One of the leaders of these youthful effete, dilettantes was a young man who lived only for himself, Henry Grew "Harry" Crosby

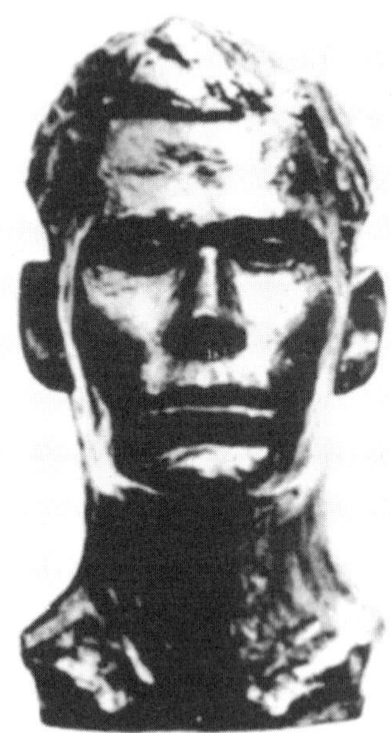

Harry Crosby in bronze; he was a Morgan heir and a playboy with a death wish.

(1898-1929). He was a sensualist and a part-time poet, a publisher of small books written by avant-guard writers. Crosby had made a career of glorious disillusionment; his fatalism was his only confidence. He was the saint of sophisticated sin, this heir to one of America's great fortunes. Crosby was the nephew and godson of billionaire J. Pierpont Morgan, and he would stain that illustrious heritage with murder and suicide.

Crosby, born into great wealth on June 4, 1898, in Boston's Back Bay, could boast of a lineage (though he expressed hatred for all that was ancestral in America) that ran to the marrow of the founding fathers. He was related to Alexander Hamilton, William Floyd, and other luminaries of the American Revolution. Riches had flowed into the Crosby coffers since the early seventeenth century when another relative, General Stephen Van Rensselaer, established a fiefdom on his land (through a Dutch grant) that ran for twenty lucrative miles along the Hudson River.

Harry's father, Stephen Van Rensselaer Crosby, a pillar of Harvard and Back Bay society, was the eternal club man who became a partner in the banking investment firm of F.S. Mosely. Harry's family ties knotted tightly about the vast fortunes of the richest man in America, if not the world at that time, J. Pierpont Morgan. It was as natural as sunrise that Harry would attend the exclusive St. Mark's preparatory school and then go on to Harvard. World War I interrupted the schedule with Harry sailing to France to become an ambulance driver just after taking his entrance examinations to Harvard in 1917.

For Crosby and his schoolmates, the war in Europe provided high adventure, an exciting excursion into danger. They looked upon the war as members of their class had earlier viewed those traditional European tours taken by the offspring of the rich before entering college. The difference became abruptly apparent when the youthful Crosby encountered horrible, mutilating death on the Western Front. The shock of recognition changed his life forever, especially after his close friends, Oliver Ames, Jr., Richard Fairchild, and Aaron Davis Weld, were killed in battle.

Worse still, on November 22, 1917, the 19-year-old Harry Crosby was hemmed in by a barrage as he attempted to rush his ambulance to a field hospital near Verdun with a friend bleeding to death inside. It was a brutalizing incident he was never to forget, writing ten years later in his diary (absent of almost all punctuation, a writing quirk): "The hills of Verdun and the red sun setting back of the hills and the charred skeletons of trees and the river Meuse and the black shells spouting up in columns along the road to Bras and the thunder of the barrage and the wounded and the ride through red explosions and the violent metamorphose from boy into man."

Crosby's abrupt loss of innocence was replaced by anger and resentment. He blamed God for the war and, in justifying his own slim survival, he concluded that there was a bit of the Superman about him; that he had been forged into a special human being who was, by birth and station, already special in his own mind, not unlike the egotistical postures assumed by Nathan Leopold, Jr. and Richard Loeb, who had attempted to commit "the perfect crime," and failed.

Crosby returned home with medals on his chest, including the Croix de Guerre, which he coveted and likened to achieving an "H" grade in college. Crosby impatient to get out of the service at war's end, begged his parents to prevail upon his omnipotent uncle, J. Pierpont Morgan, to "try and get me a discharge," according to Crosby's War Letters. "Anything can be done by means of graft." Whether or not Crosby meant for Morgan to use his considerable influence or merely buy off authorities to get him released early is not known. But there certainly was a thick venal streak in Crosby, among myriad eccentricities and vices, all of which, in his short life, he would tax to exhaustion.

When he was mustered out, Crosby arrived in New York and immediately went to the Morgan mansion where, in the

Harry Crosby is flanked by his wife Caresse (left) and his sister Kitsa, at Deauville, France, in the early 1920s.

absence of his uncle, he ordered a feast which he devoured alone while servants did his bidding. (He called them "lackeys" and "menials.") Then he began to down goblet after goblet of ancient, priceless wine until he was drunk. In that state, he later arrived by train in Boston, staggering into the arms of his waiting family.

Harry's intoxication did not alarm Mr. and Mrs. Crosby; he was their only son and his ordeal in France was excuse enough for his unpredictable behavior. Crosby was quick to take up the same rationale, using his war experience for the rest of his short life as an excuse to wallow in the libertine life.

At first, Crosby seemed to adjust, entering Harvard where his grades were less than spectacular. He studied literature and language, excelling in French in which, by virtue of his war experience, he was fluent. Crosby, like many other veterans of that day, was allowed to earn a "War Degree" at Harvard, which granted a shorter time of study in achieving a degree as compensation for serving overseas. He graduated in 1921.

A year earlier, Crosby had met and fallen in love with a married woman; he was to develop a habit that approached mania of trysting with married women for the rest of his days. The buxom, attractive female, six years older than Crosby, was Mrs. Richard Rogers Peabody (maiden name Mary Phelps Jacob), whom everybody called Polly. They met at a beach outing and both were smitten. Crosby told his parents that he intended to marry Polly, no matter what the consequences.

The Crosbys recoiled in shock. Polly would have to divorce her husband, another scion of a Back Bay fortune, to marry their son, and divorce, at that time, was inconceivable. Yet Harry persisted, telling his father that he would kill himself if he failed to have Polly as his bride. Polly reciprocated Harry's dedication. Her husband, the youthful Mr. Peabody, was a gentleman about it all. He told his wife to think it over during a trial separation. Polly did exactly that, going to New York with Crosby. At the end of six months, she still asked for a divorce and Peabody, who became addicted to alcohol (he would later write about his alcoholism in *The Common Sense of Drinking*), agreed to let his wife go.

Harry and Polly married seven months after she received her divorce. Before that time, Crosby himself took to drink. He had accepted a desk job, arranged by his father, in the Shawmut National Bank in Boston, and hated it. He told his parents that he found Boston stifling, that the environment strangled his will to write great works. He promptly went on a six-day binge and quit his job. Next he begged uncle Jack (Morgan) to get him a job in Paris, something that would allow him and Polly to live in the "City of Light" where he could follow his artistic urges.

Morgan arranged for Crosby to work in the Paris offices of Morgan, Harjes & Co. Delighted, Harry asked Polly to marry him and they were wed on September 9, 1922, in New York City. Two days later, they sailed to France on the Aquitania. It was all idyllic, a fantasy come true; but then again, Harry Crosby had been born into fantasy and he always got what he wanted.

Crosby at the Four Arts Ball in Paris, 1928, with one of his many conquests, the identify of this woman unknown.

After living in expensive Paris hotels and running up staggering bills paid for by Crosby's relatives, Harry and Polly took a series of apartments, finally renting the huge flat once occupied by Princess Marthe Bibesco in St. Germain. For a year, Crosby halfheartedly worked at his uncle's banking concern, but he spent more time during each workday strolling the boulevards, drinking in bistros, and chasing women, than he did in his office.

Another rich relative, an older cousin, Walter Van Rensselaer Berry, who had been living in European luxury for more than a decade, learned of Harry's writing ambitions and suggested that he quit his job with Morgan. Crosby, using his older cousin as a sanction of the literary life, quit, and wrote his parents that he was, from that point on, dedicating his life to the muse, so would they please sell off a few thousand shares of the great amount of stock he held and forward spending money? The money, as usual, was pro-

Crosby at the wheel of his Bugatti, 1926; like T. E. Lawrence ("Lawrence of Arabia"), he was obsessed by speed, as well as the rays of the sun.

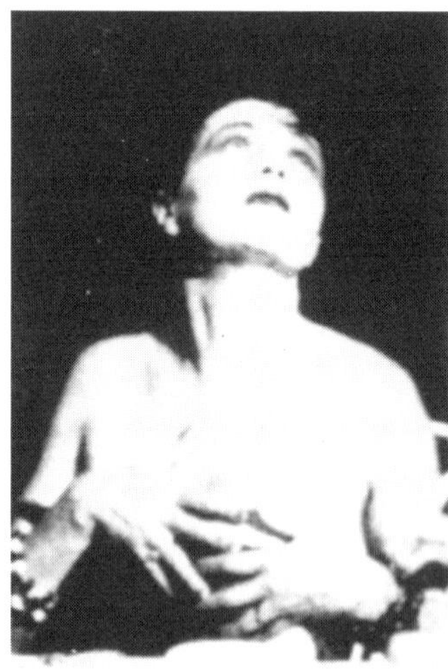

Caresse Crosby, who imagined herself a patron of the arts, shown in one of her dramatic poses.

vided. (Berry may well have been the role model for the wealthy uncle in W. Somerset Maugham's 1944 novel, *The Razor's Edge*, and his portraits of the rich young couple squandering their lives being based on the self-indulgent Crosbys.)

By 1923, the Crosbys set the style of the young rich expatriates in Paris. They exuded a sort of glossy, intellectual hedonism. Harry's new lifestyle as a self-styled artist now demanded that he seek release and "enlightenment" with women other than his wife. Among the many affairs he openly conducted was a torrid interlude with Constance Coolidge who was the niece of Frank Crowninshield, editor of *Vanity Fair*.

The darkly attractive and willful Constance, divorced from diplomat Ray Atherton, had once been the scandal of China, where her husband had been stationed. There she had raced horses and carried on in such a manner as to earn herself the sobriquet of "The Queen of Peking." Crosby, who met her at a racetrack in Paris, called her "The Lady of the Golden Horse." He was forever dubbing his mistresses with romantic names: Helen of Troy, The Tigress, The Lady of the White Polo Coat, The Sorceress, Nubile, The Youngest Princess, The Fire Princess. These were the names he used in his diaries in referring to his many sexual escapades.

Polly, whose name the Crosbys later changed to Caresse for alliterative, arcane reasons, seemed not to care about her husband's sexual adventures. She knew these "other" women well; they were social acquaintances and many of these ladies were introduced to her womanizing husband by none other than herself. Some in her careless social set went so far as to say that her indifference toward her husband's sexual adventures was rooted to her own latent lesbian nature.

Yet Harry was inexplicably loyal to Caresse. Constance Coolidge insisted Harry leave Caresse for her. When he refused, she went off to marry the Comte de Jumilhac, thereby becoming a rich and landed countess. Harry continued to see her periodically, considering her part of his stable.

There were others, many of them, including petite, dark Polia Chentoff, a Russian painter who excited the Crosbys with her weird, bizarre tales of famine in revolutionary Russia. On one occasion, she said that the people in her village were so hungry that they ate an American missionary who had brought them a little food.

While Harry's harem increased in numbers, Caresse was not idle. She, too, took on a series of lovers, boldly mentioned by Crosby in a letter to his overindulgent mother. "Caresse's boy friends are," wrote Crosby casually, "the Comte Civry, the Tartar Prince, Ortiz, Frans de Geetere (the husband of a couple who had been living on a barge docked on the Seine), Lord Lymington ..."

As early as 1923, Crosby had gotten the reputation of a crazy millionaire American who gave vent to any sensual urge and wrote poetry on the side. One of Harry's passions was attending the raucous Four Arts Balls which heralded the closing of the art academies in Paris each summer. These were nothing more than costume orgies into which Crosby hurled himself with glee.

In 1923, Crosby attended the ball wearing a Roman toga. He returned to his apartment stripped of this garment, his underpants, and all his money. Emerging completely drunk and stark naked, he staggered down the street and into his lodgings, to the amazement of his bug-eyed neighbors. Had this been the conduct of a resident Frenchman, the police would certainly have been summoned, but Crosby was too rich to arrest. Two years later, he found a monkey at the ball and got it drunk.

In 1926, Harry and Caresse shocked even the wild students attending the ball. Crosby appeared as an Incan chieftain, donning a loin cloth and coating his almost naked body with red ocher. Around his neck he wore a necklace of dead pigeons. Caresse matched Harry's abandon by appearing with a turquoise wig and was naked from the waist up, displaying her large breasts to hundreds of hooting students. (Caresse Crosby consistently complained that no female undergarments served as a proper halter for her mammae and, so she later claimed, she invented the brassiere.) The ball culminated with Caresse, breasts flopping wildly, being carried about the ballroom in the mouth of a papier-mache dragon, supported by dozens of students.

These balls were held in enormous halls, where as many as three to five thousand people jammed inside. Half of the guests were whores plying their trade. The police looked the other way on these occasions, tolerating any and all excesses, except assault and battery. It was not an uncommon sight, following the closing of the ball, to see hundreds of naked men and women dancing in the streets and atop cabs, and scores more fornicating in doorways and near the hall.

Before the balls, the Crosbys invariably gave a party which became the pre-ball party. Hundreds flocked into their spacious apartment to guzzle their gin-laced punch and fall to the floor in amorous embrace. In 1927, Crosby threw a party that alarmed even his own sense of expansive tolerance. Males in attendance mobbed his maid and almost raped her. Ushering out most of the guests, Harry retired to the bathroom with Caresse and other close friends, and all stripped and sank into the hot water held by an enormous, specially built bathtub. Then Harry painted himself green, grabbed a bag of snakes, and headed for the ball, where he distributed the reptiles as necklaces to horrified guests.

When bored with Paris, Harry would suddenly hustle Caresse off to Athens or Africa to see the sights and sample the perversions. In 1925, Harry and Caresse traveled to Tunisia, where they both made love to an 11-year-old girl named Zara. In Constantinople, on a later trip, Harry scouted the city to find just the right kind of entertainment and one night took Caresse to an enormous whorehouse, where they paid exorbitant prices to watch couples fornicate.

In Egypt, they visited a huge brothel, one of Harry's favorite visiting spots; the Crosbys sank into utter sexual perversion, seeking out young girls with which to sleep. It was here that they (especially Harry) developed an insatiable taste for opium and hashish, buying the drugs in great quantities. Crosby consumed so much opium on one occasion that he almost died from an overdose (he developed the habit of swallowing opium pills and mixing this with champagne).

The ancient land held a deep and morose fascination for the American millionaire. He collected strange artifacts from its crypts and tombs. On one occasion, he paid a large sum for three mummified hands of young girls, each having a blue ring on the forefinger. Another time he bought the skeleton of a young girl, which he pridefully hung in the library of his Paris apartment at 19 Rue de Lille. What cabalistic rites attended these purchases was never learned. Yet the mysteries of Egypt continued to hold Crosby in a trance throughout his short life.

His uncle, Walter Van Rensselaer Berry, had had an abiding interest in all things Egyptian, and his influence upon Harry to seek the answers to that land's mystical secrets was permanent. It was in Egypt that Harry Crosby became enamored with sun worship, following the ancient Egyptian rites to the sun god, Ra. He thought of the sun as God, and at every opportunity stripped naked and baked beneath its rays, absorbing its heat, its fire, until, toward the end of his life, the normally pale-skinned young man from Boston appeared to friends as a "red Indian."

Walter Berry further enriched Crosby's life when he died on October 12, 1927, leaving to Harry most of his estate and his collection of rare books, almost eight thousand tomes. This behest infuriated author Edith Wharton, who expected not only Berry's fortune, or part of it, but also Berry's library of priceless volumes. (The two had been lovers and Berry, an aristocratic, knowledgeable intellectual, had served as Mrs. Wharton's mentor.)

Crosby with a 13-year-old Berber girl in Touggpourt, Algeria, 1925; he holds an opium pipe, which provided one of his favorite pastimes.

Crosby made a mocking celebration out of his cousin's funeral. He supervised with elaborate pomp the cremation of his cousin and sneeringly greeted distinguished mourners at the funeral in Paris, while Crosby and Wharton vied for the dead man's library. Crosby feared that Mrs. Wharton, who, under the Berry will could choose whatever books she wanted, would swallow the entire library. Harry thought of her as "a bad sort," and Mrs. Wharton, according to Geoffrey Wolf, writing in *Black Sun*, told a friend that "Walter's young cousin Crosby turns out to be a sort of half-crazy cad." In the end, Mrs. Wharton selected only a few books and Harry received the bulk of the library.

That he read any of these rare volumes is debatable. What he did do with many of the books would have caused Mrs. Wharton, had she known, to collapse with apoplexy. The Berry library caused the normally spacious Crosby apartment to overflow with books; they were everywhere—in shelves on the walls and piled high on the floors of many rooms, so that the Crosbys had to move about the place through narrow paths. Harry solved the problem by giving hundreds of books away to complete strangers, cab drivers, prostitutes, bartenders, those whose interest in ancient literature was considerably less than ravenous. Crosby then amused himself by donning disguises, a rag peddler, say, and slinking through the open-air book stalls lining the Seine where cheap books were sold. He would slip from a bag slung about his shoulders many of his cousin's priceless books and secretly bury them among the tawdry novels. It amused him to think that uneducated book buyers would casually pick up one of Berry's cherished volumes for a few francs, not knowing the book's true value, which would also be the case with the unschooled book dealers along the Seine.

Crosby's own literary aspirations were grossly inflated by himself, his wife, and his friends. He and Caresse started the Black Sun Press to publish their own awkward poetry and then expanded to include the most well-known writers of the day, including Ernest Hemingway, James Joyce, Ezra Pound, and others, but these writers merely tolerated the Crosbys, giving them fragmentary works that were expensively published and for which the authors received handsome payments. D. H. Lawrence, for instance, demanded that the millionaire playboy pay him for a short work in gold pieces, and Harry dutifully complied.

Literary figures Crosby admired repeatedly told him he was a talented poet. They should have known better, but perhaps they were merely stroking the golden goose. As a result of such boulevard flattery, Crosby began to submit his material to other publications, but not before he made substantial financial contributions to such struggling expatriate periodicals as *Transition*. In this fashion, Crosby's neurotic, erotic poetry found a wider audience than the Black Sun Press could provide. To the literary set, he quickly became known as a weird playboy poet whose work screamed doom and death.

To Ernest Hemingway, Crosby was certainly nothing more than a rich social acquaintance who paid the way at the restaurant and racetrack during the author's lean years. It amused Hemingway, once he learned of Crosby's fanatical sun-worshipping, to jibe him about it. From Cuba in 1929, Hemingway sent Harry a newspaper clipping that ridiculed sun-worshippers, but it did not daunt Crosby's belief in the ancient rite.

By 1928, Harry Crosby had become hopelessly involved in himself. He lived only for pleasure. More and more, he escaped the real world to indulge in his fantasies, not unlike the time when he was on the way to a Paris bank to place Caresse's expensive jewelry in a safe deposit box. He spotted an attractive female relative, a distant cousin, and drank with her, attempting to seduce her. When Crosby departed the cafe, he left Caresse's jewels behind; they were never found. Crosby's drinking increased; he sank into prolonged stupors from drugs and great quantities of absinthe (wormwood alcohol, banned even in Paris where the deadly drink had driven poet Paul Verlaine insane and killed others).

In 1928, Caresse and Harry moved into an old mill in the Ermenonville forest, near Paris, on the 9,000 acre estate of Armand de la Rochefoucauld, renting it by the year. Renovating the place, the Crosbys turned the crumbling structure into posh spa-like quarters. They invited phalanxes of artists, writers, and bon vivants to spend weeks with them, drinking and cavorting. Hart Crane, the distinguished poet, who was published by Crosby, came to marvel at the luxury at the new Crosby dwelling and flaunt his insatiable homosexu-

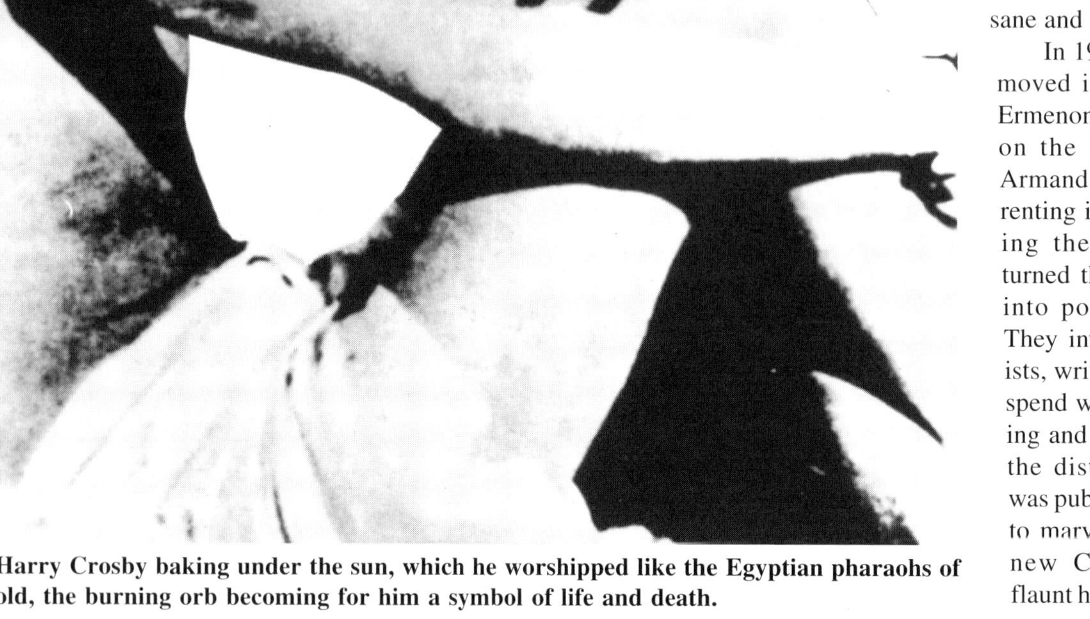

Harry Crosby baking under the sun, which he worshipped like the Egyptian pharaohs of old, the burning orb becoming for him a symbol of life and death.

ality by seducing Crosby's chauffeur. (Crane would commit suicide in 1932 by jumping from a ship while sailing from Mexico to New York, swimming directly into the propellers.)

Guests at the Crosby mill were encouraged to drink themselves blind night and day, and when not blind with booze, to amuse themselves in the gleaming, enormous pool (into which they consistently jumped fully-clothed), or participate in donkey races which Harry religiously conducted. Some of the guests stayed but briefly at Harry's wild retreat. Writers Robert McAlmon and Kay Boyle, as recalled in *Being Geniuses Together*, left one of the wild parties late at night, going from the main building to the guest cottages after a riot erupted. "It's too damned depressing," McAlmon groaned to Boyle, "so depressing that I can't even get drunk. They're wraiths, all of them. They aren't people. God knows what they've done with their realities."

Reality had long run out on Harry Crosby. He shielded himself from it with money and the rays of the sun. Crosby was forever adorning his body with pagan symbols; in Africa he had crosses tattooed on the soles of his feet. In 1928, he paid a Hindu to tattoo a huge sun on his back in the dead of night as he lay face down in a boat wallowing on the Nile. It was also in 1928 that Harry Grew Crosby began planning his suicide and that of his wife. Caresse agreed with her husband to end their lives on October 31, 1942, a date arrived at through crazy-quilt theories of Harry's own mad invention, a doomsday date approximating their twentieth wedding anniversary.

The year 1928 was momentous for Crosby. It was also in that year, on July 9, 1928, that he met at the Lido Bar in Paris 21-year-old Josephine Noyes Rotch, a darkly attractive Boston socialite. He fell madly in love with her, calling her his "Fire Princess." For three weeks they carried on a torrid affair, but when Harry refused to leave Caresse for her, Miss Rotch sailed for the U.S. The following year, on June 21, 1928, she married Albert Bigelow, a wealthy member of a distinguished East Coast family.

Crosby brooded over the loss of another mistress. His extravagances increased as did his erratic behavior. He leaped into a cab one night to drive down the Champs Elysees in Paris, hurling gold coins to startled passersby. He bought racehorses he never raced, and lost fortunes through reckless, stupid gambling, paying for his debts by selling off huge blocks of stock. (In 1929, Crosby wired his father: "Please sell ten thousand dollars worth of stock. We have decided to lead a mad and extravagant life." This wire came as no surprise; the Crosbys had led nothing but the life of wastrels to that time.)

Desperate to occupy his hours with something, anything, that would provide stimulation, Crosby suddenly became obsessed with flying. This new mania led him to take many commercial flights between Paris and England (at a time when only a handful of passengers, at great expense, could cram aboard the small planes available, traveling at about 100 m.p.h. and at an altitude of no more than 1,000 feet). Looking down from a plane on one flight, it occurred to Harry Crosby that it would "be fun to drop bombs" on the peaceful French countryside below.

Crosby took flying lessons and, in his gnawing vanity, saw himself as another Lindbergh, to whom he bore a striking resemblance. He saw himself as a hero, a pathfinder, but he never went beyond student status as a pilot. Next came fast racing cars. Crosby raced for weeks, but soon exhausted his zest for dirt tracks, sputtering engines and oil-smeared hands. For a while, the would-be literary giant decided to become the world's greatest photographer and purchased almost every known camera. He tired of this, too.

Caresse tolerated her husband's excesses and went her own way, becoming engrossed with the duties of a publisher at Black Sun Press. Harry thought only of Josephine, his fire princess, and corresponded with her. His thoughts also, more and more, turned to suicide, about which he wrote reams of poetry and talked incessantly. He had apparently little regard for his own poetry. Early in March 1929, while staying at the old mill, he dragged out eighty-some copies of his self-published book, *Red Skeletons*, and blew them to pieces with a shotgun. He then burned the remains.

On November 18, 1929, Crosby received a wire from Mrs. Josephine Rotch Bigelow, urging him to come to her in America. Harry was at first reluctant to return to his native land. His last visit in 1928 produced in him a hatred for his hometown. In one poem, he called Boston a "City of Dead Semen." Worse, on that trip Harry had barraged Boston's liter-

Writer Ernest Hemingway, who sent Crosby a newspaper clipping that ridiculed sun-worshippers in 1929, the year Crosby decided to end his life.

ary bastion, *Atlantic Monthly*, with more than fifty poems, all of which were rejected.

But Crosby did return to America, accompanied by Caresse. Keeping him company on the boat trip was an other old flame, Constance, the Comtesse de Jumilhac. After going to Boston, Harry met with Mrs. Bigelow on November 28, 1929. Caresse went to New York and registered at the Savoy-Plaza Hotel on November 25, 1929. Her husband showed up three days later but stayed only a week. Harry then took a train to Detroit, where he had arranged to meet Mrs. Bigelow. He and Josephine registered under the name of Mr. and Mrs. Harry Crane, using the name of Crosby's poet friend, Hart Crane. The love tryst lasted for two days before both returned to New York and their spouses.

Crosby began drinking heavily in early December as he and his wife prepared to return to Paris. Hart Crane gave them a party, but Harry seemed disinterested, even when Crane let in a horde of drunken sailors whom he, Crane, attempted to seduce on the spot. Unknown to Caresse, her husband had broken more than his marriage vows; it was already settled in his mind that he would not live up to their suicide pact scheduled for 1942. He intended to end it in 1929 "with a bang, not a whimper," (Harry's convolution of T. S. Eliot's premise), and with another woman, the fire princess.

December 10, 1929, was an auspicious day for the Crosbys. They were to dine in the august presence of J. Pierpont Morgan, Harry's uncle. That morning, Harry and Caresse attended an exhibition by a sculptor, who had completed a bronze sculpture of their dog, Narcisse Noir. Then Harry abruptly left his wife, kissing her and telling her he would see her and his mother at "uncle Jack's." From there, they would join Hart Crane for dinner and the theater.

Following a quick lunch, Crosby took a cab to 1 West 67th Street, the address of the Hotel des Artistes and going to the duplex studio occupied by his friend, Stanley Mortimer, a portrait painter. Here, he met Mrs. Josephine Bigelow. They had met several times at Mortimer's and the artist, an obliging friend, had given Harry a key to his ninth-floor abode. They arrived together at noon to be greeted by Mortimer. They had a few drinks and then Crosby led Josephine to an upstairs bedroom with an overhanging balcony. Mortimer continued painting, but the couple leaned over the balcony and "kidded me," according to Mortimer later. "Crosby gave me a signal and I got on my street clothes and went out."

Crosby spent unknown hours in Mortimer's place with Mrs. Bigelow, who was later described as a "strange wild girl who delighted in saying things to shock people" and who was extremely possessive of Harry. Meanwhile, Crosby's wife and mother spent an uncomfortable tea-time with uncle Jack Morgan in the financier's behemoth mansion, trying to explain the absence of the errant Harry. Caresse and Mrs. Crosby finally left the Morgan house without waiting for Harry, returning to the Savoy, where they dressed for dinner. Still, Harry did not arrive. They went to the Caviar Restaurant and met Hart Crane. Halfway through the meal, she later claimed, Caresse had a terrible premonition, and left the table to phone Stanley Mortimer at his mother's house (this, of course, made it obvious that Caresse knew all along that her husband was not only meeting with Mrs. Bigelow, but was using Mortimer's apartment as a love nest). Mortimer told Caresse that he would go by his apartment and check on Harry.

Josephine Rotch Bigelow, a married woman who became Crosby's "Fire Princess;" he murdered her in December 1929, before taking his own life.

The artist reached his studio at 9:30 p.m. and found it bolted from inside. He knocked and called, but no one answered. Desperately, he raced to the superintendent of the building and demanded that he break down the door. The man wielded an ax to batter down the door. Inside, Mortimer found Harry Grew Crosby and Josephine Rotch Bigelow—he was then thirty-one, she twenty-two—both dead on his bed. A bullet hole was in Josephine's left temple, another in Harry's right temple. Both were fully clothed, according to later newspaper reports. Their left hands were entwined and Harry's free arm was wrapped loosely about her neck, the right hand clutching a .25-caliber Belgian automatic pistol.

Police arrived to find more than $500 in cash stuffed in Harry's pockets, along with the steamship tickets which Harry and Caresse were to use on their return voyage to France. Crosby had removed a gold ring, one he called his "sun ring," which he had promised his wife he would never take off. It had been flattened, as if he had stomped on it.

Caresse learned of the suicide-murder, as it was later termed by police, late that night. She did not go to the scene of the crime, nor did the Crosbys utter a word of the disgrace their son had brought down upon the family name. It became practice for decades that none of the Crosby relatives ever mention the name of Harry Crosby again.

The bizarre end of Harry Crosby and his Bryn Mawr-trained mistress captured the nation's headlines. The Chicago *Tribune*, which bannered the deaths with the headlines, CROSBY DIED FOR A THRILL, stated that: "As a writer and publisher and a wealthy, amusing fellow besides, Crosby just about set the pace for the whole crowd of expatriates, who credit him with having 'lived more fully than any man of his generation.' None of his fast-moving crowd believe Crosby committed suicide for love, and are sure he sought death just to see what it was like ..."

But for Josephine, according to Deputy Chief Medical Examiner Thomas Gonzalez of New York City, there was no such intention. Gonzalez, along with Inspector Mulrooney, stated that, from the position of the bodies and the varying states of rigor mortis, Crosby had murdered Josephine, then spent several hours alone in the apartment before killing himself. Gonzalez was quoted as saying that homicide was obvious, along with "the expression of smiling expectancy on the dead face of the beautiful young wife, indicating that she had gone to her rendezvous expecting a caress, not deadly bullets."

Albert Bigelow arrived in New York from Boston the following day, while his wife and Harry were taken to separate mortuaries to await burial. The outraged husband, a Harvard man, told a reporter from the New York *Daily News*: "This man lured her to his apartment and murdered her. I don't believe in any suicide pact no matter what the police or anybody else says, and I believe my wife to be the victim of a mad poet who turned murderer because he could not have the woman he wanted and who was true to me."

Bigelow proved his loyalty to Josephine by having her remains buried in the family plot at Old Lyme, Connecticut. Harry's body was cremated two days later, and the remains were given to Caresse in an expensive urn which she took with her to Paris. (She would die on January 24, 1970, still promoting Harry Crosby to the world as an offbeat, misunderstood rebel poet who simply happened to be rich and had ended his young life more at the instigation of a reckless age than from his own hand.) Critic Malcolm Cowley further eulogized Crosby in his 1920s literary memoirs, *Exile's Return*, remarking about this supremely self-indulgent young man: "Harry Crosby, dead, had ...become a symbol of change ...In spite of himself he had died at the right time." It was Cowley's thought that the death of Harry Crosby signaled the close of the Roaring Twenties, the age of excess, only moments before a great night of depression and war blanketed the world.

Poet e.e. cummings (who used the lower case in his name) had the last succinct words, dealing with the murder-suicide as would a deadline-hounded newspaper editor, captioning the strange deaths with:

2 Boston
Dolls found
with
Holes in each other
's lullaby

Recently graduated from Annapolis, Ensign Thomas H. Massie is shown with his 16-year-old bride, Thalia Fortescue.

THE MASSIES OF HAWAII/January 8, 1932

In the fall of 1931, Hawaii, then an American Territory, was a wild mixture of cultures—Hawaiian, Japanese, Filipino, Portuguese, Korean, and Americans. Racial unrest was the norm. In early September, the city of Honolulu began to experience a rash of rapes in which white women were dragged into an old touring car occupied by five "little swarthy men," taken to secluded spots, and sexually attacked. On the night of September 21, 1931, attractive 20-year-old Mrs. Thalia Massie, wife of Navy officer Lieutenant Thomas Massie (1900-1944), left a party at the Ala Wai Inn to cool off by taking a walk alone down the poorly lighted John Edna Road. Suddenly an old Buick drove alongside her and stopped. Five men were inside of it, Horace Ida, a Japanese who owned the large touring car; David Takai, another Japanese; Henry Chang, a Chinese; and Hawaiians Ben Anekuelo and Joe Kahahawai, a tough, well-built young man, who was a professional boxer.

Four of the men leaped out of the car and grabbed Mrs. Massie, throwing her into the back seat of the car and speeding off to the Old Animal Quarantine Station, which Mrs. Massie recognized. She was dragged out of the car and when she offered resistance Kahahawai sent a powerful punch to her jaw, breaking it. Thalia Massie went limp and the five men pinned her to the ground and then took turns raping her.

After her attackers departed, Mrs. Massie, battered and bleeding, managed to stagger to Al Moana Drive and flagged down a car. She was taken home and Lieutenant Massie, still attending the party, was called. He rushed home to find his wife's face battered, her lips cut and bleeding, her eyes swollen and blackened. "I thought at first that she had been hit by a truck," Massie later recalled.

Thalia Massie collapsed into her husband's arms, sob-

Thalia Fortescue Massie, shortly before she was abducted while she was walking along a lonely road and brutally beaten and raped by five non-whites outside Honolulu, Hawaii, on the night of September 21, 1931.

Social grande dame of Long Island, New York, Grace Hubbard Bell Fortescue, a woman of iron will, flew to Hawaii after hearing that her daughter had been attacked and, upon arrival, took charge of exacting revenge.

bing: "It's awful, Tommy, the shame! I just want to die!" She then related the story of being raped by five natives of mixed race. She produced a scrap of paper on which she had written the number 58895, the license of the car the men had been driving. Police were summoned and the Buick was tracked down to Ida, who quickly involved the others.

These same five men had been arrested many times in the past, separately and in a group, for committing a number of sex crimes. All five had been previously accused of raping a Mrs. Peebles, but because of "lack of evidence" had been released. The five men were brought before Mrs. Massie, who identified each one of them as her attackers, adding: "I'd know those savages anywhere."

The news of this rape shocked the island and the story made front-page news in mainland U.S. newspapers. What was doubly shocking at that time was that the Massies were members of the social elite in Hawaii and came from distinguished, upper-class families. Lieutenant Thomas Massie was a quiet, gentle officer who had graduated with honors from the Naval Academy at Annapolis and came from a wealthy, much-respected Kentucky family.

Thalia had married Massie when only sixteen, but she had the blessing of her mother, Mrs. Grace Glanville-Fortescue, a wealthy society woman, whose husband was a retired army major. Mrs. Fortescue herself came from a prestigious Long Island family and was the niece of inventor Alexander Graham Bell. She and her daughter Thalia were listed in the Social Register.

While the rapists were jailed pending trial, Fortescue flew to Hawaii to be near her daughter. She was infuriated that such a brutal crime could be perpetrated against a white woman and said so publicly and to her friends in Hawaii, all members of the island's social elite. Fortescue also met with Admiral Yates Stirling, commander of the Navy base at Pearl Harbor. Stirling was livid about the attack. He told Fortescue that "our first inclination is to seize these brutes and string them up on trees, but we must give the authorities the chance to carry out the law. It will be slow and exasperating, but we must be patient."

On November 19, 1931, the five accused men were brought to trial. Hospital doctors testifying at the trial were of little help to the prosecution, stating that, indeed, Mrs. Massie had

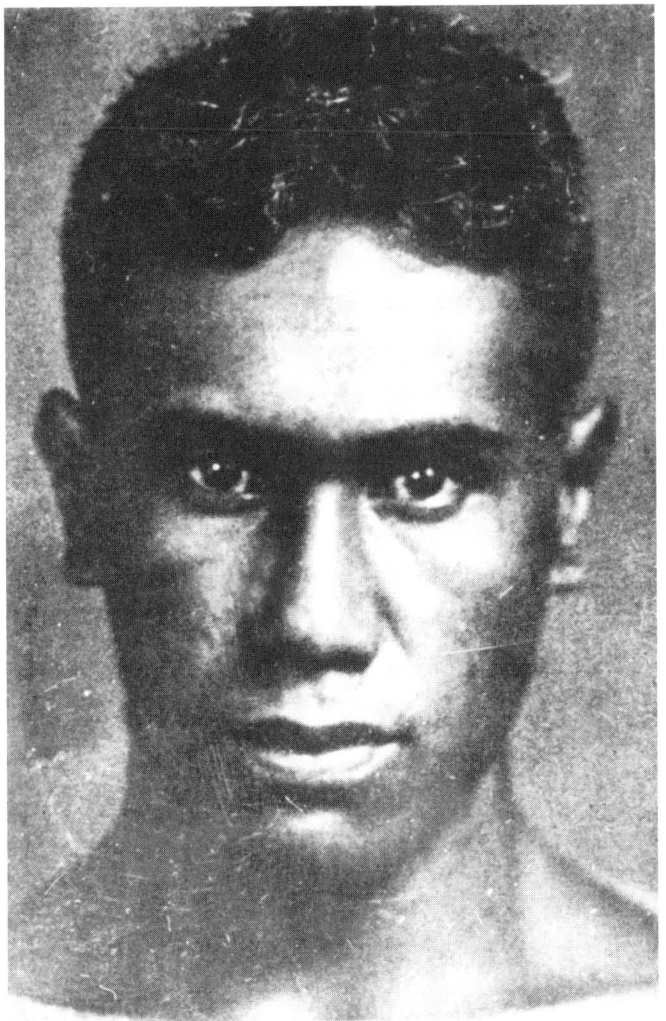

Joseph Kahahawai was accused of being one of the five men who raped Thalia Massie, but a jury set him and the others free, which incensed Massie and Mrs. Fortescue, who then planned their own brand of justice.

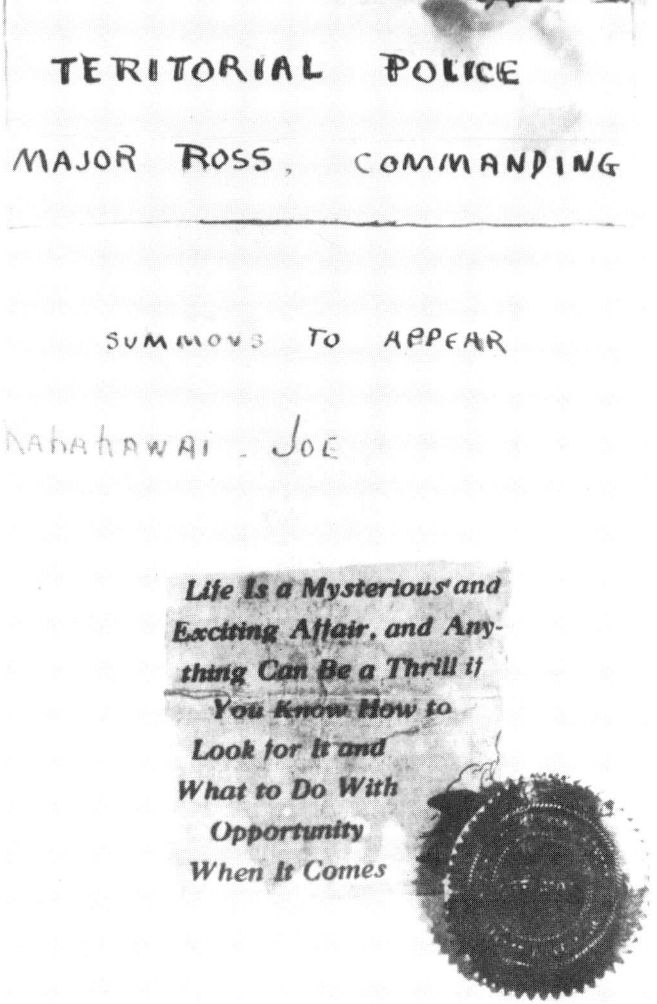

TERITORIAL POLICE

MAJOR ROSS, COMMANDING

SUMMONS TO APPEAR

KAHAHAWAI . JOE

Life Is a Mysterious and Exciting Affair, and Anything Can Be a Thrill if You Know How to Look for It and What to Do With Opportunity When It Comes

The bogus summons (created by Mrs. Fortescue, along with the cryptic newspaper text) that convinced the naive Joseph Kahahawai that he was under arrest and allowed his abductors to drive him away to his death.

been attacked, but they had found no real evidence of rape, no presence of sperm in her body. She was not, as popularly thought, pregnant at the time of the attack. Five white men and seven men of mixed races listened to arguments for fifteen days and then decided that there was not sufficient evidence to convict the defendants, even with Thalia Massie's sworn statements that each of the accused had raped her.

This travesty of justice inflamed the white community on Oahu. The rage over the jury decision was centered on the seven jurists of mixed races who, it was said, had freed the rapists because they were of their own race or nationalities (not unlike the prejudicial decision by the almost all black jury that acquitted O. J. Simpson more than sixty years later). Admiral Stirling summed up the attitude of the white community by later writing: "The criminal assault of a white woman by the five dark-skinned citizens had gone unpunished by the Courts. Sympathies have been aroused in favor of the accused men. Conviction was thus impossible."

The defendants did help their cause by making sneering remarks about Mrs. Massie and strutting about Honolulu as if they were victors of a boxing match. (These men were later portrayed in a far-from-the-truth TV movie as innocent youths who had been pilloried by a white society. In truth they all had police records as sex offenders.) The conduct of the defendants so enraged a group of Navy officers that, on the night of December 13, 1931, a group of officers seized Horace Ida and drove him to a remote spot, where he was beaten and pistol-whipped into unconsciousness and then left to make his way back to Honolulu. Ida had been dealt with in the same manner as had been Mrs. Massie, proper and ironic retribution in the minds of the men who attacked him.

Meanwhile, Mrs. Massie showed the signs of a nervous breakdown. The trial had been a tremendous strain on her and she had been held up to ridicule by defense attorneys whose snide inferences portrayed her as a loose woman, a flirt who invited the advances of white Navy officers. Groundless rumors following the trial had it that Mrs. Massie had not been raped by men of other races, but by a group of white Navy men, and that she had put the blame on the hapless Hawaiians.

Thomas Massie was also shattered during and after the

Sailors Edward J. Lord, left, and Albert O. Jones, both members of the submarine boxing team, were recruited by Massie to aid in the abduction of Joseph Kahahawai.

trial. He was a taciturn young man who said little, keeping his emotional problems to himself. On rare occasions he stated that his wife had been victimized not only by the rapists, but by the publicity attending the trial; her reputation was ruined and he sought some sort of justice beyond the court system which had failed them.

To that end, Massie enlisted the aid of two sailors, Edward Lord and Albert Jones, who served under his command and held him in great respect. Massie had learned that Joe Kahahawai, the worst offender of the rapist group, reported each day to the court as a condition of his release. On the morning of January 8, 1932, Massie drove up to the courthouse with Jones. Massie was behind the wheel of a rented Buick, disguised as a chauffeur. Jones, in civilian clothes, got out of the car when Kahahawai appeared and stopped him before the Hawaiian entered the court building, showing him a fake summons to appear before a special tribunal. Kahahawai, who understood little English, shrugged and got into the Buick. Massie drove to a bungalow Fortescue had rented in Ala Moana Valley.

Lord posted himself on guard in front of the bungalow while Massie and Jones escorted Kahahawai inside. The Hawaiian stood before a desk behind which Massie sat, acting as inquisitor, while Jones held a gun on the burly boxer. Said Massie: "Okay, we're here to get the truth out of you and to beat it out of you if necessary. If you don't talk before the police get here, we'll beat you to ribbons. Now tell me, who kicked my wife, broke her jaw, and raped her?"

Kahahawai shook his head and said he was innocent.

Massie persisted, stating: "You're a prizefighter. Of course it was you who hit her. Be a man and admit it!"

Kahahawai then broke down, according to the later statements of Massie and Jones, mumbling: "Yeah, I did it all right. We all did it, all right. We attacked your wife."

What happened next was the subject of courtroom debate and historical argument for decades to come. Massie went into a blind rage at hearing this offhand admission of a brutal crime against his wife and grabbed a revolver and shot Kahahawai

Kahahawai was taken to this bungalow, which had been rented by Mrs. Fortescue, and where Massie performed his kangaroo court, grilling the man until he admitted raping his wife, which sparked a murderous response.

Policemen remove the naked body of Joseph Kahahawai from the back seat of the Buick, which was stopped by officers after a five-mile chase, which was carrying Mrs. Fortescue, Massie, Lord and Jones; all were arrested.

once in the chest, killing him on the spot. Jones was interviewed many years later and claimed that Kahahawai leaned or lurched toward Massie at this point in the questioning, while Jones, who was holding a revolver on the man, instinctively squeezed the trigger, shooting the boxer dead.

Mrs. Fortescue and seaman Lord appeared in the living room of the bungalow at the sound of the shot and, after a hurried conference, decided to dump the body in a remote spot. At first Jones and Lord put the body in a bathtub, stripped it, and washed away all the blood. Then they wrapped it in a blanket, and placed the body in the back seat of the Buick. Massie, Fortescue, Jones, and Lord then drove toward Koko Head, thinking to dump the corpse in a canyon there.

Police, however, had already been looking for Massie, Jones, and Kahahawai, who had been seen leaving the courthouse at 8:30 a.m. by Kahahawai's cousin. They intercepted the Massie car and quickly discovered the body of the dead boxer. Fortescue, Massie, Jones, and Lord were taken into custody and charged with murder. The wealthy Fortescue immediately hired America's most famous criminal attorney, Clarence Darrow, who flew from Chicago to Hawaii to defend the foursome. The Massie case became an overnight sensation, a national cause celebre, with the races violently divided. Riots broke out in Honolulu and in various parts of the U.S., where race tension and strife was high.

Before his trial, Massie made a brief statement: "I'm sorry that this man has been shot, but it was no more than he asked for and deserved." By this statement, Massie established the line of defense in the trial, one which Darrow would vigorously pursue, that of the unwritten law, where a man defends his wife's honor at all costs and at all hazards to his own safety and well-being (the same defense that had been mounted in the notorious Harry Thaw murder case).

The U.S. Navy, rather than disavowing the actions of one of its officers, backed Massie to the hilt. Stated Admiral Stirling: "An Hawaiian rapist had been killed by the family of the tortured girl because they felt that legal justice was impossible." In Washington, D.C., Admiral William Lee Pratt, chief of Naval operations, went even further, issuing the following statement to the press: "American men will not stand for the violation of their women under any circumstances. For this crime they have taken the matter into their own hands repeatedly when they have felt that the law has failed to do justice."

Sympathies were generally with the defendants, although the Honolulu *Star Bulletin* thundered against the killing of Kahahawai, saying: "People who take the law into their own hands always make a mess of it ... There is no justification in civilized society for lynch law methods or premeditated killing of any kind." Stated the Honolulu *Advertiser*: "Vengeance which takes the form of private execution cannot be condoned."

Most were concerned with how Clarence Darrow would defend his clients, who were obviously guilty of murder. The greatest lawyer in the land had been reluctant to take the case, stating privately that he did not like "the smell of it." But his financial difficulties at the time were acute and he accepted Mrs. Fortescue's fee of $25,000 and an all-expenses paid trip to Hawaii for himself and his wife.

On April 5, 1932, Darrow appeared with his clients before Judge Charles Davis, stating that Massie had killed Kahahawai out of "mental illness brought on by extreme provocation." As usual, Darrow's magnetic presence in the courtroom held everyone in fascination. He walked about in his rumpled clothes, his silvery hair falling in front of his forehead.

Darrow intoned dramatically the series of events that led up to the killing of Kahahawai, emphasizing the awful ordeal undergone by Mrs. Massie at the hands of savage rapists, depicting how Mrs. Massie had been humiliated by the traumatic experience and how she had been emotionally unstable thereafter. The same kind of emotional instability seized the mind of Thomas Massie, Darrow pointed out, one which clouded his reason and judgment and led to the shooting of the murder victim.

Throughout Darrow's orations and the court proceedings, Mrs. Fortescue proudly held up her head. She was dressed in the height of fashion, wearing a cloche hat and a red dress. Massie sat immobile, his blank expression interrupted only

Famed criminal attorney Clarence Darrow, center, who undertook the near-impossible defense; he is shown with defendants (left to right) Edward J. Lord, Mrs. Fortescue, Thomas Massie and Albert O. Jones.

Hawaii's Governor Lawrence Judd, to avoid more racial riots, commuted the sentences of the defendants (they were all convicted of second-degree murder and faced ten years in prison) to one hour in custody.

Admiral Yates Stirling, U.S. Navy Commander at Pearl Harbor, felt that the matter should have been settled immediately after the attack on Thalia Massie by the speedy execution of the five men who attacked her.

The defendants and friends are shown with Darrow, after their release from custody; they spent only one hour in the dock, their commutation causing more widespread rioting throughout the troubled islands.

when he bit his thin lips on occasion. The sailors, Lord and Jones, sat passive, staring ahead. The burning black eyes of Joe Kahahawai's parents were constantly focused upon the defendants as they sat in the spectator's gallery. Across the aisle from them sat Thalia Massie, dressed in black. Darrow's brilliant defense worked only to reduce the status of the charge against the defendants. Prosecutor John Kelley was obviously overwhelmed by Darrow's magical addresses and confined himself to the facts in the case. That was enough for a conviction, although it was not the first-degree murder conviction Kelley had sought.

All four were convicted of second-degree murder and sentenced to ten years imprisonment. Darrow immediately stated that he would appeal the case to the U.S. Supreme Court, but officials had had enough of this case. Riots against blacks, Orientals, and Hawaiians had broken out throughout the islands and on the mainland. Further court hearings would only ferment more race riots and unrest, prosecuting attorneys told Darrow after the conviction.

Prosecutors recommended leniency toward the defendants and this plea was acted upon by the much-harassed Governor Judd who was tired of calling out hundreds of national guardsmen to quell riots taking place over the Massie case. Judd signed an order that commuted the sentences of the four convicted murderers, reducing their time to one hour to be served in the courtroom dock. The defendants were placed in the dock and sat motionless and silent for an hour and then walked free.

Fortescue and Thalia Massie immediately sailed back to the U.S. mainland. Massie and the two seaman remained on duty in the islands. Massie himself would remain in the Navy, later serving on the U.S.S. *New Mexico*, a battleship which saw heavy action in World War II. He later died in obscurity. Thalia did not remain married to Thomas Massie for long. She filed for divorce in Reno, Nevada, which was granted on February 23, 1934. At the time, she told reporters that the crime against her had caused so much strain between her and her husband that their marriage disintegrated.

"Do you think you'll marry again soon?" a reporter asked Thalia Massie.

"Sure," she snapped back sullenly. "I'm going to marry Clark Gable, didn't you hear."

That night the despondent woman went to a Reno nightclub and ordered a drink into which she poured poison. She collapsed shortly after drinking the mixture and was rushed to St. Mary's Hospital where she recovered. Thalia Massie then took a train to New York where she booked passage on the *Roma*, a liner sailing to Italy. At sea, Mrs. Massie told other passengers that she did not care to live any longer. She was found hours later bleeding to death in her cabin, her wrists slashed. She was saved by a ship's nurse and Dr. Valliga, the ship's captain.

Thalia Massie survived her deep depressions, however, and later moved to Eugene, Oregon, living under her maiden name, Thalia Bell. She later married a man many years her junior and died on July 3, 1963. Although it was not listed as such, Thalia's death may have been a suicide. According to one newspaper account, "she was found in the bathroom of her apartment, barbiturate bottles scattered about her." Her proud and aristocratic mother, Mrs. Grace Fortescue, had already died years earlier.

A TITLED VICTIM IN KENYA/ January 24, 1941

Sir Henry John Delves Broughton (AKA: Sir Jock, 1884-1942), 57-year-old British aristocrat, married the ravishing young Diana Caldwell, a 27-year-old socialite, and in a prenuptial agreement guaranteed her an estimated yearly income of £5,000. This "May-September" marriage was not expected to last. Broughton was overly possessive of his new bride and his alluring wife attracted a flock of young male (and even female) admirers with whom she would allegedly have brief affairs, further inflaming her spouse's inherent jealousy. It was a dangerous proposition for both, made more explosive when Broughton decided to lead a new lifestyle in a savage country.

With his new bride, "Sir Jock," as Broughton was known to his friends in the fashionable London clubs, arrived in Kenya on November 12, 1940, to begin a new life. His well-appointed home outside Nairobi, however, held no fascination for the vivacious Lady Broughton. In this last outpost of the crumbling British empire, Diana met Josslyn Victor Hay, the dashing twenty-second Earl of Erroll and immediately embarked on a torrid affair with the handsome swain.

Hay was eighteen years younger than Henry Broughton, and infinitely more interesting to Diana. Hay had many female admirers, most of them married to men of title, and was, in the words of an English divorce judge, a "very bad black-

Sir "Jock" Boughton (left), a wealthy sportsman, shown here at the races with friends, married a beautiful woman thirty years his junior, a union that was soon undone when she fell in love with another man.

The handsome Josslyn Victor Hay, the 22nd Earl of Erroll (shown with his wife, who died in 1939), murdered on the night of January 24, 1941, a homicide charged to the cuckolded "Sir Jock" Boughton, who, through money and influence, went free.

Greta Scacchi, right, shown with Geraldine Chaplin, left, played the role of Diana Caldwell Boughton in the 1987 film, *White Mischief*, which was faithfully based upon the sordid uppercrust society of Kenya in 1941 and the murder of Sir Josslyn Hay.

guard." On January 20, 1941, less than two months after his arrival in Africa, Broughton wrote to a friend about the futility of his situation. He knew that Diana had fallen in love with Hay. "They say they are in love with each other and mean to get married," he confided. "It is a hopeless position and I am going to cut my losses. I think I'll go to Ceylon." That same day, Broughton told the police that someone had stolen two Colt revolvers from his home.

Diana Caldwell Boughton, who moved to Kenya with her husband and where she conducted a lethal affair.

On the afternoon of January 23, 1941, Hay, Broughton, and Diana discussed their situation over drinks and dinner at the Muthaiga Country Club. "Diana tells me she is in love with you," Broughton said matter-of-factly.

"She never told me that, but I'm frightfully in love with her," Hay replied curtly. Form dictated that the two aristocrats try to arrive at some understanding. Afterward, Hay would remark to his friend Lieutenant Lezard, "Jock could not have been nicer. He has agreed to everything. As a matter of fact, he has been so nice it smells bad!"

That night, Broughton had too much to drink and was driven home by a friend, leaving his wife with Hay. At 2:30 a.m., Hay brought Diana home, said his goodnight on the porch, and then climbed back into his car and drove down the Ngong Road. A short distance from the house, his car careened into a gravel pit. The next morning, a passerby found him slumped over the steering wheel. He had been shot in the back of the head.

Several weeks later, Broughton was arrested and charged with murder. He was the only one with an obvious motive, and the bullet extracted from the victim's brain had been fired with a black powder propellant, which was unobtainable in Kenya. Broughton's African houseboy would later tell the court that he had seen Broughton take two pistols to his bedroom shortly after arriving home from the club on the night of Hay's murder.

Broughton went to trial on May 26, 1941. The prosecution was handled by the Attorney General of Kenya, W. Harrigan. Broughton's life depended on discrediting the witnesses for the prosecution. From South Africa, H.H. Morris, one of the finest legal minds in the country, accepted his case. Morris brilliantly demonstrated to the jury that the murder bullets were not necessarily fired from any of his client's guns. Further, he demonstrated through witnesses that Broughton had never uttered a public word of objection or made a single threat to or about Hay regarding the young man's affair with his wife. Sir Henry John Delves Broughton was duly acquitted on July 1, 1941.

Broughton left Kenya as planned, and took up residence with Diana in Ceylon. However, Broughton soon suffered a serious fall which partly paralyzed him. Forced to return to England, Broughton sequestered himself in a Liverpool hotel, where he committed suicide in December 1942. Physicians attributed his death to an overdose of narcotics. He left a long, rambling note about the Kenya tragedy that neither affirmed nor denied his guilt. Broughton's story became the basis for the captivating 1988 British film, *White Mischief*, a movie that aptly captured the decaying aristocratic society in Kenya at that time and most decidedly pointed to the guilt of "Sir Jock."

THE JUDGE-TO-JUDGE MURDER/ June 16, 1955

One of the world's most sensational missing persons cases involved New York Supreme Court Justice Joseph Force Crater, who vanished on August 6, 1930 and was never seen again. An equally disturbing disappearance occurred twenty-five years later, one that also involved a distinguished jurist, Florida Circuit Court Judge Charles E. Chillingworth, who seemed to dissolve into thin air in 1955. There was a marked difference between these two disappearing judges. Chillingworth, however, resurfaced, at least in the chilling testimony of his murderer.

Judge Charles E. Chillingworth, who vanished from his Manalpan, Florida, home in 1955.

Judge Chillingworth had spent thirty-four years on the bench. He had been stern, but fair, placing emphasis on the law, always the law. Most of Chillingworth's judgeship had been centered in Palm Beach and Broward counties, and he was particularly known for his promptness, an unbending trait even his wife and three grown daughters had learned to respect.

Mrs. Marjorie Chillingworth, who disappeared along with her husband in 1955.

Seldom if ever could the judge's court attendants remember Chillingworth being late; so, when he failed to appear at a hearing at his West Palm Beach chambers on June 16, 1955, the alarm was immediately sent out. Police and family members immediately converged on the judge's fashionable seaside home at Manalpan, an exclusive area twelve miles south of Palm Beach. What detectives found in the Chillingworth home—or what they did not find—stunned and amazed them.

Judge Chillingworth *and* his wife were missing, with only a few physical traces that they had returned to their home the previous night at 10:30 p.m., after dining with friends. Investigators determined that the couple had undressed and had neatly hung up their clothing, retiring in pajamas. Their money and jewelry remained untouched on bedroom bureaus. Nothing was missing except the two human beings who inhabited the home.

Outside the home, detectives found a few slim clues. A beach lamp that lighted the area leading to the water was broken, and on the wooden stairs and walkway leading to the

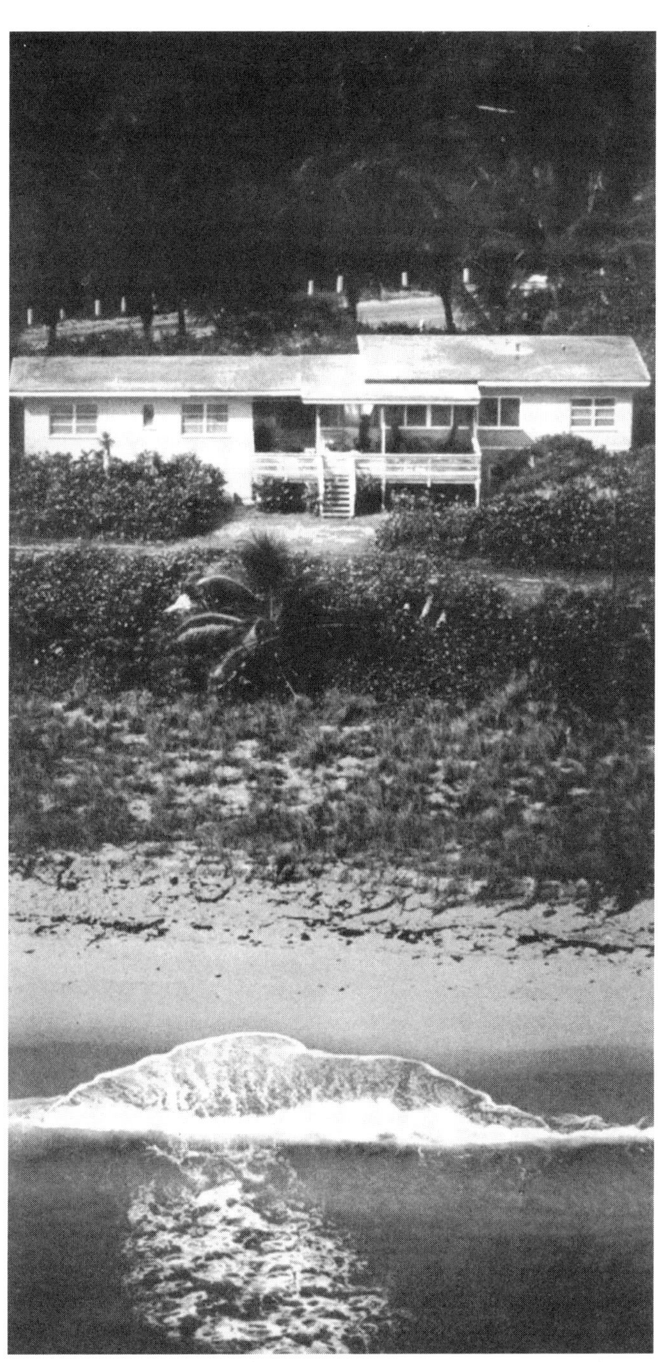
The Chillingworth ocean-front home, where the couple was abducted, then rowed out to sea and murdered, their bodies weighted and given the deep six.

Jim Yenzer, who lured one of the killers of the Chillingworths to a drinking party, where he bragged of the double murder.

Undercover police officer P. O. Wilbur was present at the drinking party where the killer's admissions were recorded.

Floyd "Lucky" Holzapfel, right, who got drunk with Yenzer and Wilbur and talked about murdering the Chillingworths; he was convicted and sent to Florida's electric chair.

The affable and scheming Judge Joseph Peel, right, convicted of ordering Holzapfel and his alleged accomplices to commit the Chillingworth murders; he was sent to prison for life.

sea, investigators found traces of blood and two rolls of adhesive tape. One footprint, distorted as if a person had been struggling, was found in the sand next to what appeared to be the marks of a boat that had been beached at the water's edge.

At first authorities deduced that the couple had drowned, even though Chillingworth and his wife were known to avoid deep water since they were poor swimmers. Planes and helicopters soon buzzed and whirred over the waters near the Chillingworth home, pilots and observers scanning the sea for floating bodies. Scores of surface vessels joined the search that extended as far as the Bahamas. Skin divers and deep-sea divers explored the depths offshore. In the end, nothing was found.

Police then concluded that the couple had been kidnapped and they expected for weeks a ransom note to arrive. Officials even went so far as to name a Methodist minister, the Reverend Harry Waller, to act as an intermediary. Others doubted the abduction theory, knowing that Chillingworth and his family did not possess the kind of money that would bring an appreciable ransom payment. A reward of $113,000 was offered by friends, family and state officials for the return of the missing couple, but no leads developed.

The Chillingworth disappearances remained a complete mystery and would have remained so, had it not been for a startling conversation between Brevard County Sheriff aide James Yenzer and an old friend, Joseph Alexander Peel, Jr. (b. 1924) in late 1960. Yenzer was told by Peel that he would receive a large amount of money if he would kill an habitual criminal named Floyd Albert Holzapfel (pronounced *holds-apple*), known to Yenzer and Peel as "Lucky."

Yenzer stalled, but later contacted the wanted felon, Holzapfel, but not for the purpose of killing him. Yenzer had told authorities about Peel's proposal and they urged Yenzer to contact the intended "hit," in order to obtain more information. To that end, Yenzer, along with P. O. Wilbur, and undercover policeman, lured the alcoholic Holzapfel into a drinking spree in a motel room that was wired for sound. Once drunk, Holzapfel spewed forth a tale that caused the flesh of his listeners to crawl.

Holzapfel and a few of his friends had murdered Judge Chillingworth and his wife, he admitted. They did it, like Hemingway's thugs in "The Killers," for "a friend," a powerful pillar of the Florida community, who was annoyed with the Judge's rigid ways. The murder had not been an easy chore, Holzapfel said. He and his accomplices had arrived late on the night of June 15, 1955, on the beach behind the Chillingworth home. They crept into the house, intent upon slaying only the Judge, but the crotchety old man struggled so fiercely and shouted so loudly in his bed that he woke up his wife, who started to scream. The killers bashed her into unconsciousness. (It was Marjorie Chillingworth's blood the investigators had found the next day on the walkway, blood gushing from her wound as she and her husband were dragged, mouths taped, out to the beach and into the waiting boat.)

Once in the boat—clouds shrouding the moon and the movements of the murderers—Marjorie Chillingworth was wrapped in chains and weights were attached. She was rolled into the sea and sank immediately. The Judge was another matter. So violently did he struggle with his assailants that he almost succeeded in knocking Holzapfel and his friends into the ocean. They barely managed to get the chains and weights about him before tossing him into the water.

Judge Chillingworth would not die easily. To the astonishment of his killers, he did not sink. Encumbered in chains and weights, the feisty jurist nevertheless began to swim to shore. The killers paddled furiously after him, and, just as he was about to reach shallow water, one of them reached out in desperation with an oar and split his skull. Only then did the Judge sink from sight.

Finishing his tale in a drunken stupor, Holzapfel passed out. He was arrested for the murder of the Chillingworths on October 4, 1960. Within hours, he tried to commit suicide by cutting his wrists, but his efforts were as awkward as his murders of the Chillingworths. He lived to stand trial. Holzapfel's employer in this and other murders was Joseph Peel, the man who had politely asked Yenzer to kill him. Investigation into Peel's background was laborious and painful. Peel came from one of the most respected families in Florida. He had been West Palm Beach's only municipal judge and from that sacrosanct position, police learned, took bribes and kickbacks from every illegal operation in the area, from moonshining gangsters to grifters selling illegal lottery tickets.

Judge Peel stood for no nonsense from those who interfered with his lucrative graft. When a 22-year-old informer named Lew Harvey caused dozens of raids on stills producing moonshine whiskey—operations in which Peel had interests—the Judge ordered Holzapfel to murder him. Harvey's bullet-ridden corpse was discovered in a canal outside of Palm Beach in November 1958. Holzapfel was sent to South America until the search for Harvey's murderer subsided. Peel sent his hired killer regular checks to South America, but when he stopped the payments, Holzapfel returned and began to blackmail his employer. This was the reason why Peel went to Yenzer and asked him to kill his troublesome henchman.

Judge Chillingworth had always been troublesome to Joseph Peel, investigators learned. During a 1952 divorce case—Peel was then a practicing attorney—Peel instructed his client to lie. That case was tried before none other than Judge Chillingworth, who helped to establish perjury that sent Peel's client to prison. The Judge's oral rebuke of Peel was so devastating that its repercussions destroyed his law practice and forced him to resign from the bar. Peel later became a municipal judge, but Chillingworth knew of his links to organized gambling and several times threatened to expose him. But, by then, Peel had professional killers like Holzapfel on his payroll and he simply eliminated a nuisance by ordering his henchman to murder Chillingworth.

Peel stood trial for his crimes and was convicted twice and sentenced to two life terms for the murders of Chillingworth and his wife. His not so dutiful stooge, Lucky Holzapfel, did not leave up to his nickname. He went to the electric chair.

"I WILL DESTROY YOUR FACE"/April 4, 1958

The violent deaths of gangsters have been common occurrences, but the killing of gangster Johnny Stompanato in 1958 drew uncommon attention from the press. He died at the hands

Johnny Stompanato, left, when he worked as a bagman and driver for Los Angeles gangster Mickey Cohen, right.

of a teenager whose actress mother had been an on-screen sex symbol for decades. The only child of Hollywood actress Lana Turner, Cheryl Crane (b. 1943), was born to Turner and Stephen Crane, the actress' second husband, a marriage that lasted only a few months. Turner had already been married to Artie Shaw and, after her annulment from Crane, went on to marry Henry J. "Bob" Topping, Lex Barker, Fred May, Robert Eaton, and Ronald Dante. The marriage to Barker, it was claimed, had been broken up by Cheryl, who continued to live with her mother through her host of husbands.

Cheryl Crane was surrounded by her mother's enormous wealth, living in a mansion peopled by servants. Always glittering before her were jewels, expensive cars, and mostly fame. Teenage jealousy of her mother prompted Cheryl, some claimed, to whisper nasty gossip to her mother about her husbands and those she dated between marriages. One of these was the handsome, smooth-talking gangster, John Stompanato, one-time chauffeur and bagman for Los Angeles gambler and gangster Mickey Cohen.

Stompanato, born in Woodstock, Illinois, in 1925, had served as a Marine during World War II. He had attended an exclusive military school and then Notre Dame briefly before enlisting in the Marines in 1944, serving three years. The ruggedly handsome Stompanato had married and divorced twice by 1948, when he went to work for Cohen in Los Angeles as Cohen's bodyguard, driver, and later as bagman, collecting the profits from Cohen's gambling and extortion rackets. He then struck out on his own, operating as a Hollywood lounge lizard, picking up lonely but wealthy women who were married, then making love to them in a room where hidden motion picture cameras recorded every move. Stompanato would then sell the film to the compromised women at staggering extortion prices.

When Lana Turner's marriage to Lex Barker ended, she received a call from Stompanato, asking her for a date. He first

Stompanato and Lana Turner at poolside; the 38-year-old actress was by then madly in love with the gangster.

used the name John Steele when introducing himself to Turner and her daughter Cheryl. The lonely 38-year-old Turner accepted and their tempestuous affair began. The gangster was nothing like Turner's husbands or previous lovers. He was loud, crude, gauche, a braggart and a bully, who wore shiny shirts open almost to his navel to reveal his hairy chest. He oozed Latin charm and earthiness, but at the same time his passions were violent and menacing.

Cheryl Crane was enamored by her mother's new lover; she and Stompanato spent hours horseback riding or swimming together in her mother's Olympic-sized pool. Stompanato played the older brother to her, writing her long letters when she was traveling with her mother. Turner, meanwhile, lavished Stompanato with expensive gifts, clothes, and then loaned him $10,000, money that was never repaid.

When he joined her and Cheryl in London, while Turner was filming *Another Time, Another Place*, Stompanato moved into the luxurious townhouse Turner and Cheryl were sharing. The gangster then asked the actress for another loan, $50,000, to secure the rights to a film script for a movie in which, he, Johnny Stompanato, would star. The gangster had long nurtured the secret ambition to become a film star.

The actress turned him down, saying that she did not have that kind of cash and that her financial advisers had ordered

Lana Turner's daughter, Cheryl Crane, right, greets her mother and Stompanato upon their return from Mexico.

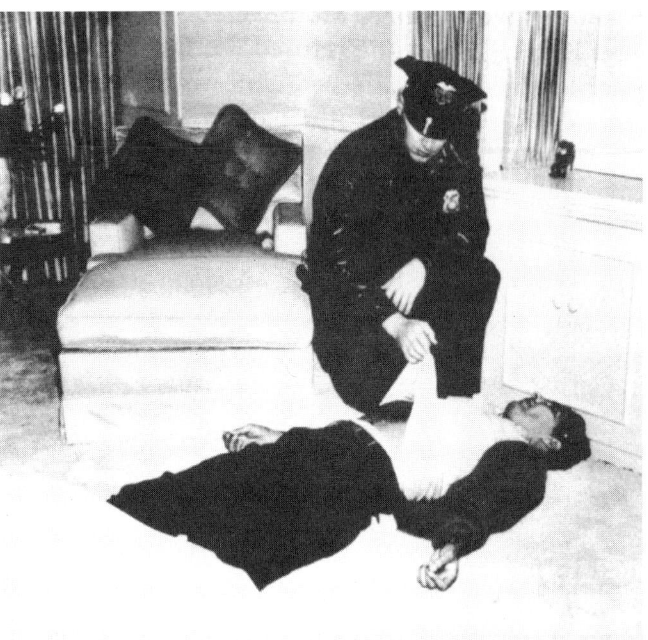

An officer examines the mortal wound in Stompanato's body, which was sprawled in the bedroom of Lana Turner's home on the night of April 4, 1958.

her not to give him any more money. Her refusal caused Stompanato to go berserk. He threatened the star, who walked out on him, going to the set of *Another Time, Another Place*, where she began to rehearse with co-star Sean Connery.

Stompanato suddenly appeared on the set, raging, ordering Connery to "stay away from Lana!" Connery turned his back on Stompanato, who grabbed the burly actor and swung him about, waving a gun in Connery's face. The burly actor's response was to land a powerful punch to the gangster's jaw, sending him to the floor in a half-conscious state. Stompanato got up and walked away, swearing revenge. Back at the townhouse, the gangster cornered Turner and shrieked: "When I say hop, you'll hop! When I say jump, you'll jump!"

The actress ordered Stompanato out of the townhouse. He yelled: "I'll mutilate you! I'll hurt you so that you'll be so repulsive you'll have to hide forever!" With that he leaped forward, grabbed the actress around the throat and began to choke her. He then threw her down to the floor and threatened her with a razor, saying that he could cut her "just a little" but he could "do worse." She pleaded with Stompanato, who then relented, but he warned her: "That's just to let you know that I'm not kidding. Don't think that you can ever get away!"

Cheryl Crane had heard the commotion and expressed fears for her mother's life. The director of the film Turner was working on called Scotland Yard, and Stompanato was politely escorted to the airport and put on the next plane to the U.S. Lana Turner had successfully gotten rid of the menacing thug, but this separation was brief.

Once the film in England was completed, however, Turner and Cheryl returned to Los Angeles and the actress made the mistake of calling Stompanato, showing herself to be much more dependent upon him than she had previously admitted. Stompanato now moved into her mansion to fully enjoy Lana Turner's luxurious lifestyle, swimming in her pool, lounging in the sunray and massage rooms, watching the latest Hollywood films in her private screening room. The couple took a seven-week vacation to Acapulco, renting a suite at the Via Vera Hotel.

When they returned to Los Angeles, Cheryl Crane, now a tall girl who towered over her mother, was present to welcome the pair home. The arguments began all over again, beginning with the Academy Awards. Turner had been nominated for an Oscar for her performance in *Peyton Place* (she did not win) and had decided to attend the ceremonies without Stompanato. When he learned that he was not invited, the gangster went into a raging tirade, accusing the actress of being ashamed of him, that she did not want to be seen in public with him.

More importantly, Stompanato had been gambling heavily in gambling spas owned by his former employer Mickey Cohen, and Cohen held several IOUs Stompanato had signed. On the evening of April 4, 1958, Stompanato demanded that Turner pay these debts. He confronted her in her lavish bedroom and she, in turn, utterly refused to give him any more money. Again the gangster lost control and began screaming that he would use a razor to disfigure her for life. Cheryl Crane, downstairs, could hear the gangster yelling: "If a man makes a living with his hands, I would destroy his hands. You make your living with your face, so I will destroy your face. I'll get you where it hurts the most! I'll cut you up and I'll get your mother and your daughter, too ... That's my business!"

Stompanato grabbed the actress by the arm and she broke away. She opened the bedroom door to see her daughter standing there. "Please, Cheryl, please don't listen to any of this," the actress told her, and closed the door. She then ordered Stompanato to return to his own room. He picked up a hanger with a jacket on it and approached her, poised it seemed, to attack her with it. The actress then told the gangster that she was finished with him and that he was to get out of her house.

Turner again opened the door and Stompanato came rushing toward her, holding the jacket and the hanger. Cheryl Crane was there, moving past her mother into the bedroom, holding a butcher knife with a nine-inch blade, which she had gotten

This photo of Lana Turner, which she had lovingly inscribed in Spanish, was found on Stompanato's body.

in the downstairs kitchen. The actress was later to testify: "I swear it was so fast; I truthfully thought she had hit him in the stomach. The best that I can remember is that they came together and they parted. I still never saw the blade."

The gangster, holding his stomach, fell backward on the thick carpet. Lana Turner went to him and pulled back his shirt to see the deep knife wound. Stompanato tried to speak but only a gurgle came out of his throat. She grabbed a towel from the bathroom and tried to staunch the flow of blood, but it was useless. Her lover was dead. Her daughter, meanwhile stood sobbing nearby as Turner called her mother and then her lawyer, the famed Jerry Giesler. She said to Giesler: "This is Lana Turner. Could you please come to my house. Something terrible has happened." Within minutes, Giesler was driving toward the Turner mansion.

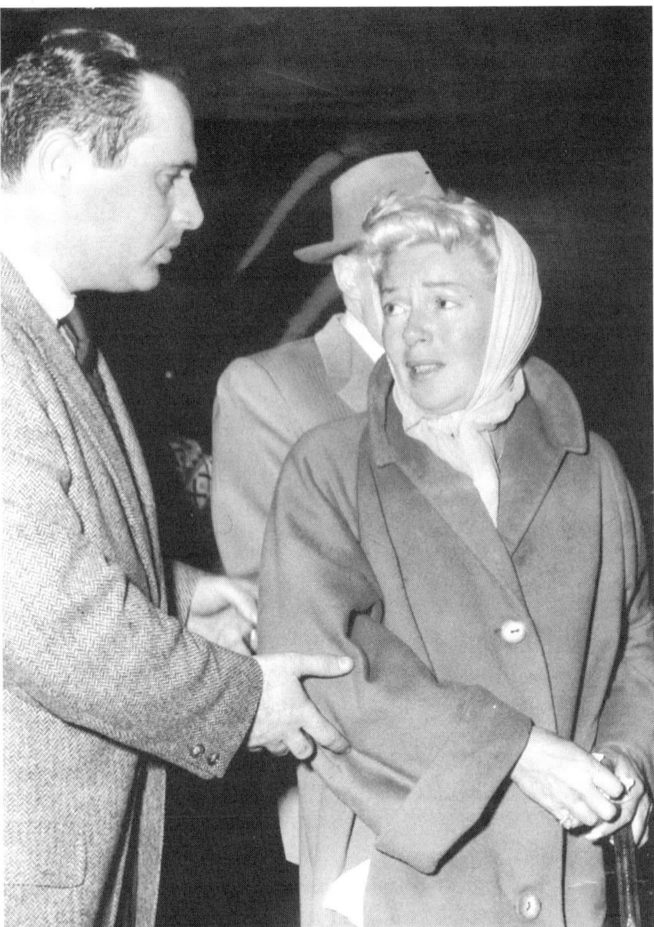

Turner is shown accompanied by Beverly Hills police detectives, begging them not to arrest her daughter; Cheryl Crane was nevertheless booked on a charge of murdering Stompanato.

Cheryl Crane then called her father and asked him to come to the house. Crane asked a patron in his restaurant to drive him to Turner's Beverly Hills home and was the first to arrive there. Cheryl met him at the door. Crane looked at Stompanato's stiffening body in the upstairs bedroom while his sobbing daughter blurted: "I did it, Daddy, but I didn't mean to. He was going to hurt Mommy. I didn't mean to, I didn't mean to."

Giesler showed up, meeting the actress for the first time, but promising her that his office would do all it could to protect her and her child. Clinton Anderson, Beverly Hills police chief, then arrived with several officers. Reporter Jim Bacon quickly appeared, gaining access to the house by telling uniformed officers stationed outside that he was from the coroner's office. Lana Turner was by then pleading with Anderson to put the blame on her, that her child only meant to protect her. "I don't want her involved, poor baby," Turner said through tears. "Please say that I did it." Stompanato was by this time examined and pronounced dead.

Giesler immediately introduced his defense by putting his arm around Turner and saying: "Your daughter has done a courageous thing. It's too bad that a man's life is gone but under the circumstances the child did the only thing she could do to protect her mother from harm." Giesler looked at Chief

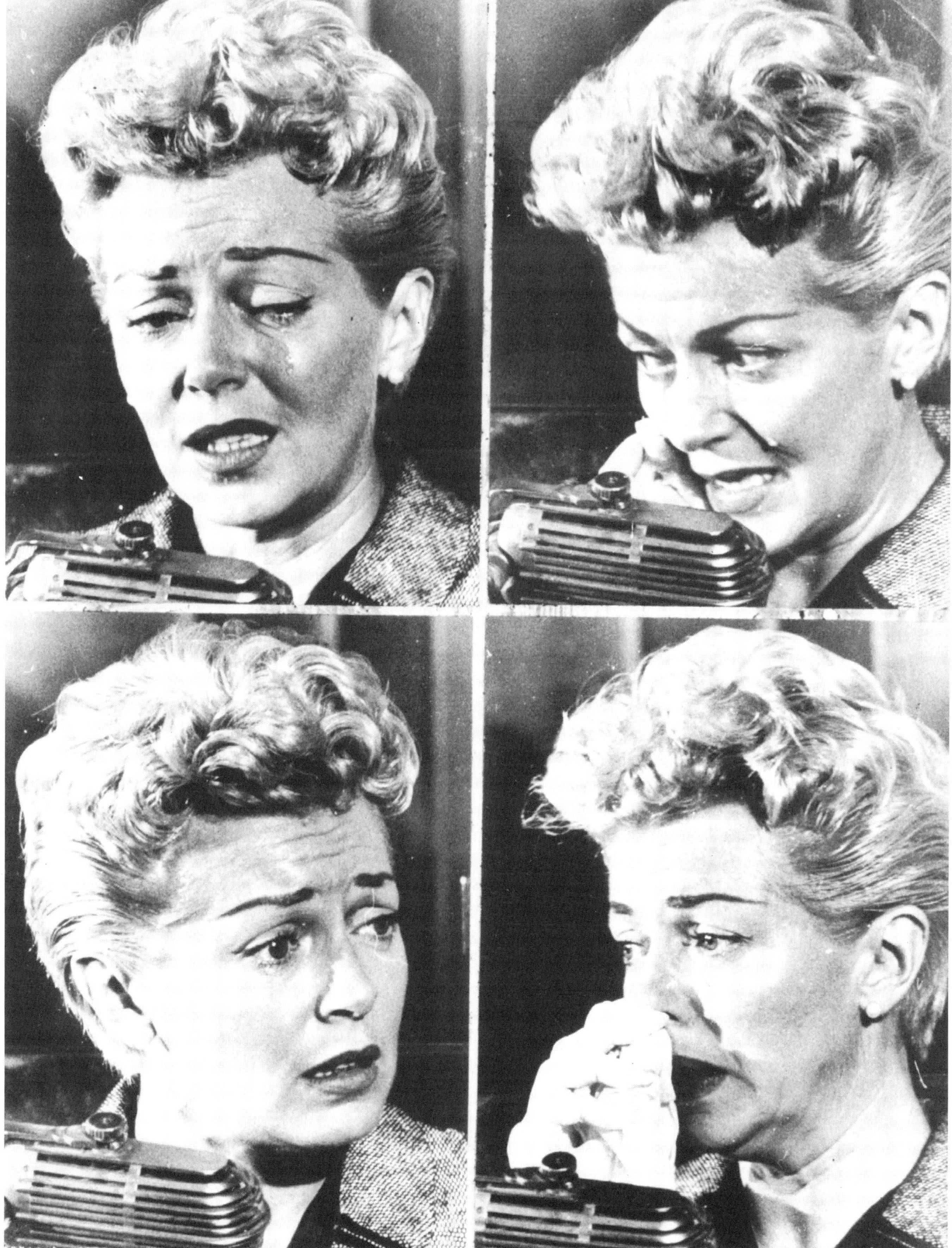

Weeping and in anguish, the above series of photos show Turner's tortured testimony before a jury in the Stompanato case.

Anderson and spoke to Turner, but kept his eyes on the police officer: "I understand your concern for the child's welfare. But you won't get anyplace by hiding the truth, will she, Chief?"

Lana Turner than gushed the whole sordid affair between herself and Stompanato while Bacon and other reporters took notes. Anderson sympathetically listened to her and then to Cheryl's description of how she had plunged the knife into the gangster who was about to attack her mother. The chief reluctantly informed the actress that he would have to lock up her 14-year-old daughter. "Can't you arrest me instead?" Turner pleaded with him. "Poor baby's not to blame for all this mess."

Cheryl Crane was nevertheless arrested and locked up in the Juvenile Section of the city jail, charged with murder. The newspapers blared the killing from coast to coast and most of the gossip columnists used the Stompanato death to parade Turner's myriad torrid love affairs in print. She was pilloried for subjecting her daughter to a series of reckless marriages and love affairs, and some even wildly speculated that Turner herself had murdered Stompanato after finding her daughter in bed with him. Only Walter Winchell came to the defense of the movie queen, asking that fans understand the tragedy and give their sympathy "to the girl with a broken heart."

Few of Turner's peers had anything to say about the killing. The outspoken Gloria Swanson, sex goddess of the silent era, did voice a scathing opinion, attacking Winchell for defending Turner, saying that his defense of the actress was "disgusting ... You are trying to whitewash Lana ... She is not even an actress ... she is only a trollop." Gangster Mickey Cohen then suddenly appeared in the editorial offices of the Los Angeles *Herald Examiner*, dumping Lana Turner's love letters to Stompanato into the editor's hands. He had ordered his goons to go to Stompanato's apartment after hearing about the killing and obtain these gushing billet doux. The cost-conscious Cohen had paid the bill for Stompanato's funeral, and when Turner reportedly refused to pay him for these expenses, he released the letters out of spite.

By the time Cheryl Crane appeared in court, the charge against her had been reduced to manslaughter. Geisler brilliantly placed Lana Turner on the stand and softly talked her through the nightmare killing. The actress detailed everything that occurred that evening, weeping, wiping away perspiration with her handkerchief, her face distorted in anguish and expressing a mother's pain. Some say it was the greatest performance of her career.

Then Cheryl Crane testified, repeating almost word for word the story her mother had given. The coroner's jury, relying exclusively on the testimony of the two females, ruled that Cheryl Crane had committed justifiable homicide. She was made a ward of the state and placed in her grandmother's custody. The press photographers had a field day with Lana Turner on the stand that day and reveled in taking photos of her kneeling at her mother's feet, a penitent pose that was no doubt meant to elicit sympathy.

Cheryl Crane did not adjust well. Her grandmother, Mildred Turner, could not control her. The girl ran away several times and was later placed by court order in the El Retiro

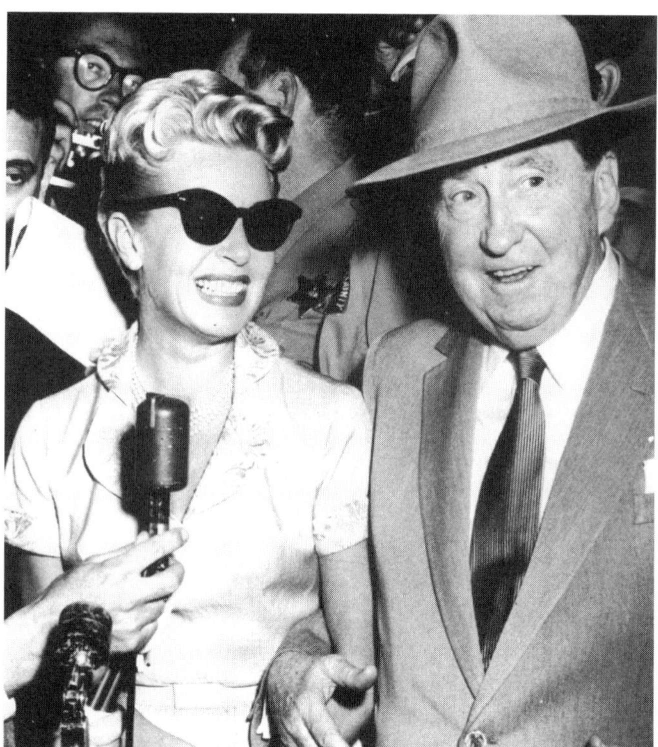

A jubilant Lana Turner is shown with criminal attorney Jerry Giesler, right, whose strategy in the Stompanato case resulted in an acquittal for Cheryl Crane, her lethal action ruled "justifiable homicide."

School for Girls in the San Fernando Valley. She later worked for her father as a hostess in his restaurant. The American public favored Lana Turner and her daughter in this sensational killing, and the actress' next few films were box office hits. She and her daughter survived the scandal, emerging as heroines. Cheryl Crane later became a success as a San Francisco real estate broker and wrote a book about her life, detailing the Stompanato murder in terms that repeated her original statements, a book in which she revealed that she was a lesbian. Only the publicity-seeking gangster Mickey Cohen angrily spoke on behalf of Johnny Stompanato, declaring to the world: "Look, everybody is forgetting something here! This was a great guy!"

TWO MURDERS IN MANHATTAN/ August 28, 1963

In the late afternoon of August 28, 1963, 21-year-old Patricia Tolles, a researcher for *Time* magazine, returned to the apartment on east 88th Street in Manhattan, New York, which she shared with 21-year-old Janice Wylie, who was employed at *Newsweek*, and 23-year-old Emily Hoffert. Both Wylie and Hoffert had the day off from work. When Tolles entered the apartment, she soon saw that objects in the hallway had been disturbed and the bathroom was spattered with blood. Alarmed, Tolles retreated from the apartment and called Janice's father, Max Wylie, distinguished author. (The victim was also the niece of famed author Philip Wylie.)

Wylie arrived shortly and explored the apartment. In the bedroom, to his horror, he found the bodies of the two young women. Although Janice's body was nude, Hoffert's was fully clothed. The two bodies bore multiple stab wounds and had been tied together with strips of cloth torn from the sheets. Further investigation revealed that Janice had been eviscerated, and there was evidences that the murderer had intended to rape her.

Police made little progress in the case, finding only a few clues. They knew that the victims had been killed on or before 7 a.m., because an electronic clock-radio had been unplugged when Janie Wylie's body fell across it, unplugging the cord leading to a wall socket. They knew that the assailant had slain the two young women with maniacal fury in that two of the three kitchen knives used by the killer broke in half during the attack. Dozens of suspects were interrogated, but released for lack of motive and having reliable alibis that placed them elsewhere at the time of the murders.

Attractive Janice Wylie, the niece of novelist Philip Wylie, was stabbed to death in 1963.

Not until April 24, 1964, did investigators get a break. On that day, George Whitmore, Jr., a 21-year-old Negro, was arrested and charged with a stabbing murder and an assault. Police found a photo among Whitmore's belongings that they believed to be of Janice Wylie. Whitmore eventually confessed to the Wylie and Hoffert murders, but recanted later, claiming the confession had been coerced by police. Regardless, Whitmore was convicted of attempted rape and sentenced to five to ten years in prison. (The Whitmore confession consisted of a 61-page statement that contained many exacting and precise details of the killings, which mystified many latter-day crime historians, who could not determine how Whitmore learned of such exacting information if, indeed, he had not been present at the murders. The only explanation was that detectives working on the case provided these details.)

The case might have ended there, except that in the fall of that year, Nathan "Jimmy" Delaney, a 37-year-old Negro junkie, was arrested on a murder charge. In order to "cut a deal," he told police that he had information regarding the two murders. He told them that 22-year-old Richard Robles, who had a heroin addiction, had been staying with him and his wife at the time of the Wylie-Hoffert murders and had returned home distraught and asking for a fix. He had also told Delaney that he had "just iced two dames" during a burglary.

The Bronx-born Robles (b. 1942) was arrested on January 26, 1965, and confessed to murdering Wylie and Hoffert. He was tried before Judge Irwin Davidson in October 1965. Max Wylie was called to the witness stand by prosecutor John Keenan. The 60-year-old father of Janice Wylie held back his emotions while he clearly described how his daughter's roommate, Patricia Tolles Smalley (she had married since the time of the murder) had called him and asked him to inspect the ramshackled apartment she had entered.

Wylie stated that he had immediately gone to the apartment and entered Hoffert's bedroom, saying: "I passed behind the foot of the second bed, and there I found the girls. They were close together. The space was very confining. They had been flung to the floor, lying side by side. Janice was nude, Emily was dressed. Emily was facing the same direction as Janice—away from the windows. I recognized Janice instantly. I didn't recognize the other girl—I had met her only once.

"Janice had been stabbed through the heart. The knife wounds round Emily's neck were noticeable. The curlers were still in Janice's hair. Emily had been frightfully cut. It was very gory. I knelt at the feet of the two girls. I put my knuckles on Janice's right calf to check if she were still alive. She looked quite peaceful. I realized she was dead. There was a dark woolen blanket on the floor near Miss Hoffert's knees. I pulled the blanket over both the girls' bodies, covering them as much as I could."

Wylie's roommate, Emily Hoffert, who was also killed in a burglary gone wrong.

Throughout this painful testimony, Richard Robles coldly stared at the witness, the father of the girl he was accused of murdering. Robles never blinked an eye. He was also passive during the testimony of Nathan Delaney, who had fingered Robles as the killer of Wylie and Hoffert. He was portrayed as a lifelong criminal by defense attorney Jack Hoffinger, who attempted to discredit Delaney's statements by pointing out that the witness was a convicted felon, a drug peddler whose white wife was also a drug addict (and that Delaney had hooked her on drugs, as well as the defendant, Robles) and a prostitute.

Delaney admitted that he had made his living from the sale of illegal drugs and lived off the proceeds, as well as the income produced by his street-hustling wife, since 1946. Yet, Hoffinger could not overturn Delaney's statements concerning Robles' own admission to him that he had committed the murders.

Supporting Delaney's statements were tape recordings police had made in Delaney's apartment, which involved conversations between Robles, Delaney and Delaney's wife, Marjorie Delaney. Attorney Hoffinger strongly objected to the admission of these tapes in the trial, but Judge Davidson ruled to admit the tapes, which were played through four large loudspeakers placed in the courtroom.

What came through to jury members was a hellish babble of three junkies babbling in almost incoherent conversation. Apparently, Robles suspected that he was being "set up" during these tapings and tried to supply his own defense by alter-

A clock radio in the apartment showed the exact time of the murders, its plug pulled from an electric socket when Wylie's naked body fell across it.

Burglar Richard Robles, a heroin addict, later confessed to the murders of Wylie and Hoffert; he was sent to prison for life.

ing his original statements to Delaney, saying that he probably "imagined" the killings of Wylie and Hoffert.

More damaging was the testimony of Detective David Downes, who first interviewed Robles when he was arrested and charged with the killings. In the witness chair, Downes emphatically recalled Robles' word-for-word statement to him at that time: "I went to pull a lousy burglary and I wound up killing two girls."

Downes said on the witness stand that he wanted to make sure of the identities of the "two girls." He turned to the jury and stated: "I said to him: 'You mean Janice Wylie and Emily Hoffert?' He said: 'Yeah.'"

On December 1, 1965, Richard Robles was found guilty of first-degree murder by a jury of eight men and four women. He was sentenced to life in prison, with eligibility for parole in twenty-six years. At the time, Robles told the judge: "All I can say, your honor, is that I did not kill those girls. I'm going to jail for something I didn't do."

Whitmore, who had confessed to the same crime, was exonerated on June 27, 1966. His "confession," which was thought to be specious and coerced, was thrown out. Many continued to believe, however, that Whitmore was somehow involved in the Wylie-Hoffert murders, even believing that Whitmore and Robles had committed the killings together during a botched burglary to support their mutual drug habits (about $40-a-day in that era).

Robles continued to insist that he was innocent for the next two decades, but after a spiritual transformation, he admitted to the two murders. He fully confessed to the killings during a parole hearing on November 5, 1986, at the Eastern Correctional Facility in New York. At that time, Robles told commissioners what actually happened on the day of the murders: "I got in through a window. Miss Wylie was in the apartment. She was in bed...I tied her up...I tied her hands up...she was nude...I wanted to have sex with her...I attempted to. She said, 'No!' I stopped." At that moment, Robles told commissioners, Emily Hoffert entered the room.

"I grabbed her," Robles continued. "I tied her up. Hoffert told him that she would remember his face, Robles recalled. "She started telling me that she was going to tell the police on me ... She would remember me ... that I was going to jail ... The thought entered my mind—I have to kill ... I killed ... I was out of it, totally out ... I felt like throwing up and I almost ran out of the room ... I noticed a mirror. I looked in that mirror. The blood had drained from my face. I was like a ghost. My eyes were like glassy."

Robles went on to tell commissioners that he could not recall all the details of that horrible moment since he felt he was in some sort of a trance. "I looked like a ghost. I felt like a ghost. I can't even describe the feelings...I think of that now ... What I had just done ... I was feeling—God knows what I was feeling—I don't know how to describe what I was feeling." Robles remains behind bars at this writing, continuing to serve two life terms at New York's Attica prison.

THE MURDER OF AN OIL TYCOON/ June 30, 1964

The marriage of a blonde, blue-eyed, curvaceous woman to a Texas oil baron twenty-four years her senior would end in tragedy, some predicted. In fact, the union ended in homicide, resulting in one of the most sensational murder cases in America. Born Candace Grace Weatherby (1914-1976) in Buchanan, Georgia, Candy Mossler was determined to escape the poverty of her childhood. At fifteen, she ran away from home to become a shoe and toothpaste model, and by her mid-twenties she owned her own modeling agency in New Orleans. In 1948, at the age of thirty-four, she met and married Texas millionaire oil tycoon Jacques Mossler.

Mossler, fifty-eight at the time he married Candy, had made millions of dollars in oil and then invested his fortune in banks and finance companies. The interest from his investments allowed Jacques and Candace Mossler to live an extravagant lifestyle which included homes in Houston, Miami, and Chicago. The couple adopted four children, all the offspring of a Chicago mental patient, who had murdered his wife.

At 1 a.m. on June 30, 1964, in Key Biscayne, Florida, Candy took her four children, ranging in age from eleven to twenty, for a ride in her car. She drove around apparently aimlessly for the next few hours, stopping once at a hospital emergency room for treatment of a migraine headache. At 4:30 a.m., she returned to the apartment she shared with her husband to find his badly beaten body lying in the living room. He had been stabbed thirty-nine times and hit over the head with a heavy object. Neighbors reported hearing voices coming from the apartment and the sounds of a man leaving it. Several suspects were picked up, but all eventually provided alibis and were released.

On July 4, 1964, police arrested Candy Mossler's strapping, darkly handsome nephew, Melvin Lane Powers (b. 1940),

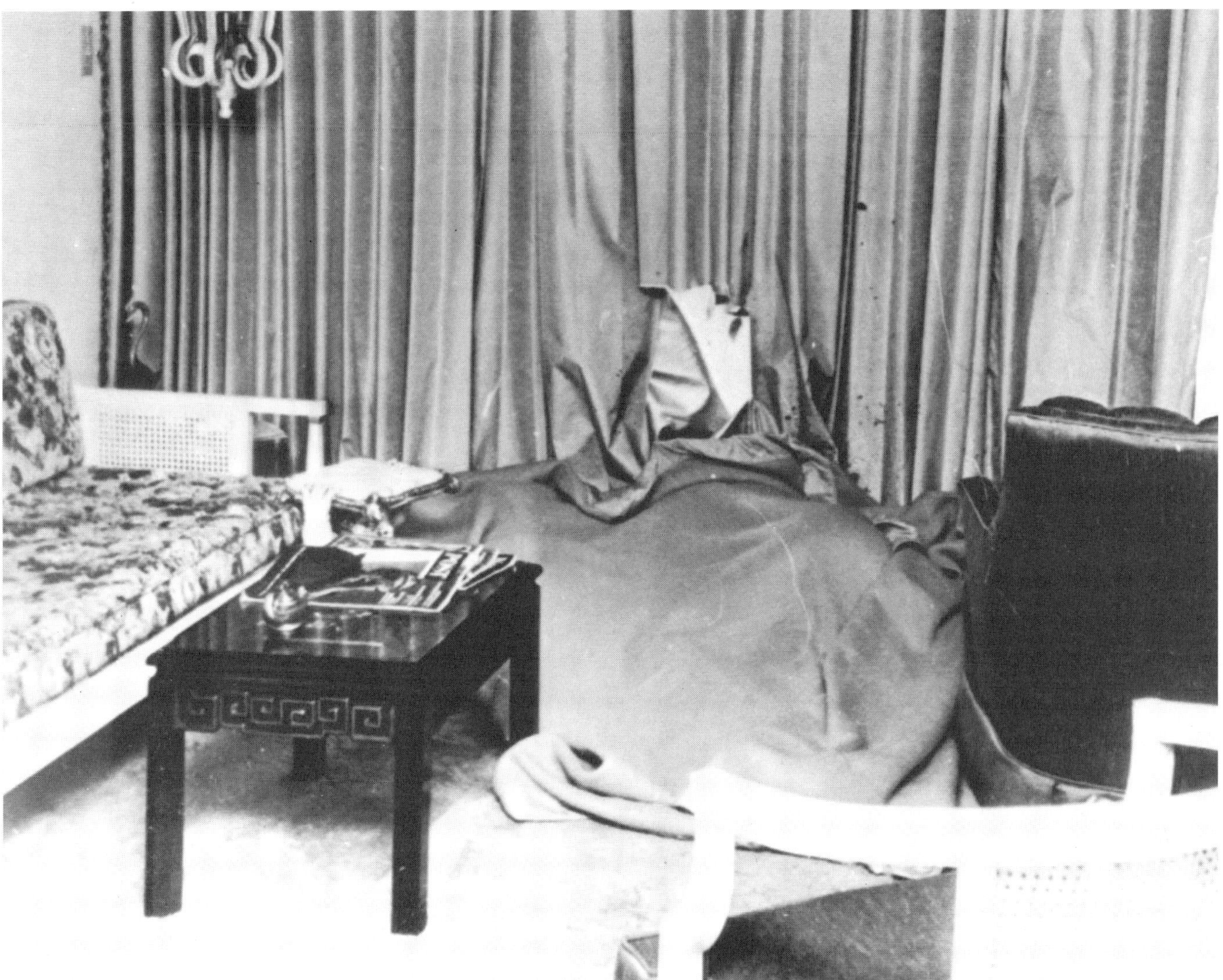

The body of oil tycoon Jacques Mossler lies beneath a blanket in his apartment in Key Biscayne, Florida; his skull had been crushed and he had been stabbed thirty-nine times.

at a trailer sales lot in Houston. The trailer lot had been financed by Jacques Mossler. Police charged that Powers and Candy Mossler were carrying on an incestuous affair that Jacques Mossler had recently discovered. When he threatened to divorce Candy and cut her out of his will, she called Powers, who flew to Miami, murdered Mossler while Candy and the children were out driving, and returned to Houston that same night.

A bloody palm print in the Mossler's kitchen matched Powers' hand. Candy went immediately to Powers' aid and hired well-known defense attorney Percy Foreman to represent him. However, Candy was soon indicted for murder along with Powers. After fighting extradition from Texas to Florida for more than a year, Powers relented and appeared before Florida Circuit Court Judge Harvie DuVal to plead not guilty.

Mossler and Powers were both released on $50,000 bonds. Prior to the trial, Candy gave countless interviews to reporters in which she claimed that the killer was a man named "Ted" who would come forward if it became necessary. She also categorically denied having an incestuous relationship with Powers. When some so-called love letters were turned up, Candy blithely dismissed them, saying, "I write to everyone, `Darlin', I love you. I want you in my arms.' I say the same thing to my lawyer. It doesn't mean I really love him."

The trial lasted seven weeks and was covered by more than fifty newspapers to which Candy gave continual interviews. She told Dr. Joyce Brothers (who was then a Hearst columnist) that her husband had invited his own murder by openly soliciting and consorting with homosexuals. Candy told Brothers that one of her husband's homosexual lovers had most probably killed the tycoon. Said Candy: "I think it was one of those strange people he used to pick up on the street all the time. He would waltz into the house with strangers by the half dozen. He would tell people that we were very wealthy and important and owned a chain of banks and then say, 'Come on over and have a drink any time!"

Another Hearst writer, Jim Bishop, described Candy Mossler as "sixty inches of wrought iron ... painted with ... many veneers of honey and passion." The press took pains to point out that Candy's brother, DeWitt Weatherby, a bartender in Georgia, had killed a man during a heated poker game in 1956, and had

Famed criminal attorney Percy Foreman consults with Candy Mossler during her trial, where the tempestuous blonde was accused of murdering her husband to gain his fortune.

Foreman whispers advice to co-defendant, Melvin Lane Powers, Candy's rugged nephew, who, it was claimed, was her incestuous lover and the person who killed Mossler on orders from his aunt.

been sent to prison for life. Candy, after marrying into Mossler's wealth, hired attorney Carl Sanders, who later became governor of Georgia, to aid her brother in getting his parole. Further, Candace was portrayed in the press as an oversexed middle-aged swinger who seduced any available male. One report held that "some claimed to have seen photos of Candace embracing her Negro chauffeur... Other photos show the swinging grandma almost nude on a bed." The most shocking elements of this sordid story involved the insistent claim that Candy had carried on an incestuous relationship with her naïve nephew, Powers. Hotel clerks and stewards later testified that the pair often met in hotels under assumed names, and, in the words of one Texas clerk, were always "a-huggin' and a-kissin'."

The prosecution, headed by Richard Gerstein, claimed the murder had been committed so that the two lovers could continue their affair and have all of Mossler's money as well. He produced a note reportedly written by the victim, which stated: "If Mel and Candace don't kill me first, I'll kill them." Moreover, prosecutors brought forth a key witness, William Frank Mulvey, a convicted felon, who stated that Candace Mossler had given him $7,500 to murder her husband so that she could inherit the tycoon's estate of $7 million. He said that he spent the money, but had no intention of ever completing the contract killing. While in prison on another offense, Mulvey said, he met Powers, who was then jailed and awaiting trial for killing Mossler. Powers had bragged to him that he had murdered the tycoon, claimed Mulvey.

When Foreman responded, he first attacked the largely circumstantial evidence upon which Gerstein had built his case, and then launched into the technique of trying everyone but his clients. He characterized Jacques Mossler as a pervert who compulsively picked up homosexuals. It was one of these "creatures," Foreman insisted, who had killed the tycoon. A powerful and dynamic attorney, Foreman stood six-feet-four inches. He was brilliant, articulate and, in delivering his summations, mesmerizing, having lost only one client to the electric chair in more than seven hundred criminal cases he handled. Although Gerstein pointed out the irrelevancy of the tactic Foreman used to defend his clients, the jury found Mossler and Powers not guilty on March 6, 1966, after sixteen-and-a-half hours of deliberation.

Candy Mossler inherited her husband's $33 million banking business. She eventually married again, this time to an electrician eighteen years her junior. The new husband, Barnett Wade Garrison, had an unfortunate accident. Locked out of their Houston home one night, he fell while attempting to climb to a third-floor window and suffered injuries, which left him mentally incapacitated.

The couple divorced in 1975. Later that year, Candy rewrote her will, excluding three of her adopted children for failing to show her the "care, love, and affection" she felt she deserved. All these errant children did, Candy pointed out, was guzzle beer, walk about barefoot, hang out at a drugstore, run up staggering bills on her credit cards, and "use dirty language." On October 26, 1976, Candace Grace Weatherby Johnson Mossler Garrison died at the Fontainebleu Hotel in Miami at the age of sixty-two.

An autopsy showed she was in a state of physical collapse caused in part by years of drug abuse. She had been addicted to the use of Placidyl, a sleeping tablet, swallowing these "like jelly beans," according to a relative. She had received thousands of injections of Demoral and Phenergan, so that her buttocks had "turned as hard as rock." Pathologists reported that Candy had overdosed on drugs, and also stated that they had removed 475 and 500 grams of silicone

Candy Mossler and Melvin Lane Powers are shown joyously waving to spectators after leaving a courtroom in 1966, where they were acquitted of slaying Jacques Mossler.

from her breasts, deposited by injection, not implant. Such injections were illegal, they pointed out.

Melvin Powers became a wealthy and successful real estate developer in Houston, Texas, his worth later set at $7 million, the very amount that represented the fortune Jacques Mossler himself had accumulated. Powers did not attend the elaborate funeral services for Candy Mossler, which were held at Arlington National Cemetery, where the remains of the incendiary blonde were put to rest next to the husband she was once accused of murdering.

"I AM THE TIGER"/April 2, 1965

Everyone in Hollywood knew that Tom Neal (1913-1972), "The King of the B Pictures," was a he-man, who took no abuse from anyone. In fact, this jealous and violent man proved to his peers and millions of fans everywhere that he would hand out abuse to anyone who displeased him. A boxer of some note, Neal first appeared as a bit actor in a number of Hollywood films in the early 1940s. His name was listed in the credits along with John Wayne in the war epic *Flying Tigers*. Neal acted in over 180 films, few of them of lasting importance, the cheaply-produced film noir production of *Detour* later becoming a minor cult classic.

Neal's first wife, the lovely Vicky Lane, divorced him in 1949 because of his obsessive jealousy. He then became involved with Barbara Payton, an aspiring actress of very mod-

Handsome Tom Neal, shown in the early 1940s, when he was "King of the B Pictures" and even during his novice days in Hollywood proved to have a violent and uncontrollable temper.

Actress Barbara Payton, shown with Neal during the late 1940s; his obsessive jealousy over her prompted Neal to viciously attack matinee idol Franchot Tone, who had been dating Payton.

est talents, who was later arrested for intoxication, passing bad checks, and prostitution. Her biggest role was that of James Cagney's girlfriend in *Kiss Tomorrow Goodbye*, a 1950 film remembered chiefly for its excessive violence. Payton reappeared in Neal's life at regular intervals. Once she tried to get him jealous enough to marry her by dating matinee idol Franchot Tone.

On September 14, 1951, Neal cornered Tone outside his residence and beat him badly enough to cause a brain concussion. Franchot Tone went on to marry the sympathetic, adoring Barbara Payton in her Minnesota hometown, a union she said she sought due to the beating he'd taken solely because he loved her, but the marriage ended disastrously after only seven weeks.

The Tone episode effectively destroyed Tom Neal's film career as lackluster as it was so he turned to landscaping, which he'd learned from his Japanese gardeners during his salad days, in order to earn a living. The business he started prospered, and within a few years Tom Neal, the man with the short temper and quick fists, was attending to the lawns and gardens of the elite in Palm Springs, California.

Neal remarried, but his second wife Patricia died of cancer in 1958. That marriage produced a son. He married for a third time in June 1961, this time to a petite brunette named Gail who worked as a receptionist at the Palm Springs Tennis Club. The one-time Hollywood bad boy dutifully attended to his wife and his successful gardening business for the next four years. He managed to keep his name out of the papers until April 2, 1965, when he fired a bullet into his wife's head behind the right ear while she reclined on the couch. Within the next several hours he wandered aimlessly around the city, visiting his most intimate friends, to whom he admitted that he had killed his wife.

Neal told a different story to Palm Springs Police. He said that he was making love to Gail, when she inexplicably produced a gun, which she aimed at him, and during the struggle to take it from her, the weapon accidentally discharged. She had obtained the weapon recently for protection, as she had developed emotional problems and believed that she was being followed, but the quarrel had stemmed from Neal's own paranoid jealousy. He had accused his wife of sleeping with other men, a story he later told to the judge and jury.

Robert Lawrence Balzer, part owner of the Tyrol Restaurant in Pine Grove and a close friend of Neal's, substantiated these statements by recounting his confession the night of the murder. While visiting Balzer hours after the shooting, Neal complained that Gail "had become my whole life and I could not live without her." Tom Neal had sought out Balzer, a Buddhist monk, the day before for spiritual advice. The two men had discussed Buddhist philosophy for hours, with Balzer advising his friend, "The problems of life are as a

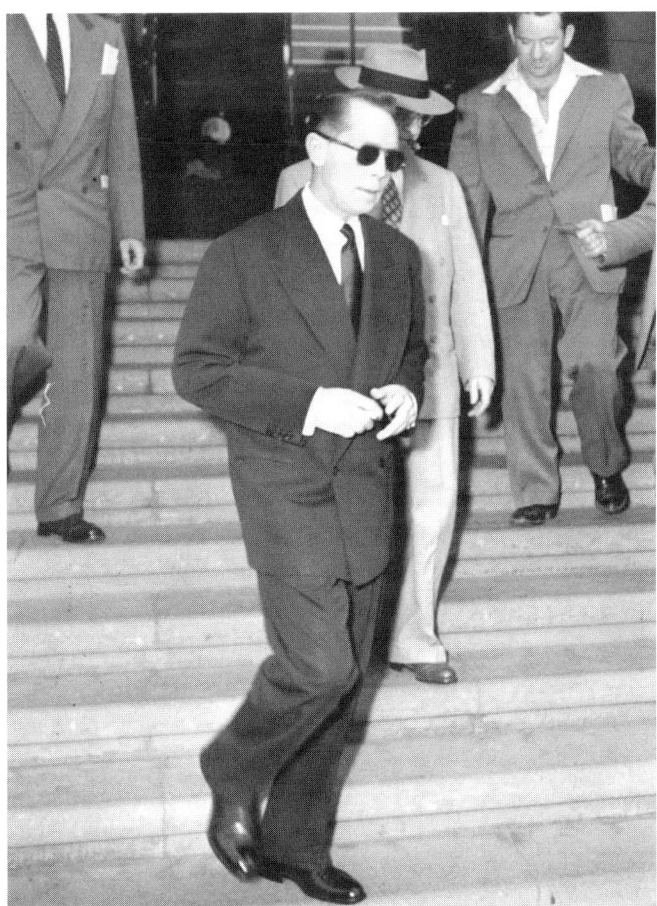

Franchot Tone leaving a hospital, where he had undergone a long recovery after the 1951 brutal beating he received from a jealous Tom Neal; Tone's face required plastic surgery.

Neal is shown with his third wife, 29-year-old Gail Neal, in 1961; he shot her to death while she was asleep on a couch in their Palm Springs, California, home on April 2, 1965.

tiger at the door." Neal reportedly answered, "I am the tiger, and the walls are all around me."

Some time before Neal reported the murder of his third wife, the gun used to end her life mysteriously disappeared and was never found. According to Police Lieutenant Richard Harries, the house was in a shambles when he arrived. Items of clothing belonging to a Steven Peck were found strewn about the rooms. Peck's address was listed as 2481 Cardillo Street, which was Neal's residence, but Peck was never called to testify. The police found the fatal bullet nestled in a plush pillow. Neal was taken into custody and held without bail for four days before being arraigned on a murder charge. No explanation was given for another peculiarity: the fact that all the windows in an adjacent apartment building had been shattered.

Although the prosecution lined up thirty prospective witnesses, they rested their case after calling only eight. No reason was ever given. The nine-woman, three-man jury spent a full day deliberating the evidence before returning their verdict on November 18, 1965. Perhaps more intrigued by the mysteries than by the testimony of the witnesses, the jury found Neal guilty only of involuntary manslaughter.

Tom Neal was sentenced to one to fifteen years at the California Institution for Men at Chino. The courts repeatedly denied Neal's appeals, but he still served less than seven years

His face ravaged by seven years of hard prison time, Neal is shown in 1971, following his parole; he had little to say to the press.

before being paroled in December 1971. He emerged from prison at age fifty-eight, his face lined and creased so deeply that he appeared to be a man in his eighties. Neal attempted a show business comeback following his release from prison. He produced a morning television show called "Apartment Hunters," but it was short-lived.

The one-time actor seldom talked about the bestial beating he had administered to Franchot Tone and the killing of his third wife. He clung to the ambition of some day going before the cameras once more, but this was not to be, despite his pleas to directors and producers that he could give fine performances since he was one "who had really lived." Said one producer: "He was kidding himself if he really thought anyone would hire him. He was too dangerous a man for that and everybody knew it." The King of the B Pictures died a forgotten man on August 7, 1972. By then he was simply a gardener looking for lawns to mow.

KILLING A SILENT SCREEN STAR/ October 30, 1968

Ramon Novarro (1899-1968) was an institution in Hollywood, hailed at the dawn of the 1920s as a great Latin lover, his handsome dark features causing legions of flappers to swoon whenever he appeared on screen. (Novarro was one of the "big three" Latin lovers on the silent screen, the other two being Rudolph Valentino and Antonio Moreno.) This surefire svengali of the box office, who was to become extremely wealthy, was born and raised in Durango, Mexico, where his father had a flowering practice as a dentist. The Novarro family fled Mexico in 1913, to escape the bloody revolution, moving to Los Angeles.

At age fourteen, Novarro worked as a grocery clerk, and later as a singing waiter in restaurants—he had a fine tenor voice—and still later as a dancer and bit player in the early-day silent movies. He went to New York and appeared on stage in some minor plays, having small parts and would have remained an obscure Broadway actor had not an enterprising talent agent spotted him and arranged for him to have a short-time Hollywood contract. He first appeared in a billed role in the film *Omar*, based upon the legendary Persian poet. Director Rex Ingram spotted him in this film and cast him in the role of Rupert of Hentzau in the 1922 silent screen version of *The Prisoner of Zenda*. He became an overnight sensation.

Novarro went on to starring roles in more big budget films—*The Arab*, *Scaramouche*, and *The Student Prince*—his career culminating in the 1925 silent epic, *Ben Hur*. Appearing bare-chested in this film, Novarro became the dream idol of every young girl in America and Louis B. Mayer's top star at MGM, which had spent an unprecedented $5 million on *Ben Hur*. Mayer made a special arrangement with Novarro—one which pleased the actor—wherein he was to act in one high-budgeted film every two years, so that he would not wear out his welcome with his adoring fans. This allowed Novarro a great deal of leisure time, which he spent training his voice for a possible operatic career (which never materialized) and appearing in plays he backed.

MGM's publicity department sent myriad press releases to magazines and newspapers in which it said Novarro spent most of his time studying philosophy and that he was consumed by spiritual thought, so much so that the studio had a difficult time in preventing him from entering a monastery. This was typical Hollywood hoakum and hype. Novarro spent most of his time drinking in Hollywood's exclusive clubs, particularly those who catered to wealthy homosexuals. His

Ramon Novarro, left, became a superstar of the silent screen when appearing in the 1925 screen epic, *Ben Hur*; Francis X. Bushman is shown battling with him in the classic chariot race.

penchant for attractive, young men was not unknown to the Hollywood community. Novarro, however, kept such liaisons very private. In the rampantly dissolute and perverted community that was Hollywood during the 1920s, Novarro was considered to be a harmless personality, a reserved gentleman, who never made scandalous headlines.

Rudolph Valentino, the Great Lover, became one of Novarro's best friends, showering gifts upon him. His sense of the ridiculous undoubtedly prompted Valentino to give Novarro an expensive lead Art Deco dildo in 1923. Novarro cherished this gift and kept it among his special belongings, an oddball object d'art, as events proved, he would have been better off without.

Though Novarro successfully made the transition from the silent era to sound movies, appearing in such smash hits as *Mata Hari* in 1932 opposite the great Greta Garbo, he knew that his career would soon come to an end. The image of the Latin Lover was fading and more rugged types—Clark Gable, James Cagney and Spencer Tracy—soon captured the attention of the fickle film fans. Following the completion of *Mata Hari*, Novarro told newshounds that "before it is too late, I want to stop."

Novarro did halt his career, and, despite occasional appearances in films and on TV years later, he spent most of his time and considerable wealth in developing a booming real estate business, growing even richer after buying up large tracts of land in San Fernando Valley. He purchased a $150,000 hillside home in remote Laurel Canyon, where he regularly entertained his party guests by performing marionette shows in the full-sized theater he had built in his home.

As the years passed, Novarro's drinking increased, as well as the number of young men he invited to his home. Two such young hustlers arrived at Novarro's home at the actor's request on the night of October 30, 1968. On the following morning, Novarro's 42-year-old secretary, Edward J. Weber, let himself into the actor's home, as had been his habit for nine years. Weber was shocked to see the house in disarray. The cushions of couches and chairs had been ripped apart, tables turned

Novarro continued his film career into the talking era, but his Latin Lover image fell from favor and he decided to quit films; he is shown above with Greta Garbo in the 1932 film, *Mata Hari*.

over, pictures torn from the walls. Souvenirs that Novarro had cherished for forty-some years lay in smashed ruins on the floor.

After calling out to Novarro and getting no response, Weber cautiously stepped into the actor's bedroom. He found his employer near the bed, naked, his body a bloody mess. Ramon Novarro was dead, suffocated, the Art Deco dildo Valentino had given him stuffed down his throat. Police were called and began an intensive investigation, questioning neighbors and relatives, but learning little about the brutal homicide. An officer routinely checked Novarro's phone, obtaining a record of all the calls placed from his number on the night of October 30, 1968. One of these was a long-distance call made to an attractive 20-year-old brunette named Brenda Lee Metcalf.

Police called Metcalf and learned that she had, indeed, talked with someone from Los Angeles on the night of the murder. She stated that her friend, Thomas Scott Ferguson, seventeen, had phoned her and told her that he was calling from Novarro's house. She also stated that Ferguson's brother, 22-year-old Paul Robert Ferguson, was with him at the time. The brothers were soon picked up and, after routine interrogation, were charged with Novarro's murder.

Paul Ferguson had been in Los Angeles for five months. Thomas Ferguson had run away from his Chicago home and joined his brother, who had already met Novarro and had introduced him to the actor. At first, Paul Ferguson admitted his guilt, telling police that he had killed the actor. He then recanted, and said that his brother Tom had murdered Novarro. It was later revealed that, to avoid the gas chamber, Paul had told Tom to admit complete guilt because, as a juvenile, he would draw no more than a six-month term and he, Paul, would go free.

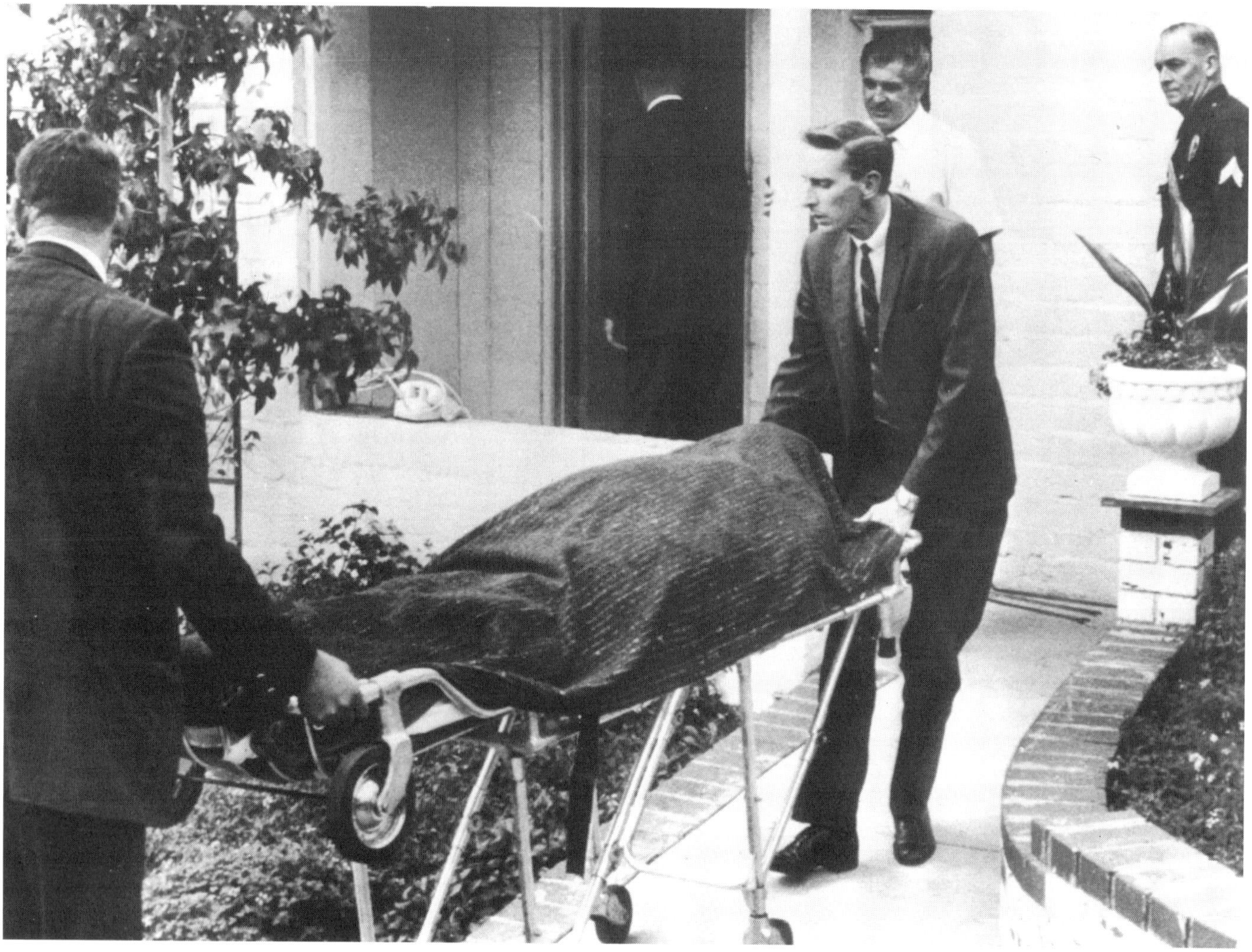

The last photo taken of Novarro before he was murdered at the age of sixty-nine.

The body of Ramon Novarro is removed from his Laurel Canyon home, following his brutal murder on October 30, 1968; his killers ransacked the home in search of money and valuables.

Thomas Ferguson agreed to the plan, telling police that he alone had battered Novarro to death. Then Julius Libow, a Juvenile Court Referee, ordered that Tom Ferguson stand trial as an adult. Hearing this and knowing that now he might face the death penalty, Tom Ferguson denied his guilt and said that his brother Paul had done the killing. No, said Paul, it was Tom.

According to Brenda Lee Metcalf, who was flown from Chicago to Los Angeles to give testimony on behalf of the prosecution, both brothers had had a hand in the killing. At least, that is what she opined after her forty-eight minute conversation with the Fergusons on the phone, which had been made at 8:15 p.m., Los Angeles time. From what the Fergusons told her at that time, she had the impression that the brothers were both abusing the actor.

Tom Ferguson told her at that time that he and his brother had gone to Novarro's home to "hustle" the actor, their visit made strictly for "sex," and that they were tearing up the actor's home in a desperate search for $5,000 in cash that Novarro reportedly kept on hand at all times.

The young hustlers told Metcalf that there were about 700 framed pictures on the walls of the house and they had been busy tearing these down because Paul Ferguson believed that the cash was hidden behind one of them. Tom Ferguson told Metcalf at the time that his brother was "up with Ramon" (in the actor's bedroom), attempting to force the actor into revealing where he had secreted the money.

Metcalf stated that she had warned Tom Ferguson "not to do anything wrong." Tom replied that he was not doing anything wrong. It was his brother, Paul, he said, who was "working" on Novarro, not he. When Tom put down the phone to look for some cigarettes, Metcalf said she could hear loud screams, as if someone were in agonizing pain. When Tom returned to the phone, Metcalf asked him what the screaming was about. Ferguson told her that his brother, Paul, was trying to force the actor into telling him where the money was hidden. "I have to go now before Paul really hurts Ramon," Tom Ferguson said to Metcalf. "I want to find out what's going on." He hung up.

Two hustling brothers from Chicago (shown in short sleeves with their defense attorneys), Tom, left, and Paul Ferguson, were convicted of beating Novarro to death and given life sentences.

During the seven-week trial of the Ferguson brothers, which began in August 1969, both brothers took the stand, squarely placing the blame on each other. Paul Ferguson told the court that Novarro had promised to make him a movie star, that he, Paul, was in Novarro's words, "a young Burt Lancaster, a superstar...another Clint Eastwood." It was his younger brother, Tom, who did the killing, not he, he insisted. After an hour at Novarro's home on the murder night, Paul Ferguson said he had consumed many beers, some tequila, and a fifth of vodka. He claimed that he had passed out dead drunk on the couch and that his brother woke him up. Paul quoted Tom as saying: "'This guy is dead, just like he might say 'hand me a pencil.'"

Tom Ferguson had a decidedly different story. He had gone into Novarro's bedroom after getting off the phone with Metcalf, he testified, to see his brother, Paul, standing over the actor, who was naked and bleeding. "Mostly in the face," said Tom. "It looked like he had a bloody nose...His lips were beat up...there was blood on his forehead." Paul ordered him to take Novarro into the shower and "clean him up," Tom said. He washed the groggy actor in the shower, telling him not to talk to his brother, that Paul "might become violent." Tom Ferguson then claimed that he returned the actor to his bedroom, placing him on the bed and leaving the room. When returning, he found Novarro in a pool of blood. "He looked dead," Tom Ferguson concluded.

"How did you know he was dead?"

"I just had that feeling," Tom Ferguson replied from the witness stand.

In the end, prosecutors placed the blame for the murder on Paul Ferguson. District Attorney James Ideman described to a jury in gruesome detail how Novarro had been "trussed up like an animal," by Paul Ferguson. "It was done for money, by torture...done cruelly by a man who had no respect for himself or others...who had no remorse, no compassion, no regrets...and who got his brother to perjure himself."

Medical experts testified that Paul Ferguson had been a practicing homosexual since the age of nine and that he was, after consuming liquor, subject to uncontrollable outbursts of violence. He was a dangerous man with homicidal tendencies, the experts agreed.

The jury was convinced that both brothers had had a hand in the murder and convicted both, returning a verdict "of guilty of murder in the first degree." The torture killers were both given life sentences by Superior Court Judge Mark Brandler, who recommended that they never be paroled.

The senseless murder of Ramon Novarro produced no fortune for the hustling brothers. They went away from the murder site without ever finding anything other than a few dollars they took from the pockets of their victim. The slain actor left in his will more than $500,000 to his four sisters and three brothers, and his secretary, Edward J. Weber.

THE SLAYING OF AN FILM ICON/ February 12-13, 1976

Teenage heart-throb Sal Mineo had died on screen several times as a juvenile delinquent and an apprentice thug. As Plato, the neurotic rich kid in *Rebel Without a Cause*, the actor died uselessly, wastefully, gunned down by police as he brandished an empty gun. Mineo went on playing homicidal, self-destructive role models, typecast into the man-child who never grew up, seemingly born for a star-crossed and violent end. In real life, the actor met that very same fate, although he was anything but the type of characters he had portrayed on screen.

On the night of February 12-13, 1976, Mineo was returning from a play rehearsal of James Kirkwood's "P. S. Your Cat is Dead," which Mineo was directing and which was scheduled to open shortly at the Westwood Playhouse. Mineo had appeared in the play during its San Francisco run, enacting the part of a bisexual burglar. The actor had left his blue Chevelle and was walking through the carport at the rear of

Sal Mineo, playing the role of a terrorist in the 1960 film, *Exodus*, a part that earned him an Academy Award nomination.

his West Hollywood apartment, just below the notorious Sunset Strip, which, for decades, had been awash with hustlers, pimps and prostitutes, including an enterprising army of petty criminals, from purse-snatchers to pickpockets.

As he was walking through the poorly lighted carport area, Mineo was confronted by a long-haired man in dark clothes. Neighbors suddenly heard the 37-year-old actor shout: "Oh, God, no! Help! Someone help!" Ray Evans, a neighbor and friend of Mineo's, ran to the carport to find the actor lying on his back, his feet in the air, and a stream of blood several yards long stemming from several wounds in Mineo's chest. He had been stabbed by what the coroner's office later described as a "heavy type knife." The wounds penetrated Mineo's heart and caused massive hemorrhaging, yet he did not die instantly.

Seeing that the actor was still breathing, Evans desperately tried to keep him alive through mouth-to-mouth resuscitation. "He kept gasping," Evans later told police, "and after about five or six minutes his last breath went into me and that was the end of it."

But it was just the beginning for the Los Angeles Police Department. Investigators were initially baffled by the murderous attack. Mineo's wallet had not been taken, and robbery as a motive for the slaying was ruled out. Acquaintances voiced wild speculations as to the motive for the murder. One mentioned "the drug angle." Another anonymous person sneeringly pointed to the kinky Sunset Strip, notorious for its queues of male hustlers waiting at curbside to be picked up, and brought up the "long-whispered reports of the actor's alleged bisexuality and fondness for sado-masochistic ritual." Another callously snickered that "It was a new boyfriend or something. They *do* have their quarrels."

None of this posthumous gossip aided the police in identifying or locating the killer. Some witnesses claimed to have seen a white man wearing dark clothes fleeing from the scene, but descriptions were vague. After weeks of tracking down hundreds of tips, Lieutenant Stanley Backman of the Los Angeles Sheriff's Department reported that the Homicide Bureau had "reached a dead end."

As Mineo's body was being shipped to Mamaroneck, New York, where it would be interred in the family plot at the Gate of Heaven Cemetery on February 17, 1976, police were still fruitlessly following trails created by rampant gossip and rumor. Critics and friends of the actor went to their typewriters and quickly eulogized Mineo in profiles that saw him as a "born-to-lose" character.

Mineo was not this kind of person at all. He began without a hope of ever becoming a world celebrity. Born Salvatore Mineo, Jr., on January 10, 1939, the son of a Sicilian-born coffin-maker, he came from a large family that struggled for survival in the Bronx. He lived on 217th Street, a tough neighborhood, and was recruited as a gang member at age eight, at a time when he was also dismissed from a parochial school for being a troublemaker. He was reinstated and went on to attend Christopher Columbus High School, but never received a diploma.

Josephine Mineo, his mother, thought to keep her boy out of trouble by enrolling him into a dancing class, where, two years later and quite by accident, he was spotted by Broadway producer Cheryl Crawford. She was then looking for two Italian-American children to appear in Tennessee Williams' play, "The Rose Tattoo." At eleven, Mineo found himself leading a goat across the stage of the Martin Beck Theatre, delivering a single line: "The goat is in the yard." He later understudied for the role of the prince in "The King and I," and subsequently took over that role.

Mineo just before the time of his murder in 1976; he had by then turned from acting to directing theatrical productions.

The doe-eyed youth with full lips and thick black hair was prey for predatory homosexuals, and Mineo knew it. He bought a gun that fired only blanks and several times brandished this harmless weapon on subways and dark New York streets to ward off molesters. By the mid-1950s, Mineo went to Hollywood, where he landed his first film role in the 1955 film, *Six Rivers to Cross*, in which he played Tony Curtis as a youth, a delinquent who grew up to rob Brink's. (The film was based upon the 1950 Brink's robbery in Boston.) His next movie, *Rebel Without a Cause*, shot him to fame and teenage idolatry. He appeared in several more blockbusters, including *Exodus*, where he enacted the role of a terrorist (another role casting him as a revenge-seeking delinquent, who had been "used as a woman" by Nazi guards in a German concentration camp during World War II).

Stabbed in the heart, Sal Mineo's body lies beneath a sheet in the carport of his West Hollywood apartment on the night of February 12-13, 1976.

Robber and killer Lionel Ray Williams, right, was convicted of second-degree murder in the Mineo slaying, serving only twelve years for taking the actor's life, being paroled in 1990.

When the Mineo fad faded in the 1960s, the actor got fewer and fewer substantial film roles and turned to the theater to support himself. In 1969, Mineo directed "Fortune and Men's Eyes," which had long runs in Los Angeles and New York and which portrayed prison life in homosexual terms, including a graphic homosexual rape scene. Clive Barnes of the New York *Times* scathingly reviewed this play, stating: "If this does sound like the kind of play you'd like, you need a psychiatrist a lot more than you need a theater ticket."

During the early 1970s, Mineo busied himself with dinner theater, but his fortunes gradually diminished with each year. His family eventually sold the $200,000 home he had purchased in 1956 for them in the exclusive Edgewater Point section of Mamaroneck, New York, with his first big film success. He himself moved from a luxurious Hollywood home to one inexpensive apartment after another, until he was living on the fringe of the West Coast's seamiest district, the Sunset Strip. This area was populated by tens of thousands of female and male prostitutes, dope peddlers, muggers, rapists, transvestites—every conceivable degenerate and pervert. Among this repulsive flotsam was the man who finally killed Sal Mineo, motivated not by sex or drugs, but for money.

After the actor's death, his friends attempted to collect $10,000 reward money for the capture of his killer, but only a few hundred dollars flowed into this coffer. Film director Peter Bogdanovich stated at the time: "In this racket when you're not hot anymore, or when you're cold, you're dead anyway, so a lot of folks turned the page on Sal's murder and shrugged."

One person, Mrs. Theresa Williams, a Los Angeles housewife, did not turn the page. In May 1977, she went to police to say that her husband had admitted to her that he had killed Mineo. He had returned home on the night of the murder covered with blood and casually saying: "I just killed this dude in Hollywood." It was never determined why Mrs. Williams took so long in deciding to report her husband's remarks.

Theresa Williams went on to state that her husband, 22-year-old Lionel Ray Williams, had used a hunting knife to stab Mineo to death, a weapon he had purchased for $5.28. Police were slow to accept the woman's statements, remembering that they had arrested Lionel Williams for robbery a short time after the actor's murder. In a move for leniency on the robbery charge, Williams had offered to provide information on the Mineo killing. The black one-time pizza-deliveryman told officers at that time that Mineo had been murdered in an argument over drugs, but the actor's background suggested that Mineo had no drug connections, so investigators dismissed Williams' story.

Detectives purchased a knife identical to the blade described by Mrs. Williams and inserted it in the wound that had been made in Mineo's chest; pathologists had preserved that part of the actor's anatomy as evidence. The knife fit perfectly. Williams, however, could not be arrested in Los Angeles, as he was then serving time in a Michigan jail for check fraud. Guards and inmates at the jail told Los Angeles investigators that Williams had often bragged about murdering Mineo, but they had not reported his statements, thinking them nothing more than jailhouse brags.

When Los Angeles detectives interviewed Williams in Michigan, the suspect denied having had anything to do with the Mineo murder. One of the detectives noticed that Williams bore a tattoo on his arm that depicted a knife almost exactly like the one used in the Mineo killing. Los Angeles County prosecutor Michael Genelin later stated that the tattoo had ominous significance: "It was almost like he put the mark of Cain on himself."

Because of lengthy legal maneuvering, Williams was not brought to trial until 1979, almost three years after the Mineo slaying. Williams' defense attorney repeatedly pointed out that Mineo's killer had been described as a white man and that his client was a Negro. Genelin then produced photos of Williams taken after the killing when he had been booked for robbery. The photos showed Williams with auburn-colored "processed" hair. The fact that Williams was a light-skinned black further convinced jurors that Williams had been mistaken for a white man by witnesses who had only a fleeting glance of the killer before he fled the murder scene.

Witnesses at that time had also stated that the killer had fled in a yellow subcompact auto. Genelin produced a loan agreement Williams had signed that allowed the suspect to drive a yellow Dodge Colt, the car the defendant was driving on the night of the murder. In his summation, Genelin said: "This man is a predator. This was a progressive process with him...He enjoyed brutalizing people. These were not just street robberies, but one incident after another, where he inflicted pain...and enjoyed it."

Williams' trial involved more than the Mineo slaying; he was also being tried for eleven street robberies in West Hollywood, Beverly Hills and the Wilshire district. The jury found him guilty and as the verdicts were slowly read aloud, the defendant turned to his lawyer, Morton Herbert, and moaned: "My God, they're going to convict me of every one of these things." He was convicted of ten of the eleven robbery charges *and* the Mineo murder.

Herbert admitted after the trial that evidence against his client "was extremely strong—and they were bad robberies ... Basically, this was a case of ten brutal robberies with Mineo tacked on. It was ironic that Mineo became a very minor part of the trial."

Williams had been convicted of second-degree murder in the Mineo slaying, but he nevertheless received a life term. Judge Bonnie Lee Martin first recounted Williams' long criminal record, beginning with four arrests when he was 14-years-old. She then stated that Williams "should be locked up as long as the law allows...I don't think he's susceptible to rehabilitation, considering his escalating conduct of committing more and more serious crimes and more and more violence." She then sentenced him to fifty-one years to life.

Defiant to the end, the stocky, muscular Williams sneered at Judge Martin and said: "I fault you for my going to the penitentiary."

Prosecutor Genelin felt exceptionally triumphant in the conviction of Lionel Ray Williams, knowing that the conviction was a rare event, especially when it came to the slaying of Sal Mineo. He told newsmen following the conviction: "If a murder is not solved within twenty-four to forty-eight hours, you generally do not get a solution. Anyone who says that people don't get away with murder is crazy. They do it all the time."

Lionel Ray Williams did not serve out his complete sentence. He was paroled in 1990, after serving only twelve years for killing Sal Mineo. Since that time and to this writing, he has been jailed many times for parole violations.

THE DANCER AND THE SKIER/ March 21, 1976

In the 1970s, Aspen, Colorado, hit its stride as the "in place" to be, a rollicking spa for wealthy swingers, whose chief ambition was pleasure. Although those who flocked to this trendy town ostensibly arrived to ski, the attraction was (and is) the expensive bars and restaurants and the chic resorts. The New York *Times* once aptly described Aspen as "a hedonistic place where the rich, the young, the haunted and the newly divorced come to find a new sense of self."

Claudine Longet (b. 1941), a French performer, who married pop singer Andy Williams in 1961, arrived there in 1974

Dancer Claudine Longet and skier Vladimir "Spider" Sabich, who lived as man and wife in idyllic Aspen, Colorado, until Sabich was shot to death on March 21, 1976.

Claudine Longet, charged with murdering Sabich, is escorted to court by her former husband, singer Andy Williams; she was convicted of "criminally negligent homicide," and served only thirty days in jail.

to be with her lover, Vladimir "Spider" Sabich, a one-time Olympic skier and a ski pro since 1971. In 1973, he lost a race to downhill champion Jean-Claude Killy, and with it, his last chance to emerge as the world's premier skier. A series of crippling injuries had ended his professional career by 1976. His relationship with Longet would follow suit.

Sabich's friends were sympathetic when he told them of the growing discord in his relationship with Longet. By early 1976, he was saying, "It's either going to end or we'll be married within a year."

The end came on March 21, 1976, when Longet returned home from a day on the slopes. She had reportedly been drinking and socializing with several men in a resort lodge. At 6:30 p.m., Roy Griffith, chief of security for the area, received a frantic call asking him to come at once to the Sabich home. He found Spider Sabich lying on the floor in the master bedroom with a bullet in his stomach. Longet said she found a .22-caliber Irma pistol in a closet, and was asking Sabich how to use it properly when it accidentally discharged. Sabich was taken to the Aspen Valley Hospital, where he died a short time later.

Longet's diary recounting the deterioration of her romance with Sabich was taken as evidence, but the presiding judge in the 1977 murder trial refused to admit it. It was also reported that Sabich had ordered Longet and her children from the house. Andy Williams rushed to Longet's side, and during her trial, lived with her in the home of singer John Denver.

At her trial, Longet pleaded not guilty to second-degree murder charges. She stuck to her story about the accidental shooting, and claimed that, as Sabich slipped into unconsciousness, she tried to revive him with mouth-to-mouth resuscitation. On January 14, 1977, the jury returned a verdict of guilty on a reduced charge of "criminally negligent homicide."

Longet left the court to await sentencing, choking back tears to tell reporters: "I have too much respect for human life to have been guilty...I am not guilty."

Facing a possible two-year sentence and a $5,000 fine, Longet pleaded hardship before district Judge George Lohr on January 31, 1977. She said she feared the "stigma" of prison would adversely affect her children, who might become resentful "against a system that would send to jail [the] mother they trust and believe in." Judge Lohr took pity on Longet and ordered her to serve thirty days in jail "at a time of her own choosing," and pay the $25 for the preparation of court documents. He then placed her on two-year probation. Lohr said that he could not in good conscience give her probation without jail because it would have "undermined the law." She served her time from April 18 to May 18, 1977.

The lenient sentence meted out to Longet enraged many of Aspen's citizens, who were embittered over Sabich's death. They summed up the affair in a flurry of bumper stickers that suddenly appeared after Longet's sentencing, one that read: "It's All Claudine's Fault."

THE BIG SLEEP/1979 TO PRESENT

Claus von Bulow (Claus Cecil Borberg, b. 1926) was born into the Danish aristocracy, learning early a great respect for wealth. Sent to a boarding school in Switzerland as a child, he returned to his native Denmark at age eleven in 1937, where he was surrounded by wealth and power. His grandfather, Fritz von Bulow, was Denmark's minister of justice, who controlled the country's treasury. It was from this penny-conscious Edwardian that Bulow learned well an appreciation for money. He would work hard to establish his own wealth, but then marry into millions that he stood to inherit upon the death of his spouse, a death he reportedly arranged with diabolical cunning.

Freedom, not wealth, was foremost in the mind of Bulow when, at the age of sixteen, he escaped the Nazi regime in Denmark in 1942 by fleeing to England to join his mother, who had escaped the Germans earlier. His father, Svend Bulow, remained behind and, following the war, was accused and stood trial for collaborating with the Nazis. He was acquitted, but the family name was stained in Denmark. Claus von Bulow, however, intended to make his mark in England, studying law at Cambridge and, following the war, attending the Sorbonne

Claus von Bulow, who became a European social lion through his legal contacts and his employment with the world's richest man, J. Paul Getty.

in Paris, where he became fluent in French, German and English.

Returning to London, Bulow became a junior executive at the Hambro bank and later practiced as a barrister. He lived an ideal bachelor's life, maintaining a luxurious apartment in Belgrave Square. He gave intimate parties at least twice a week, entertaining beautiful women, who eagerly dallied in his bedchamber. High society lions and matrons welcomed the cultured, well-mannered Bulow, inviting him to their mansions for fetes and dinners. He soon became a fixture in this elitist society and it was through these contacts, as well as those established in his banking and legal career that Bulow met the richest man in the world, J. Paul Getty III.

Getty was impressed with Bulow's diplomatic airs and careful social postures and, in 1959, he invited the enterprising Bulow to join the Getty empire as a legal negotiator in the billionaire's labyrinthine businesses. Getty demanded that Bulow give up his law practice and devote his entire time to Getty interests and this Bulow did. Friends and acquaintances correctly believed that Bulow's obsessive passion for money prompted this decision.

Since his tycoon boss refused to fly, Bulow flew about the world to negotiate and conclude Getty mergers, acquisitions and, in particular, the establishment of refineries for Getty Oil. So important did Bulow become to Getty that the tycoon repeatedly asked him to settle family squabbles between him and his sons. This he did with alacrity and with such success that he won his employer's complete confidence. It was more than a rumor that Bulow would some day become the chief executive of all Getty enterprises.

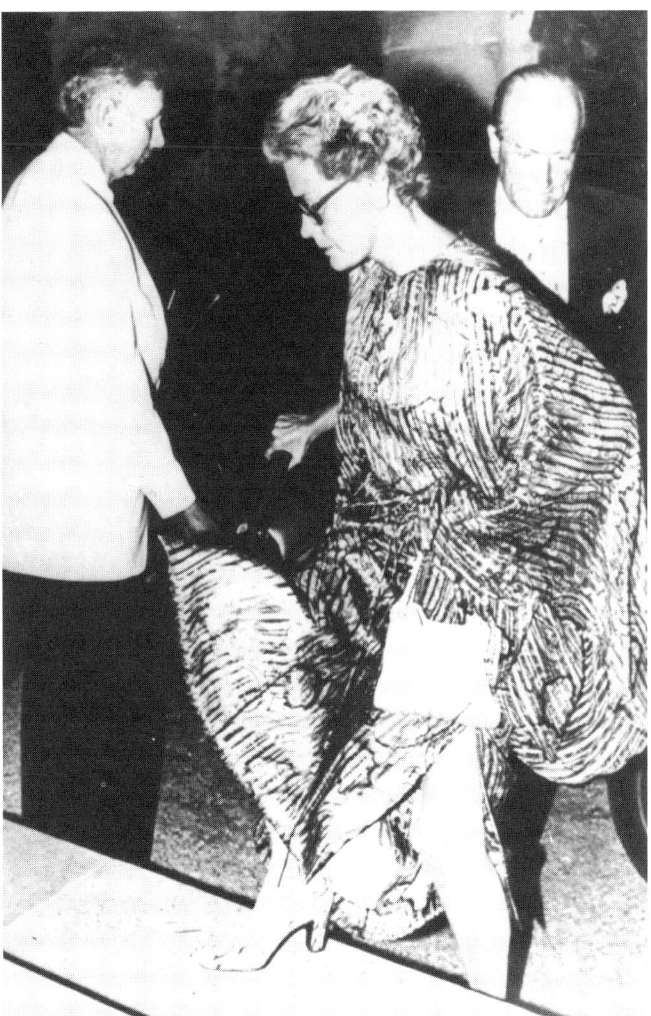

The beautiful blonde heiress, Martha "Sunny" Crawford von Auersperg von Bulow; her husband, Claus von Bulow, authorities claimed, tried to murder her in order to inherit her fortune of more than $75 million.

Then, in 1960, another opportunity presented itself in the form of an attractive blonde, Martha "Sunny" Crawford von Auersperg, whose own fortune exceeded $75 million. She was at that time married to Alfred von Auersperg, an Austrian prince. How many times Bulow saw Sunny after that first meeting can only be speculated, but it is known that the couple met again in 1964, and once more the following year. By that time, Sunny had left her husband and Bulow energetically courted her. They were married on June 6, 1966.

Bulow told his friends that "I have finally found the right girl." What he had found, of course, was a life of riches and comfort stemming from old money. Sunny, born in 1932, was the only child of George Crawford, chairman of the board of Columbia Gas and Electric Company. The utilities tycoon died when his daughter was only three, and she was left in the care of her mother, Annie-Laurie (who later married Russell Aitken), and her grandmother, Mrs. Martha Warmack.

Sunny, like her peers, attended exclusive schools as a child, Chapin School in New York, and Maryland's St. Timothy's. She made her social debut as a tall, stunning blonde in 1951, em-

The resplendent estate in Newport, Rhode Island, purchased by "Sunny" and where she was reportedly dosed with insulin shots which sent her into a permanent coma.

barking on the traditional European tour a few years later. Despite her breathtaking beauty, the youthful Sunny was shy and retiring, in awe of the European aristocrats she encountered. On a trip to an exclusive Alpine resort, Sunny met a handsome and charming ski instructor, who turned out to be Prince Alfred von Auersperg. His aristocratic lineage dated back centuries, but, like many of his class following World War II, he had little or no money. That was no problem to Sunny, who promptly fell in love with the nobleman, marrying him in 1957. The couple had two children, Alexander and Annie-Laurie, named Ala.

By the early 1960s, Sunny grew weary of supporting her penniless husband and was easy prey for Bulow, who presented himself to her as a man having his own wealth and exuding the kind of authority and worldliness her husband did not possess. She began seeing Bulow regularly long before her marriage to Auersperg ended in divorce. Bulow became Sunny's perfect traveling companion. He was every inch a man of commanding stature, having a tall frame (six feet four inches), a large head with thinning hair, a long nose and prominent jaw that jutted above tightly tied silk ties. He looked elegant in his double-breasted suits, tailor-made in Saville Row.

Bulow made a point of telling friends that he had quit Getty to devote all his time to Sunny, but this was apparently not his wife's true desire. She grew weary of Bulow's loafing—a repeat performance from her first husband—and told him to secure a high level executive post. Bulow instead relied upon the Crawford millions to support his lavish lifestyle, learning early on that of his wife's $75 million fortune, he stood to inherit at least $14 million upon her untimely death.

Sunny finally became resigned to the fact that Bulow would never acquire that high-level post and settled back into her millions. The couple appeared to have a happy and contented relationship for ten years, the union producing a girl, Cosima. They lived in luxury at Sunny's lavish Fifth Avenue co-op in New York and throughout this sprawling suite of rooms, servants scurried about to satisfy the whims and fancies of the family.

Thinking to upgrade her image, Sunny purchased Clarendon Court at Newport, Rhode Island, a resplendent mansion built in the days of the Robber Barons, its impressive acreage having priceless beach frontage. Sunny busied herself by spending a great fortune on the mansion, improving its huge pool and gardens. She and Bulow began to host sumptuous parties, complemented by large orchestras and dozens of servants serving endless quantities of champagne and stuffed pheasant. Their guests made up the cream of Eastern Establishment society and their neighbors were equally satiated with wealth and power. A short distance from Sunny's

Maria Schrallhammer, Sunny's devoted maid, testified in court that she found hypodermic needles stored by Bulow, which he used to secretly inject his wife with insulin.

estate was Hammersmith Farm, where Jacqueline Kennedy Onassis had been raised and was married.

The ideal life at Clarendon Court collapsed in 1979. It was at this time, Bulow later insisted, that Sunny came to him and abruptly told him that she "was no longer interested in having sex." This was not the truth, according to Maria Schrallhammer, Sunny's devoted maid since her marriage with Auersperg. Sunny told her that Bulow had broken off their marital relations and Sunny believed that he was having a nervous breakdown.

Bulow's nerves were fine, according to later reports. His own sexual drive was thriving, but it was channeled to another woman, Alexandra Isles, a 33-year-old socialite and actress (who had become a regular on the TV soap opera, "Dark Shadows"). Bulow, at this time, took to staying at his New York club, The Knickerbocker, and visiting Isles regularly. Her father had been a friend of Bulow's in Denmark. Mrs. Isles was divorced and had a young son. Bulow, however, did not confine his extramarital affairs to Isles, but routinely visited at this time Leslie Baxter, a 43-year-old prostitute in New York. Bulow was not suffering from mental problems, as Sunny suspected, but was simply becoming physically exhausted from his incessant bouts with Isles and Baxter.

Bulow blamed Sunny for his own problems, complaining to his children that their mother made him feel like a cheap gigolo and that his uppercrust Newport neighbors had grown hostile toward him, thinking him as nothing more than a man sponging off a wealthy woman. Bulow did try to earn some money by financially backing some Broadway shows. One of these, *Deathtrap*, became a great success and was later sold to Warner Brothers for $1.5 million, plus a percentage of the profits. It was ironic that the plot of this play involved a man and wife plotting a murder.

Alexandra Isles, TV soap opera star, testified that she had carried on a secret affair with Bulow and had given him a deadline to divorce his wife, a timeframe, prosecutors concluded, that prompted Bulow to attempt his wife's murder.

Bulow's campaign to profile his wife as a purposeful recluse increased. He told friends and relatives that she was retreating from the world to read books and consume great quantities of sweets. He made it apparent that he was contemplating divorce, asking family physician, Dr. Richard Stock, if Sunny could endure the trauma of a divorce. By this time, Alexandra Isles had given her lover a deadline—either he divorce Sunny by the end of 1979, or quit his relationship with her.

At Christmas that year, as was the family's custom, the Bulows moved from New York to Clarendon Court. There, Sunny consumed great quantities of sweets. Her sweet-tooth had caused her to drink rich eggnogs by the pint and drink ice cream sodas. She had ice cream smothered with caramel prepared for her by her cook, Irene Silvia, and these rich dishes were brought to the heiress on an hourly basis. Sunny put on weight.

Then, on December 27, 1979, after she consumed several glasses of eggnog and a large glass of ginger ale, Sunny lapsed

Bulow confers with his attorneys during a murder trial, which resulted in his conviction; he was exonerated in subsequent hearings.

into unconsciousness, which Bulow attributed to a case of the flu, aggravated by too much eggnog. At the maid's insistence, Bulow finally summoned Dr. Janis Gailitis of Newport Hospital, who revived Martha and diagnosed her illness as hypoglycemia. But Maria Schrallhammer suspected Bulow of having induced Sunny's condition.

For the next few months, Sunny was lethargic and depressed. Bulow insisted that she had a drinking problem and took barbiturates. In April 1980, tests at New York's Columbia-Presbyterian Hospital confirmed that Sunny, indeed, suffered from hypoglycemia. On Thanksgiving Day, 1980, Schrallhammer found a bottle marked "insulin" and several other containers of drugs in a black bag in Bulow's closet. She gave the bag to Dr. Stock, Martha's personal physician, for chemical analysis. He determined that an odd-looking paste found in the bag would not have been prepared by any legitimate druggist.

Sunny lapsed into a second coma on December 21, 1980, in her New York apartment. She was rushed to the hospital, where tests showed low blood sugar, but a high insulin count. She was placed on a life support system. Bulow suggested that she be allowed to die. On January 23, 1981, Schrallhammer turned the black bag over to Newport police, who found traces of Diazepam, Amobarbital, and insulin on a syringe. On July 6, 1981, Claus von Blow was indicted on two counts of assault with intent to murder.

Bulow's trial began in Newport on February 1, 1982. He pleaded not guilty before Judge Thomas Needham in a courtroom packed with journalists. The prosecution based its case on the testimony of Maria Schrallhammer. The thirty-one-day trial ended on March 16, 1982, when Bulow was found guilty. He was sentenced to thirty years in prison, but was released on $1 million bail pending appeal. Outside the courtroom, a throng of spectators chanted, "Free Claus! Free Claus!" But a year would pass before any further action.

During that time, the defense filed 100-page brief seeking a reversal of the conviction, and on April 27, 1984, the judgment of the lower court was reversed. After the U.S. Supreme Court refused a request from Rhode Island attorney general Dennis J. Roberts to review the case, the state announced plans to retry Von Blow. The second trial began in Providence on Apr. 25, 1985, and ended in a final acquittal on June 10, 1985. Claus von Bulow was at last a free man. There were allegations that he had been "framed" by his stepchildren, Prince Alexander von Auersperg and Princess Annie Laurie Kneissl. Another theory held that Bulow and his mistress, Alexandra Isles, drove Sunny to attempt suicide by taking insulin. At this writing, Martha von Bulow remains on a life support system, still in a coma that has lasted more than two decades.

THE WRATH OF A WRONGED WOMAN/ March 10, 1980

Dr. Herman Tarnower, known as "Hi," was not only a distinguished New York cardiologist, but he grew immensely rich from his best-selling book, *Scarsdale Diet,* published in 1979 and which grossed $11 million in its first printings. The long and lucrative life of Dr. Tarnower, who enjoyed a thriving practice, a resplendent home and worldwide recognition for his medical skills, was also adorned with a number of beautiful mistresses. He was not a physically attractive man, lean, balding and with a long face and nose, but his wealth and prestige were enticing to women seeking status and financial security.

One of these was Jean Struven Harris (b. 1923 or 1926, depending upon various sources). She dated and then became engaged to Tarnower in a prolonged and troubled union that ended in her murder of the dallying doctor. Tarnower's relationship with Harris began when the physician met Harris at a dinner party in Manhattan on December 9, 1966. Harris, at the time was a divorced mother of two. She had graduated *magna cum laude* from Smith College in 1945, and by 1972, was the headmistress of the exclusive Madeira School for girls in McLean, Virgina. Her students called her "Integrity Jean" because of her numerous lectures about self-control, commitment to excellence, and propriety.

Following their meeting at the home of Leslie Jacobson, Tarnower and Harris began their lengthy courtship. There was talk of marriage, but it never got past the discussion stage. Tarnower, fifty-eight at the time of his "engagement" to Harris in 1967, entertained a variety of women at his estate in Purchase, New York, his $500,000 home decorated with the heads of African beasts—kudu, lions, rhinos—he had shot on big game safaris in Africa. Though he loved to hunt such animals, Tarnower's chief hobby was hunting attractive women. One of them, Lynne Tryforos, a 38-year-old medical assistant, who was hired by Tarnower and who replaced Harris as the doctor's favorite. In 1977, Jean Harris first became aware of Tarnower's philandering. On New Year's Day, Harris was with Tarnower at a Palm Beach resort when she saw a personal notice in the New York *Times* that read "Happy New Year, Hi T. Love Always, Lynne."

A long struggle followed between the two rivals for the doctor's affections. Harris and Tryforos cut up each other's clothes, and rubbed human feces on each other's personal belongings whenever they found them in Tarnower's residence. Harris then accused Tryforos of placing anonymous obscene phone calls to her, and when she complained of this abuse to Tarnower, the doctor accused her of fabricating such tales. It was clear that Tarnower favored the younger Tryforos, but he continued to rely on Harris to help him prepare his diet book.

In fact, most of the recipes for the book were provided by Tarnower's housekeeper, Suzanne van der Vreken, although the doctor included one recipe in his book—"Spinach Delight a la Lynne" (creamed spinach made with yogurt) as a way of acknowledging his new, young mistress. This irked Harris, who served as the physician's editor on the book. She polished and improved its structure and grammar.

After twelve years of her tenuous relationship with Tarnower, Harris became increasingly disturbed and apparently made plans to either kill herself or slay the man who she later claimed was ruining her life by taunting her with the Tryforos woman. In November 1978, Harris bought a .32-caliber Harrington and Richardson revolver from Irving's Sport Shop in Tyson's Corner, Virginia, a few miles from the Madeira School. James Forst, the shop clerk, asked her why she was buying the weapon and Harris replied that it was for her own protection since she lived "back in the woods in a secluded area."

The situation between Tarnower and Tryforos became intolerable to Harris. She decided to take action on March 10, 1980. Driving in a heavy rainstorm directly from McLean to the Tarnower estate. In her purse was the .32-caliber handgun

Jean Struven Harris, educator at an exclusive Virginia school, was "engaged" for more than a decade, until she killed the man who jilted her.

Wealthy Dr. Herman Tarnower, author of the best-selling *Scarsdale Diet*, who was shot to death by Jean Harris on March 10, 1980.

Tarnower's estate in Purchase, New York, where the "Diet Doc" entertained myriad women, including Harris, who, enraged at his many assignations, shot him to death.

Harris, under arrest, is shown en route to court to be arraigned for the killing of Tarnower, March 11, 1980; she claimed that Tarnower was killed when trying to prevent her suicide.

Harris, center, confers with her defense team (left to right)—Barbara York, Joel Aurnou, Bonnie Steingart, and Victor Grossman; she got life in prison, but was later paroled.

and the amphetamines she needed for courage. At eleven that night, after Tarnower's dinner guests had left, Harris drove up the doctor's driveway in her blue 1973 Chrysler. She climbed the darkened staircase, entered the doctor's bedroom, and fired four shots. Tarnower slumped over dead and Harris fled the grounds. Rushing to the window, the startled housekeeper, Suzanne van der Vreken, saw Harris getting into her car. She called police.

Squad cars were soon on the scene. Patrolman Brian McKenna spotted Harris sitting in her car in the driveway and approached her.

"There's been a shooting in the house," she told the officer in a calm voice.

McKenna rushed into the house and raced up the stairs to see Tarnower lying on the floor of his master bedroom, mortally wounded. By that time, Harris had re-entered the house and was standing in the foyer. Patrolman Daniel O'Sullivan went to her and she looked directly at him while saying: "I shot him. I did it. He wanted to live. I wanted to die." She then said to Detective Arthur Siciliano: "I'd been through so much hell. I loved him very much. He slept with every woman he could. I had no intention of going back to Virginia alive."

Harris later stated that her intention had been to persuade Tarnower to shoot her, and she described how she had confronted the doctor, asking that he kill her. Tarnower, she said, called her "crazy," and ordered her from the house. A struggle for the revolver then ensued and Tarnower was shot four times. Police doubted from the beginning that there had been much of a struggle or no struggle at all and that Harris had simply cornered her cuckolding lover and blasted four slugs into him as he stood in his bedroom. A long, rambling letter describing her physical and mental subjugation to Tarnower corroborated her story and established a motive.

Jean Harris was charged with second degree murder. Her trial, sensationalized in tabloids, began in the White Plains, New York, courtroom of Judge Russell R. Leggett in November 1980. On February 4, 1981, the infamous "Scarsdale Letter," mailed from Virginia the day of the murder, was introduced into evidence. "Going through the hell of the past few years has been bearable only because you were still there and I could be with you," it read in part. The letter failed to sway the jury. On February 24, 1981, the jurors returned a verdict of guilty. Harris was sentenced on March 20 to life imprisonment at the Bedford Hills Correctional Facility. As an inmate there, Harris became involved in prison reform, writing a book about her prison experience, *They Always Call Us Ladies,* which was published in 1988. She was later paroled and went on writing more books and giving lectures about prison abuse, but seldom, if ever, mentioning the name of the man she murdered.

MURDER OF A PLAYMATE/August 14, 1980

Paul Snider had been on his own from childhood. Born into poverty in Vancouver, British Columbia, he was the product of a broken home and the tool of street gangs. His abiding love was for money and to turn a dollar in his early twenties he became a pimp. He grew modestly wealthy peddling only a few girls, "class ladies," in his language. He adorned himself with furs, flashy clothes and an ostentatious pinky ring, in the tradition of any successful whoremaster.

Driving about Vancouver in sports cars (either over-financed or on loan to him), Snider failed in his amateur efforts to promote auto shows and motorcycle races. He stayed with his small-time prostitution racket, carefully avoiding any traffic in drugs, although underworld contacts who protected his flesh peddling attempted to high-pressure him into that racket. He dreaded any arrest for drug violations, which he knew would draw a lengthy prison term, once telling a friend: "I will kill myself before I go to jail."

Still, Snider's expensive habits endangered his life. When he failed to pay a loan shark, he was seized by goons and taken to the top of a Vancouver hotel, where he was held by his ankles out of an open window, until he promised to repay the juice loan. This experience so terrified him that Snider imme-

Beautiful Dorothy Stratten, shown with a life-size image of herself and holding a plaque that honored her as Playmate of the year.

diately left Vancouver for the fleshpots of Los Angeles. Within days of arrival, Snider recruited several girls to work the neighborhoods in and about posh Beverly Hills. He prospered for about a year (1976-1977), maintaining a lavish Hollywood home and riding about in a gold limousine. Yet, the hordes of hustlers lining Sunset Strip soon diminished the profits his six girls could produce.

Snider took his spoils and returned to Vancouver, where he told friends that he would no longer pursue illicit activities. He vowed to go "straight" and to that end he worked several promotion schemes that brought little income and promised a limited future. All that changed on the day he walked into a Vancouver Dairy Queen, where he beheld a tall, buxom girl with a milk-white complexion. She was Dorothy Stratten (real name Dorothy Ruth Hoogstraten), eighteen, who had been working at the Dairy Queen for four years.

Like Snider, she was the offspring of divorced parents. Shy and retiring, the lovely girl lived with her mother, wrote poetry and was saving her money to pay for secretarial courses, hoping some day to become an executive secretary. David Redlick, her employer at the Dairy Queen later stated that Stratten "was the kind of girl you'd be proud to have as a sister or a daughter. She even used to take my kids to the beach sometimes, and she was the only girl I ever bought roses for when she left [the Dairy Queen. I don't even do that for my wife."

Snider was taken by the girl and, typical of his approach, did not directly ask her for a date, but got Stratten's phone number from a friend before asking her to dinner. He then began to shower her with flowers and inexpensive jewelry, flattering her over her good looks. She was overwhelmed by Snider's attention and was proud to be escorted by Snider to her high school graduation dance. Snider then began to take the impressionable girl to better restaurants and nightclubs, but this was only part of another money scheme. He told a friend: "That girl could make me a lot of money."

The hustler had recently learned that *Playboy* Magazine was about to conduct a hunt for "the perfect girl" to appear in its publication as the 25th Anniversary Playmate. Snider, through flattery and cajolery, convinced Stratten to pose naked so that he could send these photos to Playboy, telling the naïve girl that she would certainly be selected as "the perfect girl." Editors at Playboy were impressed with the photos, but turned Snider down when they learned that Stratten was underage and telling him that they could not use the graphics unless he obtained the signed permission of Dorothy's parents.

Snider then launched a campaign to persuade Stratten's mother to grant that permission, but Mrs. Hoogstraten adamantly refused. This was her daughter's one golden opportunity, he insisted. Never again would the five-foot-nine-inch Dutch blonde have such a chance at fame and fortune. Stratten's mother finally relented and signed the form that granted permission. Snider sent the form to Playboy and, in August 1978, boarded a plane with Stratten—her first ride in an airplane—and flew to Los Angeles, where photo tests were made of the aspiring model.

Playboy photographers were impressed with the girl's photogenic qualities and her natural beauty. She was selected as one of the sixteen finalists for the contest, but lost out to another girl. Still, fame beckoned when Stratten was selected as the August 1979 Playmate, and her appearance in the magazine launched her career. She was no longer Dorothy Hoogstraten, but had acquired a new name, Dorothy Stratten. She was quoted in the article about her as being "a sucker for the romantic approach. Romance is very effective for me because I'm a very sensitive person. I'm a faithful one-man woman. It might sound old-fashioned, but I have to concentrate my love on just one man."

Stratten with hustler Paul Snider, celebrating her 20th birthday; Snider became her husband and killer.

Snider, meanwhile, hustled small promotions, returning to the seamy side of the street by operating a small disco that featured nude male dancers, who titillated middle-aged women. The hustler knew that his own future was limited and banked on the opportunities presented to Stratten. To that end, he proposed marriage to her in May 1979. Though warned that Snider was merely out to use her, Stratten felt obligated to the

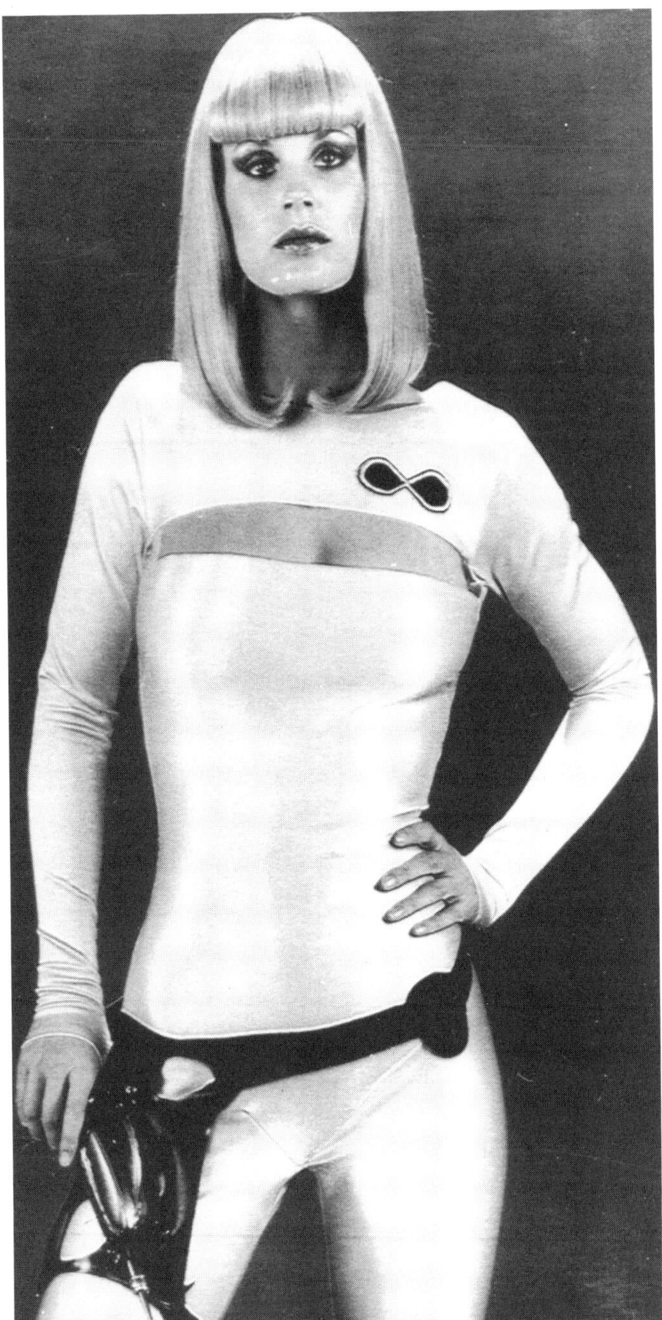

Stratten appeared in a number of low-budget films; she is shown above as a ravishing robot in *Galaxina*.

hustler and described him as her lover, friend, guide, counselor, and manager. She accepted and the couple married in Las Vegas, Nevada, on June 1, 1979.

After the *Playboy* appearance, Stratten began to get TV and movie offers, as Snider expected. She was ecstatic after appearing as a guest star on the *Buck Rogers in the 25th Century* TV series. At the time, the innocent ingénue blurted: "Seeing my name in the *TV Guide* was the most exciting thing in my life." She next appeared in a low-budget Canadian film, *Autumn Born*, but she showed little enthusiasm for her role in the movie, telling a reporter that she spent most of her time on camera "getting beat up."

The model turned actress appeared in more low-budget films, such as *Americathon* and *Skatetown, U.S.A.*, but in roles that showed she had a genuine talent for acting. Her star rose to greater heights when *Playboy* chief Hugh Hefner selected Stratten as the 1980 Playmate of the Year. From this coveted position, she gleaned more than $200,000 in jewelry and furniture gifts. Suddenly, she was followed about by Hollywood designers, managers, coaches, hairdressers, and, especially, photographers.

Snider saw that he was losing control of his wife to these entrepreneurial mentors. He became resentful and accused Stratten of cutting him out of her successful business enterprises. He became enraged when being eliminated from the invitation list to many of the *Playboy* functions at Hefner's lavish mansion. He was further frustrated by Hefner himself, who kept him at arm's distance, after Snider tried to interest the publishing mogul in some of his shady schemes.

While Snider faded into the background, Stratten continued to appear in more films, her latest being *Galaxina*, in which she appeared as a beautiful robot. "I have been programmed for love," she tells a space crew member in this film, one that was released only a few weeks after her tragic death. Although Stratten began to enjoy the company of Hollywood's movers and shakers, her life with Snider crumbled. The hustler argued with her incessantly, bickering that finally led to the couple's separation. Snider moved into a cheap bungalow in West Los Angeles next to a freeway, while Stratten flew to New York to appear in Peter Bogdanovich's new film, *They All Laughed*. She would join the company of stars Audrey Hepburn and Ben Gazarra.

Stratten fell in love with the director and when she returned to the Coast, she told Snider that she would make a comfortable settlement in a quiet divorce. Snider was having none of it. He had groomed her for stardom, nurtured her career, he said. He had created her image as a sex goddess, he yelled. Stratten ignored him and moved into Bogdanovich's Beverly Hills home, an act that enraged Snider. He reportedly vowed that he would kill the director, but he soon began to focus his revenge exclusively on Stratten.

Snider called his estranged wife on August 12, 1980, arranging a meeting with her. The following day, he bought a 12-gauge shotgun and then stopped by a photographer's studio, where he looked over some proofs showing his latest protégé, a new model he had acquired. At that time, the promoter cryptically stated to the photographer: "Sometimes, Playmates get killed and when that happens it brings about chaos."

The Playmate and movie starlet arrived at Snider's bungalow about noon on August 14, 1980. She spent about two hours with her estranged husband in the living room where her purse was later found. Inside of it was a note from Snider which demanded money. Early that evening, Snider's roommate, a physician, knocked on the promoter's bedroom door and, entering the room, reeled in horror. Paul Snider and Dorothy Stratten were dead.

The bedroom walls were spattered with blood. The naked body of the 20-year-old Stratten was draped over a bed, her beautiful face shot away. Snider was on the floor, also naked, his bleeding corpse having fallen upon the shotgun he had

May 2, 1980: Dorothy Stratten appeared with a construction worker in her hometown of Vancouver, British Columbia, Canada, on a promotion tour for *Playboy*, holding the issue in which she was featured as a Playmate; her husband, Paul Snider, shot and killed her four months later.

used to kill his wife and end his own life. News of the murder-suicide sent shockwaves through the Hollywood community. The movies had been robbed of a potential star, the gossip columnists carped, Hefner of a Playmate and Bogdanovich a future wife.

The director arranged for Stratten's funeral, having her body cremated and the ashes placed in an urn, which he would later visit with regularity. Bogdanovich, in a moving statement, said: "Dorothy looked at the world with love, and believed that all people were good down deep. She was mistaken, but it is among the most generous and noble errors we can make."

There were no eulogies for Paul Snider. His body was shipped back to his native Vancouver, where it was buried in an inexpensive grave.

THE KILLING OF A SUPERSTAR/ December 8, 1980

Although he desperately tried to disassociate himself from the most popular rock'n roll singing group in history—one that he himself created—superstar John Winston Lennon was forever linked to that celebrated foursome, even long after he was slain by a berserk fan, Mark David Chapman. "We're going to live, or we're going to die. If we're dead, we're going to have to deal with that; if we're alive, we're going to have to deal with being alive." A few hours after he said those words, rock star and former Beatle John Lennon was shot to death by Chapman.

Born into an unhappy family in Liverpool, England, on October 9, 1940, Lennon's father deserted him and his mother when he was three. His mother also deserted him later, putting him in the care of her sister, but Lennon maintained a lifelong hatred for his father. Years later, when the elder Lennon suddenly appeared as his famous son's door, the rock star took one look at him and, without a word, slammed the door in his face. He later stated with deep bitterness: "I don't feel I owe him anything. He never helped me. I got there by myself."

Lennon always took exclusive credit for his enormous success and there was about him an egotistical attitude that bordered on megalomania. At the zenith of the Beatles' career, Lennon stupidly blurted: "We're more popular than Jesus now. I don't know which will go first—rock 'n' roll or Christianity." He was to deeply regret that comment, and, always commercially minded, saw its damage when thousands of irate Beatle fans smashed and burned the albums of the singing group. While on tour in Chicago, on August 12, 1966, Lennon said he "was sorry that he opened his mouth about Jesus Christ."

It was clear that had he not made the retraction, his and the careers of his three singing companions, might well have ended right there. The group had had a rocky beginning in the first place. Lennon had the idea for such a group when he was only fifteen and after meeting Paul McCartney at a party in Liverpool in 1955. Rock 'n' roll was then beginning to emerge through the gyrating efforts of rock pathfinders Elvis Presley, Buddy Holly and Bill Haley. In 1956, Lennon formed his first

The Beatles in 1968 (left to right): Paul McCartney, John Lennon, Ringo Starr and George Harrison.

Yoko Ono and John Lennon, shortly before the singer-composer was fatally shot on December 8, 1980; they are standing outside the Dakota apartments in New York.

The upscale Dakota apartments, in New York City, where Lennon maintained a suite of rooms and outside of which a mentally disturbed fan waited to kill him.

band, the Quarrymen, which McCartney joined. Most of the members could not stand Lennon's vanity and arrogance and left, but McCartney remained and the group was joined by George Harrison and, finally, the comedic Ringo Starr.

The group was renamed Johnny and the Moondogs, then Long John and the Silver Beatles and then simply The Beatles. It was a difficult period and Lennon made it more difficult by alienating many of those who might give financial support to the group. He quickly earned a reputation of being a brash young man, who insulted almost everyone he encountered, his sarcasm passing for thin wit.

Lennon's first wife, Cynthia, with whom Lennon had a son, Julian, was to comment in her book, *A Twist of Lennon*: "I think he was the last stronghold of the Teddy Boys [British street thugs who were aptly described in Anthony Burgess' brutal novel, *A Clockwork Orange*, later a film by the same name]—totally aggressive and anti-establishment."

Critic Stanley Reynolds, who knew Lennon long before the Beatles came to fame, remarked: "John Lennon was the hardest, toughest kid I ever met. He had an uncompromising attitude that would never give an inch. He was completely unbending and it shocked you [when] meeting him, because he was, after all, a young fellow and a civilian—so why was he at war? The truth was that he was at war with the whole world." Others were even more severe in their appraisal of Lennon, one seeing him as a calculating fellow "whose sensitive ballads were contrived to milk sentiment from emotionally gullible fans—he squeezed out emotion like someone would wring out a mop. He used love to make a fortune and he was a man without the sincerity of love."

Despite Lennon's self-destructive ways, the group caught on and, in February 1963, the Beatles cut their first album, "Please, Please Me," which climbed rapidly in the charts in England. A year later, on February 8, 1964, the Beatles appeared on Ed Sullivan's enormously popular variety TV show and they were an instant success. Within months, the Beatles

Mark David Chapman, who shot John Lennon five times, and then sat down upon the cement to read a book.

became a household word in America. Many compositions followed, with McCartney providing the music and Lennon the lyrics. Their songs, style and personae dominated the popular music world for six years, its stubborn vogue continuing to this day.

Thousands aped the Beatles and their lifestyles. When Lennon donned casual clothes and dark glasses—he was myopic—hordes of fans abandoned suits and opted for sport shirts and jeans and dark glasses. Lennon grew a droopy mustache and droopy mustaches became the rage. The idolizing fans soon became to irk Lennon and he expressed his contempt for the throngs of teenage girls that grabbed, clutched and tore at his clothes during public appearances. On one occasion, he told his wife, Cynthia: "We'll have to get out of this death trap before they kill me. I had no idea it was going to be like this. It's like a bloody madhouse out there. We deserve every penny we get."

By 1966, Lennon sought relief from the crowds, having met Yoko Ono, who urged him to pursue a "more classical" kind of music. It took four more years before the group disbanded in 1970. Only Paul McCartney and the Wings saw the kind of success enjoyed by the original group and that latter day singing group did not last for long. Deluged with fame and riches, the foursome went their separate ways throughout the 1970s, experimenting with self-analysis, drugs and a search for gurus with all-knowing answers.

Yoko Ono, for whom Lennon left his first wife, persuaded the singer-composer to move to New York, where he occupied a lavish suite of rooms at the exclusive Dakota apartments. Lennon spent most of his time in New York talking about his own premature demise, which he predicted would occur in a nuclear holocaust. Every time Lennon left the Dakota, he was surrounded by loyal fans seeking autographs, which he dutifully supplied. One of these autograph-seekers was a swarthy, heavy-set young man with glasses and a mop of dark hair, Mark David Chapman.

Chapman was born in Fort Worth, Texas, on May 10, 1955. Raised in Georgia, he ran away from home when he was fourteen. He was away only a few weeks, but remained part of the drug scene for another two years. Becoming a Beatles fan as a teenager, he tried to emulate them with his own band. However, after Chapman became a born-again Christian, he was offended by Lennon's remark about Jesus.

Thus, Chapman gave up the Beatles, as he had given up drugs and used his spare time to work with children at the YMCA. Chapman's friends watched him become increasingly preoccupied with internal struggles concerning the sinfulness of the "Bad Mark." He moved around the country, working at various jobs and studying religions in his free time. He was arrested for armed robbery, kidnapping, and possession of drugs. Chapman tried to commit suicide in 1977, and received psychological care.

In 1979, he married a travel agent, Gloria H. Abe, a woman four years his senior and of Japanese descent (as was John Lennon's Yoko Ono) and moved to Hawaii, where he insisted that she never watch television or read newspapers. He frequently stood outside a Church of Scientology and shouted abuse, and month by month he became more irrational, although he kept that side of him hidden from most people. In 1980, he got a job as a security guard at a condominium and a short time later he changed the name tag on his security guard's uniform to read "John Lennon," and on October 23, 1980 he quit his job, signing out as John Lennon.

From that time, it became necessary for Chapman to get rid of the real John Lennon, since he had taken on his idol's personality and identity. Chapman first bought a .38-caliber pistol. Then he borrowed $2,500 from a credit union and flew to New York City on December 6, 1980. He began to spend long hours stationed outside the Dakota. On December 8, Lennon emerged to go to a recording studio, and Chapman had him autograph his most recent album, *Double Fantasy.* Chapman stayed where he was as Lennon and Ono drove off, then turned to continue reading a copy of J. D. Salinger's *The Catcher in the Rye.*

At 11 p.m. that night, Lennon and Yoko Ono returned to the Dakota, Chapman called out, "Mr. Lennon." Lennon looked up and Chapman dropped to a military crouch, his legs spread apart as he aimed a .38-caliber Charter Arms revolver at him. Without another word, Chapman fired five times, the bullets striking Lennon's chest, back and left arm. He took a few steps, then called out to Yoko Ono: "I'm shot!"

Opposite page, left: Mourning fans gather to honor the memory of their slain music idol; Lennon's killer went to prison for life.

Patrolman Jim Moran, who had been assigned to control the crowds outside the Dakota (many celebrities lived there in addition to Lennon, including actress Lauren Bacall, musical director Leonard Bernstein, and comic Gilda Radner), ran forward and helped Lennon into the back of his squad car. By the time Moran arrived at the emergency entrance of Roosevelt Hospital, Lennon had died from his wounds.

After killing Lennon, Chapman sat down and returned to reading the Salinger novel, seemingly unconcerned at murdering his idol. He was arrested and charged with second-degree murder. At the time, Chapman told the police: "I have a small part in me that cannot understand the world and what goes on in it. I did not want to kill anybody, and I really don't know why I did ..."

Chapman's lawyer, Jonathan Marks, wanted him to plead not guilty by reason of insanity, but Chapman told the court that God had told him to confess to murder. He was convicted and sentenced on July 24, 1981, to twenty years to life in prison, with a recommendation that he receive psychiatric treatment. Even his own attorney asked the judge not to sentence him too lightly. "All reports came to the conclusion that he is not a sane man. It was not a sane crime. It was ...a monstrously irrational killing." Chapman's only response to the sentencing was to read aloud a passage from *The Catcher in the Rye.* He was sent to Attica State Prison in upstate New York, where he was put to work as a janitor.

IN THE BELLY OF THE BEAST OF FAME/ July 18, 1981

Jack Henry Abbott (AKA: Jack Eastman, b. 1944) spent most of his adult life in prison. He committed his first murder in 1966 and, after novelist Norman Mailer worked for his release, killed a second time in 1981. At first, this convict, dedicated wholly to violence, was celebrated by New York's literati for penning a prison journal successfully published by Random House. Upon his 1981 release, Abbott was adopted by such literary lights as Norman Mailer, his sponsor, and Jerzy Kosinski.

Abbott was invited to elitist cocktail parties, where the rich and famous fawned over him. He was heralded as a "great writer" and an "insightful philosopher." Jack Henry Abbott, however, was in reality, always had been, a man who would kill anyone over the slightest annoyance. This he did, at the height of his brief literary fame, oblivious to his so-called rehabilitation, committing a cold-blooded, conscienceless murder that proved how dangerous it really was for amateur criminologists to meddle with crime.

A habitual criminal, Abbott spent all but nine months of his adult life in prison. He was convicted of forgery, bank robbery, and murder. In 1953, at age nine, Abbott proved so incorrigible in foster homes that he was sent to reform school in Utah. Released at age eighteen, Abbott was arrested and convicted of passing bad checks and sent to Utah State Penitentiary, where he killed a fellow inmate in 1966.

Tried for this murder, Abbott claimed self-defense, that he had been the victim of a violent homosexual attack. When that ploy did not appear to affect the court, Abbot assumed the role of the lunatic, throwing a pitcher of water at the judge and claiming insanity. A court psychiatrist examined him and reported that Abbott was fit to stand trial. He was sentenced to fourteen years.

Abbott escaped from Utah State Penitentiary in 1971 and was at large for six weeks, during which time he robbed a Denver bank and, upon his recapture, became a federal prisoner. While serving time in a maximum security prison, Abbott read voraciously, consuming scores of books on philosophy, enmeshing himself in the credos of Karl Marx and becoming an avowed Marxist. He read a 1977 newspaper story about Norman Mailer writing a book (*The Executioner's Song*) on Gary Gilmore, who was condemned for murder and was awaiting execution in Utah State Penitentiary.

Mailer, like his New York contemporary, Truman Capote (author of *In Cold Blood*, a novelized version of the Clutter slayings in Kansas—see Mass Murder), was suddenly departing mainstream literature to enter the world of criminology. Oddly, Mailer never got to meet Gilmore, using the taped interviews between Lawrence Schiller and Gilmore to create Gilmore's dialog.

It was to Mailer, at then a powerful influence in the media, that Abbott began addressing his letters, which were fifteen-page, handwritten missives to the author. The clever Abbott, obviously realizing that Mailer was a complete novice in perceiving prison life, offered to aid him in that understanding by detailing his own experiences as a long-term, "state-raised" prisoner.

Abbott intrigued the author by spewing forth tales of dark violence, writing in a clinically descriptive style reminiscent of Mailer's own early works, particularly certain passages from *The Naked and the Dead*, which had certainly not gone unnoticed in Abbott's endless rummaging through prison libraries.

The prisoner's literary nightmares described fourteen years of solitary confinement and unbelievable cruelty on the part of prison guards, who beat him, tortured him with antipsychotic drugs, sadistically gassed him, starved him so that he was forced to eat cockroaches in his cell to survive, and placed him in strip-and-search cells, where he had to stand naked, chained by one arm to his bed.

Abbott's relentless correspondence fed on hatred and violence, intriguing an author whose own interest in violence had always been intense. Mailer took Abbott's letters to the editors of the elitist *New York Review of Books*, and, at his urging in June 1980, an article praising Abbott's writing style appeared in that publication, along with a sample of the letters. This article was read with great interest by Errol McDonald, an editor at Random House. Within two months, McDonald had placed Abbott under a book contract, which called for a $12,000 advance, and McDonald began organizing the killer's book, which was entitled *In the Belly of the Beast*.

Almost immediately, Abbott began to energetically lobby for a parole. The Federal Bureau of Prisons made the first step easier by returning Abbott to Utah State Penitentiary to serve out his remaining time there. Once inside the walls of that institution, an automatic parole was considered. Mailer and others were influential, if not decisive, in their pleas that Abbott be released.

The chair in which condemned killer Gary Gilmore was executed in Utah, a symbol that inspired the dark ambitions of another murderer, Jack Henry Abbott.

Mailer wrote to the parole board that Abbott was really "a powerful and important American writer," urging a positive decision and offering the killer a job as his research assistant. McDonald, the Random House editor, also wrote to prison authorities, saying that he believed Abbott "could support himself as a professional writer if he were released from prison and that he could very well have a bright future."

The parole campaign was successful and Abbott was released on June 5, 1981, transferred from prison to a halfway house in Manhattan's Lower East Side. When the killer's plane arrived in New York, Norman Mailer was on hand to greet him. Almost at the same time, reviews of Abbott's recently released book gushed torrents of praise upon the killer. Wrote Colgate University Professor Terrence Des Pres in the New York *Times* Book Section: " ...awesome, brilliant, perversely ingenious; its impact is indelible and, as an articulation of penal nightmare it is completely compelling." New York's literati welcomed the killer with warm embraces, celebrating his published achievement with a number of cocktail parties and smart gatherings at which Abbott was lionized. Great things were predicted for him. He would become a literary giant of the century. His books would be read as credo by anyone needing to know about prison life. Moreover, some even said, Abbott represented the new wave of American literature and was, in fact, its leader.

Other than Mailer, many New York literary lions heaped praise on Abbott's work, and these included the brilliant writer Jerzy Kosinski of *Being There* fame. (Kosinski would later regret endorsing the lethal Abbott, being one of the few in the clique of the killer's admirers, who later concluded that the Abbott episode was a fraud, likening the literary laurels placed upon Abbott's head to the literati's support of the Black Panthers, an American terrorist group in the 1960s.)

Abbott worked briefly for Mailer by doing some scanty research, but he spent most of his time drifting aimlessly about the city, a misplaced creature, who paradoxically spent time with the elite and powerful of New York one hour, and the next walking about the worst area of the city, the Lower East Side, peopled with prostitutes, pimps, drug pushers, and hardened criminals like himself. Besides Mailer and Kosinski, Abbott found himself in the company of such sterling personalities as author Jean Malaquais, literary agent Scott Meredith, and Robert Silvers, editor of the *New York Review of Books.*

Abbott impressed them no end with his knowledge of Sartre and Camus, existentialists like himself, he said. He knew just what names and quotations would lure these Establishment personalities closer to his web, manipulating them with ease, calling loudly for entrees from their own menus, chewing upon the fat of their own philosophical beliefs, and thanking them for allowing him, Jack Henry Abbott, convicted killer, to dine at their table.

Surrounded by the protecting arms of New York's literary sachems, Abbott undoubtedly felt that his future was secure. He lobbied discreetly for an even loftier position, one which would afford him continuous recognition and financial support, not as a reformed criminal, but as a misunderstood literary giant. He expected his new friends to arrange a fellowship for him at the prestigious MacDowell Colony for accomplished artists in picturesque Petersborough, New Hampshire. Here he would preside over the novice writer, the impressionable artist, dictating the thoughts of youthful, adoring followers. None of this, thankfully, was to be.

On the morning of July 18, 1981, Abbott, accompanied by two women, entered a small, all-night restaurant, the BoniBon, on Second Avenue and Fifth Street. It was 5 a.m. After Abbott and the women took their seats, 22-year-old Richard Adan, a struggling Cuban-born actor working as a waiter, approached the table to take their order. Adan had recently appeared on public TV in Spain in a series of dramatic roles that had given his career a boost. His newly completed play about the Lower East Side was soon to be produced by an experimental stage group and the youth, known always to be polite and pleasant, was looking eagerly forward to a blossoming career in the theater. Adan had recently married a young choreographer-actress whose father had given him a job as a waiter in his restaurant so the young couple could make ends meet.

Abbott asked Adan where the washroom was located. Adan, according to customers in the restaurant, courteously explained that it was an employee-only washroom and that insurance restrictions prevented customers from using it. Abbott became incensed and began using abusive language. According to witnesses, Adan asked him to go outside with him to try to settle the argument so as not to disturb the other customers. Abbott later claimed that Adan was threatening him, but it was Abbott who did the threatening.

Once outside the restaurant, Abbott drew a knife with a medium-length blade and with one powerful thrust, drove the blade into Adan's heart. Another waiter, just at that moment, looked out of one of the restaurant's windows to see the young waiter jumping up and down, gushing blood. Abbott then returned to one of the women with him, college student Susan Roxas, and shouted: "Let's get out of here. I just killed a man!"

Author Norman Mailer was so impressed by Abbott's writing that he lobbied for his prison release, promoted Abbott's book, and even attempted to reduce Abbott's sentence after the killer murdered again.

At that moment, Jack Henry Abbott, acclaimed author, vanished. It is revealing to quote Abbott's own work, where he describes how he knifed a fellow prisoner to death fifteen years earlier, a methodical, cold-blooded act that was duplicated with the same precision in his 1981 murder of Richard Adan: "The enemy is smiling and chatting away about something. He thinks you're his fool; he trusts you. You see the spot. It's a target between the second and third button on his shirt. As you calmly talk and smile, you move your left foot to the side to step across his right-side body length. A light pivot toward him with your right shoulder and the world turns upside down; you have sunk the knife to its hilt into the middle of his chest."

For two months Abbott eluded police and federal agents who were searching for him nationwide. Using the considerable advances from his book, Abbott managed to get to Mexico and hole up near the Guatemalan border, but after some weeks, not being able to speak Spanish or find work that would cloak his activities, he moved back to the U.S., relocating in Louisiana.

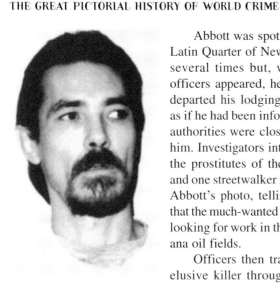

Jack Henry Abbott, heralded as a powerful new writer at the time his book was published.

Abbott was spotted in the Latin Quarter of New Orleans several times but, whenever officers appeared, he had just departed his lodgings, almost as if he had been informed that authorities were closing in on him. Investigators interviewed the prostitutes of the Quarter and one streetwalker identified Abbott's photo, telling police that the much-wanted killer was looking for work in the Louisiana oil fields.

Officers then tracked the elusive killer through the oil towns of Algiers, Harvey, and Marrero, searching through the murky bunkhouses, where hundreds of nameless itinerant workers lived, but at every turn they missed their man, sometimes only by minutes. Abbott seemed to have a sixth sense about lawmen closing in on him and would, according to fellow workers, suddenly quit whatever he was doing, grab his meager belongings, and depart. In mid-September 1981, New York Police Detective William Majeski, who had arrived at the BoniBon restaurant after the Adan killing to take charge of the investigation and had trailed Abbott with other officers to New Orleans, learned that the fugitive was using a social security card with the alias of Jack Eastman.

Abbott had selected an anonymous world into which he hoped to disappear. The boom town oil fields of Louisiana collected thousands of roughnecks and roustabouts, many with criminal records, men like Abbott, who sought obscurity. Mixing with these tough, taciturn men were illegal aliens from Mexico, refugees from Vietnam, the flotsam and jetsam of the world, men who worked for $4 an hour, sixteen hours a day, and paid a third of their salary to the company to sleep in filthy bunkhouses and eat from open-air canteens. The rest of their money they would give to the whores who visited these camps in droves.

On September 23, 1981, following a tip from Detective Carl Parsiola of St. Mary's Parish, James Riley, an intelligence agent of the sheriff's department, accompanied by Dan Dossett of the Morgan City Police, and other officers, located Abbott working in the fields of the Ramos Oil Company. He was unloading pipe from trucks that clogged the roads. Overhead helicopters buzzed about on company work and the nearby bayous belched smoke from tugs pulling freight. Where years before there had been wilderness, this area was now cluttered with humanity and the officers were concerned that their man would once again escape. Carefully, Riley, Dossett, and the others moved toward Abbott, pretending to be workers. When they saw Abbott raise his arms to comb his hair, the lawmen rushed forward, eight shotguns leveled at him.

Abbott was ordered to keep his hands in the air as officers moved forward to handcuff him. He said nothing, remaining motionless, offering no resistance. He wore cheap blue jeans and a T-shirt that were coated with oil; his boots were crusted with caked oil and were falling apart. Returned to New York and held at Riker's Island, Abbott was tried before Judge Irving Lang of the Manhattan State Supreme Court. He was defended by criminal attorney Ivan Fisher and prosecuted by James Fogel. Early on, Abbot displayed anxiety and nervousness, a pose unlike his earlier aloof attitudes.

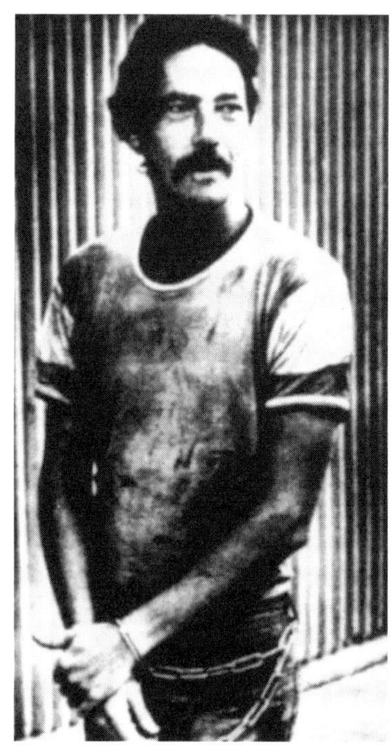

Jack Henry Abbott when was captured in the Louisiana oil fields.

In his own words, Abbott characterized the death of Adan as the result of a "tragic misunderstanding," a literary understatement without parallel. He went on to explain that he acted in self-defense, believing that Adan intended to attack him, the same plea that Abbott had employed when stabbing a fellow prison inmate to death in 1966. To that claim, a spectator in court rose and shouted, "You intended to do it, you scum!" This cry came from Henry Howard, the father-in-law of the dead Adan. Judge Lang ordered Howard removed from court, but he waited outside the courtroom throughout the trial, frustrated by his inability to see justice done.

The prosecution provided several witnesses, but one, Wayne Larsen, a 35-year-old Vietnam veteran, proved damning to Abbott's self-defense tactic. Larsen was standing at the corner of Second Avenue and Fifth Street and watched as Abbott attacked Adan. He testified that Adan was walking away from Abbott when Abbott drew his knife and raised it. He recalled that when Abbott struck Adan there was an impacting sound that "still rings in my ears."

Even though Adan was mortally wounded and helpless, Abbott, according to Larsen, acted as if he had merely scratched his victim, cursing Adan and screaming, "Do you still want to continue this?" Adan had made no move toward Abbott and, according to Larsen, was trying to back away from his assailant. Abbott "made a beeline" for the backpedaling Adan and lunged forward to make sure he killed his man and, in Larsen's words, Abbott's knife blow to Adan's chest was so powerful "that the hair swung back on his [Abbott's] head."

Abbott sat trembling in court, clutching a handkerchief. He wore glasses and his hair was combed in a meticulous pompadour. Immediately following Larsen's testimony, Abbott asked that he be allowed to leave the courtroom. "The testimony was extremely upsetting to him, reliving the event," lawyer Fisher later stated. Abbott's request was granted, although the paradox was evident. Abbott had graphically described his murder of another human being without a gnat-sting of remorse in his best-selling book, but he was visibly upset by the retelling of his murder of Adan.

The victim, however, was offered up by Abbott to be not Adan, but Abbott. He again recited the litany of his prison sufferings, the endless abuse that was heaped upon him by an unthinking, inhumane prison system, the very rationale that had brought about his much-influenced parole. Abbott wanted it both ways, first to be released from prison for what the prison system had done to him, then excused from another murder outside of prison and shielded from being returned to that system because of what the prison system had done. If nothing else, Abbott was certainly angling for a minimum sentence, after having been found guilty of first degree manslaughter.

Prosecutor Fogel was having none of it, calling for a maximum sentence, a life term. "This is a killer," Fogel argued before the bench, "a killer by habit, a killer by inclination, a killer by philosophy, and a killer by desire."

Fisher clung to Abbott's own lifelong defense, stating that his client had been warped by a lifetime of prison. "He was mistreated for so long and so horrible a way. If it was, in fact, the poison of prison that brought about these events, how can it be urged that a lot more is the cure?"

Judge Lang had earlier ruled that Abbott's previous convictions had qualified him as a "persistent violent felon." When he asked the defendant if he had anything to say before sentence was pronounced, Abbott mumbled, "No." Judge Lang then stated that the conviction of Abbott was in part "an indictment of a prison system which brutalized instead of rehabilitating ...It's perfectly clear that the defendant could not cope with the reality of a non-prison existence."

Judge Lang then sentenced Abbott to fifteen years to life, a minimum sentence. He would be returned to Utah State Penitentiary to serve out his remaining eight years for earlier convictions before serving the New York sentence of fifteen years.

Norman Mailer went before the court and implored leniency, stating, "Culture is worth a little risk. A major sentence would destroy him." Even though Abbott did not receive the maximum sentence, Mailer, following the sentencing, was disgruntled, saying that Judge Lang's sentence was so long as to be "killing." Complained the 59-year-old author, "At the point he gets out, he'll be as old as I am now." Adan's father-in-law, Henry Howard, heard the news of the sentence and was filled with rage. "In twenty-four years," he said, "Jack Abbott will be back on the street and he will kill again. Why are his rights better than Richard Adan's rights?"

This was a question answered obliquely and rather callously by Abbott's attorney, Ivan Fisher, who was quoted as saying, in responding to questions about Adan's family being entitled to the profits from Abbott's book (then estimated to be about $500,000), "If you kill a brain surgeon you're in much more trouble than if you kill a waiter working nights at the BiniBon Restaurant. That's not my judgment, that's the law."

Before being led back to prison, Abbott, through Fisher,

Jack Henry Abbott at the time of his trial for the 1981 murder of New York waiter Richard Adan; he was convicted and returned to prison, hanging himself in 2002.

announced plans to sue the state of New York for $10 million for "the mental anguish and threats to his life" while he was a prisoner on Riker's Island. Meanwhile, Abbott's book soared to best-seller status, selling more than 40,000 hardbound copies through Random House. At the time, dramatic rights to Abbott's savage tale had been purchased by a film company headed by comic Alan King in the amount of $250,000.

Jack Henry Abbott did not live to see parole. On February 10, 2002, Abbott hanged himself with a bedsheet and a shoelace at New York's Wende Correctional Facility. He reportedly left a suicide note, but this was not released by authorities. Moaned Norman Mailer: "His life was tragic from beginning to end. I never knew a man who had a worse life."

MURDER OF A MILLIONAIRE'S MISTRESS/ July 6-7, 1983

At the age of seventeen, Vicki Morgan was a tall, slender and buxom young woman with a face of classic beauty—high cheekbones, aquiline nose, wide-set expressive eyes and full lips. She drew the attention of every male that encountered her, not the least of whom was 53-year-old department store tycoon Alfred Bloomingdale, who spied the willowy Morgan walking down Sunset Boulevard in 1970. He followed her into the Old World Restaurant and immediately asked for her phone number. "He was so persistent, I had lunch with him," Morgan later said.

Within days, Morgan had become one of Bloomingdale's mistresses, learning early about his myriad perversions. According to her later statements, Morgan became the tycoon's willing pawn in sadomasochistic orgies, where she and other females were stripped naked, bound and whipped by Bloomingdale. Aroused, Bloomingdale then had sex with Morgan and other women and often he invited other males to participate in these orgies, conduct rather startling for one of America's leading businessmen.

Bloomingdale had not only established a department store empire, but had created Diner's Club and numerous other businesses that filled his coffers to the brim. His wife, Betsy, was a social grande dame who counted Nancy Reagan as her close friend and it was through this relationship that Bloomingdale befriended then California Governor Ronald Reagan, whom he called "Ron." The tycoon became part of Reagan's "kitchen cabinet," of unofficial advisors and he was one of those who helped to finance Reagan's presidential campaign, which put him into the White House in 1980.

Other than a brief affair in 1971 with another man that produced a son, Todd, Morgan remained Bloomingdale's devoted mistress for a decade. The tycoon came to love her and lavished a posh home on her, a Mercedes-Benz, furs, jewelry and an $18,000-a-month allowance. Despite his busy schedule in attending to his many businesses, Bloomingdale spent most of his time with Morgan and not until his death by cancer in August 1982, did his wife Betsy learn of the relationship. At that time, Mrs. Bloomingdale ordered Morgan from the home her husband had rented for her.

Embittered at this eviction, Morgan filed a suit against the Bloomingdale estate, claiming $10 million in palimony payments were due her. Her attorneys used as a precedent the palimony case successfully won against actor Lee Marvin by his mistress. Morgan, in her suit, said that her deceased lover had promised to pay her for "her services," as an advisor on a new business scheme, a pizza parlor chain. If the Bloomingdale

Vicki Morgan in 1970, when she caught the eye of a millionaire, who made her his sex slave and mistress.

Department store magnate Alfred Bloomingdale, who kept Morgan in style for a decade as his mistress.

family established such a chain, Morgan's attorneys said, their client was entitled to fifty percent of ownership.

Morgan and her attorneys were in for a shock. In September 1982, the case was heard before Superior Court Judge Christian Markey. Morgan told the court that she was Bloomingdale's "business confidante, companion and mistress." Judge Markey, however, determined that the relationship had been only for sex and that the *Michelle Triola Marvin v. Lee Marvin* case did not apply. Morgan was awarded nothing. Her lawyers immediately instituted new lawsuits, but these cases promised to drag through the courts for years and, meanwhile, the unemployed Morgan no longer had the funds to support her old lavish lifestyle.

The 30-year-old actress—she had appeared in a few low-budget films—could not find suitable work. Unemployed and running out of money, she rented a small $1,000-a-month condominium in Studio City in early 1983, where she and her son Todd lived. To pay bills, she began selling off her furs and jewelry and even the Mercedes-Benz Bloomingdale had bought for her. Still, her extravagant lifestyle demanded more immediate support and to that end, she invited 33-year-old Marvin Pancoast, an admitted homosexual who frequented all the stylish gay bars in Los Angeles, to become her roommate. Morgan had known Pancoast for about four years, thinking that he would share the costs of the condo with her. After Pancoast moved in, however, Morgan learned that he had lost his job as a clerk at the William Morris Agency and was himself unemployed and had little money. To compensate for his inability to pay his way, Pancoast ran errands for Morgan, baby-sat her son and functioned as her obedient servant.

When Morgan realized that Pancoast could not provide needed funds, she decided to move to a girlfriend's house, leaving her roommate with the burden of the condo. She ordered movers to pick up her furniture on July 7, 1983, but this was a move that was never made. Pancoast, who had rankled at his subservient position, decided to simply murder Morgan. "I was tired of being her slave boy," he later lamely explained.

On the late night of July 6-7, 1983, Pancoast turned down the lights in the condo's living room and turned up the stereo so that neighbors would not hear any loud noises. He then picked up a baseball bat used by Morgan's son and walked into Morgan's bedroom. He found her asleep and proceeded to savagely beat her on the head and chest for several minutes until he realized that she was dead.

Before 4 a.m., on July 7, 1983, Pancoast walked into a police precinct station in North Hollywood to tell the desk sergeant "I just killed someone." In addition to the sensational disclosures made by Morgan in her lawsuits, her murder now captured the nation's front pages. The case was further enlarged when Los Angeles attorney Robert Steinberg announced, on July 11, 1983, that he had acquired video tapes that showed Morgan, Bloomingdale and "top government

Vicki Morgan in 1982, when she filed a palimony suit following Bloomingdale's death, one that ended in failure.

Homosexual slayer Marvin Pancoast, beat Morgan to death on the night of July 6-7, 1983; he died in prison of AIDS.

officials" participating in sex orgies. He later admitted that these tapes had been stolen from his office and he could not produce them or subsequently identify those involved who posed a "high risk to the national security of the country."

Pancoast, meanwhile, went on trial and throughout it was rumored that he had been a willing pawn in a conspiracy to murder Morgan to keep her mouth shut about high-level government people involved in the Bloomingdale sex scandals. Pancoast, in truth, had a long history of mental problems and pleaded not guilty by reason of insanity to the slaying of Vicki Morgan. His brief trial ended on September 14, 1984, when he was convicted of first-degree murder. He was sentenced to twenty-six years to life.

Pancoast died of aids while serving out his term. The "Morgan conspiracy" lingers in the minds of the suspicious to this day, but Steinberg's tapes never surfaced and there is little or no evidence to substantiate the wild claims that a cabal plotted to silence the beautiful mistress by calculated murder.

THE BEDEVILED BRANDOS/May 17, 1990

One of the greatest actors of the 20th Century, Marlon Brando has heard the plaudits of the world. He has also undergone the pain and suffering of a parent whose son, Christian, went to prison for shooting his sister's lover, and then endured the agony of his daughter's suicide. On May 17, 1990, a 911 operator was startled to hear one of the world's most famous voices report a shooting. It was that of Marlon Brando.

Police drove to 12900 Mulholland Drive, a posh complex in the Santa Monica mountains that overlooked Los Angeles, and entered the twelve-room mansion of the actor. In the entertainment room of Marlon Brando's house, officers found the body of 26-year-old Dag Drollet, the Tahitian boyfriend of 20-year-old Cheyenne Brando, the pregnant half-sister of Christian Brando. They also found Christian Brando (b. 1958), who was promptly charged with killing Drollet.

Christian Brando, the son of actor Marlon Brando and actress Anna Kashfi, had been the center of a bitter custody battle that lasted sixteen years. Tahitian, like his sister (Cheyenne being the daughter of Brando and Tahitian actress Tarita Teriipia, who played the actor's sweetheart in the 1962 film *Mutiny on the Bounty*), Christian was a high school dropout and drifter, who had briefly held jobs as a tree surgeon, welder, artist and actor, having played an assassin in an Italian-made film.

During the custody battle over Christian, Brando and Anna Kashfi waged a bitter fight. At one point, Kashfi abducted the boy and spirited him to a fishing village in Mexico, where he was tracked down by a private investigator hired by Brando. The hippie keepers of the 13-year-old boy claimed at the time that Kashfi had promised to pay each of them $10,000 to hide the child from her ex-husband. In 1986, Christian himself was entangled in an ugly divorce with Mary McKenna Brando, who claimed he had physically abused her and threatened her mother with a rifle.

Volatile and unpredictable, Christian Brando had a fierce protective instinct toward his sister, Cheyenne. After she and her lover, Drollet, the son of a prominent Tahitian businessman turned banker, traveled to Los Angeles from Tahiti to stay at Marlon Brando's home, Cheyenne, pregnant with her lover's child, began to complain that Drollet was physically abusing her. After a violent argument on May 17, 1990, Christian confronted Drollet in the family room of the actor's sprawling home (Marlon Brando was elsewhere in the house at the time). The two argued and Christian produced a .45-caliber semiautomatic pistol registered to Christian Brando. Both men struggled with the gun, which went off, shooting Drollet in the face.

Christian Brando, left, with his attorney Robert Shapiro, during his 1991 trial for killing his sister's fiancé; he was convicted of manslaughter.

Hearing the gunshot, Marlon Brando rushed to the family room, where he attempted to revive Drollet with mouth-to-mouth resuscitation. It was useless. Drollet was dead. When police arrived, they arrested Christian Brando and then noted the presence of several weapons in addition to the .45-caliber pistol—a shotgun, a .44-caliber carbine, an unregistered M-14 rifle, an unregistered Uzi submachine gun and a silencer. The actor told officers, "I don't want these guns here. Take them out of here."

Charged with murder, Christian Brando was imprisoned while his father called lawyer William Kunstler to defend his son. When arraigned, Brando pleaded not guilty to premeditated murder. Before he was led

Marlon Brando, left, with Martin Sheen in the film, *Apocalypse Now*; he testified at his son's trial, telling the court that his son had been troubled as a child, blaming the boy's early problems on his mother, actress Anna Kashfi.

away, he turned to Kunstler and asked: "Will I have to spend the rest of my life in jail?" Robert Shapiro, who was to become O.J. Simpson's lawyer, later took over the defense of Christian Brando. On February 28, 1991, after his son had pleaded guilty to involuntary manslaughter, Marlon Brando took the stand to testify on Christian's behalf in a Santa Monica courtroom, explaining that his son had been a troubled youth traumatized at an early age by the vicious custody battles waged by Brando and his wife, Anna Kashfi, and that this experience had contributed to his violent behavior.

Brando also admitted that he may have failed as a parent. "Most people have some good and bad aspects," he related. "His mother came as close to being a negative person, and as cruel and unhappy a person as I've ever met ... You always tend to blame the other parent, but I know I could have done better. But I did the best I could." (Before taking the witness stand, Brando refused to take the normal courtroom oath before God to tell the truth. Instead, he said he would swear only on his children and his grandchildren.)

Superior Court Judge Robert Thomas then sentenced Christian Brando to six years on the charge of manslaughter and four years' imprisonment for aggravating circumstances in the use of a gun. While Christian Brando was serving his time at the California Men's Colony in San Luis Obispo, Cheyenne Brando's life went to pieces. As volatile and unpredictable as her half-brother Christian, she flitted between Tahiti and Los Angeles. Prior to Drollet's death, she had been involved in a traffic accident in Tahiti—she was driving a car in excess of 100 m.p.h. in a fit of pique after her father told her that she could not join him in Canada, where he was then making the film, *The Freshman*—and was so disfigured by the accident that she had to undergo several plastic surgery operations to regain her attractive appearance.

As the years went on, Cheyenne became more and more moody, introspective and depressed. She delivered Drollet's child, but grieved for her dead lover year after year. On Easter Sunday, 1995, the 25-year-old Cheyenne Brando committed suicide by hanging herself in the town of Faa'a. Ingrid Drollet, sister of the slain Dag Drollet, remarked that her family felt as if "Cheyenne had made something wonderful, beautiful—to die for love. It was like Romeo and Juliet." Irrespective of this pretentious and unnerving endorsement of suicide, Cheyenne Brando's act was not unexpected. She had attempted to kill herself many times in the past.

When Marlon Brando got the news of his daughter's death, he moaned, "Oh, God, no," and then collapsed. He later agreed with his longtime enemy, Jacques-Denis Drollet, father of the slain Dag, that Cheyenne would be buried next to the grave of Dag Drollet. Many pointed to the alcoholism that seemed inherent in the Brando family as the root cause of the tragedies that became Christian and Cheyenne Brando. Marlon Brando himself admitted that his mother, Dorothy Brando, "cared more about drinking than caring for us," and that his father's blood "consisted of compounds of alcohol, testosterone, adrenaline and anger."

Cheyenne had for years become a regular visitor to drug rehabilitation centers in Tahiti, Paris, San Francisco, and Stockbridge, Massachusetts. In addition to drugs, family members shared a common identity crisis. The actor had produced eleven children, five by his actress wives Kashfi, Teriipia and Movita Castenada, all Tahitians, three by his Guatemalan housekeeper, Christina Ruiz, and three more from other affairs. "The family kept changing shape," Christian Brando once said. "I'd sit down at the breakfast table and say, 'Who are you?'" At another time, Christian labeled the entire family "a bunch of crazy drunks."

THE O.J. SIMPSON CASE/June 12, 1994

The murder trial of former football player, actor and promoter O.J. Simpson (James Orenthal Simpson, b. 1947) was the most widely publicized in American history, with millions glued to TV sets and avidly reading printed reports on the case as it unfolded day by day. It was not "the trial of the century," as the media promoted it, but a rather shoddy, sad tale of two brutal murders and a black millionaire suspect whose black attorney managed to win him acquittal by flagrantly using race as the key issue, while playing to an almost all-black jury.

The prosecution essentially botched its presentation of the mountain of circumstantial evidence at its command. The defense tried the Los Angeles Police Department instead of defending its client. And the trial judge, Lance Ito, a smug, limelight-seeking jurist, was so overindulgent with attorneys that, in the opinion of this author, he unnecessarily prolonged an already lengthy trial and vastly contributed to the wasting of millions of dollars in taxpayer money.

Ito had been a prosecuting attorney with little will to seek the death penalty in capital cases. In one instance when prosecuting a serial killer, Ito made sure that defense attorneys got hold of a witness to one of the murders, a witness who asked the jury for mercy, instead of the death sentence. The killer was given a life sentence. When presiding over the trial of colossal swindler Charles Keating, Jr., Ito threw out half the charges against the savings and loan thief.

When hearing the pretrial motions for the murdering Menendez brothers, Ito sealed the grand jury findings and thus muzzled arguments for the prosecution. Before becoming a judge, Ito pridefully placed on his car a license plate that read "7 Bozos, 33," referring to the California Supreme Court judges. When he himself became a judge, Ito got rid of the plate. At the start, Ito said he was not in favor of televising the trial. He not only allowed a TV camera in the courtroom, albeit with a fixed point of view that prevented viewers from seeing the jurors and key evidence produced, but, during the course of the trial, gave a five-part TV interview to Tritia Toyado on a local Los Angeles station.

Ito took advantage of this situation to condemn the incarceration of Japanese in America during World War II (without fully explaining the reason for that massive internment), as well as promote his own career. Ito flagrantly likened his public status to that of Cher and Madonna. It was apparent then and now that, unlike most jurists, Ito reveled in the limelight.

From the day of the murders, June 12, 1994, until Simpson's acquittal on October 3, 1995, the world watched as the defense, led by attorney Johnnie Cochran, whipped up race hatred to the boiling point. When the not guilty verdict was announced, most of white America reeled in shock, believing Simpson to be guilty; most of black America rejoiced, insisting upon Simpson's innocence. To this day and for decades to come, these attitudes, woefully, will probably not change. The Simpson case did more to destroy race relations in America than the Dred Scott decision.

The killer or killers of Nicole Brown Simpson and Ronald Goldman, viciously slain some time during the night of June 12, 1994, have not been found at this writing, despite O.J. Simpson's vow (upon his release) that he would not rest until the killer or killers were brought to justice (albeit Simpson has been energetically searching for the killer or killers on every golf course in America). When slaying Nicole Brown Simpson and Ronald Goldman, the killer apparently hid in the bushes outside Nicole's Brentwood, California, condominium at 875 S. Bundy.

Nicole Brown Simpson and O. J. Simpson, shown early in their marriage, which later became a shambles.

When Nicole appeared outside, either to respond to the doorbell rung by Ronald Goldman (who was reportedly returning her glasses from a restaurant where he worked as a waiter) or summoned by the killer himself, the murderer most probably attacked her from behind, driving a knee into her back, pulling her head backward with an armlock over her face and then reaching around with a large, razor-sharp knife to slash her throat so deeply that she was almost decapitated. He then drove the knife into her breasts many times. The blood spurting from her undoubtedly shot away from the killer because of the murder position he had selected (much the same way Jack the Ripper killed most of his victims).

Nicole Brown Simpson shortly before she was brutally murdered in Brentwood, California, on June 12, 1994.

Police believed that Goldman was most likely killed afterward, coming upon the scene as Nicole was being murdered, and was killed because he was able to identify the killer. He was slashed to death. At 9:50 p.m. the waiter left the Mezzaluna Restaurant, where Nicole Simpson and her family, except for O.J. Simpson, had earlier dined, intending to return a pair of eyeglasses she had forgotten. His death was later signaled, according to the prosecution, by the "plaintive wail" of a neighborhood dog.

A neighbor of Nicole Simpson's, Pablo Fenjves, was distracted from watching TV by the sound of loud barking or wailing from a dog. His condominium backed onto the one owned by Nicole Simpson. The barking went on for about an hour. He later fixed the time the dog began wailing at about 10:15 or 10:20 p.m. This was the time fixed for the murders. There were others in that Brentwood neighborhood who also heard the strange wail of the dog. (Brentwood was packed with famous people or relatives of famous people, including a close friend of Nicole's, Candace Garvey, and her former baseball star husband Steve Garvey; Carl Colby, son of former CIA director William Colby; and Leif Tilden, who had played the part of Donatello in the first Ninja Turtle movie.)

Louis Karpf and Eva Stein, who were also Nicole's neighbors, pinpointed the sound of the wailing dog at about 10:15 p.m. The dog, as it turned out, belonged to Nicole, a white Akita dog named Kato, a name that also belonged to the long-haired houseguest of O.J. Simpson's, the unemployed Brian Kaelin.

The dog Kato was found wandering outside of Nicole's condominium about 11 p.m. by Steven Schwab, who thought the dog was lost. Kato, Schwab later described, kept turning up the walkway toward Nicole's condominium, barking, then turning back to Schwab as if trying to get him to follow him. Instead, Schwab took the dog home with him, where neighbors Sukru Boztepe and his wife took the dog on a walk a short time later, looking for its owner. As Kato approached Nicole's condominium, it pulled hard on the leash, leading the Boztepes up the walkway, where they saw Nicole's body sprawled in a pool of blood.

O.J. Simpson, the accused murderer, had picked up some fast-food hamburgers with Kaelin at 9:30 p.m. that night and then reportedly returned to his estate at 360 N. Rockingham Avenue, Brentwood. From that point until 11 p.m., Simpson could provide no alibi or witnesses who supported his claimed whereabouts. He said later that he was sleeping, resting up for a long-planned trip to Chicago.

Also planned was a limousine ride to the Los Angeles Airport. The limousine appeared twenty minutes earlier than expected at Simpson's estate. Its driver, Allan William Park, entered the Simpson estate and waited. While waiting, he later stated, he noticed that Simpson's white Bronco was not parked in front of the estate as later claimed by the defense.

Park would also later testify that he saw Kaelin walking about the grounds around 10:30 p.m., using a flashlight, as if searching for something or someone. At 10:45 p.m., Park also testified, he saw a well-built six-foot black man weighing, according to his estimation, about 200 pounds, rapidly cross the grounds in front of him and go to the front door. He said he could not make out the man's facial features. After the man entered the house, the house lights went on.

A few minutes later, Park said, he went to the front door and rang the bell. He got no answer. At about 11 p.m., Simpson finally responded, saying that he had been sleeping and that he would be outside soon. Simpson did appear with several bags, ready to go to the airport. One well-packed black handbag Simpson kept close to him. This bag reportedly vanished at the L.A. Airport when Simpson was waiting to check his bags and standing next to a large garbage container. Then Simpson caught an 11:45 p.m. flight to Chicago.

A few hours later, Los Angeles Police Detective Philip Vannatter called the home of Marcia Clark, a deputy district attorney, telling her of a horrible double homicide in Brentwood and that he needed a search warrant. "It's O.J. Simpson," Vannatter said.

"Who's that?" Clark responded.

"The football player? *Naked Gun*?"

"Phil, I'm sorry. I don't know him."

Vannatter explained further, how Simpson was a legendary football player, a movie star, the man who was seen in television ads jumping over luggage for Hertz rent-a-car. He went on to say how blood had been found on the door handle

Ronald Lyle Goldman, the young waiter who was also brutally murdered outside Nicole's Brentwood home.

of Simpson's white Bronco, there was blood on the driveway of his Rockingham estate, and that a bloody glove had been found on the estate by Vannatter's junior associate, Detective Mark Fuhrman.

"Jesus," Clark finally said, "it sounds like you've got enough for filing (an arrest warrant), much less a search warrant."

Vannatter got his search warrant. He and other detectives then began to build a case against Simpson, who was in Chicago. Simpson himself was awakened earlier in his hotel room in Chicago by LAPD Detective Ronald Phillips, who used the kitchen phone in Simpson's home to call him at 6:05 a.m., June 13, 1994.

As soon as Simpson picked up the phone, Phillips said, "I have some bad news for you. Your ex-wife, Nicole Simpson, has been killed."

Simpson's first words were: "Oh, my God, Nicole is killed. Oh, my God, she's dead."

When Simpson became distraught, according to Phillips, the detective said, "Mr. Simpson, try to get hold of yourself. I have your children at the ... police station. I need to talk to you about that."

Simpson then asked to speak to his adult daughter, Arnelle. He instructed her to pick up his children from the police station, his daughter, Sidney, age 8, and his son, Justin, age 6. He then resumed his conversation with Phillips, which lasted five minutes.

Phillips later testified that he never mentioned to Simpson that Nicole had been murdered. The detective later stated in court that Simpson never asked if his ex-wife had been murdered. He never asked when she had been killed or how she had been killed or any other details of her death. Just after he hung up the phone, Phillips talked with Mark Fuhrman, who reported finding a bloody glove on the Simpson estate.

Phillips did not call the coroner until 6:50 a.m., alerting him to the double murders, and again at 8:10 a.m., asking that someone from the coroner's office go immediately to the crime scene on Bundy. Simpson returned to Los Angeles to attend his wife's funeral. When Simpson met with police, he was not immediately told that he was a suspect in the case. Not until the morning of June 17 did Simpson learn that he was about to be arrested for murdering Nicole and Ronald Goldman. This information was given to him by his defense attorney, Robert Shapiro.

Shapiro and Simpson were then in the home of Simpson friend Robert Kardashian, who had held on to some luggage Simpson had taken with him on his trip to Chicago. After Simpson was told that he was going to be arrested, he went upstairs to say goodbye to family members. He then vanished with his burly friend, Al Cowlings.

According to Cowlings, he drove Simpson to the cemetery where Nicole was buried, hiding Simpson's white Bronco in an orange grove. Simpson made three calls on his cellular phone from that area before he and Cowlings fled after seeing a marked police car in the area. Police by then were frantically searching for Simpson and put out a public bulletin describing his car.

Two motorists responded to the police alert at 6:25 p.m., reporting that the Bronco was on the San Diego freeway. The infamous chase then ensued, with dozens of police cars catching up to the Bronco and pursuing it. Police ordered Cowlings, who was at the wheel, to pull the car over to the side of the freeway. He did so. Officers drew their weapons as they approached the Bronco.

Cowlings yelled, "F—- no!" He slammed his fist against the driver's door, shouting, "He's got a gun to his head!" Cowlings referred to Simpson, who sat in the back seat allegedly holding a gun to his temple with thoughts of suicide. With that, Cowlings sped off, the police in pursuit, but in a wave of squad cars that blocked all lanes behind the Bronco and remained at a respectful distance, strange, even bizarre behavior for police attempting to catch a murder suspect who was attempting to avoid arrest.

More than ninety million persons in the U.S. and around the world were glued to the televised police chase (or motorcade), watching the slow chase, which seemed to go on forever, until the Bronco turned slowly into the driveway of Simpson's Brentwood estate, where he and Cowlings finally got out of the car. Simpson was taken into custody and the Bronco was immediately inspected. It was apparent to officers that O.J. Simpson had attempted to flee the country. Items found on him and in his car at that time—these items were never made part of his subsequent trial—included his passport. Also found was $8,750 in cash and six checks in a sealed envelope. In addition, a fake beard and a mustache were found

The murder scene outside the Brentwood home of Nicole Brown Simpson; Los Angeles police officers were later accused of botching the DNA samples taken from the pavement and clumsily obscuring other evidence.

in the car, one which prosecutors believed Simpson would employ in his flight to another country. None of these items were introduced as evidence in the case against O.J. Simpson.

Oddly, Vannatter and his partner, Tom Lange, later entered these items not as Simpson's property and evidence but as the property of Al Cowlings. The chase itself was never presented to the jury at Simpson's trial. All of this, according to prosecutor William Hodgman, was a judgment call on the part of the police and the D.A.'s office. Said Hodgman later, "If you knew some of the evidence we were dealing with, you would understand what the cost--benefit analysis was." It was a poor call at that, as events later showed.

The prosecution was made up of Marcia Clark, who had never lost a case; William Hodgman, a veteran trial prosecutor; and Christopher Darden, a young black prosecutor who was portrayed by the defense as an "Uncle Tom." It was Darden who would later, bravely, take most of the abuse heaped upon the prosecution by black defense lawyer Johnnie Cochran, an attorney noted for consistently winning when defending blacks accused of various crimes. His formula was simple. He almost always played the race card to black jurors, insisting that his clients were the victims of race hatred and prejudice.

Cochran had successfully defended black singer Michael Jackson in a child molestation case, one that was reportedly settled out of court for $20 million. (Jackson was arrested and charged with child molestation in November 2003.) Cochran also represented black drug suspect Rodney King, who was videotaped as he was mercilessly beaten by LAPD officers, and won for him a $40 million settlement. Cochran was not originally part of Simpson's "Dream Team" of defense lawyers, hired at unspecified millions in fees.

The case was first headed by Shapiro. F. Lee Bailey was brought in at Simpson's request. It was later stated that Simpson wanted a superstar lawyer like Bailey to match what he considered his own status, that of a superstar. A few days after his arrest, according to Cochran, Simpson began calling him at home. "The whole thing was," Cochran later stated, "he wanted to get out and get this over with by Halloween [of 1994] so he could go trick-or--treating with his kids." It seemed to some that Simpson's only concern was his release and returning to life as usual, rather than any deep concern for solving the murder of his ex-wife.

In addition to Cochran, Bailey and Shapiro, Simpson's monolithic defense team included Alan Dershowitz, who functioned as an adviser and who, in case Simpson was found guilty, would lead the attack on appeal. It was Dershowitz who appealed the conviction of Claus von Bulow for the murder of his millionaire wife and won him freedom on technicalities. Simpson called Dershowitz his "God forbid" lawyer, meaning "God forbid I am found guilty." Dershowitz, who never let the world forget that he was a Harvard professor, promoted himself through his academic position almost every time he appeared on TV. Remaining in Cambridge, Massachusetts with his research team (made up of his students), Dershowitz viewed the televised case on a special split screen monitor and sent in advice via a fax machine that was at the defense table.

The defense team at first was showered with publicity, the wrong kind. It appeared that Shapiro had taken insult at being demoted from lead lawyer when Cochran was brought in by Simpson. He and the temperamental, flamboyant Bailey fell to arguing over the direction the defense should take. Bailey, for instance, was the only one who argued that Simpson should take the stand, telling the accused, "You've got great charisma. You'll blow them away." He also resented Cochran's undeviating intention to play the race card, to portray the prosecution as the white oppressors to a famous black athlete. Shapiro later went on TV to denounce this tactic as his fellow defense team lawyers ridiculed him shamelessly.

The real reason for Shapiro's demotion, however, was undoubtedly based on the fact that early on in the trial, he proposed a plea-bargain arrangement, one where Simpson would plead guilty to manslaughter. (Shapiro was known as "The Prince of Plea Bargains.") This was seriously considered by

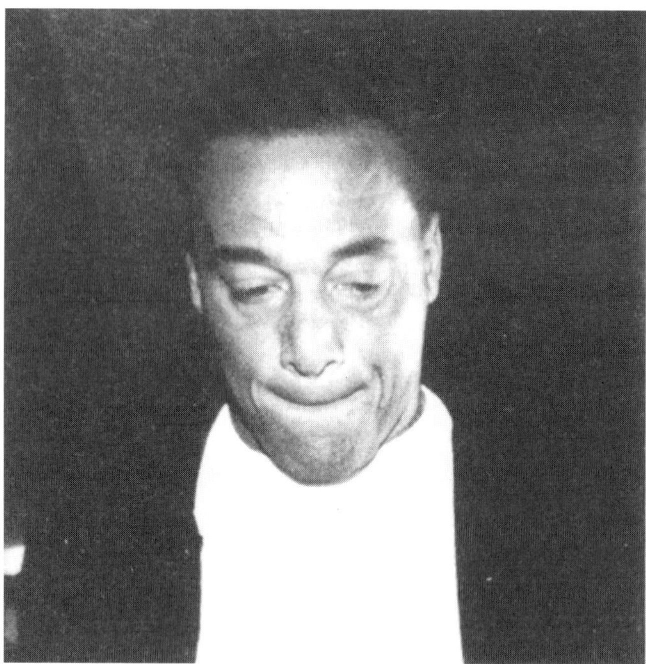

Allen C. Cowlings, Simpson's boyhood friend, who drove Simpson about in the actor's Bronco, while police searched for him.

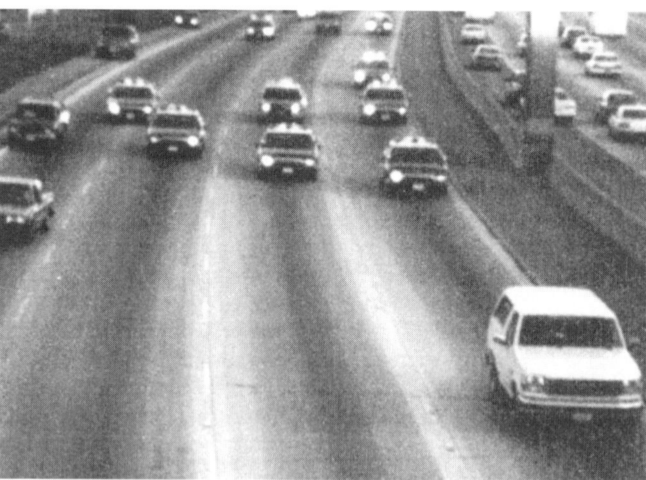

The agonizingly slow police chase after the Bronco (at right) carrying Simpson and Cowlings down the San Diego Freeway, a snail-like pursuit viewed by millions of viewers riveted to their television sets.

Simpson and his attorneys and then abandoned, mostly due to Bailey's insistence; Cochran stayed out of this debate, merely listening, it was later reported.

The prosecution, though it had at hand more circumstantial evidence than similar trials, accepted defeat as early as July 1994, less than three weeks after the double murder, when Marcia Clark concluded that, as an American hero, O.J. Simpson was "an unconvictable defendant." Moreover, according to one report, she said at that time that "they've filed this case downtown, which means they're going to get a downtown jury. A black jury will not convict this defendant. Forget it. It's all over."

Yet the prosecution went ahead with one of the most expensive trials on record, playing out legal battles and grandstanding for the television camera Judge Ito had allowed in his courtroom. Ito himself proved to be one of the most blatant publicity seekers in the whole shoddy mess. Ito was not unflappable. He focused upon details apparently to impress the court, but so much so that he often forgot procedures. He was so upset about one juror being televised that he forgot to ask the defense for certain witness information. Prosecutor William Hodgman objected thirteen times to Cochran's wild opening arguments that, rather than focusing on his client's defense, attacked the prosecution and the police department. Ito ignored the objections and let the defense ride roughshod.

A maverick judge on courtroom behavior from his judicial beginnings, Ito made a point of wearing a pair of weathered jogging shoes into court. On the bench, Ito controlled the courtroom through a special television monitoring screen, which allowed him to inspect every corner of the courtroom through security cameras hidden in the ceiling dome. And he reportedly used this device as would an aspiring but amateur film director.

One of Ito's many pet peeves was chewing gum in his courtroom. Three times, while peering at his special monitor he saw the jaws of reporters moving and had an officer chastise the newsmen for chewing gum. One might wonder, since Ito was spending so much time monitoring the conduct of everyone in court, how he could stay focused on the actual trial.

Ito's relationship with chief prosecutor Marcia Clark was strained from the start. Clark later said that she felt she had to pretend to play a submissive role with Ito. She was not alone. Defense attorney Peter Neufeld later related how he and others on the defense team were compelled to go to Ito's chambers to cater to his "petty needs."

Neufeld portrayed Ito as an egomaniac, one who was "so concerned with his status as a celebrity, his willingness to entertain personalities in his chambers, to show the lawyers little videotapes of skits on television." On one occasion, Ito called defense lawyers into his chambers to show them a video he had recently taped from Jay Leno's "Tonight Show," which parodied the trial under the title of "The Dancing Itos."

This incident later caused Neufeld to state, "He had thought it [the Leno show] was great and loved it and wanted all of us to see it in chambers. You may find that amusing on a personal level, but I can assure you that on a professional level it is so unacceptable, for a judge who is presiding over a murder where two people lost their lives in the most gruesome and horrible fashion, and where a third person has his life on the line, to bring the lawyers into chambers to show them comic revues." Ito went so far as to tell the lawyers Simpson jokes he had heard. "I found it deplorable and I was shocked," Neufeld said.

The ego of the lawyers and the judge, however, were nothing compared with the raging, bullish ego of the defendant. Simpson bossed his lawyers about mercilessly, paying mil-

Simpson (second from left) is shown under arrest after the Bronco stopped at his Brentwood estate.

lions for the privilege of posing as dictator, of course. He dictated the course of his defense and the positioning of his attorneys from his jail cell and in court. Not until one of his former long-time friends, Ron Shipp, testified in court, however, did Simpson realize that he was in real jeopardy.

Shipp, a fellow black, testified that he had been a close friend of both Simpson and Nicole. A one-time LAPD officer, Shipp had taken classes on domestic violence and at one time, at Nicole's request, had counseled both of them on Simpson's long history of physical abuse of Nicole. Shipp testified that at that time, he told Simpson that he fit the pattern of an abuser. More damaging, Shipp went on to say that he went to Simpson's house on the night he had returned from Chicago and, despite the fact that his ex--wife had just been brutally murdered, Simpson laughed and admitted to Shipp that he had thought of killing Nicole. Shipp quoted Simpson as telling him, "You know, to be honest, Shipp. I've had some dreams of killing her."

Cochran's assistant, defense attorney Carl Douglas, attacked Shipp in a bullying cross-examination, bringing up the fact that Shipp was a recovered alcoholic and claiming he was not a close friend of O.J. Simpson, but merely a Simpson groupie. This tactic backfired, most observers agreed, causing the quiet-speaking Shipp to appear sympathetic and believable rather than less credible. Simpson, a shrewd observer himself, realized this, and ordered that Douglas was never again to cross-examine witnesses. That night he held a conference call with Dream Team members and shouted, "I'll decide who the running backs are in this game!"

In the meantime, to shore up his defense fund, Simpson received a $1 million advance from Little, Brown for a quickie tell--nothing book entitled *I Want to Tell You*, a book he dictated to Lawrence Schiller from his jail cell. This was only the beginning of Simpson's self-serving promotion. He

O. J. Simpson, former football star and film/TV actor, is shown in a LAPD mug shot, taken on June 17, 1994, when he was booked for murdering his wife, Nicole, and Ronald Goldman.

autographed photos and other Simpson memorabilia to glean more millions, including an audiotape that said nothing about the trial but, like all the other propaganda he produced, brought in a great deal of money because of the trial. He was literally earning a fortune on the murders of Nicole and Ronald Goldman and receiving over the course of the trial more than 300,000 letters from fans.

As the trial proceeded, the defense tried several approaches, one being that others had killed Nicole Brown Simpson and Ronald Goldman, not their client. Simpson's attorneys implied that both had been victims of a drug buy gone wrong, or of drug dealers avenging nonpayment or some sort of betrayal, all of this linked to Faye Resnick, one-time Nicole confidante who was extremely hostile toward Simpson and who had written her own book and made a great deal of money from the case, a book that incensed Judge Ito. Resnick had stated in her book that her friend Nicole had told her that Simpson was going to kill her. Ito personally wrote many letters to the media requesting that no publicity be given to the book, stating that it might prejudice potential jurors. Extending this logic to the media at large would be the same as asking that the trial have no publicity whatsoever for the same reason.

The drug connection advocated by Cochran was a farfetched scenario, one that was never supported by any facts or actual links to a drug-inspired murder. It was just another defense smokescreen. Defense attorneys offered up the wild statements of Mary Ann Gerchas, who said that she had seen four men running from the murder scene about the time the victims had been killed. Gerchas was later thoroughly discredited as a bad-check artist who had been charged with fraud by several persons and companies. In addition, Gerchas was being sued by Marriott International, Inc. for $23,000 in unpaid room charges.

Cochran told the jury that he would call Gerchas (he did not) and some two dozen witnesses who would support the story about suspicious persons prowling about in Nicole's neighborhood on the night of the murder. Cochran was typically running off at the mouth. He did not disclose the names of these witnesses or call them, which was in violation of a 1990 requirement which demands that the defense turn over to the prosecution all the names of witnesses and their written statements. Judge Ito did nothing about this egregious, disingenuous behavior by Cochran.

Next, the defense attempted to unseat Allan Park's statements about Simpson's Ford Bronco not being present when he arrived at Simpson's estate to take him to the airport. Defense attorneys brought forth Rosa Lopez, a maid who lived next door to Simpson. Lopez, in halting English, claimed that Simpson's Bronco was parked at the estate at the time when prosecutors said he was murdering Nicole and Goldman. (Lopez was long in getting to court. She was ordered to leave a Las Vegas gambling casino to attend the trial in Los Angeles.)

Under pressure from prosecutor Chris Darden, Lopez admitted that she had lied several times in giving information on passport visas and in other instances. She, like Mary Ann Gerchas, was discredited; in fact, some observers stated that she appeared to be a "bought witness," especially when it was learned that the defense was providing her expenses.

On a day-to-day basis, the defense appeared to be

Denise Brown (shown with a photo of her murdered sister Nicole in the background) testified how Simpson, a notorious wife-beater, had repeatedly degraded his wife in public and how he physically abused her.

Marsha Clark, who led the prosecution, gave up early on getting a conviction, believing that since Simpson was "booked downtown," he would get a mostly black jury that would decide in his favor, a deliberation based on race not issues; she and her co-attorneys nevertheless conducted a half-hearted, near incompetent prosecution that greatly contributed to Simpson's acquittal.

Simpson, left, sits passively in court next to one of his high-priced attorneys, Robert Shapiro (later fired by Simpson, who bossed all of his lawyers, relying on chief counsel Johnnie Cochran to play the race card to win his freedom).

losing ground. Simpson's attorneys fought hardest against the introduction of any evidence concerning Simpson's long time abuse of his former wife. That shameful record, it was finally learned, coursed through seventeen years of the Simpson marriage, and it was a horrid litany of physical and mental abuse by a sadistically domineering O.J. Simpson. The record shows that Simpson beat his wife mercilessly and subjected her to ridicule, embarrassment and public degradation. He treated her as a possession, a thing, dehumanizing and disgracing her whenever his dark whims urged. It is the record of a crude, morally deficient bully intent upon inflicting physical and mental pain upon a long-suffering spouse who had told friends that she expected Simpson to someday lose all control and murder her.

Prosecutors found a great deal of the abuse evidence in Nicole Simpson's safe deposit box. It contained a record of all of Simpson's attacks on her, along with color photos showing her bruised and battered face from a 1989 attack for which Simpson was booked. Nicole's careful chronicle of her husband's abuse was assembled for her divorce case two years prior to her murder, but since Simpson continued to visit and terrorize her after the divorce, she kept the evidence, in case, some said, her husband might eventually murder her as she reportedly believed.

In 1986, Nicole wrote, Simpson "beat me up so bad at home, tore my blue sweater and blue slacks completely off me." Nicole's sister, Denise, echoed her sister's grim chronicle, saying that she witnessed many of Simpson's abuses of Nicole. In one instance, Denise Brown recalled how she told Simpson that he took her sister "for granted," which caused a fight. "Pictures started flying off the walls," Denise later testified, weeping, her voice trembling. "Clothes started flying down the stairs. He grabbed Nicole and told her to get out of the house. He picked her up and threw her against the wall. He picked her up and threw her out of the house. She ended up falling on her elbows and her butt."

In 1987, Denise recalled, she and a friend accompanied Nicole and Simpson to a Santa Ana bistro, The Red Onion. There, at the crowded bar of the restaurant, Simpson grabbed Nicole's crotch and shouted, "This is where my babies come from and this belongs to me!" The prosecution added that later that night Nicole asked a friend to drive her home in Simpson's Rolls Royce. As the car began to drive away, Simpson slapped his wife and pushed her out of the car and onto the pavement.

In 1988 Nicole's chronicle recounted an incident where she, her daughter Sidney, and her mother and sister attended a "Disney on Ice" show. Simpson, she wrote, was incensed, accusing Nicole of excluding him from the family outing. He got drunk and then went berserk, calling the pregnant Nicole "a fat pig ... You're a slob! I want you out of my f——g house ... I want you to have an abortion with the baby."

Nicole reportedly responded by saying, "Do I have to go tonight? Sidney's sleeping. It's late."

Simpson, Nicole stated, retorted, "Let me tell you how serious I am. I have a gun in my hand right now. Get the f— out of here."

Nicole Simpson woke her sleeping daughter, packed some clothes, and left. The key to understanding Simpson's motive for murder, one which somehow slipped through the perception of the prosecution, was in the locked fixation Simpson had for being ostracized or shut out (especially in public events, where he could strut the star).

The identical scenario occurred on the night of the 1994

Presiding Judge Lance A. Ito, a limelight-seeking jurist, who grandstanded his way through the tedious trial, manipulating the TV monitors, and causing endless delays in the procedures that made this one of the costliest trials in Los Angeles history.

Faye Resnick, a friend of the slain Nicole Simpson, who authored a quickie book about Nicole's stormy life with Simpson, which was published during the trial and caused Marsha Clark to complain that its publication would taint the jury pool. Judge Ito suspended jury selection for two days because of the book and then told jurors not to read any news stories about it, his widely published remarks helping to make this otherwise undistinguished book a best-seller.

double murders. Simpson was totally rejected by the entire Brown family on the night of his daughter's recital—all of them said he was "not invited" to a celebration party at the Mezzaluna Restaurant—a white family he had enriched by supporting his wife in style, by reportedly funding her father's enterprises, by paying for college expenses for her sisters. Now all of them, these ungrateful whites, were rejecting him, O.J. Simpson, no longer the superstar, merely a black man with money.

Moreover, that night (and not revealed until after the trial), waiting for him on his answering machine was a message from his attractive girlfriend, Paula Barbieri, a message stating that she was breaking off their relationship. (It was reported that Barbieri was with Michael Bolton on the night of the murders.) This was but another rejection from a white woman to a black man who had given her expensive gifts and trips. He had tried to enter the white world, lived inside of its Brentwood majesty, but gnawing on him—beyond his own bone marrow ego and vanity—was the fact that he was nothing more than a black man with money, mostly a black man, who was being rejected by the whole of the white power structure, which he had sought so desperately for years to enter.

Simpson struck out against these whites, it is the author's opinion, by brutally slaying Nicole and the young white man who suddenly appeared at her doorstep. (It mattered not whether Goldman was Nicole's lover, friend or merely an acquaintance—he was there, a witness to the gore.) This was the white race card the prosecution did not, or could not play in response to Cochran's black race card. It certainly would have done little good with a predominantly black jury whose black members were bent on believing from the beginning, irrespective of the reasons they later gave for the acquittal, that a black man—one of their own black heroes—was being unfairly tried by a system Cochran portrayed as white and prejudicial.

Had Simpson premeditated the murder, waiting until the right opportunity, a scheduled trip to leave town, and the correct provocation, another gross insult to his pride and ego by being shut out? He was certainly prepared. He certainly had the right tool. Simpson had purchased a knife, a fifteen-inch stiletto, from a Los Angeles cutlery store in May 1994, it was reported. (This was not brought into evidence by the prosecution.) He had told Shipp how he had dreamed of murdering his wife. The family rejection of him served as the catalyst that prompted his plan into action.

In 1989, Simpson beat his wife so badly that he was booked for assault and battery, the charges later dropped.

This was the incident, where Nicole took pains to have her bruised and battered face photographed. Following that incident, Simpson wrote to Nicole, "Let me start by expressing to you how wrong I was for hurting you. There is no exceptible [sic] excuse for what I did."

Though Simpson later shrugged at accusations of his being jealous of his ex-wife, claiming to be happily attached to Barbieri (when he knew that Barbieri had already broken off with him), his abuse of Nicole continued long after their divorce. On October 25, 1993, only eight months before Nicole was murdered, she called 911 to report that Simpson had barged into her home and was terrorizing her. The 911 tape, played in court, was chilling as it recorded Nicole telling the operator that "It's O.J. Simpson. He's going f———g nuts!" In the background the court could hear Simpson screaming, cursing, banging things about.

To all of this, Johnnie Cochran responded by saying that these were merely domestic arguments. He portrayed the violent history of O.J. Simpson's wife-beating as somehow nothing more than family spats, not the fist-pounding, body-throwing events that they actually were. According to the Los Angeles *Times*, Cochran himself had been accused by a former wife, as being a wife abuser. In divorce proceedings against Cochran twenty-eight years earlier, his former wife, Barbara Berry, accused him of assaulting her. Cochran shrugged a denial, saying that these charges were merely used as leverage in a divorce. (Berry reportedly stated that she was writing a book about her life with Cochran, joining a never-ending list of authors linking themselves to this notorious case.)

About the same time Cochran was fending off accusations of being a fellow wife-beater, a national TV talk show presented a woman named April Levalois, who insisted that while Cochran was still married to Berry, he was the lover of Levalois' mother who bore his illegitimate son, Jonathan Cochran.

The prosecution then introduced what it considered its strongest and most telling evidence. The first of these salient artifacts was a pair of black, bloodstained gloves. The left--handed glove had been found at Nicole's Bundy St. address, near the bodies. The right-handed glove had been found on a walkway near the guest house on Simpson's estate. Both gloves had been found by Detective Mark Fuhrman, who was in the company of other detectives when the gloves were found. The gloves, DNA analysis later confirmed, contained blood from Simpson, Nicole and Goldman.

A bloody sock containing Nicole's blood and found on the floor of Simpson's lavish bedroom was introduced. A navy-blue knit watch cap containing hairs from the head of a black man was found on the grounds of Nicole's residence. Some of Simpson's blood, DNA evidence later stated, was found at the murder site and more at Simpson's estate, including blood from Nicole and Goldman. More bloodstains were found inside the white Bronco. Then there were bloody shoe prints (the size of which later matched Simpson's size) leading from the murder scene on a walkway to the alley.

The defense attacked this evidence. Barry Scheck, a reported DNA expert, paraded so-called DNA experts before the court who reported that the LAPD lab experts handling the DNA and other blood analysis were sloppy, their procedures slipshod. The defense went so far as to say that some of the blood samples taken from O.J. Simpson following his arrest were missing, more than what would make up normal "spillage" in DNA testing.

O. J. Simpson awkwardly spread his fingers and arched his hands backwards to display before the jury the bloodstained gloves used in the murders to indicate that they did not fit him.

The thrust of this statement went to a full-blown claim by the defense that all of Simpson's bloodstains had been planted by a conspiracy of racist policemen and perhaps LAPD lab people, and that the chief racist cop was none other than Detective Mark Fuhrman. It was later shown that Fuhrman was, indeed, a racist who repeatedly used the word "nigger" to describe blacks, but it was never shown how this man was able to plant all of the drops of Simpson's blood throughout the Bundy and Rockingham areas, in the white Bronco, and that he also planted and then discovered the gloves, that he planted the knit cap and the bloody sock.

Fuhrman was, however, a prosecution witness who first appeared to be cool and unflappable on the witness stand. Tapes he recorded years earlier when talking to a writer about a proposed book of fiction revealed him to be one who hated blacks. The destruction of Fuhrman's credibility was complete and the most telling blow to the prosecution.

Then, in a dramatic and bold move, Cochran had his client actually try on the gloves before a riveted jury. His method in doing so was unorthodox. Those putting on gloves compress their fingers and cup their hands so as to be able to slip into gloves that are normally tight-fitting. When Simpson tried the gloves, he purposely kept his fingers wide apart, spreading his palms so that the gloves did not go on easily. He kept his fingers spread so that the gloves appeared not to fit, without snuggling the bottom ends over his palms. It was a colossal bluff that worked, since the prosecution did not take exception to the manner in which Simpson performed this procedure.

So effective did Cochran believe this demonstration to be that he harped on it until the very end of the trial, carping in his final summation a glib coinage: "If it doesn't fit, you must acquit." He repeated this phrase over and over while wearing a copy of the knit cap that had been placed in evidence, as if to contemptuously mock the evidence. And always, with almost every statement, was Cochran's insistence that O.J. Simpson was the victim of a white conspiracy.

The prosecution, on the other hand, put up a list of what it thought were convincing arguments for the jury to convict, but Marcia Clark's summation was timid, tentative, weak, unconvincing, as if she were listening to her own words of a year earlier—"A black jury will not convict this defendant. Forget it. It's all over."—and she appeared unenthusiastic, fearful of failure.

Missing from the prosecution's summation was any mention of Simpson's fantastic flight for freedom and the money, passport and false identity inside the Bronco that would pave the way for his escape. Missing was any mention of the stiletto he had purchased a month before the murders. Missing was an argument showing how Simpson had purposely manipulated the gloves to make them appear not to fit. Missing was a precise timetable that would show that O.J. Simpson had had enough time to commit murder and then return to his estate before flying to Chicago. Missing were all of the abuse offenses committed by Simpson against his wife (who had called the Sojourn shelter only five days before her death to say that Simpson was going to kill her).

The International Chiefs of Police had statistics to prove that most women—1,400 of them a year, on average—who were murdered were killed by men who knew them and that most of them were victims of consistent spousal abuse. None of that mattered to a jury of nine blacks (mostly women), two whites and one Hispanic. In less than four hours after merely glancing at the mountain of evidence, the jury acquitted Simpson. Its verdict was not made public for twenty-four hours on order of Judge Ito so that all the lawyers could be present in court, or so he said. Another reason for this delay may have been Ito's typical playing to the TV gallery in order to have the dramatic moment captured on prime time.

The verdict was read on October 3, 1995. Simpson, who had spent 473 days in jail and had defended himself at a cost of unreported millions, was set free. The trial itself had cost more than $9 million and was the most watched event in television history. Judge Lance Ito had seen to it that the trial lasted as long as it did.

Half of the trial time was consumed by endless, unimportant sidebar conferences with lawyers whom Ito allowed to squabble, argue, attack and insult each other. He grandstanded throughout the trial, seeking to impress anyone who would

O. J. Simpson wears a triumphant smile, following his acquittal and release, an acquittal that millions believed to be a travesty of justice.

listen to his nonlegal comments, which, for the most part, were neither learned nor enlightening. As a jurist, Ito was a disgrace, and, in the opinion of this author, should have been removed from the bench.

The jurors showed themselves unconcerned with the evidence. Brenda Moran, a black female jurist, labeled all of the evidence of Simpson's spousal abuse "a waste of time." One young juror posed for *Playboy*, several wrote books, all played to the media. Though they later claimed to have reached a verdict on the evidence, it was apparent that the almost all-black jury released O.J. Simpson because he was black. "It was payback," one observer stated, "for the unfair Simi Valley decision to release the cops who beat Rodney King, and for all of the LAPD oppression of blacks in Los Angeles."

One of the most repulsive reactions to the verdict was a group of televised (by NBC) black women watching TV to hear the verdict. They were all victims of marital abuse, all residing in a battered women's retreat. When the not guilty verdict was announced, the women leaped from chairs, threw their hands in the air in jubilation and screamed their joy. All that mattered to them was that a fellow black had triumphed, not justice.

The reaction to this strange and apparently unevaluated verdict was to deeply divide whites and blacks as never before, and it most likely convinced an able presidential candidate, Colin Powell, that his chances of being elected were considerably lessened by the racial division that had been drawn by the verdict. More than 80 percent of the more than 220 million whites in America believe to this writing that Simpson is guilty. Roughly 80 percent of the eighteen million blacks in the U.S. believe Simpson not guilty.

Everyone except the murder victims profited by this trial. Network television had captured viewers by the untold millions and benefited enormously. Simpson won his release, while his defense attorneys were enriched by his millions. Prosecutors Marcia Clark and Christopher Darden received multimillion-dollar contracts for books and movies about their rather uninteresting lives. Instead of the dismal failures they really were, the prosecutors were looked upon as beleaguered, heroic figures, but such is the warped perception of media-created images. The choked-up conduct of Clark and Darden during a prosecution press conference at the trial's conclusion was embarrassing and, to some observers, obviously feigned. Instead of heaping kudos on these people, District Attorney Gil Garcetti should have pointed out their ineptitude in failing to use evidence at hand to convict O.J. Simpson. But then, Marcia Clark had announced that inevitable failure more than a year earlier.

Simpson's own conduct following the trial, convinced his critics that he was guilty. He had vowed upon his release that he would spend the rest of his life seeking the killer or killers of his ex-wife and Ron Goldman. That was the last time he mentioned that crusade. On the night of his release, he returned to his Brentwood estate, where he held a champagne party to celebrate his freedom, laughing and drinking with fawning friends, hardly the expected conduct of an aggrieved wrongly accused husband.

He was seen thereafter flitting about the country to play golf at the best courses, courting new friends even among the startled strangers who saw him driving past them in golf carts. Simpson, however, did not escape his actions altogether; he next had to face civil lawsuits brought against him for damages from the Goldman family. He dodged depositions in that case, but in January 1996 accepted a reported $3 million payment to appear on a video in which he talked about the trial, attacking Marcia Clark and trying to dispute the evidence brought against him, particularly the DNA analysis.

It appeared at that time that Simpson was still attempting to regain the favor of the power structure that once made him a millionaire. The tape, however, was viewed as a staged affair, one where Simpson simply answered questions that met his beforehand approval. There was no cross-examination. It was a kangaroo court where Simpson retried his own case and turned the facts in whatever direction suited his purpose. Newsman Ross Becker, who was hired to act as Simpson's questioning stooge in this rigged scenario, was interviewed after its completion and was asked if he felt that Simpson lied to him during the staged videotaping. Becker replied, "Sure, sure." Simpson did not mention his quest for the real killers of his ex--wife on the video, nor did he state that he would be offering any portion of the $3 million he received for doing the tape as a reward for the apprehension of that killer or killers.

Many esteemed criminologists and prosecutors throughout the U.S. generally agreed that Simpson had gotten away with murder. Not the least of these was the brilliant prosecutor Vincent Bugliosi, who had won 105 out of 106 felony jury trials, while working for the district attorney's office in Los Angeles, including the notorious Charles Manson case of the Tate-LoBianca slayings of 1969. Said Bugliosi of Simpson in 1996, "I've known a lot of murderers, but this guy is the most audacious murderer I've ever known. I'm convinced that he feels that he had a right to kill Nicole and that she did something to warrant the murder."

Simpson's audacity flared throughout the subsequent wrongful death civil suit brought against him by the Goldman family in the murders of Nicole Brown Simpson and Ron Goldman. This time, most of the evidence improperly introduced or not introduced at all in Simpson's criminal trial was presented in masterful fashion by Goldman family lawyer Daniel Petrocelli. He deposed Simpson and continually caught him in stated inconsistences. (Simpson repeatedly lied to Petrocelli in stating that he had never hit or struck or abused his dead wife.)

A key piece of Petrocelli's evidence was a single photo of Simpson wearing size-12 Bruno Magli shoes, the same shoes that had reportedly left a bloody imprint at the scene of the Nicole Simpson-Ronald Goldman murders. Only 299 pairs were sold in the U.S. between 1991 and 1993, and Simpson emphatically denied that he ever owned, let alone wore, such shoes, describing them as "ugly." The single unclear photo of Simpson wearing such shoes at a September 26, 1993 football game at Rich Stadium in Buffalo, New York, was discredited by Simpson's lawyers, who stated that the photo was a fake.

Then Petrocelli found an entire series of photos taken of Simpson at the same event that were crystal clear, and by blowing up the photos he was able to pinpoint the identification of the rare shoes: Indeed, at that time, Simpson was wearing size-12 Bruno Magli shoes. He had been caught in a lie, another lie his lawyer, Robert Baker, could not undo. Baker took the unsavory approach of attacking the victim, attempting to portray the slain Nicole Brown Simpson as a promiscuous woman, a drug-taking alcoholic who abused her children by subjecting them to the company of drug dealers and perverts. His attack backfired; the jury refused to believe his argument.

Petrocelli then worked in the evidence that the black jury in the criminal trial had ignored, but this time he effectively nailed that evidence to O.J. Simpson's guilt. On February 4, 1997, the jury in the civil trial found Simpson guilty on all eight counts brought against him and that he was guilty of the wrongful deaths of Nicole Simpson and Ronald Goldman. The victims' families were awarded $33.5 million in damages.

Simpson immediately scurried about to liquidate assets, but he eventually lost everything, including his resplendent Brentwood estate, which he had occupied for twenty years

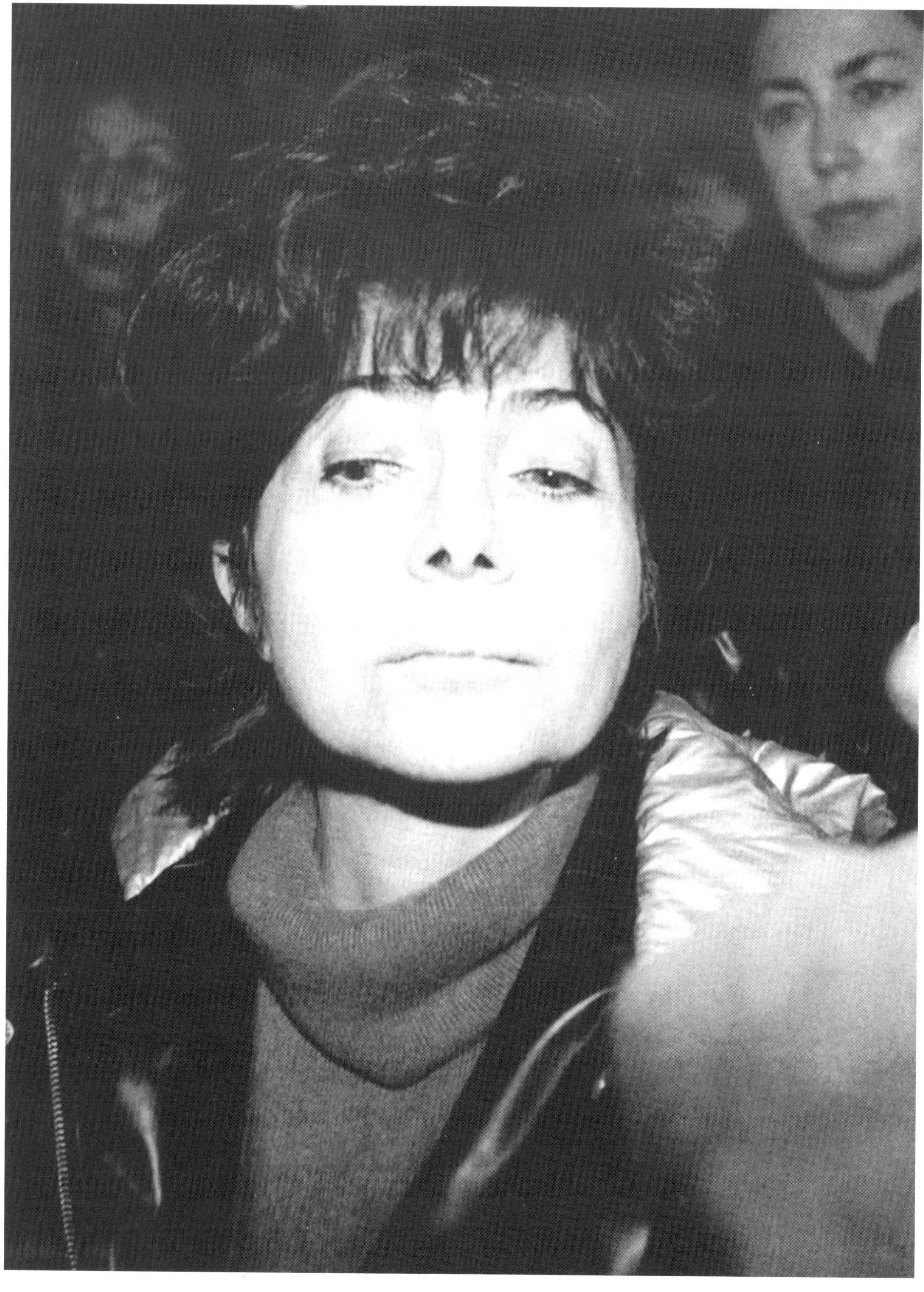

(six bathrooms, a tennis court, waterfalls, and an Olympic-sized pool). His money gone, his prestige and fame reduced to the stigma of murderer, O. J. Simpson even lost custody of his two young children, according to a November 10, 1998 appellate court decision in Santa Ana, California, based on the civil court decision that found Simpson responsible for the murder of his ex-wife. He was no longer famous, but notorious.

ITALY'S BLACK WIDOW/March 27, 1995

Milan is the chic capital of Italy's fashion industry, and no one's name in that dizzying designer world of glitz and glamour is more potent than that of Gucci. Three generations of Guccis have imprinted the founder's initials, "GG," on the most coveted leather goods and shoes to be found anywhere. Maurizio Gucci was the grandson and last of the direct descendants of Guccio Gucci to hold a stake in the company, and he sold out his interest in 1993 for $120 million following years of family discord and acrimony.

Much of that acrimony had to do with Maurizio Gucci's former wife, Patrizia Reggiani Martinelli Gucci (AKA: The Black Widow, b. 1948), a social-climbing, money-loving ex-spouse who was so unsatisfied with her $860,000-a-year alimony that she planned to obtain all of Gucci's millions through a murder-for-hire plan. Having been divorced years earlier by Gucci, the once glamorous Neapolitan, who had humble origins and who had given birth to two of Gucci's daughters, had threatened the fashion king with all sorts of terrible fates and even told him to his face that she would have him killed unless he turned over many millions to her.

Gucci waved her off. On March 27, 1995, as he was mounting the stairs to his elegant offices in Milan, Gucci was shot to death by an unknown assailant who fled in a fast car with another conspirator behind the wheel. Police doggedly worked on the killing until they identified the getaway driver, Orazio Cicala, an unemployed auto worker. Cicala led police to the gunman, Benedetto Ceraulo, the owner of a pizzeria who was swimming in debt. Ceraulo told detectives that he had received his orders from Ivano Savioni, the doorman of a broken-down Milan hotel.

The doorman was picked up and, following grueling interrogations, said that he had followed the orders of Giuseppina Auriemma, a mysterious psychic, warning officers that her spiritual powers could overwhelm and destroy any law enforcement agencies probing into her dark doings. Police then learned that Auriemma had for years been the personal psychic "adviser" to Gucci's ex-wife, Patrizia Reggiani Martinelli.

The one-time queen of Milan's social world bristled when investigators cautiously approached her, gently quizzing her about her husband's murder. She said she had nothing to do with it. She later admitted that she had for some time been seeking someone to kill her miserly ex-husband, but, she emphasized, she had never gone through with that plan. Of course,

Opposite page, left: Patrizia Reggiani Martinelli Gucci, who was convicted and sent to prison for hiring killers to slay her millionaire ex-husband, Maurizio Gucci, in 1995.

nodded the polite police inquisitors, but her personal psychic now stood accused of acting on her behalf.

Reggiani Martinelli then said that Auriemma had arranged for the murder without her approval and that the psychic had been blackmailing her ever since, taking more than $375,000. But, the ex-wife insisted, she was nevertheless innocent of having her former husband killed. "Never let even a friendly wolf into the chicken coop," she confided to police, a statement she would often repeat in months to come. "Sooner or later it will get hungry." She was, of course, referring to the scheming psychic, Auriemma, the real mastermind behind the murder of Maurizio Gucci, she said.

In June 1998, Reggiani Martinelli and her four co-conspirators were brought to trial in Milan, all charged with capital murder. The former queen bee denied having anything to do with the other four defendants, insisting that they had acted on their own under Auriemma's orders and that the psychic was an evil person, who had seized upon Reggiani Martinelli's dislike of her former husband to initiate a murder and involve her in it, so that she could become the perfect blackmail victim.

"I have been naive to the point of stupidity," Reggiani Martinelli cried out to the court, where her mother sat with a worried look on her face. "I found myself involved against my will. I deny categorically that I was an accomplice."

The costly trial dragged on for five months while the seamy side of Milan's social set was exposed. Tawdry tales of greed, intrigue, calculating social climbing and murderous betrayals were told and retold in detail, an army of reporters in the courtroom writing down every sensational word and photographing every move made by witnesses and defendants, especially the former grande dame, Reggiani Martinelli, who played the role of the discarded wife and blackmail victim to the hilt.

On November 3, 1998, Reggiani Martinelli and her four co-defendants were all found guilty of capital murder. Instead of the life term expected for her, Reggiani Martinelli was sentenced to twenty-nine years in prison. Auriemma, the scheming psychic, received a 25-year sentence. Savioni, her stooge, the doorman, got a 26-year sentence, while Cicala, the getaway driver, received a 29-year sentence and Ceraulo, the gunman who continued to shout out his innocence, was sent to prison for life.

Only Savioni, the go-between, seemed repentant, stating: "I know that I face many long years in prison for what I've done. I ask the pardon of Gucci's children. I am horrified that things went so much further than I intended."

At the announcement of the verdict and sentence, Reggiani Martinelli's two daughters, who had sat patiently through the trial, burst into tears. The defendant's mother sat stone-faced and silent. Reggiani Martinelli herself then turned to her lawyer, Giovanni Dedola, and, showing her best bewildered face, said in a soft and knowing tone: "Truth is the child of time. Evidently, they didn't believe me."

As Italy's most notorious "Black Widow" was being escorted from the courtroom and en route to prison, hordes of journalists began brawling with police. Reporters and photographers struggled, jostled, pushed, and shoved to get close to Reggiani Martinelli, to scribble down a final statement, to snap just one more photo.

A MURDEROUS MAD MILLIONAIRE/ January 26, 1996

David Schultz, 36, a wrestling coach, had the unenviable job of training an Olympic wrestling team on the grounds of John E. du Pont's sprawling Foxcatcher estate outside Philadelphia, Pennsylvania. He lived on the estate with his wife Nancy and two small children and was subject to the unnerving and eccentric behavior of tycoon John E. du Pont (b. 1939), heir to the vast chemical company fortune, whose own fortune was estimated to be $250 million. At times du Pont would appear to be affable and easygoing, and at other times he was harsh and dictatorial.

Du Pont began to develop a wrestling program on his sprawling estate in the 1980s, becoming the founder and head coach of the Team Foxcatcher Athletic Club, which sponsored programs in swimming, triathlon, modern pentathlon and wrestling, grooming the best candidates for Olympic appearances. He contributed hundreds of thousands of dollars to sponsor Olympic teams. Mark and David Schultz were two of the first wrestlers to join Team Foxcatcher. Both had been 1984 Olympic champions, with David winning a gold medal in his class. Du Pont spent more than $500,000 in establishing a wrestling center on the grounds of his estate.

On January 26, 1996, for no apparent reason, du Pont suddenly appeared before his trainer, David Shultz and his wife and shot the coach three times, killing him. He ran into his mansion and remained barricaded there for two days, while police tried to coax him into surrendering. He was captured when he emerged to fix his heating unit.

Charged with murder, du Pont was at first thought to be mentally incompetent. He claimed at different times to be the Dalai Lama and Jesus Christ. He said that he was "the last surviving heir of the ruling family of Russia." He told people that there were mechanical trees moving about on his property and trying to get into his mansion to steal his money. He said that Schultz had been "killed by Republicans because I didn't contribute [money] to them." While awaiting trial, du Pont told guards that "Bill Clinton will get me out of jail."

In September 1996, a judge ordered du Pont to the Norristown State Hospital to undergo observation in order to determine his competency to stand trial. Psychiatrists gave du Pont antipsychotic drugs to "clear his head" (of what was later described as paranoid schizophrenia) and he was later ruled competent to stand trial. Described by a prosecutor as "the wealthiest murder defendant in the history of the United States," du Pont sat passively through his three-week trial, his gray hair grown so long that it fell over his shoulders and spouting a bushy gray beard. He wore the same blue sweatshirt every day in court.

A twelve-member jury found du Pont guilty of third-degree murder on February 5, 1997, a verdict that stipulated he had acted without premeditated intent. On May 13, 1997, du Pont was sentenced to thirteen to thirty years in prison by Delaware County Court Judge Patricia Jenkins. He was to serve his time in a mental institution, or, if deemed mentally fit at any time during his sentence, to be removed to a prison to there serve out his sentence.

Millionaire John E. du Pont, beset by madness, shot and killed Olympic wrestler David Schultz, on his estate outside Philadelphia in 1996.

In 2002, the National Law Journal reported that a wrongful death suit brought against the du Pont estate by Nancy Schultz, was settled for an estimated $35 million. This was one of the largest awards ever bestowed upon an individual in wrongful death suits.

No one ever explained the motive for du Pont's strange murder of Schultz. Mental illness overtook him in 1988, one report held, after his mother died. He then allegedly began to use large quantities of cocaine and walked about his estate heavily armed. Prosecutors claimed that the millionaire killed his wrestling coach simply because he was jealous of Schultz's standing in worldwide wrestling competition. Others suggested a more sinister motive, that du Pont, who had been briefly married, was a latent homosexual and that he was incensed when Schultz rudely rebuffed his sexual advances, spurring him to shoot a reluctant lover.

In 1988, Andre Metzger, a coach at Villanova University, filed a complaint against du Pont, in which he accused the millionaire of making sexual advances toward him. Little evidence points to this claim and Metzger, at the time of the Schultz shooting, refused to make any comment.

THE HARTMAN SUICIDE-MURDER/ May 28, 1998

The life of Canadian-born comedian Phil Hartman (1948-1998) was seemingly crowded with blessings. Only days before he was shot to death by his wife Brynn (Vicki Jo Omdahl, 1958-1998) on May 28, 1998, in their comfortable Encino, California, home, the comedian, who had been a fixture on *Saturday Night Live* and other comedy TV shows, stated, "In the overall spectrum of human careers, I have what is, I'm sure, in the top 1 percent of the world's most fun jobs. I've made money beyond my wildest dreams. I have every toy I've ever wanted, I have a beautiful home, plus all the important things, the wife and two perfect kids. I've got every reason to be happy."

His wife, Brynn Hartman, an attractive, stately blonde, was not happy. Born in Thief River Falls, Minnesota, she had married young to Douglas Tourfin, moving to Arizona, where they both worked for the Bell Telephone Company. Brynn moved to California to become a model and worked at that profession, changing her name to Brynn. By that time, she was divorced and met comedian Phil Hartman, marrying him on November 25, 1987. They lived in New York for eight years, where Hartman became a fixture on the "Saturday Night Live" TV comedy show.

Then the Hartmans moved to California to raise their two children, Sean and Birgen in a comfortable ranch style home in Encino at 5065 Encino Avenue. While Brynn had ambitions to become an actress and a screenwriter, she remained a housewife, a role she did not envy. Moreover, she reportedly became intensely jealous of her husband's success, fame and popularity. The handsome Hartman, who had been married three times, was attractive to many women and Brynn often exploded, becoming hysterical whenever other women paid attention to her amiable husband. She was particularly spiteful toward Hartman's second wife, Lisa Jarvis, who had remained friendly toward the comedian following their divorce.

Steve Small, the attorney who handled that divorce, later stated that Brynn "had trouble controlling her anger. She got attention by losing her temper." He pointed out that the couple separated more than once over bitter squabbles and that "Phil had to restrain her at times."

Brynn's composure began to crumble after she increased her drinking and cocaine use, although the couple continued to appear at public affairs where they were described as "an adoring couple." Hartman, however, by 1998, had resolved to end the marriage, believing that he could not remedy the problems between Brynn and himself. It was also rumored that he had become interested in another woman and when Brynn suspected this clandestine relationship, she planned her husband's murder.

On May 28, 1998, Brynn Hartman went drinking with a friend, staying at the stylish Buca di Bepo restaurant on Ventura Boulevard and she did not return home until about 2 a.m. She found her husband sleeping in bed. Brynn then took a Smith and Wesson revolver from her purse—she had reportedly been carrying the weapon all night—when she went into the bedroom. Phil Hartman was asleep on their king-sized bed, wearing a purple T-shirt and boxer shorts with cartoon Dachshunds on them. Calmly, Brynn placed the muzzle of the revolver to her husband's head and fired a bullet into his forehead. She then shot him twice more, in the neck and forearm, the last shot proving fatal.

With her two children still sleeping in the house, Brynn went to a neighbor's home, waking up Ron Douglas, saying to him: "I shot Phil." She seemed dazed and soon fell asleep on a couch. Douglas did not initially believe her, but he searched her purse and found the revolver. Brynn woke up three hours later and took Douglas to her home, where she showed him her husband's body. Douglas immediately called 911, telling police: "Yeah, hi...I think there's been a shooting here. She came to my house and she was drunk. She said that she had killed her husband and I didn't believe her."

Police arrived at 6:20 a.m., and while they were escorting the two Hartman children from the house, Brynn locked herself in the master bedroom with the corpse of her husband. Officers tried to talk the woman from the room, but she was in hysterics, screaming incoherently. They then tried to distract her, but that did not work either. Finally, they heard a single shot explode and they broke down the door to find Brynn Hartman sprawled in a two-piece pajama outfit, next to the body of her husband. She had used a second gun (both were legal and had been purchased by Hartman to provide the household with protection) to end her life by putting the muzzle of the revolver into her mouth and pulling the trigger. One unsubstantiated report held that Brynn Hartman had become distraught that night when she read a note from her husband that suggested they end their marriage. A coroner's inquest later determined that Brynn Hartman had that night consumed considerable quantities of alcohol, cocaine and an antidepressant, Zoloft (her family members later sued the drug firm making Zoloft).

According to Phil Hartman's will, the bodies of Phil and Brynn Hartman were cremated at Forest Lawn Glendale and their ashes were reportedly scattered all over picturesque Catalina Island.

Many Hollywood friends and associates had much to say about the shocking suicide-murder of the Hartmans. "They fought a lot," said Cassandra Peterson, the voluptuous Elvira, Mistress of the Dark. "[She was] a very troubled person. I tried to talk Phil out of marrying her in 1987. She put a serious damper on our friendship."

The death of Phil Hartman shook the Hollywood community. He was a personable, well-loved comedian, a master mimic who expertly impersonated more than seventy public figures, among them President Clinton, Ed McMahon, Frank Sinatra, and Jimmy Swaggart. Like many other stars of "Saturday Night Live," including Dan Aykroyd and John Candy, Hartman was a Canadian, born in Brantford, Ontario. He worked in graphic design before choosing the world of comedy as his vocation. Many Hollywood reporters felt that Hartman's death was part of the so-called "Saturday Night Curse," recalling the premature deaths of John Belushi and Chris Farley from drug overdoses, and Gilda Radner and Danitra Vance, who both died of cancer at early ages.

Brynn Hartman, shown with her husband Phil Hartman, a comedic superstar in film and TV, murdered her spouse in 1998, after a night of drinking and drug-taking, then ended her own life.

CHAPTER TEN:

MURDER/MASS MURDER

Unlike the serial killer (see Serial Killers, this chapter), who stalks his or her prey over extended periods of time—months, years, sometimes decades—the mass murderer kills in one fell swoop, and is one who often acts on irrational impulse, or is driven to rage through the influence of drugs or alcohol. There are no set numbers of victims that qualify for a mass murder, although more than one victim is considered justifiable for such categorization. The term is applied to those who are killed in numbers at the same time, murders that take place within the framework of a short period, usually within minutes or hours of a given day.

Such wholesale killings prove to be the most shocking in the public view in that the loss of life is estimated by quantity which is easily equated with slaughter or massacre. The Indian massacres of the Old West, the so-called Fort Pillow "Massacre" of April 12, 1864 during the American Civil War, the massacres committed by troops on both sides during many wars rightly belong in the category of war crimes.

Vlad Tepes, the bloodthirsty ruler of Walachia (Romania), who committed many mass murders in the 15th Century.

It is the killing of a number of non-combatants—innocent victims—in a short period of time that truly constitutes the act of mass murder and there are thousands of such recorded events which span the troubled centuries of mankind. One of the earliest mass murderers was the savage king, Vlad Tepes (Basarab; AKA: Vlad the Impaler, prom. 1456-1462, 1476-1477), who excelled his father, Vlad Dracul, in practicing extreme cruelty in his kingdom of Walachia (later Romania).

Like all mass murderers or serial killers, the Walachian ruler had an enormous capacity for evil and sadistic cruelty. Vlad Tepes' castle, high in the Carpathian Mountains of Transylvania, later inspired novelist Bram Stoker for the location of the castle of his infamous fictional monster, profiled in the book, *Dracula*. Stoker drew from the lives of both Vlad Dracul and Vlad Tepes to create his frightening character, but most of his research is based on Vlad Tepes, also known as Vlad the Impaler.

Vlad Tepes impaled his enemies on high spikes, reportedly murdering 50,000 victims in this fashion, hundreds, if not thousands at the same time. This monster dined amidst victims impaled on spikes, reveling in their dying agonies. It was also said that he drank the blood of these hapless persons, thus giving rise to Stoker's tale of a blood-drinking vampire, who survived on the blood of the living. Vlad Tepes was a

Bela Lugosi, as Bram Stoker's horrific vampire, in the 1931 film, *Dracula*, a character based upon Vlad Tepes.

Mass murderer Edward Morgan, who slaughtered his relatives in Wales in 1756, then tried to hide his crime through arson.

hopeless pervert who enjoyed the pain of others, reserving his special wrath for Saxon invaders and Turkish merchants. He impaled the Saxons and tortured the Turks by having their turbans nailed to their heads.

Though feared as a bloodlusting maniac by foreigners, Vlad Tepes was considered a hero by his own people, a great warrior, who finally rid Walachia of foreign invaders. Historically he is remembered, thanks to novelist Stoker, as an inhuman beast whose lethal reputation conjured up images of undead spirits and bloodsucking vampire bats. In this gruesome image, Stoker was not far from the truth.

The living nightmare of Vlad Tepes was translated into evil dreams that plagued others who slew by the numbers. Superstition, the concept of a lurking Devil, often impelled deluded souls to mass murder. One such demented soul was Edward Morgan, whose routine visit to Welsh relatives ended in bloody disaster. According to Welsh custom, the Christmas feast was open to all visitors. In 1756, Edward Morgan was invited to share in the celebration at his cousin's farmhouse in Lanvabon. Rees Morgan's hospitality led to his death.

On Christmas night, Morgan retired to his bedroom with another house guest. In the middle of the night, Morgan awoke and decided to commit wholesale murder. He would later say that the devil commanded him to kill the family. Morgan found a knife. He first attacked his roommate, then went to his cousins' bedroom and slit their throats from ear to ear. Next he stabbed the couple's young daughter, then set fire to the barn, the stable, and the farmhouse to cover his tracks.

The blaze leveled the three buildings, leading authorities to believe that the entire Morgan family died in the fire. Morgan, however, failed to murder the young apprentice who shared a room with him that night. Based on his testimony, and Morgan's eventual confession, Morgan was convicted and hanged at Glamorgan on April 6, 1757.

THE RATCLIFF HIGHWAY MURDERS/ December 1811

During the early 1800s, the separate slayings of two families in the East End of London came to be known as "The Ratcliff Highway Murders." The crimes shocked and terrified all of England and were eclipsed only by the Jack the Ripper killings, which began in 1888.

Timothy Marr operated a hosier's shop on Ratcliff Highway and lived there with his wife, Cecilia, their infant daughter, an apprentice, John Goen, thirteen, and a maid, 18-year-old Margaret Jewell. On December 7, 1811, as Marr and Goen were closing up the store shortly before midnight, Jewell was sent out to buy some oysters and was told that the door would be left open for her. When she returned about twenty minutes later, the house was locked and quiet.

Jewell rang and knocked at the door, but no one answered. When neighbors arrived and entered the house, they found the entire family slain. Timothy Marr was lying behind the counter, Cecilia Marr was found in the doorway between the back room and the store, and the apprentice, Goen, was at the bottom of the stairs. The killer had battered their heads and slashed their throats. The infant's throat had also been cut.

Although the killer may have stolen some pocket change or small items, nothing valuable was taken. He apparently had been looking upstairs when he heard Jewell at the door and fled through the back door. A ship's carpenter's maul and a sledgehammer with the initials J.P. on the handle were found.

The residence and shop of Timothy Marr, where he and three others were slain on the night of December 7, 1811.

Londoners were stunned when they learned of the mass murders, and the entire country, especially the Birmingham region, was gripped with fear. People became cautious, and many equipped their homes with sturdy bolts and chain locks. Door-to-door searches were conducted in the Shadwell area, where many tramps were arrested, and rewards were offered for the killer's capture.

On December 19, 1811 the killer struck again at the King's Arms, a pub on Old Gravel Lane, a road that intersected Ratcliff Highway. The pub was operated by an old man named Williamson, who resided there with his wife; their grandchild; 14-year-old Kitty Stillwell; a maid, 50-year-old Bridget Harrington; and a journeyman carpenter John Turner. Williamson customarily closed the pub and the house door at 11 p.m. He usually left the pub's front door open until 12 a.m. for anyone who wanted a late-night drink.

Turner arrived home shortly before 11 p.m., and, exhausted from work, immediately went to his second-floor room and fell asleep. Sometime after 11 p.m. the killer entered the King's Arms and first attacked Harrington, who was setting up the fire for the next morning. When Williamson's wife entered the room, he attacked her as well. He cut both women's throats, nearly severing Harrington's head, and then killed Williamson, who had just returned from the cellar.

At 11:25 p.m., Turner was awakened by the slamming of the outside door. He went downstairs, where he saw "a tall man in a loose, shaggy coat" inside the parlor. The killer, whose back was to Turner, was hovering over a body and going through the pockets. When the killer stood up and walked away, Turner heard his boots creak. Undetected by the intruder, Turner slipped back up to his bedroom, tied some sheets together, and climbed out his window. He alerted neighbors, who broke into the house. The killer broke a window at the back of the house and escaped. Kitty Stillwell had escaped injury.

The Williamson slayings caused even greater panic. Notices were circulated, emphasizing the initials, J.P., found on the sledgehammer left at the first murder scene. A man who ran an area pub and inn called the Pear Tree, named Vermiloe, saw the flyers and thought the weapon might belong to a Nordic seaman, John Petersen, who had lodged at his inn and stored a tool chest there. Vermiloe identified the maul as Petersen's, but Petersen, it was later proven, had been at sea during the murders.

Another Pear Tree lodger, Irishman John Williams, about twenty or thirty years old, became a suspect and was taken to the Shadwell police station for questioning. Williams had been seen going toward the King's Arms the night of the slayings and was known to have returned to the inn at about 1 a.m. on the nights of the murders. On the night of the King's Arms murders, he had asked two other lodgers to snuff out their candles and then gotten into bed in the dark.

Officials discovered that Williams' shoes and socks were muddy, and he had blood on his shirt, which he said had resulted from a fight. After the first murders, Williams had purchased a new pair of boots, which creaked. Additionally, Williams' coat pocket was stained with blood, as were a pair of his pants found in an outhouse. During questioning, Williams

A contemporary print shows carpenter John Turner escaping the stalking mass murderer at the King's Arms pub by dropping to the street from knotted sheets on the night of December 19, 1811.

John Williams, shown in death, a sketch drawn by Sir Thomas Lawrence, only minutes after Williams hanged himself in his prison cell.

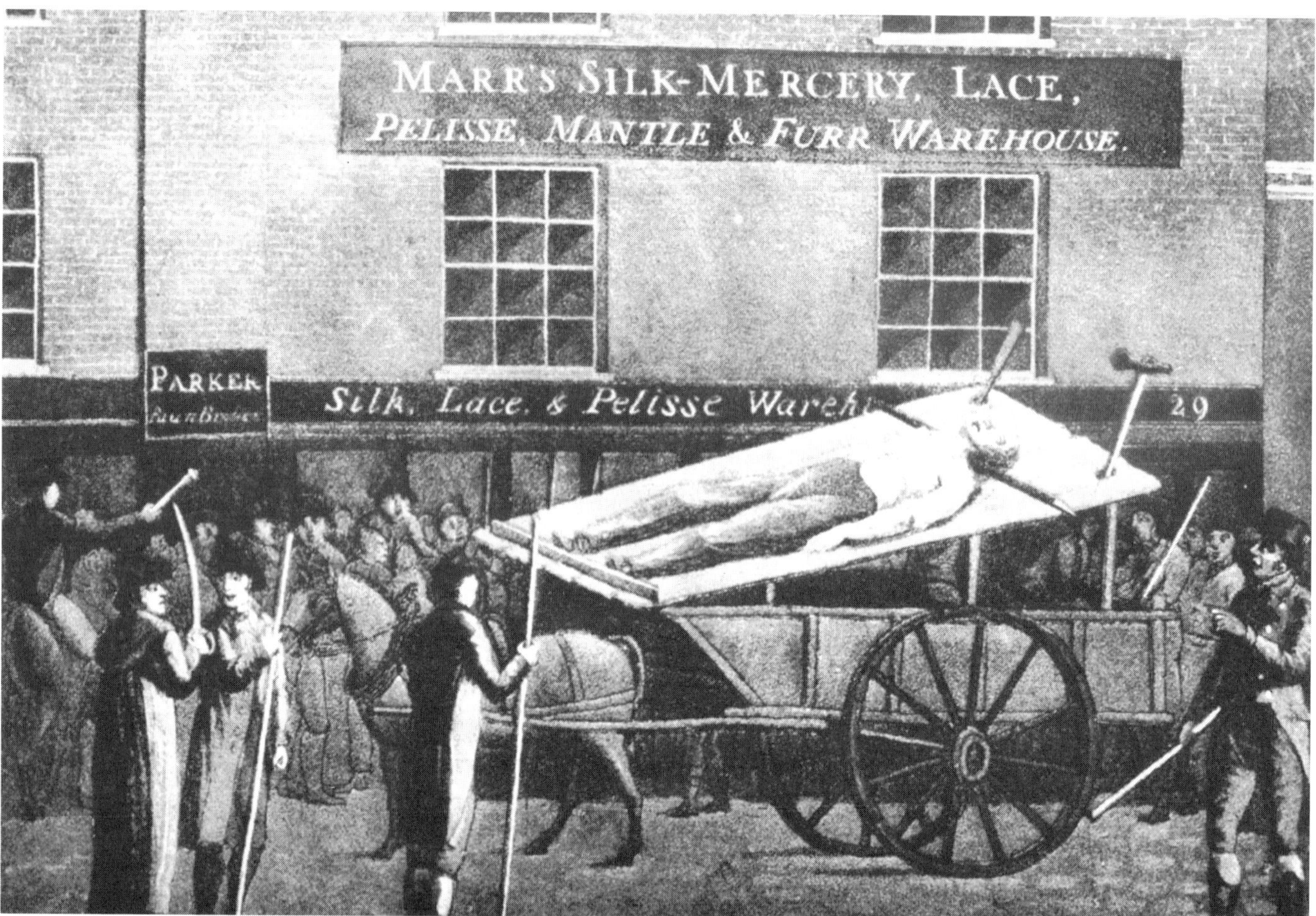

The half-naked body of John Williams, displayed on a cart, was taken to the scene of the first mass murders, the Marr shop, so convinced were authorities that Williams was the mass murderer.

admitted frequenting the King's Arms. He was arrested and taken to the New Prison at Coldbath Fields.

On December 28, 1811, Williams hanged himself in his prison cell. His corpse was placed on a cart and taken to the scene of the crime. On December 31, 1811, his body was taken to the intersection of New Road and Cannon Street, and a stake was driven through his heart before burial. About five or six weeks later, a knife covered with dried blood was discovered in Williams' former room at the Pear Tree. The weapon had been hidden in the floor of the room in a mouse hole. Although Williams was never tried, and the evidence in the case was primarily circumstantial, the slayings stopped after his arrest and officials conveniently concluded that Williams had been the killer in the Ratcliff Highway Murders. In 1849, Williams' remains were disinterred and reburied because of street repairs.

Within hours of Williams' death, Sir Thomas Lawrence made a watercolor portrait of him, showing light blue eyes and blond hair, although according to other reports, he had red hair. The case also captured the imagination of Thomas De Quincey (1785-1859), who wrote a dark, long essay entitled *On Murder, Considered as one of the Fine Arts,* published in 1827. In an appendix, he composed a descriptive piece recreating the mass murders.

"THE WORST MAN WHO EVER LIVED"/ March 16-17, 1860

On the misty morning of March 17, 1860, the sloop *E.A. Johnson* was found aimlessly drifting in the lower bay by the schooner *Telegraph.* Crew members of the *Telegraph* boarded the sloop and found no one on board. They did discover, however, evidence of widespread carnage: blood spattered on the ceiling, floor, table, and bunks in the ship's interior. Furniture was scattered and broken. Heel marks that seemed to be from a heavy body trailed from the cabin to a railing. The railing itself was coated with dark splotches of blood. Next to this spot, on the deck, were four neatly severed human fingers and a thumb.

After the tug *Ceres* towed the derelict *E.A. Johnson* to the Fulton Market slip, authorities released the story of the deserted vessel and its gory clues. The crew had obviously been killed and dumped overboard, but by whom? John Burke, who owned a boarding house on Cedar Street, and one of his boarders, Andrew Kelly, thought they had the answer. With fresh newspapers relating the strange story of the blood-soaked ship curled in their hands, these two men entered the police station commanded by Captain Weed and gushed out an accusation.

The shambles left in the cabin of the oyster sloop, *E. A. Johnson*, after a brutal killer had slain the captain and crew on March 16-17, 1860.

"Hicksey is your killer," one of them said. "Twenty-four hours before that ship was discovered, he was back in the house."

"He had a lot of money," the other put in, "but when we asked how he came by it, he talked of other things. Yes, Hicksey is your man."

The "Hicksey" the informants referred to was Albert E. Hicks (AKA: William Johnson; 1819-1860), known as Hicksey to a rare few. He had lived with his wife and child in Burke's boarding house and had inexplicably come into a large sum of money. Knowing his background, his acquaintances did little guessing as to how. A professional thief, pirate, and killer-for-hire, the large, middle-aged Hicks was a lone wolf, who sometimes, if the pay was promising, would join with one gang or another in raids for loot, but he owed no one his allegiance. This brutish but somewhat intelligent thug would fight with various gangs, sometimes on the side of the Daybreak Boys. On other occasions, he would stand with the Dead Rabbits. The highest bidder owned his knife hand.

Police had a long file on Hicks, one that told them he had run away from his home in Rhode Island, where his father had been a tenant farmer. As a teenager, he stole some money and was imprisoned. Hicks escaped twice and was recaptured and put into solitary confinement. Upon his release, Hicks, by then a broad-shouldered, towering man, hardened by long years of prison, signed on board a merchant ship and traveled around the Horn. He led a violent mutiny, which was suppressed. Hicks was flogged, tossed into the hold, and turned over to authorities, when the ship returned to port. Again, he was sent to prison. Released, Hicks pursued many criminal activities, mostly theft, while disguised as a peddler. Pickings were slim, so he again signed on board a ship, the ill-fated *E. A. Johnson,* using the alias, William Johnson.

Captain Weed selected his best patrolman, a man named Nevins, and ordered him to track Hicks down and take him into custody. Through tips, Nevins trailed the gangster to Providence and, with the aid of a local police squad, arrested him in a rooming house. (Nevins later stated that he found Hicks asleep in his room and that the sleeping suspect emitted "buckets of sweat.") Hicks and his wife and child were returned to New York. The thug was locked up in the Tombs, his hands manacled and his feet chained to a large stone block in the center of a cell. A police officer entered his cell shortly after Hicks had been chained, and held up a gold watch.

"Hicks," the officer said, "this was found in your room at Burke's place."

The thug stared at the watch which swung from a chain gripped in the officer's large hand. He said nothing.

"This watch belonged to the skipper of the *E. A. Johnson,* Captain Burr." The policeman next held out a daguerreotype of an attractive young woman. "This portrait was given to one of the two Watts boys, Oliver, by his sweetheart. This was also found in your room."

New York thug and mass murderer Albert E. Hicks, who called himself "the worst man who ever lived."

"I don't know what those things were doing in my room," Hicks growled. "I never saw those things a'fore."

"You shipped on that sloop under the name of William Johnson," the policeman said. "You then killed Captain Burr and Oliver and Smith Watts."

"My name ain't Johnson and I never been to sea on that ship."

"Oh yes you have, Hicks. And you're going to swing for it."

Hicks clenched his hands into fists and violently rattled his manacles, and with short kicks jangled his chains. He spat and cursed at the officer. He then remained silent. The questioning was brief. Officials knew Hicks' background and his reputation as being tight-lipped. They also concluded that he was violently insane. Hicks' brother, who had murdered several persons in recent years, had also been considered a lunatic and had been scheduled to die on the gallows, but had escaped and completely disappeared.

Circumstantial evidence was weighty in the Hicks trial held on May 18, 1860 in the U.S. Circuit Court before Judge Smalley. The pirate was found guilty of slaying the entire crew of the *E. A. Johnson.* Sentenced to die, Hicks suddenly decided to not only confess to this multiple killing but offer in a small-book form his biography, the proceeds of which were to keep his family "all snug." Mrs. Hicks, however, made it appear to prison warders that she had no intention of being "snug" from her husband's murder profits. When she first visited her husband in the Tombs, she held up her small child to the bars and screamed: "Look at your offspring, you rascal, and think what you have brought on us! If I could reach you, I'd tear your bloody heart out!"

"Why, my dear," Hicks replied in a quiet, soothing voice, "I've done nothing. It will be all out in a day or two." The murderer talked many times again with his wife, jailors hopelessly straining to hear their conversations. It was felt that Hicks had told his wife, where the loot from his many killings and robberies was hidden and that she eventually recovered this large amount of money.

The published confession was only a smoke screen to make it appear to authorities that Mrs. Hicks' newfound riches came by way of royalty payments for his book. These payments were paltry at best, but authorities did not learn this until much later, when Hicks had been executed and his wife moved on with her child to live out a life of relative ease. It was the last act of a scheming criminal who turned his own hanging into a plot to protect his ill-gotten fortunes.

New York's Five Points, in 1859, where Hicks and his fellow criminals operated and found a safe haven from police.

No doubt a reader of the more lurid press of the day, Hicks belched out a sensational tale of brutal killings, robberies, and licentiousness that encompassed several decades in New York's underworld. When speaking of the crime that had condemned him, Hicks insisted that he had been shanghaied. He had been drinking, he said, in one of the low dives along Cherry Street on the night of March 14, 1860. The owner was apparently unafraid of the terrible Hicks and slipped just enough laudanum in the thug's ale to knock him out (too much of this drug was fatal). Unconscious, Hicks was carted to the *E. A. Johnson,* he said, where Captain Burr threw him into the cabin. When he came to, Hicks was told to "get to work" and in a few hours found himself at the helm.

"I was steering," he told his publisher, "and Captain Burr and one of the Watts boys were asleep in the cabin. The other Watts was on lookout at the bow. Suddenly, the devil took possession of me and I determined to murder the captain and crew that very night."

Lashing the wheel to maintain course, Hicks grabbed a capstan bar and, on his hands and knees, crawled slowly toward the bow. Oliver Watts turned slightly when he noticed Hicks' shadow, but the hoodlum was quicker, leaping up and forward, crashing the bar down on the boy's head. Watts managed one scream before the blow sent him toppling to the deck. The noise had awakened the other brother, Smith, and he came running up from the cabin. Hicks waited for him with an ax, and as Watts emerged on deck, the killer took a swipe at him. "It was like chopping a small tree," gloated Hicks. "His whole head came off. The rest of him took a few steps, spouting blood like a fountain. Then it sagged down as the head rolled along the deck."

Peering into the dark cabin, Hicks leaned on the ax. He was looking for the heavyset Captain Burr. The thug took a step into the dark room and knocked over a chair. Burr awakened to see Hicks standing over him, his arms over his head, and the ax already descending. The captain moved slightly and the blow missed his head by inches, the ax thudding through the pillow and part of the wooden headrest of the bed. Rolling onto the floor, Burr took a moment to come to his senses. Hicks yanked his ax out of the wood and turned, rushing toward Burr, who also sprang forward from a crouch. Clasping the murderer's legs and driving forward, the captain was able to topple Hicks backward, but the thug obstinately clung to the ax.

Burr managed to crawl on top of the gangster and get his hands around Hicks' throat, but the killer worked his way into a roll and shoved the captain against the hot stove, stunning him. Hicks then jumped up, brought the ax down in one slashing chop, and drove it deep into Burr's skull. "The blow took away half of Burr's head...half of his eye was on the blade, a piece of his nose, some beard."

Tired from his grisly labors, Hicks went up on deck for some air. His chores were not completed, however, for Oliver Watts, whom he had attacked first, had only been knocked unconscious and was just then staggering to his feet. Hicks rushed over to him and hit him with the blunt end of his ax. He then lifted Watts to his shoulders and carried him to the rail. Again, the youth recovered and, just as Hicks was letting him over the side, Watts reached out and tenaciously clung to the rail. The gangster swore at him as he tried to pry the boy's fingers loose. Hicks then grabbed the ax and brought it down on one hand, cutting off Oliver Watts' four fingers and thumb,

The Bowery Boys and the Dead Rabbits are shown battling for control of the Five Points; Hicks fought with the Dead Rabbits.

which plopped to the deck. The youth slipped into the water and disappeared.

Such slaughter was work enough to tire any hearty man. Hicks paused to drink several tankards of ale which he filched from the captain's stores. It tasted strange, and while pouring himself a fourth drink, he finally noticed in the dim light that the tankard was coated with blood, human gore that had dripped from his own hands. He threw the tankard overboard and then tossed the bodies of Smith Watts and Captain Burr in after it. He almost forgot the decapitated head of Smith Watts and had some difficulty locating it. This, too, he hurled into the water. Rifling the lockers of the captain and crew, Hicks took all the valuables on board the sloop, including Burr's watch and the picture Oliver Watts kept over his bunk.

It was almost dawn when Hicks made out the coastline of Staten Island. He steered for it in the fog and when he neared land, he lowered a small lifeboat and rowed for shore, setting an open-sea course for the *E. A. Johnson.* The tides, however, caused the sloop to drift in the wrong direction, and the *Telegraph* spotted it before it disappeared. By then, Hicks had reached land and gone home, where he made the mistake of paying his rent and several other bills the moment he walked into Burke's boarding house. He ostentatiously withdrew the money from Burr's sea bag. The suspicious Burke and another roomer, Kelly, later went to police when the mystery of the *E. A. Johnson* was publicized.

Death by hanging was to be meted out to Hicks on July 13, 1860. It was a Friday. "That date and day have never held good for me," Hicks complained to the dozens of curious spectators, who came to gape at him through the bars of his cell, the horribly vivid details of his crimes gouged into their imaginations by his widely published memoirs. Among the many notables visiting Hicks was the irrepressible Phineas T. Barnum, who was always on the lookout for curiosities with which to enliven his museum. Barnum wanted a death mask and the condemned man's clothing to display in his building, but he was wary of dickering with the money-grubbing Hicks. Instead, he bartered with Warden Charles Sutton.

Showman and jailor haggled in the corridor outside of Hicks' cell, while the killer silently glared at them. For $25 cash, Sutton agreed to turn over Hicks' clothing to Barnum, a death mask to be thrown in for free. When Hicks protested, Barnum promised to send him two boxes "of the finest cigars." They were delivered some hours later, and Hicks happily puffed on these until the time he met his doom. The killer was less enchanted with the suit of clothes Barnum sent to replace Hicks' "murder suit."

"This suit I got in exchange for my own," Hicks complained to Sutton, "is shoddy." Oddly, with no thought to the waiting rope, he added bitterly: "It won't last." (Barnum later had a sinister-looking wax effigy made of the mass murderer, which was exhibited at his museum for decades and was catalogued thusly: Hicks - "No. 74. Life-Size Model of Albert E. Hicks, the murderer of the crew of the oyster-smack. *E. A. Johnson,* on or about March 18, 1860, attired in the very clothes worn by him when he butchered his victims with an ax. Note dark stains on jacket. The face was modeled from a plaster cast made by P.T. Barnum, of the Greatest Show on Earth, a fortnight before Hicks was hanged. Acknowledged to be a wonderful likeness of the infamous pirate.")

Sutton, hearing that the hanging was to be a gala event, decided that his star Tombs boarder should be more presentable and prevailed upon officials to provide better clothing. The day before Hicks was to hang, he was given a suit of blue cottonade with gilt buttons and needlework anchors. It pleased Hicks enormously. "I look like an admiral," he beamed.

At 5:30 p.m. on Thursday, July 12, 1860, Mrs. Hicks was shown into her husband's cell. He was free of his chains and wearing his new suit. He shook her hand briskly and then kissed her twice, murmuring each time, "Goodbye, goodbye." The woman showed no emotion whatever and only a faint smile played about the killer's lips when she departed.

True or not, Hicks manifested a spiritual change during the last hours of his life and prayed with Father Duranquet until midnight when he told the priest he was tired. He flopped onto

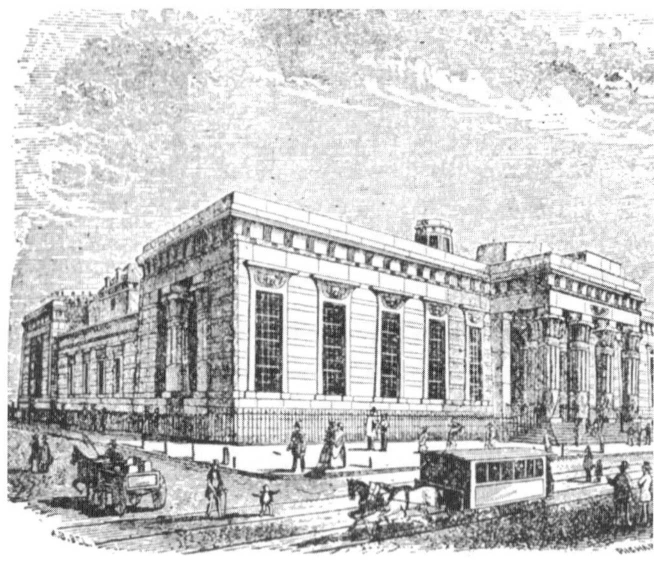

New York's old Tombs prison, where Hicks awaited execution.

Entrepreneur and showman Phineas Taylor Barnum, shown at the time he haggled with jailors for Hick's clothing and death mask, which he later displayed at his museum.

his bunk and was soon sound asleep. Guards had to shake him awake at 3 a.m. He then renewed his prayers, pronouncing his words loudly, as if he wanted his jailors to overhear his devotions.

A large breakfast was brought to Hicks and not only did he devour the eggs, bacon, and bread, washing it down with several cups of tea, but asked for more. Another meal was brought, and he finished it. He then methodically washed his face and hands, put on a clean shirt and his new sailor's suit. He brushed the dust from his shoes with a rag, saying with a grin: "Hicksey should look his best this day. My, my, won't New York be proud!"

Hicks was preening himself when the jailors opened his cell door at 6 a.m. It was time, they told him. He stepped into the corridor and signaled to a janitor who mopped out the cells: "Take what you find in there," he told the man and then quizzically looked at his jailors.

"How do you feel, Hicks?" a guard named Clackner asked.

"I feel very well," the killer responded.

Another guard reminded Hicks that Barnum wanted the empty cigar boxes, which he would also place on display with other Hicks memorabilia. Hicks jammed the last cigar into his mouth and pointed to his cell. "Under the bed...That man overlooks nothing."

Suddenly, Hicks leaned forward and firmly grasped the lapel of Officer Dugan. Looking the guard straight in the eyes, the murderer gritted: "I am the worst man who ever lived!"

Dugan gently removed Hicks' hand.

"You don't seem to think I mean what I say, Dugan."

"Yes," Dugan replied solemnly, "I believe you would not say what was not true when so near your end."

Then, they walked down to the main corridor. Awaiting them was a large group of officials headed, ironically enough, by U.S. marshal, Isaiah Rynders. Captain Rynders had for some twenty years been the political boss of the Sixth ward, and a Tammany stalwart and mentor and financial backer to dozens of New York's super criminals. Unknown to all but two present on the day of the execution, Rynders had employed Hicks on several occasions. The hooligan had handled the more unsavory jobs in the dark doings of Isaiah Rynders.

Hicks smiled when he saw Rynders, but before he could speak, the calculating politician and U.S. marshal, wearing a long, clanking sword especially for the affair, stepped forward and unraveled a long scroll, stating in stentorian tones: "Albert E. Hicks, it is now my painful duty to read to you in the presence of these officers of the law, the warrant of execution which I have received from the President of the United States." The killer was still smiling at his sometimes employer as Rynders read the document, ending with: "This is my authority for now carrying out the sentence of the law. The prisoner will prepare to depart."

Rynders, Sheriff Kelly, Father Duranquet, and Hicks then left the Tombs and got into a carriage. Several other carriages carrying dozens of guards formed the procession to the foot of Canal Street. On the way, Rynders devilishly stared at Hicks, who returned his gaze. The marshal inquired: "And what do you think the future holds for you, Mr. Hicks?"

Hicks squinted at his one-time employer, who showed no trace of apprehension that his former thug for hire would reveal their dealings. The killer mouthed his words carefully: "That is a matter I would rather leave to Father Duranquet."

A huge throng was gathered on Canal Street next to the dock. Frantic members of this curious mob pushed away the guards, and, to get a better glimpse of Hicks, smashed the carriage windows and tore away the curtains. The killer gave them his most derisive smile. Rynders and his guards shoved their way through the crowd, their prisoner in tow, and boarded the already jammed *Red Jacket,* a ship chartered by U.S. authorities to take the execution party to Bedloe's Island, where Hicks was to be hanged in full view of the harbor.

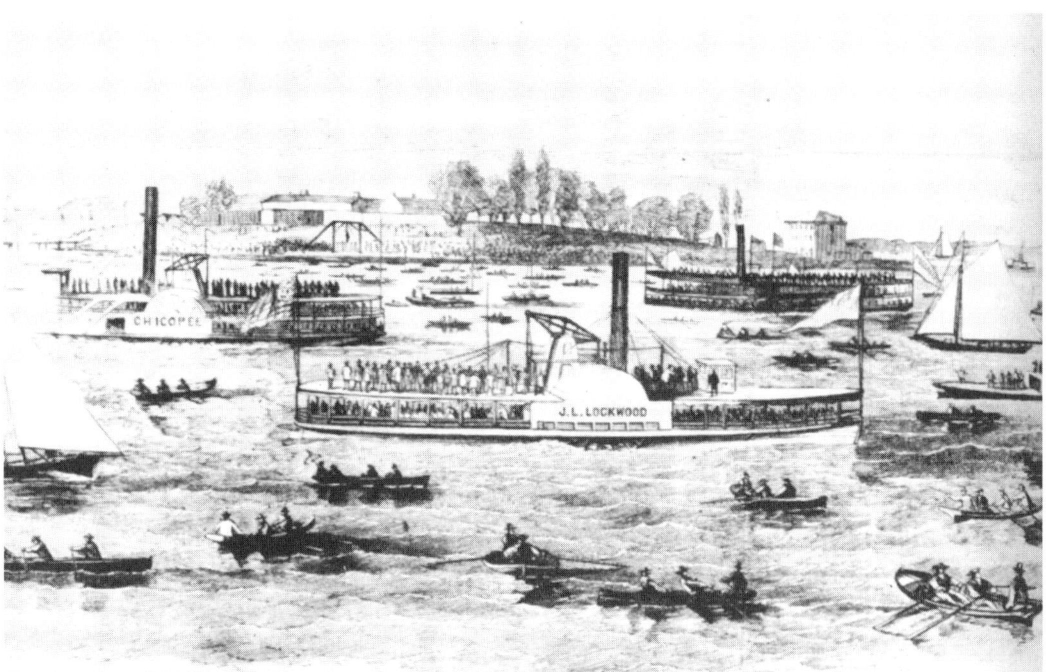

Thousands of excursionists are shown sailing in every type of vessel near Bedloe's Island, New York, to watch the hanging of Albert E. Hicks on July 13, 1860.

The killer was taken to the ladies' cabin and there held court, conversing calmly with many reputable and famous people, who wished to talk with "the worst man in the world." Hicks seemed to enjoy it all, smiling at his visitors and acting as if he were merely on a pleasant outing.

Once on Bedloe's Island, the killer was led to a scaffold, which was promptly surrounded by 200 marines. These troops formed a hollow square around the gallows. The harbor was full of tooting vessels, thousands of spectators lining the rails. All of these gapers had paid large sums to ships' captains for the privilege of witnessing the execution. Huge ships like the *Harriet Lane* and the *Great Eastern* joined the procession of bobbing vessels. The multiple decks of the *Lockwood* and the *Chicopee,* giant side-wheelers, were crammed with people. As an act of either grim irony or strange vengeance, the *E. A. Johnson,* on whose decks the blood of Hicks' victims had been spilled, had been ordered drawn up close to the island. It had been freshly painted, and Hicks was placed on the scaffold so that he could not help but see the vessel.

More than 10,000 shouting persons coated the small island and the floating ships nearby. It was an unreal scene of civilized bedlam. A reporter for the New York *Times* stood near the scaffold, which had been purposely erected on a knoll to afford a good view of the execution. The newsman took in the cacophonous spectacle, and scribbled: "Steamboats, barges, oyster sloops, yachts and rowboats swarmed everywhere in view of the gallows. Large steamers such as carry hundreds of people away on pleasure excursions were there, so laden with a living freight of curious people, that it seemed almost a wonder that they did not sink.

"There were barges there with awnings spread, under which those who were thirsty imbibed lager beer. There were rowboats with ladies no, females of some sort in them, shielding their complexions from the sun with their parasols, while from beneath the fringe and the tassels they viewed the dying agonies of the choking murderer." The ships were decked out with colored bunting, and colored flags snapped in the wind. The incessant crowd roared: "Down in front!...Get out of the way!"

On the scaffold, Hicks turned to Rynders and was heard to utter: "This is your show, isn't it, Marshal Rynders?" The remark was thought insignificant at the time, but it was later pointed out that Rynders reaped a fortune from the circus; he had issued tickets for the execution and those thousands in attendance had unwittingly purchased these from his private agents. His own man, Hicks, would perform one last service up to the moment of his death, once again lining his former employer's pockets.

The executioner, George Isaacs, came forward and placed the rope around Hicks' neck. "Mr. Isaacs," Hicks said sternly, "hang me quick, make haste!" Isaacs stalled for more time after getting a signal from Rynders, who obviously wanted the event to drag out for the edification of the spectators.

The roar of the crowd to "Stand away in front!" became deafening, and the troops, fearing a riot, moved to one side of the square so that the view from the water was better. Hicks had had enough. He jerked his head violently in the direction of Rynders, and the marshal, displaying his only signs of nervousness, perhaps thinking his one-time bully boy was about to reveal their sinister relationship, hurriedly motioned Isaacs to get on with his work.

At the drop of an arm, Isaacs cut the rope and Hicks was hanged. A thunderous din of approval went up from the throng at that moment, and cheers went on unabated for six minutes. Then, a hush fell over the crowd as doctors Woodward and

Guilmette approached the body. They determined that Hicks' third cervical vertebrae had been broken almost at once when the rope had jerked him upward. They then examined his heart. A repeated shout rippled through the crowd on land and above those gathered on the tightly-packed ships: "They found pulsations! He still lives!" And then thousands began to chant in mass hysteria: "Hang him some more...hang him some more!" The body was left to hang another twenty-eight minutes, allowing those visitors who had brought their lunch to eat in a leisurely fashion. At 11:45 a.m., Hicks' corpse was taken down and placed in a wooden box, which was carried to the tug, *Only Son*. The tug moved off to the dock of the customs house, while boat whistles whined and horns blared, signaling the end of the "grand" celebration.

Mrs. Hicks waited for her husband's body in vain. Rynders had purposely misinformed her as to the eventual whereabouts of the corpse. She sat alone on the wrong dock for hours, while officials quickly buried her husband in Calvary Cemetery without her knowledge. In a few days, the body of the mass killer and terror of New York disappeared altogether. Ghouls, it appeared, had dug up the corpse and made away with it. In reality, Isaiah Rynders had turned yet another profit on his dutifully silent protégé, Albert E. Hicks. Rynders had sold Hicks' body to medical students for dissection.

A HANDYMAN'S HANDIWORK/ April 25, 1866

Antoine (or Anton) Probst, a German immigrant, arrived in America during the Civil War. When learning that the Federal Army would pay enlistees to fight for the Union, Probst promptly volunteered. He had no intention, however, of serving in the front lines. Instead, he turned his loudly demonstrated patriotism into a business. He enlisted again and again for service in the Union Army, each time collecting a bounty of $300 with each enlistment.

After each enlistment, Probst would desert, thus becoming a professional "bounty jumper." By the end of the war he had spent all the money, so he first drifted about, committing petty thefts. Finally, he took a job as a handyman on the farm of Christopher Dearing outside Philadelphia. His laziness and his leering attitude toward Mrs. Dearing soon got him fired. Probst pretended illness and went to a charity hospital while he began to work out a plan for getting even with Dearing and for obtaining some money.

On March 2, 1866, Probst went back to Dearing, telling him that he had had a change of heart, that he believed that doing honest work was the best policy and he begged to have his job back. In a generous gesture, Dearing rehired Probst, and the man worked well for several weeks.

On April 25, 1866, the family left Probst at the farm while the Dearings traveled to Philadelphia to pick up a visitor. Probst began his revenge by hitting Cornelius Carey, a young farmhand, over the head with an axe. He beheaded the body and hid it in a haystack. When the Dearing family returned, he lured them into the barn, one at a time, where he systematically murdered Mrs. Dearing, four of the five children (the oldest was away on a visit), Mr. Dearing, and the visitor, Elizabeth Dolan. He arranged the bodies in a row sitting against the barn wall and covered them with hay.

Going into the house, Probst ransacked it for cash, finding a total of $13. Then he changed into some of Dearing's clothes, and, ironically living up to his new code of work ethics, dutifully fed the animals before leaving the farm. Neighbors found eight bodies a few days later. All of the victims had been killed with an ax, some of them partially dismembered, some of the body parts hidden beneath horse blankets and stacks of hay, as if the killer had decided to secret the gory remains and had then given up on the grisly chore. One report held that Probst "had too many bodies to hide and abandoned the idea of covering up the evidence."

Within five days, the police found Probst in Philadelphia. He was easily identified as wearing Dearing's clothes and some of the family's meager heirlooms were found on his person. Probst did not deny his mass murders, and merely shrugged when he was convicted and sentenced to death. He was hanged on June 8, 1866.

Handyman Antoine Probst, shown entering a barn with ax in hand before he slaughtered the entire Dearing family outside of Philadelphia in 1866.

This was not the end of Probst's story. Like his more infamous counterpart, Albert Hicks, Probst's body was much sought, not by P. T. Barnum, however, but by a host of physicians. "The doctors had a field day with his cadaver," said one account, "putting it through all kinds of tests, including one to test the theory that the retina of the eye of dying persons retains the last image seen." Probst's head and right arm were later exhibited in a New York museum of anatomy and science.

THE "BUSINESS" OF JEAN TROPPMANN/ 1869

It was rumored that the diabolical murders of Jean Kinck, his wife, and six children by the fiend, Jean-Baptiste Troppmann (1849-1870) were engineered by Otto von Bismarck, Germany's "Iron Chancellor," to undermine the government of Napolon III. Troppmann was the agent provocateur, according to one account, paid to do away with Kinck, a Prussian spy who had become an embarrassment to Bismarck. The story was dismissed out of hand when the true facts of the case came to light in late 1869.

Troppmann was born in Cernay (Haut-Rhin), west of Mulhouse. As a boy he was apprenticed to his father's manufacturing company, Troppmann and Kambly. In December 1868, the firm sold some heavy equipment to a Paris businessman and the son was sent to the city to supervise its installation. The young man made a good accounting of himself and was greatly admired for his thrift and ambition.

After the project was complete, Troppmann moved to Roubaix, where he made the acquaintance of Jean Kinck, an Alsatian businessman, who had risen from the status of common laborer to private entrepreneur and who successfully manufactured spindles and looms. The enterprising Kinck desired to resettle in Alsace, his ancestral home. He owned a house in Buhl, but had so far been unable to persuade his wife, a native of Roubaix, to agree to move. Troppmann exploited this gnawing ambition in Kinck, a man thirty years his senior. In time, the two became fast friends, discussing at length their ambitions to grow wealthy together in Alsace.

Kinck was convinced by Troppmann to map out a journey with him to Bollwiller, Alsace, where, presumably, they would set into motion their business plans. On August 24, 1869, Kinck left Roubaix, having told his wife that he would "be home between ten and eleven on the morning of September 2, 1869." He carried in his valise a number of blank checks issued by a bank in Roubaix. At the train station, Kinck was greeted by Troppmann, who escorted him to the village of Guebwiller by carriage. From there the trusting businessman fully expected to be taken to Bollwiller to meet some family members. But he was never seen again, at least by those family members who expected him for a visit.

Troppmann appeared in Cernay, about a dozen miles from Bollwiller, on August 25, 1869. He told of an important business contact he had made and of an impending transaction involving large amounts of money and bank-notes. Meanwhile, back in Roubaix, the anxious wife awaited some news of her husband. On August 27, she received a curious letter in Troppmann's handwriting.

Jean-Baptiste Troppmann, who murdered the Kinck family as part of his "business."

Kinck explained in the letter that he had met with an accident and was unable to hold a pen, but his young friend Troppmann was taking down his instructions. Hortense Kinck was directed to cash an enclosed check in the amount of 5,500 francs and remit the cash to her husband in Alsace. The money arrived at Guebwiller on the thirty-first, and, using Kinck's identification papers, Troppmann attempted to claim the money. A suspicious postmaster, however, refused to turn it over.

Troppmann devised a new strategy. He returned to Roubaix and presented a letter to Hortense Kinck, allegedly dictated to him by her husband, which read: "You must all of you come to Paris for two or three days. Don't fear the expense as Troppmann has given me a half a million. I insist on your coming. You, Gustave, must go at once to Guebwiller to draw out the money." The next day, Hortense Kinck received power of attorney and 500 francs as promised in the letter. The check, however, was in Troppmann's handwriting. The wife barely concealed her uneasiness about her husband's continuing disability, which prevented him from writing in his own hand, but she trusted Troppmann and followed his instructions to the letter.

Troppmann insisted that the family join him at the Hotel du Chemin de Fer du Nord in Paris, and to bring money. Troppmann's parents received several dispatches from their son, which alluded to a fabulous business transaction that was to make them all rich for the rest of their days. Puzzled, they simply waited. On September 17, 1869, Gustave Kinck met Troppmann at the railway station in Paris.

Two days later Hortense Kinck and her five children left Roubaix. Mrs. Kinck still had apprehensions, which she hoped would be diminished once she and her children were reunited with Jean Kinck. When Troppmann made his rendezvous with the Kinck family members, he told them that they must go with him by carriage to Pantin. He directed the driver to continue past several farms and fields to a secluded spot off the main road.

When the cab stopped, Troppmann, Madame Kinck, and the two youngest children made their way down a winding path toward a dark and silent building that stood nearby. The other three youngsters remained behind, talking with the driver. Half an hour later, and under the cover of darkness, Troppmann returned alone. "We have decided to stay the night here, children," he said. Thinking nothing more of it, the cabman received his fare and drove off. The following Monday morning, Troppmann returned to Paris to change into clean clothing in preparation for his journey to Le Havre, where he planned to set sail for America. His bloodstained clothes were carelessly left behind in the hotel. This mistake was to cost Troppmann his life.

The bodies of Hortense Kinck and her five children, Emile, Henri, Alfred, Achille, and Marie, were unearthed on September 20, 1869, by a farmer named Langlois, who reported his gruesome discovery to the police. Each of the victims had been bludgeoned over the head and there was evidence that the younger ones had been buried alive. The identity of Hortense Kinck and her children was quickly established by clothing labels.

In Le Havre the police quickly became suspicious of a young man shopping for immigration papers. The suspect was arrested and taken into custody after registering at two different hotels on successive nights. The man claimed to speak only German, but he was overheard conversing in French.

Placed under intense questioning, Troppmann said he was merely an accessory. Jean Kinck and his son Gustave had plotted the murders of Hortense and the five children. On September 26, 1869, a seventh body was pulled out of the Langlois field, that of Gustave Kinck who had been stabbed through the throat. When shown the grisly remains, Troppmann became indignant, saying: "The swine! He has now killed his remaining son." The police continued to interrogate Troppmann until he confessed his mass killings.

"I murdered the father," Troppmann admitted, "to get possession of the money, which he said he had in the bank and which would have been paid out to his order. That order I proposed to forge by copying his signature. Having murdered him, it was almost a matter of necessity to me to kill all the rest of the family, since they all knew that Kinck had gone with me to my home."

Jean Kinck (center foreground), with his wife and eldest son, all murdered by Jean-Baptiste Troppmann in 1869.

On November 25, 1869, what was left of Jean Kinck was found in a wooded glade outside the castle of Herinfluch, north of Cernay. Troppmann explained that he had poisoned Kinck in Alsace using prussic acid poured into a wine flask.

Following the discovery of the eighth and final body, an indictment charging Troppmann with theft, fraud, and murder was returned by the courts. The trial commenced at the Assize of the Seine on December 28, 1869. The gallery was packed with spectators from all strata of French society including politicians, artisans, and nobles. It was in many respects the gala social event of the year as people haggled for scarce tickets.

Troppmann was represented by the notable attorney Charles-Alexandre Lachaud, who attempted to portray his client as a weak, innocent knave who suffered from a diseased mind. Lachaud was a highly respected lawyer who had earned the admiration of leading political figures in the government. But the task before him proved too great.

For his part, Troppmann persisted in his assertion that he had accomplices, which gave rise to the theory that Prussian agents were behind the murders. Invasion of France was imminent, some said. Left-wing sympathizers accused the emperor of paying Troppmann to murder the Kinck family to divert public attention away from the sagging fortunes of the Second Empire. Both theories were nothing more than baseless conjecture.

Jean-Baptiste Troppmann was found guilty and executed at the Place de la Roquette on the morning of January 19,

1870, amidst solemn fanfare. The event was witnessed by scores of celebrities including the Russian writer Ivan Turgenev, who later wrote about Troppmann in one of his novels. Observing the curious solemnity of the day, Turgenev quoted a remark made by one of his friends: "It seemed to me as though we were in 1794 instead of 1870, as though we were not ordinary citizens escorting to the scaffold a common assassin, but Jacobins hurrying to his execution a [nobleman]."

"YOU'RE GOING TO HELL, BOY"/ November 10, 1904

On May 26, 1904, Adolph Weber (1884-1906), robbed the Bank of Placer County in Auburn, California. Dropping his gun during the robbery, 20-year-old Weber absconded with $5,000 and buried a five-pound can filled with $20 gold pieces in the back yard of his family's home. As evidence began to mount against Adolph, his father, Julius Weber, a wealthy, retired brewer, secured an out-of-court agreement to prevent the young man's prosecution.

In July 1904, the young Weber bought another pistol in a San Francisco pawn shop on Dupont Street from the shop owner, Henry Carr. The owner noted that Weber was accompanied by another youth, who purchased brass knuckles and a blackjack. Such items were openly sold in San Francisco and other towns, where a variety of weapons were ostensibly used for self-defense.

On November 10, 1904, the Weber home was consumed by fire. While the blaze continued, Adolph Weber suddenly appeared at a store in Auburn, where he purchased a new pair of trousers from a storeowner named Cohen. Weber quickly changed his trousers in the back room of the store and wrapped up the old ones, running from the store and back to his burning home. Here he was seen to break a window with his hand, throwing his old trousers into the flames. In breaking the window, Weber cut his hand so severely that he fainted from loss of blood and was taken to the home of Adrian Wills, where he was doctored and spent the night.

At the time of the fire, a neighbor broke down the door of the burning Weber home. He entered a room that had not been consumed by flames and here he found the bodies of Mrs. Weber and 18-year-old Bertha Weber. Both had been shot to death, their corpses apparently dragged into the room, where the killer had attempted to set fire to their clothes. Following the fire, the bodies of Julius Weber and Adolph's invalid brother Earl, who was 8-years-old, were also found. Earl Weber, officials discovered, had been beaten to death. Julius Weber, like his wife and daughter, had been shot to death.

While investigators were rummaging through the smoldering remains of the Weber house, Adolph Weber took up residence with his great aunt, a Mrs. Snowden. She questioned him about his miraculous survival from the burning building and getting no answers, suspiciously said: "I believe you know a great deal about what happened there."

Weber grew angry and snapped: "Your turn will come next!"

Mrs. Snowden reported this remark to the police, who, by then, had concluded that Weber was behind the fire. He was arrested and a coroner's inquest was held on November 12, 1904. At that time, part of Weber's old trousers had been retrieved from the ashes of the house and they proved to have bloodstains on them. Some days later, a .32-caliber pistol was found under the flooring of the barn at the rear of the Weber home. It was identified by San Francisco pawnbroker Henry Carr as the weapon he had sold to Weber five months earlier.

Adolph Weber, who murdered his entire family in Auburn, California, in 1904.

All the bullets had been fired from the pistol's chambers and on the handle was found clots of blood and some of Earl Weber's hair. On November 23, 1904, officers digging in the Weber yard found a large lard can containing $20 gold pieces, the proceeds from the bank robbery committed in Auburn. To four charges of murder, a charge of robbery was lodged against Adolph Weber.

Weber was brought to trial for murdering his mother on February 6, 1905. He was convicted on February 22, the jury recommending death. Throughout the trial, Weber said little and his attorneys found no evidence to establish his innocence. He was sentenced to death, but his attorneys filed several appeals and even obtained a stay of execution, while an insanity hearing was conducted. Determined to be sane, Weber was hanged on September 22, 1906. He went to the scaffold with the same stoic attitude he had displayed throughout his trial and imprisonment.

Before he was executed, an official visited Weber in his cell, confronting the young man with his crimes, and seeking a full confession. "Your family learned of your bank robbery, did they not?" asked the official.

Weber said nothing.

"You believed that they might later tell authorities about the robbery, did you not?"

Weber said nothing.

"To silence them and to also gain the family inheritance, which was substantial, you killed them, did you not?"

Again, Weber refused to answer, but the official thought he detected a thin smile on the youth's face.

"You murdered four people—your own family. You're going to hell, boy," the official announced and left the cell.

It was never learned from the tight-lipped Adolph Weber whether or not he had any concept of such a destination.

"HE FOUGHT LIKE A MAD WOLF"/ November 24, 1932

Explaining that he "felt funny in the head" at the time, Julian Marcelino (b. 1902) of Seattle decided to kill everyone in sight. Armed with a pair of crudely fashioned knives, the 30-year-old Filipino entered the Midway Hotel on November 24, 1932, which was centered in a skid row area. Marcelino was in

Julian Marcelino (standing right), who killed six people and wounded thirteen others in a murder rampage on the streets of Seattle, Washington in 1932; Marcelino is shown in a cell with five other murderers who are enjoying a game of cards.

a rage. He proceeded to the room of Pito Gualto, whom he had accused of stealing $300. Without warning, he stabbed Gualto in the heart and then wounded his nephew, Christolo Bayson.

"I was sitting in my room with my uncle when Marcelino came in," Bayson said. "They had been quarreling this morning about what I don't know...Marcelino said nothing. But he had that funny look. All of a sudden he pulled out his knife and stabbed my uncle."

Marcelino fled the hotel, running haywire down the crowded skid row streets. He stabbed grocer W. J. Morris on the sidewalk, and also an astonished bystander, who failed to get out of the way in time. He assaulted four more men, throwing the street into confusion as people scurried for cover.

The Seattle police arrived on the scene just as Marcelino was about to kill a Japanese man identified as L. Kitamura. Officer Gordon Jensen, driving home from a football game, helped subdue Marcelino.

"He fought like a mad wolf," Jensen recounted. "He had more than human strength." The seven-inch razor Marcelino used had been manufactured in the Philippines and was known to the local residents as a bolo. Sixth Avenue and Jackson Street resembled a combat zone as ambulances rushed fifteen people to nearby hospitals. The six murder victims were taken to the county morgue.

Julian Marcelino was led under heavy guard to the King County Jail. He was declared sane and tried for first-degree murder. Sentenced to life imprisonment, he entered Washington State Penitentiary on April 22, 1933. Three years later, on March 11, 1936, he was transferred to the Eastern State Hospital after examining psychiatrists declared him insane. Sixteen days later he was granted a conditional parole and deported to the Philippines.

It was later reported that Marcelino found work in Manila, and later joined the Philippine Scouts, an army unit that fought against invading Japanese during World War II. Marcelino survived the Bataan Death March in April 1942, escaping to the hills and, as a guerrilla, constantly attacked occupying Japanese forces. He was credited with killing scores of his nation's enemies. Following the war and the establishment of Philippine independence, Marcelino vanished.

THE KANSAS CITY MASSACRE/ June 17, 1933

Police photos of bank robber Frank "Jelly" Nash, who was in federal custody, when the Kansas City machine gunners attempted to free him at Union Station on June 17, 1933.

American gangsters had been slaughtering each other for more than a century in an effort to dominate the lucrative rackets of big cities, the most infamous of these bloodlettings being the 1929 St. Valentine's Day Massacre in Chicago, perpetrated by members of the Capone gang (see chapter on Gangs, Gangsters and Organized Crime). Found in the folklore of the Mafia is another broad-based underworld bloodletting, euphemistically called "the night of the Sicilian Vespers," when, on September 10, 1931, more than forty old-time Mafia leaders were summarily executed in several U.S. cities, including boss of bosses, Salvatore Maranzano, who had waged a prolonged underworld war in New York with Joe "The Boss" Masseria.

Killed in these mass murders were Maranzano stalwarts—called "Mustache Petes" by the young gangsters who sought to replace their authority—Samuel Monaco, Louis Russo and James Marino. The perpetrators of this slaughter included Charles "Lucky" Luciano, Albert Anastasia, Meyer Lansky, Benjamin "Bugsy" Siegel, Thomas Lucchese, Joe Adonis and other young turks, who quickly established the new U.S. crime syndicate over the bones of these old-time Mafia chiefs.

The Kansas City Massacre four years later is not to be confused with such organized crime slayings. The bloody slaughter occurring in Kansas City was at the hands of independent gunmen belonging to a loose federation of bank robbing gangs that plagued the Midwest in the early 1930s. This massacre was not inflicted by gangsters upon a rival gang, but on a bevy of lawmen attempting to take to prison one of the most notorious independent bank robbers of that era, Frank Nash, an exploit that mirrored the actions of Old West outlaws like Jesse James and the Dalton Brothers.

The plan to free Frank Nash from federal custody was impetuously hatched in Hot Springs, Arkansas, which was one of the "safe" cities for independent outlaws in the U.S. during the early 1930s. There high-rolling and much-wanted independent bank robbers, kidnappers, and members of organized crime moved about unmolested by local authorities. This pleasant southern city was one of many U.S. cities, including St. Paul, Minnesota, and Kansas City, Missouri, which catered to the needs and desires of American public enemies.

The politicians and police departments of these cities, for the most part, were heavily bribed by these outlaws. One of these, the notorious Frank "Jelly" Nash, had been robbing banks and trains since the days of Al Spencer. Spencer dated

Frank Nash's wife Frances, who asked underworld contacts to free her husband from custody, a decision that proved fatal to her errant spouse.

Gambler Dick Galatas, shown in custody with a female associate, got the "high sign" from Nash, when the bank robber was arrested by FBI men in Hot Springs, Arkansas; Galatas alerted underworld contacts to put in motion a bold plan to free Nash from his captors.

Kansas City's Boss Tom Pendergast (left), with his handpicked city manager, Henry F. McElroy; through these two men, Galatas made contact with Kansas City underworld boss Johnny Lazia, who, in turn, hired the gunmen to attack lawmen in an effort to free Frank Nash.

back to the turn of the century and had ridden on horseback with western outlaw Henry Starr. After Spencer was killed, his gang was captured, including Nash, Grover Durrell, Earl Thayer, and George Curtis. All four were tried and, on March 1, 1924, were given twenty-five-year sentences for train robbery and sent to the federal penitentiary at Leavenworth, Kansas.

Nash had escaped from Leavenworth in 1930 and, for more than three years, had robbed banks throughout the Midwest with Harvey Bailey, George "Machine Gun" Kelly, the Holden-Keating gang, and the Barker brothers. His underworld contacts were deep and wide and he had taken refuge in Hot Springs, Arkansas, when FBI agents began tracking him.

Ralph Colvin, FBI agent-in-charge of the office in Oklahoma City, Oklahoma, received a phone call from Hot Springs on June 15, 1933. An informant told Colvin that Nash was hanging about the White Front, a gambling den in Hot Springs run by Dick Galatas. Agents Joseph Lackey and Frank Smith were immediately sent to Hot Springs to arrest Nash. First, these two agents went to McAlester, Oklahoma, to see Police Chief Otto Reed, who had known Nash for decades and could recognize him on sight. They convinced Reed to accompany them to Hot Springs so he could identify the fugitive.

The FBI agents had another reason for having Chief Reed with them. By current law, all local arrests had to be made by local police before the FBI could assume jurisdiction. The police in Hot Springs, Lackey and Smith knew, were wholly corrupt. They could not trust Hot Springs chief of police Joseph Wakelin or chief of detectives Dutch Akers, whom they rightly believed were receiving bribes from Nash and others to protect, not arrest them.

On June 16, 1933, Lackey, Smith, and Reed drove to Central Avenue and parked across the street from the White Front Poolroom. At 11 a.m., a car came to a stop in front of the place and a man got out whom Reed believed to be Nash. "I'm not so sure," Smith said, squinting at the man, who sauntered into the White Front. "That guy has a mustache, is wearing glasses and has a full head of hair. Nash is bald."

Reed, however was positive. He and the agents went into the White Front. There was a bar area and a door to the back room, where the gambling hall was located. A bartender eyed the trio as they entered. One of the agents noticed a shotgun in a rack behind the bar. Although Prohibition was still enforced, customers could buy 3.2 beer in this bar. The three lawmen moved toward the back room door just as Frank Nash stepped through it holding a bottle of beer in his hands.

The two FBI agents grabbed Nash's arms as Chief Reed jammed a revolver in his back. "Come along, Nash," Agent Lackey said. Neither of the agents were armed. FBI men were not yet authorized to carry firearms and invariably relied on local lawmen to provide the necessary firepower when making arrests. The lawmen hustled Nash outside and into their car. Without returning to their hotel rooms to retrieve their luggage or contacting the Hot Springs police, they immediately headed out of the state, driving at high speeds.

Gambler Dick Galatas arrived at the White Front only

minutes after Nash was taken and called Dutch Akers, chief of detectives in Hot Springs, to ask what he knew. Akers told Galatas that he did not even know FBI agents had been in town, but he put out an alert for the car in which the agents and Nash had been seen, a Buick sedan with California license plates.

At that time, Nash and his captors were heading for Little Rock, Arkansas. Outside that town, a local sheriff, alerted by Akers, set up a roadblock. The Buick came in sight and the sheriff's posse leveled shotguns and rifles at the agents and Nash and ordered them to produce identification. They complied, but the sheriff gave them a hard time before letting them go. It appeared that the sheriff and his men were purposely delaying the FBI agents and Chief Reed from getting to their destination, Kansas City, Missouri.

Meanwhile, Dick Galatas was informed that the lawmen were taking Nash to Joplin, Missouri. He hired a plane and flew there with Nash's common-law wife, Frances Nichols Luce. In Joplin, Galatas contacted Herbert "Deafy" Farmer, who had served time with Nash in the Oklahoma State Prison in the early 1920s. Farmer was part of the underworld network used by the independent bank robbers of the day. He, in turn, tried to find the route the agents were taking back to Kansas City. Farmer knew that once Nash reached Kansas City, the gangster would be hustled back to Leavenworth. A hasty plan was put in motion to free Nash from the agents, regardless of cost. Nash had substantial sums from recent bank robberies and also had high-level contacts in Kansas City. He would gladly pay any price for his freedom, it was concluded. If he went behind bars again, Nash had repeatedly said to his associates, and at his present age of forty-five, he feared he would never come out.

On the afternoon of June 16, 1933, the FBI agents and Chief Reed, with Nash in tow, reached Fort Smith, Arkansas. It was 285 miles to Kansas City and after numerous stops by many local sheriffs and constables, at which times their papers were checked and rechecked by suspicious and uncooperative Arkansas police, the lawmen came to believe that they might never get out of the state alive. At least, that is what Frank Nash told them.

Nash also added cryptically that he himself might not survive the trip, a remark that later caused some to conclude that his underworld friends were really hunting *him* for some arcane reason. He had been wearing a red wig when arrested apparently to disguise himself from police as well as others. When the lawmen inside of the car removed Nash's red wig, he carped: "Hey, take it easy with that hairpiece. It cost me a couple of hundred bucks." The agents laughed and gave it back to him and Nash repositioned it on his head.

When the agents reached Fort Smith, Lackey called Ralph Colvin and told him they were having trouble getting Nash out of Arkansas. Colvin instructed Lackey to take Nash on to Kansas City by train, where he would arrange to have FBI agents there meet the train and escort Nash to Leavenworth. Colvin then called Reed E. Vetterli, the FBI agent in charge of Kansas City, and told him that Lackey, Smith, and Reed would be arriving at Union Station in Kansas City on the Union Pacific train at 7:15 a.m. Colvin instructed Vetterli to meet the agents when they arrived. Vetterli, in turn, called the Kansas City Police Department and informed them of Nash's arrival, requesting local officers to join him and others when they met the Nash party.

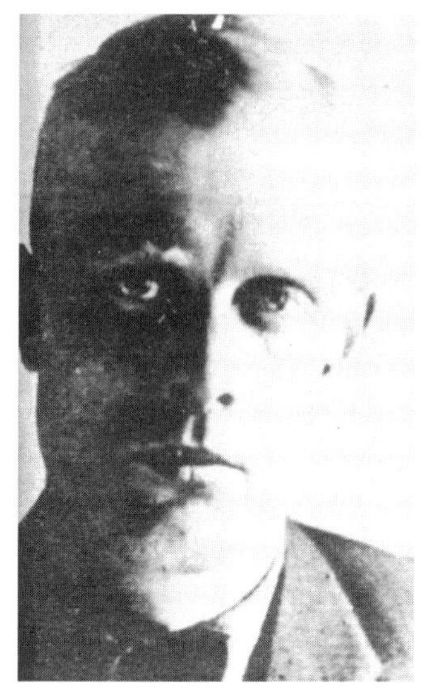

Former sheriff Vernon C. Miller, who led the attack on the lawmen at Kansas City's Union Station; he was later murdered by underworld killers.

When Agent Vetterli made that call to the Kansas City Police Department, he inadvertently informed the underworld exactly when and where gangster Frank Nash would be on Saturday morning, June 17, 1933. The KCPD was then in the grip of the corrupt Pendergast machine, a political organization that had controlled Missouri for decades. Boss Tom Pendergast ran the state, especially Kansas City, and his imperial edicts were carried out by the local politicians under the direction of Pendergast's minion, city manager Henry McElroy. Moreover, Pendergast's underworld lieutenant, Johnny Lazia, ran all the rackets in Kansas City, splitting the enormous profits from gambling, prostitution, and bootlegging with Pendergast, *after* enormous monthly payments had been made to Kansas City politicians and to the city's crooked police force.

Lazia, on the evening of June 16, 1933, received a call from his contact in the KCPD, telling him that Nash would arrive on the 7:15 train the next morning. He, in turn, called

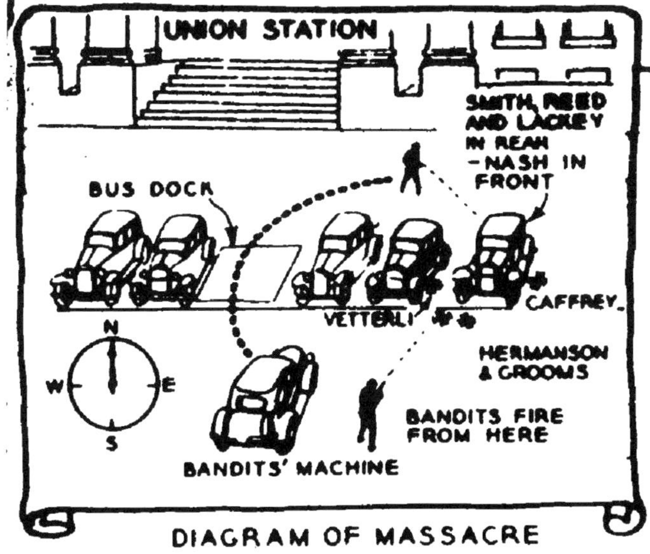

A contemporary sketch shows how the gunmen attacked the lawmen at Union Station.

The carnage following the machinegun attack at Union Station; detectives Grooms and Hermanson lie dead between the cars.

Vern Miller, a local independent bank robber and strong-arm man. Miller had already been contacted by Dick Galatas and Herb Farmer and was looking for Nash and his FBI escort. (Miller was not and never had been connected to the Capone gang, as later alleged in books and in an outlandishly fabricated film about him.)

Miller and Lazia met in a restaurant that night and Lazia assigned two of his best killers, brothers Homer and Maurice Denning, to help Miller free Nash. He also assured Miller that he would have no trouble from the local police. Only two detectives, W.J. "Red" Grooms and Frank Hermanson from the burglary squad, would be sent to meet the Nash party when they got off the train. They would not give Miller and the Denning brothers any problems, Lazia assured Miller. There would be no other police officers or detectives present at the station, Lazia said. The only difficulty might come from the FBI agents, but Lazia pointed out with a wicked smile that these men could offer no real resistance since none of them, by law, were armed.

Bright and early the following morning, Kansas City detectives Hermanson and Grooms appeared at Union Station, driving an armored car in which Nash was to be taken to Leavenworth. Both detectives noticed that all the automatic weapons in the armor-plated car had been removed, leaving the detectives with only their two police revolvers. They got out of the car and met the unarmed FBI agents, Vetterli and Raymond Caffrey. Earlier, Vetterli had mentioned to Caffrey that he had not seen one uniformed policeman in or around the station. When Vetterli checked with the station master, he learned that the Union Pacific train would be on time. The officers had about twenty minutes to wait.

At that moment, a car drove into the station parking lot and came to a stop facing a row of cars and beyond them, the station. At the wheel of the car was Mary McElroy, the impetuous daughter of City Manager Henry McElroy. She had a penchant for gangsters and took her thrills from the exploits of underworld characters such as the slick Johnny Lazia, who worked indirectly for her father and Boss Pendergast.

McElroy had asked bank robber James Henry "Blackie" Audett (who later became an associate of the notorious John Dillinger) to accompany her to the station that morning, telling him that "all hell is going to break loose." Somehow, she had heard that Frank Nash was going to be freed by gunmen planning to attack federal agents accompanying Nash on the 7:15 a.m. train. The two sat in the car like spectators awaiting a circus parade.

Union Station was crowded that Saturday morning. Cars filled the lot, depositing people who were either departing on the Union Pacific train or meeting persons arriving on it. A Chevrolet sedan pulled into a parking spot a short distance from where McElroy sat with Audett. It parked so that it faced a two-door sedan parked there earlier by agents Raymond Caffrey and Reed Vetterli.

Three men sat in the Chevrolet, the heavily armed gunmen Vern Miller and Homer and Maurice Denning. They did not get out of the car. How these men identified Caffrey's car and knew where it would be parked that morning remains a mystery. It was later speculated that police officials had identified the car for the gangsters so they would know exactly where to wait for Nash and his escorts.

Vetterli, Caffrey, Grooms, and Hermanson were waiting at Track Twelve for the train to pull in when Vern Miller got out of the Chevrolet and went into the station, peering about. He walked to the Travelers Aid counter and started to say something to Mrs. Lottie West, then stopped and nervously walked into the crowds. On the train, a conductor knocked on a Pullman drawing room door and told Agent Lackey that the train was about to reach Kansas City.

Knowing the agents' purpose for being on the train, the conductor told Lackey that he would let the lawmen and their prisoner off first. Lackey, Smith, and Chief Reed, with Nash between them, walked down the train aisle, and as the train came to a halt, stepped down onto the station platform. Vetterli, Caffrey, and the two Kansas City detectives met them, and the party of eight began walking through the station toward the parking lot. Frank Nash was surrounded by the seven lawmen, his hands manacled in front of him.

In the plaza parking lot, the group walked to Ray Caffrey's two-door sedan. Lackey, Reed, and Smith got into the back seat of the car. Nash was placed in the front seat, told to sit in the middle. Before the rest of the officers could climb into the car, Miller and the Denning brothers alighted from the Chevrolet facing Caffrey's car. They all held Thompson submachine guns and Miller shouted to the lawmen: "Up! Up! Get 'em up!"

The four lawmen outside the car, Vetterli, Caffrey, Hermanson, and Grooms, stood motionless for some seconds, their eyes riveted on the three gunmen slowly approaching them, guns aimed directly at them. Then Red Grooms' hand instinctively reached into his coat pocket and he withdrew his police revolver. He fired two shots, and although one appeared to hit a heavyset gunman in the arm, the gunman showed no signs of being wounded.

"No! No!" Frank Nash shouted from inside the car.

Vern Miller made a split-second decision. "Let 'em have it!" he shouted to the other two gunmen. "Let the bastards have it!"

Three submachine guns sent a torrent of bullets into Caffrey's car and sprayed the group of officers inside and outside the car. As Homer Denning stood in front of the Chevrolet, Miller and Maurice Denning ran around behind the Caffrey car, continuing to fire at it so that it was caught in a cross fire. People in the parking lot screamed and ran in all directions as the one-sided battle continued. Police Chief Reed was struck several times in the chest, slumping dead against the rear seat of the car. Smith and Lackey were both struck several times by bullets. Lackey managed to get Reed's weapon and tried to fire at the machine gunners from the smashed window of the car, but bullets tore the gun out of his hand.

Outside the car, all the lawmen were down. Vetterli was hit in the arm, Caffrey was shot in the head and was dying. Detectives Hermanson and Grooms received the full force of the opening barrage of submachine gun bullets, which had knocked them over on their backs, one on top of the other. Both were dead. Frank Nash, when the firing began, crouched on the front seat. He now sat up, waving his manacled hands above his head, shouting at the machine gunners: "Don't shoot me! My God! Don't shoot me!" But he was ignored and a stream of bullets crashed through the window of the car, blowing a hole in it and killing Nash instantly.

Frank Nash, dead behind the wheel of one of the cars parked at Union Station, killed by the very men who were assigned to free him from the clutches of the law.

Suddenly, a patrolman, Mike Fanning, arrived in the lot to investigate the awful racket. Mrs. West, who had run from her counter at the sound of the firing, spotted the patrolman's familiar face and she shouted to him: "They're killing everybody!" She pointed to Maurice Denning, who was spraying the ground around the fallen bodies of the lawmen, and she screamed: "Shoot the fat man, Mike! Shoot the fat man!"

Fanning pulled his revolver and fired several shots at Denning. After dropping to the ground, Denning jumped up, fired another burst of bullets into Caffrey's car, and then raced to a waiting Oldsmobile and escaped. Miller and Homer Denning got into the Chevrolet and it roared away and disappeared. Fanning ran to Caffrey's car. "It was a shambles," he later reported. "In the front seat a man was dead under the steering wheel [Nash]. On the left rear seat was another dead man [Chief Reed]. On the right was an unconscious man, but he was groaning [Smith]. A third man lay face down on the floor [Lackey]. I could see that he was alive."

Holding his wounded arm, Special Agent Reed Vetterli managed to get to his feet. He slipped on the pavement, which

FBI agent Raymond Caffrey, killed.

Detective W. J. Grooms, killed.

Police Chief Otto Reed, killed.

was running with blood. Five men were dead, FBI agent Raymond Caffrey, police chief Otto Reed, detectives Red Grooms and Frank Hermanson, and Frank Nash, the very man the attackers had intended to free during their bloody machine gun raid. Nash was not wearing the red-haired wig when found behind the wheel of the car. One witness said he saw Nash take the wig off and wave it in front of the machine gunners so that he could be properly identified. Now the officers came to believe the killers intended to murder Nash; that the raid was not intended to free Nash, but to ensure his silence about the Lazia operations in Kansas City and his underworld contacts in the Midwest.

Nash had been suspected of being an informant because he had "magically" escaped from the Old Mission Golf Course a year earlier, when FBI agents had captured bank robbers Harvey Bailey, Thomas Holden, and Francis Keating. One minute Nash had been teeing off with this trio and the next, when agents closed in to arrest the three gangsters, Nash was gone. Had he set up Bailey, Holden, and Keating for the arrest so that he would be allowed to flee? Was the Kansas City Massacre really designed to silence a dangerous informer? These questions were never really answered.

The identities of the killers were not known for some time. Miller was the only machine gunner, who was quickly identified. Mrs. West and others, with questionable coaching from FBI agents, tentatively identified bank robber Charles Arthur "Pretty Boy" Floyd and his sidekick, Adam Richetti, as the other two machine gunners, but these two outlaws were elsewhere at the time of the Kansas City Massacre.

Even though Floyd insisted, in his dying statement when being apprehended by FBI agent Melvin Purvis in 1934, that he was "not in on" the Massacre, he is to this day considered one of the killers by the Bureau. Adam Richetti, who was later executed for this crime, insisted that he was innocent to the moment of his death.

James Henry "Blackie" Audett, who watched the awful carnage that day, and clearly saw the killers, insisted decades later in interviews with the author that the true killers were Miller and the Denning brothers. He also implicated William Weissman, brother of notorious Kansas City killer and Lazia henchman, Solly Weissman. "Floyd was nowhere near that station that day," Audett told the author. "The FBI had to solve the case fast because one of their own men got killed so they pinned it on two guys, who were already wanted and widely known. They ran down Floyd and killed him over it and then they burned poor little Adam Richetti for the same crime and he wasn't there either. I know. I sat in that parking lot with Mary McElroy and saw the whole thing from less than fifty yards away."

Following the shooting, the wounded agents Caffrey and Lackey were taken to the Research Hospital. Caffrey, who was pronounced dead on arrival, left behind a young wife and a 6-year-old son, Jimmy Caffrey. Lackey recovered slowly from a near-fatal wound. A bullet lodged in his spine kept him confined for some time. When Agent Smith regained consciousness in a hospital bed and was told that his close friend, Chief Otto Reed, had died, tears came into his eyes. "I asked him to come with us," Smith said.

"You can't blame yourself, Frank," he was told by FBI agent Monte Spear, who had been called from the FBI office following the massacre to look after the wounded agents. Agent Smith was inconsolable regarding Chief Reed's death. "I took him to his death," he said. "I took him from his family."

Some hours later Vern Miller called Herb Farmer in Joplin, Missouri. He asked to talk to Frances Nash, but she would not come to the phone. She had already heard how the machine gunners had botched the escape attempt of her husband and blamed Miller for killing Nash. About the same time, J. Edgar Hoover, after hearing the news that his unarmed agents had been slaughtered in Kansas City, called Mrs. Regina Caffrey to offer her his condolences over the loss of her husband. "I promise you that these fiends, whoever they are, will be caught and punished," Hoover told Mrs. Caffrey. "The Bureau will never cease its relentless search until they are caught." Hoover then ordered agents from Texas and Oklahoma to go to Kansas City to help in the investigation. He told his field agents that catching those responsible for the Massacre was their top priority.

Eugene C. Reppert, police director of Kansas City, announced that the men responsible for the Kansas City Massacre would never get out of his city. "A net of guns and steel has been placed around the city. We expect to have them in our custody at any hour now. They simply cannot get out of Kansas City."

The Denning brothers had no intention of leaving Kansas City. They returned to their apartments and went to sleep. Vern Miller, however, believed he might be identified at any moment. He made plans to leave town, ordering the furniture in his bungalow stored with a friend and telling his mistress, Vivian Mathias, only an hour after the shooting when he arrived home in a sweat: "Things went wrong this morning. We're getting out of here." That night, Miller met with Johnny Lazia and his top henchman, James LaCapra later suspected of murdering Lazia in a grab for the crime boss' empire.

Ironically, Lazia and LaCapra were having dinner at the Fred Harvey restaurant in Union Station. This is where Miller met them, eating a sandwich and drinking coffee only a few hundred feet from the spot where, in the morning of the same day, he had stood with a blazing machine gun in his hands, shooting down officers of the law. Miller was told by Lazia to get out of town. Lazia said he would make sure that the Denning brothers also went into hiding somewhere. (Both Maurice and Homer Denning remained undetected for this crime for decades to come, continuing to work with the successive crime bosses of Kansas City and dying comfortably of natural causes, Maurice in the early 1950s, Homer Denning in the late 1970s.)

That night, after conferring with police director Reppert and Chief of Detectives Thomas J. Higgins, City Manager Henry McElroy held an amazing press conference in which he stated: "It has been definitely established that no Kansas City gangster had anything to do with the shooting at the Union Station this morning." It was as if McElroy was saying that the gangsters in Kansas City would never stoop to such bloody slaughter and even the astounding admission of the existence of these powerful criminals went unchallenged. The newspapers throughout the country headlined the grim story.

The event's only rival was the 1929 St. Valentine's Day Massacre in Chicago in which a death squad, at Al Capone's order, shot down seven rival gunmen inside a garage. The Kansas City Massacre seemed worse because the killings were committed on a beautiful Saturday morning in June, in the open, with hundreds of innocent people about. It was the most flagrant act of criminal violence on record and it shocked the nation.

In Washington, FBI director Hoover used the mass murders to convince Congress to give his agents the right to bear arms and make their own federal arrests without the interference of local police departments which might have ties to the underworld. The Kansas City Massacre was finally responsible for accomplishing those purposes for Hoover and the FBI.

Bank robber Charles Arthur "Pretty Boy" Floyd, who was named by the FBI as one of the machinegun killers at the Union Station, but he was reportedly not in Kansas City at that time.

Meanwhile, Vern Miller and Vivian Mathias went to Chicago and took an apartment and waited. James "Fur" Sammons, Capone mobster and fur thief, wanted for fur robberies in Philadelphia and Baltimore, was picked up and charged with being part of the Kansas City Massacre. He emphatically proclaimed his innocence. Sammons was later convicted of a different crime and sent to prison. When Frances Nash was picked up, she implicated Galatas and Farmer, who were tracked down and arrested and charged with complicity. Both would later be given long prison terms. These men knew only that Vern Miller had been involved in the mass slayings.

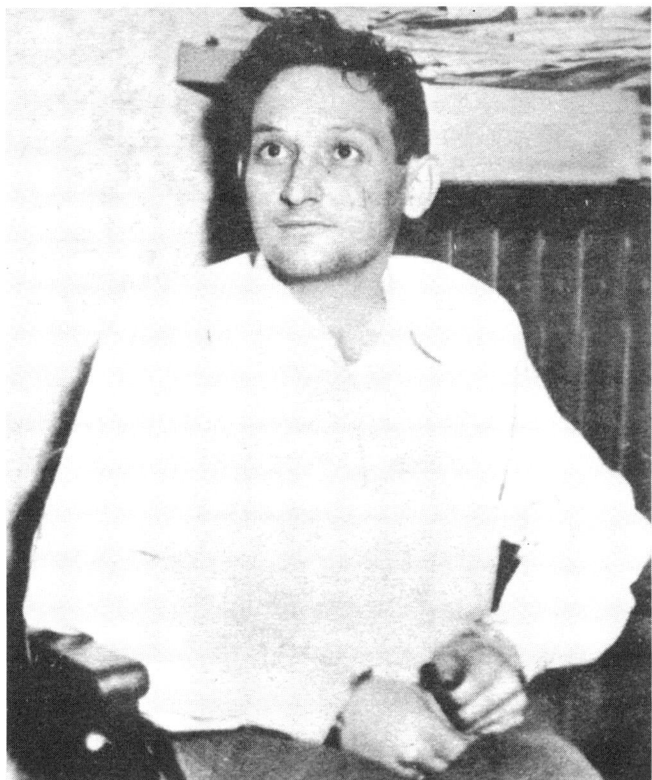

Adam Richetti, Floyd's bank robbing sidekick, shown in custody; he was later convicted as one of the Kansas City killers and executed, although he insisted to the last that he was innocent of that crime.

Miller himself was finally named as a wanted federal fugitive. He fled to New York, where he sought work from crime syndicate boss Louis "Lepke" Buchalter, but he was turned down for being too reckless. In New Jersey, Miller was taken in briefly by that state's mob boss, Abner "Longy" Zwillman. He began drinking heavily, however, and killed one of Zwillman's gunmen in an argument. He fled back to the Midwest, first going to St. Paul, Minnesota, another "safe" underworld city. But mob bosses Harry Sawyer and Jack Peifer ordered Miller to leave town. "There's federal heat everywhere because of what you pulled in K.C.," Sawyer told him.

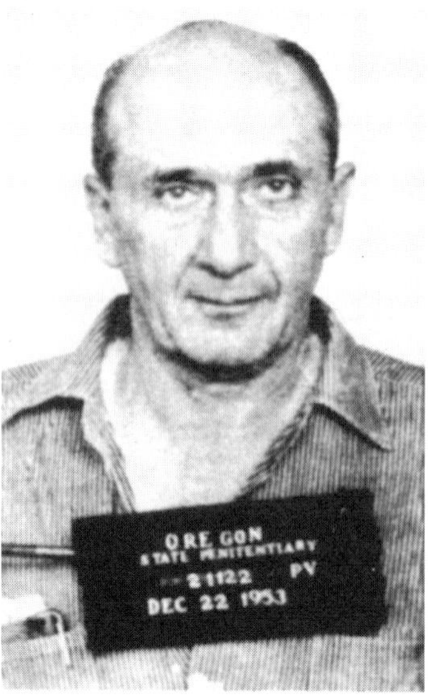

James Henry "Blackie" Audett, who was paroled to the author in June 1979, and who stated that he witnessed the mass murders at Union Station; Audett told the author that Vern Miller and the Denning brothers were the killers, not Floyd and Richetti.

After deserting Vivian Mathias, Miller went to Detroit and vanished. Vivian Mathias was tracked down some days later in Brainerd, Minnesota. She was charged with harboring a fugitive, and was convicted. Vivian Mathias was given a year and a day in prison and was sent to the federal detention farm in Milan, Michigan. She was, however, steadfastly loyal to Miller, refusing to tell FBI agents where he had gone to ground. He was, at the time, hiding in Detroit, protected by members of the old Purple Gang.

Miller had been a member of the Purples years earlier before moving to Kansas City. He was given a cheap room in a sleazy hotel and ordered not to go into the streets. Sometime during the night of November 28, 1933, Miller received a visit from two East Coast gangsters, members of Zwillman's New Jersey mob. They exacted a terrible revenge for Miller's killing of their fellow gang member.

The next morning, Vern Miller's naked body was found wrapped in a moth-eaten blanket in a ditch beneath a railroad embankment outside Detroit. The body of the once slick, bold gunman had been riddled with bullets. It also bore dozens of holes from an ice pick, along with scores of cigarette burns. Parts of Miller's body had also been mutilated. He had obviously been tortured for some time before his murderers tired of the gruesome game and shot him to death.

NIGHT OF THE LONG KNIVES/ June 30, 1934

Where the mass murders in 1933 Kansas City was a botched attempt to free a fellow outlaw by independent gunmen, the wholesale slaughter of Brownshirts in Germany the following year was strictly a ruthless political move on the part of a mesmerizing madman, Adolf Hitler. But like the Kansas City killings, where the murderers slew one of their own, Hitler ordered the killing of one of his closest associates, Ernst Roehm (Rohm, 1887-1934), head of the SA, along with that powerful organization's top leaders.

These mass murders were designed to appease an apprehensive German army, as well as eliminate a potential political rival that had the ability to unseat Hitler. The decision to order the slaughter was not a rash one, but long calculated by Hitler in estimating the result of murdering Roehm, who had become the most dangerous man in the Third Reich.

Roehm came from the lower class in Germany, joining the army at an early age. He rose through the ranks, and emerged a captain following World War I. He was tough, pig-eyed, and battle-scarred, part of his nose having been shot off during fighting on the Western Front. An ardent nationalist, Roehm was one of the first to join the National Socialist party, even before Adolf Hitler, who became its leader.

Roehm enthusiastically supported Hitler from the inception of the Nazi party and backed Hitler with the army of strong-arm thugs, the Brownshirts or the SA. When Hitler decided to take over the German government in Bavaria in 1923 in the abortive Munich Beer Hall Putsch, it was Roehm who provided his storm troopers to make the march against government offices. Roehm seized many key buildings during this putsch, but the effort failed and Roehm was tried, convicted, and sent to Stadelheim Prison to serve a short term. Hitler was also sent to prison, where he wrote his memoirs, *Mein Kampf.*

During the 1920s, Roehm remained a member of the regular German army, a captain, but he commanded an army of Brownshirts that was five times the size of the army, giving the German High Command anxious moments. The generals feared that with his great numbers of SA men, Roehm could seize the government. When Hitler was finally named chancellor, the generals went to the Nazi leader and told him that he could count on their support, but only if Roehm and his top leaders in the SA were eliminated, and if the storm troopers were disbanded and drafted into the regular army.

Hitler agreed, and made plans to exterminate the SA. The Brownshirts by 1934, had become an unruly horde of thugs, thieves, and killers. Its upper echelon leaders, like Roehm, were, for the most part, flagrantly homosexual, and they indulged in all manner of perversities and sexual orgies. Hitler, with the help of Paul Joseph Goebbels, Hermann Goering, and especially, Heinrich Himmler, head of the Gestapo and SS, moved to crush the SA on June 30, 1934.

At that time, most of the leaders of the SA, including Roehm, were on a retreat, relaxing at Wiesee at the Hanslbauer Hotel on the shores of Lake Tegernsee, outside Munich. Arriving at this hotel before dawn with a group of heavily armed SS men, Hitler marched through the rooms occupied by the SA.

In one room Hitler found Brownshirt leader Edmund Heines, head of the SA in Silesia. Heines was a notorious homosexual and convicted killer, and sleeping next to him was a young SA officer. Hitler exploded, screaming to his SS men to "drag this filth out of here and execute them!" Heines, who had a broad, burly figure and the face of a teenager, blinked in amazement

Adolf Hitler (left) conspired with the German High Command to get rid of his old ally, Ernst Roehm (shown at right at an SA/Stormtroopers rally) in 1934.

In this Nazi propaganda poster, SA stormtroopers are shown as heroic figures ready to defend the Fatherland; in truth, most were perverts and street thugs with criminal pasts.

as he and his friend were dragged naked outside behind the hotel and summarily shot. Many more SA men, who had all bedded down with other SA men, were also pulled from their beds and taken to prison. Hitler then barged into Roehm's bedroom, slamming the door. He could be heard by those in the hall as he screamed at Roehm, calling his most staunch supporter "a traitor" to the Nazi cause. Roehm, of course, was stunned and baffled; he had no idea what Adolf Hitler was talking about.

SS men then carted off Roehm to Stadelheim Prison, where he had been imprisoned ten years earlier after following the lunatic Hitler in the Munich Putsch. He was placed in a cell and then one of Himmler's SS men placed a pistol on a table in the cell, telling Roehm that Hitler was allowing his old comrade to shoot himself rather than having him placed before a firing squad. Roehm demanded to know why he and the other SA men had been arrested and shot. He was told "because you are a traitor." No specific charges were made. Roehm refused to use the pistol, shouting at the guards: "If I am to be killed, let Adolf do it himself!"

Heinrich Himmler, left, head of the SS, stands next to Ernst Roehm, center, while reviewing Roehm's stormtroopers; Himmler had by then received orders from Hitler to "eliminate" Roehm and the SA.

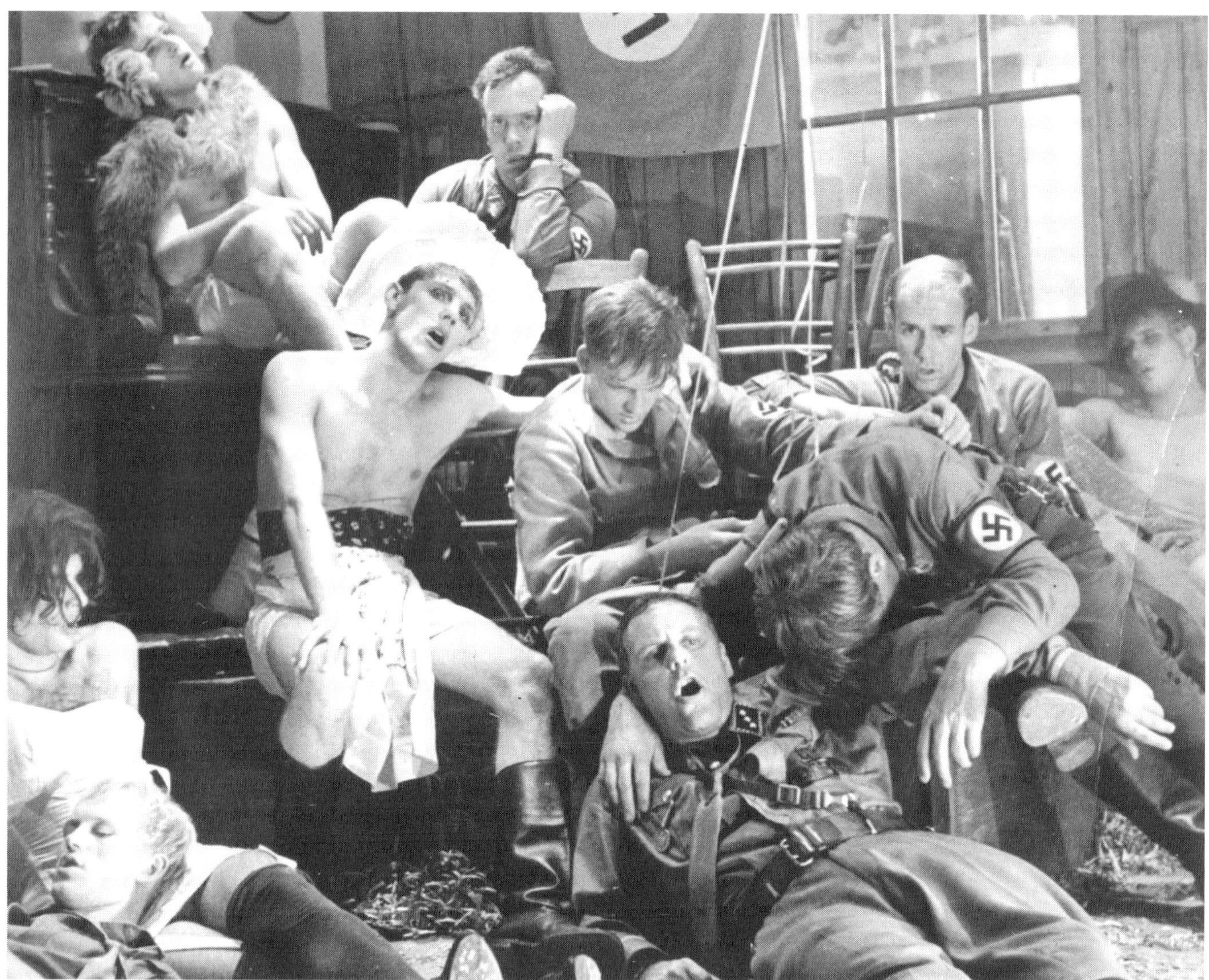

A scene from Visconti's film, *The Damned*, which depicts Roehm's homosexual stormtroopers at a cross-dressing orgy in Wiesee on the night of June 30, 1934, and where Hitler and Himmler found them, executing the leaders out of hand.

The SS men then pulled out their weapons and aimed them at Roehm. He stood defiant, bare-chested, his face scowling contemptuously at his executioners. The SS men fired point blank at him, emptying their pistols. Roehm fell dead. More than 200 SA leaders were also executed that morning, and the SA was disbanded. The odd thing about the mass murders during the SA purge of 1934 was that none of the victims realized what was happening. Most believed that the government had been seized by left-wing radicals.

Many, like Karl Ernst, the SA chief of Berlin, thought it was all a joke until the last moment when they were placed against a wall. They came to attention, giving the Nazi salute and shouting "Heil Hitler," dying as they uttered the name of the man who had ordered their murders. Ernst, like so many of the SA leaders, was a thug, who was raised from the criminal dregs of Berlin.

Ernst had been a bellhop in a seedy Berlin hotel, where he made his money by pimping whores to guests. He later became a bouncer in a notorious homosexual café in Berlin, where he was spotted by Roehm and recruited into the SA. Ernst rose high in the organization by ingratiating himself to Roehm by offering to beat up any of Roehm's political opponents, and this he did often, many such beatings resulting in death. Roehm rewarded Ernst by appointing him chief of the SA in Berlin.

On the night of June 30, 1934—known later as "the night of the long knives"—Ernst was being driven to Bremen with his new bride, planning to board ship for an extended honeymoon in the Canary Islands. His car was stopped by SS gunmen, and his armed chauffeur and bodyguard, thinking the SS men were members of a right-wing takeover of the government, drew their guns and were immediately shot to death.

Ernst was dragged from his car and handcuffed, then taken to a cadet school at Lichterfeld, a suburb of Berlin, where he and 150 other SA men were placed in a coal cellar. The men were then dragged out in groups, lined up against a wall and shot to death without trial. Ernst was also dragged to the wall and believed up to the moment of his death that his beloved leader—the man who had approved of his murder—Adolf Hitler, had himself been slain in a political coup. Ernst raised his handcuffed hands and shouted: "Heil Hitler!" Moments later bullets tore into his body, killing him.

Karl Ernst, head of the SA in Berlin, who was dragged from the side of his new wife, lined up against a wall, and shot to death; he died saluting Hitler.

Also typical of these victims was SA leader and Munich chief of police August Schneidhuber. His Nazi insignias and rank of colonel were personally ripped off by Hitler, who called him a traitor and who was later placed against a wall in the courtyard of Stadelheim Prison. Just before the firing squad sent its lethal volley into him, Schneidhuber said: "Gentlemen, I don't know what this is all about, but shoot straight."

One-time Nazi ally Gregor Strasser, who was also murdered on June 30, 1934, during a massive blood purge that took thousands of lives.

Within twenty-four hours, Adolf Hitler had slaughtered hundreds (the body count was never accurately given, but there may have been several thousand victims) of men who had made his rise to power possible and rid himself of an army of thugs to appease the German High Command, which he desperately needed to fulfill his ambition of world conquest. The deaths of Roehm and the others meant nothing to him. He later commented that "they were all filth, diseased creatures, who had disgraced our uniform."

Not only SA leaders were executed on June 30, 1934. Hitler, Goering, Goebbels and Himmler drew up lists of everyone and anyone they disliked, including fellow Nazi Party members, like Gregor Strasser, and slated them for murder. Politicians, army officers, civilian officials by the scores, were marked for death and they were summarily executed by Himmler's SS assassins, who, in their authorized bloodlust, also slew their family members—wives, children, servants.

Hitler publicly excused the mass murders of the SA by releasing information he had obtained (a false report created by SS leader Josef "Sepp" Dietrich) that showed how Roehm had made up an assassination list that included all of the officers of the Army's High Command and that Roehm intended to liquidate these commanders and seize control of the government. In Hitler's political gobbledygook—routinely accepted by the German public in that dictatorial era—the Nazi leader claimed to have saved the country from radical usurpers, who were, in reality, his own hand-picked terrorists.

"IT LOOKS LIKE A PRETTY GOOD SCORE"/September 6, 1949

One of the worst mass murderers in American history, Howard Unruh, was born (January 21, 1921) and raised in Camden, New Jersey. He had a normal, uneventful childhood and was a good student, graduating from high school during the early stages of World War II. Unruh was drafted into the army and served with an armored division. In basic training, he became a sharpshooter and his fellow GIs noticed that he had a fascination for weapons. He would spend hours each night sitting on his bunk taking apart his rifle and putting it back together again. Unruh never took advantage of weekend passes and was never seen in the company of women. He preferred to remain within the confines of his barracks and occupy himself reading his Bible or cleaning his rifle.

Religion had been deeply rooted in Unruh since childhood. He had attended church regularly, gone to Bible class and read the Bible each day at home. Unruh continued to carry his Bible with him through battle after battle as his armored unit fought its way up the boot of Italy in 1943. By this time, he had become a machine gunner in a tank turret. In the following year, Unruh's unit, part of General George Patton's Third Army, helped to liberate Bastogne in the bloody Battle of the Bulge.

Throughout these war years, Unruh kept a diary in which he daily wrote his private thoughts. A fellow GI, who later became a New York policeman, sneaked a look at Unruh's diary and was horrified to view its contents. Unruh had recorded the death of every German soldier he had killed, the hour and the place he had killed them and how they appeared in death after he had shot them.

Yet the Army looked at Unruh as a hero and before receiving his honorable discharge at war's end, he was awarded several commendations for his heroic service during battle. There was no hero's welcome for Howard Unruh when he returned to Camden. He was just another soldier, among millions, returning to civilian life.

Unruh announced to his parents that he intended to become a pharmacist and, to that end, he took some refresher

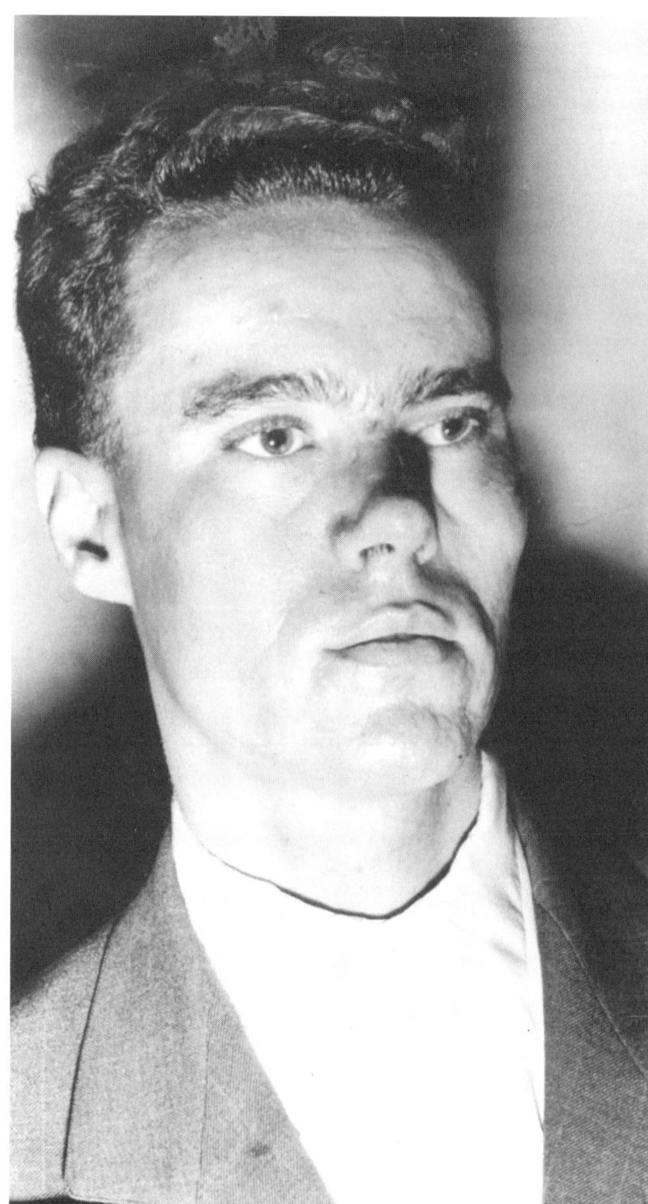

Howard B. Unruh, twenty-eight, at the time he went on his killing spree in his home town of Camden, New Jersey.

high school courses and then enrolled at Temple University in Philadelphia. He continued his Bible classes and here met the only girl he ever dated. The relationship was only a mild flirtation and quickly ended.

This brief affair left Unruh embittered. By 1949, he was considered the neighborhood recluse. He became more withdrawn and seldom spoke to his parents, keeping to his room. The only preoccupation that made him joyful was maintaining his collection of weapons, which he had begun after his military discharge. Unruh set up targets in the basement of his parents' home and practiced his marksmanship each day.

Always sensitive to criticism, Unruh began to take offense at off-handed comments made by neighbors. These became in his mind terrible insults and he suffered what doctors later termed acute paranoia and schizophrenia. He started another diary, or a hate list, wherein he jotted down every imagined and real insult made by neighbors and friends. No grievance was too small to record. This diary was no less exact than the one he had kept in service where he compiled in gruesome detail the German soldiers who had died at his hands.

The next-door neighbors, the Cohens, were particularly annoying to Unruh. Once, while taking a short-cut through the Cohen backyard, Mrs. Cohen had yelled at him: "Hey, you! Do you have to go through our yard?" The Cohens gave their 12-year-old son a bugle, which he practiced daily and Unruh looked upon this as a personal offense against him, as if the neighbors had purposely awarded their son this noisy instrument to annoy him. The list of names and those who offended Unruh grew and grew and after each offense, Unruh wrote the abbreviation "retal," meaning "retaliate."

At first Unruh tried to shut off the world that offended him, rather than attack it. He built a high wooden fence around the tiny Unruh back yard. With his father's help, he built a huge gate that was locked against the intrusions of the world. Unruh's room was another haven, where he took refuge from offensive neighbors. Here the young man kept a 9mm German Luger which he had purchased for $40, several pistols, a large quantity of ammunition, a knife and a machete, both kept razor sharp by their owner.

The shaky world of Howard Unruh collapsed on September 6, 1949. He came home at 3 a.m. that morning to find that someone had stolen the massive gate he and his father had labored so long to erect. Local pranksters had done the deed, but to Unruh, everyone living about him was responsible for this unforgivable insult. Unruh was up all night, staring at the ceiling of his room, seething with hatred. He decided to take revenge.

At 8 a.m. he sat down to a breakfast prepared by his mother. He stared at her strangely and later admitted that she was to be his first victim. He had to kill her to spare her the grief he would bring upon the family through his homicidal plans. Unruh went to the basement, then returned, eyes glaring at her, walking toward her menacingly. His mother ran from the house and to a neighbor's where she blurted her fears about her unstable son.

Going to his room, Unruh loaded his Luger and another pistol, pocketing these weapons, along with a knife. He gathered up several clips of ammunition for both guns and filled his pockets. He walked outside and scrambled over the fence instead of going through the gaping area where the gate had been. At 9:20 a.m., Unruh stood in the doorway of a small shoemaker's shop owned by John Pilarchik.

The cobbler, who had just recently finished paying off the mortgage for his shop, was busy working on children's' shoes. The 27-year-old Pilarchik looked up to see Unruh, someone he had known since boyhood. He stared in disbelief as Unruh pulled out the Luger and fired two bullets into his head. Pilarchik pitched forward dead onto his work bench.

Unruh then stepped next door, into the barbershop owned by 33-year-old Clark Hoover, who had been cutting Unruh's hair for years. Sitting on a small plastic horse in the shop was 6-year-old Orris Smith, whose mother and 11-year-old daughter stood nearby. Without a word, Unruh raised his Luger and

Police grabbed Unruh (in bow tie) after he had murdered thirteen people on September 6, 1949; he told them he was not insane and had "a good mind."

shot the boy dead and then pumped two more bullets into the startled Clark. He ignored the screams of Mrs. Smith and her daughter, who rushed forward to cradle the dead child. Unruh looked at both of them, but strangely did not fire his Luger. With a vacant stare, he wheeled about and headed for the corner drugstore, which was owned by the Cohen family, the people he most hated.

James Hutton, Unruh's insurance agent, stepped from the drugstore. "Hello, Howard," he said affably.

"Excuse me," Unruh said in a monotone. He leveled the Luger at Hutton and fired twice. The insurance agent toppled dead to the sidewalk. Cohen, who saw Unruh shoot Hutton through the window of his shop, raced upstairs to warn other members of his family. Unruh entered the drugstore, inserted another clip into the Luger and then plodded up the stairs after his mortal enemy.

Upstairs, Unruh saw no one about. He suspected that the Cohens were hiding and when he heard a noise in a closet he fired a bullet through the closet door. He opened this to see Mrs. Rose Cohen sagging to the floor. He sent another bullet into her head. Cohen and his son slipped out a window and walked along the second-story ledge of the building, scrambling to a nearby roof.

Police inspectors examine the arsenal Unruh used in his mass murders.

Unruh went into another room of the Cohen apartment and saw Cohen's elderly mother, 63-year-old Minnie Cohen, desperately calling police on a phone. He fired twice, killing her. Then he spotted Maurice Cohen and his son scrambling across a sloping roof and he leaned calmly from a window and fired a bullet that slammed into Cohen's back, causing him to slide off the roof and crash to the pavement below.

Carefully leaning out the window, Unruh fired straight down at Cohen, sending another bullet into his back, although the man was already dead. The Cohen boy had by this time worked his way down to the side of the roof and was clinging to its edge, screaming. Unruh glanced at him, but did not shoot him. He walked back downstairs and went outside. He found Alvin Day, a passerby, kneeling at the body of James Hutton, trying to help a man who was already dead. Day looked up to see the muzzle of Unruh's Luger poking into his face. Unruh fired twice, killing Day, a man he had never met before this moment.

Reloading the Luger, Unruh began to leisurely stroll across the street. A car was idling at the corner, its driver waiting for the light to change. Unruh walked up to the car and stuck the Luger through the window, shooting the female driver dead. She was Helen Wilson. He then fired at and killed the woman's mother, Emma Matlack, who was in the back seat of the car, along with her 9-year-old son, John Wilson.

Unruh then began walking down the street. He spotted a truck driver getting out of the cab of his truck a block away. Taking careful aim, Unruh shot him in the leg. By then panic had gripped the entire area. The maniac in the streets was shooting anyone he encountered. The manager of a supermarket quickly locked the front doors and told his customers to lie down on the floor. So did the manager of a bar which Unruh approached. As bar customers huddled on the floor, Unruh tried the door and found it locked. He fired twice, trying to blow away the lock but it held. He moved on, seemingly unconcerned.

Going into the tailor's shop next door, Unruh found the place empty. Tom Zegrino, the proprietor, was not present but Unruh heard a noise in the back room. He pushed back a drape to see Mrs. Helga Zegrino cringing behind a chair. "Oh, my God, please don't," she pleaded. Unruh said nothing as he sent two bullets into her, killing her instantly.

Stepping outside, Unruh looked about at the now empty street. The only persons present were those whom he had already killed or wounded. Neighbors and passersby had rushed into houses and shops and had locked themselves inside against the random rage of the lunatic. Unruh looked up to see 3-year-old Tommy Hamilton staring down at him. He fired once, killing the boy.

Walking to a nearby house, Unruh entered it by the back door which he found unlocked. Inside the kitchen, he found Mrs. Madeleine Harris and her two sons. The older son, a courageous youth, saw the gun in Unruh's hand and dashed forward, driving his shoulder into the body of the tall killer. Unruh fired twice, wounding the youth and his mother. He then stood over these two fallen victims who squirmed in pain. He leveled the Luger at them but, oddly, decided not to end their lives. He turned on his heel and walked once more outside.

Police sirens wailing from squad cars could be heard in the distance. Unruh increased his pace as he walked back to his home, where he went to his second-story room, barricading the door and reloading his Luger. He waited patiently as police surrounded his house. He looked out his window at them without firing. His identity was by then known and had been reported to Phillip Buxton, editor of the Camden *Courier Post*. Buxton ob-

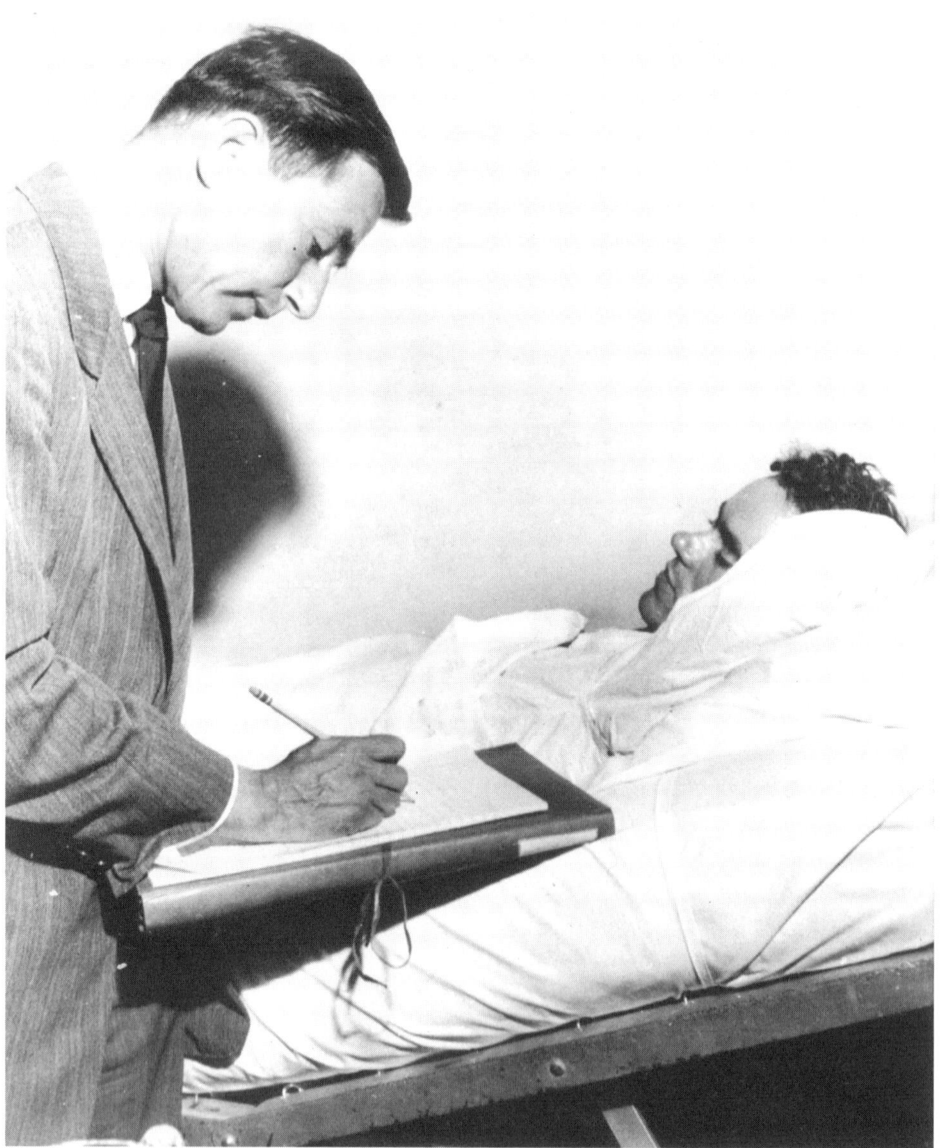

Unruh is shown bed-ridden (he had been wounded by a stray police bullet before surrendering) in Camden's Cooper Hospital, interviewed by prosecutor Mitchell H. Cohen; the mass murderer had no regrets, saying "I'd have killed a thousand if I'd had bullets enough."

tained Unruh's listed phone number and took a chance, calling the killer.

Unruh picked up the phone and one of the strangest phone conversations in the annals of murder then occurred.

"Hello," Unruh answered in a calm voice.

"Is this Howard?" Buxton inquired.

"Yes, this is Howard," Unruh replied. "What is the last name of the party you want?"

"Unruh."

"Who are you and what do you want?" Unruh asked politely.

Buxton was diplomatic: "I am a friend and I want to know what they are doing to you."

"Well, they haven't done anything to me yet," Unruh said in an even voice, as if he were chatting with an old friend. "But I am doing plenty to them."

"How many have you killed?"

"I don't know yet. I haven't counted them, but it looks like a pretty good score." (Thirteen persons had been shot to death and thirteen more had been wounded by Howard Unruh within twelve minutes.)

"Why are you killing people, Howard," Buxton asked, trying to control his own passions while writing down the murderer's every word.

He was greeted by silence. After some moments, Unruh replied in a low voice: "I don't know. I can't answer that yet. I'm too busy. I'll have to talk to you later." He hung up.

At that moment tear gas canisters fired by police outside smashed through the glass of the bedroom windows and exploded inside, filling the room with eye-searing gas. These were followed by fusillades of bullets that smacked into the walls of Unruh's room, chipping the plaster. After a few minutes, Unruh took down the barricade in front of his door and walked downstairs and outside. He put his hands slowly into the air at a command barked by a police officer. Dozens of guns were trained upon him.

Detectives rushed forward, manhandling him, manacling his large hands. Detective Vince Connelly, sickened at the sight of the bodies in the street nearby, stared at Unruh and said: "What's the matter with you? Are you a psycho?"

Howard Unruh lifted his head indignantly and snapped: "I am no psycho! I have a good mind!"

More than twenty psychiatrists, who later examined Howard Unruh disagreed. They believed him to be hopelessly and criminally insane. The mass killer was never brought to trial, but sent to the New Jersey State Mental Hospital for life. He had no remorse for his brutal, unthinking murders. In one interview with a psychiatrist, Unruh stated: "I'd have killed a thousand if I'd had bullets enough."

Unruh, alive at this writing (age seventy-eight), has repeatedly petitioned to be released from the Trenton Psychiatric Hospital (where he has spent most of his days "cowering near the nurse's station in the locked ward for the criminally insane") to another hospital for the elderly. Such petitions have thus far been denied.

DEATH OVER QUEBEC/September 9, 1949

Three days after Howard Unruh went on his berserk murder spree in Camden, New Jersey, blasted steel and flesh rained from the skies over Quebec. On September 9, 1949, Canadian Pacific Airlines Flight 108, a two-engine DC-3 (Dakota) from Quebec to Baie Comeau exploded in flight forty miles from Quebec, only twenty minutes after takeoff. All twenty-three passengers and crew members were killed in the crash, which was initially considered an accident.

Among those grieving over the lost lives in the crash was Joseph Albert Guay (1919-1951), a mild-mannered Quebec jeweler. He appeared with his small daughter, Lise, at the airport, to learn that his wife, Rita Morel Guay, a petite, dark-haired French-Canadian, had perished with all on board the ill-fated flight.

Guay was remembered earlier by workers at Quebec's Ancienne Lorette Airport, when he affectionately bid his wife goodbye earlier that day, kissing her on the cheek before she boarded the plane. He had in his pocket at that time, an insurance policy he had taken out on his wife, one calling for a $10,000 payment in the event of her death in the air. Like many other mourners that day, Guay appeared unconcerned about anything but the loss of his loved one. He was emotionally devastated, or so he appeared, weeping openly. He and his daughter were driven to one of Quebec's better hotels where they were given a room. A priest then consoled the stricken husband, who seemed to be inconsolable.

By that time, searchers struggled through dense woods to find the debris from the shattered plane, mangled body parts, luggage and twisted steel spread over a wide area. The explosion made national news across Canada and in the U.S., particularly since three of the passengers were American millionaires, who had interests in Canadian copper mines.

Inspectors examined all the remaining fragments of the plane and found that flames had touched only a section of the freight compartment where the metal walls were scorched. Items were taken from the freight compartment and closely examined by chemists, who then issued a shocking report. The plane had been sabotaged, that dynamite had been used to blow up the plane and that the twenty-three fatalities on board were victims of mass murder. Specifically, investigators had found evidence of a dry battery cell and dynamite in the wreckage, indicating that a bomb had been planted on the plane.

The cargo manifest listed a package being sent to a nonexistent address. Airport freight handlers recalled that a woman dressed in black had left the package. Ten days after the crash, a taxi driver, Paul Pelletier contacted police to say that he remembered driving a woman in black carrying a package to the airport on the day of the crash. He gave police an address that turned out to be that of Marguerite Pitre.

When police arrived to question Pitre, however, they were informed that she was in the hospital recovering from a suicide attempt. Pitre admitted taking the package to the airport, and told police that she had done so at the request of a friend

The wreckage of Canadian Pacific Airlines Flight 108, which exploded over Quebec on September 9, 1949, killing all twenty-three persons on board, including three children, the mangled doll shown in this photo belonging to one of those victims.

Joseph Albert Guay ordered the bomb to be placed on Flight 108 to rid himself of an unwanted wife and to collect her flight insurance; he was executed in 1951.

Eccentric watchmaker Genereaux Ruest, who accommodated the killer by constructing the bomb that blew up Flight 108; he was executed in 1951.

Marguerite Pitre, who delivered the bomb to the airport; she cooperated with police in exposing the murder plot but was nevertheless executed in 1951.

and former lover, Joseph Albert Guay. She explained that it was all part of a plot to kill Guay's wife, Rita Guay.

Albert Guay had become involved with 19-year-old nightclub cigarette girl, Marie-Ange Robitaille and wanted to get rid of his wife so he could marry her. He got help from Pitre, who in turn convinced her brother, Genreaux Ruest, to build the bomb. Guay managed to get his wife to take the plane flight by asking her to go to Baie Comeau to pick up two suitcases of jewelry for him. He took out the insurance policy on her life as an added bonus to his murderous plan, the $10,000 from her life insurance to be lavished upon his mistress.

Guay had long plotted the murder of his wife, Pitre insisted. In fact, he had offered a friend $500 to put poison in a bottle of wine and give it to his wife, but the friend laughed off the request as a joke. It was after this rebuff that Guay went to Pitre, who lived in the seamy side of Lower Quebec, where she was known as a petty criminal and abortionist.

It was Guay, Pitre said, who suggested that a bomb be placed on a plane carrying his wife. To construct this infernal machine, Pitre went to her brother, Genreaux Ruest, a crippled jeweler and watchmaker, who undertook to construct the bomb. He was inexpert at the job at best, struggling to put dynamite into an alarm clock at his workbench in his open shop.

At one point, when Ruest saw a miner enter his shop, he exclaimed: "Now, here's a man who can tell us about dynamite!" On another occasion, Ruest and Guay attempted to persuade a taxi driver to carry the bomb in his car while Mrs. Guay was riding in it, and leap out of the taxi after setting it off. The cab driver refused, not because of any moral qualms, but because his taxi would be destroyed. Guay finally settled on blowing up a plane carrying his unsuspecting wife.

All of this was related in Guay's trial, beginning in March 1950. He was found guilty and sentenced to death and was hanged in January 1951. His two blundering confederates, Pitre and Ruest, followed him to the scaffold.

"I WISH THEY WOULD HANG ERNIE"/ November 17, 1950

Ernest Ingenito (b. 1924) was a violent youth from the time his parents separated in 1937. Mrs. Ingenito found it impossible to control him during his childhood, and by the time he was fifteen he was known to police in Gloucester County, Pennsylvania, as an incorrigible thug. Before another year had passed, Ingenito was serving a term in the Pennsylvania State Reformatory, convicted of attempted burglary. After his release, he returned to his mother's home. Her death in 1941 created an emotional scar Ingenito carried with him for the rest of his life.

Ingenito married at seventeen, but his angry tirades were too much for his young bride and she left him while she was pregnant. He then enlisted in the army, where his habit of sleeping late did not endear him to his sergeant or the officers on the base. In 1943, during an argument, he beat up a sergeant and an officer. Imprisoned in a stockade for two years, he was dishonorably discharged in 1946. The next year he met Theresa Mazzoli, a dark-haired Italian beauty whose parents owned and operated a prosperous truck farm in Gloucester County, and though Theresa's mother objected loudly to the couple's relationship, they soon married.

Ernest Ingenito (center) is shown entering court, where he was convicted of slaughtering his in-laws in 1950; he was later sent to an insane asylum.

The impoverished young couple went to live with the Mazzolis in their home and from the start there was trouble. Pearl Mazzoli, the mother, did not care for her son-in-law and daily made a point of expressing her disapproval of him. At first Mike Mazzoli, the father, took Ingenito's side. But when he learned that Ingenito had cheated on his daughter, he immediately evicted Ingenito from his home.

Ingenito moved to a residence a short distance away, so that he could be near his two sons. When Theresa refused him visitation rights, Ingenito consulted a lawyer, Fred Gravino, of Woodbury, New Jersey, who told Ernie to get a court order to see his children. Ernie rejected the advice because it would take too long, he said. A second lawyer told him the same thing. Agitated, Ingenito selected two pistols and a carbine rifle from his extensive weapons collection and, on November 17, 1950, banged on the Mazzoli's front door armed with his guns.

Upon seeing her estranged husband approach, Theresa Ingenito fled. When Mike Mazzoli appeared, Ingenito leveled a German-made Luger and fired two times, then stepped into the house and fired at his wife, wounding her. Next, he went after Pearl Mazzoli, but was unable to locate her in the house for she had run screaming to the home of Armando and Theresa Pioppi who lived down the block. "It's Ernie!" she cried, running upstairs to hide in a bedroom closet. "He's shooting everybody!"

Before Gino Pioppi, Pearl's brother, could summon police, Ingenito burst through the door with his guns blazing. He fired on Mrs. Pioppi and Gino's wife, Marion, killing them. Ingenito fired repeatedly at Pearl Mazzoli and then fired on his 9-year-old daughter before exiting the Pioppi home. As he left, Gino's brother, John, grabbed a knife lying on the kitchen table and chased the gun-toting madman across the lawn until Ingenito turned and fired, killing John Pioppi instantly. Ingenito next drove to the home of Frank Mazzoli in Minatola, New Jersey. Screaming a torrent of curses, he shot Hilda and Frank Mazzoli and then tried to escape.

The killing spree had begun at 9 p.m., and ended shortly after midnight when a patrol car flagged Ingenito down. As the police officers approached, Ingenito tried to kill himself with the jagged edges of a tin can, but failed. Speaking from her hospital bed, Theresa told a reporter: "I wish they would hang Ernie."

In January 1951, Ingenito was tried for the murder of his mother-in-law. His severe psychological problems led to a sentence of life imprisonment at the New Jersey Hospital for the Insane, in Trenton. In 1956 he was brought to trial for four additional murders committed that same night, and received a sentence of life for each killing.

A MASS MURDER IN FRANCE/ August 4, 1952

Gaston Dominici (1877-1965), the elderly, affable patriarch of a large French farm family living near Lurs, Provence, became the hub of one of the most sensational mass murder cases in modern French history. Sir Jack Drummond, a brilliant 61-year-old British biochemist, his wife Ann, forty-six, and their daughter Elizabeth, ten, were vacationing in France, driving leisurely through the beautiful Durance Valley. They decided to camp on the night of August 4, 1952, and pulled their car off the road outside the town of Lurs, near a farmhouse.

The Drummonds pitched a tent and began to dress for bed. Someone hiding in some nearby bushes and watching them was discovered by Drummond, who berated the Peeping Tom, who, in turn, shot Drummond and his wife to death and chased the terrified Elizabeth Drummond through the tall grass and crushed her head with the butt of a carbine.

The bodies of the Drummond family were found the next morning by railway workers. Police also received a report from 33-year-old Gustave Dominici that he had also discovered the bodies on a large, sprawling farm called La Grande Terre, belonging to his father, Gaston Dominici. The deaths of the prominent Drummond and his family members made headlines in Paris, London, and New York, and Edmond Sebeille, the superintendent of police in Marseilles, was called in to personally direct the investigation.

Sebeille was convinced that the killer or killers were part of the Dominici family at La Grande Terre. The family included Gaston Dominici, seventy-five, his reticent wife Marie, his son Gustave, Gustave's wife, Yvette, and their child. Another son, 49-year-old Clovis Dominici, lived on a nearby farm. Superintendent Sebeille methodically conducted dozens of interviews with residents and workers in the area.

One of the railway workers who had discovered the bodies told the superintendent that Gustave Dominici had stated that Elizabeth Drummond was alive when he found her, although she was apparently dying of head wounds. Sebeille

British biochemist Sir Jack Drummond, shown with his wife Ann and daughter Elizabeth, all brutally slain while vacationing in France's Durance Valley on August 4, 1952.

Gustave Dominici, who was at first thought to be the mass murderer.

Clovis Dominici, who also came under suspicion as the killer of the Drummond family.

Family patriarch Gaston Dominici, who was found guilty of slaying the Drummonds.

confronted Gustave Dominici, who admitted this was the case, but he was quick to say that he had nothing to do with the murders.

Sebeille ordered Dominici's arrest for failing to come to the aid of a dying person. He was tried at Digne on November 13, 1952, convicted, and sentenced to two months in prison. The sentence was appealed and Dominici was released. Sebeille, however, persisted in visiting the Dominici family, questioning members over and over throughout 1953. Finally, with Gustave and Clovis Dominici present in the farmhouse, Sebeille openly accused Gustave of murdering the Drummonds. Gustave's nerves were frayed by the prolonged police investigation and he shouted: "It was my father!"

Sebeille looked at Clovis and the older brother nodded. Gustave then stated that he heard two shots at about 1 a.m. on the night of the murders and he ran to the field, where he saw his father with an American carbine. He had just shot the Drummonds after being caught spying on them and had bludgeoned the little girl. Gustave, terrified that his father might turn on him, fled and returned at 5:30 to find Elizabeth Drummond in a dying condition. He left her to be found later, still fearing that his father would kill him if he knew he had witnessed the murders.

The fierce old man, with a head of white hair, a droopy mustache, and dark, beady eyes, was arrested and taken to jail. He cursed his sons when he learned that they had informed on him and he later confessed to police that he had, indeed, slaughtered the Drummond family because Jack Drummond had accused him of gaping at his half-dressed wife and making lewd advances to her.

Dominici felt it was his right to do as he pleased on his own land, even to commit sexual assault and murder. The old man made several confessions, but these were later retracted and denied when Gaston Dominici was placed on trial at the Digne Assize Court in November 1954. Before that time,

Gaston Dominici is shown going to prison under heavy police guard; he was condemned to death, but his sentence was later commuted to life imprisonment.

Dominici accompanied police to the scene of the murders, which were re-enacted before him, so unnerving the hoary old killer that he tried to commit suicide by jumping off a railroad bridge.

At the end of the eleven-day trial, Gaston Dominici was found guilty and sentenced to death. As the old man was led from the dock and back to his cell, he turned to the court and hissed: "My sons! What swine!" Dominici's death sentence was commuted to life in prison. Meanwhile more developments and revelations in the case left considerable doubt about who had killed the Drummonds. One story had it that the old man killed the adults, but someone else in the Dominici family murdered the child.

Another account insisted that Gaston Dominici was a senile old man, who had confessed out of ignorance and confusion and that his sons had done the killings. The old man was released in 1960 and returned to La Grand Terre where he lived until his death in 1965, residing for six years inside a household that seethed with hostility and hatred.

"SEND IT TO HELL!"/November 1, 1955

John Gilbert Graham (1932-1957), called Jack by family and friends, was a clean-cut young man, tall, well-mannered, his hair cropped close to his head. A stranger might guess that he had played center for the local high school basketball team. His politeness and quiet voice suggested years of experience as a Boy Scout. He would be the kid down the block selling cool drinks at a cardboard stand outside his house in the summer, the boy next door who shoveled the walk in winter, cut the grass in spring. But he was none of these things, as his neighbors in Denver, Colorado, would slowly discover, along with the FBI. He was a killer, moreover a mass murderer who plotted not only the death of an overindulgent mother, but would be responsible for the first in-flight plane bombing in U.S. history.

Mrs. Daisie King, Jack's mother, doted on her only son. She had led a roller-coaster life, marrying in and out of poverty three times. Her second marriage produced her only child, Jack, who was born in Denver in 1932. When Jack was five, his father, William Graham, died, and Daisie Graham was left without a dime, forced to place her son in an orphanage. In 1943, Daisie met and married a wealthy Colorado rancher, John Earl King, and she immediately recovered her son, bringing him to an upper-middleclass home where comfort and convenience replaced Spartan discipline.

Yet the disparity of the two lifestyles young Jack had lived seemingly affected him little. He was bright, some said highly imaginative. He was an above-average student through his first year of high school. Then, at sixteen, he ran away to join the Coast Guard, lying about his age. Graham served only nine months, being AWOL for sixty-three days, which caused his detention. Officers learned that he was underage and dismissed him from the service. His mother took him back into her home and, when he said he did not want to complete school, she nodded patient understanding.

Jack Graham went to work, taking odd jobs. To his neighbors he appeared the same easygoing boy, but close friends noticed that he would become restless when talking about his mother and then sink into brooding silence. Mrs. King urged her son to return to school so that he could qualify for a white-collar job. By 1951, Graham had accumulated enough night school credits to earn himself a job as a payroll clerk for a Denver manufacturer.

Mrs. Daisie King, who, along with forty-three others, died when United Airlines Flight 629 blew up after taking off from the Denver Airport on November 1, 1955.

Though Graham had a taste for riches, his meager salary afforded few pleasures. He wanted fast, new cars and a handsome wardrobe. He insisted upon taking his girlfriends to better restaurants. He could afford little of this lifestyle on his $200-a-month salary, so Jack Graham did what had become a habit at home—he merely helped himself, in this case forging the name of his company's vice-president to checks he had stolen from his firm and cashing these to collect $4,200. He bought a fast convertible and drove away from Denver to see the sights.

For several months, Graham went on a minor crime spree, but when he took up bootlegging in Texas, the Rangers and other lawmen closed in on him. Outside of Lubbock, Texas, police set up a roadblock on a tip that a young bootlegger would be taking a certain route, his car loaded with moonshine. Graham approached the barrier at high speed, ignoring police warnings to stop. When he drove through the roadblock, officers riddled his beautiful new convertible, which Graham crashed into a house. Miraculously he was uninjured when taken into custody.

After serving sixty days in the county jail, Graham was turned over to Denver officials who intended to prosecute him for forgery. But Daisie Graham King wouldn't hear of it. She couldn't bear to see Jack behind bars and begged authorities to be lenient toward her errant son, a good boy really, who had made a mistake for which he was sorry, she said.

Rescue workers are shown carrying some of the bodies strewn over a wide area from the remains of Flight 629.

Mrs. King offered her son's former employer $2,500, saying that Jack would work off the balance of the stolen $4,200. Authorities agreed, placing the apprentice forger on probation. For a time, it seemed as if Mrs. King's unswerving belief in her son was vindicated. Graham did get a job and did make regular payments to the firm he had looted.

In 1953, Graham married Gloria Elson in Denver and settled down, working hard as a mechanic, righting his wrong. Like many another citizen, Jack Graham had his "brush with the law" and had been spared prison. It appeared that, like any other citizen having made one mistake, he was on his way to becoming a respected member of his community. His friends found him hardworking, conscientious, and a faithful husband. His relatives marveled at the consideration and affection he showered upon his mother, especially after her third husband died in 1954.

Following King's death (he had been a successful rancher), a large sum of money was left to Mrs. Daisie Graham King. Thrice widowed, Mrs. King turned to her son for consolation and, to occupy her time, proposed a business partnership between herself and her hard-working offspring. She invested $35,000 of her husband's money in a drive-in restaurant in West Denver. Jack became her partner, managing the restaurant. Graham labored to make the restaurant a success, and he continued working nights at a Hertz Drive-Ur-Self garage to further reduce the money owed against his forgery theft, until the balance remaining was no more than $106. He had learned his lesson, his mother was fond of saying. Jack was a good boy, she said, a solid citizen.

Then, on November 1, 1955, an ear-shattering event took place that would slowly strip away that upstanding image of John Gilbert Graham, penitent lawbreaker, hardworking married man, and dutiful son. At 7:03 p.m. on that day, United Airlines flight number 629, only eleven minutes from Denver's

Denver's District Attorney Bert Keating, who later led the prosecution case against John Gilbert Graham, is shown examining the crucial cargo section of Flight 629, which had been painstakingly reassembled by experts in a warehouse of the Denver Airport.

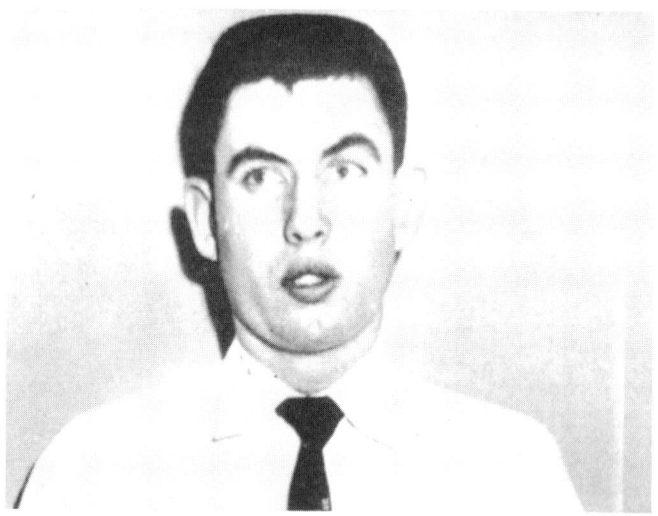

John "Jack" Gilbert Graham is shown only minutes after he signed his confession at FBI offices in Denver. He took pride in constructing the bomb that killed his mother and destroyed Flight 629.

Stapleton Airport and en route to Portland, Oregon, with forty-four passengers and crew members aboard, passed directly over a Colorado beet farm near Longmont. The farmer stood near his barn, looked up, and saw a terrific explosion that sent to earth the shattered remains of the silver plane, burning wreckage that littered his fields and sent him scampering for help when help was useless.

Within an hour, nearby citizens and National Guardsmen arrived to recover the mutilated bodies. These shattered remains were taken to the National Guard Armory at Greeley, Colorado. Responding to one of the worst air disasters in American aviation, the FBI routinely offered the aid of its Identification Division in an effort to help authorities pinpoint the identities of the victims. Two of the Bureau's fingerprint experts arrived in Greeley the following day. Of the forty-four aboard Flight 629, including one infant and five crew members, nine had already been identified by grieving relatives and friends.

The FBI experts fingerprinted the remaining thirty-five bodies, or what was left of the bodies, and twenty-one of these were identified from prints, which were in the Bureau's files. The reason why so many sets of prints were on file was explained by FBI officials: a Canadian couple had had their fingerprints taken in 1954, when applying for citizenship, another for personal identification, and many had been government workers during World War II, holding jobs requiring fingerprinting.

FBI experts also joined with investigators from United Airlines, the Douglas Aircraft Company, and the Civil Aeronautics Board to determine the cause of the crash. Mechanical failure and human error were high on the priority of probabilities; sabotage was an almost unthinkable possibility.

At the same time, other investigators looked into the unthinkable by examining the backgrounds of every passenger and crew member. They were shocked to learn that a staggering $752,000 in flight insurance had been taken out by eighteen of the passengers, almost as if these travelers had had a collective premonition of disaster, making Flight 629 one of the most heavily insured flights in the history of commercial aviation up to that time. The policies were put through the checking mill.

Other experts collected the jagged pieces of the plane, from tail to nose, which, when falling from the fireball to earth had spread over a mile-and-a-half of cropland. The pieces were carefully moved to a Denver hangar and pieced together meticulously, until the ill-fated DC-6B's fuselage was completely reassembled except for a section near the tail from Number 4 Cargo Pit. Not a fragment remained of this section of the plane. The metal shell of the fuselage surrounding the area that had once been Number 4 Cargo Pit, engineers discovered, was bent outward in jagged pieces. This could only mean that a force more powerful than any crash had torn out that part of the plane.

Moreover, bits of steel from the fuselage had been driven through the soles of some of the shoes worn by passengers sitting near the cargo section of the plane. Even the brass fittings of one suitcase had been driven through a stainless steel container known to have been in the hold. An explosion had occurred in the cargo hold and, since no gas lines or tanks were located near this section, experts concluded that *something* in the hold had exploded by accident, perhaps an illegal dynamite shipment or—and this was the last possibility any of the experts wanted to include—someone had deliberately sabotaged the plane, planting some sort of bomb on board.

The tragedy of Flight 629 was quickly known to many of those who had friends and relatives on board. One of them was John Gilbert Graham, whose mother, Mrs. Daisie Graham King, had been en route to Portland, then Seattle, and finally to Alaska, to visit her daughter. Graham and his wife Gloria, accompanied by their 2-year-old son, Allen, had driven Mrs. King to Stapleton Airport and walked her to the gate, kissing her goodbye.

After Mrs. King boarded, the Grahams went to a nearby coffee shop to have a snack. Jack got sick, rushed to the restroom, and threw up. When he returned he told his wife: "It must be this airport food." As they were leaving the airport, they heard rumors that a plane had crashed. When they returned home, Jack turned on the radio to listen for news about the supposed air crash. Said his wife later: "We finally heard his mother's name on the radio and Jack just collapsed completely."

Graham appeared to be in shock for days after learning of his mother's death. Said one neighbor: "He was really broken up about it, They were very close." While Graham was recovering from the loss of his mother, FBI lab technicians were sifting through the smallest remains of the crash found in the sections of the plane and at the crash site. One technician finally emptied the contents of an envelope onto the desk of Roy Moore, assistant special agent in charge in the Denver FBI office, saying: "These fragments were found among the wreckage but they are the only pieces of debris that we have been unable to identify in any way with parts of the airplane or with known contents of the cargo."

Before Agent Moore were five tiny pieces of sheet metal. The technician went on to say that the pieces of metal contained foreign deposits of white and dark-gray colors which consisted mainly of sodium carbonate and traces of nitrate and sulfur compounds. That added up to dynamite, and that meant a bomb had been placed in the luggage of one of the passengers on Flight 629. According to the plane's manifest, the cargo hold carried nothing that day but passengers' luggage.

The tedious job of checking every piece of luggage carried by the forty-four persons on board the flight began. The only person for whom no luggage, except tiny fragments, could be found was Mrs. Daisie King. Airport authorities then informed the FBI that Mrs. King had taken out $62,500 in flight insurance, very heavy insurance for those days and far in excess of the amounts taken out by other passengers. The beneficiary was her son, Jack. Although Mrs. King's luggage had vanished in the explosion, the handbag she carried was found intact, and inside, tucked into a small purse, yellowed and folded into a wad, was a newspaper clipping, which Mrs. King had been careful to keep with her.

The clipping reported her son's forgery of stolen checks and his subsequent arrest. Why a mother so devoted to her son would carry about such an item, as one might carry about a keepsake, remains imponderable. Perhaps, some later theorized, she kept the clipping as a reminder of what her son was capable of doing, or, it was also later said, she kept the clipping *to remind him* of his errant ways. No one ever knew for sure, but it was this very clipping, which Mrs. King may have wanted authorities to find should she ever meet with foul play, that led FBI agents to the door of Jack Gilbert Graham.

Before interviewing Graham, agents learned that he was not the penitent wrongdoer attempting to set things right. He and his mother had been arguing constantly about Jack's management of the drive-in restaurant, particularly about a strange fire from an even stranger gas explosion that had caused more than $1,200 in damages. The explosion had occurred only a few months before Flight 629 exploded in the skies of Colorado. Graham had tried to collect insurance on the restaurant after the fire, but had failed.

Insurance must have been much on Graham's mind, agents thought, when they discovered that on another recent occasion, the 23-year-old had apparently stalled his pick-up truck in front of a speeding railroad train to collect insurance. Then a neighbor told agents that Jack had boasted of his demolition work while serving in the Coast Guard.

On November 10, 1955, agents went to the home of John Gilbert Graham. Jack was cordial, offering the agents coffee and telling them the story of his life, detailing his days in the orphanage, his mother's three marriages, even his forgery of stolen checks, being careful to point out that he had just about made complete restitution.

Graham told them that his mother was going to Alaska to visit his half sister and hunt caribou. He added that she was carrying in her luggage a large amount of shotgun shells and other ammunition for hunting purposes. The agents nodded, already knowing that Mrs. King was an outdoorswoman, a woman who loved to fish and hunt.

Then one of the agents inquired: "Exactly what did she have in her luggage and did you help her pack it?"

District Attorney Bert Keating demonstrates in court where an explosive device was located on United Flight 629 in a model of the plane that blew up on November 1, 1955.

"I can describe her luggage," replied Graham in an even voice, "but I can't tell you what was in it. Mother would never allow anyone to help her pack. She always insisted upon doing it herself."

Jack's wife, Gloria, stepped forward to support her husband's statements, saying that Mrs. King, who had recently been living with them, was always particular about her things. Jack excused himself, telling the agents he was going to make some more coffee. Gloria Graham then remembered a small item about Mrs. King's luggage: "Just before Mrs. King left for the airport Jack gave her a present, or, I presume he did."

"A present?" asked one of the agents. "What kind of present?"

"Oh, I think it was a small set of tools, like drills and files. My mother-in-law used these things to make art gifts out of sea shells. Jack had talked of buying her a set for Christmas. On the day she was to leave, he came home with a package and took it to the basement, where his mother was packing. I just assumed that this contained the tool set and that he gave it to her to take along."

When the agents left the house, they immediately interviewed Graham's next-door neighbors. One woman stated that she remembered the gift Jack had bought for his mother, recalling that "he had wrapped it in Christmas paper and I was told that he put it in his mother's luggage before she left."

"What else were you told?" asked an agent.

"Nothing important...only someone told me later that Jack became suddenly ill only a short time after the plane had taken off, and was very pale. I remember also having been told that when the Grahams were informed of the crash, Jack remarked: 'That's it.' I guess he was too stunned to know what he was talking about. It was really a great blow to him...Why, the poor fellow has been unable to eat or sleep since. All he does is walk up and down the house."

John Gilbert Graham at his trial; he had little or nothing to say, having already confessed to the mass murder of his mother and forty-three others.

On November 16, 1955, agents called the Grahams and asked them to come to headquarters to identify, if possible, some fragments of luggage, which might have belonged to Mrs. King. Both appeared on time and agreed that, yes, the pieces looked like parts from a small suitcase Mrs. King had taken with her. Agents then asked Graham to stay behind for some more routine questions, while sending his wife home.

The young man stretched out his six-foot-one-inch, 190-pound frame in an office chair and smilingly agreed to answer any questions. Agent Moore conducted the interrogation, beginning slowly, detailing all the facts the agents had gathered, then stating that Jack's wife had told them about the Christmas gift he had slipped into his mother's suitcase, a package approximately eighteen inches long, fourteen inches wide, and three inches deep, as described by Gloria Graham.

Graham's attitude was cool and cooperative. Calmly, and with a smile, he replied: "Oh, you've got your facts all mixed up. I had intended buying her a tool set, but I couldn't find the right kind so I didn't buy any."

"But your wife told us you did and that you brought it home with you."

"She's wrong about that. I'd been talking a lot about the tools and I guess she just supposed I bought them. That's reasonable, isn't it?"

Moore did not respond, but asked about Graham's conduct at the airport restaurant. "You did get sick, didn't you, Jack?"

"We had a snack to eat out there," he responded quickly, "but the food was miserable and it turned my stomach."

Then Moore took the hard line, saying: "I want you to know that you have certain rights. The door there is open. You can walk out any time you wish. There is a telephone. You can call your wife or an attorney if you wish. You don't have to tell us anything and if you do, it can be used in a court of law. There will be no threats and no promises made while we talk with you." Moore stared at John Gilbert Graham for some moments, then said firmly to the smiling young man: "Jack, we have gone over what you told us. You blew up that plane to kill your mother, didn't you?"

"No, I didn't," Graham answered in a calm voice.

"Then you don't mind making any statements?"

"Of course I'll make a statement," Graham said. His voice was full of confidence. "Why shouldn't I? And I'll do a lot more. I'll take a lie detector test if you wish. What's more, you have my permission to search my house, my car or anything else. I haven't done anything wrong."

To prove his claim, Graham signed a waiver giving the agents the right to search his home, eliminating the necessity for a court-ordered search warrant. Agents went immediately to Graham's house. Within minutes one of them called to inform Moore that "Mrs. Graham says Jack told her not to tell about the Christmas present. She signed a statement." Moore immediately confronted Graham with his wife's contradiction of his statements.

Graham thought for a moment, then said: "Oh yeah, I remember now. I did get her that present." He related that he had bought an X-Acto tool set from "some guy" whose name he did not know, paying him $10 for it. Yes, he had slipped the present into his mother's luggage. It now came back to him, all of it, he said.

Agents busy searching the Graham home kept calling with more information. A small roll of copper wiring, a type used for detonating dynamite, had been found in a pocket of one of Graham's shirts. An hour later agents found the insurance policies his mother had signed at the airport, all of them making her son the beneficiary. These had been hidden in a cedar chest in Graham's bedroom. Then they found the shotgun shells and ammunition Mrs. King was supposed to have taken with her. Also left behind by Mrs. King were presents she intended to give to her daughter in Alaska.

Agent Moore outlined the discoveries to Graham, one by one, then summed up the evidence, mounting every minute, surrounding the suspect with his guilt. "Why didn't your mother take these things [the ammunition and gifts] with her?"

Graham grew solemn, then said: "I told her not to take them because her baggage was overweight."

Moore threw a report in front of Graham. "This is from our lab and it proves that the crash was caused by a dynamite explosion." The agent looked at his watch. It was past midnight. They had been at it for almost six hours.

Then Graham sat stiffly in his chair. "May I have a glass of water, please?" he said. He was given a glass of water, which he drank slowly with long gulps. He put down the glass and, in a hard voice, said: "Okay, where do you want me to start?"

"Wherever you want to," replied Moore.

"Well, it all started about six months ago. Mother was raising hell because the drive-in wasn't making any money." He then explained how he had caused the explosion that wrecked the kitchen of the restaurant.

"And what about the truck you left on the railroad tracks so that you could collect the insurance after the train had wrecked it?"

A heavily manacled John Gilbert Graham, center, entering Colorado Penitentiary; he was executed in the gas chamber on January 11, 1957, telling a newsman before entering the chamber: "I'd like you to sit in my lap as they close the door in there."

"I did that, too, for the insurance." Graham's confidence had vanished. He squirmed in the chair. Sweat welled up on his forehead and ran down his cheeks. When he wiped it away with his handkerchief, his hand visibly trembled.

Moore leaned close to Graham. "What about the plane crash? You did that, too, didn't you?"

Graham wet his lips and looked at the ceiling nervously.

"What about the plane crash, Jack?"

Graham drank some more water, spilling some on his shirt-front, but said nothing.

"Come on, Jack," Moore persisted. "The truth. You blew up that plane for your mother's insurance. We know it. Let's have the truth from you."

Graham's bloodless face greeted the question. Slowly, he nodded, as if unable to speak the words. He then asked for more water. This was brought to him and he drank slowly, then said: "I might as well tell you everything." With that, Jack Graham became calm and in a deliberate, seemingly indifferent tone, he told in exacting detail how he had made his bomb from twenty-five sticks of dynamite, two electric primer caps, a six-volt battery and a timer (the fragments of sheet metal found by the technicians were from the battery).

Graham seemed proud to announce the fact that he had worked at an electric shop for more than a week to learn how to connect and activate the timer before buying the dynamite. Yes, he had taken the ammunition and the gifts for his half sister from the suitcase and replaced them with the bomb. After twenty minutes, Graham fell silent. A stenographer was then called into the office and he repeated the entire story, and then signed the confession.

John Gilbert Graham was arrested for sabotage and mass murder and later turned over to Colorado authorities. The stores where he had purchased the dynamite and timer were checked and Graham was identified as the buyer. Graham's half sister arrived from Alaska and told how Jack had once grimly joked about the possibility of his mother's hunting ammunition exploding during one of her plane trips. She quoted him as saying: "Can't you just see those shotgun shells going off in the plane every which way? Can't you just imagine the pilots and the passengers and Mother jumping around?" She thought he was insane.

Graham was placed in the Denver jail to await trial. He refused to see his wife, to whom he had transferred all his assets, and told a guard: "You can send my mail to Canon City [Prison] until next month. After that, you can send it to hell."

Graham claimed that he was without funds on December 9, 1955, when being arraigned for murder. Three lawyers were assigned to defend him. He was then charged with murder in the first degree, but Graham, ignoring his confession, entered a plea of "innocent and innocent by reason of insanity before, during, and after the commission of the crime."

The State then sent Graham to the Colorado Psychopathic Hospital, where four psychiatrists examined him. As a way of repudiating his confession, Graham told a weird, wholly unbelievable tale. He said to the doctors sitting before him: "While the FBI men were interviewing me in Denver, I saw a photograph on the wall and it fascinated me. It showed the capture of Nazi saboteurs on the coast of Florida during World War II and FBI men were digging up dynamite. Somehow, that gave me the idea of confessing that I'd used dynamite to blow up the plane but, really, I didn't do it."

Graham's ridiculous tale failed to convince the doctors that he was insane, and he was returned to jail to await trial. On February 10, 1956, Graham was found by guards in his cell almost dead, after trying to strangle himself with a pair of socks. He was revived and made his confession all over again, almost word-for-word with the statement he had given the FBI.

Night and day in his cell, he professed his deep sorrow for the murdering of his mother and forty-three other helpless human beings, but he would often recant his confession and turn brutally callous, telling guards that the people on Flight 629 were no more than strangers to him, saying the number of dead was unimportant, that "...it could have been a thousand. When their time comes there is nothing they can do about it."

Graham's trial began on April 16, 1956, at which time the confessed killer admitted signing his confession, but said that the confession was not true. He chewed gum incessantly and shrugged indifference at the testimony of the eighty witnesses and 174 exhibits brought against him. Though he had bragged that he would take the witness stand and demolish the State's case, Graham never sat in the box. He was convicted of first-degree murder on May 5, 1956, by a jury of five women and seven men after they deliberated only seventy-two minutes.

The Colorado Supreme Court heard Graham's appeal on August 8, upholding the decision of the lower court. Graham unexpectedly did take the stand this time, but only to inform one and all that his appeal had been made by his lawyers against his wishes. He was promptly sentenced to death. His lawyers went on appealing for many months, until the state Supreme Court ordered that the bomber's execution take place on January 11, 1957.

On that Friday morning, Jack Gilbert Graham stepped coldly into the gas chamber at the Colorado Penitentiary, where he would be pronounced dead within eight minutes after the lethal gas was let loose. Only a few moments before gingerly stepping into the death chamber, Graham turned to a few reporters standing nearby. One newsman who had incurred Graham's ire because of the criticism he had heaped upon the mass murderer, asked the condemned man if he had any last words.

"Yeah," snapped Jack Graham, ending his life with a wisecrack: "I'd like you to sit on my lap as they close the door in there."

THE CLUTTER SLAYINGS/ November 15, 1959

Richard Eugene Hickock (1932-1965) and Perry Smith (1929-1965) were habitual criminals, professional burglars, and thieves. Neither man was mentally sound, according to reports. Hickock had suffered headaches since a car crash in 1950 and Smith was diagnosed a paranoid long before both men became infamous (thanks to a pervasive, novelized book treatment of their otherwise pedestrian lives by author Truman Capote) for their slaughter of the Clutter family.

While serving time in the Kansas State Penitentiary at Lansing, Hickock learned from his cellmate, Floyd Wells, of a wealthy farmer in Holcomb, Kansas, Herbert W. Clutter. Wells, who was at one time employed by Clutter, told Hickock that the farmer often kept as much as $10,000 in a safe in his home. This misinformation—Clutter never held such sums in his rural house—sparked an idea of robbery in the devious mind of Hickock.

Perry Smith, who admitted killing one or more of the Clutter family members; he hanged on April 14, 1965.

Upon his release, Hickock teamed up with Smith. Both men planned to rob the Clutter family and then retire to South America, where they would while away their lives diving for treasure from a boat they would buy from the spoils of the Clutter robbery. The two thieves entered the home of the Clutter family on the night of November 15, 1959. They stumbled about in the darkness of the large farmhouse, until they awoke family members. Both men held their victims at bay with guns and knives, deciding what to do with them.

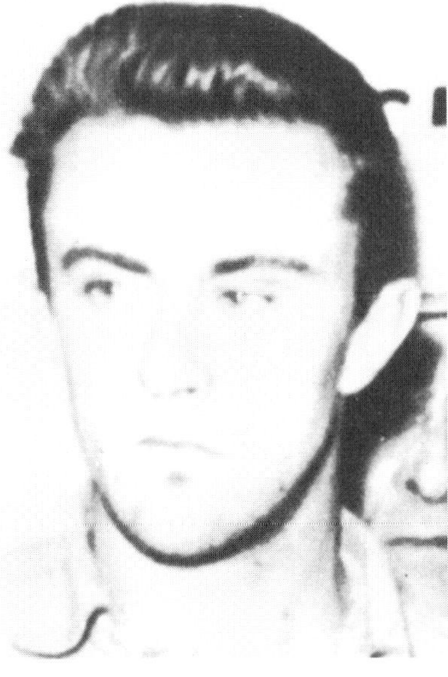

Richard Eugene Hickcock, who joined Smith on the scaffold in 1965 for the Clutter killings.

The intruders tied up the Clutters and then systematically searched the house. Failing to find anything other than about $50, Hickock and Smith turned in a rage upon the helpless Clutter family, which included Herbert Clutter, forty-eight; Bonnie Clutter, forty-five; daughter Nancy, sixteen; and son Kenyon, fifteen. They stabbed and shot the four members of the family, killing all of them before they fled.

Wells, who was still an inmate of the Kansas State Prison, heard the news of the Clutter deaths on the radio in his cell and he asked to see the warden, telling him about Hickock's talk with him earlier concerning the Clutters. Detective Al Dewey then led an exhaustive hunt for Hickock and Smith, finally running both men down in Las Vegas, where they were arrested.

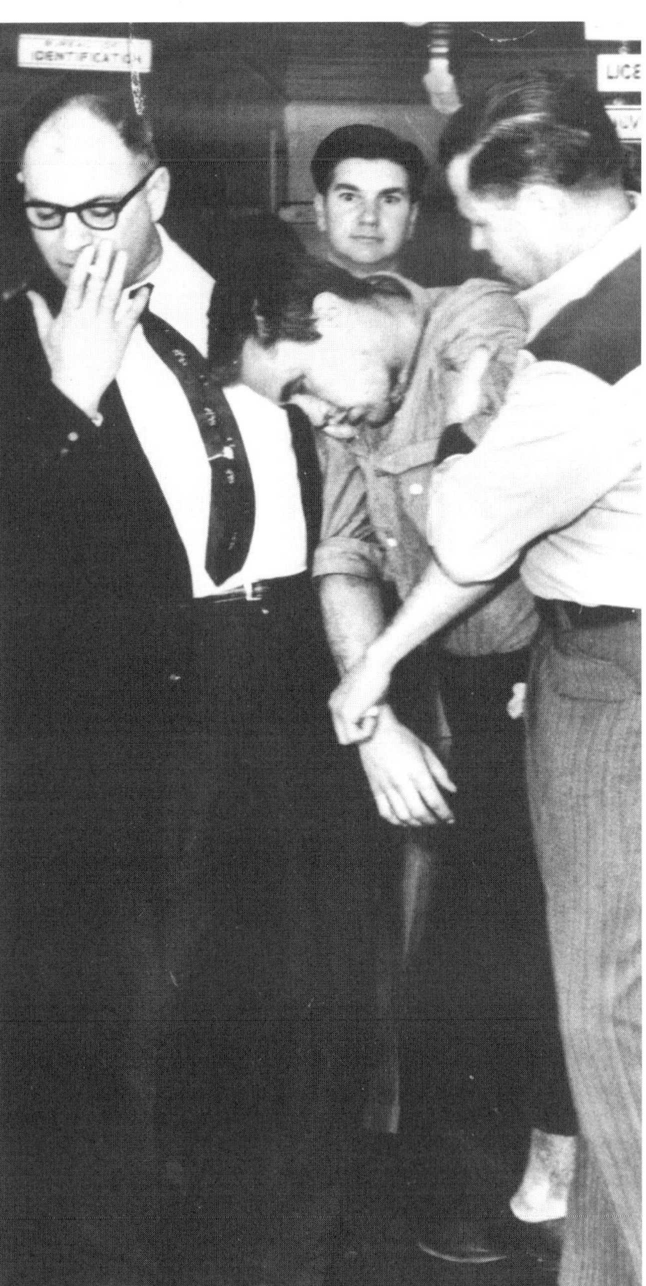

Hickcock. in custody after he and Smith were tracked down and arrested in Las Vegas; the killers had sought $10,000, but realized less than $50 for slaughtering the Clutters.

The murderous thieves immediately turned on each other. Hickock told authorities that "Perry Smith killed the Clutters. I couldn't stop him. He killed them all!"

Smith denied killing anyone. Then he said of Herbert Clutter: "He was a nice gentleman. I thought so right up to the time I cut his throat." He later said he killed only the wife, Bonnie Clutter, and that Hickock murdered the rest. Smith added, as if to make himself appear noble, that Hickock insisted upon raping the 16-year-old daughter Nancy, but he had kept Hickock from sexually abusing the girl.

Only Herbert Clutter was knifed, his throat cut from ear to ear and his body then thrown into the basement of the house. The others were murdered as they sat tied to chairs, Hickock and Smith taking turns blowing off their heads with a shotgun.

Both Hickock and Smith were tried in March 1960 in Kansas City. The prosecutor in the case aggressively pilloried the two men, aptly describing them as inhuman beasts and reminding the jury that "chicken-hearted jurors" before them had allowed ruthless murderers to go free. The jury found Hickock and Smith guilty on four counts of murder and both men were sentenced to death. Appeals were denied and each man, quaking and screaming for mercy, were half-dragged to the gallows inside the Kansas State Penitentiary at Lansing on April 14, 1965, and promptly hanged.

"BORN TO RAISE HELL"/July 13-14, 1966

When he was nineteen, mass-murderer Richard Franklin Speck (AKA: B. Brian; Richard Franklin Lindbergh; Richard Benjamin Speck, 1941-1991) emblazoned a tattoo into his left forearm which accurately summed up his emotional and mental state at the time. It read: "Born to Raise Hell." Years later, Speck burned the tattoo off using the ember of a lit cigar. From his cell in the Illinois Penitentiary (Stateville) at Joliet, Illinois, he dreamed of the day he would be paroled. By his own admission though, the convicted killer of eight student nurses believed that the chances were not good. "If he was ever freed on parole, I'd probably take up arms myself," explained John Wilkening, father of one of the women Richard Speck murdered. "I have a lot of friends and so I would probably have to wait in line."

Richard Franklin Speck was born in Kirkwood, Illinois. He was one of eight children belonging to Margaret and Benjamin Speck. In 1947, the family moved to Dallas, Texas, where Speck completed junior high school. It was the only formal education the young man received before he left home. By the time he was twenty, Speck had been arrested ten times on charges ranging from criminal trespass to burglary.

Speck had tallied thirty-seven arrests by spring 1966, when he returned to Chicago to find work as a merchant seaman. The semi-literate drifter spent his waking hours reading comic books and drinking himself into stupors. He was a habitual

Richard Franklin Speck, drifter, thief and mass murderer of eight nurses in Chicago on the night of July 13-14, 1966.

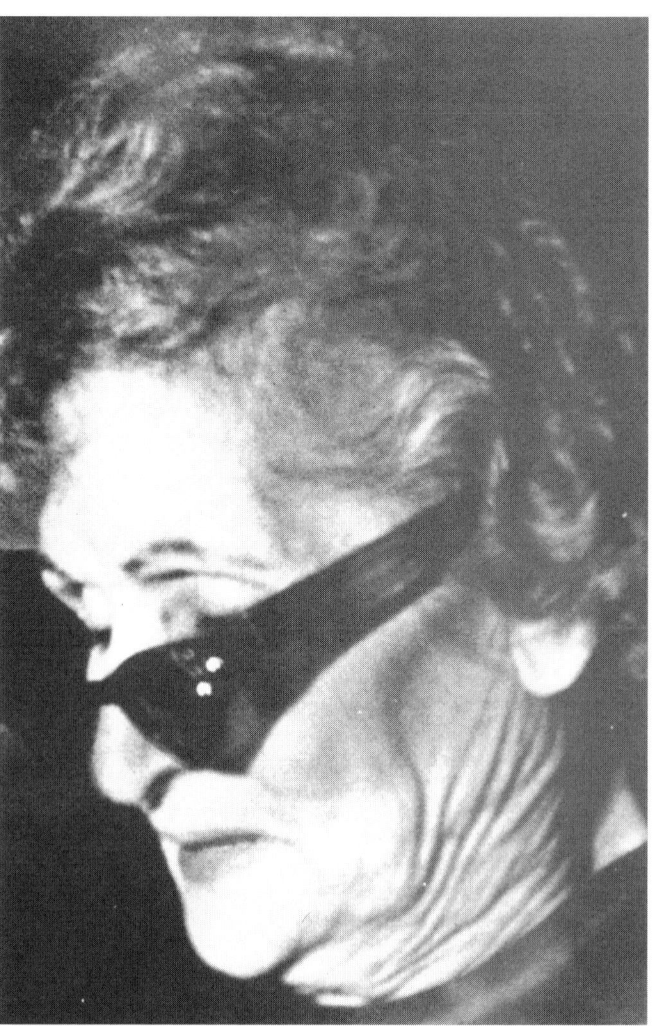

Speck's mother, Mrs. Margaret Speck Lindbergh, who raised him in Dallas, Texas, where, by 1966, he ran up 37 arrests.

One of the blood-stained bedrooms at the house in Chicago, where Speck molested and murdered some of his victims.

pill-popper with a distorted view of reality, evidenced by his total lack of recall concerning his movements the night of July 13, 1966.

Speck shipped out on the cargo vessel the *Randall,* owned and operated by the Inland Steel Company. He was discharged in June 1966 for insubordination and fighting with a superior officer. His sister Martha Thornton, who lived in Chicago, provided him with pocket money and drove him to the National Maritime Union hall, where Speck hoped to find work on a cargo ship heading to New Orleans. But there were no berths available to him on July 10, 1966, the day he made his application.

Brooding about his inability to find any work on merchant ships, Speck began drinking for the next three days. His bender took him through the lowlife taverns and skid row dives that dotted the west side of Chicago, where he plotted ways to earn enough money to pay for his trip to New Orleans. On the night of July 13, the besotted Speck injected a narcotic into his veins and headed to the South Side to see what he might steal.

Speck wandered to a two-story townhouse belonging to the South Chicago Community Hospital on East 100th Street around 11 p.m. He dug into his pockets and pulled out a handgun and a knife. He knocked on the door, and after a few seconds had passed, 23-year-old student nurse Corazon Amurao appeared. "I'm not going to hurt you," he said. "I'm only going to tie you up. I need your money to go to New Orleans." Amurao and two of her companions were directed to the upstairs bedroom, where three of their other roommates were sleeping.

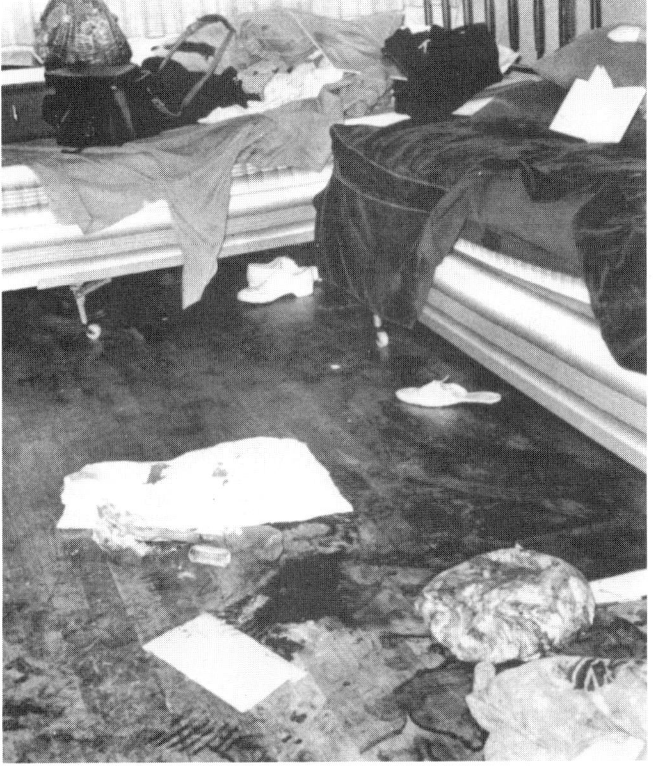

A second room of the murder house, coated with human gore, where Speck sexually attacked and then stabbed several nurses to death.

Mary A. Jordan, murdered by Speck.

Merlita Gargullo, murdered by Speck.

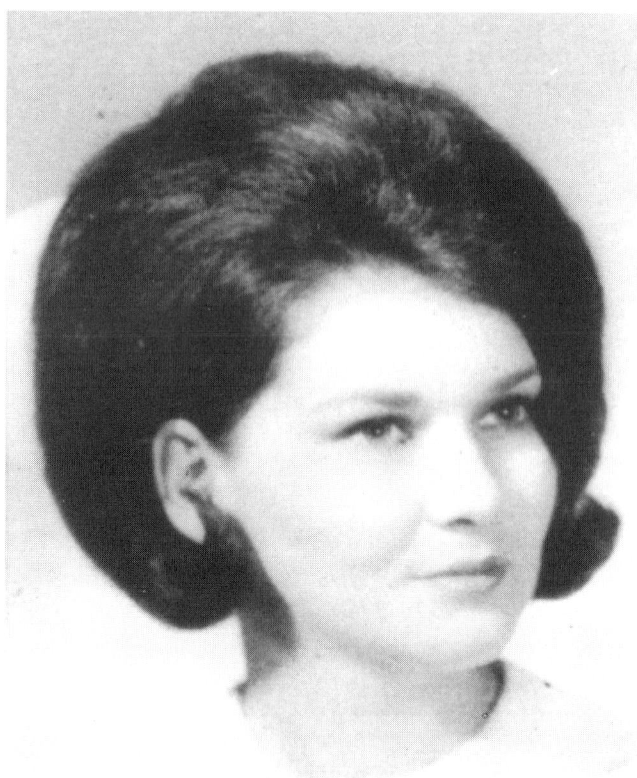

Gloria Davy, murdered by Speck.

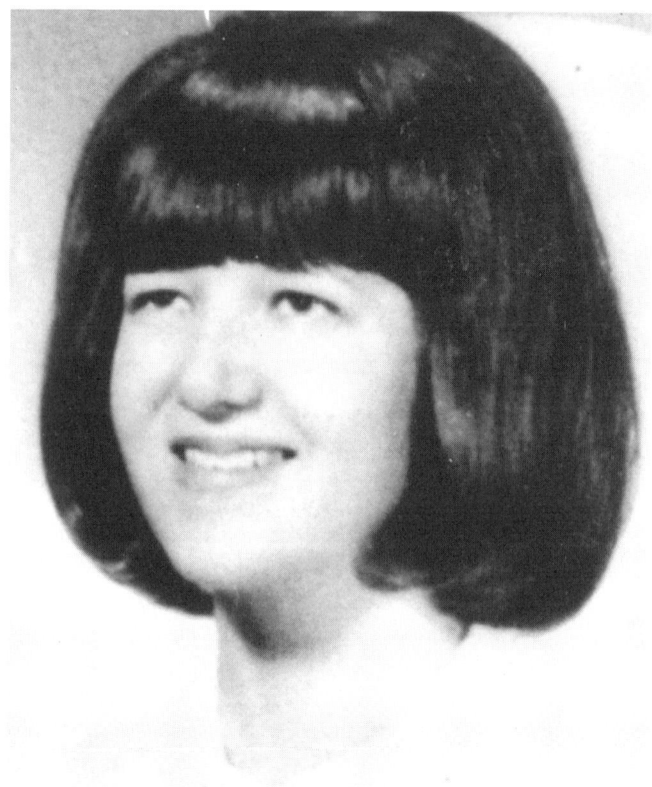

Nina Schmale, murdered by Speck.

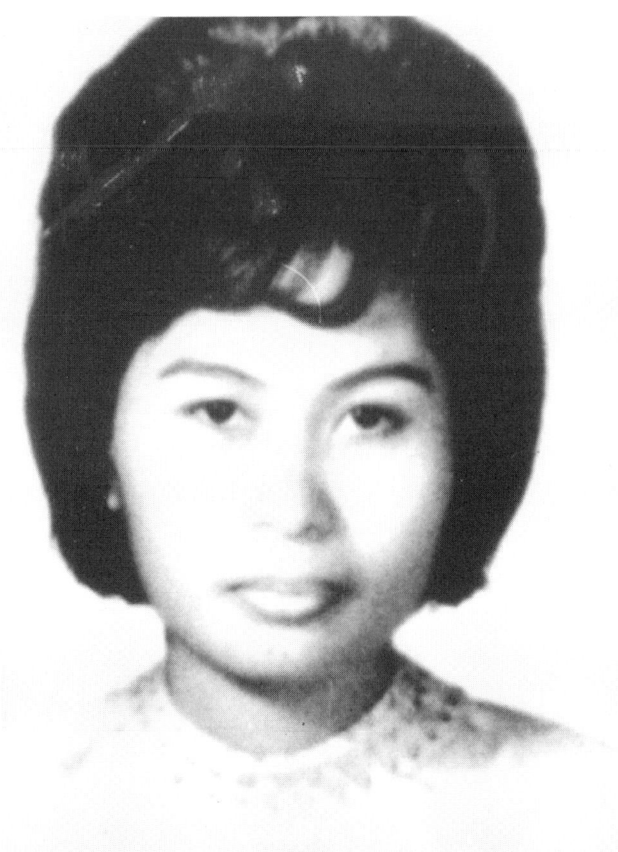

Valentina Passion, murdered by Speck.

Pamela Wilkening, murdered by Speck.

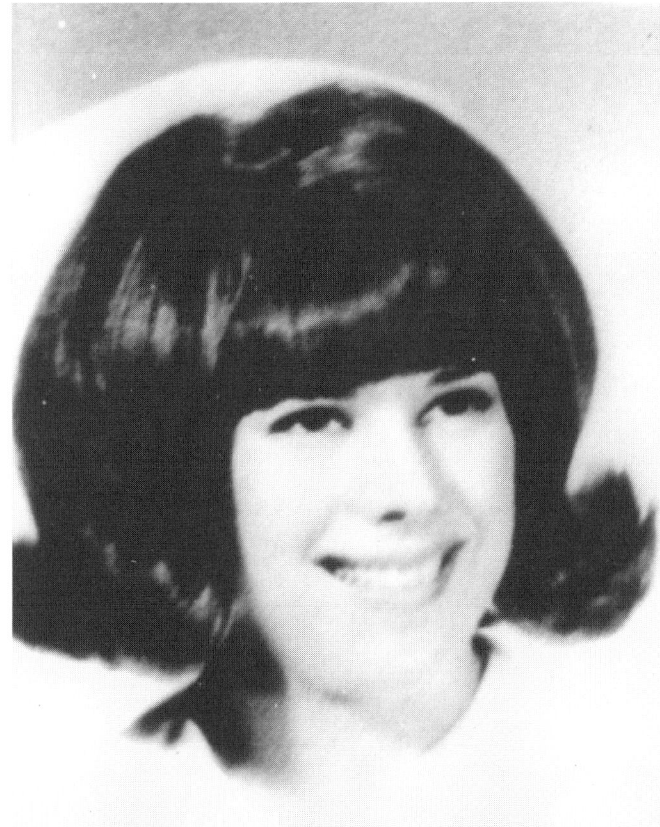

Patricia Matusek, murdered by Speck.

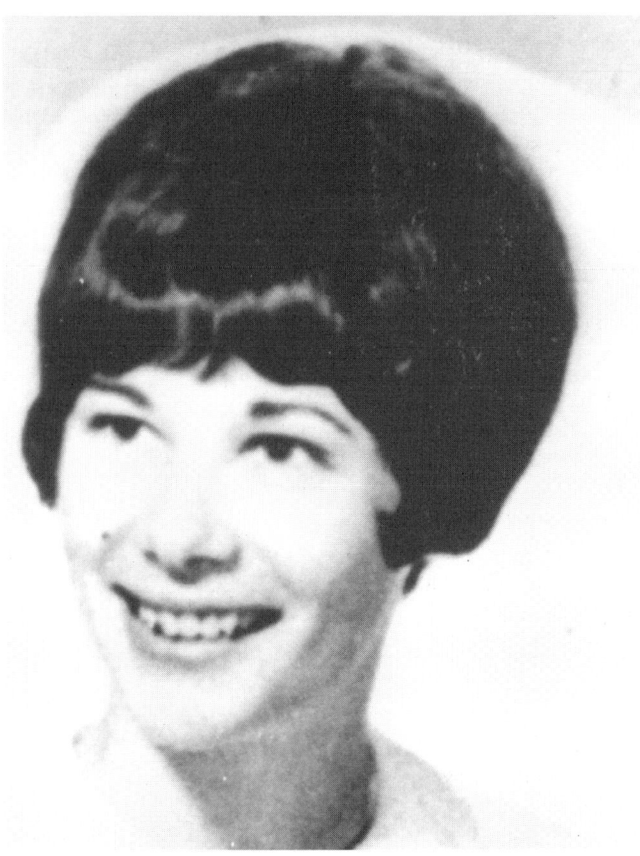

Suzanne Farris, murdered by Speck.

At gunpoint, the nurses were ordered to lie flat on the floor. The young women meekly complied with Speck's directive. He bound their hands and feet with strips torn from the bed sheets and then waited. At 11:30 p.m., Gloria Davy returned home from a date. Speck seized her at the door and led her upstairs. Then at midnight, Suzanne Farris and Mary Ann Jordan arrived home. Jordan did not live at the address; it was her tragic luck to be Farris' overnight guest.

Having tied up all nine young women, Speck then demanded their money. He restated his peaceable intentions. "Don't be afraid, I'm not going to kill you," he said. A few more minutes passed. Speck chatted with Merlita Gargullo, who was born in the Philippines. "Do you know karate?" he asked. According to the statements of Amurao the only survivor that night, Speck became increasingly agitated. He led 20-year-old Pamela Wilkening into the adjacent bedroom and stabbed her with his knife. Her muffled scream was stifled when Speck twisted her neck with a strip of sheet.

The killer was apparently sexually excited by committing this brutal murder and decided to continue killing. Speck returned moments later for Mary Ann Jordan and Suzanne Farris. The two of them were repeatedly slashed in the face, neck, and chest. Farris, the daughter of a Chicago Transit Authority employee, fought him, but was stabbed eighteen times. Afterward, Speck calmly went into the washroom, where he rinsed the blood off his hands.

The next victim was 24-year-old Nina Schmale from suburban Wheaton. He stabbed the woman in the neck and then strangled her to death. The remaining student nurses attempted to hide beneath beds, but Speck tracked them all down but one: Corazon Amurao, who succeeded in pushing herself under the bed and out of the killer's view.

Lone survivor, 23-year-old Corazon Amurao, who hid beneath a bed and went undetected by Speck; she later became the chief witness against the mass murderer.

Paralyzed with fear, Amurao heard the death cries of her two friends from the Philippines: Valentina Passion and Merlita Gargullo, who were stabbed in the next room. Twenty-year-old Patricia Matusek, a former swimming champion, was carried to the bathroom. She begged Speck to untie her ankles before he killed her. He kicked her in the stomach and then strangled her to death. This left Gloria Davy, the only one of the eight that Speck sexually molested.

Amurao remained beneath the bed for hours, fearful that Speck would find her if she attempted to escape. Not until 5 p.m. the next day did she venture out. She stepped out onto a narrow ledge outside her bedroom and called for help. Her cries were heard by two local residents. The police arrived minutes later. What they found shocked and sickened them: eight student nurses, savagely mutilated, were lying dead. Detectives found thirty fingerprints and a man's T-shirt was found beside Davy's body. Police artist Otis Rathel sketched a composite drawing of the suspect from a description provided by Amurao. The Chicago newspapers published the likeness the next day. As it turned out, Rathel's sketch bore an amazing likeness to the killer.

Speck's identity was established when a gas station attendant recognized the suspect from the police sketch. The suspect had told the attendant that he was looking for work at the National Maritime Union. The union retrieved Speck's application from a wastepaper basket. Fingerprints taken at the murder scene were matched to a set of Speck's prints on file with the Dallas police. With a name and a description of their suspect, police prepared to search for Speck. Their search was short-lived; the killer made himself easy to locate.

Following his murder spree, Speck had returned to his ninety-cent room at the Starr Hotel on West Madison Street, where he fell asleep. On July 16, 1966, the gaunt, thin-faced killer slashed his right wrist and left arm with a blade. As the blood pulsated from his arm, Speck called to the man in the next bunk. Failing to elicit sympathy, Speck stumbled into the hall. A police ambulance was summoned and he was taken to the Cook County Hospital emergency room, where Dr. LeRoy Smith attended to him. "What's your name?" Smith asked. He answered, "Richard. Richard Speck."

Dr. Smith summoned police, who promptly arrested the mass murderer. It took a Cook County jury only forty-nine minutes to convict Richard Franklin Speck of the crime of murder. On June 15, 1967, he was sentenced to die in the electric chair. After the U.S. Supreme Court set aside the death penalty, Speck was re-sentenced on November 22, 1972, to 400 to 1,200 years at the Illinois Penitentiary the longest jail term ever meted out, up to that time.

The flophouse room in which Speck cut both arms (his blood stains the floor in this photo) in an attempt to commit suicide.

Richard Speck, left, shown at the time of his 1967 trial; he was convicted and sentenced to death, but his sentence was commuted to life imprisonment following the U.S. Supreme Court's moratorium on the death penalty.

Nevertheless, Speck became eligible for parole in 1976. In 1977 and again in 1981, the convicted killer sent a tersely worded note to the state parole board saying that he was not interested in an early release. He was content to remain behind bars, where he happily pursued his hobby of oil painting. "Why don't you give parole to some of those young guys in here?" he complained. "They don't need to be in here in the first place."

In August 1987, Speck had a change of heart and asked that the Illinois Prison Review Board consider granting his application for early release. There was little chance of that occurring, however. The memory of Speck's crime was still fresh in the public's mind. According to Joseph Matusek, Patricia's father: "We can't let this go. We'll be there to oppose it."

Matusek and many other relatives of the slain nurses had no need to block the release of Richard Speck after December 5, 1991. On this day, the mass murderer died in his cell of a massive heart attack. Though dead, Richard Speck went on generating lucrative "news stories" for TV journalists such as Bill Kurtis, who exemplified the worst kind of TV's "crime journalism." One-time anchorman for the CBS affiliate in Chicago, Kurtis went on to produce and "star" as an on-screen narrator in a series of shock crime programs for the Arts and Entertainment (A&E) cable station. His show, euphemistically entitled "American Justice," and "Investigative Reports," pandered, among many unsavory subjects, a vile videotape that showed the imprisoned Speck using drugs and having oral sex with other male prisoners before his death.

Kurtis at first presented this tape to the Illinois House of Representatives in May 1996, as a way of "exposing" prisoner excesses, but he had already shown and would continue to show (with censored applications) this tape on CBS. In reality, Kurtis, having no credentials as a penologist or criminologist, or having any published works to indicate his expertise or authority in these fields, ostensibly used the tape to indict the prison system. His real purpose was obvious—he employed the tawdry tape to promote his own career and to boost viewership, typifying the tasteless brand of TV crime journalism that establishes notorious killers as media icons, recycling their rap sheets over and over again to reap large profits, ghoulishly feeding upon the rotting carcasses of society's worst criminals.

THE SHOOTIST IN THE TOWER/ August 1, 1966

A one-time altar boy, Eagle scout, and U.S. Marine, Charles Joseph Whitman (1941-1966) of Lake Worth, Fla., committed one of the most ruthless mass murder rampages in U.S. history. In July 1966, Whitman, twenty-five, was enrolled as a junior for the summer semester at the University of Texas in Austin. A student in architectural engineering, Whitman was taking an

Charles Whitman at age thirteen, top, with his two younger brothers Patrick, left forefront, and John, right forefront.

Charles Whitman as a student at the University of Texas in Austin, a quiet scholar with psychological problems.

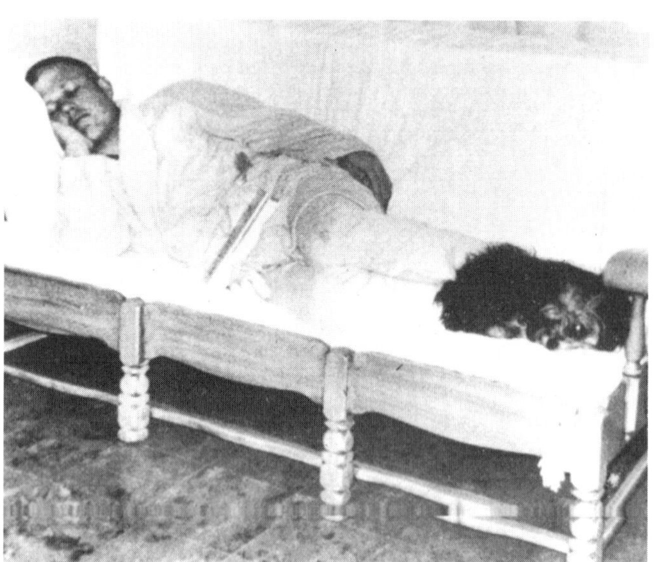

Whitman sleeps a short time before he began his mass murder spree, first killing his mother and wife.

unusually heavy class load of fourteen credit hours, the pressure from such studies, it was later thought, contributing to his mental breakdown and his illogical decision to embark upon mass murder.

Like the dark resolve of Howard Unruh in 1949, who first thought to murder his own mother, Whitman's first victims were selected from his own household. In the early morning hours of August 1, 1966, Whitman stabbed his 24-year-old wife, Kathleen Leissner Whitman, to death in his Austin apartment. He then shot and killed his mother, Mrs. C.A. Whitman.

Nothing indicated that these savage attacks were provoked. Whitman left three cryptic notes in his apartment. The first, addressed to "Roy" read: "My mother's ill and won't be at work today." The two remaining notes were addressed "To whom it may concern." In one, Whitman professed love for his wife and mother, but confusion about why they had to die, except to "save them the embarrassment" of the action he had planned. Whitman expressed contempt for his father, a plumbing contractor from Lake Worth. He said he hated him "with a mortal passion."

Whitman spent the remainder of the morning assembling an arsenal of weapons and gathering provisions. A mail carrier, Chester Arrington, watched as Whitman retooled his shotgun in the family garage. "I talked to Whitman for about twenty-five minutes on the day he did it," Arrington recalled years later. "I saw him sawing off the shotgun, and I knew that was illegal." Arrington did not call police. "All I had to do was pick up the phone and report him. I could have stopped him. I've always blamed myself."

When Whitman was finished with his preparations, his foot locker resembled an arsenal. It contained a 6-mm. rifle with a telescopic sight, a Remington .35-caliber pump rifle, a .357 magnum pistol, a 9-mm. Luger pistol, a 30.06 reconditioned army carbine, a 12-gauge sawed off shotgun, and a large Bowie knife. The locker was well stocked with food and two bottles of water.

Whitman then carried the locker to the tallest building in Austin, a twenty-seven story tower on the university campus. The granite tower housed the university library and administration offices with an observation deck on the top level. In 1966, the deck was open to the public, commanding an expansive view of the entire campus and a significant portion of Austin. Whitman entered the tower, shot and killed the woman at the visitor's registration desk, and proceeded to the elevator. He next killed a mother and her two children, who were spending the day sightseeing. Just before noon, Whitman reached the observation deck, and with his cache of weapons he began random shooting at those below who fell prey to his telescopic sights.

An office worker on the eighteenth floor of the tower, Ruth Kiykendall, heard gunshots and called a friend in a nearby building. "Somebody's up there shooting in the tower," she said. "There is blood all over the place!" The campus was thrown into an uproar as students, faculty, and visitors scur-

The observation platform of the Tower at the University of Texas campus in Austin, where Whitman began firing at people after 11 a.m. on August 1, 1966; arrow shows where responding police bullets kicked up the dust when striking the side of the building.

A female student crouches behind a statue, right, during Whitman's onslaught of fire; a man lies wounded at left, one of the thirty-one persons injured by the sniper.

A police diagram shows Austin's University of Texas campus, where sixteen persons were killed and thirty-one wounded by Whitman (the numbers next to each figure indicate the number of dead or wounded found at that location).

Whitman's arsenal was found in the tower.

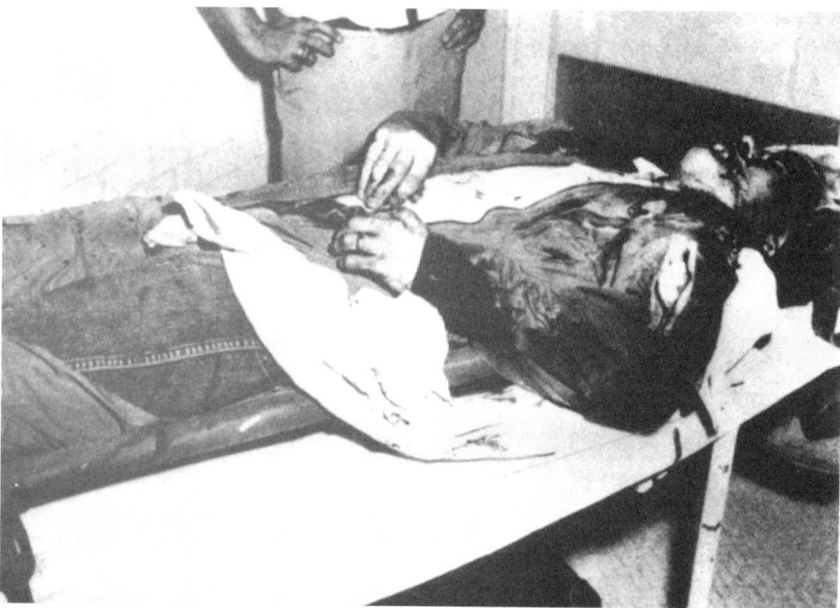

His face half shot away, the body of Charles Whitman lies on a stretcher only minutes after he was shot and killed by policemen.

ried for cover. Whitman fired his shots with unerring accuracy. He killed a student riding his bicycle near the Texas Union Building and a police officer standing behind a wooden fence. Whitman fired on a small boy and a pregnant woman, Mrs. Claire Wilson, who was taken to a hospital, where she gave birth to a stillborn baby.

Police sectioned off the campus, and tried frantically to keep 10,000 students and curiosity seekers out of the line of fire. A police airplane flew over the tower in an attempt to shoot the sniper. Armored cars were called in to rescue the wounded, several of whom lay bleeding in the 98 degree heat for more than an hour.

Whitman sprayed Guadalupe Street with bullets for eighty minutes. Police officers Romero Martinez, Houston McCoy, Jerry Jay, and George Sheppard rode up the tower elevator with civilian Allen Crum to subdue the sniper. Martinez and Crum slowly moved around the observation wall while the others covered exit doorways. Whitman spotted Martinez and fired once at him.

A few minutes later, Martinez fired six rapid shots while McCoy kicked in a door and emptied his shotgun. Martinez waved a green flag from the top of the tower signaling the all clear. Whitman lay dead on the observation deck, his head covered with blood.

"The sniper was on the northwest corner of the roof," Crum told reporters. "We rushed through the door and spread out." Whitman's body was carried out of the tower at 1:40 p.m. Later that day, administration officials allowed reporters up to the tower for a look. A pile of bloody rags was found lying in the corner. The glass face on the massive clock overlooking the campus grounds was chipped and fragmented with three bullet holes. The ex-Marine's murder spree left sixteen dead and thirty-one wounded.

School officials expressed shock over Whitman's actions. They were unable to uncover a motive. According to graduate faculty advisor Leonard F. Kreisle, Whitman "seemed to be more mature than most people his age." University Chancellor Harry Ransom released Whitman's student records, which showed that he had never been treated at the university for a psychiatric disorder, and was a "B" student. He had received an honorable discharge from the Marine Corps on December, 4, 1964, but had gone through court martial proceedings on one occasion for providing gambling loans.

Not everybody hated Charles Whitman. Hugo Ley, the owner of a Needville drug store remembered Whitman as a fine young man. "I loved Charlie," he said. "He was the kind of boy you would want for a son."

The residents of Austin were badly shaken by the slayings. Texas governor John Connally cut short a diplomatic visit to Rio de Janeiro to return home to launch a "complete and thorough investigation" into the sniper killings. Connally said that he hoped some good would result, and the inquiry would "shed light on the background and causes and give us some clues on preventing future occurrences of this nature."

In 1975, a made-for-television movie adaptation called *The Deadly Tower* starring Kurt Russell and John Forsythe aired on NBC. Martinez sued the network for $1 million, in a breach-of-contract suit, claiming the movie invaded his privacy and misrepresented his character by showing him as a radical. The same year, the University of Texas closed the observation deck, which had also been the site of several suicide attempts.

"TO MAKE A NAME FOR MYSELF"/ November 12, 1966

The summer of 1966 saw two of the most horrific mass murders in American history, the killing of eight nurses in July in Chicago by drifter Richard Speck, and the shooting deaths of sixteen persons in Austin, Texas, in August by sniper Charles Whitman. A third senseless mass murder would occur only a few months later in Mesa, Arizona, committed by a reclusive youth, who had become obsessed with the murdering Richard Speck.

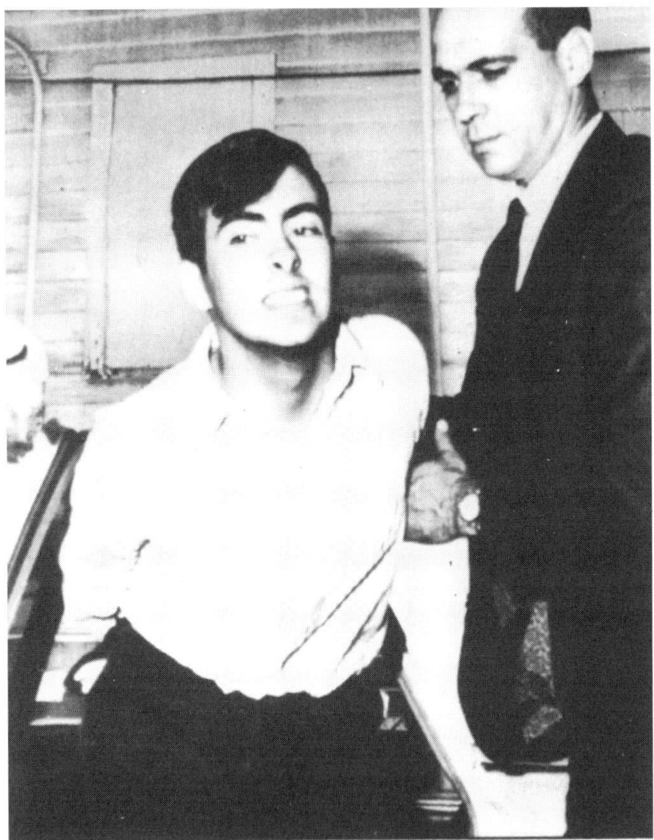

Arrogant and maniacally grinning for photographers, mass murderer Robert Benjamin Smith, eighteen, is taken into custody only minutes after he killed four women and a child and wounded two others at a beauty parlor in Mesa, Arizona, on November 12, 1966.

Robert Benjamin Smith (b. 1948), was an 18-year-old high school senior living in Mesa, Arizona in 1966. The son of a retired Air Force major, the young man was intelligent and handsome, yet extremely shy. A good student, he was elected to the student council, but he made no friends and, other than attending school, remained for the most part in his room at home, where he consumed books about the American western outlaw Jesse James and French conqueror Napoleon I. When the news about the Chicago mass murders committed by Ri-

Three-year-old Debra Sellers was shot and stabbed to death by Smith "because she was jumping around a lot."

Glenda Carter, who was killed by Smith.

Mary Margaret Olsen, who was killed by Smith.

chard Speck dominated the press, Smith read every story, keeping clippings on the killings. When the Whitman story broke, Smith avidly collected news reports on those mass murders in Austin.

Fellow students thought Smith anti-social, but his reclusive attitude was later attributed to the fact that he had recently moved with his family from Maryland to Arizona. His father had retired from the Air Force and had taken a position in an electronics plant in nearby Phoenix. It was later learned that Smith harbored a deep hatred for his father and, on one occasion, lay await for him one night with a knife but abandoned the idea of murdering him.

Psychiatrists later described Smith as schizophrenic, one saying that the boy looked upon himself "like a god, cut out to become a kind of ruler over people." Nurturing a life-and-death authority, Smith also entertained at this time, according to analysts, perverted sexual fantasies in which he shot or stabbed women. It was ironic that his parents inadvertently put into his hands on his eighteenth birthday in August 1966, the very instrument with which to murder such women. He was at that time given a gift, a .22-caliber pistol for target shooting.

On the night of November 11, 1966, Smith helped his 6-year-old sister write a letter to Santa Claus and then, following the recorded routine of Charles Whitman in Austin three months earlier, began to pack a murder case. Into this container Smith placed his target pistol, rubber gloves, two hunting knives, extra bullets and several plastic sandwich bags which he first thought to use to suffocate female victims (another fantasy he had nurtured). At the last moment, he discarded the idea of employing the bags when he realized that they were too small to fit over a human head.

Carol Farmer, who was killed by Smith.

Joyce Sellers, who was killed by Smith.

Three-month-old Tamara Lynn Sellers, though wounded, survived when her mother shielded her with her own body.

The following morning, November 12, 1966, Smith walked into the Rose-Mar College of Beauty. He immediately fired a shot into a mirror, shattering it and terrifying all of the occupants inside the beauty parlor. He ordered the five women and two children into a back room, where, according to a survivor, he laughed and frequently talked "as if he was weak in the head." He next ordered the women and children to lie on the floor head-to-head, forming a pattern that resembled the spokes of a wheel.

"Are you kidding?" one woman asked Smith.

He kneeled next to another woman and put the pistol to her head, saying: "Do you think I am?"

A third woman tried to warn him off, telling Smith that more than forty persons would shortly arrive at the beauty parlor.

He snorted: "I'm sorry, but I didn't bring enough ammunition for them."

One woman began praying and Smith asked what she was doing.

"She's praying, if you don't mind," one of his captives indignantly replied.

"I do," said Smith and he began firing, shooting each woman in the head. Killed at point blank range were Glenda Carter, eighteen; Carol Farmer, nineteen; Joyce Sellers, twenty-seven; her 3-year-old daughter Debbie, and Mary Olsen. Three-month-old Tamara Sellers was saved when her mother cradled the child as she was being shot. He also fired a bullet into the head and arm of beautician Bonita Sue Harris, but she was alive, although she pretended to be dead, waiting for the mass murderer to leave. Debbie Sellers, however was still alive, but Smith drew his hunting knife and repeatedly stabbed her to death. He later told police that he "had to do it because she was jumping around a lot."

The gunfire attracted atten-

Beautician Bonita Sue Harris, who was wounded and survived by playing dead.

tion from neighboring shopkeepers and passersby and police were summoned. They entered the shop just as a smiling Smith was about to leave. He calmly told startled officers: "I shot some people. They're back there." He pointed to the back room of the beauty parlor. "The gun is in the brown bag." The officers found four women and the three-year-old girl dead. They rushed Harris and the baby, both badly wounded, to a hospital, where they recovered.

Smith was calm about his murder spree when confronted by police. One of the horrified officers asked: "Why did you do this?"

"I wanted to make a name for myself," Smith grinned. "I wanted people to know who I was."

Arrested, Smith cooperated with police, openly admitting the mass slayings, although he stated he did not expect to find any children in the beauty parlor when he entered the place.

"Why did you shoot the baby?" he was asked.

"Well, it was going to grow up and become an adult," Smith replied. He added that if his mother and sister had been in the beauty parlor when he entered it, he would have shot and killed them, too. He expressed no regrets, adding that the shootings had "exhilarated" him.

Robert Benjamin Smith was tried and found guilty of first-degree murder on five counts on October 24, 1967. He was sentenced to death, but the U.S. Supreme Court's moratorium on the death penalty caused his execution to be commuted to life imprisonment. He is presently serving four life terms and two 99-year terms, with no hope of parole.

THE MANSON "FAMILY"/ August 8, 10, 1969

One of the worst mass murderers in America was a runt. The illegitimate son of a teenage prostitute, Charles Manson (b. 1934), never stood more than five feet, two inches, and was an unlikely candidate to lead a criminal commune, let alone a murder cult. He nevertheless became a guru to a pack of psychopathic killers whose murders shocked California and the entire U.S. in 1969.

Manson was born in Cincinnati, Ohio, on November 11, 1934. His mother, Kathleen Maddox, of Ashland, Kentucky, unable to support even herself through prostitution, left her son with his grandmother in Mc Mechen, West Virgina. He was later sent to Boys Town in Nebraska, but his incorrigible thieving and truculent manner soon caused him to leave.

Living a nomadic life, Manson drifted to Peoria, Illinois, where he was arrested for the first time for stealing food. He was sent to the Indiana Boys School in Plainfield, but Manson proved to be as surly and troublesome there as he had been at Boys Town in Nebraska. He escaped eighteen times from the

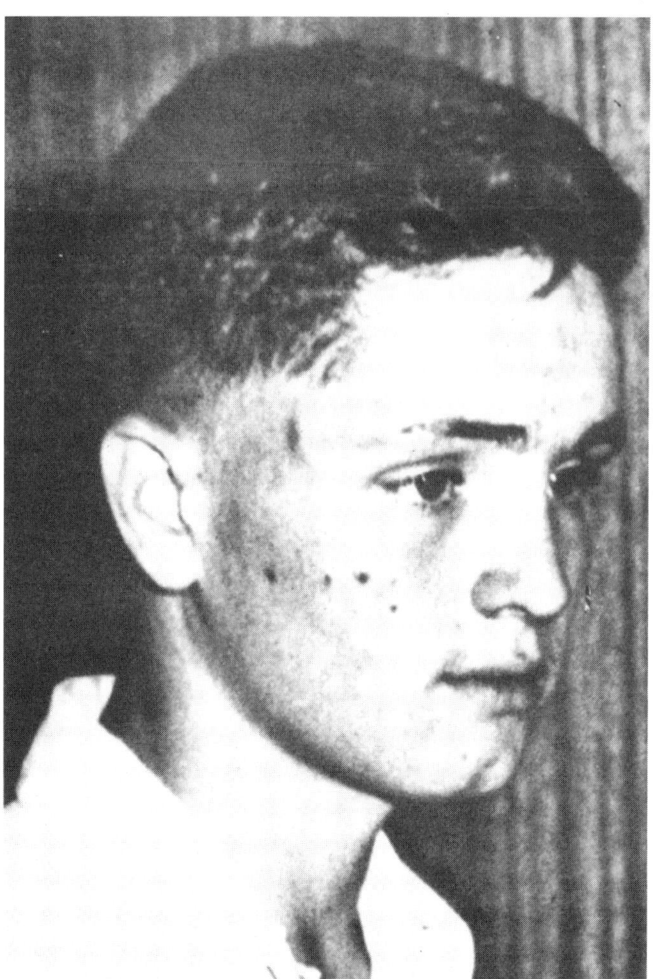

Charles Manson, fourteen, having been released from a juvenile home and made a ward of the court in Indianapolis; his mother had abandoned him.

Manson at age sixteen, a photo taken of him when he was in Philadelphia, Pennsylvania.

Charles Manson in 1969, at the time he supervised his motley "family" at the Spahn Movie Ranch and planned mass murders of whites, which he would blame on blacks to incite a race war.

Steven Earl Parent, eighteen, the first victim in the mass murders of August 8, 1969, shown at his high school prom.

school and finally fled west. He was arrested again in Beaver City, Utah, in 1951 for theft. Over the next four years, Manson spent most of his time in federal reformatories.

Manson served time in the National Training School for Boys in Washington, D.C., and he was finally paroled from the Chillicothe Federal Reformatory in November 1954. In the following year, Manson married Rosalie Jean Willis, and a short time later he was arrested and charged with transporting stolen autos across state lines. For this federal offense, Manson was sent to Terminal Island Prison outside Los Angeles to serve a three-year prison term.

In 1958, Manson was released and he immediately became a pimp, but again he was arrested, charged with violating the Mann Act for transporting females across state lines for immoral purposes. After several of these arrests, Manson resorted to forging checks and was again arrested, this time drawing a ten-year prison term in the federal penitentiary on McNeil Island, Washington. Released in March 1967, Manson bummed his way to Los Angeles. By this time he had spent seventeen years behind bars—more than half his life.

Almost illiterate and completely unschooled, prison life had nevertheless turned Manson into a shifty, cagey, and cunning creature, who had learned how to manipulate people in prison to compensate for his diminutive size. He had been used sexually by men in prison and he was bisexual, but by the time he reached California in 1967, Charles Manson had a decided taste for young women, especially the long-legged, long-haired flower children of the turbulent 1960s.

Manson mocked and sneered at convention and authority and he infused his mostly female followers with his own arrogant posture and hatred for the police and law. He labeled everyone opposed to his gypsy lifestyle an enemy of his "family," and he moved from one seamy road camp to another, first living with several young dropout women and a few docile and obedient men outside of San Francisco. Manson com-

Heiress Abigail Folger, with Voytek Frykowski; both were killed by Manson Family members invading the home at 10050 Cielo Drive.

Hair stylist Jay Sebring, who at one time dated film starlet Sharon Tate; he was murdered in the slaughter of August 8, 1969.

plained that the weather was too cold for his delicate body and insisted that his "family" follow him southward to the warmer climate of Los Angeles.

There, in 1968, Manson quickly gathered new followers who were mesmerized by his hypnotic stare and monosyllabic pronouncements, which they mistakenly took for insightful comments from an idiot savant. He mouthed platitudes and generalities that were about as enlightening as the slogans on calendars in gas stations, where he had occasionally worked in earlier years. Yet his gobbledygook and gibberish appealed to young women seeking excitement and affection.

One such was 21-year-old Patricia Krenwinkel. She had grown up in an untroubled middleclass family, had been a Camp Fire Girl and had a good education. Krenwinkel held a good job with a Los Angeles insurance company, but the moment she met Manson on Manhattan Beach, she gave up everything. She even abandoned her car and did not bother to pick up her paycheck. She was typical of the followers Manson led to the Spahn Movie Ranch, a broken down shack-cluttered dusty area in eastern Simi Valley.

Susan Atkins, twenty-one, also joined Manson. Her background rivaled his own. She had worked at seamy jobs all her life, including that of a topless dancer and bar hustler. She was unkempt, unschooled, and, like many of her repugnant ilk, proud of her ignorance, lack of hygiene and defiance to authority. Worse, she had been a practicing satanist for a number of years, an influence which was to infiltrate the deluded, receptive minds of the Manson commune. She quickly became Manson's chief aide.

The group also included tall, pretty Leslie Van Houten, nineteen, a school dropout and LSD addict, who had run away from home at an early age and had lived like a tramp in the Los Angeles area until meeting Manson and joining the commune at the Spahn ranch. In July 1969, Linda Kasabian, twenty, stole $5,000 from the home of a friend to give to Manson so he would accept her as a member of his lunatic commune. Kasabian was married and had small children, but she took her infant daughter Tanya and abandoned the rest of her family to live at the Spahn Ranch. She, like Van Houten, was addicted to LSD and was usually in a drug daze when cavorting with Manson.

Also among this motley clan was Charles "Tex" Watson, twenty-three, tall, powerfully built, a one-time high school football and track star from Farmersville, Texas. Though he had been a top student, once Watson moved to the Spahn Ranch, he became a mindless robot who slavishly followed Manson's orders. Manson's every waking moment was spent either indoctrinating his followers with his own satanic teachings or by appeasing his insatiable sexual cravings by sleeping with one or two or all of his female followers at the same time.

Manson reveled in the sexual attention his females followers lavished upon him, and he promised each of his fanatical female cohorts that he would make them pregnant with his

Actress Sharon Tate, pregnant when murdered, begged for her life and her unborn child, a plea her slayers ignored.

child as a reward for being loyal to him. As time went on, Manson began to tell his family that he was "Man-son," or "Son-of-Man," which he likened to Christ. He grew long hair and a scraggily beard and marched about Christ-like on the Spahn Ranch spouting his idiotic philosophy, telling his followers that he was not only Christ but Satan, too.

At this time Manson began to rant against blacks, saying that he had been sent to wreak divine havoc upon the earth, and against those who had allowed blacks to co-mingle with whites. The planet had to be purged of this inferior race, he said, and this could only be brought about by whites, who would rise up and slaughter all blacks. This world race war would not begin, Manson pointed out to his followers, until whites themselves had been brutally attacked, especially important white people.

His family, Manson proudly stated, had been selected as the instrument of his wrath. They would kill some important whites and blame the slaughter on the blacks. The result would be a general uprising by whites against blacks and the slaughter of blacks would ensue. Manson's hatred for blacks stemmed from his miserable life in prison, where he had been repeatedly raped by black prisoners. He would now take vengeance upon the entire race for this offense to his youthful body.

Meanwhile, Manson began playing the guitar and soon deluded himself into believing that he was one of the most accomplished guitar players in the world and a composer of great talent. He composed a monotonous song that was no more than a few notes strung together and lyrics that consisted of only two words "You Know" repeated over and over again.

Grocery store owner Leno LaBianca, murdered by Manson's people on the night of August 10, 1969.

Rosemary LaBianca, murdered with her husband in her home by the Manson killers on August 10, 1969.

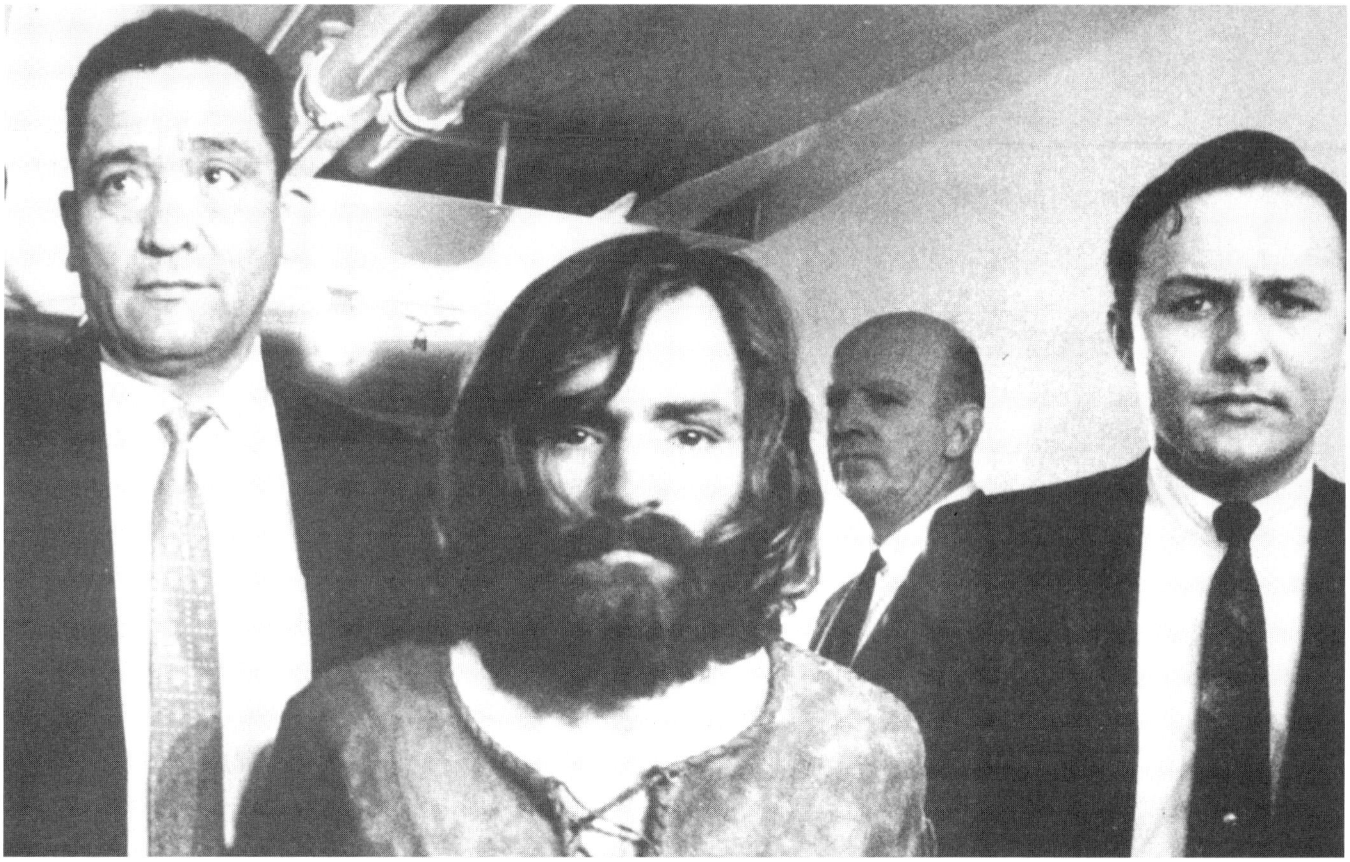

Charles Manson, under arrest and charged with the Tate-LaBianca mass murders in 1969; he taunted the court and reveled in his notoriety, making contorted faces and babbling like an idiot.

Wearing "party" dresses, left to right, Susan Atkins, Patricia Krenwinkle and Leslie Van Houten arrive at their hearing.

Linda Kasabian, twenty-one, became the star witness for the prosecution, detailing the Manson Family murders.

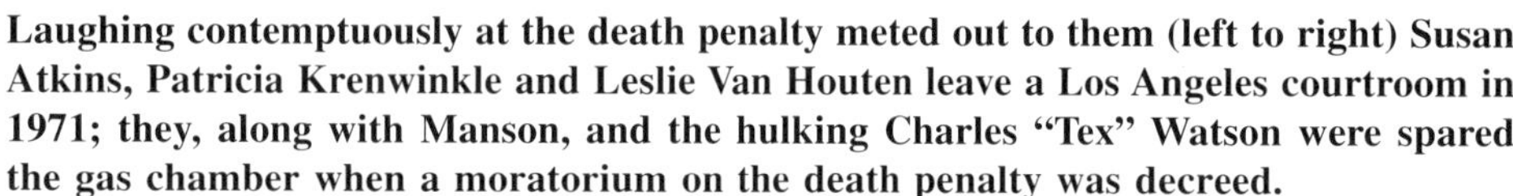

Laughing contemptuously at the death penalty meted out to them (left to right) Susan Atkins, Patricia Krenwinkle and Leslie Van Houten leave a Los Angeles courtroom in 1971; they, along with Manson, and the hulking Charles "Tex" Watson were spared the gas chamber when a moratorium on the death penalty was decreed.

Charles "Tex" Watson, who fought extradition to California, was ultimately sentenced to death.

Manson thought that his song would, if he could get it before the public, become the most popular ditty in the U.S.

Pursuing that warped ambition, Manson contacted Gary Hinman, a successful musician, badgering him to make a hit out of his song. Hinman was amused by the dogged Manson and made the mistake of allowing Manson, Susan Atkins, and Robert K. Beausoleil, another fanatical follower of Manson's, to stay in his house. Hinman did little but tolerate Manson, and he subsequently enraged the pint-sized cultist by ignoring Manson's composition.

The group moved out of Hinman's house, but Manson harbored a deep hatred for the musician, coming to believe that Hinman was jealously ignoring his song. When hearing that Hinman had recently inherited $20,000, Manson sent Atkins and Beausoleil to Hinman's house to steal the money and kill Hinman for snubbing Manson and his brilliant composition. Beausoleil and Atkins held Hinman prisoner, torturing him, while they ransacked his house in their desperate search for the inheritance money, naively believing Hinman would keep $20,000 in his home.

After two days, Atkins and Beausoleil grew disgusted and murdered Hinman. Beausoleil stabbed the musician to death, while he was bound hand and foot. Atkins then dipped her fingers in her victim's blood and wrote on the wall of his resplendent home: "Political Piggie." The killers then wiped the house clean of their fingerprints and left, but they were sloppy. Two prints were overlooked, both belonging to Beausoleil, and police quickly identified him and tracked him down, finding the killer in his car wearing a shirt stained with Hinman's blood. The knife Beausoleil used to kill the musician was found in the car with him. He was charged with murder and jailed.

Manson ignored the loss of Beausoleil. He was expendable. Manson's only concern was to have his song published, and he next approached Terry Melcher, the son of singer-actress Doris Day, asking Melcher to introduce him to the important people he knew in the music industry so that they could benefit from his musical masterpiece. Melcher apparently did nothing to help Manson, which infuriated the little cult leader. In his demented thinking, Manson came to believe that he would instill terror in the heart of Terry Melcher, so much fear that Melcher would do as Manson asked.

To create this terror, Manson would unleash his drugged up followers, instructing them to murder some innocent people. Manson drilled his cultists, organizing a death squad, telling them to put on black clothes and enter abandoned buildings in grim rehearsals which the cultists called "the Creepie Crawlies." It was all a game to these people, who had reduced themselves to moronic obedience. They become slavish cretins, all of them, blindly following the orders of their leader, Charlie Manson.

On March 23, 1969, Manson and Tex Watson went to Melcher's lavish home, a sprawling tree-lined estate in remote Benedict Canyon. Melcher no longer lived at the house on Cielo Drive. Manson saw some glamorous-looking people moving about and he labeled them "movie star types." He did not know their names, but while still brooding about how Melcher had ignored him, Manson decided that everyone now living in the house, where Melcher once lived would die. Their deaths would prove to Melcher that Manson meant business, the business of death and that next time Melcher would be more energetic in promoting the little man's long-neglected song.

On the night of August 8, 1969, Manson sent his death

In this photo series, Charles Manson is shown making faces in a Los Angeles courtroom, where, despite the pleas of his attorney, he refused to face either the judge or jury; he was finally ordered from the courtroom for his incorrigible, moronic behavior and was later condemned to the gas chamber, which he escaped, along with his fellow murderers when capital punishment was put on hold.

squad to the house on Cielo Drive. Only Linda Kasabian lost her nerve at the last minute and remained outside the house, according to her later statements. Those unsuspecting inhabitants of the house included movie star Sharon Tate, eight months pregnant. The beautiful blonde was the wife of Roman Polanski, maker of horror films, who was then in London working on a movie. Also residing at the house was Abigail Folger, coffee heiress, who was living at the house with her boyfriend, Polish writer Voyteck Frykowski, a friend of Polanski's. Present in the house that night was Jay Sebring, a celebrated hair stylist to the rich and famous. Sebring was a former boyfriend of Sharon Tate's.

Manson had made all the necessary preparations for mass murder. He had given Tex Watson a rope, a knife, and a .22-caliber revolver, ordering him to take Krenwinkel, Atkins, and Kasabian with him. The cult leader directed Watson to kill everyone in the house adding: "And make it as gruesome as possible."

As the group entered the grounds of the estate, Watson came upon 18-year-old Steven Parent, who had been visiting caretaker William Garretson. The 19-year-old Garretson lived in a small house far removed from the mansion, one completely overlooked by the killers. Watson thrust the revolver into Parent's face and the youth begged for his life. Watson fired four shots into him, killing Parent instantly. Watson then entered the house with Atkins and Krenwinkel. They ordered Tate, Sebring, Frykowski, and Folger into the living room, telling them that they were only robbing the house and would harm no one.

Sebring was tied up, but he broke free and started to flee. He was shot to death. Then Frykowski, realizing they would all be killed, leaped forward, attacking the hulking Watson. He was shot, knocked down, and kicked; then Watson beat the Polish writer with the butt of the revolver, while the girls stabbed him fifty-one times. Folger made a dash for the back door and managed to reach the lawn before Krenwinkel ran after her and knocked her down. Watson caught up to Folger and stabbed her repeatedly until she was dead.

Only Sharon Tate was left alive. She pleaded for her life, telling Susan Atkins that she was pregnant and begged for the life of her unborn child. "Woman, I have no mercy for you," sneered Atkins, who then stabbed Tate sixteen times, killing her. The slaughterhouse killers then tied a rope about Sebring's head and the other end to Tate's mutilated corpse. They spread an American flag on the couch and then wrote the word "pig" on the front door in Sharon Tate's blood.

The killers changed their bloody clothes, gathered their weapons, and drove away, later throwing their clothing and weapons into a ravine in the San Fernando Valley. It was then they realized that they had left Atkins' knife behind at the murder scene. The foursome stopped at a small house and unraveled a hose which they used to wash away the blood on their hands and faces. The homeowner then appeared and chased the killers away.

The next day Manson and his followers, now numbering almost thirty, read the gruesome newspaper accounts of the murders on Cielo Drive. While the country reeled in disgust and shock, Manson and his followers wildly celebrated this

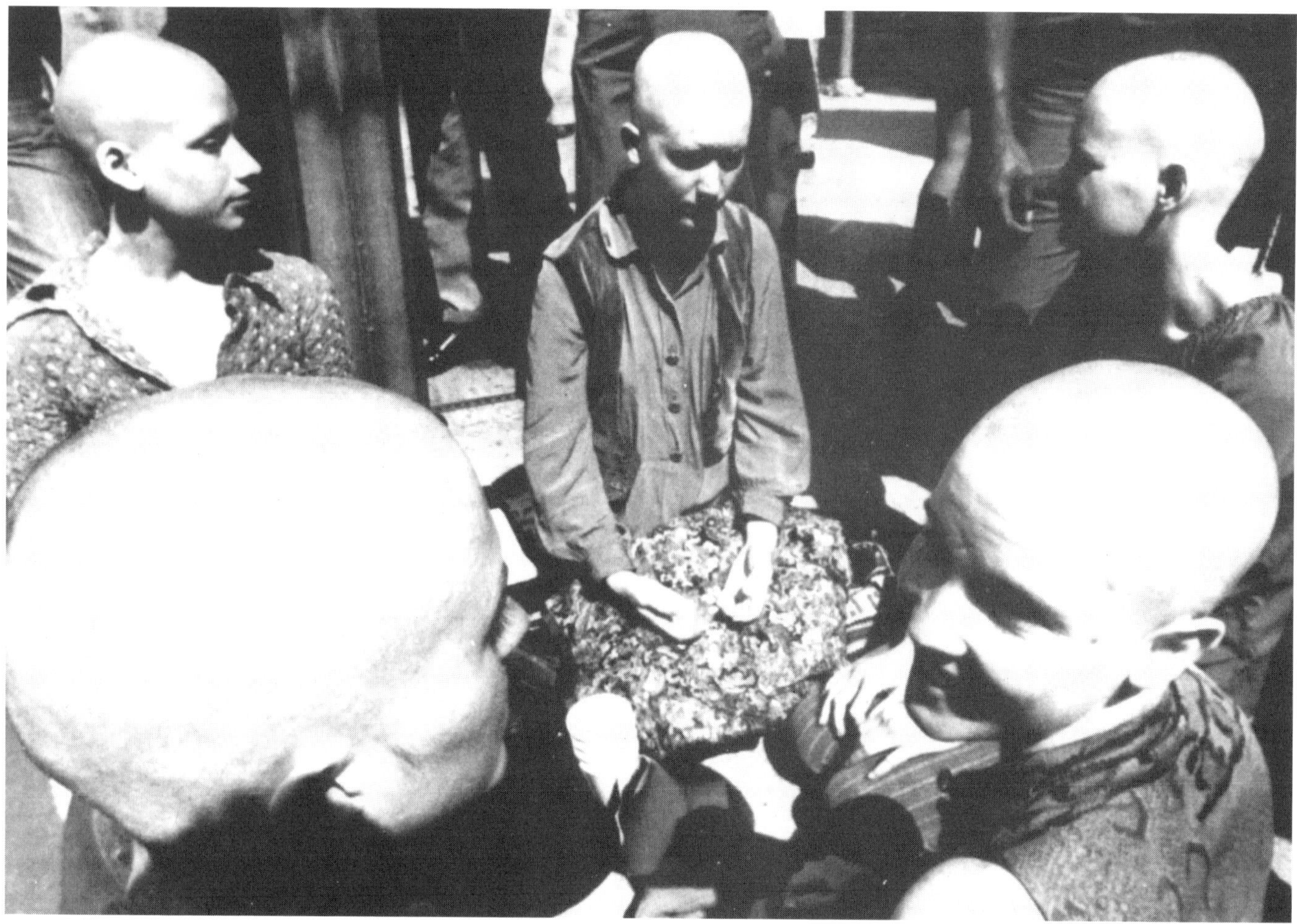

Female Manson followers not charged in the mass murders shaved their heads and sat chanting outside a Los Angeles courtroom during the murder trials of Manson and his fellow killers; these women used aliases and refused to give authorities their true identities; like those convicted, they were social dropouts and misfits.

"triumph" by having a sex orgy, with Manson at the center of the frenzied love-making, and by smoking endless marijuana cigarettes. Manson then stated that it was time to make another terror raid.

On the night of August 10, 1969, Manson led his group of killers, including Watson, Atkins, Krenwinkel, Leslie Van Houten, and 23-year-old Steve Grogan to the home of Rosemary and Leno LaBianca, a house Manson randomly selected in the Silver Lake area. The LaBianca home was large and spacious. Rosemary LaBianca, thirty-eight, ran a fashionable dress shop and her husband, 44-year-old Leno LaBianca, owned a grocery-store chain.

Manson alone invaded the home by crawling through an open window. He awoke the couple, waving a gun in their faces and tying them up with leather thongs he habitually wore about his neck. He told them that he would not harm them, only rob their house. He took LaBianca's wallet and returned to the car, where his cultists sat joking, excited at the prospect of committing more senseless murders. Manson ordered Watson, Van Houten, and Krenwinkel to go into the LaBianca house and murder the man and woman he had tied up and told them he and the others were going into the house next door to murder its occupants.

When Watson, Krenwinkel, and Van Houten went into the LaBianca home, Manson and the others drove back to the Spahn ranch. En route, Manson stopped at a gas station. He handed LaBianca's wallet to Linda Kasabian and ordered her to place it in the women's washroom. He explained that some "greedy bitch" would find the wallet, use the credit cards inside, and then be blamed for the murders. He laughed at the cleverness of his plan.

Watson, meanwhile, was dutifully murdering Leno LaBianca. He dragged the man into the living room of his house and repeatedly stabbed him until he was dead, leaving the knife sticking in his victim's neck. He then covered LaBianca's head with a pillow case. Meanwhile, Van Houten and Krenwinkel had been in the bedroom, repeatedly stabbing the helpless Rosemary LaBianca. They stabbed and chanted at the same time, making forty-one wounds in the woman, a dozen after she was long dead. They tied a cord around her neck and covered her face with a pillowcase.

On the living room wall of the LaBianca home, the slayers wrote slogans with their victim's blood, spelling out in large letters the words "Death to all pigs" and "Rise." In the kitchen they wrote, also in blood, the words "Healter [sic] Skelter" on the door of the refrigerator. The killers did not flee, but en-

Self-styled guru and mass murderer Charles Manson, manacled at hands and feet, trudges his way to prison to serve life behind bars.

joyed the home as if it was their own. They took a communal shower to wash away the blood and then helped themselves to a midnight snack by looting the refrigerator. Before the cult killers left the house, Watson took a carving knife and sliced the word "war" on Leno LaBianca's stomach. He then thrust the knife into the man's stomach and left laughing.

Many of Manson's followers left the Spahn Ranch after these incomprehensible slayings, including Atkins, who was later arrested and jailed for prostitution. She bragged to a prisoner about the killings and another inmate overheard the boastful confession. She informed police that Charles Manson had been behind the killings. On August 16, 1969, Manson and several of his demented followers were arrested at the Spahn Ranch, but then released for lack of evidence.

Manson was rearrested in a sleazy camp with some followers near Death Valley on October 15, 1969. Also in custody by that time were Atkins, Van Houten, Beausoleil, Grogan, and Kasabian. Police tracked down Krenwinkel in Mobile, Alabama, where she was hiding with an aunt. Watson had gone home to Collin County, Texas, where his influential relatives managed to fight off extradition for some time. He was finally returned to California and he, along with Manson, Krenwinkel, Atkins, Van Houten, Grogan, and Beausoleil, were placed on trial for murder.

The trial was often interrupted by the defendants who treated it as a lark. They laughed at the descriptions of their mutilations and murders and posed for newspaper photographers, especially Manson, who delighted in the limelight. He had finally found the attention he had sought all his life. Manson attempted to portray himself as the worst man on earth. He bragged to fellow prisoners that he had murdered at least thirty-five others, in addition to the Tate-LaBianca slayings, another lie from an inveterate liar.

All of the repulsive defendants were found guilty and sentenced to die in the gas chamber. When the death penalty was abolished in California in 1971, the sentences were commuted to life imprisonment, which, by California law, allows prisoners to apply for parole every seven years. Thus far, all appeals for parole by the Manson killer-cultists have been denied. At this writing, the ever-inventive Charles Manson makes extra money to buy cigarettes and candy in the prison commissary at San Quentin by selling to fans his rolled up socks upon which he draws smiling faces and autographs with the flourish of a poor man's Pablo Picasso.

FIVE SLAYINGS IN SANTA CRUZ/October 19, 1970

The coastal village of Santa Cruz, about forty miles south of San Francisco, California, was the setting for a reenactment of the 1969 Manson killings. On October 19, 1970, the home of wealthy eye surgeon, Dr. Victor Ohta went up in flames. After firemen brought the blaze under control, they found the bodies of Ohta, his wife, Virginia, their two children, Taggart, eleven, and Derrick, twelve, and the doctor's secretary, Dorothy Cadwallader. All had been shot dead, their bodies dumped into the family pool.

A note attached to the family's Rolls Royce read: "Halloween 1970. Today WWIII will begin, as brought to you by the people of the Free Universe. From this day forward, anyone and/or company of persons who misuses the natural environment or destroys same will suffer the penalty of death by the people of the Free Universe. I and my comrades from this day forth will fight until death or freedom against anyone who does not support natural life on this planet. Materialism must die or mankind will stop." The note was signed "Knight of Wands, Knight of Pentacles, Knight of Cups, Knight of Swords."

The ritualistic nature of the murders indicated that a cultist familiar with tarot cards was responsible. The groups of hippies camped in the adjacent woods suggested another Manson cult. Police came to suspect 24-year-old John Linley Frazier (b. 1946), a local car mechanic, who experimented with hallucinogenic drugs. Frazier was separated from his wife and lived near a hippie commune in Felton. He was known to be a militant ecologist and tarot card practitioner.

John Linley Frazier, half his head shaved (in a blatant attempt to project schizophrenia), murdered the Ohta family in Santa Cruz in 1970 and went to prison for life.

Frazier had a criminal record at the time of his arrest, and had been seen driving Virginia Ohta's station wagon the day after the murders. He refused to confirm or deny his guilt, but his fingerprints were found on the Rolls Royce. Police and prosecutors pieced together the method of Frazier's premeditated mass murders.

The killer had planned to "execute" all the members of this well-to-do family days in advance. First, he waited for Mrs. Virginia Ohta to return home and shot her as she entered her house. Next, he waited for Victor Ohta, his children and his secretary to arrive and Frazier shot them as they appeared, dragging their bodies to the pool, where he threw them into the water.

Frazier was ruled legally sane, tried, and convicted on five counts of murder. Frazier was sentenced to die in San Quentin's gas chamber, but California abolished the death penalty in 1971, automatically commuting his sentence to life imprisonment.

THE CANARY ISLAND RITUAL SLAYINGS/December 22, 1970

The Alexanders, a reclusive German family, were religious fanatics, who believed that only a select few of their religious cult were free of Satan's control and that all others were instruments of the Devil to be purged by violence if the "chosen one" of their cult so decreed. This is exactly what happened to the Alexanders in 1970, when 16-year-old Frank Alexander (b. 1954) decided that his mother and sisters were possessed of the Devil and had to be murdered. A horrific slaughter followed in which Frank and his equally zealous father Harald Alexander (b. 1931) destroyed their loved ones in the name of God. They later excused their grisly acts as part of their religious beliefs.

The Alexanders had originated in Dresden and later moved to Hamburg, where Harald Alexander became the ardent disciple of George Riehle, a religious zealot, who was, in turn, the self-designated leader of the Lorber Society. Jacob Lorber (1800-1864) had founded this religious group in the early part of the nineteenth century, a severe spiritual organization that taught unflinching self-denial and upheld the beliefs that all non-members were basically evil. Riehle became a member of this small sect, which never numbered more than a few hundred members through the decades.

Some time in the 1930s, Riehle came to believe that he was the Prophet of God (the same kind of delusional perspective that gripped the distorted minds of religious zealots Jim Jones and David Koresh, whose paranoid actions led to mass murders—see following entries). Alexander met Riehle in Hamburg when the old man was dying and nursed him through his last days. When Riehle died, Alexander announced to his wife that he had inherited the mantle of the Lorber Society leadership. Dagmar Alexander, equally possessed of her husband's single-minded beliefs, accepted him in his self-appointed role.

When their son Frank was born, Harald Alexander told his wife that their son was now the Prophet of God and that his every whim had to be observed and obeyed. As the boy grew up, he was served by his family members—his older sister Marina, his younger twin sisters Sabine and Petra, and his parents—as if he were a potentate. They responded to his every whim, until Frank Alexander dictated their every movement.

The boy, when reaching his teens, decided that he could never "pollute" himself with the bodies of women outside of their small sect. He informed his father that he would have sex with his mother and older sister and such incestuous relations became commonplace within the Alexander household, the father not only agreeing to such practices, but encouraging his son to have sex with his wife and daughters at any time, often joining with Frank as they both assaulted Dagmar Alexander or the older sister, Marina. The women accepted their roles as sex objects in the belief that they were serving the Prophet of God, Frank Alexander.

Such bizarre practices soon brought them to the attention of the Hamburg police, especially when the younger sisters began to talk about them to the few friends they had made. To avoid police investigation into their activities, the Alexanders moved to a reclusive society, one far apart from the rest of the world, relocating to a small apartment at 37 Calle Jesus Nazareno in Santa Cruz, the capital of Tenerife in the Canary Islands.

Neighbors soon noted that the family remained aloof and its members seldom ventured from their apartment. Harald Alexander was forever playing a small organ that had been left to him by George Riehle. For ten months the family occupied the small flat without incident, the girls and Frank supporting the family with low-paying jobs. The girls worked as domestics and Frank was a shipping clerk, though he kept irregular hours.

Then, on December 22, 1970, Harald and Frank Alexander appeared in the villa occupied by Dr. Walter Trenkler, asking to see 15-year-old Sabine Alexander. Trenkler found the girl in the kitchen preparing a meal for the family and told her that her father and brother were on the patio waiting to see her. She went to them and Trenkler, to his amazement and shock, heard Harald Alexander say to his daughter: "Sabine, dear, we wanted you to know at once that Frank and I have just finished killing your mother and your sisters."

The girl took her father's hand and put it to her cheek and replied, "I'm sure you've done what you thought necessary."

Dr. Trenkler stood in shock for a moment, staring at the Alexanders. Harald Alexander caught Trenkler's stare and said matter-of-factly: "Ah, you've overheard. We've killed my wife and other daughters. It was the hour of killing." The horrified physician then looked over the father and son carefully. What he originally thought was mud and dirt on their clothes, the result of laboring he imagined, was not what covered them from head to foot. It was human gore that smeared their clothes and faces and hands, dried and caking in the hot sun of the courtyard where they stood.

Even more frightening was the conduct of the Alexanders. There was nothing secretive or sinister about them. They were calm and reported their gruesome acts as if nothing was amiss, that the killings they had just announced were perfectly acceptable. Trenkler asked the Alexanders to wait. He raced into the villa and called the police.

Officers quickly arrived and took the Alexanders into custody, while Detective Inspector Juan Hernandez and Detective Sergeant Manuel Perera went to the Alexander flat, accompanied by a police physician, and forced open the door. They stepped into a place of carnage. All of the dishes, clothing, papers, including passports and family documents, had been torn to pieces. Everything was in shreds. The apartment was coated with blood—ceilings, walls, floors. In the middle of the living room floor were the mutilated bodies of the two daughters, 18-year-old Marina, and 15-year-old Petra. Their breasts and private parts had been hacked away and nailed to one of the walls.

The older girl had been disemboweled. In the bedroom was found the remains of 39-year-old Dagmar Alexander, also horribly mutilated, her breasts and privates also hacked away. Her heart had been cut out, bound on a cord and this was nailed to the wall. The place was a grisly slaughterhouse running blood, a sight so overwhelming that even the hardened officers grew sick to their stomachs.

The Alexanders, at the local police station, freely admitted the gruesome murders. Frank Alexander, called "The Prophet" by his father, related how he was in the bedroom when Dagmar entered it. "I saw that Mother was looking at me and I had the feeling that it was not permitted for her to look at me in this manner. I therefore took the clothes hanger and struck her over the head. After I struck her several times she fell over and lost

Religious zealots Frank (who is staring defiantly at the judge) and Harald Alexander, are shown at their mental hearings; they had slaughtered female family members for being "unclean."

consciousness. Father had gone to the living room to play the organ and I also went there. First I struck Marina on the head with the hanger, and after she lost consciousness, I struck Petra. Father continued to play the organ and praise Jesus, but when I began to remove the offending parts, he came to help me."

Harald Alexander supported every heinous detail of his son's statements, saying that the sex organs of his wife and daughters were "offending parts," and had to be removed, adding that the women in the household had expected the "hour of killing" at any time, that the family had discussed this "holy time" and its eventuality and that the women accepted their role as human sacrifices at the hands of The Prophet, Frank Alexander.

Both Frank and Harald Alexander then stated that they felt no guilt, that this was all part of their religious beliefs, that women were unclean and had to be purified by killing. They claimed that their victims had been released into heaven through their murders and they even celebrated their grisly acts by playing the organ, both taking turns, and singing hymns after slaughtering the females of their household.

Psychiatrists examined the father and son and concluded that they were both unfit to stand trial. Both were committed to an asylum for the criminally insane, where they presently reside, neither, at last report, responding to any kind of treatment and both convinced, still, that the slaughter of their family members was a purification act in keeping with their religious beliefs. Both men still believe that they are being persecuted for their beliefs and neither has expressed one thought of guilt.

Harald Alexander continues to address his son Frank as "The Prophet." Sabine Alexander, the surviving female member of the family, begged authorities to send her to the asylum with her brother and father, but this was rejected. She was sent to a convent, where she still resides, refusing to live in the outside world.

A WHITE RACIST KILLER/ February 14, 1977

His massive arms pockmarked by racist tattoos, Frederick W. Cowan is shown shortly before he embarked upon a mass murder spree on February 14, 1977.

Frederick W. Cowan (AKA: Second Hitler; 1944-1977) had three great pleasures in life: his collection of Nazi memorabilia, his weapons collection, and weightlifting. He bore tattoos of Nazi symbols on his arms, and expressed his hatred of Jews and blacks to anyone who would listen. He attributed his hatred of blacks to a time during the Vietnam War when a black man refused to help him. But Cowan was never in Vietnam. Then his neighbor in New Rochelle, New York, Theresa Schmidt, started dating a black man.

On August 2, 1975, when Schmidt walked by Cowan's house, he pointed her out to a nearby kid as a "nigger lover." Schmidt, overhearing, turned on him and demanded to know what he had said. Cowan went to the trunk of his car, grabbed a rifle, and said: "Get out of there before I blow your brains out!" Schmidt ran to call the police, but the officer, who answered the call expressed no interest in pursuing the matter when Cowan was not in sight on his arrival. Months later, when Schmidt passed Cowan's house again, he pointed a rifle at her and pulled the trigger, but the weapon was not loaded.

In January 1977, 33-year-old Cowan's opinions got him in trouble at his job. He was suspended after refusing to work for a man he thought was Jewish. The superior, who suspended him, Norman Bing, was himself Jewish, and later stated that "the guys figured he was a lot of talk. He had no history of violence. Everybody said he was a pussycat." But on Valentine's Day 1977, his first day back at work, Cowan drove to work at the Neptune Moving Company, stood in the parking lot, and armed himself as if for battle with pistols, hand grenades, bandoliers of ammunition, and a semi-automatic rifle.

Cowan then walked into the main entrance searching for Bing, and immediately shot and killed two black men passing through the office. Cowan told another employee, "Go home and tell my mother not to come down to Neptune." He continued into the company cafeteria, up the stairs, killing two more

The headquarters of the Neptune Moving Company in New Rochelle, New York, which a heavily-armed Cowan invaded for the purpose of shooting blacks and Jews.

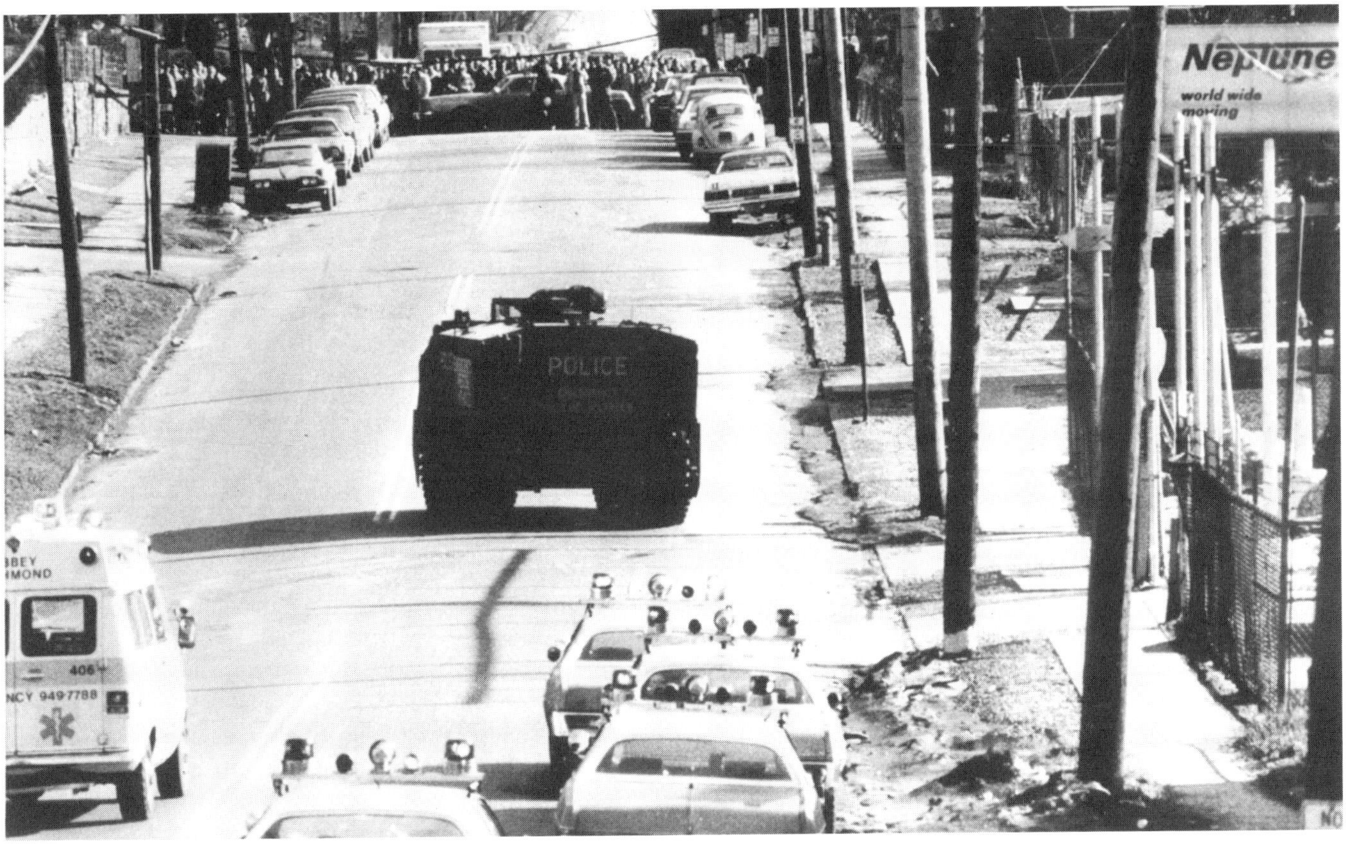

A police armored vehicle is shown arriving at the Neptune Company, where Cowan had shot five persons dead and wounded others; hundreds of spectators can be seen behind a police barricade in the distance.

Wearing flak jackets and carrying high-powered rifles, New Rochelle police are shown entering the Neptune building, where Cowan was found dead, a suicide.

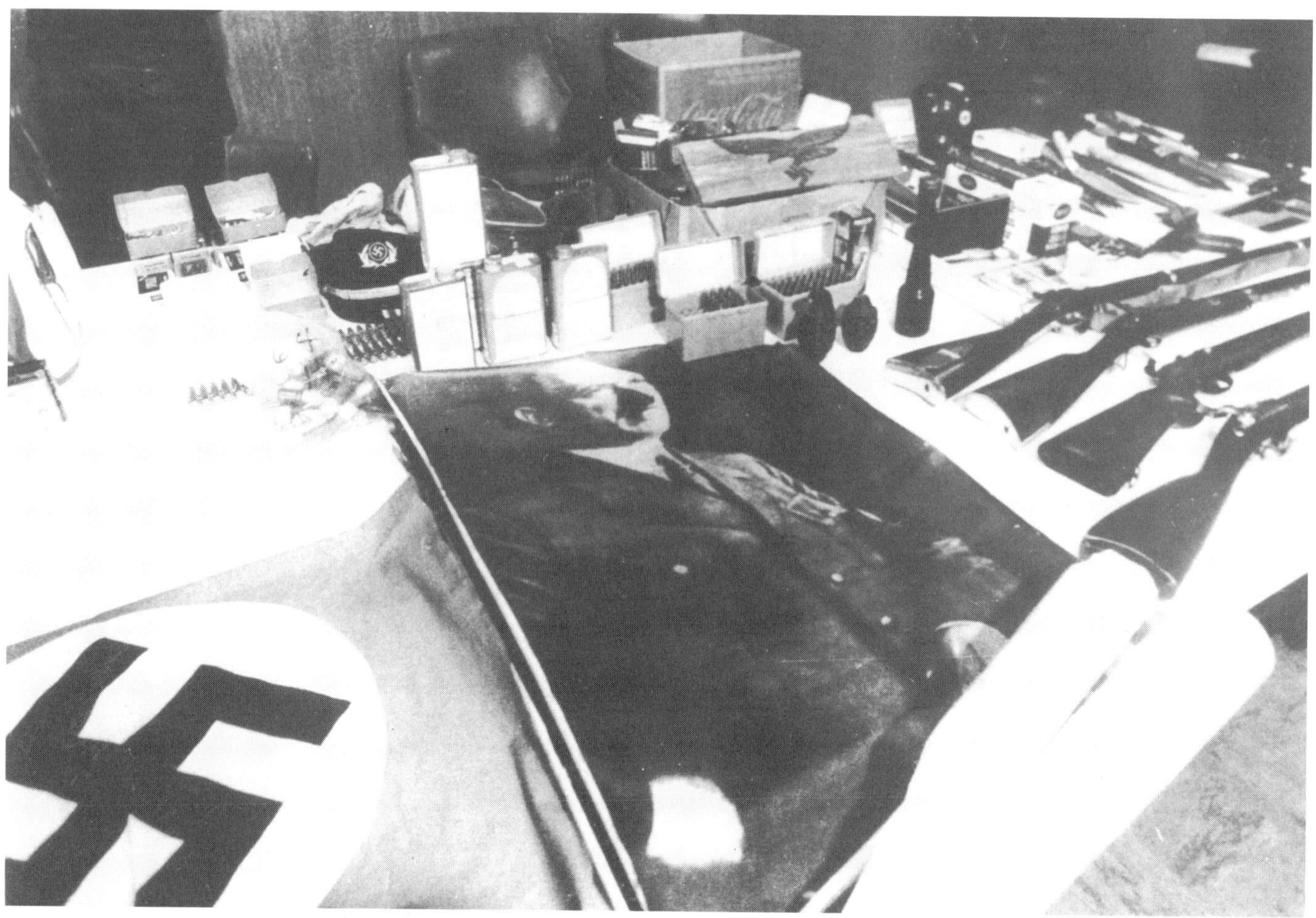

A Nazi flag and a picture of Adolf Hitler, Cowan's idol, was found with Cowan's arsenal in his home.

people on the way. When a squad car arrived, Cowan saw it from a window and shot and killed one policeman as he emerged from the car. Within minutes, the Neptune building was under siege, a New York City Police Department armored personnel carrier on hand to help.

The killer, moving back and forth from the offices to the roof, would not answer loudspeaker calls for several hours, even when his mother arrived and spoke to him. Once Cowan shouted that he had "plenty of grenades and other guns to last me all day." Another time he answered a phone and said, "I'm sorry for your trouble. Tell the mayor that I'm sorry to be causing the city so much trouble." At 2:40 p.m., a single shot sounded. As the police cleared the building, they found that Fred Cowan, killer of five, had killed himself with a gunshot to the head.

MASS MURDER IN GUYANA/November 15, 1978

Boyhood friends of the Reverend James Warren "Jim" Jones (1931-1978) would recall the times when he held mock funeral services for dead animals in his home town of Lynn, Indiana, where the cottage industry was casket making. "Some of the neighbors would have cats missing and we always thought he was using them for sacrifices," recalled Tootie Morton. Jones, whose father was a drunken Klansman unable to hold a job, became obsessed with religion. At fourteen, the Bible-toting boy delivered his first sermon. In 1949, Jones married Marceline Baldwin, his high school sweetheart.

After Jones dropped out of Indiana University, the couple moved to Indianapolis, where he started a Methodist Mission, but the church fathers found his religious pretensions objectionable. He was expelled in 1954 and then raised money by importing monkeys and selling them for $29 each. Jones accumulated $50,000, which was used to purchase a rundown synagogue in a black neighborhood of Indianapolis. During this time he and his wife adopted eight Korean and black children.

The mayor of Indianapolis, impressed with Jones' community work in the impoverished neighborhoods of the city, appointed him director of the Human Rights Commission. But when Jones found Indianapolis too provincial in its racial attitudes, he moved to Belo Horizonte, Brazil, after reading that this was the safest spot in the world to survive a nuclear holocaust. The family later relocated to Rio de Janeiro, where Jones taught in an American school. Hearing that the People's Temple in Indianapolis, which he had founded in 1957, was in the midst of a leadership crisis, Jones returned home. In 1964, he affiliated his group with the Disciples of Christ and was ordained a minister.

Influenced by the Reverend Ross Case, and half-believing that the world was about to end, Jones led a migration of 100

Rev. Jim Jones, when he was beginning his ministry in San Francisco, seemingly a forthright religious leader.

followers from Indiana to Redwood Valley, in Mendocino County, California. The minister purchased a synagogue in the deteriorating Fillmore district of San Francisco. He provided a day-care center and food kitchens for the black inner-city residents, who accounted for 80 percent of the congregation of the People's Temple and won the enthusiastic support of politicians.

Governor Jerry Brown was a visitor to the People's Temple. Mayor George Moscone (later murdered, see chapter on Assassination) appointed Jones to serve on the city's housing authority as a reward for his political support in the 1975 election. After hearing of the Jonestown horror, Moscone would say, "I proceeded to vomit and cry."

Money began to roll in. Jim Jones purchased Greyhound buses and began traveling around the country accompanied by bodyguards and press aides. At the same time, he urged sexual abstinence to his parishioners, he surrounded himself with female followers. In 1974, he purchased 27,000 acres of rain forest in Guyana on the northern coast of South America, which he hoped to turn into a socialist utopia for himself and his followers.

Despite warm endorsements from top Democratic leaders like Henry "Scoop" Jackson, Walter Mondale, and Jimmy Carter, whom Jones supported for president in 1976, he became obsessed with the notion of mass suicide as a way of escaping governmental persecution, his fascination with suicide dating back to 1953 when Ethel and Julius Rosenberg were executed in the U.S. as spies. By 1976, Jones was indoctrinating his followers in the concept of a "White Night," a mass suicide ritual that was being "rehearsed" at his People's Temple.

The first clue the public had about Jones' hidden agenda and the secret cult activities occurred at an anti-suicide rally held at the Golden Gate Bridge on Memorial Day 1977. Speaking before hundreds of spectators, Jones called for the construction of an anti-suicide barrier to be constructed on the bridge. Dr. Richard Seiden, professor of behavioral science at the University of California, later recalled how the direction of Jones' speech changed. His condemnation of suicide became almost a blanket endorsement for it. "He saw himself as the victim, persecuted and attacked, and from there proceeded to the concept of suicide as an appropriate response. We were not aware of the nuances and implications," Dr. Seiden said.

Membership in the People's Temple swelled to nearly 20,000, and as his congregation enlarged, Jones' services became increasingly bizarre. He claimed in his sermons to have the power of faith healing, and would demonstrate his powers by drawing out the "cancer" from the sufferer during ceremonies. This was a sham, the cancer actually being a bloody chicken gizzard. No longer content to be the reincarnation of Jesus, Jones began calling himself God.

Meanwhile, with the help of local authorities in Guyana and private contributions from his followers, he began clearing large sections of jungle in 1977. That year, the religious colony of Jonestown was founded and about 1,000 members made their exodus from San Francisco to the jungle retreat.

When located at the new settlement, Jones enforced his will through physical and mental coercion. The San Francisco *Examiner* reported in August 1977 that members were publicly flogged for minor infractions like smoking and falling asleep during religious sermons. Electrodes were attached to children, who were ordered to smile at the mention of the leader's name. These reports began filtering back to California congressman Leo Ryan, fifty-three, who pressured the U.S. State Department to investigate.

A delegation from the U.S. embassy in Georgetown interviewed seventy-five members of the cult, but none indicated a desire to leave. Ryan was not convinced. His friend, Robert Houston of the Associated Press, had lost a son to the cult. The young man had been murdered in San Francisco after attempting to quit the People's Temple. Ryan embarked on a fact-finding mission on November 14, 1978, accompanied by eight journalists and several relatives of Jonestown cultists.

The delegation was greeted by a congenial Jones, who led a guided tour through the compound, proudly showing off the spacious library, hospital, and living quarters. That night Congressman Ryan and his party were entertained at the pavilion. Even Ryan was impressed. He arose from his chair and announced: "From what I have seen, there are a lot of people

The People's Temple in San Francisco, where Jones had an enormous following; it was from this congregation that Jones gulled hapless parishioners into following him to Guyana.

Jim Jones in Guyana, where he oppressed his followers, holding them in virtual captivity.

After ordering Congressman Ryan and his companions killed, Jones ordered his slavish followers to commit mass suicide, although many reluctant to do so were murdered.

here who think this is the best thing that has happened in their whole lives." Jones led the thunderous applause.

The next day, NBC reporter Don Harris asked Jones about his military arsenal and if it were true that the compound was under heavy guard. Jones exploded in rage. "A bold-faced lie!" he screamed. One of the cultists slipped a note to Ryan which read "Four of us want to leave." There were other similar requests. While Ryan spoke with Jones about moving these people out, a cultist named Don Sly attacked him with a knife, but was subdued by attorney Charles Garry. Ryan and his entourage departed for the airfield at Port Kaituma and an awaiting Cessna.

As Ryan and his companions deliberated about the best way to squeeze the extra passengers into the tiny craft, a flatbed truck rumbled onto the landing field. Three armed men standing in the trailer suddenly opened fire. From inside the plane, Larry Layton produced a gun and began shooting. The crossfire left five persons dead, including Congressman Ryan, photographer Greg Robinson, NBC cameraman Bob Brown, Don Harris, and one of the departing cultists, Patricia Park.

While Ryan and his entourage were being fired upon, Jones was preparing his followers to carry out "revolutionary suicide" at the compound. His brainwashed parishioners, who had rehearsed this scenario dozens of times, were herded into the main pavilion, where they received purple Kool-Aid laced with cyanide. Mothers gave cyanide voluntarily to their children. Infants received the substance with a syringe squirting it into their mouths.

Next came the older children, who received the lethal doses in paper cups, and finally the adults, who accepted the poison as Jones intoned through a loudspeaker: "We're going to meet again in another place!" Those who refused to accept this fate

An aerial photo shows hundreds of bodies in the compound of Jonestown on November 15, 1978; most swallowed poison, but many were found shot to death by Jones' enforcers.

were prodded by heavily armed guards. Within five minutes, most of the 913 victims were dead. Not since the Japanese citizens of Saipan hurled themselves from the rocky cliffs of the island in World War II had the world witnessed such a mass suicide (or murder, as the wholesale slaughter was later termed, since most of the victims were forced to take the cyanide at gunpoint).

Jones, like Adolf Hitler years earlier, killed himself with a bullet to the head. No eyewitnesses survived. Investigators later found rows of bodies, most of them lying face down. The U.S. Air Force sent planes to retrieve the remains of the victims while experts in human behavior and sociology grappled with larger issues. "Most members have little or no sense of inner value," theorized Stefan Pasternack, associate clinical professor of psychiatry at Georgetown University. "In joining [Jones] they regress and relax their personal judgments to the point that they are supplanted by the group's often primitive feelings. With a sick leader these primitive feelings are intensified and get worse."

One person went to trial for complicity in the Jonestown Massacre. Thirty-five-year old ex-Quaker Layton, a member of Jones' death squad, was charged with injuring U.S. diplomat Richard Dwyer and conspiracy to kill Congressman Ryan. The jury in the San Francisco courtroom was unable to agree on a verdict. The courtroom was packed with relatives of the victims when, on September 23, 1981, a mistrial was declared by Judge Robert Peckham.

MASS MURDER IN WACO/ February 28, April 19, 1993

An unorthodox religious cult calling itself the Branch Davidians occupied a sprawling compound on seventy-seven acres ten miles east of Waco, Texas. Its leader called himself David Koresh (Vernon Howell, 1960-1993) and he preached an oddball dogma, which he made up more or less from biblical teachings.

Like Jim Jones before him, Koresh was paranoid and egomaniacal. Also, like Jones, he thought of himself as the Messiah. He brainwashed his followers so that they came to believe, as did the doomed apostles of Jim Jones in Guyana, that his word was law. The uneducated Koresh ordered his cult to collect a huge cache of arms, including automatic weapons of all kinds, in preparation to fight apocalyptic battles against the powers of darkness at the end of the world.

Those powers, according to the mentally unstable Koresh, were represented by the federal government. "We were thought of as God's marines," one of the cult members later said. "If you can't die for God, you can't live for God." This addlebrained philosophy summed up Koresh's warped message.

Learning that the cult had hoarded illegal weapons in violation of federal law, agents of the Bureau of Alcohol, Tobacco and Firearms conducted a raid against the Davidian compound on February 28, 1993. It proved to be a disaster. More than 100 law enforcement officers took part in the raid. When offic-

David Koresh (Vernon Wayne Howell), shown at the time he embarked upon his career as a religious zealot and leader.

An early photo of David Koresh, left, with friend Clive Doyle; Koresh was paranoid, egocentric and came to believe he was the reincarnation of Jesus Christ.

ers rushed the building, Koresh's heavily-armed cultists fired upon them. Four ATF officers were killed and at least fifteen were wounded in the resulting firefight. Several cult members were killed and wounded as well.

One of the wounded cultists was the 33-year-old Koresh, a failed rock guitarist turned religious fanatic who used the Bible for his own dictatorial ends. Born Vernon Howell in Houston, Texas, in 1960, the cult leader changed his name in 1991 to Koresh, reportedly to help his musical career, but there was a religious scheme in taking the name. Koresh is the Hebrew equivalent of Cyrus, which, along with David, is a name of historical and symbolic significance. Cyrus was the Persian king, who delivered the Jews from captivity and David became the first great king of the Jews.

The Waco *Tribune*, at the time of the ATF raid in 1993, had been running a series of articles on Koresh and the Davidians, giving the attention-seeking cult leader exactly what he incessantly craved—publicity. The paper quoted Koresh as saying "If the Bible is true, then I am Christ. But so what? Look at two thousand years ago. What's so great about being Christ? A man nailed to the cross. A man of sorrow acquainted with grief. You know, being Christ ain't nothin'."

After he was wounded in the raid, Koresh left a message on his mother's answering machine, "Hello, mama. It's your boy. They shot me and I'm dying, all right? But I'll be back real soon, okay? I'll see y'all in the skies. Bye." The message was typical of Koresh, pouty and petulant as a boy, always seeking sympathy and attention. He was not dying, as he told his mother, carelessly inflicting pain and fear upon her as was his habit with all he knew.

The seriousness of Koresh's wound was never learned, but it was reportedly superficial and he exaggerated its threat to his life to appear heroic and invincible to his followers. While agents surrounded and besieged the rural compound, Koresh continued to dominate cult members barricaded inside the large adjoining buildings. The living quarters featured a watch tower with windows facing in every direction, along with tunnels connecting smaller buildings to the main quarters.

Koresh urged his followers to fight to the death, saying that the agents would do anything to suppress the cult and kill

The Branch Davidian compound outside of Waco, where Koresh and his gun-carrying followers amassed a large arsenal.

its leader, himself. He ordered everyone to learn how to fire the many weapons available inside the compound. This arsenal was vast, according to one agent who, during the raid, was able to see into one room where weapons were stored. He said that he had never seen so many firearms in one room before.

During the 45-minute gun battle in February, cult members fired at agents with a .50-caliber machine gun, the ammunition for which one agent described as being "the size of your average banana ... It's the kind on the ground with a tripod that they also use on planes to shoot down other planes." Another agent who survived the withering crossfire from the compound stated that "I don't believe we were outmaneuvered or out-planned. The problem we had is that we were outgunned."

The raid itself was questioned by several persons, including newsmen and, later, politicians, who condemned it as being rash. The ATF stated that it intended to serve Koresh and his followers with arrest and search warrants, when they were ruthlessly attacked by the cultists. Koresh follower Paul Fatta, who was outside the compound running errands when the raid took place, later insisted that the ATF could have easily served their warrants on him and Koresh without bloodshed, that

Koresh in early 1993, at the time he defied federal officers, challenging them to attack the Branch Davidian compound.

ATF officers holding one of their wounded men during their abortive raid on the Branch Davidian compound on February 28, 1993, which resulted in ten deaths (four ATF officers and six cult members).

Tanks are shown attacking the Branch Davidian compound on April 19, 1993; the buildings were already burning and cult members died by the score inside the blaze, some by the fire, others by Koresh's execution squads.

both he and the cult leader went out jogging every day for three weeks prior to the raid and could have been approached without violence by agents at that time.

Following the raid, TV cameras representing all the networks and local press were stationed around the compound, which the cultists called Mount Carmel. They gave minute-by-minute coverage to the siege. The first day after the raid, Koresh allowed ten children to leave the compound. More than seventy-five cult members remained with him inside, most manning heavy weapons. Of the remaining members, one third were children. Koresh, who claimed to have at least fifteen wives, had sired many of these children—no one ever knew how many.

Lawmen prepared for a lengthy siege by trucking two mobile homes to the rural site. They also ordered up a national guard fuel tanker, a milk truck, two fried chicken delivery trucks that made regular food runs for them. Inside, the Davidians continued to eat well as they had stocked great quantities of food for months, some said years, in preparation for the apocalyptic vision seen by their demented leader. Hordes of media representatives who swarmed into the area received coffee, donuts, and sandwiches from the Salvation Army.

The siege became one of the year's most spectacular media events. Whenever contact was made with the Davidians, the messages—those that were released to the press—were treated as something close to Holy Scripture. Whenever a cult member could be coaxed away from the possessive Koresh, the event was treated as a major victory for law enforcement.

The reason two elderly women came out of the compound a few days after the siege began was simply that they were carrying a tape recording from Koresh, which he wanted played on local radio stations, his side of the story, he claimed. The tape contained nothing more than a ranting diatribe in which Koresh portrayed himself and his followers as persecuted victims of the ATF.

Catherine Mattson, 75, and Margaret Lawson, 77, handed the tape to ATF officers, saying that they preferred to go back to the compound and meet the fate of the others. Instead, they were charged with conspiracy, attempted murder, and murder. These charges were later dropped.

Four days after the raid, on March 3, 1993, a report flashed across the news channels that an undercover ATF agent was inside the compound and that he had been aware that Koresh received a phone call an hour before the February 28, raid that the ATF agents were moving in, a call that allowed the Davidians to arm themselves and prepare to kill federal officers.

The FBI then took over the siege and attempted to establish a dialog with the cult leader. Bureau agents sent a video to Koresh to show to parents inside the compound, one which portrayed how well their children were being treated in the custody of welfare authorities. In return for this gesture, Koresh released another child, the twenty-first permitted to leave the compound.

Meanwhile, Koresh's reputation was going to ruin. The husband of a cult member revealed that he had gotten custody of his young daughter after it was proven that Koresh had threatened the child with obligatory sex. The father stated that Koresh had had sex with compound children, who were no older than twelve and that he claimed the Bible entitled him to at least 140 wives.

Koresh and the FBI went on bantering in lengthy phone conversations that led nowhere. Koresh had no intentions of leaving the compound alive, or allowing any more members to go. His ego was such that he demanded and got national media coverage almost around the clock. He thrived on it, lived for it day to day. The FBI foolishly gave it to him. The

The entire Branch Davidian compound is shown engulfed by roaring flames, following the FBI attack on April 19, 1993; agents were fired upon by Koresh's gunmen as they attempted to enter the buildings.

The arms bunker found by FBI agents inside the gutted ruins of the Branch Davidian compound, proving the ATF claim that Koresh and his followers had hoarded a great quantity of illegal weapons.

U.S. Attorney General Janet Reno, who, most critics concluded, had thoroughly misread the character and intentions of Koresh and his deluded followers and botched an otherwise peaceful settlement by ordering a foolhardy and bloody attack on the Branch Davidians.

agents merely heard Koresh out, listening to him drone on and on about his religious beliefs. Then the Bureau ordered heavy armaments of their own.

When Koresh heard that the FBI had brought Bradley armored personnel carriers to the scene, he told agents that he had enough explosives to blow these vehicles fifty feet into the air. The FBI escalated its armaments by ordering to the scene 67-ton Abrams battle tanks. After seven frustrating weeks, on April 19, 1993, the FBI took action, under the direct orders of U.S. Attorney General Janet Reno. Agents ordered Steve Schneider, Koresh's fanatical chief lieutenant to lead the cult members out into the open and surrender. When Schneider refused, the tanks moved toward the compound, blowing holes in the sides of the buildings.

Tear gas was fired into the building. Agents later insisted that though they were fired upon by the cult members, they did not return fire. A few hours later, shortly before noon, the main buildings of the compound caught fire and a towering blaze engulfed the compound. Rather than be taken alive, the Davidians, ever loyal to their mad messiah, doused the walls and floors of the buildings with kerosene and burned themselves and their helpless children alive.

Of the seventy-two bodies recovered after the blaze, seventeen were children. Twenty adults and two children were found to have died of gunshot wounds. It took thirteen days to identify Koresh's crisply charred corpse. It was determined that he had not burned to death, but that he had been shot to death by one of his own obliging followers.

In the wake of the Waco disaster, Attorney General Janet Reno was heaped with criticism for mishandling the entire affair. She boldly confronted the press, saying that she took full responsibility for events, but this in no way ameliorated the botched siege and the resulting deaths. Reno had given the order to storm the compound, she said, in order to save children from being abused, but all of the children involved met death.

Reno's inexperience with fanatical cultists and the poor evaluations of the situation and Koresh's actual personality profile she received from erring advisers undoubtedly caused her to mishandle the entire affair. At best, Reno proved herself wholly inept and why she was not removed from office by President William Clinton remains a mystery to this day. The bombing of the ATF headquarters in Oklahoma City two years later by Timothy McVeigh was reportedly in retaliation for the Waco fiasco. (See chapter on Terrorism.)

In the end, David Koresh got from the FBI exactly what he wanted. Reno and her agents were either too ignorant or too indifferent to understand that his capture could have been facilitated by means other than a direct confrontation. Had the Bureau ordered media coverage banned and all phone and TV lines cut to the compound, isolated the place entirely and withdrew its forces to hidden positions, Koresh and his followers would certainly have come out peacefully, looking for what they needed to sustain their existence—attention.

Instead, Koresh was given what he craved most, public martyrdom. Any cursory psychological evaluation of his personality would have pinpointed for the Bureau the fact that this man was a limelight-seeker who, if ignored, would have abandoned his failed scheme for an apocalyptic end. He was an egomaniacal leader who had duped his naive, uneducated followers into believing that he was a religious icon and that their collective bloody end would have some sort of religious significance. In truth, he was only another babbling faker greedily grasping for publicity, insatiable for fame, notorious or not. He was willing to sacrifice his life and those of his followers to obtain that fame. Janet Reno and the FBI, unsophisticated and uneducated themselves when it came to really knowing people like David Koresh, gave it to him on a gory platter.

SLAUGHTERING CHILDREN IN BRAZIL/ July 23, 1993

Homeless children abound in Rio de Janeiro, Brazil. These half-starved youngsters swarmed around tourists and committed petty thievery merely to survive, and the government does little or nothing to relieve their suffering. Worse, in the early 1990s, shopkeepers and perhaps even government officials, secretly paid death squads made up of off-duty military police to get rid of these children by simply killing them.

To that end, several military policemen, including Marcus Vinicius Emmanuel (b. 1967), drove up to Rio's Candelaria Cathedral on the night of July 23, 1993. There, as they came every night to sleep, were seventy-two homeless children. They had been warned to get off the streets or else, but they had no where else to go. Huddled next to the church, the children

Leader of a Rio murder squad, Marcus Vinicius Emmanuel (center), is shown leaving a courtroom after receiving a sentence of 309 years for murdering six or more children.

suddenly came under automatic fire from Emmanuel and others. Eight children were killed and scores more wounded.

Emmanuel was later identified by one of the survivors, Wagner dos Santos, who testified against him in court. Nelson Cunha, another accused officer, confessed to helping commit the massacre and testified against Emmanuel. To the shock of everyone, Emmanuel was convicted and sentenced to 309 years in prison, a sentence later reduced to 89 years at his retrial.

These seemingly long prison terms mean little in Brazil. Emmanuel would be eligible for parole in about five years and he was sent to a military prison, where he continued to hold his rank and receive his salary.

Cunha was tried later and found guilty, sentenced to thirty years, but this prison term was also reduced when he was retried. The abuse and murder of helpless, homeless children in Rio has gone on unabated since the trials of Emmanuel and Cunha and remain the shame of Brazil.

A BLACK RACIST KILLER/ December 7, 1993

A deep hatred for whites coursed through the mind of Colin Ferguson. A native of Jamaica, Ferguson had spent some time on the West Coast, a lonely black man, who was remembered for only one thing, hating whites and Asians. He obtained an automatic pistol and went to New York. In the evening of December 7, 1993, Ferguson was riding the 5:33 local train from Penn Station in Manhattan. As it rolled into the Long Island town of Garden City, he suddenly produced the pistol and began running down aisles of the train, selecting whites to kill.

Ferguson shot and killed six persons and wounded nineteen others until three courageous passengers tackled him and held him for the police. Not until January 26, 1995, was Ferguson brought to trial. He was dissatisfied with his defense attorneys early on, including the flamboyant William Kunstler, who had planned to conduct a defense of "black rage." Such a defense seemed to be racist at best, one which Ferguson himself apparently disliked.

After his attorneys described their client as paranoid and delusional, Ferguson fired them and became his own defense lawyer. Judge Donald Belfi, presiding over the case in a Mineola, New York, courtroom, indulged the arrogant Ferguson by allowing him to defend himself. He chose fellow Jamaican Alton Rose to be his "legal adviser."

Rose described Ferguson's attempt to defend himself as similar to "a patient in a doctor's office trying to perform his own spinal cord operation." Dressed in a suit, white shirt and tie, Ferguson impersonated a lawyer (while wearing a bulletproof vest under his shirt, a protective measure he insisted upon, stating that he believed the trial was nothing more than a conspiracy to murder *him*).

Ferguson's defense of himself constituted a ridiculous shambles of legal mumbo-jumbo. He spoke as if he knew the law, saying things like "Is it your testimony that," and "Would it be fair to say that," and "Was it also your finding that," all in bad imitation of a real lawyer. He picked up legal phrases and applied them where they did not fit. He referred to himself in the third person, as "Mr. Ferguson," and "the defendant."

Black racist Colin Ferguson, center, holding documents, is shown entering court, where he awkwardly acted as his own defense counsel; he was convicted of murdering six white persons and wounding nineteen others.

Taking weeks to prepare his case, Ferguson asked Judge Belfi for more time. He wanted to summon President Clinton and New York Governor Mario Cuomo to testify, because it was reported that both had talked to witnesses in the trial. He got angry when the court ruled against these demands.

Ferguson then offered several theories as to how the mass shooting took place. First, he insisted that he was asleep when a white man stole his gun out of his bag and commenced shooting everyone in sight and that he had been arrested simply because he was black. When this argument was dismissed as ridiculous, Ferguson stated that another black man with the same name as his and looking identical to him committed the shootings.

The high point of this legal theater of the absurd was when Ferguson began raving that the killing of Jeffrey Dahmer (a notorious killer and cannibal—see chapter on Cannibalism) in a Wisconsin prison, which had recently occurred, was linked to a vast conspiracy against him, Colin Ferguson. Then one after another, the survivors of Ferguson's shooting spree confronted him in court. For the first time in any American trial, the victim confronted the criminal face to face, answering the bizarre Ferguson when he asked that the attacker be identified. Maryanne Phillips faced the killer coolly and said, "I saw you shoot me."

This was repeated time and again, twelve out of the seventeen surviving victims saying "It was you who shot me," and "You are the man who shot me." He asked one witness, "Did the gunman shoot you?" The victim replied while looking straight at Ferguson, "As soon as you had time to point the gun at me and pull the trigger." When Robert Giugliano, a burly contractor Ferguson had shot in the chest, took the witness stand, his icy stare so unnerved Ferguson that he asked for a fifteen-minute recess.

It was apparent that the strutting, posturing Ferguson was inflicting more pain upon his victims, first having shot them, then compelling them to recount in detail the horror he had inflicted upon them and then identify him as their assailant. On February 15, 1994, Ferguson had run out witnesses to identify him as a ruthless killer and he also refused to take the stand on his own behalf. It was, as Judge Belfi stated, "the moment of truth." Ferguson rested his case, which was no case at all.

On February 17, 1994, a jury deliberated ten hours and then returned six guilty verdicts in the murders of six of the train passengers. Ferguson was also convicted of twenty-two counts of attempted murder. Carolyn McCarthy, whose husband had been shot to death by Ferguson and whose son Kevin had been crippled for life by a gunshot from the killer, had sat quietly behind the defendant throughout the trial. At its conclusion she stated, "It's been a long fourteen months, but justice has been done."

Judge Belfi later sentenced Ferguson to six life terms in prison, a total of 200 years with no hope for parole. He would die behind bars. Robert Giugliano was still enraged at the mass killer, shaking his fist at an unperturbed Ferguson and shouting, "I feel this animal should suffer till the day he dies! ... Given five minutes with Colin Ferguson, this coward would know the meaning of suffering!"

SLAUGHTER BY A FAMILY FRIEND/ August 29, 1994

Residents of East Virginia Avenue in Vinton, Virginia, awoke on the morning of August 29, 1994, with the sounds of sirens in their ears. The two-story home down the block occupied by Blaine and Teresa Hodges and their two daughters, Winter and Anah, was on fire, flames shooting out of the windows. By 9 a.m., the firemen had contained the blaze, but the house was a smoldering ruin. Detectives arrived to investigate the report that four bodies had been found inside the cinders, those of 41-year-old Blaine Hodges, his 37-year-old wife Teresa, and their daughters, 11-year-old Winter and 3-year-old Anah.

In what remained of the living room, detectives discovered that Teresa Hodges had been strangled and that her corpse had been saturated with diesel oil and another accelerant thought to be gasoline. Blaine Hodges was found sprawled on the remains of a bed in the master bedroom. There was a bullet in his right temple. The two girls were found hugging each other in death. Both had been shot point blank between the eyes.

Earl Conrad Bramblett, at the time he befriended the Hodges family in Vinton, Virginia.

Police at first concluded that the family had been wiped out by a murder-suicide committed by Blaine Hodges. A recently fired .22-caliber handgun was found beside him. He had killed his wife, then shot his two daughters and finally himself, detectives believed. Blaine Hodges, they quickly learned, had been fired from his postal job after being convicted of embezzling $5,000, and was to begin a six-month prison term, all reasons, though not good ones, for prompting the destruction of his family and himself.

Disrupting police theories was a report that came from Dr. David Oxly, deputy chief medical examiner for Western Virginia. After examining the body of Blaine Hodges, he determined that he had been dead more than twenty hours before his wife and daughters died. Oxly also reported that Teresa Hodges had died a horribly painful death, that it took fifteen minutes before she died of strangulation.

Detectives then realized that someone had murdered the family and staged the murder-suicide, placing the handgun next to Hodges and a hammer next to the body of his wife. Though Blaine Hodges had problems, he and his wife had been struggling to work things out. They had been selling Amway products out of their home and had told friends the night before their murders that they were planning to hold an Amway sale at their home within a few days.

Though many leads came to the police, none proved to turn up the mass murderer. More than three years later, however, Earl Conrad Bramblett (1942-2003), a handyman who had been Blaine Hodges' friend for twenty years, was indicted

Earl Bramblett, right, at the time of his trial for the mass murder of the Hodges family in 1994. He was found guilty and sentenced to death.

for the family slayings. His background had caused prosecutors to charge him with capital murder, three counts of first-degree murder, three counts of using a firearm and arson, despite the fact that they had no murder weapon, no eyewitnesses, no informant, and no confession. Their case was wholly circumstantial, but prosecutors felt confident of a conviction.

Bramblett was born on March 20, 1942, and raised in poverty. He had been an excellent high school track star, winning a scholarship, but though he attended three colleges he never earned a degree. He married and fathered two sons, but his wife divorced him, citing his alcoholism and his abnormal fondness for little girls. It was this latter penchant of Bramblett's that caused detectives to pursue him as the primary suspect in the Hodges slayings.

Two women had accused Bramblett of sexually molesting them in 1970, and another woman claimed that he had threatened her with a gun. In 1977, he was a prime suspect in the disappearance of a 14-year-old girl, but evidence against his involvement could not be developed. A 10-year-old girl came forward in 1984 and accused Bramblett of molesting her, but she later refused to testify against him.

After Blaine Hodges was accused of embezzling $5,000 from the post office, Bramblett appeared to come to the aid of his old friend, loaning him a few dollars here and there. He began sleeping in the Hodges home for days on end. Bramblett then began making advances to 11-year-old Winter Hodges, calling her on the phone when she was in bed, asking what she was wearing, calling her when he was in the bathtub. He tape-recorded his phone conversations with the girl in what he called his "diary tapes." He recorded his innermost thoughts while he walked his dog or drove his pickup, which was white and had a black tailgate—a neighbor had described just such a pickup leaving the Hodges driveway shortly before the fire broke out in the early morning hours of August 29, 1994.

On one of the tapes, Bramblett was heard to say: "I'm trying to get her [Winter Hodges] to do things that aren't proper." He then began to imagine that Hodges wanted him to spend time at his house "so that they can manufacture some charges

Earl Bramblett, a prison photo taken a short time before his execution on April 9, 2003.

against me," in order to escape the pending prison term Hodges was facing. On the day before he was to leave for prison, Hodges had warned his wife not to let Bramblett in the house. By then Teresa and Winter had complained about the actions of the handyman, but on that day, Bramblett had taken the front and rear doors of their house off their hinges, claiming that they should be painted.

The day before the murders, a boy from the neighborhood spotted Bramblett's pickup truck in the alley in the back of the Hodges house, and Teresa, Anah and Winter were sitting inside. That afternoon a ranger at the Jefferson National Forest saw a white pickup with a black tailgate parked near Jennings Creek in Botetourt County. He saw Teresa playing with Anah on the grass and spoke to her. Winter Hodges was fishing with Bramblett at the time. With Hodges being sent to prison, it was apparent that Bramblett planned to become the head of the Hodges household, his aim being to sexually seduce 11-year-old Winter Hodges.

All of this and more was used by prosecutors to build a case against Earl Bramblett, who was put on trial in October 1997. Several persons came forward to state that they had seen Bramblett close to the Hodges home before and after the fire. Bramblett's ex-wife testified that he had called her in the afternoon following the fire to shout, "There's a fire at the Hodges house and they're going to blame me!"

Bramblett had showed up at the Vinton police station a short time later, asking to talk to the leading investigator on the Hodges case. He said that he was a friend of the family and wanted to know if anyone had been injured in the blaze. When told that all the family members were dead, Bramblett yelled, "The sorry son of a bitch! He had a beautiful family. He did them and did himself!"

The 72 tapes Bramblett had recorded which detailed his mundane movements and his attempts to seduce Winter Hodges were played before the jury. (They were retrieved from the Indiana home of Bramblett's sister after Bramblett was arrested there.) A detective report disclosed how a .22-caliber handgun had been retrieved from Bramblett's room. Also found at that time was a drawing the defendant had made of four stick figures with lines going through the heads of three of them, lines that correctly described the angle of the bullets the killer had fired into Hodges and his daughters, information known only to the police and the killer. Moreover, Bramblett had directly implicated himself when talking to police about the case, mentioning that gasoline had been sprinkled about the body of Teresa Hodges, another fact known only to the killer and investigators.

Moreover, detectives testified that Bramblett had shown up at the Vinton police station after the fire freshly bathed, shaved, even his tennis shoes washed (the tongues were sticking up and they had no shoelaces). From examining the Hodges bathroom, they later determined that he had, after killing all the family members, taken a shower, washed his clothes of any traces of blood, and shaved. He then went to the kitchen and made himself lunch, eating casually while Teresa Hodges' body lay only a few feet away from him. After eating, he set the house on fire.

Defense attorneys had a weak case. They claimed that their client was delusional. They then stated that the Hodges family had been wiped out by vicious drug dealers (the same kind of claim made by defense attorneys in the infamous O.J. Simpson case—see Celebrity Slayings). They stated that Teresa's half-brother had been an informant for the Drug Enforcement Administration and that the family had been killed in retaliation by drug-running murderers.

The jury was unimpressed. On October 31, 1997, after deliberating for only two hours, the jury returned a verdict of guilty on all counts. On November 5, 1997, Roanoke County Circuit Judge Roy Willett sentenced Earl Bramblett to death. Bramblett was executed in Virginia's electric chair on April 9, 2003. Shortly before his death, he was visited by his ex-wife and his two sons. When strapped into the oak chair (built by prison inmates), Bramblett insisted that he was innocent. "I didn't murder the Hodges family," he said. "I've never murdered anybody. I'm going to my death with a clear conscience."

"WHAT KIND OF EVIL PERSON ARE YOU?"/August 15, 1996

A native of Sacramento, California, Frederick Martin Davidson (b. 1960) was the product of a broken home, his parents divorcing when he was a child. He nevertheless proved to be a good student and his service with the army was unblemished. He moved to San Diego and studied at San Diego State University, earning a bachelor's degree in mechanical engineering in 1991. He decided to continue his studies and earn a master's degree and toward that end did research with 32-year-old Professor Chen Liang.

At times, his roommate later stated, Davidson expressed gratitude and friendship for Liang, but other times he said he considered Liang his enemy, that he was just stringing him along, using him to work long hours in research so that he, Liang, could take credit for that work. This was the classic complaint of all post-graduate students, that they performed the dirty work for researchers who later took the data, wrote papers on it, and furthered their careers through the labors of their students, even publishing books researched and written by those students.

A utilitarian and compulsive cleaner, Davidson's Spartan room was always spotless. The only thing adorning its walls were his bachelor's degree and a calendar. He was forever tidying up after himself and others.

Davidson apparently harbored a deep resentment for Liang and two other engineering professors, who were to meet him on August 15, 1996, in a room on the SDSU campus and pass review on his thesis. He had already been rejected by this panel and he believed that his master's degree was even fur-

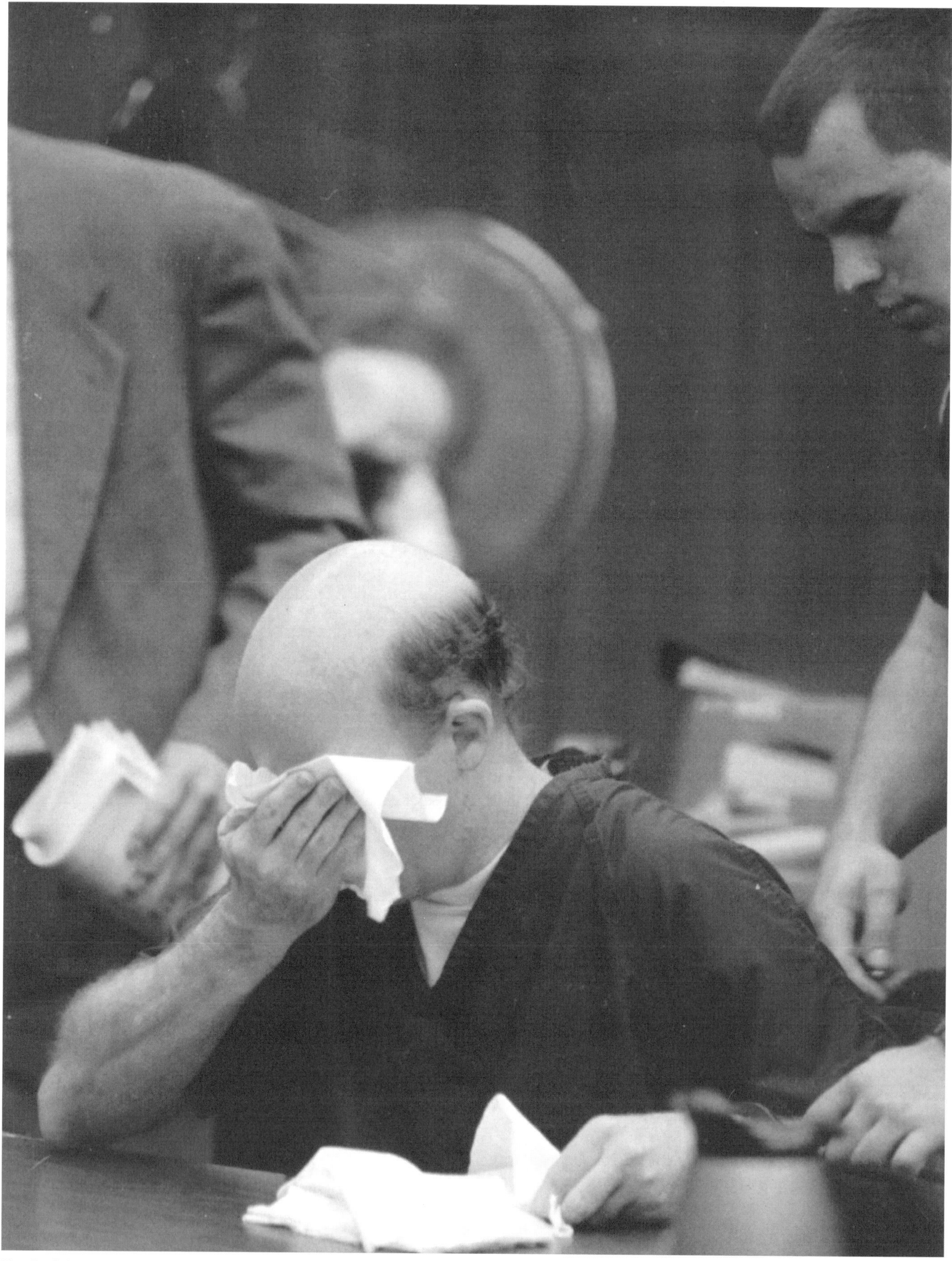

Frederick Martin Davidson wipes away tears after receiving three life terms for the mass murder of his teachers at San Diego State University on August 15, 1996.

ther beyond his reach in that Liang had been critical of his research and that 44-year-old Professor D. Preston Lowrey III had caught him using stolen notes in a recent test.

Following a careful, premeditated plan, Davidson slipped into the SDSU examination room on the third floor of the Engineering Building at about 10 a.m. on August 15. He hid a 9mm Taurus handgun with an extra clip of ammunition in the metal first-aid kit box on the wall. Returning at about 2 p.m., Davidson was greeted by three professors—Liang, Lowrey, and 36-year-old Constantinos Lyrintzis. Three student monitors stood behind the three-man thesis review panel.

Liang stood up, walked around a long table where the panel sat and went up to Davidson to state the purpose of the review. Davidson said nothing. He immediately went to the metal first-aid kit box, opened it, and withdrew the 9mm gun. He aimed this at Liang and shot him down, killing him. Lowrey and Lyrintzis, along with two students, fled. Lowrey ran toward the hall and Davidson shot him down. Lyrintzis and two students fled into a nearby computer room, but Davidson found them. He pushed away the students and fired several times into Lyrintzis' crouched body, killing him.

Campus police were by then summoned and they found Davidson standing in a hallway holding the gun at his side. He was weeping and asking the officers to shoot him. A few minutes later he dropped the gun and was arrested and taken into custody. The mass murderer never offered any excuses or reasons for the killings. He was found guilty and, on July 18, 1997, appeared in San Diego Superior Court for sentencing.

Before hearing his fate, Davidson had to face the families of the three professors he had murdered in cold blood. At that moment, 9-year-old Kendall Lowrey stood up, tears in his eyes, his words coming in gasps, saying, "In the afternoon of August 15, 1996, I lost my daddy. He used to call me 'Buddy.' No one calls me that anymore."

Baihong Liang, the wife of slain Chen Liang, looked at Davidson, whose head was bowed, eyes downcast, and said, "You have been in my home for parties and you have played with my children. How could you kill their father? What kind of evil person are you?"

Deana Lyrintzis, the widow of Professor Lyrintzis, stated, "My poor little angel will never know her daddy." She pointed at the convicted Davidson, almost yelling, "He deserves no pity, no mercy, no compassion, because he had none for my husband when he begged him not to kill him."

The widows of the slain professors, however, had endorsed a plea-bargain deal that would not result in a death penalty. When they learned that the automatic appeals process in California death penalty cases could drag on for a decade or even two, they pushed for life imprisonment. That is what they got.

Following the statements of the victims' families—this being now a ritual in most states, one that allows aggrieved family members to exorcise and exhaust their anger and hatred in the very faces of killers—Judge William Mudd sentenced Davidson to three life terms, plus ten years, in prison. There was no possibility of parole or appeal.

Mudd then asked Davidson if he had anything to say. Davidson, his back to the families of those he had slain, replied in a near whisper, "I am very sorry for what I did. I was very wrong. It should never have happened. I'm sorry."

SLAUGHTER AT HEAVEN'S GATE/March 22-23, 1997

America's junk culture has produced numerous doomsday or "escape" cults, invariably created by self-styled gurus, ministers, or glib madmen just sane enough to convince the gullible and the hopeful to throw away their lives for the sake of a leader's dream (or nightmare). Just as Jim Jones was able to con more than 900 followers into committing mass suicide with him in 1978, in Jonestown, Guyana, and David Koresh slyly convinced his naïve followers to die en masse in Waco, Texas in 1993, a smooth-talking crackbrained self-appointed space evangelist, Marshall Herff Applewhite, persuaded thirty-eight followers to kill themselves in order to spiritually board his imaginary spacecraft trailing the so-called Hale-Bopp comet on March 22-23, 1997.

Texas crackpot religious leader Marshall Applewhite, who took every dime his followers could scrape up and rewarded them with mass murder.

Son of a Texas preacher, Applewhite was a failed entertainer, who aspired to sing the lead roles in such musicals as *Oklahoma!* and *South Pacific*, but his voice was too thin and, after years of pursuing this career, he gave up on singing in the early 1970s. He had tried teaching music, but was fired from two jobs after male students complained about his homosexual advances. A report had it that he checked into a psychiatric hospital in hopes of curing his homosexuality. To a gay lover he confided that he longed for sexless passion, a "higher level" of spiritual gratification.

About this time, Applewhite began referring to himself as "Do," after the first note on the musical scale, and, as he added followers to his religious-space cult, he dubbed them with names of subsequent notes. The naive, the gullible, those tired of trying to cope with the problems of everyday life, trudged beneath Applewhite's banner for two decades. He milked them of their savings and real estate, "donations" that went to support the cult, especially after it established its headquarters in Rancho Santa Fe, a sprawling mansion (estimated to be worth $1.3 million), replete with pool, patio, and tennis court, in an upscale suburb north of San Diego, California.

Like all semi-religious cults that bilk their easily duped followers, Applewhite successfully persuaded several dozen "marks" to divorce themselves from their families, renounce all worldly goods, sex, and drugs, and to pool their resources with the cult, offering them in return the "guaranteed" promise of salvation on a spaceship.

Applewhite and his first fanatical follower, Bonnie Lu Nettles, had for years insisted that they were the Two Witnesses described in *Revelations*, the biblical prophets who would herald the end of the world and eternal salvation. In their early days they referred to themselves as Bo (Applewhite) and Peep (Nettles) to suggest that they were the shepherds

The sprawling Rancho Santa Fe, where Applewhite and his henchmen led their deluded followers to ignominious death.

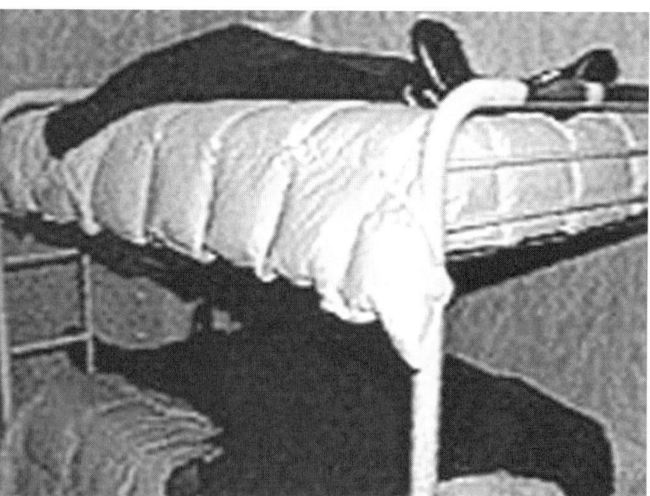

Bodies of the mass suicide-murder (some were asphyxiated by plastic bags placed over their heads) at Rancho Santa Fe, which took place on the night of March 22-23, 1997; the crackbrained Applewhite—his corpse was found among the dead—had promised his followers that they would be riding a wonderful spaceship in the wake of a comet after their deaths.

who would guide the faithful to their higher level of destiny. Later, these two would change their cult names to Do and Ti, striking a more musical posture to their lofty calling.

Those who took up residence at cult headquarters in Rancho Santa Fe were mostly semi-literate lower class whites, but a sprinkling of minorities were present. All of them were taught by Applewhite that they were "special," that they were to be grateful for having been "chosen" to make the trip from physical misery to spiritual happiness. This is the typical spiel spewed upon the lonely, the disenfranchised, or those with low self-esteem.

Applewhite knew that such persons were easily persuaded to embrace any irrational belief, as long as it gave them a sense of belonging, and, especially, importance. Actually, they were more important than anyone else in the world, he told them, for only they would be privileged to board the unseen spacecraft he said was in the milky tail of the approaching comet, Hale-Bopp. All they had to do to board this craft was to commit suicide with him, to leave their corporal bodies (shells) and he would guide them to the craft that would speed them to paradise on the eve of a century doomed to crashing oblivion. Applewhite (who had been arrested for such lowly crimes as auto theft in the early 1970s) would be their gateway to Heaven.

There was nothing new about Applewhite's millennial swindle, with one notable exception—he was selling death, presumptuously, arrogantly promising that such death was merely the first step to a finer life. At the turn of the 20th century, thousands of sharpers preyed upon the suspicious and fearful, but no one of that down-to-earth generation thought to take their own lives. They did, however, spend hundreds of thousands of dollars with confidence men who sold them tickets in crude stadiums and arenas to "watch the end of the world," as Halley's Comet approached the planet.

On the evening of March 22-23, 1997, Applewhite and thirty-eight other followers began killing themselves. The twenty-one women and eighteen men, ranging in age from 26 to 72, killed themselves, according to pathologists, in stages and in groups, all following the same procedure. The mansion was first cleaned from top to bottom and, in this spotless atmosphere, Applewhite's victims lay down on double-tiered bunks. All wore black pants, flowing black shirt, and brand new black Nikes. The first stage of suicides involved fifteen persons, the second stage another fifteen, then seven persons, then finally Applewhite and his closest male follower.

Members swallowed Phenobarbital mixed with apple-sauce or pudding, followed by a shot of vodka. An asphyxiating plastic bag was then tied over each head to assure death and complete what was in reality, mass murder. All were covered with purple shrouds, except for the 65-year-old Applewhite and his last male follower, who were found with only plastic bags tied about their heads. It was several days before this house of death was entered. When no one answered the front doorbell or the phones at the mansion, police were called. Many officers who entered the building were overcome with the putrid stench of bloated bodies.

Marshall Applewhite had another reason to end his life. One report stated he was then dying of cancer, and he urged the mass suicide before his followers learned of his terminal disease. The most insecure of all of the Heaven's Gate group, Applewhite needed to take his followers with him before cancer claimed his life. Also, he had promised this death journey for so long that, in the end, like motorcyclist Robbie Knievel who had long promised to jump the Grand Canyon (he did, in a May 1999 lunatic jump, setting a record of 228 feet), Applewhite could no longer put off his own demise. In truth, this conniving con artist proved to be a mass murderer, who, by his own cowardly suicide, put himself beyond the reach of the law.

CHAPTER ELEVEN:
MURDER/SERIAL KILLERS

The serial killer, the most bizarre of murderers has, until recent decades, made infrequent appearances in ancient and more modern eras. With the population explosions of many continents during the 20th century, however, such killers have commensurately come into existence by dint of larger numbers. These killers in all ages invariably begin with assault and rape, then kill over extensive periods of time and often their victims are selected randomly and in many locations. Though some historic serial killers like Gilles de Rais were deranged cultists, these slayers have been invariably judged sane in modern times, but having psychopathic or sociopathic personalities.

Such murderers often practice sexual perversions, translating into violent death. Consumed by inherent rage, often from childhood, and spurred by lust, the serial killer is usually without conscience or remorse. Although aware of the nature of their actions, the serial killer rarely if ever feels guilt and he is the most elusive of slayers, having no apparent motives for his murders and seldom an accomplice in his or her crimes, who might later become an informant.

The serial killer is most often apprehended through his own disclosures. German serial killer Peter Kurten, known as the Monster of Dusseldorf, might never have been detected had he not identified his myriad murders to his horrified wife over breakfast one morning. Further complicating detection of serial killers is the fact that many move from one jurisdiction to another without apparent purpose.

Most often, the serial killer is the product of a broken home, where he is set emotionally and economically adrift at an early age. Drug-addicted or alcoholic parents of such killers are commonplace. Arson and the torturing of animals in childhood mark the path of many a serial killer. Often the serial killer avenges himself or herself on hapless, random victims in an effort to punish uncaring parents or cruelty endured in childhood. In the darkest and impenetrable cases, some serial killers have sexually violated the corpses of their victims, as was the case of the coast-to-coast serial killer, Earle Leonard Nelson.

Nelson's victims, like most of those claimed by serial killers, were women and children, the most helpless of any human prey, although adult males can some time be found in the lists of such bloodletting. And like most serial killers, Nelson appeared outwardly to be friendly, retiring, gentle and harmless, beguiling and gulling the victim into trust and confidence before his lethal nature burst to the surface.

Nelson was, however, a periodic nightmare that had few peers in his age. That has changed since the traumatic 1960s, and from that point, serial killers have become horrifyingly common, scores of them, from Kenneth Bianchi and Angelo Buono (The Hillside Strangler) to Theodore "Ted" Bundy, from Henry Lee Lucas and Ottis Elwood Toole to Christopher Bernard Wilder, John Wayne Gacy and Andrew Philip Cunanan to John Allen Muhammad and Lee Boyd Malvo (who killed ten people and wounded three in senseless sniper shootings in October 2002, Muhammad sentenced to death, Malvo to life) claiming dozens if not hundreds of victims. Such serial killings are no longer phenomenal occurrences, but almost routine events.

Police are, as in the past, at a considerable disadvantage in tracking down such killers, although forensic science, ballistics and DNA has improved their abilities in identifying and subsequently apprehending a number of these elusive slayers. The police are nevertheless almost as much at the mercy of these killers as are the endless victims claimed in what has become an ongoing senseless slaughter.

FRANCE'S FIRST SERIAL KILLER/1430s

The inexplicable transformation of Gilles de Rais (Ray, Raiz, or Retz; AKA: Bluebeard; 1404-1440), from idealist and most able supporter of Joan of Arc to the slaughterhouse killer of scores of children, is one of the most chilling stories in the annals of crime. Baron Rais was born into wealth and became the richest man in France when he married Catherine de Thouars in 1620. He had been raised a devout Christian, so

A statue of France's great warrior saint, Joan of Arc in Reims Cathedral; she was the idol of Gilles de Rais, who was himself a champion of freedom, until becoming a serial killer.

Gilles de Rais when he fought alongside Joan of Arc in her crusade to rid France of English armies.

Gilles de Rais shown on his warhorse, while serving in the army of Joan of Arc.

when he heard that Joan of Arc was in search of an army to repel the British invaders, Rais met with her.

The young woman captivated and mystified Rais, and he soon pledged his sword and fortune to her cause. Rais paid for the powerful army that followed Joan to Orleans and her greatest victory. He was by her side when she captured the city and drove the British from the battlements. The young baron was ecstatic with triumph, but this euphoric attitude was short-lived. Joan was betrayed and turned over to the British, who tortured and then condemned her to death in a mock trial and executed her at the stake on May 31, 1431. Her death was devastating to Rais, who became a recluse.

Rais had already been made a marshal of France and his incredible wealth allowed him to live lavishly. He began to spend recklessly on paintings, tapestries, and sculptures, becoming the most generous patron of the arts in France. To support his sumptuous lifestyle, Rais began to sell some of his vast estates. This brought him into conflict with other family members, who claimed birthrights to these lands. Relatives went to King Charles who signed an injunction forbidding Rais from selling more estates, but he defied the powerless king and sold lands in Brittany to cover his colossal expenditures.

By 1439, Rais had become dissolute, drinking heavily and dallying with whores. His once bright and noble character had changed completely. He now sought out vice with a vengeance and was notorious for his lecheries and his obsession with alchemy, magic, and all manner of the black arts. Rais' transformation has been attributed to the painful death of the woman he most admired, St. Joan. With her death, he reportedly lost all faith in God and religion.

Rais turned to the darker side of his soul, plunging into its abyss. According to one account, "his ego had a Jekyll and Hyde variability, now urging him to depravity, now propelling him on to self fulfillment through the use of his undoubted gifts."

Suffering great financial losses because of his profligate ways, Rais turned desperately to wild schemes to create riches. He consulted Gilles de Sill, a cleric who claimed that he could change common metal into gold through alchemy. Rais financed de Sill's half-baked experiments, and when these failed to produce the expected heaps of gold, Rais consulted Francesco Prelati, a defrocked, demented priest. Prelati promised the baron that he could obtain riches for Rais through the black arts by raising Satan, and he and Rais forthwith experimented with satanic rituals.

In the baron's many castles were theaters that had been constructed years earlier for his love of drama. According to one report, Prelati used these theaters as part of his black masses dedicated to Satan, rites in which young urchin boys were brought by the dozens and viciously slain while Rais watched, fascinated, sadistically enjoying the suffering and agonizing deaths of these children.

Rais conducted the most depraved and horrid acts himself, helping the mad ex-priest to sexually abuse, torture, and mutilate to death these helpless boys. The numbers involved were staggering, reported to have been between 140 and 800. If the latter number is anywhere near correct, it would make Rais the worst serial killer in history. His defenders later claimed

The court in the trial of Gilles de Rais in 1440; the presiding judge, Bishop Jean de Malestroit, is shown top left. De Rais was accused of murdering between 140 to 800 young boys in Satanic rituals.

A contemporary sketch shows the execution of Gilles de Rais, October 26, 1440; he was strangled and burned to death before a large crowd at the Ile de Biesse, outside Nantes.

there were few deaths, that the whole trial which Rais faced on October 15, 1440, was a trumped-up affair to wrest his vast estates from him, but much of this land had already been sold and so this claim was largely invalid.

Rais was an imposing figure in court. He had a long blue-black beard, which later caused him to be named Bluebeard, a name that came to signify the serial killer in France and would later be applied to the infamous Henri Desire Landru (see The French Bluebeard, Serial Killers). Among the allegations made against him, Rais was charged with abducting a priest and killing him for his own amusement. He was also charged with sodomizing countless young boys, while they were being murdered. Rais listened as witness after witness accused him of these monstrous crimes. He then laughed loudly at the court, claiming it was all nonsense, that his enemies had fabricated these terrible stories to have him imprisoned or executed, so that they could seize his fortune.

On October 19, 1440, Rais and his closest servants were tortured and the servants confessed that all of the charges against Rais were true. They added details of Rais' unspeakable tortures and murders, some committed, they said, in front of Rais' brother. Rais himself did not break under torture, but he finally did break when threatened with excommunication from the Catholic Church.

Rais' spiritual tie was so strong that the mere threat of being set spiritually adrift from the Church compelled him to "confess everything." Rais was condemned to death and, on October 26, 1440, was publicly strangled to death, burned at the same time, while he choked out a plea for forgiveness to the parents of the murdered children witnessing his bizarre death. Two of Rais' associates were also executed at the same time, both burned alive.

HUNGARY'S MURDERING COUNTESS/1600s

Married at fifteen to Count Ferencz Ndasdy, Countess Elizabeth Bathory (or Batory; 1560-1614) lived in regal splendor inside the Castle Csejthe. Waited on hand and foot, Bathory occupied her teenage years with pleasures of the flesh and toward her twentieth year she began to display a decided taste for sadistic punishment. Her husband, while fighting the Turks, the story goes, found a rare manuscript on ancient tortures and the countess read this crusty document with avid interest which later turned to lethal fascination. She was also obsessed with flagellation, a trait learned from an unbalanced aunt, and ordered her servants to whip her for long, painful periods as would a flagellant.

The countess was an attractive woman, dark and sensuous, and she took many lovers while her husband was still alive. Upon his death in 1604, Bathory's mind seemed to snap. She slept erratically, ordered her servants to walk about naked, and developed an unpredictable appetite, demanding that she be served only exotic fruits from the Middle East.

When a servant girl dared to bring her some commonplace apples, the countess flew into a rage and struck the girl, cutting the flesh with a large ring. Some blood splashed on her face and when she wiped it off she became convinced that her aging complexion in that spot had suddenly been revitalized, made youthful again.

Hungary's Countess Elizabeth Bathory ordered the deaths of between 600 and 750 young girls, bathing in their blood to improve her complexion; she was walled up in a room of her castle, dying in 1614.

With this imagined discovery, the countess believed that eternal youth could be obtained if she bathed in the fresh virgin's blood. To this gruesome end, Bathory ordered her palace guardsmen to scour the countryside and bring her peasant girls who, upon being proved virgins, were slain, their blood drained into a hot bath in which the countess submerged herself every morning.

It was reported that, like the legendary Dracula (Vlad Tepes, see Mass Murder), Bathory turned vampire and actually sucked the blood out of her victims, but this was never supported even by her most lunatic aides, especially the cruel Dorotta Szentes, who was known as Dorka. For years the countess bathed in her human blood, but the rejuvenation process was evident only in her demented mind. Her followers, fearing for their own lives, did her bidding, murdering girls by the scores to satisfy her maniacal whim, and buried the bodies throughout the old underground passages of the castle.

Bathory, in one grim moment of reality, saw herself as the aging crone she had become and screamed to Dorka that it was the quality of blood that was missing. She was bathing in the gore of inferior humans and suddenly seized upon the idea that only the blood of aristocrats could return her youth. She devised a scheme to snare the young daughters of her peers, telling bluebloods throughout Hungary that she would take under her tutorship twenty-five of the prettiest daughters of aristocrats and teach them in the ways of social graces. Since Bathory was one of the richest and most powerful persons in the country and her horrific deeds had been kept secret, many members of the lower nobility seized upon this opportunity as a way of advancing their own positions, and sent their daughters to this monster in 1609.

At first Bathory pretended to conduct classes in manners and etiquette, but she would have the girls murdered one by one in their beds as they slept and then butchered for her gory bath. Her most trusted servants, however, grew careless and, instead of burying the bodies in the castle caverns, simply tossed the corpses over the castle wall, where peasants soon discovered and identified them. (It was conjectured that the servants intentionally made the murders apparent in order to bring Bathory's sins to public view.)

Once the murders became known a great outcry against the countess caused the arrest of her most trusted aides, Dorka, a male servant, and a captain of the palace guard. Bathory herself, under Hungarian law, could not be arrested or tried for common murder since she was a member of ranking royalty and therefore immune from criminal prosecution. Her servants were nevertheless found guilty and burned alive at the stake for their awful slayings, but this did not appease an increasingly hostile populace which demanded the punishment of Countess Bathory so vociferously that the government feared open rebellion. To sidestep laws that protected the lunatic Bathory, the Hungarian Parliament convened and passed a special law which permitted authorities to bring her to trial.

Countess Bathory was convicted of murdering scores of young girls (the count was staggering, between 600 and 750), but since she could not, under any legal circumstances, be executed in any prescribed manner, she was sent to her suite in the castle and walled up in these rooms. She was fed through an opening in the brick wall and managed to survive in her isolated castle tower for more than three years until she died screaming to be released. When the wall was broken down and officials stepped inside the suite, they beheld, as one described "a creature so hideous as to make Evil itself cringe."

MARIE DE BRINVILLIERS/1660s-1670s

Marie Marguerite de Brinvilliers (1630-1676) was responsible for at least fifty poison murders. Her fixation with poison was born out of personal greed. She was the eldest of five children and was born into nobility through the d'Aubray family. Attractive and sensuous, she reportedly had sex at an early age with several of her own brothers. After marrying the Marquis Antoine de Brinvilliers at the age of twenty-one, Marie took a lover, Gaudin de Saint-Croix, who helped her secure poison.

When Brinvilliers' father learned of the affair, he had Saint-Croix thrown into the Bastille, where the abused swain learned the dark arts of poisonings from a fellow convict named Elixi. He then plotted with Brinvilliers to murder her stern father. With the help of the conniving de Saint-Croix, Marie planned to murder her wealthy father, Dreux d'Aubray, to inherit his vast estate and live a life of ease with her lover. She was by then much in need of money, having squandered most of her husband's fortune.

Before she carried out this scheme, she "experimented"

Marie de Brinvilliers, a sketch drawn at the time she was about to be taken to her execution in 1676; she was responsible for an estimated fifty poison murders.

The executioner stands before a crowd at Notre Dame Cathedral, holding the severed head of poisoner Marie de Brinvilliers.

with Saint-Croix's poisons. The patients of the Hotel Dieu, a hospital in Paris, became her first victims. Pretending to nurse the sick and feeble, Marie de Brinvilliers murdered at least fifty patients. She disposed of her father in 1666, and later murdered two of her brothers to gain their property as well.

However, the money left behind did not satisfy her. She then turned on her peers in the French court, killing anyone that stood in her way or displeased her. Meanwhile de Saint-Croix mixed the potions as fast as he could. In a moment of carelessness, he inhaled the noxious fumes and fell over dead. Authorities then inspected Saint Croix's apartment in Paris, where they found his many poisons and extensive notes on those lethal concoctions he had prepared for the many victims selected by Marie de Brinvilliers.

Further, a servant confessed to her mistress' sinister activities under the threat of torture. In 1676, the beautiful but deadly Marie was ordered to issue a confession before the assembled multitudes at Notre Dame Cathedral, after which she was beheaded and burned.

SCOTLAND'S BURKE AND HARE/1820s

The notorious William Burke (1792-1829) and William Hare were not only early-day serial killers, but the first body snatchers of important record who, when corpses were not available for sale to anatomists for dissection, turned to murder to replenish their dwindling supply of cadavers. These killers later argued that they were only providing important research material for the advancement of medical science, a point stretched to the unbelievable. Yet in this dark age of medicine, the need to examine bodies to determine anatomical makeup was crucial.

European anatomists, or those who studied the internal structure of the human body, found that established medical schools were neither equipped nor authorized to conduct such studies. These anatomists opened schools of their own and medical students flocked to their classes. The schools, however, were limited in bodies available for study. During this time, before the Anatomy Act of 1832, British law curtailed autopsies by stipulating that all corpses must receive Christian burial.

Occasionally, the corpses of condemned felons were turned over to physicians for internal study, but these were limited in number. Doctors, particularly the successful anatomist, Dr.

Body-snatcher and serial killer William Burke, who stole bodies from graveyards for anatomical study, then resorted to murder to increase his pay for "fresh" cadavers.

William Hare, Burke's murder accomplice, eager for the shares that new bodies would bring, but reluctant to hang, saving his life by informing on Burke.

Helen McDougal, Burke's common-law wife, aided and abetted her murderous spouse in his serial-killing enterprises, encouraging him to "develop" his business.

Maggie Laird, Hare's common-law wife, who managed the boarding house where the killers plotted their murders and to which they brought some of their victims.

The Edinburgh boarding house, where Burke and Hare lived with their wives; Burke's apartment was at the bottom-right and he murdered many of his victims there before carting their bodies off to Dr. Knox's medical school for sale.

Daft Jamie, a half-witted begger boy murdered by Burke and Hare; it was this killing that eventually brought about the exposure of the serial killers.

Robert Knox of Edinburgh, had to rely upon body snatchers who ghoulishly roamed through unguarded graveyards in the murk of night, exhuming corpses and carting these gruesome burdens to medical schools where these nocturnal deliveries were received in secret. The most celebrated body snatchers of this era were Burke and Hare.

William Burke was born in County Tyrone, Ireland, a farmer's son, who received little or no education, going to work as a baker's apprentice while in his teens. He later worked as a weaver, then a cobbler, then briefly joined the British army, but was released as unfit. A surly, broad-shouldered man, Burke left Ireland after repeated quarrels with his family. He went to Scotland and worked on the Union Canal, then took a room in the Beggar's Hotel in Edinburgh, a lowly, rambling boarding house for indigent Irish laborers. By that time, he had picked up a prostitute named Helen McDougal (or Nell

William Burke in custody, shown in his prison cell wearing leg irons, while awaiting trial.

Macdougal), and both began a clothing business of sorts, collecting discarded clothes and shoes, repairing and then reselling these shabby items.

In 1826, Burke and McDougal moved to Log's boarding house in Tanner's Close, renting the basement apartment. It was here that Burke met William Hare, a lean, conniving fellow-boarder. Little of Hare's background is known. He had lived at Log's and when the owner died, he made the owner's widow, Maggie Laird, his common-law wife, and she assumed the role of boarding house proprietor.

Burke and Hare became drinking companions and would guzzle themselves into stupors while discussing get-rich-quick schemes that never materialized. Then, on November 29, 1827, Hare entered Burke's quarters while Burke was repairing a shoe and told him that one of his boarders, an army pensioner named Old Donald, had died in his room, still owing £4 in rent. Hare whispered an idea to his friend Burke: Why not sell Old Donald's corpse to Dr. Knox's medical school and make a little money on a body now useless to the world? Such an act was, of course, against the law, which required that all deaths be reported to the authorities and bodies removed for Christian burial.

Burke warmed quickly to the idea, and that night he and Hare carried the remains of Old Donald to Dr. Knox who purchased the cadaver, no questions asked, for £7. To explain the absence of Old Donald, Burke and Hare built a coffin, weighted it with bags of bark, sealed it, and turned it over to officials, who accepted this as the corpse of Old Donald and quickly buried the coffin. The porter at Dr. Knox's medical school informed Burke and Hare that good specimens for dissection might bring as much as £10 each and that these were in constant demand. They were invited to return often with such deliveries.

This transaction worked so smoothly that Burke and Hare resolved to continue selling bodies to Dr. Knox, except that some of the Log's boarders were reluctant to die. The body snatchers helped them along into eternity. The first of these was a boarder named Joe the Mumper who was dying of fever. Hare complained that such illnesses kept others from renting his rooms and the sick man was an inconvenience. Burke and Hare then smothered the man to death with a pillow, and his body was delivered to Knox's college in Surgeon's Square, bringing them £10.

William Burke, shown as a wax dummy modeled from life in Edinburgh Prison by Madame Tussaud shortly before the serial killer was executed, the dummy wearing the actual clothes worn by the murderer; Burke had grown a beard before going to the hangman, "as if to disguise himself from death," said an observer of the day.

Burke and Hare, along with their common-law wives, then went full tilt into the murder and body-selling business. Beginning in February 1828, they waylaid street peddlers and prostitutes or got them drunk, then smothered them and sold the bodies. Such was the fate of Abigail Simpson, a hawker of salt and hearthstone, Mary Paterson, a young prostitute, Mary Haldane, an aging harlot, Haldane's half-witted daughter, and an English traveler who was suffering from jaundice. There would be between fifteen and thirty victims in all, some later claimed as many as fifty or more. In most instances, Burke and Hare took turns suffocating the victims, one holding down the feet while the other smothered the victim with a pillow in the

Log's boarding house. On some occasions, Hare and Maggie Laird murdered the victims without Burke's help.

The murders were not confined to the rooms of the boarding house. Killings to obtain bodies were boldly committed in the streets of Edinburgh, especially by the cretinous and bestial Burke. He was returning to the boarding house one night with the body of an old derelict he had murdered, the body stuffed into a box carried on a cart and pulled by an ancient horse. An old Irish beggar woman made the mistake of stopping Burke to beg some money from him. He strangled her on the spot and then grabbed her grandson, a mute, and broke his back over his knee, stuffing these bodies into the box with the other corpse.

The killers became obsessed with bodies and could not find victims fast enough to fill their blood-soaked trunk. One night, their broken-down cart horse refused to budge while

A mob, enraged at the court's "not proven" verdict that freed Burke's wife, chases the terrified Helen McDougal (bottom left) through the streets of Edinburgh.

they were en route to the medical school with a delivery. Burke and Hare had to hire a porter who used a large wheelbarrow to cart their trunk to the school where the murderers were paid £16 for two bodies. So incensed were they at their horse's refusal to move their cart that they returned to the spot where the beast still stood and cut its throat.

The murder schemes of Burke and Hare began to unravel when Dr. Knox's students began to identify the corpses brought to them for dissection. One student recognized a prostitute he had patronized, but he remained silent. Knox evidently had his suspicions about Burke and Hare, but he said nothing, as long as the steady stream of bodies arrived at the door of his school. He became the most celebrated anatomist in the country and his school flourished.

Meanwhile, Burke and Hare fell out, or, at least, their women took to such arguing that Maggie Laird proposed that they kill Helen McDougal and sell her corpse to Dr. Knox. Burke drew the line at this and moved out with his wife, going to live with one of McDougal's relatives at Gibbs Close. Here the Burkes actually competed with the Hares, both operating separate murder businesses and continuing to sell the bodies to Dr. Knox. Then Burke killed an idiot beggar boy known throughout Edinburgh as Daft Jamie, who was recognized by some of Dr. Knox's students. The boy's identity was pointed out to Dr. Knox, but he denied that the body was that of the beggar boy. Again, he preferred to close his eyes and stifle his suspicions as to the real activities of his suppliers, Burke and Hare.

Burke and Hare's lucrative body racket came to an end on October 31, 1828. On the afternoon of that day, Burke was drinking in Rymer's pub when an old crone named Mary Docherty entered the pub and walked from table to table, begging. Burke sized her up and quickly concluded that her body would bring a considerable payment from Dr. Knox. He invited the woman to share some ale with him and the two got tipsy together. Then Burke invited Docherty to accompany him home to Gibbs Close where she would attend a "Halloween party." The woman accepted with alacrity and the pair went to Burke's boarding house, where Burke ordered a young couple boarding there, James and Ann Gray, to leave the premises, saying a private party was to commence. Then Hare and his wife were invited, Burke and his wife having made up with their murderous friends.

A drunken revel ensued with Burke dancing wildly with Docherty while she was periodically plied with heavy drink. (Because of this macabre revel, Burke was often called by writers a "dancing master.") In the middle of this raucous party, Burke suddenly pounced upon Docherty's bare feet with his hobnailed boots, grinning like a madman, and cut off her piercing screams of "murder!" (heard by the neighbors) by placing his paw-like hands about her throat and strangling her to death.

Docherty's naked body was then stuffed into the tea chest Burke used for his deliveries to Dr. Knox, and this was picked up by David Patterson, Dr. Knox's porter who gave Burke a disappointing £5 for the corpse. Having received so many bodies from Burke, Dr. Knox no longer waited for cadavers to be delivered to his school, but had his porter go to Burke for the corpses. Before this happened, however, James and Ann Gray, the momentarily evicted boarders at Burke's house, glimpsed Mrs. Docherty's legs protruding from the chest before it was quickly closed. Hare, realizing that the Grays had spotted the body, offered a great deal of money for their silence.

James Gray, however, went to the police and reported the murder, along with the fact that Gray had seen Patterson collect the tea chest, hearing him state that he would be taking this grim cargo to Dr. Knox's school. Police raced to the school, barged through the back door and found the tea chest with Docherty's body in it. Burke was quickly arrested and taken to jail. Then Mrs. McDougal was captured, along with the Hares.

To save himself, William Hare turned state's evidence, detailing his many murders with William Burke, or as many as he could remember. Mrs. McDougal was charged with murder, as were the Hares. Burke's trial began on December 24, 1828, but there was little to debate. He had already confessed his murders. Hare's vivid chronicle of the murders brought about a conviction for Burke, but the jury felt there was insufficient evidence to convict Helen McDougal and returned the verdict of "Not Proven" against her, a unique Scottish verdict which signified that the accused was probably guilty but not enough proof was present to allow conviction.

The execution of William Burke on January 28, 1829; more than 25,000 spectators watched the serial killer hang.

Burke phlegmatically stood in the dock throughout his trial and said very little, except to grunt derision at his one-time partner Hare. When he heard Helen McDougal's verdict he snorted: "Nelly, you're out of the scape." The court then released William Hare and his wife. The long-nosed, tall Hare, who had not been tried, but retained until Burke's trial ended, leaped from his seat in court, unable to restrain his joy at being set free; he danced a weird little jig as Burke was dragged away cursing in chains to await his execution.

While waiting for the hangman, Burke allowed artists to sketch him in his condemned cell but, ever the businessman, he charged them fees. He also complained bitterly about being cheated by Dr. Knox's porter, that many of the bodies he had turned over had been worth much more than what he had been paid. On the morning of January 28, 1829, William Burke was led to a public scaffold in Edinburgh and, in a driving rain that did not thwart 25,000 people from attending, was sent through the trapdoor. The huge crowd cheered his death and demanded that Hare, too, be hanged, but Hare had vanished from Edinburgh, as had Maggie Laird and Helen McDougal.

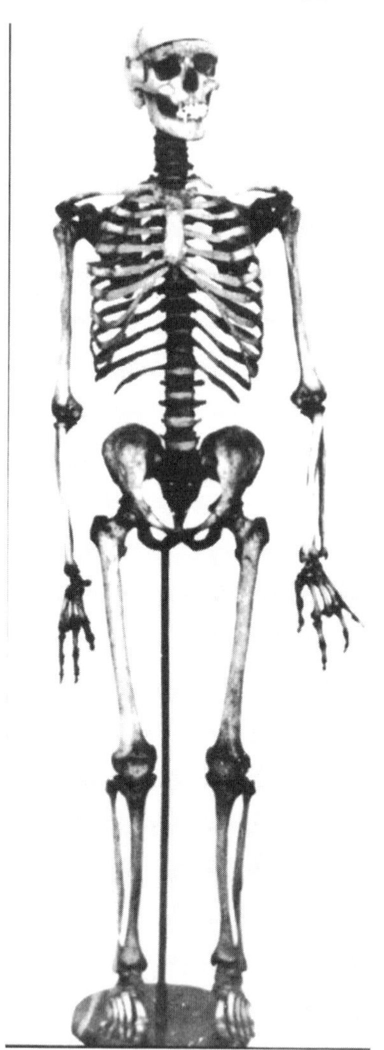

Grim irony: Burke's skeleton was later displayed at the very medical school to which he had earlier carted the bodies of his victims.

Crowds hunted them for weeks, but Helen McDougal was smuggled onto a ship and sailed for Australia, where she reportedly died many years later. Maggie Laird was given police protection and she was escorted to a ship sailing for Ireland and there she lived out her life under an assumed name. Hare fled to the Midlands where, under an assumed name, he labored in the lime pits. When his fellow workers learned who he was, one account has it, they blinded him with quicklime. He then went to London, a blind beggar last seen shaking a tin cup and begging outside the British Museum.

Dr. Robert Knox, who had paid for all the bodies and encouraged, willingly or not, the hard-working Burke and Hare to continue their murder business, was in disgrace following Burke's conviction and execution. Dr. Knox's school closed and he left Edinburgh. One report held that he became a showman with a traveling group of American Indians, but it is known that he first went to London and worked as an obstetrician and later as a general practitioner in Hackney, dying in 1862 with whatever dark memories that may have haunted him.

The gloomy deeds of his servants, however, did serve one useful purpose. The acts of Burke and Hare, dubbed Resurrectionists or Resurrection Men, so appalled the country that widespread body snatching was condemned in Parliament, where liberal politicians successfully argued that the lack of legal bodies hindered the advancement of medicine and allowed beasts like Burke and Hare to flourish. Parliament passed the Anatomy Act in 1832 which permitted relatives and officials to turn over dead bodies to medical schools for dissection and study before burial. This legislation caused the gruesome business of body snatching to go into decline and eventually cease.

It was grim irony that the day following his execution, William Burke's body would follow the same route he had in life sent so many others. His corpse was taken to the medical school operated by Dr. Knox's brilliant rival, Dr. Alexander Monro. Here, before a large audience, Burke's short, thick corpse was dissected and studied, the pieces later preserved in jars and held up during anatomical lectures. His skeleton was later reassembled and placed in a glass case that can be seen to this day as a prized exhibit at the Anatomical Museum of the University of Edinburgh. Beyond these skeletal remains, however, Burke and Hare, along with their medical mentor, Knox, would be remembered down through the annals of crime with a little ditty chanted by children for decades in the streets of Edinburgh:

> Burke's the murderer,
> And Hare's the thief,
> And Knox's the boy
> Who buys the beef.

THE POISONOUS COOK/1833-1851

Helene Jegado (d. 1851) was an illiterate French peasant with a great skill. She was, by the time she entered her thirties, known as a wonderful cook who could prepare delicious stews, roasts, salads, cakes, cuisine so savory as to make her employers drool and salivate. Orphaned at the age of seven, Jegado was taken into the home of a pastor in a small Breton village, where her two aunts worked as servants. She remained there for seventeen years, learning the arts of cooking from her aunts, then leaving with one of them to relocate in Seglien, where she was employed as a cook for the local pastor. It was here that she apparently began to experiment with poisons.

Moving to Guern, Jegado began dosing the meals she prepared for her employers with arsenic, which she had obtained to rid the place of rats. Seven persons died of mysterious causes before Jegado moved on to Bubery, where three more people succumbed to her marvelous meals. Again she moved, going to Locmine, where two persons died. Remaining in the same village, the cook moved to another home, where a person quickly died. She moved to another home still,

Shown preparing one of her lethal stews, cook Helene Jegado claimed twenty-six lives, perhaps three dozen more, a serial killer who enjoyed poisoning her victims.

and four more people died violent deaths, until Jegado came under suspicion.

The motives for Jegado's serial poisonings were obscure, but apparently she was easily offended and took quick retaliation by murdering her employers and members of each household. In Guern, where seven died, including her own sister, the industrious cook simply remarked: "Wherever I go, people die." She murdered without remorse and it was obvious to officials looking into her horrendous career later that Jegado enjoyed killing people, and that she was a thrill-killer, one who took great pleasure in bringing life to an end, appropriating a life-and-death power that was legally possessed by her superiors, whom she resented and perhaps, even hated.

Moving to a convent, Jegado remained behind these cloistered walls for some years, but she was dismissed for theft and wanton destruction of property. Further, many of the nuns had become ill after she had been repeatedly rebuked for her shameful conduct. Jegado resumed her duties as a cook in one small village after another, always moving. Painful death followed her at the towns of Plumeret, Auray, Pontivy, Hennebon, Lorient. Physicians, as had been their practice in the past with all of those who died at Jegado's poisonous hands, diagnosed the deaths as the result of drinking too much vinegar. These were country doctors with little or no skill in understanding the symptoms of poison, even the most blatant killer, arsenic.

Then, in 1841, Jegado inexplicably ceased her serial murders. It was later surmised that she had simply run out of arsenic and thought it too dangerous to secure more of the poison. Yet, it was evident from her careless conduct that she was all but indifferent to being detected, having a cynical disregard at being discovered.

Following a seven-year lull in her murderous activities, Jegado arrived in Rennes in 1848, where she became the cook for a university professor, Theophile Bidard, who was also a surgeon. When Rosalie Sarrazin, another servant in the household, was poisoned in July 1851, Bidard suspected murder—Jegado and Sarrazin had quarreled incessantly—and he called police to investigate. Upon the arrival of the officers, Jegado, who had not been accused, suddenly shouted: "I am innocent!"

Arousing suspicion, she was taken into custody and then laborious investigations ensued, trailing back two decades. Bodies were exhumed and examined and in all cases arsenic was found. Jegado was brought to trial in December 1851 in Rennes, where she was found guilty of having murdered twenty-six persons and having attempted the murder of dozens of others. Prosecutors speculated that she may have killed as many as sixty people. Jegado, showing no remorse, went to the guillotine, where she was beheaded that month.

Staggering as the number of victims were in Jegado's long career as a serial killer, other female poisoners vied for her lethal record. A woman in Holland named Van der Linden, who lived in Leyden, was reportedly responsible for poisoning 102 persons between 1869 and 1885. Like Van der Linden, who was both a nurse and cook, Anna Maria Zwangziger of Germany (1760-1811), poisoned a dozen people with arsenic in several towns, but her motive was unlike that of Jegado and Van der Linden in that she attempted to eliminate female spouses in order to marry surviving husbands. These crude murders, however, did not see her intended results. She was tried and convicted of several killings, then admitted her guilt in court: "Yes, I killed them all and I would have killed more if I had had the chance." She was beheaded by the sword in July 1811.

ENGLAND'S ARCH POISONER/1840s-1850s

William Palmer (AKA: Rugeley Poisoner; 1824-1856) of Rugeley, Staffordshire, England, was the second son of Joseph Palmer, a sawmill owner. His father died when he was thirteen, leaving a considerable fortune to his seven children. After leaving school at seventeen, William Palmer began an apprenticeship with a pharmacy in Liverpool. He met Jane Widnall, who later became pregnant. Palmer stole money from the druggists to pay for her abortion. He confessed to the theft and was fired.

Palmer then became apprenticed to Dr. Edward Tylecote in Hayward, Cheshire, where he performed abortions and reportedly had fourteen children out of wedlock. He next studied at Stafford Infirmary, and in 1842 pursued his medical work in London at St. Bartholomew's Hospital. He also acquired a reputation as a gambler and womanizer. A man named Abley, with whose wife Palmer had been having an affair, died after drinking poisoned brandy thought to have been administered by Palmer. Palmer may also have poisoned one of his illegitimate children, whose mother was Jane Mumford.

These early killings, however, went undetected, and Palmer was accepted into the Royal College of Surgeons on August 10, 1846 and on September 8 of that year, joined the staff of St. Bartholomew's Hospital as a surgeon. He resigned a month

Dr. William Palmer of Rugeley, who poisoned fourteen or more persons in murder-for-profit schemes in order to feed his gambling addiction.

The trial of William Palmer; prosecutors won a conviction on circumstantial evidence.

Dr. Palmer shown at the racetrack, where he lost in bets most of the money he received from his murderous insurance swindles.

later and returned to Rugeley, where he opened a general practice.

Palmer, possibly planning to marry for money, courted Annie Brooks, an illegitimate child of wealthy Colonel Brooks whom the Colonel had adopted. Upon the colonel's suicide, she was left with a large inheritance. Brooks had to obtain permission to marry from the Court of Chancery, whose ward she became when her mother was declared unfit. Early in the marriage, Palmer was earning an ample income and quit gambling, but eventually fell back upon his passion for gambling; he bought racing horses and stables. He suffered heavy losses at the track and had several affairs.

In 1850, he poisoned a man named Bladen, who had come to visit Palmer and collect a debt. After borrowing money from another man, named Bly, Palmer killed him too, and then lied to Bly's widow by asserting that Bly had owed *him* money. Palmer apparently next poisoned his uncle, "Beau Bently," and then tried to poison Bently's wife, who was staying with Palmer. When she complained of feeling unwell, Palmer gave her some pills, but she began to feel better, decided not to take the medicine, and tossed the pills out the window. Some chickens were discovered dead the following day, apparently killed by Palmer's poison, but the notion that the physician had attempted to murder Bently's wife was dismissed as "nonsense."

In 1853, Palmer bet heavily on a horse called *Nettle*, which lost, so he purchased life insurance policies totaling £26,000 on his wife, Annie, and his brother Walter. Next year, Annie caught a chill on a trip to Liverpool to see a concert. One of Palmer's friends, Dr. Bamford, diagnosed the sickness as "bilious cholera," and gave her some medicine. A week later, on September 29, 1854, Annie Palmer was dead. Palmer used the £13,000 insurance settlement to pay his bookmaker.

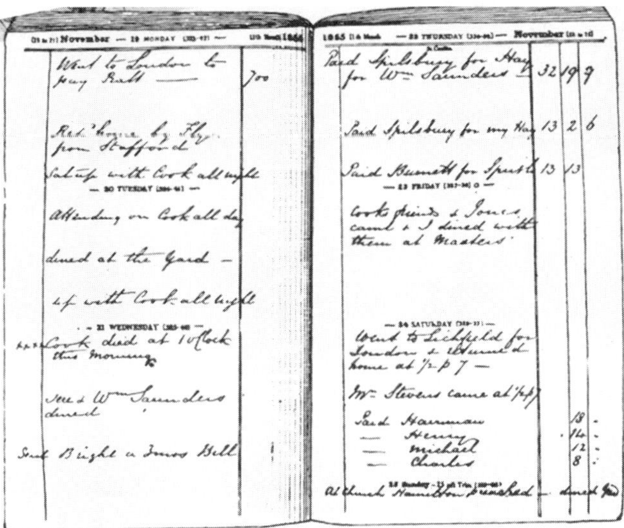
November — 19 MONDAY

Went to London to pay Pratt — 700

Rode home by Fly from Stafford

Sat up with Cook all night

— 20 TUESDAY —

attending on Cook all day

dined at the Yard —

up with Cook all night

— 21 WEDNESDAY —

Cook died at 1 o'Clock this morning

Mr & Wm Saunders dined

1855 — 22 THURSDAY — November

Paid Spilsbury for Hay for Wm Saunders 32 19 9

Paid Spilsbury for my Hay 13 2 6

Paid Burnett for Sport 13 13

— 23 FRIDAY —

Cooks friends & Jones came & I dined with them at Masters

— 24 SATURDAY —

Went to Lichfield for London & returned home at ½ p 7 —

Wm Stevens came at ½ p 7

Paid Harman 18 -

— Henry 14 -

— Michael 12 -

— Charles 8 -

— 25 Sunday —

At Church Hamilton preached — dined

Two pages from Palmer's diary, which incriminated him at his trial; his notations show payments made to bookies and others that matched insurance monies.

Nine months after his wife's death, his maid had a child that died within a few weeks of birth. William Palmer next focused on his alcoholic brother, Walter Palmer, attempting to kill him by giving him too much to drink. William promised to loan Walter as much money and buy him as much alcohol as he wanted, calculating that the life insurance policy would reimburse him for expenses after Walter's death. Walter Palmer died on August 16, 1855. The cause of death was listed as "apoplexy." The insurance company refused to pay the £13,000 policy.

Palmer also tried to purchase a policy on George Bates, a gambling crony, but the insurance company was already suspicious about Walter's death and refused to issue the policy. When Palmer heard that the company had spoken to a youth named Myatt, who claimed to have witnessed Palmer putting something into his brother's drink, Palmer invited Myatt for a drink too, after which Myatt suffered from gastric pain for the next few days.

The scheming doctor had already secured a large insurance policy on the life of his alcoholic mother-in-law, who also lived with him. Palmer poisoned her and was also thought to have poisoned four of the five children he had had with Annie Brooks. At the time of these mysterious deaths, Palmer was deeply indebted to a money-lender named Pratt, who threatened to seek out Palmer's mother whose name Palmer had forged on loan documents for settlement.

Forced to try his luck at the racetrack to settle his debt with Pratt, Palmer met up with John Parsons Cook, an old friend and fellow gambler. Cook won a considerable amount betting on *Polestar*, a mare he owned, that won a race at Shrewsbury on November 13, 1855. Cook and Palmer both

Palmer's cell at Stafford Jail, where he calmly awaited execution and chatted with guards.

The hanging execution of Dr. Palmer on June 14, 1856, where an angry crowd hooted and jeered at the condemned man before he went through the trap.

had rooms at the Raven Hotel in Shrewsbury, where Palmer gave Cook brandy and water that burned his throat and made him sick. The men returned to Rugeley, where Cook stayed at the Talbot Arms near Palmer's home. Palmer nursed Cook with some coffee and soup, and in four days Cook was feeling better. Palmer was called back when Cook became sick that night. The next day, November 20, Cook died. Palmer meanwhile, had obtained Cook's track winnings by forging Cook's signature.

Palmer was linked to Cook's death when Cook's stepfather, Stevens, became suspicious. Stevens asked to see Cook's betting records, but Palmer said his book was lost. A hotel maid told Stevens she had seen Palmer rifling Cook's pockets. The insurance company, already suspicious about the death of Palmer's brother, began to investigate Cook's death. Palmer again requested help from Dr. Bamford, who noted the cause of death on Cook's death certificate as "apoplectic seizure." He also permitted Palmer to help with Cook's autopsy, during which Palmer first tried to remove Cook's stomach and then tried to bribe the courier taking the stomach to London to drop the jar.

In London, Dr. Alfred Swayne Taylor, a poison expert, further examined Cook's organs, and determined the cause of death to be tetanus. Officials found no traces of the strychnine that might have caused this, but they did find antimony. They also learned that Palmer had bought large amounts of strychnine. A coroner's inquest returned a verdict of willful murder.

Meanwhile, the bodies of Palmer's wife and brother were exhumed. Although no poison was found in Annie's body, Palmer was indicted for murder at the inquest. Because public opinion in Stafford was so strong against Palmer, a law was introduced in the House of Lords on February 5, 1856, to allow a change of venue. The law passed and moved Palmer's trial to the Central Criminal Court.

On May 14, 1856, Palmer was brought to trial before Lord Chief Justice Campbell and two other judges at the Old Bailey in London. Palmer was defended by Sir William Shee and prosecuted by Attorney General Sir Alexander Cockburn. Dr. Taylor testified that strychnine could cause death without leaving traces in the stomach because it would be absorbed into the victim's nervous system. Palmer, who claimed he was innocent, was found guilty of murder on May 27, 1856, on strictly circumstantial evidence. He was publicly hanged on June 14, 1856, by the Stafford jail.

Rugeley citizens sought to change the town's name after Palmer's execution, so it would not be associated with the notorious serial killer. The mayor of Rugeley asked the prime minister, William Palmerston, who ironically enough, granted permission on condition that the town be named after him.

THE MARRIED MURDERERS OF FRANCE/ 1850s

For more than a decade, Martin Dumollard, a farmer living outside the French village of Montluel, attacked and murdered several young women, ravaging the bodies and taking what belongings these poor peasant girls carried. Following such barbaric attacks, Dumollard dutifully returned to his home and wife. Marie Dumollard not only knew of these myriad killings, but encouraged her husband's perverted slayings and, in return for her lethal support, was given some of the victim's clothes to wear as payment for her complicity.

Marie Dumollard, who encouraged her serial killer husband, Martin Dumollard, to commit murders; she is shown in a wax image by Madame Tussaud, and is wearing the actual clothes taken from some of her husband's victims.

Martin Dumollard often went to an employment agency in Lyons to hire new help, and sometimes he merely approached young girls himself, asking if they would like to work at his farm. Although the body of one of the maids was found in the woods in 1855, the case was left open and nothing more was said.

Six years later, however, young Marie Pichon of Lyons was approached by Dumollard, who offered her a serving position at a nearby chateau where he worked. When they did not go directly to the palatial estate Dumollard said he represented, Pichon became cautious and was ready to run when he pulled out a rope and tried to put it around her throat.

Dashing away, the girl ran frantically through the woods and down a dark lane, with Dumollard chasing her. She managed to outdistance the older man and arrived at a village, where an innkeeper offered her safety. Police were summoned and Pichon told the story of the attack. Dumollard was arrested, but he refused to admit having committed any crimes, denying that he had attacked the girl and claiming that she was a witless waif making up tales to discredit her elders.

The authorities disbelieved him, however, and investigated the Dumollard farm, where they discovered at least ten fairly new corpses of young women, along with piles of clothing. Marie Dumollard, unable to keep silent, confessed that her husband killed the girls, and she kept or sold the clothing as she chose. Some bodies were tossed into the nearby Rhone River, others were buried.

In January 1862, the Dumollards were tried at Bourg while mobs of angry townspeople tried to lynch them. Martin Dumollard was described at the time as "a strong and brutal peasant, with a large nose, thick lips, hollow eyes and brushy eyebrows. A beard fringed his hard features. His wife, thin and slight, with shifty eyes and cunning face, was placed at his side." Both were found guilty. Martin Dumollard was sentenced to be guillotined. He was executed on March 8, 1862. Marie, his accomplice, was sent to hard labor in prison for twenty years.

A FRENCH SERIAL KILLER/1860s

Like Dr. William Palmer, a French physician adopted the Rugeley Poisoner's same modus operandi, poisoning for profit. Dr. Edmond de la Pommerais (1835-1864) left Orleans, France, in 1859 at the age of twenty-four to set up a private practice in Paris. He advertised himself as the "Count de la Pommerais" at the Paris gambling tables. In 1861, he married Mademoiselle Dabizy, the daughter of one of his patients and heiress to a fortune.

The girl's mother had stipulated, however, that the Dabizy inheritance could not revert to the de la Pommerais family until her own death, a proviso that marked her for murder. She died just months later. As Madame Dabizy's physician, de la Pommerais certified the cause of death to be Asiatic cholera.

At the time, the young doctor was also conducting a secret affair with Seraphine de Pauw, the widow of one of his former patients. She had three small children, and faced financial problems. De la Pommerais proposed a scheme whereby he would insure de Pauw's life for 500,000 francs (£20,000). After several payments had been made, Madame de Pauw was to feign an illness. Fearing greater loss, the insurance company would offer to settle for 5,000 francs. When she signed the policy, the doctor persuaded her to name him as her beneficiary.

Supposedly to simulate illness de la Pommerais gave de Pauw a strong dose of digitalis, a vegetable poison. She became quite ill and soon died. The cause of death was listed as cholera, common in Paris during the summertime. The insurance company first seemed willing to pay the doctor the full 500,000 francs, but an anonymous letter to the Paris police warned them about the possibility of murder. The body was exhumed, an autopsy performed, and poison detected.

The doctor was tried for the murders of both his mistress and mother-in-law, but was acquitted for the death of Madame Dabizy. De la Pommerais was found guilty of poisoning Seraphine de Pauw, convicted mainly on the testimony of de Pauw's sister, Madame Ritter, who knew about the insurance fraud, her sister having confided the scheme to her during her illness. De la Pommerais was sentenced to die on the guillotine. To the very last moment, he expected to be reprieved, but he went to his death in 1864. Though officials were certain that de la Pommerais had poisoned at least two hapless women, they suspected that he had administered lethal doses to a half dozen other victims.

Dr. Edmond de la Pommerais, who poisoned victims in order to collect on their insurance policies; he went to the guillotine in 1864.

AMERICA'S "QUEEN POISONER"/1860s

Perhaps the most infamous female poisoner in 19th Century America, Lydia Struck Sherman (1830-1878) was an attractive housewife with a disarming manner. She killed every person she met with only one thought in mind—profit. Sherman collected insurance monies on various families and lived in high style in New York's tenderloin district.

Sherman married Edward Struck, a New York policeman, the union producing six children. Struck became a drunkard after being dismissed from the police department, and, tired of working to feed her large family, Sherman purchased ten cents worth of arsenic in the spring of 1864. When the druggist asked if she intended to use the poison to kill rats, the woman replied: "Rats? My goodness, yes, we're alive with rats!"

Sherman then poisoned her husband of seventeen years and, and later murdered her six children. Although the weapon was arsenic, New York City doctors attributed the seven deaths to various illnesses. The killer collected insurance on each of her victims. The killing of seven persons took time, but Lydia Sherman was in no hurry. She murdered her six children, ranging in ages from nine months to fourteen years, over a two-year period, from 1864 to 1866.

Lydia Sherman is shown encouraging the elderly Dennis Hurlbut to drink the wine she doctored with arsenic; he did, becoming one more of her many victims.

Lydia Sherman, shown haunted by the visions of her murders in her prison cell; she died behind bars on May 16, 1878.

Moving to New Haven, Connecticut, Sherman married elderly Dennis Hurlbut, a wealthy farmer, on November 22, 1868. After slowly poisoning the old man, she collected his estate. By April 1870, Sherman was low on funds and she went to work as a housekeeper for Horatio Nelson Sherman of Derby, Connecticut. She soon persuaded the elderly Sherman to marry her. A short time later she poisoned his two children, Frank and Addie (because they "would be better off," she said later) and then, when he became an alcoholic after their deaths, she systematically poisoned Sherman until he died on May 12, 1871.

The Shermans' physician, Dr. Beardsley, was not as indifferent to the Sherman deaths as the New York physicians who had haphazardly examined Lydia Sherman's previous victims. Beardsley became suspicious and called in other doctors to perform autopsies on the family. Finding poison, they called police, but Lydia Sherman had fled to New York. She was tracked down by detectives and returned to Connecticut, where she stood trial.

Sherman confessed to at least eleven murders, though she may have killed as many as fifteen others. Sherman, called "America's Queen Poisoner", was found guilty of second-degree murder (because all the evidence was circumstantial) and was sentenced to life in Wethersfield Prison, where she died on May 16, 1878. In her confession, Lydia Sherman took an almost lackadaisical attitude toward her many killings. In the instance of Edward Struck, she said: "I gave him the arsenic because I was discouraged. I know that that is not much of an excuse, but I felt so much trouble that I did not think about it."

Dr. Edward William Pritchard, who used aconite poisoning to rid himself of several women; he was executed on July 28, 1865, at Scotland's last public hanging.

A MEDICAL MURDERER IN SCOTLAND/ 1860s

The last public hanging in Scotland occurred on July 28, 1865, when the execution of Dr. Edward William Pritchard (1825-1865) was witnessed by 100,000 spectators at Jail Square, near Hutcheson Bridge in Edinburgh. Few among the crowd had any sympathy for this cold-blooded serial killer.

Pritchard was the son of a naval captain. At the age of twenty-one, he was commissioned an assistant surgeon in the Royal Navy. While stationed in Portsmouth he married a Scottish woman, Mary Jane Taylor. The couple settled in the village of Hunmanby, Yorkshire, where Mary Jane bore her husband five children. Pritchard opened a private practice, but soon acquired a reputation as a surly, habitual liar and a braggart. In 1858, he was forced to sell his practice.

The truculent doctor traveled abroad for a short time before moving to Glasgow, where he began a second medical practice. On the side, he delivered travel lectures and claimed to be an intimate of Garibaldi, a claim the Italian statesman denied.

Dr. Pritchard's reputation suffered further embarrassment in 1863 when one of his servant girls perished in a fire at his residence. The body was found lying in bed, which showed that she had made no effort to flee and suggested that she was unconscious at the time of the fire. The coroner's verdict exonerated Dr. Pritchard. A year later the doctor moved into more spacious quarters on Sauchiehall Street with money provided by Pritchard's mother-in-law, Mrs. Taylor of Edinburgh.

In 1864, Pritchard began an affair with 15-year-old Mary M'Cleod. She became pregnant and allowed the doctor to perform a crude abortion with the promise that he later would marry her. In November Mary Jane Pritchard became ill. She traveled to Edinburgh, where she recovered. But after rejoining her husband in Glasgow she again became sick.

Dr. Pritchard, who was attending her during this time, purchased an ounce of Fleming's Tincture of Aconite on December 8, 1864. He made three similar purchases in the next three months. Mrs. Taylor rushed to her daughter's bedside but after a few weeks in the house, the 70-year-old matron became afflicted with the same ailment after eating tapioca. She died on February 24, 1865.

Pritchard's wife died on March 17, 1865 amid growing suspicion in the community that her husband was a poisoner. The family cook and a maid who had sampled some of the food consumed by Mrs. Pritchard also suffered from the same malady, which was diagnosed as gastric fever by the ever-attentive Pritchard.

An anonymous letter, believed to have been written by Dr. Patterson, who had first thought that Mrs. Taylor was under the influence of a powerful narcotic, was sent to the police. The bodies of the two deceased women were exhumed and a quantity of antimony and aconite were found in the remains.

Dr. Pritchard was indicted for murder. His trial began at the High Court of the Judiciary in Edinburgh in July 1865, with Lord Justice Clerk John Inglis presiding. Defense attorneys attempted to shift the blame to Mary M'Cleod, but the judge rejected this argument during his summation. Pritchard was found guilty and was ordered to hang. While awaiting his execution the doctor confessed to the murders. At first, he had implicated M'Cleod, but later said she had nothing to do with killings he had so carefully planned.

THE TERRIBLE BENDERS/1872-1873

The first, most notorious of America's serial killers, who now oddly enjoy historical significance, at least in the sovereign state of Kansas, were the fierce and enigmatic Benders. Outwardly, this was a typical family of the American frontier, father, mother, daughter, son, all hardworking souls dedicated to the land, innkeepers who sought the common goals of commercial success, enough wealth to provide old age comforts, enough security to weather the storms howling down from the future.

Untypical were the methods the Bender Family employed in its mercantile practices, for the real business of the Benders was murder, and their victims, like the wayward wanderers who stumbled upon their own doom at Castle Dracula in far away Transylvania, were travelers seeking food and a bed for the night. This they received cheerfully from their sly hosts, along with an early unmarked grave.

The four Benders appeared for the first time in Labette County, Kansas, in fall 1870. The father, John Bender (some claim his name was William), was a man of about sixty, a primitive immigrant wearing a shaggy beard and possessing large, angry-looking eyes. He was accompanied by an equally robust wife whose first name is not recorded, a woman of fifty, with blue eyes and brown hair, his son John, about twenty-seven, and daughter Kate, age twenty-four.

Much was later said of the backgrounds of these four, most reports differing widely. It was later reported that John Bender, Jr., was not a Bender at all, his real name being John Gebhardt, or Liefens, and that he was Mrs. Bender's son from a previous marriage. Whether John Bender was his father or not, the younger man possessed all the traits of the old man. He was surly, sullen, and mean of spirit. His face was later described as having "had the fierce malice of a hyena." His build was slight and across thin, turned-down lips rode a light brown mustache.

John Bender spoke broken English, preferring to converse in German, the native tongue of his father. The old man never spoke anything but German, although he would make some guttural-sounding English words when angry, which was most of the time. Kate Bender, who was later described as a vicious-looking harridan or ravishing beauty, depending upon the sympathies of her ex-lovers and the editorial whims of newsmen in that day, spoke good English but with a slight German accent.

Mrs. Bender seldom spoke, and merely followed the grunted orders from the old man, working like a horse from dawn to dusk. Kate, of course, was of chief interest of this band of murderers and by most accounts she was far from ugly, although one report describes her rather brutally as "a large, masculine, red-faced woman." Others profile Kate as a very good looking red-haired girl, statuesque, buxom, with a small waist, slender hips and mesmerizing eyes, full lips and a charming manner, a cross between the subtle sirens of the Nile and the plump Broadway stars of that day.

Kate herself might not have been a Bender either, but, as was claimed by some, the mistress of John, Jr. Of this strange family, only Kate possessed a personality remembered long

The infamous Bender inn outside Cherryvale in southeastern Kansas, where dozens of travelers were slain by their hosts in 1871-1873.

John Bender, Sr., the 60-year-old patriarch of the family, who, with his son, crushed the heads of guests, while his wife and daughter prepared dinner for them.

Kate Bender, twenty-four, who claimed to be a spiritualist with powers to heal all maladies and who actively participated in her family's murder-for-profit killings.

by those who encountered the Benders. Governor Thomas Osborn of Kansas, who issued wanted posters for the family shortly after their horrendous crimes were unearthed, described Kate with some first-hand facts: "Dark hair and eyes, good looking, well-formed, rather bold in appearance, fluent talker." But when she and the other three members of her cold-hearted clan rolled across the gentle hills of southern Kansas in late 1869, she had no identity to speak of; she was just another homeless pioneer looking for a place to settle.

The first resident of Labette County to greet the Benders was a fellow German immigrant, Rudolph Brockmann, who ran a small country grocery store. How he came to know the Benders before they called on him for aid has never been learned. Brockmann had a large land claim and allowed the four strangers riding in a large wagon, all their earthly possessions piled behind, to build a shanty house on his property. They managed to endure a severe winter and moved in the spring to another hastily constructed building. In the following spring of 1871, the Benders selected a site on the main road stretching between the Kansas towns of Cherryvale and Parsons, closer to the former, their single structure squatting seven miles northeast of Cherryvale.

The Benders had studied traffic on the road, which was considerable, for along this well-beaten path hundreds of travelers made their way from Fort Scott and the Osage Mission to Independence. Beyond, to the southwest, was the Indian Territory that would later become the state of Oklahoma. The Bender Inn was only eighteen miles from what is now the Kansas-Oklahoma border.

The house was a simple affair, one which functioned as living quarters for the four Benders and was designed, with exceeding malice aforethought as later discoveries showed, to offer travelers the comforts of the crude inns of the day. The house was in a hollow, surrounded by plum and cottonwood trees, at the end of a long vale in the prairie, but it could not be seen at any great distance by those riding along the main road. Near the building was Drum Creek, a small stream seldom more than waist-high deep with water.

Behind the house, the Benders kept hogs and a few cattle in some pens. The house, or inn as it was called, had but one room that passed for two, divided as it was by a large piece of canvas. The first section of the house at the entrance was for travelers, who could sit at a large table and eat the meals prepared by Mrs. Bender and Kate. Behind the canvas was the area that functioned as sleeping quarters for the family and guests. In the back of the house was also a stable where patrons could keep their horses overnight.

In back of the inn stretched a garden, rather haphazardly kept by the Benders, and an orchard. To their meager ensemble, the Benders added a limited grocery which was nothing more than some shelves against the wall of the first room. They were lined with tinned goods and other supplies, which were purchased by overnight guests and some of the Bender neighbors, who lived quite a distance from nearby towns and found it convenient to occasionally buy some items from the Benders.

For about a year and a half the Bender Inn was no more than a waystop and its inhabitants aroused no special notice, except that Kate Bender began making a name for herself in many small towns in southern Kansas. She had moved into rural society quickly. By fall 1871 she became the desired partner of young men attending county dances and she proved an excellent dancer. Several young swains later claimed that she was also free and easy with her favors, although so aggressive a sex partner that after one night her lovers gave her up from exhaustion.

This was undoubtedly hindsight embellishment, given the monster image of Kate later favored by most portraits. For about a month Kate worked as a waitress in a Cherryvale hotel, but she resigned when male patrons began to make advances, or so she said when quitting. Only Kate of the entire Bender clan could be seen attending church on Sunday and, for a short time, she attended regular Sunday evening meetings.

Prof. Miss KATIE BENDER

Can heal all sorts of Diseases; can cure Blindness, Fits, Deafness and all such diseases, also Deaf and Dumbness.

Residence, 14 miles East of Independence, on the road from Independence to Osage Mission one and one half miles South East of Morehead Station.

KATIE BENDER.

June 18, 1872.

The handbill Kate Bender distributed in 1872, advertising herself as a "professor," who could heal all manner of diseases and afflictions.

It was at one of these meetings that Kate Bender announced that she was a genuine medium and that she had the power to call the spirits of the dead to the presence of the living. In fact, she said, her entire family possessed these powers. All of them were spiritualists, she insisted, who had direct contact with the Great Beyond. To prove it, Kate began to give lectures on the subject and hold crude séances, where she spoke for those at her table to the "Dear Departed," for a price, of course, and the spirits replied through her to the loved ones still chained to earthly life.

So popular did Kate become that she took her act on tour through the local Kansas towns, appearing in theaters, which were mostly packed with men eager to hear the secrets of the Beyond. Her success increased her capacities to make one miracle after another, until she began to place advertisements in local newspapers, which described her abilities to cure almost every human malady.

One advertisement stated: "Professor Miss Kate Bender can heal disease, cure blindness, fits and deafness. Residence: 14 miles east of Independence on the road to Osage Mission. June 18, 1872." In light of what was found at that address later one can only shudder at the thought of the sick and infirm traveling the lonely roads to Kate Bender, seeking relief from physical agonies only to be met by excruciating pain and bloody death.

During the period such advertisements were running, Kate Bender appeared to appreciative audiences in the towns of Parsons, Labette, Oswego, and Chetopa. Men flocked to see her for female lecturers were rare in that day and most men found such appearances shocking. There were occasions when men would shout to Kate across the footlights that she had no business as a woman appearing in public to lecture on any subject, that she was merely using her curing and spiritual talks as guises to stump for obtaining equal rights for women, that she was secretly lobbying for the female vote.

If this were the case, of course, Kate Bender should be entered in the female hall of fame honoring the pioneers who struggled for equal rights for women. It was not. Kate fended off such accusations with a winning smile and went on to suggest that those with real interest in employing her powers should visit her at the Bender Inn. There she would put them in touch with the Great Beyond. This claim was more than ironic as events would prove.

In the summer and fall of 1872 the conduct of the Benders began to noticeably change. Kate was off lecturing most of this time, but her brother John was absent from the wayside inn for extended periods of time, these being business trips, according to the senior Benders, who never explained what business their son was conducting. By the fall of that year both Kate and John had returned to the inn and their demeanor from that time on was later reported as decidedly strange.

It was guessed with some degree of accuracy that the murder spree in which the family indulged was confined to the six month period between October 1872 and March 1873. What caused the Benders to decide that murder for profit was the best or only course open to them remains a mystery. The decision was made. The murders began.

A man named Wetzell of Independence, Kansas, read Kate's running advertisements in a local newspaper and, because he suffered from a nagging and seemingly incurable neuralgia, decided to visit this lady of miracles. Wetzell and a friend named Gordan rode to the Bender Inn in the fall of 1872, where Kate greeted the pair warmly. She examined Wetzell's face closely and told him that she could positively cure him, but since it was near dinner time, it would be best that the visitors sit down to a good home cooked meal first. She and Mrs. Bender prepared the meal.

While they waited, Wetzell and Gordan were surprised to see old man Bender and his son John enter the inn and stare at them, saying nothing. They seemed to be scrutinizing the height and weight of the travelers. Kate Bender motioned the

Kate Bender is shown conducting a lecture on spiritualism before an enthralled audience, this at the same time she and her family members were murdering travelers at the Bender inn.

visitors to sit at the table and this they did, in the only chairs available, which had been placed tightly against the canvas partition so that when the two men sat down their heads rested against the canvas partition. By then the male Benders had walked behind the partition and were making noises that sounded as if they were dragging some heavy weights toward the canvas.

Just as the meal was being served, Wetzell and Gordan, responding to nervous impulse, stood up and grabbed their plates, telling Kate that they preferred to eat standing up. They stood away from the table, nervously munching their food at a small counter. At that moment all the charm went out of Kate Bender. Where she had earlier been pleasant and charming, she now sneered viciously at the two travelers; she was now caustic and abusive toward them.

"You two have no manners," she told them, "only farm animals eat standing up! Are you gentlemen or beasts of the field?" Neither man made a response. Her eyes widened, her prominent jaw jutted forth and her teeth showed as she spat out her words: "Disgusting! Vile!" She pointed a long finger at Wetzell and, with eyes blazing, shouted: "Cure you? You are not worth a cure!" She turned to Mrs. Bender, who stood in front of the pair, her hands on wide hips, glaring at them. "Look at these beasts," hissed Kate Bender to her mother, "two horses with their snoots in the trough!"

Suddenly, Bender and his son reappeared, coming from behind the canvas, once more staring at the visitors in stony silence. Then they shuffled outside, and Wetzell saw them go into a nearby shanty that passed for a barn, where they stood talking, looking back to the inn, as if debating what next to do. Wetzell and Gordan put down their plates, mumbled their thanks for Kate's dubious hospitality and went outside to the road, where their carriage was tied. As Gordan got into the carriage, Wetzell drew forth his pistol and kept it by his side, not knowing what to expect from his strange hosts. He later claimed that, at any moment, he thought he would see the father and son come charging out of the barn with weapons aimed at killing him and his friend.

At that moment two freight wagons en route to Independence came rumbling down the road and Wetzell waved a nervous hello to the drivers, then jumped into the carriage. Gordan whipped the horses to a full gallop so that the travelers were ahead of the wagons. Wetzell turned to look back at the inn. It was now dark, but he could see in the doorway, holding a lantern aloft, the Junoesque form of Kate Bender, peering after them; he later swore that he saw her arm go up as she shook a menacing fist in his direction.

Both Wetzell and Gordan stopped some miles down the road to discuss what had just happened and concluded that they had been unnecessarily alarmed over the mercurial temperament of a rather tempestuous female and the phlegmatic actions of the Bender males, who were, at best, cretinous types with mordant personalities. They marked their experience at the inn as misadventure and decided to forget the matter. It

A contemporary sketch shows the interior of the one-room Bender inn, with old man Bender behind a canvas wall and about to crush the head of an unsuspecting guest with a sledgehammer, while Mrs. Bender serves the victim dinner and daughter Kate Bender sits outside, on watch for intruders.

never occurred to them to notify authorities about the peculiar behavior of the Benders.

Wetzell's escape, one certainly of intuitive compulsion, was not shared by others whose sense of danger was less acute. Most prominent of these was Dr. William H. York, one of the leading citizens of Independence, Kansas. Dr. York had been visiting his brother, Colonel A. M. York, who lived in Fort Scott, Kansas, and was one of the richest men in the territory. Moreover, a third brother was a state senator, who was considered the most powerful man in southern Kansas. Dr. York left Fort Scott on March 9, 1873, returning to his Independence home. He stopped at Osage Mission and left there on March 10. Outside of Cherryvale, the doctor met some friends on the road and told them he intended to stop at the Bender Inn for his midday meal.

York was in a fine humor as he rode off on his expensive horse. He sat on a saddle of the finest leather. His clothes and boots were new and expensive. He also carried with him a considerable amount of money, as much as $1,500 some later estimated, and in his vest nestled a gold watch of great value. Dr. York was only two miles from the Bender place when more friends passed him on the road. Again he stated that he would stop at the inn to have some of Kate Bender's "fine stew." It was the last time anyone ever saw Dr. William York alive.

Days passed, and Dr. York did not arrive home. His family notified the other York brothers and soon both men organized search parties. A dozen detectives were also hired by the Yorks and these men combed the countryside between Fort Scott and Independence. In Independence, Colonel York, who announced that he would spare no expense to find his brother, encountered Wetzell, who related his nervous experience at the Bender Inn. He made no claims against the Benders, he said, but their actions had been more than suspicious.

On April 3, 1873, a large search party rode to the Bender inn to inquire as to the whereabouts of Dr. York. When they arrived, the Bender family claimed no knowledge of Dr. York. They had never set eyes on him. No amount of questioning by the searchers caused the family members to change their story. The detectives rode off, planning to search beyond Cherryvale and the Osage Mission. But all their inquiries led the search back to the Bender Inn, where Dr. York's trail vanished. When this was reported in detail to Colonel York, he decided to personally conduct the search.

On April 24, 1873, York himself visited the Benders. Accompanying him were twelve heavily armed men from Cherryvale. Before this group reached the Bender inn, they came across John Bender the younger. He was sitting alongside the road with a Bible in his hands. York questioned him while still sitting in the saddle, asking once more if he had seen his brother, Dr. York. The reply was startling. Yes, John Bender had seen him. He certainly had stopped at the inn. Bender reported that his sister Kate had prepared a good dinner for the doctor, who ate it and then left the inn.

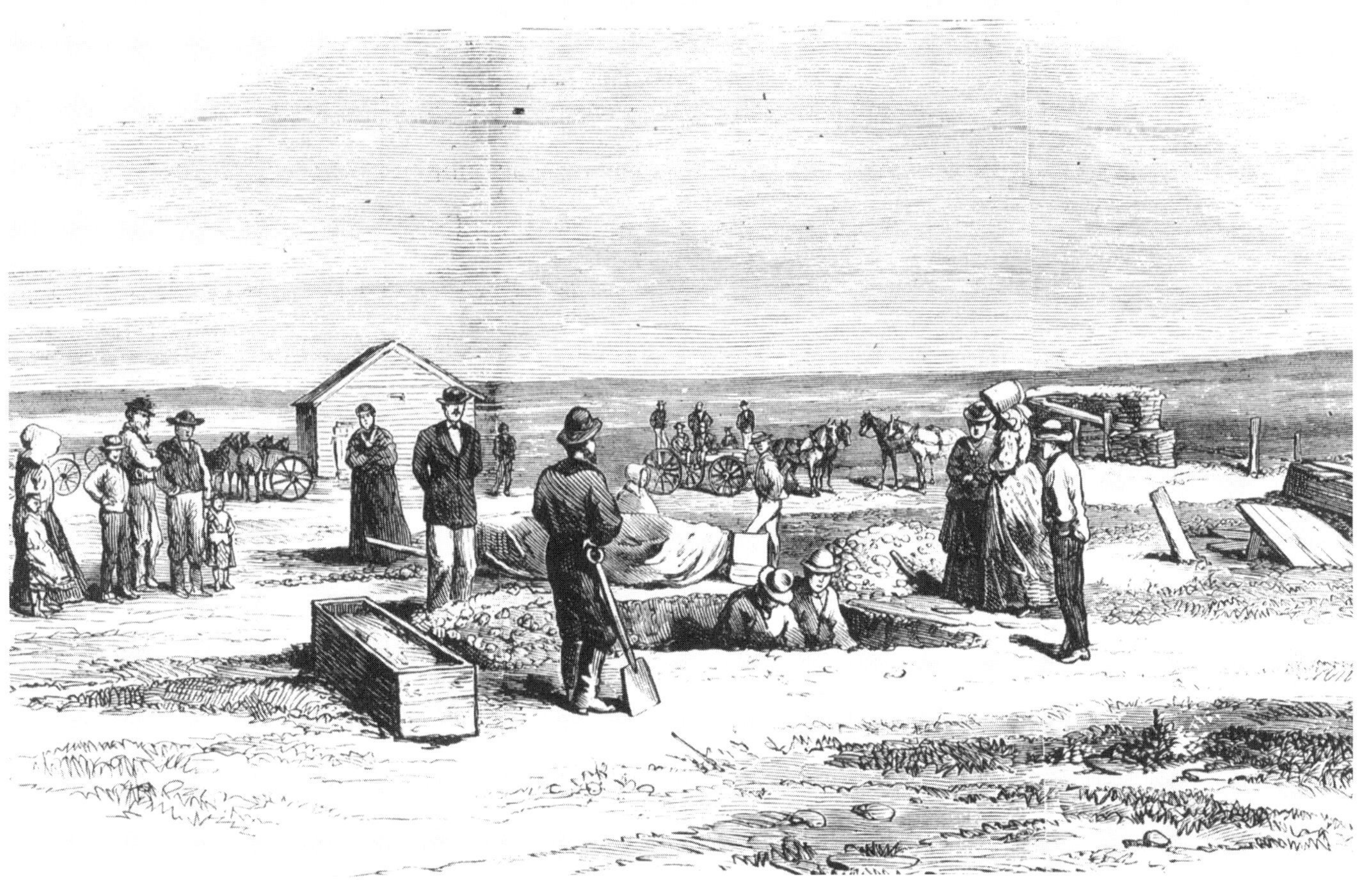

Lawmen and townspeople from Cherryvale are shown unearthing bodies outside the Bender Inn; they found twenty victims, but many more murders were attributed to the serial-killing Benders. So terrified of the Benders were travelers that for several years these pioneers refused to sleep in wayside inns.

Before any more questions could be put to Bender, the young man volunteered some harrowing information. "There are outlaws hereabouts," he told York. "I have been shot at by these people, dangerous men, border ruffians they are, the worst scum of the war." (He referred to those Civil War soldiers who, after the end of the war in 1865, had taken up outlawry along the Kansas border, raiding small villages and robbing unsuspecting travelers.) Colonel York pressed Bender for an explanation: "Why tell us this?"

Replied Bender: "You see, sir, your brother, Dr. York, was most likely robbed and killed by the same bandits who sometimes lurk around these places. Find those bandits and you will find the body of your brother most likely."

York and his men then rode on to the inn and there Kate Bender greeted them warmly, telling them that she did remember seeing Dr. York and serving him some stew. Why had she not told the first search party this, she was asked. She had simply forgotten, Kate replied. With that she and her mother served the search party a large meal.

One man with York, who had been with the first search party, walked up to Kate Bender and held her hand firmly, saying: "You claim to be able to reach the spirit world, do you not?"

"That is well known," she replied.

"Then contact the spirits now and ask them in which world Dr. York can be found, among the living or the dead."

Kate Bender pulled her hand away and shook her head. Colonel York asked her to hold a séance then and there and search the Beyond for his brother. "This I cannot do," replied Kate. "There are too many unbelievers here and the spirits resist giving aid to those who scoff at their powers." She then turned to the detective who had cynically asked her to contact the Other World and said: "If you wish to make such contact with the Beyond, then come back here in five days and come alone. I will take you and your questions into that world and you will have all the answers you require."

Both Bender males then arrived at the inn, and father and son appeared eager to aid York and his men any way they could in finding the lost doctor. It was John Bender the younger who suggested that the entire party drag Drum Creek, pointing out that "this was the place, the Creek, where the bandits shot at me in the past and that is where you will find the body of your brother if he is to be found at all." The men stepped outside and the Benders led them down to the Creek, which they dragged for hours with no success. Exhausted, the search party left that evening, convinced that the Benders knew nothing of Dr. York's disappearance. They were a cooperative and compassionate family, even if Mrs. Bender had complained during their stay that "a crowd of men like this should not disturb peaceable people like us."

As the York party rode off, only the detective who had toyed with Kate about her spiritualistic powers remained skeptical and suspicious of the Benders. Colonel York asked this young man if he actually planned to return in five days to contact the spirit world through Kate Bender. "Should I undertake that journey," he told the colonel, "I would never return to this world."

The search for the mythical bandits proved fruitless, and by May 5, 1873, York and his detectives were once again back at the Bender Inn, but this time there was no trace of the family. Neighbors had already heard the livestock moaning in pain and had investigated the area a day earlier. They found the Bender livestock mostly dead, hogs and calves having perished from thirst. The family had deserted the place, leaving in a great haste. They had not even bothered to take their cattle and hogs with them, precious property in that hardscrabble era.

Colonel York ordered his men to break a padlock that had been placed on the front door of the inn, and this was smashed open. The searchers entered the inn and then stepped back, momentarily overwhelmed by a terrific stench. A short time later they found the inside a shambles, as if the family had packed pell-mell and cleared out in manic desperation. Everywhere they stepped litter and debris greeted them. Even some of Kate's "lecture papers" were found scattered over the floor. (These papers were later carefully examined and in them were found startling statements about "the foulness of man" and how "the murder of the heart" should be explored to "expose the natural instincts of a killer race." Much of this was later attributed to inventive newspapermen enhancing the already colorful character of Kate Bender.)

Searchers soon discovered the source of the powerful stench, which had been created by the shuttered windows having been sealed by the departing Benders. A trap door toward the rear of the building was found and opened and a pit six feet deep lay beneath this. At the bottom of the pit was a thick layer of congealed human blood which, in the airless inn, had caused the stench. York and his men began to tear the place apart in their desperate search.

The colonel went to the back door of the inn and peered out at a stretch of land near the orchard. This had been plowed and harrowed meticulously by the Benders, but such industry puzzled the young detective who had originally suspected Kate Bender of foul play. He pointed to this much plowed land and said to York, who was looking at the same spot: "The Benders did not farm. They grew nothing on their land. Why then plow up the land?" It had rained the night before, and much of the furrows had been washed over, leaving peculiar looking mounds of earth in this plowed patch. Colonel York gasped and then shouted: "Boys, I see graves yonder in the orchard!"

The men raced to the plowed area and began to dig furiously. The first of these graves yielded the much sought-after Dr. William York. His body was badly decomposed but recognizable. The skull had been crushed and the throat slit. Of course, all of York's valuables, including his boots, had been taken by the killers. One after another, seven more graves were opened and bodies removed. These included W. F. McCrotty, a Cedarville resident, who had been traveling to Independence to contest a land office case six months earlier. He had undoubtedly stopped at the Bender place for food and sleep and was murdered for his money and belongings. McCrotty was, perhaps the first of the known victims to be killed by the Benders.

The next corpse was identified by a small ring the killers overlooked; his body was too badly decomposed to identify. The victim was D. Brown, a horse trader from Cedarville. Henry F. McKenzie, who had disappeared on December 5, 1872, a native of Hamilton County, Indiana, who had been traveling to Independence to relocate there with his sister, was next found and identified later by the sister, Mrs. J. Thompson who recognized the dead man's clothing. Then came the body of a man named Longoer and, found beneath his body in the shallow grave, the body of his baby girl. Longoer had lost his wife in late fall 1872, had buried her body in Cherryvale, and had then headed for Iowa with his small child, only to stop at the Benders for refreshment and untimely death. Two more bodies were then discovered, both males, but they were so badly decomposed that their identities were never established.

So far there had been eight victims in all, but several more were later added to the Bender tally. Colonel York and his men quickly pieced together the murder method employed by the sinister Benders. Guests were seated at the table in the inn and served a hearty meal. Their chairs were purposely placed so that their heads pressed against the canvas partition separating the one-room inn into two rooms. Behind the canvas curtain stood old man Bender and his son John. As soon as the victims' heads made an impression on the other side of the canvas, the two men would strike the impression with a stonemason's hammer, crushing the skulls.

There had been some occasions where, as the investigators reconstructed the Bender modus operandi, the two Bender males had struck two men at the same time with their hammers. With the victim unconscious, Kate and her mother stripped the corpses of their valuables and the men dragged the bodies to the trap door, throwing them into the pit where, to make sure of death, the throats were slit much in the manner of slitting a hog's throat, allowing the pool of blood to build up in the bottom of the pit. This was done often enough in broad daylight, the bodies kept in the pit until the cover of darkness allowed the Benders to drag the bodies outside and bury them in graves where they had furrowed the land.

The plowing was meant to hide the outlines of the graves. In the instance of the small Longoer child, a girl of about eighteen months, no marks of violence covered her body. She had merely been thrown down into the shallow grave, her father's corpse placed on top of her and she had been buried alive. This was supported by a local physician, who stated that the child had died of suffocation, smothered by the weight of her own dead father. This child killing, more than any of the others, filled the searchers with rage, causing them to vow vengeance on the serial killers. (If certain reports are to be believed, their consuming vengeance was achieved in a spectacular manner.)

The awful discoveries did not end that terrible day. The next day, May 6, 1873, searchers found another grave near the orchard. This yielded the body of a child, which was so decomposed that its sex was difficult to determine, but later doctors concluded it was the body of an 8-year-old girl whose bones had been literally pulled from their sockets and crushed by some demented fiend who took a long time to mutilate the flesh. Later, near Drum Creek, the body of a man identified as Jones was found. Again, the head had been crushed, the throat slit.

In months to come other bodies in the area were found, twenty in all, but eleven murders were definitely attributed to the Benders, who had made their inn a foul slaughterhouse. The discovery of the bodies caused hundreds of citizens from nearby communities to descend upon the inn, and so incensed were these shocked spectators that armed posses were immediately formed. Colonel York offered rewards for the Benders, as did local and state officials. As the armed bands set off in several directions to hunt down the fiends, Colonel York reportedly shouted in anger and pain: "Boys, find these monsters, if it takes you through the Indian Nation, and finish them!"

Long before the posses rode that far they stopped about a mile from the Bender Inn, at the grocery of Rudolph Brockmann, the first man to help the Benders in Kansas. By then the searchers had discovered that Brockmann had not only helped the Benders settle in the area, but that he and old man Bender had actually been partners in the grocery from 1869 to 1871. He alone would know where these butchering maniacs were, the mob concluded. Brockmann was dragged from his home and mercilessly questioned. He insisted time and again that he knew nothing of the whereabouts of the Benders. Taking Brockmann into the woods about eight miles from his home, the mob pummeled and pushed him about, attempting to get him to provide information about the fleeing fiends, information they believed he possessed.

Brockmann shook his head and said he had no idea where the Bender family had gone. Someone brought a rope and placed it about Brockmann's neck. He denied having any knowledge about the wanted killers. He was yanked upward and hanged high until his feet stopped kicking and he was about to die. Then he was lowered and revived; he was given cold coffee to drink so that he could regain his speech. Again the possemen grilled him, but they received the same answer. Brockmann knew nothing. Again Brockmann was yanked skyward, then brought down when close to death. The half-conscious grocer pleaded with the possemen: "I beg your mercy, please, I knew nothing of these people for months now. I have not seen them."

Again he was hanged, brought down, and choked out his ignorance. Once more the rope stretched his neck. He was lowered. He made his denials. A fourth time the grocer was pulled upward by the rope, lowered at the last minute, and he still gasped he knew nothing. This time, with the passion of the mob cooled, he was believed. Some of the searchers insisted that Brockmann did know, but feared the Benders more than the rope, that if he did tell what he knew, he felt the Benders would seek him out and torture him before killing him. But most of the possemen were weary of their gruesome chore, and they decided to give Brockmann his life. They rode off, to search the bottoms of Drum Creek.

It was here that the body of the man named Jones had been found, his head almost severed from his torso. More than that grisly grave offered evidence of the Benders. Nearby in the snow on the ground, still frozen in spots, were strange marks made by a wagon wheel, one that was obviously out of plumb so that, as it revolved, it made a zig-zag track through the snow. The possemen reasoned that Jones had been killed when the ground in the orchard had been so deeply frozen that a grave could not be dug. The Benders had put the body in

A contemporary sketch shows the trackless landscape that surrounded the Bender Inn and the scores of curious who flocked to the place to view the bodies found there (shown at right).

their wagon and driven to the Creek, cut a hole in the ice and shoved the body into it. Using the peculiar wagon marks to follow, the possemen followed these tracks southwest toward the Indian Territory.

Some hazy reports have it that the Vigilance Committee members did find their quarry and wreaked a horrible vengeance upon them, that old man Bender and his son John put up a fight and were riddled with bullets, that Mrs. Bender grabbed an ax and attacked several possemen and she too had to be shot repeatedly like a hard-to-kill viper before dropping dead of wounds and belching curses at her attackers. Kate Bender was saved for the last. She was tied to a small tree and branches were placed around her, as was the custom of putting witches to the torch in earlier centuries. The kindling was torched and the woman was burned alive as she shouted profanities at the possemen in a loud, long shriek that supposedly lingered in their ears for the remainder of their lives.

This tale of vengeance seemed to find support in letters received in 1910 by criminal historian Captain Thomas S. Duke. He had written the chiefs of police in Cherryvale and Independence. J. N. Kramer, Cherryvale's chief of police, informed Duke that "It so happened that my father-in-law's farm joins the Bender farm and that he helped to locate the bodies of the victims. I have often tried to find out from him what became of the Benders, but he only gave me a knowing look and said he guessed they would not bother anyone else. There was a Vigilance Committee formed to locate the Benders, and shortly afterward old man Bender's wagon was found by the roadside riddled with bullets. You will have to guess the rest."

D.M. Van Cleve, police chief of Independence, wrote: "In regard to the Bender family I will say that I have lived here forty years, and it is my opinion that they never got away. A Vigilance Committee was formed and some of them are still here, but they will not talk except to say that it would be useless to look for them, and they smile at reports of some of the family having been recently located. The family nearly got my father. He intended to stay there one night, but he became suspicious, and, although they tried to coax him to stay, he hitched up his team and left."

As late as 1910 there were those still alive who had hunted the Benders and who may have been part of the posse that reportedly caught up with the fiends. If they had participated in the summary executions of the four killers, they would have been indictable for murder, even forty years later, there being no statute of limitations on homicide. Under such legal circumstances, no one then or later could be expected to admit having taken a life, even the most despicable lives of the hated Benders.

Yet, with the absence of bodies in graves where the world could point with some relief and knowledge that the bloody Benders had finally been tracked down, there remained the many legends that blossomed in the wake of the Bender flight. The story that the family escaped completely remains persistent to this day. One tale has it that the family raced their wagon to Chanute, which was then called New Chicago, and there tied their exhausted horses to a rail and left them, buying train tickets to some unspecified destination in Texas, but that the family got off the train at Chetopa to further confuse pursuers and made their way on foot through the Indian Nation to Texas. A wagon matching the Bender vehicle was found in Chanute some days after the bodies were found at the Bender inn. The wagon, some speculated, might have been a ruse, planted by Bender associates to mislead the possemen.

There was a story that the Bender clan had been members of a very large criminal organization that stretched its evil talons through the states of Kansas and Missouri, even into the Indian Nation. This organization specialized in murdering travelers and stealing horses. The Benders were one of many murderous families, who settled in lonely places for a few years, killed until discovered and then moved off to resume their dark work elsewhere.

One book, *The Five Fiends*, published a year after the Benders fled into oblivion, claimed that Kate Bender was not one but three women, all using the same name, all appearing throughout the southwest in spiritualist lectures and all married to the same man, a satyr and murder maniac who was none other than the cunning John Bender, Jr. Bender the younger, it will be remembered, had taken long and unexplained business trips in fall 1872, and it was theorized that Bender was really acting as a booking agent for all these women known as Kate, booking their lectures and selecting victims to visit his "sisters" at several murder inns he was then operating.

This wild speculation was never proved in fact in that only one Bender murder inn was ever discovered and that was enough for anyone. The author of *The Five Fiends* obviously indulged in colorful fiction, taking pains to protect his identity against criticism by authoring this work anonymously. Such impossible fictional treatments of the Benders have continued through the decades, the most recent being *The Bloody Benders*, which adroitly mixes fact and fiction but comes to a less spectacular conclusion than what is found in *The Five Fiends,* a title which of itself is misleading in that only four Benders were ever known to have existed.

Another, final speculation was rendered by John Towers James in *The Benders of Kansas*, one that through a process of elimination, outlined the logical route the Benders used to make their permanent escape. James had them fleeing by train from Thayer, to Humboldt, Kansas, switching to another train line that ran to Venita in the Indian Territory and getting onto another railroad line there to take a train to Denison, Texas, where they may have finally vanished forever. There was much to believe in this, the best of the theories regarding the Bender escape route, in that this was the only route that was not covered by the many posses hunting the killers.

Four main posses fanned out from Cherryvale after the discovery of the bodies. One posse headed for Thayer, another toward Independence, still another toward Oswego, and a fourth, a party of seven men led by an ex-captain of the Union Army, rode straight into the Indian Territory. The first three parties returned within a week, admitting that the trails they followed led nowhere. The eight men that had crossed into the Indian Territory did not return for quite some time, about two weeks, and when they did return they refused to discuss the Benders. None of them even mentioned the name of the killers, and it was assumed that this was the posse that had caught up with the killers and destroyed them.

The silence of these men had been assured, it was claimed, when they discovered more than $7,000 on the Benders when they were caught (some later claimed the amount was as high as $10,000), all blood money taken from their victims. After killing the Benders, it was speculated, the posse members divided the money equally as a sort of bounty payment for their labors, and the possession of this loot further insured their silence once they had returned to Cherryvale.

GOVERNOR'S PROCLAMATION.

$2,000 REWARD

State of Kansas, Executive Department.

WHEREAS, several atrocious murders have been recently committed in Labette County, Kansas, under circumstances which fasten, beyond doubt, the commissions of these crimes upon a family known as the "Bender family," consisting of

JOHN BENDER, about 60 years of age, five feet eight or nine inches in height, German, speaks but little English, dark complexion, no whiskers, and sparely built;

MRS. BENDER, about 50 years of age, rather heavy set, blue eyes, brown hair, German, speaks broken English;

JOHN BENDER, Jr., alias John Gebardt, five feet eight or nine inches in height, slightly built, gray eyes with brownish tint, brown hair, light moustache, no whiskers, about 27 years of age, speaks English with German accent;

KATE BENDER, about 24 years of age, dark hair and eyes, good looking, well formed, rather bold in appearance, fluent talker, speaks good English with very little German accent;

AND WHEREAS, said persons are at large and fugitives from justice, now therefore I, Thomas A. Osborn, Governor of the State of Kansas, in pursuance of law, do hereby offer a REWARD OF FIVE HUNDRED DOLLARS for the apprehension and delivery to the Sheriff of Labette County, Kansas, of each of the persons above named.

In Testimony Whereof, I have hereunto subscribed my name, and caused the Great Seal of the State to be affixed.

[L. S.] Done at Topeka, this 17th day of May, 1873.

THOMAS A. OSBORN,
Governor.

By the Governor
W. H. SMALLWOOD,
Secretary of State

A reward poster issued by Governor Osborn for the capture of the Benders; posses searched for them in many states and one reportedly tracked down and killed the fiends.

Still, no amount of dire reports that had the Benders dead could cease the belief that the fiends were alive and well, a belief that became traditionally strong. One of the believers was a self-styled soothsayer and practitioner of spiritualistic rites, much like Kate Bender. She was Mrs. Frances McCann, of McPherson, Kansas, a small, spare woman with indefatigable energy and a suspicious eye for much wanted felons living under aliases. McCann had dreams each night that revealed marvelous and frightening truths to her about her neighbors, her relatives, and even her employees.

One night in 1888 her clairvoyance focused upon Sarah Eliza Davis, the woman who did McCann's washing. McCann's spirits clearly informed her that Sarah Davis was none other than the legendary murderess, Kate Bender, operating under a disguise. For months the dogged spiritualist investigated Sarah Davis and her elderly mother. She traveled through several states looking into the background of the family and haunted their every footstep, watching the Davis family from the distance of their outhouse, where she made night-ly notes of their suspicious activities. Then, equipped with what she thought was enough evidence to convict the Davis women, McCann went to authorities. She insisted that the Davis women be arrested and tried as the missing murderesses, Mrs. Bender and her daughter Kate.

Although local authorities were inclined to dismiss these accusations, McCann raised such a fuss and Sarah Davis acted in such a manner as to bring suspicion against her that the women were finally arraigned in November 1889 for the murder of Dr. York, sixteen long years after the Benders had vanished. This took place in the Oswego courthouse. Certain officials were convinced that finally the Bender monsters, or, at least two of them, were now in custody, but many of the chief state's witnesses were not so sure, particularly the almost hanged Rudolph Brockmann. He took one look at the Davis women and said no, these were not Mrs. Bender and Kate.

Working in favor of the accused was the fact that they were defended by John Towers James, later to write one of the best books on the Benders and Judge Webb, who had actually dined at the Bender Inn in 1873 and managed to survive being killed; he certainly remembered Mrs. Bender and daughter Kate. But Mrs. McCann, who sat at the prosecutor's table and urged the state's attorney to be more aggressive in his questioning of witnesses, relentlessly badgered the court to bring these two monsters to justice.

A trial date was set for the two women, but attorney James finally unearthed documentation from the state of Michigan proving that Sarah Davis was exactly who she said she was and her mother was Mrs. Almira Griffith, who had led a dissolute life, had been convicted of manslaughter years earlier, and had served time in prison. This was the reason why the accused women had kept their silence and refused to defend themselves, fearing that the dark past would catch up with them. The trial against Griffith and Davis was abandoned and McCann went back to her crystal ball considerably annoyed. She had, at least, smelled out a felony, even though it had nothing to do with the Benders, and secured for herself, somewhere slightly above crank status, a place in the Bender mythology.

That myth exists to this day. Were the Benders run down and killed? Did they survive to live out their lives in the West under assumed names, the memories of their days filled with the nightmares of their past? No one knows for sure and never will know, unless evidence in the future pinpoints the true facts. Over the early years of the 20th Century, several men died, claiming they had been part of the original posse that had tracked down the Benders. They admitted in deathbed confessions that they had killed the Bender family, horribly mutilating their bodies, which were then thrown down a well.

These deathbed confessions made by a man named Downer in Chicago and a man named Harker in New Mexico in 1909 and 1910 went unsubstantiated, as did a report of an old man arrested for murdering a man in Idaho in 1884. This suspect was thought to be John Bender, Sr. Officers believed that since his victim had been murdered in the modus operandi of the Benders, his skull crushed from behind, and the fact that the old man answered the loose descriptions of John Bender, Sr., that he was one and the same. He was reportedly shackled by the ankle in his cell and, after somehow obtaining a large knife, the old man tried to cut off his foot in an effort to escape and subsequently bled to death. His remains were later examined by some Kansas residents who had known John Bender, Sr., but they could not make a positive identification.

The inglorious chronicle of this mass murdering family is preserved on a Kansas State marker outside of present day Cherryvale. It reads: "On the high prairie, a mile northwest, beyond the nearby Mounds, which bear their name the Bender family, John, his wife, son, and daughter Kate in 1871 built a small house. Partitioned into two rooms by a canvas cloth, it had a table, stove and grocery shelves in front. In back were beds, a sledge hammer, and a trap door above a pit-like cellar. Kate, a self-proclaimed healer and spiritualist, and reported to be a beautiful, voluptuous girl with tigerish grace, was the leading spirit of her murderous family.

"The house was located on the main road. Travelers stopping for a meal were seated on a bench, backed tight against the canvas. In the next two years several disappeared. When suspicions were finally aroused, in 1873, the Benders fled. A search of their property disclosed eleven bodies buried in the garden, skulls crushed by hammer blows through the canvas. The end of the Benders is not known. The earth seemed to swallow them, as it had their victims."

Dr. Thomas Neill Cream, who poisoned prostitutes in London and who claimed to be the infamous Jack the Ripper just before he was hanged in 1892.

THE KILLINGS OF THOMAS NEILL CREAM/ 1880-1891

The fact that Dr. Thomas Neill Cream (d. 1892) committed his diabolical murders a few years after Jack the Ripper went on his murder spree has led many arm-chair detectives to speculate that the two killers were one and the same. The parallels were striking. The Ripper and Cream had a fixation for London prostitutes. Both men were in the habit of taunting the police with letters after the commission of a crime. Cream, however, disdained the use of knives and was never present at the moment of his victim's death.

Thomas Neill Cream was a short, squat, cross-eyed man who began his medical practice in London, Ontario, in 1878 after completing his medical studies at McGill University. He earned plaudits for his experiments with chloroform, a substance he would later find useful in murdering young women. A widower at an early age, Cream was forced to flee from the province after local pharmacists became suspicious about his over-reliance on chloroform.

The body of a young chambermaid was subsequently found in back of Cream's office on Dundas Street. The inquest showed that the girl was pregnant at the time of her death, and had solicited Cream for an illegal abortion. Letters were uncovered that indicated that Cream was attempting to blackmail a prominent citizen whom he accused of murdering the girl.

Cream was freed under a cloud of suspicion. He settled in Chicago in 1880, but got into trouble with the authorities after performing an abortion on a Canadian woman. A second patient died from a fatal dose of prescribed medicine. Cream then tried to blackmail the druggist who had fulfilled the prescription. While the police investigated his actions in connection with this case, a third patient fell victim to the poisoner.

On June 14, 1881, Daniel Stott was given a fatal dose of strychnine by his wife, who had become infatuated with Cream, who, in turn, had provided the poison to dispatch the unwanted husband. For this the doctor received a sentence of life imprisonment at the Illinois Penitentiary in Joliet. With time off for good behavior, Cream was on the streets again in July 1891.

Rumors and allegations have since come to light that Cream may have in fact been released earlier after bribing

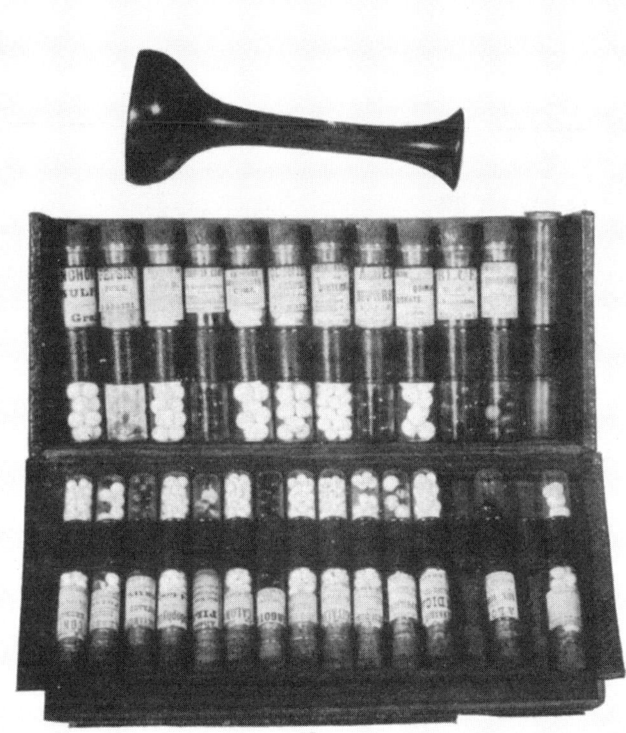

The stethoscope and medicine case carried by Dr. Thomas Neill Cream; the vials contained lethal strychnine, which Cream used to poison his victims.

prison officials. Those who believe that Cream was actually Jack the Ripper have subscribed to this unsubstantiated theory, which allowed the poisoner enough time to travel to London to commit the Ripper slayings.

There is no doubt, however, that Cream left the U.S. and took up residence in London, England, in October 1891. Within the span of a year, he murdered four prostitutes by means of strychnine poisoning, but failed in three other attempts. Cream's undoing came when he tipped the hand of the police by writing a series of extortion letters to various citizens of London. As a result he was arrested on June 3, 1892, and charged with blackmail. The charge was later expanded to include murder and attempted murder.

His well-publicized trial was held in October 1892, and a guilty verdict was duly returned. Thomas Neill Cream, one of the most famous gaslight murderers of Victorian England was executed at Newgate on November 15, 1892. According to the story the hangman later told, Cream shouted: "I am Jack—", only seconds before the trap was sprung, his final words cut short by the rope that jerked him to eternity. (See Jack the Ripper, Unsolved Murders.)

THE MAN IN "MURDER CASTLE"/1893-1894

Without a doubt the archfiend and worst serial killer of the American nineteenth century was Herman Webster Mudgett (AKA: H. H. Holmes, Henry Howard Holmes, H. M. Howard, Henry Mansfield Holmes, D. T. Pratt, Harry Gordon, Henry Gordon, Edward Hatch, J. A. Judson, Alexander E. Cook, A. C. Hayes, George H. Howell, G. D. Hale, Mr. Hall; 1860-1896), best known to his victims and to the police as the infamous H. H. Holmes. He murdered for profit and killed with such alacrity and such inhuman resolve that it is a wonder that Mudgett ever slept or ate.

Herman Webster Mudgett, alias H. H. Holmes, the worst serial killer in 19th Century America, who reportedly killed more than 200 women in his whirlwind murder-for-profit schemes.

Born in the small town of Gilmanton, New Hampshire, on May 16, 1860, Mudgett's childhood was comfortable. His father was a rich farmer and his mother, having been a teacher before her marriage, took pains to educate her son. In school he was frail and unpopular, but he excelled at his studies, graduating early and with honors at the age of sixteen. He was so bright that he earned a teaching certificate within weeks and taught school at Gilmanton and at Alton, another small town nearby. At the age of eighteen, Holmes eloped with Clara A. Lovering and was married in Alton before a justice of the

The home in Wilmette, Illinois, a surburb on Chicago's north shore, where Mudgett lived with his family, commuting to the South Side of Chicago, where he operated a pharmacy and later built his "Murder Castle."

peace, a wedding that irked his mother and father, who were devout Methodists and expected their son to be married in the Methodist church, not by a stranger in another town.

Mudgett himself later stated that his parents and his home life during his childhood had no bearing on the monstrous acts he would later commit: "That I was well trained by loving and religious parents, I know, and any deviations in my after life from the straight and narrow way of rectitude are not attributable to the want of a tender mother's prayers or a father's control, emphasized when necessary, by the liberal use of the rod wielded by no sparing hand."

The serial killer would recall only one traumatic incident in his childhood. He was deathly afraid of a doctor's office, which he had to pass daily, and the smells of strange medicines and the presence of a skeleton hanging from the ceiling in the corner frightened and nauseated him. Learning this, his classmates leaped upon him one day and dragged him screaming into the doctor's office, shoving him into the clattering skeleton whose bones flew about the Mudgett child, embracing and terrorizing him. "It was a wicked and dangerous thing to do to a child of tender years and health," he later remembered, "but it proved an heroic method of treatment, destined ultimately of curing me of my fears, and to inculcate in me, first, a strong feeling of curiosity, and, later a desire to learn, which resulted years afterwards in my adopting medicine as a profession."

Clara Mudgett gave birth to a second child while Herman was in his freshman year at Dartmouth. Planning to become a doctor, he transferred the next year to the University of Vermont in Burlington to study medicine. He then attended medical school at Ann Arbor, Michigan. It was here, in his junior year, that Mudgett committed his first crime. Working many jobs to pay for his education, Mudgett developed an insurance scheme that soon lined his pockets with cash. He stole bodies from the university's dissecting rooms and hid these in remote farmhouses. He would then take out insurance policies on a distant relative, who would suddenly turn up dead in accidental fires. The bodies of the insured relatives were actually the corpses stolen from the medical school. (It was later wrongly reported that Mudgett stole bodies from graveyards and sold these cadavers to the medical school for dissection. Michigan medical schools had no need to buy corpses as they were freely supplied with the bodies of those killed in accidents or donated by relatives.)

In 1884, Mudgett reportedly graduated from the University of Michigan at Ann Arbor, although there is some question about his insurance-corpse scheme causing him to be temporarily expelled. Apparently he was caught one night by a watchman as he was dragging a body out of the medical building. The guard demanded to know what Mudgett was doing and he jiggled the naked body of a young woman and darkly quipped: "Can't you see? Taking my girl for a walk!"

The body-snatcher was dragged before the dean of the medical school, who stood sputtering in his nightshirt as he heard the guard's story. Mudgett was expelled but apparently reinstated a short time later after giving the school authorities the story that he had been using corpses to further his dissection studies at home. This was looked upon as dedication to the profession, and Mudgett was soon back within the good graces of his academic superiors who warned him not to let his studies become so excessive.

Upon graduation, Mudgett went to Minneapolis and found work in a drugstore, where he met an attractive girl named Myrta Belknap. Despite the fact that he was still married and had his wife Clara and his child living with his parents in New Hampshire, Mudgett bigamously married Belknap. But by then he was no longer Herman Webster Mudgett. He was known in Minneapolis as Henry Howard Holmes. From Minneapolis, Mudgett moved to Philadelphia, where he worked in a drugstore. He then moved to Chicago in 1886 and, using many aliases and addresses, purchased furniture on credit and then sold off the furniture and moved to a new address. Mudgett moved to the South Side of Chicago, where he obtained a job as a pharmacist and clerk at a drugstore owned by Mrs. E. S. Holton, an attractive widow with a small daughter.

Mrs. Holton's husband, a physician, had recently died, leaving her with a lucrative drugstore on the corner of Sixty-third and Wallace streets in the upperclass suburb of Englewood. In short order, Mudgett seduced the woman, got her to sign over all her property and savings to him on the promise of marriage, and then killed her and her daughter. He disposed of the bodies by dissecting them in the back room of the drugstore and was nearly caught when depositing the remains from a wagon at a city dump by a policeman. At the

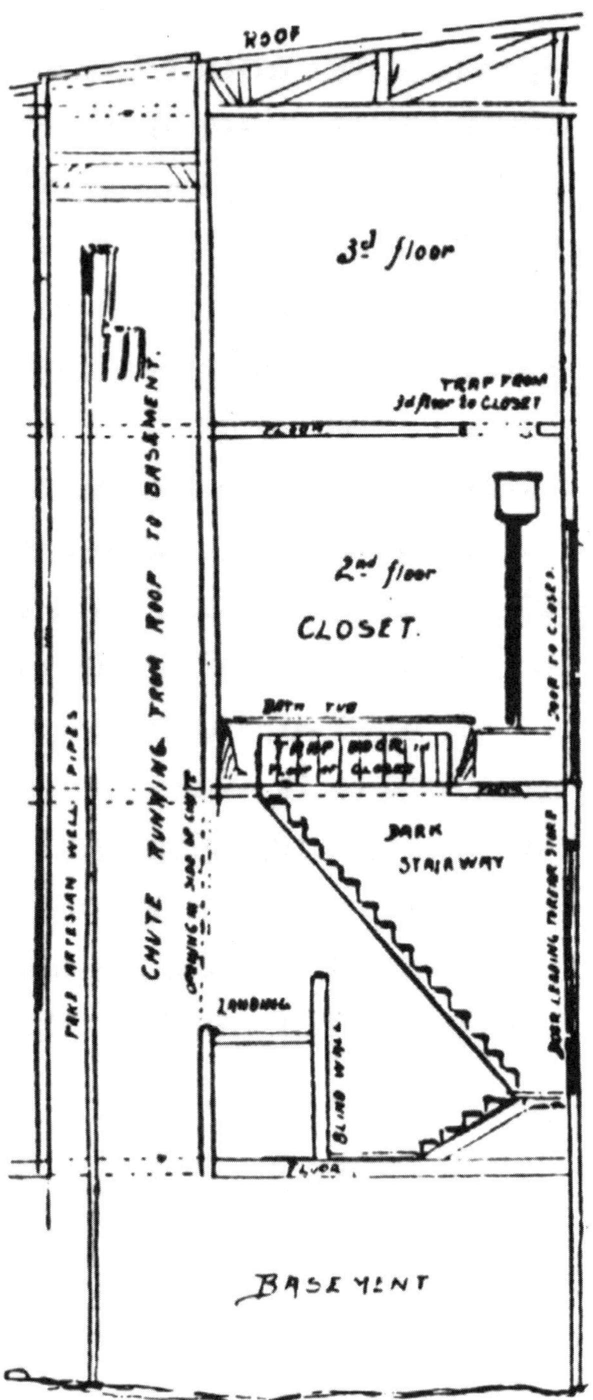

A sectional view of Mudgett's "Murder Castle," which shows how the serial killer could secretly get to the street or basement via a sliding chute (at left).

One of the trap doors Mudgett had builders construct in Murder Castle; in this passage he could view from secret hallways the female tenants of his labyrinthine building.

A vault in Murder Castle in which Mudgett gassed some of his victims to death; he had installed a glass ceiling through which he could view their death throes.

time, he explained that he was a garbage peddler and was disposing of the slaughtered remains from a hog-butchering shop nearby.

When customers, friends, and even relatives inquired about Mrs. Holton, Mudgett politely explained that the widow had sold him the business and moved away for health reasons. "She went west, poor lady," Mudgett would say with an ingratiating smile. "She was always in poor health, a frail woman, you know. She took her daughter with her. I paid her handsomely for the business." He had a bill of sale with Mrs. Holton's forged signature on it to show to the curious. "Yes, she's gone west to seek new opportunities." This remark reflected Mudgett's sinister sense of macabre humor. In the argot of the underworld to "go west" was to die.

The Grand Court of the World's Columbian Exposition, 1893, in Chicago, which, Mudgett knew, would draw enormous crowds and out-of-town single females looking for jobs and husbands, these naïve women his intended victims.

No one at the time suspected wrongdoing, particularly by the disarming druggist. Herman Webster Mudgett was tall, broad-shouldered, and intelligent, with an outwardly affable nature. He had a thick, black handlebar mustache that he took care to wax each morning. He wore a derby hat every day and he dressed in fashion, wearing tailor-made suits that were usually black or gray. He wore white shirts with soft collars and only his ties gave some life to his conservative appearance. They were striped and polka-dotted and full of color. Mudgett's eyes were the most arresting of his facial features. They were dark, penetrating, and wideset with dark arching eyebrows and when he narrowed his eyes they appeared snakelike.

For the next few years Mudgett confined himself to operating his drugstore and selling fake elixirs he claimed would cure all sorts of maladies. In the late 1880s, Mudgett had moved into a large home in the north suburb of Wilmette and here he brought his second wife, Myrta Belknap. Mudgett commuted daily to his South Side drugstore. By the early 1890s, Mudgett had separated from his wife and was living above the drugstore.

In early 1892, Mudgett began talking about acquiring the large vacant lot across the street from the drugstore. He spent hours looking at it, remarking, to customers: "I want that lot...I have plans." Mudgett had spent a good deal of time reading about the upcoming World's Fair Exposition planned for Chicago in 1893-1894. He knew that the fair would bring tens of thousands of people to the city, many of them women looking for jobs or for husbands. He made preparations.

Mortgaging the drugstore and borrowing heavily, Mudgett began to build one of the strangest buildings ever erected in Chicago or any other city for that matter, a sprawling, three-story structure that he intended to be a hotel that would house those flocking to the city to see the fair. Or, at least that was what Mudgett told neighbors and customers. The truth was that he had designed an eerie monstrosity that puzzled the various construction companies working on it. Mudgett had one crew work on a part of the building and then fired this group, hiring another firm to complete another section of the structure.

The druggist would find some excuse to fire this crew and hire yet another construction company, and another, and another. Mudgett's strange conduct was dismissed as eccentricity, but his odd behavior in the building of his "hotel" followed a careful plan. He had purposely fired the building crews one after another so that one would not know what the other had done. The result was a mad hatter's structure, one that later came to be known as Murder Castle.

Mudgett's Murder Castle, when completed, occupied a corner lot on Sixty-Third and Wallace Streets, in Chicago, a sprawling structure that offered shops on the first floor and boarding rooms on the second and third floors.

Mudgett's building appeared normal on the first floor, offering a series of streetside shops. His office was on the third floor, a corner suite, adjoined by a large bedroom. The second floor, however, ostensibly designed as a series of hotel rooms, had rooms that had no doors, and doors opening onto solid brick walls. One room opened into a steel vault with pipes leading to it, pipes that led through a wall to an adjoining room where hoses were affixed to pumps and containers of poisonous gas. There were closets that led to secret panels and corridors so that Mudgett could move through the corridor and peer through peepholes for each one of his hotel rooms.

There was an elevator that had no shaft and an elevator shaft that had no elevator. On the second and third floors, trap doors led to secret staircases that, in turn, led to the street and hidden exits from the building so that Mudgett could come and go undetected. There was a trap door in Mudgett's third-floor master bedroom, but here, instead of a staircase, was a chute that spiraled down to the building's basement. In the basement, Mudgett had installed several stoves with exhaust pipes that rose alongside the back of the building. Huge concrete pits had been built in the basement and these Mudgett later filled with lime. By the opening of the World's Fair, Herman Webster Mudgett was open for business. But what kind of business?

Shortly before the fair opened in 1893, Mudgett began to advertise the availability of his inexpensive hotel rooms. He also advertised for secretaries and stenographers to handle the heavy correspondence of his many businesses. Women flocked to the hotel, taking advantage of the incredibly cheap rates Mudgett established. Women also answered his job ads by the hundreds. He began interviewing in early 1893. Most of the young women were from small towns in the Midwest, and had arrived in Chicago, as Mudgett knew they would, looking for jobs generated by the fair.

As detailed in his extensive confession and the laborious reconstruction of events by tracking detectives, the serial killer would hire a young girl, give her some useless business letters

Mrs. Julia Conner, one of Mudgett's murder victims.

Emeline G. Cigrand, one of Mudgett's murder victims.

Minnie R. Williams, one of Mudgett's murder victims.

Nannie Williams, one of Mudgett's murder victims.

Spectators stand before Mudgett's deserted Murder Castle in 1895 as police begin removing bodies; by that time Mudgett, who had used the alias of H. H. Holmes, had fled.

to write for him and then quickly make advances. Most of the women were flattered and responded favorably to Mudgett's romantic suggestions. Those who did not were fired. Once a girl succumbed to Mudgett's charm, she was quickly wooed and taken to bed. Mudgett would then convince the girl to sign over her savings and any property deeds, and would take out an insurance policy on her. This done, he appeared to make arrangements to marry the girl, but with no real intention of doing so.

Mudgett would take his bride-to-be to bed, allowing her one night of sexual relations. When the woman fell asleep, Mudgett would rise and go to his "laboratory," a room off the master bedroom. He would take a bottle of chloroform back to the bedroom and then place a cloth soaked with the anesthetic over the sleeping woman's face so that she was completely unconscious when he lifted her body to dispose of her. Mudgett would then "eliminate" his victim according to the whim of the hour. He would sometimes, if in a lazy mood, drop the unconscious woman into the chute from the trap door of his bedroom, and she would quickly spiral downward and crash into one of the limepits in the basement. If wishing perversely to entertain himself, Mudgett would place the woman in the vault, lock it, then wait until she revived before pumping gas into the vault to watch her die in agony.

This calculating monster would then cart the body to the basement for dissection and burning in one of the many stoves there. Mudgett placed the bones and other parts of the body that could not be burned off into the limepits to allow them to dissolve, after pouring acid over the remains. The basement was always kept well-stocked with barrels of acid for the serial murder system Mudgett organized and conducted.

On some occasions, Mudgett stripped the flesh from his victims, cleaned off the skeletons, and sold these to medical laboratories in the city. He kept many barrels of bones in the basement, but mixed these with chicken bones and the bones of other animals, believing that some day this gruesome basement would be discovered and then the bones would be thought to be that of animals. Clinical and detailed as Mudgett was in the disposal of his victim's remains, he was nevertheless perversely enthralled with the process of his murder system.

The serial killer often chose to amuse himself through a bizarre routine, whereby music accompanied his murders. On some occasions, Mudgett got rid of the victim by placing her in the elevator shaft, over which he slid a large glass plate

Workers digging in Murder Castle's basement reportedly recovered the bones of 200 women; Mudgett was officially credited with twenty-seven murders.

Western outlaw Marion Hedgepeth, who shared a cell with Mudgett and who later informed on the serial killer.

Benjamin F. Pitezel, who joined with Mudgett in a murderous insurance swindle and wound up being the victim.

operated by a hydraulic motor. He would then stand above the woman and, when she revived, pump poison gas into the shaft. As the hysterical woman begged for her life, Mudgett would laugh and sometimes clog dance upon the glass plate, a death dance wherein he would accompany his wild gyrations above the dying victim by playing discordant notes from a hand organ.

There was no shortage of victims. For more than a year, Mudgett's hotel was packed with female victims and he received so many applications from female secretaries that he had to hire a real secretary to process the paperwork. He became so selective that he demanded in his advertisements that applicants submit photos of themselves. This way Mudgett could select only the prettiest of victims. He would sit for hours at his desk in his office, poring over these photos, and finally slipping those he intended to murder into a file holder on his desk, one marked "to be hired and enriched."

Other than what Mudgett himself would recall in his nonstop confessions, while he faced the executioner, few records remain as to the identities of the monster's roll call of victims. Known victims in this period include: Mrs. Holton; Julia Conner, wife of one of Mudgett's business associates and who became his mistress for a short time before he tired of her and butchered her; Emeline Cigrand, one of Mudgett's favorites, whom he used as stenographer for some months until killing her; and sisters Minnie and Nannie Williams from Texas, who arrived in Chicago seeking careers as actresses only to find horrible death at the hands of Mudgett.

Nannie Williams proved to be one of Holmes' most difficult victims. She was a tall, darkly attractive woman with ambitions to go onto the stage. She was also too inquisitive for Mudgett. After she became Mudgett's mistress, she began wandering through the enormous Murder Castle and apparently discovered some of the secret rooms and trap doors along with correspondence Mudgett maintained with other women and his many wives about the country. She confronted Mudgett with her discoveries one day and shortly disappeared down the chute to the limepits.

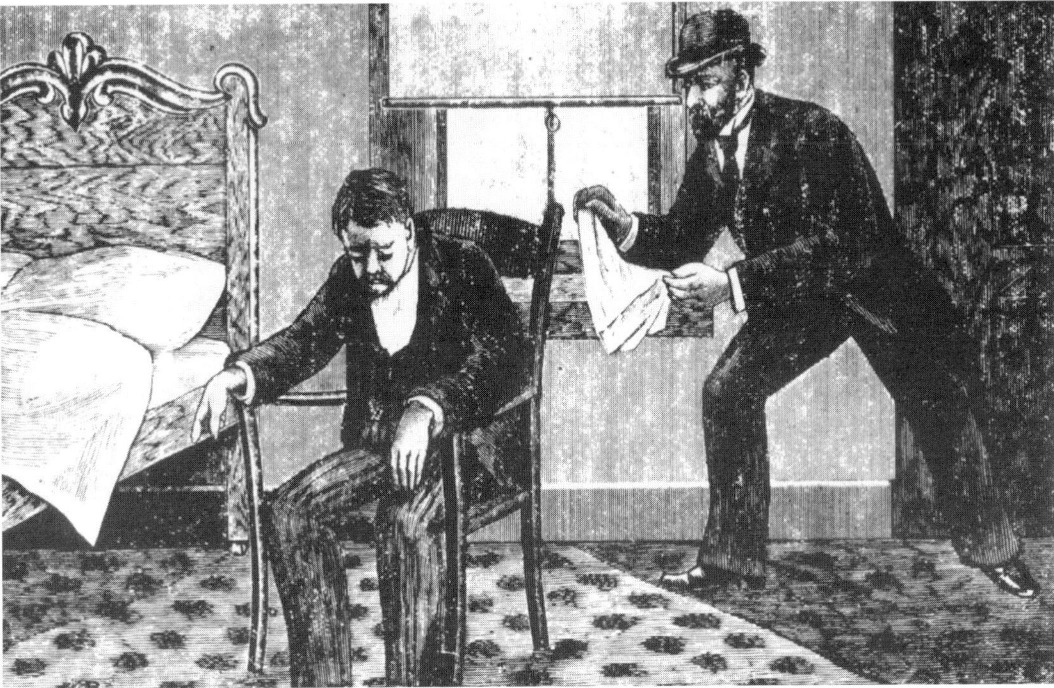

A contemporary sketch shows how Mudgett crept up behind his drugged associate Pitezel and strangled him, then tried to collect insurance money on his policy.

Patrick Quinlan, the janitor of the building, occasionally, asked Mudgett if he wanted him to clean out the basement. He was always told that this was Mudgett's private laboratory and Quinlan was not allowed beyond the locked door that led to the basement stairs. Mudgett kept the key to that door. Other areas of Murder Castle were also off limits to Quinlan, who was confined to cleaning the hotel rooms on the second floor and the shops on the street level. He often complained to Mudgett about "the awful smell" coming from the various pipe chimneys leading from the basement and suggested to Mudgett that he replace the stoves there, believing they were rusting out and causing these strange odors which the neighbors also complained about.

Quinlan began to overhear strange conversations Mudgett had with his many female friends. On one occasion the janitor heard a prospective victim ask Mudgett: "You're married, aren't you, Harry? That Mrs. Holmes in Wilmette, she's your wife, isn't she, Harry?"

"Ridiculous," Mudgett replied. "There are a lot of people named Holmes. You must be thinking about the detective character made up by that British writer, the one who solves all the cases in London." It is interesting to note that Mudgett, who was a reader of fiction and a fan of Arthur Conan Doyle, began to use the alias of H.H. Holmes shortly after Doyle published his first famous stories about the fabulous detective, Sherlock Holmes.

One of the few men Mudgett took into his confidence was a character as devious and scheming as himself, Benjamin Pitezel, who was married and had three small children. It was later claimed that Pitezel actually helped Mudgett get rid of the many bodies piling up in the lime pits of Murder Castle, routinely sawing up corpses and burning the remains at Mudgett's direction. He was certainly on Mudgett's payroll and it was this payroll and the upkeep of the building that finally caused Mudgett to abandon his Murder Castle. He later complained that the building and its mortgage payments had driven him to his murder-for-profit enterprise and that he had spent more than $50,000 in maintenance, especially on supplies like lime, acid, chloroform, all the tools of his grim enterprise.

Mudgett proposed an insurance fraud scheme one day that appealed to Pitezel. Mudgett would fund Pitezel's return to Philadelphia, his native city, and there Pitezel, using an alias, would establish himself as a rich patent agent, taking out a $10,000 insurance policy. Mudgett then explained that he would arrive in Philadelphia and steal a corpse, mutilate it beyond recognition and then place it in Pitezel's home. Following a fire, Pitezel's wife, the beneficiary, would claim the $10,000 and he would split this with the cooperative Pitezel.

While Pitezel went to Philadelphia to set up the insurance fraud, Mudgett surveyed his Murder Castle with resignation. The basement was loaded with skeletons and there seemed to be no more room for additional victims. His murder work had also exhausted him. He then realized that he could destroy the entire place, collect a great deal of money and flee. He insured the place and then set fire to it.

Before the insurance firm paid off, however, it insisted that police inspectors review the building. It had been badly damaged, but the structure remained intact. Mudgett had boarded up the windows and doors and police detectives informed him that they would have to look over the premises before the insurance claim was paid. Mudgett appeared at a police station, full of indignation and demanding his rights. "I am a tax-paying, law-abiding citizen and I am entitled to my claim," he told a detective.

"Of course you are, Dr. Holmes," the detective replied, "but we must inspect the premises. It's only a formality. You'll have to unlock your building."

"That's an insult!" roared Mudgett. "Are you accusing me of something?"

"Certainly not. It's only a formality."

Mudgett said he was busy at the time, but would return and give the detectives the keys to his building. He had no intention of doing so. Mudgett packed his clothes, gathered his money, and fled to Fort Worth, Texas, where he unsuccessfully tried to pry loose a deed to a property once owned by

Alice Pitezel, murdered by Mudgett.

Nellie Pitezel, murdered by Mudgett.

Howard Pitezel, murdered by Mudgett.

A contemporary sketch shows Mudgett strangling Howard Pitezel; the serial killer was methodical and without remorse, looking back upon his murders as a "part of the business," although he later (and insincerely) decried his crimes.

Minnie Williams. The property was worth $60,000, but lawyers shrewdly prevented Mudgett from making claim to the land. When local police began to look into Mudgett's claim, he panicked. Seeing detectives heading for his hotel room, Mudgett ran to a livery stable, stole a horse, and rode out of Fort Worth.

The serial killer arrived in St. Louis where, using the name H. M. Howard, Mudgett attempted a crude swindle and was arrested for the first time in his life. He was thrown into a cell to await trial and found himself in the company of notorious train robber, Marion Hedgepeth. Without money, the desperate Mudgett confided his insurance scheme to Hedgepeth, saying that he would pay the outlaw $500 if he would recommend a St. Louis criminal lawyer, who could help him defraud the insurance firm in Philadelphia. Hedgepeth got word to Jeptha D. Howe, a crooked lawyer, that his cellmate had a fabulous scheme that would enrich them all.

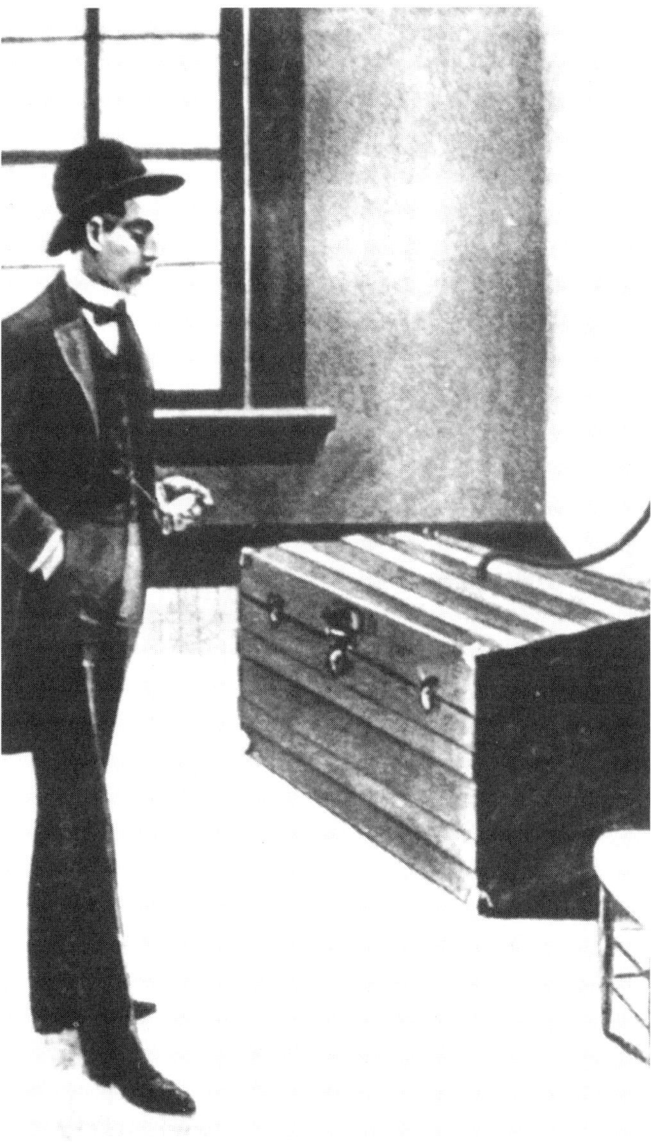

Mudgett holds a stopwatch, timing the gassing of the Pitezel girls, whom he had placed in a trunk affixed with a gas line.

Howe arranged for Mudgett's bail, and as soon as the serial killer was freed, he fled to Chicago. From there he quickly contacted his old associate, Benjamin Pitezel, and told him to go ahead with the insurance scheme in Philadelphia. Mudgett had by then involved the crooked lawyer Howe in the plan. On September 4, 1894, B.F. Perry, who operated a patent office in Philadelphia, was found dead on his porch. His face was charred almost beyond recognition. Next to him was found a pipe, some matches, and the shattered remains of a benzene bottle.

Investigators first assumed that Perry had tried to light his pipe next to the open benzene bottle and it exploded in his face. A coroner's jury ruled the death accidental and a claim for $10,000 against the Fidelity Mutual Life Insurance Company of Philadelphia was immediately filed by lawyer Jeptha D. Howe on behalf of Mrs. Carrie A. Pitezel, who was then calling herself Mrs. Perry.

Carrie Pitezel weepingly identified the corpse as her husband, but insurance investigators were hesitant in paying. Two curious doctors, Dr. William J. Scott and Dr. William K. Mattern, had since examined the body and found fluid in the stomach that they determined to be chloroform. By this time, Mrs. Pitezel, pretending to be Mrs. Perry, had threatened to sue the insurance firm through her dogged lawyer, Howe, unless she received payment. The company stalled while it contacted a Mr. H. H. Holmes in Chicago, a man, according to Perry's records, who had known the accident victim well for a number of years.

As Holmes, Mudgett was asked to go to Philadelphia and identify the corpse of Perry. He did so willingly, after getting the insurance firm to pay his round trip expenses. Mudgett arrived with one of the Pitezel daughters in tow. She stated that her name was Perry and she cried great tears as she identified the remains as her father. Mudgett himself identified the corpse, saying that his old friend Perry had a mole on the back of his neck. It was present. Mrs. Pitezel was paid the $10,000. The body was buried in Potter's Field.

The matter did not rest, however. Marion Hedgepeth, still languishing in a St. Louis jail cell, contacted officials a short time later and told them of the insurance scheme that Mudgett, his one-time cellmate, had hatched. "So I give him the name of my lawyer," carped the train robber, "and that's the last I seen of him. He got out on bail the next day and skipped out. I heard by the grapevine that he collected the insurance money, but he ain't been near me to pay me the five hundred he owes me!"

Hedgepeth's statement caused the insurance company to pressure the Philadelphia police into assigning its best detective to the case. This was Frank P. Geyer, a crafty sleuth who, once on the track of a criminal, doggedly followed the culprit, no matter how long or how far it took him. He had solved dozens of murder cases and he believed that the accidental death of B. F. Perry had been murder, that Perry had been chloroformed by the mysterious Mr. Holmes that Hedgepeth the train robber had known in jail.

Geyer traveled to Chicago to locate Mudgett, but he found that he had left town. The detective visited Murder Castle. He inspected the exterior of the building, noting the many stove-

Frank P. Geyer, the indefatigable detective, who tracked the serial killer across the country until he finally captured Herman Webster Mudgett.

Herman Webster Mudgett in his cell, where he stalled his execution by countless confessions; he was hanged in Philadelphia on May 7, 1896.

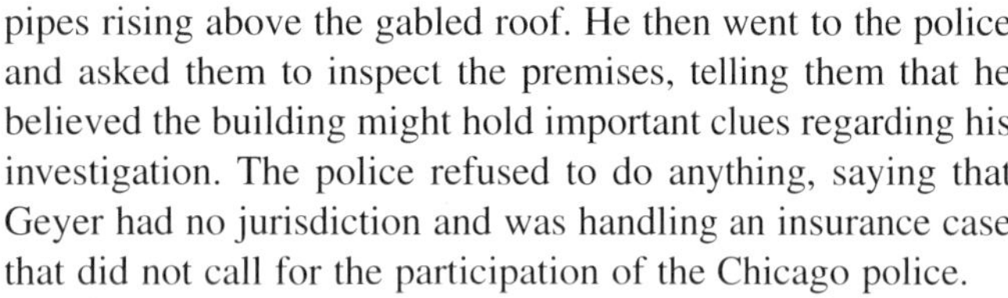

pipes rising above the gabled roof. He then went to the police and asked them to inspect the premises, telling them that he believed the building might hold important clues regarding his investigation. The police refused to do anything, saying that Geyer had no jurisdiction and was handling an insurance case that did not call for the participation of the Chicago police.

Checking the background of Mudgett-Holmes, Geyer went to the school in Ann Arbor and there learned of Mudgett's real name and birthplace. He then traveled to Gilmanton, New Hampshire, where he learned from relatives—Mudgett habitually kept in contact with family members—that Mudgett could be found in Boston where he had gone on business. On September 17, 1894, Geyer walked into a Boston hotel room to find Mudgett with Mrs. Carrie A. Pitezel. He arrested both of them, charging them with conspiracy to defraud the Fidelity Mutual Life Insurance Company.

Pitezel told Geyer that she did not have the insurance money, that she had that very day signed it over to Herman Webster Mudgett. In reality, Geyer undoubtedly saved the woman's life as Mudgett apparently had planned to murder her, too, and claim insurance money from a policy he had taken out on Mrs. Pitezel. Mudgett was returned to Philadelphia to await trail. While he waited in jail, Geyer busied himself with unearthing Mudgett's sordid past.

Mudgett, realizing he was trapped, began to talk. At first he admitted the insurance scheme, saying that Benjamin Pitezel had stolen a body and passed it off as his own and had then fled to South America. Then Mudgett changed his story, telling Geyer: "All right. The dead man was Pitezel, just as you suspected, but his death was his own doing, a result of his own stupidity! He was supposed to steal a cadaver, lost his nerve and got despondent. He drank chloroform. When I discovered his body, I decided to make it look like an accident so his poor widow could collect the insurance."

"What about the Pitezel children?" Geyer asked Mudgett pointedly. "We can't find them."

For weeks Geyer went back to the maze-like trail taken by the cagey Mudgett. The trail led him to Indianapolis, Indiana, where, in a stove inside a small cottage he found the skull and bones of a small boy, the remains of Howard Pitezel. Mudgett had murdered the child by strangling him to death and then dismembered and burned his body. Geyer found the bodies of Alice and Nellie Pitezel stuffed in a trunk in Toronto, Canada. Mudgett had stuffed the little girls into the trunk and had then inserted a small hose into it, pumping poisonous gas into the container.

Geyer returned to Philadelphia's Moyamensing Prison to tell Mudgett about the deaths of the Pitezel children. He slowly described how these innocent children had been strangled and gassed to death, watching the reaction of Mudgett. The serial killer clutched the bars of his cell and shouted through them: "It was foul murder! Who was the fiend?"

"You don't know?" Geyer replied, staring back at the handsome man in the prison cell. The detective then returned to Chicago. Without getting permission from the Chicago police, Geyer ordered a crew of workmen to break into Mudgett's Murder Castle. The stench from rotting flesh in the basement overcame so many of the workers that new crews had to be called in. Human bones by the barrel full were unearthed out of the limepits and all of the buildings strange rooms, chutes, and trap doors were discovered. The Chicago police arrived and helped in the investigation. The newspapers blared the grim truth of Murder Castle. Out of its foul depths came the remains of at least 150 to 200 corpses, according to most reliable accounts, making Herman Webster Mudgett America's all-time serial murderer a killer without conscience, without mercy. (This astounding murder record was meticulously assembled by teams of medical inspectors, who simply reconstructed as many human skeletons as the intact bones found in the basement could yield.)

When Mudgett was confronted with the discoveries at Murder Castle, he denied knowing anything about the human remains found there. "Untrue!" he roared, "a villainous lie! Vile slander!" When the press named him a murderer to rank with Gilles de Rais and other historic serial killers, Mudgett threatened to sue them for libel.

Convicted of Benjamin Pitezel's murder and sentenced to death, Mudgett thought to postpone his end on the gallows. He began to recite the long history of his crimes, detailing one vicious murder after another, precisely describing his monstrous slayings. He then contradicted himself, denying his murders. He then admitted them again, and began to relate more killings, all in an effort to stall his execution.

By May 7, 1896, the officials had had enough of Herman Webster Mudgett. He was led to the gallows in Moyamensing Prison. Detective Frank Geyer was on hand to watch Mudgett march up the thirteen steps to the hangman and the noose that awaited him. On the scaffold, as the rope was placed around his neck, Mudgett showed the first signs of mortal terror. His face drained of blood and he began to scream out in a high-pitched voice: "As God is my witness, I was responsible for the deaths of only two women!"

The executioner stepped away from the condemned man, who twisted his head about frantically looking for anyone who might come to his rescue, might forestall the inevitable. No one stood near him except the executioner, who placed his hand on the lever that would spring the trap. "Wait, wait!" Mudgett cried out. "I didn't kill Minnie Williams! Not me! Let me tell you about her." He saw the hand of the executioner snap back the lever. "Minnie killer her—" In a second, he fell downward into neck-snapping death and the everlasting infamy as America's worst killer.

THE FRENCH RIPPER/1894-1897

A lust for killing which he ascribed to the bite of a mad dog turned this frustrated army corporal into a serial killer. Between 1894 and 1897 Joseph Vacher (AKA: The French Ripper; c.1869-1898) is known to have murdered at least eleven people, though some estimates place the number much higher. The famed criminologist Professor A. Lacassagne, (author of a book on the case, titled *Vacher l'Eventreur et les Crimes Sadique*), believed that the madman was responsible for at least fifteen murders and five rapes between June 1888 and July 1897.

Vacher was the fifteenth and final child born to a respectable working class family in Beaufort, France. According to Lacassagne, except for Vacher, there was no hint of aberrant behavior in the family until his sister went insane after Vacher's death. At the age of eight Vacher was bitten by a rabid dog and was treated by a local magician, who compelled him to drink a strange potion, an event Vacher, at least, credited as transforming his normal character into a criminal personality.

In 1888, Vacher attempted to rape a male servant employed by the Marist brothers, who had educated him. In November 1890 he was drafted into the 60th Infantry Regiment at Besanon. Vacher seemed to enjoy the military life and desperately wanted to advance through the ranks. When his promotion to full corporal was denied, he attempted suicide by cut-

Joseph Vacher murdered women out of bloodlust, claiming he had turned killer after being bitten by a mad dog; he was beheaded on December 31, 1898.

ting his throat with a razor. Hearing of this incident, the colonel of the regiment authorized the promotion at once, and Vacher recovered. His persecution complex however, was soon apparent in other ways. His menacing behavior caused Vacher's roommates to go to bed each night holding their bayonets out of fear that the unstable corporal might attack them.

In May 1893, Vacher was granted a sick leave. He traveled to Baume-les-Dames in June where he met a young woman named Louise. When she spurned his advances, Vacher fired three shots at her, none of which, however, caused serious injury. He then turned the pistol on himself and fired a bullet into his face. The bullet pierced his right eye, paralyzing the right side of his face. The courts found Vacher insane and committed him to the asylum at Saint-Ylle on July 7, 1893. In the asylum, Vacher behaved like an unredeemable madman. However, when Vacher was transferred to a hospital in Saint-Rober in December his mad behavior suddenly stopped, and he began behaving normally. On April 1, 1894, the director of the institute approved his discharge papers.

Six weeks later, on May 20, the body of Eugenie Delhomme, a 21-year-old factory worker, was found on a country road near Vienne. She had been raped, knifed to death, and disemboweled. She was the first of Vacher's confirmed victims, most of whom were rural farm workers he met while he roamed from town to town begging for food and shelter. "A sort of frenzy drove me blindly forward to commit my crimes," he said. "Never did I look for victims: chance meetings decided their fates. The poor creatures need not be pitied. None of them suffered longer than ten minutes."

The second victim was 13-year-old Louise Marcel, whose mutilated remains were found in a stable near Blais. On May 12, 1895, Adele Mortureux, seventeen, was strangled and disemboweled in the Bois de Chene. In August, the serial killer, by then known as the Ripper, attacked a 60-year-old widow, Mme. Morand, killed her, and then raped the corpse.

A week later Vacher crept up on Victor Portalier, a youthful shepherd in Onglas, and stabbed him to death. The Portalier murder was the one for which Vacher would ultimately be held accountable. The killings continued for another two years and four months before Vacher was apprehended. The police had little to go on except a sketchy physical description supplied by various villagers. A vagrant with a black beard and a scarred face had been observed in the vicinity of the murders.

On August 4, 1897, Vacher encountered Marie-Eugenie Plantier in the countryside near Bois des Pelleries. Plantier was picking pine cones with her husband and children and had been separated from them. When Vacher grabbed her from behind, she fought fiercely and called for help. Plantier's husband appeared and struggled with Vacher until a peasant farm hand named Henri Nodin arrived and helped the husband subdue Vacher.

Once in custody, police began a thorough investigation of Vacher's background and concluded that he was, indeed, the much-sought Ripper. He was tried before the Tribunal Correctionel of Tournon. Subsequent interrogation, and the testimony of a score of eyewitnesses, who had seen Vacher, convinced the defendant that further resistance was useless. He confessed to his many murders and rapes, but blamed his psychological malady on the dog bite he received at age eight.

A five month inquiry into the state of his mind began on December 16, 1897. Three psychiatrists, led by Professor Lacassagne, concluded that Vacher was only pretending to be mad. His fantasy about the mad dog was dismissed as "puerile." Vacher was found guilty of murder on October 28, 1898, at the Assizes of Ain, and was guillotined on December 31, 1898.

ENGLAND'S MURDERING BARBER/ 1897-1902

George Chapman (1865-1903), born Severin Atonionivitch Klosowski in Nargonak, Poland, on December 14, 1865, was the son of a carpenter. He apprenticed at age fifteen to a surgeon in Zvolen, working at a clinic for six years, but failing to be appointed to the expected post of junior surgeon. He left the clinic at twenty-one and traveled about Poland as a barber's surgeon, or feldsher, removing warts, performing small surgeries, even bloodletting which was still, in less sophisticated societies in the late nineteenth century, considered a form of purifying the blood system. (The red and white poles outside of barber shops originally indicated that a bloodletting expert was on the premises.)

Chapman married in Poland, then worked in a Prague hospital before enlisting in the Russian army where he served for almost two years. He then migrated to England, arriving in early 1888, the year that Jack the Ripper turned loose his reign of terror in London's West End. He later became one of the prime suspects in the Ripper killings and it was rumored that Chapman had decapitated a woman in Poland, but no evidence could be found to support this claim.

Locating in London's West End, Chapman worked as a barber. He later moved to Tottingham to set up his own business, but when this failed he returned to his old job as a barber's surgeon and assistant. He married Lucy Baderski, but this marriage was compromised when Chapman's first wife arrived from Poland. Both women, oddly, lived with Chapman for a while until the first and legal wife returned to Poland. Chapman and Lucy went to the U.S. in 1890, but after constant quarreling, Lucy returned to London in 1891, Chapman himself arriving in London a year later.

The marriage floundered when Chapman went on womanizing, taking a mistress named Annie Chapman, ironically the same name as one of Jack the Ripper's victims. Lucy left her philandering husband in 1894, taking their two children with her. Chapman, who had used his real name, Klosowski, up to this time, now took the name of his mistress, Chapman, and tried to conceal his original name.

The promiscuous barber met a drunken divorcée, Mary Spinks, in 1895 in one of the many pubs he visited, and the couple lived together for two years, moving in 1897 to Hastings, where they assumed the roles of man and wife. Chapman opened a hairdresser's shop and promoted "musical shaves." His mistress-wife would play the piano while Chapman shaved his customers, a notion that caught on, and so popular was Chapman's shop that he began to turn a profit for the first time in his entrepreneurial life.

Chapman bought a sailboat and began taking his wife on sailing expeditions. A short time later the boat capsized and the Chapmans were saved by some fishermen. It was later theorized that this was the barber's first attempt at murder, since he planned to eliminate his wife. About six months later, Chapman suddenly sold his lucrative shop in Hastings and moved back to London, leasing the Prince of Wales Tavern on Bartholomew Square, near City Road.

On April 2, 1897, before leaving Hastings, Chapman bought tartar emetic from a local druggist and this he would later use to murder Mary Spinks, it was later concluded by police officials. Mary Spinks grew ill in late 1897 and suffered vomiting seizures. Doctors examining her could find no reason for these seizures. Chapman, meanwhile nursed her until Mary Spinks died on December 25, 1897. The cause of her death was listed as consumption. A few months after Mary Spinks was buried, Chapman hired a barmaid, Bessie Taylor, a naive farmer's daughter. He married Bessie some months later.

Chapman tired of Bessie and made plans to kill her. First he sold his pub and bought another tavern, The Grapes, at Bishops Stortford. Bessie was then hospitalized for a small operation never disclosed. When she was released, Chapman began mistreating her, at one point threatening to shoot her with a revolver. Again, Chapman sold his pub, and bought another, The Monument, which was located on Union Street. He continued to abuse his wife and run around with other women. Bessie's health grew steadily worse and she was finally bedridden, with Chapman nursing her; she died on February 13, 1901. Doctors examining her attributed her demise to "exhaustion from vomiting and diarrhea."

Maud Marsh, the daughter of a Croydon laborer, next went to work for Chapman as a barmaid in his pub. Maud was reluctant to become Chapman's mistress, even though he gave her a gold watch and chain. The young girl wrote to her mother that Chapman had threatened to send her home unless "I give him what he wants." She finally relented, but grew ill in the fall of 1902, suffering from severe abdominal pains. Chapman called in doctors who had her removed to Guy's Hospital where she recovered.

When Maud Marsh returned to Chapman, he moved her into quarters above his new pub, The Crown Public House, which was also on Union Street. Here the girl grew ill again, despite constant attention from Chapman. Maud's mother and a nurse arrived one evening to attend to Maud and they found at her bedside a special drink Chapman had prepared for Maud, a brandy and soda which Maud's mother and the nurse drank. Within minutes both women became ill with vomiting and diarrhea.

Serial killer George Chapman with one of his mistresses, Bessie Taylor, whom he later murdered; he visited America in 1890, which explains the U.S. flag next to the Union Jack on the wall.

Mrs. Marsh went to her own physician and told him that she believed Chapman was poisoning her daughter. This doctor went to the physician attending Maud with Mrs. Marsh's suspicions. The attending doctor and the Marsh family physician visited the ailing girl and both men were soon convinced that Maud was being poisoned. Chapman, meanwhile, panicked after this visit from the doctors and he gave Maud a massive dose of his special preparation. She died on October 22, 1902, the very day of Edward VII's coronation procession through the streets of London.

Maud's body was examined, and it was determined that she had been poisoned not with arsenic, as the Marsh family suspected, but with antimony. Chapman was arrested and charged with murder. He was tried before Justice Graham at the Central Criminal Court on March 16, 1903. Sir Edward Carson prosecuted Chapman, who was defended by George Elliott. Chapman's attorney could mount very little defense. The bodies of Chapman's other two mistresses, Mary Spinks and Bessie Taylor, were exhumed and these corpses also contained antimony, enough to have killed them. Chapman was convicted in a quick trial and condemned. He was executed on April 7, 1903.

The rumor that this serial killer might have been Jack the Ripper was strengthened by a cryptic remark from the very man who had supervised the investigation into the 1888 Ripper slayings. Just after Chapman's arrest, Scotland Yard's Inspector Frederick Abberline approached the officer in charge of the case, Inspector George Godley (who had been Abberline's assistant in the Ripper killings), telling him: "You've got Jack the Ripper at last!"

Abberline believed Chapman to be the awesome Ripper since his handling of the bewildering 1888 mass murders re-

George Chapman at the time he was tried for murder; he was convicted and executed on April 7, 1903.

mained unsolved. Why Abberline believed Chapman was the Ripper was never explained either by Abberline or anyone else. It is believed that Abberline had suspected Chapman or Klosowski during his original 1888 investigations, but could never prove his secret suspicions about the barber.

Many experts are quick to point out that Chapman's modus operandi and that of the Ripper's were widely dissimilar, the Ripper using extreme violence and a surgical knife to end his victims' lives, where Chapman had regularly chosen the slow, secret method of poison. It was later claimed that Chapman, as Klosowski, had even tried to obtain poison, when he lived in Whitechapel during the Ripper murders, perhaps planning at the time to rid himself of his first Polish wife and Lucy Baderski at the same time. Another theory held that Chapman could very well have been the Ripper and that he continued slitting throats and dismembering bodies long into the 1890s, electing to kill women he was known to associate with through poison so that the Ripper's modus operandi would not be attached to him, believing that poison would allow him to go undetected.

Even more puzzling is why Chapman chose to murder three women (or more) simply because they either came to annoy him or because he tired of them. He was not necessarily a sadist, according to his character profiles, so he took no particular pleasure in slowly murdering his common-law spouses and mistresses. Moreover, he derived no money from the deaths of these women, having already bilked his first mistress of her savings to buy his first pub.

There may be a link to the deaths in Chapman's consistent buying and selling of pubs, changes that were invariably made at the time of the murders. It was proposed by one crime writer that Chapman murdered his women when his pub business began to drop off, believing they were bringing him bad luck. A check of the consistent popularity of these pubs, however, disproves this contention. Chapman remains a murdering enigma, one who could possibly have been Jack the Ripper. He never confessed to his crimes, however, leaving frustrated criminologists to theorize and wonder in his wake. (See Jack the Ripper, Unsolved Murders.)

BELLE OF LA PORTE/1900-1908

One of America's worst female serial killers surfaced at the turn of the 20th Century in the flatlands of the Midwest. She was Belle Gunness, a woman dedicated to murder for profit. A stonemason's daughter who was born near Lake Selbe, Trondheim, Norway, Belle Gunness (AKA: Bella Poulsdatter Sorensen Gunness, Belle Brynhilde Paulsetter Sorenson Gunness, The Female Bluebeard; 1859-1908?) migrated to the U.S. in 1883, following her sister to America. (Another report has it that Belle was born Belle Paulson in Christiania (now Oslo), Norway, and that her father was a traveling magician, who taught Belle all sorts of magic and had her walk a tightrope as a child outside his tent to lure customers into his magic show.) She married Mads Albert Sorenson in 1884 in Chicago, a union that produced no children. Sorenson died in 1900, heavily insured, the cause of death listed as heart failure.

Belle immediately claimed the insurance money, $8,500, the day following her husband's funeral, a suspicious act, according to her in-laws. Sorenson's relatives claimed that Belle had poisoned her husband to collect the insurance money and an inquest was ordered, according to records. It is unclear, however, whether or not the inquest ever took place or whether Sorenson's body was exhumed to check for arsenic as his relatives had demanded.

Belle used the insurance money to open a confectionery store at Grand Avenue and Elizabeth Street, but this store mysteriously burned down just after Belle had the place heavily insured. The insurance company at first resisted paying off, but it finally relented after the outspoken Belle threatened to take the matter into court and to the newspapers.

With her insurance money, Belle moved in 1902 to La Porte, Indiana, about fifty miles east of Chicago, where she purchased a large farm, six miles outside of town. She had, while married to Sorenson, adopted three children, all girls, Jennie, Myrtle and Lucy. Just after moving into a large farmhouse, Belle met a local man, Peter Gunness, a fellow Norwegian, and they were married a short time later. This union produced a son, Philip, in 1903.

Belle Gunness as a young woman, when she arrived in the U.S. in 1883 and before she became America's female bluebeard; she left Chicago under a cloud when her first husband mysteriously died.

Belle Gunness, in 1902, when she moved to La Porte, Indiana, to marry hog butcher Peter Gunness; shown with Belle are three girls she adopted (left to right), Jennie, Myrtle and Lucy.

Gunness did not last long. He met with a "tragic accident," according to Belle's sobbing story, in 1904. While working in a shed on the farm, a meat chopper fell from a high shelf and struck Gunness square in the head, splitting his skull and killing him on the spot. Belle, still a great believer in insurance, had, of course, insured her husband Peter for just such an unforeseen event. She collected another $4,000.

Local authorities refused to believe that Gunness, who ran the hog farm and butchering shop on the property, could be so clumsy. He was an experienced butcher and the local coroner reviewed the case and announced: "This was murder!" He convened a coroner's jury to look into the matter. Meanwhile, Jennie Olson, age fourteen, the oldest of Belle's adopted children, was overheard confessing to a classmate: "My momma killed my poppa. She hit him with a cleaver." Jennie was brought before the coroner's jury but denied having made this remark.

While she testified, Belle sat nearby at a witness table, silently glowering at her adopted daughter. Then Belle took the stand and, weeping, told her tale. She managed to convince the coroner's jury that she was innocent of any wrongdoing and that she now bore the responsibility of raising her children without the help of a strong man. She was released and the matter was dropped.

In September 1906, Jennie Olson suddenly vanished. When neighbors inquired about her, Belle told them that she had sent Jennie to finishing school in Los Angeles. A short time later, Belle hired Ray Lamphere, a somber little man with a drooping mustache, to perform the chores on her farm. Next, in late 1906, she inserted the following advertisement in the matrimonial columns of all the Chicago daily newspapers and those of other large midwestern cities:

> "Personal: Comely widow who owns a large farm in one of the finest districts in La Porte County, Indiana, desires to make the acquaintance of a gentleman equally well provided, with view of joining fortunes. No replies by letter considered unless sender is willing to follow answer with personal visit. Triflers need not apply."

Several middle-aged men with comfortable bank accounts and property responded to Belle's lovelorn column ads. They traveled to Belle's La Porte farm, fat wallets and deeds to their farms tucked in their pockets, all proving that they were men of substance and worthy of Belle's attentions. One of these

Jennie Olson Gunness told classmates that her mother killed her father; the girl vanished, her body found years later, one of Belle's many victims.

Henry Gurholdt, one of Belle's suitors, who had come prepared "to stay forever"—his body parts were found buried in Belle's hogpen.

was John Moo, who arrived from Elbow Lake, Minnesota. He was a husky man of fifty and brought along with him more than $1,000 to pay off Belle's mortgage, or so he told neighbors, who were introduced to him by Belle as her cousin. He disappeared from Belle's farm within a week of his arrival. Next came George Anderson who, like Peter Gunness and John Moo, was a migrant from Norway. Anderson, from Tarkio, Missouri, was also a farmer with ready cash and a lovesick heart.

Anderson, however, did not bring all his money with him. He had been persuaded to make the long trip to see Belle in La Porte because her eloquent letters intrigued him. Once there, he realized that Belle, in her mid-forties and gone portly, was not the beauty he expected. Her face was hard, and she had a severe manner about her, but she made Anderson feel at home and provided good dinners for him while he occupied a guest room in her large farmhouse. One night at dinner Belle raised the issue of her mortgage. Anderson agreed that he would pay this off if they decided to wed. He was almost convinced to return to Tarkio and retrieve his money, then go back to Belle and eternal bliss.

But late that night, Anderson awoke "all in a cold sweat," and he looked up to see Belle standing over him, peering down with a strange look in her eyes. She held a guttering candle in her hand and the expression on her face was so foreboding and sinister that Anderson let out a loud yell. Belle, without a word, left the room.

Anderson jumped out of bed, hurriedly dressed, and fled the dark farmhouse, running up the road, trotting all the way into La Porte, peering over his shoulder down the moonlit road, expecting Belle to come chasing after him at any moment, wildly driving her carriage. Anderson reached the train station and waited with more than casual concern for the next train to take him back to Missouri.

The suitors nevertheless kept arriving in La Porte, but none, except for the apprehensive Anderson, ever left the Gunness farm. At this time, Belle began ordering huge trunks to be delivered to her home. Hack driver Clyde Sturgis delivered many such trunks to Belle from La Porte and later remarked how the heavyset woman would lift these enormous trunks "like boxes of marshmallows," tossing them onto her wide shoulders and carrying them into the house. She kept the shutters of her house closed day and night, and farmers traveling past her house at night saw Belle working in the hog pen area, digging. Her handyman, Lamphere, also spent a good deal of time digging in the hog pen and all about the house and barn.

Meanwhile, the suitors continued to arrive in the small town wearing their Sunday suits, all responding to Belle's enticing ads. Ole B. Budsburg, an elderly widower from Iolo, Wisconsin, next appeared. He was last seen alive at the La Porte Savings Bank on April 6, 1907, when he mortgaged his Wisconsin land there, signing over a deed and obtaining several thousand dollars in cash. His sons, Oscar and Mathew Budsburg, it seems, had no idea that their father had gone off to visit the widow Belle. They finally discovered his destination and wrote to Mrs. Gunness who promptly wrote back, saying she had never seen Mr. Budsburg.

Several other middle-aged men appeared and disappeared in brief visits to the Gunness farm throughout 1907. Then, in

South Dakota farmer Andrew Hegelein, another suitor who answered one of Belle's lovelorn ads, traveled to La Porte and vanished; his body was later found buried on Belle's farm.

Andrew's brother, Asle Hegelein, who grew suspicious of Belle and visited La Porte, all but accusing Belle of murdering his sibling, encouraging the sheriff to investigate.

December 1907, Andrew Hegelein, a bachelor farmer from Aberdeen, South Dakota, wrote to Belle and was warmly received. The pair exchanged many letters, until Belle unleashed her most amorous masterpiece yet, a letter that overwhelmed the simple Hegelein, written in Belle's own careful handwriting and dated January 13, 1908. (This letter was later found at the Hegelein farm in South Dakota.) It read:

> "To the Dearest Friend in the World: No woman in the world is happier than I am. I know that you are now to come to me and be my own. I can tell from your letters that you are the man I want. It does not take one long to tell when to like a person, and you I like better than anyone in the world, I know.
>
> Think how we will enjoy each other's company. You, the sweetest man in the whole world. We will be all alone with each other. Can you conceive of anything nicer? I think of you constantly. When I hear your name mentioned, and this is when one of the dear children speaks of you, or I hear myself humming it with the words of an old love song, it is beautiful music to my ears.
>
> My heart beats in wild rapture for you, My Andrew, I love you. Come prepared to stay forever."

That, of course, is exactly what the hapless Hegelein did. In response to her love-gushing letter, the farmer flew to her side in January 1908. He brought with him a check for $2,900, his savings, which he had drawn from his local bank. A few days after Hegelein arrived, he and Belle appeared at the Savings Bank in La Porte and deposited the check for cashing. Hegelein vanished a few days later, but Belle appeared at the

Joseph Maxon, Belle's second handyman, who barely escaped when the Gunness farmhouse caught fire on April 28, 1908, a blaze set by Belle herself.

The still smoking remains of the gutted Gunness farmhouse, following the devastating fire that took the lives of her children and herself, or a body she may have left in her place.

Officials search the charred remains of the Gunness farmhouse, finding eight men's watches in the cinders; by then they had already decided to thoroughly search the farm for bodies.

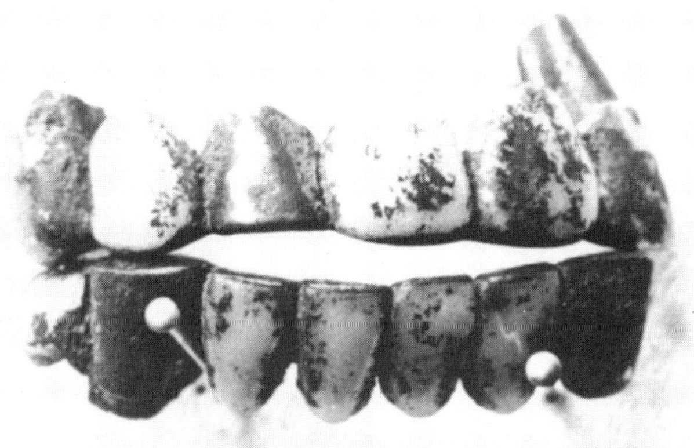

Belle's false teeth, found in the burned out house; most believed she planted them, along with a headless body she hoped would be accepted as her own.

Belle's rings, also conveniently found next to the headless corpse (the head was never found), also thought to be planted by the conniving serial killer.

Police investigators examine a sluice in which hundreds of small human bones were washed to discovery, the remains of more than forty lovesick men murdered by Belle Gunness.

One of the graves in Belle's hog pen that yielded the remains of one of her victims; most of the victims had been butchered like her hogs and were found in pieces.

By Stanley Steamer and horsedrawn carriage, curious residents and spectators from Chicago drove to the Gunness place to examine the dozens of graves discovered on the serial killer's Indiana farm.

Savings Bank to make a $500 deposit and another deposit of $700 in the State Bank.

At this time, Belle started to have trouble with her hired hand, Ray Lamphere. The hired hand was deeply in love with Belle and was an apparent slave to her ambitions, performing any chore for her, no matter how gruesome. He became jealous of the many men, who arrived to pitch woo at his employer and soon Lamphere began making scenes. Belle fired him on February 3, 1908, and then appeared at the La Porte courthouse and declared to authorities that Lamphere was not in his right mind and was a menace to the public.

Belle somehow convinced local authorities to hold a sanity hearing and the grim little Lamphere was examined. He was pronounced sane and sent on his way. Belle was back a few days later to complain to the sheriff that Lamphere had arrived at her farm, despite the fact that she had fired him, and argued with her. She felt that he posed a threat to her family and had Lamphere arrested for trespassing.

The little handyman was persistent. He returned again and again to see Belle, but she drove him away. Lamphere then began to make thinly disguised threats about Belle and, on one occasion, said to farmer William Slater that "Hegelein won't bother me no more. We fixed him for keeps." Hegelein had long since disappeared from the precincts of La Porte, or so it was believed. His brother, Asle Hegelein, however, was disturbed when Andrew failed to return home and he wrote to Belle in Indiana, asking her about his brother's whereabouts.

Belle boldly wrote back, telling Asle Hegelein that his brother was not at her farm and probably went to Norway to visit relatives. Hegelein wrote back saying that he did not believe his brother would do that and, moreover, he believed that his brother was still in the La Porte area, the last place he was seen or heard from. Belle Gunness brazened it out, telling Hegelein that if he wanted to come to La Porte and look for his brother, she would help him conduct a search for the lost brother, but she cautioned Hegelein that searching for missing persons was an expensive proposition, and if she was to be involved in such a manhunt, Asle Hegelein should be prepared to pay her well for her efforts.

Obviously worried about the turn of events, Belle went to a La Porte lawyer, M. E. Leliter, telling him that she feared for her life and that of her children. Ray Lamphere, she said, had threatened to kill her and burn her house down. She wanted to make out a will, in case Lamphere went through with his threats. Leliter complied, drawing up Belle's will. She left her entire estate to her children and then departed Leliter's offices. She went to one of the La Porte banks holding the mortgage for her property and paid this off. Oddly, she did not go to the police to tell them about Lamphere's life-threatening conduct. The reason for this, most later concluded, was that there had been no threats, but that Belle was merely setting the stage for an act of arson that would cover her escape.

Joe Maxon, who had been hired to replace Lamphere in February 1908, awoke on the night of April 28, 1908, smelling smoke in his room, which was on the second floor of the Gunness house. He opened the hall door to a sheet of flames. Maxon screamed Belle's name and those of her children, but got no response. He slammed the door and then, in his underwear, leaped from the second-story window of his room, barely surviving the fire that was closing in about him. He raced to town to get help, but by the time the old-fashioned hook and ladder arrived at the farm at early dawn, the farmhouse was a gutted heap of smoking ruins.

The floors had collapsed and four bodies were found in the cellar. The grand piano, Belle's pride and joy, was on top of the bodies. One of the bodies was that of a woman who could not be identified as Belle since she had no head. The head was never found. Nearby, after much searching, officials found Belle's false teeth. The pathetic little bodies of her children were found next to the corpse. Sheriff Albert H. Smutzer took one look at this carnage and immediately arrested Ray Lamphere, who, he knew, had made threats about Belle. Lawyer Leliter came forward to recount his tale about Belle's will and how she had expressed her fears that Lamphere would kill her and her family, and burn her house down.

Lamphere did not help his cause much. At the moment Sheriff Smutzer confronted him and before a word was uttered by the lawman, Lamphere blurted: "Did Widow Gunness and the kids get out all right?" He was then told about the fire, but he denied having anything to do with it, claiming that he was not near the farm when the blaze occurred. A youth, John Solyem, was brought forward. He said that he had been watching the Gunness place (he gave no reasons for this) and that he saw Lamphere running down the road from the Gunness house just before the structure erupted into flames.

Lamphere snorted to the boy: "You wouldn't look me in the eye and say that!"

"Yes, I will," replied Solyem bravely. "You found me hiding behind the bushes and you told me you'd kill me if I didn't get out of there."

Lamphere was arrested and charged with murder and arson. Then scores of investigators, sheriff's deputies, coroner's men and many volunteers began to search the ruins for evidence. The body of the headless woman was of deep concern to La Porte residents. C. Christofferson, a neighboring farmer, took one look at the charred remains of this body and said that it was not the remains of Belle Gunness. So did another farmer, L. Nicholson, and so did Mrs. Austin Cutler, an old friend of Mrs. Gunness. More of Belle's old friends, Mrs. Nellie Olander and Mrs. Sigurd Olson, arrived from Chicago. They had known Mrs. Gunness for years. They examined the remains of the headless woman and said the corpse was not Belle's.

Doctors then measured the remains, and making allowances for the missing neck and head, stated that the corpse was that of a woman who stood five feet three inches tall and weighed no more than 150 pounds. Belle, according to her friends and neighbors, as well as the La Porte clothiers who made her dresses and other garments, swore that Belle was more than five feet eight inches tall and weighed between 180 and 200 pounds. Physicians then made detailed measurements of the body. These measurements were compared with those on file with several La Porte stores, where Belle

Belle's first and most loyal handyman, Ray Lamphere, right, who helped Belle bury the bodies and burn down her house, claiming later that she escaped the fire and fled with a fortune filched from her lovelorn victims; Lamphere is shown with his attorney, Wirt Worden, left, while on trial for arson and murder.

purchased her apparel. When the two sets of measurements were placed side by side, the authorities reeled back in shock:

	Victim (inches)	Mrs. Gunness (inches)
Biceps	9	17
Bust	36	46
Waist	26	37
Thigh	25	30
Hips	40	54
Calf	22	14
Wrist	6	9

The headless woman, officials concluded, could not have been Belle Gunness, even when the ravages of the fire on the body were taken into account. (The flesh was badly burned but intact.) Moreover, Dr. J. Meyers examined the internal organs of the dead woman. He reported that the woman died of strychnine poisoning. Asle Hegelein then arrived in La Porte and told Sheriff Smutzer that he believed that his brother had met with foul play at Mrs. Gunness' hands. Smutzer seemed disinterested in searching the blackened grounds of the Gunness farm once again, but Hegelein persisted.

Then Joe Maxon came forward to tell the sheriff that Mrs. Gunness had had him bring loads of dirt by wheelbarrow to a large area surrounded by a high wire fence, where the hogs were fed. Maxon stated that there were many deep depressions in the ground that had been covered by dirt. These filled-in holes, Belle had told Maxon, contained rubbish. She wanted the ground made level, so Maxon filled in the depressions.

Smutzer took a dozen men back to the farm and began to dig. On May 3, 1908, the diggers unearthed the body of Jennie Olson. Then they found two more small bodies, that of unidentified children. Then the body of Andrew Hegelein was unearthed. As the days progressed and the gruesome work continued, one body after another was discovered in Belle's hog pen: Ole B. Budsburg; Thomas Lindboe of Chicago, who had left Chicago and had gone to work as a hired man for Belle three years earlier; Henry Gurholdt of Scandinavia, Wisconsin, who had gone to wed Belle a year earlier, taking $1,500 to her; Olaf Svenherud, from Chicago; John Moo (or Moe) of Elbow Lake, Minnesota; Olaf Lindbloom from Iowa. There were many others who could not be identified. In fact, the remains of more than forty men and children buried in shallow graves throughout Belle's property were found.

Ray Lamphere was arrested and tried for murder and arson on May 22, 1908. He pleaded guilty to arson, but denied murdering Belle and her children. He was sentenced to twenty years in prison. The little handyman grew ill in prison and died of consumption on December 30, 1909. On January 14,

The MRS GUINNESS MYSTERY
A THRILLING TALE OF LOVE, DUPLICITY & CRIME

1910, the Rev. E.A. Schell came forward with a confession that Lamphere had made to him while the clergyman was comforting the dying man. In it, Lamphere revealed the true nature of Belle Gunness, a human monster who killed for profit and who survived her own reported death.

Lamphere had stated to the Rev. Schell and to a fellow convict, Harry Meyers, before his death, that he had not murdered anyone, but that he had helped Belle bury many of her victims. She had her lethal system down to precise procedures, Lamphere said. When a victim arrived, Belle made him comfortable, charming him and cooking a large meal for him. She then drugged his coffee and when the man was in a stupor, she split his head with a meat chopper. Sometimes she would simply wait for the suitor to go to bed and then enter the bedroom by candlelight and chloroform her sleeping victim. A powerful woman, Belle would then carry the body to the basement, place it on a table, and dissect the body. She then bundled the remains and buried these in the hog pen and the grounds about the house.

Belle had become an expert at dissection, thanks to instruction she had received from her second husband, the butcher Peter Gunness. To save time, she sometimes poisoned her victims' coffee with strychnine. She also varied her disposal methods, sometimes dumping the corpse into the hog-scalding vat and covering the remains with quicklime. Lamphere even stated that if Belle was overly tired after murdering one of her victims, she merely chopped up the remains and, in the middle of the night, stepped into her hog pen and fed the human flesh to the hogs.

The handyman also cleared up the question of the headless female corpse found in the smoking ruins of Belle's home. This woman had been lured from Chicago by Belle to serve her as a housekeeper only days before Belle decided to make her permanent escape from La Porte. Belle, according to Lamphere, had drugged the woman, then bashed in her head and decapitated the body, taking the head, which had weights tied to it, to a swamp where she threw it into deep water. Then she chloroformed her own children, smothered them to death, and dragged these bodies, along with the headless corpse, to the basement.

She dressed the female corpse in her old clothing, and removed her false teeth, placing these beside the headless corpse to convince investigators that the corpse was indeed Belle Gunness. She then torched the house and fled. Lamphere had helped her, he admitted, but Belle had not left by the road, where he waited for her after the fire began. She had betrayed him in the end by cutting across open fields and then disappearing into the woods. He had suspected this betrayal and drove back up the road to see by moonlight the heavyset woman hurriedly making her way across an open field and disappearing into a forest.

Lamphere insisted that Belle was a rich woman, that she had murdered forty-two men by his count, perhaps more, and had taken amounts from them ranging from $1,000 to $32,000. She had accumulated more than $250,000 through her lovelorn murder schemes over the years, a great fortune for those days. She had also left a small amount in one of her savings accounts, but local banks later admitted that Belle had withdrawn most of her funds shortly before the fire.

Belle Gunness was, for several decades, seen or sighted throughout the U.S. Friends had spotted her on the streets of Chicago, San Francisco, New York, and Los Angeles. As late as 1931, Belle was reported alive and living in a Mississippi town where she owned a great deal of property and lived the life of an aging southern belle, entertaining elderly men of property. Sheriff Smutzer, for more than twenty years, received an average of two reports a month, these reports claiming that Belle had been seen in one distant city or another. She became part of U.S. criminal folklore, a female Bluebeard, who to this day, dominates the dark legends of northern Indiana. A bit of doggerel later emerged which captured the character of the horrific Belle Gunness:

Belle Gunness lived in In-di-an;
She always, always had a man;
Ten, at least, went in her door
And were never, never seen no more.
Now, all these men were Norska folk
Who came to Belle from Minn-e-sote;
They liked their coffee and their gin:
They got it, plus a mickey finn.
And now with cleaver poised so sure
Belle neatly cut their jug-u-lar
She put them in a bath of lime,
And left them there for quite some time.
There's red upon the Hoosier moon
For Belle was strong and full of doom;
And think of all them Norska men
Who'll never see St. Paul again.

Page left: A penny dreadful mystery glamorized Belle Gunness on this cover, showing a woman much more beautiful than the portly Belle, as she approaches a sleeping suitor with chloroform in hand and murder in her heart.

A FRENCH SERIAL POISONER/1910s

After being cashiered out of the French Hussars in 1897, Henri Girard (1875-1921), a petty swindler and amateur scientist, eventually turned to murder for profit. But even the many financial swindles he perpetrated between 1897 and 1910 did not provide him with a comfortable lifestyle, nor did they keep him out of the clutches of the law. In 1909, Girard's bogus insurance company, Credit General de France, was fined 1,000 francs for deceptive practices. However, in the process he met Louis Pernotte, who seemed willing to go along with Girard's schemes.

Pernotte, an insurance broker, gave Girard power of attorney. Then Girard insured Pernotte's life for 316,000 francs, which evidently didn't strike Pernotte as unusual. Meanwhile, Girard began to experiment with poison in his Paris laboratory. He realized that it was nearly impossible to come up with an untraceable poison, so he prepared a typhoid germ culture, which he planned to test on Pernotte. In August 1912, Girard poured a vial of deadly bacilli into a pitcher of water on Pernotte's dining table. Shortly afterward, the Pernotte family left for Royan, where they became ill.

Dr. Henri Girard, who poisoned his victims with deadly germs.

They returned to Paris, but Pernotte did not recover. Shortly before Pernotte's death on December 1, 1912, Girard had administered an injection of camphorated chamomile. "Notice, madame," he said to Mrs. Pernotte, "that it is quite definitely your own syringe. You observe that I have nothing in my hands." It was a curious remark, but was quickly forgotten, when Pernotte expired from what the family doctor diagnosed as an embolism resulting from typhus. Upon Pernotte's death, Girard informed the widow that her husband had owed him 200,000 francs.

Pleased with the results of this first "experiment," Girard insured the life of Mimiche Duroux and then fed him the poisonous germs. For the next three days, Girard wrote in a journal detailing the progress of the disease. However, Duroux was strong and healthy, and he did not die. Girard had to select another victim, with the help of one of his many mistresses, Jeanne Droubin. Together they chose a widow named Madame Monin, and then took out a policy on her life with the Phenix Insurance Company. Fifteen minutes after ingesting one of Girard's mushrooms in the Metro station, Madame Monin died.

The insurance company did not pay off on Monin's insurance policy, but, instead, began an investigation, which culminated in Girard's arrest on August 21, 1918. He was taken to the Fresnes Prison, where he told the guards, "Yes, I have always been unhappy, no one has ever tried to understand me. I will always be misunderstood, abnormal, as I have been called, and for all that I am good, with a very warm heart." Before the case could go to trial, this serial poisoner swallowed a germ culture and died in his cell in May 1921.

HUNGARIAN SERIAL KILLERS/1910s-1920s

Belle Gunness had a male counterpart in Hungary, who began employing her modus operandi only six years after the enigmatic Belle vanished from La Porte, Indiana. This was a hulking, heavily mustached farmer named Bela Kiss (b. 1872), who lived at Czinkota, a suburb of Budapest, Hungary. Little is known of Kiss, a reclusive type, except that his 25-year-old wife, Maria, was having an affair with a local swain, Paul Bihari. Kiss was at that time living under the alias of Hoffmann.

At this time, in February 1912, when war loomed in Europe, Kiss suddenly ordered several large metal drums in which he said he would store gas, a commodity he said would soon be in short supply when war occurred. A short time after Kiss received the huge containers, his wife Maria and her lover Bihari vanished. Kiss explained to inquiring officials that his "worthless" wife and Bihari had run off together and the matter was dropped.

As the months passed, Mrs. Anna Kalman, who was Kiss' housekeeper, noted with some alarm that her employer began to entertain a number of women, a stream of female visitors who arrived, but seemed not to leave the premises. At the same time, more and more huge gas drums also arrived, these containers carefully placed by Kiss in a storage area. Kiss explained that he was preparing for "the war effort," in purchasing these drums.

Budapest police then began to investigate the disappearances of two widows named Schmeidak and Varga, who were last seen visiting Kiss. Their whereabouts, however, were not determined until much later. Kiss, meanwhile, continued buying more gas drums. His "war effort" came to a halt in November 1914, when he was drafted into the Hungarian army and sent to the front in Serbia. Two years later, in May 1916, authorities received a report from the military that Kiss had died in an army hospital in Belgrade.

Officials recalling Kiss' remarks about the gas drums stored at his house then went to the home to closer inspect these containers. Seven drums were found, each containing the body of a woman. All had been garroted. Inspectors uncovered considerable correspondence produced by Kiss, learning that he had lured the victims to his home through newspaper advertisements, offering marriage. He had signed his missives to these hapless women as "Professor Hoffmann." Those who visited Hoffmann/Kiss, were simply murdered for the jewels and cash they carried with them.

A thorough search of the countryside near Kiss' home unearthed seventeen more gas drums stuffed with corpses. Inside of two of these containers, police found the bodies of Kiss' errant wife, Maria, and her lover, Bihari. Believing that the serial killer had died in Belgrade, police simply buried the bodies and closed the case. In 1919, however, officials received a report that Kiss was very much alive, that he had switched tags with a fallen comrade on the battlefield and had assumed a new identity.

Hungarian police conducted a decade-long search for Kiss, sending information about him to every major police department in the world, but without results. The serial killer was reported as being seen in many cities, but he always eluded police. He was last seen in New York in 1932. A man fitting Kiss' description was seen exiting the Times Square subway station by Detective Henry Oswald of the Homicide Squad. Oswald followed the suspect, he later stated, but lost him in the crowd.

While Kiss used the war in Hungary as a way to disguise his murders, the conflict oddly brought about a number of other serial killings. Unlike Kiss' murder-for-profit motive, these new murders were prompted by passion. The women of Nagyrev, Hungary, an isolated village southeast of Budapest, while their husbands were away during World War I, took lovers from among the prisoners of war in nearby camps. After several years of such promiscuity, the war ended and the husbands returned. But domesticity no longer satisfied the women of Nagyrev, and with the help of local midwife Suzanne Fazekas (d. 1929), they began poisoning their unwanted spouses.

The only known photo of Hungarian serial killer Bela Kiss, who vanished after murdering numerous women outside of Budapest before World War I.

Once the murders had begun, anyone considered inconvenient was in danger. Fazekas sold arsenic to the women, which she obtained by boiling the flypaper she purchased in bulk. Officials later learned that, for several years, Nagyrev and a neighboring village bought more flypaper than the rest of Hungary combined.

The first murder occurred as early as 1911, the beginning of a spree that lasted nearly twenty years and involved perhaps fifty women. Returning husbands, relatives who owned land, mothers-in-law, even recalcitrant children, were not exempt from Fazekas' poison. Added to the ease of perpetration was the fact that the official who approved death certificates was Fazekas' cousin, so when outsiders noted the region's high death rate, a routine check of the death certificates showed nothing amiss.

Further, the village of Nagyrev and its neighbor, Tiszakurt, were so isolated that no one paid much attention to the alarming number of premature deaths until 1929, when two potential victims of Mrs. Ladislaus Szabo claimed that she had tried to poison them. After Szabo was arrested, she implicated another woman, Mrs. Bukenoveski, who confessed to having obtained arsenic from Fazekas five years earlier to kill her mother. The mother's body was exhumed and arsenic was found in the corpse.

Fazekas was arrested, held only briefly when she refused to talk, and then released, free to run from house to house in Nagyrev, letting the women know what was happening, and telling the police whom to arrest. When officers once more approached Fazekas, she politely invited them into her house, and there promptly drank her own poison and died before their eyes. Thirty-eight women were arrested, chief among them Susanna Olah, the "White Witch of Nagyrev," who also sold arsenic and was believed to possess the power to protect the murdering women from the law.

Suzanne Fazekas, who, with other women in her Hungarian town, poisoned unwanted husbands by the droves.

Each accused woman offered reasons for their murders: Rosalie Sebestyen's husband bored her; Maria Szendi was tired of her husband always having "his own way"; Maria Varga could no longer put up with her husband, who had returned from the war blind. Varga preferred her young lover, but after five years disposed of him, too, along with his grandfather; Mrs. Kardos had an invalid son who was a burden to her—she found it easy to kill him because she had already eliminated a lover and her husband.

Juliane Lipka was an exception. She killed not for love, but for real estate. Within eight years she had disposed of seven relatives, gradually becoming the richest woman in the region. Eventually, twenty-six women were tried for murder. Eight were sentenced to death and seven to life in prison. The rest received varying prison terms. Three of the women committed suicide. The bodies of those hanged were displayed as a warning to others.

LANDRU, THE FRENCH BLUEBEARD/ 1914-1919

Henri Desire Landru (AKA: Bluebeard, M. Diard, Georges Petit, M. Dupont, M. Cuchet, Lucien Guillet, M. Fremyet, M. Forest; 1869-1922) was a lady killer whose repetitious slayings, except for the manner of disposal, were uninspired and must have been wearisome for him, if, indeed, he slew the more than 300 women estimated by French police. The number of his victims positively known was ten women and a boy, but in all probability, this systematic serial killer murdered twenty to thirty people, almost all women.

Landru, like Belle Gunness and Bela Kiss, his American and Hungarian counterparts, preyed upon the lovelorn, middle-aged people seeking comfort and loving care. Those women with means who answered Landru's enticing ads were charmed by the serial killer and readily succumbed to his magnetism and animal craving for sex, little realizing that this passionate, thickly-bearded, bald-headed lothario was planning their deaths.

Little in Landru's childhood and early life foretold the

Lady killer Henri Landru with his first victim, Mme. Izoré, in 1914.

Mme. Cuchet, murdered by Landru.

Landru's villa at Gambais, where he murdered many of his victims, although he was clever enough to destroy the corpses.

monster to come. The Paris-born Landru was educated at Ecole des Ferres and received good grades. He went on to study at the School of Mechanical Engineering and was then conscripted into the army, serving four years and reaching the rank of sergeant. In 1893, while still in the service, Landru began an affair with his cousin, Mlle. Remy. When she became pregnant with his child, Landru married the attractive young girl. Upon returning to civilian life in 1894, he obtained a job where he had to provide a deposit against goods he was to sell. He never got the goods and his employer decamped to the U. S., taking Landru's deposit with him. This so embittered (or inspired) the 24-year-old Landru that he decided to turn crook himself. He opened a second-hand furniture store in Paris, but concentrated on swindling schemes.

Landru was not an effective confidence man. He was arrested four times between 1900 and 1908, receiving prison terms that ranged between two years and eighteen months, all for various frauds. Shortly before the outbreak of World War I in 1914, Landru, using many aliases, began placing advertisements in newspapers, addressing these ads to lonely women reading the lovelorn columns. Though he remained married and had by then fathered three more children, Landru, unknown to his wife, advertised himself as a well-to-do bachelor looking for "proper" female companionship.

Landru maintained a separate address for the assignations that resulted in this lovelorn scheme. He apparently enticed the women answering his ads to his bachelor's residence and, after promising marriage and obtaining their money from small savings accounts or deeds to parcels of land or buildings, he murdered them and disposed of their bodies. The first such victim was 40-year-old Mme. Izoré, who vanished into Landru's arms in 1914, along with her dowry of 15,000 francs.

By this time police were looking for Landru, who was suspected of swindling an elderly couple out of their savings. Landru had disappeared, however, and with the coming of a disruptive war that confused and jumbled normal police procedures, he was easily able to assume other identities. What

Mme. Laborde-Line, murdered by Landru.

Mme. Guillin, murdered by Landru.

Mme. Héon, murdered by Landru.

launched Landru into a career of murdering for profit is uncertain.

The war, with its awful devastation and utter unconcern for human life, may have altered his otherwise reasonable perspectives. It was also suggested that he turned to this most atrocious form of making a living since his family ties had been severed by the deaths of his mother and father. It is also safe to assume that Landru, having failed miserably at lesser illicit schemes to make a dishonest franc, felt that he had nothing to lose in his lovelorn murder schemes.

In late 1914, Mme. Cuchet, a 39-year-old widow with a 16-year-old son, answered one of Landru's ads, thinking him to be M. Diard, a successful engineer. Falling in love with Landru, the woman informed her family that she intended to marry him and asked that her parents, sister, and brother-in-law visit the man of her dreams at a villa he kept in Chantilly. The family, unannounced, went to the villa, but found Landru absent.

The inquisitive brother-in-law looked through a chest and found it crammed with love letters from other women, who had been answering his dozens of lovelorn ads. The brother-in-law denounced Landru to Mme. Cuchet, but the woman would hear no criticism of him and she and her teenage son moved away from her family to a small villa in Vernouillet where Landru joined her. The woman and boy vanished a short time later, in January 1915, as did Diard-Landru.

Opening up new bank accounts, Landru deposited about 10,000 francs, claiming he had received an inheritance from his father. The bankers, had they checked, would have realized how unlikely this story was since Landru's father was a common laborer, who had worked in the Vulcain Ironworks and had barely eked out a living wage.

In June 1915, Landru met through his ads Mme. Laborde-Line, a widow from Buenos Aires, who moved out of her Paris apartment, telling the concierge that she was going to live in a villa at Vernouillet with a "wonderful man." She was seen picking flowers in Vernouillet on June 26, 1915, and was never seen again. Landru later sold her securities and moved Mme. Laborde-Line's furniture to a ramshackle garage he kept at Neuilly, which he called his used furniture store. From here he sold off his latest victim's household goods one by one.

Mme. Guillin, a 51-year-old widow who had just converted some insurance policies to 22,000 francs, answered one of Landru's ads on May 1, 1915, later visiting Landru at his villa in Vernouillet and then moving there to ostensibly become Landru's bride on August 2, 1915. She too vanished and on August 4, Landru moved all the furniture from the Vernouillet villa to his Neuilly garage and later cashed some of Mme. Guillin's securities.

Late in 1915, Landru, using the alias Georges Petit, forged Mme. Guillin's signature to certain bank documents in order to withdraw 12,000 francs from her account in the Banque de France. When questioned about his actions at the bank, Landru coolly explained that he was Mme. Guillin's brother-in-law and that she could no longer conduct her own business affairs since she had suffered a stroke that left her paralyzed.

Apparently, after having murdered Cuchet, Laborde-Line, and Guillin—juggling his time tables closely in the cases of the last two victims—Landru felt it was too dangerous to keep his villa at Vernouillet. He moved to the village of Gambais renting the Villa Ermitage from M. Trio in December 1915. He said his name was Dupont and that he was an engineer from Rouen. This was to be his murder headquarters for several years to come.

A few weeks later, Landru enticed 55-year-old Mme. Héon to the Gambais villa. She was a widow whose son had been killed in the war and whose daughter had just died. Landru consoled her and promised marriage. She went to Gambais with him; after December 8, 1915, Mme. Héon was seen no more. About this time, Landru's neighbors began to notice

Mme. Collomb, murdered by Landru.

Mme. Babelay, murdered by Landru.

Mme. Buisson, murdered by Landru.

that the chimney at his villa belched black smoke at odd hours. He had purchased a new stove when he occupied the villa. This stove would be one of the chief exhibits at Landru's murder trial years later.

A short time later, Landru again inserted one of his lovelorn ads in the Paris newspapers. It read:

Widower with two children, aged forty-three, with comfortable income, affectionate, serious and moving in good society, desires to meet widow with a view to matrimony.

This ad was answered by yet another widow, 45-year-old Mme. Collomb, a typist who was living with a man named Bernard who had refused to marry her. Mme. Collomb had saved more than 10,000 francs, a tidy sum Landru covetously eyed. But before this lovesick woman succumbed to Landru's persuasive ways, she insisted that he meet her family. He stalled, but then reluctantly agreed to meet the woman's relatives. Landru at the time was using the alias of one of his victims, Cuchet. None of Mme. Collomb's relatives liked Landru and her sister, especially, found him odious and offensive. Mme. Collomb nevertheless went off with Landru to his Gambais villa and, after December 24, 1916, was seen no more.

On March 11, 1917, Landru's youngest victim, Andrée Babelay, went to see her mother. The 19-year-old girl, who had lived in poverty all her life, told her mother that she had met a wonderful man in the Metro and that she intended to become his bride. Babelay accompanied Landru, who bought two tickets to Gambais and a single ticket returning to Paris. Andrée Babelay was last seen alive on April 12, 1917.

Landru's next victim was Mme. Buisson, who had been corresponding with Landru for more than two years. She was a 47-year-old widow with a nest egg of 10,000 francs. After announcing to her relatives her plans to wed Landru, she disappeared sometime after August 9, 1917. Her killer appeared in her Paris apartment with a forged note from Mme. Buisson, which demanded her furniture. This was taken to Landru's second-hand furniture store, the Neuilly garage.

Mme. Jaume was the serial killer's next victim. She had separated from her husband and gone to a marital agent who introduced her to Landru. Using the name Guillet, Landru soon took Mme. Jaume off to Gambais and her doom. She was last seen leaving her house in Rue de Lyanes with Landru on November 25, 1917. Landru appeared in Paris a few days later and withdrew Mme. Jaume's savings, 1,400 francs, from the Banque Allaume through forged documents. Mme. Pascal was next, a 36-year-old Landru had been seeing on and off since 1916. She had little money, but, like the young Babelay, she met his strong and almost incessant need for sex. Landru, using the alias of Forest, kept Mme. Pascal in a Paris apartment until he tired of her. He then took her to the Gambais villa on April 5, 1917, where she, like her predecessors, went up in smoke.

In 1918, Mme. Marchadier began corresponding with Landru, who was then using the alias of Guillet. Mme. Marchadier owned a large house on Rue St. Jacques, but she had little money. Landru promised to buy her house from her, but had little cash himself. He proposed marriage and, on January 9, 1919, Mme. Marchadier left with Landru to go to the villa at Gambais. She brought along her two small dogs and both she and the dogs were seen no more after a few days. Landru later appeared in Paris, selling off Mme. Marchadier's house and belongings.

Landru's many victims left considerable relatives searching for vanished women. This proved to be Landru's undoing. On April 11, 1919, Mme. Lacoste, the sister of Mme. Buisson, one of Landru's early victims, spotted Landru strolling down the Rue de Rivoli with a young, attractive woman on his arm. She followed Landru to a china shop where she pretended to examine items while overhearing Landru ordering some china and giving the name of Lucien Guillet and an address for the delivery of the china. Mme. Lacoste then went to police with this information and detectives returned to the shop and obtained Landru's address on the Rue de Rochechouart. Here, on April 12, 1919, officers found Landru living under the alias of Guillet with a 27-year-old clerk, Fernande Segret, who was planning to go off with

Mme. Jaume, murdered by Landru.

Mme. Pascal, murdered by Landru.

Mme. Marchadier, murdered.

Landru to his villa in Gambais. The intervention of the police undoubtedly saved her life.

In one of Landru's pockets, detectives found a black loose-leaf notebook, which contained cryptic remarks about many of the women he had taken to Gambais. Landru was arrested and charged with murdering Mme. Buisson. He was then taken to the villa in Gambais, where the gardens were dug up and the villa torn apart. Only the bodies of three dogs were found buried in the garden. The clothes and personal effects of all of Landru's known victims and those belonging to many more unknown women were found in the villa at Gambais, but the bodies of his victims were nowhere to be found. Landru was indignant at his arrest and challenged the police, as he later did the court, to "produce your bodies." He admitted to nothing and proved utterly uncooperative.

The stove in the villa was loaded with ashes and tiny bone fragments were found inside of it. The stove was removed to a Versailles court where, between November 7-30, 1921, Henri Desire Landru was tried for murder. Police had found the voluminous correspondence Landru had maintained with 283 women and almost none of them could be located. Authorities were convinced that Landru murdered them all, but busy as he was in the murder-for-profit business, it would have been humanly impossible for him to have juggled that many romances and effected that many murders from 1914 to 1919, the known period of his killings. The press, of course, made much of this arrogant, strutting serial killer, aptly dubbing him "Bluebeard," a name that had once been attached with terror to France's all-time serial killer, Gilles de Rais.

The press obtained a copy of Landru's notes, wherein he had systematically classified all those writing to him in response to his lovelorn advertisements. He had labeled each group of marital applicants:

1. To be answered *poste restante.*
2. Without money.
3. Without furniture.
4. No reply.
5. To be answered to initials *poste restante.*
6. Possible fortune.
7. In reserve. For further investigation.

It was believed that Landru drugged his victims into insensibility, then suffocated or strangled them. He then spent hours, even days, chopping the bodies into tiny pieces and exhaustively burning the remains, meticulously taking care not to leave any traceable remains. Landru's defense attorney was the brilliant Maitre Moro Giaffery, who found that his client agitated the court and defied the prosecution to convict him without the presence of bodies. Landru claimed that the whereabouts of his female friends was *his* business, and that these women had been his clients, and he had been in the furniture business with them at one time or another.

The court was filled with bulky exhibits during Landru's lengthy and volatile trial. In addition to the stove, which sat ominously before the bench, a great deal of furniture was piled up in the courtroom, all items which Landru had filched from his victims. Meanwhile, Landru became a dark *cause celebre.* Cartoons portrayed him in the newspapers and ribald songs about him and his lady killings were sung in Paris music halls. Reporters from around the world came to sit in court each day and write thousands of pages about the bald, bearded killer in the dock.

Moro Giaffery worked hard to develop a line of defense. The best he could offer was that his client was no murderer but a white slaver, who had abducted the women in question and had shipped them to brothels in South America. The prosecution destroyed this theory with ridicule. Roared Prosecu-

Henri Landru proved to be difficult in court, arrogantly posturing his self-styled expertise in criminal law; charged with murder, he shouted to prosecutors: "Produce your bodies!"

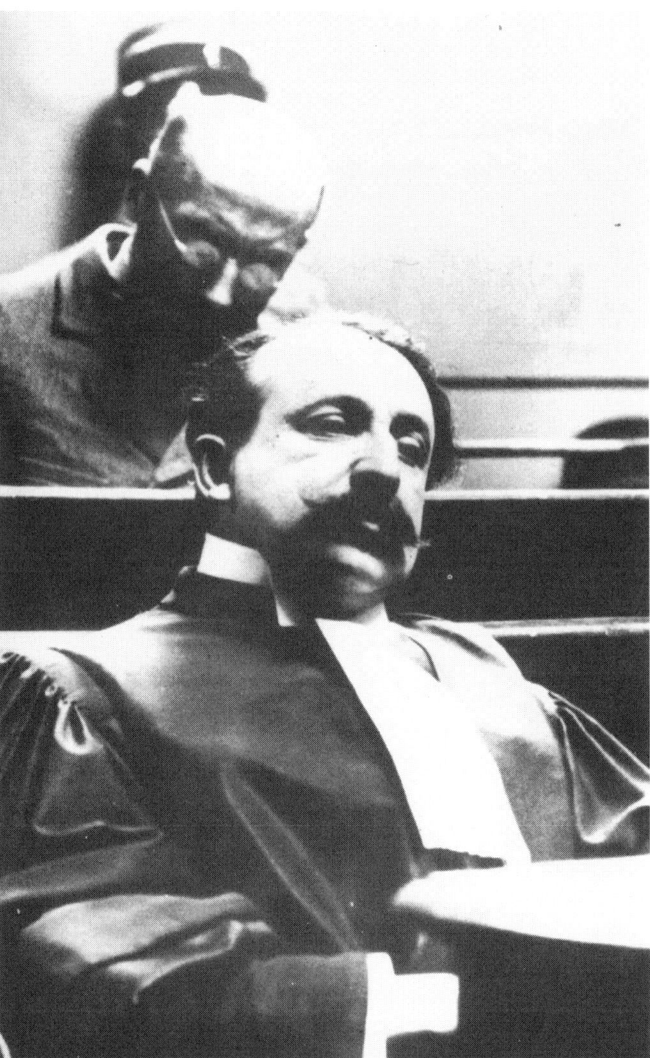

The brilliant criminal attorney, Maitre Moro Giaffery (his client is shown taking notes behind him); Landru was difficult to defend and was found guilty and sentenced to death.

tor Robert Godefroy in derision: "What? Women who were all over fifty years of age? Women whose false hair, false teeth, false bosoms, as well as identity papers, you, Landru, have kept and we captured?"

"Produce your corpses!" shouted Landru, his usual refrain. He occasionally found time for jest. At one point, the presiding judge asked Landru if he were not an habitual liar. Replied Landru: "I am not a lawyer, monsieur." He was brazen and bold to the point of shocking the court. When his notebooks with their incriminating but cryptic data were presented to him, Landru merely shrugged and then sneered that he was not obligated to interpret his codes for the court. He mockingly added: "Perhaps the police would have preferred to find on page one an entry in these words: `I, the undersigned, confess that I have murdered the women whose names are set out herein.'"

It was then pointed out to Landru that his neighbors at Gambais had often complained about the putrid smell emanating from the smoke belching from the chimney of his villa. Landru ran a bony hand over his bald head, jerked his head upward and laughed menacingly, saying: "Is every smoking chimney and every bad smell proof that a body is being burned?"

The evidence that the prosecution did produce was enough to convince a jury of Landru's guilt. He was convicted and sentenced to death. At that time, he smiled and bowed to the courtroom, which was packed with female spectators anxious to examine this strange little man. All were fascinated with the secret powers and persuasion he held over his female victims. Knowing this, Landru said, before leaving court for the last time: "I wonder if there is any lady present who would care to take my seat?"

France's modern Bluebeard was arrogant to the end. On February 25, 1922, a priest entered his cell to give him religious comfort on this, the last day of his life. He asked the serial killer if he wished to make a last confession. Landru waved him away and then pointed to the guards who had come to escort him to the waiting guillotine. "I am very sorry," he said, "but I must not keep these gentlemen waiting."

Landru left his cell to steadily walk between his guards

Landru (in white shirt, center) is led to the guillotine, where he was beheaded on February 25, 1922; he refused to confess, stoically taking his secrets with him to the grave.

into the courtyard of the Versailles prison and up the stairs of the scaffold. His hands were tied behind his back, his legs were tied together, and his shirt was ripped off. Landru was then placed upon a plank and his head was placed upon the block. In seconds the blade of the guillotine descended with terrifying suddenness, decapitating him.

"I WILL EXECUTE SOME MORE OF YOU!"/ 1910s-1920s

Carl Panzram (AKA: Jeff Rhodes, John O'Leary; 1891-1930) was devoid of all normal human emotions, save one: an obsessive hatred for the human race that bordered on the maniacal. This dislike for himself and his fellow man was manifested in a lifetime of murder and mayhem. "I have no desire to reform myself," he said in his published autobiography. "My only desire is to reform people who try to reform me. And I believe that the only way to reform people is to kill them."

Panzram was the son of immigrant Prussian farmers. He was born on a farm near Warren, Minnesota. His father deserted the family when Panzram was only a boy, leaving a heavy burden on his over-taxed mother, who had precious little time to give her children. Without a nurturing family environment, Panzram fell into bad ways. In 1899 he was brought before the juvenile court on a drunk and disorderly charge. He was only eight. This led to acts of petty thievery, which convinced a judge to send him to the Minnesota State Training School in Red Wing.

The discipline at this school was rigid, if not sadistic. Panzram toiled in workshops from dawn to dusk and spent much of his time washing dishes. On the night of July 7, 1905, he set fire to the school warehouse which housed winter blankets and clothing. "That night the whole place burned down at a cost of over $100,000," Panzram later gloated in his chilling memoirs. "Nice eh?"

Released in January 1906, Panzram was launched on his criminal career. On March 29, 1906, he hitched a ride on a west bound freight train at East Grand Forks, North Dakota. He committed a string of robberies and assaults before winding up in the Montana State Reformatory. But as future events later showed, there were few jails that could hold this hardened felon. With fellow inmate James Benson, Panzram escaped.

In the next few months he robbed and burned down several Montana churches. He joined the army in Helena, Montana, but was court-martialed on April 20, 1907, for insubordi-

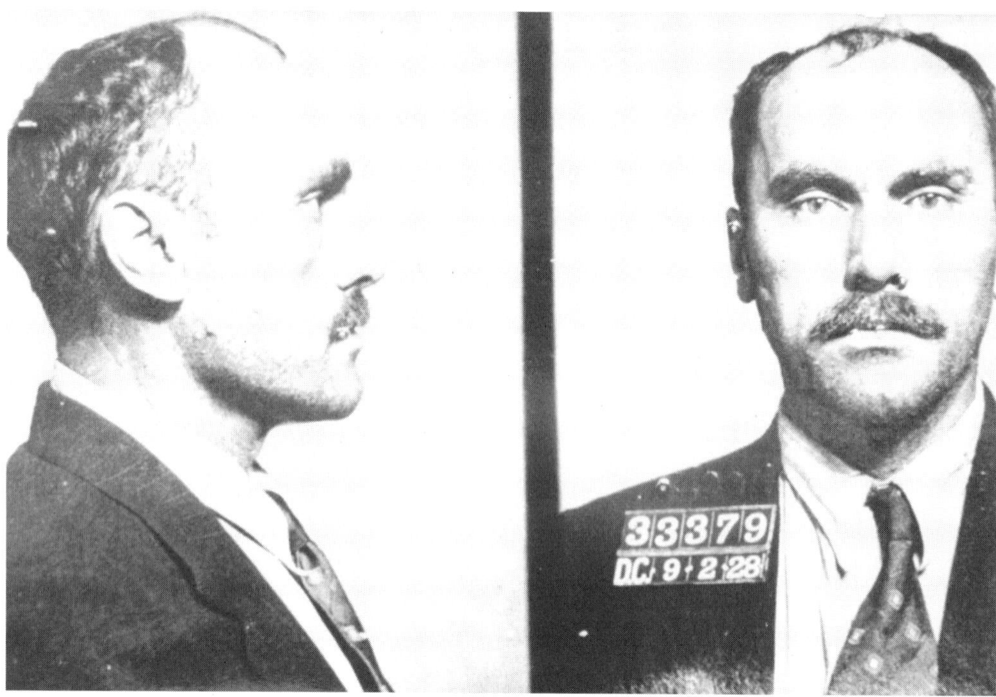

Police photos of serial killer Carl Panzram, who, by his own brutal admission, committed countless arsons and robberies, and boasted of murdering dozens of boys and men over a twenty-year period.

nation and sentenced to three years in Fort Leavenworth for pilfering government property. He spent the next thirty-seven months breaking rocks under the blazing Kansas sun, an experience that fine-tuned his razor-sharp meanness.

After receiving a discharge in 1910, Panzram went to Mexico to briefly join and fight with the rebel leader, Pascaul Orozco, who served under Venustiano Carranza. Moving on to California and the Pacific Northwest, Panzram committed various robberies, assaults, and acts of sodomy. Looking back on his career he would brag: "I have murdered twenty-one human beings. I have committed thousands of burglaries, robberies, larcenies, arson, and last but not least I have committed sodomy on more than 1,000 male human beings."

Panzram was arrested in Chinook, Montana, on a burglary charge and sentenced to a year in the Montana State Prison. He escaped eight months later. He was arrested a year later under the alias of "Jeff Rhodes." He was given a two year sentence in the Montana State Prison on burglary charges, receiving his parole in 1914. Panzram barely had time to enjoy his freedom. In Astoria, Oregon, he was arrested on a burglary charge and imprisoned in the state prison at Salem for seven years. An additional seven years was added to his sentence for attempting to lead a prison insurrection.

For this he was fed a diet of bread and water, and was beaten and sprayed with a fire hose. Panzram constructed his own tools and hacked his way to freedom in May 1918. He was next seen on the east coast, where he robbed a hotel in Frederick, Maryland of $1,200. Continuing on to New York, Panzram joined the Marine Firemen's, Oiler's, and Water Tender's Union. He signed on board the *James Whitney*, a merchant vessel bound for South America, but jumped ship in Peru in order to work in a copper mine.

From there, Panzram traveled to Chile, where he worked as a foreman for the Sinclair Oil Company. In Bocas del Toro, Panama, Panzram senselessly set fire to an oil rig. A $500 reward was posted, but Panzram eluded capture and slipped back undetected into the U.S. In 1920, he broke into a jewelry store in Bridgeport, Connecticut, making off with $7,000. Later that summer, he removed $40,000 in jewels and liberty bonds from the private residence of former president William Howard Taft in New Haven.

With this large windfall, Panzram purchased a deluxe yacht under the name of "John O'Leary." He hired ten sailors to refit the boat. After their task had been completed, Panzram invited them to spend the night in the cabin. "When they were asleep I would get my .45 Colt Army Automatic and blow their brains out," he said. The weighted bodies were taken to the middle of the harbor and dropped into the water.

Panzram was later arrested in Bridgeport on a burglary charge. He served his six months in the local jail without incident before heading on to Philadelphia, where he was imprisoned for inciting a riot during a labor dispute. After posting bond he fled the country and sailed to Europe on a tramp steamer. Afterward, he continued on to Africa. In Portuguese West Africa, Panzram got himself a job with the Sinclair Oil Company. By his own admission, he murdered a 12-year-old boy. "First I committed sodomy on him and then I killed him," he said. At Lobito Bay, Panzram committed yet another atrocity. Deciding that crocodile hunting might pose a challenge, he hired six black porters to guide him through the murky backwater. For "sport," he shot the six men in the back and tossed them to the crocodiles.

Returning to the U.S. in 1922, Panzram assaulted a 12-year-old boy in Salem, Massachusetts, Henry McMahon, killing him with a rock. "...I tried a little sodomy on him first...I left him laying there with his brains coming out of his ears." In June 1923, while working as a night watchman for the New Haven Yacht Club, Panzram stole a boat and then murdered a would-be robber, who climbed aboard in the middle of the night.

The body was tossed into the bay at Kingston, New York. Later, this one-man crime wave was arrested for attempted robbery and sentenced to five years in Sing Sing. But the

Mexican revolutionary Pascual Orozco, under whom Panzram served in the 1910 Mexican Revolution; Orozco was a savage killer, who executed thousands of captured soldiers and this bloodletting developed Panzram's desire to murder.

guards at this facility were unable to keep him in line. He was transferred to Clinton Prison in Dannemora, considered to be the end of the line for criminal hard cases.

Released in 1928, Panzram hit the Baltimore-Washington, D.C., area like a tornado, committing eleven burglaries and one murder. He was arrested by capitol police on August 16, 1928. While in jail Panzram wrote his autobiography and gave it to a sympathetic jailer, Henry Lesser. At his trial, Panzram glared at the jurors, chiding them with a deadly threat. "If I live, I'll execute some more of you!" Judge Walter McCoy sentenced the defendant to twenty-five years in Leavenworth. "Visit me!" Panzram shouted to the judge.

To the deputy warden, Fred Zerbst, Panzram issued a grim warning: "I'll kill the first man who bothers me." Zerbst assigned him to the prison laundry, which was supervised by a civilian employee, Robert G. Warnke, who minded his own business and rarely bothered the prisoners. Warnke maintained a penalty sheet, which he used to record infractions of the rules and which he turned over to the warden. Perhaps because of this, Panzram decided to make Warnke his victim, his last as it turned out.

On June 20, 1929, Carl Panzram assaulted Warnke with an iron bar. Warnke fell to the floor dead, his skull crushed. Panzram surrendered himself to the guard, accepting his fate with weary resignation. He was sentenced to die on the gallows following a hasty trial. When the Society for the Abolishment of Capital Punishment tried to intervene on his behalf, Panzram told them to forget it. Hanging, he said, would be a "real pleasure and a big relief," adding: "the only thanks you or your kind will ever get from me for your efforts on my behalf is that I wish you all had one neck and I had my hands on it...I believe the only way to reform people is to kill 'em ... My motto is: `Rob 'em all, rape 'em all and kill 'em all!'" His last epitaph was signed "Copper John II" in memory of a statue he had seen outside Auburn Prison in New York. Panzram, defiant to the end, was executed in Leavenworth on September 5, 1930. His autobiography was published forty years after his death.

THE "GORILLA MURDERER"/1926-1927

Earle Leonard Nelson (AKA: Roger Wilson, The Gorilla Murderer; 1897-1928) was one of the strangest and most evasive serial killers in U.S. history. He slew from coast to coast, selecting only women, and even here, his distinction was that he murdered first and *then* attacked his victims sexually. Nelson's victims were almost always middle-aged landladies, matronly, motherly figures who probably represented the mother he lost early in life, a fantasy figure, whom he loved and hated, and an overbearing religious aunt, whom he simply hated.

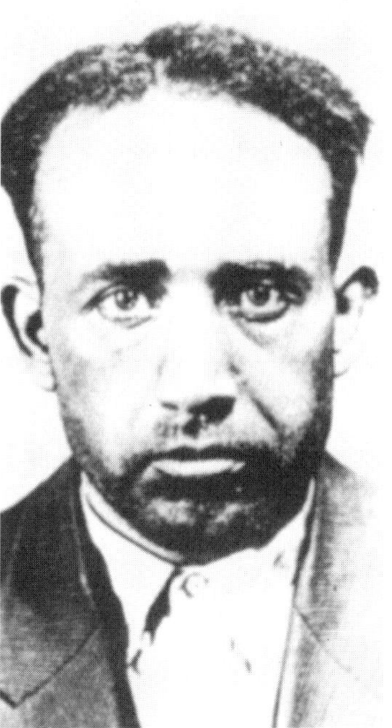

Earle Leonard Nelson posed as a Bible student in renting rooms from landladies he strangled in 1926-1927.

Born in Philadelphia, Nelson was orphaned before the age of five and was taken in by his aunt, Mrs. Lillian Fabian. She was kindly, but insisted that Earle follow her every dictate, especially when it came to his reading the Bible at least an hour every day. She often predicted to friends that Earle "will be a minister some day."

At the age of seven, Nelson was playing on a Philadelphia street with another child and ran into the street to chase a ball. A passing trolley car snared him in its cowcatcher and bounced him fifty feet. His head repeatedly struck the cobblestones. He was rushed to a hospital where he underwent a lengthy operation. Nelson survived, but he developed excruciating headaches, which, he claimed, were so severe, that they made him blind.

Although Nelson's brain had not been physically injured, the terrible accident most certainly altered the boy's thinking. He began to conjure one image of horror after another, dwelling in particular upon the crucifixions, suicides, mass slayings recorded in the Bible, passages he had avidly read under the stern direction of his aunt. He also became obsessed with the Biblical sirens of the Holy Scripture: Bathsheba, Salome, the Queen of Sheba.

He began to manifest his hatred for females by attacking little girls, including his small cousin. When his aunt scolded him for this behavior, Nelson, clever enough to use Mrs. Fabian's obsession for religion, would drop to his knees and beg his aunt's forgiveness, babbling Biblical phrases, crying and pleading so that the overwhelmed Mrs. Fabian restricted his punishment by sending him to his room. In his room Nelson passed the time searching his Bible for profiles of evil, of murder, and the darkest deeds of man. He grew up a solitary, sullen youth, graduating from high school without a single friend.

Reaching adulthood, Nelson was a powerful young man with broad shoulders and huge, muscular hands with webbed fingers. He could break solid boards with those hands and also perform amazing feats, like walking on his hands for several blocks without losing his balance. He practiced scaling the sides of buildings and claimed that he could actually use his webbed fingers as suction cups in climbing into second-story windows. On his twenty-first birthday, Nelson dragged a neighbor girl into his basement where he tried to rape her. Her screams brought help and Nelson was arrested.

Mrs. Fabian begged police to release her nephew. He was a misunderstood youth, she said, a recluse who meant no harm. Authorities disagreed. Nelson was convicted of rape and sentenced to two years in a penal farm. He escaped but was recaptured. He escaped again, but police found him a short time later, standing outside a window of his aunt's house in a heavy downpour, watching his cousin Rachel undress for bed. This time Nelson was sent to the penitentiary to serve out his sentence, but on December 4, 1918, he escaped again. Using the alias Roger Wilson, Nelson moved to San Francisco where he met a schoolteacher, marrying this unsuspecting young woman on August 12, 1919.

The marriage soon turned into a living nightmare. Whenever the couple went out, Nelson accused his wife of flirting with other men. He openly chastised her on public streets and screamed out that she was a slut and a whore. She finally had a nervous breakdown, and while she was recovering in a hospital, Nelson entered her hospital room and raped her. It took several interns and male hospital attendants to drag Nelson from his wife. Nelson ran from the hospital cursing his wife and the hospital staff and vanished for seven years.

Mrs. Clara Newman, who was murdered and raped on February 20, 1926 in San Francisco by Nelson; she was the first victim.

On February 20, 1926, Nelson appeared on the doorstep of a boarding house owned by Clara Newman in San Francisco. He told the landlady he was a college student and that he was looking for a nice clean room, where he could study in peace. As Mrs. Newman showed Nelson into a third floor room, he attacked her and strangled her to death, and then sexually attacked the dead body. He fled, leaving Newman's naked body on the floor. Richard Newman, Mrs. Newman's nephew, found his aunt's ravaged body a few hours later and called the police, telling detectives that his aunt had last been with a man about five-feet-six with a heavy torso, piercing blue eyes, and ape-like arms.

On March 2, 1926, Nelson struck again, this time strangling Mrs. Laura Beale, another landlady. He raped the dead body repeatedly before fleeing. On June 10, Mrs. Lillian St. Mary was found strangled and ravished, her body hidden under a bed in her rooming house. On June 26, Nelson arrived in

Mrs. Beta Withers (shown with her son), who was murdered and raped by Nelson in Portland, Oregon, on October 19, 1926.

Santa Barbara and strangled and raped Mrs. George Russell. By then the press was blaring headlines about a serial killer dubbed "The Gorilla Murderer" because of his long arms and monkey-like face. On August 16, after strangling and raping Mrs. Mary Nesbit in Oakland, California, Nelson was inactive for several months. Police, trying to puzzle out the killer, believed he was momentarily seized by an irresistible urge to murder, followed by the sordid acts of necrophilia, but had no clues to the killer's identity or his whereabouts. Warnings were sent out that a killer was on the loose and that unescorted women were in danger.

Nelson resurfaced in Portland, Oregon, on October 19, 1926. After renting a room from landlady Beta Withers, he strangled and raped her. On October 20, Nelson strangled and raped another Portland landlady, Mrs. Mabel Fluke. A few days later in the same city, he strangled and raped landlady Virginia Grant. He then traveled back to San Francisco, and on November 11, 1926, strangled and raped Mrs. William Edmons. Nelson then took the train back to Portland where he strangled and raped Blanche Myers on November 15, 1926.

As the manhunt for the Gorilla Murderer intensified, Nelson began traveling east. On December 23, 1926, he strangled and raped Mrs. John Berard in Council Bluffs, Iowa. He then moved southwest and in Kansas City, Missouri, Nelson strangled and raped Mrs. Germania Harpin, another landlady. Before leaving Mrs. Harpin's house, Nelson also strangled her eight-month-old daughter.

Returning to his home town of Philadelphia, Nelson strangled and raped Mary McConnell on April 27, 1927. On May 1, he strangled and raped Jennie Randolph in Buffalo, New York. By June 1, 1927, Nelson was in Detroit. Here he strangled two sisters at the same time, Minnie May and Mrs. M.C. Atorthy, raping both corpses. Nelson then moved to Chicago where, on June 3, 1927, he strangled and raped Mary Sietsome, his last victim in the U.S.

All of Nelson's victims in the U.S., with the exception of Mrs. Harpin, had been landladies. With the entire nation looking for him, Nelson crossed into Canada and took a room in Winnipeg, renting from Mrs. August Hill. He said he was a Bible student. That night, June 8, 1927, Lola Cowan, who supported her family by selling artificial flowers made by her crippled sister, vanished from the streets of Winnipeg.

On June 9, 1927, when William Patterson of Winnipeg returned home, he found his wife missing and his small children told him that they had not seen her in hours. Patterson, who knew that a strangler was loose in the city, went into the bedroom, where he saw his wife's hand protruding from beneath the bed. When he looked beneath the bed, he saw his wife's naked body. She had been strangled and raped.

A short time later, George Smith, Winnipeg's chief of detectives, gathered his best men and told them: "I think that we must operate on the assumption that the madman who has been killing all those landladies in the States has crossed over into Canada. Mrs. Patterson had been strangled by a man with extremely powerful hands, and then, after death, she had been sexually molested. It is the same pattern."

"But Mrs. Patterson was not a landlady," one of the detectives said.

"The killer has altered his *modus operandi*," Smith said. "But the method of killing and the ravishing of the corpse follows the same murder methods as that occurring in the States. This time he has stolen things, about $70, Mrs. Patterson's ring and a Bible." Smith also pointed out that the killer left behind his old clothes, and took a shirt, pants, and an old coat from the Patterson house.

Detectives began to search every rooming house and hotel in the city, interviewing every boarder and guest. Two detectives arrived at Mrs. Hill's rooming house and she admitted that she had taken in a new boarder, describing him as a serious young man with piercing blue eyes, a dark complexion, and a powerful build.

The officers were shown to the boarder's room, but he was gone. They began to search the place. One of the officers leaned down and looked beneath the bed: "Good God, man!" he shouted to his partner. "Look here!" It was the body of Lola Cowan, the flower girl. She, like the other victims, had been strangled and raped. Nelson had taken her body back to his room and hidden it. He later admitted that he made love to the corpse for two days.

By that time Nelson was heading west, hitching rides. In Regina, 200 miles west of Winnipeg, he rented a room. Only minutes after occupying it, he spotted an attractive female boarder in the hall. He shoved her into his room and began to strip her, but she screamed and the landlady and male boarders

Mrs. Mabel Fluke, who was murdered and raped by Nelson in Portland, Oregon, on October 20, 1926.

Mrs. Blanche Myers, who was murdered and raped by Nelson in Portland, Oregon, on November 15, 1926.

Serial killer Earle Leonard Nelson in custody in Manitoba, Canada; he was convicted of murder and executed on January 13, 1928, stating he was innocent as he stood on the scaffold.

ran upstairs. Nelson leaped out the window, slid down a drainpipe, and escaped. Police were on his trail within minutes. Nelson headed for the U.S. border, but two constables stopped him only a few miles outside of the border town of Killarney. Nelson stood in the road and talked casually with the officers who sat in their car, studying him.

"My name is Wilson," he told them. "I work as a stock hand on a ranch near here."

Constable Grey then thought to shock the young man into blurting a confession by saying: "We're looking for a man who is responsible for the deaths of twenty women."

Nelson gave him a little grin that was more like a sneer and said: "I only do my lady killing on Saturday night, fellas."

Said Grey: "I think you'd better ride along with us back to Killarney until we can check on your story."

"Fair enough," Nelson said, climbing easily into the back seat of the car. "I guess you fellows have to play it safe when there's a killer on the loose."

In Killarney, Nelson was placed in a small jail and Constables Grey and Sewell went down the street to call Chief Smith in Winnipeg. They described their captive. Smith told them that the killer had used the same name, Roger Wilson, in Winnipeg. Smith then asked where the man was being kept. When he heard that Nelson had been left handcuffed to a cell bar and that his shoes had been taken away, he shouted: "What! Don't let that man out of your sight! I want one of you with him at all times!" He then said that he and a dozen officers were on their way to Killarney by the next train.

When Grey and Sewell returned to the jail fifteen minutes later they found the cell door open and the handcuffs dangling from the bar. Nelson had picked the lock on the handcuffs and the cell door and had fled. The escape of the "gorilla murderer" caused panic to grip the tiny town of Killarney. All the women and children were taken to the local church where they were guarded by dozens of gun-carrying men. More than 500 men formed a huge posse and they began a desperate search for the mass murderer, going house to house, field by field, through the night, their burning torches sending up eerie shoots of light.

Meanwhile, Nelson was sound asleep in the loft of William Allen's barn, which was only a block from the jail. The next morning, wearing a pair of worn-out boots he had found in the barn, Nelson walked to the train station and sat in the waiting room for the next train. When the train pulled into the station, Nelson moved toward it, but suddenly dozens of armed detectives leaped from the cars, Chief Smith in the lead. With two dozen revolvers pointed at him, Nelson surrendered. He was led away handcuffed.

Taken to Winnipeg, Nelson was tried and convicted of Mrs. Patterson's murder. He said very little in his defense, except to claim insanity. This plea was not accepted. It was pointed out that because he had changed his clothes and addresses constantly and had made intelligent escapes from dozens of cities in the U.S. and in Canada, he was sane. On November 14, 1927, Nelson was convicted and sentenced to death.

Nelson was visited in prison by his aunt and ex-wife on the day of his execution, January 13, 1928. He showed no remorse for his many murders and refused to explain his actions to an alienist who probed the reasons for his sexual attacks on the bodies of his victims. A few minutes later, wearing a crooked smile, Earle Leonard Nelson mounted the thirteen steps to the gallows and stood on the scaffold, saying in a clear voice: "I am innocent. I stand innocent before God and man. I forgive those who have wronged me and ask forgiveness of those I have injured." Just before the black hood was placed about his head, Nelson cried out: "God have mercy!" Five seconds later, one of the worst serial killers of the early twentieth century was sent downward through the trap door, the rope instantly snapping his neck, killing him.

THE MONSTER OF DUSSELDORF/1913-1929

The 1931 courtroom appearance of the "The Monster of Dusseldorf" surprised many Germans, who expected to see a real-life incarnation of the Frankenstein monster. Far from being the hulking sadist of expectation, 48-year-old Peter Kurten (AKA: The Monster of Dusseldorf, The Vampire of Dusseldorf; 1883-1931) more clearly resembled a shy businessman. He wore a conservative, well-tailored suit and smelled of Eau de Cologne. Although Kurten was officially charged with nine murders and seven other assaults with intent to kill, he had confessed to sixty-eight other crimes during his long interrogation by police.

German serial killer Peter Kurten, shown in his late thirties, when he was imprisoned for arson.

Peter Kurten was one of thirteen children born to a sand molder and his wife in the village of Cologne-Mulheim. His father, an alcoholic, sexually abused the children and beat his wife. In 1897, the elder Kurten was sentenced to prison for attempted incest. Published reports indicate that young Peter exhibited criminal tendencies before his sixth birthday. While playing on a raft in the middle of the Rhine River, Kurten allegedly pushed one of his playmates over the side and held his head under water. His sadistic tendencies were encouraged by the local dog catcher, who taught the boy to torture animals.

Kurten allegedly derived sexual pleasure from watching the blood flow from pigs and sheep. At the age of eight he ran away from home after quarreling with his mother. Kurten slept in the woods at night and survived by stealing from the local stores before returning home. In 1894, he accompanied his family to Dusseldorf, where he went to work as a molder's apprentice.

Kurten's sexual attacks commenced when he was four-

Christine Klein, choked to death by Kurten on May 25, 1913.

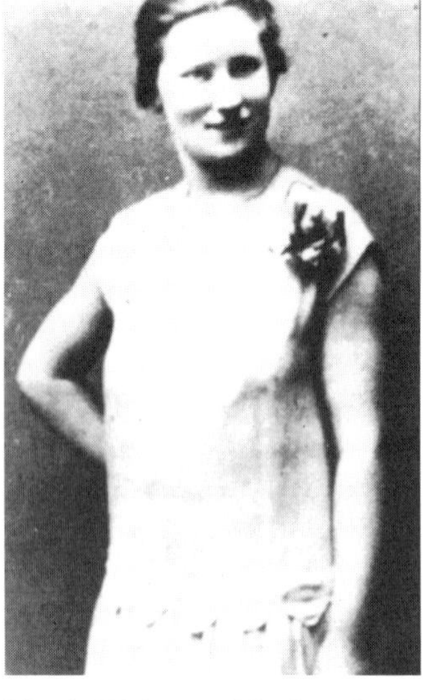

Maria Hahn, stabbed to death by Kurten on August 11, 1929.

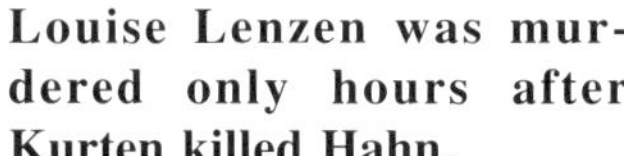

Louise Lenzen was murdered only hours after Kurten killed Hahn.

Ida Reuter, murdered by Peter Kurten on October 29, 1929.

teen. In the Grafenberger Woods outside Dusseldorf, he assaulted and choked his young girlfriend to the point of death. The experience left him sexually drained, but firmly resolved to duplicate the crime. "I thought of myself causing accidents affecting thousands of people and invented a number of crazy fantasies such as smashing bridges and boring through bridge piers," he later explained. A two-year prison sentence at age seventeen for petty theft reinforced his growing sado-sexual compulsions.

Kurten deliberately violated prison rules so that he would be put in solitary confinement, where he passed the time daydreaming about fresh new tortures. With each new jail sentence for burglary or assault, Kurten's desire to lash out at society grew. Within a few years he became an arsonist. "The sight of the flames delighted me, but above all it was the excitement of the attempts to extinguish the fire and the agitation of those who saw their property being destroyed." Kurten traced his fire fixation back to 1904 when he started three fires.

A year later, Kurten was arrested and jailed on thirty-four counts of theft and desertion. The day after Kurten began his military service, he ran away from the regiment. He would spend the next seven years at hard labor. In total, Peter Kurten spent twenty of his forty-seven years in prison.

Following his release from prison in 1913, Kurten decided to enact his murder fantasy. On May 25, 1913, he broke into the private rooms of the Klein family, owners of a public inn at Koln-Mulheim. Kurten discovered 13-year-old Christine Klein lying asleep near the window. He reached for her throat and choked her into unconsciousness before cutting her throat with a pocket knife. The next day, Kurten returned to the inn to share in the local gossip and speculation which accompanied the discovery of the body.

"People were talking about it all around me," he recalled. "All this amount of indignation and horror did me good." The girl's father, Peter Klein, was suspected by police after a bloody handkerchief bearing the initials "P.K." was found near the body. The handkerchief belonged to Peter Kurten, not Klein, who was later released.

Kurten married in 1923. There was nothing irregular about his conduct, according to his wife and neighbors. By all accounts he was a conservative, soft-spoken man with few vices. Beginning in 1925, he sexually assaulted several women, none of whom reported him to the police. In 1929, the peak year of Kurten's blood lust, twenty-three people were set upon by the "Monster," who said that he enjoyed drinking the blood of his victims and often attained sexual climax immediately afterward.

On February 2, 1929, Kurten stabbed Apollonia Kuhn with a pair of scissors. Fortunately, her screams scared off Kurten and she was saved. Six days later, he accosted 9-year-old Rosa Ohliger near the Vinzenz Church in Dusseldorf. Using the same pair of scissors, he stabbed the girl to death, and burned the body with kerosene several hours later.

On the night of February 12, 1929, Kurten attacked a drunk named Rudolf Sheer. He knocked Sheer to the ground and stabbed him repeatedly. As Sheer lay dying, Kurten drank the blood that spurted from the open wound of his victim, or so he later claimed. Maria Hahn, a housemaid who was enamored with Kurten, became the next victim on August 11, 1929. When the fiend could get no further than kissing and caressing Hahn, he produced his scissors and stabbed her in the throat, and then dumped the body in a ditch. Pleased with his work, Kurten went home whistling a tune.

Scarcely two weeks later, the "Monster" claimed his next two victims in the suburb of Flehe, outside Dusseldorf. Gertrude Hamacher, fourteen, and her 5-year-old sister, Louise Lenzen, were on their way home from a country fair when a

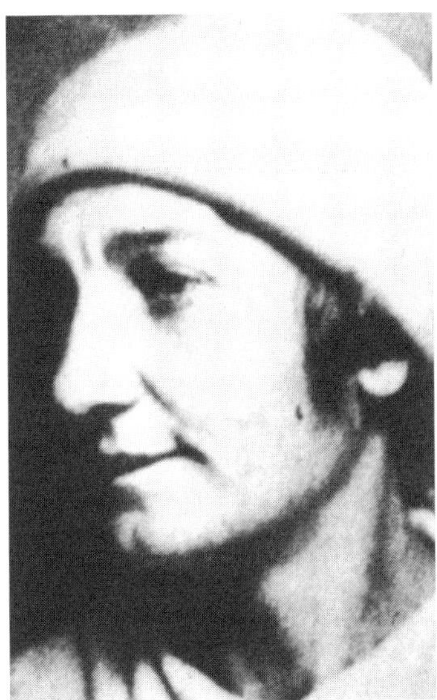

Frau Meurer, murdered by Kurten in 1929.

Frau Meiner, murdered by Kurten in 1929.

Gertrude Albermann, killed by Kurten in 1929.

Gertrude Schulte, stabbed six times by Kurten, but survived.

stranger approached. "Oh, dear," the man said. "I've forgotten to buy cigarettes. Look, would you be very kind and go to one of the booths and get some for me? I'll look after the little girl." Louise ran off to fetch the man's cigarettes. When she returned a short time later, Kurten seized the girl and dragged her to the adjacent footpath.

A dozen hours later, Kurten met up with Gertrude Schulte, a 26-year-old servant girl, whom he stopped on the way to the fairgrounds in Neuss. She agreed to accompany him to the fair, with a side trip through the woods. When Schulte refused his sexual advances, he stabbed her repeatedly, but was unable to administer the fatal blow because a passerby hearing her screams arrived on the run and Kurten took flight. These crimes, occurring in quick succession, awakened the city of Dusseldorf to the presence of a madman.

The newspapers were filled with lurid accounts of the sado-sexual murders amidst growing rumors that Satanism and vampirism—the common superstitions with many of the residents—were behind the murders. Detectives discounting these notions attributed the crimes to a "club of sadists." With no viable leads except the vague descriptions of Gertrude Schulte, the police employed a new gambit.

Believing that their killer frequented one or more of the popular Dusseldorf beer halls, detectives enacted a grisly tableaux-vivant. A coffin containing the embalmed remains of Maria Hahn was paraded into the center of one of the pubs. A detective addressed the hushed crowd: "The clay must have stuck to the murderer's clothes," he said, describing the manner in which Hahn met her death. "But he got away! He got away!" The detective threw back the lid of the coffin, and a spring mechanism enabled the corpse to sit bolt upright. "And here is Maria Hahn!"

The police carefully studied the faces of the patrons, operating under the theory that if the killer were present he would likely reveal himself through his facial expressions. When this ploy failed, the detectives sent out the first of their "decoy victims" to entrap the killer. The killings nevertheless continued.

After the blade of his scissors broke off inside one of his victims, Kurten decided the time was right to change weapons. On September 29, 1929, he used his hammer for the first time on Ida Reuter, a servant girl, in the woods outside Dusseldorf. Two more hammer murders followed. Elizabeth Dorrier was out for a walk in the woods on October 11, 1929, when she, too, was felled by hammer blows. The last victim was a 5-year-old child, Gertrude Albermann, whom Kurten stabbed thirty-six times with a new pair of scissors.

An uncharacteristic show of compassion for one of his intended victims finally led to Kurten's apprehension. Twenty-one-year-old Maria Budlick was preparing to board her train in Dusseldorf on May 14, 1930, when Kurten offered to lead her to the local youth hostel.

One of the scissors Kurten used in stabbing his 1929 victims.

The modest room Kurten shared with his wife in Dusseldorf; the serial killer took Maria Budlick to this room and gave her soup, then took her to a woods, where he tried to rape her, but inexplicably walked away, allowing her to live.

Budlick had recently lost her position as a domestic servant and had come to Dusseldorf from Cologne to meet with a Frau Brugmann, who had promised her a job. The woman failed to keep the appointment and Maria was about to return home when Kurten appeared. She went with him through the city toward the Volksgarten Park, a secluded patch of woods.

Recalling the stories about the "Monster," Maria Budlick hesitated, but Kurten coaxed her and she agreed to accompany him to his flat on the Mettmannerstrasse for a warm meal. After feeding her, Kurten offered to take her to the hostel. They rode a tram to the edge of the city and then walked together into the Grafenburg Woods.

Suddenly Kurten turned to her and said: "Do you know where you are? I can tell you! You are alone with me in the middle of the woods. Now you can scream as much as you like and nobody will hear you!" Kurten forced the girl against a tree and tried to rape her, but suddenly relaxed his grip. He asked if Maria remembered where he lived. When she cleverly said that she did not, Kurten inexplicably walked away.

Maria Budlick reported the incident to the police the next day and led detectives to his flat on the Mettmannerstrasse. Kurten saw the detectives in the foyer of the building talking to the landlady and fled. The next day, he met with his wife at a sidewalk cafe and confessed his crimes to her. (One account has it that he sat with his wife in their apartment and while the pair ate breakfast, he casually informed his spouse that he was the much-wanted "Monster of Dusseldorf.") Kurten convinced her to go to the police and report him so that she would receive the reward money. "It was not easy to convince her that this was not betraying me," he said. Frau Kurten eventually collected one-third of the reward and Kurten was arrested on

Page right: Peter Kurten on the day of his arrest, May 24, 1929, appearing as a normal businessman, instead of the serial killer that her terrorized Dusseldorf.

the morning of May 24, 1929.

Kurten cooperated fully with police. He astounded interrogating detectives and court-appointed psychiatrists with his ability to recall events dating back twenty years. The doctors learned about this extraordinary killer's childhood influences. At sixteen, he had visited the Chamber of Horrors exhibition at the Kolnerstrasse Waxworks. "I am going to be somebody famous like those men one of these days," Kurten remarked to a friend as he viewed the likenesses of some of history's greatest villains. The story of Jack the Ripper amused and delighted him. "When I came to think over what I had read, when I was in prison, I thought what pleasure it would give me to do things of that kind once I got out again," he said.

Kurten's trial began on April 13, 1931. Spectators lined the hallways of the courtroom to catch a glimpse of the murderer and the collection of skulls, knives, scissors, and clothing items placed on public display. In court, Kurten assumed a defiant posture. "I did not kill either people I hated or people I loved. I killed whoever crossed my path at the moment my urge for murder took hold of me," he said.

After nine days, the jury returned a verdict of guilty in each of the nine murders charged against him. Kurten was given the traditional last meal on July 1, 1931. The next day he was beheaded by the ax in the courtyard of the Klingelputz Prison in Cologne.

Turning to the executioner seconds before the blade fell, Kurten asked: "After my head has been chopped off, will I still be able to hear at least for a moment the sound of my own blood gushing from the stump of my neck? That would be the pleasure to end all pleasures."

AN AMERICAN BLUEBEARD/ 1930s

Born Raymond Lisemba in rural Alabama in 1895, Robert James (d. 1942) had done the back-breaking work of a cotton baler until he inherited $2,000 from each of two uncles, who had named him beneficiary of their insurance policies. Receiving such a windfall without expending any effort made a lasting and lethal impression on the young man. He took his inheritance and traveled to Birmingham, Alabama, where he attended a barbers' college and changed his name to Robert James. It was also in Birmingham, in 1921, that he met and married Maud Duncan. This first marriage ended when James' wife could no longer tolerate his demands for sadomasochistic sex. In the divorce suit, Duncan claimed that James frequently stuck hot curling irons under her nails.

James reportedly had also fathered several illegitimate children during his time in Birmingham and decided it would be healthier to move on. He relocated to Emporia, Kansas, where he opened a small barber shop and married again. He suddenly left Emporia and his wife when the father of a girl he had gotten pregnant threatened his life. Only weeks after arriving in Fargo, North Dakota, James opened another barber shop and married for a third time to Winona Wallace. The newlyweds' honeymoon trip to Colorado's Pike's Peak was marred when Winona was seriously injured in a car accident.

Robert James (Raymond Lisemba), who married many women (between five and seven, perhaps more) and murdered most of them for insurance money.

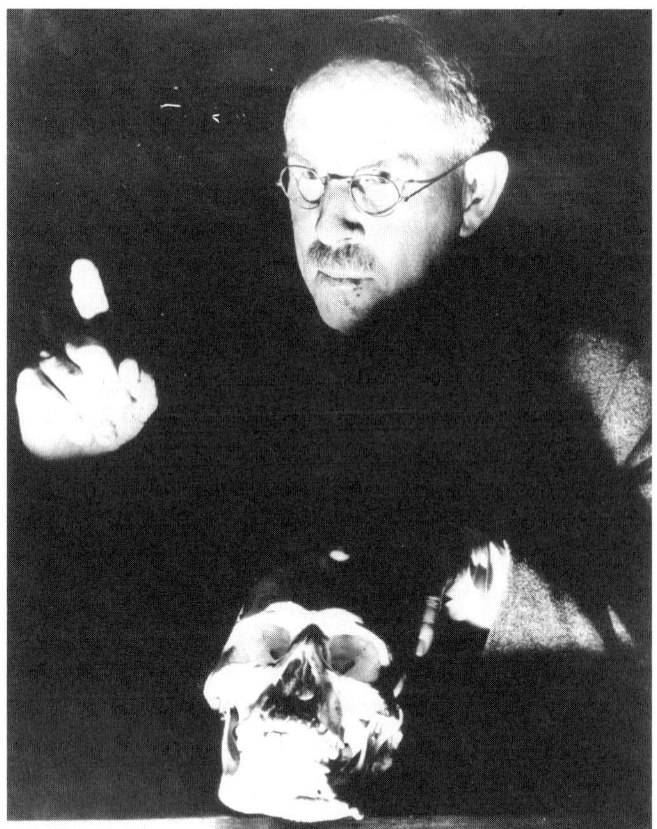

Health officer Charles W. Decker displays the skull of Winona Wallace James, describing its injuries; Winona James died in a bathtub and her husband collected the insurance money.

When she recovered sufficiently to be released, James took her to a remote cabin in Canada. A few days after their arrival, James appeared at a police station to report that his wife, dizzy from the accident, had drowned in a bathtub (shades of George Joseph Smith—see Brides of the Bath, Bigamy). Shortly after the funeral, James collected $14,000 in life insurance, a policy he had taken out on his wife's life a day before the wedding.

Mrs. Mary Bush James, who was the last wife to be killed by Robert James in one of the most bizarre murders in the annals of crime.

Returning to Alabama in 1934, James met a local girl, Helen Smith. The two were married and moved to Los Angeles. Helen Smith later told authorities that James was sexually impotent, but could be aroused if she whipped him. This fourth wife became suspicious, when James told her he wanted her to have a medical examination for a life insurance policy. She refused saying that "people who have it [insurance] always die of something strange." James resented her obstinacy and the two were soon divorced.

Next, James took out a $10,000 life insurance policy on a nephew, Cornelius Wright, then a sailor stationed at San Diego. Wright had a long history of being accident-prone. He had been hit several times by cars; some scaffolding had once collapsed on him; he had been knocked unconscious when beaned by a foul ball at a baseball game. James, playing the magnanimous uncle, loaned Wright his car to use while on leave and told him to "go off and have a good time." Three days later, Wright drove the car off a cliff near Santa Rosa, California, and was killed in the crash. Only later did the mechanic, who towed the wrecked car away, tell police that something was wrong with the car's steering wheel.

With the money he collected on his nephew's death, James opened a posh barber shop in Los Angeles and he began an affair with his manicurist, 25-year-old Mary Bush. When Bush became pregnant and insisted that James marry her, he did so. Not long after their marriage, however, James again took out another insurance policy. Then he persuaded one of his employees to find a couple of poisonous snakes, explaining that he had a friend whose wife was bothering him and he wanted the snakes to "take care of her." In July 1935, the employee, Charlie Hope, went to "Snake Joe" Houtenbrink, a reptile collector, and procured two Crotalus Atrox rattlers. James then confided to Hope his plot to kill his wife and promised him part of the insurance money if he would help in "completing the job."

After working out the details, James took Hope home with him for dinner one evening, introducing him as a doctor. After Hope had been in their home for a brief period, he told the pregnant Mrs. James that she didn't look well and

Robert James, center, handcuffed to the detective at his right, gazes down at the lily pond in which his wife Mary was found dead; at the extreme left is Charles Hope, James' handyman and murder accomplice.

A black widow spider was used to kill Mary James, but the creature did not cooperate.

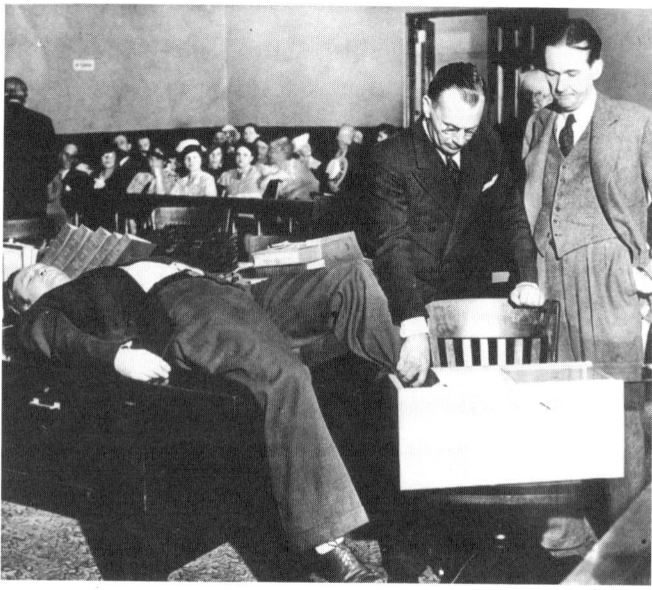

During his 1936 murder trial, James, right, is compelled to witness prosecutors demonstrating how he stuck his wife's leg (she was drunk at the time) into a box containing a rattle snake, believing the viper's poisonous bite would kill her.

Prosecutors in the James case inspect the poisonous rattle snakes rented by Charles Hope on behalf of Robert James and used in a futile effort to kill the rugged Mary James.

Charles Hope, the eager murder accomplice, is shown standing left in court as he hears his sentence—life imprisonment.

probably should not go through with her pregnancy. The naive woman agreed to let this "eminent physician" perform an abortion on her that very night. In lieu of anesthetic, James encouraged her to drink whiskey until she passed out. Once she was incoherent, he brought the snakes into the house in a specially designed box constructed so that he could insert her leg into it without letting the snakes escape. He left her for several hours with her leg stuck in the box, and she was bitten repeatedly.

Mrs. James did not die, however. When she revived and complained of a terrible pain in her leg, James assured her it was nothing important. The leg, however, swelled to twice its normal size and became increasingly painful. Early in the morning, James suggested to her that she take a bath to soothe the pain. He ran the water into the bathtub for her and stood by to help her into the tub. As she got into the tub, James pushed her down, pulling her legs up high enough that her head was submerged and held her in this fashion until she drowned, the same method employed by George Joseph Smith, the bigamous British wife-killer, a modus operandi that James himself may have studied when reviewing that decades-earlier case.

After dressing his wife's corpse, James and Hope carried Mrs. James' body to the yard, where they placed it face down in a small lily pond in such a way as to make it appear that she had become dizzy, collapsed, and accidentally drowned, duplicating the same fate that had befallen James' third wife, Winona Wallace. After going over the alibi with Hope, James went on to his barber shop. He worked through the day as though nothing at all was wrong, and that evening returned home with two friends, whom he had invited to dinner, ostensibly after clearing the impromptu dinner party with his wife. As planned, the three "discovered" his wife's body in the pond. The death was at first thought to be accidental.

Three months later, however, a Los Angeles captain of detectives, Jack Southard, saw a report that James had been arrested for mashing and thought it peculiar that a man so recently widowed should be apprehended for such a crime. Southard learned from neighbors that a green Buick sedan had been seen outside the James home and that Charles Hope had been phoning James constantly. Southard also discovered that Hope owned a green Buick sedan, so he searched Hope's apartment. There he found a receipt for two rattlesnakes. Reviewing the coroner's report on the deceased Mary Bush James, Southard saw an annotation that described how the woman had been bitten by a poisonous snake. Southard collected enough evidence against Charlie Hope to arrest him on suspicion of murder.

Once arrested, Hope confessed, implicating James. James was arrested in May 1936 and after a quick trial, was sentenced to death. Hope received a life sentence. James remained in the Los Angeles County Jail for the next four years while appealing his case. In 1940, he was finally moved to San Quentin. As it became evident that commutation of his sentence was unlikely, James fought to die in the gas chamber instead of by hanging because the law changing the manner of execution was enacted after his sentencing. In seeking what he thought would be a less painful death, Robert James met with defeat. He would go to the scaffold as originally decreed by the court. On May 1, 1942, Robert James was sent through the trapdoor at San Quentin, the last man to be hanged in California.

Confronted with the evidence by prosecutors, James squirmed in the witness chair, denying his guilt to the end; he was convicted and sentenced to death, being the last man hanged in California, on May 1, 1942.

AUSTRIA'S MONEY-LOVING MARTHA MAREK/1930s

The motive for the bizarre slayings committed by Martha Lowenstein Marek (1904-1938) was rooted in a pathological greed of astounding proportions. She resolved at an early age to live well, no matter the cost, even if the cost included human lives. Her early poverty undoubtedly kindled the dark ambitions that found reality in serial killings. Born Martha Lowenstein in Vienna, Austria, she was a foundling who was adopted by an impoverished couple. As a teenager, she went to work in a Vienna dress shop in 1919. A few years later, a kindly old man, Moritz Fritsch, took pity on the beautiful girl and made her his ward.

Fritsch was wealthy, a department store owner, and even though he was seventy-four, he had little qualms in taking the youthful Martha to bed. In exchange for her sexual favors,

An ailing Martha Marek, sitting with pillow behind her in court, pleads for her freedom; the serial killer was convicted and beheaded on September 6, 1938; the officer sitting close to her wears a Nazi armband signifying that Austria by then had been absorbed into Hitler's Third Reich.

Fritsch dressed the girl well and sent her to two elite finishing schools in France and England. She was at that time surrounded by upper-crust society girls, who came from wealth and the lifestyles of these classmates soon whetted Martha's appetite for the finer things in life.

When she returned to Vienna, Martha again went to live with Fritsch, but shortly met a handsome, young engineer, Emil Marek, with whom she carried on a secret affair. When Fritsch died, he left his stately mansion at Modling, along with all of his money, to Martha, as he had promised. Martha reveled in her new riches, but she and Marek, who married her in 1924, were extravagant and soon exhausted their new-found wealth. They were forced to sell the mansion. Out of funds, they devised a weird insurance fraud. Martha insured her spouse against any and all kinds of accidents, obtaining a £10,000 policy on Marek.

The "accident" arranged by the Mareks was a bloody one, calling for Marek to accidentally chop off one of his legs with an ax while splitting wood. Apparently, he had difficulty in finishing the job, pleading with Martha in his semi-conscious state to take off the rest of his half-severed leg. Martha managed to amputate the leg below the knee, but the gruesome effort aroused the suspicions of insurance officials. An insurance firm physician examined Marek and reported that Marek's leg showed three separate cuts and that the accident had clearly been staged. The Mareks were charged with fraud.

Martha then bribed a nurse to state that the examining doctor had falsified his report and had himself, been bribed by the insurance firm. Charges of fraud against the Mareks were dropped. The nurse, however, demanded more money and when not receiving the payoff, went to the police. The Mareks were then charged and convicted of bribery and sent to prison for four months. Oddly, the insurance firm nevertheless settled with the couple, paying £3,000 for an accident they were convinced had been falsified.

Moving to Algiers, the Mareks tried several businesses, but all failed. A few years later they returned to Vienna with two children and little money. So poor were they that Martha was reduced to selling vegetables in the streets. Emil Marek died in 1932 and Martha received a small insurance payment on his life. A few weeks later, Martha's 7-year-old daughter, Ingeborg, died of a mysterious ailment and Martha collected money on the child's small life insurance policy.

An aging aunt, Suzanne Lowenstein, then asked Martha to look after her. Martha moved in with the aunt, who died within a month. Before the aunt died, she, like Emil and Ingeborg Marek, manifested strange symptoms. She found it difficult to swallow and her limbs were numb. In all of these cases, death was attributed to tuberculosis.

Again, Martha Marek was enriched, her aunt leaving her house and modest fortune to her. Martha spent most of the money quickly and was then compelled to open her aunt's house to boarders, taking in a man named Neumann and a dowager named Kittenberger. The elderly woman died a short time later, insurance money on her life, which amounted to no more than $300, being left to Martha.

By 1937, however, Martha Marek was again in dire financial straits. She arranged for some expensive paintings in her aunt's house to be removed to a warehouse in the middle of the night. Next, she reported the paintings stolen and then made a claim for the missing artwork. The insurance firm asked a detective, Ignatz Peters, to investigate the case. Peters, ironically, had been the investigator involved in the amputated leg claim made by the Mareks years earlier and he suspected another scam. He canvassed warehouses in Vienna and soon located the hidden artwork. Martha was thrown into prison, charged with fraud.

Reading of this arrest, the son of Mrs. Kittenberger went to the police to tell them that he believed Martha Marek had poisoned his mother in order to obtain her insurance money. Detective Peters had Kittenberger's body exhumed, along with those of Emil and Ingeborg Marek and Suzanne Lowenstein. Toxicologists soon reported that all had been poisoned with thallium, a rare poisonous chemical compound first discovered in 1861.

Peters then remembered that Martha had another child, a son, and he soon found the boy boarded out in a poor district of Vienna. He was just in time. The boy, who had recently been insured by his mother, was dying from thallium poisoning. He was rushed to a hospital and saved.

Brought to trial, Martha Marek was charged with four murders (prosecutors claimed that she had killed a half dozen more people). She was convicted of murdering Lowenstein, Kittenberger and her husband and daughter, after prosecutors proved that Martha had been regularly buying thallium from a pharmacist in Vienna. Though she continued to insist upon her innocence, the serial killer was condemned to death, capital punishment having been restored in Austria after Hitler had taken over the government.

Martha Lowenstein Marek was sent to the block on December 6, 1938, where she was beheaded by an executioner wielding an ax far more accurately than the one she had used on her late husband. It took but a single stroke.

A POISONER IN CINCINNATI/1930s

German-born Anna Marie Hahn (1906-1938) moved to Cincinnati, Ohio, with her husband, Phillip Hahn, and their young son, Oscar, in 1929. With her rich contralto voice and her plump, blonde good looks, Hahn delighted the elderly German men in the immigrant community, especially when she visited the many German beer gardens in the city.

Many of these elderly German-American men were ailing and the ever caring Anna Marie Hahn volunteered to look after them, despite the fact that she had no formal training as a nurse. One by one, however, under Anna's "loving care," these men began to die. Relatives grateful for the unstinting care Hahn lavished upon her "patients," paid the self-appointed nurse thousands of dollars from the estates of the deceased.

Ernest Kohler died while under Hahn's care, in 1933, and left her a large house. Dr. Arthur Vos, a resident in that house, soon found several blank prescription forms missing from his offices and complained to the new owner, Anna Hahn, who shrugged and suggested "maybe one of your patients took them."

As the Depression deepened, Anna Hahn continued in her role of "an angel of mercy," by flitting from one house to another to nurse ailing, elderly men. Despite her indefatigable efforts, they died like flies. On June 1, 1937, 68-year-old Jacob Wagner became Hahn's patient. He died on June 2, 1937. Days later, 70-year-old George Opendorfer, seventy, died under Hahn's care. The fact that both men had died after acute stomach pains and vomiting was brought to the attention of Cincinnati police chief Patrick Hayes.

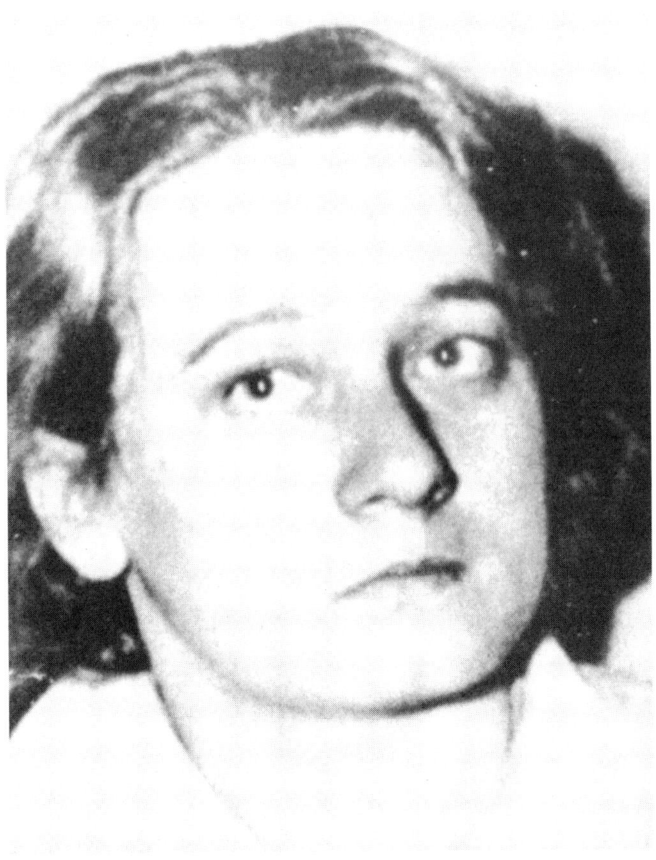

Anna Marie Hahn poisoned elderly men to obtain their wealth and went the electric chair on December 7, 1938.

Chief Hayes ordered an autopsy of Wagner's body, and poison was found. Several other bodies were exhumed—the cadavers of Hahn's "patients," and it was discovered that four types of poison were present in these corpses. Subsequent autopsies of Hahn's other patients, including a man named Palmer and another patient named George Gsellman, sixty-seven, revealed more evidence of arsenic and croton oil.

Hayes summoned Hahn to his office, where he questioned the woman. She appeared indignant at the suggestion that she had anything to do with the deaths of these elderly gentlemen. "I love to make old people comfy," she told Hayes. Because these grateful old men left her their worldly goods and fortunes was not a reason to think ill of her. The poor old fellows died from dysentery, she said, or something like that. The number of men dying under her care in such short order, she admitted as being "very peculiar, but why pick on me, chief?"

Hayes stared back at her and finally said: "We searched your place, Mrs. Hahn and we found enough poison to kill half of Cincinnati."

Anna Hahn's lips quivered and she then burst into tears, sobbing: "I have been like an angel of mercy to them. The last thing that would ever enter my head would be to harm those dear old men."

Her fate was sealed when her husband, Phillip Hahn, went to officials to inform them that not only had his wife stolen the prescription forms from Dr. Vos, but had had their 12-year-old son Oscar fetch the poisonous prescriptions from pharmacists. He went on to state that his wife had twice attempted to insure him for more than $25,000, but that he had refused. Shortly after that refusal, he said, he grew ill, having the same symptoms as the old men Anna nursed. Somehow, he said, he miraculously survived the poison she had administered to him through meals. Anna Marie Hahn was then charged with several murders.

At her trial, Hahn's history of theft, adultery, and forgery was brought out by her own defense lawyers, including Hiram Bolsinger, in an attempt to establish robbery, not murder, as her motive for her dealings with the old men. Dubbed "the beautiful blonde killer" by the press, Hahn was convicted and sentenced to die in the electric chair. The night before her execution, on December 7, 1938, Hahn refused to see her husband or son, but threw a farewell party for the newsmen who had covered her trial, treating them to punch and cakes in her cell.

"You gave me a good show at my trial," Hahn told the sheepish-looking reporters. "The least I could do was to throw a bash for you. I guess I'm not much like a 'beautiful blonde' now, huh? Well, give me a good write-up when it's all over." None of these reporters came to her execution early the next morning. Hahn was the first woman to die in the electric chair in Ohio. She was thirty-two.

LONDON'S KILLER-FOR-CASH/1942

Within four days in February 1942, four women were savagely murdered in London air raid shelters during the blackout. These brutal killings prompted British journalists to believe that London was suffering from a second "Jack the Ripper." This serial killer was Gordon Frederick Cummins (AKA: The Count, the Duke; 1914-1942). He was the illegitimate son of a member of the House of Lords. His friends called him the "Duke" or the "Count" because of his social pretensions. When the war came, he enlisted in the RAF.

Air cadet Gordon Frederick Cummins murdered four women in London during the blitz; he was hanged on June 25, 1942.

Though well-educated and coming from a good family, Cummins had long earlier gotten into trouble with the police, after being fired by a number of employers, who accused him of dishonesty and theft. Cummins affected an Oxfordian accent and was attracted to show business, marrying the secretary of a theatrical producer in 1936. He and his wife lived in North London. He was always in financial difficulties and this condition worsened when he became an air cadet early in World War II.

To obtain money, Cummins simply went on a murder spree. On the night of February 9-10, 1942, the mutilated body of Evelyn Hamilton, a 42-year-old schoolteacher, was found in the central district of London known as Marylebone. The killer placed the body in an air raid shelter. The next day, Mrs. Evelyn Oatley was found dead in her Soho apartment. Police found a blood-stained can opener nearby, which the killer had used to rip open the lower portion of her body. Oatley, under the name of Nita Wood, had turned to prostitution to support herself.

Cummins murdered his third victim, 42-year-old Margaret Lowe, on February 11, 1942, but the body was not discovered until three days later. The mutilation convinced police that the same killer was responsible. Like Oatley, Lowe was a prostitute.

The body of the fourth murder victim, 40-year-old Doris Jouannet, was found just hours later in Paddington. She was in the custom of picking up servicemen in Leicester Square. As was the case in the previous three murders, Cummins had attacked and murdered Jouannet in order to take whatever money and jewelry she carried. This was his intent when Cummins assaulted two other women, Greta Heywood and Catherine Mulcahy (or Kathleen King). Both women were fortunate to escape with their lives. In these attacks, the serial killer was frightened off by the screams of the victims and in the first instance, he was actually pursued by a passerby.

Cummins left one clue near the shelter where he accosted Heywood, a gas mask bearing an easily traceable serial number. Only twelve hours after his attack on Mrs. Catherine Mulcahy, the police arrested Cummins near St. John's Wood, where they found the 28-year-old airman returning to his barracks.

Fingerprints found at the murder locations, on a mirror and a tin-opener, matched Cummins'. He was left-handed, as had been the killer. It took a jury at the Old Bailey only thirty-five minutes to find him guilty of murder. He was condemned to death, but appealed his sentence. Lord Chief Justice Humphreys dismissed his appeal, and Cummins was taken to Wandsworth Prison, where he was hanged on June 25, 1942.

Dr. Marcel Petiot's message board at his Paris office; among his patients were many victims.

THE SERIAL KILLINGS OF PETIOT/ 1942-1944

France's worst serial killer (in respect to substantiated number of victims) committed his crimes during the German occupation, from 1942 until 1944, his many murders coming to an end when a disgusted neighbor reported him to the police. Marcel Andre Henri Felix Petiot (AKA: Henry John Felix Marcel, Henri Valery; 1897-1946) was born at Auxerre, the son of a postal official. In 1917 he enlisted in the French army, but was court-martialed for stealing drugs and then selling them on the black market. Curiously, he was granted a full pension and free ongoing treatment for his condition, diagnosed as psychoneurosis.

In 1921 Petiot qualified to become a physician at a time when he was still being treated for a mental disorder. Petiot established his practice in Villeneuve-sur-Yonne and became the town's mayor in 1928. He was accused shortly afterward of fathering a child with his housekeeper. "She told everyone she was having sexual intercourse with me," he said. "In fact I declined this honor." During the time he served as mayor of Villeneuve, the doctor was accused of drug peddling and theft, and actually served time in prison for the latter offense. In 1930 he was implicated in the murder of one of his patients, Madame Debauvre, but the principal witness against him died suddenly and the case was forgotten.

In 1933, Petiot moved to Paris. In 1936 he was arrested there for robbing book shops. The charge was dismissed, but Petiot agreed to submit to psychiatric examinations. He remained on the medical roster though, and re-established his practice at 66 Rue Caumartin. The next few years were very good for Petiot, whose practice expanded so rapidly that he numbered 3,000 patients. In 1941 he bought a fifteen-room house at 21 Rue Lesueur to use as his laboratory.

Alterations to the building were completed in September of that year. By all accounts it was designed for the peculiar needs of a serial killer (not unlike the sinister preparedness enacted by Herman Webster Mudgett, the proprietor of Chicago's Murder Castle). Among the many architectural designs created by Petiot was a triangular "death room" and a massive wall that prevented any view by curious neighbors.

No one paid much attention to the comings and goings at the Rue Lesueur in the next few years. The residents of the neighborhood were mainly concerned with surviving the ordeal of the Nazi occupation until March 11, 1944, when Jacques Marcais complained to the police about a nauseating, smoky odor coming from 21 Rue Lesueur. The police summoned the doctor to his residence to explain the smell, and while awaiting his arrival they ordered a fire brigade to extinguish a fire in the chimney.

An overhead view of Marcel Petiot's 15-room "laboratory," which he had customized, providing a "death room" for his intended victims; investigators are shown milling about the courtyard at this notorious house at 21 Rue Lesueur, where twenty-seven bodies were found following a fire.

Investigators inspect a pit in Petiot's residence; it was here that the serial killer burned the body parts of his victims, mostly Jews, whom he promised to hide from Nazi hunters. Instead, Petiot murdered these hapless fugitives and stole their cash and meager belongings.

Dr. Marcel Petiot, left, at his trial; he was convicted of murdering twenty-four persons, but he may have killed many more; he was beheaded at Santé Prison on May 26, 1946.

The firemen forced their way into the house, where they beheld an eerie, disgusting sight. Scattered about the floor of the cellar were the remains of twenty-seven human bodies in various stages of decomposition. Petiot told the police sergeant that the bodies were those of Nazi collaborators executed by the Resistance. Satisfied with this, the sergeant let him go. Petiot, his wife, and their 16-year-old son fled into the countryside and dropped out of sight, while speculation mounted that the doctor was not a loyal member of the Resistance, but a Gestapo sympathizer who had carried out atrocities for the Germans.

In October Petiot wrote a letter to the newspaper *Resistance* stating that he had been cleverly framed by the Gestapo. Because he claimed to be an officer in the Resistance, his handwriting was checked against that of all officers of the Free French forces in Paris. It was found to be that of Captain Henri Valery, a member of the Free Forces for only six weeks. Valery and Petiot were one and the same. Petiot was arrested on November 2, 1944, in a flat at the Rue Faubourg St. Denis, and taken to headquarters for questioning. He declared that the twenty-seven bodies found in the house on Rue Lesueur were mostly German soldiers, but went on to say that he had actually killed sixty-three people while working for the Resistance.

Indicted for murder, Petiot was placed on trial at the Seine Assize Court on March 18, 1946. When asked by Public Prosecutor Pierre Duval about why he refused to mention the names of his former associates in the Resistance, he had a stock answer. "I wouldn't dare name them in this court. There are too many Petainists here." The prosecution charged that Petiot had concocted a scheme to lure wealthy Jews to the mansion, promising to provide them with safe passage out of France in return for all their money and jewels.

Introduced into evidence were forty-seven suitcases seized by police in a private residence at Villeneuve. They contained an assortment of clothes that were identified by relatives of some of the victims. Petiot stole in excess of £1 million from the unfortunate Parisian Jews, who had solicited his help only to lose their lives. The jury returned a guilty verdict in twenty-four of the twenty-seven murders on April 4, 1946. The president of the court passed the death sentence. As Petiot was led from the court, he screamed to his mortified wife, "You must avenge me!" On May 26, 1946, having exhausted all his appeals, Marcel Petiot was guillotined at the Santé Prison in Paris.

LONDON'S ACID-BATH MURDERER/ 1944-1949

In 1949, John George Haigh (AKA: The Acid-Bath Murderer, the Vampire Killer; 1909-1949) burst into the headlines of the British press as an inhuman monster, who had been killing for

John George Haigh, one of England's most notorious serial killers, is shown in childhood as a choirboy.

profit for many years. Worse, according to his own statements, this serial killer had dissolved his victims in acid after drinking their blood, or so he claimed at his trial. Born in Stamford, Lincolnshire, England, on July 24, 1909, Haigh was raised with strict religious discipline. His parents were ardent members of the Plymouth Brethren, a severe religious sect for whom all manner of casual entertainment—movies, carnivals, musical shows, even the reading of magazines and newspapers—was deemed sinful.

A bright child, Haigh received a scholarship to the Wakefield Grammar School and then won another scholarship as a choirboy at Wakefield Cathedral. His life was governed by strict routines and he was allowed no freedom to enjoy the small entertainments shared by his peers. Haigh scratched for a living in his early twenties, usually working as a salesman. He was glib and somewhat flashy in his appearance, preferring loud ties and tight-fitting suits. He married Beatrice Hamer in 1934, but this marriage quickly collapsed after Haigh was arrested in November of that year for fraud. After serving a brief prison sentence, Haigh was released, and continued his illegal schemes, living hand to mouth through the 1930s and the war years.

In 1937, Haigh was convicted of his second serious crime, attempting to obtain money by false pretenses and was given a four-year prison term. He was released in 1940. In 1943, Haigh managed to make enough money through his small-time schemes to take up residence at a highly reputable address, the Onslow Court Hotel in South Kensington, where he occupied Room 404. The residents here were professional people and retired persons of some wealth. The other residents regarded Haigh as a congenial entrepreneurial businessman. However, he made few friends because he was a bit too gregarious and showy for the tastes of most residents.

In 1944, Haigh renewed his acquaintance with the McSwan family. In 1936, he had worked for W. D. McSwan as a secretary and chauffeur. The McSwans owned an arcade in an amusement center and had considerable means. At the time Haigh rented a small basement workroom at 79 Gloucester Road in Kensington, where he devoted considerable time to his "inventions." He killed the McSwans one by one. The first victim was the son, Donald McSwan, on September 9, 1944. He murdered Mr. and Mrs. W. D. McSwan the following year. When the McSwan couple expressed concern over their son's disappearance in 1944, Haigh was ready with a glib answer, explaining that their son had gone into hiding to avoid being drafted into the army, a not uncommon occurrence during the war.

Haigh's murder system was simple. He invited the McSwan family members to see his workroom on Gloucester Road and there bludgeoned them to death. He destroyed their bodies by placing them in vats of acid and disposing of the remains by simply pouring the gooey residue onto the dirt surface of an open yard behind his workshop.

By forging McSwan's name on transfer deeds, Haigh was able to obtain the McSwan properties in Raynes Park, Wimbledon Park, and Beckenham, Kent, as well as £4,000 in

Haigh is shown handcuffed and in custody, after being charged with murder on March 5, 1949; the serial killer told officers that he had sipped the blood of his victims through a lemonade straw.

Three witnesses for the prosecution in the Haigh case (left to right): Mrs. E. Robbie, manager of the Onslow Court Hotel, where Haigh lived, Mrs. M. Kirkwood, and Mrs. C. Lane.

Investigators inspect Haigh's "factory," one where he murdered victims, then soaked them with sulfuric acid to obliterate their identities.

Haigh, center foreground left of officer, leaves the courthouse while dozens of middleaged women seek his autograph; he received numerous marriage proposals during his trial.

cash. Endowed with considerable funds, Haigh tried to make a fortune through a betting system he had devised which he believed could predict regular winners at the dog track. When he lost, he turned again to murder for profit. This time his victims were Dr. Archibald Henderson and his wife, Rosalie, well-to-do middle-aged retirees, who, in August 1947, were advertising a house for sale.

Haigh, though he had no money, answered the ad and began negotiating for the purchase of the Henderson house in Ladbroke Grove. He later explained that one of his business deals had fallen through, preventing him from purchasing the house immediately. The amiable Hendersons struck up a friendship with the scheming Haigh. On February 12, 1948, he drove Dr. Henderson to his workshop, where he shot him in the head and disposed of the body by dumping it into a vat of sulfuric acid. He then returned to Mrs. Rosalie Henderson and told her that her husband had taken sick and needed her. She accompanied Haigh to his workshop where he killed and disposed of her body in the same manner.

In both the McSwan and Henderson murders, Haigh duplicated his victims' handwriting and sent notes to their servants, relatives, and friends explaining that they had moved to Australia or some other distant place, mentioning that "Mr. Haigh" would settle their affairs. The profits from this double murder exceeded those in the McSwan killings. Haigh, through clever forgeries, sold off the Henderson house and car, and obtained more than £10,000 from their bank accounts. But, within a year, Haigh had gone through most of this money, losing heavily to an army of bookies.

By early 1949, Haigh was running out of money. He was overdrawn at the bank and the manager of the Onslow Court Hotel was pressing him for back rent. Desperate for money, Haigh was looking about for more victims when his needs were answered in the dining room of the Onslow Court Hotel. Sitting opposite Haigh in the hotel dining room was a wealthy, retired matron, Mrs. Henrietta Helen Olivia Robarts Durand-Deacon. The 69-year-old widow knew that Haigh was then in the business of leasing and renting expensive cars to rich patrons and believed that, as a salesman, he might be interested in promoting a new business she envisioned, the manufacturing of plastic fingernails.

Haigh responded warmly to the idea and immediately suggested that Mrs. Durand-Deacon discuss the proposition further in his workshop. On February 18, 1949, Mrs. Durand-Deacon accompanied Haigh to the Gloucester address. As soon as she entered the basement workshop, Haigh shot the woman in the back of the head, killing her instantly. He stripped her and then dumped her body into a 40-gallon vat of sulfuric acid. Haigh drained the vat through a basement sewer and then scraped the sludge from the vat and dumped this onto the dirt of the back yard. This was hard work and Haigh, according to his later statements, paused to go to the nearby Ye Olde Ancient Prior's Restaurant, where he ate an egg on toast. He then returned to his workshop to "tidy up."

This killing produced little profit for the money-desperate Haigh. He sold Mrs. Durand-Deacon's Persian lamb coat and pawned her jewelry, obtaining only a few hundred pounds. He used this money to pay off his hotel bill and some other pressing expenses and then looked about for more victims. But Haigh had struck too close to home by killing the wealthy widow. To avoid being asked about the widow's disappearance, Haigh thought it clever that *he* make some inquiries about the missing woman. Haigh approached Mrs. Durand-Deacon's good friend, Mrs. Constance Lane, another retired lady living at Onslow Court, plying her with questions: "Do you know anything about Mrs. Durand-Deacon? Is she ill? Do you know where she is?"

Mrs. Lane shocked Haigh with her response: "Don't *you* know where she is? I understood from her that you wanted to take her to your factory."

Haigh said that he had not taken the widow with him to his factory, that he was not ready to show her his operation. "Well, I must do something about that," Mrs. Lane said.

The following morning, Haigh again asked Mrs. Lane if she had heard anything about Mrs. Durand-Deacon and she said that she had not, adding that she intended to report the matter to the police that day. In an attempt to avoid suspicion, Haigh then offered to go to the Chelsea Police Station and report the matter with her. But when Mrs. Lane and Haigh appeared in the police station, an officer recognized Haigh and had his background checked. His criminal record made the police suspicious and Haigh was brought in for question-

Jay Robert Nash with film director Alfred Hitchcock (examining crime photos together in 1969); the director told this author that he regularly attended the Haigh trial, but "all that vampire nonsense" was to convince the court that he was insane and that he hoped to be sent to Broadmoor, the prison for the criminally insane, instead of being executed.

ing on February 28, 1949. At first, he denied having had anything to do with the missing Mrs. Durand-Deacon, but the police kept grilling him and finally Haigh blurted: "Mrs. Durand-Deacon no longer exists! I've destroyed her with acid...You can't prove murder without a body."

But Haigh was wrong. Police searching his workshop uncovered enough gruesome remains of Mrs. Durand-Deacon to make an identification. Though most of her remains had been reduced to hardened sludge that coated the back yard behind Haigh's workshop, forensic investigators unearthed twenty-eight pounds of body fat, false teeth which were identified as Mrs. Durand-Deacon's, a pelvis, an ankle, gallstones, and the victim's red handbag found in the workshop beneath the acid vat. Haigh had been sloppy in his workshop, as well as in his room at Onslow Court. Here investigators found his diary in which he had kept abbreviated details of his previous murders. Some personal effects from the McSwan and Henderson families were also unearthed.

Haigh was charged with murdering Mrs. Durand-Deacon and placed on trial on July 18, 1949. Prior to this, while being held, Haigh had asked his jailors how hard it was to escape from Broadmoor, the prison where criminally insane persons were sent. Haigh then tried to convince everyone that he was insane. He stated that "in each case I had my glass of blood after I killed them." He then went on to describe in detail all sorts of ghoulish acts performed on his victims, before giving their bodies acid baths. The press, when learning of Haigh's statements, had a field day. No newspaper gave the story more sensational coverage than the London *Daily Mirror,* which, on March 4, 1949, bleated to its fifteen million readers that "the Vampire killer will never strike again. He is safely behind bars, powerless to lure his victims to a hideous death." Above this front-page story, the tabloid emblazoned the headline: "Vampire: A Man Held."

The British courts were appalled at this coverage, so much so that the *Daily Mirror* was fined £10,000 and its editor, Silvester Bolam, was given a three-month jail term for contempt of court, the paper having been previously warned by Scotland Yard not to publish details of the case before Haigh's trial. Bolam, ironically, was placed in the same prison that held Haigh. The serial killer continued to feign insanity while in prison, purposely drinking his own urine in front of guards and performing other irrational acts to convince them that he was a lunatic.

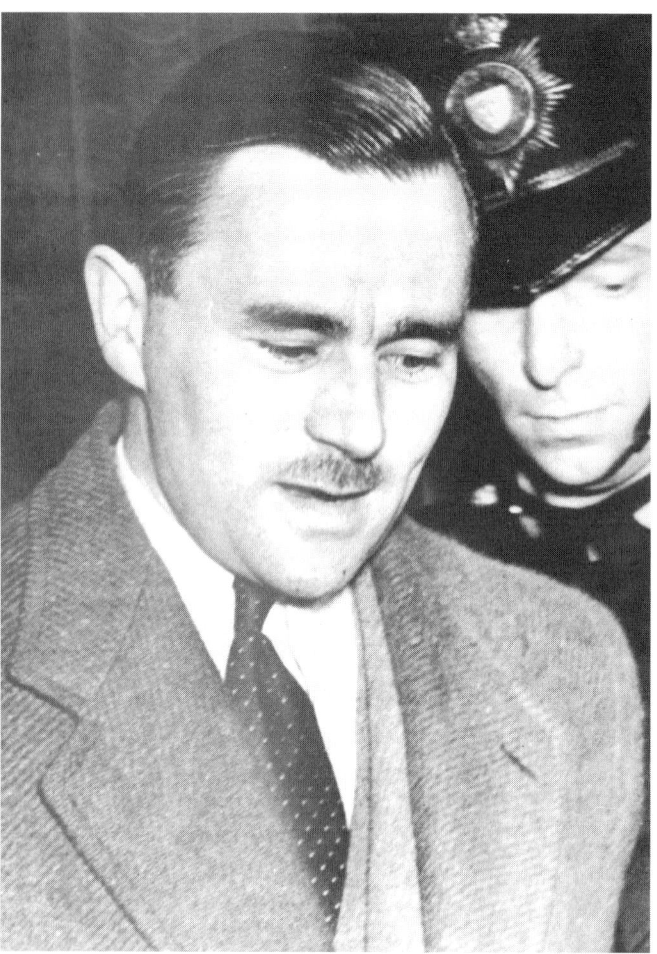

A grim-faced John Haigh leaves the courtroom after his conviction for murdering Mrs. Olivia Durand-Deacon; he was hanged at Wandsworth Prison on August 6, 1949.

Haigh was tried before Justice Travers Humphreys with Sir Henry Shawcross prosecuting. Sir David Maxwell defended, but he could do little more than plead his client insane. He brought Dr. Henry Yellowlees, a noted psychiatrist, to the stand to testify that he had examined Haigh and believed him to be a "paranoic," because of his early childhood and that he was "pretty certain" that Haigh drank the blood of his victims.

None of this impressed the jury. It took only fifteen minutes for the jury to render a verdict of guilty. He was sentenced to death. While awaiting execution, Haigh penned his brief, nightmare-filled memoirs, recounting how all his boyhood pleasures had been suppressed by his father, a religious fanatic. His father, an electrician, had had an accident which caused him to bear a blue scar down the middle of his forehead. Haigh quoted his father as telling him when he was a boy: "I have sinned and Satan has punished me. If you ever sin, Satan will mark you with a blue pencil likewise." For years, Haigh, as a child, nervously ran his fingers over his forehead, frantically looking into mirrors each morning to see if a blue scar had appeared while he had slept.

Haigh also related a recurring nightmare he had following a 1944 car accident, when he was injured and blood ran down his forehead and into his mouth, the year in which he began his murders: "I saw before me a forest of crucifixes, which gradually turned into trees. At first there appeared to be dew or rain dripping from the branches, but as I approached I realized it was blood ... A man went to each tree catching the blood. When the cup was full he approached me. 'Drink,' he said, but I was unable to move."

These horrifying words were penned by a man who undoubtedly still thought he might be reprieved and sent to Broadmoor as criminally insane. Haigh was highly intelligent and able to contrive such lunatic images for his own ends, just as he very probably researched the methods he used in disposing of his victims' bodies, most likely reading about the exploits of George Sarret of France who used similar methods in 1925 to eliminate the bodies of his victims. Haigh's horror stories did him no good in the end. He was hanged at Wandsworth Prison on August 6, 1949.

An interesting footnote to this case involved one of the many celebrities that attended Haigh's trial. That celebrity was none other than film director Alfred Hitchcock. The director told this author in 1969 that he knew that Haigh was "feigning insanity," because "he was quite sane in describing his aberrations." Hitchcock remembered at that time the many references to "sludge" that Haigh had made in his statements. "Do you know what sludge is?" Hitchcock asked rhetorically. He then answered for himself, drawing out the words with dark relish: "Half-decomposed flesh!"

AN AUSTRIAN BLUEBEARD/1946-1958

Max Gufler (b. 1910) became a confidence man and "bluebeard" serial killer after the police closed down the stand from which he had sold pornographic photos. Gufler was an illegitimate child who had moods of unpredictable violence after he was struck on the head with a stone at age nine. He drove an ambulance for the German army in World War II and suffered a second head wound. After the war, he sold books for seven years. When he met Herta Jonn, the woman who became his mistress, he began working in her father's tobacco shop, extending the inventory to include pornography.

Max Gufler killed eight persons in Austria and went to prison for life.

Gufler's sales of pornographic photos led to prison terms for Gufler, his mistress, and her father. The tobacco stand was permanently closed. Upon his release from prison, Gufler began his career as a confidence artist and bluebeard. His method was to read matrimonial advertisements, write letters to lonely widows, and propose marriage. As a test of the woman's love, he would ask her to withdraw all her savings. On the way to the marriage ceremony, he drugged the victim, disposing of the body so that the death looked like suicide.

Gufler is suspected of eighteen murders, the earliest in 1946, but was convicted of only eight. He confessed to bludgeoning to death 50-year-old prostitute Milie Meystrzik in her room in Vienna in 1952, and to giving an overdose of barbiturates to 45-year-old Josefine Kemmleitner, whose body was found in the Danube on June 3, 1958.

Gufler also confessed to killing Maria Robas three months later, and 50-year-old Juliana Nass, found in the Danube on October 15, 1958. The serial killer was arrested following the Robas killing because he made one serious mistake, and it is just such mistakes that invariably lead police to identify these most elusive murderers.

In an attempt to identify one of his murders as an accident, Gufler mailed a letter to the father of Maria Robas, a letter eventually traced to him, and one saying that he had witnessed Robas' death in a car accident. The police also found sufficient evidence to prosecute Gufler for murdering Augusta Lindebner, Theresa Wesely, Juliana Emsenhuber, and Josephine Dangl, and suspected him of murdering ten other women. They also found intended victim Marlene Buchner in tears at the registry office. Gufler's arrest had prevented him from keeping their appointment. Gufler was sentenced to life imprisonment in May 1961.

THE KILLER AT 10 RILLINGTON PLACE/ 1943-1952

One of the most horrific killers in modern British history, John Reginald Halliday Christie (AKA: Waddingham; 1898-1953) was half monster, half human, although in appearance he seemed to be nothing more than a meek-mannered middle-class citizen. He lived in a grimy, grubby little house at 10 Rillington Place in Notting Hill Gate, North Kensington, London. This small, rather run-down domicile, appeared to be identical to tens of thousands of other London homes, but it was exceptional in that it was truly a house of horrors.

In 1948, Timothy John Evans, his wife Beryl, and baby daughter Geraldine rented the top floor of the Christie house (the Christies lived on the ground floor). On November 5, 1949, Mrs. Evans' father visited with her and this was the last time she was seen alive. Police conducted a search and, on December 2, 1949, the bodies of Mrs. Evans and her infant were found in a wash house in Rillington Place, both strangled to death. Evans, a 24-year-old, dim-witted truck driver, had walked into the small police station at Merthyr Tydfil, South Wales, to inform officers that he had found his wife dead in his apartment and he had placed her body down a drain. After the bodies were found, Evans was returned to London under guard and there he confessed to murdering his wife and child.

Evans was charged with murdering his child, but before he was brought to trial at the Old Bailey, he withdrew his confession. He insisted that Christie had performed the killings. Christie emphatically denied having anything to do with the deaths of Mrs. Evans and her child. Moreover, he and his wife appeared as witnesses for the prosecution and gave evi-

John Reginald Halliday Christie, who murdered people in his own home, hiding the bodies behind false walls, under floorboards and in his small garden.

dence that helped to convict Evans. Evans was sentenced to death and hanged at Pentonville Prison on March 9, 1950.

Mrs. Christie then disappeared. She was last seen alive on December 12, 1952, and Christie gave nervous explanations for her absence, claiming she was visiting relatives or that she had gone on a vacation. He then left his apartment in early 1953, subletting the place to a couple named Reilly. These people were quickly evicted by the owner of the building, a Jamaican named Beresford Brown, who moved into the Christie residence.

On March 24, 1953, Brown went into the kitchen of the Christie apartment and began looking for a beam behind the wall into which he could screw a bracket for a wall-mounted radio. He tore away a loose piece of wallpaper and discovered an opening in the wall, a sort of large closet that had been

The shabby front of Christie's small home at 10 Rillington Place, an address that later became infamous.

covered by a thin sheet of posterboard and then covered with wallpaper. Taking out the board, Brown saw that three bodies had been stuffed inside the hollow area. He immediately called the police. Another body was discovered beneath the floorboards, and officers unearthed the skeletal remains of two more corpses found in the garden.

These gruesome remains were easy to detect when an officer noticed that a human bone was propping up a fence and the police merely dug at this spot to find the rest of the remains. All of the bodies and remains were that of women. The corpses found in the closet and the one beneath the floorboards in the front room were for the most part naked, and three had been wrapped in blankets. Contrary to most later reports, there was very little odor from the bodies and there was no "overpowering stench" which led to their discovery. All were dehydrated and the atmospheric conditions in the apartment kept the smell of the dead bodies to a minimum.

The body beneath the floorboards was Mrs. Ethel Christie, whose husband had left 10 Rillington Place three days earlier. Those in the cupboard area were all known prostitutes, Hectorina McLennan, twenty-six; Kathleen Maloney, twenty-six; and Rita Nelson, twenty-five. The remains found in the garden were subsequently identified as those of Ruth Fuerst, an Austrian girl who had been murdered by Christie in 1943, and Muriel Eady, a girl who had worked with Christie at the Ultra Radio Factory in Park Royal in 1944. The shocking story of the mild-mannered serial killer broke just at the time when police were conducting a nationwide search for Christie. He was found on March 31, 1953, by Constable Ledger as he stood near Putney Bridge, watching a group of children at play.

Timothy John Evans, who confessed to killing his wife and child and was executed; many believe that Christie was the perpetrator of those murders.

Christie, bald, wearing horn-rimmed glasses over weak eyes, with a flabby, middle-aged body, offered no resistance. He quickly confessed to the murders of the six women, saying that his first victim had been the Fuerst girl, followed by Muriel Eady. Christie calmly stated that he strangled the Fuerst girl while he was having sex with her. He had not murdered for nine years, but he suddenly went on a murder spree in late 1952, luring the prostitutes to his apartment, when his wife was away and, after killing them, raping the corpses.

In a quiet recital, Christie detailed his acts of necrophilia, which made him appear to be all the more inhuman. He had murdered his wife on December 14, 1952, Christie said, as an "act of mercy." He could no longer bear to witness her "convulsive attacks." She suffered from some sort of undefined malady and so, when she went into one of her fits while they were still in bed, Christie grabbed one of her stockings, rolled over, and strangled her with it.

Sir Francis Camps, one of England's most brilliant pathologists, examined Christie and his murders in minute detail. He learned that when Christie had brought his prostitute victims to his flat, he would ply the women with liquor. When they were drunk, he would position them in a chair with a canopy, under which he had affixed a gas pipe. He would then turn on the gas, and, when they were unconscious, strangle the women, then rape them. The trick with the gas explained the

Christie with his wife, Ethel, whom he also murdered, placing her body beneath the floorboards of his tiny home.

carbon monoxide Camps found in the blood of the three women hidden in the kitchen enclosure.

There were, however, strange sexual undertones to this case which puzzled Camps. He found that all three prostitutes were naked, but were wearing what amounted to handmade diapers. Semen had been found in them, as well as in an old pair of Christie's shoes, indicating that he had ejaculated following the murder-rapes. A tin can was found in the kitchen enclosure, and inside of this was found four separate tufts of pubic hair, which Christie had plucked from his victims and preserved, but for what purpose Camps could not determine.

Camps probed deeper into the sexual mysteries of John Reginald Halliday Christie, discovering that the myopic, always frail Christie had had psychological problems rooted in childhood. Born in Boothstown, Yorkshire, in April 1898, the son of carpet designer Ernest Christie, and one of seven children, Christie was treated with unloving harshness by his martinet father. He was disciplined often for the slightest infractions. Introverted, weak, the boy was labeled a "sissy" by his classmates, who made fun of his poor eyesight. He took to stealing small things, which caused him to be returned home by constables.

Christie's father, at these times, responded with the typical action of the era, a beating. At the age of fifteen in 1913, Christie quit school and took a job clerking for the Halifax Borough Police, but he was fired when he was suspected of stealing small items. About this time, Christie was seduced by an older girl, who later made fun of him when he could not finish the sex act. The girl spread the story and Christie was the butt of sex jokes among his peers, who called him "Can't Do It Christie." He was confined at home for a time, ill again. Christie's confession was punctuated repeatedly by statements claiming his lifelong illnesses, and it was apparent to Camps that he was a confirmed hypochondriac.

Following a severe bout with pneumonia, Christie

Christie is shown in wax by Tussaud's; he holds a brush which he used in wallpapering posterboards that hid bodies.

claimed, he went to France in 1915, serving in the trenches until he was blown out of a trench and inhaled mustard gas, which caused him to go blind for several months and lose his voice for three years. This was attributed to hysteria and not physical damage received when the artillery shell blew him out of a trench.

Whenever Christie was excited after that, he would lose his voice or it would rise to a high whine. In 1920, Christie met and married his wife Ethel, a union which produced no children. Christie claimed that he did not have sex with his wife for two years following the marriage and continued to have a pervasive feeling of inadequacy. Following a quarrel with his wife in 1923, the couple separated and Christie lost his voice completely, he claimed.

Bad luck followed Christie wherever he went, he said in his confession. In 1934, a hit-and-run driver knocked him down, injuring his head, knee, and collar bone. Worse luck, most brought about by Christie himself, dogged his work life. He seldom kept a steady job, the longest being five years while working as a clerk for a transport company. He had been a postal employee at one time, but it was proved that he filched money orders and he was sent to prison for seven months.

During his 1923 separation from his wife, Christie was imprisoned briefly for false pretense; he had falsified documents which claimed that he was a rich man at one time but had lost his money. He went to Brixton and Battersea and there put on the air of a once-wealthy man who was down on his luck. When a woman rebuffed his advances, Christie hit her on the head with a cricket bat and was arrested and sent to prison once more.

During World War II, Christie was a member of the War Reserve Police, a blackout warden who marched about his neighborhood pumped up with authority. He delighted in turning in those who ignored blackout rules. In 1943, his wife went to visit relatives in Sheffield, and it was at this time that Christie committed his first murder, bringing Ruth Fuerst home with him and murdering her, burying her corpse in the back yard. Although Christie admitted to murdering the six women, he was contradictory about Mrs. Evans and her child. He claimed that he found Mrs. Evans unconscious in her flat after she had quarreled with her husband about "a blonde woman." She had tried to commit suicide by turning on the gas, Christie said. He gave her a cup of tea and told her to calm down.

Mrs. Evans tried to kill herself once more, Christie said, and he again came to her rescue. Then she said she was pregnant and Christie, who had no medical knowledge, offered to perform the abortion she desired. She panicked when he was applying the gas to make her unconscious prior to the operation and thus died. He varied this tale by saying that Mrs. Evans, despondent over her husband's sexual escapades, asked Christie if he would kill her since she had botched two other suicide attempts. She said he could have sexual intercourse with her, Christie claimed, if he would but help her die. He strangled her, Christie said at one point, and *then* had sexual intercourse with her corpse.

When Evans returned home, Christie told him that she had gassed herself and that he had best flee since authorities would think Evans murdered his wife. Evans then reportedly murdered his child and sold off the household furniture before fleeing. His confusing statements throughout his trial concerning the death of the Evans child and his wife only further confused and complicated his actual role in the deaths of his wife and child.

Following the deaths of the three prostitutes, Christie said he sold his wife's wedding ring and the household furniture, and wandered about London with a total loss of memory. When he was arrested, he said, he had been sleeping in a cheap hotel. At the time he looked like a common tramp with dirty clothes, unshaven beard, and empty pockets. Christie was tried at the Old Bailey for three days, June 22-25, 1953, before Justice Fennemore. He was prosecuted by Sir Lionel Heald, then attorney general, and defended by Derek Curtis Bennett. Little defense could be offered on Christie's behalf, so Bennett opted to plead his client insane. Several medical experts examined Christie and testified that he was sane. The jury returned a verdict of guilty and Christie was sentenced to death. He was hanged at Pentonville Prison on July 15, 1953.

The conviction and execution of the monster Christie left many believing that Timothy Evans' conviction and hanging was a gross miscarriage of justice, that he had been executed for a crime that Christie himself had committed, the murder of Mrs. Beryl Evans, although considerable doubt exists that Christie killed the Evans child. This is the one murder that he said he did not commit, and the one murder that Evans admitted committing.

The Evans case remains a baffling mystery, which is exactly the way Christie wanted it, for he in no way cleared up the Evans murders but, through his whining statements, seemed to add even more confusion as to who was the real killer of Mrs. Evans and her child. Such were Christie's strange perversions that he would be content to go to the hangman knowing that he had created a lingering doubt in the minds of those who sent Timothy Evans to his death. From the grave, Christie would nag the consciences of good men, whereas he was himself without conscience altogether.

THE SCOTTISH GUNMAN/1956-1958

Peter Thomas Anthony Manuel (1927-1958) was born in New York in 1927 to immigrant Scottish parents. During the Depression, Manuel's parents were forced to return to Scotland where they remained. By the time Manuel was sixteen, a probation officer remarked that he had the worst juvenile record he had ever seen. By age thirty, his record included prison sentences for burglary, theft, indecent assault, and rape.

In January 1956, Manuel committed a more serious crime. In Glasgow he met 17-year-old Anne Kneilands, who was wait-

Peter Thomas Anthony Manuel, a serial killer who claimed the lives of at least nine people and who was hanged on July 11, 1958.

ing for her boyfriend. Manuel persuaded her to join him for coffee. As the two walked toward her home later, Manuel dragged the girl into a wooded area, where he bashed in her skull with a piece of iron. Manuel was routinely questioned by police, but he did not become a suspect in the murder.

The following summer, Manuel acquired a gun for the first time. In September 1956, he and two other men and a woman burglarized an unoccupied house south of Glasgow. After breaking into the first home, Manuel suggested burglarizing a second. When his companions declined, Manuel went by himself. The home he selected belonged to the Watt family. Mr. Watt, a master baker, had left that day for a fishing trip to Lochgilphead, eighty miles away.

Manuel invaded the Watt home, where he shot three people he found there, Mrs. Marion Watt, her sister, Margaret Brown, and 16-year-old Vivienne Brown, at close range. The two older women died immediately and the teenager was mortally wounded. Neighbors and a cleaning lady who discovered the bodies the next day called police. The investigation indicated that although the women's attacker had disarranged their clothing, they had not been sexually assaulted. Some valuables had been stolen.

When the police discovered that Mr. Watt had had affairs, he became a suspect. They soon proved it was possible for him to have driven back to Glasgow, murdered his family, and returned to the small fishing town by the following morning. They also located witnesses who said they had seen Watt on the ferry that night. Watt was then held at Barlinnie Prison, the very place where Peter Manuel was serving an eighteen-month sentence for burglary.

On October 8, 1956, Watt's attorney received a letter from Manuel offering information about the murders to Watt. As the attorney and Watt listened to Manuel, they became convinced Manuel was the murderer or had, at least, been present. Manuel refused to reveal the identity of the alleged perpetrator, but Watt was released from custody.

A year later, in early December, Manuel traveled to Newcastle-upon-Tyne, England. Although he was never formally charged with the crime, authorities believe he murdered cab driver Stanley Dunn, whose body was found some twenty miles from Newcastle. Dunn had been shot and his throat was slashed. Shortly after Manuel returned to Scotland, on December 28, 1957, 17-year-old Isabelle Cooke disappeared.

The girl left her home in a suburb of Glasgow to meet her boyfriend and go with him to a dance in the nearby town of Uddingston. The following day some of her belongings, including a slip and underpants, were found, but no trace of her body was discovered. As police continued the search for her, Manuel struck again. This time, on December 31, 1957 Manuel chose the home of 45-year-old Peter Smart, his wife, Doris, and their 10-year-old son, Michael. The Smarts had gone to sleep early in preparation for a trip the following day.

Apparently, as they slept, Manuel broke into their home in Uddingston and shot all of the Smart family members to death. Because they were expected to be out of town, no one contacted authorities until Smart failed to return to work on January 6, 1958. When police investigated and found the bodies, they also found evidence that the murderer had returned to the scene of the crime: the beds had been walked on with muddy boots, a mattress slashed, food eaten, and the family cat fed.

While conducting the murder investigation, police received information that Manuel, usually without funds, had been seen spending freely. Some of the crisp £5 notes he used were retrieved from a bar he frequented and traced to money Peter Smart had drawn out of his bank for his family's trip. Manuel was arrested on January 13, 1958, and confessed to the murders of the Smarts, the Watts, Isabelle Cooke, and Anne Knielands. Manuel's trial opened on May 12, 1958, before Lord Cameron. Gordon Gillies and Ronald Sutherland conducted the prosecution and Harald Leslie and Malcolm Morrison defended Manuel.

On May 22, 1958 Manuel dismissed his defense counsel and represented himself. Despite his insistence that Watt had killed his own family and that the police had forced his confession from him, he was convicted on May 26, 1958 of all but the Knielands murder. He was sentenced to death and was hanged on July 11, 1958, at Barlinnie Prison.

THE MURDER RAMPAGE OF "LITTLE RED"/ 1957-1958

Diminutive Charles Starkweather (AKA: Little Red; 1940-1959) committed the first of eleven murders at seventeen and

Caril Ann Fugate and Charles Starkweather, a photo taken only days before the serial killing began.

Eight of Starkweather's ten victims during his serial killing spree of December 1957-January 1958 (left to right, top row): Carol King, Robert Jensen, C. Lauer Ward, Clara Ward; (left to right, bottom row) Marion Bartlett, Velda Bartlett (Fugate's parents), Betty Jean Bartlett (Fugate's little sister) and August Meyer.

died in Nebraska's electric chair two years later. He and his girlfriend, Caril Ann Fugate (b. 1945), terrorized the plains states for a week in 1958 when they went on a murder rampage.

Uneducated, impressionable and resentful at his impoverished life, Starkweather spent most of his free time reading comic books, fiddling with hot rods and hunting rabbits. He emulated actor James Dean and believed he bore a striking resemblance to the actor. He followed the charismatic actor's career in films like *Rebel Without a Cause,* while working as a garbage man. In keeping with the rebel image, he took up with a much younger girl. Where girls Starkweather's age were put off by his five-foot, two-inch stature, 14-year-old Caril Ann Fugate was flattered by his attentions. She was well-developed for her age, rebellious in school, and at home.

On December 1, 1957, Starkweather robbed a service station, training a gun on attendant Robert Colvert. He took the cash from the station's register and Colvert's personal money, then kidnapped the attendant, driving him to a remote spot outside Lincoln, Nebraska, and killed him with a shot to the head. Starkweather was seventeen at the time, Colvert twenty-one.

In late January 1958, Starkweather called on Fugate at the home she shared with her mother and stepfather, Marion Bartlett. Fugate was not yet home from school, so Starkweather passed the time quarreling with Fugate's mother, Velda Bartlett. Starkweather was carrying his prize possession, a hunting rifle, with him (he was rarely without it). The quarrel mushroomed into a shouting match, which Starkweather ended by shooting the Bartletts dead. Starkweather later stated: "They said they were tired of me hanging around. I told Mrs. Bartlett off and she got so mad that she slapped me. When I hit her back, her husband started to come at me, so I had to let both of them have it with my rifle." To the hateful little Starkweather, it was the victims' fault for arguing with him.

Starkweather knew Fugate did not like her parents, or so he later claimed and she reportedly made no objection to his murdering the Bartletts. Further, she stood by without objection when Starkweather murdered her sister, choking two-year-old Betty Jean Bartlett by shoving the gun barrel down her throat. He hid the baby's body in a cardboard box, put Marion Bartlett's body in a chicken coop behind the house and wrapped it in rags and newspapers, then disposed of Velda Bartlett in an abandoned outhouse, also covering her with newspapers.

The brutal murders of the three Bartletts did not trouble the killer or Fugate, who, after the bodies had been hidden, made sandwiches and munched their lunch as they watched television. To keep away unwanted visitors, Fugate insisted Starkweather put a note on the front door. It read: "Stay Away. Every Body is Sick With the Flu."

The note failed to deter Fugate's older sister when she came to call. She knocked anyway, and Fugate warned her to stay away. The sister told her husband that Caril Ann had refused to let her in. Both of them thought her behavior strange, so they called the police. They, too, were refused entrance. The police went away unsatisfied and were called again two days later when Fugate turned away her grandmother.

Assistant Police Chief Eugene Masters sent two officers with the grandmother to check on the Bartlett house. They ignored the warning sign and entered to find the house empty except for the bodies. Police surmised that the couple had made more sandwiches, packed them in Starkweather's car, and left. They swore out arrest warrants and the search began. A short time later, a gas station attendant in nearby Bennet, Nebraska, told police that the fugitives had stopped at his station to fix a flat, fill the tank of their car, and buy shotgun and rifle ammunition.

Starkweather's next victim was farmer August Meyer, his life taken on January 29, 1958. Police received a tip that Starkweather's car was parked outside Meyer's farmhouse. Sheriff Merle Karnopp and his men surrounded the house and called through a bullhorn for Starkweather's surrender. When no answer came, police entered the building to find Meyer dead, his head torn apart by a shotgun blast.

Evert Broening, a farmer helping in the search for Starkweather, found two bodies in an storm cellar near Meyer's farm a short time later. Seventeen-year-old Robert Jensen and 16-year-old Carol King had been shot in the head. Jensen's car was missing, and King had been raped before being killed. The posse seeking Starkweather and Fugate swelled to 200 police officers.

The next victims died at the home of businessman C. Lauer Ward. A car was parked in Ward's driveway, and his own 1956 Packard was gone, although Ward had not come to work. There was no answer when officers knocked on the Ward's door. When they entered the house, police found Ward, forty-seven, dead in the foyer, shot in the head. His wife, Clara, and their maid, Lillian Fenci, were bound and gagged in a bedroom. The women had been stabbed to death and mutilated.

Alarmed police realized that Starkweather was murdering everyone he encountered. To quell this lethal epidemic, and to aid in the manhunt, 200 armed soldiers from the National Guard were called up and participated in the dragnet, which now numbered more than 1,200 searchers.

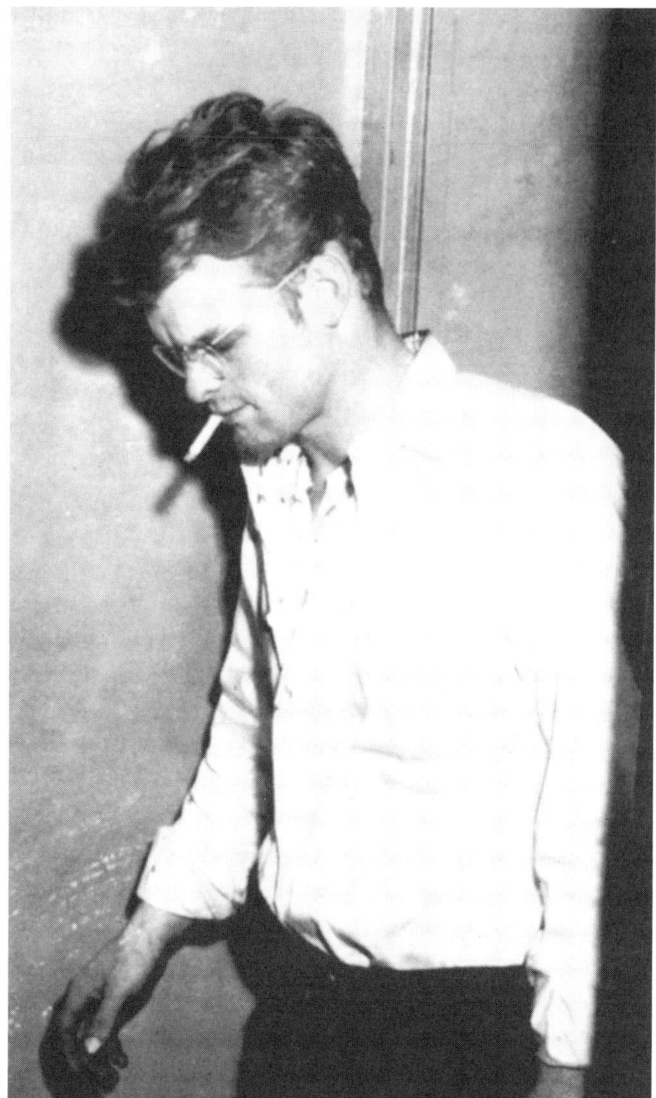

Starkweather in custody; he was caught on a highway while trying to murder a motorist.

Caril Ann Fugate shown in custody, drinking a soda pop, and unconcerned with the slaughter committed by her boyfriend Starkweather.

Starkweather in a jail cell awaiting trial; he at first shielded Fugate, then implicated her in his killings. The banty serial killer was executed on June 24, 1959.

Fourteen-year-old Caril Ann Fugate, smiling as she is sent to prison; she was later paroled.

Meanwhile, Starkweather and Fugate headed west. When they neared Douglas, Wyoming, the serial killer saw a car parked along the roadway. Shoe salesman Merle Collison was napping inside the car. Starkweather woke him up with a gunshot, firing through the window of the car and shouting: "Come on out of that car, mister!"

As the salesman stepped from the car, Starkweather fired nine bullets into him, killing him instantly and blowing his body back into the car.

"We've got us another car, honey!" Starkweather shouted to Fugate. The killer pushed Collison's body away, sitting behind the wheel, but when he tried to release the emergency break, he found it stuck. At that moment, Starkweather saw an approaching car and flagged down motorist Joseph Sprinkle, shouting: "Help me release this brake or I'll kill you!"

Sprinkle saw Collison's body and realized that his only chance was to grab Starkweather's rifle as he maneuvered around the brake. The motorist had a firm hold of the rifle, which caused the enraged Starkweather to scream: "You bastard! Gimme my rifle!"

Fugate stood in the road, watching. Starkweather called to her: "Jump him, Caril! Get my shotgun!"

As the two struggled for the gun, a police car arrived. Instead of going to Starkweather's aid, Fugate ran toward Deputy Sheriff William Rohmer's car. "Help!" she yelled. "It's Starkweather! He's going to kill me! He's crazy! Arrest him!" It was later stated by prosecutors that the clever little Fugate realized that her murderous boyfriend was about to be apprehended and she immediately played the role of the victim to dispel any image of being a murder accomplice.

The courageous Sprinkle fought wildly with the killer, finally wresting the gun away from Starkweather. The killer shoved Sprinkle away and managed to release the emergency brake, driving off in Collison's car at 115 miles per hour. In the ensuing chase, the rear window of Starkweather's getaway car was shot out by pursuing officers. He suddenly stopped the car and staggered out, complaining of a superficial cut on his ear from broken glass. "I'm hit!" he shouted to the policemen. "You lousy bastards shot me!"

Sheriff Earl Heflin leveled a shotgun on the killer, while Police Chief Robert Ainsley frisked him.

"You're a real tough guy, aren't you?" Ainsley asked the murderer.

Fugate claimed at her trial that she had been an innocent hostage all along. Starkweather was willing to support this, at first saying: "Don't take it out on the girl. She had no part of any of it." He insisted Fugate had been his hostage. Starkweather maintained this position until Fugate testified in court against him, labeling him a killer. He turned on her and painted a picture of a less-than-innocent hostage. "One time," Starkweather claimed, "she said that some hamburgers were lousy and we ought to go back and shoot all them people in the restaurant. After I shot her folks and baby sister, Caril sat and watched television while I wrapped the bodies in rags and newspapers. We just cooked up that hostage story between us."

In Fugate's defense, her attorney claimed that she refused to let her sister or the police enter her parents' house to avoid further bloodshed. The jury did not believe it. Caril Ann Fugate was sentenced to life imprisonment (she would be paroled from the Nebraska Centre for Women in June 1976). Fugate left the courtroom sobbing and insisting that she was innocent of any crimes.

Charles Starkweather was easily convicted and sentenced to death. The serial killer was electrocuted in the Nebraska State Penitentiary at midnight, June 24, 1959. Just before his execution and true to his character, he rejected a request from the Lions Club in Beatrice, Nebraska, that he donate his eyes for transplant after his death. Typical of the vicious-minded Starkweather, he replied: "Hell, no! No one ever did anything for me! Why the hell should I do anything for anyone else?"

THE SEX BEAST/1957-1959

Melvin David Rees (AKA: The Sex Beast; b. 1933), a student at the University of Maryland in 1953, was taken into custody on Mar. 12, 1955, and charged with assault after he tried to force a 36-year-old woman into his car. The victim later dropped the charges. In the meantime, Rees set up a nook in an abandoned basement in a cinderblock building near Annapolis, Maryland. He plastered the basement with pornographic pictures and also put up a yearbook picture of Wanda Tipson, a 1955 graduate of the University of Maryland.

On June 26, 1957, Rees was driving a green Chrysler near Annapolis when he passed a car in which Margaret Harold was a passenger. Rees forced the car off the road and, armed with a .38-caliber pistol, forced his way into the back seat of the car. When Harold panicked, Rees shot her in the head. The car's driver, an Army sergeant, quickly jumped from the car and ran down the road, weaving back and forth in an attempt to avoid being shot. Rees did not fire at the sergeant, however. After running a mile, the sergeant saw a farm house, where he stopped and called Annapolis authorities. Police arrived and found Harold's body in the abandoned car. Although the sergeant gave police a detailed description of the assailant, police were unable to track down the killer.

A year and a half later, Rees was driving in Virginia. He put on his car's high beam lights and closely followed another car. As the other car, driven by truck driver Carroll Jackson, speeded up or slowed, Rees did the same. Then Rees speeded up and drove alongside Jackson's car. Jackson, twenty-nine, slowed and Rees drove in front of Jackson's car, causing Jackson to stop. Jackson got out, leaving his wife, Mildred, and daughters Susan, four, and Janet, eighteen months, in the car.

Rees, armed with a pistol, got out of his car and rushed up to Jackson. Rees ordered the rest of the family out of the car, tied Jackson's hands with a necktie, and made the family get into his car trunk. The next day, Mrs. H. M. Ballard, a Jackson relative, saw Jackson's car abandoned alongside a road and notified Sheriff Willis E. Proffitt. Rees' skid marks, Mildred Jackson's purse, the car keys, and dolls were found.

On Mar. 4, 1959, Carroll Jackson's body was found by the side of a road near Fredericksburg, Virginia, by John Scott and James Beach. Jackson had been shot in the head and his daughter, Janet, also found dead on the scene, had suffocated after Rees put her under her father's body.

Shortly afterward, two boys were digging in the dirt not far from the scene of the Harold attack and uncovered some hair. They notified police, who investigated and found the corpse of 4-year-old Susan Jackson, her skull fractured. The body of her mother, Mildred Jackson, was also found; she had been raped and strangled or beaten to death. Police linked the Jackson murders to the basement in the cinderblock building where they found a button like those on Mildred Jackson's dress.

After extensive news coverage, police received many tips from citizens who had noticed a strange man driving a green or blue Ford. Police also received a letter from a man in Norfolk, Virginia, who said Rees, a musician, had killed the Jacksons and Harold and gave a description of Rees, saying he had a thin face, long dark hair, and thick eyebrows. The informant said he had been with Rees at the time of the Harold murder, and Rees had been taking Benzedrine. When the writer received a letter from Rees postmarked West Memphis, Arkansas, he notified police.

Melvin David Rees with an unknown woman; he killed motorists in Maryland and Virginia and went to prison for life.

FBI agents found Rees in this small Arkansas town, where he was selling pianos in a music store and arrested him on a charge of flight to avoid prosecution for Harold's murder. He had also violated federal law in committing interstate crimes, which had allowed federal agents to enter the case.

Rees was put into a police lineup and the army sergeant identified him as the killer of Margaret Harold. FBI officials searched Rees' parents' house and found a .38-caliber pistol in a saxophone case in the attic. Ballistics reports identified this pistol as the weapon used to murder Harold. Agents also found a picture of Mildred Jackson that had appeared in the newspaper and attached to the picture was a message that read "Caught on a lonely road...after pulling them over, leveled pistol and ordered them out and into car trunk, which was opened by husband and both bound...".

Further investigation linked Rees to the slayings of Shelby Jean Venable, sixteen, and Mary Elizabeth Fellers, eighteen, who had been found dead in rivers in Maryland. He was also linked to the sexual assaults and murders of Ann Ryan, fourteen, and Marie Shomette, sixteen, murders that occurred in the area of the University of Maryland.

After Rees was tried, convicted and sentenced to a life term in prison in 1961 in Baltimore, Maryland, he was sent to Virginia, where he stood trial for the Jackson family slayings. Once again he was found guilty and sentenced to death. Rees was convicted of federal crimes and managed to evade state death penalties. He is presently confined in the federal detention center in Springfield, Missouri.

Albert DeSalvo, the Boston Strangler, murdered thirteen or more women between 1962 and 1964; he went to prison for life, but was murdered in his prison cell in 1973.

THE BOSTON STRANGLER/1962-1964

Thirteen Boston-area women were sexually assaulted and then strangled to death between June 1962 and January 1964 by a fiend the press dubbed the "Boston Strangler." This man proved to be Albert Henry DeSalvo (AKA: The Boston Strangler, The Green Man, The Measuring Man; 1931-1973). Born in Chelsea, Massachusetts, in 1931, DeSalvo was one of six children. His father was a severe taskmaster who beat him and the other children over the smallest infraction. He did not spare his wife either, using his fists on the poor, overworked woman whenever he was displeased.

DeSalvo's father was also criminally bent and served two prison terms for theft before his wife divorced him in 1944. Like his father, DeSalvo began stealing when in his teens, and was charged with breaking and entering several times before joining the army at age seventeen. He served in the occupation forces in Germany, where he began boxing on a U. S. army team. Small, but squat and tough, DeSalvo became the U.S. Army welterweight and, while stationed in Frankfurt, Germany, met and married a petite German girl.

Returning to the U. S. with his new wife, DeSalvo was stationed at Fort Dix, New Jersey, where, in January 1955, he was charged with molesting a 9-year-old girl, his first sex offense. The child's mother, fearing publicity would affect her daughter, refused to prosecute. The Army, therefore, had no case against DeSalvo and released him. He received an honorable discharge a short time later and moved back to Boston with his wife.

DeSalvo worked as a handyman, supporting his wife and two small children. His sex drive was almost overwhelming. He exhausted his wife Irmgard, who told him to control himself. DeSalvo demanded sex from her on an almost non-stop basis. "Five or six times a day don't mean much to me," he later stated. Finally, Irmgard told her husband, "Al, you can learn by yourself to control yourself. It is just a matter of self-control."

When it came to sex, however, DeSalvo had no control. He thought about sex night and day, according to his later admissions, and he found little release. He was arrested for breaking and entering and given a suspended sentence in 1958 and a short time later he embarked on a sexual game whereby he became known to the police as "The Measuring Man."

DeSalvo would approach young, attractive women in their apartments, telling them he represented a modeling agency and that they had been selected as possible candidates for modeling in television commercials. If chosen, they could make considerable money and would become famous. Further, they might even be offered a movie contract.

Hundreds of young women opened their apartment doors to him after hearing this pitch and DeSalvo, clipboard and tape measure in hand, would then measure the woman's vital statistics. At these times DeSalvo would not make overt sexual

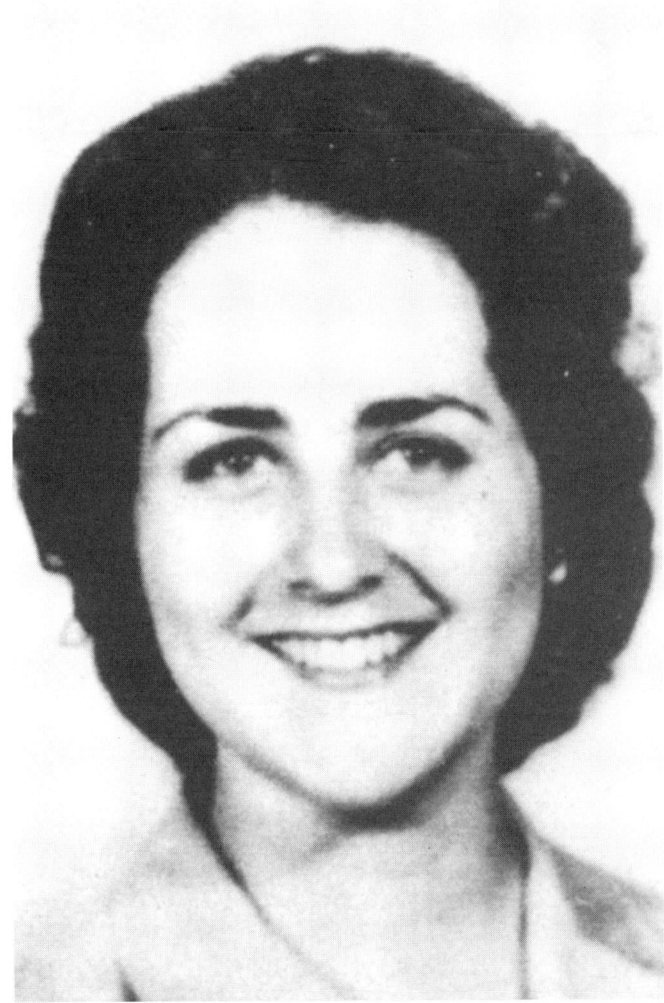

Patricia Bissette, twenty-three, was one of DeSalvo's many victims; she invited him into her apartment, where he strangled and raped her on December 8, 1962.

approaches, but he did seduce a number of these gullible females. He later claimed that many of the would-be models, however, seduced *him* and invited him back.

On March 17, 1960, police in Cambridge, Massachusetts responded to an alarm of a break-in and they chased and caught DeSalvo. He had thrown away a screwdriver, which he had been using to force apartment door locks, but this was recovered. On his person was found a pair of gloves and a tailor's measuring tape. He admitted that he was "The Measuring Man" about which the police had received scores of complaints.

DeSalvo was convicted of breaking and entering and received a two-year sentence. He was released in ten months. The police did not list him as a sexual deviant, but put him on their list of potential burglars. When DeSalvo was released from prison, he returned to his family, but he now became more aggressive, breaking into apartments and tying up and raping females. He was described by his victims at this time as "The Green Man" since he wore green work pants and shirt. DeSalvo later bragged that he tied up and raped six women in one morning. Moreover, he ranged throughout New England, assaulting, according to police in Massachusetts and Connecticut, hundreds of women. DeSalvo put the number at more than 1,000.

In the summer of 1962, DeSalvo began to add murder to his sexual attacks, raping and strangling his victims, the first of whom was 55-year-old Anna Slesers, whose body was found in her apartment on Gainsborough Street in Boston, her corpse placed in a lascivious position. DeSalvo had used a cord to strangle his victim and had tied the ends in a bow beneath her chin, a technique he would continue to employ, as if it were his trademark.

Within two weeks, DeSalvo attacked and killed 85-year-old Mary Mullen, a victim he later reluctantly talked about since she reminded him of his grandmother. On June 30, 1962, DeSalvo raped and strangled Helen Blake, a 65-year-old nurse. Nina Nichols was his next victim, a woman in her sixties. She fought her attacker, digging her nails into his arms as he strangled her from behind.

On August 19, 1962, DeSalvo raped and strangled 75-year-old Ida Irga. Jane Sullivan, sixty-seven, died at DeSalvo's hands the next day. Boston police were inundated with demands to solve the rash of horrible rape-murders. Though scores of sexual deviants were arrested and questioned, DeSalvo escaped attention. He refrained from making more attacks until December 5, 1962, his wedding anniversary. He later claimed that then, as on former attacks, he became obsessed with the image of violent sex, that the top of his head "was so hot that I thought it would explode."

On that day, DeSalvo spotted an attractive girl entering an apartment and followed her. He knocked on her door and employed the usual technique that invariably gained him access to an apartment, saying through the door that he was a repair man sent by the landlord to check the pipes and toilet. The girl, however, refused to let him inside. He went to another apartment and knocked on the door. Inside was 25-year-old Sophie Clark, a tall, attractive black woman.

Clark opened the door a crack and DeSalvo persuaded her to open the door, saying that he was from a modeling company, using his old Measuring Man technique. As he walked inside the apartment, Clark turned her back on DeSalvo, who later reported that he was stunned by her curvaceous body. He leaped on her from behind, subduing her, raping her and strangling her, leaving her as he had the others, her naked body propped upward, legs spread, the bow tied beneath the cord he had used to strangle her.

DeSalvo's next victim was Patricia Bissette, a 23-year-old secretary he had visited years earlier as The Measuring Man. On December 8, 1962, she invited him inside, gave him a cup of coffee and, when she turned her back, he placed his arm around her throat and then raped her, strangling her with her own nylons. On February 16, 1963, DeSalvo gained entrance to the apartment of a woman, who was home sick. He attacked her, but she fought so desperately, scratching him and biting him while screaming out for help, that DeSalvo fled. (This woman, whose identity is withheld, proved that by ignoring quiet submission to the rapist, as is often counseled, she had saved her life.)

On March 9, 1963, 69-year-old Mary Brown allowed DeSalvo into her apartment, thinking him a workman sent by the landlord to fix her stove. This time DeSalvo's violence was unchecked. He had brought along a lead pipe, which he used to crush his victim's head. He raped Brown *after* killing her. He then drove a fork into her breasts several times, leaving it embedded in the flesh. He also strangled her, although, by that time, she was dead.

On May 6, 1963, instead of driving to work, DeSalvo drove to Cambridge, "on an impulse" he later said, and there spotted pretty Beverly Samans, a 23-year-old undergraduate living on University Road. He gained entrance to her apartment, tying her to bedposts. He then blindfolded and gagged her and then repeatedly raped her. DeSalvo used the girl's nylon stockings to strangle her.

Before leaving his victim, DeSalvo used his jackknife to repeatedly stab the girl. An autopsy reported twenty-two stab wounds. DeSalvo later stated, "Once I stabbed her, I couldn't stop. I kept hitting her and hitting her with that knife...She kept bleeding from the throat...I hit her and hit her and hit her..." His savage bloodlust exhausted, DeSalvo walked into the kitchen, wiped off the handle of the knife and dropped it into the sink. When found by police, this knife offered no fingerprints.

DeSalvo's eleventh victim was 58-year-old Evelyn Corbin, whom he strangled and raped on September 8, 1963. When Corbin failed to keep an appointment, police were summoned and they found the woman as they had the others, except that she had been manually strangled. The killer had left his trademark, a nylon with a bow, tied about her ankle. Boston police seemed helpless to catch the killer. The city was in a near panic with thousands of husbands constantly calling their wives or staying home from work to protect them against a fiend who seemed to come and go at will. Not a single person reported seeing this serial killer and police were admittedly stymied.

A special "Strangler Bureau" was set up and a dedicated detective force began running down the slimmest clues around the clock. Dozens of sex offenders, muggers, and even peeping toms were rounded up, questioned, and subsequently released. At one point, the brilliant medium, Peter Hurkos, was brought into the case. He examined a number of personal items belonging to suspects and gave a startling and somewhat accurate description of the killer, although he never pinpointed DeSalvo or any other person as the Boston Strangler.

A number of good suspects were kept under surveillance, but proved innocent. On November 23, 1963, a day following President John F. Kennedy's assassination in Dallas, Texas, DeSalvo struck again, gaining entrance to the apartment of Joann Graff, a 23-year-old dress designer. He raped and strangled her with her own black leotards, tying these in a bow about her neck. Following the killing, DeSalvo went home, helped his wife clean up their apartment, played with his children, watched a television news report, and then sat down to dinner.

DeSalvo had watched a television report that night on the death of Joann Graff. He later stated: "I knew it was me who did it but why I did it and everything else, I don't know...I wasn't excited. I didn't think about it. I sat down to dinner and didn't think about it at all."

On January 4, 1964, DeSalvo struck for the last time, claiming his thirteenth victim, 19-year-old Mary Sullivan. Once inside her apartment, he flourished a knife, tied up the girl, and raped her. He then strangled her with his hands. He left her naked and, as a bizarre afterthought, inserted a broom into her and placed a card he found in the apartment between her toes which read, "Happy New Year."

Criminal attorney F. Lee Bailey, who defended DeSalvo, is shown looking at a photo of his client in 1967, after the Boston Strangler escaped from a mental hospital and was recaptured within thirty hours.

In fall 1964, a young woman reported being sexually assaulted in her apartment, describing a man police identified as DeSalvo, using the same technique as DeSalvo had when he was labeled as The Measuring Man. DeSalvo was arrested for breaking and entering, held on a $100,000 bond, and sent to the mental institution at Bridgewater. Amazingly, police never coupled DeSalvo with the crimes of the Boston Strangler. Officials later stated that DeSalvo's police rap sheet listed him only as a felon guilty of breaking and entering. Police records revealed nothing of his sexual offenses.

At Bridgewater, DeSalvo claimed that he was hearing voices and he was diagnosed by psychiatrists as "schizophrenic." On February 4, 1965, he was ordered to be detained indeterminately by Judge Edward A. Pecce. Another inmate at Bridgewater, George Nassar, who had killed a garage attendant and who was himself a suspect in the Strangler killings, met DeSalvo and, after listening to him talk for some time, mostly about sex and violence, came to believe DeSalvo was the Boston Strangler. He informed his young lawyer, F. Lee Bailey, and Bailey interviewed DeSalvo, recording his conversations.

DeSalvo admitted being the Strangler and even added two killings to the known murder count of thirteen. More importantly, DeSalvo related facts about the murders which the police had kept secret, the positioning of the naked bodies, the tying of bows in the strangling cords, nylons, and pantyhose, the location of the wounds inflicted, all the sordid details that only the killer would have known.

Police were still puzzled since they had no eyewitness, who could positively identify DeSalvo. Bailey was convinced that DeSalvo was the killer and said so, but officials were disinclined to officially prosecute DeSalvo as a mental patient. DeSalvo was kept in confinement and the strangulation murders stopped. Most reliable authorities considered DeSalvo the Boston Strangler, including court authorities, who transferred DeSalvo to the Walpole State Prison where, in his cell, on November 26, 1973, he was found dead, stabbed to death in his heart.

THE PIED PIPER OF TUCSON/1964-1965

Like Charles Starkweather before him, serial killer Charles Howard Schmid, Jr. (AKA: Smitty; The Pied Piper of Tucson; b. 1942) five feet, three inches tall, was bothered by his short stature. To improve his image, he became a devoted gymnast, winning a state championship in high school. Uncomfortable with his peers in his twenties, he enchanted teenagers in Tucson, Arizona, with fantastic tales. "Smitty" Schmid's dark fantasies turned to terrible reality in spring 1964. His teenage friends apparently knew when their hero turned to murder, but they told no one.

Mary Rae French was Schmid's devoted follower. The 18-year-old girl worked at his mother's nursing home and turned most of her pay over to him. She never minded when he used her small cottage for orgies, and she often joined in. On the evening of May 31, 1964, French, Schmid, and a friend, John Saunders, were talking about Smitty's exploits with girls, when, French recalled, "he suddenly got a different look on his face" and announced: "I want to kill a girl...I think I can get away with it." French suggested as their victim 15-year-old Alleen Rowe, whom she knew would be alone because her mother worked late in the evening. French called the girl and persuaded her to agree to sneak out of her house and meet the threesome.

Charles Howard Schmid, Jr., at his murder trial; he lured three teenage girls to the desert outside Tucson, Arizona, killing them in 1964-1965, and went to prison for life.

The two young men and two girls drove into the desert, stopping at a remote spot, where French stayed in the car while the men took Alleen off into the shadows and raped her. Then they killed the terrified, struggling girl by bashing in her head with rocks. French helped Schmid and Saunders dig a shallow grave into which the battered body of Alleen Rowe was placed. Everyone who knew Alleen Rowe was soon questioned about her disappearance. Schmid appeared puzzled when investigators interviewed him. He said that he had had a date with Rowe on the night of her murder, but that she was not home when he arrived to pick her up. Police kept the case open but had no leads or clues to follow in the case, which remained dormant.

Schmid soon started dating 17-year-old Gretchen Fritz, the daughter of a physician, whose wild nature seemed to match his own. Schmid became furious when Fritz informed him that she had "gone all the way" with a boy in California. "I really loved that girl! I'll kill her!" Schmid told a friend. On August 16, 1965, Gretchen and her 13-year-old sister, Wendy Fritz, went to a drive-in movie.

Schmid met them at the drive-in, and enticed them to go driving with him in the desert. As in the case of Rowe, Schmid drove to a secluded area and there he killed both girls, leaving their bodies exposed along an unfrequented road. After he bragged to his friend, Richard Bruns, that he had killed them, Schmid and Bruns returned to the desert and buried the already-decomposing bodies.

Friends of the Fritzes hired some "Mafia types" to investigate their daughters' disappearances. The men, hearing Schmid's story that the girls had run away to San Diego, insisted that he go with them to hunt for the girls. Schmid stayed in San Diego for several months, until he was arrested for impersonating an FBI agent questioning girls on the beach.

Although the police by this time listed Schmid as a strong suspect in the Fritz and Rowe killings, they did not have enough substantial evidence with which to charge him in those murders. Schmid's friends were of no help to authorities. These moronic and ghoulish teenagers reveled in Schmid's horror stories and delighted in protecting their murderous idol. However, Schmid himself began to crack under the pressure of the intense investigations.

Schmid once drove his fist through the wall of his small cottage, then ran outside shouting: "God is going to punish me!" Bruns, too, was feeling the pressure and he was beginning to get terrified that his psychopathic friend might murder Bruns' girlfriend, Kathy Morath, who had previously been enamored of Schmid. With that possibility preying on his mind, Bruns went to visit his grandmother in Ohio, and from there called the Tucson police and told them everything he knew.

On November 11, 1965, Schmid was arrested for the murders of the Fritz sisters. Mary Rae French and John Saunders, under arrest for abetting the murder of Alleen Rowe, turned state's evidence against him. Schmid was found guilty and sentenced to death, though the punishment was never carried out because of the 1971 U.S. Supreme Court decision that overturned capital punishment. Saunders received a life sentence, and French was sent to prison for four to five years.

Schmid was later tried for the murder of Alleen Rowe. He was convicted and received an additional fifty-five-year sentence on top of his life sentence in the Fritz killings.

Held in the Arizona State Prison, Schmid escaped on November 11, 1972, along with Raymond Hudgens, a convicted three-time killer. Schmid and Hudgens held four people hostage on a ranch near Tempe, Arizona, before deciding to separate. Both were caught again within days and returned to prison.

TWO SERIAL KILLERS IN SALT LAKE CITY/ 1966

Eight days before Christmas 1966, Walter Kelbach (b. 1938), twenty-eight, and his friend Myron Lance (b. 1941), twenty-five, went on a killing spree that left six people dead. A 1972 television NBC documentary titled "Thou Shalt Not Kill" profiled these two killers from Salt Lake City, Utah. The two ex-convicts were also homosexual lovers and had consumed large amounts of drugs on the night of December 17, 1966.

Kelbach drove to a Salt Lake City gas station where the two robbed an attendant of $147 and forced him into the back seat of their station wagon. They drove into the desert where, after forcing their victim to engage in sex, Kelbach stabbed him repeatedly and threw the body into a roadside ditch. Victim number two was Michael Holtz, who also worked in a filling station. He was abducted and murdered in the same fashion, this time by both Kelbach and Lance. Police issued a citywide order that all gas stations be closed at nightfall.

Serial killer Walter Kelbach, who, with Myron Lance, murdered six people in 1966.

Four days before Christmas, Kelbach and Lance got into the back seat of a taxi belonging to Grant Creed Strong. Suspicious about the two grinning men who wanted to go to the airport, Strong radioed the dispatcher. He said that if he encountered problems, he would click his microphone twice. As the taxi pulled over to the curb, Lance thrust a gun at Strong's head and demanded all his money. Strong handed over $9, which angered Lance, and he shot Strong through the head, killing him.

Myron Lance, who, like his partner, had no reservations in killing people for cash.

The two men proceeded to Lolly's Tavern, near the airport. Announcing to the stunned patrons that they were committing a robbery, Lance casually shot 47-year-old James Sizemore through the head. The killers took $300 from the till and then sprayed the bar with gunfire, killing Beverly Mace, thirty-four, and Fred William Lillie, twenty. Kelbach and Lance fled, but were soon captured at a police roadblock.

Charged with first-degree murder, Kelbach and Lance were convicted, and quickly sentenced to death. But when the Supreme Court outlawed capital punishment in 1971, the pair were spared. Neither killer ever expressed remorse. "I haven't any feelings towards the victims," Lance said. "I don't mind people getting hurt because I just like to watch it," Kelbach added. At this writing, both men are imprisoned at the Utah State Penitentiary.

A WEST COAST MURDER SPREE/1967

Thomas Eugene Braun (AKA: Mike Ford; b. 1948) was born in the state of Washington. When barely into his adolescence, he was forced to shoot the family dog because his drunken father thought the dog was "a chicken killer." On August 17, 1967, Braun left his job as a gas station attendant in Ritzville, Washington, to ride off with Leonard Maine (b. 1948). They took with them a .22-caliber Luger and a Frontier Colt single-action .22-caliber pistol.

Heading for Seattle, they overtook a late-model Skylark driven by 22-year-old Deanna Buse on Route 72 outside Richmond. They motioned her over to the side of the road on the pretense that her tires were going flat. When she got out of the car, Braun aimed a gun at her head and told her to get into their car. Maine got into the Skylark and followed Braun to a secluded spot near Echo Lake. There Braun shot Buse five times. He and Maine drove on to Seattle, where they abandoned their car, driving off in Buse's stolen Skylark.

The next day, Braun and Maine crossed into Oregon and tried to register at a resort motel. The owner was suspicious of the unkempt strangers, and asked to see their vehicle registration. They drove off, but had a flat tire a few miles away. Samuel Ledgerwood, who had just come from his favorite fishing spot, offered to help. Braun pumped two shots into Ledgerwood's head, and then set fire to the Skylark. The two killers drove off in Ledgerwood's shiny new Buick. The two then continued south to Northern California.

On Route 120, Braun stopped to pick up two 17-year-old hitchhikers, Susan Bartolomei and Timothy Luce. Early the next morning, the Mease family stopped their car on the same highway to investigate what they thought was an accident. They found Susan Bartolomei lying on the side of the road, barely conscious. She said that two men named Mike and John from Oklahoma had shot them, killing Timothy. Meanwhile, searchers found the body of Deanna Buse. Oregon police reported the murder of Samuel Ledgerwood, and soon the manhunt had begun as three states pooled their resources in searching for the serial killers.

Several days later, Maine and Braun were captured at a motel in Jamestown, California, after Constable Ed Chafin noticed Ledgerwood's stolen green Buick with Oregon plates. Chafin called for back-up and he was soon joined by several officers, who, with drawn guns, entered the room where Maine

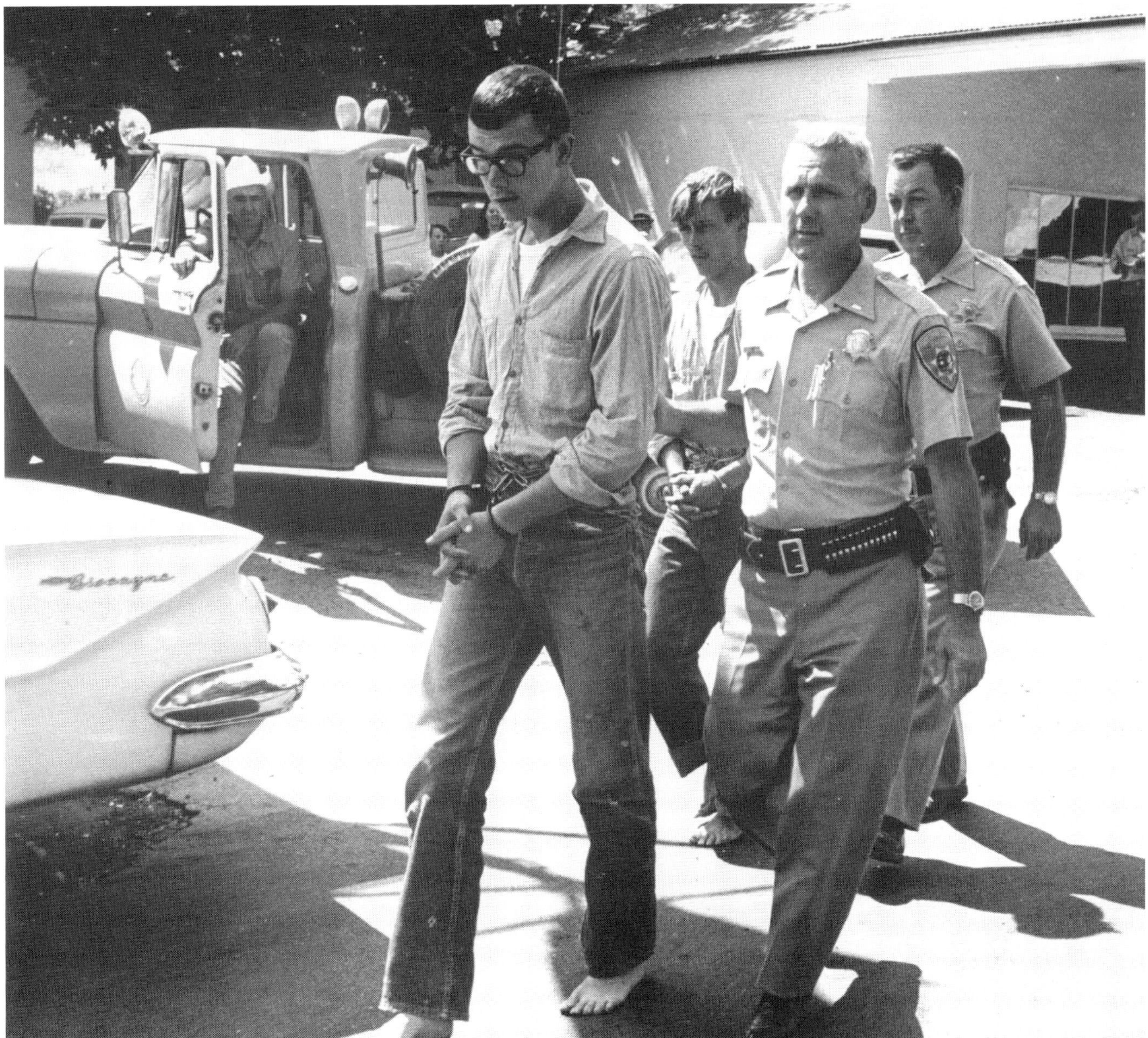

Thomas Eugene Braun (front, left) and Leonard Maine (behind Braun) are shown only minutes after they were captured at a motel in Jamestown, California (they are barefooted, having been caught napping in their rooms); both went to prison for life for senselessly murdering three people in 1967.

was sleeping. He surrendered meekly, pointing out the next room where Braun was asleep. The officers broke down the door of this room and spotted Braun in bed, his hands beneath a pillow.

"His hands, watch his hands!" shouted one of the officers. Braun reached for a gun, but an officer leaped upon him and wrested the weapon from the killer's grip. After being shown still photos and movies of the victims, they confessed to their crimes.

On December 2, 1968, Superior Court Judge Joseph Kelly of San Jose, California, sentenced Braun to die in the San Quentin gas chamber. However, the sentence was later commuted to life imprisonment. Leonard Maine also received a life sentence.

SERIAL KILLINGS IN HOUSTON/1970-1973

On Aug. 8, 1973, 17-year-old Elmer Wayne Henley (b. 1956) called the Pasadena, Texas, Police Department and said he had just shot his friend Dean Arnold Corll (1939-1973). The police found Dean Corll lying face down with six slugs in his shoulder and back. Henley then related a horrific story of serial killings perpetrated by Corlll, Henley and his friend David Owen Brooks (b. 1955), twenty-seven murders by their count. In the previous three years Corll indulged his sado-masochistic sexual fantasies by murdering teenaged boys, Henley said.

Corll had been punished harshly as a child, and when his parents divorced, he and his brother Stanley were shuttled between nursery schools and baby sitters. In 1964, Corll was drafted into the army, and by 1969 his personality disorders

Houston serial killer Dean Allen Corll, shown at home with a stuffed animal; he murdered twenty-seven people in the early 1970s.

In custody, Elmer Wayne Henley, Corll's slavish murder accomplice, turned on his mentor and killed him on August 8, 1973.

caused concern with his friends and relatives. Corll returned to Houston and went to work for the Lighting and Power Company. He began to associate with teenage boys, and sniffed glue with two of them, Elmer Wayne Henley and David Owen Brooks.

The killing began in 1970, when Corll lured hitchhiking University of Texas student Jeffrey Konen to his house in Pasadena. But Corll usually relied on Henley, a high school dropout, to find victims from the economically depressed Heights section of Houston. Corll promised to pay $200 for each victim lured into the trap, but he usually reneged. Brooks, Corll's first willing recruit, said he met the man in the schoolyard and Corll gave him some candy, after which they lived together for a time. In 1970, Brooks came home and found Corll engaged in sexual acts with two young men who had been bound and gagged. Brooks was given a car to keep silent.

Brooks and Henley soon became willing participants in murder. In the next two years, the three murdered twenty-seven young boys. Victims were lured to Corll's home for drug and alcohol parties. After the victims fell unconscious, Corll tied them up, sexually molested them, and killed them. He disposed of the bodies in either a remote spot near the Sam Rayburn Reservoir or a boat shed in southwest Houston rented for the purpose.

On August 8, 1973, Henley violated the "trust" by bringing 15-year-old Rhonda Williams to the apartment. "You weren't supposed to bring any girl!" Corll bellowed. The girl had run away from home and needed a place to stay for the night, and Henley said his friend Dean wouldn't mind. Varnish sniffing began, and Henley, Williams, and Timothy Kerley, sixteen, passed out. When he awoke and discovered that Corll had tied them up, Henley pleaded for his life. Corll released him when he promised to rape and kill Williams while Corll did the same to Kerley.

Henley, however, was too upset to perform a sexual act with the girl. He seized a .22-caliber pistol and pointed it at Corll, who taunted him. Henley fired six shots, and then called the local police. Later that day he took police to shed number eleven at the Southwest Boat Storage and the excavation began. After the twenty-seventh body was removed from the shallow graves at the boathouse and near the lake, the search stopped. A "record" had been established, eclipsing the slayings of twenty-five migrant workers in California in 1971 by serial killer Juan Corona. But Mary West, Corll's divorced mother, thought there might be more victims. The Houston police were unwilling to continue, despite hundreds of parents' requests for information about their missing children.

On August 11, 1973, the Houston district attorney filed

murder charges against Brooks and Henley. Judge Preston Dial barred the press during jury selection. The trial opened in San Antonio in July 1974. Henley and Brooks were convicted of the murders of six of the twenty-seven victims, and were each sentenced to life imprisonment.

Though their lawyers have repeatedly asked the courts to parole Henley and Brooks, these requests have been routinely denied. Meanwhile, Henley, considered to have a modest talent as an artist, produced a number of artworks while behind bars, some of these paintings exhibited in Houston art galleries in 1998.

MULLIN'S "OFFERINGS" TO THE GODS/ 1972-1973

In the early 1970s serial killers Edmund Emil Kemper III (see Cannibalism) and Herbert William Mullin (b. 1947) terrorized Santa Cruz, California, which had been known for years as a haven for drug-taking dropout hippies. Mullin, the religious-minded, schizophrenic son of a Marine colonel, spent a number of years smoking marijuana and taking LSD. When he was twenty-five, he began to hear voices that told him that if he sacrificed human lives, he would prevent the massive earthquakes predicted for Southern California.

Between October 1972 and February 1973, Mullin killed thirteen people: On October 13, 1972, Mullin gave a lift to Lawrence White, a tramp he met in the mountains. Mullin asked White to help him fix his car and while the old man's back was turned, the serial killer beat him to death with a baseball bat. Less than two weeks later, Mullin picked up coed Mary Guilfoyle. He stabbed the girl in the heart before disemboweling her and leaving her grisly remains on the shoulder of a road, where they were found in February 1973.

Apparently feeling guilt for these murders, Mullin went to St. Mary's Church in Santa Cruz, where he entered a confessional, confessing his killings to a Catholic priest, Father Henry Tomei. Mullin was suddenly seized by panic, believing that the priest would tell police. He promptly stabbed Tomei to death. Seeking revenge for his own crimes, which he attributed to marijuana, Mullin irrationally searched for James Gianera, the man who had introduced the drug to him. Unable to locate the man, he went, on January 25, 1973, to 29-year-old Kathy Francis, who gave Mullin Gianera's address.

Finding Gianera, Mullin shot him to death, then killed Gianera's wife by stabbing and shooting her. The serial killer then returned to Francis and murdered her and her two small boys, shooting them as the three lay asleep in bed. Mullin continued hunting humans, finding on February 6, 1973, four teenage boys, who were camping in the mountains. Mullin pulled his gun and shot all of them dead. On February 13, 1973, Mullin slowly cruised through the streets of Santa Cruz, spotting Fred Perez, an elderly man working in his garden. Mullin got out of his car, walked up to Perez and shot the old man dead. He then sauntered back to his car and leisurely drove off.

This time, he was positively identified by witnesses, who provided police with the license plate number of his car. He was arrested a short time later. Freely confessing to his murders, Mullin immediately mounted a defense based on insanity, telling officials that he had offered his victims to the gods to prevent devastating earthquakes in California, an absurd rationale that insisted he was actually saving lives by murdering people as sacrificial offerings.

Herbert William Mullin, center, murdered victims at random in the Santa Cruz, California, area as "offerings" to the gods, he said, in order to prevent earthquakes.

At Mullin's trial it was shown that he had voluntarily committed himself to mental hospitals five different times in the preceding years. Each time he was diagnosed as a paranoid schizophrenic with dangerous aggressive tendencies, given some drugs, and sent on his way. Yet, a close inspection of his background showed that it was unlike that of most serial killers. He had lived a relatively normal life as a teenager, participating in sports while in high school, where he was voted "most likely to succeed."

Mullin's attorneys pointed out that the accidental death of his best friend in a car crash in 1965, altered the youth's reason. At that time, the bereaved Mullin transformed his bedroom into a shrine to the dead friend, arranging furniture around a photograph of the dead boy. This traumatic experience, however, failed to convince the court that Mullin was deranged. The jury, determined that he should not be released, found him guilty on ten counts of murder, and he was sent to prison for life. He will be eligible for parole in 2020.

CALIFORNIA'S MIGRANT KILLER/1971

Few serial killers match the ruthlessness and systematic slaughter demonstrated by Juan Vallejo Corona (b. 1934), a killer who murdered at least twenty-five migrant workers in the space of six weeks during 1971. Corona, a Mexican migrant worker himself, had arrived in Yuba City, California, in the 1950s. By the early 1970s, he was a labor contractor, hiring migrant workers to pick the various fruit crops in the Yuba City area. He was also, by that time, a man who suffered from several forms of mental illness. He had been diagnosed as suffering from schizophrenia. He was also a homosexual and a brutal sadist.

As early as 1970, the Corona family was involved in violent sex. Corona's half-brother, Natividad, was charged with sexually attacking a young Mexican worker who was found bleeding in the washroom of the half-brother's Guadalajara Café, which was located in Marysville, close to Yuba City. When the youth sued the half-brother and won a $250,000 settlement, Natividad fled back to Mexico.

The odd thing about Corona's murder spree, which was decidedly connected to homosexual attacks, was the fact that he was a married man with children. Heterosexual or not, Corona also craved sex with his own gender, an uncommon but not unheard of tendency on the part of some sex killers.

As a labor contractor, Corona hired migrant workers, and housed these single men in a barracks-like building on the Sullivan ranch. These men were, for the most part, elderly alcoholics, social dropouts, and misfits. They began disappearing in early May 1971.

On May 19, 1971, a Japanese fruit farmer noticed a large hole seven feet long and three and a half feet deep that had been scooped out of his land in a peach orchard. The next night he went to the same spot and saw that the earth had been packed back into the hole. He called the police who dug into what was a fresh grave. Inside of it was Kenneth Whitacre, a hobo who had homosexual literature in his back pocket. He had been sexually assaulted and then stabbed to death, his head chopped with a machete.

Another farmer noticed what appeared to be a freshly dug grave on his ranch and police began digging again, this time finding an elderly man. More graves in this area yielded more men, all of them sodomized and stabbed to death, one having been shot and chopped viciously about the head with a machete. In one grave police found a meat market receipt made out to "Juan V. Corona."

The bodies kept turning up including that of John Henry Jackson, an elderly worker, who had been seen some weeks earlier riding in the back of Corona's pickup truck. The police kept digging until June 4, 1971, unearthing twenty-five bodies, along with more receipts that had the name of Juan Corona on them. Corona was arrested and charged with murder. He pleaded not guilty, but his defense lawyers, who maintained that another person had done the murders, had an uphill battle against the overpowering evidence of bodies, receipts, and eyewitnesses who had seen the murdered workers with Corona shortly before they disappeared.

There was speculation that Corona and another man had committed the murders, but no other suspect was ever found, let alone arrested. Psychiatrists ventured many theories about Corona, one claiming that as the spring deepened and the fruit ripened, Corona's madness increased until the climate drove him into a frenzy of murder and mutilation so that he was compelled to kill someone each day to satisfy his blood lust. The availability of victims increased as warmer weather set in and scores of migrant workers drifted into the Marysville-Yuba City area.

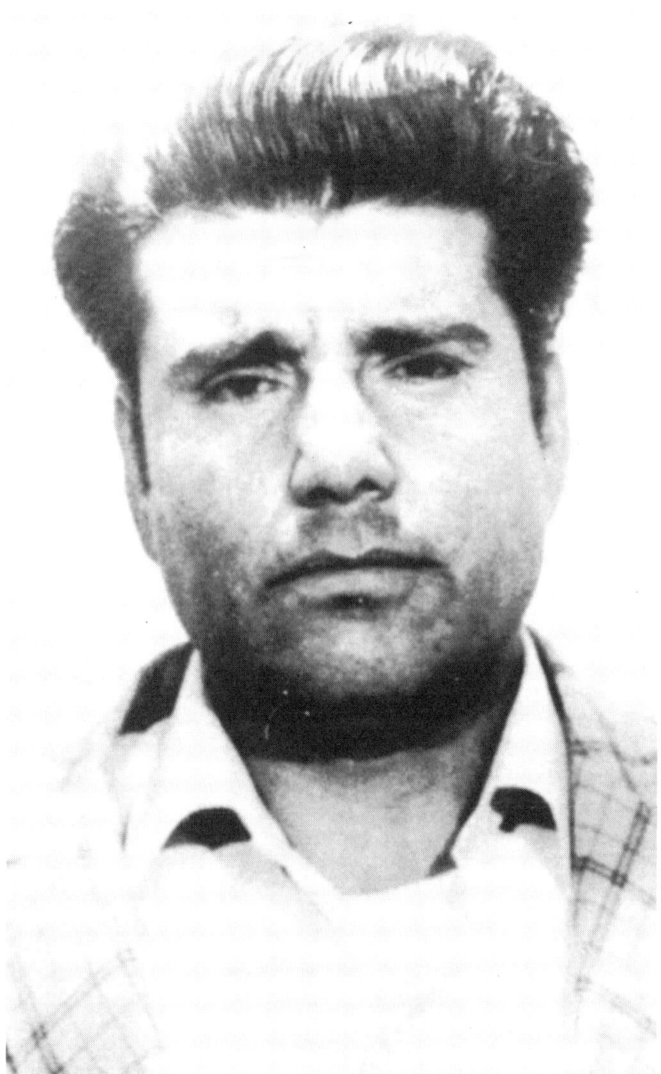

Juan Vallejo Corona murdered twenty-five or more migrant workers so that he did not have to pay their wages.

Corona simply had to stop his truck at any roadside and pick up the lonely workers, social pariahs no one would ever miss. He would work these men a few days and, when it came time to pay them, the burly, 200-pound Corona would sexually molest these men, then murder them, and bury their bodies. These included Kenneth Whitacre, Charles Fleming, Melford Sample, Donald Smith, John J. Haluka, Warren Kelley, Sigurd Beierman, William Emery Kamp, Clarence Hocking,

An aerial view of the Sullivan ranch, where more than two dozen bodies were unearthed, all victims of serial killer Juan Corona.

James W. Howard, Jonah R. Smallwood, Elbert T. Riley, Paul B. Allen, Edward Martin Cupp, Albert Hayes, Raymond Muchache, John H. Jackson, Lloyd Wallace Wenzel, Mark Beverly Shields, Sam Bonafide also known as Joe Carriveau, Joseph Maczak, and four unidentified men the court labeled "John Doe."

In several instances, the prosecution at Corona's trial was able to prove, Corona had planned his murders in advance, digging graves days before he had any victims to put into them. Added to this were the damning bloodstained knives, machete, pistol, and Corona's blood-caked clothes found in his home, along with an equally damning ledger in which Corona had officiously listed the names of his victims and the dates of their murders.

The jury in the Corona case deliberated for forty-five hours and then brought in a verdict of guilty in the case of each of the twenty-five murdered men. In January 1973, Judge Richard E. Patton sentenced Corona to twenty-five life terms to run consecutively with no hope of parole. Although Corona never publicly admitted his serial murders, he reportedly met with an official from the Mexican Consulate, who was visiting his prison and was quoted as telling this person: "Yes, I did it, but I am a sick man and I can't be judged by the standards of other men."

Corona was attacked in prison in 1980, stabbed thirty-two times. He lost the sight of one eye. He later won an appeal that claimed he had not received an adequate defense, that he should have been allowed to plead insane at his trial. He was placed in an asylum for the criminally insane. Retried in 1982, Corona met the same judicial fate, being convicted and sentenced to twenty-five consecutive life terms.

Seemingly endless conjectures have been offered by psychiatrists and psychologists studying this case, many of them contributing bizarre theories to explain the motivation for Corona's serial killings. His motivation, however shrouded in such elaborate rationales, was plain and simple. He murdered out of greed, simply killing those he did not want to pay for their work, pocketing the meager salaries of his victims like any petty crook. Juan Corona was not and is not a complicated felon, merely a thief, who stole lives and money.

THE "RECREATIONAL" SERIAL KILLERS/ 1973

Douglas Gretzler (b. 1950), from the Bronx, New York, met William Steelman (b. 1945), a former mental patient and convict from the San Joaquin Valley in California on October 11, 1973. The two shared the same perverted outlook on life and united in their murderous fantasies to become a serial killing team. They met in Denver, Colorado, and traveled to Arizona, where they randomly robbed homes and blithely killed anyone who got in their way. Arizona police attributed seven deaths to these ruthless killers, two of which were their partners in an alleged drug deal. It should be chillingly noted that both killers later stated that the many serial killings they performed were not committed for profit, but for "recreation."

Douglas Gretzler murdered people for cash and "recreation" in California and Arizona; he was executed on April 3, 1998.

The pair drove to Sacramento, California, with Michael Adshade and Ken Unrein of Phoenix and held them captive in their van near the city. There they killed and buried them by a small creek. Gretzler and Steelman then returned to Arizona, where they offered two hitchhikers a ride, then killed them. In Mesa, Arizona, on October 28, 1973, the two serial killers invaded a house trailer, where they tied up Robert Robbins, nineteen,

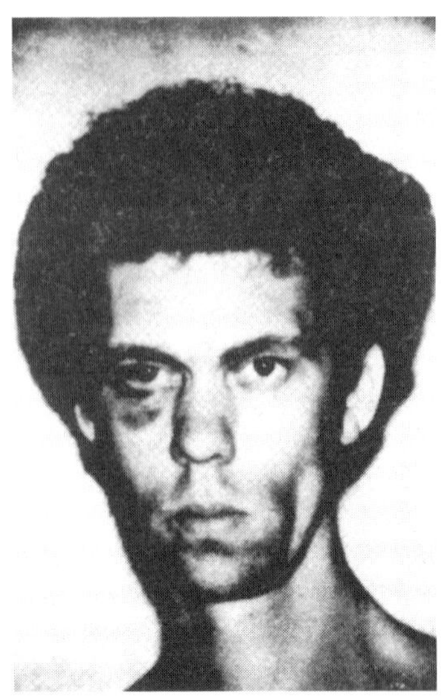

William Steelman, Gretzler's co-killer, who murdered for profit and pleasure; he is presently serving life in prison.

and Katherine Mestiter, eighteen. They shot them both to death. Shortly thereafter, the pair drove to Tucson, where they broke into the apartment of Michael and Patricia Sandberg, killing the couple and stealing their car, which they drove to the little farming community of Victor, California.

In the evening of November 6, 1973, Walter and Joanne Parkin, who owned a successful grocery store in Victor, went bowling with their friends, Dick and Wanda Earl. They left their two children with teen-aged Debbie Earl, Dick and Wanda's daughter, and the girl's brother, Rick and her boyfriend, Mark Lang. When the two couples returned, they were confronted by Gretzler and Steelman who were holding the children at gunpoint. One of the men took Parkin to his store and forced him to take $4,000 from the safe. They then returned to the Parkin's home, tied up all nine hostages and shot them to death one by one.

The next morning, Laura Carlson, a house guest who had returned late the night before and gone straight to bed, found the victims. First she saw the two children dead in their parents' bed. Then, she found the three older children and four adults all crammed into a bedroom closet. When the police arrived it was noticed that the ropes binding the victims were tied with unusual knots.

A police bulletin was widely distributed, which described the manner in which the victims had been tied up. Then word was received from Arizona police that serial killers using similar knots in that state had been identified as Gretzler and Steelman. Photos of the two were immediately published in the newspapers. A hotel clerk in Sacramento recognized the pair as they were checking in and called the police. Gretzler was easily seized, but Steelman escaped and was not captured until a SWAT team sent tear gas into the room where he had been hiding.

Gretzler confessed to the killings and pleaded guilty. Steelman did not plead before the California judge, letting his grand jury testimony speak for him. They were both found guilty of the nine murders in Victor. California had outlawed capital punishment, so the men were sentenced to life in prison, which would make them eligible for parole in seven years.

California willingly sent the men to Arizona, where the death penalty was still in use. They were sentenced to death in the gas chamber for the killing of the Sandberg couple. It is believed that Gretzler and Steelman were responsible for at least eleven other murders for which they were not tried. Steelman died in prison in 1987, and Gretzler, after his lawyers exhausted all appeals, was finally put to death by lethal injection on April 3, 1998.

MURDERING "OLD FOLKS" IN ENGLAND/ 1973-1974

Patrick David MacKay (AKA: Franklin Bollvolt the First; b. 1952) was a violent and dangerous young street thug who, at an early age, tortured animals and beat boys younger and weaker than himself. As a child, he set fire to the local Catholic church with a candle. The judge at the Dartford juvenile court placed him on probation, to the considerable alarm of neighbors, who feared MacKay would commit much worse crimes before he was through.

As a boy, MacKay roasted his pet turtle alive. Later, he became preoccupied with the Nazi regime. He decorated his room with military regalia and began calling himself "Franklin Bollvolt the First," the new world dictator. At age fifteen, MacKay, the son of an alcoholic, had a long record of violent offenses. In 1973 a Catholic priest named Father Anthony Crean took the troubled adolescent under his wing. MacKay rewarded his kindness by breaking into his residence and pilfering a check for £30. He altered the "3" and cashed the check for £80.

On St. Valentine's Day, 1974, MacKay called on 84-year-old Isabella Griffiths in Chelsea, volunteering to do her grocery shopping. When Griffiths refused, MacKay strangled her and plunged a kitchen knife into her stomach. Later that year he committed a string of muggings against elderly women. On March 10, 1975, MacKay followed Adele Price, an elderly

Patrick David MacKay, posing in a coin-operated photograph booth, wearing a Nazi swastika on his sleeve; he murdered several elderly people in 1974-1975.

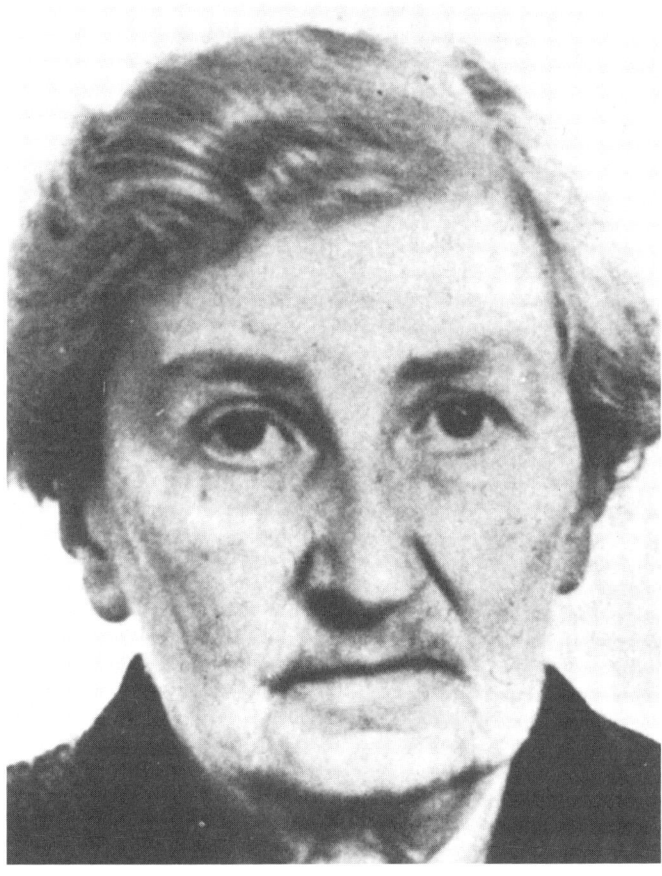

Mrs. Isabella Griffiths, stabbed to death by MacKay on February 14, 1974 in her home in Chelsea.

Mrs. Adele Price, who was strangled to death by Patrick David MacKay on March 10, 1975.

widow, to her home in Lowndes Square. Feigning illness, he won the widow's permission to enter her flat, where he strangled her. Afterward MacKay paid a call on his widowed mother, who lived in Gravesend.

Then, on March 21, 1975, he decided to visit his old benefactor, Father Crean, who had attempted to prevent his prosecution on charges of theft two years prior. Finding the priest's residence unoccupied, MacKay stepped inside. When Father Crean returned a short time later, MacKay viciously assaulted him. The priest rushed into the bathroom to shield himself from MacKay, but MacKay followed close behind, and killed him.

Two days later the police arrested MacKay. The suspect freely confessed to the three murders, and was considered the prime suspect in at least eight others committed between July 1973 and March

Father Anthony Crean, who had earlier aided the troubled youth, was murdered by MacKay on March 21, 1975.

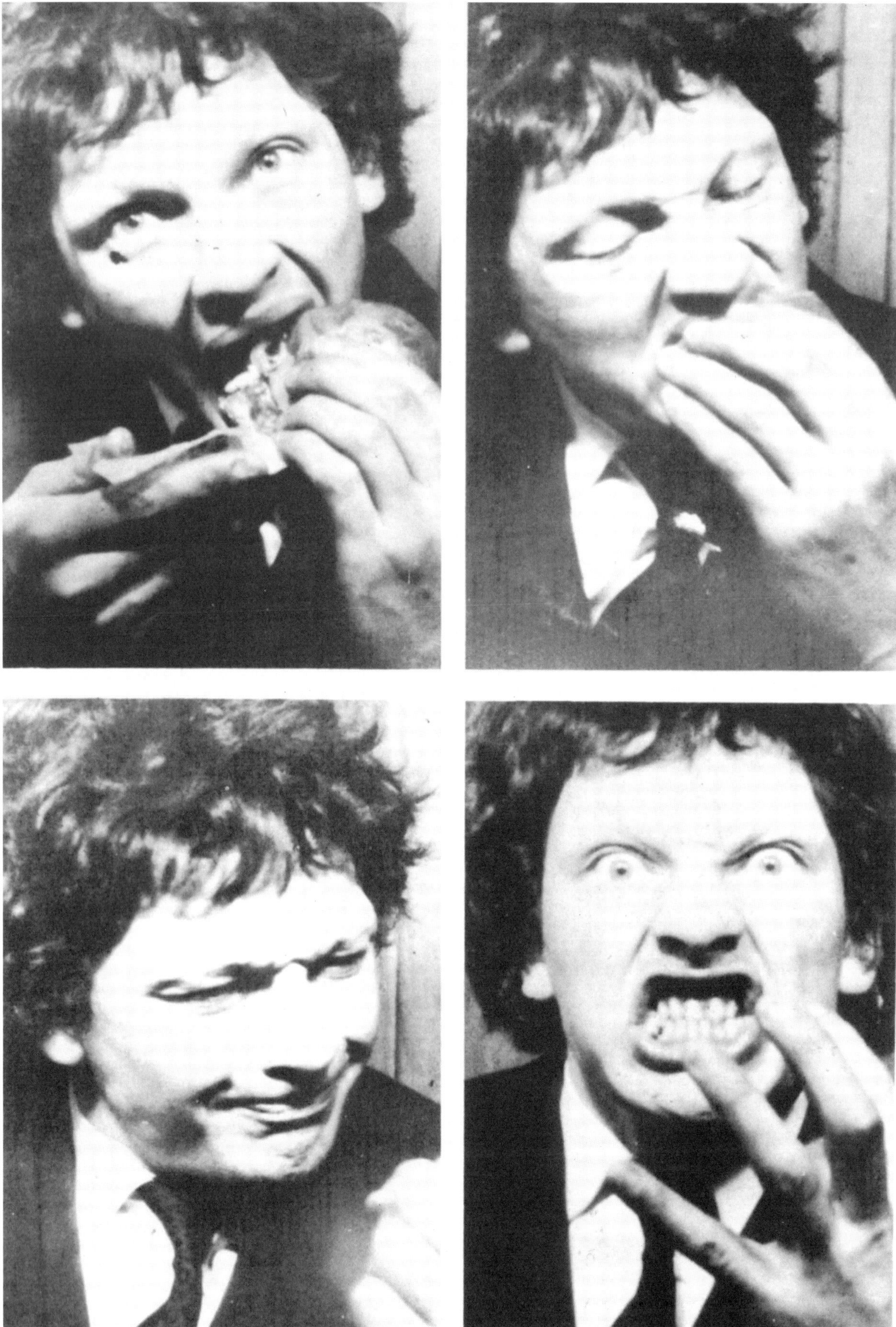

A series of photos shows a disturbed if not unbalanced MacKay in a coin-operated photograph booth, gobbling his lunch and making a menacing face; he was arrested a short time after this photo session and sent to prison for life.

1975. Patrick MacKay was tried at the Old Bailey in November 1975 for the murders of the three elderly people, whom MacKay called "the old folks." Judged to be sane at the time the murders were committed, MacKay was convicted and sentenced to life imprisonment.

PATRICK WAYNE KEARNEY/1973-1977

On July 13, 1977, Patrick Wayne Kearney (b. 1940) an electronics engineer for the Los Angeles Hughes Aircraft Co. was indicted on three counts of murder by a Riverside, California, grand jury. Charges against his roommate and homosexual lover, David D. Hill, thirty-four, were dropped because of lack of evidence. Kearney took full blame for all the serial killings attributed to him, an investigator later stating that Kearney had murdered "because it excited him and gave him a feeling of dominance." At the time, Patrick Kearney was being investigated in connection with at least twenty-eight murders of homosexual men.

Hill and Kearney, roommates for fifteen years, turned themselves in to authorities on July 1, 1977 pointing to a wanted poster with their pictures and announcing: "We're them." Most of the information about the killings came from Kearney's statements to police. Bodies of many of the victims were found in plastic garbage bags along highways from south Los Angeles to the border of Mexico and several of the corpses had been dismembered after being shot.

Kearney was indicted for the slayings of Albert Rivera, twenty-one, Arturo Marquez, twenty-four, and John Le May, seventeen. The first victim to be identified was Rivera. His corpse was found on April 13, 1975, near San Juan Capistrano, with five more bodies turning up by the end of 1976. Two more victims were discovered in March 1977. (Kearney, according to reliable reports, launched his serial killings as early as 1973.) All the victims were nude, shot in the head with a small-caliber gun, and dumped alongside the highway. Almost all were transient young men who frequented the homosexual cruising areas and hangouts in and around Los Angeles and Hollywood.

At Hill and Kearney's Redondo Beach home investigators found a hacksaw, which proved to be stained with Le May's blood, as well as hair and carpet samples which matched those on tape found on the victims' bodies. Kearney and Hill had fled to Mexico, but surrendered when persuaded by relatives to turn themselves in.

On December 21, 1977, Kearney pleaded guilty to three murders and was sentenced to life imprisonment by Superior Court Judge John Hews. On February 21, 1978, Kearney pleaded guilty before Judge Dickran Tevrizzian, Jr., to eighteen

Serial Killer Patrick Wayne Kearney in custody; he reportedly murdered at least twenty-eight homosexual men from 1973 to 1977, but may have been slaying people for fifteen years.

A recent photo of Kearney, who is serving life; Kearney was known as the "Trash Bag Murderer," because many of his victims were found in garbage bags alongside California highways.

slayings of young men and boys in exchange for a promise from the prosecution that he would not be given the death penalty. Kearney also provided details of the related killings of another eleven homosexual men, bringing the probable total to thirty-two victims.

THE MAN WHO WAS SON OF SAM/1975-1977

David Berkowitz (AKA: Son of Sam; b. 1953), an unbalanced slayer who terrorized New York for more than a year as the "Son of Sam," was born June 1, 1953, the bastard son of a woman who gave him up for adoption. Throughout his miserable life, he had a deep sense of rejection. He grew up shy and terrorized by women. His stepfather, Nat Berkowitz, ran a hardware store in the Bronx and later retired to Florida. His stepson, David, remained in New York, living on Pine Street in Yonkers. He worked at odd jobs and his room was always littered with garbage. He could not sleep, he complained in letters to his stepfather, because the sound of trucks on the street and a neighbor's barking dog kept him up every night. He became paranoid, insisting that strangers on the street displayed hatred for him and spat at him as he walked past. "The girls call me ugly and they bother me the most," he wrote his stepfather.

On Christmas Eve 1975, Berkowitz attacked two girls with a knife at separate sites. The first girl frightened him off with her wild shrieking, but he plunged the blade into the lung of the second girl, a 15-year-old schoolgirl and left her for dead. She survived. Berkowitz waited seven months before striking again, this time on the night of July 29, 1976. He found two girls, Donna Lauria and Jody Valenti talking in the front seat of a car parked on Buhre Avenue in Queens.

David Richard Berkowitz, the New York serial killer, who called himself "Son of Sam."

Calmly taking a gun from a brown paper bag, Berkowitz fired five shots into them, killing Lauria and wounding Valenti in the leg. Police were baffled by this murder, the killer apparently having no motive. Investigators quickly concluded that they were dealing with a maniac who killed for thrills. Berkowitz next shot and wounded Carl Denaro on the night of October 23, 1976, firing through the rear window of his car as Denaro sat with his girlfriend, Rosemary Keenan, in front of a bar in Flushing, New York.

On November 26, 1976, two more girls, Joanne Lomino and Donna DeMasi, sitting on the stoop of a house in the Floral Park section of Queens, were approached by Berkowitz, who began to ask them directions, but stopped in mid-sentence. He pulled his gun from a brown paper bag and fired blindly, wounding both of them before fleeing. Lomino was paralyzed by a bullet that lodged next to her spine. Other bullets dug out of the wooden stairs of the stoop matched those in the Lauria-Valenti shootings.

Police still had no clue as to the identity of the killer, despite efforts to trace the gun. Then, on January 30, 1977, Berkowitz spotted a young couple necking in a car in Ridgewood. He crept up on the car, took the gun out of the brown paper bag, and fired through the window, one of his bullets striking the head of Christine Freund, who collapsed into the arms of her boyfriend, John Diel. She was pronounced dead a few hours later.

On March 8, 1977, Berkowitz walked up to Virginia Voskerichian, an Armenian student he had never met, pulled out his gun, and fired point-blank into the girl's face, killing her as she walked down a Forest Hills street. Witnesses described Berkowitz as about five feet, ten inches tall, with black hair combed straight back. He was described by authorities as "a savage killer" and women were warned to go nowhere alone at night in the city. On April 17, 1977, Berkowitz came upon Valentina Suriani and Alexander Esau, sitting in a parked car in the Bronx, only a short distance from where he had shot Lauria and Valenti. He shot both of them at close range. Suriani was killed instantly and Esau, with three bullets in his head, died in the hospital some time later.

Following this shooting, a note was found addressed to Police Captain Joseph Borrelli, who had made several statements about the killer to the press. To Borrelli, Berkowitz wrote: "I am deeply hurt by your calling me a weman-hater [sic]. I am not. But I am a monster. I am the Son of Sam. I am a little brat...I love to hunt, prowling the streets, looking for fair game ... tasty meat ... The weman of Queens are prettyist of all."

Page right: A geographical chronology of some of the attacks by Berkowitz in 1976-1977.

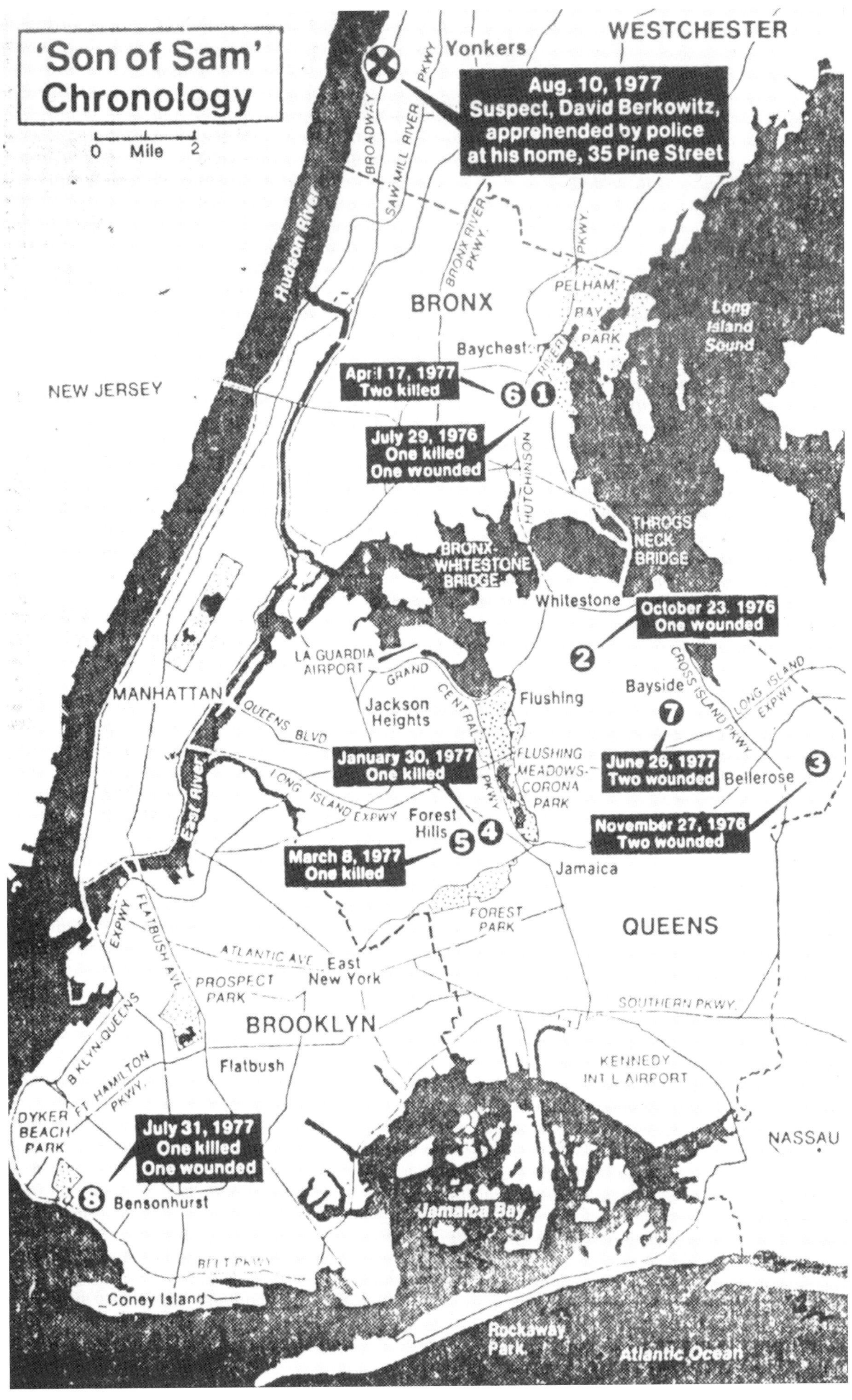

'Son of Sam' Chronology
0 Mile 2
WESTCHESTER
Yonkers
Aug. 10, 1977
Suspect, David Berkowitz, apprehended by police at his home, 35 Pine Street
Hudson River
BROADWAY
SAW MILL RIVER
BRONX RIVER PKWY.
BRONX
PELHAM BAY PARK
Long Island Sound
Baychester
NEW JERSEY
April 17, 1977
Two killed
July 29, 1976
One killed
One wounded
HUTCHINSON
THROGS NECK BRIDGE
BRONX-WHITESTONE BRIDGE
Whitestone
October 23, 1976
One wounded
LA GUARDIA AIRPORT
GRAND CENTRAL PKWY
MANHATTAN
QUEENS BLVD
Jackson Heights
Flushing
Bayside
CROSS ISLAND PKWY
LONG ISLAND EXPWY
East River
January 30, 1977
One killed
FLUSHING MEADOWS-CORONA PARK
June 26, 1977
Two wounded
Bellerose
LONG ISLAND EXPWY
Forest Hills
November 27, 1976
Two wounded
March 8, 1977
One killed
Jamaica
FOREST PARK
QUEENS
FLATBUSH AVE
ATLANTIC AVE
East New York
PROSPECT PARK
SOUTHERN PKWY.
BROOKLYN
B'KLYN-QUEENS EXPWY
FT. HAMILTON PKWY.
Flatbush
KENNEDY INT L AIRPORT
DYKER BEACH PARK
July 31, 1977
One killed
One wounded
NASSAU
Bensonhurst
Jamaica Bay
Coney Island
Rockaway Park
Atlantic Ocean

Donna Lauria, eighteen, the first fatality claimed by Berkowitz, shot to death on July 29, 1976, while she was sitting in a car with girlfriend Jody Valenti.

Christine Freund, twenty-six, was shot and killed by Berkowitz on the night of January 30, 1977, while she was sitting in a car with her boyfriend, John Diel.

A smiling, David Berkowitz, right, in custody on August 2, 1977, only minutes after his arrest.

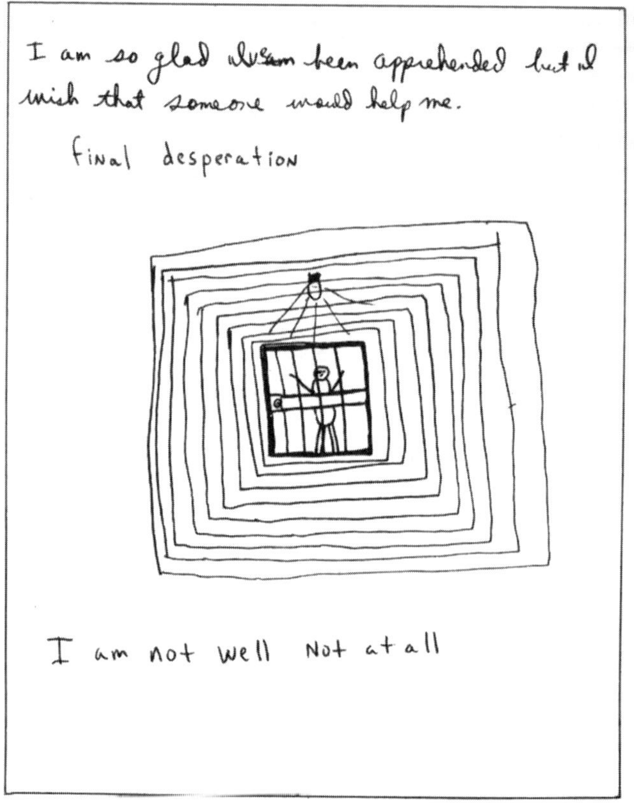

A drawing by Berkowitz after he had been jailed and was awaiting trial, one that pleaded for "help."

In this letter, Berkowitz, seeming to emulate the letters Jack the Ripper sent to authorities almost a century earlier when prowling the streets of London, claimed that he had been brutalized by his father when he was a child and that he was later ordered by his father to go into the streets and murder. Berkowitz sent a similar letter to New York columnist Jimmy Breslin, who had been writing extensively about the slayer.

Berkowitz struck again on June 26, 1977, shooting Judy Placido and Salvatore Lupo as they sat in a car in a street in Queens. This time Berkowitz had fired quickly and his aim was poor; his victims were only slightly wounded. Berkowitz nevertheless continued to roam the streets of the Bronx and Queens looking for victims, but police seemed to be everywhere and, on several occasions, he was frightened off by the presence of officers. The serial killer changed locales: He went to Brooklyn and, on July 31, 1977, found Stacy Moskowitz and Robert Violante sitting in a car. He fired four shots through the window, killing Moskowitz and blinding Violante.

A woman walking her dog saw Berkowitz run to his car and leap in, speeding away. She told police that the car had a parking violation ticket in its windshield. Police checked to find that only four parking tickets had been issued that morning and the carbon copy of one of these bore the registration number of David Berkowitz of Yonkers. Police Inspector Tim Dowd and others found the car parked near Berkowitz's apartment and waited for him to appear on August 2, 1977. Berkowitz walked toward the car at 10:15 p.m. Dowd stepped forward and said: "Hello, David."

Berkowitz stood still for a moment, then his pudgy face crinkled with his peculiar beamish smile. "Inspector Dowd!" he said, recognizing the officer from his newspaper photos. "You finally got me." He surrendered meekly and later tried to mount a defense of insanity, but psychiatrists testified at Berkowitz's trial that he was faking. The sinister Son of Sam name was an invention of Berkowitz's, taken from his neighbor, Sam Carr. It was Carr's dog who had kept him up nights. He had shot the dog, but the animal had recovered and it was later claimed by Berkowitz that the dog spoke to him as one of the voices that ordered him to murder. Berkowitz pleaded guilty to murder charges when he was arraigned on August 23, 1977, and was never tried. He was sentenced to 365 years in prison with no hope of parole. His apartment was later looted by souvenir hunters.

THE SERIAL SLAYINGS OF JOHN WAYNE GACY/1970s

John Wayne Gacy, Jr. (1942-1994) had a long record of homosexual abuse, sodomy and other acts of perversion. In 1968, at the age of twenty-six, while he was married and operating a fast food operation in Waterloo, Iowa, Gacy lured a youth into a back room after closing time and handcuffed him. He tried to pay the youth to perform oral sex on him and when this was refused, Gacy attempted to sodomize the youth. The youth escaped and reported Gacy.

Before going to trial, Gacy paid some thugs to terrorize the youth into not testifying against him, but this only strengthened the boy's resolve and he did testify. Gacy drew a ten-year sentence, but, because his past indicated no serious crime and because he proved to be a model prisoner, he was released in eighteen months.

Moving to Chicago in 1971, Gacy went into the construction business and soon developed his own contracting company. He also continued his sexual abuses. In the year he arrived in Chicago, Gacy picked up a teenage boy and attempted to force the youth to have sex with him. He was arrested, but was released when the boy failed to appear in court to testify against him. A young man later insisted that Gacy, in 1977, had held a gun on him in his Norwood Park home when he arrived to apply for work as a construction worker.

Gacy attempted to force the man to have sex with him, the applicant later said. He flourished the gun and snarled through full lips: "I killed a guy before." The construction worker did not believe Gacy, thinking he was only acting out a fantasy and nothing came of the incident. Gacy, however, had, indeed, killed several persons by this time, but not until years later would the secret of this vile serial killer be revealed.

With each sexual offense and murder that went unpunished, Gacy became more bold, daring to abduct boys from the street and force them to participate in unspeakable sexual perversions, while holding them captive in his modest

Chicago serial killer John Wayne Gacy, who reportedly killed thirty-three persons, mostly homosexual hustlers, in the 1970s.

Gacy in his clown costume and makeup; he gave performances for local children. This photo was taken in December 1976 outside of Gacy's home, at the time when the serial killer was routinely murdering people and burying the bodies beneath his home.

Norwood Park home. He then murdered them and buried their bodies. In 1977 Gacy was arrested and charged with sexually abusing a youth at gunpoint. Gacy admitted to the sexual attack and brutality, but said the youth was a willing participant and was blackmailing him. He was released with a warning.

By 1978, Gacy was operating with abandon. He earned considerable money from his contracting business and he was a small but important precinct captain for the Democratic Party in Norwood Park Township's 21st Precinct. He felt that he was insulated against detection. He would drive about in his sleek, black Oldsmobile, cruising near notorious homosexual hangouts in Chicago, such as "Bughouse Square" across from the Newberry Library, and, particularly, along North Broadway in the New Town section. On March 21, 1978, Gacy picked up 27-year-old Chicagoan Jeffrey Rignall on North Broadway in New Town.

Gacy, by then grown fat with a triple chin and bulging eyes, suggested that Rignall join him in the car to smoke some marijuana and take a drive. Rignall accepted. Gacy pulled the car over to a curb and suddenly whirled about, forcing a chloroform-soaked rag over Rignall's face. Rignall passed out and vaguely remembered later traveling at high speed and then seeing an expressway exit.

Gacy, an energetic worker for the Democratic Party, is shown at a 1978 reception with First Lady Rosalyn Carter, who autographed this photo for him.

Rignall awoke in the basement of Gacy's home, his body naked and pressed into a pillory-like rack which held his arms and head. Gacy, a powerful, heavyset man, was also naked, his fat, hairy belly bulging. Gacy showed Rignall various whips, and instruments of torture, along with a number of strange-looking sexual devices, explaining lasciviously how he intended to use these implements on his victim, Rignall.

The assaults and torture went on for hours. Gacy periodically applied the chloroform and waited sadistically until his victim regained consciousness to renew his attacks. He bragged that he was a policeman, and said to his terrorized victim: "I'd just as soon shoot you as look at you." The sexual attacks became so acutely painful that Rignall wanted to die, he later said. He begged Gacy to release him, saying he would leave town and say nothing about the incident.

Rignall finally blacked out with another dose of chloroform and woke up later beneath a statue in Chicago's Lincoln Park. He was fully clothed and his wallet and money were in his pockets, although his driver's license was missing. He discovered that he was bleeding from the rectum and medical tests showed that his liver had been permanently damaged by

Workers from the Cook County Highway Department are shown excavating Gacy's house in Norwood Park, Illinois; they found twenty bodies buried there.

the heavy doses of chloroform that had been administered by Gacy. Rignall's face had been burned by the chloroform.

Going to the police with his story, Rignall was told that there was little hope of locating his attacker since he had no name, address or license number for the man's car. Rignall was determined to bring to justice the hulking sadist who had attacked him. He rented a car and drove the route he vaguely remembered while being abducted. He sat at the expressway exit he remembered clearly, patiently waiting in his car for hours, watching for the big black Oldsmobile. Finally, his perseverance was rewarded. The car turned off the expressway and passed Rignall's parked car. He wrote down the license number, then followed the car. It turned into a driveway at 8213 West Summerdale Avenue in Norwood Park, an unincorporated area bordering on Des Plaines.

Having worked for a law firm which dealt with real estate, Rignall was able to check real estate records and he unearthed the name of his attacker: John Wayne Gacy, Jr. He went to police with this information, having performed some excellent amateur detective work. The Chicago police took his information and then told Rignall that Gacy had served time in Iowa for sodomy. Rignall had difficulty in getting the Chicago Police Department to act. but finally managed to have a warrant for Gacy's arrest issued.

Meeting CPD officers at Gacy's home, Rignall was told that since the subject lived in Norwood Park, he was beyond the jurisdiction of the Chicago Police. Rignall, through his attorney, finally had Gacy arrested on a misdemeanor charge of battery on July 15, 1978, but police refused to charge Gacy with a felony, despite the protests from Rignall and his attorney, Fred Richman. Some time later, Gacy agreed to settle $3,000 on Rignall for the medical bills incurred from his sexual attack.

Everything seemed to be closing in on John Wayne Gacy in 1978. He mentioned to his neighbors that he was running out of space in his home, where he lived alone after his wife had left him. Gacy spoke of adding more floors to his house which perplexed residents in the area. One told him that if he needed more space it was easier to sell his home and buy a new and larger house. He agreed and made plans to sell his Norwood Park house.

At 11:30 p.m. on December 11, 1978, Mrs. Elizabeth Piest appeared in the Des Plaines Police Department, asking them to check on her son Robert, age fifteen, who had been missing since 9:05 that night. She and her son had been in the Nisson Pharmacy in Des Plaines at that time. Robert, who had been looking for a job for the following summer, told his mother that he had to see a "contractor" who lived nearby. "I'll be right back," he told her, but he did not return. Mrs. Piest talked to the druggist who told her that her son might be seeing Gacy, a contractor who had given the druggist an estimate for remodeling the drugstore.

Mrs. Piest and her husband Harold, her son Ken, and daughter Kerry had searched for Robert, but could find no trace of him. Des Plaines police captain Joseph Kozenczak heard Mrs. Piest's story and believed her son had met with foul play, especially since he had left her in the pharmacy with the words "I'll be right back," and he knew he was to accompany her home to celebrate her birthday that night. Nothing in Robert Piest's background suggested he might be a runaway. Kozenczak asked Des Plaines youth officer Ron Adams to follow up. Adams interviewed the pharmacist, Phil Terf, and again talked with the Piest family members. The following morning, Adams called the contractor, Gacy, a definite suspect at that time.

Gacy picked up the phone on December 12, 1978, at 9:30 a.m. He was terse with Adams, telling him: "I don't talk to any kids. I can't help you. I don't know anything about it." Gacy had already murdered the Piest boy and the body was lying in Gacy's bedroom as he made his denials to Adams on the phone. The Des Plaines police, however, were dogged. They checked Gacy's background and found his conviction for sodomy in Iowa. Kozenczak and several officers visited Gacy that night and questioned him further. Gacy admitted nothing, merely staring back at the officers as they described the Piest boy. He then mumbled something about talking "to one of the boys about some shelves" that were discarded in the remodeling of the Nisson Pharmacy. "I don't remember who it was."

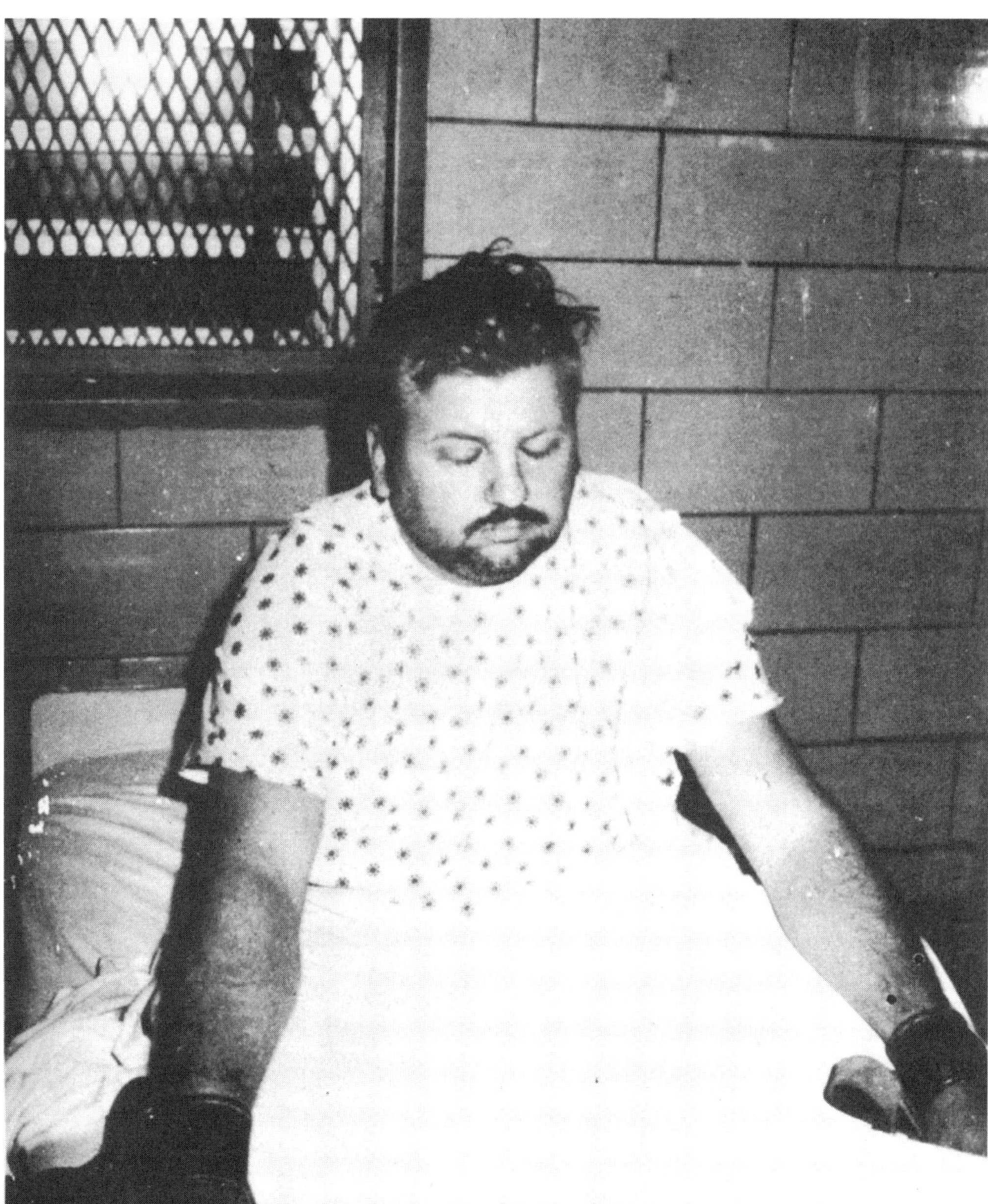

John Wayne Gacy in custody at the Cook County Jail; he was convicted and sentenced to death in 1980. After exhausting fourteen years of appeals, Gacy was put to death by lethal injection on May 10, 1994.

Kozenczak asked Gacy to go to the police station and make an official statement about the Piest boy. Gacy then received a call from a relative about an uncle who had just died. He stretched out his long distance phone conversation, but the policemen remained in his home. After hanging up the phone, Gacy started to put on his coat. Two more officers then burst through the door and Gacy suddenly became obstinate, saying loudly: "Hey, I got a lot of important work to do. I can't be going down to the police station. I know this kid is missing, but that's not important to me."

"Well, it's important to the parents," Kozenczak replied, angrily impatient. Yet, without evidence, he realized he was powerless to make a formal arrest, and left after giving Gacy his card and asking him to come to the station and make a voluntary statement. Police now put Gacy under close surveillance. On one occasion, Gacy, realizing he was being watched, jumped into his car and roared off at high speed, losing his pursuers.

Meanwhile, Gacy managed to remove the body of the Piest boy from his home. He put the corpse into his trunk and then drove to the Des Plaines River at Interstate Highway 55, where he dumped the body into the swirling waters. This undoubtedly unnerved the mass killer since, upon his return trip home, his car inexplicably went out of control and wound up in a ditch, requiring a tow.

In the afternoon of December 13, 1978, Gacy appeared at the Des Plaines police station. His clothes were disheveled and his trousers and shoes were coated with mud. His glassy-eyed appearance caused one officer on duty to describe Gacy as "spaced out on some kind of drug." He asked for Kozenczak but the police captain was not in at the time. Gacy left. Later, Assistant State's Attorney Terry Sullivan helped Kozenczak obtain a search warrant for Gacy's house from Judge Marvin Peters, a considerable feat because such warrants were nearly impossible to obtain without substantial evidence.

The police searched Gacy's home, but found little. Kozenczak spotted a receipt from the Nisson Pharmacy and took it along. As it turned out, this was the most important piece of evidence in the case. The receipt was made out to the Piest boy, indicating Gacy had had contact with the boy, possibly inside Gacy's house. The killer later admitted that he had emptied his victim's pockets, thrown the receipt into a garbage can, and forgotten about it.

The police returned to the Gacy residence to take up a round-the-clock surveillance. Gacy watched the police sitting outside of his home for days. On December 19, 1978, he boldly invited two of the officers into his house to have breakfast with him. As they sat down to eat, the policemen noticed a peculiar smell. Gacy explained that he had unplugged his sump pump. The resulting water flowing beneath the building had softened the dirt of the crawl space and disturbed the twenty-nine bodies Gacy had buried there over the years.

Another warrant was quickly obtained and the bodies were dug out of the crawl space. Four more bodies found in nearby rivers over the next four months, including that of the Piest boy, were linked to Gacy. The victims ranged from a 9-year-old boy to grown men such as John Butkovich, reportedly murdered by Gacy as early as 1976. Others included Greg Godzik, John Szyc, Billy Carrol, Randall Reffett, Samuel Stapleton, Michael Bonnin, Rich Johnston and Piest, the last victim of the thirty-four sexually abused and murdered by Gacy. The serial killer—one of the worst to ever plague Chicago—was tried in 1980 and sentenced to death. After spending fourteen years on Death Row, John Wayne Gacy, his appeals exhausted, was executed by lethal injection on May 10, 1994.

TED BUNDY, THE CHARMING SERIAL KILLER/1974-1978

The public personality of Theodore "Ted" Bundy (AKA: Chris Hagen, 1947-1989) suggested nothing of the serial killer he truly was. Handsome, apparently well educated, a glib talker, Bundy struck those who met him for the first time, if they were to think ill of him, as someone who might be guilty of practicing smooth confidence games, but never one capable of violent crime. Everything in his posture and conversation smacked of culture, and his sense of humor was instant and infectious, one that won over new friends quickly and established trust on the part of the women who found him attractive.

This was a fatal attraction for perhaps as many as forty young females, all of them brutally murdered by Ted Bundy. A number of pretty, young women began to suffer violent attacks from a strange intruder and others disappeared in western states in early 1974. The first of these was Sharon Clarke of Seattle, who was attacked in her bedroom while she slept, her head brutally smashed with a metal rod. She suffered skull fractures, but survived and the rod was found in her room. There was no explanation for the attack and Clarke could not identify her attacker, even as to whether or not the attack was made by a male or female.

The first police photo taken of the clever and manipulating serial killer, Theodore "Ted" Bundy.

While authorities pondered this strange attack, Lynda Ann Healy, a student at the University of Washington in Seattle, who lived only a few blocks from Clarke, disappeared from her rented room on January 31, 1974. Then, over the next seven months, young women began to disappear with dreadful regularity. Donna Gail Manson, a student at Evergreen State College in Olympia, Washington, went to a concert on March 12, 1974, and vanished. Susan Rancourt, a Central Washington State student, disappeared in Ellensburg while going to see a foreign film on April 17, 1974. Out for a late night walk on May 6, 1974, Roberta Kathleen Parks, an Oregon State University student living in Corvallis, disappeared. Brenda Ball left the Flame Tavern near the Seattle Airport with an unknown man at 2 a.m. on June 1, 1974, and vanished. On the evening of June 11, 1974, Georgann Hawkins left her boyfriend and began walking back to her sorority house at the University of Washington and she, too, disappeared.

At Lake Sammanish, Washington, on July 14, 1974, a number of attractive, young women were approached by a

A 1974 police sketch of a wanted rapist-killer; a remarkable likeness to the photo of Bundy at left.

good-looking, dark-haired young man, who called himself Ted. He had an arm in a sling and asked a number of women to help him load a sailboat on top of his car, a Volkswagen. One woman agreed and accompanied Ted to a parking lot, but when he told her that they had to drive to a house on a hill to load the boat, she refused. Others did the same.

Blonde-haired Janice Ott agreed to help Ted and disappeared. Some hours later Denise Naslund was seen walking toward the public washrooms at the lake and was not seen again. Other women were seen talking to the handsome young man with the arm sling and many were seen to accompany him to the parking lot that day. On September 7, 1974, two hunters near the lake found the decomposed bodies of Denise Naslund and Janice Ott, along with that of another unidentified female. The remains found were in bits and pieces, scattered by wild animals, officials later concluded.

Detectives began an extensive investigation, learning from a young woman in Ellensburg that a young man wearing a sling had tried to pick her up on the night Susan Rancourt vanished. Another Seattle woman recalled a young man wearing a sling and driving a Volkswagen, who tried to pick her up. When she refused to get into his car, he shrugged and blithely took his uninjured arm out of the sling and drove off, using both hands on the wheel. Another woman reported that a man wearing an arm sling drove onto a sidewalk, attempting to block her path, in an effort to get her into his Volkswagen, but she managed to avoid him.

During these investigations, the remains of two young women were found, one in northern Washington who was identified as Carol Valenzuela of Vancouver, Washington, who had vanished some months earlier. The second body, or what was left of it, was found in southern Washington State near the Oregon border. She remained unidentified. Both women had been apparently murdered. Police by then had many suspects they thought capable of having committed the abduction-murders.

One strong suspect was a depraved young man named Warren Forrest, a park employee who had picked up a Portland, Oregon, woman, convincing her to pose for him. In a secluded area of the park, he tied her up, taped her mouth, stripped her naked, and fired darts at her naked breasts. Forrest sexually attacked her before strangling her and leaving her for dead. She survived, however, and identified her attacker.

Another strong suspect was ex-convict Gary Taylor, who was accused of abducting Seattle females under various pretexts. Then an anonymous female caller phoned police to tell them that she believed that Ted Bundy was the man who had been abducting and killing young women in Seattle. Officers duly noted the report and filed it with the thousands of other leads they had collected. But the women continued to disappear.

On October 2, 1974, Nancy Wilcox vanished and, on October 18, 1974, after leaving an all-night party in Midvale, Utah, Melissa Smith, daughter of the local police chief, disappeared. Her raped and strangled body was found on October 27, 1974, in the Wasatch Mountains, east of Salt Lake City. In Orem, Utah, Laura Aimee went to a Halloween party after midnight on October 31, 1974, and vanished.

Then, on November 8, 1974, a young man pretending to be a police detective approached Carol DaRonch in a Salt Lake City shopping mall, demanding the license plate number of her car, explaining that someone had tried to break into it. She accompanied him to her car, but found that it was undisturbed. The fake detective persuaded her to accompany him to police headquarters to view a suspect. She got into his Volkswagen, but once they were on a quiet street, the imposter stopped the car and produced a set of handcuffs, snapping one end onto DaRonch's wrist.

DaRonch let out a scream and he pulled a gun, placing this next to her head and ordering her to keep quiet. She was not the typically submissive type of woman the serial killer had dealt with in the past. She forced the door open and jumped out. The man leaped after her with a crowbar in his hand. He tried to smash her skull with this, but she caught the bar in mid-air and struggled with him. Then DaRonch saw a car coming down the street and leaped in front of it, forcing it to come to a stop. She jumped into the auto, which drove away.

The gall of the killer knew no bounds. Even with a potential victim escaping and now able to identify him, the young man tried to pick up a pretty, young French teacher outside Viewmont High School, but she turned him down. A short time later Debbie Kent vanished when she went off to meet a brother at an ice skating rink. Police searching for Kent found a key to a set of handcuffs in the school playground where she disappeared.

Ted Bundy in custody in Salt Lake City, Utah, where he charmed his captors into relaxing their guard before his escape.

Bundy in custody in Florida; by the time of this arrest, officers took no chances with the elusive killer.

Salt Lake City police then received the name of Ted Bundy from Seattle detectives, who stated that they had received an anonymous tip that Bundy had been kidnapping and killing young females. Bundy's photograph was also sent along to the Salt Lake officials and shown to Carol DaRonch, who said that Bundy was not the man who tried to abduct her. Laura Aimee, who had vanished in Orem, Utah, on October 31, 1974, was found dead, her naked body having been tossed into a canyon.

The killings went on. In Snowmass Village, a Colorado ski resort, on January 12, 1975, Dr. Raymond Gadowsky, staying at the Wildwood Inn, went to the room of his fiancée, Caryn Campbell, only to find her gone. Her remains were not found until February 17, 1975, the naked corpse hidden in some thick underbrush. She had been raped and her skull had been crushed. In another resort town, Vail, Colorado, Julie Cunningham vanished on March 15, 1975, after going to meet a girlfriend in a bar. A short time later the remains of two missing women, Susan Rancourt and Brenda Ball, were found on Taylor Mountain, Washington.

Then Melanie Cooley of Nederland, Colorado, disappeared on April 15, 1975, her body found on April 23, 1975, only a dozen miles from her home. Unlike the other victims, she was fully clothed, but her jeans had been slipped from her waist, showing that sex was the motive for the attack that killed her. Her head had been battered with a rock found nearby. Shelley Robertson disappeared on July 1 from her Golden, Colorado, home. Three days later, Nancy Baird, a gas station attendant in Golden, Colorado, vanished from her workplace. On August 23, Shelley Robertson's naked body was found in a mine shaft outside of Berthoud Pass, Colorado.

Then police, on August 16, 1975, arrested Ted Bundy. He was stopped by a Salt Lake City patrolman, who thought he was acting suspiciously, driving his Volkswagen down a street slowly as if inspecting homes for possible break-ins; the area had suffered a rash of recent burglaries. Bundy did not stop when ordered to do so by the patrol car and a chase ensued. His car was finally brought to the curb and Bundy was placed under arrest.

Bundy's room was searched, but nothing incriminating

Lynda Healy, Bundy victim.

Donna Manson, Bundy victim.

Susan Rancourt, Bundy victim.

Roberta Parks, Bundy victim.

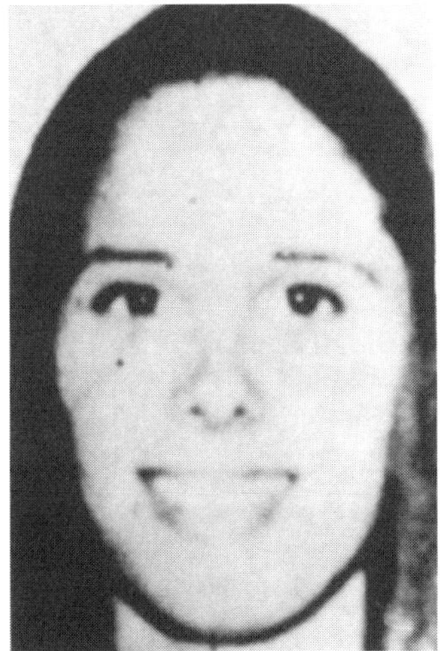

Brenda Ball, Bundy victim.

Georgann Hawkins, Bundy victim.

Denise Naslund, Bundy victim.

Jackie Ott, Bundy victim.

Melissa Smith, Bundy victim.

Laura Aimee, Bundy victim.

Debra Kent, Bundy victim.

Caryn Campbell, Bundy victim.

Lisa Levy, Bundy victim.

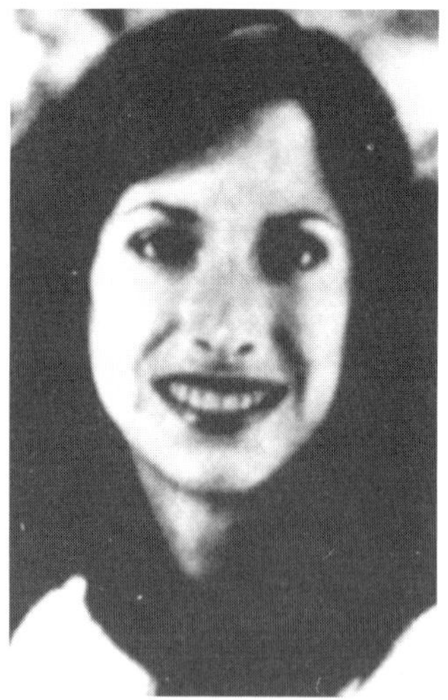

Margaret Bowman, Bundy victim.

Kimberley Leach, Bundy victim.

Bundy in custody in 1979.

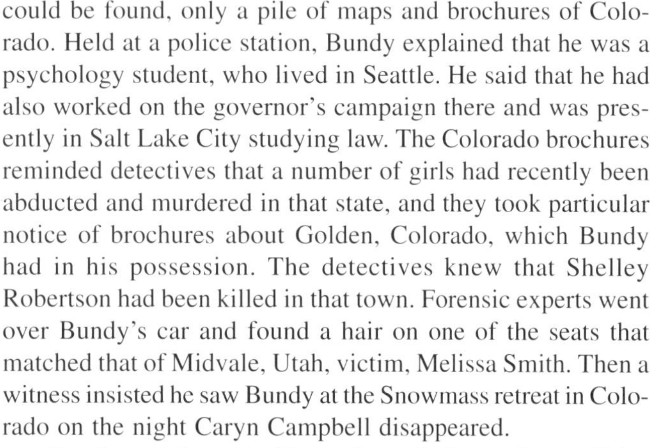

could be found, only a pile of maps and brochures of Colorado. Held at a police station, Bundy explained that he was a psychology student, who lived in Seattle. He said that he had also worked on the governor's campaign there and was presently in Salt Lake City studying law. The Colorado brochures reminded detectives that a number of girls had recently been abducted and murdered in that state, and they took particular notice of brochures about Golden, Colorado, which Bundy had in his possession. The detectives knew that Shelley Robertson had been killed in that town. Forensic experts went over Bundy's car and found a hair on one of the seats that matched that of Midvale, Utah, victim, Melissa Smith. Then a witness insisted he saw Bundy at the Snowmass retreat in Colorado on the night Caryn Campbell disappeared.

Bundy was charged with murder and taken to Aspen, Colorado, to stand trial. Here he charmed his wardens and prosecutors, affably cooperating with them, or seeming to, and giving an impression of an intelligent young man, who was anything but a berserk sex slayer. He was shown every courtesy, given special health foods to eat and allowed to attend court without being manacled. Bundy insisted that he could defend himself and received whatever law books he requested. Witnesses, however, showed Bundy for what he was, an inveterate liar, a cunning, crafty character who would go to any impossible lengths to get his way.

Carol DaRonch, who had at first failed to recognize Bundy from a photo as the man who tried to abduct her in Salt Lake City, then came forward and identified Bundy as the man who had attacked her. As the pretrial hearings dragged on, Bundy was allowed to roam about the law library in Aspen. Even though he was under guard, Bundy managed to open a window of the library and drop twenty feet to the ground, escaping. He was tracked down eight days later at a deserted shack on Smuggler's Mountain and brought back to Aspen, where he was now kept under heavy guard.

Bundy insisted that he was a victim of circumstance, that he merely *happened* to have been in the same places where all these women disappeared and that there were many young men, who bore a resemblance to him. He was also adept in using the law to create one legal motion after another to delay the case. While implementing this systematic legal stall, the insidious Bundy slowly took off weight in preparation for his next escape attempt.

Bundy somehow obtained a hacksaw and carved a hole around the light fixture of his cell, removing the fixture on December 30, 1977, and squeezing through the one-foot opening—by then he had lost enough weight to work his way through the opening. Bundy made a successful escape. He moved to Chicago, then Ann Arbor, Michigan, then on to Atlanta, and finally, he settled in Tallahassee, Florida, living only a few blocks from the sorority houses of Florida State University.

On the night of January 15, 1978, Nita Neary saw a man holding a log and lurking about the front door of her sorority house. As she thought about calling the police, a student named Karen Chandler, blood flowing from her wounds, staggered from her room. A madman had entered her room and had savagely beaten her on the head. Her roommate, Kathy Kleiner, had also been attacked in the same room, her jaw being broken.

In another room of the sorority house, police later found two other students Lisa Levy and Margaret Bowman. Both had been sexually abused. Bowman was dead, strangled with her own pantyhose. Lisa Levy had been brutally battered about the head and died en route to the hospital. Only a few hours later another female student, Cheryl Thomas, was brutally attacked in her room at another sorority house and was severely injured, but she survived the attack.

Though police began a widespread manhunt for the sorority house killer, they could find no one answering the sketchy description of the attacker. On February 9, 1979, 12-year-old Kimberley Leach left her classroom in Jacksonville and disappeared. Some days later Bundy, who had been living in Tallahassee under the name of Chris Hagen and using stolen credit cards to purchase essentials, sneaked out of his Tallahassee apartment, when his rent was long overdue. He stole an orange Volkswagen and drove to Pensacola, where a policeman stopped him and checked the license plates.

Ted Bundy dramatically addresses the court during his murder trial, serving as his own defense attorney

Discovering the car was stolen, the officer arrested Bundy. The serial killer bolted and the officer tackled him, struggling with him. When the officer fired a shot, Bundy meekly surrendered. He first identified himself as Chris Hagen, then admitted he was the fugitive, Theodore Bundy, wanted by Colorado authorities on charges of murder. He was held on charges of using stolen credit cards and stolen autos while detectives worked hard to tie Bundy-Hagen to the Tallahassee sorority house slayings. Meanwhile, the body of Kimberley Leach was found in the Suwannee River Park, her privates violated and mutilated; she had been strangled to death.

Still, the vain and strutting Bundy refused to admit to any murders. He claimed he was innocent. The police had made a terrible mistake. Detectives took Bundy on April 27, 1979, to an examining room. When he learned that they intended to take a wax impression of his teeth, Bundy went berserk, struggling violently so that a half-dozen men had to pin him down and hold his mouth open for the impression to be made. Bundy knew what the detectives were seeking. The impressions of his teeth were later perfectly matched to the bite marks found on the buttocks of the murdered student, Lisa Levy, and it was this bizarre piece of evidence that would later, more than anything else, convict Ted Bundy of the many serial murders he had so ruthlessly committed.

Charged with the Levy and Bowman murders, Bundy was taken to Miami and placed on trial. He pled innocent, again acting as his own lawyer. He smiled at jurors, swaggering before the judge as he spouted law and precedent-setting cases of the past. He exuded confidence that he would never be convicted. His demeanor changed as he was compelled to sit quietly and listen to arresting officers tell the court how he had admitted having sexual problems, that he had begun his sexual offenses in Seattle as a voyeur and quoting Bundy as having said: "Sometimes I feel like a vampire."

Dental experts then came forward to positively identify Bundy's teeth impressions with the bite marks found on the body of Lisa Levy, and this convinced the jury of Bundy's guilt. He was found guilty and sentenced to death by Judge Edward D. Cowart, who expressed regret that Bundy had gone "the wrong way" and that "you would have made a good lawyer...I'd have loved to have you practice in front of me." Bundy was also found guilty of the murder of the Leach girl and sentenced again to death.

Oddly, all of those around this vile and utterly cunning killer, his guards, arresting officers, the judges who heard his cases and ordered him executed, as well as most of those, who later devoted tedious and unrevealing books to his rather unimaginative murders, especially Ann Rule, who has established a literary career from serial killers, and Michaud and Aynesworth, who warmed too brightly to the man, showered him with the kind of attention given to Hollywood celebrities.

These writers complained about the limelight Bundy bathed in and then proceeded to flood him with it. The killer was an actor as well as an unrepentant criminal and the portrait he drew of himself caused all about him to empathize about a future he never had, as if he deserved a future. Though various crime scribes tried to point out his talents, there was nothing talented or redeeming about Ted Bundy and, more importantly, nothing to learn from him, except to recognize his pattern of serial murder as an alarmingly increasing *modus operandi* among modern killers.

Like the vicious killer Jack Henry Abbott, Theodore Bundy was undeservedly a *cause celebre,* and he played his part to the hilt, acting the pundit and even the criminologist as he waited to be executed, issuing cautionary statements to the young on how not to go wrong, to avoid pornography, to stay in school, to follow the legitimate road through life.

For a decade, this disgusting serial killer kept himself alive with one appeal after another, reaping millions of words

Theodore Bundy hears the verdict from a jury convicting him of murder; he was sentenced to death.

Ted Bundy is shown in a holding cell at Florida's state prison only a short time before he went to the electric chair on January 24, 1989.

from the nation's press about his so-called "intellectual thought process," and his "psychological makeup," but his act finally closed when all appeals, stays, and last-minute delays were exhausted. In a last ditch stand to save his miserable life, Bundy began a recital of all the murders he committed, twenty-three in all. (At least fifteen more murders were attributed to Bundy by authorities.)

The killer finally went to the electric chair at Florida's State Prison on January 24, 1989. His last nervous words were: "Give my love to my family and friends." He was taken to the execution chamber, his head and right calf shaved so that the electrical conduits would work properly. He sat down in the chair and was strapped in.

Bundy gripped the arms of the chair and his head, strapped to a stationary position, could not move, but his eyes darted about wildly and, according to witnesses: "He was totally white, very scared." His eyes rolled frantically before the twenty-four witnesses gathered to observe the awful killer's end. Then, promptly at 7:07 a.m., 2,000 volts went through his body, and he was pronounced dead four minutes later.

Outside the prison, more than 100 reporters moved through a huge crowd that had assembled, trying to milk one more story out of Theodore Bundy. But none in the crowd protested this execution. Signs were held high that read "Buckle up, Bundy, it's the law," and "Roast in Peace!" When the black flag went up to signal the serial killer's death, the throng cheered wildly and firecrackers and other fireworks were set off in celebration. One Florida resident, hoarse from cheering the execution, told a reporter: "I waited eleven years to see that creep fry."

THE YORKSHIRE RIPPER/1975-1980

The hunt for the "Yorkshire Ripper" lasted five years and nearly cost Assistant Chief Constable George Oldfield, a man obsessed with capturing the fiend, his life. The man Oldfield sought was Peter William Sutcliffe (AKA: Peter Williams, The Yorkshire Ripper; b. 1946), a vicious, elusive serial killer, who taunted the police and challenged them to catch him. Oldfield worked around the clock trying to piece together fragmented clues that might bring the killer to justice. Thirteen women were brutally murdered between 1975 and 1980, most of them prostitutes.

The British press portrayed this hulking night-stalker as a 1970s reincarnation of Jack the Ripper, who had murdered several London street-walkers in 1888. Before this latter-day Ripper was apprehended, the British police had questioned 200,000 people. They searched 30,000 houses and checked the registration on some 180,000 motor vehicles. It was without doubt the widest manhunt in British history. But then, the Yorkshire Ripper was the worst serial killer in 20th Century England.

The first attack attributed to the Ripper occurred on July 5, 1975, when Anna Rogulsky was assaulted by a man wielding a hammer. Six weeks later, on August 15, 1975, Olive Smelt was struck from behind in a similar manner. Both women recovered after surgery. Not so lucky was Wilma McCann, a 28-year-old Scotswoman who had resorted to prostitution to take care of her four children. McCann was canvassing the pubs of Leeds on the night of October 29-30, 1975 in search of customers when the Ripper pounced on her from behind. Struck on the head with a ball-headed hammer, the woman was dragged into an empty field and viciously assaulted with a knife. Her mutilated body was found the next day. The random murder of a prostitute carried little weight in the media. One of the dead woman's neighbors expressed the opinion that "Hotpants" McCann was "no better than she ought to have been."

No one knew at the time that the McCann murder would set into motion a series of these crimes, the next one occurring on January 20, 1976, when 42-year-old Emily Jackson was battered over the head and stabbed to death in a Chapeltown alley in Leeds. Jackson was married to a roofing specialist who did not know that his wife was supplementing the family income by turning "tricks" on the side.

By this time the CID (Criminal Investigation Department) and the press were aware that a serial killer might be loose. Chief Superintendent Dennis Hoban expressed concern: "I can't stress strongly enough that it is vital we catch this brutal killer before he brings tragedy to another family." The killer was dubbed the "Yorkshire Ripper" by writer George Hill, who covered the murder for the *Daily Express*.

The Ripper kept a low profile for the next year, resurfacing on February 5, 1977, when he stabbed 28-year-old Irene Richardson to death in Roundhay Park in Leeds. The murder site was scarcely a mile away from Chapeltown, the notorious red-light district where the Ripper cruised for his victims. Richardson, like Emily Jackson before her, was nominally connected to the trade. Richardson had taken to the streets after separating from her husband.

The murder count climbed to four on April 23, 1977 when Bradford prostitute Patricia Atkinson, thirty-two, was found bludgeoned to death in her apartment on Lumb Lane. This time the killer left behind an important clue: a bloody footprint identical to one found at the scene of the Jackson murder. The scarcity of eyewitnesses however, hampered the investigation.

Sixteen-year-old Jayne MacDonald was certainly no prostitute. She was a fun-loving teenager who had been dancing the night away at the Hofbrauhaus in Leeds. On June 26, 1977, she was grabbed by the Yorkshire Ripper near Roundhay Park and stabbed to death, possibly because he mistook her for a street-walker. The girl lived only a few doors down the lane from Wilma McCann.

Maureen Long narrowly avoided a similar fate on July 27, 1977. While walking through Bradford, she was accosted by the Ripper and dragged unconscious to a darkened street nearby. Before he could inflict the final fatal blows, something caused him to flee. Long was removed to a local hospital. She provided police with a sketchy description of the suspect and his car, which was proven to be inaccurate when the real killer, Sutcliffe, was arrested several years later.

In the next two years, six more women were murdered, beginning with 21-year-old prostitute Jean Bernadette Jordan on October 1, 1977, in Manchester, and followed by Yvonne Pearson, twenty-two, on January 21, 1978, in Bradford. On February 1, 1978, the body of 18-year-old Helen Rytka was found under a railroad viaduct in Huddersfield, West Yorkshire.

Next came Vera Millward, a 41-year-old prostitute from Manchester, on May 16, 1978. She was murdered on the grounds of the Manchester Royal Academy. This was followed by the bludgeoning death of Josephine Whitaker, a 19-year-old building society clerk from Halifax, Yorkshire, on the night of April 4, 1979.

Following this latest outrage, the Ripper communicated for the first time with the police. On June 26, Constable Oldfield played back a tape-recording he had received from the killer to members of the press. In a slow, recognizable Geordie accent, the killer taunted his pursuers. "I'm Jack," the voice said. "I see you are still having no luck catching me. I have the greatest respect for you, George, but, Lord, you are no nearer catching me than four years ago when I started. I reckon your boys are letting you down, George. You can't be much good, can ya? The only time they came near catching me was a few months back in Chapeltown, when I was disturbed. Even then it was a uniform copper, not a detective." The message closed with a chilling warning: "Well, I'll keep on going for quite a while yet. I can't see myself being nicked just yet. Even if you do get near I'll probably top myself [kill myself] first. Well, it's been nice chatting to you, George. Yours, Jack the Ripper."

Peter Sutcliffe, shown with his bride, Sonia, on their wedding day; though married, the burly truck driver sought sex from prostitutes, some numbering among the fourteen women he killed over a five-year period.

The next month the emotionally spent constable suffered a heart attack and was forced to temporarily withdraw from the investigation. He was replaced by veteran Leeds detective James Hobson, who seemed to have no better luck than his

Wilma McCann, murdered by Sutcliffe on October 29-30, 1975.

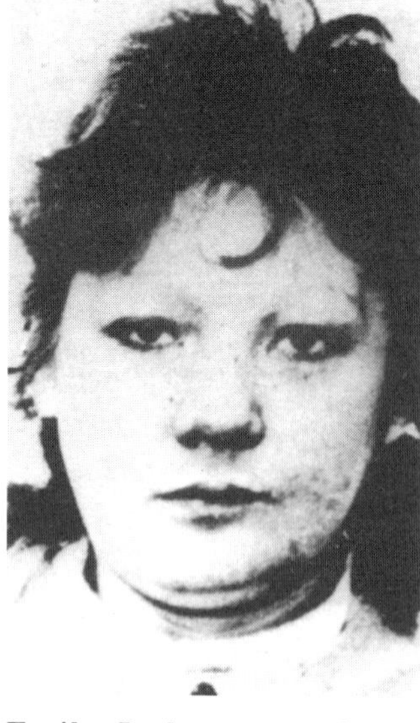

Emily Jackson, murdered by Sutcliffe on January 20, 1976.

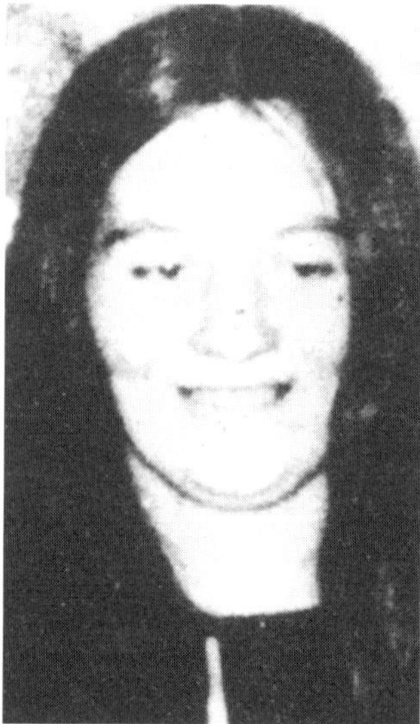

Irene Richardson, murdered by Sutcliffe on February 5, 1977.

Patricia Atkinson, murdered by Sutcliffe on April 23, 1977.

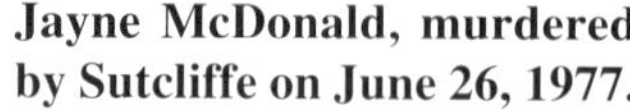

Jayne McDonald, murdered by Sutcliffe on June 26, 1977.

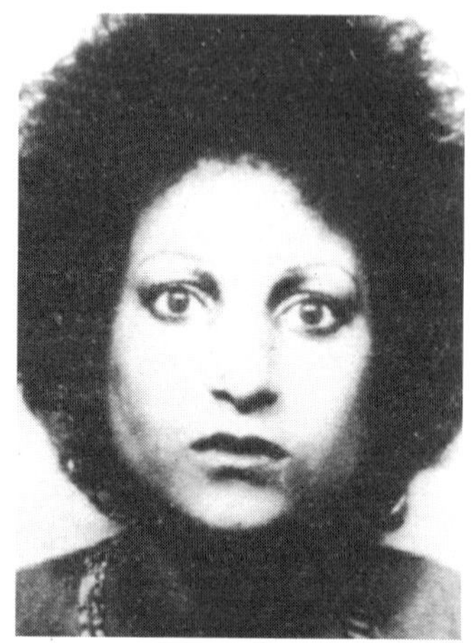

Helen Rytka, murdered by Sutcliffe on February 1, 1978.

predecessor. A toll-free number for citizens wanting to hear the voice of the Ripper was provided by the phone company, but after thousands of calls the police were no closer to identifying a suspect.

Even during this major barrage of publicity, the Ripper was able to kill again. On September 1, 1979, Barbara Leach, twenty, a student at Bradford University, told some friends she was with that evening that she was going to get some fresh air before going home. She walked away from the Mannville Arms pub and was never seen alive again. Her body was found the following afternoon next to a back-alley dustbin, covered with old carpets. The wounds showed the unmistakable mark of the Yorkshire Ripper: Leach had been stabbed with the same rusty screwdriver used in the Whitaker killing.

The police investigation was becoming so intense, that it apparently caused the Ripper to lay low for almost a year before his next attack. On August 20, 1980, a 47-year-old civil servant from the Department of Education in Pudsey named Marguerite Walls was assaulted and strangled while on her way home to her apartment in Farsley. After two more unsuccessful attacks against women in Leeds and Huddersfield, the Ripper claimed his final victim, 20-year-old Jacqueline Hill, a literature student at Leeds University. She was taking a bus back to her dormitory on November 17, 1980, when she was assaulted in the "triangle of terror," the familiar stretch of ground that included Leeds, Bradford, and West Yorkshire, the killer's favorite haunt. Hill was the madman's thirteenth victim.

On November 25, 1980, West Yorkshire Chief Constable Ronald Gregory announced the formation of a special squad to deal with the Ripper case. Hobson, who superseded Oldfield as the head of the investigation, echoed the words of the killer when he predicted that the fiend would eventually be captured by the men on patrol. His prophecy was realized on January 2, 1981, when Sergeant Robert Ring and PC Robert Hydes pulled their squad car next to a Rover V-8 parked in an office complex in Sheffield. There they found Peter William Sutcliffe, an over-the-road truck driver from Heaton, engaged in a sex act with a black prostitute named Olivia Rievers.

The driver of the car told the officers that his name was Peter Williams, but a quick check of the registration tags showed that they did not belong to the Rover. While the police were deciding what to do with Sutcliffe and Rievers, Sutcliffe asked if he could relieve himself. The officers consented, and he wandered over to some nearby bushes. It would be two days before Sergeant Ring, realizing that the man they had picked up could be the Ripper, would return to the bushes, where Sutcliffe had stood and would find the hammer and knife used in several of the murders.

Sutcliffe and Rievers were taken to the police station for further questioning. Again, Sutcliffe asked to go to the bathroom, and again, he unloaded another murder weapon: a knife, which he deposited in a cistern in the bathroom. When asked to empty his pockets, the suspect pulled out a length of clothesline. On January 4, during an interview with Sergeant Desmond O'Boyle, the officer produced the hammer and knife found where Sutcliffe had been arrested.

"I think you're in trouble," O'Boyle told Sutcliffe, "serious trouble." Sutcliffe then admitted that he was the Ripper.

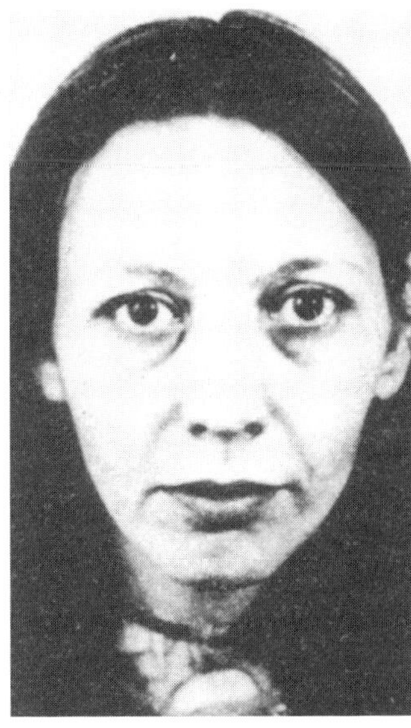
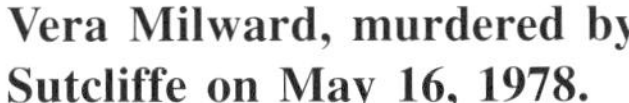

Vera Milward, murdered by Sutcliffe on May 16, 1978.

Josephine Whitaker, murdered by Sutcliffe on April 4, 1979.

Barbara Leach, murdered by Sutcliffe on September 1, 1979.

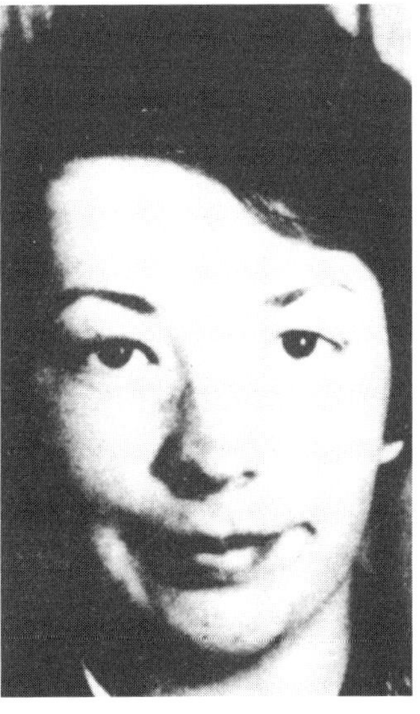

Jacqueline Hill, murdered by Sutcliffe on November 17, 1980.

He confessed to committing eleven murders, but the police charged him with thirteen, and had strong suspicions that he may have killed Joan Harrison, whose body was found in Preston, Lancashire.

Sutcliffe's motive for murdering prostitutes was tied to an unfortunate incident that occurred in 1969, when he was twenty-two years old. Sutcliffe picked up a streetwalker one night, but was unable to perform. The woman kept the £10 note he handed her, refusing to return the £5 he had coming in change. He ran into her at the same pub several weeks later, and, when asked about the £5, she laughed and rebuked him. "I developed and played up a hatred for prostitutes," Sutcliffe told the West Yorkshire Police in a confession that took seventeen hours to record. He said that he had deliberately arranged the clothes of his victims so that they "would be known for what they were."

In checking into his background, police learned that Sutcliffe had married Sonia Szurma in 1974. His wife was a Czech national he had been dating irregularly for seven years. The immigrant girl had been previously diagnosed as a schizophrenic, a mental condition that created many violent arguments in the next few years. While Sonia took teacher-training courses in London, Peter prowled the red-light districts in search of fresh-faced girls, who sold themselves on the street.

For the residents of Yorkshire, the long nightmare was over. Peter Sutcliffe went on trial at the Old Bailey on May 5, 1981, amidst the jeers of a thousand angry spectators who lined the streets outside chanting: "Hang him! Hang him!" He pleaded not guilty to the charge of murder on the grounds of diminished responsibility. He told the court about "his mission from God," but a jailer overheard the prisoner tell his wife that he would be let off with a ten-year sentence if he could convince the jurors that he was a prime candidate for the "looney bin." Consequently, the jury found him guilty of thirteen murders, and seven other assaults. On May 22, 1981, the Yorkshire Ripper was sentenced to life imprisonment with no chance for parole for thirty years by Justice Leslie Boreham.

THE HILLSIDE STRANGLERS/1977-1979

For no reason other than to satiate their sadistic lusts, two bestial killers slew ten young women and girls who were mostly part-time prostitutes, murdering them from 1977 to 1979. These victims were slain in the home of Angelo Buono, Jr. (1935-2002) in Glendale, California, serial killings that were initially attributed to a ubiquitous "Hillside Strangler." Kenneth Bianchi (AKA: Steve Walker, Anthony D'Amato, Nicholas Fontana; Billy; b. 1952) was the second serial killer in this murder tag-team. Bianchi who had been born in Rochester, New York, and had been raised by foster parents, arrived in Los Angeles in 1977 to stay with his cousin Buono, a street-tough sub-normal creature who was always trying to prove his manhood and authority.

Buono reveled in his Italian heritage and flew the Italian flag 24-hours-a-day from a flagpole on the grounds of his house. He ran an upholstery business out of his garage and was already parading prostitutes through his home by the time Bianchi arrived. One night, as the cousins sat about drinking beer, they speculated as to what it might be like to murder someone.

They started their serial killing spree by murdering Elissa Teresa Kastin, twenty-one, on October 6, 1977, dumping her naked body near Chevy Chase Drive in Glendale. Their next victim was 19-year-old Yolanda Washington; her body was found on the slopes of the distinguished Forest Lawn Cemetery, the resting place of movie stars, on the night of October 18, 1977. The body was naked, cleaned by the killers so as to leave no clues, and posed in a lascivious position.

Bianchi and Buono went on to murder eight more women. On Oct. 31, 1977, the naked body of 15-year-old Judith Lynn Miller was found on a hillside next to the road in Glendale. She had been raped, sodomized, and strangled to death. Her wrists, ankles, and neck bore the marks of the ropes that had bound her, as was the case with the Washington woman and those victims to come. Bianchi and Buono, to show their con-

Kenneth Bianchi, while being detained in Washington State, where he almost convinced examining psychiatrists that he was insane.

Bianchi in a California courtroom, where he put all the blame for the serial murders on his savage cousin, Angelo Buono.

tempt for lawmen looking for them, made sure that this body and the others had been cleaned, leaving no clues whatsoever, but placed the corpses in areas, where they could easily be found and usually close to police stations, as if to thumb their noses at police.

On November 20, 1977, the killers slew three more women: Kristina Weckler, twenty; Dolores Cepeda, twelve; and Sonja Johnson, fourteen, dumping the nude body of Weckler on a slope in Highland Park and the corpses of Cepeda and Johnson in Elysian Park. They killed Jane Evelyn King, twenty-eight, on November 23, 1977, dumping her body at the off-ramp of the southbound Golden State Freeway. On November 29, 1977, Bianchi and Buono murdered Lauren Rae Wagner, eighteen, placing her naked body on Cliff Drive in Glassell Park.

Next, on December 14, 1977, police found the naked body of Kimberly Diane Martin, eighteen. The intensity of the murders slackened but, on February 17, 1978, Cindy Lee Hudspeth's naked body was found in the trunk of a car, which had been driven off Angeles Crest Highway. The killings had all been committed in Buono's home and the bodies dumped in a rough circle around that house.

Police announced regularly that they were closing in on the Hillside Strangler and that several "good" suspects had been pulled in for questioning, but when the killings stopped, police had little to say and less to investigate, their special team of investigators reassigned to other chores. Los Angeles detectives were perplexed when the killings suddenly ended.

The reason for this was hygiene. Bianchi left Buono's home because of the filthy conditions there, going to Bellingham, Washington, where, in January 1979, he raped and strangled to death with a cord two college women, Karen Mandic and Diane Wilder, packing the bodies into the trunk of Mandic's car. Following a missing persons report, these bodies were found and Bianchi came under suspicion as having been seen with one of the women shortly before her disappearance.

Ironically, Bianchi was working as a security guard and had applied for a job with the Bellingham police department. (He had also applied for a job with the Los Angeles Police Department and, in fact, had gone along on a few rides with officers in Los Angeles, while the Hillside Strangler was being sought.) Under arrest for the Mandic and Wilder disappearances, Bianchi, who had steeped himself in psychiatric studies, played a game with doctors examining him, pretending, it was later reported, to have a split personality, or many personalities, one of which being the killer of the women.

While being examined by these psychiatrists, Bianchi claimed that he had blackouts and could not remember his actions. He presented all the symptoms of someone unbalanced, out of control, legally insane. His act, however, did not work, and he was charged with the murder of the two Bellingham women.

Then Bianchi offered prosecutors a deal. He would turn over his cousin Buono, the real Hillside Strangler, he said, if he were removed to California and did not have to face the death penalty in Washington, that of hanging. Washington authorities agreed to the deal, as long as Bianchi pleaded guilty. He did and received a life sentence, then was shipped to California to testify against his brutal cousin, Buono, after which he would serve his time in a California prison, one less austere and rigid than Washington's Walla Walla Prison.

On Bianchi's statements, Buono was charged with murder but Bianchi, who had fooled six Washington state psychiatrists into labeling him legally insane, now could not testify against Buono since he had been officially labeled a lunatic. Yet it was shown that he had planned his "insanity" position years earlier, reading endless studies on psychiatry and particularly studying the novels, *Sybil* and *The Three Faces of Eve,* preparing for his own positioning of multiple personalities, a psychological profile he assumed when confronted with the Washington murders.

Bianchi had gone so far as to claim he had a degree in psychiatry and was about to actually open up a practice in Los Angeles before going off to Washington. Bianchi also had faked being hypnotized, according to most reports, when being examined in Washington, and then released his other "identities," claiming that these personalities had done the horrible murders with his beast-like cousin Buono.

Bianchi nevertheless gave a complete profile of the murders he committed with Buono once back in Los Angeles, describing how he and Buono drove about in Buono's car, using fake badges to identify themselves to young women as policemen, ordering them into Buono's auto, which they passed off as an unmarked police car.

Once the women were in the car, they were taken to Buono's home, tortured, forced to have sex with both of them, and then tied up and murdered, usually strangled, although the killers experimented with injections and other murder methods that proved unsuccessful. Then the murderers fastidiously washed their victims and dumped their naked bodies at remote spots.

Buono was arrested in 1979 after Bianchi's Washington conviction, and he was eventually tried on November 16, 1981. A grueling two years passed during which more than 400 witnesses were heard, 55,000 pages of trial transcript were compiled, and millions of dollars were spent to convict Buono. A jury, more than two years later, convicted him of nine counts of murder on November 14, 1983. The trial was aptly labeled a "judicial extravaganza" by the press, one in which Buono insisted, in court and out, that he was innocent of the murders his cousin claimed he had performed. (He had been extremely thorough in cleaning up his home after Bianchi left, not one fingerprint of the victims, not even his own, could be found by police, although a single eyelash belonging to one of the victims was unearthed and a few strands of fiber from one of Buono's chairs was found on one of the bodies.)

A surprise prosecution witness was 27-year-old Catherine Lorre, who identified both Bianchi and Buono as the two men who had stopped her on a Hollywood street in 1977, saying they were detectives and demanding her identification. She had shown her driver's license and next to it, Bianchi saw a photo of her as a little girl sitting on her father's lap, her father being the famous character actor of films, Peter Lorre. Bianchi later admitted that he had let Lorre go, because he feared that murdering the child of a celebrity would bring more police heat down upon him and Buono.

Judge Ronald George, who had refused to drop charges against Buono "for lack of evidence," as asked by the prosecution during the initial stages of his trial when it felt it would lose the case altogether, had conducted a fair and impartial trial for more than two years. He pronounced sentence on Angelo Buono, Jr. on January 9, 1984, giving him life imprisonment without possibility of parole.

Bianchi, against his clever designs, was ordered sent back to Walla Walla Prison to serve out a life sentence, parole not

Angelo Buono is shown outside his garage, where he and Bianchi murdered many of their victims. He is talking to a female undercover investigator, who suspected him of being a serial killer.

Angelo Buono, Jr., leaving court, after being pronounced guilty of murder; he was sent to prison for life and died in his cell on September 22, 2002.

available until the year 2005. Stated Judge George after sentencing: "I'm sure, Mr. Buono and Mr. Bianchi, that you will only get your thrills by reliving over and over the tortures and murders of your victims, being incapable as I believe you to be, of ever feeling any remorse."

Angelo Buono, Jr., died in his cell at Calipatria State Prison on September 22, 2002. He was sixty-seven and though his cause of death was not stated, it was believed that he had died of heart failure, having had heart problems for several years. While imprisoned, Buono, in 1986, married Christine Kuzuka, a mother of three and a supervisor in the Los Angeles office of the State Employment Development Department.

THE RACIST SNIPER/1977-1980

Joseph Paul Franklin (James Clayton Vaughan, Jr.; b. 1950) of Mobile, Alabama, carried out a series of racially motivated sniper attacks from 1977 to 1980. Franklin shot and killed ten people in five states, and was a prime suspect in at least three other shootings, including that of Vernon Jordan, president of the National Urban League, who, on May 29, 1980, was shot in the back as he returned to his motel room in Fort Wayne, Indiana. (In 1982, Franklin was acquitted of wounding Jordan.) He also remains a suspect in the March 6, 1978, shooting of sleeze magazine publisher Larry Flynt, who was paralyzed from the waist down by a shot to the abdomen.

Franklin's father, James Vaughan, Sr., was a World War II veteran, who was unable to hold a job and was jailed on numerous occasions for public drunkenness. Vaughan was away from the house much of the time, returning briefly to torment his family emotionally and physically. In 1965, he divorced Helen Rau Vaughan, who then moved her children into low-income housing in the Oakdale section of Mobile. Franklin (his real name was James Vaughan, Jr.) was a quiet loner fascinated by organized religion. His sister said that he looked up and visited every church in the Mobile area. By his senior year of high school, the boy had abandoned religion for the American Nazi movement. (He would later change his name to Joseph Paul Franklin after Nazi propagandist and racist Joseph Paul Goebbels, who committed suicide in Hitler's underground bunker in spring 1945.)

Franklin dropped out of high school to devote his energies to the right-wing hate groups. He directed his aggression particularly toward bi-racial couples. "If he saw a black man and white woman together, he would tell them right out what he thought of them and it was never nice," his sister Carolyn recalled.

In 1968 Franklin married his high school sweetheart Bobbie Louise Dorman, age sixteen. Four months later they were divorced. Franklin moved to Arlington, Virginia, in 1970 to offer his services to the Nazis. On September 18, 1970, he stood in front of the White House passing out leaflets denouncing the state visit of Israeli prime minister Golda Meir.

On October 25, 1972, Franklin was arrested and jailed for carrying a concealed weapon in Fairfax County, Virginia. Four years later, Franklin, who had recently joined the Ku Klux Klan, sprayed Mace in the faces of a black man and a white woman in a Washington, D.C., suburb. He was arrested on September 8, 1976, for this assault, but was released on bond. When he failed to show up for a December hearing, a warrant was issued for his arrest.

After a March 1977 arrest for carrying a concealed weapon, Franklin traveled extensively through the South and the Midwest for the next two years, using eighteen different aliases. On July 29, 1977, he bombed a synagogue in Chattanooga, Tennessee, and four days later in Rockville, Maryland, set off explosives at the home of a Jewish-American lobbyist.

On August 7, 1977, in Madison, Wisconsin, a sniper shot 23-year-old Alphonse Manning, Jr. and his white girlfriend Toni Schwenn in the parking lot of a shopping mall. In his 1984 confession, Franklin told police that he had intended to kill former judge Archie Simonson of Dane County after reading about a case involving two black men, who assaulted a white woman. Franklin objected to the "lenient" sentence the judge doled out. When the plan went awry, Franklin said, he killed Manning and Schwenn. While posing as a plumber in 1979, he married Anita Carden, age sixteen. He dyed his hair and changed his cars frequently, always managing to remain one step ahead of the law.

Franklin was linked to the shooting deaths of Jesse Eugene Taylor and Marian Vira Bressette, an interracial couple gunned down outside a supermarket in Oklahoma City, Oklahoma, on October 21, 1979. The charges against Franklin in this instance were dropped for lack of evidence. In two sepa-

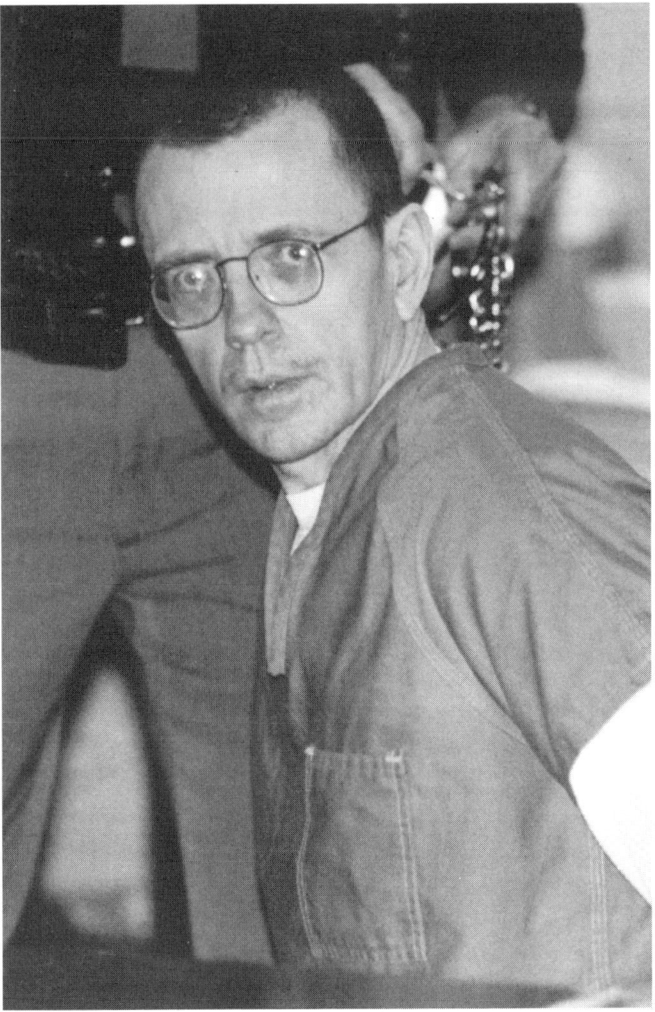

Joseph Paul Franklin, who shot and killed ten people in five states from 1977 to 1980; he was sentenced to death.

rate shootings on January 12 and January 14, 1980, two young black men, Lawrence Reese and Leo Watkins, were killed in Indianapolis. Franklin was charged with firing on the men as they stood near a window in a residential complex. Police officials had too little evidence against Franklin to sustain a conviction.

In Cincinnati, two black teenagers were shot dead near a railroad overpass on June 8, 1980. Franklin's presence in the city was confirmed by a newspaper ad he had placed in the Cincinnati *Enquirer* offering to sell a .30-06 Remington rifle, the same type used in the shooting attack on Vernon Jordan a week earlier. Suspected of these shootings, Franklin was picked up in Florence, Kentucky, and taken to the police interrogation room, but he managed to slip away from his captors.

Franklin drove his 1975 Camaro west to Salt Lake City, Utah. On August 20, 1980, he took his rifle to Liberty Park where he shot David Martin, twenty, and Ted Fields, eighteen, who had been jogging with two white women. Eyewitnesses reported seeing a brown Camaro drive away from the murder scene minutes later. Police matched the tire tread marks to those taken in Florence, Kentucky, several weeks earlier. Before he left the city, Franklin hired a prostitute to pose nude for him, surrounded by his personal arsenal of pistols and rifles.

The FBI next traced Franklin's movements to Lakeland, Florida, where he was arrested outside a local blood bank on October 28, 1980. He denied his identity, and had attempted to scrape off his tattoos when police picked him up. Franklin was extradited to Salt Lake City, where he faced federal and state charges for killing the Liberty Park joggers, and for violating their civil rights.

U.S. Assistant Attorney Steven Snarr asked for the mandatory sentence, as he assailed Franklin for having "accomplished the very evil the Civil Rights Act is designed to address." "Do you have any more lies to tell?" the defendant screamed back. Franklin was convicted and sentenced to four life terms at the federal facilty at Marion, Illinois, by Federal District Judge Bruce Jenkins in March 1981.

The case of the Madison, Wisconsin, couple murdered in 1977 went before Judge William D. Byrne in February 1986. The Dane County Circuit judge sentenced Franklin to two consecutive life terms on February 14, 1986. "The defendant's history of violence, terror, and murder prompts this court to do all it can so that he will never kill again," Byrne said.

Franklin was ultimately convicted and sentenced to death for nine murders. At this writing, he is on Missouri's Death Row, awaiting execution for a 1977 sniper attack. In 1996, the one-time white supremacist who killed Jews, blacks and interracial couples, and who claimed to have shed himself of his hateful philosophy, began admitting to many more murders that had gone uncharged to him.

Franklin confessed that he had randomly shot and killed two black teenagers, 14-year-old Darrell Lane and 13-year-old Dante Evans Brown, in 1980 in hopes of igniting a race war (which had also been the maniacal plan of mass murderer Charles Manson, see Mass Murder). A jury sifting through this old case found Franklin guilty of these killings on October 21, 1998. He also confessed to murdering 22-year-old Arthur Smothers, a black, and 16-year-old Kathleen Mikula, a white, as they walked across a bridge in Johnstown, Pennsylvania, on June 15, 1980. The interracial couple had talked about getting married.

The motivation for Franklin's confessions was unclear. Prosecutors believed that he hoped to prolong his life by admitting to more murders and thereby extend his time for appeals. Others claimed that Franklin was angling to manage an escape while being moved for trials, as he had in the past. He did not escape and still awaits execution, but he has prolonged his life through seemingly endless appeals.

THE FREEWAY STRANGLER/1978-1980

William George Bonin (1947-1996) was shuttled in and out of detention homes following his first criminal conviction at the age of ten. His father was a drunk and a gambler, and his doting mother more often than not became the servile victim of her husband's murderous rage. In 1969, the young truck driver from Downey, California, was convicted of his first sex crime, charged with molesting five boys.

William George Bonin, left, at his murder trial in 1981; he was sentenced to death, executed in the gas chamber at San Quentin on February 23, 1996. Bonin admitted to killing twenty-one boys from 1978 to 1980.

Murder accomplice Vernon Butts committed suicide in 1981.

Bonin was sent to Atascadero State Hospital, but after two years physicians concluded he was not receptive to treatment. For the next five years William Bonin moved in and out of prison on a variety of sexual offenses. A psychiatrist's report concluded that his homosexual problems were related to his mother's domination during childhood.

By his own estimate, Bonin killed at least twenty-one teenaged boys between 1978 and 1980 (authorities attributed a total of forty-four homicides to the "Freeway Strangler"). With the help of several willing accomplices including Vernon Butts, Bonin cruised the highways of Los Angeles and Orange County, targeting young homosexuals for death. Butts, at first shocked, soon became a willing participant in the killing orgy, which always accompanied "rough sex." "After the first one, I couldn't do anything about it," Butts later explained. "He [Bonin] had a hypnotic way about him."

The naked and battered bodies were deposited near the on-off ramps of the Los Angeles freeways. The press quickly dubbed the unknown assailant the "Freeway Strangler." Police from four counties assisted in the investigation which yielded no new clues. Butts grew tired of the game and temporarily dropped out of sight, but this did not deter Bonin, who recruited younger, more willing henchmen to help him locate victims. Two of these men, Greg Miley and James Monro, were drifters who wandered into Hollywood, where they met Bonin.

Police were finally tipped off to the identity of the "Freeway Strangler" by 18-year-old William Ray Pugh (no relation to 15-year-old Russell Pugh, who was abducted from Huntington Beach by Bonin on March 21, 1980, and murdered by him). William Pugh informed police that Bonin and others had been killing boys for some time and that Bonin had tried to enlist William Pugh as an accomplice. Police checked Bonin's record, which dated back to 1969, replete with many sexual offenses. The Vietnam veteran and truck driver was arrested in Hollywood after parking his van at a closed gas station near his home in Downey, California.

Charged with fourteen counts of murder, Bonin was arraigned in Los Angeles Superior Court, along with Butts, who quickly confessed to helping in five of the killings. However, the prosecution lost its star witness when Butts hanged himself in his jail cell on January 11, 1981. (Butts had earlier tried to kill himself in four unsuccessful attempts.)

Bonin was brought to trial on November 4, 1981. Accomplices Miley and Monro testified for the prosecution, telling the court that after his arrest, Bonin had instructed them to "start going around and grabbing anyone off the street and killing them," in order to convince authorities that the "Freeway Strangler" was still operating while Bonin was behind bars and that they had jailed an innocent man.

A reporter obtained and publicized an interview conducted with Bonin before his trial, one in which he reportedly admitted his serial killings: "I couldn't stop killing. It got easier with each one we did." This admission had no effect on the jury's decision, which was rendered on January 5, 1982, when, after an eight-hour deliberation, the jury found Bonin guilty on ten charges of murder and ten charges of robbery.

On March 12, 1982, Judge William Keene sentenced the serial killer to death. Bonin fought desperately for life through one appeal after another, prolonging his life for fourteen years. The serial killer was finally executed in the gas chamber at San Quentin on February 23, 1996.

THE "MISSION" OF CORAL EUGENE WATTS/ 1974-1982

Burglar Coral Eugene Watts (b. 1953), who killed an estimated forty women, felt that all women were deceitful and unfaithful. In 1974, Watts attended Western Michigan University in Kalamazoo, Michigan (admitted even though he tested with an IQ of 75). There, October 25, 1974, he attempted to strangle two women, choking them into unconsciousness. He left their apartment without molesting them or taking anything, but became incensed when he learned that both were alive.

On October 30, 1974, he attacked 19-year-old Gloria Steele, stabbing her to death and leaving her corpse close to the university campus. He was detained in the case of the two attacks on the women who had survived, but he refused to talk about the Steele killing and voluntarily admitted himself to a state hospital on the advice of his attorney. He waited fourteen months before plea-bargaining a deal, confessing to the attack of one of the two women who survived his attack and receiving a one-year prison sentence. Upon his release in 1975, he moved to Ann Arbor, Michigan.

Watts eventually became a bus mechanic, working during the week and traveling on weekends. During this time, three young women, 18-year-old Shirley Small, 20-year-old Glenda Richmond, and 29-year-old Rebecca Huff, were attacked and killed in Ann Arbor, from April to September 1980, the victims of multiple stabbings. Many of the bodies were severely mutilated, several with jagged postmortem wounds.

Police suspected Watts as the so-called "Sunday Morning Slasher." At that time, Watts was also allegedly killing women in Detroit and Windsor, Canada, as well. Not all of his associations with women were violent and fatal, however. In 1980, he married, but his wife found him peculiar and left him within two months. He had a relationship with another woman, who gave birth to his child.

In 1981, Watts lost his bus mechanic job and moved to Houston, Texas. There he worked regularly and attended a local Pentecostal church. The Ann Arbor police sent Houston law enforcement officials their suspicions of Watts, and Houston police placed surveillance on him over the weekends for about sixty days. Not finding anything peculiar about his behavior, they discontinued the surveillance.

On March 27, 1981, 34-year-old Edith Ledet, was found stabbed to death. The body of the medical student was discovered along a Houston tow path where she had been jogging. At midnight on September 12, 1981, Elizabeth Montgomery was suddenly knifed by a black man while she was walking her dog. She staggered back to her apartment, where she was discovered and rushed to a hospital. Only two hours after this attack, Susan Wolfe, twenty-one, who lived near Montgomery, was stabbed to death.

In January 1982, two women were killed. Phyllis Tam, a 27-year-old advertising art director was hanged with her own clothes in a secluded area near Rice University where she jogged every morning. Two weeks later, police found the body of a student stuffed in the trunk of her car. On January 18, student Margaret Fossi had been sideswiped on the road while driving. When she stopped, Watts had pulled her from her car and beaten her to death. In each of the attacks, Watts left no physical evidence and made sure his victims were dead.

On May 23, 1982, Watts attacked 20-year-old Lori Ann Lister in her apartment. He twisted a coat hanger around her

Woman-hater Coral Eugene Watts reportedly murdered an estimated forty females from 1974 to 1982, although prosecutors failed to convict him of a single slaying.

wrists and throttled her before attempting to drown her in the bathtub. A neighbor, Linda Aguilar, arrived and also came under attack from Watts, but she escaped by jumping from a balcony and called police.

Police arrived to see Watts fleeing from the apartment building and they arrested him, charging him with attempted murder, aggravated kidnapping, and burglary. The serial killer again arranged a plea bargain in which he would give the police information on several murders and, in exchange, he would be charged with merely first-degree burglary. In the ensuing months, he took police to the burial sites of many of his victims. He cleared up twenty-two killings in three states and two countries. After re-investigating other unsolved murders, police concluded that Watts murdered at least forty women. When asked why he killed so many women, Watts replied that women were evil and that it was his "mission" to rid the earth of them.

The district attorney could not definitely link Watts to any of the murders and proceeded with the plea-bargained charge of first-degree burglary. Judge Doug Shaver sentenced him to the maximum sentence, sixty years in prison. Because the judge ruled that the water-filled bathtub was a deadly weapon, Watts must serve at least twenty years of his sentence before he can become eligible for parole. Shaver asked that the Texas Department of Corrections and the state legislature make sure he completed the entire sentence without a chance for parole. At the sentencing on September 3, 1982, Shaver said to Watts, "I hope you serve each and every minute of the sixty years."

THE SERIAL KILLINGS OF LUCAS AND TOOLE/1951-1983

Henry Lee Lucas (b. 1936) and Ottis Elwood Toole (1947-1996), may have been the most prolific serial killers in U. S. history, if their bragging statements are to be believed, in that they murdered jointly and separately more than 300 people from 1951 to 1983. Both came from dysfunctional families and both were uneducated, having cretinous mentalities and no regard for civility, decency, or human life. They were subhuman creatures prowling through the social debris and economically depressed backwaters of America, selecting peer victims at random to murder.

Born August 23, 1936 in Blacksburg, Virginia, Lucas lived in dire poverty in a two-room shack with a dirt floor outside of town. His parents made bootleg moonshine and his mother, Viola Lucas, helped to support the family with occasional prostitution. His father, Anderson Lucas, was an alcoholic, who fell on some railroad tracks when in a drunken stupor and was run over by a freight train, leaving him with stumps for legs—he was called "No Legs Lucas" by neighbors and even his own family members. Anderson Lucas thereafter dragged himself about on the dirt floor of the family shack, slowly drinking himself to death. Disgusted by his wife's prostitution—she brought her "clients" into the shack at all hours to perform sex in front of her invalided husband, Anderson Lucas dragged himself outside one night, where he contracted pneumonia, which eventually brought about his death.

When Henry Lucas entered school in 1943, his mother sent him to class wearing a girl's dress and curling his hair in ringlets. He arrived without any shoes and a caring teacher provided a pair. When the boy returned home with the shoes, his mother—always too full of pride to accept gifts from strangers—beat him mercilessly. He was beaten routinely when he returned home with a pet. Viola Lucas killed these little animals, before again beating her son. Lucas soon came to understand through his sadistic mother that life was not only cheap but worthless.

The boy injured his eye with a knife, but his mother refused to treat it. The infected eye had to be removed and replaced with a glass eye. One of his mother's lovers taught Lucas to mistreat animals, torturing and raping them before killing them, instilling a bloodlust in the boy. By the time Lucas was fifteen, he was nothing more than a savage predator. In March 1951, the 15-year-old Lucas abducted Laura Burley, seventeen, near Lynchburg, Virginia. When the girl fought off his sexual advances, Lucas strangled her to death, taking her body to nearby Harrisburg, Virginia, where he buried it in some woods. (This murder would not be cleared up until Lucas informed authorities of the killing in 1983.)

Lucas committed a series of burglaries in June 1954, in and about Richmond, Virginia. He was captured and sent to prison for six years. Escaping from a road gang on September 14, 1954, Lucas fled to the home of a sister in Tecumseh,

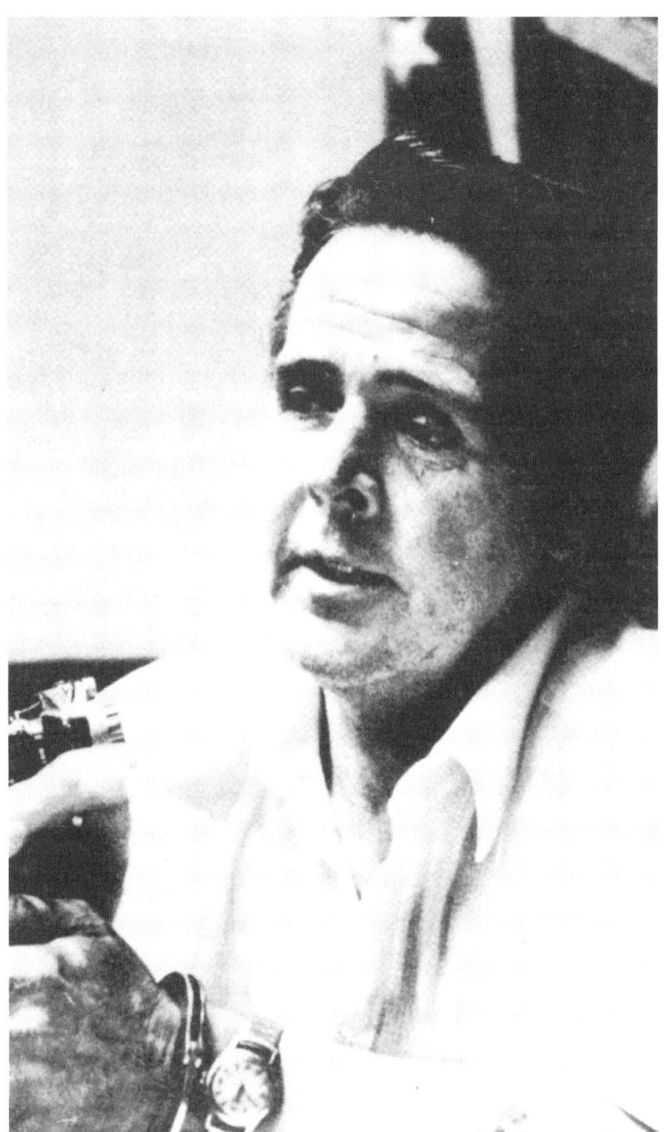

Henry Lee Lucas, who reportedly murdered as many as 300 persons over several decades, numbers inflated by his own grandiose admissions; he went to prison for life.

Michigan, where he was picked up three months later. He tried to escape again in December 1957, but was caught the same day. Lucas decided to serve out his term and was released for good behavior on December 2, 1959.

Lucas went to Tecumseh, where he became a day laborer. He became enraged when his mother arrived unexpectedly and demanded that he return to Blacksburg, to support her in her old age. Lucas, who had always hated his mother, offered her liquor and both got drunk on the night of January 11, 1960. The old harridan took some offense to her son's remarks and hit him with a broom. Lucas grabbed a knife and stabbed her to death, leaving her body on the floor of his shack before fleeing.

Police in Toledo, Ohio, arrested Lucas five days later and he quickly confessed to murdering his mother, saying that he had raped the dead corpse several times, a statement he later recanted as "something I made up." Tried in March 1960, he

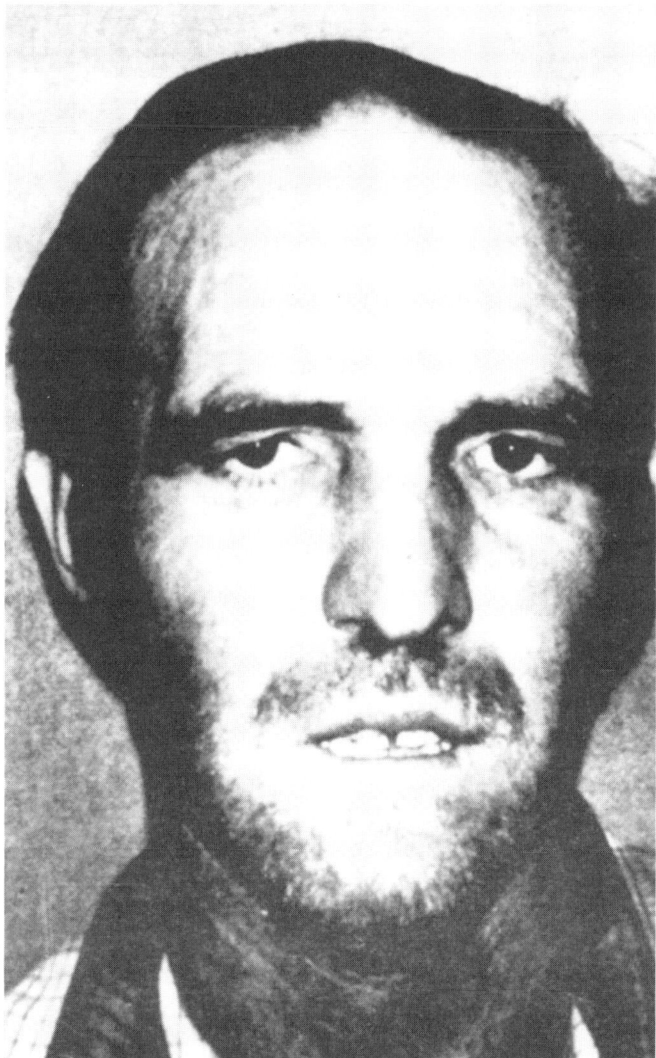

Ottis Elwood Toole, who was Lucas' sometime homosexual lover and joined Lucas in many murders, although he had reportedly committed dozens more killings on his own.

was convicted and sentenced to twenty to forty years in prison for his mother's murder. He was subsequently transferred to the state hospital for the criminally insane in Ionia, remaining there until April 1966. He was sent back to prison and paroled on June 3, 1970.

Moving back to Tecumseh to stay with relatives, he molested two teenage girls in December 1971, and was convicted of kidnapping, being sent to the prison in Jackson, Michigan. He was paroled in August 1975, despite the fact that Lucas himself protested his own release, saying that he was a dangerous person. In December of that year, Lucas married Betty Crawford, who was the widow of one of Lucas' cousins, but the union ended in 1977, when Crawford filed for divorce on charges that he had molested her two daughters from a previous marriage.

By that time, Lucas was living in Port Deposit, Maryland, and, by his later confession, had already embarked upon his serial killings, abducting young girls and women and murdering them throughout Maryland. In late 1976, he had met Ottis Elwood Toole, at a soup kitchen in Jacksonville, Florida. Toole, an arsonist and a homosexual like Lucas, bragged of having murdered many people and Lucas befriended him, embracing him as a fellow serial killer. They regaled each other with gruesome tales of each other's murders. For the next six years, the two became lovers and often roamed the country together, murdering people at will.

Toole was the most moronic of the pair, born in Jacksonville on March 5, 1947. His father, like Lucas', had been an alcoholic and had abandoned the family early on, leaving his mother, a religious fanatic, to raise Toole. He, like Lucas, was forced to wear girl's dresses. His mind, like Lucas', was twisted toward evil in childhood, chiefly by a grandmother who was a practicing Satanist, or so Toole later claimed, who dragged him through graveyards in the middle of the night in search of bones to be employed in her "black magic" rites.

By the time he was a teenager, testing proved that Toole was retarded, having an IQ of 75. Also by that time, he had, at age fourteen, murdered for the first time. He had been taken into a woods by a traveling salesman, who assaulted him. Toole knocked the man unconscious and then crushed him to death by running over him with the salesman's car, which he later sold to fund his wanderings in the western states. In 1974, he murdered four people in Colorado within six months, perhaps more, taking their cash and valuables to support his nomadic lifestyle. He married, but his wife divorced him within three days due to his flagrant homosexuality.

By the time Toole met Lucas, he was married to a woman twenty-four years his senior, forcing this woman to share her bed with Lucas and other strange men he brought to the Jacksonville, Florida, house. The woman left Toole in 1978, which pleased both Toole and Lucas, who had become lovers. The serial killers lived on and off with relatives, but, after saving some money from their day labor jobs, hopped into their old car and went off for weeks on killing and robbery sprees.

The pair split up, Lucas going to Texas, where he continued killing people on his own. Toole remained in Jacksonville, where, he burned down two houses in 1983. He was identified as the firebug by teenage accomplices and was arrested on June 6, 1983. Toole admitted the arsons and bragged that he had set fire to more than forty buildings in the last two decades. Convicted of arson, he was sent to prison for twenty years.

By that time, Lucas had gone to Texas with Toole's niece, Frieda Powell, who was called Becky. The two roamed about the countryside, until, following an argument in which Becky slapped Lucas' face, the serial killer stabbed the girl to death. As was his savage custom, he then raped the corpse, or so he later stated. On June 11, 1983, Lucas was arrested in Stoneburg, Texas, charged with having an illegal firearm. While in jail, he began to confess his many murders, so many killings that much of what he said was later discredited by officials and criminologists, although he and his partner Toole claimed to have collectively murdered more than 300 people in their long careers as serial killers.

Lucas was tried for several of these murders and was sentenced to death. Because he cooperated with authorities and cleared up dozens of old unsolved murders, his death sentence was commuted to life imprisonment. Toole was also tried and convicted of several murders and sentenced to death in Florida. He bragged that he had abducted and killed little Adam Walsh (see Kidnapping), but refused to disclose the whereabouts of the boy's body unless his father, who had become a national celebrity by hosting the TV show, "America's Most Wanted," paid him a great deal of money.

Toole never cleared up this case, dying in prison from cirrhosis in September 1996. Much of his "confession," like that of Lucas, was designed to impress the world that this worthless person at least had the distinction of murdering more people than anyone else, and in that awful and idiotic claim, Lucas vied for the same position. Toole's own illiterate comment marked the crude mentalities of both of these serial killers: "I killed people I didn't think was worth living anyhow."

Lucas confessed to killing 360 persons, but later recanted his confessional litany. In 1998, Lucas tantalized Florida law enforcement officials by claiming that he had murdered a dozen or more persons in that state, but close inspection of his claims proved that he could not have been the killer in those slayings.

THE PLAYBOY SERIAL KILLER/1984

Five hundred FBI agents trailed an elusive killer believed responsible for the murders of at least nine young women between February 26 and April 12, 1984. Christopher Bernard Wilder (1945-1984) was a wealthy playboy whose lifestyle and easy manner women found attractive. His technique was not unlike that of Ted Bundy, who raped and killed dozens of women in the 1970s before being captured. Unlike Bundy, however, Wilder's trail of death ended abruptly in Colebrook, New Hampshire, on April 13, 1984.

The state trooper who bagged the killer was not sure at the time who he was dealing with. "Hold on, we want to talk to you," ordered Detective Leo C. Jellison, who had received reports of the fugitive murderer driving a blue 1982 Firebird. Wilder reached for a .357 Magnum in the glove compartment and pointed it at Johnson. The 250-pound state trooper grabbed the serial killer in a bear hug. The gun discharged and a bullet passed through Wilder's heart, killing him. Two days later Trooper Jellison was proclaimed a hero when the FBI established that he had brought down the most dangerous man in the U.S.

Christopher Bernard Wilder was the son of a U.S. serviceman, who had emigrated to Australia to begin a construction business. In 1970, at the age of twenty-four, Wilder returned to the U. S. to make his fortune. With his partner, L. K. Kimbrell, he started Sawtel Electric and Sawtel Construction, but he paid little attention to the business, preferring to invest in Florida's booming real estate market. Using balloon notes and quit-claim deeds to buy and sell property, he made himself a small fortune by the end of the decade.

Articulate and well-mannered, Chris Wilder bought up six parcels of prime Palm Beach County real estate worth an estimated $400,000. Much of his money was used to finance an ostentatious lifestyle. He spent many happy weekends skiing in trendy Vail, Colorado, tinkering with his speedboat moored to a private dock in Boynton Beach, Florida, or participating in the amateur race-car circuit.

In 1984, Wilder raced his white Porsche 911 in the Miami Grand Prix, finishing seventeenth in the field. It was an impressive showing for a novice. When it came to attracting glamorous women, however, Wilder was in the big leagues. "I want to date and enjoy the company of women. Women with depth. I'm looking for a long-term relationship, but not marriage," he said in a 1981 interview with a Florida matchmaking service.

His first known assault was committed in 1976 against the 16-year-old daughter of a Boca Raton family that had hired him to work on their home. Using a tactic that proved successful for him in later years, Wilder lured the girl into his truck, promising to take her to someone who might offer her a job. The girl fended him off by saying she was afflicted by venereal disease.

Lucky to escape with her life, she related the story to her parents who pressed charges. Court-appointed doctors examined Wilder and concluded that he was psychotic. "Wilder is not safe except in a structured environment and should be in a resident program geared to his needs," said Dr. D. G. Boozer.

Serial killer Christopher Bernard Wilder, who raped and murdered scores of women before he was shot and killed in 1984.

Despite the warning, Wilder was acquitted on assault charges and never received the treatment he so desperately needed.

Three years later, in 1979, he was arrested and charged with assaulting a 17-year-old Tennessee girl vacationing in Florida. He told her he was a representative of the Barbizon modeling school, and was interested in giving her a tryout. During the "session," Wilder ordered her to pose for cheesecake photos holding a slice of pizza that had been laced with drugs. "He told her to chew it real slowly so that he could see what it would be like," explained Palm Beach detective Arthur Newcombe. Afterward he forced the girl to engage in sex with him in a pickup truck. Wilder was eventually sentenced to five years' probation and was ordered to see a sex therapist twice a month.

Wilder's second encounter with the police and the courts did not deter him from chasing after women. He neglected the construction business to cruise the pickup bars looking for attractive "street type" girls, who were inveigled to return with him to his photography "studio" for fashion-modeling assignments. Many were given hypnotic drugs and then forced to pose for pornographic pictures. In December 1982, Wilder violated the terms of his parole and flew to Sidney, Australia, where he was arrested for abducting and sexually assaulting two 15-year-old girls.

Released on $376,000 bail, Wilder negotiated for a postponement of the trial and returned to the U.S. "I didn't really know the man," explained his business partner Kimbrell, "but we did talk about the rape charges. He told me he didn't know the girls were only fifteen, he thought they were twenty. I told him to throw the camera away and be more careful. I could relate to his wanting sex. After all, he was single."

While in Miami for the Grand Prix, Wilder ran into 20-year-old Rosario Gonzalez, an aspiring fashion model who was handing out free samples of aspirin. She had met Wilder two years earlier in 1982, and had posed for the cover of a romance book according to her fiancé. Gonzalez was never seen after February 26, 1984. She was Wilder's first known murder victim. A week later, 23-year-old Elizabeth Kenyon vanished from a Coral Gables shopping center. The former Orange Bowl queen was a finalist in the 1982 Miss Florida contest and had been dating Wilder off and on. During the Grand Prix, Kenyon spurned his offer of marriage out of respect to the wishes of her parents, who objected to the sixteen-year age difference between the two.

Following Kenyon's disappearance, a gas station attendant told the woman's parents that he had seen Wilder in the girl's company. The distraught father pleaded with the FBI to place Wilder under surveillance, but the agents refused on the grounds of insufficient evidence and hearsay. "We couldn't understand why a man who broke probation four times couldn't be tailed," Dolores Kenyon later stated. "In our justice system the criminal has all the rights and that is why my daughter isn't here tonight."

Teresa Ferguson of Indian Harbor Beach, Florida, left her home on March 18, 1984, to shop at a nearby mall. The body of the dark-haired 21-year-old woman was found three days later in a Florida swamp. The day after the police fished the remains of Ferguson out of the swamp, Wilder claimed his

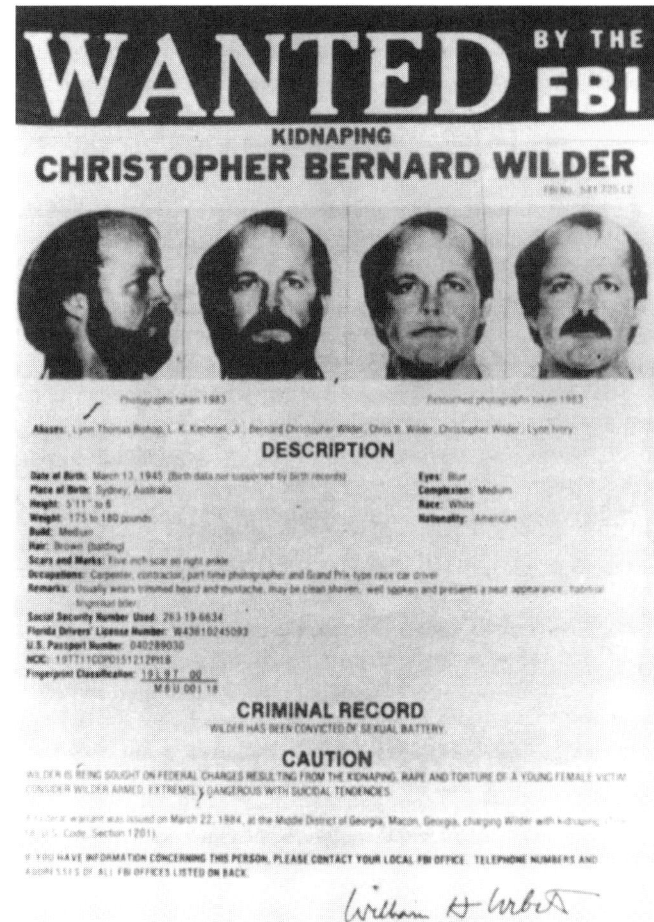

The FBI poster that declared Wilder to be the most wanted man in America.

next victim, 24-year-old Terry Diane Walden of Beaumont, Texas. When she failed to pick up her daughter at the local day-care center, school officials phoned her husband, John David, a machine operator at the Goodyear Chemical plant. Her body was found floating face down in the canal. She had been bound, gagged, and knifed to death.

By this time federal authorities were piecing together fragmented information about a dozen rapes, sexual tortures, and murders of young women committed in Florida, Texas, Nevada, and Colorado. A clear pattern had emerged, suggesting that a serial killer similar to Bundy and Seattle's Green River serial killer was loose. Several more weeks passed before the FBI assembled enough evidence to finger Wilder as the suspect. Meanwhile, the killer proceeded in a northerly direction.

On March 26, 1984, a fisherman in Milford Lake, Kansas, found the body of Suzanne Logan, a 20-year-old woman Wilder had abducted from an Oklahoma City shopping mall. Logan was another one of Wilder's modeling hopefuls. Three years earlier she had assembled her first portfolio.

Sheryl Bonaventura of Grand Junction, Colorado, became Wilder's sixth victim on March 29, 1984. Shortly before leaving for Aspen on a pleasure trip, the 18-year-old woman chided her mother for her undue concerns. "Mom, you worry too much," she said. Before meeting with a girlfriend, Sheryl stopped at a local mall where she met Wilder, who told her that he was looking for a model. She was murdered later that day.

"We were always dreaming of someone coming up and saying `You're found. You're *Vogue* material' I would have done it," said Kristal Cesario, Bonaventura's best friend. Two days later Wilder turned up at the Meadows Mall in Las Vegas, Nevada, where *Seventeen* Magazine was sponsoring a beauty contest. An amateur photographer took a candid shot of Wilder as he was leaving the mall with Michelle Korfman, the 17-year-old daughter of a casino executive. She became Wilder's eighth victim.

The serial killer continued to California. On April 4, 1984, he picked up Tina Marie Riscio, a 16-year-old girl, at a dress shop in Torrance, California. For the next three days he held her hostage, torturing her with a 110-volt prod. Under the penalty of death, Wilder made the girl his unwitting accomplice. Together they drove eastward just as the FBI added Wilder's name to its Ten Most Wanted list.

"We consider this to be the top fugitive investigation at this time," explained FBI spokesman Chris Mazzella at the time. "Unlimited resources are being poured into it. This is a truly massive manhunt, stretching from coast to coast." Wilder and Riscio arrived in Merrillville, Indiana, a few days later. At an area shopping mall Tina approached 16-year-old Dawnette Sue Wilt and asked if she would like to become a fashion model. The girl followed Riscio back to Wilder's car to sign a consent form. The killer then pulled a gun and ordered her into the car.

Wilder proceeded to Barrington, New York, where he repeatedly stabbed Dawnette and left her for dead in a patch of woods on April 12, 1984. The wounded girl, who had been trussed up by Wilder, broke free of her bonds and flagged down a passing truck. In the hospital the severely wounded girl provided police with enough detail for them to identify her assailant as Wilder.

In Victor, New York, Wilder again used Riscio to lure 33-year-old Beth Dodge to his car. "He had told Tina he would kill her if she did anything unusual," explained an investigator. "He drove the hostage car with the hostage, and Tina followed in her car. For her to try to escape then would have been foolish. He had told her he was a race-car driver and could easily catch her." Beth Dodge was shot to death near a mall and dumped in a road side gravel pit. Wilder had murdered her for her car.

Arriving in Boston, Wilder bought Tina Riscio an airplane ticket for her return trip to Los Angeles. He handed her some "going-away money" which was later used to purchase lingerie in a tourist shop on Hermosa Beach. After her shopping spree was complete, Tina Riscio notified police about her cross-country trek with the serial killer. During the entire time the girl was away, Tina's mother believed her 16-year-old daughter was out "partying."

Wilder drove Beth Dodge's Firebird north toward the Canadian border. On Friday the thirteenth he made his ill-fated stop at Vic Stanton's Getty Station in Colebrook, New Hampshire, eight miles from the Canadian border. There he was finally apprehended and shot to death by the police. Following Wilder's shooting death, a newsman commented: "Wilder thought he could do anything he wanted, murder anyone he wanted, get anything he wanted and that no one could really stop him. It was his blind arrogance that led to his murders and his own death. They say he possessed intelligence, but he was really stupid, really dumb."

THE SERIAL KILLING LANDLADY/1985-1988

One of California's most ruthless serial killers proved to be an old lady whose docile appearance suggested that she wouldn't hurt a fly, let alone poison more than a half dozen people. She reportedly murdered at least nine of her boarders and went to prison for life after being convicted of three of these serial killings. Police arrested Dorothea Montalvo Puente (b. 1929) at the boardinghouse she ran at 1426 F Street in Sacramento, California, on November 16, 1988. They had just exhumed seven bodies from the backyard of the Victorian house, including that of Alvaro "Bert" Montoya, a lodger of Mrs. Puente's, whose social caseworker had reported him missing.

California prosecutors were not ready to lodge a formal charge against her of nine counts of murder, however, until July 1990. By that time, they had formulated a case that would eventually prove that the gray-haired, grandmotherly Puente had systematically poisoned her elderly lodgers in order to receive their Social Security checks.

Defense attorneys asked for a change of venue, arguing that the extensive press coverage in Sacramento, where preliminary hearings in the case were being heard, depicted their client as a serial-killing monster, that the media had "dehumanized" her to the extent that a fair trial could not be held in that city. Superior Court Judge Michael J. Virga selected the compromise of hearing preliminary defense motions in the capital, then moving the case to Monterey, where jury selection would be made and arguments heard from both sides.

The defense immediately made a motion to ban at the trial any talk of Dalmane, a prescription sedative found in the systems of all the victims disinterred from Puente's yard. None of these victims' bodies contained enough toxicological information for the coroner to fix a cause of death. However, Ruth F. Munroe, 61, who died at Puente's boardinghouse on April 28, 1982, was determined to have died of Tylenol and codeine intoxication. This was the first death at the F Street location, and the only one reported. A macabre sequel to Munroe's death occurred on New Year's Day 1986, when the body of Everson T. Gillmouth, another lodger of Puente's, was discovered in a wooden box near the Sacramento River in Yuba County.

Puente was charged with their deaths as well as the seven found in the yard. The prosecutors, meanwhile, moved that evidence be included that Puente had also drugged three surviving lodgers in the year before the grisly backyard discovery. Defense attorney Kevin D. Clymo surprised the trial on February 11, 1993, by offering an alternative theory as to why Puente failed to report eight alleged natural deaths (the ninth allegedly being a suicide) at the boardinghouse.

"She has a touch of larceny in her heart," Clymo admitted, acknowledging that Puente had done time in a California prison for administering drugs to an older man she'd met at a bar. A condition of her parole was that she make no contact with elderly or mentally disabled people. Therefore, Clymo argued, when her friend Everson Gillmouth moved in with her, then died suddenly in 1985, Puente was afraid she would go back to prison for a parole violation if she reported it.

Another shocking development occurred six days later, when truck driver David Van Alstine, testifying for the prosecution, identified Alvaro Montoya and fellow victim Benjamin Fink as the two men who helped him unload a delivery of premixed concrete in the summer of 1988. The concrete was later used to cover some of the grave sites. Later in the trial the prosecution also introduced a videotape of Montoya talking to his social worker to give the jury a sense of the life that had been lost.

Another tenant testified that he complained to Puente about a smell "like death" in the boardinghouse four days after Fink's disappearance, only to be told that it was the smell of a sewer backing up. Puente herself testified that she saw Montoya alive after his disappearance, but a check of the sequence of events showed this to be a lie, as Montoya was already buried at the time Puente claimed to have seen him.

Former boarder Joyce Peterson testified that after her eviction, Puente pushed her down a flight of stairs when she returned for her belongings and her welfare check. Another ex-boarder, Robert S. French, said that during the winter of 1988, he witnessed Puente lifting 95-pound sacks of concrete in the front yard to move them to shelter. Puente had claimed to detectives that she had a bad heart and could not lift anything heavy, and therefore "couldn't drag a body anyplace."

One of the most gruesome pieces of testimony came from Dr. Gary A. Stuart, a pathologist who examined the remains of victim Dorothy Miller shortly after her exhumation from Puente's yard. Dr. Stuart stated that Miller's body was bound with duct tape and twine, swathed all over with plastic, then wrapped in three layers of fabric. He offered no speculation on why the body was treated this way, but could not, under cross-examination, rule out the defense contention of death by natural causes.

By April Fools Day, Social Security records were subpoeaned for use at the trial. These documents revealed that Puente, under her maiden name of Dorothea H. Montalvo, had been diagnosed as schizophrenic in 1978 and had been approved for disability benefits. She received benefits until the time of her arrest for murder—even during the years 1982-1985, when she was imprisoned after pleading guilty to forgery, grand theft, and administering stupefying drugs.

The defense, as has been the case in almost every serial killer brought to trial in recent decades, paraded the same tired argument that Puente had been abused as a child and this had been the insidious nurturing of her murderous nature. It was true that her parents were alcoholic, that she had been abused as a child and even had to scavenge for food, before she was six, when her mother died and she was placed in an orphanage. She was not one of eighteen children born in Mexico, as she later claimed, but had been born in San Bernadino County on January 9, 1929.

Puente had married for the first time in 1946, but her husband died of a heart attack two years later. To survive, she forged checks, a criminal pursuit that would become a lifelong habit, and for which she was caught and sent to prison for a year. Paroled in six months, Puente was impregnated by a stranger and she promptly put her child up for adoption. In 1952, she married Axel Johnson, a turbulent union that lasted fourteen years. During this period, she worked as a prostitute and was arrested in a brothel in 1960, convicted of prostitution and sent to the Sacramento County Jail to serve a three-month term.

Dorothea Montalvo Puente, when she became a landlady in a boarding house in Sacramento, California, murdering her elderly boarders to collect their insurance and social security money.

Puente then found work as a nurse's aide and began caring for the disabled and the elderly in private homes. It was at this time that she embarked upon thieving from her "patients," a habit enlarged when she started to manage boarding houses. She married Robert Puente in 1966 in Mexico, after divorcing Johnson, but this union lasted only two years, her husband being almost twenty years her junior. It was at this time that

Puente's boarding house at 1426 F. Street, Sacramento, where a number of bodies were later found buried.

Dorothea Puente at her 1990 trial; the jury took a record twenty-four days to return a guilty verdict on three murder charges; she went to prison for life.

Puente took control of the three-story, sixteen-bedroom care home on F. Street, the site where she would systematically poison those in her care to obtain their pension and social security payments.

By the time Puente's case went to the jury in July, 3, 1990, exhibits were amassed, including photographs of the victims' remains, scale models of the boardinghouse and its surrounding neighborhoods, maps, drawings, and graphs. Testimony and arguments had lasted five months. Jury deliberation lasted twenty-four days (a state record) over a five-week period, after which Dorothea Puente was convicted of first-degree murder in the cases of Dorothy Miller and Benjamin Fink and second-degree murder in the case of 78-year-old Leona Carpenter. The jury was deadlocked on the other six counts. At no time in her marathon trial did Dorothea Puente take the stand in her own defense. She was sentenced to life imprisonment.

THE MOLALLA RIVER KILLER/1987

A clearing in the forested hills above the Molalla River at Oregon City, Oregon, was the scene of the torture and murder of seven women, all of them known prostitutes during the summer of 1987. Three of the bodies were found with their feet cut off. These deaths were the extension of violence begun long before by serial killer Dayton Leroy Rogers.

At the 1989 trial of Rogers, Melody Dahlman Myers testified that in 1972, 19-year-old Rogers had taken her to the woods and stabbed her in the abdomen. Even though he had been married for six weeks, he said he would marry her and take her to the hospital if she would claim to have done the damage herself. He took her for help, but Myers told the truth and Rogers was arrested. He pleaded guilty to second-degree assault and was placed on probation. Thus, the violence began, interspersed with a very different life in which Rogers was active in the Seventh-Day Adventist Church and ran his own small-engine repair business.

Born in Idaho in 1954, Rogers was reared in a strict home in which he was severely punished for infractions of various rules. Whenever he or the other six Rogers children made friends with someone, their father would move elsewhere, sometimes three or four times a year. Rogers felt his first wife, Julie Miller Rogers, was physically and mentally cruel. They divorced in 1974 and he later remarried.

As demonstrated with Myers, the knife had become an important tool in Rogers' quest for sexual gratification. One woman testified at his 1989 trial that in 1976, she had been picked up by Rogers. They had sat and talked in his truck until she had to leave. At that point, he drew his knife and began to cut her clothes from her. Then he hog-tied her and began to play with her feet, finally threatening to kill her. After releasing the woman, he was charged with kidnapping and returned to prison for violating his parole.

Hog-tying became a typical method for Rogers in seeking sexual satisfaction. He began taking prostitutes to the woods where he would, usually with their permission, tie them around the wrists and ankles and then fasten the two ties together, so that they were bent over backwards. He then proceeded to cut them on the heels or breasts with a sharp knife. Forty to fifty prostitutes described his similar treatment of them.

The eleven who testified at the actual trial said that as long as they protested and fought, he would be in a frenzy and continue to cut them, but once they had given up and become submissive, he lost interest and ultimately took them back to town. A woman whom he picked up in 1986 testified that after they had several drinks, he bit her breasts and feet, drawing blood.

Police photos of serial killer Dayton Leroy Rogers, who killed and mutlitated seven women in 1987 and who awaits execution at this writing.

The increasing violence culminated during the summer of 1987. On August 6, 1987, Rogers picked up Portland prostitute Jennifer Lisa Smith in his truck. He spent the next twenty-four hours with her and at some point bound her up in the way that had become his signature. When he drove her back to town, she leapt out of his truck in front of Denny's Restaurant in Oak Grove, where he pursued her. He caught up with Smith and stabbed her to death.

Broken shoelaces used to bind her were found on her body. He was arrested and charged with aggravated murder. He called his father-in-law (his wife divorced him after he was arrested for this offense) to ask if the police had searched the stove in his workshop. They had not, but when they did, they found numerous metal bits of shoes, belts, bra hooks, and other items indicating where women's clothing had been burned. Rogers said that the bits were from Smith's and his own clothing, and the police at that time had no cause to question the sheer quantity of the metal pieces. Rogers was found guilty of the murder of Smith and sentenced to life in prison.

In the meantime, however, the nude bodies of seven women, tortured and sexually abused, had been found on an isolated lumbering road back in the forests above the Molalla River. Three of the bodies had had the feet cut off, and a fourth had been severely wounded around the ankles. A leather dog collar bound the wrists of one victim. Broken bits of shoelaces tied in the same knots that had been used on Smith's body, as well as miniature vodka bottles and orange juice containers, were found near each body.

Rogers was charged with the aggravated murder of the six women whose bodies were identified, including Christine Lotus Adams, Lisa Marie Mock, and 16-year-old Reatha Marie Gyles. An all-woman jury found him guilty on May 4, 1989. According to Oregon law, the death penalty can be imposed only if the jury believes that the killing was completely intentional and that the killer is likely to pose a threat to society if he is not put to death.

The penalty phase of Rogers' trial included the testimony of his brother-in-law, Floyd Mohr, various psychiatrists, and the women, who could demonstrate that his violent behavior had been going on for an extended period. Also testifying, however, were friends who told of his caring and devotion to a prison ministry that he had started while he was an inmate. The deputy district attorney, Andrejs I. Eglitis, said in his closing statement to the jury, "That person is a walking time bomb. That person is an act of criminal violence looking for a place to happen....He's capable of fooling psychologists. He's capable of fooling psychiatrists. I hope to God he's not capable of fooling you."

The jury deliberated for seventeen and a half hours over two days before returning a vote in favor of execution by lethal injection. Rogers awaits execution at this writing.

CONSTANZO'S SATANIC MURDER CULT/ 1988-1989

Adolfo de Jesus Constanzo (AKA: El Padrino, Godfather; 1963-1989) was born and raised in Miami, Florida. His Cuban-born mother, Delia Aurora Gonzalez del Valle, practiced

Adolfo de Jesus Constanzo, who operated a Mexican drug peddling cartel and established a murder cult in Matamoras, Mexico.

The shed at Rancho Santa Elena in Matamoras, Mexico, where Constanzo's followers took kidnapped victims and ritually murdered them.

Cult suspect Sergio Martinez was compelled, along with other cultists, to dig up bodies at Rancho Santa Elena; fifteen corpses were found.

Cult member David Serna Valdez, right, is shown in the custody of a Mexican policeman.

Santeria, a religion that mixed Catholicism with the tribal gods and ancestral spirits of African slaves. Santeria, which involves some animal sacrifice, is normally a benign religion practiced by an estimated 100 million persons, mostly in the Caribbean and South America. Gonzalez Del Valle, however, used Santeria for her own evil ends, according to her Miami neighbors, settling long-standing grudges by leaving headless animals at the doorsteps of those who had angered her.

Adolfo de Jesus Constanzo, Gonzalez's son, had only one brush with the law in Miami, being arrested for (ominously, as events proved) shoplifting a chainsaw. He was, however, widely feared in Coral Park Estates in West Miami, where he lived with his mother, two brothers, and a sister. Exactly what Constanzo did in this largely Cuban enclave to inspire deep-seated fear is not known, but one former neighbor trembled at the sound of his name and stated, "Everyone here is worried that Constanzo will come back and get them for talking."

Leaving for Mexico in 1984 to seek his drug fortune, Constanzo set up shop in Matamoras, Mexico, just over the border bridge that spans the Rio Grande linking Brownsville, Texas with Mexico. Constanzo drew several naive, uneducated followers to his ranks and launched into drug-smuggling, keeping his followers in line by practicing a warped version of Santeria, one that became a Satanic blood-lust cult where sacrifices were human beings.

Sara Maria Villarreal Aldrete, Constanzo's mistress; she served as the cult's leading "witch."

Constanzo's mini-drug cartel in Matamoras moved more than a ton of drugs a week into the U. S. and was netting more than $200,000 with each shipment. Constanzo lived high, buying a Mercedes-Benz, a lavish home, and expensive jewelry. He took a full-time mistress, 24-year-old Sara Maria Villarreal Aldrete, who led a

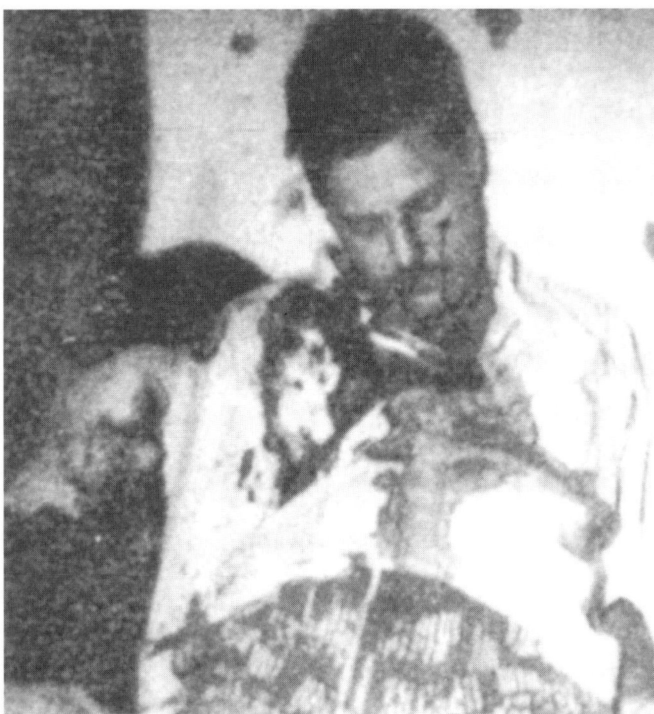

Mexican police photo showing Constanzo dead in a Mexico City apartment, along with his homosexual lover, Martin Quintana; both had been shot to death by cult members on May 8, 1989.

A Mexican detective, gun drawn, holds cult member Alvaro de Leon Valdez in a headlock as he is hustled to a police van; Valdez, called El Duby by cultists, admitted that he shot his leader Constanzo and Quintana to death, but claimed that Constanzo had ordered him to do it before police captured him.

double life. She served as the "witch" of the drug gang, as well as being an honor student at Texas College in Brownsville.

As Constanzo prospered, his perversions deepened. He demanded his henchmen round up victims to be tortured and then murdered in Santeria sacrifice at a ramshackle ranch he occupied outside of Matamoras. Cult members later claimed that Constanzo had by then mixed Santeria practices with a much more sinister tribal ritual known as Palo Mayombe, a malevolent Afro-Caribbean cult that practiced "evil for evil's sake," according to one cult expert. Further, Constanzo added Satanism and santismo, a bloody and ancient Aztec ritual involving human sacrifice.

Constanzo used his murderous rituals to bond his followers to him. He ordered his drug-runners to abduct persons in Matamoras and bring them to the ranch. Here the hapless victims were slashed with machetes, beaten senseless, shot, hanged, and even boiled alive, before their corpses were hacked to pieces and then buried about the grounds of the ranch. One of the last known victims of the Constanzo cult was Mark Kilroy, a 21-year-old University of Texas student who was abducted from a Matamoras street at about 2 a.m., on March 14, 1989, while outside of a cantina fighting off the effects of bad booze.

A teaching aid used by Constanzo was the 1987 film *The Believers*, starring Martin Sheen and Jimmy Smits, a movie that purported to investigate Santeria and Palo Mayombe, but one that blantantly employed those themes to sensationalize and graphically expose blood-lust scenes. Aldrete, one report had it, used a videotape of this film to lure men into the cult. Constanzo told his followers that by taking human life they would absorb the spirit and essence of their victims, all of which was gobbledygook, but it was the kind of mumbo-jumbo that appealed to his illiterate, almost cretinous followers, supposedly empowering them with a kind of God-like authority that fed their starving egos.

The disappearance of Kilroy, however, led to a massive police manhunt on both sides of the border. One of Constanzo's henchmen was apprehended and he began to talk, leading officials to the broken-down Rancho Santa Elena, the blood-stained floor and walls of the shack that passed for the ranch house, and the many graves that surrounded it. Other cult members were rounded up and were forced to dig up the dismembered remains of the cult's victims, fifteen persons in all. (There may have been twice that number, mostly young boys.) Body parts and bones, including the remains of Mark Kilroy, were unearthed for days at the gruesome site.

Constanzo, however, had fled, first to Mexico City, where he maintained a comfortable two-story white house. By the time police arrived, he was gone. They found baby clothing. Moreover, when police searched Aldrete's apartment they also found baby clothing. The rumor that Constanzo was kidnapping babies in revenge for being exposed soon spread across Mexico, but nothing of the kind was happening. Aldrete by then had vanished. Her purse and driver's license were found and authorities came to believe that Constanzo had murdered her and hidden her body as a way of covering his tracks.

The arch serial killer and Satanist, however, was running

for his life as hundreds of law enforcement officers sought him out. On May 8, 1989, they received a tip that he was hiding in an apartment in Mexico City and squads of heavily armed men stormed the place. Following a fierce firefight, officers burst into the apartment to find Constanzo and cult member Martin Quintana, both shot to death, their bodies stuffed into a closet. Police believed that Constanzo had ordered his followers to kill him before they fled the place.

When told that Constanzo had been killed in Mexico City, one of his former West Miami neighbors breathed a sigh of relief. He recalled how Constanzo as a child emulated the bloody Santeria practices of his mother, running wildly after chickens with a hatchet, grabbing the chicken and chopping off its head to gleefully splatter himself with its blood, laughing hysterically. The neighbor nodded solemnly and said, "Thank God, the real beast is dead."

WASHINGTON'S CHILD KILLER/1989

Westley Allen Dodd (1968-1993) was the perfect example of how therapy, counseling or any kind of treatment other than hard prison time utterly fails to shut down serial killing child molesters. A loner and drifter, Dodd was, like almost all child molesters, an obsessive recidivist. In dozens of instances, he was arrested and courts reduced the charges, suspended sentences, offered therapy in lieu of incarceration, while Dodd himself openly criticized this system as hopelessly ineffective. "Each time I entered treatment," he said, "I continued to molest children. I liked molesting children and did what I had to do to avoid jail so I could continue molesting."

Admitting that he had molested dozens of children, Dodd never served sentences longer than four months. He took every opportunity to prey on children. At one point he was babysitting the 10-year-old son of some friends and he promptly molested the boy. Arrested in Seattle, Washington, in 1987, Dodd expressly told his police interrogators that his urge to molest children was "predatory and uncontrollable." He received a one-year suspended sentence in 1989. Following that conviction, Dodd left Seattle and moved to Vancouver, Washington.

"I was getting bored," Dodd later stated, "I didn't have a TV." He took to stalking children in Vancouver parks, which he felt were "good hunting grounds." In one park he selected nineteen different children, fifteen boys and four girls, whom he marked for molestation and murder. One by one, however, he ruled out his intended victims, mostly because they were accompanied by an adult or because too many adults were near them as they played.

The next evening, September 4, 1989, Dodd appeared in the same park. He brought along shoelaces to use in tying up his victims, and beneath an Ace bandage affixed to his leg he hid a 6-inch fish filet knife. As dusk fell, Dodd hid in some bushes in the park and spotted two young brothers, Cole and William Neer, who were taking a shortcut through the park en route home to supper. He seized them both, tied them up, molested one of the boys, then stabbed them both to death.

Dodd then jogged home, listening to police and ambulance sirens wail in the distance, apparently, he thought, in response to his double slaying. "I was kind of afraid that I was going to get caught," he later told newsmen. "And then, as I watched the papers, I realized that the police didn't have any clues."

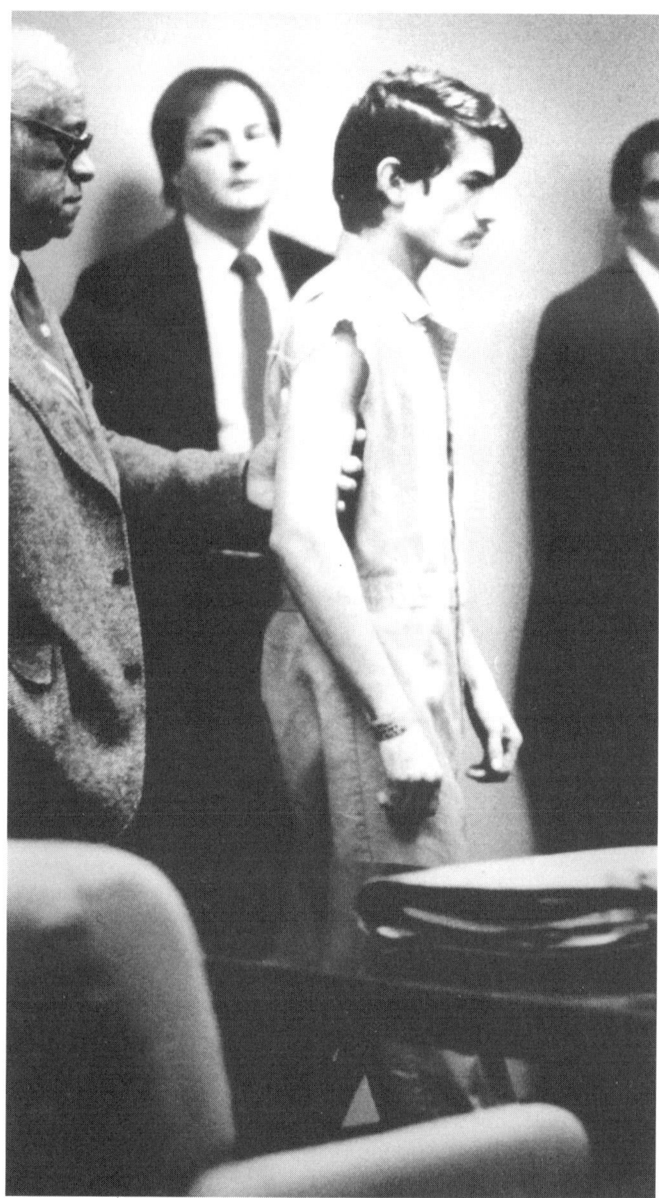

Westley Allen Dodd (sleeveless in court) murdered several children in Washington State in 1989; he was put to death at his own request on January 5, 1993.

Seven weeks went by before Dodd struck again. He stalked elementary school playgrounds and found 4-year-old Lee Iseli playing alone. He took the boy home with him under the ruse of promising to show him some new games. When in his apartment, he molested, tortured and murdered the boy. He took photos of the corpse and kept this in a pink photo album he labeled "Family Memories."

Vancouver police got onto Dodd's trail with the disappearance of the Iseli boy and upon his arrest he blurted out a full, gruesome confession. Jury members at Dodd's trial got sick while listening to his pitiless accounts of molestation and murder and hardened newsmen recoiled in nauseating shock. As the nation, and in particular, the state of Washington, reeled in shock at Dodd's remorseless statements during his trial, an incensed Governor Booth Gardner and Washington lawmakers passed one of the toughest child molester laws in the country.

The new precedent-setting law established a registry of child molesters through which their whereabouts could be tracked and monitored, a registry that dozens of other states would use as a role model in years to come. It demanded that convicted child molesters register with police wherever they moved, that authorities were obligated to notify communities into which child molesters moved, and, the most controversial aspect of all, that the state had the authority to imprison repeat offenders after they served their sentences if they were still thought to pose a threat.

By that time, Dodd had been convicted and was condemned to death. Unlike most Death Row inmates, Dodd wanted no part of a prolonged appeals process (a disgraceful average of fifteen to seventeen years), insisting that he be executed and threatening to file suit against any death penalty opponents who tried to prolong his life. "I *must* die, because I know I will kill again," Dodd stated. He got his wish on January 5, 1993, when he was put to death by hanging, the first time anyone was hanged in the U.S. since 1965 and the first person executed in the state of Washington since 1963. Many wanted him to rot in prison, to remain in a cell no larger than a car space and there be slowly crushed by boredom and vile memories.

NEW YORK'S ZODIAC KILLER/1990

A Brooklyn shooting on June 18, 1996, would not have amounted to more than a routine domestic quarrel had not a curious detective investigated further to discover that the man under arrest was the notorious Zodiac killer who had terrorized New York in 1990. A family dispute erupted when 26-year-old Heriberto Seda (AKA: Zodiac Killer; b. 1970) reportedly shot his teenage half-sister in the back for running around with members of a notorious gang.

When police were summoned to Seda's third-floor Brooklyn apartment, they were met by gunfire. Seda held off police in a raging gunfight for almost four hours before he surrendered. One of the detectives inspecting Seda's apartment after the gunman was taken into custody examined the strange scrawls on paper strewn about the apartment and recognized them as those of the mysterious Zodiac killer, who had been widely sought six years earlier.

The Zodiac killer had shot four persons, one fatally, on the Queens-Brooklyn border and in Central Park. The shootings had occurred on Thursdays, twenty-one days or a multiple of twenty-one days apart. The killer wrote taunting letters to the police, saying that he would kill someone born under each of the twelve astrological signs, thus earning the sobriquet of the Zodiac killer (not to be confused with the Zodiac killer who had terrorized San Francisco decades earlier).

Zodiac had shot a Scorpio, a Gemini, a Taurus and a Cancer, somehow learning the signs from the victims. So wide was the 1990 panic that New Yorkers were warned by the press not to divulge their birth dates to strangers. Police went on extra alert every three weeks in anticipation of Zodiac striking again. After a June 21, 1990 shooting, however, the killer vanished.

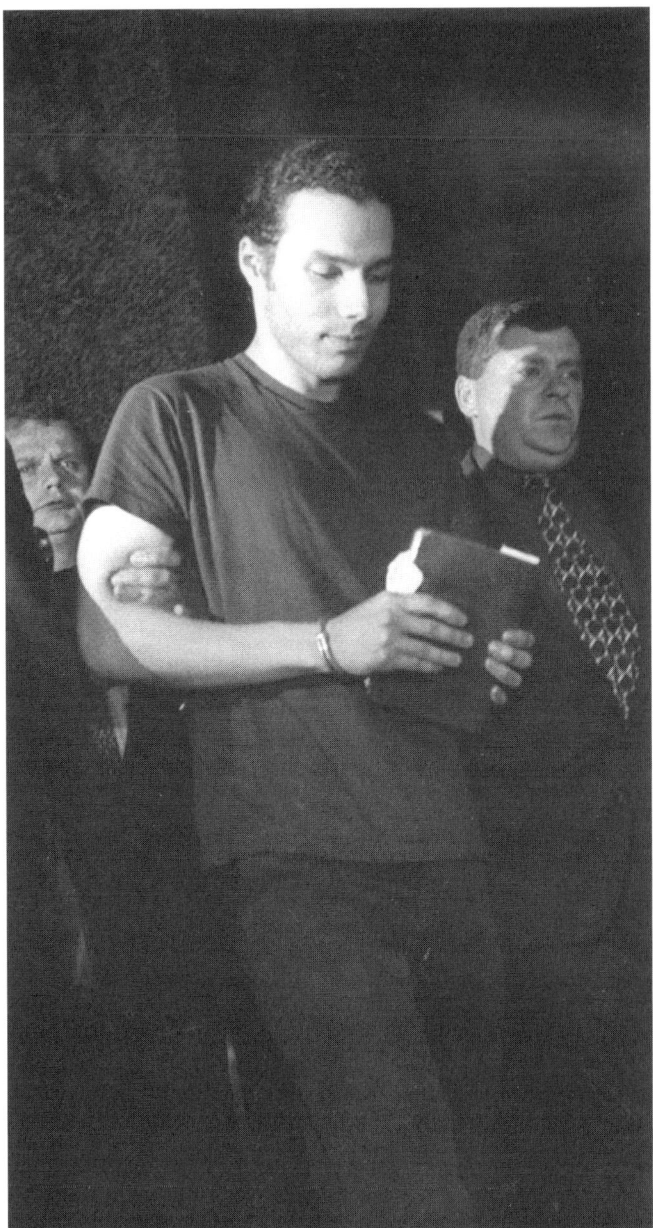

Heriberta Seda, arrested for a shootout on June 19, 1996; police then learned that he was the Zodiac killer, who had stalked New Yorkers in 1990.

When Seda was confronted with evidence from his apartment, he broke down and confessed that he was Zodiac, saying that he had been seized by "a sudden urge" to strike randomly and that he learned of his victims' astrological signs only "by chance." Seda was convicted of the 1990 shootings on June 24, 1998. He was sent to prison for life.

THE KILLER WHO WANTED TO BE HITLER/1991

The news of Jeffrey Dahmer's serial killings had no sooner burst into headlines in 1991 when an even more shocking killer was identified, Donald Leroy Evans (1957-1999). Arrested in August 1991 in Biloxi, Miss., Evans confessed to

Donald Leroy Evans murdered children in Mississippi, and later claimed to have slain sixty persons (discredited); he was stabbed to death in prison on January 5, 1999.

kidnapping, raping and murdering Beatrice Louise Routh, a homeless 10-year-old child, in Jones Park in Gulfport. He admitted dumping the body of the girl in Pearl River County.

Almost immediately after his original confession, Evans began to recite a list of murders he had committed, telling Mississippi authorities that he had been killing people since his discharge from the Marine Corps in 1977. He admitted to more than sixty murders in twenty-one states. He insisted that he had raped and murdered six women in Illinois, California, and Texas and he rattled off more victims in more states.

Evans was convicted of the Routh slaying and sentenced to death, while investigators attempted to clear up the many murders he claimed to have committed. In 1994, Evans was charged with murdering a prostitute, Ira Jean Smith, in Fort Lauderdale, Florida. He was convicted of this murder and received a second death sentence. Still, he rattled off more murders, but by this time, officials discounted most of Evans' claims, saying that he was a liar, merely attempting to postpone his own execution by being tried again and again for additional homicides, thus extending his appeals for these future convictions.

During his 1994 trial for the Smith murder, Evans, who was close to illiterate, told the court that he was a member of the Ku Klux Klan and insisted that he be allowed to wear a Klan robe during his trial (which was denied). An avowed racist, Evans then filed a motion demanding that the court address him as "Hi Hitler," a name he wished to officially adopt. Evans mistook the Nazi salute of "Heil Hitler," as the dictator's first name. This request, too, was denied.

The serial killer died in the prison at Parchman, Mississippi, knifed to death by a black inmate enraged at his racist taunts. Jimmie Mack, another death row inmate, stabbed Evans to death with a makeshift knife while both he and Evans were being taken to a shower on January 5, 1999.

AUSTRALIA'S IVAN MILAT/1991-1992

Paul Onions, an Englishman on a backpacking tour of Australia, was hitchhiking along Hume Highway, a well-traveled roadway running past the scenic Belanglo State Forest between Sydney and Melbourne, on January 25, 1990. A silver two-door Nissan four-wheel drive truck came to a stop and a strange-looking man offered him a ride. Onions got in and the driver, a man with bushy black eyebrows and a thick black mustache that curled downward around his lips, began chatting with him as they drove along. The conversation seemed friendly enough until the topic of Northern Ireland came up. Then the man became agitated. Suddenly, he pulled a gun and pointed it at Onions, saying, "This is a robbery."

Though startled, Onions tried to calm the man down. The vehicle came to a stop and the driver reached for a rope. Onions then leaped from the Nissan and began running down the middle of the heavily trafficked highway, waving frantically at drivers who refused to stop for him. The man with the thick mustache was by then running after him, ordering him to stop, saying that he would fire. The man fired his gun and Onions later swore that he heard the bullet whistle past him. Onions was slowed by the weight of his backpack and his pursuer caught up with him, pulling him by his shirt to the ground while still holding the gun.

Onions managed to break free and then throw himself in front of a van driven by a woman. She stopped and Onions jumped into the passenger seat, telling her to drive off, that a man with a gun was firing at him. The woman drove to the nearby town of Bowral, where Onions reported the bizarre incident to the police. Officers drove back to the sight of the attack on Hume Highway, but could find no trace of the Nissan or the man with the gun. The incident was filed and forgotten by police, but Paul Onions would never forget the experience, the most frightening of his life.

In September 1992, a group of backpackers going along a rocky path in Belanglo State Park were stopped by a foul odor. They at first thought the stench wafting over them came from the body of a dead kangaroo, but closer inspection revealed the decomposing bodies of two women who turned out to be 21-year-old Caroline Clarke and 22-year-old Joanne Walters, both British tourists who had disappeared between April 17 and April 19, 1992.

Pathologists determined that Clarke had died of multiple head wounds and Walters, who had been gagged, had been repeatedly stabbed. Many persons had been disappearing in this area since 1987. Naoka Onda, a 22-year-old Japanese tourist, had vanished at that time. On December 9, 1989, 19-year-old Deborah Everist, and her 19-year-old companion, James Gibson, both Australians, had disappeared. Following the discovery of Clarke and Walters, the bodies of Everist and Gibson were found, buried in a shallow grave.

A widespread search by large parties ensued, scouring the area. These searches continued for months. Three more bodies were uncovered. Simone Schmidt, a 21-year-old German tourist, had been missing since January 21, 1991. Her body was found in October 1992. After being gagged and tied, Schmidt had been repeatedly stabbed to death.

Finally, on November 4, 1993, the bodies of two more German tourists, 20-year-old Anja Habschied, and her boyfriend, 21-year-old Gabor Negebauer, were found. They had been missing since 1991. Negebauer had been shot six times in the head. Habschied, an exceptionally beautiful girl, was found naked from the waist down. She had been decapitated and her head was never found.

All of the missing backpackers, except for the Japanese tourist, Naoka Onda, had been found, but Australian police were baffled as to the identity of their murderer. The only conclusion they drew was that the serial killer most probably worked and lived in the area, since he had repeatedly used the Belanglo State Park as a dumping area for the bodies of his victims.

It was not until an article about the missing backpackers appeared in a British newspaper that Australian investigators got their break. At the time, Paul Onions, reading about the Australian serial killings, recalled the attack made on him in 1990. He contacted police in New South Wales and in response, he was flown to Australia in 1994, where he detailed the story about the man who had attacked him four years earlier. Onions gave a vivid description of the attacker, which an artist translated into a composite sketch.

Australian serial killer Ivan Robert Marko Milat, poses as an American western sheriff in his Eagle Vale home, outside of Sydney.

A police officer later saw this sketch and from it identified a road worker, who worked for the county highway maintenance department. The son of a Croatian immigrant, he was divorced and wore a thick, black mustache. His name was Ivan Robert Marko Milat (b. 1943). His photo was shown to Onions, who immediately recognized him as the man who had attacked him on Hume Highway.

Milat was arrested on May 22, 1994, in his home at Eagle Vale, a suburb of Sydney. By the time police had taken Milat into custody, they had a complete profile of the man. He had lived in Sydney all his life with his thirteen brothers and sis-

Ivan Milat leaving a courthouse on July 27, 1996, after being convicted of murdering seven backpackers in Australia's Belanglo State Forest in 1991-1992.

ters. Milat had worked as an unskilled laborer since the age of fifteen, after dropping out of school. He had married in 1983 and divorced in 1989. Milat had been accused of a date-rape in 1974, but the charges had been dropped.

Not until March 26, 1996, did Milat's trial begin. It would be one of the longest in Australian history. The evidence against Milat was strong. Items taken from the victims, including a camera, had been found in Milat's home. Several pieces of rope also found in his home matched those used to tie up the victims. A cord found in Milat's garage, it was proved, was stained with the blood of Caroline Clarke. Plastic cables found in his garage also matched those the killer had used to tie up two of the German victims.

Milat was stoic, refusing to confess. He stubbornly denied guilt at every turn. When asked to explain how the stolen items, ropes, and plastic cords came to be found in his home, Milat shrugged, saying: "I have no explanation at all." On July 27, 1996, Ivan Milat was found guilty of murdering seven backpackers by a jury of eleven persons after they had deliberated for twenty hours. The serial killer was sentenced to life in prison.

THE TAMIAMI TRAIL STRANGLER/ 1994-1995

For four months in 1994, a serial killer preyed upon prostitutes along the Tamiami Trail, a major east-west thoroughfare feeding downtown Miami, Florida. Six prostitutes in all, five women and a male cross-dresser were raped and murdered by a single killer, their bodies tossed in neighborhoods off the road. In mid-June, 1995, a prostitute who had been bound and gagged, broke free and banged on the walls of an apartment occupied by Rory Enrique Conde (AKA: The Tamiami Trail Strangler; b. 1965), a building supply salesman.

The prostitute's cries for help prompted neighbors to call police and Conde was arrested before he could claim his seventh victim. Conde, charged with six murders on June 26, 1995, in Miami, freely admitted the murders to Metro-Dade police, vaguely explaining that his compulsion to kill had something to do with his problems with his estranged wife (he was the father of two children). He was subsequently convicted on his own confession and DNA evidence and sentenced to death.

Conde, born in Barranquilla, Colombia in 1965, was orphaned at six months when his mother died of tetanus (his father had abandoned the family). He and his sister were raised by their paternal grandmother, but both went to Miami, Florida when the boy was twelve to live with their father, Gustavo Conde. The boy was reportedly sexually abused by his father, although this was a tale Conde later told the court in an effort to gain sympathy.

Wedding a 15-year-old girl in 1987, Conde mistreated his wife Carla throughout their marriage, savagely beating her for any infraction of his rules; he insisted that their apartment be immaculate and if his small son, Rory, Jr., dropped a crumb on the floor, Conde viciously beat his wife. At one point, he tried to kill her by suffocating her with a pillow.

When his wife was absent, Conde brought prostitutes to his home, where he had them lasciviously pose in his wife's lingerie, before sexually assaulting them. He often videotaped these sexual bouts, his wife later finding and viewing these tapes. The couple separated but reunited in 1992, when Carla Conde discovered herself pregnant. The family took a condominium near the Tamiami Trail. At the time, Conde worked as a building supply salesman.

After Conde refused to have sex with his wife and returned to prostitutes, his wife and children moved out, going to the home of Carla's parents. A short time later, on September 17, 1994, the first serial killings attributed to the Tamiami Strangler occurred. On that night Lazaro Comensana, a prostitute, was strangled to death. Two more similar murders quickly followed. On October 8, 1994, Elisa Martinez was strangled to death, and Charity Nava was choked to death on November 20, 1994. Conde used a black felt marker to write on the buttocks of both women: "Catch me if you can."

A short time later, Conde was discussing the case with some of his fellow employees, telling them that the Tamiami Strangler "was a smart guy. They're not going to get him." The fourth victim, Wanda Crawford, was found strangled to

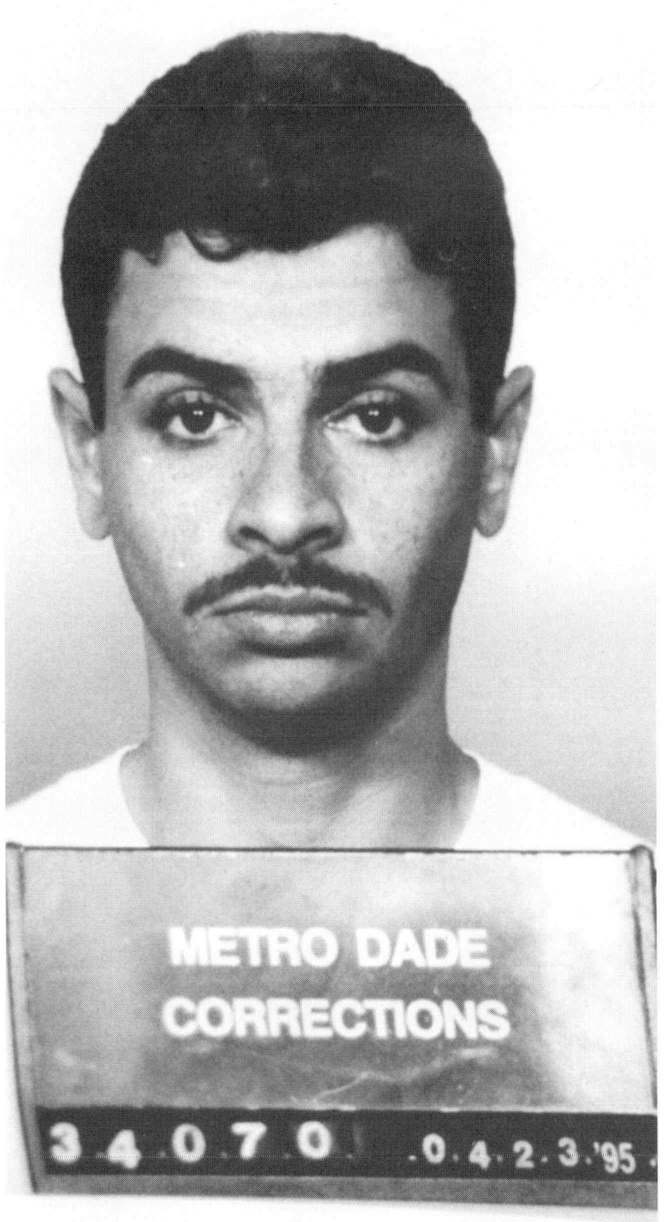

Rory Enrique Conde, who murdered six prostitutes along the Tamiami Trail in 1994-1995; at this writing he awaits execution on Florida's death row.

death on November 25, 1994. On December 17, 1994, Necole Schneider, another prostitute, was found strangled. Conde claimed his sixth victim, Rhonda Dunn, on January 12, 1995.

Brought to trial, Conde was convicted of killing one of the prostitutes, Rhonda Dunn, on October 20, 1999. On March 17, 2000, Conde was sentenced to death for this conviction. On April 5, 2001, Conde, in a plea-bargain arrangement, pleaded guilty to the murders of the five other prostitutes he had strangled. He was sentenced to five consecutive life terms by Miami-Dade Circuit Court Judge Jerald Bagley, on the condition he would never receive a parole. He nevertheless still awaits execution for the murder of Rhonda Dunn and, at this writing, is on death row in Starke, Florida.

THE MURDER ODYSSEY OF ANDREW CUNANAN/1997

One of the worst transcontinental murder sprees in American history was enacted in 1997 by a handsome homosexual hustler called Andrew Phillip Cunanan (1970-1997). He proved to be a spectacular serial killer who had the police of a dozen states hot on his heels in a day-to-day chase that culminated in the slayings of five persons and an ignominious suicide. Nothing in Cunanan's suave, intelligent character would have ever suggested that he would suddenly embark on an odyssey of murder, that he would defy local, state and federal police to catch him, to stop him from killing. He murdered with a vengeance, following what appeared to be a plan, as if he had drawn up a special hit list he had prepared long in advance.

Born and raised in San Diego County, California, Cunanan was the youngest of four children. He attended Bonita Vista Middle School in Chula Vista, proving to be a good student who, according to his mother, began reading the Bible at age 6. His father, Modesto Cunanan, who had been born in the Philippines, had served in the U.S. Navy and was a successful stockbroker, providing enough money to send Andrew to the private and expensive Bishop School in LaJolla, the upscale community of seaside homes, tony shops and expensive cars just north of San Diego.

Bishop School offered a sedate campus of sand-colored buildings constructed in the Spanish mission style in 1909, which surround a peaceful quadrangle where students play lacrosse. Cunanan did well at Bishop, maintaining high marks. He excelled in track and ran cross-country meets. He was also the only openly gay student on the campus, "flamingly gay," according to one classmate. His favorite saying was "*apres moi, le deluge*" ("after me, the deluge," a proverbial French quote often attributed to either Madame de Pompadour or King Louis XV).

Cunanan did not hide his homosexuality at Bishop. He often appeared in a tight-fitting red leather jumpsuit or other skimpy garb that would reveal his lithe body. He whistled seductively at other boys swimming in the pool or working out in the gym, but there is no evidence that he ever attempted any kind of molestation. He was forever pretending to have relatives of importance and wealth and he early on affected an air of sophistication, although classmates described his laugh as nervous and his manner edgy. At graduation, he was voted "most likely to be remembered."

In 1988, the year Cunanan enrolled as a history major at the University of California in San Diego, his world crumbled when his father fled the country, accused by investors of scamming more than $100,000 of their money in a phony stock scheme. Modesto Cunanan abandoned his family and returned to the Philippines where Andrew, at 19, tracked him down, shocked to see his father living in poverty.

Andrew Cunanan at the time he lived high in San Diego as a homosexual hustler.

Cunanan at the time his high-paying homosexual contacts stopped the cashflow.

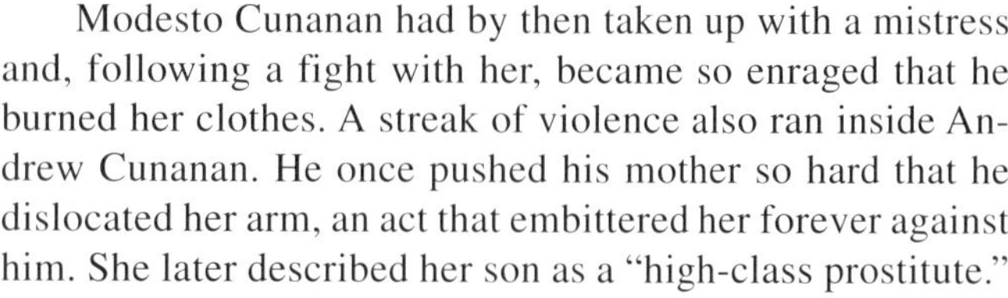

Modesto Cunanan had by then taken up with a mistress and, following a fight with her, became so enraged that he burned her clothes. A streak of violence also ran inside Andrew Cunanan. He once pushed his mother so hard that he dislocated her arm, an act that embittered her forever against him. She later described her son as a "high-class prostitute."

Cunanan was anything but that. After working as a cashier in a drugstore in Rancho Bernardo, he continued his studies at UCSD on and off until he dropped out. He appeared on the gay scene in the late 1980s in San Diego and, by 1990, in San Francisco. He was remembered by the manager of a gay bar on 18th Street as "gregarious, loud and always wanting to be the center of attention. He threw a lot of money around. Some people thought he bordered on the obnoxious. He was constantly laughing."

To others, however, Cunanan was a subtle and artful homosexual dodger, a worthy companion to older homosexuals whose art of conversation was stimulating and whose knowledge of current affairs often startling. He was by then no longer Andrew Cunanan, but Lt. Commander Cummings, he said, one-time student at Choate and Yale, who imported expensive antiques.

On other occasions, he would introduce himself as Andrew De Silva, the chief of a Hollywood production company who had a mansion on the Riviera and whose father was a rich sugar planter. He was always impeccably dressed, wearing tailored blazers and silk ascots, and always in fashion, favoring anything designed by Gianni Versace. He smoked Cohiba cigars and, according to one gay friend, "knew about the arts, the right kind of fork to use, the right cognac to drink ... He was in a class of his own as a gigolo."

Cunanan met his idol in 1990, it was reported, when designer Versace appeared in the VIP room of a San Francisco disco, in town to be feted for the costumes he had fashioned for the opera *Capriccio*. Versace spotted Cunanan standing in the crowd and walked up to him, saying: "I know you. *Lago di Como*, no?"

"Yes," Cunanan lied, "it is good to see you again, Mr. Versace."

Though he habitually frequented gay discos and clubs, Cunanan was never seen touching or kissing anyone. He talked vaguely of having an estranged wife and a child. He was never seen with gay men his own age, except in crowds, such as the gay party for Versace. It was whispered that Cunanan's wealth—he drove about in a $30,000 Infiniti, the gift of one of his elderly gay sponsors—was kept by an aging millionaire gay man, one of the business leaders of LaJolla who, like others of his ilk, remained in the closet. (It was later reported that Cunanan had unearthed through his elderly gay companion a "sugar daddy" list of aging, wealthy homosexuals throughout the country, a list that contained the names of Lee Miglin of Chicago and Gianni Versace of Miami Beach, both of whom he later murdered.)

The San Diego millionaire kept Cunanan in luxury and cash for about six years, but when he began to put on weight, he lost his gay sponsor, a wealthy art collector who was identified later by San Diego police as Norman Blanchford, who maintained a condo in LaJolla and who not only supplied

Cunanan in early 1997, discarded by sugar daddies, decided to take murderous revenge.

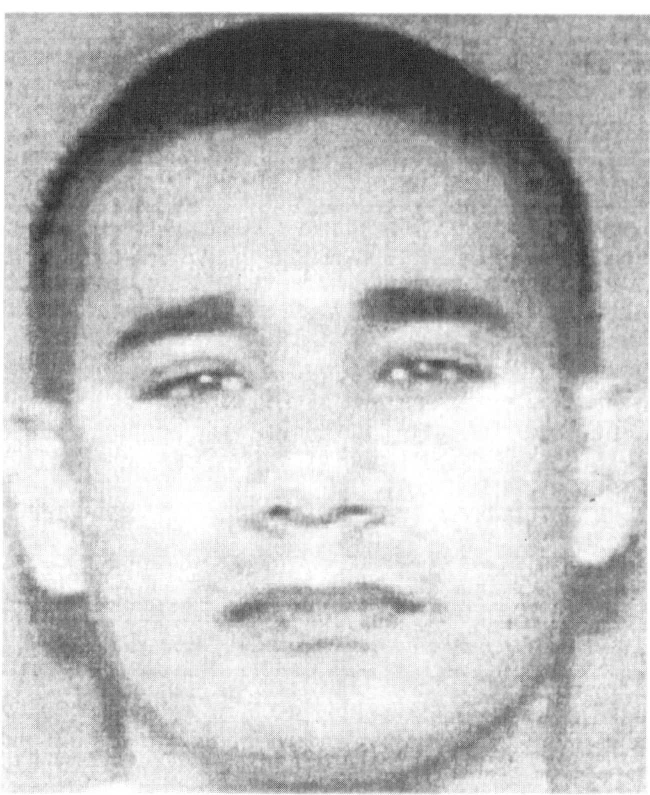

FBI photo of Andrew Cunanan, after he embarked on his murder spree in April 1997.

Cunanan with cash, but had taken him to Europe on a pleasure trip.

Down on his luck, Cunanan sold his car for cash, moved from LaJolla to Hillcrest, and began selling drugs to support himself. He also used those drugs and began drinking heavily, putting on more weight and complaining to bartenders in San Diego gay bars that he had difficulty in getting dates. He appeared despondent and worn out. In April 1997, Cunanan told a few friends that he was returning to San Francisco. "I'm not coming back," he said to one friend, almost fatalistically. "People don't know me. They think they do, but they don't."

The owner of a gay club Cunanan visited didn't know him until Cunanan called him up one day and propositioned him. The club owner declined the offer and, according to his later statements, would later see Cunanan in his club. Said the club owner: "The way he looked at me ... was pure hatred. He would just glare at me ... He was frightening. I thought, 'this guy is an evil person.' He was demonic, almost."

Cunanan had changed, drastically, some thought. His good gigolo looks were going. He had put on weight and run up $25,000 on his credit cards and had no way of paying them off. None of his sugar daddies wanted him. Worse, according to one report, he learned that he had tested positive for the HIV virus and the thought of contracting AIDS from one of his elderly gay sponsors threw him into a rage. Michael Dudley, a part-time AIDS volunteer, later reported having a safe-sex conversation with Cunanan, one that ended with Cunanan jumping to his feet and viciously kicking a wall, then screaming, "If I find out who did this to me, I'm going to get them!"

In mid-April 1997, Cunanan announced to friends that he was leaving town, that he was going to San Francisco, after he attended "to some business" in Minnesota. A few friends gathered on April 24, 1997, in a San Diego gay eatery to give him a farewell dinner—ostrich and Veuve Cliquot champagne. At that time, Cunanan gave away many of his personal belongings, sweaters, Gucci shoes, many of the gifts his sugar daddies had purchased for him on Rodeo Drive in Beverly Hills. This time, Cunanan's friends picked up the tab; he was broke. Before leaving, Cunanan looked around the table and said in a low tone, "None of you really know who I am."

When asked by a friend the next day about his trip to Minnesota, Cunanan replied that he had a friend living there, one with whom he had developed "the perfect relationship ... He lets me do anything [sexually] I want." Cunanan went on to admit that he was by then into S&M. (Police later found S&M tapes beneath his bed in his last San Diego dwelling, a dingy apartment he shared with homosexual Erik J. Greenman, who demanded and got FBI protection after Cunanan went on his killing spree, fearing that Cunanan would return to San Diego and kill him.)

On April 25, 1997, Cunanan flew to Minnesota on a first-class one-way ticket, purchased for him by his friends in San Diego, going to meet his former lover, architect David Madson, who lived a well-to-do life in Minneapolis' trendy Warehouse District, occupying an apartment at the Harmony

Lofts complex. He owned a Dalmatian named Prints and drove a red Jeep Cherokee. Madson dined out frequently in the city's better restaurants, such as the Monte Carlo Bar and Cafe, and he was fond of dancing at Nye's Polonaise Room. He worked for the architectural firm of John Ryan Co., designing banks and buildings for financial institutions.

Madson was a likeable, charming person who held a master's degree in architecture from the University of Minnesota. He had won the President's Award for a traveling exhibit on AIDS and had been a 1994 guest lecturer at Harvard, talking on assisted living for those suffering from AIDS. He had apparently had a sexual liaison with Cunanan in San Francisco. When Cunanan appeared in Minneapolis on the night of April 25, Madson took him out for drinks with some other friends.

None of Madson's gay friends liked Cunanan, who spent most of the evening bragging about driving a Rolls Royce convertible. Madson, who had told some of his gay friends that he wanted to end any kind of relationship with Cunanan because he thought he was involved with "shady dealings," nevertheless took Cunanan home with him and two nights later, Cunanan invited another gay, Jeffrey Trail, to visit him at Madson's Harmony Lofts apartment.

Trail had been born and raised in DeKalb, Illinois. His father, Stanley Trail, was a professor of mathematics at Northern Illinois University. Jeffrey Trail graduated from the U.S. Naval Academy in 1991 and was stationed in San Diego, where he reportedly met Cunanan and had a homosexual relationship. (Some later stated that Trail and Cunanan did not have a homosexual affair, that their relationship was platonic, that Trail served as a surrogate older brother to the troubled Cunanan, one whose sound advice he often took in straightening himself out.) In 1996, the 28-year-old Trail moved to Bloomington, Minnesota, to work as a district manager at a propane delivery firm.

The reunion between Trail and Cunanan was not a happy one. According to Minneapolis police, Cunanan discovered that both his former lovers, Madson and Trail, had formed a relationship and neither was available to him. This news, it was speculated, caused him to snap. Just after 10 p.m., on the night of April 27, 1997, Madson's neighbors heard a loud shout: "Get the f— out!" This was followed by several loud thuds. They did not report the commotion, however.

Two days later, on April 29, 1997, the battered body of Jeffrey Trail was found in Madson's apartment wrapped in a rug. Police had been notified by Madson's employers when he failed to report to work for two days and officers, searching for him, entered his apartment to find Trail beaten to a pulp. A bloody claw hammer was found nearby. Both Cunanan and the 33-year-old Madson were nowhere to be found. Close to the body, police found a gym bag with Cunanan's name on it. Police also found a holster that belonged to Trail and from it was missing a .40-caliber handgun.

Some time later, one of Trail's gay lovers reported that Trail nervously told him that he had tried to "straighten out" Cunanan, but that he had had "a huge falling out," adding, "I made a lot of enemies this weekend ... I've got to get out of here. They're going to kill me." This remark, made in comfortable hindsight, implied that perhaps Cunanan *and* Madson were out to murder Trail. Yet, some currency was added to this insidious conclusion in that some of Madson's neighbors insisted that they saw Cunanan and Madson strolling and chatting amiably while they walked Madson's dog a day after the time the coroner fixed for Trail's murder.

With the discovery of Trail's body, Cunanan had begun to settle his "business," which was murder, plain and simple, and from the way he left clues behind as to his identity, he didn't care who knew that he had embarked upon a killing spree. This was confirmed three days later, on May 3, 1997, when the body of David Madson was pulled limp and bloated from the reeds of a lake north of Minneapolis by two startled fishermen.

Madson had been shot twice in the back and once in the head with a .40-caliber pistol. Again, Cunanan had been sloppy, or had intentionally and arrogantly left behind a blatant clue, another empty bag with his name on it. Police by then believed that Cunanan had killed Trail and then forced Madson to flee with him, driving northward out of Minneapolis in Madson's red Jeep Cherokee. At this point or earlier, Cunanan, investigators surmised, decided to kill Madson because he was a witness to his murder of Trail.

Although this was a perfectly credible concept, it defied Cunanan's blatant scattering of clues that pinpointed him as the killer. Someone suggested that police had another serial killer like Ted Bundy on their hands, but Bundy was a meticulous murderer, for the most part, who left few clues as to his identity. Cunanan's actions better copied those of the playboy woman-killer Christopher Wilder, who drove cross-country killing at will and not much caring if the police knew he was the person they were seeking or not, almost as if daring them to hunt him down and kill him, which is what they did.

By the time Madson's body was dragged dripping from the lake, Cunanan had long left the area, driving southeast in Madson's red Jeep Cherokee. While police initiated a widespread dragnet for the killer, he had gone to Chicago and the gay bars and restaurants stretching from the Gold Coast northward to the Broadway bistros of "Gay Town."

In Chicago, Cunanan apparently made contact with 72-year-old real estate developer Lee Miglin. Though married, it was later stated that Miglin was on Cunanan's "sugar daddy" list. The Miglin family later emphatically denied that the real estate tycoon was gay and said he had never had any kind of relationship with Cunanan. Yet, the question remained as to how Cunanan knew about Miglin and how he gained the man's confidence long enough to torture and murder him, a man who zealously guarded his privacy. Miglin's mutilated body—he had been stabbed repeatedly—was found by police in the garage of his Gold Coast townhouse on May 4, 1997, after his wife Marilyn reported him missing. Miglin's head had been wrapped in masking tape with holes made for the nostrils,

Photo left page: Italian designer and fashion mogul Gianni Versace, who is shown with his sister; the designer was shot and killed in front of his posh Miami Beach villa on July 15, 1997, by Andrew Cunanan.

much in the manner of a black leather S&M head mask Cunanan had owned in San Diego, one which left room only for the nostrils. His punctured body was wrapped in plastic and brown wrapping paper.

Miglin had suffered "a worse death than Christ," according to the magnate's 96-year-old mother. His neck had almost been cut in half with a saw. He had been stabbed dozens of times and his chest jabbed with pruning shears. Cunanan had spent time torturing Miglin, apparently to learn the whereabouts of cash and jewelry in the posh townhouse.

After killing the tycoon, he prepared a sandwich in the kitchen of the townhouse, eating casually as he ransacked the place, taking his victim's jewelry and better designer clothes. He shaved in Miglin's bathroom, then took Miglin's briefcase, which contained $2,000 or more in cash, and the keys to Miglin's Lexus and drove off, leaving the stolen Jeep Cherokee a short distance from the townhouse.

Miglin's family members strenuously denied that the real estate magnate was homosexual. They pointed to the fact that he had had a lasting relationship with his wife Marilyn for thirty-two years and had raised a family.

From Chicago, Cunanan drove east to New York City. While thousands of lawmen and FBI agents were searching for him, on May 5, 1997, he checked into a West 20th Street transient hotel frequented by homosexuals and used his pet alias of De Silva. According to a receipt later found by police, the fugitive, who was fast becoming Public Enemy Number One, went shopping for clothes, buying inexpensive garb in an apparent attempt to conserve the cash he had stolen from Miglin. On the following day, Cunanan went to a movie theater on West 23rd Street where he viewed the film *Liar, Liar*. The next day, May 8, according to witnesses, he went to a different theater to view the movie *The Devil's Own*.

Something or someone apparently spooked Cunanan for he suddenly left New York City, driving Miglin's Lexus into New Jersey, and then to Philadelphia, Pennsylvania, sometime on May 9 or May 10, 1997. Police later theorized that as he drove along, he listened to news reports of his flight and heard one report that police had been tracking him through Miglin's car phone. He ripped out the cellular unit and, as he drove out of Philadelphia and across the Delaware Memorial Bridge, on May 10, he desperately looked about for another vehicle to replace the much-publicized green Lexus. He spotted a red pickup truck parked in Finn's Point Cemetery, a remote graveyard he was passing as he traveled through rural Pennsville, New Jersey. He drove into the cemetery, which was bordered by marshland and surrounded by tall foxtails.

The red pickup truck belonged to 45-year-old caretaker William Reese. While holding a full-time job, Reese maintained the small lodge in the graveyard for twenty years, but his burial duties were limited. The cemetery was chiefly reserved for the Union and Confederate dead of the Civil War. One of Reese's ancestors was buried at Finn's Point, along with about 200 Union dead and more than 2,300 Confederates who had died of starvation and disease in a Union prison fort on the Delaware River.

A Civil War re-enactor and head of the 14th Brooklyn Chapter he had founded, Reese arrived at the cemetery every morning to raise the flag, went to work, then returned in the evening to lower Old Glory. Apparently, Cunanan arrived at the cemetery and the amiable Reese showed him the lodge.

It was inside this building that Cunanan killed Reese, firing a single shot to the head. He left behind a shell casing that police later matched to the same weapon, the .40-caliber pistol, Cunanan had used to kill Trail and Madson. He also left behind Miglin's green Lexus. Reese, who left a wife and a 12-year-old son, was later buried among the graves of the fallen Civil War soldiers he had so lovingly tended.

By then Andrew Cunanan was driving Reese's red pickup truck south (he stopped to steal a license plate and replaced Reese's original plate on the pickup truck), going toward Florida, homing in on South Beach and the gay strip of bars and bistros through which sauntered millionaire sugar daddies, selecting from among thousands of young gay men with a wave of the finger their companions for the night, perverse potentates buying their ways through this fleshpot bazaar. Crashing about this island of hopeful, forlorn young homosexuals were waves of drag queens and transvestites, the diseased scum of a degenerate society, worthy now only of a bullet in the mindset of Andrew Cunanan.

For all of its glitz and glitter, its phony high tone talk and ersatz sophistication, South Beach was the homosexual heart of sun-baked Miami ("Florida's AIDs zone" remarked one police investigator), and the pantheon inspiration for this hip-swishing, limp-wristed community was 50-year-old Gianni Versace, head of a $500-million-a-year designer empire, and where Versace maintained a luxurious villa, peopled each night by "the glamorous types."

There was nothing glamorous about Cunanan when he reached his destination. On May 12, 1997, he checked into the Normandy Plaza Hotel, using an alias and a French passport and taking Room 116 at the rate of $35.73 a night. He later economized by moving into Room 201 and paying a weekly rate of $230.50. By his third week, the fugitive thought to conserve more money by moving to Room 322, paying a monthly rate of $690.50.

The Normandy, its walls festooned with photos of long-dead movie stars, had seen better days. Cunanan chose to hole up here, it was later presumed, because the hotel was only a few miles north of Versace's mansion at South Beach. It was Versace that the spree killer had come to see.

While law enforcement officers searched throughout America for him—reports had it that he was in Oklahoma, Pennsylvania, dozens of places—Cunanan whiled away the time sleeping long hours in his room, going out only for fast-service junk food, then scurrying back to his hideout at the Normandy. He kept the curtains closed to the ocean view, and often went out late at night and did not return until shortly before dawn. He made no phone calls from the hotel and never argued with anyone. "He came and went like a ghost," one hotel employee stated. He was never seen without a cap pulled low on his head and dark sunglasses covering his eyes.

The unattended houseboat in Miami Beach in which Cunanan lived out the last moments of his life; before police arrived, the serial killer (he had slain five persons) fired a bullet into his own brain on

Cunanan was fastidious. He kept his room so tidy that it hardly ever needed cleaning. He put his dirty towels in a bag and hung this outside his door for pickup. His linen, however, seemed peculiarly shaped to a hotel maid, who noted how she would find the bedsheets rolled into a tight ball each morning, as if "he had a bad sleep."

In early June 1997, he drove Reese's stolen pickup truck to a parking garage in South Beach, only a few blocks from Versace's villa on Ocean Drive. The pickup, which lawmen had been looking for all along the eastern seaboard, simply sat in the garage week after week, unnoticed. So, too, was Cunanan, although his presence was reported in Miami Beach, West Palm Beach, and other areas along the sun-drenched strip.

It is possible that Cunanan murdered again at this time. On May 12, only hours after the serial killer checked into the Normandy Plaza, Casey Patrick Sigler, a 41-year-old gay man, was beaten to death by a man who reportedly picked him up in nearby Flamingo Park, a hangout for gays. Sigler was battered to death in his apartment. One report had it that his attacker was black, but others later claimed that the man visiting Sigler answered to Cunanan's description. Moreover, Sigler's Toyota Celica was stolen that night, the kind of theft that was part of Cunanan's *modus operandi*.

It was never clear whether Cunanan was seeking to ingratiate himself into Gianni Versace's sexual favor (as if a liaison with the powerful and rich Versace might serve as a protection against inevitable murder charges) or was stalking him with the purpose of murdering him, of taking revenge against someone he thought might have infected him with the HIV virus years earlier.

Although the Versace family later denied that Cunanan ever knew Versace, reliable reports have it that Cunanan met Versace at the 1990 opera party in San Francisco and again in northern Italy after traveling there with one of his elderly sponsors, a homosexual millionaire who owned a hotel close to one of Versace's residences and who was a close "boyfriend" of the designer.

Versace's friends later rejected the idea that Cunanan was the designer's lover at any time, flippantly denigrating Cunanan's homosexual appeal to such a discriminating fashion guru, one giving Cunanan a lowball rating "a 5 out of 10, and you can find 10s all over South Beach." This was, of course, a tacit admission that Versace was *the* gourmet homosexual, the chief "sugar daddy" who took his pick of the best male flesh available in South Beach. It was no secret that the designer invited many handsome young men to his 20,000-square-foot villa, which boasted a gymnasium, pool, and a custom-designed shower large enough to accommodate more than a dozen bathers at a time.

A wealthy patron of the arts from Brazil later told FBI agents that she had attended a party at Versace's villa a short time before the designer was killed, and insisted that Cunanan was at the party and in close company with Gianni Versace. If this was the case, Cunanan was receiving no financial support from Versace. On July 7, 1997, the fugitive killer went to a pawnshop, Cash on the Beach, and pawned a gold coin, most probably stolen from Miglin (but some said given to him by Versace), obtaining $190 in return. Cunanan used his own name to make the transaction and even left a thumbprint on a receipt, which was sent to the Miami police the next day.

On July 11, 1997, Cunanan walked into the Miami Subs Grill, a fast-food sandwich shop three blocks north of his hotel, and ordered a Junior Tuna Combo. Cashier Kenneth Benjamin immediately recognized Cunanan after having viewed a recent TV show, "America's Most Wanted," which had featured the homosexual spree killer. Benjamin whispered to his boss, who told him to call 911. A police operator told Benjamin to stall the man until officers could arrive. When he returned to the counter, however, Cunanan had gone, walking south on Collins Avenue, another attendant having given the killer his sandwich.

Police came running into the sandwich shop only minutes later, guns drawn. They began to search the area, building by building, but they did not get to the Normandy until five days later and by that time Cunanan had slipped away, dodging his hotel bill and leaving a room scattered with designer magazines. He was later seen at some South Beach gay bars, attempting to engage drag queens in conversation, saying he was a newly arrived political science major doing research in the area. He had closely cropped his dark hair and wore a white shirt and jeans.

By this time, Cunanan was either sleeping on the beach, as hundreds do each night, or was curled up inside the cab of Reese's stolen pickup truck inside the garage. He was now planning only one course, the murder of his one time idol, Gianni Versace. The gay designer was oblivious to such dangers.

Unlike his homes and offices in Italy, which were surrounded with security systems and bodyguards, the Versace oceanside villa, which he had purchased in 1992 for $3.7 million and had painstakingly restored, naming it La Casuraina, had no bodyguards or alarm systems, only an iron gate to which Versace and a few others had the key. The place did have eight security cameras, but none was working on the morning of July 15, 1997, when Versace strolled outside and through the gate at about 8:30 a.m., to casually walk to the nearby News Cafe to buy magazines, a morning ritual.

After purchasing $15.07 worth of publications, the designer began slowly walking back to his villa. Andrew Cunanan, at some distance, was walking behind him. Cunanan knew Versace's habits, having surveyed the News Cafe the morning previous (the Cafe's security camera later revealed Cunanan scouting the area on that day; some later claimed that Cunanan knew about the morning stroll because he stayed with Versace earlier in the month).

Versace reached his gate and paused to insert the key into the door. Cunanan, dressed in a gray muscle T-shirt, black shorts, black cap and tennis shoes, had caught up to him and stood behind him. He lifted the .40-caliber pistol to Versace's head and pulled the trigger twice. The fashion designer sank dead to the ground, blood streaming from his open skull to stain pink coral steps. Drawn to the front of the villa by the sound of the shots, Antonio D'Amico, Versace's live-in lover at the time, let out a piercing sound that many first believed was the high-pitched wail of a woman.

Cunanan fled, walking swiftly down the avenue, then dashing down an alleyway. He went immediately to the parked pickup, where he changed clothes, leaving the gray T-shirt and the black shorts in a pile near the truck. Police found these items and Cunanan's passport in the truck, along with many newspaper clippings about the nation-wide hunt for him.

The killing of Gianni Versace sent shock waves around the world, just as Cunanan expected, or, at least, police thought he expected. The other murders he had committed were of obscure persons, but now he had killed someone of international importance. Now he had committed a murder of someone so famous that, in his twisted world, his mad act was equal to the assassination of a king or emperor.

Cunanan was now a fugitive so infamous that he knew that his only hope of escape was to leave the country. The FBI later stated that for two days following the Versace murder, Cunanan sought ways to secretly depart Florida by air or by sea, calling a friend inside the homosexual network of South Beach and discussing how to get a false identification and a passport so that he could escape the country.

While hundreds of police officers frantically searched for the spree killer, Cunanan was safely holed up and undetected in an unoccupied houseboat docked on the intracoastal waterway known as Indian Creek, a houseboat owned by Las Vegas club owner Torstein Reineck (who was wanted in Germany for fraud and tax evasion). On July 23, 1997, while the world hunted for Andrew Cunanan, 71-year old caretaker Fernando Careira entered the houseboat and found the interior in disarray. As he went outside to call police, a single shot rang out. Police arrived to find Cunanan, killer of five persons, sprawled on a bed wearing only shorts. He had committed suicide by firing a bullet into his head.

CHAPTER TWELVE:
MURDER/UNSOLVED HOMICIDES

It is a grim fact that a preponderance of murders remain unsolved. Without clues, informants, eye-witnesses or hard evidence, the police are, unfortunately, incapable of solving these capital crimes. Such slayings, however, remain on the books as "open files," and since there is no statutes of limitation regarding such offenses in most countries, the perpetrators are still sought. The search for these killers by police, however, is a haphazard affair, their efforts diminished by limited time and personnel at hand to address these aging cases.

Deep historical whodunits are some times inspected and researched by crime historians, who, for the most part, are left with little but speculation, theories and guesswork. These sifters of fact and fiction busy themselves with catching dust in the wind and rooting up human artifacts in their search for long-gone culprits. A few successfully identify such perpetrators, but for the most part, these elusive criminals are shrouded by an uncertain past that separates their mysterious identities from the factual reality of the present.

The hunt goes on for the killers involved in sensational cases that have nagged the police and criminologists for decades, some of the most perplexing cases going back for centuries, such as the mysterious murder of Sir Edmund Godfrey, one of England's most respected magistrates. Godfrey's body was found in a ditch near Primrose Hill, London, on October 17, 1678, six days after he vanished from his home in Hartshorn Lane. Godfrey, an autopsy revealed, had been beaten (or stomped), strangled with a rope and run through with a sword.

Titus Oates, a rabid anti-Catholic who had brought to Godfrey a complaint about a popish plot about to unravel—one which Godfrey dismissed as perjurous—used Godfrey's death to railroad three Catholic leaders to quick conviction and execution—Henry Berry, Lawrence Hill, and Robert Green, along with three Catholic priests and five Catholic members of the House of Lords.

Crime writer and historian John Dickson Carr concluded that Godfrey's killer was none other than the Earl of Pembroke, who had stomped a man to death only months before the magistrate's slaying and had been convicted of manslaughter by none other than Godfrey. The stomping wounds suffered by Godfrey were, as Carr pointed out, identical to those of Pembroke's victim. Yet, Carr provided only circumstantial evidence and Godfrey's murder still remains unsolved.

This case and scores more linger in the minds of crime

Sir Edmund Godfrey, a leading British magistrate, who was mysteriously murdered in 1678, some claimed by a British aristocrat never charged.

Frank Dolezal was arrested and held on suspicion of being the Mad Butcher of Cleveland; he was later released. The serial killer was never found.

Mystery writer Edgar Allan Poe, who knew Mary Rogers and who used her unsolved murder as the basis of his story, "The Mystery of Marie Roget."

Madame Ann Restell (Ann Lohman), New York's infamous abortionist—a bat devil is shown devouring an infant beneath her portrait—was suspected of having botched an abortion on Mary Rogers and then disposing of her body.

historians, such as the so-called Ax Man of New Orleans, who reportedly butchered a number of residents in that city from 1911 to 1919, these murders credited to Black Hand assassins. A similar slayer, dubbed the Mad Butcher of Cleveland, senselessly slew a number of low-life people in Kingsbury Run, the city's industrial valley (where twelve were murdered and mutilated), and also in Pittsburgh (where six more were slain), from 1935 to 1939. These killings stopped as inexplicably as they began.

The unsolved murders of attractive women have drawn riveting attention from the public of their eras and crime historians following in their musty wake. Such was the case of Gulielma Elmore Sands, known as Elma, who disappeared on December 22, 1799, and whose body was found ten days later in a well in Lispenard's Meadow, in Greenwich Village. The Elma Sands case became the first great murder mystery in New York. She helped to manage a small boarding house owned by her Quaker relatives.

A beautiful young woman, Sands drew the amorous attentions of two young men, both boarders at the house. One was Richard David Croucher, a recently arrived Englishman who proposed marriage to Sands, but was rejected. The second suitor was Levi Weeks, the nephew of a rich carpenter. He, too, proposed, and Sands accepted. She was killed, however, before taking the nuptial vows. Croucher, the rejected suitor, immediately lobbied for Weeks' arrest and brought about his trial for murder.

The case against Weeks was so weak, however, that a jury promptly returned a not guilty verdict. Croucher was later convicted of raping a young woman and sent to prison for life. He was nevertheless paroled and moved to Virginia, where he was indicted for fraud. Before his trial in that case, he slipped aboard a ship sailing for England, where, years later, he was hanged for committing a capital crime. Most historians believe Croucher to have been the culprit, but others insist that Weeks murdered Sands because he had fallen in love with another woman and wanted to escape his promise of marriage. That debate continues.

New York was rocked by a second and even more sensational unsolved murder, that of Mary Cecilia Rogers, who was known as "the beautiful cigar girl," and whose body was found floating by fishermen in the Hudson River on July 28, 1841. She had been strangled to death by an eighteen-inch piece of muslin torn from her own petticoat. The 22-year-old Rogers had worked behind the counter of Anderson's cigar store on Broadway and her customers included journalists and celebrated writers like Washington Irving and Edgar Allan Poe.

Although a few suspects—young men who had dated the girl—were detained and questioned, police were unable to pinpoint the killer. Poe avidly followed the investigation and when it appeared hopeless, the writer of the macabre found a way to solve the case himself, by using Rogers as his role model in his chilling story, "The Mystery of Marie Roget," which became a crime classic story. In his story, Poe profiled his tragic heroine as being pregnant and his readers took his tale literally, coming to believe that Rogers was, indeed, pregnant, and had died at the hands of New York's most notorious abortionist, Ann Restell,

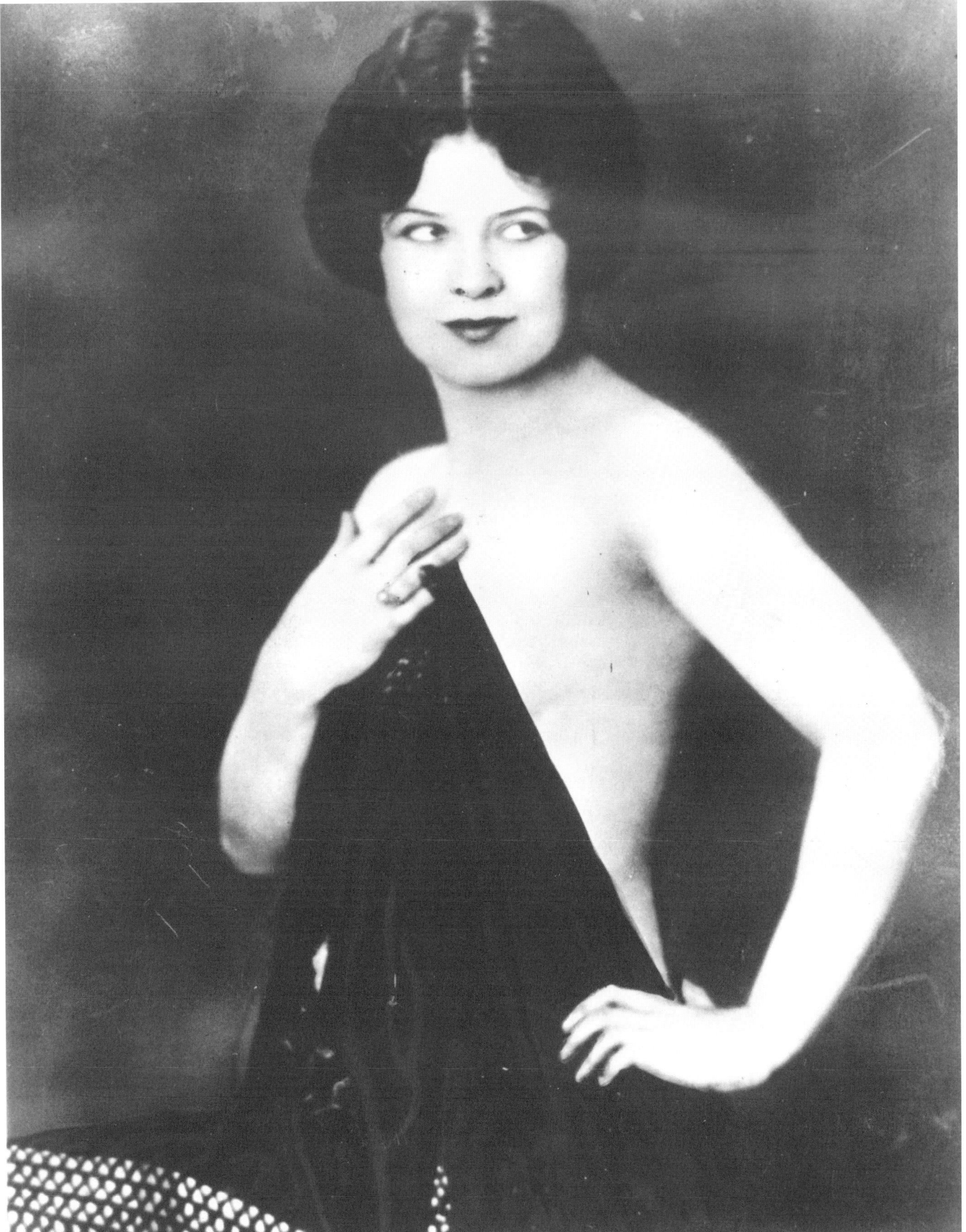

New York bordello madam Vivian Gordon, who was slain in 1931; her killer was never apprehended, even though police checked the dozens of male "friends" listed in her private ledger.

New York showgirl Dot King, who was killed in 1923.

who was known as Madame Killer because of her ineptitude with the knife.

The tale was spread that Rogers was brought to Restell by a naval officer (who later became an admiral) and that the girl died under Restell's unwieldy knife, her body then tossed into the Hudson River. This was but a piece of fiction, however, because there was no evidence of a pregnancy in the careful examination of the victim's body. Moreover, one must ask why the girl would be strangled if she had already died from Restell's botched surgery?

Rogers' unsolved homicide parallels that of the tragic Starr Faithful, whose body was found on a Long Island beach in 1931 (profiled in this chapter). Her mysterious death caused widespread publicity as did another slaying that year, that of Vivian Gordon, a sultry New York bordello madam, who flaunted her ill-gotten riches and lived extravagantly, even boasting of the "black book" she kept, which detailed the identities of her high society and underworld clients. One of these, the NYPD concluded, silenced her, but detectives were never able to pinpoint the murderer.

Another such unsolved case involved showgirl Dot King (Dorothy Keenan, 1896-1923), who was the prototype of the Jazz Age bobbed-hair flapper. King danced, drank and dallied through nighttime New York during the early 1920s. She became a hostess in a popular speakeasy and was the rival of the celebrated Texas Guinan. King was "sponsored" by a sugar daddy she called "Mr. Marshall," an alias for a high society figure. This man showered jewels upon the seductive Dot—diamond bracelets, a ruby necklace, a diamond and emerald-studded wristwatch, pearl necklaces, gems thought to be worth $30,000 (valued at ten times that much today).

At the same time, King met and fell in love with a Latin gigolo, Albert Guimares, a man without an income, who lived from the cash Dot gave him. He vanished on the day King's maid found her dead in her bedroom on March 15, 1923. A coroner's report stated that someone had held her arms behind her back while chloroforming her to death (which explained the burns on her face).

Marshall, the sugar daddy, was not suspected, but police arrested Guimares, who was suddenly flaunting cash. Though he was suspected of killing King and absconding with her missing jewelry, Guimares was released. He had an iron alibi provided by Philadelphia socialite Aurelia Dreyfus, who came forward to state that Guimares, her new lover, had been with her at the time King was murdered. The King case, like so many others, remains open.

The sensation caused by the killing of Dot King was equaled by the baffling murder of Wilma Montesi, a voluptuous, ravishing woman, whose body was found by a carpenter on a beach about twenty miles outside of Rome, Italy, on April 11, 1953. Found only in her slip at the water's edge, police first announced that the young woman had committed suicide. Investigators changed their mind when Montesi's family—her father was a wealthy sawmill owner—objected, saying that she was a happy woman and was looking forward to her upcoming marriage. Police then stated that Montesi died by accident, falling into the water and drowning.

This verdict was accepted by Montesi family members, who promptly buried the young woman in her wedding dress. Five months later, however, Silvano Muto, publisher of a gossip magazine, publicly stated that Montesi had been drugged to death by wealthy playboys at a drug party. Again, Italian police reopened the case and this time announced that Montesi had been, indeed, murdered. The killer, however, was never identified.

Italian police, a decade later, had a much more serious problem with a strange serial killer they called the "Monster of Florence." This night stalker killed and mutilated sixteen people in and about Florence, Italy, from 1968 to 1985, invariably selecting as victims couples necking in cars parked in remote areas (not unlike the *modus operandi* of David Berkowitz of New York, see Serial Killers). This fiend was never caught. Police in Kenosha, Wisconsin met with the same results in their dedicated attempt to locate the perpetrator of seven murders from 1967 to 1981.

On rare occasions, either by accident or through a misstep of the perpetrator, open murder cases are suddenly solved. This was the case of Gary Leon Ridgeway, a 54-year-old truck painter, who, in 2001, after being suspected of several murders, arranged for a plea-bargain in exchange for his confes-

Albert Guimares, a hustling gigolo, who was suspected of murdering King and stealing her jewels, but another woman provided his alibi on the night of the King murder.

Beautiful Wilma Montesi, who was found dead outside of Rome, Italy, in 1953, reportedly murdered at a playboy's drug party.

Serial killer Gary Leon Ridgeway, who solved the "Green River Killings" by confessing to forty-eight murders in 2003.

sion to being Washington State's notorious "Green River Killer." Ridgeway admitted to murdering forty-eight women—mostly runaways and prostitutes, most of his victims claimed from 1982 to 1984. He received forty-eight life sentences in November 2003, despite public consensus that such flagrant plea-bargaining was a travesty of justice and that Ridgeway should have been be put to death in a state where capital punishment was exercised.

Ridgeway calmly stated his motive for these serial killings: "I wanted to kill as many women as I thought were prostitutes as I possibly could...I hate most prostitutes and I did not want to pay them for sex...I picked prostitutes because I thought I could kill as many of them as I wanted without getting caught." From his savage mutilation murders and taunts to the press, another such killer felt the same way. He was the ubiquitous and never apprehended Jack the Ripper.

JACK THE RIPPER/1888

No other killer in British history rivaled that of the gruesome, mocking Jack the Ripper, a serial killer whose arrogance and boldness defied the entire police department of London and held in terror a great city for as long as he cared to roam its streets and slay at will. He was a murderous braggart, who gave himself his own grim name, publicly signing "Jack the Ripper" in notes and letters to the authorities to taunt them. His ability to kill whenever an evil whim urged and the inability of the police to apprehend him indelibly stamped his black fame in the minds of all, from the street urchins of the East End to Queen Victoria fretting over his identity in her palace.

From the notorious reputation the Ripper has gleaned in more than a century, one might assume that he slaughtered dozens or more helpless victims. The truth, according to most authorities past and present, is that Jack the Ripper killed five women within a ten-week period, from August 31 to November 9, 1888. Other killings before and after that were also attributed to bloody Jack, but they differed, some radically so, in style and method and were most likely the dark deeds of others.

Some diehard Ripperologists insist that this mass murderer slew as many as nine or more female victims, from April 1888 to February 1891, and perhaps beyond. But the five *definitive* Ripper slayings were unmistakably his handiwork. All five women had their throats slashed, were disemboweled and mutilated; the killer paid obsessive attention to the destruction of female organs. Not only did he dare the police to find and arrest him, but he proved his identity by proudly sending some human remains of his victims to authorities.

In one instance, he actually foretold a "double event," one in which he would murder two women on the same night, a haughty prediction which came all too true. The Metropolitan Police of London seemed inept and powerless to stop the fiend from his appointed murderous rounds. They had never before had to contend with such a monster, one that killed purely for the sadistic pleasure of killing.

Pressured by the Crown, the press, and the public, the police, under the direction of Sir Charles Warren, frantically exhausted their forces in futile searches and wild speculations unconnected to the slim facts unearthed. The East End of London, where the murders occurred, was infested with thousands of criminals and prostitutes. There were sixty-two brothels in this area in the year 1888, and 233 lodging houses catered to whores.

Inside these dirty little rooms, heated by small charcoal-burning stoves and invariably lighted by a single candle, thousands of assignations occurred each night. There was no way in which the police could monitor these one night stands and check each prostitute's customers. It was clear from the start that the Ripper had chosen one sort of person to murder, prostitutes, but these hapless, diseased creatures, ranging in age from their late teens to their seventies, outnumbered on-duty police fifty to one.

Most of those prostitutes plying their trade in the East End were middle-aged, alcoholic females. They had no education for the most part and were most often infected with myriad venereal diseases. One such was Emma Elizabeth Smith, forty-five, who, on the night of April 3, 1888, was fatally assaulted while returning to her single small room at 18 George Street, Spitafields. Earlier, Smith had been seen soliciting a well-dressed gentleman, who wore a dark suit and sported a white scarf.

A constable saw Smith staggering toward the door of her lodging house. She collapsed in his arms, babbling about being attacked earlier by four men on Osborn Street. She thought one of these assailants had been a teenager, but was not sure. The men had beaten her about the face and had slashed off her ear. Worse, these attackers had brutally inserted a foreign object in her vagina and broken it off. Emma Smith died of peritonitis a few hours later.

The next killing often attributed to the Ripper, and more in keeping with his grisly *modus operandi,* was that of Martha Tabram (or Turner), another middle-aged prostitute. Stabbed no fewer than thirty-nine times, she was discovered dead at 3 a.m. on August 7, 1888, at George Yard Landing, later Gunthorpe Street, in Whitechapel. The killer had paid particular attention to Tabram's female organs and parts, as most of the fatal wounds were administered in these areas.

Police were baffled at these first two attacks. Both occurring in the early morning hours, these killings involved women who had been seen alive only a few hours before they were found dying or dead. In neither instance was anyone seen running from the area, and neither victim had called out or given an alarm that would have been heard in the densely populated districts. It was assumed that Smith and Tabram had solicited men, who pretended to buy their sexual favors and, when they turned their backs to prepare for a street assignation, had slashed them to death and quietly left the area.

Mary Ann "Polly" Nichols, age forty-two, was the next victim, the first of the "certifiable" Ripper victims, according to dedicated Ripperologists. She was an alcoholic harridan, who was known for her barroom brawls. A tough and uncompromising harlot, Nichols could have put up a ferocious fight for her life, but she was apparently given no chance to do so by her killer. Her body was found on Buck's Row by a patrolling constable at 3:15 a.m. on August 31, 1888. The Ripper had slashed her throat twice, two incisions about an inch apart, so deep that the blade had cut to the vertebrae. The victim was almost decapitated.

When the body was taken to the Old Montague Street Workhouse morgue, further inspection revealed deep slashes on Nichols' abdomen and in the area of the vagina, but no organs had actually been removed. It was later speculated that the Ripper had had no time to perform this grisly chore since he was probably interrupted by the approaching footsteps of the constable and fled. However, five front teeth of the victim were missing. It was not reported if these teeth had been removed by the killer or lost when the victim was still alive. Again, the victim had not cried out, even though she was

Jack the Ripper is shown as a gruesome, bloodthirsty ghost-like murderer in this contemporary sketch of the serial killer, who stalked London's Whitechapel area in 1888.

A contemporary sketch shows the Ripper, left, as a furtive character observed by two characters at right bearing resemblances to the fictional sleuth, Sherlock Holmes, and his companion, Dr. Watson. Arthur Conan Doyle's great detective first appeared in "A Study in Scarlet," in 1887, a year before the Ripper killings occurred, and his popularity soared with a public that had more belief in Holmes' abilities to solve crimes than that of Scotland Yard.

St. Mary's Church, on Whitechapel Road, the site where Emma Elizabeth Smith was attacked on April 3, 1888. Smith may or may not have been a Ripper victim.

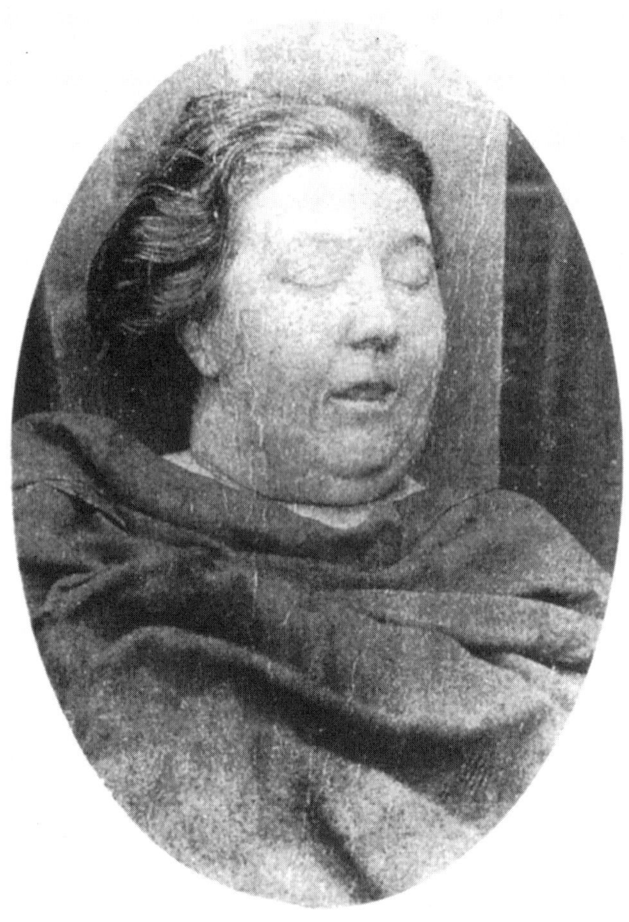

The body of Martha Tambram, shown in a mortuary after her murder on August 7, 1888. Some criminologists do not consider Tambram a Ripper victim, but others do.

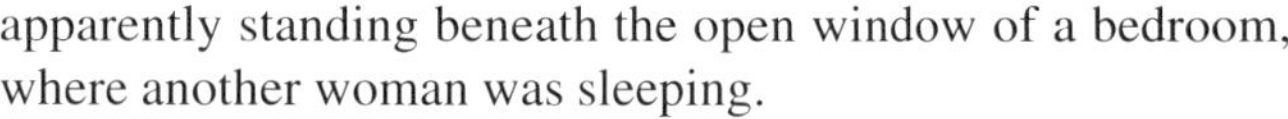

apparently standing beneath the open window of a bedroom, where another woman was sleeping.

The depth and width of the wounds, especially around the neck, caused examining doctors to believe that the killer had employed a blade from six to eight inches long. Since the incisions had been made cleanly and appropriately across the jugular vein to assure death, the examiners also speculated that the killer possessed some medical experience or knowledge of post-mortem operations.

Nichols had been married, but had left her husband, William Nichols, who was brought to the morgue to identify the mutilated remains of his estranged spouse. At first reluctant to look upon the corpse and bitterly complaining that his wife had left a good home to turn to prostitution more than three years ago, Nichols said that he did not wish to look upon her again. He did, however, view the remains and then he sobbed, while staring at the corpse and saying: "I forgive you for everything, now that I see you like this!"

After three prostitutes had been murdered, police concluded that if these victims had been slain by the same killer, he had no motive for murdering them except for an abiding hatred for prostitutes. Detectives fanned out through the East End, searching for any man who had mistreated prostitutes. The name "Leather Apron" kept recurring in their investigations. "Leather Apron" turned out to be a bootmaker named John Pizer, who had manhandled and pushed about prostitutes when he was drinking in the lowlife pubs of Whitechapel.

Pizer, who earned his sobriquet from a leather apron he wore when repairing boots, occupied his cramped workshop-lodgings, and many small, sharp knives were found on the premises. Pizer told police that the knives were essential to his bootmaking trade, and he demonstrated their uses. Moreover, his family swore that he was at home, when all three of the previous murders had occurred. He was interrogated at length and then released.

While the police had been looking for Leather Apron, constables picked up a strange-acting character named William Piggott, who bore a close resemblance to Pizer. This man had been drinking heavily in a Gravesend pub and had begun to talk to himself and chant incoherently, alarming the proprietor who called police. His clothes and one hand were bloodstained and, after considerable questioning, Piggot told detectives that he had gone to the aid of a woman who had been having some sort of fit.

As Piggott steadied her, he said, she grabbed his hand and bit it so hard that she pierced the flesh, causing blood to flow.

George Yard in Whitechapel, a dimly-lit area, where Martha Tambram was killed.

The story sounded fabricated, and Piggott was held for further questioning. He was placed in a cell, but the minute he was behind bars, he began to howl like a dog and bang his head against the walls and bars of the cell. Doctors were called and quickly pronounced Piggott insane. He was removed to a lunatic asylum.

The press by this time was screaming alarm about a berserk killer, an unnamed fiend, who lurked in the shadowy lanes and narrow streets of the East End, murdering women at random, while police seemed powerless to stop him. The slaying of Nichols was the third murder that could realistically be attributed to the Ripper. At that time, the newspapers had taken notice of the first two murders, that of Smith and Tabram, and had coupled these killings to the Nichols slaying, attributing all three killings to the same man.

Irrespective of the hindsight of Ripperologists of a century later, who insisted Nichols was the first true Ripper victim, the press of that day considered her the *third* victim and part of a one-person murder spree. All three women, Smith, Tabram and Nichols, were whores, and all three were middle-aged and down on their luck. All three were abroad in the early morning hours, and all three were found on lonely, narrow lanes with no one about.

What continued to perplex the police was the fact that not a single person had seen these women in anyone's company near the time of death and, even more puzzling, none of the victims had cried out. However, the Metropolitan Police of London did not, at that time, have investigative branches that specialized in types of crime, including prostitution. Had a vice squad as such existed at the time, police would have known *why* none of the victims before and after this time gave no call of alarm. No police officer ever came forward to describe the methods of the street whores in relationship to the murder method of Jack the Ripper.

The victims simply had no idea that they were about to be killed and never saw the long, sharp knife that Jack the Ripper wielded when he so clinically cut their throats. The practice of street whores in London at the time was to solicit customers and go to an out-of-the-way corner or back lot or alleyway to have a quick assignation. There was generally no light at all in these dark byways. Traditionally, the prostitute turned her back on the customer and flipped up her skirts, allowing entry from behind.

Standing unseen behind the victim, Jack withdrew his knife from the black surgical bag he carried, came close to the woman bending over in front of him, then reached forward, driving his knee into the small of their backs, pulling their heads back with one hand and, with the free hand, bringing the knife over the shoulder of his victim and with one or two slashes across her neck, cut her throat from behind. Pulling the knife toward him, while pushing the weight of the victim away from him, the killer unleashed great force against the blade, almost severing the necks of his victims.

Moreover, by killing in this manner, the Ripper avoided being spattered with blood. The blood shot out from the front of the victim, in the opposite direction of Jack, who was behind the victim. In this way, he avoided soaking his clothes with blood. Without being covered with blood, Jack was able to return to either his workplace or domicile without drawing

A contemporary drawing shows Constable John Neil discovering the body of Mary Ann "Polly" Nichols in Bucks Row, Whitechapel, on August 31, 1888. Many considered Nichols be the Ripper's first murder.

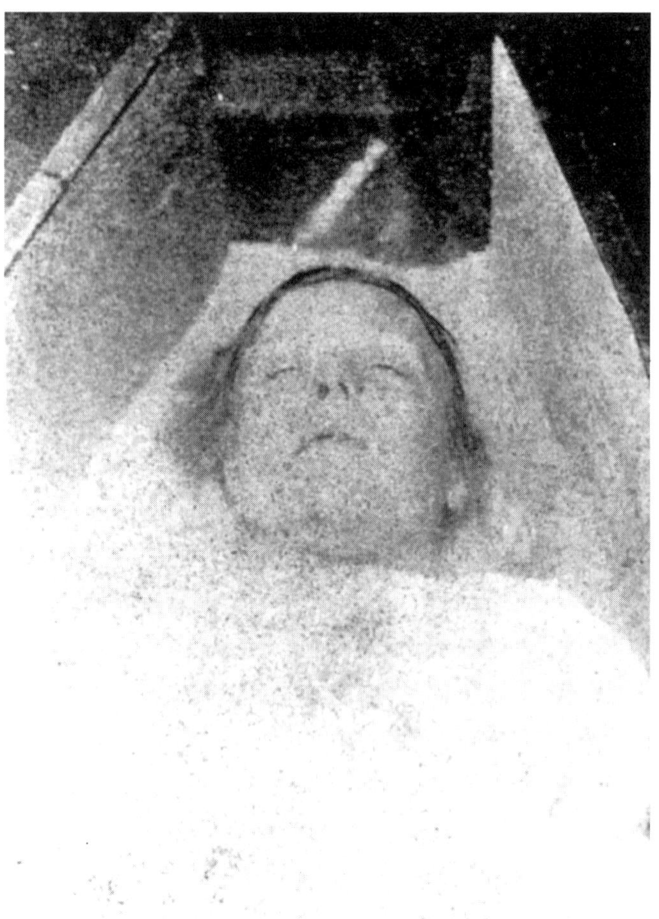

The body of Mary Ann Nichols in the mortuary (Old Montague Street Workhouse), the day after the Ripper slashed her throat to the vertebrae.

A newspaper sketch of John Pizer, who was called "Leather Apron," a suspect in the Ripper killings.

suspicion upon himself. (The murder method described by the author above is based upon coroner's reports in these cases, and, ironically, is almost identical to the method by which Nicole Brown Simpson and Ronald Goldman were murdered in Brentwood, California, on the night of June 12, 1994, by, in the author's opinion, O. J. Simpson, which allowed Simpson to escape the scene of the killings without being entirely coated with blood.)

There was much debate between investigators and medical experts at the time that the Ripper was a physician. Many doctors theorized that he could not have been so since most of his incisions were crude and often missed the mark in his search for certain organs, mistakes no professional physician would make. Yet, these long-ago observers either forgot or ignored the then training medical practices—that medical students were compelled at one time or another in those days to find and remove organs from experimental cadavers in the dark so as to become expert in locating such organs. Such was the case with the Ripper, who, after killing his victims, had to grope in the unlit byways for those organs, making his incisions as would a blind man, searching by hand over bone-protruding flesh for the location of the organs he sought.

As the Ripper killings continued, the residents of the East End, especially Whitechapel, the hub of the killing area, panicked. No one talked of anything but the deranged cutthroat, who roamed their streets, murdering at will. Police were openly jeered and derided as they made their rounds. When would the monster strike again? Terrified residents had not long to wait. Eight nights after the slaying of Nichols, on September 8, 1888, the Ripper struck again.

Annie Chapman, a 47-year-old prostitute, drunk and bragging through the pubs of Whitechapel that she would know how to deal with the killer if he came her way, staggered down Dorset Street in the early morning hours. She asked for a room at a cheap boarding house but, not having enough money, she was turned away.

Chapman lurched down the street and turned into narrow Hanbury Street. Here she was seen by a woman to stop and talk to a stranger, who was later described as about 40-years-old, wearing dark clothes, with a dark complexion, which marked him as a foreigner. He was described as a "gentleman." Chapman was seen to talk to this man in a friendly manner at 5:30 a.m. The "gentleman," according to the witness, a park keeper's wife, wore a duck-billed deerstalker hat later associated with Sherlock Holmes. The stranger was heard to say to Chapman: "Will you?" Chapman was heard to reply: "Yes." The two went down the street arm-in-arm.

A half hour later, Annie Chapman's chopped up corpse was found in a small yard behind 29 Hanbury Street. Chapman had been nearly decapitated and her head was held by a strand of flesh and some bone to her torso by a scarf she had been wearing when last seen alive. Chapman was found lying on her back with her legs drawn up, her left arm resting on her left breast. Her body had been savagely mutilated.

A doctor, who examined the corpse at the scene of the crime, tersely reported: "...small intestines and flap of the abdomen lying on the right side above right shoulder attached by a cord with the rest of the intestines inside the body, two flaps of skin from the lower part of the abdomen lying in a large quantity of blood above the left shoulder; throat cut deeply from left and back in jagged manner right around the throat." In addition, two front teeth were missing from Chapman's mouth. Even more gruesome was the fact that the murderer had removed one of the victim's kidneys and the ovaries from the body and taken these grim trophies.

A piece of leather was too conveniently left under a nearby tap. Police reasoned that the killer believed that authorities were still seeking Leather Apron, although Pizer was found and cleared two days after Chapman's murder. This seemed to be a calculated move on the part of the murderer to pin the blame for the crimes on the suspect Leather Apron (Pizer). The killer also left another false clue, a piece of a blood-soaked envelope with the crest of the Sussex Regiment upon it. The murderer was undoubtedly a newspaper reader, who kept the clips reporting all the murders.

It had been reported that several hours before her death, Martha Tabram had been seen by witnesses in the company of a soldier. Her wounds were later described as possibly having been inflicted by a soldier's knife or bayonet. It was well known that witnesses, who had seen the soldier with Tabram had scrutinized a whole company of soldiers from the Tower, who were paraded before them. Not one was identified. Obviously, the Ripper planted the torn piece of envelope to cause police to believe that a soldier still might be the culprit. Detectives, however, believed this clue was too obvious and ignored the idea of searching for a military man.

Twenty days after the slaying of Annie Chapman, the killer identified himself for the first time as Jack the Ripper by mailing a letter to the Central News Agency on September 28, 1888. Dated three days earlier, it read:

> Dear Boss,
> I keep on hearing that the police have caught me but they won't fix me just yet. I have laughed when they look so clever and talk about being on the right track. That joke is about Leather Apron gave me real fits. [This was undoubtedly a reference to the false clue the Ripper left behind after the Chapman killing.] I am down on whores and I shan't quit ripping them until I do get buckled. Grand work the last job was. I gave the lady no time to squeal. [Another reference to Chapman, the killer was taunting police with his knowledge that he murdered the woman only a short distance from a boarding house where seventeen people were sleeping in rooms with open windows.] How can they catch me now. I love my work and want to start again. You will soon hear of me with my funny little games. I saved some of the proper red stuff [blood from Chapman who had been drained of blood] in a ginger beer bottle over the last job to write with but it went thick like glue and I can't use it. Red ink is fit enough I hope *ha ha*. The next job I do I shall clip the lady's ears off and send to the police officers just for jolly wouldn't you. Keep this letter back till I do a bit more work, then give it out straight. My knife is nice and sharp and I want to get to work right away if I get a chance. Good luck.
> Yours truly, Jack the Ripper
>
> Don't mind me giving the trade name. Wasn't good enough to post this before I got all the red ink off my hands, curse it.

The postscript to this letter refers to physicians who examined the wounds made on the bodies of the Ripper's victims and stated the possibility of the killer being an unhinged doctor or a demented medical student, given the knowledge of the human anatomy and the surgical skill employed in making incisions and removing internal organs. A second letter arrived at the Central News Agency on September 30, 1888, the day of the fourth murder (or second, depending upon at which point you begin counting), a murder which Jack brazenly predicted in this missive:

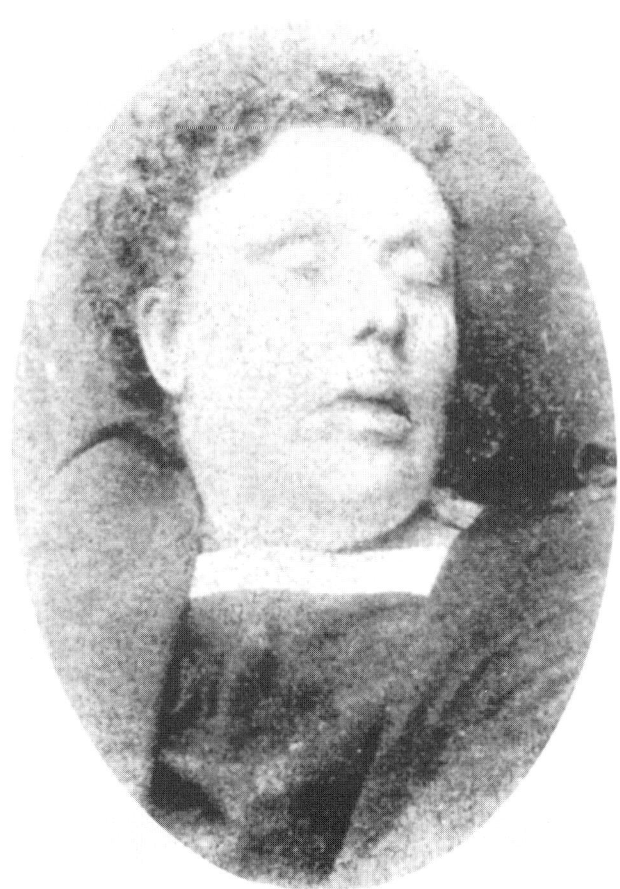

Annie Chapman, shown in a mortuary, murdered by the Ripper on September 8, 1888.

> I was not codding dear old Boss when I gave you the tip. You'll hear about saucy Jack's work tomorrow. Double event this time. Number one squealed a bit. Couldn't finish straight off. Had not time to get ears for police. Thanks for keeping last letter back till I got to work again.
> Jack the Ripper

After Jack attacked and murdered two more women in the predawn hours of September 30, 1888, the so-called "double event," he immediately sat down and wrote to the Central News Agency, boasting of the killings, couching these murders as preplanned killings. The first of these victims was Elizabeth "Long Liz" Stride, a 45-year-old Swedish prostitute. Her real name was Elizabeth Gustaafsdotter, and she was also known on police blotters as Annie Fitzgerald. At 1 a.m., Louis

The courtyard in back of 29 Hanbury Street, Spitafields, where Annie Chapman was brutally murdered and mutilated.

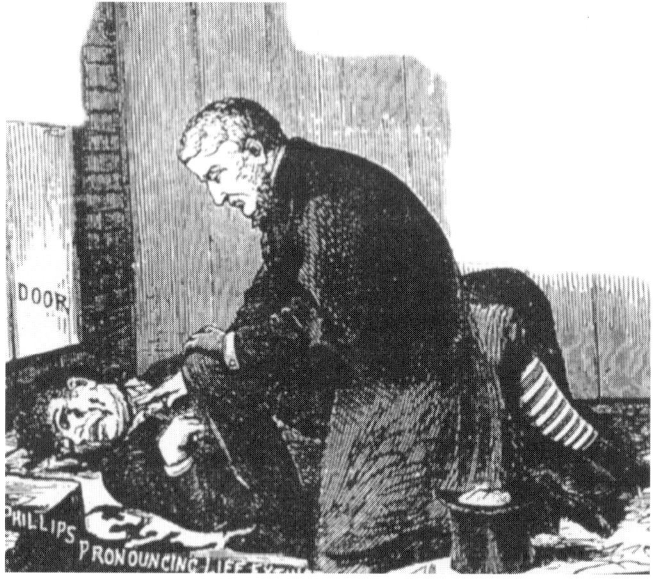

Dr. George Bagster Phillips, shown examining the mutilated corpse of Annie Chapman.

Deimschutz, a delivery man, drove his horse-drawn cart into the back yard of the International Working Men's Education Club on Berner Street, near Commercial Road. His horse's shoed hoofs clattering noisily over the cobblestones, he suddenly brought his cart to an abrupt halt when he saw a body stretched before him.

Deimschutz jumped from the cart and ran to the body of Long Liz Stride. It was warm to his touch and there was a great pool of blood, more than two quarts according to later estimates, welling about the corpse. The victim's throat had been slashed, a long, deep incision, but the Ripper had apparently been interrupted by the delivery man and had fled at the sound of his approaching cart. (He had said in his recent missive: "Couldn't finish straight off.")

At the time Jack was attacking Stride, another harlot, 43-year-old Catherine Eddowes, had been released from the Bishopsgate Police Station, where she had been placed behind bars some hours earlier for creating a drunken disturbance. Police were later criticized for turning this woman out at the very time of night, when they knew the Ripper was most actively seeking prostitutes to murder. A constable stood at the entrance to the station and saw Eddowes emerge. She turned to him and said: "Night, old cock." She then walked toward Mitre Square, Houndsditch, and painful death.

At about 1:30 a.m., Eddowes met the man known as Jack the Ripper and undoubtedly agreed to sexually service him, going off toward Mitre Square with him. Within fifteen minutes, Jack had slit her throat, viciously slashed her face, even nicking her eyelids with his slashing knife, then cut at her ears, which were left attached. ("Had not time to get ears for police," the maniac had written.) He had disemboweled Eddowes, slicing through the abdomen and removing the left kidney and entrails. The intestines, as had been the case with Annie Chapman, had been strangely thrown over the shoulder. A constable turned into tiny Mitre Square and in the corner of this dark area he thought he saw a pile of rags. He turned his light upon the heap of clothing to find the bloody remains of Catherine Eddowes.

These two killings sent the whole of London into a panic. Police Commissioner Warren sputtered apologies and promises before a disturbed Queen Victoria, who demanded action. She wanted the monster caught no matter the cost and time to the police. Warren told her that everything possible was being done to find and arrest this fiend. He stated that he had special bloodhounds out in the streets and that he was considering newly designed rubber-soled shoes for his policemen.

Warren explained to the queen that the hob-nailed boots then worn by his officers clattered loudly on cobblestones and could be heard for some distance, undoubtedly warning the Ripper of an approaching constable. The new rubber-soled shoes would allow policemen to approach in almost total silence. The queen merely clucked her disgust with such inane, straw-clutching proposals.

Meanwhile, George Lusk, a volatile resident of Whitechapel, had formed the Whitechapel Vigilance Committee, and he loudly proclaimed that if the police could not catch the Ripper then he and his bully boys, now hunting Jack in the streets in armed groups, would locate the killer and

Contemporary sketches show the "double event" in the predawn hours of September 30, 1888, the sketch above showing the discovery of the body of Elizabeth "Long Liz" Stride, on Berner Street, the sketch below showing a constable finding the mutilated corpse of Catherine Eddowes near Mitre Square.

Elizabeth Stride shown in the mortuary, her throat slashed, but otherwise unmolested—the Ripper had fled after being interrupted by an unexpected delivery man.

lynch him from the nearest lamppost. Lusk had been warned by police not to take matters into his own hands, but Lusk and his pub-crawling supporters sneered at the authorities, labeling them do-nothings. On October 16, 1888, Lusk received a small package and a note reading:

> *From Hell*
> Mr. Lusk:
> Sir I send you half the Kidne I took from one woman prasarved it for you tother piece I fried and ate it was very nise I may send you the bloody knif that took it out if you only wate a whil longer signed Catch me when you can Mishter Lusk

Inside the small package, Lusk found a human kidney and this was matched to the remains of Catherine Eddowes. This message and grisly package proved to be one of the genuine missives sent by Jack the Ripper. By this time, there were scores of pranksters and disturbed London residents inundating the police with messages and letters from the notorious Jack. The letter Lusk received was obviously disguised in ungrammatical text to convince authorities that Jack was an unschooled Irishman, particularly after the way he phonetically spelled the word "preserved" as "prasarved," giving the word a spelling in keeping with its pronunciation with a thick Irish accent.

None of this aided the police. Patrols were doubled, then tripled, and street prostitutes and inmates of bordellos were warned repeatedly to keep off the streets at night, but this was tantamount to telling these near destitute creatures to stop living. Police headquarters and Scotland Yard saw a steady stream of pickets before their entrances, all demanding action. Buckingham Palace was swamped with petitions signed by thousands of citizens from all over London. These petitions were directed at Queen Victoria and asked her to bring this horror to an end.

The queen was, of course, as powerless as the police. She spent many nervous hours deliberating over the matter. Victoria came to believe that the killer had to be a foreigner, a seaman visiting the fair city of London. It was inconceivable to her that the monster could be an Englishman. No native son, she was convinced, possessed the brutality, the bestial inclinations, to perform the kind of slaughterhouse acts committed by Jack the Ripper. He had to be an alien from foreign shores.

Victoria wrote to her home secretary: "Have the cattle boats and passenger boats been examined? Has an investigation been made as to the number of single men occupying rooms to themselves? The murderer's clothes must be saturated with blood and kept somewhere." Queen Victoria was aware of the woeful ineffectiveness of her policemen. Following the murder of Mary Kelly, supposedly the last of the Ripper's victims, Victoria wrote on November 11, 1888, to Lord Salisbury, her prime minister: "All these courts must be lit and our detectives improved. They are not what they should be."

Jack the Ripper had become a national calamity. This was never more clearly illustrated than by the fact that Lord Salisbury actually convened a cabinet meeting specifically designed to deal with him. Yet little came of the meeting. Sir Charles Warren could only shake his head, stating once more that he had taken extraordinary measures to track down the Ripper, that he had set bloodhounds on the killer's trail. He failed to mention that the two bloodhounds employed for this purpose, Barnaby and Burgho, had been trained to follow what the police thought might be the scent of the killer, taken from the piece of leather and other scraps left at the scenes of the killings.

Warren did not mention to Lord Salisbury that he himself had pretended to be Jack, having the bloodhounds following *his* scent to see if they could perform their duties and how he had run so far ahead of the dogs that he had lost them. The dogs themselves then broke loose, ran away, and had to be hunted down by other dogs and police. The use of the bloodhounds was an utter failure and was later lampooned in the press.

Warren was the worst sort of man to be in charge of this impossible case. He was an old-fashioned bureaucrat, one without imagination, who followed traditional police methods that were obviously obsolete in dealing with a killer who murdered without apparent motive, selecting victims at random. Warren's concept of catching the lunatic was simply to throw more men into the dark, labyrinthine streets of Whitechapel and surrounding areas, but these dragnets were also useless.

Four, sometimes six constables together clumped along noisily through the fog-bound alleyways, their approach so obvious that they might as well have been preceded by brass bands bleating bugles and thumping drums. The furtive and slinking Jack could easily avoid these large patrols. And who were they looking for, really? An obscure man wearing dark clothes, a "gentleman," a man wearing the commonly worn deerstalker hat? How would they know their man unless they actually caught Jack in the act, leaning over his victim, slicing away.

A medical sketch provided at an inquest shows the body of Catherine Eddowes, horribly mutilated by Jack the Ripper.

Warren also did not tell Lord Salisbury that he had wiped out clues as to the possible identity of the Ripper. Following the double killing of Stride and Eddowes, a constable had found a scrap of cloth soaked with blood, a piece of fabric torn from Eddowes' dress and apparently used to wipe off Jack's bloody knife. This bit of apron was found on Goulston Street near Mitre Square, and when the constable turned to a nearby wall and flashed his light upon it, he saw a message written there. It read:

> The juwes are not the
> men that will be blamed
> for nothing.
> Jack The Ripper

The wall writing had been done only a few hours after the Eddowes killing, according to authorities. Sir Charles Warren was called to the spot, where he looked at the writing, and then quickly ordered the words wiped off the wall. It was obvious to him, or so he later said, that the Ripper was attempting to place the responsibility for the killings on a Jew or a Jewish group of killers. Warren's apologists later claimed that the commissioner had acted in the best interest of the community and by wiping out this racial slur, had prevented anti-Semitic outbursts. There were tens of thousands of Jewish immigrants then living in London, with more arriving each day from the continent. Dislike for Jews was widespread. Yet Warren, in his zeal to keep the peace, had violated a cardinal rule of police work. He had destroyed evidence, important information that begged for analysis. By wiping away the Ripper's words, he made it impossible to have experts analyze the handwriting.

Warren had been motivated to destroy this wall note for another reason, some later argued. He was a high-ranking mem-

George Lusk, the tempestuous leader of the Whitechapel Vigilance Committee, who reportedly received a letter from Jack the Ripper.

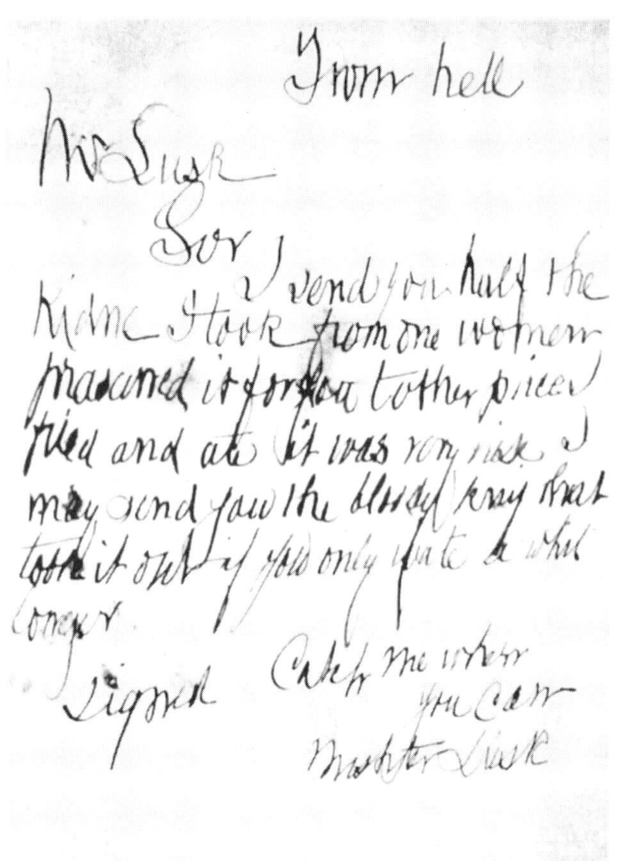

From hell

Mr Lusk
Sor
I send you half the Kidne I took from one women prasarved it for you tother piece I fried and ate it was very nise I may send you the bloody knif that took it out if you only wate a whil longer

signed Catch me when you Can Mishter Lusk

The letter reportedly written by Jack the Ripper and received by George Lusk on October 16, 1888.

ber of the Masons, the secret fraternal association, and he immediately recognized the peculiar spelling of the word "Juwes," instead of "Jews." This spelling was the ancient way of spelling the word in old Masonic rites.

Warren feared, it was later conjectured, that the true link to be made to this wall writing would be to the Masons. Moreover, the disemboweling of the victims, particularly in the instances where the entrails had been thrown over the right shoulder, was reportedly in keeping with ancient Masonic rites of sacrifice. It would be claimed, many years after, that Jack was a representative of a high-positioned radical Masonic group that had conspired to rid London of its plague of prostitutes.

On November 9, 1888, Mary Jane Kelly, another prostitute, was murdered by Jack the Ripper. This was the most gruesome killing of all. Mary Jane Kelly, also known as Mary Ann Kelly or Mary Jeannette Kelly, was unlike all the previous victims. She was only twenty-four and was attractive and intelligent. She was in the prime of life and made a good living at her unsavory trade. Kelly had lived with a fish peddler until the couple quarreled and he moved out. She then turned to full-time prostitution, although she had practiced the trade on and off, even when living with other men.

Kelly maintained her own small lodgings, a first-floor room with a separate entrance at 13 Miller's Court near Dorset Street. Behind on her rent, Mary Kelly began to solicit men with regularity on November 7, 1888. Two nights later, on November 9, at 2 a.m., Mary Kelly approached a man she knew and tried to borrow six pence. He refused and, a few moments later, the man saw Kelly standing in the street talking to "a well-dressed gentleman."

Between 3:30 a.m. and 4 a.m., Elizabeth Praten, who lived in a room above Kelly's, heard Kelly cry out: "Oh, murder!" Praten was half asleep and thought she was having a dream. She went back to sleep. Such cries in that crime-infested area were commonplace and did not necessarily mean that someone was being murdered, but that there was a domestic battle, a drunken brawl, at worst, a robbery taking place.

At 10:45 a.m. the next morning, rent collector Thomas Bowyer knocked on Kelly's door. Getting no response, he peered through the first-floor window and gasped in horror. Next to the bed close to the window, Bowyer saw two mounds of flesh, carved as if by a butcher, and on the bed, the gutted body of Mary Jane Kelly. There was a huge pool of blood beneath the bed. Bowyer ran for the owner who returned with him, looked into the window, and *then* summoned the police.

Police arrived and blocked off the small street, posting guards at the door to Kelly's small room. No officers entered the premises while detectives waited for Sir Charles Warren. The police commissioner had given strict orders that, in the event of another Ripper killing, he was to be summoned immediately and no officer was to do anything until his arrival.

This day, however, was Lord Mayor's Day, and there were festivities and parades only a few blocks from the murder scene. News of the Kelly slaying was captured in headlines within a few hours, and newsboys by the dozens raced through the streets shouting: "Murder, horrible murder!" The Ripper had chosen this particular day, it was later claimed, to upstage the lord mayor of London, such was Jack's bloated ego.

Warren could not be found, and finally other officers ordered Kelly's door broken down. A half dozen officers took turns battering the door with their shoulders and when it finally gave way, these burly men rushed inside, only to stagger outside again to retch from the awful carnage they had seen. There was very little left of Mary Kelly to examine. The Ripper had apparently spent more than an hour mutilating the corpse after murdering the woman by slitting her throat.

This was the first murder Jack had committed indoors and he had taken his time in cutting up his victim, enjoying an orgy of bloodletting. It was Jack's most vile and disgusting crime. Even the doctors who arrived to make their official report found themselves queasy at the sight of the devastated remains of Mary Kelly. The report, published in its entirety the next day in *The Illustrated Police News,* read:

> The throat had been cut right across with a knife, nearly severing the head from the body. The abdomen had been partially ripped open, and both the breasts had been cut from the body. The left arm, like the head, hung to the body by the skin only. The nose had been cut off and the forehead skinned, and the thighs, down to the feet, stripped of the flesh. The abdomen had been slashed with a knife across down-

METROPOLITAN POLICE.

Fac-simile of Letter and Post Card received by Central News Agency.

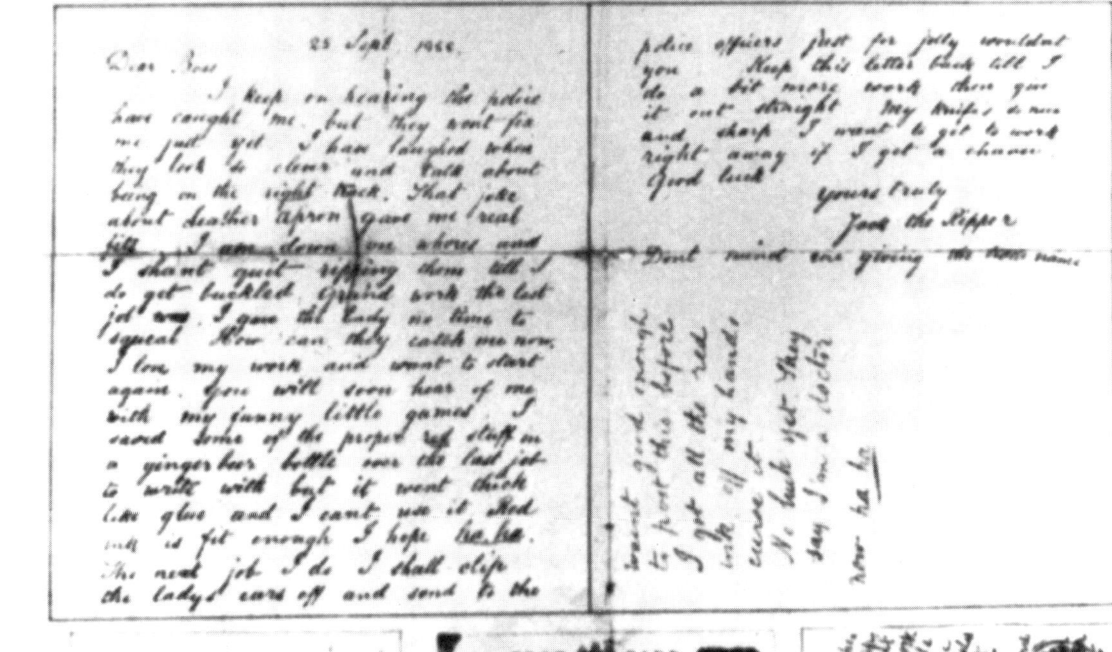

25 Sept. 1888.

Dear Boss,

I keep on hearing the police have caught me but they wont fix me just yet. I have laughed when they look so clever and talk about being on the right track. That joke about Leather Apron gave me real fits. I am down on whores and I shant quit ripping them till I do get buckled. Grand work the last job was. I gave the lady no time to squeal. How can they catch me now. I love my work and want to start again. You will soon hear of me with my funny little games. I saved some of the proper red stuff in a ginger beer bottle over the last job to write with but it went thick like glue and I cant use it. Red ink is fit enough I hope ha. ha. The next job I do I shall clip the ladys ears off and send to the police officers just for jolly wouldnt you. Keep this letter back till I do a bit more work then give it out straight. My knife's so nice and sharp I want to get to work right away if I get a chance. Good luck.

Yours truly

Jack the Ripper

Dont mind me giving the trade name

wasnt good enough to post this before I got all the red ink off my hands curse it. No luck yet. They say I'm a doctor now ha ha

The Boss
Central News Office
London City

POST CARD
Central News Office
London E.C

Any person recognising the handwriting is requested to communicate with the nearest Police Station.

The letter sent to "Dear Boss," which was postmarked September 27, 1888 and sent to the Central News Agency. It was signed "Jack the Ripper," and dated September 25, 1888, and was reproduced and distributed by the Metropolitan Police.

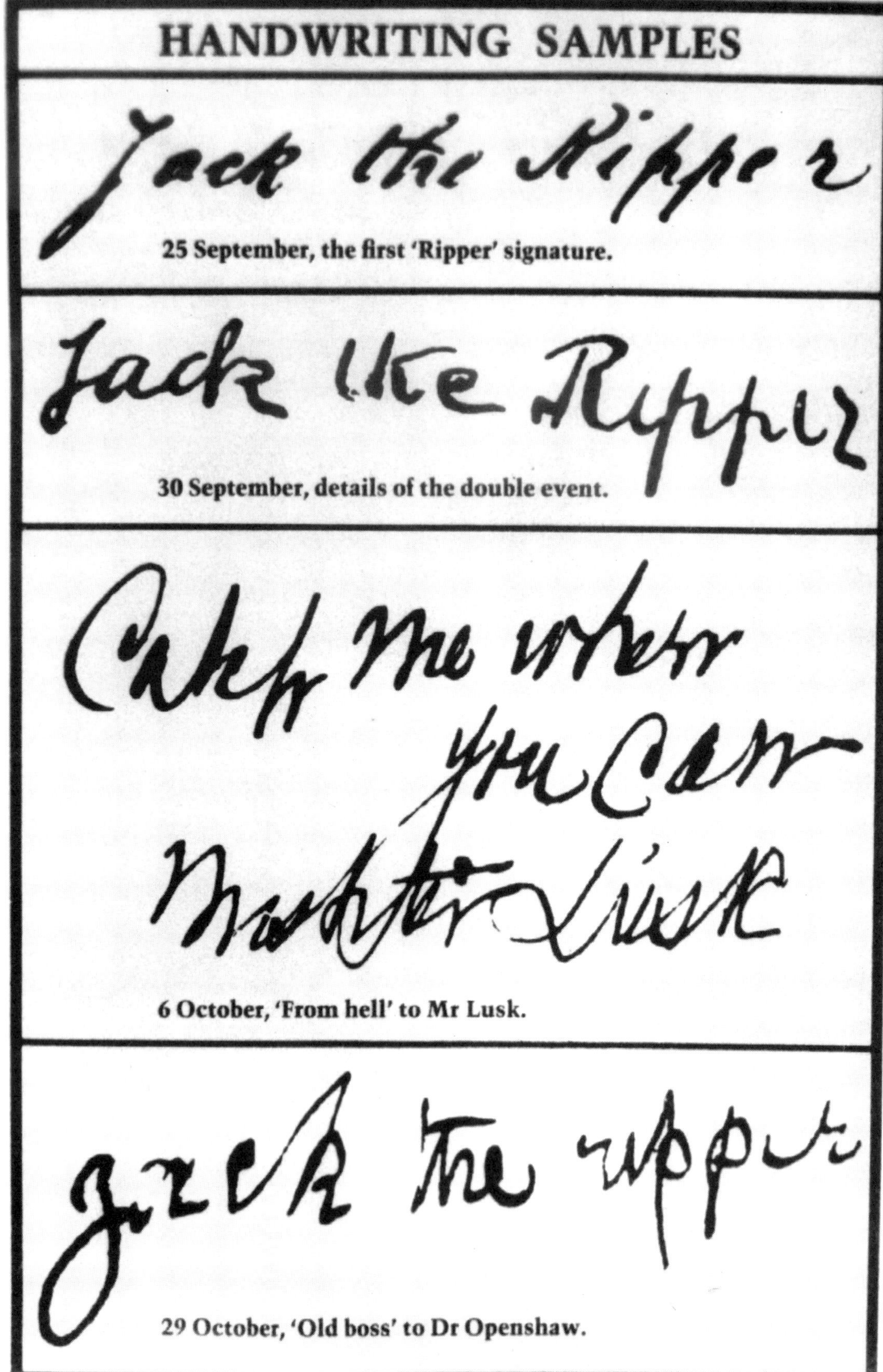

HANDWRITING SAMPLES
25 September, the first 'Ripper' signature.
30 September, details of the double event.
6 October, 'From hell' to Mr Lusk.
29 October, 'Old boss' to Dr Openshaw.

The various handwriting styles of the person(s) sending four letters purportedly sent by Jack the Ripper; each of the samples show different writing styles, but the killer may have disguised his handwriting in each or all of the letters. Graphologists studying these handwriting styles came to no revealing conclusions.

Home Secretary Henry Matthews, who could give no satisfactory answers to Queen Victoria regarding Jack the Ripper.

Sir Charles Warren, head of the Metropolitan Police, who thought to capture Jack the Ripper by ordering rubber-soled shoes for his policemen (so they could quietly creep up on the lurking maniac) and employing bloodhounds that promptly got lost in the East End. Warren also destroyed valuable evidence and otherwise confounded his own investigators in a bumbling investigation that led to his resignation.

> wards, and the liver and entrails wrenched away. The entrails and other portions of the frame were missing, but the liver, etc., were placed between the feet of this poor victim. The flesh from the thighs and legs, together with the breasts and nose, had been placed by the murderer on the table, and one of the hands of the dead woman had been pushed into her stomach.

This savage killing established a new hallmark in the history of British murder. Nothing like it had ever been seen or reported. The mutilation of Mary Kelly had been ferocious. The madman had indulged himself in the most bestial acts, taking his time as he sliced and cut away the remains. So much blood had been produced that Jack had to wipe it away with rags, which he burned in the small stove as he worked. These charred remains were later found in the grate. He had also burned a hat and portions of other clothes that may have been his own blood-soaked garments.

Mary Kelly's daily clothes were found neatly folded on a nearby chair so it was assumed that she had entered the room with Jack, disrobed in front of him, and then went conveniently to the bed, where, instead of making love, he reached out with his lethal knife. It may have been that the Ripper, coated with blood, had burned his own clothes and left by the window, where traces of blood were found, wearing only a long cloak and his boots.

When Police Commissioner Warren heard the news of the ghastly murder in Miller's Court, he only shook his head. He resigned his post a short time later, admitting his utter failure to capture the fiend. The killing of Mary Kelly, in the staunch opinion of most Ripperologists, was the last murder committed by Jack the Ripper, but there were at least two, perhaps three more murders occurring after this time, that could be attributed to Jack. They fit his *modus operandi* to some degree.

Elizabeth Jackson's headless corpse was found floating in the Thames in June 1889. She was later identified from scars and was a known prostitute operating in the Chelsea

Mary Jane Kelly, the youngest and most attractive of the Ripper's known victims; she invited him into her one-room flat on the night of November 9, 1888.

area. On the night of July 17-18, 1889, Alice McKenzie, a prostitute working in Whitechapel, was found with her throat cut from ear to ear and her sex organs cut out. The last murder of any similarity close to the time of Jack's known killings was that of Frances Coles, a street whore commonly known as "Carroty Nell" because of her red hair. She was found on February 13, 1891, in Swallow Gardens, Whitechapel, with her throat slashed and mutilations on her abdomen.

In the course of the last murder, Constable Ernest Thompson, out for the first time on night patrol, turned into Swallow Gardens and saw a man bending over Frances Coles. He stood up and fled, running at great speed and soon disappeared. Thompson rushed to the side of Coles, who was still alive. She remained unconscious for a few hours, but doctors were unable to save her or to revive her so she gave no information about her killer. This may have been the only occasion where the Ripper was seen by a police officer, but Thompson's description of the man was vague at best since he did not get a good look at the man who was quite a distance from him when Thompson entered the darkened area of Swallow Gardens.

There were descriptions of Jack the Ripper, many of them, provided by witnesses who came forward later to state that they had seen men with the women, who were killed by the maniac. Jack was described as being short and stout, standing only five feet, five inches. He was also described as tall, five feet, ten inches, and slender. He was described as wearing the clothes of a gentleman, or those worn by the upper class: tailored suits, a deerstalker hat, a dark slouch hat, a derby, an Inverness cloak or a long dark coat, and, in many instances, carrying a small black bag, the type that doctors or surgeons used.

It was speculated that inside that bag Jack carried the tools of his horrific trade, his sharp knives, perhaps scalpels and other medical instruments. Jack was described by many as a "foreigner," a man who had a dark complexion and dark hair. It was not by happenstance that Jack, observed by others while talking to his victims-to-be, stood purposely in a way as to shield his face, either turning his back to others or standing in the shadows, the brim of his hat pulled low over his forehead in order to hide his face.

One of those who gave the most detailed description of the Ripper, if he was the Ripper, was George Hutchinson, who knew Mary Jane Kelly. He told police that he had seen Kelly only an hour before her murder, at 2 a.m. Hutchinson said that Kelly picked up a man while walking to her lodgings, a slender man who stood about five feet, six inches, with a pale face and a dark, thin mustache turned up at the ends. He was well-dressed and Hutchinson made a point of saying that the man looked "Jewish" to him, and that he would estimate his age at thirty-five. He wore a long, dark, well-tailored coat that hung loosely on him. Beneath the overcoat, he wore a dark-colored jacket and a light-colored waistcoat. A gleaming gold chain crossed the waistcoat from pocket to pocket.

The man also wore dark trousers with white-buttoned gaiters, a white shirt, a black tie, and an expensive horseshoe pin affixed to the tie. It was this description that would be fixed in the minds of all who thought about Jack the Ripper for decades to come, a dashing and handsome young man, wealthy, polite, a gentleman whose good looks and fine manner lured women into the arms of a homicidal maniac.

This man, Hutchinson observed, was standing on Thrawl Street and, as Kelly passed him, he gently tapped her on the shoulder. She stopped, smiled, and began talking to him. "All right," she was heard to say to the man.

"You will be all right for what I have told you," the man said in a low, smooth voice.

"All right, my dear," Kelly told the dark man. She put her arm around his shoulder and began to lead him toward her lodgings. "Come along. You will be comfortable."

The couple strolled past Hutchinson who followed them to Kelly's first-floor lodgings. They went inside and Hutchinson saw a candle being lit through the window. He stood some distance away from the small one-room flat, curious, he told police later, about such an aristocratic-looking customer. He wanted to see how long this man would stay with Kelly. Hutchinson left, he said, after about half an hour, which would make the time about 2:30 a.m. It was a short time after this, according to police estimates, that Jack the Ripper withdrew his knife and began to carve up Mary Kelly.

A few hours after police had arrived at the gory scene of Mary Kelly's blood-spattered room, a man who matched Hutchinson's description stopped before a Mrs. Paumier, who sold roasted chestnuts. He was a gentleman wearing a long dark coat, a black silk hat, and a thin black mustache turned up at the ends. He gripped a small black bag. "Have you heard that there has been another murder?" asked this man of Mrs. Paumier.

"I have," replied the chestnut vendor.

"I know more of it than you do," the handsome stranger said through a strange grin. He then walked away. Mrs. Paumier told police that this very same man had stopped three women, all prostitutes, on the night of Mary Kelly's murder, offering them money to go with him. All three women, for various reasons, refused. The third woman asked the man: "What's in that bag you're carrying?"

The well-dressed stranger began walking away, but said in a low, menacing voice: "Something the ladies don't like." When reports of the shiny black bag carried by the man thought to be the Ripper were published, these bags, popular with doctors and professional people, suddenly went out of style. No one dared to carry this kind of bag lest he be suspected of being the worst murderer London had ever seen.

How, everyone asked, did the Ripper manage to leave Whitechapel and other murder areas? Police were everywhere in the streets after the bodies were discovered, covering all major exits of the district. One theory had it that Jack never left the district after committing murder. He simply went to one of the thousands of the small boarding houses in the area and rented a cheap room for the night. At dawn, he washed, dressed, and casually left the area. Yet the identity of the Ripper has continued to plague police, psychiatrists, amateur sleuths, and crime historians.

A contemporary sketch shows Mary Kelly taking a well-dressed Ripper into her small flat on the last night of her life. He carries the little black bag in this sketch, one which reportedly contained the knives and scalpels he used in his murders.

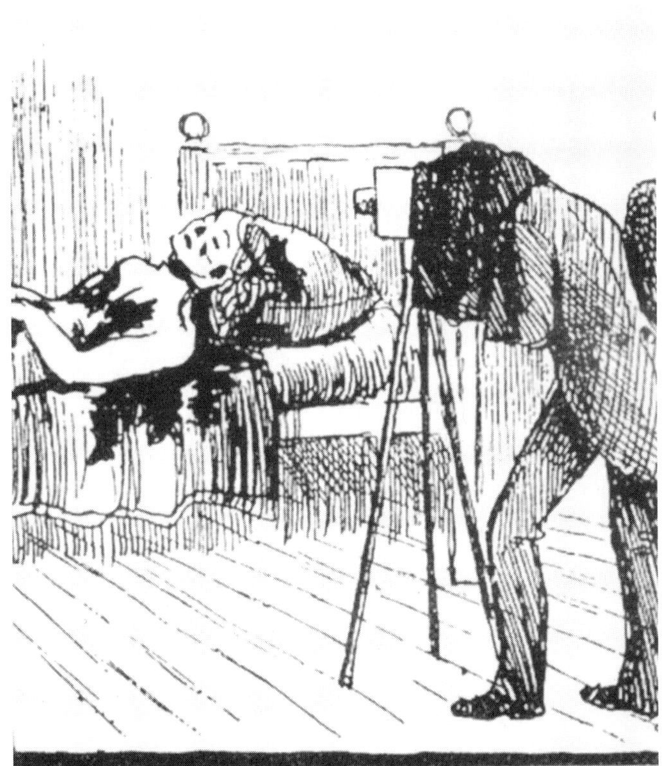

A contemporary sketch depicts a police photographer capturing the image of Mary Kelly's mutilated corpse at 13 Miller's Court. Police photos captured the savage destruction of the victim, along with the killer's bloody fingerprints.

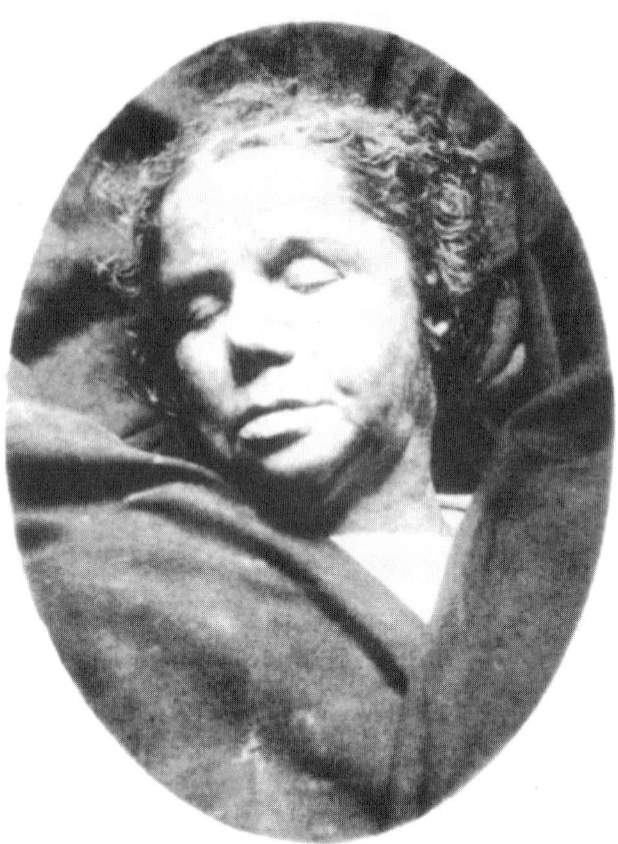

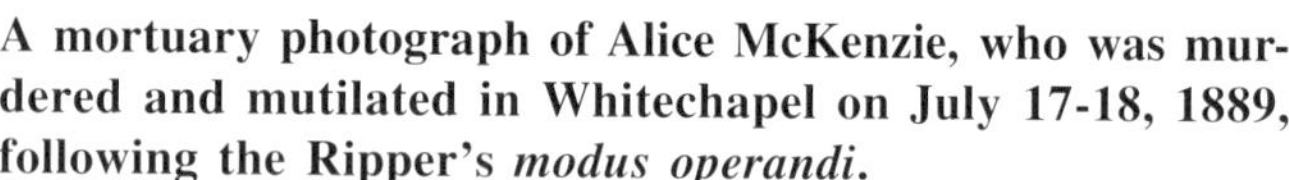

A mortuary photograph of Alice McKenzie, who was murdered and mutilated in Whitechapel on July 17-18, 1889, following the Ripper's *modus operandi*.

The body of Frances Coles, shown in the mortuary following her murder on February 13, 1891, who, like McKenzie, was killed in a Ripper-like slaying.

The police did have suspects, 176 of them, but none were charged with the killings. Theories abound to this day and many suspects were offered as likely candidates for the gory role of Jack the Ripper. None of these individuals were ever established as the real serial killer. Some had criminal records, some were mad, some were entirely innocent, but their station in life and previous indiscretions caused sensation-seeking writers to brand them guilty.

One of the most impossible of the suspects was a mad Russian physician, Dr. Alexander Pedachenko. He was reportedly sent to England by the Okhrana, the Czarist secret police, to embarrass British detectives by committing murders the London police could not solve. It was also claimed in another version of the Pedachenko tale that this madman had murdered several women in Russia after the *modus operandi* of the Ripper, but, because of his high social position, was sent to England, where he continued his slaughtering ways. He was also known as Michael Ostrog, Mikhail Ostrong, Vassily Knoovalov, and Andrey Luiskovo. Pedachenko worked at a clinic in London's East End and reportedly treated Martha Tabram, Mary Nichols, Annie Chapman, and Mary Kelly.

Pedachenko was reported to be the Ripper in a manuscript found in the basement of Gregory Rasputin after the Mad Monk's assassination in 1916. The manuscript, written in French, was examined by William Le Queux, a journalist, who had a ravenous appetite for the sensational and whose research was later discredited as shoddy. His tale was nevertheless later supported by mystery writers Sapper and E. Phillips Oppenheim. But others have pointed out that Rasputin did not have a basement in his house, neither wrote nor read French, and was not in the least interested in criminals. Dr. Thomas Dutton, a friend of Chief Inspector Frederick Abberline, who was in charge of the Ripper investigations for Scotland Yard, believed that Pedachenko was the best suspect in the Ripper case, according to one report, but his reasons were never made public.

Sometime in late 1888, Pedachenko supposedly left London, returned to Russia, and lived in St. Petersburg, where he killed a woman and was sent to a lunatic asylum for life. Sir Basil Thompson, head of Scotland Yard's Criminal Investigation Department, was convinced to his dying days that Pedachenko was Jack the Ripper.

Another medical man, Dr. Stanley by name, was another suspect. He reportedly contracted syphilis from Mary Kelly and went in search of her, killing off her friends and associates before tracking her down and cutting her body to pieces in his blind vengeance. Dr. Stanley supposedly died in Buenos Aires in 1929, from the ravages of Kelly's disease, after confessing his grim crimes to a student. Very little exists to even prove that a Dr. Stanley existed, and, according to the precise records of the General Medical Council of Great Britain, no Dr. Stanley practiced in London in 1888-1889.

A man named V. Kosminski was also a suspect. He was described as "a vice-ridden Polish Jew" and lived in Whitechapel, where he was known to have abused prostitutes whom he threatened to "slice up some day." Kosminski was arrested in March 1889 for attacking several people and he was quickly judged to have homicidal tendencies. He, like Pedachenko, was sent to an asylum, where he later died. Thomas Cutbush was arrested on March 5, 1891, a month after the murder of Coles, who was possibly the last Ripper victim.

Thomas Sadler is shown in this sketch with murder victim Frances Coles; Sadler was thought to be the Ripper, but prosecutors could not prove a case against him, although police remained convinced that he was, at least, guilty of the murder of Frances Coles.

Cutbush had been stabbing women in the buttocks. He was also determined to be insane and he was shipped off to an asylum. A painter and close friend of Oscar Wilde named Frank Miles was, many years later, also claimed by some to be the notorious Ripper. Patricia Cornwell, in a highly publicized 2002 book, claimed that another painter, Walter Richard Sickert, was the Ripper, but she based her shaky "evidence" on theories rooted to Sickert's notes, memoirs, sketches and paintings and her claim was mostly dismissed by serious criminologists.

Even a newspaper writer of the gaslight era, one Roslyn D'Onston, was, decades later, named as the Ripper. A failed physician, who was also an alcoholic and drug addict as well as a friend of black magic advocate, Aleister Crowley, D'Onston, it was said, actually killed the whores of Whitechapel in order to write about them for London's newspapers. He became a suspect when he included in his detailed reports information that only the Ripper would have known, or so it was claimed. Yet D'Onston was never charged and, if he was ever picked up by the police and questioned, records of this detention have been lost.

A resident who boarded at 27 Sun Street in Finsbury Square, G. Wentworth Bell Smith, became another strong suspect, at least as far as the killings of Nichols, Chapman, Stride, Eddowes, and Kelly were concerned. Smith, a solicitor of a trust society in Toronto, Canada, was the role model for Marie Belloc-Lowndes' *The Lodger*, her imaginative profile of Jack (which was later made into a silent film by Alfred Hitchcock). Smith was forever complaining to his landlord, E. Callaghan, about the whores in the streets and how these strumpets had the audacity to enter churches. "They should all be drowned," Smith once told Callaghan.

Smith was a nocturnal prowler who left Callaghan's house late at night, wearing rubber-soled shoes and a long dark coat. He said that he was an insomniac and would often return just before the dawn with early-edition newspapers beneath his

Inspector Frederick George Abberline, right, is shown interviewing fruit peddler Matthew Packer, who sold grapes to a young man shortly before Elizabeth Stride was murdered; a grapestalk was clutched in Stride's hand when her body was found. Abberline was in charge of the Ripper investigation, a reliable but unimaginative officer with limited perspectives.

Sergeant George Godley, who worked for Abberline in the Ripper investigations; he energetically tracked down suspects and may have inadvertently interviewed the Ripper himself when talking to one of the interns at the Whitechapel clinic.

arm. On occasions, Smith left Callaghan's boarding house with a small black shiny bag. When Smith was in his room, he paced the floor constantly, his loud treading heard by Callaghan who lived below. Smith was a paranoid and expected trouble at any moment. He kept three loaded revolvers in his bureau and would stand in front of it whenever anyone was in his room with him, ready to reach for these weapons at any moment. Smith left Callaghan's house in early 1889 and was never seen again.

Various nondescript and anonymous suspects were dredged up with considerable effort to identify the elusive Jack. One preposterous claim was that the killer was a Jewish *shochet,* the slaughtering butcher who killed animals according to Talmudic law. This theory is rooted in the fact that there was a large Jewish population in Whitechapel at the time of the murders and therefore many such workers and abattoirs performed the ritualistic butchering for Jewish meat shops. These slaughterers possessed the sharp knives and the ability used in the attacks on the murdered women, but they lacked motive. Other than technique, there was little credence in this theory.

Frederick Bailey Deeming was another suspect, a serial killer and bigamist (see chapter on Bigamy), who had killed his wife and children in England and then, in 1891, fled to Australia, where he murdered another wife and was about to kill a third woman when apprehended. Deeming, who was executed on May 23, 1892, claimed while awaiting the hangman that he was Jack the Ripper. But this was mere boasting and an attempt to prolong his own life by being sent back to England, where he hoped to be tried for the Ripper killings and then prove himself innocent, possibly evading the gallows. Deeming, nevertheless, according to his documented movements, could not have been at the scenes of the murders committed by Jack.

Michael Ostrog, also known as Dr. Alexander Pedachenko, who was a strong suspect in the Ripper case.

Another serial killer, Dr. Thomas Neill Cream (see Serial Killers), who had murdered several people in the U.S. and who poisoned London prostitutes in 1891-1892, went to the scaffold on November 15, 1892. He was heard to say by the executioner, only a moment before he dropped through the trap: "I am Jack..." The rope cut off the final words, "the Ripper." It was this last act of vanity and a final taunt to the police that caused Cream to be considered a prime suspect in the Ripper killings.

Cream, however, according to prison records in Illinois, was sent to Joliet State Prison on November 1, 1881, and was not released until July 31, 1891, long after the Ripper murders had been committed. Moreover, Cream's method of murder differed widely from that of Jack. He was a sly killer, poisoning all his victims, and his timid personality would never have permitted him to perform the slaughter that Jack so much enjoyed. Being a sickly weakling, Cream lacked psychological and physical strength, whereas Jack the Ripper was obviously in top physical condition, judging from his ability to run from the police and move with such lightning speed when murdering his victims.

One of the most popular suspects, the favorite among police officials, was Montague John Druitt, a handsome young man who came from a well-to-do family. He had graduated from Oxford and probably studied medicine for about a year, which would explain his ability to murder with surgical precision if, indeed, he was the serial killer. Druitt was left little money upon the death of his father and he became a barrister, but his practice failed. Next, Druitt took a job as a schoolteacher in Blackheath. He was dismissed in 1888 for getting "into trouble." Druitt, apparently a homosexual, had taken liberties with a young boy, according to one account, and had been summarily fired. Druitt's mother, by this time, had been institutionalized, and it was later learned that there was a streak of insanity running through Druitt's family.

Following Druitt's dismissal from his teaching job, he moved to Whitechapel and wandered its streets day and night, living hand-to-mouth. Reports of his exact whereabouts during the Ripper killings were vague at best. Some said he was present in Whitechapel at the time, while others claimed that he had

Journalist William Le Queux supported the theory that Ostrog was the Ripper.

already been sent to an asylum. Druitt was despondent but not violent. He had no criminal background and had never committed an act of violence. Druitt was released from an asylum toward the end of 1888 and wrote a note to himself, which was later found by his brother. It read: "Since Friday I felt I was going to be like mother and the best thing for me was to die." He disappeared on December 3, 1888.

A month later constables fished Druitt's badly decomposed body from the Thames River. Druitt had loaded his pockets with rocks and had drowned himself. The reason why Druitt remained the favorite suspect for police was that he committed suicide shortly after the murder of Mary Kelly, who was considered the last authentic Ripper victim. But this was merely a convenience for the police, whose officials, to quiet apprehension, concluded publicly that the Ripper killings ended after Kelly's death. Yet, as stated earlier, there were several similar deaths as late as 1891. Druitt became a suspect only by reason of the time of his death. As such, he was no suspect at all.

George Chapman was one of the most promising suspects. A Polish immigrant, Chapman's real name was Severin Antoniovich Klosowski. He had worked in a hospital in Prague before emigrating to England. He worked as a barber's surgeon in Whitechapel during the time of the Ripper killings, and possessed sharp knives with which he removed warts and moles, as well as practicing minor bloodletting to "clean the blood," a primitive medical technique that even by the 1880s had fallen into disfavor. Chapman went on to murder three women, all common-law wives or mistresses, from 1897 to 1902, but his method of murder was poison, not throat-slitting. Chapman was hanged on April 7, 1903.

After Chapman's arrest, Chief Inspector Abberline, who had been in charge of the investigations into the Ripper killings, went to his one-time assistant in that case, Inspector George Godley and told him: "You've got Jack the Ripper at last!" He never explained this remark, but it was later thought that Chapman had been on Abberline's suspect list in 1888 when he was desperately and fruitlessly searching for the evasive Jack.

It was later speculated that though Chapman murdered those women close to him with poison, he could have very well have employed the more gruesome method of slitting the throats and disemboweling whores with whom he was not associated. He may have believed that poison would not be as readily identified and that by killing those close to him with this method he could evade detection. This remained speculation. Chapman never confessed to any of his killings.

Dr. Thomas Neill Cream, who was hanged in 1892 for poisoning several women, reportedly claimed to be the Ripper just before he went through the trap.

Another latter-day suspect was the unnamed secretary of William Booth, founder of the Salvation Army. According to Booth, his secretary stated a few days before the slaying of Frances Coles in 1891: "Carroty Nell will be the next to go." The secretary disappeared after Frances "Carroty Nell" Coles was slain on Feb. 13, 1891. Thomas Sadler, an alcoholic railroad worker, was later claimed to be Coles' killer. He had been arrested as a strong suspect in the killing of Alice McKenzie in 1889 but, because of lack of evidence, he was never charged with this killing or that of Coles, whom he also knew.

There were those, including the redoubtable creator of Sherlock Holmes, Arthur Conan Doyle, who believed that a woman, a midwife, was the real Jack the Ripper, "Jill the Ripper," according to some. This theory holds that "Jill" was a midwife who had been sent to prison for performing illegal abortions. Upon her release, this powerful, unhinged woman haunted the streets of Whitechapel, taking her vengeance out on prostitutes, careful to dissect her victims with some surgical skill, which midwives then possessed, and especially mutilate the sex organs of her victims in a throwback to her previous profession.

Montague John Druitt, who drowned himself in the Thames and became a Ripper suspect in the eyes of the police, who conveniently closed the case with Druitt's death.

Woman killer George Chapman, a poisoner like Cream, who was hanged in 1903, but who was thought to be the Ripper by Inspector Frederick George Abberline.

Roslyn D'Onston (R. D. Stephenson), an alcoholic writer and drug addict, who was also thought to be the Ripper.

Spiritualist Robert James Lees, who saw the Ripper in "a vision," and later followed the "guilty" man.

Where Doyle looked for suspects in low places, others saw the Ripper as a member of the professional class, the idle rich, or even royalty. One account insists that Dr. William Gull, physician to Queen Victoria, was the Ripper. Spiritualist William Lees, who had performed séances for the queen, envisioned several Ripper murders and was so terrified that he fled to the continent.

Lees returned after these murders and, when getting off a bus, saw a man he intuitively felt was the killer. He followed this man to Gull's mansion and then confronted the man, who turned out to be Gull himself. The physician admitted that he was having blackouts, according to Lees, since suffering a stroke in 1887. Gull did visit a surgery in Whitechapel, but he was never known to have roamed the crime-ridden area at night, as some later claimed. Further, Gull's stroke had left him partially paralyzed and there was no way in which this invalid could have committed the energetic acts of Jack the Ripper.

Next, the wealthy poet and ne'er-do-well, James Kenneth Stephen was named as a strong suspect. He was eccentric and obsessed with violence, which permeated his writing. It was said that Stephen's eccentricities merely cloaked pure madness and that, as a homosexual suitor who was rejected by no less a person than Prince Albert Victor, Duke of Clarence, heir to the British crown, Stephen went berserk and took his rage out on the whores of Whitechapel, an area where Stephen and Prince Albert had reportedly visited an exclusive homosexual club.

Such a club did exist, and many distinguished British men did meet there for homosexual assignations, but none were ever arrested. This place was rarely raided, and authorities notified the proprietors far in advance so that their elegant clients could depart ahead of the police and save embarrassment all around. It was claimed that Stephen wrote the Ripper letters, affixing his own thumbprint to one of them, and purposely misspelled certain words and omitted simple punctuation to convince police that the killer was unschooled. Stephen's handwriting and that of the Ripper's were compared. A few similarities were not enough to identify Stephen as the Ripper.

It was also claimed that Stephen wrote the letters and even sent the kidney from the disemboweled Catherine Eddowes, but he was merely covering up for his dear friend, the real Jack the Ripper, who was none other than the Duke of Clarence himself. The eldest son of future king Edward VII was suffering from syphilis, it was claimed, which he had contracted through a Whitechapel whore, a disease that caused advanced paresis of the brain and the prince's premature death in 1892.

Prince Eddy, as the Duke was nicknamed, had sought out Whitechapel whores to murder as he slowly went insane, taking his vengeance out on these poor creatures. Most of this wild theory stems from the research of Dr. Thomas Stowell, who, in 1970, examined the papers of Dr. William Gull and said that Gull's own unpublished records supported this story. Stowell's research was destroyed by his family after his death and Gull's records have yet to be examined by anyone else.

Sir William Gull, the man that Robert Lees trailed to his own mansion, believing that Gull was the Ripper. Gull was beyond reproach as the personal physician to Queen Victoria; he had suffered a stroke that left him partially paralyzed and, because of that crippling stroke, most thought he could never have performed the Ripper killings.

The absurd theory expands on Prince Eddy being the culprit and the London police authorities knowing about it and using it to blackmail Queen Victoria into political sanctions for certain inept ministers. In return, they kept Prince Eddy's identity as the Ripper a secret. This is the most preposterous theory of the lot.

Though autocratic and rather cold, Queen Victoria was a person of impeccable moral conduct and high principles, who, history and her personal conduct has shown in evidence, would never have shielded even one of her own family had they been guilty of any crimes. Further, examining the records showing the whereabouts of the Duke of Clarence during the Ripper

James Kenneth Stephen, an eccentric writer, who became another strong suspect in the Ripper slayings and who was reportedly the homosexual lover of Prince Albert Victor.

Prince Albert Victor, Duke of Clarence, heir to the British throne, known as Eddy, who also came to be a suspect in the Ripper slayings, but he was an improbable candidate.

slayings proves that he could not have committed these crimes. In several instances he was out of the country at the time of the murders.

None of the above suspects really fit into the horrific mold created by the Ripper. He was not, in the opinion of the author, a vicious homosexual seeking vengeance on low-class prostitutes. Why, if this were the case, would he select only common prostitutes to murder? He was not a demented doctor or an unhinged prince. He was not one of the many poisoners who later went to the hangman.

Jack the Ripper was a young man, full of ideals, one who had once been married to a woman who had turned to prostitution, who had deserted him and her family. This was the common thread connecting all the victims. All nine women had been married one way or another and had left their husbands and their families, turning to prostitution. They had betrayed the concept of the family, then the most sacred of institutions. It should be remembered that Mary Kelly was three months pregnant when horribly murdered and butchered.

All of the prostitutes murdered from 1888 to 1891 went regularly to small clinics in the East End and their records and examinations were on file, a regular murder list for the medical man who examined them all, the man who eventually hunted all of them down, the man whose own wife had deserted him for the streets, selling her favors to other men, betraying family and motherhood.

The police, the medical experts, and the historians following in their footsteps decades later looked only, and continue to look, into Whitechapel as an area *into which* the killer went in search of victims and bloodletting. They look still for a maniac of bizarre nature, a diseased homosexual, a foreigner with odd political motives tied to serial killing, one

Painter Walter Sickert in 1884, four years before the Ripper slayings; several writers, including Stephen Knight and Patricia Cornwell, claimed that Sickert was the Ripper.

poisoner or another from a later era. None stood within Whitechapel and looked out as would an incensed husband deserted by a woman, who cuckolded him with strangers she did not know nor love.

In the opinion of this author, he was there all the while, this enigmatic Jack. He worked there. He lived there. He murdered there, this young intern at a clinic where the names and addresses of his victims were in files at his fingertips. He did not, after each murder, flee the area, but returned to the clinic where the blood on his clothes and hands counted for nothing more than the badge of his profession.

Of course, this intern would have blood on his clothes and his hands. It was part of his job, operating on the countless patients that came to his clinic with ugly lesions and festering sores. And with a knife he was an expert, preserving the living, and, on those dark nights in the streets, bringing death to those already dead in his own distorted mind. He would outlive the era of his dark fame, but not the haunting self-image which lurked inside his own shadow.

The killer crossed into the twentieth century unmolested. Comfortable and distinguished in his profession, he looked back like any other upon the gaslight era of Jack the Ripper and, like any other, beheld this serial killer as a dark barbaric stranger from another time.

NOTE TO SCOTLAND YARD: To solve this nagging and much-nurtured case, the author suggests that investigators begin with the photographs taken in Mary Kelly's first-floor, single-room lodging. Among those photographs, originally filed as glass plates, there is a close-up of the murder victim, mutilated by Jack's knife. The body, as the photograph shows, was on a small bed next to the wall of the room. The killer, his hands coated with the blood and gore of his victim, which he took considerable time to disembowel, left discernable fingerprints on the unmolested parts of the victim's flesh and on the wall next to the bed, as the glass plates will show when properly enlarged. (Discernable bloody fingerprints were also placed by the sender of the card sent to "Dear Boss" on September 25, 1888, but these prints are not directly linked to the location of any known Ripper slayings and may or may not be the killer's authentic prints.)

It is well known that fingerprinting as an identification system was not employed by your agency at the time of the Ripper slayings, so that even possessing a clear fingerprint belonging to the real Jack the Ripper would be, at that time, insignificant. Certainly, none of the many suspects interrogated by your agency were fingerprinted so that a match from any print taken in Mary Kelly's room to any of the prints of these suspects is, at this late date, not applicable. However, the author believes that a fingerprint from that terrible room, captured in your photographs, can be matched to the real killer.

The author, who does not have the time or inclination to further pursue this case, suggests that your agency match the print(s) of the Ripper to one of the interns working at the Whitechapel clinic. At the time of the murders, the clinic employed a number of young interns who, among their many chores, took smears from local prostitutes to capture types of venereal diseases for further research—Whitechapel being one of London's centers of prostitution at that time—and these smears were traditionally captured between two small, oblong glass slides. These slides, identified with the initials or names of the interns producing them, were, the author believes, part of medical research that has been preserved and stored to this day. The killer's fingerprints will be found on the slides bearing his name or initials and can be matched to the prints from the photographs taken in Mary Kelly's room.

THE LIZZIE BORDEN CASE/August 4, 1892

It is a wonder that a plump, shy, 32-year-old American spinster from an upperclass family could ever become one of the world's most celebrated murderers, especially when she was acquitted at her sensational 1893 trial and, that the heinous crimes for which she stood accused could have been easily committed by two other persons. Lizzie Borden (1860-1927) lived a quiet

Lizzie Borden at age seventeen.

Lizzie in her twenties.

Lizzie under arrest in 1892.

Lizzie in middle age.

life in Fall River, Massachusetts, residing in her father's large three-story house on Second Street. It was here, on the sizzling hot day of August 4, 1892, that Andrew Jackson Borden, sixty-nine, and his wife Abby Durfee Gray Borden, sixty-four, were found chopped to death from hatchet blows. Other tenants of the death house at the time of the grisly murders included Lizzie's sister Emma, the family maid and cook, Bridget Sullivan, and John Vinnicum Morse, sixty, brother of the first Mrs. Borden, who had come to visit.

Lizzie's mother, Sarah Morse Borden, had died when Lizzie was a small child and Andrew Borden had quickly remarried in 1865 to Abby Durfee Gray, a kind-hearted, gentle woman, who worked as hard in her own home as did the hired help. It was later claimed that Lizzie harbored a deep-seated hatred for this woman, who had replaced her own mother in her father's affections, but this could hardly have been the case since Lizzie's mother died when Lizzie was very young and it was Abby Borden who raised the child and who was the only real mother Lizzie ever knew or remembered.

Andrew J. Borden, Lizzie's father, a penny-pinching landlord, with many enemies.

Abby Durfee Gray Borden, Lizzie's hard-working stepmother with no known enemies.

In fact, as an adult, Lizzie called Abby "mother," except when angry with her and then, in minor fits of pique, called her "Mrs. Borden." Her sister Emma, an equally retiring spinster, was older than Lizzie, forty-one at the time of the murder, and could have more easily nurtured the deep-rooted resentments of Abby Borden attributed to Lizzie as motives for murder.

Later claims also insisted that Lizzie wanted her stepmother and father dead so she could claim her father's money, or that she was about to be disinherited for obscure reasons and struck quickly to preserve her inheritance. This was all nonsense. Both Lizzie and Emma stood to benefit from their father's will without concern; the will had been written a decade earlier. Andrew Borden had not altered the will nor had he any plans to change it, and this both sisters knew.

Moreover, Borden had not only set aside a handsome inheritance for both of his daughters, but he had allocated considerable land and farms for them and both enjoyed above-average allowances from which to freely draw money for clothes and other expenses. As spinsters, the Borden sisters had little to worry about; the present was comfortable and the future secure.

Andrew Borden made a visit to this site, The A. J. Borden Building, only a short time before he was horribly murdered.

Bridget Sullivan, the hard-working maid in the Borden household, was a closed-mouthed person who literally worked from dawn until dusk, cleaning, cooking three meals a day, and doing the most arduous chores for the large family, albeit Abby Borden helped with the considerable workload. It was Bridget, who prepared the heavy meal eaten by the family the night before the killings, one which caused Andrew and Abby Borden to become ill. In fact, Lizzie herself, as well as Bridget, had become slightly sick after dinner, so the later claim that Lizzie had poisoned the food in her first attempt to murder her parents was also rejected as nonsense.

John Vinnicum Morse, Lizzie's uncle, left to see friends on the day of the murders.

Borden maid Bridget Sullivan was in the house with Lizzie on the day of the murders.

Some days earlier, Lizzie had tried to purchase prussic acid. She had told the druggist that she wanted the prussic acid to clean a sealskin coat, but the local druggist had refused to sell her the acid. It was said that she nevertheless obtained poison and managed to dose the meal. The Bordens ate from common platters and therefore Lizzie could not be sure which portion would contain the lethal dose, if, indeed, she had opted for this murder plan which, since she also took her portions from those common platters, could have meant her own death.

John Vinnicum Morse, Lizzie's uncle, visited the family on August 3, 1892, taking the guest room. Early on the day of the murder, Morse left the Borden house to visit friends in Swansea. Emma Borden also left the house, renting a buggy and driving some thirty miles to visit friends in Fairhaven. Lizzie was left in the house with Bridget and her parents. Andrew Borden left the house at about 9 a.m., visiting the downtown bank of which he was president, and making several stops to collect rents from the buildings he owned.

Borden was not a well-liked man by those with whom he did business, known as a penny-pinching landlord who fought over every dollar he earned. He had enemies, it was well known, one man arguing so heatedly with Borden a week earlier in the Borden house that he was ordered to leave the premises. Also, the Bordens had, in recent months, suffered a rash of burglaries in their barn, and they had reported a daylight burglary of the house two months before the murders.

Lizzie had nightmares about impending doom because of her father's skinflint reputation and the enemies he had created through his hard business deals. She confided her fears to Alice Russell, telling the neighbor: "I feel that something is hanging over me that I cannot throw off." She felt that her father's enemies would "burn the house down over us," describing this nightmare to Mrs. Russell.

Lizzie's critics later pointed out that all of these uttered forebodings were planned by Lizzie to create the illusion of strange killers, who could later be blamed for the murders that she herself committed. Yet Lizzie Borden's character and personality had never shown her to be calculating or insidious. She was a much-protected child and her father doted upon her as an adult. She lived a sheltered life up to the time of the murders, and her fears were those of a child rather than a devious adult with a clever murder plan.

At 9:30 a.m. on the morning of the murders, Bridget Sullivan went to the Borden barn and got a pail and a brush and began washing the outside first-floor windows of the house. Abby Borden went upstairs to make the beds and Lizzie was somewhere in the house at the time. At 10:30 a.m. Andrew Borden arrived back home from his downtown business chores, but when he tried the front door of the house he found it locked. He knocked and rattled the doorknob which Bridget heard.

The maid left her window-washing and entered the house through an unlocked side door and went to the front door. Just as she did so, she later testified, she saw Lizzie standing on the first step of the front staircase leading to the bedrooms, appearing as if she had just come downstairs. When Borden was finally let into the house, he walked into the dining room, asking for Abby.

"She's gone out," Lizzie told him. "She had a note from somebody who was sick."

Borden went upstairs to his bedroom, then he returned to the main floor and rested on a small couch in the sitting room. Bridget continued washing the windows but from inside the house, while Lizzie began ironing some handkerchiefs in the kitchen. She asked the maid if she planned to go out in the afternoon, reminding Bridget, whom she called Maggie, that there was a sale of some dress goods that day at a local store. Bridget told her that she was not feeling well, that the heavy family breakfast had upset her stomach.

The meal served by Bridget that morning was extraordinary for the sweltering hot season, consisting of mutton-broth soup, johnny cakes, coffee, and cookies. The soup had been made from the mutton eaten the night before, which had obviously made everyone ill, but no one thought to question the soup. The Borden household was a frugal one and nothing was thrown away if it could serve a purpose; so consuming some slightly tainted soup would follow the family's utilitarian traits.

Lizzie then told Bridget that "if you go out, make sure and lock the door, for Mrs. Borden has gone out on a sick call and I might go out, too."

"Miss Lizzie, who is sick?" Bridget asked.

"I don't know. She had a note this morning. It must be in the town."

A few minutes before 11 a.m., Bridget climbed the back stairs to her attic room to take a short nap, her daily custom. She worked from 6 a.m., preparing breakfast, then completed other chores until her short nap before preparing the family lunch. The maid lay back on her bed and tried to sleep, but the intense heat caused her only to doze. She later testified that she could hear every noise in the old house, every creaking floorboard and that all was silent. At 11 a.m. she heard the city hall clock chime out the time. Then she heard Lizzie frantically calling her: "Maggie! Come down!"

She went to the back stairs and called down to Lizzie: "What's the matter?"

Lizzie called back with words that sent shivers of fear through the maid: "Come down! Quick! Father's dead! Somebody came in and killed him!"

Bridget raced down the stairs and found Lizzie standing at the door to the sitting room. Lizzie blocked the half-opened door to the sitting room, as if to shield the maid from the awful scene within, then said: "Oh, Maggie, don't go in. I have to have a doctor quick." She told Bridget to go to the home of Dr. Seabury W. Bowen, a house diagonally across the street from the Borden house, and bring the physician. The maid raced across the street and found that Dr. Bowen was making a house call; she returned to find Lizzie in the hallway.

"Miss Lizzie," Bridget asked, "where were you when this thing happened?"

The body of Andrew Borden lies on a couch in the living room; the victim's face was all but obliterated by numerous chops from an ax.

The body of Abby Borden lies on the floor of an upstairs bedroom in the Borden house; she, too, had been slain by a killer using an ax.

The Borden house at 92 Second Street, Fall River, Massachusetts, shown shortly after the murders; thousands of people milled about the residence only hours after Andrew and Abby Borden had been killed.

The rear of the Borden house, with the barn at right, where Lizzie said she was hunting for sinkers at the time of the murders.

The side porch of the Borden house, where Lizzie called out to her neighbor: "Oh, Mrs. Churchill, do come over! Someone has killed Father!"

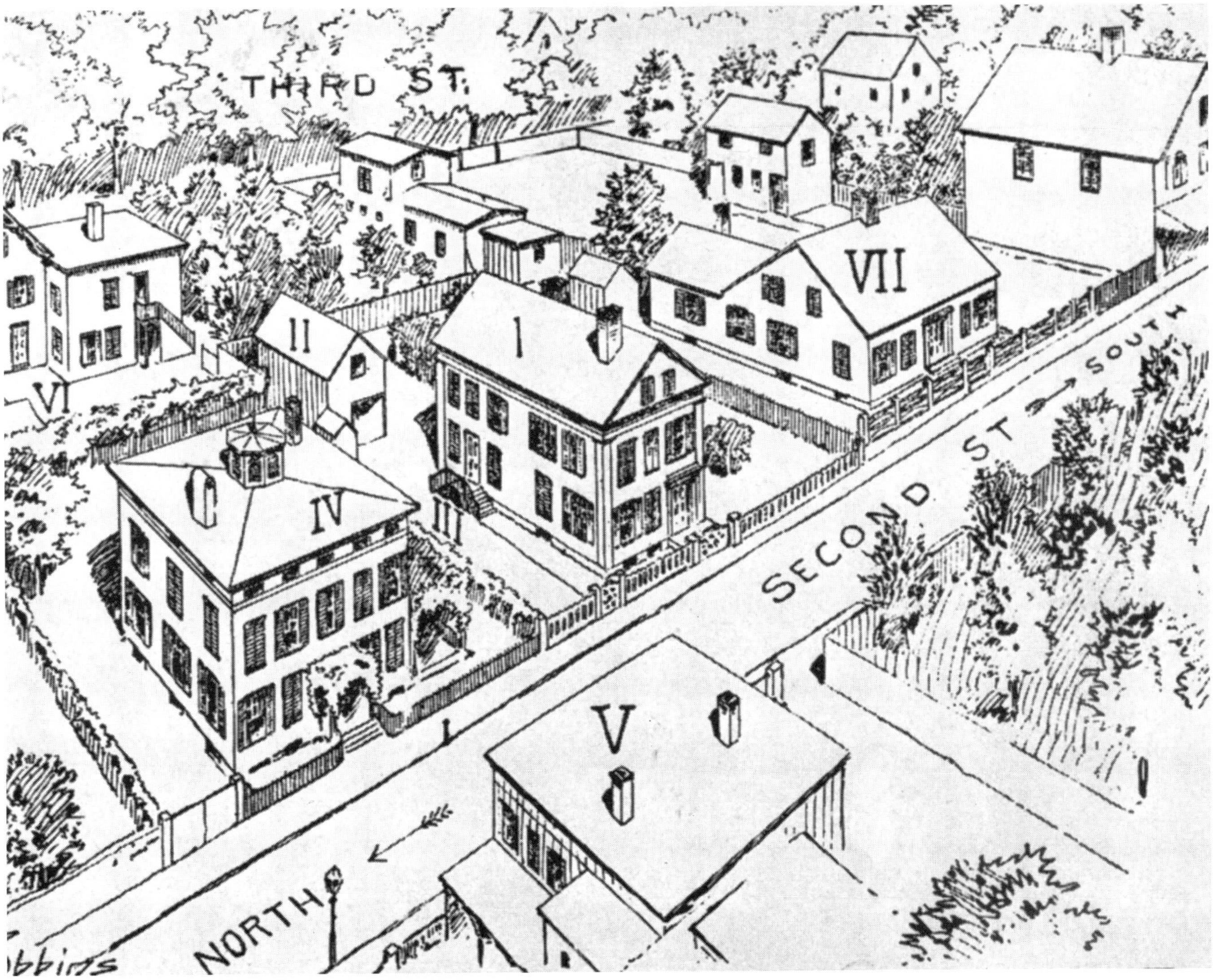

The Borden house and its neighbors: I. Borden House; II. Borden Barn; III. Side Porch Entrance; IV. Mrs. Churchill's House; V. Dr. Bowen's House; VI. Dr. Chagnon's House; VII. Dr. Kelly's House.

Mrs. Adelaide B. Churchill, the first neighbor called by Lizzie to witness the murders in the Borden house.

Mrs. Alice M. Russell, who was summoned to the Borden house by Bridget Sullivan, on Lizzie's orders.

Hosea M. Knowlton, the energetic district attorney, who vigorously prosecuted Lizzie Borden.

George D. Robinson, ex-governor of Massachusetts, who undertook the defense of Lizzie Borden.

Lizzie Borden at her murder trial, anxiously sitting forward as she listens to George Robinson present his masterful arguments on her behalf.

Mrs. Churchill hurried to Lizzie, standing with her at the side door and holding on to her arm, as if to keep her from fainting. "Where is your father?"

"In the sitting room," Lizzie responded in a dazed voice.

"Where were you when it happened?"

"I went to the barn to get a piece of iron," she replied. She later explained that by "iron" she meant a fishing sinker as she intended to go fishing when she visited the Borden farm outside of town, a trip that had been planned for a week.

"Where is your mother?" questioned Mrs. Churchill.

"I don't know. She had a note to go see someone who is sick, but I don't know but she is killed, too, for I thought I heard her come in. Father must have an enemy for we have all been sick, and we think the milk has been poisoned."

Then Mrs. Churchill went looking for a doctor, asking neighbors to call police. Oddly, given Lizzie's remark about her mother being another possible murder victim, Mrs. Churchill did not suggest to look for Mrs. Borden. Bridget then returned to the house, meeting patrolman George W. Allen, who was responding to Mrs. Churchill's alarm. Following these two was a scurrying Dr. Bowen. Both

"I was in the yard," she said, "and heard a groan, and came in and the screen door was wide open." She then ordered the maid to fetch her friend and neighbor, Mrs. Russell. Bridget went next door to bring back the neighbor. At this time, Mrs. Adelaide B. Churchill, whose house bordered the Borden home on the north, looked out an open window and saw Lizzie standing at the screen door, holding on to it, trembling. "Is there anything the matter," Mrs. Churchill asked.

"Oh, Mrs. Churchill," Lizzie said, "do come over. Someone has killed Father."

Officer Allen and Dr. Bowen entered the sitting room and found Andrew Borden sprawled on the couch, his face a river of blood, a pulpy ruin that caused even Dr. Bowen to shudder.

Shaking his head, Dr. Bowen said in a near whisper: "Physician that I am, and accustomed to all kinds of horrible sights, it sickens me to look upon the dead man's face." Patrolman Allen noticed that the sitting room was undisturbed. There had been no struggle and not a stick of furniture was out of place. The dead man lay half on the couch, his legs sticking outward to the floor. His hands were unclenched and it appeared that he had been attacked while sleeping. The couch and the wall behind it were coated with Andrew Borden's blood, as if the blows he had received, from what was later determined to be a hatchet, were savagely repeated.

While Dr. Bowen and Officer Allen were inspecting the gruesome corpse in the sitting room, Lizzie sat in the kitchen, as if in a stupor, Mrs. Churchill and Mrs. Russell comforting her. She then said that someone should look for Mrs. Borden and tell her what happened. Mrs. Churchill and Bridget then decided they would search every room in the house, believing that they would find Mrs. Borden in the same condition as her husband. Their assumptions were correct. As they climbed the front staircase, Mrs. Churchill looked into the guest room to see a body sprawled on the floor. She and Bridget went back downstairs and Mrs. Russell asked the ashen-faced Mrs. Churchill: "Is there another?"

"Yes, she is up there," replied the terrified neighbor. Officer Allen and Dr. Bowen almost bounded up the stairs to inspect the guest room where John Morse had slept the night before. Abby Borden, too, had been hacked to death, her head crushed with what looked to be numerous blows from a hatchet. She lay in an awkward position, face down, on her knees, her backside pushed upward and forward.

It appeared that Mrs. Borden had been making the bed in the guest room when attacked. Her blood had splattered the bed covers and the nearby wall. A medical examiner arrived and diligently counted nineteen head wounds to Mrs. Borden's skull, ten to Mr. Borden's head, a total of twenty-nine, not the eighty-one "whacks" later attributed to Lizzie.

While funeral arrangements were made for the Bordens, Lizzie became the focal point of a subtle police investigation. She was repeatedly questioned as to her whereabouts during the time of the murders. Her answers varied. She said she was in the yard, then she said she was in the barn, then in the loft of the barn searching for sinkers, even picking pears and eating these in the barn. Why Lizzie would even enter the hot barn on such a steamy day caused great suspicion on the part of police and Fall River Mayor John W. Coughlin, who ordered Lizzie placed under house detention.

Lizzie's confused conduct continued when she faced a coroner's jury. The inquest could not firmly establish just *where* Lizzie was at the time of the murders. She was then officially arrested, charged with the murder of her parents. Her trial began on June 5, 1893. She was defended by former Massachusetts governor George D. Robinson. Bridget Sullivan did a complete turn-about and offered herself as a witness for the prosecution, some later said because this would cast less suspicion in her direction.

The maid had as much opportunity to murder the Bordens as did Lizzie. In fact, when she went up to take her nap that fateful morning, she could have easily gone up the backstairs, entered the family area on the second floor and killed Mrs. Borden. The prosecution was handled by District Attorney Hosea Knowlton and he was anything but gentle with Lizzie.

Knowlton claimed that Lizzie hated her stepmother, believing they had secretly disinherited her, although Knowlton had no evidence whatsoever to support this idea. By presenting this line of argument, Knowlton also implicated Emma Borden, who was then above suspicion, in that she and Lizzie equally shared in Andrew Borden's will. (Some Lizzie Borden historians later claimed that Emma Borden could have easily murdered her parents, returning from out-of-town, slipping into the house to murder Abby and Andrew and then driving her buggy back to Fairhaven. Emma *did* rent a buggy which was reportedly seen outside the Borden house shortly before the murders, according to one report.)

Lizzie awaits the verdict with downcast eyes, her sister Emma, right, covering her face (her habit throughout the trial).

The district attorney then attacked Lizzie's story about the note from an anonymous sick person, a note Lizzie claimed Abby Borden had shown her, but one that she did not read. There was no note, Knowlton said. This was merely a device Lizzie employed to explain her stepmother's absence when Andrew Borden's body was found. Lizzie simply invented the note, Knowlton said.

Robinson's defense was spirited and telling. With all that blood spattering after each blow, he pointed out, why was Lizzie not coated with gore? She was seen only a few minutes before and after the discovery of Andrew Borden's body, dressed in the same dress and not a blotch of blood on her. It was also claimed that Lizzie had somehow managed to wash off the blood after murdering her parents. (In a ridiculous TV story Elizabeth Montgomery portrays Lizzie as she runs about naked to commit the murders, washes, and then puts her original dress back on).

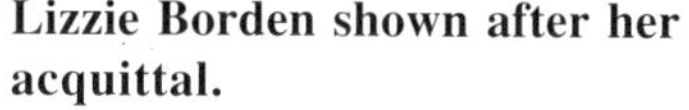

Lizzie Borden shown after her acquittal.

Maplecroft, the mansion into which Lizzie and Emma Borden moved following the acquittal; Lizzie Borden lived out a peaceful life in this home, doubling the $350,000 fortune her father left to her and her sister through shrewd investments. She died in 1927.

The washroom, however, had been thoroughly examined by police just after the murders and no trace of water existed; there had been no quick bath. Also, where was the murder weapon, Robinson wanted to know. He held up the hatchet that was exhibited in court, but this, the prosecution admitted, had been found in the Borden basement without a handle, rusted, and covered with cobwebs. Not a spot of blood could be found on it.

The *possibility* of a strange intruder entering the house, Knowlton pointed out, was a good one. The screen door was open and there was enough time for someone to come into the Borden house, kill both Abby and Andrew Borden, and escape undetected while both Lizzie and Bridget were out of the house. The defense attorney pointed to the recent burglaries suffered by the Bordens to prove that their property had been successfully invaded and looted earlier and where one burglar could go, a murderer could follow. Every word bantered between prosecution and defense was picked up and hurried into print by the more than forty newsmen covering the trial which captured national headlines for two weeks.

Lizzie Borden herself was the reason why country wide readers were fascinated with this case. She was not a low-born, uneducated slattern from the criminal dens of America. Lizzie represented mainstream America. In fact, she was of the upper middleclass. She had money, position, and was an esteemed member of Fall River society. Lizzie was a member in good standing of the Fruit and Flower Mission, the Woman's Christian Temperance Union, secretary of the Christian Endeavor Society, and, most important, a Sunday school teacher. Could such a woman cold-bloodedly murder her parents? The jury thought not.

On June 20, 1893, Lizzie Borden stood before the court and was pronounced not guilty. She sank back into her chair, exhausted, relieved. Applause and mild cheering broke out in the courtroom, mostly from Lizzie's friends and members of her social clubs. With her sister Emma at her side, Lizzie moved out of the old Borden house and purchased a handsome mansion called Maplecroft. She spent the rest of her life here, occupying her hours with social clubs and aiding stray animals. She made small but shrewd investments and she and her sister more than doubled the $350,000 left to them by her father.

Lizzie Borden, at the time of her death on June 2, 1927, left most of her estate to animal shelters. She died, in the eyes of the law, an innocent woman, but the public had long been convinced of her guilt, not from the results of the trial that freed her, but from a bit of clever doggerel written at the time of her trial, lines that pricked the imagination of the public and were passed down from one generation to another, so that history has blurred the true facts, leaving only the following wrongful but memorable ditty:

Lizzie Borden took an ax,
And gave her mother forty whacks;
And when she saw what she had done,
She gave her father forty-one.

THE DEATH OF A LADIES' MAN/June 11, 1920

Millionaire bridge expert and ladies' man extraordinaire, Joseph Browne Elwell (1875-1920) was killed by persons unknown on the morning of June 11, 1920. His violent death is considered by criminal historians to be one of the classic murder mysteries of the 20th Century. Nothing in Elwell's early life remotely suggested the inexplicable fate he would later meet. Born in Cranford, New Jersey, to middle-class parents, Elwell attended public schools and proved to be a good student, alert and enterprising. He moved to Brooklyn in 1900 at age twenty-five, seeking work. He found it in a hardware store where he was soon the most productive salesman.

Wealthy Joseph Browne Elwell at a Long Island beach shortly before his mysterious murder.

Charming, polite, and dapper, Elwell was given a sales job at $60 a month, plus commissions; he traveled from store to store with his line of hardware goods, always on the lookout for new business. To develop contacts, Elwell joined several social clubs in Brooklyn, including the Irving Republican Club, where the consuming passion of members was bridge whist. Elwell had always been good with cards, having a remarkable memory which allowed him to recall every card played in a game. He soon became so adept at bridge that he earned more money from the game than from his job.

At the suggestion of club members, he began teaching bridge whist to socially prominent people, collecting sizeable fees that soon allowed him to quit his sales job and earn a handsome living at cards. Elwell's reputation grew to the point where he was recognized as the foremost bridge expert of his day, and his social position vastly improved. He was soon invited as a celebrity into the dens and parlors of New York's rich and famous, as a teacher of bridge, the game of the social elite. In this heady circle Elwell met Helen Derby, former wife of a successful lawyer, whom he married in 1904. The couple had a son, Richard, a year later and settled down in Manhattan.

Elwell began to write books on bridge, with his wife's considerable help, and these soon headed the best-seller lists. His *Elwell on Bridge* would become one of the most widely-read books in America, returning huge royalties to his coffers, which were already burgeoning. It is estimated that as early as 1908 Elwell was earning $20,000 each year from his card tutoring, equal to ten times that sum by today's inflated dollar. He invested wisely in real estate and the stock market and his fortunes bloomed; Elwell was soon banking tens of thousands of dollars. Acting on tips from his social contacts, who assiduously worked the Market, Elwell accumulated huge fortunes in cotton futures.

The card expert purchased a handsome three-story brownstone at 244 W. 70th St. and hired a staff of servants. Traveling with the smart set, Elwell soon found it necessary to buy expensive vacation homes in Palm Beach, Florida, Saratoga Springs, and Long Island, New York. As he prospered, Elwell began to have affairs with other women, from chorus girls to social sirens, even other men's wives.

Helen Derby Elwell found this new lifestyle insufferable and the couple separated in 1916, with Elwell paying $200 a month for all of Helen's expenses, plus paying handsomely for his son's private schooling. He found the arrangement satisfying, for it permitted him to live the life of the playboy, and soon his female friendships expanded into a regular harem.

More than fifty women (some reports later gave the number as high as seventy), became "close friends" of Elwell. He carefully wrote down their phone numbers and addresses in his little black book, later found by police, along with pertinent information about their sexual abilities and deficiencies. Into another ledger, he meticulously entered amounts of money he paid to these women, either as loans or as "gifts."

With the mind of a meticulous accountant, Elwell never paid in cash,

The cover of the best-selling book that made Elwell famous and rich.

Helen Derby Elwell, who was cuckolded by Elwell as soon as he acquired wealth, causing a separation.

always by check, and these canceled checks he kept in a black metal box next to the name and address book and the ledger, tucked neatly into a top drawer of his desk. The bridge expert hid these records by stacking magazines atop the metal box, so that he could quickly access these items for additional entries to be made.

Because of the heavy female traffic in and out of his townhouse, Elwell made sure that his three house servants lived elsewhere. They included William H. Barnes, the valet and part-time secretary (he would later claim he was Elwell's business manager), Edward Rhodes, the chauffeur, and housekeeper Marie Larsen. But even the seemingly inexhaustible Elwell had to slow down, and by early summer of 1920 he became nervous about the many women in his life. He found them at his front door, on his stoop, and ringing his phone off the hook. He jokingly mentioned this avalanche of attention to a friend, remarking: "This must stop before one of these jealous ladies murders me." Mrs. Larsen, a loyal, silent type, was nevertheless kept busy collecting female underclothes in her employer's bedroom and even throughout the other rooms of the townhouse.

In late May 1920, Elwell ordered the locks changed on the front doors of his house, but Mrs. Larsen thought this move was prompted less by the bevy of women in her employer's life than by a break-in a year earlier, when three thieves smashed the basement window at the rear of the house. They looted the place, only to be arrested by detectives, while in the house, called there by an alert neighbor who had seen the burglars enter. (These men were serving prison sentences when Elwell was murdered a year later.)

For several years, in addition to his other pursuits, Elwell had taken a keen interest in horse racing and had invested in a

Elwell is shown sitting atop one of his horses at the Beach Racing Stable in Covington, Kentucky, a stable he bought, along with expensive cars, a yacht, and numerous mistresses.

small stable in Covington, Kentucky, The Beach Racing Stable, which he owned jointly with turf man William H. Pendleton. Moreover, he spent thousands of dollars to buy two great stallions with another sportsman, Phil Chinn, a track celebrity. By the spring of 1920, horse racing fascinated Elwell as much as bridge and he found himself spending more and more time at the track and making plans to enlarge his stable, hiring Lloyd Gentry, a noted trainer, to get his horses in shape to enter significant races that year.

In early June 1920, Elwell began seeing Viola Kraus, a pretty brunette, who had filed for divorce from Victor von Schlegell, a top executive at the United States Rubber Company. Schlegell had been a famous football player for Yale in 1898 and he and his estranged wife moved in the same social circles as Elwell. Viola Kraus was the sister of Mrs. Walter Lewisohn, the wife of a business tycoon and Broadway celebrity. Lewisohn managed several stock portfolios of Elwell's and it was through him that the bridge expert met and became enamored of Viola. All of these ultra-polite high society people came together on the night of June 10, 1920, although not intentionally.

That evening, Elwell accompanied Viola and the Lewisohns to the Ritz-Carlton Hotel, attending a 7:30 dinner. As they were retrieving their coats, the foursome turned to see Victor von Schlegell with Emily (Elly) Hope Anderson, a beautiful young singer from Minneapolis, who was studying in New York. Oddly, Miss Anderson had been a friend of Elwell's. The parties exchanged cordial greetings and then broke into ironic chuckles. Viola Kraus had just that day been granted a divorce from Schlegell. A few hours later the Elwell party was seated at the New Amsterdam Roof to view the "Midnight Frolics" and they were joined by a South American journalist and *bon vivant,* Octavio Figueroa.

Elwell looked to a nearby table, pointed to its occupants, and his party broke into laughter. Seated next to them was Schlegell and Miss Anderson. Schlegell grinned and said: "I can't keep away from Vi even if the judge said today that we needn't be together again." Schlegell and Miss Anderson left early, but the Elwell party stayed until closing time, leaving the New Amsterdam at 2 a.m. Elwell and Viola had some cross words, or so Viola later told police, and he therefore refused to get into the taxi carrying the Lewisohns and Viola, saying that he would get another cab. The Lewisohns later claimed that Elwell merely said the cab was too crowded and that he would talk to them the next day.

The bridge expert walked to Seventh Avenue, where he hailed a cab driven by Edgar Walters, who drove to a newsstand. There, Elwell purchased a copy of the *Morning Telegraph,* and Walters next took the bridge expert to his home on West 70th Street. Elwell gave him a thirty-five cent tip, walked across the street, and went up the three stairs to the front doors of his house, entering at exactly 2:30 a.m., according to Walters who wrote down his fare at that time.

Elwell, presumed to be alone in his townhouse, did not go directly to bed that night, but was busy on the phone. Viola Kraus later claimed that she called him about 3 a.m. to patch up the mild argument they had had. The bridge expert appar-

The chair in which Joseph Elwell was found fatally shot; he was almost unrecognizable by his own maid, appearing without his expensive toupee and false teeth.

Reporters are shown swarming about the Elwell Manhattan brownstone, where the bridge expert was slain; the NYPD had no answers.

Mrs. Marie Larsen, Elwell's maid, who found her employer slumped and dying in a locked house, presenting police with a perfect mystery.

ently made several calls himself that night, one, according to telephone company records, made to William H. Pendleton, Elwell's racetrack partner, calling Far Rockaway 1841.

Pendleton later testified that his phone, which was next to his bed, never rang that morning and his maid, who had an extension of the same number in her room, also stated that the Pendleton phone never rang that morning. At 6:09 another long distance call, to an unknown party in Garden City, Long Island, was made, ostensibly by Elwell. Obviously, Elwell was disturbed about something, as he decided to stay up all night making phone calls, and yet this is not supported by the fact that he was found mortally wounded a few hours later, dressed only in his pajamas.

It was already daylight when milkman Henry Otter, a driver for the Sheffield Dairy Company, walked up the stairs of Elwell's house, leaving a quart of milk in the small vestibule, finding the two outer doors open. Otter logged the delivery at precisely 6:15 a.m. At 7:10 a.m., Charles S. Torey, the mailman, arrived with a number of letters. He went into the vestibule, dropped the letters on the tile floor, then twice rang the buzzer which was outside the main door leading into the house. This was the mailman's usual signal that he had delivered the mail.

Mrs. Marie Larsen, the housekeeper, appeared at the front door at 8:10 a.m. She unlocked the main door inside the vestibule—only she and Elwell had keys to this door since the locks had been recently changed—and entered the house, carrying the bottle of milk. As she walked down the hall toward the kitchen to prepare Elwell's breakfast, Mrs. Larsen thought she smelled smoke. She later described the smell as "powder smoke." She passed the open doors leading to the living room and saw Elwell sitting in the large plush-upholstered chair next to a card table.

At first Mrs. Larsen thought she was staring at a stranger. The man was completely bald and he was toothless. She had never before seen her employer without his toupee or his false teeth. Before her, slumped in the chair, his chin upon his chest, was Joseph Elwell. He was wearing his pajamas, the top unbuttoned, revealing a chest of gray hair and a flabby belly. His feet were bare. In the middle of his forehead, directly between the eyes, was a hole from which blood was still oozing. The man was still alive, breathing heavily, according to Mrs. Larsen. She dropped the milk bottle and ran outside to the street.

Seeing milkman Otter in the street collecting empty bottles, Mrs. Larsen called to him: "Call an ambulance, quick! Mr. Elwell has been shot!"

Otter was a man who minded his own business. He tersely shouted back: "I'm not a policeman, I don't know how to call an ambulance! Run up to the corner and tell the cop about it!"

Mrs. Larsen raced off to blurt her discovery to a traffic cop who, in turn, accompanied her back to the Elwell house. He too noted that the man was still breathing and tried to use the phone on a small table next to the chair in which the wounded Elwell slumped. It was not working, so the officer went next door, where he called police headquarters, asking that an ambulance be sent immediately. The call was registered at exactly 8:31 a.m. The ambulance arrived within minutes and it raced off with its dying cargo to a nearby hospital. Elwell was pronounced dead two hours later, without regaining consciousness.

Before the ambulance drivers took Elwell out of his chair, Mrs. Larsen and the traffic cop noticed that a letter from the horse trainer, Lloyd Gentry, had been opened and was resting in the dying man's lap. Another letter, one from Elwell's son, then sixteen and writing from his boarding school, lay unopened on the floor with five other pieces of mail, all advertisements. By the time homicide detectives arrived, they were presented with a murder without a body to examine, as it had already been removed. They were deprived of viewing the exact position of Elwell's body, how he was sitting, the positions of his legs and arms, all important aspects of their subsequent investigation.

From the first moment the police entered the picture, this case became a *cause celebre*. As soon as it was learned that Joseph Elwell had been shot, the city's top brass appeared, including District Attorney Edward Swann, Captain Arthur Carey, later a deputy inspector in charge of the Homicide Bureau, and Inspector John Cray, of the Detective Division, one of New York's best sleuths. Following close at hand was the city's noted medical examiner, Charles S. Norris. As an army of police filed into the Elwell home, a host of reporters followed, gathering in the street and demanding answers the police could never provide.

At first Norris thought the man had committed suicide and Carey agreed with him. Then a spent bullet was found on the table next to the chair where Elwell had sat. On the wall behind the chair was a mark, which police soon realized had been caused by the bullet fired into Elwell's head. The bullet, a .45-caliber steel jacket, had gone through the victim's head, struck the wall behind him at an upward angle, ricocheted off the wall and bounced onto the table. The empty cartridge shell was found at Elwell's bare feet before he was removed from the house. The cartridge and bullet had been made in 1917 by the U.S. Cartridge Company for the U.S. Army. The weapon from which the cartridge had been fired was a .45-caliber automatic, strictly government issue. The automatic was never found.

Norris' examination of the body convinced authorities that murder had been committed. Elwell had powder burns on his face and Norris concluded that the gun firing the fatal bullet was held not closer than three and not farther than four feet from his head. Moreover, the exit wound was higher by an inch than the entry wound, causing the police to believe that the killer fired the weapon from a sitting or crouching position. This was supported by the mark on the wall behind Elwell's chair, which was above the spot where his head rested in the stuffed chair.

On the mantle across the living room, police found a cigarette stub, not the brand smoked by the victim, but without telltale lipstick marks. Though the entire house was dusted, no fingerprints were found, other than Mrs. Larsen's and that of the victim. The phone standing on the table next to the victim's chair was out of order and police reported that this had "been tampered with."

Mrs. Larsen reported that the phone had not been working for two days and yet this phone, the only one in the house, had been used by Elwell throughout the night to make long distance calls, according to the phone company. Further, Elwell had received a call from Kraus, according to Viola Kraus, only hours before he had been murdered.

The time of death was fixed by Norris, the medical examiner, at forty-five minutes before Mrs. Larsen found the dying man, or at 7:25 a.m. Captain Carey theorized that Elwell had heard the postman's ring and had gone downstairs immediately in his pajamas. Eager to read the letter from his horse trainer, Gentry, he sat down in his chair, opened the letter, and was shot only twenty minutes later. Carey later claimed that a burglar could have entered the house after Elwell opened the heavy inner door to get his mail, and left the door ajar. The man, however, would have had to inexplicably spend twenty minutes in the hallway before entering the living room to kill Elwell, and then leave the premises within forty-five minutes.

There was no way to exit or enter the place, except by the front door, which was closed and locked when Mrs. Larsen arrived at 8:10 a.m. Still, this would have been enough time to gather considerable valuables. But a thorough examination of the house revealed that nothing had been taken. On the third floor, the location of Elwell's sumptuous bedroom, the dead man's jewelry and other valuables were present. There was $400 in his tuxedo pants pocket, draped neatly over a chair. All of his clothes were as he had left them and no drawers had been opened, no closets or other rooms entered.

None of the dozens of people in the street between 7 a.m. and the time Mrs. Larsen arrived saw anyone leave the Elwell house. A painter had been working next door from 7 a.m. on, until he saw Mrs. Larsen run from the house and he insisted he saw no one else leave the building. A burglar was ruled out in that nothing had been taken and it was unlikely that even the most novice intruder would think to enter a house in broad daylight, risking quick detection. Since bars were on the basement windows and the back door was heavily bolted, no one could have entered except by the front door.

Emily Hope Anderson, one of Elwell's girlfriends, who had dinner with him on the night he was murdered.

It was thought that perhaps someone had been in the house with Elwell all along, perhaps a female companion, but there was no trace of another person having spent the night either in the guest bedroom or in Elwell's adjoining bedroom. Detectives took pains to notice that only Elwell had slept in the bed, and on top of the bedspread in his pajamas, it having been a hot night. The pillow on the other side of the bed had no indentation.

That Elwell knew his killer was not ruled out. The man allowed his killer to get very close to him, but whether that killer was male or female was never determined. Yet the victim's vanity was such that everyone who knew him realized he would never have allowed any acquaintance, let alone a lover, to see him without his toupee and teeth. No woman, including his wife or his housekeeper, had ever viewed Joseph Elwell without a toupee and his expensive false teeth. Police later found the toupee, which had been neatly put away by its owner before going to bed. His teeth were still soaking in a glass in the bathroom. There had been no house guest, police concluded; Joseph Elwell had spent his last night on earth all alone.

New York medical examiner (pathologist) Charles S. Norris, who at first thought Elwell committed suicide, then concluded he had been murdered, even saying that he knew (but never disclosed) the identity of the killer.

A heavy weapon such as the .45 used to kill Elwell was eliminated as a weapon a female would have used. Too heavy, too much of a jolt when firing, Captain Carey said, adding that it was not the kind of automatic a lady would employ. Such thinking was in accord with a predominately masculine perspective of the day that held that all women were timid and frail and if they did elect to use a handgun to kill someone, their most popular choice would be a "dainty" weapon like a derringer. Still, the police, once they discovered Elwell's list of lady friends, began to consider each a likely suspect, interviewing every one of them.

Investigators did not rule out family members, although they had been well taken care of by the wealthy Elwell. He had purchased a fine home for his parents, and his brother and two sisters, who, along with his much-ignored wife, had concrete alibis for the night of the murder. Mrs. Elwell even admitted that she was about to file for a divorce at her husband's insistence. She stood little to gain by Elwell's death, knowing he had not made provisions for her in his will.

Police investigated every one of Elwell's business and social associates, even traveling to Saratoga, Palm Springs, and Kentucky to look into his far-flung business ventures. They scoured racetracks all over the East Coast, following up leads that only led to ignorant racetrack touts. What perplexed the police even more was the obvious fact that Elwell had no dedicated enemies. He owed money to no one, was apparently generous with money, and no one begrudged him his lifestyle, not even his abandoned wife. At first, Viola Kraus became a suspect of sorts, since she called Elwell's house an hour after he had died in the hospital.

A detective answered the phone and asked her to come over. She did, confused and upset as she pushed her way through a mob of reporters at the door. She had no idea that Elwell was dead, she said, and had arrived to retrieve a pink kimono left nights earlier. This was given to her by housekeeper Larsen, who had hidden it from the police to prevent Viola from being compromised, which she was anyway. (If Mrs. Larsen could hide a kimono before investigators arrived, some sleuths later speculated, she could certainly have hidden the murder weapon, but no motive for doing so could be established.)

Others were quickly compromised. When police insinuated that Schlegell had a motive for killing Elwell because the bridge expert had taken up with his ex-wife, the businessman said he had no interest in what Viola did with her life. He then produced Miss Anderson, who testified that she was having breakfast in Schlegell's apartment at the very time someone was blowing a hole into the bridge expert's head. Viola Kraus produced the Lewisohns, who insisted that she had slept in their apartment on the morning of the murder and did not leave their apartment until almost noon on that day.

Still, the police doggedly kept after anyone associated with the dead man, running down Elwell's lover list. There was the wealthy divorcee, Mrs. Josephine E. Wilmerding, whom the press dubbed "the woman in white" and who provided a concrete alibi. (Viola Kraus was labeled "the woman in pink" because her kimono was of a pink hue.) Bridge pupil Mrs. Schuyler L. Parsons had an unshakable alibi. So did Countess Sonia Szinswaska of Poland and Princess Dalla Patra Hassan el Kammel. On and on the investigation dragged. For years the police interviewed the most casual Elwell acquaintances, following every slim clue. At one point, they grilled Mrs. Larsen's husband mercilessly because he had served in the army and may have, at one time or another, fired a .45-caliber automatic.

Police spent months looking for a disheveled soldier who had been seen talking to Elwell days before he was shot, but this man was never found. The murder weapon, along with the killer, was never found. The Elwell family did not suffer. Elwell's mother, Mrs. Jennie A. Elwell, died in February 1927 and left more than $125,000 to her surviving son and two daughters, most of this being money her murdered son had earlier given her.

Elwell's wife struggled to save her murdered husband's estate for her son and was, for the most part, successful. Wronged woman that she was, Helen Elwell even had a decent marker erected over her philandering spouse's grave in a Ridgewood, New Jersey cemetery. After the burial ceremony, Mrs. Elwell was badgered by reporters for any kind of statement. She refused, however, to make one as she walked solemnly from the scene. But before getting into a car, the woman turned and said matter-of-factly: "Mr. Elwell was a piker all his life and a chaser of women."

THE KILLING OF A FILM DIRECTOR/ FEBRUARY 1, 1922

The 1922 murder of Hollywood director William Desmond Taylor (William Cunningham Deane-Tanner, 1877-1922) has remained one of filmdom's greatest unsolved crimes, one that has baffled investigators, criminal historians, and armchair detectives for more than eighty years. The tall, ruggedly handsome 45-year-old film director was considered one of the most cultured men in Hollywood, the envy of matinee idols and the love object of a bevy of Hollywood vamps and ingénues.

Born in Mallow, County Cork, Ireland, Taylor's original name was William Cunningham Deane-Tanner. He was the oldest son of a wealthy landowner who had been a colonel in the British army. His grandfather had been a member of the British parliament. Taylor, who had been trained from childhood to become an officer in the British army, graduated from Clinton College in 1895, but instead of joining the army, shocked his family by becoming a member of a theatrical group in Manchester, England. He took the stage name of William Desmond Taylor, one that he would use thereafter as his legal name.

Taylor's acting career stalled and he immigrated to Canada. He worked briefly as an engineer and then moved to the Klondike during the gold rush. He failed to find gold and moved to New York, where he met his younger brother, Dennis Deane-Tanner. The brothers opened an antique store, but saw little profit due to Taylor's expensive tastes and habits. He was addicted to custom-made clothes and the cuisine of expensive restaurants. He was also a blatant opportunist, so when he met Ethel Harrison, a member of the Floradora Sextet and niece of real estate tycoon Daniel J. Braker, he quickly proposed. The couple married a short time later, Taylor's wife knowing him only as William Deane-Tanner.

Meanwhile, Taylor's brother, who had been living meagerly and wearing threadbare suits because of Taylor's wastrel habits, was left to run the antique shop alone. Taylor continued to spend money lavishly, borrowing heavily from his wife's uncle. The ne'er-do-well actor told his drinking companions that he expected to inherit Braker's vast estate. The millionaire died in 1908, but Taylor was shocked to learn that all that was left him was the money Taylor had already borrowed. Taylor, desperate for cash, took $600 from the antique shop till, all the cash his brother had on hand, pocketed $100, and sent the balance to his wife before deserting her. He left no forwarding address.

In 1912, Ethel Tanner was granted a divorce on charges of adultery. She claimed that shortly before her husband abandoned her and their small daughter, Daisy, he had had an affair with a Broadway showgirl, taking this woman to an Adirondacks retreat, where he used the name Townsend. Dennis Tanner (neither brother was using the full name Deane-Tanner by this time) then sold his antique shop and, imitating his brother's actions, he, too, abandoned his wife and child.

Nothing was heard of either brother until 1914, when relatives of Tanner's ex-wife attended a movie and were stunned to see the missing man on the screen dashing about as

William Desmond Taylor as an actor in the early silent period; he later became one of Hollywood's leading directors.

a cowboy hero. The missing Dennis Tanner also had a minor role in the film. The film credits revealed no William Cunningham Deane-Tanner, however. The man playing the hero in the film was called William Desmond Taylor. The relatives rushed to reveal their discovery to the ex-Mrs. Tanner, but she was unconcerned with this news. She was already remarried to the millionaire owner of Delmonico's, one of New York's finest restaurants.

Taylor's daughter Daisy, however, wrote to her father. Taylor wrote back from Hollywood, telling her he was delighted to hear from her. When he joined the Canadian air force to fight in WWI, Taylor sent his daughter a photo of himself wearing a captain's uniform of the Royal Canadian Air Force. He cut quite a dashing figure, wearing jodhpurs and boots, and carrying a walking stick. This was Taylor's favorite photo of himself and he had dozens of copies made, giving this autographed photo to his many female admirers over the years.

William Desmond Taylor at the time he had become the top director for Famous Players-Lasky, a subsidiary of Paramount Studios.

After deserting his wife in New York, Taylor took bit parts in Hollywood movies to survive, but his striking, sharp features and charming manners soon earned him bigger parts. By 1917, he was given leading roles. A few years later Taylor began directing one-reelers, then features. He was appointed the chief director for Famous Players-Lasky, a subsidiary of Paramount Studios, in 1922, working under studio manager Charles Eyton. Both Eyton and Paramount chief Adolph Zukor considered Taylor one of the most gifted directors in Hollywood. They paid him a salary of $50,000 a year, then a staggering amount, he was given hefty bonuses for bringing his pictures in on schedule, and his expense account was almost equal to his salary.

The director lived stylishly in a bungalow court on Alvarado Street. The interior of his house was adorned by tapestries and original paintings, along with thousands of books. Taylor exuded the air of the refined, urbane middle-aged gentleman. Nothing in his life outwardly reflected an excessive lifestyle, which was then the hallmark of Hollywood. Other homes of Hollywood celebrities were adorned with bearskin or tiger skin rugs, sexually suggestive paintings and sculpture, and full bars where all manner of illegal liquor was available to guests eager to break the unpopular law of Prohibition. In some homes, like that of actress Barbara La Marr, guests were invited to help themselves to trays laden with cocaine and opium.

All this William Desmond Taylor disdained. He was the epitome of good taste and noble living, or so everyone thought. Secretly, Taylor was carrying on a half-dozen affairs with some of Hollywood's greatest silent film stars, including Mabel Normand, one of the most popular comediennes in the business, and ingénue Mary Miles Minter, who looked no more than fifteen, but was thirty during her tempestuous affair with Taylor in 1922. The director, who had an enormous sexual appetite, was also seeing actress Claire Windsor, along with a number of other Hollywood personalities, from extras to stars.

Much in Taylor's life remained a mystery, however, even to his Hollywood intimates. He seldom spoke about his background, and when he did he described his past in vague, contradictory terms, his stories varying widely. At the time, Taylor also employed a truculent chauffeur named Edward F. Sands, a man who avoided cameras whenever his employer's photo was taken. Henry Peavey, Taylor's butler, was as eccentric as Sands. He was discernibly homosexual, walking in mincing steps, employing feminine gestures in an exaggerated manner by flopping limp wrists, swaying his hips, speaking in a high falsetto voice that turned to a screech when he was excited.

In early 1922, Taylor took a European vacation. Upon his return, he called one of his paramours, Mabel Normand, to invite her to his house on the evening of February 1, 1922. The two dined together, eating a supper prepared by the fussy Peavey. That night Taylor told Normand that his chauffeur, Sands, had all but destroyed him financially, explaining that Sands, who had disappeared just before Taylor returned from Europe, had stolen his jewelry, damaged the director's two expensive cars while drunk, run up bills on his charge accounts, forged checks against Taylor's bank account, and even taken a good portion of his employer's wardrobe with him.

Taylor showed Normand his desk, which was littered with cancelled checks, bills, and receipts. He explained that while he was completing his income tax forms he had discovered his chauffeur's thefts. "That contemptible Sands has almost undone me," he told Normand. "Nearly every one of those checks is forged. He did such a good job that I can't tell which are my signatures and which are his. I've been going over them all day and it's driving me mad."

"What are you going to do about him?" Normand asked.

"I'll do plenty if they ever find Sands," Taylor said in a voice full of threat and anger.

Normand left the Taylor home at 7:45 p.m. Through the opened window of her limousine, Taylor handed her two books he wanted her to read. The comedienne gave him an affectionate kiss on the cheek and was driven home. Shortly after 8 p.m., actor Douglas MacLean and his wife Faith, along with others living in the bungalow court, heard what they thought was the sound of a car's backfire. They later stated that these sounds could have been shots being fired.

Faith MacLean looked out her front window at the time and saw a man leaving the Taylor house. "I suppose it was a

Taylor is shown next to his open-air limousine; the chauffeur at the wheel is Edward F. Sands, who is none other than Taylor's brother, Dennis Tanner. Taylor later claimed that his brother financially ruined him by looting his bank accounts.

Taylor's bungalow, left, in a court of lavish homes on Alvarado Boulevard in Los Angeles, where the director was mysteriously murdered.

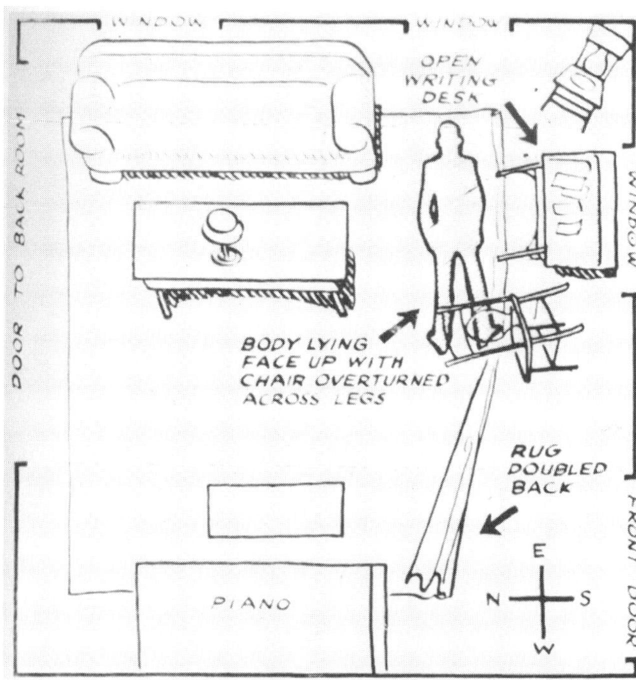

A Los Angeles Police Department diagram shows where Taylor's body was found in his bungalow, following his murder on the night of February 1, 1922.

Faith MacLean lived next door to Taylor and saw a strange figure leave his bungalow on the night of the murder, telling police: "It was dressed like a man ... but it walked like a woman."

Silent film star Mary Miles Minter, who was having a torrid affair with Taylor at the time of his murder; her career ended when her love letters to the director were discovered.

man," she later told police. "It was dressed like a man, but you know, funny-looking. It was dressed in a heavy coat with a muffler around the chin and a cap pulled down over the eyes. But it walked like a woman—quick little steps, with broad hips and short legs."

Edna Purviance, who had been Charlie Chaplin's first female costar and who occupied one of the bungalows in the court, saw lights go on in the Taylor house a few hours later and she knocked on Taylor's front door. There was no answer. Purviance thought Taylor was entertaining another one of his female friends, so she returned to her bungalow.

A short time later, Howard Fellows, Taylor's new chauffeur, knocked on the front door, but got no answer. He had been instructed by his employer to park the Taylor limousine if no one answered the door and then go home, which he did. At 7:30 the next morning, Henry Peavey, the butler, who lived elsewhere, arrived at the backdoor of the Taylor house. He picked up the morning milk bottle and, using his key, entered the bungalow. He walked into the living room and saw Taylor lying face-up on the floor. A chair rested on top of his legs. The director was fully dressed. His arms were at his sides and his legs were close together. His position was later described as "lying at attention."

A small trickle of blood had crusted about Taylor's mouth. Peavey leaned down and saw that the director was not breathing. He jumped up, raced out the backdoor, and ran through the court and down the sidewalk screaming: "Massa Taylor's dead!" (according to one Los Angeles newspaper).

Peavey was like a man possessed. He shook and twitched and jerked his body about in his frenzied flight from the murder scene, screeching in his falsetto voice as he ran down Alvarado Boulevard. Douglas MacLean and Edna Purviance

Dearest –
I love you – I
love you – I
love you – – –
XXX XXXXX X X
X
Yours always!
Mary

One of the many love notes written to Taylor by Mary Miles Minter, correspondence innocuous by today's standards, but shocking to the actress' countless fans in that innocent era.

Film comedienne Mabel Normand, who was also having an affair with Taylor at the time of his murder; her career, too, coupled to the revelation that she was addicted to drugs, was crushed.

were the first to answer his cries. They went into the Taylor house through the unlocked back door and Purviance spotted the director lying dead on the floor. She ran back to her own house and called Mabel Normand, not the police. Normand called Charles Eyton, Taylor's superior, and Eyton called Paramount mogul Adolph Zukor. Purviance, who knew about the director's many affairs, then called Mary Miles Minter. The ingénue was not available, but her protective mother, Charlotte Shelby, took the call and seemed indifferent to the news of Taylor's death.

While Purviance was making her Hollywood calls, MacLean phoned a doctor, who arrived shortly to examine Taylor. He felt for a pulse and found none. He listened for a heartbeat and heard none. "This man's dead," announced the physician.

"Of what?" MacLean asked.

"He died of gastric hemorrhage," said the doctor who then called the coroner's office to report Taylor's death. A few minutes later, Charles Eyton and his aides arrived. Edna Purviance went back to the Taylor bungalow to see Adolph Zukor, one of the most powerful men in Hollywood, arrive. By then Eyton and his aides were tidying up the bungalow. Eyton found some bottles of liquor and almost threw them at MacLean, barking: "Get rid of this booze, quick!" Zukor walked up to the body of his top director, studied it for a moment, and then turned to Eyton and said: "Find anything that might damage the studio's reputation and destroy it!"

Paramount had suffered major scandals in the recent past, including the horrendous rape-murder case against its stellar comedian, Roscoe "Fatty" Arbuckle, and Zukor did not want his studio to undergo another publicity disaster. Eyton and his men dashed around the bungalow, gathering female gar-

Actress Claire Windsor, who was also reportedly having an affair with Taylor at the time he was killed; unlike Minter and Normand, her career remained undamaged by gossip and rumor.

ments that were tucked into desk and bureau drawers, along with piles of love letters sent to the director from many of Hollywood's top female stars. A fire was started in the fireplace and Zukor, Eyton, and other studio executives began burning everything and anything that might incriminate Paramount in Taylor's untimely death.

Mabel Normand then arrived and raced into the bedroom where she began a desperate search for many of her own love letters to the philandering Taylor. As the Paramount executives and Normand were ransacking Taylor's home, Peavey, the butler, continued his hysterical screaming and gyrations up and down Alvarado Boulevard. Neighbors finally called police and Peavey, who had to be subdued, babbled out the fact that his employer was dead.

A coroner's assistant arrived and looked down on Taylor's corpse, saying: "He looks too neat lying there like that."

"Yeah," another person in the living room said, "like someone had laid him out."

Eyton stopped burning papers for a minute to glance over to the body and then he nervously shouted: "Turn him over! Turn him over!" The body was turned over and all in the living room gaped at the two bullet holes that had punctured the back of William Desmond Taylor. "Murder," gasped Eyton. A minute or so later Mabel Normand departed the Taylor house. Zukor then left, telling Eyton to remain behind and "handle this awful mess."

When detectives arrived to inspect the body, they concluded that Taylor had not been shot where his body was found. The holes in his suit coat did not line up with the holes in his back, so they propped the body up at his desk chair and hiked up the suitcoat so that the holes lined up. Taylor had been seated at his desk, working, they theorized, when his killer crept up behind him and shot him twice. Then the killer laid out the body on the floor, perhaps to rifle Taylor's pockets, which the detectives found were empty.

At the backdoor of the house were a number of cigarette butts, indicating that the killer had waited there the previous evening, until Normand and Peavey had left for the night. Edna Purviance again called Charlotte Shelby, mother of Mary Miles Minter, to tell her that Taylor had been shot to death. Shelby drove to her mother's home, where her daughter Mary had been living. Mother and daughter had been arguing for several months, mostly about Mary's clandestine affair with Taylor, and Mary had moved out of her mother's house, going to live with her grandmother, Julia Branch Miles. Shelby went to the Miles home and confronted her daughter, shouting through a locked door: "Mr. Taylor was found murdered this morning!"

Mary Miles Minter quickly grabbed the keys to her car and began to leave the house when her mother grabbed her, ordering her to stay in her room. Mary struggled free, ran to the car, and drove at high speed to the Taylor residence. Police were swarming over the place and refused to let her in. Minter then went to see Mabel Normand and stayed with her for several hours. Whatever these two movie stars had to say about their dead paramour was never revealed.

The worst they anticipated came about when detectives unearthed their gushing love letters to Taylor. The press soon acquired these and published the intimate thoughts of both Normand and Minter. Police also found, beneath a stack of film scripts, dozens of pornographic photos showing Taylor with several film actresses.

The scandal heightened when it was learned that Mabel Normand was an opium addict. A note found in the director's home from Taylor to Normand chastised her for continuing this "filthy, beastly habit." So incensed had Taylor been about Normand's drug problem that he had conducted his own investigation of drug dealers in Los Angeles' Chinatown. He had turned over his findings to the district attorney, leading investigators to speculate that Taylor might have been murdered by drug traffickers for revenge.

Even Mary Pickford, the greatest film star of the era, was

Taylor is shown in uniform with silent film star Mary Pickford; the director had served in the Canadian Royal Air Force in World War I. This photo led reporters to Pickford's door.

Dennis Deane Tanner, the director's ubiquitous brother, who vanished shortly before Taylor's murder; many believed that he had killed his famous brother after looting his bank accounts.

drawn into the case. She had merely given Taylor an autographed picture of herself, but because he had kept this on his bedstand, it was suggested that even the pristine Pickford was having an affair with the director. When asked about her relationship with Taylor, Pickford replied that she did not heed Hollywood gossip. "I will pray," was her final comment as she closed her door to reporters.

A strong suspect in the case was the missing chauffeur, Edward Sands, who turned out to be none other than Taylor's brother, Dennis Deane-Tanner. Detectives pursued the theory that Sands-Tanner had looted his brother's checking account, wardrobe, and jewelry box in retaliation for Taylor's bankrupting him in New York and later using him as a lowly servant in Hollywood. This so rankled the younger brother, one account had it, that Tanner went to the bungalow on the night of February 1-2, 1922, and shot his brother dead.

Charlotte Shelby also became a prime suspect. Taylor had been shot with a .38-caliber revolver, and Shelby was known to possess just such a weapon. In fact, she was seen practice-firing this weapon only a short time before the director was murdered. Her motive, it was said, had nothing to do with protecting her daughter's image, but that Shelby herself had been having an affair with Taylor and murdered him in revenge for having been rejected in favor of her daughter. It was Shelby, some said, who left the Taylor home that night disguised as a man.

The valet-butler Henry Peavey was a suspect briefly. Peavey had been arrested a few weeks before the murder on a morals charge, for attempting to seduce a young boy in a Hollywood park. Taylor had used his influence to save his butler from a jail term and paid his fine for him. Peavey, instead of appreciating Taylor's kindness, it was claimed, re-

Mary Miles Minter in retirement; her mother, Charlotte Shelby, left, some believed, killed Taylor after he left her for her daughter and she disguised herself as a man when leaving the bungalow that night.

sented his employer's knowing about his perversions and killed him for that knowledge. Peavey later went insane and died of paresis in a Napa mental institution in 1931.

Taylor's killer was never identified. The amorous film director was buried as the victim of an unsolved murder case, one that has caused amateur sleuths to sift through the slim evidence in the case over the years and produce wild conjecture and impossible theories. Taylor's murder and the resulting publicity ended the careers of Mabel Normand and Mary Miles Minter. Normand was branded a dope fiend and found it almost impossible to obtain movie roles. Her life was further complicated in 1923 when her chauffeur, Horace A. Greer, shot and almost killed millionaire Courtland S. Dines as the Denver oil tycoon was about to enter Normand's limousine for a night on the town with the star. Both chauffeur and tycoon had been battling over Normand's sexual favors. This scandal, hot on the heels of the Taylor murder, utterly destroyed her career. She married actor Lew Cody in 1926. A few years later she contracted tuberculosis and died in a sanitarium on February 22, 1930, at age thirty-three.

Mary Miles Minter fared better. She separated from her domineering mother, later battling Shelby in court for control of her own estate. Mary invested her savings wisely in real estate and lived out her life in comfort. To the end of her days, Mary Miles Minter kept an autographed portrait of Taylor in her bedroom. He was her one great love and her one great mistake.

THE MINISTER AND THE CHOIR SINGER/ September 16, 1922

The secret affair between the Reverend Edward Wheeler Hall (1882-1922) and Eleanor Reinhardt Mills (1888-1922), the petite, pretty woman who sang in his choir, brought these lovers to violent death, creating one of America's greatest mysteries. The trials involving the Hall family that resulted from the double murder were some of the most lurid of the sensation-ridden 1920s. The press indulged itself in a glut of garish reportage, feeding on impossible characters they dubbed "The Pig Woman," and "The Idiot." In the end, no one profited except the readers and the publishers of those sensation pandering tabloids.

It all began when an amorous couple, Raymond Schneider, twenty-two, and Pearl Bahmer, fifteen, strolled down a lover's lane three miles outside of New Brunswick, New Jersey, early on a Saturday morning, September 16, 1922. The couple walked into a famous spooning area, De Russey's Lane, then into Phillips' Lane, named after the nearby Phillips farm. Schneider and Bahmer stopped, frozen in their tracks.

Before them, under a crab apple tree, were the bodies of a man and woman. Both had been shot in the head. The man, the Reverend Hall, lay flat on his back, a wide Panama hat over his head. His own calling card was propped up against his foot, a grim joke rendered by the killer. The woman, Mills, lay with her head cradled in Hall's arm.

Schneider and Bahmer ran for the police and soon the crab apple orchard was swarming with police and detectives. The balding, chubby, once-affable Hall had been shot only once. A .32-caliber bullet had been sent into the Episcopal minister's back. His death appeared to have been swift and almost merciful. Mrs. Mills, however, was another matter. Her killer had shot her three times in the middle of the forehead.

The 34-year-old Mills had been the lead soprano in Hall's Church of St. John the Evangelist of New Brunswick. Her voice had thrilled the congregation as it lilted through one hymn after another. Someone, after shooting her to death, had undoubtedly remembered too often hearing that voice and had vindictively slashed Mills' throat from ear to ear. An autopsy, not fully described until four years later, showed that the killer had savagely cut out her tongue and then hacked out her vocal cords.

The murdered couple had obviously been caught in the middle of making love, or so police believed. Since both were married at the time, it was quickly thought that their cuckolded spouses could have been involved in the deaths. The manner in which the victims were neatly dressed also allowed some officials to speculate that they had not been killed when dressed, that they had been found naked, while making love, and killed.

After murdering them, the killer or killers had dressed the victims, investigators speculated. Mills had been clothed in her blue lawn dress with red polka dots, placing her blue velvet turban on her head, her black hose on her legs, and brown oxfords on her small feet. Reverend Hall was also neatly attired, wearing a gray worsted suit, white shirt with high stiff collar, white tie, black socks, and black shoes.

The killer had even been careful enough to button Reverend Hall's suit coat and, when the Panama hat was removed, it was noted that the clergyman's glasses had been meticulously placed on the bridge of his nose. Mills' mutilated head was covered with a long scarf. The whole gruesome scene appeared to be a setting which had been posed by a killer with a macabre sense of humor. He had mocked his victims, placing them together to signify their adulterous relationship. Scattered over the bodies and in the immediate area were dozens of love letters Mrs. Mills had written to the Reverend Hall over the years.

By leaving these love notes, torrid by that era's standards, the killer further emphasized the illicit relationship between the murdered pair, as if to vindicate the killings. Later, these letters would be published widely in the nation's press. James Mills, husband of the slain choir singer, callously sold off his wife's missives, which gushed love for another man, at $500 a letter.

As police officers, detectives, and coroner's officials stomped about the murder site, newsmen as well as curious residents, arrived and the site took on the image of a carnival. One of the reporters raced to a telephone and called Mrs. Frances Noel Stevens Hall, the pastor's wife, telling her that her husband had just been found dead, murdered, lying next to the body of his lead choir singer, Mrs. Mills. Was there anything between the couple, the naive newsman asked.

Mrs. Hall did not reply, slamming down the receiver. Mrs. Hall was the richest woman in New Brunswick, New Jersey. She lived in the largest mansion in New Brunswick and was seven years older than her slain husband. Mrs. Hall was autocratic, arrogant, and aloof to gossip and scandal, or so she maintained all of her august life.

A half hour after the newsman's phone call, Mrs. Hall's wealthy cousin, Henry de la Bruyere Carpender, a leading member of New York's Stock Exchange, appeared at the murder site. With him was William E. Florence, New Jersey state senator, and the Hall family lawyer. Carpender ignored policemen at the site and went immediately to the body of his brother-in-law, kneeling for a moment at his side. He took the hand of the corpse briefly and said: "Well, old fellow, you never did this yourself." Carpender ignored the body of Mrs. Mills. Both he and Florence then departed without uttering a single word to the police, as if their visit were merely to verify Hall's death.

The authorities at the scene did not question Carpender because they were too busy arguing over the jurisdiction of the case. Azariah Beekman, prosecutor for Somerset County, pointed out that even though the bodies of the murdered couple were inside his county by 350 feet, they had been murdered in Middlesex County, which contained New Brunswick, the home of the deceased, and the case properly belonged with Middlesex officials. Middlesex authorities shouted back that it was a Somerset case since the corpses

The Reverend Edward Wheeler Hall, of New Brunswick, New Jersey, murdered with his mistress, Eleanor Mills, in a lover's lane on the night of September 16, 1922.

Lovesick Eleanor Mills, who sang in the choir at Hall's church, and who boldly cuckolded her husband, while carrying on a torrid affair with the minister.

A detective simulates the position of Hall's body, when it was found the morning after the murders. Hall's calling card had been propped up at the feet by the killer and Mrs. Mills' love letters to him were strewn next to the two bodies.

De Russey's Lane, a spooning area, where the minister and his mistress were slain, discovered by a young couple, who later came under suspicion by baffled detectives.

were found in that county, though barely. Obviously no one wanted to assume the responsibility for this case from the beginning.

Technically, this last position was correct and Beekman had to bow to the law. Somerset County assumed responsibility for the case and the bodies were sent to the morgue. After the bodies were removed, Somerset detective George Totten scooped up several .32-caliber cartridges, the same caliber bullets that had killed the murdered couple. In a few hours, the area was overrun with hundreds of spectators. Vendors appeared, hawking hot dogs, soda pop, and popcorn. Whatever clues might have been present were trampled into the dust. The first people police interviewed that day were James Mills and Frances Hall.

Mills, eleven years older than his slain wife, was the sexton and janitor of Hall's church. He was meek and a seemingly ineffectual man who openly admitted that his wife had been seeing Reverend Hall, but he insisted that their relationship was platonic. When pressed by reporters, Mills admitted that his attractive young wife had been leaving their house at all hours of the day and night for months. It was all innocent, he said. He pointed out that Reverend Hall had visited his home many times, staying for dinner.

Pressed for more details concerning Mrs. Mills' movements on the last night of her life, the mild-mannered Mills admitted that his wife had left their house at 7:30 p.m. on Thursday and that was the last time he had seen her alive. Before she left the house, Mills asked his wife where she was going. He quoted her taunting reply: "Why don't you follow me and find out?" He said he waited until midnight for his wife to return and then went to bed. He awoke at 2 a.m. and, finding his wife still not home, went to the church, which was empty. He returned home, went back to sleep, and by 9 the next morning, he was back at the church looking for Mrs. Mills.

Mills said he saw Mrs. Hall and told her his wife had not come home the previous night. He said that Mrs. Hall had stated that her husband, too, had not returned home. But there the spouses let the matter lay. They went about their business, saying nothing to anyone, including the police. When Mrs. Mills' body was found about thirty-six hours later, Mills was found in a New Brunswick drugstore, sipping a chocolate soda. The obvious unconcern of Mills and, especially of the very proper Mrs. Hall, as to the whereabouts of their spouses, brought suspicion on both of them.

Hall had married Frances Stevens in 1911. She was then thirty-six and wealthy. He was a struggling 29-year-old clergyman who, two years after his marriage to Frances, was appointed pastor of the well-endowed St. John the Evangelist church. Members of the wealthy Stevens family were the richest supporters of this church. Frances Stevens was no prize. She was dowdy, overweight, had a decidedly unattractive face and a severe personality.

New Brunswick residents believed Hall had married Frances Stevens for her money, but the marriage proved to be happy, at least on the surface. When Mrs. Hall finally consented to answer questions from police, she said that her husband had left their home at 7:30 p.m., giving the exact time as Mills had given when explaining his wife's departure. She said that the Reverend Hall had told her he had "some business to attend to."

Mrs. Hall said she had spent a "sleepless night" when realizing that her husband had not returned home, and the next morning, she had called the police, asking if there had been any "casualties" reported. This was an odd word, but Mrs. Hall was not challenged; she was one of the most distinguished citizens in the community and authorities were cautious in interviewing her. Mrs. Hall also pointed out that police undoubtedly had a record of her call and that they had told her that no "casualties" had been reported.

Wealthy and aristocratic, Mrs. Frances Hall was aloof and almost indifferent when she was charged with the murder of her errant husband.

Jane Gibson, the so-called "Pig Woman," claimed that Mrs. Hall and her brothers were the culprits.

Ailing and wheeled into court on a stretcher, Jane Gibson shouted out her accusations at the Hall family members, while her mother screamed from the gallery: "she's a liar!"

Servants who worked in the Hall mansion emphatically stated that Mrs. Hall and her brother, Willie, who was thought to be rather dim-witted, had never left the house on Thursday night, the time of the murders. A watchman who patrolled the exclusive neighborhood, however, reported that a woman wearing a large gray coat entered the side door of the mansion at 2 a.m. on Friday, but he could not identify the woman as Mrs. Hall. Mrs. Hall then admitted that she had been the woman seen by the watchman, and that she could not sleep, and had gone with her brother, Willie, to the church in search of her husband. She then added that she believed her husband had gone to give spiritual aid to some parishioner who "might have been taken ill."

Mrs. Hall and her brother, said Mrs. Hall, then went to the Mills home, but when they saw no lights on, they returned home. It was apparent that Mrs. Hall had known for some time that her husband had been having an affair with the pert Mrs. Mills. In fact, the affair had been going on since early 1922. After eleven years of marriage, Mrs. Hall, at age forty-seven, was heavyset, gray-haired, and could have passed as her husband's matronly mother instead of his wife. Mrs. Mills, on the other hand, was young, vivacious, and attractive.

Willie Stevens, who appeared to be a big, oafish bachelor, and who was later ridiculed because of his ungainly appearance, at first insisted that he had never left the Hall mansion, but under continued police questioning, admitted accompanying his sister to the church early Friday morning. Stevens was rather comical. His thick, uncombed hair stuck outward like a porcupine and his thick-lensed glasses made him appear myopic. He wore a walrus mustache over thick, sensuous lips, and his receding chin tucked itself into a bull neck.

Willie Stevens had been left a sizeable fortune, more than $150,000, but he was given only a $40-a-week allowance so that he would not "spend away his fortune." Stevens liked costumes and was made an honorary fireman. He spent a good deal of time at the New Brunswick Fire Department. He purchased expensive steaks with his allowance and took these to a firehouse where he cooked them for the appreciative firemen, who treated him like a mascot. He was given a fireman's hat and Willie proudly wore this on strolls through the town's Hungarian quarter, where extravagant costumes were the norm and Willie in his fireman's hat did not cause undue attention.

Henry Stevens, another brother who lived in Lavallette, New Jersey, and who was enormously wealthy, came under suspicion because his ability as a hunter and marksman was well known. It was pointed out that it would not take a sharpshooter to kill Hall and Mills since they were both shot at almost point blank range. Henry Stevens was as arrogant and uncooperative with the police as his sister, conduct that made him appear that he was hiding something, but he produced an iron-clad alibi. He was at a waterfront party with a host of people when the murders occurred.

Several local suspects were picked up and questioned. Then police, seemingly helpless, promptly arrested the couple that had been unlucky enough to have found the bodies, Schneider and Bahmer. Raymond Schneider was found to have recently left a wife of only two months. He was unemployed, and described as an "idler." Pearl Bahmer was portrayed as a young vagrant. Both were arrested and charged with the murders, but were held only briefly.

Schneider, at this time, claimed that another youth, Clifford Hayes, had shot Hall and Mills, saying that Hayes thought he was killing Pearl Bahmer and her father. Hayes was arrested, but discharged after proving to be innocent. Schneider later admitted lying under oath, giving no reason for implicating Hayes. He was convicted of perjury in a later trial and sent to prison for two years.

Then the strangest person in this strange cast of characters stepped forward, Mrs. Jane Gibson, also known as Mrs. Jane Easton. She was thrice divorced, owned a hog farm near the murder site, and became the chief witness against the Stevens family. The press immediately nicknamed Mrs. Gibson "The Pig Woman" because she owned a hog farm. Gibson came forward to state that she saw the killers, or heard them, on the night of the murders, September 14, 1922.

Gisbon said she had been riding her mule Jennie in search of poachers who had been stealing corn from a field, next to the Phillips farm. She said she heard men and women arguing in the nearby crab apple orchard, then shots. She mounted faithful Jennie and fled. This was not enough to indict the Stevens family members. On November 27, 1922, a grand jury filed a "no bill" verdict, meaning no one had been indicted for the murders.

Mrs. Hall left for a year-long vacation in Italy. James Mills continued to ring the bells of the church and Mrs. Gibson returned to her hog farm. The case remained in limbo, the murders unsolved. Four years went by before New Brunswick police learned that Louise Geist, a maid in the Stevens mansion, had lied about Mrs. Stevens' whereabouts on the night of the murders. Geist had married a piano salesman, Arthur M. Riehl, who divorced his wife in 1926, charging that she was a liar, and stating that his wife had been paid $6,000 by the Stevens family to keep quiet about what she knew in connection with the Hall-Mills slayings.

This story was bannered in the New York *Mirror*. The paper's managing editor, Phillip Payne, who had wrung every detail from the 1922 murders, urged New Jersey governor A. Harry Moore to reopen the case, based on Riehl's allegations. Payne persuaded Moore and others to charge the Stevens family by saying that he had employed a fingerprint expert, who had found Henry Stevens' thumbprint on the calling card left at the murdered Reverend Hall's foot. On July 28, 1926, police marched into the Hall mansion and arrested an indignant Mrs. Hall in her nightgown, and sleepy-eyed Willie Stevens for murder. Henry Stevens was awakened at his residence and also charged with murder.

Willie Stevens, center, called an "idiot" by the press, proved himself sane and reasonable in his testimony.

James Mills, the cuckolded husband of the slain Eleanor Mills; he sold his wife's love letters to the tabloids and served as a commentator for the press in the 1926 trial.

Mrs. Hall posted a $15,000 bond and was released, but she and her two brothers went on trial on November 3, 1926, at Somerville, New Jersey. The courtroom in the small courthouse was packed with five hundred people, even though it was designed to hold no more than half that number. Scores of reporters descended upon the town to write endless stories, real and imagined, about the case. Included among these headline-hunters was Charlotte Mills, the teenage flapper daughter of the slain Mrs. Mills. Her father appeared as a prosecution witness against the Stevens, but his memory was hazy and he offered little that would convict the family members.

Again, Mrs. Gibson, the celebrated "Pig Woman," appeared for the prosecution. She had recently undergone a cancer operation and in a dramatic move, was brought into court on a hospital bed, moaning and groaning. She testified in this position, sometimes craning her head to stare at Mrs. Hall, who sat at the nearby defense table. Hall refused to set her eyes on her accuser and she remained aloof during the entire proceedings.

Mrs. Gibson seemed to recall more details in 1926 than what she could remember in 1922 and it soon became apparent that she was playing to the crowd and enjoying her fame. Croaked Gibson: "I was peeking and peeking and peeking" into the crab apple orchard, and that she saw Mrs. Stevens, and her brothers Willie and Henry get out of a car near the crab apple tree. She said she heard a woman's voice, ostensibly Mrs. Hall's, shout: "Explain these letters!" She heard the Stevens' brothers arguing with the Reverend Hall and then, she said, there was a struggle.

As she eked out her story, a nurse applied cold cream to Gibson's lips, so that she could continue to bravely unravel her murder tale. She said that there was more shouting and fighting and she became frightened and "I run for my mule." Gibson said she was fleeing from the scene when she heard "bang, bang, bang, three quick shots. Then I stumbled over a stump getting on the mule and I run for home." She went on to say that she had lost her moccasin and returned to the scene, where she saw Mrs. Hall bending "over something."

Adding to the drama and confusion at that moment was Gibson's elderly mother, who sat behind her in the first row of the visitor's gallery, yelling loudly at her daughter's every utterance: "She's a liar! She's a liar! She's a liar!" The defense attorneys attacked Gibson's memory with a vengeance. They asked her if she could remember the names of her three ex-husbands. She could not. She could not remember when she had been married or when she was divorced from these men. How then, the defense pointed out to the jury, could Gibson remember anything about a murder case that was four years old? Gibson was then taken back to a Newark hospital, but only after the ambulance stopped at her request to get her a pint of ice cream from a road vendor.

Mrs. Hall then went to the witness stand and showed remarkable confidence. She answered badgering questions from the prosecution with ease. Unruffled, she was dubbed the "Iron Widow" by the press. Willie Stevens also proved to be anything but "the Idiot," as the press had earlier profiled him. He, like his sister, was cool and calm under fire and could not be moved from his original story regarding his actions and that of his sister's on the night of the murder. The jury was impressed enough to render a not guilty verdict on December 3, 1926.

Mrs. Frances Hall on the witness stand in 1926, where she told the court that she had no idea that her husband was having an affair with Eleanor Mills; her dignified composure convinced jurors of her innocence.

The Stevens family had not escaped unscathed, having to spend more than $200,000 in a trial that cost everyone twice that amount. Then the Stevens family sued the New York *Mirror* for $3 million. The case was settled out of court for an undisclosed amount. The editor, Phillip Payne, who had brought the 1926 court battle into existence, disappeared in a transcontinental flight in 1927, taking off in a monoplane piloted by Lloyd W. Bertaud in a flight from Maine to Rome. The flamboyant editor and Bertaud vanished somewhere over the Atlantic. Payne was later profiled in two films, *Five Star Final* (1931) and *Unholy Partners* (1941) portrayed in both films by Edward G. Robinson.

Mrs. Gibson died of cancer, still a celebrity on February 7, 1930, in a Jersey City hospital. Mrs. Hall remained in New Brunswick for another twenty years, attending her husband's church and continuing her role as the grande dame of the community. Willie Stevens gave up his position as an honorary fireman in New Brunswick. He spent the remainder of his days with his sister behind the huge walls of the Stevens mansion. The murders of Reverend Hall and Mrs. Mills remained unsolved.

THE MURDER OF JULIA WALLACE/ January 20, 1931

Much like Mrs. Stevens in the Hall-Mills case, William Herbert Wallace (1878-1933) was accused and tried for murdering his spouse in a strange case that still mystifies British criminologists. Wallace was an insurance salesman and amateur chess

Attractive, sophisticated Julia Wallace, found murdered in her locked home in Liverpool, England, on the night of January 20, 1931, a homicide that baffles police to this day.

The Wallace home at 29 Wolverton Street, shown only hours after Julia Wallace was found bludgeoned to death; all the doors and windows were apparently bolted from the inside.

player, was scheduled to play in the Second Class Championship at the Liverpool Central Chess Club on January 19, 1931, the night before his wife was murdered. Julia Wallace, like her husband, was mild-mannered and refined.

The couple first met in Manchester in 1911 after he had returned from the orient, where he had done bureaucratic work in China and India while studying western stoic philosophy. The two were intellectual, sharing an interest in music and philosophy. They were married in 1913. Wallace recorded eighteen years of peaceful, happy married life in his diary.

On the night of the chess championship, club manager Samuel Beattie took a telephone message for Wallace. A man who identified himself only as R.M. Qualtrough requested that Wallace meet him at 7:30 the next night at 25 Menlove Gardens East. Although the name Qualtrough is fairly common in Liverpool, the caller spelled out his name for Beattie to make sure he got it. When Wallace, fifty-two, arrived late at the club and received the message, he remarked that he did not know anyone by that name.

Assuming the matter concerned insurance, Wallace went to meet Qualtrough, but the address proved to be fictitious. Wallace returned to his Liverpool home on January 20, 1931, at about 8:45 p.m. He was apparently unable to gain entrance. The front and back doors were bolted from the inside and his wife did not answer. His neighbors, John and Florence Johnston, were leaving their house then, and he spoke to them about his house being locked. Then he tried the door again and was able to open it.

Upstairs, Wallace found 50-year-old Julia Wallace dead. She had been bludgeoned eleven times, although the police pathologist later testified that the first blow almost certainly killed her and that all the additional blows were "gratuitous." Wallace ran back downstairs, calling out to the Johnstons, "Come and see. She has been killed."

Qualtrough was never found. Wallace told police that he had been home between "about 6:05 and 6:45 on the night of the murder. A 14-year-old milk delivery boy said he saw Julia Wallace take in the milk at 6:30 p.m., and the evening paper

Introspective, chess-playing William Herbert Wallace was tried for the murder of his wife and later released on appeal, although many believed he had killed his wife.

had been delivered at 6:35 p.m. The paper was found spread on the kitchen table. The pathologist, Professor John Edward MacFall, set the time of death at 6:10 p.m. When a locksmith was asked to check the locks on the doors, he found them inadequate. The strongest evidence against William Wallace was his normal stoicism. Police thought he was behaving too calmly. He was arrested on February 2, 1931, and went to trial on April 22, 1931.

The prosecution suggested that Wallace made the "Qualtrough" call himself to avert suspicion. Beattie said the voice on the phone was "gruff but ordinary"; surely Beattie would have recognized Wallace's voice. Wallace had no apparent motive for killing his wife and no murder weapon was found. Justice Wright instructed the jurors that all the evidence against Wallace was circumstantial, strongly suggesting that he considered the case not proven. The jury nevertheless found Wallace guilty of murder. Wright reluctantly sentenced Wallace to death.

The Court of Criminal Appeal overturned Wallace's conviction four weeks later, and Wallace was set free. A bizarre backlash of public opinion occurred. During the trial, Liverpool residents seemed to believe that Wallace had been horribly wronged, but afterward he was harassed by people who believed he had gotten away with murder. His insurance company considerately transferred him out of the field to a desk job, but his former chess playing partners refused to associate with him, and children taunted him by chanting rhymes they made up about the murder.

Wallace had had recurring stomach troubles and they returned full force in December 1932. By February 9, 1933 the pain was so severe he needed to be hospitalized, and he died of kidney disease on February 26, 1933. To this day, many believe Wallace to be the killer of a wife he ostensibly loved and cared for through most of his adult life.

THE STRANGE DEATH OF STARR FAITHFULL/June 8, 1931

On June 8, 1931, a wandering beachcomber named Daniel Moriarity, making his rounds on a Long Island, New York, beach made a gruesome discovery. Washed up on the sand was the body of a beautiful woman with long hair. Moriarity pulled the body away from the water line and summoned the police. A check of the missing persons' files turned up the oddly poetic name Starr Faithfull (Starr Wyman; 1906-1931), a 25-year-old woman, whose disappearance had been reported three days earlier by her stepfather Stanley Faithfull, a retired manufacturing chemist.

An autopsy showed that Starr had died from drowning. But the police weren't sure if it was murder or suicide. District

Starr Faithfull in 1927, a doomed flapper looking for thrills and fun and found death four years later.

Attorney Elvin Edwards was convinced she had met with foul play. There were visible lacerations on the upper arms, probably inflicted by someone with a powerful grasp, Edwards surmised. The evidence of rape was inconclusive and medical examiners debated the point for two days. Edwards, however, was certain that the girl had been criminally assaulted and was anxious to establish hard evidence to back up his belief.

A check of the woman's background revealed that she was the daughter of Frank W. Wyman, divorced from Starr's mother in the early 1920s. Mrs. Wyman was a Bostonian of high social standing. She had lived with her two daughters, Starr and Tucker, at Faithfull's home in Greenwich Village. Before the Depression, the girls had vacationed in Europe. The junket abroad only served to whet Starr's appetite for more of the good life. But the family suffered some financial reversals that put such further excursions out of reach.

Unable to join the privileged globe trotters, Starr lived vicariously in their world by crashing the last-night parties on ocean liners, slipping off the ship minutes ahead of the final call. While pursuing her own peculiar fantasy, Starr made the acquaintance of Dr. George Jameson-Carr, a ship's surgeon stationed aboard the *Franconia.* He was a serious-minded intellectual, well versed in the arts and literature.

Starr fell hopelessly in love with the doctor, but soon came to understand that not only did he not share her rapture, but he found her advances annoying. When Jameson-Carr asked her to leave his quarters, Starr stumbled out of the room in a drunken stupor and disappeared into the crowd. Unknown to the doctor, she remained on board, forcing the captain to summon a tug boat to pick her up as the ship headed down river toward the open sea.

On June 4, 1931, the date of her disappearance, Starr was observed wandering the docks where the *Mauritania* and *Ile de France* were about to set sail. After leaving home that morning, Starr went to a Manhattan department store, where she wrote a brief farewell note to Jameson-Carr, which she mailed to England via the *Olympic.* "Hello Bill, Old Thing: It's all up with me now. This is something I am going to put through. The only thing that bothers me about it, the only thing I dread, is being outwitted and prevented from doing this which is the only possible thing for me to do. If one wants to get away with murder one has to jolly well keep one's wits about one."

There was speculation that Starr had stowed away on board and then committed suicide from the deck of one of the great liners as it left the port of New York. Edwards was still insisting that she had been murdered, when new revelations about her past appeared in newspapers that had kept the case alive through myriad headlined stories. A year earlier, Starr had been found in a hotel room with a man identified as Joseph Collins, thought to be a male prostitute. Hearing her cries for help, hotel guests alerted the police.

When officers entered her room they found her naked and bleeding. Starr was taken to Bellvue Hospital, where she spent the night screaming for her parents to come and get her. "I was drinking gin as far as I know...I don't remember...I suppose somebody knocked me around a bit," she said. The police dismissed Collins, even though there was little doubt he had beaten Starr. Police found a diary, which she called her "Mem Book," several entries alluding to a man with whom she was conducting an affair.

Starr Faithfull in 1931, then haunting ocean liners before their departure and joining farewell parties, where she knew no one.

This man was identified only as "A.J.P." The entries mentioned continuing sexual torment. "Spent night A.J.P. Providence. Oh Horror, Horror, Horror!!" Stanley Faithfull provided additional details to the press, revealing that Starr had been seduced at the age of eleven by an elderly Boston financier whom he called "X." Following up on this, the press linked "X" to "A.J.P.," coming up with the name of Andrew J. Peters, former U.S. Congressman and one-time mayor of Boston.

As a young girl, Starr had played with the mayor's children. Mrs. Faithfull was distantly related. A large sum of money,

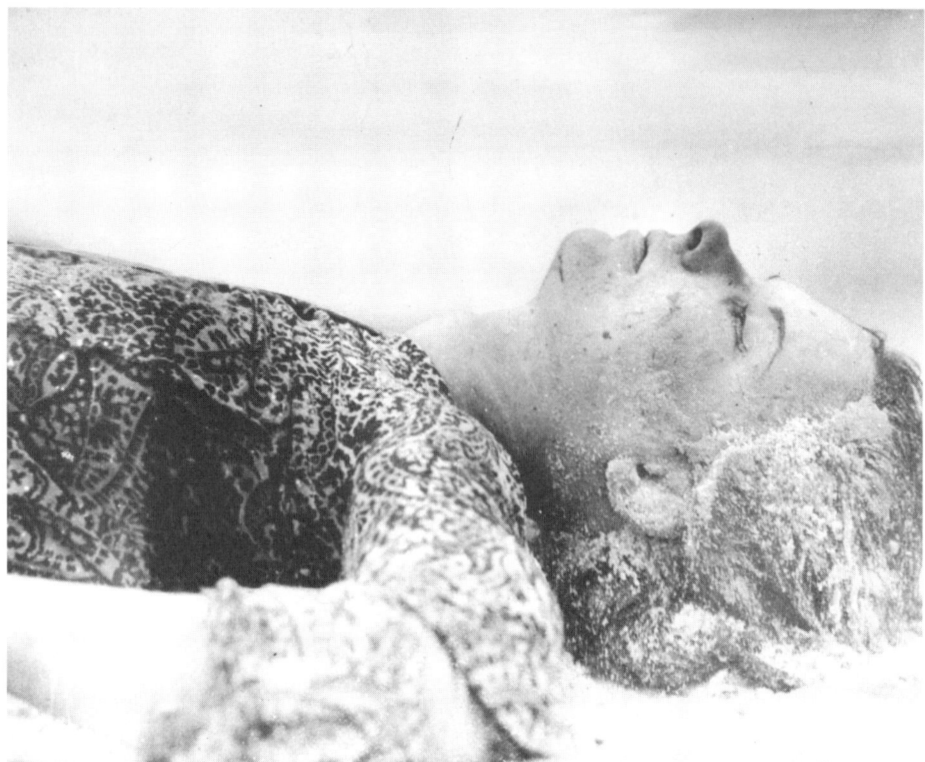

June 8, 1931: Starr Faithfull lies dead on a lonely beach in Long Island, New York; her death would plague detectives and mystery writers for decades to come.

Stanley Faithfull, Starr's eccentric stepfather, released all the family secrets to the press and sought the eerie limelight shed upon his wayward stepdaughter.

Detectives hover over the sand-blown body of Starr Faithfull; at first they believed she had either accidentally drowned or committed suicide, but an autopsy pointed to murder.

Elizabeth Taylor won an Oscar as the star-crossed call girl in the 1960 film, *Butterfield 8*, which was based upon the short and tragic life of Starr Faithfull.

estimated to be between $20,000 and $80,000 had been paid to the Faithfulls as a "settlement," for damages done to Starr. The former mayor had allegedly enticed the young girl into his home, drugged her, and raped her. Peters issued denials of wrongdoing.

District Attorney Edwards then announced that he had positively identified the killers, who had taken Starr to Long Beach, drugged her, and drowned her. He claimed that one of the killers was a prominent New York politician and he promised to arrest the culprits within thirty-six hours. However, when pressed for further details, Edwards later retreated and a follow-up statement was never issued and no suspects were taken into custody.

Suicide seemed to be the only plausible theory. Dr. Jameson-Carr returned from England and revealed the existence of three suicide letters sent by Starr between May 30 and June 4, 1931. "I am going now," she wrote to Jameson-Carr in care of the liner *Berengaria* on May 30, 1931, "to end my worthless disorderly bore of an existence before I ruin anyone else's life as well." She described in melodramatic detail what she imagined to be the perfect death experience. "I am going to drink slowly, keeping aware every second. Also I am going to enjoy my last cigarettes. I won't worry because men flirt with me in the streets. I shall encourage them. I don't care who they are."

The ship's doctor was in Belgium when he received word of her death. Jameson-Carr rushed back to New York to try to clear up the mystery. Stanley Faithfull declared that the letters Jameson-Carr claimed to have received were forgeries. After careful analysis, a battery of handwriting experts declared the letters were genuine. Those familiar with the case concurred that Starr Faithfull killed herself over an unrequited love. Her sister Tucker recalled an occasion in London when Starr attempted suicide by taking twenty-four grains of allonal, but was revived by physicians.

Morris Markey, a journalist for the *New Yorker* Magazine was not convinced by this logic. In 1948, he offered the more titillating theory that Starr had been murdered on the very same night she planned to kill herself. The unknown assailant was someone she had picked up in town. Her scribbled letter to Jameson-Carr on June 4 had, after all, promised that she would encourage any man who came her way. The killer, Markey surmised, grew frustrated by her teasing games. "And then I think she teased this unknown man beyond endurance...he mauled her...then he was frightened...and decided that she would never tell of it," Markey wrote. The assailant dragged Starr Faithfull to the water and held her head under until she was dead.

The first autopsy performed on Starr showed the presence of two grains of Veronal, not enough to induce death. There was enough food in her system to suggest that she had eaten a final meal before meeting her death. The second autopsy, ordered by District Attorney Edwards found that while she was probably not raped, Starr Faithfull had recently engaged in sexual intercourse. The presence of bruises on the corpse suggested that the love-making had turned violent. After drowning her, the killer retraced his steps in the shallow waters in order to avoid leaving incriminating footprints.

This is where the odd story of Starr Faithfull ends, with one more dangling mystery. The girl who sought pleasure and affection from strangers was later profiled in John O'Hara's fascinating novel, *Butterfield 8*. Actress Elizabeth Taylor played the tragic call girl in her Oscar-winning performance in the 1960 film of the same name.

THE TOBACCO TYCOON AND THE TORCH SINGER/July 5-6, 1932

Libby Holman (Elizabeth Lloyd Holzman, 1904-1970) was one of a handful of celebrated white torch singers in the 1920s. She will be forever remembered for singing one song. With Helen Morgan it was "My Bill," with Fannie Brice it was "My Man," and with Libby Holman it was "Moanin' Low." She was identified with other songs, of course, including "Body and Soul," which she introduced; "Can't We Be Friends;" and "Something to Remember You By," from the 1930 musical *Three's a Crowd.*

It was in this popular Broadway show that Holman selected a member of the band to sing to, the same band member each night, a man wearing a sailor suit and standing with his

Libby Holman is shown with bee-sting lips early in her career as a torch singer of such tunes as "Moanin' Low."

Libby Holman is shown between Clifton Webb and Fred Allen in the 1930 Broadway production of "Three's a Crowd," and in which Libby sang the memorable tune "Body and Soul."

back to the audience. This was Fred MacMurray in his first Broadway appearance; he would go on to become one of Hollywood's most enduring leading actors. The woman who sang to him, however, would become involved in the sensational 1932 murder of her then-husband, Zachary Smith Reynolds, tobacco tycoon and, from all reports, cuckolded spouse.

Libby Holman was born Elizabeth Lloyd Holzman in Cincinnati, Ohio, on May 23, 1904. Her father, Alfred Holzman, was a successful stock broker, her mother, Rachel (Workum) was an attractive school teacher. The couple produced three children, Marion, Elizabeth (Libby), and Alfred, Jr. A year after Libby was born, her father and his brother, Ross Holzman, declared bankruptcy. Holzman and Company had speculated too broadly in the volatile cotton market and had overextended themselves.

More than $1 million was lost by investors, according to one report, this being the biggest financial disaster to date in Cincinnati. Then it was learned that Ross Holzman had ostensibly gone to Louisville, Kentucky, to raise more funds. He was never seen again. Gone with Holzman was $150,000 in bonds he had borrowed from a Kentucky utilities firm, along with $7,000 he had embezzled from the distinguished Cincinnati Club while a member.

Alfred Holzman was left in disgrace and poverty. His brother Ross never again surfaced, but it was believed that he went to Honduras, a country he had often talked about. The Holzman family sank into debt and both parents took menial jobs to survive. Libby was raised with the rumors of her family's former wealth, and from childhood, all she thought about was becoming a millionaire. She fantasized about her thieving uncle, Ross Holzman, referring to him as Uncle Honduras, believing that one night he would appear and shower the family with money. But it was Holman's marriage to a troubled young tobacco heir that would bring her such a fortune.

Zachary Smith Reynolds, heir to one of the great tobacco fortunes, shown at age sixteen; he would become an extravagant playboy.

To rid himself of some of the taint his financial failure and his brother's thefts had heaped upon his name, Alfred Holzman, in 1918, petitioned the courts to have the family name changed to Holman. This was granted and Libby later stated that the name change delighted her. With her stage and singing ambitions, Holman was a better name, she felt, with which to forge a show business career.

Libby Holman graduated high school in 1920, still wearing the hand-me-down dresses of her older sister, Marion. She entered the University of Cincinnati to study drama and graduated in 1924. Then she was off to New York to make a name for herself on Broadway. She haunted the casting offices and stood for hours in line to try out for parts but without success. Then she got her big break, the part of a streetwalker in a play called *The Fool.*

In 1925, after taking several bit parts in Broadway plays, Holman, more because of her shapely legs than her voice, was given a part in the *Garrick Gaieties* written by Richard Rodgers and Lorenz Hart. She sang a sensuous opening number, "Ladies of the Box Office," and was suddenly the darling of the theater crowd. Her success boomed after that until she had become a top star in 1929.

In that year, youthful playboy Zachary Smith Reynolds, heir to the $40 million Reynolds tobacco fortune, went to see *The Little Show.* He sat in the first row wearing riding boots and jodhpurs and became enthralled by the singer on stage, Libby Holman, whose deep voice chanted out "Moanin' Low." She was twenty-five at the time, he eighteen. Reynolds pursued her with flowers, candy, and jewelry. She ignored him.

Reynolds was used to having his way. He and his older brother Richard, who had been raised by servants as maharajahs after their parents died early in life, spent their money along Broadway recklessly, courting statuesque chorus girls and giving lavish parties. Dick Reynolds, a heavy drinker,

Zachary Smith Reynolds at the time he married Libby Holman; he overwhelmed her with jewels, furs, expensive cars, and his millions.

went to England in 1929 and got drunk before recklessly killing a pedestrian with his sports car and spending several months in jail. Zachary, called Smith by his friends and relatives, idolized his older brother, who busily corrupted him with the thought of Broadway and its fleshpots.

Reynolds, from the first moment he saw Libby Holman, swore she would be his and Holman yielded under his constant demands to see her. They dated throughout 1931 and in that year Reynolds bought Holman a pistol, telling her that kidnappers were everywhere and that it would be a good idea if she had a weapon. He taught her how to shoot, the .32-caliber Mauser automatic he had bestowed upon her.

Meanwhile, the Depression deepened. Libby Holman's career soared. She made $2,500 a week in her Broadway shows. She bought a lavishly appointed town house and an even snappier sports car. Reynolds, meanwhile, devoted himself to aviation and planned several long-distance flights, an adventuresome hobby that captured Holman's imagination. Finally, the Depression reached Broadway and Holman's fortunes began to dip. More and more she eyed the comfort and security the Reynolds millions might bring her.

Reynolds took her for a flight over the Reynolds' ancestral estate in Winston-Salem, N.C. She gasped when she learned that the thousand acres over which they were flying all belonged to Reynolds. Moreover, Reynolda, the palatial mansion she entered, staggered her. This was real wealth, she con-

The sprawling mansion called Reynolda, on the Reynolds estate at Winston-Salem, North Carolina, where Reynolds and Libby gave one wild party after another.

The spacious living room at Reynolda, where, during a drinking party on the night of July 5-6, 1932, Zachary Smith Reynolds grew despondent, believing his wife was cheating on him.

cluded. Holman finally consented to marry Reynolds, who quickly obtained a divorce from his estranged wife, Anne Cannon, on November 16, 1931. He and Libby Holman were wed that day. After traveling around the world for months, the couple settled in Reynolda and, in the early summer of 1932, gave one lavish party after another.

The parties were non-stop affairs with catered meals, flowing liquor, and champagne. There were motorboat rides at night and car races during the day. The party never stopped. A visiting reporter from the New York *News* attended a week-long festivity at Reynolda and returned to his paper to write: "Whirligig: Speed: Faster: Crazier: Champagne cocktails...Corn liquor straight...Pour it on...Step on the gas...Shoot the works...Speed: Gin, rye, bourbon, sex. Dizzy dames. Dizzy house parties. A thousand-acre estate. Private golf course. Tennis courts. Swimming pool. Lake. Moonlight dips. Dances. Joyrides. Airplanes. Yachts. High powered car. Speed. Chasing a new thrill today. Tiring of it tomorrow. Nowhere to go but places. Nothing to do but things. Speed, with youth at the throttle. Millions to spend...and bored stiff. Life's blah. The world's a phony. The whirligig spins on."

Holman was always the center of the party, singing her Broadway hit tunes over and over again to a captive audience. Theater people like Clifton Webb and Tallulah Bankhead visited the estate. So did Blanche Yurka, Peggy Fears, and Beatrice Lillie. This crowd, according to Jim Baggs, a friend of Reynolds, was "little more than a convention of homosexuals." Holman had, in fact, cultivated homosexual friendships throughout her theater career. It was later claimed that Libby

The second floor "sleeping porch," where Zachary Smith Reynolds ended his life.

Holman really had no interest in men, but was in love with a number of women and that her marriage to Reynolds quickly fell apart when he learned the truth about her sexual inclinations.

Zachary Smith Reynolds became moody and withdrawn during the summer of 1932. His best friend, Albert "Ab" Walker, seemed to spend more time with Libby than did her husband. Walker was the son of a successful Winston-Salem realtor who had been a high school football hero. Short and well-built, Walker was outgoing while Reynolds was introverted. Walker was gregarious while Reynolds was tight-lipped.

Reynolds felt that his wife was avoiding him and accused her of evading him. Holman denied it. On July 5, 1932, another party was given at Reynolda with the guests leaving around midnight. Actress Blanche Yurka retired to her room at that time. Ab Walker, who was staying at the mansion, sat around drinking with Holman and Reynolds. Tipsy by then, Holman went outside, and Walker and Reynolds went to search

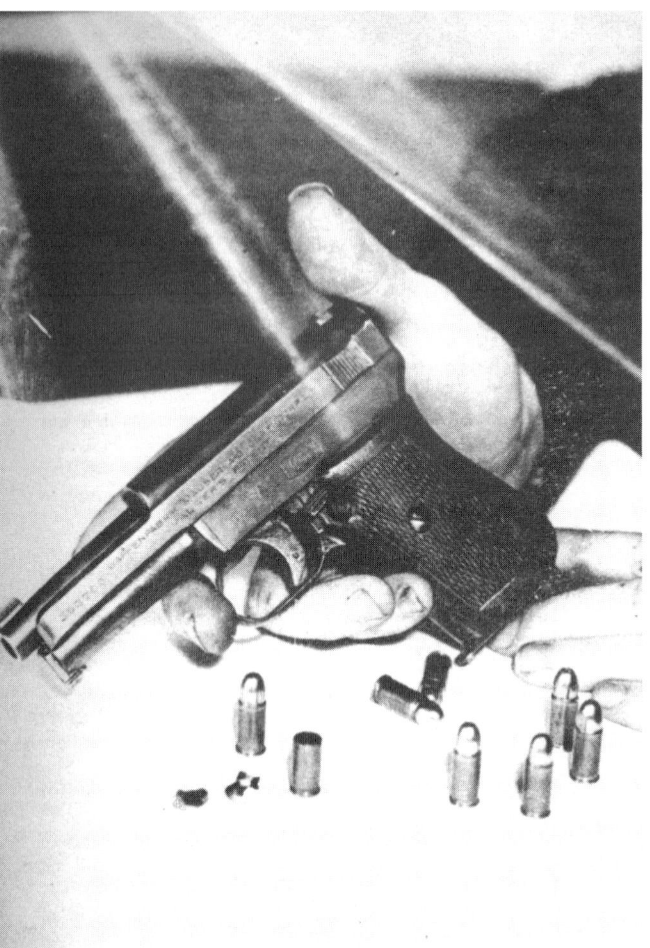

The weapon used in the shooting death of the tobacco tycoon.

Libby, extreme left, is shown heavily veiled at her murder trial; she professed her innocence publicly, stating: "I loved that boy!"

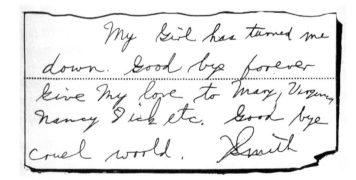

Ab Walker, who had been a lifelong friend of the tycoon, but who reportedly betrayed him with a sneaking affair with Libby, and who was later accused of murdering Zachary Smith Reynolds.

My Girl has turned me
down. Good bye forever
Give My love to Mary, Virginia
Nancy Dick etc. Good bye
cruel world. Smith

A note written by Reynolds years before he met Libby was used by the defense to prove that the tycoon was suicidal from an early age.

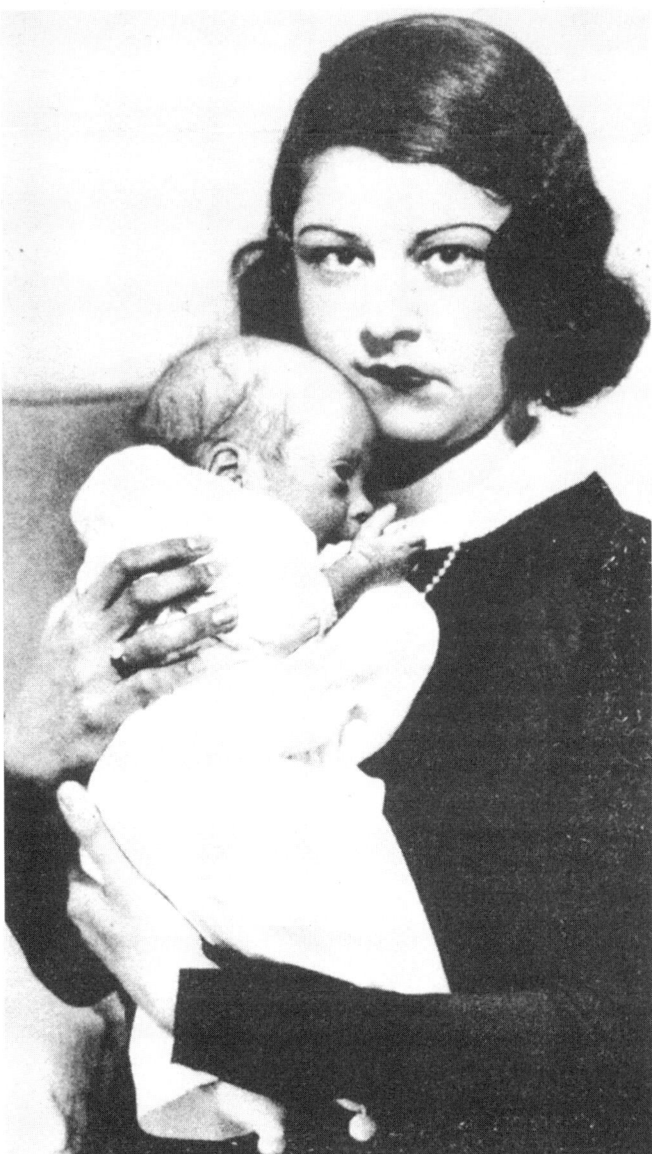

Libby is shown with her newly-born son, Christopher Smith Reynolds in 1933; the murder case against her was dropped after the Reynolds family asked that all charges be dismissed.

for her. Holman was found wandering around in her nightgown and both young men took her back to the mansion. What happened next is in doubt.

One story held that Holman and Reynolds went into Walker's bedroom and Walker followed them. A fight broke out and Reynolds was suddenly killed by a bullet. Another has it that Holman and Reynolds retired at about 12:30 p.m., but an hour later, Yurka was aroused by the sound of shrieks and yelling from their room. Holman suddenly appeared on the balcony above the living room, her gown coated with blood, and announced to Walker, who was cleaning up: "Smith, Smith shot himself!"

Walker, who was wearing only swimming trunks, raced up the stairs and found Reynolds sprawled on a bed on a sleeping porch outside the master bedroom he shared with Libby. Blood seeped from a bullet hole in his head. Yurka,

Libby is shown with her 8-year-old son Christopher and her new husband, Ralph Holmes in 1941; Holmes committed suicide in 1945 after separating from Libby, who was twenty years his senior.

The neo-Georgian mansion Libby purchased in 1938 in Connecticut; by that time, $6.5 million had been awarded to her son from the Reynolds estate, money which she freely spent on a lavish lifestyle, which also included funding the career of some of young actors like Montgomery Clift.

Tallulah Bankhead thusly described Holman's inactive career: "She is between murders."

Walker, and Libby carried his limp form to a car and rushed to the Baptist Hospital. Here, the unconscious Reynolds was taken to an operating room, while two doctors examined him. There was little that could be done other than to wait for the tycoon to die. Despite orders to leave the operating room, Ab Walker remained at his friend's side. Dr. Alexander Cox later stated that he got the idea that Walker was waiting to see if his friend Reynolds would regain consciousness and talk.

Holman was finally taken to a hospital room where her blood-soaked negligee was replaced with hospital garments. Ab Walker walked into the room, asking head nurse Ruby Jenkins to leave, saying that he had to talk to Holman alone. As she was leaving, Jenkins heard Walker tell the torch singer: "Don't talk, don't say anything. Don't say anything to anybody!"

Some minutes later Jenkins heard a noise and entered the room without knocking. She found Walker on the floor with Holman on top of him. Libby nervously explained that she had fallen out of bed and had dragged Walker with her. She then announced that she was pregnant with the child of the 20-year-old man dying in a room downstairs.

On July 6, 1932, at 5:25 a.m., Zachary Smith Reynolds died in his hospital bed. That morning, Reynolda was swarming with policemen and sheriff's deputies under the command of 34-year-old Transou Scott, who had been sheriff of Forsyth County for two years. The weapon used in Reynolds' death, a .32-caliber Mauser, the same kind Reynolds had given Holman a year earlier, was found on the sleeping porch, a few feet from the bed where Reynolds had been found.

Police also found a pair of Holman's sleeping pajamas in Ab Walker's room, which was some distance from her room and that of her husband's. Walker, by that time, had gone home to bed. Later that day he told his father that he had had nothing to do with Reynolds' death. He saw a friend, Bob Critz, later that day and explained what happened, but Critz said that he felt Walker was holding something back. "Well," Walker sighed, "there is something I'm going to take to my grave."

When Walker was later questioned by Sheriff Scott, he proved to be uncooperative and truculent, saying as little as possible. Blanche Yurka, still a guest at Reynolda, went riding with C. G. Hill that night, discussing the Reynolds death with him. Hill later went to Sheriff Scott and said that the actress had told him that no one who was in the mansion on the night of the shooting would ever reveal what had happened. When confronted with this statement, Yurka angrily denied ever having said such a thing.

A strange coroner's inquest was held on July 8, 1932, at Reynolda, in the very bedroom Holman and Reynolds had shared. The coroner's jury crammed itself into this room and questioned Walker, Yurka, and Holman. Walker was asked if he knew "if Mrs. Reynolds was a Jewess?" He said that he had not. He was then asked if he ever heard Reynolds express opinions about Jews and Walker replied that he had not. This line of questioning was peculiar and it seemed to stem from Libby Holman, that she had somehow talked to officials, saying that her husband had recently learned that she was Jewish and this put him in a suicidal mood.

It was claimed that Reynolds had always had a suicide complex. A scrap of writing he had scribbled at age sixteen, where Reynolds stated his unhappiness at being turned down by a girl, was offered up to prove this complex. "Goodbye forever," Reynolds had written, "goodbye cruel world." This, of course, was nothing more than the lovesick moanings of a teenager who, through his words, may have meant that he was running away, not committing suicide. But the effect of this kind of testimony caused Coroner W. N. Dalton to quickly close the hearing, stating that Reynolds had met death by suicide.

Sheriff Scott would have none of this. He and local officials reopened the case. Coroner Dalton suddenly changed his mind and ordered another inquest. This time Holman said that Reynolds had killed himself because he was sexually inadequate, an absurd claim in that she had already admitted that she was pregnant with Reynolds' child. The dead tycoon was also the father of a 2-year-old child through his marriage to Anne Cannon. The second coroner's inquest ended with a verdict that Reynolds died "from a bullet wound inflicted by a person or persons unknown."

Still, Forsyth County authorities were not satisfied. Neither was Richard Reynolds, the dead man's older brother. He arrived in Winston-Salem on August 24, 1932, and immediately told the press: "In view of all the facts available at this time, I believe my brother's death was murder. If it is, I want to see justice done. I do not think Smith was of a temperament that would allow him to commit suicide." W. N. "Will" Reynolds, uncle to Zachary Smith and Richard Reynolds, and chairman of the board of the R. J. Reynolds Company, echoed his nephew's beliefs, not accepting for a minute the fact that Zachary Smith Reynolds committed suicide.

Libby Holman was then charged with murdering her husband, Zachary Smith Reynolds, and Ab Walker was named as an accessory. The charge was later reduced to second-degree murder. Reynolds' body was exhumed and re-examined. The powder burns evident on his face, and the path of the death bullet indicated to experts that the victim had not committed suicide, but had been shot to death by someone other than himself. Released on bond and joined by her father and mother, Holman gave an interview to her friend, Ward Morehouse, of the New York *Sun*.

Holman sat before the newsman knitting a pink sleeping suit for her unborn child. Gushed Holman: "It's knowing that I am going to give birth to the child of the man I loved that affords me my only gleam of happiness, that gives me any desire to live at all. The fact that within four long months I will have a child, *his* child, makes me strong enough to fight for a complete and absolute vindication.

"I didn't shoot Smith Reynolds. God in heaven knows that. The Reynolds family know it in their hearts. I loved

The early career of actor Montgomery Clift, shown with Elizabeth Taylor in a scene from the 1951 film, *A Place in the Sun*, was nurtured and advanced by Libby Holman, who gave him money and set up Hollywood contacts for him.

Smith as I never loved anyone before or will ever love again. The fullest and richest hours of my life were spent with that dear boy. I loved him tenderly, dearly and completely and to him I meant everything, everything. When I realized he was gone...I didn't want to live...my life was over...And now I want to go through with the trial. I want no strings left, no doubts left in people's minds as to my innocence. I don't want only an acquittal, I want a complete apology."

She got neither. Libby's trial was scheduled for November 21, 1932, but, on October 18, solicitor Carlisle Higgins received a startling letter from W. N. Reynolds, head of the Reynolds family, in which Reynolds asked that the case against Libby Holman and Ab Walker be dropped. This was done and Libby Holman was no longer charged with murder.

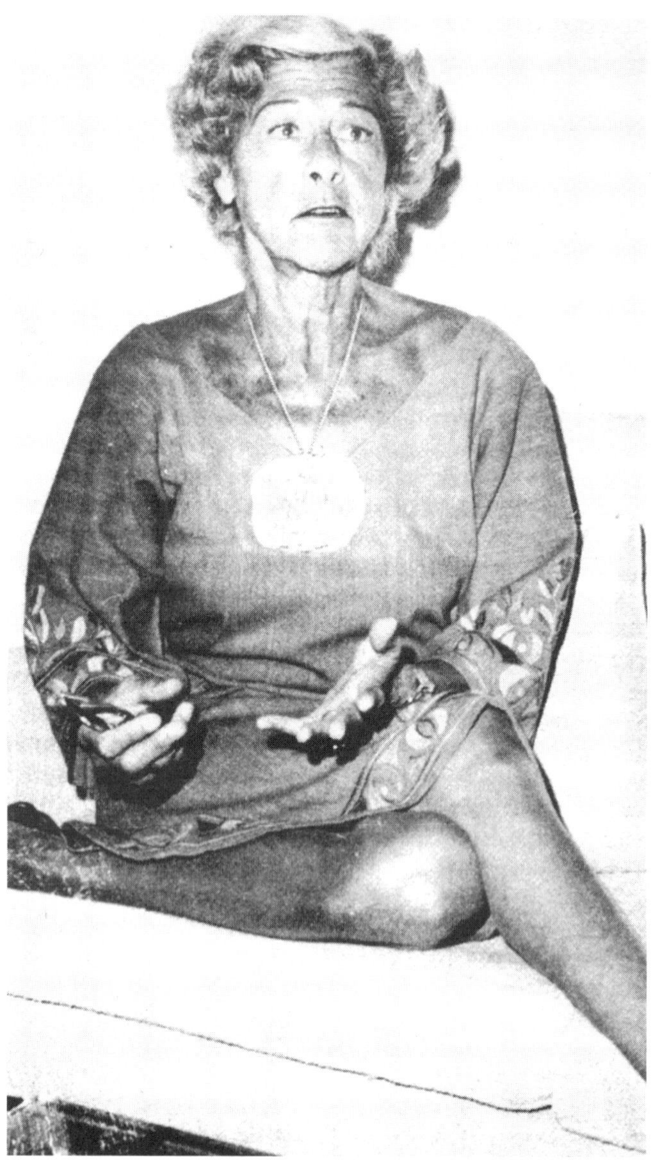

Libby Holman in 1968, two yeas before her death; she stated to a friend earlier: "I was so drunk that night that I don't know whether I shot him or not."

She was neither exonerated nor convicted, but many would form their own opinion about her guilt in the years to come. Libby Holman herself was unsure of what happened that fateful night, saying to a friend later: "I was so drunk that night I don't know whether I shot him or not."

Holman's child, a boy she named Christopher, not Smith, as she had vowed to her husband, was born two months later. She had to battle in the courts for a number of years before approximately $6.5 million was awarded her son. The singer married Ralph Holmes, another aviator, in 1941. Holmes, the son of Broadway actor Taylor Holmes and brother of screen actor Phillips Holmes, was then serving with the Royal Air Force. The couple separated in 1945 and a few months later Holmes was found dead from an overdose of sleeping pills.

Libby Holman continued to appear in public occasionally, singing the old torch songs that had made her famous. Her son grew to be a tall, strapping fellow who was killed in 1950, while climbing a mountain in California. Holman became even more reclusive, but, in the early 1960s, she did make a rare singing appearance on Broadway. During one of these appearances, Tallulah Bankhead, Holman's on-and-off friend for decades, was appearing in another play nearby. One day the outspoken Tallulah asked her co-star Patsy Kelly to invite Holman to join them for a tea break.

"Is Libby working again?" asked Kelly.

"Yes, darling," replied the acid-tongued Tallulah. "She's between murders."

In her last years, though wealthy, Libby Holman suffered repeated attacks of depression. She was at the time married to artist Louis Shanker and lived in a luxurious home in Stamford, Connecticut. She took large doses of lithium, but nothing helped to cure her deep fits of depression. On the evening of June 18, 1970, the 67-year-old Libby Holman was found by servants in her garage on the front seat of her Rolls Royce wearing only a bikini bottom. She was in a stupor. Rushed to a nearby hospital, she died without speaking a few hours later.

THE DEATH OF THELMA TODD/ December 14-15, 1935

Beautiful Thelma Todd (AKA: The Ice Cream Blonde, Blonde Venus; 1906-1935) was a gifted comedienne who lived on the wild side, corrupted, as so many stars were, by celebrity fame. Todd, the "Ice Cream Blonde" and "Blonde Venus," died in her garage above the Will Rogers Beach on December 15, 1935. Publicists at the Hal Roach studio expressed their regrets over the unfortunate death of their brightest star. It was their belief that Todd fell asleep or passed out at the steering wheel of her car and was asphyxiated by carbon monoxide fumes.

Others were not so sure. The whole thing hinted at a cover up engineered by Hollywood insiders to protect the interests of the studio. A nasty murder investigation would sully the reputation of key industry figures in the public limelight. No one, least of all Hal Roach or Joe Schenck, founder of 20th Century-Fox, wanted that to happen.

Thelma Todd in the late 1920s, when she was a rising starlet at the Hal Roach Studio in Hollywood and appearing in many one-reel comedies.

Todd, her hair dyed black, is shown as a dancing girl in the 1930 film, *Kismet*, before she became a star known as the "Blonde Venus."

Todd was born in Lawrence, Massachusetts, the daughter of a local politician named John Shaw Todd. While still in her teens, she won the crown of Miss Massachusetts. The blonde glamour girl never aspired to a career in show business. The ambitions of others, coupled with incredible happenstance, made her a star of the silver screen almost overnight. A theater manager in Lawrence who was on friendly terms with her father sent Todd's photograph to Jesse Lasky of Paramount Studios in Hollywood, urging the mogul to give the girl a chance.

Todd, who was teaching sixth grade at the time, had no prior knowledge of this. Lasky was impressed with her natural beauty and offered her the opportunity to learn acting at the Paramount school in Astoria, Queens. There she was taught the finer points of etiquette, makeup, dancing, and other necessary skills needed for a successful screen career. After six months she was one of sixteen candidates awarded a one-year contract by Paramount. They appeared together as a group in *Fascinating Youth,* a box-office hit in 1926.

Todd displayed a natural talent for light comedy. Within a year, she had taken Hollywood by storm. The studio loaned her to the Hal Roach Studio, where she starred in seventeen two-reelers with her best friend, ZaSu Pitts. By the early 1930s, she had appeared alongside Buster Keaton in *Speak Easily,* and Stan Laurel and Oliver Hardy in *The Bohemian Girl.* Todd had a beautiful speaking voice and easily made the transition to talkies in 1927. However, she wanted desperately to perform in serious drama and went so far as to change her name to "Alison Lloyd." This she did "so that no taint of comedy would cling to her skirts."

In 1930, director Roland West starred her opposite Chester Morris in *Corsair,* a gangster drama that became an immediate sensation. She appeared in several other dramas, but went back to being Thelma Todd after Roach threatened to change her name to "Susie Dinkleberry. So that no taint of drama would cling to her skirts," he said half-seriously.

In July 1932, Todd eloped with Pasquale "Pat" DeCicco, a talent agent. The marriage ended disastrously in March 1934, after Todd charged her husband with physical and mental cruelty. During this time, Todd acquired a taste for liquor, fast cars, and handsome leading men. She had affairs with actor Ronald Colman, band leader Abe Lyman, and the mercurial director Roland West who achieved critical acclaim with *The Bat Whispers,* and *Corsair,* before his career stagnated. On January 23, 1933, Todd slammed her car into a palm tree on Hollywood Boulevard, suffering severe internal injuries. Upon her recovery Roach hired a private chauffeur, Ernest Peters, to drive her to her numerous parties and social engagements.

Peters was behind the wheel on the night of December 14, 1935, when Todd was the guest of honor at the opulent Trocadero nightclub on Sunset Strip. The party was thrown by Stanley Lupino, whose daughter Ida was on the brink of stardom. DiCicco demanded inclusion on the guest list, only to show up with two glamorous starlets hanging on each arm. Ida Lupino later recalled the anger in Todd's voice as she upbraided her husband for his callous and manipulative conduct. The evening ended on that sour note, as Todd left the party. Turning to her many admirers at the nightclub, she waved before leaving.

Todd told Peters to drive her back to her "Sidewalk Cafe" on Posetano Road, a popular roadway restaurant. Her home, which she shared with her lover and business partner, West, was located up the hill from the restaurant. She urged the chauffeur to drive fast, for she believed that there were gangsters following close behind. Arriving at the cafe, Todd told Peters to go home. "Don't you want me to walk you up to your apartment?" he asked. "That won't be necessary," she replied. "Go home Ernest." It was the last time anyone saw Thelma Todd alive.

Thelma Todd in 1933, when she had become a leading actress in many major films, specializing in comedies, and known by then as "The Ice Cream Blonde."

At 10:30 a.m. on December 16, 1935, Todd's private maid, May Whitehead, arrived at the Todd's home with a load of packages. As was her usual custom, she opened the garage door to pull the 1933 Lincoln phaeton sedan into the driveway in order to leave her own car in its place. Approaching the Lincoln from the passenger side, the maid noticed her employer slumped over the wheel, dressed in the same outfit she had worn to the Trocadero two nights before.

Roused from his bed by Whitehead, West stumbled down to the garage after being informed of the tragedy by the maid. Police arrived to find traces of blood on the seat and running board, yet there was no evidence of an open wound on the body, just a facial laceration that was believed to have been caused when the actress fell forward into the steering wheel.

The police theorized that Todd, discovering that she was locked out of the apartment, decided to sleep in her car. Since it was a cold, windswept night she started the motor to keep warm. Her death by asphyxiation was called a terrible accident. It was a tidy explanation that nervous studio officials accepted at face value, despite evidence from an autopsy that showed a bruise inside her throat, the kind that a bottle might make if forced into her mouth.

A coroner's jury returned a verdict of death by carbon monoxide poisoning. The case was closed by police, but nagging questions remained. Why were her silk slippers not scuffed? If indeed Todd had trudged up 271 stairs from the restaurant to the garage as the police thought, the slippers

Thelma Todd's Roadside Café on the Pacific Highway; the actress had earned so much money in Hollywood that she established this lucrative side business. Her stylish home can be seen upon the hill above the restaurant.

Thelma Todd, second from right, is shown dining with friends; she loved nightclubbing and was last seen alive during a party at the Trocadero on the night of December 14-15, 1935.

Ida Lupino, then a rising movie star, was the honored guest at the last party attended by Thelma Todd; Lupino later stated that Todd smiled and waved to her on the night of her death.

would have borne definite marks of wear. To further confuse matters, Todd was reportedly seen alive some time after the estimated time of death. Mrs. Wallace Ford insisted that she had received a phone call from Todd on Sunday afternoon in which the actress confirmed her acceptance of an invitation to a cocktail party that night.

"And when you see who's coming with me you'll drop dead," Todd said. Jewel Carmen, the estranged wife of Todd's live-in lover Roland West, testified that she had seen Todd on the street with an unknown male companion. This person was never found. Deputy District Attorney George Johnson dismissed the accidental death theory as preposterous. "It seems too difficult to believe Miss Todd went to that garage and started the motor of her car to keep warm," he said.

But who then actually murdered the movie actress? There were several likely suspects. New York mob boss Charles "Lucky" Luciano had demanded of Todd the right to locate a gambling casino on the upper floor of her café, it was reported. When she refused, veiled threats were made against her life. Pat DeCicco, the erstwhile booking agent, was embittered by the pending divorce action and reportedly would stop at nothing to exact revenge, it was claimed.

The most likely suspect was Roland West. On December 17, 1935, three deputies from the Los Angeles County Sheriff's office allegedly had told Hal Roach that West confessed to killing Todd. "West was very possessive, very controlling," Roach admitted years later. "He told Thelma she was to be back by 2 a.m. She said she'd come and go as she well pleased. They had a little argument about it and then Thelma left for

Police Captain Bert Wallis examines the mink-wrapped body of Thelma Todd, slumped inside her 1933 Lincoln sedan.

Detectives mill about the outside of Todd's garage only a short time after the film actress was found dead.

the party. When Sid Grauman [owner of Grauman theaters in Hollywood] called West, about 2:30, to tell him Thelma was leaving, West went into her apartment and locked her out. He was going to teach her a lesson."

Then, according to one version, West followed her back to the garage and locked her inside with the engine running. "He wasn't thinking about carbon monoxide, just about teaching her a lesson about who was the boss. So he left and went back to bed," Roach added. The story was quickly suppressed by Roach to protect the integrity of his studio. Todd was still a married woman and the details of her adulterous affair with West could result in a scandal not unlike the Roscoe "Fatty" Arbuckle debacle of 1921, still fresh in everyone's mind. Such a scandal could prove ruinous for business at a time when Will Hays exerted tremendous influence over the moral climate in Hollywood.

West also had friends in high places, it was pointed out. Eugene Biscailuz, formerly of the California Highway Patrol, was the sheriff at the time. West was a 32nd Degree Mason and an esteemed lodge brother of Biscailuz. The oath-bound Ma-

Film director Roland West, left, sits on the running board of the death car while a detective questions him about Thelma Todd; he became a primary suspect in Todd's death, which was at first ruled an accident from carbon monoxide poisoning.

Pasquale "Pat" DeCicco, who wedded Todd in 1934; the marriage ended in the same year and the volatile DeCicco, it was thought, may have murdered the actress out of revenge.

Shown at Todd's funeral are, left to right, May Whitehead, the maid who first discovered Todd's body; Mrs. Alice Todd, the mother of the dead actress; and Dr. Harold Proppe.

sons were pledged to help each other whenever the need arose. Members of the Los Angeles Police Department were equally culpable, it was claimed. Under the iron-fisted rule of Mayor Frank Shaw, political corruption filtered downward through the ranks. For the good of the city, as well as the movie studio, it was deemed advisable to put the wraps on the story, though Detective Chief Thad Brown reportedly had the "goods" on West.

No indictments were returned against any of the suspects. Roland West died in 1951 after he reportedly confessed his guilt to his close friend, actor Chester Morris. Morris then later told director Alex Gordon. An ironic footnote to the tragedy can be found in a cryptic scene from one of Todd's movies with the Marx Brothers, entitled *Monkey Business*. In it, comedian Groucho Marx seizes Todd's arm and says, "Now be a good girlie or I'll lock you in the garage!"

THE MURDER OF SIR HARRY OAKES/ July 7, 1943

The society murder on July 7-8, 1943 of Sir Harry Oakes, a close personal friend of the Duke of Windsor, and the wealthiest land owner in the British Bahamas was never solved, although all the circumstantial evidence pointed to Count Alfred Marie de Fourguereaux de Marigny, Oakes' son-in-law, as his murderer. The count and his wife Nancy were the darlings of the social set in the Bahamas. They drifted from one gala party to the next, unaffected by the war raging in Europe. "The war? I do not follow the news. Why should I?" the count once remarked to a newsman.

Oakes, a self-made American aristocrat, disapproved of his daughter's decision to marry de Marigny, a divorced Frenchman, who claimed to have been born of noble stock on the island of Mauritius in the Indian Ocean. Sir Harry threatened to disown his daughter, giving his son-in-law a possible motive for murder. After a falling out with de Marigny, Oakes threatened to send his daughter back to Bennington College in Vermont, which would have left the Count virtually penniless.

Oakes was a powerful man in the Bahamas and he dictated the courses of many lives. He had created the air service that linked the islands to each other and controlled the airfields and planes that serviced travelers. He had financed hospitals and schools throughout the islands and generously gave much of his fortune to support the British war effort, funding the construction of Spitfires, the celebrated British fighter planes.

The discovery that Oakes had been murdered in his bed inside his sprawling fifteen-room home, called "Westbourne," sent shock waves through the islands. The discovery was made by Oakes' close friend and financial adviser, Harold Christie, who, when getting no response to the knock on Oakes' bedroom door, entered the large room on the morning of July 8, 1943. He found Oakes sprawled on his bed, his head caved in by what police later described as "a long blunt instrument." The killer had set the body on fire, and the corpse was badly charred.

The killer then, through some mad caprice, dumped feathers from a slashed pillow all over the body, which clung to the mottled flesh, making the body of the tycoon all the more

Sir Harry Oakes, one of the richest men in the Bahamas, who was murdered on the night of July 7, 1943.

The resplendent mansion of Sir Harry Oakes, called "Westbourne," where the millionaire businessman and philanthropist was murdered in his bed.

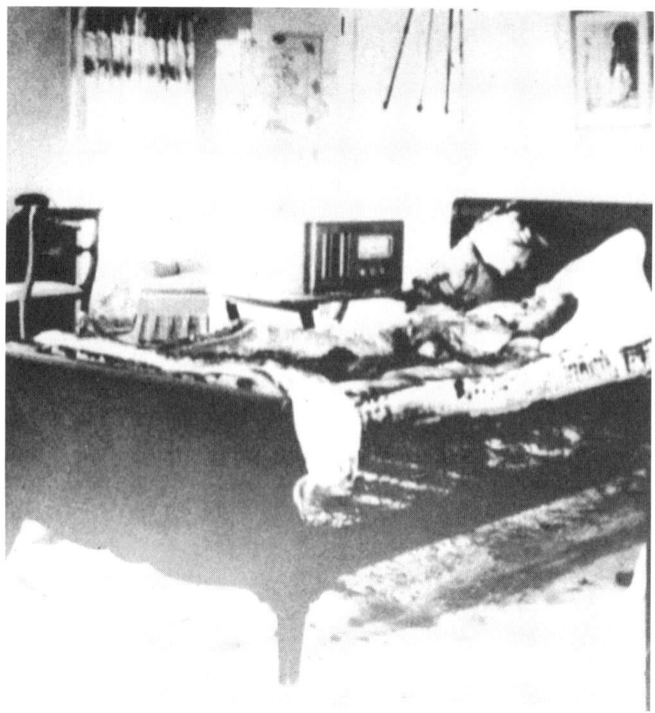

The charred body of Sir Harry Oakes on the morning after his murder; his head had been crushed, the body set on fire.

hideous in death. This was obviously the "tar-and-feathers" treatment that had been traditionally administered to confidence men by irate citizens gulled in phony business transactions.

Evidence suggested that de Marigny had killed his father-in-law, but investigators had less than a solid case against the opportunistic de Marigny. A handprint, said to be the count's, was found on a screen next to Oakes' bed, but was confused with other prints found on a piece of glassware. Following a speedy trial, de Marigny was acquitted and released on November 11, 1943. However, according to the jury's recommendation, the count was asked to leave the island. This decision was made without the permission of the Duke of Windsor, governor of the Colony.

It was commonly believed that Oakes' real killers were Mafia hit men sent by Meyer Lansky to do the job when Oakes refused to sanction a scheme to build casinos in Nassau. Oakes' close personal friend, Harold Christie, a business associate of Lansky, allegedly acted as liaison between the Duke of Windsor and the mobsters, but at the last minute, Oakes backed down and declared he would have nothing to do with such an arrangement. It was hypothesized that Lansky's people murdered Oakes in revenge, a killing that was never solved.

Harold G. Christie, a house guest on the night of the murder, found the body of his lifelong friend the following morning.

Alfred de Marigny was tried for Oakes' murder, but was found innocent; acquitted, he is shown with his wife, Nancy Oakes.

THE BLACK DAHLIA CASE/January 15, 1947

The Black Dahlia case, still unsolved to this day, proved to be one of America's most baffling and sensational murders of the 20th Century. On January 15, 1947, the horribly mutilated body of Elizabeth Ann Short was found in a vacant Los Angeles lot by a woman walking her small child on Norton Street, between Thirty-ninth and Coliseum streets. She literally stumbled over the lower half of the victim's body, which was on the sidewalk, the other half of the torso being in the high weeds of the lot. The woman ran screaming for the police and soon the nation's headlines blared the skimpy facts of the gruesome killing.

Called into the case were veteran detectives Harry "Red" Hansen and Finis Arthur Brown. They would stay on this most vexing case of their careers for many years to come, following endless leads, listening to countless crackpots confess to the murder, and, in the end, leave the file open and unsolved for generations to come. Hansen would work on the case periodically up to the time of his retirement in 1971.

The corpse the officers saw had been mutilated by a savage fiend, one who had battered the head and slashed the face almost beyond recognition by cutting the mouth at the edges from ear to ear to form a gruesome grin. The killer had made repeated cuts on the thighs, arms, and breasts, and these slashes were both straight and in circles. Scores of cigarette burns marked the flesh. Rope burns found on the hands and feet made it evident that the victim had been bound and tortured for several hours before the maniac finished his grisly work.

The initials "B.D." had been carved into one thigh. (These initials stood for Black Dahlia, as police later learned.) The killer had scrubbed the body before depositing it in the empty lot. The detectives noted the killer had meticulously cleaned the body parts with a hard brush, leaving bristles embedded in the flesh. This was undoubtedly done to eliminate any traces of the killer's identity (or, possibly, to satisfy a perverse fetish of some sort).

Identification was impossible, except for the victim's fingerprints, which were taken and sent to FBI headquarters in Washington, D. C. Within a short time, the Los Angeles Police Department was sent the results of the Bureau's search through its millions of prints—a card which identified the dead woman

Elizabeth Ann Short, who was known as "The Black Dahlia," and who was horribly murdered and mutilated on or before January 15, 1947, her unsolved killing haunting LAPD detectives to this day.

Elizabeth Ann Short, left, with a friend on a California beach some years before a maniac cut her in half, this snapshot found by detectives following her death.

as Elizabeth Ann Short, born July 29, 1924, in Hyde Park, Massachusetts, giving her last known address as Santa Barbara, California. Once the press learned of this, reporters were sent scurrying through the Los Angeles area to get more background on the victim.

One of the more enterprising scribes, Bevo Means of the Los Angeles *Herald-Express,* discovered that Short had lived in Long Beach and interviewed Short's former landlady, learning that Short had a peculiar quirk. She always dressed in black. All her shoes were black, her dresses and skirts and blouses were black. She wore a black jade ring at all times and, when her trunk was found, it was learned that all her undergarments were black.

Means talked to the owner of a drugstore in Long Beach and found out that the victim was much admired by all the young men she met at his soda fountain. "Who could forget a beautiful girl like that?" the drugstore owner told Means. "Always in black. The fellows coming in here called her The Black Dahlia." The sobriquet was used by Means in his first story, and the name electrified editors across the country. Soon every newspaper, radio station, and wire service used the arresting name, which became household words across the nation.

The name Black Dahlia also explained the initials carved on the victim's leg. Detective Hansen soon learned that Short, one of five children, had been raised in near-poverty in Medford, Massachusetts, and had left home in 1942 at age seventeen, going to Los Angeles to seek a career in show business. It was an old story, one enacted thousands of times each week as pretty, young women with no experience headed for Hollywood and wound up taking menial jobs to survive, or, worse, turned to prostitution.

Elizabeth Short made the usual rounds of the film studios and got nowhere. She landed a job at Camp Cooke, working in the post exchange as a hostess, serving coffee and doughnuts to lonely GIs, a position she held through 1944. She was a popular girl, even elected a "Cutie of the Week." She reportedly became engaged to Major Matt Gordon, Jr., an Air Corps officer, who was later killed in India. Her life went downhill after that. Short was picked up several times as underage, while drinking in Santa Barbara lounges and bars with soldiers, and finally she was shipped back to Massachusetts. She got off the bus before arriving there and returned to Hollywood, where she became a call girl.

It was at this time, while earning considerable cash from her occasional "dates," that an assistant producer at one of the studios dubbed her The Black Dahlia, after noticing that she always wore black. Short was promised many screen tests by her clients, who never kept their word. Forsaking the elusive film contract, Elizabeth Short returned home in 1946 to see her mother. Then she drifted to Florida and later Chicago, working as a cocktail waitress in both cities.

By December 1946, Short had returned to her old haunts in California, just barely avoiding the label of streetwalker. She moved to San Diego and convinced a woman to take her in, telling her that she was a destitute war widow, a story she would repeat many times to gain sympathy, lodging, and money from the kind-hearted.

In January 1947, Short was back in Long Beach, but had resolved to quit prostitution, telling her friends that she was looking for a job and had given up her dreams of becoming a movie star, that all she wanted was to find a good man, to settle down, and to have children. She mentioned that she was deeply in love with a man she referred to only as Red.

A few days later, her dissected corpse was found. Hansen began to interview Short's friends, hunting for the elusive boyfriend The Black Dahlia intended to marry. The killer then surfaced indirectly, six days following the murder. He called Jimmy Richardson, city editor of the Los Angeles *Herald-Examiner,* speaking in a voice described by Richardson as "soft and silky." The caller detailed the mutilations made on the corpse to convince Richardson that he, indeed, was the murderer. "I killed her," the caller said. "I'm going to turn myself in, but I want to have a little more fun. I want to watch the cops chase me some more." Then he added: "You can expect some souvenirs of Beth Short in the mail."

Richardson described the caller as egotistical, proud of the fact that he had eluded police, a personality with a superior attitude not unlike the fiend known as Jack the Ripper, who stalked prostitutes through London's Whitechapel fifty years earlier. A few days later, as promised, the killer sent the "souvenirs." Enclosed in the package was Short's birth certificate, her address book with more than seventy names of male clients in it, and a note which had been pieced together from newspaper headlines which read: "Here is Dahlia's Belongings. Letter to follow."

A lonely burial for a lonely girl: Only three persons, seated left to right, Mrs. Phoebe Short (Elizabeth's mother), A. C. White, a brother-in-law, and Mrs. Virginia West (sister of Elizabeth) attended the ceremonies on January 25, 1947, at a Los Angeles cemetery. Rev. G. R. White, at left, is shown conducting the services, while two LAPD detectives stand in the background.

Detectives immediately began to run down all the men listed in Short's address book, although they first thought that the killer would not have been so foolish as to send such an item with his own name in it. Later, it was reasoned that the killer, being the vain slayer that he was, could well have had his name in that little black book and had sent it on as a challenge to police to see if they could select him from all the others listed therein.

Challenging the police is a game historically played by many criminals, usually by psychopathic killers like the Ax Man of New Orleans, David Berkowitz (Son of Sam), William Heirens, and Jack the Ripper (see entries). Even Richard Loeb, who, with his love slave, Nathan Leopold (see entry in Celebrity Slayings), boldly murdered Bobbie Franks, then, with the consummate gall of the megalomaniac, insisted upon helping the police to find the killer, hunting for clues, looking for the body that he himself had hidden. The killer of Elizabeth Short was no different, except he never revealed his true identity and used the phone and the mail to make his presence known and felt.

Following the killer's contact with newsmen, Hansen and other detectives were able to track down Elizabeth Short's trunk, and inside they found many love letters from boyfriends. They began to contact these men in hopes of finding the killer. Meanwhile, as expected by some experts, the killer reneged on his promise to give himself up, sending another postcard, again made up of letters clipped from newspapers which read: "I've changed my mind. You would not give me a square deal. Dahlia killing justified."

No more mail arrived from the sender, who police believed to be the real killer. Detectives also believed that one of Short's friends, Robert Manley, who was also known as Red, was a prime suspect. Manley, a 24-year-old married hardware salesman who lived in Huntington Park, had sent a telegram to Short in San Diego only a week before she was murdered. It read: "Be there tomorrow afternoon late. Would like to see you. Red."

When Hansen picked up Manley for questioning, the suspect yelled: "I don't know her! I never met the woman!" Manley did an about-face when being grilled at police headquarters, admitting that he had picked up Short at a San Diego bus station and they had spent the night together in a motel room. He told Hansen that "she had bad scratches on both her arms and above the elbows...She told me that she had a friend

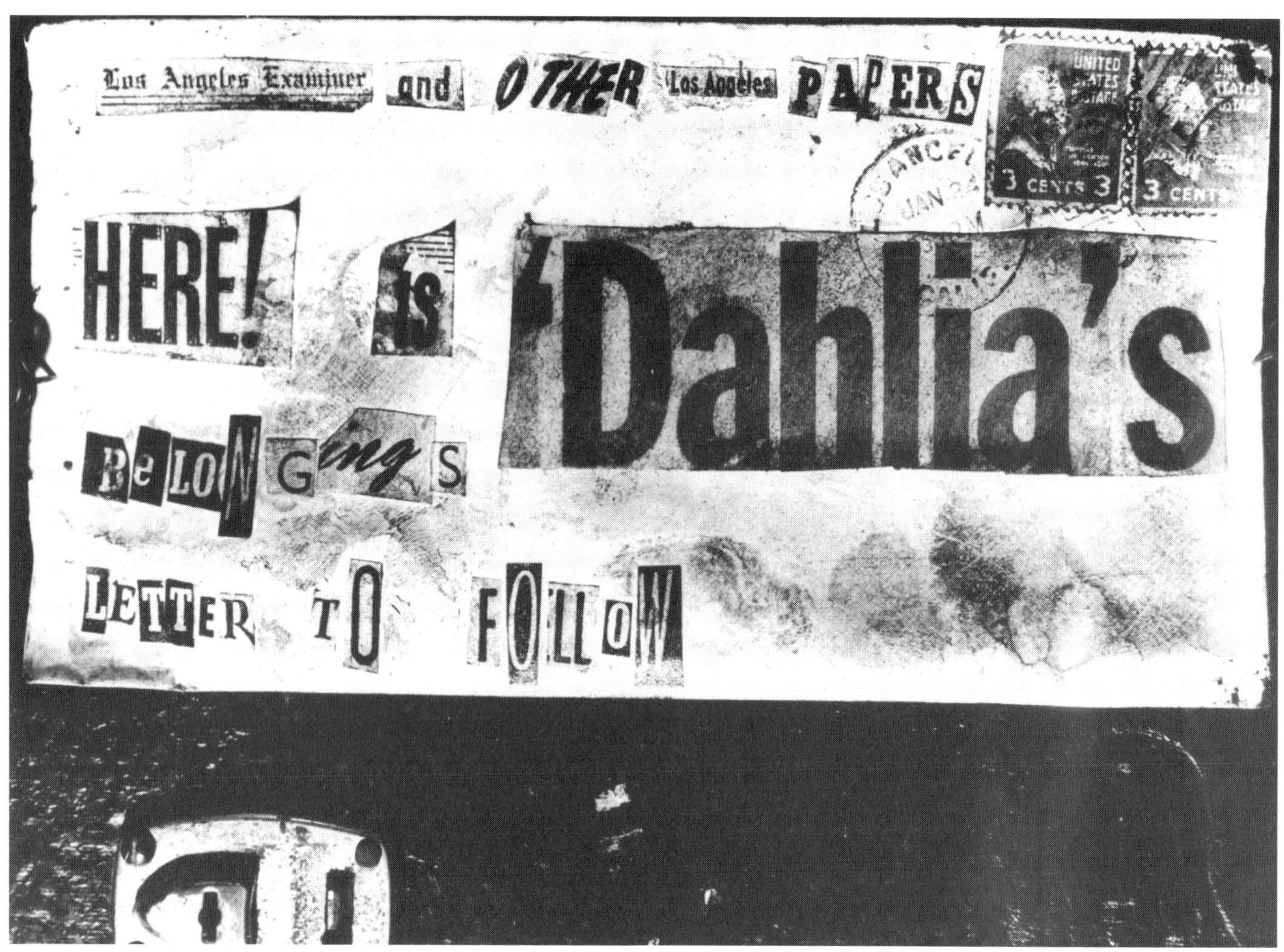

The message—pieced together by headlines clipped from newspapers—that was sent by Short's killer; the envelope held Elizabeth Short's address book and birth certificate.

who was intensely jealous of her...an Italian with black hair." Manley said that he did not know this person or even his name, only that this man lived in San Diego.

Manley told police that he had denied knowing Short at first because he and his wife had been arguing and he did not want to make matters worse by confessing his affair with Short. He went on to state that his night with Short was not pleasant, that she had gotten sick after they had been drinking and he had wound up driving her to Los Angeles and dropped her off at the Biltmore Hotel on January 9, 1947. He swore that this was the last time he had seen her, a week before her savage murder.

Manley was interrogated with considerable intensity by detectives and his whereabouts on the night of the murder were thoroughly checked. He was finally released when police were convinced that he was innocent. The image of the Black Dahlia, however, was to plague Robert Manley. In 1954, he was committed to an insane asylum by his wife who claimed that "he hears noises, writes foolish notes, and has a guilt complex." Police again questioned Manley, once again believing that he was innocent of the murder.

Dozens of other men were suspected, dragged in for questioning, and "sweated" for hours, but all proved to have solid alibis for the night of the killing. Psychiatrist J. Paul de River of the Los Angeles Police Department had predicted that the Dahlia case would cause considerable crackpots to confess to the murder, but officials were in no way prepared for the *hundreds* of psychological malcontents who came forward.

One of these was Daniel S. Voorhees, a 33-year-old unemployed waiter, who called detectives and screamed over the phone: "I can't stand it any longer! I want to confess to the murder of the Black Dahlia!" He was picked up and, while being driven to headquarters, Voorhees blurted over and over "I killed her, I killed her." Though he signed a confession, which stated that he had committed the murder, Voorhees denied ever sending the letter and postcard to newsmen and the police. Some days later Voorhees jumped up in his cell and yelled that he did not kill Short, demanding to see his attorney, adding: "I'm not gonna talk to you anymore. I've talked too much already." Voorhees was later sent to an institution for psychiatric care.

Hansen and his partner Brown answered a report from another self-confessed killer, finding Army corporal Joseph Dumais covered with blood and dozens of newspaper clippings dealing with the Dahlia slaying littering his cheap room. Said Dumais: "It's possible that I could have committed the murder. When I get drunk, I get rough with women." His claim did not hold up and he was released. Then John N. Andry, a chief pharmacist's mate in the navy, was arrested by the detectives after he bragged in a Long Beach bar that he had great skill in cutting up bodies. When grilled by police, Andry said: "Well, I'm capable of doing it," but he quickly added that he was "only kidding."

Dumais, Andry, and countless others, who confessed were questioned by Detectives Hansen and Brown, who always asked pointed questions of the many who confessed, questions to which only the murderer would have the answers and which dealt chiefly with the state of the corpse as it was left in the empty lot, as well as specific mutilations made by the killer. None had the answers.

The case slipped into the macabre over the years. At one point seers and soothsayers, who claimed to see the past and future inundated the police department with reports of where to look for the killer and how to employ magic to produce positive results. One caller, a woman phoning long distance, seriously told Detective Hansen to "bury the girl with an egg in her right hand. The killer will then be found in a week. That's the way it works in Alabama!"

A photographer insisted that if the police turned over the eyes of the dead girl he would be able to retrieve an image of the killer from the irises, this being an old myth in trapping murderers, a wayward notion that the last vision of the victim, the image of the killer, is forever trapped in the victim's eyes. Then there was the ludicrous. Hansen received a call from a hysterical waitress who reported that two men with guns had just left her restaurant, two ugly-looking thugs who had talked furtively and in suspicious detail over their sandwiches about the Dahlia killing. When she identified her restaurant, Hansen had to suppress a laugh, saying: "That was us! My partner and I ate there today."

Robert Manley, the last person known to have seen Elizabeth Short alive, is shown with an LAPD detective as he identifies a shoe and bag found in a Los Angeles city dump on January 25, 1947 as those belonging to the Black Dahlia.

Robert Manley, the prime suspect in the Black Dahlia case—he was cleared, providing a convincing alibi for the night of the murder—is shown with his wife, Harriet Manley.

LAPD Detective Harry Hansen, right, is shown with another detective investigating evidence in the Black Dahlia murder, a case that he stayed with for decades, always hoping to find the murderer.

In the wake of the Dahlia killing, there followed a series of murders that were not dissimilar in *modus operandi*. Mary Tate was sexually attacked and strangled to death with a silk stocking only three days after Short's body was found. In February 1947, the mutilated body of Mrs. Jeanne French was found, with obscenities written in lipstick on her stomach.

On March 11, 1947, the body of Mrs. Evelyn Winters was discovered, also hacked to pieces. Then police found the body of Rosenda Mondragon, who had also been strangled to death with a silk stocking. Next to be found was Mrs. Dorothy Montgomery, her body left naked and mutilated. Mrs. Laura Trelstad was found beaten to death, her naked body dumped in a vacant area. Detectives believed that at least two of these murders were committed by the same fiend who slaughtered Elizabeth Short, but these murders, like that of Dahlia, remain unsolved to this day.

Captain Jack Donahoe, overall head of the Black Dahlia investigation, developed an unusual theory, coming to believe that the killer was not a man but a *woman,* pointing out that the wounds inflicted on Short's body were similar to those, which had been performed by women in other cases. Donahoe believed that the horrible mutilations were done out of the kind of spite a female reserves for a detested rival.

Donahoe added that between male and female killers,

women were "the deadlier of the species." He also pointed out that Elizabeth Short had spent some time among a lesbian community in Long Beach and may have incurred the wrath of either one or a group of lesbian killers who took their revenge on her for deserting their sexual world. There were few women, however, who confessed to the Dahlia slaying.

A prime suspect, who was arrested in December 1947, was Donald Graeff. This man had taken in a destitute woman, Mrs. Helen Miller, and had attacked her, carving his initials on her hip. Graeff claimed he was drunk at the time of his attack and had no idea of what he was doing. He was dropped as a Dahlia suspect after an extensive investigation into his background. Year after year, the so-called killer continued to come forward. Nine years after the Dahlia murder a New York dishwasher, 44-year-old Ralph von Hiltz adamantly insisted that he knew who the killer of Elizabeth Short was, that he had no part in the killing, but had witnessed the murder and helped the slayer dissect the corpse. He was interrogated, but had no real information on the murder; he was dismissed as another crackpot.

Hansen answered every lead on the case for twenty-five years, no matter how absurd they might have been. He believed, after becoming intimate with every nuance of Elizabeth Short's life, that she may have brought about her own demise. He said: "From all accounts, Elizabeth Short liked to tease men. She probably went too far this time and just set some guy off into a blind berserk rage." Hansen also believed that he "never met the killer face to face. I know he didn't manage to slip through with the other subjects. We considered the possibility of his coming right in, making a confession, then cleverly sidestepping the key question. We watched for that, had taken measures to expose him in that advent. We never underestimated this guy. You'd never believe the amount of checking we did on this case. We followed everything as far as it would go, then we'd turn right around and walk through it all again." The bizarre motive of the killer, as well as his (or her) identity, remains as mysterious and unexplained today as it was on that first shocking day when the shattered remains of The Black Dahlia were found.

CHICAGO'S GRIMES SISTERS/ December 28, 1956

During the 1950s a series of baffling, unsolved child murders sorely tested the resources of the Chicago Police Department. In October 1955 three adolescent boys, Craig and Anton Schuessler, and their friend Robert Peterson were abducted and murdered by persons unknown (Stable worker Kenneth Hansen was convicted of these murders decades later, see Kidnapping). The horrific nature of the crime, and the fact that the police were unable to identify a suspect led to sharp criticism of Chief Timothy O'Connor and his detective force.

On December 28, 1956, two South Side girls disappeared shortly after they had exited the Brighton Theatre, where Elvis Presley's movie, *Love Me Tender* was playing. Barbara Grimes (1941-1956), fifteen, and her sister Patricia Grimes (1943-1956), thirteen, were reported missing by their parents at around midnight. There was grave concern that the same murderer who had kidnapped and killed the Schuessler boys had abducted the Grimes sisters. The police thought that the girls

Barbara Grimes, fifteen, disappeared on December 28, 1956; her body, along with that of her younger sister, was found almost a month later.

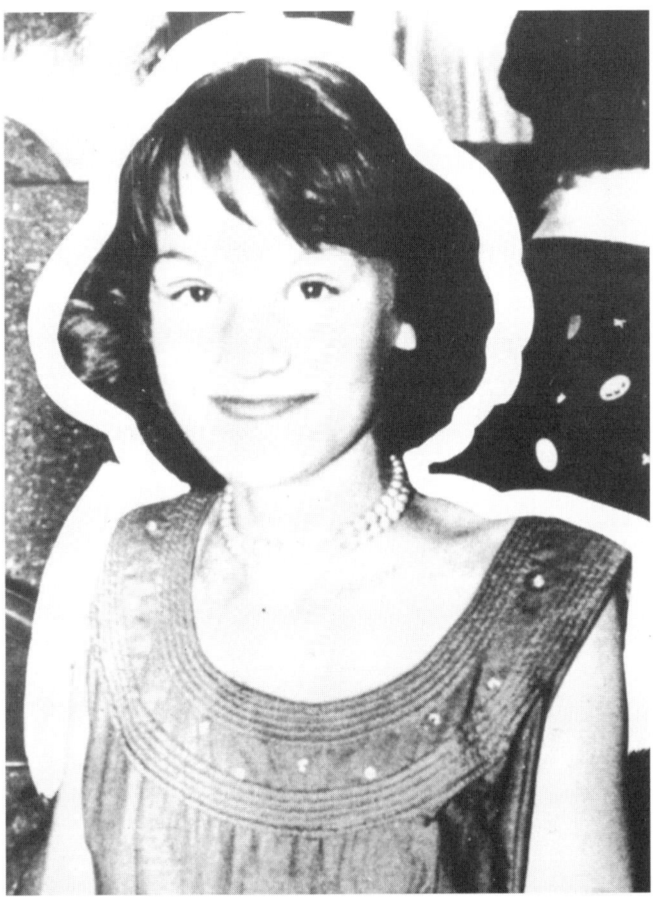

Patricia Grimes, thirteen, vanished with her older sister after seeing a movie; the girls reportedly accepted a lift from a young man.

Spectators mix with police and newsmen on German Church Road in DuPage County, where the bodies of the Grimes sisters were found on January 22, 1957.

Drifter Edward "Bennie" Bedwell, center, wearing jacket, was charged with the kidnapping-murders of the Grimes Sisters, but his confession, it was later discovered, had been beaten out of him and he was later released.

might have attempted to emulate their leather-jacketed hero Elvis Presley, by running away from home.

The singer was contacted in Memphis, where he immediately issued a statement to the girls via the press: "If you are good Presley fans, you will go home and ease your mother's worries." Barbara and Patricia were not the kind to rebel against parental authority. They were good students in the Catholic school system, and had shown no rebellious tendencies.

Newspaper columnist Ann Landers received a letter allegedly written by a young girl, who was in the Brighton Theatre that day. It read:

> "Betty asked me to go with her and her parents to visit her aunt. Later we decided to go to the movie. While looking for a seat Betty noticed Barbara and Pat Grimes sitting with some other kids. Outside the show we all got to talking and we exchanged phone numbers. When we got to the street where we turned off, we said good-by and we ran across the street. Then Betty forgot something she had to tell Barbara and we ran back to the corner. A man about twenty-two or twenty-five was talking to them. He pushed Barbara into the back seat of a car and Pat in the front seat. We got part of the license number as the car drove by us. The first four numbers were 2184. Betty thinks there were three or four numbers after that. We didn't think so much about it but it struck us as kind of funny. When we heard that they were missing we didn't know what to do."

The letter was not signed, raising suspicions that the killer might have written it. In January 1957, Police Sergeant Ernest Spiotto questioned a young man who had snipped off a lock of hair from a girl sitting in a movie house. The individual told of a troubling dream he had, in which two girls were found lying naked in a public park surrounded by trees and a tiny creek. The location that matched the description was only several miles away from the actual spot where the Grimes sisters were found on January, 22, 1957.

Motorist Leonard Prescott was driving down German Church Road, a twisting two-lane highway in remote DuPage County when he spotted two "mannequins" lying in a ditch. Their frozen, lifeless bodies were piled on top of each other. The Grimes girls had at last been found, but the answers to the puzzle still eluded the police. A pathologist determined that the cause of death was due to exposure. There was little evidence of rape or sexual abuse.

The police interrogated the young man who had described the location, where the bodies were found, but released him for lack of evidence. Though scores of Chicago detectives answered thousands of tips on the case and interviewed hundreds of suspects and so-called witnesses, not one concrete clue developed in the baffling Grimes case. The CPD still treats the case as an "open file."

Mrs. Loretta Grimes, the mother of the slain girls, is shown sobbing at a table during the inquest of her daughters' deaths as she is comforted by two of her other daughters on January 29, 1957. The killer was never found.

JACK THE STRIPPER/1964-1965

In a chilling emulation of Jack the Ripper, a psychopathic killer in London began murdering prostitutes in early 1964, strangling his victims and then stripping them. The first victim was Hannah Tailford. On February 2, 1964, her nude body was found floating in the Thames. Within the next year and a half, five more women, all prostitutes, were found either strangled or suffocated, their corpses tossed in the Thames or left along isolated roads. The killer eluded intensive police investigation. Several of the victims had their front teeth knocked out.

Irene Lockwood, discovered on April 8, 1964, had been strangled, as had Birdie O'Hara. Margaret McGowan, a prostitute, who had testified in the infamous Profumo sex scandal, was found in a pile of garbage on November 25, 1964. At first, British police thought that McGowan's death might be connected to the Profumo Affair, but upon close examination, detectives dismissed this idea, attributing the murder to a serial killer.

An army of detectives combing London for clues were unable to pinpoint the identity of the murderer. This clever maniac was very careful in covering his trail, but he left a gruesome hallmark in all of his slayings. All of his victims were found naked. He had stripped the women after killing them, earning the unsavory sobriquet of "Jack the Stripper."

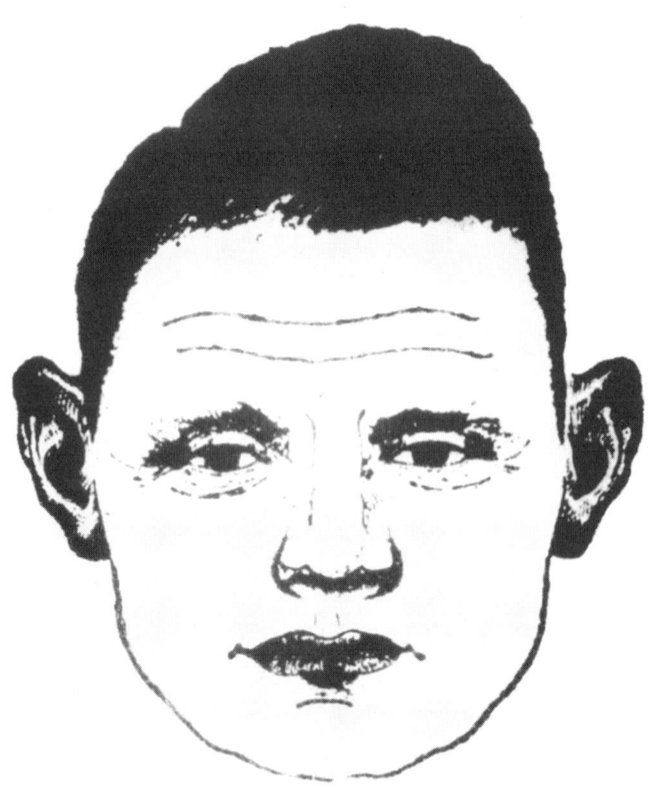

A police sketch of the serial killer who terrorized London, and who was known as "Jack the Stripper."

Detectives did learn that all of the women disappeared between 11 p.m. and 1 a.m., so it was supposed that the murderer worked a night shift. Scotland Yard Chief Superintendent John Du Rose, acting on the discovery that four of the six bodies were flecked with spray paint, launched a search of all garages and small factories in the western section of London. When the murders stopped in late 1965, Du Rose searched through records of suicides, jailings, and accidental deaths since the killing.

A night security guard had killed himself, leaving a suicide note saying, "I am unable to stand the strain any longer." Although no definitive evidence against him was established, it was conveniently assumed that he had been Jack the Stripper. The files on these cases, however, remain open.

SAN FRANCISCO'S ZODIAC KILLER/ 1960s-1970s

A serial killer whose *modus operandi* was strangely similar to that of the Monster of Florence, a killer who preyed on couples in parked cars in Italy in the 1960s and 1970s, the Zodiac Killer (not to be confused with New York's Zodiac killer of 1990, later identified as Heriberto Seda, see Serial Killers) committed a series of killings in northern California beginning in 1966. Investigators named him the Zodiac Killer due to the signs and cryptograms he mailed to the police.

Through descriptions provided by surviving victims, it is fairly certain that the Zodiac killer was male. He did not claim responsibility for several murders he most certainly committed, and police could not find bodies of several victims he claimed to have killed. Most of his victims were young women, and the Zodiac killer once claimed he was "collecting slaves for my afterlife." Body counts of Zodiac murders range from nine to more than forty.

The first killing that the Zodiac murderer confessed to occurred on a deserted road outside Vallejo, California, on December 20, 1968. The killer approached David Faraday, seventeen, and Bettilou Jensen, sixteen, who were sitting in a parked car. He shot Faraday three times in the head with a .22-caliber pistol, and then shot Jensen five times after she jumped out of the car and attempted to run away.

The killer struck again on July 4, 1969, killing a 19-year-old girl and critically wounding her companion, who survived, but could give only a sketchy description of the attacker, who had blinded him by shining a flashlight in his eyes. He said the attacker was male, fairly heavy, and wore glasses.

A particularly gruesome murder attributed to the Zodiac Killer was that of Cecelia Shephard, whom he stabbed twenty-four times in the back. He then carved the outline of a cross into her skin. The killer then shot a taxi driver in the back from the rear seat of the taxi, wiped the car clean of prints, and cut off a bloody piece of the driver's shirt to send to the police.

The driver lived and gave the most accurate description to date of the murderer. With the driver's description, a composite of the Zodiac killer was developed and circulated. Police searched for a man approximately five-feet, eight-inches tall with short reddish-brown hair and thick glasses.

Byron Hartnell, who was attacked with girlfriend Cecelia Shepard, by the Zodiac killer; though stabbed several times in the back, he survived.

Cecelia Shepard, who was stabbed twenty-four times in the back by the Zodiac killer; so savagely was Shepard slashed that there was no hope of survival.

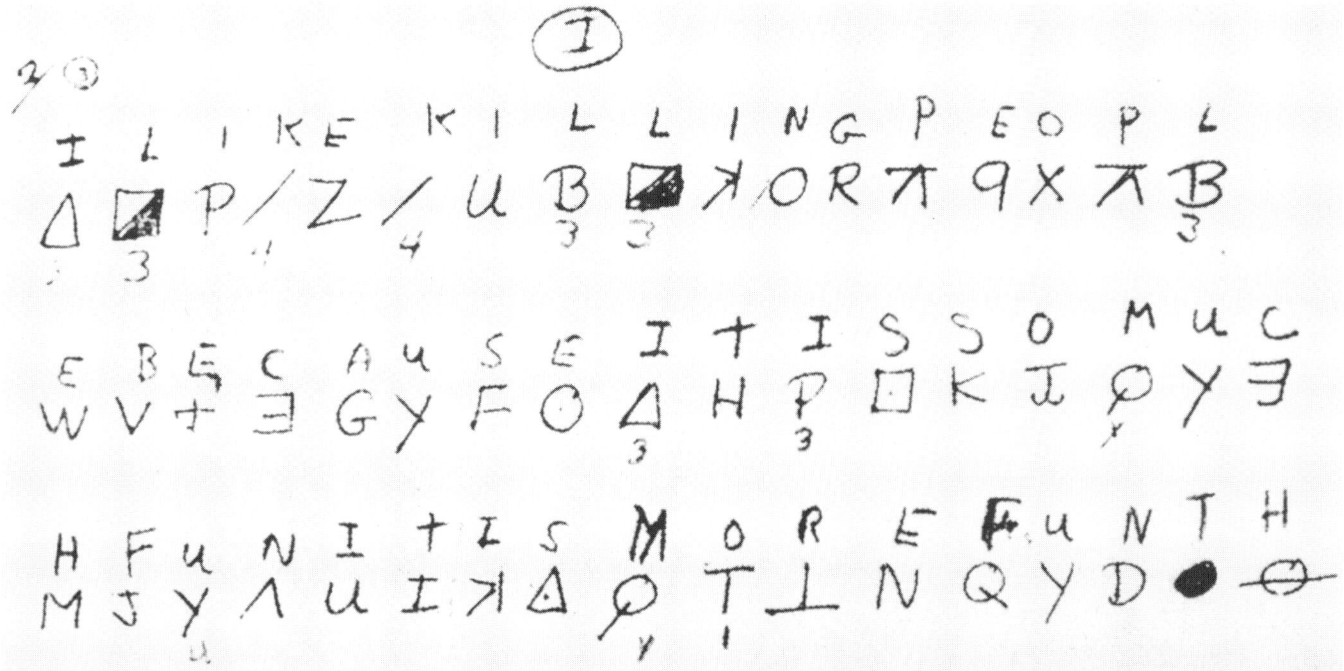

When Navy experts could not decipher the Zodiac's cryptogram shown above, amateur cryptographers decoded his gruesome message.

WANTED

SAN FRANCISCO POLICE DEPARTMENT

NO. 90-69 | WANTED FOR MURDER | OCTOBER 18, 1969

ORIGINAL DRAWING

AMENDED DRAWING

Supplementing our Bulletin 87-69 of October 13, 1969. Additional information has developed the above amended drawing of murder suspect known as "ZODIAC".

WMA, 35-45 Years, approximately 5'8", Heavy Build, Short Brown Hair, possibly with Red Tint, Wears Glasses. Armed with 9 MM Automatic.

Available for comparison: Slugs, Casings, Latents, Handwriting.

ANY INFORMATION:
Inspectors Armstrong & Toschi
Homicide Detail
CASE NO. 696314

THOMAS J. CAHILL
CHIEF OF POLICE

The wanted poster above was issued by the San Francisco Police Department and shows sketches of the Zodiac killer, as described to police artists by surviving victims. He was never apprehended.

The killer stopped communicating with police in 1975. He claimed to have killed thirty-seven people, though police believed that some of the letters were fakes. While the San Francisco police attributed only six murders to Zodiac, the sheriff of Sonoma County, Don Striepeke, placed the total slayings at more than forty, these murders occurring in four western states, based on a computer study of similar murders.

Striepeke hypothesized that the murderer worked from a large "Z" drawn over a map of several states. Police believe that the murderer either died or was committed to a psychiatric institution. Like the Monster of Florence, he simply ceased killing.

THE MICHIGAN CHILD MURDERS/1976-1977

Oakland County, Michigan, northwest of downtown Detroit, is home to moderately affluent suburban communities, well-policed, and generally free of the multitudinous crimes that plague nearby Detroit. However, suburban Oakland County was the scene of seven child murders between January 15, 1976, and March 16, 1977. These unsolved crimes defied the efforts of over fifty law enforcement agencies that joined in the hunt for the killer.

On January 15, 1976, 16-year-old Cynthia Cadieux became the first victim. The teenager was killed after leaving her girlfriend's house in suburban Roseville, and her unclad, bludgeoned body was later found on a desolate stretch of road. Less than a week later, 14-year-old Sheila Srock was shot to death by a home invader at her sister's Birmingham home. In August 1976, Jane Louise Allan, thirteen, was found on a public road outside Miamisburg, Ohio. The evidence suggested that she had been bound, gagged, and smothered. Although these first three murders seemed unconnected, the next four murders were clearly the work of one individual.

Mark Stebbins, a 12-year-old Ferndale youth disappeared shortly after leaving the American Legion Hall on February 13, 1976. He was found dead a week later in Southfield. There was evidence of sexual molestation. Similar to the Stebbins murder, Jill Robinson, twelve, vanished shortly after walking out of a hobby shop in Royal Oak on December 22, 1976.

Like the Stebbins boy, Jill Robinson's body had been washed and arranged in a funeral position. The body was found near the I-75 Freeway in Troy on December 26, 1976. Seven days later, Kristine Mihelich of Berkley left her house to buy a magazine. Her body was found adjacent to a rural road in Franklin Village on January 21, 1977. Again, the corpse had been thoroughly cleaned and arranged in the traditional funeral position.

The only eye-witness account of the killer was given to police following the disappearance of 11-year-old Timothy King on March 16, 1977. According to the witnesses, a white man between twenty-five and thirty-five driving a Blue Gremlin was seen conversing with the King boy outside a local drugstore. Timothy's body was found next to a road in suburban Livonia on March 23, 1977. He had been suffocated and sexually assaulted.

The killer was never heard from again. Investigators from over fifty police departments focused their search on the owners of blue Gremlins in the Detroit area, but not one suspect emerged. Birmingham police chief Jerry Tobin speculated that the murderer might have been an affluent businessman. At the time, Tobin stated: "We think he is a white-collar-class person or a professional man somebody who is trusted, like a doctor, a policeman, a member of the clergy."

The ritualistic nature of the crimes—the fact that the bodies had all been washed and laid in the traditional funeral position—suggested to police that the killer might have been foreign-born, perhaps Middle Eastern. An informant with a Middle Eastern accent told a local psychiatrist that he could point out the murderer in one of Detroit's gay bars. However, the informant never showed up. The investigation dragged on for months with no viable clues and these murders remain unsolved at this writing.

Three police composite sketches of the suspected killer, who kidnapped and murdered seven or more children in 1976-1977.

THE MURDER OF JONBENET RAMSEY/ December 26, 1996

On December 26, 1996, JonBenet Ramsey (1990-1996), a pretty 6-year-old girl, who had won several beauty contests—she was Little Miss Colorado for 1995—was found murdered in the basement of her parents' sprawling Boulder, Colorado, home. An autopsy revealed that the girl had been sexually attacked and then strangled to death. Her skull had also been crushed by a powerful blow to the head.

A ransom note, found on the stairwell leading to the basement of the Ramsey home, claimed that the girl had been kidnapped (even though her body was present) by a group representing "a small foreign faction" and demanded $118,000 for her release. Police and media speculated that the kidnappers—if, indeed, that's who the killers had been—had attempted to abduct the girl, but that she put up a fight and they killed her, dropping the ransom note they had prepared in advance.

Much of the case remained enigmatic in that the Boulder police, even after a prolonged investigation, never charged anyone with the rape-killing. What evidence detectives collected was never made public. Shrouding the murder further was the fact that the child's parents, John and Patsy Ramsey, shielded themselves behind expensive lawyers and talked to authorities only in carefully screened interviews, as was the case when they faced the media.

Though no suspects in the killing were ever named, John and Patsy Ramsey remained under an "umbrella of suspicion." Theories abound. One investigator surmised that an intruder killed the child in her bedroom, then attempted to hide the body in the basement, and left the note so that he would not have to risk taking the body from the home in the hope that the parents would pay the ransom before the body was discovered. Another suspected that one of JonBenet's older siblings killed her.

A scream was heard by a Ramsey neighbor on the night of the murder, one report stated. Another said there was no scream. A writing expert said that the ransom note bore a striking resemblance to Patsy Ramsey's own handwriting. Another expert said no. Then a bevy of experts tried to figure out why the so-called kidnappers would demand the odd ransom amount of $118,000, instead of a million, which her tycoon father could reportedly afford to pay. The case drowned in questions and was starved for answers.

Criticism was rampant. Police in Boulder were lambasted for allowing John Ramsey to search his own house eight hours after he had called police in response to finding the ransom note, a search that led to his discovery of his daughter's body. Moreover, police were blasted for allowing friends and relatives to roam through the house at that time. Then prosecutors and police fell out, accusing each other of bungling the case.

In fall 1997, Detective Steve Thomas of the Boulder force, who had investigated the murder, quit his position. He accused District Attorney Alex Hunter of botching the case in an extraordinary effort to protect the Ramseys. Lou Smit, a special investigator, who looked into the case, also quit, but he stated that he thought the Ramseys, who later relocated to Atlanta, Georgia, were innocent. In the end, there was no solution, only silence and wonder.

Six-year-old JonBenet Ramsey, strangled to death in the home of her wealthy parents in Boulder, Colorado, on December 26, 1996; her killer was never found.

There is every reason to believe that the killer of little JonBenet Ramsey and his/her horrible predecessors and successors look back upon their own terrible crimes with the strange perspective of manufactured innocence as they make their placid ways through life. They maintain a public posture of common virtue and respectability and in the end, convince themselves that they have had nothing to do with the hideous deeds reported in the daily press. They have their layered rationales: That was someone else, some strange creature crawling about in the past. And nestling inside this cozy rationalization, the reality of guilt and conscience becomes a hazy historical nightmare in which all the lurking slayers are conveniently anonymous.

CHAPTER THIRTEEN:

PIRACY

Although one might argue that the Vikings were the first pirates, routinely raiding the coastal towns of England, Scotland and Ireland as early as 789 A.D., the age of piracy began in earnest shortly after Columbus sailed to the New World in 1492. As virgin lands were discovered, great fleets moved across the oceans, seeking commodities and gold. Following in their wakes were the pirates, seagoing highwaymen, who plundered the rich cargoes of these vessels, often slaughtering the crews who served them, or taking these hapless prisoners to be later sold as slaves. The pirates menaced world commerce for more than three hundred years, tens of thousands of these self-styled corsairs capturing lone ships and even whole commercial fleets.

The pirates sought and found safe harbors in remote island chains in the Mediterranean and the Caribbean and off the isles of India and China. These were barbarous men, for the most part, with little or no regard for human life, except for what a life might bring them in ransom. Robbery, rape and murder were their usual pursuits, when not drowning themselves in alcohol. They considered themselves above and beyond the law.

Charles Bellamy, who flourished in the so-called "Golden Age" of piracy, in the early 18th Century, captured a Boston merchantman off the coast of South Carolina in 1717. When the captain of that ship challenged Bellamy's authority to take his vessel, the pirate declared: "I am a free prince and I have as much authority to make war on the whole world as he

Daniel Defoe, who penned the first chronicle of the pirates.

Below, Robert Newton, as pirate Long John Silver menaces Bobby Driscoll, as Jim Hawkins in the 1950 film of *Treasure Island*, faithfully based upon the Robert Louis Stevenson tale.

who has a hundred sail of ships at sea and an army of 100,000 men in the field."

The exploits of such men were heralded far and wide, the first to chronicle their deeds in detail being Daniel Defoe, who used the alias of "Captain Charles Johnson" when writing *A General History of the Robberies and Murders of the Most Notorious Pirates*. He condemned these ocean-going freebooters, but within his pages one can detect Defoe's

The great swashbuckler Errol Flynn, as the physician-turned pirate, in the 1935 film, *Captain Blood*, the first spectacular talkie about buccaneers.

Dueling pirates: Tyrone Power, left, and George Sanders in the 1942 film, *The Black Swan*, another epic about corsairs and their conquests.

sneaking admiration for these cutthroats. By any comparison, the pirates were extraordinary men, who took fierce pride in their independence and regarded their murdering and pillaging as a right granted by the gods.

These pirates took on mythical images that were nurtured and perpetuated by writers such Lord Byron in his 1814 essay, "The Corsair," one in which he profiled his piratical hero as a victim of despotic society. The pirate was romanticized by Sir Walter Scott in his 1822 novel, *The Pirate*, and Robert Louis Stevenson made his pirates into legendary characters in his 1883 tale, *Treasure Island*. The motion pictures furthered that image with such classic swashbuckling films like *Captain Blood*, starring Errol Flynn, and *The Black Swan*, with Tyrone Power. As late as 2003, the film *Pirates of the Caribbean: The Curse of the Black Pearl* vaulted pirates to fantasy figures.

To be sure, there were among these brazen thieves intelligent and (rarely) compassionate captains, such as Jean Bart, but for the most part they were wolves preying upon innocent commerce with a pathological obsession to obtain riches at any cost. The governmental navies of the world united to track down these sea wolves and destroy them, sweeping the pirates from the seas by the middle of the 18TH Century. A few sea-going rogues continued to practice piracy into the next century and some pirates exist to this day in remote areas of the China Seas, but they are furtive, hunted creatures and a far cry from the bold buccaneers who terrorized the oceans of the past.

THE TERRIBLE REDBEARDS/1500s-1540s

One of two sea-roving Turkish pirate brothers who raided Italian, Spanish, and French shipping for the Mamelukes, Barbarossa I (Arouj or Horush or Koruk; AKA: Redbeard, c.1473-1518) pillaged indiscriminately. In 1504, two heavily-laden treasure ships of the Vatican were sent from Genoa to Rome, and when they became separated, a small, fast ship, captained by Barbarossa I, intercepted the second ship and attacked it. After subduing the Vatican crew, the Turks stripped off their own garb and put on the uniforms of the captives. They quickly overtook the first Vatican ship and signaled for it to rendezvous. When the second ship caught up with the

The fierce Barbarossa brothers, Turkish pirates who sank countless ships and seized enormous treasures in the Mediterranean Sea during the 1500s.

first, the disguised pirates quickly overwhelmed the Vatican crew.

Barbarossa I then sailed with an enormous booty to Tunis, where the pirate chief, called Redbeard, gave half of the loot to the Emir for protection. But Barbarossa, who had lost one hand in his pirate battles, had no intention of sharing power with the Emir and, at an audience with the potentate, casually reached out with his one good hand and strangled his host to death, immediately proclaiming himself Emir.

Incensed at the increased raids conducted by Barbarossa I against his ships, Charles I of Spain ordered a huge armada with 10,000 men to storm Tunis and the Turkish pirates, along with their Arab allies, were slaughtered. Barbarossa I was trapped in the Emir's palace and there scores of Spanish soldiers cut the pirate to pieces. It was the terrible reputation of Barbarossa I that tainted the image of his surviving sibling, and most historians have profiled both Barbarossa brothers as fierce, merciless beasts who murdered at whim and showed not a bit of mercy to their victims. Both wore the sobriquet Redbeard but the most infamous of the pair was certainly Barbarossa I.

Upon the death of his brother, Barbarossa I, Khizr, or Barbarossa II (Khizr, Khair ed-Din or Khaireddin or Chaireddin; AKA: Redbeard, c. 1466-1546), went to Selim I, the Sultan of Turkey, and asked that he provide an army to retake Tunis from the Spanish, stating that he would make the land a present to Turkey in return. The armies and navy were provided and Barbarossa II retook all the lost lands of Tunis and was made deputy ruler in 1516 by Selim I.

For more than thirty years Barbarossa controlled the Mediterranean Sea with his hordes of Turkish and Arabic pirates, becoming as famous as Attila the Hun or Hannibal. His ships looted almost every coastal town from Spain to the Black Sea and, since he considered his raids part of a Holy War against Christians, he was inclined to show little mercy to prisoners. Those too young or old, those unfit for work as slaves, were butchered by his pirates. The rest of a town's inhabitants, thousands, were sold into slavery.

Barbarossa II, who was also known as Redbeard, heard that the Duchess of Trajetto was a rare beauty and the pirate decided she would make an excellent gift for Selim I. He raided the city of Calabria with a mighty fleet of sixty ships, but found that the Duchess, warned in advance of Redbeard's intentions, had escaped her seaside villa in her nightgown, riding her horse to death to reach safety. When she returned to Calabria, she found the city in ruins, most of the inhabitants murdered, crucified as was Barbarossa's favorite method of execution or taken off into slavery. The pirate, in his rage at not capturing the duchess, had burned the city to the ground. This incident pointed to the world the barbarous nature of the Turkish pirate.

Yet, the same man took an 18-year-old Italian girl prisoner, so the story goes, when besieging Reggio. Instead of sending the beautiful girl to one of his many harems, the pirate, who had fallen in love with the girl, begged her to marry him, saying he would abandon the siege of her city if she consented. She did, and Barbarossa retired to his magnificent palace in Constantinople, living into his sixties in wedded bliss.

Barbarossa II was far from the hedonistic, cruel tyrant the world thought him to be when he died in bed in 1546. By this time, Barbarossa had given up the black flag and sword and had become a scholar, learning several languages and becoming a patron of the arts. He did not die, as popular history has it, through sexual overindulgence with a bevy of his harem ladies surrounding him. He died with his Italian wife at his side and a book in his hands.

THE VOYAGES OF SIR FRANCIS DRAKE/ 1570s-1580s

The naval heroics of British admiral Sir Francis Drake (c.1545-1596) amounted to little more than piracy, sanctioned by the throne of England. When the Spanish demanded of Queen Elizabeth I that Drake be executed for attacking their ships, the Queen might have agreed in order to assure peace, but the Spanish also demanded a return of £1.5 million in treasure that Drake had stolen during his around-the-world voyage. When the Queen knighted Drake on board his ship, *Golden Hind,* the Spanish were outraged and began preparing for war.

Francis Drake was born in Devonshire, and apprenticed to sea as a pirate by his cousin Sir John Hawkins. In 1567, Drake stood at the helm of the *Judith* during an expedition to the Gulf of Mexico. He earned a reputation as a fearless, if not cunning, seaman during three expeditions to the New World. In 1572, he was commissioned a privateer by the Queen and was the first Englishman to see the Pacific Ocean. During this voyage, Drake sacked the town of Nombre de Dios, and played havoc with Spanish shipping in the region. Before the looting

The privateer (later admiral) Sir Francis Drake, backed and knighted by Queen Elizabeth I, wreaked havoc upon the Spanish fleets and looted great amounts of gold for England.

Drake, center, without helmet, and his men greet Indians on the Rio de la Plata during the global voyage of the *Golden Hind* (1577-1580).

Sir John Hawkins financed Drake, traded in slaves, designed the heavily-gunned, sleek ships that destroyed the Spanish Armada, and was with Drake when he died in 1596.

of that coastal town, Drake moved through the jungles of Panama, where he waylaid mule trains laden with Spanish gold, although he lost half his crew members to Yellow Fever, poisonous snakes and Spanish troops hunting the brigands. (This and many other Drake episodes were incorporated into the greatest pirate film of them all, *The Sea H*awk, starring the inimitable Errol Flynn.)

Drake returned to England to prepare for his eventual trip around the world, a journey of piracy licensed by the Queen. He embarked in December 1577, sailing through the Cape Verde Islands and past Brazil. Continuing past the Straits of Magellan and up the coast of Chile, Drake seized as many Spanish ships as he could, amassing a fortune of plundered cargo in the hold of his ship. He sailed across the Pacific, through the Indian Ocean, and around the Cape of Good Hope.

By this time the Spanish ministers demanded that "El Draque" hang for his peacetime piracies. Drake returned to Plymouth in September 1580. Elizabeth carefully weighed Drake's service to her against the irate demands of the Spanish. After six months, she went to Deptford and knighted him. In subsequent privateering missions, Drake sailed with the blessings of the throne, although the Spanish refused to consider him as anything more than a common pirate.

Drake often retired to his estates to play the country squire, and even became the mayor of Plymouth (1581). The courteous Drake thought himself a God-fearing Protestant knight errant and soon grew restless on land, wearying of his image as a national hero. He again embarked upon raiding voyages and on an ill-fated expedition to the West Indies, where he was accompanied by Sir John Hawkins, he died aboard his own ship in 1596.

Errol Flynn, center, fences with a horde of foes in the greatest pirate movie of them all, the 1940 film, *The Sea Hawk*, which was based upon the incredible exploits of Sir Francis Drake.

JEAN-DAVID NAU'S "REVENGE"/1660s

Taking his name from his ancestral birthplace in Brittany, Jean-David Nau (AKA: Lolonois, Francois Lolonois) became a pirate not to amass wealth, but to avenge his suffering at the hands of the Spanish. As a youth he had shipped out as an indentured servant and had worked long hours in the steaming tropical Caribbean heat of Hispaniola sugar plantations. He was incessantly beaten and tortured, until he became a hateful, vengeance-seeking killer. In light of his later conduct, one could easily term Jean-David Nau as a bloodthirsty psychopath.

Nau escaped his servitude by fleeing to the island of Tortuga, a safe harbor for fugitives, murderers, and pirates. Nau recruited a band of 700 pirates for the sole purpose of waging undeclared war against Spanish shipping. With Michel le Basque serving as his top aide, Nau sailed to Gibraltar, then on to New Granada, and Nicaragua, although he had no navigational experience.

Nau's raids and cruelty against the coastal towns became legendary. One account maintains that Nau cut open a Spanish prisoner's chest with a cutlass, removed the heart, and began chewing on it. He shouted to a group of terrified prisoners, who had been reluctant to tell him where treasures were hidden: "I will serve you all alike, if you don't talk!" Another favored method of torture employed by Nau was to tighten a cord around a victim's forehead until the eyes popped out of their sockets. The cruel practice was known as "woolding."

Nau's own death was equally ghastly. After being captured by Darien Indians, the pirate captain was kept alive long enough to witness his limbs being pulled from his body and thrown into a roaring bonfire.

French pirate Jean-David Nau, called Lolonois, a savage pirate, who killed for pleasure and tortured captives for entertainment.

Pirate Nau (Lolonois) is shown cutting out the heart of a captive and feeding it to another victim, bestial conduct that was routine for this corsair.

MORGAN OF THE WEST INDIES/1660s-1670s

Sir Henry Morgan (c.1634-1688), one of the most infamous of seventeenth-century British privateers, was born in Llanrhymney, Glamorganshire, Wales. He was the eldest son of Robert Morgan, who was either a farmer or a gentleman, depending on which source is cited. The issue of his father's occupation and corresponding status was apparently a matter of some concern to Morgan himself, as is evidenced by the lawsuit he filed against an English publisher. Morgan objected to the publisher's alleged descriptions of Morgan's father as a farmer and him as a "monster of cruelty."

As anxious as he was to be described favorably, Morgan never made clear what circumstances brought him to the West Indies or what he did there in the years before 1665, when he gained prominence as a buccaneer. One account stated that he went to sea as a cabin boy and ended up in Jamaica, but another suggested that he arrived there with elements of Cromwell's army in 1655. Regardless of the circumstances in which he arrived, it is clear that he had useful connections with the colonial establishment in Jamaica. Morgan's uncle, Sir Edward Morgan, was appointed deputy governor of Jamaica in 1663. The governor of the island at the time was Sir Thomas Modyford, a wealthy planter from Barbados.

Jamaica had no naval protection in the mid-1660s, so Modyford awarded privateering commissions to men like Morgan for the island's protection. Prior to 1667, this type of commission was officially sanctioned by the British because they had no treaty with Spain, their main rival in that part of the world. However, in 1667, King Charles II signed a treaty with Spain and ordered Modyford to rescind all privateering commissions. Modyford, believing that the Spaniards in Cuba were preparing to seize Jamaica, ignored the king's orders and asked a large company of buccaneers with Morgan at its head to raid Cuba, take Spanish prisoners, and torture them to obtain information regarding their invasion plans. Modyford induced Morgan and his men to take the assignment by granting them permission to plunder the towns as well.

Morgan set out with a force of 700 men both British and French in twelve ships. They landed in Cuba and marched fifty miles inland to the town of Puerto del Principe, whose citizens ransomed themselves with 1,000 cattle. Disappointed with their booty, the buccaneers sailed to the Isthmus of Panama to sack the coastal city of Porto Bello, a transit point for the treasure being taken out of Peru. The city was defended by three strong forts, but Morgan's men were fierce fighters. After taking two of the forts, Morgan and his men forced a group of captured nuns and monks to serve as shields for the buccaneers by preceding them up the scaling ladders with which they stormed the final fort.

The nuns and monks were killed, but Morgan and his men overwhelmed the last fort and proceeded to behave in typical buccaneer fashion. They looted the town, including the churches, raped the women, and tortured the prisoners including some small children to obtain information about where valuables were hidden. Morgan and his men held the town for thirty-one days, during which time his crews repulsed the at-

Sir Henry Morgan, a privateer turned pirate hunter, who was knighted and became governor of Jamaica.

A Spanish galleon of the era proved to be the easy prey of pirate Henry Morgan.

Morgan, shown right forefront holding spear, leads his pirates in the sacking of Puerto del Principe in Cuba.

Laird Cregar, center, portrayed pirate Henry Morgan, in the 1942 film, *The Black Swan*; shown with him is Tyrone Power, right, and Thomas Mitchell.

tack of a Spanish relief expedition, before sailing back to Jamaica. Despite the fact that his commission permitted him to attack only Spanish shipping, Morgan received only a mild reprimand from Modyford for the plunder. The governor reasoned that the attacks on Spanish towns kept Spanish forces engaged in self-defense, and thereby lessened their capability to attack Jamaica.

Morgan's next expedition was to Maracaibo, where he suffered a setback. As Morgan and his men planned a raid on the city on board his flagship, the *Oxford,* in the harbor of Port Royal, an explosion rocked the ship, killing over two hundred men. Only Morgan and about twenty-five officers sitting on his side of the table survived the blast. Buccaneers from other ships swarmed into the area to loot the remains, taking boots, swords, and pistols, and hacking off corpses' fingers when necessary to salvage a ring. Although the explosion was probably caused by a careless or drunken gunner, Morgan insisted that it was a French plot.

Morgan's prestige suffered temporarily because of the incident on the *Oxford,* but by 1670, he was ready to embark on another large mission. The Spanish had renewed their attacks on Jamaica, burning and looting some of the coastal towns. Modyford once again gave Morgan a commission to do whatever was necessary to drive the Spanish back. The commission was in direct disobedience of his instructions from London, but Modyford ignored this fact in order to defend the island.

Morgan gathered a force of some 2,000 men on thirty-six ships, ranging from a flagship of 120 tons and twenty-two guns to an unarmed sloop of twelve tons. Preparations for the expedition were made through the autumn of 1670. The buccaneers raided Spanish hogyards and cattle ranches and cruised the coast seizing cargoes of foodstuffs. The Council of Jamaica unanimously approved the venture on the basis of what Modyford referred to as "the old, pleasing account of no purchase, no pay." The buccaneers would take their pay in plunder.

According to the articles of the expedition, compensation for injuries would be paid first by six hundred Spanish dollars for the loss of a hand or a leg; 1,800 for both hands; 1,500 for both legs; and one hundred for an eye. (These amounts were substantially higher than for expeditions conducted completely at sea because of the greater risk of mortality and serious wounds in land campaigns.) After the injuries were paid for, the remaining spoils were to be divided into equal shares, with a certain number of shares going to each captain.

With preparations completed, the expedition set sail in December 1670, despite a treaty that had just been signed in Madrid that recognized British territorial claims in the West Indies. Morgan's force traveled first to Providence Island, which the governor surrendered to them without a fight. (The governor arranged with Morgan for a sham battle, which would be fought with powder but no shot, so that he could save face with his constituency.) Then, using Old Providence as a base, the buccaneers attacked Fort San Lorenzo at the mouth of the Chagres River.

At least one hundred buccaneers were killed and seventy severely wounded before the garrison of 350 Spanish soldiers was subdued. Leaving 300 men to guard the fort and 150 to protect the fleet, Morgan and 1,400 buccaneers sailed to Panama City in January 1671. After a grueling march through the jungle and a brief but fierce fight, Morgan and his men subdued the city and looted it before burning it to the ground. The town, reputedly one of the richest in Latin America, yielded so much treasure that it took 175 mules to haul it away. The buccaneers also took 600 prisoners to be ransomed, adding even more value to the spoils.

When the triumphant Morgan returned to Jamaica, he discovered that Spanish complaints about Modyford's violation of the "Treaty of America" had caused the governor to be sent back to England under arrest. Six months later, Morgan was also called to London to "answer for his offenses against the king, his crown, and dignity." Neither Morgan nor Modyford was punished, but they were both detained in London for three years until the king was certain that Spain would not demand their punishment. At the end of the three years, they were sent back to Jamaica, Modyford as Chief Justice and Morgan as Lieutenant-Governor and both were knighted. In his new position, Morgan hunted down buccaneers with the same ferocity he had displayed when he was one of them. Morgan himself died peacefully in his bed in 1688.

Pirate Thomas Tew, left, entertains Colonel Benjamin Fletcher, royal governor of New York, with his adventures in the Red Sea, where he seized a treasure ship from the Great Mogul of India.

THOMAS TEW, THE RED SEA PIRATE/1690s

Like Drake and Morgan before him, Thomas Tew became a pirate with the official approval of government officials. A long-time privateer, Tew was, in 1692, approached by a group of merchants and officials in Bermuda, who offered him a share in the 70-ton sloop *Amity*. After paying for his share in December of that year, Tew carefully recruited a crew of sixty hardy seaman, all adept with cutlass and musket. He then met with Isaac Richier, the governor of Bermuda, and persuaded that riches-seeking official to give him a commission to raid French trading posts on the west coast of Africa, France then being at war with England.

Such commissions were avidly sought by pirates, who, if captured, could explain their criminal deeds as "official actions," in that they had plundered on behalf of their government. Such commissions were freely given by government officials, who sought to acquire wealth for their country and for themselves. With government approval, Tew set sail, but when only a few days at sea, he called his crew members together and proposed that they abandon the plan to attack the French outposts, as these lonely bastions would yield little or no treasure. Instead, he suggested, that the *Amity* sail around the Cape of Good Hope, and into the Indian Sea and from there, sail into the Red Sea, where he was convinced rich plunder could be had. The crew agreed and the *Amity* altered its piratical course.

Tew encountered only one prize during his voyage, but it yielded him and his crew a fortune, a huge vessel of the Great Mogul of India, which was laden with enormous riches. Though guarded by hundreds of Indian troops, this ship gave up without much of a fight. Not one of Tew's men were killed. Tew and his crew members loaded into the hold of the *Amity* the equivalent of £100,000 worth of gold, silver, spices, silk and elephant ivory tusks. Sailing southward, the *Amity* took refuge in a tranquil bay on the island of St. Mary, off the Madagascar coast. Tew took on new provisions, and made repairs, then sailed leisurely to America, arriving at Newport, Rhode Island in April 1694.

The tales of treasure told by Tew and his men electrified the town, and made heroes of the pirates. Every young man along the Atlantic seaboard hearing of Tew's exploits, envisioned himself a pirate and thousands eagerly signed on board merchant vessels quickly converting to pirate ships. Tew sailed his vessel to New York, where he met with Colonel Benjamin Fletcher, the royal governor. The pirate spent several hours regaling Fletcher with his piratical feats, all of which delighted the governor.

Though the Indian prize had enriched Tew and his crew members to the point where they might retire in comfort, they, like most of their ilk, were lured back under the black flag by greed. In November 1694, Tew paid the venal Governor Fletcher £300 to obtain another "official" commission to raid the Red Sea. His next voyage was far from the success he had enjoyed in 1692. The Amity sailed into the Red Sea and, spotting another Indian vessel in September 1695, made a bold attack. Tew and his pirates boarded the ship, but they were met by hordes of hard-fighting Indian sailors and soldiers. Tew, leading his men, was greeted with a volley of musketry that tore open his belly and blew him onto the deck. He sat for moments trying to hold in his entrails and then died with a surprised look on his face.

FRANCE'S GENTLEMAN PIRATE/1690s

Jean Bart (c.1651-1702) was a French privateer from Dunkirk who operated with the secret commission of King Louis XIV. He was a gentleman pirate, elegantly attired and insisting upon the normal rules of warfare when his squadrons overwhelmed Dutch vessels and destroyed the Dutch herring fleets along the Atlantic coasts during the war between France and the Netherlands (1672-1678). He captured eighty-one ships and took enormous spoils, but did not seek the normally ruthless reprisals of those in his trade when offered resistance. So successful was Bart that King Louis XIV personally appointed him a lieutenant in the French navy.

Bart was after loot to send to his king, not slaves. The prisoners captured by his well-disciplined men were treated with consideration and put ashore at the first landfall. If Bart demonstrated any great failing, it was his vanity. He dressed in ornate clothes, strutting about the deck of his flagship, peacock-proud. He dined on the best plate and was adamant that his top mates display the proper table manners, hardly the image of the raw, uncouth pirate the world had come to dread.

Made a captain, Bart led the French corsairs against the British, engaging the enemy at Beachy Head in 1690, and defending Dunkerque in 1694-1695. After Bart's successful raids against the forts near Newcastle-on-Tyne, he attacked a 91-ship convoy of wheat and this prize relieved a famine that had gripped France for months. These feats were acknowledged by Louis XIV, who, in 1697, gave Bart the command of a royal fleet. He died a much respected captain of the French Royal Fleet, known for his courage, despite his early occupation as a desperate corsair. Bart's memory was commemorated prior to World War II, when a French battleship was named after him.

French pirate Jean Bart, who became an admiral and national hero.

HENRY EVERY, PRINCE OF BUCCANEERS/1690s

A legendary character, British pirate Henry Every (AKA: John Avery, Long Ben; b.c.1665), known to his cutthroat crews as "Long Ben," was born near Plymouth about 1665 (some reports have him born as early as 1653), and went to sea early. In the early 1690s, Every served under the pirate, Captain "Red Hand" Nichols. By 1693, Every captained a slave ship along Africa's Guinea coast. In the spring of 1694, Every truly launched his career as a pirate. He began as first mate aboard the 46-gun ship, *Charles II,* which left Bristol, commissioned by the Spanish government as a privateer, assigned to stop French smugglers from raiding Spanish colonies in the Caribbean. Every and many of his followers undoubtedly signed on board this ship with the secret plan of taking over the vessel and conducting a pirate expedition in the Indian Ocean.

Captain Gibson of the *Charles II* was a confirmed alcoholic and, while the ship was in port, he took more than his share of rum and fell into a stupor in his cabin. Every and his men quietly secured the hatches, weighed anchor, and set sail. Hours later, when Gibson was rocked to revival by the heavy swells of the Atlantic, Every appeared in his cabin and told him that he had taken over the ship, stating: "I am bound to Madagascar with a design of making my own fortune, and that of all the brave fellows joined with me." Every gave Gibson the choice of either joining him and the mutineers intent on piracy or leaving the ship in an open boat. Gibson and five or six others chose to leave the ship and were set adrift in a small boat, left to make their way to shore, which they did.

Every renamed the ship the *Fancy* and sailed to Madagascar, flying his newly designed pirate flag, four silver chevrons on a red background. Once in the Eastern seas, Every and his men attacked vessels of all nations, looting and plundering at will. Every ordered the heavy upper masts of the *Fancy* stripped so that the ship's speed was increased. He could now outrun any pursuer.

The *Fancy* made the island of Johanna its home port and when a heavily-armed French ship made the mistake of sailing into the harbor one day, the *Fancy* quickly attacked it and overwhelmed the crew, who turned out to be pirates. The French ship was loaded with plunder taken in the Red Sea from Moors and this loot greatly enriched the crew of the *Fancy*. Moreover, Every's numbers swelled when forty Frenchmen from the captured ship joined his piratical band.

So bold did Every become that he wrote a letter, or a pirate's manifesto, so to speak, and left this with a native chief at Johanna, asking that it be delivered to the captain of the first British ship to enter the port after the *Fancy* had departed. This curious document, blending English patriotism and roaring pirate bravado, declared:

> To All English Commanders:
> Let this satisfy that I was riding here at this instant in the ship *Fancy,* man of war, formerly the *Charles II* of the Spanish expedition who departed from La Carua 7th May 1694, being then and now a ship of forty-six guns, 150 men and bound to seek our fortunes. I have never as yet wronged any English or Dutch, or ever intend whilst I am commander. Wherefore, as I commonly speak with all ships I desire whoever comes to the perusal of this to take this signal, that if you or any whom you may inform are desirous to know what we are at a distance, then make your ancient (ship's flag) up in a ball or bundle and hoist him at the mizen peak, the mizen being furled. I shall answer with the same, and never molest you, for my men are hungry, stout and resolute, and should they exceed my desire I cannot help myself. As yet an Englishman's friend.
>
> At Johanna, 18th February 1695
> Henry Every

(He inserted a postscript) Here is 160 odd French armed men at Mohilla who waits for opportunity of getting any ship, take care of yourselves.

An English East Indian sailed into the harbor at Johanna a short time later and was handed this remarkable document, but instead of earning appreciation from the British, at the promise of being left unharmed, Every's bold declaration branded him a hunted pirate by the British and all nations. He would forever be pursued as a felon and became one of the few British pirates never granted amnesty. The *Fancy,* meanwhile, sailed into the Red Sea where it was met by four other pirate ships from the U. S. colonies. In August 1695 Every was elected commander of this powerful fleet.

At first Every's pirate fleet had little luck in running down its prey, the treasure ships of the Great Mogul. One fleet of twenty-five ships slipped past the pirate vessels in the night but, at dawn, Every spied two ships coming into view. The huge *Gang-i-Sawai,* one of the largest vessels on the sea at the time, was so enormous and powerful that the Indian commanders believed her to be unbeatable in battle. This ship carried 200 battle-seasoned sailors, 600 musketeers and 600 passengers. It had sixty-two guns and towered over anything on the oceans. Its lone escort, the smaller *Fatah Mohamed,* was also a

Pirate Henry Every commanded a fleet of ships that plundered the Indian seas and the waters of the Bahamas; he reportedly bought died in bed.

powerful warship. Every thought nothing of sailing after these two ships in the *Fancy,* intent upon capturing and destroying them both.

The *Fatah Mohamed* purposely lagged behind the behemoth *Gang-i-Sawai* to do battle with Every, but after the *Fancy* drew alongside the *Fatah Mohamed,* letting loose a broadside that ripped into the side of the Indian ship, the *Fatah Mohamed* quickly surrendered. It carried more than £50,000 in gold and silver and this treasure was quickly taken aboard the *Fancy.* Most of the Indian crew were slain before Every pushed off in pursuit of the lumbering *Gang-i-Sawai.* This ship was returning from Mecca after a pilgrimage and carried many high-ranking Indian officials, as well as relatives of the Great Mogul.

The *Gang-i-Sawai* was considered by Indian historian Khafi Khan to be the greatest ship ever built. It carried more than 500,000 pieces of gold and silver, which were to be delivered to the coffers of the Great Mogul at the Indian port of Surat. Eight days before it reached that destination, the fast-moving *Fancy* overtook the giant *Gang-i-Sawai.* Though the Indian ship could easily outgun Every's ship and its musketeers outnumbered the pirates five to one, its commander was a coward and, when he first glimpsed the *Fancy,* he fled below decks, hiding with twenty young women, concubines of the Great Mogul. He ordered the women to don turbans so that they might be mistaken for men and he dressed himself as a slave.

Above decks, misfortune quickly overtook the *Gang-i-Sawai* when its first salvo aimed at the *Fancy* resulted in one of its own guns blowing up and killing five or six of its crewmen. Fires broke out, causing panic among the crew and musketeers who saw it as an omen of disaster. Then Every's best gunners fired a shot which blew away the main mast of the Indian vessel, causing it to lose control.

The Indian ship maneuvered about wildly and the *Fancy* circled it like a wolf stalking an injured stag. Every ordered the *Fancy* to come alongside the great Indian ship and, when grappling hooks pulled the two ships together, the pirates literally had to climb upward to board the towering *Gang-i-Sawai.* The pirates, goaded by the lure of the fabulous riches, eagerly battled the phalanxes of musketeers, driving them overboard and killing them in large groups.

Every lost about twenty men, but more than 300 of the Indians were slain. The loot was taken aboard the *Fancy* and the women on board were raped. Most of the prisoners were tortured by the pirates into disclosing where their valuables were hidden and then left to die. Following the barbaric slaughter, Every and his men selected the most attractive women on board and took these hapless females with them when the *Fancy* sailed away, leaving the burning hulk to sink. The *Gang-i-Sawai* did not go to the bottom, however, but managed to stay afloat and later limp into port with its few surviving crewmen, who told the tale of Every's bestial attack.

The plunder from the Indian ships made the pirates rich. Every took two full shares and then spread the loot throughout his five-ship fleet. Each pirate received about £1,000 and younger seamen, ages sixteen to eighteen, received £500. Boys in the pirate crews under the age of sixteen were given £100 and set ashore to set themselves up in "honest apprenticeship." Many of Every's crew members retired then and there, leaving the ship on the tropical island of Bourbon (known as Reunion after 1793) where they quit piracy and became gentleman planters. So depleted was Every's crew that he took on ninety African slaves and converted them to seamen before setting sail for the Bahamas. The pirates anchored in St. Thomas some weeks later.

The pirate flag Henry Every's ships flew from their mastheads.

Every is shown with a slave on his island fortress in the Bahamas, where he lived like a king, governing thousands of pirates.

Every and his men were welcomed by the Bahamian governor, Nicholas Trott, whom the pirates had bribed with more than £7,000 in gold and great quantities of ivory and other precious goods. Trott gave Every and his top aides a formal dinner in the Governor's mansion and then saw them off when they set sail for Jamaica. Here Every and his men sent a request for pardon to Governor William Beeston, offering him £24,000 for the official favor. Beeston, an honest man, refused and Every sailed back to St. Thomas, where the pirates gave the *Fancy* to Governor Trott for his protection. The men got drunk and allowed the ship to be driven ashore during a gale. The vessel was a total wreck, only its guns salvaged from the storm. The pirates disbanded, many going to the U. S. colonies, where some were later imprisoned.

Every, who changed his name to Benjamin Bridgeman, and a few of his lieutenants bought sloops and sailed for England, the least likely hideout since they were all posted there as wanted felons. The sloops arrived in various Irish and English ports, but the pirates soon drew attention to themselves by swaggering about the towns and spending their stolen riches like rajahs.

One man, John Dann, was caught in Rochester, near London, wearing a coat lined with gold sovereigns and weighing more than twenty pounds. The pirates stupidly displayed rare gems and paid greatly inflated prices for horses, thus drawing attention to themselves. Twenty-four of them were captured and six were hanged. The rest were sent to penal service in the U. S. colonies. The only pirate to escape was the bold Every. He landed his sloop near Dunfanaghy, about thirty miles northwest of Londonderry in County Donegal, Ireland.

The fate of Every was never learned. Some of his men claimed he went to Dublin or Scotland, or to Exeter, near his birthplace, Plymouth. Daniel Defoe gave one account twenty years later that the shrewd Every, living under the name of Bridgeman, settled down in the town of Bideford, in Devon, where he tried to negotiate the sale of a sack of diamonds with greedy merchants. The merchants gave him a small down payment against the gems, promising the balance after they had been sold. However, they gave Every only a pittance each week so that he was finally reduced to begging and died a pauper with hardly enough money to buy a cheap coffin. Another version has it that Every lived high for many years and died in bed, the squire of a large Irish estate.

Every's looting of the *Gang-i-Sawai* became legendary and inspired thousands of British seamen to become pirates, just as Thomas Tew's first great prize in the Red Sea inspired countless American boys to sign on board pirate ships and end their premature lives in bloody sea battles. In India, the Great Mogul's advisers turned on the British East India Company, accusing it of engineering the piratical attack on their greatest ship. Dozens of British officers were thrown into prison and many died of torture and malnutrition. One was stoned to death. The East India Company lost millions in trade because of Every's actions and it took years before the Company earned back the good graces of the Indian leaders.

A portrait of William Kidd, who became one of the most notorious pirates of the 1690s.

CAPTAIN KIDD AND HIS MYTHICAL TREASURE/1690s

Captain William Kidd (c.1645-1701) has been pilloried for several hundred years as the worst pirate who ever boarded a ship. Seemingly endless tales have been written about his villainous nature and his ruthless slaughter of helpless captives. He has been depicted as a bloodthirsty plunderer and a deceitful emissary of King William III of England. He was most likely a little bit of all of these, but he was nowhere the scourge of American seaways during the late 1690s as he was later depicted and the fabulous treasures he was supposed to have buried along the east coast of the U. S. are probably as mythical as many of the horrible feats attributed to him.

William Kidd was born in Scotland, circa 1645, and he began as a small trading goods merchant, later going into shipbuilding. He migrated to New York in 1690 and, as a captain of armed merchant ships, he successfully drove off a number of French raiding vessels, more to protect his own interests than to safeguard British colonial shipping. He was nevertheless looked upon as a hero, and the state assembly gave him a reward of £150 and a citation listing him among New York's leading citizens.

Prospering through his shipping line, Kidd further enriched himself by marrying a wealthy widow. He became a leading church member and a pillar of New York society. In 1695, William III authorized a syndicate of wealthy Whigs to hire Kidd to clear the American sea lanes of pirates who had been raiding British shipping. Kidd was also authorized to attack French commercial ships since England was then at war with France. Most of the booty seized by Kidd was to be converted to cash and distributed to those participating in the syndicate. These included Sir John Somers, the lord chancellor of England, as well as Sir Edward Russell, the first lord of the admiralty, and the Duke of Shrewsbury, the secretary of state.

The king stated that he himself would participate in the syndicate, but he failed to put up the required £3,000 and was eliminated from sharing in the booty. What made Kidd's job next to impossible was the syndicate's insistence that his crew receive, instead of pay, only a quarter of the prizes, a woefully small payment, since sixty percent of the spoils was then the standard offered any privateering crew. Kidd complained about the arrangement, saying that he would not be able to sign aboard any seamen except cutthroats and fugitives.

In 1696, Kidd set sail in the 287-ton *Adventure Galley*. The first seventy crewmen he hired were all married men with

Captain Kidd's resplendent home in Manhattan at Pearl and Hanover streets, where he was visited by political leaders and aristocrats.

families, a law-abiding lot. But to this understaffed crew Kidd added another eighty men, taken from local prisons and poorhouses, all of them cutthroats and thieves, the worst sort of sailors. His ship was equipped with thirty-four guns, carried a great deal of sail, and had twenty-three oars for rowing when the ship was becalmed.

Kidd sailed to the mouth of the Red Sea, reaching the island of Perim in July 1697. While en route, he had insulted several officers of the Royal Navy by demanding additional sails and supplies and upbraiding Indian merchant ships for flying the British colors. He informed the Indian captains that only he, who possessed a royal commission, was allowed to fly such colors. The *Adventure Galley* waited for a fleet of ships to enter the narrows which, Kidd knew, was a favorite ambush point for pirates preying upon commercial ships.

On August 16, 1697, a fleet of sixteen ships sailed through these narrows and Kidd attacked it, not bothering to see if the ships were French or pirate. They were neither, being a flotilla of British and Dutch vessels. Kidd nevertheless sailed his ship alongside a British merchantman and let loose a broadside that crippled the vessel. The *Sceptre,* a British warship accompanying the fleet, gave chase and Kidd ordered his crew to evade and flee it. He had attacked the wrong kind of ship and came away without any loot, which caused resentment among his crew members.

Kidd next appeared in the Indian Ocean, where he attacked a Moorish barque and allowed his men to board this small merchant vessel. They brought back with them a bale of pepper and a sack of coffee, which he allowed them to keep for their mess. He also forced the skipper of the Moorish ship, an Englishman named Parker, to serve the *Adventure Galley* as pilot. The Moorish ship was not a legitimate prize under Kidd's charter.

Kidd next appeared at the British-controlled island of Kawar, stopping for water and wood. When British officials learned that Kidd was holding Parker, two officers of the Royal Navy boarded the *Adventure Galley,* and demanded that the captive be released. Kidd boldly lied to them, saying that he held no such captive, while all the while Parker was locked in chains in the vessel's brig. Kidd then set sail, but two of his crewmen jumped ship and informed authorities that Parker was indeed on board the *Adventure Galley* and that Kidd had turned pirate, planning to attack any kind of ship he felt was worth seizing.

In November 1697, Kidd's ship spied a large merchantman, but when the *Adventure Galley* sailed close to this coveted prize, it proved to be flying the British colors. His gunners moaned, but Kidd ordered them not to fire. The crew threatened to mutiny, but Kidd threatened to have them thrown in chains and the unruly seamen backed down. William Moore, a gunner, felt, as did many other crewmen, that Kidd was depriving them of their prizes and he upbraided the captain. Kidd exploded and struck Moore with a bucket, which fractured his skull. The captain ordered Moore, who was unconscious, to be carried below decks, shouting: "Damn him! He is a villain!" Moore died the next day and was buried at sea. The crew grew even more sullen and truculent.

Three weeks later, Kidd seemed desperate to fulfill his commission by capturing *some sort* of vessel, hopefully a French or a pirate ship. He spotted a large merchant ship and

Captain Kidd buries his family Bible at Plymouth Sound after resolving to become a pirate, an apocryphal story that nevertheless captured Kidd's true intent.

Lord Bellomont, governor of New York and New England, who defended Kidd, then, when the pirate proved unreliable, inveigled him to a meeting, where he could be arrested.

Captain Kidd fatally injures seaman William Moore, by striking him with a bucket; Moore died the next day, a fatality that caused resentment among crew members.

Kidd supervises two of his pirates in digging a hole on the beach at Gardiner's Island, where he reportedly buried a great treasure.

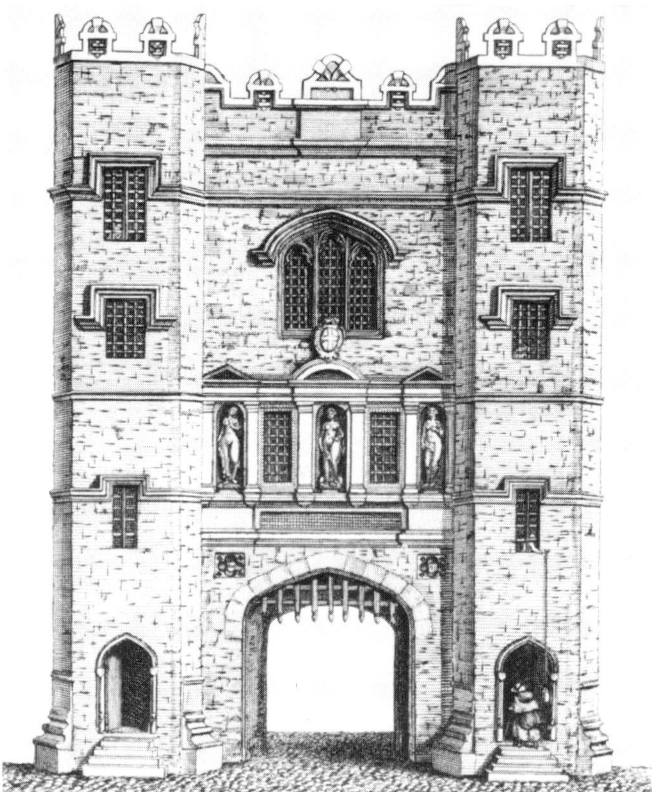

Newgate Prison, where, ironically, Kidd was held on charges of piracy and theft from the syndicate that had commissioned him as a privateer.

cleverly hoisted the French colors. The merchant ship also hoisted a French flag. Kidd boarded the ship and discovered that it was the *Maiden,* commanded by Dutch officers and a crew of Moors. The captain gave Kidd a French pass, telling him that he was sailing under the authority of the French. Kidd was elated, saying: "By God, I have catched you! You are a free prize to England!" He then set the Moorish seamen adrift in a longboat, took the *Maiden* to a port, and sold off its rich cargoes of cotton, quilts, sugar, and horses.

Kidd split this loot with his crew, keeping none for the syndicate, which had hired him, and thus broke his contract with the British authorities. He renamed the captured vessel the *November,* after the month in which he had captured it, and sailed off commanding a flotilla of two ships. One tale later reported that Kidd, the son of a Presbyterian minister, when he had actually decided to become an out-and-out pirate, went ashore on a small island and buried his Bible, thus signifying his dark dedication to the life of a freebooter.

Kidd had operated legally, according to his own reasoning, using the French pass given to him by the Dutch skipper as proof that he had captured the type of ship he was ordered to seize, but the pass proved not to be his vindication. Almost all merchantmen carried passes from all the powerful nations and the Dutch captain also had in his possession a British pass. The French pass, however, was enough to satisfy Kidd that he had not broken his contract, although, technically, he had committed piracy. Kidd proceeded to plunder several merchant ships and finally attacked an Armenian ship, the *Quedah Merchant,* off the Indian coast during a storm. This 500-ton vessel was laden with gold, rare spices, opium, gunpowder, rice, iron, beeswax, and butter. It was also commanded by an Englishman named Wright.

Kidd used the same ruse and ran up the French flag. Wright countered the ruse by sending an elderly French gunner on board the *Adventure Galley,* posing as the skipper of the *Quedah Merchant,* and showing a recently signed pass from the director general of the Royal French East India Company. This pass was enough of an excuse for Kidd to announce that he was seizing the ship in the name of England. He hoisted the British flag and took command of the merchant ship, declining an offer from its owners, who tried to buy him off with a payment of £3,000. Kidd took the vessel to a port and sold off its rich cargo and again divided this among the crew. He received forty shares of the loot.

The *Adventure Galley* was then riding at anchor in St. Mary's harbor and oddly, so was a pirate ship, the *Mocha Frigate,* a ship captained by Robert Culliford, a privateer like Kidd who had openly turned pirate. Kidd was still apparently torn between his duty and his inclinations toward piracy. He suddenly asked his men to fire upon the pirate ship and take its crew captive. His crewmen jeered and howled derisively at him, one shouting that if they fired at anyone it would be at *him!* Following this split, all of Kidd's crewmen, except thirteen, quit his service and went over to Culliford. These deserters included Joseph Palmer and Robert Bradinham. Both would later testify against Kidd at his trial for piracy.

Kidd was left with the *Adventure Galley,* which had been stripped by its former crew and was now a leaking hulk. He burned her and took her iron, equipped the *Quedah Merchant,* and then set sail with considerable spoils still on board to pacify his lofty sponsors. By then, letters had been written by British officials in India, describing Kidd's piracies to his sponsors in England, who were more indignant at not having received their shares of the spoils than at their emissary's wrongdoing. They condemned Kidd out of hand and ordered that he be arrested whenever he touched British soil. British officials in America were directed by the admiralty to capture Captain Kidd in order that "he and his associates, be prosecuted with the utmost rigor of the law."

To the Tory politicians, the Whig-backed Kidd represented a major scandal and they inflated Kidd's pirate image to the point where he appeared to be the most hellish freebooter on the high seas. Meanwhile, Kidd and his small crew lumbered across the Atlantic in the bulky *Quedah Merchant.* The vessel anchored off Anguilla in the Leeward Islands and here Kidd and his men learned in shock that they were being sought throughout the world, having been branded abominable pirates by the very men who had hired Kidd.

The captain and crew decided that the *Quedah Merchant* was too cumbersome to try and outrun any pursuing British man-of-war and Kidd bought a sleek trading sloop, the *Antonio,* transferred his considerable treasure to the new ship, and then sailed for New York, where he felt he could explain his actions. He still possessed the two French passes which he hoped would exonerate him from the label of pirate.

Kidd sailed the *Antonio* to New York and sent one of his men with a letter to Lord Bellomont, one of his closest friends and a man with great influence with the lords in England, who had condemned him. First, however, Kidd buried some of his considerable treasure in Oyster Bay, on Gardiner's Island, and reportedly in many other spots including Block Island, Rhode Island; Stratford Point, Connecticut; Clarke's Island in the Connecticut River, on Rye Beach; and on Fisher's Island in the lower Hudson River. (The spot on Gardiner's Island was later found by treasure hunters.) There was much to bury, if indeed, Kidd did bury all his loot, which consisted of many gold bars, gold dust, silver plate, precious stones, and chests of fine silks.

Lord Bellomont, who had originally gotten Kidd his commission, realized that if he championed Kidd at this time,

Captain Kidd addresses the House of Commons on March 27, 1701, without betraying his Whig backers, and blaming others for his piratical acts; he was judged guilty and sentenced to death.

he himself would be ruined by powerful men in London. He inveigled Kidd ashore for a meeting and promised that he would seek the king's pardon for Kidd's questionable acts. "I assure you on my word and honor," wrote Bellomont to Kidd, "I will perform nicely what I have promised."

Kidd first met with his wife Sarah and two daughters on board the *Antonio,* which then sailed to Boston and a meeting with Lord Bellomont. The ship landed in Boston on July 2, 1699, and Kidd went ashore, taking rooms in a comfortable boarding house. He foolishly sent several bribes to the governor's wife, including an enameled jewelry box with four diamonds set in gold and £1,000 worth of gold bars wrapped in a fine silk green bag. Lady Bellomont returned these items without comment.

The next day Lord Bellomont received Kidd not as a friend, but as a judge, ordering him to sit before a council of Whig authorities. Bellomont curtly demanded that Kidd explain his extraordinary voyage. Kidd said that his mutinous crew had burned his log. He was ordered to provide a report, but when Kidd failed to do so, he was arrested on July 6, 1699. A desperate search for Kidd's treasure by Bellomont's men commenced. John Gardiner, the man who lived on Gardiner's Island and ran a small tavern and inn there, was ordered to turn over the loot he knew Kidd had buried there.

Gardiner did turn over some of the gold and gems, but he apparently kept a considerable share for himself, including many huge Golconda diamonds. Most of Kidd's spoils were hidden by the wily captain because he believed that, if he were found guilty by a British court, he could bargain with the crown by offering to turn over his buried treasure for a royal pardon.

Bellomont sent on to the royal treasury what loot his men did recover, including more than 1,000 ounces of gold, 2,300 ounces of silver, a pound of precious stones, and more than 100 bags of goods. Kidd was returned to England on board the H. M. S. *Advice,* which left America on February 6, 1700, and arrived in the Thames on April 11, 1700. Kidd, who had been locked in his cabin throughout the voyage, was then taken aboard the royal yacht *Katherine,* which sailed to Greenwich. There an armed escort appeared on board and went to Kidd's cabin.

Upon opening the door, the guards were greeted with a sickening sight. Kidd appeared a wreck. His eyes were bloodshot and drool curled from his gaping mouth. His head sagged on his chest and he appeared unbalanced. He had not changed his clothes since leaving America and his unwashed body gave off a powerful stench. He offered one of the guards a gold coin, telling him to "give this to my wife." He then asked for a knife so he could commit suicide. When this was refused, Captain Kidd asked that he be shot, not hanged.

Captain Kidd was taken to Newgate Prison and thrown into a cell. This privately run prison was a foul pest hole, where guards routinely abused prisoners. If a prisoner could pay his guards, he could obtain enough food to stay alive, but no more. The place was permeated with the foul stench of unwashed bodies and excrement. The few visitors who braved the place entered with flowers into which to bury their noses in order not to breathe the foul air. Kidd remained in this dungeon-like fortress for more than a year. He was denied

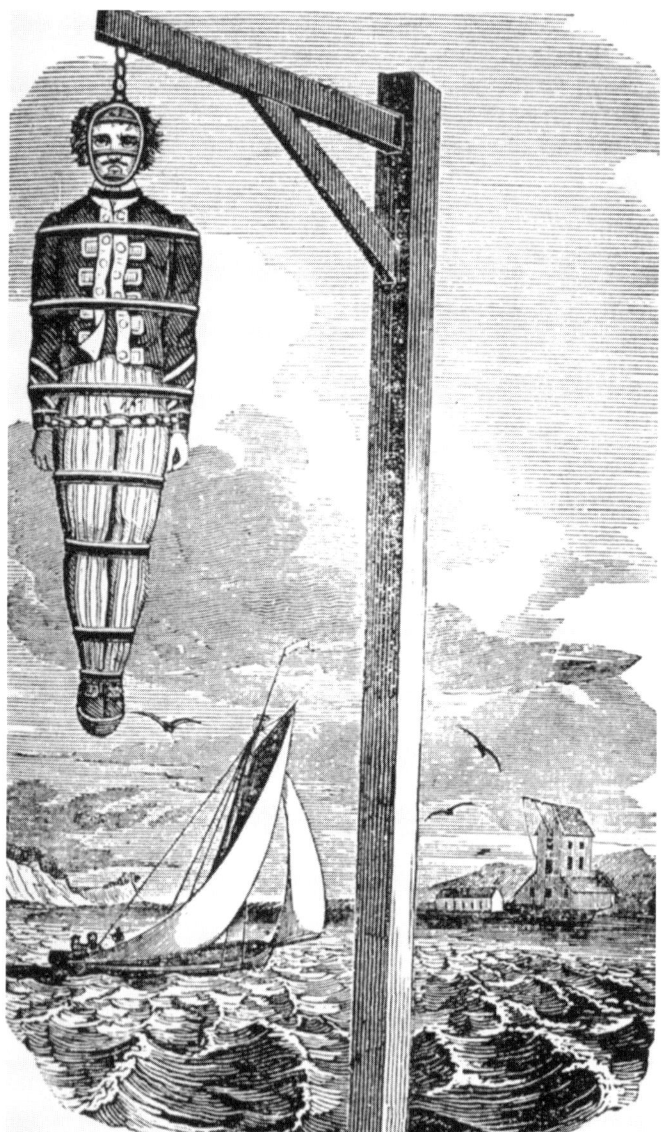

The body of Captain Kidd, encased in an iron gibbet and bound in chains, swings at Tilbury Point in the Thames estuary, as a warning to all other would-be pirates.

exercise, visitors, the right to send letters, even to his wife, and the right to receive any letters. He was not allowed to prepare his defense for his upcoming trial. Before this occurred, Kidd was ordered to appear before the Tory-controlled House of Commons. He was so filthy that he had to be bathed in vinegar and given a new suit of clothes, which hung loosely upon his now haggard, thin frame.

On March 27, 1701, Kidd appeared dazed before the Tories who sought an explanation of his activities. Had Kidd admitted his piracies, and thus implicated his sponsors, the Tories would have undoubtedly granted him a pardon and gone after his Whig sponsors. He had no head for politics, however, and, in a long-winded, ponderous, and often confusing speech read from a meandering script he had written, claimed complete innocence. The Tories were disgusted with him, one member of the house later stating: "I had thought him only a knave. Now I know him to be a fool as well." Kidd's trial was set for May 8, 1701.

Kidd had counted on using the two French passes that he had taken from the *Maiden* and the *Quedah Merchant*. These passes, he believed, would prove that the ships were French (although one was Dutch and the other Armenian) and thus justify his actions. He had, however, turned these two passes over to Bellomont and they were withheld from him by the court. Moreover, Kidd was denied legal counsel until a few hours before his trial. He was prevented from testifying at his own trial, nor were any of his loyal crew members, also under arrest, allowed to testify.

The dedicated pirates Bradinham and Palmer, however, were allowed to testify for the prosecution. Kidd was charged with murdering his gunner, William Moore, and a secondary charge of piracy was added. It appeared that his Whig sponsors, despite his clumsy attempt to claim complete innocence and thus protect them, intended to take vengeance upon Kidd for his not providing them with the expected spoils from his strange and confused expedition.

Bradinham played the loyal seaman when testifying against Kidd, who was allowed to cross-examine the witness. He did a bad job of it, making only one telling point: To save his own life, Bradinham had perjured himself in giving evidence against Kidd. Bradinham swore that Moore had done nothing to provoke Kidd's actions. Kidd admitted his guilt, saying that the death of Moore was an accident for which he was "heartily sorry." He was found guilty of the murder charge by a jury that deliberated for less than a half hour. Kidd was then found guilty of piracy and his fate was sealed. He was sentenced to be hanged. In response, Kidd declared: "My Lord, it is a very hard sentence. I am the innocentest person of all, only I have been sworn against by perjured people."

Kidd tried one last gambit. He appealed to Robert Harley, speaker of the House of Commons, saying that if he were pardoned, he would return to America under guard and reclaim the buried treasure for the crown, a fortune Kidd estimated to be worth £100,000. There was no response to this final plea. Also, there was little or no buried treasure to be dug up. On May 23, 1701, Kidd was dragged from his Newgate cell and placed in a cart draped with black cloth and driven to Wapping. In front of the rumbling cart walked a deputy marshal who carried on his shoulder the silver oar which was the emblem of the admiralty court.

Someone had taken pity on Kidd and given him all the liquor he could drink before he left his cell. He was so drunk that he could hardly stand in the cart and had to be supported as he made his way to the gallows at Execution Dock, where thousands had gathered to witness his execution. Hooting and jeering dinned into Kidd's ears as the hangman adjusted the rope. He disdained any consolation from a clergyman. He was promptly hanged, but the hangman, who was also drunk, had done a bad job and the rope broke, sending Kidd into the mud, causing the enormous crowd to howl in perverse delight.

Kidd was dragged up again to the gallows and this time, at the urging of the clergyman, Kidd "professed his charity to all the world with his hopes of salvation through the merits of his Redeemer." He was then successfully hanged. His body was then tarred, bound with chains, and the head set in a metal harness. This was done so that when Kidd's flesh rotted away, his bones and skull would remain in place. A special gibbet was constructed at Tilbury Point at a cost of £10. Every ship leaving the harbor passed this point and seamen could view the remains for years to come as a reminder to what might befall them should they break the law or defy the crown.

Charles Laughton portrayed the pirate in the 1945 film, *Captain Kidd* in a performance that brilliantly captured the brutal and sly nature of the buccaneer.

Almost all of Captain Kidd's treasure was dug up and returned to the royal treasury, about £3,000 worth of gold, gems, and goods. Yet to this day, thousands of amateur treasure hunters, from Maine to the Carolinas, spend endless time and effort digging and searching for a treasure that does not exist, recovered long ago by members of Kidd's piratical crew and returned to England's coffers or squandered in pubs, on harlots, or used to finance the kind of misadventures that brought Captain William Kidd to his doom.

BLACKBEARD, THE LUNATIC PIRATE/ 1700s-1710s

No pirate who roamed the open seas in search of booty and conquest ever matched the fierce character of Blackbeard (Edward Teach; AKA: Tach, Tatch, Thatch; d.1718), who was truly a sadistic madman, a bloody butcher of helpless victims. But he was fair in his insanity, oppressing his crews and peers with the same demoniac punishments as he inflicted upon his enemies and captives. It was later said by revisionist historians that Blackbeard blatantly performed atrocities to establish for himself an image of mercilessness, of ferocity, producing instant terror in those who faced him in combat. The truth was that Blackbeard was deranged and simply enjoyed killing, reveling before his own death in the hundreds of lives he had taken.

Blackbeard was born Edward Teach in either Bristol, England or Jamaica. His brother became a respected artillery officer in the Jamaican army, but Blackbeard went to sea early and became a pirate as a youth. His name came from the long, flowing black beard he assiduously cultivated, one which he used to create a bogeyman character. Daniel Defoe described the beard as "that large quantity of hair which like a frightful meteor covered his whole face and frightened America more than any comet."

The pirate Blackbeard (Edward Teach), put gunner's matches on his hat and at the end of his braided beard to instill fear in his enemies.

Blackbeard twisted his hair in long strands, adorning it with ribbons, and to further accent his fierce-looking beard he would, before attacking a ship or coastal city, put slow-burning gunner's matches in the ends of his waxed beard strands and in his hat so that he looked like a volcano belching fire and smoke. When going into battle, the pirate put on a glaring red sash and hung six pistols from it. Being ambidextrous, he wielded two swords in combat.

To serve with Blackbeard was to risk one's life with enemies and the captain as well. A giant of a man with seemingly endless stamina and power, he was forever testing his crews. He would pick fights with the toughest of his mates and bring the contest almost to death blows. Dozens of his pirates bore facial scars that they had received from Blackbeard's sword or knife point. On one occasion, Blackbeard suspected that one of his crews was planning a mutiny or desertion. He boarded this ship and ordered everyone into a hold where sulphur barrels were stored.

The pirate crews of Blackbeard and Charles Vane join in drinking and dancing at their hideout on Ocracoke Island off the North Carolina Coast in 1718.

The fight between Blackbeard and Lieutenant Maynard, which resulted in the death of the fierce pirate.

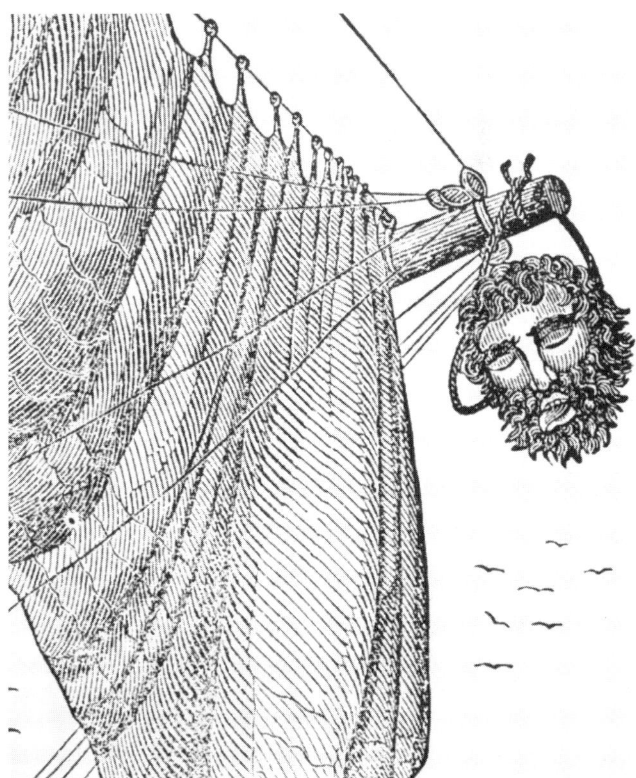

Hanging from the bowsprit of Maynard's sloop is the severed head of the dreaded pirate, Blackbeard.

Robert Newton, who played many a corsair in movies, is shown here as the fearsome buccaneer in the 1952 film, *Blackbeard the Pirate*.

"Now," he said with gleaming eyes, "we shall make our own hell!" With that he lit the sulphur and compelled the crew to stay in the hold and inhale the noxious fumes. He laughed wildly as his crew members eventually bolted for the hatch, coughing and choking, their faces streaming tears. He stayed longest in the hold and emerged to call his now submissive followers weaklings.

Captives taken after Blackbeard's crews overwhelmed a ship were usually mistreated. Women were invariably gang raped by his crews, Blackbeard believing that they were a "natural part of the spoils." He forced some of his captives to walk the traditional plank to their own watery graves, and others who looked at him in "an odd fashion" were run through with his sword, or had their eyes poked out or their ears or noses cut off. A few he disemboweled in front of his crews and fed the bloody entrails to sharks following his flagship, *Queen Anne's Revenge,* a forty-gun French frigate, which seldom found its equal in high seas combat. Oddly, when capturing a ship, Blackbeard often spared the enemy captain. He would interrogate the crew of the ship he had captured and, if these sailors swore that their captain was a fair man, the captain would be spared, put into a longboat first and shown all the courtesy of a military prisoner. Captains who received a bad report from their crew members were horribly mutilated and then murdered.

Blackbeard earned an undying reputation as the worst buccaneer in pirate history, yet he operated for only about three years before his career was brought to an end. His ships operated out of Ocracoke Inlet in North Carolina. He preyed upon shipping of all nations sailing along the coasts of Virginia and the Carolinas.

The pirate operated with impunity because of the connivance of North Carolina governor, Charles Eden and his secretary and collector of customs, Tobias Knight, both of whom secretly protected Blackbeard and shared in all his loot. One report held that the venal Eden, so thankful for one enormous delivery of loot, sent Blackbeard a 16-year-old virgin from North Carolina, whom he suggested Blackbeard marry. The pirate turned the girl over to his crew for their sexual pleasures.

Blackbeard was so bold that he would sail to the bar outside of Charleston, his favorite hunting ground, and blockade the harbor for ten days to two weeks at a time. Then he would attack and capture any ship that went in or out of the harbor. Charleston governor Robert Johnson begged Eden for help but got none. Then, in 1718, Johnson learned that two men-of-war were anchored as guard ships off the Virginia coast. Johnson asked Virginia governor Alexander Spotswood to send the two warships to attack Blackbeard.

Without authority, Governor Spotswood dispatched Lieutenant Maynard and the two men-at-war to the Carolinas with explicit instructions to wipe out the pirates. Maynard sailed his vessels to Ocracoke Inlet and attacked at dawn, but ran aground. The smaller man-of-war was nearly blown out of the water as Blackbeard's flagship raked it with a broadside. But the pirate ship also ran aground, and leaving his own stranded flagship, H.M.S. *Pearl,* Maynard and his crew boarded the *Queen Anne's Revenge,* fighting hand to hand with the pirates, overwhelming them.

Only minutes before the enemy boarded his ship, Blackbeard, undoubtedly realizing that his end was near, seized a huge jug of rum and poured it down his throat, sloppily spilling it down his front. He then roared: "Damnation to all who give or ask for quarter!" He charged into the enemy after firing off his six pistols, swords flailing. Three sailors, including Maynard himself, attacked the giant and ran him through several times with their swords.

To prove that the scourge of the seas was dead, Maynard cut off Blackbeard's ugly head, hanging this grisly trophy from the bowsprit of his ship so that all the inhabitants of the Virginia coastal towns could see that the pirate was finally dead. Governor Eden exploded and threatened to have Spotswood and Maynard arrested. When this proved futile, Eden tried to punish these gentlemen with legal action, but this, also, failed. Eden gave up and also ceased to encourage any other freebooters to plague the coast of the state he had been appointed to protect and preserve. Blackbeard remains in the fierce annals of piracy the most terrifying of his awful breed, a human monster of the high seas, who thoroughly enjoyed death and destruction, even his own.

THE PIRATE OF THE CAROLINAS/1710s

Endowed with a small fortune, a good education, and social rank, Stede Bonnet (AKA: Major Bonnet, Captain Edwards, Captain Thomas; d. 1718) relinquished these worldly advantages to plunder the coastal waters of the British colonies of North America. His social acquaintances on the island of Barbados, where he resided, believed that a disease of the mind had caused him to become a pirate.

About 1715, Stede Bonnet outfitted a fast sloop with ten guns and seventy men. He named his vessel *Revenge*, and

Stede Bonnet, a former major in the British army, who turned pirate, wearing a powdered wig and dandified clothes; he lost his ship to Blackbeard in 1718.

The capture of pirate Stede Bonnet in 1718; he was imprisoned, but later escaped.

November 8, 1718: The hanging of Stede Bonnet on the docks of Charleston, South Carolina.

sailed toward the Virginia Capes, where he soon captured the *Anne,* the *Turbet,* the *Endeavor,* the *Bristol,* and the *Young.*

Within a few months, Bonnet's cargo hold was filled with molasses, clothes, ammunition, rum, and other prizes. his own ship, however, was captured by another notorious pirate, Blackbeard (Edward Teach), and Bonnet was forced to serve aboard his ship, *Queen Anne's Revenge* When Blackbeard lost his ship at Topsail Inlet, Bonnet regained command of his sloop. He sailed to Bathtown, North Carolina, where he made his peace with the colonial authority, promising to end his crimes against the British. In return for a royal pardon, Bonnet agreed to move against the Spaniards as a privateer.

Bonnet discovered that Blackbeard had stolen a good part of his provisions. Bent on revenge, Bonnet sailed up and down the Capes but could not locate Blackbeard. In his search for Blackbeard, Bonnet was unable to pay a fair exchange rate for necessary goods, and he reverted to piracy. The *Revenge* plundered every vessel in sight and Bonnet, now called Captain Thomas, became the terror of the British colonies. The South Carolina authorities, alarmed at having a pirate in their midst, enlisted the help of Captain William Rhet, a privateer who placed his two vessels, the *Henry* and the *Sea Nymph,* at the governor's disposal.

Bonnet was at last overtaken by Rhet in September 1718 off the coast of Carolina. Bonnet and his crew were put ashore on Sept. 30, 1718 near Charlestown. The men were placed under guard by the militia, but Bonnet and David Hariot, one of his men, escaped by bribing one of the sentinels.

Fearing that Bonnet would organize a new pirate band, the governor issued a reward of £700 for his apprehension. Meanwhile, Bonnet had secured a new vessel, but was sorely in need of provisions. He laid anchor at Swillivants Island, off Charlestown. Colonel Rhet learned of Bonnet's whereabouts from the governor and, with a heavily armed band of men, he set out for the island. In a brief firefight, Hariot was killed and Bonnet was forced to surrender.

On November 6, 1718, the pirate leader was returned to Charlestown, where he was put on trial in a Vice-Admiralty Court. Indictments were sworn against Bonnet and thirty-three members of his plundering band. All but four men were found guilty and sentenced to die. The prisoners declared that their intentions were honorable, but that they were driven to piracy by the terrible shortage of provisions.

On November 8, 1718, twenty-two members of the pirate gang were executed at White Point near Charlestown, pursuant to the sentence handed down by Governor Nicholas Trott. In passing sentence on Bonnet, the Trott noted the fact that he compounded his crimes by murdering eighteen people. Trott quoted scripture, and expressed the hope that Bonnet was sufficiently repentant. On November 18, 1718 Captain Stede Bonnet was hanged.

VANE OF THE CARIBBEAN/1710s

Pirate Charles Vane (AKA: Charles of Vaughan, d.c.1719) plundered the seas around Jamaica and Barbados in the early eighteenth century. In 1717, in New Providence, an island in the Bahamas, he and many other pirates were granted conditional amnesty by Governor Woodes Rodgers. Vane refused, firing at one of the governor's man-of-war ships as he sailed away. Two days later, Vane and company captured a ship headed to Barbados, appropriating the vessel and adding its twenty-five sailors and quartermaster, Yeats, to the pirate crew. In the Spring of 1718, Vane captured sloops from Cuba, Puerto Rico, and New Providence, and through the summer and into the fall looted ships from Antigua and Guinea. Eventually, the pirates had two ships, one commanded by Yeats, the other by Vane.

Yeats, however, soon disgusted with Vane's harsh treatment of him and the men, decided to defect. He set sail with his own vessel. When Yeats neared Charleston, South Carolina, he sent a message to the governor requesting amnesty for himself and his men, promising surrender. The governor granted his request, and Yeats, to further curry favor from the governor, turned over several stolen slaves and much of his loot.

Vane was incensed by Yeats' desertion, vowing revenge. He set sail, hoping to catch his one-time associate, but, instead, he captured two ships from Charleston bound for England. The pirate then eluded several warships commissioned by the governor of South Carolina to capture Vane. In late November, 1718, Vane's ship was struck by a French man-of-war. The pirate attempted to flee, but some of his crew and his quartermaster, John Rackham, known as "Calico Jack," wanted

After defying British warships, Charles Vane lost his nerve and was abandoned by his piratical crew, replaced by John "Calico Jack" Rackham.

to board the ship and fight it out. Vane refused, saying it was "too rash and desperate an enterprise, the man-of-war appearing to be twice their force."

Robert Deal, the first mate, sided with Vane, but the rest of the crew supported Rackham. Vane, however, insisted on flight, persuading most the crew that attacking the powerful French warship was suicidal. The pirates sailed away from the French ship, but the crew branded Vane a coward and relieved him of his command the next day, sending him and his supporters off in a small sloop with provisions and ammunition. Rackham was voted captain, and Vane's flagship sailed without him for the Caribbean.

Vane sailed toward Honduras in a smaller ship. In February 1719, a typhoon destroyed this vessel and drowned most of his men, stranding Vane on a small uninhabited island near the Bay of Honduras. He survived for several weeks on fish and turtles until a Jamaican ship landed to replenish its water supplies. Holford, the ship's captain, refused, however, to transport Vane, after realizing that he was a notorious pirate.

Said Holford: "Charles," he said, "I shan't trust you aboard my ship unless I carry you a prisoner; for I shall have you caballing with my men, knock me on the head, and run away with my ship a-pirating." Captain Holford said he'd be back in

A merchant vessel is shown under attack from Vane's ship, which captured dozens of such prizes from Cuba, Puerto Rico and the Bahamas.

Woodes Rogers, right, the governor of the Bahamas, offered Vane amnesty, but the pirate answered by attacking two British warships.

a month and, if he found Vane again would take him to Jamaica and see him hang. Soon after Holford's departure, however, another ship landed and took Vane on board as a crewman. The captain of this vessel did not recognize him.

Some weeks later, Holford met up with this same ship, and was invited to dine by the captain, and noticed Vane hard at work down in the hold. Holford told the captain who Vane was and volunteered to take him prisoner and surrender him to authorities in Jamaica. Vane was taken aboard Holford's ship and taken to Jamaica, where he was promptly tried and convicted of piracy. He was then executed.

HOWELL DAVIS, THE RELUCTANT PIRATE/ 1710s

Born in Milford Haven, in Pembrokeshire, Wales, Howell Davis (d. 1720) was raised to become a seaman and became a pirate only by chance. Davis was serving as the first mate on aboard the slave ship *Cadogan,* en route from Nassau, Bahamas, to Madagascar, when it was captured by the buccaneer Edward England. The pirates murdered the captain of the *Cadogan* and attempted to force the crew to sign oaths of allegiance. When Davis refused, Captain England, impressed with his bravery, returned the ship to him, advising him to sail for Brazil, dispose of the slave cargo, and keep the profits. After England departed, Davis and the crew decided to resume their original course toward Barbados.

Howell Davis was a buccaneer who won the admiration of his crew through courage and guile, often disguising his ship as a merchant vessel.

On reaching port, the colonial authorities arrested Davis and accused him of piracy. When Davis was released from prison three months later, he sailed to New Providence, Bahamas, determined to adopt the very criminal pursuit to which he had been wrongly branded. Davis was disappointed to find that Governor Woodes Rogers had broken up the pirate colony. Rogers agreed to make an accommodation with Davis and gave him command of the *Buck,* a cargo ship laden with a rich payload earmarked for the French and Spanish traders.

With a crew of cutthroats and murderers, Davis sailed to Martinique, where he drew up articles of piracy, an open declaration of war against all nations. From Coxon Hole, Honduras, the pirate crew seized two French ships before sailing under the British flag to the Cape Verde Islands. Thus disguised, the *Buck* was welcomed into friendly ports and given the protection of the colonial powers. Davis next sailed to Gambia in western Africa, where he purported to be a Liverpool, England, trader. There he stole warehouses of gold and ivory before joining forces with two other notorious pirates of the day, Oliver La Buze and Thomas Cocklyn.

In the next few months, the *Buck* captured several English and Dutch prizes. Davis transferred his crew and cargo to a Dutch ship, the *Royal Rover.* Near the coast of Anamaboe, in western Africa, Davis seized a slave ship named the *Princess* on June 5, 1719. The second mate, also from Pembrokeshire, was 36-year-old Bartholomew Roberts. The Welsh pirate took his new-found protege along, allowing him to choose whether or not he wanted to become a pirate, an offer that Davis had himself earlier declined from pirate Edward England.

In 1720, Davis arrived at Prince's Island, a Portuguese settlement, where he planned to capture the governor and hold him for a £40,000 ransom. To lure the governor on board, Davis offered him the chance to inspect twelve slaves offered for sale. One of the slaves escaped and warned the governor. Davis and his escort were shot and killed as they made their way toward the governor's mansion. The surviving crew members of the *Royal Rover* nominated Bartholomew Roberts to succeed Davis. This he did, and with blood-thirsty effectiveness.

BARTHOLOMEW ROBERTS' BLACK FLAG/ 1710s-1720s

Bartholomew Roberts (AKA: Black Bart; c.1682-1722), one of the world's most notorious buccaneers, came late to piracy. By the time he reached his mid-thirties he had twenty years' experience as a seaman and was an expert in handling a ship, controlling a crew, and deploying the tactics of naval warfare, skills most likely acquired in active service with the British navy or aboard a privateer. Regardless of his prowess as a seaman, Roberts was excluded from the possibility of commanding a ship by virtue of his relatively low birth. He resisted the notion of piracy until Howell Davis, the captain of the *Royal Rover,* a pirate ship on which Roberts was being held captive, was killed and the crew offered him its command.

Roberts accepted the post with alacrity. Apart from a new style of dress (which included a crimson damask waistcoat

Pirate Bartholomew Roberts is shown in 1722, at the time of his greatest prize, the seizing of eleven slave ships at Whydah, his two pirate ships, the *Great Ranger* and the *Royal Fortune*, shown in foreground.

and breeches, a red feather in his tri-cornered hat, and a gold neck chain with a diamond cross suspended from it), Roberts adopted few of the habits and characteristics of most pirates. He eschewed alcohol himself and discouraged its use among his crew. He set out a list of rules and made each member of the crew swear to abide by them. He tolerated no disrespectful behavior.

Roberts and his new pirate crew set sail in July 1719. After first returning to Prince's Island, where Howell Davis had been killed in an ambush, and destroying a Portuguese settlement there by way of revenge, Roberts took his ship south along the African coast where he seized and plundered two ships, a Dutch trading ship and a Royal African Company slave boat. The crew voted then to sail to Brazil, a journey which Roberts managed to navigate in a record twenty-eight days.

In September 1719, the *Royal Rover* sighted a fleet of forty-two Portuguese merchant ships loaded with Brazilian gold, tobacco, sugar, and hides. With the audacity that was to become his signature, Roberts sailed directly into the middle of the fleet, boarded the ship with the greatest store of goods,

The black flag flown by Bartholomew Roberts, showing him astride skulls representing two island chains that defied his raids.

plundered it (a haul which included the equivalent of £50,000 in currency), and sailed away again without a confrontation.

After celebrating their victory on Devil's Island off the coast of Guyana, Roberts and his crew sailed into the Caribbean. There they were forced to retreat by the British Royal Navy and turned toward Newfoundland, a departure point for merchant ships crossing the Atlantic. In June 1720, the *Royal Rover* sailed into the port of Trepassey, where the crew plundered twenty-six merchant ships. Roberts took one of the prize ships and converted it for his own use, calling it the *Royal Fortune.* Off the Newfoundland Banks, Roberts captured another six French ships, for one of which he swapped his recent acquisition. He added twenty-eight guns to the new ship and dubbed it also the *Royal Fortune.*

From mid-summer 1720 until late in 1721, Roberts and his crew enjoyed an incredible success rate. Off the New England coast they took a number of English prizes, among them the sloop *Samuel.* They returned briefly to the Caribbean, but before long decided to return to the African coast. Weather conditions prevented the crossing and the pirates sailed to Surinam on the north coast of South America. Defiantly, Roberts decided to return to the Caribbean in spite of the presence of the Royal Navy.

There Roberts and his crew terrorized the islands so thoroughly that the residents attempted unsuccessfully to secure help in defeating the pirate. Roberts became so incensed at this move that he redesigned his personal flag to show him standing with each of his feet on a skull, one labeled "ABH" for "A Barbadian's Head," and the other labeled "AMH" for "A Martinican's Head."

After bringing Caribbean shipping to a virtual standstill, Roberts and his crew decided to return to Africa, where they could trade their booty for gold. In Sierra Leone, Roberts was informed of the presence on the coast of two British men-of-war, the *Swallow* and the *Weymouth,* each of which was equipped with sixty guns and had been sent to protect British shipping and trading interests against Roberts and others of his ilk. In August 1721 Roberts captured the Royal African Company frigate *Onslow* and after increasing her guns from twenty-six to forty, he adopted her as his third and final *Royal Fortune.*

In late December Roberts made a tactical error. He relied on the information he had been given that the British warships would be safely out of his path by the time he turned back up the coast. Due to an outbreak of dysentery, however, the British ships had been delayed at Prince's Island. On January 11, 1722, Roberts sailed into Whydah, a slaving port on the coast. In so doing, he passed directly under the guns of the British ships, which were anchored near Cape Coast Castle. The *Swallow* set out after him. On February 5, 1722, the Britsh man-of-war located Roberts in one of the inlets along the coast toward Cape Lopez.

Roberts, seeing the approaching ship, mistook it for a merchant ship and sent Captain James Skyrme off in the *Great Ranger* to pursue and capture it. The captain of the *Swallow* turned back to sea, feigning flight and allowing the pirates to gain on him slowly. When reaching a distance where the guns would not be heard on shore, the British man-of-war turned

Members of Roberts' crew celebrate a recent victory at the Old Calabar River; alcoholism was rampant among pirates and often led to their capture.

about and opened fire on the pirate ship. Finally Skyrme was forced to call for quarter. After sending their captives back to Prince's Island under guard, the *Swallow* turned back toward land and Roberts' two remaining ships.

Roberts was caught unaware and at first attempted to escape the British ship. He then decided to confront the pursuing ship. In the first round of fire, Roberts was hit in the throat and killed. Unnerved, his crew continued to fight after they had thrown his body overboard as he had requested. After several hours the crew of the *Royal Fortune* admitted defeat and asked for quarter. Of the 254 prisoners taken, 169 were charged.

All of the prisoners pleaded not guilty to charges of piracy. Seventy-four men were acquitted, fifty-four were sentenced to death (two were later reprieved), seventeen were sent to prison in London, and twenty were sentenced to seven years' hard labor in the Royal African Company's mines. Fifty-two men, including Captain Skyrme were hanged. The last hangings occurred on April 20, 1722. The bodies of eighteen of the worst offenders were dipped in tar, bound with metal straps, and hung in chains from gibbets on three hills.

THE UNLUCKY CALICO JACK/1710s

John Rackham (or Racham; AKA: Calico Jack) took command of the pirate ship *Vane* on November 24, 1718, in the Caribbean. After plundering several vessels, Rackham and his men

John "Calico Jack" Rackham's piratical exploits were studded with misfortune; he fell in love with lady pirate Anne Bonny before he was hanged.

The "Jolly Roger" flag flown brazenly from the topmast of Rackham's pirate ship.

Pirate Anne Bonny in a prison cell, consoling her condemned lover, John "Calico Jack" Rackham.

went ashore on a small island near Jamaica, where they spent Christmas drinking and carousing. When their liquor ran out they went back to sea in search of more. They plundered a number of ships over the next few months, but procured little more than provisions. Rackham did take one ship, which turned out to be full of plantation-bound thieves from Newgate Prison, but even this bounty was retaken within a few days by an English man-of-war.

Rackham's luck did not thereafter greatly improve. He sailed to Bermuda where he took two ships. However, the governor of Providence heard Rackham had docked in Bermuda and sent an armed sloop, which recaptured Rackham's prizes. Rackham escaped only to be caught by a Spanish guard ship, while at anchor off the coast of Cuba. Rackham and his men cleverly left their ship at night and boarded an English sloop commandeered earlier by the Spanish. Though forced to abandon the *Vane,* which the Spanish raked with gun and cannon fire in the morning, the pirates escaped with a ship that continued to serve their purposes.

In August 1720, Rackham attempted to replenish his crew by taking prisoners from plundered ships off the coast of Jamaica. The Jamaican governor heard of his presence there and sent out a force headed by Captain Barnet. Barnet located Rackham near Point Negril and gave chase. He had the advantage of a brisk wind and soon captured Rackham and his ship and crew, who were brought ashore on November 16, 1720, and tried before an admiralty court at Saint Jago de la Vega. Rackham, George Fetherston, Richard Corner, John Davis, John Howell, Patrick Carty, Thomas Earl, James Dobbin, and Noah Harwood were convicted and sentenced to death by Sir Nicholas Laws. Five of them were hanged the next day at Gallows Point in Point Royal.

The other four were hanged the following day at Kingston. The bodies of Rackham, Fetherston, and Corner were later taken down and hanged in chains on public display in three different sites. Nine men who had joined Rackham the same day he was captured were also tried. Though it was shown that these men had not committed any acts of piracy, they also were condemned to death and hanged on February 7, 1721. Only two pirates escaped execution, both females. Anne Bonny and Mary Read were granted stays of execution because they were pregnant.

PHILLIP ROCHE, THE IMPETUOUS PIRATE/ 1720s

Born in Ireland, Phillip Roche (d. 1723) was an accomplished sailor, who eventually advanced to the position of first mate. When acquiring that position, Roche suddenly decided to turn pirate, a decision that led him to the gallows within two years. Peter Tartoue, a Frenchman sailing to Cape Breton, hired Roche as first mate. Roche brought with him as part of the crew five Irish seamen. On the night of November 15, 1721, soon after the ship set sail, Roche ordered two seamen to furl the sails. As soon as they descended to the deck, Roche and his piratical followers stabbed them and threw them overboard.

A boy and a sailor witnessed these slayings, and the pirates threw the boy into the sea and murdered the sailor. Their cries woke the rest of the crew and, as they hurried on deck, Roche and his men murdered them all, including the captain. Roche later confessed that he and his men were "all over as wet with the blood that had been spilt, as if they had been dipped in water, or stood in a shower of rain, nor did they regard it any more."

The killers then drank up much of the former captain's rum and named Roche their new leader. They intended to sail for the Gulf of St. Lawrence but, finding themselves short of provisions, stopped at Portsmouth, where they disguised the ship by renaming it the *Mary Snow* and repainting it.

Roche and his crew then sailed for Rotterdam to dispose of their cargo and pick up a new one. An Englishman named Annesley, joined them there, brought a large quantity of goods aboard and sailed with them for London. After one day at sea, the pirates threw him overboard. Annesley swam beside the ship for a long time, begging to be rescued and promising the crew all his property. He finally drowned. When the ship arrived in the Thames, Annesley's friends sent inquiries about him. Roche denied knowing anyone by that name. But Roche's real identity was suspected, and he was arrested and detained for questioning before the secretary of state.

The pirate continued to insist that he was not Phillip Roche. But when an intercepted letter that he had written to his wife was shown to him, he confessed his crimes and was taken to Newgate Prison. Officials hinted to Roche that he might be pardoned if he could provide the names of three persons who were equally guilty of his crimes. But, as the pirate could not do so, he was tried, convicted, and sentenced to die. Roche was hanged at Execution Dock on August 5, 1723.

Mutinous Phillip Roche, holding spike, and his henchmen, are shown shoving the bodies of Captain Tartoue and a crew member into the sea.

IRELAND'S EDWARD ENGLAND/1720s

The Irish buccaneer Edward England was once described by the author Daniel Defoe as "having a great deal of good nature ... courageous, not over-avaricious, humane, but too often overruled." England's unfortunate victims probably regarded him

Pirate Edward England rampaged in the Caribbean and along the African coast, but he showed kindness toward his captives, which led to his undoing.

somewhat differently. In one instance, England lashed an enemy captain to a pole and ordered his crew members to throw broken glass at the man. Finally, England ordered that he be shot through the head.

The pirate captain began his career at sea, sailing from Jamaica as first mate on a sloop, but was pressed into pirate duty when his ship was seized by Captain Winter and taken toward New Providence. There, England voluntarily became a pirate captain. With a crew, the captain sailed from New Providence to plunder the shipping lanes off the coast of Africa. In the spring of 1719, England and his men seized ten vessels belonging to the British government. On the way to the West Indies, England continued to wreak havoc on British and Portuguese shipping. At various native settlements along the way, the pirate crew dropped anchor and engaged in debauchery before setting the towns on fire and slaughtering whole tribes.

In August 1720, the pirate captain sailed his vessel, the *Fancy,* to Johanna Island near Madagascar. There, England and a fellow pirate captain, John Taylor, encountered the *Cassandra* and the *Greenwich,* commanded by James Macrae and Richard Kirby. When Macrae spied the two pirate ships approaching, he implored Captain Kirby of the *Greenwich* to come to his aid. Instead, Kirby withdrew from the bay to observe the ensuing battle from a safe distance. Macrae and his crew withstood a merciless bombardment from the pirate ships, but at night, the crew of the *Cassandra* sailed away from their ship in a long boat. Captain England's men stormed the ship and took £75,000 from the cargo hold.

After ten days, Captain Macrae returned to the harbor to bargain for the return of his ship and its cargo. England and Taylor argued bitterly over what they should do with Macrae. Taylor, and many of the men believed he should put him to death, but England was inclined to show mercy. Macrae was soon freed. The pirates exchanged the badly crippled *Fancy* for the *Cassandra.* With the remaining crew, Macrae managed to reach India and was promoted by the East India Company for heroism. England, for showing weakness, was deposed by Captain Taylor and forced to sail in a long boat to Madagascar, where he died in poverty. Edward England lost his command for displaying mercy, a failing that brought many a pirate to ruination.

THE AMBITIONS OF GEORGE LOWTHER/ 1721-1723

In 1721 the British vessel *Gambia Castle,* owned and operated by the Royal African Company, sailed toward the African coast with a garrison of soldiers assigned to fortify the settlement at St. James Island against pirates. George Lowther (d. 1723) was the second mate and John Massey was the captain in charge of the garrison. Lowther had long nurtured the ambition of commanding a ship, but his method in taking such a command was not through promotion but through piracy.

When the *Gambia Castle* arrived in the port of St. James Island in May 1721, the crewmen discovered that the outpost had been taken over by the merchants employed by the company. They refused to supply the ship with adequate food and provisions. Massey, torn between loyalty to his country and self-preservation, was easily influenced by second mate George Lowther to refuse the direct orders of the ship's captain, Charles Russell.

Lowther and Massey decided to seize control of the ship and sail it back to England. They looted a storeroom and took the governor's son prisoner while the ship was outfitted and provisioned for sea duty. Captain Russell offered the mutineers favorable terms if they would surrender the ship. Lowther, who had emerged as the spokesman and leader of the mutiny, flatly refused the offer, but freed the governor's son.

While the *Gambia Castle* was at sea, Lowther presented the crew with the facts. A return trip to England would carry with it certain death, for mutiny was a capital offense. It was better to take their chances on the sea as pirates. The *Gambia Castle* was renamed *Delivery* because it was going to deliver the crew to freedom on the high seas. The black colors were run up the mast, and "Captain" Lowther set course for the Spanish Caribbean and the rich prizes awaiting there.

The *Delivery* plundered a French sloop of its cargo of wine and brandy, and also attacked a brigantine from Boston called the *Charles.* Captain Massey, who wanted only to return to England, quarreled with Lowther. Massey wrote a long letter explaining that his original intention was to save the

George Lowther stands guard, while some of his crew members eat a meal; on the beach, other pirates scrape the barnacles off their careened ship.

lives of his men, who faced certain starvation because of the uncompromising posture of the governor. He explained that he had never intended to plunder His Majesty's fleet.

Massey returned to England via Jamaica, and delivered the letter to the African Company. On July 5, 1723, he was brought before the Court of Admiralty at the Old Bailey on two counts of piracy. Captain Russell and the governor's son appeared as witnesses for the prosecution, refuting Massey's story. Massey was convicted, and hanged at Execution Dock three weeks later.

Meanwhile, Lowther sailed to Honduras and joined forces with Edward Low, whom he appointed his lieutenant. Natives attacked the pirate fleet anchored at Port Mayo in the Gulf of Matique. Lowther was forced to set fire to the *Delivery.* He outfitted a new ship, the *Ranger,* and parted company with Captain Low.

In the spring of 1723, Lowther and his buccaneers approached a string of Spanish islands near Tortuga. Captain Walter Moore, commander of the sloop *Eagle* spotted the pirate ship and asked it to show colors. The ship hoisted St. George's flag. Trapped in the inlet waters, Lowther and his men attempted to escape toward shore. Moore pursued them, with the full cooperation of the Spanish. Sixteen pirates were captured on the island of Blanco, but Lowther was not one of them. The pirate shot himself in the head, finding death preferable to a Spanish jail.

THE SAVAGE EDWARD LOW/1720s

Edward "Ned" Low worked in a rigging-house in Boston for several years, then signed on as a crewman on a sloop bound for Honduras. When the ship arrived in the Gulf of Honduras, the captain ordered Low to go ashore to chop wood for the return trip. It was a dangerous mission, because the Spanish army ashore shot British trespassers. When Low and his twelve mates returned, the Captain immediately ordered them back to shore for another load of wood.

This so angered Low that he grabbed a musket and fired on the captain. He missed his mark, shooting another crewman by mistake, but by then there was no turning back. Ned Low was guilty of mutiny, and would be hanged if he didn't escape. Low put the captain and most of his crew off the sloop and prepared to leave the harbor.

The next day, Low raised the black flag and set sail for the Grand Caymans as commander of a pirate ship. At the island, Low met Captain George Lowther, another rebellious sailor turned pirate, who pledged his assistance. With Lowther as chief commander, the pirate crew headed for New England, taking several ships along the way. After Edward Low and Captain Lowther captured a fast brigantine on May 28, 1722, the two men decided to divide the loot and go their separate ways.

Low and his forty-four man crew sailed the brigantine near the Rhode Island coast, where they captured the sloop *James Calquhoon* on June 3, 1722. In August, Low and his band sailed for the Cape Verde Islands, where they seized two Portuguese ships and three English sloops bound for Curacao. The pirates were lucky until they went ashore at St. Michaels for provisions. A visiting Portuguese merchant ship arrived at the same time and identified Low to the royal governor, who had Low and his crew thrown into irons.

Edward "Ned" Low turned to piracy after rebelling against the cruelty of a merchant ship's captain; he is shown escaping from one of his vessels that sank in a hurricane.

Low managed to escape, but he was deprived of his brigantine. He outfitted his old schooner, which he renamed the *Fancy,* and set sail with a new crew. They had not been at sea long when Captain Low decided to attack a Portuguese vessel called the *Nostre Signiora de Victoria.* The pirates took the ship and tortured the crewmen into revealing the location of a sack of money supposedly hidden in the bow.

The captain of the Portuguese ship had lowered the cloth sack by a rope from the window of his quarters. Just before he surrendered his crew, he cut the rope and the 11,000 gold coins fell into the sea. When Low heard of this, he ordered the captain's lips cut off and burned them in his presence. The pirates then murdered the entire crew.

Edward Low and his buccaneers watch indifferently as one of their captives is made to "walk the plank," the typical fate of those who fell into the hands of pirates.

For the next two years Ned Low plundered the coastal waters from the British colonies in North America to the Caribbean islands. In January 1724, he captured a vessel called the *Squirrel,* near the West Indies. That was the last anyone heard of him. Captain Low was rumored to have made his way to Brazil, but more probably he died when his ship was sent to the bottom of the Caribbean after a sea battle with a British frigate.

TWO FEARSOME FEMALE PIRATES/ 1710s-1720s

Anne Bonny was the illegitimate daughter of an Irish lawyer named William Cormac. The attending scandal drove Cormac to the New World, where he began a new life with his mistress and infant daughter. Cormac flourished in Charleston, South Carolina, and bought a large plantation. While in her teens, Anne disappointed her father by running off with an itinerant sailor named James Bonny.

Bonny heard of handsome subsidies paid to fortune hunters in the Bahamas by Governor Woodes Rogers, who was looking for men to track down and capture pirates that infested the area. With his wife Anne, he traveled to the island in 1716 and worked as a paid informant, picking up scraps of information on the waterfront. Anne was disgusted with her husband's seamy line of work and when the opportunity presented itself, she fled New Providence to become a pirate herself. While Bonny investigated the pirates, Anne openly consorted with them.

When Governor Rogers offered an amnesty, pirates by the dozen converged on the island, including John "Calico Jack"

Female pirates Anne Bonny and Mary Read sought their fortunes on the high seas, and were as bold and fierce as any of their male counterparts. Read was exceptionally accomplished with the sword.

Mary Read, right, is shown running a sword through a pirate, who had dared to challenge her lover to a duel.

Rackham, known for his gaudy striped pants. Rackham noticed Anne and tried to "buy" her divorce from Bonny. The husband refused and reported Rackham's intentions to the governor, who ordered Anne flogged unless she returned to her husband. Instead, Anne went to sea with Rackham. Together they outfitted a pirate ship and went in search of prey.

They soon captured a Dutch ship laden with rich cargo and a crew of healthy sailors ready to be impressed into pirate duty. Anne Bonny selected a fair youth she deemed worthy of seduction. The boy turned out to be a girl, Mary Read. Read and Bonny became fast friends. They also acquired an unsavory reputation as two of the most fearsome pirates of the Caribbean until one day in October 1720 when Captain Burnet of the Royal Navy captured their vessel, the *Queen Royal,* as it lay anchored off Jamaica.

Rackham was taken along with the rest of the crew to St. Jago de la Vega, where they were tried as pirates. Anne Bonny and Mary Read pleaded pregnancy (or in the argot of the day "pleaded their bellies") and escaped the death sentence. Mary Read died in her prison on December 4, 1720, from a fever before her child was born. Anne Bonny escaped, and was said to have lived to old age on a South Carolina plantation.

AMERICA'S PIRATE HUNTER/1810s

The pirates of North Africa, mostly Turks and Moslems who controlled Algiers, Morocco, Tripoli, and Tunis, declared open war on U.S. shipping in 1801. The Pasha of Tripoli, to extort more cash from the U.S., chopped down the flagstaff of the U. S. consulate, drawing an immediate response from President Thomas Jefferson. No longer would the U. S. continue a policy of appeasement and bribes to the North African pirates, said Jefferson, and he ordered the tiny U.S. fleet into the Mediterranean to bombard Tripoli.

On Oct. 31, 1803, the USS *Philadelphia,* a 36-gun American frigate commanded by Captain William Bainbridge, ran aground in Tripoli's harbor and was captured. The pirates turned

The heroic Stephen Decatur, who told Algerian pirates that they could have American tribute from the mouth of his cannon.

the guns of the ship against the U. S. blockading fleet commanded by Captain Edward Preble. To eliminate this threat, Lieutenant Stephen Decatur (1779-1820), a firebrand officer possessed of incredible courage, led seventy-four men into the harbor in small boats on the night of February 16, 1804.

Decatur and his men slipped aboard the *Philadelphia,* and after a wild fight with the Turkish pirates, killed all the guards on board. They then set fire to the *Philadelphia,* rendering it useless to the pirates, and escaped with only one fatality. Decatur, a fiery patriot, repeatedly proved his bravery during the Tripolitan pirate war. On another occasion, he and his men boarded a pirate ship. Decatur, wielding a cutlass and a pistol, was knocked to the deck of the enemy gunship, but before the pirate captain could cut his throat, Decatur fired a fatal shot into the pirate's throat.

At that moment, with Decatur prone on the deck, another pirate ran forward and was about to decapitate Decatur with a swing of his scimitar, but a wounded American sailor jumped forward and placed his head in the way, receiving the blow and dying in place of Decatur. The American sailor, who was

The burning of the American frigate *Philadelphia*, which was captured by Tripoli pirates; Stephen Decatur slipped a small band of U. S. sailors on board this ship and set it afire, then rowed away to safety.

almost helpless from a wound at that moment, was said to be either Daniel Frazier or, more likely, Reuben James, after whom several U. S. warships were later named. The Turkish pirates in Tripoli, due to the continuing U.S. blockade, sued for peace in 1805.

Decatur, in 1815, again led a punitive squadron to the Mediterranean Sea to prevent Algerian pirates raiding U. S. ships. The brilliant Decatur once again quelled the main Algerian pirate fleet off the coast of Spain and then forced Algiers, Tripoli, and Tunis to pay $81,000 for the American ships captured or destroyed by the pirate captains. He forced the North African potentates to sign treaties forbidding them to collect "tribute" or bribes from the U. S. When the Dey of Tripoli pleaded with Decatur for a small token of tribute in the form of gunpowder to save face, Decatur retorted: "If you insist upon receiving powder as tribute, you must expect to receive [cannon] balls with it!"

Following Decatur's expedition against the North African Turks and Moslems in 1815, U. S. ships went unmolested by pirates. Decatur, the hero of the hour, returned in triumph to the U. S. At a banquet in his honor at Norfolk, Virginia, Decatur uttered his famous toast: "Our country! In her intercourse with foreign nations may she always be in the *right,* and always successful, *right or wrong!*" The life of the brilliant Decatur came to a premature end when he was killed in a duel with naval officer James Barron on March 22, 1820.

Stephen Decatur, after boarding a Tripolitan pirate ship, was knocked to the deck by its captain; Decatur shot him dead, his life saved by wounded American sailor Reuben James (some said Daniel Frazier), who placed his head in the path of a sword being wielded by another pirate.

Decatur's squadron returns in triumph from victories over Tripoli, Tunis and Algiers in 1815; his successful campaign against the pirates established the U. S. Navy as a formidable foe feared by foreign buccaneers.

THE LAST OF THE BUCCANEERS/1810s-1820S

No power in New Orleans could control the pirates who operated freely throughout the Gulf of Mexico and made New Orleans and points south their home. In the eighteenth century, Blackbeard, Henry Morgan, and others attacked, looted, and sank hundreds of ships at will, protected by the many nations then at war. These pirates all carried letters of marque (commissions), ostensibly issued to them by small, new, independent countries that labeled them privateers. These pirates were authorized to attack vessels of any warring country and return the prize ships to home port, selling off the cargo to merchants and the crew and passengers to slave dealers.

The most notorious of these tiny countries issuing such *carte blanche* powers to sea wolves was Cartagena on the Colombian coast. The long trip to Colombia soon discouraged the pirates of the coast; they thought it more convenient to use the Bay of Barataria, between Grand Isle and Grande-Terre Island, as their base of operations. Prize ships and cargoes were brought to this natural port sixty miles south of New Orleans and the loot smuggled into the U. S. via New Orleans.

The unpredictable, sometimes chivalrous pirate, Jean Lafitte, at the time he raided throughout the Caribbean.

Lafitte, on deck, holding sword aloft, boards a merchant vessel with his pirate crew; he was a fearless leader with a subtle loyalty to the U. S.

General Andrew Jackson, who asked Lafitte and his pirates to fight with his troops against British forces in 1815.

Of all the freebooters operating from Barataria, the most infamous and legendary was Jean Lafitte (1780-1826), who, with his brother Pierre, looted and sacked his way across the Gulf and throughout the Caribbean for two decades. Little fact, however, attends his vaunted exploits. Lafitte was born in Bordeaux in 1780 and died at the early age of forty-six in 1826, broke and enraged at his obscurity. He was a slim, dark-haired man of average height, who first appeared with his brother, Pierre, in New Orleans in 1806, when he opened a blacksmith shop on St. Philip Street.

Ingratiating himself to the polite society of the city, Lafitte's smithy soon prospered, patronized by the best families. On the side, the Lafitte brothers processed smuggled goods brought up to New Orleans from Barataria by the pirates. When the news arrived in 1808 that the pirates were raiding one another's strongholds for goods and slaves, Lafitte decided to take control of the anarchists and return order to this profitable, albeit illegal, enterprise.

Lafitte journeyed to Barataria by piragua and boldly marched into the camp of pirates on Grande-Terre Island, a teeming fortress with 500 of the most vicious sea renegades ever assembled in one spot. Through his considerable charm, wit, and ability to speak several languages faultlessly—Spanish, Italian, French, and English—Lafitte soon convinced the most rowdy of the piratical band that their best interests lay in following his dictates. It was simply a matter of money, he explained; Lafitte knew best how to invest the profits of the

Lafitte's pirates joined other Americans on the ramparts at Chalmette, outside New Orleans, on January 8, 1815, to mow down with musket and cannon fire more than 2,000 attacking British soldiers in the final battle of the War of 1812 (which, unknown to both sides in this battle, had ended two weeks earlier with the signing of the Treaty of Ghent).

privateers and quickly displayed his financial ability to further enrich them.

Lafitte dealt with a rough bunch, including Ren Bluche, Cadet Bouteille, Chighizola, better known as Nez Coup ("Cut Nose") because of the horrible scar he wore across his nose as a result of a sword slash, Vincent Gambie, and the redoubtable Captain Dominique You, who had fought with the legions of Napoleon I as an artilleryman and who later distinguished himself in the battle of New Orleans. (Captain You commanded five pieces of artillery so expertly against the British, using Lafitte's pirates as gun crews, that Andrew Jackson raised him to the rank of captain in the U. S. Army and, during the historic battle, told You: "I wish I had fifty such guns on this line, with five hundred more such devils serving them." Captain You later turned his back on freebooting and became one of New Orleans' most revered citizens, dying as a patriot instead of a pirate and being buried in St. Louis Cemetery next to the finest citizens in the city.)

Lafitte did not take over the pirate community at Barataria without force. One of his reluctant lieutenants, Captain Vincent Gambie, smirked at Lafitte's authority. "I am no privateer, such as Jean Lafitte wishes to call us," Gambie shouted to his men one rum-struck night. "I am a bloody pirate!" He waved a broad ax about his head. "With this weapon I have opened the heads of more than twenty men. I have split wide women and children!" He grinned, showing a set of broken teeth. "I liked it! To hell with Jean Lafitte!" Gambie then staggered to his shack and fell into a drunken torpor.

Gambie's men thought to duplicate their captain's insubordination and shouted curses at Lafitte, who walked calmly into the glare of their campfire. Lafitte, who was by then called the Boss, stared silently at the upstarts. One of Gambie's officers jumped up, shouting: "The men of Gambie take orders only from Gambie!" He half yanked his sword from its scabbard in a menacing movement.

Lafitte casually drew a pistol and, from a distance of fifteen feet, fired its single ball. The shot killed the pirate instantly as he was struck between the eyes. The slaying served to bring Gambie and his men quickly into line and no more criticism of Lafitte was spoken. (Gambie's skull was later split open by his own men and with his own ax.)

Lafitte organized all the raids on the sea and disposed of all the stolen goods, his fifty ships flying the flag of Cartagena. As his success became known, more pirates flocked to Lafitte's banners, a thousand of the worst brigands of the seas. He improved living conditions at Barataria by having comfortable

Jean Lafitte when he fought with Jackson at New Orleans in 1815.

huts built and importing hundreds of women to the settlement to keep his men company. Brothels, gambling dives, and saloons soon dotted the area. Lafitte built an elegant mansion for himself and furnished it with the luxurious loot his privateers took from hundreds of captured ships.

Some of the most respected leaders of New Orleans, men who headed the government, cultural and civic leaders of the city, were Lafitte's willing guests at Barataria. Of course, all of these pleasantries were designed to further cement strong relationships with certain businessmen of New Orleans, those who took Lafitte's illegal goods as well as his slaves and sold them to the public at large, acting as fences.

By 1813, Lafitte had a commercial strangle-hold on the city and threatened to monopolize the entire Mississippi valley. In desperation, Governor W. C. Claiborne proclaimed all inhabitants of Barataria out-and-out pirates, not privateers, and urged all citizens to shun them and their goods. When the Lafitte brothers attempted to woo the upper crust families of New Orleans to their side of the commercial war, Claiborne proclaimed Jean Lafitte an outlaw and set a price of $500 for his arrest. Lafitte, in his typical grand manner, sent out a proclamation which appeared on almost every wall of the city, and in which he offered $1,500 for the arrest of Governor Claiborne and his delivery to the pirate's nest of Barataria.

Incensed, Claiborne also ordered Pierre Lafitte's arrest, and Jean's brother was quickly clapped in jail. Pierre Lafitte then disappeared, mysteriously breaking out of prison. The offenses of the pirates were quickly forgotten with the War of 1812 and the battle of New Orleans in 1815, a battle the pirates helped mightily to win. Following Jackson's victory, all the pirates, the Lafitte brothers included, who had fought against the British, were pardoned. Jean and Pierre Lafitte and a hundred others abandoned their fortresses at Barataria and roamed the Gulf of Mexico, finally settling at Galveston, Texas, where, it seemed, almost every wanted felon and cutthroat had gathered.

From this port, the Lafittes again began preying upon merchant ships until one of their crews was captured while looting a Spanish vessel and taken to New Orleans for trial. Seventeen of Lafitte's best men, including Robert Johnson and Jean Desfargues, were summarily hanged for piracy. It was the end of Lafitte's love affair with New Orleans. The corsair moved deeper into the hostile waters of the Caribbean and though he vanished from the public eye, he is most remembered as the mysterious pirate, who saved New Orleans from the British invaders.

Fredric March as Lafitte in the 1938 film, *The Buccaneer*.

Yul Brynner as Jean Lafitte in the 1958 film, *The Buccaneer*.

CHAPTER FOURTEEN:

ROBBERY

The criminal act of robbery dates back to the earliest periods of recorded time, with myriad biblical references citing such brigands, not the least of whom was Barabbas, the bandit who was set free in lieu of the crucified Jesus. Robbery was a way of life for scores of nomadic tribes in Asia that finally banded together under the banner of Genghis Khan, who began as a bandit until becoming leader of the so-called Golden Horde that conquered most of the then known world. In Europe, the Vikings, Goths, Huns and other invaders from Central Europe were nothing more than marauding robbers, pillaging the Roman Empire for spoils and with no thought of appropriating and governing the lands they looted. With the opening of the New World by Columbus, the most notorious bandits, beginning in the 16th Century, operated along the sea lanes of the world's great oceans as dreaded pirates (see Chapter Thirteen, Piracy).

Highwayman Claude Duval, left, is shown robbing the Master of Buck Hounds to Charles II in Windsor Forest; Duval became the most notorious highwayman of 17th Century England.

By the 17th Century, the great cities of Europe were awash with thieves, who subtly robbed their victims by picking their pockets, such as the notorious Moll Cutpurse of London. England, at this time, was plagued by a new type of robber, the highwayman, daring thieves who waylaid coaches and lone travelers on horseback and at gunpoint. One of the earliest of these brigands was Phillip Stafford, a former captain in the British army, who became a successful highwayman in the 1640s, especially preying upon wealthy clergymen for whom he held intense hatred. Stafford, ironically, gave up robbery to become a pastor, absolving himself publicly before his parishioners, until falling back on his old ways, stealing the church's gold, linen and sacramental plate. He again took to the road, but was apprehended, tried and hanged at Reading.

Another such rogue was Claude Duval, a youthful highwayman, who robbed the coaches of British aristocrats. He displayed elegant manners and danced by moonlight with his charmed female victims before taking their jewels and money. Duval was hanged at Tyburn in 1671. William Johnson, another notorious highwayman of that era, was not so polite. A failed businessman turned robber, Johnson committed robberies with the help of forger Jane Housden, his mistress, who provided him with information on travelers carrying gold and jewels. Johnson had a short temper and manhandled any victim reluctant to turn over his purse. That temperament brought about his demise when, being tried at the Old Bailey, he shot and killed a jailer in open court when he refused to allow him to speak to Housden, then on trial for coining (counterfeiting coins). Johnson and Housden were then promptly tried and convicted of murder and both were hanged in 1712.

Thomas Lympus is shown robbing a postal messenger on February 21, 1738 and getting away with a fortune.

The most legendary English highwaymen—Dick Turpin, James Maclaine and John Rann—overshadowed in the chronicles of crime the exploits of dozens of their ilk, but many of these lesser-known meandering miscreants made their memorable marks along the dark highways they haunted. Often as not, these wayward creatures became highwaymen after their own honest labors and professions failed them, such as John Everett, a salesman turned highwayman, who was hanged in 1729, or Thomas Lympus, who abandoned his position as a postal clerk to rob the very system that employed him, absconding in 1738 with a fortune after holding up a postal messenger. Lympus fled to France and lived high, until his money ran out and he made the mistake of returning to England, where he was caught following another robbery and promptly hanged.

Henry "Gentleman Harry" Simms, who robbed coaches in England and Ireland, with such alacrity that officials thought he commanded a band of hundreds. Simms, who was hanged in 1746, had been a friend of Jenny Diver (Mary Jones), London's most celebrated pickpocket, and who was immortalized in "The Beggar's Opera" (she was hanged in 1740). William Page, on the other hand, was a gentleman's gentleman, a part-time actor, livery servant and occasional body

Actor-turned highwayman, William Page committed more than 300 robberies in the 1750s.

California bandit Joachim Murieta (or Murrieta) attacks a defenseless woman in this lurid dime novel portrait; he was reportedly killed and decapitated by a bounty hunter in 1853.

servant to a wealthy aristocrat. Page witnessed his employer being robbed by a highwayman one night and thought the robbery so easy to perform that he immediately adopted that criminal pursuit. Page committed more than three hundred robberies in the late 1750s and lived like a gentleman in London, until he was caught and hanged in 1758.

Franz Muller committed the first known railway robbery on July 9, 1864.

Like Page, William Field had worked for an aristocrat, serving as a footman. He had been sold into slavery, but escaped a penal colony and returned to England to mete out his vengeance through highway robbery. Field committed as many as four to five robberies of coaches a night, until he was captured and hanged in 1773. The brothers George and Joseph Weston shared a similar background, and became highwaymen. They were hanged together in 1782.

Percy Lefoy robbed and killed a coin dealer on a London train while it steamed through Merstham Tunnel in 1881.

Bob Dalton is shown with his sweetheart, Eugenia Moore, on May 9, 1889; Moore often scouted banks and train schedules for robberies the Daltons planned. Bob Dalton led his band on an abortive raid to rob two banks in 1892 and met with disaster.

Two decades later in America, Michael Martin ("Captain Lightfoot") an Irish youth, who had learned his trade as a robber in England, migrated to the U.S., where he became the first highwaymen in Massachusetts. Far to the west, a bevy of brigands rose from the murky swamps and dense forests along the Natchez Trace, robbing and murdering travelers with such frequency that small armies tracked them to their lairs. Among these robbers were the brothers Wiley and Micajah Harpe, known as Little Harpe and Big Harpe. They were brutal men, who not only took all the valuables from their victims, but stripped them of their clothes and shoes, then, if the whim urged, murdered them out of hand. Sam Mason was another of these fierce American highwaymen, who routinely killed his victims in robberies, so that "none would look upon my face again."

The most memorable of these Natchez Trace robbers was John A. Murrel, known as "The Great Western Land Pirate," and about whom countless legends were later spun. To the south, Bras Coupé, a runaway slave, organized a band of robbers, who terrorized the Louisiana bayou country for a decade. Twenty years later, Joachim Murieta (or Murrieta), the daring Mexican bandit, robbed stagecoaches and travelers in California. His fierce exploits made him a living legend long before his reported death in 1853. While these brigands operated on the frontiers of America, the frontiers of Australia were menaced by the likes of Frank Gardiner, who robbed stagecoaches in the 1850s and 1860s, succeeded in infamy by that country's most celebrated highwayman, Edward "Ned" Kelly, who wore iron-plated armor in pitched gun battles with police.

Train robbery began not in America or Australia, but in England, the first such criminal act being conducted by Franz Muller, who, in 1864, robbed and murdered Thomas Briggs, a 70-year-old bank clerk on the North London Railway train, throwing his victim from the moving train and establishing

The end of the Dalton Gang: Brothers Bob and Grat Dalton are shown hands tied and propped up dead between peace officers after they and two others had been shot to death on October 5, 1892; a third brother, Emmett Dalton, was the only survivor of the fusillade from the citizens of Coffeyville, Kansas, who stopped the outlaw brothers from robbing two banks at the same time.

Sam Bass, shown at age sixteen in Indiana, became one of the most notorious bank and train robbers in Texas, killed by lawmen in 1878.

another "first," in that this was also the first homicide committed on a moving train in England. Muller fled to America, but a dogged Scotland Yard detective, Chief Inspector William Tanner learned that Muller had booked passage and went aboard a faster ship that arrived ahead of Muller's vessel, arresting the robber when he walked down the gangplank. (Muller was returned to England, where he was tried, convicted and condemned, hanged on November 14, 1864.) The very same technique in apprehending a fugitive was employed by Inspector Walter Dew of Scotland Yard, when he took a fast ship to the U. S., which arrived before another vessel docked, one which carried Dr. Hawley Harvey Crippen and his mistress, Ethel LeNeve. Crippin had chopped up his wife, Belle Elmore Crippen, and buried her body in the basement of his London home and then run off with his mistress (who was dressed as a boy during the voyage). Crippen was hanged on November 23, 1910.

England saw another terrible train robbery on June 27, 1881, when Percy Lefoy, a journalist and short story writer, robbed and killed 64-year-old Frederick Gold, a coin dealer, on the London to Brighton train as it passed through the Merstham Tunnel, a robbery-murder that sent Lefoy to the gallows. By then, in America, train robbing had almost become routine. As the railways pushed through the western frontiers, bands of hard-riding outlaws—many of these being the remnants of guerrilla forces used in the Civil War—began robbing trains in the Midwest. The Reno Brothers of Indiana, were the first to rob an American train, stopping a passenger train in 1866.

Many of these outlaw bands were headed by brothers who came from the South and Midwest—the Farrington Brothers; Reuben and Jim Burrow; the Younger Brothers, who rode stirrup to stirrup with the James Brothers, and the three Dalton Brothers, Robert, Gratton (Grat) and Emmett, who, in 1892, rode into their home town of Coffeyville, Kansas, and were shot to pieces, with only Emmett surviving to tell their saga. Another brother, William Dalton, who had once been a lawman, turned train robber and rode with the Bill Doolin Gang

Charles E. Boles (or Bolton), known as Black Bart, robbed stagecoaches and left doggerel in empty strong boxes

of Oklahoma. He was shot dead on the front porch of his home by officers in 1893. Brothers George and John Sontag robbed trains in California and met the same fate as that of the Daltons.

Many of the bank, stagecoach and train robbers between 1865 and 1900, this thirty-five-year period being the heyday for such western bandits, followed obediently behind the most audacious in their midst. The boldest of these included Henry Plummer, who committed countless robberies and killings in Nevada, Idaho and Montana, before he was lynched by vigilantes in 1864. Though having no regard for the law, many of these bandits clung to their own strange code of ethics. Sam Bass, the train robber, died in his abortive raid on a bank near Round Rock, Texas in 1878, but with his dying breath refused to "blow [inform] on my pals" when lawmen asked about the identities and whereabouts of his confederates.

The lawman of that day did not spend too much time racing after these bandits, who robbed a bank in one town or a train in one county and then fled on horse-

Bandit Oliver Curtis Perry committed one of the most spectacular train robberies on record.

A contemporary sketch shows how Perry employed his acrobatic technique in robbing the New York Express in 1892.

back to another county or even a state. Peace officers such as James Butler "Wild Bill" Hickok, Wyatt Earp and William Barclay "Bat" Masterson, were too busy rounding up drunks and facing down gunslingers in the wild towns where they wore the badge to lead exhaustive searches for the elusive robbers.

Rustling cattle, if this activity was confined to a local area, was another matter. Earp and his brothers Morgan and Virgil, along with their friend, gambler and gunfighter John H. "Doc" Holliday, confronted the Clanton gang of rustlers in Tombstone, Arizona, where the classic gun battle at the O. K. Corral occurred in 1881. Rustling cattle was almost a routine occurrence in the Old West, this kind of robbery meeting with terrible justice. If a rustler of cattle or a horse-thief was found, he was invariably lynched on the spot. Such was the case of Jim Averill and his sweetheart, Ella "Cattle Kate" Watson, who had rustled large herds of cattle, were caught and lynched in 1889.

Anarchists Bartolomeo Vanzetti and Nicola Sacco, who were convicted of a bloody 1920 Massachusetts robbery and who were executed in 1927 over the protests of millions who believed them innocent.

Stagecoach robberies throughout the West became a pedestrian crime. The most fascinating of these bandits was an elderly gentleman who called himself Black Bart. He was Charles E. Boles (or Bolton), a man of some refinement, who fancied himself a poet, and often left bits of doggerel at the sites of his robberies. One such ditty found in an empty strongbox read:

I've labored long and hard for bread,
For honor and for riches
But on my corns too long you've tred,
You fine-haired sons-of-bitches.

Boles robbed a number of California stagecoaches in the late 1870s before he was tracked down and sent to prison. One of his peers, William "Old Bill" Miner, robbed stagecoaches in California throughout the 1870s, then began robbing trains. In and out of prison, Minor robbed his last train in 1911 and died in a prison cell two years later. He preferred to work usually alone, distrusting associates. "They make mistakes," he complained in old age about his bumbling fellow robbers, "and this gets you caught after they inform on you."

One daring young man, Oliver Curtis Perry, would have nothing to do with other robbers. He worked alone, robbing banks in Wyoming before going East to single-handedly rob the New York Express on September 29, 1892, dropping by rope from the top of the moving train during a blinding hailstorm and crashing feet-first through the window of the express car to over-

Judge Webster B. Thayer presided with blatant prejudice at the Sacco and Vanzetti trial.

whelm a guard and conductor. He then snatched more than $100,000 in gold and jewels and jumped from the moving train. Trapped by lawmen in a railroad yard a short time later, Perry attempted to flee by driving a locomotive with one hand and firing a pistol at a posse pursuing him in another locomotive, but he was captured and sent to prison.

Perry escaped several times, but was always recaptured. He was finally sent to the maximum security prison at Dannemora, where he became despondent. He fashioned a block of wood with two protruding nails, which he used to gouge out his own eyes. He left a note that said: "I was born in the light of day against my will, of course. I now assert my right to shut out the light." Perry never spoke another word, dying silently in his cell in 1930.

Other than Butch Cassidy and members of the Wild Bunch, few bandits on horseback attempted the robbing of trains or banks by 1900. The risks were too high, with each state by then having law enforcement agencies and man power capable of tracking down these outlaws. One who defied the Texas and Arizona rangers, was Henry Starr, alleged nephew of the infamous cattle rustler Belle Starr. He robbed banks throughout the Southwest in the 1910s, and, in 1914, was the first bandit to use an automobile in robbing a bank. Starr was shot and killed in an abortive bank robbery in 1921.

The coming of the auto as a popular, inexpensive vehicle brought with it myriad car bandits, who robbed banks in small towns, for the most part, then departed in a cloud of dust. They invariably fled from one state to another, local police refusing to follow them into states where they had no jurisdiction. At that time, through the 1920s and early 1930s, there existed no federal law enforcement agency that had the authority to pursue these robbers. In the case of the Mobley-Ashley Gang, the robbers preyed upon banks in Florida, but never left the state. They simply drove to their various hideouts in the Everglades, a huge swampy area infested with snakes, alligators and poisonous insects, a state within a state that few lawmen were willing to enter. This gang, headed by John Ashley, robbed banks from 1914 to 1924, and gleaned an estimated $1 million from their heists. Ashley and three of his gunmen were captured in 1924 and all four were killed while "resisting arrest," but evidence indicates that the bandits were murdered while handcuffed.

A similar fate befell (in the nature of a "judicial execution") two other suspected robbers, Nicola Sacco and Bartolomeo Vanzetti, immigrant Italians, who were avowed anarchists in a day when the "Red Menace" was a reality. Sacco and Vanzetti were accused of robbing a shoe company payroll in South Braintree, Massachusetts in 1920, cold-bloodedly killing two guards and taking $16,000 in cash. They were convicted in a controversial trial at which arch-conservative Judge Webster Thayer presided. Thayer reportedly convicted the pair out-of-hand before the trial ever began. He was quoted as saying: "Did you see what I did to those anarchist bastards?" Both were condemned to death and a worldwide campaign ensued to save their lives. Sacco and Vanzetti were nevertheless executed in the electric chair on August 22-23, 1927.

Charles Arthur "Pretty Boy" Floyd, the Oklahoma bank robber known as the "Robin Hood of the Cookson Hills." He was shot to death in 1934 when cornered by FBI agents in Ohio.

During the 1920s, U. S. banks were plagued with scores of "professional" bank robbers, such as Al Spencer (who had been robbing banks and trains in the horseback era), Harvey Bailey, the brothers Matthew and George Kimes, Jake Fleagle,

A composite photo shows the lethal Barker Brothers (left to right), Herman, Arthur ("Dock") and Freddie, notorious bankrobbers and kidnappers of the early 1930s.

Ray Terrill and Wilbur Underhill (the "Tri-State Terror"). When economic chaos gripped the nation in the early 1930s, bank robbery increased at an alarming rate. At the nadir of the Depression, a new breed of bank robbers sprang from the Midwest and Southwest, emulating the western outlaws, but using cars and submachine guns instead of horses and six-guns. Most of these robbers were from rural areas, farm boys, such as Charles Arthur "Pretty Boy" Floyd, from Oklahoma.

Floyd was a romantic figure to the back county people of his native Cookson Hills. He robbed dozens of banks in Oklahoma and elsewhere and was encouraged to do so by his impoverished fellow citizens, who felt that banks and bankers had created their economic woes. Bank foreclosures of farms and small businesses had driven thousands of hard-working families onto the road, and these homeless drifters saw Floyd, whom they called "Chock," as an avenger of their plight. At one point, Floyd walked down the main street of a small Oklahoma town holding several guns. Some friends asked him where he was going. "To rob the bank," Floyd replied. Some of these citizens applauded and one shouted: "Give 'em hell, Chock!" That day, as he had on many another, Floyd not only robbed

Arizona Donnie Clark Barker, called "Ma," at left with her elderly paramour, Arthur Dunlop, who was murdered by Ma's boys. FBI chief Hoover said Ma led the gang, but one gang member said she was merely "an old lady we kept around for laughs."

The bungalow at Lake Weir, Florida, where FBI agents battled with Ma and Freddie Barker for four hours; the Barkers fired submachine guns at the agents, until both were shot to death.

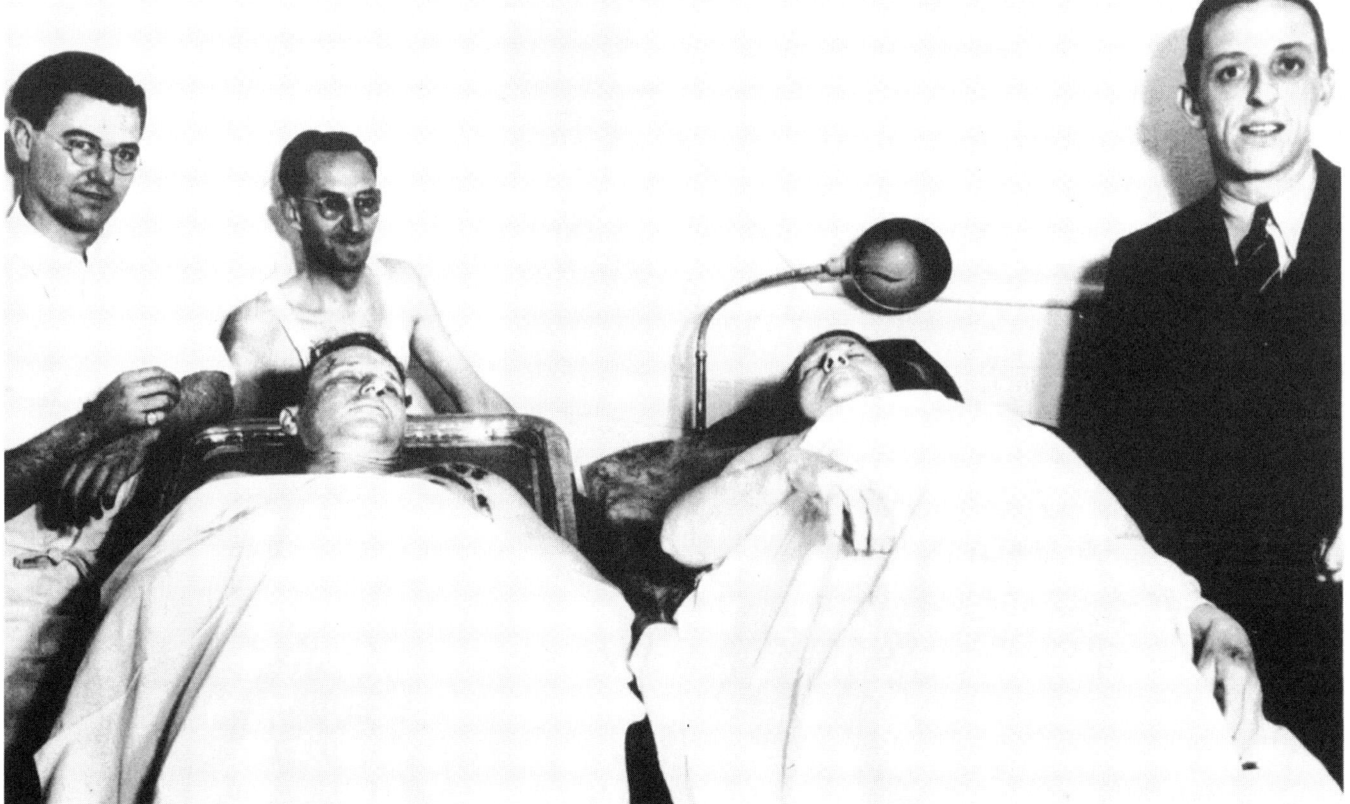

January 17, 1935, Oklawaha, Florida: The bodies of Fred Barker (left) and Ma Barker lie on slabs in the local morgue; both were riddled with bullets, but Freddie may have ended the battle after his mother was shot to death by committing suicide.

the local bank, but took pains to burn all of the unrecorded mortgages the bank held on local stores and farms. Floyd's own family had been dispossessed by a bank that had foreclosed on the Floyd farm.

Often as not, Floyd gave some of the money he took from banks to his neighbors and friends, earning the sobriquet: "The Robin Hood of the Cookson Hills." To FBI agents, however, he was a cold-blooded killer, and was blamed for the 1933 Kansas City Massacre (see Murder/Mass Murder), which took the lives of several lawmen in an abortive attempt to free bank robber Frank Nash. Floyd was shot down by FBI agents under the command of Melvin Purvis, while trying to escape across a field on an Ohio farm, on October 22, 1934. Purvis stood over the fatally shot bank robber and asked him: "Were you at the Kansas City Massacre?" Floyd replied with his dying breath: "I didn't do it. I wasn't in on it." (One report held that Purvis ordered one of his men to execute the bank robber on the spot and a coup de grace bullet was then fired into Floyd's head.)

Other bank robbers of that day were less charismatic than Floyd. The Barker Brothers—Herman, Lloyd, Arthur (known as "Dock") and Fred Barker were the lethal sons of Arizona Donnie Clark Barker, the infamous "Ma" Barker (1872-1935). They robbed scores of banks in the late 1920s and early 1930s, and added many kidnappings to their crimes (see Kidnapping). Encouraged in their criminal pursuits, one Barker after another went behind bars. Herman Barker, after being trapped by a posse in 1927 following a bank robbery outside of Newton, Kansas, committed suicide by firing a bullet into his brain, rather than be captured and go back to prison.

Barker gang member Alvin "Creepy" Karpis, so named because botched plastic surgery drastically altered his facial features, FBI chief Hoover named him "Public Enemy Number One" until his 1936 capture in New Orleans; he was paroled in 1968 and went to Europe, dying ten years later.

As a teenager Clyde Barrow had already committed several thefts and was a habitual criminal.

Bonnie gets the drop on Clyde, a snapshot of the two lethal bandits clowning; this and many other photos were left in an apartment the gang abandoned in Joplin, Missouri, on April 13, 1933, where they killed two officers when escaping police.

Bonnie Parker posing with gun on hip and cigar in mouth, trying to look as tough as she really was, although she did not smoke cigars.

Clyde Barrow holding several rifles; he was fascinated with weapons and kept a large arsenal in the stolen cars he drove.

Bonnie and Clyde are shown at a picnic area outside of Dexter, Iowa on the morning of July 24, 1933 (Barrow is cleaning weapons); only minutes after this photo was taken, a huge posse attacked the gang, wounding both Parker and Barrow, who escaped.

In this startling photo, taken only minutes after a posse attacked the Barrow gang outside Dexter, Iowa, Blanche Barrow (left) is shown screaming for the life of her fatally shot husband while officers hold her; Marvin "Buck" Barrow, is shown kneeling in his underwear at right, dying from several wounds. Bonnie and Clyde had escaped only minutes earlier.

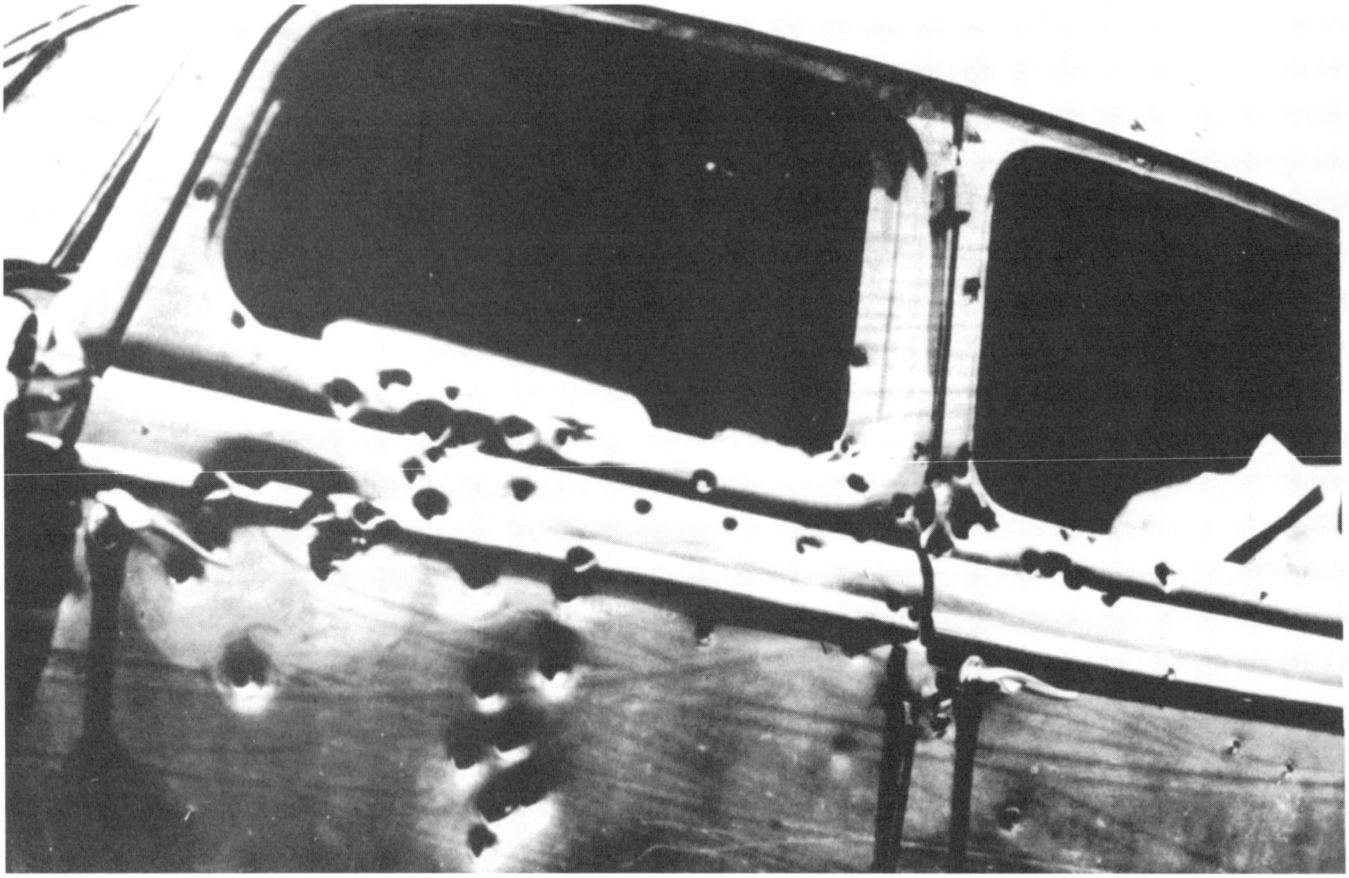

The car in which Bonnie and Clyde were driving when they were ambushed by a posse of Texas rangers, who riddled the auto as it drove down a dirt road outside of Gibsland, Louisiana on May 23, 1934; the murderous bandits were shot to pieces.

The six Texas Rangers who killed Bonnie and Clyde: (top row, left to right) Ted Hurton, P. Moakley, B. M. Gault; (bottom row, left to right), Bob Alcorn, Henderson Jordan and the leader, Frank Hamer. They had no regrets.

Clyde Barrow and Bonnie Parker in the morgue, only an hour after they were slain by a posse of Texas Rangers; their bodies had been pierced by dozens of submachine gun and Browning Automatic Rifle bullets. "They were the worst killers of the Southwest," one of the Rangers said. "We weren't about to take any chances with those two. Others did, and they died. A lot of folks can rest easy now...even Bonnie and Clyde."

A scene from the 1967 film, *Bonnie and Clyde*, showing the gang escaping a police trap; (left to right), Michael J. Pollard (head down), Faye Dunaway (as Bonnie) and Warren Beatty (as Clyde). A fine period production, this film nevertheless misrepresented the true nature of the homicidal bandits.

Ma Barker accused officials of executing her son on the spot. In reviewing the Barkers, FBI Chief J. Edgar Hoover later said that Herman's suicide altered Ma Barker's personality "from an animal mother of the she-wolf type to veritable beast of prey." Hoover credited Ma Barker as the mastermind behind all of the gang's robberies and kidnappings, although this was later discredited by Alvin "Creepy" Karpis (or "Old Creepy," a gangland nickname derived from his having botched plastic surgery that resulted in a grotesque appearance). Karpis (1908-1979), who was Freddie Barker's homosexual lover and later went to Alcatraz, said that Ma Barker was only "an old woman the boys carried around for laughs."

Yet the Barkers, with or without Ma's influence, were well-connected to corrupt politicians in St. Paul, Minnesota and Hot Springs, Arkansas, where they often hid while planning their next bank robberies, shielded by local authorities and paying huge protection money. A small army of experienced gunmen were on call for many of the bank robberies scouted by bank caser Eddie Bentz. These heist experts included Larry Devol, Volney Davis, Earl Christman, Harvey Bailey, Jess Doyle, Phil Courtney.

By early 1935, however, the Barker gang, their whereabouts betrayed by politicians and gang informants, were tracked down and either arrested or killed. Arthur "Dock" Barker was arrested on a Chicago street on January 8, 1935, by FBI Agent Melvin Purvis. He went to Alcatraz for life and was killed while trying to escape "The Rock," in 1939. Ma Barker and her psychopathic son Freddie were trapped by FBI agents at a house outside the resort town of Lake Weir, Florida, and both were killed after a prolonged firefight in which Freddie and Ma Barker, both wielding submachine guns, fought to the death on January 16, 1935.

Less than a year earlier, two other bank robbers, Clyde Barrow and Bonnie Parker, who had become infamous in the Southwest, were shot to death by a posse outside Gibsland, Louisiana on May 23, 1934. Barrow and Parker were Texas misfits from rural towns. Bonnie Parker had been a waitress in a café and Barrow was a petty thief. They joined with Barrow's older brother, Marvin "Buck" Barrow and his wife, Blanche, and a few adolescent thieves to commit several robberies of grocery stores and small banks in the Southwest from 1932 to 1934.

The Barrow Gang was notorious for murdering their robbery victims out-of-hand. Clyde and Bonnie were ruthless killers, who reveled in taking human life. They shot and killed several lawmen while escaping dragnets. Bonnie Parker shot a traffic cop dead in Oklahoma City "just for fun," as she later stated. Unlike the 1967 film, *Bonnie and Clyde*, which glorified Barrow and Parker, these two bank robbers "were psychopaths who would murder you if you looked cross-eyed at them," according to James Henry "Blackie" Audett. While visiting Herb Farmer, who supplied weapons to the independent bank robbing gangs of the era from his Joplin, Missouri, home, Audett encountered Barrow and Parker. "I walked into Herb's house," he told the author in 1978, "and saw these two kids sitting on the sofa. They were fondling a Browning Automatic Rifle and a submachine gun, like they were making love to those guns, cooing and kissing the stocks." Herb took me into the kitchen and I stood there with Farmer, whose knees were knocking. 'That's Bonnie and Clyde in there,' he said. 'Don't say a word to those two—they're crazy. They told me that on the way up here from Oklahoma, they passed a motorcycle cop and shot him. They stopped to dump gas all over him and his cycle and burned him to a crisp and then danced around the burning body.'"

Said Audett to Farmer: "Well, sell them the guns and they'll get out of here."

"*Sell* them!" Farmer replied. "Hell, if I don't just give 'em those guns, they'll kill me and you, too!"

Farmer gave Barrow and Parker the guns "as gifts," and when Barrow complained that his car was low on gas, Farmer and Audett gave Barrow some cash to buy more gas. "I would have given them my shoes, if they wanted them," Audett added. "Clyde was a snake, waiting to bite someone and Bonnie was worse, giggling about blowing the top of someone's head off. They both smelled bad and their clothes were dirty and torn, because they lived in the cars they stole. They shot and robbed from their own people. Nobody wanted to be around these two nuts. Before I left Farmer's place, Herb said to me: 'I swear I'm gettin' out of this business, before those two come back and shoot me for fun!"

After Buck Barrow was killed in a police ambush at a picnic field outside of Dexter, Iowa, on July 24, 1933, and Blanche Barrow was captured, Clyde and Bonnie escaped. They lived like hunted animals on the back roads of the Southwest, stealing cars, holding up small banks and waiting for the "laws" to close in on them. They shared a deathwish, which Bonnie Parker summarized in a lengthy poem that was later widely published and ended with:

Some day they will go down together,
And they will bury them side by side.
To a few it means grief,
To the law it's relief,
But it's death to Bonnie and Clyde.

The posse that ambushed Clyde Barrow and Bonnie Parker took no chances with these killers. They loosed a fusillade of bullets on their passing car and riddled the auto and its two occupants, making sure that these two homicidal bank robbers were, indeed, dead. The killing of Bonnie and Clyde not only gave law enforcement officers the "relief" Bonnie Parker predicted, but edified many another bank robber, who felt that these psychopathic thieves had so focused the nation on bank robbery that state and federal law enforcement considerably increased its efforts to apprehend such criminals. "All they did was to bring more heat down on us," said Charles Arthur Floyd. Another bank robber of that era, the most infamous of them all, John Herbert Dillinger (see entry, this chapter, IN THE DAYS OF DILLINGER), had no respect for Barrow and Parker. When reading about one of their robberies and attendant murders, Dillinger commented: "These two are giving bank robbery a bad name."

With the destruction of the "super gangs" in the 1930s, bank robberies diminished, and with America's eventual economic recovery, fewer desperate bandits took to the roads to rob

French robber and killer Emile Buisson, beheaded at Santé Prison on February 28, 1956.

William Liebscher, Jr., was a used-car salesman who robbed California banks "on the side." When in custody in 1957, he called his wife, telling her: "I won't be home for a long time… I hate to tell you this, but I have been robbing banks for a year and a half."

banks, although bank robbery increased following World War II, and through the turbulent 1960s, when terrorist organizations began robbing banks to fund their operations. In Europe and elsewhere, the number of bank robberies nowhere equaled those in the U. S., although there were periods in which some spectacular bank robbers emerged, such as France's Emile Buisson, who robbed banks from the 1930s to the 1950s, and who committed a number of murders in the process. He was beheaded in 1956.

Bank robbery became, to a great extent, a "lone wolf" operation, where even normally law-abiding citizens embarked on such criminal excursions. Typical was William Liebscher, Jr., a used car salesman in California, who robbed banks "on the side" for eighteen months, until he was captured by FBI agents in 1957. Underpaid blue collar workers, unemployed white collar workers, and others in financial trouble, took to bank robbing. There were few "organized" bank robbing gangs willing to risk their operations with tighter security measures taken by law enforcement. Offbeat robberies, outside of banks, were more conveniently conducted by such gangs. This was the case of the 1978 Lufthansa heist at that airline's cargo terminal in New York, where members of the Gambino crime family stole a reported $6 million and which was profiled in the film *Goodfellas*.

Since that time, bank robberies have actually increased. According to FBI statistics, the year 2000 saw 7546 bank robberies, burglaries and larcenies in the U. S. Banks today, however, are heavily protected by armed guards, and, most importantly, electronic cameras and alarms that will summon police to the site of the robbery within a few minutes, thus dissuading potential bank robbers from foolishly testing those security systems. Such a system, however, was reportedly not in place when, on August 11, 1994, three men armed with submachine guns (as in the days of the Barkers), robbed the Carlton Hotel in Cannes, France, making off with $45 million worth of gems from the hotel's jewelry shop, the largest jewelry heist on record to date. This well-organized robbery was far from the conniving efforts of England's most celebrated pickpocket, Moll Cutpurse, who was satisfied with stealing a few coins from wealthy passersby in the streets of London almost four hundred years earlier.

MOLL CUTPURSE OF ENGLAND/1600s

The most notorious female criminal in early British history was Moll Cutpurse (AKA: Mary Markham, c.1589-1662), born Mary Frith on London's Aldersgate Street around 1589. Her parents were hard-working, law-abiding middle-class citizens and there is little or nothing to suggest a criminal influence in Moll's background. The little girl was, however, extremely homely and, as she aged, Cutpurse would develop a decidedly masculine-looking face. Moll's parents denied her nothing, even providing tutors for her, but from an early age she rebelled against them. One historian described her as "above breeding and instruction. She was a very tomrig, rumpscuttle, or hoyden."

Despairing of ever having a man find interest in her, Moll, by her early teens, took to playing with the roughest boys in her neighborhood, and standing outside of pubs and contorting her already repulsive features into hideous faces at the men entering and leaving. Physically powerful, Moll could best any boy in acrobatic feats and could run and jump faster and higher than any of her male peers. She was also feared for her ability to use her large fists and had the reputation of beating up any boy or man who displeased her.

The family realized that they could not control the wild girl, so her rich uncle made arrangements to send her to the American colonies, believing that once she arrived in Virginia, the rigorous pioneer life would tame her. Moll acquiesced and boarded a ship bound for America but, as the ship pulled away from the Gravesend dock, she dove overboard and swam to shore. "I escaped the voyage," she sardonically remarked later, "alike hating Virginia and my virginity."

Donning men's clothing, Moll struck out on her own, becoming a fortune teller and befriending the members of the lowest criminal element in London. Most of her friends belonged to the Society of Divers, a diver being one who dove into the pockets of wealthy passersby to pick wallets and purses. One of the most adept of these was Mary Jones who was later celebrated in *The Beggar's Opera* as Jenny Diver (see entry).

Moll learned the art of pickpocketing so well that she soon became one of the most successful thieves in London. Those purses too difficult to pluck from a pocket, Moll learned, had to be cut away, and often as not this meant cutting away an entire pocket in the coat of a victim without being detected. Pickpockets who could successfully perform this delicate act were known as "cutpurses." Such techniques required special dexterity and skill, which Moll expertly demonstrated time and again. So adept did she become at this method of pickpocketing that she quickly earned the esteemed underworld sobriquet Moll Cutpurse.

Moll reveled in her legendary exploits, such as cutting away the purses of more than fifty victims in a single day, and became rich. Even law-abiding citizens looked upon Moll as a sort of cult heroine. She played the part, dressing in elegant men's apparel, brocaded breeches, doublet, plumed hat, and smoking a pipe, a habit she was addicted to until her death at age seventy-three. So rich did Moll Cutpurse become that she bought stores and property, but she never deserted her underworld friends, continuing to fence their stolen wares for a handsome profit into old age.

Seehere the Preſideſſe o'th pilfring Trade
Mercuryes ſecond; Venus's onely Mayd
Doublet and breeches in a Uniform dreſſe
The Female Humurriſt a Kickſhaw meſſe
Heres no attraction that your fancy greets
But if her FEATURES pleaſe not read her FEATS..

Moll Cutpurse (looking better than she actually did) was England's most notorious pickpocket and robber.

Not until she decided to blatantly publicize her wicked image did she run afoul of the law. In 1605, she leaped upon the stage of London's Fortune Theatre, dressed, of course, as a man, and puffing heavily on a pipe, and loudly sang bawdy songs while strumming a lute. She regaled the raucous crowd with lascivious stories until watchmen arrived to place her under arrest. The charge was a minor one, that of a female wearing the garb of a man. She was fined and released.

More serious punishment came with her being branded four times on the hands after she was somehow caught with her fingers working loose the pocketbooks of unsuspecting victims. These rare arrests and subsequent brandings were badges of honor to Moll, but as she grew older and her fingers were less adept in picking purses, she abandoned the practice. She put together a band of roughnecks and embarked on the career of highway robbery. She would ride wildly down a road in pursuit of a coach and order the driver to halt while training a brace of pistols on him. Her confederates would then order the passengers to step out and they would be robbed of their jewelry and purses. Moll was even bold enough to stop the coach of General Fairfax. The general resisted and Moll shot him in the arm. When he tried to flee by grabbing the reins of the horses, Moll shot two of the horses to death, then climbed onto the coach, knocked the general unconscious, took his purse bulging with gold coins, and fled.

Fairfax returned to Hounslow, where a company of troopers were alerted. They pursued Moll and found her in the middle of the road, cursing her horse, which had gone lame. Surrounded by fifty guardsmen with drawn swords, Moll threw down her empty pistols and surrendered. Taken to Newgate Prison, she was tried and sentenced to be hanged. Moll asked to see General Fairfax, who was astounded to discover that a woman had robbed and shot him. When meeting Fairfax, Moll proposed a deal.

Moll would pay Fairfax £2,000, she said, if he would drop the charges against her and arrange for her release. Fairfax, at the time, was in need of funds, Moll knew, because he was helping to finance Cromwell and his roundheads, who were in revolt against King Charles I. The general accepted the deal, and after the money was paid, released Moll. The experience so frightened Moll that she gave up highway robbery. With her considerable fortune, she retired to her lavish Fleet Street residence, but kept active by opening the Globe Tavern, which became the center of all criminal activities in London, the meeting place for every pickpocket, highwayman, and cutthroat in the city.

At the Globe, Moll gave advice on planned robberies and burglaries and also established herself as the most important fence in the city, buying stolen silver and gold and other valuables and then reselling them at a considerable profit, often to the original owners. She was referred to at this time in her life by the aristocrats of London as "The Queen of Misrule." Moll then established a bevy of beautiful harlots on her premises and used these women to compromise wealthy nobles, making sure the aristocrats wrote letters to her girls that Moll later used in effective and lucrative blackmail schemes. Further, because no man, not even the lowest of her criminal associates, would involve himself with Moll due to her repulsive face and body, she grew to hate all females and horribly abused her barmaids and female servants. Moll later established brothels, where clients were encouraged to abuse the strumpets.

Moll's hatred for women ran so deep that she took to prowling the streets of London, picking up young girls from rural towns, who had come to London to seek honest employment. She cajoled and lured these girls to her brothels, where they were made white slave captives and forced into a life of prostitution. Those who resisted the powerful Moll were beaten senseless by her and physically carried to her bordellos. If a girl proved truculent after having been held captive for more than a week and refused to service Moll's noblemen clients, Moll personally administered severe whippings. Denied the love of men, Moll perversely watched through peepholes as her captive whores were ravished by her clients, cackling with joy over each debasement and debauchery.

Reveling in her role of criminal overlord, Moll swaggered through the elegant areas of Drury Lane and St. Giles, richly bedecked in her men's clothing, puffing her pipe and roaring out ribald stories to aristocrats who squirmed at being in her company. She was once again arrested for "indecently and publicly wearing male attire." Tried and convicted in February 1612 at the Court of the Arches, Moll was sentenced to do public penance. She was forced to stand before St. Paul's Church on a Sunday morning after services, dressed only in a white sheet, making public apologies to passersby for daring to dress like a man.

Moll wept openly, but it was later learned that these were not penitent tears. Moll had downed three bottles of rum before doing her penance and she was sloppy drunk while standing in the square pretending to be a remorseful sinner. Thousands filled the square to witness this spectacle, as Moll knew

Moll Cutpurse (Mary Frith) is shown smoking her pipe; she was repeatedly arrested for dressing like a man and shouting obscenities in public.

they would. They hooted and jeered at her, cursing her, calling her every vile name. Meanwhile, as Moll had arranged it, scores of her best pickpockets roamed through the crowd, picking the purses of the very persons who stood about deriding her.

As the decades rolled by, Moll Cutpurse amassed one of England's great fortunes. She purchased grand manor houses, even estates. Her wealth was fabulous and her criminal career so notorious that every child in the country knew her name. She grew more hideous with each passing year, and by her late sixties, gluttony had made her obese. She never bathed and the stench of her body became so overpowering that even her closest associates crossed the street, when they saw her approaching. In the next few years, Moll's once keen mind became muddled. She lost track of her affairs and her associates bled her accounts, stole her valuables, and looted her houses. At the age of seventy-three, afflicted by severe dropsy, Moll Cutpurse had but a few hundred pounds left and this money she bequeathed in her will to the three maids still working for her. She left a small amount to a distant relative, a Captain Frith.

Moll's last wish was that she be buried face down in her coffin "as because I am unworthy to look upwards, and that, as I have in my life been preposterous, so I may be in my death." In 1662, her diseased, bloated body relaxed into death, and she was buried in St. Bride's churchyard, face down, according to her request, so that God would not have to look upon her withering ugliness at Judgment Day.

COLONEL BLOOD AND THE CROWN JEWELS/1671

Born in Ireland, Thomas Blood (c.1618-1680) was the son of a blacksmith and his life was full of intrigue and adventure, both real and imagined. During England's Civil War, beginning in 1642, he served in the Parliamentary forces of Cromwell and, through dashing battle feats rose to the rank of colonel. He later obtained forfeited estates which gave him a yearly income of £500. He subsequently lost these estates and the lucrative income, which turned him into an ardent Republican. He led an abortive coup to overthrow the crown in Ireland by seizing Dublin Castle and capturing the Duke of Ormonde in 1663. Defeated, Blood fled to Holland, where he went into hiding.

Blood became a legendary conspirator, involved in the plots of the Fifth Monarchy Men in London and the revolutionary Conventeers of Scotland. In 1666, he fought in the battle of Pentland Hills, but he managed to escape, as usual. Blood's successive and miraculous escapes from these conspiracies and other misadventures, led most to believe that he had been allowed to flee by government officials, who had made a secret pact with him: his freedom in exchange for information about the rebels with whom he worked.

In 1671, Blood put together the most fantastic plot of his life, the stealing of the British Crown Jewels from the Tower of London. Oliver Cromwell had stolen the jewels in 1649 after Charles I had been executed and, upon their recovery, great care was shown in protecting the royal heirlooms from ever being stolen again. The jewels consisted of crowns, state swords, scepters, orbs, and spurs of chivalry, which were of gold and silver and richly ornamented and inlaid with rare gems. These priceless jewels had been placed in the Tower of London with a strong and loyal detachment of guards ordered to protect the jewels around the clock from any thief.

Colonel Thomas Blood, the Irish adventurer, who stole the British crown jewels out of revenge in 1671.

That thief was none other than the daring Colonel Blood. In April 1671, Talbot and Dolly Edwards, official caretakers of the jewels, who lived in the Martin Tower rooms directly above the heavily guarded jewel room, were approached by a traveling minister and his wife. The Edwards couple was obligated to show the jewels to distinguished visitors, and they conducted a tour of the jewel room for the visiting clergyman and his wife.

The clergyman and his wife befriended the Edwards couple and the minister stated that he knew of a wealthy young man who would be a good suitor for the Edwards' daughter. When next he visited the Tower, the parson promised, he would bring the young man along. The Edwards couple delighted in the

Colonel Blood and his fellow robbers are shown looting the crown jewels from the Tower of London; all were captured and the jewels retrieved. Blood escaped the hangman through his glib tongue and charming personality.

prospect of meeting the young man. The parson returned on May 9, 1671, bringing along two friends and telling Edwards that his nephew, the young suitor, would be along shortly. Said the parson: "Until he gets here, why don't we visit the jewel room? My friends are most anxious to see the ensigns of the king."

Once inside the jewel room, the parson, who was none other than Colonel Blood, seized the gullible Talbot Edwards, while his two friends tried to bind him with ropes. Edwards struggled and Blood pulled out a mallet and struck the caretaker on the head three times, knocking him unconscious. Then a gag was stuffed in Edwards' mouth and he was tied to a pillar.

Blood and his two fellow thieves then began to steal the most valuable jewels in the room. The Colonel used his mallet to smash the largest crown flat so that it would fit in his pouch. The second man slipped the royal orb into a large pocket in his coat. The royal scepter was too long to conceal, so the third man quickly filed the scepter into halves and slipped these into the specially made pockets of his cloak. Just as the filing of the scepter was completed, the alarm was given and guards swarmed through the many passageways of the Tower.

Blood and his two friends dashed from the jewel room and down flights of stairs, slipping past guards going upward. The guards thought the three men were officials also looking for the thieves. Blood and his men got to the main gate, where their horses awaited them, held by a confederate. Mounting, they rode wildly away with a detachment of guards riding after them. The thief carrying the orb found the gold ball too cumbersome to carry and threw it into a large crowd which had assembled along the escape route. Then he dismounted his horse and vanished.

Colonel Blood rode on, but the leather pouch holding the crown slipped from his saddle horn and he stopped to retrieve it. As he did so, the mounted guards overtook him and a wild sword fight ensued, which ended with Blood being disarmed and made prisoner. He was taken back to the Tower and imprisoned there, along with the other three men. The jewels were recovered and were thereafter guarded night and day by specially trained soldiers, who were stationed inside the jewel room as well as outside.

Blood proved to be a recalcitrant captive. He refused to cooperate with his captors, telling them that he would not answer any questions "unless they are put to me by the king himself." When King Charles II was told of this, he was as staggered by the arrogance of Blood's demands as he was by the daring robbery. The king could not resist meeting the adventurer, who was expected to be executed.

King Charles went to the Tower and visited with the bold Colonel Blood, listening to his eloquent explanation for attempting the robbery. The amazing thief told the king that in taking the Crown Jewels he was merely retaliating against an oppressive system that had wrongfully deprived him of his estates. Charles was so enthralled by the colorful Blood that he not only reprieved him from the gallows, but pardoned him and his companions. The king restored Blood's estates and even awarded the great conspirator with a pension of £300 a year (some said as a bribe to Blood for not continuing his conspiratorial ways). Charles' generosity did little to curb Blood's appetite for intrigues and plots. He continued to be involved in all manner of conspiracies. When he died on August 24, 1680, Blood was deeply enmeshed in a lawsuit brought against him by the Duke of Buckingham.

THE INIMITABLE DICK TURPIN/1730s

Richard "Dick" Turpin (AKA: Dick Palmer, John Palmer, Tom Palmer; 1706-1739) was a British highwayman whose exploits became legendary. He was reportedly born in "The Crown Inn," the son of John Turpin, an Essex innkeeper. Turpin served an apprenticeship under a Whitechapel butcher and set up his own business by the time he was twenty-one. Accused of stealing livestock, Turpin left the area. In Essex, he became a member of a smuggling gang and then joined a gang that stole live deer, primarily in Epping Forest. When the group began committing robberies, Turpin became its leader.

England's infamous highwayman Dick Turpin vaults a cart in his wild ride through Edmonton with his great horse, Black Bess.

The robbers' first target was a man called Strype, who ran a Watford chandler's store. They robbed Strype's house of money, but did not harm him. They next broke into the home of a Loughton woman, blindfolding her and her maid. When the woman refused to tell the robbers where she kept her money, they allegedly tortured her by placing her hand over a fire until she provided the information. Then the robbers stole more than £400.

At a farm in the Barking area, the gang tied up a farmer, his son-in-law, wife, and maid, and stole more than £700. The thieves' next target was the house of a man named Mason, an official in charge of Epping Forest. Turpin, however, had gone to London, gotten drunk, and apparently forgotten about the plans. The gang went ahead without him. They broke in, kicked and hit Mason, and vandalized the house. After finding 120 guineas, they left and went to London, where they found Turpin and gave him some of the loot.

On January 11, 1735, the Turpin gang raided a farmer's house at Charlton, Kent, interrupting a card game. They forced the farmer, a man named Saunders, to take them through the house, where they found more than £100. They also allegedly ate mince pie and drank wine before leaving with threats to return if the robbery was reported too quickly. The gang attacked the Surrey home of a Mr. Sheldon on January 18, 1735, tied up Sheldon's coachman in the stable, captured Sheldon, and robbed his home of jewelry, eleven guineas, and other valuables.

On February 4, 1735, the bandits burst into the home of a Mr. Lawrence of Edgware, Middlesex, and stole money, silver, and other valuables. Before leaving one of the gang members also raped the maid. Following the Lawrence robbery, the king was notified, and a reward of fifty guineas was offered for the arrest and conviction of any of the gang members.

The gang set out to rob a farmer's house in the Marylebone region on February 7, 1735. They tied up two servants and the farmer, Mr. Francis, in the stable. In the house, they tied up and beat the farmer's daughter, wife, and maid before making off with jewelry, money, and other valuables. After this attack, the reward for their capture was increased to 100 guineas. Two of the leaders were arrested, tried, convicted, and hanged in chains, effectively discouraging the rest of the gang. When the gang disbanded, Turpin decided to become a highwayman.

Turpin met Tom King (d. 1737), a notorious highwayman, on Cambridge Road in February 1735. Turpin reportedly did not recognize King and ordered him to hand over his valuables. When King identified himself, the two agreed to begin robbing together. They were successful in robbing many travelers, and were thought to have operated from a cave in Epping Forest. On May 4, 1737, Turpin shot and killed Thomas Morris, a servant, who intended to capture him for a reward. After that incident, additional reward money was offered for Turpin, who was described as "...about thirty ... marked with the smallpox, his cheekbones broad, his face thinner towards the bottom...." Turpin and King nevertheless continued their robberies without interruption.

Dick Turpin is shown relaxing in his hideout, a remote cave officials found impossible to locate.

Close to the Green Man Inn in Epping Forest one evening, the highwaymen caught up with another traveler, a man named Major. Turpin's horse was exhausted, so he took Major's horse. Major reported the theft to authorities, who learned that a similar horse had been spotted at the Red Lion in Whitechapel.

A constable went to investigate and when he attempted to question King, the highwayman pulled out his pistol, which misfired. King shouted to Turpin, who was approaching, telling him to shoot the lawman. Turpin's shot missed the constable and instead fatally wounded King, who died a week later. While he lingered, King told officials about likely places to find Turpin, and huntsmen and bloodhounds searched the region guided by this information.

Turpin fled to Long Sutton, Lincolnshire, and then traveled to Welton, Yorkshire, where he assumed the name John Palmer. He made repeated trips to Lincolnshire, stole horses, and brought them back to Yorkshire to trade or sell. He was arrested and confined in York Castle on suspicion of stealing horses in early February 1739. He allegedly was identified as Richard Turpin after he sent a letter to his brother in Essex that was seen by his former teacher, a Mr. Smith, who traveled to York and identified Palmer as Turpin.

On March 22, 1738, Turpin was brought to trial at the York Assizes with Sir William Chapple presiding. The highwayman was convicted of stealing a foal and a mare at Welton and given the death penalty. He admitted to a few robberies and to one murder. Turpin reportedly bought some new clothes while awaiting execution and hired five men as mourners. When he was hanged at York on April 7, 1739, he reportedly spoke with the hangman for about half an hour and then jumped off the ladder. He was buried at the cemetery of St. George's church, but the body was later found in the garden of a city surgeon. A crowd carried it back to St. George's, where it was re-interred.

Richard Turpin was immortalized in the novel, *Rookwood,* published in 1834 by William Harrison Ainsworth (1805-1882). Ainsworth, who primarily wrote historical novels, was fascinated by highway robbers, especially Turpin. In the preface to *Rookwood,* he stated "I had always had a strange passion for highwaymen and have listened by the hour to their exploits, as narrated to me by my father, and especially to those of `Dauntless Dick', that `chief minion of the moon' ... Turpin was the hero of my boyhood."

THE "GENTLEMAN HIGHWAYMAN"/1749

The British robber known as the "Gentleman Highwayman" appears to have acquired his fame for his good looks and the fact that he almost killed the English writer Sir Horace Walpole. James Maclaine (1724-1750), a Scotsman, was raised in Ireland by his father, a Presbyterian minister. He showed his propensity for laziness, extravagance, and womanizing early in life and, instead of going into the business career for which he had trained, he set out to win a wealthy wife.

Using a legacy from his father, Maclaine established himself as a man of fashion, but went through the money before finding himself a wife. Reluctantly, he went into domestic service, but regarded it as an opportunity to steal, so the job did not last long. He went to London, where he married a Miss MacGlegno, an innkeeper's daughter, and quickly failed at being a grocer. When his wife died, he left their child with his in-laws and went away with William Plunkett, the Irish apothecary who had attended his dying wife and who recognized Maclaine's capacity for crime.

Maclaine became a gentleman dandy, attended by his servant Plunkett, and the two set about stealing from the gentry. When Maclaine lost all he had at gambling, Plunkett acquired pistols and horses and the two set out as highwaymen. Apparently Maclaine tended to hang back from the action, especially if danger threatened, but Plunkett did not seem to mind, willingly sharing the take. Maclaine made a point of repaying borrowed money, only to have Plunkett steal it back.

In November 1749, the two men held up Horace Walpole as he was riding through Hyde Park. Maclaine's pistol went off by accident, scorching Walpole's face. The next day, when

James Maclaine, the "Gentleman Highwayman," who was courteous to victims he robbed, especially women. One of the masks he used in his robberies is at his feet.

James Maclaine and his fellow highwayman William Plunkett rob a coach containing the Earl of Eglinton, the proceeds of this theft later sent Maclaine to the gallows.

Maclaine learned the identity of the man he had almost shot, he wrote a letter of apology to Walpole and even agreed to return what he had taken, but Walpole did not appear at the designated site to retrieve his belongings.

A few months later, the Gentleman Highwayman and his faithful Plunkett robbed a coach en route to Salisbury. Unusually, one of the victims advertised for his lost items in a newspaper. When Maclaine tried to pawn them, the fence recognized the items from the paper. On July 27, 1750, Maclaine was arrested. Terrified, he tried to place all the blame on Plunkett, but then confessed.

At his trial, he tried to retract his confession, saying it was the result of "a delirium and confusion in the brain" at the shock of being arrested. But the jury did not believe him, and he was found guilty. The following Sunday, more than 3,000 people came to Newgate Prison to visit him. When he was sentenced to death, public support for the handsome 26-year-old was amazing, but it failed to change the outcome. The Gentleman Highwayman was hanged on October 3, 1750.

SIXTEEN STRING JACK/1770s

Born to poor parents in a village near Bath, England, John Rann (AKA: Sixteen String Jack; d. 1774) was hired at age twelve by a woman visiting a local spa. When he displayed an aptitude for work, she took him to London. By the time he turned twenty, he had been promoted to the position of coach driver. He also had acquired tastes for clothes and women, however, neither of which his coachman's salary could support. After working briefly as a pickpocket, Rann decided that he was better suited to the life of a highwayman. He bought a horse, two pistols, a mask, and a fancy new suit. It was a detail of his breeches with no fewer than sixteen silk strings that earned him the name of "Sixteen String Jack."

In total, Rann was arrested seven times and acquitted, generally for lack of evidence, six times. Arrested first in 1772 for robbing a coach on Hounslow Heath, he was committed to Bridewell, but was later released. In December 1773, he and three other highwaymen, William Davis, David Monro, and John Saunders, held up the Hampstead stagecoach and robbed one of its passengers of the small sum of one guinea, three shillings, and sixpence. When informed of the crime, Bow Street (the contemporary police department) sent out one of its more competent "runners," John Clarke, who arrested the four the following evening. Again the evidence proved insufficient and Rann won acquittal.

In these and subsequent arrests that resulted in acquittals, two facets of Rann's method of operation figured prominently. Rann's victims were rarely able to identify him in court because when he worked he dressed in clothes decidedly different from the finery he wore to trial. Additionally, he never sold his stolen goods, leaving that dangerous work to Eleanor Roche, a prostitute, and his frequent companion. Despite the care with which he performed his crimes, Rann came close to being caught in May 1774.

After robbing John Devall of a watch and a small sum of money, Rann turned the watch over to Roche, who, in turn, gave it to Catherine Smith to take to a pawnbroker. The pawnbroker became suspicious, called police, and both Rann and

Highwayman John Rann, called Sixteen String Jack because of the strings dangling on his breeches.

Roche were arrested. Rann confidently denied Smith's accusations and again was released. In November of the same year, he was caught one night entering a house through a window. He appeared before Sir John Fielding, explaining to the magistrate that he had had a date with the owner of the house, one Doll Frampton, and, when he arrived late, had found the house locked. He was entering through the window to "surprise" Frampton, he said. When Frampton was called into court and upheld his story, Rann was released.

Rann did actually spend some time in prison for running up debts he could not pay. Due to the pressure of these debts he returned to robbery. In September, Rann and a partner, William Collier, stole a watch from a Dr. Bell, chaplain to Princess Amelia. He gave the watch as usual to Roche, to sell. Roche sent her servant, Christian Stewart, to a pawnbroker, who accepted the watch, but contacted the manufacturer, who, in turn, revealed that it had been made for Dr. Bell. John Clarke, eager to finally make a charge stick against Rann, arrested him as he and Collier were getting ready to commit another robbery. Roche and Stewart were arrested soon thereafter.

Confident as ever, Rann invited a group of his friends to a supper to celebrate his expected acquittal. The prosecution, however, produced a witness named William Hills, who had seen Rann and Collier going up the hill at Acton just twenty minutes before Dr. Bell was robbed. He positively identified the robbers as they had not yet put on their masks. Hill's testimony convinced the jury and Rann and Collier were found guilty and sentenced to death. Collier's sentence was later commuted, but Rann's condemnation was allowed to stand. Eleanor Roche, for her part in the crime, was sentenced to fourteen years in a penal colony.

Rann continued entertaining his friends while he awaited his execution at Newgate. Shortly before his execution, he staged a farewell dinner attended by a number of his prostitute friends. He reportedly went to his execution at Tyburn bravely attired in a new green suit.

ADVENTURES OF CAPTAIN LIGHTFOOT/ 1700s-1720S

For many impoverished youths in England or Ireland in the eighteenth century, the life of the highwayman was alluring. Michael Martin (AKA: Captain Lightfoot; 1775-1822) of Connehy, Ireland, was no different. At age seventeen he ran away from the family farm to seek his fortune. In the large city of Dublin, he met many dissolute characters, including the notorious highwayman "Captain Thunderbolt." Martin became his associate for the next twenty-six years, staging many highway robberies together in Scotland and Ireland.

In 1818, Martin decided to strike out on his own, as authorities were on his heels. He fled to the U. S. on board the brig *Maria,* landing in Salem, Massachusetts, on June 17, 1818. At first, he decided to earn his living honestly. He purchased a farm in the country, but the venture bankrupted him. Then he

America's first highwayman, Captain Lightfoot (Michael Martin) robbed the coach of the governor of Massachusetts, which caused his downfall.

opened a brewery that also failed. A failed love affair finally convinced him to resume his former occupation of highwayman. He disguised himself as an itinerant Quaker and set off on the Connecticut highway. In early 1819, he held up a merchant for $70 and struck the man over the head.

For the next three years Martin, who called himself "Captain Lightfoot," meandered through New England, copying the techniques of his former mentor. He made no distinctions in the selection of his victims, although he claimed he did not rob women. After he robbed the governor's coach in 1821, the Massachusetts governor demanded Martin be tracked down and arrested. Rewards were soon posted for any man who could bring "the most notorious scoundrel" to justice.

A posse of local farmers caught up with Martin as he lay sleeping in a hay barn outside Springfield, Massachusetts. He surrendered meekly to the farmers and was taken to Letchmere Point, near Cambridge, Massachusetts. Tried as a horse thief, Martin was convicted and sentenced to die on December 22, 1822. He was taken to the hanging tree, where hundreds of spectators had gathered. Martin removed a handkerchief from his pocket. "When shall I drop the handkerchief?" he asked his executioner. "Whenever you are ready," was the answer. Martin let the cloth slip from his hands and the prison wagon lurched into motion. Michael Martin, alias Captain Lightfoot, was dead at age forty-seven.

THE GREAT WESTERN LAND PIRATE/ 1820s-1830s

John A. Murrel (b. 1794) was lionized in fictional tales that described him as The Great Western Land Pirate. He was no American Robin Hood, however, but a vicious cutthroat and robber. He had the distinction of being the first bandit to terrorize and rob travelers along the Natchez Trace, the only trail through the wilderness from the Ohio Valley to Natchez, Miss.

Murrel befriended a young traveler named Virgil Stewart in 1834. Traveling along the Trace under another name, Murrel amused himself by telling Stewart about his older brother, who had become a bandit. He described countless robberies and murders committed by the older brother. By the campfire one night, Murrel leaned his scarred and frightening face close to Stewart and said: "I might as well be out with it. I'm the older brother I've been telling you about."

Bandit John A. Murrel on horseback stealing a slave for his black army, one to be used in a revolt in the South.

Murrel (wearing hat) rows across a lake in a storm with his captive, Virgil Stewart, en route to his secret camp in the Natchez Trace.

Murrel told Stewart that he and his bandits had been stealing slaves and reselling them. "I have carried off more than a thousand slaves," Murrel told Stewart proudly, adding that he kept the fiercest, most powerful slaves for himself to add to the ranks of his slave army. Murrel believed that Stewart was his friend and would join him in his dark enterprises.

In grim detail, Murrel outlined his plans to attack Natchez and New Orleans with thousands of armed slaves. The bandit hated the landed gentry of New Orleans, he said, and the Southern aristocracy that somehow in the past had injured him and his family. Murrel not only vowed to have his revenge, but meant to control the entire states of Louisiana and Mississippi.

To preserve his own life, Stewart not only placated Murrel but pretended to join his revolt. On the way to Murrel's camp, which was deep in the wilderness of the Trace, Stewart learned the real reason for Murrel's hatred of the southern landowners. Years earlier, he had been caught horse-stealing and had been whipped and branded. He was a preacher at the time, and the humiliation of the public whipping caused him "to abandon the work of the Lord." Murrel blamed the very landowners he preyed upon as having caused him to turn outlaw and bandit. "My blacks will cut all their throats!" he vowed. "We will swim in rivers of blood!"

At Murrel's camp, Stewart witnessed scores of blacks marching about, heavily armed, preparing for the invasion of Natchez and New Orleans. Stewart took his opportunity to escape the camp in the middle of the night. Upon reaching Nashville, he told his horror story of John A. Murrel and the impending slave revolt. Stewart then led a small, heavily armed posse to the outlaw's camp, where they captured Murrel and his men. Murrel was returned to Nashville, where he stood trial for slave stealing and banditry. He was convicted and sent to prison for ten years, being released in 1842, and once more disappeared into the Natchez Trace. Though rumors persisted of his continuing robberies and murders, no one ever again saw John A. Murrel alive.

THE BRIGAND OF THE SWAMPS/1830s

A product of the antebellum South, Bras Coupé (AKA: Squier, The Brigand of the Swamp, d. 1837) was a giant slave, about six-foot-six-inches, owned by General William de Buys, who also owned one of the largest plantations outside of New Orleans. First known as Squier, the giant black was a marvel to behold when he performed African tribal dances such as the bamboula and the calinda, the latter requiring incredible gyrating, leaping, and contortionist movements, all stemming from voodoo ceremonial rites.

Bras Coupé would perform his wild dances with hundreds of other slaves, who were brought to New Orleans' ancient Circus Square. Here, once a week, between 4 and 6 p.m., slaves were allowed to vent their frustration and anger in wild, abandoned dancing. This custom began in 1817 and continued until the Civil War. The square itself was renamed Congo Square for obvious reasons, and Bras Coupé became the star attraction. He would select a new black female slave each week and whirl, toss, and throw her about until she fell exhausted, but he would continue leaping and stomping until overseers called the curfew and ended the frenetic celebration.

De Buys was tolerant of his prized possession, teaching Bras Coupé to shoot and hunt, and even loaning him his best rifles to hunt wild game in the swamps and bayous about New Orleans. He learned to fire a weapon with both hands because, he said, he had had a dream where he lost an arm. In 1834 he was shot in a swamp by whites, who thought he was a runaway slave, the bullet shattering his arm which had to be amputated. The loss of his arm embittered Bras Coupé; he became moody and developed an explosive temperament. Then he tried to run away, but when he was captured and returned to his owner, the indulgent de Buys refused to have him whipped or punished.

Instead, the general lectured his errant slave on the proper behavior for a favored possession. The one-armed giant stood mute, then ran away permanently to the swamps, where he formed a band of other runaway blacks, who preyed on white travelers and made robbing forays into small villages and hamlets. (Bras Coupé would later serve as the role model for Robert Penn Warren's character Rau-Ru in his novel of the Old South, *Band of Angels.*)

Soon the once-esteemed slave became known as The Brigand of the Swamp. So notorious did Bras Coupé's reputation become that unruly children all over Louisiana were warned that if they did not mind their manners they would "be trimmed by Bras Coupé." The outlaw's band swelled to several dozen cutthroats, and Bras Coupé led his men into New Orleans itself on raids, where he attacked districts of the city, looting

The educated slave Bras Coupé is shown dancing the Bamboula in New Orleans' Congo Square before he turned bandit and killer.

Sidney Poitier, shown at right with Clark Gable and Yvonne de Carlo, profiled a sanitized Bras Coupé in the 1957 film, *Band of Angels*, which was based upon the Robert Penn Warren novel.

homes, murdering helpless whites, including women and children. More than fifty deaths were attributed to his murderous gang within three years.

The outlaws, which even included some renegade whites, would strike in the middle of the night, race through houses and scoop up valuables, then torch the house and shoot and knife to death all the occupants, while they slept in their beds. Bras Coupé became the most notorious black outlaw in the U. S., and it was believed that if he could have called enough dissident blacks and disenfranchised whites to his banner, the South would have suffered another slave revolt, worse than the 1831 uprising led by Nat Turner.

To the oppressed blacks, Bras Coupé became a heroic and legendary creature. He could not be shot, it was said at their campfire meetings, since Bras Coupé's skin was as hard as iron and no bullet could penetrate it. He could not be burned since he used voodoo herbs to cover his flesh. He could not be caught by the vigilantes and troops following him into the swamps since mystical fogs would envelop the pursuers and whisk them off to far countries.

Those who hunted the bandit through the eerie bayou country told bone-chilling tales about this fierce brigand. If they stumbled upon him in the gloom, hunters were cautioned to never look into his eyes since his stony stare could wither the limbs or even kill. Pursuers camping in the swamps could hear his booming, sinister laughter echoing through the mangroves. Worse, the brigand had turned cannibal by 1836, or so it was claimed. One eyewitness vigilante reported that while hiding in thick brush he watched Bras Coupé kill four pursuing soldiers with his one hand, then tear them limb from limb and make a meal of them, hideously devouring their uncooked flesh.

Such ghastly tales, along with very real accounts of the brigand's murders and robberies, caused New Orleans Mayor Dennis Prieur to place a $2,000 reward on Bras Coupé's head. The New Orleans *Picayune* urged the capture or killing of the outlaw, describing him in one editorial as a "semi-devil and a fiend in human shape whose life was one of crime and depravity."

The myth of this outlaw evaporated on July 18, 1837. Fisherman Francisco Garcia was sitting in a boat, the *Bayou St. John,* when he was spotted by Bras Coupé, who shot at him. Garcia quickly paddled ashore and, grabbing a club, attacked the giant. Bras Coupé staggered back from the blows, weakened by a bullet wound he had received on April 6, 1837, when two white bounty hunters shot him. Garcia clubbed the outlaw to death, then put the huge body into a sack and drove with it to New Orleans in his cart.

Garcia uncovered the body as he entered the city so that thousands of slaves could see his trophy. The blacks wept to see their hero slain and carted to city hall. Here the fisherman jumped from the cart and ran inside to claim the $2,000 reward. After much haggling with Mayor Prieur, Garcia was paid $250. (There was a claim that Garcia deserved no reward at all and that he should have been locked up instead; some said he had actually been a member of Bras Coupé's band and had betrayed his leader, killing the outlaw as he slept in Garcia's hut.)

The brigand's badly beaten corpse was taken to the Place d'Armes and dumped next to the fountain. For days the carcass rotted in the hot sun, while thousands of slaves were forced to march past it in single file and view the remains. This was to teach all slaves that revolt against the white South meant death. (A similar action was taken by Mexican authorities following the 1919 assassination of the great Mexican leader Emiliano Zapata, whose body was gruesomely exhibited to dissuade his followers from continuing their struggle for independence.) The display of Bras Coupé's corpse did nothing but anger slaves, and many resolved to escape their brutal masters. The legend of Bras Coupé was passed on from one generation of blacks to another, until few of the real facts remained inside of what is now a traditional image of a black Robin Hood.

ENGLAND'S GREAT GOLD ROBBERY/1855

The Great Gold Robbery of 1855 in England was engineered by Edward Agar, one of the most brilliant thieves of the nineteenth century. Agar, strikingly handsome with a thick head of black hair and heavy sideburns, was an ingenious man whose clever abilities at forgery and robbery earned him a small fortune and, eventually, a long prison sentence. Early in life, the well-educated Agar pursued a business career, but realized eventually that his station would not lead to a great fortune, his driving ambition in life.

Through underworld contacts in London, Agar met James Townsend Saward, a successful barrister who was also a master forger and the underworld czar who organized London crime for more than two decades. Saward, considered the greatest forger of his day, was known as "Jim the Penman" to his cronies, and taught his techniques to the affable Agar.

In 1848, through Saward's underworld contacts, Agar met William Pierce, a lean man with a long, somber face, who worked for the South Eastern Railway in London as a ticket printer, a man of expensive tastes and little money. Pierce was as venal as Agar, but lacked Agar's intellect. Almost at once, Agar began to ask Pierce about the gold shipments that passed from London to Paris via the railroads. Pierce immediately realized that Agar was planning to rob one of these trains and excitedly told the forger all he knew about these gold shipments.

Undoubtedly, Agar had developed a deep interest in these shipments after reading about the 1848 theft of £1,500 in gold sovereigns from a British train. The gold shipment, locked in a strongbox and under guard, was being transported from London to Bristol. Yet, when the box was delivered in Bristol, it was discovered to have been broken open and the sovereigns were missing. Agar admired the theft, which was never solved.

In long talks with Pierce, Agar learned how gold shipments were sent by train from London to Paris, and what rigid security measures were taken to protect the gold. The forger decided the risk was too great. He told Pierce that he would have to think of a method by which they could obtain the gold without use of force. He gave up the plan and traveled to the U. S. Some time in 1854, Agar returned to London. He looked up Pierce, and again began discussing the possibility of robbing the South Eastern Railway.

Agar's plan was to bribe certain railway staff members to obtain copies of two keys to the safe containing the gold shipments on the night train from London to Folkestone. Agar had done his research well. He knew that gold from London goldsmiths was sent to railway officials in heavy wooden boxes bound with iron hoops. These boxes were weighed and sealed by South Eastern Railway officials and then put on board the night train to Folkestone in an iron safe in the express car. The safe could only be opened by *two* keys, one held in London, the other in Folkestone by railway security chiefs. The captain of the ship taking the shipment across the Channel to Boulogne had a set of keys, as did the bank officials receiving the shipment in Boulogne and in Paris. Once the shipments

Edward Agar, who masterminded the robbery of the London gold train in 1855.

Railway official William George Tester helped the thieves to rob a fortune in gold.

Railway guard James Burgess helped Agar loot the gold from the safes on the train.

London Bridge Station, where the gold was shipped to European banks; it was here that Agar and Pierce boarded the gold train to rob its safes on May 15, 1855.

reached Boulogne, the boxes and their seals were again checked and then sent by train to the banks of Paris.

By the time Agar proposed this plan, Pierce had already been discharged from South Eastern Railway on suspicion of committing petty theft. Pierce, however, still knew key railway staff members and quickly contacted William George Tester, the station master at Margate. Tester was brought into the plot in the early summer of 1854. He was a vain dandy with a full head of thick hair. He primped before mirrors in public houses and prided himself on his trimmed beard.

Tester wore a monocle and thought of himself as a man of destiny. He was given money by the well-off Agar and soon saw that his fortune lay in robbing a gold train. Through Tester, Agar, and Pierce secretly visited the railway offices in Folkestone at night, where they studied the procedures of the arriving night trains and the transfer of gold shipments to the Channel steamers.

Agar hung about Folkestone, befriending railway workers in the local pubs. He came under the scrutiny of local policemen who warned railway men to stay away from him, saying that he was probably a clever pickpocket. Agar, learning of this, left for London immediately, where Pierce had lined up another key railway employee, James Burgess, one of the guards in the train car that carried the gold shipments. Burgess also joined the plot, believing that he would soon retire with his portion of the loot. Agar then went to work on the seemingly impossible job of obtaining the two separate keys to the train safe.

Tester involuntarily solved half of the problem. Without making the request, he was suddenly transferred from Margate Station to London and promoted to an executive position. Once in London, he saw an opportunity to obtain the first of the two keys. One of the safes used in the train shipments had to be sent to Chubb's for replacement, a chore which Tester handled personally. He made a wax impression of the single London key used for the replacement safe and gave this to Agar. To obtain the second key, the one held in Folkestone, Agar devised a clever scheme. In October 1854, he sent a shipment of £200 in gold from London to himself in Folkestone, using the alias C. E. Archer.

At the Folkestone station, Agar asked for his gold shipment. He watched carefully as the clerk retrieved the key to the safe, seeing that it was stored in a cupboard inside the station master's office. He then stayed in Folkestone, visiting the station often. Agar noticed that the night clerk regularly left the office unattended for a brief period each night. One night, with the clerk gone for only a few minutes, the bold Agar slipped into the office, retrieved the key to the safe and made a wax impression of it. He left the office undetected.

Returning to London, Agar and the others spent months perfecting the two keys made from the wax impressions, filing and shaping these. Next the thieves spent weeks cutting duplicate dies for resealing the bullion boxes. Then, with all in readiness, the thieves waited for their opportunity. The train guard, Burgess, notified Agar that a large gold shipment, £14,000 in gold sovereigns, would be shipped from London to Folkestone on the night of May 15, 1855.

Agar and Pierce bought first class tickets on this train and arrived that night at London Bridge station. Pierce wore a wig and a false beard so that none of the railway workers he knew

Agar and Burgess pack the gold from the sealed boxes into satchels, replacing the gold with lead; they later collected the satchels when the gold train arrived in Folkstone.

would recognize him. Agar and Pierce carried several satchels that were weighted with lead shot to the exact weight of the gold shipment, as given to them by station official Tester. Agar also carried the two keys to the safe, chisels, a mallet, dies for the resealing of the iron bands clamped about the gold boxes, sealing wax and tapers. A porter labored to carry the satchels onto the train and placed them in the baggage car where the gold safes were located. The guard on duty in the car that night was Burgess.

Agar and Pierce went to separate compartments and waited for the train to get up steam. As soon as the train pulled out of the station, Agar went to the gold car and Burgess let him inside. While Burgess acted as lookout, Agar went swiftly to work on the safes, opening them with his handmade keys, which fit perfectly. Next he removed the iron bands clamped around the boxes and removed the gold, placing it in his satchels and replacing it with the lead from the satchels. The transfer completed, Agar nailed the iron clasps around the boxes and placed new seals on them.

After the train reached Redhill, Agar stepped off the train for a few minutes, with two satchels full of stolen gold sovereigns. He handed these to the waiting Tester. Then Agar got back on the train which rolled away toward Folkestone. Pierce next joined Agar and Burgess in the gold car, where both men worked furiously to remove the many remaining gold boxes from the safes, replacing the sovereigns with the lead and then re-clamping and sealing the boxes.

When all the gold had been removed and was in the satchels stored next to the safes and the lead-filled gold boxes were locked in the safes, Agar and Pierce returned to their separate compartments and rested after their labors. When the train arrived in Folkestone, they simply got off the train and waited for the porter to carry their satchels from the gold car. The porter delivered several satchels to them and they then returned to London with the stolen gold.

Meanwhile, the two safes from the gold train were transferred, as usual, to a steamer, *Lord Warden,* which sailed for Boulogne. Once in Boulogne, the captain of the steamer opened the safes, and the boxes were weighed and the seals checked. They were pronounced secure and shipped on to Paris. The next day, bank officials opened the boxes and stepped back in shock to find nothing but worthless lead instead of the gold.

Authorities in Paris and London began a frantic investigation. Railroad employees in England and in France were interrogated. Scores of detectives investigated the theft, but not a clue was found leading them to the thieves. The French indignantly insisted that the theft had been committed in England. The British police sternly claimed that the robbery had occurred in France. Six months went by and still authorities found no trace of the thieves or the gold. They were prepared to give up the hunt.

While an intensive investigation ensued, the thieves gathered every day in Agar's large rented house at Cambridge Villas in Shepherd's Bush, London. They spent many hours melting down the gold sovereigns. Some of this they sold off and the rest they buried beneath the pantry floor. The four thieves split the profits equally and then went on their separate ways.

Pierce retired, buying a house in Kilburn. Burgess remained a guard on the railroad. Tester banked his stolen loot and then improved his position mightily. The nervy Tester asked for and received a testimonial from the South Eastern Railway company. Their glowing recommendation aided him in obtaining an appointment as general manager of the Royal Swedish Railways.

Perhaps this robbery would never have been solved had it not been for the womanizing Agar. He had been living with his mistress, Fanny Kay, with whom he had a young son. Yet, he began spending time and money on another woman, attempting to steal her affections from a thief named Humphreys. In revenge, Humphreys framed Agar on forgery charges. Agar was sentenced to transportation for life to Australia. Before Agar was sent to Australia, he arranged to have Pierce take £1,500 of his own money and about £3,500 from the gold robbery and give this to his mistress Fanny so that she and his son would have some security.

Pierce, however, reneged on his promise to turn over these sums to Fanny Kay. Moreover, he cruelly refused to pay the rent for Agar's mistress and son and they were thrown into the street, left destitute, except for a few sovereigns. The mistress went to Newgate Prison to see Agar, but he had already been sent to a prison ship about to sail for Australia. Fanny, in despair, cried out her desperate plight to the warden of Newgate, who realized that the money Agar had promised Fanny might be the loot from the gold robbery and ordered Agar back to Newgate. When Agar heard how Pierce had betrayed him, he took his revenge by informing on Pierce and the others, detailing the entire gold robbery to officials.

Pierce was arrested at his home in Kilburn and thousands of pounds were unearthed beneath the front step of his house. In the same month, November 1856, Burgess was also arrested. Tester was arrested a short time later when he returned from Sweden to meet with his family. All four men were placed on trial on January 12, 1857, and, with Agar testifying against his fellow thieves, all were found guilty of robbery. Tester and Burgess were sentenced to fourteen years transportation to a penal colony. Pierce, however, hired a crafty lawyer who found a flaw in the indictment against him, and he received only a two-year prison term. Agar was sent off to serve his life term.

Some justice existed for Fanny Kay and her son, however. Although all the recovered loot from the robbery was returned to the South Eastern Railway, Agar's own money, about £1,500, was put in trust for Fanny and the boy. Thus ended England's great gold robbery. Its brilliant architect, Agar, died in an Australian penal colony many years later. Before he died, broken in spirit, a new prisoner arrived to tell him that he had become a legend in England's underworld. Replied Agar: "That means nothing, nothing at all!"

Where infamy offered nothing to England's Edward Agar, the notoriety earned from his many robberies excited and nurtured America's foremost bandit of the 19th Century. He was Jesse James.

THE OUTLAW JESSE JAMES/1860s-1880S

Born on his father's farm near Kearney, Clay County, Mo., on September 5, 1847, Jesse Woodson James (AKA: Dingus, Thomas Howard, 1847-1882) would become America's most famous bandit, rivaling in lore and legend that of England's Robin Hood. Millions of words would be written about this handsome, dashing, and utterly ruthless bank and train robber. To many of his peers, he appeared a folklore hero who took vengeance in their name upon an industrial society that was grinding the old agrarian lifestyle to ashes. To others, he and his band represented the last vestiges of the Old South and its lost cause of secession.

A good deal of truth was in the tale that Jesse James the bandit was created by oppressive troops of the Union Army, and worse, operatives working for the then widely disliked Pinkerton Detective Agency. Detectives of this agency killed innocent members of the James family and thus unified the rural communities of Missouri in protecting and nurturing this greatest of outlaws. Beyond the myriad propaganda and countless myths about this western legend, lived a farm boy who became a professional thief and a cold-blooded killer. He was at large for sixteen years. He committed dozens of daring robberies and killed at least a half dozen or more men. He died at the age of thirty-four.

Jesse James was raised with little formal education. His father, Robert James, was a Baptist preacher and his mother, Zerelda Cole Mimms, was a hard-working, strong-willed farm woman. Jesse's older brother, Frank (Alexander Franklin James, 1843-1915), a taciturn, withdrawn, and Bible-reading youth later followed his younger, more aggressive brother into banditry.

Teenager Jesse Woodson James, by then a marksman.

Alexander Franklin James at twenty, by then an outlaw.

It was because of the notorious and celebrated exploits of the James Brothers, the Younger Brothers who rode with them, and the Dalton Brothers who came later, that the state of Missouri, their home state, became known as "The Mother of Bandits." The James and Younger boys were products of what was then known as the Middle Border, the wild and still unsettled states of Missouri and Kansas.

The parents of the James boys were hardy pioneers. Robert James married Zerelda Cole Mimms when she was seventeen. The couple moved from Kentucky to western Missouri, where James became the pastor of a small Baptist Church outside of Kearney, Missouri. He and his wife, with the help of neighbors, built a log cabin in the wilderness and began to carve out a farm. On January 10, 1843, the couple's first child, Alexander Franklin James, was born. Jesse was born four-and-a-half years later. Robert James, though a cleric, was consumed by the gold fever, and in 1850, when Jesse was only three, left his family and went to California to seek his fortune, telling his wife that he would send for her as soon as he struck it rich. He slaved in the gold fields and found nothing but an early death from pneumonia.

A short time later, Zerelda James married a man named Simms, but their marriage dissolved within a few months. She was a woman of strong opinions, who fiercely guarded her sons from criticism, one of the contributing factors in the breakup of her second marriage. In 1855, she married a third time, to Dr. Reuben Samuels. The physician was well-to-do, docile, and allowed his wife to make important family decisions. When it came to the boys, Mrs. Samuels made all the decisions. A third child, Archie Samuels, was born. He was retarded and was kept close to home, his older brothers doting upon him.

The James brothers stayed on the farm begun by their father, and through Dr. Samuels' acquisition of adjoining property, the James holdings grew. The family bought some slaves to work the land, and Frank and Jesse also farmed through their teenage years. When the Civil War broke out, the James brothers sided with the Confederacy. First Frank, then Jesse, rode off to fight with Confederate guerrillas under the command of William Clarke Quantrill. Frank later fought with William "Bloody Bill" Anderson and was part of the guerrilla band that attacked and sacked Lawrence, Kansas. In 1863, Union soldiers swooped down on the James farm and looted the place, setting fires to crops and driving the slaves off the property. When the teenage Jesse attempted to stop the soldiers, he was beaten almost to death.

When he recovered, 17-year-old Jesse rode off to join his brother Frank and Cole Younger, who were fighting Union troops and raiding Union towns with Quantrill. Jesse was by then an expert horseman and crack shot with pistols and rifles. He was part of Anderson's contingent when it raided and burned Centralia, Kansas, in 1864, helping to shoot down seventy-five Union prisoners in what later became known as the Centralia Massacre. A large Union force pursued Anderson's detachment, but the Confederates turned about and ferociously attacked the Union troops, routing them and slaying dozens. Jesse James was seen riding pell-mell into the Union ranks, the reins of his horse held by his teeth, firing two pistols. He shot down six northern soldiers and was credited with killing three of them.

That night, Jesse James sat at a campfire, taking no part in the discussion about the day's battle. He spent his time cleaning his pistol. Suddenly, the gun's hair trigger went back and a bullet took off the tip of James' left middle finger. He stared momentarily at the bloody finger, then said as he wrapped a kerchief about it: "Well, if that ain't the dingus-dangest thing!" His fellow guerrillas laughed with him and nicknamed him "Dingus" James. The James boys grew to such prominence that the Samuels were singled out for persecution by Union troops, who raided the farm and compelled the Samuels family to move to Nebraska. Following the end of the war, the James brothers returned to a ruined and vacant farm. As guerrillas that were not part of regular Confederate armed forces, they were still considered outlaws and rewards were posted for them dead or alive.

Jesse James when he rode with Quantrill's guerrillas.

In early 1865, when a general amnesty was offered guerrillas, Jesse James led a small band toward Lexington, Missouri, intending to surrender. The group included his brother, Frank James, and Cole Younger. A company of Union troops ignored the amnesty, and waiting in ambush, opened fire on the Confederate guerrillas. Jesse, in the lead, was shot off his horse, a bullet puncturing his lung. As the guerrillas fled, James crawled to the nearby underbrush. Two Union soldiers pursued him, but he shot and killed one of their horses and they thought better of trying to capture James, who escaped. He was found by a friendly farmer the next day in a creek bed, trying to tend to his severe gunshot wound. The

Zerelda James Samuels, mother of the James boys.

John Younger, who was killed in an 1874 gun duel with Pinkerton agents.

Cole Younger in 1876, at the time of the Northfield, Minnesota, raid.

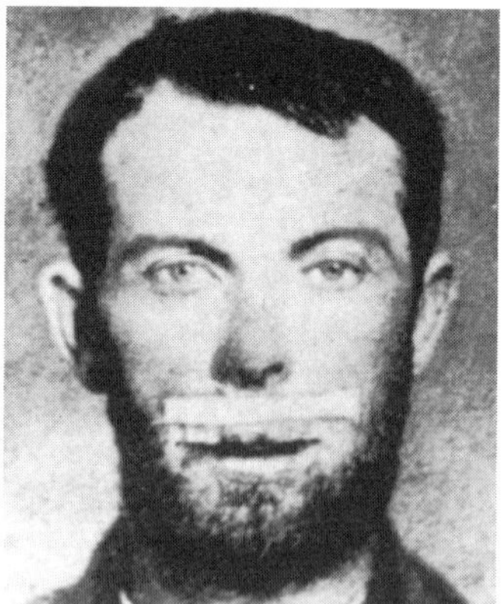

Jim Younger, a bandage covering a gun wound over his lip, in 1876.

Bob Younger in 1876, at the time of the Northfield, Minnesota, raid.

farmer bandaged James' wound and then helped him travel to Nebraska, where his mother and stepfather nursed him back to health.

James, believing he would not recover, begged his mother to take him back to Missouri, saying: "I don't want to die in a northern state." She and her husband put him into a wagon and rode slowly to Harlem, Missouri, taking Jesse to a boarding house owned by Mrs. Samuels' brother, John Mimms. There, Jesse met young Zerelda Mimms, his cousin, who had been named after his mother. She nursed him back to health and the two fell in love. Zee, as she was called, was too young to marry, but the two promised to wed in the future (they would take their wedding vows nine years later).

When Jesse was almost well, his mother and stepfather took him back to the family farm near Kearney. He worked sporadically with Frank in the fields, although he had relapses from his wounded lung and was often bedridden. Both he and Frank, when in the fields, wore guns on their hips, and kept saddled horses nearby, in the event Union troops acting as occupying forces in Missouri after the war swooped down to arrest or even shoot them, such was the bitterness that survived the war.

The war had changed much in the national character of the U. S. and it had also changed the perspective of the farm boys, who had fought in it. The James boys had tasted battle and blood, adventure, and danger. They had survived the worst car-

Jesse James in 1876, when he led his band to Northfield, Minnesota, and disaster.

The First National Bank in Northfield, where the James gang was decimated by armed citizens.

nage ever seen in the country, and either out of boredom or an ambition that went beyond the dull chores of their farm, they, like many others in that turbulent era, buckled on gun belts, mounted horses, and rode into small towns to rob banks. The rationale the raiders later said was "we were driven to it." They blamed Yankee bankers and railroad magnates for impossible farm mortgages and threatening foreclosure in underhanded land-grabbing schemes. And to some small degree it was true.

The first bank robbery attributed to the James Brothers occurred on February 13, 1866. Ten men rode into Liberty, Missouri. While eight waited outside with the horses, two went into the Clay County Savings Bank. One of these men was later identified as Frank James. The other was Cole Younger, the oldest and most daring of the Younger Brothers (this included three out of thirteen children, who later took up robbery, Coleman, James, and Robert).

One of the robbers, allegedly Frank James, approached father and son cashiers Greenup and William Bird, and said: "If you make any noise, you will be shot." He then demanded that all the money behind the teller's cage and in the vault be stuffed into a wheat sack. Both robbers held pistols aimed at the Birds. The robbers emerged from the bank without incident a few minutes later. Inside the wheat sack was more than $60,000 ($15,000 in gold and $45,000 in nonnegotiable securities).

The men outside joined the two coming from the bank and the ten rode slowly out of town. Then George "Jolly" Wymore, en route to classes at William Jewell College, paused in the town square and stared at one of the riders as if he knew him. The rider slowed his horse, rode a few feet away from Wymore, then wheeled in his saddle, drawing his pistol and firing three shots into the startled Wymore, who collapsed and died on the spot. Apparently, the rider realized that Wymore had recognized him. As Wymore fell, the entire gang drew weapons and began firing wildly into the air as they spurred their horses down the street and out of town. A posse was quickly formed, but it lost the bandits, who had crossed the Missouri River on a ferry and disappeared in a raging snowstorm.

The Liberty raid was the first daylight bank robbery in the U.S. by an organized band of robbers. (The first U.S. bank robbery was committed by lone postal employee Edward W. Green, who held up a bank in Malden, Massachusetts, on December 15, 1863.) Whether or not Jesse James was present at the Liberty bank robbery was debated by several western historians. Some claimed he was at home nursing his old lung wound. Others insist that Jesse was outside the bank with the other riders, waiting for his brother Frank and Cole Younger to emerge. However, Jesse was certainly a member of the same gang that robbed the Alexander Mitchell Bank in Lexington, Missouri, on October 30, 1866.

In a dramatic contemporary sketch, Cole Younger, center, on horseback, waits for his brother Bob to climb onto his horse after Bob Younger's mount had been killed by Northfield citizens, who unexpectedly attacked the bandits.

REWARD!

- DEAD OR ALIVE -

$5,000.00 will be paid for the capture of the men who robbed the bank at

NORTHFIELD, MINN.

They are believed to be Jesse James and his Band, or the Youngers.

All officers are warned to use precaution in making arrest. These are the most desperate men in America.

Take no chances! Shoot to kill!!

J. H. McDonald.

A "shoot to kill" reward poster issued immediately after the Northfield raid, offering $5,000 for the capture of the bandits.

A tall young man, who stood a little under six feet entered the bank, while another young man stood outside the front entrance. The first young man went to a teller's cage and held out a $50 bill to cashier J. L. Thomas. "Can you change this for me?" he asked.

"No," the suspicious Thomas replied, remembering the Liberty bank had just been robbed and that a man first asked to change a large bill during that robbery.

The young man then drew a gun and leveled it at Thomas. Three other men entered the bank and also drew guns, training these on the bank employees. The tall young man said: "You've got $100,000 in this bank. Unless you turn it over to me, you'll be killed."

"That's not true," Thomas said, denying the bank had that much money.

"Let's have the key to the vault," the tall young man demanded.

"I don't have it," Thomas told him.

The bandits went through Thomas' pockets and found nothing. They then stuffed $2,011 into a wheat sack and left cursing. Actually, the vault held considerably more cash. The tall young man was identified as Jesse James and this was the first time the bandit was linked to robbery.

On March 2, 1867, the James-Younger gang rode into Savanna, Missouri, and went into the local bank. They aimed guns at bank president, Judge John McClain, who refused to turn over the vault keys. One bandit stepped forward and shot McClain in the chest. The bandits ran from the bank and rode quickly from the town. McClain survived. On May 22, 1867, it was a different story. The James-Younger gang decided to adopt guerrilla tactics, when raiding the Hughes and Wasson Bank of Richmond, Missouri. They rode into town shooting their weapons and whooping like drunken cowboys. Pedestrians ran in all directions while six men—Jesse and Frank James, Cole, Jim, and Bob Younger, and James White—broke down the locked front door of the bank. The bandits stuffed $4,000 into a wheat sack and then raced to the street.

Citizens grabbed their guns and began firing on the bandits as they mounted their horses and attempted to flee. Mayor John B. Shaw tried to rally residents as he ran to the bank with a pistol in his hand. The bandits fired many shots at him and Shaw fell to the street dead, seven bullets in him. Impetuously, the bandits decided to attack the jail instead of fleeing, having heard that former Confederate guerrillas were being held there. They tried to batter down the jail's front door. Frank Griffin, the 15-year-old son of the jailer, ran behind a tree with a rifle and began shooting at the bandits. They rode past him and riddled his body, killing him. His father, B. G. Griffin, then raced forward, but a bandit caught him and fired a bullet into his head, leaving him dead beside his son.

The gang then rode quickly out of town, but a large posse caught up with them at sundown. A pitched battle ensued and the bandits escaped under the cover of darkness. Several were tracked down. The first was Payne Jones. A young girl guided a posse to the Jones farm and Jones came running out of his farmhouse with two guns blazing. He shot down the girl and killed a posse member. Jones was captured but later killed in a gun battle. Next, Richard Burns was tracked to his farmhouse near Richmond. Vigilantes took him to a large tree, and with torches flickering, quickly tried and convicted him of the Richmond robbery and murders. He was then hanged. Andy Maguire and Tom Little, identified as Richmond raiders, were apprehended and lynched.

The James brothers were also identified and several vigilante groups assembled. Before the vigilantes rode to the James farm, "alibi cards" were sent to the vigilante leaders. The cards bore signed statements from Frank and Jesse James saying they had no part in the Richmond bank raid, and incredibly, their word was accepted.

If the James brothers said they were innocent, then that was the end of the matter, such was their reputation in western Missouri. Nowhere in Clay or Ray counties would a Missourian betray these men. Anyone who continued to insist that they had robbed the bank risked being shot and killed while traveling lonely roads. Merchants who labeled the boys thieves and murderers risked boycotts and being put out of business. This fierce loyalty to the ex-guerrillas lasted until the day Jesse Woodson James was executed by two traitorous men.

The James-Younger gang continued robbing banks despite the threat of Union soldiers, lawmen, and vigilantes. There were always farmers, men who had fought in the Civil War on the southern side, who were willing to ride with them

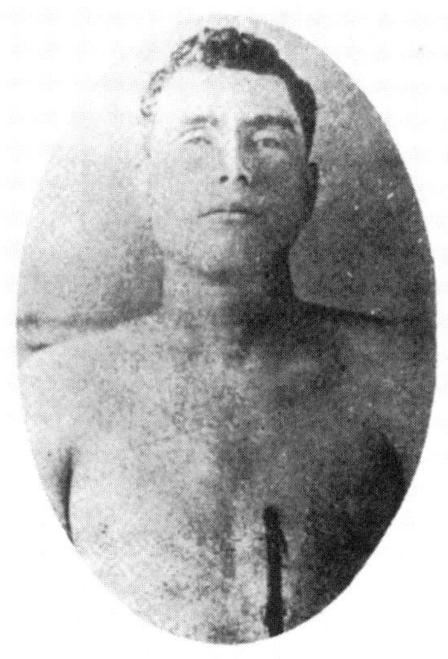

James gang member William Stiles, alias Bill Chadwell, shown dead, killed at Northfield.

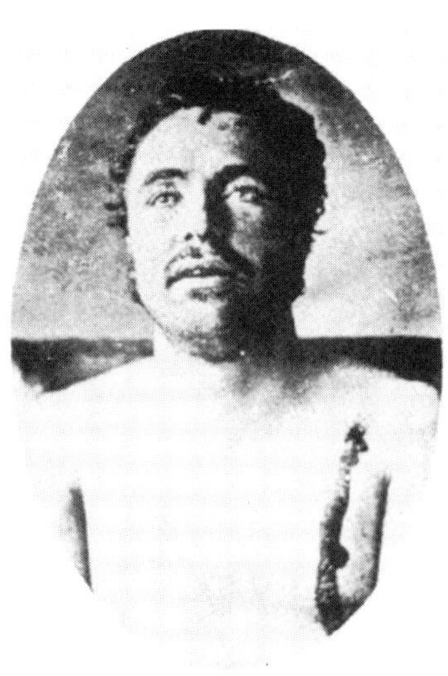

Clell Miller rode for years with the James boys; he is shown dead, killed at Northfield.

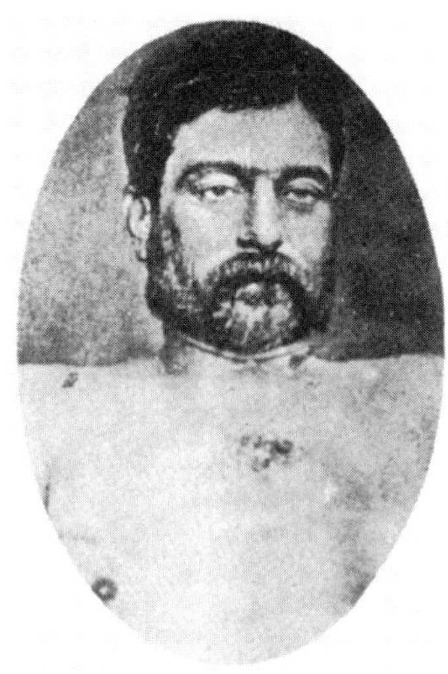

Samuel Wells, alias Charlie Pitts, shown dead, killed in flight from Northfield.

on a raid or two to get enough money to pay off a mortgage or support a family. The James and Younger brothers were the professionals and kept most of the loot.

After the Richmond raid, the James boys were careful to select banks some distance from their homes and made only a few attacks each year, then returning to their farms to resume peaceful, law-abiding ways. In these early years they robbed with leisure, but later they became desperate, infamous and much-wanted. In those later years, they sought the "big strike," a robbery that would yield a great sum and allow them to permanently retire, to resettle in California or to flee to Mexico or even South America.

Jesse and Frank James and Cole and Jim Younger, along with four other men, rode a far distance on March 21, 1868, arriving in Russellville, Kentucky. Actually, Frank James had been in the area for some days, scouting the Southern Bank of Kentucky. He had used the alias Frank Colburn, pretending to be a cattle buyer from Louisville. He entered the bank and approached the managers, Nimrod Long and George Norton. He asked Long to cash a $100 bill, but Long became suspicious. Frank James pointed to a tall, blue-eyed man standing in the door of the bank. "I've got to pay off one of my hired hands," he said.

Long looked over the bill carefully and then said: "This bill is counterfeit, Mr. Colburn."

Frank James laughed, took the bill back and tucked it into his vest pocket, saying: "I reckon it is." He then drew his pistol and aimed it at Long. "But this isn't, Mr. Long. Open the vault."

The young man in the doorway was also holding a pistol and aiming it at him. Long turned and then dashed for the rear door of the bank, but Jesse fired a single shot that grazed the banker's scalp and sent him unconscious to the floor. Then Jesse ran to him and hit Long on the head repeatedly with his gun butt. Long, a burly man, rolled over and grabbed the bandit's hands. Frank James stood next to the struggling men, shouting for Jesse to "finish him!" He aimed his pistol at the banker, but could not fire for fear of hitting his brother.

Suddenly, Long found enough strength to throw off Jesse and jump up. He ran to the door and outside into an alley. Jesse and Frank fired at him, but the two bullets merely struck the door frame. Once outside, Long raced down the alley, yelling: "They're robbing my bank! They're robbing my bank!" Citizens misunderstood Long's message and thought his bank was on fire. Several raced about the streets grabbing water buckets. Meanwhile, Frank and Jesse James dragged two sacks full of gold from the bank, about $14,000, and put the heavy sacks on the saddles of the gang's horses.

An old man, half blind, wandered into the middle of the street. Cole Younger rode up to him, saying: "Old man, we're having a little serenade here, and there's danger of you getting hurt. Just get behind my horse here and you'll be out of the way." Younger moved his horse gently next to the old man so that he edged him out of the road. The bandits then formed a single line and raced out of the town hollering and firing their weapons as if in a cavalry charge. A fifty-man posse gave pursuit, but lost the experienced riders in the wilderness.

The Pinkerton Detective Agency was then hired by an association of bankers and the agency began its long crusade to capture the James-Younger band. Their detectives interviewed George Hite, a neighbor of the James Brothers, but he insisted he knew nothing of the Russellville raid and that the James Brothers were innocent. He was lying. His own sons often rode with Jesse and Frank James.

One of those sons, Clarence Hite, upon Jesse's assassination in 1882, explained how the gang met in barns and in kitchens of farmhouses to plan their robberies. They would scout a town and determine whether or not the local bank held a sub-

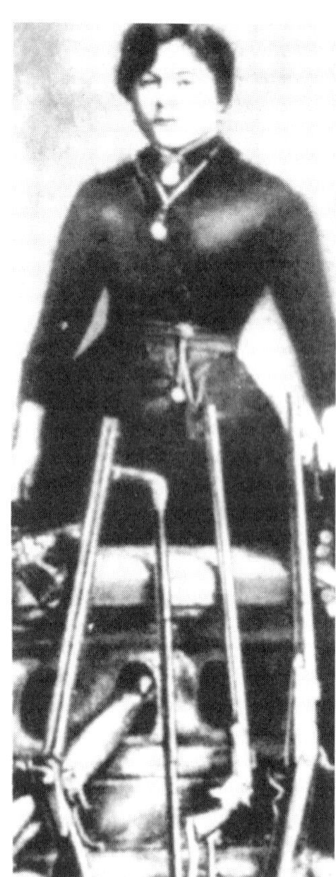

Zee James, the wife of Jesse James, shown with her husband's arsenal.

The rural James house near Kearney, Missouri; Jesse briefly returned to his mother's home after the Northfield raid.

stantial amount of cash. They might send someone from the gang to make deposits, who, as a depositor, would ask questions about security and whether or not the bank was solvent and thus learn from the bankers the amount of money usually kept on hand.

In these days, the gang operated democratically, its members selecting a target bank and then casting their votes to rob it or not. Jesse James was not then the leader of the gang, although he was considered by its members as the most daring and the one most likely to kill anyone who interfered in a robbery. Not until the gang's disastrous raid on Northfield, Minnesota, in 1876 did Jesse become the overall leader, and by then his authority rested upon his widespread reputation, which he enjoyed and used to advance his own image among his fellow outlaws. He was also by then a deadly killer, who even threatened to shoot his own brother Frank at one time for disagreeing with him.

Frank James was almost as much an enigma as his younger brother Jesse. Well-read, Frank liked to quote the Bible and Shakespeare, but his fellow bandits thought him sanctimonious, hypocritical, and overly cautious to the point of annoyance. He vexed the impetuous Younger brothers, especially the good-natured Cole Younger. But Frank James was no mere toady to Jesse. He was resolute and a deadly marksman, as feared a gunman as his younger brother. It was Cole Younger, however, who was the most experienced horseman and gunman, and it was Cole who lent balance and authority to the gang. Jesse and Frank James showed their murderous natures on December 7, 1869, when they rode into Gallatin, Missouri, going into the Davies County Savings Bank.

Frank James offered a $100 bill to cashier John W. Sheets, asking him to change it. Sheets began walking to his desk. Sheets had been a Union officer during the Civil War and the brothers apparently held a deep hatred for him. It was later claimed that it had been Sheets who had commanded the Union troops that had fired on Jesse and wounded him when he had attempted to surrender in 1865. Jesse James, without warning, suddenly shot and killed Sheets as he stood next to his desk. Jesse fired twice, hitting Sheets in the head and chest.

Frank James then ran behind the counter and gathered up about $500, which he threw into a wheat sack. William McDowell, a clerk, ran toward the front entrance of the bank and Frank shot him in the arm. The wounded clerk staggered to the street and shouted an alarm. The bandit brothers raced to their horses. Frank mounted, but Jesse's foot was snagged in the stirrup of his horse and the animal bolted, dragging the outlaw almost forty feet down the middle of the street. Frank turned back, stopped Jesse's horse, allowing the younger James to jump on Frank's horse. They then rode from town with bullets smacking at their single horse's hoofs. They later stole another horse and completed their escape.

The horse the bandits left behind was identified as having belonged to Jesse James, but he reported that his horse had been stolen just before the Gallatin robbery. Jesse had earlier established another identity for himself after robbing the Gallatin bank. As he and Frank left town, they stopped a Methodist minister named Helm, and Jesse told the pastor that he was "Bill Anderson's brother. I just killed S. P. Cox, who works back there in the bank at Gallatin. He killed my brother in the war and I got him at last!" Jesse had purposely lied about himself and his victim, wrongly identifying Sheets, to cover his murder. But this ruse did not work.

A large posse headed for the James farm on December 15, 1869, and when they arrived, Jesse and Frank James, mounted two fast horses and raced from the barn. The posse pursued them, with Deputy Sheriff John Thomason in the lead. Thomason dismounted and trained his rifle on the two fleeing James boys, but his horse bolted and spoiled his shot. Thomason's horse then caught up with the James brothers and Jesse shot the animal dead. The boys escaped.

The house in Nashville, Tennessee, where Jesse James and his family hid following the Northfield raid.

Somehow, the James boys managed to convince local authorities that they were not the bandits responsible for the bloody Gallatin holdup, even though most citizens were certain they were. For almost two years, the James gang remained inactive. Then, on June 3, 1871, Jesse and Frank James, Cole, Jim and Bob (or John) Younger, Jim Cummins, Charlie Pitts (alias Samuel Wells), and Ed Miller took a leisurely ride to the sleepy little hamlet of Corydon, Iowa.

Jesse and Frank James and Cole Younger entered the Ocobock Brothers Bank and found only one clerk. The other bandits waited outside the bank and noticed the streets were empty. Frank asked the clerk where everyone had gone and the clerk explained that Henry Clay Dean, a celebrated Methodist preacher, was giving a lecture at the local church, and the entire town had turned out to hear him.

"All the better," Jesse said, drawing his pistol and aiming it at the clerk. Within a few minutes the bandits had cleaned out the bank, taking with them more than $45,000 in gold and bills. The bandits rode slowly out of town, but when they came to the church, where the townspeople had gathered, Jesse smiled and told his men to wait. He got off his horse and went into the church, standing in the middle of the aisle at the back of the church, where he loudly announced: "Folks, you should know that some riders were just down to the bank and tied up the cashier. All the drawers are cleaned out. You folks best get down there in a hurry!" He then began to laugh loudly and, while the congregation stared in awe at the tall young man with piercing blue eyes, he slowly turned and walked back to his horse. He and his men rode out of town slowly, all laughing.

Finally, one man in the church shouted: "For God's sake! It's the James gang! They've just robbed the bank!" After finding the cashier bound, the citizens of Corydon hastily formed a posse and rode after the bandits, but the gang outdistanced them and the pursuers lost all trace of the thieves by the time they reached Clay County, Missouri. The gang did not wait long to plan and execute its next raid, this time riding to Columbia, Kentucky, on April 29, 1872. Jesse and Frank James entered the bank.

Outside waiting with the horses were Clell Miller and Cole Younger. Jesse demanded the key to the safe but cashier R. A. C. Martin balked and Jesse shot him three times, killing him. Frank James casually stepped over Martin's body and cleaned out the cash drawers, taking $600. The gang rode quickly out of town. A huge posse seeking vengeance for the Martin slaying rode after the bandits, but the James gang, old hands at evasion by then, doubled back on their own trail twice, circled Columbia, and then rode on to Missouri, completely confusing the pursuing lawmen.

On May 23, 1872, Jesse James, Cole and Bob Younger, Clell Miller and Bill Chadwell (alias Bill Stiles) rode into Ste. Genevieve, Missouri, entering the local bank where cashier O. D. Harris recognized the bandits. He quickly complied with their demands and filled a grain sack with more than $4,000 in gold and bills, and the gang left town at a gallop. No posse pursued the robbers. By then, it seemed inevitable that every town in Missouri would receive a visit from the James-Younger gang and most local lawmen became apathetic in their efforts to catch the thieves, knowing that the bandits were protected by almost everyone in Clay and Ray counties. A short distance outside of Ste. Genevieve, Jesse dismounted to readjust the gold sack hanging from his saddle and, at that moment, his skittish horse ran off into a field.

A farmer appeared on the road and Jesse asked him to go after the animal. He refused but quickly changed his mind when the other members of the gang aimed six-guns at him. The farmer chased the horse across the field and returned him to Jesse. He grinned at the outlaw chief with a toothless smile and then asked with a thick accent: "I catch der horse. Vot do I get for dot, yah?"

Jesse mounted the animal and replied: "Your life, Dutchy. Vot you tink, yah?" He rode off laughing. By then Jesse James

A contemporary sketch shows Jesse James in 1881, when he organized a new gang and planned more train and bank robberies.

was very much aware of his growing reputation and he enjoyed his notoriety. He even played up to his self-image of the unbeatable bad man, a daring bandit with a sense of humor and intelligence to outwit any country bumpkin posse. He demonstrated his belief in his fame on September 26, 1872, when he, Frank James, and Cole Younger rode to the fairgrounds outside of Kansas City, Missouri. At the main gate, Jesse dismounted and went to the cashier. He smiled at Ben Wallace, the cashier, and then said in a pleasant voice: "What if I was to say that I was Jesse James and I told you to hand out that tin box of money? What would you say?"

"I'd say I'd see you in hell first," snapped Wallace.

"Well, that's just who I am and you'd better hand it out pretty damned quick or..." He aimed a pistol at Wallace. The cashier handed over the money in the tin box, $978. Stuffing this in the traditional sack, Jesse mounted his horse. The feisty Wallace ran from the cashier's box and grabbed the stirrup on Jesse's horse, holding on to it. "It's the James gang!" he shouted, but few in the crowd heard him. Jesse turned the horse away from Wallace, drawing his pistol and firing a shot that went wild and struck a girl in the leg.

The three men then galloped into some nearby woods and vanished. En route home, Jesse cursed the bad luck. Frank James said nothing. He had scouted the fair and had reported that as much as $10,000 was kept on hand with the cashier. He had been right, but shortly before the bandits arrived to rob the cashier, thousands of dollars had been taken from the strongbox and sent to a local bank for safekeeping.

The paltry sum taken at Kansas City caused the bandits to believe that bank robbery simply was not worth the effort anymore. Even banks were unreliable in having large sums of cash on hand. Trains, however, always carried large amounts of gold, silver, and currency. They knew well that the first train robbery had been committed by the ill-fated Reno Brothers of Indiana, but they felt themselves superior to the Hoosier bandits and believed they would have no trouble in successfully looting trains.

To that end, the gang rode to Adair, Iowa, in mid-July 1873. Frank James had taken several trains west, as far as Omaha, Nebraska, riding the Chicago, Rock Island, and Pacific Express (while reading *Pilgrim's Progress*). He reported to the rest of the gang that when the Express reached Adair on July 21, 1873, it would be carrying more than $100,000 in gold, destined for eastern banks.

Gang members arrived outside Adair on that day and removed a section of track. These riders included Jesse and Frank James, Cole and Jim Younger, Clell Miller, Bob Moore, and Commanche Tony. As the Express came around a bend, its engineer, John Rafferty, saw the break and reversed the engine. It was too late. The engine raced into the open track and crashed onto its side, crushing Rafferty to death. Jesse and his men rode from a nearby wood and went to the baggage car, pointing guns at the clerks, who opened the safe to give them not $100,000 but only $2,000 in federal reserve notes.

The gold that was supposed to have been on board had been rescheduled that morning and had gone through Adair four hours earlier on a fast Express. The bandits rode back to Missouri discouraged. They decided to go back to farming and for six months, the James-Younger gang was inactive.

Before attacking their next train, the James-Younger gang committed a vintage holdup. On January 15, 1874, the bandits rode south to Arkansas and, outside of Malvern, held up the Concord Stagecoach, one of their few such robberies. Cole Younger, who was the experienced hand and practical hub of the gang, proved during this robbery that he, too, had his moments of caprice.

After the gang stopped the stage, driver and passengers were ordered to step down and line up before the gang as guns were trained on them. More than $4,000 in gold, bills, and jewels were taken from the well to-do passengers. When Cole Younger took a gold watch from a man who protested in a strong southern accent, the bandit paused. "Are you a southerner?" he asked, a rather ridiculous question since there were few northerners traveling in Arkansas at that time.

"Yes, suh," replied the gentleman traveler.

"Were you in the Confederate Army?"

"I had that distinction, suh."

"State your rank, regiment, and commanding officer," Younger demanded.

When the passenger gave Younger this information, he was startled to see Younger hand him back his watch. "We are all Confederate soldiers," Younger said with some pride, enjoying his magnanimity. "We don't rob southerners, especially Confederate soldiers." He pointed his finger at the rest of the passengers and said in a solemn voice: "But Yankees and detectives are not exempt."

In fifteen days, the gang had ridden back to Missouri, and on January 31, 1874, entered the small flag station at Gadshill, Missouri, a depot along the line of the Iron Mountain Railroad. The bandits, which included Jesse and Frank James, Cole, Jim, and Bob Younger, Jim Cummins, Clell and Ed Miller, Sam Hildebrand, Arthur McCory, and Jim Reed, flagged down the Little Rock Express. As the train came to a stop, the bandits jumped into the baggage car and quickly opened the safe, shooting off its locks. They took from it more than $22,000 in gold and bills. Some of the bandits went through the cars, robbing the passengers. Jesse James then mounted his horse and rode up to the engineer's cabin where Cole Younger held the engineer under his gun. "Give her a toot, Cole!" Jesse shouted to him. Cole Younger grabbed the whistle cord and yanked on it. As the whistle shrieked, Younger laughed like a small boy with a new toy.

Before the gang departed, Jesse threw a stick to the engineer. Around it was wrapped a piece of paper. James told the engineer: "Give this to the newspapers. We like to do things in style." The scrap of paper contained Jesse's own press release of the robbery, which he had written only a few hours before the train had been stopped. It read:

THE MOST DARING TRAIN ROBBERY
ON RECORD!

> The southbound train of the Iron Mountain Railroad was stopped here this evening by five [there were ten bandits] heavily armed men and robbed of _____ dollars. The robbers arrived at the station a few minutes before the arrival of the train and arrested the agent and put him under guard and then threw the train on the switch. The robbers were all large men, all being slightly under six feet. After robbing the train they started in a southerly direction. They were all mounted on handsome horses.
>
> PS: They are a hell of an excitement in this part of the country.

After the Gadshill raid the robberies stopped, and it seemed as if the James-Younger gang had been swallowed by the earth. There was no trace of any of the bandits for almost a year. With the spoils from the robbery, Jesse decided to finally wed Zerelda Mimms, his cousin. They had met often in wooded retreats

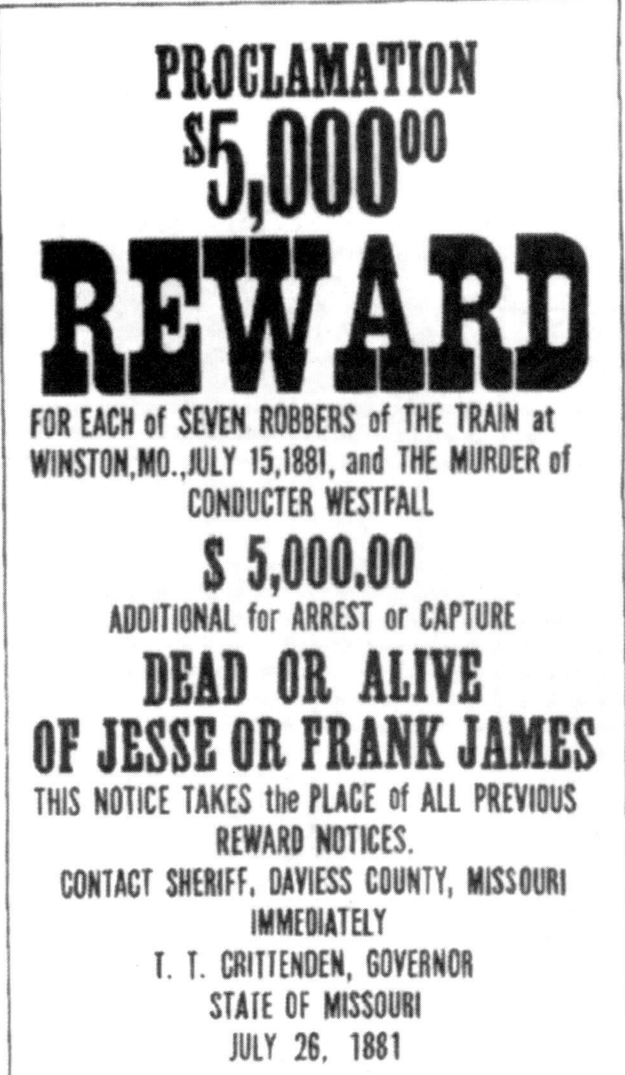
PROCLAMATION
$5,000.00
REWARD
FOR EACH of SEVEN ROBBERS of THE TRAIN at WINSTON, MO., JULY 15, 1881, and THE MURDER of CONDUCTER WESTFALL
$ 5,000.00
ADDITIONAL for ARREST or CAPTURE
DEAD OR ALIVE
OF JESSE OR FRANK JAMES
THIS NOTICE TAKES the PLACE of ALL PREVIOUS REWARD NOTICES.
CONTACT SHERIFF, DAVIESS COUNTY, MISSOURI
IMMEDIATELY
T. T. CRITTENDEN, GOVERNOR
STATE OF MISSOURI
JULY 26, 1881

The $5,000 reward for the James boys issued by Missouri Governor T. T. Crittenden in 1881, one which attracted the eye of Robert Ford, a member of the James gang.

and lonely cabins in the wilderness. Now Zee Mimms insisted that they either marry or never see each other again. Jesse and Zee went to Kansas City and were married. They then traveled to Galveston, Texas, where a reporter for the St. Louis *Dispatch* interviewed Jesse before he and Zee boarded a steamer headed for Vera Cruz, where they planned to honeymoon. Jesse candidly told the reporter: "On the 23rd of April, 1874, I was married to Miss Zee Mimms, of Kansas City, and at the house of a friend there.

"About fifty of our mutual friends were present on the occasion and quite a noted Methodist minister [Reverend William James, Jesse's uncle] performed the ceremonies. We had been engaged for nine years and through good and evil report, and not withstanding the lies that had been told upon me and the crimes laid at my door, her devotion to me has never wavered for a moment. You can say that both of us married for love, and that there cannot be any sort of doubt about our marriage being a happy one."

Jesse and Zee James, however, did not take ship for Vera

The home in St. Joseph, Missouri, where Jesse James was murdered by Bob Ford in 1882.

Cruz, but traveled back to Missouri and settled on a small farm near Kearney, living in a log cabin. Jesse James was by then dedicated to a way of crime and had no thought to retire or reform. His wife's attitude about his criminal ways was never learned, but Wood Hite, a family friend, later stated that "she looked the other way ... out of love." Hite went on to say that Jesse James was a devoted husband and loved his wife very much. The couple produced two children, Jesse, Jr., and Mary James. The outlaw spent a great deal of time with his children, playing with them whenever he was home. The couple continued to travel, living in Texas, then Tennessee, and even in the heart of Kansas City.

Frank James would also marry two years later, eloping with 17-year-old Annie Ralston, a union that would produce a son, Robert, in 1878. While Jesse was settling down to a farming life, the Pinkerton Detective Agency increased its efforts to arrest the James boys for their past crimes. Detectives roamed in pairs and in groups through western Missouri, seeking the James brothers and their allies, the Youngers. The detective agency had been waging a private war with the James-Younger clan for sometime.

On March 16, 1874, Jim and John Younger were riding through the woods near Osceola, Missouri. Two Pinkerton detectives, Louis J. Lull and E.B. Daniels, who had been trailing them, suddenly found themselves faced by the two Youngers. The detectives claimed they were cattle buyers, but Jim Younger correctly guessed them to be Pinkertons. The detectives and the Youngers both drew their guns at the same time and Lull and Daniels were killed. So was John Younger. A month later, Jesse James, Clell Miller, and James Latche, killed another Pinkerton agent, John W. Whicher. From that day on, the Pinkertons hounded the James-Younger gang.

The Pinkertons watched the Samuels farm on and off, believing that Jesse and Frank would pay their mother a visit. Detectives learned, on January 26, 1875, that the boys would arrive at the Samuels farm after sundown. They stationed men near the farmhouse and then shouted for Jesse and Frank to come outside. A light in the window went out and then a bomb of some sort was thrown through the window by one of the Pinkerton men. It exploded with a deafening roar. The bomb blew off Mrs. Samuels' arm and a fragment of the bomb tore through the side of Archie Peyton Samuels, the 8-year-old half-brother of Jesse and Frank. The child died within an hour in great pain and agony.

No other act than this "inexcusable and cowardly deed," as the press termed it, could have earned more sympathy for the James boys. The newspapers vilified the Pinkertons, who were universally hated, and labeled them child-killers and inhuman monsters that attacked defenseless women and children. Even though Allan Pinkerton repeatedly denied that any of his men had thrown a bomb into the Samuels' home, his agency fell into disgrace. Jesse was so incensed at the killing of his little half-brother and the mutilation of his mother that he spent long hours planning the execution of Allan Pinkerton.

According to Wood Hite, he actually took a train to Chicago and spent hours waiting for Pinkerton to show up at his headquarters there, planning to shoot the detective on sight. He did see Pinkerton, but did not shoot him on a crowded Chicago street. He later told Hite: "I had a dozen chances to kill him when he didn't know it. I wanted to give him a fair chance, but the opportunity never came."

For some time after this, Jesse and Frank James fell out. Frank had apparently tried to convince his younger brother to retire, that bank and train robbing were getting too dangerous. Jesse, on the other hand, called Frank a coward, especially since he refused to try to track down Allan Pinkerton and take vengeance on him for the death of his half-brother.

Frank James refused to associate with Jesse or the rest of the gang for some time. He remained on a farm, reading and writing letters to Missouri newspapers, attempting to vindicate himself and stating that he was not responsible for the robberies attributed to him. He went on to say that he and his brother Jesse "were not good friends [at the time of the Kansas City fairgrounds robbery] and have not been for several years."

By early 1875, the brothers were reunited and led the Youngers to Texas where, on May 12, they robbed the San Antonio stage of $3,000. Cole Younger reportedly had to be persuaded to join the band. He was busy romancing Belle Starr, the daughter of Collins County rancher John Shirley. Cole Younger then had the notion to quit banditry. He told Jesse and Frank James that he was thinking of settling in Dallas, where he had a job offer as a census taker. Jesse talked him out of this idea and Younger followed the James boys back to Missouri, where an important train robbery was planned.

Through a bribed railroad clerk, the gang learned that the United Express Company would be shipping more than $100,000 on the Missouri Pacific Railroad. On July 7, 1875, Jesse and Frank James, Cole, Jim and Bob Younger, Clell Miller, Charlie Pitts, and Bill Chadwell were waiting for the train as it slowed to cross an old railroad bridge east of

Crowds assembled at the James house in St. Joseph, Missouri, after learning that the notorious bandit had been killed; souvenir-hunters stripped the house within hours.

Otterville, Missouri. The gang trained pistols on the engineer who brought the engine to a halt. The bandits then approached the Adams Express car and entered it, ordering guard John Bushnell to open the safe. "It can't be done," Bushnell nervously told Jesse. "I don't have the keys to it. It's locked all the way through and the keys are at the other end of the run."

"Get an ax," Jesse told Bob Younger, who took a fire ax from the wall of the baggage car and began chopping away at the safe. It was useless. All Younger succeeded in doing was making a few dents in the heavy iron safe. Then Cole Younger demanded the ax. A tall, powerful man, Younger repeatedly swung his 200 pounds against the safe for ten minutes, finally making a small hole in the top of the safe. Jesse reached through the hole and pulled up a leather pouch from which the bandits took more than $75,000. They stuffed the money into a grain sack and then tossed it to Frank James and the others waiting outside. Jesse, Cole, and Bob Younger then climbed on their horses, but before riding off, Jesse told Bushnell: "If you see any of the Pinkertons, tell 'em to come and get us."

This strike, the gang's largest to date, convinced Jesse and the others that with the proper information they could commit robberies that would bring them quick fortunes and enough money to retire. Bill Chadwell, a native of Minnesota, was sent to scout the large First National Bank in Northfield, Minnesota, reputedly one of the wealthiest banks in the Midwest. Though far from their regular haunts, the Northfield bank promised as much as $200,000 in cash and gold, perhaps more. The gang members were further lured to rob this bank because its two principal stockholders were Benjamin Butler and W. A. Ames, who had been Union officials in the Civil War and were still much hated for the oppressive measures they employed when occupying southern cities.

Butler, the general in charge of conquered New Orleans, had issued an order which allowed his soldiers to treat women there as common streetwalkers. Ames was considered the worst carpetbagger to ever plague the South. Both men had enriched themselves through the spoils of war and the misfortune of the devastated southerners.

In August 1876, the James-Younger band began its ride north, moving slowly and with great confidence. They had never experienced any serious setbacks and their members had remained unharmed in ten years of robbery. The bandits were all mounted on the finest horses available and looked prosperous. All wore new suits, shiny black boots, and long linen dusters like those worn by cattle buyers. They carried new carbines and heavy Colt pistols on their hips. Jesse wore two more Colts in shoulder holsters.

The eight men rode into Northfield, Minnesota, on September 7, 1876. To the bandits, Northfield looked like any other town they had raided, with a main street and small stores nestled next to the bank. Yet Northfield was unlike any town the gang had ever visited. Its residents were industrious pioneers, who placed great value on thrift and an even greater value on the law.

Minnesota was not Missouri, where roving bands of outlaws were commonplace. The state was relatively free of such

The James children, Mary and Jesse James, Jr., were playing outside the house when Bob Ford killed their father.

bandits and the natives of Northfield were fiercely protective of their town and the savings in their bank. And, as they proved with lethal dedication, they would battle anyone who tried to take what they had earned by the sweat of their brows.

At 2 p.m., Jesse, Charlie Pitts, and Bob Younger entered the First National Bank, while Cole Younger and Clell Miller waited outside the bank, holding the horses. At the end of the street Frank James, Bill Chadwell, and Jim Younger sat on their horses, guarding the exit of the town, ready to protect the gang when it fled Northfield. Trouble began almost immediately. J. A. Allen, a hardware store owner, spotted the men outside the bank and walked over to investigate. Clell Miller grabbed his arm and said: "Keep your goddamned mouth shut!" Allen broke free of Miller's grip and began to run down the street, shouting: "Get your guns, boys! They're robbing the bank!"

Henry Wheeler, a university student home on vacation, saw Allen and took up the alarm. He, too, began to shout: "Robbery! Robbery! Robbery! They're all at the bank!" Cole Younger and Miller quickly mounted their horses and they were joined by Frank James, Jim Younger and Chadwell. The five outlaws began racing up and down the street, shouting to the startled residents: "Get in! Get in!" This technique had worked many times in Missouri where gun-shy natives raced for cover. But the citizens of Northfield did just the opposite. Dozens of men, young and old, grabbed pistols, rifles, and shotguns and ran to the street or took positions in windows, behind doors, and at the corners of buildings.

Inside the bank, Jesse James held his pistol on acting bank cashier Joseph Lee Heywood, telling him: "Don't holler! There's forty men outside the bank." Heywood nodded as Jesse added in a menacing voice: "Open the goddamned safe before I blow your head off!"

"I can't do that," Heywood said, "there's a time lock on it."

Pitts ran forward with a knife and cut the cashier's throat slightly. He and Bob Younger both stuck their pistols into Heywood's stomach. The cashier kept insisting that the safe was on a time lock. None of the bandits bothered to check the safe. Heywood was lying. The safe was unlocked and had no time lock. Then a clerk, A. E. Bunker, ran into a back room. Pitts fired a shot at him, but his bullet missed its mark. Bob Younger went through the cash drawers and found only a small amount of money. Firing could be heard in the street and Pitts went to the front entrance of the bank. He turned to Jesse and shouted: "The game's up! Pull out or they'll be killing our men!"

Bob Younger and Jesse James followed Pitts out the front door, but one of them—it was never determined which—turned and shot Heywood in the head. He fell dead to the bank floor. The scene that greeted Jesse as he stepped into the street was as bloody as any battle he had experienced in the Civil War. Clell Miller was riding crazily about, his face blasted to pulp and gushing blood. Elias Stacy, a resident, had rushed him moments earlier and let loose a shotgun blast that caught Miller full in the face. He was unrecognizable. His flesh hung in shreds from his jaw and his shirt front was soaked with blood. He moaned and screamed wildly, firing his six-gun indiscriminately. One of Miller's wild shots struck and killed Nicholas Gustavson, a terrified immigrant, who was trying to reach the cover of a building.

A bullet smacked into Cole Younger's shoulder. Then A. B. Manning fired a shot that struck Bill Chadwell square in the heart. The outlaw stood straight up in his saddle for a moment, then toppled to the earth, dead. Wheeler, the university student, had gotten a gun and repeatedly shot the already wounded Clell Miller until he also fell from his horse dead. Bob Younger raced forward on his horse, firing at Manning, and Wheeler fired a shot at him, wounding him in the hand. Younger switched his weapon to the other hand and fired back at Wheeler.

By that time the citizens had blocked both ends of the street and dozens of men were firing at the outlaws, who rode up and down the street through a murderous cross fire, looking desperately for an escape route. A bullet struck Charlie Pitts, then Jim Younger, then Cole Younger. The gang was being shot to pieces. "It's no use, men!" Jesse shouted to the others. "Let's go! Let's go!" Bob Younger, who had been shot from his horse, managed to climb up behind his brother Cole and what was left of the gang rode wildly down the street through heavy fire. Scores of citizens, who did not have weapons threw rocks at them.

Some miles outside Northfield, the gang rested for a few minutes. Jesse looked at Bob Younger's wounds and then told his cousin Cole Younger that Bob was too seriously wounded to continue. He suggested that either Bob be left behind or "we put him out of his misery." Reaching for his six-gun, Cole Younger, who had taken Jesse's orders for years, glared at Jesse and told him that he would not leave his brother behind. "Maybe it's best we split up," he said. Jesse and Frank, the only bandits in the gang not wounded, nodded and then rode off in one direction.

The Younger Brothers and Pitts headed in another direction. The Youngers were slowed by their wounds and left a clear trail for pursuing lawmen to follow. Fourteen days later they were trapped in a swamp outside of Madelia, Minnesota.

Bob Ford, killer of Jesse James, who holds the pistol that slew the infamous bandit; Ford would later be killed in Creede, Colorado.

More than fifty men surrounded them and a full-scale battle ensued. An hour later, Sheriff Glispen shouted to the outlaws who were behind a large fallen tree: "Do you men surrender?" As the lawmen waited for an answer, they reloaded their weapons and prepared for further battle.

Then the silence was pierced by a voice from behind the large tree. "I surrender!" Bob Younger, bleeding from five wounds, stood up unsteadily and waved the possemen forward. "They're all down, except me." The lawmen came forward cautiously, guns at the ready. They found Cole Younger wounded seven times and Jim Younger wounded five times. Both were still alive. Charlie Pitts lay flat on the ground, his six-guns and rifle empty of bullets. There were five bullet wounds in his chest. He was dead.

The Younger Brothers were taken into custody, and as they rode in an open cart through the small Minnesota towns, en route to medical attention, citizens came out by the thousands to see them, curious about these strange men from Missouri who had traveled hundreds of miles to risk their lives. All three brothers were tried and sentenced to life imprisonment. As they entered the state penitentiary at Stillwater, Minnesota, Cole Younger was asked why he and his brothers had turned to crime. "We were victims of circumstances," he explained, not half believing his own oft-repeated words. "We were drove to it, sir."

Charlie Ford later had nightmares about Frank James hunting him; he committed suicide.

The Northfield raid made national headlines and Jesse and Frank James became the most sought-after outlaws in the U. S. But they were nowhere to be found. Hundreds of possemen scoured Minnesota, Wisconsin, and Iowa for them as the brothers moved slowly south. They traveled on foot, stole horses, and then abandoned them. They slept in abandoned farm buildings during the day and moved only at night. They ate raw vegetables and hid from sight, believing that all were their enemies. It took them three weeks to reach Missouri and by then they looked like scarecrows, their clothes in rags.

Jesse and Frank realized that they were too notorious now to remain in Missouri. The murders they had committed in Northfield had branded them cold-blooded killers. Even many of their former supporters in Missouri found it hard to excuse their actions. Hiding in a covered wagon, Jesse and Frank were driven to Tennessee. Both purchased small farms outside of Nashville and lived there in obscurity for three years with no thought of returning to the outlaw trail.

Jesse, however, ran low on money and organized a new gang in Fall 1879 that included his brother Frank, Bill Ryan, Dick Liddell, Ed Miller, Tucker Basham, and Wood Hite. On October 7, 1879, the gang held up the Alton Express near Glendale, Missouri, and took more than $35,000 from the baggage car safe. The outlaws were inactive for almost a year and a half before they robbed a stage in Muscle Shoals, Alabama, of $1,400.

On July 10, 1881, Jesse led the same men to Riverton, Iowa, where they held up the Sexton Bank, looting it of $5,000. Five days later, they stopped the Chicago, Rock Island, and Pacific train at Winston, Missouri. When Frank McMillan tried to interfere with the robbery, Jesse shot him dead. The train engineer, William Westfall (or Westphal), refused to do as Jesse ordered and the bandit chief shot him dead in the engine cabin. The outlaws got only $600 from this bloody robbery, which caused Missouri governor Thomas T. Crittenden to offer a $10,000 reward for the capture and conviction of Frank and Jesse James.

The amount of money offered in this reward was staggering for its day. In earlier times, however, this kind of reward would not have tempted any member of the James gang. The Younger brothers, cousins to the James boys, were blood kin and absolutely loyal. Other earlier members were fellow veterans of the guerrilla battles of the Civil War and were tied to the James and Younger brothers through old associations and loyalties. But the new gang members Jesse had recruited for the band had little or no allegiance to them. This included Robert and Charles Ford, two young men, who had learned of the reward and planned to murder Jesse.

Bob Ford, the younger of the Ford Brothers was not a

Frank James in 1882 after he surrendered to Governor Crittenden; he would be tried for many robberies and murders, but would be acquitted.

regular member of the gang. He spent time around gang members, clamoring to ride with the bandits, but was mostly used to run errands, a fact which caused him to become resentful and embittered. Charlie Ford rode with Jesse and Frank James, however, on August 7, 1881, in a strange robbery that occurred near Blue Cut, outside Glendale, Missouri, near the site where the gang had stopped a train two years earlier. The gang, consisting of Jesse and Frank James, Charles Ford, Wood and Clarence Hite, and Dick Liddell, stopped a train by piling large timbers across the track.

Engineer Jack Foote brought the train to a halt and the bandits used a pickax to chop their way into the locked express car. They hammered open the safe, but were disappointed at the small amount of money in the safe. The outlaws then walked through the train, robbing the passengers. Jesse, wearing a thick, black beard, and the only bandit without a mask, made no effort to disguise himself. In fact, he reveled in his notoriety. He had taken to collecting the dime novels that Eastern presses had churned out about his exploits. "I'm Jesse James," he said to several stunned passengers and then he boldly introduced other members of the gang. The bandits rode off grumbling about the meager loot, less than $1,500. This was Jesse James' last robbery.

Following this robbery, Frank rode back to his farm near Nashville. Jesse, accompanied by the Ford Brothers, rode to Missouri to visit his mother. The three men slept in the Samuels barn. Jesse kept his pistols at the ready, believing that the Pinkertons might arrive at any moment. When he fell asleep, the Ford Brothers began discussing how to kill the man they followed. They had been planning to murder Jesse for months, but were cautious and fearful of this deadliest of outlaws. Robert Ford was already in contact with Governor Crittenden, promising him that he would kill Jesse James in the near future.

After having breakfast at his mother's home for the last time, Jesse, still accompanied by the Ford Brothers, rode to St. Joseph, Missouri, where he was living under the name of Thomas Howard with his wife and two children. The family occupied a small but comfortable house atop a hill and in this quiet community, Jesse went on planning robberies. He sent the Ford boys out to scout several banks he was thinking of robbing.

The second James gang began to disintegrate quickly. Ed Miller was found dead, his body shot to pieces and dumped on a rural Missouri road. Jim Cummins later claimed that Jesse had murdered Miller after learning that Miller planned to turn himself in and inform on the rest of the gang. Wood Hite was then killed by Dick Liddell and Bob Ford over a split of the loot from the second Glendale train robbery at Blue Cut. Liddell, thinking that the Ford brothers intended to murder him, surrendered and confessed all he knew. His statements led to the arrest of Clarence Hite, who was tried and convicted of robbery and sent to prison for twenty-five years.

Only four active members of the James gang were now at large: Jesse, Frank, and the Ford brothers. Still, Jesse was undaunted and planned another robbery, summoning the Fords to his St. Joseph home on the morning of April 3, 1882. Zee James made breakfast for the three men and the two small James children were sent out to play in the back yard. Following the meal, Jesse and the Fords went into the small parlor to further plan the robbery of the Platte County bank. When Jesse glanced at a newspaper containing Dick Liddell's confession, Charlie Ford, according to his later statements, was suddenly gripped by fear that Jesse would learn of the Fords' secret meeting with Governor Crittenden. Bob Ford also became nervous, and later stated at James' inquest: "I knew then that I had placed my head in the lion's mouth. How could I safely remove it?"

James put the newspaper aside, stood up, walked to the window and looked outside to see his children playing. He then turned and spotted a picture that was hanging crooked on the wall. According to the Fords, he then removed two gun belts, one about his hips, another around his shoulders. Each belt contained two big Colts, four guns in all. James looped the gun belts around a chair. Why he took the belts off was never known. The Fords may have told this story to make their target all the more dangerous. Some claimed that Jesse wore no guns in the house at any time, at least not *four* weapons, especially in the company of men he trusted. Given his belief in his invulnerability, it is most likely that Jesse was never armed that morning.

The outlaw chief stood upon a small stool to reach the picture on the wall. As he adjusted the picture, Jesse exposed his back to the Fords. Robert pulled his pistol and aimed it squarely at the bandit's back. His hand shook so that he had to steady it with the other. At a distance of about four feet, he fired several times. James turned slightly to give his assassin a fierce look and then fell lifeless to the floor. Zee James rushed in from the kitchen, and kneeling at her husband's side, cradled his head in her arms, sobbing. Robert Ford sputtered that his gun went off by accident.

The Fords raced from the house. As Bob Ford ran down the hill toward the telegraph station he yelled loudly to anyone who would listen: "I killed him! I killed Jesse James! I killed him! I killed him! I killed Jesse James!" Only a few minutes later, he wired Governor Crittenden that the most wanted man in the U. S. was dead, that he, Bob Ford, had killed the infamous Jesse James. He immediately demanded his reward. The Ford Brothers were later charged with murder, but Crittenden, keeping his word, had the charges dropped and the reward money sent to the Fords.

The news of the bandit's murder was bannered in almost

every newspaper in the U.S., from New York to California, from Maine to Texas. "Jesse by Jehovah!" read the front page headline in the St. Joseph *Gazette*. "Goodbye, Jesse!" read the Kansas City *Journal*. The newspapers and the dime novelists, who had churned out endless copy on the outlaw for sixteen years lamented his passing, if only for commercial reasons. Almost immediately, the legend and lore of Jesse James began to be embellished so that within a few months, he was known as a hero. The ruthless killer and thief, the real Jesse James, was somehow forgotten and in his place sprang up a sterling, enviable Robin Hood.

The heavily bearded body of the outlaw was officially identified by his wife and by Mrs. Zee Samuels, his mother. The old woman appeared the next day at an inquest where the Ford Brothers and Dick Liddell testified. When Mrs. Samuels took the stand, she wept and said: "I live in Clay County and I am the mother of Jesse James ... My poor boy ... I have seen the body since my arrival and I have recognized it as that of my son Jesse ... The lady by my side is my daughter-in-law and the children hers ... He was a kind husband and son." Then she fixed her eyes on the Fords and Dick Liddell. She held up the stump of her arm and shook an empty sleeve in their direction, shouting: "Traitors!" The Fords and Liddell were hurried out of the courtroom by officers. Their lives were thought to be in great jeopardy, and Frank James would appear at any moment, leading a large band of men, with the single thought of killing the Fords.

Mrs. Samuels took Zee Mimms and her children back with her to the Clay County farm and with them the body of her son, which had been placed in a $500 coffin, an expensive casket for that day. The outlaw was buried on the Samuels farm and a white marble headstone was placed over the grave. It read:

Jesse Woodson James, shown dead after having been shot in the back by Bob Ford on April 3, 1882.

> Jesse W. James
> Died April 3, 1882
> Aged 34 years, 6 months, 28 days
> Murdered by a traitor and a coward
> Whose name is not worthy to
> appear here.

On October 5, 1882, five months after his brother's murder, Alexander Franklin James, last of the outlaw band, surrendered to Governor Crittenden. The 39-year-old bandit marched into the governor's office and took off his gun belt, placing it before Crittenden and saying: "Governor Crittenden, I want to hand over to you that which no living man except myself has been permitted to touch since 1861." The governor promised James protection and a fair trial. James was a celebrated prisoner and reporters flocked to interview him. One asked: "Why did you surrender? No one knew where you were hiding."

"What of that," James replied. "I was tired of an outlaw's life. I have been hunted for twenty-one years. I have literally lived in the saddle. I have never known a day of perfect peace. It was one long, anxious, inexorable, eternal vigil. When I slept it was literally in the midst of an arsenal. If I heard dogs bark more fiercely than usual, or the hooves of horses in a greater volume than usual, I stood to my arms. Have you an idea of what a man must endure who leads such a life? No, you cannot. No one can unless he lives it for himself."

Universal sympathy for Frank James and the James family was exhibited. The cowardly way the Ford brothers had killed Jesse almost assured Frank James an acquittal. After a number of long trials, that is exactly what he received. He returned to the Samuels farm and took up peaceful pursuits, working as a horse trainer and a racetrack starter. After the turn of the century, he appeared in a small Wild West show with his friend, Cole Younger, who, by then, had been released from prison. Frank James died in a small bedroom of the Samuels farmhouse on February 18, 1915.

Cole and Jim Younger were not released from the penitentiary at Stillwater, Minnesota, until July 10, 1901. Bob Younger had died in prison of pneumonia on September 16, 1889. Jim Younger fell in love with a young woman in St. Paul, but she rejected him when he asked her to marry him. Younger went to his hotel room and shot himself to death. Cole Younger returned to Lee's Summit, Missouri, where he lived a quiet life. He became a farmer and later appeared at

THE DAILY GRAPHIC

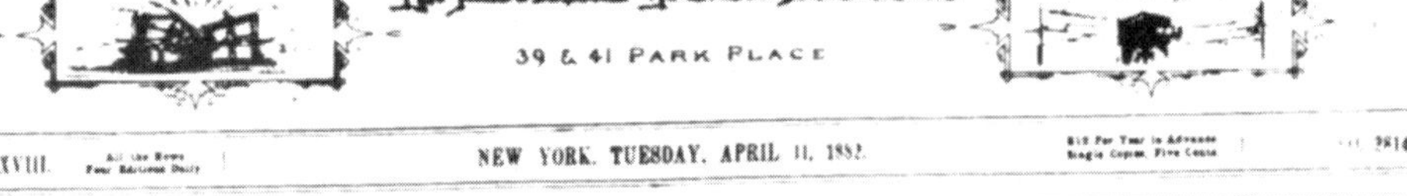

An Illustrated Evening Newspaper

39 & 41 Park Place

XXVIII. All the News Four Editions Daily | NEW YORK, TUESDAY, APRIL 11, 1882. | $12 Per Year in Advance Single Copies, Five Cents | 2814

An editorial cartoon shows how the public built a monument to Jesse James, glorified in death for American boys inspired to follow in his footsteps.

local fairs, sometimes with Frank James. As the two bandits aged, they gave lectures to Sunday school classes and at ladies tea parties, thundering their condemnation of the outlaw life. The tall and muscular Cole Younger was the last of the outlaw band to die, suffering a fatal heart attack on March 21, 1916.

The Ford brothers, following Jesse's death, enjoyed some brief notoriety, but were mostly shunned as "vile cowards." Charlie Ford was consumed by fear that Frank James or some of Jesse's other relatives would hunt him down and kill him. He was plagued by nightmares and became an insomniac. He finally committed suicide. Bob Ford moved west, traveling from town to town, opening up several saloons with the reward money he had received. He was shot to death in Creede, Colorado, a decade after he became the most infamous "traitor" in the U.S. by shooting Jesse James in the back. Ford's shooting of Jesse James was challenged by J. Frank Dalton, who appeared in the late 1940s to claim that he was Jesse James and that the man shot in 1882 in St. Joseph, Missouri, was an imposter. But it was generally agreed that Dalton was the impersonator and that the man buried in James' grave was indeed Jesse (as DNA tests in the 1980s and 1990s proved).

From the moment Jesse Woodson James was put into his grave, his life became a great fiction and he was lionized as a hearty pioneer, a brave son of the Middle Border, an embodiment of the spirit of adventuresome America. Fabulous tales were told of his kindliness and generosity. One abiding canard involved a widow woman who had given the James boys breakfast as they fled from a bank robbery. She informed her guests that she was about to lose her farm, that she did not have the money to pay the mortgage.

Jesse reportedly gave her the money and then hid as the land owner appeared and collected this sum from the woman, signing back the deed to the farm to her. Jesse then rode after the landlord and held him up, recouping his loan to the widow woman. Jesse was kind to children and chivalrous to women. Journalists of the day took pains to point out that he never robbed a woman in a bank, in a stagecoach, or on a train. They omitted the many murders he was known to have committed.

Most of these tales had no foundation, but generations of small boys were thrilled by these stories and Jesse James became their tarnished idol, much to the chagrin of lawmen and parents. A decade later, the Dalton Brothers tried to emulate the James boys and were destroyed at Coffeyville, Kansas. In the next century, the likes of John Dillinger and Charles Arthur "Pretty Boy" Floyd, who both admired Jesse James in their youth, not only followed his career closely, but copied his

Tyrone Power portrayed the famous bandit in the 1939 film, *Jesse James*, a beautifully filmed production that failed to realistically show the bandit as a cold-blooded killer.

bank robbing techniques. The bandit's myth deepened so that it became part of the core of the American character or psyche, one of dash and quick action, one of fearless adventure. A song created by an amateur composer came into existence almost overnight following the bandit's death and did much to perpetuate the legend of this strange and mysterious man whom few called friend and whom no one really knew. This melodramatic ballad captured the myth if not the reality of Jesse Woodson James:

Jesse James was a lad who killed many a man.
He robbed the Glendale train.
He stole from the rich and he gave to the poor,
He'd a hand and a heart and a brain.

(Chorus)
Jesse had a wife to mourn for his life,
Two children, they were brave,
But that dirty little coward that shot Mister Howard
Has laid poor Jesse in his grave.

It was Robert Ford, that dirty little coward,
I wonder how does he feel,
For he ate of Jesse's bread and he slept in Jesse's bed,
Then he laid Jesse James in his grave.

Jesse was a man, a friend to the poor.
He'd never seen a man suffer pain,
And with his brother Frank, he robbed the Gallatin bank
And stopped the Glendale train.

It was on a Wednesday night, the moon was shining bright.
He stopped the Glendale train.
And the people all did say for many miles away,
It was robbed by Frank and Jesse James.

It was on a Saturday night, Jesse was at home,
Talking to his family brave.
Robert Ford came along like a thief in the night,
And laid Jesse James in his grave.

The people held their breath when they heard of Jesse's death
And wondered how he ever came to die.
It was one of the gang called little Robert Ford,
Who shot Jesse James on the sly.

Jesse went to his rest with his hand on his breast,
The devil will be upon his knee.
He was born one day in the County of Shea
And he came from a solitary race.

This song was made by Billy Garshade,
As soon as the news did arrive,
He said there was no man with the law in his hand

Could take Jesse James when alive.

NED KELLY OF AUSTRALIA/1870s

Edward "Ned" Kelly, Australia's most notorious bandit.

Edward "Ned" Kelly (1854-1880), Australia's most infamous desperado, is often referred to by historians as the "last of the bushrangers." Kelly was wrongfully imprisoned as a young man, and he left prison bitter and vengeful. His hatred of police bordered on the maniacal, finally manifesting itself in the wanton murders of three police constables at Stringybark Creek in 1878. Kelly was the son of an Irish farmer and former convict who was transported from Belfast to the Tasmania pri-son colony in 1841. His father quickly earned a reputation as a mean-spirited horse thief and cattle rustler.

The body armor Ned Kelly fashioned and used in attacking police.

One of seven children, Kelly grew up on his father's farm near Melbourne. In his roughneck childhood, criminal activity was fairly normal. His father, his uncles, and their friends were frequently being arrested for rustling and horse theft and sent off to prison. Kelly himself was first imprisoned for assault and indecency for allegedly attacking a man named McCormack and later sending the man's wife a pair of bull testicles accompanied by an obscene note.

Kelly was convicted of the crime and sent to prison for six months, despite the fact that McCormack tried to withdraw the charges and another man confessed to the "prank." He returned from prison embittered and hardened, developing a reputation as a barroom brawler. Before long he was convicted of horse stealing and sentenced to three years in prison. When he was released after serving nearly the entire term, Kelly was determined to live a criminal life.

Ned Kelly demonstrated his body armor for his fellow bandits, but gang members were disinclined to use similar shields, which they believed cumbersome.

At this point, the 22-year-old Kelly, already a skilled marksman and rider, teamed up with his 16-year-old brother, Dan, and formed what would soon become the notorious Kelly Gang. In April 1878, Police Constable Fitzpatrick came to the Kelly farm to arrest Dan Kelly on charges of stealing livestock. The entire family joined in the battle against the single constable. Family members, including the Kelly women, fought Fitzpatrick off and he left wounded and without his man.

When arrest warrants were subsequently issued for Ned and Dan, they fled to the bush, where they were joined by two other young men, Joe Byrne and Steve Hart. (Joe Byrne, a young, aspiring poet wrote the first popular ballads celebrating the Kelly Gang's adventures.) In the meantime, Mrs. Kelly and the other members of the family were arrested, convicted, and sent to prison for their parts in the attack on Constable Fitzpatrick. Mrs. Kelly was sentenced to three years for hitting the officer over the head with a shovel.

In October 1878, a £100 bounty was offered for the arrest of the Kelly gang. Disguised as gold prospectors, Constables Scanlon, Lonigan, Kennedy, and McIntyre set out across the

Wombat Ranges to bring the bandits to justice. Armed with Remington .44s, they were under constant surveillance by Kelly. Finally Kelly and his gang ambushed the officers.

Two of the four police officers were killed in the shoot-out and a third was killed later. Only McIntyre escaped with his life. The ambush made the Kelly Gang the talk of Victoria, and a special Felon's Apprehension Act was passed in the state parliament in response to the attack on the constables. Additionally, the bounty on the gang was increased to £2,000, then a staggering sum.

Ned Kelly is shown battling Australian police while wearing his body armor in 1880; twenty-five bullets bounced off the crude iron shield, but he was captured after falling to the ground when shot several times in his unprotected legs.

For the next few months the gang rampaged through the area. They managed to evade capture because they were intimately familiar with the countryside and also because they received continual information regarding the whereabouts of the police from their many sympathizers. On December 9, 1878, the police received a tip that the gang was to be in a particular location. While they waited for Kelly and his men to show up, Kelly and his cohorts were actually 100 miles away at Euroa.

There the gang took twenty prisoners while they raided the bank and made off with £2,000. On February 10, 1879, the Kellys arrived in Jerilderie, New South Wales, where they took thirty people hostage in a local hotel. Police arrived and attempted to capture the gang, but while the siege continued, the bandits robbed the local bank of £2,141 before making a clean getaway.

Criticism against the police intensified after this episode and the rewards offered for the capture of the Kelly Gang increased. However, the police were again foiled in their attempts to stop the gang. When they attempted to invoke the Felon's Apprehension Act to arrest the gang's sympathizers they discovered that many of their supporters were women and public opinion prevented them from being arrested.

The Kelly gang kept a low profile until June 1880 when they took some plowshares from some farms in the countryside. On June 26, 1880, at Beechworth, Joe Byrne murdered a former gang member, Aaron Sherritt, who had turned informant. Sherritt's murder was an intentional ploy to draw the police posses into the open. By this time, Kelly had become determined to shoot it out with the constables or perish. Just outside of Glenrowan, Kelly forced two railroad workers to remove a section of track so that the train carrying the police superintendent would crash.

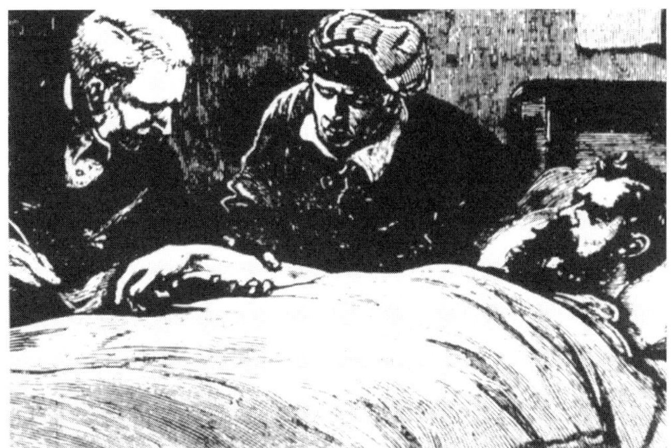

Kelly is shown recovering from his wounds in a Melbourne hospital. He was later condemned to death for his many robberies and murders and hanged on November 11, 1880, at age twenty-four.

At Glenrowan Kelly and his men rounded up sixty-two hostages and locked them inside a hotel owned and operated by a sympathetic Englishwoman named Ann Jones. Kelly's plan probably would have worked except that a schoolteacher slipped out of town and warned the approaching train of the danger. The police, once alerted, advanced on the town and surrounded the hotel. The Kelly brothers, Byrne, and Hart held them at bay for nearly seven hours in a protracted gun battle. Dan Kelly and Hart poisoned themselves and Joe Byrne died from gunshot wounds.

During the siege Ned escaped into the bush where he donned a suit of armor he had earlier constructed from plough moldboards. He emerged from the bush and slowly advanced on the police line, garbed in his ninety-two pounds of armor. The police scarcely knew what to think of this strange apparition. They fired on Kelly, but he continued to advance, firing two pistols at the officers.

Twenty-five bullets struck Kelly's armor. The armor saved his life, but he was finally wounded in the legs and fell to the ground. When asked why he decided to confront the police rather than running, Kelly replied, "A man gets tired of being hunted like a dog ... I wanted to see the thing end."

The last of the bushrangers was taken to Melbourne, where he was tried and convicted of robbery and murder. Kelly was only twenty-four years old when he was hanged on November 11, 1880, after stoically remarking: "It has come to this. Such is life." Kelly's spectacular criminal career brought about an investigation by the Royal Commission, which produced a report in 1881 that made many recommendations about police administration, equipment, and training of the police force in Victoria. In the report, Ned Kelly, whose capture alone was estimated to have cost the police approximately £115,000, was described as a "quiet, self-possessed man with a fanatical hatred of the police."

BUTCH CASSIDY AND THE WILD BUNCH/ 1890s-1900s

Butch Cassidy (Robert Leroy Parker; AKA: George Cassidy, William T. Phillips, Ingerfield, Lowe Maxwell; 1866-c.1908) and his Wild Bunch members were the last of the old time western bank and train robbers, a motley group of outlaws with distinctive personalities and a flair for the flamboyant. Cassidy was no mean-minded desperado, but a fun-loving, easygoing bandit who preferred to use his brains rather than his six-gun. He was backed up in most of his gun play by the lightning fast-draw artist, the Sundance Kid. His gang members included Will Carver, addicted to reading press notices about the gang; Ben Kilpatrick, the towering bandit known as the Tall Texan; and the most deadly of the group, Harvey Logan, who was also known as Kid Curry, a dead-eyed killer who vowed he would never be taken alive by the law and kept his word.

Born Robert Leroy Parker in Beaver, Utah, on Apr. 13, 1866, Cassidy was one of ten children and had no formal education. He became a cowboy while still in his teens when he met outlaw Mike Cassidy, adopting Cassidy's name after he joined him in rustling cattle in Utah and Colorado. Cassidy taught Butch how to shoot so that he was able to hit a playing card dead center at fifty paces and his draw was much faster than historians later described. Mike Cassidy led a small band of robbers and rustlers but, after he shot a Wyoming rancher, he disappeared. Butch Cassidy took over the gang.

Butch Cassidy (George Leroy Parker), an affable robber who, with his Wild Bunch bandits, made up the last outlaw band of the Old West.

The gang's hideout was at Robber's Roost, located in the southwest corner of Utah, a rough, mountainous area which was difficult to find, even by the outlaws who returned again and again to the rocky haven. In early 1887, Cassidy met Bill and Tom McCarty, hard-riding outlaws who headed up their own gang, which included Matt Warner (real name Willard

Christiansen), Tom "Peep" O'Day, Silver Tip (Bill Wall), Gunplay Maxwell, and Indian Ed Newcomb.

When the McCarty boys suggested Cassidy join them in a train robbery, the apprentice outlaw happily agreed. On November 3, 1887 Cassidy and the McCartys stopped the Denver and Rio Grande express near Grand Junction, Colorado. The stubborn express guard refused to open the safe in the mail car and Bill McCarty put a six-gun to his head. "Should we kill him?" he asked.

"Let's vote," Cassidy said.

The gang members voted not to kill the guard and the train moved off leaving the bandits with not a dime in loot. Cassidy became disheartened with train robbery and went back to rustling and occasional work as a cowboy or a miner in the local Colorado and Utah mines. It was almost a year and a half before Cassidy agreed to once more accompany the McCartys on another raid. This time the gang picked out the First National Bank of Denver, robbing it of $20,000 on March 30, 1889. Tom McCarty approached the bank president that day and, expressing his sense of macabre humor, stated: "Excuse me, sir, but I just overheard a plot to rob this bank."

The bank president trembled so that he appeared to be undergoing an apoplectic fit, then managed to say: "Lord! How did you learn of this plot?"

"I planned it," McCarty said, pulling his six-gun. "Put up your hands."

Four men, Cassidy, Tom and Bill McCarty, and Matt Warner rode out of Denver with $5,000 each from the robbery, a fortune for those days. Warner immediately opened a saloon. Cassidy and the McCartys, however, decided to raid another bank and, on June 24, 1889, robbed the

Butch Cassidy at the time he worked as a cowboy, robbing banks on the side; he took the name Butch Cassidy from an old-time outlaw.

A famous photo shows the leaders of the Wild Bunch; (standing, left to right) William "News" Carver, Harvey "Kid Curry" Logan; (sitting, left to right) Harry "The Sundance Kid" Longbaugh (or Longabaugh), Ben "The Tall Texan" Kilpatrick, and Butch Cassidy.

The express car blown to pieces during the train robbery committed by Cassidy and others at Wilcox, Wyoming, on June 2, 1899; the guard, a man named Woodcock, defied the gang and was almost killed when Cassidy set off the dynamite, which had been placed at the door of the car.

bank of Telluride, Colorado, taking $10,500. Like the bank robbery in Denver, the gang never fired a shot. They merely trained guns on the bank employee, emptied the tellers' cages and looted the opened vault, then rode quietly out of town. Lawmen, however, formed huge posses and conducted wide and long searches for the bandits. This caused Cassidy and the others to go into hiding.

Cassidy decided to follow the straight and narrow path and he took several jobs with ranches as a cowboy. He even worked as a butcher in Rock Springs, Wyoming, which is where he earned his sobriquet "Butch." But such legitimate pursuits never worked out for Cassidy. A drunk picked a fight with him, while he was serving customers and Cassidy knocked the man cold which caused his arrest. He was convicted of disturbing the peace and served a short term in the local jail. When released, Cassidy vowed he would never again work for a living.

Cassidy and Al Hainer, another cowboy, then began an extortion racket, selling Colorado ranchers protection, telling them that they would make sure that cattle was not rustled nor any of their property damaged by fire or other man-made hazards. Cassidy and Hainer were the man-made hazards, of course, and any rancher who did not pay monthly protection fees had his cattle rustled by Cassidy and Hainer. Complaining cattlemen caused Wyoming lawmen John Chapman and Bob Calverly to hunt Cassidy and Hainer down to their cabin hideout near Auburn, Wyoming.

The lawmen crept up on Hainer as he was tending to the horses, wrestled him to the ground and tied him to a tree. Calverly then entered the cabin, his six-gun drawn. As soon as Cassidy spotted him he leaped for his two six-guns and gun belt, which were on a chair. Calverly fired four shots, one of which creased Cassidy's scalp and knocked him unconscious. Both men were quickly tried for extortion, sentenced to two years, and sent to the penitentiary at Rawlins, Wyoming, on July 15, 1894. The man who had sworn out the arrests for Cassidy and Hainer, rancher Otto Franc, of the Big Horn Basin, was mysteriously murdered in 1903. Cassidy was released on January 19, 1896, and immediately headed for a place called Hole-in-the-Wall, the last great hideout of the western outlaws. He had learned of this place behind the walls of the penitentiary and he resolved to put together the last super-bandit gang.

Hole-in-the-Wall was located in Colorado, more of a fortress than Cassidy's old Utah haven, Robber's Roost. At Hole-in-the-Wall, Cassidy was welcomed by the notorious Logan brothers, Harvey and Lonnie. Harvey Logan was the worst killer of the Wild Bunch, a brooding, small-bodied man with piercing black eyes, who had taken the name of Kid Curry, after another bandit, Big Nose George Curry. Cassidy also met

The posse that set out after Butch Cassidy and the Wild Bunch after the train robbery at Tipton, Wyoming on August 29, 1900; (identified by numbers, left to right) 1) George Hiatt; 2) T. T. Kelliher; 3) Joe Lefors, the lawman the Wild Bunch most feared; 4) H. Davis; 5) Si Funk; 6) Jeff Carr.

such gunmen and outlaws as Bob Meeks and William Ellsworth "Elzy" (or "Elza") Lay. Cassidy talked long and hard to these men about the mistakes he and others had made which resulted in imprisonment or death. He talked about how his friend Bill McCarty and another McCarty brother, Fred, had been shot to pieces in Delta, Colorado, on September 27, 1893, when they attempted to rob the bank there and how Matt Warner had been captured and sent to prison for a long prison term. (Warner would later reform and lecture against crime, dying in 1937.)

Cassidy warned his fellow bandits that it was no good to merely ride into a town and rob the bank, unless the town was scouted and it was learned whether or not a local vigilante group existed, or how strong the local sheriff's force was, how many deputies were in that town, and chiefly, how much money was really in the bank. Usually, he pointed out, such information could be easily learned by merely visiting the bank in advance and asking a few questions of its employees.

On August 13, 1896, Cassidy led Bob Meeks and Elzy Lay to the Montpelier Bank, which they successfully robbed of $7,165. Butch had scouted this bank some weeks ahead of the robbery, learning that money would be transferred to this bank a few days before he raided it. Next, Cassidy, with Elzy Lay and Joe Walker, rode to the large mining camp at Castle Gate, Utah, on April 21, 1897, a camp where Butch had once worked as a miner. He knew when payrolls were received and paid and he and his fellow bandits arrived just in time to scoop up $8,000. Before the outlaws fled, Cassidy had Walker cut the telegraph wire so that the local lawmen could not be warned.

Cassidy then rode to a New Mexico ranch with Lay where the two of them took jobs as cowboys. This was part of Butch's plans. He no longer drew attention to himself by freely spending the money he had robbed. He would put up a good "front" by pretending to work while posses were searching for shiftless thieves. Cassidy and Lay left the ranch in early June, rode back to Hole-in-the-Wall and gathered more men, Harvey Logan, Walt Putney, Tom "Peep" O'Day, and Indian Billy Roberts. These men then rode to Belle Fourche, South Dakota, on June 27, 1897, and robbed the bank there, taking about $5,000.

On May 13, 1898, Joe Walker was killed with another man by a posse seeking cattle rustlers near Thompson, Utah. When the two bodies were brought in, the entire town of Thompson turned out to cheer, thinking that the other man was the dreaded Butch Cassidy, but the corpse was that of Johnny Herring, a lesser-known outlaw who bore some resemblance to Butch. Cassidy was far from dead. In fact, he had, by then, carefully planned a train robbery at Wilcox, Wyoming, on June 2, 1899.

This robbery was conducted by a gang consisting of

Hole in the Wall, a natural fortress surrounded by mountains in Wyoming, where Cassidy and the Wild Bunch routinely took refuge.

Cassidy, George "Flatnose" Curry, Elzy Lay, Harvey Logan, Lonny Logan, Ben Kilpatrick, the Sundance Kid (Harry Longbaugh or Longabaugh), and Ben Beeson. The bandits stopped the Union Pacific's Overland Flyer on a small trestle which was barricaded. When the train came to a halt, Cassidy ordered the engineer, W. R. Jones, to uncouple the express car. He refused and Harvey Logan pistol-whipped the engineer. He still refused and Lay took the controls in the engine's cab and forced the train forward.

Just as the train crossed the trestle the small bridge blew up. Cassidy and his men had forgotten a small charge of dynamite they had placed there. Once the train was some distance from the smashed trestle, the gang stood outside the express car and called out to the guard inside, a man who identified himself as Woodcock. He was ordered to open the express car door and come out.

"Come in and get me!" the defiant guard shouted to the bandits. A charge of dynamite was placed next to the door and the fuse lighted. The bandits dove into a nearby ditch and the resulting explosion tore the express car in half, sending Woodcock hurling outward. He was injured but alive. Harvey Logan ran up to the stubborn guard, pulling his six-gun and putting this next to the man's head. "This damned fellow is going to hell!" Logan shouted.

Cassidy ran up to him and brushed his gun aside, saying: "Now, Harvey, a man with that kind of nerve deserves not to be shot." Meanwhile the rest of the bandits ran about wildly, picking up more than $30,000 in bank notes and securities which had been blown every which way. This spectacular raid caused the Union Pacific to enlist the Pinkerton Detective Agency, which sent scores of agents after the outlaws. Lawmen also, in dozens of posses led by such famous manhunters

The beautiful and mysterious Etta Place, who was Harry Longbaugh's sweetheart and accompanied him to South America, where they joined Cassidy.

as Charles Siringo and N. K. Boswell, were on the trail of the gang.

Cassidy decided that the best way for the outlaws to escape was for the Wild Bunch to split up. He, the Sundance Kid, who had become Cassidy's most loyal companion, and Ben Kilpatrick rode toward Hole-in-the-Wall while Logan, Curry, and Lay took a more circuitous route and were cornered by a large posse near Teapot Creek, Wyoming.

The outlaws took refuge behind boulders while several possemen, including Sheriff Joe Hazen, charged their position. Hazen was shot off his horse, dead, by the sharpshooting Harvey Logan. The outlaws then mounted their horses and, blazing away with their six-guns, shot their way through the ranks of the disorganized posse. Logan and Curry rode on alone while Lay joined notorious bandits, Thomas "Black Jack" Ketchum and G. W. Franks, and held up a Colorado Southern train on July 11, 1899, at Twin Mountains, New

Mexico, stealing $30,000.

The next day, the three bandits were surrounded at Turkey Creek Canyon, New Mexico, by a determined posse. A gunfight ensued and Lay was wounded twice and Ketchum once. The outlaws shot and killed Sheriff Edward Farr, Tom Smith, and W. H. Love before escaping. Ketchum was later captured and hanged for train robbery in a gruesome execution. (Ketchum was hanged on April 25, 1901 at Clayton, New Mexico, telling the hangman to "let her rip!" before going through the trap; the knot about his neck, however was inexpertly fixed and during the drop, Ketchum's head was separated from his body). Lay was trapped by lawmen in August 1899 and was subdued after a desperate fight; he was sent to the New Mexico Territorial Prison on October 10, 1899, being given a life term. He would be paroled in 1906 and reform, living until 1934.

A sketch indicates where Butch Cassidy and Harry "The Sundance Kid" Longbaugh reportedly died (shown in the hut at top left) after a shootout with Bolivian troops in San Vicente in 1908. Many tales claimed that Cassidy or both outlaws escaped and lived into old age.

Despite losing some of his best riders, Cassidy put together another band of outlaws for another train raid. These bandits included Harvey Logan, who had managed to ride through several posses and return to Hole-in-the-Wall following the wild Wilcox robbery, the Sundance Kid, Ben Beeson, Ben Kilpatrick, and Laura Bullion, the Tall Texan's girlfriend. They stopped the Union Pacific's Train Number 3 at Tipton, Wyoming, on August 29, 1900.

Ironically, the express guard, Woodcock, was in the mail car and he again refused to open the door to the bandits. Butch shook his head in disgust and then said to the engineer: "You tell that iron-headed Woodcock that if he doesn't open the door *this* time, we're going to blow up him and the whole damned car sky high!" When the engineer pleaded with Woodcock, the plucky guard finally relented and threw open the door. The bandits blew open the safe and took more than $50,000, the largest haul taken by the gang up to that time.

Joe Lefors, one of the most feared lawmen of the era, was then assigned by the Union Pacific to track down Cassidy and his gang at all costs. He wore out fifty men and twice as many horses chasing the Wild Bunch across Wyoming, but lost them when they slipped into their mountainous hideout, Hole-in-the-Wall. The gang rode out again to strike the bank at Winnemucca, Nevada, taking $30,000 on September 19, 1900. Next the gang rode all the way to Wagner, Montana, where Cassidy, Logan, Kilpatrick, the Sundance Kid, and Deaf Charley Hanks stopped the Great Northern Flyer on July 3, 1901. (The Sundance Kid had robbed a train near this spot almost ten years earlier.)

Two of the men boarded the train, and as the train got up steam, Logan climbed into the engineer's cab by crawling over the coal tender, dropping down with two six-guns in his hands and ordering the engineer to stop the train. The Sundance Kid and Ben Kilpatrick raced through the passenger cars, firing their six-guns into the ceiling and shouting to the startled passengers: "Keep your heads inside the car!"

When the train came to a small trestle, it ground to a stop where Cassidy and Hanks were waiting. Cassidy planted a charge of dynamite beneath the Adams Express car and blew off its side. More than $40,000 was taken from the safe, but most of it was in unsigned bank notes. This never bothered the Wild Bunch. Bill Carver or someone else with good penmanship merely signed the notes and these were quickly cashed or passed. During this holdup, Laura Bullion was present, tending to the horses.

Laura Bullion was Ben Kilpatrick's girl, although she had been a mistress to many an outlaw before him. Following the Wagner robbery, the Wild Bunch split up for the last time. Ben Kilpatrick and Laura Bullion rode east and were later arrested in Memphis with part of the loot taken from the Wagner robbery. Both were given long prison terms. When Kilpatrick was released in 1912, he attempted another train robbery and was killed by an aggressive express car guard, who crushed the Tall Texan's skull with a large wooden mallet. Harvey Logan was later trapped by a posse and, rather than be taken captive, sent a bullet into his brain.

The fate of Butch Cassidy and the Sundance Kid after that has been much in debate. It is known that Cassidy and Sundance rode to Fort Worth, Texas, to relax in Fannie Porter's luxurious brothel. The Sundance Kid then took up with a bored teacher and housewife, Etta Place, a beautiful statuesque brunette, who longed for adventure and left with Cassidy and Sundance, when they decided that the West was too "hot" for them, all three going first to New York to stay in the finest hotels, eat in the best restaurants, and have their photos taken

Paul Newman and Robert Redford are shown in the shootout at San Vicente, Bolivia, in the memorable 1969 film, *Butch Cassidy and the Sundance Kid*, which faithfully followed the facts and appropriately closed with an ambiguous ending.

while wearing evening attire.

The trio then traveled to Bolivia where they hid out by taking jobs as miners for the American-owned Concordia Tin Mine. While living in employee quarters (Sundance and Etta living as man and wife), the three went off on several raids. They reportedly took a vacation to Argentina and robbed a bank in Mercedes, San Luis Province, in 1906. Once more in Bolivia, Etta decided to leave the outlaws and returned to the U. S., where she changed her name and drifted into oblivion. Butch and Sundance, however, continued their errant ways.

In Spring 1908 they robbed a Bolivian payroll in Aramayo and were trapped in the small village of San Vincente by a regiment of troops searching for the "gringo" bandits. After a fierce gun battle in which Cassidy and Sundance killed a number of troopers, the bandits were finally killed, shot full of holes. A variation of this report has Cassidy wounded, looking upon his dead friend, and, rather than falling into the hands of the Bolivian soldiers, he put his six-gun to his temple and pulled the trigger.

Another story has it that only Sundance was killed in the murderous crossfire and that he gave his money belt and a letter to his best friend Cassidy, telling him to give these items to Etta Place, whom he had married. Cassidy reportedly watched the mortally wounded Sundance die and then, under the cover of darkness, escaped, returning to the U.S. There are many unsupported stories claiming that Cassidy returned to his birthplace of Circleville, Utah, and changed his name, living out his life there and dying in 1929. Another story held that he moved to Johnnie, Nevada, and lived there until 1937, running, of all things, a western curiosity shop. Still another tale insists that the celebrated outlaw survived until 1943 or 1944, dying in either California or Washington.

FRANCE'S BONNOT GANG/1910s

Jules Joseph Bonnot had been one of the most daring racecar drivers in the early era of autos. He turned anarchist about 1911 and then decided to form a gang of thieves who would use cars for fast getaways, Bonnot being the first to cmploy the motorized escape in Europe. (Henry Starr was the first American bandit to use the car in a robbery in the U.S., see entry). On December 21, 1911, Bonnot and others waylaid a bank messenger named Gaby of the Societé Générale in Paris' Rue Ordener, shooting him and taking a pouch stuffed with a half million francs, then the equivalent of £25,000 or $200,000, an enormous haul that stunned the French police.

After escaping in a Delaunay-Belleville car, the bandits then raided an arsenal on the Grand Boulevard, taking scores of rifles, revolvers, and many boxes of ammunition. As usual, the bandits made their escape in a car driven by race driver and gang leader Bonnot. Following several more robberies where great sums were taken, more than ten thousand reward posters for the gang were distributed throughout Paris and neighboring cities. Prime Minister Raymond Poincaré stated: "Bonnot must be brought to justice by whatever means and at whatever cost."

Jules Joseph Bonnot, race-car driver and the first French bandit to use an auto when robbing banks.

To capture the elusive bandits, the French Garde Mobile, or Flying Squad, also employing cars, were assigned to track down the murderous band. Bonnot, meanwhile, robbed a factory and shot several persons, then motored to Belgium. When Bonnot and his men drove back into Paris, a policeman recognized the Dion-Bouton car in which they were riding and leaped onto the running board as the car sped along. Bonnot and his men fired three bullets into his chest, killing him. The French bandit leader seemed to be emulating the tactics of the American western bandits, except that he used cars instead of horses to make his escapes.

Police at the time were aided by author H. Ashton-Wolfe, who ironically specialized in penny dreadful-type books of fanciful tales that claimed to report about real criminals. Ashton-Wolfe had actually employed Bonnot as a chauffeur, and he had had a photo taken of himself in the car and Bonnot at the wheel. This photo was the first to be used in identifying the bandit chieftain.

Since his car had now been identified, Bonnot fielded about for another fast auto and decided to obtain the fast new touring car owned by the Marquis de Roug. The gang scouted the routes driven by the Marquis, a well-known sporting figure, and, in March 1912, drove their car into the path of the auto driven by the Marquis' chauffeur. They brutally shot the Marquis and the chauffeur to death and threw their bodies into a ditch, abandoning the Dion-Bouton for the touring car. Bonnot, Francois Callemin, and others then drove to Chantilly, where they raided the local bank, firing rifles as they entered, killing one clerk and injuring two others. The bandits leaped over the tellers cages and scooped up the money in the drawers, a technique that John Dillinger and others would duplicate in the U. S. two decades later.

Bonnot henchman Pierre Garnier taunted police and died in a gun battle with officers in 1913

Outside the bank, Callemin and others fired their rifles in the air to frighten off the citizens, who came running toward the bank at the sound of the first gunfire. The scene was something out of the American West a half century earlier. With Bonnot and his men rushing from the bank, those bandits outside the bank fired wildly into the air and at scurrying citizens. Then the bandits leaped into the touring car and Bonnot jerked the car forward as if he were in a race, speeding out of town. A policeman fired at the retreating car, wounding Callemin, but this only served to make the bandit angry and he fired a random shot at a motorist traveling in the opposite direction.

The Sureté Nationale, one of France's four police forces, made an all-out effort to capture the ruthless bandits, assigning hundreds of its men to track down Bonnot. Poincaré announced that Bonnot was "the most dangerous criminal of this century, or the last." A short time later, Bonnot and his men struck again, this time raiding the ancient fortress of Vincennes, where they shot one guard and wounded others while looting the arsenal of guns and ammunition.

The gang was now hunted everywhere in France, police and even military units on the trail of its members. Bonnot was all bravado and threatened to kill anyone who dared to get near him or his men. One of his henchmen, Pierre Garnier, wrote challenging letters to the Sureté. One missive said: "I know that you will get the better of me in the long run. All the strength is on your side. But I will make you pay for it dearly."

In March 1913 Bonnot's top aide, Callemin, was arrested as he peddled down a Paris street on a bicycle. As he was dragged away, the anarchist robber-murderer screamed: "I was ready for you! But you had all the luck! You will find that my three revolvers are all loaded!" A few days later, one of the gang members contacted police and told them that they could find Bonnot in his hideout at Choisy-le-Roi, adding: "I hope you get the skunk! He killed one of my best friends." More than 200 policemen and soldiers closed in on the bandit chief's lair, using carts filled with hay and mattresses to approach the house.

As the policemen and troopers moved forward, Bonnot began firing at them, dozens of rounds that killed one man and wounded many others. He ran from window to window firing and screaming oaths, a lethal maniac. The police and troops fired back and the gun battle raged for more than six hours until there was no more gunfire from the house. Cautiously, police crept forward, entered the house and climbed

Jules Bonnot is shown as a chauffeur at the wheel of an electric Brougham before he began his bank robberies; the man in the back seat is crime writer H. Ashton Wolfe.

Police assemble next to a large hay cart which they used as a shield in attacking Bonnot's rural hideout; they found the bandit dead after a prolonged battle.

the stairs. They found Bonnot on the floor, hit by four bullets, bleeding to death. He was in a half coma and with his dying breath he cursed the officers staring down at him. Nailed to a wall was a letter he had written during the gun battle. It read: "I am famous. My name is trumpeted to the four corners of the globe and the publicity given to my humble person must make all those people jealous who try in vain to get into the papers. As far as I am concerned, I could well have done without it."

Bonnot added that certain persons who had harbored him were innocent of his crimes. Police inspecting the bandit's dead body soon realized that Bonnot had inflicted the wound that killed him, committing suicide before he could be taken into custody. Several other gang members chose the same inglorious exit, including a gang member named Carouy who drank prussic acid. Callemin, Soudy, and Monier were tried for murder, found guilty, and sentenced to the guillotine. They were all beheaded on April 21, 1913. Garnier and another gang member shot it out with police on May 14, 1913, and were killed. The rest of the gang members were quickly rounded up and given long prison terms. It was the end of Bonnot's reign of robbery and terror.

THE "INVINCIBLE" GERALD CHAPMAN/ 1920s

Brooklyn-born Gerald Chapman (AKA: G. Vincent Caldwell, Waldo W. Miller; 1890-1926) would have remained an obscure petty crook had it not been for a prison education that inspired him to commit the infamous robberies that would bring him wealth and an early death. Before he was ten, Chapman was an accomplished pickpocket and sneak thief. He was often sent to reformatories, but he was just as quickly paroled. When he was sent to New York's House of Refuge in 1904 at the age of fourteen, the judge remarked that he was a likely candidate for the electric chair, a prophetic remark as it later turned out.

In 1908 Chapman, at eighteen, was sent to Sing Sing Prison for the first time, after being convicted of a robbery. He was later transferred to Auburn Prison, where he met his new cell mate and future mentor, a confirmed professional thief from Denmark named Ivan Dahl von Teller, who was known in the U.S. as George "Dutch" Anderson.

Anderson, who was highly educated, having attended the European universities at Heidelberg and Uppsala. He spoke five languages fluently, and so impressed Chapman that the youth began to read voraciously, improving his manners and affecting a British accent. Anderson taught his protegé the use of a "good front" to throw off suspicion, and under which criminal pursuits were best achieved. Anderson tried to convince Chapman that nonviolent crimes such as swindling and embezzlement, the crimes of which Anderson had been convicted, were preferable to armed robbery, where murder was often part and parcel.

When Chapman was released, however, he went back to the kind of crime he understood best and committed several robberies. With his loot, Chapman purchased expensive clothes, donned a homburg, and carried a walking cane, appearing to be every inch a gentleman. He rented an expensive Manhattan apartment and began dining in better restaurants. After committing another robbery in 1912, Chapman was caught and sent back to Sing Sing. Here he met another habitual criminal, Charles Loeber, who believed that the only way to obtain fast money was with a gun.

In 1919, Chapman, Loeber, and Anderson were all paroled. At first, Chapman followed Anderson's advice, accompanying the con man through the Midwest where several quick swindles netted the pair more than $100,000. Chapman and Anderson moved back to New York and took a lavish apartment in Gramercy Park. Here, as they planned several involved confidence games, Loeber arrived and convinced Chapman to rob a mail truck on Wall Street.

Loeber explained that he had been watching these unguarded mail trucks make pickups along Wall Street. "Inside of these trucks," Loeber announced, "are millions of dollars in money orders, securities, checks, and bonds." Chapman agreed

Gerald Champman, center, one of the most daring American bandits of the 1920s, who thought he could achieve the impossible and almost did.

Composite photos show disguises used by Chapman's dedicated accomplice, George "Dutch" Anderson, who turned from confidence games to robbery.

Frank Havernack (inset) is shown with the mail truck he drove when Chapman and others robbed it of more than $1 million worth of registered mail on October 14, 1921.

son and Loeber opened the back doors of the truck and climbed inside, rummaging through the thirty-three regular mail sacks to find five sacks of registered mail, which they dragged to the Cleveland and tossed into the back seat. Within minutes the robbers roared off on Leonard Street. Once in their hideout, they were amazed to discover that they had stolen $1,424,129, the largest mail theft in U. S. history to that date. Only $27,000 in cash was present, however, the rest being securities which the gang later fenced for 40¢ on the dollar. The return was still staggering.

After fencing hundreds of thousands of dollars in securities through Anderson's Midwest contacts, Chapman and Anderson, with Loeber acting as their butler and chauffeur, moved back to Gramercy Park. Here they lived like drunken millionaires, spending more than $1,000 a day on lavish parties, new cars, and tall blonde chorus girls from the Follies.

The Leonard Street Mail Robbery, as it came to be known, caused a sensation in the press and alarmed federal and New York law enforcement officials. Heavily armed guards were assigned to guard the mail trucks, and an intensive manhunt for the robbers ensued, but their identities could not be determined. A few months later the gang again struck, taking more than $70,000 in money orders from an American Express office in Niagara Falls.

The bandits continued their high living in Gramercy Park, but Loeber proved to be their undoing. He did not have the same contacts as Anderson and Chapman had in fencing his portion of the stolen securities taken in the Leonard Street Robbery. Instead, Loeber tried to fence these highly publicized securities with some Broadway touts and was turned in to the police. Once under arrest, Loeber, to earn a lesser sentence, informed on his associates.

to rob one of these trucks and, on October 14, 1921, Chapman, Loeber, and a reluctant Anderson waited in a stolen Cleveland car. A mail truck driven by Frank Havernack shortly appeared, moving along Wall Street.

The Cleveland suddenly shot forward when the truck passed and raced alongside the truck, swerving in front of it, suddenly causing Havernack to brake his vehicle. As the truck stopped, Chapman leaped on its running board, holding a pistol in his hand, which he shoved into Havernack's stomach. "Pull over and don't make any noise," the bandit ordered. Havernack brought the truck to a full stop.

While Chapman held him prisoner, placing a mail sack over the driver's head and tying him with draw-ropes, Ander-

Both Chapman and Anderson were arrested.

Chapman, while awaiting trial in New York, tried to escape jail by climbing along a 75-foot ledge to freedom but was caught in the act. The bold escape attempt, coupled with the daring mail robbery, caused the tabloid newspapers of the day to make Gerald Chapman into a modern-day Robin Hood, a spectacular criminal with amazing abilities to commit holdups and make escapes. Chapman delightedly posed for newspaper photographers, dressed in his imported tailor-made suits, puffing on a cigar and exuding a nonchalant air. He soon came to believe that he was a special kind of crook, one who could never be held long in any prison.

Following a quick trial and conviction, Chapman and

Anderson were sent to the federal penitentiary at Atlanta to begin serving twenty-five-year prison sentences. Chapman arrogantly informed the warden at Atlanta that he would escape, that no prison could hold a man like him. "The publicity you have acquired recently has gone to your head, Chapman," the warden told him. "You won't be getting out of Atlanta until you've either served your time or if you die inside these walls." Chapman merely smirked.

Then, once in his cell, Chapman quickly swallowed a full bottle of disinfectant, which made him violently ill and caused him to be removed to the prison hospital. Once there, he knocked a guard unconscious and, with several bed sheets tied together, managed to lower himself from a hospital window to the yard, then climbed over the wall with a handmade rope-ladder. His escape made national headlines, but he was captured two days later when police cornered him. Rather than surrender, Chapman shot it out and was wounded three times before being dragged back to Atlanta.

Undaunted, the determined Chapman recovered from his wounds and then made another escape, again employing bed sheets and ropes to get over the prison walls. Some weeks later, Anderson, who also escaped Atlanta by tunneling his way out, joined Chapman. The two began committing a series of burglaries and robberies from Boston to Savannah. In New Britain, Connecticut, the pair robbed a large department store but made two mistakes. The first was to take along a small-time hoodlum named Walter Shean, and the second and most important error was to shoot a policeman, Officer John Skelly, who interrupted the pair while they were cracking the safe on October 12, 1924. Chapman and Anderson made good their escape, but Shean was found standing next to a Lincoln auto, waiting for the pair to show up when police surrounded him. He boasted to police that the robbery had been masterminded by "my pal, Gerald Chapman."

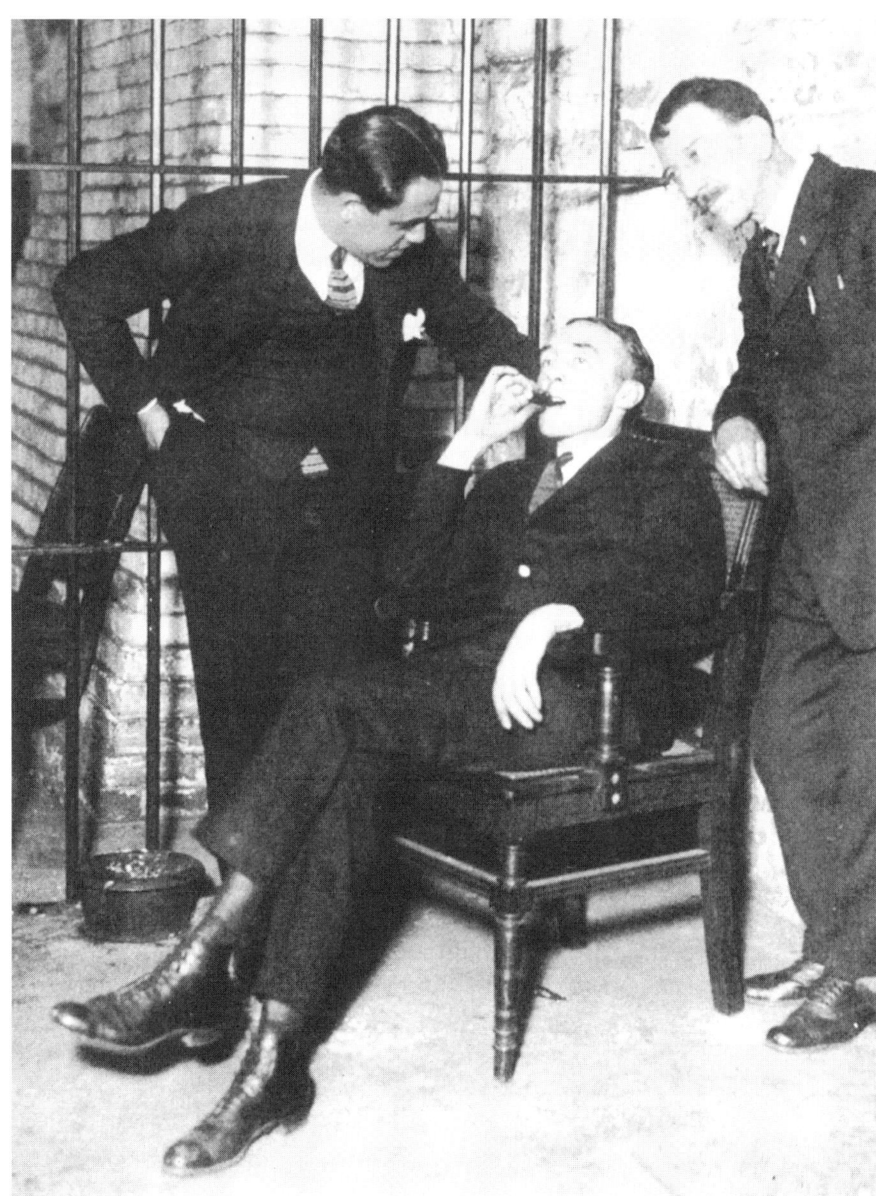

Condemned to death, Gerald Chapman sits arrogantly puffing a cigar, while jailers listen as he promises to escape once again; he did not, going to the hangman on April 6, 1926.

With police searching every known hideout along the Eastern seaboard for Chapman, he and Anderson, both in disguises, traveled by train to Muncie, Indiana, where they stayed at the home of Ben Hance, one of Anderson's underworld contacts. Somehow police learned of this hideout and closed in when Chapman was in the house alone. He was apprehended without a struggle in January 1925.

Again, millions of tabloid readers were thrilled by the exploits of Chapman and most expected the "super bandit" to once again escape. But there would be no more daring flights from justice for Gerald Chapman. President Calvin Coolidge approved a commutation for Chapman on the federal conviction of the Leonard Street Mail Robbery to the time he had already served so that Chapman could be extradited to Connecticut where he would stand trial for killing Officer Skelly.

Tried in Connecticut for Skelly's murder, Chapman insisted at his trial that he was in Holyoke, Massachusetts, on the day Skelly was killed, but Shean testified in court that Chapman was the man who shot and killed the officer. Ben Hance, in whose farm home Chapman had been found, appeared at the bandit's trial and also testified against him, saying that Chapman had paid him to hide out in his home.

Hance provided some of the stolen money from the New Britain department store safe which clearly placed Chapman at the scene of the crime. He was convicted and sentenced to death, then sent to the state prison at Wethersfield, Connecticut, to await execution. Chapman's lawyers filed every appeal available, but were unable to postpone their client's inevitable hanging on April 6, 1926.

To the time of his execution, Chapman was a model prisoner, remaining silent and always obedient and courteous. He was "the perfect gentleman," according to one report. On the day of his execution, Chapman quietly allowed guards to pinion his arms with straps and lead him into the execution chamber, the hanging room. A row of witnesses watched as he entered the room with a slight smile on his lips. His legs were tied and the rope placed about his neck, then a black hood was placed over his face.

Chapman muttered a few words no one could hear since the hood muffled his voice. The warden then pulled a lever and weights shot downward, causing the rope to yank Chapman upward, jerking him to death. The bandit's body hung suspended twelve feet above the floor, dangling. Death was instantaneous, Chapman's neck being snapped. It took only fifteen seconds to execute the "super bandit" from the time he entered the death chamber. Silence pervaded the death chamber, interrupted by the sound of pencils scratching across paper as newspapermen wrote their grim stories.

When George "Dutch" Anderson read these stories of Chapman's gruesome death, he went berserk. First he attempted to kill Shean, but the informer was too heavily guarded. Anderson traveled to Indiana and there confronted Ben Hance, calling him a traitor. Anderson shot and killed Hance and his wife and then burned their house down around them. He fled to Michigan and was surrounded by police in Muskegon. An officer approached the bandit cautiously, thinking him unarmed. Anderson laughed loudly, then pulled a revolver and fired at the officer just as the policeman fired. Both men fell dead, shooting each other in the heart. It was the end of the Gerald Chapman gang.

DILLINGER, THE INDIANA BANDIT/1930s

Audrey Dillinger with little John, at age two.

No bandit in twentieth century America so captured the public imagination and frustrated the efforts of police and federal agents as did John Herbert Dillinger (AKA: John Hall, John Donovan, Frank Sullivan, Carl Hellman; 1903- ?), a shrewd farm boy from the flatlands of Indiana whose name is synonymous with bank robbery. The history of his notorious reputation is varied and few writers have bothered to investigate his real nature, exploits, and eventual fate, preferring to repeat the lurid newspaper tales of the day. The real story of this strange and unpredictable criminal is more astounding than the fictional profiles created about him in countless detective magazines.

Delivered by a midwife on June 22, 1903, in his father's Indianapolis home, Dillinger's birth was surrounded with some mystery. His mother and father, John and Mollie Dillinger were already middle-aged at this time and Mollie Dillinger was not a well woman, dying of apoplexy in 1906 when John was only four years old. Audrey Dillinger, his 15-year-old sister, took care of the child, while his father, John Wilson Dillinger, maintained his thriving grocery store on Bloyd Street and looked after several houses he owned and rented. One claim later insisted that the closeness between Audrey and her little brother, fiercely maintained throughout Audrey's lifetime, was maternal, that Audrey had really given birth to John out of wedlock, and his father was an unknown Indianapolis youth. Then considered a rigid social taboo, the elderly Mrs. Dillinger assumed responsibility for John's birth.

Photos of Audrey Dillinger and little John show a marked similarity in features, but those with young Dillinger and the elder Dillinger show decided differences in physical makeup. Audrey married Emmett Hancock in 1906 at the age of nineteen, living next door to her father in one of his houses on Cooper Street. When her mother died, Audrey, with her husband, gave up her own house and moved into her father's house to take care of little Johnny. Audrey Dillinger Hancock gave birth to seven children, beginning in 1908, but she continued to watch over John until her father remarried.

The elder Dillinger wedded Elizabeth Fields of Mooresville, Indiana, in 1912. This union produced two children, Hubert, born in 1914 and Doris, born in 1916. Little John lived a normal life, playing outside his home on Cooper Street with a favorite tricycle. The elder Dillinger often took him to his grocery store, where the child would sit on the seat of a horse-drawn wagon and travel the streets of Indianapolis while deliveries were made. Even after the elder Dillinger remarried, Audrey Dillinger Hancock spent as much time with little John as she did with her own children.

While teaching piano, Audrey tried to interest little John in the instrument, but his interest and abilities were limited. He entered Public School 38 in Indianapolis and proved to be an average student, not brilliant, according to his teachers, but one who was quiet and caused little or no trouble. After fourth grade, Dillinger attended Public School 55.

Though teachers and classmates later reported Dillinger to be an average student, his peers did notice that he seemed "tougher" than most of the other boys. No one was able to best him in a fight, even when he was opposed by more than one

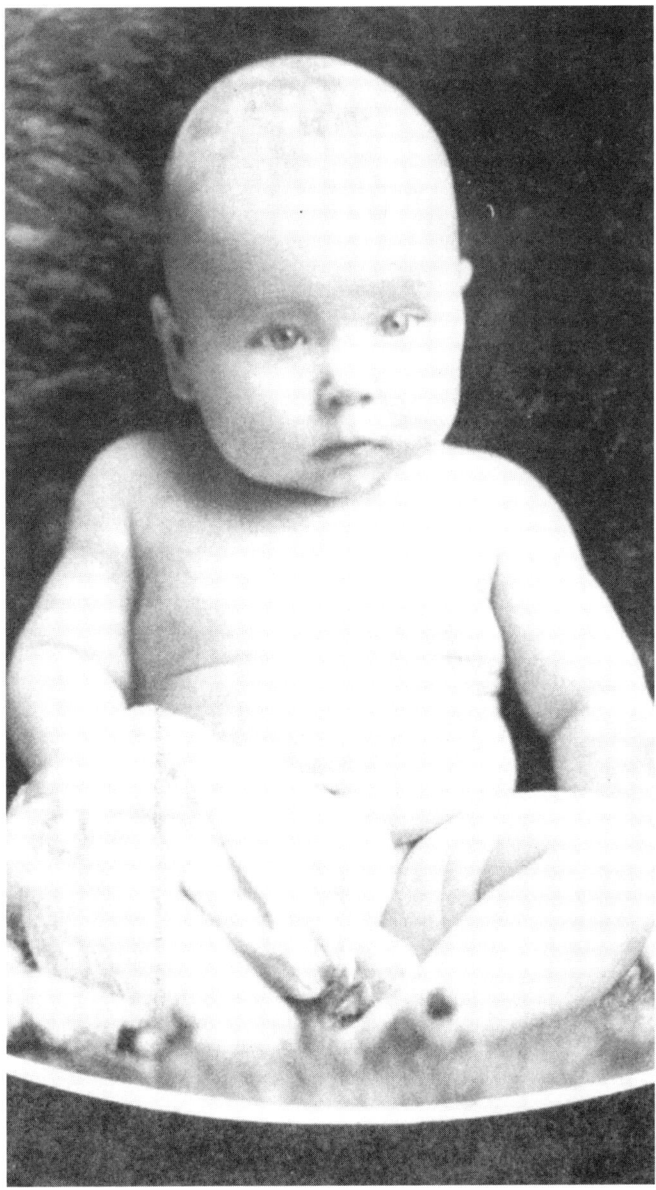

John Herbert Dillinger, seven months old.

John Dillinger, shown at age seven, lonely and quiet.

boy, although by nature, he was easygoing and did not look for trouble. One classmate remembered Dillinger, in sixth grade, going to the class bully and telling him to stop picking on smaller children or "I'll give you something to remember." He was occasionally truant from school, like the other boys and stole berries from a nearby orchard, like the other boys and went swimming in Fall Creek, like the other boys. He loved baseball and, unlike the other boys, excelled at the game, proving to be a good pitcher and a swift infielder. His aim in throwing out runners was deadly accurate. Along with the other boys, classmates later remembered, Dillinger played cops and robbers and did not care which side he was on.

In grammar school, Dillinger showed little interest in academic subjects but became intensely interested in anything mechanical, according to Elizabeth O'Mara, one of his teachers. Unlike some of the other boys in her class, she later pointed out, he never stole the small change she kept in her desk. The boy had a wry sense of humor and played subtle, harmless pranks that secretly amused O'Mara. Dillinger was a polite child, tipping his hat to teachers and adults he knew when on the street. When he received some bad grades, Dillinger signed the elder Dillinger's name to a report card and this earned him severe punishment from the elder Dillinger, a strict taskmaster who, it was claimed, locked John in a bedroom on occasions.

Another report had it that little John was, at one time, chained to a bed when he refused to obey, but this is not to be believed given the boy's usually quiet and unassuming ways. Another story, offered up by writer John Toland, reports John giving some gum to a pretty girl in his father's store and, being caught in the act, hit so hard by the elder Dillinger that the boy flew over a counter, his lip running blood. This is fiction.

While in sixth grade, Dillinger, part of a small gang of boys but not its leader, stole some coal from the Pennsylvania Railroad yards and sold it to neighbors. He and the other boys were dragged out of bed one night and taken before a local magistrate, who lectured the boys about stealing and then

Little John Dillinger sits in a delivery wagon, while his father holds the horse, next to the Dillinger store in Indianapolis, Indiana.

placed them in the custody of their parents. It was reported that Dillinger was the only defiant one in the gang, staring back at the judge, arms folded, his cap pulled low over his eyes, his jaw slowly working a piece of gum. The judge ordered him to remove the gum and Dillinger took it out of his mouth and slowly stuck it on the bill of his cap while grinning at the judge who remarked: "Your mind is crippled." This, too, is a piece of Toland's fiction.

Dillinger was not wearing a cap, nor was he chewing gum at this hearing. He was just as frightened as the other boys, having been dragged out of bed by a policeman, who barely allowed him to put on his shirt, pants, and shoes. He did not defy the judge nor was he singled out in any way before the magistrate released the boys.

Following his graduation from grade school, Dillinger was suddenly uprooted and went with the elder Dillinger to live on a farm in Mooresville, Indiana, seventeen miles south of Indianapolis. The elder Dillinger sold his store and houses and bought the farm, a lifetime ambition. He also wanted his children to grow up on a farm, rather than in the city, which he felt held too many corruptive influences. John continued his education, entering high school, but he dropped out at sixteen, taking a job at a veneer mill, where he was considered a good worker, one who helped out his fellow workers when needed and was called a "right guy" by his co-workers.

After five months, he grew bored with this job and went to work as a runner for the Indianapolis Board of Trade, a job he held for four months. He then went to work for the Reliance Specialty Company, a machine shop where he worked, on and off, for several years. Dillinger was thought to be "honest and industrious" by his employer, James P. Burcham, but he lost interest in the work and would not appear for some months, preferring to take odd jobs and ride about on his beloved motorcycle.

More to please his stepmother than to fulfill his own ambitions, Dillinger returned to school, but he dropped out of his first semester at Mooresville High. The elder Dillinger asked that he help out on the small farm the Dillingers were then working, but John made up one excuse after another and went back to his machinist job. Said the elder Dillinger years later: "My people have been farmers for generations. I liked the land. John never did. Said it was too slow ... I guess the city kind of got hold of him." In nearby Martinsville, Dillinger watched a local amateur baseball team go through its workouts and then joined the squad, proving to be an expert infielder. He was assigned the position of second base.

At about the same time, he fell in love with Frances Thornton, the stepdaughter of his uncle Everett Hancock, and he asked for her hand, but the uncle ended the affair, when he informed Dillinger that he and his stepdaughter were too young to think of getting married. Everett Hancock did not tell his nephew that he really wanted Frances to marry a boy from Greencastle, Indiana.

Dillinger, angry and feeling rejected, returned to Indianapolis where he began drinking heavily. His father was alarmed to hear neighbors tell him that they had seen Johnny patronizing whores in Indianapolis. John later went to a doctor for treatment of gonorrhea. It was then, on the night of July 21, 1923, the day before his twentieth birthday, Dillinger committed his first serious crime. He was standing outside the Friends Church in Mooresville, thinking to attend, when he saw a key in the ignition of a car belonging to Oliver P. Macy. Friends saw him get into the car and drive away. John Dillinger had stolen his first car.

Dillinger drove the car to Indianapolis and parked it on a quiet street, then began walking about aimlessly. A policeman stopped him at midnight and he gave his real name. As the officer was calling the station house from a call box, Dillinger disappeared. Nothing came of the car theft. Macy refused to press charges and only a few people knew about the incident.

The theft made Dillinger nervous and, thinking he might be arrested for taking Macy's car, he enlisted in the U. S. Navy at an Indianapolis recruiting office, giving his real name, but a fake St. Louis, Missouri, address. He was sent to Great Lakes, Illinois, for basic training and from there wrote a letter to Macy, insisting that he did not steal his car and that he had a girlfriend in Indianapolis, who would vouch for his statements. Macy did not respond.

On October 4, 1923, Dillinger's basic training was completed and, as a fireman third class, he was assigned to duty on the U. S. S. *Utah,* one of the United States' great battleships, destined to be destroyed by the Japanese at Pearl Harbor on December 7, 1941. Dillinger's navy experiences would be brief and unrewarding.

No sooner was Dillinger on board the *Utah* than he went AWOL, on October 28, 1923, disappearing for a full day. He was reprimanded when he returned and he went AWOL again, drawing a deck court-martial on November 7, 1923, resulting in ten days' solitary confinement on bread and water, which allowed a full ration of food every third day. He also lost $18 in pay. Defiant, Dillinger went AWOL again and another five days punishment was added to his sentence. He served all his time, but when the battleship anchored in Boston on December 4, 1923, Dillinger left the *Utah* forever, deserting the U.S. Navy. He was posted as a deserter, and a $50 reward for his apprehension was offered, but never collected.

Dillinger did not return home until March 1924, telling his family and friends that he did not like the navy and that he had received an honorable discharge because of illness. He went back to occasional work as a machinist and that spring played baseball for the St. Martinsville team. Watching one of the games in which Dillinger made some spectacular plays as a second baseman was 16-year-old Beryl Hovious. The two dated, fell in love, and were married on April 12, 1924. Dillinger and his young bride lived at the Mooresville farm and at Hovious family's home in Martinsville. Dillinger was still restless and spent little time at home with his wife, going out late to poolrooms and bars in Martinsville. Often, his wife would go looking for him, tracking him down and dragging him home.

In Gebhardt's poolroom, Dillinger befriended the man who would set him on the road to a criminal career, Edgar Singleton, thirty-one, married with several children. Singleton was an ex-convict, who was one of the umpires for the Martinsville baseball team, and had a criminal record of thefts dating back several years. It was Singleton who suggested that he and Dillinger pick up "some easy money" by robbing a Mooresville grocer, Frank Morgan. Singleton told Dillinger that Morgan took his weekly receipts home every Saturday night and it would be easy to relieve him of his money.

Both men lay waiting for Morgan on Saturday night at 10:30 p.m. on September 6, 1924. As Morgan passed the Mooresville Christian Church, Singleton and Dillinger attacked him. It was never made clear which one struck Morgan with the heavy bolt wrapped in a cloth, but the grocer was hit several times and knocked to the sidewalk. He got up and Dillinger pulled a revolver from his pocket, waving it at Morgan while demanding that he turn over his money.

The feisty 65-year-old Morgan, however, was not about to surrender his hard-earned cash, and he boldly knocked the gun from Dillinger's hand. It went off when it struck the sidewalk and the sound echoed down the deserted Mooresville street. Morgan then began to yell for help, and both would-be robbers panicked and bolted for Singleton's car, which was parked in a nearby alley. Singleton got in and drove off, leaving Dillinger, who had stopped to retrieve the gun and who fled on foot.

Sheriff John Hayworth answered Morgan's distress calls and took the injured grocer to a doctor; it took eleven stitches to seal Morgan's head wounds. Then Hayworth questioned several youths in Mooresville, who told him that the most likely suspect was John Dillinger. Hayworth drove out to the Dillinger farm and retrieved Dillinger, taking him to see Morgan. The grocer was unsure of the identity of his attackers and was surprised to see Dillinger, who had often visited his store. "You wouldn't hurt me, would you, John?" he asked the 20-year-old.

"No, Mr. Morgan," Dillinger said.

Hayworth's information, however, led him to believe Dillinger was guilty and he placed Dillinger in the Martinsville jail. On September 9, 1924, Dillinger was brought before the grand jury in Morgan County and indicted for attempted robbery. He was placed in jail again, pending trial, and the elder Dillinger visited him there. John broke down, admitting the robbery and the elder Dillinger urged John to tell the whole truth to the county prosecutor, Fred Steiger, which he did, on the promise of receiving a lenient sentence. Edgar Singleton was arrested on September 15, 1924, after Dillinger implicated him in his confession.

It was Dillinger's misfortune (and that of the entire Midwest's as events of a decade later proved) to be tried before Judge Joseph Williams, the most severe, uncompassionate jurist in the county. With no lawyer to defend him, Dillinger pled guilty to conspiracy to commit a felony and assault with intent to rob. Judge Williams ignored the fact that Dillinger was a first offender and had made a full confession. He gave

John Dillinger at age twelve, with his father, on the front porch of the farm in Mooresville.

Dillinger as a teenager; a fair student, he dropped out of school to take a job.

the youth the maximum sentence under the law, two concurrent sentences of two to fourteen years and ten to twenty years in prison, fining him $100 and disenfranchising him for twelve years. Prosecutor Steiger reneged on his promise of leniency, never mentioning the deal he had made with the elder Dillinger and his son. Edgar Singleton was also convicted a few weeks later, but he had the presence of mind to hire a lawyer and received a much lighter sentence, being paroled in two years.

Russell Peterson, the deputy sheriff who delivered Dillinger to the Indiana State Reformatory at Pendleton, sympathized with Dillinger and his family, telling the elder Dillinger that he did not agree with the brutal sentence handed down by Judge Williams. Said Peterson later: "He was just a kid. He got a raw deal. You just can't take ten years away from a kid's life." Dillinger quickly added six months to his sentence by trying to escape from Pendleton, where he had been sent to serve his sentence.

On October 10, 1924, Dillinger slipped out of a work detail, returned to the cells, and hid in a large pile of excelsior inside one of the work sheds. When he was discovered missing that night, all the lights in the reformatory were turned on and Dillinger was forced from the excelsior when it was lighted by guards and it began to burn around him.

As had been the case in the Navy, escape was constantly on Dillinger's mind. When first being brought before A. F. Miles, warden of Pendleton, Dillinger calmly listened to Miles instruct him in the rules and regulations. Then Dillinger said: "I won't cause you any trouble except to escape."

"I've heard that kind of talk before," Miles replied.

"Yeah, well I'll go right over the administration building," Dillinger promised.

After he testified at Singleton's trial, Dillinger, escorted again by Deputy Peterson, was sitting at a soft drink stand in Indianapolis, waiting for a train to take him back to Pendleton. He suddenly kicked the table over on Peterson, sending the deputy crashing to the ground, and ran across the capital lawn, across Senate Avenue, and into a rundown tenement area. Peterson followed, gun in hand, trapping Dillinger in a blind alley. He fired his gun in the air and Dillinger quietly surrendered and was taken back to Pendleton. Here, the kind deputy agreed to tell the warden of the incident only after getting a promise that Dillinger would not be punished for trying to escape. But Dillinger kept trying. In November 1924, Dillinger fashioned a homemade hacksaw and cut through the bars of his cell, slipping into a corridor. He was quickly caught and

Dillinger is shown extreme left in his sailor's uniform; he was assigned to the battleship U. S. S. *Utah*, but went A. W. O. L., when the ship anchored at Boston, and he never returned to the service.

six more months were added to his sentence.

Dillinger's list of offenses grew. On January 31, 1925, Dillinger was charged with being disorderly and was reprimanded. On February 26, 1926, he was caught gambling and thirty days were added to his sentence. In August 1926, he was again charged with being disorderly and another thirty days were added to Dillinger's term. He grew sullen and depressed and, on December 27, 1926, he started a fight and was sent to solitary confinement. He was released in a few days, but started another fight on December 31, 1926, and went back into solitary. Warden Miles described Dillinger at this time as troublesome, adding: "There is very little I can say in his favor." Meanwhile, the U.S. Navy, informed of Dillinger's imprisonment, dropped its fugitive warrant for him and issued him a dishonorable discharge. Also, his wife of five months, Beryl Hovious, who visited and wrote to him for a few years, slowly turned against him, writing him less, and less, and finally divorced him in 1929.

Before that time, however, Dillinger established two friendships that were to continue in his bank robbing heyday. The first was with a man who would deeply influence Dillinger's thoughts and behavior. Harry Pierpont was a well-educated, shrewd, and tough young bank robber, who was sent to Pendleton after single-handedly robbing a Kokomo, Indiana, bank. The second friendship was with Homer Van Meter, a wild young man, who had also been sent to Pendleton for bank robbery.

Dillinger, to earn the respect of these men, acted tough and got into trouble, almost as if to show Pierpont and Van Meter that he was worthy of their admiration, that he was "tough enough" to endure solitary confinement or any other punishment authorities gave him. Pierpont and Van Meter disliked each other, however, and, after several vicious fist fights, they had to be separated in different cell blocks. Both proved so incorrigible that they were sent to the state prison at Michigan City, Indiana.

The Martinsville, Indiana, baseball team in the early 1920s; Dillinger, who played second base, is shown standing second from the right; Edgar Singleton, his first accomplice in crime, is shown seated, without uniform, at extreme left.

In 1929, Dillinger expected a favorable response from the parole board. He had maintained a good record for several years and believed that he would be released, particularly with Indiana governor Harry Leslie sitting in on the hearing in July 1929. Dillinger had played well for the Pendleton baseball team and had heard that Governor Leslie, after watching him perform in some games, had remarked: "That kid ought to be playing major league baseball!" He appeared before Leslie, Warden Miles, and board member John Hoy. Miles reviewed his file and a brief discussion was held. Dillinger was told by Leslie: "Maybe you ought to go back for a few years." Realizing that he would not get his parole, Dillinger asked the board to grant a special request, startling Leslie, Miles, and Hoy by asking if he could be sent to the state prison.

"Why do you want to go to Michigan City?" Governor Leslie asked him.

Dillinger remembered Leslie's interest in him as a baseball player and shrewdly replied: "Because they have a real baseball team up there."

The governor nodded and then told Miles and Hoy that such a notion might not be a bad idea, that if he got better experience playing baseball at Michigan City "it might lead to an occupation for him later." The request was granted, but Dillinger's desire to go to the state prison had nothing to do with his playing baseball. His wife had recently divorced him and his two best friends, Pierpont and Van Meter, had been sent to Michigan City. He undoubtedly felt that, if his parole was denied, he would have nothing more to live for than to get into the state prison with the top professionals in crime, especially the expert bank robbers to whom he was instinctively drawn. He had, at that moment, decided to become a professional criminal whenever he managed to get out and that when he did, it would be with the benefit of an education taught by the country's top bank robbers.

The gates of the Big House opened for John Dillinger on July 15, 1929, and he happily took his place among the prison population, renewing his friendships with Pierpont and Van Meter. Pierpont introduced Dillinger to experienced bank robbers John Hamilton, Charles Makley, Russell Lee Clark, and others, who would form the core of the super bank robbing gang that would later operate under the nominal leadership of Pierpont and Dillinger. Hamilton, at thirty-four, was the most experienced of the group, having robbed banks throughout the Midwest. He was known as "Three-Fingered Jack" Hamilton, having lost the index and middle fingers of his right hand in an accident years earlier.

Intelligent and tough, Hamilton taught Dillinger the necessity of "casing" a bank, learning about its assets and its security measures before robbing it. He also outlined the need to inspect the town in which the bank was located and the best escape routes from it. Special maps had to be made of the back roads going in and out of the area. Hamilton was considered one of the "tough cons" in Michigan City, but he seldom got into trouble, his worst offense occurring in 1932 when he was caught and punished for, of all things, skipping rope in the machine shop.

From Walter Dietrich, another hard case bank robber who had been part of the gang once led by Hermann K. Lamm before being smashed in a police dragnet in 1930, Dillinger, Pierpont, and the others learned additional techniques. Dietrich, the only survivor of the gang, detailed Lamm's methods of robbing banks, intricate casing, surveillance of the bank, mapping escape routes, and the ever-important aspect of timing yourself when inside the bank, allowing for just enough time to perform the robbery before the estimated arrival of police. It had been Lamm's unswerving discipline that had allowed him to operate for a decade before mishap brought about his end.

Dietrich proudly told his fellow inmates at Michigan City how Lamm would stand at the entrance of a bank with a stopwatch and, at the required moment, shout orders for gang members inside the bank to drop whatever they were doing and leave immediately, strictly adhering to his timetable. If the schedule demanded that a gang member not reach for another wad of bills when the time allotted for the robbery was up, that gang member retreated, obeying orders. Lamm, of course, was used to giving orders, having been an officer in the Prussian Army before World War I.

Charles "Fat Charley" Makley was another important member of Dillinger's coterie. At forty-four, he was long on experience as a bank robbery. Born in Ohio, Makley had been robbing banks since the early 1920s and had been sent to Michigan City after robbing a bank in Hammond, Indiana. He was also a natural comic and vied with Van Meter at being the gang's clown. Russell Clark was a big, brooding man, impris-

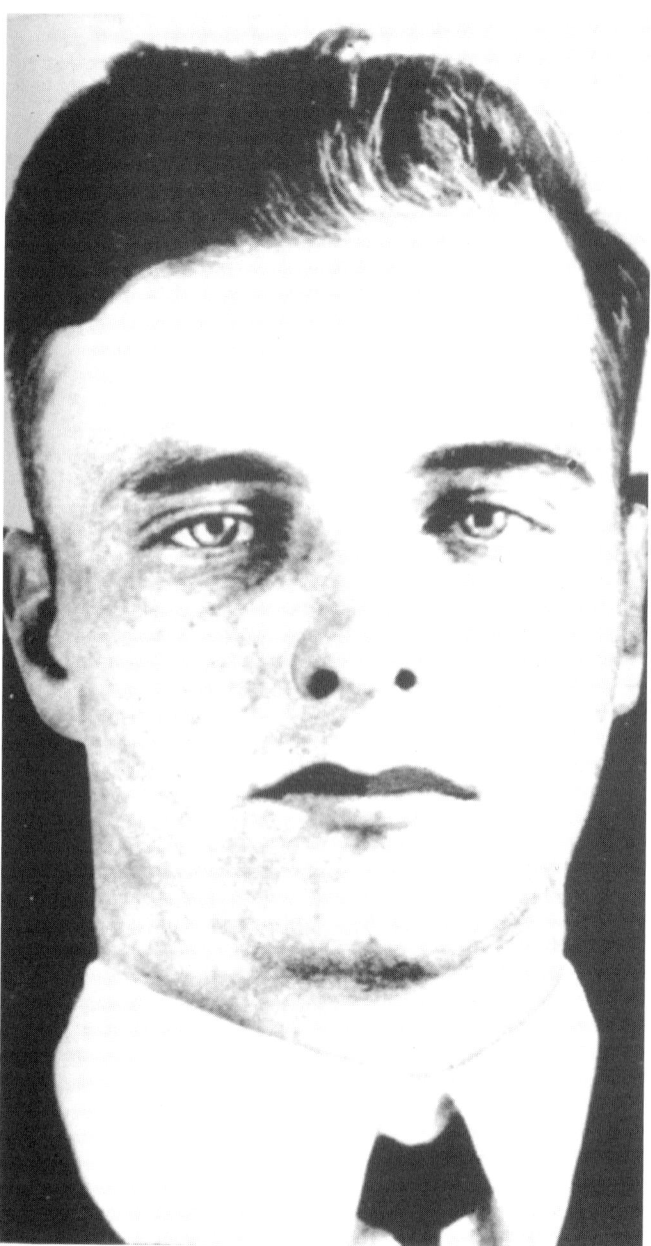

Harry "Pete" Pierpont, the brainy bankrobber Dillinger met and befriended in prison and who, along with other experienced bandits, taught him the techniques of robbery.

oned for bank robbery in 1927. He was the strong man of the bunch and his record at Michigan City was peppered with prison breaks, instigating riots, and several attempts to kill guards who displeased him.

Pierpont and the others groomed Dillinger well and for a purpose. All of his mentors were serving long prison terms with little hope of parole, but Dillinger was due to go before the parole board shortly and it was planned that once he was outside the walls, he would perform several robberies of banks Pierpont, Makley, and Hamilton had mapped out with great detail. Dillinger would use the proceeds of these robberies to finance a mass prison break, which would allow all of his closest friends to escape and join him.

With that constant thought in mind, Pierpont taught Dillinger to assume the penitent posture, telling him that the authorities would be watching his every move. Officials would read his letters to family members to see if he had truly reformed and actually meant to go straight once he was released, Pierpont pointed out. If censoring officials believed these intentions, they would be taken into account by the parole board.

Dillinger's letters became more and more contrite. He wrote mostly to Audrey Dillinger, the closest family member, telling her how much he was looking forward to getting out of prison and helping out at the farm. To a niece, he wrote: "I know right from wrong and I intend to do right when I get out. I suppose you think that I do not try to make my time clear [without trouble] but, honey, I do try, and a lot of times when I want to start something that might get me into trouble I think of Sis [Audrey] and don't do it."

In April 1933, Indiana governor Paul McNutt received an amazing petition seeking the parole of John Dillinger from the state prison at Michigan City. There were 180 names signed to the petition, which the elder Dillinger had obtained and sent on. Among those signing was grocer Frank Morgan, the very man Dillinger had attacked in 1924. Most important was the signature of Judge Williams, who had rendered the harsh sentence to Dillinger, undoubtedly regretting the lengthy term he had assigned to the farm boy.

Judge Williams even attached a solicitous letter which read, in part: "I have read the petition on behalf of J. H. Dillinger for clemency. I see that B. F. Morgan signs the petition. He was the party that was assaulted. I join in the recommendation for clemency petitioned for. Mr. Singleton, his partner, only received a sentence of from two-to-fourteen years and has been out of prison for about six years. As the trial judge I am entirely free to say that I think he should receive clemency as you in your judgment may see fit to grant, and trust that he may be paroled without delay to his father who will act, if appointed, as his parole officer ... The father of this prisoner is getting up in years and needs the assistance of his son on the farm ... I believe the prisoner has learned his lesson and that he will go straight in the future and make a useful and honorable citizen."

Governor McNutt sent the petition on to the parole board in May 1933 and, on May 9, 1933, it was reviewed by Delos Dean, J. Tom Arbuckle, and Wayne Coy. Dean voted to parole Dillinger and Arbuckle agreed with him. Despite the petition and the positive stance of his fellow board members, Coy was disinclined to make a recommendation. Instead of voting against the parole, however, he merely abstained and the order was given to release John Herbert Dillinger, Inmate 13225, from the custody of the Michigan City, Indiana, State Prison. The prison received the order on May 10, 1933, but for some reason it was not acted upon. A short time later, Elizabeth Dillinger suffered a stroke and was dying.

The elder Dillinger wired the prison on May 20, asking why the parole had not been put into effect. The parole was put through two days later and Dillinger's half brother, Hubert, picked up John as he stepped through the gates and to freedom on May 22, 1933, after serving almost nine years. Both immediately drove to the Dillinger farm in Mooresville, but they were too late. They saw the undertaker pulling into the yard just as they arrived. Elizabeth Dillinger had died an hour earlier.

The man that appeared at the farm that night was not the boy who had gone bewildered to prison almost nine years earlier. He had a man's rough face and a smile that seemed twisted, when he smiled at all which was seldom. He was depressed over the death of his stepmother, a kindly, giving woman he felt he had disappointed. The man sitting in the Dillinger parlor that night was worldly, self-assured, and distant, so much so that Audrey Dillinger Hancock, who stayed close to him, noticed the difference. He caught her staring at him and said: "Don't worry. Everything's going to be all right."

As if to assure the family that he meant to stay out of trouble, Dillinger visited with Mrs. Gertrude M. Reinier, pastor of the Friends Church in Mooresville, having several talks with her. On Father's Day, a month later, John sat in church with the elder Dillinger and the rest of the family while Mrs. Reinier delivered a moving sermon on the Prodigal Son, directing most of her statements at John Dillinger. He was seen to weep openly during the sermon and, following the services, Dillinger went to Mrs. Reinier and said to her: "You will never know how much good that sermon has done me."

A few weeks later Dillinger embarked on a series of petty holdups in the Indianapolis area. He teamed up with a 19-year-old hoodlum named William Shaw and another thug simply called Sam. The trio robbed an all-night supermarket of a small amount and split the loot in a local tavern. Dillinger, who had told Shaw that his name was Dan Dillinger, left early, saying he had to report to his parole officer. Shaw, a vain thief, insisted that gang members wear white caps and glasses and that they would strike terror among victims once they were known as the "White Cap Gang."

Dillinger was amused by these antics and went along with the disguise, but soon opted for a straw boater. The man named Sam dropped out of the gang and was replaced by Paul "Lefty" Parker, supposedly an expert wheelman, claiming he could outrun any police car. After borrowing revolvers from a saloon keeper, the trio robbed a number of drugstores and supermarkets before Dillinger drove off to Kentucky in a stolen car to see friends.

Dillinger returned to Indianapolis on July 7, 1933, and met with Shaw in the home of Shaw's mother. Shaw took Dillinger to his room where Dillinger asked for a knife to cut open a briefcase he had been carrying. It was full of wadded big-numbered bills. Although he never asked, Shaw was convinced that Dillinger had robbed a bank. Dillinger had stuck up a bank in Kentucky which had been on Pierpont's list of "ripe" banks to be robbed. This list was hopelessly outdated, however, since the Depression was deepening and many of the banks on Pierpont's list had gone under or were in receivership. Dillinger, Parker, and Shaw robbed the bank of New Carlisle, Indiana, of $10,500, but the gang was suddenly dissolved when Parker and Shaw were arrested by police.

By then Dillinger had been joined by Harry Copeland, whom he had known at Michigan City and who had recently been paroled from the state prison. Dillinger was driving a stolen Chevrolet with Copeland in the passenger seat. In the alley behind Shaw's home, they saw a police car and officers with guns drawn. Standing in front of the officers, hands in the air, were Shaw and Parker. Dillinger immediately threw the car into reverse and backed out of the alley at high speed. Shaw saw Dillinger escape, later commenting: "He drove faster backward than some people drive forward."

Homer Van Meter, who committed several bank robberies with Dillinger in 1934.

On July 17, 1933, Dillinger selected another bank from Pierpont's list, driving with Copeland to tiny Daleville, Indinana. The bank was a one-story, redbrick building with a single teller, Margaret Good. That morning, a young man wearing a pressed blue suit and a straw boater walked casually into the bank and looked around. He then produced a gun and said: "This is a stickup, honey." He startled Good by vaulting over the five-foot wooden barrier surrounding the teller's cage and once inside, scooped up the money from the drawer.

Bankrobber John Hamilton, who taught Dillinger the ropes in many 1933-1934 robberies.

Copeland, who had parked a stolen car in front of the bank, also walked inside and stood by the door, gun drawn, lining up customers as they entered. Dillinger entered the vault and took everything of value, including a collection of antique coins and two diamond rings left there by bank president, J. M. Barnard's daughter, who had taken them off to play tennis.

After collecting about $3,500, Dillinger herded the customers and Margaret Good into the vault and shut the door, after seeing that it could be opened from the inside. The 22-year-old Good opened the door a few minutes later. When police and a newspaperman arrived, she described the robbery in dramatic terms, speaking kindly of the leader, Dillinger, saying: "I think he knew I was a kid and was sorry to scare me. He didn't want to scare me any worse than he had to." This almost-sympathetic attitude toward John Dillinger would become a familiar refrain over the next year, mostly due to Dillinger's polite manner when robbing a bank and his soft-spoken promises not to injure those he was holding at gun point, an attitude that would change drastically when he later associated with the likes of Lester Gillis, better known as Baby Face Nelson.

A few days after the Daleville robbery, Dillinger drove to Dayton, Ohio, and there called on Mary Longnaker, a married

Dillinger, released from prison and already robbing banks, is shown with Mary Longnaker at Chicago's World Fair in 1933; this snapshot was taken by a policeman, who was asked by Dillinger to take the photo.

woman estranged from her husband, and the sister of James Jenkins, one of Dillinger's friends still doing time in the state prison at Michigan City. He invited Mary to go to the World's Fair in Chicago. She happily accepted on the condition that they also take her girlfriend, Mary Ann Bucholz. Dillinger drove to Chicago with the two women and registered at the Crillon Hotel, where the women shared one room and Dillinger had a room to himself. Miss Bucholz became alarmed when she walked into Dillinger's room and saw a pistol on his bureau, but Mary seemed to know that her new boyfriend was a man of the underworld and she delighted in showing her girlfriend his wallet, which was bulging with large bills.

Mary and Dillinger attended the fair for several days and posed for photos, which Dillinger asked passing policemen to snap for them, such was his offbeat sense of humor. He even took several photos himself of policemen patrolling the fair grounds. He and Mary dined in the better restaurants and went dancing in such nightclubs as the Island Queen. On their way back to Dayton, Mary asked if they could stop at the state prison in Michigan City and visit her brother, Jenkins. Dillinger agreed. The trio stopped in Michigan City and here Dillinger bought a large basket of fruit, telling Mary to give it to her brother. He cut a small hole in the top of a banana and inserted several $50 bills into it. He then wrote a note, which Mary was to read to Jenkins while talking with him through the cage in the visitor's room. This she did, the message ending with the words "sit tight." Mary also told Jenkins to "eat the banana first."

Before the trio left the prison parking lot, Dillinger handed $50 to a guard and told him to "give it to Jenkins, so he can have his teeth fixed." It is not known whether the guard recognized Dillinger, but it is presumed that he did and said nothing. Many of the guards at the prison were corrupt and their confidence could be purchased easily.

After Dillinger returned Mary Longnaker and Mary Ann Bucholz to Dayton, he was off on another bank raid. He, Copeland, and an unidentified bandit (who may have been Glen "Big Foot" Zoll), on August 4, 1933, raided the First National Bank of Montpelier, Indiana. Dillinger and Copeland entered the bank and Dillinger, carrying a sugar sack turned inside out, vaulted the guard rail, an action that was fast becoming his trademark. He scooped up the cash while Copeland trained a .38-caliber revolver on the employees and customers.

Dillinger took $3,900 from the counter cages and another $6,200 from a small safe in the corner. The vault was closed and Dillinger seemed to accept the word of bank president M. D. Tewksberry when he said that nothing was in the vault and that the government bonds held by the bank were stored in a Fort Wayne vault. Dillinger found a .45-caliber automatic in the safe and took it, remarking: "This is a good gun." When he was leaving the bank he patted the sack bulging with currency and coin and said: "This is a good haul."

The bandits fled in a stolen car and were seen changing license plates by farmer Albert Stoll ten miles outside of town. Although police set up roadblocks at several points on roads leading from Montpelier, the bandits escaped using rural routes that had been obviously mapped earlier. Ironically, they had just missed being slaughtered.

The First National Bank at Montpelier had been the target of several other bank robbers and, in 1931, local officials had taken precautions. The office above the bank contained a corner office facing the street, which was occupied by the local sheriff, mayor, and an attorney, all equipped with high-powered rifles. These three men had cut down a gang of bandits in 1931, killing one and wounding others. However, on the day Dillinger and his men struck the bank in 1933, all three men were elsewhere.

Some days later, Mary Longnaker received a letter from Dillinger in which he talked about taking her and her two daughters to South America with him, saying they could all live well and be happy in some South American country. This was a recurrent desire expressed by the bandit. Forrest Huntington, a former Pinkerton detective, was hired by the American Surety Company which had to repay the Montpelier bank loss.

It was Huntington's job to find the bandit who had already been identified as Dillinger. He learned that the bank robbers had eaten lunch at Barr's Restaurant only an hour before robbing the bank. Moreover, one of the bandits, who

Mary Kinder, who helped Dillinger plan the escape of her brother and nine other inmates at the Indiana State Prison in 1933.

had worn a Panama hat, had visited an ex-convict in town three days before the robbery.

On August 14, 1933, five men in a long green sedan pulled up in front of the Citizens National Bank of Bluffton, Ohio. One man stayed behind the wheel of the car, which was parked the wrong way, two men remained on the sidewalk in front of the bank as sentinels, and two more entered the bank. Inside the bank, Dillinger and Copeland, both wearing expensive suits and straw hats, pulled guns.

Dillinger ordered cashier Roscoe Lingler to "stand back, this is a stickup!" He vaulted the barrier and began stuffing money into a sack. He turned and said to Oliver Locher, the bookkeeper: "You've got more money in here. Where is it?" As Locher pointed to a huge vault, the bank alarm went off. Copeland shouted to Dillinger: "They're after us! Let's go!"

Dillinger ignored Copeland and the alarm. He tugged at a locked drawer, demanding the key. At the same time the two men on the sidewalk, seeing curious crowds assembling down the street in response to the bank alarm, began to fire their guns high, bullets chunking into second-story windows and walls. Finally, Dillinger and Copeland emerged and the five men piled into the sedan and roared away. The take was meager, only $2,100. Angered, Dillinger vowed to obtain more cash quickly, telling Copeland that he needed money to finance "something big," this being the mass breakout of his friends from Michigan City State Prison. Still using Pierpont's list of banks, a "soft jug" was selected, the large Massachusetts Avenue State Bank in Indianapolis.

On September 6, 1933, Dillinger, Copeland, and Hilton Crouch, a professional dirt track race driver, drove up to the bank and Dillinger and Copeland went into the bank. Copeland, opening a long coat, produced a submachine gun and trained it on the customers and tellers, ordering everyone to keep quiet and saying "this is a stickup." Dillinger again vaulted the guard rail and scooped up every dime he spotted, including $500 in heavy coin. Copeland kept glancing at the street as more customers entered the bank, ten in all. He herded them away from the windows. "Hurry up, will you?" he called to Dillinger. Minutes later both men left the bank and slipped into the De Soto which Crouch then drove up the street. This time the take was considerable, the largest haul yet, $24,800. Dillinger took half of this amount as the major share going to the planner and leader of the raid.

A few days later, Dillinger drove alone to the state prison and crept along one of the outer walls, throwing several loaded revolvers over the wall. These weapons landed on the baseball field and were found the next morning and taken to Warden Louis Kunkel. This had been according to plan. Dillinger, a clever convict-trained criminal, reasoned that someone would have leaked information to the warden of an impending break. He also reasoned that after the revolvers were found, prison officials would believe that the delivery of the weapons constituted the intended break and would relax their guard for the real break to come. He then went to the home of Mary Kinder in Indianapolis, leaving money with her and telling her to buy clothes and food for fourteen men who would be coming to visit her soon, including her brother, Earl Northern and her sweetheart, Harry Pierpont, then both still in state prison.

In Chicago, Dillinger contacted the foreman of a thread-making company, one which supplied the state prison at Michigan City with thread for its shirt-making factory. The bandit bribed the foreman to allow him to doctor a barrel of thread inside which Dillinger placed three automatic pistols. He then marked the barrel with a small red "X," the prearranged signal to Pierpont and others that the barrel contained weapons. On September 24, 1933, several barrels of thread were delivered to the prison. Walter Dietrich, alerted to the special shipment, spotted the barrel marked with the red "X" and placed it in a button box in the factory and alerted Pierpont, Makley, Clark, and others. By then, however, Dillinger was already back in police custody.

In September, Dillinger visited his girlfriend, Mary Longnaker, in Dayton, Ohio. Her house had been watched for weeks since Detective Forrest Huntington had learned her identity, from photos and some letters Dillinger had somehow dropped following the Montpelier robbery. Police showed the landlady, Lucille Stricker, photos of Dillinger, and she was asked to call if he visited Mary Longnaker. When Dillinger appeared on the night of September 20, 1933, Stricker called Dayton detectives Russell K. Pfauhl and Charles E. Gross who rushed to the Longnaker home on West First Street, arriving at

Captain Matt Leach, chief of the Indiana State Police, who led the hunt for Dillinger and became the bandit's self-appointed nemesis.

about 1:30 a.m.

Carrying shotguns, the detectives kicked open the door to the Longnaker apartment and there, in the middle of the room stood Dillinger, showing Mary photos that had been taken at the World's Fair. "Stick 'em up, Johnnie," ordered Pfauhl. The photos fell from his grasp as Dillinger's hands went upward and then momentarily stopped and began to slowly drop toward his vest where a revolver was nestled in a shoulder holster. Pfauhl lifted his shotgun and aimed it directly at Dillinger's head, saying in a low but firm voice: "If you do, John, I'll kill you on the spot."

Mary Longnaker tried to distract the detectives by pretending to faint, but Pfauhl was having none of it. "Stop that play-acting," he said to her as she lay on the floor between Dillinger and the detectives. "Get up on your hands and knees and crawl out of the way," ordered Pfauhl. "Right now!" Mary, on hands and knees, crawled out of the way and the detectives stepped forward and clamped handcuffs on Dillinger, while removing his revolver from its holster.

The detectives found another .38-caliber revolver stuffed between some cushions on the couch and two more in Dillinger's luggage in the trunk of Dillinger's 1933 Ford Terraplane car parked outside. They also found a large supply of roofing nails in the back seat, these nails were thrown in the wake of Dillinger's car when being pursued. He would simply throw them out of the window, covering the roadway behind him and causing police car tires to be punctured into instant flats.

As the detectives took more than $2,000 in cash from Dillinger's pockets, the bandit began to relax, saying: "When you fellows came in I didn't know if you were part of another gang or not. I know uniformed police, but not plainclothesmen. I thought you were somebody else." The bandit kept up this pleasant chatter, but refused to admit to any robberies. He was wanted mostly by the state of Indiana, but Dillinger wanted to avoid being taken to the state prison at all costs, one which might jeopardize the prison break he had set in motion.

The bandit suddenly admitted to robbing the bank in Bluffton, Ohio, and was removed to the Lima, Ohio, Jail, an old, lightly guarded building. Dillinger correctly reasoned that his friends from Michigan City, once outside the walls, would return the favor and he was selecting the easiest jail from which they could affect his release.

On September 26, 1933, after Walter Dietrich notified Pierpont that Dillinger's smuggled guns had arrived and were hidden in the shirt factory, the leader of the gang approached other members of the plot in the prison yard. The 31-year-old, blue-eyed, sandy-haired Pierpont, called "Handsome Harry" by his friends, told the group: "All right boys, if you want to go and take a chance, we will go now."

G. H. Stevens, superintendent of the shirt factory, and Albert Evans, assistant warden, were taken prisoner and used as hostages as ten men made their way across the yard to the first steel gates. Here guard Frank Swanson challenged the group, but Evans whispered to him: "They've got guns. Open the gate or they'll kill us." Swanson opened the gate and he, too, was taken prisoner and marched in front of the convicts.

At a second gate, guard Fred Wellnitz refused to open up and was slugged unconscious by the convicts, who took his keys and opened the gate. The procession then walked solemnly into the administration building where eight clerks, including two women, were herded into a vault, along with Warden Kunkel who was not recognized by the convicts. When 72-year-old Finley Carson, one of the clerks, moved too slowly to please one of the convicts, he was shot in the stomach. Lawrence Mutch, superintendent of prison industries, was spotted and was ordered to open up the adjacent arsenal so the convicts could seize submachine guns and shotguns. Mutch refused and was beaten senseless.

Then the ten convicts, Harry Pierpont, Charles Makley, Russell Clark, John Hamilton, Walter Dietrich, Edward Shouse, Joseph Fox, Joseph Burns, Jim "Oklahoma Jack" Clark (no relation to Russell Clark), and James Jenkins, Mary Longnaker's brother, rushed out of the administration building and into the parking lot, where they bumped into Sheriff Charles Neel of Harrison County, who had just delivered a prisoner. Burns, Fox, Dietrich, and James Clark grabbed Neel and pushed him into his own car and drove it out of the lot. Pierpont and the others ran to the street and stopped the first passing car, one driven by Herbert Van Valkenberg. They forced Van Valkenberg, his wife, and 89-year-old grandmother from the car, and sped off with it.

Dillinger with Mary Longnaker; he was captured in her apartment in Dayton, Ohio, on September 20, 1933.

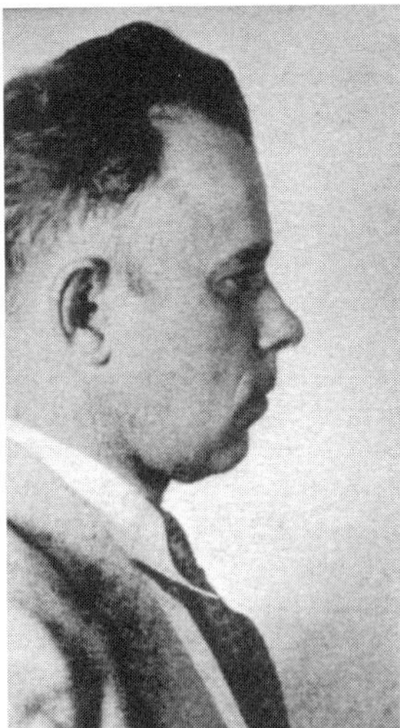

Police photos of Dillinger, taken on September 22, 1933, after he had been arrested in Mary Longnaker's apartment in Dayton, Ohio; he was imprisoned at the Lima, Ohio, jail, where, on October 12, 1933, Pierpont and others freed Dillinger, killing Sheriff Jess Sarber in the process.

Captain Matt Leach of the Indiana State Police, who was later to become obsessed with hunting Dillinger, organized several posses and set up roadblocks to recapture the escaped prisoners. The car in which Dietrich, Fox, Burns, and James Clark were traveling with their hostage, Sheriff Neel, crashed into a ditch and was abandoned. This group, heading for Chicago, struck out on foot, hiding in thick underbrush and moving at night through torrential rains. Fox and Burns suggested that they tie Neel up to a tree, but James "Oklahoma Jack" Clark told them that if they did that the elderly sheriff would die of exposure.

Dietrich, Burns, and Fox then told Clark that he could take care of Neel. They parted company near Hobart, Indiana. Clark took Neel to Gary on an interurban train and, once in Gary, the sheriff bought them both dinner. Neel gave Clark his topcoat to hide his prison denims and the bandit left his hostage. Sheriff Neel walked into a police station a short time later, shocking officials, who had assumed he was dead. Three companies of armed militia were milling about the place, demanding to know which way the convicts went. The exhausted Neel gave so many vague answers to questions that searchers had no idea where to look and it was later suggested that he had purposely avoided pinpointing Clark, still in the area, in gratitude for saving his life.

Clark, however, did not get far. He reached Hammond where he took a cab to a boarding house. The taxi driver led police to him the next day. Clark was returned to the Gary police station, where he was warmly greeted by Sheriff Neel, who slipped him $5 before he was taken back to the state prison at Michigan City. "I might as well be dead now," Clark said en route back to prison. "I just wanted to be free a couple of years so I could get proper medical attention." He suffered from stomach ulcers and would die of them. Fox and Burns would be recaptured in a short time and Walter Dietrich, after joining up with the College Kidnapper Gang headed by handsome Jack Klutas in Chicago, would be arrested and returned to prison in January 1934.

The other six men roared toward Indianapolis and the home of Mary Kinder. Longnaker's brother James Jenkins, however, never got home. As the car in which the six convicts raced around a curve, a door flew open and Jenkins fell out. The car started to back up to retrieve Jenkins but sounds in the nearby woods were thought to come from posses moving toward the convicts and the car suddenly sped off. Jenkins made his way alone to the outskirts of Bean Blossom, Indiana.

There Jenkins encountered three farmers armed with shotguns, who were part of the dozens of posses looking for the escaped prisoners. With one of Dillinger's smuggled pistols in his hand, Jenkins ran up an alley after wounding one of the farmers in the shoulder, and the farmers chased after him, blasting away with their shotguns. Jenkins received a barrel load in the side of the head and he fell mortally wounded and died a few hours later. His father, the Reverend George Jenkins, arrived to identify the body and said: "I'm glad it's like this. Better like this than that he killed somebody else."

On September 28, 1933, Pierpont, Russell Clark, Hamilton, Makley, and Shouse arrived at the home of Mary Kinder, remaining there to plan a bank robbery to fund the prison release of John Dillinger. Makley suggested that they rob the bank in St. Marys, Ohio, his home town, a bank he knew would yield considerable cash. Pierpont, Makley, Clark, Hamilton, and Shouse raided the First National Bank of St. Marys on October 3, 1933, parking their stolen green Hudson in front of the bank. Pierpont and Makley went inside while Hamilton and Clark covered the street and Shouse stayed at the wheel of the car. Pierpont cleaned out the tellers' cages while Charley Makley stood next to the door and herded customers at gunpoint to the vault as they entered the bank.

Several persons recognized Makley, including the bank's president, W. O. Smith. Makley, smiling and chewing gum, casually talked with Smith of old days in St. Marys, while courteously ushering him to the vault. Smith appeared just as friendly, asking Makley innocuous questions about the health of his family, stalling, of course, to prevent the bandits from getting at the cash inside the vault. "It's on a time lock, Charley," Smith told his old friend, "and it won't open for hours." Just then the time mechanism loudly clicked off and Smith realized that his ruse had failed.

"Looks like it decided to open early today," Makley said through a wide grin. He opened the vault and motioned the customers and employees inside. He also entered and cleaned out the cash on the shelves with Pierpont, while Clark stepped inside the bank to act as lookout. More than $14,000 was stuffed into a sack and as the bandits closed the vault door, Pierpont said: "If anyone steps out of this vault and cries an alarm before we leave we'll blow the side of this building out with machine gun fire!" He, Makley, and Clark stepped into the street and, joined by Hamilton, got into the Hudson which Shouse drove off at moderate speed.

Dillinger, meanwhile, awaited trial for the Bluffton, Ohio, bank robbery in a cell in the Lima, Ohio, Jail. The decrepit building was poorly guarded. Dillinger was a celebrated prisoner, having had his name in the headlines for months as newsmen chronicled his crime wave. Sheriff Jess Sarber was a kind lawman whose wife Lucy made delicious meals for Dillinger, but the Sarbers thought Dillinger was just another farm boy gone wrong and attached no particular importance to him. He was placed in the small cell block at the rear of the building. In adjoining cells were Art Young, awaiting sentencing for a second-degree murder conviction, and George Miller and Claude Euclid, two prisoners who had committed minor offenses. Dillinger had told Miller that he expected his friends to "spring" him but he was uncertain when they would make their move.

Harry Pierpont made his move on the night of October 12, 1933. First, he and Russell Clark visited attorney Chester M. Cable, in Lima, Ohio, asking him to call the jail so that Dillinger's sister, who was outside in a car, could visit him. Cable thought the two men looked like "tough customers," and he said that it would take some days to arrange such a visit. When the two men left, Cable called Sheriff Sarber, who was sitting in the front office in his shirt sleeves, reading some reports at his desk.

Sarber took Cable's warning lightly, thinking that reports about Dillinger's gangster friends nothing more than "a lot of nonsense, cartoon nonsense." In the same office, Lucy Sarber sat in a nearby chair piecing a crossword puzzle together. In another chair, reading a newspaper, was Deputy Wilbur Sharp. He and Sarber were both unarmed, although Sarber's revolver was in the center drawer of his desk.

At 6:25 p.m., Pierpont and Clark boldly walked to the front of the jail and saw that it was unguarded. Across the street and down the block, at various posts assigned to them by Pierpont, stood John Hamilton, Charles Makley, Ed Shouse, and Harry Copeland, recently arrived from Indiana to help in the freeing of John Dillinger.

Shouse later told lawmen, when captured that there was no real plan that night, only "to free Dillinger, and stick together and help each other if we could, and, if we couldn't, make a break for it, and go for ourselves." This fierce loyalty to one of their own was a singular trait of the 1930s bank robbers, the independent bandits of the day who, thinking themselves superior to the city gangster, retained certain values and friendships even at the risk of their lives. Dillinger had earlier freed them. They were obligated to free him.

Bankrobber Charles Makley, who would later die in the Ohio's electric chair along with Pierpont for murdering Sheriff Jess Sarber in releasing Dillinger from a jail at Lima, Ohio.

Pierpont, Makley, and Clark went up the stairs of the jail while Copeland, Shouse, and Hamilton stayed with the escape car. The three men, all well-dressed and wearing hats with wide brims pulled low over their faces, went inside and approached Sheriff Sarber, who looked up from his desk. "Can I help you?" he said.

"We're officers from Michigan City," Pierpont said. "We want to talk to the prisoner John Dillinger."

Deputy Sharp kept reading his paper and Mrs. Sarber never looked up from her puzzle. Sheriff Sarber nodded and said: "I guess that will be all right. But first you will have to show me your credentials."

Pierpont's eyes narrowed as he pulled out a pistol and aimed it at Sarber's head. "Here's our credentials."

"Oh, you can't do that," Sarber said, his mouth agape and he instinctively tried to push the gun aside.

Pierpont fired two shots quickly, one striking Sarber in the hip and one ploughing into the sheriff's stomach. He fell out of his chair and onto the floor. Sharp and Lucy Sarber were frozen in shock in their chairs. Pierpont then barked: "Give us the keys to the cells." When Sarber tried to rise on his elbow, Makley dashed forward and hit him on the head with his gun butt, splitting the skull to the bone. He hit him once more.

Lucy Sarber jumped up screaming: "I'll get the keys! Don't hurt him anymore!"

Inside the cellblock, Art Young and Dillinger, who had been playing cards through the bars of their adjoining cells, suddenly sat up and Young said: "John, your gang has come for you." Dillinger slipped on his coat and stood by the cell door. He asked Young if he wanted to "come along," but Young declined the offer.

Pierpont, grinning, entered the cellblock and unlocked the door of Dillinger's cell. Both men then ran into the office, but Pierpont stuck his head back inside the door and looked down the corridor, where the other prisoners were yelling to be set free. "Get back there, you bastards," shouted Pierpont. "We

Russell Clark, a towering bank robber, helped free Dillinger from the Lima, Ohio, jail; he, Pierpont, Makley, Hamilton and Van Meter joined Dillinger in robbing banks in late 1933.

came for John. The rest of you can leave when we've gone."

In the office Dillinger saw Sheriff Sarber on the floor, bleeding to death, his wife holding him, sobbing. The bandit knelt close to the sheriff, the man who had been so kind to him and said without looking at his liberators: "Did you have to do this?"

"Men," moaned Sarber to his attackers, "why did you do this to me?" He turned his head slightly to look up at his weeping wife and said: "Mother, I believe I am going to have to leave you."

Pierpont and Makley then forced Mrs. Sarber and Deputy Sharp into the cell block and locked the door. All of the gang members then left the office while Sheriff Sarber died within minutes. Outside, Dillinger climbed into the long sedan with the rest of the gang and sped away. The super gang that would terrorize the Midwest was now united. Only minutes after Sarber's body was found, dozens of motorized posses chased after the Dillinger gang, but they found no trace of the bandits.

By midnight, the gang reached Indianapolis and stayed with Mary Kinder. Also waiting for Dillinger was Evelyn "Billie" Frechette, a Menominee Indian girl, daughter of the chief, who had run away from the reservation in northern Wisconsin to become a hat check girl at the World's Fair. Dillinger had met her while visiting the fair with Mary Longnaker and had seen her briefly before his capture at Longnaker's apartment. The gang made immediate plans to arm its members and then quickly raid a number of banks.

On October 14, 1933, Dillinger, Pierpont, and Makley entered the police station at Auburn, Indiana, drawing guns and holding at bay police officers Henry West and Fred Kreuger. The bandits seemed to know that Chief of Police Charles Davis and Sheriff John P. Hoff would be absent at that time. Dillinger walked up to Kreuger, who had been sitting with his back to the front door of the station, eating popcorn, before he turned around to see a revolver poked into his face. Said Dillinger: "You might as well sit still. We don't want to kill anyone unless we have to. Have you got any guns?" Kreuger started to reach for the gun on his hip, but Dillinger's hand went quickly to the holster and withdrew it while he remarked: "Oh, no! I'll get it." West was disarmed by Pierpont, while Makley stood at the door, casually leaning against the wall, watching the street, where Hamilton and Clark chatted on the sidewalk and Shouse sat at the wheel of a car.

West and Kreuger surrendered the keys to the gun cabinet and the bandits took turns carrying out weapons, including a Thompson submachine gun with several pans of ammunition, two .38-caliber revolvers, a .30-caliber Springfield rifle, a Winchester automatic rifle, a shotgun, a .45-caliber Colt automatic, a .44-caliber Smith and Wesson, a .44-caliber Spanish, and a German Luger. The bandits also grabbed three bulletproof vests and many boxes of ammunition. The police officers were then locked in a cell. As he left, Dillinger turned to the elderly Kreuger and said: "I have heard of you for thirty years," a strange remark that was obviously intended to flatter the policeman. The invaders then fled.

Swarms of police in Indiana and Ohio were now frantically searching for what the newspapers had termed The Terror Gang. Dillinger's home in Mooresville was staked out but this only served to annoy the elder Dillinger, who stated that "Johnny would not have caused all this trouble if Judge Williams had never given him such a harsh sentence" in 1924 and if the prosecutor at that time had lived up to his promise of a lenient sentence in exchange for a plea of guilty. "It was Judge Williams' fault, all of it."

Ohio police also searched and then watched the homes of Harry Pierpont and Charles Makley, but saw no sign of these men. Newspapers throughout the Midwest gave over their front pages to the daring bandits, who could so easily defy the law, marching right into jails and police stations to free comrades and loot arsenals. On October 20, 1933, the Dillinger gang did it again, this time raiding the police station at Peru, Indiana.

At 11 p.m. that night, Leo "Red" Eakins, who worked as a porter at the Model Restaurant a few doors away from the Peru police station, walked into the station and was greeted by a tall, young man, fastidiously dressed in a three-piece suit and wearing a wide-brimmed hat. He held a gun in his hand. The stranger, Pierpont, grabbed Eakins by the arm and pulled him into the back room, saying: "Come back here. I want to show you something." Eakins thought it was some sort of joke until he stepped into the back room to see three police officers, Eddie Roberts, Eldon Chittun, and Ambrose Clark sitting in chairs, looks of terror on their faces as another gunman, Dillinger, held a gun on them. Said Eakins later: "I still thought they were in fun until I noticed the cops' knees shaking. Then I knew it was a holdup."

To make the policemen even more uneasy, Pierpont said without humor: "I haven't killed anybody for a week and I'd just as soon shoot one of you as not. Go ahead and get funny." The policemen remained motionless as another man appeared with a robe, spreading this out on the floor. Onto this gang members dumped two Thompson submachine guns, two sawed-off shotguns, four .38-caliber Police Specials, two .30.30 Winchester rifles, six bulletproof vests, three police badges and many boxes of ammunition. The robe was then tied about the cache of weapons and carried outside, while Makley marched the officers and Eakins into the basement where they were locked up. As Deputy Robert Tillett arrived in front of the

Evelyn "Billie" Freschette, the Menominee Indian girl, who became Dillinger's favorite girlfriend and escaped several police traps with the bandit, until she was arrested and jailed in Chicago in 1934.

station, he saw a blue Hudson pull away from the curb and a good-looking young man wave at him.

News of the Peru raid stunned law enforcement officials in the state and elsewhere, the second raid on a police arsenal within a week. Funds were quickly collected to build special security posts, install barbed wire, and put in barred windows around all Indiana police stations. Security at the state prison in Michigan City and at the reformatory in Pendleton was beefed up, as authorities believed that the Dillinger gang was assembling enough weapons for an army of gangsters to attack these institutions in order to free the entire prison populations.

Edward Shouse, one of the ten convicts, who escaped in the Indiana State Prison break engineered by Dillinger; a one-time dirt track racer, he became the gang's getaway driver.

The American Legion offered to put 30,000 volunteers onto Indiana highways in armed patrols to look for the bandits and the National Guard was put on active status, its officers reporting on the availability of poison gas, airplanes, and tanks in combating the Terror Gang. The U.S. Army provided local police with dozens of armored cars with heavy-caliber machine guns mounted on top.

Attorney General Homer Cummings received a message from the Indianapolis *Times* requesting FBI help for Indiana since the local and state police seemed helpless to stop or capture the Dillinger gang. J. Edgar Hoover was alerted to have his field agents cooperate with local police, but there was little the Bureau could do on its own at this time.

No federal laws then existed, which allowed agents to pursue the Terror Gang. Bank robbery, stealing cars and transporting them across state lines, and other offenses committed by bandits of the day were state offenses and federal authorities had no jurisdiction in such crimes. It was John Dillinger and his henchmen who would bring about federal legislation that would allow Hoover's G-Men to act, but this would not happen for some time.

When details of the Peru raid were released to the press, the public fascination with Dillinger and his gang members increased, mostly due to the inventiveness of the gangsters. It was later learned that Dillinger and Pierpont had brazenly walked into the Peru station and informed the armed policemen there that they were tourists, thinking of depositing considerable money in the local bank. They were apprehensive, they said, of risking their money in a bank that might not be able to withstand an attack of the Dillinger gang. What types of weapons did the police have, they asked, to repel such an attack?

Ambrose Clark proudly took Dillinger and Pierpont to the police arsenal to display its weaponry and it was at this moment that Dillinger and Pierpont pulled guns and put the policemen under guard. Pierpont's girlfriend, Mary Kinder, later reported that she had driven along with the gang on this raid and was sitting in the back seat of the big Hudson when Pierpont, Dillinger, and others ran from the Peru station and filled the back floor of the car with guns and ammunition. "My God," she exclaimed at the time, "what are you going to do? Start a young army?"

On the morning of October 23, 1933, Charles Makley appeared in the bustling town of Greencastle, Indiana. He asked a town official for a permit to sell Oriental rugs, saying that he was a sailor who had obtained these rugs in the Far East. He planned, he said, to keep his deposits in the local bank and then made inquiries about its security measures. He was not issued the permit. At 2:45 p.m. that day, five men, including Makley, arrived in front of Greencastle's Central National Bank, double-parking a black Studebaker. Five men got out, one, Russell Clark, going down the street and standing near the local police station, another, John Hamilton, standing at the entranceway to the bank, acting as "the tiger" or sentinel.

The other three, Dillinger, Pierpont, and Makley, went into the bank. Makley stood inside the door of the bank, while Dillinger and Pierpont went to the tellers' cages. Pierpont went to a window and asked Ward Mayhall, assistant trust officer of the bank, to change a twenty-dollar bill. Mayhall told him to go to the next window and be served by Harry Wells. From beneath his long coat, Pierpont produced a submachine gun, sticking the muzzle through the window at Mayhall. "*You* change it, bub, and give me everything else you have in the drawer."

A second later Dillinger shouted to everyone in the bank: "Don't press anything or there will be a lot of dead people in here!" He vaulted the barrier, smashed a glass pane in the door leading to the tellers' cages and went inside, going from cage to cage, scooping money into a sugar sack. Makley pushed the eight customers inside the bank to a wall, lining them up and the bank's dozen employees were herded to the same wall while Makley trained a submachine gun on them. The robbery went smoothly and was obviously well-planned. It was later learned that Pierpont had once worked in Greencastle at one of the plants and knew the town well.

Makley, in his early rounds of the town, had inspected the bank and had learned that the guard in a cage above the tellers' windows would be leaving that cage at about 2:30 p.m. to stoke the furnace downstairs. That is precisely what happened. The elderly guard, Leo Ratcliff, left the cage only moments before the gangsters entered the bank. The bandits also knew that each teller's cage was equipped with an alarm button, which is why Dillinger warned them not to "press anything" at the onset of the robbery.

As Dillinger forced Wells to open the vault, Pierpont surveyed the customers and employees lined up against the wall. All had their hands high in the air. Pierpont realized that these cowed victims could be seen through the bank's large open windows and he shouted to them: "Put your hands down and keep them at your sides and don't move! We're not advertising." Makley held a stopwatch in his hand and kept glancing at it and then to the street and to Hamilton, who stood outside. One middle-aged woman started to go into the bank and then apparently changed her mind. Hamilton gently held her arm for a moment and said: "Better go inside, lady." The foreign-born woman jerked her arm away and turned on her heel, saying angrily: "I go to Penny's and you go to hell!"

Makley pressed the top of the stopwatch and then yelled out to Dillinger: "It's five minutes!" Dillinger had completed cleaning out the vault and the tellers' cages and he jumped onto a ledge, sailing in spectacular fashion over the ten-foot barrier of the teller's windows, to the public side of the bank. As he was about to leave, he noticed a farmer standing in the line of customers next to the wall. The man held some bills in his hand.

"Is that your money or the bank's?" Dillinger asked the farmer.

"Mine," the farmer said.

"Keep it," Dillinger told him. "We only want the bank's." This gesture was undoubtedly made by Dillinger the farmboy remembering his youth and the farm in Mooresville and the old man who struggled to bring crops out of the flat stubborn earth of Indiana. (This gesture was later wrongly attributed to Clyde Barrow in the movie *Bonnie and Clyde*, but anyone knowing the true nature of Barrow and his prostitute lover would realize that Barrow was incapable of such a beau geste, that the Texas bandit and killer would have snatched the farmer's meager savings and shot him to death for "kicks.")

Within minutes, Dillinger and Pierpont had gathered $18,428 in cash and $56,300 in bonds, which the gang would later fence for 50¢ on the dollar, after paying a commission to mastermind Eddie Bentz, who had reportedly provided information on the bank and its holdings at the time, Bentz being the master bank "caser" for almost all the notorious bank robbing gangs of that era. As the gang members left the bank, Dillinger, carrying the sugar sack stuffed with the money, including $400 in halves, $200 in quarters and $18 in silver dollars, bumped into Rex Thorlton, a grocery store manager, who was about to make a deposit.

Thorlton, as he was entering the bank, was reaching for his bankbook and money in a back pocket and Pierpont believed he was reaching for a gun. Pierpont brought his gun butt down hard on Thorlton's head. The grocer fell, striking Dillinger and knocking his hat off. Realizing who the bandits were, Thorlton, according to one story, apologized to "Mr. Dillinger," handing him back his hat.

The robbers got into the Studebaker and drove down to the end of the block, picking up Clark, who was still standing lookout, and then drove along dirt roads and disappeared, avoiding all roadblocks set up a short time later. They followed routes they had specially mapped, which would allow them to drive for fifty miles without ever using a highway and thus evade pursuers.

The Greencastle robbery was one of the best-planned and executed crimes committed by the Terror Gang, one which displayed an extraordinary amount of precaution and sophisticated planning. This, more than the awful reputation the gang had earned within a few weeks, alarmed local, state, and federal officials. They realized that they were dealing not with bungling thugs but with intelligent, crafty men who were well-armed and prepared to kill anyone who stood in their way. Much of this posture was due to the style and attitude of Harry Pierpont, the real brains of the gang.

Pierpont was also a better-than-average amateur psychologist. He proved to be the most daring of the gang and had steel nerves, but he was also impulsive and knew it, so he preferred that Dillinger take the limelight during the robberies, knowing that Dillinger enjoyed showing off by vaulting the tellers' cages. When Dillinger's name began to be a household word through his exposure in the nation's press and on radio, the bandit told Pierpont that he intended to write to certain radio announcers to correct their mispronunciation of his name. The name Dillinger was Germanic and contained a hard "g." The press and public pronounced the name with a soft ending and Pierpont persuaded Dillinger to let it stand that way, telling his fellow bandit that it was better that way, that his name sounded like the pistol, "derringer," and was thus synonymous with a lethal weapon.

With large funds at their disposal, gang members rented expensive apartments in Chicago, which they used as a base, much to the annoyance of the Capone gang and other members of organized crime in the city, since these urban gangsters felt that independent bandits like Dillinger brought too much police attention to their area and, often enough, police raids of suspected Dillinger hideouts snared members of organized crime in illegal gambling dens and bordellos. Members of the Dillinger gang enjoyed their stolen loot by taking their girlfriends to musical shows, nightclubs, and the better restaurants. They bought tailor-made suits and imported ties and hats. They purchased fast cars, using only stolen autos for robberies. They planned carefully each of their robberies, holding long meetings and studying their targets, buying information from such expert bank casers as Eddie Bentz.

During their meetings, only Dillinger and Pierpont talked, describing the approach to the bank, and how it was protected and how much money it would probably be holding. Hamilton, the "old pro" of the group, occasionally made remarks about techniques to be employed. Makley, Clark, Copeland, and Shouse invariably kept silent and listened as their mentors outlined their next move. None of these men were heavy drinkers. Dillinger himself was a light cigarette smoker and drank mostly beer, taking an occasional shot of whiskey. They were also in excellent physical condition after having undergone years of prison discipline.

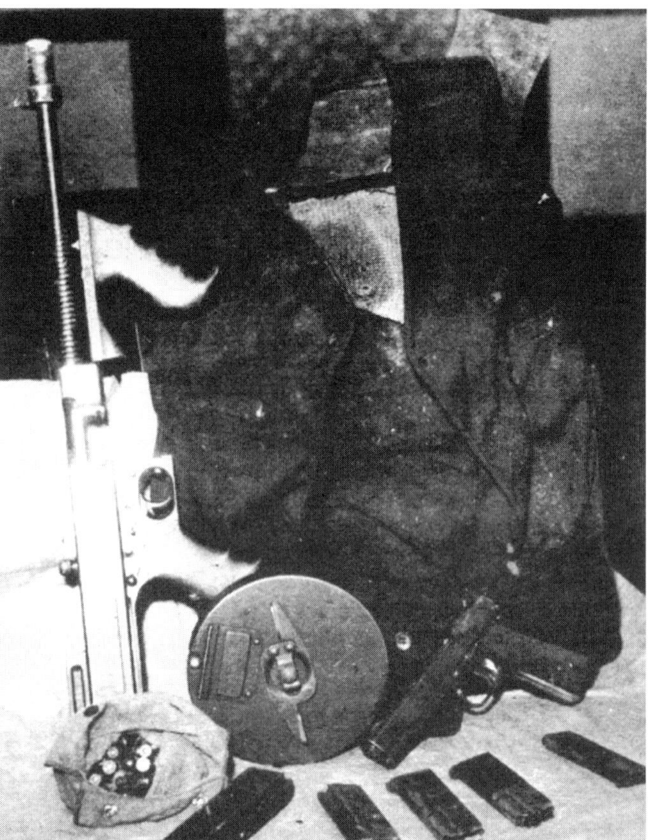

This submachine gun, bullets, a .45-caliber automatic and bullet proof vest (taken in a raid by the Dillinger gang from the arsenal room of the Auburn, Indiana, Police Department on October 14, 1933) were found in Dillinger's room in Tucson.

Opposing the gang were a number of competent lawmen in several states, the most dogged being Captain Matt Leach, head of a special Dillinger force of the Indiana State Police. Leach was a rather pompous, self-serving officer, who believed he could outsmart the Terror Gang. He thought to undermine the gang by publicly naming Pierpont as the gang leader, believing this would cause dissension among members and eventually cause them to split up, but nothing of the kind ever happened. Leach insulted Dillinger in print at every opportunity and Dillinger, more than once, called Leach to threaten him. The captain once insisted that Dillinger had called him on the phone and said: "We'll get you! Watch your ass!" Sergeant Frank Reynolds, a member of the "Dillinger Squad" headed by Captain John Stege of the Chicago Police Department, also claimed to have received an identical call from Dillinger.

Leach, however, remained in the news as the law enforcement watchdog on Dillinger's trail. The captain had his photo taken at every opportunity, mostly in heroic poses, as he made sweeping statements about how he and his men would soon have the Dillinger gang in custody. At one point, Leach called a press conference to report that he had re-

John Dillinger, center, is shown under guard in a police car as he arrives in Chicago from Tucson, en route to the so-called "escape-proof" jail in Crown Point, Indiana, where he was held pending a murder charge in a bank robbery.

ceived in the mail an 1896 publication entitled "How To Be a Detective," which he said the taunting Dillinger had sent to him. This later proved to be untrue; the author later learned that newspaperman William L. "Tubby" Toms of the Indianapolis *News* had sent the publication to humiliate Leach for his strutting ways.

Leach was forever giving newsmen profiles of Dillinger, who had, for him, become the arch criminal of the century. It was Leach's belief that Dillinger's own inflated self-confidence and "wise guy" posturing would bring about his ruination. It is true that Dillinger placed phone calls to Leach and, on one occasion, said: "This is John Dillinger. How are you, you stuttering bastard?" (In the 1973 motion picture *Dillinger,* such phone calls are shown to be made from Dillinger to Melvin Purvis, but this was pure fiction, as was most of the idiotic script for this film.)

Dillinger became a Midwest mania. Every robbery of note was attributed to him and the Terror Gang. When the Western State Bank of South Bend was robbed of $5,000 on October 24, 1933, the robbery was credited to Dillinger, but the actual thieves were apprehended a short time later. Even small jobs such as the robbery of the tiny bank in Fillmore, Indiana, which yielded robbers only $130, and the theft of $400 from the People's Loan and Trust Company in Modoc, Indiana, were at first attributed to Dillinger. Moreover, the public was fascinated with John Dillinger and his friends simply because they were robbing banks in an era when bank reputations were at an all-time low. Banks were looked upon as mean-spirited institutions that ruthlessly foreclosed on farmers and shopkeepers, that put decent families into the street, that made of a hardworking middleclass a nation of hobos and bums during the Depression.

To many living in that dark economic Depression, bankers were economic despots and tyrants, unthinking, uncaring, and without compassion, hateful creatures who preyed upon the misery and misfortune of good people. Dillinger avenged these real or imagined wrongs, it was thought by many, when he raided a bank; a farm boy striking back, as it were, against a bureaucratic system, rooted not in the good earth of an agrarian America, but in the corrupt foundations of the cities, where venal politicians and bankers squandered the country's wealth, gluttonously consuming the product of honest toil.

Letters by the thousands objecting to any smear of this offbeat folk hero poured into newspapers that editorialized against Dillinger and his men. One letter to an Indianapolis newspaper attacked an editorialist who had lambasted Dillinger: "This person calls Dillinger cheap. He isn't half as cheap as a crooked banker or a crooked politician because he did give the bankers a chance to fight, and they never gave the people a chance." Another said: "I am for John Dillinger. Not that I am upholding him in any of his crimes, that is, if he did any. Why should the law have wanted John Dillinger for bank robbery? He wasn't any worse than bankers and politicians who took the poor people's money."

Meanwhile, all was not well within the ranks of the Terror Gang. Ed Shouse had begun drinking heavily and his nerves seemed shattered. He was a supposed expert getaway driver, yet he handled the wheels of cars so nervously as of late that gang members feared driving with him. Worse, gang members believed that Shouse might be informing lawmen about their movements. Shouse had been asking many questions concerning the day to day movements of gang members.

The suspicions of Dillinger and Pierpont were correct. Shouse had turned informer. He, along with another police informant, Art McGinnis, who knew Dillinger and sometimes provided him with guns, tipped police that Dillinger was suffering from an irritating rash, and that he was taking treatment from Dr. Charles Eye, whose offices were located at 4175 W. Irving Park Boulevard, in Chicago.

Chicago Police Department Captain John Stege ordered several men from his Dillinger Squad to stake out Dr. Eye's office, and on November 15, 1933, Dillinger, indeed, showed up. He was driving his favorite car, a Hudson Terraplane, with Evelyn Frechette at his side. As he approached the physician's office, Dillinger noticed several unmarked police cars parked nearby, all of them parked the wrong way. He changed gears and roared off down the boulevard. Detectives saw the Terraplane turn about abruptly and they gave chase. In a frightening burst of speed, Dillinger quickly outdistanced all the squad cars except one occupied by Sergeant John Artery and officer Art Keller. Both cars raced along Irving Park Boulevard at 80 m.p.h., narrowly missing pedestrians, street trolleys, and parked cars. When the cars were hood to hood, Keller leaned out a window and began pumping shells from his shotgun at Dillinger.

"Hey," Evelyn Frechette said to her lover, "somebody's shooting at you." Dillinger grinned, seeming to enjoy the chase and the hazard of the shotgun bursts, which exploded the glass of his car but left him uninjured. He jammed his foot down on the accelerator. The Terraplane, a powerful car, seemed to jerk in mid-flight and then surge suddenly forward. Dillinger saw a narrow side street and, when almost at

Crown Point, Indiana: While posing for scores of news photographers, the impudent John Dillinger, in vest, center, puts his arm onto the shoulder of Indiana Prosecutor Robert Estill, while Sheriff Lillian Holley looks at her famous prisoner with what the press thought to be admiration; Estill, exhausted after escorting Dillinger from Tucson, instinctively put his arm around Dillinger, a friendly gesture that destroyed his political career.

the corner, he spun the wheel of the car, which took the corner almost on two wheels as the police squad roared past it down Irving Park. By the time Artery turned the car around and returned to the side street, Dillinger had vanished. Keller threw his shotgun into the back seat in disgust and grudgingly complimented Dillinger by saying: "That bird can sure drive!"

Shouse later appeared in Mary Kinder's apartment, a meeting place for the gang and here Kinder overheard him tell Hamilton that they might do better if they robbed a few banks on their own. Kinder shouted at Shouse: "You ain't gonna do a damned thing, Ed. There ain't nobody going no place until we all talk it over! This has always been a friendly bunch and you ain't gonna take no two or three and go rob a bank." Dillinger had no love for Shouse, believing that Shouse, when drunk on earlier occasions, had made a play for his girlfriend, Evelyn Frechette. He took a wad of bills from his pocket and tossed this to Shouse. "There's your money. You're through. Now get your ass out!" Shouse left the gang and was later captured and jailed.

For some time, gang members had been eyeing the American Bank and Trust Company in Racine, Wisconsin. The gang moved to a hideout in Milwaukee and from there made plans to rob this bank. The resulting successful robbery was so well planned that its intricate preparations smacked of Eddie Bentz's techniques. Someone, perhaps the master bank caser himself, arrived in Racine in early November 1933, staying at the Hotel Racine, only a block from the bank. Bentz undoubtedly checked the bank's current assets by visiting the local library and reading the banking reports published by law in the local press. He then went to the bank every day at 2:30 p.m., the time that the actual bank robbery would occur, to check conditions at that time, noting the movements of guards, city police and employee activity inside the bank, along with the number of customers to be expected at that hour. Escape routes were carefully planned. He noted stoplights, traffic police, and the distance from the bank to the city limits and how much time, at normal driving speed, it would take to get out of town.

On November 20, 1933, a brand new blue Buick sedan with yellow wire wheels pulled up in front of Racine's American Bank and Trust Company at Main and Fifth Streets. Harry Pierpont, looking dapper and elegant in a new custom-tailored suit, entered the bank with a roll of paper tucked under his arm. Without a word to anyone, Pierpont went to the large bay window and, unraveling a Red Cross Poster, pasted this on the window.

The poster was designed to obstruct any view of the inside of the bank by passersby outside, but Mrs. Henry Patzke, the bank's bookkeeper, merely noticed a handsome young man putting up the poster and thought he had been given permission to do so. She went back to her work. Then, in quick order, Dillinger, Makley, and Hamilton entered the bank. Makley went to the head teller, Harold Graham, who was in a cage and was busily counting coins.

"Stick 'em up," Makley ordered, poking a submachine gun at Graham.

The head teller did not look up, thinking someone was kidding him. He merely said: "Go to the next window, please."

Makley, annoyed, repeated his demand: "I *said* stick 'em up!"

Then Graham looked up and made a sudden movement which caused Makley to instinctively fire a burst from the gun. A bullet struck Graham in the arm and another in the hip, sending him crashing to the floor, where he reached up and pressed an alarm button beneath the ledge of the teller's cage. The alarm did not sound inside the bank, but did go off at Racine Police headquarters. Officers Cyril Boyard and Rudy Speaker got the report of the bank alarm going off, but they took their time responding, driving slowly toward the bank in a circuitous route. The alarm had gone off many times in the past, mostly when a clerk or teller accidentally hit the alarm button.

Inside the bank, Dillinger, Pierpont, and Hamilton ran down the aisle behind the tellers' cages. Pierpont carried a submachine gun. Dillinger shouted: "Everybody flat on their stomachs!" L. C. Rowan, an assistant cashier, who was sitting at a front desk, hit an alarm button, which caused another bell to go off in the police station and this also started a bell clanging outside the bank. Just at that moment police officers Franklin Worsley and Wilbur Hansen, answering the alarm, walked into the bank and Pierpont began to disarm them. Hansen tried to back out of the door, but Clark, who was standing guard outside, shoved him back into the bank. Then Hansen appeared to go for his gun and Makley let loose a burst from his submachine gun which wounded the officer and caused the women in the bank to begin screaming.

Dillinger and Pierpont had walked Grover Weyland, the president of the bank, to the vault where Weyland took his time unlocking it, stalling until the police arrived. Pierpont jammed a submachine gun into Weyland's stomach and shouted: "Get into the vault and open it up, and you'd better not miss it. We don't like bank presidents. We'd as soon shoot you as look at you!" Weyland finally managed to open the vault and Dillinger and Pierpont stepped inside with the bank president. Pierpont, who had fired a burst from his gun at Officers Worsley and Hansen when they first entered the bank, took time to reload his weapon, slipping another pan of ammunition onto the Thompson. As he was doing so, he pointed the gun in the direction of George Ryan, a young bank teller who was flat on the floor.

Some of the hundreds of guards outside of the so-called "escape-proof" jail at Crown Point, Indiana, which Dillinger escaped from on March 3, 1934.

"For God's sake, mister," Ryan implored, "point that gun the other way!"

Pierpont smiled at him and said: "As long as you're a good boy, you don't have to worry."

Outside crowds were gathering in front of the bank and Clark fired several warning shots for passersby to stay away. No one seemed to understand that the bank was being robbed. Dillinger finally emerged from the vault and he leaped over the tellers' cages, shouting triumphantly: "I've got it all." He did not have it all. While hurriedly going through the drawers of the tellers' cages, Pierpont and Dillinger had overlooked more than $50,000 in cash which was wadded up and in the back of a drawer, covered with deposit receipts. The gang, however, took $27,789 before leaving the bank. When the gang emerged, police officers across the street fired, aiming high so as not to hit the crowd members in front of the bank. Clark, Makley, and Hamilton fired back, raking the buildings across the street, smashing second-story windows. Then the gang pushed several female bank employees onto the running

Criminal attorney Louis Piquett, Dillinger's lawyer, intended to prove that his client could not have committed the bank robbery and murder in East Chicago, for which Dillinger was charged. Reportedly, Dillinger told Piquett that he intended to escape the jail at Crown Point, believing he would be railroaded into the electric chair.

board of the a Buick, got inside and roared down the street, the hostages hanging on the car and preventing police from firing at it.

Following their own maps, the gang sped along dirt roads and later deposited their hostages in a lonely spot. Dillinger jocularly asked one of the females if she could cook. She replied: "After a fashion."

"Some other time," Dillinger said and the car shot forward, quickly disappearing over a rise. The gang then cut south and headed for Florida, driving to Daytona Beach, where members rented several cottages. They chartered fishing boats and fished for marlin. They sat about playing cards and listening to the radio. Mary Kinder and Evelyn Frechette cooked for them. From Daytona, the gang moved west, driving to Tucson, Arizona. About the time the gang arrived in Tucson, on January 15, 1934, the First National Bank of East Chicago was robbed of more than $20,000. A 43-year-old motorcycle policeman, William Patrick O'Malley, tried to stop two men, when they fled the bank and he was cut in half by their machine gun fire. The robbery and murder were attributed to John Dillinger and John Hamilton, although it is improbable that either man could have participated in this robbery since both were in Arizona at the time, according to most reliable accounts. This was, however, the first and only murder ever credited to John Dillinger.

Convicted murderer Herbert Youngblood escaped with Dillinger from the Crown Point Jail; he was later killed in Michigan.

In Tucson, the gang's luck went bad. A fire broke out in the Congress Hotel, where Clark and Makley were staying and they gave hundreds of dollars to firemen to carry their bags out of their rooms. A fireman lugging one of the heavy suitcases became suspicious and opened it up to discover a submachine gun and several pistols. He notified local police and both Clark and Makley were arrested without a fight. Then Dillinger, Pierpont, and their girls, Opal Long, Clark's girl friend, Mary Kinder, using the alias Bernice Thompson, and Evelyn Billie Frechette, using the alias Anne Martin, were captured. Pierpont and Makley were quickly extradited to Ohio to stand trial for the murder of Sheriff Sarber, while Dillinger was sent back to Indiana to stand trial for the killing of Officer O'Malley. The girls were also shipped back east, charged with obstructing justice, and in Mary Kinder's case, aiding in the prison escape at Michigan City. John Hamilton was not apprehended, having left Tucson a few days earlier, ostensibly to case another bank in the Midwest.

The gangsters were placed in the Pima County Jail while their hastily hired attorney, John Van Buskirk of Los Angeles unsuccessfully fought against several writs demanding extradition to Indiana and Ohio. The first arriving to demand extradition was a large delegation from Indiana, including Captain Matt Leach, Prosecutor Robert Estill of Lake County, Indiana, Sheriff Lillian Holley and her nephew, Under-sheriff Carroll Holley, and Police Chief Maker of East Chicago, Indiana. One in this group saw Dillinger in a cell and shouted: "He's the one who killed O'Malley," a point too sorely made in that Estill and others from Indiana knew there was considerable doubt about Dillinger actually being in East Chicago, Indiana, when the motorcycle policeman was killed. (Police Chief Maker's presence in Tucson was strange in that he had no official capacity. It was later claimed that Maker was present to make sure that the O'Malley killing was, indeed, pinned on Dillinger, even though he knew that someone else had killed the policeman. Maker represented a small but widely corrupt police force, with several of its officers being in the pay of gangsters, including Sergeant Martin Zarkovich, who would later be deeply involved in Dillinger's so-called execution and permanent escape.)

Dillinger had repeatedly denied being in East Chicago on January 15, 1934, and said he could prove it; so did attorney Van Buskirk. They knew that if convicted of the O'Malley killing, it would mean a death sentence. Matt Leach, in a confidential interview with the press, all but admitted that certain politicians in Indiana planned to have "Johnny executed for the East Chicago robbery and killing, no matter what it cost." Leach beamed with triumph when he entered the lockup at the Pima County Jail.

Leach walked straight to Dillinger's cell and stuck his hand through the bars. Dillinger lamely took it in a brief shake. As Leach walked past the cell holding Pierpont, Handsome Harry exploded: "I should have killed you when I had the chance, you dirty son-of-a-bitch! You put my mother in jail in Terre Haute, you bastard! If I ever get out of this, the first thing I going to do is kill you, you rat!"

Dillinger later told newsmen on his plane trip back to Indiana that Pierpont and he had been walking down an Indianapolis street one night some weeks earlier and discovered that Matt Leach, their pursuer, was walking directly in front of them and it was all Dillinger could do to prevent Pierpont from killing the lawman on the spot. The statement Pierpont made about his mother referred to a time when Indiana officers had arrested Mrs. Pierpont and Fred Pierpont and held them in the Terre Haute Jail for questioning for some days. Leach, however, had nothing to do with this. After officials inspected the prisoners, crowds of curious citizens clamoring for a view of the notorious Terror Gang were allowed to go into the Pima Jail lockup in small groups.

By this time, Dillinger had tired of all the bravado. He snarled at a guard: "if anyone one of those bozos or besocks gets close to my cell I'll brain them." He lay on his bunk, face to the wall. Ever the clown, Makley convinced a young Texan locked up in the cell opposite to impersonate Dillinger for the crowd. The Texan happily agreed to do so, as long as he was paid by those posing with him for photos next to his cell. He earned so much money that he was able to pay off his attorney and the fine for his minor offense and was released the next day.

Dillinger stands outside his father's farmhouse near Mooresville, Indiana in early March 1934, holding the wooden gun he used to effect his jail escape. He holds a real submachine gun in his left hand, one that he took from the jail at the time he broke free.

Fat Charley Makley, though he knew he and Pierpont were wanted for the murder of Sheriff Jess Sarber, acted as if he were being detained on a speeding charge. A newspaperman, Jack Weadock, stood by Makley's cell and reminded him that they had known each other as youths in St. Marys, Ohio: "You once shoed horses in my father's blacksmith stable," he reminded Makley.

"So you're George's kid," Makley said. And then he became conspiratorial, telling Weadock that the most dangerous man in the gang was Harry Pierpont, whom everyone in the gang called Pete. "If anything happens here, you watch out for Pete. He's a wild man." He said that Dillinger was not as tough as Pierpont but "every one of us trusts Johnny ... He's got a level head and he's the smart one." Makley then lapsed into childhood memories and nostalgically remembered the hardworking members of his family. "They were honest, at least, even if never rich. But I could not take that kind of life. Look at my dad. He worked like the devil all his life and what did he get out of it? I've lived as long in forty minutes at times as my dad did in forty years."

Clark, the towering giant of the gang, had been hit twice in the head with gun butts by arresting officers and his head had been opened up and had required several stitches. He wore a bloody bandage around his head and sat quietly in his cell, his eyes furtively darting back and forth, as if looking for an opportunity to escape. He refused to talk to anyone, but he did make a remark to one guard, a feeble joke: "When I get out of here I'm gonna wear a football helmet. Every time we get in trouble, I get hit over the head." Of all of the gang members, only Clark could look forward to surviving a trial in that he was the only member of the gang not charged with murder.

Dillinger was by then so notorious that his capture made national headlines. An army of newsmen descended on Tucson and he was interviewed endlessly, saying nothing of importance and denying that he had anything to do with the East Chicago robbery and O'Malley's death. Newsmen accompanied him on the plane back to Chicago and Sol Davis (the father of novelist Marc Davis, and grandfather of journalist and author Kevin Davis), a photographer for the Chicago *Times,* who bought all four vacant seats on the plane, took endless photos of the bandit while engaging him in chatty conversation. When the plane landed in Chicago, dozens of gun-carrying guards were on hand to surround the prisoner who was led through a phalanx of newsmen to a waiting car, which would take Dillinger to the Crown Point Jail, the so-called "escape-proof jail."

Dillinger with Evelyn Freschette outside his father's farmhouse at a family reunion.

Dillinger's father sits on plough at his farm during the time his bandit son visited him after his jail break from Crown Point; he felt his son had received a "raw deal" from the courts.

It appeared that the Dillinger Terror Gang was smashed, finished once and for all. A great show of force was displayed in Crown Point with newsreel photographers recording the dozens of armed vigilantes roaming the grounds and streets in front and back of the jail, while national guardsmen, state and local police paraded back and forth, thousands of men arrayed to prevent Dillinger associates from again releasing him. But there were few Dillinger gang members still at large. John Hamilton had gone into hiding. Homer Van Meter, who had been released from Michigan City, Indiana, was somewhere in St. Paul, Minn. All the rest, Copeland, Shouse, Makley, Clark, Pierpont, and Shaw were in custody.

Dillinger was photographed upon his arrival with Prosecutor Estill and Sheriff Holley. In an act of brazenness, Dillinger leaned his arm on Estill's shoulder and the prosecutor, exhausted by the trip, paid no attention to it. This photo, however, later proved to be disastrous for Estill, making him appear chummy with the very man he was to prosecute. This photograph would cost Estill his next election. Scores of newsmen took photos and motion pictures for the newsreels. Questions were pumped at Dillinger like bullets spitting out of a submachine gun. He was treated like a visiting movie star.

"How long does it take for you and your men to rob a bank?" one newsman asked.

"Oh, about one minute and forty seconds flat," Dillinger bragged.

"How did you get caught in Tucson?"

"Makley and Clark. They paid those firemen too much money to carry their bags down from that burning hotel. If those saps had made it only a couple of bucks, we'd still be safe and happy."

"Weren't you almost caught in Chicago by the police there?"

"Yeah, in November of last year when I was going to see a doctor on Irving Park Boulevard. That was because a stool pigeon turned me up to the police." Dillinger narrowed his eyes and looked directly into the cameras, as if hoping McGinnis would

FBI Director J. Edgar Hoover named Dillinger Public Enemy Number One after the Crown Point Jail break, but the bandit had broken only one federal law at that time—taking a stolen car across a state line.

FBI Agent Melvin Purvis, left, with Attorney General Homer Cummings, was in charge of the Chicago Bureau and ordered by Hoover to "get Dillinger at all costs." Purvis was reckless in his pursuit of the bandit.

see the newsreel and hear his chilling words, knowing what to expect if Dillinger ever regained his freedom: "His name is Art McGinnis. I fed him and clothed him when he was broke, but he squealed on me."

"How did you live, you, Pierpont, Clark, Makley, and the others?"

Dillinger grew nostalgic for a period of time that was only a few months in the past, almost as if he were talking about deep time, decades earlier: "Those were exciting times. We moved from house to house. Rented one, stayed a few days, and moved on when the neighborhood got too hot. But we used to go downtown [in Chicago] to the theaters whenever we wanted to."

"What's your favorite movie?"

"*The Three Little Pigs.*"

The interview ended and Dillinger was taken to a cell on the third floor of the jail. The newsmen joined the thirty Chicago police officers and their leader, Captain John Stege, who had escorted Dillinger to the Crown Point Jail in a motorcade brimming with machine guns. The Chicago police were sitting in the jail's dining room, eating a roast beef dinner. There was a huge barrel of beer in the center of the long table at which they ate. Hoosier hospitality was in full force.

The following day, front page stories in all the newspapers reported how Crown Point had been turned into an impregnable fortress. Said one story: "The measures taken by Sheriff Holley to guard her noted prisoner makes it almost impossible to stage an attempt to rescue him and none will be tried ... The jail is floodlit and in a protected corner a special police officer sits night and day with a machine gun trained on Dillinger's cell, ready to repel any attempt to liberate him."

The day after Dillinger's arrival at Crown Point, he availed himself of the one phone call to which he was entitled, calling Chicago criminal attorney, Louis Piquett. The attorney visited Dillinger the next day. The 53-year-old Piquett was a most unusual criminal lawyer with a colorful past. He had been a lead miner in Platteville, Wisconsin, before moving to Chicago to become a bartender. He studied law at night and, without a college degree, passed the Chicago bar in 1916 at the age of twenty-six.

From 1920 to 1924, Piquett was a prosecuting attorney for the city and proved to be a spellbinder in court. He went into private practice and effectively represented a host of criminals, mostly those on Al Capone's payroll. It was Piquett who had, in spite of overwhelming evidence of guilt, saved Leo Brothers from the electric chair when defending him in 1931 on the charge of killing the corrupt Chicago *Tribune* reporter, Jake Lingle. Piquett was a close associate of the crooked politicians and gangsters, who ran Chicago at that time and his contacts with the underworld were widespread.

After conferring with his client, Piquett announced that Dillinger would never go to the electric chair for killing Officer O'Malley. "We have an ironclad alibi," boasted Piquett to the press, "which will prove that John was in Florida on January 14, 1934, and could therefore not have been in East Chicago on the following day when the officer was killed."

Psychopathic Lester Gillis, known as Baby Face Nelson, joined the gang Dillinger assembled after his March 1934 jail break.

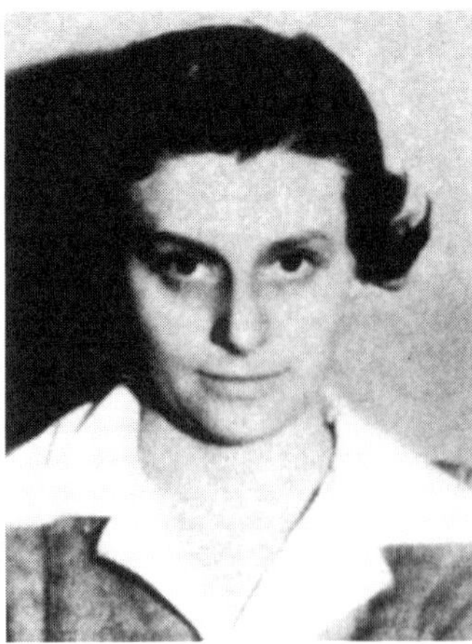

Baby Face Nelson's wife, Helen, was with him when FBI agents attacked Little Bohemia Lodge on April 22, 1934.

On February 9, 1934, a pretrial hearing before Judge William J. Murray proved to be explosive. Prosecutor Estill demanded that Dillinger be tried within ten days for the killing of O'Malley, but Piquett demanded more time, saying it would take at least four months to round up all the witnesses in Florida, who would testify to his client's being in that state at the time of the O'Malley killing. Estill continued to insist on ten days and Piquett leaped from his seat, yelling: "That would be legal murder! There's a law against lynching in this state!"

Estill also rose and yelled back: "There's a law against murder, too!"

Judge Murray set the date of the trial for March 12, 1934. Estill was edgy about the possibility of Dillinger being freed. He asked Judge Murray to transfer the prisoner to Michigan City, Indiana, for safekeeping at the state prison. Judge Murray refused to move Dillinger, saying: "a hundred men couldn't take him out of that jail." He added that he could not, under the law, transfer Dillinger, unless there was a threat of mob violence and no vigilantism threatened the prisoner. Guards around the jail had proved to be alert.

A sightseer was stopped while driving slowly past the front of the jail. His car was searched and his identity determined him to be an innocent man. A photographer took a photo of the rear of the jail and was suddenly surrounded by six gun-toting guards, his camera confiscated. This was returned to him after his credentials were checked, but the film he had exposed was kept by the jail guards.

No one was trusted near the jail and guards were all too aware of the subtle ways in which the Dillinger gang operated; how its members had posed as newsmen in robbing banks, boldly interviewing bank presidents about their security systems and measures, thus learning the bank's weak points; how they had also posed as policemen and sheriffs, obtaining vital information from legitimate lawmen. Several hundred men kept an around-the-clock vigil, expecting an army of gangsters to come roaring into Crown Point at any moment to free America's most celebrated bandit.

The army of guards, however, were looking the wrong way. Dillinger's deliverance would not come from without, but from within. The notorious prisoner sat in his cell most of the time whittling and chatting with other prisoners. He was permitted by Judge Murray to visit with his lawyer, Piquett, at least five or six times, in a private room with no one else present. Moreover, Evelyn Billie Frechette, out on bail, was permitted to visit Dillinger on February 26, 1934. She went to the jail accompanied by Piquett, but was thoroughly searched by Sheriff Holley. Piquett was never searched. Dillinger also met briefly with the elder Dillinger, an awkward meeting where the bandit apologized for creating such notoriety for his family.

Piquett was confident that he could successfully defend his client against the murder charge, having put together an impressive list of witnesses, who were willing to swear that Dillinger was in Florida at the time of the East Chicago robbery and shooting. Moreover, he had given Estill the names of three Indiana citizens who would also swear that Dillinger was not the machine gun killer of O'Malley, that they had seen the shooting and would identify another man. This information sent shock waves through the East Chicago Police Department, where a case against Dillinger had been a foregone conclusion. Still, Dillinger apparently felt that no number of alibi witnesses could save him from a murder conviction the state insisted on having. He decided to escape on his own.

Dillinger had spent hours each day whittling, working with a penknife on a piece of wood he took from the top of a washboard. He fashioned an automatic pistol, according to the best reports, and then, using a razor, cut out the fine details of the gun, blackening it with boot polish, so that it looked very real. At 9:15 a.m., on March 3, 1934, Dillinger and fourteen other prisoners were walking about the exercise room in the rear of the second floor of the jail. Sam Cahoon, a 64-year-old turnkey, unlocked the bullpen holding the prisoners and was about to enter, carrying buckets of hot water and soap for the prisoners' morning wash-up, when Dillinger rushed to Cahoon's side as the bullpen door swung open, and jammed the wooden gun into his ribs, saying: "Get inside quick or I'll kill you." He quickly took Cahoon and two porters prisoner, placing them in a cell. He then crept down a deserted corridor and, around the corner, spotted Ernest Blunk. He forced Cahoon to call Blunk to the exercise area and when the turnkey did so, Blunk was made a prisoner, believing Dillinger was holding a ".45-caliber automatic."

Little Bohemia Lodge, at Manitowish Waters, Wisconsin, where FBI agents attacked on the night of April 22, 1934, shooting the front of the lodge to pieces after killing an innocent guest and wounding two others; the Dillinger gang offered no resistance, escaping from the back of the lodge into nearby woods.

Blunk was then sent to call up three more guards and Warden Lou Baker, as Dillinger, menacing him with the fake gun, hid in a nearby corridor. The guards, turnkey Cahoon, Blunk and then Warden Baker, along with thirteen prisoners were all locked into cells by the energetic Dillinger. He was joined by a black prisoner, Herbert Youngblood, awaiting trial for murder. Dillinger had asked Youngblood and Harry Jelinek, awaiting trial for robbery, if they wanted to join him. Jelinek declined, but Youngblood replied: "Yes, sir, Mr. Dillinger, I believe I do." Youngblood grabbed a heavy mop handle and used this to corral prisoners with Dillinger. The wooden gun employed by Dillinger throughout this time appeared to be different to each guard he intimidated with it. To Deputy Kenneth Houk, the gun was "a .38-automatic," and Houk later insisted that it was real: "When I hear people say that he got out with a wooden gun I get so mad I could spit. You look down the barrel of one and you know the difference between a wooden gun and a good one. There's, a difference between metal and wood covered with shoe blacking."

The problem was that none of the guards stared at the gun for more than a few seconds and none of them at the time, including Houk, would have been foolish enough to challenge the gun's genuineness. All of the prisoners up to this point were unarmed and Dillinger was desperate to obtain a real gun before his ruse was discovered. Pushing Blunk in front of him, Dillinger went downstairs through a side corridor and spotted Warden Hiles, who was carrying a real .45-caliber automatic. He quickly disarmed Hiles and marched him and Blunk back to the cells on the second floor. He then went back downstairs while Youngblood guarded the prisoners and walked into the empty front office.

Dillinger found two Thompson submachine guns lying on a window sill and grabbing these, returned to the second floor. He handed one of the submachine guns to Youngblood and then took up a collection, getting $15 from the guards. He then produced his wooden gun and ran its barrel slowly along the bars of the cell holding the guards and Warden Baker. "I did it all with my little toy pistol, gentlemen," he told them. All but Houk would later agree that the gun Dillinger held up to them was a clever fake. Blunk later stated: "It was the best imitation of a gun I ever saw." It was later claimed that Louis Piquett, or even Evelyn Frechette had smuggled a real automatic to Dillinger during one of their jailhouse conferences, but most evidence points to the use of a wooden gun.

Again using Blunk as a shield, Dillinger and Youngblood went downstairs and through the side corridor to the open yard and crossed this to the jail garage. None of the cars inside the garage had keys in the ignition. Dillinger locked up several jail employees in a laundry room, including Mrs. Mary Linton, Warden Baker's mother-in-law, who had just returned from a shopping trip, having been driven by a bailiff. Mrs. Linton took one look at the man holding the submachine gun and said: "My God! You're John Dillinger!"

Dillinger motioned to her and the bailiff to join the others in the laundry room, saying: "Right. You do as I tell you." After locking these two up, Dillinger asked Blunk where the nearest public garage was located. Blunk told him three doors down from the back of the jail garage and the three men stepped outside, Dillinger wearing Blunk's overcoat. They walked down the street in full view of patrolling guardsmen and passersby, none taking note of the trio. They then stepped into the rear of the Main Street Garage, where Dillinger saw mechanic Edwin Saager leaning at work on a car, his head beneath the car's hood.

"Which car in here is the fastest?" Dillinger asked.

Saager glanced at him, thinking Dillinger to be a deputy and pointed to a black Ford V-8 with a red headlight and a siren. It was parked facing toward the garage doors. "That one," said Saager, "the Sheriff's car."

"Come on, let's go," Dillinger ordered Saager.

"I can't," replied the mechanic, still thinking he was talking to a deputy, who was going out on a routine patrol. "I'm working on a car."

Dillinger hit Saager's leg with the machine gun and the mechanic straightened up and then went white. Trembling, he got into the back seat of the car as ordered. Dillinger got in beside him and ordered Blunk to get behind the wheel and drive. Youngblood climbed in next to Blunk and the car rolled slowly out of the garage. Robert Volk, a postal employee, who was part of the vigilante force and carried a .45-caliber automatic, was in the garage at the time and watched the whole scene, but was frozen with fear at the sight of Dillinger and did nothing.

Blunk drove slowly, but purposely went through a red light to attract the attention of police lining the street. The police, however, believing the occupants of the car to be Sheriff Holley and deputies, merely smiled and waved them on. When the V-8 reached the city limits, Dillinger ordered Blunk to drive onto the macadam road running alongside the Pennsylvania Railroad tracks. Meanwhile, Volk regained his composure and raced to a phone, calling the police department. "Dillinger's escaped!" he screamed over the phone.

"What?" said an incredulous voice at the other end. "You're nuts! You want us to lock you up?" Finally, Volk managed to convince some jail authorities that the most desperate outlaw in America was once more free. The news stunned Sheriff Lillian Holley, who sank into a chair in near collapse. Some minutes later she called the state police to report the escape.

"How did it happen?" she was asked.

"It's too ridiculous for words," she replied. Later she met the press, almost in a state of shock, saying: "Dillinger took one chance in a million and all the breaks were with him and against me ... How this could have happened I don't quite see." Sheriff Holley was a rare exception in 1934 America, a female sheriff. She was actually filling out the term vacated when her husband died. But she came under criticism as a female, being too soft with Dillinger and other prisoners. It was even pointed out that she had, in photos taken with Dillinger, looked at her prisoner with a look of admiration.

"You think your job is too big for a woman?" one reporter asked her.

"Oh, hell's fire, of course not," she replied in disgust.

Deputy Houk did show a certain amount of admiration for the desperado, saying of Dillinger: "I never heard him cuss or be abusive in any way, shape or fashion. The morning he came out, he was tough, but not the tough "killer" type. He would have killed if his life had been at stake, but as far as being a deliberate killer, I can't believe John Dillinger was that way. I'm skeptical as to whether they would ever have found him guilty of that East Chicago charge ... I don't believe the man *was* there."

As posses fanned out in every direction looking for Dillinger, the bandit sat in the back seat of the V-8, telling Blunk to "take your time, take your time. Thirty miles an hour is enough. There's no hurry." The bandit chatted freely with his hostages. Youngblood said nothing, sitting like a wooden Indian next to Blunk, his submachine gun trained on the driver. Dillinger grew philosophical, saying to Blunk, an educated penologist: "You know, a prison is like a nut with a worm in it. The worm can always get out."

Dillinger then directed Blunk to take many turns, following gravel roads. He then jocularly asked Blunk and Saager: "How would you like to go to Ohio and get those other guys [Pierpont and Makley] out?" His hostages did not respond. Near Peotone, Illinois, the car ran into muddy roads washed out by heavy rains the night before. Dillinger ordered everyone out of the car and chains were put on the back wheels. "Take your time, boys," Dillinger said in a low voice. "What's time to me?"

After the chains were fixed on the wheels, Dillinger reached into his pocket and handed Saager $4, telling him that this money was for carfare for himself and Blunk. "I'd give you more, but I only got fifteen dollars. I'll remember you at Christmas." He got behind the wheel and told Youngblood, who was in the back seat, to lie down in the back. The V-8 slowly moved down the road, going south. Saager and Blunk stood in the middle of the road, listening to Dillinger whistle, hum and then sing a few lines from the song, "I'm Heading for the Last Roundup."

News announcing the spectacular escape held the nation in suspense and wonder. It appeared that no prison, no matter how strong, how well fortified and guarded, could hold John Dillinger. He became a living legend, his fame broader than that of Jesse James in the 19th Century, because Dillinger struck with electrifying speed, using fast cars and machine guns, utilizing all the techniques and inventions of modern society to best law enforcement agencies that appeared helpless before him. Indiana attorney general Philip Lutz stated: "The nation is horrified and shocked at the escape of this notorious bank robber and I am surprised that Lake County officials let him get away."

Tough, old Captain Stege of the Chicago Police Department shook his head in amazement, saying: "How in the name of common sense could a prisoner go through six barred doors to freedom?...But I told them it would happen. I pleaded with Governor McNutt's secretary to put him in the penitentiary. Now, bright and early Monday, Dillinger will rob a bank to get funds. Then, when he gets together with John Hamilton, the two of them will raid a police station some place and get guns and ammunition. Then maybe they'll come back to Chicago for another game of tag."

Stege was right. Dillinger did contact John Hamilton as soon as he drove Sheriff Holley's souped-up car across the Illinois line, making arrangements to meet him not in Chicago but in St. Paul, Minnesota, then one of the "safe" cities for the independent bank robbers of the era, a town where heavily bribed politicians and police looked the other way. This was the safe haven of the Barker gang and Alvin Karpis, a town filled with underworld bosses with strong political connections, such as Harry Sawyer and Boss John J. McLaughlin. But by driving the stolen Sheriff's car from Indiana to Illinois, Dillinger had violated a new federal law, illegally transporting a stolen vehicle across a state line, and this then put him under the jurisdiction of the FBI. J. Edgar Hoover promptly made Dillinger Public Enemy Number One and ordered his agents in all bureaus to make the Indiana outlaw their primary duty.

Dillinger soon abandoned the stolen car and separated from Youngblood, giving him a few dollars and wishing him well. Youngblood made his way to Michigan where he was later cornered and killed when he decided to shoot it out with lawmen. Dillinger, driving another stolen car, met with his attorney Piquett on a Chicago street. Piquett later reported this meeting and he claimed that he pleaded with the bandit to surrender. "I told him that it was impossible for him to defeat the law. I told him that it was my duty to advise him to surrender, and let me take him to Town Hall station. He said he would do all that later."

The bandit then met Evelyn Frechette, who had already rented a room where Dillinger stayed for a short time before going on to St. Paul. Here Dillinger met with Hamilton who gave him $1,500. Dillinger bought a new wardrobe, a new car, and rented a nice apartment for himself and Frechette in Minneapolis.

The new Dillinger gang was then formed. Homer Van Meter arrived with two new tough recruits, Eddie Green, a nerveless getaway driver, and Tommy Carroll, an ex-boxer and experienced bank robber, who had looted banks in Iowa and Nebraska. Another man was needed, the gang felt, and, against Van Meter's wishes, Dillinger brought Lester Gillis into the gang. Gillis, better known as Baby Face Nelson, had worked for some Chicago gangsters such as Bugs Moran. He was a West Coast bank robber, who stood five foot, four inches high, and had a streak of murderous insanity. A hot-head, Nelson's idea of bank robbing was to roar up to a bank shooting, enter shooting, and escape shooting. "Kill everybody in sight, mostly the cops, and take off," he told Dillinger. "That way, they know you mean business!"

"This rooster is nuts," Van Meter said, sneering at Nelson.

"You say that again and we'll settle it with guns," Nelson sneered back.

Dillinger stepped between the two men, saying: "We'll do it my way, Nelson, or you can look for work somewhere else." Nelson nodded and kept silent. Then Hamilton outlined plans for the new gang's first robbery. On March 6, 1934, driving a large green Packard, which had been stolen from a St. Paul car dealer, the gang entered Sioux Falls, South Dakota, parking the car next to the Security National Bank and Trust Company at 10 a.m. A secretary in the bank looked out the bank window and noticed the six men in the car and joked to a clerk: "Look, there's a bunch of holdup men." The clerk placed his finger over a button that would trigger the bank alarm.

Dillinger, Hamilton, Van Meter, and Nelson entered the bank, while Carroll took the "tiger" position of lookout just outside the bank entrance, a submachine gun beneath his long winter coat. Eddie Green sat behind the wheel of the Packard, waiting. Before Dillinger could make his customary announcements, Nelson whipped out his submachine gun and screamed shrilly: "This is a holdup! Lay down on the floor!" As Hamilton, Nelson, and Van Meter trained guns on the customers and employees, Dillinger ran behind the teller's cages, to that of the head teller, Robert Dargen.

The bandit put his automatic down on the counter and began to scoop up bills, shoving these into the sugar sack he held in his other hand. Dargen looked at the automatic and thought for a moment of grabbing it, then decided that such a move would be suicide. Meanwhile, the clerk pressed the alarm button and a bell began to clang loudly outside the bank.

The bank robbers remained calm. Dillinger continued emptying the drawers from the tellers' cages then ordered Dargen to open the vaults at the rear of the bank. Dargen said that it was a complicated affair, that each vault required five different combinations to open them. Van Meter then proved that he was as volatile as Nelson. He ran forward and jammed the barrel of his submachine gun into Dargen's ribs, shouting: "Open it up, you son-of-a-bitch, or I'll cut you in two." Dillinger said nothing. Dargen told Van Meter if he took the gun away, he'd open the vault.

When the vault was opened, Van Meter filled another sack with about $14,000 in bills. Van Meter then ordered Dargen to open the next vault, but the head teller told him that he did not have the combination and that the vault contained only nonnegotiable bonds. "Get the damned bank president out here now!" yelled Van Meter.

Someone called the local police station and said there was trouble at the bank but neglected to tell the desk sergeant that the alarm was ringing. The sergeant turned to an officer and told him to "go up to the bank. Probably some drunk bothering the customers." The officer strolled up to the bank and when he entered, walking past Carroll, the ex-boxer whipped out his submachine gun and prodded the officer into the bank, where Hamilton disarmed him and told him to lie on the floor.

The constant clang of the alarm bell outside the bank made Nelson jittery. He began to move erratically about the foyer of the bank, screaming: "I'm going to kill the man who hit that damned alarm!" He pointed his machine gun at a teller and screamed: "I know it was you!"

"No, no," the teller said, trembling. "Look, my button here is sticking up. If I had pressed it down it would still be down."

Dillinger called from the vault area to Nelson: "Forget that! Just get the money!"

At that moment, Nelson saw off-duty policeman Hale Keith get out of a car near the bank and cross the street. He had seen large crowds swelling about the bank and thought he should investigate. As he approached the bank he hitched up his belt and Nelson thought he was drawing a gun. The diminutive gangster jumped a guard railing and leaped onto the top of a

The car driven by Eugene Boiseneau, a CCC worker killed in a hail of FBI bullets as he and two friends attempted to drive from the parking lot of the Little Bohemia Lodge.

One of the windows at the Little Bohemia Lodge, riddled with FBI bullets. Agents led by Melvin Purvis sent hundreds of rounds into the lodge without any response from the gang members.

The arsenal left by the Dillinger gang when hastily departing the lodge; all of their female companions were captured, but none of the bank robbers were apprehended in the FBI debacle.

desk, letting loose a burst of machine gun fire which shattered the plate glass window and cut down Keith, sending him wounded to the pavement. Nelson, his face flushed red, turned and screamed: "I got one of them! I got one of them!"

In the street Tommy Carroll, a cool-headed gunman, rounded up the entire police force of twelve officers, who had arrived in small groups to learn the cause of the alarm bell. Even the embarrassed chief of police, M. W. Parsons, stood with his men against the wall of a building with his men as Carroll guarded them. A short distance away more than a thousand curious spectators milled about. The gang finally emerged carrying about $49,000. They took five female hostages and a teller, Leo Olson with them.

Nelson, though there was no reason for it, stood at the bank's entrance and shot out the glass of the window in the door, then swaggered outside and ordered the women to hang onto the running boards of the big Packard. The gang members got inside and the car labored up the street. A shot fired by patrolman Harley Chrisman punctured the radiator and the car stopped. The hostages leaped off but Nelson shouted: "Get back here!" The hostages again took their positions hanging onto the car, but one girl complained, saying she could no longer hold on. Dillinger told her to get off and the car lumbered around a corner, then another.

The Packard slowly made its way out of town, loaded down with six bank robbers and five hostages, while its radiator steamed and huffed. Dillinger stopped the car several times to have roofing nails spread over the road behind them. Outside of town, the bandits stopped a motorist and switched cars, leaving the hostages to stand freezing along the muddy road. They were picked up by a sheriff's car some time later, the officers complaining that they had to stop several times to repair flat tires, one officer carping: "Some damned fool spilled roofing nails from his truck all over the road."

Taking back roads, the gang did not arrive back in Minneapolis until midnight. There, in Dillinger's apartment, the gang split up the loot. Nelson insisted on counting it so that he would not be "cheated," reminding the others that "I shot the cop, didn't I?" His petite wife Helen, a dark-featured young woman, sat some distance away, saying nothing. Van Meter objected to Nelson counting the money, but Dillinger, who was recognized as the leader of this gang, decided the argument, saying: "Let Lester count the money." Nelson sat down, his submachine gun on his lap, and carefully counted out six even amounts of money.

Dillinger later called Louis Piquett and told him he was sending several thousand dollars to Mary Kinder and that he and Mary should arrange to hire "the best attorneys you can get for Harry and Charley." At that time Pierpont and Makley were about to be tried for the murder of Sheriff Sarber. He then told Eddie Green to scout another bank, "one with a lot of cash. We are taking big chances and we should be getting big amounts." He told Billie Frechette that once he had accumulated enough money, they would travel to South America or Mexico and live out their lives in comfort. Green returned in a few days, reporting a bank stuffed with money, the First National Bank of Mason City, Iowa, which reportedly held more than $240,000.

The gang struck the bank in Mason City on March 13, 1934. This time, at Dillinger's insistence, Nelson stayed outside, near the getaway car, which Eddie Green was driving. Carroll once again took the position of the "tiger," standing outside the bank entrance with a submachine gun hidden beneath his gray overcoat. Dillinger, Hamilton, and Van Meter entered the bank, but Van Meter suddenly went running about, screaming for the bank president.

Willis Bagley, the president, saw Van Meter racing about the lobby and ran for his office, thinking "a crazy man was loose" inside the bank. He ran to the office and Van Meter ran after him, jamming the barrel of his gun into the door opening just as Bagley slammed it shut. Bagley leaned against the door and Van Meter yanked on the gun, freeing it. Bagley slammed the door shut and locked it, but Van Meter, who knew Bagley had the key to the vault, angrily fired through the door, wounding Bagley. He then joined Hamilton and Dillinger to help clean out the tellers' cages.

Hamilton went into the vault with cashier Harry Fisher, but a door with bars slammed shut, separating Hamilton from the teller. On the shelves around Fisher, Hamilton could see more than $200,000 in neat stacks. He ordered the teller to shove the stacks of money through the bars, but Fisher purposely selected the stacks of one-dollar bills, then five-dollar bills, until Hamilton, flourishing his automatic shouted: "Just give me the big bills!" Crowds were assembling in the street. Gas bombs fired by a guard in a cage high above the tellers' cages had filled the bank with smoke which poured out of the bank entrance. Bank alarm bells went off everywhere. Dillinger and Van Meter shouted to Hamilton: "We have to go! We're going!" Hamilton begged for more time, shouting: "It's hell to leave all that money back there!" With only $52,000 in their sacks, the bandits finally left the bank, but they were greeted by a street packed with curious citizens.

Nelson, who was standing at a nearby alley entrance, was approached by a middle-aged woman who wagged her finger at him. "Young man, do something, can't you see the bank is being robbed?" He produced a submachine gun and waved her away, saying: "Lady, you're telling me?" Down the street, Dillinger was lining up citizens, waving a submachine gun. From an upstairs window, John Shipley, an elderly policeman, fired a single shot that wounded Dillinger in the arm. Dillinger switched the submachine gun to his good hand, then his gun stuttered and its bullets raked the walls and windows of the building in which Shipley had taken cover. Shipley retreated after firing his one shot.

Police did not respond to the robbery with great speed. When the alarm went off, officers believed that a motion picture company, which had been shooting a film the day earlier around the bank, was at work re-enacting a bank robbery, that all of it was make-believe. (It is quite possible that the bandits themselves had arrived a day earlier and had photographed the bank and the surrounding area, explaining that they were making a Hollywood film in order to disguise the real bank robbery the next day.)

Taking more than a dozen hostages, the robbers left in an overloaded Buick. So many hostages were clinging to the car that Dillinger asked a few women to step off the running boards. Before the car lumbered out of town, one of the female bank employees yelled: "This is where I live! Let me off!" Dillinger let the woman go. Outside town, on a paved road, Dillinger ordered Nelson to spread roofing nails behind them. The bantamweight gangster leaped from the car and tossed nails recklessly in all directions. Dillinger leaned out a window and said to him in disgust: "You're spreading nails under our own car, Lester."

A police car containing Police Chief E. J. Patton and other officers inched up the road after the Buick. Inside, officers urged Patton to open fire on the escaping Buick. "We can't do that," Patton said, "or we might hit the hostages." Nelson spotted the police car and let loose a burst from his submachine gun. The police turned off the road and stopped.

Two hours later, the Buick stopped to let off the last hostages. The gang drove back to Minneapolis, Hamilton brooding all the way over how the cashier Fisher had tricked him. "I should have killed that man," he said. Both Hamilton and Dillinger had received slight wounds and were treated in St. Paul by Dr. N. G. Mortenson, the city health officer. Both went on their way to mend quickly and plan their next robbery. But FBI agents in St. Paul, who had been diligently tracking Dillinger's movements, believed he was living under the alias of Carl Hellman with Billie Frechette in a St. Paul rooming house.

Dillinger and Frechette took a trip back to Indiana and, incredible as it may seem, drove right into the yard of the Dillinger farm in Mooresville without anyone taking note. No lawmen had been posted to stake out the home of the most wanted man in the country. A family reunion was held with Audrey Dillinger and her family present. The elder Dillinger tried to persuade his son to surrender, but John put him off. The family ate a large dinner, talked about old times and John posed for photos outside the house. He stood with Frechette as Audrey took snapshots and there was talk of marriage and, again, South America. In one snapshot, Dillinger posed with the wooden gun he had made in Crown

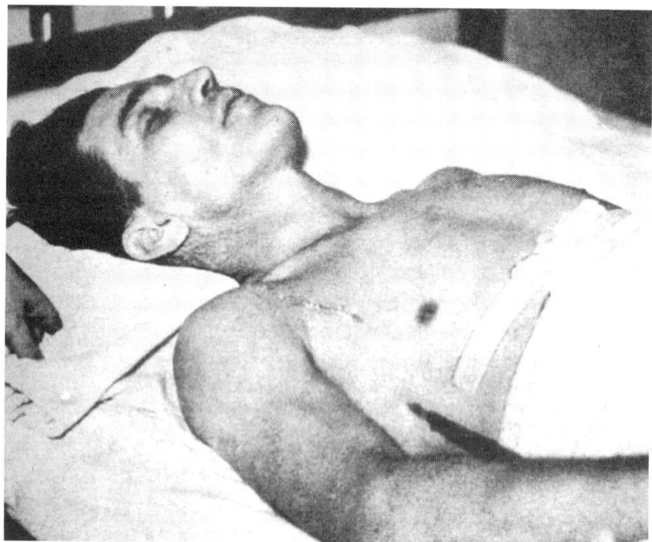

Dillinger gang member Tommy Carroll lies dying after being fatally shot in a police trap.

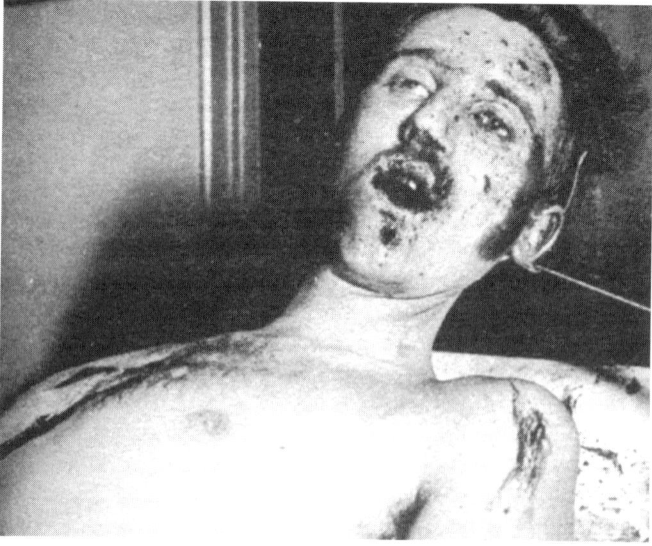

Homer Van Meter, Dillinger gang member, shot to death by police in St. Paul, Minnesota following a running gunfight.

Point in one hand and a real submachine gun in the other. Dillinger left the wooden gun with Audrey and she kept this crime relic until the day she died in 1988.

Meanwhile, the Ohio trial of Harry Pierpont and Charles Makley for the murder of Sheriff Sarber had ended in conviction, despite the testimony of Pierpont's mother that her son was eating dinner with her in their Leipsic, Ohio, home on the night Sarber was killed. Mrs. Pierpont, who had coddled Harry throughout his life, hid his face with her scarf when newsmen in court tried to photograph him. Pierpont did not help his own cause on the witness stand, shouting at the prosecutor: "I'm not the kind of man you are, robbing widows and orphans. You'd probably be like me if you had the nerve!" Handsome Harry was condemned to die in the electric chair, as was Charles Makley. Russell Clark was also tried but received a life sentence. (Clark would die of cancer only a few weeks after his release from prison in 1973.) Both Pierpont and Makley were not surprised at receiving death sentences. When Pierpont returned from his sentencing, Makley, sitting in the next cell of the Lima, Ohio, Jail, asked him: "What was it, Harry?"

"Well, what would it be?" Pierpont replied.

A day later, Makley returned after being sentenced. "What did you get, Charley?" asked Pierpont.

Makley sat down on the bunk in his cell, shoved an entire pack of gum into his mouth and then replied: "I got everything." He added a moment later: "We all have to die once."

Still, authorities believed that Dillinger might try to rescue his close friends Pierpont and Makley before they were transferred to the state prison. The Lima jail was surrounded by guards, and searchlights played over every square inch of the building at night. Vigilantes, local and state police, and national guardsmen were everywhere, waiting for Dillinger to arrive. Dillinger, meanwhile, barely escaped an FBI trap on March 31, 1934.

FBI Agents R. L. Nalls and R. C. Coulter had finally pinpointed his address in St. Paul. They went to the Lincoln Court Apartments and knocked on the door of Carl Hellman, the alias Dillinger was then using. Billie Frechette opened the door a crack and told the two agents that her husband, Mr. Hellman, was asleep, and that she was not dressed. She said she would wake him and put on some clothes. She closed the door and locked it, then ran to the bedroom and told Dillinger that police were in the hallway.

The agents were waiting nervously in the hall when they noticed a man walking up the stairs to the third floor, where they stood. It was Homer Van Meter.

"Who are you?" Agent Coulter asked him.

Van Meter gave him a broad smile and said: "I'm a soap salesman."

Coulter looked him over closely. "Yeah, well if you are, where are your samples?"

"In my car outside," Van Meter said glibly. "Come on downstairs, fella, and I'll be glad to show them to you."

Coulter followed Van Meter down the stairs, but at the landing on the second floor the bandit pulled an automatic and wheeled about, shouting at the FBI agent: "You asked for it, so I'll give it to you!"

The agent, helpless, opted for a quick retreat. He bolted straight past Van Meter, going down the stairs three at a time and through the front doors. Van Meter was about to go upstairs again, but remembered the other lawman and left the building. He ran into the street, where he spotted a horse-drawn delivery wagon, its driver gone. Van Meter jumped onto the seat of the wagon, put the driver's cap on his head and then whipped the horse wildly so that it leaped forward at a gallop with Van Meter making an unorthodox, clattering escape.

Agent Nalls heard the commotion downstairs and went to investigate. When Dillinger stepped into the hallway carrying a submachine gun, he saw the hallway empty. He went to the front stairs and fired a burst from the gun, then retreated with Frechette down a back staircase to the rear door of the apartment building. Just as he and Frechette reached his Hudson

Terraplane, Nalls appeared and fired a shot at Dillinger, wounding him in the leg. Dillinger jumped into the car, Frechette at his side, and roared away down the alley, escaping. He and Frechette went to Eddie Green's apartment and Green brought an underworld doctor to patch up Dillinger's leg.

The gang then decided to leave St. Paul immediately, realizing that FBI agents had them spotted. Pat Reilly, who did odd jobs for the gang, suggested that everyone go to a resort in northern Wisconsin, a backwoods retreat where no one, including the FBI, would think to look for them. Before going to this retreat, Dillinger and Frechette made a quick "business" trip to Chicago. On April 9, 1934, Dillinger and Frechette had a mysterious meeting with someone at a tavern located at 416 N. State Street.

Dillinger was apprehensive and sent Billie Frechette into the tavern to await a contact person, while he stood across the street. A few minutes later, three men who seemed to Dillinger to be "feds" rushed into the tavern and arrested Frechette. She was hustled out of the tavern to a waiting car and she looked at Dillinger from the car window as he sank back into the shadows of a doorway. Frechette was jailed, charged with harboring Dillinger, a fugitive.

Dillinger soon returned to St. Paul, and with Van Meter, Carroll, Hamilton and Nelson, along with three women, he traveled southeast to the Little Bohemia Lodge in Manitowish Waters, Wisconsin. Its owner, Emil Wannatka, reportedly welcomed the visitors, although he later claimed that the gang members were strangers to him and had forced their way into his lodge, which was not yet officially open. Wannatka later insisted that the gang barged in on him and his family unannounced and they were more or less prisoner-hosts to the gang, but it is likely that Wannatka, who had once owned a Chicago speakeasy and was associated with gangsters Terry Druggan and Frankie Lake, knew the gang was going to use his lodge as a hideout.

The bandits sat drinking and playing cards. Marie Conforti, Van Meter's girl, helped to make meals with Helen Gillis and Jean Delaney Crompton Carroll, the wife of Tommy Carroll. Everybody spent a good deal of time trying to cheer up Dillinger, who was depressed and sullen over the arrest of Billie Frechette.

Melvin Purvis, the FBI agent in charge of the hunt for Dillinger in Chicago, received a tip that Dillinger and his gang were hiding out in the Little Bohemia. On the night of April 22, 1934, he and other agents flew to Rhinelander, Wisconsin, and then commandeered several cars and drove down the narrow roads surrounded by dense forests to the lodge. By then FBI agents had been armed, but their training in weaponry was limited and their judgment in using firearms worse. Purvis himself was a shoot-from-the-hip lawman, excitable, impulsive, even reckless, the very type J. Edgar Hoover wanted to weed out of the bureau. Purvis was also a man who craved the limelight and cultivated publicity. He put himself before the Bureau and the only man in the FBI able to take such a position was Hoover himself. In reality, Purvis was a ruthlessly ambitious agent who may have harbored thoughts of replacing Hoover.

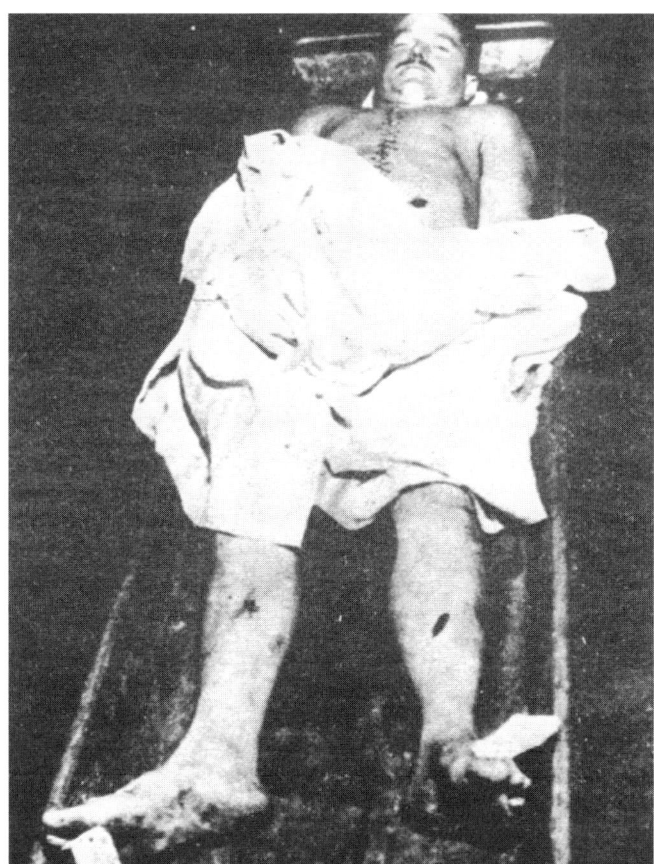

Dillinger gang member Baby Face Nelson, in the morgue with 17 slugs in his body, following a gun battle with two FBI agents. Nelson killed both agents before he died of wounds.

The FBI under Purvis' leadership in Chicago underestimated Dillinger, believing him to be a dim-witted outlaw, who resorted to the gun first and last. Purvis did not study Dillinger's habits and character, but followed the machine gun image of him the press had created. Agents in this era were either lawyers or accountants with little or no street experience dealing with gangsters or the independent bank robbers of the 1930s. They relied on tips from newsmen and informants passed along to them from local police departments to track federal fugitives. They learned much of their search and seizure technique, according to the author's contacts inside the Bureau, from watching Hollywood movies, and they emulated movie police grilling suspects by using the third degree.

Hoover, desperate to prove the FBI effective during the crime wave of the 1930s, had made Dillinger Public Enemy Number One, mostly due to Dillinger's national publicity. Technically, Hoover overreached himself in making Dillinger Public Enemy Number One. As a federal fugitive, Dillinger's most serious crime was crossing a state line with a stolen auto, and that offense was the only one which allowed Hoover and his agents to pursue Dillinger. It certainly was not a crime that would win Dillinger the dubious honor of being named the most sought criminal in America. Ironically, Hoover increased Dillinger's notoriety by naming him Public Enemy Number

Special FBI Agent Sam Cowley, who was killed by Baby Face Nelson.

One, perhaps with the thought that once the Bureau had captured or killed Dillinger, its own status would surpass that of Dillinger's or any other infamous gangster.

When Purvis led his men through the dark woods toward the Little Bohemia Lodge, he had no idea how many gang members might be inside, what their fire power might be, or the possible escape routes they might use. He merely assembled his eight heavily armed agents in front of the lodge and advanced like General Custer charging in a frontal attack into the valley of the Little Big Horn. As the agents went forward, three men emerged from the lodge, wobbly-legged, to get into a coupe parked in front of the lodge.

The driver turned on the radio and Purvis ordered the men to get out of the car, but got no response. (Two survivors later denied Purvis' claim that he shouted such a command to the men.) When the men in the car did not respond, Purvis and his men opened fire with submachine guns, automatics and automatic rifles, riddling the car and blowing its occupants to pieces. All three men in the car were CCC workers and one of them, Eugene Boiseneau, was killed outright, a slaying that was, immediately after the abortive raid, attributed to Dillinger.

The gunfire outside the lodge alerted Dillinger and his men to the presence of the FBI. They had been playing cards with Wannatka and they jumped up and peered through the front windows, turning off the lights. Inside the lodge were Dillinger, Hamilton, Van Meter, Carroll and their women. Baby Face Nelson and his wife Helen were sleeping in a cottage nearby. Dillinger and the others raced upstairs without a thought of fighting it out with lawmen.

The bandits had no idea that the front area of the lodge was crawling with FBI men since Purvis never identified himself or his men to the occupants of the lodge. The attackers could have been local vigilantes, national guardsmen, state troopers, or local lawmen for all the Dillinger gang knew. As Dillinger and the other men grabbed their weapons, coats, hats and cash, Purvis and his men let loose a deafening fire that raked the front of the lodge, smashed windows and destroyed china and bric-a-brac in the first floor rooms.

At that moment, Dillinger and the others slipped out a back window on the second floor, lowering themselves to a small roof and then dropping about ten feet to the ground. They ran single file to Little Star Lake behind the lodge and ran along the water's edge and into the trees, going north. The only member of the gang to offer resistance was Nelson. He leaped half-dressed from his bed at the sound of gunfire, grabbed a submachine gun, and ran outside to see from a flanking position the FBI men charging the front of the lodge. Believing his associates were still inside and returning fire, he joined in, letting loose a burst from his Thompson, which drew fire from Purvis and other agents. The agents stopped their attack on the lodge and angled toward Nelson, who soon realized that he was hopelessly outnumbered. He fled into the woods, abandoning his wife.

Purvis resumed his attack on the lodge. Its occupants, the women who had accompanied the gang, and Wannatka and his family, had taken refuge in the basement. They huddled there for hours as the FBI blasted the lodge with automatic fire and tear gas bombs. Some time later, oblivious to the one-sided battle that was going on, Pat Reilly, with Patricia Cherrington at his side, drove into the long driveway leading to the parking lot in front of the lodge.

The agents wheeled about and opened fire on the car after Reilly realized he was driving into a trap and threw the auto into a quick reverse. One tire was shot flat and the windows of the car were shot out, but Reilly and Cherrington remained unharmed. Back on the highway, Reilly threw the car into gear and shot ahead, weaving crazily up the road on the flat.

Dillinger, Van Meter, and Hamilton reached the home of E. J. Mitchell and there tried to start an old truck parked in the yard, but it would not turn over. They spotted a coupe parked in a neighbor's yard and took it, heading for St. Paul. Tommy Carroll, who had gotten lost in the woods, wandered into Manitowish Waters, a small town about a mile from the Little Bohemia, and stole a Packard and began driving to St. Paul.

Nelson, who had gone in the opposite direction from the rest of the gang, stopped a car carrying G.W. Lang and his wife and forced the elderly couple at gunpoint to drive him out of the area. The car broke down near the home of Alvin Koerner, and Nelson raced to the house. Koerner, however, suspicious after hearing the gunfire from the nearby lodge, called police to tell an officer that a strange car had parked in his yard and a man with a gun was approaching the house. He hung up just as Nelson reached his front door.

Another car containing Emil Wannatka, his two bartenders and his brother-in-law, George LaPorte, then arrived at the Koerner house. LaPorte had driven to the lodge in response to a desperate phone call from Wannatka. When LaPorte arrived on a side road near the lodge, Wannatka and his two bartenders escaped and LaPorte drove them away, while the FBI agents continued to pepper the lodge.

Once in the Koerner house, Wannatka saw Nelson, his former guest, and he tried to placate the jittery gangster. Nelson told Wannatka to shut up and lined everyone in the house up against a wall. He then ordered Wannatka and Koerner outside, telling them they were his hostages. He told Wannatka to start LaPorte's car, but Wannatka flooded the engine.

At that moment, about 11 p.m., another car drove into Koerner's lot. In it were two FBI agents Jay Newman and H. Carter Baum, along with Constable Carl C. Christiansen. Newman was driving and Baum sat next to him, cradling a submachine gun in his lap. The car stopped just behind and to the right of LaPorte's car. Christiansen, who was sitting in the back seat, later remembered how "this little jack rabbit flew right out of nowhere." Nelson had leaped from the front of the LaPorte car and raced up to the FBI auto, just as Newman opened the door and was about to step out.

Nelson held a machine pistol, described later by Christiansen as "a forty-five Colt converted into a machine gun with a long clip and a pistol grip." The little bandit screamed: "I know you bastards are wearing bulletproof vests so I'll give it to you high and low!" With that he began firing point blank into the car. First Newman fell, hit over the eye. He collapsed onto the dirt lot.

Baum struggled to hold up the submachine gun as he stepped from the other door, but Nelson's bullets tore through his neck and killed him instantly. Christiansen, fumbling for his .38-caliber Smith & Wesson, jumped from the car and ran for the cover of a nearby wood pile, but he was floodlit by the headlights of Newman's idling car and Nelson shot him in the back several times, knocking him down. Christiansen crawled back to Baum's side but saw that he was dead.

Newman somehow came to, and while holding his bleeding head, the courageous agent lifted his automatic and fired a wild shot in Nelson's direction. Nelson was by then berserk, screaming and cursing and firing in all directions. Wannatka ran to a snow bank and Nelson fired at him, shouting: "You traitor, you informed on us!" Wannatka was unharmed and he managed to crawl over the bank and into some woods. He got up and began running back to the Little Bohemia.

Nelson then jumped into the Ford that had been driven by Newman and backed out of the yard so violently that Koerner's house was showered by gravel kicked up by the tires. Nelson roared onto the highway and raced southward. Newman staggered to his feet and went to Koerner's house. He knocked on the door, but those inside refused to let him in, thinking he was another bandit bent on havoc. Christiansen later remembered that those in the house "let us lie there for about an hour before anyone dared to come outside."

Wannatka emerged from the woods near Little Bohemia, his hands and legs bleeding from the thorny underbrush. The noise of his movements caused the agents still positioned in front of the lodge to train their guns on him. "Hands up, you! Hands up!" shouted an agent in his direction. Wannatka staggered forward, exhausted, panting, as Purvis and other agents surrounded him, guns aimed at his head. "All your men are dead at Koerner's," gasped Wannatka.

Purvis squinted at Wannatka, saying: "How do you spell your name and address?"

"What?" Wannatka said, amazed at Purvis' seeming indifference to the news that his agents had been killed. "Are you crazy? I told you that all your men have been killed at Koerner's house! Did you come here for Dillinger or for me?" Wannatka then filled a truck with hay and, after another argument with Purvis, drove back to Koerner's to retrieve the dead and wounded. The body of the 29-year-old Baum was placed on the hay and driven to a nearby mortuary. Newman and Christiansen were taken to a clinic where they would survive their wounds.

Martin Zarkovich, at the wheel of a car, shown with his close friend, Anna Sage, in the 1920s. Zarkovich set up the man shot at the Biograph on July 22, 1934; Sage led him to his death.

By dawn, the one-sided battle of Little Bohemia was over. The inside of the lodge was thick with teargas and the three mob women, Marie Conforti, Helen Gillis and Jean Carroll, staggered choking from the building, their hands in the air. The real quarry had fled and escaped. Purvis' embarrassment was thorough, but that of his boss, J. Edgar Hoover, was increased by the fact that the director had announced at 2 a.m. Washington, D. C., time (midnight at Little Bohemia) that the Dillinger gang was surrounded and its members had no chance of escape. Then the bad news came in that Dillinger and the others had escaped. Hoover finally got hold of Purvis and told him how disappointed he was.

There was more bad news to come. When it was discovered that the agents had wounded several innocent persons and killed Eugene Boiseneau, newspapers across the country ran banner headlines attacking Hoover and the Bureau for recklessness, some even charging manslaughter. Senator Kenneth McKellar later held hearings investigating the Little Bohemia fiasco and charged Hoover and Purvis with irresponsible acts that had caused the death of an innocent man. Several Republican senators began campaigns to have Hoover demoted or even removed from office.

Instead of being portrayed as heroes, the FBI agents were held up to ridicule. Hoover, privately incensed at Purvis for being disgraced, gave orders to Purvis and other agents to get Dillinger "at all costs." So driven were Hoover and Purvis to right their wrong and to recapture public opinion that they would grasp at any straw to deliver John Herbert Dillinger. Their desperation would lead them into an even greater debacle.

The killing of innocent men by the FBI created a scandal that provided material for Will Rogers, then America's favorite humorist. Wrote Rogers: "Well, they had Dillinger sur-

Anna Sage at the time she met FBI Agent Melvin Purvis and explained how she would accompany "Dillinger" to a movie theater, where Public Enemy Number One could be apprehended. Purvis promised that Sage, a notorious brothel-keeper, would not be deported, but she was nevertheless sent back to Romania.

rounded and was all ready to shoot him when he come out, but another bunch of folks come out ahead, so they shot them instead. Dillinger is going to accidentally get in with some innocent bystanders some time, then he will get shot."

Some side benefits came of the Little Bohemia failure, however, in that twelve anticrime bills in Congress, which had long been delayed were finally enacted. Throughout the Midwest, the Dillinger mania caused local legislators to provide their police departments with new equipment, including city-wide and state-wide radio systems, the lack of which allowed Dillinger and bandits like him to escape police dragnets and roadblocks. Indirectly, Dillinger had caused speedy improvements in U. S. law enforcement procedures.

The Dillinger gang was still on the run. Hours after leaving Wisconsin in the stolen car, Dillinger, Van Meter and Hamilton were about to drive across a bridge spanning the Mississippi near Hastings, Minnesota, about twenty miles south of St. Paul. Deputy Sheriff Norman Dieter and three other lawmen were guarding the bridge, alerted that Dillinger might try to escape along that route to St. Paul. A fast-moving Ford then came into sight and the lawmen leveled their automatic weapons in its direction. The driver, Dillinger, saw the roadblock across the bridge and spun the car about, driving away.

Dieter and the others jumped into their car and gave pursuit, catching up with the Ford some miles down the road. They saw that it had Wisconsin license plates, the same as one of the cars having been stolen near the Little Bohemia shootout. Dieter fired a shot at the tires and this caused Van Meter, sitting in the back seat, to smash the back window of the Ford and thrust forth an automatic. Van Meter began shooting at the officers, who returned fire. One of the bullets fired by the officers ploughed into the back of John Hamilton before Dillinger was able to outdistance and lose the lawmen.

The car driven by the bandits was too shot up to continue and Dillinger drove it off the road twenty or so miles outside of St. Paul. He then stopped a car driven by Roy Francis. Francis, his wife and small boy were in the car and the bandit ordered them into the back seat. Dillinger, Van Meter, and Hamilton climbed into the car. The badly-wounded Hamilton said he needed something to drink and Dillinger pulled into a gas station, where he bought Hamilton and the Francis boy bottles of soda pop. Francis and his family were left unharmed at a farmhouse down the road, while the gangsters drove the new V-8 toward St. Paul.

Dillinger and Van Meter met Reilly later that day, but Hamilton was not with them. Reilly later told police that Hamilton had died before Dillinger could find a doctor and that his body was buried in a stone quarry by Dillinger and Van Meter. Quicklime had been poured over the body to obliterate the face and fingers and thus prevent identification.

Dillinger and Van Meter reportedly returned to Chicago but Public Enemy Number One was no longer his easygoing self, telling Van Meter that he was a jinx. He had been unnerved by the harrowing escape from Little Bohemia and he vowed to "get away for keeps." Everyone around him had died or wound up in prison. He had heard that Billie Frechette had been convicted of harboring him in St. Paul and had been given an eighteen-month prison term. From May to July 1934, Dillinger's movements were in deep shadows and little activity was reported, although it was claimed that on June 30, 1934, Dillinger, Van Meter, and Nelson were joined by Charles Arthur "Pretty Boy" Floyd and that this formidable group of bank robbers raided the Merchants National Bank of South Bend, Indiana, taking a $18,000 in cash, but it is doubtful that any of these men participated in that robbery.

Floyd was elsewhere in the Midwest at the time and Nelson was in California. In June 1934, Dillinger did rob, with James

Henry "Blackie" Audett and others, some banks in Iowa, Kansas, and Nebraska, according to Audett's statements to the author forty-five years later. Audett claimed that Dillinger was looking to make a "permanent escape" and that arrangements for such would be costly. This necessitated the string of bank robberies Dillinger, Audett, and other lesser known bandits committed.

It is known that Dillinger spent a good deal of time in Chicago in June and July of 1934, talking several times to Louis Piquett while making those escape arrangements, but the escape was not to South America or Europe, but an escape from the world of the living. The FBI later claimed that during June 1934, Dillinger went into deep hiding, and that a minor hoodlum, Arthur O'Leary, took Dillinger and Van Meter to the home of James Probasco in Chicago, a hideout set up by Louis Piquett. Here, according to the Bureau, Dillinger and Van Meter had plastic surgery performed on their faces and had their fingerprints burned away with acid, these operations conducted by two underworld physicians, Dr. Harold B. Cassidy and Dr. Wilhelm Loesser.

Probasco, however, was not picked up until July 25, 1934, days after a shooting at Chicago's Biograph Theater, one in which Melvin Purvis insisted John Dillinger was killed. Probasco was held incommunicado at the Bureau Headquarters in the Banker's Building and, on July 30, 1934, suddenly fell, jumped, or was pushed from a nineteen-story window in

The Biograph Theater on Lincoln Avenue in Chicago a few minutes after the shooting on July 22, 1934, after which the FBI claimed to have killed John Dillinger.

FBI offices, crashing to his bloody death in an alley below. His death was ruled a suicide. (It was later claimed that Probasco died when agents trying to get him to inform, dangled him by the legs from one of the Bureau's office windows, a third-degree routine they had earlier practiced from seeing gangster movies in that era, and that they had lost their hold on the suspect, who then "accidentally" fell to his death.)

Investigation into the shooting at the Biograph on July 22, 1934, occupied the author for a number of years in the research and writing of two previously published works, *Dillinger: Dead or Alive?* and *The Dillinger Dossier.* The mysterious, and to some degree, still baffling events occurring at that time are these: Dillinger, for all purposes of the FBI manhunt, had utterly disappeared sometime in June 1934. Law enforcement officials combed the country for him, but no trace could be found, even though dozens of men looking like Dillinger were arrested and later released. Since most of his known associates were either dead or in prison, and since he had stopped seeing his usual contacts, except for the underworld lawyer, Piquett, lawmen became more frustrated with each day's search.

Polly Hamilton Keele accompanied Anna Sage and her "friend" to the Biograph.

The author's research revealed that Dillinger was, indeed, residing in the Chicago area, but that he had, in early June, entered into a scheme that would bring about his permanent escape. He would be killed, or, more precisely, someone else would be killed in his place and he would thus be free to live out his life with the aid of considerable cash he had accumulated within the last six to nine months, more than $250,000, according to one estimate. Through Piquett, Dillinger met with Martin Zarkovich, a crooked police sergeant with the East Chicago, Indiana, Police Department.

For more than a decade, Zarkovich had been taking bribes and kickbacks from bootleggers and brothel owners in Lake County, Indiana, and he had persuaded several of his fellow officers to also enjoy such underworld spoils. Zarkovich, since about 1920, had known a notorious bordello keeper, Anna Sage, a Romanian immigrant who ran several whorehouses in northern Indiana. The enterprising sergeant had even supplied her with runaway girls and had seen to it that her operations were protected, receiving a cut of her take.

When Anna Sage was run out of northern Indiana, she set up shop in Chicago, running a bordello out of a sprawling North Side home. Zarkovich continued to supply her with girls, driving them from Indiana to Chicago, where he was still on Anna's payroll. Martin Zarkovich was a money man, a cop on the take, and, if the subtle scheme arranged by Louis Piquett worked, he would not only enjoy a large fee for his services, but collect a considerable chunk of the $20,000 reward money offered for John Dillinger, as long as *he made sure* that Dillinger was officially declared dead.

In mid-July, Zarkovich met with Anna Sage, who had a customer deeply involved with one of her girls, Polly Hamilton Keele, a slender, attractive brunette. Zarkovich studied this man from afar, watching him go in and out of Anna Sage's place. He used the name James Lawrence, but Polly Hamilton called him Jimmy. Lawrence, who told people he worked at the Board of Trade, was a minor hoodlum and pimp who actually worked on and off for Anna Sage bringing Hamilton customers. He lived on Pine Grove Avenue and was always looking for a dishonest dollar. Further investigation of his background, according to Audett, revealed that he had no known living relatives in the Midwest. He was an ideal candidate.

According to Audett, Piquett then contacted Lawrence and made a deal. He would pay this young man $30,000 to pretend to be Public Enemy Number One, John Dillinger. The crafty lawyer explained that this would take no effort at all and certainly would not be dangerous. He would simply go on with his normal activities, but drop a little hint here or there. If arrested, he could easily prove he was not Dillinger. Piquett held up his hands to wiggle his fingers. Lawrence's fingerprints would prove he was not the wanted outlaw. Lawrence asked why he was being asked to do this. Piquett told him that he would be only one of several "decoys" who would be used to give the real Dillinger enough time to leave the country. Lawrence accepted his odd assignment and received a $5,000 down payment with a promise to receive additional payments each week.

Unknown to Lawrence, there were many others involved in the plot to pass Lawrence off as Dillinger, and this included Martin Zarkovich and Anna Sage. A few days later, Sage began to make remarks to Lawrence about his striking resemblance to newspaper photos of Dillinger. "A lot of people tell me that," Lawrence replied. He began to swagger a bit, even occasionally talk out of the side of his mouth in the best gangster tradition of the movies. Meanwhile, Ray McCready, a mortician who maintained a funeral home at 4506 N. Sheridan Road, sat down at his desk on July 14, 1934, and opened his ledger to a blank page to record a death that had not yet occurred. McCready entered the name of John Dillinger in his ledger, using the July 14, 1934, *twice* on the same page, though the shooting outside the Biograph Theater would not happen until July 22, 1934, six days later. From later events, it can be assumed that McCready had already been contacted by someone and told that he would be handling the body.

On July 20, Martin Zarkovich, a lynch pin in the conspiracy, appeared in the offices of Chicago Police Department Captain John Stege, who headed the Dillinger Squad. In front of Sergeant Frank Reynolds, Stege's aide, Zarkovich offered to provide information that would lead Stege and his men to Dillinger. But there was a condition, Zarkovich said, explaining that he wanted revenge for the killing of his good friend Pat O'Malley, the cop killed in the East Chicago bank robbery in January of that year. There could be no live capture of Dillinger, Zarkovich insisted. He, Martin Zarkovich, must be allowed to execute the man, once the trap that he, Zarkovich, devised, was sprung.

John Stege was an old hand at fighting criminals and one of the best cops in Chicago, an honest and upright lawman who liked to believe that, after so many years in dealing with the worst elements of society, he still maintained scruples and a sense of decency. Stege stood up and said angrily to Zarkovich: "I'd give even John Dillinger a chance to surrender." He then ordered Zarkovich out of his office, as Zarkovich knew he would, for this meeting was a setup, a reference point to which another man, Melvin Purvis, would be directed. Purvis would naively accept the murderous motivation of Martin Zarkovich and subsequently accept the East Chicago cop's story about Dillinger as being genuine. Some hours later, Zarkovich called Melvin Purvis, who was desperate to apprehend Dillinger and, according to one report, had a deadline from his boss Hoover to do so or begin looking for another career.

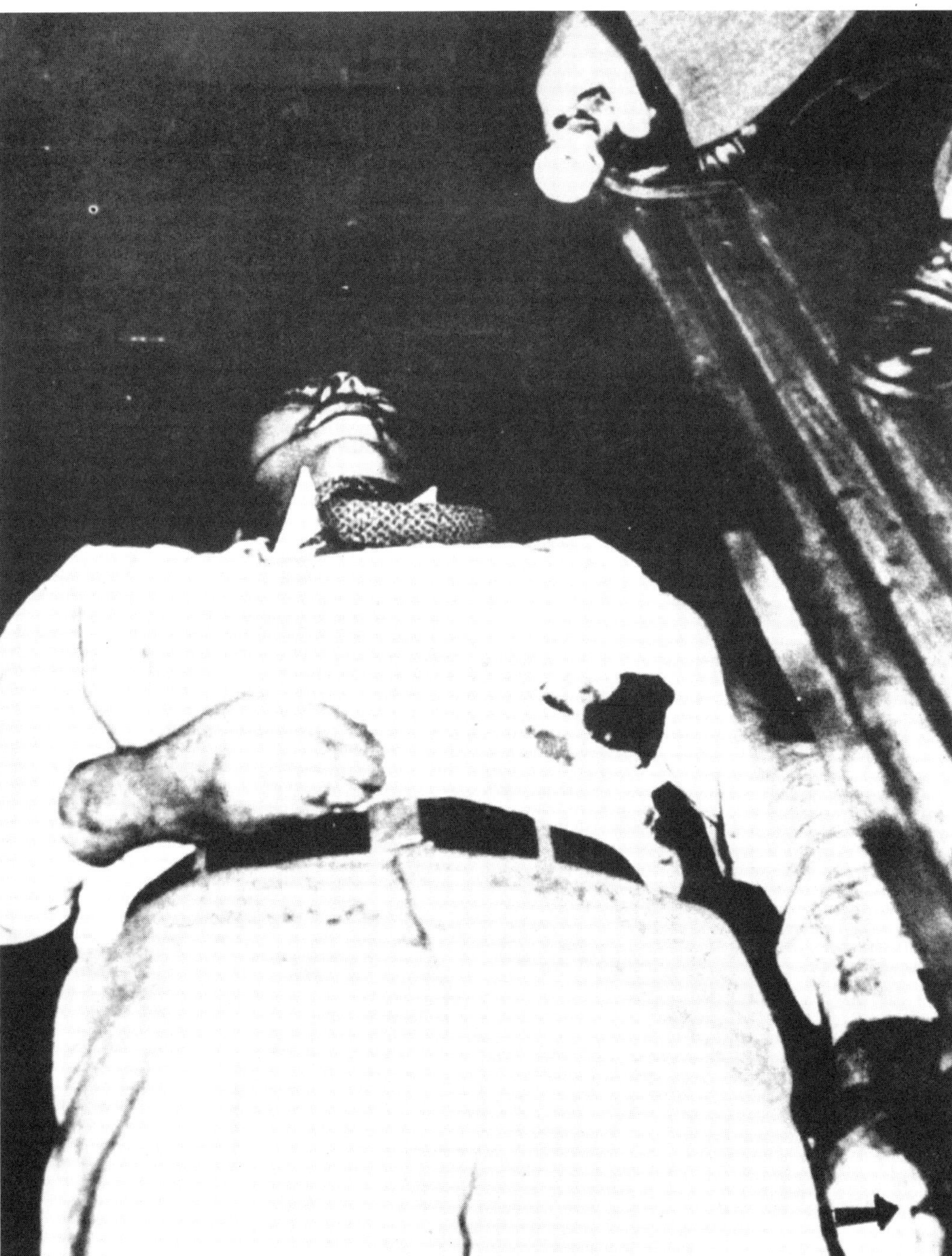

The body of the man shot outside the Biograph Theater, claimed by the FBI to be John Dillinger, in a Chicago police wagon at the scene of the shooting. Purvis saod that he reached for a gun and an unspecified FBI agent killed him. The man killed, however, had no gun and was killed by Martin Zarkovich, who set up the execution. The arrow at bottom right shows a ring on the left finger, one which disappeared.

Zarkovich was thoroughly familiar with the dilemma facing the trigger-happy Purvis and he also knew that the FBI chief was reckless and easily deceived. Purvis' erratic and lethal conduct at Little Bohemia had proved that to the world. He informed Purvis that he could "set up Dillinger" for him and Purvis leapt at the opportunity, arranging to meet Zarkovich the next afternoon in the lobby of the Great Northern Hotel. This was the residence of Sam Cowley, who recently had been placed in the Chicago Bureau of the FBI, a special agent with powers equal to Purvis. Purvis ran the office, but Cowley had veto power over his activities and served as Hoover's watchdog. Yet, Sam Cowley, an experienced and intelligent agent, was just as desperate as Purvis to arrest John Dillinger.

Zarkovich met with the two agents the next day and told them that he knew a brothel keeper through his official capacities, not mentioning his personal relationship with Anna Sage. Dillinger, he had learned, was patronizing one of Sage's girls and he believed he could set up Public Enemy Number One for the Bureau. He could arrange a meeting that night with Anna Sage if the agents wanted to meet her. There were a few conditions to this deal, however, Zarkovich added. One, he must be allowed revenge for the killing of his pal, Patrolman O'Malley; he must be allowed to execute John Dillinger. The agents said nothing. The second condition involved Anna Sage, who was not a U.S. citizen. She had been designated by the immigration authorities as "an undesirable alien" and there were proceedings against her to deport her back to Romania. Sage, for her cooperation, would want these proceedings dropped. Again the agents said nothing, but Purvis agreed to meet with Anna Sage that night.

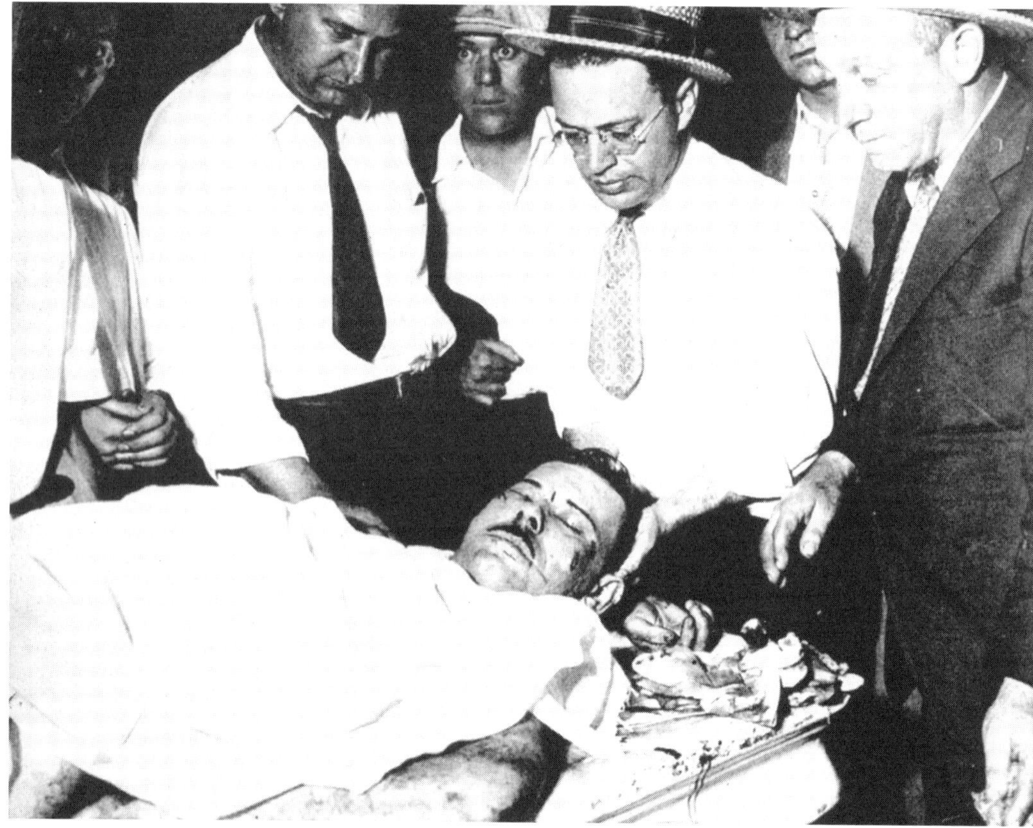

The head of the body of the man slain at the Biograph is held by Dr. Charles D. Parker (wearing glasses and straw hat), who told the author that no one ever fingerprinted the deceased on the night of July 22, 1934; a Chicago police fingerprint card later purported to have Dillinger's prints on it.

So frantic were these agents to apprehend Dillinger that they took at face value whatever Martin Zarkovich told them and without bothering to check on this rural policeman, a man they had not met up to this moment. Neither Purvis nor Cowley ordered the customary background check on Zarkovich. If they had, they would have easily seen that they were dealing with a man whose word and reputation was suspect.

The agents could have looked into their Bureau files to see that Zarkovich had been involved in a federal conspiracy in 1931, and local records would have revealed his ties to organized crime in northern Indiana, Anna Sage's brothel operations, and a close association to Louis Piquett, Dillinger's lawyer. Zarkovich, guessing this might be the case, gave the agents very little time to think about his proposition or his background, telling them that if they were to move on his information, it would have to be in a matter of hours.

Three decades later, Virgil Peterson, a member of the Chicago Bureau of the FBI who worked with Purvis on the Dillinger case, was asked by the author why FBI agents, particularly Purvis and Cowley, had not checked the backgrounds of Zarkovich and Sage. Peterson, indignant, responded angrily: "That has nothing to do with it! These people had information and we had to get this guy! You don't go around asking questions when you're after someone like Dillinger! And these people had information. No, their backgrounds had nothing to do with it!"

Purvis did call Captain Stege, however, and learned that Zarkovich had been to see him with the same offer concerning Dillinger, but that Stege had declined on the grounds that he would not sanction legal murder. Purvis, by then, undoubtedly felt that if he did not accept Zarkovich's proposition, some other law enforcement agency might and the FBI would be deprived of closing its most important criminal case, a cornerstone case, as events proved, upon which the reputation of the FBI and the image of the "G-Man" was later built.

The *kind* of information Zarkovich and Sage were peddling also had nothing to do with the real John Dillinger. That night, Melvin Purvis sat in a Pierce-Arrow with Martin Zarkovich, who was sitting in the back seat. The car was parked on a quiet, tree-lined north side Chicago street. Behind Purvis' car was another car with Sam Cowley in it. As planned, at 9 p.m. sharp, the thick, fast-walking figure of Anna Sage appeared. She walked past the car looking straight ahead. "She's making sure there's no trap," said the ever-dramatic Purvis to Zarkovich. Then Zarkovich put his hand out the window and signaled to Sage and she got in, sitting next to Purvis.

Cowley was surprised to see Purvis suddenly drive away. This lone car later parked at the lakefront. Zarkovich remained silent in the back seat while Anna Sage told Purvis that a man named James Lawrence, who had been visiting one of her girls, Polly Hamilton, had admitted to her that he was John Dillinger (this was, of course, untrue). Lawrence had a lot of money, wore the best clothes, and had mentioned the names of many Dillinger gangsters. She said Keele did

Author's recreation of the Biograph shooting, based upon the entry and angle of bullets fired by two men while the victim was prone, an out-and-out execution, supported by the path of the fatal bullets described in Dr. J. J. Kearns' elusive autopsy.

not know Lawrence's true identity. She could deliver this man into the hands of the FBI, Sage told Purvis, if the Bureau persuaded the immigration authorities to drop deportation proceedings against her.

The ever-impetuous Purvis wasted no time in accepting Sage's terms, leaping at the opportunity to finally catch the elusive Dillinger. As far as immigration officials were concerned, Purvis promised to set things right. "I'll call them off," he said, but Melvin Purvis had no authority to make such a promise. Moreover, he arbitrarily raised the reward for Dillinger then and there, stating that $25,000 would be paid to everyone involved in delivering Dillinger, with shares going to Zarkovich, his boss, Captain Tim O'Neill, who had helped set up the FBI meeting, Sage, and even Polly Hamilton Keele. The reward was to be paid through the U.S. attorney general's office, but Attorney General Homer Cummings had not authorized Melvin Purvis to increase the reward. In light of later events, it is obvious that Purvis would say or do anything in order to capture Dillinger.

Purvis then drove Anna Sage back to her Halsted Street address. By driving off with Anna Sage and leaving Cowley behind and in the dark, Purvis had made the Dillinger case exclusively his since no one but Zarkovich and he could identify Anna Sage. Before he dropped her off, Purvis was told by Sage that she would be calling him some time next day, that she, Keele, and Lawrence-Dillinger would be going to a movie, probably the Marbro Theater, and she would phone Purvis as soon as she knew what show they would be attending. Purvis nodded agreement. After he drove off, Purvis had a little talk with Zarkovich and it was then that the FBI man undoubtedly agreed that Zarkovich, in return for set-

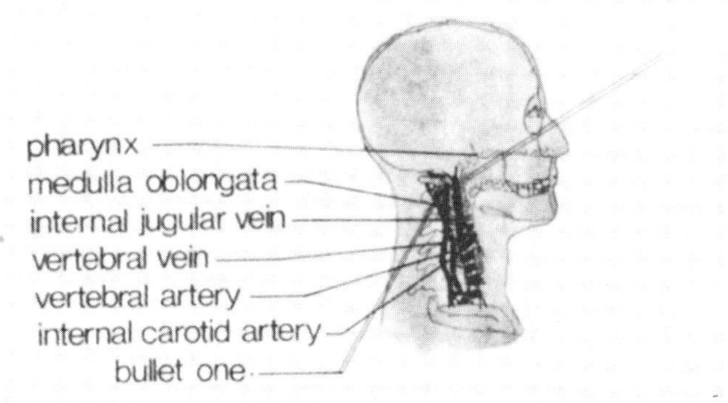

Author's recreation of the real angle of the death bullet as described in Kearns' meticulous autopsy, confirming an execution-style killing.

ting up Lawrence-Dillinger through Sage, would be allowed to execute the man. Purvis now felt that the disgrace and blunder of the abortive Little Bohemia Lodge raid would be wiped out and that he would be redeemed in the eyes of J. Edgar Hoover and the country that thought of him as a reckless, trigger-happy lawman.

Zarkovich's real motive for killing Lawrence, of course, had nothing to do with seeking revenge for the dead policeman, O'Malley. Lawrence could only be accepted as Dillinger if he were dead, and if later identification of him proved him someone else, it would be Melvin Purvis' responsibility. Zarkovich and the men behind him, Louis Piquett, Blackie Audett, and even Dillinger himself correctly figured that when

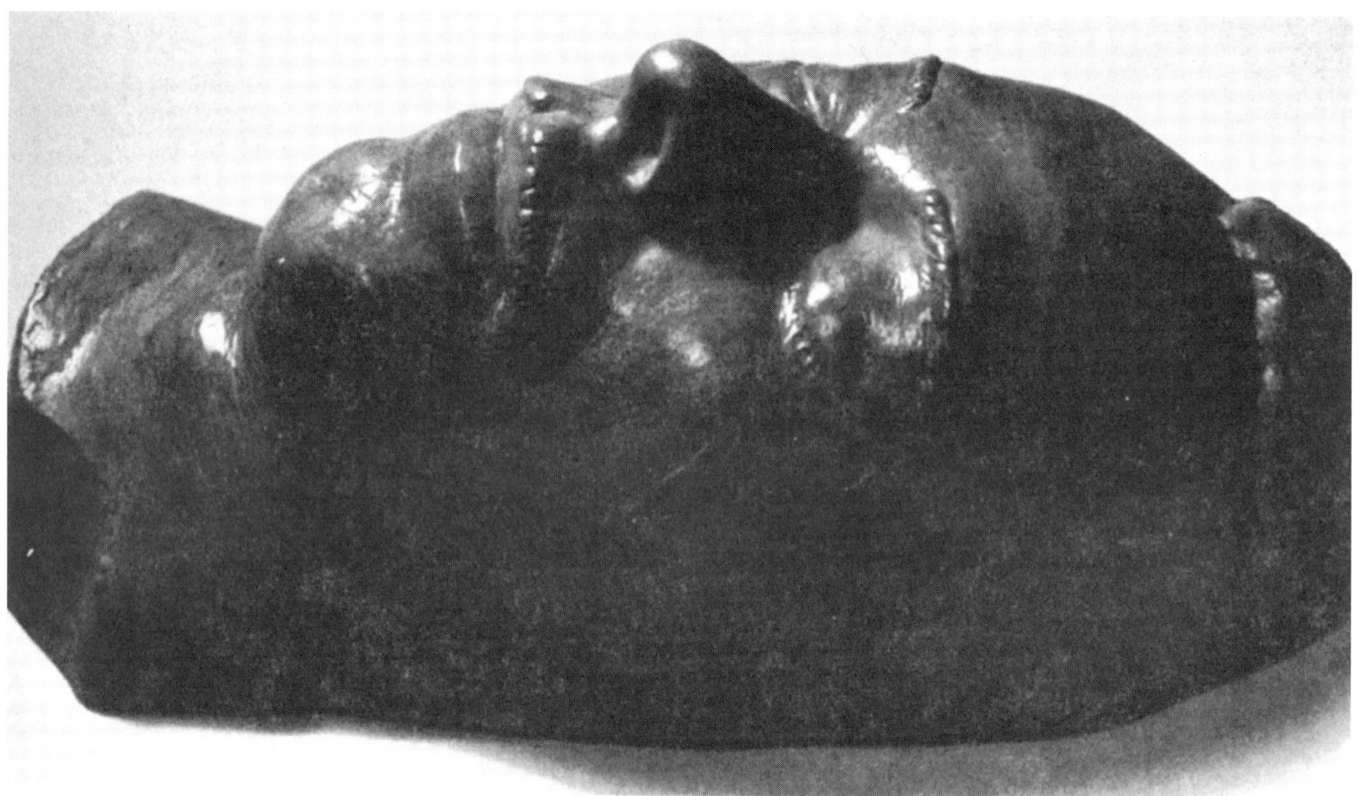

The death mask made of the corpse in the morgue, one of two copies. One of these masks hung on the wall of J. Edgar Hoover's office for years.

and if the FBI did realize the wrong man had been killed, Hoover and company would be disinclined to make such information public, especially after the recent fiasco at Little Bohemia.

Dillinger, through his emissaries, could then make arrangements with certain federal authorities to let the matter lay and quietly make his "permanent escape," living a comfortable life under another identity. Zarkovich also knew that he would never be named as Lawrence's killer, according to his agreement with Purvis, since this was an FBI operation and Purvis would not embarrass the Bureau by admitting that he allowed a non-FBI person to kill Lawrence. (The shooter at the Biograph was never revealed by the Bureau, who insisted that, indeed, an agent did kill Lawrence, but used the lame excuse to hide his identity by saying that they did not want to place this "agent" in jeopardy from revenge-seeking Dillinger associates. The Bureau knew such a threat did not exist since all known Dillinger gang members were by then dead or in prison.)

The next morning, July 22, 1934, Purvis assembled about twenty FBI agents and told them to be prepared to rendezvous at a Chicago theater, where they would apprehend John Dillinger. Agents were sent to the Marbro Theater where they checked the streets and the theater, detailing positions they would later take. Purvis and Cowley decided that they would let Anna Sage, Polly Hamilton Keele, and Lawrence-Dillinger go into the theater and wait until after the movie to make their move. When Anna Sage did call the anxious Purvis, she upset his careful plans by telling him that she, Polly, and Lawrence-Dillinger would be going to *either* the Marbro or the Biograph that night, she wasn't certain.

This presented a terrible dilemma for Purvis. Zarkovich was on hand to solve it for him. Since only Zarkovich and Purvis knew what Anna Sage looked like, he, Zarkovich, would go to the Marbro and Purvis would go to the Biograph, with agents stationed at both theaters. Whomever spotted Sage first would call the other and the forces would join.

This, too, was part of Zarkovich's (or perhaps Piquett's) subtle, crafty plan. Zarkovich knew that the trio would appear at the Biograph, which is why he suggested that he go to the Marbro. In that way, Purvis and only Purvis would identify Anna Sage and thus take full responsibility. It would then be *an FBI identification,* not one made by an East Chicago policeman and the killing of Lawrence would also be the exclusive responsibility of the FBI and Agent-in-Charge, Melvin Purvis.

That night the two groups of lawmen waited at the two theaters and Purvis, standing next to the Biograph on Lincoln Avenue, saw Anna Sage turn a corner at 8:30 p.m. and head toward the theater. She was with a young woman, Polly Hamilton Keele, and a young man wearing glasses, a straw hat and no coat, only a white shirt and slacks. As they paid for their tickets and went into the theater, Purvis called Cowley and Zarkovich at the Marbro and told them to come with their men to the Biograph.

More than twenty agents were positioned outside the Biograph while Sage, Hamilton, and Lawrence watched Clark

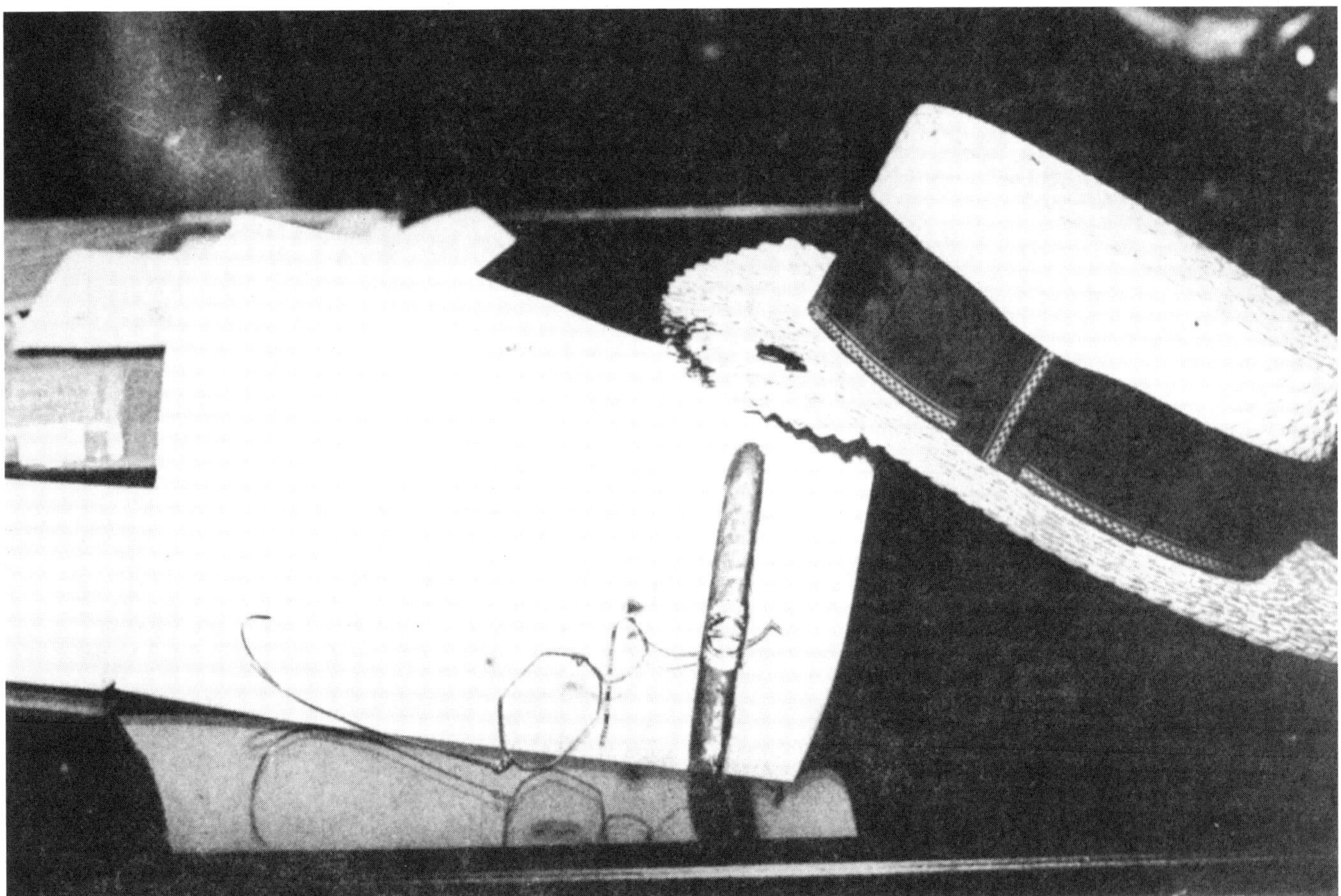

The dead man's effects on Purvis' desk. Note bullet hole through bent part of hat brim; the broken glasses worn by the dead man have prescription rims.

Gable, William Powell, and Myrna Loy star in *Manhattan Melodrama,* a gangster film. Purvis had assumed full responsibility for the stakeout and had made the identification of Anna Sage on his own, as well as the man he believed to be Dillinger. This identification was the most absurd aspect of the entire Biograph affair. Contrary to all FBI procedures, the man about to be shot was not identified prior to his appearance that night. In fact, so reliant on the word of Anna Sage was Melvin Purvis that whomever she showed up with that night at the Biograph, he, Melvin Purvis, would accept as John Dillinger.

Purvis was sitting in his car in front of the theater when the trio appeared. Said Purvis later: "He had passed my car before I saw him, but I had studied every available photograph of him so carefully that I recognized the back of his head immediately." There were no known photographs of *the back of John Dillinger's head,* so Purvis' identification remains all the more mystifying and ridiculous.

At a little before 10:30 p.m., Purvis got out of his car and took up a position near the box office of the theater, standing a little south of this cubicle. Further south, hidden in a doorway of a closed and dark shop stood Martin Zarkovich, a .45-caliber gun in an unbuttoned holster. At 10:30 p.m., the movie ended and the crowd inside began to spill out onto the sidewalk. Anna Sage, Polly Hamilton Keele, and Lawrence-Dillinger suddenly appeared and Purvis nervously lit a cigar, the prearranged signal to Zarkovich that the prey was heading his way, going south down Lincoln Avenue. The direction the trio took, of course, was engineered by Anna Sage, who led the way out of the theater, taking Polly and Lawrence, walking behind her, straight past Zarkovich, a detail worked out between Zarkovich and his good friend Sage. She would later describe her fifteen-foot walk to the death spot and how she glanced to the side to see the tall, burly East Chicago policeman, hat pulled low on his face, lurking in the shadows of the doorway. "I saw Zarkovich," she told newsmen, just before the trio reached the alleyway.

At that point, Anna Sage dropped back, pulling Polly Hamilton Keele with her, so that the young man took several steps forward, alone. At that point Zarkovich, a man of six-feet-four-inches, swiftly came up from behind Lawrence and violently pushed him to the ground. The young man fell forward, crashing to the cement so that his head was over the lip of the sidewalk and into the gutter of the alley. Zarkovich already had his .45 in his hand and quickly pumped two bullets into the prone figure, the bullets smashing into the man's head, one bullet emerging from beneath the right eye, the other entering the neck and embedding in the skull. The big policeman fired another shot that went wild and ricocheted off the pavement. (The autopsy later performed on the deceased meticulously describes the path of the bullets, both fired at a forty-five degree angle, proving the victim to be prone when shot.) Zarkovich then slipped his gun back into its holster and joined the milling crowds as Purvis and his men rushed forward.

Women in the crowds began to scream (two had been superficially wounded by Zarkovich's bullets) and several male voices, including Zarkovich's, were heard to shout: "They got Dillinger! They got Dillinger!" A large crowd ringed the man on the sidewalk. He did not move, and a pool of blood from his head wounds swelled around his smashed straw boater and broken glasses. Some people leaned down and dipped their handkerchiefs into the blood for grim souvenirs. At this moment, James Henry "Blackie" Audett, by his own later admission to the author, left his car, which had been parked across Lincoln Avenue since early that day, and joined the crowd. "It was my job to make sure that Lawrence was dead, that Zarkovich had killed him," Audett told the author in 1979.

Purvis broke through the crowd, holding his gun, and, with his foot, rolled the body over, realizing that the man was dead. He also realized, despite his prior "identification" of Lawrence as Dillinger when he passed his car that night, that the dead man did not look like John Dillinger. Reporters had already arrived and heard Purvis blurt in surprise: "That's not Dillinger's nose." He quickly caught himself and then said: "Neat bit of plastic surgery that," thus introducing for the first time the FBI theory of Dillinger having had plastic surgery, an excuse, really, to explain away the fact that the dead man did not look like John Dillinger. FBI agent Alan E. Lockerman stated to the author in 1968: "Identification was made there. I believe it was made later, at the morgue. Of course, his identification was perfectly well established when he came out of the theater. Otherwise, he wouldn't have been killed."

The FBI later claimed that one of its agents had shot down Lawrence-Dillinger because "he drew a gun and fired at agents closing in on him." This was an outright lie. The man shot at the Biograph had no gun. An FBI historian later said that the man "pulled a .38 from his waistband." Another fabrication. The dead man would have had to walk down a public street, go into a theater filled with people, emerge in a dense crowd, all while wearing a .38, in plain sight, tucked into his trousers. A short time later, when Hoover was building a monument to the FBI around the apprehension of John Dillinger, FBI Headquarters in Washington, D.C., set up an FBI museum with many showcases for the public to inspect. In one was placed the so-called weapon pulled by the man at the Biograph on July 22, 1934. This weapon, a .38 Colt automatic, bore the serial number 119702 and a check of the records of Colt's Patent Fire Arms Manufacturing Company, revealed that this weapon was sold for the first time to the L. H. Kurz Company, located in Des Moines, Iowa, on December 19, 1934, *five months after the death of the man the FBI insisted was John Dillinger.*

Identification of the dead man was not made at the morgue, as Agent Lockerman supposed. The body arrived without any personal identification and was accepted by Dr. Charles D.

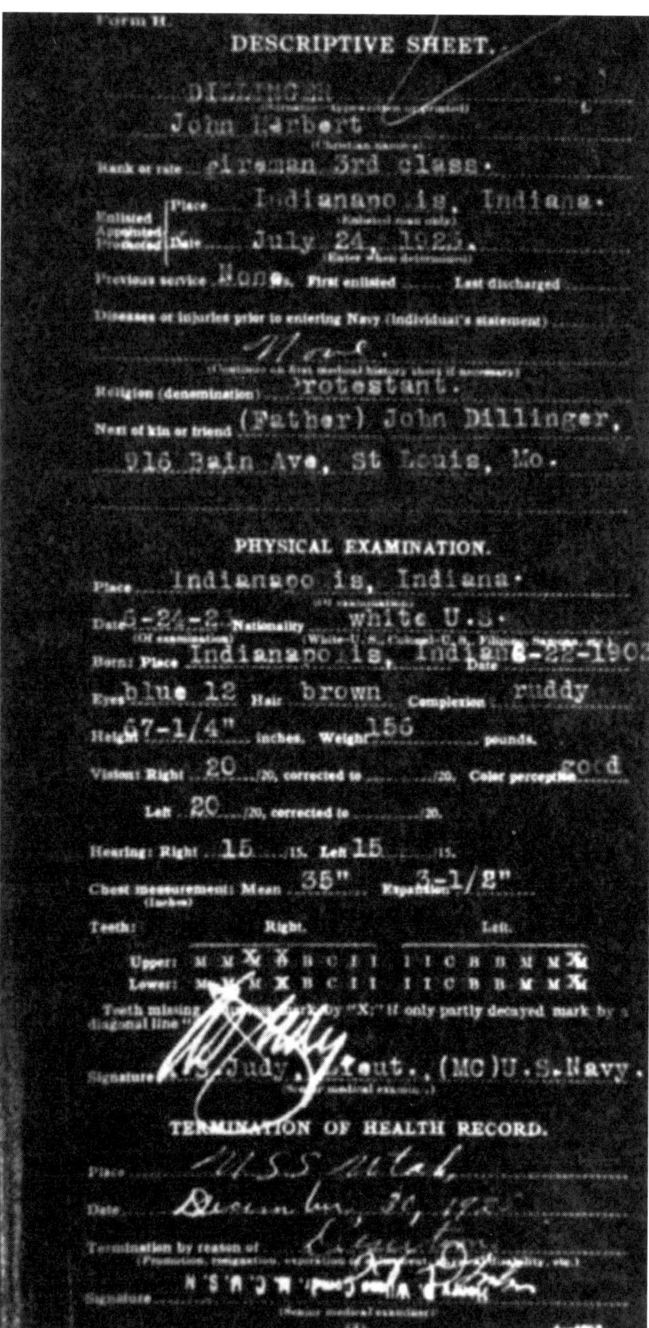

Form H.

DESCRIPTIVE SHEET.

DILLINGER

John Herbert

Rank or rate Fireman 3rd class.

Enlisted / Appointed / Promoted — Place Indianapolis, Indiana. Date July 24, 1923.

Previous service None. First enlisted ... Last discharged ...

Diseases or injuries prior to entering Navy (individual's statement) None.

Religion (denomination) Protestant.

Next of kin or friend (Father) John Dillinger, 916 Bain Ave, St Louis, Mo.

PHYSICAL EXAMINATION.

Place Indianapolis, Indiana.

Date 6-24-2 Nationality white U.S.

Born: Place Indianapolis, Indiana Date 6-22-190

Eyes blue 12 Hair brown Complexion ruddy

Height 67-1/4" inches. Weight 156 pounds.

Vision: Right 20/20, corrected to /20. Color perception good

Left 20/20, corrected to /20.

Hearing: Right 15/15. Left 15/15.

Chest measurement: Mean 35" Expansion 3-1/2"

Teeth: Right. Left.

Signature ... Judy, Lieut. (MC) U.S. Navy.

TERMINATION OF HEALTH RECORD.

Place ...

Date ...

Termination by reason of ...

Signature ...

Part of John Dillinger's U. S. Navy records. His eyes are recorded as "blue."

Parker, an assistant coroner's physician. A ring, a watch made in 1907 and worth very little, a wallet with unknown contents, and about $7 was taken from the body in the Chicago police wagon before the body arrived at the city morgue. Dr. Parker stayed with the body from the moment it arrived at the morgue at about 11 p.m. until the next morning, July 23, 1934, and, in his statements to the author, saw no one take fingerprints of the dead man.

A fingerprint card showing altered fingerprints identified as John Dillinger's was later introduced to support identification, but this card is dated "July 22, 1934," a date on which no

CORONER'S PROTOCOL

FRANK J. WALSH—CORONER—COOK COUNTY, ILL. [illegible]

NAME John Dillinger DATE OF DEATH 7/[illegible]/34

ADDRESS Unknown AUT. Yes CERT. [illegible] INQ [illegible]

DATE OF EXAM 7/23/34 COR. PHY. J. J. Kearns

SEX Male AGE 32 LENGTH 5'7" WEIGHT [illegible]

RACE White NAT'L'TY American EXAM. AT Cook County Morgue

AUTOPSY PERFORMED BY J. J. Kearns, M.D.

SIGNATURE OF IDENTIFIER Cook County Morgue Records

HISTORY OF CAUSE OF DEATH:

Gunshot. Removed from sidewalk at 2450 Lincoln Ave. 37th District Police.

ANATOMIC DIAGNOSIS:

1. Multiple (4) (3 superficial: two of the face and one of the chest) and (1) thru and thru of the face, causing laceration of the soft tissues of the neck, comminuted fractures of the lateral processes of the 3rd, 2nd and 1st cervical vertebrae and body of the 2nd cervical vertebra, laceration of the vertebral artery and veins, lower portion of the medulla oblongata and spinal cord to the level of the 5th cervical segment.
2. Anemia and edema of the brain and lungs.
3. Hemorrhagic softening of the myocardium, liver, kidneys and spleen.
4. Multiple healed scars of the face, chin and volar surface distal phalanges of the fingers of both hands.
5. Healed thru and thru bullet wound of the left thigh.
6. Healed scars in the left thigh and leg.
7. Rheumatic mitral (partly stenosing) verrucous endocarditis.
8. Eccentric hypertrophy of the myocardium.

The three pages of Dr. J. J. Kearns' thorough autopsy (he was aided by another physician who checked and repeated all findings to a medical stenographer). Among the pertinent facts, Kearns lists the corpse's eyes as "brown" and states that the dead man suffered from a rheumatic heart complaint (that may have been terminal, a condition that would have prevented the energetic Dillinger from ever playing baseball, as he did, or vaulting over six-foot bank tellers' cages).

one took the dead man's prints; it also contains several technical errors dealing with the whorl and ridge counts of Dillinger's prints which indicates that the card was a plant later used to shore up the shaky identification of the dead man, a fingerprint identification made on a Chicago Police Department Print Card, not an official FBI card, a card that anyone like Louis Piquett could easily obtain.

Purvis later proudly displayed the dead man's artifacts on his desk for newsmen to photograph, but these were items that spoke for the innocence of the dead man, not the claimed disguise of John Dillinger. The straw hat the dead man had been wearing had had its brim smashed and bent, further proving that the man had been pushed down while wearing the hat. A bullet hole had *then* been made through the bent part of the brim, which would not have occurred had the man been upright when shot. Moreover, the glasses the man was wearing were also displayed. These were gold-rimmed octagonal prescription glasses, not the cheap dark sunglasses one would use in a disguise. Dillinger's eyesight was, of course, 20-20.

The following order of description will be followed on this and succeeding pages:

1. External findings (in detail)	7. Blood Vessels	13. Spleen	19. Skull
2. Thoracic Cavity	8. Upper Digestive Tract	14. Lymph Glands	20. Meninges
3. Abdominal Cavity	9. Stomach	15. Adrenals	21. Brain
4. Upper Respiratory Tract	10. Intestines	16. Kidneys	22. Miscellaneous
5. Lungs	11. Liver—Gall Bladder	17. Pelvic Organs	23. Chemical Microscopic
6. Heart Aorta	12. Pancreas	18. Testicle—Ovary	24. Bacteriologic

EXTERNAL EXAMINATION (Inspection)

Development of skeleton: Slender / Medium xx / Powerful / Deformed

Musculature well developed Panniculus adiposus (subcutaneous) 2 cm.

Skin—Color white Edema none

Pigmentation none Bed Sores none

SIGNS OF DEATH

Body Heat absent Lividity dorsal Rigor-mortis present

Cornea cloudy Putrefaction none

Color of hair brown scalp hair and mustache (dyed black)

Size of pupils dilated Color of Iris brown Color of Sclera gray

Size and shape of neck medium

Size and shape of thorax symmetric

Abdomen flat

Evidences of External Injury, with description:

There were two superficial "gutter-like" abrasions of the skin, such as a bullet would make: #1—adjacent to the outer angle of the left eye; #2—in the cheek over the zygoma, on the left side.

#3—Bullet wound of entrance at the level of the 6th cervical vertebra 5 cm. to the right of the midline. This bullet passed upward in the neck causing laceration of the soft tissues, comminuted fractures of the lateral processes of the 3rd, 2nd and 1st cervical vertebrae, comminuted fracture of the body of the 2nd cervical vertebra, laceration of the vertebral artery and vein, laceration of the meninges of the spinal cord, posterior, lateral and anterior tracts from the level of the 4th thru the medulla oblongata on the right side, from here the bullet passed upward along the postero-lateral pharynx causing hemorrhage around the internal jugular and internal carotid arteries, leaving thru an opening in the lower lid of the right eye at its outer angle. There was an extensive sub-periosteal hemorrhage from the level of the jugular foramen to the 6th cervical vertebra, in the spinal canal. The spinal canal contained clotted and fluid blood.

#4—Bullet wound of entrance in the mid-clavicular line over the 7th costal interspace. This bullet passed superficially leaving thru an opening in the mid-axillary line over the 8th rib on the left side.

There were superficial abrasions of the skin of the nose and face. There were healed scars in the chin, oblique in direction, 2 cm. on either side of the midline. There were healed verticle scars over the temporo-mandibular joint, 3 cm. long, on either side. There was a purple-red area in the skin, 2½ cm. square, over the sternum at the level of the 7th costal cartilage just to the right of the midline. This was covered with a thin parchment-like membrane. There were roughly circular scars in the skin, up to 1 cm. in diameter, in the middle of the volar surface of the distal phalanges of the fingers of both hands. There was a linear scar, 10 cm. long, in the left thigh, antero-lateral aspect, lower third. There was a healed semi-lunar scar in the antero-medial aspect, calf of the left leg. There was a wound, such as a bullet wound of entrance and exit would make, the former at the junction of the middle and lower thirds antero-lateral aspect, the latter in the postero-lateral aspect, slightly above the wound of entrance, in the left thigh. There was a healed wound in the neck, roughly circular in outline, 1 cm. in diameter, posterior aspect 2 cm. to the left of the midline at the level of the 7th cervical vertebra.

HEAD: The scalp, cranial bones and meninges showed no traumatic changes. The brain, on multiple surfaces made by cutting, was pale. The lower portion of the medulla oblongata and the spinal cord to the level of the 5th cervical segment was studded with petechial and ecchymotic hemorrhages.

NECK: The soft tissues of the neck, including the mucous membrane of the buccal cavity, esophagus, pharynx and larynx, were pale.

CHEST: The lungs were subcrepitant and on surfaces made by cutting covered with pale bloody frothy fluid. The trachea and bronchi contained bloody frothy fluid. The tracheo-bronchial lymph nodes were soft and anthracotic.

HEART: The pericardial sac contained straw colored fluid. The myocardium was thickened, pale, soft. The mitral leaflets were thickened, the commissures partly obliterated. The corda tendinae and papillary muscles were thickened. There were pin point to pin head sized semi-firm warty vegetations on the auricular surface of the free margins of the mitral leaflets. The intima of the aorta and coronary arteries contained a few atheromatous plaques.

ABDOMEN: The abdominal surfaces were smooth and dry. The liver, kidneys and spleen were pale, soft, the markings were indistinct. The gall bladder and biliary passages were patent. The adrenals, pancreas and lower genito-urinary tract were not remarkable. The stomach contained a partly digested meal consisting of particles of red peppers, and fragments of meat and vegetables.

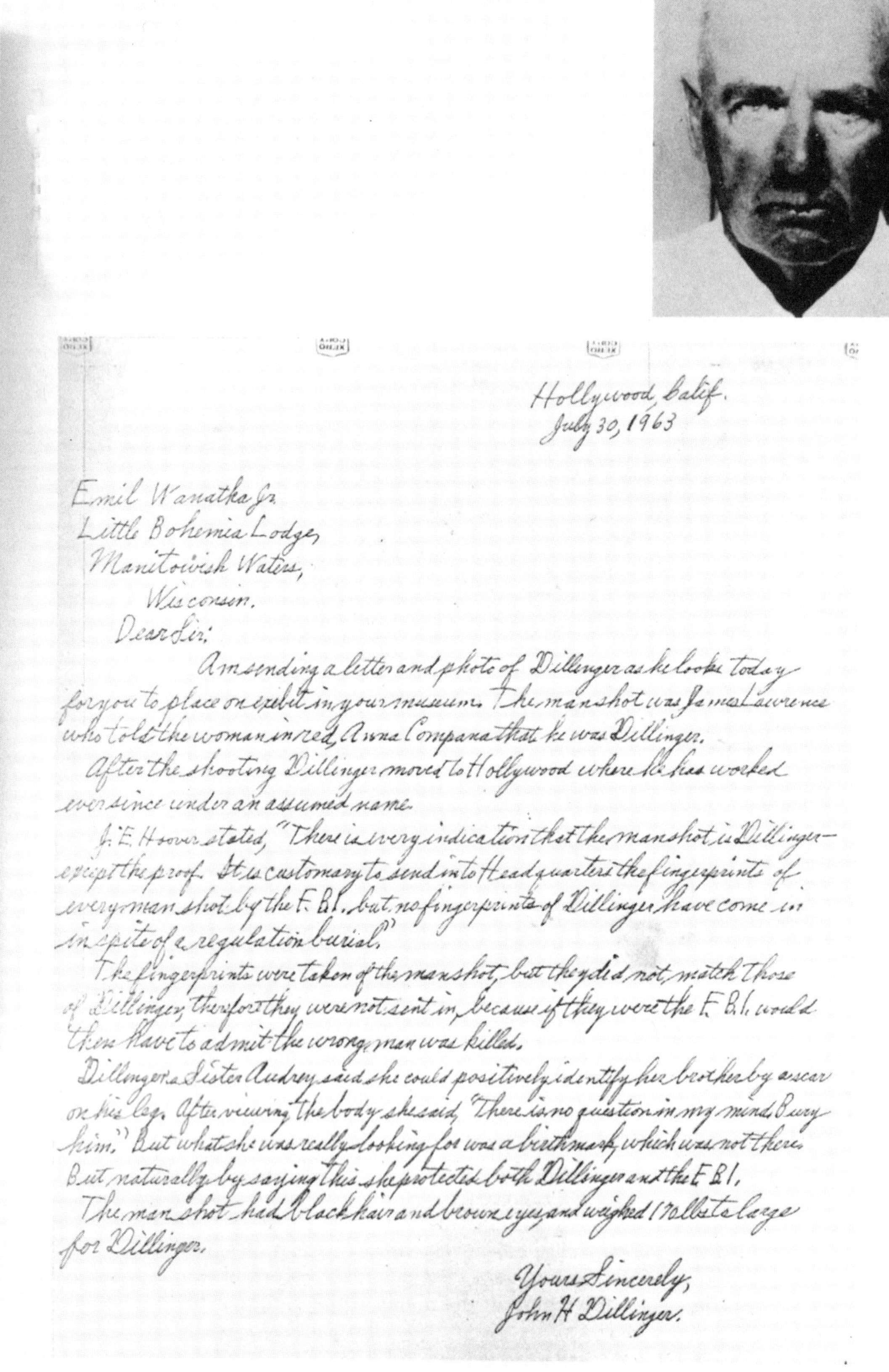

Hollywood Calif.
July 30, 1963

Emil Wanatka Jr
Little Bohemia Lodge,
Manitowish Waters,
Wisconsin.

Dear Sir:

Am sending a letter and photo of Dillinger as he looks today for you to place on exebit in your museum. The man shot was James Lawrence who told the woman in red, Anna Compana that he was Dillinger.

After the shooting Dillinger moved to Hollywood where he has worked ever since under an assumed name.

J. E. Hoover stated, "There is every indication that the man shot is Dillinger— except the proof. It is customary to send in to Headquarters the fingerprints of every man shot by the F.B.I., but no fingerprints of Dillinger have come in in spite of a regulation burial."

The fingerprints were taken of the man shot, but they did not match those of Dillinger, therfore they were not sent in, because if they were the F.B.I. would then have to admit the wrong man was killed.

Dillinger's Sister Audrey said she could positively identify her brother by a scar on his leg. After viewing the body she said, "There is no question in my mind. Bury him." But what she was really looking for was a birthmark, which was not there. But, naturally by saying this she protected both Dillinger and the F.B.I.

The man shot had black hair and brown eyes and weighed 170 lbs to large for Dillinger.

Yours Sincerely,
John H Dillinger.

The photo and letter sent to the son of the owner of Little Bohemia Lodge dated July 30, 1963, by a man who said he was John Dillinger, pointing out that "the man shot had black hair and brown eyes..." details that only Dillinger, who had blue eyes, would know.

A sample of Dillinger's handwriting while he was an inmate at Pendleton Reformatory, one that shows a marked similarity to that written by the man who claimed to be Dillinger in 1963.

The most telling document was the autopsy performed on the slain man by Dr. J. J. Kearns, chief pathologist for the Cook County coroner. The original document disappeared almost the moment it was completed (confiscated from public records, one might assume, by Melvin Purvis or other federal authorities, once it was realized that the FBI under Purvis had again killed the wrong man, Eugene Boisineau being the first). Kearns' autopsy was meticulously conducted and could not later be challenged by the FBI or Hoover. It was performed with another doctor checking Kearns' every discovery and a medical nurse writing down what both doctors verbally described. Dozens of medical students were in attendance, watching every move made by Kearns, one of the top pathologists in America at the time. The author obtained through Kearns a copy of this autopsy in 1968, and its startling revelations include the fact that the dead man had brown eyes, and all of Dillinger's records (also obtained by the author from the files of the U.S. Navy, local and state governments in Indiana, Illinois, Arizona, and Ohio, and FBI documentation) show him to have blue or blue-gray eyes. The color of the iris does not change after death and color contact lenses were not available until four decades later.

A photo taken from Evelyn Freschette's purse when she was arrested by Melvin Purvis on April 9, 1934. The photo shows Dillinger's girlfriend in younger days with a young man who bears an amazing resemblance to the man shot at the Biograph Theater in 1934. Note (arrow) the man is wearing the same kind of heavy ring as indicated on the left third finger of the man shot at the Biograph, a ring that vanished. This young man wears a very real gun belt across his chest, placing him somewhere in the murky realm of the underworld.

The burial marker where Dillinger's double is buried in Crown Hill Cemetery, Indianapolis. It is oddly marked "John H. Dillinger, Jr." Dillinger was not "junior" to his father, John Wilson Dillinger. The "Jr." may have been the bandit's last bit of macabre humor, a reference to the man, who assumed his identity and died with his name.

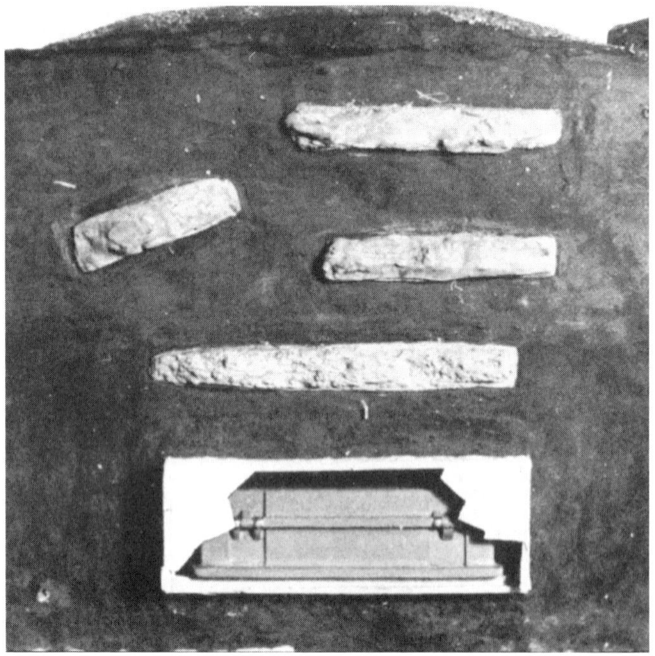

A side view mockup showing the buried casket containing the body of the Biograph victim. Surrounding the wooden casket is poured concrete, mixed with scrap iron and chicken wire. Slabs of concrete mixed with scrap iron are shown above the concrete-encased casket at staggered levels to prevent exhumation, an expensive bit of work Dillinger paid for, according to James H. Audett, who also stated that the capricious Dillinger was one of the workers at the gravesite who mixed and poured the concrete.

Also, the dead man was missing Dillinger's known scars, a half-inch scar on the back of his left hand and another pronounced scar on his upper lip. Known birthmarks were missing as were two bullet wounds Dillinger was known to have received in recent months, one in the arm, the other in the leg. The dead man was shorter and heavier than Dillinger would have been and he possessed a top right incisor tooth which is clearly missing from the mouth of John Dillinger in motion picture footage taken of him at Crown Point, Indiana, only four months earlier. The tooth in the dead man's mouth was real, not false.

Dr. Kearns removed the dead man's heart and studied it, noting that it was in a severe rheumatic condition, a chronic condition that had existed since childhood. Dillinger had never had a rheumatic heart. Such a condition would have prevented Dillinger from playing baseball, joining the Navy, or performing the running and scaling feats he was seen to enact when robbing banks. The man on the slab in the morgue who Kearns examined had been executed, according to the angle of the bullets entering his body as carefully charted by the pathologist.

But the FBI announced that John Dillinger was dead and that news was welcomed by Dillinger himself, according to Blackie Audett. After seeing that Zarkovich had performed his duty and that the man on the sidewalk outside the Biograph was, indeed, dead, Audett walked across Lincoln Avenue, got into his car and drove to Aurora, Ill., and parked in front of a small rented cabin. He entered the cabin and said to the man sitting at a table, playing solitaire: "You're dead now, John." Dillinger, according to Audett, got up and shook his hand. Audett urged him to leave the Midwest, but Dillinger told him he wanted to "see the folks just once more." He also wanted to make sure that the body being passed off as his own would not be disturbed.

The body was shipped from the morgue to the far north side mortuary of Ray McCready, the man who had entered Dillinger's death date in his ledger six days before the shooting at the Biograph. It was thought by the conspirators that this would be a safe place for it, out of the reach of prying newsmen. When the elder Dillinger and Audrey Dillinger Hancock arrived to pick up this body and take it back to Mooresville, Indiana, for burial, they both immediately denied that it was John Dillinger, but quickly overcame their shock and, prodded by a member of the conspiracy, suddenly remembered a scar on the leg which Dillinger had received when a child, a scar that did appear on the body but one that Dillinger himself never received.

Following the burial of this body in Crown Hill Cemetery, Indianapolis, Dillinger arranged to have the coffin dug up and reburied, this time surrounded by tons of cement mixed with chicken wire and scrap iron. The director of the cemetery later told the author: "The only way to get that body out of there now is to blow it up and there wouldn't be enough left to put into a cookie jar."

Dillinger paid several thousand dollars to have this chore performed. The Dillinger family was nearly broke and the elder Dillinger had to borrow the $50 to cover McCready's embalming fees. Following the reburial, Dillinger climbed into a car and was driven to the West Coast by Blackie Audett, who told the author that he left Dillinger at the Indian reservation in Klamath Falls, Oregon, just north of the California border and that he later married an Indian girl. "Evelyn Frechette was an Indian, a Menominee," Audett stated, "and John was partial to Indian ladies." Audett, who corresponded with Audrey Dillinger to the day of his death in 1979, claimed that up to that time, John Herbert Dillinger was still alive, living on the West Coast.

The question remained: Why would he not surface after all these years? The answer is that there is no statute of limitations on the capital offense of murder and he would still have to stand trial for the murder of Officer O'Malley. He would also have to stand trial for his part in the conspiracy to murder an innocent man, James Lawrence, the patsy who took his place and unwittingly sealed his own fate. Others knew well the existence of the conspiracy, including Harry Pierpont who, according to Audett, was informed by the prison grapevine of John's "permanent escape" before he and Makley went to the electric chair in Ohio in September 1934 for the murder of Sheriff Sarber. Pierpont was smiling as he sat in the chair and he said cryptically: "Today, I am the only man who knows the `whos and hows' and, as my end comes very shortly, I'll take this little story with me."

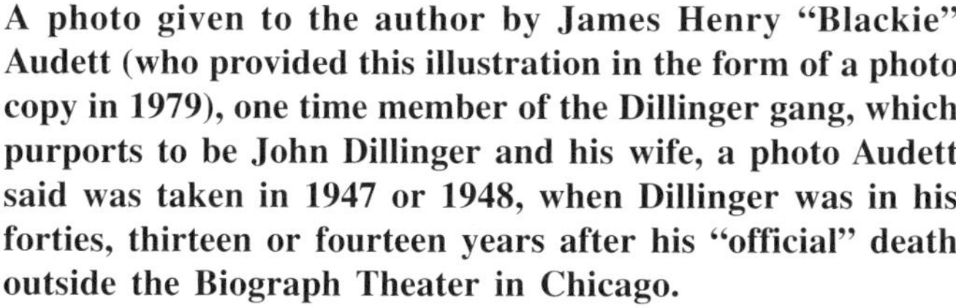

A photo given to the author by James Henry "Blackie" Audett (who provided this illustration in the form of a photo copy in 1979), one time member of the Dillinger gang, which purports to be John Dillinger and his wife, a photo Audett said was taken in 1947 or 1948, when Dillinger was in his forties, thirteen or fourteen years after his "official" death outside the Biograph Theater in Chicago.

Though condemned to death, bank robber Harry Pierpont smiled to himself, as if enjoying his own secrets, saying before he went to the electric chair for the murder of Sheriff Sarber in September 1934 (two months *after* the shooting at the Biograph Theater): "Today, I am the only man who knows the 'whos' and 'hows', and, as my end comes very shortly, I'll take this little story with me."

Most of the Dillinger gang had been destroyed by that time. Tommy Carroll was shot to death by detectives outside Waterloo, Iowa, in the summer of 1934. Eddie Green had been shot in the back by FBI agents while trying to escape a dragnet on April 3, 1934. Homer Van Meter was trapped by FBI agents on August 23, 1934, and he died in a gun battle as he ran up a St. Paul alley. Baby Face Nelson, the worst of the lot, would go to his death in a blazing machine gun battle with FBI agents Sam Cowley and Herman Hollis, killing both of them, in Barrington, Illinois, on November 27, 1934. Russell Clark would be paroled from prison and die a short while later of cancer. Evelyn Billie Frechette (extensively interviewed by the author) would die about the same time of cancer. So, too, would Martin Zarkovich (extensively interviewed by the author), who received $5,000 of the federal reward money.

Anna Sage, who had worn an orange skirt on the night of the Biograph shooting, one that was made to appear red beneath the bright lights of the marquee and was thus called The Lady in Red, was given $5,000 in reward money and then shipped back to Romania. Before leaving the U.S., she cursed Melvin Purvis for lying to her, and she later threatened while living in Bucharest, "to tell the real story about the Dillinger shooting." She died mysteriously a short time later, murdered, according to Audett, "to keep her mouth shut."

Melvin Purvis, the most spectacular FBI agent in the Bureau during the early 1930s, went on to greater glory, tracking down and killing Charles Arthur "Pretty Boy" Floyd in the fall of 1934. But by June of 1935, he and his boss Hoover had such harsh words that he left the Bureau. Following his resignation, all Purvis could murmur was: "I'm glad to be out of here!" He later went on the radio, peddling an inflated G-Man image and became the chief of the Post-Toasties Junior G-Man Squad. Still later Purvis tried his hand at running a radio station and other enterprises which more or less failed.

On February 29, 1960, Purvis called his doctor and said he was despondent over an unstated matter. He made an appointment with the physician but never appeared. Instead, he looked over his extensive weapon collection and selected the .38 Police Special he had carried on the night of the Biograph shooting. He then stepped into his backyard and blew out his brains. Purvis had reportedly received a letter a short time earlier, one from an elderly man in California who claimed to be John Dillinger.

In the early 1960s, this old man sent several letters (and snapshots of himself) from California, one to the Indianapolis *Star* and one to Emil Wannatka, Jr., son of Dillinger's host at Little Bohemia in 1934. Both letters claimed that "the wrong man" had been killed at the Biograph and contained information that only Dillinger would seem to know, one line reading: "The dead man had brown eyes and black hair." This man was never found and it is not known if he was Dillinger or not.

WILLIE SUTTON: "WHERE THE MONEY WAS"/1930S-1940s

No American bank robber ever employed the dramatic techniques and the inventiveness displayed by William Francis Sutton (AKA: Edward Lynch; 1901-1980), better known as "Willie the Actor." Born in Brooklyn, New York, the son of a blacksmith, Sutton, like John Dillinger, Charles Arthur "Pretty Boy" Floyd, and many a bank robber before and after him, quit school at an early age and earned his living by shoplifting and, in his late teens, burglary. He preferred to operate alone, although he often took in a partner or two when robbing banks, which became his specialty in the late 1920s. Sutton was not only a student of other people—their mannerisms, quirks, facial expressions—but a student of his own face and body.

A 1930 police photo of bankrobber Willie "The Actor" Sutton.

While working for a munitions plant in New York during World War I, Sutton made good money and purchased a handsome wardrobe. He then began hanging around clubs off Broadway, befriending actors. He was intrigued with the theater and was soon backstage, where he watched avidly as performers made up their faces. An old trouper gave him his old makeup box and Sutton cherished this gift, keeping it all his life. What came out of that makeup box were as many faces and characters as Lon Chaney, Sr., ever created (Chaney was the silent film star who was called "The Man of a Thousand Faces.")

Sutton would use his makeup to create a different face for every robbery he committed. He would insert cork into his nostrils to make his nose appear wider, powder his hair to make himself appear older, and, just as often, use different dyes to color his hair, changing it from its natural black. Sutton would insert pads into his cheeks to broaden his face and use gum arabic to create longer earlobes or to fill in the bridge of his nose or add more chin and jowls to his face.

In 1920, Sutton fell in love with Bessie Hurley, daughter of a Brooklyn shipyard magnate. At the time, Sutton was helping to build ships in the Brooklyn Navy Yard. He also helped himself to $16,000 of Hurley's money in the paymaster's office and ran off with Bessie. The couple was tracked down to a Poughkeepsie, New York, hotel a short time later and Sutton was arrested. Bessie's father interceded on Sutton's behalf and saved him from serving a jail term.

Sutton then went to bootlegger Jack "Legs" Diamond and was hired as a collector for various rackets Diamond was operating. He continued to work in this capacity for such bootlegging crime czars as Dutch Schultz and Arnold Rothstein (See Gangs, Gangsters and Organized Crime). By 1922, Sutton met and became the willing pupil of Edward "Doc" Tate, one of the foremost safecrackers in the U. S. Tate approached safes as if giving a solo performance before royalty. He never used an acetylene torch or nitroglycerin, preferring to work exclusively with his fingers, "feeling out" the quirks of a safe's tumblers.

Tate gave Sutton a set of golden rules by which Sutton was to live as a professional thief and burglar. "Plan every detail in advance," Tate told his pupil. "Always use ordinary tools and leave them behind when you finish a job, except for your jimmy. Keep that with you until you are clear. Never overlook the possibility of locked doors barring your escape."

On their first night together, Tate took Sutton along to four different shops, where they broke into safes and went away with more than $10,000. Tate, in a typical gesture of bow-taking, left his jimmy on the outside window sill of a police station. Sutton worked with Tate for four years and was never caught, but his first solo safecracking job in 1925 was a disaster. He forgot Tate's advice and got trapped in a locked hallway and was apprehended. He drew a four-year sentence in Sing Sing. Upon his release, Sutton teamed up with Jack Bassett and, in 1930, went into bank robbery.

Sutton appeared at the bank in Jamaica, Long Island, at 8 a.m. A guard answered his knock and opened the door to see Sutton dressed as a Western Union messenger, wearing the complete uniform. Sutton informed the guard that he had a telegram for the bank president. The guard began to sign for the telegram, when Sutton jammed a gun into the guard's stomach and said: "Now be a good boy and you won't get hurt." He backed the guard into the bank, with Bassett slipping in behind them and locking the door.

The president of the bank was summoned and Sutton, his face made up to look much younger than his twenty-eight years, ordered him to open the vault. He did, and Sutton scooped up $48,000. As he and Bassett were about to depart, Sutton said: "We're leaving now. But I have a third man outside. If anyone goes through this door in the next five minutes, he will be shot."

Sutton and Bassett slipped outside only a few minutes before the bank was scheduled to open. There was no third man waiting outside, but Sutton correctly figured that the bank employees would believe him and wait several minutes before giving the alarm, just enough time for Sutton and Bassett to blend in with the heavy crowds on the street.

Sutton had planned this robbery well, obtaining a Western Union uniform and then sending a telegram to himself. He steamed open the envelope and substituted a telegram he had typed himself on Western Union stationery, one showing the bank president's name. He then resealed the envelope and was ready to rob the bank. At the time, Sutton was married. He explained to his wife that the $24,000 he brought home was an inheritance from a rich uncle, who had just died in Ireland.

A few days later Sutton and Bassett used the same Western Union ruse to gain entrance to the Rosenthal Jewelry store on Broadway in Manhattan. The manager was so terrified that he completely forgot the combination to the safe that held the company jewels. A janitor was forced at gunpoint to call the firm's owner to get the combination. Sutton and Bassett took more than $130,000 in rare gems from the Rosenthal store. In all, Sutton and Bassett robbed thirteen banks and jewelry stores within a few weeks. Their take was staggering.

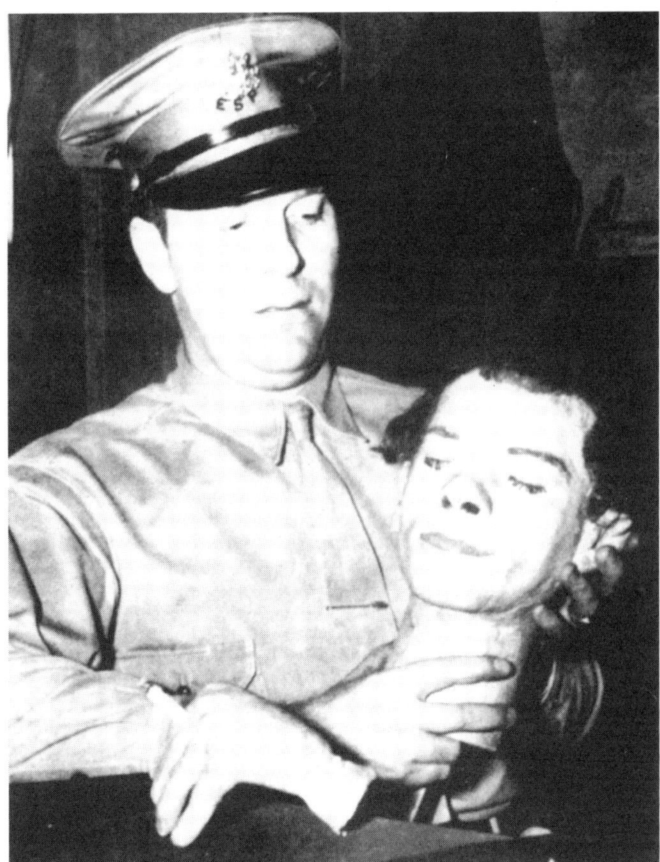

The dummy head Sutton fashioned and left behind during one of his many prison escapes.

Bassett's wife, however, was jealous over her husband's mistress and informed police that her husband and Sutton were the bandits they were seeking. Both men were arrested. Sutton withstood five days of rubber-hosing from the police without confessing. Witnesses from his robberies were brought forth, but they failed to recognize him. One witness told police that Sutton was "far from the man you want." One victim said: "No, no, the man who robbed my place had a flat nose and puffy cheeks." Another stated: "The robber was taller and heavyset. This guy is puny." Of course Sutton, when robbing this last man, had worn elevator shoes and had padded his stomach.

Only the porter made a positive identification of Sutton as the man who robbed the Rosenthal store. Sutton was sent back to Sing Sing for thirty years. In less than two years he was again outside. In December 1932, Sutton picked four locks in Sing Sing's "escape-proof" block house, used a rope ladder of his own making to get over the wall, and fled in a car which had been left near the prison by an associate. He returned to robbery immediately.

Within weeks, Sutton by himself had robbed a number of banks and jewelry stores, using various disguises in each robbery. At one bank, where he got away with more than $18,000, Sutton was dressed as a policeman, speaking with a thick Irish

Sutton shown under arrest, captured in 1952, after a citizen reported his whereabouts to police.

accent, and wearing a red wig. He turned up at an exclusive Fifth Avenue jewelers dressed as a fireman carrying city credentials. He informed the jewelers that he was there to check on possible fire code violations, so he was allowed to inspect every corner of the place freely.

When he was inside the vault, Sutton held up the owners, taking jewels worth hundreds of thousands of dollars. At a Manhattan bank a few days later, Sutton appeared outside the locked door dressed as a postman carrying a large package that was too big to slip through the mail slot. The guard opened the door to take the package, and Sutton backed him into the bank at the point of a gun. Sutton looted this bank of more than $130,000.

Though he was rich, Sutton was also one of the most wanted men in the East. He could not go near his wife, who had given birth to a daughter, because he knew police would be watching her residence. He flitted from hideout to hideout, paying enormous amounts of money for these havens, but he was told to "keep moving" because he was "too hot to stay in one spot" for any length of time. He lived a lonely, furtive life. His only enjoyment was reading books.

By 1934, Sutton realized just how alone he was. One of his partners, Johnny Eagan, was killed by gangsters in New York for not turning in part of his loot from a burglary. Another partner, Eddie Wilson, was trapped inside a store and was blinded for life by a police bullet. Jack Bassett was captured and sent to prison for fifty years. Then Sutton's mentor, Doc Tate, was sent to prison, where he died of lung problems.

Sutton did not remain inactive. He and Joseph Pelango robbed a bank in Philadelphia. Sutton used his policeman's routine to gain entrance to the bank and, within minutes, had taken more than $160,000 out of the vault. But Pelango was arrested and he informed on Sutton, who was trapped inside his small apartment by a half dozen policemen wielding Thompson submachine guns.

On February 4, 1934, Sutton, following a conviction for bank robbery, entered Eastern State Penitentiary to serve twenty to fifty years. This was a maximum security prison, one of the toughest in the U. S., and its administrators prided themselves on its thick steel doors, double teams of guards, and an informer system whereby convicts were rewarded with substantial time off for turning in other convicts planning to escape. Sutton's reputation preceded him. He was placed in solitary confinement for the first eighteen months of his stay at Eastern. Guards told him that he would never be able to escape from Eastern like he had from Sing Sing.

When Sutton was placed in a regular cell, he carefully planned his escape. During an exercise period, he slipped into the prison's 200-foot underground drainage system. He crawled some distance until he reached a second tunnel, which was filled with water. Stripping, Sutton swam under water for several feet until he reached an underwater iron door. He dove repeatedly downward in an attempt to find the handle to the door, but realized, almost too late, that the door was controlled by an automatic device. His lungs nearly bursting, Sutton barely managed to get to the surface and returned to the first conduit. He put on his clothes and returned to his cell only a few minutes before roll call.

For two years Sutton collected materials, piecing together a plaster of Paris head, which was almost a perfect likeness of himself. He painted the skin area a sallow flesh tone and pasted hair from his own head onto the skull and eyebrows, using the cuttings from the prison barber shop. Then he made a plaster of Paris arm. On a winter night, he positioned the fake head and arm in his bunk so that he appeared to be sleeping. By then Sutton had also acquired a rope, a hacksaw blade, and a grappling hook. He sawed through the bars of his cell window, then worked himself through the opening and onto a ledge of the cell block.

Sutton flung the grappling hook attached to the rope to the outer wall and was about to swing out to it, where it would be a simple matter to let himself down the other side and escape. At that moment, however, prison alarms went off. Another group of convicts were making an escape attempt in another part of the prison. Sutton, realizing his ridiculous position, crawled back into his cell. A short time later, the severed bars and fake head and arm were discovered and he was sent to the isolation block for two years. Sutton decided to settle into prison life, serve his time, and work toward an early release as a model prisoner.

The bandit learned shorthand and was made assistant to the prison psychiatrist. After ten years, however, Sutton realized there was little hope for parole. He and twelve other inmates began digging a tunnel at the end of 1945. Within six months the convicts had dug ninety-seven feet and broken the earth on the other side of the prison wall. The convicts leaped from the hole and ran in all directions. As Sutton arrived at ground level he found himself looking into the muzzle of a guard's revolver. He was sent back to the isolation ward, another ten to twenty years added to his sentence.

In August 1946, Sutton was transferred to Holmesburg County Prison outside of Philadelphia. On February 9, 1947, Sutton and other inmates, using a smuggled .38-caliber revolver and a hacksaw, worked their way out of their cells and into a guardhouse. They marched the guards to the fire house, where they obtained two ladders. Sutton and the others, using the guards as hostages, carried the ladders into the yard, placing them against the wall. It was snowing heavily, and the convicts hoped that the swirling snow would hide them from the guards in the towers.

One of the tower guards, however, fired a shot at the group. The quick-thinking Sutton shouted up to the tower guard: "Stop that! Can't you see we're guards?" The guard ceased firing and the convicts raced up the ladders and dropped to freedom on the other side of the wall. They commandeered a milk truck and drove it to Philadelphia.

Sutton was free after thirteen years in prison. All of the other convicts went to underworld gathering spots and were soon caught, but the wily Sutton found the perfect hiding spot. He took a low-paying job as a hospital porter at Farm Colony, a home for retired persons operated by the City of New York. Giving the name Edward Lynch, Sutton was hired at $20 a week and was also given room and board. The City of New York had provided him with a hideout and walk-about money as well! Sutton worked hard, minding the rules, and living quietly. He planned to spend the rest of his days working at Farm Colony, but in August 1949, one of the nurses showed him a picture of himself in a newspaper, saying that he looked enough like Willie Sutton the bank robber to be Willie Sutton.

"If I were Willie Sutton," said Sutton, "I wouldn't be working here for $80 a month." The nurse and Sutton laughed at the joke, but Sutton, shaken by the experience, decided to quit. Some days later Sutton entered the Manufacturer's Trust Company bank in Sunnyside, New York, a suburb of New York City. He longed to rob it, but according to his later claims, he resisted the temptation that had for years compelled him to steal (years earlier, Sutton admitted in his memoirs, he once robbed a bank even though he had more than $40,000 in his pockets; the temptation was too strong to resist).

Sutton further claimed that he passed information about the Sunnyside bank to some bank robbers he knew, and the bank was robbed of $64,000 some weeks later. The thieves used Sutton's techniques so well that he was blamed for the robbery (if, indeed, he did not commit it).

While riding the subway on February 18, 1952, Sutton was identified by 24-year-old clothing salesman Arnold Schuster. The young man followed Sutton off the subway at the Bergen Avenue station and trailed him to a garage. He then went to the nearest precinct station and told officers that he believed he had recognized one of the most wanted men in the country, Willie "The Actor" Sutton, saying that the man he had followed looked just like a photo of Sutton on a wanted poster he had recently seen.

Two uniformed officers investigated, finding Sutton tinkering on an old car in his garage. They asked to see his driver's license and he politely showed them a license with the name Edward Lynch on it. The officers left but returned with a detective minutes later. "You better come along with us to the station," the detective told him. "You look too much like Sutton to be wandering about loose." At first, Sutton insisted that it was merely a case of mistaken identity, but when his fingerprints were taken and checked, he knew the game was over. "I might as well be dead now," sighed Sutton, tired of running from the law. "You can shoot and kill me for all I care."

Schuster was hailed as a hero. He was given a reward and he was interviewed on television, lauded for his civic action in bringing a desperate criminal to justice. Watching the TV program was one of the worst killers in New York, Albert Anastasia. The New York Mafia/syndicate chief jumped to his feet and shouted to several of his goons: "I hate squealers. Hit that guy!" On March 9, 1952, a gunman shot and killed Schuster as he was walking home. A bullet was sent into each eye of the victim, the ritualistic shooting of an informer.

Author Jay Robert Nash, left, interviewed Willie "The Actor" Sutton in 1979, when the bank robber detailed his many elaborate prison escapes.

Sutton claimed for the rest of his life, emphasizing in a 1979 interview with the author that, "I had nothing to do with that. I didn't even know Anastasia or the man he sent out to kill Schuster. He was a nice boy and he thought he was doing his duty as a citizen. I don't blame him and what was done to him was terrible, awful. It was that maniac Anastasia. He would kill anyone he didn't like. If he hadn't liked my looks he would have killed me! That's the kind of nut he was."

Sutton was tried for the robbery of the Sunnyside bank, and witnesses swore that he was the man who led the bank raid. Sutton argued that they had looked at so many photos of him in newspapers and mug shots of him from files that these witnesses had been "conditioned" to recognize him. He was nevertheless convicted and sent back to prison to serve an additional thirty years. The irony of all this, according to Sutton, was that he was convicted of the one crime he had not committed.

At the time of his arrest, more than $7,000 was taken out of Sutton's pocket. He explained that this money was his life savings. He was asked why he had not placed the money in a bank. Sutton replied: "It's never safe in a bank!" Sutton spent several more years in prison but was finally paroled. He wrote his autobiography, entitled "Where the Money Was," and earned enough money to move to a retirement village in Spring Hill, Florida, where he died peacefully in bed of natural causes on November 7, 1980.

In his 1979 interview with the author, Sutton emphasized his dedicated unwillingness to shoot any person involved in his many robberies. "Sure, I used a gun to intimidate, but I would never have shot anyone, never! Robbing banks is one thing, shooting and killing someone is another and I knew right from the beginning what that would mean—I would fry in the electric chair like Two-Gun Crowley and a lot of other guys. [Francis "Two-Gun" Crowley committed several robberies and murders with Rudolph "Fats" Duringer and went to Sing Sing's electric chair in 1931.] Anyone who shoots someone in a robbery is just asking to get burned."

GIULIANO, THE SICILIAN BANDIT/1940s

Just as American bandits Jesse James and John Dillinger captured the public imagination of their country, the most romanticized modern bandit of the Old World was Salvatore Giuliano (Turiddu; 1922-1950). He was born on November 16, 1922, the fourth child of Salvatore and Maria Giuliano. The elder Giuliano had worked in the U. S., in New York, Texas, and California and saved enough money to return to his native village of Montelepre, outside of Palermo, Sicily, where he bought a small farm. Young Salvatore, a bright boy with a vivid imagination, attended school until the age of thirteen, when he dropped out and went into the fields to help his father raise crops. After that he transported olive oil, worked as a telephone repairman, and worked on road construction.

During World War II, Giuliano returned to the transporting of olive oil. He also began to trade in the black market. He went armed since the hills about Montelepre were crawling with bandits. On September 2, 1943, Giuliano was returning home with two sacks of black market grain when two

Salvatore Giuliano, the bandit who controlled a large section of Sicily by 1945, wanting that island to become part of the U. S.

carabinieri (state policemen) stopped him near Quattro Molini to inspect his cargo. Giuliano pulled his pistol and shot one of the officers dead. He fled into a cane field, a bullet smacking into his side.

Wounded, Giuliano managed to escape to his home. His family sent him to a doctor in Palermo and there the bullet was removed from his side. When authorities began searching for him, Giuliano fled to the hills around Montelepre, where he found scores of homeless men, army deserters, smugglers, black marketeers, murderers and bandits, the flotsam of war.

A born leader, Giuliano organized these directionless men into a guerrilla force of more than fifty men. He trained them to shoot so that they killed with their first shot, hitting the chest or head. He marched them in formations around the mountaintops, as he had watched soldiers drilling when he was a boy. Then he led them in raids into villages and towns where stores were robbed and wealthy landowners were kidnapped and held for ransom.

Giuliano established headquarters in some caves high in the Sagana Mountains towering above Montelepre. These were bald, low mountains which the police would normally have secured, but Giuliano and his band knew every inch of the terrain and when *carabinieri* did comb the hills for the bandits, they were invariably met with deadly machinegun fire which raked their ranks and took a great toll of lives.

Giuliano, right, is shown with his cousin, Gaspare Pisciotta, who turned informant and later assassinated the bandit.

As time went on, a number of legends about Giuliano were created by his romantic notion of himself. He learned that a postal official was stealing letters containing money that was sent from poor Sicilian families to their relatives in the U. S. Giuliano shot the postal employee and sent the money on to the correct recipients. He marked the letters "Divine Providence." He also shared his spoils with the tenant farmers and poor of the countryside, sending these people money and food. He became their "protector" and "benefactor."

On one occasion, Giuliano invaded the villa of the Duchess of Pratameno. When she found him in her palatial rooms, she thought he was the son of a duke, so polished were his manners. Not until he politely asked for her jewelry, did she realize that Giuliano was a common bandit. He left her wedding ring and kissed her hand, and, as he was about to depart, asked for the loan of a book she was reading, *In Dubious Battle* by John Steinbeck. He later returned the book with a thank you note, telling her that Steinbeck was his favorite author. Such gallantry and charm quickly made the handsome Giuliano into a local folk hero.

Giuliano's greatest ambition was to see Sicily annexed by the U. S. He wrote letters to President Harry Truman in which he urged Truman to make Sicily the forty-ninth state. He even drew a map showing how Sicily would appear as an American state. Though he sided with the peasants, in the end Giuliano's support came from the landed gentry and the Mafia. He received his money and supplies from rightist groups who convinced the altruistic Giuliano that the peasants were being controlled by evil Communists. On May 1, 1947, Giuliano and his men ambushed a peasant parade near Portellella della Ginestra, his men firing into the crowd. Eleven innocent people were killed, including a woman and three children.

Mafia boss Calogero Vizinni first supported Giuliano, then ordered his execution.

The bandit's image was forever tarnished after this slaughter, although his authority in the mountains and countryside was more widespread and accepted than that of the police and government. Grown vain and pompous, the youthful bandit began issuing decrees and regulations, threatening to punish by death all who disobeyed him. From 1947 through 1949, Giuliano was the most powerful force in Sicily, but the government resolved to put an end to him.

More than 300 police and national guardsmen invaded the mountains, where Giuliano and his men had their retreat. Their main cave was located and a terrific battle ensued. Grenades and cannon shells were hurled into the cave, but when the smoke cleared, police found no one. The bandits had fled through a rear crevice in the rocks.

In late 1949, Giuliano's kidnappings and terror raids increased drastically. On August 14, 1949, seven policemen were killed and twenty more seriously wounded when Giuliano's men exploded mines under a police barracks outside of Palermo. With thousands of police and military troops looking for him, the defiant Giuliano dressed in his finest clothes and drove to Palermo, where he boldly dined in the best restaurants for two days, leaving notes under his plates with large tips. One note read: "This is to show that Giuliano, the Champion of Sicily, can still come into Palermo whenever he likes." He wrote letters to the press in which he compared himself to Benito Mussolini and Napoleon Bonaparte.

The government of Sicily finally made an all-out effort to get rid of Giuliano, but this time they only sent one man to kill him, 26-year-old Gaspare Pisciotta, Giuliano's former chief lieutenant and cousin. Pisciotta had been captured earlier and, rather than face prison or execution, he agreed to be a police spy and then to kill Giuliano on the promise that he would receive a large reward and a full pardon for past crimes. Apparently, the planned killing of Giuliano was done with the collusion and approval of Don Calogero Vizinni, Mafia overlord of Sicily, who had first backed the bandit and then condemned Giuliano, when he realized he could not control him.

Pisciotta found his way to Giuliano's hideout and, while the 27-year-old bandit slept, he shot him in the head, killing him. The body was then taken to Palermo and dumped in a square. A gun was placed next to the body to make it appear that Giuliano had been shot while resisting arrest. The authorities claimed, when the body was found and photographed,

Giuliano's body, top left, is shown in a square at Palermo, Sicily, 1950.

that Captain Antonio Perenze, of the *carabinieri,* had killed the fierce Giuliano.

Then, reneging on its promise, the government put Pisciotta on trial, along with a dozen other Giuliano lieutenants. Pisciotta, in the dock, thundered in court: "It was *I* who killed Giuliano, under a personal agreement with the Minister of Interior, Mario Scelba!" This bombshell created havoc in court and denials and charges flew in all directions.

Maria Giuliano, then sixty, settled the arguments by informing the press that, indeed, the treacherous Pisciotta had murdered her beloved son while he slept. She took the witness stand in 1951 and shouted: "Pisciotta and Giuliano were blood brothers and wrote their names with drops of each other's blood. Pisciotta became a traitor, worse than Cain. His heart was always bad and Turridu's was open and generous. My son Turridu often had to tie Pisciotta to a tree and beat him to teach him manners."

Pisciotta was not released, nor given any reward. He and eleven other Giuliano bandits were sent to prison for life. On February 9, 1954, Pisciotta sat in his spartan cell in Palermo's Ucciardone Prison and sipped his coffee. He suddenly screamed, fell on the floor and his body bowed in horrible agony. He died within minutes. Officials stated that Pisciotta died of a sudden heart attack, but the truth was finally made known. Pisciotta had died of a massive dose of strychnine. Another Giuliano aide, Angelo Russo, also died of poisoning in prison.

The vast fortune Giuliano had accumulated through his kidnappings and robberies was never uncovered. This was estimated to be as high as £2 million, but was more likely about £500,000. This amount, it was suspected, went mostly to his family and friends, along with the bandits who served him loyally. But today, Giuliano's treasure is still sought throughout the Sagana Mountains by the poor peasants of Sicily, and little boys who dream of fortune, fame and adventure.

THE BRINK'S ROBBERY/January 17, 1950

Anthony "Tony" Pino, a New England petty thief who had a criminal record dating back to 1928, began to develop the idea of robbing the Brink's headquarters in Boston as early as 1948 when he noticed that he could enter the building almost at will and, because of the slack security, approach the upper level area where millions of dollars were processed behind an easily penetrated wire barrier. Pino took into his confidence Joseph F. "Big Joe" McGinnis, a Boston saloon keeper, who helped organize a robbery gang, all culled from Boston's underworld and most of whom were, like Pino, small-time crooks looking to commit "the robbery of the century." These included Vincent J. Costa, who was said to be an expert getaway driver; James Ignatius Flaherty, bartender and burglar; Henry J. Baker, a lock specialist; and gunmen and professional burglars Thomas F. Richardson, Michael V. Geagan, Adolph "Jazz" Maffie, John S. Banfield, Stanley H. Gusciora, and Joseph James "Specs" O'Keefe, a clever thief and burglar whose nickname, one he hated, came from the freckles that coated his face when he was in his teens.

Anthony Pino, the jovial mastermind of the 1950 Brink's robbery.

The North Terminal Garage of the Brink's company was cased daily by members of the gang. They studied the comings and goings of employees from the street during the day and from rooftops with binoculars at night. This surveillance went on for eighteen months. Brink's shipment schedules were noted each day and when and where the biggest cash shipments would be made. Knowing the routines of the watchmen, gang members, in twos and threes, brazenly entered the Brink's building almost every night, going through their own routine of mock robbery, sneaking through doors, up stairways and down corridors to the money room so that all the gang members could find their ways through this building in the dark. Baker, the locksmith, removed locks from five separate doors in the Brink's building, one each night between the rounds of the watchmen. He made keys for the locks and replaced a lock each night without being detected.

Then the gang practiced their robbery with the precision of a Ranger unit penetrating a high-security military operation. Seven of the men, led by O'Keefe, entered the building, went through the five doors and right up to the money room where Brink's employees were busy counting cash. Two others remained on rooftops with high-powered binoculars and a telescope to watch for police and guards. Another was at the wheel of a truck parked nearby, waiting for the loot to be thrown into the back.

The robbers went through this routine twenty times, but waited until Pino thought the moment was right, the moment being when the largest amount of cash would be on hand. The seven men entering the building were to look identical.

A sketch showing how robbers entered and looted the Brink's building in Boston on January 17, 1950.

Those chosen were all about five-feet-ten-inches tall, weighed between 170 and 180 pounds, and all would wear Navy pea jackets, halloween masks, rubber-soled shoes, and gloves.

Pino finally selected the night of January 17, 1950, a murky, rainy night which would keep people off the streets. The seven men entered the Brink's building shortly before 7 p.m., went through the five locked doors using the keys made by Baker, walked silently upstairs and through halls, until they came to the counting room.

O'Keefe and the others reached the wire mesh door of this room at exactly 7:10 p.m. They had no key to this door. O'Keefe and the others pulled out guns and aimed them through the wire mesh at Thomas P. Lloyd, head cashier, as he came out of the vault. "This is a stickup," O'Keefe said in a low, menacing voice. "Open the gate and don't give us any trouble."

Only guard Charles Grell was armed; the weapons belonging to the four other men in the cage were in a gun rack. Grell did as he was ordered and opened the gate without reaching for his weapon. Lloyd later told Boston police commissioner Thomas F. Sullivan that "it would have been sheer death for him (Grell) to reach for it." The five Brink's men were ordered to lie on the floor, faces down. They were then tied hands and feet behind their backs and adhesive tape was placed over their mouths by some of the thieves, while other members of the robbery gang went directly into the vault and began filling large sacks with big bills. Each man knew his job.

As one pulled the money off the shelves in the vault, another held open a sack and the sacks were passed from hand to hand from one robber to the next. The thieves scooped up $2,775,395 including $1,218,211.29 in cash and coins and $1,557,183.83 in money orders and checks. The sacks filled with all this loot weighed about 1,200 pounds and each man dragged two of these from the money room. Before leaving, the thieves looked at a large metal security box and thought to take it with them but, at the last minute, they decided it was too heavy to drag down corridors and steps. They left it behind and the more than $1 million in cash it contained.

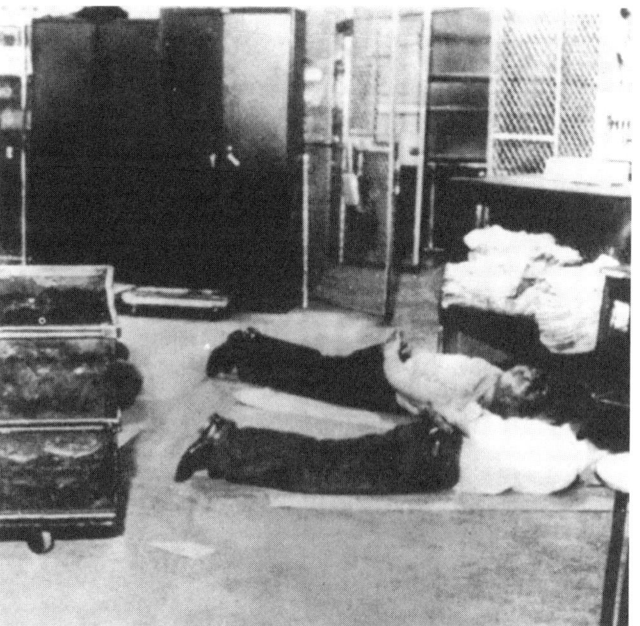

Brink's guards took prone positions in re-enacting the $2.7 million robbery.

By 7:27 p.m., the gang had left the premises with the largest cash haul in an American robbery to that time, accomplishing the massive theft within seventeen minutes. The money was thrown into the truck which was driven to Roxbury and to the home of Adolph "Jazz" Maffie. Here the robbers destroyed more than $90,000 in new bills which the thieves suspected were marked, along with the negotiable securities. The balance was kept by Maffie to be split up later, $1,100,000.

Pino and McGinnis had ordered that the money was not to be taken by anyone since any considerable spending by gang members would surely draw suspicion. They would wait until the inevitable police "heat" dissipated and then take their shares. Each gang member returned to the various jobs they held. Most of them, along with hundreds of other suspects, were detained for questioning since almost all the gang members had long police records. They were routinely grilled and released. State and local police, along with the FBI, had no idea where to look for the robbers. The clues left behind at the scene of the robbery were scant: two pieces of white cotton line and a visored cap with its lining and label torn from it.

Joseph "Specs" O'Keefe talked to police after being shorted on his share of the loot.

The Brink's robbers under arrest in 1956, left to right, Jim Flaherty, Mike Geagan, Thomas Richardson, Joe McGinnis, Tino Pino, Vincent Costa, Jazz Maffie, Henry Baker; all went to prison.

A month later, the gang members took their shares of the stolen money, about $100,000. O'Keefe entrusted about $90,000 of his money to a fellow mob member, and when he was sent to prison for another robbery, he demanded but never got his money. Facing a long prison term and incensed at being stalled on getting his money, O'Keefe contacted authorities and tried to plea bargain his sentence in return for information about the celebrated Brink's robbery.

Though Banfield died of natural causes in 1955, the other thieves were arrested, convicted, and given long prison sentences. Several of them were later released. What angered surviving gang members was the fact that a Boston *Globe* crime reporter, Joseph F. Dineen, wrote a novel about the Brink's robbery, entitled *Six Rivers to Cross* and reportedly made $150,000 on a movie sale of this book, more money than any of the robbers ever enjoyed from their elaborate and shocking robbery.

ENGLAND'S GREAT TRAIN ROBBERY/ August 8, 1963

Like the Brink's robbery thirteen years earlier, the Great Train Robbery in England was conducted and engineered by a bevy of thieves and would-be bandits. On August 8, 1963, fifteen men, some with criminal backgrounds, some with no records at all, stopped the Royal Mail train from Glasgow to London, near Cheddington Station, and committed the largest robbery in England up to that time, looting mail sacks containing more than £2.5 million. This amazing crime caper, one which shocked the world with its suddenness and efficiency, had been in the planning a long time.

The men involved, all known to each other and having had long associations, for the most part, in shady London deals, met more than a year before the train robbery at Cheddington. To finance the train robbery, several of the leaders decided to commit another, similar theft. On November 27, 1962, three businessmen appeared in London's Heathrow Airport. They wore conservative pin-striped suits and bowler hats, and they carried walking canes or umbrellas. These men somehow got into a security area and then permitted five more men wearing balaclava helmets to enter the area.

Security guards were overpowered and £62,500 in old bank notes, then en route to a London bank, were quickly taken. Of the eight men involved in the robbery, three were apprehended, but only one, Mickey Ball, was convicted, and then sentenced to five years imprisonment. As he was being led away, Ball sneered and said: "Well, at least you won't get me for the big job!" This remark confused police at the time, but they knew full well what Ball meant eight months later.

Bruce Reynolds, mastermind of England's great train robbery.

The two men who were acquitted of the airport robbery, Charles Frederick Wilson and Gordon Goody, went on to participate in "the big job," the Cheddington train robbery. Using the loot from the airport robbery to finance the train heist, the thieves gathered in a large farmhouse in Leatherslade, Buckinghamshire, near Cheddington. Here, Bruce Reynolds, the mastermind of the robbery, outlined the details of the operation, running his men through their duties as would a drill sergeant. The methods and procedures employed by Reynolds and his top aides were decidedly military in nature.

The Royal Mail train robbed of $7 million on August 8, 1963.

When all was ready, this paramilitary band pinpointed August 8, 1963, as the day for the robbery. From inside information, the leaders, Bruce Reynolds, Ronald Biggs, Buster Edwards, Charles Wilson, and others, knew that on that day the Royal Mail train would be carrying in its baggage car 120 bags stuffed with old, unmarked surplus bills. These notes were being sent from Scottish banks to their London offices for recycling or destruction, depending upon wear and tear. It was estimated that this regular shipment would contain between £2 million and £3 million, an enormous prize.

The mail train appeared on schedule a half-hour from its destination, Euston Station, and was stopped by a simple railroad procedure. The thieves merely blacked out the green "go" signal, and affixed a wire to a battery so that the red "stop" signal, would remain on. The engineer, seeing the red light, brought the train to a halt. Several men waiting alongside the tracks jumped into the engineer's cab and slugged the engineer. Others piled into the two mail cars immediately behind the engine, overpowered the guards, and then threw the sacks of money to others waiting outside. The sacks were hurriedly dumped into Land Rovers parked nearby. Then the engineer was forced to drive the train on to its destination as one of the masked robbers cavalierly waved to him and shouted "cheery-bye!"

The bandits drove to the Leatherslade farmhouse and there divided the spoils, lesser members of the gang each given a small amount, "a drink" of the take, as one of the robbers later put it. The chief bandits received equal shares, £150,000 each. The entire amount came to a staggering £2,631,684, or about $7,000,000. After the split, the gang members, who had each made plans for individual getaways, went their separate ways. London police, when hearing the news, sent an army of investigators to the site of the robbery, but they found no clues. The world's press heralded the robbery as the greatest theft of the century.

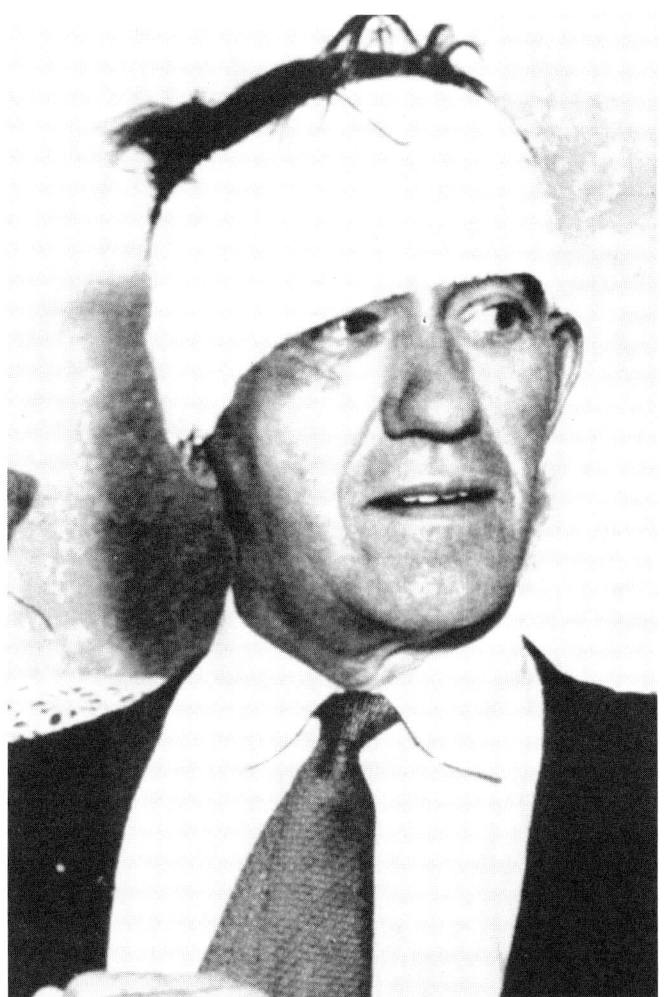

Engineer Jack Mills, with a bandage covering a head wound received during the train robbery.

An aerial photo shows the farmhouse where the bandits met to divide the loot following the train robbery.

Charles Frederick Wilson, one of the co-leaders of the train robbery, at left when apprehended following the robbery and, right, when recaptured following a prison escape.

In five days, the police discovered the abandoned farmhouse in Leatherslade. Suspicious neighbors had seen a number of Land Rovers, and many men arriving at the building carrying sacks. Detectives found the place a mess. For all their careful planning, the thieves apparently panicked after the robbery and hurried their final arrangements. They left fingerprints everywhere and they had not taken the trouble to disguise the license plates of the Land Rovers, which were traced. England's greatest manhunt then began, and, one by one, the bandits were tracked down and arrested. They had brought further suspicion upon themselves by not remaining at their jobs, but by disappearing immediately after the robbery, going into hiding.

The small-timers were caught first and they cracked under interrogation, naming others. Most of the top men in the robbery ring were brought to trial a year after the robbery and, on March 26, 1964, they received sentences that were considered harsh, even for their sensational crime. Thirty-year prison sentences were meted out to Reynolds, a car and antique dealer and the brains of the gang, Charles Wilson, a small-time bookie (who later escaped prison and was then recaptured), Thomas Wisbey, James Hussey, Robert Welch, Roy James, Douglas Goody, and Ronald Biggs. Roger Cordrey received twenty years, but this was later reduced to fifteen. William Boal, Brian Field, and Leonard Field (the Fields were not related) received twenty-four-year sentences each. The Fields appealed their sentences, as had Cordrey, and their prison terms were reduced to five years each. These punishments were considered severe in that there was only one injury involved in the robbery, that of the engineer, who recovered.

Only £336,524 of the stolen money, however, was recovered. It took several years to capture the leaders of the gang. James White, a cafe proprietor, was not arrested until 1966 and he drew an eighteen-year sentence. Buster Edwards was then tracked down and sent to prison for fifteen years. Bruce Reynolds, who had led the gang and escaped from prison, was finally recaptured in 1969 and sent back to prison for twenty-five years. Ronald Biggs also escaped from prison in 1965.

Biggs led authorities in an around-the-world chase through a dozen countries, until he landed in Brazil. He managed to fight off extradition and lived well with his wife and son on his ill-gotten money. Most of the missing money, officials concluded, had been spent by the gang members in their flight from police. They had paid enormous amounts to underworld contacts for hiding places. In the end, the robbery got the thieves nothing more than long prison terms.

The most astounding tale connected with the Great Train Robbery emerged in the mid-1970s when informants stated that the real brains and financier behind this robbery was none other than the one-time Nazi super commando, Otto Skorzeny, who had fled to Spain after World War II and had there organized Odessa, a secret organization of former SS officers, one that had taken great sums of money out of Germany before the collapse of the Third Reich. Odessa financed the escapes and maintenance of wanted Nazi war criminals, and according to the story connected to England's great train robbery, financed enormous robberies to continually refill its coffers.

Some of the train robbers had reportedly met with Skorzeny or his representatives in Cologne, and it was Skorzeny, who originally put up £80,000 to finance the first robbery at London Airport and helped to set up other details of the train robbery. One of his men was even in the Leatherslade farmhouse helping Reynolds and Biggs direct their men, according to one account. Skorzeny and his men went even further. Following the robbery, Skorzeny, who reportedly received £1 million of the stolen loot, arranged for his own men to smuggle Charles Wilson out of Winston Green prison. He also arranged for Buster Edwards to have his face altered through plastic surgery, and it was Otto Skorzeny who helped the elusive Ronald Biggs reach a safe haven in Brazil. Fantastic as this story might be, there is some evidence to make it credible. Skorzeny, however, was long dead by the time this tale was told.

THE NORTH HOLLYWOOD BANK ROBBERY/ February, 28, 1997

One of the most violent bank robberies in record occurred at the Branch of America Bank in North Hollywood, California, on February 28, 1997. Two men, Emil Matasareanu and Larry Phillips, wearing black hoods, body armor and carrying AK-47 rifles and handguns, along with considerable ammunition, invaded the bank shortly after 9 a. m. They ordered the bank employees and customers in the bank, located at Archwood Street and Laurel Canyon Boulevard, to line up, while one of the robbers looted the tellers' cages.

Placing cash in bags which they dumped into a rolling cart, the bank robbers began to leave the bank as an alarm went off. Police immediately responded, dozens of officers arriving in squad cars that surrounded the bank. Matasareanu and Phillips emerged from the bank to see officers pointing revolvers at them. One of the robbers turned and fired several rounds into the foyer of the bank, apparently in retaliation against someone in the bank, who set off the alarm. A female teller was shot in the foot and a bank customer was wounded in this burst.

At the same time, the other robber opened fire on the police officers, wounding several of them. The two robbers then attempted to get into their getaway car, firing at officers all the while. Some of the first LAPD officers struck by bullets included Stuart Guy and his female partner, Tracey Angeles. Guy, seriously wounded and bleeding profusely, was guarded by the also wounded Angeles, who kept firing back at the robbers while shouting to her partner to "hold on," and that "help is on the way."

(This courageous officer would receive the LAPD Police Commissioner/City Council Women of Courage Award the next month.)

By then the two robbers unleashed a terrible onslaught of firepower against the police (nine officers would be wounded, along with three civilians). As more than 350 police officers arrived to battle the robbers in an hour-long firefight, the bandits fired more than 1,100 rounds from their semiautomatic assault rifles. In addition to the AK-47s, the robbers had a .223 fully automatic Bushmaster rifle, a .308 semiautomatic H&K and a semiautomatic 9mm Beretta handgun.

Police poured a devastating fusillade into the two men, but their bullets bounced harmlessly off the thick body armor worn by the robbers as they stoically plodded down the street. One, Matasareanu, got into the getaway car, while Phillips walked beside it as it slowly moved down the street, Phillips using the car as a shield as he continued to fire at police. Phillips suddenly left the car and began plodding alone down Archwood Street, firing at police following him and while police and TV news helicopters hovered over him. He was shot several times, but again, the bullets merely bounced off his bullet-proof armor. Running out of ammunition for his AK-47, Phillips drew a handgun and fired off several rounds. A police bullet found its mark, striking Phillips in the head and killing him.

Meanhwile, Matasareanu slowly drove his getaway car two blocks from the bank, all the while under terrific fire from hundreds of police officers. He returned the fire, and, when seeing a pickup abandoned in the middle of the street, decided to leave his own car, which had been riddled. While firing many bursts from his AK-47, Matasareanu transferred his weapons to the pickup and got into the truck.

Dozens of heroic officers closed in on the truck from all sides and the robber got out of the truck and began firing at them. The firefight was fierce, with many officers being wounded. Matasareanu, however, was struck by several bullets—he would be hit twenty-nine times—and finally collapsed. He was pronounced dead upon arrival at a nearby

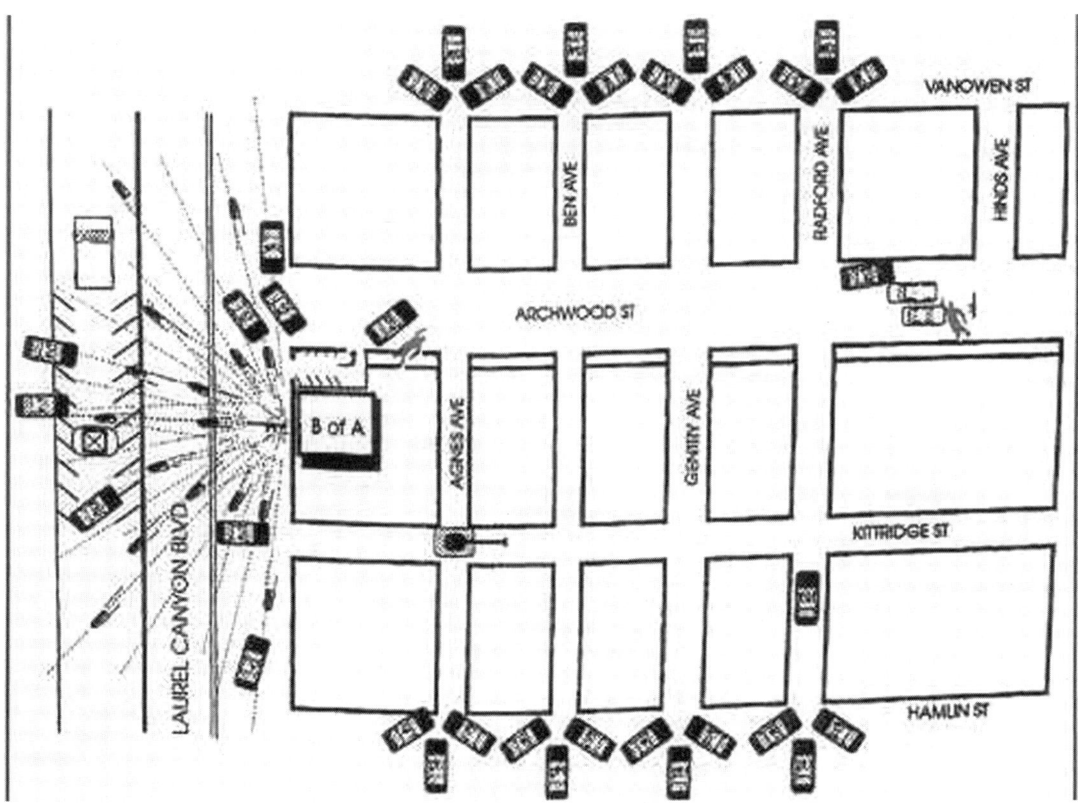

Police sketch shows the location of the robbers and the firefight they launched when emerging from the North Hollywood Branch Bank of America on February 28, 1997.

Two LAPD officers in SWAT gear are shown advancing on the robbers, who shot a dozen people in their prolonged gun battle following the robbery.

LAPD officers are shown next to the riddled getaway car, one pointing a weapon downward at one of the robbers, fatally wounded Emil Matasareanu.

hospital. (Matasareanu's relatives later filed a suit, charging that LAPD officers let the bank robber die before summoning an ambulance.)

Both dead bandits, police later stated, had been suspects in several California bank robberies that had taken place in 1996. "These guys were ready for war," said Bob McKibben, a manager at an appliance store near the bank, and who witnessed the bloody battle. "They had black masks over their faces and full black gear, with belts and ammo around their waists." He watched Matasareanu casually shoot at pursuing police, then "going to the trunk of the car and getting more ammo. He was like in a trance. He was walking like there was nothing going on. He had everyone pinned down. It was like he didn't have a care in the world."

To the police, the bandits were "well organized," and had planned to murder anyone who interfered with the bank robbery. "They were killers," said LAPD spokesman Tim McBride. "The suspects continued to fire at officers who were undergunned for over an hour." McBride, as was the case with everyone else, had no regard for the dead bandits, whom he aptly described as having "no sense of conscience, no sense of dignity, no sense of respect for life."

The mindless North Hollywood Bank robbery typified the new breed of robbers in the 1990s and into the 21st Century, killers thinking to rob at any cost, including their own lives, suicidal robberies where dead thieves might claim an extraordinary number of lives while sacrificing their own. It was claimed by some that the robbers had emulated a scene in the 1995 film, *Heat*, starring Robert De Niro and Al Pacino, one in which bandits rob a downtown Los Angeles bank in full body armor and are then killed in a running gun battle through the streets.

The movies have, particularly in the last two decades, been held responsible for molding many spectacular and gruesome crimes. Oliver Stone's mindless 1994 film, *Natural Born Killers*, most certainly inspired Eric Harris and Dylan Klebold to kill thirteen people and wound another twenty-five persons at Columbine High School in Littleton, Colorado, in 1999. These bloodlusting teenagers were so enamored of Stone's gratuitously violent film that they made a homemade version of the movie and then used this as a blueprint in their mass murder spree on April 20, 1999.

Teenager Natasha Cornett, who established a Satanic cult and moved about the country murdering people in 1997, stated that she was inspired to kill people after viewing Stone's film. The same movie, according to Washington State prosecutors, inspired 14-year-old Barry Loukaitas to kill two classmates and a teacher on February 2, 1996.

In his much-lauded documentary, *Bowling at Columbine*, Michael Moore makes no mention of Stone's terrible and culpable influence, but then again, the inclusion of such a justifiable indictment might have injured Moore's box office receipts, let alone the residual returns Stone's awful film continues to enjoy.

CHAPTER FIFTEEN:
SECRET CRIMINAL SOCIETIES

From the beginning of time, men and women of all races and nations have banded together to create fraternal societies, invariably dedicated to healthy socializing and works of good will that are designed to aid and nurture their fellow humans. Parallel to these well-intentioned organizations sprang a number of secret societies dedicated to self-serving criminal pursuits designed to either enrich members with spiritual or corporal rewards. Clotted with cabalistic rites, blood oaths, life-or-death loyalties, many of these secret criminal organizations infiltrated high level government and business positions that gave them virtual control of their governments.

Through blackmail, extortion and threat of death, these societies seized banks and other financial institutions, appropriated corporations and industries, either compelling business leaders to join their shrouded ranks or embedding their own members into those organizations. These criminal societies established their own murder squads to mete out justice to those members who betrayed their organizations and for centuries ruled whole populations with the weapons of fear and terrorism.

No country was immune to the influence of these sinister groups that invariably sprang to life out of patriotism and national pride. Nationalism, not unlike the right-wing dictatorships of the 19th and 20th centuries, first attracted members to organizations that ostensibly vowed to repel foreign invaders from their lands. Such was the case of the Mafia, which was originally founded to evade Arab conquerors, and later, to drive from Sicily the legions of French invaders in 1282.

A hatred of foreigners, xenophobia with a will to murder, gave birth to Japan's Yakuza, China's Boxers and Triads and Kenya's Mau Mau. In the U. S., the Ku Klux Klan, which, in its 20th Century rebirth, expanded its violent bigotry to include blacks, Catholics, Jews, and just about anyone who was not a white citizen.

In the desperate fight for economic survival, immigrating foreigners made up their own secret societies in order to acquire better jobs and working conditions. Thus, the Irish secret society in America known as the Molly Maguires, came into existence. Its members employed bombings and murder of company police and business leaders to improve their poverty-level lot. A century later, in Detroit, the Black Legion was formed to drive blacks and foreigners from jobs in the automotive industry and those who would not leave town were kidnapped and killed.

In the Middle East, at the time of the Third Crusade, right-wing Moslem leaders created secret societies dedicated to the assassination of Western leaders invading the Arab world. Those enlisting in their cause, which was (and still in existence under the leadership of Osama bin Laden) rooted in a reactionary form of Moslem religion, became dedicated to spilling the blood of "nonbelievers." Osama bin Laden has imbued his terrorist followers of Al Qaeda with the concept that their widespread murders are justified in the eyes of Allah. This same credo was indoctrinated into the fanatical and suicidal members of the Order of the Assassins of the 11th Century.

An Indian bazaar painting of 1830 depicts the Hindu goddess Kali, consort of Shiva, who, in the eyes of its worshippers, the Thugs, was transformed into a blood-lusting deity.

Perverted religion was also at the inspirational core of the worst secret criminal society to ever plague India—Thuggee. This religious organization was made up of tens of thousands of fanatics, who worshipped a goddess that demanded the sacrificial lives of others, or so their evil gurus insisted. In taking these lives, members were given their heavenly "rewards" by stealing any valuables their victims might possess. The true cause of Thuggee was and is that of any secret criminal society then or now—to loot the riches of the earth at any cost.

THE THUGS OF INDIA/700-1900s

The mystic and murderous killer cult of Thuggee (pronounced "Tugee"; c.700-1900s?) plagued India for twelve centuries, a religion within religions that insisted upon human sacrifice to its gory goddess, Kali (Bhowani or Bhawani). Its fanatical followers were known in southern India as Phansigars, stemming from the Hindustani term *Phansi,* meaning noose. These killers employed strangling cords or nooses and were known as "noose operators." In northern India, the same sect of killers was commonly called Thugs (pronounced "Tugs"), after the Sanskrit word *othag,* meaning to conceal, or *othaga,* one who cheated.

To the rest of the world, when the existence of this cult was recognized in shock by western civilization, Thugs were known as the most sinister of human creatures, clandestine, bizarre, utterly unconscionable. They took lives, tens of thousands a decade, to edify their blood lusting goddess and to enrich themselves with spoils taken from their unsuspecting victims.

Operating in strict secrecy, Thugs were known to Indian civilization as early as 700 or earlier, but they conducted their cabalistic rites with such controlled stealth that local chiefs and sultans had no real idea of the sect's widespread influence or so it was claimed, though some historians insist that many Indian leaders protected the Thugs in order to receive part of the spoils from their murder raids.

Further assuring the murder cult's anonymity was the rigidly enforced rule of death to any who revealed its secret rites and practices. Uniting all the bands of Thugs throughout India was its totemic goddess, Kali, who, through its high priests, established strict codes that dictated the murder methods of its worshippers.

In mythology, Kali, the wife of the God Shiva (or Siva), is the Hindu goddess of Destruction and Death. She was also known as a deity of war and to the Thugs, Kali was worshipped as "the divine mother." Surviving images of Kali present a frightful picture of a black-skinned goddess with three glaring eyes, many arms, and an open mouth displaying long teeth, blood-soaked lips, and an extended, drooling tongue coated with human gore. (Only when appearing alone does Kali transform into her true and hideous nature; when appearing with Shiva the goddess is beautiful and fair.)

Kali, according to myth, first appeared on the banks of the Hooghli River, a site now called Kali Ghat (whence Calcutta) where her most venerated shrine stood for eons. The goddess, through its gurus, encouraged its earliest apostles to go forth and destroy unbelievers. With each murder, the killer Thug would thus attain a higher status in the hereafter. Moreover, the goddess was obligingly protective of her killers, disposing of the bodies of their victims so they could go on undetected.

Legend has it that after depositing several bodies at the foot of Kali's statue, a band of Thugs retreated, turning their backs to Kali, forbidden, according to tradition, to cast eyes upon the goddess and witness how she destroyed the human remains. An apprentice Thug, however, unable to control his curiosity, turned to see Kali eating the body.

This 1843 sketch shows a Thug with his murder weapons—a pickax, a knife and a rope—although Thugs used their waistcloths, not ropes, to strangle their victims.

Her grisly custom exposed, the goddess thereafter refused to hide the evidence of the cult's murders and would consume no more corpses. The high priests pleaded for forgiveness and aid. Kali responded by spitting out one of her teeth, which took the form of a pickax. One of her ribs became a long knife and from the hem of her sari she provided a noose. All these items became sacred in the tradition of Thuggee. The noose was the instrument of death, to be employed as a strangling cord. The knife was to dismember the limbs of victims and the pickax, the most sacred of all these lethal instruments, was to be used to gouge out the eyes of the murdered victims and dig their unhallowed graves.

Ironically, the eternal rifts between Muslim and Hindu were put aside in that both religious sects joined the Thugs, worshipping a Hindu goddess and putting her before all other gods, although members went on practicing their separate religions. Even stranger was the fact that before its wholesale eradication by the British, the sect was predominately Muslim, followers risking everything to pay homage to this ancient Hindu image.

Initiates were brought into the Thuggee fold from their own families or by older Thugs, who had taken young boys, usually under ten, in a raid, and raised them to become Thugs, not unlike the methods of Hitler and Mussolini in the 20TH Century, when these dictators began training their legions almost from the cradle to follow fascism to the grave. Initiates into the cult were brought together in a row, stretching from the towering image of the goddess in a hidden temple, usually in a remote mountainous area. They faced veteran Thugs, kneeling before them. As the veterans chanted out an oath to preserve the customs of Kali, the initiates repeated the vow. From their waists the veterans unwound their *rumals,* long handkerchiefs, holding these forth. The initiates would take the strangling cords, accepting these as instruments of death.

Each was then given a pickax, which was held aloft, announced to be sacred as the burial tool used to dig the graves of victims. A long knife was handed to each and these were then used to slaughter small animals, especially sheep. The initiates dipped their hands into the gore and, one by one, stepped up to the goddess, smearing the blood on its figure. (The statue of Kali, often towering twenty feet, usually had a large base which, after each initiation ceremony, was given another coat of gore, so that this dried gore was often several feet thick over the eons; often enough, the blood preserved from the bodies of recently killed victims was used instead of the animal blood on such occasions.)

A similar ritual was enacted before every raid by a band of Thugs. A party of between ten and twenty Thugs would gather before Kali and seek the goddess' approval. Fresh fruit, cakes, and wine would be placed before the statue, along with flowers. The Thug priest would then have a sheep brought before the image and ordered its head to be cut off. The right forefoot of the decapitated sheep would be placed in its mouth and a lighted lantern placed upon the disembodied head. Oil that had been blessed by the priest would then be poured down onto the head of the sheep while the priest chanted his invocation, asking Kali to approve of the band's murder mission.

If the nostrils and mouth of the sheep's head gave any sign of movement, usually a convulsive, nerve-ending quiver, it was seen as a sign from Kali that she had given her consent to launch another murder attack. Seldom, if ever, would Kali withhold her approval and the body of Thugs would then leave their local village under cover of darkness and gather in a lonely spot, then travel to a well-used trade route, where they would lay in wait for caravans of merchants or, most desired, rich princes en route from one palace to another.

The absence of the Thugs from their villages was, of course, noticed, but family members knew full well the purpose of their spouses and other male members. Wives had no voice in the sinister pursuits of their husbands, nor had any other member of the family. All knew that if one of their number was ever exposed, the entire family would suffer. Moreover, the local chieftains of the villages said nothing when residents vanished for long periods of time, knowing they were off on a murder raid for Kali and also knowing that when these killers returned to resume normal law-abiding existences, they, the chieftains, would be enriched with part of their spoils.

The Thugs only practiced their murderous religion during the winter months in India, so that during the rest of the year they were at home in their villages, toiling as honest laborers and craftsmen. Many of them were pillars of their communities, holding minor offices, observing and enforcing the local laws, appearing to be upright citizens. On the road, looking for sacrificial quarry, however, they were the worst kind of lethal cutthroats in the history of murder.

The long success enjoyed by the Thugs was due to their clever deceits, practiced with care. They cunningly convinced any gullible traveler that they were themselves seeking protection against the marauding bands of Dacoits, nomadic tribes, who practiced armed robbery but not ritualistic murder. Ten of the twenty Thugs would position themselves along a trade route and plead with some passing merchant that they be allowed to join his party for protection.

Sir William Sleeman became a major-general and headed the British government's department for the suppression of Thuggee in India.

The other ten Thugs would be miles distant, already digging the graves of the intended victims. When the merchant's party would stop to make camp for the evening, at a spot invariably suggested by one of the accompanying Thugs, the band would wait until the merchants were asleep and then, with those members laying in wait outside the campfires, leap upon their victims, strangling them to death. (The victim could only be murdered with the *rumal,* not the knife or pickax, to meet the religious requirements of Kali.)

Once all the victims had been slain, some of the Thugs would dismember the bodies and disembowel them so no gasses or odors would be forthcoming from the shallow graves into which they would be placed. It was necessary that no wild animals, jackals and other scavengers, seek out the graves and accidentally reveal the hiding place of Thug corpses. Sometimes young boys of ten were taken to these murder scenes and forced to watch their elders kill, dismember, and bury their victims so they would acquaint themselves with the methods of their teachers, be indoctrinated into the looting of the victims, and share the responsibility of the act.

While several Thugs divert the attention of an unsuspecting merchant, another Thug creeps up behind the victim with his strangling cloth.

The Thugs earned their reputation as sly deceivers. If a party traveling on the road inadvertently came upon a group of Thugs kneeling next to their victim, the Thugs would instantly send up a chant, pretending to mourn the loss of one of their own tribesmen, who had suddenly taken ill and died. In carrying out their gruesome rituals, the Thugs doggedly maintained strict rules. No robbery could occur unless the victim was murdered, and no goods or money could be taken unless the victim was murdered in the proper fashion.

Even the way in which the Thugs strangled their victims had to follow an exact code. According to one report "two *Phansigars* are considered to be indispensably necessary to effect the murder of one man, and commonly three are engaged. While traveling along, one of the *Phansigars* suddenly puts the cloth round the neck of the person they mean to kill, and retains hold of one end, while the other end is seized by an accomplice; the instrument crossed behind the neck is drawn tight, the two *Phansigars* pressing the head forwards; at the same time the third villain, in readiness behind the traveler, seizes his legs, and he is thrown forward upon the ground. In this situation he can make little resistance. The man holding the legs of the miserable sufferer, now kicks him in those parts of the body endowed with most sensibility (the scrotum), and he is quickly dispatched."

Just *who* the Thugs would kill was also a matter of strict regulation. Their selection of victims was rife with superstition and mixed with the laws of their separate religions, along with their worship of the dreadful Kali. Since their murder goddess was a woman, the Thugs killed no women and allowed any caravan with women in it to pass unmolested. They never killed male children under the age of ten, taking these as hostages to their cult. Also spared from their strangling cords were any craftsmen who worked with gold, brass, and iron. Carpenters, smiths, stonecutters, dancing masters, shoemakers, pot makers, and washer men also went unharmed.

It was also forbidden to molest any infirm person, particularly the blind or anyone who had suffered mutilation. No herder leading cows or female goats was ever molested by Thugs. Lepers were never approached as was the case with pariahs. It was often told in the campfires of the Thugs how one band of their cult had attacked a caravan carrying a beau-

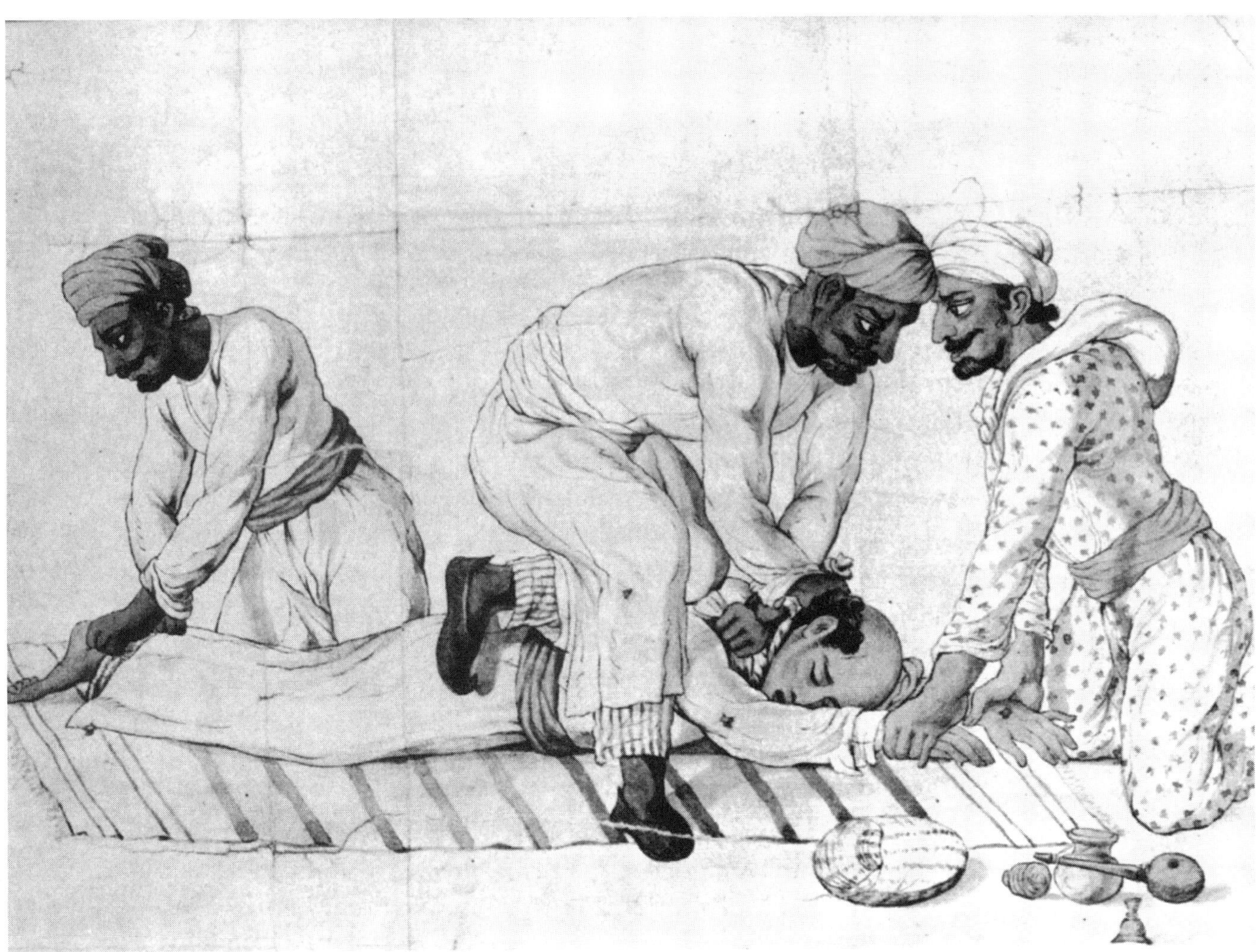

A Thug is shown tightening the noose around a victim to make sure he is dead, while others bind the body, preparing to carry it to an awaiting grave.

tiful princess and how the twenty some Thugs, after slaughtering her retainers, had each raped the woman before strangling her to death. Kali's fortunes no longer smiled on this band, the story went, and each member shortly thereafter fell upon hard times, each of them dying premature and painful deaths, their families destroyed.

It was also important for any band of Thugs to operate at least one hundred miles from their native village. Once the decision had been made to attack a traveling party, it was mandatory that all in the party, except those exempted, must be killed. As each band set out to perform its ritual murders, its members were ever mindful of the images that surrounded their demanding Kali, that of the lizard and the snake. If the members heard a lizard chirping while en route to kill, it meant that the raid would be a success. If a snake crossed the road in front of them, it meant that the attack would fail or bad luck would ensue. Crows and partridges cawing to each other from either side of the road meant good luck.

The most fortuitous sign any Thug band could encounter was the sight of a tiger. This wild beast reflected in the eyes of the Thugs their own way of life and survival, cunning and savagery without remorse. There were bad omens that included the sight of an ass braying, a hare crossing the road, a lone jackal howling, an owl screeching, a crow sitting on the back of another animal cawing, and, the very worst, a dog shaking its head. If three or more of these signs were present on a murder raid, the superstitious Thugs would invariably turn back or take another road.

All of this ritualistic murder, as high as a million victims a century, according to one account, went on in India without detection by the western world, a thousand years of mass slayings in a country that could apparently afford to lose ten million souls in ten centuries without giving pause to look for the vanished. In the teeming subcontinent of India such numbers of missing persons meant little or nothing, but to the western mind the loss of life is staggering, unthinkable. And when the presence of the Thugs and their sweeping activities were first revealed to Europeans, the mere concept, let alone the reality of such serial murders, was thought to be nothing more than a dark fantasy.

Shortly after the turn of the 19th Century, as Britain flexed her military muscles in support of its East India Company to

Thugs mutilate the bodies of their victims by gouging out their eyes as part of their ritualistic murders.

Thugs carrying bodies to pre-arranged graves, which had been dug up long before the victims had been murdered.

capture the commerce of India, the new authorities were brought reports by its soldiers and officials that gave vague but terrifying descriptions of bands of stranglers operating throughout the country. British troops were sent out to investigate and returned with more reports of missing travelers, mostly merchants. At first it all seemed confusing and as unreal as the mystical people who had come under British domination, but then more than 100 Thugs were rounded up near Bangalore. They wore long *rumals* and carried knives with ornate handles carved with the images of snakes and lizards, along with pickaxes.

These men refused to speak, admitting to nothing. In 1810, near Jumna, bodies were discovered at the bottom of wells, more than thirty of them, all mangled and disfigured, limbs torn out, eyes gouged. Though the British authorities suspected that the bodies and a strange strangling sect were one and the same, it proved almost impossible to develop anything but a loose and unbelievable theory. Their first breakthrough followed six years later in Madras.

Dr. Richard Sherwood, stationed at Fort St. George, interrogated several Thugs, who had been picked up on suspicion and managed to isolate in their number some who were willing to talk. Exactly how Dr. Sherwood convinced the Thugs to break their oath of silence was not recorded by Sherwood, but later reports had it that he threatened several with execution, unless they revealed the nature of their secret criminal society. Sherwood had discovered a pickax with strange markings on it, one that the Thugs treated as a holy relic. When he asked one Thug about its use, the cultist shrugged.

An 1825 sketch shows a British officer leading his Sepoy troops (right) in a surprise raid, where Thugs, shown around a campfire, were captured

The Prince of Wales, touring India in 1877, was "entertained" by elderly Thugs at Jubbulpore, who demonstrated their strangling techniques from days of old

Sherwood told him that he would be hanged immediately, unless he revealed the true nature of his cult. The Thug was then shown a large tree where ropes with nooses had been tied to high limbs. He shrank back in fear and, trembling, began to talk, explaining that the pickax was the most sacred tool of his faith, Thuggee, and that "it could fly into the hands of its user" when necessary. Slowly he and a few others began to detail the cult of Kali. Every ritual was outlined, every murder freely admitted without any sense of guilt displayed. Sherwood carried on his investigation for months and subsequently wrote a shocking paper entitled *Of the Murderers Called Phansigars.*

Sherwood not only pinpointed the oaths, the superstitions, and the murder procedures of Thuggee, but he even provided a brief lexicon exclusively used by the cultist killers. The secret language included such phrases as "Sweep the place" ("See that no one is about"), "Bring firewood" ("Take up your positions"), "Eat betel" ("Kill him"), "Look after the

This 1840 sketch by Mrs. Fanny Parks depicts the interior of a Thuggee temple, the goddess Kali at the center; Parks was unimpressed by the idol, believing it to be "more of a child's toy than a redoubtable goddess."

straw" ("Bury the corpse and watch for strangers"), "Descendants of bhowani?" ("Are you also Phansigars?").

There were numerous secret signs that provided warnings to other Thugs. According to Sherwood "drawing the back of the hand along the chin, from the throat outward, implies that caution is requisite that some stranger is approaching. Putting the open hand over the mouth and drawing it gently down implies that there is no longer cause for alarm." The sacred knife was called *cathini,* the revered pickax was called *mahi.*

The Thugs interviewed by Sherwood reported the killing of their victims without expressing any regret, and the numbers of victims were staggering. One killer "stopped counting when he reached the thousand." Sherwood's western morality was numbed by the admissions of the Thugs: "What constitutes the most odious feature in the character of these murderers is, that prodigal as they are of human life, they can rarely claim the benefit of even the palliating circumstance of strong pecuniary temptation. They are equally strangers to compassion and remorse. They are never restrained from the commission of crimes by commiseration for the unfortunate traveler and they are exempted from the compunctious visits of conscience, which usually follow, sooner or later, the steps of guilt."

Phansigari, Sherwood went on to explain "is their *business.*" (In the latter part of the same 19th Century the Mafia would excuse its ceaseless murders with the same word, *business.*) They were not, the Thugs patiently told Sherwood, the cause of countless deaths. These murders were ordained by Kali, the blameless goddess of destruction. The Thugs were merely the instruments of a goddess that could only survive through killing.

A young British officer in the Bengal army, William Sleeman, read Sherwood's paper with obsessive interest. He had already learned four Indian dialects and was much interested in the country's natives. At Sleeman's request, he was transferred to civil service in 1818, continuing his own investigation of Thuggee, which the military authorities still considered an infrequent problem occurring in the most remote areas of India. High officials refused to accept Sherwood's evaluation of the killer cult, believing that the surgeon had exaggerated the extent of the sect.

Sleeman's own discoveries not only enforced Sherwood's evaluation of the secret criminal society as a massive and controlled menace, but they pinpointed the areas, mostly the well-traveled trade routes, where the Thugs operated with abandon. Now the killer bands had discarded much of Kali's traditions, killing women and children, motivated by the promise of loot. Their numbers increased so that the marauding bands often exceeded 150 to 200 armed men.

When Sleeman was given control over the entire Nerbudda Valley in 1822, he increased his probes into the mysteries of Thuggee, preparing exhaustive reports on Thug activities. In 1826, he was ordered to explore the possibility of Thuggee being an organized murder cult throughout India. In 1830, Sleeman was able to convince his immediate superior, Lord William Bentinck, governor general, that Thuggee was a nationwide secret criminal society that wielded vast power and influence. After reading Sleeman's reports, Bentinck became convinced that Thuggee was real and a national threat. He gave Sleeman his orders: Wipe out the Thugs.

This was no easy task, despite the number of men put under Sleeman's command. As had been the case for centuries, the Thugs operated under the guise of marauding Dacoits when Sleeman's men arrested them and invariably most were released since the bodies of their victims were seldom discovered. No local police system then existed in India, other than that newly established by the British, and these poorly organized constabularies operated in only a few districts that were under strict British control. Sleeman carefully selected his own men, both British and Indian, trusting only these specially trained paramilitary sleuths to ferret out Thugs. When suspected Thugs were arrested, Sleeman's force was hampered by local courts who balked at trying Thugs accused of murders in far flung areas.

To understand the motivations and methods of this secret murder sect, Sleeman learned from imprisoned Thugs the language of Thuggee, called *Ramasi.* Further, Sleeman recorded the history of this astounding killer cult, tracing its existence as far back as 700, according to some reports from informing members. Feringheea, a Thug priest who confessed his membership to Sleeman under pain of execution, boasted of the long and distinguished history of Thuggee, saying that its activities were accurately recorded in the cave drawings and carvings discovered at Ellora; these early etchings and sculptures could be dated back to the early eighth century. Said Feringheea: "In one place [of the cave drawings] you see men strangling; in another burying the bodies, in another carrying them off to the graves. There is not an operation in Thuggee that is not exhibited in the caves of Ellora."

Sleeman believed that the sect may have developed as early as four centuries before the gruesome artistry of the Ellora caves when discovering in Herodotus reports of the tribe called Sagartii, Persian nomads known for their horsemanship, and were depicted by Herodotus as using a dagger and a noose of twisted leather to dispatch their enemies.

Much that Sleeman found in his own history of Thuggee pointed to the strong possibility that the religious murder sect was an offshoot of the dreaded Order of the Assassins, founded in the late eleventh century by Hasan Sabah, a clever Persian, who fused the Moslem faith with political murder (as has today's Osama bin Laden) as a way of wielding enormous power. This sect was developed in its most fanatical period by a bloodthirsty elder of Sabbah's sect known simply to western Crusaders in the twelfth century as The Old Man of the Mountains.

A century later more than 1,000 Thugs were captured after a pitched battle near Delhi, according to one historian, but the local sultan released them, either through bribery or believing their plea that their group had nothing to do with the invading army that had been defeated. The Thugs were set free and shortly thereafter this formidable band spread murder and terror throughout Bengal. The existence of the Thugs in succeeding centuries became known to local and even European historians who erratically recorded their presence in India.

Sleeman learned that though the orthodox Hindus regarded Kali as a goddess that licked the blood from wounds they received in battle, the Thugs believed that the deity had grown tired epochs earlier of giving succor to a mankind persecuted by demons and had made two men from her own person, instructing these creations to murder the demons with handkerchiefs, shedding no blood in the act of murder so that she would no longer have to consume the blood. Thus sprang forth the cult of Thuggee, bloodless, methodical killers believing that they were killing not humans, but the reincarnation of ancient demons, anyone, actually, who did not follow Thuggee. This, of course, was but a cold-blooded rationale, according to other historians, to excuse murder for profit, irrespective of the fact that Thugs paid offhand homage to Kali by placing in the hands of her priests some portion of the loot they took from their victims.

In Sleeman's era, it became evident that Thuggee was no longer the "pure" murder sect of ancient times. It was basically a murder-for-profit organization that briefly nodded in Kali's direction before its avaricious followers enriched themselves through murder. The number of members in each murder raid, by the 1830s, was no longer strictly controlled. Instead of ten to twenty Thugs carefully planning their ambushes, the bands were bloated to several hundred, all eager to enrich themselves under the religious umbrella of Kali.

A gang of Thugs are shown pulling a wealthy merchant from his horse; some times these murder bands numbered in the hundreds.

A portrait of several Thugs captured in 1854.

Decorum and protocol were ignored by priests demanding a share of the spoils and the sect, perhaps numbering as high as 500,000 in 1830, was populated by known criminals,

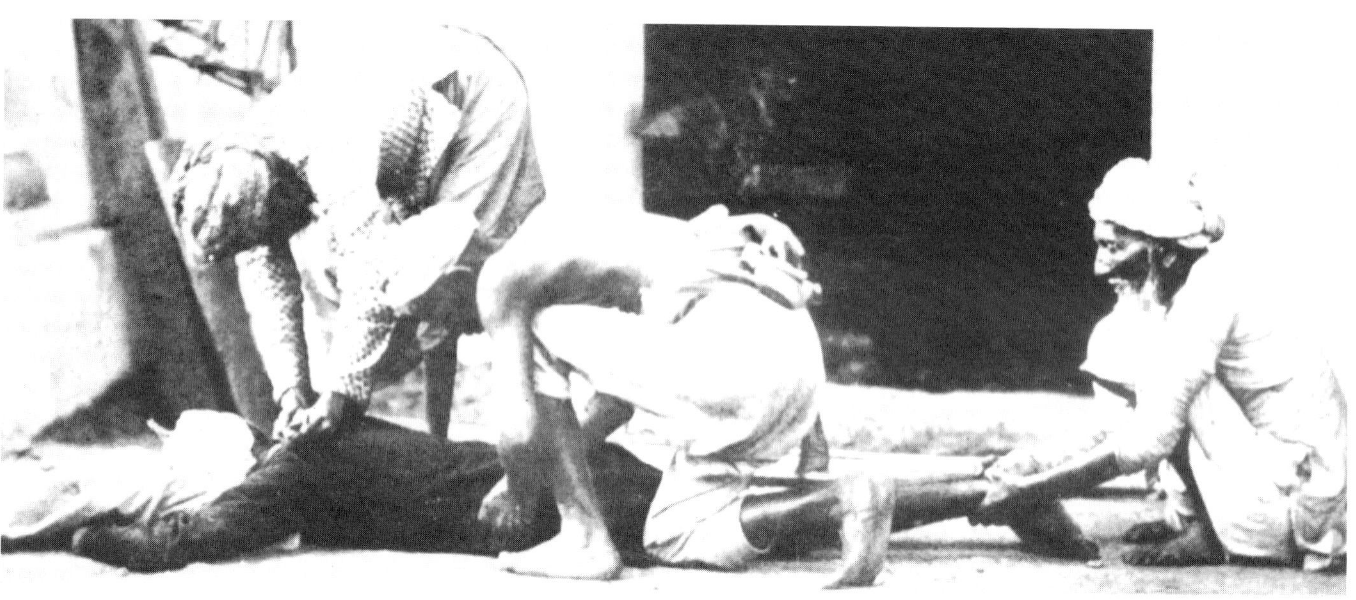

Captured Thugs demonstrate how they prepared bodies for burial for visiting British dignitaries; to save themselves from execution, many Thugs informed on other members of the sect.

who later informed on Thug operations to save themselves from the hangman's noose. The devout Thug was quickly intimidated into cooperation with Sleeman and his men when told that he would not only be hanged if he did not confess his crimes and point out other Thugs, but that his corpse would be left to dangle from a tree limb and would be covered with the sacred blood of cows or pigs, depending upon whether the Thug was Hindu or Muslim, thereby assuring eternal damnation for his soul.

Muslim members of the sect puzzled Sleeman, especially since Thuggee was more Muslim than Hindu in numbers. He confronted one Muslim Thug, telling the accused murderer that he was disloyal to his own religion by worshipping a Hindu goddess. The Muslim shrugged and said that Kali was the twin of Fatima, daughter of Muhammad, and therefore a Muslim deity as well. To the Thugs, Sleeman was the embodiment of the avenger of their transgressions, as foretold by their own priests.

The Thugs had long believed that because they had murdered the *wrong* people, from sweepers to tradesmen, and because they had ignored or misinterpreted Kali's dictates, the Europeans would be the cause of their destruction. Sleeman was thought to be the avenger and so well versed in Thug language and custom had he become that he was recognized by the Thugs as one who possessed as much knowledge of their secret society as the most respected of their high priests.

William Sleeman, to his prey, was not a foreign demon, but a European guru seemingly gifted with the ability to look into the heart and soul of a Thug and know his secrets. By the time Sleeman began to round up Thugs in great numbers, thanks to his countless informers from their sect, the sect believed that their days were ending, that Kali had abandoned them for breaking her taboos. Sleeman and his men compelled informers to reveal hundreds of murder sites, known as *beles,* where thousands of bodies were unearthed along trade routes that traversed North India for thousands of miles. For a decade Sleeman's men counted corpses and skeletons, then estimated that within the last hundred years the Thugs had murdered more than a million travelers.

The Thugs truly believed that their serial murders were not immoral and that they had committed no real offenses, except to Kali, when breaking her sacred rites. Buhram, one of the most notorious Thugs to be captured, freely admitted to murdering 931 people, saying, as did most of the Thugs interrogated, that he was merely following the fate decreed by Kali. She had thrown the travelers into his hands, commanding him to kill them. Had he refused, his family and friends would have suffered want and misery for the rest of eternity.

Buhram went stoically to the gallows in 1840, convinced that he was being executed not for his wholesale slaughter of fellow humans, whom he still considered demons, but because he had displeased Kali in the manner of his murders. Nasir, another Thug extensively interrogated by Sleeman, endorsed Buhram's rigid perspective, stating: "I have a hundred times heard my father and other old and wise men say when we had killed a sweeper and otherwise infringed their rules, that we should be some day punished for it; that the European rulers would be made the instruments to chastise us for our disregard of omens and neglect of the rules laid down for our guidance."

Sleeman learned from another Thug that the pickax, once consecrated in a temple of Kali, was so sacred that no Thug could swear a falsehood when touching it. He employed the pickax with great effect thereafter, bringing Thugs to him and having them place their hands on their own pickax, then demanding they tell him what he wanted to know. When a Thug shrank back from the pickax, holding his hands behind him, this was tantamount to a confession that he was a practicing Thug. But most Thugs were so obsessed with their own ritual that, once placing their hands on the pickax, unblinkingly admitted their countless murders, pointing out the graves of their victims and quickly identifying their fellow members in village after village. Next to Kali herself, the pickax was the most worshipped symbol of Thuggee.

Every bizarre ceremony conducted by the Thugs was recorded by Sleeman as he pried revelations from Thug informers. From Feringheea he learned of the ritual murder feast, *Tuponee.* Following the mass slayings of travelers in a caravan, a band of Thugs would erect a ten-foot tent so as to shield themselves from other travelers and inside gather in a circle and pass *goor* from hand to hand, this being lumpy pieces of coarse sugar. Each Thug, who had committed a murder that night, licked and consumed a portion of the *goor.* If any of this substance fell accidentally to the ground, it had to be buried immediately with the murder victims in their nearby graves.

Only Thugs, who had performed the murders, were permitted to partake of the *goor,* and if a novice Thug ate any of this sacred substance, he was ordered to immediately go forth and strangle a victim so as to be worthy of consuming the *goor.* As the Thugs licked and swallowed this substance they would chant to Kali, asking her to provide more demon travelers for them, so they could share in more loot, a moaning prayer for gain repeated over and over again. As often as not, this murder feast was performed directly upon the graves of the victims killed only hours earlier. Some far-reaching historians have likened this ritual to that of communion where bread and wine are consumed.

The pickax was ever present, placed on a sheet. Sitting next to the pickax was the Thug leader of the band, always facing west, with other elders ringed about him, leading the prayer to Kali, placing some silver next to the pickax, this was meant to be an offering to Kali, part of treasures stolen that day from the murder victims. The leader would then sprinkle holy water on the pickax, still chanting, pleading with Kali to provide more victims, more treasure, and to present good omens the next day that would assure them of success. Other Thugs of lower rank and accomplishment sat in several circles about the inner circle of elders, repeating the prayer to Kali.

Such rituals made a indelible impression on any novitiate. To the younger untried Thugs this murder feast bonded them to the older men and to Thuggee itself. Said Feringheea: "We all feel pity sometimes, but the *goor* of the *Tuponee* changes our nature. It would change the nature of a horse. Let any man once taste of that *goor,* and he will be a Thug though he know all the trades and have all the wealth in the world. I never wanted food; my mother's family was opulent, her relations high in office. I have been high in office myself and become so great a favorite wherever I went that I was sure of promotion. Yet I was always miserable when absent from my gang, and obliged to return to Thuggee. My father made me taste of that fatal *goor* when I was a mere boy, and if I were to live a thousand years, I would never be able to follow any other trade."

Sleeman discovered that dozens of leading Thugs were also leaders in their local communities, men who were respected for their upstanding and law-abiding ways, such as Makeen Lodhi, who had murdered innumerable travelers. As one of his aides put it, Lodhi considered his victims fair game, an attitude any hunter had for his prey, one shared by all Thugs: "They all look upon travelers as a sportsman looks upon hares and pheasants; and they recollect their best sporting grounds, and talk of them, when they can, with the same kind of glee!"

It was this kind of gregarious talk that led many Thugs into Sleeman's traps. He had a small army at his command by

Thugs turned carpet weavers are shown in 1874, sitting on one of their elaborate rugs, which were much in demand at that time.

The resplendent carpet shown in the Waterloo Chamber at Windsor Castle, was made by Thugs and presented as a gift to Queen Victoria.

begging to join a caravan to seek protection were invited to do so, but that night British soldiers would round up the stranglers and put them under arrest to prevent their wholesale slaughter of the caravan.

This protective system, coupled with later improvements in communication and travel, particularly the coming of the railroad to India, made the murder methods of Thuggee obsolete. In the late 1830s, Thugs by the hundreds were tried and quickly convicted of murder. By 1840, about 3,700 Thugs, most of them cult leaders and the worst serial murderers, had been tried. About 500 were hanged and these were public executions, where the body was defiled so that such executions served as effective propaganda, implanting real fear into the hearts of other still unexposed Thugs.

the mid-1830s, which he used in sweeping wide areas of India. So well briefed were Sleeman's men that they easily ferreted out the Thugs from villages and towns. Sleeman had prepared precise charts and genealogical maps that documented Thug families, from grandfathers to babes in arms. Using regular British troops, European volunteers, and loyal Sepoy soldiers, Sleeman was able to arrest thousands of Thugs.

The British government allowed him a free hand, and Sleeman's kangaroo courts quickly convicted and condemned hundreds of Thugs. Those who cooperated with Sleeman were called "Approvers" and were spared. They were given minor government jobs and were re-educated, along with their children. Sleeman's army of bureaucrats then taught these reformed Thugs new trades, new concepts of morality. Feringheea proved to be the most informative of Sleeman's captured Thugs and he was spared the gallows, despite the fact that he had murdered more than 100 people by January 1831, when he was arrested.

Even the older Thugs, most dedicated to Kali's teachings, refuted the blood goddess in the end, accepting the ways of the Europeans, attending schools established for them, where they, along with their children, learned bricklaying and the art of weaving. Some of these Thugs, serial killers all, became the most accomplished carpet weavers in the world, and one of their products was later given to Queen Victoria, a massive two-ton, 40-foot-wide, 80-foot-long carpet which later decorated the mammoth dining hall in the Waterloo Chamber at Windsor Castle.

Further aiding Sleeman in breaking up the Thug gangs was the rapid expansion of British-controlled commerce. No longer did the followers of Kali find easy prey in unprotected caravans. British and Sepoy troops accompanied these merchants, guarding against the Thug techniques. Groups of Thugs

To those witnessing their public executions, the condemned Thugs showed no concern for their own horrible fate, stoically accepting their grim destiny. One eyewitness to a public execution of twenty-five Thugs in 1831, a friend of Sleeman's, Mrs. Fanny Parks, later wrote: "It would be impossible to find in any county a set of men who meet death with more indifference than these wretches; and had it been in a better cause, they would have excited universal sympathy. As it was, there was something dreadful in the thought that men, who had so often imbrued their hands in blood, should meet their death with such carelessness. I believe that they had previously requested to be allowed to fasten the cord about their necks with their own hands; certain it is that each individual as soon as he had adjusted the noose, jumped off the beam and launched himself into eternity; and those who first mounted the ladder selected their ropes, rejecting such as did not please them. One of them who had leaped off the beam and had been hanging for more than three seconds put his hands up and pulled his cap over his face."

Fifty-six Thugs, some of them known serial murderers, were spared execution, because they had turned informer. These "Approvers" survived only because they allowed Sleeman to unearth thousands more of active members. Sleeman found himself battling for the lives of these Approvers since the British government insisted upon executing them. In the end, Sleeman had his way, explaining that without his informers he would never have been able to break Thuggee's stranglehold on Indian commerce.

The rest of the leading Thugs were sent to prison for life,

The dreaded Thugs of India were grimly depicted in the 1939 adventure film classic, *Gunga Din*; three British soldiers (left to right) Douglas Fairbanks, Jr., Victor McLaglen and Cary Grant) have captured the Thug high priest (Eduardo Ciannelli), while their regimental water-boy, Gunga Din (Sam Jaffe, behind Grant's right shoulder) looks on in terror.

or, as was the case with half of them, were transported to other countries, where they were sentenced to penal servitude for life. By 1848, another 650 Thugs were tried, half of these being executed, the remainder imprisoned for life. By then the religion of Thuggee as a practicing murder cult was all but finished.

By the 1870s, the cult of Thuggee held interest to British dignitaries visiting India only as a curiosity. Ancient stranglers who had been imprisoned for forty years were brought from their miserable jails to amuse British royalty by reenacting their strangling methods. This then was the residue of the most feared murder sect in ten centuries, skeletal creatures with long white beards, holding up anachronistic *rumals* and pickaxes, while chanting dead prayers to the fallen idol of now bloodless Kali.

This secret criminal society, however, did not completely die out for there were isolated reports that Thuggee was still being practiced in remote northern regions of India as late as the early 1900s, but these tales went unsubstantiated. Thuggee is thought to be, mercifully, at this writing a defunct sect, its nightmare rites and horrible murders buried long ago with its sacrificial victims.

MAFIA: BROTHERHOOD OF DEATH/ 800s-present

The secret criminal society known as the Mafia of the present day has little or nothing to do with the ancient tribal concept of the Mafia that dates back to the ninth century, when Sicily was ruled by Arab invaders. The Arabic word *mafia* means "place of refuge," and this term originally applied to those hillside refuges to which oppressed inhabitants of the island fled. When Norman invaders overran Sicily in the 11th century, all of the small farms were seized and made into great estates. The islanders were used as farm slaves, and to escape this miserable existence, thousands took to the hills, seeking the sanctuaries of the Mafia strongholds.

In the fifteenth century, the Spaniards conquered the island and brought the Inquisition to Sicily with all its sadistic punishments and tortures. Again the inhabitants sought the Mafia strongholds to escape this new oppression. Another version of the organization's beginnings stems from the invasion of the French in 1282 and the patriotic resistance to French armies by Sicilian forces was symbolized in the motto: "Morte alla Francia Italia anela!" ("Death to the French is Italy's cry!") The initial letters of this motto form the word Mafia, although it appears that this explanation for the existence of one of the world's most dreaded underworld fraternities was created in hindsight. For several centuries, the Mafia in Sicily was a patriotic clandestine society, a band of nationalists that conducted guerrilla warfare against foreign invaders. The society created a hierarchy of dons (chiefs), who commanded separate Mafia families in each village and town with the overall don residing in Sicily's capital, Palermo.

The original concept for this secret society was to liken it to a family, related not by blood but by Sicilian nationality. By an oath, members vowed never to reveal Mafia secrets under pain of death. The discipline that kept the Mafia together one century after another was *omerta,* meaning "manliness," or, more generally, "silence." This was the code of the Mafia then as it is now. Betrayal was likened to the act of Judas and no authority, church or state, was superior to or held in more respect than the Mafia itself.

As time passed, the Mafia was slowly perverted into a secret criminal organization that controlled all manner of vice, rackets, and murder in Sicily. By the middle of the 19th Century, Sicily was utterly controlled by the Mafia, then a completely criminal secret society. Mafia dons had replaced feudal lords and they virtually controlled the island's government.

Before their teens, Mafia members—all male—were taught how to use a sword, knife, and rope in expertly mur-

Fascist leader Cesare Mori, who was sent to Sicily to stamp out the Mafia in the 1920s by Italian dictator Benito Mussolini; his extraordinary efforts yielded little results.

New Orleans Police Chief David Hennessey, who led a crusade against the Mafia and was shot to death by Mafia gunmen while walking home on the night of October 15, 1890.

dering victims. Mafia chiefs also taught their apprentices how to torture victims to extract information. Members were indoctrinated in the use of fear and savage reprisals against those who betrayed the Mafia. Hatred for all authority except the Catholic Church was and is fostered to this day. The Church is tolerated by the Mafia, which considers it a spiritual organization with no temporal authority and therefore no instructional value to the living. The primitive and superstitious natives of Sicily, poorly paid and poorly educated, remain mystically captive to this vile and utterly dictatorial organization. Secrecy is the hallmark of the Mafia. Violent death is its promise to all informers.

In the early part of the 19th Century, Sicily, following the example of the feudal city states, established loosely organized Mafia gangs in each province and in most towns and villages, an organization similar to the structure of the Camorra, the criminal secret society of southern Italy, which had its roots in 15th Century Bourbon Spain. In Monreale, Sicily, the Mafia was known as the *Stuppaghieri;* in Bagheria, it was called the *Fratuzzi.* In other towns the society was called *Cudi Chiatti* (Flat Tails), the *Mano Fraterna* (the Brotherly Hand), and the *Birritti* (The Caps). By the middle of the 19th Century, Mafia overlords, who were nothing more than glorified bandits, realized that effective power could be wielded only after Mafia leaders infiltrated the very government of Sicily.

To that end, Mafia Don Raffaele Palizzolo, in 1876, ran for political office in Caccamo and won an overwhelming victory. At gunpoint, voters signed open ballots that could be checked on the spot. Palizzolo became the first Mafia don to rule in national government and secretly direct the operations of the Mafia at the same time. Within a decade, all of western Sicily was under his control. Palizzolo, in turn, worked for the election of Francesco Crispi as prime minister of Sicily. Crispi, also

The Old Parish Prison in New Orleans, where more than a dozen members of the Mafia were held while being tried for the murder of Police Chief Hennessey and other crimes.

William S. Parkerson, standing before a statue of Henry Clay, addresses a crowd of ten to twenty thousand New Orleans citizens, urging an attack on the Old Parish Prison and the destruction of the Mafia members held there on March 14, 1891.

a Mafia don, took this high office in 1887, and the whole country came under Mafia domination. Crispi became the first national don of the Mafia and ruled the secret criminal society with an iron hand, dispensing legitimate national business on one hand and directing overall Mafia operations on the other. He blithely looted the national treasury and used these funds to build up Mafia operations throughout Sicily.

Those who opposed the Mafia politician-dons were invariably from the landed gentry and were members of the conservative party. These courageous men were financially ruined by the Mafia or were assassinated. Typical of this fate was that which befell the Marquis Commendatore Emanuel Notarbartolo, former director of the Bank of Sicily. Notarbartolo had publicly vowed to eradicate the Mafia and use his great fortune to back all anti-Mafia political candidates. On February 1, 1893, Notarbartolo was dragged from his private train suite by a gang of Mafia killers and stabbed to death. Then his body was mutilated and dumped onto some railroad tracks.

Notarbartolo was succeeded as director of the Bank of Sicily by none other than Palizzolo, who had orchestrated Notarbartolo's assassination and was by then representing Sicily as a member of the Italian parliament in Rome. Palizzolo busied himself with directing the bank's funds into Mafia coffers. When Notarbartolo's son, Leopoldo, a Sicilian Navy officer, began to investigate his father's murder, he was reassigned to the China Seas.

Giuseppe Fontana, a notorious Mafia killer, was accused of leading the murder gang which slew Notarbartolo, but his trial was a farce. Magistrates hearing this case, who proved to be uncooperative with the Mafia dons, were simply replaced until a cooperative presiding judge dismissed the charges against Fontana. This became the typical Mafia ploy in court cases involving the society.

Palizzolo, who had been decorated by King Humbert I for his so-called outstanding civic services, was accused of masterminding Notarbartolo's murder by the victim's son, Leopoldo Notarbartolo, who had since resigned his commission and had become a private detective, dedicating his life to solving his father's murder. Deputy Palizzolo was imprisoned on December 8, 1899, along with his chief henchman Fontana, and held for trial.

This court proceeding was a mockery of justice, as had been Fontana's earlier trial. After several trials, Palizzolo and Fontana were released on July 25, 1904. The many witnesses against them had lost their memories. Documents disappeared and even police reports were not available to the court. The central police department in Palermo (its chief a Mafia stooge) actually refused to turn over documents to the court in the Palizzolo proceedings.

At the turn of the 20th Century, the Mafia secretly ruled Sicily. They had infiltrated the local police, the small Sicilian army, and all branches of government. Honest government officials, who tried to combat or even stamp out the Mafia were invariably murdered. During the 1920s, Italian dictator Benito Mussolini attempted to wipe out the Mafia by sending to Sicily his top police official, Cesare Mori, with instructions to destroy the leadership and operations of the Mafia, which proved to be an impossible task.

For years, Mori arrested scores of suspected Mafia leaders and jailed them, but he found few witnesses willing to risk their lives by testifying against these men. The lyrics of a popular Sicilian ballad of that day summed up the insidious, death-dealing society which Mori battled: "I am an herb which poisons all, who picks me cannot eat me. Put me in your mouth and you won't be able to swallow me, and whoever swallows me, I suffocate."

Thousands of vigilantes stormed the Old Parish Prison on March 14, 1891, where they dragged Mafia members from their hiding places, lynching them from lampposts.

The Mafia attempted to expand into other countries, but met with little success on mainland Italy, where the Camorra had long been in power. Its operations in France, Spain, and other Latin-language countries were limited to cooperating with already-established criminal gangs and organizations, and they were usually confined to the trafficking of narcotics or white slavery operations. The most lucrative opportunities for the Mafia were in the U. S. Hundreds of Mafia killers and thieves migrated to the U.S. in the 1890s, joining the hundreds of thousands of Italians and Sicilians resettling in this land of opportunity.

Beginning in the late 1880s, the greatest Mafia enclave was New Orleans. Here the Mafia successfully transplanted itself and was soon terrorizing the local Italian-Sicilian community through Black Hand operations. It also controlled the considerable vegetable markets, and the dockside shipping, and was encroaching upon local politics. The same code of death to informers was meted out in New Orleans as it had been in Sicily. One Mafia member, Vincenzo Ottumvo, was disgruntled at having been cut out of the group's spoils and threatened to go to the authorities. On January 24, 1889, his throat was slit while he was playing cards.

New Orleans police investigated the case and Police Chief David Hennessey took particular interest in the murder, personally questioning Italian and Sicilian inhabitants of the Italian quarter. Hennessey was biased and had openly criticized Italians in general, boldly stating that he had no use for them. He was the first in the U. S. to learn of the Mafia's existence, when several Italians whispered darkly about a "secret society" operating in the city.

While Hennessey was conducting his investigation, Mafia dons learned that another defector from their ranks, Giuseppe Mataino, was about to turn informer. He was found by police with his throat slit. His savage killers had jammed Mataino's head into a stove and had burned it beyond recognition. In June 1899, Camillo Victoria, another person Hennessey had interviewed, was executed by Mafia killers. He was shot through the head, while he sat in his home with his family, his murderers firing shotguns through a window.

Dozens of mob members used a battering ram to break down the doors of the prison to get to the Mafia prisoners, while guards stood by and did nothing.

Some of the Mafia members who were shot are shown lying dead or dying in the courtyard of the Old Parish Prison after the mob broke inside.

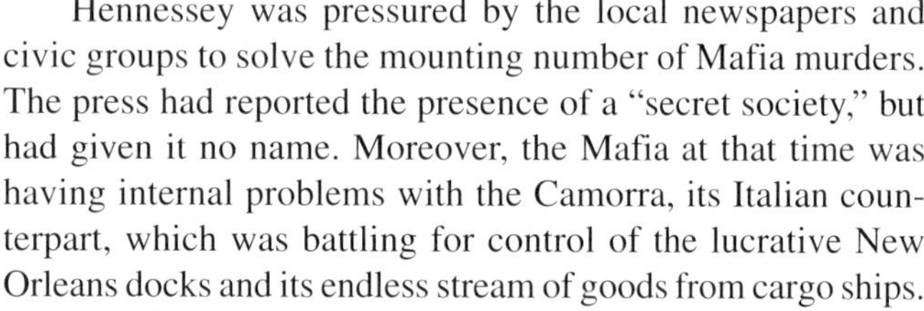

Hennessey was pressured by the local newspapers and civic groups to solve the mounting number of Mafia murders. The press had reported the presence of a "secret society," but had given it no name. Moreover, the Mafia at that time was having internal problems with the Camorra, its Italian counterpart, which was battling for control of the lucrative New Orleans docks and its endless stream of goods from cargo ships.

The Camorra was headed by the Provenzo family while the Mafia was controlled by Anthony and Charles Matranga. These two deadly secret societies then began to make war upon each other. On May 1, 1890, Anthony Matranga was attacked while driving a horse-drawn wagon on Esplanade Avenue. He was shot and wounded by several Camorra thugs whom Matranga drove off with gunfire from his own revolver.

Chief Hennessey investigated this shooting and learned of the word Mafia for the first time, along with its ongoing feud with the Camorra, an organization that had been identified long before. The police chief decided that the Camorra was the lesser of the two evils and he went to the Provenzos to make a pact with the family leaders. If they helped to stamp out this new secret society, he would be tolerant of Camorra rackets. The Provenzos provided Hennessey with detailed information on the Mafia, its origins, its local structures, its bosses in New Orleans, and their ties to Mafia dons in Sicily. Hennessey wrote to the police in Palermo and sent names and descriptions of suspected criminals in New Orleans.

Police authorities in Sicily cooperated, even though their ranks had been infiltrated by Mafia members. Hennessey received dossiers on more than one hundred Sicilians, who were escaped Mafia convicts in Sicily and now resided in New Orleans. It was later speculated that the Sicilian police had been ordered by Mafia dons Crispi and Palizzolo to cooperate with Hennessey and turn over this information as a way of punishing the Matranga faction for its lack of obedience to the Sicilian Mafia board. The Matrangas had refused to send tribute to Sicily from the spoils of its extensive rackets. The dossiers sent by the Palermo police involved small-time Mafia members who would be sacrificed to American law in order to teach the Matrangas a lesson.

Thus gulled, Hennessey was nevertheless elated at this discovery and informed the press that he would expose the Mafia and its entire organization at a special upcoming hearing. "I am now prepared to break the Mafia in New Orleans," he stated. "The Mafia doesn't scare me. I will tear it out by the roots before I'm finished!" He declared war on the Mafia, which had already made plans for Hennessey's assassination. Hennessey would never make his public address against the criminal secret society. On the night of October 15, 1890, the tall, burly policeman was walking unescorted toward his home when a small boy, Aspero Marchese, darted in front of him and began whistling loudly, skipping down the street, heralding Hennessey's approach. Close to his house, Hennessey was sud-

Antonio Scaffidi was shot by a friend of the murdered Chief Hennessey in the prison's visitor's room; he was lynched.

Manuel Polizziadmitted to a Pinkerton agent that he and other Mafia members killed Chief Hennessey; he was lynched.

Antonio Marchese raced to the third floor of the prison, but was caught by the mob and dragged to a street and lynched.

Pietro Monastero (or Monasterio) hid from the mob, but was found and taken to a street, where he was hanged from a post.

denly struck by several shotgun blasts, the small pellets tearing through his clothes.

Hennessey drew his service revolver and turned, firing at the dark figures hovering across the street. He staggered down the block, firing at the dozen or more Mafia gunmen running across the street and parallel to their victim, and firing blast after blast from their shotguns. The running gun battle ended when Hennessey, hit a half dozen times, collapsed onto the pavement. A Mafia gunman ran across the street, leveled a shotgun at his back, and fired almost point-blank into the fallen man. To the Mafioso's surprise, Hennessey, a powerful man, suddenly raised himself erect, roaring curses, and emptied his revolver at his assailants. He took a few more steps and collapsed again.

Police Captain William J. O'Connor, who was walking in the next block, heard the roaring gunfire and came on the run to find Hennessey slumped on a curb. O'Connor held the police chief in his arms, asking: "Who did this?"

The half-conscious Hennessey said: "The Dagoes ... Billy, oh, Billy, they have given it to me ... and I gave them back the best I could!" A few hours later Police Chief Hennessey was dead from his horrible wounds. The news of this killing shocked and enraged the city. Civic groups and vigilantes began to meet on street corners. They demanded action and cried out for Sicilian blood. The Mafia members went into hiding. The society had broken its own rule of never attacking local authorities and it soon felt the repercussions. Nineteen members of the Mafia, whose names were prominent in Hennessey's

Antonio Bagnetto hid in a dog house in a prison corridor, but was discovered and taken to a lamppost and lynched.

Joseph P. Marcheca was shot to death when the mob saw him at a third-floor window of the prison.

Bastiano Incardona successfully hid inside the prison and escaped the mob; he was set free after March 14, 1891.

Charles Matranga (or Mantranga), Mafia don in New Orleans; he hid from the mob and was set free after March 14, 1891.

NYPD Lt. Joseph Petrosino, who headed the "Italian Squad" that tracked down Black Hand extortionists and who was killed in Palermo, Sicily, in 1909, after identifying Mafia members who had migrated to the U. S.

Mafia chief of Sicily, Don Vito Cascio Ferro (or Cascioferro), shown with his son in 1902; he bragged of ordering Petrosino's murder, supervising the execution of the NYPD detective or shooting him himself.

files, were indicted for the police chief's murder, including the small boy, Aspero Marchese.

Those indicted included Charles "Millionaire Charlie" Matranga, who had given the orders for Hennessey's assassination, J. P. Macheca, Antonio Bagnetto, Antonio Marchese, Bastiano Incardona, Pietro Monastero, Antonio Scaffidi, and Manuel Polizzi. The district attorney already had a confession from Polizzi, who said that he alone had murdered Hennessey, but officials felt that Polizzi was acting as the sacrificial lamb in order to protect the other, more important Mafia killers. The confession was not accepted so that all of those indicted could stand trial.

The grand jury pored over Hennessey's files on the Mafia and then revealed the existence of the secret criminal society to a shocked nation, which had been following the details of the brazen murder in the press. A spokesman for the grand jury announced that "the extended range of our researches has developed the existence of the secret organization styled 'Mafia.' The evidence comes from several sources fully competent in themselves to attest its truth, while the fact is supported by the long record of bloodcurdling crimes. As if to guard against exposure, the dagger or the stiletto is selected as the deadly weapon to plunge into the heart or back of the victim and silently do its work ... The officers of the Mafia and many of the members are known ... The larger number of the Society is composed of Italians or Sicilians [investigators then did not know that the Mafia was an exclusive Sicilian society] who have left their native land, in most instances under assumed names to avoid conviction for crimes there committed."

The statement shocked and terrified the public, and officials in New Orleans came to believe that even Italian members of the city police force might be members of the insidious society. Because of that fear, private detectives from the Pinkerton Agency were hired and placed in cells next to the Mafia prisoners at the Old Parish Prison, at Conti and Orleans streets. One of these Pinkerton operatives, Frank Dimaio, posing as an Italian counterfeiter with the alias of Anthony Ruggiero, was placed in a cell next to Mafia member Manuel Polizzi. Dimaio gained Polizzi's confidence, the frightened Mafioso admitting: "We killed Hennessey, but they think I

J. Carrol Naish, left, with Gene Kelly (in one of his best dramatic roles) played a detective based upon Petrosino in the 1950 film *The Black Hand*.

In the 1960 film, *Pay or Die*, Ernest Borgnine, left, played the part of the intrepid Joseph Petrosino, a movie that accurately portrayed the extortion, blackmail and murders of the Mafia in the 1900s.

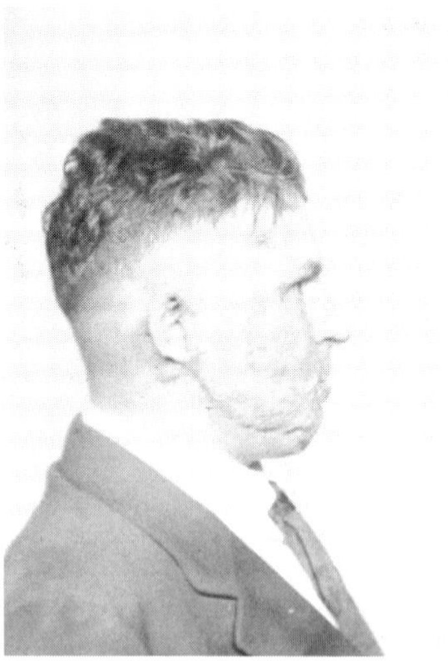
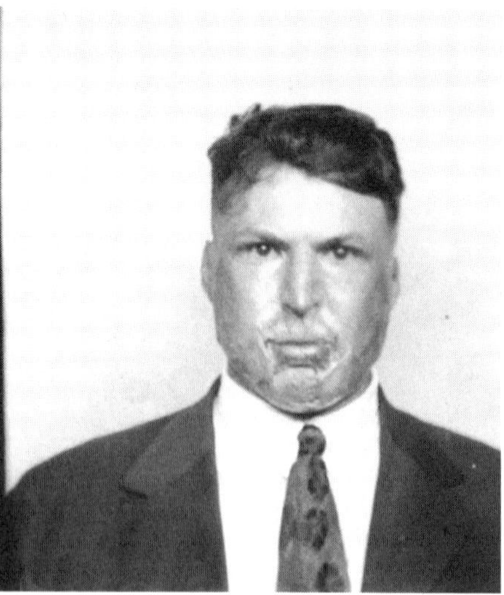

Police photos of Joseph "Scarface" DiGiovanni, the Mafia chief of Kansas City, Missouri, for several decades, his power exceeding that of Boss Pendergast and crime boss Johnny Lazia. The horrible scars on DiGiovanni's face resulted when a homemade still blew up during his early years as a bootlegger.

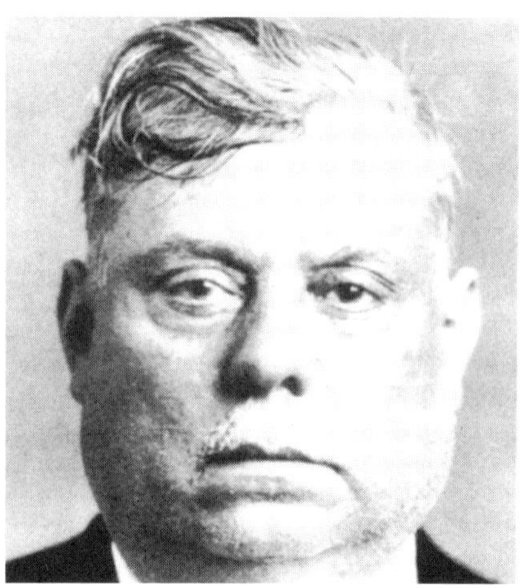
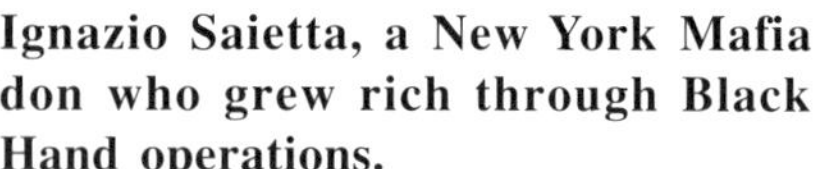

Ignazio Saietta, a New York Mafia don who grew rich through Black Hand operations.

Deported, Charles "Lucky" Luciano continued to direct the U. S. Mafia from Italy.

will betray the society." Dimaio fed officials information he gathered from Polizzi as the case was built against the accused nineteen Mafia members.Meanwhile, matters worsened when Thomas Duffy, the 18-year-old son of a prominent New Orleans businessman and a close friend of Hennessey's, entered the prison and asked to see Antonio Scaffidi. When Scaffidi was brought into the visiting room, Duffy pulled a gun and shot the Mafioso in the neck, a wound which Scaffidi survived. Duffy later received a six-month sentence. When he was taken to the Old Parish Prison to serve his sentence, Duffy shouted: "I'm willing to hang if one of those Dagoes die and I wish there were seventy-five more men like me!"

The Sicilians were kept in a separate wing of the prison since many of the other convicts had threatened to murder them. Duffy's plea for mob violence did not go unheeded, especially when another boatload of 1,800 Italian and Sicilian immigrants landed on the docks of New Orleans a few days later. When Mayor Shakspeare publicly stated that he believed that most of the newly arrived immigrants were "known criminals" (a rash and unfounded statement), panic seized the whole city. The situation was further aggravated when a jury exonerated nine of the nineteen men charged with the Hennessey killing. The nine suspected Mafiosi, however, continued to remain behind bars at the prison while their files were slowly processed.

The news of this court decision caused several citizens' groups to hurriedly meet. Posters were plastered to the walls of buildings all over New Orleans, asking "all good citizens to appear at Clay Statue to remedy the failure of Justice in the Hennessey case." The date of the meeting was scheduled for March 14, 1891. On that day, thousands of angry citizens met to see W. S. Parkerson, a New Orleans lawyer and inspired orator, leap on top of a tree stump and harangue the already boiling mad crowd. "When courts fail, the people must act!" he shouted. "What protection or assurance of protection is there left us when the very head of our police department, our chief of police, is assassinated in our very midst by the Mafia society, and his assassins again turned loose on the community?

"The time has come for the people of New Orleans to say whether they are going to stand these outrages by organized bands of assassins, for the people to say whether they permit it to continue." He paused, surveying the anxious crowd, sensing its willingness to do what he felt necessary. Then, with a booming voice, Parkerson asked: "Will every man here follow me and see the murder of Hennessey vindicated? Men and citizens of New Orleans follow me!" The crowd responded with a roar that was deafening and then followed Parkerson as he quickly walked to the city arsenal.

The mob broke into the arsenal and took armloads of rifles, revolvers, and ammunition. The mob then raced to the Old Parish Prison, knocking down the few guards on duty. (There was a noticeable absence of guards at the prison this day and those who were present offered little or no resistance to the mob. None of the guards drew their weapons.)

"We want the Dagoes!" cried some members of the mob as they ran through the corridors of the ancient prison. Captain Lem Davis, in charge of the prison, ordered all of the prisoners, except the Mafiosi held on the second floor, to be herded out into the prison courtyard, where they were kept under guard. He then went through the second-floor cellblock, unlocking the cells of the Mafia prisoners, telling them: "Hide yourselves as best as you can."

Davis, feeling that his duty was done, then vanished, leaving the Mafiosi to their fates. The Sicilians dashed from their cells, desperately looking for hiding places, which did not exist. Scaffidi, who was easily identified from the large bandage on his neck, along with Macheca and Marchese, climbed the stairs to the third floor, thinking to hide with the other prisoners. When they found all the cells empty, they realized that they were trapped. They ran to the windows where the mob below quickly spotted them and fired at them. Macheca was struck by several bullets and killed.

The mob was already inside the prison, having broken through the huge iron doors at the front entrance where a towering black man had used an enormous paving stone to hammer down the doors. A man named Ross started to run up some stairs, when he noticed some movement in a small wooden doghouse, where Polizzi was hiding. He was dragged screaming from the doghouse by the mob and quickly taken to a lamppost at the corner of St. Anne and Treme streets, where his body soon swayed and dangled.

Scores of mob members used his lifeless body for target practice, shooting the corpse repeatedly, and cheering when a bullet found its mark. Next came Bagnetto and then nine more, all of them hanged from lampposts at this corner. Two of these helpless victims were not even under indictment for Hennessey's murder, but they were Sicilian and this was enough to seal their fates on this black, vengeance-filled day.

Luciano's corpse is driven in the same hearse that was used to carry the body of Italian singer Enrico Caruso; his 1962 funeral ceremonies in Italy were on the level of those given to national heroes.

After the mob had shot and abused the dangling corpses, Parkerson again addressed the crowd, shouting out to its members: "Mob violence is the most terrible thing on the face of the earth. I called you together for a duty. You have performed that duty ... I have performed the most painful duty of my life today ... Now go to your homes and if I need you, I will call you. If you have confidence in me and the gentlemen associated with me, I ask you to disperse and go quietly to your homes. God bless you."

A loud "God bless you, Mr. Parkerson!" came roaring back to the leader. With that, the lynch mob put down its arms and moved off in separate groups or alone, each man thinking he had performed his civic duty and cleansed the city of an evil force. There was no thought of murder, of ignoring all established laws and proceedings. The Mafia, as far as New Orleans citizens were concerned, had been obliterated and no foreign secret society would ever again dare to sully the city with its slinking criminals.

The mass hangings, however, had tremendous international repercussions, and in Washington, D. C., the representative of Italy lodged formal protests against the way in which its resettled people had been treated. No mention of the Mafia was made in these protests, which claimed that men who had been found innocent in a U. S. court had been hanged simply because they were Italian.

Tensions ran high in New Orleans following the hangings. As news of the regrettable tragedy filtered through the U. S., various Italian organizations staged protest meetings. Then on April 3, 1891, a New Orleans grand jury returned indictments against two jurors, who had allegedly accepted bribe money during the deliberations. A private detective named Dominick O'Malley, and five other persons were also indicted on similar charges.

One of the accused, Thomas McCrystal, implicated O'Malley, but his testimony could not be proven and he was dismissed. None of the ringleaders of the lynch mob that stormed the Parish Prison were ever formally charged. Official protests were filed by the Italian ambassador, Baron Fava, with the White House, but no further actions were taken to bring

The bullet-ridden car and corpse of Dr. Michelle Navarra, who headed the Mafia in Corleone, Sicily, in 1958, an execution ordered by rival Mafia don Luciano Liggio.

the perpetrators to justice. When Fava demanded some form of retribution from Secretary of State James G. Blaine, he was met with cold indifference. No doubt fearing international repercussions over this matter, President Benjamin Harrison went before Congress on December 19, 1891, to denounce the tragic affair.

Later, Secretary Blaine would put the matter to rest by announcing a $25,000 award, which was divided among the families of the victims. The hangings of 1891 did little to deter the growth of the Mafia in New Orleans. By the turn of the century, the Mafia was stronger than ever in the city and worked in silence, with members belonging to one powerful family with an overall boss. This was the same structure as used in Sicily, where town Mafia chiefs known as *capofamiglias* answered in turn to the boss of bosses in Palermo, a chief called the *capo dei capi.*

The strict family code of the Mafia was kept intact as new chapters were established throughout the U. S., in the great metropolitan cities of New York, Chicago, Boston, Philadelphia, Cleveland, New Orleans, St. Louis, Kansas City, San Francisco—anywhere a sizeable Italian-Sicilian population was present. The Mafia depended then, as it does today, upon its ability to prey upon its own ethnic people.

In Sicily, the Mafia survives as the second most powerful (if not *the* most powerful) entity in the land, basing its power wholly upon a protection racket. The people in Sicily are taxed first by the government and then by the Mafia, which assures them that no harm will befall them and that they will suffer no theft of livestock or goods if one is a farmer, or merchandise if one is a merchant. Petty crime in Sicily was thus eliminated, but the population as a whole exchanged their larger profits for the security the Mafia provided on the level of the farm, the village, the town, and finally the city.

This protection racket flourished in the U. S. as practiced by the Black Hand, wherein Sicilians preyed upon their fellow immigrants from the 1890s to the 1920s, until other more lucrative rackets overshadowed this primitive extortion system. Black Hand extortionist Ignazio Saietta, known as Lupo the Wolf, headed the Mafia in New York in the first two decades of the 20th Century, until he was sent to prison. It was the Black Hand in New York that was so energetically battled by the valiant NYPD Lieutenant Joseph Petrosino, who traveled to Sicily to gather information from the files of the Palermo police department in identifying fugitives wanted in Sicily who had fled to New York and were known to Petrosino.

Only at the last minute, on the night of his murder in Palermo, did Petrosino, who represented a forerunner to Interpol as an information-gathering agent, learn that the Black Hand was not an organization but a system employed by the Mafia and the existence of the Mafia badly unnerved Petrosino. He was killed in 1909 while on a rendezvous to meet the then *capo dei capi* of all Sicily, Don Vito Cascio Ferro. Petrosino was shot and killed by one of Cascio Ferro's *caporegimes,* Paul di Cristina, while Ferro watched from a distance. Later Ferro himself, credited with more than twenty-five murders, claimed to have killed the feared Petrosino. "My action was a disinterested one," he was later quoted, "in response to a challenge I could not afford to ignore." This Mafia don was later sent to prison on Mussolini's orders, convicted of smuggling, but Don Vito Cascio Ferro continued to issue orders as boss of the Sicilian Mafia until he died in his cell.

Given the heterogeneous nature of the U. S., the Mafia system as practiced in Sicily did not fare well in America, where the Mafia had to control various vices and rackets to survive. Many U. S. cities were dominated by Italian or Sicilian gang chiefs and behind these men were the Mafia chiefs, extracting tribute from the gangsters for their operations through bogus brotherhoods such as the Unione Siciliane. In Chicago during the 1920s, Al Capone dominated the rackets, but behind him, taking tribute from Capone in the millions of dollars each year was the Unione Siciliane.

In Kansas City, Missouri, where politics was controlled

by the Pendergast Machine, the rackets were directed by gangsters Johnny Lazia, Frank "Chee Chee" DeMayo, and later Vincenzo Carrollo and Charles Binaggio. The real power behind these men were Mafia dons Joseph "Scarface" DiGiovanni and his brother, Pete "Sugarhouse" DiGiovanni. These brothers not only ran their own rackets but took a share of the spoils from the operations controlled by the more public gangsters such as Lazia and Carrollo. When the racket czars were either eliminated by rival gangs or were sent to prison, the more secretive Mafia dons survived through the decades unmolested for the most part by the police and the courts.

In St. Louis, the early-day Mafia was headed by John and Vito Giannola and Alphonse Palizzola, who had migrated from rural Sicily and were called "The Green Ones," in reference to their former occupations as farmers. New York during the Prohibition era was dominated by non-Italian gangs led by British-born Owen "Owney" Madden, Dutch Schultz, Jack "Legs" Diamond, Louis "Lepke" Buchalter, and Meyer Lansky. Only Lansky survived and thrived in the post-war era as a director of the board of the national syndicate that came to be dominated by Sicilians, who followed the strict Mafia structure of the family. Until his death in 2002 (even then behind bars) John Gotti, according to most reliable reports, was the *capo dei capi* in New York, with all five Mafia families representing the five different boroughs, paying tribute and allegiance to his family.

The traditions of the Mafia in the U.S., however, remain essentially the same as in days of old. Murder and other crimes are still viewed by Mafia members as "business," while these same members attend church on Sunday with their blood families. The oath of allegiance remains the same, a brief ceremony in which the initiate Mafia member is taken into a room and surrounded by Mafia members. A piece of paper with the image of a saint is then placed in the initiate's outstretched hand and the middle finger of the right hand is pricked and a few drops of blood spread across the paper. The paper is crumpled in the hand and set on fire while the initiate repeats the words: "I swear to be loyal to my brothers, never to betray them, and if I fail, may I burn and be turned to ashes like the ashes of the image."

This oath was taken by many Mafia members who later betrayed the criminal secret society, and was reported word for word by Nicola Gentile in the late 1920s in the U. S., by Joseph Valachi in the early 1930s in New York, and by Dr. Mechiore Allegra in Sicily in 1937. Moreover, the new Mafia member had to learn and accept the five cardinal rules of the society: 1) Reciprocal assistance to any Mafia faction in need without question (unless the factions were warring, of course), 2) Total obedience to the boss, 3) An attack on any Mafia member to be considered an attack on all members, to be avenged irrespective of circumstance, 4) No dealings with authorities in any circumstances, 5) The code of *omerta* (silence) to be maintained under penalty of death; the identities of Mafia members and the brotherhood's rites to be kept secret at all costs.

By the end of the 1920s, the U.S. Mafia had purged itself of such old-fashioned Mafia dons as the warring Joe "The Boss" Masseria and Salvatore Maranzano, replacing them with new, young gang bosses like Charles "Lucky" Luciano, Thomas "Three Finger Brown" Lucchese, Albert Anastasia, and Vito Genovese. These men, in turn, were replaced by even more subtle Mafia chiefs such as Carlo Gambino in New York, Carlos Marcello in New Orleans, Santo Trafficante in Florida, and Jack Dragna in California. The Mafia in Sicily had made inroads in establishing small chapters in Marseilles, in southern Italy, on Corsica, and in the coastal towns of Spain, but it remained a small-town society in Sicily and U. S. loyalty to Sicilian authority waned following World War II.

An early-day police photo of Luciano Liggio, who became Sicily's top Mafia don in the early 1960s after eliminating scores of rivals.

The U. S. Mafia (also known as the Cosa Nostra, meaning "this thing of ours"), by the 1980s, had invested billions of its illegal earnings from gambling, prostitution, and especially drug trafficking into legitimate businesses that produced even more profits. Today the Mafia in the U. S. is enormously rich and powerful and its tentacles reach into almost all areas of U.S. business. It works in cooperation with non-Sicilian criminals who are members of the same crime cartel known as the syndicate, which was once aptly described by one of its leading exponents, Meyer Lansky: "We are bigger than U. S. Steel."

From the time of the Mafia "maxi trials" in 1986-1987, in which 338 Mafiosi were convicted of organized crime, kidnapping, political corruption and murder, the Mafia in Sicily and Italy has gone into sharp decline. Although Mafia dons continue to control certain labor organizations and contracting firms throughout Italy and Sicily, their numbers have been winnowed down by the efforts of the Anti-Mafia Commission and law enforcement officials.

Mafia henchmen under arrest in Palermo, Sicily, 1935.

Mafia bosses await trial in Palermo, Sicily, in 1938, guarded by Cesare Mori's special police.

Mass trial of Mafia members in Palermo, Sicily, 1972; all went free.

The commission had induced many Mafia members to inform on their leaders in the 1980s, particularly chief informant Tommaso Buscetta, who was brought back to Italy from the U. S. In 1992, the commission again brought about sweeping arrests and convictions of the dreaded society members. More than ninety high-ranking Sicilian Mafia dons and their lieutenants were arrested and placed on trial, along with three members of Italy's Parliament and many small-town mayors, who had worked in collusion with the Cosa Nostra.

Most of the accused were convicted after it was proved that they had bribed politicians to award lucrative government contracts to Mafia-controlled construction companies, or had diverted government funds with the help of Mafia bankers from government accounts to those controlled by the Mafia as bogus loans. Buscetta had persuaded many middle-level Mafiosi to break the criminal brotherhood's code of *omerta* (silence), and testify against their superiors, with the guarantee from national police chief Vincenzo Parisi that they would be given new identities and homes outside of Italy, most likely in the U. S., as had been the case with Buscetta in 1984, when he began testifying for the government.

The successful campaign against the Mafia in 1992 was not without losses on the side of honest government. The two leading criminal prosecutors, Paolo Borsellino and Giovanni Falcone, who had grown up together in a Palermo slum and who dedicated their lives to eradicating the Mafia, proved so successful that the Mafia marked them for murder. Both were killed within two months of each other in 1992 bomb attacks. These brazen slayings shocked the nation and galvanized the anti-Mafia forces as never before, marking the turning point of Italy's struggle against the Mafia.

Tens of thousands marched in protest against the Mafia in the streets of Palermo, Messina and all over Sicily, as well as in southern towns of the Italian mainland. Mafia hoodlums were punched and kicked down the streets by mobs of angry citizens. Suddenly, it was no longer safe for Mafiosi to prowl and prey their ways through the narrow byways of Palermo, the dark domains they once controlled. In retaliation for the murders of Borsellino and Falcone, Leoluca Orlando, an avowed lifetime enemy of the Mafia, was swept into office as mayor of Palermo with a resounding seventy-five percent of the vote.

Orlando had been elected mayor of Palermo in 1985, following the first wave of Mafia convictions, holding the office until resigning in 1990 after breaking with the Mafia-controlled Christian-Democratic Party. With the zeal of a fundamentalist preacher, Orlando's stepped-up crusade against the criminal brotherhood saw good results. Palermo's inner city, once home to about 125,000, had dwindled to 39,000 by the mid-1990s, but Orlando helped to reclaim the center of the town by spending more than $250 million for renovation and clean-up, chanting his slogan into the ears of his fellow citizens: "The only way to beat the Mafia is for us to take the place of the Mafia."

Up to this time, the Mafia had been responsible for the urban shift of Palermo's population. From 1950 to 1980, the Mafia was responsible for building cheap concrete high rises through the building trades it controlled at the outskirts of the

A military policeman (carabiniere) and a Mafia gunman share equal authority at a polling place in Brancaccio, Sicily, a situation that did not change until anti-Mafia politician Leoluca Orlando was swept into office in the 1990s.

city, neglecting the expensive restoration of Palermo's historic inner city. The one exception was Palermo's once magnificent Teatro Massimo, Italy's largest opera house. Closed in 1974 for "minor repairs," the Mafia used this most wonderful of opera houses as a money pit. More than twenty billion lire was dumped into its renovation, with most of the money lining the pockets of Mafia-controlled contractors and their bosses, the Mafia dons of Sicily.

Orlando and his supporters stopped the flow of cash into that sinkhole, fired the Mafia contractors and brought in legitimate firms and craftsmen to restore the grand old opera house to its former magnificence. The freshly restored Teatro Massimo reopened in April 1998 to present a lavish production of Giuseppe Verdi's *Aida*.

Years before the opera reopened, the inner city of Palermo began to come to life with younger people moving back into the core of the town, artisans and craftsmen and new businesses opening everywhere. Orlando streamlined city services—installing a new lighting system to illuminate the once forbidding narrow backstreets, and picked up the trash and garbage, these services having formerly been controlled by Mafia contractors.

Moreover, Orlando, traveling about with forty bodyguards and in a bulletproof car (he was forever mindful of the fates that befell Falcone and Borsellino), replaced half of Palermo's police force with officers specially trained in combating Mafia tactics. As a result, the murder rate in Palermo, which averaged 130 to 140 each year, dropped to fewer than ten murders a year beginning in 1997.

Much of this was due to the considerable efforts of Guido Marino, head of Palermo's police mobile squad, which instantly responded to any street disturbance. The Mafia was not only in remission, it was going broke. Mafia dons resorted to the brazen kidnapping of wealthy businessmen all over Italy, holding these victims for millions, but most of its income trickled from petty crimes—loan-sharking, fencing stolen goods, extortion by selling protection to local shopkeepers, the old Black Hand technique, pay or suffer the destruction of goods and services and even death.

In Palermo, the protection racket was termed *pizzo*, but even this racket diminished under police pressure. Most merchants approached by Mafiosi demanding payments for *pizzo*, unlike their quaking predecessors, reported these incidents to the police and the extortionists were later ensnared in police stings and sent to prison.

The Mafia's fortunes throughout the world mirrored the hobbled Cosa Nostra in Sicily. In Europe, the Russian Mafia grabbed off rackets long controlled by the Italian-Sicilian Mafia—drugs, prostitution, gambling, arms-running to terrorist groups and rogue nations, even the stealing of nuclear fuels for the building of nuclear bombs. In the Far East, from Hawaii to Japan, the rackets were taken over by the Chinese Triads and Japan's Yakusa.

In the U. S., the Mafia lost ground everywhere to local street gangs, which took over control of illegal gambling and prostitution. The Colombian and Mexican drug cartels locked up the drug trade. The Mafia was reduced to operating penny ante rackets, specializing in loan sharking and extortion, but these rackets were repeatedly exposed and local dons, such as John Gotti in New York, were eventually jailed, mostly through money-grubbing confederates or plea-bargaining murderers who turned informer, such as Salvatore "Sammy the Bull" Gravano, who informed on his boss, Gotti.

The once powerful Genovese family in New York was ruled in the 1990s by a former hitman, Vincent "The Chin" Gigante, who had risen in status after his attempted murder of Mafia/syndicate chief Frank Costello. Gigante, however, was no "dapper don." He shuffled through the streets of Italian neighborhoods wearing slippers and a bathrobe, pretending to be mentally feeble, bodyguards leading him by the arm. This shabby idiot act did not fool law enforcement officials, or prosecutors, who convicted the Mafia boss of conspiracy and sent him to prison in 1997.

In California, Salvatore "Bill" Bonanno, the son of the once-powerful Mafia boss, Joe "Bananas" Bonanno, was reduced to running sleazy building repair rackets and went to jail for it. "Joe Bananas" Bonanno, could not lift a finger to prevent his son's incarceration. He had retired to Tucson, Arizona, puttering about his backyard, dying there powerless. In Chicago, top Mafia hitmen like Harry Aleman were sent to prison, as were mob bosses like Gus Alex, also sold out by former associates. Though the Mafia lingers, it is a sinister giant suffering from arthritis, gout and rheumatism, one that loses more ground each day as it crawls from reality to legend.

Many legends surround the Mafia in the U. S., but none more cruel nor misleading than that which was put forth by Mario Puzo in his crime fantasy, *The Godfather,* one where certain members of the Mafia are shown to be humane, patriotic, considerate, compassionate, fair, and honorable, at least in loyalty to their blood families and to their Mafia families, irrespective of the horrid crimes they commit, and these crimes are offered up as expediencies to business.

Nothing, of course, could be further from the truth. The Mafia is criminal to the core and continues to prey on the unsuspecting and the innocent, murdering its way through the ages to preserve a secret criminal society that has, unfortunately, become part of the American fabric and the American myth itself.

THE ORDER OF THE ASSASSINS/1100s-1200s

The Order of the Assassins (AKA: Alamut, Ismaili, Hashashin, Old Men of the Mountains) had its origin in the Ismaili sect of Islam, then Persia, later Syria-Iraq, in the late eleventh century. Hasan ibn-al-Sabah, the spiritual leader of the Ismailis, pioneered the use of political murder in his quest to unify Islamic lands under his leadership. His elaborate plans for the deaths of his enemies and the use of mind control techniques to manipulate his followers are commonly employed in the modern world, especially by his self-appointed successor, Osama bin Laden, leader of the terrorist group, Al Qaeda.

Hasan, known to his contemporaries and to history as "The Old Man of the Mountains," had vision to match his ambition. Hasan had a garden constructed in his fortress of Alamut ("Eagle's Nest"), in the Elburz Mountains, which Marco Polo described in detail: "He had caused a certain valley between two mountains to be enclosed, and had turned it into a garden, the largest and most beautiful that was ever seen, filled with every variety of fruit. In it were erected pavilions and palaces the most elegant that can be imagined, all covered with gilding and exquisite painting. And there were runnels too, flowing freely with wine and milk and honey and water; and numbers of ladies and of the most beautiful damsels in the world, who could play on all manner of instruments, and sung most sweetly, and danced in a manner that it was charming to behold. For the Old Man desired to make his people believe that this was actually Paradise."

Volunteers for Hasan's murder assignments (suicide missions) were drugged and taken to the garden, where their sensual desires were indulged for days. (Although these future assassins did not take drugs while committing their crimes, their use of hashish or opium, as Marco Polo believed led to the group being called Hashashin. This name was later corrupted by Europeans during the Crusades to the present day designation: assassin.) Later, Hasan told his assassins that this was the paradise that awaited anyone who died in his service. Since they would go to paradise whether or not they were successful in killing their intended victims, the volunteers fought without fear of death or injury. Hasan had so much control of his followers that if he ordered it, they would jump from windows to their death, just to impress visitors.

The first victim of one of Hasan's assassins was Nizam-al-Mulk, grand vizier of Turkey and author of the *Book of Government,* a work on political economy. At the beginning of his administration, Nizam had his predecessor, Wazir Kundruri, assassinated. Before he died, Kundruri sent Nizam the message that he hoped that the same fate would befall him. Hasan dispatched one of his fanatics to kill Nizam in 1092. The assassin, disguised as a holy man, stabbed the Vizier in the chest when allowed access to "bless" Nizam. Subsequently, a member of the sect disguised as a beggar murdered Nizam's son, Fakhri, who had sworn to avenge his father's death.

Fakhri's brother Ahmed, besieged Hasan's mountain fortress, but could not break through its defenses, and ultimately became a target for assassination himself. He survived, but never avenged his father's and brother's deaths. Another leader preparing to attack Hasan was convinced to negotiate a truce with him when he awoke one morning to find a knife buried to the hilt in the ground beside his bed.

Hasan was born in Rey, Persia, (now a suburb of Tehran, Iran). The fanaticism he cultivated among his followers sharply contrasted his early life. He was raised in the Shiite faith, which his family practiced in secret for fear of Sunnite persecution, but he converted to Ismailiism as a young man, attracted by the sect's concept of equating heaven with wisdom and hell with ignorance.

Hasan traveled widely during his youth, visiting Egypt in 1078, when it was beset with extreme religious factional-

Hasan, shown wearing crown, administers drugged wine to his fanatical followers at his mountain stronghold, Alamut; he founded the sect known as the Order of the Assassins and was called "the Old Man of the Mountain."

The first significant assassination committed on Hasan's order, the murder of Nizam-al-Mulk, stabbed to death by a fanatical member of the Order of the Assassins in 1092.

Alamut under siege by Hulagu's forces in 1256; the stronghold was taken, but the assassins retook the city two decades later and were not extinguished for another fifty years; Osama bin Laden resurrected the Order of the Assassins as Al Qaeda in the 1980s.

ism. It was during this time that he began formulating the principles of his sect, which included hostility to anyone with different views and a demand of absolute blind obedience from his adherents. By the time he returned to Persia, he was adept at both political manipulation and proselytizing. He took over the Alamut fortress in a bloodless coup in 1090.

Hasan's followers, the *fidais,* were chosen for their good health, inventiveness, and intelligence, as well as their devotion to him. Hasan was an elitist, who believed that the common people had to be controlled with a firm hand. Those in whom he saw the special qualities he sought received extensive training in killing techniques, the cultural backgrounds of their enemies, and the Koran's description of paradise.

With this ultimate control of his followers, Hasan was unassailable in his mountain fortress, and caused great fear in religious and political foes. Hasan, however, never succeeded in his ambitions, though he lived until about the age of ninety. Historians have theorized that the success of his terrorism actually caused his failure. Though no one dared to actively oppose his leadership, neither did the common people actively support him in consolidating additional power.

Another Old Man of the Mountain, Hasan's spiritual descendant Sheik Sinan, prevented Sultan Saladin from gaining control over the Islamic world. Saladin was the Fatimid Khalif's grand vizier and ruler of Egypt. Sinan's political influence extended over Syria, Egypt, and other countries, while at the same time, Saladin was attempting to unify these lands under one Muslim rule. To stop such a plan, Sinan teamed his assassins with Latins, Shiites, and Sunnites. Sinan's fidais continually beleaguered Saladin, but the conqueror escaped death just as often. After repeated failed assassination attempts, a truce was agreed upon. Sinan agreed to call off his men and Saladin agreed not to attack Sinan's territories.

The skill of the fidais during this era was reflected in the assassination of the crusader Conrad of Montferrat. Along with their accomplishments in stealth, martial arts, and disguise, these assassins were fluent in the Frankish language and intimate with Christian liturgical ritual, allowing them to infiltrate the Crusaders' camps disguised as monks. Just such a group of assassins lived among their enemies for six months before killing Conrad in a church. Many other Western leaders of the Third Crusade, especially Richard the Lionheart, king of England, had been marked for a similar fate, but Richard was so well protected that the assassins could not approach him.

The power of the Old Men of the Mountain was broken when Hulagu, grandson of Genghis Khan and leader of the Mongol Empire's western front, marched upon assassin strongholds. The fortresses in Syria were subjugated by the Mamluk Sultan of Egypt, Baybars, and henceforth governed by Mamluk overlords. In the east, Hulagu captured one after another of the sect's fortresses, culminating with the fall of Alamut in 1256. The last Old Man of the Mountain, Rukn al-Din Khurshah, surrendered to Hulagu, who later had Khurshah and 12,000 of his people killed. Alamut was recaptured by the assassins in 1275, but was lost again the following year.

The assassin sect all but vanished (some scholars contend that the Thuggee sect of India was possibly an offshoot of the Ismailite assassins) and was no longer a threat to governing bodies. Today, Ismailis still thrive in central Asia, Syria, and Iran under the spiritual guidance of Osama bin Laden (see Terrorism).

THE CHINESE TRIADS/1674-present

The Triads of China and greater Southeast Asia (AKA: Dagger Society, Heaven & Earth Society, Hung Society, Red Society) pose as great a threat to law and order in their corner of the world as does the Mafia in the U. S. The Triads date back to the late seventeenth century, the time of the Ch'ing dynasty.

The Triads were sects organized to overthrow the oppressive yoke of the Ch'ing emperors, whose armies originated in Manchuria and marched south to conquer and subjugate the

Ming dynasty. The Chinese in the southern provinces regarded the Ch'ings, and their emperor K'ang-Hsi, as foreign invaders. They took refuge at the Siu Lam monastery in the Fukien Province, where the Buddhist monks aided and abetted the military uprising fomented by the Mings. The monastery, according to popular legend, was surrounded by the Ch'ing army and blown up.

There were only eighteen survivors, of which thirteen eventually died from starvation and powder burns. The remaining five crossed the Yangtze River, managing to stay one step ahead of the pursuing Ch'ing armies. The fugitives of the Siu Lam monastery were henceforth known as the "First Five Ancestors," a story that is more allegory than fact. Continuing on to Muk Yeung in the Fukien Province, these five survivors joined five other loyal supporters of the cause being known as the "Second Five Ancestors," who estab-

A Triad leaflet distributed in the 1890s shows a xenophobic China as a lion about to devour pigs and goats, labeled in Chinese "Christians and Westerners."

European troops who have relieved Peking, are "entertained" by the decapitation of a captured Boxer in 1900; the Boxers worked in cooperation with the Triads to unsuccessfully drive out the European armies from China.

The San Francisco *Call* portrayed this "hatchet man" in 1900, one of the many executioners of the Chinese tongs (Triads) in San Francisco's Chinatown, who "dispatched" the society's enemies.

This sketch claims to show the initiation of a new member to a Chinese Triad in 1898; the initiate holds aloft a bowl containing blood and wine, which he will drink after chanting his vows of secrecy and loyalty to the criminal society.

Triad leader Fong Ching (Little Pete), an inmate at Folsom Prison, 1887; released, he reclaimed his old tong, but was killed in 1894.

A typical opium den operated by a Triad in the 1900s; the distribution of this drug, and later heroin, made untold millions for the "Chinese Mafia."

Sun Yat-Sen, China's first president, shown center of approaching officers in 1911, overthrew the Ch'ing dynasty; as a Triad official, he backed the secret criminal society in expanding its opium growth and distribution throughout Asia.

General Kot Siu-wong, founder of the 14K Association, the most feared of all Chinese Triads.

A handcuffed Triad member under arrest in Singapore, identified as a member of the Chinese secret criminal society by the tattoos on his arms.

Chung Mon, Triad boss in Amsterdam, who was shot to death on March 3, 1975, by three assassins from another Triad before he could get into his bullet-proof Mercedes.

Police photo of a Hong Kong heroin factory seized in 1978. Thousands of such factories operate around the clock throughout Asia, producing a billion-dollar business.

lished a city as a home base of operations for the fledgling "Triad Society." The Triad, symbolizing heaven, earth, and man, was divided into five lodges in five provinces of China, each under a separate banner.

The initial aim of the Triad movement was to overthrow the brutally oppressive Manchus. Their motto was "Overthrow Ch'ing; Restore Ming." But in 1736, the society was suppressed and driven into exile throughout the provinces. In the next sixty years there were a series of bloody insurrections, notably by the Eight Diagrams and Nine Mansions Sects in 1786-88, the Heaven and Earth Society in 1786-89, and the White Lotus sect in 1794 that dragged on for eight years. The influential White Lotus was a religious sect that took up arms only in times of extreme persecution. Such was the case in 1794.

According to a Chinese imperial decree published in 1813, the White Lotus "was engaged in daily worship ... and reading scripture, claiming thereby to make its members invulnerable to weapons, fire or drowning; but in times of famine and disorder they might plot for the Great Enterprise." Future Triads called the Big Swords, Red Spears, Yellow Beards, Small Daggers, and Dragon Flowers were organized on this principle.

The power of the Triads continued to grow and in 1851 the great Taiping Rebellion nearly toppled the government of the Manchus. With the popular support of villagers in the southern provinces, the Taipings, led by Hung Hsiu-Chu'an, scored a series of impressive military victories over the Manchu armies. In 1853, Hung seized Nanking, where he declared himself emperor. The Triads conquered Shanghai, Amoy, and several other important cities in a ten-year rebellion that cost 20,000 lives and decimated some of the richest land in the country. In 1864, Hung Hsiu-Ch'uan committed suicide after his military forces were crushed by the combined forces of the British and Chinese statesman Li Hung-Chang.

Triad enforcer Georgie Pai (Yau Lap Leun) attempted to take over London's Chinatown by establishing a widespread protection racket; he was imprisoned, then deported back to his native Hong Kong in 1979.

The focus of the secret societies began to shift in the next fifty years as the Manchu base of power was eroded by the foreign interventionists. The Boxer rebellion, or the *I Ho Chuan,* meaning "The Fists of Righteous Harmony," began in Shantung in 1898 and was aimed at the final expulsion of

Triad heroin dealers May Wong and her lover, Li Mah, who were sent to prison for fourteen years.

Triad boss Ng Sik-ho, right, under arrest, worked with the Sicilian Mafia to distribute heroin and cocaine worldwide; he was sent to prison for thirty years.

European and American interests which had encroached on the economic and social life of the nation. The Boxers' reliance on mysticism and the power of the supernatural did them little good, for the mainland of China was soon back in Western hands following the capture of Peking on August 14, 1900. (The Boxers represented another type of Chinese Triad or criminal secret society, one which was, like the Order of the Assassins in Persia, dedicated to the assassination of all foreign leaders.)

In 1911, the Manchus were deposed and the Triads were recognized by Dr. Sun Yat-Sen, himself a former member. The Republican Revolution provided them with a degree of legitimacy previously unheard of in China. Bureaucrats and politicians scrambled to join the secret societies in order to enhance their prestige and reputation in the government. Triad influence was soon felt in Hong Kong, Malaya, and Singapore. In 1925, a power struggle in Malaya resulted in a five-way split between the 18, 24, 36, 108, and Independent Groups. (The five groups honored the five founding monks. Eighteen and thirty-six are the number of monks who escaped the massacre at the monastery, and the number 108 corresponds to the number at Shaolin).

From its revolutionary beginnings, the Triads evolved into secret criminal societies, embracing organized crime, extortion, drug trafficking, prostitution and white slavery. Following the 1949 Communist takeover, British Hong Kong became the center of the criminal activity in Southeast Asia. Seven Triad groups masquerading under the guise of trade guilds and fraternal societies vied for the control of the criminal rackets. Before 1941 only eight percent of the population in Hong Kong belonged to Triad societies. This figure grew to a staggering fifteen percent by 1958.

After the 1949 Communist Revolution, the Green Pang Triad, made up of political refugees from the mainland, who had fought with the Nationalists, dominated prostitution, labor unions, and the narcotics trade on a large scale. The Green Pang was one of the oldest established Triads whose members belonged to the higher socio-economic classes. By the mid-1950s, the 14K Association, originally organized to do battle with the Communists, had become Hong Kong's second-most powerful criminal gang. Conservative estimates placed total membership in the area at 80,000 by 1954. The threat posed by the 14K Association compelled the other Triads to bolster their memberships.

To be admitted into a Triad carried with it a heavy obligation, the penalty of death for violating the tenets of the secret oath-bound brotherhood. There are thirty-six such oaths a new member must swear. Those who refused to join the Triads were branded as pro-Communist, a tactic encouraged by the Nationalist government led by Generalissimo Chiang Kai-shek.

The growth of the Triads during this period led to serious incidents of rioting and gang wars in 1956, forcing the Hong Kong police to enact stern measures to deal with the problem. The Triads pillaged more than $25 million worth of goods during the civil disturbance. There were 900 murders in Hong Kong in 1958, most of them attributed to the Triad societies.

An example of the ferocious bloodletting that went on in Hong Kong during those troubled times involved a prosperous merchant named Ko Sun Wei, who lived in the city of Kowloon. Wei, two daughters, one son, and his wife were found dead in their home. The women were raped repeatedly and then tortured to death with knives. The Ko Sun Wei family were but five of the 350 murder victims entered into the police records for September 1958.

Today the Triads control the bulk of the drug trade and street prostitution in Hong Kong (even after the Communist take-over of that city) and Singapore. Though they were outlawed by the British colonial government as far back as 1845, the Triads continue to operate with impunity. In Singapore alone, there are at least 9,000 active members belonging to six different groups. Despite the thrust of technology and profound Western influence, the Triads endure as a formidable criminal network.

THE YAKUZA OF JAPAN/1600s-present

In 1988, the citizens of Ebitsuka, Japan, launched a campaign to rid their community of some unwanted neighbors. A five-story green building housed what they believed to be the headquarters of a formidable criminal Yakuza gang known as *Ichiriki Ikka,* or "One Power Family." The citizens of Ebitsuka erected a two-level shack across the street and videotaped the movements of all visitors entering and leaving the building. After one surly gangster attacked the surveillance team with a sword, the townspeople gathered outside the green building they referred to as the *burakku biru* or "black building." "Get out!" they chanted. "Seek an honorable life!" National media attention was focused on the case, as the town's eight-member police force was bolstered with an additional 300 officers from other communities.

The nearby city of Hamamatsu set up a police task force of 120 officers to stand guard against illegal activities. Eventually, half of the Yakuza in the town were jailed or put in detention. In April 1988, Tetsuya Aono, the chief of the *Ichiriki-Ikka,* agreed to settle the suit out of court and abandon the Yakuza headquarters building in Ebitsuka. The anti-yakuza banners were taken down by the happy residents as the gangsters sneaked out of town. It was a small, but important victory in an escalating war against organized crime in Asia, a growing menace with larger implications for the industrial nations of the west.

The history of the Yakuza can be traced back to 1612, during the time of the *machi-yakko* a popular band of young rebels who defied the murderous Samurai warlords. According to criminologist Kanehiro Hoshino of Japan's Police Science Research Institute, the shogunate rounded up and executed the last of the *machi-yakko* in 1686. The exploits of this gang of "Robin Hoods" are kept alive in the folk tales and kabuki plays of the Japanese.

Yakuza gangs first appeared in the mid-1700s. Like the Italian Mafia, the gangs were divided into families; however, in the Yakuza, the father-child role, or *oyabun-kobun,* which mirrored traditional Japanese society, played an important role. Just as the father was the supreme authority figure in the family, he was also the master of the apprentice's destiny in the yakuza. *Oyabun-kobun* provided strength and cohesion, which ultimately translated into blind obedience to the "boss" or criminal ruler. "If the boss says that a passing crow is white, you must agree," states a Yakuza adage.

In the late 19th Century, as Japan threw off the last vestiges of feudalism, a schism developed within the Yakuza. Many of its members sided with the Tokugawa shogunate; others joined with the emperor. The ultimate victor was Jirocho no Shimizu, the boss of the *bakuto* or gambling empire. When Jirocho died in 1893, he was revered by the peasant classes as a wise and just bandit leader. In the early years of the 20th Century, Japan modernized, and within a few decades, became the leading industrial power of Southeast Asia.

The Yakuza also adapted to the profound social changes around them and many of its members joined the sinister Black Dragon Society, headed by Mitsuru Toyama. The Black Dragon Society was dedicated to nationalism and the development of what Japanese officials later termed the "co-prosperity sphere," which meant that Japan intended to invade and dominate all of Southeast Asia. Before its aggressions into Korea and China, however, Yakuza gangs gained a toehold in the big cities by organizing groups of industrial workers for construction projects. The bosses of the lucrative *bakuto* gangs organized legitimate business fronts to cover their illegal activities, while the *tekiya* factions, which controlled thousands of peddler's stalls in the large cities, cultivated important ties to the politicians and police officials.

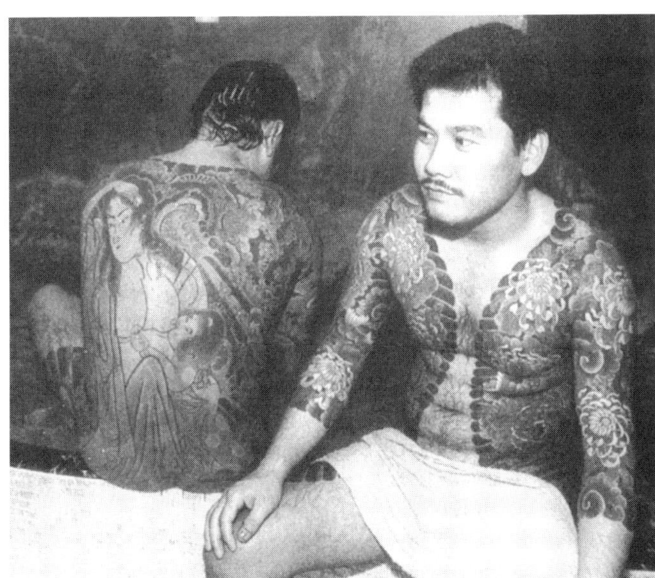

Two members of Yakuza show the extensive tattoos coating their bodies, a mark of rank in this criminal secret society.

Yakuza chief Kodama Yoshio, left, with aides; he was the supreme crime boss in Japan throughout the 1960s-1970s.

Yakuza gangsters battling during a meeting at the Mitsubishi Shoji Corporation.

Takeshi Takagi, left, the Yakuza boss in Honolulu, Hawaii, beginning in 1978.

The nationalist fervor that swept Japan in the first two decades of the 20th Century started in the 1880s, when Mitsuru Toyama organized a group of right-wing toughs from Fukuoka into the *Genyosha,* Black Dragon Society or "Dark Ocean Society," the latter a reference to the narrow passage of water separating Japan from Korea and China. This group spawned hundreds of secret societies in East Asia including the "Blood Pledge Corps," the "Association for Heavenly Action," and the "Death-Defying Corps" terrifying names for an organized crime network that oversaw prostitution, gambling, extortion, drugs, and street peddling. The Yakuza gangs realized that their success was intrinsically tied to the fortunes of the political right.

Neither the Yakuza nor the right-wingers wished to see their influence diminished by socialist coalitions. After World War II, such pre-war nationalists as Kodama Yoshio, Kishi Nobu-suke, and Sasakawa Ryoichi forged alliances with the Yakuza to vanquish their enemies on the left. In 1960, for example, the rightists assassinated Socialist Party leader Asanuma Inejiro, his killers being Yakuza assassins.

The very nature of the Yakuza changed after World War II. Swords were replaced by guns and the gangsters assumed a more western appearance. The *kobun* abandoned traditional folk dress in order to copy their counterparts in the Mafia. Dark suits and sunglasses became the preferred attire among a new generation of toughs. By 1958, the Tokyo police estimated that there were 70,000 Yakuza in the whole of Japan. Five years later this figure grew to 184,000, by far the largest organized crime network in the world. The most formidable of the gangs to emerge after the war was the *Yamaguchi-gumi*, originally a small waterfront mob in Kobe before it was given direction by Taoka Kazuo, Japan's Al Capone.

Taoka bossed 343 different gangs by 1964. His influence in the Osaka region was particularly strong. Here the syndicate was said to control eighty percent of all cargo loading on the Kobe docks. Across Japan there were other Yakuza gangs of lesser stature, which nonetheless employed the same viciousness in their methods. In Yokohama, the ruler of the criminal underworld was Inagawa Kakuji, whose *Kakusei-kai* gang (later called *Kinsei-kai*) claimed 2,700 members by the mid-1960s. The most important source of revenue for Kakusei was gambling.

On October 24, 1972, the Inagawa gang and the powerful Yamaguchi were united in a federation by the visionary gangster Kodama Yoshio. As a ranking member of the rightist Liberal-Democratic Party, Kodama desired to bring about permanent harmony between the warring clans. More than anything, he feared that the leftists would exploit the factional rivalries and eventually eclipse the LDC in power. The amalgamation of the Yamaguchi and Inagawa empires brought the majority of Japanese gangs under their control.

By the 1970s, Yakuza gangs were reported to be active in Thailand, Malaysia, Hong Kong, and Taiwan, where they forged important links with the Chinese Triads. The specter of an all-powerful Chinese-Japanese Mafia controlling the international drug trade alarmed western observers, who feared that the gangs were on the brink of funding large-scale shipments to the U.S. and Europe. In September 1985 for example, the U.S. and the Hong Kong police took ten people into custody, who were charged with smuggling fifty-two pounds of amphetamines and twelve pounds of heroin into the states.

Two high-ranking members of *Yamaguchi-gumi* were picked up in Hawaii where they were to serve as "point men" for the deal. As Inagawa Kakuji explained: "Ultimately the Yakuza will become like the U.S. Mafia. In the future there'll be one national mob. Like my organization the biggest firms will take over. You can see the move towards a more corporate structure." He warned of a lack of respect for traditional morality, a concern reflected in an ever-increasing murder rate in Japan. By the 1990s, the Yakuza accounted for about one-third of all the murders committed in Japan and some sixty percent of blackmail cases.

A decade earlier, Yakuza all but wrecked Japan's once-booming economy. During the 1980s, Japan's banking system, with many Yakuza members at the helms of banks, made enormous loans to developers and building firms that were nothing more than fronts for the Yakuza's illegal operations, loans the bankers knew would never be repaid. This led to the establishment of ultra-secret banking records, where such loans could not be disclosed. By the mid-1990s, intelligence reports held that the top bankers in Japan, chiefly those in Tokyo, had come under suspicion of being members (high-echelon directors) of the secret criminal society, Yakuza, and had umbilical ties to Yakuza's enforcement-collection arm, Sokaiya.

The more than $600 billion in defaulted loans, which caused the Far East economic crisis of the late 1990s, were made by Japanese bankers and chiefs of security firms, who were Yakuza members themselves, to Yakuza directors of development firms and other businesses in the private sector. In some cases, huge, unsecured loans were made directly to Yakuza members. Kunjii Miyazaki, chairman of the Dai-Ichi Kangyo Bank (which claimed to have had more assets than Citibank and Bankers Trust combined), loaned 30 billion yen to Ryuichi Koike, chief extortionist of Yakuza's strong-arm organization, Sokaiya. When confronted with this loan by Japanese regulators, Miyazaki excused himself, went to his study and promptly committed suicide.

The Japanese banks had lamely attempted to collect the bad debts by seizing collateral, but this measure utterly failed. One report held that such collections were intended to fail, that such attempts were merely lame-duck gestures by bankers, who were themselves Yakuza members attempting to pacify the demands of banking investigators. The regulators themselves may have been Yakuza members, who were compelled to act because "outsiders" unearthed information on the criminal loans. When Sumitomo Bank *appeared* to aggressively seize collateral for an outstanding loan in Nagoya, its branch manager, who had been instructed to seize assets, was murdered by Yakuza thugs.

In August 1997, Koichiro Tarutani, an executive of Yamaichi Securities (this firm having loaned crime boss Koike 79 million yen), was murdered in Tokyo, while walking home, slashed to death, as if his killers had employed a Samurai sword—the traditional weapon of the Yakuza. (The shopkeeper, who found Tarutani crying for help, stated: "His guts were spilling out. I was so shocked I couldn't sleep that night.") This murder, like so many others dealing with Japan's financial community, remained unsolved. One report insisted that the investigations into such murders were purposely sluggish in that they were directed by high-ranking police officials, who were also Yakuza members.

For years, Japanese bankers used Yakuza and Sokaiya members as collection enforcers on bad debts. Real estate developers used Yakuza thugs to forcibly evict tenants from desirous locations. Over time, however, Yakuza placed members inside the banks and then recruited the top banking officials, as well as top officials in real estate, business, manufacturing, finance, securities firms, government, police and military to its ranks (under penalty of death).

The control of Japan's finances, banking and government was considered by many to essentially be in the hands of the Yakuza by the late 1990s. Much like the Masons, there are degrees of rank in the Yakuza, signified by the number and type of tattoos to be found on the bodies of Yakuza members, and this would include leading bankers, financiers and government officials. When Dai-Ichi chairman Miyazaki's body was examined following his suicide, it was reported that his body was coated, from neck to ankles, with Yakuza tattoos.

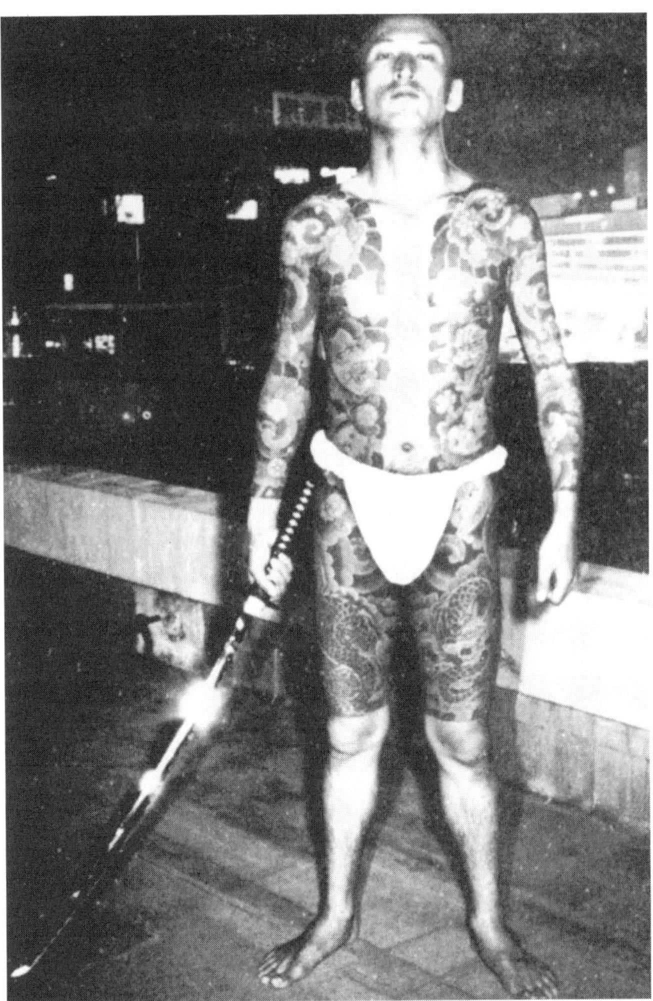

A tattooed Yakuza gangster in Tokyo, Japan, holding a samurai sword, the very kind of weapon that was used in the 1990s to murder bank inspectors and officials examining the staggering loans made by Japan's banks to Yakuza firms and members.

Japan's Ministry of Finance (MOF) was rife with Yakuza members at that time. MOF had a practice of "arm-twisting" in the back rooms of its government offices. Japan's entire economy was, in intelligence parlance, run "extralegally." One report stated that Hideo Sakamaki, one-time president of Nomura Securities, was a Yakuza member, as was Tadashi Okuda, former chairman of the Dai-Ichi Kangyo Bank. The more than $600 billion in loans made by Japanese banks in recent years went largely to real estate developers, the bankers and the developers both being reported as Yakuza members.

These loans made up more than half of Japan's bad real estate loans.

Some of the Yakuza-controlled banks attempted to "re-package" their bad debts in the form of bonds to be sold to investors. One such overseas deal by Japanese banks involved $1 billion in medium-term notes, which were reportedly backed by Yakuza loan-shark assets, as well as other illegal operations (brothels and opium distribution that trail to Hawaii and Mexico). Japan's Ministry of Finance had unofficially admitted that its country was in the grip of the Yakuza, one of its top officials stating (off the record): "I do not think it can be rooted out." At this writing, that official's estimation of this all-powerful secret criminal society still applies.

THE MURDEROUS MAU MAU OF KENYA/ 1950-1956

In response to the British annexation of lands traditionally held by members of the Kikuyu tribe in Kenya, a secret criminal society called Mau Mau was formed for the purpose of removing European settlers from the natives' lands. The disputed area, a fertile Highland region bounded by Mount Kenya, Nairobi, the Aberdare Mountains, and Nyeri, had been inhabited by the Kikuyu since the late sixteenth century. Much of the land had previously belonged to a smaller tribe of hunter-gatherers called the Wanderobo. In some cases, a single Wanderobo family would own as much as forty square miles. Although the Kikuyu had the numbers and the strength to take the Wanderobo's land by force, their religious beliefs and legal customs precluded it. Consequently, Kikuyus who wanted land negotiated for it by bartering animals or other goods. The Kikuyu would also propose a ceremony of "mutual adoption" which, by making the Wanderobo an adopted Kikuyu, validated the transaction.

Kikuyu settlements had sprung up throughout Nyeri, Muranga, and the Kiambu district by the late 19th Century. Toward the turn of the century, the country was stricken with an epidemic of smallpox, an outbreak of rinderpest, and a severe drought leading to famine and a locust plague. From twenty to fifty percent of the population died.

Most of the Kikuyu who had settled in the Kiambu district left their farms and moved to Nyeri and Fort Hall. Despite the fact that by 1902 many Kikuyu farms had reverted to bush, the owners of the property considered their separation from the land to be only a temporary condition. In 1902, the Kenya-Uganda railroad, begun six years earlier, reached the Kikuyu territory, bringing large numbers of European settlers.

Seeing what appeared to be virgin land, the European colonists began dividing the area into farms. Where a Kikuyu farmer had remained on the land, the colonist purchased the land. For the Europeans, this constituted legal ownership of the land, whereas for the Kikuyu, as demonstrated by the practice of mutual adoption they went through with the Wanderobo, it did not. This misunderstanding was greatly compounded by the British ignorance of Kikuyu law and custom.

Because other African tribes with whom they had experience did not have private land ownership, the British settlers assumed that no African tribe did. All of the uncultivated land was designated as "Crown Land," with the exception of areas called "Reserves" that were set aside for the native population. Large areas of the Kiambu district were given to European farmers.

Kenya's foremost leader Jomo Kenyatta, shown in 1945 at the Pan African Congress, held in Manchester, England.

At first the Kikuyu attempted to adjust to the situation by seeking jobs in the cities. Those who went to Nairobi, however, found they were unable to find employment that would support them. When they sought political help in balancing the obviously unequal conditions between whites and natives, they encountered the Kenya Civil Service, an agency of government officers set up ostensibly to protect native Kenyans' interests against the settlers. This paternalistic structure, if benignly intentioned, nonetheless ultimately served white interests over that of the native Kenyans.

In 1923, when European and Indian settlers lobbied for greater representation in the legislative council, the British government stated: "The interests of the African natives must be paramount. If, and when, those interests, and the interests of the immigrant races should conflict, the former should prevail." As supportive of the native Africans as this statement sounded, the reality of their position was tenuous at best. Eleven council members represented 10,000 Europeans, five members represented more than 2,300 Indians, while only one member each represented the Arab and African communities. The African representative, however, was not African himself until 1944.

The Lancashire Fusilliers, flown from Egypt in Britain's longest military airlift, arrive in Nairobi, assuring whites and intimidating black Mau Mau members after British authorities declared a state of emergency in Kenya on October 20, 1952.

The growing skepticism of the African nationalists about the possibility of equitable treatment at the hands of the British increased after World War I. Following the war, many Kikuyu attempted to return to their lands in Kiambu only to discover that they had been taken over by white settlers. A group of ex-servicemen and ex-mission school students formed the Kikuyu Central Association (KCA) in 1922.

The KCA began operating after the arrest of Harry Thuku, president of the Young Kikuyu Association, for leading a protest against the government. Its activities were forced underground when colonial police shot and killed followers of Thuku during a demonstration in March 1922. The basis of their organization—the recovery of the lands traditionally held by the Kikuyu—foreshadowed the aims and battle cry of Mau Mau.

In 1940, the KCA was outlawed by the government, which claimed that the group had established treasonable ties with Italian agents in Ethiopia. In 1944, Eliud Mathu (recently nominated as the first African representative in the legislature) founded the Kenyan African Union (KAU). The aims of the KAU were the same as the KCA, and former KCA members, along with many new recruits, filled the ranks of the new organization.

In 1946, Jomo Kenyatta (or Johnstone Kamau), who was named general secretary of the KCA in 1928, returned to Kenya after a sixteen-year stay in England. Kenyatta, born in the Kiambu district, had entered politics in 1922 by joining the Young Kikuyu Association. When he returned to Kenya, he was appointed principal of the Kenya Teacher's College in Githunguri and he offered his services to the legislative council, but Governor Sir Philip Mitchell suggested Kenyatta re-

Esme Ruck and her son Michael were hacked to pieces at their ranch, along with Roger Ruck in 1953 by invading Mau Mau assassins.

Mau Mau members are shown surrendering to British troops after a pitched battle in the jungle. The Mau Mau forces fought with the zeal of fanatics, but had poor leadership and limited arms.

Black Kenyan troops, members of the King's African Rifles, are shown whipping Kikuyu women with switches in an effort to obtain information on the sect's hiding places.

While Dana Wynter looks down in horror, Rock Hudson discovers the body of a white female settler in Kenya, who has been slaughtered by Mau Mau killers in the 1957 film, *Something of Value*.

Boys and men rounded up in a Nairobi shantytown by British troops went through severe interrogations to determine actual Mau Mau members; suspects were given starvation rations and many were beaten to death.

A Kikuyu medicine man is shown conducting a ceremony where Mau Mau members can be released from their vows and thus identify themselves as sect members to British authorities.

familiarize himself with Kenyan politics on the local level before entering into them nationally. Kenyatta started recruiting for the KAU and was elected its president in 1947. At this point Kenyatta's power as a leader of the KAU depended completely on his willingness to follow the will of the group.

The secret society known as the Mau Mau (a phrase which was a corruption of "*Uma, Uma*" meaning "Out! Out!") had its beginning during this period. The KAU was allegedly used by the early Mau Mau to propagate their own organization, and it was likely that Kenyatta was not the leader of the Mau Mau movement. The Mau Mau oath, called the Oath of Unity, *Ndemwa Ithatu,* was administered in a ceremony that incorporated many tribal elements.

The first oath a Mau Mau inductee took was a pledge of his loyalty to the cause of restoring the Kikuyu's lands. The only specific requirement of this level of membership was a small donation to the organization's funds. Successive levels of membership were accompanied by different oaths requiring greater commitment. The most extreme level of oath was the *Batuni* or Platoon oath, which required the initiate to kill.

By 1952, the KAU was merely a front for Mau Mau. The goals of Mau Mau, as viewed by whites, were to recover lost lands, self govern, wipe out Christianity, restore tribal customs, force out all foreigners, end soil terracing, and increase secular education. As the organization became more and more widespread, recruitment methods became more aggressive. In many cases, reluctant Kikuyu were forced to take the oath under threat of death if they refused.

Mau Mau also began using arson to intimidate others

The Kikuyu village of Lani, which had rebelled against the Mau Mau and was burned to the ground, its inhabitants murdered to the last child on March 26. 1953.

Mau Mau leader Waruhiu Itote, center, who called himself "General China," and who commanded forces on Mount Kenya, is shown standing trial in Nyeri in 1954; he saved his life by informing on other Mau Mau leaders.

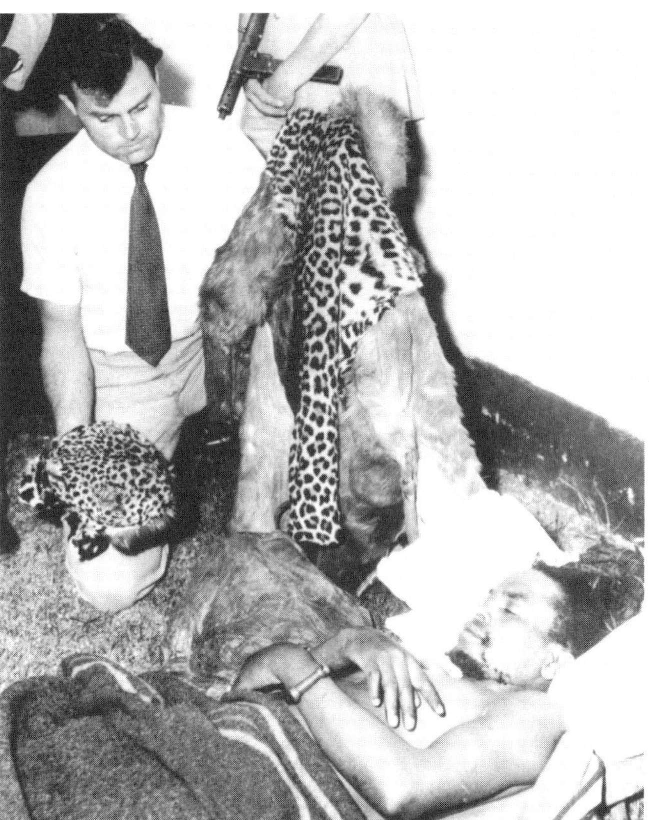

Top Mau Mau military commander Dedan Kimathi, is shown wounded and in handcuffs after his capture, a British official holding the leopard-skin uniform he wore in battle; found with him was a Bible and Napoleon's Book of Charms, the latter consulted by Kimathi in strategizing his moves; he was hanged on February 19, 1957.

into joining their ranks. Until 1948, the British were largely unaware of the Mau Mau organization, and even when they knew of its existence, its highly secretive nature prevented them from learning much about it. As the violence employed in recruitment became more common and more obvious, the colonial government began to perceive the danger of the situation. When it launched an effort to remove the oath from Mau Mau members, using tribal medicine men to perform the ceremonies, the Mau Mau escalated their activity. On May 15, 1952, the first murders occurred. Two Kikuyu, one of whom had informed against the Mau Mau, were found dead in the Kirichwa River near Nairobi. Six people were brought to trial in these murders, but the man who found the bodies and notified the authorities was himself later assassinated.

Immediately prior to the declaration of a State of Emergency on October 21, 1952, Mau Mau recruiting efforts were massively increased, with motorized "oathing" teams driving out from Nairobi to the Reserve. Some of the assemblies recruited as many as 800 people at a time. The crimes of murder, arson, and destruction of resisting Kikuyu's property proliferated. A new governor, Sir Evelyn Baring, had arrived in Nairobi on September 29, 1952.

After a tour of the troubled land, during which a government official was assassinated in broad daylight, Baring recommended the declaration of the State of Emergency. On October 20, twelve RAF troop carriers arrived with reinforcements from the Lancaster Fusiliers. Eighty-three Mau Mau suspects, including Kenyatta, were arrested, and the following day the State of Emergency became reality. With this, the attacks against government officials and white settlers escalated.

The settlers and loyal Kikuyu fought back by organizing a Kikuyu Home Guard that worked with the African tribal police. By mid-January 1953, the Home Guard numbered 10,000. On March 26, 1953, the Mau Mau staged two attacks, one at the police station at Naivasha, in which they stole guns and ammunition, and the other, a particularly brutal massacre at Lari, in which they attacked families of men in the Kikuyu Home Guard. Eighty-four people were killed.

In April, Kenyatta and five comrades were found guilty of "managing" Mau Mau. Kenyatta was sentenced to seven years in prison at hard labor. The government continued to increase its military presence but the conflict did not reach a turning point until Waruhiu Itote, a Mau Mau operative, was captured. With the help of a Kenyan-born Englishman, Ian Henderson, the British finally gained important intelligence regarding the Mau Mau activities.

Through this intelligence, Henderson gradually infiltrated individual groups of Mau Mau, converted them, and used them to convert or capture their fellow Mau Mau. On October 26, 1956, an important Mau Mau leader, Dedan Kimathi, was captured. His subsequent execution apparently

Mau Mau members are marched into a British prison camp in 1954, the year in which the backbone of the secret criminal society was broken by British forces, predominately native black troops.

Jomo Kenyatta, center, holding book aloft, takes the oath when becoming Kenya's first black prime minister (president) in 1963, when the country gained its independence.

marked the end of the militant Mau Mau. A total of 10,527 Mau Mau were killed, in contrast to thirty-two white settlers. Another new governor, Sir Patrick Rension, formally proclaimed the end of the Emergency in January 1960.

Mau Mau, however, survived. There were rumors of new, secret oath-taking ceremonies in the 1960s. Just before Kenya's independence in 1963, Mau Mau activity increased in hopes of driving out the white settlers once and for all. When Kenyatta was declared prime minister of the newly independent Kenya, many former Mau Mau members were elected to seats in the National Assembly.

Two separate periods of amnesty were declared that year in an effort to reclaim the remaining Mau Mau. Those who did come forward to take advantage of these amnesties, as well as a later one in 1964, returned to the forests instead of settling on the farmland allotted to them by Kenyatta's government. The failure to reintegrate them into the mainstream population suggested that Mau Mau would remain alive in Kenya for years to come.

KKK: UNDER THE WHITE ROBE/ 1865-1877; 1915-present

At the close of the American Civil War, the South lay devastated in political and economic ruins. Carpetbagging northerners swarmed into the South to seize rich farmlands through exorbitant taxes levied upon the once powerful slave-owning gentry by northern-controlled state houses. In most of the southern states, former land owners were disenfranchised. The old Democrat party was in shambles, unable to govern. With the assassination of the moderate Abraham Lincoln, conditions in the South worsened. Republican hardliners in the U. S. Congress put through measures that were obviously designed to punish the South for its attempted secession, rather than initiate the healing process during the so-called Reconstruction Period.

A Freedman's Bureau was established that ostensibly worked for the benefit of former slaves. However, the corrupt organization placed uneducated blacks in positions of authority over whites, giving blacks full opportunity to take vengeance upon former slave owners or whites. Moreover, hordes of blacks invaded small towns and plantations, looting and pillaging, while Union occupation troops stood by idle or even encouraged them. Women were raped and those apprehended were locked up for a few days and then freed.

To combat these dreadful conditions, ex-Confederate General Nathan Bedford Forrest, a fearsome, relentless cavalry commander, founded and organized the first Ku Klux Klan in 1865. Forrest, who never admitted his leadership of

Confederate General Nathan Bedford Forrest, who was credited with founding the Ku Klux Klan in 1865.

Klan members in costume during the Reconstruction Period; many riders used false heads to frighten blacks.

Klan members without their robes dragged a Negro girl named Phillis into some North Carolina woods and whipped her into unconsciousness for striking a white girl.

John Campbell, a reconstructionist, is shown in 1871 with a rope about his neck and about to be hanged by a group of North Carolina klansmen; he was rescued by federal agents.

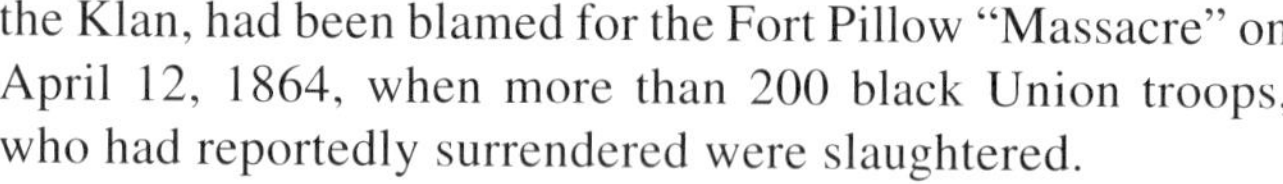

the Klan, had been blamed for the Fort Pillow "Massacre" on April 12, 1864, when more than 200 black Union troops, who had reportedly surrendered were slaughtered.

Forrest was not present at the actual founding of the Klan, but had apparently given his approval when six young ex-Confederate soldiers in Pulaski, Tennessee created a hooded secret society that was intended to be a short-lived guerrilla organization. The society was called the Ku Klux Klan, a name that derives from the combination of the Greek word *kuklos* (circle) with the Scottish word "clan."

The organization adopted white hoods and robes, and even the horses its members rode were covered in white shrouds. All of this paraphernalia was designed to frighten the uneducated and superstitious blacks. The night riders of the Ku Klux Klan (KKK) terrified the blacks, whom they suspected of harassing and oppressing whites. Blacks were confronted with what they thought were the ghosts of dead Confederate soldiers, and the KKK riders played upon this eerie concept. Many of the KKK riders wore false heads, and they handed these skulls to quaking blacks. On other occasions, riders clutched the hand of the black with a skeleton's hand.

The Klan grew in great numbers as dispossessed and disenfranchised southern whites flocked to its banners. The society adopted formal rules and regulations, and it quickly established a secret oath. New members were brought into a circle of robe-wearing Klansmen, and by torchlight, repeated the following vows:

I, before the immaculate Judge of Heaven and Earth, and upon the Holy Evangelists of Almighty God, do, of my own free will and accord, subscribe to the following sacredly binding obligation:

1. We are on the side of justice, humanity, and constitutional liberty, as bequeathed to us in its purity by our forefathers.
2. We oppose and reject the principles of the radical party (the Republican Party, then rulers of the U.S. Congress).
3. We pledge mutual aid to each other in sickness, distress, and pecuniary embarrassment.
4. Any member divulging, or causing to be divulged, any of the foregoing obligations shall meet the fearful penalty and traitor's doom, which is Death! Death! Death!

Hundreds of Klan groups sprang up in great force throughout the South and many operated under self-styled names: Knights of the White Camelia, Order of the White Rose, The White Caps, White League, Palefaces, White Brotherhood. These groups thought themselves reincarnated knights based on the Arthurian legends of old. KKK riders believed themselves the champions of the oppressed and of damsels in distress. They rode to the rescue of all that was sacred to the white culture of the antebellum South. They thought themselves noble and inspired with a glorious mission. They also began to administer beatings and whippings to blacks accused of offending whites. Phillis, a black girl who had struck a white girl, was seized by KKK members and dragged to a woods in North Carolina. There dozens of men took turns whipping her. Six of these brutes were later jailed.

As the whites began to wrest back control of southern state legislatures during the late 1860s, new "Black Codes" designed to keep blacks out of the election process and within a sub-economic and non-educational position were put into effect. Under these unjust codes, blacks were arrested in wholesale lots and jailed for vagrancy, drunkenness, and disorderly conduct. Some were guilty, but many were not. The Black Codes served as a catchall to legally punish blacks who sought to supplant white politicians, land owners, and businessmen.

The Republican radicals in Congress retaliated by sending new Union troops into the South to enforce its edicts, and in particular, to protect the operations of the hated Freedman's Bureau. When former Union Army commander Ulysses S. Grant became president in 1868, he proved to be a

Negroes in New Orleans are shown in custody, arrested for vagrancy under the newly-established Black Codes, used to keep freed blacks poor, uneducated and without voting rights.

The frontispiece of Thomas Dixon's novel, *The Clansman* (1905), a popular book that whitewashed the exploits of the KKK and portrayed its early-day members as heroes.

do-nothing administrator, allowing the radical Republicans to overrun the South.

Grant's disinterest in true Reconstruction of the South only served to increase the strength of the KKK, which began to ride in great numbers, its hooded legions burning the homes and communities of blacks. They shot and hanged blacks by the hundreds. They waged open warfare for almost three years. By 1871, however, the radical wing of the Republican Party had lost political support in the North, and many of its leaders either retired or were replaced in senatorial elections.

In that year, however, the KKK was recognized as a powerful force in the South, and a U.S. Senate committee investigated the operations of this secret society. Nathan Bedford Forrest was summoned to Washington, D. C., and testified before the committee. He did not admit that he had given the orders to establish the KKK or that he was its nominal leader.

Forrest had always provided colorful copy for newspapers. During the Civil War, he had been asked by newsmen how he won his cavalry battles, and the uneducated Forrest replied: "I get there first with the most." (In the north, this remark was altered to: "I get there furstest with the mostest.") Forrest had given many interviews with the press, telling reporters about the wonderful and brave Klan, which had sprung up throughout southern states and how he had traveled through those states, ostensibly organizing its chapters and planning its paramilitary operations.

Before the Senate committee, the tall, dark-bearded Forrest stated that the Klan had been founded upon high principles and that it was a necessity in preserving law and order in a land made helpless and vulnerable by oppressive forces. Said Forrest in his homespun way: "There was a great deal of insecurity felt by the southern people. There were a great many northern men coming down there, forming Leagues all over the country. The Negroes were holding night meetings, were going about, were becoming very insolent, and the southern people all over the states were very much alarmed. I think that many of the organizations did not have any name. Parties organized themselves so as to be ready in case they were attacked. Ladies were ravished by some of these Negroes, who were tried and put in the penitentiary, but were turned out a few days afterwards. There was a great deal of insecurity in the country, and I think this organization (the KKK) was got up to protect the weak, with no political intention at all."

In 1868, Klan membership was estimated to be more than 500,000 throughout the South and by the early 1870s this number had doubled. But the Klan, led by ex-Confederate officers, was getting out of control. Its leaders found that members swelling its ranks refused to take orders and went their own way. They were no more than terrorist gangs bent on burning, looting, and robbing. They murdered blacks in large numbers and operated as bandits. One of their leaders characterized his men as "rash, impudent, and bad men." The white-robed legions, intended as a chivalrous society, had turned into packs of marauding night-riders who brought murderous terror to the countryside.

Black militia was organized and fought pitched battles with the KKK, but usually these poorly trained and equipped blacks got the worst of it. In a six-month period in 1872, the KKK lynched or shot thirty-five blacks and had "chastised"

Black troops occupying a Southern town are shown retreating in panic before charging Klansmen in D. W. Griffith's epic 1915 film, *The Birth of A Nation*, a movie that inspired the rebirth of the Klan.

262 men and women by whipping them. More than 100 others had been shot, raped, and mutilated, according to the findings of the Senate committee. Meanwhile, the Klan took root at the local level, following Forrest's original paper plans, where he had organized the society as an army.

Forrest had termed the entire South as the Invisible Empire; each state was termed a Realm, each congressional district a Dominion, each county a Province, and each locality or town a Den. The leaders all had glorious titles. The Grand Wizard was General Forrest. The ten men who made up Forrest's staff were called Genii. Every Realm had a Grand Dragon and eight Hydras, each Dominion had a Grand Titan and six Furies, each Province a Grand Giant and four Goblins, each Den a Grand Cyclops and two Night Hawks.

Forrest realized that he could not control the Klan since the very hoods and robes he had originally designed to hide the identities of his avenging riders were now used to mask all sorts of inhuman offenses and outrages. When local KKK units were accused of acting simply as terrorists and thieves, those same riders claimed innocence, insisting that the offenses had been committed by blacks dressed in robes and hoods and pretending to be Klansmen. By 1872, Forrest and his staff quit the secret society in disgust, stating that it had become a lawless organization lost in myriad Halloween gibberish and vicious acts of outlawry.

The Grant administration and U. S. Congress, to combat the ever-increasing Klan outrages, passed the Ku-Klux Acts in 1870 and 1871, more or less outlawing the organization and branding it a criminal secret society. A wave of vigilantism against the Klan then swept its leaders into jail, where they were allowed to languish without trials since white juries invariably freed any Klan member accused of crimes. Moderate white leaders then began openly denouncing the Klan as an anarchistic secret society, labeling it "foolish and childish."

The Democrats won back the state legislatures and the Klan died for lack of purpose. Political compromise was reached wherein the South was allowed to regain supremacy over the black populations, reducing them to sharecropper status without voting rights and little or no education. In return, the southern Democrats supported all the Congressional measures of northern business interests, which included enormous profits in cotton and tobacco crops grown in the South. By 1877, the Ku Klux Klan was virtually dead, its local and state memberships disbanded, its white and red robes and hoods stored away as social artifacts of a bygone era.

Twenty-three years went by before the Klan stirred again, and this time only in the fitful dreams of a back county preacher named "Colonel" William Joseph Simmons. As he would later recall it, Simmons, who had been exposed to the fearsome tales of the old Klan since boyhood, obtained a book of anec-

Master film director David Wark Griffith was shocked to learn that the KKK used his film in promoting enlistment to its ranks.

Mary Phagan, thirteen, who was murdered in the basement of Atlanta's National Pencil Company on April 26, 1913, ironically Confederate Memorial Day. Her death was used by Simmons and others to establish the Knights of Mary Phagan, which dedicated itself to hunting down and punishing the killer.

dotes about the secret society in 1900. He fell asleep one night while reading this volume and dreamed of the old galloping night riders. "On horseback in their white robes," Simmons later told a newsman, "they rode across the wall in front of me and as the picture faded out I got down on my knees and swore that I would found a fraternal organization which would be a memorial to the Ku Klux Klan."

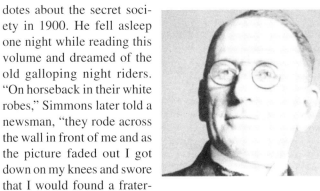

William Joseph Simmons, who called himself the "Imperial Wizard" of the reborn Klan of 1915 in Georgia.

Simmons took his time to do so. He encouraged the idea of the Klan wherever he traveled, but he concentrated upon saving souls at this time. A self-righteous person, Simmons traveled through the South as a Methodist preacher, using his fists to bully unruly flocks to church on Sunday. The strong-armed tactics of preacher Simmons were condemned by Methodist Bishop Wilson, who eventually suspended him from all religious activities for "inefficiency." Simmons defied this church edict and continued his circuit-riding and fiery sermons. Bishop Wilson, enraged at this defiance, tracked Simmons down to a lonely backwoods church and, using a strong switch, whipped Simmons from the pulpit and out of the church.

Simmons established his own brand of religion and collected some malcontent Methodists to serve as his disciples. To supplement his income, Simmons sold women's garters and undergarments to small-town general stores. Meanwhile, Simmons and his self-styled preachers continued their rural religious activities for years until a startling event took place on December 6, 1915.

On that day, the greatest motion picture of the era, *The*

Leo M. Frank, the mild-mannered manager of the pencil factory, who was railroaded into a conviction for murdering Mary Phagan, mostly because he was a "Yankee Jew."

Birth of a Nation, opened to enormous crowds in Atlanta. It was based on the best-selling novel, *The Clansman* by Thomas Dixon, which portrayed the old Klan of Nathan Bedford Forrest as a champion of female honor and a noble defender of the weak and helpless.

While thousands of Atlantans queued for the premiere showing of the film, Simmons and his disciples circulated in the crowds. Wearing a cutaway frock coat and striped trousers, the traditional garb of the southern preacher, Simmons addressed the throngs: "I am he who from the realms of the unknown wrested the solemn secret from the grasp of the night and became the sovereign Imperial Master of the Great Lost Mystery." It was all gobbledygook, of course, but citizens eagerly responded to the racism and bigotry put forth by Simmons and his followers.

Actually, Simmons had been hard at work reorganizing the old Klan since 1913 when a Jewish businessman transplanted from the north, Leo Max Frank, was wrongly accused and later wrongly convicted of raping and murdering 14-year-old Mary Phagan, who worked in his Atlanta pencil factory. At that time, Simmons and others had organized a secret group which called itself the Knights of Mary Phagan. One night they went to the top of Stone Mountain, set fire to a giant wooden cross, and by its fiery light vowed vengeance on "the Yankee Jew."

It was this group that later dragged Frank out of prison and lynched him in 1915 near Marietta, Georgia, some months before *The Birth of a Nation* opened in Atlanta. The film's appearance followed closely behind the sensational Frank case and only served to aid Simmons in his reorganization of an ancient evil. Simmons would later admit: "I went to see *Birth of a Nation.* It made a tremendous impression on everybody. Yes, *Birth of a Nation* helped the Klan tremendously."

The film, directed by the master filmmaker David Wark Griffith, did extol the dubious virtues of the old Reconstruction era Klan, and Simmons used the invaluable publicity surrounding this epic film to promote the rebirth of his own self-styled Klan. The victimized director, Griffith, was astounded when he discovered that Simmons had exploited his film to establish the Klan.

In a 1928 interview, Griffith stated: "That ends a thirteen-year-old mystery. I have been accused of having made *Birth of a Nation* as propaganda for the Klan. What's more, throughout the years, I have been constantly asked to explain the relationship between the picture and the Klan. That accusation seemed foolish to me. So did the question. But if Simmons actually used *Birth of a Nation* to raise membership in the Klan, as he says he did, running his Klan advertising simultaneously with advertising of the picture, I can see how many persons may have been confused."

Simmons and his henchmen organized the confusion into a terrorist fraternity which swelled to more than seven million during its heyday in the 1920s. Simmons and others incorporated the Klan in Atlanta and the visionary leader placed advertisements in newspapers and on billboards throughout Georgia. "A Classy Order for Men of Character," one ad was headlined. It went on to state: "No Roughnecks, Rowdies, nor Yellow Streaks Admitted. It is of and for men who are in all things 100 percent American and no other."

Simmons did not advertise the real reason for the Klan—race and religious hatred and bigotry. The Klan opposed the immigration of all foreigners to American shores. It condemned Catholics, Jews, and especially blacks. The hatred for blacks was rampant among its members and Simmons made no excuses for the rabid racism he and his followers embraced. Simmons opened his KKK meetings by placing a brace of pistols and a horsewhip on a table and then shouting to his hooting supporters: "All right! Now bring on your niggers!"

The old night riders on horseback were replaced by hooded thugs in autos who raced about the Georgia countryside, dragging blacks and Jews from their beds in the middle of the night and administering whippings or worse to these hapless victims. The Klan spread through the Carolinas, Alabama, Virginia, Arkansas, Mississippi, Louisiana, Florida, Texas, Tennessee, and then crept into northern states with large rural populations and finally into the industrial cities of the Mid-

August 17, 1915: The dangling barefooted body of Leo Frank, lynched by the Knights of Mary Phagan (some of whom proudly posed in this grim photo), the precursor to the new Ku Klux Klan; Frank's death penalty had been commuted to life imprisonment by Georgia Governor John Slaton, who believed Frank innocent, so Klansmen kidnapped Frank from a farm prison and hanged him.

Omaha, Nebraska, 1919: A Negro accused of raping a white woman was burned to death by Klansmen; Klan supporters gather about the grisly remains.

west, where blacks and minorities had made headway into the normally white forces on assembly lines. Detroit was infected by the secret society, and the Klan in Chicago, by the mid-1920s, boasted of 50,000 dues-paying members.

The Klan adopted brutal, medieval methods to quash opposition to its whippings and lynchings. Its members took to branding unruly blacks and whites who openly opposed them. The Reverend Orrin Van Loon, pastor of a community church outside of Detroit, openly criticized the Klan in 1924 from his pulpit; the next night a gang of hooded men forced their way into his home and dragged him to a waiting car which sped off to a lonely spot where Van Loon was branded on the back with three large letters: KKK. The shootings, mutilations, burnings, and lynchings spread unchecked.

For the Klansmen of the early 1920s, life was, in the words of one of its hooded leaders "roaming through the clover." Simmons and the top leaders of the Klan grew enormously

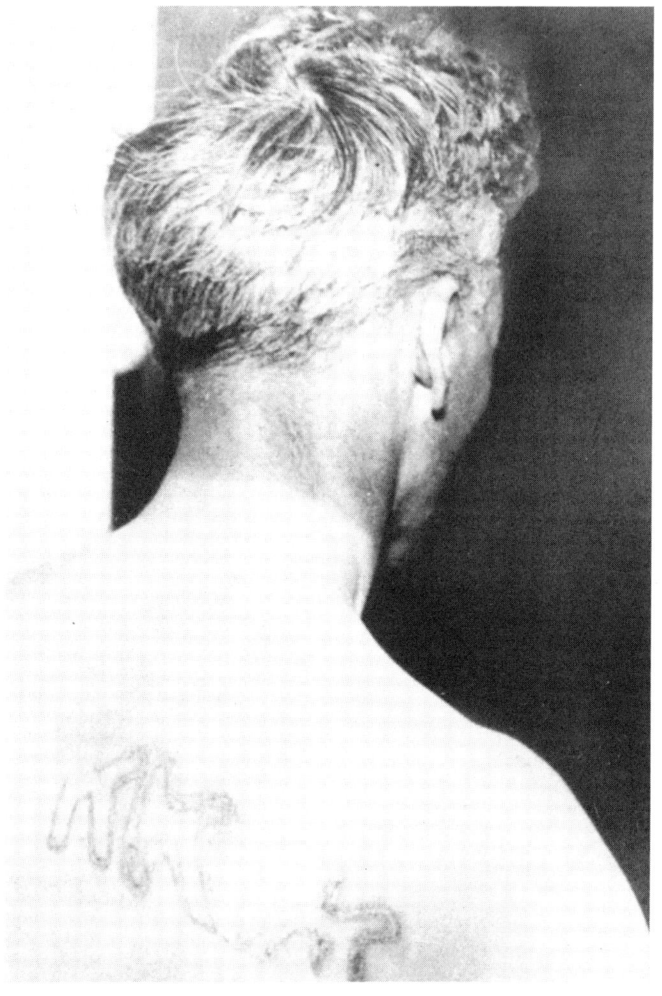

Detroit, Michigan, 1924: Reverend Orrin Van Loon, who had openly opposed the Klan from his pulpit, was kidnapped by Klansmen who branded "KKK" on his back.

The Klan was at the peak of its power in the mid-1920s, with more than five million dues-paying members; here, in wave after wave of white-robed Klansmen, the KKK shows its sinister might with more than 50,000 members marching down Pennsylvania Avenue in Washington, D. C.

Hooded Klan members march through a small town in 1925 in Indiana, a state where the government and law enforcement agencies were controlled by Klan members.

Hiram Wesley Evans, who took over the Klan from Simmons, is shown in 1929 in his Imperial Wizard costume during a Klan rally.

rich by charging their members a $10 initiation fee, $1-a-month dues, and $6.50 for a simple white robe and hood with peaked cap. (Later, from the 1950s on, the Klan would not sell these costumes, but rent them for each meeting to get maximum cash flow from Klan trappings.) Simmons also made money by selling titles to the richest of his bigoted followers. It was the secret society's best fund-raising device and through the Klan's haphazard rites, a member with enough money could

Elizabeth Tyler, assistant publicity director of the Klan, whose drunken affair with her Klan boss, Edward Young Clarke, disgraced Simmons' administration of the KKK; she and Clarke were dismissed.

Klan publicity director Edward Young Clarke, who had an affair with his assistant, Elizabeth Tyler, and who misappropriated Klan funds in a scandal that caused widespread desertions from the Klan.

Indiana KKK chief David C. Stephenson went to prison for life for the rape and murder of a young woman; his 1925 conviction shattered the image of a Klan claiming to uphold public morality.

Arthur A. Bell, right, New York's KKK grand dragon, at a New Jersey rally with Nazi Bund leader Arthur Klapprott on August 18, 1940; during World War II, the Bund vanished and the Klan went into decline.

quickly become a Nighthawk, Klokann, Klexter, Klagaro, Kladd, Klabee, Kligrapp, Kludd, Klokard, or Klaliff. Seniority brought august titles such as Exalted Cyclops, Kleagle, King Kleagle, and Grand Goblin. There was, of course, only one Imperial Wizard. That was Simmons.

The "Colonel" (a title Simmons conferred upon himself) was soon living in a resplendent mansion and was banking tens of thousands of dollars each month. Simmons and some of his supporters spewed forth nonstop propaganda. Said one Klan spokesman in 1924: "The Klan is for a Christian country,

Unconcerned Klansmen Sheriff Lawrence Rainey and deputy Cecil Price, at an arraignment where they listen to prosecutors indicting them for the murders of three young civil rights workers in Mississippi; Rainey, Price and sixteen others went free.

free, clean, and Democratic. We want clean politics. We want the elimination of the bootlegger. [This was a joke in that many Klan leaders were becoming rich through their bootlegging activities during Prohibition.] We want the elimination of the prostitute, gambler, niggers, Mexicans, Irish, Jews, Germans, Huns, and, in fact, all foreigners, so they will not be able to appropriate to themselves the policies and destinies of the Great and Glorious American Republic." It was the Know-Nothing Party all over again, only this time it clutched a shotgun and a whip and hid beneath a sheet.

Slogans exploded from the mouths of the Atlanta Klan leaders night and day. "Will you faithfully strive for the eternal maintenance of white supremacy?" they asked their grunting followers. "Jesus Christ is the leader of the Ku Klux Klan, and we are for him. The Jew is not for him and therefore the Jew has shut himself out of the Klan," they decreed. "The Pope will sit in the White House when Hell freezes over," they fulminated.

The power of the Klan spread from rural communities and small towns to the metropolitan areas of the country. Men in high public office, as well as hundreds of thousands of white workers afraid of losing their jobs to immigrants willing to work for less, subscribed to and supported Simmons' criminal secret society. Klansmen defied the law and laughed. In Hammond, Indiana, a Klansman murdered an immigrant for saying "to hell with the United States." He was acquitted by an all-white jury whose members were all Klansmen.

When Congress edged toward investigating the operations of the Klan, Simmons bombastically condemned easterners as being bigoted against the Klan and the South. He influenced several congressmen, chiefly Representative W. D. Upshaw from Atlanta, to threaten to begin similar investigations of the Catholic Knights of Columbus. The congressional investigation was still-born, but a probe conducted by the New York *World* did expose the debaucheries of Klan leadership. The newspaper revealed how, in 1919, Imperial Kleagle Edward Young Clarke had been arrested for drunkenness and indecent behavior. (Clarke's brother, Francis Clarke, was managing editor of the Atlanta *Constitution;* the newspaper never published a word of the arrest.)

What made this scandal doubly damaging was that Clarke's debauchery was performed with Mrs. Elizabeth Tyler, who was associated with the Klan and vice chairman of the Georgia Committee of the Republican Party. Both Clarke and Tyler had been arrested on a disorderly charge, but the story of the arrest, as retold by the *World,* was never seen in Atlanta. The Klan purchased every one of the 3,000 copies of the *World* distributed there and destroyed them. One of the Klan publications retorted that the attack on Mrs. Tyler indicated to its members that their "mothers, sisters, and daughters were unsafe from the millionaire newspaper owners."

While Klansmen marched down Atlanta's streets at night bearing torches and singling out blacks along the parade route as if marking them for extermination, Simmons and other Klan leaders lined their pockets with hundreds of thousands of dollars pilfered from the Klan treasury. Simmons became an alcoholic and was not fit to appear in public. In Fall 1922, Hiram Wesley Evans, who called himself "the most 100 percent American," ousted Simmons from Klan leadership. Evans, an overweight dentist from Texas, had been made the Klan's national secretary, or Imperial Kligrapp, by Simmons and bided his time until Simmons overreached himself. Simmons objected to the ouster and threatened to create a schism in the Klan, but Evans bought him off with an official Klan severance payment of $146,000.

Activist Lemuel Penn, murdered in Georgia by two Klansman in 1964; an all-white jury acquitted his accused killers.

Activist Mrs. Viola Liuzzo, who was shot and killed following the 1965 march on Selma, Alabama, by a Klansman.

By then the Klan was one of the biggest businesses in Atlanta. The organization had purchased a stately antebellum mansion six miles out of town for $75,000 and went about its fanatical routine of oppressing minorities with big-budget advertising programs. Klan leaders tried to pressure Atlanta's Board of Education into firing all of the city's Catholic teachers. Those who resisted

Klansman Collie Leroy Wilkins, center, under arrest, was charged with murdering Viola Liuzzo, but was acquitted; he nevertheless went to prison for ten years for depriving Liuzzo of her civil rights.

Dale Reusch, Imperial Wizard of the Klan, addresses a hostile crowd on the steps of the Statehouse in Columbus, Ohio, on Labor Day, 1977; the Klan by then had little funds to advance their racist cause.

Hooded Klan members are shown carrying burning torches to a KKK meeting in the late 1980s.

this move were threatened with death. In September 1922, the city council denounced in a formal resolution the Knights of Columbus as an un-American fraternity. Its passage was blocked at the last minute by Mayor James Key, who angrily vetoed the measure.

One of the more rabid Klan movers and shakers was Imperial Kludd Caleb A. Ridley, a pastor of the Central Baptist Church and national chaplain for the Klan. Though he openly expressed his hatred for Jews and Catholics, Ridley reserved his special venom for the Pope, saying: "I can't help being what I am racially. I am not a Jew, nor a Negro, nor a foreigner. I am an Anglo-Saxon white man, so ordained by the hand and will of God, and so constituted and trained that I cannot conscientiously take either my politics or my religion from some secluded ass on the other side of the world."

The same kind of hysteria that had afflicted those in Salem, Massachusetts, during the witch hunts more than two hundred years earlier, gripped the country at the height of the Klan fever. Atlanta ministers, who addressed blacks as "mister," or treated them as equal to whites, such as Dr. Plato Durham and the Reverend M. Ashby Jones, were openly branded "Negrophiles." Plans were put in motion to create a Klan college to be called the University of America, which would boast an endowment of $1 million, but the money was not forthcoming (most of these funds were raked off by Klan leaders).

In the 1920s, the Klan made great political headway, Atlanta's police force was honeycombed with Klan members. The city council was almost all pro-Klan and one of its members, Walter Sims, ran for mayor on an anti-Catholic ticket and won in 1922. Atlanta had gone over to the Klan. The state of Indiana was another stronghold of the Klan in the 1920s. Here the Klan, under the direction of David C. Stephenson, became all-powerful, controlling the governorship and all important political and police positions in the state. Evans, in Atlanta, organized the southern Democrat Party as the political arm of the Klan. It was Stephenson's own corruption and criminal acts that would bring down the Klan in Indiana. Stephenson would be convicted of rape and murder and sent to prison for life.

For a brief period in the 1930s, the Klan was replaced in Detroit by a rival organization called the Black Legion, which consisted of white auto workers who beat and even killed foreigners, fearing these immigrants would take their jobs. The Black Legion was really more of a terrorist group, designed for enormous profit by its leaders. It was finally destroyed when its murderous chiefs were tracked down, convicted, and sent to prison.

The Atlanta headquarters, however, remained the national headquarters of the Klan. From this headquarters, Evans issued an endless stream of hate literature. Evans stated in one Klan publication that blacks could never become good Americans since they were utter primitives, incapable of being educated or civilized. Stated Evans: "They have not, they cannot obtain the Anglo-Saxon level. Both biology and anthropology prove it, and the experience of centuries confirms that conclusion. The low mentality of savage ancestors, of jungle environment, is inherent in the bloodstream of the colored race in America. No new environment can more than superficially overcome this age-old hereditary handicap."

Said Evans of the Jews: "They are a people from all other peoples ... Not only because of the forbidden intermarriage, but also in an actual sense, is the Jew unmergeable. By every patriotic test he is an alien and unassimilable ... The evil influence of persecution is upon him ... He does not tie himself to the land. Jews owning farms are almost negligible; and it is largely only the Hebrew bankers and long-established merchants that have their homes."

Said Evans of Catholics: "They demand and increasingly

seek to exercise the dominion outside the spiritual. To them the presidency in Washington is subordinate to the priesthood in Rome ... Do you realize, my friends, that the illiteracy of Europe is practically confined to Catholic countries?" During 1928, Evans was able to increase Klan activities and funds through a vicious campaign against New York's Al Smith who was running for the presidency. Smith was Catholic, favored repeal of Prohibition, was a liberal, and was from a big city, "all good reasons" for the Klan to condemn him. Klan political pressure and voting power were largely why Smith's candidacy collapsed.

Backing every one of Evans' bigoted statements and racist programs in Georgia was E. D. Rivers, later the governor of Georgia, while maintaining the Klan position of Exalted Cyclops. Rivers and Evans would eventually be disgraced in the 1930s, when it was revealed that these two men had illegally controlled the state sale of emulsified salt used in highway construction.

Klan excesses nevertheless continued in Atlanta and throughout the country. Deputy Sheriff W. W. Scarbrough raided Atlanta homes throughout the 1930s. He and other Klansmen administered brutal punishments to those breaking the so-called Klan Moral Code. Two white men, who had patronized black prostitutes were beaten unconscious and hurled into an Atlanta garbage dump in 1939. A short time later, an Atlanta theater owner was dragged from his own office in the theater and whipped and branded for serving "no account niggers." A white girl and her black lover were found by patrolling Klansmen in a car parked in a lover's lane. Both were whipped for "immoral behavior."

Sam H. Bowers, Klan leader in Hattiesburg, Mississippi, directed the January 10, 1966 firebombing of the home of black supporter Vernon Dahmer. Dahmer burned to death and Bowers was tried five times, not convicted for the slaying until August 1998; he was sent to prison for life.

Other Klansmen invaded the Atlanta barbershop of Ike Gaston and abducted him. He was charged with "cutting the hair of an inferior race with the same scissors used to cut the hair of white men." Gaston was stretched between two trees and beaten so unmercifully with a cleated belt that he died of his injuries. The beatings and lynchings continued throughout the South, but Klan membership declined with the coming of the Great Depression. By the time World War II began, the Klan had shrunk drastically. It was all but dissolved when the U. S. entered the war. Most Klan members resigned from the organization or simply did not attend meetings or went into the armed forces during the war. It was then felt that membership in the Klan was unpatriotic.

Evans quit the Klan in 1939, selling its charter, property, and trappings to Samuel Green and Dr. James H. Colescott, a veterinarian from Terre Haute, Indiana. Klan power, however, had ebbed so drastically that Colescott joined forces with the American Nazi Bund in 1940. When the Bund was branded as un-American and broken up, the Klan quickly severed its ties to the Bund. Following the attack on Pearl Harbor by the Japanese, all of America was united in a common cause that obliterated the racist purposes of the Klan. The U. S. government dealt the Klan a great blow in 1944 when the IRS charged the Klan with owing $685,305 in back taxes.

Colescott and Green held a final Klan convention in Atlanta on April 23, 1944, and officially dissolved the Klan, surrendering its titles and abandoning its charter and membership. But in the late 1940s the Klan reared its head again when old members collected on Stone Mountain outside Atlanta and gave rebirth to the organization. Its membership remained scattered and ineffectual, however, except in rural areas. All over the South during the mid-1950s, again mostly in rural areas, the Klan sprang up, usually under the banner of White Citizen's Councils. In the turbulent 1960s, the Klan found support in the deep South among those diehard racists who opposed mandatory integration.

Again the Klan rose with considerable support, while Freedom Riders invading the southland were mauled, beaten, and even killed. The Klan's murderous opposition to school integration was so violent and blatant that it no longer drew white support from the rest of the country, but rather general condemnation. In this period, black leaders such as Martin Luther King, Jr., emerged victorious over the Klan. Still, this secret society enjoyed a resurgence in the early 1960s when young northerners called Freedom Riders went into the South to support black voter registration. These Freedom Riders were met by hordes of Klan members, who beat and persecuted them while local police did nothing. Three of them were murdered in Mississippi.

Medgar Evers, a black activist was, shot and killed outside his Jackson, Mississippi, home in 1963, but his killer, Byron de la Beckwith, a Klan leader, escaped punishment when two white juries in separate trials were hopelessly deadlocked. All that changed in the 1990s. Beckwith was tried a third time in 1994 and a jury of eight blacks and four whites convicted him of slaying Evers and sent him to prison (see Assassination). Other Klan leaders fell beneath the gavel of American justice in the 1990s.

Sam H. Bowers, the Klan leader in Hattiesburg, Mississippi, led a KKK group to the home of Vernon Dahmer, Sr., another black activist and set his home on fire in 1966. Dahmer died of his burns. Bowers, tried five times, was finally convicted in 1998 and sent to prison. In Mobile, Alabama, Henry Francis Hays, the son of Klan leader Bennie Jack Hays, and James "Tiger" Knowles, went in search of a black to kill in 1981. They abducted and murdered 19-year-old Michael Donald. Both men were later tried; Knowles was sent to prison for life and Hays received a death sentence. Hays was put to death on June 6, 1997, the first white man in the state to be executed for murdering a black person since 1913.

More devastating to the Klan was a suit filed by Donald's mother, Beulah Donald, charging the Klan with wrongful death.

The lynching of Michael Donald in 1981 by Klansmen Henry Francis Hays and James "Tiger" Knowles; Knowles went to prison for life and Hays was executed, the first white man put to death since 1913 for a crime against an American Negro.

Beulah Mae Donald filed a wrongful death suit against the United Klans of America for killing her son, Michael Donald; she surprisingly won her case, being awarded $7 million on July 24, 1998, a decision that, coupled to other such successful suits, broke the financial back of the Klan.

She was awarded $7 million in damages against the United Klans of America. On July 24, 1998, the Christian Knights of the Ku Klux Klan of South Carolina, as the result of a civil suit involving the Klan burning of the black Macedonia Baptist Church, was ordered to pay a whopping $37.8 million in damages to the church ($300,000 was in actual damages, the balance in punitive damages). A jury of nine blacks and three whites in Manning, South Carolina, took only forty-five minutes to deliberate and return their message to the Klan.

Elderly Horace King, the Klan leader in South Carolina, ran Klan headquarters from a shed on his rural property. He denied having anything to do with the 1995 church burning, although three men went to prison for committing the arson. During the civil trial, a lawyer for the church played a videotape of Klan leader King speaking at a Klan rally, saying, "It's time, people, to wake up and shape up and say this is our country, white people, take it back." King, who was not criminally prosecuted for the burning, was made liable for $15 million of the judgment, but his lawyer pointed out that he was on disability and, of course had no way of paying the damages, which were considered largely symbolic. King had been described by a church lawyer as a Klan leader, who got younger men to do his bidding and then "like a yellow-bellied dog, he runs."

Three men were sent to prison for the church burning (two testified against King, stating that the arson was done on Klan orders). One of the convicted arsonists was Timothy Adron Welch, who received a twelve-year sentence. Following the end of the civil trial, Welch's younger brother, Richard Welch stated, "I hope this trial right here is a sign for every Klan member to stay away from our town. We don't put up with this. We're not going to put up with this."

The judgments won by Beulah Donald and the Macedonia Baptist Church were actually more than symbolic. They literally bankrupted the KKK and broke the financial back and spirit of the worst terrorist organization in America. Although the Klan exists to this day, it is but a shell of its former organization. Like the Thugs of India and Kenya's Mau Mau, its ranks were devastatingly diminished with the coming of an enlightened public that viewed the members of these secret organizations as nothing more than common criminals.

CHAPTER SIXTEEN: TERRORISM

Since the beginning of the human race, individuals and organizations have practiced terrorism to achieve political, religious or economic dominance over their fellow creatures. Other, more arcane motives had spurred terrorists to their violent acts. In reality, terrorism defies exact definition. It has been invariably described as wanton acts of violence; irrational and senseless acts of barbarism, and insidious vandalism. Terrorism markedly differs from other crimes in that its main objective is to evoke panic, disorder and intimidation within society. Terrorist tactics are calculated to destroy order, paralyze activity within a community and inflict suffering and pain. The governmental view of terrorism includes any act of violence committed by political opponents to the in-power administration.

International terrorism has traditionally been an issue necessarily and inextricably intertwined with international politics. That perspective on the part of Osama bin Laden and his Al Qaeda group (along with myriad right-wing Islamic organizations allied with that group) was radically altered in the 1970s. These fanatics appropriated the Islamic religion, twisting its credo to its own destructive dogma, in order to conduct a religious "holy war" against all Western cultures not embracing their warped faith.

These terrorists are dedicated not to the destruction of any specific government, but to the violent eradication of all religions other than their own, wrongly pitting all third-world Arab nations against the rest of their global neighbors. Rooted to this fundamentalist belief is the history of the Order of the Assassins of the 11th Century (see Secret Criminal Societies), the murderous procedures and rites of this ancient, suicidal group being wholly embraced by the misanthropic and lethally xenophobic Al Qaeda.

Modern-day terrorist tactics, such as skyjackings, were employed in ancient eras in the form of massacres, sacked cities, kidnappings and enslavement of whole populations. The fierce nomadic tribes of Asia and Europe that invaded orderly kingdoms and even the well-organized empires of Greece and Rome, were basically terrorist raiders seeking loot. Latter day terrorists had more specific goals. In the Medieval era, rulers of fiefdoms practiced terrorism through men-of-arms, who branded and flogged farmers delinquent in paying taxes or delivering foodstuffs.

During the four centuries of the Spanish Inquisition, where Catholicism was as criminally altered by Spanish prelates as Al Qaeda later twisted Islamism, terrorism was practiced through horrible methods of torture to compel accused heretics into confessing or to force others into pointing out heretics, who were then burned at the stake. The chief Inquisitor of this draconian institution was Tomas Torquemada (1420-1498), a Dominican monk who became the confessor and adviser to Queen Isabella and King Ferdinand, and who practiced religious terrorism not only in Spain, but imported his persecution to the New World through his appointees traveling with Christopher Columbus and who, in turn, inflicted horrible punishments upon those natives in new lands reluctant to embrace the Catholic religion.

Catholic prelates of the Spanish Inquisition supervise a torture chamber, while suspected heretics are compelled to confess "offenses" against the Church. The worst terrorist of the Inquisition was religious fanatic Tomas Torquemada, the Grand Inquisitor, who was responsible for at least two thousand deaths.

Clerics representing the Inquisition accompanied explorer Hernan Cortes to Latin and South America, intimidating natives as well as Cortes' own men with savage punishment for any interpreted offense to their religion. Protestant monarchs of Europe embraced the same terrorist tactics in their persecution of anyone practicing a faith other than their government-backed religions, giving rise to the innumerable witchcraft trials in France and England, where dozens were burned alive at the stake.

The same type of religious terrorism occurred in the New World in 1692 during the Salem (Massachusetts) Witchcraft trials, where twenty persons were wrongly accused of heresy, black magic, consorting with the Devil, by other settlers, chiefly neurotic young females, and were put to death by hanging and pressing. Oddly enough, if one confessed to being a witch or warlock (both females and males were tried), their life was spared, but all of their land and property was seized and given to their accuser.

Many of the accused, such as Giles Corey, refused to admit to heresy or witchcraft, knowing that they would be put to death but that they would also preserve their assets for their families. Many of the accusers were used as instruments to gain that property. The young girls who had falsely accused other settlers later recanted their accusations, admitting that they had, for various reasons, wrongly accused their neighbors, but this provided little comfort to the families of those who had been executed.

Accusations were at the root of France's Reign of Terror in 1793-1794, wherein revolutionists named thousands of aristocrats as being counter-revolutionaries, and, through kangaroo-type tribunals, sending them to the guillotine. The chief terrorist of that era was Maximilien Francois Marie Isidore de Robespierre, who headed the Committee of Public Safety and decreed almost by whim the guilt of countless victims and sentencing them to death.

So bloodthirsty was Robespierre that he condemned his closest friends as betraying the revolution and sending Camille Desmoulins and Georges-Jacques Danton to the guillotine. Robespierre's followers, gripped by the paranoia, fear and terrorism he had created, turned on him and sent him also to the guillotine on July 28, 1794. His death literally ended the Reign of Terror in France, the guillotine claiming the lives of more than 17,300 people, while 3,000 more victims died in prison from disease and malnutrition.

Almost seven decades later, during the American Civil

Bridget Bishop was the first to hang on June 10, 1692 as a result of the notorious Salem Witch trials; she was a victim of superstition and hysteria that created a reign of terror in New England, not unlike the House of Un-American Activities Committee three centuries later that punished the innocent with the guilty in its obsessive hunt for Communists.

War, a new kind of military terrorism visited the U. S. in the form of raiding guerrillas on both sides of the conflict in Missouri and Kansas. James Lane headed the Union Redlegs that attacked and looted settlements occupied by pro-Confederate residents, where William Clarke Quantrill headed a Confederate force of guerrillas that invaded towns occupied by pro-Union citizens. The worst of these raids occurred at Lawrence, Kansas on August 21, 1863. Quantrill and 450 of his men rode into Lawrence and shot down 185 men and boys, while burning 154 homes and businesses to the ground.

Ironically, their arch enemy, James Lane, went unnoticed. He was in Lawrence at the time, but survived the massacre by fleeing at the sound of the Rebel Yell and hiding in a cornfield throughout the raid. Gathering up their loot, the guerrillas, most of them drunk, took the precaution of hiding their terrorist massacre by throwing the bodies of their victims into the burning buildings. Quantrill and his top aide, William "Bloody Bill" Anderson, were later tracked down by Union troops and killed. Others belonging to this Confederate terrorist band, like Jesse and Frank James and the Younger Brothers, survived the war to become the most notorious bandits in American history (see Robbery).

Following the war and with the coming of a flood of Irish immigrants to the U. S., labor terrorists reared their heads in West Virginia and Pennsylvania. During the 1870s, these immigrants formed a secret organization called the Molly Maguires, which employed terrorist tactics to intimidate coal mine owners into paying better wages and improving conditions in the dangerous mines. To that end, the Mollies killed mine officials and policemen, as well as blowing up the mines and company stores that workers were compelled to patronize. Their leader, John "Black Jack" Kehoe, and nineteen others were convicted of these terrorist acts and were sent to the

Robespierre, who headed the Committee of Public Safety following the French Revolution and unleashed the Reign of Terror, 1793-1794, causing the deaths of more than 20,000 persons, chiefly aristocrats, until he himself was sent in 1794 to the very instrument of death he so admired, the guillotine.

Confederate guerrilla William Clarke Quantrill led the terrorist raid on Lawrence, Kansas in 1863, slaughtering 185 men and boys.

The gutted remains of Lawrence, Kansas following Quantrill's murderous raid on August 23, 1863, when the Rebel terrorists burned down dozens of homes.

John "Black Jack" Kehoe (center, holding cross), leader of the Molly Maguires, and some of his fellow terrorists, go to the gallows in 1877.

gallows in 1877. They had been identified by James McParland, an undercover agent for the Pinkerton Detective Agency, which was then employed by the mine owners to track down the terrorists. This story was movingly depicted in the 1970 film, *The Molly Maguires*.

Twenty years later, Alexander Berkman (1870-1936), an avowed anarchist, emulated the Mollies in his attempt to murder industrial leaders. Born and raised by Jewish bourgeois parents in Russia, Berkman immigrated to the U. S. in 1890, where he met and allied himself with Emma Goldman. Berkman worked with Goldman and Johann Most, who published an anarchist weekly, *Freiheit*, a newspaper published in New York City that explicitly urged open revolt against the government and the violent destruction of capitalism. These anarchists focused their hatred upon Andrew Carnegie, a steel magnate that would not tolerate unions in his firms.

In June 1892, Carnegie steel workers organized and struck

Anarchist Alexander Berkman, standing, aiming pistol, tried to assassinate steel magnate Henry Clay Frick, sitting and facing John Leishman (back shown) in Frick's office, on July 23, 1892.

the plants at Homewood, Pennsylvania. Carnegie retaliated by hiring hundreds of non-union members. He then took a vacation to his native Scotland, leaving the crisis in the hands of his general manager, Henry Clay Frick. Taking the same hard line as his boss, Frick announced that unless the striking workers returned to their jobs on a non-union basis, the firm would evict them and their families from the housing Carnegie provided. Incensed, Berkman arrived at Frick's office in Homewood on July 23, 1892, announcing that he represented a New York firm that would help Carnegie break the strike.

Gaining access to Frick's office, Berkman produced a pistol and firing at the executive as he sat behind his desk. Two bullets ploughed into Frick's neck. He collapsed on the desk as John Leishman, a vice president of the firm grabbed Berkman so that he could not fire the weapon again, wresting the pistol from his hand. Berkman fought like a wild man, drawing a knife, which he thrust into Frick's side and legs seven times before Pinkerton guards rushed into the office and knocked him senseless.

Frick regained consciousness and, wiping the blood from his face, demanded that Berkman stand before him so that he could see his face. He had only glanced at his assailant before Berkman unleashed his attack. When the gunman was held by guards in front of Frick, the steel boss shook his head and said: "Why, I have never met this man before in my life!" He turned to Leishman, saying: "Why would this man want to take my life?"

"To take the life of capitalism," Berkman said.

During his trial, Berkman attempted to use the court as a podium for his anarchistic beliefs, but he was silenced. He then tried to commit suicide before the judge as his final political statement, but he was prevented from taking his own life. Berkman was sentenced to sixteen years in prison. Upon his release in 1906, Berkman rejoined Goldman, both publishing an anarchist magazine, Mother Earth. They openly objected to America's entrance into World War I and, during the "Red Menace" scare, were arrested as dangerous aliens. They were deported to Russia, sailing on the *Buford* on December 2, 1919.

William J. Flynn, chief of the Bureau of Investigation (the precursor to the FBI) personally escorted Berkman on board the ship, giving him a lecture and then handing him a cigar, saying: "Aww, don't be so glum. You're alive, aren't you? You better enjoy that cigar, because you won't get any where you're going."

Watching as the ship moved away from the dock was J. Edgar Hoover, a young attorney with the Department of Justice, who would, in 1924, become chief of the Bureau. Hoover had been the lawyer who had drawn up the legal briefs used by the government to deport Berkman, Goldman and hundreds of other anarchists and socialists. "Merry Christmas, Emma! Happy New Year, Alexander!" one of the U. S. officials shouted to the anarchists as they stood at the ship's rail.

Berkman shook his fist at the man, shouting: "We'll come back! And when we do, we'll get you bastards!"

Berkman and Goldman did not come back. Emma Goldman died in Russia, venerated as a Communist saint. Berkman, however, became disillusioned with communism and immigrated to Paris, France, where he haunted cheap bistros and cafes, vainly attempting to interest strangers in his anarchist movement. He died in France, committing suicide on June 28, 1936, little remembered in America where he once thought to bring about a total revolution.

Bureau of Investigation Chief William J. Flynn escorted Berkman and Emma Goldman on a ship when the anarchists were deported in 1919 to Russia; Flynn gave Berkman a cigar, saying: "You won't get any where you're going."

At the time Berkman shot Frick in America, another anarchist in France was busy trying to kill government officials with his home-made bombs. France in the early 1890s was plagued by labor terrorists, who, like the Mollies, tried to improve their income and working conditions by bombing offices and the homes of officials. Many of these terrorists were either socialists or anarchists, who thought to use the labor strife as a means of toppling the government.

One of these was a fierce bomber called Ravachol. A waiter in a Paris café overheard this man boasting that he had set off

French terrorist and bomber Ravachol is seized by Paris detectives in 1892.

A photo and measurements of Ravachol made by French criminologist Alphonse Bertillon, identifying him as Claudius Francois Koeningstein, a wanted murderer.

the bomb that had destroyed the home Prosecutor Bulot, on March 27, 1892. Bulot had earlier won a conviction of three anarchists who had attacked policemen, sending them to prison for five years.

The waiter summoned police and several gendarmes captured Ravachol after a wild fight. To establish the identity of this man, who was considered to be the most dangerous terrorist on the continent, Alphonse Bertillon, the inventor of the criminal identification system that bore his name, was brought into the case. Using his set of anthropometric measuring devices, Bertillon compared Ravachol's physical characteristics to other criminal suspects on file. He was able to establish that Ravachol and Claudius Francois Koeningstein, a man wanted for several murders, were the same person. Ravachol was tried, found guilty and sentenced to death, being executed in July 1892. Ten years later a crafty little terrorist with an appetite for murder, repeated Ravachol's *modus operandi* with devastating effectiveness in America.

AMERICAN UNION TERRORISTS/ 1900s-1910s

Harry Orchard (Albert E. Horsely) was a bomb specialist dedicated to the IWW (Industrial Workers of the World, or "Wobblies"), a violently radical labor organization that surfaced at the beginning of the twentieth century. Orchard was responsible for a string of terrorist bombings for the Wobblies throughout the West, beginning in 1903, when he killed two men by blowing up a mine shaft opening at the Vindicator Mine in Cripple Creek, Colorado, because its owners had locked out the Wobblies.

After that, IWW president William "Big Bill" Haywood sent Orchard to Independence, Colorado, where strikebreaking miners had also rejected the Wobblies. Haywood instructed Orchard that "something ought to be blown up." Orchard went about his work methodically, but viciously. He timed his detonation for a change of shift when tired workers were waiting on a railroad platform to be shuttled back to their quarters.

Orchard planted a hundred pounds of dynamite that he had stolen from the mine at Cripple Creek under the Independence railroad platform and rigged a triggering device with a bottle of acid to set off the charge when he turned a windlass. When the platform filled up, he set off the charge, killing twenty-six workers and maiming more than fifty others. Haywood was reported to be pleased with Orchard's accomplishment.

Orchard next went to San Francisco to murder Fred Bradley, a member of the Mine Owners Association. The charge he set in the Bradley family's front door went off when Bradley opened it, ripping off the facade of the house and blowing Bradley across the street. Bradley survived, and Orchard was dispatched to attempt another assassination soon after.

The Wobblies marked Judge Luther M. Goddard of the Colorado Supreme Court for death because he had ruled against them in a case, but Goddard also survived. Orchard dropped a purse with an explosive charge inside it on a path he knew the judge always took to work, but an innocent bystander picked it up first and was killed by mistake.

Orchard finally succeeded in killing an intended victim in December 1905. Former Idaho Governor Frank Steunenberg had called in federal troops to restore the peace, when Wobblies rioted during his administration. In dynamiting the front door of Steunenberg's home in Caldwell, Idaho, Orchard used the same technique he had tried unsuccessfully against Bradley, but this time Steunenberg was killed. As he attempted to leave the area, though, Orchard was recognized by a visiting sheriff from Oregon, Harvey K. Brown. Brown knew of Orchard's terrorist activities and identified him to the local authorities, for which Brown himself was later blown up.

Harry Orchard (Albert E. Horsley), chief terrorist for the IWW.

Orchard was convicted of Steunenberg's murder, but his death sentence was commuted to life in prison due to lobbying from labor representatives. Haywood was implicated in Orchard's confession, but, due to Clarence Darrow's representation in his defense, Haywood was acquitted for lack of corroborative evidence, as were all of the rest of the IWW leaders. Haywood, however, was arrested and jailed in 1917 for sabotaging America's war effort. Posting bond, Haywood fled to Russia, where he was hailed as a Bolshevik hero. Upon his death in 1928, he was given a state funeral and buried in the Kremlin, near the mummified body of his hero, Lenin.

Where the IWW targeted mine owners and their managers, leaders of the Bridge and Structural Iron Union workers aimed at one of the most powerful anti-Union tycoons in America—Harrison Gray Otis, publisher of the Los Angeles *Times*. For years, Otis used the Merchants and Manufacturers Association and the editorial pages of his influential newspaper to oppose unionism. "We employ no union men!" was his motto.

For twenty years, Otis and his coterie enforced his edicts and during that suppressive era open shops prevailed throughout Los Angeles industry. Union terrorists began setting bombs at plants and threatening the lives of bosses. Otis himself repeatedly received death threats, causing him to strap a small cannon to the side of his car and travel about with an army of well-armed guards.

In the early hours of October 1, 1910, a huge explosion blew apart the Los Angeles *Times* building, decimating the six-story structure. Twenty persons were killed and dozens more injured. Otis immediately announced that it had been the work of union terrorists and, as events unfolded, his accusations were hammered into truth. To find that truth, William J. Burns of the Burns Detective Agency was hired to investi-

IWW officers (left to right) Charles Moyer, William "Big Bill" Haywood and George Pettibone, who were successfully defended by Clarence Darrow in their 1907 murder trial.

The smoldering ruins of the Los Angeles *Times* Building, October 1, 1910, where twenty persons died and dozens more were injured in a terrorist bombing.

Another view of the destroyed Los Angeles *Times* Building, owned by publisher Harrison Gray Otis, a virulently anti-union boss, who had been targeted by Union terrorists.

James and John McNamara, union bosses who ordered the bombing of the Los Angeles *Times* Building; James went to prison for life, John for fifteen years.

Detective William J. Burns, left, who operated the Burns Detective Agency, is shown with Los Angeles *Times* owner Harrison Gray Otis; Burns tracked down the terrorist-bomber of the *Times* building, which led to the conviction of two union bosses.

Clarence Darrow was tried on charges of bribery in the McNamara case; he was acquitted by the efforts of another brilliant criminal attorney, Earl Rogers.

gate. Burns, then considered to be the greatest sleuth in America, directed a massive investigation, his workers sifting through the ruins of the *Times* building to find bomb fragments.

Burns and his workers soon concluded that the bombing had followed a pattern of previous bombings committed by members of the Bridge and Structural Workers Union, which was closely allied with the IWW. Burns then learned that one of the union's terrorists, Ortie McManigal, had fled to Detroit, Michigan, only hours after the explosion. Burns tracked him down and warned McManigal that existing conspiracy laws would bring him to trial and either send him to prison or to the hangman. McManigal quickly signed a confession in which he stated that his bosses, John J. McNamara, twenty-eight, secretary and treasurer of the Bridge and Structural Workers Union, and his brother, James McNamara, had ordered him to blow up the *Times* building.

The McNamara brothers were charged with murder and held for trial, defended by Clarence Darrow, who had successfully defended Big Bill Haywood and his IWW officers. The esteemed lawyer soon found himself in a quagmire of corruption. Burns and Otis, as well as members of the Los Angeles district attorney's office began bribing court officials and investigators in the case. Darrow's people did the same thing. Darrow realized that his clients were guilty and that he was about to conduct a losing case where both of his clients would be executed. He persuaded the court and Otis to cooperate if his clients pleaded guilty, which they did. Before the trial began, James McNamara admitted that he ordered McManigal to blow up the *Times* building "for moral purposes." He was sentenced to life imprisonment. His brother John was sentenced to fifteen years behind bars.

Darrow himself was tried six months later on charges of bribery, but he was brilliantly defended by the heavy-drinking Earl Rogers, who, in a masterful summary to a jury, won an acquittal for Darrow. In his conclusion, Rogers stated: "Will you tell me how any sane, sensible man, who knows anything about the law business—and the defendant [Darrow] has been at this for thirty-five years—could make himself go to a detective and say to him: 'Just buy all the jurors you want. I put my whole life, my reputation, I put everything I have into your hands. I trust you absolutely. I never knew you until two or three months ago and I don't know much about you now. But there you are. Go to it!"

Early in the year that the *Times* building was exploded, another terrorist arrived in Los Angeles. He was Joel Emmanuel Hagglund, a Swedish immigrant and devout union man. He called himself Joe Hill and he reportedly helped McManigal build the bomb that blew up the *Times* building. Hill was an IWW man, and, like Orchard a decade earlier, had been handpicked by Big Bill Haywood to spread terrorism and kill staunch anti-laborites. To that end, Hill went to Utah, where, on the night of January 10, 1914, accompanied by fellow wobbly, Otto Applequist, shot and killed John Morrison and his son Arling Morrison, both anti-union men.

Hill and Applequist, wearing masks, invaded the Morrison store in Murray, Utah, just outside Salt Lake City, firing pistols as they entered the place. The Morrisons fired back. The attackers fled, leaving only the owner's youngest son, Merlin Morrison, alive. Hill was later located at the home of Dr. Frank P. McHugh, where he asked that he be treated for a gunshot wound, claiming that he had been in a domestic squabble. McHugh, hearing of the Morrison shootings, contacted police and Hill was arrested. (Applequist was never located.) He was found guilty and sentenced to death. Though his boss, Haywood, attempted to mount a campaign to save his life, Hill had no misgivings. "Don't waste any time mourning—organize!" he wired Haywood from prison.

IWW terrorist Joe Hill (Joel Emmanuel Hagglund) murdered two anti-Union men in Utah and was executed in 1915, becoming a union martyr.

Officials offered Hill a choice of execution (the only U. S. state to provide alternate ways of being put to death), by hanging or shooting. "I'll take shooting," Hill said. "I'm used to that. I have been shot a few times in the past and I guess I can stand it again."

Before dawn on November 19, 1915, guards took Hill kicking and screaming from his cell. He was taken to the prison courtyard, where he was strapped into a wooden chair. A firing squad faced him twenty yards away. "Fire!" shouted Hill. "Go on and fire!" The volley exploded and one bullet struck Hill dead center in his heart, killing him. Hill became a union martyr—Haywood saw to that—and, during the 1960s, a coffeehouse hero, whose songs (he had composed several union tunes) were wailed by singers who, for the most part, had never heard of the IWW, or John or Arling Morrison, who had been killed in cold blood by Hill, and for whom no poignant songs had been written.

Six months after Joe Hill was executed, a terrific explosion took place on a street in San Francisco, one that killed ten persons and seriously injured another fifty people. Weeks before that terrorist attack took place, San Francisco businesses had been advertising Preparedness Day, scheduled for July 22, 1916. The day was fast approaching, these business leaders concluded, when the U. S. would enter the war in Europe on the side of the Allies. A parade was planned to display patriotic support for the Allied cause, despite President Woodrow Wilson's reelection slogan of "Too Proud to Fight."

As bands blared and veterans marched, a dynamite bomb exploded near the intersection of Market and Steuart streets, causing a searing blast that took the lives of ten spectators and wounded another fifty people. The blast could be heard blocks away. The explosion indiscriminately killed men, women and children. The huge fireball from the explosion shot upward and a sickening cloud of black smoke towered above the tallest buildings, so that it could be seen from any place in San Francisco.

Police and officials inspect some of the ten dead spectators killed by a terrorist bomb at Market and Steuart streets during San Francisco's Preparedness Day Parade on July 22, 1916.

Police worked night and day to identify the terrorists, rounding up German citizens, who might be working on behalf of the Kaiser Wilhelm II. They arrested Mexicans, who might be resentful of the incursion into Mexico by General John J. Pershing, then searching for the bandit, Pancho Villa. Italians were arrested, who might have been members of Black Hand rings. All were released. Officials settled on IWW union leaders Thomas J. Mooney and Warren Knox Billings, who had openly opposed America's entry into World War I. Both were arrested and charged with setting off the Preparedness Day Parade bomb.

Mooney and Billings were brought to trial on January 3, 1917, before Judge Frank Griffin. Mooney was unruffled, providing the court with an iron-clad alibi. He showed photos of him and his wife watching the parade from the roof of the Eilers Building, with a large clock nearby that showed their presence at that building at 2:04 p.m. The explosion, several blocks away, took place two seconds later. It appeared that Mooney and Billings would quickly be dismissed, but the prosecution had a star witness, Frank C. Oxman, a traveling salesman from Durkee, Oregon.

Imprisoned union leader Tom Mooney was wrongly convicted for the Preparedness Day Parade bombing, spending twenty years behind bars, until pardoned in 1939.

Oxman took the stand to emphatically state that he saw Mooney and Billings place a large black suitcase against the wall of a saloon and that only a few minutes after the explosion took place, which was at the site of the saloon, Mooney and Billings fled. This eyewitness testimony resulted in convictions. Mooney was sentenced to death and Billings to life at Folsom Prison. Awaiting execution at San Quentin, Mooney's sentence was commuted to life after President Woodrow Wilson intervened.

Following these events, it was then learned that Oxman had lied, that he had been nowhere near the Preparedness Day Parade on July 22, 1916, but had been doing business on that day in Woodlands, California, more than 100 miles distant from San Francisco. He was tried for perjury, but was acquitted in 1921, due to the efforts of the prosecutors, who had originally induced him to lie against Mooney and Billings.

Embarrassed state officials, however, later offered Mooney and Billings paroles. Billings accepted and was released, but Mooney said that by accepting a parole, he would be admitting to having set off the 1916 explosion. He demanded a full pardon, but he did not get it until twenty years later. He was released on October 15, 1939, having spent two decades behind bars for a terrorist act committed by someone else.

THE SIEGE OF SIDNEY STREET/ January 3, 1911

The anarchy practiced by the Wobblies was embraced by many European political groups, not the least of which was a murderous anarchist clan that committed violent robberies in London in late 1910 that resulted in a full-scale battle on the city streets only weeks later. Though Winston Churchill would later point to England's finest hours with justifiable pride, his actions during the shootout on Sidney Street on the dank morning of January 3, 1911, were not among them. "The police can hardly be congratulated upon their success in dealing with this formidable conspiracy," exclaimed the *Daily Mail* afterward. Home Secretary Churchill committed a major public relations *faux pas* by appearing in the streets with an army of police officers—never had it taken so many to bring down so few.

The events leading up to the Sidney Street battle had caused a sensation among conservatives, who sought to quell the tide of foreigners with anarchist leanings entering the country. Five Russian and Eastern European nationals attempted to rob a jeweler's store in the Exchange Buildings in Houndsditch, a section of London's East End, on December 16, 1910. The police were summoned by a resident complaining of loud noises in the middle of the night. The burglars were attempting to bore a hole through a wall to reach a jeweler's safe in an adjacent office.

The five robbers were political refugees who had been driven out of their respective countries for subversive activities. The leader of the gang was George Gardstein, otherwise known as Mouremtzov. His accomplices included Max Smoller, a fugitive from the Crimea; Nina Vassileva, Gardstein's mistress, who stood watch outside the store; Jacob Peters, a Communist ideologue, who had been tortured by the Okhrana, the czar's secret police; and

Anarchist leader Peter the Painter eluded police during the Siege of Sidney Street.

British constables carrying shotguns proceed along Sidney Street to confront the anarchists waging an open battle with them on January 3, 1911.

Yourka Dubof, a locksmith who was to open the jeweler's safe for the gang. Vassileva alerted Gardstein when the police arrived.

The men ceased drilling, as Sergeant Bentley positioned his men around the perimeter of the building. Bentley cautiously approached the door of number eleven and knocked. When Gardstein opened the door, Bentley asked, "Have you been working or knocking about inside?" Gardstein indicated that he understood no English, then disappeared into the rear of the building.

Police officers entered the premises, but it was too dark for them to see. Suddenly, the rear door swung open and a man with a gun opened fire. Bentley was shot in the neck and shoulder and Constable Woodhams was also shot, when he tried to assist Bentley. A third man, Constable Tucker, was shot through the chest and died instantly. Gardstein attempted to flee. He pushed past Constable Choat, who was knocked to the ground, and who was shot by Peters and Dubof.

One policeman was dead and two others were mortally wounded. Gardstein, who also suffered a serious gunshot wound, escaped with his gang intact. The anarchists retreated to the dwelling of Fritz Svaars, a cousin of Peters and an instigator of the aborted robbery, where Gardstein was judged a liability and left to die in his bedroom. The police, meanwhile, launched an intensive manhunt. The field of suspects was quickly narrowed, and the trail of blood left by Gardstein led investigators to Svaars' room.

Jacob Peters, Yourka Dubof, and Svaars' mistress, Luba Milstein, were arrested. Smoller disappeared, and Svaars became a fugitive from justice despite having taken no direct part in the robbery-murder. Fearing deportation back to Russia, he took the greatest care not to fall into a police trap.

For the next several weeks, the police focused their efforts on the East End, rousting all suspected anarchists from their known haunts. Detective-Superintendent John Ottaway and Inspector Frederick Wensley were particularly effective in this regard. On New Year's Day 1911, they received a tip that Svaars and a jeweler known as "Joseph" were hiding out at 100 Sidney Street with a woman named Betsy Gershon.

Ottaway and Wensley's plan to approach the dwelling with caution was complicated because the building was one of ten four-story abodes, each divided by fireproof walls. A full complement of 200 policemen was deployed throughout the neighborhood to prevent any escapes. Safely removing

Soldiers and police mass for a charge at the buildings occupied by the battling anarchists on Sidney Street.

British Home Secretary Winston Churchill, first man left wearing top hat, peers apprehensively around a corner during the battle; he was later criticized for mishandling the bloody confrontation.

Peter Lorre, left, is shown as the anarchist leader in Alfred Hitchcock's 1935 film, *The Man Who Knew Too Much*, which depicted the disastrous Siege of Sidney Street.

the other residents of 100 Sidney Street proved to be the most difficult aspect of the operation, and this was not accomplished until 4 a.m. The police then tightened their cordon around the tenement building. Inside remained only two men, one of whom was believed to be the notorious Peter the Painter, an anarchist who had been involved in several robberies and shootings.

The conflict began at 7:30 on the morning of January 3, 1911. One of the sergeants from the detail hurled pebbles at the window to draw the attention of the men inside while a second officer pounded on the door. Suddenly, a stream of gunfire came from one of the upper windows. The street scene was chaotic as the police took cover. For the next two hours the police traded shots with the anarchists.

Winston Churchill was interrupted in his bath and informed of the situation. He instructed the police to "use whatever force necessary" to bring the situation under control. At 10:15 a.m., a detachment of Scots Guards arrived from the Tower of London. There was furious debate among the officers about the proper way of ending the siege, but nothing was accomplished.

Churchill decided on an impulse to go to Sidney Street and take charge of the situation. It was a serious breach of protocol that would be severely criticized in the days to come. The home secretary gave the order to bring in field artillery and bring down the house if necessary, but it was decided to storm the building first.

Before the Scots Guards could mount their attack, however, an onlooker pointed to a thin wisp of smoke coming from the roof. The house was on fire. The blaze apparently started on the upper floors and worked its way downward. As one of the gunmen poked his head out the window, bullets from the street pierced his head, but neither Churchill nor the police knew that at the time.

The fire spread quickly inside the bullet-riddled building. The fire brigade arrived on the scene, but Churchill ordered them to stand by and wait before turning their hoses loose. When the upper floors of the tenement collapsed in flames, the firemen quickly moved in. From the massive pile of rubble the police pulled out the charred remains of Fritz Svaars and Jacob Vogel, both of whom worked for Peter the Painter. Vogel had been shot, and Svaars had killed himself in the flames. The Sidney Street shootout became a lively topic of debate in the world press, while the British government struggled with the immigration issue. Ironically, the remaining members of the gang, who had been arrested for the Houndsditch murders, were acquitted for lack of evidence. The Siege of Sidney Street was recreated with considerable accuracy by film director Alfred Hitchcock, in his first outing of *The Man Who Knew Too Much*, produced in 1935.

DAYS OF THE ANARCHISTS/1919-1920

In an all-out campaign to provoke a widespread revolution in America, anarchists and Communists in the U. S. unleashed terrorist campaigns that led to public panic. Through bombings and attempted assassinations, these terrorists only provoked heavy-handed repression from governmental agencies, which would later be known as the notorious Red Raids (1919-1921).

The anarchists launched their terrorist campaign on June 2, 1919, when one of their members left a bomb on the front doorstep of the home of U. S. Attorney General A. Mitchell Palmer. The bomb prematurely exploded at 11:15 p.m., destroying the façade of Palmer's house and killing the anarchist who had placed it there. The terrorist could not be identified as the bomb blew him into tiny pieces. The largest fragment remaining was a bloody foot, still encased in a shoe, blown across the street, where it landed at the front door of the assistant secretary of the Navy, Franklin Delano Roosevelt.

On that same night, anarchists planted eight more bombs throughout Washington, D. C. The facades of several government buildings were destroyed, but no one was killed. At all of the sites the police found the same message left behind by the terrorists: "The powers that be make no secret of their wills to stop the worldwide spread of revolution. The powers that be must reckon that they will have to accept the fight they have provoked. A time has come when the social question's solution can be delayed no longer; class war is on and cannot cease but with a complete victory for the international proletariat."

Thirty-eight more bombs were sent in following days to government leaders, who had denounced anarchists and Communists. None were killed, but the bomb explosions and mailings of bombs terrified the country and promptly created a national fear of what was called the Red Menace. Palmer took quick measures, having a young Department of Justice attor-

A 1919 cartoon shows a threatening "Red" creeping from beneath an American flag clutching a knife labeled "Bolshevism," and a torch entitled "anarchy."

Police and militia round up hundreds of suspected anarchists and Communists in Boston, at the beginning of the Red Raids.

U. S. Attorney General A. Mitchell Palmer, responding to accusations that he overreached his authority in launching the Red Raids.

Youthful J. Edgar Hoover prepared the briefs that gave Palmer the rationale to launch the oppressive Red Raids.

ney write a history and evaluation report about the terrorists. He was J. Edgar Hoover, who also began preparing thousands of briefs that would allow the seizure of left-wing groups and individuals. Thousands of street brawlers and saloon thugs were deputized as U. S. marshals, who, without warrants, invaded the homes of suspected anarchists and Communists, beating them and dragging them to jails. Hundreds were later deported after kangaroo court hearings, including leading anarchists Alexander Berkman and Emma Goldman.

The anarchists retaliated with more bombs, the worst of these explosions occurring on September 16, 1920. On that day a lone terrorist drove a horse-drawn wagon to the corner of Broad and Wall streets in New York City. He stepped from the wagon and began to run. A few minutes later, at 11:59 a.m.—undoubtedly timed to kill the many people crowding the area at lunch time—the entire wagon, which was packed with explosives, blew up with a terrific roar. Thirty-eight persons were found dead in the smoking debris. Hundreds more had been injured, dozens crippled for life.

The offices of J. P. Morgan, America's foremost banker and financier, the epitome of the American capitalist system, had been widely damaged, but only one clerk, Thomas Joyce, had been killed. The blast had blow cars onto their sides, reduced other cars to skeletal frames and blown out thousands of windows blocks away. Reporter Edmund Gilligan was at the site, later stating: "The gentle sound of tinkling glass falling and slipping from sill to ledge and then to the pavement came like music." Then high piercing screams from injured women could be heard.

Police learned that the terrorist had delivered a bomb that was carefully constructed to take many lives. The wagon had been filled with sash weights that had been chipped into small pieces so that when the dynamite exploded, these metal fragments served as shrapnel tearing through the lunchtime Wall Street crowds. Police launched a manhunt for the terrorist, but since his wagon and horse was blown to pieces, little evidence remained. A reward of $100,000 was posted for his capture, but no one claimed it. The terrorist was never found.

The government stepped up its Red Raids and, in 1920-1921, arrested more than 10,000 suspected anarchists and Communists, deporting 446 of these persons. These repressive measures were denounced in Congress and labor leaders accused Attorney General Palmer of acting in "absolute ignorance of American principles." Palmer was summoned to explain his actions before the House Rules Committee, where he said he had been pressured to act prematurely, admitting that his untrained marshals had been sent out to conduct raids with little or no evidence because of the lack of time involved.

"I say that I was shouted at from every editorial sanctum in America from sea to sea!" thundered Palmer. "I was preached upon from every pulpit. I was urged—I could feel it dinned into my ears—throughout the country to do something and do it now, and do it quick, and do it in a way that would bring results to stop this sort of thing [bombings] in the United States!" He called his rowdy marshals patriots, who had exercised their authority with understandable excessive zeal. "I forgive them," he said. "I do not defend it, but I am not going to make a row about it."

September 16, 1920: Death at Broad and Wall Streets in New York City, where a terrorist left a horse-drawn wagon filled with explosives and shrapnel-like metal, which blew up at lunch time, killing thirty-eight and injuring hundreds more.

The offices of banker J. P. Morgan, ripped to pieces by the Wall Street Bombing in 1920; Morgan's chief clerk, Thomas Joyce was killed by flying metal that blew out the windows.

The man who had prepared the so-called "evidence" that launched the Red Raids, young J. Edgar Hoover, not only survived this scandal, but was privately lauded for his efforts by many government officials. It was Hoover's diligent "research" (culled from a two-week crash course in leftist philosophy at the Library of Congress) that directly resulted in Palmer's Red Raids and propelled Hoover into a position at the Bureau of Investigation, which he took over in 1924, later renaming it the Federal Bureau of Investigation or FBI.

HUNGARY'S TRAIN BOMBER/1931-1932

Hungarian businessman Sylvestre Matuschka prospered after World War I, until he was accused of fraud. He was acquitted, but the scandal wrecked his reputation, so he sold his businesses in Budapest and moved to Vienna. There he developed an interest in causing train crashes. His first attempt was on New Year's Day, 1931, when he tried unsuccessfully to derail the Vienna-Passau train near Ansbach.

Matuschka's first success came at Juelerboy, Hungary, where he managed to overturn several coaches, which then rolled down an embankment, injuring seventy-five people on August 8, 1932. Then, on September 12, 1932, he used an explosive device to blow up a Hungarian Railways express as it crossed a viaduct at Bia-Torbagy. Twenty-two people were killed when cars fell off the elevated track. As the dust settled, he bloodied his own face and lay down among the victims.

Matuschka was taken to a hospital where he quickly recovered from his "wounds." He then promptly sued the Hungarian Railways over his supposed injuries. But the police could find no one who had seen him on the train. After further investigation, Matuschka was arrested. In his house, police found plans for similar disasters in France, Italy, and the Netherlands. Matuschka soon confessed to having wrecked trains in order to collect insurance money on non-existent injuries he claimed to have sustained.

The first of several trials began on June 15, 1932. The only believable motive offered at the trials was that Matuschka derived from the crashes some deep sexual satisfaction that he could not find elsewhere. Matuschka himself blamed his condition on a hypnotist he met at a country fair, or on orders from an invisible spiritual being named Leo. Prosecutors felt that all of these "visions" were created by the train bomber to convince the court that he was insane.

Sylvestre Matuschka, bearded man center, blew up trains in Hungary in order to collect insurance money.

Matuschka, however, was judged sane and, after the second trial, was found guilty and sentenced to hang. His sentence was then commuted to life imprisonment, and he was reportedly released during World War II by the Soviets, who employed him as an explosives expert.

NEW YORK'S MAD BOMBER/1940s-1950s

George Metesky (AKA: The Mad Bomber, b. 1903), the man who terrorized New York City for two decades, was a squat, unassuming man with a receding hairline and a very sharp ax to grind. On September 5, 1931, Metesky was working for Consolidated Edison as a generator wiper at its Hell Gate plant, when a sudden rush of hot, noxious gasses threw him to the ground. Doctors who examined him found nothing seriously wrong. In the coming months, he argued unsuccessfully for permanent disability pay, claiming the accident had brought on serious headaches.

Metesky raged against Consolidated Edison for the next nine years. On November 16, 1940, police removed an unexploded pipe bomb from the Edison building on West Sixty Fourth Street in Manhattan. The device was wrapped inside a toolbox, with a note that read: "Con Edison crooks, this is for you." It was the first of thirty-seven bombs Metesky was to plant in the next sixteen years at scattered sites throughout Manhattan.

The second bomb was recovered from a location on Nineteenth Street in September 1941. It was also a dud. When war was declared in December, a note was received at police headquarters, which said: "I will make no more bomb units for the duration of the war my patriotic feelings have made me decide this later I will bring the Con Edison to justice they will pay for their dastardly deeds." It was signed "F.P.," which police later found out stood for "Fair Play."

During the war, Metesky sent a series of anonymous letters to newspapers, theaters, and restaurants promising reprisals against the city of New York, but no more bombs were planted until March 29, 1950, when one was found at Grand Central Station.

The bomb squad detonated it before it could do any damage. Bombs four and five exploded in a phone booth near the New York Public Library and the Grand Hotel a month later, but no one was killed or injured. The next three bombs were duds, but the police noted with alarm that each was more dangerous than the last.

In 1954, a bomb exploded under a seat at the Radio City Music Hall, resulting in two injuries and substantial property damage. A year later four of six bombs planted by Metesky exploded in New York. One device in Grand Central Station seriously injured a redcap. By this time, the press dubbed the unknown terrorist the "Mad Bomber." Macy's Department Store, the Paramount Theatre in Brooklyn, and the Radio Corporation of America—all high visibility public buildings—became Metesky's next targets.

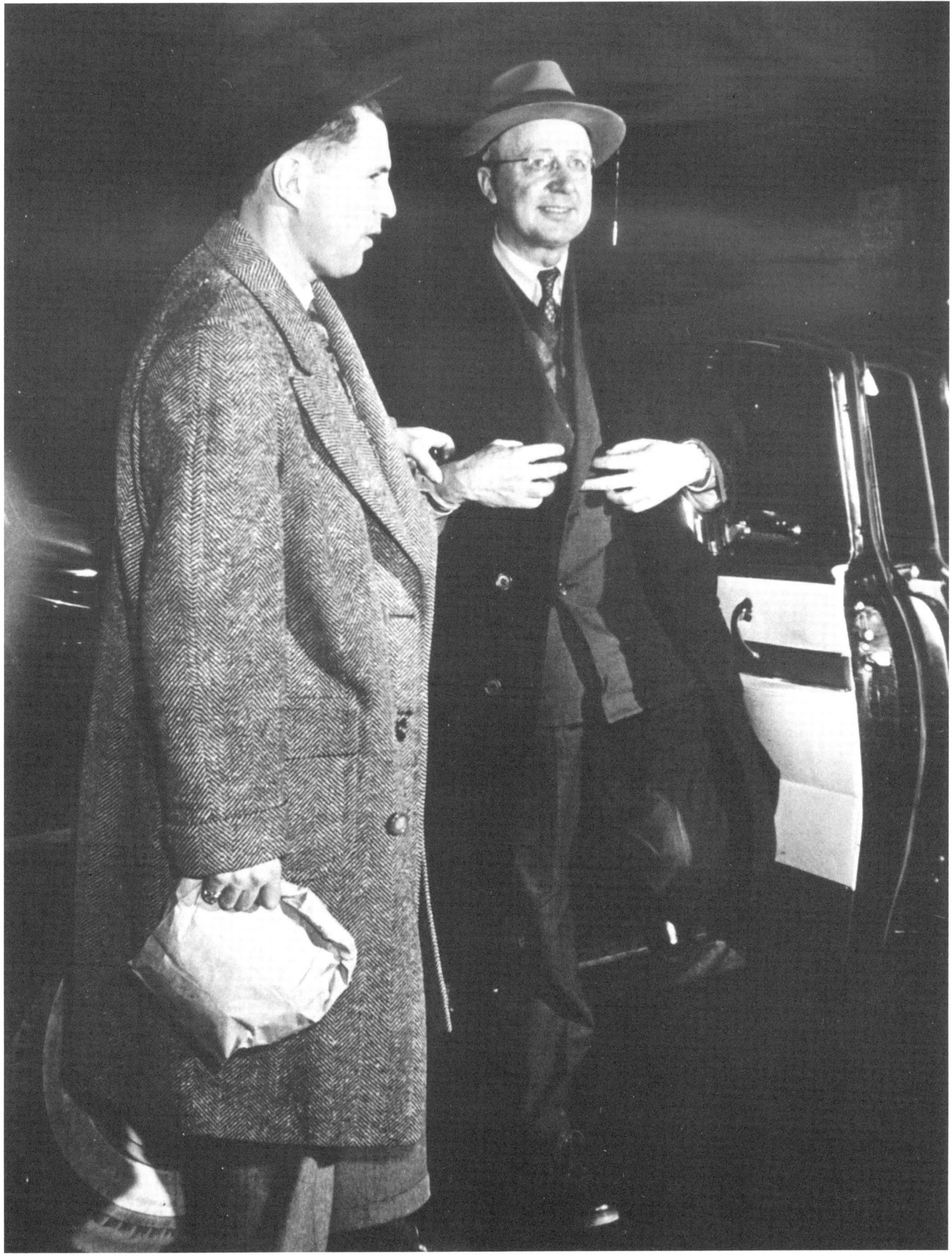

George Peter Metesky, right, under arrest; New York's Mad Bomber was identified by a clerk at the Edison company and was sent to an insane asylum.

Stymied, the police asked James A. Brussel, assistant commissioner of mental health for the state of New York, to construct a psychological profile of the suspect. Brussel concluded that "F.P.", or whoever he pretended to be, was undoubtedly Slavic since, he said, these people had a long history of this kind of activity and a chronic paranoid. "When you find this man he'll be wearing a double-breasted suit," Brussel added.

The police organized a special bomb investigation unit, but before police could identify the bomber, the collective efforts of Alice Kelly and several other employees of Consolidated Edison fingered Metesky as the terrorist. His file contained the pertinent history. Metesky was picked up in Waterbury, Connecticut, at the residence of his two spinster sisters.

"I think I know why you fellows are here," Metesky said unconcernedly to the officers. "You think I'm the Mad Bomber." The 54-year-old bachelor put on a pinstripe, double-breasted suit and accompanied detectives to the police station. Metesky was deemed of unsound mind, and was committed to the state hospital by Judge Samuel Leibowitz in April 1957.

Metesky spent the next sixteen years in various mental health facilities before earning a final release from custody on December 13, 1973. At the time, the man who had terrorized New York for almost two decades met briefly with newspapermen and gave them a wide smile. "I don't look like a mad bomber, do I," he asked them before stepping into a car that took him to the home of his elderly sisters.

"That guy is right out of the movie, *Arsenic and Old Lace*," quipped one newsman. "The character Jonathan, the monster brother fooling around in the basement and making plans you don't want to hear about."

THE SLA AND PATTY HEARST/1973-1977

Within a four-month period, the public image of Patricia Campbell Hearst, granddaughter of the wealthy and powerful newspaper publisher William Randolph Hearst, went from tragic kidnap victim to leftist sympathizer to bank robber, and finally to "armed and dangerous fugitive." Hearst was the most prominent victim of a group of half-baked intellectuals and hard-core criminals called the Symbionese Liberation Army, or SLA.

The SLA was founded by Donald David DeFreeze, a terrorist who had escaped from prison in March 1973 after being sentenced four years earlier for possession of a bomb. In prison DeFreeze learned both the rhetoric and strategy of revolutionary action. He called himself Field Marshal Cinque and advocated equality and the abolition of capitalism. Upon his release, DeFreeze began to collect followers, chiefly academic dropouts and social misfits, recruits for his revolutionary army, the SLA.

Fielding about for terrorist prey, DeFreeze selected a by-the-book educator to be murdered in the name of his crazy-quilt revolutionary theories. SLA members shot to death Marcus A. Foster, the school superintendent of Oakland on November 6, 1973, because Foster endorsed the use of mandatory student identification cards to control juvenile crime. The bullets found in Foster's body proved to be tipped with cyanide.

Two months later, on January 10, 1974, a policeman stopped a van in Concord, California. The van's occupants, Russell Little and Joseph Remiro, both SLA members, pulled guns. Little was apprehended. Remiro got away but was caught later. When the SLA headquarters was set on fire that night, police found records listing names of members, and a written entry alluding to Patricia Hearst.

On February 4, 1974, Steven Weed, Patricia Hearst's fiancé answered a knock at the door of their shared townhouse in Berkeley, California. As a woman engaged Weed in conversation, two men appeared and pushed the door open. Weed was beaten on the head and 19-year-old Hearst, dressed in a bathrobe, was carried screaming to a waiting car. Three days after Hearst's abduction, authorities received word that the SLA was demanding the donation of millions of dollars worth of food to the poor of California. In a tape recording delivered to a radio station, Hearst said in a monotone: "These people aren't just a bunch of nuts. They're perfectly willing to die for what they're doing."

Randolph Hearst, Patricia's father, organized a quick give-away of packaged foods, but the SLA said the shipment was inadequate. Another tape on which Patricia criticized her father's lack of generosity caused speculation that the kidnapping had been planned by Patricia Hearst and her friends. Although Hearst gave away more food totaling another $2 million, the SLA did not release his daughter. DeFreeze then made a statement that she would be held until SLA members Remiro and Little were released.

In Patricia Hearst's own version of the kidnapping, told seven years later, she said that she spent the first fifty-seven

Patricia Campbell Hearst was reportedly recruited by SLA terrorists while attending the University of California at Berkeley.

days of her captivity in a closet, blindfolded and bound. She was raped repeatedly and gradually brainwashed into believing that the SLA members were the only people who cared about her, she said.

Just as her parents believed that she was about to be released, they received another tape in which their daughter stated: "I have never been forced to say anything on any tape. Nor have I been brainwashed, tortured, hypnotized or in any way confused....My love has...grown into an unselfish love for my comrades here, in prison and on the streets. A love that comes from the knowledge that `no one is free until we all are free.'...I have been given the choice of (1) being released in a safe area, or (2) joining the forces of the Symbionese Liberation Army...I have chosen to stay and fight."

While the public continued to believe that Patricia Hearst was being coerced, the SLA robbed a branch of the Hibernia Bank in San Francisco's Sunset District of more than $10,000. Hidden cameras in the bank showed "Tania," as Hearst was called by SLA members, holding a semiautomatic carbine and apparently giving orders. It would later be discovered that Hearst had early on joined the SLA, perhaps as early as 1973, while attending the University of California at Berkeley, then a hotbed of radicals and had play-acted her own abduction to coerce her father into providing food and money.

Hearst later participated in the robbery of a sporting goods store in Inglewood, California, with white SLA members Emily and William Harris, spraying the façade with machine gun bullets. Three days later, on May 17, 1974, police received a tip from a former SLA member that the gang was holed up in a small stucco house at 1466 East 54th Street in Los Angeles. More than 400 heavily-armed officers, including FBI agents, attacked the place after the occupants refused to surrender.

A terrific firefight ensued, with more than 6,000 shots being fired on both sides before the house caught fire. The next day, the bodies of four women and two men were found in the ruins. The dead were identified as DeFreeze and William Wolfe, purported to be Hearst's lover, Camilla Hall, Nancy Ling Perry, and Patricia Soltysik. At the time of the shootout, Hearst was with William and Emily Harris in Las Vegas. Following the destruction of the main gang, Hearst and the Harris couple traveled eastward and tried to keep the SLA going even when its original leaders were dead.

In 1975, the remaining SLA members robbed a bank in Carmichael, California. Emily Harris reportedly killed a

Steven Weed and Patty Hearst were living in Berkeley, California, where Weed was beaten by SLA members and Hearst "abducted."

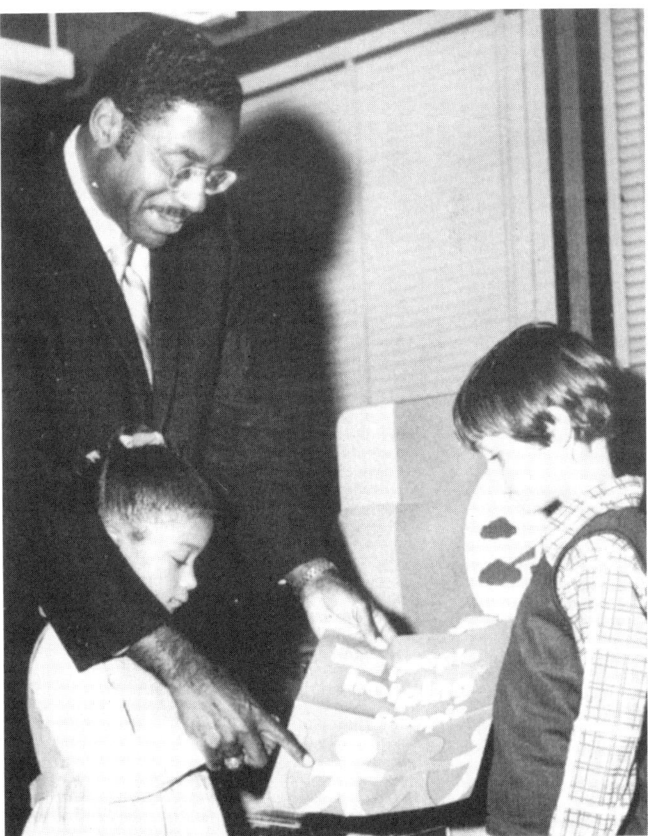

Marcus A. Foster is shown with school children shortly before he was murdered by SLA terrorists on November 6, 1973.

Patty Hearst, who later claimed that she was kidnapped and held hostage by terrorists, poses with the SLA symbol (a hydra-headed cobra) and an automatic weapon.

SLA leader Donald DeFreeze died in the 1974 L. A. shootout.

SLA member Patricia Soltysik died in the 1974 L. A. shootout.

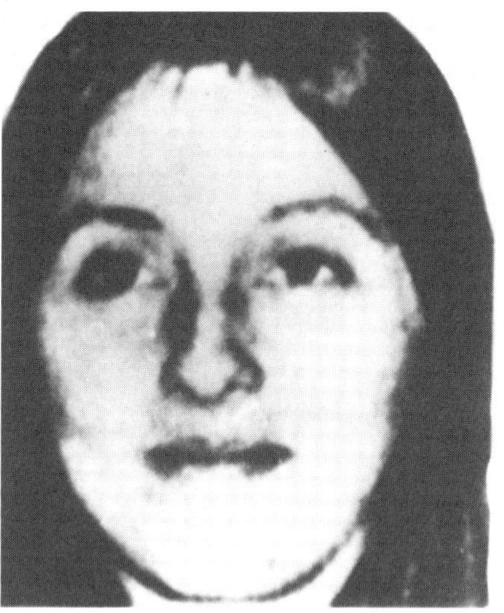

SLA member Angela Atwood died in the 1974 L. A. shootout.

SLA member William Wolfe died in the 1974 L. A. shootout.

SLA member Nancy Ling Perry died in the 1974 L. A. shootout.

SLA member Camilla Hall died in the 1974 L. A. shootout.

Catherine and Randolph Hearst after hearing their daughter's "plea" on a tape that food be distributed to the poor before her captors set her free.

Parcels are tossed wildly from a truck to blacks in Richmond, California, following the People in Need program launched by Randolph Hearst to effect the release of his "captive" daughter.

Captured on video tape, Patty Hearst is shown brandishing an automatic weapon during the robbery of the Hibernia Bank in San Francisco on April 15, 1974. She later claimed that she was compelled to aid the terrorists in this and other robberies.

A SWAT officer fires at the Los Angeles bungalow, where six SLA heavily armed terrorists fired back in a prolonged battle.

The burning bungalow in which the SLA terrorists died following a firefight on May 17, 1974; six SLA members were later found dead in the burning wreckage.

LAPD Sergeant Charles Loust shows the site of the 1974 firefight with SLA members and the huge arsenal retrieved from the rubble, including machine guns, shotguns, handguns, and pipe bombs.

SLA terrorist William Harris was imprisoned for kidnapping and paroled in 1983.

SLA terrorist Emily Harris was imprisoned for kidnapping and paroled in 1983.

woman in the robbery. On a third attempt to bomb a police station on September 18, 1975, Patricia Hearst and Wendy Yoshimura were caught by the police. The rest of the group was apprehended within a few days.

Patricia Hearst was tried and found guilty of armed robbery. She was sentenced to seven years in prison, but her sentence was commuted by President Jimmy Carter after two years. The Harrises, jailed for kidnapping, were paroled in 1983. In June 1977, Michael Remiro and Russell Little were sentenced to life in prison for the killing of Marcus Foster, and six months to twenty years for the attempted murder of Robert Blackburn, Foster's deputy, who was wounded at the time of Foster's murder.

DAYS OF THE JACKAL/1970s-1980s

The father of the man who came to be known as Carlos, or the Jackal, the world's most feared terrorist, was a wealthy Venezuelan attorney in Caracas. He and his wife were devout Communists and raised their son on communism, indoctrinating the boy at an early age with unswerving Marxist theory and philosophy, as had been the case with his brothers, Vladimir and Lenin Ramirez Sanchez. Illich Ramirez Sanchez (Carlos, The Jackal, b. 1949)—his parents gave him Lenin's middle name—joined the Communist student movement in Venezuela in 1964 and was then sent to Cuba, where, under the wing of Communist dictator Fidel Castro, he was trained to become a terrorist.

Castro saw to it that Ramirez Sanchez, coming from an elitist Communist family in Venezuela, received special attention from experts in the Cuban Direccion General de Inteligencia (DGI). He was then known to his fellow trainees as "Pudgy" or "Fatty." So eager did the apprentice terrorist appear, however, that he was brought to the attention of KGB General Simenov, a Russian spymaster who was overseeing DGI training inside Cuba. Simenov arranged for the overweight youth to travel to Moscow, where his talent for murder and mayhem could be sharpened to razor-like effectiveness.

In 1968, Ramirez Sanchez received more intense training at Patrice Lumumba University in Moscow, an institution notorious for educating terrorists in the bloody techniques of their trade, as well as KGB agents who were used exclusively in covert operations. In 1970, he joined the most deadly terrorist organization in the Middle East, the Popular Front for the Liberation of Palestine, or the PFLP, which had, throughout the 1960s, been responsible for countless bombings, assassinations, kidnappings and mass murders.

A willing and eager PFLP disciple, Ramirez Sanchez soon became a group leader and then a PFLP strategist engineering terrorism against Israel and Western democracies. His code name of Carlos became widely known, as well as his sobriquet among his enemies, the Jackal, so much so that author Frederick Forsyth used him as a role model in his devastating portrait of the terrorist-assassin who stalks French President Charles de Gaulle in his 1971 novel, *The Day of the Jackal*. This book, and the 1973 film by the same name, more than any of his actual exploits to that time, elevated Ramirez Sanchez to the high and unenviable rank of international terrorist, a position he would soon occupy in reality.

Illich Ramirez Sanchez, in his early twenties, before he became known as Carlos, the international terrorist.

In 1972, Carlos was linked to the massacre of eleven Israeli athletes at the Munich Olympics. He was also connected to the takeover of the French Embassy in The Hague, Netherlands, in 1974, along with the bombing of a drugstore in Paris, France, that same year, an explosion that took the lives of two people and wounded another thirty.

In early 1975, Ramirez Sanchez had engineered attacks against Israel's El Al airlines at Paris' Orly Airport. Two French intelligence agents, members of the DST, France's version of the FBI, got on to Carlos through one of his friends, a Lebanese informer, and were tracking down the terrorist in Paris, when he turned the tables on them. Carlos lured the three to a Paris apartment and then shot and killed the two French agents, Raymond Dous and Jean Donatini, along with his former Lebanese colleague, Michel Moukharbal.

This triple murder vaulted Carlos to the top of the terrorist heap in the estimation of his ruthless peers, but it also set upon his trail scores of dogged DST agents who would not give up the hunt for him. Defying capture, Ramirez Sanchez then performed his most spectacular terrorist coup on December 21, 1975, when he and six other heavily armed terrorists invaded an OPEC conference in Vienna, Austria, holding eighty-one members hostage.

Austrian negotiators were informed by Carlos, in the name of the "Arm of the Arab Revolution," that if his demands were not met, he would slaughter the entire OPEC membership, representing the richest men in the world, who controlled the global flow of oil. Forty-one Austrian hostages were released through negotiations, but the other African, South American and Arab delegates were forced to accompany Carlos on a flight to Algiers and then on to Tripoli, where they were released unharmed, but only after the Shah of Iran and King Khaled paid Ramirez Sanchez an estimated $50 million in cash. (The terrorist had reportedly demanded $1 billion.)

Ernesto "Che" Guevara, and Fidel Castro; the Cuban dictator took Ramirez Sanchez under his wing and had him trained as a terrorist.

Carlos (Illich Ramirez Sanchez), also known as the Jackal, at the time he was the world's most notorious terrorist kidnapper and killer.

Almost immediately after completing this terrorist coup, Carlos vanished, the most reliable reports having him in Libya, where he was protected by one of his employers and fellow terrorist, Muammar Qadaffi, the country's Islamic fundamentalist dictator, who reportedly received a goodly share of the loot from the OPEC kidnappings. Ramirez Sanchez did not remain inactive for long. On June 24, 1976, Carlos sent seven terrorists, five PFLP members and two German Communists, to skyjack an Air France airbus en route from Tel Aviv to Paris.

The plane was ordered to fly to Entebbe, Uganda, where it re-

A surveillance photo of Carlos (Ramirez Sanchez) just before French agents seized him in Khartoum, Sudan, and took him back to France in 1994. He was convicted of murder and given a life sentence in 1997.

mained grounded with the collusion of Ugandan dictator Idi Amin, the mostly Jewish passengers held hostage in a nearby building complex. Israeli commandos, ordered to Entebbe by Israel's then-prime minister, Yitzhak Rabin, effected the release of the hostages by storming the complex and the plane. Thirty-one persons were killed, including two hostages, all seven of the terrorists, and Colonel Netanyahu, leader of the Israeli commandos and the older brother of future Prime Minister Benjamin Netanyahu.

For almost five years Carlos appeared to be inactive, but during 1982-1983 he resumed his terrorist campaigns with a vengeance. Carlos directed the March 29, 1982, bombing of a Paris-to-Toulouse express train that killed six persons and wounded another fifteen. He was thought to be behind the August 9, 1982, bombing of a Jewish restaurant in Paris and the machine-gunning of fleeing patrons, a massacre that killed six people and wounded another twenty-two. Carlos was also behind a Paris bombing on the Champs Elysees that killed a pregnant woman and injured another sixty-three persons.

In 1982, Ramirez Sanchez was himself almost killed when Palestinian guerrillas were driven out of Beirut by Israeli forces, but he managed to escape. Carlos renewed his attacks in 1983, directing the bombing of the main terminal in Marseille, France, an explosion that killed five people and wounded another fifty. He was also behind the bombing of the French cultural center in West Berlin, a blast that killed one person and injured another twenty-three.

Again, Carlos went underground. In 1992, a French court convicted Ramirez Sanchez *in absentia* of killing the two French counterintelligence agents and the Lebanese informer. He was sentenced to thirty-two years in prison, but this mattered little to the terrorist, who remained at large, becoming an arms merchant and hiding in Khartoum, Sudan. There he drank the best whiskey in the capital's nightclubs. Though married to a new Jordanian wife, Carlos was infamous throughout Khartoum as a woman-chaser.

To the strict Islamic Sudanese government, the high-living Carlos was an embarrassment, and through its tacit cooperation, Ramirez Sanchez was seized on a hospital operating table in August 1994 by French agents. He was reportedly injected with an incapacitating drug and stuffed into a sack before he was bundled aboard a plane and flown to France, where he sat in solitary confinement for two years, awaiting a retrial for the three murders for which he had already been convicted.

Carlos demanded that retrial, even though he condemned the right of any French court to try him because he had been illegally seized in the Sudan. He was finally brought before a French court in 1997, wearing an ascot and proudly stating, "My name is Illich Ramirez Sanchez. My profession is professional revolutionary."

To one observer, the fat, balding terrorist was a thing of the past: "He knows he's a has-been. His mental universe is the Palestinian guerrilla movement. He's nothing but a dinosaur of the Cold War stranded in the 1990s."

Ramirez Sanchez insisted that he was a "political prisoner" and that "there is no law for me." He could not refute the evidence brought forth that eventually convicted him of the 1975 killing of the two French agents and his former Lebanese friend. Carlos stood smug and smirking as the French tribunal announced his conviction on December 24, 1997. He shook his fist in the air four times and shouted, "Viva la revolución!" He was then sentenced to life in prison.

Before he was led away, Carlos stated, "They want to sentence me to life in prison. I'm 48 years old, so it could be another forty or fifty years. That doesn't horrify me."

THE JAPANESE TERRORIST CULT/1995

During the early 1990s, many dissatisfied members of the Japanese criminal and terrorist society known as the Yakuza (see Secret Criminal Societies) left the society's ranks to join a strange cult. This organization first came to international attention on March 20, 1995, when several packages left inside moving subway cars in the vast subway system of Tokyo began to spurt a powerful nerve gas that soon overwhelmed thousands of terrified passengers. Victims ran, tumbled, and staggered from the train cars and subway stations in wild panic. At the end of the day, twelve persons had died (eleven official deaths, one death unofficially related) from the poison gas attacks and 3,789 persons were injured or contaminated.

The terrorists behind the horrific attack were quickly identified by police as members of Aum Shinri Kyo (Supreme Truth). This doomsday cult believed that the end of the world

Bodies taken from the Tokyo subway system on March 20, 1995, victims of a sarin gas attack by Aum Shinri Kyo terrorists.

Almost all of Tokyo's paramedics and hospitals were used to treat the more than 3,000 people stricken by the gas attack.

Japanese police are shown rounding up cult members, which numbered in the tens of thousands.

Japanese police raided a cult site in a mountainous area and seized large quantities of deadly gas.

was coming soon and that only its organization would survive and rule over a mostly devastated planet.

Swarms of police teams began ferreting out cult members following the attack, making raids on their various headquarters throughout Japan and arresting hundreds. In the village of Kamikuisiki, nestled at the foot of Mt. Fuji, sixty-three miles west of Tokyo, police assaulted a cult compound in a televised raid, taking fifty-three children belonging to cult members, fearing that these children might be somehow injured by their doomsday-obsessed parents.

The parents chased after buses carrying the children, shouting: "This is kidnapping! Return our children!" The children were taken to a welfare facility, while bomb experts examined the compound. They found tons of chemicals, including trimethylphosphate and methuylphosphon acid dimethyl, byproducts of sarin, a gas decomposition the Nazis invented before World War II.

The use of sarin, the deadliest nerve gas ever created, caused the people of Japan to live for weeks in nerve-wracking terror, especially after cultists predicted a terrible calamity about to again engulf Japan. Cult spokesman Hirofumi Joyu, a youthful lawyer, tried to calm national fear by appearing on TV news and talk show programs, saying: "Please rest assured that Aum Shinri Kyo will not be taking any action."

Masato Yokoyama planted two packets of sarin in the Tokyo subway system; he was sentenced to death.

More than 100 cult members were meanwhile arrested in raids against more than 130 cult facilities throughout Japan. Members were charged with possession of guns, kidnapping, and even driving without a license, any offense that would allow police to take them into custody and interrogate them about cult leaders, such as the 40-year-old Shoko Asahara, who was then being widely sought. (The children of cult leaders wore electrode caps that reportedly put them directly in touch with the ever-expanding brain waves of the cult leader and thus benefited from Asahara's thoughts.)

Though lawyer Joyu had promised that the cult would "not be taking any action," Takaji Kunimatsu, chief of the National Police Agency, was shot and gravely wounded on March 30, 1995. It would take a year before the police rooted out the perpetrator, a 31-year-old police officer who was a cult member and who told his interrogators that Aum Shinri Kyo leaders ordered him to make the assault on Kunimatsu and he simply obeyed. (As is usually the case—and despite the claim that Japan claims to have an "open society"—Japanese law enforcement officials seldom provide information to the press, secreting their investigations and, even after trials, secreting judicial determinations. Thus, police would not release the name of the officer who had shot their chief.)

On April 24, 1995, police were able to locate and arrest 36-year-old Hideo Murai, one of the five top cult leaders and head of the cult's "Science and Technology Ministry," a department of the cult's shadow government that had been established to control Japan following doomsday. As Murai was being escorted out of the Tokyo offices of Aum Shinri Kyo, surrounded by a mob of press photographers and onlookers, an assassin named Hiroyuki Yo, a 29-year-old South Korean, pushed his way through the crowd and fatally stabbed the cult leader in the abdomen.

As Murai clutched his abdomen and screamed in pain, police seized Yo, who later told them that he wanted to punish Murai because he believed him responsible for creating the sarin attack of March 20, and for other crimes. Murai died of his wounds a short time later. The assassin, Yo, was believed by police to be connected to the vast Japanese underworld society, Yakuza. Only two days after Murai's murder, a man wielding a two-foot-long sword appeared outside the cult's offices in Kyoto, shouting: "Come out, you guys!"

When no one appeared, the sword-wielder broke into the offices while four Aum Shinri Kyo cultists locked themselves inside a room. Police arrived to subdue the swordsman before he could injure anyone. He, too, police believed, was a member of Yakuza, a killer from one of the society's execution squads, who traditionally employ swords to dispatch enemies.

Exactly why Yakuza was demonstrating against the cult was never explained, but one official speculated that the criminal society, which claims more than a million members worldwide at this writing, was attempting to show its disapproval and disassociation with cultists, who had once been members of Yakuza. On April 25, 1995, several Aum Shinri Kyo cultists, all adorned in white satin costumes, placed flowers at the site of Murai's assassination and then performed a ritual dance.

Meanwhile, more than 10,000 police officers rummaged through thousands of homes suspected of housing cult weapons and bombs. They unearthed evidence of widespread rifle production, biological warfare labs, and plans to purchase nuclear weapons from Russia. Two days later, police learned of a secret basement beneath the Mt. Fuji headquarters of Aum Shinri Kyo.

Following this tip, officers found the much-sought Masami Tsuchiya and six other cult leaders hiding inside of the basement. Considered to be one of Japan's scientific elite, Tsuchiya was the chemical expert who was thought to have created the sarin used in the massive poison gas attack in the Tokyo subway system.

Shoko Asahara, left, leader of Aum Shinri Kyo, shown with his top disciple, Yoshihiro Inoue, was charged with masterminding the gas attack on the Tokyo subway.

The 30-year-old Tsuchiya was reported to be a brilliant scientist who quit a five-year chemistry doctoral program at Tsukuba University, one of the top schools in Japan, to join the doomsday cult. (Eight weeks later, Tsuchiya admitted that he and others had, indeed, made the poison gas sarin, but he would not admit that the gas had been created specifically for the purpose of the subway attack.) Also taken into custody was 34-year-old Seiichi Endo, cult leader and former genetics and virus researcher. These cult chiefs and their followers held by police universally denied having anything to do with the gas attacks in Tokyo and elsewhere. The lone exception was cultist Katsuhiko Kobayashi, who confessed that the sect produced poisoned gas at its headquarters.

More insidious were the revelations that came from two sergeants in the Japanese Army. They admitted to being cult members and said they had staged firebomb raids against their own cult headquarters before the March 20, 1995 attack to disrupt an ongoing police investigation into cult activities.

Despite the widespread police raids and arrests, cultists continued to spread terror in Japan by engineering three more gas attacks in subway stations. The attacks sent more than 500 people to the hospital, but caused no deaths. On May 5, 1995, cultists left two burning plastic bags of chemicals in a men's room. Four fast-acting train employees rushed into the men's room and extinguished the fires; they were all injured and were hailed as heroes.

One bag contained sodium cyanide and the other diluted sulfuric acid. Had the vapors combined properly (as was no doubt the design of the cultists), enough hydrogen cyanide

A Japanese police photo of Skoko Asahara, who was found guilty of orchestrating the gas attack of March 20, 1995; he was sentenced to death in 2004.

would have been formed to kill more than 10,000 people. The terrorists had selected Japan's "Children's Day" for the attack.

On May 15, police stopped a car at a roadblock outside of Tokyo and took into custody 25-year-old Yoshihiro Inoue, the cult's so-called "intelligence minister." By then police had assembled a great deal of evidence against the cult, including the confessions of more than 200 cult members, who detailed how ten of their leaders had developed the sarin gas and how another ten top members had placed the gas containers in three strategic places in the Tokyo subway system on March 20. These confessions led to the discovery of Inoue's notebook, which contained a record of timetables and numbers of passengers, who used the three subway lines where the sarin nerve gas was released.

The following day, an army of policemen stormed the cult compound at the base of Mt. Fuji. This time officers were successful in unearthing and arresting the top cult leader, 40-year-old Shoko Asahara, along with fourteen of his top lieutenants, who were all charged with mass murder. Asahara was found sitting "in meditation" in a hidden room beneath the third floor of "Truth Building" Number Six. He wore long, black, flowing hair and an elegant robe.

The terrorist campaign was over, according to police. Said Metropolitan Police Chief Yukihiko Inoue of the cult attacks: "This is an unprecedented crime in our history—killing people indiscriminately by spreading gas in the subway. We devoted all our strength to investigate this case to relieve the Japanese people of their anxiety. We will continue to make efforts to prevent any recurrence of such incidents."

Hundreds of cult leaders were jailed, along with all of their top leaders, many of whom being former members of Japan's organized criminal society, Yakuza, as well as thirty members of the Japanese army, who had acted as secret agents for the cult, tipping off its members to impending police and army raids.

Asahara, whose real name is Chizuo Matsumoto, along with forty of his top followers, were charged with murder, assisting murder, and a host of other charges. Many were convicted and sent to prison. Asahara, who is partially blind, had predicted that in 1997, nuclear war would destroy most of the world and his sect would be the only organized body left living. The reasons he had ordered the gas attacks remain obscure.

Asahara was like many another false prophet. He had been educated at a school for the blind, where he was known as a terrible bully. He had experimented with acupuncture to cure his own blindness and failed. He and his wife opened a health food store where he was arrested in 1982 for selling fake medicines. He started a cult, The Heavenly Blessing Association, in that same year, but he attracted few followers. After traveling to Nepal in 1987, he returned to Japan with a new credo, one made up of Hindu and Buddhist beliefs and practices, which he funneled into Aum Shinri Kyo, a cult that appealed to the insecure and the paranoid.

Asahara played upon the fears of the public and in Japan, where superstition, legends and the prophesizing of dire events have been historically popular and nurtured his ridiculous sect. The cult leader ran for office in 1992, but he was soundly defeated. Bitter over this setback, Asahara ranted against the United States, Europe, and the Japanese government for the country's recent economic recessions.

Most of Asahara's followers were youthful college students who came from middleclass or wealthy families. Through them, the cult amassed more than $1 billion in assets, which allowed Asahara to build a network of warehouses, chemical plants, computer firms, and compounds, where cultists could hide weapons and themselves, while they experimented with deadly chemicals and kinetic energy, seeking at the same time to purchase nuclear weapons and develop mental telepathy, which would allow them to read the minds of their enemies. Cult branches sprang up in Germany, Hawaii, and the United States.

Cult activities were fiercely guarded by members. As reported in 1996, those who dared to criticize Aum Shinri Kyo came under attack from members. Some cult critics, like lawyer Tsutsumi Sakamoto, were murdered. In 1989, producers of a talk show for the Tokyo Broadcasting System, then filming training exercises for inductees into the cult outside of Tokyo, mentioned that they had taped an interview with Sakamoto in which he had been critical of the cult. Aum Shinri Kyo leaders asked to see the videotape and were shown the interview, but were warned by TBS to keep quiet about the private screening. A few days later Sakamoto, his wife, and his infant child were all murdered.

It is not known whether or not Asahara actually ordered Sakamoto's death, but he did continue to deny having anything to do with the March 20, 1995 poison gas attack. At the time of his arrest, the cult leader snickered, "How can a blind person like me commit such a crime?" When police grabbed him and began leading him into custody, the fanatical cult leader shouted, "Don't touch me! I don't even allow my followers to touch me!"

During his lengthy trial, Asahara was portrayed by prosecutors as a cold-blooded killer. In a ninety-nine-page opening statement, prosecutors described how the cult leader had ordered the subway assault in March 1995 "to set off massive confusion in the Tokyo area" in order to divert the attention of police he believed were about to raid cult sites. Following the subway attack, Asahara welcomed his cultist perpetrators at his headquarters, providing them with sweet rice cakes and juice. He told them at the time: "Meditate. And chant 10,000 times the phrase: 'This is good, with the blessing of the guru, the great god Shiva, and all the victors of truth.'"

At the opening of the trial, Asahara refused to enter a plea and read a long, rambling statement in which he claimed that all he intended to achieve was to provide "ultimate freedom, ultimate happiness, and ultimate joy." He was defiant in answering any questions from the court, stating: "I don't care about the inconvenience and pain inflicted on me. I have no intention of saying anything else." He infuriated many Japanese by his aloof and arrogant attitude, showing no remorse for the widespread suffering he had caused. He was found guilty of mass murder and, like many of the cult's top leaders, Asahara was sent to prison for life.

For years afterward, officials continued to unearth guilty cultists, as well as huge caches of dangerous weapons and chemicals. On July 7, 1997, Masahiro Tominaga, a former cult member, testified against Seiichi Endo, another cult leader, in Tokyo, stating that Aum Shinri Kyo planned to ship the deadly nerve gas sarin to the United States, hiding tons of the gas in sculpted ice or concrete. It would then be released in congested areas of major cities. Endo, who confessed to helping make the sarin gas, stated that the murder cult did not carry out its plan to ship the gas to the United States.

On April 19, 1998, 45-year-old Tochiyasu Ouchi, a former member of Aum Shinri Kyo, who was traveling on board a Japanese airline, was arrested when the plane entered Japan's airspace. Ouchi had been a fugitive since February 1989, when he reportedly murdered 21-year-old Shuji Taguchi, to prevent her from leaving the cult. Ouchi fled to Russia, but he was expelled from Moscow and went to Cyprus after the devastating cult attack on the Tokyo subway system in 1995.

On May 27, 1998, Japanese police unearthed eight large cylinders containing 353 pounds of hydrogen fluoride, which had been buried seventy miles north of Tokyo. Aum Shinri Kyo cultists had hidden the cylinders in order to conceal evidence; hydrogen fluoride is an ingredient of the deadly nerve gas sarin.

The day before this latest discovery, on May 26, 1998, Ikuo Hayashi, the cult's former physician, had been sentenced to prison for life for his role in helping to release sarin inside the Tokyo subway system in 1995. Hayashi had testified against Asahara during his 1996 trial, admitting that the cult leader had given him detailed instructions concerning the subway attack and that he had unleashed one gas attack by piercing a package of sarin with his umbrella.

Typical of the many convicted cultists, Hayashi admitted his guilt but, at the same time, blamed Asahara for his own actions, stating: "Even though it was under Asahara's orders, our cruel acts took the lives of many people." Hayashi went on to claim that he had somehow been duped into committing mass murder: "I regret that I did not become aware of Asahara's falsehoods sooner."

This strange, self-excusing posture has been typical of those charged with crimes in Japan since that country embarked upon world conquest at the direction of its war-seeking emperor, Hirohito, in the late 1920s. For example, Japanese war criminals, put on trial after World War II for war crimes and countless atrocities, assumed the same inexplicable and inexcusable posture, always attempting to portray themselves as victims rather than criminals.

THE OKLAHOMA CITY BOMBING/ April 19, 1995

During the late 1980s and through the early 1990s, a paranoid fear of the U. S. government was nurtured by rural militants, one that insisted that the federal government was the enemy of the common man and that it might, at any moment, send troops through the land to disarm the simple farmer and workman in an insidious conspiracy to change the social order of democracy into a totalitarian state. Many uneducated whites responded by joining paramilitary groups, most calling themselves state militias, and preparing for the imagined threat of federal encroachment.

Militia members armed themselves with assault weapons and donned battlefield fatigues. They drilled at regular meetings, going through rigorous commando exercises, visiting ranges where they fired their automatic weapons. The basic philosophy put forth by these militant groups was one of the extreme right. It branded the federal government a dictatorial power bent on destroying the individual rights of Americans, particularly the right to own and bear arms. It labeled the FBI and the Bureau of Alcohol, Tobacco and Firearms (ATF) enemies of the people and, by the early 1990s, it openly defied federal, state, and local law enforcement agencies seeking to disarm and disband the militias.

One of their number was dissatisfied with the apparent inability of the militias to effect any real change or to move against the government in open rebellion. He thought to change all that, and to strike back in particular at the ATF for its 1993 attack and destruction of the Branch Davidian compound in Waco, Texas (see Mass Murder).

At 9:04 a.m. on April 19, 1995, Secretary's Day, a truck

Its façade vertically sheared away by a tremendous blast, the Alfred P. Murrah Building in Oklahoma City, Oklahoma, stands in ruins.

bomb went off next to the Alfred P. Murrah Federal Building in Oklahoma City, Oklahoma, vertically shearing off one third of the building, killing 168 men, women, and children and injuring hundreds more. Initially, the impact of this colossal explosion suggested at first that foreign terrorists, part of a vast anti-American conspiracy, had done the horrible deed. Then a penny-ante protestor and drifter, 27-year-old Timothy James McVeigh (1968-2001), was identified as the chief bombing suspect.

Only an hour and fifteen minutes after the Oklahoma City explosion, McVeigh had been stopped by state trooper Charles Hangar, who had spotted a beat-up yellow Mercury Marquis without license plates outside of Perry, Oklahoma. When Hangar pulled the driver to the side of the roadway he noticed a suspicious bulge beneath his jacket. He discovered that the driver, McVeigh, was carrying a concealed 9mm pistol, along with a 6-inch knife. He placed McVeigh under arrest and took him to the Perry courthouse, where he was charged with traffic violations and carrying concealed weapons.

On April 21, 1995, Hangar saw a composite sketch of the suspected Oklahoma City bomber on TV and realized that it bore a strong resemblance to the man he had arrested two days earlier. Rushing to the Perry lockup, Hangar was just in time to prevent McVeigh from being released on a $500 bond. Turned over to the FBI, which had been conducting a massive, desperate search for the bomber, McVeigh was placed in federal custody and charged with the bombing.

Wearing a crew-cut and dressed in orange prison garb and shackled, the tall, lean-faced McVeigh was implacable as he was taken from the Perry courthouse by FBI agents to a

An aerial photo shows the devastation of the Murrah Building in the blast of April 19, 1995, that killed 168 people and injured dozens more.

waiting army helicopter en route to Tinker Air Force Base. Dozens of heavily armed agents accompanied McVeigh through angry throngs in Perry who screamed, "Baby killer! Murdering bastard!" Once at the base, McVeigh was hurried to a makeshift courtroom in the supply building, where he was formally charged with the bombing.

At the time, the taciturn McVeigh refused to admit anything. He did, however, express militant right-wing views and said that he had visited the devastated one-time Branch Davidian compound in Waco. He stated bitter resentment against the federal government for attacking the suicidal cult members who followed David Koresh into a fiery doomsday in 1993. He told investigators that the government "should never have done what it did in Waco."

The explosion in Oklahoma City took place on the second anniversary of the destruction of the Davidian compound in Waco, where Koresh and more than 80 fanatical followers, including many innocent, helpless children, died of self-inflicted gunshot wounds, were executed by fellow members, or were incinerated when the complex was consumed in a towering blaze. The Waco incident had served as a rallying point for right-wing extremists and paramilitary groups in the U.S. who believed Waco served as a symbol of a tyrannical federal government.

The same day McVeigh was identified and arrested, his cousin, 40-year-old Terry Nichols (b. 1955), was arrested in Herington, Kansas, and identified as the second person involved in the Oklahoma City bombing. At the same time, federal investigators swarmed onto a small farm outside of Deckerville, Michigan, sixty miles north of Detroit. The farm

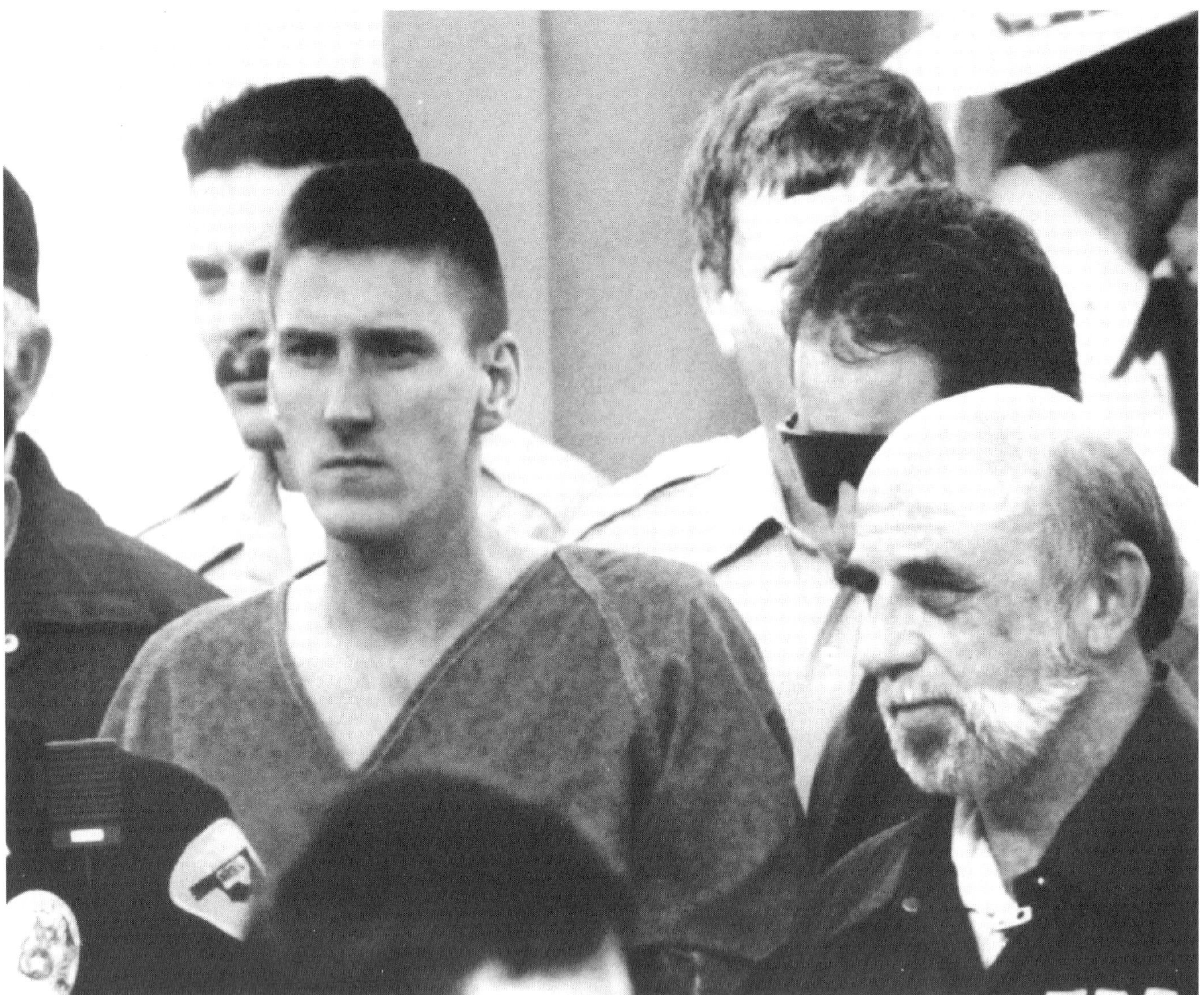

Timothy James McVeigh, center, wearing crewcut, under arrest and charged with delivering the truck bomb in front of the Murrah Building in Oklahoma City.

was owned by James Douglas Nichols, Terry Nichols' brother. The federal agents searched for ingredients that might be used in the making of bombs, particularly fertilizer and fuel oil, the components used in creating the enormous bomb that destroyed the federal building in Oklahoma City.

James Nichols' neighbors thought him to be a crank, a man who bathed in peroxide (for the oxygen, he claimed), and, for the fun of it, made and exploded small bombs on his property. James' younger brother Terry was once described by an ex-army buddy as a "spastic, nerdy kind of guy who walked with an odd waddle." Both belonged to extremist groups that were linked by fax machines and the Internet. They were, like many of the oddball militants in the U. S., playing at militia, part of what was aptly called the lunatic fringe.

McVeigh stood solidly in their ranks after living with the Nichols brothers in Michigan and where he was indoctrinated at meetings of the paramilitary group called the Michigan Patriots, headed by Mark Koernke, a janitor turned militia leader. Koernke preached the credo of the extreme right, urging America to arm in order to fend off an impending coup d'etat planned by bankers, politicians, and media moguls.

Terry and James Nichols were later indicted as suspects in the Oklahoma bombing. Michael Fortier, a friend of McVeigh's and the Nichols brothers, was also later indicted as having transported stolen property, chiefly guns, which were sold to raise money. The cash was used to buy explosives in preparing the huge bomb used in Oklahoma City. Fortier later pleaded guilty to this charge, as well as to the charge of perjury, agreeing to testify against McVeigh and Terry Nichols.

Fortier told federal investigators that he had accompanied McVeigh to the Alfred P. Murrah Federal Building, where they closely examined the structure. McVeigh picked out the spot in the parking lot, where he planned to park a rented truck filled with explosive materials some days later. The parking lot was directly in front of the building and beneath

McVeigh confers with his attorneys; the evidence against their client assured his conviction and death sentence; he was executed on June 11, 2001.

a daycare center packed with children, and, above that, the offices of the ATF, the supposed object of the bombing attack.

Taken to the federal corrections center at El Reno, Oklahoma, McVeigh was watched night and day. TV cameras monitored his every move in his 8-foot by 12-foot cell. Meanwhile, government officials studied the backgrounds of McVeigh and Nichols, homegrown terrorists, who had reportedly committed one of the worst terrorist atrocities in American history.

McVeigh had grown up in Lockport, New York, and was an above-average student with an IQ of 128. He was known as a "pleasant, cooperative" boy. He enjoyed the comfort of a middle-class home and the affection of his parents and two sisters. Following his high school graduation, McVeigh entered the army, joining up the same day as Terry Nichols in 1988. They went through basic training together at Fort Benning, Georgia, and they were stationed together at Fort Riley, Kansas. Both apparently held the same political views, and told one and all that they were staunchly against any federal government controls. In May 1989, Nichols was discharged for undisclosed reasons. McVeigh, however, remained in the service and achieved the rank of sergeant. He served in Operation Desert Storm, being awarded several medals, including a Bronze Star.

Exactly what McVeigh did in the Gulf War to earn that medal is not known. He was a gunner on a Bradley Fighting Vehicle in the First Division, the "Big Red One," as that unit was known during World War II when it stormed onto beaches in Italy and later at Normandy. He told friends that he "blew up" an Iraqi soldier, which prompted more than 500 more Iraqis soldiers to surrender to him. An army buddy said that McVeigh shot several Iraqi soldiers, who attempted to surrender. Taking prisoners was not foremost in the minds of McVeigh and others. In some reported instances, hundreds of Iraqi soldiers were simply buried alive in their sand bunkers by U.S. bulldozers.

Obsessed with guns, McVeigh spent most of his service

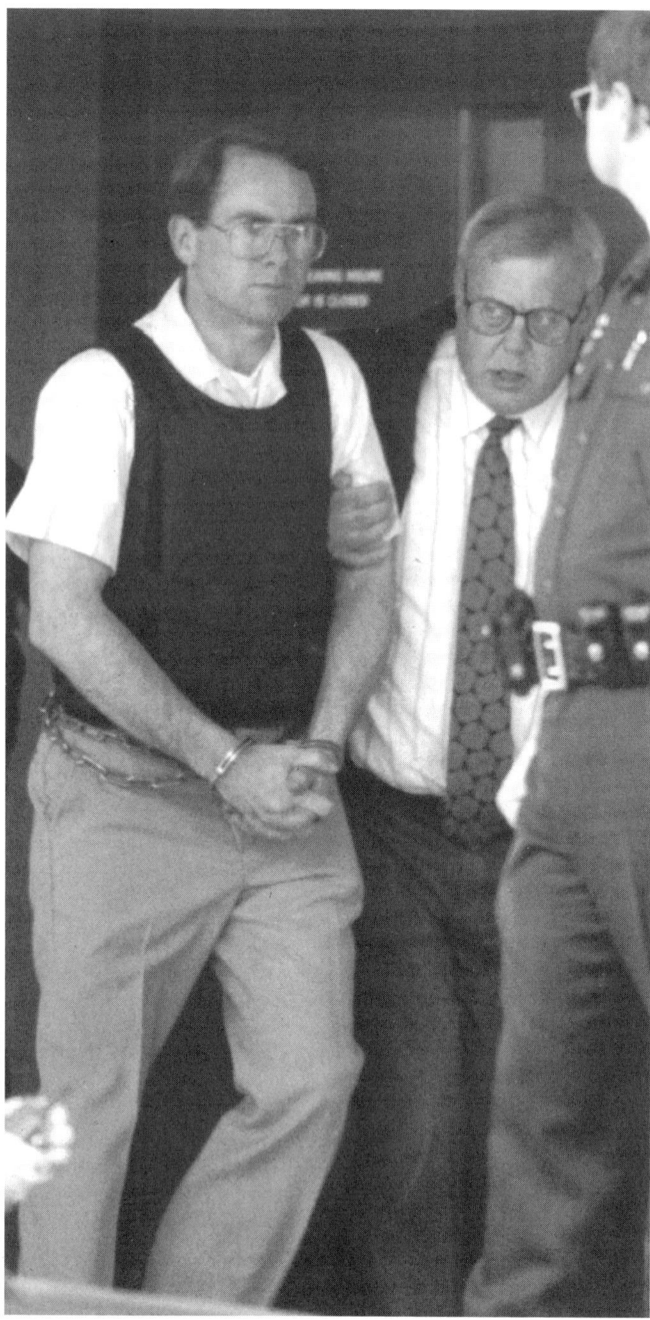

Terry Nichols, McVeigh's associate, who was sent to prison for life in the Oklahoma City bombing.

time in the barracks reading *Guns and Ammo* magazine. Against the rules, he kept a 9mm Glock pistol with him at all times. In the trunk of his car, parked on the post, McVeigh kept pistols, rifles, shotguns, and a Czech-made machine gun. Yet, he was not then thought of as a terrorist. "Something happened to Tim McVeigh between the time he left the army and the Oklahoma City bombing," said one army buddy.

Something happened before that. As early as 1989, McVeigh became obsessed with right-wing revolts in the U.S. as postured in the more absurd action fiction of the day. At one point he loaned a book he was reading, *The Turner Diaries*, to an army friend, saying, "Don't let anybody see it. I don't want to get into trouble." This hack fiction story begins with the bombing of the FBI headquarters in Washington and describes a bloody right-wing revolt and race war in America.

The actual turning point for McVeigh may have been when he applied for Special Services and was rejected, a rejection that embittered him against the army. He sought his release and was discharged a short time later. On December 31, 1991, a friend received a disturbing card from McVeigh, one which showed a skull and crossbones and a pistol aimed at the viewer. It read, "So many victims, so little time." During this period McVeigh worked for the National Guard in New York and he also served as a part-time security guard.

To add to his income, McVeigh, according to Terry Nichols' later statements, sold army surplus goods with Nichols throughout the country. Nichols also told authorities that McVeigh at one point called him at his home in Herington, Kansas, and asked that he pick him up in Oklahoma City. This occurred a short time before the bombing. Nichols did pick up McVeigh, driving him to Junction City, 240 miles away. On this trip, McVeigh told Nichols several times, "Something big is going to happen."

It was in Junction City where McVeigh, along with "John Doe No. 2," rented the Ryder truck, which was then packed with explosives and driven to Oklahoma City, according to authorities. (Several witnesses later told federal investigators that they saw McVeigh near the federal building in Oklahoma City only minutes before the bomb went off.)

Nichols, however, could not distance himself from his close friend McVeigh as to their common interests. He, too, investigators quickly proved, was not only a gun enthusiast but a collector. His home in Herington yielded a 60mm antitank rocket, thirty-three assorted firearms, non-electric detonators, four 55-gallon plastic drums, and three empty 50-pound bags that had contained ammonium nitrate fertilizer, the very material used in the Oklahoma City bombing. Also found in Nichols' home was literature concerning the Waco incident and considerable anti-tax and anti-government literature.

McVeigh made no secret of his hatred for federal controls. He had written a letter to his hometown newspaper in Lockport, New York, in which he stated, "Is civil war imminent?" His older sister Jennifer shared his views about Waco and also wrote letters to the local paper condemning government action in that affair. She reportedly told friends in early 1995 that "something big is going to happen in March or April and Tim's involved."

For some time in 1994, McVeigh lived with the Nichols brothers on their Michigan farm. Then Terry Nichols moved to Kansas and McVeigh to Kingman, Arizona where he roomed in a mobile home with former army chum Michael Fortier, the very man who later agreed to testify against McVeigh and Nichols. It was conjectured that McVeigh and Nichols made their moves to Kansas and Arizona in preparation for their bombing of the federal building in Oklahoma City.

In Kingman, McVeigh supported himself by selling weapons, using the alias of T. Tuttle in his mail order advertisements. This alias may be a play on the name "Harry Tuttle," a terrorist played by Robert De Niro in the 1985 offbeat futuristic movie, *Brazil*, one in which De Niro explodes a bomb that destroys a building housing government bureaucrats. Like De

Niro in the movie, McVeigh wore combat boots and fatigues while living in Kingman and was so attired when regularly picking up his mail. In late February and early March 1995, McVeigh was absent, his mail being picked up by Michael Fortier. On one occasion, another man, who was later described as "John Doe No. 2," also picked up McVeigh's mail.

In hindsight, Kingman seemed to be a logical base of operations for McVeigh. In the mid-1980s, a paramilitary group calling itself the Arizona Patriots, with an agenda similar to that of Koernke's Michigan Patriots, planned to blow up federal buildings in Phoenix and Los Angeles, and execute a machine gun attack on Internal Revenue Service offices in Ogden, Utah. The Arizona group expected to finance these terrorist operations by robbing an armored car en route from a Nevada casino. The conspiracy was unearthed by the FBI and three of the plotters were sent to prison.

During his absence from Kingman, McVeigh reportedly scouted federal buildings in Phoenix, Arizona; Omaha, Nebraska; and Dallas, Texas. He apparently chose the federal building in Oklahoma City to bomb because he could more easily park the truck planted with explosives directly in front of the place, assuring himself that, when the bomb went off, the explosion would thoroughly damage the structure. Upon his return to Kingman, some time in March 1995, McVeigh went to a local video store and rented the film, *Blown Away*, a psycho-bomber movie starring Jeff Bridges and Tommy Lee Jones. He viewed this film many times.

McVeigh is thought to be the person most responsible for the ghastly Oklahoma City bombing. Reports have it that McVeigh's destruction of the daycare center in the federal building was intentional and that he purposely sought to kill as many children as possible in retaliation for the children

Robert De Niro, playing the role of a terrorist bomber in the 1985 futuristic movie *Brazil*, one which Timothy McVeigh repeatedly viewed, emulating De Niro's character in dress and manner.

killed in the Waco firestorm. To that end, nineteen helpless children in Oklahoma City were murdered in the towering blast.

Some authorities believe that McVeigh had more help than that given by Nichols and Fortier, that he was not able to construct the mammoth bomb himself. According to explosive experts, the bomb was made up of 4,800 pounds of ammonium nitrate fertilizer mixed with fuel oil packed in twenty blue plastic drums. This was "boosted" with metal containers of hydrogen or acetylene to make the bomb even more devastating. It would have taken several persons to load this material into the large Ryder truck McVeigh had rented.

The far right militias and paramilitary groups throughout the U. S. ranted that the Oklahoma City bombing was actually performed by federal agents at the behest of a government that intended to use this terrible carnage to destroy the militias. Militia leaders pointed out that this was the same technique employed by Adolf Hitler when he had Hermann Goering set fire to the German government building housing its parliament, the Reichstag, in 1933, in order to blame political opponents for the blaze.

To many right-wing militia members, McVeigh was a hero. Phil Markowski of the Michigan Militia said of him, "I consider Tim McVeigh to be a good guy. If I were in a war, I would want him on my side. He's the kind of a guy who forms allegiances to the death." To the surviving family members of those senselessly slaughtered in Oklahoma City, McVeigh is no hero. The mere mention of his name evokes incredible pain. Edye Smith was only one example. She lost her two small sons, Colton, two, and Chase, three, in the horrible blast, found it impossible to watch little blonde boys at play without thinking back on her own slain children. "There's a hole in her heart," Smith's mother stated, "that can never be replaced."

McVeigh and Nichols were granted separate trials, with McVeigh going to court first. In March 1997, a month before McVeigh went to trial, the Dallas *Morning News* reported that one of his defense attorneys had interviewed him, asking why he had not bombed the Alfred P. Murrah Federal Building at night, when fewer persons would have been killed. "That would not have gotten the point across to the government," the *News* quoted McVeigh's response. "We needed a body count to make our point."

Stephen Jones, McVeigh's chief defense attorney, denied that McVeigh had made the statement to anyone working on his defense and went on to charge the *News* with "jury pool contamination." When McVeigh's trial began, the accused terrorist and mass murderer chatted casually with paralegals in court and smiled and nodded at members of the press and prosecutors, enjoying, it seemed, his moment of high drama.

Jury selection began on March 31, 1997, and the case then went to court before Judge Richard Matsch, with opening statements made on April 24, 1997. A parade of witnesses came forth to state that they had seen one or two men driving the Ryder truck. Fred Skerdla, a gas station attendant in Billings, Oklahoma, reported how he had seen McVeigh driving the Ryder truck at between 1 a.m. and 3 a.m. on the morning of the bombing.

Another witness, Mike Moroz, insisted that he saw McVeigh driving this truck, when he stopped at Johnny's Tire Company on Tenth Street in Oklahoma City—only seven blocks from the Murrah Building—about a half hour before the explosion on April 19, 1995, where McVeigh asked directions to the building.

The most damaging testimony came from McVeigh's close friends, Michael Fortier and his wife, Lori Fortier, who both stated that McVeigh had confided his plans to them, that he had told them that he intended to blow up the Murrah Building in retaliation for the destruction of the Branch Davidians in Waco, Texas. Nothing defense attorney Jones did in his cross-examination of these witnesses caused them to change their stories.

In June 1997, a jury of seven men and five women found 29-year-old McVeigh guilty and decreed the death penalty. The emotional burden endured by these jurors was deep and painful. Before rendering their decision, the jurors were all reduced to tears. Vera Chubb, one of the jurors, later explained that the tears were not for the convicted McVeigh. "We were thinking about the families that were left in Oklahoma City ... how their lives would never be the same and how mothers and fathers had to bury their loved ones."

Juror Diane Faircloth had been moved by McVeigh's mother, Mildred "Mickey" Frazier, who had earlier appeared in court to sobbingly beg for her son's life. Faircloth nevertheless felt no sympathy for McVeigh, stating, "What he represents to me is a terrorist—someone with no regard for human life. He represents a twisted view of the intentions of the government and the principles that this country was founded upon."

Terry Nichols, McVeigh's friend and cohort in the plot to destroy the Murrah Building, was next to go to trial, even though he was not present at the time of the bombing. In fact, Nichols was seen on the morning of April 19, 1995, working on his lawn in Herington, Kansas. He was dusting the grass with fertilizer—ammonium nitrate—the same substance used in the horrendous bomb that destroyed the Murrah Building. Federal authorities insisted that Nichols was not merely fertilizing his lawn—he was destroying evidence, the remainder of the fertilizer that had not been used in the bomb packed into the Ryder truck left outside of the Murrah Building.

The prosecution in Nichols' separate case convinced a jury that Nichols had, indeed, aided McVeigh in building the bomb and then drove McVeigh's car to Oklahoma City and left it there so that McVeigh, after parking the Ryder truck next to the Murrah Building, had the auto available for his escape. Nichols was also convicted of being an accessory to McVeigh's crime; he was given a life sentence.

Timothy James McVeigh remained a quiet prisoner behind bars while awaiting his execution. He dissuaded his lawyers from energetically pursuing appeals that would prolong his life (and by today's agonizingly slow court procedures such appeals might prolong a condemned person's life for as long as twenty years). He was put to death by lethal injection at 7:14 a.m., on June 11, 2001. There is no record of anyone mourning his passing.

THEODORE KACZYNSKI, UNABOMBER/ 1980s-1990s

The ubiquitous terrorist and serial killer the press dubbed the Unabomber began murdering and maiming American citizens at will in 1978. Apparently driven by a seething hatred for modern technology, specifically computer science and the changes it brings about, he struck out at corporations, institutions and individuals.

On April 20, 1995, the terrorist sent a letter to Nobel Prize Winner Richard J. Roberts, one of four letters he mailed from Oakland, California, along with a bomb, which, on April 24, 1995, killed Gilbert Murray, the president of the California Forestry Association, an industry trade group located in Sacramento. (The package containing the bomb was addressed to Murray's associate, William Dennison.) The contents of the letters received by geneticist Roberts at New England Biolabs in Beverly, Massachusetts, were not disclosed. Roberts helped to launch the field of biotechnology and brought definition to the makeup of DNA.

Up to that time, the Unabomber had sent sixteen bombs that killed three persons and seriously injured twenty-three people in the U.S. The first to be killed was Hugh Scrutton, owner of a computer store in Sacramento, California, who discovered a bag left behind in his store on December 11, 1985. When he picked it up, it blew him to pieces. The second person murdered by the Unabomber was advertising executive Thomas Mosser of North Caldwell, New Jersey, who was killed on December 10, 1994 when he opened a package delivered to his home. The last fatality was timber lobbyist Gilbert Murray, killed when he opened a package on April 24, 1995.

The FBI sketch of the Unabomber, pieced together from descriptions given by witnesses glimpsing the ubiquitous terrorist.

In one of the letters the Unabomber sent to the New York *Times*, he stated in a typewritten note: "Clearly, we are in a position to do a great deal of damage." This was the second note the terrorist had sent to the *Times*, the first missive having been sent in 1993. In both notes, the killer described himself as an "anarchist" representing a group called "FC" (standing for "Freedom Club," according to the terrorist's later letters).

The FBI believed that the terrorist was striking back at anyone who had polluted the environment. In his 1995 note to the *Times*, the Unabomber referred to Burson-Marsteller, an agency that represented Exxon following the *Exxon-Valdez* oil spill in Alaska. Bureau experts pointed out that the terrorist's hatred for institutions was exemplified early on when, in his first attack, he mailed a bomb that exploded on the campus of Northwestern University in Evanston, Illinois, on May 26, 1978.

In the 1995 note, the Unabomber inexplicably claimed that he had "nothing against universities or scholars as such ... All the university people we have attacked have been specialists in technical fields" who were involved "in certain areas of applied psychology, such as behavior modification." He added that "we would not want anyone to think that we have any desire to hurt professors who study archaeology, history, literature or harmless stuff like that."

Then the Unabomber stated that he would stop killing people if a national publication would print his manuscript, one which he said he had been working on for some time and consisted of between 29,000 and 37,000 words. The terrorist added (either jocularly or as a way to gain unthinkable sympathy) that "it's no fun having to spend all your evenings and weekends preparing dangerous mixtures, filing trigger mechanisms out of scraps of metal or searching the sierras for a place isolated enough to test a bomb."

In another April 20, 1995, letter, the Unabomber taunted one of his own victims, David Gelernter, a noted computer science professor at Yale University, who received serious injuries when a bomb exploded in his hands in June 1993. Gelernter was blinded in one eye and deafened in one ear, lost part of his right hand, and was injured in the chest when the terrorist's bomb went off.

"People with advanced degrees aren't as smart as they think they are," taunted the Unabomber in his letter to Gelernter. "If you had any brains you would have realized that there are

David Kaczynski recognized the writings of the Unabomber as that of his brother, Ted Kaczynski, and contacted the FBI.

a lot of people out there who resent bitterly the way technonerds like you are changing the world and you wouldn't have been dumb enough to open an unexpected package from an unknown source."

The letter went on to criticize Gelernter's book, *Mirror Worlds*, which predicted the inevitability of widespread computerization. Remarked the Unabomber, "In the epilogue of your book you tried to justify your research by claiming that the developments you describe are inevitable, and that any college person can learn enough about computers to compete in a computer-dominated world.

"Apparently people without a college degree don't count ... In any case, being informed about computers won't enable anyone to prevent invasion of privacy (through computers), genetic engineering, environmental degradation through excessive economic growth and so forth ... If the developments you describe are inevitable, they are not inevitable in the way old age or bad weather are inevitable. They are inevitable only because technonerds like you make them inevitable. If there were no computer scientists there would be no progress in computer science."

The Unabomber's hatred for academics like Gelernter was evident, emphasized in his letter to the *Times* in which he clearly stated that he was "out to get" computer and genetic scientists, whom he felt were ruining the world and that he was dedicated to the "destruction of the worldwide industrial system." After studying the letters, the FBI stated that though the Unabomber claimed to be part of a group, agents did not "have a shred of evidence that he is connected with other people in the placing of the bombs."

It was evident, however, that the terrorist insisted upon establishing a frightening personal image. Before he sent a bomb on June 22, 1993 to geneticist Charles Epstein at the University of California in San Francisco, the Unabomber spray-painted the initials "FC" and the word "anarchy" in the campus area of the Sacramento State University. Epstein lost several fingers and suffered a broken arm when he opened the package containing the bomb. Two days later, the Unabomber mailed his bomb to Gelernter.

In one of the letters the terrorist sent in 1995, he showed his return address as being the headquarters of the FBI in Washington, D.C., a way of sneering his contempt at those he knew were avidly pursuing him. Smugly, in his letter to the *Times*, the killer bragged about how his expertise at bomb-making had improved, "Since we no longer have to confine the explosive in pipe, we are now free of limitations on the size and shape of our bombs. We are pretty sure we know how to increase the power of our explosives.

"And, we think we now have more effective fragmentation material. So we expect to be able to pack deadly bombs into ever smaller, lighter and more harmless-looking packages ... we believe we will be able to make bombs much bigger than we've made before."

Further, the Unabomber said that he represented a movement that hoped to promote "instability in industrial society, propagate anti-industrial ideas and give encouragement to those who hate the industrial system ..." To some academics studying the Unabomber's letters, it seemed as if he were echoing the early 19th century beliefs of the Luddites, an anti-industrial sect in England.

At one point in 1995, the mysterious Unabomber brought panic to air travelers and airlines when he threatened to blow up an airliner at the Los Angeles Airport. For days, FBI agents swarmed throughout southern California airports, where all passengers were stopped and ordered to identify themselves. Postal authorities announced that no mail weighing more than three-quarters of an ounce would be accepted or delivered.

Then, to placate the terrorist, the New York *Times* and the Washington *Post*, offered to publish the Unabomber's manifesto. Both publications received his 35,000-word manuscript entitled "Industrial Society and Its Future." Along with the manuscript, which the FBI certified as genuine, was a letter in which the Unabomber decried the Oklahoma City bombing, stating, "We strongly deplore the kind of indiscriminate slaughter that occurred in the Oklahoma City event."

The remote one-room cabin in Montana, where hermit Kaczynski plotted death and made his bombs.

In a precedent-setting move, the *Times* and the *Post* published a segment of the Unabomber's rambling, raving manuscript in September 1995, one in which the terrorist condemned a corrupt technocracy responsible for stamping out human freedom on behalf of the corporate and governmental elite. Said a *Times* spokesman, "We are absolutely not trying to appease the Unabomber by publishing the excerpts. It was only 3,000 words." The *Post* stated, "We thought we owed our readers the relevant excerpts. For all we know it could wind up in the Internet next week."

Hundreds of FBI agents were assigned to tracking down the elusive terrorist. As is the case with most such manhunts, FBI agents got a break when a tipster contacted them in January 1996. The unlikely informant was David Kaczynski, who had found papers with Unabomber-like rhetoric in the home of his mother, Wanda Kaczynski, in Lombard, Illinois. The papers had been written by his brother, one-time academic, social dropout, and Montana hermit, Theodore "Ted" Kaczynski (b. 1942).

David Kaczynski, a social worker, lived quietly with his wife in Schenectady, New York. He had read the excerpts of the Unabomber's diatribes in the *Times* and realized that the writing was strikingly similar to that written by his brother over the years. Moreover, when helping his mother move from her Lombard home in January 1996, he found hundreds of letters his brother had written, all brimming with the same invective. The loyalty-torn Kaczynski agonized for some time over his decision to contact the FBI through a Washington, D.C., attorney. He offered to help the Bureau only if his name was not disclosed and that his brother, if found guilty, would not receive the death penalty. Neither promise could be kept.

Agents investigated every square inch of the Lombard home. An around-the-clock stakeout kept vigil on the house and neighborhood, while other agents scoured the remote regions of Stemple Pass, Montana, where Kaczynski lived in a crude cabin. Agents kept the cabin under close surveillance while they monitored the movements of the hermit, a shaggy-haired, heavily bearded Ted Kaczynski.

Kaczynski had lived in the cabin for twenty-five years and seldom went to the town of Lincoln, which was six miles distant. When he did go to Lincoln, he peddled a battered bicycle to a dry goods store to buy meager supplies, seldom talking to store owner Becky Garland, who described him as a "hermit kind of guy. Over the years we had a few conversations about things, but we didn't talk long. Mostly, I saw him maybe every six months or so ..."

After observing Kaczynski for almost two months, FBI agents finally took him into custody. He offered a scuffling resistance and then went meekly, silently behind bars. Inside his cabin, agents found ten three-ring binders full of detailed writings and diagrams of explosive devices and sketches of boxes meant to conceal the devices. They also found handwritten notes in Spanish and English describing how chemical compounds could create explosive charges. Kaczynski had also filled logs that described his experiments in determining the optimal design for pipe bombs and their effectiveness in various weather conditions. The cabin was also filled with books on chemistry and electrical circuitry.

The Kaczynski cabin had no toilet facilities or running water, but it contained a treasure trove of terrorist devices, including one finished package bomb that bore no address and had not been mailed; copper, plastic and galvanized metal pipes, some having plates at one end, a preliminary step in the construction of pipe bombs; containers with aluminum, zinc, lead, and potassium chlorate, which can be used in constructing bombs; solid cast ingots; batteries and electrical wire that could be used to detonate explosives; and assorted drills, drill bits, wirecutters and hacksaw blades. It also had two manual typewriters, which Kaczynski used to write the Unabomber messages, according to law enforcement experts.

While Kaczynski remained in custody, his strange background was pieced together by law enforcement officials. Born on May 22, 1942, to Wanda and Theodore R. Kaczynski in Evergreen Park, Illinois, he was the first of two sons, his brother David born eight years later. Kaczynski's father worked in a Chicago sausage factory until managing a firm called Cushion Pak in Cedar Rapids, Iowa. (The elder Kaczynski committed suicide in 1990 after he was diagnosed with cancer.)

The Kaczynski family, according to Evergreen Park neighbors, kept to themselves. Ted Kaczynski was a bright lad who spent most of his time in the family basement, tinkering. He was so brilliant that he skipped one grade in grade school and his junior year of high school, entering Harvard on a scholarship at age sixteen. During high school, Kaczynski showed a decided interest in creating homemade bombs. One school chum remembered that "he was very intelligent and had a flair for pyrotechnics." One of Kaczynski's classmates asked him how to make a bomb and Kaczynski told him; the bomb went off in a chemistry class and caused a girl to lose her hearing.

Kaczynski did not adjust well to Harvard. Though he was a brilliant math student, he was shy and retiring, wanting to be alone most of the time. He shut himself up in a single room at a fraternity house, one which was later described by a fellow student as "the messiest room I've ever seen ... a foot or two deep in trash. And it smelled, because there was spoiled milk and sandwiches underneath all that stuff."

Never outgoing, Kaczynski did not date girls and had no close friends at Harvard. He did sit in on some "bull sessions," where the more brilliant math students met in the cafeteria and espoused the idealist philosophy of Immanuel Kant. (The Unabomber's published manifesto contains many allusions to Kantian thinking.) Following his graduation from Harvard in 1962, Kaczynski attended the University of Michigan from 1962 to 1967, receiving his doctorate in mathematics. He displayed brilliance and solved problems that stumped professors. His articles were published in academic reviews and he was one of ten young math graduates to be hired in 1967 at the University of California in Berkeley, where he was thought to be one of the few who would get tenure.

At Berkeley, Kaczynski taught without incident. Here, too, he did not mix with faculty, but remained reclusive. Though Berkeley had always been known to be a hotbed of leftist political activities, Kaczynski took no part in partisan politics. In 1969, Kaczynski shocked the staff at Berkeley by resigning, saying that he was giving up math and was uncertain

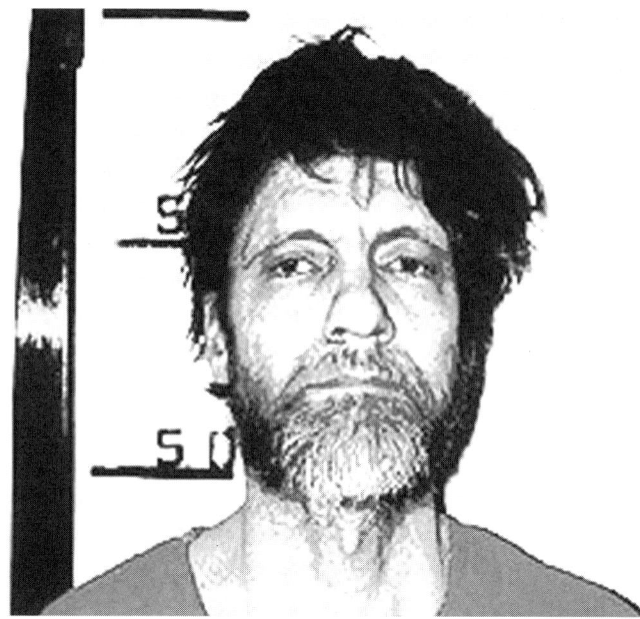

Police photo of Theodore Kaczynski at the time of his arrest in 1996.

Kaczynski was a brilliant student and teacher, who dropped out of society to become the Unabomber.

as to what he might do. No amount of persuasion could compel him to reconsider.

It was later pointed out that he was feeling "inner tension" at this time as a result of his disgust with leftist activism. (The Unabomber's manifesto is highly critical of leftist political philosophies.) To family members, Kaczynski later confided that he quit Berkeley because he feared that what he taught to engineers would later be used to destroy the environment.

Kaczynski surfaced briefly in Salt Lake City where he took menial jobs before moving to the wilds of Montana in 1970 or 1971. In 1971, Kaczynski and his brother (who apparently provided the financing) bought 1.4 acres of land outside Lincoln, Montana, next to a dirt road. Here Kaczynski built a small shack, ten feet by twelve.

From that time on, Kaczynski lived the hermit's life. He nurtured a small vegetable garden. He lived on a dollar a day, going to Lincoln only to buy supplies and visit the library. Occasionally, he traveled by bus to Helena, where he bought and sold used books, staying at the $14-a-night Park Hotel. He did not remain away from his shack for long. Most of his hours he spent inside the shack, which FBI officials described as a low-tech bomb factory where Kaczynski meticulously pieced together his bombs from scraps of metal and wood, scavenged some distance from his home, which made them impossible to trace.

Not until October 1996 was Kaczynski indicted by a grand jury in Newark, New Jersey, for the 1994 murder-bombing of ad executive Thomas Mosser. By then, the FBI had put together a strong case to convict Kaczynski in the Unabomber killings. They expected to prove that the suspect's saliva matched that taken from the stamps on the packages mailed by the Unabomber, as well as matching his fingerprints to the one Unabomber print found on one of the bomb packages and that one of the two typewriters found in Kaczynski's cabin would match perfectly to the Unabomber's manifesto.

An "intellectual" match of the Unabomber's philosophy can be found in the works of novelist Joseph Conrad, who was Ted Kaczynski's favorite author. Kaczynski read and reread every novel ever written by Conrad, whose real name was Teodor Jozef Konrad Korzeniowski. More than the name similarities, Kaczynski undoubtedly took over the lifestyle of one of Conrad's fictional protagonists.

In Conrad's 1907 novel, *The Secret Agent*, a brilliant but mad professor abandons academia and takes up residence in a "hermitage," where he fashions a bomb, which he intends to use in destroying "that idol of science," an observatory. He eats raw carrots; Kaczynski ate raw turnips. The professor-turned-anarchist vows revenge against the advocates of modern science; so did the Unabomber.

The anarchists of *The Secret Agent* use the initials "FP" ("Future of the Proletariat") in their leaflets; the Unabomber used the initials "FC" as a signature. Like Conrad's mad professor, who lived a lonely life of isolation, Kaczynski dwelled in total alienation from society. Conrad had written that the bomb-making professor saw science and technology as nefarious forces exalted by a naive public, as did the Unabomber. As Conrad wrote, "Explosives were his faith, his hope, his weapon and his shield." For Ted Kaczynski, these weapons of destruction also powered an arrogance and vanity that led to his eventual identification, arrest and indictment as America's most wanted terrorist.

Following his arrest, Kaczynski refused to talk with his 80-year-old mother, Wanda, and his 47-year-old brother, David. He had not seen either of them in fifteen years, and when first appearing in the Sacramento, California, court of Judge Garland Burrell, Jr., he walked past them without looking at them or uttering a single word. He pleaded not guilty to the charges of having killed three persons and seriously injuring another twenty-nine people over his eighteen-year course of terrorism. Only four persons, all residents of tiny Lincoln, Montana, visited the terrorist in jail.

In the second week of January 1998, Kaczynski attempted to hang himself with his underwear in his jail cell, a clumsy attempt that failed. The suicide attempt, in fact, was so awkward that it was thought that Kaczynski had purposely planned to fail in taking his own life, but, in attempting to do so, try to convince authorities that he was mentally unbalanced.

Yet, Kaczynski had been fighting with his attorneys, who wanted to portray him as mentally ill. He insisted that he was sane and ordered them to abandon all efforts to profile him as unbalanced. The defense lawyers agreed, but said that they would use the insanity plea during the expected death penalty phase of their client's trial. Then Kaczynski insisted that he be allowed to fire his lawyers and that he be permitted to act as his own attorney.

In an effort to prove that he was sane enough to represent himself, Kaczynski agreed to be examined by court-appointed psychiatrists. The court was frustrated in that, by allowing Kaczynski to act as his own attorney, the trial might become the same kind of farce created by killer Colin Ferguson (see Mass Murder). Many close to the case thought that Kaczynski was simply attempting to remain in control, to continue to battle the entire government arraigned against him—the federal judiciary, the FBI, the Department of Justice, all representing a social system he had vowed to destroy with his bombs.

At the end of January 1998, Kaczynski agreed to a deal. He would plead guilty in exchange for a life sentence with no right to appeal, but on the condition that Judge Burrell deny his petition to represent himself in court. This was agreed. Appearing before Judge Burrell, the defendant's bid to represent himself was denied. He was then asked if he was responsible for all the murders and bombings of which he stood accused. "Yes, your honor," replied Theodore Kaczynski. On May 4, 1998, the terrorist was sentenced to four life terms, plus thirty years behind bars without the possibility of parole.

Judge Burrell later stated that Kaczynski made a conscious decision "to employ trickery" in order to prevent any jury of ever hearing the details of his many crimes. Burrell went on to openly state that Kaczynski had faked the arguments with his attorneys and staged a suicide attempt to improve his chances of striking a deal with prosecutors and avoiding the death penalty. Everything was a ploy, said Burrell, because the terrorist "wanted to live." Kaczynski knew that the government planned to introduce 22,000 journal pages in which Kaczynski described his numerous bombings. Judge Burrell pointed out that these revelations might have so enraged a jury that conviction was a certainty.

Theodore Kaczynski at the time of his 1997 trial; he cleverly engineered the court into giving him a life sentence.

Kaczynski was sent to the federal maximum-security prison in Florence, Colorado (U.S. Penitentiary, Administrative Maximum Facility). His climate-controlled cell is actually larger than the hermit's cabin he inhabited in rural Montana and a great deal more luxurious, having shower, toilet, electric lamp, concrete desk and stool, cigarette lighter, and a 13-inch television. He can order books of all kinds from a well-stocked library without ever leaving the cell. Breakfast, lunch, and dinner (he can choose several culinary options for each meal) are delivered to his cell. Freshly laundered bedding and clothing are delivered to his cell three times each week.

This prison, however, is no garden spot. Completed in 1994 at a cost of $190 million, the prison holds "the worst of the worst," or "the folks who simply cannot function in open institutions," according to one source. Warden John Hurley stated, "We don't send out invitations to this place. They earn the right to be here." More than twenty-two percent of those housed at this prison, which has replaced the U.S. federal penitentiary at Marion, Illinois, as the top federal maximum security prison (Marion having replaced Alcatraz after that institution was closed in 1963) are men who have murdered fellow inmates in other federal prisons. About thirty-five percent have been involved in violent attacks on inmates or guards.

Other infamous prisoners at this federal prison included Oklahoma City bomber Timothy McVeigh until his execution in 2001, who, up to that time, was the first federal prisoner to be executed in thirty-eight years, and Ramzi Ahmed Yousef, mastermind of the 1993 World Trade Center bombing. None of the men have contact with each other or other convicts. They are shackled and escorted by at least two guards every time they leave their cells, which is no more than two hours every day. Beyond the bars of their cells, none have a future.

THE ISLAMIC TERRORISTS/1980s-2000s

Beginning in the 1970s-1980s, many right-wing Islamic terrorist sects were organized in the Middle East, first to destroy Israel by establishing a Palestinian state, and then to combat Israel's foremost ally, the United States. Bombings, kidnappings and assassinations by these groups were committed so frequently that their terrorist atrocities became com-

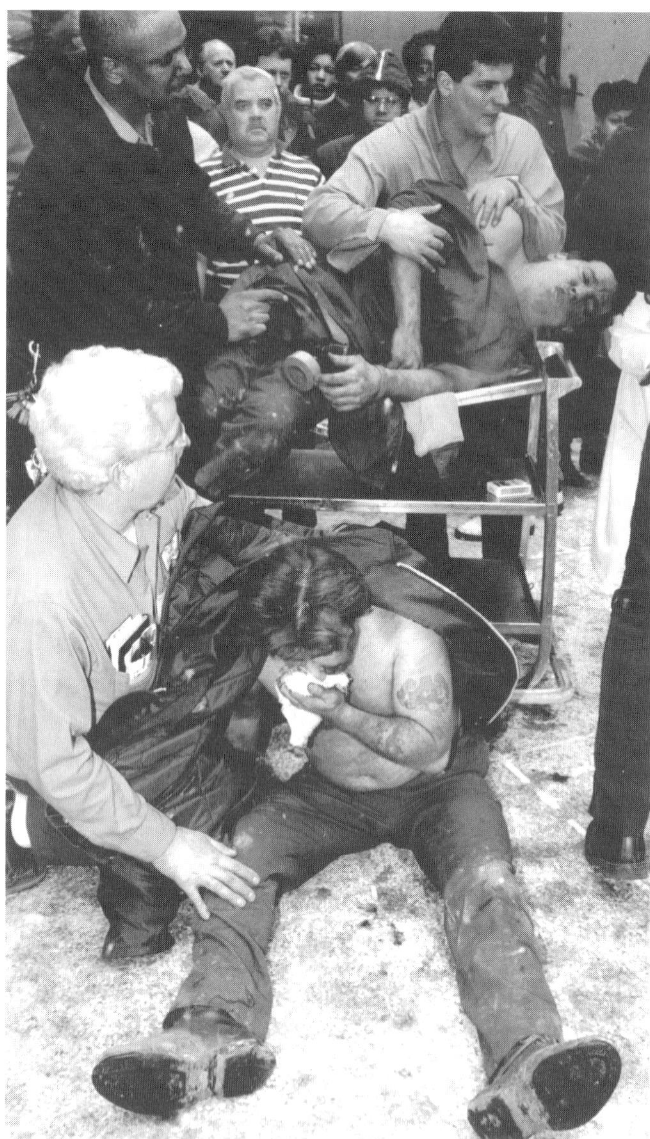

Victims of the fire and smoke from the 1993 bombing of New York's World Trade Center; six persons were killed and more than 1,000 others injured.

FBI photos of Ramzi Ahmed Yousef, mastermind the 1993 World Trade Center bombing; he fled to Pakistan, living in a house owned by Osama bin Laden, until captured and sent to prison for life.

mon occurrences. The PFLP (Popular Front for the Liberation of Palestine), Hamas, Hezbollah (or Hezballah; Party of God), and later Al Qaeda became the most significant terrorist organizations, recruiting and indoctrinating countless Moslems to their warped causes. These fanatics were trained to destroy buildings and kill people, taking as many lives as possible while sacrificing their own in countless suicidal missions. Typical was the bomb set by a fanatic pro-Iranian Moslem group that exploded in the U. S. Embassy in Beirut, Lebanon, on April 18, 1983.

Sixty-three people were killed, their mutilated bodies found buried in the rubble. The bomb had been placed inside a van, allegedly driven by a suicide driver, who drove past Lebanese guards and through the front door of the embassy during lunch hour. The bomb blew apart the front wall of the central section of the embassy from ground level to the top floor and caused severe damage in the visa section on the ground floor of the northern wing.

Robert S. Dillon, the U.S. ambassador to Lebanon, was sitting in his office when the bomb exploded. The office collapsed under him, burying him in the rubble. Freed by rescuers, he climbed out a window and down to the ground unscathed. Robert C. Ames, a senior CIA analyst, was killed in the blast, along with twenty-three other Americans, including several U.S. Marines. The remaining dead were Lebanese citizens, many of whom worked in the embassy or were applying for visas. The pro-Iranian group, Islamic Jihad (Muslim Holy War), Lebanese Shiite Muslims, first claimed responsibility but were quickly followed by two other radical organizations claiming to have detonated the bomb.

By the early 1990s, these terrorist organizations imported their assassins to Europe and the U. S. In 1993, Islamic terrorist Ramzi Ahmed Yousef planned to destroy the symbol of American finance and corporate world power, the World Trade Center, in New York City. Yousef employed techniques that would later be gruesomely mimicked by Timothy McVeigh two years later in his destruction of the federal building in Oklahoma City, Oklahoma.

Yousef or one of his followers drove a Ryder rental truck into the underground parking area of the World Trade Center on February 26, 1993. The truck was packed with 1,200 pounds of explosive material, along with three cylinders of hydrogen gas. The entire truck was one huge bomb and when it exploded, six persons were killed and more than 1,000 others were injured. Officials evacuated the twin towers of more than 50,000 people and then inspected the near-catastrophic damage the bomb had made.

The terrorists, engineers determined, had planned to blow up the support columns and base structure of one of the WTC towers so as to topple it into the other, thus killing tens of thousands of persons. They almost succeeded. Engineers worked night and day to support the weakened columns to avoid a collapse. The terrorist knew, it was surmised, that the twin WTC towers sat on a large landfill, primarily a mud basin, and the bomb was positioned so that it could blow a hole in the mud fill. Had that occurred, the Hudson River would have crashed through the opening and flooded lower Manhattan.

Experts believed that the bombing had been the work of any number of Islamic terrorist groups, in that it followed the *modus operandi* of earlier bombings known to have been exploded by such groups. They thought that the terrorists were immigrants from one of several countries—Libya, Iraq or Iran—all right-wing Islamic countries that supported terrorism. Investigators nevertheless were left guessing until an important clue was discovered.

On February 28, 1993, investigators uncovered a three-foot piece of truck chassis that had been hurled from the center of the blast. An identification number on the chassis led agents to a truck rental agency in Jersey City, New Jersey. This firm had, on Febraury 23, 1993, rented the Ryder truck to Mohammed Salameh, a resident of the Little Egypt section of town. Salameh was a 25-year-old Islamic follower of Sheik Omar Abdel Rahman, a blind fundamentalist leader of fanatical Islamic groups in Manhattan.

Salameh was a man made stupid by greed. He refused to forfeit the $400 deposit he had placed on the truck. When the money-grubbing terrorist appeared to report the vehicle stolen and collect his deposit on March 4, 1993, he was arrested by FBI agents, who had staked out the truck rental agency. On that same day, agents arrested Ibrahim Elgabrowny in his Brooklyn, New York, apartment, where they found bomb-making materials. Elgabrowny did not go gentle into custody, kicking and punching agents as they tried to subdue him. His address appeared on Salameh's New York driving license.

Six days later, on March 10, 1993, agents located and arrested Nidal Ayyad in Maplewood, New Jersey. Ayyad was a chemical engineer and a friend of Salameh's, who, according to officials, possessed the expertise to make the bomb that exploded at the World Trade Center. The terrorist cell to which Salameh, Elgabrowny and Ayyad belonged, officials concluded, was headed by Sheik Omar Abdel Rahman, the blind Egyptian cleric, who often preached at a storefront in Jersey City, New Jersey, ceremonies, it was determined, that were often attended by Salameh and Ayyad.

Checking the background of these suspects, agents learned that Salameh had often visited a prison that housed Sayyid Nosair, who had been acquitted of the 1990 assassination of Rabbi Mein Kahane in New York City, but who went to jail on weapons charges. Nosair was closely associated with all of the suspects. On March 17, 1993, Salameh, Elgabrowny and Ayyad were indicted for the World Trade Center bombing. The following day, Sheik Omar Abdel Rahman was visited by press members, asking about his involvement with these men.

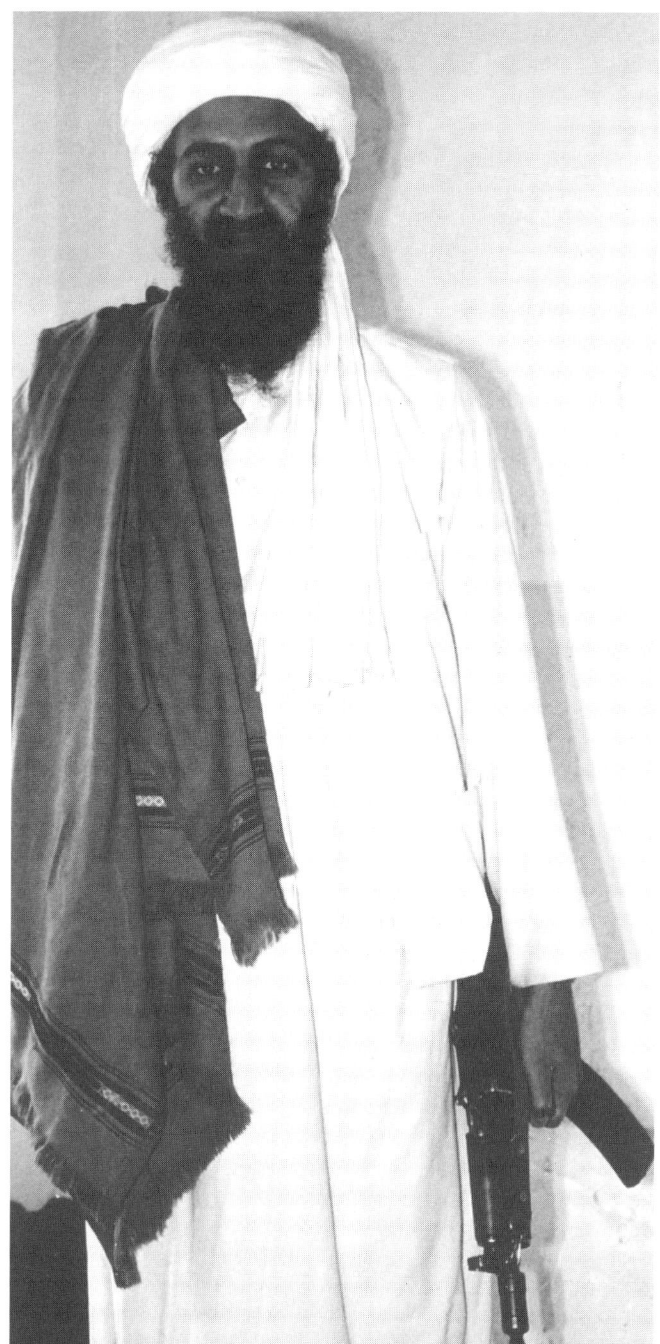

International terrorist Osama bin Laden, a Saudi oil-millionaire, financed the 1993 WTC attack, orchestrated the 1998 U. S. embassy attacks in Kenya and Tanzania and directed the destruction of the World Trade Center on September 11, 2001. He is, at this writing, the most wanted man in the world, an unparalleled mass murderer.

He denied having anything to do with the WTC bombing. To one reporter he stated: "Did anyone intercept any kind of a letter or any kind of written statement or anything else? I'm asking, what is the clue that they [law enforcement officers] have based their accusations on?"

Two more suspects, Mahmud Abouhalima and Bilal Alkaisi, were arrested in connection with the bombing on

The destruction created at the U. S. Embassy in Nairobi, Kenya, on August 7, 1998; more than 200 people were killed and thousands more injured from a blast set off by members of Osama bin Laden's Al Qaeda.

March 24-25, 1993, but by then, the mastermind of the bombing, Ramzi Ahmed Yousef, a 26-year-old Iraqi, had been identified. He was indicted in absentia on March 31, 1993 for the bombing. By June, the media announced that Emad Salem, a translator and bodyguard for Sheik Omar Abdel Rahman, had been an FBI informer. Salem had gone wired for many months among the Islamic fundamentalists working with Rahman and Yousef. On August 25, 1993, Rahman was arrested and jailed for the WTC bombing.

Yousef, however, had fled the country, and FBI and CIA officials scoured the world for him. A 20-man FBI team found him in Pakistan, where he may have been hidden on orders of Al Qaeda leader Osama bin Laden. (It was later speculated that Yousef had set off the 1993 WTC bomb at Osama bin Laden's direct orders.) Yousef was extradited to the U. S., where he was tried.

In the end, all of the indicted Islamic terrorists connected to the 1993 WTC bombing were convicted and sent to prison. Yousef and four others were given life sentences. During Yousef's trial, it was learned that three men had driven the truck into the parking area at the World Trade Center—Siddig Ibrahim Siddig Ali, who had turned state's evidence, Yousef, and one other man. The man reportedly orchestrating the 1993 bombing, however, was at large and was conducting a "holy" war against the West. This was Osama bin Laden, who, with Muhammad Atef, had established Al Qaeda in 1989.

A leader against Russian troops in the attritional war in Afghanistan, bin Laden was initially given support by the U.

The U. S. Embassy at Dar es Salaam, Tanzania, partially destroyed by a bomb on August 7, 1998, planted by Al Qaeda terrorists under Osama bin Laden, where eleven were killed and hundreds injured.

S., but he earmarked America as the number one enemy when U.S. aid was given to Iraq during the Iraq-Iran war. Bin Laden showed great empathy for the fundamentalist regime of Iran, but, in typical contradiction, obliquely supported Iraq's dictator Saddam Hussein, since he represented an Islamic state. In establishing Al Qaeda, bin Laden's chief plan was to oppose with force and violence all non-Islamic governments and western nations, chiefly the U. S.

In addition to Iran, bin Laden's support came from Iraq, the fundamentalist Islamic Taliban government of Afghanistan, Pakistan, Syria, Somalia and Kenya. Many of his expensive terrorist operations were funded through his own fortune. Bin Laden, born and raised in a rich Saudi oil family, had personal wealth exceeding $300 million. In 1991, bin Laden established one of his headquarters in Khartoum, Sudan, operating a number of businesses that served as "fronts" for his terrorist operations. These businesses consisted of investment companies and other firms dealing with agriculture, transportation and construction, but chiefly financed procurement of explosives, weapons, chemicals, as well as travel expenses for Al Qaeda operations and personnel.

In the early 1990s, bin Laden—recognized by his peers as the chief Islamic terrorist leader—issued a series of orders, called fatwahs (edicts interpreting Islamic law to Al Qaeda's terrorist ends) that called for attacks on U. S. forces in Saudi Arabia, Yemen and the Horn of Africa, especially Somalia. On October 3-4, 1993, Al Qaeda terrorists led the attacks on U. S. peacekeeping forces in revolution-torn Mogadishu, Somalia.

Al Qaeda terrorist Mohammed Atta led the team that seized American Airlines Flight 11, when leaving Logan Airport in Boston, this plane crashing into the North Tower of the World Trade Center.

Al Qaeda terrorist Marwan al-Shehhri, who led the team that seized United Airlines Flight 175, flying it to New York and crashing it into the South Tower of the World Trade Center.

Al Qaeda terrorist Mohammed Jaweed, who helped to skyjack one of the four planes in the suicide attacks of September 11, 2001.

Ayub Ali Khan, another Al Qaeda terrorist, who died on board one of the suicide planes on September 11, 2001.

In devastating firefights, eighteen American soldiers were killed. In December 1993, bin Laden worked with Omar Abdel Rahman and Ramzi Ahmed Yousef to attack the World Trade Center. When those twin towers were not destroyed, bin Laden vowed that he would later demolish the buildings, a threat he would keep.

In 1994, bin Laden marked Pope John Paul II for death, ordering a murder squad to assassinate the spiritual leader when he arrived on a state visit in Manila, Philippines. This assassination went awry, but the terrorist group did, in that year, set off bombings at the U. S. and Israeli embassies in Manila and Asian capitals. In the following year, Al Qaeda terrorists succeeded in setting off mid-air explosions on several U.S. trans-Pacific flights. In mid-1998, bin Laden planned two simultaneous attacks in Africa, both aimed at the United States.

One of the worst terrorist attacks against the U. S. occurred when two U.S. embassies in Nairobi, Kenya, and Dar es Salaam, Tanzania, were bombed on August 7, 1998, both gigantic explosions taking place within seconds of each other at 10:40 a.m. The bomb in Tanzania exploded some distance from the U.S. Embassy, thanks to the building having been constructed far from the street. Eleven Tanzanians were killed and many injured. In Nairobi, however, the explosion was catastrophic, claiming the lives of twelve Americans and 213 Kenyans. The entire building next to the embassy was collapsed by the massive explosion and hundreds of windows in scores of buildings nearby were blown out, causing more than 5,000 persons to be injured by flying glass.

Almost immediately after the smoke cleared, American intelligence and other foreign agencies scurried to identify those behind the horrific bombings. Investigators were at a loss to identify the culprits until the apprehension of Mohammed Sadeek Odeh, also known as Abdull Bast Awadh and Mohammad Sadig Howaida. Odeh had been arrested by Pakistani officials on August 7, 1998, the very day of the explosion, after arriving in Karachi, Pakistan, from Nairobi. After being promptly extradited back to Nairobi, Kenya, Odeh was relentlessly interrogated by Kenyan investigators, as well as interrogation experts from the FBI who had flown to Nairobi from the U.S.

At first, Odeh would admit nothing, even though he had earlier told Pakistani officials that the bombings had been ordered by Osama bin Laden. It was at this time, that bin Laden's background was fully examined, investigators learning much about the 42-year-old Saudi Arabian millionaire and terrorist leader. Bin Laden, whose father was a billionaire in Saudi Arabian construction, had studied engineering in England. Backed by his father's millions, bin Laden, a shrewd investor, amassed his own fortune—between $200 and $300 million. He volunteered his services to the CIA in the Afghan war against Soviet Russia, financing and organizing his own mountain guerrillas, who defeated the Russians at almost every turn.

Following the war, bin Laden reorganized his Afghan forces into his own terrorist organization, which he called the Islamic Front for Jihad Against Jews and Crusaders, later retitled Al Qaeda. He was suspected of being behind the bombing of the World Trade Center in 1993, the prime suspect in that case, Ramzi Ahmed Yousef, being convicted of the bombing in 1996. Yousef had reportedly been captured in a bin Laden family guest house in Pakistan.

In studying the background and rigid Islamic beliefs of Osama bin Laden, it became apparent that bin Laden had become as fanatical a terrorist as the mystical figure he sought to emulate—the Old Man of the Mountain (Hasan ibn-al-Sabah), creator of the Order of the Assassins, an eleventh-century killer cult seeking to murder the Christian leaders of the Third Crusade, which invaded the kingdoms of Islam. (This explained why bin Laden labeled his enemies "crusaders.")

Since the early 1990s, bin Laden posed as an "agriculturalist," and began expanding his terrorist organization into Egypt, Saudi Arabia and Sudan. Saudi officials became so unnerved by his activities that he was "denaturalized" in 1991.

American Airlines Flight 11 crashes into the North Tower of the World Trade Center, 8:45 a. m., September 11, 2001.

United Flight 175 crashes into the South Tower at 9:05 a. m., creating a huge fireball.

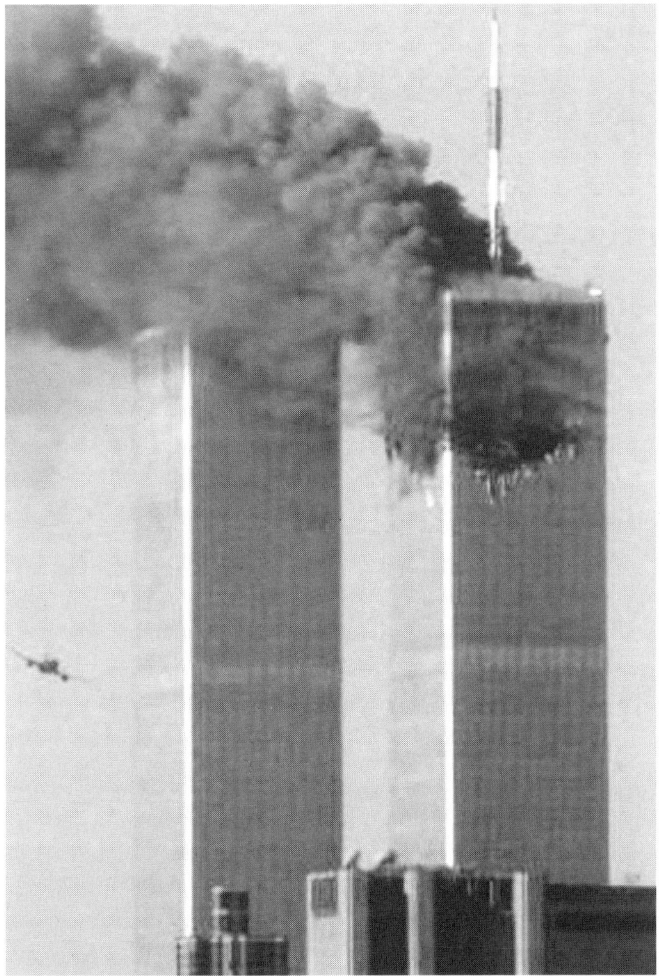

While the North Tower burns and belches smoke, United Flight 175, lower left, approaches the South Tower on its suicide course.

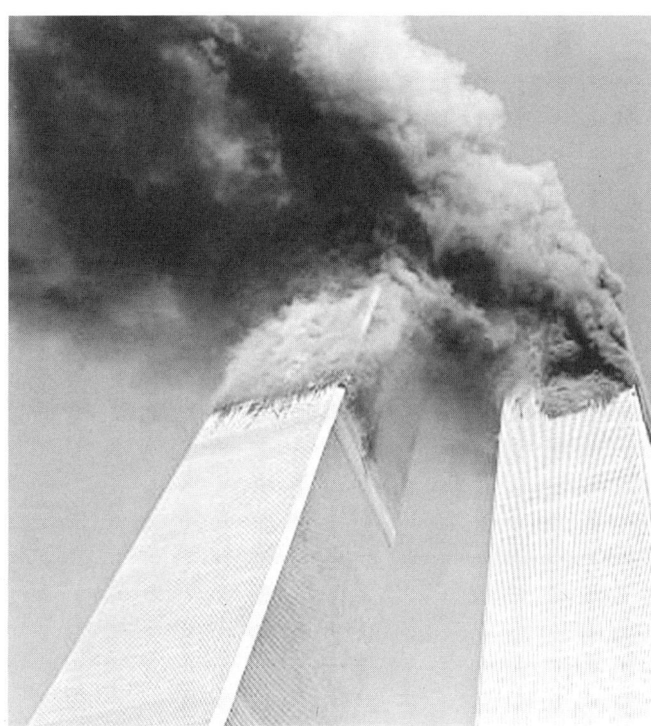

Both North and South Towers are shown burning and belching smoke; they would crash to earth within a few hours, taking with them thousands of lives.

Fighting back smoke, occupants of the North Tower make their way down the endless flights of stairs, seeking safety; thousands would not reach the ground floor.

Bin Laden then moved to the Sudan where, through a front, he invested in, the Military Complex, an industrial compound in Khartoum, where the plant for Shifa Pharmaceutical Industries was located. It was in this plant, U.S. officials later claimed, that the deadly nerve gas VX was to be produced and then later used in terrorist attacks against the U. S. and its allies.

Bin Laden's terrorist activities intensified throughout the 1990s. In addition to funding the bombing of the World Trade Center, bin Laden was pinpointed as the person behind several bombings of U.S. facilities in Saudi Arabia in 1995 and 1996, although these attacks still remain officially unsolved. The U.S. pressured Sudan to expel him (and his three wives) in 1996. He then established a terrorist training compound at Zhawar Kili, Afghanistan, near the Pakistan border. Bin Laden had long endeared himself to the fundamentalist Islamic Taliban regime controlling Afghanistan and its leader, Mullah Mohammad Omar.

From his mountain retreat, bin Laden granted interviews and publicly condemned Western "non-believers," telling a reporter from the ABC-TV network that U. S. forces should "leave Saudi Arabia or die." He proudly led the reporter and others on a tour of his terrorist compound, which boasted anti-aircraft missile systems, radar, and a sophisticated communications systems allowing bin Laden to uplink faxes and video by satellite and to tap into the Internet. It was from this remote staging area that bin Laden ordered the bombings of the U. S. embassies in Africa.

In 1994, Saudi authorities froze many of his bank accounts for fear that bin Laden would employ these millions to fund terrorism inside Saudi Arabia. (This was, of course, the official Saudi posture, but many believed that this was only lip service to the West and that the Royal Saudi family that controlled oil-rich Saudi Arabia, secretly backed bin Laden as an economic-political wedge against Western incursions into Islamic countries, or, to preserve their own autocratic positions, as well as protect their own lives, tacitly endorsed the terrorist.)

Once U.S. intelligence had pinpointed bin Laden's stronghold, President Clinton retaliated on August 20, 1998, ordering American warships in the Red Sea to launch cruise missiles into Khartoum, utterly destroying the Shifa Pharmaceutical plant. At the same time, U.S. warships in the Arabian Sea unleashed long-range Tomahawk missiles that targeted bin Laden's camp at Zwahar Kili. The damage inflicted was reported to be considerable, but bin Laden survived the attack. One of the reasons why the camp was targeted was to disrupt a conference of many top-level Islamic terrorists who were to meet on that day, including members of the Islamic Jihad.

U.S. intelligence was not able to determine if, indeed, the conference had taken place, but it was believed that among those scheduled to attend were representatives of the PFLP (Popular Front for the Liberation of Palestine), a terrorist arm of the Al Fatah Council (as is Islamic Jihad), which was directly linked to the Palestine Liberation Organization and Yasir Arafat. Although he was profiled as the director of the August 1998 bombings, it was obvious to trained observers that bin Laden's posturing and threats, his willingness to give interviews and be photographed and filmed in his Afghanistan hideout, made him too much of a public figure to be the actual mastermind of the bombings. To some observers, bin Laden was simply another high-profile PFLP front man. None of the real Islamic terrorist leaders in the past two decades would ever think to seek the limelight.

The Islamic terrorist leaders have always opted for the shadows, as has been the case with Abu Abbas (Mohammed Zaidan Abbas; AKA: Abu Khalid), the insidious PFLP leader and one of Arafat's foremost aides and advisers, who engineered the Black September killings of the Israeli Olympic team in 1972, the seizing of the cruise ship *Achille Lauro* in 1985 and the destruction of Pan Am Flight 103 over Lockerbie, Scotland, in 1988. The bomb that destroyed the plane was placed by two of Abbas' hand-picked terrorists who for years took refuge in Libya, guests of Muammar Qaddafi. It was Abbas who directed countless terrorist attacks against Israel, usually from Lebanon bases, as well as numerous skyjackings through the 1970s and 1980s. Abbas was captured in Iraq by U. S. forces that destroyed Saddam Hussein's troops and occupied the country in 2003; he died in 2004.

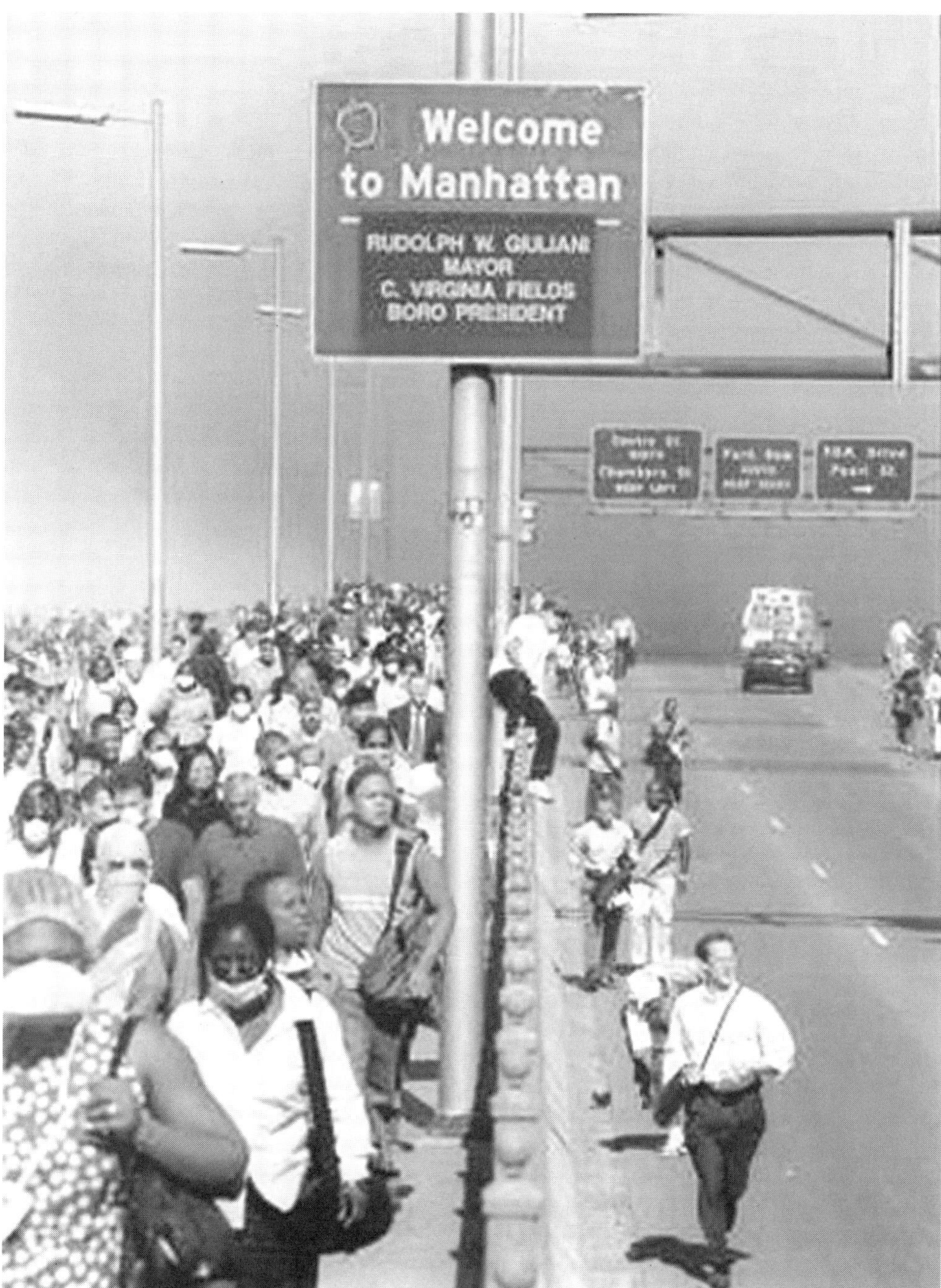

As huge dust clouds from the collapsed towers roll toward them, thousands flee Manhattan on September 11, 2001, a day that lives in infamy.

By the mid-1990s, the PFLP/Al Fatah had flattered the strutting, arrogant bin Laden into taking up their terrorist causes. Bin Laden's gnawing vanity, these shrewd manipulators knew, would insist that he take center stage as the successor to the legendary Old Man of the Mountain (which undoubtedly explained bin Laden's proclivity for residing in mountaintop caves). Bin Laden would not only help fund PFLP operations, but would happily take credit for its heinous crimes in the name of "holy Jihad."

There could be no doubt that bin Laden certainly represented the terrorist arm that launched the August 1998 embassy bombings, but he was not the catalyst that inspired those deadly attacks; that distinction belonged most certainly to the PFLP, which has historically directed and approved of almost all major Islamic terrorist attacks against the U.S. and Israel in the last three decades. Through this attack, a PFLP message was sent to both the U.S. and one of its most ardent allies, Israel: Give up the territories along the West Bank demanded by the Palestinians and Arafat, and give them up quickly.

The historical precedent, *modus operandi* and motive for the August 1998 bombings in Kenya and Tanzania were deeply rooted to the PFLP, not to the publicity-seeking bin Laden. Two months before the attacks in Nairobi and Dar es Salaam, on June 19 and June 21, 1998, two bomb attacks in Beirut were made by PFLP terrorists, a car bomb killing two persons and, two days later, rocket-propelled grenades that were exploded near the U.S. Embassy, which brought about no injuries. These attacks were symbolic demonstrations against the U. S. to compel America to further pressure Israel into giving up West Bank territory. Prime Minister Benjamin Netanyahu's government, despite U.S. pressure, resolved not to give up territory until the Palestinians (Arafat) cracked down on terrorism.

The PFLP's answer was to urge bin Laden's attacks in Africa, returning to the very city, Nairobi, where the PFLP had exploded a tremendous bomb on December 31, 1980, destroying the Zionist-owned Norfolk Hotel, an explosion that killed between sixteen and twenty persons and injured another eighty-five. In that explosion, as well as those of August 7, 1998, the PFLP left its calling card—traces of Semtex, an explosive manufactured in Czechoslovakia and used consistently by the PFLP in its terrorist bombings over the years.

The 1980 and 1998 bombings followed an identical attack plan, a vehicle packed with explosives driven close to a parking area before the explosives were detonated. The 1980 Nairobi bombing was conducted by the PFLP in retaliation for the successful raid by Israeli commandos at Entebbe four years earlier when Israeli hostages were rescued. (More than irony can be found in the fact that only one fatality among the commandos was inflicted by the PFLP terrorists—that of its heroic leader, Col. Netanyahu, the brother of Israel's former prime minister.)

Moreover, the August 1998 attacks against U.S. embassies occurred in the year marking the fiftieth anniversary of Israel as a sovereign state, the U.S. being one of the first nations to acknowledge it as such. To Yasir Arafat, the PFLP and its allied terrorist groups, Israel and the U.S. were one and the same, a common enemy; they were the "Jews and Crusaders" Osama bin Laden has vowed to destroy.

The West Side of the Pentagon in Washington, D. C., was hit by American Flight 77 at 9:40 a. m., collapsing the side of the building and causing many deaths. Fifteen of the nineteen Al Qaeda suicide terrorists were Saudis.

Intensive searches and manhunts for the terrorists resulted in the September 21, 1998 arrests in Tanzania of two men identified as part of bin Laden's terrorist organization—Mustafa Mahmoud Said Ahmed, an Egyptian, and Rashid Saleh Hemed, a Tanzanian. Both men were charged in Dar es Salaam with eleven counts of murder, the number of deaths brought about by the Tanzanian bombing. On November 4, 1998, Osama bin Laden was indicted by a federal grand jury in New York for directing a worldwide terrorist network that launched the August 7, 1998 bombings in Nairobi and Dar es Salaam. The charges also named bin Laden's group, Al Qaeda, as the one directly responsible for the bombings, specifying that Al Qaeda maintained terrorist cells in Kenya, Tanzania, Britain and the U.S.

In addition to Odeh, who was arrested and charged with the blast in Nairobi the day after the Kenyan explosion, authorities located Mohamed Rashed Daoud al-'Owhali in a hospital where he was being treated for wounds from the bombing and placed him under arrest as one of the terrorists who helped set off the bomb. Two more men, Wahid Hage and Fazul Abdullah Mohammed were also arrested and charged with the Nairobi bombing. All of these suspects held low level positions in bin Laden's organizations, according to officials. Mamdough Mahmoud Salim, however, who handled some of the group's finances, was located in Germany in December 1998, and U.S. extradition efforts were made to have Salim sent to the U.S. for trial. He and others were later convicted and sent to prison.

Bin Laden, however, continued his war on the U. S., on October 12, 2000, targeting an American destroyer, the U.S.S. *Cole*, one of the country's most modern vessels equipped with the most sophisticated equipment in the U.S. Navy. The ship was anchored at the ancient port of Aden, Yemen. The destroyer was under repairs, after having been gouged by a small ship in what was first thought to be an accident. This was followed by a suicidal attack by two Al Qaeda terrorists who set off a bomb where the ship had originally been damaged. The explosion killed seventeen American sailors and injured another thirty persons, out of a crew of 346.

This and subsequent terrorist attacks paled by comparison to Al Qaeda's horrendous attacks against American landmarks on September 11, 2001. Osama bin Laden prepared long and hard to make these attacks, recruiting his most fanatical followers on what they all knew to be suicide missions. Sup-

The gutted remains of the World Trade Center, where more than 2,500 people lost their lives in the world's worst terrorist attack, one that would bring overwhelming retaliation from America and its allies.

plied with abundant cash, nineteen Al Qaeda members went circuitously to the U. S., where they took up residences along the East Coast and as far south as Florida. Some had training as pilots and others enrolled in U. S. flying schools. Al Qaeda had no air force so the insidious and clever bin Laden thought to simply borrow American planes for his attacks.

To that end, on the morning of September 11, nineteen Islamic terrorists boarded four separate planes, coordinating their movements so that all would hijack U. S. commercial flights at about the same time. Five terrorists boarded American Flight 11 at Boston's Logan Airport. This plane was en route to Los Angeles, leaving Boston at 7:59 a.m., but the terrorists commandeered the plane and diverted its course to New York City. Muhammed Atta led this team.

United Airlines Flight 175 was seized by five other Islamic fanatics led by Marwan al-Shehhri. This plane left Boston's Logan Airport one minute before American flight 11, also bound for Los Angeles. Another five Arab terrorists seized American Airlines Flight 77, as it left Dulles International Airport at 8:10 a.m., en route to Los Angeles and diverting its course. A fourth plane, United Airlines Flight 93, was hijacked by four more Islamic terrorists as it took off from Newark International Airport at 8:01 a.m., en route to San Francisco, but that course, too, was altered. Instead of pilots from these planes routinely answering traffic controllers, the voices from the four seized planes chattered excitedly in Arab tongues. One shouted in glee: "We have the plane! We have the plane!"

But what did they intend to do with these planes? Within two hours, their maniacal plans were revealed in awesome horror. They planned to crash these planes into the largest structures containing the most people and kill as many human beings as possible, while taking their own lives in suicide crashes, not unlike the kamikaze pilots crash-diving onto American ships in the Pacific during World War II. It would later be said that Osama bin Laden had studied films of these WW II crashes and realized the devastating effect that these kamikaze planes had created on capital ships, not to mention the gigantic loss of life they claimed.

The hijackings became clear to officials when the first plane, American Airlines Flight 11, with an Al Qaeda pilot at the controls, purposely crashed into the North Tower of the World Trade Center in New York City at 8:45 a.m., killing all ninety-two persons, including nine flight attendants and two pilots. The structure was apparently hit at a level intended to weaken the core supporting the building, as had been bin Laden's plan in planting the car bomb that exploded at the WTC in 1993. While this tower belched flames and billowed smoke, its thousands of occupants trying to flee down endless staircases, an Al Qaeda pilot approached the South Tower in United Airlines Flight 175, aiming it at about the same level where the first plane had struck the North Tower. This flight crashed with a terrific explosion into the South Tower at 9:05 a.m., killing all sixty-five people on board, including seven flight attendants and two pilots.

The South Tower had been hit with such force that it gave up tremendous clouds of smoke. The terrified thousands of this building also began to run down staircases, but most of them would never reach the ground level. As armies of police and firemen raced to the smoking buildings, tens of thousands of citizens ran from the area in a sea of panicking human flight. As police tried to evacuate the buildings, many courageous firemen entered the stricken buildings to fight the raging fires the crashes had started, as well as aid fleeing occupants, some of these heroic men losing their lives only a hour or so later.

While the country stood by in shock and horror—most having seen the second plane crash into the South Tower of the WTC, which had been recorded on numerous video cameras—a third plane, American Flight 77, with an Al Qaeda pilot at the controls, dove at the Pentagon in Washington, D. C., crashing into its West Side at 9:40 a.m., killing sixty-four people, including five flight attendants and two pilots. The crash caused widespread destruction of the Pentagon and claimed many lives. The fourth plane, United Airlines Flight 93, had flown almost to Cleveland, but had turned about and was on a course toward Washington, D. C. The terrorists on this plane, however, encountered unexpected problems in that the passengers refused to go meekly to their deaths. Several passengers called their loved ones on cellular phones to tell them that the plane had been hijacked and one brave young man told his wife that he and some others were "going to rush them."

This flight, apparently due to the struggle put up by the passengers, did not reach the destination planned by the terrorists. Apparently in the struggle for the controls of the plane between Al Qaeda fanatics and heroic passengers, the plane was sent out of control, crashing in Stony Creek Township, about eighty miles south of Pittsburgh, Pennsylvania, at 10:10 a.m. Forty-five persons were killed, including five flight attendants and two pilots.

By then the towers of the World Trade Center were giving way, first the South Tower, then the North Tower, and when they telescoped to earth in gigantic crashes, they took with them the lives of thousands of victims. Nearly 3,000 lives were lost in the combined Al Qaeda attacks of September 11, 2001. Osama bin Laden had achieved his goal through his fanatical Islamic followers, killing as many Americans as possible and on a scale that horrified the world and brought down upon the Islamic fundamentalists the wrath of America and its allies.

The Taliban regime in Afghanistan, which had supported bin Laden and his terrorists, making a home for them in its country, proved culpable in the attacks. The U. S. and its allies invaded the country and, with the help of dissident Afghan forces, overthrew the Taliban regime. This UN-supported invasion was followed by the U. S. invasion of Iraq, which toppled dictator Saddam Hussein in 2003 and diminished another part of the Arab world in which Osama bin Laden could hide.

The search for the most wanted terrorist continues at this writing. It is not known whether or not he is alive or dead. Most believe the world's worst terrorist is still cave-hiding in remote mountains either in Afghanistan or Pakistan. A relentless, justifiable search goes on for him. If alive, he should be aware that he is no longer the hunter, but the hunted one, well-branded by the free nations of the world as one of the worst mass murderers in human history.

OTHER NOTABLE TERRORIST ATTACKS, 1951-2000

1951

MARCH 8: General Ali Razmara, prime minister of Iran, is assassinated by terrorists in Iran.

JULY 16: Riad Al-Sulh (Riad Solh Bey), prime minister of Lebanon, is assassinated.

1952

FEBRUARY 16: Hussein Fatemi, Iran's minister of foreign affairs, is assassinated in Iran.

SEPTEMBER 25: Gangs of Mau Mau terrorists attack fellow blacks in the Kenya village of Timau, setting fire to the place and slaughtering 120 cattle in an effort to intimidate villagers into joining their secret criminal society.

NOVEMBER 26: Tom Mbotela, a black councillor in Nairobi City, is murdered by Mau Mau terrorists after having publicly denounced the secret society.

DECEMBER 30: An Tie Cho skyjacks a Philippines DC-3 traveling from Laong to Aparii, killing the pilot and purser, and demanding to go to Red China. The co-pilot lands the plane at Quemoy and Tie Cho is arrested.

1953

JANUARY 11: George Peter Metesky, New York's "Mad Bomber," explodes a bomb in New York's Pennsylvania Station injuring several people.

MARCH 26: Mau Mau terrorists attack and capture the police station at Naivashi, Kenya, slaughtering all the officers and their families.

APRIL 15: Juan Domingo Perón, president of Argentina, is the target of a failed assassination attempt in Argentina.

APRIL: Mau Mau leader Jomo Kenyatta and other leaders of the secret criminal society are identified and tried. Kenyatta is given a seven-year prison sentence.

SEPTEMBER 11: Sidi Muhammad ben Moulay Arafa, sultan of Morocco, is the target of a failed assassination attempt in Morocco by Allal ben Abdallah, a Moroccan terrorist who is shot during the attack.

1954

MARCH 1: Puerto Rican nationalists terrorize the U.S. House of Representatives in Washington, D.C. by spraying gunfire into the assembly, injuring Congressmen Alvin Morell Bentley, Clifford Davis, George Hyde Fallon, Benton Franklin Jensen, and Kenneth Allison Roberts. The attackers, including Lolita Lebron, are sent to prison.

MARCH 22: Sir Winston Churchill, prime minister of England, is the target of a failed assassination attempt when a bomb arrives in the mail at 10 Downing Street, London. It is disarmed.

AUGUST 5: Carlos Lacerda, an outspoken journalist who has openly criticized the Brazilian government, is injured during a failed assassination attempt on his life in Brazil by terrorists thought to be backed by the regime in power. An air force major accompanying Lacerda is killed.

OCTOBER 27: Gamal Abdel Nasser, president of Egypt, is the target of a failed assassination attempt in Egypt.

1955

MARCH 12: Jawaharlal Nehru, prime minister of India, is the target of an unsuccessful assassination attempt in India.

APRIL 2: Sir Robert Armitage, governor of Cyprus, is the target of a failed assassination attempt in Cyprus.

APRIL 11: A bomb placed in the wheel well of an Air India Constellation jet explodes over Great Naturna Island in the South China Sea, killing sixteen. Three passengers survive.

APRIL 22: Lieutenant Colonel Adan Al-Malki, ruler of Syria, is assassinated in Syria by terrorist members of the Syrian army.

Winston Churchill was targeted for assassination when a bomb was mailed to his office at 10 Downing Street.

MAY 7: Reverend George W. Lee, a fifty-one-year-old Negro preacher who refuses to withdraw his name from a voting list, is shot to death by Ku Klux Klan members in Belzoni, Mississippi.

MAY 14: Konrad Adenauer, chancellor of Germany, is the target of an unsuccessful assassination attempt in Germany.

JUNE 16: Juan Perón, president of Argentina, is the target of an unsuccessful assassination attempt in Argentina.

JUNE 25: William Vacanarat Shadrach Tubman, president of Liberia, is the target of an unsuccessful assassination attempt in Liberia.

JULY 14-17: Following a terrorist bomb explosion on Bastille Day which destroys a cafe in Casablanca, Morocco, killing six Europeans, widespread rioting ensues for three days

AUGUST 6: Lamar D. Smith, a sixty-three-year-old Negro who has been encouraging blacks to register to vote, is shot to death by white supremacists on the courthouse lawn of Brookhaven, Mississippi.

AUGUST 31: Emmett Louis Till, a fifteen-year-old black youth who has reportedly whistled at an attractive white woman, is shot to death by white supremacists and his body thrown into the Tallahatchie River near Greenwood, Mississippi.

NOVEMBER 17: Hussein Ala, premier of Iran, is the target of an unsuccessful assassination attempt in Iran.

1956

FEBRUARY 28: Mao Tse-tung, Communist dictator of China, is the target of an unsuccessful assassination attempt in China.

JUNE 26: Fulgencio Batista, dictator and president of Cuba, is the target of an unsuccessful assassination attempt in Havana, Cuba.

OCTOBER 10: Chinese triads in Hong Kong create riots that last for several days, committing many murders and causing more than $25 million in damages.

OCTOBER 26: Dedan Kimathi, the last of the important Mau Mau leaders still at large, and who has been one of the most ruthless mass murderers of the secret criminal society in Kenya, is captured. He is later executed for his countless murders and the Mau Mau movement is broken (10,527 Mau Maus have been killed, and an equal number of blacks killed by Mau Maus, as well as thirty-two white settlers in the five-year reign of terror in Kenya.)

1957

FEBRUARY 23: Ngo Dinh Diem, president of South Vietnam, is the target of an unsuccessful assassination attempt by Communist terrorists.

MARCH 13: Fulgencio Batista, dictator and president of Cuba, is the target of an unsuccessful assassination attempt in Cuba.

APRIL 17: Nnamdi Azikiwe, premier of the Eastern Region of Nigeria, is the target of a failed assassination attempt by terrorists.

MAY 25: Kliment Efremovich Voroshilov, chairman of the Russian presidium, is the target of an unsuccessful assassination attempt in Indonesia.

JULY 12: Mohammed Zahir Shah, king of Afghanistan, along with Sadar Mohammed Daud Khan, the country's prime minister, are the targets of unsuccessful assassination attempts in Afghanistan.

Indonesian strong-man Sukarno survived an assassination attempt on December 1, 1957.

AUGUST 4: Three men—Clyde Bates, Manuel Chavez and Manuel Hernandez—firebomb a neighborhood bar in Los Angeles, California, killing six people. All three men will be convicted of murder on August 16, 1956.

DECEMBER 1: Terrorists attack Ahmad Sukarno (Kusnasosro), president of Indonesia, in Jakarta, Indonesia, spraying the president's entourage with gunfire and hurling grenades into the group. Sukarno escapes injury, but ten other persons are killed, including the terrorists.

1958

JANUARY 23: More than 100 persons are killed in widespread street rioting in Caracas, Venezuela, as militants oppose the dictatorship of General Marcos Perez Jimenez, whose regime will be toppled.

FEBRUARY 8: Jacques Soustelle, minister of information for France, is the target of a failed assassination attempt. Another attempt by terrorists will be made on Soustelle's life on September 15, 1958.

AUGUST 12: Twenty-one segregationists are arrested outside Central High School in Little Rock, Arkansas, for refusing an order to disperse when protesting integration by black students.

SEPTEMBER 20: Rev. Martin Luther King, Jr., civil rights leader, is the target of an unsuccessful assassination attempt in New York City.

1959

APRIL 12: James Lindsay Almond, Jr., governor of Virginia, is the target of an unsuccessful assassination attempt, possibly by segregationists.

APRIL 10: Six skyjackers force a Haitian DC-3 traveling from Auxcayes to Port-au-Prince to fly to Cuba. The pilot is killed and the co-pilot takes the plane to Havana.

APRIL 16: Three Cubans skyjack a Cuban Aerovias DC-3 flying from Havana to the Isle of Pines, landing the plane in Miami, where the skyjackers are taken into custody.

APRIL 25: Antonio Rodrigues Diaz, a general under the deposed Cuban dictator Fulgencio Batista, and several others, skyjack a Cuban Vickers Viscount flying from Varadero Beach to Havana, ordering the pilot to fly to Miami, Florida. The plane, lacking fuel, lands at Key West, Florida.

SEPTEMBER 26: Hurricane Vera ravishes Nagoya, Japan, killing more than 5,000 persons, prompting scores of criminals to rape and loot at will. Police arrive to shoot and kill at least 100 looters and rapists.

1960

JANUARY 6: A National Airlines jet, flying from New York to Miami, explodes over Bolivia, North Carolina, and crashes after a passenger sets off a dynamite bomb in the forward fuselage. Thirty-four persons are killed.

FEBRUARY 18: Norodom Sihanouk, king of Cambodia, is the target of a failed assassination attempt in Cambodia.

MARCH 8: Felton Turner, a twenty-seven-year-old Negro accused of improprieties with white women, is abducted outside of Houston, Texas, by four members of the Ku Klux Klan and hanged by his heels from a tree, while a series of KKK's is carved into his chest and stomach.

MARCH 9: Ahmad Sukarno, president of Indonesia, is the target of a failed assassination attempt in Indonesia.

MARCH 28: Arturo Frondizi, president of Argentina, is the target of a failed assassination attempt in Argentina.

APRIL 9: Hendrik Frensch Verwoerd, prime minister of South Africa, is critically wounded (he will survive) by gunshots fired by a white farmer opposed to apartheid in Johannesburg.

APRIL 28: A bomb explodes in the cockpit of a Linea Aeropostal jet bound from Caracas to Puerto Ayacucho, Venezuela. Thirteen people are killed.

JUNE 17: Japanese socialist leader Jotaro Kawakami is stabbed to death in Japan.

JUNE 24: Romulo Betancourt, president of Venezuela, is wounded by a bomb set off by terrorists in Caracas. One of Betancourt's aides is killed and many others are wounded.

JULY 8: Patrice Lumumba, prime minister of the Congo, is the target of an unsuccessful assassination attempt in the Congo. It is later claimed that the CIA has been behind this murder plot.

JULY 14: Nobusake Kishi, premier of Japan, is stabbed in a failed attempt to assassinate him in Japan.

JULY 19: Alex Hildebrant skyjacks a Trans-Australia Electra L-188 headed for Brisbane, Australia. He is overpowered by the co-pilot and taken into custody in Singapore, and imprisoned.

AUGUST 29: Hazza Majali, premier of Jordan, and ten others, are killed when terrorists bomb government offices in Amman, Jordan.

SEPTEMBER 15: Patrice Lumumba, prime minister of the Congo, is the target of an unsuccessful assassination attempt in the Congo. It is later claimed that the CIA has been behind this second attempt on Lumumba's life.

OCTOBER 12: Inejiro Asanuma, secretary-general of the Socialist Party in Japan, is stabbed to death by a terrorist.

OCTOBER 29: A Cubana DC-3 is skyjacked by nine men who shoot and kill a security guard. The plane lands in Key West, Florida. The pilot, co-pilot and one passenger are injured.

DECEMBER 8: Five skyjackers take over a domestic Cuban flight, but the pilot crash-lands. One is killed and four injured.

1961

JANUARY 1: Two skyjackers wave pistols at the pilot of a Cubana domestic flight in the Havana terminal, forcing the plane to fly to New York. The skyjackers are Batista supporters fleeing Communist Cuba and dictator Fidel Castro.

JANUARY 17: Patrice Lumumba, prime minister of the Congo (now Zaire), is kidnapped by agents of President Joseph Kasavubu and is assassinated in the back of a truck in Katanga Province.

MAY 27: Imam Ahmed Ibn Yahya of Yemen is shot and critically wounded at Hodeida, but he will survive. Five terrorists making the attack receive the death penalty.

MAY 30: Rafael Leónidas Trujillo y Molina, dictator of the Dominican Republic, is traveling in his car when he is shot to death from ambush by Pedro Cedeno and Amado Garcia in an unsuccessful coup.

MAY: Freedom Riders arrive in Alabama to aid blacks in securing their civil rights. One of their buses is burned in Anniston by KKK members. Another bus is boarded by KKK thugs who club and beat occupants, who suffer concussions and broken ribs and arms.

JULY 31: Bruce Britt skyjacks a DC-3 Chico, California, to San Francisco flight, shooting and injuring the pilot and a ticket agent. Britt will be arrested and imprisoned.

AUGUST 9: Albert Cadon skyjacks a Pan American DC-8 with seventy-nine aboard, flying from Mexico City to Guatemala, ordering the pilot to land in Cuba. He is deported from Cuba back to Mexico where he is imprisoned.

AUGUST 9: Five skyjackers take over a Cuban C-46 on its way to the Isle of Pines. The pilot and two others are killed, and six are wounded. The co-pilot makes a crash landing.

SEPTEMBER 10: Three skyjackers skyjack a U.S.S.R. Yak-12 plane which crashes in Armenia, killing one of the skyjackers. The other two skyjackers are captured and put to death.

NOVEMBER 27: Five men skyjack a Venezuelan DC-6B on its way to Maracaibo. It lands in Curacao. The skyjackers will be extradited and imprisoned.

1962

APRIL 13: David Healy and Leonard Oeth skyjack a chartered plane over Miami to Cuba. They will be deported back to the U.S. and imprisoned.

APRIL 16: Edgar Da Silva skyjacks a Royal Dutch Airlines plane heading for Lisbon, demanding to go to East Berlin. The plane lands in Holland where Da Silva is taken into custody.

MAY 22: A bomb placed inside the towel holder in the rear lavatory of a Continental Airlines jet bound from Chicago, Illinois, to Kansas City, Missouri, explodes and kills all forty-five persons on board.

SEPTEMBER 30: Two persons are killed and more than seventy others are injured when a mob attacks U.S. marshals escorting Negro student James Meredith to the University of Mississippi, during federally mandated intergration. A fifteen-hour attack by white supremacists is finally halted when 3,000 U.S. troops and the Mississippi National Guard are called to the scene.

James Meredith's entrance to the University of Mississippi touched off KKK terrorist riots, on September 30, 1962.

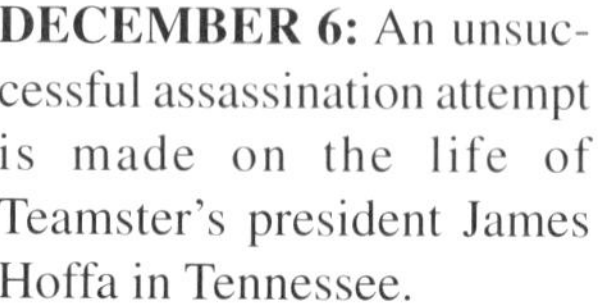

DECEMBER 6: An unsuccessful assassination attempt is made on the life of Teamster's president James Hoffa in Tennessee.

1963

JANUARY 13: Sylvanus Olympio, president of Togo, is assassinated at Lomé, Togo, by terrorists who have been former soldiers serving Olympio.

FEBRUARY 8: General Abdul Karim Kassem, prime minister of Iraq, is ousted and assassinated in a military coup in Baghdad, Iraq.

MARCH 8: Members of the Front de Libération du Québec (FLQ) throw Molotov cocktails at military establishments in Canada, marking the start of a wave of FLQ bombings throughout the country.

APRIL 11: Mohammed Khemisti, foreign minister of Algeria, is shot to death in Algiers, Algeria, by a Muslim terrorist.

APRIL 20: An FLQ bomb explodes at an army recruiting center in Montreal, Canada, killing a guard.

JUNE 12: Medgar W. Evers, Mississippi field secretary for the National Association for the Advancement of Colored People, is shot to death in front of his Jackson, Mississippi home. Though the assailant is never apprehended, the Ku Klux Klan is thought to be behind the murder. (Not until 1994 will Evers' killer, Byron de la Beckwith, be convicted of the terrorist murder.)

SEPTEMBER 15: White supremacists thought to be members of the Ku Klux Klan bomb the 16th Street Baptist Church in Birmingham, Alabama, killing four black school girls.

NOVEMBER 28: Six skyjackers take over a Venezuelan Convair twin engine plane, landing it in Trinidad where the skyjackers are taken into custody. They will be extradited and imprisoned.

1964

JANUARY 10: Provoked by inflammatory radio broadcasts, anti-American riots break out throughout Panama, in which dozens are killed.

FEBRUARY 4: Hassan II, king of Morocco, is the target of an unsuccessful assassination attempt in Morocco.

JUNE 21: Three northern civil rights workers, Michael Schwerner, Andrew Goodman and James Chaney, while traveling at night between Philadelphia and Meridian, Mississippi, are stopped by Neshoba County Deputy Sheriff Cecil R. Price, a Klan member, who turns the trio over to KKK leader Sam H. Bowers, Jr., and other Klan members. All three are shot and killed, their bodies dumped into shallow graves that have been prepared in advance of the premeditated murders.

Three Freedom Riders murdered by KKK members in Mississippi on June 21, 1964 (left to right): Michael Schwerner, James Chaney and Andrew Goodman.

JULY 1: Race riots take place in Philadelphia, Pennsylvania, in which 150 persons are injured and 165 (mostly blacks) are arrested for attacking police.

JULY 16: After a Negro youth is shot and killed for attacking a policeman in Harlem, New York, widespread rioting and looting by blacks ensues. One looter will be killed, dozens arrested, and 140 others will be injured.

OCTOBER 9: U.S. Air Force Lieutenant Colonel Michael Smolen is abducted in Caracas, Venezuela., by Castroite terrorists demanding the release of a terrorist held in Saigon, Vietnam. The prisoner's execution will be delayed and Smolen released.

DECEMBER 8: A dynamite charge apparently planted by a passenger who has insured himself for a large amount of money kills fifteen passengers aboard an ALAS Airline jet bound from Tipuani to LaPaz, Bolivia.

DECEMBER 20: Simon Wiesenthal, the celebrated Nazi hunter, is the target of an unsuccessful assassination attempt in Vienna, Austria.

1965

FEBRUARY 9: Colonel Harold Hauser, head of the U.S. military mission to Guatemala, is the target of an unsuccessful assassination attempt by terrorists of the Movimiento Revolucionario.

A black looter lies dead, while police patrol a damaged store in Watts, a section of Los Angeles, where Negroes rioted; 4,000 blacks were arrested, thirty-four died and more than $34 million in damage was done.

JULY 8: A Canadian Pacific airline flying over British Columbia crashes en route to Whitehorse in the Yukon. A bomb planted in the fuselage is blamed for the terrorist act which kills all fifty-two passengers on board.

JULY 20: General Maxwell D. Taylor is the target of an unsuccessful assassination attempt in Vietnam.

JULY 27: Fidel Castro, Communist dictator and premier of Cuba, is the target of an unsuccessful assassination attempt in Havana, Cuba, one which is later attributed to the CIA.

AUGUST 8: Widespread rioting in the Los Angeles suburb of Watts takes place. Blacks run amuck, starting hundreds of fires (even their own homes), then severing the hoses of firemen who arrive to fight the fires, stoning the firemen. Half the entire area will be gutted, thirty-four persons will die, and 1,032 will be injured. More than 4,000 blacks will be arrested and damages will exceed $34 million.

AUGUST 11: A widespread race riot in Cape Town, South Africa, results in seventeen blacks being killed and another fifty more injured.

AUGUST 31: Harry S. Fergerstrom, armed with a knife and glass from a broken bottle, skyjacks a Hawaiian DC-3 scheduled to fly from Honolulu to Kauai, Hawaii. He orders the pilot to return to Honolulu where he is taken into custody and sent to a correctional school.

OCTOBER 11: Lawrence D. Heisler and Richard K. Boyd, both U.S. Navy seaman, skyjack an Aloha F-27 en route from Molokai, Hawaii, to Honolulu. They will be dishonorably discharged and imprisoned.

OCTOBER 20: John Kilpatrick, president of the United Industrial Workers' Union, is fatally shot by Dana H. Nash, who will be sent to prison.

OCTOBER 26: Luis Medina Perez attempts to skyjack a National L-188 with thirty-three aboard, heading from Miami to Key West, Florida. He uses a "BB" pistol to order the pilot to land in Cuba. He will later be found mentally incompetent.

OCTOBER 29: Diosdado Macapagal, president of the Philippines, is the target of an unsuccessful assassination attempt in the Philippines.

NOVEMBER 17: Thomas H. Robinson, brandishing two revolvers, skyjacks a National DC-8 flight carrying ninety-one people from Houston to New Orleans. He orders the pilot to fly to Cuba. Robinson will later be sent to a correctional school.

1966

JANUARY 10: Negro activist Vernon Dahmer is killed by a Ku Klux Klan bomb in Hattiesburg, Mississippi.

JANUARY 15: Sir Abubakar Tafawa Balewa, prime minister of Nigeria, is assassinated in Nigeria.

JANUARY 29: Five Yugoslavian consulates in the U.S. are bombed by political dissidents.

MARCH 27: Angel Betancourt Gueto, a flight engineer, attempts to flee Communist Cuba by skyjacking a Cubana IL-18 heading for Havana. After the plane lands in Cuba, the pilot and a guard are killed, and the co-pilot wounded. Gueto, who thinks he has landed in Miami, is captured.

MAY 6: A FLQ bomb explodes in a Quebec arms manufacturing plant, killing one employee, Therese Marin.

MAY 18: General Maximiliano Hernandez Martinez is assassinated in Honduras.

JUNE 6: James Meredith, civil rights worker, is the target of a failed assassination attempt.

JUNE 19: Arthur Caldwell, head of the Labor Party, is the target of an unsuccessful assassination attempt in Australia by Peter R. Kocan, who will be sent to prison for life.

JUNE 30: Thomas Albert Tarrant and Kathy Ainsworth, two anti-semitic terrorists, attempt to plant a bomb at the home of a Jewish businessman in Meridian, Mississippi, but are interrupted by police. Ainsworth flees and is shot and killed.

JULY: Race riots in Chicago, Cleveland and New York, leave dozens injured.

SEPTEMBER 28: Maria Varrier and nineteen others skyjack an Argentine DC-4, which lands in the Falkland Islands. The three leaders of the skyjacking group are sentenced to death, the others imprisoned.

SEPTEMBER 29: National Guardsmen are called into San Francisco to quell widespread race rioting, where dozens are injured.

NOVEMBER 13: A bomb blows up on the Grand Integrity five days after the ship sails from Portland, Oregon. Captain Ho Lien-Siu and a motorman are killed as they inspect the device just before it explodes, but the ship is not seriously damaged.

NOVEMBER 22: An Aden Airways jetliner crashes in Southern Yemen after an explosive device hidden in a piece of carry-on luggage is detonated. Twenty-eight persons are killed.

1967

JANUARY 7: Army deserter Richard James Paris detonates a dynamite bomb with a .38-caliber pistol in the honeymoon suite of the Orbit Inn, in Las Vegas, Nevada, killing himself, his wife, and five other newlyweds.

FEBRUARY 7: Terrorist Riyad Kamal Hajjaj skyjacks an Egyptian AN-24 domestic flight, forcing the plane to land in Jordan. Hajjaj will escape to Sweden, but later be arrested and imprisoned for other crimes.

APRIL 19: Sheik Salem Al-Amoodi is assassinated in Aden.

JUNE 2: Massive riots by students protesting the visit of the Shah of Iran result in widespread injuries and damage in Berlin. The riots are used by Ulrike Meinhof, a Marxist, and playboy student Berndt Andreas Baader, to form the dreaded terrorist group known as the Baader-Meinhof Gang.

JUNE 9: Charles Eustis Bohlen, U.S. Ambassador to France, is the target of a failed assassination attempt on his life in Paris.

JUNE 22: Roy Wilkins, civil rights leader, is the target of an unsuccessful assassination attempt in New York City.

JUNE 25: Francois Duvalier, dictator and president of Haiti, is the target of a failed assassination attempt on his life in Port-au-Prince.

JUNE 30: Francois Bodenan skyjacks a private United Kingdom jet carrying Moise Tshombe, former prime minister of the Congo. The plane lands in Algeria where Tshombe is held captive until his death on June 29, 1969.

JULY 12-18: Race riots break out across the U.S. (127 separate riots) in a six-day period, which will leave dozens injured and millions of dollars in property damage.

JULY 23: Angered over police raids on black nightclubs breaking mandatory closing times, Negro rioters take to the streets of

Police battle armed looters in Detroit, Michigan, where thousands of blacks and some whites committed widespread looting on July 23, 1967.

More than $46 million in damage was done before military units were ordered into Detroit to restore order.

Detroit, Michigan, and begin looting stores. Police and National Guardsmen battle the enormous black crowds, and thirty-three blacks and ten whites are killed, with more than 600 injured, and 3,800 persons, mostly blacks, arrested. Property damage attributed to black rioters is estimated at $46 million.

SEPTEMBER 28: Levi Eshkol, prime minister of Israel, is the target of an unsuccessful assassination attempt in Israel.

OCTOBER 12: A British European Airways jet flying over the Mediterranean Sea explodes in midair when a bomb planted in the passenger cabin goes off. Sixty-six lives are lost.

NOVEMBER 20: Louis G. Babler takes control of a chartered Piper Apache, taking three persons from Hollywood, Florida, to Bimini, Bahama Islands. He demands that the plane be flown to Cuba where he will escape.

1968

JANUARY 16: Colonel John D. Webber, Jr., commander of a U.S. special service squad in Guatemala, and Lieutenant Commander Ernest A. Munro, are shot to death by terrorists in Guatemala.

FEBRUARY 9: William Clark, a Marine, skyjacks a Pan American military chartered DC-6, flying from South Vietnam to Hong Kong. Clark will be court-martialed and sentenced, but charges will be dropped when he is diagnosed as schizophrenic.

FEBRUARY 18: James Boynton skyjacks a private plane to Cuba, but he is returned by the Castro government and is sent to prison.

FEBRUARY 18: One person is killed and fourteen others are injured when a terrorist bomb explodes in the basement of the Yugoslav ambassador's home in Paris, France.

FEBRUARY 21: Lawrence M. Rhodes skyjacks a Delta DC-8 flying from Tampa to West Palm Beach, Florida, demanding that he be taken to Cuba. He will be committed to a mental institution.

APRIL 3: Four members of the Baader-Meinhof gang—Berndt Andreas Baader, Gudrun Ensslin, Thorwald Proll and Horst Sohnlein, all heavily drugged, plant firebombs in Berlin's largest department stores. One bomb, planted in the toy department, causes a small fire that will be extinguished; another firebomb fails to ignite. All four terrorists will be captured and sent to prison for three years. All will be released on bond on June 13, 1969, to await an appeal hearing. They flee to France while Ulrike Meinhof, who emerges as the leader of the terrorist gang, begins organizing.

APRIL 5-9: In response to the assassination of black leader Martin Luther King, Jr., Negro rioters swarm through the streets of Chicago, Baltimore, Washington, and Cincinnati, looting stores and attacking police and National Guardsmen. Thirty-one will die in the various city riots and millions of dollars in damage will be done.

APRIL 23-28: Students belonging to the radical Students for a Democratic Society, seize five buildings on the Columbia University campus in New York. After six days of occupation, the students are dispersed by police. More than 130 persons are injured and 600 are arrested

MAY 6: A drunken patron ejected from a Fort Worth, Texas, nightclub, returns to firebomb the place, killing seven customers and horribly burning six others.

MAY 21-22: After four students are suspended for their roles in the April Columbia University riot in New York, SDS members seize the main classroom building on May 21, holding it for forty-eight hours before they are dislodged. Sixty-eight persons are injured, 177 more are arrested, and damage is put at $300,000.

Members of the SDS seized Columbia University in New York on May 21-22, 1968 (the man with the briefcase is a professor climbing over bodies to get to his classroom), where $300,000 damage was done.

JUNE 29: E. H. Carter, armed with a revolver, skyjacks a Southeast Airlines DC-3 carrying seventeen people from Miami to Key West, Florida, to Cuba where he remains.

JULY 1: Mario Velasquez Fonseca skyjacks a Northwest Airline B-727, carrying eighty-five passengers and crew, from Chicago to Cuba.

JULY 4: John H. Morris boards a TWA B-727 in Kansas City, telling the crew that he was carrying dynamite and will ignite the explosives unless he is taken to Cuba. When it is learned that he has no weapons, Morris is overpowered and later sent to prison.

JULY 12: A private Cessna-210 with two persons on board is skyjacked in Miami by Leonard S. Bendicks and taken to Cuba on his orders. The Castro government will return Bendicks to the U.S. where he will be imprisoned.

JULY 12: Boarding a Delta CV-880 in Baltimore, Oran D. Richards orders the pilot to fly to Cuba instead of Houston. Richards is later returned to the U.S. where he is judged insane and confined in an asylum.

JULY 22: Three Habash Front terrorists skyjack an El Al plane traveling from Rome to Tel Aviv, Israel, forcing the pilot to land in Algeria. They will be imprisoned.

JULY 27: Armed with a pistol, Rogelio Hernandez Leyva skyjacks a National Airlines DC-8, ordering the pilot to fly to Cuba with his fifty-seven passengers. Leyva, identified as a Communist terrorist, disappears after the plane arrives in Havana.

AUGUST 4: Willis Jesse and his three-year-daughter board a chartered private plane in Naples, Florida. Jesse skyjacks the plane to Cuba. He is later returned, charged and convicted of kidnapping, and sent to prison.

AUGUST 13: George Papadopoulis, premier of Greece, is the target of a failed assassination attempt in Greece.

AUGUST 21: Antonio LoBianco, twenty-nine, and Barbara Locci, who sit in a parked car in a cemetery fifteen miles outside of Florence, Italy, are shot and killed by a terrorist who will be dubbed the Monster of Florence and whose killings will be almost identical to the New York's "3-X," Son of Sam (David Berkowitz), San Francisco's Zodiac, and the Texarkana, Texas, slayer of the 1940s. The Monster of Florence follows an identifiable pattern: After shooting his victims through car windows, he will use a scalpel to remove the sex organs of his female victims.

AUGUST 22: Bill McBride forces the pilot of a chartered Cessna-182, flying from Naples, Florida, to fly to Cuba, where he vanishes.

AUGUST 26: Thousands of anti-establishment youths, led by radical leftists Abbie Hoffman, Jerry Rubin and others, begin three days of violent opposition to the Democratic National Convention then convening in Chicago, labeling the Democrats as being members of "a war party." The protestors hurl rocks, bricks and other objects against police and national guardsmen, as well as use razors affixed to their shoes to bloody the shins of officers. Police retaliate with mass clubbings. Hundreds on both sides are injured.

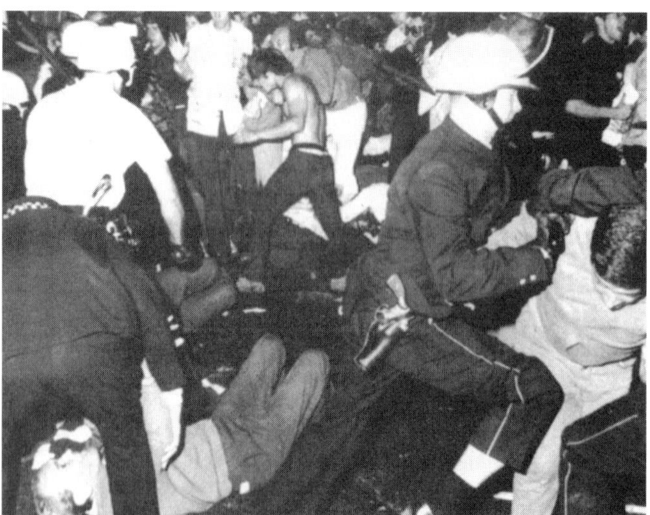

Police and anti-establishment youth clash at the Democratic Convention in Chicago on August 26, 1968; hundreds were injured on both sides and seven radical leftists were later tried for inciting to riot.

SEPTEMBER 11: Charles Beasley skyjacks an Air Canada plane flying to Toronto, demanding to be flown to Cuba. He will be imprisoned.

SEPTEMBER 20: Jose A. Suarez Garcia skyjacks an Eastern B-720, flying from San Juan, Puerto Rico to Miami, Florida, with forty-six passengers on board, diverting it to Cuba where he will vanish.

OCTOBER 12: Captain Charles R. Chandler of the U.S. Army, is slain outside his home in Sao Paulo, Brazil, by Vanguarda Popular Revolucionaria (VPR) terrorists.

OCTOBER 23: Anti-Castro El Poder Cubano terrorists are arrested in New York for attempting to assassinate the Cuban ambassador to the United Nations.

OCTOBER 26: Three Croatian leaders opposed to communism are killed by Communist terrorists in Munich, Germany.

NOVEMBER 2: Roger A. Pastorcich takes control of an Eastern DC-9 with fifty-four persons on board, flying to Chicago from Birmingham, Alabama. He demands to be flown to South Vietnam, demands which are rejected. He will later be captured and placed in a juvenile detention center.

NOVEMBER 4: Raymond Johnson, Jr., skyjacks a National B-727 carrying sixty-five people from New Orleans to Miami, ordering the plane to fly to Cuba, where he will disappear.

NOVEMBER 22: Twelve people are killed and fifty-two more injured when a bomb explodes in Jerusalem's busiest open-air market.

NOVEMBER 23: Six Latin-Americans armed with four pistols skyjack an Eastern B-727 Chicago to Miami flight with ninety persons on board, taking the plane to Cuba, where they escape.

DECEMBER 11: James and Gwendolyn Patterson, armed with a revolver, skyjack a St. Louis to Miami TWA B-727 flight carrying thirty-nine persons to Cuba, where they disappear.

DECEMBER 14: Charles Senecal, director of Chanbly Transport, is the target of a terrorist bombing in Canada.

DECEMBER 19: Thomas G. Washington, carrying a fake pistol and phony nitro, takes 142 passengers and nine crew members hostage when he skyjacks a Miami-bound Eastern DC-8 to Cuba. He will be returned to the U.S. and imprisoned.

DECEMBER 20: The terrorist who would be called the Zodiac Killer, and whose body count would range between nine to more than forty (depending upon lawmen who credited killings to him), struck for the first time on a deserted road outside Vallejo, California, shooting and killing David Faraday, seventeen, and Bettilou Jenson, sixteen, as they sit in a parked car.

DECEMBER 26: Two Habash Front terrorists, armed with hand grenades and small arms, attack an El Al jetliner in Athens, Greece, killing one Israeli passenger, before being captured by police.

1969

JANUARY 2: Tyrone and Linda Austin, armed with a pistol, skyjack a 138-passenger Eastern DC-8 heading for Miami from New York. They order the pilot to fly to Cuba, where they escape. Tyrone Austin will later be killed in a bank robbery.

JANUARY 2: George Flamourides (AKA: G. Paravolidakis) skyjacks a Greek DC-6B flying to Athens, Greece. The plane lands in Cairo, where Flamourides is captured and imprisoned.

JANUARY 9: Ronald T. Bohle, wielding a knife, skyjacks a seventy-three passenger Nassau-bound Eastern B-727 to Cuba. He will later be imprisoned.

JANUARY 11: Robert M. Helmey, brandishing a revolver, skyjacks a B-727 Jacksonville to Miami flight, taking twenty persons to Cuba. He will later be found insane and acquitted.

JANUARY 17: Kenneth E. McPeek takes over a Delta CV-880 en route from Detroit to Miami carrying seventy-seven people. Wielding a shotgun, McPeek unsuccessfully attempts to force the pilot to fly to Cuba. He will be captured and imprisoned.

JANUARY 28: Clinton R. Smith and Byron V. Booth, armed with a revolver and dynamite, skyjack a National DC-8 Miami-bound flight with thirty-two persons aboard to Cuba. They will escape.

JANUARY 28: Larry F. Brooks, Noble B. Mason, and Everett L. White, wielding three pistols, skyjack an Eastern DC-8 Atlanta to Miami flight and its 105 passengers. They force the pilot to fly to Cuba, but they will later be imprisoned.

JANUARY 31: Allan C. Sheffield skyjacks fifty-five passengers on board a National DC-8 en route from San Francisco to Tampa, Florida, forcing it to land in Cuba. He will be arrested and imprisoned.

FEBRUARY 3: Michael Anthony Peparo and Tasmin Rebecca Fitzgerald, armed with a knife and an aerosol insecticide cylinder, attempt to skyjack a National B-727 New York to Miami flight carrying seventy passengers and crew to Cuba. They will be arrested and sent to prison.

FEBRUARY 14: A number of people are injured and substantial damage done when an FLQ bomb demolishes part of the Montreal Stock Exchange building.

FEBRUARY 18: Four terrorists armed with guns and hand grenades, and belonging to the Habash Front attack an El Al jet in Zurich, Switzerland, killing the co-pilot and injuring five passengers. One skyjacker will be killed and the other three arrested and later imprisoned.

FEBRUARY 21: Two persons are killed and eight more are injured when a bomb explodes in a Jerusalem food store.

FEBRUARY 25: Lorenzo Ervin, Jr. uses a revolver to take over an Eastern DC-8 Atlanta to Miami flight carrying sixty-seven people and forcing the pilot to land in Cuba. He will later be imprisoned.

MARCH 1: Clay Shaw, a wealthy entrepreneur in New Orleans, is acquitted on charges of conspiring to assassinate President John F. Kennedy.

MARCH 5: Anthony G. Bryant skyjacks a National B-727 New York to Miami flight carrying twenty-six people, threatening the pilot with a revolver and forcing him to fly to Cuba. Bryant will later be imprisoned.

MARCH 17: Robert L. Sandlin, who will later be sent to an insane asylum, skyjacks a Delta DC-9, carrying sixty-three persons from Atlanta to Augusta, Georgia, diverting the plane to Cuba. Sandlin threatens the crew with a bomb which turns out to be a fake.

MARCH 19: Dallas A. Dickey skyjacks a Delta CV-880, with ninety-seven people on board, scheduled to fly from New Orleans to Dallas, Texas. He orders the pilot to fly to Cuba. Dickey will later be sent to an insane asylum.

MARCH 25: Luis A. Frese skyjacks a Delta DC-8 scheduled to fly 114 people to San Diego from Dallas, Texas. At gunpoint, Frese orders the pilot to fly to Cuba, where he will be imprisoned and die in his cell.

MARCH 30: The New African Organization, a militant group in Detroit, Michigan, erupts in a gun battle after a meeting. One policeman is killed and four blacks are injured, while 135 others (mostly blacks) are arrested for rioting.

APRIL 15: Terrorist Cameron David Bishop is placed on the FBI's Ten Most Wanted List for bombing a defense plant in Colorado in January 1969.

MAY 5: Jean P. Charrette and Alain Allard use two revolvers and a knife to skyjack a National B-727 flying from New York to Miami, with seventy-five people on board, ordering the pilot to fly to Miami. They will later be imprisoned in Canada.

MAY 13: Race rioting in Kuala Lumpur, Malaysia, results in more than 100 deaths.

MAY 30: Terrance Niemeyer attempts to skyjack a Texas International CV-600 New Orleans to Alexandria, Louisiana, carrying forty-four people, to Cuba. Niemeyer, who falsely claims to have a hand grenade, will later be sent to an insane asylum.

JUNE 17: William L. Brent uses a revolver to skyjack a TWA B-707 Oakland, California, to New York flight, carrying ninety people, to Cuba. He will escape.

JUNE 26: Thoroughly drunk and wearing only shorts, a T-shirt and sandals, Anthony Raymond boards an Eastern Airlines 727 in Miami. He suddenly flashes a penknife and is able to terrify the entire crew and passengers, although it was later admitted that he could easily have been overpowered. Once in the cockpit, Raymond orders the pilot to fly to Cuba which he does. Raymond is welcomed in Havana but when he sobers up he demands that he be returned to the U.S. When he does return, Raymond is sent to prison for fifteen years.

JUNE 26: The Fuerzas Armadas Rebeldes (FAR) bombs fourteen minimax supermarkets in Argentina, causing $3 million in damage.

JUNE 26: Joseph C. Crawford skyjacks a Continental DC-9 destined for Midland from El Paso, Texas. Brandishing a knife, he forces the pilot to land in Cuba. He will be returned to the U.S. and imprisoned.

JULY 4: The Zodiac Killer shoots and kills a nineteen-year-old girl and wounds her companion as they sit in a car near San Francisco. The terrorist will later stab Cecelia Shephard twenty-four times in the back when killing her, and carve an outline of a cross on her skin. Zodiac still later tries to kill a cabdriver who survives and gives the only description of this maniac—a man approximately five feet eight-inches tall with short reddish-brown hair and thick glasses. Zodiac will send dozens of taunting letters to police and leave cryptograms at the scenes of his many murders, one reading: "I like killing people because it is so much fun." By 1975, Zodiac will cease to communicate with police and authorities will believe him dead or committed to an insane asylum. San Francisco police estimate his murders at six, but Don Striepeke, sheriff of Sonoma County, believes the Zodiac is responsible for more than forty slayings.

JULY 30: A. H. Meyer, U.S. ambassador to Japan, is the target of a failed assassination attempt when he is accosted by a Japanese citizen armed with a knife in Tokyo.

JULY 31: Lester E. Perry, wielding a razor blade, skyjacks a TWA B-727, flying 123 passengers from Pittsburgh to Los Angeles, forcing the pilot to fly to Cuba where he will escape.

AUGUST 5: A Philippine Airlines jet explodes over Zamboanga, Philippines. The bomb is detonated in one of the restrooms, killing the person setting it off and injuring four others.

AUGUST 5: John S. McCreery attempts to skyjack an Eastern DC-9 flying from Philadelphia to Tampa, Florida. McCreery, who wields a knife and a razor blade, will later be sent to an insane asylum.

AUGUST 29: Leila A. Khaled and Salim K. Essawai of the PFLP skyjack a TWA B-707 flying from Rome to Athens with 127 persons on board. Armed with pistols and hand grenades, the terrorists order the pilot to fly to Syria. In Damascus, two passengers are exchanged for two Syrian pilots. Everyone aboard deplaned and the skyjackers demolish the cockpit before escaping.

SEPTEMBER 3: Three terrorists of ELF skyjack an Ethiopian DC-6 flying from Addis Ababa to Djibouti, French Territory of the Afars and Issas. When the plane lands at Aden, South Yemen, one skyjacker is shot and the other two captured.

SEPTEMBER 4: Charles Burke Elbrick, U.S. ambassador to Brazil, is abducted in Rio de Janiero by MR-8 (Revolutionary Movement of the Eighth) and ALN terrorists who demand that several political prisoners be freed and the group's manisfesto be printed. Some of the demands will be met and Elbrick set free.

SEPTEMBER 21: Muslims and Hindus in western India riot over alleged mistreatment of sacred Hindu cows and Hindu spiritual leaders by Muslims. More than 1,000 persons are killed.

Seven of the original defendants in the 1969 Chicago riots trial are shown left to right (standing) Abbie Hoffman, John Froines, Lee Weiner, David Dellinger, Rennie Davis, Tom Hayden and (sitting) Jerry Rubin clowning at a microphone, with his girlfriend, Nancy Kurshan sitting next to him.

SEPTEMBER 26: The trial of the so-called "Chicago Eight" (Jerry Rubin, Abbie Hoffman, Rennie Davis, David Dellinger, Thomas Hayden, John Froines, Lee Weiner and Bobby Seale of the Black Panther Party) commences in Chicago before Judge Julius Hoffman. The defendants are charged with intent to commit a conspiracy and inciting to riot earlier to and during the Democratic National Convention. The five-month trial is a farce with the defendants and their attorneys creating mayhem and confusion in the court.

SEPTEMBER 29: Two Habash Front terrorists skyjack a TWA plane flying from Rome to Lodi, Italy, forcing it to land in Damascus, where two Israeli passengers are freed in exchange for the release of two Syrian pilots being held in Israel.

OCTOBER 6: José Strassle, son of the Swiss consul in Cali, Colombia, and Hermann Bluff, consul secretary, are kidnapped by a terrorist group called the Invisible Ones, but are later set free. Officials deny media reports that a ransom of several thousand dollars has been paid.

OCTOBER 17: Abdirashid Ali Shermarke, president of Somalia, is assassinated at Las Anos, Somalia.

OCTOBER 21: Henry Shorr skyjacks a Pan American B-720 scheduled to carry its twenty-eight passengers from Mexico City to Merida, Mexico. Shorr wields a revolver to divert the plane to Cuba. He will commit suicide a year later.

NOVEMBER 10: Fourteen-year-old David Booth, wielding a knife, attempts to skyjack a Delta DC-9 en route from Cincinnati, Ohio, to Chicago, with seventy-five persons on board. Booth demands to be flown to either Sweden or Mexico but he is unsuccessful and is later sent to a juvenile detention center.

NOVEMBER 27: Two Jordanian terrorists launch a grenade attack on the El Al Airlines office in Athens, Greece, killing a Greek child and wounding thirteen others.

DECEMBER 12: Red Brigadists explode a bomb in the Piazza Fontana, in Milan, Italy, that kills sixteen people. Seven persons are later put on trial, five acquitted, and on March 20, 1981, two others sentenced to prison on lesser charges.

DECEMBER 2: Benny R. Hamilton, armed with a knife, skyjacks a TWA B-707, flying from San Francisco to Philadelphia, forcing the pilot to fly to Cuba. He will later be imprisoned in the U.S.

DECEMBER 21: Three Habash Front terrorists plan to skyjack a TWA plane arriving at Athens, Greece from Tel Aviv, but they are apprehended by police and will be imprisoned until July 1970.

DECEMBER 22: A bomb explodes in a lavatory on an Air Vietnam jet, killing thirty-two people near Nha Trang, South Vietnam. The landing brakes are damaged by the bomb and the plane careens into a school when landing.

1970

JANUARY 6: Anton Funjek skyjacks a Delta DC-9 taking sixty passengers from Orlando to Jacksonville, Florida. Brandishing a knife, Funjek attempts to force the pilot to land in Switzerland. He will later be imprisoned.

JANUARY 8: Christian Belon "to spite Americans and Israelis for their aggression in the Middle East," skyjacks a TWA 707 carrying twenty persons from Paris to Rome. Belon orders the pilot at gunpoint to fly to Beirut, where he will be arrested and imprisoned.

JANUARY 30: A state of siege is declared in Guatemala following the attempted assassination of a presidential candidate and the murder of a newspaper editor opposed to communism by Communist terrorists.

FEBRUARY 10: A bus at the airport in Munich, Germany, is attacked with grenades by three Arab terrorists. An Israeli citizen is killed and eleven other passengers are injured.

FEBRUARY 15: Some of the members of the original "Chicago Eight" trial in Chicago are acquitted of the charge to commit a conspiracy before and during the 1968 Democratic National Convention but Jerry Rubin, Abbie Hoffman, Rennie Davis, David Dellinger and Thomas Hayden are convicted of crossing a state line to incite a riot. Further, Judge Hoffman has sentenced several of the defendants, along with their attorneys, William Kunstler and Leonard Weinglass, to long terms for contempt of court. None of the terms are served. A federal district judge will overturn the convictions on a technicality—that Hoffman waited too long to impose sentencing.

FEBRUARY 21: A Swissair jet flying from Zurich, Switzerland, to Tel Aviv, Israel, is blown up in midair, claiming forty-seven lives. It is believed that the bomb had been planted by Abu Ibrahim of the Popular Front for Liberation of Palestine (PFLP).

FEBRUARY 27: Fuentes Mohr, Guatemalan foreign minister, is abducted by leftist FAR terrorists. He will be released after a terrorist is set free from prison.

MARCH 3: Takeshi Okamoto, a fanatical member of the terrorist Japanese Red Army, boards a Japanese jet and, brandishing a sword, forces the pilot to fly to North Korea.

MARCH 6: Sean M. Holly, U.S. labor attaché in Guatemala, is abducted by FAR terrorists and is later released when three terrorists are set free from prison.

MARCH 11: Nobuo Okuchi, Japanese consul general in Sao Paulo, Brazil, is kidnapped in Brazil by VPR terrorists, who demand the release of prisoners. The diplomat is released after the prisoners are set free.

MARCH 11: Clemmie Stubbs skyjacks a United B-727, scheduled to fly from Cleveland to Atlanta. Stubbs threatens the 106 passengers and crew members with a revolver and compels the pilot to fly to Cuba, where he is imprisoned. He will later be killed while attempting to escape his Cuban jail cell.

MARCH 17: John Divivo unsuccessfully tries to skyjack an Eastern DC-9 flight taking seventy-three persons and crew from Newark, N.J. to Boston. Divivo shoots and kills the pilot and wounds the co-pilot who resists his orders. He is overpowered and later imprisoned, committing suicide in his cell.

MARCH 21: Joaquin Waldemar Sanchez, Paraguayan consul in Ituzaingo, Argentina, is kidnapped by FAL terrorists. When their demand for the release of two other terrorists in prison is refused, Sanchez is released.

MARCH 24: Lieutenant Colonel Donald J. Crowley, U.S. air attaché to the Dominican Republic, is kidnapped. Crowley will be released later after twenty political prisoners are allowed to leave the country.

MARCH 29: MANO terrorists kidnap Yuri Pivovarov, U.S.S.R. assistant commercial attaché in Argentina, but police rescue Pivovarov after a harrowing car chase.

MARCH 31: Count Karl von Spreti, West German ambassador to Guatemala, is abducted, his terrorist kidnappers demanding the release of twenty-two political prisoners, along with $700,000. When the Guatemalan government refuses, Spreti will be slain.

MARCH 31: Nine URA terrorists skyjack a Japan Airlines plane, ordering it to fly to Pyongyang, North Korea. The plane instead flies to Seoul, where the airport has been quickly disguised to look like the Pyongyang airport. The terrorists are not deceived, but allow the passengers to deplane, then order the pilot to fly them to Pyongyang, where they vanish.

APRIL 5: Curtis S. Cutter, U.S. consul general in Brazil, is nearly kidnapped in Pôrto Alegre, but he escapes and three UPR terrorists are arrested.

APRIL 21: Seventy-five miles north of Manila, Philippines, a bomb hidden in the lavatory of a Philippine Airlines jet explodes in midair, killing all thirty-six passengers.

APRIL 22: Ira D. Meeks and Diane V. McKinney, wielding a revolver, skyjack a chartered Cessna-172 from Gastonia, North Carolina, to Cuba. Both will later be captured; Meeks will be found mentally incompetent and charges against both skyjackers will be dropped.

APRIL 23: Using a toy pistol and an alleged bomb, Joseph A. Wagstaff unsuccessfully attempts to skyjack a DC-9 en route from Pellston to Sault St. Marie, Michigan, to Detroit. He will be seized and sent to an insane asylum.

MAY 4: Students at Kent State University protesting the Vietnam war are fired upon by nervous National Guardsmen and four students are killed.

MAY 4: Al Fatah terrorists invade the Israeli Embassy in Asunción, Paraguay and shoot to death the wife of the first secretary and another person.

MAY 11: Rioting blacks in Augusta, Florida, are dispersed by police who shoot and kill six black demonstrators.

MAY 14: Ulrike Meinhof and other terrorists free Andreas Baader from prison guards in Berlin's Tegel Library where Baader had been allowed to do research. The terrorists fire submachine guns, injuring the guards and several employees and patrons.

MAY 22: Members of the Feyedeen cross Lebanon into Israel and fire three bazooka rockets into a school bus, killing eight Israeli children and injuring twenty-two others.

MAY 25: Nelson Molina skyjacks an American Airlines B-727 en route from Chicago to New York. Molina brandishes a pistol when ordering the pilot to fly the seventy-four passengers and crew to Cuba, where he will escape.

MAY 25: Graciella C. Quesada Zamora skyjacks a ninety-six passenger Delta CV-880 en route from Chicago to Miami. Flashing a revolver, she forces the pilot to fly to Cuba. She will be returned to the U.S. in 1980 and imprisoned.

JUNE 2: One person is killed and twelve others are injured when a hand grenade explodes beneath a seat on a Philippine Airlines jet en route to Bacolod, Negros Island. The plane lands safely at Roxas, Philippines.

JUNE 4: Arthur Barkley attempts to hold hostage the fifty-six people aboard a TWA B-727 en route from Phoenix, Arizona, to St. Louis, Missouri. Brandishing a revolver, razor blade and a bottle of gasoline, Barkley demands a $100 million ransom. He is seized, then found temporarily insane and acquitted.

JUNE 7: Morris Draper, U.S. political secretary, is abducted in Amman, Jordan, by PFLP terrorists. He will later be released.

JUNE 10: Major Robert Perry, U.S. military attaché in Amman, Jordan, is at home when he is fatally shot by terrorists.

JUNE 11: Ehrenfried von Holleben, West German ambassador to Brazil, is kidnapped by terrorists who demand that forty prisoners be released. The demands are met and Holleben is set free.

JUNE 18: The Parke-Davis plant in Buenos Aires, Argentina, is bombed, killing three employees.

JUNE 22: Terrorist Haxhi H. Xhaferi skyjacks a Pan American plane carrying 133 passengers from Beirut to Rome. Flashing a pistol, Xhaferi orders the plane flown to Cairo. He will be tried and sent to prison three years later.

JULY 3: Five persons are killed in Belfast, Ireland, in a clash between IRA forces and British troops.

JULY 9: Fernando Londone y Londone, ex-foreign minister of Colombia, is kidnapped by Colombian terrorists who demand and receive $200,000.

JULY 21: Two West Germans are kidnapped in Teoponte, Bolivia, by ELN terrorists whose demands for the release of prisoners will be met and the Germans will be set free.

JULY 24: Quick-acting police arrest several terrorists who are about to abduct Donner Lyon, U.S. consul in Recife, Brazil.

JULY 31: Aloisio Mares Dias Gomide, Brazilian vice consul in Uruguay, is kidnapped by Tupamaro terrorists who allegedly receive a $250,000 ransom. Gomide is then released.

JULY 31: U.S. diplomat Daniel A. Mitrione is kidnapped by Uruguayan terrorists, who demand the release of all Tupamaros held in prison. The demand will be refused and Mitrione will be slain by his captors.

JULY 31: Michael Gordon Jones, second consul to the U.S. embassy in Montevideo, Uruguay, along with cultural attaché Nathan Rosenfeld are kidnapped by Tupamaro terrorists, but they manage to escape.

AUGUST 2: Rudolfo Rivera Rios skyjacks a Pan American B-747 scheduled to fly from New York to San Juan, Puerto Rico. Rios threatens 360 passengers and seventeen crew members with a pistol and alleged nitroglycerin, ordering the pilot to fly to Cuba. He will later be imprisoned.

AUGUST 7: Claude L. Fly, U.S. agronomist, is abducted in Montevideo, Uruguay, by Tupamaro terrorists who demand that 150 political prisoners be freed. Fly will suffer a heart attack and be set free.

AUGUST 15: Alfredo Stroessner, president of Paraguay, is the target of a failed assassination attempt.

AUGUST 20: Gregory A. Graves skyjacks a Delta DC-9 scheduled to fly from Atlanta to Savannah, Georgia, to Cuba. Graves threatens the eighty-two passengers and crew with an alleged bomb. He will be returned to the U.S. in 1975 and be imprisoned.

AUGUST 24: Karleton Armstrong, David S. Fine, and other members of the Students For a Democratic Society (SDS), detonate a bomb at the University of Wisconsin in Madison, Wisconsin, killing Robert Fassnacht and injuring several other persons. Armstrong will later be sent to prison for this terrorist act.

AUGUST 24: Robert J. Labadie skyjacks a TWA B-727, scheduled to fly from Chicago to Philadelphia, to Cuba. Labadie claims to have a bomb while threatening the eighty-six passengers and crew. He will later be sent to an insane asylum.

AUGUST 30: Johan Huber unsuccessfully attempts to skyjack a Pan American B-727 en route from Munich to West Berlin with 125 persons on board. Using a starter pistol, Huber tries to force the pilot to fly to Budapest, Hungary. He will be sent to an insane asylum.

George Habash, terrorist leader of the PFLP (Popular Front for the Liberation of Palestine); he orchestrated countless skyjackings, kidnappings and murders.

SEPTEMBER 6: Terrorists of the Habash Front skyjack a Pan American 747 to Beirut, and then to Cairo, where its 171 passengers and crew are disembarked. The terrorists then blow up the plane. The same terrorist organization will skyjack three other planes this same day, one of these being an El Al plane on which terrorists Patrick Arguello will be killed and Leila Khalid will be injured. An Israeli flight attendant is injured, along with four passengers.

SEPTEMBER 12: Members of the Jewish Defense League take three hostages at the Egyptian embassy in London, England. The captors demand the release of airplane passengers held hostage in Jordan by Arab terrorists.

SEPTEMBER 15: Donald B. Irwin attempts to skyjack a TWA B-707 scheduled to fly from Los Angeles to San Francisco. Irwin flashes an unloaded pistol to control fifty-nine passengers and crew members, ordering the pilot to fly to North Korea. He will be thwarted and imprisoned.

SEPTEMBER 19: Richard D. Witt skyjacks a 727 jet flying from Pittsburgh to Philadelphia. Using a pistol and an alleged bomb, Witt commandeers the aircraft and its ninety-eight passengers and crew, having the pilot fly to Egypt and then to Cuba. He will later be imprisoned in the U.S.

SEPTEMBER 22: David W. Donovan fails to skyjack an Eastern DC-8 en route from Boston to San Juan, Puerto Rico. Donovan threatens to set the plane on fire if his demands are not met but he will not state his demands. He is seized and skyjacking charges dropped, but he will be imprisoned for an unrelated robbery and murder.

OCTOBER 5: Four FLQ terrorists kidnap James Richard Cross, the British trade commissioner for Canada, in Quebec in the country's first political kidnapping. The kidnappers demand $500,000 in gold, the reinstatement of recently fired postal workers and safe passage to Cuba or Algeria. When the government fails to comply, the terrorists kidnap Pierre Laporte, Quebec's Minister of Labor, threatening to kill Laporte unless their demands are met.

OCTOBER 18: When their demands are refused by the Canadian government, FLQ terrorists murder hostage Pierre Laporte; his bullet-riddled body is found in the trunk of a car parked at St. Hubert's Airport near Montreal. Three of Laporte's kidnappers and killers will be sent to prison for life.

NOVEMBER 6: The central bus station in Tel Aviv, Israel, is devastated by two explosions which kill two persons and injure twenty-four others.

DECEMBER 1: Eugen Beihl, a West German consul, is abducted in San Sebastián, Spain, by ETA Basque terrorists. Biehl will be set free on December 25.

DECEMBER 2: The FLQ terrorists still holding James Richard Cross are located in a Montreal house and are surrounded by police who agree to allow them safe passage to Cuba if they release Cross. The terrorists release their hostage and are flown safely out of the country.

DECEMBER 7: Giovanni Enrico Bucher, Swiss ambassador to Brazil, is abducted in Rio de Janeiro by members of the National Liberation Alliance (ALN). After seventy political prisoners are released, Bucher will be set free.

1971

JANUARY 3: Arthur J. Wilson, Lolita K. Graves, Carl White, and Norma Jean White skyjack a National DC-8, scheduled to fly eighty-nine passengers from Los Angeles to Tampa, Florida, to Cuba. All four will later be apprehended. Charges against Norma White will be dropped, but the other three terrorists will be sent to prison.

JANUARY 8: Tupamaro terrorists kidnap Geoffrey M. S. Jackson, British ambassador to Uruguay, in Montevideo. Jackson will be released after 106 political prisoners are set free.

JANUARY 15: The Baader-Meinhof gang robs two banks in Kassel, Germany, using the money to buy guns from Al Fatah, an Arab terrorist organization.

JANUARY 22: Garland J. Grant skyjacks a Northwest B-727, scheduled to fly sixty people from Milwaukee, Wisconsin, to Detroit, Michigan, to Cuba. Grant has boarded the plane with a hatchet and an alleged bomb. He will be returned to the U.S. and imprisoned.

FEBRUARY 1: Jibril Front terrorists attempt to blow up an El Al plane flying from London, England. A bomb is planted in the luggage of an unwitting woman and is located. The woman is released.

FEBRUARY 4: Walter C. Hines, allegedly armed with nitroglycerin, skyjacks a Delta DC-9, set to fly twenty-seven people from Chicago to Nashville, Tennessee, to Cuba. He will be imprisoned.

FEBRUARY 10: Two Croatian terrorists take over the Yugoslavian consulate in Gothenburg, Sweden, demanding that prisoners in Yugoslavia be freed. When their demands are not met, the terrorists surrender.

FEBRUARY 15: James Finlay, U.S. air force security officer in Ankara, Turkey., is abducted by TPLA terrorists who make no demands. Finlay will be released a short time later.

FEBRUARY 25: Chapin S. Paterson, allegedly carrying a bomb, skyjacks a B-737, scheduled to fly ninety-eight people from San Francisco to Seattle, to Cuba and then Canada. He will be deported from Canada to the U.S. and imprisoned.

MARCH 4: Four U.S. air force members are kidnapped in Ankara, Turkey, by TPLA terrorists who demand but do not receive $400,000 ransom. The airmen will be set free and the terrorists captured and convicted.

MARCH 6: Colonel Delgado Villegas, former prominent Guatemalan police official, is fatally shot following three previous attempts on his life by terrorists.

MARCH 8: Thomas K. Marston, seventeen, attempts to skyjack a B-727 flying forty-six persons from Mobile, Alabama, to New Orleans. Marston, armed with a pistol, orders the pilot to fly to Canada, but he is overpowered. He will later be sent to prison.

MARCH 10: Berro Oribe, attorney general of Uruguay, is kidnapped by Tupamaro terrorists, who grill him about legal cases against terrorists and then, surprisingly, set him free.

MARCH 31: John M. Matthews, Jr., fourteen, armed with a pistol, attempts to skyjack a Delta DC-9 Birmingham, Alabama, to Chicago flight, to Cuba. He is seized and later put on a three year probation for carrying a weapon aboard an airplane.

APRIL 7: The Yugoslavian ambassador to Sweden is killed and other Yugoslavian statesmen are injured in Stockholm, Sweden by Croatian terrorists.

MAY 17: Ephraim Elrom, Israeli consul general in Istanbul, Turkey, is kidnapped by terrorists who demand the release of imprisoned terrorists. When the demand is refused, Elrom is shot and killed.

MAY 21: Three members of the Black Liberation Army (BLA), a Negro terrorist organization, shoot and kill two police officers in Harlem who have answered a bogus call for help placed by the terrorists. Members of the same group will, five months later, shoot and kill a police desk sergeant at Ingleside, California and two more NYPD officers in January 1972. The killers will be apprehended and the BLA will soon go out of existence.

MAY 23: Stanley Sylvester, honorary British consul and administrator of Swift & Co., in Rosario, Argentina, is kidnapped by ERP terrorists whose demands for the distribution of $62,500 in goods and foodstuffs to the poor are met. Sylvester will be released.

MAY 29: Henri Wolimer, French consul in San Sebastian, Spain, evades a kidnapping attempt by Basque terrorists.

JUNE 11: Gregory L. White skyjacks a TWA B-727 en route from Chicago to New York. Holding twenty-six persons hostage with a pistol, White demands $75,000 ransom and to be flown to North Vietnam. He is seized and sent to an insane asylumn where he will later kill himself.

JUNE 23: Alfredo Cambron, legal adviser to U.S.-financed companies in Uruguay, is kidnapped by OPR-33 terrorists, but he will later be set free.

JULY 2: Robert L. Jackson and Ligia Sanchez Archila skyjack a 707 en route from Mexico City to San Antonio, Texas. Wielding pistols and alleged nitroglycerin, they terrorized the 110 passengers and crew, demanding a $100,000 ransom and to be flown to Brazil, Argentina and Algeria. They will later be imprisoned.

JULY 15: Petra Schelm and Werner Hoppe, two members of the Baader-Meinhof gang who have just stolen a BMW, are

Guards and state police identifying the dead following the police onslaught of rioting prisoners at Attica Prison on September 9, 1971.

halted by a police roadblock outside of Hamburg. The terrorists fire upon the officers. Schelm is killed by return fire and Hoppe is captured and later sent to prison.

JULY 23: Richard A. Obergfell is killed while attempting to skyjack a TWA B-727 New York to Chicago flight to Italy with sixty-one people on board. Although Obergfell has claimed to have a pistol and a bomb, no weapons are found on his dead body.

AUGUST 9: Twelve persons are killed, 300 arrested and 150 houses burned in widespread rioting in Belfast, Ireland.

SEPTEMBER 3: Armed only with an icepick, Juan M. Borges Guerra attempts to skyjack an Eastern DC-9 Chicago to Miami flight, to Cuba. He is overpowered and later sent to prison.

SEPTEMBER 9: Inmates at Attica Prison near Buffalo, New York, seize the facility, taking fifty hostages and demanding better conditions. Twenty-nine inmates and ten hostages are killed when state police and military units storm the prison. Eighty-five inmates, three hostages and a state trooper are wounded. None of the surviving prisoners will be punished.

SEPTEMBER 24: Barbara H. Pliskow attempts to skyjack an American Airlines B-727 Detroit to New York flight, to Algeria, wielding a pistol and dynamite, and demanding that some prisoners be released. She will be captured and put on probation for two years.

SEPTEMBER 25: Holger Meins and Magrit Schiller, two members of the Baader-Meinhof gang, are stopped by two police officers on the Freiburg-Basel motorway. The terrorists shoot and kill the officers and speed off.

OCTOBER 4: George Giffe, Jr., and Bobby Wayne Wallace, armed with pistols, try to skyjack a Big Brother, Inc. Aero Commander Hawk 681 to the Bahamas. Giffe kills his wife and the pilot of the Nashville, Tennessee, to Atlanta flight, before committing suicide.

OCTOBER 9: Richard F. Dixon skyjacks an Eastern B-727 Detroit to Miami flight, to Cuba, terrorizing the forty-six passengers and crew members with a revolver. He will be imprisoned five years later.

OCTOBER 18: Del L. Thomas skyjacks a B-737 Anchorage, Alaska, to Bethel, Arkansas, flight to Cuba. He overpowers thirty-five passengers and crew with a pistol. Thomas will later be imprisoned.

OCTOBER 25: Angel Lugo Casado skyjacks an American Airlines B-747 New York to San Juan, Puerto Rico flight, to Cuba. He terrorizes the 236 passengers and crew members with a pistol that turns out to be fake. He will be returned to the U.S. in 1978 and be imprisoned.

NOVEMBER 19: Jaime Castrejon Diez, rector of the State University of Guerrero, Mexico, is abducted by terrorists. After nine political prisoners are set free and the kidnappers paid $500,000 ransom, Diez will be released.

NOVEMBER 20: An explosion rips apart a China Airlines Caravelle over the South China Sea, killing twenty-five persons. There are no survivors.

NOVEMBER 27: Michael R. Finney, Charles R. Hill, and Ralph L. Goodwin commandeer a TWA B-727 en route from Albuquerque, New Mexico, to Chicago. Brandishing two pistols and a knife, the terrorists divert the flight to Cuba. Goodwin will later drown and Finney and Hill become fugitives.

NOVEMBER 30: French reporter Michele Ray claims to have been kidnapped by OPR-33 terrorists in Uruguay, but officials believe she has arranged the abduction in order to interview the terrorists and sell a sensational, though faked, story.

DECEMBER 15: Zaid Rifai, Jordan's ambassador to England, is injured by gunshots in a failed attempt on his life in London by Black September Palestinian terrorists.

DECEMBER 22: Klaus Junschke and three other members of the Baader-Meinhof terrorist gang rob the Bavarian Mortgage and Exchange Bank in Kaiserslautern, Germany, killing policeman Herbert Schoner before fleeing.

DECEMBER 24: Everett L. Holt skyjacks a B-707 taking thirty-five persons from Minneapolis, Minnesota, to Chicago. He wields a revolver and alleged bomb, demanding a $500,000 ransom. He will be captured and sent to an insane asylum.

DECEMBER 26: Donald L. Coleman attempts to skyjack an American Airlines B-707 en route from Chicago to San Francisco, carrying eighty-five persons. Using a knife, toy pistol, and a fake bomb, Coleman also demands $200,000 ransom. He will be captured and imprisoned.

1972

JANUARY 7: Brandishing a pistol and a shotgun, Allen G. Sims and Ida P. Robinson skyjack a B-727 San Francisco to Los Angeles flight, with 151 persons on bo ard, to Africa and then to Cuba. Sims will later be imprisoned, but Robinson will escape.

JANUARY 12: Billy E. Hurst, Jr., skyjacks a B-727 en route from Houston to Dallas, Texas, with 100 persons on board. Waving a pistol and an alleged bomb, Hurst demands $1 million ransom and ten parachutes. He will later be imprisoned.

JANUARY 20: Richard C. LaPoint skyjacks a DC-10 Las Vegas to Reno, Nevada, flight with seventy-three persons on board. Claiming to have a bomb, LaPoint demands $500,000 and two parachutes. He will parachute from the in-flight plane, be captured, and imprisoned.

JANUARY 26: A bomb explodes in the luggage compartment of a Yugoslavian jet en route from Copenhagen, Denmark, to Zagreb, Yugoslavia, killing twenty-seven persons. One person survives.

JANUARY 26: Croatian terrorists explode a bomb aboard a Stockholm-to-Belgrade jetliner, killing twenty-six passengers.

JANUARY 26: Members of the Jewish Defense League (JDL) firebomb the New York City offices of entertainment empressario Sol Hurok, who has managed the performances of Soviet entertainers in the U.S. Considerable damage is done but no injuries are reported.

JANUARY 26: Merlyn L. St. George, armed with a starter pistol and an alleged bomb and demanding $200,000 ransom and four parachutes, is killed while attempting to skyjack an FH-227 plane flying forty-six people from Albany to New York.

JANUARY 26: Patrick H. McAlroy, brandishing a pistol, attempts to skyjack an SFO helicopter about to leave Berkeley, California, for San Francisco, to Cuba. He is seized and sent to a mental institution.

JANUARY 27: Croation terrorists explode a bomb aboard a train en route from Vienna, Austria, to Zagreb, Yugoslavia, injuring six passengers.

JANUARY 29: Garrett B. Trapnell, armed with a pistol and phony bomb, fails to skyjack a B-707 en route from Los Angeles to New York, with 101 people aboard. Trapnell demands $306,800 ransom, the release of a prisoner in Dallas, Texas, and flight to Europe. He is shot, captured and imprisoned.

FEBRUARY 22: The IRA sets off a bomb at the Parachute Regiment headquarters at Aldershot, England, killing nine soldiers and civilians and injuring three others.

FEBRUARY 22: Habash Front terrorists skyjack a Luthansa Airlines plane en route from New Delhi to Athens, and order it to fly to Aden, South Yemen, where the passengers and crew are released after the West German government has paid the terrorists $5 million, and allow them to go free.

MARCH 2: Wolfgang Grundmann and Manfred Grashof, two members of the Baader-Meinhof gang, are captured after a wild shootout in their Hamburg apartment.

MARCH 3: Members of Italy's Red Brigades, a terrorist group, kidnap businessman Idalgo Macchiarini but release him a short time later.

MARCH 3: Black September Palestinian terrorists try to assault the London headquarters of Hussein I, King of Jordan, or so it is reported. (Some terrorist authorities believe that Hussein is a secret backer of Palestinian terrorists and that the feeble attack is only a ruse to convince the West that Hussein is opposed to Arab terrorism.)

MARCH 7: James W. Brewton and Joseph T. Bennett, armed with guns, skyjack to Cuba a Chalk's Flying Service Grumman 73 scheduled to fly to the Bahamas from Miami. Bennett will escape to Cuba. Brewton will be fatally shot in Jamaica three years later.

MARCH 21: Oberdan Sallustro, president of Fiat in Argentina, is kidnapped by ERP terrorists in Argentina, who demand $1 million in ransom and the release of political prisoners. Fiat agrees to pay the ransom, but the government refuses to release the prisoners. Sallustro is killed

MARCH 27: One Canadian and two British NATO radar technicians are kidnapped in Turkey by TPLA terrorists whose demands for the release of prisoners are refused. All three captives will be slain, along with the terrorists, who are gunned down as police raid their hideout.

APRIL 4: The Cuban Trade Office in Montreal is bombed, killing one person and injuring seven others.

APRIL 7: Richard F. McCoy skyjacks a United 727 taking ninety-one persons from Denver to Los Angeles. McCoy brandishes a pistol, a hand grenade and a phony bomb when demanding $500,000 ransom and six parachutes. He escapes but will later be killed when resisting arrest.

APRIL 9: Stanley H. Speck, claiming to have a hand grenade, attempts to skyjack a B-727 with ninety-two aboard and which was en route from Oakland to San Diego, California. He demanded four parachutes and $500,000 ransom. Speck will be captured in San Diego and sent to an insane asylum.

APRIL 17: Kenneth L. Smith forces his way on board a B-727 scheduled to fly from Seattle to Annette Island, Arkansas. Claiming to have a pistol, Smith orders the pilot to fly to Cairo, Egypt, but his plans are foiled. He will be sent to an insane asylum.

APRIL 17: William H. Greene III attempts to skyjack a Delta CV-880 en route from West Palm Beach, Florida to Chicago. Threatening the seventy-six persons on board with a phony gun, Greene demands $500,000 ransom and a flight to Nassau, Bahamas. He will surrender and be imprisoned.

MAY 3: Four TPLA members demanding the release of three prisoners in Turkey, skyjack a Turkish plane to Sofia, Bulgaria, where they surrender.

MAY 5: Frederick W. Haneman, armed with a pistol and fake bomb, skyjacks an Eastern B-727 carrying forty-nine passengers from Allentown, Pennsylvania, to Washington, D.C.

The officer's mess at U. S. Army headquarters in Frankfurt, Germany, was bombed on May 11, 1972 by members of the Baader-Meinhof terrorist gang.

Haneman demands $303,000 ransom, six parachutes, and a flight to Central America. He will later surrender and be imprisoned.

MAY 5: Michael L. Hansen, armed with a pistol, skyjacks a B-737 en route from Salt Lake City, Utah, to Los Angeles, diverting the seventy-five passenger craft to Hanoi, North Vietnam, and then Cuba. He will later be imprisoned.

MAY 7: Ulrich Schmucker, a member of the Baader-Meinhof gang, is captured by German police but released. He is later thought to have turned police informant and is murdered by gang members.

MAY 11: Four members of the Baader-Meinhof terrorist gang—Ulrike Meinhof, Gudrun Ensslin, Andreas Baader and Jan-Carl Raspe—plant bombs at the U.S. Army headquarters in Frankfurt. Lt. Col. Paul Abel Bloomquist is killed by one of the exploding bombs and twelve other U.S. servicemen are injured. The blasts cause more than $1 million in damage.

MAY 24: The Baader-Meinhof gang explodes two car bombs outside the U.S. Army's European headquarters in Heidelberg, Germany, killing one soldier and wounding two others.

MAY 30: Three members of the Japanese terrorist oganization known as the Red Army (who have been recruited by Black Septemberists), machine gun and blow up with grenades innocent travelers at Lod Airport terminal. They kill twenty-four persons and wound another twenty-six, four of whom later die. Police kill two of the suicidal terrorists and capture the third, Kozo Okamoto, who will be sent to prison for life.

JUNE 1: An informant gives police in Frankfurt, Germany, the address of the "bomb factory" used by the Baader-Meinhof terrorist gang. Officers capture Jan-Carl Raspe and surround

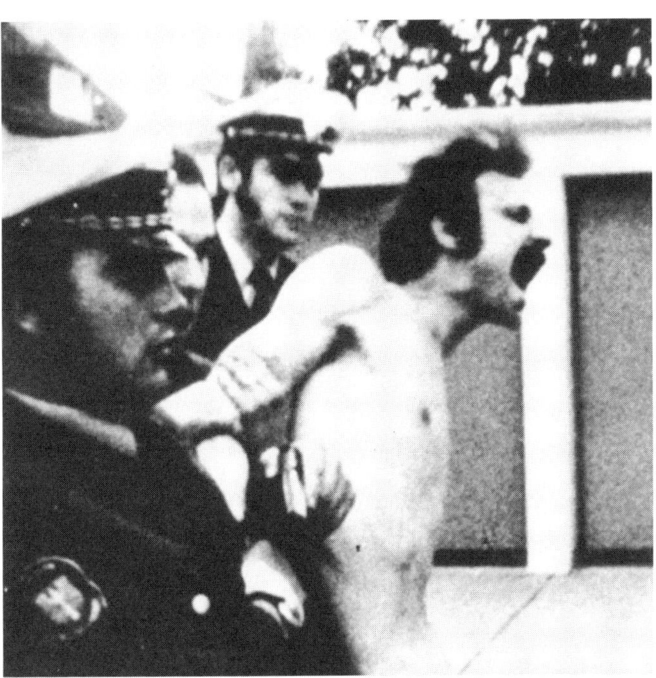

Baader-Meinhof terrorist Holger Meins struggles with police after he attempted to escape naked down a street in Frankfurt, Germany.

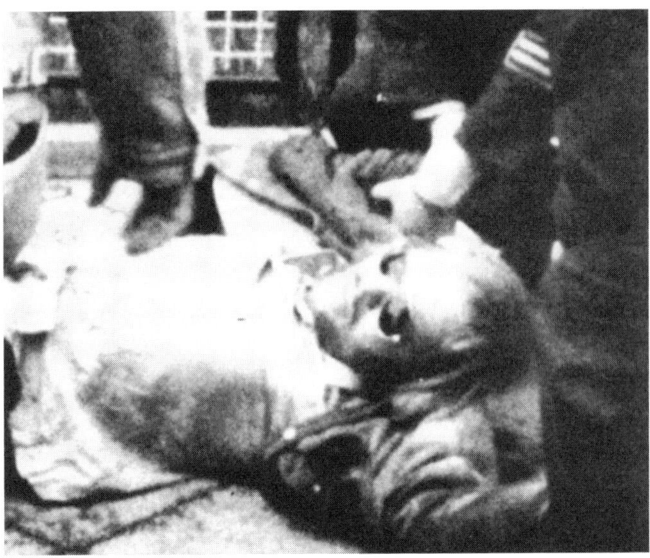

Andreas Baader, leader of the Baader-Meinhof terrorist gang in Germany, is wrestled into submission by police in Frankfurt, Germany on June 1, 1972.

the garage containing the bombs and two of the terrorists—Andreas Baader and Holger Meins. After a shootout, both terrorists are wounded and captured. A short time later, gang leader Ulrike Meinhof is captured in Hanover.

JUNE 2: William Holder and Katherine Kerkow, armed with a fake bomb, skyjack a B-727 en route from Los Angeles to Seattle carrying ninety-seven people. They demand to be flown to Algeria, a $500,000 ransom, and five parachutes. The ransom will be returned. Holder will be given a suspended sentence and Kerkow will escape.

JUNE 15: A bomb placed beneath a passenger seat of a CV-880 jet of Cathay Pacific Airways (Hong Kong), reportedly by a police officer whose fiancee and daughter are on board, explodes over the central highlands of South Vietnam, killing eighty-one people.

JUNE 23: Martin J. McNally and Walter J. Petlikowsky, wielding a submachine gun, a hand grenade, and a phony bomb, skyjack an American B-727 en route with 101 people from St. Louis to Tulsa, Oklahoma. They demand $502,000 and five parachutes. Both will later be captured and imprisoned.

JUNE 30: Daniel B. Carre, claiming to have a knife, skyjacks a DC-9 en route to Portland, Oregon, from Seattle. He demands $50,000 and a parachute. Carre will later be sent to an insane asylum.

JULY 2: Thai Binh Nguyen, wielding a knife and showing alleged hand grenades, skyjacks a Pan American B-747 en route from Honolulu, Hawaii, to Saigon, South Vietnam, with 135 passengers on board. The terrorist demands to be flown to Hanoi, North Vietnam, but he is killed by another passenger when the plane first lands in Saigon.

JULY 5: Dimitz K. Alexiev and Michael D. Azmanoff, armed with pistols, skyjack a B-737 en route with eighty-six people aboard from Sacramento to San Francisco, California. The terrorists demand $800,000 and two parachutes. Both terrorists and one passenger will be killed. Lubomir Peichev, a conspirator, will be imprisoned.

JULY 8: Members of Israel's Mossad detonate a car bomb that kills PFLP terrorist leader Ghassan Kanafani in Beirut.

JULY 21: IRA terrorists explode twenty-two bombs in downtown Belfast, Ireland, killing eleven people and injuring 130 more; the day is thereafter known as Bloody Friday.

JULY 28: Hector Menoni, director of United Press International in Uruguay, is abducted by OPR-33 terrorists. He will later be set free.

JULY 31: Wielding handguns, Melvin and Jean McNair, George Wright, George Brown and Joyce Burgess, all members of the terrorist Black Panther Party, skyjack a Delta DC-8 en route from Detroit to Miami with 101 people aboard. They demand $1 million ransom and a flight to Algeria. All but Wright will later be imprisoned.

AUGUST 4: A murderous Negro gang styling itself after the terrorist Mau Maus of Kenya of the 1950s, calling itself the De Mau Mau Gang, invades the western suburbs of Chicago. The gang kills four members of the Corbett family in Barrington Hills and then, in Monee, slaughters the Stephen Hawtree family. In Highland Park, gang members murder William Richter. In Frankfort, they kill Michael Gerschenson. After claiming nine victims, the six bloodthirsty gang members are captured. Tried and convicted, the gang members escape the death penalty and are given long prison terms.

SEPTEMBER 5: Eight Black September terrorists, all Syrian-trained commandos, invade the Olympic compound housing athletes participating in the XX Olympiad in Munich, Germany. (Black September is the official enforcement arm of Al Fatah which is directed by Yasir Arafat.) The terrorists kill two members of the Israeli team and hold the rest hostage, demanding the release of the imprisoned Ulrike Meinhof and other members of the Baader-Meinhof gang, along with 234 other Arab terrorists then in jail. When the terrorists are provided a jet to fly them out of the country, they are attacked by German police. The terrorists immediately kill nine more members of the Israeli team. Five of the Arab terrorists are killed and three taken prisoner. The organizer of the massacre, Ali Hassan Salemeh, will be killed in reprisal by Mossad agents in 1979.

SEPTEMBER 5: Jan J. Van de Panne, Dutch chief of Philips Electronics Co., in Argentina, is kidnapped by Montoneros terrorists. When the firm pays $500,000 ransom, Panne is set free.

SEPTEMBER 9: Dr. Ami Shachori, agricultural adviser to the Israeli Embassy in London is slain by a mail bomb sent by Black September terrorists. Forty nine other letter bombs mailed by Black September are intercepted and disarmed.

SEPTEMBER 11: Salvador Allende Gossens, president of Chile, is ousted in a military coup led by General Augusto Pinochet Ugarte. Allende either commits suicide or is assassinated in this supposedly CIA-backed coup.

OCTOBER 16: Wael Zuaiter, Al Fatah official in Rome, is fatally shot near his apartment, reportedly by Mossad agents.

OCTOBER 16: Two Americans are injured and a Canadian is killed by a bomb blast at the Sheraton Hotel in Buenos Aires, Argentina. The bombing is attributed to Maximo Mena Command.

OCTOBER 29: Black Septembrists skyjack a Lufthansa Boeing jet bound from Beirut, Lebanon, to Ankara, Turkey, demanding that three terrorists imprisoned for the 1972 massacre of the Israeli atheletes during the XX Olympiad in Munich, Germany, be released. The plane lands in Libya and, following negotiations, the three terrorists are first arrested and then set free.

NOVEMBER 2: Three terrorists bomb the French consulate in Zaragoza, Spain, killing one person.

NOVEMBER 3: A French woman is killed while attempting to plant a bomb at the U.S. Embassy in Amman, Jordan.

NOVEMBER 7: Enrico Barrella, Italian industrialist, is abducted in Buenos Aires by terrorists who later release him after collecting $500,000 in ransom money.

Ali Hassan Salameh, chief of Black September, directed the murders of some of the Israeli athletes in Munich, Germany, during the XX Olympiad on September 5, 1972; he was killed in 1979 by Israeli forces.

DECEMBER 7: Imelda Marcos, wife of Philippine President Ferdinand Edralin Marcos, is stabbed and critically injured, but survives the terrorist attack in Pasay City, Philippines.

DECEMBER 8: Mahmoud Hamshari, the primary official of Al Fatah and the Palestinian Liberation Organization (PLO) in France, dies when a bomb explodes in his Paris apartment. Mossad agents are allegedly responsible.

DECEMBER 8: Seven terrorists attempt to skyjack an Ethiopian Airlines craft over Addis Ababa, Ethiopia, a grenade blast injuring eleven persons, before the plane safely lands.

DECEMBER 28: Black September terrorists hold six hostages at the Israeli embassy in Bangkok, Thailand. They demand the release of terrorists imprisoned in Israel. When the demands are not met, the terrorists later back down and are allowed to leave the country.

1973

JANUARY 23: Three armed terrorists abduct U.S. ambassador Clinton Knox and U.S. consul general Ward Christensen, demanding the release of prisoners and ransom. The demands are met and the prisoners set free.

FEBRUARY 3: Norman Lee, administrator of a Coca-Cola plant in Buenos Aires, Argentina, is abducted by terrorists who later release him after collecting a ransom.

FEBRUARY 20: Three Pakistani terrorists take hostages at the Indian High Commission offices in London, England, demanding that Pakistanis imprisoned in India be released. Their demands will not be met and two of the three terrorists will be killed by police, the third captured.

FEBRUARY 23: Believing that a Libyan Boeing 727 jet is "a flying bomb," Israelis shoot the plane down over the Sinai, killing 106 passengers and crew.

MARCH 1: Black September terrorists take ten hostages at the Saudi Arabian embassy in Khartoum, Sudan, demanding the release of several imprisoned terrorists in several countries. When their demands are not met, the terrorists will kill three diplomats and then surrender to authorities.

MARCH 8: Two IRA bombs explode in London, England, killing one person and injuring more than 200 others.

MARCH 19: An Air Vietnam passenger jet is blown apart over Ban Me Thuot when a bomb explodes in the cargo area, killing all fifty-nine persons aboard.

MARCH 28: Gerardo Scalmazzi, manager of the First National Bank of Boston's Rosario branch, is kidnapped by terrorists in Rosario, Argentina and will later be released after the terrorists receive between a reported $500,000 to $1 million in ransom money.

APRIL 2: Anthony R. DaCruz, a technical operations manager for Eastman Kodak, is abducted by terrorists in Argentina. He will later be released after a $1.5 million ransom is paid.

APRIL 8: Francis Victor Brimicombe, president of Nobleza Tobacos, a subsidiary of the British-American Tobacco Co., is kidnapped by terrorists in Argentina. He will be set free after the firm pays between $1.5 and $1.8 million.

APRIL 9: Al Fatah chief Kamal Adwan is assassinated in Beirut, Lebanon, by Israeli terrorists.

APRIL 12: An Arab terrorist carrying a Jordanian passport is killed when a bomb in his luggage accidentally explodes in his hotel room in Athens, Greece.

MAY 4: Terrance G. Leonhardy, U.S. consul general in Guadalajara, Mexico, is abducted by terrorists of the People's Revolutionary Armed Forces, who demand that political prisoners be released and an $80,000 ransom be paid. The demands are met and Leonhardy is later released.

MAY 21: Oscar Castel, president of a Coca-Cola bottling plant in Córdoba, Argentina, is kidnapped by terrorists who later set him free after collecting $100,000 ransom.

MAY 21: ERP terrorists kidnap and fatally shoot Luis Giovanelli, the administrator of a Ford Motor plant, in Buenos Aires, Argentina. ERP states that they will continue kidnapping Ford employees until a $1 million ransom is paid. The company later complies.

JUNE 2: Lieutenant Colonel Lewis Hawkins, U.S. military adviser in Iran, is shot to death by Iranian terrorists.

JUNE 6: Charles Lockwood, a British executive of an Acrow Steel division in Argentina, is kidnapped by terrorists. He will later be set free after a $2 million ransom is paid.

JUNE 18: Roberto Galvez, manager of a U.S. company in Guatemala, is kidnapped by FAR terrorists. He will be released later after a ransom of $50,000 is paid.

JUNE 18: West German businessman Hans Kurt Gebhardt is kidnapped in Argentina by terrorists. He will be set free after a $100,000 ransom has been paid.

JUNE 18: ERP terrorists abduct John R. Thompson, president of a Firestone subsidiary in Buenos Aires, Argentina. After a $3 million ransom is paid, Thompson will be released.

JUNE 25: Mario Baratella, vice president of the Italian-owned Bank of Rio de la Plata in Buenos Aires, Argentina, is abducted and released after the terrorist kidnappers receive and undisclosed ransom (reported to be $2 million).

JUNE 28: Mohammed Boudia, most prominent Arab terrorist in Europe, is slain by a car bomb in Paris, one planted by Mossad agents.

JULY 1: Colonel Josef Alon, Israeli military attaché in Washington, D.C., is fatally shot by Arab terrorists in his Chevy Chase, Maryland home.

JULY 2: Terrorists kidnap Raul Bornancini, assistant manager of the Córdoba, Argentina branch of the First National City Bank of New York. He will later be set free after the kidnappers receive a reported $1 million ransom.

JULY 21: A Japan Airlines plane traveling from Paris via Amsterdam to Tokyo with 137 passengers is skyjacked by four terrorists who force the pilot to land in Dubai. The plane is then flown to Libya, the passengers deplaned and the plane blown up.

AUGUST 2: Juan Felipe de la Cruz Serafin, a leading member of the anti-Castro Cuban Revolutionary Directorate, is killed by a bomb explosion in his hotel room in Avrainville, France.

AUGUST 4: A train station in Belgrade, Yugoslavia is bombed by terrorists, killing one person and injuring seven others.

AUGUST 5: The Libyan-based National Arab Youth for the Liberation of Palestine (NAYLP) carries out a machine gun and hand grenade attack against a TWA jet at the airport in Athens, Greece, killing five passengers and injuring fifty-five others.

AUGUST 27: Ian Martin, British manager of a meat firm, is abducted by terrorists in Asunción, Paraguay. Police raid the terrorist hideout and rescue Martin, killing two terrorists and arresting others.

SEPTEMBER 5: Palestinian terrorists take thirteen hostages at the Saudi Arabian embassy in Paris, France, demanding that Jordan free the imprisoned Abu Daoud, a terrorist leader. Daoud is not released and the terrorists free their hostages, then surrender.

SEPTEMBER 8: Three persons are injured when IRA terrorists explode bombs at the King's Cross and Euston railway stations in London, England.

OCTOBER 10: Anthony Williams, British consul in Mexico, is kidnapped by terrorists who demand the release of political prisoners. The prisoners are not released but a ransom of $200,000 is reportedly paid and Williams is set free.

OCTOBER 22: Kurt Schmid, an executive for Swissair, is abducted by ERP terrorists in Argentina, who demand a $10 million ransom. An unspecified ransom is later paid and Schmid is released.

OCTOBER 23: David Wilkie, Jr., president of an Amoco International Oil Co. subsidiary, is abducted by terrorists in Buenos Aires, Argentina. He will be set free after a reported $3.5 million ransom is paid.

NOVEMBER 6: Marcus Foster, the black superintendent of schools in Oakland, California, who has proposed that all students be photographed for identification purposes, is shot to death by cyanide-tipped bullets by members of the Symbionese Liberation Army (SLA).

NOVEMBER 22: John A. Swint, general manager of a Ford subsidiary, is shot to death with his three bodyguards in Cordorba, Argentina by terrorist members of the Fuerzas Armadas Peronistas (FAP).

DECEMBER 6: Victor E. Samuelson, U.S. administrator of Exxon Co., is kidnapped by ERP terrorists in Buenos Aires, Argentina. He will later be released after a staggering $14.2 million ransom is paid.

DECEMBER 13: George Peter Metsky, the infamous "Mad Bomber" of New York, is released from a mental facility.

DECEMBER 17: Five NAYLP terrorists carry out an unauthorized operation in Rome, Italy, by hurling thermite bombs into a Pan Am jetliner, burning thirty-two passengers to death, and injuring eighteen others.

DECEMBER 18: Sixty persons are injured when two car bombs and a parcel bomb explode in London, England.

DECEMBER 30: Teddy Seiff, prominent British Zionist, is slain in London by a PFLP terrorist.

DECEMBER 29: FAR terrorists abduct Yves Boisset, director of Peugeot in Argentina, who demand a $4 million ransom. An unspecified ransom is paid and Boisset is set free.

1974

JANUARY 10: Two members of the SLA are stopped by police near Concord, California, and shoot it out; Russell Little is wounded and Joseph Remiro escapes, only to be captured a short time later. The SLA's bomb-making factory catches fire in Concord a few days later and police find revolutionary pamphlets and a note (later determined to be the handwriting of SLA leader Donald DeFreeze), reading: "Patricia Campbell Hearst on the night of the full moon of January 7." Little and Remiro will later be convicted of murdering Marcus Foster in 1973 and will be sent to prison for life.

JANUARY 24: The international terrorist Carlos (Illich Ramirez Sanchez) throws a bomb into the Israeli Bank in London, England. A woman is injured.

FEBRUARY 4: Publishing heiress Patricia Campbell Hearst is reportedly kidnapped from a San Francisco, California, apartment she shares with fiancé Stephen Weed by members of the Symbionese Liberation Army (SLA), in liaison with the Black Muslims, and headed by Negro terrorist Donald DeFreeze. She is held for $70 million in foodstuffs that are to be distributed to the poor. The distribution of food will be begun in Oakland, California, but a near-riot ensues when 13,000 persons arrive to obtain the food parcels. It will later be concluded that Hearst has faked her own kidnapping and has been part of the SLA conspiracy all along.

FEBRUARY 22: Samuel J. Byck, armed with a gun and a bomb, kills a policeman in the Baltimore, Maryland, terminal before forcing his way aboard a Delta DC-9 scheduled to fly to Atlanta with fourteen people aboard. Byck kills the co-pilot, wounds the pilot, then kills himself.

FEBRUARY 23: Two demolition experts are killed in an explosion while trying to defuse a bomb placed in the Dow Chemical plant in Lavrion, Greece.

MARCH 20: Ian Ball attempts to kidnap Princess Anne of England in London, planning to demand a £3 million ransom. Ball shoots three persons before he is captured. He will be sent to an institution for the criminally insane.

MARCH 23: A disgruntled bar patron ejected from an Allentown, Pennsylvania, bar returns to hurl a Molotov cocktail inside, killing eight persons and injuring a dozen more. The mass murderer is never found.

APRIL 12: Alfred Albert Laun III, chief of the U.S. Information Service section in Córdoba, Argentina, is severely injured when he is abducted by ERP terrorists. He will be set free the next day, apparently due to his injuries.

APRIL 18: Members of the Red Brigades kidnap deputy prosecutor Mario Sossi, demanding the release of eight imprisoned terrorists. The demand is agreed to by Genoa prosecutor Francesco Coco and Sossi is released. Coco reneges on his promise and is murdered by the terrorists two years later.

MAY 17: Acting on a tip, more than 400 heavily armed police surround a small house at 1466 E. 54th Street, a hideout for SLA terrorists. A fierce fight ensures with more than 6,000 shots exchanged by the terrorists and police. The building catches fire and police later find in the smoldering ruins the bodies of SLA leader Donald DeFreeze, William Wolfe (reported to be Patricia Hearst's lover), Nancy Ling Perry, Camilla Hall and Patricia Soltysik.

JULY 17: An IRA bomb explodes in the Tower of London, killing one person and injuring forty-one others.

JULY 26: Small-time thief Paul John Knowles breaks out of a Jacksonville, Florida jail and immediately kills Alice Curtis. He will go on to murder another seventeen persons in four states until he is captured. He will be killed by a police detective on November 18, 1974 while attempting to escape.

John Paul Knowles, center, escaped from a Florida jail and went on a murder-terrorist spree, killing seventeen persons before he was captured.

AUGUST 4: The neo-fascist Ordine (Black Order) of Italy explodes a bomb on a Rome-to-Munich train near Bologna, Italy, killing twelve persons and injuring forty-eight others.

AUGUST 15: Park Chung Hee, president of South Korea, is the target of a failed assassination attempt on his life by terrorists who fatally shoot his wife instead.

SEPTEMBER 4: Marshall Collins III skyjacks an Eastern DC-9 en route with 100 people from New York to Boston. Collins uses a razor blade and a nail to intimidate the crew, demanding a $10,000 ransom. He will be sent to an insane asylum.

SEPTEMBER 7: Barbara Hutchinson, chief of the U.S. Information Service in the Dominican Republic, and six others, are abducted by terrorists, who demand that prisoners be freed and a $1 million ransom be paid. The demands will not be met, and the terrorists release their hostages before being allowed to leave the country.

SEPTEMBER 8: The NAYLP plants a bomb on board a TWA jet bound from Athens to Rome. The explosion damages the plane's engines and the jet crashes into the Ionian Sea, killing all eighty-five persons on board.

SEPTEMBER 13: Terrorists of the Japanese Red Army, the German RAF and the PFLP take eleven hostages at the French embassy in the Hague, Netherlands, demanding that a hostage held in France be set free. Following negotiations, the hostages will be set free and the terrorists allowed to leave the country.

SEPTEMBER 14: Pasqauale Gentilcore, nineteen, and his girlfriend, Stefania Pettini, eighteen, are shot to death as they sit in their car fifteen miles outside of Florence, Italy, by the Monster of Florence, who has used the same weapon, a .22-caliber pistol, as he has used on two victims in 1968.

SEPTEMBER 15: An Air Vietnam jet is hijacked over Phan Rang, a terrorist suicidally exploding two hand grenades and causing the plane to crash, killing all seventy persons on board.

SEPTEMBER 16: Jorge and Juan Born, sons of the chairman of Argentina's largest firm, Bunge Born, are kidnapped by Monteneros terrorists who receive a $60 million ransom. The brothers are set free.

OCTOBER 5: Three British soldiers and two women are killed when IRA bombs explode in several pubs in Guildford, England, which cater to military personnel. Fifty-four patrons are injured.

NOVEMBER 14: Gunter von Drenckmann, president of the West German Supreme Court, is shot to death at his Berlin home by members of the Baader-Meinhof gang on orders from the imprisoned Ulrike Meinhof who has marked the jurist for death as an example of the power she still wields even behind bars.

NOVEMBER 21: The IRA explodes a series of bombs in Birmingham, England, which kill twenty-one people and wound another 168 persons.

DECEMBER 1: Charles Jackson, forty-six, is the first of eight victims who fall victim to the lone terrorist known as the Los

Seen through a shattered window is a pub which was blown up by IRA terrorists in Guildford, England, on October 5, 1974, one of several pub bombings which killed five people.

Angeles Slasher or the Skid Row Slasher. Jackson is found sprawled on the lawn of the Los Angeles Public Library with his throat slashed.

DECEMBER 8: Moses August Yakanak, forty-seven, is found slashed to death in a Los Angeles alley, another victim of the Los Angeles slasher.

DECEMBER 11: Drifter Arthur Dahlstedt, fifty-four, is found dead in the doorway of an abandoned Skid Row building, the third known victim of the Los Angeles slasher.

DECEMBER 22: The Los Angeles Slasher kills David Perez, whose sliced-up body is found in some bushes on Flower Street.

1975

JANUARY 8: Casimir Strawinski, fifty-eight, is found slashed to death in his third-floor room at the Pickwick Hotel, the fourth victim of the Los Angeles Slasher. Strawinski has earlier remarked to a friend: "I won't be around too long," and police believe he was predicting his own murder. It is later learned that the murder victim has made reference to his advanced cancer and not to the murdering Skid Row terrorist.

JANUARY 15: Robert "Tex" Shannahan, forty, is found slashed to death in a Skid Row room, another Los Angeles slasher victim.

JANUARY 25: Samuel Suarez is found cut to pieces in his fifth-floor room at the Barclay Hotel, the seventh victim of the Los Angeles Slasher.

JANUARY 31: Clyde C. Hay, thirty-four, is found slashed to death in his cheap Hollywood apartment, another Los Angeles Slasher victim. The slasher, originally described as a wiry man with long, blond hair, is portrayed by LAPD Lieutenant Dan Cooke as a "human jackal...We're dealing with a real monster." In each murder, the terrorist has performed a strange ritual, sprinkling salt about the bodies, removing the victim's shoes and pointing them at the feet, facts kept secret by the police to prevent copycat killings.

FEBRUARY 3: Vaughn Greenwood, a thirty-one-year old Negro, is arrested and charged with the deaths committed by the Los Angeles Slasher. He is indicted for the eight known slasher murders and three more homicides, two of these dating back to 1964.

FEBRUARY 27: German politician Peter Lorenz is kidnapped in Berlin by terrorists. The West German government releases five members of the Baader-Meinhof gang and pays a ransom for Lorenz's release.

MARCH 27: Susan Edith Saxe, a leader of a student terrorist organization that has looted a federal arsenal and robbed a Boston bank in 1970, is arrested in Philadelphia. She later pleads guilty and receives a long prison sentence.

APRIL 24: Members of the Baader-Meinhof gang invade the West German Embassy in Stockholm, holding hostages and demanding that their leader Ulrike Meinhof and others be

Ulrike Marie Meinhof, co-leader of the German terrorist Baader-Meinhof gang, was charged with hundreds of bombings, kidnappings and murders; she committed suicide in her prison cell on May 9, 1976.

released from prison. The terrorists kill Lt. Col. Andreas Baron von Mirbach, a military attaché and an official before Swedish police storm the building, killing two terrorists, including Ulrich Wessel, the leader, and capturing four other terrorists.

APRIL 25: Francis P. Covey skyjacks a United B-727 en route with sixty-seven people from Raleigh, North Carolina, to Newark, New Jersey. Covey demands to be flown to Cuba. He will be later imprisoned.

MAY 15: Deborah L. Crawford attempts to skyjack a United B-737 en route from Eugene, Oregon, to San Francisco with eighty people aboard. Claiming she has a knife, she forbids the pilot from landing in San Francisco. She will be institutionalized.

MAY 21: The trial of German terrorists Ulrike Meinhof, Andreas Baader, Gudrun Ensslin and Jan-Carl Raspe begins, with more than 600 capital offenses charged against them. The trial will go on for almost two years.

JUNE 3: A Philippines Airlines passenger jet makes an emergency landing 200 miles south of Manila, after a bomb planted in the lavatory explodes, killing one person and injuring forty-five others.

JUNE 6: Morris E. Colosky, wielding a knife, skyjacks a chartered helicopter en route from Plymouth to Lansing, Michigan. Colosky forces the pilot, Richard Jackson, to fly to the Southern State Prison at Jackson, Michigan, and land inside the walls on the athletic field where a red handkerchief has been placed by prisoner Dale Otto Remling. Seconds after the helicopter lands, Remling dashes forth and leaps inside. Jackson is then ordered by Colosky to land the helicopter on a roadway where two cars are waiting. After landing, Colosky and Remling disable Jackson by spraying him with mace, and then make their escape in the cars. Both Remling and Colosky will later be captured, along with six accomplices, and imprisoned. Remling has schemed up the helicopter escape, modeling it after a prison escape by helicopter as shown in the trailers for a new movie, Breakout, which Remling has seen on the prison TV only weeks earlier.

AUGUST 3: Fifty-three hostages are taken at the U.S. embassy in Kuala Lumpur, Malaysia, by Japanese Red Army terrorists who demand that Japan release imprisoned terrorists. The dema nd is agreed to by Genoa prosecutor Francesco Coco and Sossi is released. Coco reneges on his promise and is murdered by the terrorists two years later.

AUGUST 15: Seven patients at the Veterans Administration Hospital in Ann Arbor, Michigan suffer lung and heart failure within the same hour, and, despite the frantic efforts of physicians, four patients die. FBI agents will determine that between July 1 and August 15, eleven suspicious deaths have occured (out of fifty-six patients stricken with beathing failures in the six-week period). The victims have been given Pavulon, a powerful muscle relaxant, which has been added to the dextrose and water solutions administered to these patients. (Pavulon is a derivative of curare, a vegetable poison South American Indians ritualistically use on blow-gun darts to paralyze enemies and animals.) Though two Filipino nurses are later charged with the killings, they are exonerated and the culprit is not found.

SEPTEMBER 15: Arab terrorists take the Egyptian ambassador and others hostage in the Egyptian embassy in Madrid, Spain, insisting that Egypt repudiate the Sinai Agreement with Israel. After several Egyptian diplomats sign such a statement, the hostages are released. Egypt then refuses to recognize the statement as valid.

SEPTEMBER 15: Frederick Saloman attempts to skyjack an out-of-service B-727 in San Jose, California. Saloman takes four hostages, two of whom escape. He releases another hostage and wounds the fourth before he is fatally shot by police officers.

SEPTEMBER 27: A bombing in a Lowell, Massachusetts, cafe injures twenty-three people and causes considerable damage to Jake's Cafe and sixty-eight neighboring businesses. The bomb has been set off by two persons who open a gas main in the cafe under the directions of a terrorist who is later sent to prison.

SEPTEMBER 30: A bomb explodes inside a Hungarian passenger jet en route from Budapest to Beirut, causing it to crash into the Mediterranean Sea, killing all sixty-four persons on board.

OCTOBER 3: IRA terrorists abduct and hold hostage the manager of a steel plant in Limerick, Ireland, demanding that prisoners be released. After the hostage is released, the IRA terrorists are captured.

NOVEMBER 8: A suicidally-bent Jack R. Johnson skyjacks a chartered Tri State Aero Cessna flying over Evansville, Idaho. Wielding a pistol, Johnson orders the pilot to dive straight into the ground below. The pilot struggles with Johnson, finally pushing him out of the in-flight plane. Johnson is killed by the fall.

DECEMBER 2: Six South Moluccan terrorists take about fifty persons hostage on a train near Beilen, Netherlands, demanding independence for their homeland. Three hostages will be killed before the terrrorists surrender on December 14, 1975.

DECEMBER 4: Forty-seven hostages are taken at the Indonesian consulate in Amsterdam, Netherlands, by South Moluccan terrorists who demand autonomy for their homeland. The demand is refused and, on December 19, 1976, the hostages will be set free and the terrorists surrender.

DECEMBER 21: Illich Ramirez Sanchez, an infamous terrorist better known as Carlos or The Jackal, leads seven other PFLP terrorists in a raid on an OPEC conference in Vienna, Austria, holding eighty-one representatives hostage. Sanchez, his men and hostages are given a $50 million ransom and flown safely to Algiers.

DECEMBER 29: Eleven persons are killed and seventy more are injured when a bomb explodes in one of the terminals at New York's LaGuardia Airport. The terrorist is not found.

1976

JANUARY 1: A bomb explodes in the luggage compartment of a Lebanese jetliner flying between Saudi Arabia and Kuwait, killing all eighty-two persons on board.

FEBRUARY 27: Business executive William Niehous is kidnapped by terrorists from his home in Caracas, Venezuela. The abductors demand $3.5 million ransom and concessions for Niehous' employees. After negotiations, Niehous is released.

MARCH: Five Negro terrorists, who make up San Francisco's Death Angels, are tried for the random murders of fifteen whites, slain in the city as part of the group's "initiation" rites. After 371 days, the terrorists are convicted and sent to prison for life.

MAY 4: Gudrun Ensslin of the Baader-Meinhof Gang confesses to three bombings for which her group has been charged.

MAY 21: Moslem terrorists skyjack a Philippines Airlines jetliner at Zamboanga, Philippines, exploding hand grenades on board and killing thirteen persons and injuring fourteen others.

MAY 23: Armed Vanguard of the Proletariat terrorists abduct Gayle Moony, daughter of a U.S. businessman, in Acapulco, Mexico, and she is held for ransom. She will later be set free unharmed.

JUNE 16: Anti-apartheid riots take place in Soweto, South Africa, in which 176 persons, mostly blacks, are killed. Rioting will spread to Transvaal, Natal, and Pretoria.

JUNE 24: Seven terrorists, two West Germans and five PFLP members, skyjack an Air France Airbus en route from Tel Aviv to Paris with 245 passengers on board. They order the pilot to fly to Entebbe, Uganda, where, through the collusion of military dictator Idi Amin, the mostly Israeli passengers will be held hostage at the airport until rescued by Israeli commandos. Two captives will die while being held hostage and all of the terrorists will be killed in the commando raid, after which the passengers are flown to safety.

Wailing grief are relatives of the seven terrorists who skyjacked an Air France Airbus and were slain at Entebbe by Israeli forces.

JULY 21: An IRA bomb kills British Ambassador Christopher Ewart-Biggs as he drives from his residence outside of Dublin, Ireland to the embassy in Merrion Square.

SEPTEMBER 28: An Army bomb expert is killed and a state arson expert wounded while attempting to defuse one of five dynamite bombs blown up at the Quincy Compressor Company at Quincy, Illinois, shortly after a visit from vice presidential candidate Robert Dole. Three men are later sent to prison, after being convicted of murder and arson.

OCTOBER 6: Nine minutes after taking off from Barbados, West Indies, a Cuban jet bound for Kingston, Jamaica, explodes, killing all seventy-three passengers on board.

OCTOBER 11: Three Palestinian terrorists attempt to seize the Syrian embassy in Islamabad, Pakistan, but are foiled by police who kill two terrorists and capture the third.

OCTOBER 11: Palestinian terrorists belonging to the Black June group, hold five hostages at the Syrian embassy in Rome, Italy, stating that Syria has not treated their terrorist groups fairly. After injuring one hostage, the terrorists surrender to police.

OCTOBER 17: A movie theater in Buenos Aires, Argentina, is destroyed and fifty persons are injured when a bomb explodes during a Peronist "Loyalty Day" celebration.

OCTOBER 20: Members of the People's Revolutionary Front kidnap financier Tulio Oneto in Buenos Aires, Argentina. Oneto will be murdered after his family refuses to pay the $2 million ransom.

DECEMBER 15: Fifteen persons are killed and thirty more are injured when a dynamite bomb planted by leftist Montoneros terrorists explodes in the Defense Ministry building in Buenos Aires, Argentina.

1977

JANUARY 11: William Saupe attempts to skyjack a TWA B-747 en route from New York to London, with 333 persons on board. Saupe claims to have hand grenades and demands to be flown to Uganda. He will be seized and later put on probation.

JANUARY 19: Vaughn Greenwood, who has been tried and convicted for eleven murders, including those 1974-1975 murders committed by the Los Angeles Slasher, is sentenced to life imprisonment.

JANUARY 31: Following a heavy snowfall in Buffalo, New York, dozens of homes, businesses and vehicles are looted by thieves. Police attempt to track them down on snowmobiles but are largely unsuccessful.

MARCH 9: Haamas Abdul Khaalis, a Negro whose real name is Ernest Timothy McGhee, leads a group of black terrorists calling themselves the Hanafi Muslims (a splinter group of the Black Muslims), in a terror campaign in Washington, D.C., invading three buildings, killing one person and wounding eleven others. Khaalis and his terrorists hold 100 hostages and demands that the movie, *Mohammad, Messenger of God*, which he deems sacrilegious, be banned, and that five Black Muslims responsible for the 1973 slayings of seven Khaalis family members in 1973 be turned over to him for execution. Some of the demands are met and Khaalis releases the hostages.

MARCH 15: Luciano Pocari skyjacks an Iberia Airlines B-727 scheduled to take thirty-seven people from Barcelona to Palma, Majorca, forcing the pilot to fly to the Ivory Coast. Pocari demands $120,000 to recover his daughter from her mother. He will be arrested and imprisoned.

MARCH 27: Nine persons are injured when six bombs are exploded in the Sheraton Hilton Hotel in Buenos Aires, Argentina.

APRIL 15: Luchino Rewvelli-Beaumont, head of a French Fiat subsidiary is kidnapped near his apartment in Paris by nine South American terrorists calling themselves the Committee for Socialist Revolutionary Unity. A $2 million ransom is reportedly paid for the executive's release.

APRIL 17: David Berkowitz (Son of Sam) shoots Alexander Esau and Valentina Suriani, who sit in a parked car in the Bronx. Suriani dies instantly and Esau dies three hours later.

APRIL 28: Ulrike Meinhof (tried in absentia; she has committed suicide in 1976 inside her cell), Andreas Baader, Gudrun Ensslin and Jan-Carl Raspe, the leadership core of the dreaded Baader-Meinhof terrorist gang, are all convicted of murder, robbery and terrorism and sent to prison for life. The three remaining terrorists will commit suicide in their cells.

Jan-Carl Raspe, one of the worst killers of the German Baader-Meinhof terrorist gang, was sentenced to life; he would commit suicide.

MAY 8: Bruce J. Trayer, armed with a razor blade, tries to skyjack a Northwest B-747 en route from Tokyo to Honolulu with 262 persons on board. He demands to be taken to Moscow, but Trayer is overpowered and the plane returns to Tokyo. Trayer will be sent to an insane asylum.

MAY 23: South Moluccan terrorists take fifty-five persons hostage on board a train close to Glimmen, Netherlands, and demand the release of imprisoned terrorists and an escape bus. Police storm the train and the resulting shootout leaves two hostages and six terrorists dead. On the same day, South Moluccan terrorists seize an elementary school in Bovensmilde, Netherlands, holding 125 children and five teachers hostage. The children will be freed by the terrorists and the police will rescue the teachers while capturing the terrorists.

JUNE 6: Nasser Mohammed Ali Abu Khaled skyjacks a Lebanon Middle East Airways B-707 bound for Baghdad, Iraq with 115 passengers aboard. The terrorist demands $5 million ransom. He will be subdued by commandos and later released for health reasons.

JULY 23: Hanafi Muslim terrorist Haamas Abdul Khaalis and seven of his followers are convicted of kidnapping and murder during their March 9, 1977 terrorist spree in Washington, D.C. They are all given long prison terms.

JULY 30: Jürgen Ponto, a prominent German banker, is slain in Frankfurt, Germany, by Red Army Faction (RAF) terrorists.

AUGUST 6: A bomb explodes in a Woolworth store in Salisbury, Rhodesia, killing eleven people and and injuring antoher seventy-six.

OCTOBER 13: Four PFLP terrorists skyjack a Lufthansa 737 jet from Palma, Majorca, to Frankfurt, Germany. The plane lands in Rome for refueling and then flies to several Middle Eastern countries where it is refused the right to land. During the flight the Arab terrorists demand that eleven political prisoners be released and $15 million paid to them. After fatally shooting the pilot, the terrorists order the co-pilot to fly to Mogadishu where German commandos storm the plane, killing three of the terrorists. Other than the pilot, the passengers and other crew members miraculously remain unharmed.

OCTOBER 18: Yolanda Washington is slain by Kenneth Bianchi (the Hillside Strangler) and Angelo Buono, her naked body, scrubbed clean to eliminate clues, dumped on the slopes of Forest Lawn Cemetery.

OCTOBER 19: German industrialist Hans Martin Schleyer, who has been kidnapped in Cologne, Germany, is murdered by members of the Baader-Meinhof gang after authorities refuse to exchange Schleyer for imprisoned B-M gang members.

OCTOBER 20: Thomas M. Hannan skyjacks a B-737 en route from Grand Island to Lincoln, Nebraska, with thirty-four persons on board. He wields a shotgun and demands to be flown to Atlanta, Georgia, to pick up a convict. Hannan also demands $3 million ransom, parachutes and weapons. The hostages will be released and Hannan will fatally shoot himself.

OCTOBER 31: Judith Lynn Miller, fifteen, is abducted, raped and strangled by Kenneth Bianchi (the Hillside Strangler) and Angelo Buono, her naked body, scrubbed clean, dumped close to a road on a hillside in Glendale, California.

OCTOBER: Sayf bin Sa'id al-Ghubash, the foreign minister of the United Arab Emirates, dies in an assault at the Abu Dhabi airport, apparently assassinated by Abu Nidal terrorists in an unsuccessful attempt to kill Abd al-Halim Khaddam, the Syrian foreign minister.

NOVEMBER 15: Muhammed Salah, director of the Arab Library in Paris, France, is slain by Abu Nidal terrorists.

DECEMBER 14: Achilleas Kypianou, son of the Cyprus president, is abducted by terrorists. He will be released after political concessions are made to the terrorists.

DECEMBER 25: Nikolai Wischnewski skyjacks an Eastern DC-9 en route from Jacksonville, Florida, to Atlanta, with thirty-six people aboard. He wields a toy pistol and phony bomb, and demands to be flown to Cuba. He will later be imprisoned.

1978

JANUARY 1: Said Hammami (Hamami), Palestinian Liberation Organization agent in London, is slain in London by Abu Nidal terrorists.

JANUARY 10: Pedro Chamorro, an editor and publisher who publishes an anti-government newspaper, is murdered by terrorists in Managua Nicaragua.

FEBRUARY 2: Seven hostages are taken at the United Nations office in San Salvador by Popular Revolutionary Bloc terrorists whose demands for the release of political prisoners are not met. The hostages are released after the U.N. promises to make an official inquiry into human rights violations in El Salvador.

FEBRUARY 3: Ten persons are killed in widespread rioting in Nicaragua by those opposing the Somoza regime.

FEBRUARY 17: The naked body of Cindy Lee Hudspeth is found by Los Angeles officers in the trunk of a car; she has been abducted, raped and strangled by Kenneth Bianchi (the Hillside Strangler) and Angelo Buono.

FEBRUARY 18: Yusuf Siba'i (Yousseff el-Sebai), leader of the Committee for Afro-Asian Solidarity and editor of *Al Ahram*, an Egyptian newspaper, is murdered in Nicosia, by Abu Nidal Palestinian terrorists.

MARCH 12: PLO terrorists from South Lebanon blow up a public bus in Tel Aviv, Israel, killing thirty-seven people.

MARCH 13: Seventy-two hostages are taken at government offices in Assen, Netherlands, by South Moluccan terrorists who demand the release of fellow imprisoned terrorists, a $12 million ransom, and an escape bus. The demands are refused and police storm the offices. One hostage is slain and three terrorists are apprehended.

MARCH 16: Aldo Moro, who has served as Italy's prime minister, is kidnapped as five of his bodyguards are shot and killed by Red Brigades terrorists. The terrorists demanded the release of all Communist prisoners to guarantee Moro's safe return.

MARCH 27: Chief Kapuuo, who has been appointed president of Namibia by South African officials, is slain by terrorists.

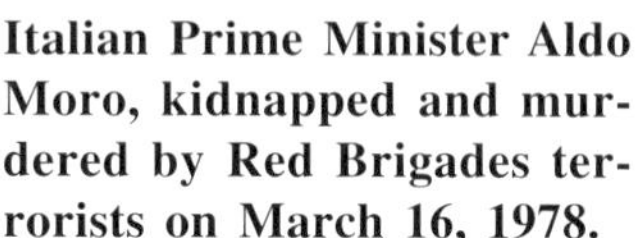

Italian Prime Minister Aldo Moro, kidnapped and murdered by Red Brigades terrorists on March 16, 1978.

Prospero Gallinari, the Red Brigade leader who fired 11 shots into the heart of Italian Prime Minister Aldo Moro.

APRIL 1: Richard Bland, sixteen, attempts to skyjack a B-737 en route from Richmond to Norfolk, Virginia, with sixty-six persons aboard. Brandishing a rifle, Bland demands $1 million ransom and a flight to New York, and then France. He will be captured and later put under psychiatric care.

MAY 8: After the Italian government refused to yield to the Red Brigades kidnappers of Aldo Moro, the body of the former prime minister is found in Rome, stuffed into the trunk of a car. Moro, his hands and feet bound with chains, had been shot eleven times in the heart.

MAY 11: Mario Astarita, Italian manager of the Chemical Bank of New York, is shot in the legs in Milan, Italy, apparently by a terrorist group calling itself the Front Line and Fighting Communist Formations, a faction of the Red Brigades. The shooting is apparently a reprisal against the Italian Government's refusal to exchange Aldo Moro (the former prime minister who has been killed days earlier by Red Brigadists) for imprisoned terrorists.

MAY 24: Four persons flying in a small Piper Aztec plane are killed by an explosion over Nairobi, Kenya.

MAY 24: Barbara A. Oswald, armed with three pistols, skyjacks a chartered helicopter out of St. Louis. She demands the release of G. Trapnell, a federal prisoner. The pilot struggles with her, grabs her pistol, and fatally shoots her.

JUNE 15: Ali Yasin, an agent of the Palestinian Liberation Organization, is slain in Kuwait by Abu Nidal terrorists.

JUNE 24: President Ghashmi of North Yemen is assassinated by terrorists at a conference in Beirut, Lebanon.

JULY 21: General Juan Sanchez and Lieutenant Colonel Juan Perez Rodriguez are assassinated in Spain by a terrorist who will be sent to prison.

AUGUST 3: Ezzedine Kalak, director of the Palestinian Liberation Organization in Paris, and Adnan Hamid, a journalist for the Palestine news organization, are both slain in Paris by Abu Nidal terrorists.

AUGUST 17: Two Croatian terrorists take eight persons hostage at the West German consulate in Chicago, Illinois, demanding that a Croatian in Cologne, West Germany, be set free. The terrorists later give themselves up and free the hostages.

AUGUST 18: A terrorist accidentally sets off a bomb he is planting in the lavatory of a Philippines Airlines jetliner en route from Cebu to Manila, killing himself and wounding three others.

AUGUST 27: Diana L. Benson skyjacks a United DC-8 en route from Denver to Seattle with 159 people aboard. Claiming to possess a bomb, Benson demands to be flown to Vancouver, Canada. She will be captured and found to be mentally incompetent before being released.

NOVEMBER 23: John R. Prindle attempts to skyjack a DC-9 en route from Madison to Milwaukee, Wisconsin, with twenty-three persons on board. Prindle brandishes a knife and claims to have a bomb, but when asked for his demands, Prindle only grins and babbles incoherently—"Take me to Paris...no, no, maybe New York is better...What do you think about Dallas?" He will be seized and found to be mentally incopetent.

DECEMBER 7: Abdul Wahhab Kayali, former leader of the pro-Iraqi Liberation Front, is shot by terrorists in his office in Beirut, Lebanon.

DECEMBER 11: Ayatollah Abdol Hossein Dastgheib, an aide to militant Iranian religious leader Ayatollah Ruhollah Khomeini, is killed by a bomb blast set off by terrorists near his home in Shiraz, Iran.

DECEMBER 11: Fifteen-year-old Robert Piest is abducted, sodomized and murdered by serial killer John Wayne Gacy. The search for Piest will lead to Gacy's arrest, conviction and life sentence for killing the boy and twenty-six others over many years.

DECEMBER 17: U.S. President Ronald Reagan is the target of an assassination attempt when he receives a letter bomb which is disarmed.

DECEMBER 21: Robyn S. Oswald, claiming to carry a bomb, skyjacks a TWA DC-9 en route from St. Louis to Kansas City, Missouri, to help G. Trapnell escape from prison—her mother has attempted the same thing in skyjacking a St. Louis helicopter seven months earlier—but she is seized, and will be put into a juvenile home and then placed on probation.

DECEMBER 23: Paul Grimm, manager of the Oil Service Company of Iran, is shot to death by terrorists as he drives to work in Ahwaz, Iran.

1979

JANUARY 12: Ali Hassan Salemeh, organizer of the Black September (the enforcement arm of Al Fatah) massacre of Israeli athletes at the XX Olympiad in Munich, Germany, on July 18, 1972, is slain by a car bomb planted by members of the Mossad, Israeli intelligence, which has sought Salemeh for seven years. Six passersby are also killed in the blast.

JANUARY 16: More than 100 hostages are taken from the Mexican Embassy, Red Cross and the Organization of American States in El Salvador by United Popular Action Front terrorists who demand the release of prisoners and other political concessions. The hostages will be released and the terrorists will leave the country.

JANUARY 27: Irene McKinney, claiming to have nitroglycerin, skyjacks a United B-747 carrying 131 persons from Los Angeles to New York. She demands that a number of celebrities read a message on television. She will be seized and placed on probation.

FEBRUARY 14: About 100 hostages at the U.S. Embassy in Teheran are seized for about two hours by Iranian terrorists. An Iranian embassy worker is slain before the terrorists leave the embassy grounds.

MARCH 16: John C. Kivlen, claiming to have a knife, skyjacks a B-727 en route from Los Angeles to Tuscon, Arizona, carrying ninety-four people. He demands $200,000 ransom and a flight to Cuba. He will be seized and sent to an insane asylum.

MARCH 30: Airey Neave, Tory member of the British parliament, is slain when a bomb explodes in his car, one reportedly planted by IRA terrorists.

APRIL 4: Zulfikar Ali Bhutto, former president and prime minister of Pakistan, overthrown in 1977, is put to death in Rawalpindi, Pakistan.

APRIL 4: Domenico Speranza attempts to skyjack a Pan American B-747 in Sydney, Australia, which is scheduled to fly to Auckland, New Zealand. Wielding a knife and showing two cans of gunpowder, Speranza demands to be flown to Rome and then on to Moscow. He will be killed before the plane leaves Sydney.

MAY 4: The Metropolitan Cathedral in San Salvador is seized by Popular Revolutionary Bloc terrorists, who demand the release of five political prisoners and an investigation into human rights violations in El Salvador. Seventeen persons will die and another thirty-five are injured when police storm the building.

MAY 15: Farabundo Marti Popular Liberation Forces terrorists fail to take over the South African Embassy in San Salvador. Two police officers die in a shootout and the terrorists escape.

MAY 29: U.S. District Judge John H. Wood, Jr., is shot to death by Charles B. Harrelson in San Antonio, Texas. Harrelson, a professional killer, who previously served time for a 1968 murder-for-hire, is convicted of killing Wood and given two consecutive life sentences. His employer, drug king James Chagra, who was to appear before Wood on a drug conviction, is also sent to prison for life.

JUNE 11: Eduardo Guerra Jimenez skyjacks a Delta L-1011 en route from New York to Fort Lauderdale with 204 people on board. Jimenez carries a pocketknife and claims to have a bomb and a gun. He demands to go to Cuba, where he will escape.

JUNE 20: Nikola Kavaja skyjacks an American Airlines B-727 en route from New York to Chicago with 136 people aboard. Claiming to have dynamite, he demands the release of a prisoner and a flight to Ireland. He will be seized and imprisoned.

JUNE 29: U.S. General Alexander Haig, NATO commander, is the target of a failed attempt on his life with a car bomb in Belgium.

JUNE 30: Rigoberto Gonzalez Sanchez attempts to skyjack an Eastern Airlines L-1011 en route from San Juan, Puerto Rico, to Miami carrying 306 people. Threatening to ignite a bottle of gasoline (it is rum), he orders the pilot to fly to Cuba. Gonzalez Sanchez is overpowered and will later be institutionalized.

JULY 15: Thousands of San Francisco homosexuals enraged at the lenient sentence given to former Supervisor Daniel James White for his killing of gay Supervisor Harvey Milk (and straight Mayor George Moscone), create widespread rioting which results in millions of dollars in damage to businesses.

JULY 20: Ronald A. Rimerman skyjacks a United B-727 en route from Denver to Omaha, Nebraska carrying 126 people. He claims to have plastic explosives and orders the pilot to fly to Cuba. He will be seized and sent to an insane asylum.

JULY 25: Zuhair Moshin, head of the Syrian-dominated Sa'ika, is fatally shot near his apartment in Cannes, France, by Abu Nidal terrorists acting for Al Mukharabat, the Iraqi secret service.

AUGUST 16: Alfred R. Kagan skyjacks an Eastern B-727 en route from Guatemala City, Guatemala, to Miami with ninety-one people on board. Brandishing a penknife and claiming to have a bomb, Kagan demands he be flown to Cuba. He will be seized and institutionalized.

AUGUST 22: James R. Albee will become a convicted skyjacker, sentenced to sixty years in prison in Oregon for threatening with a bomb the pilot of a United B-727 en route from Portland, Oregon, to Los Angeles with 120 people on board.

AUGUST 27: World War II hero First Earl Louis Mountbatten is blown up and killed on his boat as he fishes in Donegal Bay, off the coast of County Sligo, Ireland; the cause of the explosion is an IRA bomb.

AUGUST 27: Eighteen British soldiers are killed by two IRA bombs exploding in Warrenpoint, Ireland.

SEPTEMBER 12: Rafael Keppel, employing a toy pistol, skyjacks a Lufthansa B-727, flying from Frankfurt, Germany with 119 persons and eight crew members. Keppel forces the pilot to land at the Bonn-Cologne airport, holding all on board hostage for seven hours while reading a rambling manifesto demanding a "more humane world." Keppel will later surrender and be imprisoned.

OCTOBER 30: John E. Gray skyjacks a B-727 en route from Los Angeles to San Diego, California with 108 people on board, ordering the pilot to fly to Mexico. He will be seized and imprisoned.

OCTOBER 30: About 300 leftwing terrorists attempt to storm the U.S. Embassy in San Salvador but are repulsed by U.S. Marines and local police and troops. Two Marines are injured and the terrorists driven off.

NOVEMBER 4: Sixty-three hostages are taken at the U.S. Embassy in Teheran by Iranian terrorists who demand the return of the Shah of Iran to Iran for trial. Though the demands of the terrorists will not be met, and a poorly organized rescue attempt of the hostages will fail, the American hostages, after enduring prolonged captivity, will eventually be released, their freedom negotiated by officials of President Ronald Reagan's administration. (The failure of President Jimmy Carter to effect the release of the hostages greatly contributes to Reagan's election as president.)

NOVEMBER 13: Efraim Eldar, Israel's ambassador to Portugal, is the target of an unsuccessful assassination in Lisbon, by Abu Nidal terrorists.

NOVEMBER 21: A bomb thrown from a passing car into Junior's Lunch Cafe in Lynchburg, Virginia, injures three people and causes $28,000 worth of damage.

NOVEMBER 21: Thousands of Muslim terrorists attack and burn the U.S. Embassy in Islamabad, Pakistan. Local troops manage to rescue more than 100 U.S. citizens. One U.S. Marine is killed while defending the embassy.

British hero Earl Mountbatten of Burma, assassinated by an IRA bomb on August 27, 1979.

NOVEMBER 24: Gerald J. Hill, claiming to carry a knife and dynamite, skyjacks an American Airlines B-727 en route from San Antonio to El Paso, Texas with seventy-four persons aboard. Hill demands to be flown to Iran but he is seized and imprisoned.

NOVEMBER 29: A seventeen-year-old boy is killed while attempting to place a bomb inside a soda-pop machine in St. Stephens, South Carolina.

NOVEMBER: Five Communist Workers Party members are killed by terrorists in

Greensboro, North Carolina. Six members of the Ku Klux Klan are indicted for the slayings but they will be acquitted a year later.

DECEMBER 3: Eleven persons are trampled to death in a riot created by fans trying to enter a crowded Cincinnati, Ohio, rock concert given by the rock-and-roll group, The Who.

1980

JANUARY 25: Samuel A. Ingram, claiming to have a bomb and a pistol, skyjacks a Delta L-1011, compelling the pilot to fly sixty-three people to Cuba, where the crew and most of the passengers escape. Ingram insists that he then be flown to Iran, but he surrenders and will be imprisoned.

JANUARY 31: Left-wing terrorists seize the Spanish Embassy in Guatemala City, Guatemala, holding eight hostages. The police do not negotiate but storm the building which catches fire. Only one of the terrorists and the Spanish ambassador will survive the blaze.

FEBRUARY 3: Thirty-two persons are killed and scores more injured when inmates of the New Mexico State Prison riot over conditions.

FEBRUARY 27: Fifty-seven hostages are taken at the Dominican Republic Embassy in Bogatá, Colombia, by M-19 terrorists who demand $50 million ransom and political concessions. They will accept $2 million and be given permission to leave the country.

MARCH 10: Four persons are killed in a Paris synagogue bombed by the PFLP, the explosive device placed on the back of a motorcycle parked in front of the temple.

APRIL 14: Indira Gandhi, prime minister of India, is the target of an unsuccessful assassination when a terrorist hurls a knife at her in New Delhi.

APRIL 14: Thomas C. Wiltgen, carrying a knife and claiming to be an IRA member, skyjacks a Continental B-727 in Denver, demanding to be flown to Libya. He allows the seventy-five passengers to deplane before surrendering. He will be sent to prison.

APRIL 30: Five Arab terrorists from Iran take twenty-six hostages at the Iranian embassy, demanding the release of political prisoners in Iran. Two hostages will be slain, five set free and the others rescued when British forces storm the embassy, killing two of the terrorists and taking the other three prisoner.

MAY 1: Stephen W. Bilson sneaks onto a Pacific Southwest B-727 in Stockton, California, taking the flight engineer hostage. He reads a rambling statement about Iran and hostages in Iran before he is overpowered by the flight engineer and arrested. He will be imprisoned.

MAY 10: Omran el-Mehdawi, second secretary of the Libyan Embassy in Bonn, Germany, is killed by terrorists.

MAY 19: Race riots in Miami see eighteen persons killed, scores injured, more than 1,300 people, mostly blacks, arrested, and more than $100 million in damage. Only when 3,500 National Guardsmen are called to the scene will the riots be quelled.

MAY 29: Vernon E. Jordan, Jr., civil rights leader and president of the National Urban League, is shot and injured in Fort Wayne, Indiana, but survives the attack.

JUNE 12: FAR terrorists kidnap the president of a subsidiary of Nestle Company in Guatemala, receiving a reported $4.7 million for the executive's release.

JUNE 27: A bomb, or a ground-to-air missile, explodes a DC-9 jetliner, causing it to crash ninety miles southwest of Naples, Italy, killing eighty-one persons.

JULY 11: Glen K. Tripp, threatening to blow up a Northwest B-727 about to depart for Portland, Oregon with sixty-four people, demands $100,000 and two parachutes. He later changes his mind, and demands a car. While walking to the auto he is arrested. He will be imprisoned.

JULY 22: Silvio Mesa Cabrera skyjacks a 144-passenger Delta L-1011 en route from Miami to San Juan, Puerto Rico. He demands that the plane be flown to Havana but poor weather conditions force the craft to land at Camaguey, Cuba, where he vanishes.

JULY 22: Thousands of blacks riot in Chattanooga, Tennessee, after two Ku Klux Klan members are acquitted by an all-white jury of shooting four black women. Eight policemen are injured and widespread damage done.

AUGUST 2: The Armed Revolutionary Nuclei (NAR), a neo-fascist Italian terrorist group, causes the bombing of the Bologna railway station, killing seventy-five persons and injuring another 186 people.

AUGUST 10: Manuel Soto, threatening to blow up a Key West-bound Air Florida plane carrying thirty passenges and five crew members, orders the pilot to fly to Cuba. Upon landing in Havana, Soto surrenders to local police. His "bomb" turns out to be a box of soap.

AUGUST 20: More than 150 are killed and a dozen towns in Northern India are left in smoldering ruins following riots between Hindus and Muslims.

AUGUST 27: A well-constructed homemade bomb explodes in Harvey's Casino in Stateline, Nevada, causing $18 million in damages. There are no injuries.

AUGUST 27: Thousands of blacks riot in Philadelphia, Pennsylvania, after a police officer shoots and kills a black youth.

SEPTEMBER 26: A member of the neo-Nazi Wehrsportsgruppe (Military Sports Group) explodes a bomb during the bierfest in Munich, Germany, killing himself and twelve bystanders. More than 300 people are injured.

NOVEMBER 14: Sixteen children, a school bus driver and a teacher are taken hostage in Vielsalm, Belgium, by Mark Frank, Michael Stree and another terrorist, who demand social reforms. The terrorists will drive the bus to Brussels where police capture them and free the hostages.

NOVEMBER: Countess Giovanna di Porta Puglia is rescued from the castle of Castell Arguanto, south of Milan, Italy, after she has been held captive for more than forty years by her brothers Luigi and Alfredo Puglia, and Luigi's wife, who are all arrested and imprisoned.

DECEMBER 7: Clifford Bevens, U.S. manager of a Goodyear subsidiary, Ginsa Tire, is kidnapped from his Guatemala City apartment by terrorists who demand $10 million ransom. Soldiers will locate the terrorist hideout and, when storming this place, Bevens and his five kidnappers are killed.

DECEMBER 28: Members of the Red Brigades, a terrorist organization responsible for countless kidnappings, robberies and assassinations, imprisoned at Trani, Italy, lead a mass breakout attempt, holding hostages. Two days later Italian commandos in helicopters land inside the prison yard and free the hostages.

DECEMBER 31: The PFLP avenges itself for the Entebbe raid by blowing up the Zionist-owned Norfolk Hotel in Nairobi, Kenya, killing between sixteen and twenty people. Eighty-five others are injured in the resulting fire.

1981

JANUARY 3: Jose Rodolfo Viera, president of the Salvadoran Institute for Agrarian Transformation, Michael Peter Hammer, U.S. agrarian reform authority, and Mark David Pearlman, U.S. attorney, are all shot to death by terrorists in San Salvador, El Salvador.

JANUARY 12: Sheik Hammad Abu Rabia, chief of one of the largest Negev tribes, is shot to death by terrorists in Jerusalem.

JANUARY 12: Muslim rioting in Kano, Nigeria, leaves between 7,000 and 10,000 dead.

JANUARY 13: Bernadine Dohrn, the most fanatical of the Weathermen terrorist organization of the 1960s and 1970s, goes to trial for organizing the infamous "Days of Rage" riots in Chicago in 1969 and other crimes. She pleads guilty and is given a three-year suspended sentence and is fined $1,500.

JANUARY 16: Bernadette Devlin McAliskey, Irish political activist, and her husband, Michael, survive an attack after they are shot and wounded in County Tyrone, Ireland, by three members of a Protestant paramilitary organization.

JANUARY 18: Facundo Guardado, Salvadoran terrorist, is apprehended by Honduras' National Intelligence Division. After he is later set free, the terrorist will claim that he has been kidnapped and tortured.

JANUARY 19: Chester A. Bitterman III, a U.S. linguist, is abducted from the Summer Institute of Linguistics in Bogatá, Colombia, by terrorists who claim he is a CIA agent. Bitterman will be slain.

JANUARY 27: More than 400 imprisoned IRA terrorists riot at Maze Prison, smashing furniture and windows and creating widespread damage.

FEBRUARY 6: Mahmut Dikler, deputy director of police for Istanbul, Turkey, and a bodyguard, are shot to death in Istanbul by left-wing terrorists.

FEBRUARY 6: Jose Maria Ryan, head engineer of a nuclear plant being built at Lemoniz, Spain, is killed by members of the Basque Fatherland and Liberty Group (ETA), a terrorist organization.

Hooded members of the Basque terrorist organization ETA, who killed a nuclear engineer in Spain on February 6, 1981.

FEBRUARY 9: Eighteen peasants are killed when a bomb strikes the truck in which they are riding in Suchitoto, El Salvador. Thirty others are injured.

FEBRUARY 16: Pope John Paul II is the target of a failed assassination attempt when a bomb explodes just before his appearance in Pakistan. Muslim terrorists are suspected.

FEBRUARY 17: Muslim terrorists are suspected of exploding a bomb in Davao, Mindanao, Philippines, two days before Pope John Paul II is to arrive. One person is killed and eleven are wounded.

FEBRUARY 17: Luigi Maragoni, head of the state-run Polyclinic Hospital in Milan, is fatally shot by four attackers.

FEBRUARY 19: A bomb explosion at KGB headquarters in Moscow, U.S.S.R., kills an officer and his driver, an event the Soviet government officially denies.

FEBRUARY 20-21: Three separate bomb explosions in Teheran, Iran, kill two persons and injured thirty-one others.

FEBRUARY 23: The Munich, Germany, offices of Radio Free Europe and Radio Liberty are bombed and eight persons are injured.

MARCH 7: PFLP terrorist leader Mohammed Zaidan Abbas, and top adviser to Yasir Arafat, sends two suicidal terrorists over Israeli territory in hand gliders and to drop explosives on a refinery in Haifa. Both terrorists missed their objectives and fell into the hands of Israeli soldiers.

MARCH 17: A bazooka shot is fired at a U.S. Embassy van in San Jose, Costa Rica, injuring three Marines and their Costa Rican driver.

MARCH 28: Jihad Command terrorists skyjack an Indonesian Airways jet flying within Sumatra, taking the fifty-seven persons on board hostage and demanding the release of eighty political prisoners. When the plane lands, a shootout with police ensues and four of the terrorists are killed before the hostages are set free.

MARCH 30: U.S. President Ronald Reagan, press secretary James Brady, police officer Thomas Delahanty, and Secret Service agent Timothy J. McCarthy, are shot and wounded (all survive) in Washington, D.C. by John W. Hinckley, Jr., who will be sent to an institution for the mentally ill.

APRIL 2: A bomb demolishes a garage in Newport, Kentucky, killing two persons, injuring twenty-one others, and causing $1 million in property damage.

APRIL 3: Scattered bombings and rioting in West Bengal, India, kill eight persons and injure another 200 people.

APRIL 6: Under orders from PFLP director Mohammed Zaidan Abbas, two terrorists attempt to infiltrate Israel in a hot-air balloon, but they are shot down by Israeli troops and killed.

APRIL 14: Giuseppe Salvia, deputy director of Poggioreale Prison, is shot to death in his car in Naples, Italy, by Red Brigadists.

APRIL 16: Joseph Munhangi, member of the Ugandan parliament, is assassinated by terrorists in Kampala, Uganda.

APRIL 19: Thirteen people are killed and 177 injured when terrorists of the New People's Army of the outlawed Communist Party throw hand grenades into a Roman Catholic Church in Davao, Philippines, during an Easter Mass.

APRIL 19: Two eighteen-year-old youths are killed in Londonderry, Ireland, when a British army vehicle rams into a crowd throwing gas bombs.

APRIL 23: Naser Almaneih, a former Iranian police chief, is sentenced to fifty years in prison in California for the August 20, 1980 bombing of a high school in Berkeley, California, and for conspiring to bomb an Iranian meeting at San Jose State University.

APRIL 25: A car bomb kills seven people and injures another thirty-five in the Iranian city of Kermanshah.

MAY 1: Heinz Nittel, Vienna Councilman and president of the Austrian-Israel Friendship League, is shot to death near his apartment in Vienna, Austria by terrorists who later identify themselves as members of Al-Asifa.

MAY 2: Laurence James Downey, an Australian, skyjacks an Aer Lingus B-737 flying from Dublin, Ireland, demanding publication of "The Third Secret of Fatima," a prophecy of global war held secret by the Vatican. Police will capture Downey upon the plane's landing.

MAY 4: General Andreas Gonzalez de Suso is shot to death by leftist terrorists near his home in Madrid, Spain.

MAY 7: Three Spanish military officers are killed and eleven passersby injured when Basque separatists lob a bomb into a staff car waiting for a red light in Madrid, Spain.

MAY 11: Heinz Herbert Karry, minister of econcomics of Hesse, West Germany, is shot to death in the bedroom of his apartment by terrorists in Frankfurt, Germany.

MAY 12: Otto Walter Garcia, one of the leaders of the Leftist United Revolutionary Front, is killed in Guatemala.

MAY 14: Carlos Humberto Mendez Lopez, deputy commander of the private army of the National Liberation Movement, is fatally shot by two terrorists in Guatemala City, Guatemala.

MAY 15: Following the death of hunger striker Francis Hughes, the IRA fires a rocket through the roof of a police car in West Belfast, Ireland, killing one officer and wounding three others.

MAY 16: The Puerto Rican Armed Resistance Group claims responsibility for a pipe-bomb explosion that kills Alex McMilan, an employee at Kennedy Airport in New York. Two other bombs are found in the airport within the next twenty-four hours.

MAY 20: New York Police receive 487 bomb threats in the wake of the May 16 bombing by Puerto Rican terrorists at Kennedy Airport.

MAY 20: Giuseppe Tagliercio, an administrator of a Montedison petrochemical firm, is kidnapped from his apartment in Mestre, Italy, by Red Brigades terrorists. Tagliercio will be murdered by his captors.

MAY 24: A Turkish Airlines DC-9 with 112 persons on board flying from Ankara to Istanbul, Turkey, is skyjacked by two Dev Sol terrorists who demand $500,000 ransom and the release of prisoners held in Turkey. The plane will land in Burgas, Bulgaria, where no demands will be met and the siege ended.

MAY 30: Zia Ur-Rahman, president of Bangladesh, is assassinated in Chittagong, Bangladesh, along with six bodyguards and two aides in a short-lived coup under General Abul Manzur who will be killed by guards on June 1, 1981.

MAY 31: Warrant Officer Michael O'Neill, a member of a British bomb disposal unit, is killed near Newry, Ireland, while he is examining an auto.

JUNE 1: Na'im Khadir, agent for the Palestinian Liberation Organization in Brussels, Belgium, is killed by Abu Nidal terrorists.

JUNE 3: Though no injuries occur, damage in the millions of dollars is done when time bombs destroy two huge department stores and six adjacent buildings in Athens, Greece. The Revolutionary Anti-Capitalist Action and the New Organization claim responsibility.

JUNE 6: The Monster of Florence kills again by shooting Giovanni Foggi, twenty-one, and his fianceé, Carmela Di Nuccio, nineteen, as they sit in a car in the southwest Florence suburb of Scandicci. The killer removes Di Nuccio's genitalia with a scalpel or razor-sharp knife.

JUNE 11: A bomb explosion at the Arab Socialist Union building in Tyre, Lebanon, kills twenty-five people.

JUNE 23: An explosion at the Qom Railroad Station in Iran kills four persons and wounds fifty-eight.

JUNE 28: The headquarters of the Islamic Republican Party in Teheran, Iran, is bombed, killing seventy-two persons, including Ayatollah Behesti, chief justice of the Supreme Court, and four cabinet ministers.

JUNE 28: Muhammed Kacu'i, governor of Evin Prison, is murdered in Teheran by terrorists.

JULY 5: More than 200 persons are injured in Liverpool, England, when thousands riot in protest over the policies of Prime Minister Margaret Thatcher.

JULY 10: Kenneth Rex McElroy, a towering, beefy man, has, since dropping out of school thirty years earlier, terrorized the town of Skidmore, Missouri, picking fights, shoving people off the sidewalks, barreling his pickup truck down roads to force others into ditches, firing shotgun pellets into the ceiling of the local grocery store. He has shot two residents and escaped punishment. He has even bullied the local police into shunning him and ignoring his constant abuses. On this day more than eighty residents hold a a town hall meeting to discuss McElroy and his incessant terror tactics. A short time later, as McElroy parked his pickup truck outside a local bar, dozens of residents surrounded his truck, while a man fired four rifle bullets into McElroy, killing him. All in the town refuse to identify McElroy's killer.

JULY 14: Three persons are killed by a bomb explosion in a movie theater in Banqui, in the Central African Republic.

Black September chief Abu Da'ud (Daoud; Mohammed Daoud Machmud Auda),was murdered on August 1, 1981.

AUGUST 1: Abu Da'ud (Abu Daoud), a leader of Black September and the Palestinian Liberation Organization (PLO), is slain in Warsaw, Poland, by Abu Nidal terrorists.

AUGUST 2: A bomb explodes during a wedding ceremony at the Christian Coptic Church in Cairo, Egypt, killing three people and injuring fifty-six others. The Arab Steadfastness Front, a terrorist organization, is held responsible.

AUGUST 22: Forty-eight persons are injured by two IRA bombs set off in Belfast, Ireland, following the death of hunger striker Michael Devine.

AUGUST 30: Eighteen people are injured when a bomb explodes at the Intercontinental Hotel in Paris, France.

AUGUST 31: A car bomb planted by the German Red Army at the U.S. Air Force Base in Ramstein wounds twenty persons.

SEPTEMBER 3: A car bomb explodes in front of Syrian Air Force Headquarters in Damascus, killing twenty persons and wounding fifty others.

SEPTEMBER 4: Louis Delamare, French ambassador to Lebanon, is shot to death by terrorists while driving his car in Beirut.

SEPTEMBER 17: A car bomb explodes in Sidon, Lebanon, killing twenty-three persons. The Front for the Liberation of Lebanon, a right-wing terrorist group, takes credit.

SEPTEMBER 18: A car rigged with bombs explodes in West Beirut on a street infested with drug-dealers. Three persons are killed and many more injured. A group calling itself The Front for the Liberation of Lebanon from Foreigners takes credit for the explosion. The Palestinian Liberation Organization (PLO) claims the group is an Israeli front.

SEPTEMBER 20: A bomb explodes in the Muslim section of Beirut, killing four persons and thirty-five others are injured. The Front for the Liberation of Lebanon from Foreigners takes credit.

SEPTEMBER 28: A car bomb explodes at the Palestinian checkpoint in Zrariyeh, Lebanon, killing fifteen patrons in a nearby restaurant. The pro-Amal Shi'ites are believed to be responsible.

SEPTEMBER 29: Hojatoleslam Abdulkarim Hashemi-Nejad, secretary general of the Islamic Republic Party, is killed and others are wounded in Mashad, Iran, by a hand grenade held by Hadi Alavai Fitilechi, a Mujahedeen terrorist.

SEPTEMBER 29: An India Airlines B-737 is skyjacked by five Sikhs after takeoff from New Delhi and forced to land in Lahore, Pakistan. The skyjackers demand $500,000 ransom and the release of Sant Jarnail Singh Bhindranwale and others. The terrorists will be overpowered and arrested.

OCTOBER 1: A car bomb explodes next to the PLO offices in Beirut, Lebanon, killing fifty persons and wounding another 250 people. The attackers are believed to be members of The Front for the Liberation of Lebanon from Foreigners.

OCTOBER 6: Khaled Islambouli, an Egyptian army officer and leader of the terrorist sect, Takfir Wal-Hajira, and four others, attack the reviewing stand in which Anwar Sadat, President of Egypt, and other Egyptian notables are sitting, watching a Cairo military parade. The terrorists hurl grenades and spray the reviewing stand with bullets from automatic weapons. Sadat is fatally struck by four bullets, and eleven other dignitaries are killed, along with many guards. Scores are wounded. The terrorists are quickly captured and it is later learned that they have been backed by Libyan strongman Muammar Qaddafi, who considers Sadat a traitor to the Arab cause because of Sadat's friendly relations with Israel.

OCTOBER 10: A nail bomb attack is launched by the IRA on a bus in London, England, killing two persons and injuring thirty-five others.

OCTOBER 17: Sir Stuart Pringle, general and ex-commandant of the British Marines and Northern Ireland commando leader, loses part of a leg when a bomb planted by IRA terrorists explodes in his car.

Egyptian President Anwar Sadat sought peace between his country and Israel and was slain by Islamic terrorists on October 6, 1981.

OCTOBER 22: The Monster of Florence again murders a couple spooning in their car twelve miles northwest of Florence, shooting twenty-four-year-old Stefano Baldi and Susanna Cambri. The woman is sexually mutilated as has been the case with previous victims. Police conclude from footprints that the killer is a large, heavyset man. Several suspects will be taken into custody but none will prove to be the serial killer.

NOVEMBER 4: Roland Smith receives a three-year prison sentence for threatening the life of U.S. President Ronald Reagan.

NOVEMBER 6: Israel Borquez, president of the Supreme Court of Chile, is slightly wounded in Santiago by terrorist gunmen.

NOVEMBER 14: Reverend Robert Bradford, member of the British parliament and Ulster unionist, is fatally shot in Belfast, Ireland, reportedly by IRA gunmen.

NOVEMBER 21: Terrorist Khaled Islambouli, killer of Egyptian President Anwar Sadat and many others, is tried in Cairo, along with twenty-two others of his terrorist organization, Takfir Wal-Hajira. All are found guilty of assassination. Islambouli and four others are condemned to death; seventeen others are given prison sentences.

DECEMBER 15: A suicide car loaded with explosives is driven into the Iraqi Embassy in Beirut, Lebanon, killing thirty-seven people and injuring another fifty. The Kurdistan Liberation Army takes credit.

DECEMBER 17: U.S. Brigadier General James Lee Dozier is kidnapped from his Verona apartment on orders of Antonio Savasta, fanatical leader of the Red Brigades terrorists in Italy. Savasta demanded that hundreds of Red Brigadists be released from prison in exchange for Dozier.

DECEMBER 18: The headquarters of the Zimbabwean African National Union in Salisbury is destroyed by a bomb, killing six persons and injuring another 150 people.

DECEMBER 19: Libyan dictator Muammar Qaddafi, is injured and his driver slain by Khalifa Khadir, a Libyan army colonel.

DECEMBER 19: A time bomb placed inside a pick-up truck explodes in Beirut, Lebanon, killing five policemen and injuring six persons.

1982

JANUARY 1: Terrorists kidnap fifty residents of San Francisco El Tablon, Guatemala. Most will be tortured and shot to death.

JANUARY 5: Jose Lipperheide, a Basque businessman, is abducted near Bilbao, Spain by ETA terrorists. He will be released after the kidnappers receive a $1.2 million ransom.

JANUARY 13: Rabeh Jerwa, minister plenipotentiary of the Algerian Embassy in Beirut, Lebanon, is kidnapped from his apartment by terrorists and assassinated, three bullets being fired into his head.

JANUARY 15: Twenty-five persons are injured by an explosion at the Migash-Israel Restaurant in Berlin, Germany. The 15th of May Arab Organization for the Liberation of Palestine explodes the bomb.

JANUARY 18: Lieutenant Colonel Charles Robert Ray, U.S. military attaché, is shot to death near his apartment by FARL terrorists in Paris, France.

JANUARY 26: Jacobo Ramon Larach, general manager of the Pepsi Cola botting company in San Pedro Sula, Honduras, is fatally shot when terrorists attempt to kidnap him.

JANUARY 28: Members of Italy's Nucleo Operativo Centrale, a crack anti-terrorist organization, locate the apartment in Padua where American General James Dozier is being held by Antonio Savasta and other members of the Red Brigade. They break down the door just in time to prevent Savasta from killing Dozier, rescuing the hostage and taking the Red Brigadists prisoner.

JANUARY 28: Kemal Arikan, consul general of Turkey, is shot to death in his car in Los Angeles, California, by Armenian terrorists who claim responsibility for the assassination.

JANUARY 29: John McKeague, Loyalist leader and possibly chief of clandestine Red Hand Commandos, is shot to death in Belfast, Ireland.

FEBRUARY 5: Roberto Giron Lemus, editor of La Nacion, is going to work when he is assassinated by terrorists in Guatemala City, Guatemala.

FEBRUARY 22: Fifteen people are killed and sixty-one injured when a bomb explodes in a garbage truck in Teheran's Seapah Square during rush hour.

FEBRUARY 24: Several badly informed Shiite Muslim terrorists skyjack a Kuwaiti Boeing 707 in Beirut as a protest against Libya's arrest of Shiite Muslim leader Imam Moussa Sadr. The plane will be flown to Iran, where the terrorists will surrender after learning that the plane they have skyjacked is not Libyan.

FEBRUARY 27: Eight are killed and thirty-five are injured when a car bomb planted by The Front for the Liberation of Lebanon from Foreigners explodes at the Syrian Army checkpoint in West Beirut.

MARCH 14: The trial of Red Brigades leader Antonio Savasta and sixteen others begins and will end in conviction and imprisonment of the defendants. The power of Italy's worst terrorist organization is finally broken.

MARCH 15: An eleven-year-old boy is killed and two women injured by an IRA bomb exploding in Banbridge, Ireland.

MARCH 18: Several terrorists hurl gasoline bombs at a political rally for the Functional Groups Party in Jakarta, Indonesia, killing seven persons and injuring more than 100 others.

MARCH 29: The international terrorist Carlos (Illich Ramirez Sanchez) bombs a Paris-Toulouse express train near Limoges, killing six persons and injuring another fifteen.

APRIL 3: Yacov Barsimantov, second secretary of the Israeli Embassy in Paris, is shot to death in his Paris apartment.

APRIL 3: Wandee Throngprapa, managing editor of *Tawan Siam,* a Bangkok newspaper, is shot to death by terrorists in his office.

APRIL 9: Kani Gungor, a commercial officer of the Turkish Embassy in Ottawa, is injured by gunshots fired by terrorists. The Secret Army for the Liberation of Armenia takes credit for the shooting.

APRIL 15: Khaled Islambouli and four other conspirators of the Egyptian terrorist organization Takfir Wal-Hajira are hanged for their part in the 1981 assassination of President Anwar Sadat.

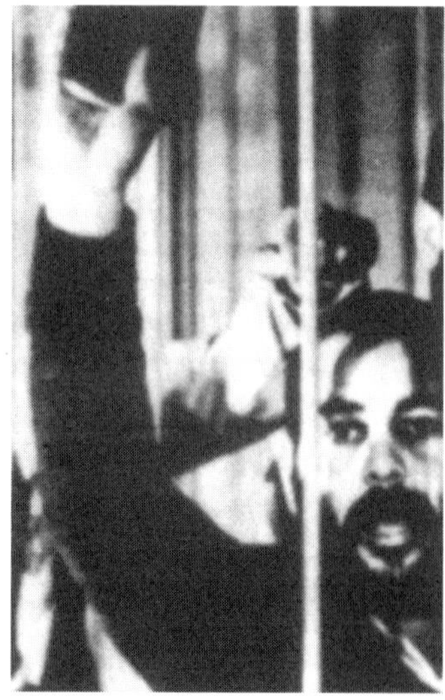

Khaled Islambouli, shown shouting obscenities from a cage at his trial, was executed on April 15, 1982 for assassinating Anwar Sadat.

APRIL 27: Raffaele de Cogliano, Christian Democrat and commissioner of the Campania administration, and his driver, are fatally shot by terrorists in Naples, Italy.

APRIL 28: Pio La Torre, member of parliament and leader of the Communist Party in Sicily, and his driver, are shot to death in Palermo.

MAY 4: Orhan R. Gunduz, honorary Turkish consul to New England, is shot to death in Sommerville, a Boston suburb. The Justice Commandos of the Armenian Genocide claim credit.

MAY 5: Angel Pascual Mugica, general manager of the Lemoniz nuclear plant, is driving outside of Bilbao, Spain, when he is shot to death by terrorists.

MAY 21: Juan Cleano skyjacks a Philippine Airlines BAC-111 before it lands at Cebu, demanding a ransom of 60,000 pesos ($7,270, the amount of his mortgage), and political reforms (added to make his crime appear politically-motivated). He will be overpowered and imprisoned.

MAY 24: A bomb hidden in a car belonging to the secretary of the French Embassy in Beirut is detonated as the vehicle enters the embassy gates, killing fourteen persons and injuring twenty-one.

MAY 27: Hamid Alaou skyjacks a Royal Air Morocco B-727 after it departs Athens, Greece, demanding a flight to Tunis and improvements in the morality of observance of Islam in Morocco. He will surrender to Tunisian officials.

JUNE 4: Mustafa Marzook, first secretary of the Kuwaiti Embassy in New Delhi, India, is shot to death in his home. The Arab Brigades Movement takes credit.

JUNE 4: Petrus Nyaose, secretary general of the African National Congress, and his wife, Jabu, are murdered by a car bomb in Swaziland.

JUNE 17: Kamal Hussein, deputy director of the Palestinian Liberation Organization, is slain by terrorists in Rome, Italy.

JUNE 18: The terrorist known as the Monster of Florence strikes again fifteen miles southwest of Florence where he shoots and kills Paolo Mainardi, twenty-two, and Antonella Migliorini, nineteen. Police will later conclude from the tire tracks of Mainardi's car that Mainardi apparently saw the killer approaching and attempted to drive away; the killer leaped in front of the car and fired several shots through the front window of the car with his .22-caliber Beretta pistol, killing the victims, but left before performing his usual mutilations.

JUNE: General Yekotiel Adam, former deputy chief of staff and leader of Israel's intelligence agency, Mossad, is murdered by members of the Palestinian Liberation Organization.

JULY 17: Fifteen terrorists kill Peruvian governor Zenon Palomino Flores in Callera and then loot stores and rape women at will in the mountain village.

JULY 20: IRA bombs exploding in Hyde Park and Regent's Park, London, kill eight persons and injure forty-seven others.

JULY 25: Five workers from Xian take control of a Chinese passenger plane heading from Xian to Shanghai and demand

Dead horses are shown in Hyde Park, London, after IRA bombs claimed the lives of eight people and wounded forty-seven others.

to go to Hong Kong. The passengers and crew members will overpower the skyjackers, causing a bomb one of the skyjackers is carrying to go off, damaging the plane and forcing it to make an emergency landing. The terrorists will be arrested and imprisoned.

AUGUST 7: A bomb thrown by two members of the Armenian Secret Army for the Liberation of Armenia into a crowded waiting room at the Esenboga Airport in Ankara, which kills three Turkish policeman and one American, as well as injuring seventy-two others.

AUGUST 9: A terrorist flings a bomb into the Jo Goldenberg kosher restaurant in Paris, France. As patrons flee, the gunman opens fire with a machine gun, killing six persons and injuring another twenty-two people.

AUGUST 10: Members of The Mozambique Resistance Movement fire a bazooka shell at a passing train near Beira, in Mozambique, killing fourteen persons and wounding another fifty people.

AUGUST 13: Dr. Hector Zevalloses, abortion clinic operator, and his wife, are abducted in Edwardsville, Illinois, but later freed by anti-abortionist Army of God terrorists led by Don Benny Anderson. Several of the terrorists will be sent to prison.

AUGUST 27: Colonel Atilla Atikat, the Turkish military attaché in Ottawa, Canada, is fatally shot in his car. The Justice Commandos of the Armenian Genocide takes credit.

SEPTEMBER 3: General Carlo Alberto Dalla Chiesa, chief of an anti-Mafia task force, is slain, along with his wife and bodyguard, in Sicily, by Mafia killers.

SEPTEMBER 6: A truck bomb explodes on the Avenue Khayyam, opposite the ministries of Justice and Interior, in Teheran, Iran, killing twenty people and injuring 100 more.

SEPTEMBER 11: A bomb blast outside an employment agency in Manila, Philippines, kills two employees and injures twenty-five people.

SEPTEMBER 14: Hamad Jutaili, acting consul general of the Kuwaiti Embassy, is shot by terrorists when he stops his car in a service station in Karachi, Pakistan.

SEPTEMBER 16: Najeeb Sayeb Refai, first secretary of the Kuwaiti Embassy in Madrid, is fatally shot by gunmen, including Abu Nidal terrorist Ibrahim Nasser Hamdan.

SEPTEMBER 27: Abu Walid (Kafr Kalil), general and Palestinian Liberation Organization chief of operations, is slain in Lebanon.

OCTOBER 1: A TNT-bomb blast at the Iman Square in Teheran, Iran, kills sixty or more persons riding on a double-decker bus, and a nearby five-story hotel is completely leveled.

OCTOBER 15: Ashrafi Isfahani, ayatollah, is hugged by an assassin carrying a grenade and both are blown up in Bahtaran, Iran. The assassin may have been a member of the Mujahedeen Khalq.

OCTOBER 22: The FBI announces that five Armenian terrorists have been arrested for assaults on Turkish statesmen in southern California.

NOVEMBER 7: Three Russian terrorists skyjack a Soviet plane flying from Novorossisk to Odessa. They stab the pilot, wound two passengers and force the plane to land in Sinop, Turkey, where they are arrested.

NOVEMBER 14: Four restaurants in Kabul, Afghanistan, that are frequented by Soviet officials are hit by terrorist bombs, killing twenty-four persons.

NOVEMBER 17: Edwin Wilson, former CIA agent and arms dealer, is found guilty of sending explosives to Libya and sent to prison for thirty years.

NOVEMBER 23: A bomb wrecks a building in the suburb of Shiyah, outside Beirut, killing six persons and injuring another twenty people.

NOVEMBER 25: Two terrorist bombs explode in a shopping center in Kabul, Afghanistan, killing five persons and injuring thirty-two others.

DECEMBER 1: Walid Jumblatt, Druse Muslim leader, is injured with thirty-eight others and four are killed when a bomb explodes near his car in Lebanon.

DECEMBER 5: Salvadoran terrorists kidnap 136 persons on a bus bound for a soccer game in an attempt to recruit members to their ranks. One captive tries to escape and is killed, and the other hostages will be released when no one volunteers to become a terrorist.

DECEMBER 8: Norman Mayer, an anti-nuclear protestor, drives his truck to the base of the Washington Monument in Washington, D.C., threatening to blow it up unless a ban on nuclear weapons is discussed in Congress. Mayer tries to drive away in the afternoon, but police open fire and he is fatally wounded. There are no explosives in his truck.

DECEMBER 9: Zola Ngini, Adolph Mpongosohe, and Jackson Tayo, leaders of the African National Congress, are slain with thirty-nine others when South African raiders attack an ANC camp in Lesotho.

DECEMBER 14: Dr. Judith Xionara Suazo Estrada, daughter of the president of Honduras, while going to the hospital in Guatemala City, Guatemala, is kidnapped by terrorists. She will be released after the government publishes a left-wing manifesto.

DECEMBER 15: A pressure-sensitive bomb placed under the driver's seat of a car seriously injures U.S. Army Captain Howard Bromberg in Darmstadt, Germany. This is the sixtieth terrorist attack against Americans on German soil in 1982.

1983

JANUARY 10: More than 550 prisoners at Sing Sing Prison in New York riot, holding seventeen guards hostage for twenty-four hours, until prison officials promise reforms.

JANUARY 13: Robert S. Hester, a Memphis, Tennessee, police officer, is taken hostage by six religious cult members led by Lindberg Sanders. Hester will be murdered by the terrorists, and a Memphis SWAT team will later kill all of the kidnappers.

FEBRUARY 14: Riots between Hindus and Muslims during the elections throughout India cause more than 1,500 deaths.

FEBRUARY 20: A Libyan Arab Airways B-727 en route from Sebha, Libya to Tripoli is skyjacked by two Libyan army officers who hold the 158 passengers hostage at the airport in Valletta, Malta for three days. They will surrender on the promise of political asylum.

APRIL 10: Dr. Issam Sartawi, prominent Palestinian Liberation Organization moderate, is shot to death in Albufeira, Portugal, by Abu Nidal terrorists.

APRIL 18: Forty-seven persons are killed in a bomb explosion at the U.S. Embassy in Beirut, The bomb has been planted by the Islamic Jihad.

MAY 5: Tjou Chang-Jen skyjacks a jet en route from Manchuria to Shanghai, China, demanding that he be flown to Taiwan. Instead, the pilot hoodwinks the skyjacker and flies to South Korea, where the terrorist is seized and imprisoned.

MAY 14: Serial killer Randolph Kraft (the Freeway Killer) is stopped by police in California and the body of Terry Lee Bambrei, a Marine, is found in his trunk. Kraft will be convicted of murdering sixteen men in California between 1982-1983 (and he has committed pershaps as many murders in five other states). He will be sentenced to death.

MAY 22: A bomb explodes in downtown Pretoria, South Africa. The outlawed African National Congress (ANC) takes credit for the blast, which kills nineteen people and injures another 200.

JULY 15: Orly Airport in Paris, France, is bombed by a terrorist group known as the Armenian Secret Army (ASALA). Seven persons are killed and sixty more are injured.

SEPTEMBER 9: The Monster of Florence enters a van parked alongside a road outside of Florence and murders two homosexual lovers in their sleep, killing Horst Meyer and Uwe Rusch Sens. He does not perform his usual mutilations but tears up the couple's homosexual magazines before fleeing.

SEPTEMBER 29: A Gulf Air jetliner of the United Arab Emirates is blow up in midair by Abu Nidal terrorists, killing all 122 persons on board.

OCTOBER 9: Four cabinet ministers of South Korea and fifteen others die in a bomb explosion in Rangoon, Burma. One of the assassins is killed by Burmese guards. Two North Korean military officers will be sentenced to death on December 8, 1983, by a Burmese court for the attack.

OCTOBER 19: Maurice Bishop, premier of Grenada, who has been placed under house arrest on October 13, is slain by insurgent military members.

OCTOBER 21: Judge Henry A. Gentile is murdered and divorce attorney James A. Piszcor is wounded by ex-police officer Hutchie T. Moore, in a Chicago, Illinois courtroom.

OCTOBER 23: A suicidal terrorist drives a TNT-packed truck into Marine headquarters at Beirut International Airport, the

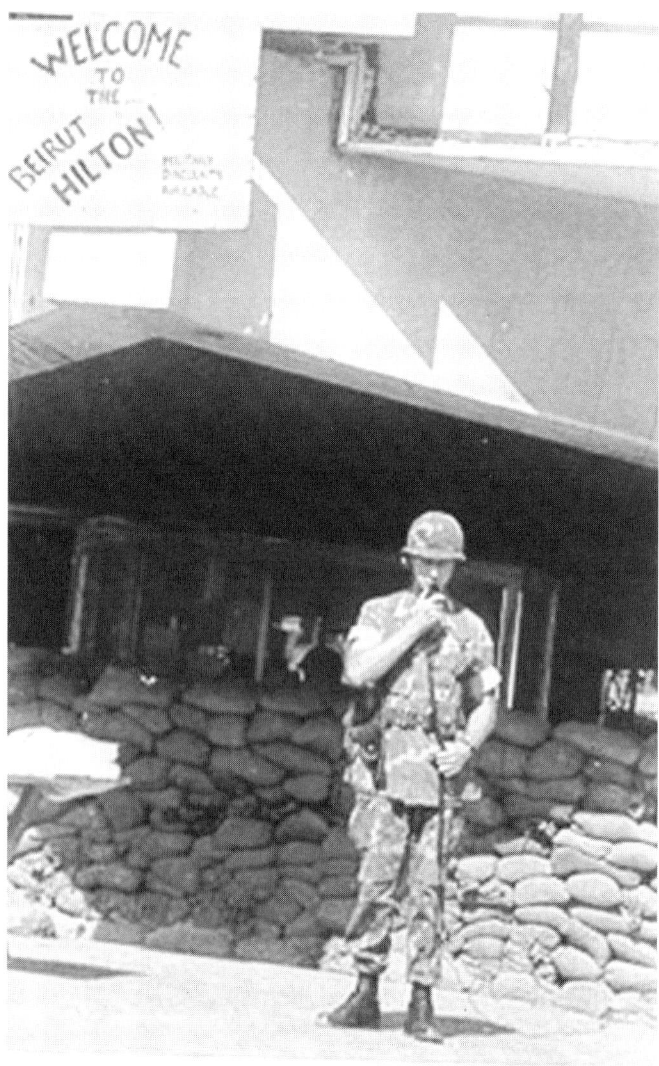

Lt. Colonel Larry Gerlach addresses Marines near the airport in Beirut, Lebanon on October 9, 1983. Many of those present would be among the 241 murdered U. S. Marines and sailors in the terrorist bombing of October 23, 1983.

Visible from many miles distant is towering smoke rising from the blast that tore apart the Marine barracks in Beirut on October 23, 1983.

The ruined Marine barracks in Beirut, where 241 U. S. Marines and sailors lost their lives on October 23, 1983 from a terrorist bombing.

horrific explosion killing 241 U.S. Marines and sailors who are part of the multi-national peace-keeping force. Another suicidal terrorist drives a second truck with explosives into a barracks two miles away, killing fifty-eight French paratroopers. The attacks have been made by terrorists belonging to the Islamic Jihad in an effort to rid Lebanon of the multi-national peace-keeping force in Lebanon.

NOVEMBER 4: Sixty Israelis are killed when a suicide truck bomb explodes in Tyre. Islamic Jihad terrorists are blamed.

NOVEMBER 15: George Tsantes, U.S. Navy captain, is shot to death by left-wing terrorists in Athens, Greece.

DECEMBER 12: A suicide truck driven by members of the Al-Dawa movement attacks the U.S. Embassy in Kuwait. The French Embassy is also attacked, leaving four persons dead and at least fifty injured.

DECEMBER 17: A car bomb explodes outside of Harrods, the famous department store in London, England, killing six persons and wounding ninety-four others. The IRA disclaims responsibility after universal condemnation for the terrorist outrage is expressed by world leaders.

1984

JANUARY 29: Guillermo Lacaci, Spanish general, is fatally shot in Madrid by terrorists.

FEBRUARY 2: Judge Braxton Kittrell, Jr., after an Alabama jury of eleven whites and one black have found racial terrorists Henry Francis Hays and James Llewellyn Knowles guilty of the 1981 murder of Michael Donald, a black, sentences Hays to death and Knowles to life imprisonment.

MARCH 8: Kiichi Miyazawa, prominent political figure in Japan, is attacked and wounded by knife-wielding terrorist Hirosato Higashijama.

MARCH 10: Several bombings attributed to the Libyan Secret Service are set off at Arab businesses in London, England, the most serious incident occurring in Berkeley Square, where twenty-seven persons are injured.

MARCH 24: Elizbeth II, queen of England, receives threats on her life on her trip to Jordan, reportedly from Abu Nidal terrorists.

MARCH 28: Kenneth Whitty, first secretary of the British Embassy in Athens, is fatally shot in Athens, Greece. The Revolutionary Organization of Socialist Muslims take credit for the assassination.

APRIL 3: A car bomb thought to be planted by the outlawed African National Congress (ANC) explodes in Durban, South Africa, killing three people and wounding sixteen others.

MAY 10: Prompted by terrorists, Hindu-Muslim riots break out in Bombay, India, causing more than 230 deaths in eleven days.

MAY 29: Two Negro serial killers Alton Coleman and Debra Brown, kidnap and strangle Vernita Wheat of Kenosha, Wisconsin, one of many murders committed in several states by these terrorists who will later be convicted of several killings and sentenced to death, executed on April 26, 2002.

JUNE 5: PFLP terrorist leader Mohammed Zaidan Abbas sends four of his most ruthless terrorists to attack the Israeli kibbutz of Ein-Gev, but all are captured and imprisoned.

JUNE 16: Hardayal Singh, chief of the Jullundur district committee of the Congress Party, is shot to death in Goraya, India, by Sikh terrorists.

JUNE 18: Alan Berg, controversial talk show host in Denver, Colorado, is shot and killed by members of the Order, a terrorist organization loosely structured after the Ku Klux Klan.

JULY 6 (through AUGUST 5, 1987): Serial killer and terrorist Robert Berdella, abducts and kills his first of six victims in the Kansas City, Missouri, area. Berdella will be apprehended when his seventh victim manages to escape. He will be sent to prison for life.

JULY 29: The Monster of Florence shoots and kills Claudio Stefanacci, twenty, and Pia Rontini, eighteen, as they sit in their car near Vicchio.

JULY 31: Islamic Jihad terrorists skyjack an Air France B-737 en route from Frankfurt to Paris, to Teheran, Iran. The terrorists demand the release of terrorists jailed in France. Two persons are killed, but the demands are not met.

SEPTEMBER 20: The Islamic Jihad attempts another suicide bombing of the U.S. Embassy in Beirut, the driver aiming his bomb-packed truck at the embassy annex, but alert guards open up on the speeding vehicle, killing the driver. The truck swerves off course and explodes, killing at least fourteen people.

OCTOBER 19: Jerzy Popieluzsko, one of the leaders of the Polish trade union Solidarity, is kidnapped by Polish secret police. He will be killed and his body later found.

NOVEMBER 4: More than 2,000 Sikhs are killed in rioting throughout India, sparked by the assassination of Prime Minister Indira Gandhi by her two Sikh bodyguards.

NOVEMBER 27: Percy Morris, British deputy high commissioner, is fatally shot in Bombay, India, by Abu Nidal terrorists.

DECEMBER 3: Five Arab terrorists skyjack a Kuwaiti jet flying from Dubai to Karachi and order it flown to Teheran, demanding freedom for Shiites held in Kuwait for bombing the U.S. embassy. The terrorists will murder two U.S. officials before Iranian troops take them into custody.

DECEMBER 22: Bernard Goetz, who has suffered earlier beatings by terrorists in New York, and who is armed with an unlicensed.38-caliber pistol, shoots four Negro youths who have attempted to rob him at knifepoint on a New York subway train.

1985

JANUARY 25: General René Audran, chief of the French international arms sales group, is fatally shot in Paris, France, by members of Action Directe.

FEBRUARY 3: A terrorist bomb explodes near the U.S. air base near Athens, Greece, injuring seventy-nine persons.

FEBRUARY 7: Enrique Camarena Salazar, U.S. drug enforcement agent, and Alfredo Azaval Avelar, his pilot, are kidnapped in Mexico, tortured and then slain by Raul López Alvarez and two other terrorists acting on the orders of drug trafficking king Rafael Cáro Quintero.

MARCH 16: Journalist Terry Anderson is kidnapped in Lebanon by Islamic Jihad terrorists. He will be held many years before being released.

MARCH 24: Arthur Nicholson, U.S. army major whom the U.S.S.R. claims to be a spy, is slain in Ludwigslust, Germany, by a Soviet guard.

MARCH 26: A Turkish terrorist group sets off a bomb on a train en route to Sofia, killing seven persons.

MARCH 25: Bruce Carroll Pierce, leader of the neo-Nazi group calling itself the Order, is arrested in Rossville, Georgia, and charged with the murder of radio talk-show host Alan Berg.

MARCH 31: In Winston-Salem, North Carolina, FBI agents arrest David Lane, the Denver-based leader of the neo-Nazi group called the Order, charging him, along with Bruce Carroll Pierce, with the murder of Denver talk show host Alan Berg. Lane, Pierce and ten other Order members are also charged with conspiring to overthrow the U.S. government.

MAY 10-12: Two days of terrorist bombings in New Delhi and other cities in northern India cause eighty-five deaths and hundreds of injuries.

JUNE 14: TWA flight 847 is skyjacked by two radical Shiites, members of Hezbollah—the Party of God—just after the plane takes off from Athens. The Arab terrorists, who have smuggled guns on board, beat passengers, then order the plane to land at Beirut. Refused the right to land, the TWA plane is then flown to Algiers, refueled, then flown back to Beirut. Before landing, the terrorists kill passenger Robert Stethem, a U.S. Navy diver, throwing his body onto the tarmac upon landing. The flight then flies back and forth between Algiers and Beirut for seventeen agonizing days, while the skyjackers unsuccessfully attempt to have 700 Shiite and Palestinian prisoners released from Israeli prisons. On June 30, 1985, the terrorists finally release their hostages in Beirut, which includes thirty-nine Americans. Mohammed Ali Hamadi, leader of the two-man terrorist team, will later be imprisoned.

JUNE 23: Sikh terrorists are held responsible for the in-flight explosion of an Air India 747, bound from Toronto to London. All 329 persons on board are killed.

JULY 11: Fifteen persons are killed and ninety more are wounded by bombs set off in Kuwait cafes by Abu Nidal terrorists.

AUGUST 20: Albert Atrakchi, first secretary of the Israeli Embassy in Cairo, Egypt, is shot to death. The Egyptian Revolution, a terrorist group, will take credit.

AUGUST 14: A car bomb in the Christian section of East Beirut kills fifteen persons and injures about 120 others.

AUGUST 17: A second car bomb in the Christian section of East Beirut kills fifty-five persons and injures seventeen others.

AUGUST 19: Christian Lebanese retaliate against Arab terrorists by exploding a bomb in the Muslim suburbs of Beirut, killing twenty-nine persons and injuring nineteen.

AUGUST 20: Forty-four persons are killed when a car bomb explodes in Tripoli.

SEPTEMBER 8: The Monster of Florence shoots and kills French tourists Jean-Michel Kraveichvili, twenty-five, and Nadine Mauriot, thirty-six. As with the previous 1984 killings, the killer not only removes the genitalia of the female victim but her left breast. The terrorist later mails two strips of skin from Mauriot's breast to an attorney. Although the terrorist has not struck since this last killing, the authorities of Florence, Italy, take precautions by posting signs on all roads outside the city, warning children and lovers not to stop in isolated areas.

SEPTEMBER 18: Michel Namri, publisher of the anti-Syrian Arab News Letter in Athens, Greece, is slain by Abu Nidal terrorists.

Hezbollah terrorists are shown in Beirut, after releasing hostages from TWA Flight 847, which they skyjacked on June 14, 1985, murdering one American.

SEPTEMBER 30: Four diplomats of the U.S.S.R. are kidnapped in Beirut, Lebanon, by Sunnis terrorists, who demand that the U.S.S.R. force Syria to halt attacks on Tripoli. One diplomat, Arkady Kathov, is slain. The other three hostages will be set free.

OCTOBER 7: Four PFLP terrorists, on orders from Mohammed Zaidan Abbas, seize the Italian cruise ship, *Achille Lauro*, but their intentions are unclear. The terrorists randomly select an American passenger, Leon Klinghoffer, shooting and killing the 69-year old invalid—he is confined to a wheelchair—and ordering other passengers at gunpoint to dump his body into the sea. The vessel sails to Port Said, where the terrorists surrender to Egyptian authorities. Accompanied by Abbas, they then flew to Sicily. Abbas is allowed by Italian authorities to escape to Belgrade, where he disappears. The four terrorists who have taken over the ship are tried, convicted and given prison sentences, the longest being thirty years, given to Yussef Magid Molqi, the killer of Leon Klinghoffer. A 1990 made-for-television miniseries, *Voyage of Terror: The Achille Lauro Affair,* starring Burt Lancaster in the role of Klinghoffer, and using the actual ship and its route, painfully recaptures this tragedy.

Leon Klinghoffer, an invalided American (shown with his wife Marilyn), was shot to death in his wheelchair and dumped into the sea by the Islamic terrorists who seized the *Achille Lauro*.

The Italian cruise ship, *Achille Lauro*, seized by four PFLP terrorists on October 7, 1985; they held passengers hostage while negotiating the release of other terrorists.

NOVEMBER 23: Libyan Abu Nidal terrorists skyjack an Egyptair 737 bound from Athens to Cairo. The plane is forced to land at Luga, Malta, where it is stormed by an Egyptian anti-terrorist task force. The task force blows open the cargo doors, killing all fifty-nine persons, including the skyjackers, except for one terrorist.

DECEMBER 11: The Unabomber, a lone terrorist, strikes for the first time, planting a bomb outside a Sacramento, California computer store, where owner Hugh Scrutton picks it up and is blown to bits.

DECEMBER 15: African National Congress (ANC) terrorists plant a land mine in Transvaal, South Africa, which kills six whites, prompting an angry warning from President P. W. Botha to officials of Zimbabwe.

DECEMBER 23: African National Congress (ANC) terrorists cause a bomb explosion at a shopping center in Durban, South Africa, that kills six whites and injures forty-eight others.

1986

FEBRUARY 6: Vice admiral Cristobal Colon, a descendant of Christopher Columbus, is murdered by ETA terrorists who throw grenades at his car in Madrid, Spain.

FEBRUARY 6: A terrorist bomb injures twenty-one persons in Paris, France.

FEBRUARY 14: Jean-Claude "Baby Doc" Duvalier, dictator of Haiti, flees the country after looting government coffers of more than $400 million. Duvalier's reign, and that of his father, Francois "Papa Doc" Duvalier, begun in 1957, has been a horrific dictatorship supported by the Duvaliers' terrorist organization, the Ton Ton Macoutes. The terrorist regime is profiled in the 1967 film, *The Comedians,* a far-fetched drama with Richard Burton and Elizabeth Taylor who gather their tourist friends on Haiti to plot the overthrow of the Duvaliers.

Francois "Papa Doc" Duvalier established the terrorist police, Ton Ton Macoutes, who were overthrown when Jean-Claude "Baby Doc" Duvalier fled Haiti on February 14, 1986.

MARCH 2: Zafr al-Masri, mayor of Nablus, is fatally shot by Palestinian terrorists.

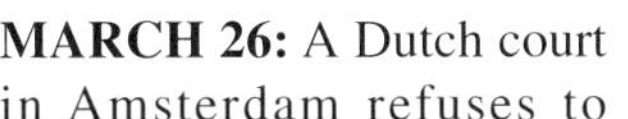

MARCH 26: A Dutch court in Amsterdam refuses to extradict IRA terrorist Gerard Kelly on the grounds that his crimes are political. The Netherlands is accused, as have been Germany, Italy and other European countries, of being intimidated by terrorists into equivocational postures, in order to avoid retaliation.

APRIL 3: PFLP terrorists plant a bomb on board TWA Flight 840, flying from Athens to Cairo. The explosion blows a hole in the side of the 727 jet and kills four Americans, including an infant, and injures nine others. May Mansur, the widow of a Syrian militant leader, is held responsible. Mansur was a passenger on the flight and present at the time of the explosion. She denies any responsibility.

APRIL 5: A bomb blast at the La Belle disco in West Berlin, Germany, kills a U.S. soldier and a Turkish woman, injuring 204 others. Intercepted messages from the Libyan Embassy in East Berlin indicate that Libya is responsible for the explosion.

APRIL 17: Two British citizens and a U.S. citizen are kidnapped and slain in Beirut, Lebanon by Libyan terrorists after the U.S. and England bomb Libya in response to the Libyan bombing of the La Belle disco in West Berlin on April 5, 1986.

MAY 3: The Liberation Tigers of Tamil Eelam (LTTE) explode a bomb on board an Air Lanka Tristar in Colombo, killing seventeen. The attack is aimed at pressuring Margaret Thatcher, Prime Minister of England, into aiding the Sri Lankan government.

MAY 3: Seamus McElwaine and Kevin Lynch, two IRA terrorists, are shot in an ambush in Dublin, Ireland, as they are about to set off an 800-pound boobytrap bomb.

MAY 7: The Central Telegraph office in Colombo, Sri Lanka, is bombed by LTTE terrorists. Fourteen persons are killed and 100 more are injured.

JUNE 9: Rival black groups riot at the Crossroads, South Africa, leaving twenty dead, hundreds wounded and 20,000 homeless.

JUNE 14: A car bomb explosion in Durban, South Africa, kills three people and injures another sixty-nine.

JUNE 23: IRA terrorist Patrick Magee is sentenced to thirty-five years in a British prison for bombing a hotel in Brighton, England, on October 12, 1984, in an attempt to assassinate Prime Minister Margaret Thatcher and her entire cabinet.

JUNE 26: Seven tourists are killed in a terrorist attack by the Sendero Liminoso aboard a train en route to the Inca ruins of Machu Picchu in Cuzco, Peru.

AUGUST 18: Blacks protesting evictions of rent boycotters clash with police in Soweto, South Africa, which leads to rioting, causing twenty-one deaths and more than 100 injuries.

SEPTEMBER 5: Four Abu Nidal terrorists skyjack a Karachi Pan American B-747 carrying 389 passengers. The crew escapes and the plane immobilized, and the terrorists murder twenty of the passengers before they are seized and imprisoned.

SEPTEMBER 7: General Augusto Pinochet Ugarte, president of Chile, is riding in a car when he is assaulted by insurgents armed with grenades, guns, and rockets. Ugarte survives but six bodyguards die.

SEPTEMBER 17: A bomb blast in a crowded department store in Paris kills five persons and injures another sixty-one people. The Lebanese Armed Revolutionary Faction (FARL) has carried out the attack in order to force the French to release their imprisoned leader, Georges Abdallah.

OCTOBER 15: Palestinian terrorists throw hand grenades in front of the Wailing Wall in Jerusalem, killing one person and injuring sixty-nine people.

OCTOBER 27: Two children, Samuel Johnson, Jr., and Emmanuel Dalieh, are abducted at a parade in Harper City, Liberia, Africa, for sacrificial use by a murder cult led by Joshua Bedell and Samuel Cummings. The terrorists will be tracked down, convicted and sentenced to death.

DECEMBER 25: An Iraqi plane is skyjacked while en route from Baghdad to Amman. It crashes and sixty-two persons are killed.

1987

JANUARY 16: Ecuadorian President Leon Febres Cordero Rivadeira is abducted by terrorists who demand the release of insurgent General Vargas. Cordero will be set free when the general is released.

JANUARY 20: Terry Waite, a special envoy of the Archbishop of Canterbury, meets in Beirut, Lebanon, with terrorists who have kidnapped Terry Anderson in 1985, in an effort to negotiate his release and that of others. Instead, Waite himself is taken hostage by the treacherous Islamic Jihad terrorists.

JANUARY 24: Four professors at the University College in Beirut, Lebanon (Alaan Steen, Mithileshwar Singh, Jesse Turner, and Robert Polhill), are kidnapped by Islamic Jihad, working hand-in-glove with Yasir Arafat and his PLO, demanding that the U.S. acknowledge Palestinian rights.

MARCH 20: Licio Giorgieri, chief air force general in charge of space research for Italy, is slain by Italian terrorists.

JULY 24: Hussein Ali Hariri, a Lebanese Shiite terrorist, skyjacks a plane to Geneva, Switzerland, where he demands the release of a Lebanese terrorist held in West Germany. One French passenger is killed, and the rest escape when Swiss police storm the plane, taking Hariri prisoner.

JULY 30: Sixty-eight persons are injured in the terrorist bombing of a military barracks in Johannesburg, South Africa.

JULY 31: Iranian pilgrims to Mecca, some of these being terrorists, clash with Saudi Arabian security forces, resulting in riots that leave 400 dead.

AUGUST 18: A bomb explodes in the Sri Lankan parliament building, killing one person and injuring fifteen others.

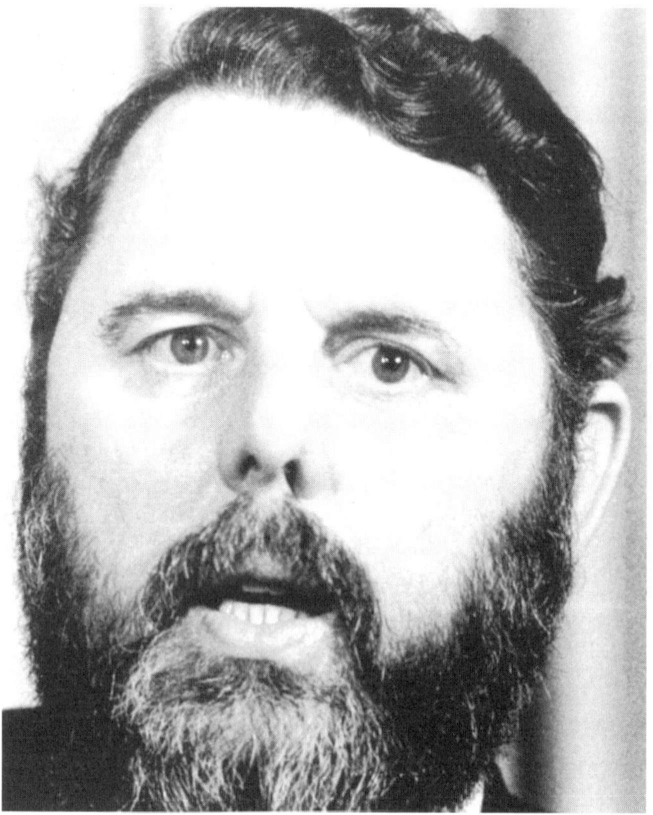

Terry Waite, sent to negotiate the release of American Terry Anderson, kidnapped in 1985, was himself kidnapped by double-dealing Islamic Jihad terrorists on January 20, 1987.

NOVEMBER 8: Remembrance Day ceremonies in Northern Ireland are disrupted by a bomb blast that kills eleven persons and wounds sixty-one others.

DECEMBER 3: David Lane and Bruce Carroll Pierce, leaders of the neo-Nazi terrorist group, the Order, are convicted of murdering Denver talk show host Alan Berg and each receives a 150-year prison sentence.

DECEMBER 9: Palestinian terrorists instigate anti-Israeli rioting on the East Bank and in the Gaza Strip in which two dozen Palestinians will be killed by January 9, 1988. Nine of the terrorists will be identified and deported.

DECEMBER 23: Zino Scioni, falsely claiming to carry a bomb, skyjacks a KLM B-737 en route to Milan from Amsterdam. Holding the ninety-seven people aboard hostage, Scioni demands $1 million ransom. He will be arrested four hours later.

1988

FEBRUARY 10: More than 200 persons are killed and thousands injured during riots between rival factions, fueled by terrorists on either side, in Bangladesh during the nationwide elections in 4,376 villages.

MARCH 6: The British Special Air Service (SAS) shoots and kills three suspected IRA terrorists in Gibraltar as they are about to detonate a car bomb with a remote control device.

MARCH 29: Dulcie September, European agent of the outlawed African National Congress, is fatally shot near her office in Paris, France, by terrorists.

APRIL 5: Eight Arab terrorists skyjack a Kuwaiti B-747 flying from Thailand to Kuwait, demanding the release of Arab terrorists imprisoned in Kuwait. Two passengers will be released and others freed as the plane lands in Iran, Cyprus, and Algeria, where the skyjackers will be allowed to leave the country.

APRIL 7: Albie Sachs, a well-known South African lawyer opposed to apartheid, is the target of an assassination attempt when he is critically wounded by a car bomb in Maputo, Mozambique.

APRIL 12: Yu Kikumura, a Japanese citizen who is thought to be a leader of the terrorist Red Army, is arrested in New Jersey with three pipe bombs in his possession.

APRIL 14: Five persons are killed in a Naples, Italy, nightclub which caters to U.S. servicemen, when a car packed with explosives is driven into the club by Junzo Okudaira, a suicidal member of the Red Army terrorist group

APRIL 23: A truck carrying 300 pounds of TNT explodes in a crowded marketplace in Tripoli, Lebanon, killing scores of people.

AUGUST 22: At least 5,000 persons are killed during a week of ethnic violence between the majority Hutu tribe and the smaller Tutsi tribe of Burundi, many of the clashes prompted by terrorists on both sides.

The wreckage of Pan Am Flight 103, which was blown up over Lockerbie, Scotland on December 21, 1988 by PFLP terrorists, killing all 259 people on board and another eleven persons on the ground; the terrorists would hide out for years in Libya, protected by terrorist dictator Muammar Qaddafi.

SEPTEMBER 24: Raimundo Alves da Conceicao skyjacks a Brazilian B-737 en route from Porto Velho to Rio de Janeiro. He shoots the co-pilot, and, when landing and attempting to flee to another, smaller plane, is himself shot and wounded by police.

DECEMBER 21: Pan Am Flight 103, a 747 jumbo jet en route to New York with 259 passengers, blows up over Lockerbie, Scotland, after PFLP terrorists plant a bomb aboard, apparently at Frankfurt, Germany. All on board, as well as eleven persons on the ground, are killed in one of the worst terrorist attacks on record.

1989

JANUARY 24: Theodore Bundy, who has been convicted of the 1978 murders of Lisa Levy, twenty, and Kimberly Leach, twelve (and, according to best reports a terrorist killer who abducted and murdered as many as ten to twenty more young girls and women from 1974 to 1978 and has fought off his execution through eleven years of appeals) is executed in Florida's electric chair.

JANUARY 31: Alvin Antonio Siu, a Nicaraguan Indian exiled in Colombia, skyjacks a Costa Rican Ace Airline B-727 carrying 122 people to Medellin, Colombia, by threatening to set a passenger on fire. An anti-terrorist squad storms the plane in Costa Rica and captures Siu.

FEBRUARY 7: Sources in the international terrorist movement report that Ahmed Jibril, a former Syrian military intelligence officer and head of the PFLP, at the urging of Libyan strongman Muammar Qudaffi (who seeks revenge for the U.S. air raids in his country in 1986), is responsible for ordering Pan Am's Flight 103 blown up. The PFLP denies the allegation, although best information confirms the PFLP as responsible. A subsequent report has it that Iran paid $1 million to Jibril to destroy Flight 103.

JULY 5: Sikh terrorists skyjack an Indian Airlines A-300 Airbus carrying 225 passengers from Srinagar, Kashmir to New Delhi, to Pakistan. The terrorists have threatened to blow up the plane unless their demands for ransom money and release of prisoners are not met. They are later taken into custody.

NOVEMBER 16: Terrorists of the Martí National Liberation Front (FMLN) shoot to death six Jesuit priests, as well as a cook and her daughter in José Simeón Cañas University of Central America in San Salvador, El Salvador.

NOVEMBER 21: Twelve members of a U.S. Special Forces group (Green Berets) are trapped in a San Salvador hotel and are forced, under threat of death, to surrender to FMLN terrorists.

NOVEMBER 27: FMLN terrorists seize several homes of U.S. diplomats in San Salvador, causing the U.S. to order all U.S. citizens to leave El Salvador.

NOVEMBER 27: An Avianca Airlines jetliner explodes over Colombia, killing 110, including some persons on the ground. Government officials state that the explosion has been the result of a bomb planted by drug-trafficking terrorists.

NOVEMBER 30: Terrorists plant a bomb beneath the presidential palace in Manila, as well as seizing several radio stations in an attempted coup but they fail.

DECEMBER 6: In the worst mass killing in Canadian history, lone terrorist Marc Lepine, armed with a hunting rifle, shoots and kills fourteen women (six in one classroom) on the campus of the University of Montreal, before killing himself. Police state the following day that Lepine has left a note in which he states that women have ruined his life.

DECEMBER 6: Drug-trafficking terrorists defying government efforts to eradicate their operations explode a half ton of dynamite in front of the Administrative Security building in Bogatá, Colombia, killing sixty persons and seriously injuring another 1,000 persons.

DECEMBER 16: Judge Robert Vance of the U.S. Court of Appeals for the 11th District, is killed in his surburban Birmingham, Alabama, home when he opens a package that explodes a pipe bomb, one reportedly sent by white supremacists angered at Vance's recent rulings against them.

DECEMBER 18: White supremacists (reportedly Ku Klux Klan members), kill Robert Robinson, a black alderman and lawyer who has represented the NAACP, in Savannah, Georgia, by sending him a pipe bomb.

DECEMBER 18: Two unexploded bombs are defused in the federal court building in Atlanta, Georgia, reportedly planted by KKK terrorists.

DECEMBER 19: Bomb experts defuse a bomb planted in the NAACP headquarters in Jacksonville, Florida, reportedly sent by white supremacists. The FBI claims that the bombs which have killed Judge Robert Vance in Birmingham, Alabama, and black lawyer Robert Robinson in Savannah, Georgia, along with those found in a federal court building in Atlanta, Georgia, and the Jacksonville bomb, are all linked through "hard forensic evidence."

1990

JANUARY 19: Nine soldiers (three officers and six enlisted soldiers), one of whom is still being sought, are indicted in El Salvador, for the murders of six Jesuit priests and two others on November 16, 1989 in San Salvador. All are reported members of the terrorist group, FMLN.

FEBRUARY 4: Palestinian terrorists attack a bus carrying Israeli academics and their wives en route to Cairo on the main highway east of the city, killing eight and wounding another seventeen persons.

FEBRUARY 11: Nelson Mandela, imprisoned (in 1964) in South Africa, for more than twenty-seven years for plotting to overthrow the government and for terrorist activities, is released. He urges pressure be applied against white minority government.

MARCH 25: Police arrest Julio Gonzalez in New York City, charging him with deliberately setting fire to a Bronx social club, where eighty-seven persons perish from burning or asphyxiation in a blazing inferno.

MARCH 27: William Robinson, a U.S. missionary, is slain in the Israeli-designated "security zone" in Lebanon by Palestinian terrorists to deter the establishment of Israeli settlements.

APRIL 9: IRA terrorists explode a bomb which wrecks two vehicles of a British army patrol on a country road near Downpatrick, County Down, killing four British soldiers.

APRIL 10: Arab terrorists release three hostages—a French woman, her Belgian companion, and daughter, who had been kidnapped on a Mediterranean cruise two years earlier.

APRIL 22: Robert Polhill, a fifty-five-year-old American taken hostage by pro-Iranian terrorists two years earlier, is released in Beirut, Lebanon.

APRIL 30: Frank Herbert Reed, a fifty-seven-year-old American abducted by Arab terrorists almost four years earlier, is released in Beirut, Lebanon.

MAY 13: Communist terrorists shoot and kill two U.S. airmen near Clark Air Force Base in the Philippines.

MAY 20: An mentally unbalanced Israeli in the occupied Gaza Strip, opens fire on Arab construction workers, killing seven before being subdued.

MAY 21: Islamic leader Maulvi Mohammed Farooq, forty-five, is assassinated in Srinagar, Kashmir.

MAY 30: PLO terrorists attempt raids along the coast of Israel, but Israeli troops wreck the attacking speedboats, killing four and capturing twelve of the raiders. Yasir Arafat denies PLO involvement.

JULY 20: The London Stock Exchange is bombed by IRA terrorists, who give warning, allowing the safe evacuation of more than 300 persons; no one is injured.

JULY 24: IRA terrorists are blamed for the explosion of a bomb that kills three policemen in a car and a Catholic nun near Armagh in Northern Ireland.

JULY 30: An IRA bomb claims the life of Ian Gow, fifty-three, a Conservative member of the British parliament who has repeatedly condemned the IRA terrorists.

AUGUST 1: Muslim terrorists in Trinidad, after seizing Prime Minister Arthur N. R. Robinson and others, surrender to local authorities, releasing their hostages.

Brian Keenan, center, who was held hostage in Lebanon by Islamic terrorists, is shown at the time of his release on August 25, 1990.

AUGUST 25: Brian Keenan, fifty-two, a Belfast-born teacher who has been held for four years as a hostage in Lebanon, is released by Arab terrorists.

SEPTEMBER 9: President of the Republic of Liberia, Samuel K. Doe, thirty-eight, who had murdered his predecessor in 1980, is himself assassinated. His mutilated body will later be put on display.

SEPTEMBER 28: A Filipino general and fifteen soldiers are convicted of killing Benigno S. Aquino, Jr., in 1983, and are all sent to prison for life.

OCTOBER 22: The White Aryan Resistance, a group of supremacist terrorists are found liable by a Portland, Oregon, jury of inciting the 1988 beating death of an Ethiopian man, and assesses damages against the leaders in the amount of $12.5 million, along with the two skinheads responsible for the beating.

1991

JANUARY 14: Two PLO leaders are shot dead in Tunis, along with a bodyguard, by rival Arab terrorists.

FEBRUARY 7: IRA terrorists fire three rounds at 10 Downing Street, residence of the British Prime Minister, but no one is injured.

FEBRUARY 16: Drug-trafficking terrorists explode a car bomb in Medellín, Colombia, killing twenty-two and injuring another 140 persons near a bullfighting ring.

FEBRUARY 18: IRA terrorists bomb two railway stations, Victoria and Paddington terminals in London, England, killing one person and injuring another forty people.

MAY 13: A South African judge in Johannesburg brands as a terrorist Winnie Mandela, wife of Nelson Mandela, leader of the outlawed African National Congress, finding her guilty of kidnapping four youths, who had been taken to her home and beaten for not supporting her political cause. She is sentenced to six years in prison the following day.

MAY 21: Mengistu Haile Mariam, president and dictator of Ethiopia, who has led a hard-line Marxist government employing terrorism, flees the country as rebels approach the capital of Addis Ababa.

MAY 26: An Austrian Boeing 767-300 jetliner explodes over the jungle in Thailand, killing all 223 persons on board; a terrorist bomb is suspected but remains unproven.

JULY 31: Six Lithuanian border guards are slain by terrorists, who challenge Lithuania's claim of independence from the Soviet Union.

AUGUST 8: Pro-Iranian terrorists release hostage John McCarthy, a British journalist.

AUGUST 11: Edward Austin Tracy, an American who has been held hostage for five years by Lebanese terrorists, is released in Beirut. Only hours earlier, French hostage Jèrome Leyraud, abducted a week before, has been released by the same terrorist group.

AUGUST 30: Federal agents storm the Federal Correctional Institution at Talladega, Alabma, freeing nine hostages from prison inmate terrorists and capturing 121 rebelling prisoners.

SEPTEMBER 13: Police in Phoenix, Arizona, arrest six persons, charging them with the terrorist slayings of nine persons at a Buddhist temple outside of Phoenix.

SEPTEMBER 24: Pro-Iranian terrorists release British hostage Jack Mann, seventy-seven and in poor health, to Syrian officials. Mann has been held captive for more than two years.

SEPTEMBER 30: Colonel Guillermo Benevides Moreno, a Salvadoran officer, is found guilty of ordering the terrorist slayings of six Jesuit priests, their cook and her daughter in 1989.

NOVEMBER 4: The trial of Arab terrorist El Sayyid Nosair opens in New York City. Nosair shot and killed former head of the Jewish Defense League, Rabbi Meir Kahane, outside a New

York hotel in November 1990. Nosair will be found guilty only of assault with a deadly weapon and be sentenced to a term of seven to twenty-two years in prison.

1992

JANUARY 4: Members of a black teenage gang who terrorized a tourist family on a New York subway platform, killing one, are sentenced to twenty-five years in prison.

JANUARY 5-6: IRA terrorists attack civilians working at a British army base in Ulster, with a bomb that kills eight persons and wounds another six people as they are riding home.

JANUARY 10: IRA terrorists explode a bomb less than 300 yards from 10 Downing Street, the prime minister's residence in London, England. No one is injured.

JANUARY 15: Joseph Doherty, IRA terrorist and convicted killer of a British soldier, who has taken refuge in the U.S., is ordered deported back to Great Britain after a court rules that he is not entitled to political asylum.

FEBRUARY 17: Serial killer, cannibal and terrorist, Jeffrey Dahmer, who has claimed insanity in the torture and sex murders of fifteen victims, mostly homosexual youths in Milwaukee, Wisconsin, is sentenced to fifteen consecutive life terms.

FEBRUARY 19: IRA terrorist Joseph Doherty, convicted in 1980 of killing a British soldier and jailed in the U.S. in 1983 after fleeing to that country, is deported to Great Britain, his claim for political asylum earlier denied.

MARCH 17: A powerful car bomb explodes at the Israeli embassy in Buenos Aires, Argentina, killing at least fourteen persons and injuring another 252 people. The bomb has been planted by Islamic terrorists.

APRIL 10: IRA terrorists explode a bomb inside of a van parked in London's financial district, killing three and wounding ninety-one others. A second IRA bomb exploding in northwest London causes no injuries.

APRIL 29-MAY 1: Three days of widespread violence in minority sections of Los Angeles that claims fifty lives, injures thousands and causes millions of dollars in damages, erupts after a jury acquits four white LAPD officers charged in the terror beating of black motorist Rodney G. King.

An IRA bomb blew out every window in London's Commercial Union Tower, killing three people and wounding another ninety-one persons on April 10, 1992.

JUNE 8: Atef Bseiso, considered to be a PLO terrorist leader by the Mossad (Israeli intelligence), is shot dead outside of his hotel in Paris, France.

JUNE 29: Mohammed Boudiaf, the seventy-three-year-old president of Algeria (installed in January 1992, following a coup), is assassinated, shot in the back and head by terrorists as he delivers a speech.

JULY 19: Mafia terrorists kill Paolo Borsellino, fifty-four, an Italian prosecutor responsible for convicting Mafia members, by blowing him up with a bomb when he visits his mother in Palermo, Sicily.

JULY 28: Giovanni Lizzio, forty-seven, who heads investigations into Mafia extortions, is slain by Mafia terrorists in Catania, Sicily.

AUGUST 13: ABC-TV news producer David Kaplan, forty-five, is shot in the back and killed in Sarajevo, by terrorist snipers firing on a caravan carrying Milan Panic, prime minister of Yugoslavia, into Sarajevo.

AUGUST 12: An Amtrak train is derailed near Newport News, Virginia, with seventy-four passengers injured. Federal investigators state that criminal vandalism to a switch has caused the wreck.

AUGUST 25: Neo-Nazi terrorists bomb a hotel housing refugees seeking asylum from communism in the Baltic seaport of Rostock, Germany, in an effort to drive out all foreigners. No serious injuries occur.

Neo-Nazis bombed a hotel in Rostock, East Germany, to drive out aliens seeking asylum from communism on August 25, 1992.

AUGUST 31: Randall "Randy: Weaver, forty-four-year-old member of a white supremacist group, and a fugitive on gun charges, surrenders after a long siege to federal agents at Ruby Ridge in northern Idaho, where William Degan, who is a deputy marshal, Weaver's wife Vicki, and son, Samuel, have been killed. Weaver is a hero of terrorist hate groups in the far American West because of his defiance of gun laws.

SEPTEMBER 7: Twenty-four protestors are machine gunned to death as they flee Ciskei troops in South Africa where terrorist tactics are enacted to support oppressive military rule.

SEPTEMBER 13: Abimael Gutzmán Reynoso, leader of the Shining Path terrorist organization of Peru, is captured after a twelve-year search, along with about a dozen of his top aides. Reynoso's decade-long terror campaign has cost 25,000 lives and $22 billion in damages.

OCTOBER 3: To mark the second anniversary of Germany's reunification, more than 1,000 neo-Nazis march through the streets of Arnstadt, Germany and another 500 neo-Nazis march through downtown Dresden, Germany, shouting "Foreigners Out!" and "Germany for Germans!"

OCTOBER 9: An engineer in a Russian nuclear plant is caught just before leaving for Moscow to sell to terrorists 1,538 kilos of highly enriched uranium (HEU).

OCTOBER 14: Ex-hostages Joseph Cicippio and David Jacobsen file suit against the government of Iran, claiming that their abductions and others were directed and financed by Iran in order to force the U.S. into freeing frozen Iranian assets.

1993

JANUARY 8: A European inquiry board reports that more than 20,000 Muslim women in Bosnia and Hercegovina have been raped by mostly Serbian terrorists in an effort to drive them from their homes.

JANUARY 8: Hakija Turajlic, one of three Bosnian deputy prime ministers, is assassinated after a U.N. vehicle is halted. Serbian military leaders later apologize, saying that an over-anxious Serbian draftee responsible for the killing has been detained.

FEBRUARY 24: Mobs in Mogadishu spread terror for hours, creating widespread destruction and looting, along with firing guns for more than six hours in challenge to the presence of U.N. peacekeeping forces, which eventually return fire.

FEBRUARY 26: A powerful bomb explodes in the parking garage beneath the World Trade Center in New York City. Six persons are killed and more than 1,000 are injured in the worst terrorist attack on U.S. soil to date. Four Islamic terrorists, and their leader, Ramzi Ahmed Yousef, will later be sent to prison for life.

MARCH 12: Terrorists kill 232 persons and injure hundreds more with several bomb explosions in Bombay's financial district. Fifty persons, mostly brokers, are killed at the Stock Exchange.

MARCH 17: Terrorists set off a bomb in the central residential area of Calcutta, India, killing forty-five persons and injuring dozens more, when two apartment buildings are leveled by the blast.

MARCH 30: Two Serbian terrorists are sentenced to death by firing squad on orders of a military tribunal that has found them guilty of mass rape and genocide against Muslims.

APRIL 1: U.S. indicts four Palestinian terrorists on charges of plotting to blow up the Israeli Embassy in Washington, D.C., as part of a terror campaign against Jews in the U.S. and abroad by the Abu Nidal network.

APRIL 12: Neo-Nazi racist Larry Wayne Shoemake terrorizes a Jackson, Mississippi mall by invading a restaurant with an arsenal and randomly shooting black passersby, killing one and wounding seven others before police arrive and a gun battle ensues. Shoemake is killed (or committed suicide) as the restaurant catches fire.

APRIL 17: After the four LAPD officers in the Rodney King beating have been acquitted by a California jury, a federal trial has ensued against the four men and two of these, Sgt. Stacey C. Koon, and Officer Laurence M. Powell are found guilty by a federal jury, the other two officers being acquitted.

LAPD Sergeant Stacey Koon was found guilty of beating Rodney King on April 17, 1993.

APRIL 19: The Branch Davidian cult compound outside of Waco, Texas, is stormed by federal officers, battering holes in buildings and injecting tear gas. Cult members set fire to the buildings, while cult leader David Koresh, who has held many of his followers captive through terrorist tactics (his heavily armed aides reportedly threatening to kill any deserters) dies along with seventy-two followers in the inferno, ending the 51-day federal siege. Koresh and some of his top aides are found dead with bullets in their heads, apparent suicides. U.S. Attorney General Janet Reno, along with the FBI agents in charge, are severely criticized for mishandling the Waco siege and attack.

APRIL 24: An IRA bomb explodes in London's financial district, killing one person and wounding forty-four others.

MAY 15: A terrorist takes six children hostage in a Paris nursery, but he is killed by French police who catch him asleep. The children are rescued without injury.

MAY 22: An Egyptian court sentences six Muslim terrorists to death and two others to life sentences for attacks on tourists and plotting to assassinate Egyptian officials.

MAY 27: A terrorist bomb explodes outside of an art gallery in Florence, Italy, killing six persons and injuring dozens more, as well as causing damage to priceless art works.

MAY: Lithuanian police raid a bank vault and discover a rod of beryllium with about 150 grams of high enriched uranium (HEU), which is apparently intended for sale to terrorists planning on the construction of a nuclear bomb.

JUNE 22: The Unabomber sends a bomb to geneticist Charles Epstein at the University of California. The scientist losing several fingers when the bomb blows up.

JUNE 24: Federal agents seize eight Muslim terrorists in New York City before they can execute their planned campaign of political bombings and assassinations.

JUNE 29: Two Russian seaman are apprehended after stealing 1.8 kilos of highly enriched uranium and before they can sell the HEU to terrorists planning on constructing a nuclear bomb.

JULY 2: FBI agents arrest Omar Abdel Rahman, Islamic fundamentalist leader and suspected organizer of terrorist operations, outside of a mosque in Brooklyn, New York. His followers have been linked to bombing plots.

JULY 17: Egypt hangs five more Islamic terrorists who have been found guilty of bombings and mass killings, a government campaign that has shut down terrorist operations of militant fundamentalists.

JULY 27: Terrorists (reportedly Red Brigadists) explode a car bomb in downtown Milan, Italy, killing at least five persons. Another bomb exploding in the center of Rome, Italy, injures twenty-four persons, and damages the basilica of St. John Lateran, the Pope's See.

AUGUST 4: A U.S. federal judge sentences Sgt. Stacey C. Koon, and Officer Laurence M. Powell who have been found guilty by a federal jury of the terrorist beating of black motorist Rodney G. King to two-and-a-half years in prison. The judge explains the lenient sentence by stating that King had provoked the police violence.

AUGUST 15: Gold miners invading Brazil's Yanomami Indian reservation, kill seventy-three Indians and terrorize whole communities in the nation's largest massacre of the century.

AUGUST 18: Four are killed and fifteen others are injured when Islamic terrorists attack the new Egyptian security chief (he is wounded and survives) in downtown Cairo, Egypt.

NOVEMBER 7: Three Russian naval officers steal 4.5 kilos of highly enriched uranium (HEU), apparently intent on selling this to terrorists who plan to construct a nuclear bomb. The thieves and fuel are located by authorities six months later.

1994

MARCH 4: Four Islamic terrorists responsible for the bombing of the World Trade Center in New York City on February 26, 1993, are sent to prison for life. Charges will be brought against their leader, a near-blind religious fanatic, Ramzi Ahmed Yousef, mastermind behind the attack which has killed six persons and injured more than 1,000 others.

MAY 10: Police in Bavaria discover 5.6 grams of pure plutonium-239 in the garage of a professional criminal who has links to the KGB and Bulgarian terrorists. It is believed that this fuel was to be used by the terrorist for the construction of a nuclear bomb.

JUNE 13: German police seize 800 milligrams of highly enriched uranium (HEU) which has been smuggled from Prague to Bavaria.

AUGUST 10: Police in Munich, Germany, intercept at the airport a suitcase shipped from Moscow, one containing lithium-6 and nuclear fuel which are apparently intended for terrorists planning on building a nuclear bomb.

DECEMBER 10: Advertising executive Thomas Mosser opens a package delivered to his North Caldwell, New Jersey home and is killed when its contents, a bomb, goes off. This terrorist act is attributed to the Unabomber.

DECEMBER 14: Investigators in Prague, Czechoslovakia, discover 2.72 kilos of highly enriched uranium (HEU) in the back seat of a parked car. They will find another kilo of the same shipment in January 1995, all of this fuel apparently intended for delivery to terrorists planning on constructing a nuclear bomb.

1995

JANUARY 22: Two Palestinian terrorists kill eighteen Israeli soldiers, a civilian, and themselves by exploding a bomb outside a military camp in central Israel. The bomb also injures sixty-five other persons. The Islamic Jihad terrorist group claims responsibility for the bombing.

JANUARY 30: A terrorist car bomb explodes on a crowded Algiers street, killing forty-two persons and injuring another 300 people.

FEBRUARY 6: Twelve Islamic terrorists are tried in U.S. federal court in New York for the 1993 bombing of the World Trade Center. Siddig Ibrahim Siddig Ali, one of the accused, changes his plea from not guilty to guilty, saying that the Sheik Omar Abdel Rahman, one of his fellow defendants and for whom he has served as bodyguard and translator, has played a significant role in the bombing conspiracy. In addition to the UN building in New York, Siddig Ali tells the court, the terrorists had planned the destruction of an FBI office, a bridge and two tunnels.

FEBRUARY 7: Ramzi Ahmed Yousef, the Islamic terrorist leader who has masterminded the 1993 bombing of the World Trade Center in New York, is arrested in Islamabad, Pakistan, and will be flown to New York the following day to face trial. He will, on February 9, 1995, plead not guilty to eleven counts.

MARCH 20: Members of the Aum Shinri Kyo, a fanatical terrorist organization and offshoot of the Japanese criminal society, Yakuza, plant several packages inside the Tokyo subway system which emit a powerful nerve gas (sarin, which can paralyze the central nervous system and cause death) that kills twelve persons and injures another 5,500 people. A massive hunt ensues as police search for the cult leaders.

APRIL 2: The Islamic Resistance Movement of Hamas explodes a bomb in Gaza that kills eight persons and wounds another thirty. Police report that the terrorists were assembling a bomb that went off by accident.

APRIL 4: Francisco Duran, twenty-six, of Colorado Springs, Colorado, is convicted of attempting to assassinate President William Clinton by firing several shots with an assault rifle at the White House in Washington, D.C., in October 1994. Duran will be convicted and, on June 29, 1995, sentenced to forty years in prison.

APRIL 9: Two suicide terrorists kill themselves, seven Israeli soldiers and an American student, and wounding another forty-five persons, mostly Israeli soldiers, when they detonate bombs in the Gaza Strip. Both Hamas and Islamic Jihad take credit for the terrorist explosions.

APRIL 19: A powerful truck bomb explodes at **9:**02 a.m., outside the Alfred P. Murrah Federal Building in Oklahoma City, Oklahoma, sheering away half the nine-story building and killing 168 men, women and children, the worst terrorist attack in U.S. history. About an hour later Timothy McVeigh, who will become the prime suspect in the bombing, is arrested near Perry, Oklahoma, for carrying concealed weapons.

APRIL 21: FBI agents charge Timothy McVeigh, in custody in Perry, Oklahoma for carrying concealed weapons, with blowing up the Murrah Building in Oklahoma City. McVeigh's cousin, Terry Nichols, is arrested the same day in Herington, Kansas, charged with aiding McVeigh in blowing up the Murrah Building.

APRIL 24: Police locate the hideout of Hideo Murai, one of the five top leaders of the terrorist cult, Aum Shinri Kyo, which is responsible for planting the nerve gas bombs that have killed twelve persons and injured thousands more on the Tokyo subway system a month earlier. Murai is the cult's chemist, who packaged the deadly sarin nerve gas. As he is being escorted from the hideout, the thirty-six-year-old Murai is fatally stabbed by Hiroyuki Yo, a South Korean.

APRIL 24: Gilbert Murray, president of the California Forestry Association, is killed in Sacramento, California, by a package bomb which was sent by the Unabomber. Murray will be the third and final fatality claimed by the terrorist. Two dozen others will be injured and maimed by bombs sent by the Unabomber.

MAY 15: At a roadblock outside of Tokyo, police apprehend Yoshihiro Inoue, head of "intelligence" for the murderous Aum Shinri Kyo cult. Officers obtain Inoue's notebook, which details timetables and numbers of passengers using Tokyo's three subway lines where the sarin gas attacks were unleashed on March 20.

MAY 16: Police and paramilitary units storm the secret compound of Aum Shinri Kyo, located at the base of Mt. Fuji. The terrorist cult is responsible for the poison gas attacks in the Tokyo subway system on March 20. Police capture, among others, the cult leader, Shoko Asahara, who is later sent to prison. With Asahara's capture Aum Shinri Kyo is no longer an effective terrorist organization.

JUNE 26: Islamic terrorists attack the limousine carrying Egyptian President Hosni Mubarak during his visit to Addis Ababa, Ethiopia. The attackers fire from rooftops, on the street and in a passing Jeep, but they fail to injure the Egyptian leader, killing two Ethiopian policemen. Two of the terrorists are killed and many passersby are wounded in the gunfight.

JULY 25: Algerian separatists, as part of a terrorist campaign, plant a bomb in a subway car of the Paris metro system; it explodes in the Latin Quarter stop, killing seven persons and wounding dozens more.

JULY 29: Leon Bor, an Israeli citizen, boards a tourist bus in Cologne, Germany, shooting the driver and holding twenty-six sightseers hostage. He randomly shoots and kills an elderly woman who identifies herself as a German. After terrorizing the passengers for several hours, Bor is shot and killed by police.

AUGUST 11: FBI director Louis Freeh suspends four Bureau officials, including agent Larry Potts, after it is disclosed that the Bureau either withheld or destroyed documents relating to the 1992 Ruby Ridge siege in Idaho in which three persons had been killed.

AUGUST 15: The Department of Justice agrees to pay $3.1 million to Randall Weaver and his daughters, who have filed a $200 million wrongful death suit against the Department for the shooting deaths of Weaver's wife Vicki and son Samuel during the FBI's 1992 siege of Randall's cabin in Idaho.

AUGUST 16: An unexploded bomb is discovered on board the high-speed train racing between Lyon and Paris, France. Forensic specialists lift a fingerprint which identifies Khaled Kelkal, an Algerian separatist leader and terrorist.

AUGUST 29: Eduard Shevardnadze, the head of Georgia, escapes an assassination attempt in Tbilisi, the capital, when a terrorist bomb explodes close to his motorcade. Shevardnadze is slightly wounded.

SEPTEMBER 19: On the recommendations of U.S. Attorney General Janet Reno and FBI director Louis Freeh, the Washington *Post* publishes the 35,000-word manifesto which has been sent by the Unabomber, in the hopes that someone will recognize the writing style of the terrorist and identify him. The manifesto is a rambling tirade of intellectual gobbldygook that essentially attacks the Industrial Revolution.

SEPTEMBER 24: Eric Borel, a sixteen-year-old French youth, enters the village of Cuers with a hunting rifle and terrorizes the town for several hours as he hunts down residents, randomly killing nine persons and wounding another eight before killing himself when he runs out of ammunition.

SEPTEMBER 28: Outside Lyon, French police and paramilitary units locate a hideout of Algerian separatists led by Khaled Kelkal, shooting it out with the terrorists, wounding one of three who are captured; Kelkal escapes.

SEPTEMBER 30: French commandos hunting for terrorist Khaled Kelkal find him waiting at a bus stop five miles outside of Lyon, France. Following a shootout, Kelkal is killed.

OCTOBER 1: Ten Islamic fundamentalist terrorists tried before a federal court in New York, are convicted of conspiracy to

Algerian terrorist Khaled Kelkal was trapped outside Lyon, France, and killed on September 30, 1995.

destroy U.S. public buildings and structures. One of their leaders, Sheik Omar Abdel Rahman, a blind Egyptian cleric and Islamic fanatic, is convicted of directing the conspiracy and attempting to assassinate Egyptian president Hosni Mubarak. El Sayyid Nosair is convicted of the 1990 murder of Rabbi Meir Kahane (he was acquitted of murder charges in a state court in 1991 and convicted at that time only of assault). The case has been won for the prosecution largely on tapes secretly recorded by undercover FBI informant, Emad Salem. One of these tapes showed four of the Islamic terrorists making a bomb by mixing diesel oil and fertilizer in a Queens, New York, garage.

OCTOBER 3: Terrorists attempt to assassinate Macedonian President Kiro Gilgorov, in Skopje, the capital, as Gilgorov is being driven to the National Parliament building. Gilgorov is seriously wounded in the head, his driver and three bystanders being killed.

OCTOBER 9: According to federal investigators, a terrorist group calling itself Sons of the Gestapo, derails an Amtrak train southwest of Phoenix, Arizona, which kills one of the twenty crew members and injures 100 of the 248 passengers.

1996

JANUARY 15: Ramzi Ahmed Yousef, Islamic terrorist and mastermind behind the bombing of the World Trade Center in New York City on February 26, 1993, a terrorist attack in which six persons had been killed and more than 1,000 others injured, is sentenced in Manhattan to life imprisonment plus 240 years. Before his sentence, Yousef screamed out a diatribe, saying: "I am a terrorist, and I am proud of it!" To federal judge Kevin Duffy, he ranted: "Your God is not Allah. You worship death and destruction." Yousef has been sentenced for two crimes—the attack on the World Trade Center and an unsuccessful plot to blow up a dozen U.S. airliners in Asia.

JANUARY: David Kaczynski, who has read the Unabomber's rambling manifesto published, in part, by the New York *Times*, finds similar writings in his mother's Lombard, Illinois home, those written by his brother, Theodore "Ted" Kaczynski. He will later inform authorities. Six months later Kaczynski will be arrested by FBI agents at his remote cabin in Montana, identified as the Unabomber and charged with the terrorist's many crimes.

FEBRUARY 17: Mass murderer and terrorist Colin Ferguson, who has acted as his own lawyer in defense of his shooting spree aboard a New York commuter train in 1993, is convicted of murdering six persons and attempting to murder twenty-two others. He is given a life sentence with no hope for parole.

MARCH 7: A bomb explodes on a bus in Beijing, China, killing two people and injuring many others. Communist authorities blame "hooligans," but others report the explosion being created by anti-Communist terrorists.

JUNE 18: After a four-hour gunfight with police in Brooklyn, Heriberto Seda surrenders to police; evidence found in Seda's apartment pinpoints him as the lone terrorist known as "Zodiac," who had, in 1990, shot four persons. Before going to prison, Seda confesses, saying he has been moved to murder by a "sudden urge."

JUNE 25: Sentries posted on the roof of Khobar Towers in Dhahran, Saudi Arabia spot two men positioning a tanker truck in an adjacent lot, parking it next to a chain-link fence, eighty feet distant from the Towers. The sentries, suspecting sabotage, conduct a rapid evacuation of the top three floors, but within four minutes, a tremendous explosion takes place, blowing away the front of the building and damaging five other nearby structures. Nineteen U. S. Air Force men, members of the 4404th Wing, were killed and hundreds more injured by flying debris. The American servicemen were part of Operation Southern Watch which had been flying sorties over Iraq to enforce UN sanctions. The bomb used by the terrorists went off with the power of 20,000 pounds of TNT, leaving a crater thirty-five feet deep and eighty-five feet wide. On June 4, 2000, Ahmad Behbahani, an Iranian-born terrorist, told a "60 Minutes" reporter that he had been responsible for orchestrating the Khobar Towers explosion, as well as the 1988 destruction of Pan Am Flight 103 over Lockerbie, Scotland, in which 270 people were murdered. Behbanhani was later exposed by the FBI and CIA to be a fraud; two Libyan terrorists were by then identified as the Lockerbie killers.

The remains of Khobar Towers in Dhahran, Saudi Arabia, blasted by an Islamic terrorist bomb that killed nineteen U. S. airmen on June 25, 1996.

JULY 17: TWA Flight 800, a jumbo 747 jetliner, just after taking off, blows up over the ocean off Long Island, with all 230 persons on board killed. It will later be claimed that the airplane was downed by a missile, fired accidentally by a U.S. military training plane or by terrorists from shore or a ship at sea.

JULY 27: At **1:**25 a.m., Atlanta's Centennial Park is rocked by a pipe bomb explosion which kills one and injures another 112 persons. Richard Jewell, a guard, earlier reported a suspicious knapsack placed in the area where hundreds of persons were dancing to rock music and helped other guards clear the area just before the explosion. Jewell is, at first, hailed as a hero, but he later becomes the chief suspect of the FBI.

OCTOBER 26: The Department of Justice officially announces that Richard Jewell is no longer a suspect in the bombing of Atlanta's Centennial Park. Jewell's life has been thoroughly disrupted and he has been all but charged as being the terrorist bomber by the nation's press.

NOVEMBER 5: Haitian police shoot and kill five men, one in handcuffs, in Port-au-Prince, another example of terrorist tactics by what has been described as a "constabulary of thugs." The Haitian police force, poorly trained in a crash four-month course by U.S. advisers, following the free election of President Jean Bertrand Aristide (with the help of a strong U.S. military presence in Haiti in 1994), has sadistically beaten prisoners, some to death, and indiscrimately used deadly force, firing after autos (killing a small girl riding in one).

DECEMBER 2: Martin Bryant, twenty-nine, the gunman who has terrorized a Tasmanian resort, killing thirty-five and wounding nineteen in a wild shooting spree in April 1996, is sentenced to thirty-five life terms in Hobart, Tasmania.

DECEMBER 11: The U.S. Air Force clears General Terry J. Schwalier of responsibility for the terrorist bombing of the U.S. military camp in Saudi Arabia bombed in June 1996, in which nineteen Americans were killed and another 500 wounded, saying that Schwalier had taken reasonable steps to protect the base. Terrorist Hani al-Sayegh, a Saudi citizen, is later arrested and held in Canada, as being the mastermind behind the attack.

DECEMBER 17: In the worst terrorist attack in the 133-year history of the Red Cross, five women, four being nurses, and a construction worker are shot to death while they sleep in a hostpital compound in Chechnya. Veselin Sljivancanin, a Serbian terrorist, is thought to have led the raid against the hospital.

DECEMBER 18: Túpac Amaru Revolutionary Movement (MRTA) fourteen terrorists, led by Néstor Cerpa Cartolini, swarm into the Japanese Embassy in Lima, Peru, during a party, taking 490 hostages, many of these being top-ranking international diplomats, threatening to kill the hostages unless imprisoned terrorists are released by the Peruvian government.

DECEMBER 23: MRTA terrorists occupying the Japanese Embassy in Lima, Peru, release 225 of their 490 hostages as a Christmas gesture, but keep the remainder under threat of death while they continue negotiating with Peruvian officials for the release of fellow imprisoned terrorists.

DECEMBER 28: MRTA terrorists occupying the Japanese Embassy in Lima, Peru, release more hostages but the Peruvian government will not agree to release imprisoned terrorists, offering only a safe passage to Cuba for the terrorists inside the embassy.

DECEMBER 30: Separatist Bodo terrorists explode two bombs beneath the tracks of a packed train as it leaves Kokrajhar, India, killing eighteen persons and injuring sixty more.

1997

JANUARY 16: Two bombs explode at an abortion clinic in Atlanta, Georgia, the first explosions creating only damage,

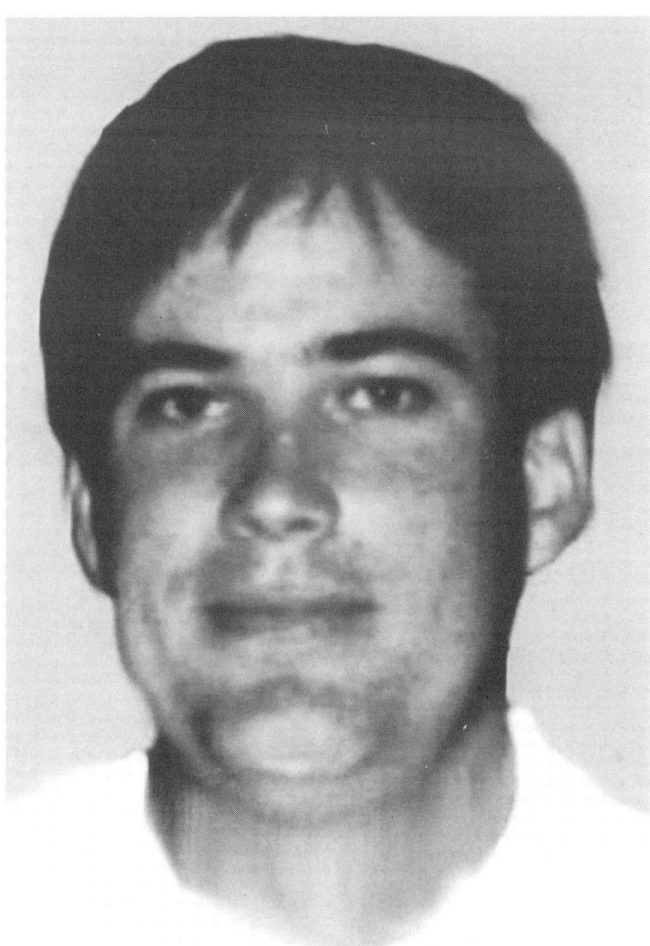

Anti-abortionist terrorist Eric Robert Rudolph reportedly set off two bombs at clinics in Atlanta, Georgia, injuring six persons; he hid for six years in the Appalachian wilderness, until captured in Murphy, N. C., while scavenging for food in a garbage can on May 31, 2003.

the second injuring six persons, including investigators and reporters covering the first explosion. Eric Robert Rudolph will become a suspect in this and the Atlanta Centennial bombings and will be widely sought by FBI and police, with a $1 million pricetag on his head.

JANUARY 20: Islamic terrorists raid a village south of Algiers, murdering thirty-six residents, decapitating some of these victims. Hours later, these same terrorists explode a car bomb outside of a cafe in Algiers, killing more than thirty persons and wounding scores more.

FEBRUARY 23: A Palestinian gunman terrorizes tourists and sight-seers on the 86th floor observation deck of New York's Empire State Building, murdering one tourist and wounding seven others before killing himself.

FEBRUARY 28: A gay and lesbian bar in Atlanta is bombed and five persons are injured; it is believed that this terrorist act is the work of the same person or persons who have bombed Atlanta's Centennial Park.

MARCH 13: A Jordanian soldier, an Islamic fanatic and terrorist, fires at Israeli school girls in the area of the Jordan Valley shared by Jordan and Israel, killing seven before his gun jams and he is seized. The soldier is allegedly imprisoned.

MARCH 21: A suicide bomber kills himself, four others and wounds dozens more when exploding a bomb in a cafe in Tel Aviv, Israel, setting back the Israeli-Palestinian peace negotiations.

APRIL 22: In a dramatic rescue, 170 Peruvian shock troops blow down doors and walls and dash into the terrorist-held Japanese Embassy in Lima, Peru, liberating all the diplomats held hostage, while killing all fourteen MRTA terrorists. Two soldiers are slain by the terrorists, along with one of the hostages.

APRIL 24: Opening statements are made in the trial of Timothy McVeigh for the 1995 terrorist bombing of the Murrah Building in Oklahoma City, Oklahoma. Within two months, McVeigh will be convicted and receive the death sentence for committing the worst terrorist act in U.S. history.

MAY 7: In the first war crimes trial dealing with the civil strife in Bosnia, Dusan Tadic, a Bosnian Serb, forty-one, is found guilty by a U.N. panel of killing two policemen and torturing and terrorizing scores of Muslim civilians in Bosnia.

JUNE 13: A federal jury in Denver, Colorado, votes uninamimously to sentence twenty-nine-year-old Timothy McVeigh to death for the 1995 terrorist bombing of the federal building in Oklahoma City, Oklahoma.

JUNE 16: IRA terrorists kill two policemen in Northern Ireland which prompts the British government to call off peace talks.

JUNE 17: Pakistani officials and Afghan tribal leaders are instrumental in capturing a fugitive who is suspected of the terrorist killings of two CIA officials outside of the agency's headquarters in Virginia, in 1993.

MRTA terrorist leader Nestor Cerpa Cartolini was killed, along with thirteen of his followers, when Peruvian troops invaded the Japanese Embassy in Lima on April 22, 1997, freeing many diplomatic hostages.

JULY 14: A U.N. tribunal sentences Bosnia-Serb terrorist Dusan Tadic to twenty years in prison for terrorist murders and "crimes against humanity" in "ethnic cleansing" terrorist campaigns in Bosnia.

JULY 15: Celebrated fashion designer Gianni Versace, fifty, is shot dead outside his mansion by serial killer Andrew P. Cunanan, in Miami Beach, Florida.

JULY 24: Andrew P. Cunanan, twenty-seven, a pronounced homosexual who has killed five persons, including gay fashion designer Gianni Versace, and terrorized the gay community nationwide (by reportedly stalking wealthy gays on an exclusive "sugar daddy" list throughout the country), is killed (either by his own hand or by police gunfire) in a deserted Miami Beach, Florida, houseboat.

JULY 30: Two terrorists carrying bombs in a crowded Jerusalem marketplace explode (on purpose or accidentally) the devices, killing themselves and thirteen other innocent passersby, along with seriously injuring another 150 persons. Hamas, an Islamic terrorist organization, takes credit for the mass murder.

JULY: The National Transportation Safety Board announces that TWA Flight 800, which blew up over the ocean on July 7, 1996, killing all 230 persons on board, has been destroyed, most probably, by an explosion in the center fuel tank, one resulting in an accident. Others still persist in believing that the plane was purposely exploded by a terrorist missile.

JULY: The FBI states that there were at least five potential members of the bombing conspiracy involved in planting the bomb that killed four Negro school girls in Birmingham, Alabama, in 1963, agents naming three living members—Robert "Dynamite Bob" Chambliss, Thomas E. Blanton, Jr., and Bobby Frank Cherry.

AUGUST 14: Timothy McVeigh, convicted terrorist bomber of the federal building in Oklahoma City, Oklahoma, in which 168 persons perished and scores were injured, is sentenced to death by a federal judge in Denver, Colorado, expediting a jury decree. After hearing his death sentence, McVeigh, cryptically quotes a dissenting opinion of the late U.S. Supreme Court justice, Louis Brandeis: "'Our government is the potent, the omnipotent teacher. For good or for ill, it teaches the whole people by its example,' That's all I have to say." Terry Nichols, who had aided McVeigh, will receive a life sentence.

AUGUST: Koichiro Tarutani, an executive of Yamaichi Securities, is murdered in Tokyo while walking home, slashed to death as if his killer(s) have employed a Sumarai sword, which is the traditional weapon of the secret Japanese criminal society, Yakuza. Tarutani has been killed by Yakuza thugs, according to one report, because he has attempted to collect on bad loans to crime boss Ryuchi Koike (who runs the Yakuza's enforcement and extortionist arm, Sokaiya). Koike has been loaned 79 million yen by Yamaichi Securities, and as much as 30 billion yen by the huge Dai-Ichi Kangyo Bank, its chairman, Kunjii Miyazaki, when confronted with this loan, committing suicide by hanging. It is believed that many top government leaders, business and banking executives, are all members of Yakuza's hierarchy (members of high standing being covered from neck to ankles by tattoos which signify their rank). Yakuza, which may have as many as a million members, is the offshoot of the old Black Dragon Society which secretly aided Emperor Hirohito in his plans to begin World War II in the Pacific. One intelligence source privately states: "Japan from top to bottom is thoroughly polluted by Yakuza, which has corrupted its government and financial institutions, not unlike the Mafia in Sicily."

AUGUST: Carl Drega, sixty-seven, shoots and kills four residents in Colebrook, New Hampshire, before police shoot him to death. Drega has been amassing pipe bombs (eighty-six empty pipe bombs, 400 pounds of ammonium nitrate, sixty-one gallons of diesel fuel and a small arsenal will be found in his home), apparently as part of an intended but unfulfilled terrorist campaign.

SEPTEMBER 4: Three terrorists suicidally explode a bomb in a Jerusalam marketplace, killing themselves and one other, while seriously wounding another 200 Israelis and tourists. Hamas, an Islamic terrorist organization, is thought to be responsible.

SEPTEMBER 23: Terrorists of the Islamic Salvation Front are held responsible for widespread attacks on civilians, killing eighty-five and injuring another sixty-seven persons.

SEPTEMBER 25: Two Israeli agents try to kill Hamas leader Khalid Mashaal, in Amman, Jordan, but are foiled in their attempt.

SEPTEMBER 30: Israel, in a concessionary gesture, releases twenty terrorists from prison, including Hamas founder, Sheik Ahmed Yassin.

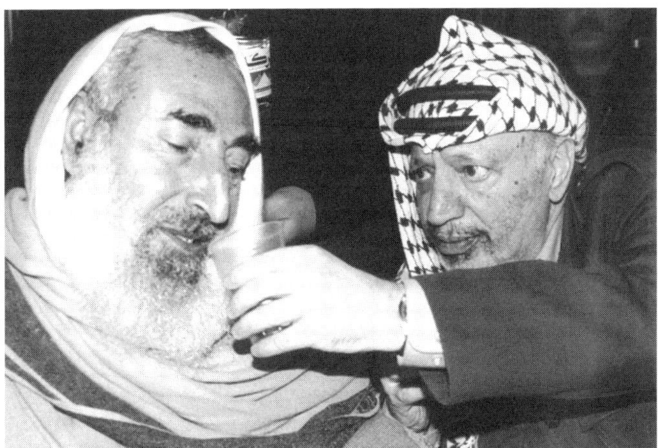

Hamas leader Sheik Ahmed Yassin, left, released from an Israeli prison on September 30, 1997, continued to urge followers to commit terrorist attacks against Israel and the West; he is shown being given a drink by his strong supporter, Yasir Arafat, chief of the PLO.

OCTOBER 8: The U.S. government labels thirty international groups as terrorist groups and bans contributions to these foreign organizations, making it illegal for any member of such terrorist groups to enter the U.S.

DECEMBER 22: Terrorists of the Institutional Revolutionary Party are blamed for killing forty-five Zapatista members in San Cristobal de Las Casas, Mexico.

DECEMBER 24: After having been captured in Sudan in 1994 and extradited to France, Illich Ramirez Sanchez, the notorious Carlos (or Jackal), is convicted of kidnapping and murder in Paris and is sent to prison for life.

1998

JANUARY 29: An abortion clinic in Birmingham, Alabama, is bombed by an unknown terrorist, killing Robert Sanderson, an off-duty policeman and injuring a nurse.

JANUARY: Theodore "Ted" Kaczynski, the notorious Unabomber, attempts to hang himself in his jail cell. He survives to cut a deal with prosecutors, confessing to his many bombings in exchange for receiving a life sentence behind bars.

FEBRUARY 9: Eduard Shevardnadze, seventy, the head of Georgia, escapes another assassination attempt in Tbilisi, the capital, when terrorists fire a rocket-propelled grenade at his passing car. Seven suspected terrorists will be arrested and charged with the attack, these being supporters of Shevardnadze's predecessor, Zviad Gamsakhurdia, a former Soviet foreign minister, overthrown in a 1992 coup and who had died in mysterious circumstances in 1993.

FEBRUARY 14: A bomb explodes aboard a bus in the central Chinese city of Wuhan, killing at least sixteen persons (one report has thirty fatalities) and injuring scores more. Two taxis and three other buses are badly damaged by the explosion which is attributed to anti-Communist terrorists.

FEBRUARY 14: The FBI announces that Eric Robert Rudolph is sought as a fugitive suspect in the January 29, 1998 bombing of a Birmingham, Alabama abortion clinic. Media reports have it that traces of explosives have been found in Rudolph's truck and storage locker.

FEBRUARY 14: Milan Simic and Miroslav Tadic, two Bosnian Serb leaders accused of conducting a "campaign of terror," turn themselves into a United Nations war crimes tribunal at Bosanski Samac, Bosnia-Herzegovina.

FEBRUARY 14: Thirteen bombs are exploded by Muslim terrorists in several crowded sections of Coimbatore, India, prior to a speech by Hindu leader Lal Krishna Advani. Hindu-Muslim clashes have increased in this city since a Hindu policeman had been killed by two Muslims in November 1997.

Cars blown up in Islamic terrorist bombings in Coimbatore, India, on February 14, 1998.

FEBRUARY 15: The bodies of seven men, Zapatista sympathizers, are found in a pit near San Cristobal de Las Casas, Mexico, victims, it is reported of terrorists from the Institutional Revolutionary Party.

FEBRUARY 17: Milan Simic and Miroslav Tadic, accused of conducting a "campaign of terror" in Bosnia, plead innocent before a court in The Hague, Netherlands. Another accused terrorist mastermind, Simo Zaric, agrees to surrender to the court.

MARCH 9: A time-activated bomb explodes inside of a compartment on the Chiltan Express train as it is crossing a bridge over a canal forty-five miles southwest of Lahore en route to Quetta, Punjab, India. Seven persons are killed and thirty-five are wounded by the terrorist explosion. Another terrorist bomb explodes the same day outside a court building in the province of Sind, injuring thirteen, six of whom are policemen.

MARCH 9: Serbian terrorist Dragoljub Kunarac, thirty-seven, admits before a court in The Hague, Netherlands, that he has raped several Muslim women in 1992 during the Bosnian war. Human rights groups state that more than 30,000 Muslim women have been raped during the 1992-1995 Bosnian conflict by Serbian terrorists, many of them telling their victims that it was their purpose to impregnate them with Serbian babies and thus increase the Serbian population (and its voting power) in the area.

MARCH 25: Salvador Valdez and Jose Santos Vasquez, two men who have been jailed for attempting to abduct small girls in Huejutla, Mexico, and are about to be released on bond, are seized by a crowd of more than 1,000 persons and lynched. It has been reported that the two victims have been kidnapping small girls in order to kill them and sell their organs on the black market.

MARCH 29: Mohiyedine Sharif, chief bomb maker for the Hamas terrorist organization, is killed in a premature car bombing in the West Bank town of Ramallah. Officials for the Palestinian Authority claim that Sharif was murdered by gunfire before the bomb exploded, shot to death by Adel Awadallah, a rival member of his own terrorist group involved in an Islamic power struggle with Sharif. Awadallah and Ghassan Addasi, a

Hamas terrorist brothers, Imad, left, and Adel Awadallah, who murdered a rival bomb-maker before both brothers were killed by Israeli forces on September 10, 1998.

teenage bombmaker, drove Sharif to a remote spot, shot and killed him, then packed his body in the car, driving to Ramallah. The terrorists then placed their leader's body near the bomb-laden car and detonated the explosives with a timer to make it appear that he was killed by Israelis. Hamas will deny this report.

MARCH 31: Gocha Esebua, leader of a 20-man terrorist group opposed to Eduard Shevardnadze, leader of Georgia, is shot and killed by police. Esebua and others had captured United Nations observers and held them hostage for more than a week in February 1998, before releasing them and escaping. Esebua has been a fugitive for several weeks.

APRIL 5: Terrorists open fire and throw a grenade at a funeral procession for rebel militant Gocha Esebua, killing five persons and wounding another eight in Zugdidi, Georgia, a former province of Soviet Russia. Esebua, killed in a shootout with police a week earlier, had been an ardent foe of Eduard Shevardnadze, whom he apparently tried to assassinate on Febuary 9, 1998.

APRIL 5: Terrorists explode two bombs—one on the terrace of the Speke Hotel, the other at the Nile Grill restaurant in Kampala, Uganda. Five persons are killed and five others are injured in the blasts.

APRIL 6: A terrorist bomb explodes outside the Russian Embassy in Riga, Latvia. An anti-personnel mine has been detonated, officials claim, by right-wing terrorists, who have recently bombed a synagogue in Riga, an act reportedly inspired by SS veterans of World War II. Fascism is reportedly on the rise again in Latvia.

APRIL 23: James Earl Ray, convicted and imprisoned for life for assassinating civil rights leader Martin Luther King, Jr., dies in prison of liver failure.

MAY 4: Theodore "Ted" Kaczynski, the notorious Unabomber who has confessed to mailing many bombs over two decades, is officially sentenced by a California judge to four consecutive life terms in prison. Susan Mosser, whose husband, Thomas Mosser, an advertising executive of North Caldwell, New Jersey, had been killed by one of Kaczynski's mail bombs in 1994, tells the court sentencing the Unabomber to "lock him so far down he'll be closer to hell." David Kaczynski, the Unabomber's brother and the man responsible for identifying the terrorist, says to the families of his brother's bomb victims: "The Kaczynski family offers its deepest apologies. We are very, very sorry."

MAY 12: Akin Birdal, fifty, Turkey's most outspoken human rights activist, who has publicly supported the much-oppressed Kurdish communities, is shot and seriously wounded by two terrorists in his office after the would-be assassins pretend to seek legal advice. The shootists escape and later state that they are members of the ultranationalist Turkish Revenge Brigade, a terrorist organization.

MAY 12: General G. Landazabal Reyes, seventy-six, a conservative political activist, is shot dead in front of his Bogotá, Colombia, residence by terrorists.

MAY 12: U.S. President William Clinton announces that he will ask Congress to pass legislation providing for $280 million more in combating terrorism and drug trafficking.

MAY 12-15: Thousands riot in Jakarta, Indonesia against the thirty-two-year authoritarian regime of President Suharto. On May 12, more than 5,000 students formed on the campus of the Trisatki University in West Jakarta, encouraged, one report has it, by radical instructors and student terrorists. Taking to the streets, the students throw rocks and other items at police who first fire rubber bullets (that can be fatal at less than 150 feet), and then change to real bullets after a police spy is publicly beaten by students. By Friday, May 15, tens of thousands invade the Chinese district, destroying whole blocks of Chinese businesses, which represent the richest minority in Indonesia. This section catches fire and several hundred looters are trapped in the flames and killed. Suharto, away on a state visit, returns to call out more than 10,000 troops and police to quell the worst rioting in Indonesian history.

MAY 15: A federal judge in New York sentences Abdul Hakim Murad, thirty, a commercial pilot who was born in Kuwait and has lived in Pakistan, to life in prison for bombing a Philippines Airlines jet in 1994 in which a Japanese passenger died, and for plotting to bomb eleven U.S. airliners over the Far East in January 1995.

MAY 17: At least ten persons are killed and twenty more injured by right-wing terrorists who swept through Barrancabermeja, in northeastern Santander province of Colombia. The country's main oil town has been plagued by "death squads" intent upon sowing terror throughout the province prior to the May 31, 1998 presidential elections.

MAY 25: A pro-democracy rally by 2,000 students in Teheran, Iran, demonstrating against the rigid Islamic government, is broken up by 400 right-wing Islamic thugs, reportedly members of the terrorist group Hezbollah, who wielded pipes and chains, injuring several of the students.

MAY 26: In France, Belgium, Italy, Germany and Switzerland, more than 450 anti-terrorist police specialists conduct raids that rounded up scores of Islamic terrorists, confiscating cash and weapons. The chief terrorist group in France, the Armed Islamic Group, is all but broken up when dozens of its members are arrested in Lyon, Marseilles, Paris and on the island of Corsica.

AUGUST 8: Officials in Washington, D. C., announce that Osama bin Laden, a multimillionaire Saudi, who heads the terrorist group Al Qaeda in Afghanistan, was responsible for the two deadly U. S. embassy bombings of August 7, 1998 in Nairobi, Kenya and Dar es Salaam, Tanzania and that bin Laden had most probably been behind the bombings of U. S. military facilities in Saudi Arabia in 1995 and 1996.

AUGUST 15: After police received two phone warnings that a bomb would explode near the courthouse in Omagh, Northern Ireland, police evacuate the building and move scores of people hundreds of yards from the building. The bomb explodes, killing twenty-eight men, women and children and seriously

Widespread destruction was created by the IRA bomb exploding in Omagh, Northern Ireland, on August 15, 1998, where twenty-eight men, women and children were killed and more than 300 others seriously wounded.

wounding another 300 persons. This is the worst terrorist bombing in the last twenty-nine years in Northern Ireland. The Real IRA, a splinter group of the IRA took responsibility for the terrorist attack.

SEPTEMBER 10: Two brothers, Adel and Imad Awadallah, both Palestinian terrorists, are shot in Hebron, West Bank by Israeli soldiers as they were reportedly planning another terrorist attack on Israeli installations. Imad Awadallah had only a short time earlier escaped from a Palestinian jail. At the urging of Sheik Ahmed Yassin, leader of the Hamas terrorist group, widespread rioting by Palestinians ensued.

NOVEMBER 6: A car bomb explodes in a busy marketplace in Jerusalem, Israel, killing two terrorist bombers, who set off the explosive, and wounding twenty-five others. The terrorist group Hamas takes credit for the bombing.

DECEMBER 25: Briefly released from confinement by the Palestinian Authority, Hamas founder and leader Sheik Ahmed Yassin addresses a crowd of 10,000 Palestinians, urging them to continue their terrorist campaign against Israel and the West.

1999

FEBRUARY 4: Palestine police arrest forty Islamic extremists allegedly planning Iranian-financed terrorist attacks against Jewish settlers in the Gaza Strip. Major-General Ghazi al-Jabali states that police also seized weapons and explosives collected by members of Izzedine al-Qassam, an underground terrorist wing of Hamas.

FEBRUARY 16: Fourteen people are killed and more than 100 others are injured when six car bombs explode outside government headquarters and other buildings in Tashkent, Uzbekistan. No one claimed responsibility for the attacks, which were apparently aimed at President Islam Karimov, who has been the nation's leader since it gained independence in the 1991 breakup of the Soviet Union. Karimov is not injured in the blasts.

FEBRUARY 19: Grand Ayatollah Mohammed Sadiq al-Sader, supreme religious leader of Iraq's Shiite Muslim majority, and his two sons are killed in a drive-by shooting in Najaf, Iraq. Iranian and Iraqi exiles blame President Saddam Hussein's government for the murders.

FEBRUARY 21: A mine explodes near the motorcade of Chechen President Aslan Maskhadov as he is returning to his residence in Grozny, Chechnya, Russia. One person is killed and eight others injured. Maskhadov is unharmed in an apparent assassination attempt.

MARCH 1: Jean-Yvon Toussaint, 47, a senator from Haiti's main political opposition party, is shot in the head and killed in front of his home in Port-Au-Prince. The assassin is not identified or captured.

MARCH 17: Herzi Mazuz, 44, is banished from Jerusalem, Israel, for planning to blow up two of the city's holiest Muslim shrines.

MARCH 23: Luis Maria Argana, 66, Paraguay's vice president, is shot to death in Asuncion by three gunmen driving alongside the car in which Argana is sitting. The assassins are not identified.

MARCH 28: Raul Cubas Grau, the impeached president of Paraguay, who has been blamed for ordering the assassination of Vice President Argana on March 23, resigns from his post.

APRIL 10: Brigadier General Ali Sayyad Shirazi, deputy chief of the joint staff command of the Iranian armed forces, is killed on his way to work in Teheran, Iran, allegedly assassinated by terrorists from the Iraq-based group Mujahedeen Khalq.

APRIL 24: Seven people are injured when a car bomb explodes in Brick Lane, London, England, the city's largest Bangladeshi community. A caller claims responsibility by Combat 18, a right-wing terrorist group.

APRIL 30: Two persons are killed and seventy-three others injured when a nail bomb explodes in a gay pub in Soho, London, England. An anonymous phone call to police claims that the bombing is the work of the White Wolves, a racist group that recently sent threatening letters to Asian, black and Jewish members of Parliament. Police suspect that the White Wolves are linked to an anti-gay terrorist group, Combat 18.

MAY 9: Barbara Meyer, 42, a suspected Red Army Faction terrorist and one of Germany's most wanted fugitives for a decade, is arrested upon her arrival at the airport in Frankfurt, Germany, after a flight from Lebanon, where she had been living.

JULY 14: Rebel leader Oscar Ramirez Durand, 46, known as "Commandante Feliciano" while chief of Peru's infamous Shining Path terrorist organization, is captured at his hideout near Huancayo in a remote jungle gorge at the base of the Andes Mountains. Hunted since 1980, Durand is the last top Shining Path leaders to be arrested. More than 30,000 Peruvians have died from the hands of this terrorist group and others plaguing the nation for two decades.

AUGUST 21: A smoke bomb exploded in a theater in Merriam, Kansas, one which prompted an investigation by FBI agents. The bombing, which took no lives, is thought to be related to numerous other incidents by local terrorists.

AUGUST 27: Jahair Joel Navarro, 18, a native of Panama, reportedly admits sending e-mail bomb threats to IBM, saying he would demolish the company's headquarters unless he received $5 million. He is charged with threatening to use a weapon of mass destruction, a crime falling under the federal anti-terrorism statutes.

SEPTEMBER 6: Egyptian President Hosni Mubarak suffers a light arm wound by a knife-wielding attacker in an assassination attempt that leaves the assailant dead during a motorcade in Port Said, Egypt.

SEPTEMBER 9: A military weaponry explosive is detonated at an apartment building in Moscow, Russia, killing thirty-two people. Investigators suspect the bombing was a terrorist attack stemming from fighting between Russian troops and Islamic separatists in the Caucasus republic of Dagestan.

OCTOBER 1: Lawrence Michael Lombardi, 41, a white former vending machine company employee, whose route included Florida A&M University, is arrested for allegedly exploding two bombs at the predominately black school. No one was injured in either terrorist explosion.

OCTOBER 15: Mourad Topalian, 56, Chairman of the Armenian National Committee of America, is indicted for allegedly helping lead a group that plotted bomb attacks against Turkish targets in the U. S. over the past two decades. Topalian is indicted on charges of conspiracy, weapons and explosives violations.

NOVEMBER 7: Thirty-three persons are injured by shrapnel when three pipe bombs explode in Netanya,, Israel. The bombings are blamed on Islamic terrorists attempting to disrupt the Oslo peace process.

NOVEMBER 11: A car bomb explodes in the commercial district of Bogota, Columbia, killing eight persons and injuring forty-five others. Police believe that the terrorist bombings stem from members of the Medellin Drug Cartel and are aimed at stopping extradition of its members to the U. S.

DECEMBER 25: Police are searching for a terrorist suspected of luring seven police officers to investigate a bomb threat outside a restaurant in Cape Town, South Africa, and then detonating an explosive device when they arrived. All of the officers were injured by the blast.

DECEMBER 31: Police discover 2,200 pounds of explosives belonging to suspected Basque terrorists in an overnight raid in Pau, France.

2000

JANUARY 5: Masood Azhar, one of three Kashmiri terrorists freed as part of a deal to end an Indian Airlines hijacking, gives an inflamed speech to 10,000 of his followers to destroy India and the United States.

JANUARY 7: Defense Minister Pavle Bulatovic, a loyal aide to President Slobodan Milosevic, is fatally shot in the dining area of a soccer club in Belgrade, Yugoslavia. A Yugoslav official states that Bulatovic "was the victim of a classic terrorist act."

JANUARY 21: Two car bombs devastated a neighborhood in Madrid, Spain, killing a Spanish army officer, the attack attributed to ETA, a terrorist group seeking Basque separatism.

FEBRUARY 17: Fourteen followers of Saudi terrorist Osama bin Laden are arrested in Amman, Jordan, and charged with planning terrorist attacks, the terrorists being twelve Jordanians, one Iraqi and one Algerian, all members of the Al Qaeda terrorist organization.

MARCH 2: Israeli forces kill three suspected Palestinian terrorists in a firefight in Taibeh, Israel. The dead terrorists were reportedly members of Hamas and had been targeting terrorist attacks on Israeli installations.

MARCH 18: Four members of the Japanese terrorist group, Red Army, are arrested in Tokyo, Japan, after they were expelled from Lebanon and denied entry into Jordan. The four, wanted in connection with aircraft hijackings, bombings and other terrorist attacks are Haruwo Wako, fifty; Masao Adachi, fifty; Mariko Yamamoto, fifty-eight; and Kazuo Tohira, forty-six.

MARCH 28: Police in Amman, Jordan, arrest twenty-eight Arabs linked to terrorist leader Osama bin Laden on charges of conspiracy to attack Americans and Israelis with bombs during New Year's celebrations.

APRIL 6: Nawaz Sharif, ousted as Pakistan's prime minister in a military coup in October 1999, is convicted of skyjacking a commercial airliner and is sentenced to prison for life.

APRIL 16: Seven people are killed and sixty-five others are injured when bombs with toxic gas are thrown into a crowded nightclub in Lisbon, Portugal. The motive for the terrorist attack is not immediately known.

MAY 3: Four hostages are found dead, shot execution-style, after Muslim terrorists holding twenty-seven captives came upon Filipino troops by a river crossing near Isabela, Philippines. Many of the hostages, used as human shields by the terrorists, had been seized from a school.

JUNE 30: David Copeland, twenty-four, a self-styled Nazi and terrorist, is convicted of murdering three people and injuring more than 100 others in nail bombings that targeted gay and black communities in London, England. His bombings had resulted with a baby with a nail in his skull, a dead woman with her unborn child, amputated limbs and horrific lacerations from flying glass.

JULY 5: Mahmoud Rizq Deeb, of Tartous, Syria, is killed while attempting to hijack a Syria bound jetliner from Amman, Jordan. Security guards on board the plane shoot and kill the terrorist after he explodes a grenade which wounds fifteen passengers. The pilot of the Royal Jordanian Airbus with ninety-six persons on board, returns safely to Amman.

JULY 17: Two members of the terrorist doomsday cult Aum Shinri Kyo, are sentenced to death by hanging for their roles in the 1995 sarin nerve gas attack on the Tokyo subway that killed twelve persons and injured more than 1,000 others. Condemned are Toru Toyoda, thirty-two, and Kenichi Hirose, thirty-six. On July 28, Kiyohide Hayakawa, fifty-one, is also sentenced to death for his role as "construction minister" in the terrorist cult.

AUGUST 8: Eleven people are injured when a bomb explodes in Madrid, Spain. In Zumaia, Jose Maria Korta, a prominent critic of the terrorist group, ETA, which has been working for Basque separatism, is killed in a car bombing.

AUGUST 22: Twenty-three Islamic militants from a terrorist cell are arrested in Jerusalem, Israel. Among the accused terrorists is Nabil Oukal, head of the cell and reported associate of Osama bin Laden.

SEPTEMBER 13: Unidentified terrorists set off a car bomb that kills fifteen persons and wounds dozens more people in the parking garage of the Indonesian stock exchange building in Jakarta.

OCTOBER 30: Jose Francisco Querol, 69, a Supreme Court judge, and his bodyguard, are killed when a car bomb explodes in Madrid, Spain. ETA terrorists are blamed for the attack.

NOVEMBER 5: Christos Kendiras, forty-eight, who is arrested for killing two people and hijacking a busload of Japanese tourists, leaps to his death from a seventh-story window at police headquarters in Athens, Greece.

NOVEMBER 9: Police arrest three Kuwaiti terrorists in Kuwait City, Kuwait, after seizing a large quantity of explosives in an alleged plot directed at U. S. targets in other countries, these terrorists having links to Osama bin Laden's Al Qaeda.

DECEMBER 8: Abbas al-Baqer Abbas appears at a mosque in Khartoum, Sudan, during evening prayers and opens fire with automatic weapons, killing twenty people before he is shot to death by police. The terrorist was a member of Takfir wal Hijra.

DECEMBER 17: Fifteen teenage students are machine gunned to death, along with a teacher by Islamic terrorists opposed to peace efforts as they sleep in the dormitory of the Lycee Technique of Medea near Algiers, Algeria. Six other students are wounded, the terrorists, adorned in military uniforms, fleeing.

DECEMBER 24: Ten people are killed when five Catholic and Protestant churches in Jakarta, Indonesia, are exploded by bombs set off by Islamic terrorists, who have vowed to kill all Christians.

DECEMBER 30: Islamic terrorists explode five bombs in Manila, Philippines, killing fourteen persons and injuring another 100 people.

BIBLIOGRAPHY

Tens of thousands of sources have been employed by the author in researching this work over the last decade, primary and secondary sources that include court, coroner and police documents, books, periodicals, reports and newspapers, all but books too numerous to cite here. The author also conducted in his exclusive research extensive correspondence and interviews with many of the subjects profiled herein. What follows are the basic published reference sources used in the researching, compiling, writing and overall preparation of this work. This bibliography is the most comprehensive ever assembled on this subject.

Aaron, Daniel (ed.). *America in Crisis.* New York: Alfred A. Knopf, 1952.

Abadinsky, Howard. *The Criminal Elite: Professional and Organized Crime.* Westport, Conn.: Greenwood, 1983.

_____. *Organized Crime.* Chicago: Nelson-Hall, 1985.

Abbait, A. H. *The Mafia in America: An Oral History.* New York: Praeger, 1981.

_____. *Organized Crime.* Chicago: Nelson-Hall, 1990.

_____. *Probation and Parole: Theory and Practice.* Englewood Cliffs, N. J.: Prentice-Hall, 1977.

Abbas, Mahmoud (Mohammad), and Mazen, Abu. *Through Secret Channels.* Reading, England: Garnet Publishing, Ltd., 1997.

Abbot, Willis J. *Life of Carter H. Harrison.* New York: Dodd, Mead, 1895.

Abbott, Edith. *The Tenements of Chicago.* Chicago: University of Chicago Press, 1936.

Abbott, Jack Henry. *In the Belly of the Beast: Letters from Prison.* New York: Random House, 1981.

Abbott, John Reginald. *Footwear Evidence.* Springfield, Ill.: Charles C. Thomas, 1964.

Abel, Ernest L. *Marihuana, The First Twelve Thousand Years.* New York: McGraw-Hill, 1982.

_____. *The Scientific Study of Marihuana.* Chicago: Nelson-Hall, 1978.

Abell, L. E. *Recollections of the Emperor Napoleon.* London: John Murray, 1848.

Abell, Tyler (ed.). *Drew Pearson: Diaries, 1949-1959.* New York: Holt, Rinehart & Winston, 1974.

Abinger, Edward. *Forty Years at the Bar.* London: Hutchinson, 1930.

Abott, Abott A. *The Assassination and Death of Abraham Lincoln.* New York: American News, 1865.

Abraham, Henry J. *The Judicial Process.* New York: Oxford University Press, 1975.

Abrahams, Gerald. *According to the Evidence.* London: Cassell, 1958.

Abrahams, Sally. *Children in the Crossfire: The Tragedy of Parental Kidnapping.* New York: Atheneum, 1983.

Abrahamsen, David. *Confessions of Son of Sam.* New York: Columbia University Press, 1985.

_____. *Crime and the Human Mind.* New York: Columbia University Press, 1949.

_____. *The Murdering Mind.* New York: Harper & Row, 1973.

_____. *The Psychology of Crime.* New York: Columbia University Press, 1960.

_____. *Report on a Study of 102 Sex Offenders at Sing Sing Prison.* Utica, N. Y.: State Hospital Press, 1950.

Abramovitch, Raphael R. *The Soviet Revolution.* New York: International Universities Press, 1962.

Abrecht, Mary Ellen, and Stern, Barbara L. *The Making of a Woman Cop.* New York: William Morrow, 1976.

Abt Associates. *An Evaluation of the Training Provided in Correctional Institutions Under the Manpower Development Act, Section 251, Final Summary Report.* Cambridge, Mass.: Abt Associates, 1971.

_____. *Prison Populations and Policy Choices.* Washington, D. C.: Law Enforcement Assistance Administration, 1977.

An Account of the Curtis Homicide. Richmond, Va.: Dispatch Steam Presses, 1879.

An Account of the Execution of Samuel Green. Boston: N. Coverly, 1822.

Account of the Terrific and Fatal Riot at the New York Astor Place Opera House. New York: n.p., 1849.

Acheson, Dean. *Present at the Creation.* New York: W. W. Norton, 1969.

Acheson, Patricia C. *The Supreme Court.* New York: Dodd, Mead, 1961.

Ackroyd, Peter. *London: The Biography.* London: Chatto & Windus, 2000.

Acland, Theodore Dyke. *William Withey Gull, A Biographical Sketch.* London: Adlard & Son, 1896.

Acton, William. *The Functions and Disorders of the Reproductive Organs in Childhood, Youth, Adult Age and Advanced Life, Considered in their Physiological, Social and Moral Relations.* Philadelphia: Blakiston, 1857.

_____. *Prostitution.* London: Frederick A. Praeger, 1968.

Adair, James. *James Adair, The History of the American Indians.* London: Johnson Reprint, 1968.

Adam, H. Pearl. *Paris Sees It Through: A Diary, 1914-19.* London: Hodder & Stoughton, 1919.

Adam, Hargrave Lee. *C.I.D.* London: Sampson, Low, 1931.

_____. *The Indian Criminal.* London: John Milne, 1909.

_____. *Murder by Persons Unknown.* London: Collins, 1931.

_____. *Murder Most Mysterious.* London: Sampson, Low, 1932.

_____ (ed.). *Notable British Trials: Trial of George Chapman.* London: William Hodge, 1930.

_____. *The Police Encyclopedia.* London: Blackfriars Publishing Co., 1908?

_____. *Trial of George Chapman.* London: William Hodge, 1930.

_____. *Woman and Crime.* London: T. W. Laurie, 1912.

_____. *Dynamite: The Story of Class Violence in America.* New York: Viking Press, 1931.

Adams, Andrew. *Ninja: The Invisible Assassins.* Burbank, Calif.: Ohara, 1976.

Adams, Caren, and Fay, Jennifer. *No More Secrets.* San Luis Obispo, Calif.: Impact, 1981.

Adams, Franklin P. *The Diary of Our Own Samuel Pepys.* New York: Simon & Schuster, 1935.

_____. *Nods and Becks.* New York: Whittlesey House, 1944.

Adams, Graham, Jr. *Age of Industrial Violence 1910-15: The Activities and Findings of the U.S. Commission on Industrial Relations.* New York: Columbia University Press, 1966.

Adams, James. *The Financing of Terror: The PLO, IRA, Red Brigades and M-19 Stand the Paymasters.* New York: Simon and Schuster, 1986.

Adams, Raymond [Ramon] F. (ed.). *The Best of the American Cowboy.* Norman: University of Oklahoma Press, 1957.

_____. *Burs Under the Saddle.* Norman: University of Oklahoma Press, 1964.

_____. *A Fitting Death for Billy the Kid.* Norman: University of Oklahoma Press, 1960.

_____. *From the Pecos to the Powder.* Norman: University of Oklahoma Press, 1965.

_____. *The Old-Time Cowhand.* New York: Macmillan, 1961.

_____. *Six-Guns and Saddle Leather.* Norman: University of Oklahoma Press, 1969.

Adams, S. *The Sociology of Punishment and Corrections.* New York: John Wiley & Sons, 1962.

Adams, Samuel Hopkins. *Alexander Woollcott: His Life and His World.* New York: Reynal & Hitchcock, 1945.

_____. *The Great American Fraud.* Chicago: Press of the American Medical Association, 1907.

_____. *Incredible Era: The Life and Times of Warren Gamaliel Harding.* Boston: Houghton Mifflin, 1939.

Adams, Terry, and Brooks-Mueller, Mary, and Shaw, Scott. *Eye on the Beast.* Omaha: Addicus Books, 1998.

Adams, Thomas F. *Police Patrol.* Englewood Cliffs, N. J.: Prentice-Hall, 1971.

Adams, Virginia. *Crime.* New York: Time-Life, 1976.

Adams, W. S. *Edwardian Portraits.* London: Secker and Warburg, 1957.

Adams, Ward R. *History of Arizona.* Phoenix, Ariz.: Record, 1930.

Adams, William Henry Davenport. *Witch, Warlock, and Magician.* London: Chatto & Windus, 1889.

Adamson, Iain. *The Forgotten Men.* London: G. Bell, 1965.

_____. *The Great Detective.* London: Frederick Muller, 1966.

_____. *A Man of Quality: A Biography of the Hon. Mr. Justice Cassels.* London: F. Muller, 1964.

Adcock, Thomas Larry. *Precinct 19.* Garden City, N. Y.: Doubleday, 1984.

Addison, Christopher, et al. *Problems of a Socialist Government.* London: Victor Gollancz, 1933.

Addy, Ted. *The Dutch Schultz Story.* New York: Tower, 1962.

Ade, George. *The Old-Time Saloon: Not Wet-Nor Dry-Just History.* New York: Ray Long & Richard Smith, 1931.

Adelman, Howard, and Suhrke, Astri (eds.). *The Path of a Genocide: Crisis from Uganda to Zaire.* Somerset, N. J.: Transaction Publishers, 2000.

Adey, R. *Locked Room Murders and Other Impossible Crimes.* London: Ferret, 1979.

Adleman, Robert H. *Alias Big Cherry.* New York: Dial Press, 1973.

_____. *The Bloody Benders.* New York: Stein & Day, 1970.

_____. *The Champagne Campaign.* Boston: Little, Brown, 1969.

_____, and Walton, George. *Rome Fell Today.* Boston: Little, Brown, 1968.

Adler, Alfred. *Billy the Kid: A Case Study in Epic Origins.* Berkeley: University of California Press, 1951.

Adler, Bill (ed.). *The Wisdom of Martin Luther King.* New York: Lancer Books, 1968.

Adler, Freda, and Simon, R. J. (eds.). *The Criminology of Deviant Women.* Boston: Houghton Mifflin, 1979.

_____. *Sisters in Crime: The Rise of the New Female Criminal.* New York: McGraw-Hill, 1975.

Adler, Friedrich. *The Witchcraft Trial in Moscow.* New York: Pioneer, 1937.

Adler, J.A. *Elsevier's Dictionary of Criminal Science in Eight Languages.* Amsterdam, Neth.: Elsevier, 1960.

Adler, Polly. *A House is Not a Home.* New York: Rinehart, 1953.

Adler, Ruth (ed.). *The Working Press.* New York: G. P. Putnam's Sons, 1966.

Advisory Committee on Drug Dependence. *Cannabis.* London: H. M. Stationery Office, 1968.

Ady, Thomas. *A Candle in the Dark.* London: T. Newberry, 1656.

_____. *A Perfect Discovery of Witches.* London: H. Browne, 1661.

Africa, Thomas W. *Rome of the Caesars.* New York: John Wiley & Sons, 1965.

Agabekov, Georges. *OGPU: The Russian Secret Terror.* New York: Brentano's, 1931.

Agee, George W. *Rube Burrows, King of Outlaws, and His Band of Train Robbers.* Chicago: Hennebery, 1890.

Agee, Phillip, and Wolf, Louis (eds.). *Dirty Work: The CIA in Western Europe.* Secaucus, N.J.: Lyle Stuart, 1978.

_____. *Inside the Company: CIA Diary.* New York: Stonehill, 1975.

Agel, Jerome, and Boe, Eugene. *22 Fires.* New York: Bantam Books, 1977.

Agourtine, Leq eon. *Le Geq eneq eral Soukhomlinov.* Clichy, Fr.: l'Auteur, 1951.

Aguilar Olmos, Rafael. *Madero sin meq ascara.* Mexico City: Imprenta Popular, 1911.

Ahearn, Danny. *How to Commit a Murder.* New York: Ives Washburn, 1930.

Ahern, James F. *Police in Trouble.* New York: Hawthorn, 1972.

Ahern, M. L. *The Great Revolution.* Chicago: Lakeside Press, 1874.

_____. *Political History of Chicago, 1837-1887.* Chicago: Donohue & Henneberry, 1886.

Ahlstrom, Sydney E. *A Religious History of the American People.* New Haven, Conn.: Yale University Press, 1972.

Ahlstrom, W. M., and Havighurst, R. J. *Four Hundred Losers: Delinquent Boys in High School.* San Francisco: Jossey-Bass, 1971.

Ahuja, Ram. *Female Offenders in India.* Meerut, India: Menanakshi Prakashan, 1969.

Aichhorn, August. *Wayward Youth.* New York: Viking, 1935.

Aiken, Albert W. *Rocky Mountain Rob, the California Outlaw; or the Vigilantes of Humburg Bar.* New York: Beadle & Adams, 1871.

Aikman, Duncan. *Calamity Jane and the Lady Wildcats.* New York: Henry Holt, 1927.

_____ (ed.) *The Taming of the Frontier.* New York: Prospect Press, 1925.

Ainslie, Rosalynde. *The Press in Africa.* New York: Walker, 1966.

Ajami, Fouad. *The Vanished Imam: Musa Al Sadr and the Shia of Lebanon.* Ithaca, N. Y.: Cornell University Press, 1992.

Akeny, Nesmith. *The West as I Knew It.* Lewiston, Idaho: R. G. Bailey Printing, 1938.

Akhmedov, Ismail. *In and Out of Stalin's KGB.* Frederick, Md.: University Publications, 1984.

Akimoto Shunkichi. *Exploring the Japanese Ways of Life.* Tokyo: Tokyo News Service, 1961.

Akita, George. *Foundations of Constitutional Government in Modern Japan, 1868-1900.* Cambridge, Mass.: Harvard University Press, 1967.

Alan, A. J. *Great Unsolved Crimes.* London: Hutchinson, 1935.

Alba, Victor. *The Mexicans.* London: Pall Mall Press, 1967.

Albach, James R. *The Annals of the West.* Pittsburgh: W. S. Haven, 1857.

Albanese, Jay S. *Organizational Offenders: Why Solutions Fall to Political, Corporate, and Organized Crime.* Niagara Falls, N. Y.: Apocalypse, 1982.

_____. *Organized Crime in America.* Cincinnati: Anderson, 1989.

Albini, Joseph L. *The American Mafia: Genesis of a Legend.* New York: Appleton-Century-Crofts, 1971.

Albion, Robert G. *The Rise of New York Port 1815-1860.* New York: Scribner's, 1939.

Albrecht-Carrieq e, Reneq e. *Italy from Napoleon to Mussolini.* New York: Columbia University Press, 1960.

Album of American History. 3 vols. New York: Scribner's, 1945.

Alcatraz. San Francisco: E. Crowell Mensch, 1937.

Alciphron. *Letters of Courtesans.* eds. Allen Rogers Benner and Frances H. Forbes. London: William Heinemann, 1962.

Alden, John Richard. *The American Revolution, 1775-1783.* New York: Harper & Row, 1962.

Aldington, Richard. *Frauds.* London: William Heinemann, 1957.

Alex, Nicholas. *Black in Blue: A Study of the Negro Policeman.* New York: Appleton-Century-Crofts, 1969.

_____. *New York Cops Talk Back: A Study of a Beleaguered Minority.* New York: John Wiley & Sons, 1976.

Alexander, C. W. *Career and Adventures of John H. Surratt.* Philadelphia: Published by Author, 1866.

Alexander, Charles C. *The Ku Klux Klan in the Southwest.* Lexington: University of Kentucky Press, 1965.

Alexander, David. *Panic! The Day the Money Stopped.* Evanston, Ill.: Regency Books, 1962.

_____. *Terror on Broadway.* New York: Random House, 1954.

Alexander, DeAlva Stanwood. *Four Famous New Yorkers: The Political Careers of Cleveland, Platt, Hill, and Roosevelt.* New York: Henry Holt, 1923.

_____. *A Political History of the State of New York.* 3 vols. New York: Henry Holt, 1906.

_____, and Healy, William. *Roots of Crime.* New York: Alfred A. Knopf, 1935.

Alexander, Gilchrist. *After Court Hours.* London: Butterworth, 1950.

_____, and Staub, M. *The Criminal, the Judge and the Public.* Glencoe, Ill.: Free Press, 1956.

Alexander, H. H. *The Life and Trial of Guiteau the Assassin.* Detroit, Mich.: F. H. Drake, 1882.

Alexander, Henry A. *Some Facts About the Murder Notes in the Phagan Case.* Atlanta, Ga.: Published by Author, n.d.

Alexander, Herbert E., and Caiden, Gerald E. *The Politics and Economics of Organized Crime.* Lexington, Mass.: D.C. Heath, 1985.

Alexander, M. E. *Jail Administration.* Springfield, Ill.: Charles C. Thomas, 1957.

Alexander, Marc. *Royal Murder.* London: Frederick Muller, 1978.

Alexander, Robert J. *Communism in Latin America.* New Brunswick, N. J.: Rutgers University Press, 1960.

Alexander, Shana. *Anyone's Daughter.* New York: Viking Press, 1978.

_____. *The Pizza Connection: Lawyers, Money, Drugs, Mafia.* New York: Weidenfeld & Nicolson, 1988.

_____. *When She Was Bad: The Story of Bess, Hortense, Sukhreet and Nancy.* New York: Random House, 1990.

Alexander, William Menzies. *Demonic Possession in the New Testament.* Edinburgh, Scot.: T. and T. Clara, 1902.

Alexander, William T. *History of the Colored Race in America.* Kansas City: Palmetto, 1887.

Alexander, Yonah (ed.). *International Terrorism: National, Regional and Global Perspectives.* New York: AMS Press, 1976.

_____. *Palestinian Secular Terrorism: Profiles of Fatah, Popular Front for the Liberation of Palestine.* Ardsley, N. Y.: Transactional Publishers, 2003.

_____. and Kilmarx, Robert A. (eds.). *Political Terrorism and Business: Threat and Response.* New York: Praeger, 1979.

_____.and Finger, Seymour Maxwell (eds.). *Terrorism: Interdisciplinary Perspectives.* New York: John Jay Press, 1977.

_____. *Terrorism: PLO Connection.* New York: Crane, Russak, 1989.

_____. *Terrorism in Italy.* New York: Crane, Russak, 1979.

_____.and Swetnam, Michael S. *Usama bin Laden's Al-Qaida: Profile of a Terrorist Network.* Ardsley, N. Y.: Transnational Publishers, 2001.

Alexandra, Empress of Russia. *Letters of the Tsaritsa to the Tsar, 1914-16.* London: Duckworth, 1923.

Alexandrov, Vistor. *Journey Through Chaos.* New York: Crown, 1945.

Alfange, Dean. *The Supreme Court and the National Will.* Garden City, N. Y.: Doubleday, 1937.

Alfers, Kenneth. *Law and Order in the Capital City: A History of the Washington Police 1800-1886.* Washington, D. C.: George Washington University Press, 1976.

Alfieri, Dino. *Dictators Face to Face.* trans. David Moore. London: Elek Books, 1954.

Alger, Horatio, Jr. *From Canal Boy to President, or the Boyhood and Manhood of James A. Garfield.* New York: J. R. Anderson, 1881.

Alger, John Goldworth. *Paris in 1789-94.* London: G. Allen, 1902.

Alinsky, Saul D. *Reveille for Radicals.* New York: Vintage Books, 1969.

_____. *Rules for Radicals.* New York: Random House, 1971.

Alioshin, Dimitri. *Asian Odyssey.* New York: Henry Holt, 1940.

Ali Shah, Sirdah Ikbal. *Mohammed the Prophet.* London: Wright & Brown, 1932.

Alibrandi, Tom, and Armani, Frank. *Privileged Information.* New York: Harper Collins, 1984.

Alix, Ernest Kahlar. *Ransom Kidnapping in America, 1874-1974.* Carbondale: Southern Illinois University Press, 1975.

Allbury, A. G. *Bamboo and Bushido.* London: Robert Hale, 1955.

Allen, Allyn. *The Real Book About the Texas Rangers.* Garden City, N. Y.: Garden City Books, 1952.

Allen, Clifford. *Sexual Perversions and Abnormalities.* London: Oxford University Press, 1949.

_____. *A Textbook of Psychosexual Disorders.* London: Oxford University Press, 1962.

Allen, D.H. (ed.). *Essex Quarter Sessions Order Book, 1652-1661.* Chelmsford, Eng.: n. p., 1974.

Allen, David D. *The Nature of Gambling.* New York: Coward-McCann, 1952.

Allen, Edward J. *Merchants of Menace: The Mafia.* Springfield, Ill.: Charles C. Thomas, 1962.

Allen, Everett S. *The Black Ships.* Boston: Little, Brown, 1965.

Allen, F. *Whitechapel Murder.* New York: Ogilvie, 1927.

Allen, Francis A. *The Borderland of Criminal Justice.* Chicago: University of Chicago Press, 1974.

Allen, Frederick Lewis. *The Big Change.* New York: Harper & Brothers, 1952.

_____. *The Great Pierpont Morgan.* New York: Harper & Brothers, 1949.

_____. *The Lords of Creation.* New York: Harper & Brothers, 1935.

_____. *Only Yesterday, An Informal History of the Nineteen Twenties.* New York: Harper & Brothers, 1931.

_____. *Since Yesterday.* New York: Harper & Brothers, 1940.

_____, and Donnithorne, Audrey. *Western Enterprise in Far Eastern Economic Development: China and Japan.* New York: Macmillan, 1954.

Allen, Gardner W. *Our Navy and the West Indian Pirates.* Salem, Mass.: Essex Institute, 1929.

Allen, H.C. *Great Britain and the United States.* London: Odhams, 1954.

Allen, H. Warner. *Italy from End to End.* London: Methuen, 1927.

Allen, Harry E., and Simonsen, Clifford E. *Corrections in America: An Introduction.* Beverly Hills, Calif.: Glencoe, 1975.

_____, et al. *Crime and Punishment: An Introduction to Criminology.* New York: Free Press, 1981.

Allen, Hervey. *Israfel: The Life and Times of Edgar Allan Poe.* New York: G. H. Doran, 1926.

Allen, J. L. *The Reign of Law: A Tale of Kentucky Hemp Fields.* New York: Macmillan, 1900.

Allen, John. *Assault with a Deadly Weapon: The Autobiography of a Street Criminal.* New York: Pantheon Books, 1977.

Allen, John Logan. *Passage Through the Garden: Lewis and Clark and the American Northwest.* Urbana: University of Illinois Press, 1975.

Allen, Louis. *Japan: The Years of Triumph.* London: Purnell & Sons, 1971.

Allen, Lucas Benjamin. *Brief Considerations on the Present State of the Police of the Metropolis.* London: J. Butterworth & Son, 1821.

Allen, Mary S. *The Pioneer Policewoman.* London: Chatto & Windus, 1925.

Allen, Peter. *The Crown and the Swastika.* London: Hale, 1983.

Allen, Peter. *Interesting Times: Life in Uganda Under Idi Amin.* Philadelphia: Trans-Atlantic Publications, 2000.

Allen, Robert S. *Lucky Forward.* New York: Vanguard, 1947.

_____, and Shannon, William. *The Truman Merry-Go-Round.* New York: Vanguard Press, 1950.

Allen, Trevor. *Ivar Kreuger.* London: John Long, 1932.

_____. *The Ukraine: A History.* Cambridge, Eng.: Cambridge University Press, 1941.

Allen, William. *Starkweather: The Story of a Mass Murderer.* Boston: Houghton Mifflin, 1976.

Allen, William Harvey. *Al Smith's Tammany Hall, Champion Political Vampire.* New York: Institute For Public Service, 1928.

_____. *Rockefeller, Giant, Dwarf, Symbol.* New York: Institute for Public Service, 1930.

_____. *Why Tammanies Revive.* New York: Institute For Public Service, 1937.

Alliluyeva, Svetlana. *Only One Year.* New York: Harper, 1969.

_____. *Twenty Letters to a Friend.* Trans. Priscilla Johnson. New York: Harper, 1967.

Allman, James J. *Police and the Changing Community.* Washington, D. C.: International Association of Chiefs of Police, 1965.

Allon, Yigal. *Shield of David.* London: Weidenfeld & Nicolson, 1970.

Allou, Roger (ed.). *Discours et plaidoyers d'Edouard Allou.* 2 vols. Paris: Durand et Pedone-Lauriel, 1884.

_____, and Chenu, Charles. *Grands avocats du sieq ecle.* Paris: A. Pedone, 1894.

Allsop, Kenneth. *The Bootleggers.* Garden City, N. Y.: Doubleday, 1961.

An Almanac of Jim Garrison's Investigation: The Crime of Silence. Austin, Texas: Research, 1968.

Almandos, Luis. *Bertillon et Vucetich.* La Plata, Argen.: n. p., 1928.

Almedingen, E. M. *The Emperor Alexander I.* London: Bodley Head, 1964.

_____. *The Emperor Alexander II.* London: Allen Lane, 1962.
_____. *The Empress Alexandra.* London: Hutchinson, 1961.
_____. *The Romanovs, Three Centuries of an Ill-Fated Dynasty.* New York: Holt, Rinehart & Winston, 1966.
_____. *An Unbroken Unity.* London: Bodley Head, 1964.
Almira, J., and Stojan, Z. *Le deq eclic de Sarajevo.* Paris: n. p., 1934.
Alois, Louis. *The Homicidal Maniac, Ten Studies.* Paris: Published by Author, 1967.
Aloutte. *Quantrell: The Terror of the West.* New York: M. J. Ivers, 1881.
Alper, Benedict. *Prisons Inside-Out: Alternatives in Correctional Reform.* Cambridge, Mass.: Ballinger, 1974.
Alsop, Em Bowles (ed.). *The Greatness of Woodrow Wilson: 1856-1956.* New York: Rinehart, 1956.
Alsop, Joseph, and Catledge, Turner. *The 168 Days.* Garden City, N. Y.: Doubleday, 1938.
Alternative Draft of the German Penal Code. South Hackensack, N. J.: Fred B. Rothman, 1977.
Altick, Richard D. *Victorian Studies in Scarlet.* London: J. M. Dent & Sons, 1970.
Altman, Jack, and Ziporyn, Marvin. *Born to Raise Hell.* New York: Grove Press, 1967.
Altrocchi, Julia Cooley. *The Spectacular San Franciscans.* New York: E.P. Dutton, 1949.
_____. *Traces of Folklore and Furrow.* Caldwell, Idaho: Caxton Printers, 1945.
Alvarez, A. *The Savage God: A Study of Suicide.* New York: Bantam Books, 1973.
Alvarez, Alfredo. *El limantourismo de Francisco Madero.* Mexico City: Talleres Tipogreq aficos de la Casa de Orientacieq on para Varones, 1934.
Alvarez, N. *The James Boys in Missouri.* Clyde, Ohio: Ames, 1907.
Alverstone, Viscount. *Recollections of Bar and Bench.* London: Arnold, 1914.
Alvisi, Eduardo. *Cesare Borgia.* Imola, Italy: Tip d'Ignazio Galeati e Figlio, 1878.
Amado, Enrique. *La Revolucion Mexicana de 1913.* Valencia, Spain: Prometeo Sociedad Editorial, 1914.
Amaya, General Juan Gualberto. *Madero y los Auteq enticos Revolucionarios de 1910.* 3 vols. Mexico City: Published by Author, 1946.
_____. *Venustiano Carranza: caudillo constitucionalista.* Mexico City: Published by Author, 1947.
Amaya Moreq an, Arturo. *Examen histeq orico-juridico del gobierno de Herta.* Mexico City: Published by Author, 1952.
Ambedkar, B. R. *Ranade, Gandhi and Jinnah.* Bombay, India: Thacker, 1943.
Ambler, Eric. *The Ability to Kill and Other Pieces.* London: Bodley Head, 1963.
Ambrose, Stephen E. *Eisenhower, The President.* New York: Simon & Schuster, 1984.
Ambrosino, Lillian. *Runaways.* Boston: Beacon Press, 1971.
American Bar Association. *Code of Professional Responsibility and Canons of Judicial Ethics.* Washington, D. C.: American Bar Association, 1970.
_____. *Final Report of the Committee on Economic Offenses.* Washington, D. C.: American Bar Association, 1976.
_____. *The Prosecution Function and the Defense Function.* New York: Institute for Judicial Administration, 1970.
_____. *Report on Organized Crime.* New York: American Bar Association, 1952.
The American Bloody Register. Boston: W. Russell, 1784.
American Correctional Association. *Correctional Officers' Training Guide.* College Park, Md.: American Correctional Association, 1959.
American Enterprise Institute. *The American Presidency: A Discussion with Gerald R. Ford.* Washington, D. C.: AEI, 1977.
American Friends Service Committee. *Struggle for Justice: A Report on Crime and Punishment in America.* New York: Hill & Wang, 1971.
American Historical Association. *Papers of the American Historical Association.* New York: Putnam, 1886.
American Humane Association Children's Division. *Trends in Officially Reported Child Neglect and Abuse in the United States.* Denver: American Humane Association, 1984.
American Law Institute. *Model Penal Code.* Philadelphia: American Law Institute, 1962.
_____, and American Bar Association. Joint Committee on Continuing Legal Education. *The Problem of Punishing Homicide.* Philadelphia: American Law Institute, 1962.
American Medical Association. *Digest of Official Action: 1846-1958,* Chicago: American Medical Association, 1959.
_____. *Drug Dependence: A Guide for Physicians.* Chicago: American Medical Association, 1969.
American Psychiatric Association. *Biographical Directory of the Fellows and Members.* New York: R. R. Bowker, 1973.
American vs. Italian Brigandage. Philadelphia: Barclay, 1875.
Ames, James E. *Theodore Roosevelt: Hero to His Valet.* New York: John Day, 1927.
Ames, Walter L. *Police and Community in Japan.* Berkeley: University of California Press, 1981.
Amies, Hardy. *Just So Far.* London: Collins, 1954.
Amir, Menachem. *Patterns in Forcible Rape.* Chicago: University of Chicago Press, 1971.
Amort, R., and Jedlicka, M. *The Canaris File.* London: Wingate, 1970.
Amory, Cleveland, and Bradlee, F. *Cavalcade of the 1920's and 30's.* London: Bodley Head, 1961.
_____. *The Last Resorts.* New York: Harper & Brothers, 1948.
_____. *The Proper Bostonians.* New York: E. P. Dutton, 1947.
_____. *Who Killed Society?* New York: Harper & Brothers, 1960.
Amrine, Michael. *This Awesome Challenge: The Hundred Days of Lyndon Johnson.* New York: G. P. Putnam's Sons, 1964.
Amster, Gerald, and Asbell, Bernard. *Transit Point Moscow.* New York: Holt, Rinehart and Winston, 1984.
Anatomy of a Murder. London: John Lane, 1936.
Andenaes, Johannes. *Punishment and Deterrence.* Ann Arbor: University of Michigan Press, 1974.
Anders, Karl. *Murder to Order.* New York: Devin, 1967.
Anders, Wladyslaw. *Hitler's Defeat in Russia.* Chicago: Regnery, 1953.
Andersen, Christopher P. *The Serpent's Tooth.* New York: Harper & Row, 1987.
Andersen, Hartvig. *The Dark City.* New York: Rinehart, 1954.
Anderson, Annelise G. *The Business of Organized Crime: A Cosa Nostra Family.* Stanford, Calif.: Hoover Institution Press, 1979.
Anderson, Chris, and McGehee, Sharon. *Bodies of Evidence.* New York: Lyle Stuart, 1991.
Anderson, Clinton H. *Beverly Hills Is My Beat.* New York: Popular Library, 1962.
Anderson, David, and Benjaminson, Peter. *Investigative Reporting.* Bloomington: Indiana University Press, 1976.
Anderson, Frank W. *Bill Miner: Train Robber.* Calgary, Alberta, Can.: Frontiers, 1963.
_____. *The Dark Strangler.* Calgary, Alberta, Can.: Frontiers, 1974.
Anderson, Galuska. *A Border City during the Civil War.* Boston: Little, Brown, 1908.
Anderson, George B. (ed.). *History of New Mexico: Its Resources and People.* Los Angeles: Pacific States, 1907.
Anderson, J. *This Was Harlem: A Cultural Portrait, 1900-1950.* New York: Farrar, Straus & Giroux, 1982.
Anderson, Jack. *The Anderson Papers.* New York: Random House, 1973.
_____, and Boyd, James. *Confessions of a Muckraker.* New York: Random House, 1979.
_____, and Blumenthal, Fred. *The Kefauver Story.* New York: Dial Press, 1956.
Anderson, Kristin. and DeBreuil, Linda. *The Wholesome Hooker.* New York: W. W. Norton, 1973.
Anderson, Margaret. *My Thirty Year's War.* New York: Alfred A. Knopf, 1930.
Anderson, Sir Robert. *Criminals and Crime: Some Facts and Suggestions.* London: James Nisbet, 1907.
_____. *The Lighter Side of My Official Life.* London: Hodder & Stoughton, 1910.
Anderson, Thornton (ed.). *Masters of Russian Marxism.* New York: Appleton-Century-Crofts, 1963.
_____. *Rule of Terror: Russia Under Lenin and Stalin.* New York: Holt, Rinehart & Winston, 1969.
Ando Yoshio (ed.). *Showa Keizai-shi e no shogen. [Evidence Pertaining to Economic History in the Reign of Hirohito].* Tokyo: Mainichi Shinbunsha, 1966.
Andreq eadeq es, A. *History of the Bank of England.* London: P. S. King, 1909.
Andreae, Percy. *The Prohibition Movement in its Broader Bearings upon our Social, Commercial and Religious Liberties.* Chicago: Felix Mendelsohn, 1915.
Andreski, Stanislav. *The African Predicament.* New York: Atherton, 1968.
Andrew, C. F. *Mahatma Gandhi: At Work.* London: George Allen & Unwin, 1931.
_____. *Mahatma Gandhi: His Own Story.* New York: Macmillan, 1931.
_____. *Mahatma Gandhi's Ideas.* London: George Allen & Unwin, 1929.
Andrew, Christopher. *Her Majesty's Secret Service: The Making of the British Intelligence Community.* New York: Penguin, 1987.
_____, and Gordievsky, Oleg. *KGB: The Inside Story.* New York: Harper Collins, 1990.
_____. *The Sword and the Shield: The Mitrokhin Archive and the Secret History of the KGB.* New York: Basic Books, 2000.
Andrew, Roland G. *Through Fascist Italy.* London: George Harrap, 1935.
Andrewes, Antony. *The Greek Tyrants.* London: Hutchinson's University Library, 1965.
Andrews, Bert and Peter. *A Tragedy of History.* Washington, D.C.: Robert B. Luce, 1962
Andrews, C. L. *The Story of Alaska.* Caldwell, Idaho: Caxton Printers, 1938.
Andrews, C. M. *The Colonial Period of American History.* 4 vols. New Haven, Conn.: Yale University Press, 1934.
Andrews, E. Benjamin. *The History of the Last Quarter-Century in the United States, 1870-1895.* 2 vols. New York: Charles Scribner's Sons, 1896.
Andrews, Frank, and Dickens, Albert. *Over the Wall.* New York: Pyramid, 1974.
Andrews, George, and Vinkenoog, Simon (eds.). *The Book of Grass.* New York: Grove Press, 1967.
_____, and Solomon, David. *The Coca Leaf and Cocaine Papers.* New York: Harcourt, Brace, 1975.
Andrews, K. H. *Elizabethan Privateering: English Privateering During the Spanish War, 1585-1603.* New York: Cambridge University Press, 1964.
Andrews, Ralph W. *Historic Fires of the West.* New York: Bonanza Books, 1966.
Andrews, Wayne. *Battle for Chicago.* New York: Harcourt, Brace, 1946.
_____. *The Vanderbilt Legend.* New York: Harcourt, Brace, 1941.
Andrews, William. *Old-Time Punishments.* London: Tabard Press, 1960.
Andreyev, A. *Lenin v Kremle.* Moscow: Politicheskoi Literaturi, 1960.
Andric, Ivo. *Bosnian Story.* London: Lincolns-Praeger, 1948.
_____. *The Bridge on the Drina.* New York: New American Library, 1961.
Angel, S. *Discouraging Crime Through City Planning.* Berkeley: University of California Press, 1969.
Angelella, Michael. *Trail of Blood.* New York: New American Library, 1979.
Angell, Norman. *The Story of Money.* New York: Frederick A. Stokes, 1929.
Anger, Kenneth. *Hollywood Babylon.* New York: Dell, 1965.
Angle, Paul M. *Bloody Williamson: A Chapter in American Lawlessness.* New York: Alfred A. Knopf, 1952.
_____. *The Great Chicago Fire.* Chicago: Chicago Historical Society, 1946.
_____, and Miers, Earl Schenck (eds.). *The Living Lincoln.* New Brunswick, N. J.: Rutgers University Press, 1955.
_____ (ed.). *A Portrait of Abraham Lincoln in Letters by His Oldest Son.* Chicago: Chicago Historical Society, 1968.
_____. *A Shelf of Lincoln Books.* New Brunswick, N. J.: Rutgers University Press, 1946.
Angley, Edward. *Oh, Yeah?* New York: Viking, 1931.

Ankaloo, Bengt, and Clark, Stuart (eds.). *Witchcraft and Magic in Europe: The Period of the Witch Trials.* Philadelphia: University of Pennsylvania Press, 2003.
Anker, Kurt. *Kronprinz Wilhelm.* Berlin: E. S. Mittler & Sohn, 1919.
Annals of San Francisco. New York: Western Press, 1855.
Annan, N. G. *Leslie Stephen.* London: MacGibbon & Kee, 1951.
Annin, Robert E. *Woodrow Wilson: A Character Study.* New York: Dodd, Mead, 1924.
Annual Report of Commissioners of Prisons and Directors of Convict Prisons 1911-12. London: H. M. Stationery Office, 1912.
Anslinger, Harry J., and Oursler, Will. *The Murderers.* New York: Farrar, Straus & Cudahy, 1961.
_____. *The Protectors.* New York: Farrar, Straus, 1964.
_____, and Tompkins, W. F. *The Traffic in Narcotics.* New York: Funk & Wagnalls, 1953.
Anson, Robert Sam. *"They've Killed the President".* New York: Bantam Books, 1975.
Anthiny, Evelyn. *The Assassin.* New York: Coward McCann, 1970.
Anthony, Irving. *Paddle Wheels and Pistols.* Philadelphia: Macrae Smith, 1929.
Anthony, K. S. *Catherine the Great.* Garden City, N. Y.: Alfred A. Knopf, 1925.
_____ (ed.). *Memoirs of Catherine the Great.* New York: Alfred A. Knopf, 1927.
Anti-Masonic Almanac for 1833. Baltimore: n. p., 1834.
Antommarchi, Dr. F. *The Last Days of Napoleon.* London: H. Colburn, 1826.
Antonius, George. *The Arab Awakening.* London: Hamish Hamilton, 1938.
Anwar, Raja. *The Terrorist Prince: The Life and Death of Murtaza Bhutta.* London: Verso, 1977.
Aoyama Koji. *Yakuza no Seikai: Kanka, Jingi, Tobaku, Sono Onna [Yakuza Society: Fighting, Chivalry, Gambling, and Women].* Tokyo: Kofusha, 1979.
Apell, George C. *Belle's Castle.* New York: MacMillan Co., 1959.
Apenszlak, Jacob (ed.). *The Black Book of Polish Jewry: An Account of the Martyrdom of Polish Jewry Under the Nazi Occupation.* New York: Roy Publishers, 1943.
Applegate, Rex. *Riot Control.* Harrisburg, Pa.: Stackpole, 1969.
Appleman, Roy E. *Charlie Siringo, Cowboy Detective.* Washington, D.C.: Potomac Corral, the Westerners, 1968.
Appler, Augustus C. *The Guerrillas of the West; or The Life, Character and Daring Exploits of the Younger Brothers.* St. Louis: Eureka, 1876.
_____. *The Younger Brothers.* New York: Frederick Fell, 1955.
Apsche, Jack. *Probing the Mind of a Serial Killer.* Morrisville, Penn.: International Information Associates, 1993.
Aptheker, Herbert. *American Negro Slave Revolts.* New York: International, 1943.
_____. *History and Reality.* New York: Cameron, 1955.
_____. *Nat Turner's Slave Rebellion.* New York: Grove Press, 1966.
_____. *Negro Slave Revolts in the United States, 1526-1860.* New York: International, 1939.
_____. *To Be Free: Studies in American Negro History.* New York: International, 1948.
Arahara Bokusui. *Dai Uyoku Shi [Great History of the Right Wing].* Tokyo: Dai Nippon Kokumin To, 1966.
Arbman, Holger. *The Vikings.* New York: Praeger, 1961.
Archambeau, Ernest R. (ed.). *Old Tascosa, 1885-1888.* Canyon, Texas: Panhandle Plains Historical Society, 1966.
Archer, Fred. *Ghost Detectives: Crime and the Psychic World.* London: W.H. Allen, 1970.
_____. *Killers in the Clear.* New York: W.H. Allen, 1971.
Archer, Jules. *Angry Abolitionist: William Lloyd Garrison.* New York: Julian Messner, 1969.
_____. *The Extremists.* New York: Hawthorn Books, 1969.
_____. *Fighting Journalist: Horace Greeley.* New York: Julian Messner, 1966.
_____. *Hawks, Doves and the Eagle.* New York: Hawthorn Books, 1970.
_____. *Mexico and the United States.* New York: Hawthorn Books, 1973.
_____. *1968: Year of Crisis.* New York: Julian Messner, 1971.
_____. *The Plot to Seize the White House.* New York: Hawthorn Books, 1973.
_____. *Resistance.* Philadelphia: Macrae Smith, 1973.
_____. *Revolution In Our Time.* New York: Julian Messner, 1971.
_____. *Riot! A History of Mob Action in the United States.* New York: Hawthorn Books, 1974.
_____. *Strikes, Bombs and Bullets.* New York: Julian Messner, 1972.
_____. *They Made a Revolution: 1776.* New York: Scholastic, 1973.
_____. *Treason in America.* New York: Hawthorn Books, 1971.
_____. *The Unpopular Ones.* New York: Crowell-Collier, 1968.
Archer, William. *America Today.* London: William Heinemann, 1900.
Arenberg, Gerald S. *Crime Prevention Handbook.* Washington, D.C.: National Association of Chiefs of Police, 1979.
Arendt, Hannah. *Between Past and Future.* New York: Meridian Books, 1963.
_____. *Crisis of the Republic.* Harmondsworth, Eng.: Pelican, 1973.
_____. *Eichmann in Jerusalem: A Report on the Banality of Evil.* New York: Viking, 1963.
_____. *On Revolution.* New York: Viking, 1963.
_____. *On Violence.* New York: Harcourt Brace & World, 1969.
_____. *The Origins of Totalitarianism.* London: George Allen & Unwin, 1958.
Arens, Richard, and Lasswell, Harold D. *In Defense of Public Order.* New York: Columbia University Press, 1961.
Arensberg, Conrad. *The Irish Countryman: An Anthropological Study.* New York: P. Smith, 1950.
Argall, Phyllis. *The Truth About Jesse James.* Sullivan, Mo.: Lester B. Dill & Rudy Turilli, 1953.
Argument of Hon. Edwards Pierrepont to the Jury on the Trial of John H. Surratt for the Murder of President Lincoln. Washington, D. C.: U. S. Government Printing Office, 1867.
Argyll, J.G.E.H.D.S. Campbell, Ninth Duke of. *V.R.I. Queen Victoria.* New York: Harper & Brothers, 1901.
Arianus, Flavius. *The Campaigns of Alexander.* New York: Viking, 1976.
Arieq es, Phillipe. *Western Attitudes Toward Death: From the Middle Ages to the Present.* trans. Patricia M. Ranum. Baltimore: Johns Hopkins University Press, 1974.
Arieti, S., and Meth, J.A. *American Handbook of Psychiatry.* New York: Basic Books, 1959.
Arizona, The Grand Canyon State. New York: Hastings House, 1940.
Arlacchi, Pino. *Mafia Business: The Mafia Ethic and the Spirit of Capitalism.* London: Verso, 1986.
Arm, Walter. *Pay-Off.* New York: D. Appleton, 1951.
Armbruster, Eugene L. *Brooklyn's Eastern District.* New York: Brooklyn, 1942.
Armitage, G. *History of the Bow Street Runners.* London: Wishart, 1932.
Armor, Samuel (ed.). *History of Orange County, California.* Los Angeles: Historic Record, 1911.
Armour, W. S. *Facing the Irish Question.* London: Gerald Duckworth, 1935.
Arms, Mear. *The Samuel Colt Biography.* New York: Beinfield, 1978.
Armstrong, Donald. *The Reluctant Warrior.* New York: Thomas Y. Crowell, 1966.
Armstrong, F. E. *The Book of the Stock Exchange.* London: Sir Isaac Pitman & Sons, 1934.
Armstrong, Hamilton Fish. *The New Balkans.* New York: Harper & Brothers, 1926.
_____. *Peace and Counter-Peace.* New York: Harper & Row, 1971.
_____. *Tito and Goliath.* New York: Macmillan, 1951.
_____. *Where the East Begins.* New York: Harper & Brothers, 1929.
Armstrong, J. B. *The Raw Edge.* Missoula: Montana State University Press, 1964.
Armstrong, John A. *The Politics of Totalitarianism.* New York: Random House, 1961.
Army Times (eds.). *Heroes of the Resistance.* New York: Dodd, Mead, 1975.
_____. *The Tangled Web.* Washington, D. C.: Robert B. Luce, Inc., 1963.
Arneson, Ben Albert. *The Democratic Monarchies of Scandinavia.* New York: Van Nostrand, 1939.
Arnett, Alex Mathews. *The Populist Movement in Georgia.* New York: Columbia University Press, 1922.
Arnold, David O. (ed.). *The Sociology of Subcultures.* Berkeley, Calif.: Glendessary Press, 1970.
Arnold, Oren, and Hale, John P. *Hot Irons: Heraldry of the Range.* New York: Macmillan, 1940.
_____. *Thunder in the Southwest: Echoes from the Wild Frontier.* Norman: University of Oklahoma, 1937.
_____. *Wild Life in the Southwest.* Dallas: Banks Upshaw, 1935.
Arnold, Peter. *How To Protect Your Child Against Crime.* New York: Association Press, 1977.
Arnold, Samuel Bland. *Defense and Prison Experiences of a Lincoln Conspirator: Statements and Autobiographical Notes.* Hattiesburg, Miss.: Book Farm, 1943.
Arnold, Thurman. *Fair Fights and Foul.* New York: Harcourt, Brace & World, 1965.
_____. *The Folklore of Capitalism.* New Haven, Conn.: Yale University Press, 1937.
Arnot, Hugo. *A Collection and Abridgement of Celebrated Criminal Trials in Scotland, 1563-1784.* Edinburgh, Scot.: W. Smellie, 1785.
Aronson, Harvey. *Deal.* New York: Ballantine Books, 1978.
_____. *The Killing of Joey Gallo.* New York: G. P. Putnam's Sons, 1973.
Aronson, Theo. *Prince Eddy and the Homosexual Underworld.* London: John Murray, 1994.
Arribavene, Count Charles. *Italy under Victor Emmanuel.* London: Hurst & Blackett, 1862.
Arrington, A. W. *Desperadoes of the Southwest.* New York: W. H. Graham, 1847.
_____. *The Rangers and Regulators of the Tanaha.* New York: R. M. Dewitt, 1856.
Arthur, George. *George V.* New York: Cape, 1930.
_____. *Life of Lord Kitchener.* New York: Macmillan, 1920.
Arthur, George Clinton. *Bushwhacker.* Rolla, Mo.: Rolla Printing, 1938.
Arthur, Herbert. *All the Sinners.* London: John Long, 1931.
Arthur, Timothy Shay. *Grappling with the Monster.* New Haven, Conn.: Edgewood, 1877.
_____. *Six Nights With the Washingtonians.* Philadelphia: T. B. Peterson & Brothers, 1871.
Artrip, Louise and Fullen. *Memoirs of Daniel Fore (Jim) Chisholm and the Chisholm Trail.* Boonville, Ark.: Published by Authors, 1949.
Asbury, Herbert. *The Barbary Coast: An Informal History of the San Francisco Underworld.* New York: Garden City, 1933.
_____. *Carry Nation.* New York: Alfred A. Knopf, 1929.
_____. *The French Quarter, An Informal History of the New Orleans Underworld.* New York: Alfred A. Knopf, 1936.
_____. *The Gangs of New York.* New York: Alfred A. Knopf, 1927.
_____. *Gem of the Prairie: An Informal History of the Chicago Underworld.* New York: Alfred A. Knopf, 1940.
_____. *The Great Illusion: An Informal History of Prohibition.* New York: Doubleday, 1950.
_____. *A Methodist Saint: The Life of Bishop Asbury.* New York: Alfred A. Knopf, 1927.
_____. *Sucker's Progress: An Informal History of Gambling in America From the Colonies to Canfield.* New York: Dodd & Mead, 1938.
_____. *Up from Methodism.* New York: Alfred A. Knopf, 1926.
_____. *Ye Olde Fire Laddies.* New York: Alfred A. Knopf, 1930.
Asch, Sidney H. *Criminal Investigation Rights of the Individual.* New York: Arco, 1967.
Aschaffenburg, G. *Crime and Its Repression.* Boston: Little, Brown, 1913.
Ascoli, Max, and Feiler, Arthur. *Fascism for Whom?* New York: W. W. Norton, 1938.
_____. *Fascism: Who Benefits?* London: George Allen & Unwin, 1939.
_____ (ed.). *Our Times: The Best from the Reporter.* New York: Farrar, Straus & Cudahy, 1960.
Asfa Yilma, Princess. *Haile Selassie.* London: Sampson Low, 1936.

Ashbaugh, Don. *Nevada's Turbulent Yesterday.* Los Angeles: Westernlore Press, 1963.
Ashe, Geoffrey. *Gandhi.* New York: Stein & Day, 1968.
Ashe, Samuel A'Court. *History of North Carolina.* Greensboro, N.C.: E.M. Uzzell, 1908.
The Ashland Tragedy...A History of the Killing of Fanny Gibbons. Ashland, Ky.: J. M. Huff, 1883.
Ashley, F.W. *My Sixty Years in the Law.* London: Bodley Head, 1936.
Ashley, Richard. *Cocaine: Its History, Uses and Effects.* New York: St. Martin's Press, 1975.
_____. *Heroin: The Myths and the Facts.* New York: St. Martin's Press, 1972.
Ashman, Charles. *The CIA-Mafia Link: The Inside Secrets of Assassination.* New York: Manor Books, 1975.
_____. *The Finest Judges Money Can Buy.* Los Angeles: Nash, 1973.
Ashman, Chuck, and Trescott, Pamela. *Diplomatic Crime.* Washington, D. C.: Acropolis Books, 1987.
Ashton, John. *The Devil in Britain and America.* London: Ward & Downey, 1896.
Ashton, Wendall J. *The Voice of the West: Biography of a Pioneer Newspaper.* New York: Duell, Sloan, & Pearce, 1950.
Ashton-Wolfe, H. *The Cask of Death.* New York: E. P. Dutton, 1932.
_____. *Crimes of Love and Hate.* Boston: Houghton Mifflin, 1927.
_____. *Crimes of Violence and Revenge.* New York: E. P. Dutton, 1932.
_____. *The Forgotten Clue.* Boston: Houghton Mifflin, 1930.
_____. *Outlaws of Modern Days.* London: Cassell, 1927.
_____. *The Underworld.* New York: George H. Doran, 1926.
Asinof, Eliot. *Eight Men Out: The Black Sox Scandal.* New York: Holt, Rinehart & Winston, 1963.
Askew, Garrett L. *The Pageant of the Packets.* New York: D. Appleton, 1929.
Askins, Charles. *Texans: Guns and History.* New York: Winchester Press, 1970.
Askwith, T.G. *Kenya's Progress.* Nairobi, Kenya: East African Literature Bureau/Eagle Press, 1958.
Asmodeus in New York. New York: Longchamp, 1868.
Asprey, Robert B. *The German High Command at War: Hindenburg and Ludendorff Conduct World War I.* New York: Morrow, 1991.
_____. *War in the Shadows.* New York: Doubleday, 1975.
Asquith, Earl of Oxford and. *Memories and Reflections.* 2 vols. London: Cassell, 1928.
The Assassination and History of the Conspiracy. New York: J. R. Hawley, 1865.
The Assassination Story: Newspaper Clippings from the Two Dallas Dailies. Dallas: American Eagle, 1964.
Assassination U. S. A. New York: Herald House, 1968.
The Assassin's Doom, Full Account of the Jail Life, Trial and Sentence of Charles J. Guiteau. New York: Richard K. Fox, 1882.
Assersohn, Roy. *The Biggest Deal: Bankers, Politics, and the Hostages of Iran.* London: Methuen, 1982.
Associated Professional Services (ed.) *The Complete Kennedy Saga.* Los Angeles: Associated Professional Services, 1964.
_____. *Four Dark Days in History.* Los Angeles: Special Publications, 1963.
_____. *Highlights of the Warren Report.* Hollywood, Calif.: Associated Professional Services, 1964.
_____. *In Memoriam . . . 365 Days Later.* Los Angeles: Matador Magazine, 1964.
_____. *A Salute to Jacqueline Kennedy.* Los Angeles: James P. Matthews, 1964.
_____. *Who Killed Kennedy?* Covina, Calif: Collectors, 1964.
Astley, John Bright. *The Inner Circle.* London: Hutchinson, 1971.
Astor, Gerald. *The Charge is Rape.* New York: Playboy Press, 1974.
_____. *The New York Cops.* New York: Scribner's, 1971.
Atholl, Justin. *The Reluctant Hangman: The Story of James Berry, Executioner 1884-1892.* London: John Long, 1956.
_____. *Shadow of the Gallows.* London: John Long, 1954.
Atiyah, Edward. *The Arabs.* London: Penguin Books, 1955.
_____. *The Thin Line.* New York: Harpers, 1952.
Atkin, Ronald. *Revolution! Mexico 1910-20.* New York: John Day, 1970.
Atkins, Burton M., and Glick, Henry R. *Prisons, Protest and Politics.* Englewood Cliffs, N. J.: Prentice-Hall, 1972.
Atkins, Gordon. *Health, Housing, and Poverty in New York City, 1865-1898.* Ann Arbor, Mich.: Edwards Brothers, 1947.
Atkinson, Eleanor. *Story of Chicago.* Chicago: Little Chronicle, 1911.
Atlay, James Beresford. *Famous Trials of the Century.* London: G. Richards, 1899.
The Attempted Assassination of President Garfield: A Full Graphic and Only Complete Account, with the Life of Our President, and the Life of Guiteau, the Assassin. Philadelphia: Barclay, 1881.
Attica Commission. *Attica: The Official Report of the New York State Special Commission on Attica.* New York: Bantam Books, 1973.
Attorney General's Task Force on Organized Crime. *Phase I, Phase II Recommendations.* Washington, D. C.: U. S. Department of Justice, 1981.
Atwell, Benjamin H. *The Great Harry Thaw Case.* Chicago: Laird & Lee, 1907.
Aubrey, Arthur S. Jr., and Caputo, Rudolph R. *Criminal Interrogation.* Springfield, Ill.: Charles C. Thomas, 1965.
Aubrey, Octave. *Sainte-Heq eleq ene.* Paris: Flammarion, 1835.
Audett, James Henry ("Blackie"). *Rap Sheet: My Life Story.* New York: William Sloane, 1954.
Auerbach, Ann. *The Untold Story of International Kidnapping.* New York: Henry Holt, 1998.
Auletta, Ken. *The Underclass.* New York: Random House, 1982.
Austin, John. *Hollywood's Unsolved Mysteries.* New York: Ace Star, 1970.
Ausubel, David P. *Drug Addiction.* New York: Random House, 1958.
The Authentic Confession of Jesse Strang. New York: E. M. Murden & A. Ming, Jr., 1827.
Authentic History of Sam Bass and His Gang. Denton, Texas: Monitor Job Office, 1878.
Auzies, Ceq elestin. *De la surveilance de la haunte police.* Paris: E. Thorin, 1869.
Averbuch, Bernard, and Noble, John Wesley. *Never Plead Guilty.* New York: Farrar, Straus & Cudahy, 1955.
Averso, Nino. *Napoli sotto il terrore tedesco.* Naples, Italy: 'Le Quattro Giornate', 1943.
Avetta, Ida. *Mussolini e la folla.* Mantua, Italy: Paladino, 1927.
Aviel, Ehud. *Open the Gates.* New York: Atheneum, 1975.
Avinov, Marie. *Marie Avinov: Pilgrimage Through Hell.* Englewood Cliffs, N. J.: Prentice-Hall, 1968.
Avirgan, Tony, and Honey, Martha. *War in Uganda: The Legacy of Idi Amin.* Chicago: Lawrence Hill and Co. (Lawrence Hill Books/Chicago Review Press), 1983.
Avner. *Memoirs of an Assassin.* New York: Yoseloff, 1959.
Avrich, Paul. *Kronstadt: 1921.* Princeton, N.J.: Princeton University Press, 1970.
_____. *The Russian Anarchists.* Princeton, N. J.: Princeton University Press, 1967.
Axford, Joseph Mack. *Around Western Campfires.* New York: Pageant Press, 1964.
Aydelotte, Frank. *Elizabethan Rogues and Vagabonds.* Oxford, Eng.: Clarendon Press, 1913.
Ayer, Frederick Jr. *Yankee G-Man.* Chicago: Henry Regnery, 1957.
Ayers, D. *The Guardian.* London: Collins, 1971.
Ayers, John H., and Bird, Carol. *Missing Men: The Story of The Missing Persons Bureau of the New York Police Department.* New York: G. P. Putnam's Sons, 1932.
Ayers, Nathaniel M. *Building a New Empire.* New York: Broadway, 1910.
Ayscough, Florence. *Chinese Women Yesterday and Today.* Boston: Houghton Mifflin, 1937.

Baader Meinhof Report, Der. Mainz, Ger.: Hase & Keq ohler Verlag, 1972.
Babington, Anthony. *The English Bastille: A History of Newgate Gaol and Prison Conditions in Britain, 1188-1902.* London: Macdonald, 1971.
_____. *A House in Bow Street: Crime and the Magistracy in London, 1740-1881.* London: McDonald, 1969.
Babst, Dean V., and Gale, Joseph C. *Wisconsin County Jails, 1958-1960.* Madison: Wisconsin Division of Corrections, 1962.
Babyak, Jolene. *Breaking the Rock: The Great Escape from Alcatraz.* San Francisco: Ariel Vamp Press, 2003.
_____. *Eyewitness to Alcatraz: Life on the Rock as Told by the Guards, Families and Prisoners.* San Francisco: Ariel Vamp Press, 1988.
Baca, Carlos Cabeza de. *Vicente Silva, New Mexico's Vice King of the Nineties.* n. p., 1938.
Bach, George R. *The Intimate Enemy.* New York: Avon, 1968.
Bacon, G. W. *Life of Andrew Johnson.* London: Bacon, n. d.
Bacon, James. *Hollywood Is a Four-Letter Town.* New York: Avon Books, 1977.
Bacon, Sir Reginald. *Life of Lord Fisher.* London: Hodder & Stoughton, 1929.
Baddeley, John H. *Russia, Mongolia, China.* 2 vols. London: Macmillan, 1919.
Baden, Michael. *Unnatural Death.* New York: Ivy Books, 1989.
Badian, Ernest. *Foreign Clientele, 264-70 B.C.* Oxford, Eng.: Clarendon Press, 1968.
Badillo, Herman, and Haynes, Milton. *A Bill of No Rights: Attica and the American Prison System.* New York: Outerbridge & Lazard, 1972.
Baehr, Harry W., Jr. *The New York Tribune Since the Civil War.* New York: Dodd, Mead, 1936.
Baerlein, Henry. *The Birth of Yugoslavia.* London: Parsons, 1922.
_____. *Mexico, the Land of Unrest: Being Chiefly an Account of What Produced the Outbreak of 1910.* London: Herbert & Daniel, 1913.
Bagdikian, Ben H. *The Shame of the Prisons.* New York: Pocket Books, 1972.
Baghdadi, Abdul Latif al-. *The Eastern Key.* London: Allen & Unwin, 1965.
Bailey, F. Lee, and Rothblatt, Henry B. *Crimes of Violence, Rape and Other Sex Crimes.* Rochester, N.Y.: Lawyers Co-Operative, 1973.
_____. *Defending Business and White Collar Crimes: Federal and State.* Rochester, N. Y.: Lawyer's Co-operative, 1969.
_____. *The Defense Never Rests.* New York: Signet Books, 1972.
_____, and Greenya, John. *For the Defense.* New York: Atheneum, 1975.
Bailey, Guy. *The Fatal Chance.* London: Peter Davies, 1969.
Bailey, Harry H. *When New Mexico Was Young.* Las Cruces, N. M.: Las Cruces Citizen, 1948.
Bailey, Kenneth P. *The Ohio Company of Virginia and the Westward Movement, 1748-1792.* Glendale, Calif.: Arthur H. Clark, 1939.
Bain, Donald. *War in Illinois.* Englewood Cliffs, N. J.: Prentice-Hall, 1978.
Bain, R.N. *The Daughter of Peter the Great.* London: Constable, 1899.
_____. *Peter III, Emperor of Russia.* London: Constable, 1902.
Bainton, Roland H. (ed.). *Castellioniana.* Leiden: E. J. Brill, 1951.
_____. *Hunted Heretic: The Life and Death of Michael Servetus.* Boston: Beacon, 1953.
Bakal, Carl. *The Right to Bear Arms.* New York: McGraw-Hill, 1966.
Bakan, David. *The Slaughter of the Innocents.* San Francisco: Jossey-Bass, 1975.
Bakeless, John. *Lewis and Clark: Partners in Discovery.* New York: William Morrow, 1947.
Baker, Bobby. *Wheeling and Dealing.* New York: W. W. Norton, 1978.
Baker, Dean C. *The Assassination of President Kennedy: A Study of the Press Coverage.* Ann Arbor: University of Michigan Press, 1965.
Baker, George Melville. *Mysterious Disappearances.* Boston: Published by Author, 1876.
Baker, J. E. *The Right to Participate: Inmate Involvement in Prison Administration.* Metuchen, N. J.: Scarecrow Press, 1974.
Baker, Leonard. *Back to Back: The Duel Between FDR and the Supreme Court.* New York: Macmillan, 1967.
_____. *The Johnson Eclipse.* New York: Macmillan, 1966.
Baker, Marilyn. *Exclusive.* New York: Macmillan, 1974.
Baker, Mark. *Cops.* New York: Simon and Schuster, 1985.
Baker, Nancy C. *Baby Selling.* New York: Vanguard, 1978.
Baker, Pearl. *The Wild Bunch at Robbers Roost.* New York: Abelard-Schuman, 1971.

Baker, R.K., and Ball, S. J. *Mass Media and Violence.* Washington, D.C.: Government Printing Office, 1969.

Baker, Ray Stannard. *American Chronicle: The Autobiography of Ray Stannard Baker (David Grayson).* New York: Scribner's, 1945.

_____. *The Capture, Death and Burial of J. Wilkes Booth.* Chicago: The Poor Richard Press, 1940.

_____. *Woodrow Wilson, Life and Letters.* London: Heinemann, 1932.

Bakos, Susan Crain. *Appointment for Murder: The Story of the Killing Dentist.* New York: Putnam, 1988.

Balchin, Nigel. *The Anatomy of Villainy.* London: St. James's Place, 1950.

_____. *Fatal Fascination.* Boston: Little, Brown, 1964.

Baldwin, Charles C. *Stanford White.* New York: Dodd, Mead, 1938.

Baldwin, H. W., and Stone, Shepard. *We Saw It Happen.* New York: Simon & Schuster, 1938.

Baldwin, J., and Bottoms, A. E. *The Urban Criminal.* London: Tavistock, 1976.

Baldwin, Joseph G. *The Flush Times of Alabama and Mississippi.* San Francisco: Sumer Whitney, 1883.

Baldwin, Leland D. *Keelboat Age on Western Waters.* Pittsburgh, Pa.: University of Pittsburgh Press, 1941.

Baldwin, W. W. *Mau Mau Manhunt: The Adventures of the Only American Who Fought the Terrorists in Kenya.* New York: E. P. Dutton, 1957.

Bales, William Alan. *A Tiger in the Streets.* New York: Dodd, Mead, 1962.

Balfour, J. S. *My Prison Life.* London: Chapman & Hall, 1907.

Balfour, Michael. *The Kaiser and His Times.* Boston: Houghton Mifflin, 1964.

Balfour, Neil, and Mackay, Sally. *Paul of Yugoslavia.* London: Hamish Hamilton, 1980.

Balfour, Patrick. *Society Racket: A Critical Survey of Modern Social Life.* London: John Long, 1933.

Balkan, S., Berger, R. J., and Schmidt, J. *Crime and Deviance in America.* Belmont, Calif: Wadsworth, 1980.

Ball, John C., and Chambers, Carl D. (eds.). *The Epidemiology of Opiate Addiction in the United States.* Springfield, Ill.: Charles C. Thomas, 1970.

_____. *Social Deviancy and Adolescent Personality: An Analytic Study with the MMPI.* Lexington: University of Kentucky Press, 1962.

Ball, Larry D. *The United States Marshals of New Mexico and Arizona Territories, 1846-1912.* Albuquerque: University of New Mexico Press, 1978.

Ballantine, William. *Some Experiences of a Barrister's Life.* London: Richard Bentley and Sons, 1822.

Ballert, Marion. *Complete & Authentic Life of Jesse James.* New York: Frederick Fell, 1953.

_____. *Younger Brothers.* San Antonio, Texas: Naylor, 1961.

Ballinger, Kenneth. *Miami Millions.* New York: Hastings House, 1936.

_____. *Shinto: The Unconquered Enemy.* New York: Viking Press, 1945.

Balsan, Consuelo Vanderbilt. *The Glitter and the Gold.* New York: Harper & Brothers, 1952.

Balsdon, J. P. V. D. *The Emperor Gaius.* New York: Oxford University Press, 1934.

_____ (ed.). *The Romans.* New York: Basic Books, 1965.

Balsinger, David, and Sellier, Charles E., Jr. *The Lincoln Conspiracy.* Los Angeles: Schick Sunn Classic Books, 1977.

Baltzell, Digby E. *Philadelphia Gentlemen: The Making of a National Upper Class.* Glencoe, Ill.: Free Press, 1973.

_____. *The Protestant Establishment: Aristocracy and Caste in America.* New York: Vintage, 1964.

Bamm, Peter. *Alexander the Great: Power as Destiny.* New York: McGraw-Hill, 1968.

Banay, Ralph S. *We Call Them Criminals.* New York: Appleton-Century-Crofts, 1957.

Bancroft, George Pleydell. *Stage and Bar.* London: Hutchinson, 1936.

Bandini, Franco. *Claretta.* Milan, Italy: Sugar, 1960.

Bane, Bernard M. *Is John F. Kennedy Alive...And Well?* Boston: BMB, 1973.

Banfield, Edward C. *Big City Politics: A Comparative Guide to the Political Systems of Nine American Cities.* New York: Random House, 1965.

Bankhead, Tallulah. *Tallulah: My Autobiography.* London: Victor Gollancz, 1952.

Bankoff, George Alexis. *Rasputin Speaks.* London: Faber & Faber, 1941.

Banks, Harold. *The Strangler!* New York: Avon, 1967.

Bankson, Russell A. *The Klondike Nugget.* Caldwell, Idaho: Caxton Printers, 1935.

Banning, Captain William, and George Hugh. *Six Horses.* New York: Century, 1930.

Bannorris, Amanda. *The Female Land Pirate.* Cincinnati, Ohio: E. E. Barclay, 1848.

Banta, R. E. *The Ohio.* New York: Rinehart, 1949.

Banton, Michael. *Policeman in the Community.* New York: Basic Books, 1964.

Baragwanath, John. *A Good Time Was Had.* New York: Appleton-Century-Crofts, 1962.

Baral, Robert. *Revue: A Nostalgic Reprise of the Great Broadway Period.* New York: Fleet, 1962.

Barante, Amable G. P. B., Baron de. *Jeanne d'Arc.* Paris: Payot, 1935.

Barba Gonzeq alez, Silvano. *La lucha por la tierra. Emiliano Zapata.* Mexico City: n. p., 1960.

Barbash, Jack. *The Practice of Unionism.* New York: Harper & Row, 1956.

Barber, Elinor G. *The Bourgeoisie in the 18th Century France.* Princeton, N. J.: Princeton University Press, 1955.

Barber, James David. *The Presidential Character.* Englewood Cliffs, N. J.: Prentice-Hall, 1972.

Barber, Richard. *The Knight and Chivalry.* London: Longman, 1970.

Barbican, James. *The Confessions of a Rum-Runner.* New York: Ives Washburn, 1928.

Barbier, Edmond Jean François. *Chronique de la req egence et du req egne de Louis XV, 1718-1763.* Paris: Charpentier, 1857-1885.

Barbour, Philip L. *Dimitry, Called the Pretender: Tsar and Great Prince of All Russia, 1605-1606.* Boston: Houghton, Mifflin, 1966.

Barboza, Joe, and Messick, Hank. *Barboza.* New York: Dell Books, 1975.

Barclay, S. *Bondage.* New York: Funk and Wagnalls, 1968.

Bard, Morton, and Sangrey, Daw. *The Crime Victims Book.* New York: Basic Books, 1979.

_____, and Shellow, Robert. *Issues in Law Enforcement.* Reston, Va.: Reston, 1976.

Bardens, Dennis. *The Ladykiller.* London: P. Davies, 1972.

_____. *Lord Justice Birkett.* London: Robert Hale, 1962.

Baridon, Philip C. *Addiction, Crime and Social Policy.* Lexington, Mass.: Lexington Books, 1976.

Baringer, William E. *A House Dividing. Lincoln as President Elect.* Springfield, Ill.: Abraham Lincoln Association, 1945.

_____. *Lincoln's Rise to Power.* Boston: Little, Brown, 1937.

Baring-Gould, Sabine. *The Book of Werewolves.* London: Smith, Elder, 1865.

Baring-Gould, William S. *Sherlock Holmes: A Biography of the World's First Consulting Detective.* London: Hart-Davis, 1962.

Barja, Julio Caro. *World of Witches.* Chicago: University of Chicago Press, 1965.

Barkas, J.L. *Victims.* New York: Scribner's, 1978.

Barker, Dudley. *Lord Darling's Famous Cases.* London: Hutchinson, 1936.

Barker, Elizabeth. *Macedonia: Its Place in Balkan Power Politics.* London: Royal Institute of International Affairs, 1950.

Barker, John T. *Missouri Lawyer.* Philadelphia: Dorrance, 1949.

Barker, Richard H. (ed.). *The Fatal Caress and Other Accounts of English Murders from 1551 to 1881.* New York: Duell, Sloan and Pearce, 1947.

Barlay, Stephen. *The Secret Business.* New York: Thomas Y. Crowell, 1973.

Barlett, Donald L., and Steele, James H. *Empire: The Life, Legend, and Madness of Howard Hughes.* New York: W. W. Norton, 1979.

Barlow, Hugh D. *Introduction to Criminology.* Boston: Little, Brown, 1984.

Barnard, Allan (ed.). *The Harlot Killer: The Story of Jack the Ripper in Fact and Fiction.* New York: Dodd, Mead, 1953.

Barnard, Harry. *Eagle Forgotten: The Life of John Peter Altgeld.* Indianapolis: Bobbs-Merrill, 1938.

_____. *Rutherford B. Hayes and His America.* Indianapolis, Ind.: Bobbs-Merrill, 1954.

Barnard, Henry. *Armsmear: The Samuel Colt Biography.* New York: Beinfeld, 1976.

Barnard, William F. *Forty Years at the Five Points.* New York: Five Points House of Industry, 1893.

Barnes, David. *The Draft Riots in New York. July, 1863. The Metropolitan Police: Their Services During Riot Week. Their Honorable Record.* New York: Baker & Godwin, 1863.

_____. *Trial of John Hendrickson, Jr.* Albany, N. Y.: Barnes & Hevenor, 1853.

Barnes, Gilbert Hobbes. *The Antislavery Impulse: 1830-1844.* New York: Harcourt, Brace & World, 1964.

Barnes, Margaret. *Murder in Coweta County.* New York: Pocketbooks, 1976.

Barnes, Robert Earl. *Are You Safe From Burglars?* Garden City, N. Y.: Doubleday, 1971.

Barnes, T. S. *Memoir of Thurlow Weed.* Boston: Houghton Mifflin, 1884.

Barnes, Viola F. *The Dominion of New England: A Study in British Colonial Policy.* New Haven, Conn.: Yale University Press, 1923.

Barnett, D.L., and Njama, Karari. *Mau Mau for Within: Autobiography and Analysis on Kenya's Peasant Revolt.* New York: Monthly Review Press, 1966.

Barnett, David, and Wooding, Ray. *Uganda Holocaust.* Chicago: Chicago Review Press (Zondervan), 1980.

Barnett, Michael N. *Eyewitness to a Genocide: The United Nations and Rwanda.* Ithaca, N. Y.: Cornell University Press, 2002.

Barnhart, Russell T. *Casino Gambling.* New York: E. P. Dutton, 1978.

Barnum, G. H. *Rube Burrow, The Famous Outlaw, Murderer, and Train Robber.* Chicago: Published by Author, 1890.

Baroja, Julio Caro. *The World of the Witches.* Chicago: University of Chicago Press, 1965.

Baron, R. A. *Human Agression.* New York: Plenum, 1977.

Baron, Samuel H. *Plekhanov: The Father of Russian Marxism.* Stanford, Calif.: Stanford University Press, 1963.

Baron, Stanley. *Brewed in America.* Boston: Little, Brown, 1962.

Baron, Wendy. *Sickert.* London: Phaidon, 1973.

Barone, Francesco. *Una vita per Giuliano.* Genoa, Italy: Immordino, 1968.

Barr, Jennifer. *Within a Dark Wood.* New York: Doubleday, 1979.

Barr, Martin. *Mental Defectives.* Philadelphia: Blackerson's and Sons, 1904.

Barr, Stringfellow. *The Mask of Jove.* New York: J. B. Lippincott, 1966.

Barracato, John. *Arson.* New York: Avon Books, 1976.

Barraclough, Geoffrey. *The Medieval Empire: Idea and Reality.* London: Historical Association, 1950.

Barrett, Ethel. *A Street Cop Who Cared.* Old Tappan, N. J.: Rerell, 1978.

Barrett, James Wyman (ed.). *The End of the World.* New York: Harper & Bros., 1931.

_____. *Joseph Pulitzer and His World.* New York: Vanguard, 1941.

_____. *The World, the Flesh, and Messrs. Pulitzer.* New York: Vanguard Press, 1941.

Barrett, Marvin. *The Jazz Age.* New York: Putnam, 1959.

Barrett, Walter. *The Old Merchants of New York City.* New York: Carleton, 1864.

Barrett, Wilfred Phillips. *The Trial of Jeanne d'Arc.* New York: Gotham House, 1932.

Barrett, William. *Irrational Man.* Garden City, N. Y.: Doubleday, 1962.

Barrett, William E., et al. *Denver Murders.* New York: Duell, Sloan, & Pearce, 1946.

Barron, John. *KGB: The Secret Work of Soviet Secret Agents.* New York: Dutton, 1974.

Barrow, Sir John. *The Eventful History of the Mutiny on the Bounty.* London: John Murray, 1831.

_____. *A Voyage to Cochinchina, 1792-1793.* London: T. Cadell and W. Davies, 1806.

Barrows, William. *The United States of Yesterday and of Tomorrow.* Boston: Roberts Brothers, 1887.

Barry, Iris. *D. W. Griffith, American Film Master.* New York: Museum of Modern Art, 1940.

Barry, James P. *The Noble Experiment, 1919-1933.* New York: Franklin Watts, 1972.

Barry, John Brooks. *The Michaelmas Girls.* London: Deutsch, 1975.

Barry, Commandant General Tom. *Guerilla Days in Ireland.* Cork: Mercier Press, 1955.

Barstow, Anne. *Witchcraze: A New History of the European Witch Hunts.* San Francisco: Harper, 1995.

Barth, Alan. *Government by Investigation.* New York: Viking, 1952.

_____. *The Loyalty of Free Men.* New York: Viking, 1951.

_____. *Prophets with Honor.* New York: Knopf, 1974.

Barthel, Joan. *A Death in Canaan.* New York: E. P. Dutton, 1977.

Bartholomew, Ed. *A Biographical Album of Western Gunfighters.* Houston: Frontier Press of Texas, 1958.

_____. *Black Jack Ketchum: Last of the Hold-Up Kings.* Houston: Frontier Press of Texas, 1955.

_____. *Cullen Baker: Premier Texas Gunfighter.* Houston: Frontier Press of Texas, 1954.

_____. *Henry Plummer: Montana Outlaw Boss.* Ruidoso, N. M.: Frontier Books, 1960.

_____. *Jesse Evans: A Texas Hideburner.* Houston: Frontier Press of Texas, 1955.

_____. *Kill or Be Killed: A Record of Violence in the Early Southwest.* Houston: The Frontier Press of Texas, 1953.

_____. *Some Western Gunfighters.* Toyahvale, Texas: Frontier Book, n. d.

_____. *Western Hardcases.* Ruidoso, N. M.: Frontier Book, 1960.

_____. *Wild Bill Longley: A Texas Hard-Case.* Houston: Frontier Press of Texas, 1953.

_____. *Wyatt Earp, 1879-1882: The Man and the Myth.* Toyahvale, Texas: Frontier Book, 1964.

_____. *Wyatt Earp, 1848-1880: The Untold Story.* Toyahvale, Texas: Frontier Books, 1963.

Bartholomew, Paul C. *Summaries of Leading Cases on the Constitution.* N. J.: Littlefield, Adams, 1961.

Barthorp, Michael. *The Jacobite Rebellions.* New York: Osprey, 2000.

Bartlett, Evan. *Love Murders of Harry F. Powers.* New York: Sheftel Press, 1931.

Bartlett, F. *Remembering.* London: Cambridge University Press, 1932.

Bartol, C.L. *Criminal Behavior: A Psychosocial Approach.* Englewood Cliffs, N. J.: Prentice-Hall, 1986.

Bartollas, Clemens, Miller, Stuart J., and Dinitz, Simon. *Juvenile Victimization.* New York: Sage & Halsted Press, 1976.

Barton, George. *The True Stories of Celebrated Crimes.* New York: McKinlay Stone & Mackenzie, 1909.

Barton, O.S., and McCorkle, John. *Three Years with Quantrell.* Armstrong, Mo.: Armstrong Herald Printing, 1914.

Barton, Roy F. *The Half-Way Sun.* New York: Brewer & Warren, 1930.

Barton, William E. *The Life of Abraham Lincoln.* 2 vols. Indianapolis, Ind.: Bobbs-Merrill, 1925.

Bartz, Karl. *Die Trageq odie der deutschen Abwehr.* Salzburg, Aust.: Pilgram Verlag, 1955.

Baruch, Bernard. M. *Baruch: My Own Story.* New York: Henry Holt, 1957.

_____. *The Public Years.* New York: Holt, Rinehart & Winston, 1960.

Barzini, Luigi. *From Caesar to the Mafia.* New York: The Library Press, 1971.

_____. *The Italians.* New York: Atheneum, 1964.

_____. *O America!* London: Hamish Hamilton, 1977.

Barzman, Sol. *Madmen and Geniuses.* Chicago: Follett, 1974.

Bar-Zohar, Michael. *Armed Prophet.* London: Davis & Poynton, 1966.

_____. *Spies in the Promised Land.* London: Davis & Poynton, 1972.

Barzun, Jacques. *Burke and Hare: The Resurrection Men.* Metuchen, N.J.: Scarecrow, 1974.

Basedow, H. *The Australian Aboriginal.* Adelaide, Aus.: F. W. Preece & Sons, 1925.

Basham, A.L. *The Wonder That Was India.* New York: Grove Press, 1954.

Basichis, Gordon. *Beautiful Bad Girl.* Santa Barbara, Calif.: Santa Barbara Press, 1985.

Basin, Thomas (ed.). *Histoire de Louis XI.* trans. Charles Samaran. Paris: Socieq eteq e d'eq Edition "Les Belles Lettres," 1963.

Baskerville, Beatrice. *What next, O Duce?* London: Longmans, 1937.

Baskin, R.N. *Reminiscences of Early Utah.* Salt Lake City, Utah: *Tribune-Reporter*, 1914.

Basler, Roy P. *Abraham Lincoln: His Speeches and Writings.* New York: World, 1946.

_____ (ed.). *The Collected Works of Abraham Lincoln.* 8 vols. New Brunswick, N. J.: Rutgers University Press, 1953.

_____ (ed.). *The Collected Works of Abraham Lincoln, Supplement 1832-1865.* Westport, Conn.: Greenwood Press, 1974.

Bass, U. F., et al. *A Study of Narcotics Addicted Offenders at the D.C. Jail.* Washington, D. C.: Narcotics Treatment Administration, 1971.

Basserman, Lujo. *The Oldest Profession: the History of Prostitution.* New York: Stein & Day, 1968.

Bassiouni, M. Cherif. *Criminal Law and Its Process.* Springfield, Ill.: Charles C. Thomas, 1969.

_____. *International Terrorism and Political Crimes.* Springfield, Ill.: Charles C. Thomas, 1975.

Basutoland Medicine Murder. London: Her Majesty's Stationary Office, 1958.

Bataille, A. *Les Causes criminelles et mondaines.* 18 vols. Paris: Dentu, 1881-1898.

Bataille, Georges. *Death and Sensuality.* New York: Walker, 1962.

_____. *Le Proces de Gilles de Rais.* Paris: Jean-Jacques Pauvert, 1965.

Bataille, Michel. *Gilles de Rais.* Paris: Editions Planete, 1966.

Bates, David Homer. *Lincoln in the Telegraph Office.* New York: Century, 1907.

Bates, Edmund Franklin. *History and Reminiscences of Denton County.* Denton, Texas: McNitzky, 1918.

Bates, Ernest, and Carlson, Oliver. *Hearst: Lord of San Simeon.* New York: Viking, 1936.

Bates, Ernest Sutherland. *The Story of the Supreme Court.* New York: Bobbs-Merrill, 1936.

Bates, Finis L. *The Escape & Suicide of John Wilkes Booth; or The First True Account of Lincoln's Assassination.* Atlanta: J. L. Nichols, 1907.

Bates, Harbin E.H. (ed.). *Quarter Sessions Records for the County of Somerset.* London: Harrison and Sons, 1907.

Bates, J.C. (ed.). *History of the Bench and Bar of California.* San Francisco: Bench and Bar, 1912.

Bateson, Charles. *The Convict Ships, 1787-1868.* Glasgow, Scot.: Brown, Son & Ferguson, 1959.

Batsell, Walter R. *Soviet Rule in Russia.* New York: Macmillan, 1929.

Battaglia, Roberto. *Story of the Italian Resistance.* trans. P. D. Cummins. London: Odhams Press, 1958.

Battiscombe, Georgina. *Queen Alexandra.* London: Constable, 1969.

Battle, Brendan P., and Weston, Paul B. *Arson: Detection and Investigation.* New York: Arco, 1978.

Battley, H. *Single Finger Prints.* London: H. M. Stationery Office, 1930.

Baudin, Louis. *Daily Life in Peru Under the Last Incas,* trans. Winifred Bradford. London: Allen & Unwin, 1961.

_____. *The Socialist Empire, The Incas of Peru.* trans. Katherine Woods. Princeton, N. J.: D. Van Nostrand, 1961.

Baudin, Robert. *Confessions of a Promiscuous Counterfeiter.* New York: Harcourt Brace, 1979.

Baudrillart, Henri. *Jean Bodin.* Paris: Guillaumin, 1853.

Bauer, Charles J. *So I Killed Lincoln.* New York: Vantage, 1976.

Bauer, Yehuda. *From Diplomacy to Resistance: A History of Jewish Palestine, 1939-1945.* trans. Alton M. Winters. New York: Atheneum, 1973.

Baugh, Jack W., and Morgan, Jefferson. *Why Have They Taken Our Children?* New York: Delacorte Press, 1978.

Baughman, E. U., and Robinson, Leonard Wallace. *Secret Service Chief.* New York: Harper & Brothers, 1961.

Baughman, Laurance. *Southern Rape Complex.* Atlanta: Pendulum Books, 1966.

Baulch, Lawrence. *Return to the World.* Valley Forge, Pa.: Judson Press, 1968.

Baumann, Ed. *Step Into My Parlor.* Chicago: Bonus Books, 1991.

Baur, Hans. *Hitler's Pilot.* London: Frederick Muller, 1958.

Baverstock, Keith. *Footsteps Through London's Past.* London: Shire, 1972.

Baxter, Beverley. *Men, Martyrs and Mountebanks.* London: Hutchinson, 1940.

Bayer, Oliver Weld (ed.). *Cleveland Murders.* New York: Duell, Sloan & Pearce, 1947.

Bayley, David H. *Forces of Order: Police Behavior in Japan and the United States.* Berkeley: University of California Press, 1976.

_____. *The Police and Political Development in India.* Princeton, N. J.: Princeton University Press, 1969.

_____ (ed.). *Police and Society.* Beverly Hills, Calif.: Sage, 1977.

_____, and Mendelsohn, Harold. *Minorities and the Police.* New York: Free Press, 1968.

Baynes, N. H. *Byzantine Studies and Other Essays.* New York: DeGraff, 1955.

_____, and Moss, H. St. L. B. *Byzantium: An Introduction to East Roman Civilization.* New York: Oxford Press University, 1948.

Bayor, Ronald H. *Neighbors in Conflict: The Irish, Germans, Jews and Italians of New York City.* Baltimore: The Johns Hopkins University Press, 1978.

Beach, Frank A. (ed.) *Sex and Behavior.* New York: Wiley, 1965.

Beach, Sylvia. *Shakespeare and Company.* New York: Harcourt, Brace & World, 1959.

Beacher, Milton Daniel, and Perfit, Diane Beacher. *Alcatraz Island: Memories of a Rock Doc.* San Francisco: Pelican Island Publishing, 2001.

_____. *Alcatraz Justice: The Rock's Most Famous Murder Trial.* San Francisco: Creative Arts Book Co., 2002.

_____. Birdman: *The Many Faces of Robert Stroud.* San Francisco: Ariel Vamp Press, 1994.

Beal, Erica. *Royal Cavalcade.* London: Paul, 1939.

Beal, Fred. *Proletarian Journey.* New York: De Capo, 1971.

Beal, M.D. *A History of Southeastern Idaho.* Caldwell, Idaho: Caxton Printers, 1942.

Beal, S. *Fo-sho-hing-tsan-king.* Oxford, Eng.: Clarendon Press, 1883.

Bealle, Morris A. *Guns of the Regressive Right.* Washington, D. C.: Columbia, 1964.

Beals, Carleton. *American Earth.* Philadelphia: J. B. Lippincott, 1939.

_____. *Brass Knuckle Crusade: The Great Know-Nothing Conspiracy, 1820-1860.* New York: Hastings House, 1960.

_____. *Nomads and Empire Builders, Native People and Cultures of South America.* New York: Chilton, 1961.

_____. *Porfirio Diaz, Dictator of Mexico.* New York: J. B. Lippincott, 1932.

_____. *Rome or Death!* New York: Century Press, 1923.

_____. *The Story of Huey P. Long.* Westport, Conn.: Greenwood Press, 1971.

Bean, Philip. *The Social Control of Drugs.* New York: Wiley, 1974.

Bean, Walton. *Boss Ruef's San Francisco.* Berkeley: University of California Press, 1952.

Beard, Dan. *Hardly a Man Is Now Alive.* New York: Doubleday, Doran, 1939.

Beard, James Melville. *K. K. K. Sketches: Humorous and Didactic.* Philadelphia: Claxton, 1877.

Beard, Ross E., Jr. *Carbine, the Story of David Marshall Williams.* Lexington, S. C.: The Sandlapper Store, 1977.

Beardsley, Isaac. *Echoes From Peak and Plain.* Cincinatti, Ohio: Curts & Jennings, 1898.

Bearss, Edwin C., and Gibson, A. M. *Fort Smith, Little Gibraltar on the Arkansas.* Norman: University of Oklahoma Press, 1969.

Beaslai, Piaras. *Michael Collins.* Dublin, Ire.: Phoenix, 1926.

Beasley, W. G. *The Modern History of Japan.* New York: Frederick A. Praeger, 1963.

_____. *Modern Japan.* London: Allen & Unwin, 1975.

Beatly, George W. *The Background and Causes of the 1943 Detroit Race Riot.* Princeton, N. J.: n. p., 1954.

Beattie, John. *The Yorkshire Ripper Story.* London: Quartet, 1981.

Beattie, Kim. *Brother! Here's A Man.* New York: Macmillan, 1940.

Beatty, Bessie. *The Red Heart of Russia.* New York: Century, 1918.

Beauchamp, Thomas L. (ed.). *Case Studies in Business, Society and Ethics.* Englewood Cliffs, N. J.: Prentice-Hall, 1983.

Beaumont, Charles (ed.). *The Fiend in You.* New York: Ballantine, 1962.
Beaumont, F. A. *The Fifty Most Amazing Crimes of the Last 100 Years.* London: Odhams, 1936.
Beaumont, G. H. *G. H. Beaumont's Railroad Stories.* Kansas City: Seip Printing, 1912.
Beaumont, Gustave, and de Tocqueville, Alexis. *On the Penitentiary System in the United States and Its Application in France.* Carbondale, Ill.: Southern Illinois University Press, 1964.
Beauvoir, Simone de. *America, Day by Day.* New York: Grove Press, 1953.
_____. *The Long March.* London: Deutsch & Weidenfeld & Nicolson, 1958.
_____. *The Second Sex.* New York: Random House, 1974.
Beaver, Ninette. *Caril.* New York: Bantam, 1976.
Beaverbrook, Lord. *The Decline and Fall of Lloyd George.* London: Collins, 1963.
_____. *Men and Power.* London: Hutchinson, 1956.
Beccaria, Cesare Bonesana. *An Essay on Crime and Punishments.* Philadelphia: Philip H. Nicklin, 1819.
_____. *On Crimes and Punishment.* trans. Henry Paolucci. Indianapolis, Ind.: Bobbs-Merrill, 1963.
Bechdolt, Frederick Ritchie. *Tales of the Oldtimers.* New York: Century, 1924.
_____. *When the West Was Young.* New York: Century, 1924.
Bechhofer, Robert. *Famous American Trials.* London: Jarrolds, 1947.
Bechhofer Roberts, C. E. *Lord Birkenhead.* London: Mills & Boon, 1926.
_____. *Sir Travers Humphreys.* London: The Bodley Head, 1936.
Beck, Warren A. *New Mexico: A History of Four Centuries.* Norman: University of Oklahoma Press, 1962.
Becker, Ernest. *Escape From Evil.* New York: Free Press, 1975.
Becker, Howard. *German Youth: Bond or Free.* London: Routledge & Kegan Paul, 1946.
Becker, Howard S. (ed.). *Campus Power Struggle.* Chicago: Aldine, 1970.
_____. *The Other Side: Perspectives on Deviance.* New York: Free Press, 1964.
Becker, Jillian. *Hitler's Children: The Story of the Baader-Meinhof Terrorist Gang.* New York: J. B. Lippincott, 1977.
_____. *The PLO: The Rise and Fall of the Palestine Liberation Organization.* New York: St. Martin's (paper), 2000.
Beckett, V.B. *Baca's Battle.* Houston, Texas: Stagecoach Press, n.d.
Bedau, Hugo Adam, and Pierce, Chester M. (eds.). *Capital Punishment in the United States.* New York: AMS Press, 1976.
_____. *The Case against the Death Penalty.* New York: American Civil Liberties Union, 1973.
_____ (ed.). *The Death Penalty in America.* New York: Oxford University Press, 1982.
Bedford, Sybille. *The Faces of Justice.* New York: Simon & Schuster, 1961.
_____. *The Trial of Dr. Adams.* New York: Time Books, 1958.
Beebe, Lucius, and Clegg, Charles. *The American West.* New York: E. P. Dutton, 1955.
_____. *The Big Spenders.* New York: Doubleday, 1966.
_____. *Boston and the Boston Legend.* New York: Appleton-Century, 1935.
_____. *Comstock Commotion, The Story of Territorial Enterprise.* Palo Alto, Calif.: Stanford University Press, 1954.
_____. *Hear the Train Blow.* New York: E. P. Dutton, 1952.
_____. *Shoot if You Must.* New York: D. Appleton Century, 1943.
_____. *U. S. West: The Saga of Wells Fargo.* New York: E. P. Dutton, 1949.
Beecher, William C., and Scoville, Rev. Samuel. *A Biography of Rev. Henry Ward Beecher.* New York: Charles L. Webster, 1888.
Beeching, Jack. *The Chinese Opium Wars.* New York: Harcourt, Brace, Jovanovich, 1975.
Beeding, Francis. *Death Walks in Eastrepps.* London: Hodder & Stoughton, 1931.
Beedle, Susannah. *An Essay on the Advisability of Total Abolition of Capital Punishment.* London: Nichols & Son, 1867.
Beer, George Louis. *The Old Colonial System 1660-1688.* 2 vols. New York: Macmillan, 1912.
Beer, Thomas. *Hanna.* New York: Knopf, 1929.
_____. *The Mauve Decade.* New York: Knopf, 1926.
Beers, George A. *Vasquez; or the Hunted Bandits of San Joaquin.* New York: Robert M. DeWitt, 1875.
Begg, Paul, and Fido, Martin, and Skinner, Keith. *The Jack the Ripper A-Z.* London: Headline, 1996.
_____. *The Scotland Yard Files: 150 Years of the C.I.D., 1842-1992.* London: Trafalgar Square, 1993.
Beggs, Thomas. *The Royal Commission and the Punishment of Death.* London: Society for the Abolition of Capital Punishment, 1866.
Begin, Menachem. *The Revolt: Story of the Irgun.* New York: Henry Schuman, 1951.
Begnac, Yvon de. *Palazzo Venezia.* Rome: 'La Rocca', 1950.
_____. *Trent'anni di Mussolini.* Rome: Arti Grafiche Menaglia, 1934.
_____. *Vita di Mussolini.* 3 vols. Milan, Italy: Mondadori, 1936-40.
Behn, Noel. *Big Stick-up at Brinks.* New York: Putnam, 1977.
Behrens, John C. *Reporting Work Test.* Columbus: GRID, 1974.
_____. *The Typewriter Guerrillas.* Chicago: Nelson-Hall, 1977.
Beidler, X. *Vigilante.* Norman: University of Oklahoma Press, 1965.
Beigel, Herbert and Allan. *Beneath the Badge.* New York: Harper & Row, 1977.
Beigel, Hermann. *The Examination and Confession of Certain Witches at Chelmsford.* London: Philobiblon Society, 1864.
Beisner, Robert L. *Twelve Against Empire: The Anti-Imperialists, 1898-1900.* New York: McGraw-Hill, 1968.
Bejerot, Nils. *Addiction: An Artificially Induced Drive.* Springfield, Ill.: Charles C. Thomas, 1972.
_____. *Addiction and Society.* Springfield, Ill.: Charles C. Thomas, 1970.
Bekker, Balthasar. *De Betoverde Weereld.* Amsterdam, Neth.: D. von der Dalen, 1691.
_____. *The World Bewitched.* London: R. Baldwin, 1695.
Belbenoit, Rene. *Dry Guillotine.* New York: Dutton, 1938.
_____. *Hell on Trial.* New York: Dutton, 1940.
Belcher, Lady. *The Mutineers of the Bounty and Their Descendants on Pitcairn and Norfolk Islands.* London: John Murray, 1870.
Belden, H.M. (ed.). *Ballads and Songs Collected by the Missouri Folk-Lore Society.* Columbia: University of Missouri, 1940.
Belden, Jack. *China Shakes the World.* New York: Harper and Bros., 1949.
Belfrage, Cedric. *The American Inquisition 1945-1960.* Indianapolis, Ind.: Bobbs-Merrill, 1973.
Belfry Murder in Boston. Philadelphia: Old Franklin, 1875.
Belgrave, Sir Charles. *The Pirate Coast.* New York: Roy, 1967.
Belin, David W. *November 22, 1963: You Are the Jury.* New York: Quadrangle Books, 1973.
Belin, Jean. *My Work at the Seq ureteq e.* trans. Eric Whelpton. London: Harrap, 1950.
_____. *Secrets of the Sureteq e.* New York: Putnam, 1950.
Bell, Alan P., and Hall, Calvin S. *The Personality of a Child Molester: An Analysis of Dreams.* Chicago: Aldine-Atherton, 1971.
Bell, Arthur. *Kings Don't Mean a Thing.* New York: William Morrow, 1978.
Bell, Daniel (ed.). *The End of Ideology.* New York: Free Press, 1962.
_____. *Marxian Socialism in the United States.* Princeton, N. J.: Princeton University Press, 1967.
_____ (ed.). *The New American Right.* New York: Criterion, 1955.
_____. *The Radical Right.* New York: Anchor, 1964.
Bell, Edward A. *Those Meddlesome Attorneys.* London: Martin Secker, 1939.
Bell, Edward I. *The Political Shame of Mexico.* New York. McBride, Nast, 1914.
Bell, Ernest A. *Fighting the Traffic in Young Girls.* New York: Walter, 1911.
_____. *War on the White Slave Trade.* Chicago: Thompson, 1909.
Bell, Horace. *On the Old West Coast.* New York: William Morrow, 1930.
_____. *Reminiscences of a Ranger.* Los Angeles: Yarnell, Caystile, & Mathes, 1881.
Bell, J. Bowyer. *Assassin!: The Theory and Practice of Political Violence.* New York: St. Martin's Press, 1979.
_____. *The Secret Army: The IRA, 1916-1979.* Cambridge, Mass.: MIT Press, 1980.
_____. *Terror Out of Zion.* New York: St. Martin's Press, 1977.
_____. *Transnational Terror.* Washington, D. C.: American Enterprise Institute for Public Policy Research, 1975.
Bell, Maria. *The Life and Times of Lucrezia Borgia.* trans. Bernard and Barbara Wall. New York: Harcourt Brace, 1953.
_____. *Lucrezia Borgia.* Rome: Arnoldo Mondadori Editore, 1974.
Bellamy, J. G. *Crime and the Public Order in England in the Later Middle Ages.* London: Routledge & Kegan Paul, 1973.
Belle, Frances P. *Life and Adventures of the Celebrated Bandit Joaquin Murieta.* Chicago: Reagan, 1925.
Belli, Melvin. *Blood Money.* New York: Grosset & Dunlap, 1956.
_____, and Carroll, Maurice C. *Dallas Justice.* New York: David McKay, 1964.
_____. *The Law Revolution.* Los Angeles: Sherbourne Press, 1968.
_____, and Kaiser, Robert Blair. *My Life on Trial.* New York: William Morrow, 1976.
Bellini, Delle Stelle, et al. *Dongo: The Last Act.* London: MacDonald, 1964.
Belloc, Hilaire. *The French Revolution.* New York: Oxford University Press, 1966.
_____. *Joan of Arc.* New York: Declan X. McMullen, 1929.
_____. *Richelieu.* Philadelphia: J. B. Lippincott, 1929.
Bellotti, Felice. *La Repubblica di Mussolini.* Milan, Italy: Zagara, 1947.
Belon, Marie Joseph. *Jean Breq ehal, grand inquisiteur de France et la req ehabilitation de Jeanne d'Arc.* Paris: P. Lethielleux, 1893.
Belson, William A. *Juvenile Theft: The Causal Factors.* London: Harper & Row, 1975.
_____. *The Public and the Police.* London: Harper & Row, 1975.
_____. *Television Violence and the Adolescent Boy.* Farnborough, Eng.: Saxon House, 1978.
Beman, Lemar T. (ed.). *Selected Articles on Captial Punishment.* Minneapolis, Minn.: H. W. Wilson, 1913.
Bemis, George. *Report of the Case of John W. Webster.* Boston: Little, Brown, 1850.
Benckendorff, Count Paul. *Last Days at Tsarskoe Selo.* London: Heinemann, 1927.
Benda, Harry J. *The Crescent and the Rising Sun: Indonesian Islam Under the Japanese Occupation, 1942-1945.* The Hague, Neth.: W. van Hoeve, 1958.
Bendiner, Robert. *Just Around the Corner.* New York: Harper & Row, 1967.
Benedetti, Jean. *Gilles de Rais.* New York: Stein & Day, 1971.
Benedict, Michael Les. *A Compromise of Principle: The Politics of Radicalism.* New York: W. W. Norton, 1974.
_____. *The Impeachment and Trial of Andrew Johnson.* New York: W. W. Norton, 1973.
Benedict, Ruth. *The Chrysanthemum and the Sword.* Boston: Houghton Mifflin, 1946.
_____. *Patterns of Culture.* Boston: Houghton Mifflin, 1959.
Benet, William Rose. *Golden Fleece.* New York: Dodd, Mead, 1935.
Benger, G. *Rumania in 1900.* London: Asher, 1900.
Bengham, Theodore A. *The Girl That Disappears.* New York: Gorham, 1911.
Bengston, Hermann. *The Greeks and the Persians.* New York: Delacorte Press, 1965.
Ben Gurion, David. *Israel: A Personal History.* New York: Funk & Wagnalls, 1971.
_____. *Israel: Years of Challenge.* New York: Holt, Rinehart & Winston, 1963.
_____. *Rebirth and Destiny of Israel.* New York: Philosophical Library, 1954.
Benjamin, Harry, and Masters, R.E.L. *Prostitution and Morality.* New York: Julian, 1964.
_____. *The Transsexual Phenomenon.* New York: Julian, 1966.

Benjamin, Reneq e. *Mossolini et son Peuple.* Paris: Plon, 1937.
Bennecke, Heinrich. *Hitler und die SA.* Munich: Geq unter Olzog Verlag, 1962.
Bennet, H. S. *Life on the English Manor: A Study of Peasant Conditions, 1150-1400.* Cambridge, Eng.: University Press, 1960.
Bennet, J. H. E., and Dewhurst, J.C. (eds.) *Quarter Sessions Records with Other Records of the Justices of the Peace for the County Palatine of Chester, 1559-1760.* Chester, Eng.: n. p., 1940.
Bennet, Richard. *The Black and Tans.* London: Paperback Four Square, 1959.
Bennett, Arnold. *Jackie, Bobby and Manchester: The Story Behind the Headlines.* New York: Bee-Line Books, 1967.
Bennett, Benjamin. *The Evil That Men Do.* Cape Town, S. Afri.: Howard B. Timmins, n. d.
_____. *Famous South African Murders.* London: T. Werner Laurie, 1938.
_____. *Freedom or the Gallows.* Cape Town, S. Afri.: Howard B. Timmins, 1956.
_____. *Genius for the Defense, Life of Harry Morris, K.C.* Cape Town, S. Afri.: Howard B. Timmins, 1959.
_____. *Murder is my Business.* London: Hodder and Stoughton Ltd., 1951.
_____. *Murder Will Speak.* Cape Town, S. Afri.: Howard B. Timmins, 1962.
_____. *The Noose Tightens.* Cape Town, S. Afri.: Howard B. Timmins, 1974.
_____. *This Was a Man.* Cape Town, S. Afri.: H. B. Timmins, 1958.
_____. *Too Late for Tears.* Cape Town, S. Afri.: Howard B. Timmins, 1948.
_____. *Up for Murder.* London: Hutchinson, 1934.
_____. *Was Justice Done?.* Cape Town, S. Afri.: Howard B. Timmins, 1975.
_____. *Why Did They Do It?* Capetown, S. Afri.: Howard Timmins, 1953.
Bennett, Daphne. *Vicki, Princess Royal of England and German Empress.* New York: St. Martin's Press, 1971.
Bennett, David H. *The Party of Fear: From Nativist Movements to the New Right in American History.* Chapel Hill: University of North Carolina Press, 1988.
Bennett, Edwin Lewis. *Boom Town Boy in Old Creede Colorado.* Chicago: Sage Books, 1966.
Bennett, Estelline. *Old Deadwood Days.* New York: J. H. Sears, 1928.
Bennett, Fremont O. *Politics and Politicians of Chicago, Cook County, and Illinois.* Chicago: Blakely, 1886.
Bennett, Georgette. *A Safe Place to Live.* New York: Insurance Information Institute, 1982.
Bennett, Harry Herbert. *We Never Called Him Henry.* New York: Gold Medal Books, 1951.
Bennett, James V. *I Chose Prison.* New York: Knopf, 1970.
_____. *Of Prisons and Justice.* Washington, D. C.: U. S. Government Printing Office, 1964.
Bennett, Lerone, Jr. *What Manner of Man.* New York: Pocket Books, 1968.
Bennett, Richard. *The Black and Tans.* Boston: Houghton Mifflin, 1960.
Bennett, Wendell C., and Zing, Robert M. *The Tarahumara.* Chicago: University of Chicago Press, 1935.
Benoist-Meq echin, Jacques. *Alexander the Great: The Meeting of East and West.* New York: Hawthorn Books, 1966.
Benoeq it-Leq evy, Edmond. *Jules Favre.* Paris: Picard-Bernheim, 1884.
Ben-Porath, Yoram. *The Arab Labor Force in Israel.* Jerusalem: Israeli University Press, 1966.
Benson, E.F. *The Kaiser and English Relations.* London: Longmans, 1936.
_____. *Queen Victoria's Daughters.* New York: D. Appleton-Century, 1938.
Benson, Captain L. *The Book of Remarkable Trials.* London: Chatto and Windus, 1924.
Benson, Luther. *Fifteen Years in Hell; An Autobiography.* Indianapolis, Ind.: Tilford & Carlon, 1877.
Bent, Alan Edward. *The Politics of Law Enforcement.* Lexington, Mass.: D. C. Heath, 1974.
Bent, Silas. *Ballyhoo: The Voice of the Press.* New York: Boni & Liveright, 1927.
_____. *Justice Oliver Wendell Holmes.* Garden City, N. Y.: Vanguard Press, 1932.
_____. *Newspaper Crusaders.* New York: McGraw-Hill, 1939.
_____. *Strange Bedfellows.* New York: Horace Liveright, 1928.
Bentinck, Lady Norah Ida Emily. *The Ex-Kaiser in Exile.* London: Hodder & Stoughton, 1921.
Bentley, Elizabeth. *Out of Bondage.* New York: Devin-Adair, 1951.
Bentley, George R. *A History of the Freedmen's Bureau.* Philadelphia: University of Pennsylvania Press, 1955.
Bentley, W. G. *My Son's Execution.* London: W. H. Allen, 1957.
Bentwich, Norman. *Israel.* New York: McGraw-Hill, 1953.
Ben-Veniste, Richard, and Frampton, George Jr. *Stonewall.* New York: Touchstone, 1978.
Bequai, August. *Computer Crime.* Lexington, Mass.: Lexington Books, D. C. Heath, 1978.
_____. *Organized Crime: The Fifth Estate.* Lexington, Mass.: D. C. Heath, 1979.
_____. *White Collar Crime: A Twentieth Century Crisis.* Lexington, Mass.: Lexington Books, D. C. Heath, 1978.
Berber, John. *Historical Collections of the State of New York.* New York: Austin, 1851.
Bercovici, Konrad. *That Royal Lover.* New York: Brer & Warren, 1931.
Beq erence, Fred. *Les Borgias.* Paris: Pierre Aliffe, 1966.
_____. *Lucreq ece Borgia.* Paris: Payot, 1937.
Berg, Charles, and Allen, Clifford. *The Problem of Homosexuality.* New York: Citadel, 1958.
Berg, Karl. *The Sadist.* London: Heinemann, 1932.
Berg, L.L., Hahn, H., and Scmidhauser, J. R. *Corruption in the American Political System.* Morristown, N. J.: General Learning Press, 1976.
Bergamini, David. *Japan's Imperial Conspiracy.* New York: William Morrow, 1971.
Bergamini, John. *The Tragic Dynasty.* New York: William S. Konecky Associates, 1999.
Bergen, Peter. *Holy War, Inc.: Inside the Secret World of Osama bin Laden.* New York: Free Press, 2001.
Berger, Earl. *The Covenant and the Sword.* Toronto, Ontario, Can.: University of Toronto Press, 1965.
Berger, Meyer. *The Eight Million.* New York: Simon & Schuster, 1942.
_____. *The Story of the New York Times.* New York: Simon & Schuster, 1951.
Berger, Morroe. *The Arab World Today.* Garden City, N. Y.: Doubleday, 1962.
Berger, Raoul. *Death Penalties: The Supreme Court's Obstacle Course.* Cambridge, Mass.: Harvard University Press, 1984.
Bergier, Jacques. *Secret Armies: The Growth of Corporate and Industrial Espionage.* trans. Harold J. Salemson. Indianapolis, Ind.: Bobbs-Merrill, 1975.
Berglar, Peter. *Walther Rathenau: Seine zeit, sein Werk, seine Perseq onlichkeit.* Bremen: Universitatsverlag, 1970.
Bergman, Andrew. *We're in the Money.* New York: New York University Press, 1972.
Berio, Alberto. *Missione Segreta.* Milan, Italy: Dall'Oglio, 1947.
Berkeley, George. *The Democratic Policeman.* Boston: Beacon Press, 1969.
Berkman, Alexander. *Prison Memoirs of an Anarchist.* New York: Mother Earth, 1912.
Berkow, Ira. *The Man Who Robbed the Pierre.* New York: Atheneum, 1987.
Berkowitz, Leonard. *Aggression: A Social Psychological Analysis.* New York: McGraw-Hill, 1962.
Berkson, Seymour. *Their Majesties!* New York: Stackpole Sons, 1938.
Berky, Andrew S., and Shenton, James P. *The Historian's History of the United States.* New York: Putnam, 1966.
Berle, Beatrice B., and Jacobs, Travis B. (eds.). *Navigating the Rapids, 1918-1971: From the Papers of Adolf A. Berle.* New York: Harcourt, Brace, Jovanovich, 1973.
Berman, Harold J. *Justice in Russia.* Cambridge, Mass.: Harvard University Press, 1950.
_____ (ed.). *Soviet Criminal Law and Procedure.* Cambridge, Mass.: Harvard University Press, 1972.
_____ (ed.). *Talks on American Law.* New York: Random House, 1961.
Bermant, Chaim. *Point of Arrival: A Study of London's East End.* London: Methuen, 1975.
Bermant, G., et al. *Psychology and the Law.* Toronto, Ontario, Can.: Lexington Books, 1976.
Bernaldo de Quiros, C. *Modern Theories of Criminality.* trans. Alfonso de Salvio. Boston: Little, Brown, 1911.
Bernard, Richard. *A Guide to Grand Jurymen.* London: E. Blackmore, 1627.
Bernardy, Francoise de. *Albert and Victoria.* New York: Harcourt, Brace, 1953.
Bernays, Robert. *Naked Fakir.* London: Victor Gollancz, 1931.
Bernelle, Freq edeq eric Henri. *La Psychose de Gilles de Rais.* Paris: Jouvet et Cie., 1910.
Bernheimer, Richard. *Wild Men in the Middle Ages: A Study in Art, Sentiment, and Demonology.* Cambridge, Mass.: Harvard University Press, 1952.
Berns, Walter. *For Capital Punishment: Crime and the Morality of the Death Penalty.* New York: Basic Books, 1979.
Bernstein, Barton J. (ed.). *Towards a New Past: Dissenting Essays in American History.* New York: Vintage Books, 1969.
Bernstein, Carl, and Woodward, Bob. *All the President's Men.* New York: Simon & Schuster, 1974.
_____. *The Final Days.* New York: Simon & Schuster, 1976.
Bernstein, David. *The Philippine Story.* New York: Farrar, Straus, 1947.
Bernstein, Irving. *Turbulent Years.* Boston: Houghton Mifflin, 1970.
Bernstein, Marver H. *The Politics of Israel.* Princeton, N. J.: Princeton University Press, 1957.
Bernstein, Saul. *Youth on the Streets: Work with Alienated Youth Gangs.* New York: Association Press, 1964.
Berrett, James. *When I Was at Scotland Yard.* London: Sampson, Low, Marston, 1932.
Berridge, Virginia and Edwards, Griffin. *Opium and the People.* New York: St. Martin's Press, 1961.
Berrigan, Darrel. *Yakuza no Sekai: Nihon no Uchimaku (Yakuza Society: Behind the Japanese Curtain).* Tokyo: Kindai Shisosha, 1948.
Berry, J. *My Experiences as an Executioner.* Devon, Eng.: David & Charles Reprints, 1972.
Berry, John A., and Berry, Carol Pott. *Genocide in Rwanda: A Collective Memory.* Washington, D. C.: Howard University Press, 1999.
Berry, Wendell, and Shahn, Ben. *November Twenty-Six Nineteen Hundred Sixty-Three.* New York: George Braziller, 1964.
Berryer, Pierre-Antoine. *Les Oeuvres conpleq etes.* 9 vols. Paris: Didier, 1872-1878.
Berteaut, Simone. *Piaf.* New York: Dell, 1973.
Berthet, Elie. *Le loup-garou.* Brussels: Hetitiens Doorman, 1843.
Bertram, James. *Beneath the Shadow.* New York: John Day, 1947.
_____. *First Act in China: The Story of the Sian Mutiny.* New York: Viking, 1938.
Bertrand, Ameq edeq ee. *Etude Meq edico-leq egale au sujet de Troppmann.* Paris: Published by Author, 1869.
Bertrand, Geq eneq eral. *Cahiers de Sainte-Heq eleq ene.* Paris: Flammarion, Albin Michel & Sulliver, 1959.
Bertrand, Isidore. *Les posseq edeq ees de Loudun et Urbain Grandier.* Paris: Bloud, 1905.
Bertrand, L., and Petrie, C. *The History of Spain.* London: Appleton Century, 1945.
Besant, Walter. *East London.* Chatto & Windus, 1903.
_____. *London in the Time of the Stuarts.* London: Adam & Black, 1903.
Besharov, Douglas J. *Juvenile Justice Advocacy.* New York: Practicing Law Institute, 1974.
Best, Geoffrey. *Mid-Victorian Britain, 1851-1875.* New York: Schocken, 1972.
Best, Harry. *Crime and the Criminal Law in the United States.* New York: Macmillan, 1930.
Best, S. Payne. *The Venlo Incident.* London: Hutchinson, 1950.
Best, Werner. *Die Deutsche Polizei.* Darmstadt, Ger.: L. C. Wittich, 1941.
Besterman, Lujo. *Men Against Women: A Study of Sexual Relations.* London: Methuen, 1924.
Besterman, Theodore. *Voltaire Essays, and Another.* New York: Oxford University Press, 1962.
Betenson, Lula. *Butch Cassidy, My Brother.* Provo, Utah: Brigham Young University Press, 1975.

Bethell, Nicholas. *The Last Secret.* New York: Basic Books, 1974.

Betts, Tony. *Across the Board.* New York: Citadel Press, 1956.

Beucler, Andreq e, and Alexinsky, G. *Les amours secreq etes de Leq enine.* Paris: Editions Baudinieq ere, 1937.

Bevan, Edwyn. *German Social Democracy During the War.* New York: E. P. Dutton, 1919.

_____. *Indian Nationalism.* New York: Macmillan, 1914.

Beveridge, Albert Jeremiah. *Abraham Lincoln, 1809-1858.* 2 vols. Boston: Houghton Mifflin, 1928.

_____. *The Life of John Marshall.* 4 vols. Boston: Houghton Mifflin, 1916.

Beveridge, Peter. *Inside the C.I.D.* London: Evans, 1957.

Beyeler, E. *Alcatraz: The Rock.* Flagstaff, Ariz.: Northland Publishing, 1987.

Beyen, J. W. *Money in a Maelstrom.* New York: Macmillan, 1949.

Beyens, Baron. *Deux Anneq eeseq a Berlin, 1912-14.* 2 vols. Paris: Plon, 1931.

Beyer, William Gilmore. *On Hazardous Service.* New York: Harper & Brothers, 1912.

Beyle, Marie Henri. *Oeuvres Compleq etes.* Paris: Librairie Honoreq e Champion, 1932.

Bezymenski, Lev A. *The Death of Adolf Hitler: Unknown Documents from Soviet Archives.* New York: Harcourt, Brace & World, 1968.

_____. *Martin Bormann.* Zurich, Switz.: Aurora Verlag, 1965.

Bialer, Seweryn (ed.). *Stalin and His Generals: Soviet Military Memoirs of World War Two.* New York: Pegasus, 1969.

Bianchi, Giuseppe. *The Work of the Fascist Government and the Economic Reconstruction of Italy.* Milan, Italy: Unione Economica Italiana, 1925.

Bianchi, Lorenzo. *Mussolini scrittore e oratore.* Bologna, Italy: Zanichelli, 1937.

Bianco, Mirella. *Gadaffi, Voice from the Desert.* London: Longman, 1975.

Bibesco, Martha Lucie. *Royal Portraits.* New York: D. Appleton, 1928.

_____. *Some Royalties and a Prime Minister.* New York: D. Appleton, 1930.

Bickel, Alexander M. *The Least Dangerous Branch: The Supreme Court at the Bar of Politics.* New York: Bobbs-Merrill, 1962

_____. *Politics and the Warren Court.* New York: Harper & Row, 1965.

_____. *The Supreme Court and the Idea of Progress.* New Haven, Conn.: Yale University Press, 1978.

Bickerman, E.J. *The Maccabees.* trans. Moses Hadas. New York: Schocken, 1947.

Biddle, Francis. *In Brief Authority.* New York: Doubleday, 1962.

_____. *Mr. Justice Holmes.* New York: Scribner's, 1942.

Biddulph, Colonel John. *The Pirates of Malabar.* London: Smith, Elder, 1907.

Bidwell, Austin. *From Wall Street to Newgate Via the Primrose Way.* Hartford, Conn.: Bidwell, 1895.

Biegel, Herbert and Allan. *Beneath the Badge: A Story of Police Corruption.* New York: Harper & Row, 1977.

Bienstock, J.W. *Rasputin la fin d'un req egime.* Paris: A. Michel, 1918.

Bierstadt, Edward Hale. *Curious Trials and Criminal Cases.* Garden City, N. Y.: Garden City Publishing, 1928.

_____. *Enter Murderers!* Garden City, N. Y.: Doubleday, Doran, 1934.

_____. *Satan Was a Man.* New York: Doubleday, Doran, 1935.

Bigelow, L. J. *Bench and Bar.* New York: Harper & Bros., 1871.

Bigelow, Poultney. *History of the German Struggle for Liberty.* New York: Harper & Brothers, 1896-1903.

Bigelow, W. E. *The Boston Tragedy: An Expose of the Parkman Murder.* Boston: n. p., 1850.

Biggs, Earl R. *How to Protect Your Child From the Sex Criminal.* Portland, Ore.: New Science Book, 1950.

Biggs, J., Jr. *The Guilty Mind.* New York: Harcourt, 1955.

Bilby, Kenneth. *New Star in the East.* Garden City, N. Y.: Doubleday, 1950.

Bilderman, Albert D., et al. *Report on A Pilot Study in the District of Columbia on Victimization and Attitudes Toward Law Enforcement.* Commission on Law Enforcement and Administration of Justice. Washington, D. C.: U. S. Government Printing Office, 1967.

Biles, J. Hugh. *The Early History of Ada.* Ada: Oklahoma State Bank, 1954.

Billingsley, A. *Black Families in White America.* Englewood Cliffs, N. J.: Prentice-Hall, 1969.

Billington, James H. *The Icon and the Axe: An Interpretive History of Russian Culture.* New York: Knopf, 1966.

Billroth, Theodore. *Historical Studies on the Nature and Treatment of Gunshot Wounds from the Fifteenth Century to the Present Time.* New Haven, Conn.: Nathan Smith Medical Club, 1933.

Billy the Kid: Las Vegas Newspaper Account of His Career, 1880-81. Waco, Texas: W. M. Morrison, 1958.

Binchy, D. A. *Church and State in Fascist Italy.* Oxford, Eng.: Oxford University Press, 1941.

Bingham, Caroline. *The Life and Times of Edward II.* London: Weidenfeld & Nicolson, 1973.

Bingham, Hiram. *Lost City of the Incas.* New York: Atheneum, 1963.

Bingham, J.A. *Trial of the Conspirators for the Assassination of President Lincoln.* Washington, D.C.: U. S. Government Printing Office, 1865.

Bingham, John, and Muncie, William. *The Hunting Down of Peter Manuel, Glasgow Multiple Murderer.* London: Macmillan, 1971.

Bingham, General Theodore A. *The Girl That Disappears. The Real Facts About the White Slave Traffic.* Boston: R. G. Badger, 1911.

Binkley, Wilfred E. *American Political Parties. Their Natural History.* New York: Knopf, 1944.

Binney, Cecil. *Crime and Abnormality.* Oxford, Eng.: Oxford University Press, 1949.

Binney, Horace. *The Privilege of the Writ of Habeas Corpus Under the Constitution.* Philadelphia: C. Sherman & Sons, 1862.

Binsfield, Peter. *Tractatus de Confessionibus Maleficorum et Sagarum.* Treves: Henricus Bock, 1591.

Biographical Dictionary of the American Congress 1774-1927. Washington, D. C.: U. S. Government Printing Office, 1928.

Biographical and Historical Memoirs of Louisiana. 2 vols. Chicago: Goodspeed, 1892.

Biography of Mr. Jason Fairbanks and Miss Elizabeth Fales. Boston: n. p., n. d.

Biondi, Dino. *La Fabbrica del Duce.* Florence, Italy: Vallecchi, 1967.

Biondi, Ray, and Hecox, Walt. *All His Father's Sins.* New York: Pocket Books, 1988.

_____. *The Dracula Killer.* New York: Pocket Books, 1992.

Bird, Caroline. *The Invisible Scar.* New York: David McKay, 1966.

Bird, Eric, and Docking, Stanley. *Fire in Buildings.* London: Adam & Charles Black, 1949.

Birkenhead, Lord. *America Revisited.* Boston: Little, Brown, 1924.

_____. *Contemporary Personalities.* London: Cassell, 1924.

_____. *Famous Trials of History.* London: Hutchinson, 1926.

_____. *F. E.: The Life of F.E. Smith, First Earl of Birkenhead.* London: Eyre & Spottiswoode, 1960.

_____. *Frederick Edwin Earl of Birkenhead.* London: Thornton Butterworth, 1933.

_____. *More Famous Trials.* London: Hutchinson, 1928.

_____. *My American Visit.* London: Hutchinson, 1918.

_____. *Points of View.* London: Hodder & Stoughton, 1922.

Birmingham, George A. *From Dublin to Chicago.* New York: George H. Doran, 1914.

_____. *Murder Most Foul!* London: Chatto & Windus, 1929.

Birney, Herman Hoffman. *Vigilantes.* Philadelphia: Penn, 1929.

Birnbaum, Martin. *Oscar Wilde: Fragments and Memories.* London: n. p., 1920.

Biron, Sir Chartres. *Without Prejudice.* London: Faber, 1936.

Bishop, C. *Women and Crime.* London: Chatto & Windus, 1931.

Bishop, Cecil. *From Information Received.* London: Hutchinson, 1932.

Bishop, Ernest S. *The Narcotic Drug Problem.* New York: Macmillan, 1919.

Bishop, George. *Executions.* Los Angeles: Sherbourne Press, 1965.

_____. *Witness to Evil.* Los Angeles: Nash, 1971.

Bishop, Jim. *A Bishop's Confession.* Boston: Little, Brown, 1981.

_____. *The Day Kennedy Was Shot.* New York: Funk & Wagnalls, 1968.

_____. *The Day Lincoln Was Shot.* New York: Harper & Brothers, 1955.

_____. *The Days of Martin Luther King, Jr.* New York: Putnam, 1971.

_____. *FDR's Last Year.* New York: William Morrow, 1974.

_____. *The Mark Hellinger Story.* Englewood Cliffs, N. J.: Prentice-Hall, 1952.

_____. *The Murder Trial of Judge Peel.* New York: Simon & Schuster, 1962.

_____. *Theodore Roosevelt and His Time.* New York: Scribner's, 1923.

Bishop, Morris. *Petrarch and His World.* Bloomington: Indiana University Press, 1963.

Bishop, Nathaniel H. *Four Months in a Sneak Box.* Boston: Lee & Shephard, 1879.

Bishop, William. *Old Mexico and Her Lost Provinces.* New York: Harper, 1883.

Bismarck-Sconhausen, Prince Otto Eduard Leopold von. *Bismarck: The Man and the Statesman.* trans. A. J. Butler. London: Smith, Elder, n. d.

Biss, Andreas. *Der Stopp der Endleq osung. Kampf gegen Himmler und Eichmann in Budapest.* Stuttgart, Ger.: Seewald, 1966.

Bisson, T.A. *Japan in China.* New York: Macmillan, 1938.

Bittner, Egon. *The Functions of the Police in Modern Society.* Rockville, Md.: National Institute of Mental Health Center for Studies of Crime and Delinquency, 1970.

Bixley, William. *The Guilty and the Innocent: My Fifty Years at the Old Bailey.* London: Souvenir Press, 1957.

Black, Algernon D. *The People and the Police.* New York: McGraw-Hill, 1968.

Black, B. J., and Glick, S. J. *Recidivism at the Hawthorne Cedar Knolls School: Predicted vs. Actual Outcome for Delinquent Boys.* New York: Jewish Board of Guardians, 1952.

Black, Charles L., Jr. *Capital Punishment: The Inevitability of Caprice and Mistake.* New York: W. W. Norton, 1974.

_____. *The People and the Court: Judicial Review in a Democracy.* New York: Macmillan, 1960.

Black, David. *Murder at the Met.* Garden City, N. Y.: Doubleday, 1984.

Black, Donald. *The Behavior of Law.* New York: Academic Press, 1976.

Black, George F. *A Calendar of Cases of Witchcraft in Scotland, 1510-1727.* New York: New York Public Library, 1938.

_____. *List of Works in the New York Public Library Relating to Witchcraft in Europe.* New York: New York Public Library, 1911.

_____. *List of Works in the New York Public Library Relating to Witchcraft in the United States.* New York: New York Public Library, 1908.

_____. *Some Unpublished Scottish Witchcraft Trials.* New York: New York Public Library, 1941.

Black, Henry Campbell (ed.). *Black's Law Dictionary.* St. Paul, Minn.: West, 1968.

Black, Ian, and Morris, Benny. *Israel's Secret Wars: A History of Israel's Intelligence Service.* New York: Grove Press, 1992.

Black, J.B. *The Reign of Queen Elizabeth, 1558-1603.* Oxford, Eng.: Clarendon Press, 1936.

Black, Jack. *You Can't Win.* New York: Macmillan, 1926.

Blackburn, Daniel. *Human Harvest.* Los Angeles: Knightsbridge, 1990.

Blacker, Erwin R. (ed.). *The Old West in Fact.* New York: Ivan Obolensky, 1962.

_____. *Prescott's Histories: The Rise and Decline of the Spanish Empire.* New York: Viking, 1963.

Blackmore, John. *The London by Moonlight Mission.* London: Robson & Avery, 1860.

Blackstock, Nelson. *Cointelpro: The FBI's Secret War on Political Freedom.* New York: Random House, 1976.

Blackwell, William L. *The Beginnings of Russian Industrialization, 1800-1860.* Princeton, N. J.: Princeton University Press, 1968.

Blackwood, A. *The Tales of Algernon Blackwood.* New York: E. P. Dutton, 1939.

Blaine, James G. *Twenty Years of Congress from Lincoln to Garfield.* Norwich, Conn.: Henry Bill, 1884.

Blair, Clay, Jr. and Joan. *The Search for JFK.* New York: Berkeley-Putnam, 1976.

_____. *The Strange Case of James Earl Ray.* New York: Bantam Books, 1969.

Blair, Walter, and Meine, Franklin J. (eds.). *Half Horse, Half Alligator: The Growth of the Mike Fink Legend.* Chicago: University of Chicago Press, 1956.

_____. *Mike Fink.* New York: Henry Holt, 1933.

_____. *A Raft Pilot's Log.* Glendale, Calif.: Arthur H. Clark, 1930.

Blake, Aldrich. *The Ku Klux Kraze.* Oklahoma City: n. p., 1924.

Blake, Euphemia Vale. *History of the Tammany Society From Its Organization to the Present Time, 1901.* New York: Souvenir, 1901.

Blake, James. *The Joint.* Garden City, N. Y.: Doubleday, 1971.

Blake, Robert. *Disraeli.* Garden City, N. Y.: Doubleday, 1968.

Blakeney, T. S. *Sherlock Holmes: Fact or Fiction?* Morristown, N.J.: Baker Street Irregulars, 1954.

Blakeslee, G.H. (ed.). *Mexico and the Caribbean.* New York: G. E. Stechert, 1920.

Blakey, G. Robert. *The Development of the Law of Gambling: 1776-1976.* Washington, D. C.: National Institute of Law Enforcement and Criminal Justice, 1977.

_____, and Billings, Richard. *The Plot to Kill the President.* New York: Times Books, 1981.

_____, Goldstock, Ronald, and Rogovin, Charles H. *Rackets Bureau: Investigation and Prosecution of Organized Crime.* Washington D.C. U. S. Government Printing Office, 1978.

Blanchard, Claude. *Dames de Coeur.* Paris: Editions du Preq e aux clercs, 1946.

Blanchard, Robert E. *Introduction to the Administration of Justice.* New York: John Wiley & Sons, 1975.

Blanckeq e, W. Wendell. *Jueq arez of Mexico.* New York: Frederick A. Praeger, 1971.

Blanco Moheno, Roberto. *Creq onica de la Revolucieq on Mexicana: de la Decena Treq agica a los campos de Celaya.* Mexico: Libros Mexicana, 1957.

Bland, J.O.P. *China: The Pity of It.* New York: Doubleday, 1932.

Blankenship, Russell. *And There Were Men.* New York: Knopf, 1942.

Blanshard, Paul. *An Outline of the British Labor Movement.* New York: Doran, 1923.

Blanshard, Paul. *Personal and Controversial.* Boston: Beacon Press, 1973.

Blasco, E. *Historia de Corte de Madrid.* Madrid: n. p., 1904.

_____. *Mexico in Revolution.* New York: E. P. Dutton, 1920.

Blau, Joseph Leon. *The Christian Interpretation of the Cabala in the Renaissance.* New York: Columbia University Press, 1944.

Blaustein, A., and Porter, C. *The American Lawyer.* Chicago: University of Chicago Press, 1954.

Blauvelt, Mary Taylor. *Oliver Cromwell: A Dictator's Tragedy.* New York: Putnam, 1937.

Blaxland, G. *The Regiments Depart: A History of the British Army, 1945-1970.* London: William Kimber, 1963.

Bleackley, Horace. *The Hangmen of England.* London: Chapman & Hall, 1929.

_____. *Ladies Fair & Frail: Sketches of the Demi-Monde During the Eighteenth Century.* London: Bodley Head, 1909.

_____. *Some Distinguished Victims of the Scaffold.* London: Kegan Paul, Trench, Trubner, 1905.

Bleau, Alphonse. *Preq ecis d'histoire sur la ville et les posseq edeq ees de Loudun.* Poitiers, Fr.: H. Oudin, 1877.

Bledsoe, Jerry. *Bitter Blood.* New York: E. P. Dutton, 1988.

Blesh, Rudi. *Keaton.* New York: Macmillan, 1966.

Bleyer, Willard Grosvenor. *Main Events in the History of American Journalism.* New York: Houghton Mifflin, 1927.

Bligh, Lieutenant William. *A Narrative of the Mutiny on Board H.M.S. Bounty and the Subsequent Voyage of Part of the Crew in the Ship's Boat from Tofoa... to Timor.* London: George Nichol, 1790.

Blinder, M. *Lovers, Killers, Husbands and Wives.* New York: St. Martin's Press, 1985.

Bliss, Douglas Percy (ed.). *The Devil In Scotland.* London: A. MacLehose, 1934.

Bliss, E.L. (ed.). *Roots of Behavior.* New York: Harper & Row, 1962.

Bloch, H.S., and Niederhofer, A. *The Gang.* New York: Philosophical Library, 1958.

Bloch, Herbert A. (ed.). *Crime in America.* New York: Philosophical Library, 1961.

_____, and Geis, Gilbert. *Man, Crime, and Society.* New York: Random House, 1962.

Bloch, Ivan. *Anthropological Studies in the Strange Sexual Practices of All Races in All Ages.* New York: Anthropological Press, 1933.

Bloch, Marc. *Feudal Society.* trans. L. A. Manyon. Chicago: University of Chicago Press, 1961.

Bloch, Max, and Kenner, Ron. *Max the Butcher.* Secaucas, N. J.: Lyle Stuart, 1982.

Bloch, Robert. *American Gothic.* New York: Simon & Schuster, 1974.

Block, Alan A. *East Side-West Side: Organizing Crime in New York, 1930-1950.* Swansea, U.K.: Christopher Davis, 1979.

_____, and Chambliss, William J. *Organizing Crime.* New York: Elsevier, 1981.

_____, and Scarpitti, Frank R. *Poisoning for Profit: The Mafia and Toxic Waste.* New York: William Morrow, 1985.

Block, Eugene B. *And May God Have Mercy...The Case Against Capital Punishment.* San Francisco: Fearon, 1962.

_____. *The Fabric of Guilt.* Garden City, N. Y.: Doubleday, 1968.

_____. *Fifteen Clues.* Garden City, N.Y.: Doubleday, 1965.

_____. *Great Stagecoach Robbers of the West.* New York: Doubleday, 1962.

_____. *Great Train Robberies of the West.* New York: Coward-McCann, 1959.

_____. *Lie Detectors.* New York: David McKay, 1977.

_____. *Science Vs. Crime.* New York: Caroline House, 1980.

_____. *Voiceprinting.* New York: David McKay, 1975.

_____. *The Wizard of Berkeley.* New York: Coward-McCann, 1958.

Block, Irvin. *Violence in America.* New York: Public Affairs Committee, 1970.

Block, Peter, Anderson, Deborah, and Gervais, Pamela. *Policewomen on Patrol.* Washington, D.C.: Police Foundation, 1973.

Blok, Anton. *The Mafia of a Sicilian Village, 1860-1960.* New York: Harper & Row, 1975.

Blom, Eric. *Mozart.* New York: Colliers, 1966.

Bloom, Murray Teigh. *The Man Who Stole Portugal.* New York: Scribner's, 1953.

_____. *Money of Thier Own.* New York: Scribner's, 1957.

_____. *Rogues to Riches.* New York: Warner, 1973.

Bloomberg, Charles. *Christian Nationalism and the Rise of the Afrikaner Broederbond in South Africa, 1918-1948.* Bloomington, Ind.: Indiana University Press, 1989.

Bloomfield, L. M. *Egypt, Israel and the Gulf of Aqaba in International Law.* Toronto, Ontario, Can.: Carswell, 1957.

Bloomgarden, Henry S. *The Gun: A "Biography" of the Gun That Killed John F. Kennedy.* New York: Grossman, 1975.

Bloomquist, Edward R. *Marijuana.* New York: Macmillan, 1970.

Blos, Peter. *On Adolescence.* New York: Free Press, 1962.

Bloss, Roy S. *Pony Express-the Great Gamble.* Berkeley, Calif.: Howell-North, 1939.

Blum, J. *Lord and Peasant in Russia from the 9th to the 19th Century.* New York: Atheneum, 1964.

Blum, John M. *From the Morgenthau Diaries.* 3 vols. Boston: Houghton Mifflin, 1959-1967.

Blum, Richard H. *Deceivers and Deceived.* Springfield, Ill.: Charles C. Thomas, 1972.

_____, et al. *The Dream Sellers.* San Francisco: Jossey-Bass, 1972.

_____. *Horatio Alger's Children: The Role of the Family in the Origin and Prevention of Drug Risk.* San Francisco: Jossey-Bass, 1973.

_____. *Offshore Haven Banks, Trusts, and Companies: The Business of Crime in the Euromarket.* New York: Frederick A. Praeger, 1984.

_____, et al. *Society and Drugs.* San Francisco: Jossey-Bass, 1969.

_____, et al. *Students and Drugs.* San Francisco: Jossey-Bass, 1969.

_____. *Surveillance and Espionage in a Free Society.* New York: Praeger, 1972.

Blumberg, Abraham S. *Criminal Justice.* Chicago: Quadrangle Books, 1970.

_____ (ed.). *Current Perspectives on Criminal Behavior.* New York: Knopf, 1974.

_____. *Problems of American Society Criminal Justice.* Chicago: Quadrangle Books, 1967.

_____ (ed.). *The Scales of Justice.* Chicago: Aldine, 1970.

Blumenthal, Ralph. *Last Days of the Sicilians: At War with the Mafia: The FBI Assault on the Pizza Connection.* New York: Times Books, 1988.

Blumenthal, Sid, and Yazijian, Harvey (eds.). *Government by Gunplay: Assassination Conspiracy Theories From Dallas to Today.* New York: Signet Books, 1976.

Blumenthal, Walter Hart. *Brides from Bridewell: Female Felons Sent to Colonial America.* Westport, Conn.: Greenwood Press, 1962.

Blumer, H. A., Sutter, S. Ahmed, and Smith, R. *The World of Youthful Drug Use.* Berkeley: University of California, 1967.

Blumstein, Alfred, Cohen, Jacqueline, and Nagin, Daniel (eds.). *Deterrence and Incapacitation: Estimating the Effects of Criminal Sanctions on Crime Rates.* Washington, D. C.: National Academy of Sciences, 1978.

Blundell, Sir M. *So Rough a Wind: Kenya Memoirs.* London: Weidenfeld & Nicolson, 1964.

Blundell, Nigel. *The World's Greatest Mysteries.* London: Octopus, 1980.

Blundell, William E. *Crime at the Top.* Philadelphia: J. B. Lippincott, 1978.

Blyth, A.W. *Poisons: Their Effects and Detection.* London: Charles Griffin, 1884.

Blyth, Henry. *Hell and Hazard.* Chicago: Regnery, 1969.

Blythe, Ronald. *The Age of Illusion: England in the Twenties and Thirties.* London: Hamish Hamilton, 1963.

Boar, Roger, and Blundell, Nigel. *The World's Most Infamous Murders.* New York: Exeter Books, 1983.

Boas, Ralph P. and Louise. *Cotton Mather, Keeper of the Puritan Conscience.* Hamden, Conn.: Archon, 1964.

Bobby: The Robert F. Kennedy Story . . . The Man and His Dream. New York: MacFadden-Bartell, 1968.

Bodansky, Yossef. *Bin Laden: The Man Who Declared War on America.* New York: Prima Publishing, 1999.

Bode, William. *Lights and Shadows of Chinatown.* San Francisco: H. S. Crocker, 1896.

Boettcher, Robert. *Gifts of Deceit: Sun Myung Moon, Tongsun Park, and the Korea Scandal.* New York: Holt, Rinehart & Winston, 1980.

Boettiger, John. *Jake Lingle.* New York: E. P. Dutton, 1931.

Boffa, Giuseppe. *Inside the Khrushchev Era.* New York: Marzani & Munsell, 1963.

Bogardus, E. S. *The Mexican in the United States.* Berkeley: University of California Press, 1934.

Bogdanovich, Peter. *The Cinema of Alfred Hitchcock.* New York: Doubleday, 1963.

_____. *The Killing of the Unicorn: Dorothy Stratten, 1960-1980.* New York: William Morrow, 1984.

Boggs, Mae Helene Bacon. *My Playhouse was a Concord Coach.* Oakland, Calif.: Howell-North Press, 1942.

Bohannan, P. *African Homicide and Suicide.* Princeton, N.J.: Princeton University Press, 1960.

Bohlen, Charles E. *Witness to History: 1929-1969.* New York: W. W. Norton, 1973.

Bois, Jules. *Le Satanisme et la magie.* Paris: L. Chailley, 1895.

Bojano, Filippo. *In the Wake of the Goose-Step.* London: Cassell, 1944.

Bok, Curtis. *Star Wormwood.* New York: Knopf, 1959.

Bok, Edward William. *The Americanization of Edward Bok.* New York: Scribner's, 1920.

Bok, Sissela. *Lying.* New York: Vintage Books, 1978.

Boland, Charles Michael. *They All Discovered America.* Garden City, N. Y.: Doubleday, 1963.

Boldt, Gerhard. *In the Shelter With Hitler.* London: Citadel Press, 1948.

Bolitho, Hector. *A Biographer's Notebook.* New York: Macmillan, 1950.

_____ (ed.). *Further Letters of Queen Victoria from the House of Brandenburg-Prussia.* London: Thornton Butterworth, 1938.
_____. *Jinnah.* London: John Murray, 1954.
_____. *Roumania Under King Carol.* London: Eyre & Spottiswood, 1939.
Bolitho, William. *Italy Under Mussolini.* New York: Macmillan, 1926.
_____. *Murder for Profit.* New York: Harper & Brothers, 1926.
Bolla, Nino. *Colloqui con Umberto II - Colloqui con Vittorio Emanuele III.* Rome: Fantera, 1949.
Bolling, Richard. *House Out of Order.* New York: E. P. Dutton, 1965.
_____. *Spanish Exploration in the Southwest, 1542-1706.* New York: Scribner's, 1916.
Bolz, Frank, and Hershey, Edward. *Hostage Cop.* New York: Rawson Wade, 1980.
Bonanno, Joseph. *A Man of Honor: The Autobiography of Joseph Bonanno.* New York: Simon & Schuster, 1983.
Bonaparte, Joseph. *Lettres d' exil.* Paris: Charpentier, 1912.
Bonaparte, Louis-Napoleon. *Oeuvres de Napoleon III.* 5 vols. Paris: Henri Plon, 1869.
_____. *The Political and Historical Works of Louis Napoleon Bonaparte, President of the French Republic, with an Original Memoir of His Life, brought down to the Promulgation of the Constitution of 1852.* 2 vols. London: Illustrated London Library, 1852.
Bonavita, Francesco. *Mussolini Svelato.* Milan, Italy: Sonzogno, 1933.
_____. *Il Padre del Duce.* Rome: Pinciana, 1933.
Bond, E.A. (ed.). *Russia at the Close of the Sixteenth Century.* London: Hakluyt Society, 1856.
Bond, John. *An Essay on the Incubus or Nightmare.* London: D. Wilson & T. Durham, 1753.
Bond, John. *Mussolini the Wild Man of Europe.* Washington, D. C.: Independent Publicity, 1929.
Bonewits, P. E. I. *Real Magic.* New York: Coward, McCann & Geoghegan, 1971.
Bonger, W. A. *Race and Crime.* New York: Columbia University Press, 1943.
Bonger, Willem. *Criminality and Economic Conditions.* Bloomington: Indiana University Press, 1969.
Bonhoeffer, Dietrich. *Letters and Papers From Prison.* London: S. C. M. Press, 1953.
_____. *Prayers From Prison.* Philadelphia: Fortress Press, 1977.
Bonilla, Policarpo. *Wilson Doctrine.* New York: Published by Author, 1914.
Bonn, John L. *The Gates of Dannemora.* New York: Doubleday, 1951.
Bonner, Judy Whitson. *Investigation of a Homicide: The Murder of John F. Kennedy.* Anderson, S. C.: Drake House, 1969.
Bonner, Thomas Neville. *Medicine in Chicago, 1850-1950.* Madison, Wis.: American History Research Center, 1957.
Bonnet, Theodore F. *The Regenrators: A Study of the Graft Prosecution in San Francisco.* San Francisco: Pacific Printing, 1911.
Bonney, Edward. *Banditti of the Prairies.* Chicago: Homewood, 1890.
Bonnie, Richard J., and Whitebread, Charles H., II. *The Marihuana Conviction: A History of Marihuana Prohibition in the United States.* Charlottesville: University of Virginia Press, 1974.
Bonnin, Charles (ed.). *Bismarck and the Hohenzollern Candidature for the Spanish Throne.* trans. Isabella M. Massey. London: Chatto & Windus, 1957.
Bonomi, Ivanoe. *Diario di unanno.* Milan, Italy: Garzanti, 1947.
_____. *From Socialism to Fascism: A Study of Contemporary Italy.* trans. John Murray. London: Martin Hopkinson, 1924.
Bontemps, Arna W. *Black Thunder.* New York: Macmillan, 1936.
_____. *100 Years of Negro Freedom.* New York: Dodd, Mead, 1961.
Bontham, Alan. *Sex Crimes and Sex Criminals.* New York: Wisdom House, 1961.
Booker, Anton S. *Wildcats in Petticoats.* Girard, Kan.: Haldeman-Julius, 1945.
Booker, Edna Lee. *News Is My Job.* New York: Macmillan, 1940.
Boole, Ella A. *Give Prohibition Its Chance.* New York: Fleming H. Revell, 1929.
Booth, Charles. *Conditions and Occupations of the People of the Tower Hamlets, 1886-7.* London: Stanford, 1887.
_____. *Life and Labour of the People of London.* London: Macmillan, 1897.
Booth, Ernest. *Stealing Through Life.* New York: Knopf, 1929.
Booth, Mary L. *History of the City of New York.* New York: E. P. Dutton, 1880.
Booth, William. *In Darkest England and the Way Out.* Montclair, N. J.: Patterson Smith, 1974.
Bopp, William J. *O. W. Wilson and the Search for a Police Profession.* Port Washington, N. Y.: Kennikat Press, 1977.
_____. *Police Administration: Selected Readings.* Boston: Holbrook Press, 1975.
Bor, Robert. *Passenger Behavior.* Burlington, Ver.: Ashgate Publishing Co., 2003.
Borah, William Edgar. *Haywood Trial: Closing Arguments of W. E. Borah.* Boise, Idaho: Statesman Shop, 1907.
Borchard, Edwin Montefiore. *Convicting the Innocent.* New Haven, Conn.: Yale University Press, 1932.
Bordeux, V.J. *Benito Mussolini-The Man.* London: Hutchinson, 1927.
Bordoni, Francesco. *Sacrum Tribunal Judicum in Causis Sanctae Fidei.* Rome: Haeredum Corbelletti, 1648.
Bordua, David J. (ed.). *The Police: Six Sociological Essays.* New York: John Wiley & Sons, 1967.
Borel, Thomas. *The White Slavery of Europe.* trans. Joseph Edmondson. London: Dyer Brothers, 1880.
Boren, Henry C. *The Gracchi.* New York: Twayne, 1968.
Borg, Dorothy. *American Policy and the Chinese Revolution, 1925-28.* New York: Institute of Pacific Relations, 1947.
_____. *The United States and the Far Eastern Crisis of 1933-38.* Cambridge, Mass.: Harvard University Press, 1964.
Borgese, G.A. *Goliath, The March of Fascism.* New York: Viking, 1938.
Borghi, Armando. *Mussolini Red and Black.* London: Wishart Books, 1935.
Borkenau, Franz. *Austria and After.* London: Faber & Faber, 1938.
_____. *European Communism.* New York: Harper, 1953.
_____. *The New German Empire.* New York: Viking, 1939.
_____. *Socialism, National and International.* London: Routledge, 1942.
_____. *The Spanish Cockpit.* London: Faber & Faber, 1937.
Borkin, Joseph. *The Crime and Punishment of I. G. Farben.* New York: Free Press, 1978.
Borniche, Roger. *Flic Story.* Garden City, N. Y.: Doubleday, 1975.
Bornstein, Joseph. *The Politics of Murder.* New York: William Sloan, 1950.
Borowitz, Albert. *Innocence and Arsenic Studies in Crime and Literature.* New York: Harper & Row, 1977.
_____. *The Woman Who Murdered Black Satin.* Columbus: Ohio State University Press, 1981.
Borrell, Clive, and Cashinella, Brian. *Crime in Britain Today.* London: Routledge & Paul, 1975.
Borreson, Ralph. *When Lincoln Died.* New York: Appleton-Century, 1965.
Borstein, Edward. *Allende's Chile: An Inside View.* New York: International Publishers, 1977.
Borthwick, J.D. *The Gold Hunters.* New York: Outing, 1927.
Bortner, M.A. *Inside a Juvenile Court.* New York: New York University Press, 1984.
Bortolotto, Guido. *Storia del fascismo.* Milan, Italy: Ulrico Hoepli, 1938.
Borton, Hugh. *Japan's Modern Century.* New York: Ronald Press, 1955.
Bose, Nirmal Kumar. *My Days With Gandhi.* Calcutta, India: Nishana, 1953.
_____. *Selections From Gandhi.* Ahmedabad, India: Navajivan, 1948.
_____. *Studies in Gandhism.* Calcutta, India: Indian Associated, 1947.
Bose, Partha. *Alexander the Great's Art of Strategy.* New York: Gotham Books, 2003.
Bose, Subhas Chandra. *The Indian Struggle.* London: Wishart, 1935.
Bosher, J.F. (ed.). *French Government and Society, 1500-1850: Essays in Memory of Alfred Cobban.* London: Athlone, 1973.
Bossard, l'Abbeq e Eugene. *Gilles de Rais, Marechal de France Dit Barbe-Bleue.* Paris: H. Champion, 1886.
The Boston Fiend! Many Long Hidden Mysteries at Last Disclosed! Full Account of the Atrocious Crimes of Thomas W. Piper. Boston: n. p., 1875.
Boswell, Charles, and Thompson, Lewis. *Advocates of Murder.* New York: Collier Books, 1962.
_____. *The Girl in Lovers Lane.* New York: Fawcett, 1953.
_____. *The Girls in Nightmare House.* New York: Gold Medal, 1955.
_____. *Practitioners of Murder.* New York: Collier Books, 1962.
Boswell, James. *London Journal: 1762-1763.* New York: McGraw-Hill, 1950.
Bosworth, Patricia. *Montgomery Clift.* New York: Harcourt, Brace, Jovanovich, 1977.
Botkin, Gleb. *The Real Romanovs.* New York: Putnam, 1931.
Botting, Douglas. *The Pirates.* New York: Time-Life, 1978.
Bottomley, A. Keith. *Criminology in Focus: Past Trends and Future Prospects.* New York: Barnes & Noble, 1979.
_____. *Decisions in the Penal Process.* London: Martin Robertson, 1973.
_____. *Prison Before Trial.* London: Bell, 1970.
Bottons, A.E., and McClintock, F. H. *Criminals Coming of Age.* London: Heinemann Educational, 1973.
_____, and McClean, J.D. *Defendants in the Criminal Process.* London: Routledge & Kegan Paul, 1978.
Bouchardon, Pierre. *L'Assassinat de l'archeveq eque.* Paris: Artheq eme Fayard, 1926.
_____. *Troppmann.* Paris: Albin Michel, 1932.
Boucher, Anthony (ed.). *The Pocket Book of True Crime Stories.* New York: Pocket Books, 1943.
_____. *Police Intelligence.* New York: AMS Press, 1976.
_____. *The Quality of Murder.* New York: E. P. Dutton, 1962.
Boudin, Louis B. *Government by Judiciary.* New York: William Godwin, 1932.
Boudreau, John F. et al. *Arson and Arson Investigations: Survey and Assessment.* Washington, D. C.: U. S. Department of Justice, 1977.
Bougainville, Louis Antoine de. *Voyage Round the World.* trans. J. R. Forster. London: J. Norse, 1772.
Boulton, David. *The Grease Machine.* New York: Harper & Row, 1979.
_____. *The Making of Tania: The Patty Hearst Story.* London: New English Library, 1975.
Boulton, Richard. *A Complete History of Magic.* London: E. Curll & W. Taylor, 1715.
Bourg, Edme-Theq eodore. *Proceq es du prince Napoleq eon-Louis et de ses coaccuseq es devant la Xour des Pairs.* Paris: A. Levavasseur, 1840.
Bourjaily, Vance Nye. *The Man Who Knew Kennedy.* New York: Dial Press, 1967.
Bourke, John G. *On the Border with the Crook.* Lincoln: University of Nebraska Press, 1971.
Boutros-Ghali, Boutros. *The United Nations and Rwanda, 1993-1996.* New York: United Nations Press, 1996.
Bouza, Anthony V. *Police Administration, Organization & Performance.* New York: Pergamen Press, 1979.
_____. *Police Intelligence: The Operations of an Investigative Unit.* New York: AMS Press, 1976.
Boveri, Margret. *Treason in the Twentieth Century.* New York: Putnam, 1963.
Bovet, Richard. *Pandaemonium, or the Devil's Cloister, Being a Further Blow to Modern Sadducism, Proving the Existence of Witches and Spirits.* London: Malthus, 1684.
Bowden, Tom. *The Men in the Middle—The UK Police.* London: Institute for the Study of Conflict, 1976.
Bowen, Walter S., and Neal, Harry Edward. *The United States Secret Service.* Philadelphia: Chilton, 1960.
Bowen-Rowlands, Ernest. *In Court and Out of Court.* London: Hutchinson, 1925.
_____. *In the Light of the Law.* London: Grant Richards, 1931.
_____. *Seventy-Two Years at the Bar.* London: Macmillan, 1924.
Bower, Tom. *The Perfect English Spy: Sir Dick White and the Secret War, 1935-90.* New York: St. Martin's, 1995.

Bowers, William. *Executions in America.* Lexington, Mass.: D. C. Heath, 1974.

Bowker, A. E. *Behind the Bar.* London: Staples Press, 1949.

_____. *A Lifetime with the Law.* London: W. H. Allen, 1961.

Bowman, Hank W. *Famous Guns from the Smithsonian Collection.* New York: Arco, 1967.

Bowman, Lynn. *Los Angeles, Epic of a City.* Berkeley, Calif.: Howell-North Books, 1974.

Bowyer, J. Barton. *Cheating.* New York: St. Martin's Press, 1982.

Bowyer Bell, J. *Transnational Terror.* Washington, D. C.: AEI Hoover Policy Studies, 1975.

Box, Steven. *Deviance, Reality and Society.* London: Holt, Rinehart & Winston, 1971.

Boyce, S.S. *Hemp.* New York: Orange & Judd, 1900.

Boyd, Belle. *In Camp and Prison.* New York: Blelock, 1867.

Boyd, James. *Above the Law.* New York: New American Library, 1968.

Boyer, Glenn G. (ed.) *I Married Wyatt Earp: The Recollections of Josephine Sarah Marcus Earp.* Tucson: University of Arizona Press, 1976.

Boyer, Richard O., and Morais, Herbert M. *A History of the American Labor Movement.* London: John Calder, 1955.

Boyle, Kay. *My Next Bride.* New York: Harcourt, Brace, 1934.

Boyle, Kevin. *Law and the State: The Case of Northern Ireland.* London: Martin Robertson, 1975.

Brace, Charles Loring. *The Dangerous Classes of New York and Twenty Years' Work Among Them.* New York: Wynkoop & Hallenbeck, 1880.

Brackett, L.P. *Our Western Empire.* Philadelphia: Bradley, Garretson, 1881.

Brackman, Arnold C. *The Last Emperor.* New York: Scribner's, 1975.

Braddy, Haldeen. *Cock of the Walk: The Legend of Pancho Villa.* Alburquerque: University of New Mexico Press, 1955.

_____. *Pancho Villa at Columbus.* El Paso: Texas Western College Press, 1965.

_____. *Pershing's Mission in Mexico.* El Paso: Texas Western College Press, 1966.

Bradford, Ernle. *The Sundered Cross: The Story of the Fourth Crusade.* Englewood Cliffs, N. J.: Prentice-Hall, 1967.

Bradford, Gamaliel. *D. L. Moody: A Worker In Souls.* Garden City, N. Y.: Doubleday, Doran, 1928.

_____. *Union Portraits.* New York: Houghton Mifflin, 1916.

Bradford, Kermit. *Miracle on Death Row.* Waco, Texas: Chosen Books, 1977.

Bradford, Sarah. *Cesare Borgia.* New York: Macmillan, 1976.

Bradford, S.B. *Prohibition in Kansas and the Kansas Prohibitory Law.* Topeka, Kan.: Crane, 1889.

Bradford, William. *An Enquiry How Far the Punishment of Death is Necessary in Pennsylvania.* Philadelphia: T. Dobson, 1793.

Bradlee, Ben, Jr. *The Ambush Murders.* New York: Dodd, Mead, 1979.

Bradlee, Francis B.C. *Piracy in the West Indies and Its Suppression.* Salem, Mass.: Essex institute, 1923.

Bradley, Glenn Danford. *The Story of the Santa Fe.* Boston: R. G. Badger, 1920.

Bradley, Hugh. *Such Was Saratoga.* Garden City, N. Y.: Doubleday Doran, 1940.

Bradley, John L. (ed.). *Rogues Progress.* Boston: Houghton Mifflin, 1965.

Bradley, Omar. *A Soldier's Story.* New York: Modern Library, 1999.

Bradley, R. T. *Lives of Frank and Jesse James.* St. Louis: J. W. Marsh, 1882.

_____. *The Outlaws of the Border.* St. Louis: J. W. Marsh, 1880.

Bradshaw, Jon. *Dreams That Money Can Buy.* New York: William Morrow, 1985.

Brady, Katherine. *Father's Days: A True Story of Incest.* New York: Seaview Books, 1979.

Brady, Robert A. *The Spirit and Structure of German Fascism.* New York: Viking, 1937.

Bragge, Francis. *A Defense of the Proceedings Against Jane Wenham.* London: E. Curll, 1712.

_____. *A Full and Impartial Account of the Discovery of Sorcery and Witchcraft Practiced by Jane Wenham.* London: E. Curll 1712.

_____. *Witchcraft Further Diaplayed.* London: E. Curll, 1712.

Bragin, Charles. *Dime Novels, Bibliography, 1860-1928.* New York: Published by Author, 1938.

Braithwaite, J. *Inequality, Crime and Public Policy.* London: Routledge & Kegan Paul, 1979.

Braithwaite, Max. *The Hungry Thirties.* Toronto, Can.: McClelland, 1977.

Braly, Malcolm. *False Starts.* Boston: Little, Brown, 1976.

_____. *On the Yard.* Greenwich, Conn.: Fawcett Publications, 1967.

Braly, William C. *The Hard Way Home.* Washington, D. C.: Infantry Journal Press, 1947.

Brampton, Baron Henry Hawkins. *The Reminiscences of Sir Henry Hawkins.* London: E. Arnold, 1904.

Bramstedt, Ernest Kohn. *Dictatorship and Political Police: The Technique and Control of Fear.* London: Kegan Paul, 1945.

Brancale, Ralph, and Ellis, Arthur. *Psychology of Sex Offenders.* Springfield, Ill.: Charles C. Thomas, 1956.

Branch, Edgar Marquess. *The Literary Apprenticeship of Mark Twain.* Urbana: University of Illinois Press, 1950.

Branch, Taylor, and Propper, Eugene M. *Labyrinth.* New York: Viking Press, 1982.

Brand, Donald D. *Mexico: Land of Sunshine and Shadow.* New York: D. Van Nostrand, 1966.

Brandeis, L. D. *Other People's Money and How the Bankers Used It.* New York: Frederick A. Stokes, 1932.

Brandenburg, Erich. *From Bismarck to the World War.* trans. Annie Elizabeth Adams. London: Oxford University Press, 1927.

Brandon, R., and Davies, C. *Wrongful Imprisonment.* London: George Allen & Unwin, 1973.

Brandt, Fred. *Fascinating San Francisco.* San Francisco: Published by Author, 1924.

Brannon, William T. *The Fabulous Drake Swindle.* New York: Mercury Press, 1955.

Brant, House. *Crimes That Shocked America.* New York: Ace, 1961.

Brantingham, Paul and Patricia. *Patterns in Crime.* New York: Macmillan, 1984.

Brantley, C. *The Giriama and Colonial Resistance in Kenya, 1800-1920.* Berkeley: University of California Press, 1981.

Braude, M.C., and Szara, S. (eds.). *Pharmacology of Marihuana.* New York: Raven Press, 1976.

Braudel, Fernand. *The Mediterranean and the Mediterranean World in the Age of Philip II.* trans. Sian Reynolds. New York: Harper & Row, 1972.

Brayer, Herbert O. *Range Murder.* Evanston, Ill.: Branding Iron Press, 1955.

_____. *William Blackmore: the Spanish-Mexican Land Grants of New Mexico and Colorado 1863-1878.* Denver: Bradford-Robinson, 1949.

Brayley, F.A. *Arrangement of Finger Prints.* Boston: Worcester Press, 1910.

Brayman, Harold. *The President Speaks Off the Record.* Princeton, N. J.: Dow Jones Books, 1976.

Breakenridge, William M. *Helldorado: Bringing the Law to the Mesquite.* Boston: Houghton Mifflin, 1928.

Brearley, H. C. *Homicide in the United States.* Chapel Hill: University of North Carolina Press, 1932.

Breasted, James Henry. *Ancient Records of Egypt.* Chicago: University of Chicago Press, 1907.

_____. *A History of Egypt.* New York: Scribner's, 1951.

Breatnach, Seamus. *The Irish Police.* Dublin, Ire.: Anvil Books, 1974.

Bradlee, Ben, Jr., and Van Atta, Dale. Prophet of Blood. New York: Putnam, 1981.

Breceda, Alfredo. *Meq exico Revolucionario, 1913-1917.* Madrid: Tipografia Artistica Cervantes, 1920.

Brecher, Edward M. *Licit and Illicit Drugs.* Boston: Little, Brown, 1972.

Breen, Timothy H. *The Character of the Good Ruler: A Study of Puritan Political Ideas in New England, 1630-1730.* New Haven, Conn.: Yale University Press, 1970.

Breihan, Carl W. *Badmen of Frontier Days.* New York: Robert M. McBride Co., 1957.

_____. *The Complete and Authentic Life of Jesse James.* New York: Frederick Fell, 1953.

_____. *The Day Jesse James Was Killed.* New York: Frederick Fell, 1961.

_____. *Escapades of Frank & Jesse James.* New York: Frederick Fell, 1974.

_____. *Great Gunfighters of the West.* San Antonio, Texas: Naylor, 1962.

_____. *Great Lawmen of the West.* New York: Signet, 1978.

_____. *The Killer Legions of Quantrill.* Seattle, Wash.: Hangman Press, 1971.

_____. *The Man Who Shot Jesse James.* New York: A. S. Barnes, 1979.

_____. *The Outlaw Brothers: The True Story of Missouri's Younger Brothers.* San Antonio, Texas: Naylor, 1961.

_____. *Outlaws of the Old West.* New York: Bonanza Books, 1967.

_____. *Quantrill and His Civil War Guerrillas.* Denver: Sage Books, 1959.

_____. *Younger Brothers.* San Antonio: Naylor, 1961.

Bremer, Arthur. *An Assassin's Diary.* New York: Harper Magazine Press, 1972.

Brenan, Gerald. *The Spanish Labyrinth.* New York: Macmillan, 1943.

Brend, W. A. *A Handbook of Medical Jurisprudence and Toxicology.* New York: Griffin, 1941.

Brener, Milton E. *The Garrison Case.* New York: Clarkson N. Potter, 1969.

Brenner, Anita R., and Leighton, George. *The Wind That Swept Mexico.* New York: Harper, 1943.

Brenner, Walter C. *The Ford Theatre Lincoln Assassination Playbills.* Los Angeles: American Scene, 1985.

Brent, Rafer (ed.). *Great Western Heroes.* New York: Bartholomew House, 1957.

Breo, Dennis, and Martin, William. *The Crime of the Century.* New York: Bantam, 1993.

Breshko-Breshkovskaya. *Hidden Springs of the Russian Revolution.* Stanford, Calif.: Stanford University Press, 1931.

Bresler, Fenton. *The Chinese Mafia.* New York: Stein & Day, 1981.

_____. *Reprieve: A Study of a System.* London: Harrap, 1965.

_____. *Lord Goddard.* London: Harrap, 1971.

_____. *Scales of Justice.* London: Weidenfeld & Nicolson, 1973.

Breslin, Jimmy. *The Gang That Couldn't Shoot Straight.* New York: Viking, 1969.

Bressler, F. *Reprieve.* London: Harrap, 1965.

Brewer, John Francis. *The Curse Upon Mitre Square AD 1530-1888.* London: Simpkin Marshall, 1888.

Brewerton, G. Douglas. *The War in Kansas.* New York: Derby & Jackson, 1856.

Brewster, Sir David. *Letters on Natural Magic.* London: John Murray, 1832.

Brian, Denis. *Tallulah, Darling.* London: Sidgwick & Jackson, 1972.

Brice, A. H. M. *Look Upon the Prisoner: Studies in Crime.* London: Hutchinson, 1933.

Brice, R. *Le secret de Napoleq eon.* Paris: Payot, 1936.

_____. *Cities in the Wilderness: Urban Life in America, 1625-1742.* New York: Capricorn, 1966.

_____. *Mitre and Sceptre.* New York: Oxford University Press, 1962.

_____. *Vexed and Troubled Englishmen 1590-1642.* New York: Oxford University Press, 1968.

Bridge, J. H. *The Inside History of the Carnegie Steel Company.* Chicago: Aldine, 1903.

Bridges, B.C. *Practical Fingerpainting.* New York: Funk & Wagnalls, 1942.

_____, and Boolsen, F.M. *Fifty-one Fingerprint Systems.* Privately Printed, 1935.

Bridges, Yseult. *Saint with Red Hands.* London: Jarrolds, 1954.

_____. *The Tragedy at Road-Hill House.* New York: Rinehart, 1955.

_____. *Two Studies in Crime.* London: Hutchinson, 1959.

A Brief Relation of the Cruel Murder of Betsy Van Amburgh. Jersey City, N.J.: n. p., 1805.

A Brief Summary of Some of the Principal Incidents Relative to the Life of Ursula Newman and the Intercourse Subsisting Between Her and Richard Johnson. New York: Elam Bliss, 1829.

Briggs, C. W. *The Reign of Terror in Kansas.* Boston: n. p., 1856.

Briggs, I. Vernon. *The Manner of Man That Kills: Spencer, Czolgosz, Richeson.* Boston: Richard G. Badger, The Gorman Press, 1921.

Briggs, L. Vernon. *Arizona and New Mexico, 1882.* Boston: Privately Printed, 1932.

Bright, John. *A History of Israel.* London: SCM Press, 1972.

_____. *Hizzoner Big Bill Thompson.* New York: J. Cape & H. Smith, 1930.

Brill, Steven. *The Teamsters.* New York: Simon & Schuster, 1978.

Brimble, E. Lillian. *In the Eyrie of the Hohenzollern Eagle.* London: Hodder & Stoughton, 1916.

Bringuier, Carlos. *Red Friday: November 22, 1963.* Chicago: C. Hallberg, 1969.

Brininstool, Earl Alonzo. *Fighting Red Cloud's Warriors.* Columbus, Ohio: Hunter-Trader-Trapper, 1926.

Brinley, John. *A Discovery of the Impostures of Witches and Astrologers.* London: J. Wright, 1680.

Brissard, Andreq e. *Les Agents de Lucifer.* Paris: Peq erin, 1975.

Brissenden, Paul F. *The I. W. W.: A Study of American Syndicalism.* New York: Columbia University Press, 1919.

Bristed, Charles Astor. *The Upper Ten Thousand.* New York: Stinger & Townsend, 1852.

Bristow, E. J. *Prostitution and Prejudice: The Jewish Fight Against White Slavery 1870-1939.* New York: Oxford University Press, 1982.

British Museum. *Murders (A Collection of Broadsides Containing Accounts in Prose and Verse of Murders and Executions).* London: n. p. 1794-1860.

Britton, Nan. *The President's Daughter.* New York: Elizabeth Ann Guild, 1927.

Brixton, Charles (ed.). *Memoirs of Sir Thomas Fowell Buston.* London: J. M. Dent & Sons, 1925.

Brock, Alan. *A Casebook of Crime.* London: Watmoughs, 1948.

Brockelmann, Carl. *History of the Islamic Peoples.* New York: Putnam, 1947.

Brockway, A. Fenner. *African Socialism.* Chester Springs, Pa.: Dufour, 1963.

Brockway, Z.R. *Fifty Years of Prison Service.* New York: Charities Publication Committee, 1912.

Brodie-Innes, John William. *Scottish Witchcraft Trials.* London: Chiswick Press, 1891.

Brodsky, Annette, M. (ed.). *The Female Offender.* Beverly Hills, Calif.: Sage, 1975.

Brody, Stephen R. *The Effectiveness of Sentencing.* London: H. M. Stationery Office, 1976.

Broehl, Wayne. *The Molly Maguires.* Cambridge, Mass.: Harvard University Press, 1964.

Broeker, Galen. *Rural Disorder and Police Reform in Ireland.* London: Routledge & Kegan Paul, 1970.

Brogan, Denis W. *The Era of Franklin D. Roosevelt.* New Haven, Conn.: Yale University Press, 1950.

Brogger, A.W., and Shetelig, Haakon. *The Viking Ships.* trans. Katherine John. Oslo, Nor.: Dreyer, 1953.

Brolaski, Harry. *Easy Money.* Cleveland: Searchlight Press, 1911.

Bromage, Mary C. *De Valera and the March of a Nation.* London: Hutchinson, 1956.

Bromberg, Walter. *Crime and the Mind.* Philadelphia: J. B. Lippincott, 1948.

Brommel, Bernard. *Eugene V. Debs: A Spokesman for Labor and Socialism.* Chicago: Charles H. Kerr, 1978.

Bronaugh, Warren C. *The Youngers' Fight for Freedom.* Columbia, Mo.: E.W. Stephens, 1906.

Brondsted, Johannes. *The Vikings.* Baltimore: Penguin Books, 1970.

Bronowski, J. *The Face of Violence.* New York: World, 1967.

Bronson, Edgar Beecher. *The Red-Blooded Heroes of the Frontier.* New York: A. C. McClurg, 1910.

_____. *The Vanguard.* New York: George H. Doran, 1914.

Brooke, Henry K. *Book of Pirates.* New York: J. B. Perry, 1847.

_____. *The Highwaymen and Pirates' Own Book.* New York: J. B. Perry, 1845.

Brooke, Hugh. *Man Made Angry.* New York: Longmans, 1932.

Brooke, John. *King George III.* New York: McGraw-Hill, 1972.

Brooke, T.H. *A History of the Island of St. Helena.* London: Black, Parry & Kingsbury, 1808.

Brookes, Cannon J.R. *Murder in Fact and Fiction.* London: Hurst & Blackett, 1926.

Brookes, Dame Mabel. *St. Helena Story.* London: William Heinemann, 1960.

Brooks, Benjamin S. *Appendix to the Opening Statement and Brief of B.S. Books, on the Chinese Question.* San Francisco: Women's Cooperative Printing Union, 1877.

Brooks, Eugene C. *Woodrow Wilson as President.* New York: Row, Peterson, 1916.

Brooks, Graham (ed.). *Trial of Captain Kidd.* London: William Hodge, 1930.

Brooks, Noah. *Washington in Lincoln's Time.* New York: Holt, Rinehart & Winston, 1958.

Brooks, Robert C. *Corruption in American Politics and Life.* New York: Dodd, Mead, 1910.

Brooks, Stuart M. *Our Assassinated Presidents.* New York: Bell, 1985.

_____. *Our Murdered Presidents: The Medical Story.* New York: Frederick Fell, 1966.

Brooks, Thomas R. *Toil and Trouble: A History of American Labor.* New York: Dell, 1971.

Brook-Shepherd, Gordon. *The Anschluss.* Philadelphia: J. B. Lippincott, 1963.

_____. *Prelude to Infamy.* New York: Ivan Obolensky, 1961.

Brophy, John. *The Meaning of Murder.* London: Ronald Whiting & Wheaton, 1966.

Brosnan, Cornelius James. *History of the State of Idaho.* New York: Scribner's, 1918.

Bross, William. *History of Chicago.* Chicago: Jansen, McClurg, 1880.

Brosse, Jacques. *Great Voyages of Discovery: Circumnavigators and Scientists, 1764-1843.* trans. Stanley Hochman. New York: Facts on File, 1983.

Brougher, William E. *The Long Dark Road.* Privately Published, 1946.

_____. *South to Bataan, North to Mukden.* Athens, Ga.: University of Georgia Press, 1971.

Broughton, Lord. *Recollections of a Long Life.* London: John Murray, 1911.

Broun, Heywood, and Leech, Margaret. *Anthony Comstock: Roundsman of the Lord.* New York: Boni, 1927.

_____. *The Boy Grew Older.* New York: Putnam, 1922.

_____. *Collected Edition of Heywood Broun.* New York: Harcourt, Brace, 1941.

_____. *It Seems to Me.* New York: Harcourt, Brace, 1935.

Browder, Robert P., and Kerensky, Alexander F. (eds.). *The Russian Provisional Government Documents.* 3 vols. Stanford. Calif.: Stanford University Press, 1961.

Brown, A. Theodore. *The Politics of Reform: Kansas City's Municipal Government, 1925-1950.* Kansas City: Community Studies, 1958.

Brown, Delmer M. *Nationalism in Japan.* New York: Russell Brown & Russell, 1955.

Brown, F. Yeats (ed.). *Escape.* New York: Macmillan, 1933.

Brown, Fredric. *The Screaming Mimi.* New York: E. P. Dutton, 1949.

_____ (ed.). *Valentine's Manual of Old New York.* New York: Valentine's Manual, 1919.

Brown, Ivor. *Dickens in His Time.* New York: Thomas Nelson, 1963.

Brown, John Henry. *Reminiscences and Incidents of the Early Life of San Francisco.* San Francisco: Mission Journal, 1929.

Brown, Michael. *Marked to Die.* New York: Simon & Schuster, 1984.

Brown, Michael K. *Working the Street.* New York: Russell Sage Foundation, 1981.

Brown, Richard M. *The South Carolina Regulators.* Cambridge, Mass.: Belknap Press of Harvard University Press, 1963.

Brown, Richard Maxwell. *Strain of Violence.* New York: Oxford, 1977.

Brown, Robert. *Demonology and Witchcraft.* London: J. F. Shaw, 1889.

Brown, Wenzell. *Introduction to Murder: The Unpublished Facts behind the Lonelyhearts Killers, Martha Beck and Raymond Fernandez.* New York: Greenberg, 1952.

Brown, Will C. *Sam Bass and Company.* New York: New American Library, 1960.

Browne, Douglas G., and Tullett, E. V. *Bernard Spilsbury: His Life and Cases.* London: Harrap, 1951.

_____, and Brock, Alan. *Fingerprints, Fifty Years of Scientific Crime Detection.* New York: E. P. Dutton, 1954.

_____. *The Rise of Scotland Yard.* New York: Putnam, 1956.

_____. *The Scalpel of Scotland Yard.* New York: E. P. Dutton, 1952.

_____. *Sir Travers Humphreys.* London: Harrap, 1960.

Browne, G. Lathom, and Stewart, C. G. *Trials for Murder by Poisoning.* London: Stevens & Sons, 1883.

Browne, Junius Henri. *The Great Metropolis: A Mirror of New York.* Hartford, Conn.: American Publishing, 1869.

Browne, Waldo Ralph. *Altgeld of Illinois: A Record of His Life and Work.* New York: B. W. Huebsch, 1924.

Brownell, Blaine A, and Stickle, Warren E. *Bosses and Reformers: Urban Politics in America 1880-1920.* Boston: Houghton Mifflin, 1973.

Browning, B.L. *Chemistry of Wood.* New York: John Wiley & Sons, 1963.

Browning, Frank, and Gerassi, John. *The American Way of Crime.* New York: Putnam, 1980.

Brownlow, Kevin. *The Parade's Gone By.* New York: Alfred A. Knopf, 1968.

Brownlow, W. G. *Sketches of the Rise, Progress, and Decline of Secession.* Philadelphia: George W. Childs, 1862.

Brownmiller, Susan. *Against Our Will: Men, Women, and Rape.* New York: Simon & Schuster, 1975.

Browse, Lillian. *Sickert.* London: Hart-Davis, 1960.

Bruce, George. *The Stranglers: The Cult of Thugee and Its Overthrow in British India.* London: Longmans, Green, 1968.

Bruce, J. Campbell. *Escape from Alcatraz.* New York: McGraw-Hill, 1963.

Bruce, John. *Gaudy Century.* New York: Random House, 1948.

Bruce, Robert V. *1877: Year of Violence.* Indianapolis, Ind.: Bobbs-Merrill, 1959.

Brunswig, H., Montroe, Charles E., and Kibler, Alton L. *Explosives.* New York: John Wiley & Sons, 1922.

Brussel, James A. *Casebook of a Crime Psychiatrist.* New York: Bernard Geis Associates, 1968.

Bruun, Kettil, et al. *The Gentlemen's Club: International Control of Drugs and Alcohol.* Chicago: University of Chicago Press, 1976.

Bryan, George S. *The Great American Myth.* New York: Carrick & Evans, 1940.

Bryan, Helen. *Inside.* New York: Houghton Mifflin, 1953.

Bryant, Louise. *Mirrors of Moscow.* New York: Thomas Seltzer, 1923.

Bryant, Samuel. *The Sea and the States: A Maritime History of the American People.* New York: Thomas Y. Crowell, 1947.

Bryant, Will. *Great American Guns and Frontier Fighters.* New York: Grosset & Dunlap, 1961.

Bryce, John. *The Gaudy Century: The Story of San Francisco's Hundred Years of Robust Journalism.* New York: Random House, 1948.

Bryson, John. *Evil Angels.* New York: Summit Books, 1985.

Brzezinski, Zbigniew K. *Permanent Purge, Politics in Soviet Totalitarianism.* Cambridge, Mass.: Harvard University Press, 1966.

Buchanan, Meriel. *The Dissolution of an Empire.* London: John Murray, 1932.

_____. *Queen Victoria's Relations.* London: Cassell, 1954.

Buchanan, Thomas. *Who Killed Kennedy?* New York: Putnam Sons, 1964.

Buchholz, E., et al. *Socialist Criminology.* Lexington, Mass.: D. C. Heath, 1974.

Buck, Pearl. *The Honeymoon Killers.* London: Sphere Books, 1970.

Buckingham, J.E. *Reminiscences and Souvenirs of the Assassination of Abraham Lincoln.* Washington, D. C.: Darby, 1894.

Buckle, George Earle (ed.). *The Letters of Queen Victoria: Third Series.* London: John Murray, 1930.

Buckley, Margaret. *The Jangle of Keys.* Dublin, Ire.: James Duffy, 1938.

Buckley, Marie. *Breaking Into Prison.* Boston: Beacon Press, 1974.

Buckley, William F., et al. *The Committee and Its Critics: A Calm Review of the House Committee on Un-American Activities.* New York: Putnam, 1962.

_____, and Bozell, L. Brent. *McCarthy and His Enemies.* Chicago: Henry Regnery, 1954.

Bucknill, Sir Alfred. *The Nature of Evidence.* London: Skeffington, 1953.

Buehlman, William. *Saint with a Gun.* New York: New York University Press, 1974.

Buel, James William. *The Border Bandits.* Chicago: Donohue, Henneberry, 1893.

_____. *The Border Outlaws.* St. Louis: Historical, 1881.

_____. *Heroes of the Plains.* St. Louis: Historical, 1881.

_____. *The James Boys.* Chicago: M. A. Donohue, n.d.

_____. *Jesse and Frank James and Their Comrades in Crime, the Younger Brothers, the Notorious Border Outlaws.* Baltimore: I. & M. Ottenheimer, 1902.

_____. *Life and Marvelous Adventures of Wild Bill, the Scout.* Chicago: Belford, Clarke, 1880.

_____. *The True Story of Wild Bill Hickok.* New York: Atomic Books, 1946.

Buffum, Peter C. *Homosexuality in Prison.* Washington, D. C.: U. S. Government Printing Office, 1971.

Bugge, Brian K. *The Mystique of Conspiracy.* New York: Published by Author, 1978.

Bugliosi, Vincent. *Helter Skelter.* New York: W. W. Norton, 1974.

_____. *Till Death Us Do Part.* New York: Norton, 1978.

Beq uhler, G. (ed.). *Sacred Books of the East.* Delhi, India: Motilala Banarasidass, 1964.

Buitrago, Ann Mari, and Immerman, Leon Andrew. *Are You Now or Have You Ever Been in the F.B.I. Files.* New York: Grove Press, 1980.

Bullard, Sir Reader. *Britain and the Middle East.* London: Hutchinson, 1951.

Bullard, Scott R., and Collins, Michael Leo. *Who's Who in Sherlock Holmes.* New York: Taplinger, 1980.

Bullock, Alan. *Hitler: A Study in Tyranny.* New York: Harper & Row, 1962.

Bullough, Vern L. and Bonnie. *The History of Prohibition.* New Hyde Park, N. Y.: University Books, 1965.

_____. *The History of Prostitution.* New Hyde Park, N. Y.: University Books, 1964.

_____, and Bonnie. *An Illustrated Social History of Prostitution.* New York: Crown, 1978.

_____. *Sexual Variance in Society and Culture.* New York: Wiley Interscience, 1976.

_____. *Sin, Sickness and Sanity.* New York: New American Library, 1977.

_____. *The Subordinate Sex.* Urbana: University of Illinois Press, 1973.

Bulygin, Paul, and Kerensky, Alexander. *The Murder of the Romanovs.* London: Hutchinson, 1935.

Buncher, Judith F. (ed.). *Crime and Punishment in America.* New York: Facts on File, 1978.

Bundy, Mary Lee, and Harmon, Kenneth R. (eds.). *The National Prison Directory.* College Park, Md.: Urban Information Interpreters, 1975.

Bunyan, James, and Fisher, H.H. *The Bolshevik Revolution, 1917-1921.* 2 vols. Stanford, Calif.: Stanford University Press, 1934.

Burchard, Johann. *At the Court of the Borgia.* trans. and ed. Geoffrey Parker. London: Folio Society, 1963.

_____. *Pope Alexander and His Court.* New York: N. L. Brown, 1921.

Burchell, Robert A. *The San Francisco Irish, 1848-1880.* Berkeley: University of California Press, 1980.

Burckhardt, Carl J. *Richelieu and His Age.* trans. Bernard Hoy, 4 vols. London: George Allen & Unwin, 1967.

Burckhardt, Jacob. *The Age of Constantine.* Garden City, N. Y.: Doubleday, 1956.

_____. *The Civilization of the Renaissance in Italy.* trans. S. G. C. Middlemore. New York: Oxford University Press, 1944.

Burckhardt, Titus. *Alchemy.* Baltimore: Penguin, 1971.

Bureau of the Census. *Characteristics of American Children and Youth: 1976.* Washington, D.C.: U. S. Government Printing Office, 1978.

_____. *Historical Statistics of the United States.* Washington, D. C.: U. S. Government Printing Office, 1975.

_____. *Statistical Abstract of the United States.* Washington, D. C.: U. S. Government Printing Office, 1984.

Bureau of Justice Statistics. *Computer Crime: Criminal Justice Resource Manual.* Washington, D. C.: U. S. Department of Justice, 1979.

_____. *Criminal Victimization, 1983.* Washington, D. C.: Government Printing Office, 1984.

_____. *Family Violence-Special Report.* Washington, D. C.: Government Printing Office, 1984.

_____. *Report to the Nation on Crime and Justice.* Washington, D. C.: Government Printing Office, 1983.

Burges, S.H. (ed.). *The New Police Surgeon.* London: Hutchinson, 1978.

Burgess, Anne Wolbert, and Holmstrom, Lynda Lytle. *Rape: Victims of Crisis.* Bowie, Md.: Robert J. Brady, 1974.

_____, et al. *Sexual Assault of Children and Adolescents.* Lexington, Mass.: Lexington Books, 1975.

Burke, Merle. *United States History.* Chicago: American Technical Society, 1970.

Burke, T. *Limehouse Nights.* New York: Robert M. McBride, 1926.

Burkitt, Miles C. *Our Early Ancestors.* Cambridge, Eng.: University Press, 1924.

Burks, A.L. *The Mayberry Murder Mystery of Bonita City.* Alamogordo, N.M.: Alamogordo News, n.d.

Burks, Richard V. *The Dynamics of Communism in Eastern Europe.* Princeton, N. J.: Princeton University Press, 1961.

Burland, C. A. *The Arts of the Alchemist.* New York: Macmillan, 1968.

Burn, Gordon. *Somebody's Husband, Somebody's Son.* New York: Viking, 1984.

Burnaby, Evelyn. *Memories of Famous Trials.* London: Sisley's, 1907.

Burnett, H. L. *The Controversy between President Johnson and Judge Holt.* New York: D. Appleton, 1891.

_____. *Some Incidents in the Trial of President Lincoln's Assassins.* New York: D. Appleton, 1891.

Burney, James. *The History of the Buccaneers of America.* New York: W. W. Norton, 1950.

Burnham, David. *The Role of the Media in Controlling Corruption.* New York: John Jay Press, 1976.

_____. *Taking Chances.* Los Angeles: Haynes, 1944.

Burnham, George Pickering. *American Counterfeits.* Boston: A. W. Lowering, 1879.

Burnham, James. *Congress and the American Tradition.* Chicago: Regnery, 1959.

_____. *The Web of Subversion: Underground Networks in the U.S. Government.* New York: John Day, 1954.

Burnley, James. *Millionaires and Kings of Enterprise.* Philadelphia: J.B. Lippincott, 1901.

Burnes, John. *MI5.* New York: Pocket, 2003.

Burns, Alan. *The Angry Brigade.* London: Quartet, 1973.

Burns, E.L. *Between Arab and Israeli.* London: Harrap, 1962.

Burns, Emile. *Abyssinia and Italy.* London: Victor Gollancz, 1935.

Burns, Henry, Jr. *Corrections: Organization and Administration.* St. Paul, Minn.: West, 1975.

Burns, Robert E. *I Am A Fugitive From A Georgia Chain Gang.* New York: Vanguard Press, 1932.

Burns, Walter Noble. *The One-Way Ride: The Red Trail of Chicago Gangland from Prohibition to Jake Lingle.* Garden City, N. Y.: Doubleday, Doran, 1931.

_____. *The Robin Hood of El Dorado.* New York: Coward-McCann, 1932.

_____. *Tombstone, An Iliad of the Southwest.* Garden City, N. Y.: Doubleday, Page, 1927.

Burns, William J. *The Masked War: The Story of a Peril That Threatened the U.S., by the Man Who Uncovered the Dynamite Conspirators and Sent Them to Jail.* New York: George H. Doran, 1913.

Burr, George Lincoln (ed.). *Narratives of Witchcraft Cases, 1648-1706.* New York: Barnes & Noble, 1959.

Burroughs, John Rolfe. *Where the Old West Stayed Young.* New York: William Morrow, 1962.

Burrows, Millar. *Palestine Is Our Business.* Philadelphia: Westminster Press, 1949.

Burrows, William E. *Vigilante!* New York: Harcourt, Brace, Jovanovich, 1976.

Burt, Cyril. *The Young Delinquent.* London: University of London Press, 1944.

Burt, Commander Leonard. *Commander Burt of Scotland Yard.* London: William Heinemann, 1959.

Burt, Olive Woolley. *American Murder Ballads.* New York: Oxford University Press, 1958.

Burton, Anthony M. *Urban Terrorism.* London: Leo Cooper, 1975.

Burton, Jeff. *Black Jack Christian, Outlaw.* Santa Fe, N. M.: Press of the Territorian, 1967.

_____. *Dynamite and Six-Shooter.* Santa Fe, N. M.: Palomino Press, 1970.

Burtt, M. *Legal Psychology.* Englewood Cliffs, N. Y.: Prentice-Hall, 1931.

Buruma, Ian. *Behind the Mask.* New York: Pantheon Books, 1984.

Bury, J.B. *A History of the Freedom of Thought.* London: Oxford University Press, 1913-52.

Bury, J.C. *The Cambridge Ancient History.* Cambridge, Mass.: Cambridge University Press, 1927.

_____. *The History of the Eastern Roman Empire.* London: Macmillan, 1912.

_____. *The History of the Later Roman Emprie.* London: Macmillan, 1889.

_____. *The History of the Roman Empire.* New York: Harper & Brothers, 1893.

Busch, Alva. *Roadside Prey.* New York: Pinnacle, 1996.

Busch, Francis X. *Casebook of the Curious and True.* Indianapolis, Ind.: Bobbs-Merrill, 1957.

_____. *Enemies of the State.* Indianapolis, Ind.: Bobbs-Merrill, 1954.

_____. *Guilty or Not Guilty.* Indianapolis, Ind.: Bobbs-Merrill, 1952.

_____. *In and Out of Court.* Chicago: De Paul University Press, 1942.

_____. *Prisoners at the Bar.* Indianapolis, Ind.: Bobbs-Merrill, 1952.

_____. *They Escaped the Hangman.* London: Arco, 1957.

_____. *The Emperor's Sword.* New York: Funk & Wagnalls, 1969.

Buse, Renee. *The Deadly Silence.* Garden City, N. Y.: Doubleday, 1965.

Businelli, Alberto. *Octtobre 1922.* Rome: Novissima, 1932.

Bussy, Frederick Moir. *Irish Conspiracies.* London: Everett, 1910.

Bustamante, Luis F. *Bajo el terror Huertista.* San Luis Potosi, Mexico: Published by Author, 1916.

Butler, Charles Henry. *A Century at the Bar of the Supreme Court of the United States.* New York: Putnam, 1942.

Butler, Eliza Marian. *Ritual Magic.* Cambridge, Eng.: University Press, 1949.

Butler, Ivan. *Murderers' England.* London: Robert Hale, 1973.

Butler, Pierce. *The Unhurried Years.* Baton Rouge: Louisiana State University Press, 1948.

Butler, P. T. T., and Lord Dunboyne (eds.). *The Trial of John George Haigh.* London: Hodge, 1953.

Butler, Richard J., and Driscoll, Joseph. *Dock Walloper.* New York: Putnam, 1933.

Butler, Rohan. *The Roots of National Socialism.* New York: E. P. Dutton, 1942.

Butler, W. E. *The Magician.* London: Aquarian, 1963.

Butow, Robert J. C. *Japan's Decision to Surrender.* Stanford, Calif.: Stanford University Press, 1954.

_____. *Tojo and the Coming of the War.* Princeton, N. J.: Princeton University Press, 1961.

Butt, Ernest. *Chicago Then and Now.* Chicago: Aurora, Finch & McCullouch, 1933.

Butterfield, Herbert. *The Origins of History.* New York: Basic Books, 1981.

Butterfield, Roger. *The American Past.* New York: Simon & Schuster, 1947.

Buxton, Thomas Fowell. *An Inquiry Whether Crime and Misery are Produced or Prevented by Our Present State of Prison Discipline.* London: J. M'Creery, 1818.

Bwengye, Francis Aloysius Wazarw. *The Agony of Uganda, from Idi Amin to Obote: Repression, Rule and Bloodshed: Cause, Effects, and the Cure.* New York: Regency Press, 1985.

Byas, Hugh. *Government By Assassination.* New York: Alfred A. Knopf, 1942.

Byck, Robert (ed.). *Cocaine Papers: Sigmund Freud.* New York: Stonehill, 1974.

Bye, Raymond T. *Capital Punishment in the United States.* Philadelphia: Committee on Philanthropic Labor of Philadelphia Yearly Meeting of Friends, 1919.

Byers, Ann. *Lebanon's Hezbollah.* New York: Rosen Publishing Co., 2003.

Byington, Lewis F., and Lewis, Oscar (eds.). *The History of San Francisco.* San Francisco: S. J. Clarke, 1931.

Bykov, P.M. *The Last Days of Tsar Nicholas.* New York: International, 1934.

Byrne, Gerald. *Borstal Boy.* London: J. Hill, 1954.

_____. *John George Haigh, Acid Killer.* London: J. Hill, 1954.

Byrnes, Thomas. *Professional Criminals of America.* New York: G. W. Dillingham, 1895.

Byrum, E. E. *Behind Prison Bars.* Moundsville, W.Va.: Gospel Trumpet, 1901.

Cabal, Juan. *Piracy and Pirates.* London: Jarrolds, 1957.

Cadiou, Yves, and Richard, Alphonse. *Modern Firearms.* New York: William Morrow, 1977.

Cadogan, Edward. *The Roots of Evil.* London: John Murray, 1937.

Cady, John Henry. *Arizona's Yesterday.* Los Angeles: Privately Published, 1916.

Caesar, Gene. *Incredible Detective: The Biography of William J. Burns.* Englewood Cliffs, N. J.: Prentice-Hall, 1968.

Cagan, Philip. *Determinants and Effects of Changes in the Stock of Money, 1875-1960.* New York: Columbia University Press, 1965.

Cahalane, Cornelius F. *The Policeman.* New York: E. P. Dutton, 1923.

Cahill, Bette. *Butterbox Babies.* Toronto: McClelland-Bantam, 1992.

Cahill, Tim. *Buried Dreams.* New York: Bantam, 1985.

Cahn, Edmond. *The Crest Rights.* New York: Macmillan, 1963.

_____ (ed.). *Supreme Court and Supreme Law.* Bloomington: Indiana University Press, 1954.

Calahan, E. W. (ed.). *List of Officers of the Navy of the United States, 1775-1900.* New York: L. R. Hamersly, 1900.

Caldwell, Robert Graham. *Criminology.* New York: Ronald Press, 1965.

_____. *Red Hannah, Delaware's Whipping Post.* London: Oxford University Press, 1947.

Calef, Robert. *More Wonders of the Invisible World.* London: N. Hillar & J. Collyer, 1700.

Calic, Edouard (ed.). *Secret Conversations with Hitler.* New York: John Day, 1971.

Calincourt, Gen. *Memoires.* Paris: Plon, 1933.

Callaghan, Morley. *That Summer in Paris.* New York: Coward-McCann, 1963.

Callahan, James Morton. *American Foreign Policy in Mexican Relations.* New York: Macmillan, 1932.

Callan, Luke B. *Ireland After Forty Years.* Boston: Angel Guardian, 1933.

Callaway, Lewis L. *Montana's Righteous Hangmen.* Norman: University of Oklahoma Press, 1982.

Callon, Milton W. *Las Vegas, New Mexico, the Town That Wouldn't Gamble.* Las Vegas, N. M.: Las Vegas *Daily Optic*, 1962.

Callow, Alexander (ed.). *The City Boss in America: An Interpretive Reader.* New York: Oxford University Press, 1976.

_____. *The Tweed Ring.* New York: Oxford University Press, 1965.

Calvert, Roy. *Capital Punishment in the Twentieth Century.* New York: Putnam, 1936.

_____. *The Death Penalty Inquiry.* London: Victor Gollancz, 1931.

_____. *Executions.* London: National Council for the Abolition of the Death Penalty, 1926.

Cambridge Department of Criminal Science. *Sexual Offenses.* New York: St. Martin's Press, 1957.

Cambridge Ancient History. London: Cambridge University Press, 1970.

Camerero, Julio. *Chessman.* Madrid: Pueblo, 1960.

Cameron, Charlotte. *Mexico in Revolution.* New York: Seeley, 1925.

Cameron, Mary Owen. *The Booster and the Snitch: Department Store Shoplifting.* New York: Free Press, 1964.

Cameron, William E. (ed.). *History of the World's Columbian Exposition.* Chicago: Columbian History, 1893.

Caminda, Jerome. *Twenty-Five Years of Detective Life.* London: John Heywood, 1895.

Cammaerts, Emile. *Albert of Belgium.* New York: Macmillan, 1935.

Cammell, Charles R. *Aleister Crowley: The Man, The Magic, The Poet.* New Hyde Park, N.Y.: University Books, 1962.

Campanelli, Paolo. *Mussolini.* London: Pallas, 1939.

Campbell, Anne. *The Girls in the Gang: A Report From New York City.* New York: Basil Blackwell, 1984,

Campbell, Edna Fay, Smith, Fanny R., and Jones, Clarence F. *Our City%%Chicago.* New York: Scribner's, 1930.

Campbell, Helen, Knox, Thomas W., and Byrnes, Thomas. *Darkness and Daylight.* Hartford, Conn.: A. D. Worthington, 1897.

_____. *Prisoners of Poverty.* Boston: Roberts Brothers, 1887.

Campbell, Helen Jones. *The Case for Mrs. Surratt.* New York: Putnam, 1943.

Campbell, John Gregorson. *Superstitions of the Highlands.* Glasgow, Scot.: J. MacLehose & Sons, 1900.

_____. *Witchcraft and Second Sight in the Highlands and Islands of Scotland.* Glasgow, Scot.: J. MacLehose & Sons, 1902.

Campbell, Marjorie Freeman. *A Century of Crime.* Toronto, Can.: McLelland & Stewart, 1970.

Campbell, N. Reason. *Dead Man Walking.* New York: Marek, 1978.

Campbell, Rodney. *The Luciano Project.* New York: McGraw-Hill, 1977.

Campbell, W. P. *Oklahoma, the Mecca for the Man of Mystery. John Wilkes Booth, Escape and Wanderings Until Final Ending of the Trial by Suicide in Enid, Oklahoma, January 12, 1903.* Oklahoma City: Published by Author, 1922.

Campbell, Will D., and Holloway, James Y. (eds.). *"... And the criminals with him ...," Luke 23:33.* New York: Paulist Press, 1973.

Camps, Professor Francis E. *Camps on Crime.* Newton Abbot, Eng.: David & Charles, 1973.

_____, and Barber, Richard. *The Investigation of Murder.* London: Michael Joseph, 1966.

_____. *Medical and Scientific Investigations in the Christie Case.* London: Medical Publications, 1953.

Canby, Henry Seidel. *American Memoir.* Cambridge, Mass.: Houghton Mifflin, 1947.

Canfield, Alyce. *God in Hollywood.* New York: Wisdom House, 1961.

Canfield, Michael, and Weberman, Alan J. *Coup d'Etat in America; The C.I.A. and the Assassination of John F. Kennedy.* New York: Third Press, 1975.

Canler, Louis. *Memoires de Canler, ancien chef du service duset.* Paris: J. Herzel, 1862.

Cannell, J.C. *When Fleet Street Calls.* London: Jarrolds, 1932.

Canning, John. *50 True Tales of Terror.* New York: Bell, 1972.

Cannon, Miles. *Toward the Setting Sun.* Portland, Ore.: Columbian Press, 1953.

Canton, Frank M. *The Autobiography of Frank M. Canton.* Norman: University of Oklahoma Press, 1954.

_____. *Frontier Trails.* Boston: Houghton Mifflin, 1930.

Cantonwine, Alexander. *Star Forty-Six, Oklahoma.* Oklahoma City: Pythian Times, 1911.

Cantor, Norman. *The Age of Protest.* London: George Allen & Unwin, 1970.

Caplan, Lincoln. *The Insanity Defense and the Trial of John W. Hinckley, Jr.* Boston: David R. Godine, 1984.

Capon, Paul. *The Seventh Passenger.* London: Ward Lock, 1953.

Capote, Truman. *In Cold Blood.* New York: Random House, 1965.

Capozzi, Gennaro. *Venti giorni di terrore.* Naples, Italy: 'La Floridiana', 1943.

Caprio, Frank S., and Brenner, Donald R. *Sexual Behavior: Psychological Aspects.* New York: Citadel, 1961.

Capstick, J. *Given in Evidence.* London: John Long, 1960.

Caputo, David A. *Organized Crime and American Politics.* Morristown, N. J.: General Learning Press, 1974.

Carcopino, Jrome. *Daily Life in Ancient Rome.* New Haven, Conn.: Yale University Press, 1940.

Cardozo, Benjamin N. *The Nature of the Judicial Process.* New Haven, Conn.: Yale University Press, 1921.

Careless, J.M.J., and Brown, R. Craig (eds.). *The Canadians, 1867-1967.* Toronto, Ontario, Can.: Macmillan, 1967.

Carena, Caesar. *Tractatus de Officio Sanctissimae Inquisitionis et Modo Procendo in Causis Fidei.* Cremona, Italy: M.A. Balpierum, 1631.

Carerio, Luigi. *Practica Causarum Criminalium...Tractatus de Haereticis.* Lyons, Fr.: Gulielmum Rouillium, 1550.

Carey, Arthur A. *Memoirs of a Murder Man.* Garden City, N. Y.: Doubleday, Doran, 1930.

Carey, Henry L. (ed.). *The Thrilling Story of Famous Boot Hill and Modern Dodge City.* Dodge City, Kan.: Herbert Etrick, 1937.

Carey, James T. *The College Drug Scene.* Englewood Cliffs, N. J.: Prentice-Hall, 1968.

_____. *Introduction to Criminology.* Englewood Cliffs, N. J.: Prentice-Hall, 1978.

Carey-Jones, N. S. *The Anatomy of Uhuru: An Essay on Kenya's Independence.* Manchester, Eng.: Manchester University Press, 1966.

Cargill, David, and Holland, Julian. *Scenes of Murder: A London Guide.* London: Heinemann, 1964.

Carlen, Pat. (ed.). *Criminal Women.* Oxford, Eng.: Polity Press, 1985.

Carlisle, William L. *Bill Carlisle, Lone Bandit: An Autobiography.* Pasadena, Calif.: Trail's End, 1946.

Carlson, John Roy. *Undercover.* New York: E. P. Dutton, 1943.

Carlson, Kenneth. *American Prisons and Jails. Population Trends and Projections.* Cambridge, Mass.: Abt Associates, 1980.

Carlson, Kurt. *One American Must Die.* New York: Congdon & Weed, 1986.

Carlson, Oliver. *Brisbane, A Candid Biography.* New York: Stackpole Sons, 1937.

_____, and Bates, Ernest Sutherland. *Hearst: Lord of San Simeon.* New York: Viking Press, 1936.

Carlyle, R. W. and A. J. *A History of Medieval Political Theory in the West.* New York: Barnes & Noble, 1932.

Carlyle, Thomas. *The French Revolution: A History.* New York: American Book Exchange, 1881.

_____. *History of Frederick II of Prussia.* 6 vols. London: Chapman & Hall, 1858-1865.

Carman, H. J., and Luthin, R. H. *Lincoln and the Patronage.* New York: Columbia University Press, 1943.

Carmer, Carl. *Stars Fell on Alabama.* New York: Farrar & Rinehart, 1934.

Carney, Louis. *Introduction to Correctional Science.* New York: McGraw-Hill, 1974.

Caro, Robert A. *The Years of Lyndon Johnson: The Path to Power.* New York: Vintage Books, 1983.

Caroll, John Alexander (ed.). *Pioneering in Arizona.* Tucson: Arizona Pioneers Historical Society, 1964.

Caron, Roger. *Go Boy.* Toronto, Ontario, Can.: McGraw-Hill, 1978.

Carothers, J. C. *The Psychology of Mau Mau.* Nairobi, Kenya: Government Printer, 1955.

Carpenter, Mary. *Our Convicts.* London: W. & F. G. Cash, 1864.

Carpenter, Rhys. *Beyond the Pillars of Hercules.* New York: Delacorte Press, 1966.

Carpozi, George Jr. *Bugsy.* New York: Pinacle, 1973.

_____. *Gangland Killers.* New York: Manor Books, 1979.

_____. *Ordeal By Trial: The Alice Crimmins Case.* New York: Walker, 1972.

_____. *Red Spies In The U.S.* New York: Arlington House, 1973.

_____. *Son of Sam.* New York: Manor Books, 1977.

Carr, Edward Hallett. *A History of Russia: The Bolshevik Revolution, 1917-1923.* 3 vols. New York: Macmillan, 1951.

_____. *Studies in Revolution.* London: Macmillan, 1950.

Carr, Gordon. *The Angry Brigade.* London: Victor Gollancz, 1975.

Carr, Harry. *Los Angeles, City of Dreams.* New York: D. Appleton-Century, 1935.

_____. *Riding the Tiger: An American Newspaperman in the Orient.* Boston: Houghton Mifflin, 1934.

_____. *The West Is Still Wild.* Boston: Houghton Mifflin, 1932.

Carr, John Dickson. *The Life of Sir Arthur Conan Doyle.* New York: Harper, 1949.

Carr, Robert K. *Federal Protection of Civil Rights.* Ithaca, N.Y.: Cornell University Press, 1947.

_____, *The House Committee on Un-American Activities, 1945-1950.* Ithaca, N.Y.: Cornell University Press, 1952.

_____. *The Supreme Court and Judicial Review.* New York: Holt, Rinehart & Winston, 1942.

Carr, William H.A. *Hollywood Tragedy.* New York: Fawcett-Crest, 1962.

_____. *JFK: A Complete Biography 1917-1963.* New York: Lancer Books, 1968.

Carrigan, E. C. *John P. Phair, A Complete History of Vermont's Celebrated Murder Case.* Boston: Carrigan, 1879.

Carrington, Frank G. *Crime and Justice: A Conservative Strategy.* Washington, D. C.: Heritage Foundation, 1983.

_____. *Neither Cruel nor Unusual.* New Rochelle, N. Y.: Arlington House, 1978.
_____. *The Victims.* New Rochelle, N. Y.: Arlington House, 1977.
Carrington, Hereward. *Gambler's Crooked Tricks: A Complete Exposure of Their Methods.* Girard, Kan.: Haldeman-Julius, 1928.
Carroll, Joseph C. *Slave Insurrections in the United States, 1800-1865.* Boston: Chapman & Grimes, 1938.
Carroll, Leo. *Hacks, Blacks, and Cons: Race Relations in a Maximum Security Prison.* Lexington, Mass.: Lexington Books, 1974.
Carruthers, Douglas. *Beyond the Caspian.* London: Edinburgh, Oliver & Boyd, 1949.
Carse, Robert. *Rum Row.* New York: Holt, Rinehart & Winston, 1959.
Carsten, F. L. *The Origins of Prussia.* London: Oxford University Press, 1954.
Carswell, John. *The South Sea Bubble.* Stanford, Calif.: Stanford University Press, 1960.
Carte, Gene E. and Elaine H. *Police Reform in the United States: the Era of August Vollmer.* Berkeley: University of California Press, 1975.
Cartel, Michael. *Serial Mass Murder.* Toluca Lake, Cal.: Pepperbox Books, 1985.
Carter, Boake, and Healy, Thomas. *Why Meddle in the Orient?* New York: Dodge, 1938.
Carter, Dagny. *The Symbol of the Beast.* New York: Ronald Press, 1957.
Carter, Dan T. *Scottsboro: A Tragedy of the American South.* New York: Oxford University Press, 1969.
Carter, Dyson. *Sin and Society.* New York: Heck Cattell, 1946.
Carter, E. C. *Notes on Whitechapel.* London: Cassell, n. d.
Carter, Hodding. *The Angry Scar.* New York: Doubleday, 1959.
_____. *Lower Mississippi.* New York: Farrar & Rinehart, 1942.
_____ (ed.). *The Past as Prelude, New Orleans, 1718-1968.* New Orleans, La.: Tulane University Press, 1968.
Carter, Robert, et al. (eds.). *Correctional Institutions.* Philadelphia: J. B. Lippincott, 1972.
Carter, Robert M., and Klein, Malcolm W. *Back on the Streets.* Englewood Cliffs, N. J.: Prentice-Hall, 1976.
Carter, Robert M., and Wilkins, Leslie T. (eds.). *Probation and Parole: Selected Readings.* New York: John Wiley & Sons, 1970.
Carter, Ronald L. *The Criminal's Image of the City.* New York: Pergamon, 1980.
Carter, Samuel, III. *The Riddle of Dr. Mudd.* New York: Putnam, 1974.
Carter, W.N. *Harry Tracy, The Desperate Outlaw.* Chicago: Laird & Lee, 1902.
Cartland, Barbara. *The Scandalous Life of King Carol.* London: Frederick Muller, 1957.
Cartwright, Gary. *Blood Will Tell.* New York: Harcourt, Brace, 1979.
Cartwright, Joe, and Patterson, Jerry. *Been Taken Lately?* New York: Grove Press, 1974.
Cartwright, Otho G. *The Middle West Side: A Historical Sketch.* New York: Survey Associates, 1914.
Carty, James. *Ireland.* Dublin, Ire.: C. J. Fallon, 1957.
Carus, Paul. *The History of the Devil and the Idea of Evil.* New York: Bell, 1969.
Carver, Leonard D. *Capital Punishment.* Augusta, Ga.: n. p., 1899.
Casamayor, Serge Fuster. *Le bras sculier-justice et police.* Paris: Editions de Sueil, 1960.
Casey, Lee (ed.). *Denver Murders.* New York: Duell, Sloan & Pearce, 1947.
Casey, Robert J. *The Black Hills and Their Incredible Characters.* Indianapolis, Ind.: Bobbs-Merrill, 1949.
_____. *Chicago, Medium Rare.* Indianapolis, Ind.: Bobbs-Merrill, 1949.
_____, and Douglas, W.A.S. *The Texas Border and Some Borderliners.* New York: Bobbs-Merrill, 1950.
Cash, W.J. *The Mind of the South.* London: Thames & Hudson, 1971.
Cashman, John. *The Gentleman from Chicago: Being an Account of the Doings of Thomas Neill Cream.* London: Hamish Hamilton, 1974.
_____. *The LSD Story.* Greenwich, Conn.: Fawcett, 1966.
Cashman, Sean D. *Prohibition.* New York: Free Press, 1981.
Caso, Alfonso. *The Aztecs: People of the Sun.* trans. Lowell Dunham. Norman: University of Oklahoma Press, 1958.
Casper, Jonathan D. *American Criminal Justice: The Defendant's Perspective.* Englewood Cliffs, N. J.: Prentice-Hall, 1972.
Cassels, Lavender. *The Struggle for the Ottoman Empire 1717-1740.* New York: Thomas Y. Crowell, 1966.
Casserly, John J. *The Ford White House, Diary of a Speechwriter.* Boulder: Colorado Associated University Press, 1977.
Cassin, Herbert N. *Cyrus Hall McCormick.* Chicago: McClurg, 1909.
Cassity, John Holland. *The Quality of Murder.* New York: Julian Press, 1958.
Casswell, J. D. *Lance for Liberty.* London: Harrap, 1961.
Castel, Albert. *A Frontier State at War: Kansas, 1861-1865.* Ithaca, N. Y.: Cornell University Press, 1958.
_____. *William Clarke Quantrill: His Life and Times.* New York: Frederick Fell, 1962.
Castellani, Aldo. *Microbes, Men and Monarchs.* London: Victor Gollancz, 1960.
Castellanos, I. *Identification Problems, Criminal and Civil.* New York: R. V. Basuino, 1939.
Castellucci, John. *The Big Dance.* New York: Dodd, Mead, 1986.
Castle, H. G. *Case for the Prosecution.* London: Naldrett Press, 1956.
Castleman, Harvey N. *The Bald Knobbers.* Girard, Kan.: Haldeman-Julius, 1944.
_____. *Sam Bass, The Train Robber.* Girard, Kan.: Haldeman-Julius, 1944.
_____. *The Texas Rangers.* Girard, Kan.: Haldeman-Julius, 1944.
Castleman, Michael. *Crime Free.* New York: Simon & Schuster, 1984.
Catalano, Michele. *Lucrezia Borgia, duchessa di Ferrara.* Ferrara, Italy: A. Taddie, 1920.
Cater, D. *The Fourth Branch of Government.* Boston: Houghton Mifflin, 1959.
_____. *TV Violence and the Child: The Evolution and Fate of the Surgeon General's Report.* New York: Russell Sage Foundation, 1975.
Cathcart, Helen. *Lord Snowdon.* London: W. H. Allen, 1968.
Cather, Helen Virginia. *The History of San Francisco's Chinatown.* San Francisco: R & E Research Associates, 1974.
Catlin, George. *In the Path of Mahatma Gandhi.* London: Macdonald, 1948.
Catterall, R. D. *The Veneral Diseases.* London: Evans, 1967.
Caughey, John Walton. *California.* New York: Prentice Hall, 1953.
_____. *History of the Pacific Coast.* Los Angeles: Published by Author, 1933.
_____. *Their Majesties the Mob.* Chicago: University of Chicago Press, 1960.
Caughey & Caughey. *Los Angeles: Biography of a City.* Berkeley: University of California Press, 1976.
Caulaincourt, General de, Duke of Vicenza. *With Napoleon in Russia: Memoirs.* New York: William Morrow, 1935.
Caulfield, Max. *The Easter Rebellion.* London: Frederick Muller, 1964.
Caute, David. *The Fellow Travellers.* New York: Macmillan, 1973.
_____. *The Great Fear: The Anti-Communist Purge Under Truman and Eisenhower.* New York: Simon & Schuster, 1978.
Cavan, Ruth Shonle. *Criminology.* New York: Thomas Y. Crowell, 1955.
_____. *Suicide.* Chicago: University of Chicago Press, 1928.
Cavan, Sherri. *Liquor License: An Ethnography of Bar Behavior.* Chicago: Aldine, 1966.
Cavanaugh, Sandy. *Airborne to Suez.* London: Kimber, 1965.
Cave Brown, Anthony. *Bodyguard of Lies.* New York: Harper & Row, 1975.
Cavendish, Lady Frederick. *Diary.* ed. J. Bailey. London: John Murray, 1927.
Cavendish, Richard. *The Black Arts.* New York: Putnam, 1967.
Cawelti, John G. *Focus on Bonnie and Clyde.* Englewood Cliffs, N. J.: Prentice-Hall, 1973.
Cawley, Elizabeth Hoon. *American Diaries.* Princeton, N. J.: Princeton University Press, 1952.
Ceballos Dosamantes, Jess. *Antinomia Politica de D. Francisco I. Madero.* Mexico City: Imprenta de A. Carranza Hijos, 1911.
Cecil, Richard. *Alcatraz.* West Lafayette, Ind.: Purdue University Press, 1992.
Cederblom, J.B., and Blizek, William L. (eds.). *Justice and Punishment.* Cambridge, Mass.: Ballinger, 1977.
The Celebrated Chicago Anarchists' Case. Rochester, N. Y.: Lawyers Cooperative, 1887.
Celebrated Murders. Chicago: Belford, Clarke, 1879.
Celebrated Trials of All Countries. Philadelphia: E. L. Carey & A. Hart, 1843.
Celler, Emanuel. *You Never Leave Brooklyn.* New York: John Day, 1953.
Celsus. *De Medicina.* trans. W. G. Spencer. London: William Heinemann, 1935-1938.
Center for Research on Criminal Justice. *The Iron Fist and the Velvet Glove: An Analysis of the U.S. Police.* Berkeley, Calif.: Center for Research on Criminal Justice, 1975.
Ceram, C.W. *Gods, Graves and Scholars: The Story of Archaeology.* New York: Alfred A. Knopf, 1967.
Cervantes, Federico. *Francisco Villa y la Revolucion.* Mexico City: Ediciones Alonso, 1960.
Ceylon Commission of Inquiry on Capital Punishment. *Report.* Colombo, Sri.: Government Press, 1959.
Chabod, Federico. *A History of Italian Fascism.* trans. Muriel Grindrod. London: Weidenfeld & Nicolson, 1963.
Chadbourn, James Harmon. *Lynching and the Law.* Chapel Hill: North Carolina University Press, 1933.
Chadwick, N. K. *Celtic Britain.* London: Thames & Hudson, 1963.
_____. *The Mooney-Billings Report Suppressed by the Wickersham Commission.* New York: Gotham House, 1932.
Chafetz, Henry. *Play the Devil: A History of Gambling in the United States from 1692 to 1955.* New York: Clarkson N. Potter, 1960.
Chaffin, Lorah B. *Sons of the West: Biographical Account of Early-Day Wyoming.* Caldwell, Idaho: Caxton Printers, 1941.
Chaiken, J. M. and M. R. *Varieties of Criminal Behavior.* Santa Monica, Calif.: Rand, 1982.
Chaiken, Marcia R., and Johnson, Bruce D. *Characteristics of Different Types of Drug-Involved Offenders.* Washington, D. C.: National Institute of Justice, 1988.
Chakravarty, Amiya. *Mahatma Gandhi and the Modern World.* Calcutta, India: Book House, 1945.
Chalidze, Valery. *Criminal Russia.* New York: Random House, 1977.
_____. *To Defend These Rights: Human Rights and the Soviet Union.* New York: Random House, 1975.
Chalmers, David Mark. *Hooded Americanism.* New York: Doubleday, 1965.
_____. *The Social and Political Ideas of the Muckrakers.* New York: Citadel Press, 1964.
Chamberlain, B. P. *The Negroes and Crime in Virgina.* Charlottesville: University of Virginia, 1936.
Chamberlain, John. *Farewell to Reform.* New York: Liveright, 1932.
Chamberlin, William Henry. *Blueprint for World Conquest.* Washington, D. C.: Human Events, 1946.
_____. *Japan over Asia.* Garden City, N. Y.: Blue Ribbon, 1942.
_____. *The Russian Enigma.* New York: Scribner's, 1943.
_____. *The Russian Revolution, 1917-1921.* 2 vols. New York: Macmillan, 1952.
_____. *Russia's Iron Age.* London: Duckworth, 1935.
_____. *Soviet Russia: A Living Record and a History.* Boston: Little, Brown, 1930.
Chambers, Homer S. *The Enduring Rock.* Blackwell, Okla.: Blackwell Publications, 1954.
Chambers, Julius. *The Book of New York.* New York: Book of New York, 1912.
Chambers, Robert. *Domestic Annals of Scotland.* Edinburgh, Scot.: W. & R. Chambers, 1858.
Chambers, Walter. *Samuel Seabury.* New York: Century, 1932.
Chambers' Guide to London The Secret City. London: Ocean Books, 1974.
Chambliss, William J. *Box Man: A Professional Thief's Journey.* New York: Harper & Row, 1972.

_____. *Crime and the Legal Process.* New York: McGraw-Hill, 1969.
_____. *Functional and Conflict Theories of Crime.* New York: MSS Modular Publications, 1973.
_____, and Seidman, Robert B. *Law, Order, and Power.* Reading, Mass.: Addison-Wesley, 1971.
_____. *On the Take.* Bloomington: Indiana University Press, 1978.
Champion, Pierre. *Splendeurs et Miseres de Paris.* Paris: Calmann-Lvy, 1934.
Chandler, Billy Jaynes. *The Bandit King: Lampio of Brazil.* College Station: Texas A & M University Press, 1978.
_____. *King of the Mountain: The Life and Death of Giuliano the Bandit.* DeKalb: Northern Illinois University Press, 1988.
Chandler, David Leon. *Brothers in Blood: The Rise of the Criminal Brotherhoods.* New York: E. P. Dutton, 1975.
Chandler, Edna Walker. *Women in Prison.* Indianapolis, Ind.: Bobbs-Merrill, 1973.
Chandler, Frank W. *The Literature of Roguery.* 2 vols. Boston: Houghton Mifflin, 1907.
Chandler, Lester V. *America's Greatest Depression.* New York: Harper & Row, 1970.
Chandler, Peleg W. *American Criminal Trials.* Boston: Little, Brown, 1841-1844.
Chandler, R. *Raymond Chandler Speaking.* London: Hamish Hamilton, 1962.
Chaney, Margaret. *The Co-Ed Killer.* New York: Walker, 1976.
Chang Chung-li. *The Chinese Gentry, Studies on Their Role in Nineteenth Century Chinese Society.* Seattle: University of Washington Press, 1955.
Chapel, Charles Edward. *Fingerprinting.* New York: Coward-McCann, 1941.
Chapin, Bradley. *Provincial America.* New York: Free Press, 1966.
Chapin, Charles. *Charles Chapin's Story.* New York: Putnam, 1920.
Chapin, Louella. *Round About Chicago.* Chicago: Unity, 1907.
Chaplain, Ray. *God's Prison Gang.* Old Tappan, N. J.: Fleming H. Revell, 1977.
Chaplin, Dr. A. *A St. Helena Who's Who.* London: A. Humphreys, 1919.
Chaplin, Charles. *My Autobiography.* New York: Simon & Schuster, 1964.
Chaplin, J.P. *Rumor, Fear and the Madness of Crowds.* New York: Ballantine Books, 1959.
Chaplin, Patrice. *By Flower and Dean Street and the Love Apple.* London: Duckworth, 1976.
Chaplin, Ralph. *Wobbly: The Rough-and-Tumble Story of an American Radical.* Chicago: University of Chicago Press, 1948.
Chapman, Arthur. *The Pony Express.* New York: G. P. Putnam's Sons, 1932.
Chapman, Brian. *Police State.* New York: Praeger, 1970.
Chapman, Gil and Ann. *Was Oswald Alone?* San Diego, Calif.: San Diego Export, 1967.
Chapman, Guy. *The Dreyfus Case.* London: Rupert Hart-Davis, 1955.
Chapman, John. *Incredible Los Angeles.* New York: Harper & Row, 1960.
_____. *Tell It to Sweeney.* Garden City, N. Y.: Doubleday, 1961.
Chappell, Duncan, et al. (eds.). *Forcible Rape: The Crime, the Victim, and the Criminal.* New York: Columbia University Press, 1977.
_____, and Monahan, John (eds.). *Violence and Criminal Justice.* Lexington, Mass.: Lexington Books, D.C. Heath, 1975.
Chappell, Joseph Mitchell. *Life and Times of Warren G. Harding.* Boston: Chapple, 1924.
Charles, Mrs. Tom. *More Tales of Tularosa.* Alamogordo, N. M.: Bennett Printing, 1961.
Charles-Picard, Gilbert. *Augustus and Nero: The Secret of Empire.* New York: Thomas Y. Crowell, 1965.
Charnwood, Lord. *Abraham Lincoln.* Garden City, N. Y: Garden City, 1917.
Charques, R. D. *The Twilight of Imperial Russia.* Fairlawn, N. Y.: Essential Books, 1959.
Charroux, Robert. *Forgotten Worlds.* New York: Walker, 1973.
Chassaigne, M. *La lieutenance generale de police Paris.* Paris: Arthur Rousseau, 1906.
Le Chateau de Gilles de Retz et Son Histoire. Olonne-Beauvoir, Fr.: Lussaud Freres, 1957.
Chatfield, W.H. *The Twin Cities of the Border.* New Orleans, La.: E. P. Brandao, 1893.
Chatfield-Taylor, Hobart C. *Chicago.* New York: Houghton Mifflin, 1917.
Chatterton, E. Keble. *The Romance of Piracy.* Philadelphia: J. B. Lippincott, 1915.
Chatterton, Fenimore C. *Yesterday's Wyoming.* Aurora, Colo.: Powder River, 1957.
Chavarria-Aguilar, O.L. (ed.). *Traditional India.* Englewood Cliffs, N. J.: Prentice-Hall, 1964.
Chein, Isidor, et al. *The Road to H: Narcotics, Delinquency, and Social Policy.* New York: Basic Books, 1964.
Chenault, Price. *Diagnostic and Remedial Teaching in Correctional Insitutions.* Albany: New York State Department of Correction, 1945.
Chenery, William L. *Freedom of the Press.* New York: Harcourt, Brace, 1953.
_____. *So It Seemed.* New York: Harcourt, Brace, 1952.
Cheney, M. *The Coed Killer.* New York: Walker, 1976.
Cherniak, Laurence. *The Great Book of Hashish.* Berkeley, Calif.: University Press, 1979.
Cherrill, Fred. *Cherrill of the Yard.* London: Popular Book Club, 1955.
Chruel, Pierre. *Histoire de France pendant la minorit de Louis XIV.* 4 vols. Paris: Hachette, 1880.
Cheshire, Maxine. *Reporter.* Boston: Houghton Mifflin, 1978.
Chesler, P. *Women and Madness.* London: Allen Lane, 1974.
Chesney, Kellow. *The Anti-Society: An Account of the Victorian Underworld.* Boston: Gambit, 1970.
Chessman, Caryl. *Cell 2455, Death Row.* Englewood Cliffs, N. J.: Prentice-Hall, 1954.
_____. *The Face of Justice.* Englewood Cliffs, N. J.: Prentice-Hall, 1957.
_____. *Trial by Ordeal.* Englewood Cliffs, N. J.: Prentice-Hall, 1956.
Chester, Lewis, Leitch, David, and Simpson, Colin. *The Cleveland Street Affair.* London: Weidenfeld & Nicolson, 1976.
Chetwynd-Hayes, R. *The Unbidden.* London: Tandem, 1971.
Chevigny, Hector. *Lord of Alaska.* New York: Viking Press, 1943.
Chevigny, Paul. *Police Power: Public Abuse in New York City.* New York: Random House, 1969.
Chiang, Monlin. *Tides from the West: A Chinese Autobiography.* New Haven, Conn.: Yale University Press, 1947.
The Chicago Anarchists and the Haymarket Massacre. Chicago: Blakely, 1887.
Chick, N. A. *In Memoriam. . .a Complete Record of the Assassination of Lord Mayo.* Calcutta, India: T. S. Smith, 1872.
Chidsey, Donald Barr. *On and Off the Wagon.* New York: Cowles, 1969.
Chien, I. *Narcotics, Delinquency and Social Policy.* London: Tavistock, 1964.
Chikao Fujisawa. *Kotonarism: An Introduction to the Study of Japanese Global Philosophy or Kotonarism.* Tokyo: Society for the Advancement of Global Democracy, 1954.
Childers, Erskine B. *Commonsense about the Arab World.* London: Victor Gollancz, 1960.
_____. *The Road to Suez.* London: MacGibbon & Kee, 1962.
Children in Custody: A Report on the Juvenile Detention and Correctional Facility Census of 1971. Washington, D. C.: National Criminal Justice Information and Statistics Service, 1974.
Chintamani, C. Y. *Indian Politics Since the Mutiny.* London: George Allen & Unwin, 1939.
Chisholm, Joe. *Brewery Gulch.* San Antonio, Texas: Naylor, 1949.
_____, and Cohn, Alfred. *Take the Witness.* New York: Frederick A. Stokes, 1934.
Chittenden, Hiram Martin. *The American Fur Trade of the Far West.* 2 vols. Stanford, Calif.: Academic Reprints, 1954.
Chittenden, L. E. *Recollections of President Lincoln and his Administration.* New York: Harper & Brothers, 1891.
Chitwood, Oliver Perry. *Justice in Colonial Virginia.* Baltimore: Johns Hopkins Press, 1905.
_____. *Psychoanalysis of the Prostitute.* New York: Philosophical Library, 1961.
Chrisman, Harry E. *Fifty Years on the Owl Hoot Trail.* Chicago: Sage Books, 1969.
_____. *The Ladder of Rivers: The Story of I.P. (Print) Olive.* Denver: Sage Books, 1962.
_____. *Lost Trails of the Cimarron.* Denver: Sage Books, 1961.
Christie, Agatha. *An Autobiography.* New York: Dodd, Mead, 1977.
_____. *Evil under the Sun.* New York: Pocket Books. 1975.
Christie, John (ed.). *Witchcraft in Kenmore (Perthshire), 1730-57: Extracts from Kirk Session Records.* Aberfeldy: D. Cameron & son, 1893.
Christie, Octavius F. *Dickens and His Age.* London: Heath, Cranton, 1939.
Christie, Richard, and Jahoda, Marie. *Studies in the Scope and Method of 'The Authoritarian Personality.'* Glencoe, Ill.: Free Press, 1954.
Christie, Trevor L. *Etched in Arsenic.* Philadelphia: J. B. Lippincott, 1968.
Christoph, James B. *Capital Punishment and British Politics.* Chicago: University of Chicago Press, 1962.
Chronology of Japan's Foreign Relations and Major Documents. Tokyo: Diet Library, 1955.
Chroust, Anton-Hermann. *The Rise of the Legal Profession in America.* 2 vols. Norman: University of Oklahoma Press, 1965.
Chubb, Judith. *Patronage, Power and Poverty in Southern Italy.* Cambridge, Eng.: Cambridge University Press, 1982.
Chunn, Calvin E. *Of Rice and Men.* Los Angeles: Veteran's, 1946.
The Church Belfry Murder in Boston. Philadelphia: Old Franklin, 1875.
Churchill, Allen. *The Incredible Ivan Kreuger.* London: Weidenfeld & Nicolson, 1957.
_____. *Park Row.* New York: Rinehart, 1958.
_____. *The Year the World Went Mad.* New York: Thomas Y. Crowell, 1960.
Churchill, Winston. *A History of the English Speaking Peoples.* New York: Dodd, Mead, 1957.
_____. *Thoughts and Adventures.* London: Macmillan, 1942.
Chute, William J. *The American Scene: 1600-1860.* New York: Bantam Books, 1964.
_____. *The American Scene: 1860 to the Present.* New York: Bantam Books, 1966.
Chynowerth, Rena, and Shapiro, Dean. *The Blood Covenant.* Austin, Tex.: Diamond Books, 1990.
Ciano, Count Galeazzo. *Ciano's Diaries, 1939-1943.* New York: Doubleday, 1946.
_____. *Ciano's Diplomatic Papers.* trans. Stuart Hood. London: Odhams Press, 1948.
_____. *Diary, 1937-8.* trans. Andreas Mayor. London: Methuen, 1952.
Ciba Foundation. *Medical Care of Prisoners and Detainees.* Amsterdam, Neth.: Elsevier, 1973.
Cicero. *Murder Trials (c. 80-60 B.C.).* trans. Michael Grant. Harmondsworth, Middlesex, Eng.: Penguin Books, 1975.
Cinel, Dino. *From Italy to San Francisco: The Immigrant Experience.* Palo Alto, Calif.: Stanford University Press, 1982.
Cini, Zelda, and Crane, Bob. *Hollywood, Land & Legend.* New Rochelle, N. Y.: Arlington House, 1980.
Cipes, Robert M. *The Crime War.* New York: New American Library, 1967.
Citizens Police Committee. *Chicago Police Problems.* Chicago: University of Chicago Press, 1931.
Citizens' Research and Investigating Committee, and Tackwood, Louis E. *The Glass House Tapes.* New York: Avon Books, 1973.
City of New York Criminal Justice Coordinating Council. *A Community Self-Study of Organized Crime.* New York: Institute for Social Analysis, 1974.
Clairmonte, Glenn. *Calamity Jane Was Her Name.* Denver: Sage Books, 1959.
Clancy, Herbert J. *The Presidential Election of 1880.* Chicago: Loyola University Press, 1958.
Clancy, Thomas H. *Papist Pamphleteers: The Allen Person Party and the Political Thought of the Counter-Reformation in England, 1572-1615.* Chicago: Loyola University Press, 1964.

Clapham, Sir John. *The Bank of England: A History*. Cambridge, Eng.: University Press, 1945.
Clark, Allen C. *Abraham Lincoln in the National Capitol*. Washington, D. C.: W. F. Roberts, 1925.
Clark, Charles L., and Eubank, Earle E. *Lockstep and Corridor*. Cincinnati, Ohio: University of Cincinnati Press, 1927.
Clark, David G., and Hutchinson, Earl R. *Mass Media and the Law*. New York: John Wiley & Sons, 1970.
Clark, G. (ed.). *Notable British Trials: Trial of James Camb*. London: William Hodge, 1949.
Clark, Sir George. *The Later Stuarts, 1660-1714*. Oxford, Eng.: Clarendon Press, 1955.
Clark, Gerald. *Impatient Giant: Red China Today*. London: W. H. Allen, 1960.
Clark, Henry W. *History of Alaska*. New York: Macmillan, 1930.
Clark, Ira G. *Then Came the Railroads*. Norman: University of Oklahoma Press, 1958.
Clark, Kenneth B. *Dark Ghetto: Dilemmas of Social Power*. New York: Harper & Row, 1965.
Clark, Loremne. *Rape*. Toronto, Ontario, Can.: Womens Press, 1977.
Clark, Marjorie Ruth. *Organized Labor in Mexico*. Chapel Hill: University of North Carolina Press, 1934.
Clark, Martin. *Modern Italy, 1871-1982*. London: Longman, 1984.
Clark, Norman H. *Deliver Us from Evil: An Interpretation of American Prohibition*. New York: W. W. Norton, 1976.
_____. *The Dry Years*. Seattle: University of Washington Press, 1965.
Clark, O.S. *Clay Allison of the Washita*. Attica, Ind.: G. M. Williams, 1920.
Clark, Phyllis Elperin, and Lehrman, Robert. *Doing Time*. New York: Hastings House, 1980.
Clark, R.T. *The Fall of the German Republic*. London: George Allen & Unwin, 1935.
Clark, Ramsey. *Crime in America*. New York: Simon & Schuster, 1970.
Clark, Tim, and Penycate, John. *Psychopath*. London: Routledge & Paul, 1976.
Clark, Tom. *The World of Damon Runyon*. New York: Harper & Row, 1978.
Clarke, Asia Booth. *Booth Memorials*. New York: Carleton, 1866.
_____. *The Elder and the Younger Booth*. Boston: James R. Osgood, 1882.
_____. *The Unlocked Book: A Memoir of John Wilkes Booth by His Sister*. New York: G.P. Putnam's Sons, 1938.
Clarke, Comer. *Eichmann: The Man and His Crimes*. New York: Ballantine Books, 1960.
Clarke, Donald Henderson. *In the Reign of Rothstein*. New York: Vanguard Press, 1929.
_____. *Man of the World: Recollections of an Irreverent Reporter*. New York: Vanguard Press, 1950.
Clarke, F. G. *Scarlet and Ermine*. London: William Kimber, 1960.
Clarke, James. *Last Rampage*. New York: Houghton Mifflin, 1988.
Clarke, James W. *American Assassins: The Darker Side of Politics*. Princeton, N. J.: Princeton University Press, 1982.
Clarke, Stevens H. *The New York City Criminal Court*. New York: Report to the Mayor's Criminal Justice Coordinating Council, 1970.
Clarke, Thurston, and Tigue, John J., Jr. *Dirty Money, Swiss Banks, The Mafia, Money Laundering, and White Collar Crime*. New York: Simon & Schuster, 1975.
Clarkson, Jesse D. *A History of Russia*. New York: Random House, 1961.
Clary, Prince. *A European Past*. New York: St. Martin's Press, 1978.
Clay, Lucius D. *Decision in Germany*. New York: Doubleday, 1950.
Clay-Clopton, Virginia. *A Belle of the Fifties*. New York: Da Capo Press, 1969.
Clayton, A. *Counter-Insurgency in Kenya, 1952-1960*. Nairobi, Kenya: Transafrica, 1975.
Clayton, James E. *The Making of Justice: The Supreme Court in Action*. New York: E. P. Dutton, 1964.
Clayton, Merle. *Union Station Massacre*. Indianapolis, Ind.: Bobbs-Merrill, 1975.
Cleary, James Mansfield (ed.). *Proud Are We Irish*. Chicago: Quadrangle Books, 1966.
Cleaveland, Agnes Morley. *No Life for a Lady*. Boston: Houghton Mifflin, 1941.
_____. *Satan's Paradise, from Lucien Maxwell to Fred Lambert*. Boston: Houghton Mifflin, 1952.
Cleaver, Charles. *Early Chicago Reminiscences*. Chicago: Fergus, 1882.
Cleaver, Eldridge. *Soul on Ice*. New York: McGraw-Hill, 1968.
Clbert, Jean-Paul. *The Gypsies*. Middlesex, Eng.: Penguin Books, 1970.
Cleckley, H. *The Mask of Sanity*. St. Louis: Mosby, 1964.
Clegg, A. and Megson, B. *Children in Distress*. London: Penguin Books, 1968.
Clegg, Eric. *Return Your Verdict*. Sydney, Aus.: Angus & Robertson, 1965.
Clegg, Reed K. *Probation and Parole: Principles and Practices*. Springfield, Ill.: Charles C. Thomas, 1975.
Cleland, Robert Glass. *California in Our Time: 1900-1940*. New York: Knopf, 1947.
_____. *California Pageant, the Story of Four Centuries*. New York: Knopf, 1946.
Clemens, Samuel Langhorne (Mark Twain, Pseud.). *The Adventures of Huckleberry Finn*. New York: Charles L. Webster, 1885.
_____. *Life on the Mississippi*. Boston: James R. Osgood, 1883.
_____. *Roughing It*. Chicago: F. G. Gilmer, 1872.
Clement, Trover, and Symes, Lillian. *Rebel America: The Story of Social Revolt in the United States*. New York: Harper & Brothers, 1934.
Clemmer, Donald. *The Prison Community*. Boston: Christopher, 1940.
Clendenen, Clarence C. *The United States and Pancho Villa: A Study in Unconventional Diplomacy*. Ithaca, N. Y.: Cornell University Press, 1961.
Clifford, Brian R. *The Psychology of Person Identification*. London: Kegan Paul, 1978.
Clifford, W. *Crime Control in Japan*. Lexington, Mass.: Lexington Books, 1976.
Clifton, Alan S. *Time of Fallen Blossoms*. London: Cassell, 1950.
Clinard, Marshall B. (ed.). *Anomie and Deviant Behavior*. New York: Free Press of Glencoe, 1964.
_____. *The Black Market: A Study of White Collar Crime*. New York: Holt, Rinehart & Winston, 1952.
_____, and Yeager, Peter C. *Corporate Crime*. New York: Macmillan, 1978.
_____, and Abbott, Daniel J. *Crime in Developing Countries*. New York: John Wiley & Sons, 1973.
_____, and Quinney, Richard. *Criminal Behavior Systems: A Typology*. New York: Holt, Rinehart & Winston, 1967.
_____, et al. *Illegal Corporate Behavior*. Washington, D. C.: U.S. Government Printing Office, 1979.
_____. *Sociology of Deviant Behavior*. New York: Holt, Rinehart & Winston, 1962.
Cline, Howard F. *The United States and Mexico*. Cambridge, Mass.: Harvard University Press, 1963.
Cline, Ray S. *Secrets, Spies & Scholars*. Washington, D. C.: Acropolis Books, 1976.
Clinton, Henry Lauren. *Celebrated Trials*. New York: Harper & Brothers, 1896.
_____. *Extraordinary Cases*. New York: Harper & Brothers, 1896.
Clissold, Stephen. *The Barbary Slaves*. Totowa, N. J.: Rowman & Littlefield, 1977.
Close, Upton. *Behind the Face of Japan*. New York: Appleton-Century-Crofts, 1951.
Clough, Frank C. *William Allen White of Emporia*. New York: McGraw-Hill, 1941.
Clough, M. S. *Chiefs and Politicians: Local Politics and Social Change in Kiambu, Kenya 1918-1936*. Palo Alto, Calif.: Stanford University Press, 1977.
Cloward, Richard A., and Ohlin, Lloyd E. *Delinquency and Opportunity*. New York: Free Press, 1960.
_____, et al. *Theoretical Studies in Social Organization of the Prison*. New York: Social Science Research Council, 1960.
Clubb, O. Edmund. *Twentieth Century China*. New York: Columbia University Press, 1966.
_____. *The Witness and I*. New York: Columbia University Press, 1974.
Club-Fellow & Washington Mirror Consolidated. *To The City of Chicago*. New York: Club-Fellow, 1912.
Clugston, W. G. *Rascals in Democracy*. New York: Richard R. Smith, 1940.
Clum, John P. *It All Happened in Tombstone*. Flagstaff, Ariz.: Northland Press, 1965.
Clune, F. *The Kelly Hunters: The Authentic Impartial History of the Life and Times of Edward Kelly, the Ironclad Outlaw*. Sydney, Aus.: Angus & Robertson, 1955.
Clurman, Harold. *The Fervent Years*. New York: Knopf, 1945.
Cluseret, Gustave Paul. *Memoires*. 3 vols. Paris: Jules Lvy, 1888.
Clutterbuck, Richard. *Guerrillas & Terrorists*. London: Faber & Faber, 1977.
_____. *Kidnap & Ransom*. Boston: Faber & Faber, 1978.
_____. *Living with Terrorism*. New Rochelle, N. Y.: Arlington House, 1975.
_____. *The Media and Political Violence*. London: Macmillan, 1981.
_____. *Riot and Revolution in Singapore and Malaya*. London: Faber & Faber, 1973.
Clyne, Peter. *An Anatomy of Skyjacking*. London: Abelard-Schuman, 1973.
Coakley, Leo J. *Jersey Troopers*. New Brunswick, N. J.: Rutgers University Press, 1971.
Coale, Edward J. *Trials of the Mail Robbers*. Baltimore: E. J. Coale, 1818.
Coan, Charles Florus. *A History of New Mexico*. Chicago: American Historical Society, 1925.
Coates, Robert M. *The Outlaw Years: The History of the Land Pirates of the Natchez Trace*. New York: Literary Guild of America, 1930.
Coatman, J. *Police*. New York: Oxford University Press, 1959.
Cobb, Belton. *Critical Years at the Yard*. London: Faber & Faber, 1956.
_____. *The First Detectives*. London: Faber & Faber, 1957.
_____. *Murdered on Duty: A Chronicle of the Killing of Policemen*. London: W. H. Allen, 1961.
_____. *Trials and Errors, 11 Miscarriages of Justice*. London: W. H. Allen, 1962.
Cobb, Joseph B. *Mississippi Scenes*. Baltimore: A. Hart, 1851.
Cobbe, Hugh. *Cook's Voyages and Peoples of the Pacific*. London: British Museum, 1974.
Cobbe, William Rosser. *Doctor Judas: A Portrayal of the Opium Habit*. Chicago: S. C. Griggs, 1895.
Coben, Stanley. *A. Mitchell Palmer, Politician*. New York: Columbia University Press, 1963.
Coblentz, Edmund D. (ed.). *William Randolph Hearst: A Portrait in His Own Words*. New York: Simon & Schuster, 1952.
Coblentz, Stanton Arthur. *Villains and Vigilantes*. New York: Thomas Yoseloff, 1957.
Cochran, Hamilton. *Freebooters of the Red Sea*. Indianapolis, Ind.: Bobbs-Merrill, 1965.
Cochran, Louis. *FBI Man: A Personal History*. New York: Duell, Sloan & Pearce, 1966.
Cochran, Thomas C., and Miller, William. *The Age of Enterprise, A Social History of America*. New York: Macmillan, 1942.
Cockburn, A., and Blackburn, R. (eds.). *Student Power*. London: Penguin Books, 1969.
Cockburn, Claude. *In Time of Trouble*. London: Rupert Hart-Davis, 1956.
Cockburn, J.S. (ed.). *Crime in England, 1550-1800*. London: Methuen, 1977.
_____. *A History of English Assizes, 1558-1714*. Cambridge, Eng.: University Press, 1964.
Cockburn, Leslie. *Out of Control: The Story of the Reagan Administration's Secret War in Nicaragua, the Illegal Arms Pipeline, and the Contra Drug Connection*. New York: Morgan Entrekin/Atlantic Monthly Press, 1987.
Coe, Charles H. *Juggling a Rope*. Pendleton, Ore.: Hamley, 1927.
Coe, George Washington. *Frontier Fighter: The Autobiography of George W. Coe*. Boston: Houghton Mifflin, 1934.
Coffey, Alan R., et al. *Administration of Criminal Justice*. Englewood Cliffs, N. J.: Prentice-Hall, 1974.
Coffey, Thomas M. *The Long Thirst: Prohibition in America: 1920-1933*. New York: W. W. Norton, 1975.
Coffin, Joshua. *An Account of Some of the Principal Slave Insurrections*. New York: American Anti-Slavery Society, 1860.
Coggeshall, E. W. *Assassination of Lincoln*. Chicago: W. M. Hill, 1920.

Cogley, John. *Report on Blacklisting.* New York: Fund for the Republic, 1956.
Cogswell, Jonathan. *A Treatise on the Necessity of Capital Punishment.* Hartford, Conn.: E. Geer, 1843.
Cohen, Albert K. *Delinquent Boys: The Culture of the Gang.* Glencoe, Ill.: Free Press, 1955.
_____. *Deviance and Control.* Englewood Cliffs, N. J.: Prentice-Hall, 1966.
Cohen, Bernard. *Police Internal Administration of Justice in New York City.* Santa Monica, Calif.: Rand, 1970.
_____, and Chaiken, Jan M. *Police Background Characteristics and Performance.* Santa Monica, Calif.: Rand, 1972.
Cohen, Felix (ed.). *Felix Cohen's Handbook of Federal Indian Law.* Albuquerque: University of New Mexico Press, 1971.
Cohen, Fred. *The Legal Challenge to Corrections.* Washington, D. C.: Joint Commission on Correctional Manpower and Training, 1969.
Cohen, Israel. *Contemporary Jewry.* London: Methuen, 1950.
_____. *The Zionist Movement.* New York: Zionist Organization of America, 1946.
Cohen, Jerry, and Murphy, William S. *Burn, Baby, Burn!* New York: Avon Books, 1966.
Cohen, Louis H. *Murder, Madness and the Law.* New York: World, 1952.
Cohen, M. R. and F. S. *Readings in Jurisprudence and Legal Philosophy.* Boston: Little, Brown, 1951.
Cohen, Mickey. *In My Own Words.* Englewood Cliffs, N. J.: Prentice-Hall, 1975.
Cohen, Rich. *Tough Jews: Fathers, Son and Gangster Dreams.* New York: Vintage, 1999.
Cohen, S. A. *British Zionists and British Jews.* Princeton, N. J.: Princeton University Press, 1982.
Cohen, Sam. D. *100 True Crime Stories.* New York: World, 1946.
Cohen, Stanley. *Folk Devils and Moral Panics.* London: Paladin, 1973.
_____. *The Game They Played.* New York: Farrar, Straus and Giroux, 1977.
_____. *Images of Deviance.* London: Penguin Books, 1971.
Cohen, Stephan. *Reporting Child Abuse and Neglect.* Cambridge, Mass.: Ballinger, 1975.
Cohn, Alfred, and Chisholm, Joe. *Take the Witness!* New York: Frederick A. Stokes, 1934.
Cohn, Art. *The Joker Is Wild: The Story of Joe E. Lewis.* New York: Random House, 1955.
Cohn, D. L. *Life and Times of King Cotton.* New York: Oxford University Press, 1956.
Cohn, Norman. *Europe's Inner Demons.* New York: Basic Books, 1975.
Cohn, S.I. (ed.). *Law Enforcement Science and Technology.* Washington, D. C.: Port City Press, 1969.
Colby, Robert. *The California Crime Book.* New York: Pyramid Books, 1971.
The Cold Springs Tragedy. Indianapolis, Ind.: A. C. Roach, 1869.
Cole, George R. (ed.). *Criminal Justice: Law and Politics.* North Scituate, Mass.: Duxbury Press, 1976.
Cole, Hubert. *Christophe: King of Haiti.* New York: Viking Press, 1967.
_____. *Laval.* London: William Heinemann, 1963.
Cole, Peter, and Pringle, Peter. *Can You Positively Identify This Man?* London: Deutsch, 1974.
Cole, S. *Counterfeit.* London: John Murray, 1955.
Coleman, J. S. *The Criminal Elite.* New York: St. Martin's Press, 1985.
Coleman, James Covington. *Abnormal Psychology and Modern Life.* Glenview, Ill.: Scott, Foresman, 1976.
Coleman, James S. *Power and the Structure of Society.* New York: W. W. Norton, 1974.
Coleman, Jonathan. *At Mother's Request.* New York: Atheneum, 1985.
Coleman, Lee. *The Reign of Terror.* Boston: Beacon Press, 1984.
Coleman, McAlister. *Eugene V. Debs: A Man Unafraid.* New York: Greenberg, 1930.
_____. *Report of the Trial of Levi Weeks, On an Indictment for the Murder of Gulielma Sands, on Monday the thirty-first day of March, and Tuesday the first day of April, 1800. Taken in Short Hand by the Clerk of the Court.* New York: John Furman, 1800.
Coles, H.L. *The War of 1812.* Chicago: University of Chicago Press, 1965.
Coles, Robert. *Children of Crisis.* Boston: Atlantic-Little, Brown, 1977.
_____, Brenner, Joseph H., and Meagher, Dermot. *Drugs and Youth.* New York: Liveright, 1970.
_____. *The Grass Pipe.* Boston: Little, Brown, 1969.
_____. *The Old Ones of New Mexico.* Garden City, N. Y.: Anchor Books, 1975.
Coletta, Paolo E. *William Jennings Bryan.* 3 vols. Lincoln: University of Nebraska Press, 1964-1969.
Coley, Nathan. *Lockerbie Trial.* Princeton, N. J.: Princeton University Press, 2001.
Colina, Federico de la. *Madero y el Gral Diaz.* Mexico City: Guerra y Vaquez, 1913.
A Collection of Rare and Curious Tracts on Witchcraft and the Second Sight. Edinburgh, Scot.: D. Webster, 1820.
Colleoni, Angelo. *Claretta Petacci: rivelazioni sulla vita, gli amore, la morte.* Milan, Italy: Lucchi, 1945.
_____. *Porfirio Diaz, Su Vida Militar, Sus Perfidias Politicas.* Mexico City: Talleres del Diario Republicano, 1911.
Collier, John. *Indians of the Americas.* New York: New American Library, 1947.
Collier, Peter, and Horowitz, David. *The Rockefellers%%An American Dynasty.* London: Jonathan Cape, 1976.
Collier, Richard. *The Great Indian Mutiny.* New York: E. P. Dutton, 1964.
_____. *Ten Thousand Eyes.* New York: E. P. Dutton, 1958.
_____, and Westrate, Edwin Victor. *The Reign of Soapy Smith, Monarch of Misrule.* Garden City, N. Y.: Doubleday, Doran, 1935.
Collins, Frederick Lewis. *The F.B.I. in Peace and War.* New York: Putnam, 1943.
_____. *Glamorous Sinners.* New York: Ray Long & Richard R. Smith, 1932.
Collins, Irene. *The Government and the Newspaper Press in France.* London: Oxford University Press, 1959.
Collins, James J. Jr. (ed.). *Drinking and Crime.* New York: Guilford Press, 1981.
Collins, Philip. *Dickens and Crime.* New York: Macmillan, 1962.
Collins, Robert O., and Tignor, Robert L. *Egypt and the Sudan.* Englewood Cliffs, N. J.: Prentice-Hall, 1967.
Collins, Ted (ed.). *New York Murders.* New York: Duell, Sloan & Pearce, 1944.
Collins, Winfield H. *The Truth About Lynching and the Negro in the South.* New York: Neale, 1918.
Collinson, Patrick. *The Elizabethan Puritan Movement.* London: Jonathon Cape, 1967.
Collison-Morley, Lacy. *The Story of the Sforzas.* New York: E. P. Dutton, 1934.
Colman, Edna M. *Seventy-Five Years of White House Gossip.* Garden City, N. Y.: Doubleday, Page, 1925.
Colman, Elizabeth. *Chinatown U. S. A.* New York: John Day, 1946.
Colombos, C. John. *The International Law of the Sea.* London: Longmans & Green, 1954.
Colquhoun, Patrick. *A Treatise on the Commerce and Police of the River Thames.* Montclair, N. J.: Patterson Smith, 1969.
_____. *A Treatise on the Police of the Metropolis.* Montclair, N. J.: Patterson Smith, 1969.
_____. *A Treatise on the Public Metropolis.* London: Joseph Mawman, 1800.
Colvin, D. Leigh. *Prohibition in the United States: A History of the Prohibition Party and of the Prohibition Movement.* New York: George H. Doran, 1926.
Colvin, Ian. *Chief of Intelligence.* London: Victor Gollancz, 1951.
Combs, Joseph F. *Gunsmoke in the Redlands.* San Antonio, Texas: Naylor, 1968.
Commager, Henry Steele. *The American Mind.* New Haven, Conn.: Yale University Press, 1950.
Commission on Obscenity and Pornography. *Report.* New York: Random House, 1970.
Commission on the Review of the National Policy Toward Gambling. *Gambling in America.* Washington, D. C.: U.S. Government Printing Office, 1976.
Committee for Economic Development. *Reducing Crime and Assuring Justice.* New York: Committee for Economic Development, 1972.
Committee on Un-American Activities. *Guerrilla Warfare Advocates in the United States.* Washington, D. C.: U.S. Government Printing Office, 1968.
Commons, M.L., et al. (eds.). *Quantitative Analyses of Behavior.* Cambridge, Mass.: Ballinger, 1982.
Commonwealth of Massachusetts by Indictment vs. Thomas W. Piper. Boston: Alfred Mudge & Son, 1876.
Complete Account of the Horrid Murder of James Murray! New York: n. p., 1823.
A Complete History of the Murder of Mrs. Ruth Fyler. Syracuse, N. Y.: Smith & Hough, 1855.
Complete Official History of Rube Burrows and His Celebrated Gang. Birmingham, Ala.: Lyman & Stone, n. d.
Comstock, Anthony. *Frauds Exposed; or How the People are Deceived and Robbed, and Youth Corrupted.* New York: J. Howard Brown, 1880.
_____. *Traps for the Young.* New York: Funk & Wagnalls, 1883.
Conant, Ralph W. *Problems in Research: Community Violence.* Washington, D. C.: Institute on Mental Health, Research Branch, 1969.
_____. *The Prospects for Revolution.* New York: Harper & Row, 1971.
Conconi, Charles, and House, Toni. *The Washington Sting.* New York: Coward, McCann & Geoghegan, 1979.
A Condensed Report of the Trial of James Albert Trefethen, and William H. Smith for the Murder of Deltena J. Davis. Boston: Wright & Potter, 1895.
Condon, John F. *Jafsie Tells All.* New York: Jonathan Lee, 1936.
Condor, Stella. *Woman on the Beat.* London: Hale, 1960.
The Confession and Dying Words of Samuel Frost. Worcester, Mass.: Thomas, n. d.
Confession of Adam Horn. Baltimore: James Young, 1843.
Confession of Adam Jones. Louisville, Ky.: D. Holcomb, 1837.
Confession of Augustus Otis Jennings. St. Joseph, Mo.: K. J. Bastin, 1853.
The Confession of Benjamin Bailey. Reading, Pa.: J. Schneider, 1798.
Confession of Charles Gibbs, the Pirate. New York: Christian Brown, 1831.
Confession of Edward Donnelly. Carlisle, Pa.: A. Louden, 1808.
Confession of Elizabeth Van Valkenburgh. Johnstown, N. Y.: G. Henry & W. N. Clark, 1847.
Confession of Henry Green. Troy, N. Y.: R. Rose & R. Belcher, 1845.
Confession of John Battus. Philadelphia: Richard Folwell, 1800.
Confession of John Haggerty. Lancaster, Pa.: John H. Persol, 1847.
Confession of John Joyce. Philadelphia: Bethel Church, 1808.
Confession of Joseph Baker. Philadelphia: Richard Folwell, 1800.
Confessions of an American Opium Eater. Boston: J. H. Earle, 1895.
Confessions of Two Malefactors, Teller & Reynolds. Hartford, Conn.: Hamer & Comstock, 1833.
Congdon, Don (ed.). *The Thirties.* New York: Simon & Schuster, 1962.
Conger, Roger N. *Texas Rangers: Sesquicentennial Anniversary, 1823-1973.* Fort Worth, Tex.: Heritage Publications, 1973.
Congress and the Nation, 1945-1964. Washington, D. C.: Congressional Quarterly Service, 1965.
Congressional Committee Staff Study. *Political Kidnappings 1968-1973.* Washington, D.C.: n. p., 1973.
Conklin, John E. *The Crime Establishment.* Englewood Cliffs, N. J.: Prentice-Hall, 1977.
_____. *The Impact of Crime.* New York: Macmillan, 1975.
_____. *Robbery and the Criminal Justice System.* Philadelphia: J. B. Lippincott, 1972.
Connable, Alfred, and Silberfarb, Edward. *Tigers of Tammany Hall: Nine Men Who Ran New York.* New York: Holt, Rinehart & Winston, 1967.
Connell, John and Sutherland, Douglas. *Fraud.* New York: Stein & Day, 1979.
Connell, Noreen, and Wilson, Cassandra (eds.). *Rape: The First Sourcebook for Women.* New York: Plume Books, 1974.
Connell, Robert, Sr. *Arkansas.* New York: Paebar, 1947.

Connelley, William Elsey. *Quantrill and the Border Wars.* Cedar Rapids, Iowa: Torch Press, 1909.
_____. *Wild Bill and His Era.* New York: Press of the Pioneers, 1933.
Conners. Bernard F. *Don't Embarrass the Bureau.* Indianapolis, Ind.: Bobbs-Merrill, 1972.
Connery, Donald S. *Guilty Until Proven Innocent.* New York: Putnam, 1977.
Connolly, C. P. *The Truth About the Frank Case.* New York: Vail-Ballou, 1915.
Connolly, Christopher P. *The Devil Learns to Vote.* New York: Covici Friede, 1938.
Connor, Walter. *Deviance in Soviet Society.* New York: Columbia University Press, 1972.
Conot, Robert. *Rivers of Blood, Years of Darkness.* New York: Bantam Books, 1967.
Conquest, Robert. *The Great Terror: Stalin's Purge of the Thirties.* London: Macmillan, 1968.
Conrad, Barnaby. *A Revolting Transaction.* New York: Arbor House, 1983.
Conrad, Earl. *Scottsboro Boy.* Garden City, N. Y.: Doubleday, 1950.
Conrad, J.P., and Dintz, S. (eds.). *In Fear of Each Other.* Lexington, Mass.: Lexington Books, 1977.
Conrad, John P. *Crime and Its Correction: An International Survey of Attitudes and Practices.* Berkeley: University of California Press, 1967.
Conradi, Peter. *The Red Ripper.* New York: Dell, 1992.
Considine, Bob. *The Man Who Robbed Brinks.* New York: Random House, 1961.
Constant, l'abbé Alphonse-Louis. *La Clef des grands mystères.* Paris: G. Baillire, 1861.
Constantine, King of Greece. *A King's Private Letters.* New York: Everleigh Nash & Grayson, 1925.
Constantine-Quinn, Max. *Doctor Crippen.* London: Duckworth, 1935.
Conway, Moncure Daniel. *Demonology and Devil Lore.* London: Chatto & Windus, 1879.
Conwell, Russell H. *Acres of Diamonds.* New York: Harper & Brothers, 1915.
Coogan, Tim Pat. *The I. R. A.* London: Fontana, 1980.
_____. *The I. R. A: A History.* Niwot, Colo.: Roberts Rinehart, 1994.
Cook, Adrian. *The Armies of the Streets.* Lexington: University Press of Kentucky, 1974.
Cook, David J. *Hands Up; or Twenty Years of Detective Life in the Mountains and on the Plains.* Denver: W. F. Robinson Printing, 1897.
Cook, E. T. *Delane of the Times.* London: Constable, 1915.
Cook, Ezra A. *Ku Klux Klan Secrets Exposed.* Chicago: Published by Author, 1922.
Cook, Fred J. *The Corrupted Land: The Social Morality of Modern America.* New York: Macmillan, 1966.
_____. *The FBI Nobody Knows.* New York: Macmillan, 1964.
_____. *The Great Energy Scam.* New York: Macmillan, 1982.
_____. *Mafia!* Greenwich, Conn.: Fawcett, 1973.
_____. *The Nightmare Decade.* New York: Random House, 1971.
_____. *The Secret Rulers: Criminal Syndicates and How They Control the U.S. Underworld.* New York: Duell, Sloan & Pearce, 1966.
_____. *A Two Dollar Bet Means Murder.* New York: Dial Press, 1961.
Cook, Frederick Francis. *Bygone Days in Chicago.* Chicago: McClurg, 1910.
Cook, James. *The Journals of Captain James Cook in His Voyages of Discovery: The Voyage of the Resolution and Discovery 1776-1780.* 3 vols. Cambridge, Eng.: Hakluyt Society, 1955-67.
Cook, Theodore P. *The Life and Public Services of the Hon. Samuel J. Tilden.* New York: D. Appleton, 1876.
Cook, Thomas. *Early Graves.* New York: E. P. Dutton, 1990.
Cook, Warren. *Flood Tide of Empire.* New Haven, Conn.: Yale University Press, 1973.
Cooke, Alistair. *A Generation on Trial.* New York: Knopf, 1950.
_____ (ed.). *The Vintage Mencken.* New York: Vintage Books, 1955.
Cooke, T. Dickerson. *The Blue Book of Crime.* Chicago: Institute of Applied Science, 1959.
Cookridge, E. H. *The Baron of Arizona.* New York: John Day, 1967.
_____. *Set Europe Ablaze.* London: Author Baker, 1966.
Cooley, John K. *Libyan Sandstorm.* New York: Holt, Rinehart & Winston, 1982.
Coolidge, Dane. *Arizona Cowboys.* New York: E. P. Dutton, 1938.
_____. *Fighting Men of the West.* New York: E. P. Dutton, 1932.
_____. *Gringo Gold: A Story of Joaquin Murieta, the Bandit.* New York: E. P. Dutton & Co., 1939.
Coolidge, Mary Roberts. *Chinese Immigration.* New York: Henry Holt, 1909.
Coons, William R. *Attica Diary.* New York: Stein & Day, 1972.
Cooper, Alfred Duff. *Old Men Forget.* London: Hart-Davis, 1953.
Cooper, C. S. *Understanding Italy.* New York: Century, 1923.
Cooper, Courtney Riley. *Designs in Scarlet.* Boston: Little, Brown, 1939.
_____. *Here's to Crime.* Boston: Little, Brown, 1937.
_____. *High Country, the Rockies Yesterday and Today.* Boston: Little, Brown, 1926.
_____. *Ten Thousand Public Enemies.* Boston: Little, Brown, 1935.
Cooper, David D. *The Lesson of the Scaffold.* Athens: Ohio University Press, 1974.
Cooper, R. W. *The Nuremberg Trial.* Harmondsworth, Eng.: Penguin Books, 1947.
Cooper, Thomas. *The Mystery of Witchcraft.* London: N. Oakes, 1617.
Cooper, William. *Shall We Ever Know? The Trial of the Hosein Brothers for the Murder of Mrs. McKay.* London: Hutchinson, 1971.
Coopers and Lybrand. *The Cost of Incarceration in New York City.* Hackensack, N. J.: National Council on Crime and Delinquency, 1978.
Coote, A., and Gill, T. *The Rape Controversy.* London: NCCL, 1975.
Copetas, A. Craig. *Metal Men.* New York: Putnam, 1985.
Copeland, James. *The Butler.* London: Granada, 1981.
Copple, Neale. *Depth Reporting.* Englewood Cliffs, N. J.: Prentice-Hall, 1964.
Coppolino, Carl A. *The Crime That Never Was.* Tampa, Florida: Justice Press, 1980.
Corbett, James J. *The Roar of the Crowd.* New York: Gosset & Dunlap, 1925.
Corbin, Charles R. *Why News Is News.* New York: Roland Press, 1928.
Corbin, Jane. *Al-Qaeda: In Search of the Terror Network that Threatens the World.* New York: Thunder's Mouth Press, 2002.
Corbitt, Robert L. *The Holmes Castle.* Chicago: Corbitt & Morrison, 1895.
Corcoran, Jean. *Folk Tales of England.* Indianapolis, Ind.: Bobbs-Merrill, 1968.
Corder, Eric (ed.). *Murder My Love.* Chicago: Playboy Press, 1973.
Cordley, Rev. Richard D. *History of Lawrence, Kansas.* Lawrence, Kan.: E. F. Caldwell, 1895.
Coremans, P. *Van Meegeren's Faked Vermeers and de Hooghs: A Scientific Examination.* trans. C. M. Hutt. London: Cassell, 1949.
Corey, Herbert. *Farewell, Mr. Gangster!* New York: Appleton-Century-Crofts, 1936.
Corey, Lewis. *The Decline of American Capitalism.* New York: Covici Friede, 1934.
_____. *The House of Morgan.* New York: Grosset & Dunlap, 1930.
_____. *The Unfinished Task.* New York: Viking Press, 1942.
Corfe, Tom. *The Phoenix Park Murders: Conflict, Compromise and Tragedy in Ireland 1979-1882.* London: Hodder & Stoughton, 1968.
Corfield, I. D. *Historical Survey of the Origins and Growth of Mau Mau.* London: H. M. Stationery Office, 1960.
Corley, T. A. B. *Democratic Despot: A Life of Napoleon III.* London: Barrie & Rockliff, 1961.
Corliss, Carlton J. *Main Line of Mid-America.* New York: Creative Age, 1950.
Cornelius, Wayne A. *Mexican Migration to the United States: Causes, Consequences and U.S. Responses.* Cambridge, Mass.: MIT Press, 1978.
Cornick, Martyn. *The French Secret Service.* New York: Transaction, 1993.
Cornish, G. W. *Cornish of the "Yard".* London: John Lane, 1935.
Cornish, M. *An Introduction to Violence.* London: Cassell, 1960.
Cornwallis-West, Mrs. George. *The Reminiscences of Lady Randolph Churchill.* New York: Century, 1908.
Cornwell, John. *Earth to Earth.* New York: Ecco Press, 1982.
Corpechot, L. *Memories of Queen Amlie of Portugal.* London: Evelyn Nash, 1915.
Corpuz, Orofre D. *The Philippines.* Englewood Cliffs, N. J.: Prentice-Hall, 1965.
A Correct and Concise Account of the Interesting Trial of Jason Fairbanks, for the Barbarous and Cruel Murder of Elizabeth Fales. Boston: n. p., 1801.
A Correct Copy of the Trial & Conviction of Richard Johnson, for the Murder of Ursula Newman. New York: Christian Brown, 1829.
The Correct, Full and Impartial Report on the Trial of Rev. Ephraim K. Avery. Providence, R. I.: Marshall & Brown, 1833.
Corry, John. *The Manchester Affair.* New York: Putnam, 1967.
Corts, J. B., and Gatti, F. M. *Delinquency and Crime.* New York: Seminar Press, 1972.
Corti, Egon Caesar, Count. *The Downfall of Three Dynasties.* New York: Books for Libraries Press, 1970.
_____. *The English Empress.* London: Cassell, 1957.
_____. *Maximilian and Carlotta.* trans. Catherine Alison Philips. New York: Knopf, 1928.
_____. *The Romanovs.* New York: Harper & Row, 1971.
_____. *The Russian Dagger.* New York: Harper & Row, 1969.
Cortwright, David. *Soldiers in Revolt.* New York: Doubleday, 1975.
Corum, Bill. *Off and Running.* New York: Holt, Rinehart & Winston, 1959.
Cory, Donald Webster. *The Homosexual in America.* New York: Greenberg, 1951.
Cosgrave, E. D. *The True History of the Phoenix Park Murders.* London: n. p. 1937.
Cosgrove, Nicholas. *The Cosgrove Report: Being the Private Inquiry of a Pinkerton Detective into the Death of President Lincoln.* New York: Rawson, Wade, 1979.
Cosio Villegas, Daniel (ed.). *Historia moderna de Mexico.* 7 vols. Mexico City: Editorial Hermes, 1955.
Cossley-Batt, Jill Lillie Emma. *The Last of the California Rangers.* New York: Funk & Wagnalls, 1928.
Cossu, Antonio. *The Sardinian Hostage.* trans. Isabel Quigly. London: Hollis & Carter, 1971.
Costello, Augustine E. *History of the Police Department of Jersey City.* Jersey City, N. J.: Published by Author, 1891.
_____. *Our Police Protectors: A History of the New York Police.* New York: C.F. Roper, 1885.
Costello, John Benjamin (ed.). *Swindling Exposed: From the Diary of William B. Morrow.* Syracuse, N. Y.: Published by Author, 1907.
Costigan, Giovanni. *A History of Modern Ireland, with a Sketch of Earlier Times.* New York: Pegasus, 1969.
Costikyan, Edward N. *Behind Closed Doors: Politics in the Public Interest.* New York: Harcourt, Brace & World, 1966.
Coston, John. *To Kill and Kill Again.* New York: Onyx, 1992.
Cosulich, Gilbert. *Adult Probation Laws of the United States.* New York: National Probation Association, 1940.
Cotta, John. *The Trial of Witchcraft Showing the True and Right Method of Discovery.* London: Samuel Rand, 1616.
Cottle, Thomas J. *Children in Jail.* Boston: Beacon Press, 1977.
Cottrell, John. *Anatomy of an Assassination: The Murder of Abraham Lincoln.* New York: Funk & Wagnalls, 1966.
_____. *Assassination! The World Stood Still.* London: New English Library, 1964.
Couchoud, P. L. *Voix de Napolon.* Geneva, Switz.: Milieu du Monde, 1949.
Coulange, Louis. *The Life of the Devil.* London: Knopf, 1929.
Coulter, J. *Approaches to Insanity: A Philosophical and Sociological Study.* London: Martin Robertson, 1973.
_____. *The Death Penalty for Heresy.* London: Simpkin, Marshall, Hamilton, & Kant, 1924.

_____. *Five Centuries of Religion.* Cambridge, Eng.: Cambridge University Press, 1927

_____. *The Inquisition and Liberty.* London: William Heinemann, 1938.

_____. *Medieval Panorama.* Cambridge, Eng.: Cambridge University Press, 1949.

Countant, C. G. *The History of Wyoming.* Laramie, Wyo.: Chaplin, Spafford & Mathison, 1899.

Countryman, Vern (ed.). *Douglas of the Supreme Court.* Garden City, N. Y.: Doubleday, 1959.

_____, and Finman, T. *The Lawyer in Modern Society.* Boston: Little, Brown, 1966.

Coupland, R. *The Constitutional Problem in India: A Restatement.* London: Oxford University Press, 1944.

Courlander, Harold (ed.). *A Treasury of Afro-American Folklore.* New York: Crown, 1976.

Course, Capt. A. G. *Pirates of the Eastern Seas.* London: Frederick Muller, 1968.

The Courtesan's Jewel Box. trans. Yang Hsien-Yi and Gladys Yang. Peking, China: Foreign Language Press, 1957.

Courtwright, David T. *Dark Paradise: Opiate Addiction in America Before 1940.* Cambridge, Mass.: Harvard University Press, 1982.

Covarrubias, Miguel. *The Eagle, the Jaguar, and the Serpent.* New York: Knopf, 1954.

Cowan, C.D. (ed.). *The Economic Development of China and Japan.* New York: Frederick A. Praeger, 1964.

Cowan, Frank. *Andrew Johnson.* Greensburg, Pa.: n. p., 1894.

Cowan, Paul, et al. *State Secrets.* New York: Holt, Rinehart & Winston, 1974.

Cowdery, Ray R. *Capone's Chicago.* Lakeville, Minn.: Northstar-Maschek, 1987.

Cowie, J., Cowie, V., and Slater, E. *Delinquency in Girls.* London: William Heinemann, 1968.

Cowles, Virginia. *The Great Swindle.* New York: Harper & Brothers., 1960.

_____. *The Kaiser.* New York: Harper & Row, 1963.

Cowles Education, and UPI. *Assassination, Robert F. Kennedy, 1925-1968.* New York: Cowles Education, 1968.

Cowley, Malcolm. *Exile's Return.* New York: W. W. Norton, 1932.

Cox, Archibald. *The Warren Court.* Cambridge, Mass.: Harvard University Press, 1968.

Cox, Arthur Macy. *The Myths of National Security.* Boston: Beacon Press, 1975.

Cox, J.R. *Kenyatta's Country.* London: Hutchinson, 1965.

Cox, Michael. *The Confessions of Henry Lee Lucas.* New York: Ivy Books, 1991.

Cox, Robert V. *Deadly Pursuit.* New York: Cameron House, 1977.

_____, and Peiffer, Kenneth L. *Missing Person.* Harrisburg, Pa.: Stackpole Books, 1979.

Cox, William R. *Luke Short and His Era.* Garden City, N. Y.: Doubleday, 1961.

Coxe, William. *Account of the Russian Discoveries Between Asia and America.* London: T. Cadell, 1780.

Coyne, F. E. *In Reminiscence: Highlights of Men and Events in the Life of Chicago.* Chicago: Excella Press, 1941.

Crabb, Richard E. *Empire on the Platte.* New York: World, 1967.

Craig, Albert M. *Choshu in the Meiji Restoration.* Cambridge, Mass.: Harvard University Press, 1967.

Craig, Gordon A. *The Battle of Kniggrtz.* London: Weidenfeld & Nicolson, 1964.

_____, and Gilbert, Felix. *The Diplomats, 1919-39.* Princeton, N. J.: Princeton University Press, 1953.

_____. *The Politics of the Prussian Army 1640-1945.* New York: Oxford University Press, 1964.

Craig, Richard B. *The Bracero Program: Interest Groups and Foreign Policy.* Austin: University of Texas Press, 1951.

Craig, William. *The Fall of Japan.* New York: Dial Press, 1967.

Craighead, Erwin. *Mobile: Fact and Tradition.* Mobile, Ala · Powers Printing, 1930.

Craigie, Sir Robert. *Behind the Japanese Mask.* London: Hutchinson, 1945.

Craigmyle, Lord. *John Marshall in Diplomacy and Law.* New York: Scribner's, 1933.

Craine, J. V. *The Conspirators' Victims.* Sacramento, Calif.: Gardiner & Kirk, 1855.

Cramer, James. *The World's Police.* London: Cassell, 1964.

Cramer, James A. (ed.). *Preventing Crime.* Beverly Hills, Calif.: Sage, 1978.

Crandall, A. W. *The Early History of the Republican Party 1854-1856.* Boston: R. G. Badger, 1930.

_____. *The Growth of Southern Nationalism 1848-1861.* Baton Rouge: Louisiana State University Press, 1953.

Crane, Milton (ed.). *Sins of New York.* New York: Boni & Gaer, 1947.

Crane, Paul S. *Korea Patterns.* Seoul, S. Kor.: Royal Asiatic Society, 1978.

Crane, Stephen. *Maggie.* Gainesville, Fla.: Scholars' Facsimiles and Reprints, 1966.

Crane, Verner Winslow. *The Southern Frontier 1670-1732.* Durham, N. C.: Duke University Press, 1928.

Crane, Walter R. *Gold and Silver.* New York: John Wiley & Sons, 1908.

Crankshaw, Edward. *Cracks in the Kremlin Wall.* New York: Viking Press, 1951.

_____. *Gestapo, Instrument of Tyranny.* New York: Viking Press, 1956.

_____. *Khrushchev Remembers.* Boston: Little, Brown, 1970.

Cranworth, L. A. *Colony in the Making, or Sport and Profit in British East Africa.* London: Macmillan, 1912.

Crapsey, Edward. *The Nether Side of New York; or The Vice, Crime and Poverty of the Great Metropolis.* New York: Sheldon, 1872.

Crater, Stella Force, with Fraley, Oscar. *The Empty Robe.* Garden City, N. Y.: Doubleday, 1961.

Craton, Michael. *A History of the Bahamas.* London: Collins, 1962.

Craven, Wesley Frank. *The Colonies in Transition 1660-1713.* New York: Harper & Row, 1967.

Crawford, Alan. *Thunder on the Right: The New Right and the Politics of Resentment.* New York: Pantheon, 1980.

Crawford, Francis Marion. *Southern Italy and Sicily and the Rulers of the South.* London: Macmillan, 1900.

Crawford, Mary Caroline. *Famous Families of Massachusetts.* Boston: Little, Brown, 1930.

Crawford, P. L., et al. *Working with Teenage Gangs.* New York: Welfare Council of New York City, 1950.

Crawford, Samuel J. *Kansas in the Sixties.* Chicago: A. C. McClurg, 1911.

Crawford, Thomas Edgar. *The West of the Texas Kid, 1881-1910.* Norman: University of Oklahoma Press, 1962.

Crawford, William. *Report on the Penitentiaries of the United States.* Montclair, N. J.: Patterson Smith, 1969.

Crawley, C. W. *The Question of Greek Independence: A Study of British Policy in the Near East, 1821-1833.* Cambridge, Eng.: Cambridge University Press, 1930.

Crawley, Ernest. *The Mystic Rose.* New York: Meridian Books, 1960.

Cray, Ed. *The Big Blue Line.* New York: Coward McCann, 1967.

_____. *Burden of Proof.* New York: Macmillan, 1973.

Creel, George. *Ireland's Fight for Freedom.* New York: Harper, 1919.

_____. *The People Next Door.* New York: John Day, 1926.

_____. *Rebel at Large: Recollections of Fifty Crowded Years.* New York: Putnam, 1947.

_____. *Wilson and the Issues.* New York: Century, 1916.

Creelman, James. *Diaz, Master of Mexico.* New York: D. Appleton, 1911.

Creer, Leland. *Utah and the Nation.* Seattle: University of Washington Press, 1929.

Creger, Ralph and Carl. *This Is What We Found.* New York: Lyle Stuart, 1960.

Creighton, Mandell. *A History of the Papacy From the Great Schism to the Sack of Rome.* New York: Longmans, Green, 1911.

_____. *Memoir of Sir George Grey Bart.* London: Longmans, Green, 1901.

Crelinstein, Ronald D., and Szabo, Denis. *Hostage-Taking.* Lexington, Mass.: Lexington Books, 1979.

_____, et al. *Terrorism and Criminal Justice.* Lexington, Mass.: D. C. Heath, 1978.

Cremeans, Charles D. *The Arabs and the World.* New York. Praeger, 1963.

Crenshaw, Files, and Miller, Kenneth A. *Scottsboro: The Firebrand of Communism.* Montgomery, Ala.: Brown Printing, 1936.

Cressey, Donald R. *Crime and Criminal Justice.* New York: Quadrangle, 1971.

_____. *Criminal Organization: Its Elementary Forms.* New York: Harper & Row, 1972.

_____. *Criminal Psychology.* Philadelphia: J. B. Lippincott, 1974.

_____. *Delinquency, Crime and Differential Association.* The Hague, Neth.: Martinus Nijhoff, 1964.

_____, and McDermott, Robert A. *Diversion from the Juvenile Justice System.* Washington, D. C.: National Institute of Law Enforcement and Criminal Justice, 1974.

_____. *Organized Crime Task Force Report.* Washington, D. C.: U.S. Government Printing Office, 1967.

_____. *Other People's Money.* New York: Free Press, 1953.

_____ (ed.). *The Prison: Studies in Institutional Organization and Change.* New York: Holt, Rinehart & Winston, 1961.

_____. *Theft of the Nation.* New York: Harper & Row, 1969.

Cresson, Ernest. *Cent jours du sige la prefecture de police.* Paris: Plon-Nourrit, 1901.

Crew, Albert. *The Old Bailey.* London: Ivor Nicholson & Watson, 1933.

Crichton, Kyle S. *Law and Order, Ltd.: The Rousing Life of Elfego Baca of New Mexico.* Glorieta, N. M.: Rio Grande Press, 1928.

Crichton, Michael. *Terminal Man.* New York: Knopf, 1972.

Crichton, Robert. *The Great Impostor.* New York: Random House, 1959.

The Crime Avenged or Guiteau on the Gallows. New York: Richard K. Fox, 1882.

Crime Prevention Officers' Handbook. Santa Rosa, Calif.: California Crime Prevention Institute, 1978.

Crimes and Punishment. London: BPC Publishing, 1973.

Crimes and Victims: A Report on the Dayton-San Jose Pilot Survey of Victimization. Washington, D. C.: National Criminal Justice Information and Statistics Service, 1974.

The Criminal Investigation Process: A Dialogue on Research Findings. Washington, D. C.: National Institute of Law Enforcement and Criminal Justice, 1977.

Criminal Statistics, England and Wales. London: H. M. Stationery Office, 1950.

Criminal Victimization in the United States. National Criminal Justice Information and Statistics Service, annual volumes since 1973.

Criminal Victimization in the United States, 1973. A National Crime Survey Report. U. S. Department of Justice, Law Enforcement Assistance Administration. Washington, D. C.: U. S. Government Printing Office, 1976.

Criminal Victimization in the United States, A Comparison of 1973 and 1974 Findings. A National Crime Survey Report. Washington, D. C.: Government Printing Office, 1976.

Crisis at Columbia: Criminal Victimization in the United States, A Comparison of 1974 and 1975 Findings. National Crime Survey Report. Washington, D. C.: U.S. Government Printing Office, 1977.

Crispe, T.E. *Reminiscences of a K. C.* London: Methuen, 1909.

Critchley, M. (ed.). *The Trial of Neville George Clevely Heath.* London: Hodge, 1951.

_____, and James. P. D. *The Maul and the Pear Tree.* London: Constable, 1971.

Critchley, T. A. *The Conquest of Violence.* London: Constable, 1970.

_____. *A History of Police in England and Wales 1900-1966.* London: T. & A. Constable, 1967.

Crites, Laura (ed.). *The Female Offender.* Lexington, Mass.: D. C. Heath, 1976.

Critical Reactions to the Warren Report. New York: Marzani & Munsell, 1965.

Crittenden, Henry Huston. *The Crittenden Memoirs.* New York: Putnam, 1936.

Crocker, W. C. *Far From Humdrum: A Lawyer's Life.* London: Hutchinson, 1967.

Crockett, Albert Stevens. *Peacocks on Parade.* New York: Sears, 1931.

Crockett, George Louis. *Two Centuries in East Texas.* Dallas: Southwest Press, 1932.

Croffut, W. A. *The Vanderbilts, and the Story of Their Fortune.* New York: Belford, Clarke, 1886.

Croker, John W. *The Croker Papers. The Correspondence and Diaries of the Late Right Honourable J. W. Croker.* 3 vols. London: John Murray, 1885.

Croker, Richard. *Some Things Richard Croker Has Said and Done.* New York: City Club of New York, 1901.

Croly, David G. *Seymour and Blair: Their Lives and Services.* New York: Richardson, 1868.

Croly, H.A. *Marcus Alonzo Hanna.* New York: Macmillan, 1912.

Cromer, Earl of. *Modern Egypt.* 2 vols. London: Macmillan, 1908.

Cromie, Robert, and Pinkston, Joseph. *Dillinger, A Short and Violent Life.* New York: McGraw-Hill, 1962.

Cromwell, Helen, and Dougherty, Robert. *Dirty Helen.* Los Angeles: Sherbourne Press, 1966.

Cromwell, John Wesley. *The Negro in American History.* New York: Johnson Reprints, 1968.

Cronin, Bernard Cornelius. *Father Yorke and the Labor Movement in San Francisco, 1900-1910.* Washington, D. C.: Catholic University of America Press, 1943.

Cronin, Harley. *The Screw Turns.* London: Long, 1967.

Cronin, Thomas E., et al. *U. S. v. Crime in the Streets.* Bloomington: Indiana University Press, 1981.

Cronon, E. David (ed.). *The Cabinet Diaries of Josephus Daniels: 1913-1921.* Lincoln: University of Nebraska Press, 1963.

Crook, G. T., and Rayner, John L. (eds.). *The Complete Newgate Calendar.* London: Navarre Society, 1926.

Crook, Wilfred H. *The General Strike.* Chapel Hill: University of North Carolina, 1931.

_____. *Memories of the White House.* Boston: Little, Brown, 1911.

_____. *Through Five Administrations.* New York: Harper & Brothers, 1907.

Crosby, A. W. *America, Russia, Hemp and Napoleon.* Columbus: Ohio State University Press, 1965.

Crosby, Caresse. *The Passionate Years.* Carbondale: Southern Illinois University Press, 1968.

Cross, A. R. N. *Punishment, Prison and the Public.* London: Stevens & Sons, 1971.

Cross, Colin. *The Fall of the British Empire, 1918-1968.* New York: Coward-McCann, 1968.

Cross, Ira Brown. *Financing an Empire.* 4 vols. Chicago: S.J. Clarke, 1927.

_____. *A History of the Labor Movement in California.* Berkeley: University of California Press, 1935.

Cross, R. *The English Sentencing System.* London: Butterworth, 1971.

_____. *Evidence.* London: Butterworth, 1958.

_____, and Jones, P. A. *An Introduction to Criminal Law.* London: Butterworth, 1959.

_____. *Precedent in English Law.* Oxford, Eng.: Clarendon, 1968.

Cross, Roger. *The Yorkshire Ripper.* London: Granada, 1981.

Cross, S. H. *Slavic Civilization through the Ages.* Cambridge, Mass.: Harvard University Press, 1948.

Crosskey, W. C. S. *The Single Fingerprint Identification System.* San Francisco: Privately Printed, 1923.

Crossman, Richard (ed.). *The God That Failed.* New York: Bantam, 1954.

_____. *Palestine Mission.* New York: Harper, 1947.

Crosthwait, William L., and Fisher, Ernest G. *The Last Stitch.* Philadelphia: J. B. Lippincott, 1956.

Crotty, William J. (ed.). *Assassination and the Political Order.* New York: Harper & Row, 1972.

Crouch, Nathaniel. *The Kingdom of Darkness.* London: A. Bettesworth, 1738.

Crouse, Russel. *It Seems Like Yesterday.* Garden City, N. Y.: Doubleday, Doran, 1931.

_____. *Murder Won't Out.* Garden City, N. Y.: Doubleday, Doran, 1932.

_____. *Twelve Unsolved New York Murders.* Garden City, N. Y.: Doubleday, Doran, 1936.

Crow, Carl. *Foreign Devils in the Flowery Kingdom.* New York: Harper, 1940.

_____. *400 Million Customers.* New York: Harper, 1937.

_____ (ed.). *Japan's Dream of World Empire: The Tanaka Memorial.* New York: Harper & Brothers, 1942.

Crow, Duncan. *The Victorian Woman.* London: Allen & Unwin, 1972.

Crow, W. B. *A History of Magic, Witchcraft, and Occultism.* London: Aquarian, 1968.

Crowe, Pat. *Pat Crowe, His Story, Confession and Reformation.* New York: G.W. Dillingham, 1906.

_____. *Spreading Evil.* New York: Branwell, 1927.

Crowell, Chester Theodore. *Liquor, Loot and Ladies.* New York: Knopf, 1930.

Crowley, Aleister. *The Book of Thoth.* New York: Lancer Books, 1971.

_____. *The Confessions of Aleister Crowley: An Autobiography.* London: Cape, 1969.

_____. *Diary of a Drug Fiend.* London: William Collins Sons, 1922.

Crowley, James B. *Japan's Quest for Autonomy: National Security and Foreign Policy 1930-1938.* Princeton, N. J.: Princeton University Press, 1966.

Croy, Homer. *Corn Country.* New York: Duell, Sloan & Pearce, 1947.

_____. *He Hanged Them High.* New York: Duell, Sloan & Pearce, 1952.

_____. *Jesse James Was My Neighbor.* New York: Duell, Sloan & Pearce, 1949.

_____. *Last of the Great Outlaws: The Story of Cole Younger.* New York: Duell, Sloan & Pearce, 1956.

_____. *Trigger Marshal: The Story of Chris Madden.* New York: Duell, Sloan & Pearce, 1958.

Crozier, Brian (ed.). *Annual of Power and Conflict.* London: Institute for the Study of Conflict, 1976.

_____. *Strategy of Survival.* New Rochelle, N. Y.: Arlington House, 1978.

Crozier, Emmet. *Yankee Reporters, 1861-65.* New York: Oxford University Press, 1956.

Crozier, Frank P. *Ireland Forever!* London: Cape, 1932.

_____. *The Men I Killed.* New York: Doubleday, Doran, 1938.

Crozier, R. H. *The Bloody Junta.* Little Rock, Ark.: Woodruff & Blocher, 1869.

Cruickshanks, Eveline. *The Stuart Court in Exile and the Jacobites.* London: Hambledon Press, 1995.

Crum, Bartley. *Behind the Silken Curtain.* New York: Simon & Schuster, 1947.

Crump, Irving, and Newton, John W. *Our G-Men.* New York: Dodd, Mead, 1937.

Cruz, Nicky. *Satan on the Loose.* Old Tappan, N. J.: Fleming H. Revell, 1973.

Cull, John G., and Hardy, Richard E. (eds.). *Types of Drug Abusers and Their Abuses.* Springfield, Ill.: Charles C. Thomas, 1970.

Cullen, Robert. *The Killer Department.* New York: Pantheon, 1993.

Cullen, Tom. *Autumn of Terror: Jack the Ripper, His Crimes and Times.* London: Bodley Head, 1965.

_____. *The Mild Murderer: The True Story of the Dr. Crippen Case.* Boston: Houghton Mifflin, 1977.

_____. *A Playful Panther: The Story of J. Maundy Gregory.* Boston: Houghton Mifflin, 1975.

_____. *When London Walked In Terror.* Boston: Houghton Mifflin, 1965.

Culpin, Howard. *The Newgate Noose.* London: Frederick Muller, Ltd. 1951.

Cumberland, Charles Curtis. *Mexican Revolution: The Constitutionalist Years.* Austin: University of Texas Press, 1974.

_____. *Mexican Revolution: Genesis Under Madero.* Austin: University of Texas Press, 1952.

_____. *Mexico: The Struggle for Modernity.* New York: Oxford University Press, 1968.

Cumming, Sir John (ed.). *Political India, 1832-1932.* New York: Oxford University Press, 1932.

Cummings, Homer, and McFarland, Carl. *Federal Justice: Chapters in the History of Justice in the Federal Executive.* New York: Da Capo, 1970.

_____. *Selected Papers.* New York: Scribner's, 1939.

Cummins, Jim. *Jim Cummins' Book.* Denver: Reed, 1903.

_____. *Jim Cummins the Guerrilla.* Excelsior Springs, Mo.: The *Daily Journal*, 1908.

Cummins, Harold, and Midlo, Charles. *Finger Prints, Palms and Soles.* New York: Dover Publications, 1961.

Cunha, W. de B. *Eight Centuries of Portuguese Monarchy: A Political Study.* London: Stephen Swift, 1911.

Cunliffe, Marcus. *The Age of Expansion: 1848-1917.* Springfield, Mass.: G. and C. Merriam, 1973.

_____. *Soldiers & Civilians: The Martial Spirit in America, 1775-1865.* Boston: Little, Brown, 1968.

Cunningham, Barry, Pearl, and Mike. *Mr. District Attorney.* New York: Mason/Sharter, 1977.

Cunningham, Eugene. *Famous in the West.* El Paso, Texas: Hicks-Haywood, 1926.

_____. *Triggernometry: A Gallery of Gunfighters.* New York: Press of the Pioneers, 1934.

Cunningham, James Charles. *The Truth About Murietta: Anecodotes and Facts Related by Those Who Knew Him and Disbelieve His Capture.* Los Angeles: Wetzel, 1938.

Cunningham, Robert E. *Trial by Mob.* Stillwater, Okla.: Redland Press, 1957.

Cupta, Manmathnat. *History of the Indian Revolutionist Movement.* Bombay: Somaiya Publications, 1972.

Curbing the Repeat Offender: A Strategy for Prosecutors. Washington, D. C.: Institute for Law and Social Research, 1977.

Curley, James Michael. *I'd Do It Again.* Englewood Cliffs, N. J.: Prentice-Hall, 1957.

Curling, J. *Janus Weathercock: The Life of Thomas Griffiths Wainewright.* New York: Nelson, 1938.

Curran, Henry H. *Pillar to Post.* New York: Scribner's, 1941.

Curran, James, Boyce, George, and Wingate, Pauline (eds.). *Newspaper History.* London: Constable, 1978.

Current, Richard N., et al. *American History: A Survey.* New York: Knopf, 1975.

Currey, J. Seymour. *Chicago: Its History and Builders.* 5 vols. Chicago: S. J. Clarke, 1912.

Curry, J. C. *The Indian Police.* London: Faber & Faber, 1935.

Curry, Jesse. *Personal JFK Assassination File.* Dallas: American Poster and Printing, 1969.

Curry, Leroy A. *The Ku Klux Klan under the Searchlight.* Kansas City, Mo.: Western Baptist, 1924.

Curry, Richard O. (ed.). *The Abolitionists: Reformers or Fanatics?* New York: Holt, Rinehart & Winston, 1965.

_____. *The Mongols: A History.* Boston: Little, Brown, 1908.

Curtin, Philip (Marie Belloc-Lowndes). *Noted Murder Mysteries.* London: Simpkin, Marshall, Hamilton, Kent, 1914.

Curtin, Philip D. *Africa Remembered: Narratives by West Africans from the Era of the Slave Trade.* Madison: University of Wisconsin Press, 1967.

Curtis, Lynn A. *Criminal Violence: National Patterns and Behavior.* Lexington, Mass.: D. C. Heath, 1974.

_____. *Violence, Race, and Culture.* Lexington, Mass.: D. C. Heath, 1975.

Curtiss, Arthur F. *The Law of Arson.* Buffalo, N. Y.: Dennis, 1936.

Curtiss, John S. *Church and State in Russia: The Last Years of the Empire, 1900-1917.* New York: Columbia University Press, 1940.

_____. *The Russian Army Under Nicholas I (1825-1855).* Durham, N. C.: Duke University Press, 1965.

_____. *The Russian Church and Soviet State, 1917-1950.* Boston: Little, Brown, 1953.

_____. *The Russian Revolutions of 1917.* Princeton, N. J.: Van Nostrand, 1957.

Curzon, Sam. *Legs Diamond.* New York: Tower, 1962.

Cushing, Marshall. *The Story of Our Post Office.* Boston: A. N. Thayer, 1893.

Cust, Sir Lionel. *King Edward and His Court: Some Reminiscences.* London: Murray, 1930.

Custine, Astolphe L. L. *The Empire of the Czar.* London: Longmans, 1843.

Cuthbert, C. R. M. *Science and the Detection of Crime.* New York: Philosophical Lib., 1958.

Cuthbert, Norma B. (ed.). *Lincoln and the Baltimore Plot 1861.* San Marino, Calif.: Huntington Library, 1949.

Cutler, James E. *Lynch-Law: An Investigation into the History of Lynching in the United States.* New York: Longmans, Green, 1905.

Cutler, R. B. *Seventy-Six Seconds in Dealey Plaza.* Manchester, Mass.: Cutler Designs, 1978.

Cutrera, Antonio. *La Mafia e i mafiosi: origini e manifestazioni studio di sociologia criminale.* Palermo, Italy: Alberto Reber, 1900.

Cutright, Paul Russell. *Lewis and Clark: Pioneering Naturalists.* Urbana: University of Illinois Press, 1969.

Cuyler, Jacob S. *Trial of Reuben Dunbar for the Murder of Stephen V. Lester and David L. Lester.* Albany, N. Y.: P. L. Gilbert, 1850.

Dabney, Virginius. *Dry Messiah: The Life of Bishop James Cannon, Jr.* New York: Alfred A. Knopf, 1949.

Dacus, Joseph A. *Life and Adventures of Frank and Jesse James, the Noted Western Outlaws.* St. Louis: N.D. Thompson, 1880.

_____. *Illustrated Lives and Adventures of Frank and Jesse James and the Younger Brothers, The Noted Western Outlaws.* St. Louis: N.D. Thompson, 1882.

Daggett, Mabel Potter. *Marie of Roumania.* New York: George H. Doran, 1926.

Daggett, Stuart. *Chapters on the History of the Southern Pacific.* New York: Ronald Press, 1922.

Daggett, Thomas F. *The Outlaw Brothers, Frank and Jesse James.* New York: Richard K. Fox, Police Gazette, 1881.

D'Agostini, Bruno. *Colloqui con Rachele Mussolini.* Rome: OET, 1946.

Dahlberg, Angela. *Air Rage: The Underestimated Safety Risk.* Burlington, Vermont: Ashgate Publishing Company, 2001.

Dahlberg, Jane. *The New York Bureau of Municipal Research: Pioneer in Government Administration.* New York: New York University Press, 1966.

Dahlinger, John Cote. *The Secret Life of Henry Ford.* New York: Bobbs-Merrill, 1978.

Dahmer, Lionel. *A Father's Story.* New York: Morrow, 1994.

Dahrendorf, Ralf. *Class and Class Conflicts in Industrial Society.* Stanford: Stanford University Press, 1959.

Daigon, Arthur. *Violence U.S.A.* New York: Bantam, 1975.

Dale, Edward Everett. *Cow Country.* Norman: University of Oklahoma Press, 1965.

_____, and Lytton, Gaston. *Cherokee Cavaliers.* Norman: University of Oklahoma Press, 1939.

_____, and Wardell, Morris L. *History of Oklahoma.* New York: Prentice-Hall, 1948.

Dale, Henry. *Adventures and Exploits of the Younger Brothers, Missouri's Most Daring Outlaws, and Companions of the James Boys.* New York: Street & Smith, 1890.

Daley, Robert. *Prince of the City.* Boston: Houghton Mifflin, 1978.

_____. *Target Blue.* New York: Dell, 1971.

_____. *The Year of the Dragon.* New York: Signet Books, 1981.

Dallas, Gregor. *At the Heart of the Tiger: Clemenceau and His World.* New York: Carroll & Grat, 1993.

Dallin, Alexander. *German Rule in Russia, 1941-1945.* New York: Macmillan, 1957.

d'Alquen, Gunter. *Die SS, Geschichte, Aufgabe und Organisation der Schutzstaffel der NSDAP.* Berlin: Junker & Dnnhaupt, 1939.

Dalton, Emmett. *Beyond the Law.* New York: J.S. Ogilvie, 1918.

_____. *The Dalton Brothers and Their Astounding Career of Crime.* New York: Frederick Fell, 1954.

_____, and Jungmeyer, Jack. *When the Daltons Rode.* Garden City, N.Y.: Doubleday, Doran, 1931.

Dalton, Kit. *Under the Black Flag.* Memphis, Tenn.: Lockhart, 1914.

Dalton, Michael. *Country Justice.* London: Society of Stationers, 1618.

Dalyell, Sir John Graham. *The Darker Superstitions of Scotland.* Edinburgh, Scot.: Waugh and Innes, 1834.

Damio, Ward. *Urge to Kill.* New York: Pinnacle, 1974.

Damore, Leo. *The Crime of Dorothy Sheridan.* New York: Arbor House, 1978.

_____. *In His Garden.* New York: Arbor House, 1981.

Dana, James. *The Intent of Capital Punishment: A Discourse.* New Haven, Conn.: T.& S. Green, 1790.

Dana, Julian. *A.P. Giannini: A Giant in the West.* New York: Prentice-Hall, 1947.

Dana, J.G. *The Man Who Built San Francisco.* New York: Macmillan, 1937.

_____, and Thomas, R.S. *A Report of the Trial of Jereboam O. Beauchamp.* Frankfort, Ky.: Albert G. Hodges, 1826.

_____. *Sutter of California.* New York: Halcyon House, 1938.

Dana, Richard Henry. *Two Years Before the Mast.* New York: Modern Library, 1936.

Dancy, J.C. *A Commentary on I Maccabees.* Oxford, Eng.: Basil Blackwell, 1954.

Dando, S. *The Japanese Law of Criminal Procedure.* trans. F.J. George. South Hackensack, N.J.: F.B. Rothman, 1965.

Dandolo, Tullio. *La Signiora di Monza e le Streghe del Tirolo, processi famosi des secolo decimosettimo.* Milan, Italy: E. Besozzi, 1855.

Daneau, Lambert. *Les Sorciers.* Geneva, Switz.: I. Bourgeois, 1574.

Danelski, David J., and Tulchin, Joseph S. (eds.). *The Autobiographical Notes of Charles Evans Hughes.* Cambridge, Mass.: Harvard University Press, 1973.

d'Anethan, Baroness E.M. *Fourteen Years of Diplomatic Life in Japan.* New York: McBride, Mast, 1912.

Danforth, Harold R., and Horan, James D. *The D.A.'s Man.* New York: Crown, 1957.

Dangerfield, George. *The Awakening of American Nationalism 1815-1828.* New York: Harper & Row, 1965.

_____. *Era of Good Feelings.* New York: Harcourt, Brace, 1952.

Daniels, Jonathan. *The Devil's Backbone.* New York: McGraw-Hill, 1962.

_____. *Frontier on the Potomac.* New York: Macmillan, 1946.

_____. *Prince of Carpetbaggers.* Philadelphia: Lippincott, 1958.

_____. *The Time Between the Wars: Armistice to Pearl Harbor.* Garden City, N.Y.: Doubleday, 1966.

Daniels, Josephus. *The Wilson Era: Years of Peace, 1910-1917.* Chapel Hill: University of North Carolina Press, 1944.

Daniels, Les. *Living in Fear: A History of Horror in the Mass Media.* New York: De Capo Press, 1983.

Daniels, Robert (ed.). *A Documentary History of Communism.* New York: Random House, 1960.

Daniels, Robert V. *The Conscience of the Revolution.* Cambridge, Mass.: Harvard University Press, 1960.

_____. *Red October: The Bolshevik Revolution of 1917.* New York: Charles Scribner's Sons, 1965.

Dansette, Adrian. *L'Attentat d'Orsini.* Paris: Editions Mondiales, 1964.

_____. *Louis-Napoleon la conquete du pouvoir.* Paris: Hachette, 1961.

The Dansville Poisoning Case. Dansville, N.Y.: George A. Sanders, 1858.

Danto, B.L., et al. *The Human Side of Homicide.* New York: Columbia University Press, 1982.

Dantwalala, M.L. *Gandhism Reconsidered.* Bombay, India: Padma Publications, 1944.

Da Orta, G. *Colloquies on the Simples and Drugs of India.* London: Henry Southern, 1913.

Daraul, Arkon. *A History of Secret Societies.* New York: Pocket Books, 1969.

Darby, Ada Claire. *"Show Me" Missouri.* Kansas City: Burton, 1938.

D'Arcy, William. *The Fenian Movement in the United States, 1858-1886.* Washington, D.C.: Catholic University Press, 1947.

D'Aroma, Nino. *Mussolini segreto.* Bologna, Italy: Cappelli, 1957.

Darrow, Clarence. *Crime, Its Cause and Treatment.* New York: Thomas Y. Crowell, 1922.

_____. *Crime and Criminals.* Chicago: Charles H. Kerr, 1902.

_____, and Yarros, V.S. *The Prohibition Mania.* New York: Boni & Liveright, 1927.

_____. *The Story of My Life.* New York: Charles Scribner's Sons, 1932.

_____. *Verdicts Out of Court.* Chicago: Quadrangle, 1963.

Dartnell, Michael Y. *Action Directe; Ultra Left Terrorism in France, 1979-1987.* New York: Frank Cass & Co., 1995.

Darwin, Charles. *The Descent of Man, and Selection in Relation to Sex.* New York: D. Appleton, 1876.

Dash, S., et al. *The Eavesdroppers.* New Brunswick, N.J.: Rutgers University Press, 1959.

Datta, Dhirendra M. *The Philosophy of Mahatma Gandhi.* Madison: University of Wisconsin Press, 1961.

Daughen, Joseph R., and Binzen, Peter. *The Cop Who Would Be King.* Boston: Little, Brown, 1977.

Daugherty, Harry M. *The Inside Story of the Harding Tragedy.* New York: Churchill, 1932.

Davenport, E.H., and Cooke, Sidney Russell. *The Oil Trusts and Anglo-American Relations.* New York: Macmillan, 1924.

Davenport, Guiles. *Zaharoff: High Priest of War.* Boston: Lothrop, Lee and Shepard, 1934.

Davenport, Jacob. *The Witches of Huntingdon.* London: R. Clutterbuck, 1646.

Davenport, John I. *The Election and the Naturalization Frauds in New York City, 1860-1870.* New York: n.p., 1894.

David, Andrew. *Famous Criminal Trials.* Minneapolis, Minn.: Lerner Publications, 1979.

David, David Brian. *The Problem of Slavery in Western Culture.* Ithaca, N.Y.: Cornell University Press, 1966.

_____. *The Slave Power Conspiracy and the Paranoid Style.* Baton Rouge: Louisiana State University Press, 1970.

David, Henry. *The History of the Haymarket Affair.* New York: Farrar & Rinehart, 1936.

David, Jay. *The Scarsdale Murder.* New York: Leisure Books, 1980.

_____ (ed.). *The Weight of the Evidence.* New York: Meredith Press, 1968.

David, Rene, and Brierley, John E.C. *Major Legal Systems in the World Today.* New York: Free Press, 1978.

David, Robert B. *Malcolm Campbell, Sheriff.* Casper, Wyo.: Wyomingana, 1932.

Davidoff, Leonore. *The Best Circles.* London: Croom Helm, 1973.

Davidson, B. *The People's Cause: A History of Guerillas in Africa.* London: Longman, 1981.

Davidson, Bill. *Collura.* New York: Simon & Schuster, 1977

_____. *To Keep and Bear Arms.* Boulder, Colo.: SIB, 1979.

Davidson, Eugene. *The Making of Adolf Hitler.* New York: Macmillan, 1977.

_____. *The Nuremberg Fallacy.* New York: Macmillan, 1973.

_____. *The Trial of the Germans.* New York: Macmillan, 1966.

Davidson, Marion. *Making It Legal.* New York: McGraw-Hill, 1979.

Davidson, R. Theodore. *Chicano Prisoners: The Key to San Quentin.* New York: Holt, Rinehart & Winston, 1974.

Davidson, Terry. *Conjugal Crime.* New York: Hawthorn, 1978.

Davidson, Thomas Douglas. *Rowan Tree and Red Thread.* Edinburgh, Scot.: Oliver and Boyd, 1949.

Davidson-Houston, J.V. *Russia and China From the Huns to Mao Tse-tung.* London: Robert Hale, 1960.

Davies, Hunter (ed.). *The New London Spy.* London: Blond, 1967.

_____, et al. *Further Studies of Female Offenders.* London: HMSO, 1976.

Davies, J., and Goodman, N. *Girl Offenders Aged 17 to 20 Years.* London: HMSO, 1972.

Davies, James C. *When Men Revolt And Why.* New York: Free Press, 1969.

Davies, John D. *Phrenology, Fad and Science.* New Haven, Conn.: Yale University Press, 1955.

Davis A., and Dollard, J. *Children of Bondage.* Washington, D.C.: American Council on Education, 1940.

Davis, Allen F. *American Heroine: The Life and Legend of Jane Addams.* New York: Oxford University Press, 1973.

_____, and Haller, Mark H. (eds.). *The Peoples of Philadelphia.* Philadelphia: Temple University Press, 1973.

_____. *Spearheads for Reform.* New York: Oxford University Press, 1967.

Davis, Bernice Freeman. *Assignment San Quentin.* London: Peter Davies, 1962.

_____, and Hirschberg, Al. *The Desperate and the Damned.* New York: Thomas Y. Crowell, 1961.

Davis, Judge Charles G. *The Conduct of the Law in the Borden Case.* Boston: Boston Daily Advertiser, 1893.

_____. *Report of the Trial of Samuel M. Andrews.* New York: Hurd & Houghton, 1869.

Davis, Christopher. *Waiting For It.* New York: Harper & Row, 1980.

Davis, Don. *Death Cruise.* New York: St. Martin's Press, 1996.

_____. *Death of an Angel.* New York: St. Martin's Press, 1994.

_____. *The Milwaukee Murders.* New York: St. Martin's, 1991.

Davis, Elmer. *But We were Born Free.* Indianapolis, Ind.: Bobbs-Merrill, 1954.

_____. *History of the New York Times, 1851-1921.* New York: New York Times, 1921.

Davis, F. James, and Stivers, Richard (eds.). *The Collective Definition of Deviance.* New York: The Free Press, 1975.

Davis, Forrest, and Lindley, Ernest K. *How War Came: An American White Paper from the Fall of France to Pearl Harbor.* New York: Simon and Schuster, 1942.

Davis, Hamilton E. *Mocking Justice.* New York: Crown, 1978.

Davis, John H. *The Bouviers.* New York: Farrar, Straus & Giroux, 1969.

_____. *The Kennedys: Dynasty and Disaster.* New York: McGraw-Hill, 1984.

Davis, John H. *Mafia Kingfish: Carlos Marcello and the Assassination of John F. Kennedy.* New York: McGraw-Hill, 1989.
Davis, Kenneth C. *Discretionary Justice.* Baton Rouge: Louisiana State University Press, 1969.
_____. *Discretionary Justice in Europe and America.* Urbana: University of Illinois Press, 1976.
_____. *Police Discretion.* St. Paul, Minn.: West, 1975.
Davis, Kenneth S. *FDR: The Beckoning of Destiny, 1882-1928.* New York: G.P. Putnam's Sons, 1971.
The Hero: Charles A. Lindbergh and the American Dream. Garden City, N.Y.: Doubleday, 1959.
Davis, Marc, and Matthews, Jim. *Highlights of the Warren Report.* Los Angeles: Associated Professional Services, 1964.
Davis, Nathaniel. *The Last Two Years of Salvador Allende.* Ithaca, N. Y.: Cornell University Press, 1985.
Davis, Paul K., and Jenkins, Brian Michael, and King, Stephen M. *Deterrence and Influence in Counterterrorism: A Component in the War on Al Qaeda.* New York: Rand Corporation, 2002.
Davis, Reuben. *Recollections of Mississippi and the Mississippians.* Boston: Houghton Mifflin, 1889.
Davis, Susan Lawrence. *Authentic History: Ku Klux Klan, 1865-1877.* New York: American Library Service, 1924.
Davis, W.W.H. *El Gringo: Or New Mexico and Her People.* Santa Fe, N.M.: Rydal Press, 1938.
Davis, W. Hardy. *Aiming for the Jugular in New Orleans.* Port Washington, N.Y.: Ashley Books, 1976.
Davison, Jean. *Oswald's Game.* New York: W.W. Norton, 1983.
Davison, M. H. Armstrong. *The Casket Letters.* Washington, D.C.: University of Washington Press, 1965.
Davison, R.H. *Reform in the Ottoman Empire, 1856-1876.* Princeton, N.J.: Princeton University Press, 1963.
Davitt, Michael. *The Fall of Feudalism in Ireland.* London: Harper, 1919.
Dawdley, David. *A Nation of Lords: An Autobiography of the Vice Lords.* Garden City, N.Y.: Doubleday/Anchor Books, 1973.
Dawes, C.R. *The Marquis de Sade: His Life and Works.* London: Holdern, 1927.
Dawson, John D. (ed.). *American State Trials.* St. Louis: Thomas Law, 1923.
Dawson, John P. *A History of Lay Judges.* Cambridge, Mass.: Harvard University Press, 1960.
Dawson, Raymond. *The Chinese Chameleon.* London: Oxford University Press, 1967.
Dawson, Robert MacGregor. *William Lyon Mackenzie King.* London: Methuen, 1959.
Dawson, Robert O. *Sentencing.* Boston: Little, Brown, 1969.
Dawson, William Harbut. *The German Empire, 1867-1914, and the Unity Movement.* London: George Allen & Unwin, 1919.
Day, Donald. *Will Rogers: A Biography.* New York: David McKay, 1962.
Day, Oscar F.G. *The Ging Murder and the Great Hayward Trial.* Minneapolis: Minnesota Tribune, 1895.
Dayan, Moshe. *The Story of My Life.* London: Weidenfeld & Nicolson, 1976.
Dayton, Frederick E. *Steamboat Days.* New York: Stokes, 1947.
Deacon, John, and Walker, John. *Dialogical Discourses of Spirits and Devils.* London: G. Bishop, 1601.
_____. *A Summary Answer.* London: G. Bishop, 1601.
Deacon, Richard. *The Chinese Secret Service.* New York: Taplinger, 1972.
_____. *A History of the British Secret Service.* New York: Taplinger, 1969.
_____. *A History of the Russian Secret Service.* London: Muller, 1972.
_____. *Kempei Tai: The Japanese Secret Service, Then and Now.* Boston: Charles E. Tuttle, 1990.
de Acosta, Mercedes. *Here Lies the Heart.* New York: Reynal, 1960.
Deakin, F.W. *The Brutal Friendship.* New York: Anchor Books, 1966.
_____, and Storry, G.W. *The Case of Richard Sorge.* New York: Friends of the Soviet Union, 1935.
_____. *The Six Hundred Days of Mussolini.* New York: Anchor Books, 1966.
Deale, Kenneth E.L. *Beyond Any Reasonable Doubt.* Dublin, Ire.: Gill & Macmillan, 1971.
_____. *Memorable Irish Trials.* London: Constable, 1960.
Dean, Henry Clay. *Crimes of the Civil War.* Baltimore: William T. Smithson, 1868.
Dean, John W. *Blind Ambition.* New York: Simon & Shuster, 1976.
_____. *The Indiana Torture Slaying.* Chicago: Beeline Books, 1967.
Dean, Stanley R. (ed.). *Psychiatry and Mysticism.* Chicago: Nelson-Hall, 1975.
Dean, Vera Micheles. *Fascist Rule in Italy.* London: Nelson, 1934.
Deane, John R. *The Strange Alliance.* New York: Viking Press, 1946.
Deans, R. Story. *Notable Trials: Difficult Cases.* London: Chapman & Hall, 1932.
Dearden, Harold. *Aspects of Murder.* London: Staples Press, 1951.
_____. *Death Under a Microscope.* London: Hutchinson, 1934.
_____. *The Mind of the Murderer.* London: Geoffrey Bles, 1930.
_____. *Queer People.* London: Hutchinson, 1935.
_____. *Some Cases of Sir Bernard Spilsbury and Others.* London: Hutchinson, 1934.
Dearden, R.L. *The Autobiography of a Crook.* New York: Dial Press, 1925.
The Dearing Tragedy. Philadelphia: C.W. Alexander, 1866.
Dearment, Robert K. *Bat Masterson: The Man and the Legend.* Norman: University of Oklahoma Press, 1979.
DeBary, W.T., Jr. (ed.). *Sources of Chinese Tradition.* New York: Columbia University Press, 1960.
de Beaumont, Gustave, and de Tocqueville, Alexis. *On the Penitentiary System in the United States and Its Application in France.* Carbondale: Southern Illinois University Press, 1964.
Debray, Rgis. *Che's Guerrilla War.* London: Penguin Books, 1975.
_____. *Revolution in the Revolution.* New York: Grove Press, 1967.
_____. *Strategy for a Revolution: Essays on Latin America.* New York: Monthly Review, 1970.
De Camp, L. Sprague. *The Great Monkey Trial.* New York: Garden, 1968.
_____. *Lost Continents.* New York: Dover, 1970.
De Castro, J.P. *The Gordon Riots.* London: Oxford University Press, 1926.
Decker, Peter R. *Fortunes and Failures.* Cambridge, Mass.: Harvard University Press, 1978.
Dedijer, Vladmir. *The Road to Sarajevo.* New York: Simon & Schuster, 1966.
Dedmon, Emmett. *Fabulous Chicago.* New York: Random House, 1953.
Dee. D. *Lowdown on Calamity Jane.* Rapid City, S.D.: Rapid City Guide, 1932.
Deeley, Peter. *The Manhunters.* London: Hodder & Stoughton, 1970.
_____, and Walker, Christopher. *Murder in the 4th Estate.* New York: McGraw-Hill, 1971.
_____. *Mussolini: Man of Destiny.* London: J.M. Dent, 1928.
Defoe, Daniel. *The Anatomy of Change-Alley.* London: E. Smith, 1719.
_____. *A General History of the Robberies and Murders of the Most Notorious Pirates, 1717-1724.* Columbia: University of South Carolina Press, 1972.
_____. *History of the Devil.* London: T. Warner, 1726.
de Ford, Miriam Allen. *Murderers Sane & Mad!* New York: Abelard-Schuman, Ltd., 1965.
_____. *The Real Ma Barker.* New York: Ace, 1970.
_____. *Stone Walls.* Philadelphia: Chilton Books, 1962.
_____. *They Were San Franciscans.* Boise, Idaho: Caxton Printers, 1947.
DeFrancis, Vincent. *Protecting the Child Victim of Sex Crimes Committed by Adults.* Denver: The American Humane Society, 1969.
DeFranco, Edward J. *Anatomy of a Scam: A Case Study of a Planned Bankruptcy by Organized Crime.* Washington, D.C.: U.S. Government Printing Office, 1973.
De Givry, E.G. *Illustrated Anthology of Sorcery, Magic and Alchemy.* New York: Causeway Books, 1973.
_____. *Witchcraft, Magic & Alchemy.* Boston: Houghton Mifflin, 1931.
de Grunwald, H. *Peter the Great.* trans. Viola Garvin. New York: Macmillan, 1956.
de Guistino, David. *Conquest of Mind, Phrenology and Victorian Social Thought.* London: Croom Helm, 1975.
Dehn, Lili. *The Real Tsaritsa.* London: Thornton Butterworth, 1922.
Deighton, Len. *London Dossier.* London: Cape, 1967.
Deindorfer, Robert G. *The Spies.* New York: Fawcett, 1949.
Deiss, Joseph Jay. *Captains of Fortune: Profiles of Six Italian Condottieri.* New York: Thomas Y. Crowell, 1967.
DeJonge, Alex. *The Life and Times of Grigori Rasputin.* New York: Coward, McCann & Geoghegan, 1982.
Dekel, Efraim. *Shai: Exploits of Haganah Intelligence.* London: Yoseloff, 1959.
Deladurantey, J., and Sullivan D. *Criminal Investigation Standards.* New York: Harper & Row, 1980.
Delano, Anthony. *Slip-up.* New York: Quadrangle, 1975.
Delaney, John P. *The Blue Devils in Italy.* Washington, D.C.: Infantry Journal Press, 1947.
Delany, Ed, and Rice, M. T. *The Blood Stained Trail. A History of Militant Labor in the United States.* Seattle, Wash.: The Industrial Worker, 1927.
Delany, Edmund T. *New York's Greenwich Village.* Barre, Mass.: Barre Publishers, 1967.
Delarue, Jacques. *The History of the Gestapo.* trans. Marvyn Savill. London: Mcdonald, 1964.
De la Torre, Lillian. *Elizabeth Is Missing.* London: Michael Joseph, 1947.
_____. *Goodbye, Miss Lizzie Borden.* New York: Sheridan House, 1948.
_____. *The Truth About Belle Gunness.* New York: Gold Medal Books, 1955.
_____. *Villainy Detected.* London: D. Appleton-Century, 1947.
Delbene, Thomas. *De Officio Sanctae Inquisitionis Circa Haeresim.* Lyons, Fr.: Jaomis Antoni Hugueton, 1666.
De Leeuw, Hendrik. *Sinful Cities of the Western World.* New York: Julian Messner, Inc., 1938.
_____. *Underworld Story: The Rise of Organized Crime and Vice-rackets in the U.S.A.* New York: Burns MacEachern, 1955.
Delgado, James P. *Alcatraz Island: The Story Behind the Scenery.* San Francisco: KC Publications, 1985.
Delin, Bart. *The Sex Offender.* Boston: Beacon, 1978.
Dell, S. *Silent in Court.* London: Bell, 1971.
Dellin, L.A.D. (ed.). *Bulgaria.* New York: Mid-European Studies Center, 1957.
Dellinger, Dave. *More Power Than We Know.* New York: Anchor Press/Doubleday, 1975.
Delony, Lewis S. *40 Years a Peace Officer.* Abilene, Texas.: Published by Author, 1937.
Delord, Taxile. *Histoire du second empire.* 6 vols. Paris: Germer Baillire, 1869-75.
Delzwll, C.F. *Mussolini's Enemies.* Princeton, N.J.: Princeton University Press, 1961.
De Madariaga, Salvador. *Bolivar.* Coral Gables, Fla.: University of Miami Press: 1952.
_____. *Hernan Cortes: Conqueror of Mexico.* Coral Gables, Fla.: University of Miami Press, 1942.
Demaris, Ovid. *America the Violent.* New York: Cowles Book, 1970.
_____. *American Military History.* Washington, D.C.: U.S. Government Printing Office, 1956.
_____. *Brothers In Blood: The International Terrorist Network.* New York: Charles Scribner's Sons, 1977.
_____. *Captive City: Chicago in Chains.* New York: Lyle Stuart, 1969.
_____. *Dillinger.* New York: Tower, 1968.
_____. *The Dillinger Story.* Derby, Conn.: Monarch Books, 1961.
_____. *The Director: An Oral Biography of J. Edgar Hoover.* New York: Harper's Magazine Press, 1976.
_____. *Dirty Business.* New York: Harper's, 1974.
_____, and Reid, Ed. *The Green Felt Jungle.* New York: Trident Press, 1963.
_____. *The Last Mafioso: The Treacherous World of Jimmy Fratianno.* New York: Times Books, 1981.
_____. *The Lindbergh Kidnapping Case.* Derby, Conn.: Monarch, 1961.
_____. *Lucky Luciano.* Derby, Conn.: Monarch Books, 1960.
Demeter, Anna. *Legal Kidnapping.* Boston: Beacon Press, 1977.
Demeter, Karl. *The German Officer Corps.* trans. Angus Malcolm. London: Weidenfeld & Nicolson, 1965.

de Mille, Agnes. *Dance to the Piper.* New York: Grosset & Dunlap, 1952.

Deming, Richard. *Women: The New Criminals.* New York: Thomas Nelson, 1977.

Demos, John Putnam. *Entertaining Satan.* New York: Oxford University Press, 1982.

_____. *A Little Commonwealth.* New York: Oxford University Press, 1970.

Demosthenes. *The Crown, The Philippics, and Ten Other Orations.* trans. C. Rann Kennedy. New York: Everyman's Library, 1911.

Dempewolf, Richard. *Famous Old New England Murders.* Brattleboro, Vt.: Stephen Daye Press, 1942.

Denarques, Edmond. *Ravachol: Crimes Anarchistes.* Paris: Bernardin-Bechet, 1931.

De Nerval, G. *The Women of Cairo, Scenes of Life in the Orient.* New York: Harcourt & Brace, 1956.

DeNevi, Don. *Alcatraz "46".* San Rafael, Calif.: Leswing Press, 1974.

_____. *The Riddle of the Rock: The Only Successful Escape from Alcatraz.* Amherst, N. Y.: Prometheus Books, 1991.

Denfield, Duane. *Streetwise Criminology.* Cambridge, Mass.: Schenkman, 1974.

Denikin, Anton. *The Russian Turmoil.* London: Hutchinson, 1922.

_____. *The White Army.* London: Cape, 1930.

Denisoff, R. Serge, and McCaghy, Charles H. (eds.). *Deviance, Conflict, and Criminality.* Chicago: Rand McNally, 1973.

Denison, Merrill. *Klondike Mike.* New York: Morrow & Co., 1943.

Dennen, Leon. *White Guard Terrorists in the U.S.A.* New York: Friends of the Soviet Union, 1935.

Dennett, Tyler. *Americans in Eastern Asia.* New York: Macmillan, 1922.

Dennis, Anthony J. *Osama bin Laden: A Psychological and Political Profi*le. London: Wyndham Hall Press, 2002.

Dennis, Charles H. *Victor Lawson, His Time and His Work.* Chicago: University of Chicago Press, 1935.

Denson, R.B. *Destiny in Dallas.* Dallas: Denco, 1964.

Densmore, G.B. *The Chinese in California.* San Francisco: Pettit & Russ, 1880.

Denton, B.E. *A Two-Gun Cyclone.* Dallas: B.E. Denton, 1927.

Denton, Sally, and Morris, Roger. *The Money and the Power: The Making of Las Vegas and Its Hold on America, 1947-2000.* New York: Knopf, 2001.

Department of Health and Human Services. *For Patients Only: What You Need to Know About Marijuana.* Washington, D.C.: U.S. Government Printing Office, 1981.

_____. *Television and Behavior.* Washington, D.C.: U.S. Government Printing Office, 1982.

Department of Justice. *Report on the National Conference on Organized Crime.* Washington D.C.: U.S. Government Printing Office, 1975.

_____, and Department of Transportation. *Cargo Theft and Organized Crime.* Washington D.C.: U.S. Government Printing Office, 1972.

Departmental Committee on the Employment of Prisoners. *Department Committee on the Employment of Prisoners Report.* London: H.M. Stationery Office, 1933.

Depperman, W.H. *Shooter's Choice.* New York: World, 1952.

de Quille, Dan. *The Big Bonanza.* New York: Thomas Y. Crowell, 1947.

De Quincey, Thomas. *Confessions of an Opium Eater.* New York: American Library, 1966.

_______. *Miscellaneous Essays.* Boston: Ticknor, Reed, Fields, 1851.

de Quirs, C Bernaldo. *Modern Theories of Criminality.* Boston: Little, Brown, 1911.

Derby, Caroline Rosina. *Salem.* New York: Harper & Brothers, 1874.

deRhram, Edith. *How Could She Do That?* New York: Clarkson N. Potter, 1969.

Deriabin, Peter, and Gibney, Frank. *The Secret World.* Garden City, N.Y.: Doubleday, 1959.

De River, J. Paul. *Crime and the Sexual Psychopath.* Springfield, Ill.: Charles C. Thomas, 1968.

_____. *The Sexual Criminal: A Psychoanalytic Study.* Springfield, Ill.: Charles C. Thomas, 1950.

_____. *Watchdogs of Terror: Russian Bodyguards from the Tsars to the Commissars.* New Rochelle, N. Y.: Arlington House, 1972.

Derleth, August. *Wisconsin Murders.* Sauk City, Wis.: Mycroft & Moran, 1968.

Dermenghem, Emile. *The Life of Mohammed.* London: George Routledge & Sons, 1930.

De Roo, P. *Materials for a History of Alexander VI.* 5 vol. Bruges: Desclee, DeBrower, 1924.

Dershowitz, Alan M. *The Best Defense.* New York: Vintage Books, 1983.

_____. *Reversal of Fortune.* New York: Random House, 1986.

De Sade, Marquis. *The 120 Days of Sodom.* New York: Grove Press, 1966.

Desai, Mahadev. *Gandhi In Indian Villages.* Madras, India: S. Ganesan, 1928.

_____. *The Gita According to Gandhi.* Ahmedabad, India: Navajivan Publishing House, 1946.

_____. *A Righteous Struggle.* Ahmedabad, India: Navajivan Publishing House, 1951.

_____. *With Gandhi in Ceylon.* Madras, India: S. Ganesan, 1928.

Des Forges, Alison Liebhavsky. *Leave None to Tell the Story: Genocide in Rwanda.* New York: Human Rights Watch, 1999.

Desmond, Hugh. *Death Let Loose.* London: Wright & Brown, 1956.

_____. *A Scream in the Night.* London: Wright & Brown, 1955.

Desmond, Shaw. *The Drama of Sinn Fein.* New York: Charles Scribner's Sons, 1923.

De Sola, Ralph. *Crime Dictionary.* New York: Facts on File, 1982.

Despert, Louise J. *The Emotionally Disturbed Child.* New York: Doubleday Anchor, 1970.

Desprs, A. *La Prostitution en France.* Paris: J.B. Baillire et fils, 1883.

Destexhe, Alain. *Rwanda and Genocide in the 20th Century.* New York: University Press, 1996.

Destler, Chester McArthur. *Henry Demarest Lloyd and the Empire of Reform.* Philadelphia: University of Pennsylvania Press, 1963.

Dethloff, Henry C. (ed.). *Huey P. Long.* New York: Heath, 1967.

Dettlinger, Chet, with Prugh, Jeff. *The List.* Atlanta, Ga.: Philmay Enterprises, 1983.

Deutsch, Albert. *The Trouble With Cops.* New York: Crown Publishers, 1954.

Deutsch, Helene. *The Psychology of Women.* New York: Grune & Stratton, 1944.

Deutsch, Hermann B. *The Huey Long Murder Case.* New York: Doubleday, 1969.

Deutsch, Julius. *The Civil War in Austria.* New York: Socialist Party, 1934.

Deutscher, Isaac. *The Prophet Armed; Trotsky: 1879-1921.* New York: Oxford University Press, 1954.

_____. *The Prophet Outcast.* London: Oxford University Press, 1963.

_____. *The Prophet Unarmed.* New York: Oxford University Press, 1959.

_____. *Stalin: A Political Biography.* New York: Oxford University Press, 1949.

_____. *The Unfinished Revolution, Russia, 1917-1967.* New York: Oxford University Press, 1967.

Deutschmann, Paul J. *Communication and Change in Latin America.* New York: Frederick A. Praeger, 1968.

De Veny, William. *The Establishment of Law and Order on Western Plains.* Portland, Ore.: Optimist Print, 1915.

Devine, Philip E. *The Ethics of Homicide.* London: Cornell University Press, 1978.

Devji, Mantoshe Singh. *The Mad Massiah: Osama bin Laden and His Seeds of Terror.* New York: Inkwell Press, 2002.

Devlin, Patrick. *Easing the Passing.* London: Bodley Head, 1985.

_____. *The Enforcement of Morals.* London: Oxford University Press, 1965.

_____. *The Judge.* Chicago; University of Chicago Press 1981.

_____. *Trial by Jury.* London: Stevens, 1956.

DeVol, George. *Forty Years a Gambler on the Mississippi.* New York: Henry Holt, 1926.

Devol, Kenneth. *Mass Media and the Supreme Court.* New York: Hastings House, 1976.

Devonshire, R.L. *Rambles in Cairo.* Cairo, Egypt: Constable, 1917.

DeVoto, Bernard. *The Course of Empire.* Boston: Houghton Mifflin, 1952.

_____. *Mark Twain's America.* Boston: Little, Brown, 1932.

Devoy, John. *Recollections of an Irish Rebel.* New York: Chas. P. Young, 1929.1111

Dew, Walter. *I Caught Crippen.* London: Blackie & Son, 1938.

Dewar, Douglas. *Bygone Days in India.* London: John Lane, 1922.

_____. *In the Days of the Company.* Calcutta: Thacker, Spink, 1920.

Dewar, Hugo. *Assassins at Large.* Boston: Beacon Press, 1952.

Dewar, Michael. *Internal Security Weapons and Equipment of the World.* London: Ian Allan, 1979.

Dewes, Simon. *Doctors of Murder.* London: John Long, 1962.

Dewey, John. *The Case of Leon Trotsky, Preliminary Commission of Inquiry.* New York: Harper & Row, 1937.

_____. *Freedom and Culture.* New York: G.P. Putnam's Sons, 1939.

Dewey, Thomas E. *In the Two-Party System.* New York: Doubleday, 1966.

_____. *Twenty Against the Underworld.* Garden City, N.Y.: Doubleday, 1974.

Dewhurst, Jack. *Royal Confinements.* New York: St. Martin's Press, 1980.

DeWilde, J.C. *Building the Third Reich.* New York: Foreign Policy Association, 1939.

Dewitt, David Miller. *The Assassination of Abraham Lincoln and Its Expiation.* New York: Macmillan, 1909.

_____. *The Impeachment and Trial of Andrew Johnson.* Madison: State Historical Society of Wisconsin, 1967.

_____. *The Judicial Murder of Mary E. Surratt.* Baltimore: John Murphy, 1895.

De Wyss, M. *Rome Under The Terror.* London: Robert Hale, 1945.

Dexter, Walter (ed.). *The Letters of Charles Dickens, 1845-1847.* 3 vols. London: Nonesuch Press, 1938.

Dhawan, G.N. *The Political Philosophy of Mahatma Gandhi.* Ahmedabad, India: Navajivan Publishing House, 1951.

Diamond, Martin. *Socialism and the Decline of the American Socialist Party.* Chicago: University of Chicago Press, 1956.

Diamond, Sander A. *The Nazi Movement in the United States, 1924-1941.* Ithaca, N.Y.: Cornell University Press, 1974.

Diaz, Carlos Flix. *Genesis de la revolucion mexicana.* La Paz, Bolivia: Litografia Imprenta "Moderna," 1918.

Dibb, Djamabatan. *The Arab Bloc in the United Nations.* Amsterdam, Hol.: Djambatan, 1956.

Dibble, Roy Floyd. *Strenuous Americans.* New York: Boni & Liveright, 1923.

Dicey, Albert Venn. *Lectures on the Relation Between Law and Public Opinion in England During the Nineteenth Century.* London: Macmillan, 1914.

Dickens, Charles. *American Notes For General Circulation.* London: Oxford University Press, 1957.

_____. *The Complete Writings of Charles Dickens.* 40 vols. Boston: C.E. Lauriat, 1923.

Dicker, Laverne Mau. *The Chinese in San Francisco.* New York: Dover, 1979.

Dickerson, Robert B., Jr. *Final Placement: A Guide to the Deaths, Funerals and Burials of Notable Americans.* Algonac, Mich.: Reference, 1982.

Dickinson, P.L. *The Dublin of Yesterday.* London: Methuen, 1929.

Dicks, Henry V. *Licensed Mass Murder; A Socio-Psychological Study of Some S.S. Killers.* New York: Basic Books, 1972.

Dickson, Grierson. *Murder By Numbers.* London: Robert Hale, 1958.

Dickson, Col. H.R.P. *The Arab of the Desert.* London: Allen & Unwin, 1952.

Diederich, Bernard. *Trujillo, The Death of the Goat.* Boston: Little, Brown, 1978.

Dies, Martin. *Trojan Horse in America.* New York: Dodd, Mead, 1940.

Diesel, Eugen. *Germany and the Germans.* London: Macmillan, 1931.

Dietz, Howard. *Dancing in the Dark.* New York: Quadrangle, 1974.

Diggins, John P. *Mussolini and Fascism: The View from America.* Princeton, N.J.: Princeton University Press, 1972.

Dill, Sir Samuel. *Roman Society from Nero to Marcus Aurelius.* New York: Meridian, 1956.

_____. *Roman Society in the Last Century of the Western Empire.* New York: Macmillan, 1899.

Dillman, John. *Blood Warning.* New York: Putnam's, 1990.

_____. *The French Quarter Killers.* New York: Macmillan, 1987.

Dillon, M., and Lehane, D. *Political Murder in Northern Ireland.* London: Penguin Books, 1973.

Dillon, Martin. *The Shankill Butchers: A Case Study of Mass Murder.* London: Hutchinson, 1989.

Dillon, Merton L. *Elijah P. Lovejoy, Abolitionist Editor.* Urbana: University of Illinois Press, 1961.

Dillon, Richard H. *The Hatchet Men.* New York: Coward-McCann, 1972.

_____. *Wells Fargo Detective, A Biography of James B. Hume.* New York: Coward-McCann, 1969.

Dilnot, George. *The Bank of England Forgery.* New York: Charles Scribner's Sons, 1929.

_____. *Celebrated Crimes.* London: Stanley Paul, 1925.

_____. *Great Detectives and Their Methods.* Boston: Houghton Mifflin, 1928.

_____. *Man Hunters: Great Detectives and Their Achievements.* London: Robert Hale, 1937.

_____. *The Real Detective.* London: Geoffrey Bles, 1933.

_____. *Rogues' March.* London: Geoffrey Bles, 1934.

_____. *Scotland Yard: Its History and Organization, 1829-1929.* London: Geoffrey Bles, 1929.

_____. *The Story of Scotland Yard.* Boston: Houghton, Mifflin, 1927.

_____. *Triumphs of Detection.* London: Geoffrey Bles, 1929.

Dimsdale, Thomas J. *The Vigilantes of Montana.* Helena, Mont.: State Publishing, 1915.

Dinale, Ottavio. *Tempo di Mussolini.* Verona, Italy: Mondadori, 1934.

Dinges, John, and Landau, Paul. *Assassination on Embassy Row.* New York: Pantheon, 1980.

Dinneen, Joseph F. *Underworld U.S.A.* New York: Farrar, Straus, 1956.

Dinnerstein, Leonard. *The Leo Frank Case.* New York: Columbia University Press, 1968.

Dio Cassius. *Roman History.* trans. Ernest Cary. New York: Loeb Classical Library, 1927.

DiPerna, Paula. *Juries On Trial.* New York: Dembner Books, 1984.

Dirks, Raymond L., and Gross, Leonard. *The Great Wall Street Scandal.* New York: McGraw-Hill, 1974.

DiSalle, Michael V. *The Power of Life or Death.* New York: Random House, 1965.

Divall, Tom. *Scoundrels and Scallywags.* London: Benn, 1929.

Divine, David. *Indictment of Incompetence.* London: McDonald, 1970.

Divine, Robert A. *American Immigration Policy, 1924-1952.* New York: Da Capo Press, 1972.

Diwakar, R.R. *Glimpses of Gandhi.* Bombay, India: Hind Kitabs, 1949.

Dix, Dorothea L. *Remarks on Prisons and Prison Discipline in the United States.* Philadelphia: Joseph Kite, 1845.

Dix, Tenille. *The Black Baron.* Indianapolis, Ind.: Bobbs-Merrill, 1930.

Dixon, Thomas. *The Clansman.* New York: William Heinemann, 1906.

Dmytryshyn, Basil (ed.). *Imperial Russia: A Source Book, 1700-1917.* New York: Holt, Rinehart & Winston, 1967.

Dobash, R. E., and Dobash, R. *Violence Against Wives.* New York: Free Press, 1979.

Dobie, Charles Caldwell. *San Francisco's Chinatown.* New York: D. Appleton-Century, 1936.

_____. *San Francisco: A Pageant.* New York: D. Appleton Century, 1939.

Dobratz, Betty A., and Shanks-Meile, Stephanie L. *The White Separatist Movement in the United States: White Power, White Pride.* Baltimore: Johns Hopkins University Press, 2000.

Dobson, Christopher. *Black September: Its Short, Violent History.* New York: Macmillan, 1974.

_____, and Payne, Ronald. *The Carlos Complex: A Study in Terror.* New York: Putnam, 1977.

_____. *Counterattack: The West's Battle Against the Terrorists.* New York: Facts on File, 1982.

_____. *The Terrorists: Their Weapons, Leaders and Tactics.* New York: Facts on File, 1982.

Dobson, Terry, and Shepherd-Chow, Judith. *Safe and Alive.* Los Angeles: Tarcher, 1981.

Dobyns, Fletcher. *The Amazing Story of Repeal.* Chicago: Willett, Clark, 1940.

_____. *The Underworld of American Politics.* New York: Published by Author, 1932.

Dodge, Calvert R. (ed.). *A Nation Without Prisons.* Lexington, Mass.: D.C. Heath, 1975.

Dodge, Daniel. *Trial of Peter Robinson.* Newark, N.J.: Aaron Guest, 1841.

Dodge, I.F. *Our Arizona.* New York: Scribner's, 1929.

Doherty, Edward J. *Gall and Honey.* New York: Sheed and Ward, 1941.

Doke, Joseph J. *M.K. Gandhi.* Madras, India: G.A. Natesan, 1909.

Dolan, J.R. *The Yankee Peddlers of Early America.* New York: Clarkson N. Potter, 1964.

Dolfin, Giovanni. *Con Mussolini nella tragedia.* Milan, Italy: Garzanti, 1949.

Dolgoff, Sam (ed.). *Bakunin on Anarchy: Selected Works by the Activist-Founder of World Anarchism.* New York: Alfred A. Knopf, 1972.

Dollinger, Hans. *The Decline and Fall of Nazi Germany and Imperial Japan: A Pictorial History of the Final Days of World War II.* New York: Crown, 1968.

Dombrowski, Roman. *Twilight and Fall.* London: Heinemann, 1956.

Domestic Council Drug Abuse Task Force. *White Paper on Drug Abuse.* Washington D.C.: U.S. Government Printing Office, 1975.

Domhoff, G. William. *The Higher Circles: The Governing Class in America.* New York: Random House, 1970.

Donahue, William A. *The Politics of the American Civil Liberties Union.* New Bruswick, N.J.: Transaction Books, 1985.

Donald, David. *Lincoln Reconsidered.* New York: Alfred A. Knopf, 1956.

_____. *Lincoln's Herndon.* New York: Alfred A. Knopf, 1948.

Donald, Jay. *Outlaws of the Border.* Philadelphia: Douglas Brothers, 1882.

Donaldson, Gordon. *The Edinburgh History of Scotland.* New York: Frederick A. Praeger, 1966.

Donaldson, Thomas. *Idaho of Yesterday.* Caldwell, Idaho: The Caxton Printers, 1941.

Donaldson, William. *Don't Call Me Madam.* New York: Mason/Charter, 1975.

Donnelly, Richard C., Goldstein, Joseph, and Schwartz, Richard D. *Criminal Law.* New York: The Free Press, 1962.

Donner, Frank J. *The Age of Surveillance.* New York: Alfred A. Knopf, 1980.

_____. *The Un-Americans.* New York: Ballantine, 1961.

Donoghue, Mary Agnes. *Assassination: Murder in Politics.* Chatsworth, Calif. Major Books, 1975.

Donovan, Robert J. *The Assassins.* New York: Harper & Brothers, 1955.

_____. *The Assassins of American Presidents.* New York: Harper & Brothers, 1956.

_____. *Conflict and Crises: The Presidency of Harry S. Truman, 1945-1948.* New York: W.W. Norton, 1977.

_____. *Tumultuous Years: The Presidency of Harry S. Truman, 1949-1953.* New York: W.W. Norton, 1982.

Donovan, Frank. *River Boats of America.* New York: Thomas Y. Crowell, 1966.

Doolittle, J. *Social life of the Chinese.* New York: Harper & Brothers, 1865.

Dore, R.P. *Aspects of Social Change in Modern Japan.* Princeton, N.J.: Princeton University Press, 1967.

D'Orleans, P.J. *History of the Two Tartar Conquerors of China.* London: Hakluyt Society, 1854.

Dorman, Michael. *King of the Courtroom: Percy Foreman for the Defense.* New York: Delacorte Press, 1969.

_____. *The Secret Service Story.* New York: Delacorte Press, 1967.

_____. *We Shall Overcome.* New York: Delacorte Press, 1964.

Dorman, Peter. *Dictionary of the Law.* Philadelphia: Running Press, 1978.

Dorough, C. Dwight. *Mr. Sam.* New York: Random House, 1962.

Dorries, Christopher. Coroner's Courts: A Guide to the Law and Practice. New York: John Wiley & Sons, 1999.

Dorsen, N., and Friedman, L. *Disorder in the Courts.* New York: Pantheon, 1973.

_____, and Gillers, Stephen (eds.). *None of Your Business.* New York: Penguin Books, 1975.

Dorsett, Lyle W. *The Pendergast Machine.* New York: Oxford University Press, 1968.

_____. *The Queen City.* Boulder, Colo.: Pruet Publishers, 1977.

Dorsey, Florence. *Master of the Mississippi.* Boston: Houghton Mifflin, 1941.

_____. *Road to the Sea.* New York: Rinehart, 1947.

Dorsey, George A. *Traditions of the Arikara.* Washington, D.C.: Carnegie Institution, 1904.

Dorson, Richard M. (ed.). *American Rebels.* New York: Pantheon, 1953.

Dosch, Henry Ernst. *Vigilante Days at Virginia City.* Portland, Ore.: Fred Lockley, 1924.

Dos Passos, John. *In All Countries.* New York: Harcourt, Brace, 1934.

Dostoevsky, Fdor. *Crime and Punishment.* Middlesex, Eng.: Penguin, 1966.

_____. *The House of the Dead.* New York: Dell, 1959.

Douglas, Arthur. *Will the Real Jack the Ripper.* Chorley, Eng.: Countryside, 1979.

Douglas, Clarence Brown. *History of Tulsa, Oklahoma.* Chicago: S.J. Clarke, 1921.

Douglas, Claude Leroy. *Cattle Kings of Texas.* Dallas: Cecil Baugh, 1939.

_____. *Famous Texas Feuds.* Dallas: Turner, 1936.

_____. *The Gentlemen in White Hats.* Dallas: South-West Press, 1934.

Douglas, Ford. *The Cattle Rustlers of Wyoming.* Nwe York: J.S. Ogilvie, 1916.

Douglas, George William. *The Many-Sided Roosevelt, An Anecdotal Biography.* New York: Dodd, Mead, 1907.

Douglas, Hugh. *Jacobite Spy Wars: Moles, Rogues and Treachery.* New York: Sutton, 2000.

Douglas, Jack D. (ed.). *Deviance and Respectability.* New York: Basic Books, 1970.

_____. *Investigative Social Research.* Beverly Hills, Calif.: Sage, 1976.

_____, and Johnson, John M. (eds.). *Official Deviance.* Philadelphia: J.B. Lippincott, 1977.

_____. *The Social Meanings of Suicide.* Princeton, N.J.: Princeton University Press, 1967.

Douglas, John, and Olshaker, Mark. *The Anatomy of Motive.* New York: Scribner's, 1999.

_____. *Journey Into Darkness.* New York: Scribner's, 1997.

_____. *Mind Hunter.* New York: Scribner's, 1995.

_____. *Obsession.* New York: Scribner's, 1998.

Douglas, John E., and Burgess, Ann W., and Burgess, Allen G., and Ressler, Robert. *Crime Classification Manual.* New York: Lexington Books, 1992.

Douglas, William O. *The Court Years 1939-1975.* New York: Random House, 1980.

_____. *The Douglas Opinions.* New York: Random House, 1977.

_____. *We the Judges.* Garden City, N.Y.: Doubleday, 1956.

Douglass, Earl L. *Prohibition and Commonsense.* New York: Alcohol Information Committee, 1931.

Douthit, Nathan. *Police Forces in History.* Beverly Hills, Calif.: Dage, 1975.

Douthwaite, L. C. *Mass Murder.* New York: Holt, 1929.

Dow, George Francis, and Edmonds, John Henry. *The Pirates of the New England Coast.* New York: Argosy-Antiquarian, 1968.

Dow, George Francis (ed.). *The Probate Records of Essex County, Mass.* Newbury, Mass.: Parker River Researchers, 1988.

Dowell, Eldridge Foster. *A History of Criminal Syndicalism Legislation in the United States.* Baltimore: Johns Hopkins Press, 1939.

Dower, J.W. *Empire and Aftermath: Yoshida Shigeru and the Japanese Experience.* Cambridge, Mass.: Harvard University Press, 1979.

Down, Thomas. *Murder Man.* New York: Dell, 1984.

Downes, David M. *The Delinquent Solution.* London: Routledge & Kegan Paul, 1966.

Downes, Donald. *The Scarlet Thread.* London: Derek Verschoyle, 1953.

Downie, Leonard, Jr. *The New Muckrakers.* Washington, D.C.: New Republic, 1976.

Downie, Robert Angus. *Murder in London: A Topographical Guide to Famous Crimes.* London: A. Barker, 1973.

Downing, David. *Yasser Arafat.* London: Heinemann, 2002.

Downs, Thomas. *Murder Man.* New York: Dell, 1984.

Doyle, Adrian Conan. *The True Conan Doyle.* New York: Coward McCann, 1946.

Doyle, James. *Not Above the Law.* New York: Morrow, 1977.

Dozy, Rinehart. *Spanish Islam.* London: Chatto & Windus, 1913.

Dragnich, Alex N. *Tito's Promised Land: Yugoslavia.* New Brunswick, N.J.: Rutgers University Press, 1954.

Drago, Harry Sinclair. *Great American Cattle Trails.* New York: Dodd, Mead, 1965.

_____. *The Great Range Wars.* New York: Dodd, Mead, 1970.

_____. *Lost Bonanzas.* New York: Dodd, Mead, 1966.

_____. *Notorious Ladies of the Frontier.* New York: Dodd, Mead, 1969.

_____. *Outlaws on Horseback.* New York: Dodd, Mead, 1964.

_____. *Red River Valley.* New York: Clarkson N. Potter, 1962.

_____. *Road Agents and Train Robbers.* New York: Dodd, Mead, 1973.

_____. *Roads to Empire.* New York: Dodd, Mead, 1968.

_____. *The Steamboaters.* New York: Dodd, Mead, 1967.

_____. *Wild, Woolly & Wicked.* New York: Clarkson N. Potter, 1960.

Drake, St. Clair, and Cayton, Horace R. *Black Metropolis.* New York: Harcourt, Brace, 1945.

Drake, Samuel G. *Annals of Witchcraft in New England.* Boston: W.E. Woodward, 1866.

_____. *Biography and History of the Indians of North America.* Philadelphia: Charles de Silver, 1860.

_____ (ed.). *The Witchcraft Delusion in New England.* Roxbury, Mass.: W. Elliot Woodward, 1866.

Drapkin, Israel, and Viano, Emilio (eds.). *Victimology.* Lexington, Mass.: Lexington Books, D.C. Heath, 1974.

_____. *Victimology: A New Focus.* Lexington, Mass.: Lexington Books, D.C. Heath, 1975.

Dreher, Robert H., and Kammler, Linda. *Criminal Registration Statutes and Ordinances in the United States: A Compilation.* Carbondale: Center for the Study of Crime, Delinquency and Corrections, Southern Illinois University, 1969.

Dreifus, Claudia. *Woman's Fate.* New York: Bantam, 1973.

Dreiser, Theodore. *An Amercan Tragedy.* New York: New American Library, 1964.

_____. *A Book About Myself.* New York: Boni & Liveright, 1922.

_____. *The Color of a Great City.* New York: Boni and Liveright, 1923.

Dresler, Adolf. *Rasputin.* Munich, Ger.: B. Funck-verlag, 1929.

Dressler, David. *Practice and Theory of Probation and Parole.* New York: Columbia University Press, 1969.

Drewry, W.S. *Slave Insurrections in Virginia, 1830-1865.* Washington, D.C.: Neale, 1900.

Driggs, Howard Roscoe. *Westward America.* New York: G.P. Putnam's Sons, 1942.

The Drinker's Farm Tragedy. Richmond, Va.: V.L. Fore, 1868.

Drinnon, Richard. *Rebel in Paradise: A Biography of Emma Goldman.* Chicago: University of Chicago Press, 1961.

Driver, G.R., and Miles, John C. (eds.) *The Assyrian Laws.* Oxford, Eng.: Clarendon Press, 1955.

Driver, Harold E. *Indians of North America.* Chicago: Chicago University Press, 1961.

Droge, Edward. *The Patrolman: A Cop's Story.* New York: New American Library, 1973.

Dromundo, Baltasar. *Francisco Villa y la Adelita.* Mexico City, Mex.: n.p., 1920.

Drucker, S., and Hexter, H.B. *Children Astray.* Cambridge, Mass.: Harvard University Press, 1923.

Drug Abuse Council. *The Facts About "Drug Abuse".* New York: Free Press, 1980.

Drug Use and Crime. Report of the Panel on Drug Use and Criminal Behavior. Washington, D.C.: The National Institute on Drug Abuse, assisted by Research Triangle Institute, 1976.

Drug Use in America: Problem in Perspective. 2nd Report of the National Commission on Marijuana and Drug Abuse. Washington, D.C.: U.S. Government Printing Office, 1973.

Drummond, A.L. *True Detective Stories.* Chicago: M.A. Donohue, 1909.

Drury, Luke. *A Report of the Examination of Rev. Ephraim K. Avery, Charged with the Murder of Sarah Maria Cornell.* Providence, R.I.: n.p., 1833.

Drzazga, John. *Sex Crimes and Their Legal Aspects.* Springfield, Ill.: Charles C. Thomas, 1960.

_____. *Wheels of Fortune.* Springfield, Ill.: Charles C. Thomas, 1963.

Dubnov, Simon. *History of the Jews.* New York: Thomas Yoseloff, 1971.

Dubofsky, Melvyn, and Theoharis, Athan. *Imperial Democracy: The United States Since 1945.* Englewood Cliffs, N.J.: Prentice-Hall, 1983.

Dubois, Abb J.A. *Hindu Manners and Customs.* Oxford, Eng.: Oxford University Press, 1906.

Dubreuil, Auguste. *Cours d'assises du Rhne. Assassinat de M. Carnot.* Lyon, Fr.: Mougin-Rusand, 1894.

Dubu, Marc. *Gilles de Rays, magicien et sodomiste.* Paris: Les Presses de la Cit, 1945.

du Cane, Sir Edmund. *An Account of the Manner in Which Sentences of Penal Servitude Are Carried Out in England.* London: Millbank Prison, 1882.

_____. *The Punishment and Prevention of Crime.* London: Macmillan, 1885.

Du Chaillu, Paul Belloni. *Explorations and Adventures in Equatorial Africa.* London: John Murray, 1861.

Duchess of Atholl. *Searchlight on Spain.* London: Penguin Books, 1938.

Duckett, Eleanor. *Alfred the Great: The King and His England.* Chicago: Chicago University Press, 1958.

_____. *Death and Life in the Tenth Century.* Ann Arbor: University of Michigan Press, 1967.

_____. *Gateway to the Middle Ages: France and Britain.* Ann Arbor: University of Michigan Press, 1938.

Du Clos, Bernard. *Fair Game.* New York: St. Martin's Press, 1993.

Dudden, F. Homes. *Henry Fielding: His Life, Work and Times.* 2 vols. London: Oxford University Press, 1952.

Duff, A.M. *Freedmen in the Early Roman Empire.* Cambridge, Eng.: Heffer, 1958.

Duff, C. *Ireland and the Irish.* New York: Boardman, 1952.

Duff, Charles. *A New Handbook on Hanging.* Chicago: Regnery, 1955.

Duff, David. *Hessian Tapestry.* London: Frederick Muller, 1967.

_____. *Victoria and Albert.* New York: Taplinger, 1972.

Duffee, David. *Using Correctional Officers in Planned Change.* Washington, D.C.: National Institute of Law Enforcement, National Technical Information Service, 1972.

Duffus, Robert L. *The Santa Fe Trail.* New York: Tudor Publishing, 1930.

_____. *The Tower of Jewels: Memories of San Francisco.* New York: W. W. Norton, 1960.

Duffy, Warden Clinton T. *The San Quentin Story, As Told to Dean Jennings.* Garden City, N.Y.: Doubleday, 1950.

_____, with Hirschberg, Al. *88 Men and Two Women.* Garden City, N.Y.: Doubleday, 1962.

Duffy, John. *A History of Public Health in New York City, 1625-1866.* New York: Russell Sage Foundation, 1968.

_____. *A History of Public Health in New York City, 1866-1966.* New York: Russell Sage Foundation, 1974.

Dugdale, Blanche E.C. *Arthur James Balfour.* 2 Vols. New York: Putnam, 1937.

Duggan, Christopher. *Fascism and the Mafia.* New Haven, Conn.: Yale University Press, 1989.

Duhamel, Pierre. *Henry of Guise.* Paris: Librairie Acadmique Perrin, 1974.

Duke, Thomas S. *Celebrated Criminal Cases of America.* San Francisco: James H. Barry, 1910.

Duke, Winifred (ed.). *Notable British Trials: Trial of Field and Gray.* London: William Hodge, 1939.

_____. *Notable British Trials: Trials of Frederick Nodder.* London: William Hodge, 1950.

_____. *Six Trials.* London: Victor Gollancz, 1934.

_____. *Skin for Skin.* London: Gollancz, 1935.

_____. *The Stroke of Murder.* London: R. Hale, 1937.

Dull, Paul S., and Umemura, Michael T. *The Tokyo Trials: A Functional Index to the Proceedings of the International Military Tribunal for the Far East.* Ann Arbor: University of Michigan Press, 1957.

Dulles, Allen. *The Craft of Intelligence.* New York: Harper & Row, 1963.

_____. *Germany's Underground.* New York: Macmillan, 1947.

Dulles, Eleanor L. *Depression and Reconstruction.* Philadelphia: University of Pennsylvania Press, 1937.

_____. *America in the Pacific: A Century of Expansion.* Boston: Houghton Mifflin, 1938.

Dulles, Foster Rhea. *America Learns to Play.* New York: D. Appleton-Century, 1940.

_____. *China and America: The Story of Their Relations Since 1784.* Princeton, N.J.: Princeton University Press, 1946.

_____. *The Imperial Years.* New York: Thomas Y. Crowell, 1956.

_____. *The United States Since 1865.* Ann Arbor: University of Michigan Press, 1959.

Dulles, John W. *Yesterday in Mexico: A Chronicle of the Revolution, 1919-1936.* Austin: University of Texas Press, 1961.

Dumas, Alexandre. *Celebrated Crimes.* Translator: Jacques Wagrez. Philadelphia: Rittenhouse Press, 1895.

Dumenil, Lynn. *Freemasonry and American Culture.* Princeton, N.J.: Princeton University Press, 1985.

Dumond, Dwight Lowell. *America in Our Time 1896-1946.* New York: Henry Holt, 1947.

Dumont, Ren. *False Start in Africa.* London: Sphere Books, 1966.

Dunaway, W.F. *A History of Pennsylvania.* New York: Prentice-Hall, 1948.

Dunbar, Dorothy. *Blood in the Parlor.* New York: A.S. Barnes, 1964.

Dunboyne, Lord (ed.). *Notable British Trials: Trial of J.G. Haigh.* London: William Hodge, 1953.

Duncan, Lee. *Over the Wall.* New York: E.P. Dutton, 1936.

Duncan, Otis Dudley and Beverly. *The Negro Population of Chicago.* Chicago: University of Chicago Press, 1957.

Duncan, Ronald (ed.). *Selected Writings of Mahatma Gandhi.* London: Faber & Faber, 1951.

Dunham, Allison, and Kurland, Philip B. (eds.). *Mr. Justice.* Chicago: University of Chicago Press, 1964.

Dunlap, Carol. *California People.* Salt Lake City, Utah: Peregrene Smith Books, 1982.

Dunn, Arthur Wallace. *From Harrison to Harding.* 2 vol. New York: Putnam, 1922.

Dunn, Christopher S. *Patterns of Robbery Characteristics.* Washington, D.C.: National Criminal Justice Information and Statistics Service, 1976.

Dunn, Delmer. *Public Officials and the Press.* Reading, Mass.: Addison-Wesley, 1969.

Dunn, Donald H. *Ponzi, the Boston Swindler.* New York: McGraw-Hill, 1975.

Dunn, H.H. *The Crimson Jester: Zapata of Mexico.* London: Harrap, 1939.

Dunn, J.B. *Perilous Trails of Texas.* Dallas: Southwest Press, 1952.

Dunn, Richard S. *Puritans and Yankees: The Winthrop Dynasty of New England 1630-1717.* Princeton: Princeton University Press, 1962.

Dunne, Edward F. *Illinois: The Heart of the Nation.* 5 vols. Chicago: Lewis, 1933.

Dunne, Gerald T. *Hugo Black and the Judicial Revolution.* New York: Touchstone, 1978.

Dunner, Joseph. *The Republic of Israel.* New York: McGraw-Hill, 1950.

Dunning, John. *The Arbor House Treasury of True Crime.* New York: Arbor House, 1981.

Dunphy, Thomas, and Cummins, Thomas J. *Remarkable Trials.* New York: Ward & Peloubet, 1878.

Dunshee, Tom, and Duncan, Richard. *Motorcade: November 22, 1963.* Trenton, N.J.: Published by Author, 1975.

Duples-Agier, H. *Registre criminel du Chatelet de Paris.* Paris: C. Lahure, 1861.

Duran, Fray Diego. *The Aztecs: The History of the Indies of New Spain.* Trans. Doris Heyden and Fernando Horcasitas. New York: Orion, 1963.

Durand, Mortimer. *Crazy Campaign.* London: George Routledge, 1936.

Durant, M.,et al. *Crime, Criminals and the Law.* London: Office of Population Censuses and Surveys, 1972.

Durant, Will. *The Renaissance.* Vol. V. New York: Simon and Schuster, 1953.

Durden, Robert F. *The Gray and the Black.* Baton Rouge: Louisiana State University Press, 1972.

Durham, M.E. *The Sarajevo Crime.* London: G. Allen & Unwin, 1925.

Durk, David, and Silverman, Ira. *The Pleasant Avenue Connection.* New York: Harper & Row, 1977.

DuRose, John. *Murder Was My Business.* London: W.H. Allen, 1971.

Dutch, Andrew K. *Hysteria: The Lindbergh Kidnap Case.* Philadelphia: Dorrance, 1975.

Dutt, R. Palmer. *Fascism and Social Revolution.* New York: International Publishers, 1935.

Dutt, Romesh. *India in the Victorian Age.* London: Kegan Paul, Trench, Trubner, 1904.

Duus, Peter. *The Rise of Modern Japan.* Boston: Houghton Mifflin, 1976.

Dvorchak, Robert, and Holewa, Lisa. *Milwaukee Murders.* New York: Dell, 1991.

Dvornik, Francis. *The Slavs in European History and Civilization.* New Brunswick, N.J.: Rutgers University Press, 1962.

Dwivedy, S., and Bhargava, G.S. *Political Corruption in India.* New Delhi: Popular Book Services, 1967.

D'Ydewalle, Charles. *Albert and the Belgians.* New York: Morrow, 1935.

Dye, John Smith. *History of the Plots and Crimes to Overthrow Liberty in America.* Freeport, N.Y.: Books for Libraries Press, 1969.

Dyer, Alfred. *The European Slave Trade in English Girls.* London: Dyer Brothers, 1880.

The Dying Confession of John Lechler. Lancaster, Pa.: S.T. Stambaugh, 1822.

Dykstra, Robert R. *The Cattle Towns.* New York: Alfred A. Knopf, 1968.

Dyne, D.G. *Famous New Zealand Murders.* London: Collins, 1969.

Dyos, Harold James, and Wolff, Michael (eds.). *The Victorian City.* Boston: Routledge & Kegan Paul, 1973.

Eames, Hugh. *Sleuths, Inc.* Philadelphia: J.B. Lippincott, 1978.

Earl, D.C. *Tiberius Gracchus: A Study in Politics.* Brussels, Belgium: Collection Latomus, LXVI, 1963.

Earl, David Mafarey. *Emperor and Nation in Japan.* Seattle: University of Washington Press, 1964.

Earle, Alice Moore. *Stage Coach and Tavern Days.* London: Macmillan, 1927.

Earle, Peter. *Corsairs of Malta and Barbary.* Annapolis, Md.: U.S. Naval Institute, 1970.

East, John M. *'Neath the Mask: The Story of the East Family.* London: George Allen and Unwin, 1967.

East, Norwood. *Sexual Offenders.* London: Delisle, 1955.

_____. *Society and the Criminal.* London: H.M. Stationery Office, 1949.

East, William. *Society and the Criminal.* Springfield, Ill.: Charles C. Thomas, 1951.

Easterlin, R.A. *Birth and Fortune.* New York: Basic Books, 1980.

Easterman, A.L. *King Carol, Hitler and Lupescu.* London: Victor Gollancz, 1942.

Easum, Chester Verne. *The Americanization of Carl Schurz.* Chicago: University of Chicago Press, 1929.

Easum, Chester. *Prince Henry of Prussia, Brother of Frederick the Great.* Madison: University of Wisconsin Press, 1984.

Eaton, Harold. *Famous Poison Trials.* London: W. Collins Sons, 1923.

Eaton, Jeanette. *Bucky O'Neill of Arizona.* New York: William Morrow, 1949.

_____. *Gandhi, Fighter Without a Sword.* New York: William Morrow, 1950.

Eaton, Peggy. *Autobiography.* New York: Charles Scribner's Sons, 1932.

Eayrs, James (ed.). *The Commonwealth and Suez.* London: Oxford University Press, 1963.

Eban, Abba. *The Tide of Nationalism.* New York: Harper, 1959.

Ebbinghaus, H. *Memory.* trans. H. Ruyer and C.E. Bussenius. New York: Teachers College Press, 1913.

_____. *The Voice of Israel.* New York: Harper, 1957.

Ebenstein, William. *Fascist Italy.* New York: American Book, 1939.

Ebin, D. (ed.). *The Drug Experience.* New York: Orion, 1961.

Ebon, Martin (ed.). *The Psychic Scene.* New York: Signet, 1974.

_____. *Reincarnation in the Twentieth Century.* New York: Signet, 1967.

_____. *The Satan Trap.* New York: Doubleday, 1976.

Eccentricities and Anecdotes of Albert John Tirrell. Boston: n.p., 1846.

Echardt, Carl C. *The Papacy and World Affairs.* Chicago: University of Chicago Press, 1937.

Eckhardstein, Baron H. von. *Ten Years at the Court of St. James, 1895-1905.* London: Butterworth, 1921.

Eckhardt, H. *Ivan the Terrible.* New York: Charles Scribner's Sons, 1949.

Echols, Mike. *I Know My First Name is Steven.* New York: Pinnacle, 1991.

Eddowes, John. *The Man on Your Conscience.* London: Cassell, 1955

_____. *The Two Killers of Rillington Place.* London: Little, Brown, 1994.

Eddowes, Michael. *Khrushchev Killed Kennedy.* Dallas: Published by Author, 1975.

_____. *The Man on Your Conscience,* London: Cassell, 1955.

_____. *November 22: How They Killed Kennedy.* London: Neville Spearman, 1976.

_____. *The Oswald File.* New York: Potter, 1977.

Eddy, George Sherwood. *Revolutionary Christianity.* New York: Willett, Clark, 1939.

Eddy, J.P. *Mystery of Peter the Painter.* London: Stevens & Sons, 1946.

_____. *Scarlet and Ermine.* London: William Kimber, 1960.

Eddy, Paul, Sabogal, Hugo, and Walden, Sara. *The Cocaine Wars.* New York: W.W. Norton, 1988.

Eddy, Thomas. *An Account of the State Prison or Penitentiary House in the City of New York:* New York: Isaac Collins & Son, 1801.

Edelhertz, Herbert. *The Nature, Impact and Prosecution of White-Collar Crime.* Washington D.C.: Government Printing Office, 1970.

_____. and Geis, Gilbert. *Public Compensation to Victims of Crime.* New York: Praeger, 1974.

Eden, Sir Anthony. *Facing the Dictators.* London: Cassell, 1962.

Edgar, P. *Children and Screen Violence.* St. Lucia, Aus.: University of Queensland Press, 1977.

Edge, L.L. *Run The Cat Roads.* New York: Dembner Books, 1981.

Eden, William (First Baron Auckland). *Principles of Penal Law.* London: B. White & T. Codell, 1771.

Edgerton, Robert B. *The Cloak of Competence.* Berkeley: University of California Press, 1967.

_____. *Mau Mau: An African Crucible.* New York: The Free Press, 1989.

Edholm, Charlton. *Traffic in Girls and Work of Rescue Missions.* Oakland, Calif.: Sierra, 1900.

Edman, Irwin. *Philosopher's Holiday.* New York: The Viking Press, 1938.

Edmonds, C.J. *Kurds, Turks and Arabs.* London: Cambridge University Press, 1957.

Edmonds, I.G. *Hollywood R.I.P.* New York: Regency Books, 1963.

Edwards, Allen. *The Royal Whore.* New York: Chilton Books, 1970.

Edwards, Alison. *Rape, Racism, and the White Woman's Movement.* Chicago: Sojourner Truth Organization, 1976.

Edwards, Francis. *The Dangerous Queen.* London: G. Chapman, 1964.

Edwards, Jerome. *The Foreign Policy of Colonel McCormick's Tribune.* Reno: University of Nevada Press, 1971.

Edwards, J.B. *Early days in Abilene.* Abilene, Texas: C.W. Wheeler, 1896.

Edwards, John Newman. *Noted Guerrillas, or the Warfare of the Border.* St. Louis: Bryan, Brand, 1877.

Edwards, Kenneth. *The Grey Diplomatists.* London: Rich & Cowan, 1938.

Edwards, L. Fielding. *Profane Pilgrimage.* London: Duckworth, 1938.

_____. *A Wayfarer in Yugoslavia.* New York: McBride, 1939.

Edwards, Loren E. *Shoplifting and Shrinkage Protection for Stores.* Springfield, Ill.: Charles C. Thomas, 1958.

Edwards, Monroe. *The Life and Adventures of the Accomplished Forger and Swindler, Colonel Monroe Edwards.* New York: H. Long & Brother, 1848.

Edwards, Samuel. *The Vidocq Dossier.* Boston: Houghton Mifflin, 1977.

Eells, George. *The Life That Late He Led.* New York: G.P. Putnam & Sons, 1967.

Egen, Frederick W. *Plainclothesman: Handbook of Vice and Gambling Investigation.* New York: Arco Publishing Co., 1959.

Egger, Steven. *The Killers Among Us.* Upper Saddle River, N. J.: Prentice Hall, 1998.

_____. *Serial Murder: An Exclusive Phenomenon.* New York: Praeger, 1990.

Egginton, Joyce. *From Cradle to Grave.* New York: W. Morrow, 1989.

Egyptian Society of International Law. *Egypt and the United Nations.* New York: Manhattan, 1957.

Ehlers, Dieter. *Technik und Moral einer Verschwrung, 20 Juli 1944.* Frankfurt, Ger.: Athenum, 1964.

Ehrenwald, Jan. *The ESP Experience: A Psychiatric Validation.* New York: Basic Books, 1978.

Ehrlich, Blake. *London on the Thames.* London: Cassell, 1968.

Ehrlich, J.W. *A Life in My Hands.* New York: Putnam, 1965.

Ehrlichman, John. *Witness to Power.* New York: Simon & Schuster, 1982.

Ehrmann, Herbert B. *The Untried Case: The Sacco-Vanzetti Case and the Morelli Gang.* New York: Vanguard, 1933.

Eichmann in Jerusalem: A Report on the Banality of Evil. New York: Viking, 1964.

Eichstaedt, J. *Von Dollfuss zu Hitler.* Wiesbaden: F. Steiner, 1955.

Einstein, Alfred. *Mozart: His Character, His Work.* trans. Arthur Mendel and Nathan Broder. New York: Oxford University Press, 1945.

Einstein, Izzy. *Prohibition Agent No. 1.* New York: Frederick A. Stokes, 1932.

Eisele, Wilbert E. *The Real "Wild Bill" Hickok.* Denver: William H. Andre, 1931.

Eisenberg, Daniel M., as told to Beffel, John Nicholas. *I Find the Missing.* New York: Farrar & Rinehart, 1938.

Eisenberg, Dennis, Dan, Uri, and Landau, Eli. *Meyer Lansky.* London: Paddington Press, 1979.

Eisenhower, Dwight D. *The White House Years: Waging Peace, 1956-1961.* Garden City, N.Y.: Doubleday, 1965.

Eisenmenger, V. *Archduke Francis Ferdinand.* London: Selwyn & Blount, 1931.

Eisenschiml, Otto, and Bishop, Jim. *The Day Lincoln Was Shot.* New York: Harper & Brothers, 1955.

_____. *In the Shadow of Lincoln's Death.* New York: Wilfred Funk, 1940.

_____. *Why Was Lincoln Murdered?* Boston: Little, Brown, 1937.

Eisenstadt, S.N. *The Decline of Empires.* Englewood Cliffs, N.J.: Prentice-Hall, 1967.

Eisenstein, James, and Jacob, Herbert. *Felony Justice.* Boston: Little, Brown, 1977.

Eisenstein, Louis, and Rosenberg, Elliot. *A Stripe of Tammany's Tiger.* New York: R. Speller, 1966.

Eisler, Robert. *Man into Wolf: An Anthropological Interpretation of Sadism, Masochism and Lycanthropy.* London: Routledge, 1951.

Eissler, K. R. *Searchlights on Delinquency.* New York: Int. Univs. Press, 1949.

Ejiri Susumu. *Characteristics of the Japanese Press.* Nihon Shinbun Kyokai, 1972.

Ekins, H. R., and Wright, Theon. *China Fights for Her Life.* New York: McGraw-Hill, 1938.

Elath, Eliahu. *Israel and Her Neighbors.* Cleveland: World, 1957.

Elder, Donald. *Ring Lardner.* Garden City, N.Y.: Doubleday, 1956.

Elder, G.H. *Children of the Great Depression.* Chicago: University of Chicago Press, 1974.

Elderkin, John, et al. (eds.) *After Dinner Speeches at the Lotos Club.* New York: Printed for the Lotos Club, 1911.

Eldridge, Benjamin P., and Watts, William B. *Our Rival the Rascal.* Boston: Pemberton, 1897.

Eldridge, William Butler. *Narcotics and the Law: A Critique of the American Experiment in Narcotic Drug Control.* Chicago: University of Chicago Press, 1967.

Eliade, Mircea. *Rites and Symbols of Initiation.* New York: Harper & Row, 1958

_____. *Shamanism.* New York: Pantheon Books, 1964

Elias, Christopher. *Fleecing the Lambs.* Chicago: Henry Regnery, 1971.

Elias, C.E. Jr., et al. *Metropolis: Values in Conflict.* Belmont, Calif.: Wadsworth, 1964.

Elias, R. *Victims of the System.* New Brunswick, N.J.: Transaction, 1983.

Elich, Philipp Ludwig. *Daemonomagia.* Frankfort, Ger.: C. Nebemii, 1607.

Eliel, Paul. *The Waterfront and General Strikes, San Francisco, 1934.*

Eliot, Sir Charles. *Hinduism and Buddhism: An Historical Sketch.* 3 vols. New York: Longmans, Green, 1921.

_____. *Turkey in Europe.* London: Edward Arnold, 1908.

Elkind, Peter. *The Death Shift.* New York: Viking, 1989.

Ellen, Mary, Murphy, Mark, and Weld, Ralph Foster. *A Treasury of Brooklyn.* New York: William Sloane Associates, 1949.

Ellenberger, Henri. *Criminologie du Passe et du Present.* Montreal, Can.: Presses de L'Universite de Montreal, 1965.

Ellet, Charles. *The Mississippi and Ohio Rivers.* Philadelphia: J.B. Lippincott, Grambo, 1853.

Elliff, John T. *Crime, Dissent, and the Attorney General: The Justice Department in the 1960s.* Beverly Hills, Calif.: Sage, 1971.

Elliff, John T. *The Reform of F.B.I. Intelligence Operations.* New Jersey: Princeton, 1979.

Elliott, Bateman M. *Revolt to Revolution.* Manchester, Eng.: Manchester University Press, 1974.

Elliott, David Stewart. *Last Raid of the Daltons.* Coffeyville, Kan.: Coffeyville Journal, 1892.

Elliott, Delbert S., and Voss, H.L. *Delinquency and Dropout.* Lexington, Mass.: Lexington, 1974.

Elliott, Mabel A. *Conflicting Penal Theories in Statutory Criminal Law.* Chicago: University of Chicago Press, 1931.

_____. *Coercion in Penal Treatment.* Ithaca, N.Y.: Pacifist Research Bureau, 1947.

Elliott, Robert G., and Beatty, Albert R. *Agent of Death: The Memoirs of an Executioner.* New York: E. P. Dutton, 1940.

Ellis, Albert. *The Folklore of Sex.* New York: Charles Boni, 1951.

_____, and Brancale, Ralph. *The Psychology of Sex Offenders.* Springfield, Ill.: Charles C. Thomas, 1956.

_____, and Gullo, John. *Murder and Assassination.* New York: Lyle Stuart, 1971.

Ellis, Anthony L. *Prisoner at the Bar.* London: Heath Cranton, 1934.

Ellis, David, et al. *A Short History of New York State.* Ithaca, N.Y.: Cornell University Press, 1957.

Ellis, Edward Robb. *The Epic of New York City.* New York: Coward-McCann, 1966.

_____. *A Nation in Torment: The Great American Depression, 1929-1939.* New York: Coward-McCann, 1970.

Ellis, Harry B. *Challenge in the Middle East.* New York: Ronald, 1960.

_____. *Heritage of the Desert.* New York: Ronald, 1956.

_____. *Israel and the Middle East.* New York: Ronald, 1957.

Ellis, Havelock. *The Criminal.* New York: Scribner's, 1900.

Ellis, J.C. *Black Fame: Stories of Crime and Criminals.* London: Hutchinson, 1926.

_____. *Blackmailers & Co.* London: Selwyn and Blount, 1928.

Ellis, John. *The Social History of the Machine Gun.* New York: Pantheon Books, 1976.

Ellis, Dr.John B. *The Sights and Secrets of the National Capital.* New York: U.S. Publishing, 1869.

Ellis, Steve. *Alcatraz Number 1172.* Los Angeles: Holloway House Publishing Co., 1969.

Ellis, William T. *Billy Sunday.* Philadelphia: John C. Winston, 1914.

Ellison, E. Jerome, and Brock, Frank W. *The Run for Your Money.* New York: Dodge, 1935.

Ellison, Herbert J. *History of Russia.* New York: Holt, Rinehart & Winston, 1964.

Ellms, Charles. *The Pirates Own Book, or Authentic Narratives of the Lives, Exploits and Executions of the Most Celebrated Sea Robbers.* Salem, Mass.: Marine Research Society, 1924.

Elman, Robert. *Fired in Anger: The Personal Handguns of American Heroes and Villains.* Garden City, N.Y.: Doubleday, 1968.

_____. *Badmen of the West.* Secaucus, N.J.: Ridge Press, 1974.

Elmer, E. *Children in Jeopardy: A Study of Abused Minors and Their Families.* Pittsburgh, Pa.: University of Pittsburgh Press, 1967.

Elsberry, Terence. *Marie of Romania.* New York: St. Martin's, 1972.

Elsbree, Willard H. *Japan's Role in Southeast Asian Nationalist Movements, 1940-45.* Cambridge, Mass: Harvard University Press, 1953.

Elst, Baron Joseph van der. *The Last Flowering of the Middle Ages.* Port Washington, N.Y.: Kennikat Press, 1969.

Elton, G.R. (ed.). *The Tudor Constitution.* New York: Cambridge University Press, 1982.

Elton, Lord. *Gordon of Khartoum: The Life of General Charles George Gordon.* New York: Alfred A. Knopf, 1955.

Elwin, V., and Winslow, J. *The Dawn of Indian Freedom.* London: Allen & Unwin, 1931.

Elworthy, Frederic Thomas. *The Evil Eye.* London: J. Murray, 1895.

Ely, Richard T. *French and German Socialism.* New York: Harper, 1898.

Emard, Paul, and Fournier, Suzanne. *Les annees criminelles de Madame de Montespan.* Paris: Les editions Denoel, 1939.

Emboden, W.A. *Flesh of the gods.* New York: Praeger, 1974.

Emerit, Marcel. *L'Algrie a l'Epoque d'Abd el-Kader.* Paris: Editions Larose, 1951.

Emerson, K.C. *Guest of the Emperor.* Privately published, 1977.

Emerson, R. *Judging Delinquents: Context and Process in the Juvenile Court.* Chicago: Aldine Press, 1969.

Emerson, Steven. *American Jihad: The Terrorists Living Among Us.* New York: Free Press, 2002.

_____. *The Fall of Pan Am 103: Inside the Lockerbie Investigation.* New York: Putnam, 1990.

Emery, Edwin, and Smith, Henry Ladd. *The Press and America.* New York: Prentice-Hall, 1954.

Emery, Fred E. *Freedom and Justice Within Walls.* London: Tavistock Publications, 1970.

Emery, J. Gladston. *Court of the Damned.* New York: Comet Press, 1959.

Emery, Richard W. *Heresy and the Inquisition in Norbonne.* New York: Columbia University Press, 1941.

_____. *Shanghai Pierce, a Fair Likeness.* Norman: University of Oklahoma Press, 1953.

Emmons, Dr. Robert. *The Life and Opinions of Walter Richard Sickert.* London: Faber and Faber, 1941.

Empey, Lamar T., and Lubeck, Steven G. *Delinquency Prevention Strategies.* Washington, D.C.: U.S. Government Printing Office, 1970.

Emrich, Duncan. *It's An Old Wild West Custom.* New York: Vanguard Press, 1949.

Encyclopedia Americana. 30 vols. Montreal: Americana Corporation of Canada, 1962.

Endelman, T.M. *The Jews of Georgian England 1714-1830.* Philadelphia: Jewish Publication Society of America, 1979.

Engel, Barbara Alpern, and Rosenthal, Clifford N. (eds. and trans.). *Five Sisters: Women Against the Tsar.* New York: Alfred A. Knopf, 1975.

Engel, Madeline H. *The Drug Scene.* Rochelle Park, N.J.: Hayden Book, 1974.

Engel, Major. *Heeresadjutant bei Hitler, 1938-1943.* Stuttgart, Ger.: Deutsche Verlags-Anstalt, 1974.

Engelbrecht, H.C. *Merchants of Death.* New York: Dodd, Mead, 1934.

Engelmann, Larry. *Intemperence: The Lost War Against Liquor.* New York: Free Press, 1979.

Engels, Donald W. *Alexander the Great and the Logistics of the Macedonian Army.* Berkeley, Calif.: University of California Press, 1981.

Englade, Ken. *Cellar of Horror.* New York: St. Martin's, 1988.

England, Ralph W. *Prison Labour.* New York: United Nations Department of Economic and Social Affairs, 1955.

Ennis, Philip H. *Criminal Victimization in the United States: A Report of a National Survey.* Washington, D.C.: U.S. Government Printing Office, 1967.

Enright, Richard T. (Earl Buell). *Al Capone on the Spot.* Graphic Arts, 1931.

Ensor, David. *I Was a Public Prosecutor.* London: Robert Hale, 1958.

Ensor, R.C.K. *England, 1870-1914.* London: Cambridge University Press, 1936.

Eptein, Robin, et al. *The Legal Aspects of Contract Parole.* College Park, Md.: American Correctional Association, 1976.

Epois, Jean. *L'affaire Corday-Marat: Prelude a la Terreur.* Les Sables d'Olonne: Cercle d'Or, 1980.

Epstein, Benjamin R., and Forster, Arnold. *The Radical Right.* New York: Vintage Books, 1967.

Epstein, Edward Jay. *Agency of Fear: Opiates and Political Power in America.* New York: G.P. Putnam's Sons, 1977.

_____. *Counterplot.* New York: The Viking Press, 1969.

_____. *Inquest.* New York: The Viking Press, 1966.

_____. *Legend: The Secret World of Lee Harvey Oswald.* New York: Readers Digest Press, 1978.

_____. *News From Nowhere.* New York: Random House, 1973.

Epstein, Israel. *The Unfinished Revolution in China.* Boston: Little, Brown, 1947.

Epstein, Jason. *The Great Conspiracy Trial.* New York: Random House, 1970.

Epstein, Klaus. *Matthias Erzberger and the Dilemma of German Democracy.* Princeton, N.J.: Princeton University Press, 1959.

Epstein, Louis M. *Sex Laws and Customs in Judaism.* New York: KTAV, 1967.

Epstein, Melech. *The Jew and Communism.* New York: Trade Union Sponsoring Committee, 1959.

_____. *Jewish Labor in U.S.A.* 2 vols. New York: Trades Union Sponsoring Committee, 1950-53.

Erbstein, Charles E. *The Show-Up: Stories Before the Bar.* Chicago: Pascal Covici, 1926.

Ercole, F. *Storia del Fascismo.* Milan, Italy: Mondadori, 1939.

Erdman, Paul E. *The Billion Dollar Sure Thing.* New York: Scribner's Sons, 1973.

Erdstein, Erich. *Inside the Fourth Reich.* New York: St. Martins Press, 1977.

Erickson, Gladys A. *Warden Ragen of Joliet.* New York: Dutton, 1957.

Ericson, Richard V. *Making Crime: A Study of Detective Work.* Toronto, Ontario, Can.: Buttersworth, 1981.

Erie, Steven P. *Rainbow's End: Irish-Americans and the Dilemmas of Urban Machine Politics, 1840-1985.* Berkeley: University of California Press, 1988.

Erikson, Kai T. *Everything in Its Path.* New York: Simon & Schuster, 1976.

_____. *Wayward Puritans.* New York: John Wiley, 1966.

Eriksson, Torsten. *The Reformers.* New York: Elsevier, 1976.

Erlanger, Rachel. *Lucrezia Borgia: A Biography.* New York: Dutton, 1978.

Erman, Adolf. *The Ancient Egyptians.* trans. Aylward M. Blackman. New York: Harper Torchbooks, 1966.

Ermann, M. David, and Lundmann, Richard J. *Corporate Deviance.* New York: Holt, Rinehart, Winston, 1982.

Ernest II, Duke Saxe-Coburg-Gotha. *Memoirs.* 4 vols. London: Remington, 1888.

Ernst, Morris L. *A Love Affair with the Law: A Legal Sampler.* New York: Macmillan, 1968.

Ernst, Robert A. *Immigrant Life in New York City, 1825-1863.* New York: King's Crown Press, 1949.

Erskine, Gladys. *Broncho Charlie: A Saga of the Saddle.* New York: Thomas Y. Crowell, 1934.

Erskine, Margaret. *Give Up the Ghost.* London: Hammond, 1949.

Ervin Sam J., Jr. *The Whole Truth: The Watergate Conspiracy.* New York: Random House, 1980.

Erwin, Allen A. *The Southwest of John H. Slaughter, 1841-1922.* Glendale, Calif.: Arthur H. Clark, 1965.

Erwin, Carol, and Miller, Floyd. *The Orderly Disorderly House.* Garden City, N.Y.: Doubleday, 1960.

Erwin, John R. *The Man Who Keeps Going to Jail.* Fullerton, Calif.: Cook Press, 1978.

Eshelman, Byron. *Death Row Chaplain.* Englewood Cliffs, N.J.: Prentice-Hall, 1962.

Eskew, Garnett. *The Pageant of the Packets.* New York: Henry Holt, 1929.

Esmein, A. *A History of Continental Criminal Procedure.* Boston: Little, Brown, 1913.

Esquirol, Jean tienne. *Des maladies mentales.* Paris: J. and B. Baillire, 1838.

Essas, Bey. *Nicholas II Prisoner of the Purple.* London: Hutchinson, 1936.

Essien-Udom, E.U. *Black Nationalism.* Chicago: University of Chicago Press, 1962.

Estol, Horacio. *Realidad y Leyenda de Pancho Villa.* Buenos Aires, Arg.: Libreria Hachette, 1944.

Estrada, Rogue. *La Revolucion y Francisco I. Madero.* Guadalajara, Mex.: Impreta Americana, 1912.

Estrella, Manuel M. Jr., and Forest, Martin L. *The Family Guide to Crime Prevention.* New York: Beaufort Books, 1981.

Ethus, Raymond A. *Double Eagle and Rising Sun: The Russians and Japanese at Port Arthur in 1905.* Durham, N. C.: Duke University Press, 1988.

Ettinger, Clayton. *The Problem of Crime.* New York: Ray Long and Richard R. Smith, 1932.

Ettlinger, Harold. *The Axis on the Air.* Indianapolis, Ind.: Bobbs-Merrill, 1943.

Eulalia, H.R.H. *Court Life from Within.* London: Cassell, 1915.

_____. *Courts and Countries After the War.* New York: Dodd, Mead, 1925.

Eulenberg, Herbert. *The Hohenzollerns.* London: George Allen & Unwin, 1929.

Evan, William M. *Law and Sociology, Exploratory Essays.* New York: Free Press of Glencoe, 1962.

_____. (ed). *The Sociology of the Law.* New York: Free Press, 1980.

Evans, Alona, and Murphy, John (eds.). *Legal Aspects of International Terrorism.* London: Heath, 1978.

Evans, Sir Arthur. *Through Bosnia and Herzegovina on Foot During the Insurrection, 1875, With Historical Review of Bosnia.* London: Longman, 1876.

Evans, Christopher. *Cults of Unreason.* New York: Farrar, Straus and Giroux, 1973.

Evans, Clyde (ed.). *Adventures of Great Crime Busters.* New York: New Power, 1943.

Evans, Daniel. *When Crime Strikes.* Olympia, Wash.: State Printing Plant, 1974.

Evans, Edward Payson. *The Criminal Prosecution and Capital Punishment of Animals.* London: William Heinemann, 1904.

Evans, George G. *Illustrated History of the United States Mint.* Philadelphia: George G. Evans, 1890.

Evans, M. Stanton. *The Law Breakers.* New Rochelle, New York: Arlington House, 1968.

Evans, P. *Law and Disorder, or Scenes of Life in Kenya.* London: Secker & Warburg, 1956.

Evans, Peter (ed.). *The Police Revolution.* London: George Allen & Unwin, 1974.

Evans, Stewart P., and Skinner, Keith. *Jack the Ripper and the Whitechapel Murders.* London: Casemate Publishing, 2002

_____. *Jack the Ripper: Letters from Hell.* Stroud, Eng.: Sutton Publishing Ltd., 2001.

_____. *The Ultimate Jack the Ripper Sourcebook.* London: Constable and Robinson, 2000.

Everest, Allen S. *Rum Across the Border.* New York: Syracuse Univ., 1978.

Everitt, David. *Human Monsters.* Chicago: Contemporary Books, 1993.

Everson, William K. *The Detective in Film.* Secaucus, N.J.: Citadel Press, 1972.

Everett, Marshall. *Life of William McKinley and Story of His Assassination.* Chicago: Donohue, 1901.

Every, Edward Van. *Sins of America as 'Exposed' by the Police Gazette.* New York: Frederick A. Stokes, 1931.

Ewen, Cecil H. L'Estrange. *Some Witchcraft Criticism.* London: Published by Author, 1938.

_____. *Witchcraft and Demonianism.* London: Heath, Crouton, 1933.

_____. *Witchcraft in the Norfolk Circuit.* London: Published by Author, 1939.

_____. *Witchcraft in the Star Chamber.* London: Published by Author, 1939.

_____. *Witch Hunting and Witch Trials.* New York: Dial, 1930.

Ewens, G.F.W. *Insanity in India.* Calcutta, India: Thacker, Spink, 1908.

Ewing, A.C. *The Morality of Punishment.* London: K. Paul, Trench, Trubner, 1929.

Ewing, Charles. *Kids Who Kill.* Lexington, Mass.: Lexington Books, 1990.

The Execution and Last Moments of Henry G. Green. New York: n.p., 1845.

Execution of Richard Johnson. New York: n.p., n.d.

Exner, Judith. *My Story.* New York: Grove, 1977.

Exquemelin, Alexander. *The Buccaneers of America.* Baltimore: Penguin Books, 1969.

The Extraordinary Life and Character of Mary Bateman, the Yorkshire Witch. Leeds, Eng.: Edward Baines, 1809.

The Extraordinary Life and Trial of Madame Rachel. London: Diprose and Bateman, 1868.

Eyman, Joy Satterwhite. *How to Convict a Rapist.* New York: Stein & Day, 1980.

Eysenck, H.J. *Crime and Personality.* London: Routledge and Kegan Paul, 1977.

Eytan, Walter. *The First Ten Years: A Diplomatic History of Israel.* New York: Simon & Schuster, 1958.

Ezell, J. *Fortune's Merry Wheel: The Lottery in America.* Cambridge, Mass.: Harvard University Press, 1960.

Fabian, Robert. *Fabian of the Yard.* London: Naldrett Press, 1950.

_____. *London After Dark.* London: Naldrett Press, 1954.

Fabre, Joseph. *Proces de condamnation de Jeanne d'Arc.* Paris: C. Delagrave, 1884.

_____. *Proces de rehabilitation de Jeanne d'Arc.* Paris: Hachette, 1913.

Fabre, Lucien. *Jeanne d'Arc.* Paris: J. Tallandier, 1948.

Fabre, M.A. *Jerome Bonaparte.* Paris: Hachette, 1952.

Fabre, Maurice. *A History of Communication.* New York: Hawthorn Books, 1963.

Fagg, John Edwin. *Cuba, Haiti and The Dominican Republic.* Englewood Cliffs, N.J.: Prentice-Hall, 1965.

Fa-Hsien. *The Travels of Fa-Hsien (391-414 A.D.) or Record of the Buddhist Kingdoms.* trans. H.A. Giles. Cambridge, Eng.: Cambridge University Press, 1923.

Fain, Tyrus G. (ed.). *The Intelligence Community.* New York: R.R. Bowker, 1977.

Fair, Laura D. *Wolves in the Fold.* San Francisco: n.p., 1873.

Fair and Certain Punishment. Report of the Twentieth Century Task Force on Criminal Sentencing. New York: McGraw-Hill, 1976.

Fairbank, J.K., Reischauer, E.O., and Craig, A.M. *East Asia: The Modern Transformation.* Boston: Houghton Mifflin, 1965.

_____. *A History of East Asian Civilization.* Boston: Houghton Mifflin, 1964.

Fairchild, Henry Pratt. *The Melting Pot Mistake.* Boston: Little, Brown, 1926.

_____. *This Way Out.* New York: Harper, 1936.

Fairfield, L. (ed.). *Notable British Trials: Trial of Peter Barnes and Others.* London: William Hodge, 1953.

Fairlie, Gerard. *The Reluctant Cop.* London: Hodder & Stoughton, 1958.

Fairman, Charles. *Mr. Justice Miller and the Supreme Court, 1862-1890.* Cambridge, Mass.: Harvard University Press, 1939.

Fairstein, Linda A. *Sexual Violence.* New York: William Morrow, 1993.

Falco, Mario. *The Legal Position of the Holy See before and after the Lateran Treaty.* Oxford, Eng.: Oxford University Press, 1935.

Falcon, W.D. (ed.). *Witness Cooperation.* Lexington, Mass.: D.C. Heath, 1976.

Falk, Candace. *Love, Anarchy, and Emma Goldman.* New York: Holt, Rinehart & Winston, 1984.

Falls, C.B. *The Birth of Ulster.* London: Methuen, 1936.

Fallwell, Gene. *The Texas Rangers.* Texarkana, Texas: Connell Printing, 1959.

Falola, Togin. *The History of Nigeria.* Westport, Conn.: Greeenwood Press, 1999.

_____. *Violence in Nigeria: The Crisis of Religious Politics and Secular Ideologies.* Rochester, N. Y.: University of Rochester Press, 1998.

Falzone, Gaetano. *Histiore de la Mafia.* Paris: Fayard, 1973.

Fang, John T. *Chinatown Handy Guide.* San Francisco: Chinese Publishing House, 1959.

Fanning, Clara E. (ed.). *Selected Articles on Capital Punishment.* Minneapolis, Minn.: H.W. Wilson, 1913.

Fanning, Pete. *Great Crimes of the West.* San Francisco: Ed Barry, 1929.

Faralicq, Ren. *The French Police from Within.* London: Cassell, 1933.

Farber, James. *Texans with Guns.* San Antonio, Texas: Naylor, 1950.

_____. *Those Texans.* San Antonio, Texas: Naylor, 1945.

Farge, Arlette, and Revel, Jacques. *The Vanishing Children of Paris.* Cambridge, Mass.: Harvard University Press, 1988.

Faris, Robert E.L. *Chicago Sociology 1920-32.* San Francisco: Chandler, 1967.

Farish, G.H. *History of Arizona.* San Francisco: Filmer, 1915.

Farjeon, Eleanor (ed.). *The Unlocked Door.* New York: G.P. Putnam's Sons, 1938.

Farley, James A. *Behind the Ballots.* New York: Harcourt, 1938.

_____. *Jim Farley's Story: The Roosevelt Years.* New York: McGraw-Hill, 1948.

Farley, Philip. *Criminals of America; or Tales of the Lives of Thieves.* New York: Published by author, 1876.

Farmer, William R. *Maccabees, Zealots and Josephus.* New York: Columbia University Press, 1956.

Farnsworth, Majorie. *The Ziegfeld Follies: A History in Text and Pictures.* New York: G.P. Putnam's Sons, 1956.

Farr, Finis. *Chicago.* New Rochelle, N.Y.: Arlington House, 1973.

_____. *Fair Enough: The Life of Westbrook Pegler.* New Rochelle, N.Y.: Arlington House, 1975.

_____. *Frank Lloyd Wright.* New York: Charles Scribner's Sons, 1961.

_____. *O'Hara.* Boston: Little Brown, 1973.

Farr, Louise. *The Sunset Murders.* New York: Pocket Books, 1992.

Farr, Samuel. *Elements of Medical Jurisprudence.* London: J. Callow, 1814.

Farran, Roy. *Winged Dagger.* London: Collins, 1948.

Farrell, Cullom Holmes. *Incidents in the Life of General Pershing.* New York: Rand, McNally, 1918.

Farson, Daniel. *The Hamlyn Book of Horror.* London: Hamlyn, 1977.

_____. *Jack the Ripper.* London: Michael Joseph, 1972.

Farson, N. *Last Chance in Africa.* London: V. Gollancz, 1953.

Farwell, Willard B. *The Chinese at Home and Abroad.* San Francisco: A.L. Bancroft, 1885.

Fast, Howard Melvin. *The Passion of Sacco Vanzetti.* New York: Blue Heron Press, 1953.

Faulds, H. *Guide to Finger Print Identification.* Hanley: Wood, Mitchell, 1905.

Faulk, Odie B. *Dodge City.* New York: Oxford Univ. Press, 1977.

_____. *Tombstone: Myth and Reality.* New York: Oxford University Press, 1972.

Faure, Edgar. *The Serpent and the Tortoise.* London: Macmillan, 1958.

Fawcett, Edgar. *The Evil That Men Do.* New York: Belford, 1889.

Fawcett, Jan (ed.). *Dynamics of Violence.* Chicago: American Medical Association, 1972.

Fawkes, Sandy. *Killing Time.* New York: Taplinger, 1979.

Fay, Bernard. *Louis XVI, or The End of a World.* Chicago: Henry Regnery, 1966.

Fay, E.S. *The Life of Mr. Justice Swift.* London: Methuen, 1939.

Fay, Peter W. *The Opium War: 1840-1842.* Chapel Hill: University of North Carolina Press, 1975.

Fay, Stephen, et al. *Hoax: The Inside Story of the Howard Hughs Affair.* New York: Viking Press, 1972.

Fea, Allan. *Secret Chambers and Hiding Places.* London: Bousfield, 1901.

Feck, Luke. *Yesterday's Cincinnati.* Miami: E.A. Seemann, 1975.

_____, and Joesten, Joachim. *The Luciano Story.* New York: David McKay, 1954.

Federal Bureau of Investigation. *Classification of Fingerprints.* Washington, D.C.: U.S. Government Printing Office, 1941.

_____. *Crime in the United States.* Washington, D.C.: U.S. Government Printing Office, 1983.

_____. *Handbook of Forensic Science.* Washington, D.C.: U.S. Government Printing Office, 1984.

_____. *Uniform Crime Reports.* Washington, D.C.: U.S. Government Printing Office, n.d.

Feeley, Malcolm M. *Court Reform on Trial.* New York: Basic Books, Twentieth Century Fund, 1983.

Fehrenberg, Don E. *Chicago Giant.* Madison, Wis.: American History Research Center, 1957.

Feifer, George. *Justice in Moscow.* New York: Delta, 1965.

Fei Hsiao-tung. *China's Gentry, Essays in Rural-Urban Relations.* Chicago: University of Chicago Press, 1953.

Fein, Judith. *Are You a Target?* Belmont, Calif.: Wadsworth, 1981.

Fein, Leonard J. *Politics in Israel.* Boston: Little, Brown, 1967.

Feitlowitz, Marguerite. *A Lexicon of Terror: Argentina and the Legacies of Torture.* New York: Oxford University Press, 1998.

Feldman, Harold. *Fifty-One Witnesses: The Grassy Knoll.* San Francisco: Idlewild, 1965.

Feldman, Herman. *Prohibition.* New York: D. Appleton, 1927.

Feldman, M.P. *Criminal Behaviour.* New York, John Wiley, 1977.

Felix, David. *Protest.* Bloomington: Indiana University Press, 1965.

Fell, James. *British Merchant Seamen in San Francisco, 1892-1898.* London: E. Arnold, 1899.

Felony Arrests: Their Prosecution and Disposition in New York City's Courts. New York: The Vera Institute of Justice, 1977.

Felstead, Sidney Theodore. *Sir Richard Muir.* London: John Lane, 1927.

_____. *Shades of Scotland Yard.* London: John Long, 1950.

Felt, Jeremy P. *Hostages of Fortune.* Ithaca, N.Y.: Cornell University Press, 1965.

Felt, Joseph B. *The Annals of Salem from Its First Settlement.* Salem, Mass.: W. & S.B. Ives, 1827.

Felt, Mark. *The FBI Pyramid.* New York: G.P. Putnam's Sons, 1979.

Fennell, J.L.I. *Ivan the Great of Muscovy.* New York: St. Martin's Press, 1961.

Fenton, Norman. *Treatment in Prison: How the Family Can Help.* Sacramento: State of California, 1959.

Fenwick, Robert W. *Alfred Packer.* Denver: Denver Post, 1963.

Fenyvesi, Charles. *Splendor in Exile.* Washington, D.C.: New Republic Books, 1970.

Ferber, Elizabeth. *Yasir Arafat: A Life of War and Peace.* Brookfield, Conn.: Millbrook Press, 1995

Ferber, Edna. *A Peculiar Treasure.* New York: Doubleday, 1960.

Ferber, Nat. *I Found Out.* New York: Dial Press, 1939.

Ferguson, Ian. *The Philosophy of Witchcraft.* London: G.G. Harrap, 1924.

Ferguson, W.J. *I Saw Booth Shoot Lincoln.* New York: Houghton Mifflin, 1930.

Fergusson, Adam. *When Money Dies-The Nightmare of the Weimer Collapse.* London: William Kimber, 1975.

Fergusson, Erna. *Murder & Mystery in New Mexico.* Albuquerque, N.M.: Armitage Editions, 1948.

Fermi, Laura. *Mussolini.* Chicago: University of Chicago Press, 1963.

Fernandez Rojas, Jos. *De Porfirio Diaz a Victoriano Huerta, 1910-1913.* Mexico City: F.P. Rojas y Campaia, 1913.

Fero, Kelly. *The Zani Murders.* Austin, Tex.: Texas Monthly Press, 1990.

Ferracuti, Franco, Lazzari, Renato, and Wolfgang, Marvin E. *Violence in Sardinia.* Rome: Mario Bulzoni, 1970.

Ferraironi, Francesco. *Le Streghe e l'Inquisizione.* Rome: Sallustiann, 1955.

Ferrara, Orestes. *The Borgia Pope.* trans. F.J. Sheed. New York: Sheed and Ward, 1940.

_____. *The Last Spanish Pope.* London: Williams & Norgate, 1937.

Ferrari, Santo. *L'Italia Fascista.* Turin, Italy: Ed Libraria Italiana, 1942.

Ferrarotti, Franco. *Rapporto sulla mafia.* Naples, Italy: Liguori, 1978.

Ferrer, R. *Manual de Identification Judicial.* Madrid: Reus, 1921.

Ferrer de M., Gabriel. *Vida de Francisco I. Madero.* Mexico City: Secretaria de Educacion Publica, 1945.

Ferrero, Guglielmo. *Four Years of Fascism.* trans. E.W. Dickes. London: P.S. King, 1942.

Ferri, Enrico. *Criminal Sociology.* New York: D. Appleton, 1896.

Ferro, Marc, and Pearce, Brian. *Nicholas II: Last of the Tsars.* New York: Oxford University Press, 1995.

Ferry, Jon, and Inwood, Damian. *The Olson Murders.* Langley, B. C.: Cameo Books, 1982.

Fest, Joachim C. *Hitler.* London: Weidenfeld & Nicolson, 1974.

Fethering, Doug. *The Five Lives of Ben Hecht.* London: Lester & Orpen, 1977.

Fetherstonhough, R.C. *The Royal Canadian Mounted Police.* New York: Carrick & Evans, 1938.

Feuerlicht, Roberta S. *The Desperate Act.* New York: McGraw-Hill, 1968.

Feuerwerker, Albert (ed.). *Modern China.* Englewood Cliffs, N.J.: Prentice-Hall, 1964.

Fewtrell, Malcolm. *The Train Robbers.* London: Arthur Barker, 1964.

Fiaschetti, Michael. *You Gotta Be Rough.* Garden City, N.Y.: Doubleday, Doran, 1930.

Fiedler, George. *The Illinois Law Courts in Three Centuries 1673-1973.* Berwyn, Ill.: Physicians' Record, 1973.

Fiedler, Leslie. *An End to Innocence: Essays on Culture and Politics.* Boston: Beacon, 1955.

_____. *On Being Busted.* New York: Stein & Day, 1970.

Fiedler, Mildred. *Wild Bill and Deadwood.* New York: Bonanza Books, 1965.

Field, Carter. *Bernard Baruch.* New York: Whittlesey House, 1944.

Fieldhouse, D.K. *The Colonial Empires.* New York: Delacorte Press, 1965.

Fielding, Cecil. *Justice Triumphant.* London: John Long, 1958.

Fielding, Henry. *An Enquiry into the Causes of the Late Increase in Robbers.* New York: AMS Press, 1975.

Fielding, John. *An Account of the Origin and Effects of a Police Set on Foot by His Grace the Duke of Newcastle in the Year 1753.* London: A. Millar, 1758.

Fielding, Xan. *The Money Spinner.* Boston: Little, Brown, 1977.

Fields, Howard. *High Crimes and Misdemeanors.* New York: W.W. Norton, 1978.

Figgis, Darrell. *A Chronicle of Jails.* Dublin, Ire.: Talbot, 1918.

_____. *A Second Chronicle of Jails.* Dublin, Ire.: Talbot, 1919.

Filler, Louis. *The Anxious Years: America in the Nineteen Thirties.* New York: Capricorn, 1964.

_____. *The Muckrakers.* University Park: Pennsylvania State University Press, 1976.

Filmer, Sir Robert. *An Advertisement of the Jurymen of England Touching Witches.* London: R. Royston, 1653.

Final Report, Commission to Investigate Allegations of Police Corruption and the City's Anti-Corruption Procedures. New York: The Fund for the City of New York, 1972.

Finch, Sir Henry. *Law.* London: Henry Lintot, 1759.

Fine, Ralph Adam. *Escape of the Guilty.* New York: Dodd, Mead, 1986.

Finegan, James E. *Tammany at Bay.* New York: Dodd, 1933.

Finer, Herman. *Mussolini's Italy.* New York: Holt, 1935.

_____. *Road to Reaction.* Boston: Little, Brown, 1945.

Fines and Imprisonments in Counterfeiting Cases. Washington, D.C.: U.S. Government Printing Office, 1935.

Fingarette, Herbert. *The Meaning of Criminal Insanity.* Berkeley: University of California Press, 1972.

_____, and Hasse, A.F. *Mental Disabilities and Criminal Responsibility.* Berkeley: University of California Press, 1979.

Fink, Joseph, and Sealy, Lloyd G. *The Community and the Police.* New York: John Wiley & Sons, 1974.

Finkelhor, David, and Hotaling, Gerald, and Sedlak, Andrea. *Missing, Abducted, Runaways, and Throwaway Children in America.* Washington, D. C.: U. S. Department of Justice, 1990.

_____. *Sexually Victimized Children.* New York: Free Press, 1979.

Finkelstein, M. Marvin, et al. *Prosecution in the Juvenile Court: Guidelines for the Future.* Washington, D.C.: National Institute of Law Enforcement and Criminal Justice, 1973.

Finlay, George. *A History of Greece from its Conquest by the Romans to the Present Time, 146 B.C. to 1864 A.D.* Oxford, Eng.: Clarendon Press, 1877.

Finley, John H. *Thucydides.* Cambridge, Mass.: Harvard University Press, 1942.

Finley, M.I., Smith, Denis Mack, and Duggan, Christopher. *A History of Sicily.* New York: Viking Press, 1987.

Finn, John T. *History of the Chicago Police.* Chicago: Police Book Fund, 1887.

Finney, Ben. *Feet First.* New York: Crown, 1971.

Finney, Charles G. *The Old China Hands.* New York: Doubleday, 1961.

Firmin, Stanley. *Crime Man.* New York: Hutchinson, 1950.

_____. *Murderers in Our Midst.* London: Hutchinson, 1955.

_____. *Scotland Yard: The Inside Story.* London: Hutchinson, 1948.

Firth, Charles H. *The Last Years of the Protectorate.* London: Longman, Green, 1909.

_____. *Oliver Cromwell and the Rule of the Puritans in England.* New York: G.P. Putnam's Sons, 1900.

Firth, James Brierley. *A Scientist Turns to Crime.* London: W. Kimber, 1960.

Fischer, Ben B. Okhrana: *The Paris Operation of the Russian Imperial Police.* Washington, D. C.: Central Intelligence Agency, Center for the Study of Intelligence, 1997.

Fischer, George. *Russian Emigre Politics.* New York: Free Russia Fund, 1951.

_____. *Russian Liberalism.* Cambridge, Mass.: Harvard University Press, 1958.

_____. *Soviet Opposition to Stalin.* Cambridge, Mass.: Harvard
University Press, 1952.

Fischer, Louis. *The Life and Death of Stalin.* New York: Harper & Brothers, 1962.

_____. *The Life of Lenin.* New York: Harper & Row, 1964.

_____. *The Life of Mahatma Gandhi.* New York: Harper & Brothers, 1950.

_____. *Russia Revisited.* Garden City, N.Y.: Doubleday, 1957.

_____. *The Soviets and World Affairs.* New Jersey: Princeton University Press, 1951.

Fischer, Ruth. *Stalin and German Communism.* Cambridge, Mass.: Harvard University Press, 1948.

Fischer-Galanti, Stephen. *Eastern Europe in the Sixties.* New York: Frederick A. Praeger, 1963.

_____ (ed.). *Twentieth Century Rumania.* New York: Columbia University Press, 1970.

Fischle, Ernst. *Kidnapped in China.* trans. Marie S. Christlieb. Mangalore, India: Basel Mission Book and Tract Depository, 1932.

Fishbein, Morris. *Fads and Quackery in Healing.* New York: Covici, Friede, 1932.

Fishburne, Patricia, et al. *National Survey on Drug Abuse.* Washington, D.C.: U.S. Government Printing Office, 1980.

Fisher, Carol, and Krinsky, Fred. *Middle East in Crisis.* Syracuse, N.Y.: Syracuse University Press, 1959.

Fisher, Sir Godfrey. *Barbary Legend: War, Trade and Piracy in North Africa, 1415-1830.* Oxford, Eng.: Clarendon Press, 1957.

Fisher, Irving. *The Nobel Experiment.* New York: Alcohol Information Committee, 1930

_____. *Prohibition at Its Worst.* New York: Macmillan, 1926.

_____, and Brougham, H.B. *Prohibition Still at Its Worst.* New York: Alcohol Information Committee, 1928.

_____. *The Stock Market Crash-and After.* New York: Macmillan, 1930.

Fisher, Jim. *The Ghosts of Hopewell: Setting the Record Straight in the Lindbergh Case.* Carbondale, Ill.: Southern Illinois University Press, 1999.

_____. *The Lindbergh Case.* New Brunswick, N. J.: Rutgers University Press, 1987.

Fisher, John. *The Elysian Fields: France in Ferment, 1789-1804.* London: Cassell, 1966.

Fisher, Joseph. *Killer Among Us.* West Port, Conn.: Praeger, 1997.

Fisher, Lord. *Memories.* London: Hodder & Stoughton, 1919.

Fisher, Paul L, and Lowenstein, Ralph L. (eds.). *Race and the News Media.* Frederick A. Praeger, 1967.

Fisher, S.G. *The Making of Pennsylvania.* Philadelphia: J.B. Lippincott, 1932.

Fisher, Sydney. *The Middle East: A History.* New York: Alfred A. Knopf, 1959.

_____ (ed.). *The Military in the Middle East.* Columbus: Ohio State University Press, 1963.
Fisher, W.B. *The Middle East.* New York: E.P. Dutton, 1950.
Fishman, Joseph F. *Sex in Prison.* National Library Press, 1934.
Fishman, William J. *East End 1888.* London: Hanbury, 2001.
_____. *East End Jewish Radicals 1875-1914.* London: Duckworth, 1975.
_____. *Jewish Radicals.* New York: Pantheon Books, 1974.
_____. *The Streets of East London.* London: Duckworth, 1979.
Fisk, James G. *The Police Community.* Pacific Palisades, Calif.: Palisades, 1974.
Fiske, Stephen. *Off-hand Portraits of Prominent New Yorkers.* New York: G.R. Lockwood & Son, 1884.
_____. *Tobacco and Alcohol.* New York: Leypoldt & Holt, 1869.
Fitch, J.A. *The Pittsburgh Survey.* New York: Russell Sage Foundation, 1911.
Fitzgerald, C.P. *The Birth of Communist China.* Baltimore: Penguin, 1964.
_____. *Flood Tide in China.* London: Cresset Press, 1958.
_____. *Revolution in China.* London: Cresset Press, 1952.
Fitzgerald, F. Scott. *The Crack-Up.* New York: New Directions, 1945.
_____. *The Great Gatsby.* New York: Charles Scribner's Sons, 1925.
Fitzgerald, Maurice. *Criminal Investigations.* New York: Greenberg, 1953.
Fitzgerald, Percy H. *Chronicles of the Bow Street Police Office.* London: Chapman & Hall, 1888.
Fitzharris, Timothy L. *The Desirability of a Correctional Ombudsman.* Berkeley, Calif.: Institute of Governmental Studies, 1973.
Fitzjames Stephen, Sir James. *A History of the Criminal Law of England.* London: Macmillan, 1883.
Fitzlyon, Kynil, and Browning, Tatiana. *Before the Revolution: Russia and Its People Under the Czar.* New York: Random House, 1983.
Fitzpatrick, George (ed.). *This Is New Mexico.* Santa Fe, N.M.: Rydal Press, 1948.
Fitzpatrick, John C. (ed.). *The Writings of George Washington.* Washington, D.C.: U.S. Government Printing Office, 1931-1944.
Fitzpatrick, Joseph P. *Puerto Rican Americans.* Englewood Cliffs, N.J.: Prentice-Hall, 1971.
The Five Fiends, or the Bender Hotel Horror in Kansas. Philadelphia: Old Franklin, 1874.
Flaherty, David H. *Essays in the History of Early American Law.* Chapel Hill: University of North Carolina Press, 1969.
Flamm, Jerry. *Good Life in Hard Times.* San Francisco: Chronicle Books, 1978.
Flammonde, Paris. *The Kennedy Conspiracy.* New York: Meredith Press, 1969.
Flanagan, Mike. *Out West.* New York: Harry N. Abrams, 1987.
Flanders, Henry. *Lives and Times of the Chief Justices of the Supreme Court of the United States.* 2 vols. Philadelphia: Lippincott, Crambo, 1855-1858.
Fleming, Alice. *New on the Beat: Woman Power in the Police Force.* New York: Coward, McCann & Geoghegan, 1975.
Fleming, D.F. *The United States and the League of Nations, 1918-20.* New York: G.P. Putnam's Sons, 1932.
Fleming, John S. *What Is Ku Kluxism?* Goodwater, Ala.: Masonic Weekly Recorder, 1923.
Fleming, Karl and Anne Taylor. *The First Time.* New York: Simon & Schuster, 1975.
Fleming, Macklin. *The Price of Perfect Justice.* New York: Basic Books, 1974.
Fleming, Peter. *The Fate of Admiral Kolchak.* London: Hart Davis, 1963.
Fletcher, Ernest M. *The Wayward Horseman.* Denver: Sage Books, 1958.
Fleuret, Fernand. *De Gilles de Rais a Guillaume Apollinaire.* Poitiers, Fr.: Marc Tzier, 1933.
Fleury, Marurice, comte (ed.). *Memoirs of the Empress Eugnie.* 2 vols. New York: D. Appleton, 1920.
Flew, Antony. *Crime or Disease?* London: Macmillan, 1973.
Flexner, Abraham. *Prostitution in Europe.* New York: Century, 1914.
Flexner, Eleanor. *Century of Struggle.* Cambridge, Mass.: Harvard University Press, 1959.
_____. *The Traitor and the Spy.* New York: Little, Brown, 1953.
Flick, Alexander C. (ed.). *The History of the State of New York.* New York: Columbia University Press, 1933.
_____. *Samuel Jones Tilden: A Study in Political Sagacity.* New York: Dodd, 1939.
Flinn, John. *A History of the Chicago Police.* Chicago: W.B. Conkey, 1887.
Flinn, John J., and Wilkie, John E. *History of the Chicago Police.* Montclair, N.J.: Patterson Smith, 1973.
Flippen, Charles C., II. *Liberating the Media.* Washington, D.C.: Acropolis Books, 1974.
Flohery, John J. *Inside the F.B.I.* Philadelphia: J.B. Lippincott, 1943.
Florence, Ronald. *Fritz, The Story of a Political Assassin.* New York: Dial Press, 1971.
Florida. Special Commission for the Study of Abolition of Death Penalty in Capital Cases. *Report.* Tallahassee: State of Florida, 1965.
Florin, Lambert. *Boot Hill: Historic Graves of the Old West.* Seattle, Wash.: Superior, 1966.
Florinsky, Michael T. *The End of the Russian Empire.* New York: Collier Books, 1961.
_____. *Fascism and National Socialism.* New York: Macmillan, 1938.
_____. *Russia, a History and an Interpretation.* 2 vols. New York: Macmillan, 1953.
Flower, Benjamin Orange. *Civilization's Inferno.* Boston: Arena, 1893.
Flower, Desmond, and Mans, Henry. *The Letters of Ernest Dowson.* London: Cassell, 1967.
_____. *Voltaire's England.* London: Folio Society, 1950.
Flower, Frank A. *Edwin McMasters Stanton.* New York: Saalfield, 1905.
Floyd, N.J. *Thorns in the Flesh.* Philadelphia: Edwards & Broughton, 1884.
Flusser, Martin. *The Squeal Man.* New York: William Morrow, 1977.
Flynn, Edward J. *You're the Boss.* New York: Viking Press, 1947.
Flynn, Elizabeth Gurley. *The Rebel Girl.* New York: International Press, 1955.
Flynn, John T. *God's Gold: John D. Rockefeller and His Times.* New York: Harcourt, Brace, 1932.
_____. *Men of Wealth: The Story of Twelve Significant Fortunes from the Renaissance to the Present Day.* New York: Simon & Schuster, 1941.
_____. *The Roosevelt Myth.* New York: Devin-Adair, 1948.
Flynn, Robert DeShields. *The Poor Man in Politics.* Danville, Va.: Dance Brothers, 1894.
Flynt, Josiah. *World of Graft.* New York: McClure Phillips, 1901.
Foat, Ginny. *Never Guilty, Never Free.* New York: Random House, 1985.
Foerster, Robert. *Italian Emigration of Our Times.* Cambridge, Mass: Harvard University Press, 1919.
Foerster, Wolfgang. *Generaloberst Ludwig Beck.* Munich: Isar, 1953.
Fogarty, Kate Hammond. *The Story of Montana.* New York: A.S. Barnes, 1916.
Fogel, David. *". . . We Are the Living Proof. . ."* Cincinnati, Ohio: W.H. Anderson, 1975.
Fogelson, Robert M. *Big City Police.* Cambridge, Mass.: Harvard University Press, 1977.
_____. *The Los Angeles Riots.* New York: Arno Press & The New York Times, 1969.
_____. *Violence as Protest: A Study of Riots and Ghettos.* New York: Doubleday, 1971.
Foix, Pere. *Pancho Villa.* Mexico City: Ediciones Xochitl, 1950.
Folley, Vern F. *American Law Enforcement.* Boston: Holbrook Press, 1973.
Folmsbee, Stanley J., et al. *History of Tennessee.* New York: Lewis Historical, 1960.
Folwell, William Watts. *A History of Minnesota.* St. Paul: Minnesota Historical Society, 1921-30.
Foner, Philip S. *The Bolshevik Revolution: It's Impact on American Radicals, Liberals, and Labor.* New York: International, 1967.
_____. *Business and Slavery: The New York Merchants and the Irrepressible Conflict.* Chapel Hill: Univeristy of North Carolina Press, 1941.
_____. *Frederick Douglass.* New York: Citadel Press, 1964.
_____. *History of the Labor Movement in the United States: From Colonial Times to the Founding of the American Federation of Labor.* New York: International, 1947.
_____. *The Industrial Workers of the World, 1905-1917.* New York: International, 1965.
Fong, Mak Lau. *The Sociology of Secret Societies: A Study of Chinese Secret Societies in Singapore and Peninsular Malaysia.* Oxford, Eng.: Oxford University Press, 1981.
Fontana, Vincent J. *Somewhere a Child Is Crying.* New York: Macmillan, 1973.
Fontenay, Charlos. *Estes Kefauver.* Knoxville, Tenn: 1980.
Fontenelle, Monsignor Ren. *His Holiness Pope Pius XI.* London: Burns, Oates & Washbourne, 1933.
Fooner, Michael. *A Guide to Interpol.* Washington, D.C.: U.S. Government Printing Office, 1985.
_____. *INTERPOL.* Chicago: Henry Regnery, 1973.
Foot, M.R.D. *Resistance.* New York: McGraw-Hill, 1977.
Foot, Michael, and Jones, Mervy. *Guilty Men.* London: Victor Gollancz, 1957.
Foot, Paul. *Who Killed Hanratty?* London, Cape, 1971.
Foote, H.C. *Universal Counterfeiter and Bank Note Detector, at Sight.* New York: Oliver & Brother, 1851.
Footman, David. *Balkan Holiday.* London: William Heinemann, 1935.
_____. *Civil War in Russia.* New York: Frederick A. Praeger, 1962.
_____. *Red Prelude.* New Haven: Yale University Press, 1945.
_____ (ed.). *Soviet Affairs.* London: Chatto & Windus, 1962.
Foran, W.R. *The Kenya Police, 1887-1960.* London: R. Hale, 1962.
Forbes, Abner, and Green, J.W. *The Rich Men of Massachusetts.* Boston: W.V. Spencer, 1851.
Forbes, Archibald. *William of Germany.* New York: Cassell, 1888.
Forbes, Colin. *The Palermo Ambush.* London: William Collins & Sons, 1972
Forbes, Esther. *A Mirror for Witches.* New York: Houghton Mifflin, 1928.
Forbes, Gerald. *Guthrie: Oklahoma's First Capital.* Norman: Univesity of Oklahoma Press, 1938.
Forbes, Ian. *Squad Man.* London: W.H. Allen, 1973.
Forbes, Nevill, et al. *The Balkans.* London: Oxford, 1915.
Ford, Betty., and Chase, Chris. *The Times of My Life.* New York: Harper Row/Readers Digest, 1978.
Ford, Ford Madox. *Return to Yesterday.* London: Victor Gollancz, 1931.
Ford, Franklin L. *Political Murder.* London: Harvard University Press, 1985.
Ford, Gerald R. *A Time To Heal: The Autobiography of Gerald R. Ford.* New York: Harper & Row, 1979.
_____, and Stiles, John. *Portrait of the Assassin.* New York: Simon & Schuster, 1965.
Ford, James. *Slums and Housing With Special Reference to New York City.* Cambridge, Mass. Harvard University Press, 1936.
Ford, John Salmon. *Rip Ford's Texas.* Austin: University of Texas Press, 1963.
Ford, Patrick H. (ed.). *The Darrow Bribery Trial with Background Facts of McNamara Case and Including Darrow's Address to the Jury.* Whittier, Calif.: Western Printing, 1956.
Ford, Paul Leicester. *The Many-Sided Franklin.* New York: Century, 1921.
_____ (ed.). *The Writings of Thomas Jefferson.* New York: G.P. Putnam's Sons, 1892-99.
Fordham, Edward Wilfred. *Notable Cross-Examinations.* London: Constable, 1951.
Fordham, Peta. *The Robbers' Tale.* London: Hodder & Stoughton, 1965.
Foreman, Grant. *Advancing the Frontier.* Norman: University of Oklahoma Press, 1933.
_____. *Fort Gibson.* Norman: University of Oklahoma Press, 1936.
_____. *A History of Oklahoma.* Norman: University of Oklahoma Press, 1942.
Forensic Science Society. *World List of Forensic Science Laboratories.* North Yorkshire, Eng.: n.p., n.d.
Forer, Lois G. *Criminals and Victims.* New York: W.W. Norton, 1980.

_____. *No One Will Listen.* New York: John Day, 1970.
Forester, C.S. *The Barbary Pirates.* New York: Random House, 1953.
_____. *Union of Italy.* New York: Dodd, 1927.
Fornaro, Carlo de. *Carranza and Mexico.* New York: Mitchell Kennerley, 1915.
Forrest, Alan. *Italian Interlude.* London: Bailey Brothers & Swinfen, 1964.
Forrest, Earle R. *Arizona's Dark and Bloody Ground.* Caldwell, Idaho: Caxton Printers, 1953.
Forrest, Jay W., and Malcolm, James. *Tammany's Treason.* Albany, N.Y.: Fort Orange Press, 1913.
Forrestal, James. *The Forrestal Diaries.* New York: Viking Press, 1951.
Forrester, Izola. *This One Mad Act; the Unknown Story of John Wilkes Booth and his Family.* Boston: Hale, Cushman & Flint, 1937.
Forsee, Peter A. *Five Years of Crime in California.* Ukiah City, Calif.: Forsee, 1867.
Forshufvud, Sten. *Who Killed Napoleon?* London: Hutchinson, 1962.
Forster, Arnold, and Epstein, Benjamin R. *Danger on the Right.* New York: Random House, 1964.
Forster, E.S. *A Short History of Modern Greece, 1821-1956.* London: Methuen, 1958.
Forster, Johann Reinhold. *The "Resolution" Journal of Johann Reinhold Forster, 1772-1775.* 4 vols. London: Hakluyt Society, 1982.
Forster, John. *The Life of Charles Dickens.* 3 vols. London: Chapman & Hall, 1873.
Forster, Joseph. *Studies in Black and Red.* London: Ward & Downey, 1896.
Forsyth, Frederick. *Day of the Jackal.* London: Hutchinson, 1971.
Forsyth, J.S.F. *Demonologia.* London: A.K. Newton, 1831.
Forsyth, William. *History of the Capivity of Napoleon at St. Helena.* London: John Murray, 1853.
Fort, Charles. *Wild Talents.* New York: Kendall, 1932.
Fortas, Abe. *Concerning Dissent and Civil Disobedience.* New York: Signet Press, 1968.
Forter, Norman L., and Rostovsky, Demeter B. *The Roumanian Handbook.* London: Simpkin Marshall, 1931.
Fortes, M., and Evans-Pritchard, E.E. (eds.). *African Political Systems.* London: Oxford University Press, 1940.
Fortier, Alce. *A History of Louisiana.* New York: Manz & Joyand, 1904.
Fortune, Jan I. (ed.). *The True Story of Bonnie & Clyde: As Told by Bonnie's Mother and Clyde's Sister.* New York: Signet Books, 1968.
Forzano, Giovacchino. *Mussolini, autore drammatico.* Florence, Italy: Barbera, 1954.
Fosburgh, Lacey. *Closing Time.* New York: Delacourt Press, 1977.
Fosdick, Raymond B. *American Police Systems.* New York: Century, 1920.
_____. *Chronicle of a Generation.* New York: Harper, 1958.
_____. *European Police Systems.* Montclair, N.J.: Patterson Smith, 1969.
Foster, Frank. *Comrades in Bondage.* London: Skeffington & Son, 1946.
Foster, George G. *Fifteen Minutes around New York.* New York: De Witt & Davenport, 1954.
_____. *New York by Gas-Light.* New York: M.J. Ivers, 1850.
Foster, Stephen. *Their Solitary Way.* New Haven, Conn.: Yale University Press, 1971.
Foster-Harris. *The Look of the Old West.* New York: Viking Press, 1955.
Fotieva, Lydia. *Pages from Lenin's Life.* Moscow: Foreign Languages Publishing House, 1960.
Foucault, Michel. *Discipline & Punishment: The Birth of the Prison.* New York: Vintage Books, 1979.
_____. *The History of Sexuality.* New York: Pantheon, 1978.
_____. *Madness and Civilization.* New York: Random House, 1965.
Fowler, F.J., and Magione, T.W. *Neighborhood Crime, Fear and Social Control.* Washington, D.C.: National Institute of Justice, 1982.
Fowler, Gene. *Beau James: The Life and Times of Jimmy Walker.* New York: The Viking Press, 1949.
_____. *Father Goose: The Story of Mack Sennett.* New York: Covici-Friede, 1934.
_____. *Goodnight, Sweet Prince: The Life and Times of John Barrymore.* New York: Viking, 1944.
_____. *The Great Mouthpiece: The Life Story of William J. Fallon.* New York: Covici-Friede, 1931.
_____. *Skyline: A Reporter's Reminiscences of the 1920's.* New York: Macmillan Books, 1962.
_____. *Timber Line.* New York: Covici-Friede, 1933.
Fowler, Kenneth. *The Hundred Years War.* New York: Macmillan, 1971.
Fowler, Robert H. *Album of the Lincoln Murder.* Harrisburg, Pa.: Stackpole Books, 1965.
Fowler, Samuel Page. *Salem Witchcraft.* Salem, Mass.: H.P. Ives & A.A. Smith, 1861.
Fowler, Will. *The Young Man from Denver.* Garden City, N.Y.: Doubleday, 1962.
Fowles, A.J. *Prison Welfare.* London: H.M. Stationery Office, 1978.
Fox, Dixon Ryan. *The Decline of Aristocracy in the Politics of New York, 1801-1840.* New York: Columbia University Press, 1919.
Fox, Frank. *The Balkan Peninsula.* London: A. & C. Black, 1915.
Fox, James. *White Mischief.* New York: Random House, 1982.
Fox, James Allen. *Forecasting Crime Data.* Lexington, Mass.: Lexington/D.C. Heath, 1978.
_____, and Levin, Jack. *Mass Murder: America's Growing Menace.* New York: Plenum Press, 1985.
Fox, Lionel. *English Prison and Borstal Systems.* London: Routledge, 1952.
Fox, R.M. *Green Banners: The Story of the Irish Struggle.* London: Secker & Warburg, 1938.
Fox, Ralph. *Lenin, A Biography.* New York: Harcourt, Brace, 1934.
Fox, Richard Kyle. *The History of the Whitechapel Murders.* New York: Fox, 1888.
Fox, Stephen. *Blood and Power: Organized Crime in the Twentieth Century.* New York: William Morrow, 1989.
Fox, Sylvan. *The Unanswered Questions About President Kennedy's Assassination.* New York: Award Press, 1965.
Fox, Vernon. *Introduction to Corrections.* Englewood Cliffs, N.J.: Prentice-Hall, 1985.
_____. *Introduction to Criminology.* Englewood Cliffs, N.J.: Prentice-Hall, 1976.
Fox, Victor J. *The White House Case.* Pleasantville, N.Y.: Fargo Press, 1968.
Foxe, Arthur N. *Crime and Sexual Development.* Glens Falls, N.Y.: The Monogram Editions, 1936.
Fracastoro, Girolamo. *The Sinister Shepherd.* trans. William van Wyck. Los Angeles: Primavera Press, 1934.
Fraenkel, Franz. *Missing Persons.* Dobbs Ferry, N.Y.: Oceana, 1950.
Fraenkel, Osmond K. *The Sacco and Vanzetti Case.* New York: Alfred A. Knopf, 1931.
Fraley, Oscar. *Four Against the Mob.* New York: Popular Library, 1961.
France, Johnny, and McConnell, Malcolm. *Incident at Big Sky.* New York: W.W. Norton, 1986.
Frances, Jose-Maria. *Vida y Aventuras de Pancho Villa.* Mexico City: Olimpa, 1956.
Francis, Dorothy B. *Shoplifting.* New York: Elsevier-Nellen, 1980.
_____. *Vandalism.* New York: E.P. Dutton, 1983.
Francis, Francis, Jr. *Saddle and Moccasin.* London: Chapman & Hall, 1887.
Francois-Poncet, Andr. *The Fateful Years.* trans. Jacques Le Clercq. London: Victor Gollancz, 1948.
_____. *Au Palais Farnese, 1938-40.* Paris: Fayard, 1961.
Francovich, Carlo. *La resistenza a Firenze.* Florence, Italy: La Nuova Italia, 1961.
Frank, Anne. *Diary of a Young Girl.* New York: Doubleday, 1952.
Frank, Gerold. *An American Death: The True Story of the Assassination of Dr. Martin Luther King, Jr. and the Greatest Manhunt of Our Time.* Garden City, N.Y.: Doubleday, 1972.
_____. *The Boston Strangler.* New York: New American Library, 1967.
_____. *The Deed.* New York: Simon & Schuster, 1963.
Frank, J. and B. *Not Guilty.* London: Victor Gollancz, 1957.
Frank, Jerome. *Courts on Trial.* Princeton, N.J.: Princeton University Press, 1950.
_____. *Law and the Modern Mind.* New York: Brentano, 1930.
_____, and Frank, Barbara. *Not Guilty.* New York: Doubleday, 1957.
Frank, John P. *Marble Palace.* New York: Alfred A. Knopf, 1958.
_____. *Mr. Justice Black: The Man and His Opinions.* New York: Alfred A. Knopf, 1949.
_____, and Karsh, Yousuf. *The Warren Court.* New York: Macmillan, 1964.
Frank, Joseph. *The Beginnings of the English Newspaper, 1620-1660.* Cambridge, Mass.: Harvard University Press, 1961.
Frank, Tenney (ed.). *An Economic Survey of Ancient Rome.* 5 vols. Baltimore: Johns Hopkins Press, 1940.
Franke, David. *The Torture Doctor.* New York: Hawthorn Books, 1975.
Franke, Paul. *They Plowed Up Hell in Old Cochise.* Douglas, Ariz.: Douglas Climate Club, 1950.
Frankel, Marvin E. *Criminal Sentences: Law without Order.* New York: Hill & Wang, 1973.
_____, and Naftalis, Gary P. *The Grand Jury: Institution on Trial.* New York: Hill & Wang, 1977.
Frankenberg, Lloyd (ed.). *A James Stephens Reader.* New York: Macmillan, 1962.
Frankfurter, Felix, and Landis, James. *The Business of the Supreme Court.* New York: Macmillan, 1927.
_____. *The Case of Sacco and Vanzetti.* Boston: Little, Brown & Little, 1927.
_____, and Phillips, Dr. Harlow B. *Felix Frankfurter Reminiscences.* New York: Reynal, 1960.
_____. *Law and Politics.* New York: Harcourt, Brace, 1939.
_____. *Mr. Justice Brandeis.* New Haven, Conn.: Yale University Press, 1932.
_____ (ed.). *Mr. Justice Holmes.* New York: Coward-McCann, 1931.
_____. *Mr. Justice Holmes and the Supreme Court.* Cambridge, Mass.: Harvard University Press, 1938.
_____. *Of Law and Men.* New York: Harcourt, Brace & World, 1956.
Frankfurter, Marion, and Gardner, Jackson (ed.). *The Letters of Sacco and Vanzetti.* New York: Viking Press, 1928.
Frankland, Mark. *Khrushchev.* New York: Stein & Day, 1967.
Frankland, Noble. *Imperial Tragedy.* New York: Coward-McCann, 1961.
Franklin, Benjamin. *Autobiography.* New York: Washington Square Press, 1975.
_____. *Satires and Bagatelles.* Detroit, Mich.: Fine Book Circle, 1937.
Franklin, Charles. *Woman in the Case.* New York: Taplinger, 1968.
_____. *World Famous Acquittals.* London: Odhams Books, 1970.
_____. *The World's Worst Murderers: Exciting and Authentic Accounts of the Great Classics of Murder.* New York: Taplinger, 1965.
Franklin, Fabian. *What Prohibition Has Done to America.* New York: Harcourt, Brace, 1922.
Franklin, John Hope. *From Slavery to Freedom.* New York: Alfred A. Knopf, 1947.
_____. *The Militant South 1800-1861.* Cambridge, Mass.: Harvard University Press, 1956.
Franklin, Julian H. *Jean Bodin.* New York: Columbia University Press, 1963.
Franks, J.M. *The American Cowboy: The Myth and the Reality.* Norman, Okla.: University of Oklahoma Press, 1955.
Frantz, Joe B., and Choate, Julian Ernest, Jr. *The American Cowboy: The Myth and the Reality.* Norman: University of Oklahoma Press, 1955.
Franzero, C.M. *Inside Italy.* London: Hodder & Stoughton, 1941.
Franzius, Enno. *History of the Order of Assassins.* New York: Funk & Wagnalls, 1969.
Frarken, Glenn L. *Inside Nevada Gambling.* New York: Exposition, 1965.
Frasca, Don. *Vito Genovese: King of Crime.* New York: Avon Books, 1963.
Fraser, Antonia. *Cromwell, The Lord Protector.* New York: Alfred A. Knopf, 1973.
Fraser, George MacDonald. *Flashman: From the Flashman Papers, 1839- 1842.* New York: World, 1969.
Fraser, Morris. *Children in Conflict.* Harmondsworth, Middlesex, Eng.: Penguin Books, 1974.

Frazier, E. Franklin. *The Negro Family in Chicago.* Chicago: University of Chicago Press, 1932.

Frederick II. *Memoirs of the House of Brandenborg from the Earliest Accounts to the Death of Frederick I, King of Prussia.* London: J. Nourse, 1757.

_____. *Posthumous Works of Frederick II, King of Prussia.* trans. Thomas Holcroft. 13 vols. London: G.G.J. & J. Robinson, 1789.

Frederick III. *The Crown Prince, Frederick William, A Diary.* London: Sampson Low, 1886.

_____. *Diaries of the Emperor Frederick During the Campaigns of 1866 and 1870-71 as Well as His Journeys to the East and to Spain.* London: Chapman & Hall, 1902.

_____. *The Emperor Frederick: A Diary.* London: Sampson Low, 1888.

_____. *The War Diary of the Emperor Frederick III, 1870-1871.* London: Stanley Paul, 1927.

Frederick, James Vincent. *Ben Holladay, the Stagecoach King.* Glendale, Calif.: Arthur H. Clark, 1940.

Freeborn, Richard. *A Short History of Modern Russia.* New York: Hodder & Stoughton, 1966.

Freed, Donald, and Lane, Mark. *Executive Action.* New York: Dell Books, 1973.

_____. *The Killing of RFK.* New York: Dell Books, 1975.

Freed, Leonard. *Police Work.* New York: Simon & Schuster, 1980.

Freedman, Marcia, and Pappas, Nick. *The Training and Employment of Offenders.* Washington, D.C.: President's Commission on Law Enforcement and Administration of Justice, 1967.

Freedman, Marlene. *Alcatraz.* San Francisco, Calif.: Smith Novelty, n.d.

Freedman, Max (ed.). *Roosevelt and Frankfurter: Their Correspondence.* Boston: Little, Brown, 1967.

Freeland, Richard M. *The Truman Doctrine and the Origins of McCarthyism.* New York: Alfred A. Knopf, 1972.

Freeman, D.S. *George Washington: A Biography.* 6 vols. New York: Charles Scribner's Sons, 1948-1954.

Freeman, E.H. *The Veil of Secrecy Removed, The Only True and Authentic History of Edward H. Ruloff.* Binghamton, N.Y.: Carl & Freeman, 1871.

Freeman, G.D. *Midnight and Noonday, or Dark Deeds Unraveled.* Caldwell, Kan.: G.D. Freeman, 1890.

Freeman, Howard E., and Sherwood, Clarence C. *Social Research and Social Policy.* Englewood Cliffs, N.J.: Prentice-Hall, 1970.

Freeman, Kathleen. *The Murder of Herodes and Other Trials from the Athenian Law Courts.* New York: W.W. Norton, 1963.

Freeman, Lucy. *Before I Kill More.* New York: Crown, 1955.

_____, and Hulse, Wilfred C. *Children Who Kill.* New York: Berkley, 1962.

_____. *Ordeal of Stephen Dennison.* Englewood Cliffs, N.J.: Prentice-Hall, 1970.

Freemantle, Brian. *The Fix, Inside the World Drug Trade.* New York: Tom Doherty Associates, 1986.

Freidel, Frank. *Franklin D. Roosevelt: The Apprentice Years.* Boston: Little, Brown, 1952.

Fremantle, Anne. *This Little Band of Prophets-The British Fabians.* New York: New American Library, 1960.

French, Allen. *Charles I and the Puritan Upheaval.* London: George Allen & Unwin, 1955.

French, Harvey M. *The Anatomy of Arson.* New York: Arco, 1979.

French, John A. *Trial of Professor John W. Webster for the Murder of Dr. George Parkman in the Medical College.* Boston: Herald Steam Press, 1850.

French, Joseph Lewis. *The Book of the Rogue.* New York: Boni & Liveright, 1926

_____ (ed.). *A Gallery of Old Rogues.* New York: Alfred H. King, 1931.

_____. *Gray Shadows.* New York: Century, 1931.

_____ (ed.). *The Pioneer West.* Boston: Little, Brown, 1923.

French, Stanley. *Crime Every Day.* Chichester, Eng.: Rose, 1976.

French, Wild James. *Wild Jim, the Texas Cowboy and Saddle King.* Antioch, Ill.: W.J. French, 1890.

Freud, Sigmund. *Civilization and Its Discontents.* New York: W.W. Norton, 1962.

_____. *Cocaine Papers.* New York: Stonehill, 1974.

_____. *Collected Papers.* London: Hogarth Press, 1953.

_____. *The Complete Introductory Lectures on Psychoanalysis.* New York: W.W. Norton, 1966.

_____. *The Ego and the Id.* trans. Joan Riviere. London: Hogarth Press, 1947.

_____. *A General Introduction to Psychoanalysis.* trans. Joan Riviere. New York: Garden City, 1943.

_____. *A Neuosis of Demoniacal Possession in the Seventeenth Century.* London: International Pscycho-Analytical Press, 1924.

_____. *The Origins of Psycho-Analysis, Letters to Wilhelm Fliess.* New York: Basic Books, 1954.

_____. *The Sexual Enlightenment of Children.* New York: Collier, 1963.

_____. *Studies on Hysteria.* trans. A.A. Brill. New York: Nervous and Mental Disease Publishing, 1920.

_____. *Three Contributions to the Theory of Sex.* New York: E.P. Dutton, 1962.

_____. *Totem and Taboo.* trans. James Strachey. New York: W.W. Norton, 1950.

Freund, Paul. *On Understanding the Supreme Court.* Boston: Little, Brown, 1949.

_____. *The Supreme Court of the United States, Its Business, Purposes and Performance.* Cleveland: World, 1961.

Freyre, Gilberto. *The Masters and the Slaves.* New York: Alfred A. Knopf, 1956.

Freytag, Gustav. *The Crown Prince and the German Imperial Crown: Reminiscences.* London: G. Bell & Sons, 1890.

Fricke, Charles W. *California Criminal Evidence.* Los Angeles: O.W. Smith, 1957.

_____. *California Criminal Law.* Los Angeles: O.W. Smith, 1956.

_____. *California Criminal Procedure.* Los Angeles: O.W. Smith, 1955.

_____. *California Peace Officers Manual.* Los Angeles: O.W. Smith, 1955.

_____. *5000 Criminal Definitions, Terms and Phrases.* Los Angeles: Legal Book, 1968.

_____. *Planning and Trying Cases.* St. Paul: West, 1959.

_____. *Sentence and Probation: The Imposition of Penalties Upon Convicted Criminals.* Los Angeles: Legal Book, 1950.

Fridge, Ike. *History of the Chisum war.* Electra, Texas: J.D. Smith, 1927.

Fried, Albert. *The Rise and Fall of the Jewish Gangster in America.* New York: Holt, Rinehart & Winston, 1980.

Fried, Charles. *Right and Wrong.* Cambridge, Mass.: Harvard University Press, 1977.

Friedan, Betty. *The Feminine Mystique.* New York: W.W. Norton, 1974.

Friede, Donald. *The Mechanical Angel.* New York: Alfred A. Knopf, 1948.

Friedel, Hans. *Der Tyrannenmord in Gesetzgebung und Volksmein*

ung der Griechen. Stuttgart, Ger.: W. Kohlhammer, 1937.

Friedland, M.L. *Detention before Trial.* Toronto, Ontario, Can.: University of Toronto Press, 1965.

Friedlander, Kate. *The Psychoanalytic Approach to Juvenile Delinquency.* London: Kegan Paul, 1947.

Friedlander, Ludwig. *Roman Life and Manners Under the Early Empire.* trans. Leonard Magnus. London: Routledge, 1940.

Friedlander, Saul. *Prelude to Downfall: Hitler and the United States, 1939-1941.* New York: Alfred A. Knopf, 1967.

Friedman, K., et al. *Victims and Helpers: Reactions to Crime.* Washington, D.C.: National Institute on Crime, 1982.

Friedman, Lawrence M. *A History of American Law.* New York: Simon & Schuster, 1973.

_____. *The Legal System.* New York: Russell Sage Foundation, 1975.

Friedman, Leon, and Israel, Fred (eds.). *The Justices of the Supreme Court of the United States.* New York: Chelsea House, 1969.

_____. *The Wise Minority.* New York: Dial Press, 1971.

Friedman, Michael (ed.). *The New Left of the Sixties.* Berkeley, Calif.: Independent Socialist Press, 1972.

Friedman, Morris. *The Pinkerton Labor Spy.* New York: Wilshire Book, 1907.

Friedrich, Carl J. *The Pathology of Politics.* New York: Harper & Row, 1972.

Friedrich, Otto. *Before the Deluge-A Portrait of Berlin in the 1920's.* New York: Harper & Row, 1972.

Friendly, Alfred, and Goldfarb, Ronald L. *Crime & Publicity.* New York: Twentieth Century Fund, 1967.

Frieze, Irene H., et al. *Women and Sex Roles.* New York: W.W. Norton, 1978.

Friis, Herman. *The Pacific Basin.* New York: American Geographical Society, 1967.

Frillman, Paul, and Peck, Graham. *China: The Remembered Life.* Boston: Houghton Mifflin, 1968.

Frischauer, Willi. *Himmler.* London: Odhams, 1953.

Fritz, Percy Stanley. *Colorado, the Centennial State.* New York: Prentice-Hall, 1941.

Frost, R. *Race Against Time: Human Relations and Politics in Kenya Before Independence.* London: Rex Collings, 1978.

Frost, Richard H. *The Mooney Case.* Stanford, Calif.: Stanford University Press, 1968.

Fry, M. *Sex, Vice and Business.* New York: Ballantine, 1959.

Fry, Margery. *Arms of the Law.* London: Victor Gollancz, 1951.

Frye, Richard N. *The Heritage of Persia.* Cleveland: World, 1963.

_____ (ed.). *Islam and the West.* The Hague, Neth.: Mouton, 1957.

Fuchs, Martin. *A Pact with Hitler.* trans. Charles Hope Lumley. London: Victor Gollancz, 1939.

Fuess, Claude M. *Carl Schurz, Reformer, 1829-1906.* New York: Dodd, Mead, 1932.

_____. *Daniel Webster.* Boston: Little, Brown, 1930.

Fugate, F.L. *The Spanish Heritage of the Southwest.* El Paso, Texas: Western Press, 1952.

Fuld, Leonard. F. *Police Administration.* New York: G.P. Putnam's Sons, 1910.

A Full Account, The Lives and Crimes of the "Molly Maguires". Philadelphia: Barclay, 1877.

Fuller, Daniel. *Trial of John Lechler.* Lancaster, Pa.: Hugh Maxwell, 1822.

Fuller, Edgar I. *The Visible of the Invisible Empire.* Denver: Maelstrom, 1925.

Fuller, George W. *A History of the Pacific Northwest.* New York: Alfred A. Knopf, 1931.

_____. *The Inland Empire of the Pacific Northwest.* Denver: H.G. Linderman, 1928.

Fuller, Henry C. *Adventures of Bill Longley.* Nacogdoches, Texas: Baker Printing, n.d.

_____. *A Texas Sheriff.* Nacogdoches, Texas: Baker Printing, 1931.

Fuller, John. *The Gentleman Conspirators.* New York: McGraw-Hill, 1971.

Fuller, Loie. *Fifteen Years of a Dancer's Life.* Boston: Small, Maynard, 1913.

Fuller, Margaret. *Woman in the Nineteenth Century.* New York: W. W. Norton, 1971.

Fuller, Robert H. *Jubilee Jim: The Life of Colonel James Fisk, Jr.* New York: Macmillan, 1928.

Fullerton, W.Y. *The Romance of Pitcairn Island.* London: Harrap, 1923.

Fulop-Muller, Rene. *Power and Secret of the Jesuits.* New York: George Braziller, 1956.

_____. *Rasputin, The Holy Devil.* New York: Viking Press, 1928.

Fulton, Maurice Garland. *History of the Lincoln County War.* Tucson: University of Arizona Press, 1968.

_____ (ed.). *Maurice Garland Fulton's History of the Lincoln County War.* Tucson: University of Arizona Press, 1968.

_____, and Horgan, Paul. *New Mexico's Own Chronicle.* Dallas: Banks Upshaw, 1937.

Fultz, Hollis B. *Famous Northwest Manhunts and Murder Mysteries.* Elma, Wash.: Elma Chronicle, 1955.

Funck-Brentano, Frantz. *Lucrce Borgia.* Paris: La Nouvelle Revue Critique, 1930.

_____. *The Middle Ages.* London: William Heinemann, 1922.

_____. *Princes and Poisoners.* London: Duckworth, 1901.

Furer, Howard B. *Chicago: A Chronological and Documentary History: 1784-1970.* Dobbs Ferry, N.Y.: Oceana, 1974.

Furlong, Thomas. *Fifty Years A Detective.* St. Louis: C.E. Barnett, 1912.

Furnas, J.C. *The Life and Times of the Late Demon Rum.* New York: G.P. Putnam's Sons, 1965.

Furneau, Rupert. *Courtroom USA-1.* Baltimore: Penguin Books, 1963.

_____. *Courtroom USA-2.* Baltimore: Penguin Books, 1963.

_____. *Famous Criminal Cases, Vols. I - VII.* London: Allan Wingate, 1959.

_____. *Guenther Podola.* London: Stevens, 1960.
_____. *The Medical Murderer.* London: Elek Books, 1957.
_____. *The Murder of Lord Erroll.* London: Stevens, 1961.
_____. *Robert Hoolhouse.* London: Stevens, 1960.
_____. *They Died By A Gun.* London: Herbert Jenkins, 1962.
_____. *The World's Most Intriguing True Mysteries.* New York: Arco, 1966.
_____. *The Two Stranglers of Rillington Place.* London: Panther, 1961.

Gabert of Bruges. *The Murder of Charles the Good.* trans. James Bruce Ross. New York: Columbia University Press, 1960.
Gabory, Emile. *Alias Bluebeard.* trans. Alvah C. Bessie. New York: Brewer & Warren, 1930.
_____. *La vie et la mort de Gilles de Rais.* Paris: Perrin et Cie, 1926.
Gaddis, Thomas E. *The Birdman of Alcatraz.* New York: Random House, 1955.
_____, and Long, James O. *Killer, A Journal of Murder.* New York: Macmillan, 1970.
Gage, Nicholas. *The Mafia Is Not an Equal Opportunity Employer.* New York: McGraw-Hill, 1971.
_____. *Mafia, USA.* Chicago: Playboy Press, 1972.
Gager, Nancy, and Schurr, Cathleen. *Sexual Assault: Confronting Rape in America.* New York: Grosset & Dunlap, 1976.
Gagnon, John H., and Simon, William. *Sexual Conduct: The Social Sources of Human Sexuality.* Chicago: Aldine, 1973.
_____ (eds.). *Sexual Deviance.* New York: Harper & Row, 1967.
_____ (eds.). *The Sexual Scene.* Chicago: Aldine, 1970.
Gainer, B. *The Alien Invasion.* London: Heinemann, 1972.
Galaway, B., and Hudson, J. *Perspectives on Crime Victims.* St. Louis: C.V. Mosby, 1981.
Galbraith, John Kenneth. *The Affluent Society.* Boston: Houghton Mifflin, 1958.
_____. *The Great Crash, 1929.* Boston: Houghton Mifflin, 1955.
_____. *The New Industrial State.* New York: Signet Books, 1968.
Galliher, Hohn F., and McCartney, James L. *Criminology.* Homewood, Ill.: Dorsey, 1977.
Gallo, Max. *Mussolini's Italy, Twenty Years of the Fascist Era.* trans. Charles Lam Markmann. New York: Macmillan, 1973.
Gallo, Patrick J. *Old Bread, New Wine: A Portrait of the Italian-American.* Chicago: Nelson-Hall, 1981.
Galloway, John. *Criminal Justice & the Berger Court.* New York: Facts on File, 1978.
Galton, Sir Francis. *Finger Prints.* London: Macmillan, 1892.
_____. *Fingerprint Directories.* London: Macmillan, 1895.
_____. *Hereditary Genius.* London: Macmillan, 1869.
_____. *Inquiries into Human Faculty.* New York: Dent, 1906.
_____. *Method of Indexing Finger-Marks.* London: Proc. Royal Society of London, 1891.
Galvin, John. *The Minute Men.* New York: Hawthorn, 1967.
Gambino, Richard. *Blood of My Blood: The Dilemma of the Italian-American.* Garden City, N.Y.: Doubleday, 1974.
_____. *Vendetta.* Garden City, N.Y.: Doubleday, 1977.
Gambino, Sharo. *La Mafia in Calabria.* Reggio Calabria, Italy: Edizioni Parallelo, 1971.
Gandhi, Mohandas K. *All Men Are Brothers: Life and Thoughts of Mahatma Gandhi As Told in His Own Words.* New York: Columbia University Press, 1958.
_____. *Bapu's Letters to Mira (1924-1948).* Ahmedabad, India: Navajivan Publishing House, 1949.
_____. *Christian Missions.* Ahmedabad, India: Navajivan Publishing House, 1948.
_____. *Delhi Diary.* Ahmedabad, India: Navajivan Publishing House, 1948.
_____. *Gandhi's Correspondence With the Government (1942-1944).* Ahmedabad, India: Navajivan Publishing House, 1945.
_____. *Jail Experiences.* Madras, India: Tagore, 1922.
_____. *My Early Life.* Bombay, India: Oxford University Press, 1932.
_____. *My Soul's Agony.* Ahmedabad, India: Navajivan Publishing House, 1932.
_____. *Non-violence in Peace and War.* Ahmedabad, India: Navajivan Publishing House, 1945.
_____. *Self-restraint vs. Self-indulgence.* Ahmedabad, India: Navajivan Publishing House, 1947.
_____. *Songs From Prison.* London: Allen & Unwin, 1934.
_____. *Speeches and Writings.* Madras, India: G.A. Natesan, 1933.
Ganey, Terry. *St. Joseph's Children.* New York: Lyle Stuart, 1989.
Gamji, Manouchehr. *Defying the Iranian Revolution: From a Minister of the Shah to a Leader of Resistance.* New York: Praeger, 2003.
Gantt, Paul H. *The Case of Alfred Packer, the Man Eater.* Denver: University of Denver, 1952.
Ganzhorn, Jack. *I've Killed Men.* London: Robert Hale, 1940.
Gard, Wayne. *The Chisholm Trail.* Norman: University of Oklahoma Press, 1954.
_____. *Frontier Justice.* Norman: University of Oklahoma Press, 1949.
_____. *Rawhide Texas.* Norman: University of Oklahoma Press, 1965.
_____. *Sam Bass.* New York: Houghton Mifflin, 1936.
Gardiner, A.G. *The War Lords.* London: Dent, 1915.
Gardiner, A.W. *The Life of Sir William Harcourt.* London: Constable, 1923.
Gardiner, Alexander. *Canfield, The True Story of the Greatest Gambler.* Garden City, N.Y.: Doubleday, 1930.
Gardiner, Dorothy, and Walker, Katherine (eds.). *Raymond Chandler Speaking.* London: Hamish Hamilton, 1962.
Gardiner, Gerald. *Capital Punishment as a Deterrent and the Alternative.* London: Victor Gollancz, 1956.
Gardiner, John A. *The Politics of Corruption: Organized Crime in an American City.* New York: Russell Sage Foundation, 1970.
_____. *Traffic and the Police.* Cambridge, Mass.: Harvard University Press, 1969.
Gardiner, John, and Olson, David. *Theft of the City.* Bloomington: Indiana University Press, 1974.
Gardiner, Muriel. *The Deadly Innocents, Portraits of Children Who Kill.* New York: Basic Books, 1976.
Gardner, Charles W. *The Doctor and the Devil, or Midnight Adventures of Dr. Parkhurst.* New York: Warren, 1894.
Gardner, Erle Stanley. *The Court of Last Resort.* New York: W. Sloane, 1952.
Gardner, Gerald Brosseau. *Witchcraft Today.* New York: Citadel, 1955.
Gardner, Martin. *Fads and Fallacies in the Name of Science.* New York: Dover Publications, 1957.
Gardner, Raymond Hatfield. *The Old Wild West.* San Antonio, Texas: Naylor, 1944.
Gardner, Roy. *Hellcatraz, The Rock of Despair.* New York: Hearst, 1939.
Garfield, Brian (ed.). *I Witness.* New York: Quadrangle, 1978.
Garnel, Donald. *The Rise of Teamster Power in the West.* Berkeley: University of California Press, 1972.
Garofalo, James. *Local Victim Surveys: A Review of the Issues.* Washington, D.C.: National Criminal Justice Information and Statistics Service, 1977.
Garofalo, Raffaele. *Criminology.* Boston: Little, Brown, 1914.
Garrard, J.A. *The English and Immigration 1880-1910.* London: Oxford University Press, 1971.
Garrat, G.T. *Mussolini's Roman Empire.* London: Penguin Books, 1938.
Garrett, Charles. *The La Guardia Years: Machine and Reform Politics in New York City.* New Brunswick, N.J.: Rutgers University Press, 1961.
Garrison, Jim. *A Heritage of Stone.* New York: G.P. Putnam's Sons, 1970.
_____. *The Star Spangled Contract.* New York: Warner Books, 1977.
Garrison, Omar V. *The Hidden Story of Scientology.* New York: Citadel Press, 1974.
_____. *The Secret World of Interpol.* New York: Ralston-Pilot, 1976.
Garrity, Donald. *The Prison.* New York: Holt, Rinehart & Winston, 1961.
Garrow, David J. *The FBI and Martin Luther King, Jr.: From "Solo" to Memphis.* New York: Norton, 1981.
Garry, Charles, and Goldburg, Art. *Streetfighter in the Courtroom.* New York: Dutton, 1977.
Garsia, Marston. *Criminal Law and Procedure in a Nutshell.* Sweet & Maxwell, 1953.
Gartner, L.P. *The Jewish Immigrant in England 1870-1914.* Detroit, Mich.: Wayne State University Press, 1960.
Gartner, Michael (ed.). *Crime and Business.* Princeton, N.J.: Dow Jones, 1971.
Garwood, Darrel. *Crossroads of America: The Story of Kansas City.* New York: W.W. Norton, 1948.
Garza, Hedda. *Salvador Allende.* New York: Chelsea House, n. d.
Gasciogne, Bamber. *The Great Moghuls.* London: Cape, 1971.
Gash, Norman. *Mr. Secretary Peel: The Life of Sir Robert Peel to 1830.* Cambridge, Mass.: Harvard University Press, 1961.
_____. *Reaction and Reconstruction in English Politics, 1832-1852.* Clarendon Press, 1965.
Gates, John D. *The Du Pont Family.* New York: Doubleday, 1979.
Gatti, Arthur. *The Kennedy Curse.* Chicago: Henry Regnery, 1976.
Gaucher, Roland. *The Terrorists: From Tsarist Russia to the O.A.S.* trans. Albin Michel. London: Secker & Warburg, 1968.
Gaxotte, Pierre. *Frederick the Great.* New Haven, Conn.: Yale University Press, 1942.
_____. *German Diplomatic Documents, 1871-1914.* trans. E.T.S. Dugdale. London: Methuen, 1928.
Gay, H. Nelson. *Strenuous Italy.* Boston: Houghton Mifflin, 1927.
Gaylord, Otis H. *The Rise and Fall of Legs Diamond.* New York: Bantam Books, 1960.
Gayn, Mark J. *Japan Diary.* New York: William Sloan Associates, 1948.
Gaynor, William J. *Some of Mayor Gaynor's Letters and Speeches.* New York: Greaves, 1913.
Gebhard, Paul H., Gagnon, John H., Pomeroy, Wardell B., and Christenson, Cornelia V. *Sex Offenders: An Analysis of Types.* New York: Harper & Row, 1965.
Gehl, J. *Austria, Germany and the Anschluss.* New York: Oxford University Press, 1963.
Geis, Gilbert. *Not the Law's Business: An Examination of Homosexuality, Abortion, Prostitution, Narcotics, and Gambling in the United States.* Rockville: National Institute of Mental Health, 1972.
_____. (ed.). *White Collar Crime.* New York: Atherton, 1968.
_____, and Meier, Robert F. (eds.). *White-Collar Crime: Offenses in Business, Politics, and the Professions.* New York: Free Press, 1977.
Geiser, Robert L. *Hidden Victims.* Boston: Beacon Press, 1979.
Gelb, Barbara. *On the Track of Murder.* New York: William Morrow, 1975.
Geller, Alan, and Boas, Maxwell. *The Drug Beat.* New York: Cowles, 1971.
Gelles, Richard J., and Cornell, C.P. *Intimate Violence in Families.* Newbury Park, Calif.: Sage, 1985.
_____. *The Violent Home.* Beverly Hills, Calif.: Sage, 1974.
Gellner, John. *Bayonets in the Streets.* Canada: Collier Macmillan, 1974.
Gelluis, Aulus. *Attic Nights.* trans. John C. Rolfe. London: William Heinemann, 1952-1960.
Gelzer, Matthias. *Caesar: Politician and Statesman.* Cambridge, Mass.: Harvard University Press, 1968.
Gemmill, W.N. *Salem Witchtrials.* Chicago: A.C. McClurg, 1924.
Genoud, Francois (ed.). *The Testament of Adolf Hitler.* trans. Col. R.H. Stevens. London: Cassell, 1961.
Genthe, Arnold. *As I Remember.* New York: Reynal & Hitchcock, 1936.
_____, and Irwin, Will. *Pictures of Old Chinatown.* New York: Mills College, 1908.
Gentry, Curt. *Frame-Up: The Incredible Case of Tom Mooney and Warren Billings.* New York: Norton, 1967.
_____. *The Madams of San Francisco.* New York: Doubleday, 1964.
Genung, Abram Polhemus. *The Frauds of the New York City Government Exposed. Sketches of the Members of the Ring and Their Confederates.* New York: Published by Author, 1871.
Geoffrey of Monmouth. *The History of the Kings of Britain.* Penguin Books, 1966.

George, Andrew L. *The Texas Convict: Thrilling and Terrible Experiences of a Texas Boy.* Austin, Texas: Ben C. Jones, 1893.
George, Earl Lloyd. *Lloyd George.* London: Muller, 1960.
George, S.K. *Gandhi's Challenge to Christianity.* London: Allen & Unwin, 1939.
George, Todd Menzies. *Just Memories, and Twelve Years with Cole Younger.* Kansas City: Quality Hill Printing, 1959.
Georgetown University Law Center. *The Role of Prison Industries Now and In the Future.* Washington, D.C.: Institute of Criminal Law and Procedure, 1974.
Gerard, John. *The Autobiography of a Hunted Priest.* New York: Pellegrini & Cudahy, 1952.
Gerhart, Eugene C. *America's Advocate: Robert H. Jackson.* Indianapolis, Ind.: Bobbs-Merril, 1958.
Germann, A.C., et al. *Introduction to Law Enforcement and Criminal Justice.* Springfield, Ill.: Charles C. Thomas, 1968.
_____. *Police Personnel Management.* Springfield, Ill.: Thomas, 1958.
Germino, Dante L. *The Italian Fascist Party in Power.* Minneapolis: University of Minnesota Press, 1959.
Gertz, Elmer. *A Handful of Clients.* Chicago: Follett, 1965.
_____. *Moment of Madness: The People vs. Jack Ruby.* Chicago: Follett, 1968.
_____. *To Life.* New York: McGraw Hill, 1974.
Gest, John Marshall. *The Old Yellow Book.* Philadelphia: University of Pennsylvania Press, 1927.
Geva, Tamara. *Split Seconds.* New York: Harper & Row, 1972.
Gevel, Claude. *Deux carbonari: Orsini et Napoleon III.* Paris: Emile-Paul freres, 1934.
Geyer, Frank P. *The Holmes-Pitezel Case.* Philadelphia: Frank Geyer, 1896.
Geyl, Pieter. *The Netherlands in the Seventeenth Century, pt. l: 1609-1648.* New York: Barnes & Noble, 1961.
_____. *The Revolt of the Netherlands, 1555-1609.* London: Ernest Benn, 1962.
Ghirshman, Roman. *Iran from the Earliest Times to the Islamic Conquest.* London: Penguin, 1954.
Ghisalberti, Alberto M. (ed.). *Lettere di Felice Orsini.* Rome: Vittoriano, 1936.
Giallombardo, Rose. *The Social World of Imprisoned Girls.* New York: Wiley, 1974.
_____. *Society of Women: A Study of a Women's Prison.* New York: Wiley, 1966.
Giancana, Antoinette, and Renner, Thomas C. *Mafia Princess: Growing Up in Sam Giancana's Family.* New York: Avon, 1985.
Gibb, Hamilton A.R., and Bowen, H. *Islamic Society and the West: A Study of the Impact of Western Civilization on Moslem Culture in the Near East.* London: Oxford University Press, 1950.
_____. *Modern Trends in Islam.* Chicago: University of Chicago Press, 1947.
_____. *Studies on the Civilization of Islam.* London: Routledge & Keegan Paul, 1962.
Gibbens, T.C.N., and Prince, J. *Child Victims of Sex Offences.* London: Instutute for the Study and Treatment of Delinquency, 1963.
_____, and Ahrenfeldt, R.H. (eds.). *Cultural Factors in Delinquency.* Philadelphia: J.B. Lippincott, 1966.
_____. *Psychiatric Studies of Borstal Lads.* London: Oxford University Press, 1963.
_____. *Shoplifting.* London: ISTD, 1962.
Gibbon, Edward. *The History of the Decline and Fall of the Roman Empire.* New York: Everyman's Library, 1936.
Gibbon, Thomas Edward. *Mexico Under Carranza.* New York: Doubleday, Page, 1919.
Gibbons, Don C. *Changing the Lawbreaker.* Englewood Cliffs, N.J.: Prentice-Hall, 1965.
_____. *Crime and Criminal Careers.* Englewood Cliffs, N.J.: Prentice-Hall, 1968.
_____. *The Criminological Enterprise.* Englewood Cliffs, N.J.: Prentice-Hall, 1979.
_____. *Delinquent Behavior.* Englewood Cliffs, N.J.: Prentice-Hall, 1970.
_____. *Society, Crime, and Criminal Careers.* Englewood Cliffs, N.J.: Prentice-Hall, 1977.
_____, and Garrity, Donald L. *The Study of Deviance.* Englewood Cliffs, N.J.: Prentice-Hall, 1975.
Gibbs, Angelica. *New York Murders.* New York: Duell, Sloan & Pearce, 1944.
Gibbs, Jack P. *Crime, Punishment, and Deterrence.* New York: Elsevier, 1975.
Gibbs, Sir Philip. *Since Then.* London: William Heinemann, 1930.
Gibney, B. *The Beauty Queen Killer.* New York: Pinnacle, 1984.
Gibney, Frank. *Five Gentlemen of Japan: The Portrait of a Nation's Character.* New York: Farrar, Straus & Young, 1953.
_____. *Japan: The Fragile Superpower.* New York: W.W. Norton, 1975.
_____. *The Operators.* New York: Harper & Bros., 1960.
Gibran, Kahlil. *The Prophet.* New York: Alfred A. Knopf, 1963.
Gibson, Arrell M. *A Political Crime. The History of the Great Fraud.* New York: William S. Gottsberger, 1885.
Gibson, Brian. *The Birmingham Bombs.* London: Barry Rose, 1976.
Gibson, Evelyn, and McClintock, W.H. *Robbery in London.* London: Macmillan, 1961.
_____. *Time Spent Awaiting Trial.* London: Her Majesty's Stationery Office, 1960.
Gibson, Rev. Otis. *Chinaman or White Man, Which?* San Francisco: Alta Printing House, 1873.
_____. *The Chinese in America.* Cincinnati, Ohio: Hitchcock & Walden, 1877.
Gibson, Sonny. *Mafia Kingpin.* New York: Grossett & Dunlap, 1981.
Gibson, Walter B. and Litzka R. *The Fine Art of Swindling.* New York: Grosset & Dunlap, 1966.
Gicaru, M. *Land of Sunshine: Scenes of Life in Kenya Before Mau Mau.* London: Lawrence & Wishart, 1958.
Gieroff, Alex K. *Sexual Deviations in the Criminal Law: Homosexual, Exhibitionistic, and Pedophilic Offences in Canada.* Toronto, Ontario, Can.: University of Toronto Press, 1968.
Gies, Joseph. *The Colonel of Chicago: A Biography of the Chicago Tribune's Legendary Publisher Colonel Robert McCormick.* New York: E.P. Dutton, 1979.
Giesler, Jerry, as told to Pete Martin. *Hollywood Lawyer—The Jerry Giesler Story.* New York: Simon & Schuster, 1960.
Gifford, Denis. *Chapin.* Garden City, N.Y.: Doubleday, 1974.
Gifford, Edward S., Jr. *The Evil Eye.* New York: n.p., 1958.
Gifford, George. *A Dialogue Concerning Witches and Witchcrafts.* London: H. Milford, 1931.
_____. *A Discourse of the Subtle Practices of Devils by Witches and Sorcerers.* London: Toby Cooke, 1587.
Giglio, Giovanni. *The Triumph of Barabbas.* London: Victor Gollancz, 1937.
Giglio, James N. *Harry M. Daugherty and the Politics of Expediency.* Kent, Ohio: Kent State University Press, 1978.
Gil, David C. *Violence Against Children.* Cambridge, Mass.: Harvard University Press, 1970.
Gilbert, Clinton W. *The Mirrors of Washington.* New York: Putnam, 1921.
Gilbert, Felix (ed.). *Hitler Directs His War.* New York: Oxford University Press, 1950.
Gilbert, Frank. *Centennial History of the City of Chicago: Its Men and Institutions.* Chicago: Inter Ocean, 1905.
Gilbert, G.M. *Nuremberg Diary.* New York: New American Library, 1947.
Gilbert, Martin. *The Arab-Israeli Conflict: Its History in Maps.* London: Weidenfeld and Nicolson, 1974.
_____. *Winston S. Churchill.* London: William Heinemann, 1976.
Gilbert, Michael F. *Dr. Crippen.* London: Odhams Press, 1953.
Gilbert, Paul Thomas, and Bryson, Charles Lee. *Chicago and Its Makers.* Chicago: University of Chicago Press, 1929.
Gilberth, Vernon. *Practical Homicide Investigation.* Bacon Raton, Fla.: CRC Press, 1993.
Gilchrist, David T. (ed.) *The Growth of the Seaport Cities, 1790-1825.* Charlottesville: University of Virginia Press, 1967.
Gilder, Rodman. *The Battery.* Boston: Houghton Mifflin, 1956.
Gildrie, Richard. *Salem, Massachusetts.* Charlottesville: University of Virginia, 1975.
Giles, F.T. *The Criminal Law.* London: Penguin Books, 1954.
Gilio, Maria Esther. *The Tupamaros.* London: Secker & Warburg, 1972.
_____. *The Tupamaro Guerrillas.* trans. Anne Edmondson. New York: Saturday Review Press, 1972.
Gill, Brendan. *Tallulah.* New York: Holt, Rinehart & Winston, 1972.
Gill, John. *Tide Without Turning: Elijah P. Lovejoy and Freedom of the Press.* Boston: Starr King Press, 1958.
Gill, John. *Stolen Children: How and Why Parents Kidnap Their Kids.—and What to Do About It.* New York: Seaview, 1981.
Gillen, Mollie. *Assassination of the Prime Minister: The Shocking Death of Spencer Perceval.* New York: St. Martin's Press, 1972.
Gillespie, Joan. *Algeria: Rebellion and Revolution.* London: Ernest Benn, 1960.
Gillespie, R.W. *Economic Factors in Crime and Delinquency.* Washington, D.C.: National Institute of Law Enforcement and Criminal Justice, 1975.
Gillett, James Buchanan. *Six Years With the Texas Rangers, 1875 to 1881.* Lincoln: University of Nebraska Press, 1976.
Gillette, Paul J., and Tillinger, Eugene. *Inside the Ku Klux Klan.* New York: Pyramid Books, 1965.
Gilliam, Harold. *San Francisco Bay.* Garden City, N.Y.: Doubleday, 1957.
Gilliam, Olive Kuntz. *The Memoirs of Augustus.* New York: Vantage Press, 1965.
Gilliard, Pierre. *Thirteen Years at the Russian Court.* New York: Doran, 1921.
Gillis, O.J. *To Hell and Back Again, Its Discovery, Description, and Experiences; or, Life in the Penitentiary of Texas and Kansas.* Little Rock, Ark.: Democrat Printing, 1906.
Gilliver, L. *Select Trials at the Sessions-House in the Old Bailey.* London: n.p., 1747.
Gillmor, Donald M. *Free Press and Fair Trial.* Washington, D.C.: Public Affairs Press, 1966.
Gilmore, Al-Tony. *Bad Nigger!* Port Washington, N.Y.: Kennikat Press, 1975.
Gilmore, John. *The Tucson Murders.* New York: Dial Press, 1970.
Gilmour, Walter, and Hale, Leland. *Butcher, Baker.* New York: Oynx, 1991.
Ginger, Raymond. *The Age of Excess.* New York: Macmillan, 1965.
_____. *Altgeld's America.* Chicago: Quadrangle Books, 1965.
_____. *The Bending Cross: A Biography of Eugene Victor Debs.* New Brunswick, N.J.: Rutgers University Press, 1949.
_____. *Eugene V. Debs: The Making of an American Radical.* New York: Macmillan, 1949.
Ginsburg, Philip. *Poisoned Blood.* New York: Warner, 1987.
_____. *The Shadow of Death.* New York: Jove Books, 1993.
Ginzburg, Ralph. *100 Years of Lynchings.* New York: Lancer Books, 1962.
Gipson, Lawrence Henry. *The British Empire before the American Revolution.* 9 vols. New York: Alfred A. Knopf, 1936-56.
Giraud, Victor. *Vie de Jeanne d'Arc.* Avignon: G. Aubanel, 1948.
Girling, J.L.S. *People's War.* London: George Allen & Unwin, 1969.
Gisevius, Hans Bernd. *Adolf Hitler: Versuch einer Deuting.* Munich: Rutten-Loening Verlag, 1963.
_____. *To the Bitter End.* trans. Richard and Clara Winston. Boston: Houghton Mifflin, 1947.
Gish, Anthony. *American Bandits.* Girard, Kan.: Haldeman-Julius, 1938.
Gish, Lillian, with Pinchot, Ann. *The Movies, Mr. Griffith and Me.* New York: Prentice-Hall, 1969.
Glaister, John. *Final Diagnosis.* London: Hutchinson, 1964.
_____., and Rentoul, E. *Medical Jurisprudence and Toxicology.* London: Livingstone Press, 1953.
_____. *The Power of Poison.* New York: William Morrow, 1954.
_____., and Smith, S.A. *Recent Advances in Forensic Medicine.* London: Churchill, 1931.
Glaser, D. *Adult Crime and Social Policy.* Englewood Cliffs, N.J.: Prentice-Hall, 1972.
Glaser, Daniel. (ed.). *Crime in the City.* New York: Harper & Row, 1970.

_____. *Crime in Our Changing Society.* New York: Holt, Rinehart, Winston, 1978.
_____. *The Effectiveness of a Prison and Parole System.* Indianapolis: Bobbs-Merrill, 1964.
_____ (ed.). *The Handbook of Criminology.* Chicago: Rand-McNally, 1974.
_____. *Strategic Criminal Justice Planning.* Rockville, Md.: National Institute of Mental Health Center for Studies of Crime and Delinquency, 1975.
_____, et al. *The Violent Offender.* Washington, D.C.: U.S. Printing Office, 1968.
Glasscock, Carl Burgess. *Bandits of the Southwest Pacific.* New York: Frederick A. Stokes, 1929.
Glazer, Nathan, and Moynihan, Daniel Patrick. *Beyond the Melting Pot: The Negroes, Puerto Ricans, Jews, Italians, and Irish of New York City.* Cambridge, Mass.: M.I.T. Press, 1964.
_____. *The Justices of the Peace in England.* Oxford, Eng.: Clarendon Press, 1969.
Gleeson, James. *Bloody Sunday.* London: Davies, 1962.
Glib, Corinne L. *Hidden Hierarchies.* New York: Harper & Row, 1966.
Glick, Carl, and Hong, Sheng-Hwa. *Chinese Secret Societies.* New York: Whittlesey House, 1947.
Glick, Rush G., and Newsom, Robert S. *Fraud Investigation.* Springfield, Ill.: Charles C. Thomas, 1974.
Glikes, Erwin A., and Schwaber, Paul, (eds.). *Of Poetry and Power: Poems Occasioned by the Presidency and by the Death of John F. Kennedy.* New York: Basic Books, 1964.
Glover, E. *The Psycho-pathology of Prostitution.* London: Instutute for Study and Treatment of Delinquency, 1945.
_____. *The Roots of Crime.* New York: International Universities Press, 1960.
Glubb, Lt. Gen. Sir John. *Britain and the Arabs.* London: Hodder & Stoughton, 1957.
_____. *The Empire of the Arabs.* London: Hodder & Stoughton, 1963.
_____. *The Great Arab Conquests.* London: Hodder & Stoughton, 1963.
Gluckman, Max. *Custom and Conflict in Africa.* New York: Barnes & Noble, 1973.
Glueck, B. *Studies in Forensic Psychiatry.* London: Heinemann, 1916.
Glueck, B.C., Jr. *New York Final Report on Deviated Sex Offenders.* Albany, N.Y.: Department of Mental Hygiene, 1956.
Glueck, Sheldon, and Eleanor T. *Criminal Careers in Retrospect.* New York: Commonwealth Fund, 1943.
_____. *Criminal Law and Its Enforcement.* St. Paul: West, 1951.
_____. *Delinquents and Nondelinquents in Perspective.* Cambridge, Mass.: Harvard University Press, 1968.
_____. *500 Criminal Careers.* New York: Alfred A. Knopf, 1930.
_____. *500 Delinquent Women.* New York: Alfred A. Knopf, 1934.
_____. *Juvenile Delinquents Grown Up.* New York: Commonwealth Fund, 1940.
_____. *Later Criminal Careers.* New York: Commonwealth Fund, 1937.
_____. *1000 Juvenile Delinquents.* Cambridge, Mass.: Harvard University Press, 1934.
_____. *Physique and Delinquency.* New York: Harper, 1956.
_____, and Eleanor T. *Predicting Delinquency and Crime.* Cambridge, Mass.: Harvard University Press, 1959.
_____. *Toward a Typology of Juvenile Offenders.* New York: Grune and Stratton, 1970.
_____. *Unraveling Juvenile Delinquency.* Cambridge, Mass.: Harvard University Press, 1950.
Goddard, Donald. *Joey.* New York: Harper & Row, 1974.
Goddard, Henry. *The Memoirs of a Bow Street Runner.* New York: William Morrow, 1956.
Goddard, Henry H. *Feeble-Mindedness.* New York: Macmillan, 1914.
_____. *Juvenile Delinquency.* New York: Dodd, Mead, 1921.
Godfrey, E. Drexel, Jr., and Harris, Don R. *Basic Elements of Intelligence.* Washington, D.C.: U.S. Government Printing Office, 1971.
Godspeed, G. S. *A History of the Babylonians and Assyrians.* New York: Charles Scribner's Sons, 1906.
Godwin, George. *Crime and Social Action.* London: Watts, 1956.
_____. *Killers Unknown.* London: Jenkins, 1960.
_____. *Peter Kurten, A Study in Sadism.* London: Acorn Press, 1938.
_____. *The Trial of Peter Griffiths: The Blackburn Baby Murderer.* London: W. Hodge, 1950.
Godwin, John. *Alcatraz 1868-1963.* New York: Doubleday, 1963.
_____. *Killers in Paradise.* London: Herbert Jenkins, 1962.
_____. *Murder U.S.A.: The Ways We Kill Each Other.* New York: Ballantine Books, 1978.
Goebbels, Josef. *Diaries.* trans. Louis P. Lochner. London: Hamish Hamilton, 1948.
_____. *The Early Goebbels Diaries.* London: Nicolson & Weidenfeld, 1962.
Goebel, Julius, and Naughton, T. Raymond. *Law Enforcement in Colonial New York: A Study in Criminal Procedure.* Montclair, N.J.: Patterson Smith, 1970.
Goerlitz, Walter. *History of the German General Staff, 1657-1945.* trans. Brian Battershaw. New York: Fredrick A. Praeger, 1953.
Goff, John S. *Robert Todd Lincoln.* Norman: University of Oklahoma Press, 1969.
Goff, Kenneth. *Crackpot or Crackshot.* Englewood, Colo.: Published by Author, 1965.
Goffman, Erving. *Asylums.* New York: Doubleday, 1961.
_____. *Encounters.* Indianapolis, Ind.: Bobbs-Merrill, 1961..
_____. *Essays on the Social Situation of Mental Patients and Other Inmates.* New York: Doubleday, 1961.
Gold, Mark S. *800-Cocaine.* New York: Bantam Books, 1984.
Gold, Martin. *Delinquent Behavior in an American City.* Belmont, Calif.: Brooks/Cole, 1970.
_____. *Deviant Behavior in an American City.* Belmont, Calif.: Brooks-Cole, 1970.
Goldberg, Alfred. *Conspiracy Interpretations of the Assassination of President Kennedy.* Los Angeles: University of California Security Studies Project, 1968.
Goldberg, Harvey. *American Radicals: Some Problems and Personalities.* New York: Monthly Review Press, 1957.
Goldberg, Isaac. *Queen of Hearts.* New York: Day, 1936.
Goldberg, Jacob A., and Rosamond W. *Girls of the City Streets.* New York: Foundation Books, 1940.
Goldberg, Robert Alan. *Hooded Empire.* Chicago: The University of Illinois Press, 1981.
Golden, Harry. *A Little Girl Is Dead.* New York: World Publishing, 1965.
Goldenberg, Boris. *The Cuban Revolution and Latin America.* New York: Frederick A. Praeger, 1965.
Goldfarb, Ronald L. *Jails: The Ultimate Ghetto.* Garden City, N.Y.: Anchor Press/Doubleday, 1975.
_____, and Singer, Linda R. *After Conviction.* New York: Simon & Schuster, 1973.
Goldman, Alex J. *John Fitzgerald Kennedy: The World Remembers.* New York: Fleet Press, 1968.
Goldman, E. *The Traffic in Women and Other Essays on Feminism.* Washington, D.C.: Times Change Press, 1970.
Goldman, Emma. *Anarchism and Other Essays.* New York: Mother Earth Publishing, 1911.
_____. *Living My Life.* New York: Alfred A. Knopf, 1931.
Goldman, Eric F. *The Crucial Decade.* New York: Alfred A. Knopf, 1956.
_____. *Rendezvous with Destiny: A History of Modern American Reform.* New York: Alfred A. Knopf, 1952.
_____. *The Tragedy of Lyndon Johnson.* New York: Alfred A. Knopf, 1969.
Goldman, Nathan. *The Differential Selection of Juvenile Defenders for Court Appearance.* New York: National Council on Crime and Delinquency, 1963.
Goldsmith, Gloria. *Rape.* Beverly Hills, Calif.: Wollstonecraft, 1974.
Goldsmith, Jack and Sharon (eds.). *The Police Community.* Pacific Palisades, Calif. Palisades, 1974.
Goldstein, Abraham S., and Joseph (eds.). *Crime, Law and Society.* New York: The Free Press, 1971.
_____. *The Insanity Defense.* New Haven, Conn.: Yale University Press, 1967.
Goldstein, Arnold P. *Police & The Elderly.* New York: Pergamon, 1980.
Goldstein, Herman. *Police Corruption: A Perspective on its Nature and Control.* Washington, D.C.: Police Foundation, 1975.
_____. *Policing a Free Society.* Cambridge, Mass.: Ballinger, 1977.
Goldstein, Jeffrey H. *Aggression and Crimes of Violence.* New York: Oxford University Press, 1975.
Goldstock, Ronald, and Coenan, Dan T. *Extortionate and Usurious* Credit Transactions: Background Materials. Ithaca, N.Y.: Cornell Institute on Organized Crime, 1978.
Goldston, Robert. *Satan's Disciples.* New York: Ballantine Books, 1962.
_____. *The Negro Revolution.* New York: Signet Books, New American Library, 1968.
Goldsworthy, D. *Tom Mboya: The Man Kenya Wanted to Forget.* London: William Heinemann, 1982.
Gollmar, Judge Robert H. *Edward Gein: America's Most Bizzarre Murderer.* Delavan, Wis.: Chas. Hallberg, 1981.
Gollomb, Joseph. *Crimes of the Year.* New York: Liveright, 1931.
_____. *Master Highwaymen.* New York: Macaulay, 1927.
Gompers, Samuel. *The McNamara Case.* Washington, D.C.: American Federation of Labor, 1911.
_____. *Seventy Years of Life and Labor: An Autobiography.* 2 vols. New York: E.P. Dutton, 1925.
Gong, Eng Ying, and Grant, B. *Tong War.* Boston: Little, Brown, 1930.
Gonzlez Blanco, Edmundo. *Carranza y la Revolucin de Mexico.* Madrid: Imprenta Helnica, 1916.
Gonzalez Blanco, Pedro. *De Porfirio Diaz a Carranza.* Madrid: Imprenta Helenica, 1916.
Gooch, George P. *Catherine the Great and Other Studies.* New York: Longmans, 1954.
_____. *Franco-German Relations, 1871-1914.* New York: Russell & Russell, 1923.
_____. *Frederick the Great: The Ruler, the Writer, the Man.* New York: Alfred A. Knopf, 1947.
_____. *Germany.* London: Ernest Benn, 1925.
_____. *History of Modern Europe.* New York: Henry Holt, 1923.
Good, Milton. *Twelve Years in a Texas Prison.* Amarillo, Texas: Russell Stationery, 1935.
Goode, E. (ed.). *Marijuana.* New York: Atherton Press, 1969.
Goode, Erich. *Deviant Behavior.* Englewood Cliffs, N.J.: Prentice-Hall, 1984.
_____. *The Drug Phenomenon: Social Aspects of Drug Taking.* New York: Bobbs-Merrill, 1973.
_____. *Drugs in American Society.* New York: Alfred A. Knopf, 1972.
Goodell, Charles. *Political Prisoners in America.* New York: Random House, 1973.
Goodman, Derick. *Crime of Passion.* New York: Greenberg, 1958.
_____. *Villainy Unlimited.* London: Elek Books, 1957.
Goodman, Edward J. *The Explorers of South America.* New York: Macmillan, 1972.
Goodman, Ezra. *The Fifty-Year Decline and Fall of Hollywood.* New York: Simon & Schuster, 1961.
Goodman, Jonathan. *Bloody Versicles: The Rhymes of Crime.* Newton Abbott, Eng.: David & Charles, 1971.
_____. *The Killing of Julia Wallace.* New York: Charles Scribner's Sons, 1969.
_____. *Posts-Mortem: The Correspondence of Murder.* New York: St. Martin's Press, 1971.
_____. *The Railway Murders.* London: Allison & Busby, 1984.
_____. *Trial of Ian Brady and Myra Hindley.* Newton Abbott, Eng.: David and Charles, 1973.
Goodman, Walter. *All Honorable Men: Corruption and Compromise in American Life.* Boston: Little, Brown, 1963.
_____. *The Committee: the Extraordinary Career of the White House Committee on Un-American Activities.* New York: Farrar, Straus & Giroux, 1968.
Goodnow, Frank J., and Bates, Frank G. *Municipal Government.* New York: Century, 1919.
Goodrich, Charles Augustus. *The Land We Live In.* Cincinnati, Ohio: H.M. Rulison, 1857.
Goodstone, Tony (ed.). *The Pulps.* New York: Chelsea House, 1970.
Goodwin, Jean, et al. *Sexual Abuse.* Boston: John Wright, 1982.

Goodwin, John G. *Insanity and the Criminal.* London: Hutchinson, 1923.

Gora, Joel. *The Rights of Reporters.* New York: Discus, Avon, 1974.

Goran, Morris. *Fact, Fraud and Fantasy: The Occult and Pseudosciences.* New York: A.S. Barnes, 1979.

Gordeaux, Paul. *Le Docteur Petiot.* Paris: Editions J'ai lu, 1970.

Gordon, Alexander. *The Lives of Pope Alexander VI and his Son Caesar Borgia.* 2 vols. London: C. Davis & T. Green, 1929.

Gordon, B.L. *Medicine throughout Antiquity.* Philadelphia: T.A. Davis, 1949.

Gordon, Charles. *The Old Bailey and Newgate.* London: T. Fisher Unwin, 1903.

Gordon, David F. *Decolonization and the State of Kenya.* Boulder, Colo.: Westview, 1986.

Gordon, Harold J. *The Austrian Empire, Abortive Federation?* Lexington, Mass.: D.C. Heath, 1974.

_____. *The Reichswehr and the German Republic.* London: Oxford University Press, 1947.

Gordon, Mike. *I Arrest Pearl Starr, and Other Stories of Adventure as a Policeman in Fort Smith, Arkansas, for 40 Years.* Fort Smith, Ark.: Press-Atgus, 1958.

Gordon, R.A. *Proceedings of the II International Symposium on Criminology.* San Paulo, Braz.: International Center for Biological and Medico-forensic Criminology, 1975.

Gordon, Rosalie. *Nine Men Against America.* New York: Devon-Adair, 1958.

Gordon, Welche. *Jesse James and His Band of Notorious Outlaws.* Chicago: Laird & Lee, 1891.

Gordon, Mrs. Will. *Roumania Yesterday and Today.* London: John Lane, The Bodley Head, 1919.

Gore, John. *King George V.* London: John Murray, 1941.

Gore, Leroy. *Joe Must Go.* New York: Julian Messner, 1954.

Gores, Joe. *Hammett.* New York: G.P. Putnam's Sons, 1975.

Goriachkin, F.T. *Pervy Russky Fashist: Pyotor Arkadievich Stolypin.* Harbin, U.S.S.R.: Merkury, 1928.

Goring, Charles. *The English Convict.* London: H.M. Stationery Office, 1913.

Gorky, Maxim. *Days with Lenin.* trans. V.I. Lenin. New York: International Publishers, 1932.

Grlitz, Walter, and Quint, Herbert A. *Adolf Hitler. Eine Biographie.* Stuttgart, Ger.: Steingruben Verlag GmbH, 1952.

_____. *Generalfeldmarschall Keitel. Verbrecher oder Offizier?* Berlin: Musterschmidt, 1961.

_____. *Die Waffen-SS.* Berlin: Arani, 1960.

Gorman, Joseph Bruce. *Kefauver: a Political Biography.* New York: Oxford University Press, 1971.

Gosch, Martin A., and Hammer, Richard. *The Last Testament of Lucky Luciano.* Boston: Little, Brown, 1974.

Gosling, John, and Craig, Dennis. *The Great Train Robbery.* Indianapolis, Ind.: Bobbs Merrill, 1964.

_____, and Warner, Douglas. *The Shame of a City.* London: W.H. Allen, 1960.

Gosnell, Harold F. *Boss Platt and His New York Machine.* Chicago: F. Mendelsohn, 1933.

_____. *Machine Politics: The Chicago Model.* Chicago: F. Mendelsohn, 1937.

_____. *Negro Politicians: The Rise of Negro Politics in Chicago.* Chicago: University of Chicago Press, 1967.

Gosse, Philip. *The History of Piracy.* New York: Longmans, Green, 1932.

_____. *The Pirates' Who's Who.* Boston: E. Lauriat, 1924.

Gosset, Pierre, and Gosset, Rene. *Adolph Hitler.* Paris: Juillard, 1961.

Gotlieb, Alan M. *The Rights of Gun Owners.* Aurora, Ill.: Caroline House, 1981.

Goto Takao. *Koria Uochiya (Korea Watcher).* Tokyo: Gendai no Rironsha, 1982.

Gott, Richard. *Guerrilla Movements in Latin America.* Garden City, N.Y.: Doubleday, 1971.

Gottesman, Ronald (ed.). *Violence in America.* 3 vols. New York: Charles Scribner's Sons, 1999.

Gottfredson, Don M., Wilkins, Leslie T., and Hoffman, Peter B. *Parole Decision Making.* Washington, D.C.: National Institute of Law Enforcement and Criminal Justice, 1973.

Gottfried, Alex. *Boss Cermak of Chicago.* Seattle, Wash.: University of Washington Press, 1962.

Gottlieb, Gerald H. *Capital Punishment.* Santa Barbara, Calif.: Center for the Study of Democratic Institutions, 1967.

Goubert, Pierre. *Louis XIV and the Twenty Million Frenchmen.* New York: Random House, 1972.

Gough, John B. *Platform Echoes: or, Living Truths for Head and Heart.* Hartford, Conn.: A.D. Worthington, 1886.

_____. *Sunlight and Shadow, or Gleanings From my Life Work.* Hartford, Conn.: A.D. Worthington, 1881.

Gough, William Charles. *From Kew Observatory to Scotland Yard.* London: Hurst & Blackett, 1927.

Goulart, Ron. *An Informal History of the Pulp Magazine.* New York: Ace Books, 1972.

_____. *Line Up, Tough Guys.* Nashville, Tenn.: Sherbourne Press, 1966.

Gould, E.W. *Fifty Years on the Mississippi.* St. Louis, Mo.: Nixon-Jones, 1889.

Gould, Leroy C., and Walker, Andrew L., and Crane, Lansing E. *Connections: Notes from the Heroin World.* New Haven, Conn.: Yale University Press, 1974.

_____, et al. *Crime as a Profession.* Washington, D.C.: Final Report to the Office of Law Enforcement Assistance and President's Commission on Law Enforcement and Administration of Justice, 1967.

Gould, Leslie. *The Manipulators.* New York: David McKay, 1966.

Goulden, Joseph C. *The Benchwarmers: The Private World of the Powerful Federal Judges.* New York: Ballantine, 1974.

_____. *The Best Years, 1945-1950.* New York: Atheneum, 1976.

_____. *Million Dollar Lawyers.* New York: G.P. Putnam's Sons, 1978.

_____. *The Superlawyers.* New York: Weybright & Talley, 1972.

Gourevitch, Philip. *We Wish to Inform You That Tomorrow We Will be Killed With Our Families.: Stories from Rwanda.* New York: Picador, 1999.

Gourko, Basil. *War and Revolution in Russia, 1914-1917.* New York: Macmillan, 1919.

Gourko, Vladimir. *Features and Figures of the Past.* Palo Alto, Calif.: Stanford University Press, 1939.

Gourley, Douglas. *Public Relations and the Police.* Springfield, Ill.: Charles C. Thomas, 1953.

Government of India. *Congress Responsibility for the Disturbances (1942-1943).* New Delhi: Government of India, 1943.

_____. *Gandhian Outlook and Techniques.* New Delhi: Government of India, 1953.

_____. *Homage to Gandhi.* New Delhi: Government of India, 1948.

Governor's Commission on the Los Angeles Riots. *Watts Report: Violence in the City-An End of a Beginning.* Los Angeles: Published by Author, 1965.

Gower, Lord Ronald. *Joan of Arc.* London: J.C. Nimmo, 1893.

Gowers, Andrew. *Behind the Myth: Yasir Arafat and the Palestinian Revolution.* Northampton, Mass.: 1992.

Gowers, Sir Ernest. *A Life for a Life.* London: Chatto & Windus, 1956.

Grady, Henry F., and Carr, Robert M. *The Port of San Francisco.* Berkeley: University of California Press, 1934.

Graebner, N.A. *Empire on the Pacific.* New York: Ronald, 1955.

Graham, Evelyn. *Fifty Years of Famous Judges.* London: John Long, 1930.

_____. *Lord Darling and His Famous Trials.* London: John Long, 1953.

Graham, Fred P. *The Alias Program.* Boston: Little, Brown, 1978.

_____. *The Self-Inflicted Wound.* New York: Dell, 1972.

Graham, Hugh D., and Gurr, Ted Robert. *The History of Violence in America: A Report to the National Commission on the Causes and Prevention of Violence.* New York: Bantam Books, 1969.

_____ (ed.). *Huey Long.* Englewood Cliffs, N.J.: Prentice-Hall, 1970.

Graham, Jory. *Chicago, an Extraordinary Guide.* Chicago: Rand McNally, 1967.

Graham, Stephen. *Alexander of Yugoslavia.* New Haven, Conn.: Yale University Press, 1939.

_____. *New York Nights.* New York: G.H. Doran, 1927.

_____. *Peter the Great.* London: Benn, 1929.

Gramling, Oliver. *AP: The Story of the News.* New York: Farrar & Rinehart, 1940.

Gramont, Sanche de. *The Secret War.* New York: G.P. Putnam's Sons, 1962.

Granet, Marcel. *Chinese Civilization.* New York: Meridian Books, 1958.

Granier, Camille. *La Femme criminelle.* Paris: Doin, 1906.

Granlund, Nils T. *Blondes, Brunettes and Bullets.* New York: David McKay, 1957.

Grant, Hamil. *Spies and Secret Service.* New York: Frederick A. Stokes, 1915.

Grant, Joanne. *Black Protest.* Greenwich, Conn.: Fawcett, 1968.

Grant, Michael. *The Jews in the Roman World.* London: Weidenfeld & Nicolson, 1973.

_____. *The World of Rome.* New York: Mentor, 1960.

Graper, Elmer D. *American Police Administration.* Montclair, N.J.: Patterson Smith, 1969.

Gratacap, Louis Pope. *The Political Mission of Tammany Hall.* New York: A.B. King, 1894.

Grathwohl, Larry. *Bringing Down America.* New Rochelle, N.Y.: Arlington House, 1976.

Grattan, Hartley. *Introducing Australia.* New York: John Day, 1942.

Gravel, Senator Mike (ed.). *The Pentagon Papers.* Boston: Beacon Press, 1971.

Graves, Richard. *Experiment in Anarchy.* London: Victor Gollancz, 1949.

Graves, Richard S. *Oklahoma Outlaws.* Fort Davis, Texas: Frontier Books, 1968.

Graves, Robert. *They Hanged My Saintly Billy; the Life and Death of Dr. William Palmer.* New York: Doubleday, 1957.

_____. *The Twelve Caesars.* Baltimore: Penguin Books, 1957.

Graves, Robert, and Hodge, Alan. *The Long Week-End: A Social History of Great Britain, 1918-1939.* London: Faber & Faber, 1940.

Graves, Sally. *A History of Socialism.* London: Hogarth Press, 1939.

Gray, Alexander. *The Socialist Tradition.* London: Longmans, 1946.

Gray, Arthur Amos. *Men Who Built the West.* Caldwell, Idaho: Caxton Printers, 1945.

Gray, F.C. *Prison Discipline in America.* London: John Murray, 1848.

Gray, James H. *The Roar of the Twenties.* Toronto, Ontario, Can.: Macmillan, 1975.

_____. *The Winter Years.* Toronto, Ontario, Can.: Macmillan, 1966.

Graysmith, Robert. *The Sleeping Lady.* New York: E. P. Dutton, 1990.

_____. *Unabomber.* Washington, D. C.: Regnery, 1997.

_____. *Zodiac.* New York: St. Martin's, 1986.

Great Britain, Home Office. *The Length of Prison Sentences: Interim Report of the Advisory Council on the Penal System.* London: H.M. Stationary Office, 1977.

_____. *A Review of Criminal Justice Policy 1976.* London: H.M. Stationary Office, 1977.

_____. *The Sentence of the Court: A Handbook for Courts on the Treatment of Criminal Offenders.* London: H.M. Stationary Office, 1964.

Great Britain, Royal Commission on Capital Punishment. *Report, Together With the Minutes of Evidence and Appendix.* London: H.M. Stationery Office, 1866.

_____. *Minutes of Evidence.* London: H.M. Stationery Office, 1949-1951.

_____. *Report.* London: H.M. Stationery Office, 1953.

The Great Guiteau Trial. Philadelphia: Barclay, 1882.

The Great Impeachment and Trial of Andrew Johnson, President of the United States. Philadelphia: J.B. Peterson & Brothers, 1868.

Great True Stories of Crime, Mystery and Detection. Pleasantville, N.Y.: Reader's Digest Association, 1965.

The Great Trunk Mystery of New York. Philadelphia: Barclay, 1871.

Greeley, Horace. *The American Conflict.* Hartford, Conn.: O.D. Case, 1864.

_____. *Greeley on Lincoln.* New York: Baker & Taylor, 1893.

_____. *Hints Toward Reforms.* New York: Fowler & Wells, 1853.

_____. *An Overland Journey from New York to San Francisco in the Summer of 1859.* New York: C.M. Saxon, Barker, 1860.

_____. *Recollections of a Busy Life.* New York: J.B. Ford, 1868.

Green, Constance McLaughlin. *Washington: Capital City, 1879-1950.* Princeton, N.J.: Princeton University Press, 1963.
_____. *Washington: Village and Capitol, 1800-1878.* Princeton, N.J.: Princeton University Press, 1962.
Green, E. *Psychology for Law Enforcement.* New York: John Wiley & Sons, 1976.
Green, Edward. *Judicial Attitudes in Sentencing.* London: Macmillan, 1961.
Green, Gil. *Cold War Fugitive.* New York: International, 1984.
Green, J.H. *Gambling Unmasked! or The Personal Experience of J. H. Green, the Reformed Gambler.* Philadelphia: Privately Published, 1847.
_____. *Report of Gambling in New York.* New York: Privately Published, 1851.
_____. *The Secret Band of Brothers; or The American Outlaws.* Philadelphia: Privately published, 1847.
Green, Jonathon. *The Directory of Infamy: The Best of the Worst.* London: Mills and Boon, 1980.

Green, V.H.H. *Medieval Civilization in Western Europe.* New York: St. Martin's Press, 1971.
Greenberg, Bradley S., and Parker, Edwin B. (eds.). *The Kennedy Assassination and the American Public: Social Communication in Crisis.* Stanford, Calif.: Stanford University Press, 1965.
Greenberg, David F. *Crime and Capitalism.* Palo Alto, Calif.: Mayfield, 1981.
_____. (ed.). *Corrections and Punishment.* Beverly Hills, Calif.: Sage, 1977.
Greenberg, Michael. *British Trade and the Opening of China 1800-1842.* Cambridge, Eng.: Cambridge University Press, 1951.
Greenberg, Norman. *The Man with a Steel Guitar: Portrait of Desperation, and Crime.* Hoover, N.H.: University Press of New England, 1981.
Greenberger, Richard. *Red Rising in Bavaria.* New York: St. Martin's Press, 1973.
Greene, Felix. *China: The Country Americans Are Not Allowed to Know.* New York: Ballantine Books, 1962.
Greene, Capt. Jonathan H. *A Desperado in Arizona, 1858-1860.* Santa Fe, N.M.: Stagecoach, 1964.
Greene, Laurence. *America Goes to Press, The News of Yesterday.* Indianapolis, Ind.: Bobbs Merrill, 1936.
_____. *The Era of Wonderful Nonsense: A Casebook of the 'Twenties.* Indianapolis, Ind.: Bobbs Merrill, 1939.
Greene, Mark H., Kozel, Nicholas J., and Hunt, Leon G. *An Assessment of the Diffusion of Heroin Abuse to Medium Sized American Cities.* Washington, D.C.: U.S. Government Printing Office, 1974.
Greene, Robert W. *The Sting Man.* New York: E.P. Dutton, 1981.
Greenhaw, Wayne. *Flying High.* New York: Dodd, Mead, 1984.
_____. *Watch Out for George Wallace.* Englewood Cliffs, N.J.: Prentice-Hall, 1976.
Greeno, Edward. *War On the Underworld.* London: John Long, 1960.
Greenwald, Dr. Harold. *The Call Girl: A Social and Psychoanalytic Study.* New York: Ballantine, 1958.
_____. *The Elegant Prostitute.* New York: Walker, 1970.
_____ (ed.). *The Prostitute in Literature.* New York: Ballantine, 1960.
Greenwall, Harry J. *They Were Murdered in France.* London: Jarrolds, 1957.
Greenwood, James. *The Seven Curses of London.* London: Stanley Rivers, 1869.
Greenwood, Peter W. *An Analysis of the Apprehension Activities of the New York City Police Department.* New York: New York City Rand Institute, 1970.
Greenwood, William. *Guilty or Not Guilty.* London: Hutchinson, 1931.
Greenya, John. *Blood Relations.* New York: Harcourt Brace Jovanovich, 1987.
Gregg, Richard B. *A Discipline for Non-violence.* Ahmedabad, India: Navajivan, 1941.
Gregory, George H. *Alcatraz Screw: My Years as a Guard in America's Most Notorious Prison.* Columbia, Mo.: University of Missouri Press, 2002.
Gregory, J.D. *Dollfuss and His Times.* London: Hutchinson, 1935.
Gregory, Lester. *True Wild West Stories.* London: Andrew Dakers, n.d.
Gregory of Tours. *History of the Franks.* trans. Ernest Brehaut. New York: W.W. Norton, 1969.
Greif, Geoffrey and Hegar, Rebecca. *When Parents Kidnap: The Families Behind the Headlines.* New York: Free Press, 1993.
Grellin, Richard. *J'Accuse.* New York: Doran, 1915.
Grenfell, Russell. *Main Fleet to Singapore.* London: Faber & Faber, 1951.
Gresh, Alain. *The PLO: The Struggle Within: Towards an Independent Palestinian State.* London: Zed Books, 1985.
Gresham, Otto. *The Greenbacks.* Chicago: Book Press, 1927.
Grey, Ian. *Catherine the Great: Autocrat and Empress of All Russia.* New York: J.B. Lippincott, 1961.
_____. *The First Fifty Years.* New York: Coward-McCann, 1967.
_____. *Ivan the Terrible.* New York: J.B. Lippincott, 1964.
_____. *Peter the Great, Emperor of All Russia.* New York: J.B. Lippincott, 1960.
Gribble, Francis H. *Emperor and Mystic: The Life of Alexander I of Russia.* London: Nash & Grayson, 1931.
Gribble, Leonard. *Adventures in Murder.* London: John Long, 1954.
_____. *The Black Maria or the Criminal's Omnibus.* London: Victor Gollancz, 1935.
_____. *Clues That Spelled Guilty.* London: John Long, 1961.
_____. *Compelled to Kill.* London: John Long, 1977.
_____. *The Dead End Killers.* London: John Long, 1978.
_____. *The Deadly Professionals.* London: John Long, 1978.
_____. *Detection and Deduction.* Garden City, N.Y.: Doubleday, 1934.
_____. *Famous Feats of Detection and Crime.* Garden City, N.Y.: Doubleday, Doran, 1934.
_____. *Famous Judges and Their Trials.* London: John Long, 1957.
_____. *Famous Manhunts: A Century of Crime.* London: John Long, 1953.
_____. *Famous Stories of the Murder Squad.* London: Barker, 1974.
_____. *Great Detective Exploits.* London: John Long, 1958.
_____. *Great Manhunters of the Yard.* New York: Roy, 1966.
_____. *Hallmark of Horror.* London: John Long, 1973.
_____. *Murders Most Strange.* London: John Long, 1959.
_____. *Queens of Crime.* London: Hurst & Blackett, 1932.
_____. *Sisters of Cain.* London: John Long, 1972.
_____. *Stories of Famous Detectives.* New York: Hill & Wang, 1963.
_____. *Stories of Famous Modern Trials.* London: Barker, 1973.
_____. *Strange Crimes of Passion.* London: John Long, 1970.
_____. *Such Was Their Guilt.* London: John Long, 1974.
_____. *Such Women are Deadly.* London: John Long, 1965.
_____. *They Challenged the Yard.* London: John Long, 1963.
_____. *They Conspired to Kill.* London: John Long, 1975.
_____. *They Got Away with Murder.* London: John Long, 1971.
_____. *They Had A Way with Women.* London: John Long, 1967.
_____. *Triumphs of Scotland Yard.* London: John Long, 1955.
_____. *When Killers Err.* London: John Long, 1962.
Grieb, Kenneth J. *The United States and Huerta.* Lincoln: University of Nebraska Press, 1969.
Grier, William H., and Cobbs, Price M. *Black Rage.* New York: Bantam Books, 1969.
Grierson, Francis. *Famous French Crimes.* London: Frederick Muller, 1959.
Griffin, Bulkley S. (ed.). *Offbeat History.* New York: World, 1967.
Griffin, John I. *Statistics Essential for Police Efficiency.* Springfield, Ill.: Charles C. Thomas, 1958.
Griffin, Susan. *Rape.* New York: Harper & Row, 1979.
Griffith, A. Kinney. *Mickey Free: Manhunter.* Caldwell, Idaho: Caxton Press, 1969.
Griffith, Lippon R. *Mugging.* Englewood Cliffs, N.J.: Spectrum, 1978.
Griffith, Robert. *The Politics of Fear: Joseph McCarthy and the Senate.* Lexington: University of Kentucky Press, 1970.
Griffiths, Major Arthur. *Early French Prisons.* London: Grolier Society, n.d.
_____. *English Prisons.* Vols. I, II, III. London: Grolier Society, n.d.
_____. *German and Austrian Prisons.* London: Grolier Society, n.d.
_____. *Italian Prisons.* London: Grolier Society, n.d.
_____. *Modern French Prisons.* London: Grolier Society, n.d.
_____. *Mysteries of Police and Crime.* Vols. I, II, III. London: Cassell, 1902.
_____. *Non-Criminal Prisons.* London: Grolier Society, n.d.
_____. *Oriental Prisons.* London: Grolier Society, n.d.
_____. *Over Seas Prisons.* London: Grolier Society, n.d.
_____. *Russian Prisons.* London: Grolier Society, n.d.
_____. *Secrets of the Prison-House or Gaol Studies and Sketches.* London: Chapman & Hall, 1894.
_____. *Spanish Prisons.* London: Grolier Society, n.d.
_____. *The World's Famous Prisons.* 12 vols. London: Grolier Society, 1894.
Griffiths, John. *Resurrection: The Kidnapping of Abby Drover.* Toronto: Insomniac Press, 1999.
Grimal, Pierre (ed.). *Hellenism and the Rise of Rome.* trans. A.M. Sheridan Smith. New York: Delacorte Press, 1965.
Grimshaw, Allen A. (ed.). *Racial Violence in the United States.* Chicago: Aldine, 1969.
Grimshaw, Eric, and Jones, Glyn. *Lord Goddard: His Career and Cases.* London: Allan Wingate, 1958.
Grinspoon, Lester, and Bakalar, James B. *Cocaine: A Drug and Its Evolution.* New York: Basic Books, 1976.
_____. *Marihuana Reconsidered.* Cambridge, Mass.: Harvard University Press, 1977.
_____. *Psychodelic Drugs Reconsidered.* New York: Basic Books, 1979.
_____, and Hedblom, Peter. *The Speed Culture: Amphetamine Use and Abuse in America.* Cambridge, Mass.: Harvard University Press, 1975.
Grisham, Noel. *Tame the Reckless Wind: The Life and Legends of Sam Bass.* Austin, Texas: San Felipe Press, 1968.
Griswold, H. Jack, et al. *An Eye for an Eye.* New York: Henry Holt, Rinehart & Winston, 1970.
Grodzins, Morton. *Americans Betrayed, Politics and the Japanese Evacuation.* Chicago: University of Chicago Press, 1949.
Grombach, John. *The Great Liquidator.* New York: Doubleday, 1980.
Gross, Feliks. *The Seizure of Political Power.* New York: Philosophical Library, 1958.
Gross, Felix. *Violence in Politics.* New York: Mouton, 1972.
Gross, Gerald (ed.). *Masterpieces of Murder: An Edmund Pearson True Crime Reader.* Boston: Little, Brown, 1963.
Gross, H.G.A. *Criminal Investigation: A Practical Textbook for Magistrates, Police Officers and Lawyers.* trans. J. Adam and J. Collyer Adam. London: Sweet & Maxwell, 1949.
Gross, Hans. *Criminology Psychology.* Boston: Little, Brown, 1915.
Gross, L. *Sexual Behavior.* New York: John Wiley & Sons, 1974.
Grosser, Alfred. *Germany in Our Time.* London: Pelican Books, 1974.
Grossman, Edwina Booth. *Edwin Booth: Recollections by His Daughter.* New York: Century, 1894.
Grosso, Sonny, and Devaney, John. *Murder at the Harlem Mosque.* New York: Crown, 1977.
Grote, George. *History of Greece.* London: John Murray, 1853.
Groth, A. Nicholas. *Men Who Rape.* London: Plenum, 1980.
Grover, David H. *Debaters and Dynamiters: The Story of the Haywood Trial.* Corvallis, Ore.: Oregon State University Press, 1964.
_____. *Diamondfield Jack: A Study in Frontier Justice.* Reno: University of Nevada Press, 1968.
Grover, G.W. *Shadows lifted or sunshine restored on the hori -of human lives.* Chicago: Stromberg, Allen, 1894
Grover, William C. *The Tammany Hall Democracy of the City of New York, and the General Committee for 1875.* New York: n.p., 1875.
Grunberger, Richard. *A Social History of the Third Reich.* London: Penguin Books, 1974.

Grund, Francis J. *Aristocracy in America.* New York: Harper & Brothers, 1959.

Grunder, Garel A., and Livezey, William E. *The Philippines and the United States.* Norman: University of Oklahoma Prss, 1951.

Grnebaum, Gustave E. von. *Medieval Islam.* Chicago: University of Chicago Press, 1946.

Grnhut, Max, *Penal Reform.* Oxford, Eng.: Clarendon Press, 1948.

_____, Sieverts, Rudolf, and Bemmelen, Jacob M. *Sexual Crime Today.* The Hague, Neth.: Martinus Nijhoff, 1960.

Grunwald, Constantine. *Peter the Great.* Philadelphia: Saunders, 1956.

_____. *Tsar Nicholas I.* New York: Macmillan, 1955.

Grupp, Stanley E. (ed.). *Theories of Punishment.* Bloomington: University of Indiana Press, 1972.

Gsovski, V., and Grzybowski, K. *Government, Law and Courts in the Soviet Union and Eastern Europe.* London: Stevens, 1959.

Guardian Newspapers. *Windscale: A Summary of the Evidence and the Argument.* London: Guardian Newspapers, 1977.

Gue, Benjamin F. *History of Iowa.* New York: Century History, 1903.

Guedalla, Philip. *The Queen and Mrs. Gladstone.* Garden City, N.Y.: Doubleday, Doran, 1934.

Guerin, Daniel. *Fascism and Big Business.* New York: Pioneer, 1929.

Guerin, Eddie. *I Was a Bandit.* Garden City, N.Y.: Doubleday, Doran, 1929.

Guerin, Thomas. *Caps and Crowns of Europe.* Montreal, Quebec, Can.: Louis Carrier, 1929.

Guriot, Paul. *Napolon III.* 2 vols. Paris: Payot, 1933-34.

Guest, Ivor. *Napoleon III in England.* London: British Technical & General Press, 1952.

Gugas, Chris. *The Silent Witness.* Englewood Cliffs, N.J.: Prentice-Hall, 1979.

Gugliotta, Guy, and Leen, Jeff. *Kings of Cocaine: Inside the Medellin Cartel-An Astonishing True Story of Murder, Money, and International Corruption.* New York: Simon & Schuster, 1989.

Guicciardini, Francesco. *History of Italy and History of Florence.* New York: Washington Square Press, 1964.

Guild, June Purcell. *Black Laws of Virginia.* New York: Negro University Press, 1969.

Guild, Leo. *The Fatty Arbuckle Case.* New York: Paperback Library, 1962.

Guiles, Fred Lawrence. *Marion Davies.* New York: McGraw Hill, 1972.

Guinn, J.M. *A History of California, and an Extended History of Its Southern Coast Counties.* Los Angeles: Historic Record, 1907.

_____. *Historical and Biographical Record of Southern California.* Chicago: Chapman, 1902.

_____. *History of the State of California and Biographical Record of Sacramento Valley, California.* Chicago: Chapman, 1906.

_____. *History of the State of California and Biographical Record of San Joaquin County.* Los Angeles: Historic Record, 1909.

Guiteau's Confession: The Garfield Assassination, Being a Full History of the Cruel Crime. Philadelphia: Old Franklin, 1881.

Guiteau's Crime: The Full History of the Murder of President James A. Garfield. New York: Richard K. Fox, 1881.

Guiteau Trial. New York: John Polhemus, 1882.

Gullick, C.A. *Austria from Habsburg to Hitler.* Berkeley: University of California, 1950.

Gumina, Deanna Paoli. *The Italians of San Francisco, 1850-1930.* New York: Center for Migration Studies, 1978.

Gummere, Amelia Mott. *Witchcraft and Quakerism.* Philadelphia: Biddle, 1908.

Gun, Nerin. *Eva Braun: Hitler's Mistress.* New York: Hawthorne Books, 1968.

_____. *Red Roses From Texas.* London: Fredrick Muller, 1964.

Gunn, John. *Violence.* New York: Frederick A. Praeger, 1973.

Gunn, John W. *Wisdom of Clarence Darrow.* Girard, Kan.: Haldeman-Julius, 1947.

Gunther, Jack D., and Charles O. *The Identification of Firearms.* New York: John Wiley & Sons, 1935.

Gunther, John. *Inside Asia.* New York: Harper & Brothers, 1939.

_____. *Inside Europe.* New York: Harper & Brothers, 1938.

_____. *Inside U.S.A.* New York: Harper & Brothers, 1947.

_____. *Riddle of MacArthur: Japan, Korea and the Far East.* New York: Harper & Brothers, 1951.

_____. *Roosevelt in Retrospect.* New York: Harper and Brothers, 1950.

_____. *Taken at the Flood.* New York: Harper, 1960.

Gunther, Max. *D.B. Cooper, What Really Happened?* Chicago: Contemporary Books, 1985.

Gurko, Miriam. *Clarence Darrow.* New York: Thomas Y. Crowell, 1965.

Gurko, V.I. *Features and Figures of the Past.* Stanford, Calif.: Stanford University Press, 1939.

Gurr, Ted Robert. *Rogues, Rebels, and Reformers: A Political History of Urban Crime and Conflict.* Beverly Hills, Calif.: Sage, 1976.

Gurr, Tom, and Cox, H.H. *Famous Australasian Crimes.* London: Frederick Muller, 1957.

Gurvitch, Georges. *Sociology of Law.* New York: Philosophical Library, 1941.

Gurwell, John K. *Mass Murder in Houston.* Houston, Texas: Cordovan Press, 1974.

Gutierres de Lara, L. and Pinchon, Edgcumb. *The Mexican People: Their Struggle for Freedom.* New York: Doubleday, Page, 1914.

Gutman, Richard J.S., and Kellie O. *John Wilkes Booth Himself.* Dover, Mass.: Hired Hand Press, 1979.

Guttmacher, Manfred. *The Mind of the Murderer.* New York: Farrar, Straus, 1960.

_____, and Weihofen, Henry. *Psychiatry and the Law.* New York: W.W. Norton, 1952.

_____. *Sex Offenses: The Problem, Causes and Prevention.* New York: W.W. Norton, 1951.

Guzman, Martin Luis. *The Eagle and the Serpent.* New York: Doubleday, 1965.

_______. *Memoirs of Pancho Villa.* trans. Virginia H. Taylor. Austin: University of Texas Press, 1965.

Gwatkin, H.M. and Whitney J.P. (eds.). *The Cambridge Medieval History.* New York: Macmillan, 1911-1936.

Gwyn, David. *Idi Amin: Death Light of Africa.* Boston: Little, Brown, 1977.

Gwynn, D.R. *Pius XI.* London: Holme Press, 1932.

Haas, Ben. *KKK.* Evanston, Ill.: Regency, 1963.

Habas, Bracha. *The Gate Breakers.* New York: Thomas Yoseloff, 1963.

Habermas, Ju¨rgen. *Toward a Rational Society: Student Protest, Science and Politics.* Boston: Beacon Press, 1971.

Hacker, Frederick J. *Crusaders, Criminals, Crazies: Terror and Terrorism in Our Time.* New York: W.W. Norton, 1976.

Hackett, Charles Wilson. *The Mexican Revolution and the United States, 1910-1926.* New York: World Peace Commission, 1926.

Hadawi, Sami. *The Arab-Israeli Conflict.* Beirut, Leb.: Institute for Palestine Studies, 1967.

_____. *Palestine Before the United Nations: Annual Documentary, 1965.* Beirut, Leb.: Institute for Palestine Studies, 1965.

_____. *UN Resolutions on Palestine, 1947-1972.* Beirut, Leb.: Institute for Palestine Studies, 1974.

Hadfield, R.L. *Picturesque Rogues.* London: H.F. & G. Witherby, 1931.

Hadley, Harold. *Come See Them Die.* New York: Julian Messner, 1934.

Hadley, Henry H. *The Blue Badge of Courage.* Akron, Ohio: Saalfield, 1902.

Hadley, Norman. *The Viking Process.* New York: Avon Books, 1977.

Hadley, Samuel H. *Down in Water Street.* New York: Fleming H. Revell, 1902.

Haestier, Richard. *Dead Men Tell Tales.* London: John Long,1934.

Haft, Marilyn G., and Hermann, Michelle (eds.). *Prisoners' Rights.* New York: Practicing Law Institute, 1972.

Hagan, Frank E. *Introduction to Criminology.* Chicago: Nelson-Hall, 1986.

_____. *Research Methods in Criminal Justice and Criminology.* New York: Macmillan, 1982.

Hagan, William T. *Indian Police and Judges: Experiences in Acculturation and Control.* New Haven, Conn.: Yale University Press, 1966.

Hagedorn, Hermann. *Roosevelt in the Badlands.* Boston: Houghton Mifflin, 1921.

_____. *The Roosevelt Family at Sagamore Hill.* New York: Macmillan, 1954.

_____. *The Theodore Roosevelt Treasury.* New York: G.P. Putnam's Sons, 1957.

Hahn, Jon K., and McKenney, Harold C. *Legally Sane.* Chicago: Regnery, 1972.

Haimson, Leopold H. *Russian Marxists and the Origins of Bolshevism.* Cambridge, Mass.: Harvard University Press, 1955.

Haines, Max. *Bothersome Bodies.* Toronto, Ontario, Can.: McClelland & Stewart, 1977.

_____. *Crime Flashback.* Toronto, Ontario, Can.: Toronto Sun, 1981.

Haldeman-Julius, Marcet. *Clarence Darrow's Two Great Trials.* Girard, Kan.: Haldeman-Julius, 1927.

_____. *The Lindbergh-Hauptmann Kidnap-Murder Case.* Girard, Kan.: Haldeman-Julius, 1937.

Hale, John. *A Modest Inquiry into the Nature of Witchcraft and How Persons Guilty of that Crime may be Convicted.* Boston: B. Eliot, 1702.

_____. *Narratives of the Witchcraft Cases, 1648-1706.* New York: Barnes & Noble, 1959.

Hale, Leslie. *Hanged in Error.* London: Penguin Books, 1961.

_____. *Hanging in the Balance.* London: Jonathan Cape, 1962.

Hale, Sir Matthew. *Pleas of the Crown.* London: Richard Tonson, 1678.

Hale, William Harlan. *Horace Greeley: Voice of the People.* New York: Harper, 1950.

Haley, Alex. *Autobiography of Malcolm X.* New York: Grove Press, 1964.

Haley, Kenneth H.D. *The First Earl of Shaftsbury.* Oxford, Eng.: Clarendon Press, 1968.

Haley, P. Edward. *Revolution and Intervention: The Diplomacy of Taft and Wilson with Mexico, 1910-1917.* Cambridge, Mass.: MIT Press, 1970.

Halifax, Lord. *Fullness of Days.* London: Collins, 1957.

Hall, A.C. *Crime in Its Relation to Social Progress.* New York: Columbia University Press, 1902.

Hall, Angus (ed.). *The Crime Busters.* London: Verdict Press, 1976.

Hall, Frank O., and Whitten, Lindsey H. *Jesse James Rides Again.* Lawton, Okla.: LaHoma, 1948.

Hall, Gladys M. *Prostitution in the Modern World.* New York: Emerson Books, 1965.

Hall, James. *The Harpe's Head: A Legend of Kentucky.* Philadelphia: Key & Biddle, 1833.

Hall, James O. *Notes on the John Wilkes Booth Escape Route.* Clinton, Md.: Surratt Society, 1980.

Hall, Jerome, and Mueller, G.O.W. *Cases and Readings on Criminal Law and Procedure.* Indianapolis, Ind.: Bobbs-Merrill, 1965.

_____. *General Principles of Criminal Law.* Indianapolis, Ind.: Bobbs-Merrill, 1947.

_____. *Theft, Law and Society.* Indianapolis, Ind.: Bobbs-Merrill, 1952.

Hall, Livingston, et al. *Modern Criminal Procedure.* St. Paul, Minn.: West, 1969.

Hall, Trevor H. *The Late Mr. Sherlock Holmes and Other Literary Studies.* New York: St. Martin's Press, 1971.

_____. *Sherlock Holmes and His Creator.* New York: St. Martin's Press, 1977.

Hallett, Benjamin F. *Trial of Rev. Mr. Avery.* Boston: Daily Commercial Gazette, 1833.

Hall-Quest, Olga W. *Wyatt Earp, Marshal of the Old West.* New York: Farrar, Straus & Cudahay, 1956.

Hallworth, Rodney, and Williams, Mark. *Where There's a Will—.* Jersey, England: Capstans Press, 1983.

Halper, Albert (ed.). *The Chicago Crime Book.* Cleveland: World, 1967.Halper, Andrew, and Ku, Richard. *New York City Police Street Crime Unit.* Washington, D.C.: U.S. Department of Justice, 1972.

Halperin, Ernst. *Terrorism in Latin America.* Washington, D.C.: Sage, 1976.

Halperin, Morton H., et al. *The Lawless State: The Crimes of the U.S. Intelligence Agencies.* New York: Penguin, 1976.

Halpern, Joel M. *A Serbian Village.* New York: Columbia University Press, 1958.

Halpern, John. *Los Angeles, Improbable City.* New York: E.P. Dutton, 1963.

Halstead, Murat. *The Illustrious Life of William McKinley.* Chicago: n.p., 1901.

_____, and Beale, J.F. *Life of Jay Gould: How He Made His Fortune.* New York: Edgewood, 1892.

_____. *Life and Distinguished Services of William McKinley, Our Martyr President.* Chicago: Vosbrink Mercantile, 1901.

Hambly, Charles R. *Hold Your Money.* Los Angeles: Monitor, 1932.

Hambrook, Walter. *Hambrook of the Yard.* London: R. Hale, 1937.

Hamby, Alonzo L. *Beyond the New Deal: Harry S. Truman and American Liberalism.* New York: Columbia University Press, 1973.

_____ (ed.). *Harry S. Truman and the Fair Deal.* Lexington, Mass.: Heath, 1974.

Hamel, Frank. *Human Animals.* London: W. Rider & Son, 1915.

Hamer, Alvin C. (ed.). *Detroit Murders.* New York: Duell, Sloan & Pearce, 1948.

Hamilton, Alice. *Exploring the Dangerous Trades.* Boston: Little, Brown, 1943.

Hamilton, Charles (ed.). *Men of the Underworld.* New York: Macmillan, 1952.

Hamilton, Henry Raymond. *The Epic of Chicago.* Chicago: Willett, Clarke, 1932.

Hamilton, James. *Negro Plot.* Boston: Ingraham, 1822.

Hamilton, Mary E. *Policewoman: Her Service and Ideals.* New York: Frederick A. Stokes, 1924.

Hammer, Richard. *Gangland U.S.A.* Chicago: Playboy Press, 1975.

Hammerschlag, H.E. *Hypnotism and Crime.* London: Rider, 1956.

Hammett, Nina. *Laughing Torso.* London: Constable, 1921.

Hammon, J.L. *Gladstone and the Irish Nation.* London: Longmans, 1938.

Hammond, J.L. *C.P. Scott of the Manchester Guardian.* New York: Harcourt, Brace, 1934.

Hammond, John L. and Foot, M.R. *Gladstone and Liberalism.* London: English University Press, 1952.

Hamon, Alain. *Action Directe.* Paris: Sevil, n. d.

Hanayama Shinsho. *The Way of Deliverance: Three Years With the Condemned Japanese War Criminals.* New York: Charles Scribner's Sons, 1950.

Hanbury-Williams, Sir John. *The Emperor Nicholas as I Knew Him.* New York: E.P. Dutton, 1923.

Hanchett, Lafayette. *The Old Sheriff.* New York: Margent Press, 1937.

Hanchett, William. *The Lincoln Murder Conspiracies.* Chicago: University of Illinois Press, 1983.

Handlin, Oscar. *Al Smith and His America.* Boston: Little, Brown, 1958.

_____. *Boston's Immigrants.* Cambridge, Mass.: Harvard University Press, 1941.

Hane, Michiso. *Peasants, Rebels, and Outcasts: The Underside of Modern Japan.* New York: Random House, 1982.

Hanes, Colonel Bailey C. *Bill Doolin Outlaw O.T.* Norman: University of Oklahoma Press, 1968.

Hanfstaengl, Ernst. *Unheard Witness.* Philadelphia: J.B. Lippencott, 1957.

Hanged by the Neck Until You Be Dead. Brooklyn, N.Y.: W.C. Wilton, 1877.

Hanna, D. O'D. *The Face of Ulster.* New York: Devin-Adair, 1952.

Hanna, David. *Harvest of Horror.* New York: Belmont Tower, 1975.

Hannibal, Edward, and Boris, Robert. *Blood Feud.* New York: Ballantine, 1979.

Hanny, David. *Diaz.* London: Constable, 1917.

Hansen, Alvin H. *Business Cycles and National Income.* New York: W.W. Norton, 1957.

Hansen, Chadwick. *Witchcraft at Salem.* New York: New American Library, 1970.

Hansen, Gladys C., and Heintz, William F. *The Chinese in California.* Portland, Ore.: Richard Abel, 1970.

Hansen, James. *Japanese Intelligence: The Competitive Edge.* New York: NIBC Press, 1996.

Hansen, Marcus L. *The Atlantic Migration 1607-1860.* Cambridge, Mass.: Harvard University Press, 1940.

_____. *The Immigrant in American History.* Cambridge, Mass.: Harvard University Press, 1940.

Hanser, Richard. *Putsch: How Hitler Made a Revolution.* New York: Peter H. Wyden, 1970.

Hanson, William H. *The Shooting of John F. Kennedy: One Assassin, Three Shots, Three Hits%%No Misses.* San Antonio, Texas: Naylor, 1969.

Hanway, Jonas. *Letters Written Occasionally on the Customs of Foreign Nations in Regards to Harlots.* London: John Rivington, 1761.

Hapgood, Hutchins. *Autobiography of a Thief.* New York: Fox, Duffield, 1903.

_____, and Moskowitz, Henry. *Up From the Streets: Alfred E. Smith.* New York: Harcourt, Brace, 1927.

Harbaugh, William H. *Lawyer's Lawyer: The Life of John W. Davis.* New York: Oxford University Press, 1973.

Harcave, Sidney. *First Blood: The Russian Revolution of 1905.* New York: Macmillan, 1964.

Harderode, Peter. *Fighting Dirty: The Inside Story of Covert Operations from Ho Chi Minh to Osama bin Laden.* New York: Sterling, 2002.

Hardie, James. *An Impartial Account of the Trial of Mr. Levi Weeks for the Supposed Murder of Miss Julianna Elmore Sands at a Court Held in the City of New York.* New York: N. McFarlane, 1800.

Harding, Thomas Swann. *Aren't Men Rascals?* New York: Dial Press, 1930.

_____. *Fads, Frauds and Physicians.* New York: Dial Press, 1930.

_____. *The Popular Practice of Fraud.* London: Longmans, Green, 1935.

Hardmon, William. *A Trip To America.* London: T.V. Wood, 1884.

Hardwick, Elizabeth. *Seduction and Betrayal.* New York: Random House, 1974.

Hardwick, Michael. *Doctors on Trial.* London: Herbert Jenkins, 1961.

Hardwick, Mollie. *Emma, Lady Hamilton.* New York: Holt, Rinehart & Winston, 1969.

Hardy, Allison. *Kate Bender, The Kansas Murderess.* Girard, Kan: Haldeman-Julius, 1944.

_____. *Wild Bill Hickok, King of Gun-Fighters.* Girard, Kan.: Haldeman-Julius, 1943.

Hare, F.A. *The Last of the Bushrangers: The Capture of the Kelly Gang.* Chicago: Weeks, 1892.

Hare, R.D., and Schalling, D. (eds.). *Psychopathic Behaviour.* Chichester, Eng.: John Wiley & Sons, 1978.

Hargrave, Francis (ed.). *A Collection of Tracts Relative to the Laws of England.* Dublin, Ire.: E. Lynch, W. Colles, 1787.

Hargreaves, Reginald. *Red Sun Rising: The Siege of Port Arthur.* Philadelphia: J.B. Lippincott, 1962.

Haring, C.H. *The Buccaneers in the West Indies in the Seventeenth Century.* New York: E.P. Dutton, 1910.

Haring, J. Vreeland. *The Hand of Hauptmann: The Handwriting Expert Tells the Story of the Lindbergh Case.* Plainfield, N.J.: Hamer, 1937.

Harkey, Dee. *Mean as Hell.* Albuquerque: University of New Mexico Press, 1948.

Harlow, Alvin. *Murders Not Quite Solved.* New York: Julian Messner, 1938.

_____. *Old Bowery Days: The Chronicles of a Famous Street.* New York: D. Appleton, 1931.

_____. *Old Waybills.* New York: Appleton-Century, 1934.

Harlow, Victor Emmanuel. *The Most Picturesque Personality in Oklahoma, Al Jennings.* Oklahoma City, Okla.: Harlow, 1912.

Harman, Samuel W. *Belle Starr, the Female Desperado.* Houston: Frontier Press of Texas, 1954.

_____. *Cherokee Bill, the Oklahoma Outlaw.* Houston: Frontier Press of Texas, 1954.

_____. *Hell on the Border.* Fort Smith, Ark.: Phoenix, 1898.

Harmer, Ruth Mulvey. *American Medical Avarice.* New York: Abelard-Schuman, 1975.

Harnden, Harvey. *Narrative of the Apprehension in Rindge, N.H. of the Rev. E.K. Avery, Charged with the Murder of Sarah M. Cornell.* Providence, R.I.: W. Marshall, 1833.

Harney, Malachi L., and Cross, John C. *The Informer in Law Enforcement.* Springfield, Ill.: Charles C. Thomas, 1960.

Harolow, Ralph Volney. *The Growth of the United States.* New York: Henry Holt, 1943.

Harpending, Asbury. *The Great Diamond Hoax.* San Francisco: James Barry, 1913.

Harper, Charles G. *Half-Hours with the Highwaymen.* London: Chapman & Hall, 1908.

Harriman, Margaret Case. *The Vicious Circle.* New York: Rinehart, 1951.

Harrington, Alan. *Psychopaths.* New York: Simon & Schuster, 1972.

Harrington, Fred Harvey. *Hanging Judge.* Caldwell, Idaho: Caxton Printers, 1951.

Harrington, Michael. *The Accidental Century.* New York: Macmillan, 1965.

Harris, Charles Townsend. *Memories of Manhattan in the Sixties and Seventies.* New York: Derrydale Press, 1928.

Harris, Larry A. *Pancho Villa and the Columbus Raid.* El Paso, Texas: McMath, 1949.

Harris, Larry R., and Shaw, J. Gary. *Cover-Up: The Governmental Conspiracy to Conceal the Facts About the Public Execution of John Kennedy.* Cleburne, Texas: Shaw, 1976.

Harris, Leon. *Upton Sinclair: American Rebel.* New York: Thomas Y. Crowell, 1975.

Harris, Richard. *The Fear of Crime.* New York: Praeger, 1969.

_____. *Freedom Spent.* Boston: Little, Brown, 1976.

_____. *Justice: The Crisis of Law, Order, and Freedom in America.* New York: E.P. Dutton, 1970.

_____. *The Police Academy: An Inside View.* New York: John Wiley & Sons, 1973.

Harris, T.M. *Assassination of Lincoln: A History of the Great Conspiracy.* Boston: American Citizen, 1892.

Harris, Thomas O. *The Kingfish: Huey P. Long, Dictator.* Baton Rouge, La.: Baton Rouge Clator, 1938.

Harrison, Carter H. *Growing Up With Chicago.* Indianapolis, Ind.: Bobbs-Merrill, 1944.

_____. *Recollections of Life and Doings in Chicago.* Chicago: Normandie House, 1945.

_____. *Stormy Years.* Indianapolis, Ind.: Bobbs-Merrill, 1935.

Harrison, Charles Yale. *Clarence Darrow.* New York: Jonathan Cape & Harrison Smith, 1931.

Harrison, Fred. *Hell Holes and Hangings.* New York: Ballentine Books, 1968.

_____. *The West's Territorial Prisons, 1861-1912.* New York: Ballantine Books, 1973.

Harrison, Fred. *Brady & Hindley.* London: Ashgrove Press, 1986.

Harrison, George Bagshawe. *Elizabethan Journal, 1591-94.* New York: Cosmopolitan, 1929.

Harrison, H.D. *The Soul of Yugoslavia.* London: Hodder & Stoughton, 1941.

Harrison, Harry P. *Culture Under Canvas: The Story of Tent Chautauqua.* New York: Hastings House, 1958.

Harrison, Henry. *The Neutrality of Ireland: Why It Was Inevitable.* London: R. Hale, 1942.

_____. *Ulster and the British Empire.* London: R. Hale, 1939.

Harrison, Leonard V. *Police Administration in Boston.* Cambridge, Mass.: Harvard University Press, 1934.

Harrison, Michael. *Clarence: The Life of the Duke of Clarence and Avondale.* London: W.H. Allen, 1972.

_____. *In the Footsteps of Sherlock Holmes.* London: Cassell, 1958.

_____. *The London of Sherlock Holmes.* New York: Drake, 1972.

_____. *The World of Sherlock Holmes.* New York: Drake, 1973.

Harrison, Richard. *Criminal Calendar.* London: Jarrolds, 1951.

_____. *Criminal Calendar II.* London: Jarrolds, 1952.

_____. *Foul Deeds Will Rise.* London: John Long, 1958.

_____. *Whitehall 1212: The Story of the Police of London.* London: Jarrolds, 1947.

Hart, Alan. *Arafat: A Political Biography.* Bloomington, Ind.: Indiana University Press, 1989.

Hart, Christine. *The Devil's Daughter.* South Woodham, England: New Author, 1993.

Hart, Henry H. *Marco Polo.* Norman: University of Oklahoma Press, 1967.

Hart, Herbert L.A. *Law, Liberty, and Morality.* London: Oxford University Press, 1963.

_____. *Punishment and Responsibility.* Oxford, Eng.: Oxford University Press, 1968.

Hart, J.M. *The British Police.* New York: Macmillan, 1951.

Hart, Smith. *The New Yorkers.* New York: Sheridan House, 1938.

Hart, W.C. *Confessions of an Anarchist.* London: Richards, 1906.

Hartjen, Clayton A. *Crime and Criminalization.* New York: Holt, Rinehart, Winston, 1978.

Hartman, Mary S., and Banner, Lois W. (eds.). *Victorian Murderesses.* New York: Schocken Books, 1977.

Hartmann, Franz. *Buried Alive.* Boston: Occult, 1895.

_____. *Magic: White and Black.* New Hyde Park, N.Y.: University Books, 1970.

Hartmann, L. M. *The Cambridge Medieval History.* Cambridge, Eng.: Cambridge University Press, 1926.

Hartmann, Robert T. *Palace Politics.* New York: McGraw-Hill, 1980.

Hartung, Frank E. *Crime, Law, and Society.* Detroit, Mich.: Wayne State University, 1965.

Harumi Maeda. *History of Rebellion in the Reign of Hirohito.* Tokyo: Nihon-sho Hosha, 1964.

Harvey, Allen. *Israfel: The Life and Times of Edgar Allen Poe.* New York: Rinehart, 1934.

Harvey, G.B. *Henry Clay Frick, the Man.* New York: Charles Scribner's Sons, 1928.

Harwell, Fred. *A True Deliverance: The Joan Little Case.* New York: Alfred A. Knopf, 1980.

Harwick, J.M.D. *The Sherlock Holmes Companion.* London: John Murray, 1962.

Hasbrouck, Louise S. *Mexico From Cortez to Carranza.* New York: D. Appleton, 1918.

Haskell, Henry C., and Fowler, Richard B. *City of the Future: A Narrative History of Kansas City, 1850-1950.* Kansas City: Frank Glenn, 1950.

Haskell, Martin R., and Yablonsky, Lewis. *Crime and Delinquency.* Chicago: Rand-McNally, 1974.

_____. *Criminology: Crime and Criminality.* Chicago: Rand-McNally, 1974.

Haskins, C.H. *The Renaissance of the Twelfth Century.* Cambridge, Mass.: Harvard University Press, 1927.

Haskins, George Lee. *Law and Authority in Early Massachusetts.* New York: Macmillan, 1960.

Haskins, James. *Profiles in Black Power.* Garden City, N.Y.: Doubleday, 1972.

_____. *Street Gangs.* New York: Hastings House, 1974.

Haskins, Jim. *The Cotton Club.* New York: Random House, 1977.

Haslip, Joan. *Catherine the Great.* New York: G.P. Putnam's Sons, 1977.

_____. *The Crown of Mexico.* New York: Holt, Rinehart & Winston, 1971.

Hassell, Ulrich von. *Vom anderen Deutschland.* Frankfurt, Ger.: Fischer Bu¨cherei, 1964.

_____. *The Von Hassell Diaries 1938-1944.* New York: Doubleday, 1947.

Hassler, Alfred. *Diary of a Self-Made Convict.* Chicago: Regnery, 1954.

Hastings, Macdonald. *The Other Mr. Churchill: A Lifetime of Shooting and Murder.* New York: Dodd, Mead, 1963.

Hastings, Max. *Yoni, Hero of Entebbe.* New York: Dial Press, 1979.

Hastings, Sir Patrick. *The Autobiography of Sir Patrick Hastings.* London: William Heinemann, 1948.

_____. *Cases in Court.* London: William Heinemann, 1947.

Haswell, Jock. *Spies & Spymasters.* New York: Thames & Hudson, 1977.

Hata Ikuhiko. *Army Fascism.* Tokyo: Kawade Shobo, 1962.

_____. *History of the Sino-Japanese War.* Tokyo: Kawade Shobo, 1962.

Hatch, Alden P. *Citizen of the World: Franklin D. Roosevelt.* London: Skeffington & Son, 1948.

Hatcher, Julian S., and Jury, Frank J., and Weller, Jac. *Firearms Investigation, Identification, and Evidence.* Harrisburg, Pa.: Stackpole, 1957.

Hatherill, George H. *A Detective's Story.* New York: McGraw Hill, 1972.

Haupe, Theodore. *Crime and Punishment in Germany.* New York: E.P. Dutton, 1926.

Hausser, Paul. *Waffen-SS im Einsatz.* Go¨ttingen, Ger.: Plesse Verlag K.W. Schu¨tz, 1953.

Haven, Charles, and Belden, Frank. *A History of the Colt Revolver and Other Arms by Colt's Patent Fire Arms Manufacturing Co. from 1936 to 1940.* New York: William Morrow, 1940.

Haven, Violet Sweet. *Gentlemen of Japan.* New York: Ziff-Davis, 1944.

Havens, Murray, Leiden, Carl, and Schmitt, Karl. *The Politics of Assassination.* Englewood Cliffs, N.J.: Prentice-Hall, 1970.

Havighurst, Walter. *Voices on the River, The Story of the Mississippi Waterways.* New York: Macmillan, 1964.

Havill, Adrian. *The Mother, the Son, and the Socialite.* New York: St. Martin's Press, 1999.

Hawes, Harry B. *Frank and Jesse James in Review for the Missouri Society.* Washington D.C.: n.p., 1939.

Hawkes, Harry. *The Capture of the Black Panther.* London: Harrap, 1978.

Hawkeye, Harry. *The Dalton Brothers and Their Gang: Fearsome Bandits of Oklahoma and the Southwest.* Philadelphia: Kerner & Getts, 1908.

_____. *Rube Burrows, the Outlaw.* Baltimore: I.& M. Ottenheimer, 1908.

Hawkins, Gordon J., and Zimring, Franklin E. *Deterrance: The Legal Threat in Crime Control.* Chicago: University of Chicago Press, 1973.

_____. *The Prison: Policy and Practice.* Chicago: University of Chicago Press, 1977.

Hawkins, Hugh (ed.). *The Abolitionists: Immediatism and the Question of Means.* Boston: D.C. Heath, 1964.

_____. *The Abolitionists: Means, Ends and Motivations.* Boston: D.C. Heath, 1972.

Hawley, Lowell S., and Bushnell, Ralph Potts. *Counsel for the Damned.* Philadelphia: J.B. Lippincott, 1953.

Hawthorne, Nathaniel. *American Note-Books.* Boston: James R. Osgood, 1817.

Haxthausen-Abbenburg, August F. *The Russian Empire: Its People, Institutions and Resources.* London: Chapman & Hall, 1856.

Hay, Denys. *The Italian Renaissance in Its Historical Background.* Cambridge, Eng.: University Press, 1961.

Hay, John. *Lincoln and the Civil War in the Diaries and Letters of John Hay.* New York: Dodd, Mead, 1939.

Hayashi Masayoshi (ed.). *Hidden History of Hirohito's Regime.* Tokyo: Mainichi Shimbun-ki, 1965.

Haycraft, Howard. *Murder for Pleasure.* New York: Appleton-Century, 1941.

Hayes, William C. *The Scepter of Egypt.* Cambridge, Mass.: Harvard University Press, 1953.

Hayes-McCoy, G.A. (ed.). *The Irish At War.* Cork, Ire.: Mercier, 1964.

Hayman, Leroy. *The Assassination of John and Robert Kennedy.* New York: Scholastic Book Service, 1976.

_____. *The Death of Lincoln: A Picture History of the Assassination.* New York: Scholastic Book Service, 1968.

_____. *O Captain! The Death of Abraham Lincoln.* New York: Four Winds Press, 1968.

Haynes, Fred E. *The American Prison System.* New York: McGraw-Hill, 1939.

Haynes, Roy A. *Prohibition Inside Out.* Garden City, N.Y.: Doubleday, Page, 1923.

Hays, Arthur Garfield. *City Lawyer.* New York: Simon & Schuster, 1942.

_____. *Trial By Prejudice.* New York: Covici, Friede, 1933.

Hays, Will. *The Memoirs of Will Hays.* New York: Doubleday, 1955.

Hayter, Alethea. *Opium and the Romantic Imagination.* Berkeley: University of California Press, 1968.

Hayward, Arthur L. (ed.). *A Complete History of the Lives and Robberies of the Most Notorious Highwaymen, Footpads, Shoplifts, and Cheats of Both Sexes.* London: George Routledge & Sons, 1926.

_____. *Lives of the Most Remarkable Criminals Who Have Been Condemned and Executed.* London: George Routledge & Sons, 1927.

Hayward, C. *The Courtesan.* London: Casanova Society, 1926.

Hayward, J. *The Case of Israel Lipski, Now Lying Under Sentence of Death for the Murder of Miriam Angel.* London: n.p., 1887.

Haywood, William D. *Bill Haywood's Book.* New York: International, 1929.

Hazelrigg, Lawrence (ed.). *Prison Within Society.* New York: Doubleday, 1968.

Hazeltine, Rachel C. *Aimee Semple McPherson's Kidnapping.* New York: Carlton Press, 1965.

Head, Richard. *The English Rogue.* London: George Routledge & Sons, 1928.

Headlam, George. *Yasir Arafat.* Minneapolis, Minn.: Lerner Publications, 2003.

Headley, Joel Tyler. *The Great Riots of New York: 1712-1873.* New York: E.B. Treat, 1873.

_____. *Napoleon and His Marshals.* New York: Baker & Scribner, 1847.

Headley, John W. *Confederate Operations in Canada and New York.* New York: Neale, 1906.

Healy, Paul F. *Cissy, A Biography of Eleanor M. "Cissy" Paterson.* Garden City, N.Y.: Doubleday, 1966.

Heaney, Frank, and Machado, Gay. *Inside the Walls of Alcatraz.* Palo Alto, Calif.: Bull, 1987.

Heaps, Willard A. *Assassination: A Special Kind of Murder.* New York: Meredith, 1969.

Hearn, Lafcadio. *Japan: An Interpretation.* New York: Grosset & Dunlap, 1904.

Hearst, Patricia Campbell. *Every Secret Thing.* Garden City, N.Y.: Doubleday, 1982.

Heath, Carl. *Gandhi.* London: Allen & Unwin, 1944.

Heath, James. *Eighteenth Century Penal Theory.* New York: Oxford University Press, 1963.

Heath, Peter. *Assassins From Tomorrow.* New York: Prestige Books, 1967.

Hecht, Ben. *Charlie: The Improbable Life and Times of Charles MacArthur.* New York: Harper & Bros., 1957.

_____. *A Child of the Century.* New York: Simon & Schuster, 1954.

_____. *Gaily, Gaily, The Memoirs of a Cub Reporter in Chicago.* New York: Doubleday, 1963.

Heckerthorn, Charles. *The Secret Societies of All Ages and Countries.* New Hyde Park, N.Y.: University Books, 1965.

Hegemann, W. *Napolean, or Prostration Before the Hero.* London: Constable, 1931.

Heiden, Konrad. *The Birth of the Third Reich.* Zurich, Switz.: Europa, 1934.

_____. *Der Fuehrer.* Boston: Houghton Mifflin, 1944.

_____. *A History of National Socialism.* Berlin: Rowohlt, 1932.

Heilbron, W.C. *Convict Life at the Minnesota State Prison.* St. Paul, Minn.: W.C. Heilbron, 1909.

Heilbrunn, O.J. *Soviet Secret Service.* New York: Praeger, 1956.

Heimer, Mel. *The Cannibal: The Case of Albert Fish.* New York: Lyle Stuart, 1971.

Heindel, R.H. *The American Impact on Great Britain, 1898-1914.* Philadelphia: University of Pennsylvania Press, 1940.

Heintz, William F. *San Francisco's Mayors: 1850-1880.* Woodside, Calif.: Gilbert Richards, 1975.

Heinz, G., and Donnay, H. *Lumumba: The Last Fifty Days.* New York: Grove Press, 1969.

Heinz, Heinz A. *Germany's Hitler.* London: Hurst & Blackett, 1934.

Heise, Kenan and Frazel, Mark. *Hands on Chicago.* Chicago: Bonus Books, 1987.

_____. *Is There Only One Chicago?* Richmond, Va.: Westover, 1973.

_____. *This Is Chicago.* Richmond, Va.: Westover, 1973.

Helbrant, Maurice. *Narcotic Agent.* New York: Vanguard Press, 1941.

Helfer, Ray E., and Kempe, C. Henry (eds.). *The Battered Child.* Chicago: University of Chicago Press, 1974.

Hellerman, Michael, and Renner, Thomas C.. *Wall Street Swindler.* Garden City, N.Y.: Doubleday, 1977.

Helm, P.J. *Alfred the Great.* New York: Thomas Y. Crowell, 1963.

Helmer, William J. *The Gun That Made the Twenties Roar.* New York: Macmillan, 1969.

_____, and Bilek, Arthur J. *The St. Valentine's Day Massacre: The Untold Story of the Gangland Bloodbath That Brought Down Capone.* Nashville, Tenn.: Cumberland House, 2003.

Helmreich, Ernst C. *The Diplomacy of the Balkan Wars, 1912-1913.* Cambridge, Mass.: Harvard University Press, 1938.

Helpern, Milton, and Knight, Bernard. *Autopsy.* New York: St. Martin's Press, 1977.

Hemingway, Ernest. *By-Line.* New York: Charles Scribner's Sons, 1967.

_____. *A Moveable Feast.* New York: Charles Scribner's Sons, 1964.

Hendel, Samuel. *Charles Evans Hughes and the Supreme Court.* New York: King's Crown Press, 1951.

Henderson, Bruce, and Summerlin, Sam. *In Memoriam: John F. Kennedy.* New York: Cowles Education, 1968.

_____. *The Super Sleuths.* New York: Macmillan, 1976.

Henderson, George C. *Keys to Crookdom.* New York: D. Appleton, 1924.

Henderson, I., and Goodhart, P. *Man Hunt in Kenya.* Garden City, N.Y.: Doubleday, 1958.

Hendrick, Burton J. *The Age of Big Business.* New Haven, Conn.: Yale University Press, 1919.
_____. *Life of Andrew Carnegie.* New York: Doubleday, Doran, 1932.
Hendricks, George David. *The Bad Man of the West.* San Antonio, Texas: Naylor, 1941.
Hennessy, W.B. *Tracy, the Bandit; or, the Romantic Life and Crimes of a Twentieth Century Desperado.* Chicago: M.A. Donohue, 1902.
Henriques, Fernando. *Modern Sexuality: Prostitution and Society.* London: MacGibbon, 1968.
_____. *Prostitution and Society.* London: MacGibbon, 1968.
_____. *Prostitution in Europe and the Americas.* New York: Citadel Press, 1965.
Henriques, Robert. *A Hundered Hours to Suez.* New York: Viking, 1957.
Henry, Andrew F., and Short, James F. *Suicide and Homicide.* Glencoe, Ill.: Free Press, 1954.
Henry, E.R. *Classification and Uses of Finger Prints.* London: H.M. Stationery Office, 1937.
Henry, Jack. *Detective-Inspector Henry's Famous Cases.* London: Hutchinson, 1942.
Henry, Jules. *Pathways to Madness.* New York: Random House, 1965.
Henry, Will. *Death of A Legend.* New York: Random House, 1954.
_____. *The Raiders.* New York: Bantam Books, 1956.
Henson, Allen L. *Confessions of a Criminal Lawyer.* New York: Vantage Press, 1959.
Hentig, Hans von. *Crime: Causes and Conditions.* New York: McGraw-Hill, 1947.
_____. *The Criminal and His Victim.* New Haven, Conn.: Yale University Press, 1948.
_____. *Punishment: Its Origin, Purpose, and Psychology.* London: Hodge, 1937.
Hentze, Margot. *Pre-Fascist Italy.* London: George Allen & Unwin, 1939.
Henze, Paul B. *The Plot to Kill the Pope.* New York: Charles Scribner's Sons, 1983.
Heppenstall, Rayner. *Bluebeard and After, Three Decades of Murder in France.* London: Peter Owen, 1972.
_____. *French Crime in the Romantic Age.* London: Hamish Hamilton, 1970.
_____. *A Little Pattern of French Crime.* London: Hamish Hamilton, 1969.
_____. *The Sex War and Others.* London: Peter Owen, 1973.
Herald, George W., and Rabin, Edward D. *The Big Wheel.* New York: William Morrow, 1963.
Hergesheimer, Joseph. *Swords and Roses.* New York: Alfred A. Knopf, 1929.
He´ritier, Jean. *Catherine De Midici.* trans. Charlotte Haldane. New York: St. Martin's Press, 1963.
Herlihy, David. *The History of Feudalism.* New York: Walker, 1971.
Herman, Robert D. *Gambling.* New York: Harper & Row, 1967.
Hermann, Donald H.J. *The Insanity Defence.* Springfield, Ill. Charles C. Thomas, 1983.
Herndon, William H., and Weik, Jesse W. *Abraham Lincoln: The True Story of a Great Life.* New York: D. Appleton, 1893.
Hersh, Seymour. *Cover-up.* New York: Random House, 1972.
Hershkowitz, Leo. *Tweed's New York: Another Look.* New York: Anchor, 1978.
Hertogs, Renatus, and Freeman, Lucy. *The Two Assassins.* New York: Thomas Y. Crowell, 1965.
Hertz, Wilhelm. *Der Werwolf.* Stuttgart, Ger.: A Kro¨ner, 1862.
Hertzog, Peter. *A Dictionary of New Mexico Desperadoes.* Santa Fe, N.M.: Press of the Territorian, 1965.
_____. *Legal Hangings.* Santa Fe, N.M.: Press of the Territorian, 1966.
Herzog, Arthur. *Vesco.* New York: Doubleday, 1987.
Herzog, Asa S., and Erickson, A. J. *Camera, Take the Stand.* Englewood Cliffs, N.J.: Prentice-Hall, 1940.
Herzog, Robert. *Die Volksdeutschen in der Waffen-SS.* Tu¨bingen, Ger.: Institut fu¨r Besatzungsfragen, 1955.
_____. *From Dreyfus to Petain.* New York: Creative Age Press, 1947.
Hess, Henner. *Mafia and Mafiosi: The Structure of Power.* trans. Ewald Osers. Lexington, Mass.: D.C. Heath, 1970.
Heumann, Milton. *Plea Bargaining: The Experience of Prosecutors, Judges and Defense Attorneys.* Chicago: University of Chicago Press, 1978.
Heymann, Robert. *Rasputin.* Leipzig, Ger.: P. List, 1917.
Hibbert, Christopher. *Benito Mussolini.* London: Longmans, Green, 1962.
_____. *Garibaldi and His Enemies.* Boston: Little, Brown, 1966.
_____. *Highwaymen.* New York: Delacorte Press, 1967.
_____. *King Mob: The Story of Lord George Gordon and the London Riots of 1780.* New York: World, 1958.
_____. *The Roots of Evil.* Boston: Little, Brown, 1963.
Hichborn, Franklin. *The System: The San Francisco Graft Prosecution.* Montclair, N.J.: Patterson Smith, 1969.
Hickey, John J. *Our Police Guardians: History of the Police Department of the City of New York Compiled and Written by Officer "787" John J. Hickey, Retired.* New York: Published by Author, 1925.
Hickey, Neal. *The Gentleman Was A Thief.* New York: Holt, Rinehart, Winston, 1962.
Hicks, Edwin P. *Belle Starr and Her Pearl.* Little Rock, Ark.: Pioneer Press, 1963.
Hicks, Seymour. *Not Guilty M'Lord.* London: Cassell, 1939.
Hidalgo, O.C. *Spy for Fidel.* Miami: Seeman, 1971.
Higdon, Hal. *The Crime of the Century.* New York: G.P. Putnam's Sons, 1975.
_____. *The Union vs. Dr. Mudd.* Chicago: Follett, 1964.
Higgins, Robert. *In the Name of the Law.* London: John Long, 1958.
Higginson, Thomas Wentworth. *Travellers and Outlaws: Episodes in American History.* New York: C.T. Dillingham, 1888.
Higham, Charles. *The Adventures of Conan Doyle: The Life of the Creator of Sherlock Holmes.* New York: W.W. Norton, 1976.
_____. *Trading with the Enemy.* New York: Delacorte Press, 1982.
_____. *Ziegfeld.* Chicago: Regnery, 1972.
Higham, John. *Strangers in the Land: Patterns of American Nativism, 1860-1925.* New York: Atheneum, 1973.
Hilberg, Raul. *The Destruction of the European Jews.* Chicago: Quadrangle, 1961.
Hilberman, Elaine. *The Rape Victim.* Washington, D.C.: American Psychiatric Association, 1976.
_____. *A Report on the Trial of Emphraim K. Avery.* Boston: Russell, Odiorne, 1833.
Hill, Rev. Albert Fay. *The North Avenue Irregulars: A Suburb Battles the Mafia.* New York: Cowles, 1968.
Hill, Christopher. *The Century of Revolution, 1603-1714.* New York: W.W. Norton, 1982.
_____. *Lenin and the Russian Revolution.* London: English Universities Press, 1957.
Hill, Douglas, and Williams, Pat. *The Supernatural.* New York: Hawthorn, 1966.
Hill, John, Jr. *Gold Bricks of Speculation.* Chicago: Lincoln Books, 1904.
Hill, Matthew Davenport. *Suggestions for the Repression of Crime.* London: John W. Parker & Sons, 1837.
Hill, Paul. *Portrait of a Sadist.* New York: Avon, 1960.
Hill, Robert A. (ed.). *Marcus Garvey and Universal Negro Improvement Association Papers.* Berkeley: University of California Press, 1983.
Hillebrand, Karl. *France and the French in the Second Half of the Nineteenth Century.* London: Tru¨bner, 1881.
Hillel, Marc, and Henry, Clarissa. *Children of the SS.* London: Hutchinson, 1976.
_____. *Of Pure Blood.* trans. Eric Mossmacher. New York: McGraw-Hill, 1977.
Hillmayr, Heinrich. *Roter und Weisser Terror in Bayern.* Munich: Nusser, 1974.
Hills, Stuart L. (ed.). *Corporate Violence: Injury and Death for Profit.* New York: Barnes & Noble, 1987.
_____. *Crime, Power and Morality.* Scranton, Pa.: Chandler, 1971.
Hilton, J. *A Popular Account of the Thugs and Dacoits: The Hereditary Gang Robbers and Garrotters of India.* London: Allen, 1857.
Hilton-Young, Wayland. *The Italian Left.* London: Longmans, 1949.
Himmelstein, Jerome L. *The Strange Career of Marijuana: Politics and Ideology of Drug Control in America.* Westport, Conn.: Greenwood, 1983.
Himmler, Heinrich. *Die Schutzstaffel als antibolschewistische Kampf-organisation.* Munich: Zentralverlag der NSDAP, Franz Eher II, 1936.
Hinckle, Warren, and Turner, William. *The Fish is Red: The Story of the Secret War Against Castro.* New York: Harper & Row, 1981.
Hinckley, Jack and Jo Ann, and Sherrill, E. *Breaking Points.* New York: Berkley Books, 1986.
Hinde, R.S.E. *The British Penal System, 1773-1950.* London: Duckworth, 1951.Hinde, Wendy. *Richard Cobden: A Victorian Outsider.* New Haven, Conn.: Yale University Press, 1987.
Hindlip, L. *British East Africa: Past, Present, and Future.* London: T. Fisher Unwin, 1905.
Hine, Robert V. *The American West: An Interpretive History.* Boston: Little, Brown, 1973.
Hingley, Ronald. *Nihilists: Russian Radicals and Revolutionaries in the Reign of Alexander II, 1855-1881.* London: Weidenfeld & Nicolson, 1967.
Hinshaw, David. *A Man From Kansas: The Story of William Allen White.* New York: G.P. Putnam's Sons, 1974.
Hinton, Arthur Cherry, and Godsell, Philip H. *The Yukon.* New York: Macrae Smith, 1955.
Hirning, L. Clovis. *The Sex Offender in Custody: Handbook of Correctional Psychology.* New York: Philosophical Library, 1947.
Hirsch, Foster. *The Dark Side of the Screen: Film Noir.* Cranbury, N.J.: A.S. Barnes, 1981.
Hirsch, Kurt. *SS, Gestern, heute und...* Darmstadt, Ger.: Progress Verlag Johann Fladung, 1960.
Hirsch, Phil. *Death House.* New York: Pyramid Books, 1966.
_____. *Fires.* New York: Pyramid Books, 1971.
_____. *Hollywood Uncensored.* New York: Pyramid Books, 1965.
_____. *The Killers.* New York: Pyramid Books, 1971.
_____. *The Law Enforcers.* New York: Pyramid Books, 1969.
_____. *Men Behind Bars.* New York: Pyramid Books, 1962.
_____. *The Racketeers.* New York: Pyramid Books, 1969.
Hirshson, Stanley P. *Farewell to the Bloody Shirt: Northern Republicans and the Southern Negro, 1877-1893.* Bloomington: Indiana University Press, 1962.
Hirst, David. *The Gun and the Olive Branch.* London: Faber & Faber, 1977.
History of the New Orleans Police Department. New Orleans: n.p., 1900.
Hitler, Adolf. *Hitler's Secret Book.* New York: Grove Press, 1961.
_____. *Mein Kampf.* trans. Ralph Manheim. Boston: Houghton Mifflin, 1943.
Hittell, Theodore H. *History of California.* San Francisco: N.J. Stone, 1898.
Hitti, Philip. *History of the Arabs.* London: Macmillan, 1937.
_____. *History of Syria.* London: Macmillan, 1951.
Hoare, Sir Samuel. *Nine Troubled Years.* London: William Collins, 1954.
Hobby, E.W. *Eastern Uganda.* London: Anthropological Institute of Great Britain, 1902.
Hobhouse, S., and Brockway, A.F. *English Prisons Today.* London: Longmans, 1922.
Hobley, C.W. *Kenya: From Chartered Company to Crown Colony.* London: H.F. & G. Witherby, 1929.
Hobsbawm, Eric J. *The Age of Revolution, 1789-1848.* New York: New American Library, 1962.
_____. *Bandits.* New York: Delacorte Press, 1969.
_____. *Primitive Rebels: Studies in Archaic Forms of Social Movement in the 19th and 20th Centuries.* New York: W.W. Norton, 1965.
_____. *The Revolutionaries.* New York: New American Library, 1975.
_____. *Social Bandits and Primitive Rebels.* Glencoe, Ill.: Free Press, 1959.
Hobson, H., et al. *The Pearl of Days: An Intimate Memoir of the Sunday Times.* London: Hamish Hamilton, 1972.
Hochstedler, Ellen C. *Corporations as Criminals.* Beverly Hills, Calif.: Sage, 1984.
Hodder, Alfred. *A Fight for the City.* New York: Macmillan, 1903.
Hodder, Edwin. *The Life and Work of the Seventh Earl of Shaftesbury.* London: Cassell, 1886.
Hodge, Harry. *The Black Maria, or the Criminal's Omnibus.* London: Victor Gollancz, 1935.

_____ (ed.). *Famous Trials.* Baltimore: Penguin Books, 1941.

Hodgetts, Edward A.B. *The House of Hohenzollern.* London: Methuen, 1911.

_____. *Life of Catherine the Great of Russia.* London: Methuen, 1914.

Hodgson, M.G.S. *The Order of Assassins.* The Hague, Neth.: Mouton, 1959.

Hodson, H.V. *Slump and Recovery, 1929-1937.* Oxford, Eng.: Oxford University Press, 1938.

Hoehling, Mary D. *The Real Sherlock Holmes.* New York: Julian Messner, 1965.

Hoff, Harry Summerfield. *Shall We Ever Know? The Trial of the Brothers Hosein for the Murder of Mrs. McKay.* New York: Harper & Row, 1971.

Hoff, Sidney. *Scarface Al and His Uncle Sam.* New York: Putnam, 1980.

Hoffer, A., and Osmond, H. *The Hallucinogens.* New York: Academic Press, 1967.

Hofman, Hans Hubert. *Der Hitlerputsch.* Munich: Nymphenburger Verlagshandlung, 1961.

Hoffman, A. *Unwanted Mexican Americans.* Tucson: University of Arizona Press, 1974.

Hoffman, Dennis E. *Scarface Al and the Crime Crusaders: Chicago's Private War Against Capone.* Carbondale, Ill.: Southern Illinois University, 1993.

Hoffman, F.L. *The Homicide Problem.* Newark, N.J.: Prudential Press, 1925.

Hoffman, Frederick J. *The Twenties: American Writing in the Postwar Decade.* New York: Free Press, 1962.

Hoffman, George W. *The Balkans in Transition.* New York: D. Van Nostrand, 1963.

Hoffman, P. *Lions in the Street.* New York: Saturday Review Press, 1973.

Hoffman, Paul. *Courthouse.* New York: Hawthorn Books, 1979.

_____. *To Drop a Dime.* New York: G.P. Putnam's Sons, 1976.

Hoffman, Robert. *More Than a Trial: The Struggle of Captain Dreyfus.* New York: Free Press, 1980.

Hoffmann, Peter. *The History of the German Resistance, 1933-1945.* trans. Richard Barry. Cambridge, Mass.: MIT Press, 1977.

_____. *Hitler's Personal Security.* London: Macmillan, 1979.

Hoffmann, Peter, and Wallace, Michael. *American Violence.* New York: Alfred A. Knopf, 1970.

Hogarth, Georgina (ed.). *The Letters of Charles Dickens, 1833-1870.* London: Chapman & Hall, 1909.

Hogarth, John. *Sentencing as a Human Process.* Toronto, Ontario, Can.: University of Toronto Press, 1971.

Hogg, Gary. *Cannibalism and Human Sacrifice.* New York: Citadel Press, 1966.

Hogg, Ian V. *The Complete Encyclopedia of World Firearms.* New York: A & W, 1978.

Hogg, Thomas E. *Authentic History of Sam Bass and His Gang.* Denton, Texas: Monitor Job Office, 1878.

Hohenberg, John. *The New Front Page.* New York: Columbia University Press, 1966.

_____. *The Professional Journalist.* New York: Holt, Rinehart & Winston, 1961.

Hohimer, Frank. *The Home Invaders.* Chicago: Chicago Review Press, 1975.

Hohne, Heinz. *The Order of the Death's Head.* New York: Coward-McCann, 1970.

Holbrook, D. *Sex and Dehumanization.* London: Pitman, 1972.

Holbrook, Stewart H. *The Age of Moguls.* Garden City, N.Y.: Doubleday, 1954.

_____. *Let Them Live.* New York: Macmillan, 1938.

_____. *Wild Bill Tames the West.* New York: Random House, 1952.

Holcombe, Arthur N. *The Spirit of the Chinese Revolution.* New York: Alfred A. Knopf, 1930.

Holden, Anthony. *The St. Albans Poisoner.* London: Hodder & Stoughton, 1974.

Holdredge, Helen. *Mammy Pleasant.* New York: G.P. Putnam's Sons, 1953.

_____. *The Woman in Black.* New York: G.P. Putnam's Sons, 1955.

Holdsworth, W.S. *A History of English Law.* London: Methuen, 1903.

Hole, Christina. *Haunted England.* London: B.T. Batsford, 1940.

_____. *A Mirror of Witchcraft.* London: Chatto & Windus, 1957.

_____. *Witchcraft in England.* New York: Charles Scribner's Sons, 1947.

Holiday, Billie. *Lady Sings the Blues.* New York: Doubleday, 1956.

Holland, Claude V. *Tortugas Run.* Bonita Springs, Fla.: Holland Books, 1972.

Holland, Henry. *A Treatise Against Witchcraft.* Cambridge, Eng.: J. Legatt, 1590.

Holland, J.G. *Life of Abraham Lincoln.* New York: Paperback Library, 1961.

Hollick, F. *Murder Made Moral: Or An Account of the Thugs and Other Secret Murderers of India.* Manchester, Eng.: A. Heywood, 1840.

Hollingsworth, Claire. *The Arabs and the West.* London: Methuen, 1952.

Hollis, C. *Shadow of the Gallows.* London: Victor Gollancz, 1951.

Hollon, W. Eugene. *Frontier Violence: Another Look.* New York: Oxford University Press, 1974.

Holmes, the Arch Fiend. Cincinnati, Ohio: Barclay, 1890.

Holmes, Clive. *The Eastern Association in the English Civil War.* Cambridge, Eng.: Cambridge University Press, 1974.

Holmes, Colin. *Anti-Semitism in British Society, 1876-1939.* London: Edward Arnold, 1979.

Holmes, Paul. *The Candy Murder Case.* New York: Bantam, 1966.

Holmes, Ronald M., and DeBurger, James. *Serial Murder.* Newbury Park, Calif.: Sage, 1988.

Holmes, Thomas James. *Cotton Mather.* Cambridge, Mass.: Harvard University Press, 1940.

_____. *Cotton Mather and His Writings on Witchcraft.* Chicago: University of Chicago Press, 1926.

Holmes, William Gordon. *The Age of Justinian and Theodora.* London: G. Bell & Sons, 1912.

Holroyd, James Edward. *Baker Street Byways: A Book about Sherlock Holmes.* London: George Allen & Unwin, 1959.

_____. *The Gaslight Murders.* London: George Allen & Unwin, 1960.

_____. *The Sheppard Murder Case.* New York: David McKay, 1961.

Holt, Don. *The Justice Machine.* New York: Ballantine, 1972.

Holt, Edgar. *Protest in Arms: The Irish Troubles, 1916-1923.* London: G.P. Putnam's Sons, 1960.

Holt, J. *Finger Prints Simplified.* Chicago: F.J. Drake, 1941.

Holt, J. *Report of the Judge Advocate General on the Order of American Knights, or Sons of Liberty.* Washington, D.C.: U.S. Government Printing Office, 1864.

Holt, Sir John. *Modern Cases Argued and Adjudged.* London: J. Walthoe, 1725.

_____. *A Report of All the Cases Determined by Sir John Holt, 1681-1710.* London: J. Hazard, 1738.

Holtzman, Jerome (ed.). *No Cheering in the Press Box.* New York: Holt, Rinehart & Winston, 1973.

Holtzoff, H. (ed.). *Encyclopedia of Criminology.* New York: Philosophical Library, 1949.

Holyst, B. *Comparative Criminology.* Lexington, Mass.: Lexington Books, 1979.

Holz, Denice (ed.). *Conspiracy in Dallas.* Shreveport, La.: Fairchild, 1981.

Home Office. *Report of the Departmental Committee on Legal Aid in Criminal Proceedings.* London: HMSO, 1966.

_____. *Report of the Working Party on Bail in Magistrates' Courts.* London: HMSO, 1974.

_____. *The Sentence of the Court.* London: HMSO, 1969.

Homer. *The Iliad.* trans. William Cowper. New York: G.P. Putnam's Sons, 1850.

_____. *The Odyssey.* trans. W.H.D. Rouse. New York: New American Library, 1963.

Homer, Frederick D. *Guns and Garlic.* West Lafayette, Ind.: Purdue University Press, 1974.

Honeycombe, Gordon. *The Murders of the Black Museum, 1870-1970.* London: Hutchinson, 1982.

Hood, R.G. *Sentencing in Magistrates' Courts.* London: Stevens, 1962.

Hood, Roger, and Sparks, Richard. *Key Issues in Criminology.* New York: McGraw-Hill, 1970.

Hoogenboom, Ari. *Outlawing the Spoils.* Urbana: University of Illinois Press, 1961.

Hoole, W. Stanley. *The James Boys Rode South.* Tuscaloosa, Ala.: Published by Author, 1955.

Hooper, Osman C. *History of Ohio Journalism, 1793-1933.* Columbus, Ohio: Published by Author, 1933.

_____. *Ohio Journalism Hall of Fame.* Columbus: Ohio State University, 1929.

Hooper, William Eden. *The History of Newgate and the Old Bailey.* London: Underwood Press, 1935.

Hooton, Earnest A. *The American Criminal.* Cambridge, Mass.: Harvard University Press, 1939.

_____. *Crime and the Man.* Cambridge, Mass.: Harvard University Press, 1939.

Hoover, Calvin B. *Germany Enters the Third Reich.* New York:Macmillan, 1933.

Hoover, Herbert. *Addresses Upon the American Road, 1941-1945.* New York: Charles Scribner's Sons, 1946.

_____. *The Memoirs of Herbert Hoover: The Cabinet and the Presidency, 1920-1933.* New York: Macmillan, 1952.

Hoover, J. Edgar. *Criminal Identification and the Functions of the Identification Division.* Washington, D.C.: U.S. Department of Justice, 1938.

_____. *J. Edgar Hoover on Communism.* New York: Random House, 1969.

_____. *J. Edgar Hoover Speaks.* Washington, D.C.: Capitol Hill, 1971.

_____. *Masters of Deceit.* New York: Henry Holt, 1958.

_____. *Persons in Hiding.* Boston: Little, Brown, 1938.

_____. *A Study of Communism.* New York: Holt, Rinehart & Winston, 1962.

Hopkins, Ernest Jerome. *Our Lawless Police.* New York: Viking Press, 1931.

_____. *What Happened in the Mooney Case?* New York: Brower, Warren & Putnam, 1932.

Hopkins, Matthew. *The Discovery of Witches.* Great Toham, Eng.: Charles Clark, 1837.

Hopkins, R.C. *Muniments of Title of the Barony of Arizona and Translation into English.* San Francisco: Bancroft, 1893.

Hopkins, R. Thurston. *Life and Death at the Old Bailey.* London: Herbert Jenkins, 1935.

Hopper, Columbus B. *Sex in Prisons.* Baton Rouge: Louisiana State University Press, 1969.

Hoptner, Jacob B. *Yugoslavia in Crisis, 1934-1941.* New York: Columbia University Press, 1962.

Horan, James D. *Across the Cimarron.* New York: Crown, 1956.

_____. *The Authentic Wild West%%The Gunfighters.* New York: Crown, 1976.

_____. *The Authentic Wild West%%The Lawmen.* New York: Crown, 1980.

_____. *The Authentic Wild West%%The Outlaws.* New York: Crown, 1977.

_____. *Desperate Men: Revelations from the Sealed Pinkerton Files.* New York: G.P. Putnam's Sons, 1949.

_____. *Desperate Women.* New York: G.P. Putnam's Sons, 1952.

_____. *The Desperate Years.* New York: Crown, 1962.

_____. *The Great American West.* New York: Crown, 1959.

_____. *The Mob's Man.* New York: Bantam, 1966.

_____, and Sann, Paul. *Pictorial History of the Wild West.* New York: Crown, 1954.

_____. *The Pinkertons, The Detective Dynasty That Made History.* New York: Crown, 1967.

_____, and Swiggett, Howard. *The Pinkerton Story.* New York: G.P. Putnam's Sons, 1951.

_____. *The Trial of Frank James Brown.* New York: Crown, 1978.

_____. *The Wild Bunch.* New York: New American Library, 1958.

Horan, J.W. *On the Side of the Law: Biography of J.D. Nicholson.* Edmonton, Alberta, Can.: Institute of Applied Arts, 1944.

Horman, Richard E., and Fox, Allen M. *Drug Awareness: Key Documents on LSD, Marijuana and the Drug Culture.* New York: Avon Books, 1970.

Horn, Calvin. *New Mexico's Troubled Years: The Story of the Early Territorial Governors.* Albuquerque, N.M.: Horn & Wallace, 1963.

Horn, David Bayne. *Frederick the Great and the Rise of Prussia.* Mystic, Conn.: Verry Lawrence, 1964.

Horn, Stanley F. *Invisible Empire: The Story of the Ku Klux Klan 1866-1871.* Boston: Houghton Mifflin, 1939.

Hornung, Rick. *Al Capone: A Biography*. New York: Park Lane, 1998.

Horos, Carol. *Rape: The Private Crime, a Social Horror.* New Canaan, Conn.: Tobey, 1974.

Horowitz, Daniel L. *The Italian Labour Movement.* Cambridge, Mass.: Harvard University Press, 1963.

Horowitz, Donald L. *The Courts and Social Policy.* Washington, D.C.: Brookings Institute, 1977.

Horowitz, Elinor. *Capital Punishment, U.S.A.* Philadelphia: J.B. Lippincott, 1973.

Horowitz, Irvin M. *Assassination.* New York: Harper & Row, 1972.

Horsky, C. *The Washington Lawyer.* Boston: Little, Brown, 1952.

Horton, Philip. *Hart Crane: The Life of an American Poet.* New York: Compass Books, 1957.

Horton, Rushmore G. *A Brief Memorial of the Origin and Earlier History of the Tammany Society, or Columbian Order.* New York: New York Printing, 1867.Horton, Sue. *The Billionaire Boys Club.* New York: St. Martin's Press, 1989.

Horwell, John E. *Horwell of the Yard.* London: Andrew Melrose, 1947.

Hoskins, Percy. *The Sound of Murder.* London: Long, 1973.

_____. *They Almost Escaped.* London: Hutchinson, 1938.

Hostetter, Gordon L., and Beesley, Thomas Quinn. *It's A Racket.* Chicago: Les Quin Books, 1929.

Hotchkiss, A.S. *The Manchester Homocide.* Hartford, Conn.: Hartford *Daily Courant*, 1866.

Hot Corn. Boston: Jewett, 1854.

Ho-t'ien Ma. *Chinese Agent in Mongolia.* trans. John De Francis. Baltimore: Johns Hopkins Press, 1949.

Hougan, James. *Spooks.* New York: William Morrow, 1978.

Hough, Richard (ed.). *Advice to a Grand-Daughter: Letters from Queen Victoria to Princess Victoria of Hesse.* London: William Heinemann, 1975.

Hough, Richard. *The Potemkin Mutiny.* Englewood Cliffs, N.J.: Prentice-Hall, 1960.

Hourani, Albert. *Great Britain in the Arab World.* London: John Murray, 1946.

House, Brant (ed.). *Crimes That Shocked America.* New York: Ace Books, 1961.

House, Humphrey. *The Dickens World.* London: Oxford University Press, 1960.

House, Jack. *Square Mile of Murder.* London: W. & R. Chambers, 1961.

Housman, Clemence. *The Werewolf.* London: J. Lane, 1896.

Houts, Marshall. *From Gun to Gavel: The Courtroom Recollections of James Mathers of Oklahoma.* New York: William Morrow, 1954.

_____. *They Asked for Death.* New York: Cowles, 1970.

_____. *Where Death Delights: The Story of Dr. Milton Helpern and Forensic Medicine.* New York: Dell, 1968.

Hoveyda, Fereydoun. *The Shak and the Ayatollah: Iranian Mythology and Islamic Revolution.* New York: Praeger, 2003.

Howard, Clark. *American Saturday.* New York: Richard Marek, 1981.

_____. *Brothers in Blood.* New York: St. Martin's/Marek, 1983.

_____. *Six Against the Rock.* New York: Dial, 1977.

_____. *Zebra.* New York: Richard Marek, 1979.

Howard, D.L. *John Howard, Prison Reformer.* London: Johnson, 1958.

Howard, H.R. *The History of Virgil A. Stewart.* New York: Harper & Brothers, 1836.

Howard, Harry N. *The King-Crane Commission.* Beirut, Leb.: Khayat, 1963.

_____. *The Partition of Turkey: A Diplomatic History 1913-1923.* Norman: Oklahoma University Press, 1931.

Howard, John. *The State of the Prisons in England and Wales.* New York: E.P. Dutton, 1929.

Howard, John R. (ed.). *Awakening Minorities.* New Brunswick, N.J.: Transaction Books, 1970.

Howarth, Henry. *History of the Mongols Part III: Mongols of Persia.* London: Longmans, Green, 1888.

Howe, Cliff. *Scoundrels, Fiends and Human Monsters.* New York: Ace Books, 1958.

Howe, Elvon L. (ed.). *Rocky Mountain Empire.* Garden City, N.Y.: Doubleday, 1950.

Howe, Frederic C. *The Confessions of a Reformer.* New York: Charles Scribner's Sons, 1926.

Howe, Irving and Coser, Lewis. *The American Communist Party: A Critical History.* New York: Frederick A. Praeger, 1962.

Howe, Mark De Wolfe. *Justice Oliver Wendell Holmes.* Cambridge, Mass.: Harvard University Press, 1957.

_____. *Readings in American Legal History.* Cambridge, Mass.: Harvard University Press, 1949.

Howe, Sir Ronald. *The Pursuit of Crime.* London: A. Barker, 1962.

_____. *The Story of Scotland Yard.* London: A. Barker, 1965.

Howe, William F., and Hummel, Abraham. *In Danger; or Life in New York, A True History of a Great City's Wiles and Temptations.* New York: J.S. Ogilvie, 1888.

Howell, Ann Chandler. *Kidnapping in the U.S.* Ann Arbor, Mich.: University Microfilms, 1975.

Howell, Thomas Bayly. (ed.). *A Complete Collection of State Trials and Proceedings for High Treason.* London: Longman, 1816.

Howells, William Dean. *A Hazard of New Fortunes.* New York: Boni & Liveright, 1889.

_____. *Impressions and Experiences.* New York: Harper & Brothers, 1896.

Howgrave-Graham, H.M. *Light and Shade at Scotland Yard.* London: John Murray, 1947.

Howson, Gerald. *The Thief-Taker General: The Rise and Fall of Jonathan Wild.* London: Hutchinson, 1970.

Hoyt, Edwin P. *The Guggenheims and the American Dream.* New York: Funk & Wagnalls, 1967.

_____. *The House of Morgan.* London: Frederick Muller, 1968.

_____. *The Vanderbilts and Their Fortunes.* Garden City, N.Y.: Doubleday, 1962.

Hoyt, Ken, and Leighton, Frances Spatz. *Drunk Before Noon: The Behind-the-Scenes Story of the Washington Press Corps.* Englewood Cliffs, N.J.: Prentice-Hall, 1979.

Hrdlicka, A. *Peoples of the Soviet Union.* Washington, D.C.: Smithsonian, 1942.

Hsiung, S.I. *The Life of Chiang Kai-shek.* London: Davies, 1948.

Hsu, Francis L.K. *Under the Ancestors' Shadow: Chinese Culture and Personality.* New York: Columbia University Press, 1948.

Hsu", Immanuel C.Y. *The Rise of Modern China.* Oxford, Eng.: Oxford University Press, 1975.

Hsu Kai-yu. *Chou En-lai.* Garden City, N.Y.: Doubleday, 1968.

Hsu-Shu-hsi. *The War Conduct of the Japanese.* Shanghai, China: Kelley & Walsh, 1938.

Hubbard, David G. *The Skyjacker: His Flights of Fantasy.* New York: Macmillan, 1971.

Hubbard, Frederick Heman. *The Opium Habit and Alcoholism.* New York: A.S. Barnes, 1881.

Hubbs, Barney. *Robert Clay Allison: Gentleman Gunfighter, 1840-1887.* Pecos, Texas: n.p., 1966.

Huber, Leonard V. *Louisiana.* New York: Charles Scribner's Sons, 1975.

_____. *New Orleans.* New York: Crown, 1971.

Hudson, Frederic. *Journalism in the United States from 1690 to 1872.* New York: Harper, 1873.

Hudson, Joe, and Galaway, Burt (eds.). *Considering the Victim.* Springfield, Ill.: Charles C. Thomas, 1975.

Huggett, Renee, and Berry, Paul. *Daughters of Cain.* London: George Allen & Unwin, 1956.

Hughes, Charles Evans. *The Supreme Court of the United States.* Garden City, N.Y.: Garden City, 1928.

Hughes, Helen MacGill (ed.). *Delinquents and Criminals.* Boston: Holbrook Press, 1970.

_____. *News and the Human Interest Story.* Chicago: University of Chicago Press, 1940.

Hughes, Pennethorne. *Witchcraft.* Baltimore, Md.: Penguin, 1967.

Hughes, Rupert. *The Complete Detective: Being the Life and Strange and Exciting Cases of Raymond Schindler, Master Detective.* New York: Sheridan House, 1950.

Huie, William Bradford. *Did the FBI Kill Martin Luther King?* Nashville, Tenn.: Thomas Nelson, 1977.

_____. *He Slew the Dreamer.* New York: Delacorte Press, 1968.

Hullah, John. *The Train Robber's Career: A Life of Sam Bass.* Chicago: Belford, Clarke, 1881.

Humbert, W.H. *The Pardoning Power of the President.* Washington, D.C.: American Council on Public Affairs, 1941.

Hume, James B. and Thacker, John N. *Report of Jas. B. Hume and Jno. N. Thacker, Special Officers, Wells, Fargo & Co.'s Express, Covering a Period of Fourteen Years.* San Francisco: H.S. Crocker, 1885.

Humes, Edward. *Buried Secrets.* New York. E. P. Dutton, 1991.

Humphreys, Christmas. *The Great Pearl Robbery of 1913.* London: William Heinemann, 1929.

_____. *Seven Murders.* London: William Heinemann, 1931.

Humphreys, Sir Travers. *A Book of Trials.* London: William Heinemann, 1953.

_____. *Criminal Days.* London: Hodder & Stoughton, 1946.

Hungerford, Edward. *Wells Fargo: Advancing the American Frontier.* New York: Random House, 1949.

Hunt, Sir David. *A Don at War.* London: William Kimber, 1966.

_____. *On the Spot.* London: Peter Davies, 1975.

Hunt, Gaillard. *Impeachment Trial of Andrew Johnson.* 3 vols. Washington: U.S. Government Printing Office, 1868.

Hunt, Henry T. *The Case of Thomas J. Mooney and Warren K. Billings.* New York: C.G. Burgoyne, 1929.

Hunt, Lenoir. *Bluebonnets and Blood.* Houston: Texas Books, 1938.

Hunt, Leon Gibson. *Recent Spread of Heroin Use in the United States: Unanswered Questions.* Washington, D.C.: Drug Abuse Council, 1974.

_____, and Chambers, Carl D. *The Heroin Epidemics.* New York: Spectrum, 1976.

_____, and Zinberg, Norman E. *Heroin Use: A New Look.* Washington, D.C.: Drug Abuse Council, 1976.

Hunt, Morton. *The Mugging.* New York: Signet, 1972.

Hunt, William R. *Dictionary of Rogues.* New York: Philosophical Library, 1970.

Hunter, Diana, and Anderson, Alice. *Jack Ruby's Girls.* Atlanta: Hallux, 1970.

Hunter, John Marvin, and Rose, Noah H. *Album of Gunfighters.* Bandera, Texas: n.p., 1951.

Hunter, Lillie Mae. *The Moving Finger.* Borger, Texas: Plains Printing, 1956.

Hunter, Louis C. and B.J. *Steamboats on the Western Rivers.* Cambridge, Mass.: Harvard University Press, 1949.

Hunter, Robert. *Violence and the Labor Movement.* New York: Macmillan, 1919.

Hunter, Sir W.W. *The Life of the Earl of Mayo.* London: n.p., 1875.

Huntington, George. *Robber and Hero: The Story of the Raid on the First National Bank, Minnesota.* Northfield, Minn.: Christian Way, 1895.

Huntington, S. *Political Order in Changing Societies.* New Haven, Conn.: Yale University Press, 1968

Hurd, Charles and Eleanor (eds.). *A Treasury of Great American Letters.* New York: Hawthorn, 1961.

_____. *Washington Cavalcade.* New York: E.P. Dutton, 1948.

_____. *When the New Deal Was Young and Gay.* New York: Hawthorn Books, 1965.

_____. *The White House: A Biography.* New York: Harper, 1940.

Hurewitz, J.C. *Diplomacy in the Near and Middle East.* Princeton, N.J.: Van Nostrand, 1956.

_____. *Middle East Dilemmas.* New York: Harper, 1952.

_____. *The Struggle for Palestine.* New York: W.W. Norton, 1950.

Hurley, Donald. *Alcatraz Island: Maximum Security.* San Francisco: Published by author, 1989.

_____. *Alcatraz Island: Memories.* San Francisco: Published by author, 1998.

Hursch, Carolyn. *The Trouble with Rape.* Chicago: Nelson-Hall, 1977.

Hurt, Henry. *Reasonable Doubt.* New York: Holt, Rinehart & Winston, 1985.

Hurwitz, Howard L. *Theodore Roosevelt and Labor in New York State, 1800-1900.* New York: Columbia University Press, 1943.

Hurwitz, Stephen. *Criminology.* London: George Allen & Unwin, 1952.

Hurwood, Bernhardt J. *Society and the Assassin.* New York: Parent's Magazine Press, 1970.

Huson, Richard (ed.) *Sixty Famous Trials.* London: Daily Express, 1967.
Hussey, J.M. *The Byzantine World.* New York: Rinehart, 1957.
Hussey, Robert. *Murderer Scot-Free.* New York: Great Albion Books, 1972.
Hutchinson, H.F. *Edward II, The Pliant King.* London: Eyre & Spottiswood, 1971.
Hutchinson, John. *The Imperfect Union: A History of Corruption in American Trade Unions.* New York: E.P. Dutton, 1972.
Hutchinson, John F. *Late Imperial Russia, 1890-1917.* London: Longman, 1999.
Hutchinson, W.H. *Another Notebook of the Old West.* Chico, Calif.: Hurst & Yount, 1954.
_____. *A Notebook of the Old West.* Chico, Calif.: Hurst, 1947.
_____. *The Rhodes Reader: Stories of Virgins, Villains, and Varmints.* Norman: University of Oklahoma Press, 1957.
Hutto, Nelson A. *The Dallas Story, from Buckskins to Top Hat.* Dallas: William S. Henson, 1953.
Hutton, James. *A Popular Account of the Thugs and Dacoits, and the Hereditary Garotters and Gang-Robbers of India.* London: William A. Allen, 1857.
Hutzel, Eleanor. *The Policewoman's Handbook.* New York: Columbia University Press, 1933.
Huxley, Aldous. *The Devils of Loudun.* New York: Harper & Row, 1952.
Hyams, Edward. *Killing No Murder, A Study of Assassination as a Political Means.* London: Thomas Nelson & Sons, 1969.
Hyde, H. Montgomery. *Carson: The Life of Sir Edward Carson, Lord Carson of Duncairn.* London: William Heinemann, 1953.
_____. *Cases That Changed The Law.* London: William Heinemann, 1951.
_____. *The Cleveland Street Scandal.* New York: Coward, McCann & Geoghegan, 1976.
_____. *Crime Has Its Heroes.* London: Constable, 1976.
_____. *An International Casebook of Crime.* London: Barrie & Rockcliff, 1962.
_____. *Norman Birkett: The Life of Lord Birkett, of Ulverston.* London: Hamish Hamilton, 1964.
_____. *Room 3603.* New York: Farrar, Straus & Giroux, 1962.
_____. *Sir Patrick Hastings, His Life and Cases.* London: William Heinemann, 1960.
_____. *Their Good Names.* London: Hamish Hamilton, 1970.
_____. *United in Crime.* New York: Roy, 1955.
Hyde, Margaret O. *Hotline!* New York: McGraw-Hill, 1976.
_____. *Juvenile Justice and Injustice.* London: Watts, 1978.
Hyland, William, and Shryock, Richard W. *The Fall of Krushchev.* New York: Funk & Wagnalls, 1968.
Hyman, Harold M. *A More Perfect Union.* New York: Alfred A. Knopf, 1973.
_____. *With Malice Toward Some.* Springfield, Ill.: Abraham Lincoln Association, 1978.
Hynd, Alan. *Brutes, Beasts and Human Fiends.* New York: Paperback Library, 1964.
_____. *Con Man.* New York: Paperback Library, 1961.
_____. *The Giant Killers.* New York: Robert M. McBride, 1945.
_____. *Murder, Mayhem and Mystery.* New York: A.S. Barnes, 1958.
_____. *Sleuths, Slayers, and Swindlers.* New York: A.S. Barnes, 1959.
_____. *Violence in the Night.* New York: Fawcett, 1955.
_____. *We are the Public Enemies.* New York: Fawcett, 1949.
Hynds, Ernest C. *American Newspapers in the 1970s.* New York: Hastings House, 1975.
Hynes, Samuel. *The Edwardian Turn of Mind.* Princeton, N.J.: Princeton University Press, 1968.

Ianni, Francis A.J. *The Black Mafia: Ethnic Succession in Organized Crime.* New York: Simon & Schuster, 1974.
_____. *Ethnic Succession in Organized Crime.* Washington, D.C.: U.S. Government Printing Office, 1973.
_____, and Reuss-Ianni, Elizabeth. *A Family Business: Kinship and Social Control in Organized Crime.* New York: Russell Sage Foundation, 1972.
Iannone, N.F. *Supervision of Police Personnel.* Englewood Cliffs, N.J.: Prentice-Hall, 1975.
Ibn Batuta. *Travels in Asia and Africa, 1325-1354.* trans. H.A.R. Gibb. New York: R.M. McBride, 1929.
Ibn Khaldun. *The Muqaddimah: An Introduction to History.* trans. Franz Rosenthal. New York: Pantheon Books, 1958.
Iceberg Slim. *Pimp: The Story of My Life.* Los Angeles: Holloway House, 1969.
Ickes, Harold L. *America's House of Lords, An Inquiry into the Freedom of the Press.* New York: Harcourt, Brace, 1935.
_____. *Autobiography of a Curmudgeon.* New York: Reynal & Hitchcock, 1943.
Ide, Arthur Frederick, and Auliff, Jacob Ronald. *Jihad Mujahideen, Taliban, Osama bin Laden, George W. Bush & Oil: A Study in the Evolution of Terrorism & Islam.* New York: Liberal Press, 2002.
Ide Hideo. *Jissho: Nihon no Yakuza (Documented Account: The Japanese Yakuza).* Tokyo: Tatsukaze, 1972.
Igwara. *Ethnic Hatred and Genocide in Rwanda.* London: London School of Economics and Political Science, 1996.
Ignatieff, Michael. *A Just Measure of Pain.* New York: Pantheon Books, 1978.
Ike Nobutaka. *The Beginnings of Political Democracy in Japan.* New York: Alfred A. Knopf, 1950.
_____ (trans. and ed.). *Japan's Decision for War: Records of the 1941 Political Conferences.* Palo Alto, Calif.: Stanford University Press, 1967.
Ileana, Princess of Roumania and Archduchess of Austria. *I Live Again.* New York: Rinehart, 1952.
Iliodor. *The Mad Monk of Russia.* New York: Century, 1918.
Illinois Legislative Council. *Bills to Abolish the Death Penalty in Illinois.* Springfield: State of Illinois, 1951.
_____. *Capital Punishment for Serious Sex Offences.* Springfield: State of Illinois, 1954.
Imai Takeo. *Reminiscences of the China Affair.* Tokyo: Misuzu Shobo, 1964.
Inbau, Fred, and Reid, J.E. *Criminal Interrogations and Confessions.* Baltimore: Williams & Wilkins, 1976.
_____. *Criminal Investigation and Criminal Law.* Radnor, Pa.: Chilton, 1972.
_____ (ed.). *Criminal Law for the Layman.* Radnor, Pa.: Chilton, 1978.
_____. *Criminal Law for the Police.* Radnor, Pa.: Chilton, 1969.
_____. *Evidence Law for the Police.* Radnor Pa.: Chilton, 1972.
_____, and Reid, J.E. *Lie Detection and Criminal Interrogation.* Baltimore: Williams & Wilkins, 1953.
_____. *Scientific Police Investigation.* Radnor, Pa.: Chilton, 1972.
Inciardi, James A. *Careers in Crime.* Chicago: Rand McNally College, 1975.
_____. *The Drugs-Crime Connection.* Beverly Hills, Calif.: Sage, 1981.
_____, and Chambers, Carl D. (eds.). *Drugs and the Criminal Justice System.* Beverly Hills, Calif.: Sage, 1974.
_____. *A History and Sociology of Organized Crime.* Ann Arbor: University of Michigan Microfilms, 1974.
_____ (ed.). *Radical Criminology.* Beverly Hills, Calif.: Sage, 1980.
_____. *Reflections on Crime.* New York: Holt, Rinehart & Winston, 1979.
_____. *The War on Drugs: Heroin, Cocaine, Crime, and Public Policy.* Palo Alto, Calif.: Mayfield, 1986.
Inderwick, F.A. *Side-Lights on the Stuarts.* London: Low, Marston, Searle & Rivington, 1888.
Ingham, K. *A History of East Africa.* London: Longmans, 1962.
Ingle, Don. *Fall Forward, My Son.* New York: Carlton Press, 1974.
Ingleton, Roy D. *Police of the World.* New York: Charles Scribner's Sons, 1979.
Inglis, Brian. *The Forbidden Game: A Social History of Drugs.* New York: Charles Scribner's Sons, 1975.
_____. *Private Conscience))Public Morality.* London: Andr Deutsch, 1964.
_____. *The Story of Ireland.* London: Faber & Faber, 1956.
_____. *West Briton.* London: Faber & Faber, 1962.
Ingraham, Abijah A. *A Biography of Fernando Wood, A History of the Forgeries, Perjuries, and Other Crimes of Our "Model Mayor."* New York: n.p., 1856.
Inman, Samuel Guy. *Intervention in Mexico.* New York: Charles Scribner's Sons, 1919.
Innerst, J. Stewart. *Is Capital Punishment the Answer?* Richmond, Ind.: The Five Years Meeting of Friends, 1959.
Innes, Brian. *The Book of Pirates.* London: Bancroft, 1966.
Ino Kenji. *Kodama Yoshio no Kyozo to Jitsuzo (The Image and Reality of Yoshio Kodama).* Tokyo: Sokon Shuppan, 1970.
_____. *Nihon no Uyoku (Japan's Right Wing).* Tokyo: Nisshin Godo Shuppan, 1973.
_____. *Yakuza to Nihonjin (Yakuza and the Japanese).* Tokyo: Mikasa Shoto, 1974.
In Prison and On the Scaffold. Indianapolis, Ind.: Ned Reed, 1879.
Institute for Mediterranean Affairs. *The Palestine Refugee Problem.* New York: St. Martin's, 1958.
Institute for the Study of Drug Dependence. *Drug Abuse Briefing.* London: Published by Author, 1987.
International Association of Chiefs of Police. *An Organizational Study of the Police Department.* New York: IACP, 1967.
International Business Publications. *Osama bin Laden in Jihad Against Us.* New York: International Business Publications USA, 2001.
International Parental Child Abduction. Washington, D. C.: U. S. Department of State, Bureau of Consular Affairs, 1993.
The Interocean. *A History of Chicago: Its Men and Institutions.* Chicago: Interocean, 1900.
The Investigation of the Assassination of President Kennedy. Washington, D.C.: U.S. Government Printing Office, 1976.
Iorizzo, Luciano. *Al Capone: A Biography.* Westport, Conn.: Greenwood Press, 2003.
Ireland, Alleyne. *Joseph Pulitzer: Reminiscences of a Secretary.* New York: Mitchell Kennerley, 1914.
Ireland, William Henry. *Memoirs of Jeanne d'Arc.* London: R. Triphook, 1824.
Irey, Elmer L., and Slocum, William T. *The Tax Dodgers.* Garden City, N. Y.: Doubleday, 1948.
Irons, Peter. *Justice at War.* New York: Oxford University Press, 1983.
Iroshnikov, Mikhail Parlovich, et al. *The Sunset of the Romanov Dynasty.* New York: Melissa Media, 1992.
Irving, Clifford. *Fake!* New York: McGraw-Hill, 1969.
Irving, David. *Hitler's War.* New York: Viking Press, 1977.
_____. *The Mare's Nest.* London: William Kimber, 1964.
Irving, Henry Brodribb. *A Book of Remarkable Criminals.* New York: George H. Doran, 1918.
_____. *French Criminals of the Nineteenth Century.* London: William Heinemann, 1901.
_____. *The Trial of Franz Muller.* London: William Hodge, 1911.
Irving, Joseph. *The Annals of Our Time, 1837-1868.* London: Macmillan, 1869.
Irving, Washington. *Life of George Washington.* New York: G.P. Putnam's Sons, 1857.
_____. *Life of Mohammed.* London: J.M. Dent, 1849.
_____. *Lives of the Successors of Mohammed.* London: John Murray, 1850.
Irwin, Inez Haynes. *Angels and Amazons: A Hundred Years of American Women.* Garden City, N.Y.: Doubleday, Doran, 1934.
Irwin, John. *The Felon.* Englewood Cliffs, N.J.: Prentice-Hall, 1970.
Irwin, Will. *The City that Was: A Requiem of Old San Francisco.* New York: B.W. Huebsch, 1906.
_____. *Confessions of a Con Man.* New York: B.W. Heubsch, 1909.
_____. *Pictures of Old Chinatown.* New York: Moffat, Yard, 1908.
Isaac, Paul E. *Prohibiton and Politics.* Knoxville: University of Tennessee Press, 1965.
Isaacs, G. R. *The South Sea Bubble.* New York: G.P. Putnam's Sons, 1933.
Isaacs, Harold R. *No Peace for Asia.* Cambridge, Mass.: MIT Press, 1967.
_____. *Scratches on Our Minds: American Images of China and India.* New York: John Day, 1958.
_____. *The Tragedy of the Chinese Revolution.* Palo Alto, Calif.: Stanford University Press, 1938.
Isely, Bliss, and Richards, W.M. *Four Centuries in Kansas.* Wichita, Kan.: McCormick-Mathers, 1936.

Isidore of Seville. *History of the Kings of the Goths.* trans. Guidi Donini and Gordon B. Ford, Jr. Leiden, Neth.: E.J. Brill, 1966.
Iskander, Marwan. *The Arab Boycott of Israel.* Beirut, Leb.: Research Center, Palestine Liberation Organization, 1966.
Israel, Fred L. *The Chief Executive.* New York: Crown, 1965.
Israel, Lee. *Kilgallen.* New York: Delacorte, 1957.
_____. *Miss Tallulah Bankhead.* New York: G.P. Putnam's Sons, 1972.
Issawi, Charles. *Egypt at Mid-Century.* New York: Oxford University Press, 1954.
Issel, William, and Cherny, Robert W. *San Francisco, 1865-1932.* Berkeley: University of California Press, 1986.
Ito Kanejiro. *Military Men of My Native Land.* Tokyo: Kyo no Mondai-sha, 1939.
Ivanov, Miroslav. *Target: Heydrich.* New York: Macmillan, 1972.
Ives, George. *A History of Penal Methods.* Montclair, N.J.: Patterson Smith, 1972.
Izzeddin, Nejla. *The Arab World: Past, Present and Future.* Chicago: Regnery, 1953.

Jaber, Hala. *Hezbollah.* New York: Columbia University Press, 1997.
Jackman, Tom, and Cole, Troy. *Rites of Burial.* New York: Windsor, 1992.
Jacks, Irving, and Cox, Steven G. (eds.). *Psychological Approaches to Crime and Its Correction.* Chicago: Nelson-Hall, 1984.
Jackson, Bruce. *Death Row.* Boston: Beacon Press, 1980.
_____. *In The Life.* New York: Macmillan, 1972.
_____. *Killing Time.* Ithaca, N.Y.: Cornell University Press, 1977.
_____. *A Thief's Primer.* New York: Macmillan, 1969.
_____ (ed.). *Letters of the Lewis and Clark Expedition.* Urbana: University of Illinois Press, 1962.
Jackson, E.L. *St. Helena.* London: Ward, Lock, 1903.
Jackson, Geoffrey. *People's Prison.* London: Faber & Faber, 1973.
_____. *Surviving the Long Night: An Autobiographical Account of a Political Kidnapping.* New York: Vanguard Press, 1974.
Jackson, George. *Soledad Brothers: The Prison Letters of George Jackson.* New York: Coward-McCann, 1970.
Jackson, H.H. *A Century of Dishonor.* New York: Harper & Brothers, 1881.
Jackson, Herbert G., Jr. *The Spirit Rappers.* New York: Doubleday, 1972.
Jackson, Joseph Henry. *Bad Company.* New York: Harcourt, Brace, 1949.
_____. *The Creation of Joaquin Murieta.* n.p., 1948.
_____. *The Portable Murder Book.* New York: Viking Press, 1945.
_____. *San Francisco Murders.* New York: Duell, Sloan & Pearce, 1947.
_____. *Tintypes in Gold: Four Studies in Robbery.* New York: Macmillan, 1939.
Jackson, Joy J. *New Orleans in the Gilded Age.* Baton Rouge: Louisiana State University Press, 1969.
Jackson, Kenneth T. *The Ku Klux Klan in the City.* New York: Oxford University Press, 1970.
Jackson, Luther P. *Negro Office-Holders in Virginia, 1865-1895.* Norfolk, Va.: Guide Quality Press, 1945.
Jackson, Mary E. *Bank and Train Robbers.* Chicago: Henneberry, 1881.
Jackson, R. *The Chief.* London: Harrap, 1959.
Jackson, R.M. *The Machinery of Justice in England.* London: Cambridge University Press, 1964.
Jackson, Sir Richard. *Occupied with Crime.* London: Harrap, 1967.
Jackson, Robert. *Case for the Prosecution: A Biography of Sir Archibald Bodkin, Director of Public Prosecutions, 1920-1930.* London: Arthur Barket, 1962.
_____. *The Crime Doctors.* London: Frederick Muller, 1966.
_____. *Francis Camps: Famous Case Histories of the Celebrated Pathologist.* London: Hart Davis, 1975.
Jackson, Robert H. *The Struggle for Judicial Supremacy.* New York: Alfred A. Knopf, 1941.
_____. *The Supreme Court in the American System of Government.* Cambridge, Mass.: Harvard University Press, 1955.
Jackson, Stanley. *The Life and Cases of Mr. Justice Humphreys.* London: Odhams Press, 1951.
_____. *Mr. Justice Avory.* London: Victor Gollancz, 1935.
Jackson, T.A. *Ireland Her Own.* New York: International, 1947.
Jackson, W.A. Douglas. *Russo-Chinese Borderlands.* New York: D. Van Nostrand, 1962.
Jackson, W.T.H. *The Literature of the Middle Ages.* New York: Columbia University Press, 1960
Jacob, Herbert. *Justice in America: Courts, Lawyers, and the Judicial Process.* Boston: Little, Brown, 1972.
_____ (ed.). *The Potential for Reform of Criminal Justice.* Beverly Hills, Calif.: Sage, 1974.
Jacobs, Clyde. *Justice Frankfurter and Civil Liberties.* Berkeley: University of California Press, 1961.
Jacobs, Harold. *Weatherman.* New York: Ramparts Press, 1970.
Jacobs, James B. *Stateville: The Penitentiary in Mass Society.* Chicago: University of Chicago Press, 1977.
Jacobs, Jane. *The Death and Life of Great American Cities.* New York: Random House, 1961.
Jacobs, Norman (ed.). *Culture for the Millions: Mass Media in Modern Society.* Boston: Beacon Press, 1964.
Jacobs, Paul. *Prelude to Riot: A View of Urban America from the Bottom.* New York: Vintage Books, 1968.
Jacobs, T.C.H. *Aspects of Murder.* London: Stanley Paul, 1956.
_____. *Cavalcade of Murder.* London: Stanley Paul, 1955.
_____. *Pageant of Murder.* London: Stanley Paul, 1956.
Jacobson, David J. *The Affairs of Dame Rumor.* New York: Rinehart, 1948.
Jacobson, Lauri. *Hollywood Heartbreak.* New York: Simon & Schuster, 1984.
Jacobson, Richard, and Zinberg, Norman E. *The Social Basis of Drug Abuse Prevention.* Washington, D.C.: Drug Abuse Council, 1975.
Jacoby, Jean. *Raspoutine.* Paris: Flammarion, 1934.
Jacoby, Joseph E. (ed.). *Classics of Criminology.* Oak Park, Ill.: Moore, 1979.
Jacoby, Neil H., Nehemkis, Peter, and Eells, Richard. *Bribery and Extortion in World Business.* New York: Macmillan, 1977.
Jacoby, Susan. *Wild Justice.* New York: Harper & Row, 1983.
Jacquard, Roland. *In the Name of Osama bin Laden: Global Terrorism and the Bin Laden Brotherhood.* Durham, N. C.: Duke University Press, 2002.
Jaeger, Richard, and Balousek, M. William. *Massacre in Milwaukee.* Oregon, Wis.: Waubesa Press, 1991.
Jaensch, E. *Eidetic Imagery and Topological Methods of Investigation.* trans. O. Oeser. New York: Harcourt Brace, 1930.
Jaffe, F.A. *A Guide to Pathological Evidence.* Toronto, Ontario, Can.: Carswell, 1976.
Jaffe, Julian F. *Crusade Against Radicalism.* Port Washington, N.Y.: Kennikat, 1972.
Jaffe, Louis. *English and American Judges as Lawmakers.* New York: Oxford, 1969.
Jaffe, Philip J. *The Rise and Fall of American Communism.* New York: Horizon, 1975.
Jaher, Frederick C. *Doubters and Dissenters.* London: Free Press of Glencoe, 1964.
_____. *The Rich, the Well Born, and the Powerful.* Urbana: University of Illinois Press, 1973.
Jahns, Pat. *The Frontier World of Doc Holliday.* New York: Hastings House, 1957.
Jamal Mohammed Ahmed. *Intellectual Origins of Egyptian Nationalism.* London: Oxford University Press, 1960.
James, C.L.R. *A History of Negro Revolt.* London: Fact, 1938.
James, Daniel. *Mexico and the Americas.* New York: Frederick A. Praeger, 1963.
James, David H. *The Rise and Fall of the Japanese Empire.* London: George Allen & Unwin, 1951.
James, E.O. *Myth and Ritual in the Ancient Near East.* New York: Frederick A. Praeger, 1958.
James, Edgar. *James Boys: Deeds and Daring.* Baltimore: I. & M. Ottenheimer, 1912.
_____. *The Lives and Adventures, Daring Hold-ups, Train and Bank Robberies of the World's Most Desperate Bandits and Highwaymen)) The Notorious James Brothers.* Baltimore: I. & M. Ottenheimer, 1913.
James, Frank. *Frank James and His Brother Jesse.* Baltimore: I. & M. Ottenheimer, 1915.
James, Grace. *Japan: Recollections and Impressions.* London: George Allen & Unwin, 1936.
James, H.K. *The Destruction of Mephisto's Greatest Web; or All Grafts Laid Bare.* Salt Lake City, Utah: Raleigh, 1914.
James, Henry. *American Scene.* New York: Charles Scribner's Sons, 1907.
_____. *The Bostonians.* New York: Macmillan, 1886.
James, Howard. *Children in Trouble: A National Scandal.* New York: David McKay, 1969.
_____. *The Little Victims: How America Treats Its Children.* New York: David McKay, 1975.
James, Jesse Edward, Jr. *Jesse James, My Father.* Independence, Mo.: Sentinel, 1899.
James, Jesse Lee. *Jesse James and the Lost Cause.* New York: Pageant Press, 1961.
James, John T. *The Benders of Kansas.* Wichita, Kan.: Kan.-Okla., 1913.
James, Marquis. *Andrew Jackson: The Border Captain.* New York: Literary Guild, 1933.
_____, and Bessie. *Biography of a Bank.* New York: Harper & Row, 1954.
_____. *The Cherokee Strip: A Tale of an Oklahoma Boyhood.*
New York: Viking Press, 1945.
_____. *The Life of Andrew Jackson.* Indianapolis, Ind.: Bobbs-Merrill, 1938.
_____. *The Raven: A Biography of Sam Houston.* Indianapolis, Ind.: Bobbs-Merrill, 1929.
_____. *They Had Their Hour.* Indianapolis, Ind.: Bobbs-Merrill, 1934.
James, Ralph and Esther. *Hoffa and the Teamsters.* Princeton, N.J.: D. Van Nostrand, 1965.
James, Rosemary, and Wardlaw, Jack. *Plot or Politics?: The Garrison Case and Its Cast.* New Orleans, La.: Pelican, 1967.
James, T.E. *Prostitution and the Law.* London: William Heinemann, 1951.
Jameson, Henry B. *Heroes by the Dozen.* Abilene, Kan.: Shadinger-Wilson, 1961.
_____. *Miracle of the Chisholm Trail.* Abilene, Kan.: Tri-State Chisholm Trail Centennial Commission, 1967.
Jameson, John Franklin. *Privateering and Piracy in the Colonial Period.* New York: Macmillan, 1923.
Janke, Peter, and Price, D.L. *Ulster: Coercion and Concensus.* London: Institute for the Study of Conflict, 1974.
Janov, Arthur. *Primal Scream.* New York: G.P. Putnam's Sons, 1970.
Janowitz, Morris. *The Last Half Century: Societal Change and Politics in America.* Chicago: University of Chicago Press, 1978.
Janowsky, Oscar I. *Foundations of Israel.* Princeton, N.J.: D. Van Nostrand, 1959.
Jansen, G.H. *Nonalignment and the Afro-Asian States.* New York: Frederick A. Praeger, 1966.
Jansen, Godfrey. *Why Robert Kennedy Was Killed.* New York: Third Press, 1970.
Jansen, Marius B. *The Japanese and Sun Yat-sen.* Cambridge, Mass.: Harvard University Press, 1954.
Japan Biographical Encyclopedia and Who's Who. Tokyo: Rengo Press, 1958.
Japan Biographical Outlines. Tokyo: Asakura Shobo, 1960.
Jaramillo, Cleofas M. *Shadows of the Past.* Santa Fe, N.M.: Seton Village Press, 1941.
Jarcke, Carl. *Carl Ludwig San, usw: Eine psychologisch-criminalistische Eroertung aus der Geschichte unserer Zeit.* Berlin: Ferdinand Dummler, 1831.
Jardin Birnie, Rene. *Le Cahier Rouge d'Eugene Weidmann.* Paris: Gallimard, 1968.
Jarman, T.L. *The Rise and Fall of Nazi Germany.* New York: New American Library, 1961.
Jaszi, Oscar, and Lewis, John D. *Against the Tyrant: The Tradition and Theory of Tyrannicide.* Glencoe, Ill.: Free Press, 1957.
Jaworski, Leon. *Files of Evidence Connected With the Investigation of the Assassination of President John F. Kennedy.* Washington, D.C.: Microcard Editions, 1967.
Jean, Albert. *Le Secret de Barbe-Bleue.* Paris: SFELT, 1950.
Jebb, Sir Joshua. *Report of the Surveyor-General of Prisons on the Construction, Ventilation and Details of Pentonville Prison.* London: W. Clowes & Sons, 1844.

Jedlicka, Ludwig. *Der 20 Juli 1944 in sterreich.* Munich: Verlag Herold, 1965.

Jeffers, H. Paul. *Who Killed Precious?* New York: Pharos Books, 1991.

Jeffery, C. Raymond. *Crime Prevention Through Environmental Design.* Beverly Hills, Calif.: Sage, 1977.

Jeffries, Sir Charles. *The Colonial Police.* London: Max Parish, 1952.

Jeffries, Joseph M.N. *Palestine: The Reality.* New York: Longmans, 1939.

Jefremovas, Villia. *Brickyards to Graveyards: From Production to Genocide in Rwanda.* Albany, N. Y.: State University of New York Press, 2002.

Jelavich, Barbara. *A Century of Russian Foreign Policy, 1814-1914.* Philadelphia: J.B. Lippincott, 1964.

Jelavich, Charles and Barbara. *The Balkans.* Englewood Cliffs, N.J.: Prentice-Hall, 1965.

_____. *Tsarist Russia and Balkan Nationalism: Russian Influence in the Internal Affairs of Bulgaria and Serbia, 1876-1886.* Berkeley: University of California Press, 1958.

Jenkins, Alan. *The Stock Exchange Story.* London: William Heinemann, 1973.

_____. *The Twenties.* New York: Universe Books, 1974.

Jenkins, Brian. *Dr. Gully's Story.* New York: Coward, McCann & Geoghegan, 1972.

_____. *High Technology Terrorism and Surrogate War.* Santa Monica, Calif.: Rand, 1975.

_____. *Hostage Survival: Some Preliminary Observations.* Santa Monica: Rand, 1976.

_____, and Johnson, Janera. *International Terrorism: A Chronology 1968-1975.* Santa Monica, Calif.: Rand, 1975.

_____. *International Terrorism: A New Kind of Warfare.* Santa Monica, Calif.: Rand, 1974.

_____. *Numbered Lives: Some Statistical Observations from 77 International Hostage Episodes.* Santa Monica, Calif.: Rand, 1977.

_____. *Should Corporations Be Prevented From Paying Ransom?* Santa Monica, Calif.: Rand, 1974.

_____. *Will Terrorists Go Nuclear?* Santa Monica, Calif.: Rand, 1975.

Jenkins, Elizabeth. *Six Criminal Women.* London: Pan Books, 1949.

Jenkins, John H., and Frost, Gordon. *I'm Frank Hamer: The Life of a Texas Peace Officer.* New York: The Pemberton Press, 1968.

_____. *Neither the Fanatics nor the Faint-Hearted.* Austin, Texas: The Pemberton Press, 1963.

Jenkins, Malinda, and Lilienthal, Jesse. *Gambler's Wife.* Boston: Houghton Mifflin, 1933.

Jenkins, Philip, and Potter, Gary W. *The City and the Syndicate: Organizing Crime in Philadelphia.* Lexington, Mass.: Ginn, 1985.

_____. *Crime and Justice: Issues and Ideas.* Belmont, Calif.: Brooks/Cole, 1984.

Jenkins, W.S. *Proslavery Thought in the Old South.* Chapel Hill: University of North Carolina Press, 1935.

Jennings, Alphonso J. *Beating Back.* New York: D. Appleton, 1914.

_____. *Number 30664, by Number 31539.* Hollywood, Calif.: Pioneer Press, 1941.

_____. *Through the Shadows with O. Henry.* New York: H.K. Fly, 1921.

Jennings, Dean. *We Only Kill Each Other: The Life and Bad Times of Bugsy Siegel.* Englewood Cliffs, N.J.: Prentice-Hall, 1967.

Jennings, Jesse D., and Norbeck, Edward (eds.). *Prehistoric Man in the New World.* Chicago: University of Chicago Press, 1963.

Jennings, Napoleon A. *A Texas Ranger.* New York: Charles Scribner's Sons, 1899.

Jennings, Peter. *An End To Terrorism.* London: Lion Paperback, 1985.

Jensen, Ann (ed.). *Texas Ranger's Diary and Scrapbook.* Dallas: Kaleidograph Press, 1936.

Jensen, Joan M. *Military Surveillance of Civilians in America.* Morristown, N.J.: General Learning Press, 1975.

_____. *The Price of Vigilance.* Chicago: Rand McNally, 1968.

Jensen, Richard. *The Winning of the Midwest.* Chicago: University of Chicago Press, 1971.

Jensen, Vernon H. *Heritage of Conflict.* Ithaca, N.Y.: Cornell University Press, 1950.

Jerome, Thomas J. *Ku Klux Klan No. 40.* Raleigh, N.C.: Edwards & Broughton, 1895.

Jerrold, Blanchard. *The Life of Napoleon III.* London: Longmans, Green, 1874.

Jersild, Jens. *Boy Prostitution.* Copenhagen: G.E.C. Gad, 1956.

Jervis, Eustace. *Twenty-Five Years in Six Prisons.* London: T. Fisher Unwin, 1925.

Jervis, John. *On the Office and Duties of Coroners, with Forms and Procedures.* London: Sweet & Maxwell, 1854.

Jesse, F. Tennyson. *Comments on Cain.* London: William Heinemann, 1948.

_____. *Murder and Its Motives.* New York: Alfred A. Knopf, 1924.

_____. *Trials of Timothy John Evans and John Reginald Halliday Christie.* London: William Hodge, 1957.

Jessor, Richard, et al. *Society, Personality, and Deviant Behavior.* New York: Holt, Rinehart & Winston, 1968.

JFK Assassination Solved: Special Report. North West Assassination Research Committee, n.d.

JFK Murder Solved: Killing Coordinated by CIA. Los Angeles: Los Angeles Free Press, 1978.

Jimenez, Janey. *My Prisoner.* Kansas: McMillan, 1977.

Job, Joseph (ed.). *The Great Age of Sail.* New York: New York Graphic Society, 1967.

Jol, Ernst, and Frnkel, Fritz. *Der Cocainismus.* Berlin: Springer, 1924.

Joeston, Joachim. *The Biggest Lie I Ever Told: The Kennedy Fraud and How I Helped Expose It.* Munich: Published by Author, 1968.

_____. *The Case Against the Kennedy Clan in the Assassination of President John F. Kennedy.* Munich: Published by Author, 1968.

_____. *The Case Against Lyndon B. Johnson in the Assassination* of President Kennedy. Munich: Published by Author, 1967.

_____. *The Dark Side of Lyndon Baines Johnson.* London: Peter Dawnay, 1968.

_____. *De Gaulle and His Murders.* Isle of Man, Brit.: Times Press, 1964.

_____. *The Garrison Enquiry.* London: Peter Dawnay, 1967.

_____. *Marina Oswald.* London: Peter Dawnay, 1967.

_____. *Oswald: Assassin or Fall Guy?* Marzani & Munsell, 1964.

Joey. *Hit #29.* New York: Pocket Books, 1975.

_____. *Joey Kills.* New York: Pocket Books, 1975.

_____. *Killer.* New York: Pocket Books, 1975.

Johannsen, Albert. *The House of Beadle and Adams and Its Nickel and Dime Novels.* Norman: University of Oklahoma Press, 1950.

John Fitzgerald Kennedy, 1917-1963, and the Federal City He Loved. Washington, D.C.: Tatler, 1963.

A John F. Kennedy Memorial. New York: MacFadden Books, 1964.

John of Joinville. *The Life of St. Louis.* trans. Ren Hague. New York: Sheed & Ward, 1955.

Johns, A. Wesley. *The Man Who Shot McKinley.* South Brunswick, N.J.: A.S. Barnes, 1970.

Johnsen, Julia E. (ed.). *Capital Punishment.* New York: H.W. Wilson, 1939.

_____. *Palestine: Jewish Homeland.* New York: H.W. Wilson, 1946.

Johnson, Allen (ed.). *Chronicles of America.* New Haven, Conn.: Yale University Press, 1918.

Johnson, Andrew: Trial of an Impeachment by the House of Representatives for High Crimes and Misdemeanor. Washington, D.C.: U.S. Government Printing Office, 1868.

Johnson, B.B. *Abraham Lincoln and Boston Corbett.* Waltham, Mass.: Byron Berkeley Johnson, 1914.

Johnson Charles. *Lives of the Most Noted Highwaymen.* Dublin, Ire.: Tegg, 1839.

Johnson, Claudius O. *Borah of Idaho.* Longmans, Green, 1936.

_____. *Carter Henry Harrison I.* Chicago: University of Chicago Press, 1928.

Johnson, David R. *American Law Enforcement.* St. Louis: Forum Press, 1981.

Johnson, Diane. *Dashiell Hammett, A Life.* New York: Random House, 1983.

Johnson, Donald Bruce, and Walker, Jack L. (eds.). *The Dynamics of the American Presidency.* New York: John Wiley & Sons, 1964.

Johnson, Dorothy. *Famous Lawmen of the Old West.* New York: Dodd, Mead, 1963.

_____. *Some Went West.* New York: Dodd, Mead, 1965.

Johnson, E. *Justice and Reform: The Formative Years of the OEO Legal Services Program.* New York: Russell Sage Foundation, 1974.

Johnson, Elmer H. *Crime, Correction, and Society.* Homewood, Ill.: Dorsey Press, 1964.

Johnson, Francis. *Famous Assassinations.* Chicago: A.C. McClurg, 1903.

Johnson, G.C. *Wagon Yard.* Dallas: William T. Tardy, 1938.

Johnson, Gerald W. *The Lunatic Fringe.* New York: J.B. Lippincott, 1957.

_____. *Woodrow Wilson.* New York: Harpers, 1944.

Johnson, Haynes. *The Bay of Pigs.* New York: W.W. Norton, 1964.

Johnson, James, and Miller, Floyd. *The Man Who Sold The Eiffel Tower.* Garden City, N.Y.: Doubleday, 1961.

Johnson, John. *Trial and Sentence of John Johnson.* New York: Joseph Desnoues, 1824.

Johnson, John. *Doing Field Research.* New York: Free Press, 1974.

Johnson, John J., and Douglas, Jack D. (eds.). *Crime at the Top: Deviance in Business and the Professions.* Philadelphia: J.B. Lippincott, 1978.

Johnson, Julia E. (ed.). *Capital Punishment.* New York: H.W. Wilson, 1939.

Johnson, K. *Guatemala: From Terrorism to Terror.* London: Institute for Study of Conflict, 1972.

Johnson, L.F. *Famous Kentucky Tragedies and Trials.* Louisville, Ky: Baldwin Law Books, 1916.

Johnson, Lyndon B. *The Vantage Point.* New York: Popular Library, 1971.

Johnson, Malcolm. *Crime on the Labor Front.* New York: McGraw-Hill, 1950.

Johnson, Pamela Hansford. *On Iniquity: Some Personal Reflections Arising Out of the Moors Murder Trial.* New York: Charles Scribner's Sons, 1967.

Johnson, R.A. *Report of the Surveyor General upon the Alleged Peralta Grant.* Phoenix: Arizona Gazette Book and Job Office, 1890.

Johnson, R.E. *Juvenile Deliquency and Its Origins.* Cambridge, Eng.: Cambridge University Press, 1979.

Johnson, Ray. *Too Dangerous to Be at Large.* New York: Quadrangle, 1975.

Johnson, Robert, and Toch, Hans (eds.). *The Pains of Imprisonment.* Beverly Hills, Calif.: Sage, 1982.

Johnson, Walter (ed.). *Selected Letters of William Allen White, 1899-1943.* New York: Henry Holt, 1947.

_____. *William Allen White's America.* New York: Henry Holt, 1947.

Johnson, William Weber. *Heroic Mexico.* New York: Doubleday, 1968.

_____. *Mexico.* New York: Life World Library, 1961.

Johnston, Alva. *The Legendary Mizners.* New York: Farrar, Straus & Young, 1953.

Johnston, James A. *Alcatraz Island Prison.* New York: Charles Scribner's Sons, 1949.

Johnston, James P. *Grafters I Have Met.* Chicago: Thompson & Thomas, 1906.

Johnston, Lloyd D., Bachman, Jerald G., and O'Malley, Patrick M. *Student Drug Use, Attitudes and Beliefs.* Washington, D.C.: U.S. Government Printing Office, 1983.

Johnston, Michael. *Political Corruption and Public Policy in America.* Monterey, Calif.: Brooks/Cole, 1982.

Johnston, Norman. *The Human Cage: A Brief History of Prison Architecture.* New York: Walker, 1973.

_____, Savitz, Leonard, and Wolfgang, Marvin E. (eds.). *The Sociology of Punishment and Corrections.* New York: John Wiley & Sons, 1962.

Johnston, Reginald F. *Twilight in the Forbidden City.* London: Victor Gollancz, 1934.

Johnston, William Davidson. *T.R.: Champion of the Strenuous Life.* New York: Farrar, Straus & Cudahy, 1958.

Joint Center for Political Studies. *A Policy Framework for Racial Justice.* Washington, D.C.: Joint Center for Political Studies, 1983.

Joll, James. *The Anarchists.* New York: Grosset & Dunlap, 1964.

Jonas, George, and Amiel, Barbara. *By Persons Unknown.* Toronto, Ontario, Can.: Macmillan, 1977.

Jonas, Hans. *The Gnostic Religion.* Boston: Beacon Press, 1958.

Jonas, Klaus. *The Life of Crown Prince William.* trans. Charles W. Bangert. London: Routledge & Kegan Paul, 1961.

Jones, A.B., and Llewellyn, J. *Malingering.* London: William Heinemann, 1917.

Jones, Ann. *Women Who Kill.* New York: Holt, Rinehart & Winston, 1980.

Jones, Aphrodite. *Cruel Sacrifice.* New York: Pinnacle, 1994.

Jones, C. Sheridan. *The Story of the Hohenzollern.* London: Jarrold & Sons, 1915.

Jones, David A. *The Health Risks of Imprisonment.* Lexington, Mass.: D.C. Heath, 1976.

Jones, Eliot. *The Trust Problem in the United States.* New York: Macmillan, 1921.

Jones, Elwyn. *The Last Two to Hang.* New York: Stein-Day, 1966.

_____, and Lloyd, John. *The Ripper File: A Documentary Investigation.* London: Barker, 1975.

Jones, Ernest. *The Life and Work of Sigmund Freud.* New York: Basic Books, 1961.

_____. *Nightmares, Witches, and Devils.* New York: W.W. Norton, 1931.

_____. *On the Nightmare.* London: International Psycho-Analytic Library, 1931.

Jones, F.C. *Japan's New Order in Asia.* New York: Oxford University Press, 1954.

_____. *Manchuria Since 1931.* London: Royal Institute of International Affairs, 1949.

Jones, Francis P. *History of the Sinn Fein and The Irish Rebellion of 1916.* New York: P.J. Kenedy, 1917.

Jones, Frank. *Trail of Blood.* Toronto: McGraw-Hill-Ryerson, 1981.

Jones, Gareth Stedman. *Outcast.* London: Clarendon Press, 1971.

Jones, H. *Crime, Race, and Culture.* New York: John Wiley & Sons, 1981.

Jones, Hardin B. and Helen B. *Sensual Drugs.* Cambridge, Eng.: Cambridge University Press, 1977.

Jones, Harry (ed.). *The Courts, the Public, and the Law Explosion.* Englewood Cliffs, N.J.: Prentice-Hall, 1965.

Jones, Howard. *Crime and Penal System.* London: University Tutorial Press, 1956.

_____. *Open Prisons.* London: RKP, 1979.

Jones, J. Elbert. *The Mysteries of Famous Crimes Solved by St. Louis Policemen.* St. Louis: Moinster, 1924.

Jones, J. Harry, Jr. *The Minutemen.* Garden City, N.Y.: Doubleday, 1968.

Jones, James. *Andrew Johnson.* Greeneville: East Tennessee, 1901.

Jones, Janie, and Clerk, Carol. *The Devil and Miss Jones.* London: Smith Gryphon, 1993.

Jones, Katherine M. *The Plantation South.* New York: Bobbs-Merrill, 1957.

Jones, Lewis Wade. *Cold Rebellion: The South's Oligarchy in Revolt.* London: MacGibbon & Kee, 1962.

Jones, Maldwyn Allen. *American Immigration.* Chicago: University of Chicago Press, 1960.

Jones, M.E. *Gandhi Lives.* London: Hodder & Stoughton, 1948.

Jones, Pamela. *Under the City Streets.* New York: Holt, Rinehart & Winston, 1978.

Jones, Penn, Jr. *Forgive My Grief, Volume I.* Midlothian, Texas: Midlothian *Mirror*, 1966.

Jones, Richard Glyn (ed.). *Unsolved Classic True Murder Cases.* New York: Peter Bedrick Books, 1987.

Jones, Robert W. *Journalism in the United States.* New York: E.P. Dutton, 1947.

Jones, Thomas. *Lloyd George.* London: Oxford University Press, 1951.

_____. *Whitehall Diary, 1916-1930.* London: Oxford University Press, 1969.

Jones, Thomas A. *J. Wilkes Booth.* Port Tobacco, Md.: Society for the Restoration of Port Tobacco, 1955.

Jones, Virgil Carrington. *The Hatfields and the McCoys.* Chapel Hill: University of North Carolina Press, 1948.

Jones, W.F. *The Experiences of a Deputy U.S. Marshal of the Indian Territory.* Tulsa, Okla.: n.p., 1937.

Jones, Willoughby. *James Fisk, Jr.: The Life of a Green Mountain Boy.* Philadelphia: W. Flint, 1872.

_____. *The Life of James Fisk, Jr.* Cincinnati, Ohio: Union, 1872.

_____. *Weighed and Found Wanting: The Stupendous Schemes and Enterprises that Make Rich Men Poor and Poor Men Rich in a Day.* Philadelphia: W. Flint, 1872.

Jones, Winfield. *Knights of the Ku Klux Klan.* New York: Tocsin, 1941.

_____. *Story of the Ku Klux Klan.* Washington, D.C.: American Newspaper Syndicate, 1921.

Jordan, David P. *The King's Trial.* Berkeley: University of California Press, 1979.

Jordan, Winthrop D. *The White Man's Burden.* New York: Oxford University Press, 1974.

_____. *White Over Black: American Attitudes Toward the Negro, 1550-1812.* Chapel Hill: University of North Carolina Press, 1968.

Jorre, Georges. *The Soviet Union: The Land and Its People.* London: Longmans, 1961.

Joselit, Jenna W. *Our Gang: Jewish Crime and the New York Jewish Community, 1900-1940.* Bloomington: Indiana University Press, 1983.

Josephson, Matthew. *Al Smith: Hero of the Cities.* Boston: Houghton Mifflin, 1969.

_____. *Life Among the Surrealists.* New York: Holt, Rinehart & Winston, 1962.

_____. *The Politicos.* New York: Harcourt, Brace, 1938.

_____. *The President Makers.* New York: Harcourt, Brace, 1940.

_____. *The Robber Barons.* New York: Harcourt, Brace, 1934.

Josephus, Flavius. *The Jewish War and Other Selections.* trans. H. St. J. Thackeray and Ralph Marcus. New York: Twayne, 1965.

Joughin, G. Louis, and Morgan, Edmund M. *The Legacy of Sacco and Vanzetti.* New York: Harcourt, Brace, 1948.

Jouve, Nicole. *The Street Cleaner.* London: Marion Boyers, 1986.

Joyce, James Avery. *Capital Punishment, A World View.* New York: Nelson, 1962.

_____. *Justice at Work.* London: Chapman & Hall, 1952.

Joyce, Michael. *Edinburgh: The Golden Age.* London: Longmans, Green, 1951.

Joyneville, C. *Life of Alexander of Russia.* n.p., 1883.

Judas, Elizabeth. *Rasputin: Neither Devil nor Saint.* Los Angeles: Wetzel, 1942.

Judd, Denis. *Eclipse of Kings.* London: Macdonald & Jane's, 1976.

_____. *The Victorian Empire.* New York: Frederick A. Praeger, 1970.

Judge, Arthur V. *The Elizabethan Underworld.* London: George Routledge & Sons, 1930.

Judson, Horace Freeland. *Heroin Addiction in Britain.* New York: Harcourt, Brace, Jovanovich, 1974.

Judson, Katherine Berry. *Montana: The Land of Shining Mountains.* Chicago: A.C. McClurg, 1909.

Jue, George K. *Chinatown: Its History, Its People, Its Importance.* San Francisco: San Francisco Chamber of Commerce, 1951.

Juergens, George. *Joseph Pulitzer and the New York World.* Princeton, N.J.: Princeton University Press, 1966.

Jukes, Geoffrey. *The Russo-Japanese War, 1904-1905.* New York: Osprey Publishing Co., 2002.

Julian, G.W. *Political Recollections.* Chicago: Jansen, McClurg, 1884.

Jumpertz Tried and Convicted. Chicago: Norris & Hyde, 1859.

Justice, Jean. *Murder vs. Murder: The British Legal System and the A.6 Murder Case.* Paris: Olympia Press, 1964.

Juvenile Violence: A Study of the Handling of Juveniles Arrested for Crimes Against Persons in New York City, July 1, 1973-June 30, 1974. New York: Office of Children's Services, Division of Criminal Justice Services, 1976.

Kadish, S.H. (ed.). *Encyclopedia of Crime and Justice.* New York: Free Press, 1983.

Kahler, Heinz. *The Art of Rome and Her Empire.* New York: Crown, 1962.

Kahn, Albert E., and Sayers, Michael. *The Great Conspiracy.* Boston: Little, Brown, 1946.

_____. *High Treason.* New York: Hour, 1950.

Kahn, David. *The Codebreakers.* New York: Macmillan, 1967.

Kahn, E.J., Jr. *The China Hands.* New York: Viking, 1975.

_____. *Fraud.* New York: Harper & Row, 1954.

_____. *The World of Swope.* New York: Simon & Schuster, 1965.

Kahn, Judd. *Imperial San Francisco.* Lincoln: University of Nebraska Press, 1979.

Kahn, S. *Mentality and Homosexuality.* Boston: Meadow, 1937.

Kahn, Samuel. *Sing Sing Criminals.* Philadelphia: Dorrance, 1936.

Kaiser, Georg. *Gilles und Jeanne.* Potsdam, Ger.: Gustav Kiepenheuer Verlag, 1923.

Kaiser, Robert Blair. *RFK Must Die! A History of the Robert Kennedy Assassination and Its Aftermath.* New York: E.P. Dutton, 1970.

Kai-shek, Chiang. *A Summing Up at Seventy: Soviet Russia in China.* London: George C. Harrap, 1957.

Kajima Morinosuke. *Emergence of Japan as a World Power, 1895-1925.* Rutland, Vt.: Charles E. Tuttle, 1968.

Kakuzo Okakura. *The Awakening of Japan.* New York: Japan Society, 1921.

Kalb, Marvin and Bernard. *Kissinger.* Boston: Little, Brown, 1974.

Kalikar, Kakar. *Stray Glimpses of the Bapu.* Ahmedabad, India: Navajivan, 1950.

Kalven, Harry, Jr., and Zeisel, Hans. *The American Jury.* Chica-go: University of Chicago Press, 1966.

Kamau, Joseph. *Lust to Kill: The Rise and Fall of Idi Amin.* Oceanside, Calif.: Transworld, n. d.

Kameji Fukumoto. *True Story of the Secret Record of the February 26 Incident.* Tokyo: Ozei Shindun-sha, 1958.

Kamiyama Shigeo. *Theoretical Problems Concerning the Emperor System.* Tokyo: Ashi-kai, 1947.

Kane, Harnett T. *Louisiana Hayride: The American Rehearsal For Dictatorship 1928-1940.* New York: William Morrow, 1941.

Kane, Harry H. *Drugs That Enslave.* Philadelphia: P. Blakiston, 1881.

_____. *The Hypodermic Injection of Morphia.* New York: C.L. Bermingham, 1880.

_____. *Opium Smoking in America and China.* New York: G.P. Putnam's Sons, 1881.

Kaneko Harushi. *The Face of the Imperial Family.* Tokyo: Imperial Household Ministry, 1962.

Kanfer, Stefan. *A Journal of the Plague Years.* New York: Athe-neum, 1973.

Kanjia, R.K. *The Mind of Mr. Nehru.* London: George Allen & Unwin, 1960.

Kanogo, T. *Squatters and the Roots of Mau Mau, 1905-63.* London: James Currey, 1987.

Kanowitz, Leo. *Sex Roles in Law and Society.* Albuquerque: University of New Mexico Press, 1973.

_____. *Women and the Law.* Albuquerque: University of New Mexico Press, 1971.

Kantor, Seth. *The Ruby Cover-Up.* New York: Zebra Books, 1978.

_____. *Who Was Jack Ruby?* New York: Everest House, 1978.

Kaplan, David E., and Dubro, Alec. *Yakuza: The Explosive Account of Japan's Criminal Underworld.* Reading, Mass.: Addison-Wesley, 1986.

Kaplan, J.D. (ed.). *The Dialogues of Plato.* New York: Wash-ing-ton Square Press, 1963.

Kaplan, John. *Criminal Justice: Introductory Cases and Materials.* Mineola, N.Y.: Foundation Press, 1973.

_____. *The Hardest Drug: Heroin and Public Policy.* Chicago: University of Chicago Press, 1983.

_____. *Marihuana: The New Prohibition.* New York: World, 1970.

_____, and Waltz, Jon R. *The Trial of Jack Ruby.* New York: Macmillan, 1965.

Kaplan, Justin. *Lincoln Steffens: A Biography.* New York: Simon & Schuster, 1974.

Kaplow, Jeffry. *The Names of Kings: The Parisian Laboring Poor in the Eighteenth Century.* New York: Basic Books, 1972.

Kapunscinski, Ryszand. *Shah of Shahs.* New York: Vintage Books, 1992.

Kariuki, J., and Ochieng, P. *Mau Mau Detainee: The Account by a Kenya African of his Experience in Detention Camps, 1953-1960.* London: Oxford University Press, 1963.

Karlen, Delmar. *Anglo-American Criminal Justice.* Oxford: Clarendon Press, 1967.

_____. *The Citizen in Court.* New York: Holt, Rinehart & Winston, 1964.

Karlin, Arno. *Sexuality and Homosexuality.* New York: W.W. Norton, 1971.

Karmel, Roberta S. *Regulation By Prosecution.* New York: Simon & Schuster, 1982.

Karmen, A. *Crime Victims.* Belmont, Calif.: Brooks/Cole, 1984.

Karol, K.S. *Guerillas in Power.* trans. Arnold Pomerans. New York: Hill & Wang, 1970.

Karolevitz, Robert F. *Newspapering in the Old West.* Seattle, Wash.: Superior, 1965.

Karpis, Alvin, and Trent, Bill. *The Alvin Karpis Story.* New York: Coward McCann & Geoghegan, 1971.

_____, and Livesey, Robert. *On The Rock.* New York: Beaufort Books, 1980.

Karpmen, Benjamin. *Case Studies in the Psychopathology of Crime.* Washington, D.C.: Mimeotorm Press, 1933.

_____. *The Individual Criminal.* Washington, D.C.: Nervous & Mental Diseases, 1935.

_____. *The Sexual Offender and His Offenses: Etiology, Pathology, Psychodynamics, and Treatment.* New York: Julian, 1954.

Karpovich, M.M. *Imperial Russia, 1801-1917.* New York: Henry Holt, 1932.

Karraker, Cyrus H. *Piracy Was a Business.* New York: Richard R. Smith, 1953.

Karski, Jan. *Story of a Secret State.* Kingsport, Tenn.: Kingsport Press, 1944.

Kassebaum, Gene, Ward, D., and Wilner, D. *Prison Treatment and Parole Survival.* New York: John Wiley & Sons, 1971.

Kaster, Joseph (trans. and ed.). *Wings of the Falcon: Life and Thought of Ancient Egypt.* New York: Holt, Rinehart & Winston, 1968.

Katcher, Leo. *The Big Bankroll: The Life and Times of Arnold Rothstein.* New York: Harper & Brothers, 1959.

_____. *Earl Warren: A Political Biography.* New York: McGraw-Hill, 1967.

Kates, Brian. *The Murder of a Shopping Bag Lady.* New York: Harcourt, Brace, Jovanovich, 1985.

Kates, George N. *The Years Were Fat: Peking, 1933-40.* New York: Harper, 1952.

Katkin, Daniel. *The Nature of Criminal Law.* Monterey, Calif.: Brooks/Cole, 1982.

Kato, Wycliffe. *Escape from Idi Amin's Slaughterhouse.* New York: Quartet, 1989.

Katz, Herbert and Marjorie. *Museums U.S.A.* New York: Doubleday, 1965.

Katz, L., Litwin, L., and Bamberger, R. *Justice is the Crime.* Cleveland: Case Western Reserve University Press, 1972.

Katz, Leonard. *Uncle Frank: The Biography of Frank Costello.* New York: Drake, 1973.

Katz, Robert. *Days of Wrath.* New York: Doubleday, 1980.

Katz, Samuel M. *Relentless Pursuit: The DDS and the Manhunt for the Al Qaeda Terrorists.* New York: Forge, 2002.

Katz, Stanley, and Kutler, Stanley (eds.). *New Perspectives on the American Past.* Boston: Little, Brown, 1969.

Katzman, Gary. *Inside the Criminal Process.* New York: W. W. Norton, 1990.

Kauffman, Reginald Wright. *The House of Bondage.* New York: Grosset & Dunlap, 1912.

Kaufman, Beatrice, and Hennessey, Joseph (eds.). *The Letters of Alexander Woollcott.* New York: Viking Press, 1944.

Kaufman, Michael T. *The Gun.* New York: Award Books, 1974.

Kaufmann, Jacques. *L'Internationale Terroriste.* Paris: Librairie Plon, 1976.

Kaus, Gina. *Catherine, Portrait of an Empress.* New York: Viking Press, 1935.

Kavanagh, Marcus. *The Criminal and His Allies.* Indianapolis, Ind.: Bobbs-Merrill, 1928.

_____. *You Be The Judge.* Chicago: Reilly & Lee, 1929.

Keane, Fergal. *Season of Blood: The Rwandan Journey.* New York: Viking Press, 1996.

Kearns, Doris. *Lyndon Johnson and the American Dream.* New York: Harper & Row, 1976.

Kearns, Phil, and Wead, Doug. *People's Temple??People's Tomb.* New York: Logos International, 1979.

Keating, Bern. *The Flamboyant Mr. Colt.* New York: Doubleday, 1978.

_____. *Texas Rangers.* New York: Promontory Press, 1975.

Keats, John. *Howard Hughes.* New York: Random House, 1966.

_____. *You Might as Well Live.* New York: Simon & Schuster, 1970.

Kedourie, Elie. *England and the Middle East.* London: Bowes & Bowes, 1956.

Kedward, H. Roderick. *Fascism in Western Europe, 1900-1945.* New York: New York University Press, 1971.

Keeley, Leslie E. *An Essay Upon the Morphine and Opium Habit.* Dwight, Ill.: Published by Author, 1882.

_____. *The Morphine Eater; or From Bondage to Freedom.* Dwight, Ill.: C.L. Palmer, 1881.

Keene, M. Lamar. *The Psychic Mafia.* New York: Dell, 1977.

Keeps, J.L.H. *The Rise of Social Democracy in Russia.* New York: Oxford University Press, 1963.

Keeton, George Williams. *Guilty But Insane.* London: McDonald, 1961.

_____. *Lord Chancellor Jeffreys and the Stuart Cause.* London: McDonald, 1965.

Kefauver, Estes. *Crime in America.* New York: Doubleday, 1951.

_____. *In a Few Hands.* New York: Pantheon, 1965.

_____. *Second Interim Report.* Washington, D.C.: U.S. Govern-ment Printing Office, 1951.

_____. *Third Interim Report.* Washington D.C.: U.S. Government Printing Office, 1951.

_____, and Levin, Jack. *A 20th Century Congress.* New York: Duell Sloan, 1947.

Kefauver Committee Report on Organized Crime. New York: Didier, 1951.

Keil, Charles. *Urban Blues.* Chicago: University of Chicago Press, 1966.

Keilitz, Ingo, and Fulton, Junius P. *The Insanity Defense.* Wil-liamsburg, Va.: National Center for State Courts, 1984.

Kelleher, Michael, and Kelleher, C. I. *Murder Most Rare.* Westport, Conn.: Praeger, 1998.

Keller, Morton. *The Art and Politics of Thomas Nast.* New York: Oxford University Press, 1968.

_____. *In Defense of Yesterday.* New York: Coward-McCann, 1958.

_____ (ed.). *Theodore Roosevelt: A Profile.* New York: Hill & Wang, 1967.

Kelley, Clarence M. *Crime in the United States, 1976.* Washing-ton, D.C.: U.S. Government Printing Office, 1977.

Kelley, Thomas P. *Jesse James.* New York: Export, 1950.

Kelling, George L., et al. *The Kansas City Patrol Experiments: A Technical Report* Washington, D.C.: Police Foundation, 1974.

_____, et al. *The Kansas City Preventive Patrol Experiment: A Summary.* Washington, D.C.: Police Foundation, 1974.

Kellogg, Charles Flint. *National Association for the Advancement of Colored People.* Baltimore, Md.: Johns Hopkins Press, 1967.

Kellogg, Grace. *The Two Lives of Edith Wharton: The Woman and Her Work.* New York: Appleton-Century, 1965.

Kelly, Alexander. *Jack the Ripper: A Bibliography and Review of the Literature.* London: Association of Assistant Librarians, 1973.

Kelly, Charles, and Hoffman, Birney. *The Outlaw Trail.* New York: Devin-Adair, 1959.

Kelly, Edward James. *The Crime at Ford's Theatre.* Alexandria, Va.: Action, 1944.

Kelly, Florence Finch. *Flowing Stream: The Story of Fifty-Six Years in American Newspaper Life.* New York: E.P. Dutton, 1939.

Kelly, G.G. *The Gun in the Case.* Christchurch, N. Zea.: Whitcombe & Tombs, 1963.

Kelly, Jack. *On The Street.* Chicago: Henry Regnery, 1974.

Kelly, Joseph "Bunco". *Thirteen Years in the Oregon Penitentiary.* Portland, Ore.: Published by Author, 1908.

Kelly, Kitty. *His Way: The Unauthorized Biography of Frank Sinatra.* New York: Bantam, 1986.

Kelly, Michael J. *Police Chief Selection.* Washington, D.C.: Police Foundation, 1975.

Kelly, Robert J. (ed.). *Organized Crime: An International Perspec-tive.* Totowa, N.J.: Rowman & Littlefield, 1986.

Kelly, Thomas P. *Jesse James, His Life and Death.* New York: Export, 1950.

Kelly, Vince. *The Charge is Murder.* London: Angus & Robert-son, 1965.

Kemble, James. *Napolean Immortal.* London: John Murray, 1959.

Kemechey, L. *Il Duce.* trans. Magda Vamos. London: Williams & Norgate, 1930.

Kemler, Edgar. *The Irreverant Mr. Menken.* Boston: Little, Brown, 1950.

Kemp, P.H., and Lloyd, Christopher. *The Brethren of the Coast: Buccaneers in the South Seas.* New York: St. Martin's Press, 1961.

Kemp, T. *Prostitution: An Investigation of its Causes, Especially with Regard to Hereditary Factors.* trans. E.M. Werner. New York: Stechert, 1936.

Kempe, Ruth and C. Henry. *Child Abuse.* London: Fontana/Open Books, 1978.

Kempner, Robert M.W. *Eichmann und Komplizen.* Stuttgart, Ger.: Europa-Verlag AG, 1961.

Kempton, Murray. *Part of Our Time: Some Monuments and Ruins of the Thirties.* New York: Simon & Schuster, 1955.

Kendall, John S. *History of New Orleans.* New York: Lewis, 1922.

Kendall, L. *The Phantom Prince: My Life With Ted Bundy.* Seattle, Wash.: Madrona, 1981.

Keniston, Kenneth. *The Uncommitted: Alienated Youth in Ameri-can Society.* New York: Dell, 1967.

_____. *Youth and Dissent: The Rise of the New Opposition.* New York: Harcourt Brace Jovanovich, 1971.

Ken Kurigara. *The Emperor: Notes of the Reign of Hirohito.* Tokyo: Yushin-do Bunka Shinsho, 1955.

Kennan, George. *American Diplomacy: 1900-1950.* Chicago: New American Library, 1951.

_____. *American Foreign Policy: 1900-1950.* Chicago: University of Chicago Press, 1951.

_____. *Decision to Intervene.* Princeton, N.J.: Princeton Univer-sity Press, 1958.

_____. *E.H. Harriman: A Biography.* Boston: Houghton Mifflin, 1922.

_____. *Russia Leaves the War.* Princeton, N.J.: Princeton University Press, 1956.

_____. *Russia and the West Under Lenin and Stalin.* Boston: Little, Brown, 1961.

_____. *Siberia and the Exile System.* New York: Century, 1891.

_____. *Soviet-American Relations: The Decision to Intervene.* Princeton, N.J.: Princeton University Press, 1958.

_____. *Soviet-American Relations: Russia Leaves the War.* Prince-ton, N.J.: Princeton University Press, 1956.

Kennaugh, Robert. *Contemporary Murder.* Johannesburg, S. Afri.: Hugh Keartland, 1968.

Kennedy, Captain. *Jesse James' Mysterious Warning: or, the Raid That Almost Failed.* Baltimore: I. & M. Ottenheimer, 1915.

_____. *Jesse James' Thrilling Raid: or the Daylight Robbery of the Harkness Bank.* Baltimore: I. & M. Ottenheimer, 1913.

_____. *Jesse James' Wild Leap: or, the Hold-Up of the Through Express.* Baltimore: I. & M. Ottenheimer, 1915.

Kennedy Confidential. Washington, D.C.: Metro, 1969.

Kennedy, D. *Islands of White: Settler Society and Culture in Kenya and Southern Rhodesia, 1890-1939.* Durham, N.C.: Duke University Press, 1987.

Kennedy, Dolores. *William Heirens: His Day in Court.* Chicago: Bonus Books, 1991.

_____, and Nolin, Robert. *On a Killing Day.* Chicago: Bonus Books, 1992.

Kennedy, John. *Fire Investigation.* Chicago: Investigations Institute, 1977.

Kennedy, John F. *The Burden and the Glory.* New York: Harper & Row, 1964.

_____. *Profiles in Courage.* New York: Harper & Brothers, 1956.

Kennedy, Lionel, and Parker, Thomas. *An Official Report of the Trials of Sundry Negroes Charged with an Attempt to Raise an Insurrection in the State of South Carolina.* Charleston, S.C.: Published by Authors, 1822.

Kennedy, Ludovic. *The Airman and the Carpenter.* New York: Viking Penguin, 1985.

_____. *Ten Rillington Place.* New York: Simon & Schuster, 1961.

Kennedy, Malcolm D. *A History of Japan*. London: Weidenfeld & Nicolson, 1963.
_____. *The Problem of Japan*. London: Nisbet, 1935.
_____. *Some Aspects of Japan and Her Defense Forces*. Kobe, Japan: J.L. Thompson, 1928.
Kennedy, Robert F. *The Enemy Within*. New York: Popular Library, 1960.
_____. *Thirteen Days: A Memoir of the Cuban Missle Crisis*. New York: New American Library, 1969.
Kennedy, Rose Fitzgerald. *Times to Remember.* Garden City, N.Y.: Doubleday, 1974.
Kennedy, William Sloane. *Italy in Chains*. West Yarmouth, Mass.: Stonecroft Press, 1927.
Kennett, Lee, and Anderson, James Laverne. *The Gun in Ameri-ca*. Westport, Conn.: Greenwood Press, 1975.
Kenney, John P. *The California Police*. Springfield, Ill.: Charles C. Thomas, 1964.
_____, and Pursuit, Dan G. *Police Work with Juveniles and the Administration of Juvenile Justice*. Springfield, Ill.: Charles C. Thomas, 1954.
Kenny, C.S. *Outlines of Criminal Law.* London: Cambridge University Press, 1947.
Kent, Arthur. *The Death Doctors*. London: New English Library, 1975.
Kent-Hughes, W.S. *Slaves of the Samurai*. Melbourne, Aus.: Ramsey Ware, 1946.
Kentucky Legislative Research Commission. *Capital Punishment*. Frankfort: State of Kentucky, 1965.
Kenworthy, Aubrey Saint. *The Tiger of Malaya: The Inside Story of the Japanese Atrocities*. New York: Exposition Press, 1953.
Kenyatta, J. *Facing Mt. Kenya: The Tribal Life of the Gikuyu*. New York: Vintage Books, 1962.
_____. *Suffering Without Bitterness: The Founding of the Kenya Nation*. Nairobi, Kenya: East African, 1968.
Kenyon, F.W. *The Naked Sword: The Story of Lucrezia Borgia*. New York: Dodd, Mead, 1968.
Kenyon, John Philippe. *The Popish Plot*. New York: St. Mar-tin's Press, 1972.
Keogh, James Edward. *Burglarproof.* New York: McGraw-Hill, 1976.
Keppel, Robert. *The Riverman*. New York: Pocket Books, 1995.
_____. *Serial Murder*. Cincinnati, Ohio: Anderson Publishing, 1989.
Kerby, Phil. *With Honor and Purpose*. New York: St. Martin's Press, 1998.
Kerensky, Alexander. *The Catastrophe: Kerensky's Own Story.* New York: D. Appleton, 1927.
_____. *The Crucifixion of Liberty.* New York: John Day, 1934
_____, and Bulygin, Paul. *The Murder of the Romanovs*. London: Hutchinson, 1935.
Kern, Erich. *Dance of Death*. New York: Charles Scribner's Sons, 1951.
Kerner, Dieter, Dalchow, Johannes, and Duda, Gunther. *Mozart's Tod: 1791-1971*. Pahl, Verlag Hohe Warte Bebenberg, 1971.
Kerner, Otto. *Supplemental Studies for the National Advisory Commission on Civil Disorders*. Washington, D.C.: U.S. Government Printing Office, 1968.
Kerner Committee. *Report of the National Advisory Commission on Civil Disorders*. New York: E.P. Dutton, 1968.
Kerns, Phil. *People's Temple, People's Tomb.* Plainfield, N.J.: Logos, 1979.
Kerry, The Earl of (ed.). *The Secret of the Coup D'Etat*. New York: G.P. Putnam's Sons, 1924.
Kershaw, Alister. *A History of the Guillotine*. London: J. Calder, 1958.
_____. *Murder In France*. London: Constable, 1955.
Kerzhentsev, P. *Life of Lenin*. New York: International, 1939.
Kessler, Count Harry. *Walther Rathenau: His Life and Work*. New York: Harcourt, Brace, 1930.
Ketchiva, Paul. *The Devil's Playground*. London: Sampson Low, 1934.
Keup, Wolfram (ed.). *Drug Abuse: Current Concepts and Research*. Springfield, Ill.: Charles C. Thomas, 1972.
Keve, Paul W. *Prison Life and Human Worth*. Minneapolis: University of Minnesota Press, 1974.
Kevorkian, Jack. *Medical Research and the Death Penalty.* New York: Vantage Press, 1960.
Keyes, Daniel. *Unveiling Claudia*. New York: Bantam, 1986.
Keyes, Edward. *The Michigan Murders*. New York: Thomas Y. Crowell, 1976.
Keyes, Harold C. *Tales of the Secret Service*. Cleveland: Britton Gardner, 1927.
Keylin, Arleen, and DeMirjian, Arto, Jr. *Crime: As Reported by the New York Times*. New York: Arno Press, 1976.
_____. *The Fabulous Fifties*. New York: Arno Press, 1978.
Khaled, Leila. *Autobiography*. London: Hodder & Stoughton, 1973.
_____. *My People Shall Live*. London: Hodder & Stoughton, 1973.
Khalaf, Samir. *Prostitution in a Changing Society*. Beirut, Leb.: Khayats, 1965.
Khalil, Mohammed. *The Arab States and the Arab League*. Beirut, Leb.: Khayat, 1962.
Khouri, Fred J. *The Arab-Israeli Dilemma*. Syracuse, N.Y.: Syracuse University Press, 1968.
Kibera, S. *Voices in the Dark*. Nairobi, Kenya: East African, 1970.
Kidd, W.R. *Police Interrogation*. New York: Basuino, 1940.
Kidder, T. *The Road to Yuba City: A Journey Into the Juan Corona Murders*. New York: Doubleday, 1974.
Kidner, John. *Grimaldi: Contract Killer.* Washington, D.C.: Acropolis Books, 1976.
Kido Koichi. *Additional Writings*. Tokyo: Tokyo University Press, 1966.
_____. *Diary of Koichi Kido*. Tokyo: Tokyo University Press, 1966.
Kiefer, Otto. *Sexual Life in Ancient Rome*. London: Routledge & Kegan Paul, 1934.
Kiernan, Thomas. *Yasir Arafat: The Man and the Myth*. New York: W. W. Norton, 1976.
Kiester, Edwin. *Crimes With No Victims*. New York: Alliance for a Safer New York, 1972.
Kilbracken, Lord. *Van Meegeren: Master Forger.* New York: Charles Scribner's Sons, 1967.
Kilduff, Marshall, and Javers, Ron. *The Suicide Cult*. New York: Bantam Books, 1978.
Kilgallen, Dorothy. *Murder One*. New York: Random House, 1967.
Killinger, George G., and Cromwell, Paul F., Jr. (eds.). *Penology: The Evolution of Corrections in America*. St. Paul, Minn.: West, 1973.
Kilroe, Edwin P. *Saint Tammany and the Origin of the Society of Tammany or Columbian Order in the City of New York*. New York: M.B. Brown, 1913.
Kilroy, Jim, and Stewart, Bob. *Sacrifice*. Dallas, Tex.: Word Publishing, 1990.
Kimball, Nell. *Her Life as an American Madam, by Herself.* New York: Macmillan, 1970.
Kimeldorf, Howard. *Reds or Rackets? The Making of Radical and Conservative Unions on the Waterfront*. Berkeley: University of California Press, 1988.
Kimmel, Stanley. *The Mad Booths of Maryland*. Indianapolis, Ind.: Bobbs-Merrill, 1940.
_____. *Mr. Lincoln's Washington*. New York: Bramhall House, 1957.
Kimmens, A.C. (ed.). *Tales of Hashish*. New York: William Morrow, 1977.
Kinberg, Olof. *Basic Problems of Criminology*. Copenhagen: Levin & Munkgaard, 1935.
Kinchen, Oscar A. *Confederate Operations in Canada and the North*. North Quincy, Mass.: Christopher, 1970.
Kind, Stewart. *Science Against Crime*. New York: Doubleday, 1972.
Kinder, Gary. *Victim: The Other Side of Murder.* New York: Delacorte Press, 1982.
Kindleberger, Charles P. *Manias, Panics and Crashes*. New York: Basic Books, 1978.
_____. *The World in Depression: 1929-1939*. Berkeley: University of California Press, 1973.
King, Coretta Scott. *My Life With Martin Luther King, Jr.* New York: Holt, Rinehart & Winston, 1969.
King, Francis. *The Magical World of Aleister Crowley.* New York: Coward, McCann & Geoghegan, 1977.
King, Gary. *Blood Lust: Portrait of a Serial Killer*. New York: Oynx, 1992.
King, Grace. *New Orleans: The Place and the People*. New York: Macmillan, 1937.
King, Gregory. *The Fate of the Romanovs*. New York: Wiley, 2003.
King, Harry. *Box Man*. New York: Harper & Row, 1972.
King, Leonard. *A History of Babylon*. New York: Frederick A. Stokes, 1915.
King, Lester S. *The Medical World of the Eighteenth Century*. Chicago: University of Chicago Press, 1958.
King, M. *Bail or Custody*. London: Cobden Trust, 1971.
King, P.D. *Law and Society in the Visigothic Kingdom*. Cam-bridge, Eng.: Cambridge University Press, 1972.
King, Rosa E. *Tempest Over Mexico: A Personal Chronicle*. New York: Methuen, 1936.
King, Rufus. *The Drug Hang-Up: America's Fifty Year Folly.* New York: W.W. Norton, 1972.
_____. *Gambling and Organized Crime*. Washington, D.C.: Public Affairs Press, 1969.
King, Veronica and Paul. *Problems of Modern American Crime*. London: Heath Cranton, 1924.
King-Hall, Sir Stephen. *Three Dictators*. London: Faber & Faber, 1964.
Kingsmill, Joseph. *Chapters on Prisons and Prisoners and the Prevention of Crime*. London: Longman, Brown & Green, 1854.
_____. *A History of the Guillotine*. New York: Taplinger, 1959.
Kingston, Charles. *The Bench & The Dock*. London: Stanley Paul, 1925.
_____. *Dramatic Days At the Old Bailey*. New York: Frederick A. Stokes, 1927.
_____. *Enemies of Society*. London: Stanley Paul, 1927.
_____. *Famous Judges and Famous Trials*. New York: Frederick A. Stokes, 1923.
_____. *A Gallery of Rogues*. London: Stanley Paul, 1924.
_____. *The Judges and the Judged*. London: John Lane, Bodley Head, 1926.
_____. *Law-Breakers*. London: John Lane, Bodley Head, 1930.
_____. *Remarkable Rogues: Some Notable Criminals of Europe and America*. New York: John Lane, 1921.
_____. *Rogues and Adventuresses*. London: John Lane, Bodley Head, 1928.
Kinney, Jay, and Mavrides, Paul. *Cover-Up Lowdown*. San Fransico: Rip Off Press, 1977.
Kinsey, Alfred C., et al. *Sexual Behavior in the Human Female*. London: Saunders, 1953.
_____, Pomeroy, W.B., and Martin, C.E. *Sexual Behavior in the Human Male*. London: Saunders, 1948.
Kinsley, David R. *The Sword and the Flute: Kali and Krasna*. Berkley: University of California Press, 1978.
Kinsley, Philip. *The Chicago Tribune: Its First Hundred Years*. Chicago: Chicago *Tribune*, 1943.
Kinzer, Stephen. *All the Shah's Men: The Hidden Story of the CIA's Coup in Iran*. New York: Wiley, 2003.
Kiplinger, Austin H., and Knight A. *Washington Now.* New York: Harper & Row, 1975.
Kiplinger, W. M. *Washington is Like That*. New York: Harper & Brothers, 1942.
Kipnis, Ira. *The American Socialist Movement, 1897-1912*. New York: Columbia University Press, 1952.
Kirby, Cecil, and Renner, Thomas C. *Mafia Enforcer.* New York: Villard Books, 1987.
Kirby, S. Woodburn, et al. *The War Against Japan*. London: HMSO, 1957.
Kirchheimer, Otto. *Political Justice*. Princeton, N.J.: Princeton University Press, 1961.
Kirk, George E. *Contemporary Arab Politics*. New York: Frederick A. Praeger, 1961.
_____. *The Middle East, 1945-50*. London: Oxford, 1954.
_____. *The Middle East in the War.* London: Oxford, 1952.
_____. *A Short History of the Middle East*. New York: Frederick A. Praeger, 1960.
Kirk, Paul L., and Bradford, L.W. *The Crime Laboratory.* Springfield, Ill.: C.C. Thomas, 1965.
_____. *Fire Investigation??Including Fire-Related Phenomena: Arson, Explosion, Asphyxiation*. New York: John Wiley & Sons, 1969.
Kirkbride, Sir Alec. *A Crackle of Thorns*. London: John Murray, 1956.
Kirkham, James F. *Assassination and Political Violence*. Washing-ton, D.C.: U.S. Goverment Printing Office, 1969.
Kirkland, Joseph. *The Story of Chicago*. Chicago: Dibble, 1892.
Kirkpatrick, Clifford. *Capital Punishment*. Philadelphia: Philadel-phia Committee on Philanthropic Labor, 1945.
Kirkpatrick, Ernest E. *Crime's Paradise: The Authentic Inside Story of the Urschel Kidnapping*. San Antonio, Tex.: Naylor, 1934.

_____. *Voices from Alcatraz.* San Antonio, Tex.: Naylor, 1947.
Kirkpatrick, Sir Ivone. *Mussolini: Study of a Demagogue.* Lon-don: Odhams Books, 1964.
_____. *The Inner Circle.* London: Macmillan, 1959.
Kirkpatrick, Lyman B., Jr. *The Real CIA.* New York: Macmillan, 1968.
_____. *The U.S. Intelligence Community.* New York: Hill & Wang, 1973.
Kirkpatrick, Sidney D. *A Cast of Killers.* New York: E.P. Dutton, 1986.
Kirkwood, James. *American Grotesque: An Account of the Clay Shaw-Jim Garrison Affair in the City of New Orleans.* New York: Simon & Schuster, 1970.
Kirpalani, K.R. *Tagore, Gandhi and Nehru.* Bombay, India: Hind Kitabs, 1947.
Kisch, C.H. *The Portuguese Banknote Case.* New York: Macmil-lan, 1932.
Kitchin, John. *Jurisdictions.* London: J. Place, 1663.
Kitson, Frank. *Bunch of Five.* London: Faber & Faber, 1977.
_____. *Gangs and Counter-Gangs.* London: Barrie & Rockliffe, 1960.
Kittredge, George Lyman. *Witchcraft in Old and New England.* Cambridge, Mass.: Harvard University Press, 1929.
Kittrel, Norman G. *Governors Who Have Been and Other Public Men of Texas.* Houston, Texas: Dealy-Adey-Elgin, 1921.
Kittrie, Nicholas N. *The Right to be Different: Deviance and Enforced Therapy.* Baltimore: Johns Hopkins Press, 1971.
Klare, Hugh J. *Anatomy of Prison.* London: Hutchinson, 1960.
_____ (ed.). *Changing Concepts in Crime and Its Treatment.* Elmsford, N.Y.: Pergamon Press, 1966.
Klasne, William. *Street Cops.* Englewood Cliffs, N.J.: Prentice-Hall, 1980.
Klasner, Lily. *My Girlhood Among Outlaws.* Tucson: University of Arizona Press, 1972.
Klaus, Samuel (ed.). *The Molineux Case.* New York: Alfred A. Knopf, 1929.
Klausner, Lawrence D. *Son of Sam.* New York: McGraw-Hill, 1981.
Klebba, A. Joan. *Homicide Trends in the United States, 1900-1974.* Washington, D.C.: U.S. Government Printing Office, 1975.
Klein, Alexander (ed.). *Double Dealers.* Philadelphia and New York: J.B. Lippincott, 1958.
_____ (ed.). *The Empire City: A Treasury of New York.* New York: Rinehart, 1955.
_____. *Grand Deception.* New York: J.B. Lippincott, 1955.
Klein, Henry H. *Sacrificed.* New York: Isaac Goldman, 1927.
Klein, Herbert T. *The Police.* New York: Crown, 1968.
Klein, Malcolm W. *Juvenile Gangs in Context.* Englewood Cliffs, N.J.: Prentice-Hall, 1967.
_____ (ed.). *The Juvenile Justice System.* Beverly Hills, Calif.: Sage, 1976.
_____. *Street Gangs and Street Workers.* Englewood Cliffs, N.J.: Prentice-Hall, 1971.
Klein, Maury. *Life and Times of Jay Gould.* Baltimore: Johns Hopkins University Press, 1986.
Klein, P. *Prison Methods in New York State.* New York: Colum-bia University Press, 1920.
Kleindienst, Richard. *Justice: The Memoirs of an Attorney General.* Ottawa, Ill.: Jameson, 1985.
Klement, Frank L. *The Copperheads in the Middle West.* Chicago: University of Chicago Press, 1960.
Klette, Ernest. *The Crimson Trail of Joaquin Murieta.* Los Angeles: Wetzel, 1928.
Klinefelter, W. *Sherlock Holmes in Portrait and Profile.* Syracuse, N.Y.: Syracuse University Press, 1963.
Kling, Samuel G. *Sexual Behavior and the Law.* New York: Bernard Geis, 1965.
Klinghoffer, Arthur J. *The International Dimension of Genocide in Rwanda.* New York: New York University Press, 1998.
Klockars, Carl B. *The Professional Fence.* New York: Free Press, 1974.
Kluchevsky, V.O. *History of Russia.* trans. C.J. Hogarth. New York: Russell & Russell, 1960.
_____. *Peter the Great.* New York: E.P. Dutton, 1963.
Kluger, Richard. *Simple Justice.* New York: Alfred A. Knopf, 1975.
Klurfeld, Herman. *Winchell: His Life and Times.* New York: Frederick A. Praeger, 1976.
Knapp, Arthur May. *Feudal and Modern Japan.* Yokohama, Japan: Kelly & Walsh, 1906.
Knapp, Whitman. *Knapp Commission Report on Police Corrup-tion.* New York: George Braziller, 1972.
Knappen, M.M. *Tudor Puritanism.* Chicago: University of Chicago Press, 1939.
Knappman, Edward W. (ed.). *Watergate and the White House.* New York: Facts on File, 1973.
Kneeland, George J. *Commercialized Prostitution in New York City.* New York: Century, 1913.
Knieriem, August von. *The Nuremberg Trials.* Chicago: Henry Regnery, 1959.
Knight, Edward. *Wild Bill Hickok.* Franklin, N.H.: Hillside Press, 1959.
Knight, Janet M. *Three Assassinations.* New York: Fonf, 1980.
Knight, Oliver. *Fort Worth: Outpost on the Trinity.* Norman: University of Oklahoma Press, 1953.
Knight, Robert Edward Lee. *Industrial Relations in the San Francisco Bay Area, 1900-1918.* Berkeley: University of California Press, 1960.
Knight, Stephen. *The Brotherhood The Secret World of the Freemasons.* London: Granada, 1984.
_____. *The Final Solution: Jack the Ripper.* New York: David McKay, 1976.
Knight, Thomas A. *The Strange Disappearance of William Morgan.* Becksville, Ohio: Published by Author, 1932.
Knott, George H. (ed.). *Trial of William Palmer.* London: W. Hodge, 1912.
Knowles, Graham. *Bomb Security Guide.* Los Angeles: Security World, 1976.
Knowles, Horace (ed.). *Gentlemen, Scholars and Scoundrels.* New York: Harper & Brothers, 1959.
Knowles, Leonard. *Court of Drama: Famous Truals at Lewes Assizes.* London: John Long, 1966.
Knox, Bill. *Court of Murder: Famous Trials at Glasgow High Court.* London: John Long, 1968.
Knox, John. *Works.* Edinburgh, Scot.: James Thin, 1895.
Knox, Thomas W. *Underground, or Life Below the Surface.* Hartford, Conn.: J.B. Burr, Hyde, 1873.
Knudten, Richard D. *Crime in a Complex Society: An Introduction to Criminology.* New York: Dorsey Press, 1970.
_____ (ed.). *Criminal Controversies.* New York: Appleton-Century-Crofts, 1968.
Kobetz, Richard W. *The Police Role and Juvenile Delinquency.* Gaithersburg, Md.: IACP, 1971.
_____, and Cooper, H.H.A. *Target Terrorism: Providing Protective Services.* Gaithersburg, Md.: International Association of Chiefs of Police, 1978.
Kobler, John. *Ardent Spirits: The Rise and Fall of Prohibition.* New York: G.P. Putnam's Sons, 1973.
_____. *Capone: The Life and World of Al Capone.* New York: G.P. Putnam's Sons, 1971.
_____. *Some Like It Gory.* New York: Dodd, Mead, 1940.
Kobre, Sidney. *The Development of American Journalism.* Dubuque, Iowa: William C. Brown, 1972.
_____. *The Yellow Press and Gilded Age Journalism.* Tallahassee: Florida State University, 1964.
Kobylinsky, Colonel Eugene. *The Last Days of the Romanovs.* London: Thornton Butterworth, 1920.
Koch, Peter, and Hermann, Kai. *Assault at Mogadishu.* London: Corgi Books, 1977.
Kochan, Lionel. *The Making of Modern Russia.* London: Jonathan Cape, 1962.
Koen, Ross Y. *The China Lobby in American Politics.* New York: Macmillan, 1960.
Koenigberg, Moses. *King News:?An Autobiography.* New York: Frederick A. Stokes, 1941.
Kofoed, Jack. *Moon Over Miami.* New York: Random House, 1955.
Kogan, Herman, and Wendt, Lloyd. *Chicago: A Pictorial History.* New York: E.P. Dutton, 1958.
_____. *The First Century: The Chicago Bar Association, 1874-1974.* Chicago: Rand-McNally, 1974
_____ and Rick. *Yesterday's Chicago.* Miami, Fla.: E.A. Seemann, 1976.
Kogan, Rick, and Possley, Maurice. *Everybody Pays: Two Men, One Murder and the Price of Truth.* New York: Berkley Publishing Group, 2002.
Kogon, Eugen. *The Theory and Practice of Hell.* trans. Heinz Norden. London: Secker & Warburg, 1950.
Kohl, James, and Litt, John. *Urban Guerrilla Warfare in Latin America.* Cambridge, Mass.: MIT Press, 1974.
Kohlmeier, Louis. *The Regulators.* New York: Harper & Row, 1969.
Kohlsaat, H.H. *From McKinley to Harding: Personal Recollections of Our Presidents.* New York: Charles Scribner's Sons, 1923.
Kokovtsov, V.N. *Out of My Past.* Stanford, Calif.: Stanford University Press, 1933.
Kolarik, Gera-Lind, and Klatt, Wayne. *Freed to Kill.* Chicago: Chicago Review Press, 1990.
Kolb, Lawrence. *Drug Addiction: A Medical Problem.* Springfield, Ill.: Charles C. Thomas, 1962.
Kolko, Gabriel. *The Politics of War.* New York: Random House, 1968.
_____. *Wealth and Power in America: An Analysis of Social Class and Income Distribution.* New York: Frederick A. Praeger, 1962.
Koller, Larry (ed.). *The American Gun.* New York: Madison Books, 1961.
Komatsu Isao. *The Japanese People: Origins of the People and the Language.* Tokyo: Kokusai Bunka Shinkokai, 1962.
Konefsky, Samuel J. *Chief Justice Stone and the Supreme Court.* New York: Macmillan, 1945.
_____. *The Legacy of Holmes and Brandeis.* New York: Collier Books, 1961.
Konig, David Thomas. *Law and Society in Puritan Massachusetts, Essex County, 1629-1692.* Chapel Hill: University of North Carolina Press, 1979.
Konopka, Gisela. *The Adolescent Girl in Conflict.* Englewood Cliffs, N.J.: Prentice-Hall, 1966.
Konoye Fumimaro. *The Konoye Diary.* Tokyo: Kyodo Press, 1968.
_____. *First Amendment Freedoms.* Ithaca, N.Y.: Cornell University Press, 1963.
Koral, Mark. *The Zionist Conspiracy Behind the President Kennedy Assassination.* Rochester, N.Y.: Published by Author, 1976.
Korn, Richard R., and McCorkle, Lloyd W. *Criminology and Penology.* New York: Henry Holt, 1959.
Korngold, R. *The Last Years of Napoleon.* London: Victor Gollancz, 1960.
Kornilov, Alexander. *Modern Russian History.* New York: Alfred A. Knopf, 1952.
Kornitzer, Bela. *The Real Nixon.* New York: Rand-McNally, 1960.
Kostov, Vladimir, and Reynolds, Ben. *The Bulgarian Umbrella: The Soviet Direction and Operations of the Bulgarian Secret Service in Europe.* New York: Palgrave Macmillan, 1988.
Koszyk, K. *Die Deutsche Presse im 19. Jahrhundert.* Berlin: Colloquium, 1966.
_____. *Die Deutsche Presse 1914-1945.* Berlin: Colloquium, 1972.
Koukoules, P. *The Private Lives of the Byzantines.* Athens, Gr.: n.p., 1947.
Kouwenhoven, John A. *Adventures of America, 1857-1900.* New York: Harper & Brothers, 1938.
_____. *The Columbia Historical Portrait of New York.* Garden City, N.Y.: Doubleday, 1953.
Kovalevski, M.M. *Russian Political Institutions.* Chicago: University of Chicago Press, 1902.
Koyama Itoko. *Nagako, Empress of Japan.* New York: John Day, 1958.
Kraemer, William, et al. *The Normal and Abnormal Love of Children.* Kansas City: Sheed Andrews & McMeel, 1976.
Krafft-Ebing, Richard von. *Psychopathia Sexualis.* New York: G.P. Putnam's Sons, 1965.
Kraines, Oscar. *Government and Politics in Israel.* Boston: Houghton Mifflin, 1961.
Kramarz, Joachim. *Stauffenberg: The Life and Death of an Officer.* trans. R.H. Barry. London: Andr Deutsch, 1967.
Kramer, Caspar J., Jr. (ed.). *The Complete Works of Horace.* New York: Modern Library, 1936.
Kramer, Heinrich, and Sprenger, James. *Malleus Malificarum.* New York: Dover, 1971.
Kramer, Martin S. *Hezbollah's Vision of the West.* Washington, D. C.: Washington Institute for Near East Policy, 1989.
Kramer, Noah Samuel. *History Begins at Sumer.* Garden City, N.Y.: Doubleday, 1959.

_____ (ed.). *Mythologies of the Ancient World.* New York: Doubleday Anchor, 1961.

_____. *Sumerian Mythology.* New York: Harper, 1961.

Krannhals, Hanns von. *Der Warschauer Aufstand 1944.* Frankfurt, Ger.: Bernard & Graefe Verlag fr Wehrwesen, 1962.

Kraus, Michael. *The Atlantic Civilization: Eighteenth Century Origins.* Ithaca, N.Y.: Cornell University Press, 1949.

_____. *A History of American History.* New York: Farrar & Rinehart, 1937.

_____. *Immigration: The American Mosaic.* Princeton, N.J.: Princeton University Press, 1966.

_____. *Intercolonial Aspects of American Culture on the Eve of the Revolution.* New York: Columbia University Press, 1928.

_____. *The United States to 1865.* Ann Arbor: University of Michigan Press, 1959.

Krause, Charles. *Guyana Massacre.* New York: Berkeley, 1978.

Krausse, Alexis. *Russia in Asia, 1558-1899.* New York: Henry Holt, 1900.

Kravchinski, S.M. *Russian Under the Tsars.* New York: Charles Scribner's Sons, 1885.

_____. *Underground Russia.* New York: Charles Scribner's Sons, 1883.

Krebs, Albert. *Fritz-Dietlof Graf von der Schulenburg.* Hamburg, Ger.: Leibnitz, 1964.

_____. *Tendenzen und Gestalten der NSDAP.* Stuttgart, Ger.: Deutsche Verlagsanstalt, 1959.

Krehbiel, Henry Edward. *Mozart: The Man and the Artist Revealed in His Own Words.* New York: Dover, 1965.

Kreighbaum, Hillier. *Pressures on the Press.* New York: Thomas Y. Crowell, 1972.

Krippner, S. *Song of the Siren.* New York: Harper & Row, 1975.

Krisberg, Barry. *Crime and Privilege.* Englewood Cliffs, N.J.: Prentice-Hall, 1975.

Krivich, Mikhail, and Olgin, Olgert. *Comrade Chikatilo.* Fort Lee, N. J.: Barricade Books, 1993.

Krivitsky, Walter. *I Was Stalin's Agent.* Bristol, Eng.: Right Book Club, 1940.

Krock, Arthur. *In the Nation: 1932-1966.* New York: McGraw-Hill, 1966.

Kroll, Harry Harrison. *Rogue's Company: A Novel of John Murrell.* Indianapolis, Ind.: Bobbs-Merrill, 1943.

Kronenberger, Louis. *No Whippings, No Gold Watches.* Boston: Atlantic, Little Brown, 1970.

Kroninger, Robert H. *Sarah and the Senator.* Berkeley, Calif.: Howell-North, 1964.

Krooss, Herman E. (ed.). *Documentary History of Banking and Currency in the United States.* New York: Chelsea House, 1969.

Kropotkin, Piotr A. *Conquest of Bread.* New York: G.P. Put-nam's Sons, 1907.

_____. *In Russian and French Prisons.* London: Ward & Down-ey, 1887.

_____. *Memoirs of a Revolutionist.* Boston: Houghton Mifflin, 1930.

Krummer, R. *Rasputin ein Werkzeug der Juden.* Berlin: n.p., 1939.

Krupskaya, N.K. *Izbrannie Pedagogicheskie Proizvedeniya.* Moscow: Izdatelstvo, Akademii Pedagogicheskikh Nauk, 1955.

_____. *O Lenine: Sbornik Statei.* Moscow: Gosudarstvennoe Izdatelstvo, 1960.

_____. *Vospominaniya o Lenine.* Moscow: Partizdat, 1933.

Khrushchev, Nikita Sergeevich. *Khrushchev Remembers.* trans. Strobe Talbott. Boston: Little, Brown, 1970.

Krutch, Joseph Wood. *The Modern Temper.* New York: Harcourt, Brace, 1929.

_____. *More Lives Than One.* New York: William Sloan, 1962.

K.S. *Agent in Italy.* London: Hutchinson, 1943.

Kschessinska, Mathilde. *Dancing in Petersburg.* trans. Arnold Haskel. Garden City, N.Y.: Doubleday, 1961.

Kubizek, August. *Young Hitler: The Story of Our Friendship.* Maidstone, Eng.: Mann, 1973.

Kucherow, Samuel. *Courts, Lawyers, and Trials under the Last Three Tsars.* New York: Frederick A. Praeger, 1953.

Kuczynski, Jurgen. *The Rise of the Working Class.* New York: McGraw-Hill, 1967.

Kuebert, Hans. *Zauberwahn, die Greuel der Inquisition und Hexenprozesse.* Munich: Buchhandlung Nationalverein, 1913.

Kugel, Yerachmiel, and Gruenberg, Gladys W. *International Payoffs: Dilemma for Business.* Lexington, Mass.: Lexington Books, 1977.

Kugler, Franz Theodor. *Life of Frederick the Great.* trans. E.A. Moriarty. New York: George Routledge & Sons, 1877.

Kuhn, Thomas S. *The Structure of Scientific Revolutions.* Chicago: University of Chicago Press, 1962.

Kuhne, F. *The Finger Print Instructor.* New York: Munn, 1942.

Kunhardt, Dorothy and Philip, Jr. *Twenty Days.* New York: Castle Books, 1965.

Kunnes, Richard. *The American Heroin Empire.* New York: Dodd, Mead, 1972.

Kunstler, William M. *Beyond A Reasonable Doubt? The Original Trial of Caryl Chessman.* New York: William Morrow, 1961.

_____. *The Case for Courage.* New York: William Morrow, 1962.

_____. *First Degree.* New York: Ocean Press, 1960.

_____. *The Minister and the Choir Singer.* New York: William Morrow, 1964.

Kuper, Leo. *Genocide: Its Political Use in the Twentieth Century.* New Haven, Conn.: Yale University Press, 1981.

Kupperman, Robert, and Trent, Darrell (eds.). *Terrorism: Threat, Reality, Response.* Stanford, Calif.: Hoover Institution Press, 1979.

Kurenberg, Joachim von. *The Kaiser.* trans. Russell and Hagen. New York: Simon & Schuster, 1955.

Kurland, Gerald. *Clarence Darrow, Attorney for the Damned.* Charlotteville, N.Y.: SamHar Press, 1972.

Kurland, Philip. *The Constitution and the Warren Court.* Chicago: University of Chicago Press, 1970.

_____. *Supreme Court Review.* Chicago: University of Chicago Law School, 1960.

Kurth, Ann. *Prescriptions: Murder.* New York: Signet, 1976.

Kurtz, Harold. *The Empress Eugnie, 1826-1920.* London: Hamish Hamilton, 1964.

Kurtz, Michael L. *Crime of the Century: The Kennedy Assassination From a Historian's Perspective.* Knoxville: University of Tennessee, 1982.

Kurzman, Dan. *Kishi and Japan: The Search for the Sun.* New York: Ivan Obolensky, 1960.

Kutler, Stanley I. *The American Inquisition: Justice and Order in the Cold War.* New York: Hill & Wang, 1982.

Kwartler, Richard (ed.). *Behind Bars.* New York: Random House, 1974.

Kwitney, Jonathan. *The Fountainhead Conspiracy.* New York: Alfred A. Knopf, 1971.

_____. *The Mullendore Murder Case.* New York: Warner Books, 1976.

_____. *Vicious Circles: The Mafia in the Marketplace.* New York: W.W. Norton, 1979.

Kyemba, Henry. *A State of Blood.* New York: Ace, 1977.

La Bern, Arthur. *Haigh: The Mind of a Murderer.* London: W. H. Allen, 1973.

_____. *The Life and Death of a Ladykiller.* London: Published by Author, 1967.

Laborde, Jean. *The Dominici Affair.* New York: William Morrow, 1974.

Lackey, B. Roberts. *Stories of the Texas Rangers.* San Antonio, Texas: Naylor, 1955.

Lacroix, Paul. *France in the Middle Ages.* New York: Frederick Ungar, 1963.

_____. *History of Prostitution.* trans. Samuel Putnam. New York: Covici-Friede, 1931.

Ladd, Robert E. *Eight Ropes to Eternity.* Tombstone, Ariz.: Tombstone Epitaph, 1965.

Ladies of the Mission. *The Old Brewery and the New Mission House at Five Points.* New York: Arno Press, 1970.

LaFave, Wayne R. *Arrest.* Boston: Little, Brown, 1965.

_____, and Scott, A.W., Jr. *Handbook on Criminal Law.* St. Paul, Minn.: West, 1972.

Laferte, V. *Alexandre II.* Bale, Fr.: H. Georg, 1882.

Laffan, Robert George. *The Serbs, Guardians of the Gates.* Oxford, Eng.: Clarendon Press, 1918.

Lagrange, Francis, and Murray, William. *Flag on Devil's Island.* Garden City, N.Y.: n.p., 1961.

Laguer, Walter. *Terrorism.* Boston: Little, Brown, 1977.

Lait, Jack, and Mortimer, Lee. *Chicago Confidential.* New York: Crown, 1950.

_____. *New York Confidential.* Chicago: Ziff-Davis, 1948.

_____. *U.S.A. Confidential.* Crown, 1952.

_____. *Washington Confidential.* New York: Crown, 1951.

Lake, Carolyn (ed.). *Under Cover for Wells Fargo.* Boston: Houghton Mifflin, 1969.

Lake, Stuart N. *He Carried a Six-Shooter: The Biography of Wyatt Earp.* New York: Peter Nevill, 1952.

_____. *Wyatt Earp, Frontier Marshal.* Boston: Houghton Mifflin, 1931.

Lamar, Howard Roberts. *Dakota Territory, 1861-1889: A Study of Frontier Politics.* New Haven, Conn.: Yale University Press, 1956.

_____. *The Far Southwest, 1846-1912: A Territorial History.* New Haven, Conn.: Yale University Press, 1966.

_____ (ed.). *The New Encyclopedia of the American West.* New Haven, Conn.: Yale University Press, 1998.

_____ (ed.). *A Reader's Encyclopedia of the American West.* New York: Thomas Y. Crowell, 1977.

Lamb, Ruth DeForest. *American Chamber of Horrors.* New York: Farrar & Rinehart, 1936.

Lambert, R.S. *When Justice Faltered.* London: Methuen, 1935.

Lambton, Arthur. *Echoes of Causes Celebres.* London: Hurst & Blackett, 1931.

_____. *Thou Shalt Do No Murder.* London: Hurst & Blackett, 1930.

Lamond, John. *Arthur Conan Doyle.* London: John Murray, 1931.

Lamott, K. *The Moneymakers: The Great Big New Rich in Ameri-ca.* Boston: Little, Brown, 1969.

Landau, Henry. *The Enemy Within.* New York: G.P. Putnam's Sons, 1937.

Landau, Jacob M. *Radical Politics in Modern Turkey.* Leiden, Neth.: E.J. Brill, 1974.

Landau, Ron. *Moroccan Drama.* London: Robert Hale, 1956.

_____. *Morocco Independent.* London: George Allen & Unwin, 1961.

Lander, C. *My Kenya Acres: A Woman Farms in Mau Mau Country.* London: Harrap, 1957.

Lander, Ernest McPherson, Jr. *A History of South Carolina, 1865-1960.* Chapel Hill: University of North Carolina Press, 1960.

Landesco, John. *Organized Crime in Chicago.* Chicago: Univer-sity of Chicago Press, 1968.

Landress, M.M., with Dobler, Bruce. *I Made It Myself.* New York: Grosset & Dunlap, 1973.

Landreth, Helen. *Dear Dark Head.* New York: Whittlesey House, 1936.

_____. *The Pursuit of Robert Emmett.* New York: Whittlesey House, 1948.

Landru, H.C. *The Blue Parka Man.* New York: Dodd, Mead, 1980.

Lane, Margaret. *Edgar Wallace: The Biography of a Phenomenon.* London: William Heinemann, 1938.

Lane, Mark. *Rush to Judgment.* New York: Holt, Rinehart & Winston, 1966.

_____. *The Strongest Poison.* New York: Hawthorn Books, 1980.

Lane, R. *Violent Death in the City: Suicide, Accident, and Murder in Nineteenth-Century Philadelphia.* Cambridge, Mass.: Harvard University Press, 1979.

Lane, Roger. *Policing the City: Boston, 1822-1885.* Cambridge, Mass.: Harvard University Press, 1967.

Lane, Wheaton J. *Commodore Vanderbilt, An Epic of the Steam Age.* New York: Alfred A. Knopf, 1942.

Lang, Rev. Gordon. *Mr. Justice Avory.* London: Herbert Jenkins, 1935.

Lange, Johannes. *Crime and Destiny.* New York: Charles Boni, 1930.

Langford, Gerald. *Alias O. Henry: A Biography of William Sidney Porter.* New York: Macmillan, 1957.

Langford, Gerald. *The Murder of Stanford White.* Indianapolis: Bobbs-Merrill, 1962.

Langguth, A.J. *Hidden Terrors: The Truth About U.S. Police Operations in Latin America.* New York: Pantheon Books, 1978.

Langlois, Janet. *Belle Gunness.* Bloomington, Ind.: Indiana University Press, 1985.

Lanphear, Roger Glenn. *Freedom from Crime.* New York: Nellen, n.d.

Lansford, William Douglas. *Pancho Villa.* Los Angeles: Sher-bourne Press, 1965.
Lapide, Pinchas. *The Last Three Popes and the Jews.* London: Souvenir Press, 1967.
Lapidus, Edith J. *Eavesdropping on Trial.* Rochelle Park, N.J.: Hayden, 1974.
Laqueur, Walter. *Guerrilla.* London: Weidenfeld & Nicolson, 1976.
_____. *The Guerilla Reader.* Philadelphia: Temple University Press, 1977.
_____, *Terrorism.* Boston: Little, Brown, 1977.
_____ (ed.). *The Terrorism Reader: A Historical Anthology.* New York: Meridian, 1978.
Lara Pardo, Dr. Luis. *De Porfirio Diaz a Francisco I. Madero.* New York: Polyglot Publishing and Commercial, 1912.
Lardner, Ring, Jr. *The Lardners: My Family Remembered.* New York: Harper & Row, 1976.
Larsen, Otto. *Violence and the Mass Media.* New York: Harper & Row, 1968.
Larsen, Richard W. *Bundy, The Deliberate Stranger.* Englewood Cliffs, N.J.: Prentice-Hall, 1980.
Larson, J.A. *A Single Fingerprint System.* New York: D. Ap-pleton, 1924.
Larson, T.A. *History of Wyoming.* Lincoln: University of Nebras-ka Press, 1965.
Lasch, Christopher. *The Agony of the American Left.* New York: Vintage Books, 1969.
_____. *The Culture of Narcissism.* New York: Warner Books, 1979.
_____. *The New Radicalism in America, 1889-1963.* New York: Alfred A. Knopf, 1965.
Lash, Joseph P. (ed.). *From the Diaries of Felix Frankfurter.* New York: W.W. Norton, 1975.
Lasky, Victor. *It Didn't Start With Watergate.* New York: Dell, 1978.
_____. *Jimmy Carter: The Man & the Myth.* New York: Richard Marek, 1979.
Lasswell, Harold D., and McKenna, Jerimiah B. *The Impact on Organized Crime on an Inner-City Community.* New York: Policy Sciences Center, 1972.
_____, and Rogow, Arnold A. *Power, Corruption, and Rectitude.* Englewood Cliffs, N.J.: Prentice-Hall, 1963.
Last Dying Words and Confession of Charles Gibbs, the Pirate. New York: n.p., 1831.
Latan, B., and Darley, J.M. *The Unresponsive Bystander.* New York: Appleton, 1970.
Latham, Earl *The Communist Controversy in Washington.* Cambridge, Mass.: Harvard University Press, 1966.
_____ (ed.). *The Meaning of McCarthyism.* Lexington, Mass.: Heath, 1973.
Latimer, Dean, and Goldberg, Jeff. *Flowers in the Blood: The Story of Opium.* New York: Franklin Watts, 1981.
La Torre, Ferdinando. *Del conclave di Alessandro VI, papa Borgia.* Rome: Olschki, 1933.
Latouche, Robert. *Histoire des Francs.* Paris: Les Belles Lettres, 1963.
Latour, Anny. *The Borgias.* trans. Neil Mann. New York: Abelard-Schuman, 1963.
Lattimer, Dr. John K. *Kennedy and Lincoln: Medical and Ballistic Comparisons of Their Assassinations.* New York: Harcourt, Brace, Jovanovich, 1980.
Lattimore, Owen. *Manchuria, Cradle of Conflict.* New York: Macmillan, 1932.
_____. *Ordeal by Slander.* Boston: Little Brown, 1950.
_____, and Eleanor (eds.). *Silks, Spices and Empire: Asia Seen Through the Eyes of Its Discoverers.* New York: Delacorte Press, 1968.
Latourette, Kenneth S. *The Chinese: Their History and Culture.* New York: Macmillan, 1934.
Lauder, Ronald S. *Fighting Violent Crime in the United States.* New York: Dodd, Mead, 1985.
Laughlin, Clara E. *The Death of Lincoln: The Story of Booth's Plot, His Deed, and the Penalty.* New York: Doubleday, Page, 1909.
Laughlin, Clarence John, and Cohn, David L. *New Orleans and Its Living Past.* Boston: Houghton Mifflin, 1941.
Laurence, John A. *Extraordinary Crimes.* London: Low, Mars-ton, 1931.
Laurence, John. *A History of Capital Punishment.* New York: Citadel Press, 1963.
Laurent, Charles. *Sainte Jeanne d'Arc.* Paris: Haton, 1920.
Laurie, Peter. *Drugs.* Middlesex, Eng.: Penguin, 1967.
_____. *Scotland Yard: A Study of the Metropolitan Police.* Mid-dlesex, Eng.: Penguin, 1972.
Laurie, T. Werner. *The Newgate Calendar.* New York: G.P. Putnam's Sons, 1932.
LaValley, Albert (ed.). *Focus on Hitchcock.* Englewood Cliffs, N.J.: Prentice-Hall, 1972.
Lavender, David. *The American Heritage History of the Great West.* New York: American Heritage, 1965.
LaVey, Anton Szandor. *The Satanic Bible.* New York: Avon, 1969.
Lavigne, Frank C. *Crimes, Criminals and Detectives.* Helena, Mont.: State, 1921.
Lavigne, Yves. *Hells Angels: Taking Care of Business.* Toronto, Can.: Deneua and Wayne, 1987.
Lavine, Emanuel H. *Gimme??or How Public Officials Get Rich.* New York: Vanguard Press, 1931.
Lavine, Sigmund. *Allan Pinkerton, America's First Private Eye.* New York: Dodd, Mead, 1963.
Lavisse, Ernest. *Histoire de France.* Boston: D.C. Heath, 1919.
Law Enforcement Assistance Administration. *Criminal Justice Monograph.* Washington, D.C.: U.S. Department of Justice, 1973.
Lawes, Warden Lewis Edward. *Cell 202 Sing-Sing.* New York: Farrar & Rinehart, 1935.
_____. *Man's Judgment of Death.* New York: G. P. Putnam's Sons, 1924.
_____. *Meet the Murderer!* New York: Harper & Bros., 1932.
_____. *Twenty Thousand Years In Sing Sing.* New York: R. Long & R. R. Smith, 1932.
Lawrence, Lt.-Gen. Sir George. *Forty Years' Service in India.* London: John Murray, 1874.
Lawrence, J. *A History of Capital Punishment with Special Refer-ence to Capital Punishment in Britain.* Port Washington, N.Y.: Kennikat Press, 1932.
Lawrence, John, Sir. *A History of Russia.* New York: New American Library, 1978.
Lawrence, Joseph Stagg. *Wall Street and Washington.* Princeton, N.J.: Princeton University Press, 1929.
Lawrence, T.E. *The Seven Pillars of Wisdom.* London: Cape, 1973.
Lawson, John D. (ed.). *American State Trials.* 17 vols. St. Louis: Thomas, 1914-1937.
Lawson, W.B. *The Indian Outlaw, or Hank Starr: the Log Cabin Bandit.* Orrville, Ohio: Frank T. Fries, n.d.
_____. *Jesse James at Long Branch; or, Playing for a Million.* New York: Street & Smith, 1898.
Lawton, Harry. *Willie Boy, a Desert Manhunt.* Balboa Island, Calif.: Paisano Press, 1960.
Lawton, Lancelot. *The Russian Revolution.* London: Macmillan, 1927.
Layman, Richard. *Shadow Man: The Life of Dashiell Hammett.* New York: Harcourt, Brace, Jovanovich, 1981.
Lea, Henry Charles. *History of the Inquisition in Spain.* New York: Macmillan, 1906.
_____. *History of the Inquisition of the Middle Ages.* New York: Harper & Brothers, 1887.
Leach, Charles E. *On Top of the Underworld.* London: Sampson, Low, Marston, 1933.
Leacock, Eleanor Burke (ed.). *The Culture of Poverty: A Critique.* New York: Simon & Schuster, 1971.
League of Nations. *Prostitutes: Their Early Lives.* The League of Nations Report, 1938.
Leake, Chauncey. *The Amphetamines.* Springfield, Ill.: Charles C. Thomas, 1959.
Leakey, L.S.B. *Defeating Mau Mau.* London: Methuen, 1954.
_____. *Mau Mau and the Kikuyu.* London: Methuen, 1953.
_____. *White African.* London: Hodder and Stoughton, 1937.
Learsi, Rufus. *The Jews in America: A History.* Cleveland: World, 1954.
Leary, John J., Jr. *Talks With T.R.* Boston: Houghton Mifflin, 1920.
LeAveux, William. *Things I Know About Kings, Celebrities and Crooks.* London: Everleigh, Nash & Grayson, 1923.
Leavitt, Ruby Rohrlich. *The Puerto Ricans.* Tucson: University of Arizona Press, n.d.
Lebey, Andre. *Les Trois coups d'tat de Louis-Napoleon Bona-parte.* Paris: Perrin, 1906.
LeBlanc, Jerry, and Davis, Ivor. *5 to Die.* Los Angeles: Holloway House, 1970.
Le Brun, George P. *Call Me If It's Murder.* New York: William Morrow, 1962.
_____. *It's Time to Tell.* New York: William Morrow, 1962.
Le Clere, Marcel. *L'Assassinat de Jean Jaures.* Paris: Mame, 1969.
_____. *Histoire de la police.* Paris: Presses Universitaires de France, 1947.
Lee, Alan J. *The Origins of the Popular Press, 1855-1914.* Totowa, N.J.: Rowman & Littlefield, 1976.
Lee, Alfred McClung. *The Daily Newspaper in America: The Evolution of a Social Instrument.* New York: Macmillan, 1937.
_____, and Humphrey, Norman Daymond. *Race Riot.* New York: Dryden, 1943.
Lee, Clark. *Douglas MacArthur: An Informal Biography.* New York: Henry Holt, 1952.
Lee, Henry. *How Dry We Were: Prohibition Revisited.* Englewood Cliffs, N.J.: Prentice-Hall, 1963.
Lee, Ida. *Captain Bligh's Second Voyage to the South Seas.* London: Longmans, Green, 1920.
Lee, Maurice, Jr. *James I and Henry IV.* Urbana: University of Illinois Press, 1970.
Lee, Peter G. *Interpol.* New York: Stein and Day, 1976.
Lee, Raymond. *Those Scandalous Sheets of Hollywood.* Venice, Calif.: Venice, 1972.
Lee, Raymond, and Van Hecke, B. C. *Gangsters and Hoodlums, The Underworld and the Cinema.* New York: Barnes & Noble, 1971.
Lee, Robert E. *Blackbeard the Pirate.* Winston-Salem, N. C..: John F. Blair, 1974.
Lee, Rose Hum. *The Chinese in the United States of America.* Hong Kong: Hong Kong University Press, 1960.
Lee, Samuel D. *San Francisco's Chinatown.* San Francisco: Central District Coordinating Council, 1940.
Lee, Sir Sydney. *King Edward VII.* New York: Macmillan, 1925.
Lee, W.L.M. *A History of Police in England.* London: Methuen, 1901.
Leech, Margaret. *In the Days of McKinley.* New York: Harper & Brothers, 1959.
_____. *Reveille in Washington 1860-1865.* New York: Harper, 1941.
Leek, Sybil and Sugar, Bert R. *The Assassination Chain.* New York: Corwin Books, 1976.
_____. *Phrenology.* New York: Macmillan, 1970.
Leeson, Benjamin. *Lost London: The Memoirs of an East End Detective.* London: Stanley Paul, 1934.
LeFave, Wayne. *Arrest: The Decision to Take a Suspect Into Custody.* Boston: Little, Brown, 1965.
Lefebure, Constant. *Souvenirs d'un ancien directeur des prisons de Paris.* Paris: H. Louvet, 1894.
Lefebure, Molly. *Evidence for the Crown.* London: Heinemann, 1955.
_____. *Murder with a Difference.* London: Heinemann, 1958.
Lefevre, Edwin. *Reminiscences of a Stock Operator.* Garden City, N.Y.: Doubleday, Doran, 1931.
Lefkowitz, B. *The Victims.* New York: G.P. Putnam's Sons, 1969.
Lefler, Hugh T. *North Carolina History Told by Contemporaries.* Chapel Hill: University of North Carolina Press, 1934.
LeHardy, William (ed.). *County of Middlesex: Calendar to the Sessions Records.* London: Sir E. Hart, 1935.
Lehman, R.C. (ed.) *Charles Dickens as Editor. Being Letters Written by Him to William Henry, His Sub-editor.* London: Smith, Elder, 1912.
Lehovich, Dimitry V. *White Against Red.* New York: W.W. Norton, 1974.
Leigh, I. *In the Shadow of the Mau Mau.* London: W.H. Allen, 1955.
Leigh, Norman. *Thirteen Against the Bank.* London: Weidenfeld & Nicolson, 1976.
Leighton, George R. *Five Cities. The Story of Their Youth and Old Age.* New York: Harper, 1939.
Leighton, Isabel (ed.). *The Aspirin Age, 1919-1941.* New York: Simon and Schuster, 1949.
Leitch, David. *The Discriminating Thief.* New York: Holt, Rinehart & Winston, 1968.
Leiter, Robert D. *The Teamsters Union.* New York: Bookman Associates, 1957.
Leith, Rod. *The Prostitute Murders.* New York: Pinnacle, 1983.
Lekachman, Robert. *The Age of Keynes.* New York: Random House, 1966.

_____. *Greed Is Not Enough.* New York: Pantheon Books, 1982.
Lemert, Edwin M. *Human Deviance, Social Problems, and Social Control.* Englewood Cliffs, N.J.: Prentice-Hall, 1967.
_____. *Social Action and Legal Change: Revolution with the Juvenile Court.* Chicago: Aldine Press, 1970.
_____. *Social Pathology.* New York: McGraw-Hill, 1951.
Lemire, Charles. *L'Episode de Barbe-Bleue au Theatre.* Paris: Trebse et Stock, 1898.
_____. *Un Marechal et un Connetable de France.* Paris: E. Leroux, 1886.
Lemke, William. *The Crime Against Mexico.* Minneapolis, Minn.: Great-West Printing, 1915.
Lemkin, Raphael. *Axis Rule in Occupied Europe.* Washington, D.C.: Carnegie Endowment for International Peace, 1944.
Lemley, Vernon. *The Old West, 1849-1929.* Osborne, Kan.: n.p., 1929.
Lemon, John J. *The Northfield Tragedy; or, the Robber's Raid.* St. Paul, Minn.: Published by Author, 1876.
Lenczowski, George. *The Middle East in World Affairs.* Ithaca, N.Y.: Cornell University Press, 1962.
Lend, Evelyn. *The Underground Struggle in Germany.* New York: League for Industrial Democracy, 1938.
LeNeve, Ethel. *Ethel LeNeve: Her Life Story.* Manchester, Eng.: Daisy Bank Printing, 1910.
Lenin, V.I. *Collected Works.* trans. Bernard Isaacs and Isidor Laker. Moscow: Progress, 1962.
Lening, Gustav. *The Dark Side of New York Life.* New York: F. Gerhard, 1873.
Lenotre, G. *The Guillotine and Its Servants.* trans. Mrs. Rudolph Stawell. London: Hutchinson, 1929.
Leo, Africanus. *History and Description of Africa.* trans. Pory. London: Hakluyt Society, 1896.
Leo, C. *Land and Class in Kenya.* Toronto, Ontario, Can.: University of Toronto Press, 1984.
Leonard, Royal. *I Flew for China: Chiang Kai-shek's Personal Pilot.* New York: Doubleday, 1942.
Leonard, V.A. *The Police, the Judiciary and the Criminal.* Springfield: Charles C. Thomas, 1969.
Leonard, V.A. *Police Organization and Management.* New York: Foundation Press, 1951.
Leonard, Wolfgang. *The Kremlin Since Stalin.* New York: Praeger, 1962.
Leonardi, Dell. *The Reincarnation of John Wilkes Booth: A Study in Hypnotic Regression.* Old Greenwich, Conn.: Devin-Adair, 1975.
Leone, Mario, and Pasetti, John. *Inchiesta sulla morte di Mus-solini.* Rome: Aletti, 1962.
Leong, Gor Yum. *Chinatown Inside Out.* New York: B. Mussey, 1936.
Leon-Portilla, Miguel (ed.). *The Broken Spears: The Aztec Account of the Conquest of Mexico.* Boston: Beacon Press, 1962.
Leopold, Nathan F. *Life Plus 99 Years.* Garden City, N.Y.: Doubleday, 1958.
Lepper, J.H. *Famous Secret Societies.* London: Low, Marston, 1932.
Le Queux, William. *Things I Know about Kings, Celebrities and Crooks.* London: Everleigh, Nash & Grayson, 1923.
Lermolo, Elizabeth. *Face of a Victim.* New York: Harper & Brothers, 1955.
Lerner, Max. *America as a Civilization.* New York: Simon & Schuster, 1957.
LeRoy, Dave. *Gerald Ford: Untold Story.* Arlington, Va.: R.W. Beatty, 1974.
Leroy-Beaulieu, Anatole. *The Empire of the Tsars.* trans. Z. Ragozin. New York: Putnam, 1898.
Lesberg, Sandy. *Assassination in Our Times.* London: Peebles Press, 1976.
Lescadieu, A., and Laurant, A. *Histoire de Nantes.* Paris: A. Pougin, 1836.
Le Shan, Edna. *The Roots of Crime.* New York: Four Winds Press, 1981.
Le Shan, Lawrence. *The Medium, the Mystic and the Physicist.* New York: Viking, 1974.
Leslie, Anita. *The Remarkable Mr. Jerome.* New York: M. Holt, 1954.
Leslie, Robert C. (ed.). *The Journal of Captain Woodes Rogers 1708-11.* London: Chapman and Hall, 1894.
Lester, David, and Lester, Gene. *Crime of Passion.* Chicago: Nelson-Hall, 1975.
_____. *Serial Killers.* Philadelphia: The Charles Press, 1995.
Lester, John C., and Wilson, D.C. *Ku Klux Klan: It's Origin, Growth and Disbandment.* New York: Neale, 1905.
Lester, Muriel. *Entertaining Gandhi.* London: Ivor Nicholson & Watson, 1932.
Le Strange, G. *Baghdad during the Abbasid Caliphate.* Oxford, Eng.: Clarendon, 1900.
Letere edite ed inedite de Felice Orsini. Milan: Francesco Sanvito, 1962.
Lethbridge, Thomas Charles. *Witches: Investigating an Ancient Religion.* London: Routledge & Kegan Paul, 1962.
Letkemann, Peter. *Crime as Work.* Englewood, N.J.: Prentice-Hall, 1973.
Leto, Guido. *OVRA, Fascismo e antifascismo.* Bologna, Italy: Cappelli, 1951.
_____. *Polizia segreta in Italia.* Rome: Vito Bianco, 1961.
A Letter from Richard P. Robinson, as Connected with the Murder of Ellen Jewett. New York: n.p., 1837.
Leuchtenburg, William E. *Franklin D. Roosevelt and the New Deal.* New York: Harper & Row, 1963.
_____. *The Perils of Prosperity 1914-1932.* Chicago: University of Chicago Press, 1958.
Leuret, Franois. *Fragments Psychologiques sur la Folie.* Paris: Crochard, 1834.
Lever, Harry, and Young, Joseph. *Wartime Racketeers.* New York: G.P. Putnam's Sons, 1945.
Leverkuehn, Paul. *German Military Intelligence.* trans. R.H. Stevens and C. Fitzgibbon. New York: Praeger, 1954.
Levi, Eliphas. *The History of Magic.* London: Rider, 1913.
Levin, Alfred. *The Second Duma.* New Haven, Conn.: Yale University Press, 1940.
Levin, David. *What Happened in Salem?* New York: Harcourt, Brace, 1956.
Levin, Jack, and Fox, James Alan. *Mass Murder.* New York: Plenum, 1985.
Levin, Meyer. *Compulsion.* New York: Simon & Schuster, 1956.
_____. *The Obsession.* New York: Simon & Schuster, 1973.
Levin, Murray. *Political Hysteria in America: The Democratic Capacity for Repression.* New York: Basic Books, 1971.
Levin, Nora. *The Holocaust, The Destruction of European Jewry, 1933-1945.* New York: Thomas Y. Crowell, 1968.
Levine, Edward M. *The Irish and Irish Politicians.* Notre Dame, Ind.: University of Notre Dame Press, 1966.
Levine, Gary. *Anatomy of a Gangster.* New York: Barnes, 1979.
Levine, Issac Don. *Eyewitness to History.* New York: Hawthorn, 1973.
_____. *The Man Lenin.* New York: Thomas Seltzer, 1924.
_____. *The Mind of an Assassin.* New York: New American Library, 1960.
Levine, Richard M. *Bad Blood.* New York: New American Library, 1982.
Levine, Stephen (ed.). *Death Row.* San Francisco: Glide, 1972.
Levinson, Horace C. *The Science of Chance.* London: Faber, 1952.
Levitsky, Serge L. *The Russian Duma: Studies in Parliamentary Procedure, 1906-1917.* New York: Fordham, 1958.
Levy, Leonard, and Nelson, Harold. *Freedom of the Press. Vol. 1, From Zenger to Jefferson; Vol. 2, From Hamilton to the Warren Court.* New York: Bobbs-Merrill, 1966.
Levy, Newman. *My Double Life.* Garden City, N.Y.: Doubleday, 1958.
_____. *The Nan Patterson Case.* New York: Simon & Schuster, 1959.
Levy, Reuben. *The Social Structure of Islam.* Cambridge, Eng.: Cambridge University Press, 1957.
Lewin, K. *Field Theory in the Social Sciences.* New York: Harper & Row, 1951.
Lewin, Malcolm. *The Government of the East India Company and Its Monopolies.* London: James Ridgway, 1857.
Lewinsohn, Richard. *A History of Sexual Customs.* New York: Harper & Bros., 1959.
_____. *The Mystery Man of Europe: Sir Basil Zaharoff.* Philadel-phia: J.B. Lippincott, 1929.
Lewis, Alfred Allan, with Mac Donell, Herbert Leon. *The Evidence Never Lies.* New York: Holt, Rinehart and Winston, 1984.
Lewis, Alfred Henry. *The Apaches of New York.* New York: G.W. Dillingham, 1912.
_____. *The Boss: And How He Came to Rule New York.* New York: A. S. Barnes, 1903.
_____. *Confessions of a Detective.* New York: A.S. Barnes, 1906.
_____. *Nation-Famous New York Murders.* New York: G.W. Dillingham, 1914.
_____. *Richard Croker.* New York: Life, 1901.
Lewis, Anthony. *Gideon's Trumpet.* New York: Random House, 1964.
_____. *Portrait of a Decade.* New York: Random House, 1964.
Lewis, Bernard. *The Arabs in History.* London: Hutchinson, 1956.
_____. *The Assassins.* New York: Oxford University Press, 1967.
_____. *The Emergence of Modern Turkey.* London: Oxford University Press, 1961.
_____. *The Origins of Ismailism.* Cambridge, Eng.: W. Heffner & Sons, 1940.
Lewis, Charles Lee. *The Romantic Decatur.* Philadelphia: University of Pennsylvania Press, 1937.
Lewis, David L. *When Harlem Was in Vogue.* New York: Alfred A. Knopf, 1981.
Lewis, Dominic B. Wyndham. *Franois Villon.* New York: Literary Guild, 1928.
_____. *The Soul of Marshal Gilles de Raiz.* London: Eyre & Spottiswoode, 1952.
Lewis, Flannery. *Suns Go Down.* New York: Macmillan, 1937.
Lewis, Jerry D. *Crusade Against Crime.* New York: Bernard Geis Associates, 1962.
Lewis, John L., et al. *Heywood Broun As He Seemed to Us.* New York: Random House, 1940.
Lewis, Leonard. *Trunk Crimes Past and Present.* London: Hutchinson, 1934.
Lewis, Lloyd, and Smith, Henry Justin. *Chicago: The History of Its Reputation.* New York: Harcourt, Brace, 1929.
_____, *It Takes All Kinds.* New York: Harcourt, Brace, 1947.
_____. *Myths After Lincoln.* New York: Harcourt, Brace, 1929.
Lewis, Meriwether, and Clark, William. *The Journals of Lewis and Clark.* Boston: Houghton Mifflin, 1953.
_____. *The Letters of the Lewis and Clark Expedition.* Urbana: University of Illinois Press, 1962.
Lewis, Norman. *The Honored Society.* New York: G.P. Putnam's Sons, 1964.
Lewis, Orlando F. *The Development of American Prisons and Prison Customs, 1776-1845.* Montclair, N.J.: Patterson Smith, 1967.
Lewis, Oscar. *Bay Window Bohemia.* New York: Doubleday, 1956.
_____. *This Was San Francisco.* New York: David McKay, 1962.
Lewis, R.W.B. *Edith Wharton: A Biography.* New York: Harper & Row, 1975.
Lewis, Richard Warren, and Schiller, Lawrence. *The Scavengers and Critics of the Warren Report.* New York: Delacorte Press, 1967.
Lewis, Sasha G. *American Exploitation of Illegal Aliens.* Boston: Beacon Press, 1979.
Lewis, W. David. *From Newgate to Dannemora: The Rise of the Penitentiary in New York, 1796-1848.* Ithaca, N.Y.: Cornell University Press, 1965.
Lewis, W.H. *The Splendid Century.* New York: Sloane, 1953.
Lexow Investigation. *Report and Proceedings of the Senate Committee Appointed to Investigate the Police Department of the City of New York.* 5 vols. Albany, N.Y.: J.B. Lyon, 1895.
Leys, N.M. *A Last Chance in Kenya.* London: Hogarth, 1931.
Liceaga, Luis. *Felix Diaz.* Mexico City: Editorial Jus, 1958.
Licht, Hans. *Sexual Life of Ancient Greece.* London: The Abbey Library, 1971.
Liddell, R. *Byzantium and Istanbul.* New York: Macmillan, 1956.
Liebling, Abbott J. *Chicago: Second City.* New York: Alfred A. Knopf, 1952.
_____. *The Press.* New York: Ballantine, 1964.
Lieck, Albert (ed.). *Notable British Trials: Trial of Benjamin Knowles.* London: William Hodge, 1933.

Lieven, D. C. B. *Nicholas II: Twilight of the Empire*. New York: St. Martin's Press, 1996.

Life and Confessions of Henry G. Green. Troy, N.Y.: n.p., 1845.

The Life and Confessions of Mrs. Henrietta Robinson, the Veiled Murderess. Boston: Dr. H.B. Skinner, 1855.

The Life and Conversations of Richard P. Robinson, the Supposed Murderer of Ellen Jewett. New Haven, Conn.: n.p., 1840.

The Life and Death of Mrs. Maria Bickford, a Beautiful Female Who was Inhumanly Murdered in the Moral and Religious City of Boston. Boston: n.p., 1845.

Life and Execution of Jack Kehoe, King of the "Mollie Maguires." Philadelphia: Barclay, 1881.

The Life, Character and Career of Edward W. Green, Postmaster of Malden. Boston: Benjamin F. Russell, 1864.

The Life, Confession, and Atrocious Crimes of Antoine Probst. Philadelphia: Barclay, 1866.

The Life of Ellen Jewett. New York: n.p., 1836.

Life of Henry Phillips. Boston: Russell, Cutler, 1817.

Life of Jesse H. Pomeroy, the Boy Fiend. Taunton, Mass.: Taun-ton, 1875.

Life of Samuel Green. Boston: David Felt, 1822.

The Life of Ursula Newman, and the Intercourse Subsisting Between Her and Richard Johnson. New York: Elam Bliss, 1829.

Life, Trial and Adventures of John H. Surratt, the Conspirator. Port Tobacco, Md.: James L. Barbour, 1988.

Life, Trial and Conviction of Edward Stokes. Philadelphia: Barclay, 1873.

Life, Trial and Execution of Edward H. Ruloff. Philadelphia: Barclay, 1871.

Life, Trial, Confession and Execution of Albert W. Hicks. New York: Robert M. DeWitt, 1860.

Lifflander, Mathew L. *Final Treatment, The File on Dr. X*. New York: W. W. Norton, 1979.

Lifton, David S. *Best Evidence: Disguise and Deception in the Assassination of John F. Kennedy*. New York: Macmillan, 1980.

Ligotti, Gene. *Dark Eagle*. New York: XLibris, 2000.

Likimani, M. *Passbook Number F.47927: Women and Mau Mau in Kenya*. London: Macmillan, 1985.

Lilly, Marjorie. *Sickert, The Painter and His Circle*. London: Elek, 1971.

Liman, Paul. *Der politische Mord im Wandel der Geschichte*. Berlin: A. Hofmann, 1912.

Limborch, Philip van. *Historia Inquisitionis*. Amsterdam, Neth.: H. Westenium, 1692.

Limpus, Lowell J. *Honest Cop: Lewis J. Valentine*. New York: Dutton, 1939.

Lincoln, C. Eric. *The Black Muslims in America*. Boston: Beacon Press, 1961.

Lincoln, Victoria. *Disgrace: Lizzie Borden by Daylight*. New York: G. P. Putnam's Sons, 1967.

Lindbergh, Anne Morrow. *The Flower and the Nettle: Diaries and Letters, 1936-1939*. New York: Harcourt, Brace, Jovanovich, 1974.

_____. *Hour of Gold, Hour of Lead: Diaries and Letters, 1929-1932*. New York: Harcourt, Brace, Jovanovich, 1973.

_____. *Locked Rooms and Open Doors: Diaries and Letters, 1933-1935*. New York: Harcourt, Brace, Jovanovich, 1974.

Lindemann, Albert S. *The Red Years: European Socialism versus Bolshevism, 1919-1921*. Berkeley: University of California Press, 1974.

Linder, Ronald L., Lerner, Steven E., and Burns, R. Stanley. *PCP: The Devil's Dust*. Belmont, Calif.: Wadsworth, 1981.

Lindley, Ernest K. *Franklin D. Roosevelt: A Career in Progressive Democracy*. New York: Bobbs Merrill, 1931.

_____. *The Roosevelt Revolution: First Phase*. New York: Viking, 1933.

Lindsay, Jack. *Cleopatra*. London: Constable, 1971.

Lindsay, Philip. *The Mainspring of Murder.* London: John Long, 1958.

Lindsey, Benjamin B., and O'Higgins, Harvey J. *The Beast*. New York: Doubleday, Page, 1911.

Linebarger, Paul, *The China of Chiang Kai-shek*. Boston: World Peace Foundation, 1941.

Linedecker, Clifford L. *Children in Chains*. New York: Everest House, 1981.

_____. *Hell Ranch*. Austin, Tex.: Diamond Books, 1989.

_____. *The Man Who Killed Boys*. New York: St. Martin's Press, 1980.

_____. *Night Stalker*. New York: St. Martin's Press, 1991.

_____. *Serial Thrill Killers*. New York: Knightsbridge, 1990.

_____. *Smooth Operator*. New York: St. Martin's Press, 1997.

_____. *Thrill Killers*. New York: Paperjacks, 1987.

_____, and Burt, William. *Nurses Who Kill*. New York: Pinnacle, 1990.

Linklater, Eric. *The Corpse on Clapham Common*. London: Macmillan, 1971.

Linn, James Weber. *James Keeley, Newspaperman*. New York: Bobbs-Merrill, 1937.

Lintott, Andrew W. *Violence, Civil Strife and Revolution in the Classical City, 750-330 B.C.* Baltimore: Johns Hopkins Press, 1982.

_____. *Violence in Republican Rome*. Oxford: Clarendon Press, 1968.

Lipman, Mark, and Daley, Robert. *Stealing*. New York: Harper's Magazine Press, 1973.

Lippmann, Walter. *American Inquisitors: A Commentary on Dayton and Chicago*. New York: Macmillan, 1928.

Lipsig, Frances. *Murder-Family Style*. New York: Collier Books, 1962.

Lister, Richard Percival. *The Secret History of Genghis Khan*. London: P. Davies, 1969.

Liston, Robert H. *The Edge of Madness: Prisons and Prison Reform in America*. New York: Franklin Watts, 1972.

_____. *Great Detectives*. New York: Platt & Munk, 1966.

_____. *Terrorism*. New York: Thomas Nelson, 1977.

Little, Tom. *Egypt*. New York: Praeger, 1959.

Litvinoff, Barnett. *Ben Gurion of Israel*. New York: Praeger, 1954.

Liu, F.F. *A Military History of Modern China, 1924-1949*. Prince-ton, N.J.: Princeton University Press, 1956.

Livermore, H.V. *A History of Portugal*. Cambridge: Cambridge University Press, 1947.

The Lives of Helen Jewett, and Richard P. Robinson. New York: Police Gazette, 1836.

Lives: The Dryden Plutarch. New York: Everyman's Library, 1910.

Livingston, Armstrong, and Stein, Captain John G. *The Murdered and the Missing*. New York: Stephen-Paul, 1947.

Livingstone, Neil C. *Inside the PLO: Covert Units, Secret Funds, and the War Against Israel and the United States*. New York: William Morrow, 1990.

_____. *The War Against Terrorism*. London: Heath, 1982.

Livsey, Clara. *The Manson Women*. New York: Marek, 1980.

Livy. *Summary*. trans. B.O. Foster. Cambridge, Mass.: Harvard University Press, 1963.

Llorente, Juan Antonio. *Histoire critique de l'Inquisition d'Es-pagne*. Paris: Treuttel et Wurtz, 1817.

Lloyd, Benjamin Estelle. *Lights and Shadows in San Francisco*. San Francisco: Published by Author, 1876.

_____. *Lights and Shadows of Chinatown*. San Francisco: Published by Author, 1896.

Lloyd, Christopher. *Sir Francis Drake*. London: Faber and Faber, 1957.

Lloyd, Everett. *Law West of the Pecos: The Story of Roy Bean*. San Antonio, Texas: Naylor, 1936.

Lloyd George, Earl. *Lloyd George*. London: Frederick Muller, 1960.

Lloyd, H.E. *Alexander I*. London: Treuttel & Wurtz, 1826.

Lloyd, John. *The Invaders: A Story of the "Hole-in-the-Wall" Country*. New York: R.F. Fenno, 1910.

Lloyd, Lord. *Egypt Since Cromer.* London: Macmillan, 1933.

Lloyd, Robin. *For Money or Love: Boy Prostitution in America*. New York: Vanguard, 1976.

Locard, E. *L'Enquete Criminelle et les Methodes Scientifiques*. Paris: Flammarion, 1920.

_____. *La Preuve Judiciaire par les Empreintes Digitales*. Lyons, Fr.: A. Rey, 1914.

_____. *Traite de Criminalistique*. Lyons, Fr.: Desvigne, 1931.

Lochner, Louis Paul. *Always the Unexpected*. New York: Macmillan, 1956.

_____ (ed. & trans.). *The Goebbels Diaries*. Garden City, N.Y.: Doubleday, 1948.

Lockhart, B.H. Bruce. *British Agent*. New York: G.P. Putnam's Sons, 1933.

Lodge, Juliet (ed.). *Terrorism, A Challenge to the State*. London: Martin Robertson, 1981.

Loewen, James. *Lies Across America*. New York: New Press, 1999.

Loewy, Arnold H. *Criminal Law in a Nutshell*. St. Paul, Minn.: West, 1975.

Lofland, John. *Analyzing Social Settings*. Belmont, Calif.: Wadsworth, 1971.

Logan, Andy. *Against the Evidence: The Becker-Rosenthal Affair.* New York: McGraw-Hill, 1970.

_____. *The Man Who Robbed the Robber Barons*. New York: W.W. Norton, 1965.

Logan, Guy. *Dramas of the Dock*. London: Stanley Paul, 1928.

_____. *Great Murder Mysteries*. London: Stanley Paul, 1931.

_____. *Guilty or Not Guilty?* London: Stanley Paul, 1928.

_____. *Masters of Crime: Studies of Multiple Murders*. London: Stanley Paul, 1928.

_____. *Rope, Knife and Chair.* London: Stanley Paul, 1930.

_____. *Verdict and Sentence*. London: Eldon Press, 1935.

_____. *Wilful Murder.* London: Eldon Press, 1935.

Logan, John A. *The Great Conspiracy*. Philadelphia: Barclay, 1866.

Lohbeck, Don. *Patrick J. Hurley*. Chicago: Regnery, 1956.

Lomask, Milton. *Andrew Johnson, President on Trial*. New York: Farrar, Straus & Cudahy, 1960.

Lombroso, Caesar. *Crime, Its Causes and Remedies*. Boston: Little, Brown, 1911.

_____. *Criminal Man According to the Classification of Cesare Lombroso*. New York: Putnam, 1911.

_____, and Ferrero, William. *The Female Offender.* New York: Appleton, 1897.

London, Jack. *The People of the Abyss*. New York: Macmillan, 1901.

Long, E. Hudson. *Mark Twain Handbook*. New York: Hendricks House, 1957.

_____. *O. Henry, the Man and His Work*. Philadelphia: University of Pennsylvania Press, 1949.

Long, Huey P. *Every Man a King. The Autobiography of Huey P. Long*. New Orleans: National Books, 1933.

Longford, Elizabeth. *Queen Victoria: Born to Succeed*. New York: Harper, 1965.

Longford, Joseph H. *The Evolution of New Japan*. Cambridge: Cambridge University Press, 1913.

Longgood, William. *Suez Story: Key to the Middle East*. New York: Greenberg, 1957.

Longman, F.W. *Frederick the Great and the Seven Years War.* London: Longmans, 1888.

Longrigg, Stephen H. *Iraq, 1900-1950*. London: Oxford Univer-sity Press, 1953.

Longsford, Elizabeth (ed.). *Queen Victoria*. New York: Harper & Row, 1964.

Longstreet, Stephen. *All Star Cast, an Anecdotal History of Los Angeles*. New York: Thomas Y. Crowell, 1977.

_____. *Chicago, 1860-1919*. New York: McKay, 1973.

_____. *Sportin' House*. Los Angeles: Sherbourne Press, 1965.

_____. *The Wilder Shore*. New York: Doubleday, 1968.

_____. *Win or Lose*. Indianapolis: The Bobbs-Merrill, 1977.

Longstreth, T. Morris. *In Scarlet and Plain Clothes*. New York: Macmillan, 1933.

_____. *The Silent Force: Scenes From the Life of the Mounted Police of Canada*. New York: Century, 1927.

Longworth, Alice Roosevelt. *Crowded Hours*. New York: Charles Scribner's Sons, 1933.

Longworth, David. *A Brief Narrative of the Trial for the Bloody and Mysterious Murder of the Unfortunate Young Woman in the Famous Manhattan Well*. New York: Published by Author, 1800.

Longworth, Philip. *The Cossacks*. New York: Holt, Rinehart and Winston, 1969.

Looker, Earle. *The White House Gang*. Old Tappan, N.J.: Fleming H. Revell, 1929.

Loomis, Stanley. *A Crime of Passion*. Philadelphia: Lippincott, 1967.

_____. *Du Barry*. Philadelphia: J.B. Lippincott, 1959.

_____. *Paris In The Terror.* New York: J. B. Lippincott, 1964.

Lopez-Ray, Manuel. *Crime: An Analytical Appraisal*. New York: Praeger, 1970.

Lord, Walter. *Day of Infamy*. New York: Holt, Rinehart & Winston, 1961.

_____. *The Good Years, From 1900 to the First World War.* New York: Harper & Bros., 1960.

Los Angeles, City of. *Dangerous Chemicals Code*. Los Angeles: Los Angeles Fire Department, 1951.

Loseby, Charles Edgar. *Witches, Mediums, Vagrants, and Law*. Manchester, Eng.: Spiritualists' National Union, 1946.

Lot, Ferdinand. *Les Invasions Barbares*. Paris: Paynot, 1937.

Lotchin, Roger W. *San Francisco - 1846-1856*. New York: Oxford University Press, 1974.

Loth, David. *Public Plunder: A History of Graft in America*. New York: Carrick & Evans, 1938.

_____. *Swope of G.E.* New York: Simon & Schuster, 1958.

Loucks, Emerson Hunsberger. *The Ku Klux Klan in Pennsylvania*. Harrisburg, Pa.: Telegraph Press, 1936.

Louderback, Lew. *The Bad Ones*. New York: Fawcett, 1968.

Louria, Donald B. *The Drug Scene*. New York: McGraw-Hill, 1968.

_____. *Nightmare Drugs*. New York: Pocket Books, 1966.

Lourie, Richard. *Hunting the Devil*. New York: Harper Collins, 1993.

Love, Nat. *The Life and Adventures of Nat Love, Better Known in the Cattle Country as "Deadwood Dick", by Himself*. Los Angeles: Wayside Press, 1907.

Love, Robertus. *The Rise and Fall of Jesse James*. New York: G. P. Putnam's Sons, 1926.

Lovett, Sir H. Verney. *The Cambridge History of India*. Cam-bridge: The University Press, 1932.

Lovett, Robert Morss. *All Our Years*. New York: Viking, 1948.

Lowdermilk, Walter C. *Palestine Land of Promise*. New York: Harper, 1944.

Lowe, David. *KKK: Invisible Empire*. New York: W.W. Norton, 1967.

Lowe, David. *Lost Chicago*. Boston: Houghton Mifflin, 1975.

Lowe, Frank M., Jr. *A Warrior Lawyer*. New York: Fleming H. Revell, 1942.

Lowenthal, Max. *The Federal Bureau of Investigation*. New York: William Sloane Associates, 1950.

Lowndes, Marie Belloc. *Lizzie Borden: A Study in Conjecture*. New York: Longmans, Green, 1930.

_____. *The Lodger*. New York: Scribner, 1911.

Lowndes, Susan (ed.). *Diaries and Letters of Marie Belloc Lowndes 1911-1947*. London: Windus, 1971.

Lowry, Edward G. *Washington Close-ups*. Boston: Houghton Mifflin, 1921.

Lowther, Charles C. *Dodge City, Kansas*. Philadelphia: Dor-rance, 1940.

Lu, David J. *From the Marco Polo Bridge to Pearl Harbor*. Washington, D.C.: Public Affairs Press, 1961.

Lubbock, Percy. *Portrait of Edith Wharton*. New York: D. Appleton-Century, 1947.

Lubin, Martin, (as told to Coe, Phyllis). *Good Guys, Bad Guys*. New York: McGraw-Hill Book, 1982.

Lubove, Roy. *The Progressives and the Slums*. Pittsburgh, Pa.: University of Pittsburgh Press, 1936.

Lucas, A. *Forensic Chemistry and Scientific Criminal Investigation*. New York: Longmans, Green, 1935.

Lucas, Norman. *The Child Killers*. London: Barker, 1972.

_____. *Laboratory Detectives*. New York: Taplinger, 1972.

_____. *The Sex Killers*. New York: W. H. Allen, 1974.

_____, and Davies, Phil. *The Monster Butler*. London: Arthur Barker, 1979.

Lucas, Scott. *The FDA*. Millbrae, Calif.: Celestial Arts, 1978.

Lucas-Dubreton, J. *The Borgias*. trans. Philip John Stead. New York: E.P. Dutton, 1956.

Lucia, Ellis. *Tough Men, Tough Country*. Englewood Cliffs, N.J.: Prentice-Hall, 1963.

Lucie-Smith, Edward. *The Dark Pageant: A Novel About Gilles de Rais*. London: Blond & Briggs, 1977.

_____. *Joan of Arc*. London: Allen Lane, 1976.

Luckenbill, David. *Other People's Lives*. Santa Barbara: Univer-sity of California, Santa Barbara, 1973.

Ludecke, Winifred. *Behind the Scenes of Espionage*. London: Mellifont Press, 1949.

Ludeke, Kurt. *I Knew Hitler*. New York: Charles Scribner's Sons, 1937.

Ludlow, Fitzhugh. *The Hasheesh Eater*. New York: Harper Brothers, 1857.

_____. *The Heart of the Continent*. New York: Hurd and Houghton, 1870.

Ludlow, J.M. *British India: Its Races and Its History*. 2 vols. Cambridge, Eng.: Macmillan, 1858.

Ludwig, Emil. *The Davos Murder*. trans. Eden and Cedar Paul. New York: Viking Press, 1936.

_____. *The Germans*. trans. Heinz and Ruth Norden. Boston: Little, Brown, 1941.

_____. *Napoleon*. Garden City, N.Y.: Garden City, 1926.

_____. *Roosevelt: A Study in Fortune and Power*. New York: Viking Press, 1938.

_____. *Talks with Mussolini*. trans. Eden and Cedar Paul. London: George Allen & Unwin, 1933.

_____. *Three Portraits*. London: Alliance, 1940.

_____. *Wilhelm Hohenzollern*. New York: G.P. Putnam's Sons, 1926.

Luhan, Mabel Dodge. *Intimate Memoirs*. 4 vols. New York: Harcourt, Brace, 1933.

Lukas, J. Anthony. *Don't Shoot - We Are Your Children!* New York: Dell, 1972.

_____. *Nightmare, the Underside of the Nixon Years*. New York: Viking Press, 1976.

Lunday, Todd. *The Mystery Unveiled: The Truth about the Borden Tragedy*. Providence: J.A. & R.A. Reid, 1893.

Lundberg, Ferdinand. *America's 60 Families*. New York: Citadel Press, 1937.

_____. *Imperial Hearst*. New York: Modern Library, 1937.

_____, and Farnham, Marynia F. *Modern Women, The Lost Sex*. New York: Harper & Brothers, 1947.

_____. *The Rich and the Super-Rich: A Study of Power and Money Today*. New York: Lyle Stuart, 1969.

Lunde, Donald T. *The Die Song*. New York: Playboy Press, 1980.

_____. *Murder and Madness*. New York: W.W. Norton, 1975.

Lunden, Walter A. *The Death Penalty*. Anamosa, Iowa: Iowa State Reformatory Printing Department, 1960.

Lundsgaarde, Henry P. *Murder in Space City: A Cultural Analysis of Houston Homicide Patterns*. New York: Oxford University Press, 1977.

Lussu, Emilio. *Enter Mussolini*. trans. Marion Rawson. London: Methuen, 1936.

Lustgarten, Edgar. *The Business of Murder*. New York: Charles Scribner's Sons, 1968.

_____. *A Case to Answer*. London: Eyre and Spottiswoode, 1947.

_____. *A Century of Murders*. London: Eyre Methuen, 1975.

_____. *Defender's Triumph*. London: Wingate, 1951.

_____. *The Illustrated Story of Crime*. Chicago: Follett, 1976.

_____. *The Judges and the Judged*. London: Odhams, 1961.

_____. *The Murder and the Trial*. New York: Charles Scribner's Sons, 1958.

_____. *Prisoner at the Bar*. London: Andre Deutsch, 1951.

_____. *Verdict in Dispute*. New York: Scribner, 1950.

_____. *The Woman in the Case*. London: Andre Deutsch, 1955.

Lutz, Alma. *Created Equal: A Biography of Elizabeth Cady Stanton, 1815-1902*. New York: John Day, 1940.

_____. *Susan B. Anthony*. Boston: Beacon Press, 1959.

Lutz, Ralph Haswell (ed.). *The Fall of the German Empire, 1914-1918*. Stanford, Calif.: Stanford University Press, 1932.

Luxemburg, Rosa. *The Russian Revolution*. Ann Arbor: Univer-sity of Michigan Press, 1961.

Lybyer, Albert Howe. *The Government of the Ottoman Empire in the Time of Suleiman the Magnificent*. Cambridge, Mass.: Harvard University Press, 1913.

Lydon, James G. *Pirates, Privateers and Profits*. Upper Saddle River, N.J.: Gregg Press, 1971.

Lyford, Joseph P. *The Airtight Cage*. New York: Harper & Row, 1966.

Lyle, Jack. *The News in Megalopolis*. San Francisco: Chandler, 1967.

Lyle, Judge John H. *The Dry and Lawless Years*. Englewood Cliffs, N.J.: Prentice-Hall, 1960.

Lyle, Katie Letcher. *The Man Who Wanted Seven Wives*. Chapel Hill, N.J.: Algonquin Books, 1986.

Lyman, Abbott. *Reminiscences*. Boston: Houghton Mifflin, 1923.

Lyman, Albert R. *Indians and Outlaws: Settling of the San Juan Frontier*. Salt Lake City, Utah: Bookcraft, 1962.

Lyman, George Dunlap. *Ralston's Ring*. New York: Charles Scribner's Sons, 1937.

Lyman, Stanford M. *Chinese Americans*. New York: Random House, 1974.

Lyman, Susan Elizabeth. *The Story of New York*. New York: Crown, 1964.

Lynch, Denis Tilden. *Boss Tweed, the Story of a Grim Generation*. New York: Boni and Liveright, 1927.

_____. *Criminals and Politicians*. New York: Macmillan, 1932.

_____. *An Epoch and a Man. Martin Van Buren and His Times*. New York: Horace Liveright, 1929.

_____. *The Wild Seventies*. New York: Appleton-Century, 1941.

Lynch, P.P. *No Remedy for Death*. London: Long, 1970.

Lynch, W. Ware. *Rape! One Victim's Story*. Chicago: Follett, 1974.

Lynx, J. J. *The Prince of Thieves*. New York: Atheneum, 1964.

Lyons, Arthur. *The Second Coming, Satanism in America*. New York: Dodd, Mead, 1970.

Lyons, Eugene. *Assignment in Utopia*. New York: Harcourt, Brace, 1937.

_____. *Herbert Hoover: A Biography*. New York: Doubleday, 1964.

_____. *The Life and Death of Sacco and Vanzetti*. New York: International, 1927.

Maas, Peter. *King of the Gypsies*. New York: Bantam, 1975.

_____. *Manhunt*. New York: Random House, 1986.

_____. *Serpico*. New York: Viking Press, 1973.

_____. *The Valachi Papers*. New York: G.P. Putnam's Sons, 1968.

Maas, Walter B. *Assassination in Vienna*. New York: Charles Scribner's Sons, 1972.

McAdoo, William G. *Crowded Years*. Boston: Houghton Mifflin, 1931.

McAleavy, Henry. *A Dream of Tartary: The Origins and Misfor-tunes of Henry Pu Yi*. London: George Allen & Unwin, 1963.

McAlmon, Robert. *Being Geniuses Together*. Garden City, N.Y.: Doubleday, 1968.

McAlpine, R.W. *The Life and Times of Col. James Fisk, Jr.* New York: New York Books, 1872.

Macardle, Dorothy. *The Irish Republic*. New York: Farrar, Straus & Giroux, 1965.

Macarthur, Douglas. *Reminiscences*. New York: McGraw-Hill, 1964.

Macartney, C.A. *The Habsburg Empire: 1790-1918*. New York: Macmillan, 1969.

McBain, Howard Lee. *Prohibition: Legal and Illegal*. New York: Macmillan, 1928.

McBrien, Richard. *Lives of the Popes: The Pontiffs from St. Peter to John Paul II*. New York: Harper Collins, 2000.

McCabe, James D. *The History of the Great Riots*. Philadelphia: National, 1877.

_____. *Lights and Shadow of New York Life*. Philadelphia: National, 1872.

McCabe, John. *Charlie Chaplin*. Garden City, N.Y.: Doubleday, 1978.

McCabe, Joseph. *The Story of the World's Oldest Profession*. Kansas City: Girard, 1932.

McCabe, S., and Purves, R. *By-passing the Jury*. Oxford, Eng.: Basil Blackwell, 1972.

McCafferty, James A. (ed.). *Capital Punishment*. Chicago: Aldine, Atherton, 1972.

McCaghy, C.H. *Crime in American Society*. New York: Macmil-lan, 1980.

_____. *Deviant Behavior*. New York: Macmillan, 1976.

McCague, James. *The Second Rebellion: The Study of the New York City Draft Riots of 1863*. New York: Dial Press, 1968.

McCall, Andrew. *The Medieval Underworld*. New York: Barnes & Noble, 1979.

McCallum, John D. *Crime Doctor*. Mercer Island, Wash.: Writing Works, 1978.

McCarthy, Burke. *The Suppressed Truth about the Assassination of Abraham Lincoln*. Washington, D.C.: Published by Author, 1922.

McCarthy, Dennis V.N., and Smith, Philip W *Protecting the President: The Inside Story of a Secret Service Agent*. New York: William Morrow, 1985.

McCarty, Lea Franklin. *The Gunfighters*. Berkeley, Calif.: Mike Roberts, 1959.

Maccarty, Thaddeus. *The Guilt of Innocent Blood Put Away*. Norwich, Conn.: John Trumbull, 1778.

Maclean, Fitzroy. *Bonnie Prince Charlie*. New York: Macmillan, 1989.

MacLean, Rick, and Veniot, Andre. *Terror*. Toronto: McClelland & Stewart, 1990.

_____. *Terror's End*. Toronto: McClelland & Stewart, 1992.

McCleery, Richard H. *Policy Change in Prison Management*. East Lansing: Michigan State University Bureau of Social and Political Research, 1957.

McClellan, Grant S. (ed.). *Capital Punishment*. New York: H.W. Wilson, 1961.

McClellan, John L. *Crime Without Punishment*. New York: Duell, Sloan & Pearce, 1962.

McClintick, David. *Stealing From the Rich*. New York: Quill, 1983.

McClintock, Frederick H. *Crimes of Violence*. New York: St. Martin's Press, 1963.

_____, and Avison, N.H. *Crime in England and Wales*. London: William Heinemann, 1968.

_____, and Gibson, Evelyn. *Robbery in London*. New York: St. Martin's Press, 1961.

McCloskey, Robert J. *The American Supreme Court*. Chicago: University of Chicago Press, 1960.

_____. *The Modern Supreme Court*. Cambridge, Mass.: Harvard University Press, 1972.

McCloy, John J. *The Great Gulf Oil Spill: The Inside Report: Gulf Oil's Bribery and Political Chicanery*. New York: Chelsea House, 1976.

McClure, James. *Killers*. London: Fontana, 1976.

_____. *Spike Island*. New York: Pantheon, 1980.

McClure, Stanley W. *Ford's Theatre and the House Where Lincoln Died*. Washington, D.C.: U.S. Government Printing Office, 1969.

McComas, J. Francis. *The Graveside Companion*. New York: Obelensky, 1962.

McConaughy, John. *From Cain to Capone: Racketeering Down the Ages*. New York: Brentano's, 1931.

McConnell, Brian. *Assassination*. London: Leslie Frewin, 1969.

_____. *Found Naked and Dead*. London: New English Library, 1974.

_____. *The History of Assassination*. Nashville, Tenn.: Aurora, 1969.

_____, and Bence, Douglas. *The Nilsen File*. London: Futura, 1983

McConnell, J.L. *Western Characters*. New York: Redfield, 1853.

McConnell, Jean. *The Detectives: Turning Points in Criminal Investigation*. Newton Abbot, Eng.: David & Charles, 1976.

McConnell, William J. *Early History of Idaho*. Caldwell, Idaho: Caxton Printers, 1913.

McConnell, William John. *Frontier Law: A Story of Vigilante Days*. New York: World Book, 1924.

McConville, Michael, and Baldwin, John. *Courts, Prosecution and Conviction*. Oxford, Eng.: Clarendon Press, 1981.

McCool, Grace. *So Said the Coroner: How They Died in Old Cochise*. Tombstone, Ariz.: Tombstone Epitaph, 1968.

McCord, W., and McCord, J. *Origins of Crime*. New York: Columbia University Press, 1959.

_____. *The Psychopath: An Essay on the Criminal Mind*. Princeton, N.J.: D. Van Nostrand, 1964.

McCorkle, John. *Three Years with Quantrill: A True Story*. Armstrong, Mo.: Armstrong Herald, 1914.

MacCormick, A.H. *Education of Adult Prisoners*. New York: National Society of Penal Information, 1931.

McCormick, Donald. *The Identity of Jack the Ripper*. London: Arrow Books, 1970.

_____. *Murder by Witchcraft*. London: John Long, 1968.

_____. *Peddler of Death*. London: McDonald, 1965.

McCormick, Robert R. *The American Empire*. Chicago: Chicago Tribune, 1952.

McCoy, Alfred W. *The Politics of Heroin in Southeast Asia*. New York: Harper & Row, 1972.

McCready, Albert L. *Railroads in the Days of Steam*. New York: American Heritage, 1960.

McCullagh, Francis. *Red Mexico: A Reign of Terror in America*. New York: L. Carrier, 1928.

McDade, Thomas. *Annals of Murder*. Norman: University of Oklahoma Press, 1961.

McDaniel, Ruel. *Vinegaroon*. Kingsport, Tenn.: Southern, 1936.

Macdermott, Mercia. *A History of Bulgaria, 1393-1885*. London: George Allen & Unwin, 1962.

McDermott, M.J., and Hindelang, M.J. *Juvenile Criminal Behavior in the United States*. Washington, D.C.: Office of Juvenile Justice and Delinquency Prevention, 1981.

_____. *Rape Victimization in 26 American Cities*. Washington, D.C.: U.S. Government Printing Office, 1979

MacDonald, Alan. *Al Capone and His Gang*. New York: Scholastics Paperbacks, 2000.

MacDonald, Arthur. *Criminology*. New York: Funk & Wagnalls, 1893.

McDonald, Donald. *The Police*. Santa Barbara, Calif.: Center for the Study of Democratic Institutions, 1962.

McDonald, Forrest. *Insull*. Chicago: University of Chicago Press, 1962.

McDonald, Hugh C., and Bocca, Geoffrey. *Appointment in Dallas: The Final Solution to the Assassination of JFK*. New York: Published by Author, 1975.

_____, and Moore, Robin. *L.B.J. and the J.F.K. Conspiracy*. Westport, Conn.: Condon, 1979.

MacDonald, John M. *Armed Robbery*. Springfield, Ill.: Charles C. Thomas, 1975.

_____. *Homicidal Threats*. Springfield, Ill.: Charles C. Thomas, 1968.

_____. *Indecent Exposure*. Springfield, Ill: Charles C. Thomas, 1973.

_____. *The Murderer and His Victim*. Springfield, Ill.: Charles C. Thomas, 1961.

_____. *Psychiatry and the Criminal*. Springfield, Ill.: Charles C. Thomas, 1958.

_____. *Rape: Offenders and Their Victims*. Springfield, Ill.: Charles C. Thomas, 1971.

MacDonald, Philip. *Mystery of the Dead Police*. New York: Doubleday, 1933.

McDonald, R. Robin. *Black Widow*. New York: St. Martin's, 1986.

MacDonald, Robert. *The League of Arab States*. Princeton, N.J.: Princeton University Press, 1965.

McDonald, William A. *Progress Into the Past: The Rediscovery of Mycenaean Civilization*. Bloomington, Ind.: Indiana Univer-sity Press, 1967.

McDonald, William F. (ed.). *Criminal Justice and the Victim*. Beverly Hills, Calif.: Sage, 1976.

McDougal, Dennis. *Angel of Darkness*. New York: Warner, 1981.

_____. *The Yosemite Murders*. New York: Ballantine, 2000.

MacDougall, Curtis D. *Hoaxes*. New York: Macmillan, 1940.

MacDougall, Ernest D. (ed.). *Crime for Profit: A Symposium on Mercenary Crime*. Boston: Statford, 1933.

Mace, Gustave. *Les Femmes criminelles*. Paris: Charpentier, 1904.

_____. *My First Crime*. London: Vizetelly, 1886.

_____. *La Police parisienne*. Paris: Charpentier, 1884.

Mace, Ellis C. *River Steamboats and Steamboat Men*. Cynthiana, Ky.: Hobson Book Press, 1944.

McElderry, Andrea Lee. *Shanghai Old-Style Banks 1800-1935*. Ann Arbor: University of Michigan Press, 1935.

Macfarlane, A.D.J. *Witchcraft in Tudor and Stuart England*. New York: Harper & Row, 1970.

McFarlane, Ian. *Proof of Conspiracy in the Assassination of President Kennedy*. Melbourne: Book Distributors, 1974.

Macfarlane, Leslie. *Violence and the State*. London: Nelson, 1974.

McGarvey, Patrick J. *C.I.A.: The Myth and the Madness*. Bal-timore, Md.: Penguin Books, 1973.

McGloin, John Bernard. *San Francisco: The Story of a City*. San Rafael, Calif.: Presidio Press, 1978.

McGovern, James. *Martin Bormann*. New York: William Morrow, 1968.

MacGovern, William. *From Luther to Hitler*. London: George Harrap, 1946.

McGowan, Helen. *Big City Madam*. New York: Lancer Books, 1965.

McGrady, Mike. *Crime Scientists*. Philadelphia: J.B. Lippincott, 1961.

McGrath, W.T. *Should Canada Abolish the Gallows and the Lash?* Winnipeg, Manitoba, Can.: Stovel-Advocate Press, 1956.

McGregor, Douglas. *The Human Side of Enterprise*. New York: McGraw-Hill, 1960.

MacGregor, Geddes. *Thundering Scot*. London: Macmillan, 1958.

_____. *The Tichborne Impostor*. Philadelphia: J.B. Lippincott, 1957.

MacGregor, George. *The History of Burke and Hare*. Glasgow, Scot.: Thomas D. Morison, 1884.

MacGregor-Hastie, Roy. *The Day of the Lion, The Rise and Fall of Fascist Italy, 1922-1945*. New York: Coward-McCann, 1963.

McGuigan, Patrick B., and Rader, Randall R. (eds.). *Criminal Justice Reform*. Chicago: Henry Regnery, 1983.

McGuire, Christine, and Norton, Carla. *Perfect Victim*. New York: Dell, 1988.

McGuire, E. Patrick. *The Forgers*. Bernardsville, N.J.: Padrie, 1969.

McGuire, Maria. *To Take Arms*. London: Macmillan, 1973.

Machiavelli, Niccolò. *The History of Florence and Other Selections*. trans. Judith A. Rawson. New York: Washington Square Press, 1940.

_____. *The Prince and the Discourses*. New York: Modern Library, 1940.

Machlin, Milton. *Libby*. New York: Tower, 1980.

McHugh, Hugh [George Vere Hobart]. *You Can Search Me*. New York: G. W. Dillingham, 1905.

McIlvaine, Mabel (ed.). *Reminiscences of Chicago during the Forties and Fifties*. Chicago: R.R. Donnelley, 1913.

_____ (ed.). *Reminiscences of Early Chicago*. Chicago: Lakeside Press, 1912.

McIlwaine, Shields. *Memphis Down in Dixie*. New York: E.P. Dutton, 1948.

McIntire, James. *Early Days in Texas: A Trip to Hell and Heaven*. Kansas City: McIntire, 1902.

McIntire, Josephine. *Boot Hill*. Boston: Chapman & Grimes, 1945.

McIntosh, Arthur T. *Chicago*. Chicago: Press of G.G. Renneker, 1921.

McIntosh, Mary. *The Organization of Crime*. London: Macmil-lan, 1975.

McIntyre, Tommy. *Wolfe in Sheep's Clothing*. Detroit: Wayne State University Press, 1988.

Mackaness, George. *The Life of Vice-Admiral William Bligh*. New York: Farrar & Rinehart, 1936.

MacKay, Charles. *Extraordinary Popular Delusions and the Madness of Crowds*. Boston: L.C. Page, 1932.

McKay, Claude. *Home to Harlem*. New York: Pocket Books, 1965.

McKay, Henry D., and Shaw, Clifford R. *Juvenile Delinquency and Urban Areas*. Chicago: University of Chicago Press, 1942.

Mackay, Margaret. *Los Angeles Proper and Improper*. New York: Goodwin, 1938.

Mackaye, Milton. *Dramatic Crimes of 1927*. Garden City, N.Y.: Crime Club, 1928.

_____. *The Tin Box Parade*. New York: Robert M. McBride 1934.

McKean, Dayton. *The Boss*. Boston: Houghton Mifflin, 1940.

McKee, Alexander. *H.M.S. Bounty*. New York: William Morrow, 1962.

MacKellar, Jean Scott. *Rape: The Bait and the Trap*. New York: Crown, 1975.

McKelvey, Blake. *American Prisons*. Montclair, N.J.: Patterson Smith, 1977.

McKelway, St. Clair. *The Big Little Man Brooklyn*. Boston: Houghton Mifflin, 1969.

_____. *True Tales from the Annals of Crime and Rascality*. New York: Random House, 1950.

_____. *True Tales of Crime and Rascality*. New York: Random House, 1933.

McKennon, C.H. *Iron Men: A Saga of the Deputy United States Marshals Who Rode the Indian Territory*. Garden City, N.Y.: Doubleday, 1967.

Mackenzie, Colin. *Biggs, The World's Most Wanted Man*. New York: William Morrow, 1975.

McKenzie, Donald. *Occupation: Thief*. Indianapolis, Ind.: Bobbs-Merrill, 1955.

Mackenzie, Frederic A. *Landru*. New York: Charles Scribner's Sons, 1928.

_____. *"Pussyfoot" Johnson*. New York: Fleming H. Revell, 1920.

_____. *The Trial of Harry Thaw*. London: Geoffrey Bles, 1928.

_____. *Twentieth Century Crimes*. Boston: Little, Brown, 1927.

_____. *World Famous Crimes*. London: Geoffrey Bles, 1927.

Mackenzie, Sir George. *Laws and Customs of Scotland in*

Matters Criminal. Edinburgh, Scot.: George Swinton, 1678.
Mackenzie, Jeanne and Norman. *The Murder of Maria Marten.* New York: Pellegrini & Cudahy, 1948.
MacKenzie, K.P. *Operation Rangoon Jail.* London: Christopher Johnson, 1954.
Mackenzie, Norman. *Secret Societies.* New York: Holt, Rinehart & Winston, 1967.
McKeon, Richard (ed.). *The Basic Works of Aristotle.* New York: Random House, 1941.
McKernan, Maureen. *The Amazing Crime and Trial of Leopold and Loeb.* New York: New American Library, 1957.
MacKey, Philip English. *Voices Against Death.* New York: Artemis, 1978.
McKinley, James. *Assassination in America.* New York: Harper & Row, 1977.
McKitrick, Eric L. *Andrew Johnson and the Reconstruction.* Chicago: University of Chicago Press, 1960.
McKnight, Gerald. *The Mind of the Terrorist.* London: Michael Joseph, 1974.
_____. *The Murder Squad.* London: W.H. Allen, 1967.
_____. *The Terrorist Mind.* Indianapolis, Ind.: Bobbs-Merrill, 1975.
Mack, John A. *The Crime Industry.* Westmead, Eng.: Saxon House, 1974.
Mack Smith, Denis. *A History of Sicily: Modern Sicily after 1713.* New York: Viking Press, 1968.
McLaren, Malcolm, Jr. "Tyranny," *The Greek Political Experience.* Princeton, N.J.: Princeton University Press, 1941.
Maclay, Edgar Stanton. *A History of American Privateers.* New York: D. Appleton, 1899.
McLellan, Vin, and Avery, Paul. *The Voices of Guns.* New York: G.P. Putnam's Sons, 1977.
MacLeod, Donald. *Biography of Hon. Fernando Wood, Mayor of the City of New York.* New York: O.F. Parsons, 1858.
Macleod, Malcolm. *History of Witches.* Washington, D.C.: C.A. Beckert, 1894.
McLoughlin, Emmett. *An Inquiry into the Assassination of Abraham Lincoln.* New York: Lyle Stuart, 1963.
McMillan, George. *The Making of an Assassin.* Boston: Little, Brown, 1976.
Macmillan, James. *The Honors Game.* London: Leslie Frewin, 1969.
McMillan, Priscilla Johnson. *Marina and Lee.* New York: Harper & Row, 1977.
Macmunn, G.F. *Religions and Hidden Cults of India.* London: Sampson, Low, 1931.
Macnaghten, Sir Melville. *Days of My Years.* London: Edward Arnold, 1914.
MacNair, Harley Farnsworth (ed.). *China.* Berkeley: University of California Press, 1951.
McNally, Raymond. *Dracula Was a Woman.* New York: McGraw-Hill, 1983.
MacNamara, Donald E.J., and Sagarin, Edward. *Sex, Crime and the Law.* New York: Free Press, 1978.
McNamara, Joseph D. *Safe and Sane.* New York: G.P. Putnam's Sons, 1984.
McNeal, Robert H. (ed.). *Lenin, Stalin, Khrushchev: Voices of Bolshevism.* New York: Prentice-Hall, 1963.
McNeal, Thomas Allen. *When Kansas Was Young.* New York: Macmillan, 1922.
McNeill, John T., and Gamer, Helena M. *Medieval Handbooks of Penance.* New York: Columbia University Press, 1938.
McNeill, William H. *The Greek Dilemma: War and Aftermath.* Philadelphia: J.B. Lippincott, 1947.
_____. *A World History.* New York: Oxford University Press, 1967.
McNelly, Theodore. *Politics and Government in Japan.* Boston: Houghton Mifflin, 1972.
McPhaul, John J. *Deadlines and Monkeyshines: The Fabled World of Chicago Journalism.* Englewood Cliffs, N.J.: Prentice-Hall, 1962.
_____. *Johnny Torrio.* New Rochelle, N.Y.: Arlington House, 1970.
McPherson, J.W. *The Moulids of Egypt.* Cairo, Egypt: Ptd. N.M. Press, 1941.
McQuillan, Alice. *They Call Them Grifters.* New York: Oynx, 2000.
McRill, Albert. *And Satan Came Also.* Oklahoma City, Okla.: Britton, 1955.
MacShane, Frank. *The Life of John O'Hara.* New York: E.P. Dutton, 1980.
_____. *The Life of Raymond Chandler.* London: Jonathan Cape, 1976.
McTaggart, Lynne. *The Baby Brokers.* New York: Dial Press, 1980.
McWatters, George S. *Detectives of Europe and America, or Life in the Secret Service.* Chicago: Laird & Lee, 1892.
_____. *Forgers and Confidence Men, or The Secrets of the Detective Service Divulged.* Chicago: Laird & Lee, 1892.
_____. *The Gambler's Wax Finger and Other Startling Detective Experiences.* Chicago: Laird & Lee, 1892.
_____. *Knots Untied, or Ways and Byways in the Hidden Life of American Detectives.* Hartford, Conn.: J.B. Burr & Hyde, 1871.
McWilliams, Carey. *Ambrose Bierce, A Biography.* New York: A. & C. Boni, 1929.
Madden, David (ed.). *Tough Guy Writers of the Thirties.* Carbon-dale: Southern Illinois University Press, 1968.
Mader, Julius. *Who's Who in CIA.* Berlin: Published by Author, 1968.
Madison, Arnold. *Great Unsolved Cases.* London: Franklin Watts, 1978.
Madison, Charles A. *Critics and Crusaders: A Century of American Protest.* New York: Henry Holt, 1947.
Madow, Leo, et al. *The Dangerous Sex Offender.* Philadelphia: General Assembly of the Commonwealth of Pennsylvania, 1963.
Maeder, Thomas. *Crime and Madness.* New York: Harper & Row, 1985.
_____. *The Unspeakable Crimes of Dr. Petiot.* Toronto, Ontario, Can.: Atlantic, Little, Brown, 1980.
Magee, D. *What Murder Leaves Behind: The Victim's Family.* New York: Dodd, Mead, 1983.
Magee, John. *Northern Ireland: Crisis and Conflict.* London: Routledge & Kegan Paul, 1974.
Magnus, Philip. *Gladstone: A Biography.* London: John Murray, 1954.
_____. *King Edward the Seventh.* London: John Murray, 1964.
Maher, George F. *Hostage: A Police Approach to a Contemporary Crisis.* Springfield, Ill.: Charles C. Thomas, 1977.
Maiken, Peter T. *Rip-Off.* Kansas City: Andrews & McMeel, 1979.
Maier, Karl. *This House Has Fallen: Nigeria in Crisis.* New York: Westview Press, 2003.
Mailer, Norman. *The Executioner's Song.* Boston: Little, Brown, 1979.
Maina, P. *Six Mau Mau Generals.* Nairobi, Kenya: Gazelle Books, 1977.
Maine, C.E. (ed.). *The World's Strangest Crimes.* New York: Hart, 1967.
Maire, G.F. *Raspoutine.* Paris: n. p., 1934.
Mairs, G.T. *Fingerprint Study Data.* New York: Delehanty Institute, 1938.
Majdalany, Fred. *State of Emergency: The Full Story of Mau Mau.* Boston: Houghton Mifflin, 1963.
Majumdar, R.C., et al. *An Advanced History of India.* New York: Macmillan, 1946.
Makins, John R. (ed.). *Boston Murders.* New York: Duell, Sloan & Pearce, 1947.
Malaparte, Curzio. *Kaputt.* trans. Cesare Foligno. New York: E.P. Dutton, 1946.
_____. *Technique du Coup d'Etat.* Paris: Bernard Grasset, 1948.
Malcolm, Lady. *A Diary of St. Helena.* London: George Allen & Unwin, 1899.
Maldonado R., Calixto. *Los asesinatos de los Senores Madero y Pino Suarez.* Mexico City: n.p., 1922.
Malinowski, Bronislaw. *Crime and Custom in Savage Society.* Totowa, N.J.: Littlefield, Adams, 1966.
_____. *Magic, Science and Religion.* New York: Doubleday Anchor Books, 1954.
_____. *Sex and Repression in Savage Society.* London: Kegan, Paul, Trench, Trubner, 1927.
_____. *The Sexual Life of Savages.* London: George Routledge & Sons, 1932.
Mallet, M.E. *The Borgias.* London: Bodley Head, 1969.
Mallet, Victor (ed.). *Life with Queen Victoria: Marie Mallet's Letters from Court 1887-1901.* Boston: Houghton Mifflin, 1968.
Maltz, Michael D. *Evaluation of Crime Control Programs.* Washington, D.C.: National Institute of Law Enforcement and Criminal Justice, 1972.
Mamdani, Mahmod. *When Victims Become Killers: Colonialism, Nativism and the Genocide in Rwanda.* Princeton, N. J.: Princeton University Press, 2002.
Manchester, William. *American Caesar: Douglas MacArthur, 1880-1964.* Boston: Little, Brown, 1978.
_____. *The Death of a President.* New York: Harper & Row, 1967.
_____. *Disturber of the Peace.* New York: Harper & Bothers, 1951.
_____. *The Glory and the Dream.* Boston: Little, Brown, 1973.
_____. *Portrait of a President - John F. Kennedy in Profile.* Boston: Little, Brown, 1962.
Mancini, Jean-Gabriel. *Prostitutes and Their Parasites.* London: Elek Books, 1963.
Mandelbaum, Seymour J. *Boss Tweed's New York.* New York: John Wiley & Sons, 1965.
Mangan, Frank J. *Bordertown.* El Paso, Texas: Carl Hertzog, 1964.
Mann, Arthur. *La Guardia Comes to Power: 1933.* Philadelphia: J.B. Lippincott, 1965.
_____. *Yankee Reformers in the Urban Age.* Cambridge, Mass.: Harvard University Press, 1954.
Mann, Kenneth. *Defending White-Collar Crime.* New Haven, Conn.: Yale University Press, 1985.
Mann, William B. *Trial, Life and Execution of Anton Probst.* Philadelphia: T.P. Peterson & Brothers, 1866.
Mannheim, Hermann. *Comparative Criminology.* Boston: Houghton Mifflin, 1965.
_____. *Criminal Justice and Social Reconstruction.* New York: Oxford University Press, 1946.
_____. *The Dilemma of Penal Reform.* London: George Allen & Unwin, 1939.
_____. *Group Problems in Crime and Punishment.* New York: Humanities Press, 1955.
_____ (ed.). *Pioneers in Criminology.* London: Stevens, 1961.
_____, and Wilkins, L.T. *Prediction Methods in Relation to Borstal Training.* London: H.M. Stationery Office, 1955.
_____. *Social Aspects of Crime in England Between the Wars.* London: George Allen & Unwin, 1940.
Manning, Peter K. *The Narc's Game.* Cambridge, Mass.: MIT Press, 1980.
_____. *Police Work: The Social Organization of Policing.* Cam-bridge, Mass.: MIT Press, 1977.
Mannix, Daniel P., and Cowley, Malcolm. *Black Cargoes: A History of the Atlantic Slave Trade, 1518-1865.* New York: Viking Press, 1962.
_____. *The Hell Fire Club.* New York: Ballantine, 1959.
Mansfield, Justine. *True Tales of Kidnappings in America - in China - in Mexico.* New York: Business Bourse Press, 1932.
Mansfield, Peter. *Nasser's Egypt.* Baltimore: Penguin Books, 1965.
Manvell, Roger, and Fraenkel, Heinrich. *The Conspirators: 20th July, 1944.* London: Bodley Head, 1964.
_____, and _____. *Goebbels.* New York: Pyramid Books, 1960.
_____. *Heinrich Himmler.* New York: G.P. Putnam's Sons, 1965.
_____. *Hermann Goring.* London: William Heinemann, 1962.
_____, *Hess.* London: MacGibbon & Kee, 1972.
_____, *The Men Who Tried to kill Hitler.* New York: Coward-McCann, 1964.
_____. *SS and Gestapo: Rule by Terror.* London: Macdonald, 1970.
Manzour, Anatole G. *Rise and Fall of the Romanovs.* Princeton, N.J.: D. Van Nostrand, 1960.
_____. *Russia, Past and Present.* New York: D. Van Nostrand, 1951.
Marchbanks, David. *The Moors Murders.* London: Frewin, 1966.
Marchetti, Victor, and Marks, John D. *The CIA and the Cult of Intelligence.* New York: Alfred A. Knopf, 1974.
_____. *The Rope-Dancer.* New York: Grossett & Dunlap, 1971.
Marcus, Sheldon. *Father Coughlin.* Boston: Little, Brown, 1973.
Marcus, Steven (ed.). *The Continental Op.* New York: Random House, 1974.

_____. *Engels, Manchester, and the Working Class.* New York: Random House, 1974.
_____. *The Other Victorians.* New York: Basic Books, 1966.
Marcuse, Maxwell F. *This Was New York.* New York: Lim Press, 1969.
Marden, Charles F. *Minorities in American Society.* New York: American Book, 1952.
Mardin, Serif. *The Genesis of Young Ottoman Thought: A Study in the Modernization of Turkish Political Ideas.* Princeton, N.J.: Princeton University Press, 1962.
Margulies, Phillip. *Al Qaeda: Osama bin Laden's Army of Terrorists.* New York: Rosen Publishing Group, 2003.
Mariani, Angelo. *Coca and Its Theraputic Application.* New York: J.N. Jaros, 1890.
Marie, Grand Duchess of Russia. *Education of a Princess: A Memoir.* trans. Russell Lord. New York: Viking Press, 1931.
_____. *A Princess in Exile.* New York: Viking Press, 1932.
Marie, Queen of Romania. *The Country That I Love: An Exile Memories.* London: Duckworth, 1925.
_____. *Crowned Queens.* London: Heath Cranton, 1929.
_____. *Masks.* New York: E.P. Dutton, 1937.
Marighela, Carlos. *For the Liberation of Brazil.* London: Pen-guin, 1971.
The Marijuana Problem in the City of New York. New York: Mayor's Committee on Marijuana, 1944.
Marine, Gene. *The Black Panthers.* New York: New American Library, 1969.
Marinoni, Antonio. *Italy: Yesterday and Today.* New York: Macmillan, 1931.
Marjoribanks, Edward. *For The Defense The Life of Sir Edward Marshall Hall.* London: Victor Gollancz, 1926.
_____. *The Life of Lord Carson.* Volume one. London: Victor Gollancz, 1932.
_____. *The Life of Sir Edward Marshall Hall.* London: Victor Gollancz, 1931.
Marks, Harry H. *Small Change, or Lights and Shadows of New York.* New York: Standard, 1882.
Marks, Stanley J. *Coup d'Etat! Three Murders That Changed the Course of History: President Kennedy, Reverend King, and Senator Robert F. Kennedy.* Los Angeles: Bureau of Interna-tional Affairs, 1970.
_____. *Murder Most Foul! The Conspiracy That Murdered President Kennedy.* Los Angeles: Bureau of International Affairs, 1967.
_____. *Two Days of Infamy: Relating to the Murder of President Kennedy.* Los Angeles: Bureau of International Affairs, 1969.
Marlowe, John. *Arab Nationalism and British Imperialism.* New York: Frederick A. Praeger, 1961.
_____. *A History of Modern Egypt and Anglo-Egyptian Relations.* New York: Frederick A. Praeger, 1954.
Maroger, D. (ed.). *The Memoirs of Catherine the Great.* New York: Macmillan, 1955.
Marriott, John A.R. *The Eastern Question: A Historical Study in European Diplomacy.* Oxford, Eng.: Clarendon Press, 1951.
Marsden, G.V. *Rasputin and Russia, the Tragedy of a Throne.* n.p., 1920.
Marsh, Ngaio. *Singing in the Shrouds.* Boston: Little, Brown, 1958.
Marsh, Thomas O. *Roots of Crime.* Newton, N.J.: Nellen, 1981.
Marshall, Carrington T. *A History of Courts and Lawyers of Ohio.* New York: American Historical Society, 1934.
Marshall, John A. *American Bastille.* Philadelphia: Thomas W. Hartley, 1877.
Marshall, Jonathan. *Drug Wars: Corruption, Counterintelligence and Covert Operations in the Third World.* Forestville, Calif.: Cohan & Cohen, 1991.
Marshall, Otto Miller. *The Wham Paymaster Robbery.* Pima, Ariz.: Pima Chamber of Commerce, 1967.
Marshall, S.L. *Sinai Victory.* New York: William Morrow, 1958.
_____. *Swift Sword: The Historical Record of Israel's Victory, June, 1967.* New York: American Heritage, 1967.
Marshall, Theodora Britton, and Evans, Gladys Crail. *They Found It In Natchez.* New Orleans, La.: Pelican, 1939.
Marten, Manuel Edward. *The Doctor Looks at Murder.* Garden City, N.Y.: Doubleday, Doran, 1937.
Martienssen, Anthony. *Crime and the Police.* London: Martin Secker & Warburg, 1951.
Martin, Charles L. *A Sketch of Sam Bass, The Bandit.* Norman: University of Oklahoma Press, 1956.
Martin, Del. *Battered Wives.* New York: Pocket Books, 1977.
Martin, Douglas D. *An Arizona Chronology: The Territorial Years, 1846-1912.* Tucson: University of Arizona Press, 1963.
_____. *The Earps of Tombstone.* Tombstone, Ariz.: Tombstone Epitaph, 1959.
_____. *Silver, Sex and Six Guns: Tombstone Sage of the Life of Buckskin Frank Leslie.* Tombstone, Ariz.: Tombstone Epitaph, 1962.
_____. *Tombstone's Epitaph.* Albuquerque: University of New Mexico Press, 1951.
Martin, Edward Winslow. *The Secrets of the Great City.* Philadelphia: n.p., 1868.
Martin, Edwin M. *The Allied Occupation of Japan.* New York: American Institute of Pacific Relations, 1948.
Martin, Frederick Townsend. *The Passing of the Idle Rich.* Garden City, N.Y.: Doubleday, Page, 1912.
_____. *Things I Remember.* New York: John Lane, 1913.
Martin, George. *Causes and Conflicts: The Centennial History of the Association of the Bar of the City of New York, 1870-1970.* Boston: Houghton Mifflin, 1970.
Martin, John Bartlow. *Break Down the Walls.* New York: Ballantine, 1954.
_____. *Butcher's Dozen and Other Murders.* New York: Harper & Row, 1950.
_____. *My Life in Crime.* New York: Harper & Brothers, 1952.
Martin, John M., and Fitzpatrick, Joseph P. *Delinquent Behaviour.* New York: Random House, 1965.
Martin, John P. *Juvenile Vandalism.* Springfield, Ill.: Charles C. Thomas, 1961.
_____. *Offenders as Employees.* London: Macmillan, 1962.
Martin, L. John. *International Propaganda.* Minneapolis: University of Minnesota Press, 1958.
Martin, Mildred Crowl. *Chinatown's Angry Angel.* Palo Alto, Calif.: Pacific Books, 1977.
Martin, Ralph G. *Ballots and Bandwagons.* Chicago: Rand McNally, 1964.
Martin, Raymond V. *Revolt in the Mafia.* New York: Duell, 1963.
Martin, Sir Theodore. *Life of the Prince Consort.* London: Smith, Elder, 1880.
Martineau, Gilbert. *Napoleon's St. Helena.* trans. Frances Partridge. Chicago: Rand McNally, 1968.
Martineau, Harriet. *The History of England During the Thirty Years' Peace, 1816-1846.* 2 vols. London: Charles Knight, 1849.
Martinez, Al. *Jigsaw John.* Los Angeles: J.P. Tarcher, 1975.
Martingale, Moira. *Cannibal Killers.* New York: St. Martin's, 1993.
Martini, John A. *Fortress Alcatraz: Guardian of the Golden Gate.* San Francisco: Pacific Monograph, 1991.
Marvin, Richard. *The Kennedy Curse.* New York: Belmont Books, n.d.
Marye, George Thomas. *Secrets of the Great City; the Virtues and the Vices, the Mysteries, Miseries and Crimes at New York City.* New York: Published by Author, 1868.
Masefield, John. *On the Spanish Main.* New York: Macmillan, 1925.
Maser, Werner. *Hitler: Legend, Myth and Reality.* New York: Harper & Row, 1974.
_____. *Hitler's Mein Kampf: An Analysis.* London: Faber & Faber, 1970.
_____. *Nuremberg: A Nation on Trial.* trans. Richard Barry. New York: Charles Scribner's Sons, 1979.
Maskelyn, John Nevil. *Sharps and Flats, A Complete Revelation of the Secrets of Cheating at Games of Chance and Skill.* New York: Longmans, Green, 1894.
Mason, Alpheus Thomas. *Brandeis: A Free Man's Life.* New York: Viking Press, 1946.
_____. *Harland Fiske Stone: Pillar of the Law.* New York: Viking Press, 1956.
_____. *Security through Freedom.* Ithaca, N.Y.: Cornell Univer-sity Press, 1955.
_____. *The Supreme Court from Taft to Warren.* Baton Rouge: Louisiana State University Press, 1958.
_____, and Beaney, William M. *The Supreme Court in a Free Society.* Englewood Cliffs, N.J.: Prentice-Hall, 1959.
Mason, Edward Gay (ed.). *Early Chicago and Illinois.* Chicago: Fergus Printing, 1890.
Mason, Herbert. *To Kill the Devil, Attempts on the Life of Adolf Hitler.* New York: W.W. Norton, 1978.
Mason, James. *The Anatomy of Sorcery.* London: I. Legatte, 1612.
Mason, John Alden. *The Ancient Civilizations of Peru.* London: Penguin Books, 1957.
Mason, Philip. *Call the Next Witness.* New York: Harcourt, Brace, 1945.
Massie, Robert K. *Nicholas and Alexandra.* New York: Athene-um, 1967.
_____. *The Romanovs.* New York: Ballantine, 1996.
Masson, Ren. *Number One: A Story of Landru.* trans. Gillian Tindall. London: Hutchinson, 1964.
Mast, Blaine. *K.K.K. Friend or Foe: Which?* Pittsburgh, Pa.: Herbrick & Held Printing, 1924.
Masters, Brian. *Killing For Company.* New York: Stein & Day, 1985.
_____. *The Shrine of Jeffrey Dahmer.* London: Hodder & Stoughton, 1993.
Masters, Edgar Lee. *Lincoln the Man.* New York: Dodd, Mead, 1931.
_____. *The Tale of Chicago.* New York: G.P. Putnam's Sons, 1933.
Masters, R.E.L. *Patterns of Incest.* New York: Ace, 1963.
_____, and Lea, Eduord. *Perverse Crimes in History.* New York: Julian Press, 1963.
_____. *Sex Crimes in History: Evolving Concepts of Sadism, Lust-Murder, and Necrophilia from Ancient to Modern Times.* New York: Julian Press, 1963.
Mastny, Vojtch. *The Czechs under Nazi Rule: The Failure of the National Resistence, 1939-1942.* New York: Columbia University Press, 1971.
Matsumoto Seicho. *Nihon no Kuroikiri* (Black Mist over Japan). Tokyo: Bungei Shunju, 1974.
Matters, Leonard. *The Mystery of Jack the Ripper.* London: W.H. Allen, 1948.
Matthews, Jim. *Four Dark Days in History: November 22, 23, 24 and 25, 1963.* Los Angeles: Special, 1963.
Matusow, Allen J. (ed.). *Joseph McCarthy.* Englewood Cliffs, N.J.: Prentice-Hall, 1971.
Matz, Mary Jane. *The Many Lives of Otto Kahn.* New York: Macmillan, 1963.
Maurer, David W. *The Big Con.* New York: Bobbs-Merrill, 1940.
_____. *Whiz Mob.* Gainesville, Fla.: American Dialect Society, 1955.
Maurois, Andre. *Edwardian Era.* New York: Appleton-Century, 1933.
Maverick, Augustus. *Henry J. Raymond and the New York Press.* Hartford, Conn.: A.S. Hale, 1870.
Mavity, Nancy Barr. *Sister Aimee.* Garden City, N.Y.: Double-day, Doran, 1931.
Maxwell, G.S. *Highwayman's Heath.* London: Middlesex Chron-icle, 1935.
Maxwell, Gavin. *Bandit.* New York: Harper & Brothers, 1956.
Maxwell, Gilbert. *Helen Morgan: Her Life and Legend.* New York: Hawthorn Books, 1974.
May, Betty. *Tiger-Woman: My Story.* London: Duckworth, 1929.
May, Henry John. *Murder by Consent.* London: Hutchinson 1968.
Maycock, Sir Willoughby. *Celebrated Crimes and Criminals.* Maidstone, Eng.: George Mann, 1973.
Mayer, Henry. *The Press in Australia.* New Rochelle, N.Y.: Soccer Associates, 1964.
Mayer, J.E., and Timms, N. *The Client Speaks.* London: Rout-ledge & Kegan Paul, 1970.
Mayer, Martin. *The Bankers.* New York: Ballantine Books, 1974.
_____. *The Lawyers.* New York: Harper & Row, 1967.
Mayer, Robert. *The Dreams of Ada.* New York: Viking Press, 1987.
_____ (ed.). *San Francisco.* Dobbs Ferry, N.Y.: Oceana Publica-tions, 1974.
_____. *Los Angeles, a Chronological and Documentary History.* Dobbs Ferry, N.Y.: Oceana, 1978.
Mayers, Lewis. *The American Legal System.* New York: Harper & Row, 1964.
Mayhew, Henry, and Binny, John. *The Criminal Prisons of London and Scenes of Prison Life.* London: Griffin, Bohn, 1862.

_____. *London Labour and the London Poor.* London: Frank Cass, 1967.
_____. *London's Underworld.* London: William Kimber, 1950.
Mayo, John B. *Bulletin fron Dallas: The President is Dead.* New York: Exposition Press, 1967.
Mayo, Katherine. *The Face of Mother India.* New York: Harper & Brothers, 1936.
_____. *Justice to All: The Story of the Pennsylvania State Police.* Boston: Houghton Mifflin, 1920.
_____. *Mother India.* New York: Harcourt, Brace, 1927.
_____. *Mounted Justice.* Boston: Houghton Mifflin, 1922.
_____. *Slave of the Gods.* New York: Harcourt, Brace, 1929.
Mazour, Anatole G. *The Rise and Fall of the Romanovs.* Princeton, N.J.: D. Van Nostrand, 1960.
Mazzula, Fred and Jo. *Al Packer, a Colorado Cannibal.* Denver: Published by Authors, 1968.
_____. *Brass Checks and Red Lights.* Denver: Published by Authors, 1966.
_____. *Outlaw Album.* Denver: A.B. Hirschfeld Press, 1966.
Mead, John Clark. *The New World War: A Behind-the-Scenes Look at Why and How Militant Muslims Plan to Destroy Western Civilization.* New York: Xulon Press, 2002.
Meagher, Sylvia. *Accessories After the Fact.* New York: Bobbs-Merrill, 1967.
_____. *Subject Index to the Warren Report and Hearings and Exhibits.* New York: Scarecrow Press, 1966.
Means, Gaston B. *The Strange Death of President Harding.* New York: Gold Label Books, 1930.
Mearns, David C. *The Lincoln Papers.* 2 vols. Garden City, N.Y.: Doubleday, 1948.
Mecklin, John M. *The Ku Klux Klan: A Study of the American Mind.* New York: Russell & Russell, 1963.
Medalie, Richard J. *From Escobedo to Miranda.* Washington, D.C.: Lerner Law Book, 1966.
Medbery, J.K. *Men and Mysteries of Wall Street.* New York: Osgood, 1870.
Medea, Andrea, and Thompson, Kathleen. *Against Rape.* New York: Farrar, Straus & Giroux, 1974.
Mee, Charles L., Jr. *The Ohio Gang.* New York: M. Evans, 1981.
Meek, Victor. *Cops and Robbers.* London: G. Duckworth, 1962.
_____. *Private Enquiries: A Handbook for Detectives.* London: G. Duckworth, 1967.
Meeker, Arthur. *Chicago With Love.* New York: Alfred A. Knopf, 1955.
Megaro, Gaudens. *Mussolini in the Making.* Boston: Houghton, Mifflin, 1938.
Mehling, Harold. *The Scandalous Scamps.* New York: Henry Holt, 1959.
Meir, Golda. *My Life.* New York: G.D. Putnam's Sons, 1975.
Mellwain, David. *The Bizarre and the Bloody.* London: Hart, 1972.
Melman, Yossi. *The Master Terrorist.* New York: Adami, 1986.
Melnicoe, William B., and Menning, Jan. *Elements of Police Supervision.* New York: Glencoe Press, 1969.
Meltzer, Milton. *Slavery: A World History.* New York: Da Capo Press, 1993.
Melvern, Linda. *A People Betrayed: The Role of the West in Rwanda's Genocide.* London: Zed Books, 2000.
Melville, Herman. *The Confidence Man.* London: Constable, 1923.
Melville, L. *The South Sea Bubble.* Boston: Small, Maynard, 1923.
Melville, Samuel. *Letters from Attica.* New York: William Morrow, 1972.
Melville-Lee, Capt. W.L. *A History of Police in England.* London: Methuen, 1901.
Memoirs of King Abdullah of Transjordan. New York: Philosoph-ical Library, 1950.
Memorial to Greatness: The Presidential Years of John F. Kennedy. Island Park, N.Y.: Aspen, 1964.
Mencken, August. *By the Neck.* New York: Hastings House, 1942.
Mencken, H.L. *The American Language.* New York: Alfred A. Knopf, 1945.
_____. *The Bathtub Hoax.* New York: Alfred A. Knopf, 1958.
_____. *A Carnival of Buncombe.* Baltimore: Johns Hopkins University Press, 1956.
_____. *The Days of H.L. Mencken (Heathen Days: 1890-1936).* New York: Alfred A. Knopf, 1947.
_____. *Newspaper Days, 1899-1906.* New York: Alfred A. Knopf, 1941.
_____. *Prejudices.* New York: Alfred A. Knopf, 1926.
_____. *The Vintage Mencken.* New York: Vintage Books, 1955.
Mendel, Arthur P. *Dilemmas of Progress in Tsarist Russia: Legal Marxism and Legal Populism.* Cambridge, Mass.: Harvard University Press, 1961.
Mendelson, Mary A. *Tender Loving Greed.* New York: Vintage Books, 1975.
Mendelssohn, Peter de. *Japan's Political Warfare.* London: George Allen & Unwin, 1944.
_____. *The Nuremberg Documents.* London: George Allen & Unwin, 1946.
Mensch, Earnest Cromwell. *Alcatraz.* San Francisco: San Francisco Books, 1937.
Mercer, Asa Shinn. *The Banditti of the Plains.* Cheyenne, Wyo.: Published by Author, 1894.
Mercier, C. *Criminal Responsibility.* London: Oxford, 1935.
Merrill, Frederick T. *Japan and the Opium Menace.* New York: Institute of Pacific Relations and the Foreign Policy Associa-tion, 1942.
Merrill, John C. *The Elite Press: Great Newspaper of the World.* New York: Pitman, 1968.
Merrow, Smith, Harris, L.W., and Harris, James. *Prison Screw.* London: Jenkins, 1962.
Merry, S.E. *Urban Danger.* Philadelphia: Temple University Press, 1981.
Merz, Charles. *The Dry Decade.* New York: Doubleday, Doran, 1931.
_____. *The Great American Bandwagon.* New York: John Day, 1928.
Meskil, Paul S., with Callahan, Gerard M. *Cheesebox.* Prentice-Hall, 1974.
_____. *Don Carlo: Boss of Bosses.* New York: Popular Library, 1973.
Messick, Hank. *John Edgar Hoover.* New York: David McKay, 1972.
_____, and Goldblatt, Burt. *Kidnapping.* New York: Dial Press, 1974.
_____. *Lansky.* New York: G.P. Putnam's Sons, 1971.
_____. *The Mobs and the Mafia.* New York: Ballantine Books.
_____. *Of Grass and Snow: The Secret Criminal Elite.* Englewood Cliffs, N.J.: Prentice-Hall, 1979.
_____. *The Only Game in Town.* New York: T.Y. Crowell, 1976.
_____. *The Politics of Prosecution.* Ottawa, Ill.: Caroline House Books, 1978.
_____. *The Private Lives of Public Enemies.* New York: P.H. Wyden, 1973.
_____. *Secret File.* New York: G.P. Putnam's Sons, 1969.
_____. *The Silent Syndicate.* New York: Macmillan, 1967.
_____. *Syndicate in the Sun.* New York: Macmillan, 1968.
Meunier, Georges. *Gilles de Rais et son temps.* Paris: Nouvells Editions Latines, 1949.
Meyer, Gerald. *The Memphis Murders.* New York: Seabury, 1974.
Meyer, Michael C. *Huerta: A Political Portrait.* Lincoln: Univer-sity of Nebraska, 1972.
Meyer, Peter. *The Yale Murder.* New York: Berkley Books, 1983.
Meyer, Philip. *Precision Journalism.* Bloomington: Indiana University Press, 1973.
Meyers, Gustavus. *Great American Fortunes.* New York: Modern Library, 1936.
Mezzrow, Milton, and Wolfe, Bernard. *Really the Blues.* New York: Random House, 1946.
Michael, Jerome, and Adler, Mortimer J. *Crime, Law and Social Science.* New York: Harcourt, Brace, 1933.
Michalowski, Raymond J. *Order, Law, and Crime.* New York: Random House, 1985.
Michaud, Stephen, and Aynesworth, Hugh. *Murderers Among Us.* New York: Signet, 1991.
_____. *The Only Living Witness.* New York: Simon and Schuster, 1983.
_____. *Ted Bundy: Conversations with a Killer.* New York: New American Library, 1989.
Michelet, Jules. *Histoire de France.* 5 vols. Paris: Hetzel et cie, 1870.
_____. *Joan of Arc.* trans. Albert Gurard. Ann Arbor: University of Michigan Press, 1957.
Mickolus, Edward. *Transnational Terrorism.* Westport, Conn.: Greenwood Press, 1980,
Mijatovich, C. *A Royal Tragedy: Assassination of King Alexander and Queen Draga of Serbia.* London: Eveleigh Nash, 1906.
Milito, Lynda. *Mafia Wife.* New York: Harper Collins, 2003.
Millard, Bailey. *History of the San Francisco Bay Region.* Chica-go: American Historical Society, 1924.
Millard, Mara. *Hail to Yesterday.* New York: Farrar & Rinehart, 1941.
Millard, Joseph. *No Law But Their Own.* Evanston, Ill.: Regency Books, 1967.
Millard, Oscar E. *Burgomaster Max.* London: Hutchinson, 1936.
Millen, Ernest. *Specialist in Crime.* London: Harrap, 1972.
Miller, David. *The PLO.* New York: Praeger, 1983.
Miller, Douglas T. *The Fifties: The Way We Really Were.* Garden City, N.Y.: Doubleday, 1977.
Miller, Ernest C. *John Wilkes Booth in the Pennsylvania Oil Region.* Warren, Pa.: Crawford County Historical Society, 1987.
Miller, Floyd. *Bill Tilghman: Marshal of the Last Frontier.* New York: Doubleday, 1968.
Miller, Frank W. *Prosecution: The Decision to Charge a Suspect With a Crime.* Boston: Little, Brown, 1969.
Miller, Gene, with Mackle, Barbara Jane. *83 Hours Till Dawn.* Garden City, N.Y.: Doubleday, 1971.
Miller, George, Jr. *Trial of Frank James for Murder.* Columbus, Mo.: E.W. Stephens, 1898.
Miller, John, and Stone, Michael, and Mitchell, Chris. *The Cell: Inside the 9/11 Plot, and Why the FBI and CIA Failed to Stop It.* New York: Thordike Press, 2002.
Miller, Joseph. *Arizona, A State Guide.* New York: Hastings House, 1956.
_____. *Arizona, The Last Frontier.* New York: Hastings House, 1956.
_____. *The Arizona Rangers.* New York: Hastings House, 1972.
_____. *The Arizona Story.* New York: Hastings House, 1952.
Miller, L.L. (ed.). *Marijuana.* New York: Academic Press, 1974.
Miller, N.M. *Kenya: The Quest for Prosperity.* Boulder, Colo.: Westview Press, 1984.
Miller, Nyle H., and Snell, Joseph W. *Great Gunfighters of the Kansas Cowtowns, 1867-1886.* Lincoln: University of Nebraska Press, 1963.
_____, Langsdorf, Edgar, and Richmond, Robert W. *Kansas, a Pictorial History.* Topeka: Kansas State Historical Society, 1961.
_____. *Kansas Frontier Police Officers Before TV.* Topeka: Kansas State Historical Society, 1958.
_____ et al. *Kansas in Newspapers.* Topeka: Kansas State Historical Society, 1963.
Miller, Ronald Dean. *Shady Ladies of the West.* Los Angeles: Westernlore Press, 1964.
Miller, Tom. *The Assassination Please Almanac.* Chicago: Henry Regnery, 1977.
Miller, Walter B. *Violence by Youth Gangs and Youth Groups as a Crime Problem in Major American Cities.* Washington, D.C.: U.S. Government Printing Office, 1975.
Miller, Wilbur R. *Cops and Bobbies: Police Authority in New York and London, 1830-1870.* Chicago: University of Chicago Press, 1973.
Miller, William. *The Balkans: Romania, Bulgaria, Serbia, and Montenegro.* London: T. Fisher Unwin, 1923.
_____. *A History of the Greek People, 1821-1921.* London: Methuen, 1922.
Miller, William D. *Mr. Crump of Memphis.* Baton Rouge: Louisiana State University Press, 1964.
Milligan, Maurice M. *The Inside Story of the Pendergast Machine by the Man Who Smashed It.* New York: Charles Scribner's Sons, 1948.
_____. *Missouri Waltz.* New York: Charles Scribner's Sons, 1948.
Millis, Walter (ed.). *The Forrestal Dairies.* New York: Viking Press, 1951.
Mills, C. Wright. *The Power Elite.* New York: Oxford University Press, 1956.
Mills, James. *The Prosecutor.* New York: Pocket Books, 1970.
_____. *The Underground Empire: Where Crime and Governments Meet.* New York: Dell, 1986.

Millspaugh, Arthur. *Crime Control by the National Government.* Washington, D.C.: Brookings, 1937.

Milner, Alan (ed.). *African Penal Systems.* London: Routledge & Kegan Paul, 1969.

Milton, George Fort. *Abraham Lincoln and the Fifth Column.* New York: Vanguard Press, 1942.

_____. *Age of Hate.* New York: Coward-McCann, 1930.

Minear, Richard H. *Victors' Justice: The Tokyo War Crimes Trial.* Princeton, N.J.: Princeton University Press, 1973.

Minehan, Thomas. *Boy and Girl Tramps of America.* New York: Farrar, 1934.

Miner, Maude E. *Slavery of Prostitution.* New York: Macmillan, 1916.

Minney, Rubeigh James. *Rasputin.* London: Cassell, 1972.

Minnigerode, Meade. *Certain Rich Men.* New York: G.P. Putnam's Sons, 1927.

_____. *The Fabulous Forties 1840-1850.* Garden City, N.Y.: Garden City, 1924.

Minot, G.E. *Murder Will Out.* Boston: Marshall Jones, 1928.

Minton, Robert J. (ed.). *Inside Prison American Style.* New York: Random House, 1971.

Mironenko, Segei, et al. *Nicholas & Alexandra: The Last Imperial Family of Tsarist Russia.* New York: Harry N. Abrams, 1998.

Mishal, Shaul. *The PLO Under Arafat: Between Gun and Olive Branch.* New Haven, Conn.: Yale University Press, 1986.

Mitchell, Allan. *Revolution in Bavaria, 1918-1919.* Princeton, N.J.: Princeton University Press, 1965.

_____. *Depression Decade: From the New Era through the New Deal.* New York: Rinehart, 1947.

Mitchell, C. Ainsworth. *Science and the Criminal.* London: Pitman, 1911.

_____. *The Scientific Detective and the Expert Witness.* London: Heffer, 1931.

Mitchell, David. *The Light of Synomon.* New York: Seaview Books, 1980.

_____. *1919: Red Mirage.* New York: Macmillan, 1970.

_____. *Pirates.* New York: Dial Press, 1976.

Mitchell, Edward P. *Memoirs of an Editor: Fifty Years of Jour-nalism.* New York: Charles Scribner's Sons, 1941.

Mitchell, Edwin Valentine (ed.) *The Newgate Calendar.* Garden City, N.Y.: Garden City, 1926.

Mitchell, Lige. *Daring Exploits of Jesse James and His Band of Border Train and Bank Robbers.* Baltimore: I. & M. Otten-heimer, 1912.

Mitchell, Sandra. *The Miramichi Axe Murder.* Halifax, N. S.: Nimbus, 1992.

Mitford, Jessica. *The American Way of Death.* New York: Paperback Library, 1963.

_____. *Kind and Usual Punishment: The Prison Business.* New York: Alfred A. Knopf, 1973.

Mitford, Nancy. *Frederick the Great.* New York: Harper & Row, 1970.

_____. *Madame de Pompadour.* London: Reprint Society, 1954.

Mitgang, Herbert. *America at Random.* New York: Coward-McCann, 1969.

_____. *Lincoln as They Saw Him.* New York: Holt, Rinehart & Winston, 1956.

_____. *The Man Who Rode the Tiger, The Life and Times of Judge Samuel Seabury.* Philadelphia: J.B. Lippincott, 1963.

Mitrione, Dan. *Suddenly Gone.* New York: St. Martin's Press, 1995.

Mitsuko Iolana. *Honolulu Madame.* Los Angeles: Holloway House, 1969.

Mix, Tom. *The West of Yesterday.* Los Angeles: Times-Mirror Press, 1923.

Miyatovitch, Cheddo. *A Royal Tragedy.* London: E. Nash, 1906.

_____. *Serbia of the Serbians.* London: Pitman, 1915.

Mizner, Addison. *The Many Mizners.* New York: Sears, 1932.

Moats, Alice-Leone. *Lupescu.* New York: Henry Holt, 1955.

Moats, Leone B. *Thunder In Their Veins.* London: George Allen and Unwin, 1933.

Mochulsky, Knostantin. *Dostoevsky: His Life and Work.* trans. Michael A. Minihan. Princeton, N.J.: Princeton University Press, 1967.

Model, F. Peter, and Groden, Robert J. *JFK: The Case for Conspiracy.* New York: Manor Books, 1976.

Moenssens, Andre A. *Fingerprint Techniques.* Radnor, Pa.: Chilton, 1971.

Moers, Ellen. *The Dandy.* New York: Viking, 1960.

Moffett, Cleveland. *True Detective Stories.* New York: G.W. Dillingham, 1898.

Moffitt, Dona (ed.). *Swindled.* New Jersey: Dow Jones Books, 1976.

Mogelever, Jacob. *Death to Traitors: The Story of General Lafayette C. Baker, Lincoln's Forgotten Secret Service Chief.* Garden City, N.Y.: Doubleday, 1960.

Mohammed Ali. *The Prophet Mohammed.* London: Cassell, 1947.

Mohr, James C. *The Radical Republicans in New York During Reconstruction.* Ithaca, N.Y.: Cornell University Press, 1973.

Mohr, Johan W., et al. *Pedophilia and Exhibitionism.* Toronto, Ontario, Can.: University of Toronto Press, 1964.

Moiseiwitsch, Maurice. *Five Famous Trials.* Connecticut: New York Graphic Society, 1962.

Mokhiber, Russell. *Corporate Crime and Violence: Big Business Power and the Abuse of the Public Trust.* San Francisco: Sierra Club Books, 1989.

Moldea, Dan E. *The Hoffa Wars.* New York: Charter Books, 1978.

Moley, Raymond. *After Seven Years.* New York: Harper & Cross, 1939.

_____. *Politics and Criminal Prosecution.* New York: Minton, Balch, 1929.

Moll, Kendall D. *Arson, Vandalism and Violence: Law Enforce-ment Problems Affecting Fire Departments.* Washington, D.C.: U.S. Department of Justice, 1974.

Mollenhoff, Clark R. *The Man Who Pardoned Nixon.* New York: St. Martin's Press, 1976.

_____. *Strike Force: Organized Crime and the Government.* Englewood Cliffs, N.J.: Prentice-Hall, 1972.

_____. *Tentacles of Power.* Cleveland: World, 1965.

Molley, Pat. *Not the Moors Murders: A Detective's Story of the Biggest Child-Killer Hunt in History.* Llandysfyl, Wales: Gomer Press, 1988.

The Mollie Maguires. Tamaqua, Pa.: Eveland & Harris, 1876.

Momigliano, Arnaldo. *Claudius, the Emperor and his Achievement.* New York: Barnes & Noble, 1961.

Mommsen, Wolfgang, and Hirschfeld, Gerhard (eds.). *Social Protest, Violence and Terror in Nineteenth and Twentieth Century Europe.* London: Macmillan, 1982.

Monaghan, Frank. *John Jay, Defender of Liberty.* New York: Bobbs-Merrill, 1935.

_____, and Lowenthal, Marvin. *This Was New York.* New York: Doubleday, Doran, 1943.

Monaghan, Jay (ed.). *The Book of the American West.* New York: Julian Messner, 1963.

_____. *The Great Rascal.* New York: Bonanza Books, 1951.

_____. *Last of the Bad Men.* New York: Bobbs-Merrill, 1946.

Monahan, Florence. *Women in Crime.* New York: Washburn, 1941.

Monahan, J. *Predicting Violent Behaviour.* Beverly Hills, Calif.: Sage, 1981.

Monahan, John and Steadman, Henry J. (eds.). *Mentally Disor-dered Offenders: Perspectives from Law and Social Science.* New York: Plenum Press, 1983.

Monas, Sidney. *The Third Section: Police and Society in Russia under Nicholas II.* Cambridge, Mass.: Harvard University Press, 1961.

Monelli, Paolo. *Mussolini: An Intimate Life.* trans. Brigid Maxwell. London: Thames & Hudson, 1953.

Mongredien, Georges. *Madame de Montespan et l'affaire des poisons.* Paris: Hachette, 1953.

Monkkonen, E.H. *Police in Urban America, 1860-1920.* Cam-bridge, Eng.: Cambridge University Press, 1981.

Monoghan, James. *The Great Rascal.* Boston: Little, Brown, 1952.

Monroe, David G. *State and Provincial Police.* Evanston, Ill.: International Association of Chiefs of Police and Northwest-ern University Traffic Institute, 1941.

Monroe, Elizabeth. *The Mediterranean in Politics.* London: Oxford University Press, 1939.

Monroe, Russell R. *Brain Dysfunction in Aggressive Criminals.* Lexington, Mass.: D.C. Heath, 1978.

Montague, Joseph. *Wild Bill, a Western Story.* New York: Chelsea House, 1926.

Montarron, Marcel. *Histoire des Crimes Sexuels.* Paris: Plon, 1970.

_____. *Histoire du Milieu.* Paris: Plon, 1969.

_____. *Les Grande Proces d'Assises.* Paris: Planete, 1967.

_____. *Tout Ce Joli Monde.* Paris: La Table Ronde, 1965.

Monteil, Vincent. *Les Officiers.* Paris: Editions du Seuil, 1958.

Monteiro, John B. *Corruption: Control and Maladministration.* Bombay, India: P.C. Manaktla & Sons, 1966.

Montell, William Lynwood. *Killings Folk Justice in the Upper South.* Lexington: University Press of Kentucky, 1986.

Montespan, Madame. *Memoirs of Madame la Marquise de Montespan.* trans. P.E.P. London: Grover Society, 1904.

Monteval, Marion. *The Klan Inside Out.* Claremore, Okla.: Monarch, 1924.

Montgomerie, Hastings Seton. *William Bligh of the Bounty in Fact and Fable.* London: Williams & Norgate, 1937.

Montgomery, John. *The Twenties.* London: George Allen & Unwin, 1957.

Montgomery, Robert H. *Sacco-Vanzetti: The Murder and the Myth.* New York: Devin-Adair, 1960.

Moody, Ralph. *Stagecoach West.* New York: Thomas Y. Crow-ell, 1967.

_____. *Wells Fargo.* Boston: Houghton Mifflin, 1961.

Moody, Richard. *The Astor Place Riot.* Bloomington: Indiana University Press, 1958.

Moody, Samuel B. *Reprieve From Hell.* New York: Pageant Press, 1961.

Moon, Parker Thomas. *Imperialism and World Politics.* New York: Macmillan, 1944.

Mooney, M. *Crime Incorporated.* New York: McGraw-Hill, 1935.

Mooney, M. *Crime, Unincorporated.* New York: Whittlesey House, 1935.

Mooney, Michael Macdonald. *Evelyn Nesbit and Stanford White, Love and Death in the Gilded Age.* New York: William Morrow, 1976.

Mooney-Billings Report Suppressed by the Wickersham Commission. New York: Gotham House, 1932.

Moorad, George. *Lost Peace in China.* New York: Dutton, 1949.

Moore, Barrington Jr. *Soviet Politics: The Dilemma of Power.* Cambridge, Mass.: Harvard University Press, 1950.

_____. *Terror and Progress U.S.S.R.* Cambridge, Mass.: Harvard University Press, 1954.

Moore, Dan Tyler. *Wolves, Widows and Orphans, An Expose of the Ways and Wiles of Con Men, Card Sharps, Swindlers and Rogues.* New York: World, 1967.

Moore, George. *Confessions of a Young Man.* London: William Heinemann, 1926.

_____. *Parnell and His Island.* London: Swan Sonnenschein, Lowrey, 1887.

Moore, Guy W. *The Case of Mrs. Surratt: Her Controversial Trial and Execution for Conspiracy in the Lincoln Assassination.* Norman: University of Oklahoma Press, 1954.

Moore, Kelly, and Reed, Dan. *Deadly Medicine.* New York: St. Martin's Press, 1988.

Moore, Kenneth C. *Airport, Aircraft and Airline Security.* Los Angeles: Security World, 1976.

Moore, Maurice E. *Frauds and Swindles.* London: Gee, 1933.

Moore, Robin, with Barbara Fuca. *Mafia Wife.* New York: Macmillan, 1977.

Moore, William H. *The Kefauver Committee and the Politics of Crime.* Columbia: University of Missouri Press, 1974.

Moore, William T. *Dateline Chicago.* New York: Taplinger, 1973.

Moorehead, Alan. *African Trilogy.* London: Hamish Hamilton, 1965.

_____. *The Blue Nile.* London: Hamish Hamilton, 1962.

_____. *The Russian Revolution.* New York: Harper, 1958.

_____. *The White Nile.* London: Hamish Hamilton, 1960.

Moorehead, Caroline. *Hostages To Fortune.* New York: Athene-um, 1980.

Moquin, Wayne. *The American Way of Crime.* New York: Frederick A. Praeger, 1976.

Morain, Alfred. *The Underground of Paris.* New York: Blue Ribbon Books, 1931.

Moran, Richard. *Knowing Right from Wrong: The Insanity Defense of Daniel McNaughtan.* New York: Free Press, 1981.

Moray, Alastair. *The Diary of a Rum Runner.* London: Philip, Alan, 1929.

Mordecai, Samuel. *Richmond in Bygone Days.* Richmond, Va.: Dietz Press, 1946.

Mordell, Albert. *Clarence Darrow, Eugence V. Debs and Hal-deman-Julius: Incidents in the Career of an Author, Editor and Publisher.* Girard, Kan.: Haldeman-Julius, 1950.

Moreland, Nigel. *Background to Murder.* London: Werner Laurie, 1955.

_____. *Hangman's Clutch.* London: Werner Laurie, 1954.

_____. *Science in Crime Detection.* London: Robert Hale, 1958.

Moreland, Roy. *The Law of Homocide.* Indianapolis, Ind.: Bobbs-Merrill, 1952Morgan, Edward E.P. *God's Loaded Dice; Alaska, 1897-1930.* Caldwell, Idaho: Caxton Printers, 1948.

Morgan, H. Wayne. *William McKinley and His America.* Syracuse, N.Y.: Syracuse University Press, 1963.

Morgan, John. *Prince of Crime.* New York: Stein and Day, 1985.

Morgan, Leon. *Shooting Sheriffs of the Wild West.* Racine, Wis.: Whitman, 1936.

Morgan, Lewis Henry. *Ancient Society.* Cleveland: World, 1877.

Morgan, Murray. *Skid Road: An Informal Portrait of Seattle.* New York: Viking Press, 1951.

Morgan, Richard E. *Domestic Intelligence: Monitoring Dissent in America.* Austin, Tex.: University of Texas Press, 1980.

Morgan, Ted. *FDR: A Biography.* New York: Simon and Schuster, 1985.

Morgan, Thomas B. *Spurs on the Boot.* New York: Longmans, 1941.

Morgan, W.P. *Triad Societies in Hong Kong.* Hong Kong: Government Press, 1960.

Morgan, Wayne H. *Drugs in America.* New York: Syracuse University Press, 1981.

_____. *The Gilded Age: A Reappraisal.* Syracuse, N.Y.: Syracuse University Press, 1970.

_____. *William McKinley and His America.* Syracuse, N.Y.: Syracuse University Press, 1963.

_____. *Yesterday's Addicts.* Norman: University of Oklahoma, 1980.

Morgan, William. *Morgan's Freemasonry Exposed and Explained.* New York: L. Fitzgerald, 1882

Morgenthau, Henry. *All in a Life-Time.* Garden City, N.Y.: Doubleday, Page, 1922.

_____. *Ambassador Morgenthau's Story.* New York: Doubleday, Page, 1918.

Morgenthau, Henry, Jr. *Morgenthau Diary, China.* 2 vols. Washington, D.C.: GPO, 1965.

Mori, Cesare. *The Last Struggle of the Mafia.* trans. Orlo Wil-liams. New York: G.P. Putnam's Sons, 1933.

Moriarty, C.C.H. *Police Procedure and Administration.* London: Spottiswoode, Ballantyne, 1950.

Morin, Relman. *Assassination: The Death of President John F. Kennedy.* New York: New American Library, 1968.

Morison, Elting E. et al. (eds.). *Letters of Theodore Roosevelt.* Cambridge, Mass.: Harvard University Press, 1951.

_____. *Turmoil and Tradition: The Life and Times of Henry L. Stimson.* Boston: Houghton Mifflin, 1960.

Morison, S. *The English Newspaper, 1622-1932.* New York: Macmillan, 1932.

Morison, Samuel Eliot. *Admiral of the Ocean Sea.* Boston: Little, Brown, 1942.

_____. *Builders of the Bay Colony.* Boston: Houghton Mifflin, 1930.

_____, and Commager, Henry Steele. *The Growth of the American Republic.* New York: Oxford University Press, 1942.

_____. *Harvard College in the Seventeenth Century.* Cambridge, Mass.: Harvard University Press, 1936.

_____. *John Paul Jones: A Sailor's Biography.* New York: Time, 1959.

_____. *The Maritime History of Massachusetts 1783-1860.* Boston: Houghton Mifflin, 1921.

_____. *The Oxford History of the American People.* New York: Oxford University Press, 1965.

_____. *The Parkman Reader.* Boston: Little, Brown, 1955.

_____. *The Rising Sun in the Pacific.* Volume 4. Boston: Little, Brown, 1948.

Morland, Nigel. *Background to Murder.* London: Werner Laurie, 1955.

_____. *Death for Sale.* London: Hale, 1957.

_____. *Hangman's Clutch.* London: Werner Laurie, 1954.

_____. *An Outline of Scientific Criminology.* London: Cassell, 1950.

_____. *An Outline of Sexual Criminology.* New York: Hart, 1967.

_____. *Pattern of Murder.* London: Elek Books, 1966.

_____. *Science In Crime Detection.* London: Robert Hale, 1958.

_____. *That Nice Miss Smith.* London: Muller, 1957.

_____. *This Friendless Lady.* London: Frederick Muller, 1957.

Morley, James William. *The Japanese Thrust into Siberia, 1918.* New York: Columbia University Press, 1957.

Morley, John. *The Life of Richard Cobden.* London: T.F. Unwin, 1903.

_____. *Life of William Ewart Gladstone.* New York: Macmillan, 1903.

_____. *Voltaire.* London: Macmillan, 1872.

Morley, Sylvanus G. *The Ancient Maya.* Stanford, Calif.: Stan-ford University Press, 1946.

Morrel, Ed. *The Twenty-fifth Man.* Montclar, N.J.: New Era, 1924.

Morrell, Parker. *Diamond Jim.* New York: Simon & Schuster, 1934.

Morrell, William P. *Gold Rushes.* New York: Macmillan, 1941.

Morris, B.F. (ed.). *Memorial Record of the Nation's Tribute to Abraham Lincoln.* Washington D.C.: W.H. & O.H. Mor-rison, 1865.

Morris, Charles, and Halstead, Murat. *Life and Reign of Queen Victoria.* Chicago: International Publishing Society, 1901.

Morris, Ed. *Born to Lose.* New York: Mason & Lipscomb, 1974.

Morris, Dr. I.I. *Nationalism and the Right Wing in Japan.* London: Oxford University Press, 1960.

Morris, Ivan. (ed.). *Japan, 1931-1945: Militarism, Fascism, Japanism?* Boston: D.C. Heath, 1963.

_____. *The World of the Shining Prince.* New York: Alfred A. Knopf, 1964.

Morris, J. *The Age of Arthur.* London: Weidenfeld & Nicolson, 1973.

Morris, James. *The Hashemite Kings.* New York: Pantheon, 1959.

Morris, Joe Alex. *First Offender.* New York: Funk & Wagnalls, 1970.

_____. *What a Year!* New York: Harper Bros., 1956.

Morris, John. *An Exposure of the Arts & Miseries of Gambling.* Cincinatti: n.p., 1843.

Morris, Lerona Rosamond (ed.). *Oklahoma-Yesterday, Today, Tomorrow.* Guthrie, Okla.: Co-Operative, 1930.

Morris, Lloyd R. *Incredible New York.* New York: Random House, 1951.

_____. *Not So Long Ago.* New York: Random House, 1949.

_____. *Postcript to Yesterday.* New York: Random House, 1947.

Morris, Lucile. *Bald Knobbers.* Caldwell, Idaho: Caxton Printers, 1939.

Morris, Norval, and Tonry, Michael. *Crime and Justice.* Chicago: University of Chicago Press, 1980.

_____. *The Future of Imprisonment.* Chicago: University of Chicago Press, 1974.

_____. *The Habitual Criminal.* Cambridge, Mass.: Harvard University Press, 1951.

_____, and Hawkins, Gordon. *The Honest Politician's Guide to Crime Control.* Chicago: University of Chicago Press, 1970.

_____, and Hawkins, Gordon. *Letter to the President on Crime Control.* Chicago: University of Chicago Press, 1977.

_____. *Madness and the Criminal Law.* Chicago: University of Chicago Press, 1982.

Morris, Roger. *The Devil's Butcher Shop.* New York: Franklin Watts, 1983.

Morris, Terence, and Blom-Cooper, Louis. *A Calendar of Murder.* London: Michael Joseph, 1964.

_____. *The Criminal Area.* New York: The Humanities Press, 1958.

_____, and Pauline. *Pentonville: A Sociological Study of an English Prison.* London: Routledge & Kegan Paul, 1963.

Morris, Virginia, and Scharf, Michael P. *The International Criminal Tribunal for Rwanda.* 2 vols. Ardsley, N. Y.: Transnational Publishers, 1998.

Morris, W.R. *The Men Behind the Guns.* Lexington, Tenn.: Angel Lea Books, 1975.

Morrison, Samuel Elliot. *The Story of the Old Colony of New Plymouth.* New York: Alfred A. Knopf, 1956.

Morrissey, John. *John Morrissey, His Life, Battles and Wrangles, from His Birth in Ireland Until He Died a State Senator.* New York: n.p., 1881.

Morrow, Honore W. *Tiger! Tiger! The Life Story of John B. Gough.* New York: William Morrow, 1930.

Morrow, Robert D. *Betrayal.* Chicago: Henry Regnery, 1976.

Morse, Arthur D. *While Six Million Died: A Chronicle of Ameri-can Apathy.* New York: Hart, 1967.

Morse, Frank P. *Cavalcade of Rails.* New York: E.P. Dutton, 1940.

Morse, John T. *Abraham Lincoln.* 2 vols. Boston: Houghton Mifflin, 1893.

Morse, John Torrey. *Famous Trials: The Tichborne Claimant.* Boston: Little, Brown, 1874.

Mortimer, Lee. *Washington Confidential Today.* New York: Paperback Library, 1962.

Mortimer, W. Golden. *Peru: History of Coca.* New York: J.H. Vail, 1901.

Morton, A.A. *Literary Detection.* New York: Scribners, 1980.

Morton, R.S. *Venereal Diseases.* London: Peguin Books, 1966.

Morton, W. Scott. *Japan: Its History and Cultures.* New York: Thomas Y. Crowell, 1970.

Mosca, Gaetano. *Encyclopedia of the Social Sciences.* New York: Macmillan, 1933.

Moscow, Alvin. *The Rockefeller Inheritance.* Garden City, N.Y.: Doubleday, 1977.

Moscow, Warren. *Politics in the Empire State.* New York: Knopf, 1948.

_____. *What Have You Done for Me Lately? The Ins and Outs of New York City Politics.* Englewood Cliffs, N.J.: Prentice-Hall, 1961.

Mosedale, John. *The Men Who Invented Broadway.* New York: Richard Marek, 1981.

Moser, Don, and Cohen, Jerry. *The Pied Piper of Tucson.* New York: Signet Books, 1967.

Moses, David. *Who Shot Kennedy?* England: Church of God, 1973.

Moskowitz, Henry. *Alfred E. Smith. An American Career.* New York: Thomas Seltzer, 1924.

Mosley, Leonard. *Haile Selassie: The Conquering Lion.* Engle-wood Cliffs, N.J.: Prentice-Hall, 1964.

_____. *Hirohito: Emperor of Japan.* Englewoood Cliffs, N.J.: Prentice-Hall, 1966.

_____. *Lindbergh.* New York: Doubleday, 1976.

_____. *On Borrowed Time: How World War Two Began.* New York: Random House, 1959.

Mosley, Nicholas. *The Assassination of Trotsky.* London: Michael Joseph, 1972.

Mosolov (Mossolov, A.A.) *At the Court of the Last Tsar.* London: Methuen, 1935.

Moss, Frank. *The American Metropolis, From Knickerbocker Days to the Present Time, New York City Life in All Its Various Phases.* 3 vols. New York: Peter Fenelon Collier, 1897.

Moss, Robert. *Urban Guerrillas.* London: Temple Smith, 1972.

Moss, Thelma. *The Probability of the Impossible.* Los Angeles: J. P. Tarcher, 1974.

Moss, William Paul. *Rough and Tumble: The Autobiography of a West Texas Judge.* New York: Vantage Press, 1954.

Mosse, Werner E. *Alexander II and the Moderization of Russia.* New York: Macmillan, 1958.

Mossiker, Frances. *The Affair of the Poisons.* New York: Knopf, 1969.

Motley, John Lothrop. *The Rise of the Dutch Republic.* New York: Harper & Bros., 1883.

Mott, Frank Luther. *American Journalism: A History, 1690-1960.* New York: Macmillan, 1969.

_____. *American Journalism: A History of Newspapers in the United States.* New York: Macmillan, 1950.

_____. *Golden Multitudes.* New York: Macmillan, 1947.

_____. *A History of American Magazines 1741-1850.* New York: D. Appleton-Century, 1930.

Mott, Harper Striker. *The New York of Yesterday.* New York: G.P. Putnam's Sons, 1908.

Mottram, R.H. *Trader's Dream: The Romance of the East India Company.* New York: Appleton-Century, 1939.

Mouneyrat, Edmond. *La Prefecture de police.* Paris: Bonvalot-Jouve, 1906.

Mousnier, Roland. *The Assassination of Henry IV.* trans. Joan Spencer. New York: Scribner, 1973.

Mousset, Albert. *L'Attentat de Sarajevo.* Paris: Payot, 1930.

Mowry, George E. *The Era of Theodore Roosevelt 1900-1912.* New York: Harper & Bros., 1958.

_____. *Theodore Roosevelt and the Progressive Movement.* Madison: University of Wisconsin Press, 1946.

The Moyer-Haywood Case and the United States Supreme Court. New York: n.p., 1907.

Moylan, John F. *Scotland Yard and the Metropolitan Police.* London: Putnam, 1929.

Mudd, Nettie. *The Life of Dr. Samuel A. Mudd.* Saginaw, Mich.: Richard D. Mudd, 1962.

Mudd, Dr. Richard D. *Dr. Samuel Alexander Mudd and His Descendants.* Freeland, Mich.: Bastian Brothers, 1982.

_____. *The Mudd Family of the United States.* 2 vols. Saginaw, Mich.: Published by Author, 1951.

Mudd, Samuel A. *The Life of Dr. Samuel A. Mudd.* ed. Nettie Mudd. New York: Neale, 1906.

Muddiman, J.G. (ed.). *The Bloody Assizes.* Edinburgh: William Hodge, 1929.

Mudgett, Herman. *Holmes' Own Story.* Philadelphia: Burk & McFetridge, 1895.

Mueller, Gerhard O.W. (ed.). *Essays in Criminal Science.* New York: Rothman, 1961.

_____. *Legal Regulation of Sexual Conduct.* New York: Oceana, 1961.

_____. *Sentencing.* Springfield, Ill.: Charles Thomas, 1977.

Muggeridge, Malcolm. *The Thirties.* London: Hamish Hamilton, 1940.

Mugglebee, Ruth. *Father Coughlin of the Shrine of the Little Flower.* Boston: L.C. Page, 1933.

Muir, Florabel. *Headline Happy.* New York: Henry Holt 1950.

Muir, Helen. *Miami, U.S.A.* New York: Holt, 1953.

Muir, Sir William. *The Caliphate, Its Rise, Decline and Fall.* Edinburgh, Scot.: John Grant, 1924.

_____. *The Mameluke Dynasty of Egypt.* London: Smith & Elder, 1896.

Mukerjee, Dilip. *Zulfikar Ali Bhutto: Quest for Power.* Delhi-Bombay: Vikes Publishing House, 1972.

Mukerjee, Hirendranath. *Indian Struggle for Freedom.* Bombay: Kutub, 1946.

Mulgrew, Ian. *Final Payoff.* Toronto: McClelland-Bantam, 1990.

Muller, Georg Alexander von. *The Kaiser and His Court.* tran. Mervyn Savill. London: Macdonald, 1961.

Mullins, Claud. *Fifteen Years' Hard Labour.* London: Victor Gollancz, 1949.

_____. *Why Crime?* Philadelphia: Saunders, 1945.

Munoz, Rafael F. *Pancho Villa: Rayo y Azote.* Mexico City: Populibros La Prensa, 1955.

Munro, Andrew Keith. *Autobiography of a Thief.* London: Michael Joseph, 1972.

Munro, Dana Carleton. *The Middle Ages.* New York: Century, 1922.

Munsterberg, H. *On the Witness Stand.* New York: Clark, Boardman, 1908.

Murchison, C. *Criminal Intelligence.* Worcester, Mass.: Clark University, 1926.

Murdock, Eugene Converse. *Patriotism Limited, 1862-1865: The Civil War Draft and the Bounty System.* Kent, Ohio: Kent State University Press, 1967.

Murdock, Kenneth B. *Increase Mather: The Foremost American Puritan.* New York: Russell & Russell, 1966.

_____. *Selections from Cotton Mather.* New York: Harcourt, Brace, 1926.

Muret, Maurice. *L'archduc Franois-Ferdinand.* Paris: B. Gras-set, 1932.

Muriithi, J.K., Ndoria, P.N. *War in the Forest: An Autobiography of a Mau Mau Leader.* Nairobi: East African Publishing House, 1971.

Murofushi Tetsuro. *Japan's Terrorists.* Tokyo: Kobunsho, 1963.

Murphy, Harry J. *Where's What: Sources of Information for Federal Investigators.* New York: Warner Books, 1979.

Murphy, John T. *A Manual on the Rise and Fall of Italy's Fascist Empire.* London: Crowther, 1943.

_____. *Stalin, 1879-1944.* London: Lane, 1945.

Murphy, Rhoads. *Shanghai: Key to Modern China.* Cambridge, Mass.: Harvard University Press, 1953.

Murray, Charles A., and Cox, I.A. *Beyond Probation.* Beverly Hills, Calif.: Sage, 1979.

_____. *Days in Court.* Washington, D.C.: American Institutes for Research, 1980.

Murray, Jesse George. *The Legacy of Al Capone.* New York: Putnam, 1975.

_____. *The Madhouse on Madison Street.* Chicago: Follett, 1965.

Murray, Margaret Alice. *The God of the Witches.* London: Faber & Faber, 1931.

Murray, Norbert. *Legacy of an Assassination.* New York: Pro-People Press, 1964.

Murray, Robert H. *The History of Political Science from Plato to the Present.* Cambridge, Eng.: W. Heffer & Sons, 1926.

Murray, Robert K. *Red Scare: A Study in National Hysteria, 1919-1920.* New York: McGraw-Hill, 1964.

Murray-Brown, J. *Kenyatta.* London: George Allen, 1972.

Murrell, John A. *Life and Adventures of John A. Murrell.* Phila-delphia: T.B. Peterson & Brothers, 1845.

Murrow, Edward R (ed.). *Talks.* New York: Columbia Broadcasting System, 1937.

Murtagh, John M., and Harris, Sara. *Cast the First Stone.* New York: McGraw-Hill, 1957.

_____. *Who Live in Shadow.* New York: McGraw-Hill, 1959.

Murton, Thomas, and Hyams, Joe. *Accomplices to the Crime: The Arkansas Prison Scandal.* New York: Grove Press, 1969.

_____. *The Dilemma of Prison Reform.* New York: Holt, Rinehart & Winston, 1976.

Mushanga, Tibamanya. *Crime and Deviance.* Nairobi, Kenya: East African Literature Bureau, 1976.

Mushkat, Jerome. *Tammany: The Evolution of a Political Ma-chine, 1789-1865.* Syracuse, N.Y.: Syracuse University Press, 1971.

Musick, John R. *Mysterious Mr. Howard.* New York: G.W. Dillingham, 1896.

_____. *Stories of Missouri.* New York: American Book, 1897.

Musmanno, Michael A. *After Twelve Years.* New York: Alfred A. Knopf, 1939.

_____. *Verdict!* Garden City, N.Y.: Doubleday, 1958.

Mussolini, Benito. *The Corporate State.* Florence, Italy: Valle-cchi, 1938.

_____. *Fascism: Doctrines and Institutions.* Rome: Ardita, 1935.

_____. *My Autobiography.* trans. Richard Washburn Child. London: Hutchinson, 1928.

Mussolini, Rachele, and Chinigo, Michele. *My Life with Mussolini.* London: Hale, 1959.

Mustain, Gene, and Capeci, Jerry. *Mob Star: The Story of John Gotti, the Most Powerful Criminal in America.* New York: Franklin Watts, 1988.

Musto, David. *The American Disease: Origins of Narcotic Control.* New Haven, Conn.: Yale University Press, 1973.

_____. *Narcotics and America.* New Haven, Conn.: Yale Univer-sity Press, 1972.

Muusmann, Carl. *Hvem var Jack the Ripper?* Copenhagen: Hermann-Petersen, 1908.

Muzumdar, H.T. *Gandhi Triumphant! The Inside Story of the Historic Fast.* New York: Universal, 1939.

Muzzey, David Saville. *History of the American People.* Boston: Ginn, 1929.

_____. *James G. Blaine: A Political Idol of Other Days.* New York: Dodd, Mead, 1934.

Myers, Gustavus. *History of Bigotry in the United States.* ed. Henry M. Christman. New York: Random House, 1943.

_____. *History of Public Franchises in New York City.* New York: The Reform Club, 1900.

_____. *History of the Great American Fortunes.* 3 vols. New York: Charles H. Kerr, 1910.

_____. *History of the Supreme Court of the United States.* Chicago: Charles H. Kerr, 1918.

_____. *History of Tammany Hall.* New York: Boni & Liveright, 1901.

Myers, John Myers. *The Death of the Bravos.* Boston: Little, Brown, 1962.

_____. *Doc Holliday.* Boston: Little, Brown, 1955.

_____. *The Last Chance: Tombstone's Early Years.* New York: E.P. Dutton, 1950.

_____. *San Francisco's Reign of Terror.* New York: Doubleday 1966.

Myers, Margaret G. *A Financial History of the United States.* New York: Columbia University Press, 1970.

Myers, Starr, and Newton, Walter H. *The Hoover Administration.* New York: Charles Scribner's Sons, 1936.

The Mysteries and Miseries of San Francisco. New York: Dick & Fitzgeraldm 1853.

Nadeau, Reni. *City-Makers: The Men Who Transformed Los Angeles from Village to Metropolis During the First Great Boom, 1868-76.* Garden City, N.Y.: Doubleday, 1948.

_____. *Los Angeles, from Mission to Modern City.* New York: Longmans, Green 1960.

Nadel, Siegfried F. *A Black Byzantium: The Kingdom of Nupe in Nigeria.* London: Oxford University Press, 1942.

Nader, Ralph. *The Consumer and Corporate Accountability.* New York: Harcourt, Brace, Jovanovich, 1973.

_____, and Green, Mark J. (eds.). *Corporate Power in America.* New York: Grossman, 1973.

_____, Green, Mark J., and Seligman, Joel. *Taming the Giant Corporation.* New York: W.W. Norton, 1976.

Nadler, Susan. *Good Girls Gone Bad.* New York: Freundlich Books, 1987.

Nag, Kalidas. *Tolstoy and Gandhi.* Patna, India: Pustak Bhan-dar, 1950.

Nagel, William G. *An American Archipelago....: The United States Bureau of Prisons.* Philadelphia: The American Foundation, 1974.

_____. *The New Red Barn: A Critical Look at the Modern Ameri-can Prison.* New York: The American Foundation, 1973.

Nagy, Ferenc. *The Struggle Behind the Iron Curtain.* New York: Macmillan, 1948.

Nahm, Milton C. *Las Vegas and Uncle Joe.* Norman: University of Oklahoma Press, 1964.

Naidu, Sushil K. *Osama bin Laden: The Patron Saint of Terrorism.* New York: Kalinga Publications, 2002.

Naimark, Norman M. *Terrorists and Socialists: The Russian Revolutionary Movement Under Alexander III.* Cambridge, Mass.: Harvard University Press, 1983.

Nair, C. Sankaran. *Gandhi and Anarchy.* Madras, India: Tagore, 1922.

Nakane, Chie. *Japanese Society.* Berkeley: University of Cali-fornia, 1973.

Namier, L.B. *England in the Age of the American Revolution.* New York: Macmillan, 1930.

Nanda, B.R. *Mahatma Gandhi: A Biography.* Boston: Beacon Press, 1958.

Naotoshi Todani. *Walk in the Mountains, Rot as a Corpse in the Grass.* Osaka, Japan: Bunsho-in, 1965.

Narell, Irena. *Our City: The Jews of San Francisco.* San Diego, Calif.: Howell-North, 1981.

Narishkin-Kurakin, Elizabeth. *Under Three Tsars.* New York: E.P. Dutton, 1931.

Nash, Harry C. *Citizen's Arrest: The Dissent of Penn Jones, Jr., in the Assassination of JFK.* Austin, Texas: Latitudes Press, 1977.

Nash, Jay Robert. *Almanac of World Crime.* New York: Doubleday, 1981.

_____. *Among the Missing, An Anecdotal History of Missing Persons from the 1800s to the Present.* New York: Simon & Schuster, 1978.

_____. *Bloodletters and Badmen, A Narrative Encyclopedia of American Criminals From the Pilgrims to the Present.* New York: M. Evans, 1973.

_____. *Citizen Hoover, A Critical Study of J. Edgar Hoover and His FBI.* Chicago: Nelson-Hall, 1972.

_____. *A Crime Story.* New York: Delacorte Press, 1981.

_____. *The Dark Fountain.* New York: A & W, 1982.

_____. *Darkest Hours, A Narrative Encyclopedia of Worldwide Disasters from Ancient Times to the Present.* Chicago: Nelson-Hall, 1976.

_____. *Dictionary of Crime, Criminal Justice, Criminology & Law Enforcement.* New York: Paragon House, 1992.

_____. *Dillinger: Dead or Alive?* Chicago: Henry Regnery, 1970.

_____. *The Dillinger Dossier.* Highland Park, Ill.: December Press, 1983.

_____. *Encyclopedia of Western Lawmen and Outlaws.* New York: Paragon House, 1992.

_____. *Encyclopedia of World Crime.* 8 vols. Wilmette, Ill.: History, Inc., 1999.

_____. *Hustlers and Con Men, An Anecdotal History Of the Confidence Man and His Games.* New York: M. Evans, 1976.

_____. *The Innovators: Sixteen Portraits of the Famous and the Infamous.* Chicago: Regnery Gateway, 1982.

_____. *Jay Robert Nash's Crime Chronology: A World-wide Record, 1900-1983.* New York: Facts on File, 1884.

_____. *Look for the Woman: A Narrative Encyclopedia of Female Poisoners, Kidnappers, Thieves, Extortionists, Terrorists, Swindlers and Spies from Elizabethan Times to the Present.* New York: M. Evans, 1981.

_____. *The Mafia Diaries.* New York: Delacorte Press, 1984.

_____. *The Motion Picture Guide.* 17 vols. Chicago/Evanston, Ill.: Cinebooks, 1984-1990.

_____. *Murder, America, Homicide in the United States from the Revolution to the Present.* New York: Simon & Schuster, 1980.

_____. *Murder Among the Mighty: Celebrity Slayings That Shocked America.* New York: Delacorte Press, 1983.

_____. *Open Files: A Narrative Encyclopedia of the World's Greatest Unsolved Crimes.* New York: McGraw-Hill, 1983.

_____. *People to See: An Anecdotal History of Chicago's Makers and Breakers.* Piscataway, N.J.: New Century, 1981.

_____. *Spies: A Narrative Encyclopedia of Double Dealing and Dirty Tricks from Biblical Times to the Present.* New York: M. Evans, 1997.

_____. *Terrorism in the 20th Century: A Narrative Encyclopedia from the Anarchists Through the Weathermen to the Unabomber.* New York: M. Evans, 1998.

_____. *World Encyclopedia of Organized Crime.* New York: Paragon House, 1992.

_____. *World Encyclopedia of 20th Century Murder.* New York: Paragon House, 1992.

_____. *Zanies: The World's Greatest Eccentrics.* Piscataway, N.J.: New Century, 1982.

Nassau Daily Tribune (eds.). *The Murder of Sir Harry Oakes, BT.* Nassau, Bah.: Nassau Daily Tribune, 1959.

Nathan, George Jean. *The Intimate Notebooks of George Jean Nathan.* New York: Alfred A. Knopf, 1932.

The Nation Encyclopedia of American Biography. New York: White, 1904.

National Advisory Commission on Civil Disorders. *U.S. Riot Commission Report.* New York: Bantam, 1968.

National Advisory Committee on Criminal Justice Standards and Goals. *Community Crime Prevention.* Washington, D.C.: U.S. Government Printing Office, 1973.

_____. *Criminal Justice Research and Development.* Washington, D.C.: National Institute of Law Enforcement and Criminal Justice, 1976.

_____. *A National Strategy to Reduce Crime.* Washington, D.C.: U.S. Government Printing Office, 1973.

_____. *Organized Crime.* Washington, D.C.: Law Enforcement Assistance Administration, 1976.

_____. *Report of the Task Force on Disorders and Terrorism.* Washington, D.C.: U.S. Government Printing Office, 1976.

_____. *Task Force Report on Corrections.* Washington, D.C.: U.S. Government Printing Office, 1973.

National Broadcasting Company. *There Was a President.* New York: Random House, 1966.

National Commission on the Causes and Prevention of Violence. Staff Report. *Crimes of Violence.* Washington, D.C.: U.S. Government Printing Office, 1969.

_____. Staff Report. *Law and Order Reconsidered.* Washington, D.C.: U.S. Printing Office, 1969-71.

_____. *Task Force on Violent Aspects of Protest and Confrontation.* Washington, D.C.: U.S. Government Printing Office, 1969.

_____. Staff Report. *To Establish Justice, To Insure Domestic Tranquility.* Washington, D.C.: U.S. Government Printing Office, 1969.

_____. *Violence in America: Historical and Comparative Perspec-tives.* Washington D.C.: U.S. Government Printing Office, 1969.

_____. *Walker Report.* Washington, D.C.: U.S. Government Printing Office, 1969.

National Commission on Law Observance and Enforcement. *Report on Penal Institutions, Probation and Parole.* Washing-ton, D.C.: U.S. Government Printing Office, 1931.

National Commission on Obscenity and Pornography. *Commis-sion on Obscenity and Pornography Report.* New York: Bantam Books, 1970.

National Council on Crime and Delinquency. *Four Thousand Lifetimes: A Study of Time Served and Parole Outcomes.* Davis, Calif.: NCCD Research Center, 1973.

_____. *Guided Group Interaction.* Hackensack, N.J.: Training Center, 1972.

_____. *Model Act for the Protection of Rights of Prisoners.* Washington, D.C.: National Council on Crime and Delin-quency, 1972.

_____. *Residential Corrections: Alternatives to Incarceration.* Davis, Calif.: NCCD Research Group, 1973.

_____. *Standard Act for State Correctional Services.* Washington, D.C.: National Council on Crime and Delinquency, 1966.

National Crime Survey. *Criminal Victimization in the United States, 1979.* Washington, D.C.: U.S. Government Printing Office, 1981.

National Criminal Justice Reference Service. *We Are All the Victims of Arson.* Washington, D.C.: U.S. Government Printing Office, 1979.

The National Cyclopedia of American Biography. New York: J.J. White, 1893.

National Institute on Drug Abuse. *National Household Survey on Drug Abuse.* Washington, D.C.: U.S. Government Printing Office, 1982.

Natori Junichi. *A Short History of Nippon.* Tokyo: Hokuseido Press, 1943.

Nauroy, Charles. *Le Curieux.* Paris: 6 rue de Seine, 1883-88.

_____. *Les Secrets des Bonaparte.* Paris: Emile Boullion, 1889.

Navasky, Victor S. *Kennedy Justice.* New York: Atheneum, 1971.

_____. *Law Enforcement: The Federal Role.* New York: Mc-Graw-Hill, 1976.

_____. *Naming Names.* New York: Viking, 1980.

Neal, Daniel. *The History of the Puritans.* London: R. Hett, 1732.

Neale, Walter. *The Life of Ambrose Bierce.* New York: W. Neale, 1929.

Neatby, H. Blair. *Mackenzie King, Vol. II., 1924-1932.* London: Methuen, 1963.

Neave, Airey. *On Trial at Nuremberg.* Boston: Little, Brown, 1979.

Nechkina, M.V. (ed.). *Russia in the Nineteenth Century.* Ann Arbor, Mich.: Edwards, 1953.

Nee, Victor G., and deBary, Brett. *Longtime Californ': A Docu-mentary Study of an American Chinatown.* New York: Pantheon Books, 1973.

Needham, Joseph. *Science and Civilization in China.* Cambridge, Eng.: Cambridge University Press, 1956.

Needham, Ted and Howard. *Alcatraz.* Millbrae, Calif.: Celestial Arts, 1976.

Neely, Mark E., Jr. *The Abraham Lincoln Encyclopedia.* New York: McGraw-Hill, 1982.

Neely, Richard. *How Courts Govern America.* New Haven, Conn.: Yale University Press, 1981.

_____. *Why Courts Don't Work.* New York: McGraw-Hill, 1983.

Neese, Robert. *Prison Exposures.* New York: Chilton, 1959.

The Negro in Chicago: A Study of Race Relations and a Race Riot. Chicago: University of Chicago Press, 1922.

Neguib, Mohammed. *Egypt's Destiny.* London: Victor Gollancz, 1953.

Nehru, Jawaharlal. *An Autobiography.* London: John Lane, 1936.

_____. *The Discovery of India.* Calcutta, India: Signet, 1941.

_____. *Eighteen Months in India.* Allahabad, India: Kitabistan, 1938.

_____. *Mahatma Gandhi.* Calcutta, India: Signet Press, 1949.

Neiderhoffer, Arthur, and Blumberg, Abraham S. (eds.). *The Ambivalent Force: Perspectives on the Police.* San Francisco: Rinehart Press, 1973.

_____. *Behind the Shield: The Police in Urban Society.* New York: Doubleday, 1967.

Neier, Aryeh. *Crime and Punishment: A Radical Solution.* New York: Stein & Day, 1975.

Neil, Arthur Fowler. *Forty Years of Man-Hunting.* London: Jarrolds, 1932.

_____. *Man-Hunters of Scotland Yard.* New York: Doubleday, Doran, 1933.

Nelli, Humbert S. *The Business of Crime: Italians and Syndicate Crime in the United States.* New York: Oxford University Press, 1976.

Nelson, Jack. *Terror in the Night: The Klan's Campaign Against the Jews.* University, Miss.: University Press of Mississippi, 1996.

Nelson, Jack E., and Ostrow, Ronald J. *The FBI and the Berrigans.* New York: Coward, McCann, 1972.

Nelson, Rick. *The Cop Who Wouldn't Quit.* New York: Ballantine, 1983.

Nelson, U. K. *Story of Scotland Yard.* London: Longmans Group, 1999.

Nelson, Victor. *Prison Days and Nights.* Boston: Little, Brown, 1933.

Nelson, Walter Henry. *The Berliners: Their Saga and Their City.* New York: McKay, 1969.

_____. *The Soldier Kings, The House of Hohenzollern.* New York: G.P. Putnam's Sons, 1970.

Nelson, William (ed.). *Out of the Crocodile's Mouth.* Washington, D.C.: Public Affairs Press, 1949.

Nenni, Pietro. *Ten Years of Tyranny in Italy.* trans. Anne Steele. London: George Allen & Unwin, 1932.

Nese, Marco. *Nel Segno della Mafia Storia di Luciano Liggio.* Milan, Italy: Rizzoli, 1975.

Ness, Eliot, with Fraley, Oscar. *The Untouchables.* New York: Julian Messner, 1957.

Nettler, Gwynn. *Criminal Careers.* Cincinnati, Ohio: Anderson, 1982.

_____. *Explaining Crime.* New York: McGraw-Hill, n.d.

_____. *Killing One Another.* Cincinnati, Ohio: Anderson, 1982.

Neubauer, David W. *Criminal Justice in Middle America.* Morris-town, N.J.: General Learning Press, 1974.

Neufield, E. *The Hittite Laws.* London: Luzac, 1951.

Neumann, Franz. *Behemoth: The Structure and Practice of National Socialism.* New York: Oxford University Press, 1942.

Neumann, Robert. *Zaharoff, the Armaments King.* trans. R.T. Clark. George Allen & Unwin, 1938.

Neumann, William L. *America Encounters Japan: From Perry to MacArthur.* Baltimore, Md.: The Johns Hopkins Press, 1963.

Neustatter, W. Lindsay. *The Mind of the Murderer.* London: Christopher Johnson, 1957.

_____. *Psychological Disorder and Crime.* London: Christopher Johnson, 1953.

Neusss-Hunkel, Ermenhild. *Die SS.* Hannover, Ger.: Norddeutsche, 1956.

Neutter, Elizabeth. *The Key to My Neighbor's House: Seeking Justice in Bosnia and Rwanda.* London: Picador, 2002.

Neutzel, Charles. *Whodunit? Hollywood Style.* Beverly Hills: California Book Company of America, 1965.

Neville, Amelia Ransome. *The Fantastic City: Memoirs of the Social and Romantic Life of Old San Francisco.* Boston: Houghton Mifflin, 1932.

Nevins, Allan (ed.). *American Press Opinion: Washington to Coolidge.* New York: D.C. Heath, 1928.

_____. *The Evening Post: A Century of Journalism.* New York: Boni & Liveright, 1922.

Nevins, Winfield Scott. *Witchcraft in Salem Village in 1692.* Boston: Lee & Shepard, 1892.

Newfield, Jack. *The Abuse of Power.* New York: Viking, 1977.

_____. *A Prophetic Minority.* New York: New American Library, 1967.

_____. *Robert Kennedy: A Memoir.* New York: E.P. Dutton, 1969.

New Forms of Juvenile Delinquency, Their Origin, Prevention, and Treatment. New York: United Nations, 1960.

The Newgate Calendar. London: T. Werner Laurie, 1932.

The Newgate Calendar, or Malefactors' Bloody Register. London: Capricorn Books, 1961.

New Jersey Commission to Study Capital Punishment. *Report.* Trenton: State of New Jersey, 1964.

Newman, Albert H. *The Assassination of John F. Kennedy: The Reasons Why.* New York: Clarkson N. Potter, 1970.

Newman, Donald J. *Conviction: The Determination of Guilt or Innocence Without Trial.* Boston: Little, Brown, 1966.

_____. *Introduction to Criminal Justice.* Philadelphia: J.B. Lippincott, 1975.

Newman, G. *Comparative Deviance.* New York: Elsevier, 1976.

Newman, Graeme. *Just and Painful: A Case for the Corporal Punishment of Criminals.* New York: Macmillan, 1983.

_____. *The Punishment Response.* Philadelphia: J.B. Lippincott, 1978.

_____. *Understanding Violence.* New York: J.B. Lippincott, 1978.

Newman, O. *Defensible Space: Crime Prevention through Urban Design.* New York: Macmillan, 1972.

Newsam, Sir Frank Aubrey. *The Home Office.* London: George Allen & Unwin, 1954.

Newsom, J.A. *The Life and Practice of the Wild and Modern Indian.* Oklahoma City, Okla.: Harlow, 1923.

Newton, A.P. *A Hundred Years of the British Empire.* London: Methuen, 1940.

Newton, George D., and Zimring, Franklin E. *Firearms and Violence in American Life.* Washington D.C.: U.S. Govern-ment Printing Office, 1969.

Newton, H. Chance. *Crime and the Drama or Dark Deeds Drama-tized.* London: Stanley Paul, 1927.

New York City Youth Board. *Reaching the Fighting Gang.* New York: New York City Youth Board, 1960.

New York Commission on Capital Punishment. *Report.* Albany, N.Y.: Argus, 1888.

New York Legislature. *Report and Proceedings of the Senate Committee on the Police Department of the City of New York.* Albany, N.Y.: State Printing Office, 1932.

New York in Slices, by an Experienced Carver. New York: W.F. Burgess, 1849.

New York, State of. *The Code of Criminal Procedure.* New York: The Eagle Library, 1965.

New York, State of. *The Penal Law of the State of New York.* New York: The Eagle Library, 1965.

New York State Special Commission on Attica. *Attica.* New York: Bantam, 1972.

Ney, Richard. *The Wall Street Jungle.* New York: Grove Press, 1971.

Nice, Richard (ed.). *Crime and Insanity.* New York: Philosophi-cal Library, 1958.

_____. *Dictionary of Criminology.* New York: Philosophical Library, 1965.

Nicolaevsky, Boris I. (ed.). *The Crimes of the Stalin Era.* New York: The New Leader, 1962.

Nicholls, Ernest. *Crime Within the Square Mile.* London: John Long, 1935.

Nichols, Alice. *Bleeding Kansas.* New York: Oxford University Press, 1954.

Nichols, C.W. *The Ulta-Fashionable Peerage of America.* New York: George Harjes, 1904.

Nicholson, George, Condit, Thomas W., Greenbaum, Stuart. *Forgotten Victims.* Sacramento, Calif.: California District Attorneys Association, 1977.

Nicholson, Harold. *King George the Fifth: His Life and Reign.* London: Constable, 1952.

_____. *Peacemaking.* New York: Grosset & Dunlap, 1965.

Nicholson, Michael. *The Yorkshire Ripper.* London: W. H. Allen, 1979.

Nicolson, Nigel (ed.). *Harold Nicolson, Diaries and Letters 1930-1939.* New York: Atheneum, 1966.

Nickel, Steven. *Torso.* Winston-Salem, N. C.: J. F. Blair, 1989.

Nic Shiublaigh, Marie. *The Splendid Years.* Dublin, Ire.: Duffy, 1955.

Niebuhr, Reinhold. *Moral Man and Immoral Society.* New York: Charles Scribner's Sons, 1933.

_____. *Reflections on the End of an Era.* New York: Charles Scribner's Sons, 1934.

Niederhoffer, Arthur. *Behind the Shield: The Police in Urban Society.* Garden City, N.Y.: Anchor Doubleday, 1969.

Niemetschek, Franz Xaver. *W.A. Mozart's Laben, nach Original-quallen Beschreiben.* Prague: Taussig, 1905.

Niemoeller, Adolph F. *Sexual Slavery in America.* New York: Panurge Press, 1935.

Nietzel, Michael T. *Crime and Its Modification.* New York: Pergamon, 1980.

Niles, Blair. *Condemned to Devil's Island.* New York: Grosset & Dunlap, 1928.

Nimmer, Raymond T. *Diversion: The Search for Alternative Forms of Prosecution.* Chicago: American Bar Foundation, 1974.

_____. *Two Million Unnecessary Arrests.* Chicago: American Bar Foundation, 1971.

Nimrod, Dan (ed.). *The PLO Terrorism and National Security.* London: Dawn Publishing Co., Ltd., 1985.

Nixon, Edgar B. *Franklin D. Roosevelt and Foreign Affairs.* Cambridge, Mass.: Harvard University Press, 1969.

Nixon, Edna. *Voltaire and the Calas Case.* London: Victor Gollancz 1961.

Nixon, Richard M. *RN: The Memoirs of Richard Nixon.* New York: Grosset & Dunlap, 1978.

Nizer, Louis. *The Implosion Conspiracy.* Garden City, N.Y.: Doubleday, 1973.

_____. *The Jury Returns.* New York: Pocket Books, 1968.

_____. *My Life in Court.* New York: Pyramid, 1963.

Noble, John, and Cronin, John F. (eds.). *Records of the Court of Assistants of the Colony of Massachusetts Bay.* Boston: Published by Author, 1901.

Noble, John Wesley, and Averbuch, Bernard. *Never Plead Guilty.* New York: Farrar, Strauss, Cudahy, 1955.

Noggle, Burl. *Teapot Dome: Oil and Politics in the 1920's.* Baton Rouge: Louisiana State University Press, 1962.

Nolan, William F. *Hammett: A Life at the Edge.* New York: Congdon and Weed, 1983.

Nolte, Ernst. *Three Faces of Fascism.* New York: Holt, Rinehart & Winston, 1965.

Nomad, Max. *Rebels and Renegades.* New York: Macmillan, 1932.

Noonan, John T., Jr. *Persons and Masks of the Law.* New York: Farrar, Straus & Giroux, 1976.

Nord, David Jr. *Dallas Conspiracy.* Hollis, N.H.: n.p., 1968.

Nordholt, J.W. Schulte. *The People That Walk in Darkness.* New York: Ballantine Books, 1960.

Nordon, Pierre. *Conan Doyle, A Biography.* New York: Holt, Rinehart & Winston, 1966.

Norfleet, J. Frank. *The Amazing Experiences of An Intrepid Texas Rancher With an International Swindling Ring (as told to Gordon Hines).* Sugar Land, Texas: Imperial Press, 1927.

_____. *Norfleet: The Actual Experiences of a Texas Rancher's 30,000-Mile Transcontinental Chase after Five Confidence Men.* Fort Worth: W.F. White, 1924.

North, Robert C. *Moscow and Chinese Communists.* Palo Alto, Calif.: Stanford University Press, 1953.

Northrop, H.D. *The Life and Achievements of Jay Gould.* New York: National, 1892.

Northrup, William B., and Northrup, John B. *The Insolence of Office: The Story of the Seabury Investigation.* New York: Putnam 1932.

Norton, Carla. *Disturbed Ground.* New York: William Morrow, 1994.

Notestein, W. *A History of English Witchcraft from 1558-1718.* Washington, D.C.: American Historical Association, 1911.

Nott-Bower, Sir William. *Fifty-two Years a Policeman.* London: Edward Arnold, 1926.

Novak, William. *High Culture: Marihuana and the Lives of Americans.* New York: Alfred A. Knopf, 1980.

Novotny, Ann. *Strangers at the Door.* Riverside, Conn.: Chatham Press, 1972.

Nowak, Frank. *Medieval Slavdom and the Rise of Russia.* New York: Henry Holt, 1930.

Nowlis, Helen H. *Drugs on the College Campus.* New York: Doubleday, 1969.

Noyes, Peter. *Legacy of Doubt.* New York: Pinnacle, 1963.

Nozick, Robert. *Anarchy, State, and Utopia.* New York: Basic Books, 1974.

Nugent, John Peer. *White Night.* New York: Rawson, Wade, 1979.

Nunn, W.C. *Texas Under the Carpetbaggers.* Austin: University of Texas Press, 1962.

Nuseibeh, Hazem Z. *The Idea of Arab Nationalism.* Ithaca, N.Y.: Cornell University Press, 1956.

Nute, Grace Lee. *Caesars of the Wilderness.* New York: D. Appleton-Century, 1943.

Nu Thakin (U Nu). *Burma Under the Japanese: Pictures and Portraits.* London: Macmillan, 1954.

Nuttall, Chris P., et al. *Parole in England and Wales.* London: H.M. Stationery Office, 1977.

Nutting, Anthony. *The Arabs: A Narrative History from Moham-med to the Present.* New York: Clarkson N. Potter, 1964.

_____. *Nasser.* New York: E. P. Dutton, 1972.

Nye, Russel B. *The Cultural Life of the New Nation 1776-1830.* New York: Harper and Row, 1960.

_____. *Fettered Freedom.* East Lansing: Michigan State College Press, 1945.

Nye, Captain W.S. *Carbine and Lace.* Norman: University of Oklahoma Press, 1937.

O'Ballance, Edgar. *The Arab-Israeli War, 1948.* New York: Frederick A. Praeger, 1957.

_____. *Language of Violence: The Blood Politics of Terrorism.* San Rafael, Calif.: Presidio Press, 1979.

_____. *The Sinai Campaign, 1956.* London: Faber & Faber, 1959.

_____. *Terror in Ireland: The Heritage of Hate.* Novato, Calif.: Presidio Press, 1981.

Oberholtzer, Ellis Paxson. *Abraham Lincoln.* Philadelphia: George W. Jacobs, 1904.

_____. *A History of the United States since the Civil War.* New York: Macmillan, 1917-1937.

_____. *Jay Cooke, Financier of the Civil War.* 2 vols. New York: George W. Jacobs, 1907.

O'Brian, John L. *National Security and Industrial Freedom.* Cambridge, Mass.: Harvard University Press, 1955.

O'Brien, C. Bickford. *Muscovy and the Ukraine.* Berkeley: University of California Press, 1963.

_____. *Russia Under Two Tsars, 1682-1689, Regency of Sophia Alekseevna.* Berkeley: University of California Press, 1952.

O'Brien, Conor Cruise. *Herod, Reflections on Political Violence.* London: Hutchinson, 1978.

_____. *Parnell and His Party, 1880-1890.* Oxford, Eng.: Oxford University Press, 1957.

O'Brien, Darcy. *Murder in Little Egypt.* New York: William Morrow, 1989.

_____. *Two of a Kind: The Hillside Stranglers.* New York: New American Library, 1985.

O'Brien, Frank M. *Murder Mysteries of New York.* New York: W.F. Payson, 1932.

_____. *The Story of the Sun, 1833-1918.* New York: George H. Doran, 1918.

O'Brien, John T. *Crime and Justice in America.* New York: Pergamon, 1980.

O'Brien, R.B. *The Life of Parnell.* 2 vols. London: Smith, Elder, 1898.

O'Brien, Robert. *California Called Them: A Saga of Golden Days and Roaring Camps.* New York: McGraw-Hill, 1951.

_____. *This Is San Francisco.* New York: Whittlesey House, 1948.

O'Brien, William V. *Law and Morality in Israel's War With the PLO.* New York: Routledge, 1991.

O'Callaghan, Sean. *Damaged Baggage: The White Slave Trade and Narcotics Trafficking in the Americas.* New York: Roy, 1969.

_____. *The Jackboot in Ireland.* London: Wingate, 1958.

_____. *The Slave Trade Today.* New York: Crown, 1961.

_____. *The Triads.* London: W.H. Allen, 1978.

_____. *The Yellow Slave Trade.* London: Anthony Blond, 1968.

O'Casey, Sean. *Drums Under the Windows.* New York: Macmil-lan, 1947.

_____. *Inishfallen Fare Thee Well.* New York: Macmillan, 1949.

_____. *The White Slave Trade.* London: Robert Hale, 1965.

Ochieng', W.R. *A History of Kenya.* London: Macmillan, 1985.

O'Connell, Marvin R. *The Counter Reformation, 1559-1610.* New York: Harper & Row, 1974.

O'Connor, Frank. *The Big Fellow.* New York: Nelson, 1937.

_____. *Michael Collins and the Irish Revolution.* Dublin, Ire.: Clonmore & Reynolds, 1965.

_____. *An Only Child.* New York: Alfred A. Knopf, 1961.

O'Connor, Harvey. *The Astors.* New York: Alfred A. Knopf, 1941.

_____. *Mellon's Millions.* New York: John Day, 1933.

O'Connor, John J. *Broadway Racketeers.* New York: Liveright, 1928.

O'Connor, Len. *Clout: Mayor Daley and His City.* Chicago: Henry Regnery, 1974.

O'Connor, Richard. *Ambrose Bierce.* London: Victor Gollancz, 1968.
_____. *Bat Masterson.* New York: Doubleday, 1957.
_____. *Black Jack Pershing.* New York: Doubleday, 1961.
_____. *The Cactus Throne: The Tragedy of Maximilian and Carlotta.* New York: G.P. Putnam's Sons, 1971.
_____. *Courtroom Warrior: The Combative Career of William Travers Jerome.* Boston: Little, Brown, 1963.
_____. *Gould's Millions.* Garden City, N.Y.: Doubleday, 1962.
_____. *Hell's Kitchen.* Philadelphia: J.B. Lippincott, 1958.
_____. *Heywood Broun.* New York: G.P. Putnam's Sons, 1975.
_____. *High Jinks on the Klondike.* Indianapolis, Ind.: Bobbs-Merrill, 1954.
_____. *Pat Garrett.* New York: Ace Books, 1960.
_____. *The Scandalous Mr. Bennett.* Garden City, N.Y.: Double-day, 1962.
_____. *Wild Bill Hickok.* New York: Doubleday, 1959.
Oddie, S. Ingleby. *Inquest.* London: Hutchinson, 1941.
Oddone, Jacinto. *Historia de Socialismo Argentine.* Buenos Aires: La Vanguardia, 1934.
O'Dell, Paul, with Slide, Anthony. *Griffith and the Rise of Hol-lywood.* New York: A.S. Barnes, 1970.
Odell, Robin. *Exhumation of Murder: The Life and Trial of Major Armstrong.* London: Harrap, 1975.
_____. *Jack the Ripper in Fact and Fiction.* London: Harrap, 1965.
Odens, Peter. *Outlaws, Heroes and Jokers of the Old Southwest.* Yuma, Ariz.: Southwest Printers, 1964.
O'Donnell, Bernard. *Cavalcade of Justice.* London: Clerke & Cockeran, 1951.
_____. *Crimes That Made News.* London: Burke, 1954.
_____. *Great Thames Mysteries.* London: Harrap, 1965.
_____. *The Old Bailey and Its Trials.* London: Clerke & Cock-eran, 1950.
_____. *Should Women Hang?* London: W.H. Allen, 1956.
_____. *The Trials of Mr. Justice Avory.* London: Rich & Cowan, 1935.
_____. *The World's Strangest Murders.* London: Frederick Muller, 1957.
_____. *The World's Worst Women.* London: W.H. Allen, 1953.
O'Donnell, Elliott. *Confessions of a Ghost Hunter.* London: Thornton Butterworth, 1928.
_____. *Great Thames Mysteries.* London: Selwyn & Blount, 1929.
_____. *Haunted Britain.* London: Rider, 1948.
_____. *Strange Disappearances.* New Hyde Park, N.Y.: University Books, 1972.
_____. *Trial of Kate Webster.* London: William Hodge, 1925.
_____. *Werewolves.* London: Methuen, 1912.
O'Donnell, John A., and Ball, J.C. (eds.). *Narcotic Addiction.* New York: Harper & Row, 1966.
_____. *Narcotic Addicts in Kentucky.* Washington, D.C.: U.S. Public Health Service, 1969.
O'Donnell, Kenneth P., Powers, David F., with McCarthy, Joe. *"Johnny, We Hardly Knew Ye."* Boston: Little, Brown, 1972.
Odorico, Federico. *Le Streghe di Valtellina e la Santa Inquisizione.* Milan, Italy: n.p., 1862.
O'Faolain, Julian, and Martines, Laura. *Not in God's Image.* New York: Harper Torchbooks, 1973.
O'Faolain, Sean. *Constance Markievicz or The Average Revolution-ary.* London: Jonathan Cape, 1934.
_____. *De Valera.* Harmondsworth, Eng.: Penguin, 1939.
_____. *An Irish Journey.* London: Longmans, 1940.
Ofer, Yehuda. *Operation Thunderbolt: The Entebbe Raid.* London: Penguin Books, 1976.
O'Flaherty, Liam. *The Informer.* London: Jonathan Cape, 1949.
_____. *Insurrection.* London: Victor Gollancz, 1950.
O'Flaherty, Michael. *Have You Seen This Woman?* London: Corgi, 1971.
O'Flaherty, Wendy D. *The Origins of Evil in Hindu Mythology.* Berkeley: University of California Press, 1978.
Ogata, Sadako N. *Defiance in Manchuria: The Making of Japanese Foreign Policy, 1931-1932.* Berkeley: University of California Press, 1964.
Ogburn, Charlton, Jr. *The Marauders.* New York: Harper, 1959.
Ogilvie, J.S. *History of the Assassination of J.A. Garfield.* New York: Published by Author, 1881.
O'Hara, Albert R. *Position of Women in Early China.* Wash-ing-ton, D.C.: Catholic University of America Press, 1945.
O'Hara, Charles. *Fundamentals of Criminal Investigation.* Springfield, Ill.: Charles C. Thomas, 1969.
O'Hea, Patrick. *Reminiscences of the Mexican Revolution.* Mexico City, Mex.: Editorial Fournier, 1966.
O'Hegarty, P.S. *A History of Ireland Under the Union.* Dublin, Ire.: Talbot, 1922.
_____. *A Short Memoir of Terence MacSwiney.* Dublin, Ire.: Talbot, 1922.
_____. *Ulster.* Dublin, Ire.: Maunsel, 1919.
_____. *The Victory of Sinn Fein.* Dublin, Ire.: Talbot, 1924.
Ohio Legislative Service Commission. *Capital Punishment.* Columbus: State of Ohio, 1961.
Ohlin, Lloyd E. (ed.). *Prisoners in America.* Englewood Cliffs, N.J.: Prentice-Hall, 1973.
_____. *Selection for Parole.* New York: Russell Sage, 1951.
Ohrwalder, Joseph. *Ten Years Captivity in the Mahdi's Camp.* London: Sampson Low, Marston, 1893.
Ohtani Keijiro. *The Beginning of Sunset: History of the Japanese Army in the Reign of Hirohito.* Tokyo: Yakumo Shoten, 1959.
_____. *History of the Secret Police During the Reign of Hirohito.* Tokyo: Misuzu Shobo, 1966.
Okamoto Aisuke. *White Paper on the Emperor.* Tokyo: Bungei Shunju, 1956.
Okonta Ike, and Oronto, Douglas. *Where Vultures Feast: Shell Human Rights and the Oil in the Niger Delta.* San Francisco: Sierra Club Books, 2001.
Olcott, C. *The Life of William McKinley.* 2 vols. New York: Houghton Mifflin, 1916.
Oldekop, Justus. *Observationes Criminales Practicae.* Frankfort, Ger.: J.Schrey & John Christ, 1698.
Olden, Marc. *Cocaine.* New York: Lancer Books, 1973.
Olden, Rudolf. *Hitler.* New York: Covici-Friede, 1936.
Oldenberg, Hermann. *Buddha: His Life, His Doctrine, His Order.* trans. William Hoey. London: Williams & Norgate, 1882.
Oldenburg, Z. *Catherine the Great.* New York: Pantheon Press, 1965.
Older, Cora. *Love Stories of Old California.* New York: Coward-McCann, 1940.
_____. *San Francisco: Magic City.* New York: Longmans, Green, 1961.
_____. *William Randolph Hearst, American.* New York: D. Appleton-Century, 1936.
Older, Fremont and Cora. *George Hearst: California Pioneer.* Los Angeles: Westernlore, 1966.
_____. *Growing Up.* San Francisco: Call-Bulletin, 1931.
_____. *My Own Story.* New York: Macmillan, 1926.
Oldroyd, Osborn H. *The Assassination of Abraham Lincoln.* Washington D.C.: Published by Author, 1901.
Oliver, John Rathbone. *Foursquare.* New York: Macmillan, 1929.
Oliver, N.T. *The Whitechapel Mystery: Jack the Ripper, A Psycholo-gical Problem.* Chicago: Continental, 1891.
Oliver, Roland and Caroline. *Africa in the Days of Exploration.* Englewood Cliffs, N.J.: Prentice-Hall, 1965.
Oliver, Thomas. *Disease of Occupation.* New York: Methuen, 1916.
Ollestad, Norman. *Inside the FBI.* New York: Lancer, 1968.
Olmstead, A.T. *History of Assyria.* New York: Charles Scribner's Sons, 1923.
Olmsted, Frederick Law. *The Cotton Kingdom.* New York: Alfred A. Knopf, 1953.
Olsen, Gregg. *Abandoned Prayers.* New York: Warner, 1990.
Olsen, Jack. *The Man with the Candy: The Story of the Houston Mass Murders.* New York: Simon & Schuster, 1974.
_____. *The Misbegotten Son.* New York: Delacorte Press, 1993.
_____. *Son: A Psychopath and His Victims.* New York: Dell, 1983.
O'Mahony, Peter Tynan (ed.). *Eamon de Valera 1882-1975.* Dublin, Ire.: The Irish Times, 1979.
O'Malley, Ernie. *On Another Man's Wound.* London: Rich & Cowan, 1936.
Oman, Sir Charles. *Seven Roman Statesmen of the Later Republic.* Freeport, N.Y.: Books for Libraries, 1971.
O'Meara, James. *The Vigilance Committee of 1856.* San Francis-co: Nash, 1932.
Omura Bunji. *The Last Genro: Prince Saionji, The Man Who Westernized Japan.* Philadelphia: J.B. Lippincott, 1938.
Omura Takeshi. *Prince Saionji in the Full Moon of Life.* Tokyo: Denki Kanko-kai, 1937.
O'Neal, Bill. *Encyclopedia of Western Gunfighters.* Norman: University of Oklahoma Press, 1979.
O'Neal, James Bradas. *They Die But Once.* New York: Knight, 1935.
O'Neill, Bard E. *Armed Struggle in Palestine: A Political-Military Analysis.* Boulder, Colo.: Westview Press, 1978.
_____. *Revolutionary Warfare in the Middle East.* Boulder, Colo.: Palatine Press, 1974.
O'Neill, Gerard, and Lehr, Dick. *The Underboss: The Rise and Fall of a Mafia Family.* New York: St. Martin's, 1989.
O'Neill, William L. *Coming Apart: An Informal History of America in the 1960s.* New York: Quadrangle, 1971
Oppenheimer, Ernest J. *The Inflation Swindle.* Englewood Cliffs, N.J.: Prentice-Hall, 1978.
Oppenheimer, H. *The Rationale of Punishment.* London: University of London Press, 1913.
Orano, Paolo. *Mussolini da vicino.* Rome: Pinciana, 1928.
Orchard, Harry (Albert E. Horsley). *The Confessions and Autobiography of Harry Orchard.* New York: Doubleday, Page, 1907.
O'Reilly, James T. *Federal Information Disclosure: Procedures, Forms and the Law.* Springs, Colo.: Shepard's, 1977.
O'Reilly, Kenneth. *Hoover and the Un-Americans.* Philadelphia: Temple University Press, 1983.
Orfield, Lester. *Criminal Appeals in America.* Boston: Little, Brown, 1939.
_____. *Criminal Procedure from Arrest to Appeal.* New York: New York University Press, 1947.
_____. *Criminal Procedure from Arrest to Trial.* New York: New York University Press, 1947.
_____. *Criminal Procedure Under Federal Rules.* Rochester, N.Y.: Lawyers Cooperative, 1967.
Organized Crime Task Force Report. Washington, D.C.: U.S. Government Printing Office, 1967.
Orland, Leonard. *Prisons: Houses of Darkness.* New York: The Free Press, 1975.
Orlansky, Harold. *The Harlem Riot: A Study in Mass Frustration.* New York: Social Analysis, 1943.
Orloski, Richard J. *Criminal Law.* Chicago: Nelson-Hall, 1977.
Orlov, Alexander. *Handbook of Intelligence and Guerrilla Warfare.* Ann Arbor: University of Michigan Press, 1965.
Orlow, Dietrich. *The History of the Nazi Party.* 2 vols. Pittsburgh, Pa.: University of Pittsburgh Press, 1969.
Orman, Richard A. van. *A Room for the Night: Hotels of the Old West.* Bloomington: Indiana University Press, 1966.
Ormerod, Henry. *Piracy in the Ancient World.* London: Hodder & Stoughton, 1924.
Ormsby, W.L.A. *A Description of Bank Note Engraving.* New York: Published by Author, 1852.
Oron, Yitzhak (ed.). *Middle East Record.* New York: Daniel Davey, 1966.
Orr, Tamra. *Egyptian Islamic Jihad (Inside the World's Most Infamous Terrorist Organization).* New York: Rosen Publishing Group, 2003.
Orsini, Felice. *The Austrian Dungeons of Italy.* Trans. J. Meriton White. London: George Routledge & Sons, 1856.
_____. *Memoirs and Adventures of Felice Orsini.* Trans. George Carbonel. Edinburgh, Scot.: Thomas Constable, 1857.
Ortega Y Gassett, Jose. *Revolt of the Masses.* New York: W.W. Norton, 1932.
Orth, Samuel P. *The Boss and the Machine: A Chronicle of the Politicians and Party Organizations.* New Haven, Conn.: Yale University Press, 1920.
Osaghae, Eghosa. *Crippled Giant: Nigeria Since Independence.* Bloomington, Ind.: Indiana University Press, 1998.
Osborn, Albert D. *Questioned Document Problems.* Albany, N.Y.: Boyd Printing, 1944.
Osborne, John. *The Second Year of the Nixon Watch.* New York: Liveright, 1971.
_____. *The White House Watch: The Ford Years.* Washington, D.C.: New Republic, 1977.

Osborne, Thomas Mott. *Prisons and Common Sense.* Philadel-phia: J.B. Lippincott, 1924.

Osgood, Cornelius. *The Koreans and Their Culture.* New York: The Ronald Press, 1951.

Osgood, Herbert Levi. *The American Colonies in the Eighteenth Century.* New York: Columbia University Press, 1924.

_____. *The American Colonies in the Seventeenth Century.* 3 vols. New York: Macmillan, 1904-07.

Osgood, Robert E., and Tucker, Robert W. *Force, Order, and Justice.* Baltimore: Johns Hopkins Press, 1967.

Oshinsky, David M. *A Conspiracy So Immense: The World of Joe McCarthy.* New York: Free Press, 1983.

Osofsky, Gilbert. *Harlem: The Making of a Ghetto.* New York: Harper & Row, 1968.

Ossendowski, Ferdinand. *Beasts, Men and Gods.* New York: E.P. Dutton, 1922.

Oster, John E. *Political and Economic Doctrines of John Marshall.* New York: Neals, 1914.

Osterburg, James W. *The Crime Laboratory.* Bloomington: Indiana University Press, 1968.

Ostermann, Peter. *Commentarius Juridicus.* Cologne, Ger.: Petrum Metternich, 1659.

Ostermann, Robert. *Crime in America.* New York: Dow Jones, 1966.

Ostrander, Gilman M. *The Prohibition Movement in California, 1848-1933.* Los Angeles: University of California Press, 1957.

Ostrogorsky, Georgije. *History of the Byzantine State.* New Brunswick, N.J.: Rutgers University Press, 1957.

Ostrovsky, Victor. *A Rogue Agent Exposes the Mossad's Secret Agenda.* New York: Harper Collins, 1994.

O'Sullivan, Donal. *The Irish Free State and Its Senate.* London: Faber & Faber, 1940.

O'Sullivan, F. Dalton. *Crime Detection.* Chicago: O'Sullivan, 1928.

O'Sullivan, Noel (ed.). *Terrorism, Ideology,and Revolution.* Boulder, Colo.: Westview Press, 1986.

Oswald, Marguerite. *Aftermath of an Execution: The Burial and Final Rights of Lee Harvey Oswald as Told by His Mother.* Dallas: Published by Author, 1964.

Oswald, Robert L., Myrick, and Land, Barbara. *Lee: A Portrait of Lee Harvey Oswald.* New York: Coward-McCann, 1967.

Oswald, Russel G. *Attica: My Story.* Garden City, N.Y.: Double-day, 1972.

Oswald: Assassin or Fall Guy? New York: Marzani & Munsell, 1964.

O'Toole, George. *The Assassination Tapes: An Electronic Probe into the Murder of John F. Kennedy and the Dallas Cover-up.* New York: Penthouse Press, 1975.

Ottenberg, Miriam. *The Federal Investigators.* Englewood Cliffs, N.J.: Prentice-Hall, 1962.

Oursel, Raymond. *Jeanne d'Arc.* Tours, Fr.: Maue, 1952.

Ousler, W. *Marijuana: The Facts, The Truth.* New York: Paul S. Eriksson, 1968.

Outlawry and Justice in Old Arizona. Tucson, Ariz.: L.A. Printers, 1965.

Outler, Albert C. (ed.). *Confessions.* London: SCM Press, 1955.

Overholser, Winfred. *The Psychiatrist and the Law.* New York: Harcourt, Brace, 1953.

Overly, Don H., and Schell, Theodore H. *New Effectiveness Measures for Organized Crime Control Efforts.* Washington, D.C.: U.S. Government Printing Office, 1973.

Overstreet, Harry A., and Overstreet, Bonaro. *The FBI in an Open Society.* New York: W.W. Norton, 1969.

Overton, Grant (ed.). *Mirrors of the Year.* New York: F.A. Stokes, 1927-28.

Owen, Collinson. *King Crime, an English Study of America's Greatest Problem.* New York: Henry Holt, 1932.

Owen, David E. *English Philanthropy, 1660-1960.* Cambridge, Mass.: Harvard University Press, 1964.

Owen, Frank. *Tempestuous Journey: Lloyd George, His Life and Times.* London: Hutchinson, 1954.

_____. *The Three Dictators.* London: George Allen & Unwin, 1941.

Owen, Launcelot A. *The Russian Peasant Movement, 1906-1917.* London: King, 1937.

Owen, Mary Cameron. *The Booster and the Snitch.* New York: Free Press, 1964.

Owens, William A. *Slave Mutiny.* New York: John Day, 1953.

Owing, Chloe. *Women Police.* Montclair, N.J.: Patterson Smith, 1968.

Oya Soichi. *Japan's Longest Day.* Tokyo: Bungei Shunju, 1965.

Ozaki Yoshiharu. *The Men Who Moved the Army.* Odawara, Japan: Hachi-ko-do Shoten, 1960.

Packard, Reynolds and Eleanor. *Balcony Empire.* London: Chatto & Windus, 1943.

Packard, Vance. *The Hidden Persuaders.* New York: Simon & Schuster, 1966.

_____. *The Naked City.* New York: David McKay, 1964.

Packe, Michael St. John. *The Bombs of Orsini.* London: Secker & Warburg, 1957.

_____. *Orsini: The Story of a Conspirator.* Boston: Little, Brown, 1957.

_____. *The Limits of the Criminal Sanction.* Palo Alto, Calif.: Stanford University Press, 1968.

The Pageant of America. 15 vols. New Haven, Conn.: Yale University Press, 1925.

Paget, R.T., and Silverman, Sydney. *Hanged-And Innocent?* London: Victor Gollancz, 1953.

Paine, Lauran. *The Assassin's World.* New York: Taplinger, 1975.

Paine, Ralph D. *Lost Ships and Lonely Seas.* New York: Century, 1922.

Pakenham, F.A., (assisted by R. Opie). *Causes of Crime.* Lon-don: Weidenfeld & Nicolson, 1958.

Pakula, Hannah. *The Last Romance: A Biography of Queen Marie of Roumania.* New York: Simon & Schuster, 1984.

Palacios, Porfirio. *Emiliano Zapata.* Mexico City: n.p., 1960.

Palologue, Maurice. *An Embassador's Memoirs.* 3 vols. trans. F.A. Holt. New York: Doran, 1925.

_____. *The Enigmatic Czar: The Life of Alexander I of Russia.* London: Harper & Brothers, 1938.

_____. *The Tragic Empress.* New York: Harper & Brothers, 1928.

_____. *The Tragic Romance of Alexander II.* London: Hutchin-son, 1926.

Palmer, Edwin O. *History of Hollywood.* Hollywood, Ca-lif.: Arthur H. Cawston, 1937.

Palmer, H.A., and Palmer, H. (eds.). *Wilsheve's Criminal Proce-dure.* London: Sweet & Maxwell, 1954.

Palmer, Stuart. *The Prevention of Crime.* New York: Behavioral, 1973.

_____. *The Psychology of Murder.* New York: Thomas Y. Crowell, 1960.

Pantaleone, Michele. *The Mafia and Politics.* New York: Coward-McCann, 1966.

Papadatos, Peter. *The Eichmann Trial.* New York: Frederick A. Praeger, 1964.

Parent-Duchtelet, A.J.B. *De la Prostitution dans la ville de Paris.* Paris: J.B. Baillire, 1836.

Pares, Sir Bernard. *The Fall of the Russian Monarchy.* New York: Alfred A. Knopf, 1939 (reissued, 2001, London: Phoenix Press).

_____. *A History of Russia.* New York: Alfred A. Knopf, 1953.

_____. *Russia and Reform.* London: Constable, 1907.

Pares, Richard. *King George III and the Politicians.* Oxford, Eng.: Clarendon Press, 1953.

_____. *Yankees and Creoles.* Cambridge, Mass.: Harvard University Press, 1956.

Parish, Joe. *Coffins, Cactus and Cowboys.* El Paso, Texas: Superior, 1954.

Park, Alexander. *Bolshevism in Turkestan, 1917-1927.* New York: Columbia University Press, 1957.

Parker, Alfred E. *August Vollmer: Crime Fighter.* New York: Macmillan, 1961.

_____. *The Berkeley Police Story.* Springfield, Ill.: Charles C. Thomas, 1972.

Parker, Donn B. *Crime by Computer.* New York: Scribners, 1976.

Parker, Frank. *Caryl Chessman, the Red Light Bandit.* Chicago: Nelson-Hall, 1975.

Parker, John Lloyd. *Unmasking Wall Street.* Boston: Stratford, 1932.

Parker, L. Craig, Jr. *The Japanese Police System Today.* New York: Kodansha International, 1984.

Parker, Theodore. *Sermon of the Dangerous Classes in Society.* Boston: Spear, 1847.

_____. *The Hidden World of Sex Offenders.* New York: Bobbs-Merrill, 1969.

Parker, Willie J. *Halt! I'm A Federal Game Warden.* New York: McKay, 1977.

Parkes, Henry Bamford. *A History of Mexico.* London: Eyre & Spottiswoods, 1962.

Parkes, James W. *A History of Palestine from 135 A.D. to Modern Times.* New York: Oxford University Press, 1949.

Parkhill, Forbes. *The Law Goes West.* Denver: Sage Books, 1956.

_____. *The Wildest of the West.* New York: Henry Holt, 1951.

Parkhurst, Rev. Charles H. *My Forty Years in New York.* New York: Macmillan, 1923.

_____. *Our Fight with Tammany.* New York: Charles Scribner's Sons, 1895.

Parkinson, Roger. *Zapata.* New York: Stein & Day, 1975.

Parkinson, Sydney. *A Journal of a Voyage to the South Seas, in His Majesty's Ship, the Endeavour.* London: Published by Author, 1773.

Parks, Charles Caldwell. *A Plaything of the Gods.* Boston: Sherman, Finch, 1912.

Parks, Melvin. *Musicals of the 1930s.* New York: Museum of the City of New York, 1966.

Parminter, Geoffrey de C. *Reasonable Doubt.* London: Arthur Baker, 1938.

Parrinder, Geoffrey. *Witchcraft: European and African.* Bal-timore: Penguin Books, 1958.

_____. *Main Currents in American Thought.* 3 vols. New York: Harcourt, Brace, 1927-1930.

Parrish, J.M., and Crossland, J.R. *The Fifty Most Amazing Crimes of the Last Hundred Years.* London: Odhams, 1936.

Parris, John. *Most of My Murders.* London: Frederick Muller, 1960.

Parrish, Joe. *Coffins, Cactus and Cowboys: The Exciting Story of El Paso, 1536 to Present.* El Paso, Texas: Superior, 1964.

Parrot, Cecil. *The Tightrope.* London: Faber & Faber, 1975.

Parry, Albert. *Terrorism: From Robespierre to Arafat.* New York: The Vanguard Press, 1976.

Parry, Sir Edward Abbott. *The Drama of the Law.* New York: Charles Scribner's Sons, 1924.

Parry, John Horace, and Sherlock, P.M. *A Short History of the West Indies.* New York: St. Martin's Press, 1956.

Parry, Dr. Leonard. *Some Famous Medical Trials.* London: Churchill, 1927.

Parsons, Philip Archibald. *Crime and the Criminal.* New York: Alfred A. Knopf, 1926.

Partridge, Burco. *A History of Orgies.* New York: Avon, 1958.

_____. *Memoirs of an Assassin, Confessions of a Stern Gang Killer.* New York: Thomas Yoseloff, 1959.

Partridge, Ralph. *Broadmoor: A History of Criminal Lunacy and its Problems.* London: Chatto & Windus, 1953.

Paschal, Joel F. *Mr. Justice Sutherland.* Princeton, N.J.: Prince-ton University Press, 1951.

Pasley, Fred D. *Al Capone: The Biography of A Self-Made Man.* New York: Ives Washburn, 1930.

_____. *Muscling In.* New York: Ives Washburn, 1931.

Passant, Ernest J. *A Short History of Germany 1815-1945.* New York: Columbia University Press, 1962.

Passy, Colonel. *Deuxime bureau—Londres.* Monte Carlo, Monaco: Solar, 1947.

Pasternack, S.A. (ed.). *Violence and Victims.* New York: Spec-trum, 1975.

Pastor, Ludwig. *The History of the Popes.* London: Routledge & Kegan Paul, 1950.

Pate, Tony, et al. *Police Response Time: Its Determinants and Effects.* Washington, D.C.: The Police Foundation, 1976.

_____, and Bowers, Robert A., and Parks, Ron. *Three Approaches to Criminal Apprehension in Kansas City: An Evaluation Report.* Washington, D.C.: The Police Foundation, 1976.

Patmore, Derek. *Balkan Correspondent.* New York: Harper & Brothers, 1941.

Patrick, Ted. *Let Our Children Go!* New York: E.P. Dutton, 1976.

Pattenden, Rosemary. *The Judge, Discretion, and the Criminal Trial.* Oxford, Eng.: Clarendon Press, 1982.

Patterns of Global Terrorism: 1983. Washington, D.C.: U.S. Dept. of State, 1984.

Patterson, C.L. *Sensational Texas Manhunt.* San Antonio, Texas: Sid Murray & Son, 1939.

Patterson, Jerry E. *The City of New York.* New York: Harry N. Abrams, 1978.

Patterson, Robert T. *The Great Boom and Panic, 1921-1929.* Chicago: Henry Regnery, 1965.

Patti, Ercole. *Roman Chronicle.* London: Chatto & Windus, 1965.

Payne, Howard C. *The Police State of Louis Napoleon Bonaparte, 1851-1860.* Seattle: University of Washington Press, 1966.

Payne, Les, and Findley, Tim. *The Life and Death of the SLA.* New York: Ballantine Books, 1976.

Payne, Ransom. *The Dalton Brothers and Their Astounding Career of Crime.* Chicago: Laird & Lee, 1892.

Payne, Robert. *Chungking Diary.* London: William Heinemann, 1945.

_____. *The Holy Sword.* London: Robert Hale, 1961.

_____. *The Life and Death of Adolf Hitler.* New York: Frederick A. Praeger, 1973.

_____. *The Life and Death of Lenin.* New York: Simon & Schuster, 1964.

_____. *Portrait of a Revolutionary: Mao Tse-tung.* New York: Abelard-Shuman, 1961.

Payne, William. *Deep Cover: An FBI Agent Infiltrates the Radical Underground.* New York: Newsweek Books, 1979.

Pearce, Charles. *Unsolved Murder Mysteries.* New York: Stokes, 1924.

Pearl, Jack. *The Dangerous Assassins.* Derby, Conn.: Monarch Books, 1964.

Pearlman, Moshe. *Ben-Gurion Looks Back.* New York: Simon & Schuster, 1965.

Pearsall, Ronald. *The Worm in the Bud: The World of Victorian Sexuality.* New York: Macmillan, 1969.

Pearson, Drew. *Diaries 1949-1959.* New York: Holt, Rinehart, Winston, 1974.

_____, and Allen, Robert S. *The Nine Old Men.* Garden City, N.Y.: Doubleday, Doran, 1936.

Pearson, Edmund. *Five Murders.* Garden City, N.Y.: Doubleday, Doran, 1928.

_____. *Instigation of the Devil.* New York: Charles Scribner's Sons, 1930.

_____. *Masterpieces at Murder.* Boston: Little, Brown, 1924.

_____. *More Studies in Murder.* New York: Smith & Haas, 1936.

_____. *Murder at Smutty Nose and Other Murders.* Garden City, N.Y.: Doubleday, 1927.

_____. *Studies in Murder.* New York: Macmillan, 1924.

_____ (ed.). *The Trial of Lizzie Borden.* New York: Doubleday, Doran, 1937.

Pearson, Geoffrey. *The Deviant Imagination.* London: Macmil-lan, 1975.

_____. *The New Heroin Users.* Oxford, Eng.: Basil Blackwell, 1987.

Pearson, Jim Berry. *The Maxwell Land Grant.* Norman: Univer-sity of Oklahoma Press, 1961.

Pearson, John. *The Profession of Violence.* London: Weidenfeld & Nicolson, 1972.

Pearson, Michael. *Age of Consent.* London: David & Charles, 1972.

_____. *The Millionaire Mentality.* London: Secker & Warburg, 1961.

Pease, E.R. *The History of the Fabian Society.* New York: E.P. Dutton, 1925.

Pease, Margaret. *Jean Jaures, Socialist and Humanitarian.* New York: Huebsch, 1917.

Peattie, Mark R. *Ishiwara Kanji and Japan's Confrontation with the West.* Princeton, N.J.: Princeton University Press, 1975.

Peavy, Charles D. *Charles A. Siringo, a Texas Picaro.* Austin, Texas: Steck-Vaughn, 1967.

Pecora, Ferdinand. *Wall Street Under Oath.* New York: Simon & Schuster, 1939.

Pedrick, W.E. *New Orleans As It Was.* Cleveland: W.W. Williams, 1885.

Peel, Mrs. C.S. *How We Lived Then, 1914-1918.* London: John Lane, 1929.

Peel, Roy V. *The Political Clubs of New York.* New York: G.P. Putnam's Sons, 1935.

Peffer, Nathaniel. *The Far East.* Ann Arbor: University of Michigan Press, 1958.

Peixotto, Jessica B. *The French Revolution and Modern French Socialism.* New York: Thomas Y. Crowell, 1901.

Pekelis, Alexander H. *Law and Social Action.* Ithaca, N.Y.: Cornell University Press, 1950.

Pekkanen, John. *Victims: An Account of Rape.* New York: Popular Library, 1976.

Pelcovits, N.A. *Old China Hands and the Foreign Office.* New York: King's Crown Press, 1948.

Pelfrey, William V. *The Evolution of Criminology.* Cincinnati, Ohio: Anderson, 1980.

Pelham, Camden. *The Chronicles of Crime, or the New Newgate Calendar.* 2 vols. London: Reeves and Turner, 1886.

Pelissier, Roger (ed.). *The Awakening of China, 1783-1949.* New York: Putnam, 1967.

Pell, Eve (ed.). *Maximum Security: Letters from Prison.* New York: E.P. Dutton, 1972.

Pellew, J. *The Home Office 1848-1914: from Clerks to Bureaucrats.* London: Heinemann Educational Books, 1982.

Pember, A. *Ivan the Terrible.* London: A.P. Marsden, 1895.

Pember, Ron, and de Marne, Denis. *Jack the Ripper: A Musical Play.* London: French, 1976.

The Penal Code of the RSFSR. London: H.M. Stationery Office, 1925.

Penal Reform in England: Introductory Essays on Some Aspects of English Criminal Policy. London: Macmillan, 1946.

Penfield, Thomas. *Western Sheriffs and Marshals.* New York: Grossett & Dunlap, 1955.

Pennsylvania Crime Commission. *A Decade of Organized Crime: 1980 Report.* St. Davids, Pa.: Pennsylvania Crime Commis-sion, 1980.

_____. *Report on Organized Crime.* Harrisburg, Pa.: Com-mon-wealth of Pennsylvania, 1970.

Penrose, Charles Bingham. *The Rustler Business.* Douglas, Wyo.: Douglas Budget, 1959.

Penrose, Valentine. *The Bloody Countess.* London: Calder & Boyars, 1970.

Pepinsky, Harold. *Crime and Conflict.* New York: Academic Press, 1976.

_____. *Crime Control Strategies.* New York: Oxford, 1980.

Pepper, Curtis Bill. *Kidnapped! 17 Days of Terror.* New York: Harmony Books, 1978.

Percy, William Alexander. *Lanterns on the Levee.* New York: Alfred A. Knopf, 1941.

Peres, Shimon. *David's Sling.* New York: Random House, 1970.

Peretz, Don. *Israel and the Palestine Arabs.* Washington, D.C.: Middle East Institute, 1958.

_____. *The Middle East Today.* New York: Holt, Rinehart & Winston, 1963.

Perkin, Harold J. *The Origins of Modern English Society, 1780-1880.* London: Routledge & Kegan Paul, 1969.

Perkins, Dexter. *A History of the Monroe Doctrine.* Boston: Little, Brown, 1955.

Perkins, William. *A Discourse of the Damned Art of Witchcraft.* Cambridge, Eng.: Thomas Pickering, 1608.

Perkus, Cathy (ed.). *Cointelpro: The FBI's Secret War on Political Freedom.* New York: Monad, 1975.

Perley, Sidney. *The History of Salem, Massachusetts.* Salem, Mass.: Published by Author, 1924.

Perlman, Selig, and Taft, Philip. *History of Labor in the United States 1896-1932.* New York: Macmillan, 1935.

Pernikoff, Alexandre. *Bushido: The Anatomy of Terror.* New York: Liveright, 1943.

Pernoud, Rgine. *Joan of Arc.* trans. Edward Hyams. New York: Stein & Day, 1966.

Perowne, Stewart. *Death of the Roman Republic.* Garden City, N.Y.: Doubleday, 1968.

Perrett, Geoffrey. *America in the Twenties.* New York: Simon & Schuster, 1982.

_____. *Days of Sadness, Years of Triumph.* New York: Coward, McCann, 1973.

_____. *Dream of Greatness.* New York: Coward, McCann, 1979.

Perreux, Gabriel. *Les Conspirations de Louis Napoleon Bonaparte.* Paris: Hachette, 1926.

Perrin, Noel. *Giving Up the Gun.* Boston: Shambhala, 1979.

Perrow, Charles. *Complex Organizations.* Glenview, Ill.: Scott, Foresman, 1979.

Perroy, Edouard. *The Hundred Years War.* Bloomington: Indiana University Press, 1962.

Perry, J., and Chabert, J. *L'Affaire Petiot.* Paris: Gallimard, 1957.

Perry, Lewis. *Radical Abolitionism: Anarchy and the Government of God in Antislavery Thought.* Ithaca, N.Y.: Cornell University Press, 1973.

Perry, Louis B., and Perry, Richard S. *A History of the Los Angeles Labor Movement, 1911-1941.* Berkeley: University of California Press, 1963.

Persons, Stow. *The Decline of Gentility.* New York: Columbia University Press, 1973.

Petacci, Clara. *Il mio diario.* Milan, Italy: Editori Associati, 1946.

Petacco, Arrigo. *Joe Petrosino.* New York: Macmillan, 1974.

Peters, Charles, and Branch, Taylor. *Blowing the Whistle.* New York: Frederick A. Praeger, 1972.

Peters, Hugh. *Good Work for a Good Magistrate.* London: W. Du Gard, 1651.

Peters, Jim. *The Nigerian Military and the State.* London: I .B. Tavris and Co., Ltd., 1997.

Petersen, David M., and Truzzi, Marcello (eds.). *Criminal Life: Views from the Inside.* Englewood Cliffs, N.J.: Prentice-Hall, 1972.

Petersen, Neil H. *From Hitler's Doorstep: The Wartime Intelligence Reports of Allen Dulles, 1942-1945.* University Park, Pa.: Pennsylvania State University Press, 1996.

Petersen, William. *Japanese Americans.* New York: Random House, 1971.

Petersen, William J. *Steamboating on the Upper Mississippi.* Iowa City: Iowa State Historical Society, 1937.

Petersilia, Joan, Greenwood, Peter W., Lavin, Marvin. *Criminal Careers of Habitual Felons.* Santa Monica, Calif.: The Rand Corporation, 1977.

_____, et al. *Granting Felons Probation.* Santa Monica, Calif.: The Rand Corporation, 1985.

_____. *Racial Disparities in the Criminal Justice System.* Santa Monica, Calif.: The Rand Corporation, 1983.

Peterson, Mark A. *Doing Crime: A Survey of California Prison Inmates.* Santa Monica, Calif.: The Rand Corporation, 1980.

_____, and Braiker, Harriet B. *Who Commits Crimes.* Cambridge: Oelgeschlager, Gunn & Hain, 1981.

Peterson, T.B. *The Trial of the Alleged Assassins and Conspirators.* Philadelphia: T.B. Peterson & Brothers, 1865.

Peterson, V.W. *Crime Commissions in the United States.* Chicago: Chicago Crime Commission, 1945.

Peterson, Virgil. *Barbarians in Our Midst: A History of Chicago Crime and Politics.* Boston: Little, Brown, 1952.

_____. *The Mob: 200 Years of Organized Crime in New York.* Ottawa, Ill.: Green Hill, 1983.

Petherick, Maurice. *Restoration Rogues.* London: Hollis Carter, 1951.

Petit, Mark. *A Need to Kill.* New York: Ivy Books, 1990.

Petrie, Sir Charles. *Lords of the Inland Sea.* London: Lovat Dickson, 1937.

_____. *Mussolini.* London: Holme Press, 1931.

Petrie, W. M. Flinders. *Social Life in Ancient Egypt.* New York: Houghton Mifflin, 1923.

Petronius. *New York Unexpurgated.* New York: Matrix House, 1966.

Petrov, V.M., and E. *Empire of Fear.* New York: Frederick A. Praeger, 1956.

Petrovich, Michael Boro. *The Emergence of Russian Panslavism, 1856-1870.* New York: Columbia University Press, 1956.

Pettigrew, R.F. *The Course of Empire: An Official Record.* New York: Boni & Liveright, 1920.

Petty, George Eugene. *The Narcotic Drug Diseases and Allied Ailments.* Philadelphia: F.A. Davis, 1913.

Peyton, George. *How to Detect Counterfeit Bank Notes.* New York: Published by Author, 1856.

Pfeffer, Leo. *Church, State, and Freedom.* Boston: Beacon Press, 1953.

_____. *God, Caesar, and the Constitution.* Boston: Beacon Press, 1975.

___. *The Liberties of an American: The Supreme Court Speaks.* Boston: Beacon Press, 1963.

_____. *Religious Freedom.* Skokie, Ill.: National Textbook, 1977.

_____. *This Honorable Court.* Boston: Beacon Press, 1965.

Phares, Ross. *Bible in Pocket, Gun in Hand.* Garden City, N.Y.: Doubleday, 1964.

_____. *Reverend Devil, A Biography of John A. Murrell.* New Orleans, La.: Pelican, 1941.

Philadelphia Society for Alleviating the Miseries of Public Prisons. *Extracts and Remarks on the Subjects of Punishment and Reformation of Criminals.* Philadelphia: Z. Poulson, 1790.

Phillips, Cabell. *Dateline Washington.* Garden City, N.Y.: Doubleday, 1949.

_____. *From the Crash to the Blitz 1929-1939: The New York Times Chronicle of American Life.* New York: Macmillan, 1969.

_____. *The 1940's: Decade of Triumph and Trouble.* New York: Macmillan, 1975.

Phillips, Charles. *Vacation Thoughts on Capital Punishment.* London: W.& F.G. Cash, 1856.

Phillips, Charles, and Axelrod, Alan. *Cops, Crooks and Criminologists.* New York: Checkmark Books, 2000.

Phillips, Conrad. *Murderer's Moon.* London: Arthur Baker, 1956.

Phillips, David. *Skyjack: The Story of Air Piracy.* London: Harrap, 1973.

Phillips, Harlan B. *Felix Frankfurter Reminisces.* New York: Reynal, 1960.

Phillips, James Duncan. *Salem in the Seventeenth Century.* Boston: Houghton Mifflin, 1933.

Phillips, Sir Percival. *The Red Dragon and the Black Shirts.* London: Daily Mail, 1923.

Phillips, Steven. *No Heroes, No Villains.* New York: Random House, 1977.

Phillips, Ulrich Bonnell. *American Negro Slavery.* Baton Rouge: Louisiana State University Press, 1966.

Phillips, W. Alison. *The Revolution in Ireland 1906-1923.* London: Longmans, Green, 1926.

Phillips, Wendell. *Oman: A History.* New York: William Morrow, 1967.

Phillips, William. *The Short Stories of Dostoevsky.* trans. Con-stance Garnett. New York: Dial Press, 1946.

Phillipson, Coleman. *Three Criminal Law Reformers: Beccaria, Bentham, Romilly.* London: J.M. Dent & Sons, 1923.

Phillipson, M. *Sociological Aspects of Crime and Delinquency.* London: Routledge & Kegan Paul, 1971.

Philpin, John. *Stalemate: A Shocking True Story of Child Abduction and Murder.* New York: Bantam, 1997.

Piatnitsky, O. *Memoirs of a Bolshevik.* New York: International, 1934.

Pichon, J.E. *Le complot de Sarajevo, 1914.* Paris: Bossard, 1918.

Picigallo, Philip R. *The Japanese on Trial: Allied War Crimes Operations in the East, 1945-1951.* Austin: University of Texas Press, 1979.

Pickering, Clarence R. *The Early Days of Prohibition.* New York: Vantage Press, 1964.

Pierce, Bessie Louise. *As Others See Chicago: Impressions of Visitors, 1673-1933.* Chicago: University of Chicago Press, 1932.

_____. *A History of Chicago.* 3 vols. New York: Alfred A. Knopf, 1937.

Pike, Frederick B. *Chile and the United States: 1880-1962.* South Bend, Ind.: University of Notre Dame Press, 1963.

Pike, Luke Owen. *A History of Crime in England.* 2 vols. Montclair, N.J.: Patterson Smith, 1962.

Pike, Royston. *Hard Times.* New York: Frederick A. Praeger, 1966.

Pileggi, Nicholas. *Blye, Private Eye.* Chicago: Playboy Press, 1977.

_____. *Wiseguy, Life in a Mafia Family.* New York: Simon & Schuster, 1985.

Pilkington, Ian D.B. *The King's Pleasure.* London: Jarrolds, 1957.

Pilot, Oliver. *Drew Pearson.* New York: Harper's Magazine Press, 1973.

Pin, Tao Hsu. *A History of Shanghai.* Taiwan: China Book Translation, 1968.

Pinchon, Edgcumb. *Viva Villa! A Recovery of the Real Pancho Villa, Peon, Bandit, Soldier, Patriot.* New York: Harcourt, 1933.

_____. *Zapata, the Unconquerable.* New York: Doubleday, Doran, 1941.

Pink, Louis Heaton. *Gaynor: The Tammany Mayor Who Swal-lowed the Tiger.* New York: International Press, 1931.

Pinkerton, A. Frank. *Jim Cummins: Or, the Great Adams Express Robbery.* Chicago: Laird & Lee, 1887.

_____. *The Whitechapel Murders: or American Detective in London.* New York: Laird & Lee, 1889.

Pinkerton, Allan. *Bankrobbers and the Detectives.* New York: G.W. Carleton, 1883.

_____. *Criminal Reminiscences and Detective Sketches.* New York: G.W. Dillingham, 1878.

_____. *History and Evidence of the Passage of Abraham Lincoln from Harrisburg, Pa., to Washington D.C., on the Twenty Third of February, 1861.* New York: Rode & Bravel, 1868.

_____. *Mississippi Outlaws and the Detectives.* New York: G.W. Carleton 1881.

_____. *The Mollie Maguires and the Detectives.* New York: G.W. Carleton, 1877.

_____. *Professional Thieves and Detectives.* New York: G.W. Carleton, 1880.

_____. *The Somnambylist and Detectives.* New York: G.W. Dillingham, 1903.

_____. *Spy of the Rebellion.* New York: G.W. Carleton, 1883.

Pinkerton, Matthew W. *Murder in All Ages.* Chicago: A.E. Pinkerton 1898.

Pinkerton, William A. *Train Robbers.* Jamestown, Va.: Interna-tional Chiefs of Police Association, 1907.

Pinkney, Alphonso. *The American Way of Violence.* New York: Random House, 1972.

Pinkowski, Edward. *The Latimer Massacre.* Philadelphia: Sunshine Press, 1950.

Pipes, Richard. *The Russian Revolution.* New York: Vintage, 1991.

_____. *Russia Under the Old Regime.* New York: Collier Books, 1992.

Pistone, Joseph D. *Donnie Brasco: My Undercover Life in the Mafia.* New York: New American Library, 1987.

Pistrak, Lazar. *The Great Tactician: Khrushchev's Rise to Power.* New York: Frederick A. Praeger, 1961.

Pitcairn, R. (ed.). *Criminal Trials in Scotland from A.D. 1488 to A.D. 1624.* Edinburgh, Scot.: William Tait, 1833.

Pitkin, John. *The Prison Cell in Its Lights and Shadows.* London: S. Low, Marston, 1918.

Pitkin, Thomas M., and Cordasco, Francesco. *The Black Hand: A Chapter in Ethnic Crime.* Totawa, N.J.: Littlefield, Adams, 1977.

Pitt, Roxane. *The Courage of Fear.* London: Jarrolds, 1957.

Pittau, Joseph. *The Meiji Political System.* Tokyo: Sophia University, 1963.

Pittenger, W. *Secret Service.* Philadelphia: J.B. Lippincott, 1882.

Pittman, Benn. *The Assassination of President Lincoln and the Trial of the Conspirators.* New York: Moore, Wilstach, Baldwin, 1865.

Pitts, Dr. J.R.S. *Life and Bloody Career of the Executed Criminal James Copeland.* Jackson, Miss.: Pilot, 1874.

Pitts, John Linwood. *Witchcraft and Devil Lore in the Channel Islands.* Guernsey, Can.: Guille-Alls Library, 1886.

Pius XII, Pope. *The Pope Speaks.* London: Faber, 1940.

_____. *Selected letters and addresses.* London: Catholic Truth Society, 1949.

Pizzey, Erin. *Scream Quietly.* Short Hills, N.J.: Ridley Easlow, 1977.

Planel, Alome. *Docteur Satan ou l'Affaire Petiot.* Paris: Editions Robert Laffont, 1978.

Platanov, S.F. *Boris Godunov.* trans. L. Rex Pyles. Gulf Breeze, Fla.: Academic International Press, 1973.

_____. *History of Russia.* trans. E. Aronsberg. New York: Macmillan, 1929.

_____. *Ivan the Terrible.* trans. J.L. Wieczynski. Gulf Breeze, Fla.: Academic International Press, 1974.

_____. *The Time of Troubles.* trans. John T. Alexander. Lawrence: University Press of Kansas, 1970.

Plate, Thomas. *Crime Pays!* New York: Simon and Schuster, 1975.

_____. *The Mafia at War.* New York: Magazine Press, 1972.

_____, and Darvi, Andrea. *Secret Police: The Inside Story of a Network of Terror.* Garden City, N.Y.: Doubleday, 1981.

Platnick, Kenneth B. *Great Mysteries of History.* Harrisburg, Pa.: Stackpole, 1971.

Plato. *Cratyllus 400C.* trans. H.N. Fowler. London: William Heinemann, 1953.

_____. *The Last Days of Socrates.* trans. Hugh Tredennick. Baltimore: Penguin Books, 1969.

Platt, Sir T.C. *The Abyssinian Storm.* London: Jarrolds, 1935.

Playfair, Giles, and Sington, Derrick. *Crime, Punishment and Cure.* London: Secker & Warburg, 1965.

_____. *The Offenders.* New York: Simon & Schuster, 1957.

Playfair, Sir Robert Lambert. *The Scourage of Christendom; Annals of British Relations with Algiers Prior to the French Conquest.* London: Smith, Elder, 1884.

Pleasants, Mrs. J.E. *History of Orange County, California.* Los Angeles: J.R. Finnell & Sons, 1931.

Pleasants, Samuel Augustus. *Fernando Wood of New York.* New York: Columbia University Press, 1948.

Ploscowe, Morris. *Organized Crime and Law Enforcement.* New York: Grosby Press, 1952-53.

_____. *Sex and the Law.* New York: Prentice-Hall, 1951.

Plowden, David. *Lincoln and His America 1809-1865.* New York: Viking Press, 1970.

Plumb, J.H. *England in the Eighteenth Century, 1714-1815.* London: Penguin Books, 1959.

_____. *The Horizon Book of the Renaissance.* New York: American Heritage, 1961.

Plunkitt, George W. *Plunkitt of Tammany Hall.* New York: Alfred A. Knopf, 1948.

Poe, Edgar Allan. *The Complete Works of Edgar Allan Poe.* 17 vols. New York: G.D. Sproul, 1902.

_____. *The Letters of Edgar Allan Poe.* 2 vols. Cambridge, Mass.: Harvard University Press, 1948.

Pogue, Forrest C. *George C. Marshall: Ordeal and Hope.* New York: Viking, 1963.

Pohl, Frederick J. *Atlantic Crossings Before Columbus.* New York: W.W. Norton, 1961.

_____. *The Lost Discovery.* New York: W.W. Norton, 1952.

_____. *The Viking Explorers.* New York: Thomas Y. Crowell, 1966.

_____. *The Vikings on Cape Cod.* Pictou, Nova Scotia, Can.: n.p., 1957.

Pointer, Larry. *In Search of Butch Cassidy.* Norman: University of Oklahoma, 1977.

Pointer, Michael. *The Public Life of Sherlock Holmes.* New York: Drake, 1975.

The Poison Fiend! Life, Crimes, and Conviction of Lydia Sherman. Philadelphia: Barclay, 1872.

Pol, Heinz. *Suicide of a Democracy.* New York: Reynal and Hitchcock, 1940.

Poldervaart, Arie W. *Black-Robed Justice.* Albuquerque, N.M.: Historical Society of New Mexico, 1948.

Police Gazette, Editor of. *The Pictorial Life and Adventures of John A. Murrel.* Philadelphia: T.B. Peterson & Brothers, 1848.

Politics and Political Parties in Roumania. London: International Reference Library, 1936.

Polk, William. *The United States and the Arab World.* Cambridge, Mass.: Harvard University Press, 1965.

Polk, William R., Stamler, David M., and Asfour, Edmund. *Backdrop to Tragedy.* Boston: Beacon Press, 1957.

Pollack, Emanuel. *The Kronstadt Rebellion.* New York: Philo-sophical, 1959.

Pollack, Jack Harrison. *Dr. Sam, an American Tragedy.* Chicago: Henry Regnery, 1972.

Pollack, Otto. *The Criminality of Women.* Philadelphia: Univer-sity of Pennsylvania Press, 1950.

Pollard, Hugh B.C. *A Busy Time in Mexico.* New York: Duffield, 1913.

_____. *The Secret Societies of Ireland.* London: P. Allan, 1922.

Pollard, James E. *The Presidents and the Press,* New York: Macmillan, 1947.

Pollard, Joseph. *Mr. Justice Cardozo.* New York: Yorktown Press, 1935.

Pollens, B. *The Sexual Criminal.* New York: Macaulay, 1938.

Polley, Robert L. (ed.). *Lincoln, His Words and His World.* New York: Hawthorn Books, 1965.

Pollock, Channing. *Harvest of My Years.* New York: Bobbs-Merrill, 1943.

Pollock, Frederick, and Maitland, Frederic William. *The History of English Law.* Cambridge, Mass.: Cambridge University Press, 1899.

Polo, Marco. *Travels.* New York: Book League of America, 1929.

Polsky, Ned. *Hustlers, Beats, and Others.* Chicago: Aldine, 1967.

Pomerantz, Sidney I. *New York, An American City: 1783-1803.* New York: Columbia University Press, 1938.

Pomeroy, Jesse H. *Autobiography of Jesse H. Pomeroy.* Boston: J.A. Cummings, 1875.

Pomfret, John E. *Founding the American Colonies, 1583-1660.* New York: Harper & Row, 1970.

Ponsonby, Arthur. *Henry Ponsonby, Queen Victoria's Private Secretary: His Life from His Letters.* New York: Macmillan, 1943.

Ponsonby-Fane, Richard A.B. *Imperial House of Japan.* Kyoto, Japan: Ponsonby Memorial Society, 1959.

_____. *Sovereign and Subject.* Kyoto, Japan: Ponsonby Memorial Society, 1962.

Poole, Ernest. *Giants Gone: Men Who Made Chicago.* New York: McGraw-Hill, 1943.

Poore, Ben Perley (ed.). *The Conspiracy Trial for the Murder of the President.* New York: Arno Press, 1972.

_____. *Perley's Reminiscences of Sixty Years in the National Metropolis.* 2 Vols. Philadelphia: Hubbard Brothers, 1886.

Pope, Jennie Barnes. *The Rise of New York Port.* New York: Charles Scribner's Sons, 1939.

Pope-Hennessy, James. *Queen Mary: 1867-1953.* New York: Alfred A. Knopf, 1960.

Popkin, Richard H. *The Second Oswald.* New York: Avon Books, 1966.

Porges, Irwin. *The Violent Americans.* Derby, Conn.: Monarch Books, 1963.

Porter, Edwin H. *The Fall River Tragedy.* Fall River, Mass.: George R.H. Buffington, 1893.

Porter, Garnett Clay. *Strange and Mysterious Crimes.* New York: McFadden, 1929.

Porter, Mary W. *The Surgeon in Charge.* Concord, N.H.: Rumford Press, 1949.

Porterfield, Austin L., and Talbert, Robert W. *Crime, Suicide and Social Well-Being in Your State and City.* Fort Worth: Texas Christian University, 1948.

Portigliotti, Giuseppe. *The Borgias.* trans. Bernard Miall. London: George Allen & Unwin, 1928.

Posner, Gerald L. *Warlord of Crime: Chinese Secret Societies - The New Mafia.* New York: McGraw-Hill, 1988.

Posner, Richard. *The Economics of Justice.* Cambridge, Mass.: Harvard University Press, 1981.

_____. *The Federal Courts: Crisis and Reform.* Cambridge: Harvard University Press, 1985.

Pospelov, P.N. (ed.). *Vladimir Ilyich Lenin: Biographiya.* Moscow: Institut Marksizma-Lenina, 1960.

Postgate, Raymond. *Murder, Piracy and Treason.* New York: Houghton Mifflin, 1925.

Poston, Richard W. *The Gang and the Establishment.* New York: Harper & Row, 1971.

Potter, David M. *Lincoln and His Party in the Secession Crisis 1860-1861.* New Haven, Conn.: Yale University Press, 1942.

Potter, John Deane. *The Art of Hanging.* New York: A.S. Barnes, 1969.

_____. The Monsters of the Moors. New York: Ballantine, 1966.

_____. *A Solider Must Hang: The Biography of an Oriental General.* London: Frederick Miller, 1963.

_____. *Yamamoto: The Man Who Menaced America.* New York: Viking Press, 1965.

Potter, John Mason. *Plots Against Presidents.* New York: Astor-Honor, 1968.

_____. *The Fatal Gallows Tree.* London: Elek Books, 1965.

_____. *13 Desperate Days.* New York: Ivan Obslensky, 1964.

Potts, Thomas. *The Wonderful Discovery of the Witches in the County of Lancaster.* London: John Barnes, 1613.

_____. *The Trial of the Lancaster Witches.* London: P. Davies, 1929.

Pound, Arthur. *The Golden Earth: The Story of Manhattan's Landed Wealth.* New York: Macmillan, 1935.

Pound, Roscoe. *Criminal Justice in America.* New York: Da Capo Press, 1972.

_____. *An Introduction to the Philosophy of Law.* New Haven, Conn.: Yale University Press, 1959.

_____. *The Lawyer from Antiquity to Modern Times.* St. Paul, Minn.: West, 1953.

Powel, Gretchen and Peter. *New York 1929.* Paris: Black Sun Press, 1930.

Powell, D.M. *The Peralta Grant.* Norman: University of Okla-homa Press, 1960.

Powell, Hickman. *Lucky Luciano: Ninety Times Guilty.* New York: Citadel Press, 1975.

Powell, John B. *My 25 Years in China.* New York: Macmillan, 1945.

Power, Samantha. *"A Problem from Hell": America and the Age of Genocide.* New York: Harper, 2003.

Powers, Edwin. *Crime and Punishment in Early Massachusetts.* Boston: Beacon Press, 1966.

Powers, Richard. *Secrecy and Power: The Life of J. Edgar Hoover.* New York: The Free Press, 1987.

Powers, Thomas. *Intelligence Wars: American Secret History from Hitler to Al Qaeda.* New York: New York Review of Books, 2002.

_____. *The Man Who Kept Secrets.* New York: Alfred A. Knopf, 1979.

Poynter, J.W. *Forgotten Crimes.* New York: Macaulay, 1928.

Prabhu, R.K. and Rao, U.R. *India of My Dreams.* Bombay, India: Hind Kitabs, 1947.

_____. *The Mind of Mahatma Gandhi.* Bombay, India: Oxford University Press, 1945.

_____. *Mahatma Gandhi and Bihar.* Bombay, India: Hind Kitabs, 1949.

Prall, Robert H., and Mockridge, Norton. *This is Costello.* New York: Gold Medal Books, 1951.

Prassel, Frank Richard. *The Western Peace Officer. A Legacy of Law and Order.* Norman: University of Oklahoma Press, 1972.

Pratt, Fletcher. *The Cunning Mulatto and Other Cases of Ellis Parker, American Detective.* New York: Smith & Haas, 1930.

_____. *Stanton: Lincoln's Secretary of War.* New York: W.W. Norton, 1953.

Pratt, Julius W. *American Secretaries of State and Their Diplo-macy.* 2 vols. New York: Cooper-Square, 1964.

_____. *America's Colonial Experiment: How the United States Gained, Governed, and In Part Gave Away a Colonial Empire.* New York: Prentice-Hall, 1950.

Prawdin, Michael. *The Mongol Empire.* London: George Allen & Unwin, 1953.

Preece, Harold. *The Dalton Gang, End of An Outlaw Era.* New York: Hastings House, 1963.

Prendergrass, W. *The Z-Car Detective.* London: John Long, 1964.

Prescott, William Hinkling. *Histories: The Rise and Decline of the Spanish Empire.* New York: The Viking Press, 1963.

President's Commission on the Assassination of President John F. Kennedy. *Investigation of the Assassination of President John F. Kennedy: Hearings Before the President's Commission.* 26 vols. Washington, D.C.: U.S. Government Printing Office, 1964.

President's Commission on Law Enforcement and Administration of Justice. *The Challenge of Crime in a Free Society.* Wash-ington, D.C.: U.S. Government Printing Office, 1967.

_____. *Task Force Report: Corrections.* Washington, D.C.: U.S. Government Printing Office, 1967.

_____. *Task Force Report: Crime and Its Impact: An Assessment.* Washington, D.C.: U.S. Government Printing Office, 1967.

_____. *Task Force Report: Juvenile Delinquency and Youth Crime.* Washington, D.C.: U.S. Government Printing Office, 1967.

_____. *Task Force Report: Organized Crime.* Washington, D.C.: U.S. Government Printing Office, 1967.

_____. *Task Force Report: Science and Technology.* Washington, D.C.: U.S. Government Printing Office, 1967.

_____, Task Force on the Police. *Task Force Report: The Police.* Washington, D.C.: U.S. Government Printing Office, 1969.

President's Science Advisory Committee. *Youth: Transition to Adulthood.* Washington, D.C.: U.S. Government Printing Office, 1973.

President's Task Force on Prisoner Rehabilitation. *The Criminal Offender.* Washington, D.C.: U.S. Government Printing Office, 1970.

President's Task Force on Victims of Crime. *Final Report.* Washington, D.C.: U.S. Government Printing Office, 1982.

Presley, James, and Getty, Gerald W. *Public Defender.* New York: Grosset & Dunlap, 1974.

Presnall, Judith Jauda. *Life on Alcatraz.* San Diego, Calif.: Lucent Books, 2000.

Press, S. James. *Some Effects of An Increase in Police Manpower in the 20th Precinct of New York City.* Santa Monica, Calif.: Rand Corporation, 1971.

Presseisen, Ernst L. *Germany and Japan: A Study in Totalitarian Diplomacy, 1933-1941.* The Hague, Neth.: Martinus Nijhoff, 1958.

Preston, John Hyde. *A Short History of the American Revolution.* New York: Pocket Books, 1952.

Preston, William, Jr. *Aliens and Dissenters.* Cambridge, Mass.: Harvard University Press, 1963.

Prettyman, Barrett, Jr. *Death and the Supreme Court.* New York: Harcourt, Brace & World, 1961.

Price, D.L. *Jordan and Palestinians: The PLO's Prospects.* London: Instutute for the Study of Conflict, 1975.

Price, Ernest Batson. *The Russo-Japanese Treaties of 1907-1916 Concerning Manchuria and Mongolia.* Baltimore: The Johns Hopkins Press, 1933.

Price, G. Ward. *Extra Special Correspondent.* London: Harrap, 1957.

_____. *I Know These Dictators.* London: Harrap, 1937.

_____. *Year of Reckoning.* London: Cassell, 1939.

Price, Willard. *Japan and the Son of Heaven.* New York: Duell, Sloan & Pearce, 1945.

Priest, Loring Benson. *Uncle Sam's Stepchildren.* New Brunswick, N.J.: Rutgers University Press, 1942.

Priestland, Gerald. *The Future of Violence.* London: Hamish

Hamilton, 1974.

Priestley, Herbert Ingram. *The Coming of the White Man, 1492-1848.* New York: Macmillan, 1929.

Primakov, Eugenii (ed.). *Studies in the History of Foreign Intelligence.* 6 vols. Moscow: Mezhdunarodnye, 1996.

Pringle, Patrick. *Hue & Cry, The Birth of the British Police.* London: Museum Press, 1955.

_____. *Jolly Roger: The Story of the Great Age of Piracy.* New York: W.W. Norton, 1953.

_____. *Stand and Deliver.* London: Museum Press, 1951.

Prisoners in America. New York: American Assembly, Columbia University, 1973.

Pritchard, James B. (ed.). *The Ancient Near East.* Princeton, N.J.: Princeton University Press, 1973.

Pritchett, V.S. *Midnight Oil.* New York: Random House, 1972.

Pritt, D.N. *Spies and Informers in the Witness Box.* London: Bernard Harison, 1958.

Proal, Louis. *Political Crime.* New York: D. Appleton, 1898.

Proceedings of the White House Conference on Narcotic and Drug Abuse. Washington, D.C.: U.S. Government Printing Office, 1962.

A Prodigious and Tragical History of Six Witches at Maidstone. London: R. Harper, 1629.

Pron, Nick. *Lethal Marriage.* New York: Balantine, 1993.

Prothero, James Warren. *The Dollar Decade.* Baton Rouge: Louisiana State University Press, 1954.

Prothero, Margaret. *The History of the Criminal Investigation Department of Scotland Yard from Earliest Times until Today.* London: Jenkins, 1931.

Protess, David, and Warden, Rob. *Gone in the Night.* New York: Dell, 1993.

Prouty, L. Fletcher. *The Secret Team: The CIA and Its Allies in Control of the World.* n.p., n.d.

Provost, Gary. *Across the Border.* New York: Pocket Books, 1989.

Pruiett, Moman. *Moman Pruiett: Criminal Lawyer.* Oklahoma City, Okla.: Harlow, 1944.

Prunier, Gerard. *The Rwanda Crisis.* New York: Columbia University Press, 1997.

Puente, Ramn. *La dictadura, la Revolucin, y sus hombres.* Mexico City, Mex.: Ediciones Bocetas, 1938.

_____. *Pascual Orozco y la revulta de Chihuahua.* Mexico City, Mex.: Eusebio Gmez de la Puente, 1912.

_____. *Vida de Francisco Villa, Contada por El Mismo.* Los Angeles: O. Paz, 1919.

_____. *Villa en Pie.* Mexico City, Mex.: n.p., 1937.

Pugh, Ralph B. *Imprisonment in Medieval England.* Cambridge, Eng.: Cambridge University Press, 1968.

Pulling, Christopher. *Mr. Punch and the Police.* London: Butterworths, 1964.

Puntoni, Gen. Paolo. *Parla Vittorio Emanuele III.* Milan, Italy: Aldo Palazzi, 1958.

Purkiss, Diane. *At the Bottom of the Garden: A Dark History of Fairies, Hobgoblins, Nymphs and Other*

Troublesome Things. New York: New York University Press, 2001.

_____. The Witch in History: Early Modern and Twentieth Century Representations. New York: Routledge, 1996.

Pursley, Robert D. *Introduction to Criminal Justice.* Encino, Calif.: Glencoe, 1977.

Purvis, James. *Great Unsolved Mysteries.* New York: Grosset & Dunlap, 1978.

Purvis, Melvin. *American Agent.* New York: Doubleday, Doran, 1936.

Pusey, Merlo J. *Charles Evans Hughes.* 2 vols. New York: Macmillan, 1952.

_____. *The Supreme Court Crisis.* New York: Macmillan, 1937.

Pusey, William Allen. *The History and Epidemiology of Syphilis.* Springfield, Ill.: Charles C. Thomas, 1933.

Putnam, Carleton. *Theodore Roosevelt: The Formative Years.* New York: Charles Scribner's Sons, 1958.

Putnam, Samuel. *History of Prostitution.* 3 vols. Chicago: P. Covici, 1926.

_____. *Paris Was Our Mistress.* Carbondale: Southern Illinois University Press, 1970.

Putterman, Jaydie, and Lesur, Rosalyn. *Police.* New York: Holt, Rinehart and Winston, 1983.

Putzel, Max. *The Man in the Mirror: William Marion Reedy and His Magazine.* Cambridge, Mass.: Harvard University Press, 1963.

Pu Yi, Aisin Gioro. *From Emperor to Citizen.* 2 vols. Peking: Foreign Language Press, 1965.

Pyarelal. *The Epic Fast.* Ahmedabad, India: Navajivan, 1950.

_____. *Gandhian Techniques in the Modern World.* Ahmedabad, India: Navajivan,1953.

_____. *Mahatma Gandhi, The Last Phase.* 2 vols. Ahmedabad, India: Navajivan, 1956.

Pye, Lucian. *Guerrilla Communism in Malaya.* Princeton, N.J.: Princeton University Press, 1956.

Pyle, G.F. et al. *The Spatial Dynamics of Crime.* Chicago: University of Chicago Department of Geography Research Paper, 1974.

Pyle, J.G. *The Life of James J. Hill.* New York: Doubleday, Doran, 1917.

Pyzur, Eugene. *The Doctrine of Anarchism of Michael A. Bukunin.* Milwaukee, Wis.: Marquette University Press, 1955.

Quackery in Twentieth Century America. Princeton, N.J.: Prince-ton University Press, 1967.

Quaranta di San Serverino, Baron Bernardo (ed.). *Mussolini as Revealed in his Political Speeches.* London: Dent, 1923.

Queen, Ellery. *A Study in Terror.* New York: Lancer, 1966.

Queens Bench Foundation. *Rape: Prevention and Resistance.* San Francisco: Queens Bench Foundation, 1976.

Quertermous, R.S. *Modern Guns.* New York: Crown, 1979.

Quicherat, J. *Proces de Condemnation et de Rehabilitation de Jeanne d'Arc.* 5 vols. Paris: Renouard, 1841-1849.

Quigley, Harold S. *Far Eastern War, 1937-1941.* Boston: World Peace Foundation, 1942.

Quillen, Jim. *Alcatraz from Inside: The Hard Years, 1942-1952.* San Francisco: Golden Gate National Park Association, 1992.

Quimby, Myron J. *The Devil's Emissaries.* New York: Modern Library, 1969.

Quinby, G.W. *The Gallows, the Prison and the Poor House.* Cincinatti, Ohio: Quinby, 1856.

Quinby, Ione. *Murder for Love.* New York: Covici-Friede, 1931.

Quinn, Arthur Hobson. *Edgar Allan Poe: A Critical Biography.* New York: Alfred A. Knopf, 1941.

Quinn, David B. *Raleigh and the British Empire.* London: Hodder & Stoughton, 1947.

Quinn, John Philip. *Fools of Fortune, or Gambling and Gamblers.* Chicago: W.B. Conkey, 1890.

_____. *Gambling and Gambling Devices.* Canton, Ohio: J.P. Quinn, 1912.

Quinney, Richard. *Class, State and Crime: On the Theory and Practice of Criminal Justice.* New York: David McKay, 1977.

_____. *Crime and Justice in Society.* Boston: Little, Brown, 1969.

_____. *Criminal Justice in America: A Critical Understanding.* Boston: Little, Brown, 1974.

_____. *Criminology: Analysis and Critique of Crime in America.* Boston: Little, Brown, 1975.

_____. *Critique of Legal Order: Crime Control in Capitalist Society.* Boston: Little, Brown, 1974.

_____, and Wildeman, John. *The Problem of Crime.* New York: Harper & Row, 1977.

_____. *The Social Reality of Crime.* Boston: Little, Brown, 1970.

Quirk, Robert E. *An Affair of Honor: Woodrow Wilson and the Occupation of Veracruz.* Lexington: University of Kentucky Press, 1962.

_____. *The Mexican Revolution, 1914-1915: The Convention of Aguascalientes.* Bloomington: Indiana University Press, 1960.

Rabie, Mohammed, and Saunders, Harold H. *U. S.-PLO Dialogue: Secret Diplomacy and Conflict Resolution.* Gainesville, Fla.: Florida University Press, 1995.

Rabin, Yitzhak. *The Rabin Memoirs.* Boston: Little, Brown, 1979.

Rabinowicz, Oscar K. *Fifty Years of Zionism.* London: Robert Anscome, 1952.

Rabutaux, A.P.E. *De la Prostitution en Europe.* Paris: Lebigre-Duquesne Fre'res, 1851.

Raby, R. Cornelius. *Fifty Famous Trials.* Washington, D.C.: Washington Law Books, 1937.

Rachlin, Harvey. *The Kennedys: A Chronological History, 1823-Present.* New York: World Almanac Books, 1986.

Radin, Edward D. *Crimes of Passion.* New York: G.P. Putnam's Sons, 1953.

_____. *Headline Crimes of the Year.* Boston: Little, Brown, 1952.

_____. *The Innocents.* New York: William Morrow, 1964.

_____. *Lizzie Borden: The Untold Story.* New York: Simon & Schuster, 1961.

_____. *12 Against Crime.* New York: G.P. Putnam's Sons, 1953.

_____. *12 Against the Law.* New York: Duell, Sloan & Pearce, 1942.

Radkey, Oliver Henry. *The History of the Russian Revolution.* Ann Arbor: University of Michigan Press, 1957.

Radzinowicz, Leon, and Wolfgang, Marvin E. (eds.). *Crime and Justice.* 3 vols. New York: Basic Books, 1971.

_____. *Crime and Society.* New York: Basic Books, 1977.

_____, and Hood, Roger. *Criminology and the Administration of Criminal Justice.* London: Mansen Information, 1976.

_____, and King, Joan. *The Growth of Crime.* New York: Basic Books, 1977.

_____. *A History of English Criminal Law and Its Administration from 1750.* 4 vols. London: Stevens & Sons, 1948-68.

_____. *Ideology and Crime.* New York: Columbia University Press, 1966.

_____. *In Search of Criminology.* Cambridge, Mass.: Harvard University Press, 1962.

_____, and Turner, J.W.C. (eds.). *The Modern Approach to Criminal Law, English Studies in Criminal Science.* London: Macmillan, 1945.

_____ (ed.). *Sexual Offences.* London: Macmillan, 1957.

_____. *Sir James F. Stephens and his Contributions to the Development of Criminal Law.* London: B. Quaritch, 1957.

Radziweill, Catherine. *Nicholas II: The Last of the Tsars.* London: Cassell, 1931.

Rae, George. *Confessions of the Boston Strangler.* New York: Pyramid, 1967.

Ragen, Joseph E., and Finston, Charles. *Inside the World's Toughest Prison.* Springfield, Ill.: Charles C. Thomas, 1962.

Raine, William McLeod, and Barnes, Will C. *Famous Sheriffs and Western Outlaws.* Garden City, N.Y.: Doubleday, Doran, 1929.

_____. *45-Caliber Law: The Way of Life of the Frontier Peace Officer.* Evanston, Ill.: Row, Peterson, 1941.

_____. *Guns of the Frontier: The Story of How Law Came to the West.* Boston: Houghton Mifflin, 1940.

Rainey, George. *The Cherokee Strip.* Guthrie, Okla.: Cooperative, 1933.

_____. *No Man's Land.* Guthrie, Okla.: Cooperative, 1937.

Rak, Mary Kidder. *Border Patrol.* Boston: Houghton Mifflin, 1938.

Ramparts Magazine (ed.). *In the Shadow of Dallas: A Primer on the Assassination of President Kennedy.* San Francisco: Ramparts, 1967.

Ramsauer, E.E. *The Young Turks: Prelude to the Revolution of 1908.* Princeton, N.J.: Princeton University Press, 1957.

Ramsay, David. *History of South Carolina.* Newberry, S.C.: W.J. Duffie, 1858.

Ramsay, Marion Livingston. *Pyramids of Power: The Story of Roosevelt, Insull, and the Utility Wars.* New York: Bobbs-Merrill, 1937.

Rand, Michael, Loxton, Howard, and Deighton, Len. *The Assassination of President Kennedy.* London: Jonathan Cape, 1967.

Randall, Leslie. *The Famous Cases of Sir Bernard Spilsbury.* London: I. Nicholson & Watson, 1936.-Randall, Terry. *Hooker.* New York: Award Books, 1969.

Randel, William Pierce. *The Ku Klux Klan: A Century of Infamy.* New York: Chilton Books, 1965.

Randell, Captain Jack. *I'm Alone.* London: Jonathan Cape, 1931.

Rankin, Hugh F. *Criminal Trial Proceedings in the General Court of Colonial Virginia.* Williamsburg: University Press of Virginia, 1965.

_____. *The Golden Age of Piracy.* New York: Holt, Rinehart & Winston, 1969.

Ransom, Rev. A. *A Terrible History of Fraud and Crime: The Twin Brothers of Texas.* Philadelphia: M.A. Milliette, 1858.

Ransom, Harry Howe. *Central Intelligence and National Security.* Cambridge, Mass: Harvard University Press, 1959.

_____. *The Intelligence Establishment.* Cambridge, Mass.: Harvard University Press, 1970.

Rao, R. Venugopal. *Facets of Crime in India.* Bombay, India: Allied, 1963.

_____. *Gandhian Institutions of Wardha.* Bombay, India: Thackus, 1947.

_____. *Murder: A Pilot Study with Particular Reference to the City of Delhi.* New Delhi: Government of India, 1968.

Raper, A.F. *The Tragedy of Lynching.* Chapel Hill: University of North Carolina Press, 1933.

Rapoport, David C. *Assassination and Terrorism.* Toronto, Ontario, Can.: Canadian Broadcasting, 1971.Rashid, Amed. *Taliban: Militant Islam, Oil and Fundamentalism in Central Asia.* New Haven, Conn.: Yale University Press, 2000.

Rascoe, Burton. *Before I Forget.* Garden City, N.Y.: Doubleday, Doran, 1937.

_____. *Belle Starr, The Bandit Queen.* New York: Random House, 1941.

_____. *We Were Interrupted.* Garden City, N.Y.: Doubleday, 1947.

Rasputin, Maria and Barham, Patte. *Rasputin: The Man Behind the Myth.* London: W.H. Allen, 1977.

_____. *The Real Rasputin.* London: John Long, 1929.

Rathbone, Perry T. (ed.). *Mississippi Panorama.* St. Louis, Mo.: St. Louis City Art Museum, 1950.

Rathenau, Walther. *Walther Rathenau in Brief und Bild.* Frankfort, Ger.: M.A. Leber, 1967.

Rathlef-Keilmann, Harriet von. *Anastasia, Survivor of Ekaterinberg.* New York: Putnam, 1928.

Rauch, Basil. *The History of the New Deal 1933-1938.* New York: Creative Age, 1944.

Rauch, Georg Von. *A History of Soviet Russia.* New York: Frederick A. Praeger, 1957.

Rauschning, Hermann. *Hitler Speaks.* London: Thornton Butterworth, 1939.

Raushenbush, Stephen. *The March of Fascism.* New Haven, Conn.: Yale University Press, 1940.

Rautenstrauch, Walter. *Who Gets the Money?* New York: Harper, 1934.

Ravaisson, Francois. *Archives de La Bastille.* Paris: A Durant Et Pedone-Lauriel, Libraires, 1873.

Raven, S.S. *The Feathers of Death.* London: Anthony Blond, 1959.

Ravitz, Abe C. *Clarence Darrow and the American Literary Tradition.* Cleveland: Press of Western Reserve University, 1962.Rawcliffe, D.H. *Illusions and Delusions of the Supernatural and Occult.* New York: Dover, 1959.

_____. *The Struggle for Kenya.* London: Victor Gollancz, 1954.

Rawson, Geoffrey. *Bligh of the "Bounty".* London: Philip Allan, 1930.

Ray, Chaplain, with Wagner, Walter. *God's Prison Gang.* Old Tappan, N.J.: Revell, 1976.

Ray, Clarence E. *The Alabama Wolf: Rube Burrow and His Desperate Gang of Highwaymen.* Chicago: Regan, 1910.

_____. *The Border Outlaws, Frank & Jesse James.* Chicago: Regan, n.d.

_____. *The Dalton Brothers.* Chicago: Regan, n.d.

_____. *The James Boys.* Chicago: Regan, n.d.

_____. *The James Boys and Bob Ford.* Chicago: Regan, 1893.

_____. *Jesse James' Daring Raid.* Chicago: Regan, n.d.

_____. *Jesse James and His Gang of Train Robbers.* Chicago: Regan, n.d.

_____. *Life of Bob and Cole Younger with Quantrell.* Chicago: Regan, 1916.

_____. *The Oklahoma Bandits: The Daltons and Their Desperate Gang.* Chicago: Regan, n.d.

_____. *Rube Burrow, King of Outlaws and Train Robbers.* Chicago: Regan, n.d.

_____. *The Younger Brothers.* Chicago: Regan, n.d.

Ray, G.B. *Murder at the Corners.* San Antonio, Texas: Naylor, 1957.

Ray, James Earl. *Tennessee Waltz: The Making of a Political Prisoner.* Saint Andrews, Tenn.: Saint Andrew's Press, 1987.

Read, Piers Paul. *The Train Robbers.* New York: J.B. Lippincott, 1978.

Reagen, Michael V., and Stoughton, Donald M. *School Behind Bars.* Metuchen, N.J.: Scarecrow Press, 1976.

Reasons, Charles E. *The Criminologist: Crime and the Criminal.* Pacific Palisades, Calif.: Goodyear, 1974.

_____, and Kuykendall, Jack L. (eds.). *Race, Crime and Justice.* Pacific Palisades, Calif.: Goodyear, 1972.

Reckless, Walter. *American Criminology: New Directions.* New York: Appleton-Century-Crofts, 1973.

_____. *The Crime Problem.* New York: D. Appleton, 1950.

_____. *The Etiology of Delinquent and Criminal Behavior.* New York: Social Science Research Council, 1943.

_____, *Vice in Chicago.* Chicago: University of Chicago Press, 1933.

The Record of Crimes in the U.S. Buffalo, N.Y.: Faxon, 1834.

Records of the Monthly Meeting of the Society of Friends. New York: Havilland Records Room, n.d.

Reddaway, W.F., et al. (eds.). *Cambridge History of Poland.* Cambridge, Eng.: Cambridge University Press, 1941.

_____ (ed.). *Documents on Catherine the Great.* Cambridge, Eng.: Cambridge University Press, 1931.

_____. *Frederick the Great and the Rise of Prussia.* New York: Haskell House, 1904.

Reddig, William M. *Tom's Town.* New York: J.B. Lippincott, 1947.

Redding, Jay Saunders. *The Lonesome Road: the Story of the Negro's Part in America.* New York: Doubleday, 1958.

_____. *They Came in Chains.* Philadelphia: J.B. Lippincott, 1950.

Redfield, Horace V. *Homicide: North and South.* Philadelphia: J.B. Lippincott, 1880.

Redford, Robert. *The Outlaw Trail.* New York: Grosset & Dunlap, 1979.

Redmond, Frank. *The Younger Brothers.* St. Louis: Dramatic, 1901.

Redston, George, and Crossen, Kendall F. *The Conspiracy of Death.* New York: Random House, 1952.

Reed, Adolf Frank. *The Case of General Yamashita.* Chicago: University of Chicago Press, 1949.

Reed, Douglas. *Nemesis: The Story of Otto Strasser and the Black Front.* Boston: Houghton Mifflin, 1940.

Reed, George Irving (ed.). *Bench and Bar of Ohio.* Chicago: Century Publishing and Engraving, 1897.

Reed, John. *Ten Days That Shook the World.* New York: Modern Library, 1935.

Reed, John Silas. *Insurgent Mexico.* New York: D. Appleton, 1914.

Reed, Lear B. *Human Wolves: Seventeen Years of War on Crime.* Kansas City, Mo.: Brown-White, Lowell Press, 1941.

Rees, Goronwy. *The Great Slump - Capitalism in Crisis, 1929-1933.* London: Weidenfeld & Nicholson, 1970.

_____. *The Multi-Millionaires.* London: Chatto & Windus, 1961.

Rees, J.R. *Sexual Perversions.* London: Practitioner, 1936.

Reeve, Simon. *The New Jackal: Ramzi Yousef, Osama bin Laden and the Future of Terrorism.* Boston, Mass.: Northeastern University Press, 1999.

Reeves, Col. Ira L. *Ol' Rum River.* Chicago: Rockwell, 1931.

Regis, E. *Les re´gicides dans l'histoire.* Lyon, Fr.: A. Storck, 1890.

Regler, Gustav. *A Land Bewitched.* New York: G.P. Putnam's Sons, 1955.Reid, Ed. *The Green Felt Jungle.* New York: Cardinal, 1964.

_____. *The Grim Reapers, The Anatomy of Organized Crime in America.* Chicago: Henry Regnery, 1969.

_____. *Mafia.* New York: Random House, 1952.

_____. *The Mistress and the Mafia.* New York: Bantam, 1972.

_____. *The Shame of New York.* New York: Random House, 1953.

Reid, I.D.A. *The Negro Immigrant.* New York: Columbia University Press, 1939.

Reid, John E., and Inbau, Fred E. *Truth and Deception, the Polygraph.* Baltimore: Williams & Wilkins, 1977.

Reid, Mildred I. *The Devil's Handmaidens.* Boston: Humphries, 1951.

Reid, Susan Titus. *Crime and Criminology.* New York: Holt, Rinehart, 1976.

_____. *Crime and Criminology.* New York: Holt, Rinehart & Winston, 1982.

Reiff, Robert. *The Invisible Victim.* New York: Basic Books, 1979.

Reik, Theodor. *The Compulsion to Confess.* New York: Farrar, Straus, 1959.

_____. *Myth and Guilt.* New York: Braziller, 1957.

Reilly, Michael F., and Slocum, William J. *I Was Roosevelt's Shadow.* London: W. Foulsham, 1946.

Reiman, Jeffrey H. *In Defense of Political Philosophy.* New York: Harper & Row, 1972.

_____. *The Rich Get Richer and the Poor Get Prison.* New York: John Wiley & Sons, 1979.

Reiners, Ludwig. *Bismarck.* 3 vols. Munich: Beck, 1956-1958.

_____. *Frederick the Great: An Informal Biography.* trans. Lawrence P.R. Wilson. London: Oswald Wolff, 1960.

Reinhardt, James Melvin. *The Murderous Trail of Charles Starkweather.* Springfield, Ill.: Charles C. Thomas, 1962.

_____. *The Psychology of Strange Killers.* Springfield, Ill.: Charles C. Thomas, 1962.

_____. *Sex Perversions and Sex Crimes.* Springfield, Ill.: Charles C. Thomas, 1957.

Reischach, Baron Hugo von. *Under Three Emperors: Being Court Reminiscences Under William I, Frederick III and William II.* trans. Prince Blu¨cher. London: Constable, 1927.

Reischauer, Edwin O. *Japan Past and Present.* New York: Alfred A. Knopf, 1964.

_____. *Japan: The Story of a Nation.* New York: Alfred A. Knopf, 1970.

_____. *The Japanese.* Cambridge, Mass.: Harvard University Press, 1977.

_____, *The United States and Japan.* Cambridge, Mass.: Harvard University Press, 1950.

Reisman, W. Michael. *Folded Lies: Bribery, Crusades, and Reforms.* New York: Free Press, 1979.

Reiss, Albert J., Jr. *The Police and the Public.* New Haven, Conn.: Yale University Press, 1971.

_____. *Studies in Crime and Law Enforcement in Major Metropolitan Areas.* Washington, D.C.: U.S. Government Printing Office, 1967.

Reiter, P.J. *Antisocial or Criminal Acts and Hypnosis.* Springfield, Ill.: Charles C. Thomas, 1958.

Reith, Charles. *The Blind Eye of History.* London: Faber & Faber, 1952.

_____. *A New Study of Police History.* London: Oliver, 1956.

_____. *The Police Idea, its History and Evolution in England in the Eighteenth Century and After.* London: Oxford University Press, 1938.

_____. *A Short History of the British Police.* London: Oxford University Press, 1940.

Reitlinger, Gerald. *The Final Solution.* New York: Thomas Yoseloff, 1961.

_____. *The House Built on Sand.* New York: Viking Press, 1960.

_____. *The SS. Alibi of a Nation.* London: William Heinemann, 1956.

Reitman, Ben L. *The Second Oldest Profession.* New York: Vanguard Press, 1931.

Reiwald, P. *Society and Its Criminals.* New York: International University Press, 1950.

Remak, Joachim. *The First World War: Causes, Conduct, Consequences.* New York: John Wiley & Sons, 1971.

_____. *The Origins of World War I, 1871-1914.* Hinsdale, Ill.: Dryden Press, 1967.

_____. *The Nazi Years.* Englewood Cliffs, N.J.: Prentice-Hall, 1969.

_____. *Sarajevo: The Story of a Political Murder.* New York: Criterion Press, 1959.

Remarkable Trials of all Countries. New York: S.S. Peloubet, 1882.

Remick, Peter as told to Shuman, James B. *In Constant Fear.* New York: Reader's Digest Press, 1975.Remy, Oliver E., et al. *The Attempted Assassination of Ex-President Theodore Roosevelt.* Milwaukee: Progressive, 1912.

Rennert, Vincent Paul. *Western Outlaws.* New York: Crowell-Collier Press, 1968.

Reno, John. *Life and Career of John Reno.* Indianapolis , Ind.: Indianapolis Journal, 1879.

Renshaw, Patrick. *The Wobblies.* Garden City, N.Y.: Doubleday, 1967.

Rentoul, Sir Gervaise. *Sometimes I Think.* London: Hodder & Stoughton, 1940.

_____. *This Is My Case.* London: Hutchinson, 1944.

Renvoize, Jean. *Web of Violence.* London: Rootledge, 1978.

Report of the Committee Appointed to Investigate Revolutionary Conspiracies in India. Parliamentary Papers, No. 9190. London: H.M. Stationery Office, 1918.

Report of the Trial of Jason Fairbanks. Boston: Russell & Cutler, 1801.

Reporter, The. *The Trial of John H. Surratt.* Washington D.C.: The Reporter, 1867.Reppetto, Thomas A. *The Blue Parade.* New York: Free Press, 1978.

_____. *Residential Crime.* Cambridge, Mass.: Ballinger Press, 1974.

Ressler, Robert, and Burgess, Ann, and Douglas, John. *Sexual Homicide.* Lexington, Mass.: Lexington Books, 1988.

_____, and Schachtman, Tom. *I Have Lived in the Monster.* New York: St. Martin's Press, 1997.

_____. *Whoever Fights Monsters.* New York: St. Martin's Press, 1994.

Reuter, Peter. *Disorganized Crime.* Cambridge, Mass.: Massachusetts Institute of Technology, 1983.

_____, and Rubinstein, Jonathan. *Illegal Gambling in New York.* Washington, D.C.: National Institute of Justice, 1982.

_____. *Racketeering in Legitimate Industries: A Study in the Economics of Intimidation.* Santa Monica, Calif.: Rand, 1987.

Reynolds, Gerald W., and Judge, Anthony. *The Night the Police Went on Strike.* London: Weidenfeld & Nicolson, 1968.

Reynolds, Michael. *Dead Ends.* New York: Warner Books, 1992.

Reynolds, Quentin R. *Courtroom: The Story of Samuel S. Leibowitz.* New York: Farrar, Straus & Cudahy, 1950.

_____. *I, Willie Sutton.* New York: Farrar, Straus, 1953.

_____. *Minister of Death. The Eichmann Story.* New York: Viking Press, 1960.

_____. *Police Headquarters.* New York: Harper, 1955.-Reynolds, Richard. *Cry for War.* San Francisco: Squibob Press, 1987.

Reynolds, Ruth. *Murder 'Round the World.* New York: Justice Books, 1953.

Rhodes, Henry Taylor-Fowkes. *Alphonse B. Bertillon.* New York: Abelard-Schuman, 1956.

_____. *Clues and Crime.* London: John Murray, 1933.

_____. *The Criminals We Deserve.* London: Methuen, 1937.

_____. *In the Tracks of Crime.* London: Turnstile Press, 1952.

_____. *The Satanic Mass: A Sociological and Criminological Study.* London: Rider, 1954.

_____. *Science and the Police Officer.* London: Police Chronicle, 1934.

Rhodes, Robert P. *The Insoluble Problem of Crime.* New York: John Wiley & Sons, 1977.

_____. *Organized Crime: Crime Control vs. Civil Liberties.* New York: Random House, 1984.

Riasanovsky, Nicholas V. *A History of Russia.* New York: Oxford University Press, 1969.

_____. *Nicholas I and Official Nationality in Russia, 1825-1855.* Berkeley: University of California Press, 1959.

Ribbentrop, Joachim von. *The Ribbentrop Memoirs.* trans. Oliver Watson. London: Weidenfeld & Nicolson, 1954.

Rice, Arnold S. *The Ku Klux Klan in American Politics.* Washington D.C.: Public Affairs Press, 1962.

Rice, Craig. *45 Murderers.* New York: Simon & Schuster, 1952.

_____. *Los Angeles Murders.* New York: Sloan & Pearce, 1947.

Rice, Cy. *Defender of the Damned: Gladys Trowles Root.* New York: Citadel Press, 1964.

Rice, George G. *My Adventure With Your Money.* Boston: R.G. Badger, 1913.

Rice, Grantland. *The Tumult and the Shouting.* New York: A.S. Barnes, 1954.

Rice, John R. *What Was Back of Kennedy's Murder?* Murfreesboro, Tenn.: Sword of the Lord, 1964.

Rice, Otis K. *The Hatfields and the McCoys.* Lexington: University Press of Kentucky, 1979.

Rice, Robert. *The Business of Crime.* New York: Farrar, Straus & Cudahy, 1956.

Rich, Everett (ed.). *The Heritage of Kansas.* Lawrence: University of Kansas Press, 1961.

Rich, Everett. *William Allen White, the Man from Emporia.* New York: Farrar & Rinehart, 1941.

Richard, Emile. *La Prostitution a' Paris.* Paris: J.B. Bailliere, 1890.

Richards, Guy. *The Hunt for the Czar.* Garden City, N.Y.: Doubleday, 1971.

Richards, Stanley. *Black Bart.* Wolfebord, N.H.: Christopher Davies, 1966.

Richards, William C. *The Last Billionaire.* New York: Charles Scribner's Sons, 1948.

Richardson, Albert D. *Beyond the Mississippi.* Hartford, Conn.: American, 1867.

_____. *The Secret Service: The Field, The Dungeon, and Escape.* Hartford, Conn.: American, 1865.

Richardson, Jack. *Memoir of a Gambler.* New York: Simon & Schuster, 1979.

Richardson, James F. *The New York Police: Colonial Times to 1901.* New York: Oxford University Press, 1970.

_____. *Urban Police in the United States.* Port Washington, N.Y.: Kennikat Press, 1974.

Richardson, Joanna. *The Courtesans.* Cleveland: World, 1967.

Richardson, Joseph Hall. *From the City to Fleet Street: Some Journalistic Experiences.* London: Stanley Paul, 1927.

Richardson, R.N. *Texas, the Lone Star State.* New York: Prentice-Hall, 1943.

Richardson, William Payson. *The Law of Evidence.* Brooklyn, N.Y.: Prince, 1955.

Richelieu. *Memoires.* Paris: Collection des memoires relatifs a l'histoire de France, 1823.

Richette, Lisa Aversa. *The Throwaway Children.* Philadelphia: J.B. Lippincott, 1969.

Richman, Harry. *A Hell of a Life.* New York: Duell, Sloan & Pearce, 1966.

Richter, D.C. *The Riotous Victorians.* n.p.: Ohio University Press, 1981.

Rickard, Mrs. "Tex", with Oboler, Arch. *Everything Happened to Him.* New York: Frederick A. Stokes, 1936.

Rickards, Colin. *The Man from Devil's Island.* London: Dawnay, 1968.

Rickles, N.K. *Exhibitionism.* Philadelphia: J.B. Lippincott, 1950.

Rickman, John. *Journal of Captain Cook's Last Voyage to the Pacific Ocean.* New York: Da Capo Press, 1967.

Ridge, John Rollin (Yellow Bird). *The Life and Adventure of Joaquin Murieta, the Celebrated California Bandit.* Norman: University of Oklahoma Press, 1969.

Ridings, Sam P. *The Chisholm Trail.* Guthrie, Okla.: Cooperative, 1936.

Ridolfi, Roberto. *The Life of Niccolò Machiavelli.* trans. Cecil Grayson. Chicago: University of Chicago Press, 1963.

Ridpath, John Clark. *Life and Trial of Guiteau the Assassin.* Cincinnati, Ohio: Jones Brothers, 1882.

Riegel, Robert E. *America Moves West.* New York: Henry Holt, 1930.

Rignall, Jeff, and Wilder, Ron. *29 Below.* Chicago: Wellington Press, 1979.

Rihan, Ameen. *Ibn Saud of Arabia.* London: Constable, 1928.

Riis, Jacob August. *The Battle With the Slum.* New York: Macmillan, 1902.

Ringel, W. *Identification and Police Line-Ups.* New York: Gould, 1968.

Ringgold, Gene, and LaManna, Roger. *Assassin: The Lee Harvey Oswald Biography.* Hollywood, Calif.: Associated Professional Services, 1964.

Riordan, William L. *Plunkitt of Tammany Hall.* New York: E.P. Dutton, 1963.

Ripka, Hubert. *Czechoslovakia Enslaved.* London: Victor Gollancz, 1950.Ripley, Thomas. *They Died with Their Boots On.* Garden City, N.Y.: Doubleday, Doran, 1935.

Rischin, Moses. *The Promised City: New York's Jews, 1870-. 1914.* Cambridge, Mass.: Harvard University Press, 1962.

Ritchie, Jean. *Myra Hindley.* London: Agnus & Robertson, 1988.

Ritter, Gerhard. *Carl Goerdeler und die deutsche Widerstandsbewegung.* Stuttgart, Ger.: Deutsche Verlagsanstalt, 1956.

River, J. Paul (ed.). *Crime and the Sexual Psychopath.* Springfield, Ill.: Charles C. Thomas, 1958.

_____. *The Sexual Criminal.* Springfield, Ill.: Charles C. Thomas, 1950.

Robbins, Lionel. *The Great Depression.* New York: Macmillan, 1934.

Robbins, Russell Hope. *The Encyclopedia of Witchcraft and Demonology.* New York: Crown, 1965.

Robert of Clari. *The Conquest of Constantinople.* trans. Edgar Holmes McNeal. New York: W.W. Norton, 1964.

Roberts, Alexander. *A Treatise of Witchcraft.* London: N.O., Samuel Man, 1616.

Roberts, C.E.B. *The New World of Crime, Famous American Trials.* London: Burrows, Eyre & Spottiswoode, 1933.

Roberts, Cecil. *The Bright Twenties.* London: Hodder & Stoughton, 1970.

Roberts, Chalmers M. *Washington, Past and Present.* Washington D.C.: Public Affairs Press, 1949-50.

_____. *The Washington Post: The First 100 Years.* Boston: Houghton Mifflin, 1977.

Roberts, Charles. *The Truth About the Assassination.* New York: Grosset & Dunlap, 1967.

Roberts, M. Elizabeth. *Outlines of Balkan History.* London: Arthur H. Stockwell, 1943.

Roberts, Stephen H. *The House That Hitler Built.* New York: Harper, 1938.

Roberts, Sydney. *Holmes and Watson: A Miscellany.* New York: Oxford University Press, 1953.

Roberts, W. Adolphe. *Sir Henry Morgan.* New York: Covici, Friede, 1933.

Robertson, Angus. *Mussolini and the New Italy.* London: Allenson, 1929.

Robertson, Frank C., and Harris, Beth Kay. *Soapy Smith, King of the Frontier Con Men.* New York: Hastings House, 1961.

Robertson, George. *The Discovery of Tahiti: A Journal of the Second Voyage of H.M.S. Dolphin...Written by Her Master George Robertson.* London: Hakluyt Society, 1948.

Robertson, Mrs. Harriet M. (ed.). *Dishonest Elections and Why We Have Them.* Chicago: Published by Author, 1934.

Robertson, John A. *Rough Justice: Perspectives on Lower Criminal Courts.* Boston: Little, Brown, 1974.

Robertson, Ruth T. *Famous Bandits; Brief Accounts of the Lives of Jesse James, Cole Younger, Billy the Kid and Others...* Washington D.C.: Washington Bureau, 1928.

Robinson, Adam. *Bin Laden: Behind the Mask of a Terrorist.* New York: Arcade Publishing, 2002.

Robinson, Charles. *The Kansas Conflict.* New York: Harper & Brothers, 1882.

Robinson, Cyril E. *Apollo History of Greece.* New York: Thomas Y. Crowell, 1965.

_____. *Apollo History of the Roman Republic.* New York: Thomas Y. Crowell, 1965.

_____. *Apollo History of Rome.* New York: Thomas Y. Crowell, 1965.

Robinson, David. *Hollywood in the Twenties.* New York: A.S. Barnes, 1968.

Robinson, Geroid T. *Rural Russia under the Old Regime.* New York: Macmillan, 1949.

Robinson, Henry Morton. *Fantastic Interim.* New York: Harcourt, Brace, 1943.

_____. *Science Catches the Criminal.* Indianapolis, Ind.: Bobbs-Merrill, 1935.

Robinson, Jerry. *The Comics: An Illustrated History of Comic Strip Art.* New York: G.P. Putnam's Sons, 1974.

Robinson, L.N. *Penology in the United States.* Philadelphia: Winston, 1921.

Robinson, Louis Newton. *History and Organization of Criminal Statistics in the United States.* New York: Hart, Schaffner & Marx, 1911.Robinson, Stuart. *Infamous Perjuries of the Bureau of Military Justice.* Louisville, Ky.: Published by Author, 1865.

Robinson, Victor. *An Essay on Hasheesh.* New York: Dingwall-Rock, 1925.

Robinson, W.W. *Bombs and Bribery.* Los Angeles: Dawson's Book Shop, 1969.

_____. *Lawyers of Los Angeles.* Los Angeles: Los Angeles Bar Association, 1959.

Robleto, Hernan. *La Mascota de Pancho Villa.* Mexico City: Ediciones Botas, 1934.

Roche, Philip Q. *The Criminal Mind.* New York: Farrar, Straus & Cudahy, 1958.

Roches, A. (ed.). *Encyclope'die nationale de la police.* Paris: Compagnie Nationale de Diffusion du Livre, 1955.

Rochester, Anna. *The Populist Movement in the United States.* New York: International, 1943.

Rockefeller Commission Report. *Report to the President by the Commission on CIA Activities Within the United States.* New York: Manor Books, 1975.

Rockhill, William W. *The Land of the Lamas.* New York: Century, 1891.

Rockwell, Wilson (ed). *Memoirs of a Lawman: Autobiography of Cyrus Wells Shores.* Denver: Sage Books, 1962.

Rodell, Fred. *Nine Men.* New York: Random House, 1955.

_____. *Woe Unto You, Lawyers!* Brooklyn: Pageant-Poseidon, 1937.

Rodell, Marie F. (ed.). *Boston Murders.* New York: Duell, Sloan & Pearce, 1948.

_____. *Charleston Murders.* New York: Duell, Sloan & Pearce, 1947.

_____. *Chicago Murders.* New York: Duell, Sloan & Pearce, 1945.

_____. *Cleveland Murders.* New York: Duell, Sloan & Pearce, 1947.

_____. *Denver Murders.* New York: Duell, Sloan & Pearce, 1946.

_____. *Detroit Murders.* New York: Duell, Sloan & Pearce, 1948.

_____. *Los Angeles Murders.* New York: Duell, Sloan & Pearce, 1947.

_____. *New York Murders.* New York: Duell, Sloan & Pearce, 1944.

_____. *San Francisco Murders.* New York: Duell, Sloan & Pearce, 1947.

Rodgers, Richard. *Musical Stages.* New York: Random House, 1975.

Rodwell, Sir Cecil. *Report on a Visit to Pitcairn Island.* London: H.M. Stationary Office, 1921.

Rodzianko, M.V. *The Reign of Rasputin.* New York: Frederick A. Stokes, 1927.

_____, and Steadwell, B.S. *The Great War on White Slavery.* Oakland, Calif.: Smithsonian, 1911.

Roe, Clifford. *Panderers and Their White Slaves.* Chicago: Revell Pub., 1910.

Roe, Edward Thomas. *The James Boys.* Chicago: A.E. Weeks, 1893.

Roe, G.M. (ed.). *Our Police: A History of the Cincinnati Police Force, From the Earliest Period Until the Present Day.* Cincinnati: n.p., 1890.

Roeburt, John. *Sex Life and Criminal Law.* New York: Belmont Books, 1963.

Roebuck, Julian B. *Criminal Typology.* Springfield, Ill.: Charles C. Thomas, 1967.

_____, and Frese, Wolfgang. *The Rendezvous: A Case Study of an After Hours Club.* New York: Free Press, 1976.

Roeburt, John. *Al Capone*. New York: Pyramid, 1959.
_____. *Tough Cop*. New York: Simon & Schuster, 1949.
Roemer, William. *Accardo: The Genuine Godfather*. Chicago: Fine, 1995.
_____. *The Enforcer: Chicago Mob's Man Over Las Vegas*. Chicago: Fine, 1994.
_____. *Mob Power Plays*. New York: SPI Books, 1998.
_____. *Roemer: Man Against the Mob*. Chicago: Fine, 1989.
_____. *War of the Godfathers*. Chicago: Fine, 1990.
Roesche, Roberta with De La Roche, Harry, Jr. *Anyone's Son*. Kansas City, Kan.: Andrews & McNeel, 1979.
Roffman, Howard. *Presumed Guilty: How and Why the Warren Commission Framed Lee Harvey Oswald*. New York: A.S. Barnes, 1976.
Rogers, Agnes, and Allen, Frederick Lewis. *I Remember Distinctly*. New York: Harper & Brothers, 1947.
Rogers, Kenneth Paul. *For One Sweet Grape*. New York: Playboy Press, 1974.
Rogers, Robert. *A History of Babylonia and Assyria*. Cincinnati: Abingdon Press, 1915.
Rogers, R.S. *Studies in the Reign of Tiberius*. Baltimore: Johns Hopkins Press, 1943.
Rogers, W.A. *America's Black and White Book*. New York: Cupples & Leon, 1917.
Rogers, W.C. *Ladies Bountiful*. New York: Harcourt, Brace & World, 1968.
Rogers, Will. *The Autobiography of Will Rogers*. Boston: Houghton Mifflin, 1949.
Rogge, O. John. *Why Men Confess*. New York: Nelson, 1959.
Roggendorf, Joseph (ed.). *Studies in Japanese Culture*. Tokyo: Sophia University Press, 1963.
Rogin, Michael Paul. *The Intellectuals and McCarthy: The Radical Specter*. Cambridge, Mass.: M.I.T. Press, 1967.
Rogo, D. Scott. *Parapsychology: A Century of Inquiry*. New York: Taplinger, 1975.
Rolland, Romain. *Mahatma Gandhi*. London: George Allen & Unwin, 1924.
Rolle, Andrew F. *California, A History*. Arlington Heights, Ill.: Harlan Davidson, 1978.
Rolph, Cecil Hewitt. *Common Sense About Crime and Punishment*. London: Victor Gollancz, 1961.
_____ (ed.). *The Police and the Public*. London: William Heinemann, 1962.
_____. *Women of the Streets*. London: Secker & Warburg, 1955.
Romain, Wiley-Paul. *Le dossier de la police*. Paris: Librairie Acade´mique Perrin, 1966.
Romano, Salvatore Francesco. *Storia dei Fasci Siciliani*. Bari, Italy: Laterza, 1959.
Romanov, Boris A. *Russia in Manchuria, 1892-1906*. Ann Arbor, Mich.: Edwards, 1952.
Rome, Florence. *The Tatooed Men*. New York: Delacorte, 1975.
Rommel, Erwin. *The Rommel Papers*. trans. Paul Finley. New York: Harcourt, Brace, 1953.

Roosevelt, Blanche. *Elisabeth of Roumania: A Study*. London: Chapman & Hall, 1891.
Roosevelt, Eleanor. *Autobiography*. New York: Harper & Row, 1961.
_____. *This I Remember*. New York: Harper & Row, 1949.
_____. *This Is My Story*. New York: Harper, 1936.
Roosevelt, Elliott. *As He Saw It*. New York: Duell, Sloane & Pearce, 1946.
Roosevelt, Franklin D. *His Personal Letters*. ed. Elliott Roosevelt. 2 vols. New York: Duell, Sloan & Pearce, 1950.
_____. *Public Papers and Addresses of F.D.R.* New York: Random House, 1938-1950.
Roosevelt, James and Shalett, Sidney. *Affectionately, F.D.R.* New York: Harcourt, Brace, 1959.
Roosevelt, Kermit. *The Happy Hunting Grounds*. New York: Charles Scribner's Sons, 1921.
_____. *The Overseas Target: War Report of the OSS*. New York: Walker, 1976.
Roosevelt, Theodore. *Autobiography*. New York: Macmillan, 1913.
Root, Gladys and Rice, Cy. *Defender of the Damned*. New York: Citadel Press, 1964
Root, Jonathan. *The Life and Bad Times of Charlie Becker*. London: Secker & Warburg, 1962.
_____. *One Night in July*. New York: Coward-McCann, 1961.
Roper, A.F. *The Tragedy of Lynching*. Chapel Hill: North Carolina University Press, 1933.
Rorabaugh, W.J. *The Alcoholic Republic*. New York: Oxford University Press, 1979.
Rorick, Eleanor. *The Notorious Benders*. Cherryvale, Kan.: n.p., n.d.
Rosa, Joseph G. *The Gunfighter, Man or Myth?* Norman: University of Oklahoma Press, 1969.
_____. *They Called Him Wild Bill*. Norman: University of Oklahoma Press, 1964.
_____. *The West of Wild Bill Hickok*. Norman: University of Oklahoma Press, 1982.
Rosa, Joseph, and May, Robin. *Gun Law*. Chicago: Contemporary Books, 1977
Rosberg, Robert R. *Game of Thieves*. New York: Everest House, 1980.
Roscoe, Jesse. *The Treasure Album of Pancho Villa*. El Paso, Tex.: Toyahvale Press, 1962.
Roscoe, Theodore. *The Lincoln Assassination, April 14, 1865*. New York: Franklin Watts, 1971.
_____. *True Tales of Bold Escapes*. Englewood Cliffs, N.J.: Prentice-Hall, 1965.
_____. *The Web of Conspiracy: The Complete Story of the Men Who Murdered Lincoln*. Englewood Cliffs, N.J.: Prentice-Hall, 1959.
Rose, Clarkson. *Red Plush and Greasepaint*. London: Museum Press, 1964.
Rose, Colin (ed.). *The World's Greatest Rip-Offs*. New York: Sterling, 1978.
Rose, G.N.G. *Royal Commission on Assizes and Quarter Sessions 1966-69*. London: Special Statistical Survey, HMSO, 1971.
Rose, J.H. *Life of Napoleon*. London: George Bell, 1901.
Rose, Kenneth. *King George V*. London: Weidenfeld & Nicolson, 1983.
Rose, T. *Violence in America*. New York: Random House, 1969.
Rose, William Ganson. *Cleveland: The Making of a City*. Cleveland: World, 1950.
Rosebery, Lord. *Napoleon, The Last Phase*. London: A. Humphreys, 1900.
Rosebury, Theodore. *Microbes and Morals*. New York: Viking Press, 1971.
Rosefsky, Robert S. *Frauds, Swindles, and Rackets*. Chicago: Follett, 1973.
Rosen, George. *Madness in Society*. New York: Harper & Row, 1968.
Rosen, Ruth. *The Last Sisterhood: Prostitution in America, 1900-1918*. Baltimore: Johns Hopkins University Press, 1983.
Rosenbaum, H. Jon, and Sederberg, Peter C. (eds.). *Vigilante Politics*. Philadelphia: University of Philadelphia, 1976.
Rosenbaum, Julius. *The Plague of Lust*. New York: Frederick Publications, 1955.
Rosenberg, Arthur. *Democracy and Socialism*. New York: Alfred A. Knopf, 1939.
_____. *A History of the German Republic*. London: Methuen, 1936.
Rosenberg, Charles E. *The Trial of the Assassin Guiteau*. Chicago: University of Chicago Press, 1968.
Rosenberg, Philip. *The Spivey Assignment*. New York: Holt, Rinehart & Winston, 1979.
Rosenblatt, Stanley M. *Trial Lawyer*. Secaucus, N.J.: Lyle Stuart, 1984.
Rosenstein, Jaik. *Hollywood Leg Man*. Los Angeles: Madison Press, 1950.
Rosenstone, Robert A. *Romantic Revolutionary: John Reed*. New York: Alfred A. Knopf, 1975.
Rosenthal, D. *Genetic Theory and Abnormal Behavior*. New York: McGraw-Hill, 1970.
Rosenthal, E.I.J. *Political Thought in Medieval Islam*. Cambridge: Cambridge University Press, 1962.
Rosenthal, Eric. *Gold Bricks and Mortar*. Johannesburg, S. Afri.: Printing House, 1946.
Rosenthal, M.A. *Thirty-Eight Witnesses*. New York: McGraw-Hill, 1964.
Rosinski, Herbert. *The German Army*. London: Hogarth, 1939.
Rosmond, Babette. *Robert Benchley, His Life and Good Times*. New York: Doubleday, 1970.
Rosow, Eugene. *Born to Lose, The Gangster Film in America*. New York: Oxford University Press, 1978.
Ross, Anne. *Everyday Life of the Pagan Celts*. New York: G.P. Putnam's Sons, 1970.
Ross, Caroline, and Lawrence, Ken. *J. Edgar Hoover's Detention Plan*. Jackson, Miss.: American Friends Service Committee, 1978.
Ross, Christian. *The Father's Story of Charley Ross, The Kidnapped Child*. Philadelphia: John E. Potter, 1876.
Ross, D. *Hitler und Dollfuss*. Hamburg, Ger.: Leibniz, 1966.
Ross, Edith Connelley. *The Bloody Benders*. Kansas State Historical Society, 1926-28.
Ross, Edmund G. *History of the Impeachment of Andrew Johnson*. Santa Fe, N.M.: New Mexican Printing, 1896.
Ross, Joel H. *What I Saw in New York; Or, A Bird's eye View of City Life*. Auburn, N.Y.: Derby & Miller, 1852.
Ross, Robert. *The Trial of Al Capone*. Chicago: Robert Ross, 1933.
Ross, Stanley R. *Francisco I. Madero: Apostle of Mexican Democracy*. New York: Columbia University Press, 1955.
Rossi, Angelo T. *The Rise of Italian Fascism*. trans. Peter and Dorothy Wait. London: Methuen, 1938.
Rossiter, Clinton. *Seedtime of the Republic*. New York: Harcourt, Brace, 1953.
Rosskam, Edwin and Louise. *Towboat River*. New York: Duell, Sloan & Pearce, 1948.
Rossum, Ralph A. *The Politics of the Criminal Justice System*. New York: Marcel Dekker, 1978.
Rosten, Leo C. *The Washington Correspondents*. New York: Harcourt, Brace, 1937.
Rostovtzeff, Michael I. *The Social and Economic History of the Roman Empire*. 2 vols. Oxford, Eng.: Clarendon Press, 1957.
Roth, Andrew. *Japan Strikes South*. New York: American Council, Institute of Pacific Relations, 1941.
Rothbard, Murray N. *America's Great Depression*. Princeton, N.J.: D. Van Nostrand, 1963.
Rothblatt, Henry B. *That Damned Lawyer*. New York: Dodd, Mead, 1983.Rothert, Otto A. *The Outlaws of Cave-in-Rock*. Cleveland: Arthur H. Clark, 1924.
_____. *The German Opposition to Hitler: An Assessment*. Krefeld, Ger.: Scherpe-Verlag, 1949.
Rothman, David J. *Conscience and Convenience*. Boston: Little, Brown, 1980.
_____. *The Discovery of the Asylum: Social Order and Disorder in the New Republic*. Boston: Little, Brown, 1971.
Rothschild, Joseph. *Communist Eastern Europe*. New York: Walker, 1964.
Rothstein, William G. *American Physicians in the Nineteenth Century: From Sects to Science*. Baltimore: Johns Hopkins University Press, 1973.
Roughead, William. *The Art of Murder*. New York: Sheridan House, 1943.
_____. *Bad Companions*. New York: Duffield & Green, 1931.
_____. *Burke and Hare*. London, Hodge, 1948.
_____. *Classic Crimes*. London: Cassell, 1951.
_____. *Famous Crimes*. London: Faber & Faber, 1935.
_____. *The Fatal Countess*. London: Green, 1924.
_____. *In Queer Street*. London: Green, 1924.
_____. *Mainly Murder*. London: Cassell, 1937.
_____. *Malice Domestic*. New York: Doubleday, Doran, 1929.
_____. *The Murderer's Companion*. New York: Readers Club, 1941.
_____. *Neck or Nothing*. London: Cassell, 1939.
_____. *Reprobates Reviewed*. London: Cassell, 1941.
_____. *The Riddle of Ruthvens*. Edinburgh, Scot.: W. Green & Son, 1919.
_____. *Rogues Walk Here*. London: Cassell, 1934.
_____. *The Seamy Side*. London: Cassell, 1938.
_____. *Tales of the Criminous*. London: Cassell, 1956.
_____. *Twelve Scots Trials*. London: Green, 1913.
Rounds, Frank. *Window on Red Square*. Boston: Houghton Mifflin, 1953.
Rovere, Franco. *Vita amorosa di Claretta Petacci*. Milan, Italy: Lucchi, 1946.
Rovere, Richard H. *The American Establishment and Other Reports, Opinions, and Speculations*. New York: Harcourt, Brace & World, 1962.
_____. *Howe and Hummell: Their True and Scandalous History*. New York: Farrar, Straus, 1947.
_____. *Senator Joe McCarthy*. New York: Harcourt, Brace, 1959.
______. *The Weeper and the Blackmailer*. New York: New American Library, 1950.

Rowan, David. *Famous American Crimes.* London: Frederick Muller, 1957.

_____. *Famous European Crimes.* London: Frederick Muller, 1956.

Rowan, Ford. *Techno Spies.* New York: G.P. Putnam's Sons, 1978.

Rowan, Richard Wilmer. *A Family of Outlaws.* Fort Wayne, Ind.: n.p., 1955.

_____. *The Pinkertons, A Detective Dynasty.* Boston: Little, Brown, 1931.

_____, with Deindorfer, Robert. *Secret Service, 33 Centuries of Espionage.* New York: Hawthorn Books, 1967.

_____. *The Story of Secret Service.* New York: Garden City, 1939.

Rowe, Gary Thomas, Jr. *My Undercover Years With the Ku Klux Klan.* New York: Bantam Books, 1976.

Rowell, Earle A. and Robert. *On the Trail of Marijuana: The Weed of Madness.* Mountain View, Calif.: Pacific Press, 1939.

Rowell, Henry T. *Rome in the Augustan Age.* Norman: University of Oklahoma Press, 1962.

Rowland, John. *A Century of Murder.* London: Home & Van Thal, 1950.

_____. *Criminal Files.* London: Arco, 1957.

_____. *More Criminal Files.* London: Arco, 1958.

_____. *Murder by Persons Unknown.* London: Mellifont Press, 1941.

_____. *Murder Mistaken.* London: J. Long, 1963.

_____. *Murder Revisited: A Study of Two Poisoning Cases.* London: John Long, 1961.

_____. *Poisoner in the Dock.* London: Arco, 1960.

_____. *The Wallace Case.* London: Carroll & Nicholson, 1949.

_____. *Unfit to Plead?* London: John Long, 1965.

Rowse, Arthur Edward. *Slanted News.* Boston: Beacon Press, 1957.

Royal College of Psychiatrists. *Drug Scenes: A Report on Drug Dependence.* London: Gaskell, 1987.

The Royal Commission and the Punishment of Death. London: Society for the Abolition of Capital Punishment, 1866.

Royal Commission On Capital Punishment, 1949-1953: Report. London: H.M. Stationery Office, 1953.

Royal, H.W. *Gambling and Confidence Games Exposed: showing How the Proprietors of Gambling Houses and the Players can be Cheated.* Chicago: Published by Author, 1896.

Royal Institute of International Affairs. *Great Britain and Palestine, 1915-1945.* London: Oxford University Press, 1946.

_____. *The Impact of the Russian Revolution, 1917-1967.* London: Institute, 1967.

_____. *The Middle East: A Political and Economic Survey.* London: Oxford University Press, 1958.

Royce, Josiah. *California From the Conquest in 1846 to the Second Vigilance Committee in San Francisco.* New York: Houghton Mifflin, 1886.

Royko, Mike. *Boss: Richard J. Daley of Chicago.* New York: E.P. Dutton, 1971.

_____. *I May Be Wrong, But I Doubt It.* Chicago: Henry Regnery, 1968.

_____. *Up Against It.* Chicago: Henry Regnery, 1967.

Royster, Vermont. *A Pride of Prejudices.* New York: Alfred A. Knopf, 1968.

Ruark, Robert. *Something of Value.* New York: Doubleday, 1955.

Rubenstein, or The Murdered Jewess. Philadelphia: Old Franklin, 1876.

Rubenstein, Richard E. *Rebels in Eden: Mass Political Violence in the United States.* Boston: Little, Brown, 1970.

Rubin, Barry. *Revolution Until Victory?: The Politics and History of the PLO.* Cambridge, Mass.: Harvard University Press, 1996.

Rubin, David. *The Law of Criminal Corrections.* St. Paul, Minn.: West, 1963.

Rubin, Vera (ed.). *Cannabis and Culture.* The Hague, Neth.: Mouton, 1975.

_____, and Comitas, Lambros. *Ganja in Jamaica.* Garden City, N.Y.: Anchor Press/Doubleday, 1976.

Rubinstein, Jonathan. *City Police.* New York: Ballantine, 1973.

_____, and Reuter, Peter. *Numbers: The Routine Racket.* New York: Policy Sciences Center, 1977.

Rublowsky, John. *The Stoned Age: A History of Drugs in America.* New York: G.P. Putnam's Sons, 1975.

Ruck, S.K. (ed.). *Paterson on Prisons.* London: Frederick Muller, 1951.

Rude, George F.E. *The Crowd in History: A Study of Popular Disturbances in France and England, 1730-1848.* New York: John Wiley & Sons, 1964.

_____. *Hanoverian London 1714-1808.* Berkeley: University of California Press, 1971.

Rudenko, S.I. *Frozen Tombs of Siberia.* Berkeley: University of California Press, 1970.

Rudensky, Morris ("Red"), and Riley, Don. *The Gonif.* Blue Earth, Minn.: Piper, 1970.

Ruehlmann, William. *Saint with a Gun.* New York: New York University Press, 1974.

Ruggles, Eleanor. *Prince of Players: Edwin Booth.* New York: W.W. Norton, 1953.

Ruggles-Brise, Sir Evelyn. *The English Prison System.* London: Macmillan, 1938.

Ruhm, Herbert (ed.). *The Hard-Boiled Detective.* New York: Vintage Books, 1977.

Rule, Ann. *The I-5 Killer.* New York: New American Library, 1984.

_____. *Lust Killer.* New York: New American Library, 1983.

_____. *The Stranger Beside Me.* New York: New American Library, 1980.

_____. *The Want-Ad Killer.* New York: New American Library, 1983.

Rumbelow, Donald. *The Complete Jack the Ripper.* Boston: New York Graphic Society, 1975.

_____. *The Houndsditch Murders: The Siege of Sidney Street.* London: Macmillan, 1973.

_____. *I Spy Blue: Police and Crime in the City of London from Elizabeth I to Victoria.* London: Macmillan, 1971.

_____. *Jack the Ripper: The Complete Casebook.* New York: Berkley, 1988.

Runciman, Steven. *Byzantine Civilization.* New York: Longmans, Green, 1933.

_____. *History of the Crusaders.* 3 vols. London: Cambridge University Press, 1951-1954.

Runyon, Damon. *Guys and Dolls.* New York: Frederick A. Stokes, 1931.

_____. *More Guys and Dolls.* New York: Garden City Books, 1951.

_____. *A Treasury of Damon Runyon.* New York: Random House, 1958.

_____. *Trials and Other Tribulations.* New York: J.B. Lippincott, 1933.

Rush, Florence. *The Best Kept Secret.* Englewood Cliffs, N.J.: Prentice-Hall, 1980.

Rush, M. *Khrushchev and the Stalin Succession.* Santa Monica, Calif.: Rand, 1957.

Rush, N. Orwin. *Mercer's Banditti of the Plains.* Tallahassee: Florida State University Library, 1961.

Rusher, William. *Special Counsel.* New Rochelle, N.Y.: Arlington House, 1968.

Rushing, William (ed.). *Deviant Behavior and Social Process.* Chicago: Rand McNally, 1969.

Russell, Brian, and Sellier, Charles E. *Conspiracy to Kill a President.* New York: Bantam Books, 1982.

Russell, Diana E.H. *Crimes Against Women.* Millbrae, Calif.: Les Femmes, 1977.

_____. *The Politics of Rape.* New York: Stein & Day, 1975.

Russell, Dick. *Closing In: The Search for JFK's Assassins.* New York: Dial Press, 1977.

Russell, Donn (ed.). *Best Murder Cases.* London: Faber & Faber, 1958.

_____. *Lizzie Borden, The Untold Story.* New York: Simon & Schuster, 1961.

Russell, Lady Dorothea. *Medieval Cairo and the Monasteries of the Wadi Natrun.* London: Weidenfeld & Nicolson, 1962.

Russell, Edward Frederick Langley, Baron, of Liverpool. *The French Corsairs.* London: Robert Hale, 1970.

_____. *Knights of Bushido: The Shocking History of Japanese War Atrocities.* New York: E.P. Dutton, 1958.

_____. *Though the Heavens Fall.* London: Cassell, 1956.

Russell, Francis. *A City in Terror.* New York: Viking Press, 1975.

_____. *The Shadow of Blooming Grove: Warren G. Harding in His Times.* New York: McGraw-Hill, 1968.

_____. *Tragedy in Dedham.* New York: McGraw-Hill, 1962.

Russell, George K. *Marihuana Today.* New York: Myrin Institute, 1976.

Russell, Guy. *Guilty or Not Guilty?* London: Hutchinson, 1931.

Russell, Harold E., and Beigel, Allan. *Understanding Human Behavior For Effective Police Work.* New York: Basic Books, 1982.

Russell, Jeffrey Burton. *The Devil.* Ithaca, N.Y.: Cornell University Press, 1977.

Russell, Oland D. *The House of Mitsui.* Boston: Little, Brown, 1939.

Russell, R.V., and Lal, Hira. *Tribes and Castes of the Central Provinces of India.* London: Macmillan, 1916.

Russell, Ray. *Unholy Trinity.* New York: Bantam, 1967.

Russell, Sue. *Damsel of Death.* London: True Crime, 1992.

Russell, Thomas H. *The Illustrious Life and Work of Warren G. Harding.* Chicago: n.p., 1923.

Russo, Gus. *The Outfit: The Role of Chicago's Underworld in the Shaping of America.* New York: Bloomsbury USA, 2003.

Russo, Robert J. *Amphetamine Abuse.* Springfield, Ill.: Charles C. Thomas, 1972.

Rutherford, Andrew, et al. *Prison Population and Policy Choices.* Washington, D.C.: National Institute of Law Enforcement and Criminal Justice, 1977.

Rutherford, L. *John Peter Zenger.* New York: Peter Smith, 1941.

Rutledge, Lyman V. *Moonlight at Murder Smuttynose.* Boston: Star King Press, 1958.

Rutter, Owen. *The Pirate Wind: Tales of the Sea Robbers of Malaya.* London: Hutchinson, 1930.

Rutter, Owen (ed.). *Notable British Trials: Trial of Bounty Mutineers.* London: William Hodge, 1931.

Ruud, Charles A., and Stepanov, Sergei A. *Fontauka 16: The Czar's Secret Police.* London: Sutton, 1999.

Ryan, John A. *Distributive Justice.* New York: Macmillan, 1942.

Ryan, Michael. *Prostitution in London.* London: Bailliere, 1838.

Ryan, N.J. *A History of Malaysia and Singapore.* Oxford University sity Press, 1976.

Ryan, William. *Blaming the Victim.* New York: Vintage Books, 1976.

Rynning, Thomas H. *Gun Notches.* New York: Frederick A. Stokes, 1931.

Rysan, Joseph. *Wilhelm Meinhold's Bernsteinhexe.* Chicago: University of Chicago, 1948.

Saad-Ghorayeb, Amal. *Hizbu'llah* [Hezbollah]: *Politics and Religion.* London: Pluto Press, 2002.

Sabin, Edwin LeGrand. *Wild Men of the Wild West.* New York: Thomas Y. Crowell, 1929.

The Sacco-Vanzetti Case: Transcript of the Record of the Trial. New York: Henry Holt, 1928-1929.

Sacks, Benjamin. *Arizona's Angry Man.* Tempe: Arizona Histori-cal Foundation, 1970.

Sackville-West, Vita. *Saint Joan of Arc.* New York: Doubleday, Doran, 1936.

Sadat, Anwar. *Revolt on the Nile.* New York: Day, 1957.

Saferstein, R. *Criminalistics: An Introduction to Forensic Science.* Seventh Edition. Englewood Cliffs, N.J.: Prentice-Hall, 2001.

Sagarin, Edward. *Criminology: New Concerns.* Beverly Hills, Calif.: Sage, 1979.

_____ (ed.). *Taboos in Criminology.* Beverly Hills, Calif.: Sage, 1980.

Saggs, H.W.F. *The Greatness That Was Babylon.* New York: New American Library, 1968.

St. Aubyns, Giles. *Edward VII: Prince and King.* New York: Atheneum, 1979.

_____. *Infamous Victorians.* London: Constable, 1971.

St. John, Robert. *Ben Gurion.* Garden City, N.Y.: Doubleday, 1959.

_____. *The Boss: The Story of Gamal Abdel Nasser.* New York: McGraw-Hill, 1960.

St. Johns, Adela Rogers. *Final Verdict.* Garden City, N.Y.: Doubleday, 1962.

Saito, Dr. Yoshie. *Deceived History: An Inside Account of Matsuoka and the Tripartite Pact.* Tokyo: Yomiuri Shimbun, 1955.

Sakolski, A.M. *The Great American Land Bubble.* New York: Harper & Brothers, 1932.

Sakomizu Hisatsune. *The Prime Minister's Official Residence under Machine-Gun Fire.* Tokyo: Kobun Sha, 1965.

Sakran, Frank C. *Palestine Dilemma: Arab Rights versus Zionist Aspirations.* Washington, D.C.: Public Affairs Press, 1948.

Sale, Kirkpatrick. *SDS.* New York: Vintage Books, 1974.

Salerno, Ralph, and Tompkins, John. *The Crime Confederation.* New York: Doubleday, 1969.

Salgado, Gamini. *Cony-Catchers and Bawdy Baskets.* New York: Penguin Books, 1972.

_____. *The Elizabethan Underworld.* London: J.M. Dent & Sons, 1977.

Samenow, Stanton E. *Inside the Criminal Mind.* New York: Times Books, 1984.

Sammon, Bill. *Fighting Back: The War on Terrorism from Inside the Bush White House.* Washington, D. C.: Regnery, 2002.

Sampson, Anthony. *The Arms Bazaar.* London: Coronet Books, 1977.

Samuel, Raphael. *East End Underworld.* Boston: Routledge & Kegan Paul, 1981.

Samuel, Ray, Huber, Leonard, and Ogden, Warren C. *Tales of the Mississippi.* New York: Hastings House, 1955.

Samuels, Charles. *Death was the Bridegroom.* New York: Fawcett, 1955.

_____. *The Girl in the House of Hate.* New York: Fawcett, 1953.

_____. *The Girl in the Red Velvet Swing.* New York: Fawcett, 1955.

_____. *The Magnificent Rube: The Life and Gaudy Times of Tex Rickard.* New York: McGraw-Hill, 1957.

_____. *Night Fell on Georgia.* New York: Dell, 1956.

Sandburg, Carl. *Abraham Lincoln: The Prairie Years.* 2 vols. New York: Harcourt, Brace, 1926.

_____. *Abraham Lincoln: The War Years.* 4 vols. New York: Harcourt, Brace, 1939.

Sanders, Bruce. *Murder Behind the Bright Lights.* London: Herbert Jenkins, 1958.

_____. *Murder in Big Cities.* New York: Roy, 1962.

_____. *Murder in Lonely Places.* London: Jenkins, 1960.

_____. *They Caught These Killers.* New York: Roy, 1968.

_____. *They Couldn't Lose the Body.* London: Jenkins, 1966.

Sanders, Ed. *The Family.* New York: E.P. Dutton, 1971.

Sanders, Ronald. *The Downtown Jews: Portraits of an Immigrant Generation.* New York: Harper & Row, 1966.

Sanders, Wiley B. *Juvenile Offenders of 1000 Years.* Durham: University of North Carolina Press, 1970.

Sanders, William B. *Criminology.* Reading, Mass.: Addison Wesley, 1983.

_____. *Detective Work.* New York: Free Press, 1977.

_____ (ed.). *The Socialogist as Detective.* New York: Praeger, 1976.

Sandmeyer, Elmer C. *The Anti-Chinese Movement in California.* Urbana: University of Illinois Press, 1939.

Sandoe, James (ed.). *Murder: Plain & Fanciful.* New York: Sheridan, 1948.

Sands, Bill. *My Shadow Ran Fast.* Englewood Cliffs, N.J.: Prentice-Hall, 1964.

Sanger, Joan. *The Case of the Missing Corpse.* New York: Green Circle Books, 1936.

Sanger, William W. *History of Prostitution.* New York: Harper, 1858.

Sann, Paul. *The Angry Decade: The Sixties.* New York: Crown, 1979.

_____. *Kill the Dutchman!* New Rochelle, N.Y.: Arlington House, 1971.

_____. *The Lawless Decade.* New York: Crown, 1957.

Sansom, George. *A History of Japan.* 3 vols. Stanford, Calif.: Stanford University Press, 1958.

_____. *Japan: A Short Cultural History.* New York: Appleton-Century-Crofts, 1962.

_____. *The Western World and Japan.* New York: Alfred A. Knopf, 1950.

Santayana, George. *Character and Opinion in the United States.* New York: Charles Scribner's Sons, 1920.

Santesson, H.S. *The Locked Room Reader: Stories of the Impos-sible Crimes and Escapes.* New York: Random House, 1968.

Sapte, W. *A Century's Sensations.* London: George Routledge, 1893.

Sarfatti, Margherita. *Dux: The Life of Benito Mussolini.* trans. Frederic Whyte. London: Thornton Butterworth, 1925.

Sarp-Wiwa, Ken, and Boyd, William. *A Month and a Day: A Detention Diary.* New York: Penguin, 1996.

Sauvage, Leo. *The Oswald Affair: An Examination of the Con-tradictions and Omissions of the Warren Report.* Cleveland: World, 1966.

Savage, Edward H. *Police Records and Recollections or Boston by Daylight and Gaslight.* Montclair, N.J.: Patterson Smith, 1971.

Savage, Henry, Jr. *Discovering America, 1700-1875.* New York: Harper & Brothers, 1979.

Savage, John. *Life of Andrew Johnson.* New York: Derby & Miller, 1866.

Savage, Percy. *Savage of Scotland Yard.* London: Hutchinson, 1934.

Savitz, Leonard D., and Johnston, Norman. *Crime in Society.* New York: John Wiley & Sons, 1978.

_____. *Dilemmas in Criminology.* New York: McGraw-Hill, 1967.

Sawyer, Joseph Dillaway. *Washington.* 2 vols. New York: Macmillan, 1927.

Saxon, Lyle. *Fabulous New Orleans.* New York: D. Appleton-Century, 1928.

Sayer, James Edward. *Clarence Darrow: Public Advocate.* Dayton, Ohio: Wright State University, 1978.

Sayers, Dorothy L. *Tales of Detection, Mystery and Horror.* London: Gollancz, 1928.

Scacco, Anthony M. *Rape in Prison.* Springfield, Ill.: Charles C. Thomas, 1975.

Scaduto, Anthony. *Scapegoat: The Truth about the Lindbergh Kidnapping.* New York: G.P. Putnam's Sons, 1976.

Scarr, Harry A. *Patterns of Burglary.* Washington, D.C.: Depart-ment of Justice, 1972.

Schaack, Michael J. *Anarchy and the Anarchists.* Chicago: F.J. Schulte, 1889.

Schafer, Robert S. *Introduction to Criminology.* Englewood Cliffs, N.J.: Prentice-Hall, 1926.

Schafer, Stephen. *Introduction to Criminology.* Reston, Va.: Reston, 1976.

_____. *The Political Criminal.* New York: Free Press, 1974.

_____. *The Political Prisoner: The Problem of Morality and Crime.* New York: Free Press, 1974.

_____. *Restitution to Victims of Crime.* London: Stevens & Sons, 1960.

_____. *Theories in Criminology.* New York: Random House, 1969.

_____. *The Victim and His Criminal: A Study in Functional Responsibility.* New York: Random House, 1968.

Schakovsky, Zinida. *Precursors of Peter the Great.* London: Jonathan Cape, 1964.

Schecter, Harold. *Bestial.* New York: Pocket Books, 1998.

_____. *Deranged.* New York: Pocket Books, 1990.

_____. *Deviant.* New York: Pocket Books, 1989.

Schecter, Jerrold, and Schecter, Leona P, and Strobe, Talbot. *Sacred Secrets: How Soviet Intelligence Operations Changed American History.* Dulles, Va.: Brassey's, 2002.

Schecter, Leonard, and Phillips, William. *On the Pad.* New York: Berkeley, 1973.

Scheim, David E. *Contract on America: The Mafia Murders of John and Robert Kennedy.* Silver Springs, Md.: Argyle Press, 1983.

Schellenberg, Walter. *The Labyrinth.* New York: Harper & Brothers, 1956.

_____. *The Schellenberg Memoirs.* trans. Louis Hagen. London: Andre Deutsch, 1961.

Scherrer, Christian P. *Genocide and Crisis in Central Africa: Conflict, Roots, Mass Violence and Regional War.* Westport, Conn.: Praeger, 2001.

Schiavi, Allessandro. *La vita e l'opera di Giacomo Matteotti.* Rome: Opere Nuove, 1957.

Schiavo, Giovanni. *The Truth About the Mafia.* El Paso, Texas: Vigo Press, 1962.

Schiavo, Giovanni Erminegildo. *Italians in Chicago.* Chicago: Italian-American, 1928.

Schiller, Lawrence, and Atkins, Susan. *The Killing of Sharon Tate.* New York: New American Library, 1970.

_____. *Perfect Murder, Perfect Town.* New York: Harper Collins, 1999.

Schlabrendorff, Fabian von. *The Secret War Against Hitler.* New York: Pitman, 1965.

Schlapp, Max G., and Smith, Edward H. *The New Criminology: A Consideration of the Chemical Causation of Abnormal Behavior.* New York: Boni & Liveright, 1928.

Schlesinger, Arthur Meier. *The American as Reformer.* Cambridge, Mass.: Harvard University Press, 1951.

_____. *The Colonial Merchants and the American Revolution 1763-1776.* New York: Columbia University Press, 1918.

_____. *Paths to the Present.* New York: Macmillan, 1949.

_____. *The Rise of the City, 1878-1898.* New York: Macmillan 1933.

Schlesinger, Arthur M., Jr. *The Age of Jackson.* Boston: Little, Brown, 1945.

_____. *The Age of Roosevelt.* London: William Heinemann, 1957.

_____. *The Coming of the New Deal.* Boston: Houghton Mifflin, 1960.

_____ (ed.). *The Cotton Kingdom.* New York: Alfred A. Knopf, 1953.

_____. *The Crisis of the Old Order 1919-1933.* Boston: Houghton Mifflin, 1957.

_____. *Robert Kennedy and His Times.* Boston: Houghton Mifflin, 1978.

_____. *A Thousand Days: John F. Kennedy in the White House.* Boston: Houghton Mifflin, 1965.

_____. *Violence: America in the Sixties.* New York: New American Library, 1968.

Schmaltz, William H. *Hate: George Lincoln Rockwell and the American Nazi Party.* Dulles, Va.: Brassey's, 2001.

Schmeckebier, Laurence F. *The Bureau of Prohibition: Its History, Activities and Organization.* Washington, D.C.: Brookings Institution, 1929.

Schneider, Reinhold. *Die Hohenzollern.* Leipzig, Ger.: Hegner, 1933.

Schneir, Walter and Miriam. *Invitation to an Inquest.* Garden City, N.Y.: Doubleday, 1965.

Schoenberg, Harris Okun. *A Mandate for Terror: The United Nations and the PLO.* New York: SPI Books, 1989.

Schoenberg, Robert J. *Mr. Capone.* New York: William Morrow, 1992.

Schoenberger, Dale T. *The Gunfighters.* Caldwell, Idaho: Caxton Printers, 1971.

Schott, Joseph L. *No Left Turns, the FBI in Peace and War.* New York: Frederick A. Praeger, 1975.

Schramm, Percy Ernst. *Hitler: The Man and the Military Leader.* Chicago: Quadrangle Books, 1971.

Schreiber, Flora Rheta. *The Shoemaker, Anatomy of a Psychotic.* New York: Simon & Schuster, 1983.

Schriftgiesser, Karl. *The Lobbyists.* Boston: Little, Brown, 1951.

_____. *This Was Normalcy.* Boston: Atlantic, Little, Brown, 1948.

Schultz, Jim. *Cauldron of Blood.* New York: Avon, 1989.

_____. *Preacher's Girl.* New York: William Morrow, 1993.

Schultz, Leroy G. *Rape Victimology.* Springfield, Ill.: Charles C. Thomas, 1975.

Schultz, R.L. *Crusader in Babylon: W.T. Stead and the Pall Mall Gazette.* Omaha: University of Nebraska Press, 1972.

Schuman, Frederick L. *Europe on the Eve.* London: Robert Hale, 1939.

_____. *The Nazi Dictatorship.* New York: Alfred A. Knopf, 1936.

Schuschnigg, Kurt von. *Austrian Requiem.* New York: G.P. Putnam's Sons, 1946.

_____. *Im Kampf gegen Hitler.* Vienna, Aust.: Molden, 1969.

_____. *My Austria.* New York: Alfred A. Knopf, 1938.

Schuster, Ernest Otto. *Pancho Villa's Shadow.* New York: Exposition Press, 1947.

Schwartz, Ann. *The Man Who Could Not Kill Enough.* Secaucus, N. J.: Carol, 1992.

Schwartz, Stephen. *The Two Faces of Islam: The House of Sa'Ud from Tradition to Terrorism.* New York: Doubleday, 2002.

Schwartz, Ted. *The Hillside Strangler: A Murderer's Mind.* Garden City, N.Y.: Doubleday, 1981.

Sciascia, Leonard. *L'Affaire Moro.* Palermo, Italy: Sellerio Editore, 1978.

_____. *Mafia Vendetta.* New York: Alfred A. Knopf, 1963.

Scott, Arthur P. *Criminal Law in Colonial Virginia.* Chicago: University of Chicago Press, 1930.

Scott, George Ryley. *The History of Capital Punishment.* London: Torchstream Books, 1950.

_____. *A History of Prostitution.* London: T. Werner Laurie, 1936.

_____. *Such Outlaws as Jesse James.* London: Gerald S. Swann, 1943.

Scott, Sir Harold (ed.). *The Concise Encyclopedia of Crime and Criminals.* New York: Hawthorn Books, 1961.

_____. *Scotland Yard.* London: Andre Deutsch, 1954.

Scott, Kenneth D. *Belle Starr in Velvet.* Tahlequah, Okla.: Pan Press, 1963.

Scott, Peter Dale, et al. (eds.). *The Assassinations: Dallas and Beyond - A Guide to Cover-ups and Investigations.* New York: Random House, 1976.

_____. *Crime and Cover-Up: The CIA, the Mafia, and the Dallas-Watergate Connection.* Berkeley, Calif.: Westworks, 1977.

Scott, W.S. *Jeanne d'Arc.* London: George G. Harrap, 1974.

Scoundrels & Scalawags. New York: Reader's Digest, 1968.

Seabury, Paul. *The Wilhelmstrasse.* Berkeley: University of California Press, 1954.

Seagle, William. *Acquitted of Murder.* Chicago: Henry Regnery, 1958.

Seagrave, Sterling. *The Soong Dynasty.* New York: Harper & Row, 1985.

Searcher, Victor. *The Farewell to Lincoln.* New York: Abingdon Press, 1965.

Sears, Donald. *To Kill Again.* Wilmington, Del.: Scholarly Resources, 1991.

Seccombe, Thomas (ed.). *Lives of Twelve Bad Men.* London: T. Fisher Unwin, 1894.

Segal, Ronald. *Race War.* New York: Viking Press, 1967.

Segrave, Kerry. *Women Serial and Mass Murderers.* Jefferson, N. C.: McFarland, 1992.

Seidenberg, D.A. *Uhuru and the Kenya Indians: The Role of a Minority Community in Kenya Politics, 1939-1963.* Delhi, India: Vikas, 1983.

Seidman, Harold. *Labor Czars: A History of Labor Racketeering.* New York: Liveright, 1938.

Seitz, Don Carlos. *The Dreadful Decade...1869-1879.* Indianapolis, Ind.: Bobbs-Merrill, 1926.

_____. *The James Gordon Bennetts: Father and Son, Proprietors of the New York Herald.* Indianapolis, Ind.: Bobbs-Merrill, 1928.

_____. *Joseph Pulitzer, His Life & Letters.* New York: Simon & Schuster, 1924.

_____. *Lincoln the Politician: How the Rail-Splitter and Flat-Boatman Played the Great American Game.* New York: Coward-McCann, 1931.

_____. *Uncommon Americans.* Indianapolis, Ind.: Bobbs-Merrill, 1925.

_____. *Under the Black Flag.* New York: Gryphon Books, 1971.

Sela, Auraham, and Maoz, Moshe. *The PLO and Israel: From Armed Conflict to Political Solution, 1964-1994.* New York: Palgrave Macmillan, 1997.

Seldes, George. *Lords of the Press.* New York: Julian Messner, 1938.

_____. *Sawdust Caeser.* New York: Harper, 1938.

_____. *The Vatican: Yesterday, Today and Tomorrow.* London: Kegan Paul, Trench, Trubner, 1934.

_____. *You Can't Print That.* New York: Payson & Clarke, 1929.

Seldes, Gilbert. *The New Mass Media: Challenge to a Free Society.* Washington, D.C.: Public Affairs Press, 1968.

_____. *The Stammering Century.* New York: Harper Colophon Books, 1965.

Select Committee on Intelligence. *The Investigation of the Assassination of President John F. Kennedy: Performance of the Intelligence Agencies.* Washington, D.C.: U.S. Govern-ment Printing Office, 1976.

Sellers, Ann. *The Leopold-Loeb Case.* Brunswick, Ga.: n. p., 1926.

Sellers, Alvin V. *Classics of the Bar: Stories of the World's Greatest Legal Trials and Forensic Masterpieces.* Washington, D.C.: Washington Law Books, 1942.

Sellin, Thorsten (ed.). *Capital Punishment.* New York: Harper & Row, 1967.

_____. *Culture Conflict and Crime.* New York: Social Science Research Council, 1938.

_____. *The Death Penalty.* Philadelphia: American Law Institute, 1959.

Selwyn, Francis. *Rotten to the Core.* London: Routledge, 1988.

Semmler, Rudolf. *Goebbels: The Man Next to Hitler.* London: Westhouse, 1947.

Seng, R.A., and Gilmour, J.V. *Brink's the Money Movers.* Chica-go: R.R. Donnelley & Sons, 1959.

Senzel, Howard T. *Cases: A Courthouse Chronicle of Crime and Wit.* New York: Viking Press, 1982.

_____. *Men in Prison.* London: Writers & Readers, 1969.

Sereny, Gitta. *The Case of Mary Bell.* London: Methuen, 1972.

Sergeant, Philip Walsingham. *Witches and Warlocks.* London: Hutchinson, 1936.

Servadio, Gaia. *Angelo LaBarbera: The Profile of a Mafia Boss.* London: Quartet Books, 1974.

_____. *Mafioso: A History of the Mafia from Its Origins to the Present Day.* New York: Dell, 1976.

Seth, Ronald. *Encyclopedia of Espionage.* London: New English Library, 1972.

_____. *Petiot, Victim of Chance.* London: Hutchinson, 1963.

_____. *The Sleeping Truth.* New York: Hart, 1968.

_____. *Unmasked: The Story of Soviet Espionage.* New York: Hawthorn Books, 1965.

_____. *Witches and Their Craft.* New York: Taplinger, 1967.

Seton-Watson, Hugh. *Decline of Imperial Russia, 1855-1914.* New York: Frederick A. Praeger, 1953.

_____. *The Russian Empire, 1801-1917.* Oxford, Eng.: Clarendon, 1967.

Seton-Watson, R.W. *Sarajevo: A Study in the Origins of the Great War.* London: Hutchinson, 1925.

Seton-Williams, M.V. *Britain and the Arab States.* London: Luzac, 1948.

Settle, William A., Jr. *Jesse James Was His Name.* Columbia: University of Missouri Press, 1966.

Seward, Frederick W. *Andrew Johnson.* Philadelphia: J.B. Lippincott, 1890.

_____. *Reminiscences of a War-Time Statesman and Diplomat.* New York: G.P. Putnam's Sons, 1916.

_____. *Seward at Washington.* New York: Derby & Miller, 1891.

Seymour, L. *Finger Print Classification.* Los Angeles: Privately Printed, 1913.

Seymour-Smith, Martin. *Fallen Women.* London: Thomas Nelson, 1969.

Shaaber, M.A. *Some Forerunners of the Newspaper in England, 1476-1622.* New York: Octagon Books, 1966.

Shackleford, William Yancey. *Belle Starr, The Bandit Queen.* Girard, Kan.: Haldemann-Julius, 1943.

_____. *Gunfighters of the Old West.* Girard, Kan.: Haldemann-Julius, 1943.

Shadwell, Thomas. *The Lancaster Witches.* London: J.Starkey, 1682.

Shanani, Ranju. *Mr. Gandhi.* New York: Macmillan, 1961.

Shaner, Dolph. *The Story of Joplin.* New York: Stratford House, 1948.

Shannon, David A. (ed.). *The Great Depression.* Englewood Cliffs, N.J.: Prentice-Hall, 1960.

_____ (ed.). *The Great Imposter.* New York: Prentice-Hall, 1960.

Shannon, Elaine. *Desperados: Latin Drug Lord, U.S. Lawmen, and the War America Can't Win.* New York: Viking Press, 1988.

Shannon, William V. *The American Irish.* New York: Macmillan, 1963.

Shapiro, Fred C., and Sullivan, James W. *Race Riots: New York 1964.* New York: Thomas Y. Crowell, 1964.

Shapiro, Harry Lionel. *Descendants of the Mutineers of the Bounty.* Honolulu, Hawaii: The Museum, 1929.

Shapiro, Nat, and Hentoff, Nat. *Hear Me Talkin' to Ya: The Story of Jazz and the Men Who Made It.* New York: Rinehart, 1955.

Shapiro, Stanley. *A Time to Remember.* New York: Random House, 1986.

Shapland, J.J. Williams, and Duff, P. *Victims in the Criminal Justice System.* Brookfield, Vt.: Gower, 1985.

Shaplen, Robert. *Kreuger: Genius and Swindler.* New York: Alfred A. Knopf, 1960.

Sharabi, Hisham B. *Nationalism and Revolution in the Arab World.* Princeton, N.J.: D. Van Nostrand, 1966.

Sharman, Lyon. *Sun Yat-sen.* New York: John Day, 1934.

Sharpe, Charles Kirkpatrick. *Witchcraft in Scotland.* New York: Barnes & Noble, 1972.

Sharpe, May Churchill. *Chicago May: Her Story.* New York: Macaulay, 1928.

Shaw, A.G.L. *Convicts and the Colonies.* London: Faber & Faber, 1966.

Shaw, Albert H. (ed.). *The Lincoln Encyclopedia.* New York: Macmillan, 1950.

Shaw, Arnold. *The Street That Never Slept.* New York: Coward, McCann & Geoghegan, 1971.

Shaw, Clifford R. *Brothers in Crime.* Chicago: University of Chicago Press, 1938.

_____, et al. *Delinquency Areas.* Chicago: University of Chicago Press, 1929.

_____. *The Jackroller.* Chicago: University of Chicago Press, 1930.

Shaw, J. Gary, and Harris, Larry R. *Cover-Up: 'The Governmental Conspiracy to Conceal the Facts About the Public Execution of John Kennedy.'* Cleburne, Texas: Published by Authors, 1976.

Shawcross, Tim, and Young, Martin. *Men of Honour: The Confessions of Tommaso Buscetta.* London: Collins, 1987.

Shay, Frank. *More Pious Friends and Drunken Companions.* New York: Macaulay, 1928.

_____, and Held, John, Jr. *My Pious Friends and Drunken Com-panions.* New York: Macaulay, 1927.

Shea, John Gilmary (ed.). *The Lincoln Memorial: A Record of the Life, Assassination, and Obsequies of the Martyed President.* New York: Bruce & Huntington, 1865.

Shearing, Joseph. *Airing in a Closed Cottage.* New York: Harper & Brothers, 1943.

_____. *So Evil My Love.* New York: Harper, 1947.

Sheehan, Susan. *A Prison and a Prisoner.* Boston: Houghton, 1978.

Sheldon, Addison Erwin. *Nebraska Old and New: History, Stories, Folklore.* Lincoln: University of Nebraska, 1937.

Sheldon, Walter J. *The Honorable Conquerors: The Occupation of Japan 1945-1952.* New York: Macmillan, 1965.

Shelley, L.E. *Crime and Modernization.* Carbondale: Southern Illinois University Press, 1981.

Shelton, Vaughan. *Mask for Treason: The Lincoln Murder Trial.* Harrisburg, Pa.: Stackpole Books, 1965.

Shemesh, Moshe. *The Palestinian Entity, 1959-1974: Politics and the PLO.* New York: Frank Cass, 1996.

Shepard, Gordon. *Dollfuss.* New York: Macmillan, 1961.

Shepard, Odell. *Connecticut, Past and Present.* London: Alfred A. Knopf, 1939.

Sheperd, Charles R. *The Ways of Ah Sin.* New York: Revell, 1923.

Sheresky, Norman. *On Trial.* New York: Viking Press, 1977.

Sheridan, James E. *Chinese Warlord: The Careen of Feng Yuh-siang.* Stanford, Calif.: Stanford University Press, 1966.

Sheridan, Leo W. *I Killed for the Law.* New York: Stackpole Sons, 1938.

Sheridan, Martin. *Comics and Their Creators.* Boston: Hale, Cushman & Flynt, 1942.

Sheridan, Walter. *The Rise and Fall of Jimmy Hoffa.* New York: Saturday Review Press, 1972.

Sherrard, P. *Constantinople.* New York: Oxford University Press, 1965.

Sherrill, Robert. *Gothic Politics in the Deep South.* New York: Grossman, 1968.

_____. *The Saturday Night Special.* New York: Charterhouse, 1973.

Shew, E. Spencer. *A Companion to Murder.* New York: Knopf, 1960.

_____. *Hands of the Ripper.* London: Sphere, 1971.

_____. *A Second Companion to Murder.* New York: Knopf, 1961.

Shields, Robert William. *Seymour, Indiana and the Famous Story of the Reno Gang.* Indianapolis, Ind.: H. Lieber, 1939.

Shigemitsu, Mamoru. *Japan and Her Destiny: My Struggle for Peace.* New York: E.P. Dutton, 1958.

Shimada Toshihiko. *The Kwantung Army.* Tokyo: Chuo Koron-sha, 1965.

Shinn, Charles Howard. *Graphic Description of Pacific Coast Outlaws.* Los Angeles: Westernlore Press, 1958.

Shirer, William L. *Berlin Diary.* New York: Alfred A. Knopf, 1941.

_____. *The Collapse of the Third Republic.* New York: Simon & Schuster, 1969.

_____. *End of a Berlin Diary.* New York: Alfred A. Knopf, 1947.

_____. *Gandhi: A Memoir.* New York: Simon & Schuster, 1979.

_____. *The Rise and Fall of the Third Reich.* New York: Simon & Schuster, 1960.

_____. *20th Century Journey: A Memoir of a Life and the Times of William L. Shirer.* New York: Simon & Schuster, 1976.
Shirley, Glenn. *Belle Starr and Her Times.* Norman: University of Oklahoma Press, 1982.
_____ (ed.). *Buckskin and Spurs: A Gallery of Frontier Rogues and Heroes.* New York: Hastings House, 1958.
_____. *Henry Starr, Last of the Real Bad Men.* New York: David McKay, 1965.
_____. *Law West of Fort Smith.* New York: Henry Holt, 1957.
_____. *Outlaw Queen: The Fantastic True Story of Belle Starr.* Derby, Conn.: Monarch Books, 1960.
_____. *Shotgun for Hire: The Story of "Deacon" Jim Miller, Killer of Pat Garrett.* Norman: University of Oklahoma Press, 1970.
_____. *Six-Gun and Silver Star.* Albuquerque: University of New Mexico Press, 1955.
_____. *Temple Houston.* Norman: University of Oklahoma Press, 1980.
_____. *Toughest of Them All.* Albuquerque: University of New Mexico Press, 1953.
_____. *West of Hell's Fringe: Crime, Criminals, and the Federal Peace Officer in Oklahoma Territory, 1889-1907.* Norman: University of Oklahoma Press, 1978.
Shirovama Saburo. *War Criminal.* Tokyo: Kodansha, 1980.
Shoenfeld, Dudley D. *The Crime and the Criminal: A Psychiatric Study of the Lindbergh Case.* New York: Covici-Friede, 1936.
Shogan, Robert, and Craig, Tom. *The Detroit Race Riot: A Study in Violence.* Philadelphia: Chilton Books, 1964.
Shoham, S. *Crime and Social Deviation.* Chicago: Henry Regnery, 1966.
_____. *Society and the Absurd.* Oxford, Eng.: Blackwell, 1974.
Shonle Cavan, Ruth. *Criminology.* New York: Thomas Y. Crowell, 1955.
Shore, W. Teignmouth (ed.). *Crime and Its Detection.* London: Gresham, 1931.
_____. *The Trials of Charles Frederick Peace.* London: William Hodge, 1926.
_____. *Trial of Thomas Neill Cream.* London: Hodge, 1923.
Short, Anthony. *The Communist Insurrection in Malaya.* Prince-ton, N.J.: Princeton University Press, 1956.
Short, James F., Jr. (ed.). *Delinquency, Crime and Society.* Chicago: University of Chicago Press, 1976.
_____ (ed.). *Gang Delinquency and Delinquent Subcultures.* New York: Harper & Row, 1968.
Shridharani, Krishnalal. *The Mahatma and the World.* New York: John Day, 1939.
Shub, David. *Lenin, A Biography.* New York: Doubleday, 1948.
Shugg, Roger W. *Origins of the Class Struggle in Louisana.* New York: n.p, 1953.
Shultz, Gladys Denny. *How Many More Victims?* New York: J.B. Lippincott, 1965.
Shulvass, Moses A. *The History of the Jewish People.* Chicago: Regnery Gateway, 1982.
Siberman, Charles E. *Crisis in Black and White.* New York: Random House, 1964.
Sichel, Joyce L., et al. *Women on Patrol. A Piot Study of Police Performance in New York City.* New York: Vera Institute of Justice, 1977.
Sichel, Walter. *Emma Lady Hamilton.* New York: Dodd, Mead, 1907.
Siciliano, Vincent. *Unless They Kill Me First.* New York: Haw-thorn Books, 1970.
Sickels, H.E. *Reports on the Cases decided in the Court of Appeals of the State of New York.* Albany, N.Y.: James B. Lyons, 1893.
Sicot, Marcel. *Servitude et Grandeur Policieres.* Paris: Les Productions de Paris, 1959.
Sieburg, F. *Napolon.* Paris: Robert Laffont, 1957.
Siegel, Larry J. *Criminology.* St. Paul, Minn.: West, 1983.
Sigler, Robert T. *Furlough Programs for Inmates.* Washington, D.C.: National Institute for Law Enforcement and Criminal Justice, 1976.
_____. *Furlough Programs for Inmates: Final Report.* Washington, D.C.: National Institute for Law Enforcement and Criminal Justice, 1976.
Silberman, Charles E. *Criminal Violence, Criminal Justice.* New York: Random House, 1978.
Silverman, David. *Pitcairn Island.* New York: World, 1967.
Silverman, Kenneth. *The Life and Times of Cotton Mather.* New York: Harper & Row, 1970.
Simanovich, Aron. *Rasputin der allmchtige Bauer.* Berlin: Hensel, 1928.
Simis, Konstantin M. *The Corrupt Society: The Secret World of Soviet Capitalism.* New York: Simon & Schuster, 1982.
Simmons, J.L. *Marihuanna: Myths and Realities.* North Hol-lywood, Calif.: Brandon House, 1967.
Simmons, Jerry L. *Deviants.* Berkeley, Calif.: Glendessary Press, 1969.
Simmons, Lee. *Assignment Huntsville: Memoirs of a Texas Prison Official.* Austin: University of Texas Press, 1957.
Simon, Edith. *The Making of Frederick the Great.* Boston: Little, Brown, 1963.
Simon, Paul. *Lovejoy, Martyr to Freedom.* St. Louis: Concordia, 1964.
Simon, Rita James. *As We Saw the Thirties.* Urbana: University of Illinois Press, 1967.
_____. *The Contemporary Women and Crime.* Rockville, Md.: National Institute of Mental Health, 1975.
_____. *The Jury System in America: A Critical Overview.* Beverly Hills, Calif.: Sage, 1975.
_____. *Women and Crime.* Lexington, Mass.: D.C. Heath, 1978.
Simonelli, Frederick James. *American Fuehrer: George Lincoln Rockwell and the American Nazi Party.* Urbana, Ill: University of Illinois Press, 1999.
Simpson, Alan. *Puritanism in Old and New England.* Chicago: University of Chicago Press, 1955.
Simpson, Anthony. *The Literature of Police Corruption.* New York: John Jay Press, 1977.
Simpson, C.H. *Life in the Far West; or, a Detective's Thrilling Adventures Among the Indians and Outlaws of Montana.* Chicago: Rhodes & McClure, 1893.
Simpson, C. Keith. *Modern Trends in Forensic Medicine.* London: Butterworth, 1952.
Simpson, F.A. *Louis Napoleon and the Recovery of France.* London: Longmans, Green, 1923.
_____. *The Rise of Louis Napoleon.* London: Longmans, Green, 1909.
Simpson, Helen (ed.). *The Anatomy of Murder.* New York: Macmillan, 1934.
Simpson, Keith. *Forensic Medicine.* London: Arnold, 1964.
_____. *Forty Years of Murder.* New York: Charles Scribner's Sons, 1979.
Simpson, Lesley Byrd. *Many Mexicos.* Berkeley: University of California Press, 1952.
Sims, George Robert. *The Mysteries of Modern London.* London: Pearson, 1906.
Sims, Judge Orland L. *Gun-Toters I Have Known.* Austin, Texas: Encino Press, 1967.
Sims, Patsy. *The Klan.* New York: Stein & Day, 1978.
Sinclair, Andrew. *The Available Man.* New York: Macmillan, 1965.
_____. *Era of Excess: A Social History of the Prohibition Movement.* New York: Harper & Row, 1964.
_____. *Prohibition: The Era of Excess.* Boston: Little, Brown, 1962.
_____. *Satan's Invisible World Discovered.* London: J. Bailey, 1915.
Sinclair, Robert. *East London.* London: Robert Hale, Ltd., 1950.
Sinclair, Upton. *The Autobiography of Upton Sinclair.* New York: Harcourt, Brace & World, 1962.
_____. *The Book of Life.* Long Beach, Calif.: Published by Author, 1926.
_____. *Boston.* Pasadena, Calif.: Published by Author, 1928.
_____. *The Brass Check: A Study of American Journalism.* Pasadena, Calif.: Published by Author, 1920.
_____. *The Cup of Fury.* Great Neck, N.Y.: Channel Press, 1956.
_____. *The Jungle.* New York: Doubleday Page, 1906.
_____. *Presidential Agent.* New York: Viking Press, 1944.
Sindler, Allan P. *Huey Long's Louisiana.* Baltimore,: Johns Hopkins, 1956.
Singer, Kurt (ed.). *Crime Omnibus.* London: W.H. Allen, 1961.
_____, and Sherrod, Jane. *Great Adventures in Crime.* Minneapolis, Minn.: T.S. Denison, 1962.
_____ (ed.). *My Greatest Crime Story.* London: W.H. Allen, 1956.
_____. *My Strangest Cases.* Garden City, N.Y.: Doubleday, 1958.
Sion, Abraham. *Prostitution and the Law.* Winchester, Mass.: Faber, 1977.
Siragusa, Charles. *The Trail of the Poppy.* Englewood Cliffs, N.J.: Prentice-Hall, 1966.
Siringo, Charles A. *A Cowboy Detective, an Autobiography.* Chicago: W.B. Conkey, 1912.
Sites, Paul. *Lee Harvey Oswald and the American Dream.* New York: Pageant Press, 1967.
Sitwell, Sir Osbert. *A Free House! or The Artist as Craftsman, being the Writings of Walter Richard Sickert.* London: Macmillan, 1947.
Size, Mary. *Prison I Have Known.* London: George Allen & Unwin, 1957.
Sjorquist, Captain Arthur W. *Los Angeles Police Department, 1869-1984.* Los Angeles: LAPD Revolver and Athletic Club, 1984.
Skendi, Stavro (ed.). *Albania.* New York: Mid-European Studies Center, 1956.
Skene, Anthony. *The Ripper Returns.* Manchester, Eng.: Pemberton, 1948.
Skinner, Cornelia Otis. *Elegant Wits and Grand Horizontals.* Boston: Houghton Mifflin, 1962.
Skinner, Otis. *The Mad Folk of the Theater.* New York: Bobbs-Merrill, 1928.
Skogan, W.G. *Issues in the Measurement of Victimization.* Washington, D.C.: Bureau of Justice Statistics, 1981.
_____ (ed.). *Sample Surveys of the Victims of Crime.* New York: Ballinger, 1976.
_____. *Victimization Surveys and Criminal Justice Planning.* Washington, D.C.: National Institute of Law Enforcement and Criminal Justice, 1978.
Skolnick, Jerome H., Forst, Martin L., and Scheiber, Jane L. (eds.). *Crime and Justice in America.* Del Mar, Calif.: Publishers, 1977.
_____, and Currie, Elliot (eds.). *Crisis in American Institutions.* Boston: Little, Brown, 1982.
_____. *House of Cards: Legalization and Control of Casino Gambling.* Boston: Little, Brown, 1978.
_____. *Justice Without Trial.* New York: John Wiley and Sons, 1966.
_____. *The Police and the Urban Ghetto.* Chicago: American Bar Foundation, 1968.
_____. *The Politics of Protest.* New York: Ballantine Books, 1969.
Skorzeny, Otto. *Skorzeny's Special Missions.* London: Robert Hale, 1957.
Slate, Sam, and Cook, Joe. *It Sounds Impossible.* New York: Macmillan, 1965.
Slater, M. *Trial of Jomo Kenyatta.* London: Secker & Warburg, 1955.
Slatin, Rudolph C. *Fire and Sword in the Sudan.* New York: Edward Arnold, 1896.
Sleeman, W.H. *A Journey Through the Kingdom of Oude.* London: Richard Bentley, 1858.
_____. *Ramaseeana, or A Vocabulary of the Peculiar Language Use by the Thugs.* Calcutta, India: G.H. Huttmann, Military Orphan Press, 1836.
_____. *Rambles and Recollections.* London: Hatchard, 1884.
_____. *Report on the Budhuk Dacoits.* Calcutta, India: J.C. Sheriff, 1949.
_____. *Report on the Depredations Committed by the Thug Gangs of Upper and Central India.* Calcutta, India: G.H. Huttmann, Bengal Military Orphan Press, 1840.
_____. *The Thugs or Pansigars of India, Comprising a History of the Rise and Progress of That Extraordinary Fraternity of Assassins.* Philadelphia: Carey & Hart, 1839.
Slingerland, Peter van. *Something Terrible Has Happened: The Account of the Sensational Thalia Massie Affair which Burst from Prewar Hawaii to Incense the Nation.* New York: Harper & Row, 1966.
Sloan, Irving J. *Our Violent Past: An American Chronicle.* New York: Random House, 1970.
Sloan, Stephen. *The Anatomy of Non-Territorial Terrorism.* Gaithersburg, Md.: Bureau of Operations and Research, International Association of Chiefs of Police, 1978.
_____. *Simulating Terrorism.* Norman: University of Oklahoma Press, 1981.
_____. *A Study in Political Violence: The Indonesian Experience.* Chicago: Rand McNally, 1971.

Small, Joe Austell (ed.). *The Best of True West.* New York: Julian Messner, 1964.

Smart, Carol. *Women, Crime and Criminology.* London: RKP, 1977.

Smart, Charles Allen. *Viva Juarez!* London: Eyre & Spottis-woode, 1964.

Smith, Aaron. *The Atrocities of the Pirates.* Guilford, Conn.: Lyons Press, 1999.

Smith, Adam. *Supermoney.* New York: Random House, 1972.

Smith, Alan G.R. *The Government of Elizabethan England.* New York: W.W. Norton, 1967.

Smith, Captain Alexander. *History of the Highwaymen.* London: George Routledge & Sons, 1926.

Smith, Alson Jesse. *Syndicate City: The Chicago Crime Cartel and What to Do about It.* Chicago: Henry Regnery, 1954.

Smith, Ann D. *Women in Prison.* Chicago: Quandrangle, 1962.

Smith, Anthony. *The Newspaper An International History.* Lon-don: Thames & Hudson, 1979.

Smith, Arthur. *Lord Goddard.* London: Weidenfeld and Nicol-son, 1959.

Smith, Arthur D. Howden. *Commodore Vanderbilt: An Epic of American Achievement.* New York: Robert M. McBride, 1927.

_____. *John Jacob Astor: Landlord of New York.* Philadelphia: J.B. Lippincott, 1929.

Smith, Bill. *A Hog Story: From the Aftermire of the Kennedy Assassination.* Washington, D.C.: L'Avant Garde, 1968.

Smith, Bradley F. *Adolf Hitler: His Family, Childhood and Youth.* Stanford, Calif.: Stanford University Press, 1967.

_____. *Reaching Judgment at Nuremberg.* New York: Meridian, 1979.

_____. *The Shadow Warriors.* New York: Basic Books, 1983.

Smith, Bruce. *Police Systems in the U.S.* New York: Harper, 1960.

_____. *The State Police.* Montclair, N.J.: Patterson Smith, 1969.

Smith, C. Alphonso. *Edgar Allan Poe.* Indianapolis, Ind.: Bobbs-Merrill, 1921.

_____. *O. Henry Biography.* Garden City, N.Y.: Doubleday, Page, 1916.

Smith, Carlton. *Killing Season.* New York: Oynx, 1994.

_____. And Guillen, Thomas. *The Search for the Green River Killer.* New York: Oynx, 1990.

Smith, Cecil. *Musical Comedy in America.* New York: Theatre Arts Books, 1950.

Smith, Colin. *Carlos: Portrait of a Terrorist.* New York: Holt, Rinehart & Winston, 1977.

Smith, D.B. *Two Years in the Slave-Pen of Iowa.* Kansas City: H.N. Farey, 1885.

Smith, Dennis Mack. *Garibaldi.* New York: Alfred A. Knopf, 1956.

_____. *A History of Sicily: Modern Sicily (after 1713).* London: Chatto & Windus, 1968.

Smith, Dwight C., Jr. *The Mafia Mystique.* New York: Basic Books, 1975.

Smith, E.W. *Baker Street and Beyond: A Sherlockian Gazetteer.* New York: Pamphlet House, 1940.

_____. *The Incunabular Sherlock Holmes.* New York: Morrison, 1957.

_____. *Profile by Gaslight: An Irregular Reader about the Private Life of Sherlock Holmes.* New York: Simon & Schuster, 1944.

Smith, Edward Henry. *Famous American Poison Mysteries.* New York: Dial Press, 1927.

_____. *Mysteries of the Missing.* New York: Dial Press, 1927.

_____. *You Can Escape.* New York: Macmillan, 1929.

Smith, Elizabeth Oakes. *The Newsboy.* New York: J.C. Derby, 1854.

Smith, Frank Meriweather (ed.). *San Francisco Vigilance Committee of '56.* San Francisco: Barry, Baird, 1883.

Smith, Gene, and Smith, Jayne Barry. *The National Police Gazette.* New York: Simon & Schuster, 1972.

_____. *When the Cheering Stopped.* New York: William Morrow, 1964.

Smith, George Ivan. *Ghosts of Kampala: The Rise and Fall of Idi Amin.* New York: Harper Collins, 1980,

Smith, Gibbs M. *Joe Hill.* Salt Lake City: University of Utah Press, 1969.

Smith, Gerald L.K. *The Mysterious and Unpublicized Facts Behind the Assassination of John F. Kennedy.* Los Angeles: Christian Nationalist Crusade, 1965.

Smith, Greg. Made Men: *The True Rise and Fall of a New Jersey Mob.* New York: Berkley Publishing, 2003.

Smith, H. Allen. *The Life and Legend of Gene Fowler.* New York: William Morrow, 1977.

Smith, Sir Henry. *From Constable to Commissioner: The Story of Sixty Years, Most of Them Misspent.* London: Chatto & Windus, 1910.

Smith, Henry Justin. *Chicago's Great Century, 1833-1933.* Chica-go: Consolidated, 1933.

_____. *Deadlines and Josslyn.* Chicago: Sterling North, 1934.

Smith, Homer W. *Man and His Gods.* Boston: Little, Brown, 1952.

Smith, Horace. *Crooks of the Waldorf.* New York: Macaulay, 1929.

Smith, J.C., and Hogan, B. *Criminal Law.* London: Butterworth, 1973.

Smith, Laurence Dwight. *Counterfeiting, Crime Against the People.* New York: W.W. Norton, 1944.

Smith, Malcolm E. *The Real Marijuana Danger.* Smithtown, N.Y.: Suffolk House, 1981.

Smith, Margaret Bayard. *The First Forty Years of Washington Society.* New York: Charles Scribner's Sons, 1906.

Smith, Matthew Hale. *Sunshine and Shadow in New York.* Hartford, Conn.: J.B. Burr, 1868.

Smith, Mortimer. *William Jay Gaynor: Mayor of New York.* Chicago: Henry Regnery, 1951.

Smith, R. Harris. *OSS: The Secret History of America's First Central Intelligence Agency.* Berkeley: University of Califor-nia Press, 1972.

Smith, Ralph Lee. *The Tarnished Badge.* New York: Thomas Y. Crowell, 1965.

Smith, Randolph Wellford. *Benighted Mexico.* New York: John Lane, 1916.

Smith, Richard Norton. *Thomas E. Dewey and His Times.* New York: Simon & Schuster, 1982.

_____. *An Uncommon Man: The Triumph of Herbert Hoover.* New York: Simon & Schuster, 1984.

Smith, Sydney. *Mostly Murder.* London: Harrap, 1959.

Smith, Wallace. *Prodigal Sons: The Adventures of Christopher Evans and John Sontag.* Boston: Christopher, 1951.

Smith, Wilfred Cantwell. *Islam in Modern History.* Princeton, N.J.: Princeton University Press, 1957.

Smith, Zay N., and Zekman, Pamela. *The Mirage.* New York: Random House, 1980.

Smith-Hughes, Jack. *Eight Studies in Justice.* London: Cassell, 1953.

_____. *Unfair Comment Upon Some Victorian Murder Trials.* London: Cassell, 1951.

_____. *Nine Verdicts on Violence.* London: Cassell, 1956.

_____. *Six Ventures in Villainy.* London: Cassell, 1956.

Smyth, Alfred P. *King Alfred the Great.* New York: Oxford University Press, 1996.

Snares of New York, or Tricks and Traps at the Great Metropolis, Being a Complete, Vivid and Truthful Exposure of the Swin-dles, Humbugs and Pitfalls of the Great City. New York: n.p., 1879.

Snell, Joseph W. *Painted Ladies of the Cowtown Frontier.* Kansas City: Kansas City Posse of Westerners, 1965.

Snow, Edward Rowe. *Mysteries and Adventures Along the Atlantic Coast.* New York: Dodd, Mead, 1948.

_____. *Mysterious Tales of the New England Coast.* New York: Dodd, Mead, 1961.

_____. *Piracy, Mutiny and Murders.* New York: Dodd, Mead, 1959.

_____. *True Tales and Curious Legends.* New York: Dodd, Mead, 1969.

_____. *Unsolved Mysteries of Sea and Shore.* New York: Dodd, Mead, 1963.

Snow, Peter, and Phillips, David. *Leila's Hijack War.* London: Pan, 1965.

Snyder, Louis L., and Morris, Richard B. (eds.). *They Saw it Happen.* Harrisburg, Pa.: Stackpole Books, 1951.

_____, and Morris, Richard B. (eds.). *A Treasury of Great Report-ing.* New York: Simon & Schuster, 1949.

Sobel, Lester A. *Corruption in Business.* New York: Facts on File, 1977.

Sobel, Robert. *The Age of Giant Corporations.* Westport, Conn.: Greenwood Press, 1972.

_____. *The Big Board - A History of the New York Stock Market.* New York: Free Press, Macmillan, 1965.

_____. *The Great Bull Market - Wall Street in the 1920's.* New York: W.W. Norton, 1968.

_____. *The Manipulators.* Garden City, N.Y.: Anchor Press/Dou-bleday, 1976.

_____. *Panic on Wall Street.* New York: Macmillan, 1972.

Sobell, Morton. *On Doing Time.* New York: Bantam, 1976.

The Social Evil in New York City, A Study of Law Enforcement by the Research Committee of the Committee of Fourteen. New York: A.H. Kellogg, 1910.

The Social Evil, With Special Reference to Conditions Existing in the City of New York. A Report Prepared under the Direction of the Committee of Fifteen. New York: G.P. Putnam's Sons, 1912.

Soderman, Harry, and O'Connell, J.J. *Modern Criminal Investigation.* New York: Funk & Wagnalls, 1952.

_____. *Policeman's Lot.* New York: Funk & Wagnalls, 1956.

Solomon, George. *Among the Red Autocrats.* New York: Arno C. Gaebelein, 1935.

Solomon, Peter H. Jr. *Soviet Criminologists and Criminal Policy.* New York: Columbia, 1978.

Soloveytchik, George. *Potemkin: A Picture of Catherine's Russia.* New York: W.W. Norton, 1947.

Solzhenitsyn, Alexander. *The Gulag Archipelago.* New York: Harper & Row, 1973.

Soman, Alfred (ed.). *The Massacre of St. Bartholomew: Reap-praisals and Documents.* The Hague, Neth.: Nijhoff, 1974.

Somerville, Charles. *The Master Rogue.* Philadelphia: J.B. Lippincott, 1935.

Sondern, Frederic, Jr. *Brotherhood of Evil: The Mafia.* New York: Farrar, Straus & Cudahy, 1959.

Sorel, Georges. *Reflections on Violence.* Glencoe, Ill.: Free Press, 1950.

_____. *The Kennedy Legacy.* New York: New American Library, 1970.

Sorenson, Alfred R. *Hands Up! or The History of a Crime.* Omaha, Neb.: Barkalow Brothers, 1877.

Sorenson, Theodore C. *Kennedy.* New York: Harper, 1965.

Soustelle, Jacques. *The Daily Life of the Aztecs on the Eve of the Spanish Conquest.* trans. Patrick O'Brian. New York: Macmillan, 1962.

Souvarine, Boris. *Stalin, A Critical Survey of Bolshevism.* New York: Longmans, Green, 1939.

Sowle, Claude R. (ed.). *Police Power and Individual Freedom.* Chicago: Aldine, 1962.

Soyinka, Wole. *The Open Sore of a Continent: A Personal Narrative of the Nigerian Crisis.* New York: Oxford University Press, 1997.

Spaggiari, Albert. *Fric-Frac.* Boston: Houghton Mifflin, 1979.

Spalding, Thomas Alfred. *Elizabethan Demonology.* Chatto & Windus, 1880.

Spargo, John. *The Bitter Cry of the Children.* New York: Macmil-lan, 1916.

Sparhawk, E.V. *Report of the Trial of Richard Johnson.* New York: n.p., 1829.

Sparks, R.F. *Local Prisons: The Crisis in the English Penal System.* London: Heinemann Educational, 1971.

Sparling, Earl. *Mystery Men of Wall Street.* New York: Green-burg, 1930.

Sparrow, Judge Gerald. *Crimes of Passion.* London: Barker, 1973.

_____. *The Great Abductors.* London: John Long, 1964.

_____. *The Great Assassins.* New York: Arco, 1969.

_____. *The Great Swindlers.* London: John Long, 1959.

_____. *Murder Parade.* London: Robert Hale, 1957.

_____. *Satan's Children.* London: Odhams, 1966.

_____. *Vintage Edwardian Murder.* London: Arthur Barker, 1971.

_____. *Vintage Victorian Murder.* New York: Hart, 1972.

_____. *Women Who Murder.* New York: Abelard-Schuman, 1970.

Sparrow, John. *After the Assassination: A Positive Appraisal of the Warren Report.* New York: Chilmark Press, 1967.

Spear, Percival. *The History of India.* London: Penguin Books, 1965.

Speare, Dr. David. *Jack the Ripper: Crime Scene Investigation.* London: Xlibris, 2003.

Spears, John R. *The American Slave Trade.* New York: Ballan-tine Books, 1960.

Spee, Friedrich von. *Cautio Criminalis*. Weimar, Ger.: H. Bhlaus, 1939.

Speer, Albert. *Infiltration: How Heinrich Himmler Schemed to Build an SS Industrial Empire*. New York: Macmillan, 1981.

_____. *Inside the Third Reich*. New York: Macmillan, 1970.

Speer, W. Harold. *The Secret History of Great Crimes*. London: Arthur H. Stockwell, 1931.

Speidel, Hans. *Invasion 1944: Rommel and the Normandy Cam-paign*. trans. Ian Colvin. Chicago: Regnery, 1950.

Spergel, Irving. *Racketville, Slumtown, Haulberg*. Chicago: University of Chicago Press, 1964.

_____. *Street Gang Work*. Reading, Mass.: Addison-Wesley, 1966.

Spicer, Edward H. *Cycles of Conquest*. Tucson: University of Arizona Press, 1960.

Spiegel, Lawrence D. *A Question of Innocence*. Parsippany, N.J.: Unicorn, 1986.

Spiel, Hilde. *The Congress of Vienna*. trans. Richard H. Weber. Philadelphia: Chilton Book, 1968.

Spiering, Frank. *Lizzie*. New York: Random House, 1984.

_____. *The Man Who Got Capone*. Indianapolis, Ind.: Bobbs-Merrill, 1976.

_____. *Prince Jack: The True Story of Jack the Ripper*. New York: Doubleday, 1978.

Spigelgass, Leonard. *Hello, Hollywood*. Garden City, N.Y.: Doubleday, 1962.

Spink, J.G. Taylor. *Judge Landis and Twenty-Five Years of Baseball*. New York: Thomas Y. Crowell, 1947.

Spinka, Matthew. *A History of Christianity in the Balkans*. Chicago: American Society of Church History, 1933.

Spinks, Sarah. *Cardiac Arrest*. Toronto: Doubleday, 1985.

Spiridovitch, Gen. Alexandre. *Les Dermieres Annees de la Cour de Tsarkoie-Selo*. 2 vols. Paris: Payot, 1928.

_____. *Raspoutine, 1863-1916*. Paris: Payot, 1935.

Spiro, Edward. *From Battenberg to Mountbatten*. London: Arthur Barker, 1966.

Spivak, J.L. *Europe under the Terror*. London: Victor Gollancz, 1936.

Spooner, Mary. *Soldiers in a Narrow Land: The Pinochet Regime in Chile*. Berkeley, Calif.: University of California Press, 1994.

Spray, John Campbell *Chicago's Great South Shore*. Chicago: South Shore, 1930.

Squiers, Granville. *Secret Hiding Places*. Tower, 1971.

Stafford, Jean. *A Mother in History: Mrs. Marguerite Oswald*. New York: Farrar, Straus & Giroux, 1966.

Stafford, Marshall P. *A Life of James Fisk, Jr*. New York: Polhemus, 1873.

Stang, Alan. *They Killed the President: Lee Harvey Oswald Wasn't Alone*. Belmont, Mass.: American Opinion, 1976.

Stanley, Leo. *Men at Their Worst*. New York: D. Appleton-Century, 1940.

Staples, William R. *A Correct Report of the Examination of Rev. Ephraim K. Avery*. Providence, R.I.: Marshall & Brown, 1833.

Starhemberg, E.R. Von. *Between Hitler and Mussolini*. London: Hodder & Stoughton, 1941.

Starkey, Larry. *Wilkes Booth Came to Washington*. New York: Random House, 1976.

Starkey, Marion L. *The Devil in Massachusetts*. New York: Alfred A. Knopf, 1949.

Starr, John. *The Purveyor: Shocking Story of Today's Illicit Liquor Empire*. New York: Holt, Rinehart & Winston, 1961.

Starr, John W. *Lincoln's Last Day*. New York: Frederick A. Stokes, 1922.

Starr, Lando. *Blue Book of San Franciscans in Public Life*. San Francisco: McLaughlin, 1941.

Starrett, Vincent. *The Private Life of Sherlock Holmes*. New York: Macmillan, 1933.

Staudenraus, P.J. (ed.). *Mr. Lincoln's Washington: Selections from the Writings of Noah Brooks, Civil War Correspondent*. New York: Thomas Yoseloff, 1967.

Stave, Bruce M. (ed.). *Urban Bosses, Machines, and Progressive Reformers*. Lexington, Mass · D.C. Heath, 1972.

Stavrianos, Leften S. *Balkan Federation: A History of the Move-ment Toward Balkan Unity in Modern Times*. Northamton, Mass.: Smith College, 1944.

_____. *The Balkans, 1815-1914*. New York: Holt, Rinehart & Winston, 1963.

_____. *The Balkans since 1453*. New York: Holt, Rinehart & Winston, 1958.

_____. *Greece: American Dilemma and Opportunity*. Chicago: Henry Regnery, 1952.

Stead, Christina. *House of All Nations*. New York: Alfred A. Knopf, 1938.

Stead, Philip J. (ed. and trans.). *Second Bureau*. London: Evans, 1959.

_____. *The Memoirs of Lacenaire*. London: Staples, 1952.

_____. *Pioneers in Policing*. Montclair, N.J.: Patterson Smith, 1977.

_____. *The Police of Paris*. London: Staples, 1951.

_____. *Vidocq*. New York: Roy, 1954.

Stead, William T. *If Christ Came to Chicago: A Plea for the Union of All Who Love in the Service of All Who Suffer*. Chicago: Laird & Lee, 1894.

Steadman, Robert F. (ed.). *The Police and the Community*. Baltimore: John Hopkins University Press, 1972.

Stealey, O.O. *Twenty Years in the Press Gallery*. Published by Author, 1906.

Stearn, Gerald Emanuel, and Fried, Albert (eds.). *The Essential Lincoln*. New York: Collier Books, 1962.

Steele, Robert V.P. *The Vanishing Evangelist: The Aimee Semple McPherson Kidnapping Affair*. New York: Viking Press, 1959.

Steffan, Jack. *The Long Fellow: The Story of the Great Irish Patriot, Eamon De Valera*. New York: Macmillan, 1966.

Steffen, Jerome Q. *The American West*. Norman: University of Oklahoma Press, 1979.

Steffens, Lincoln. *Autobiography*. New York: Harcourt, Brace, 1931.

_____. *The Letters of Lincoln Steffens*. New York: Harcourt, Brace, 1938.

_____. *The Shame of the Cities*. New York: McClure, Phillips, 1904.

Steidel, Stephen (ed.). *Missing and Abducted Children: A Law Enforcement Guide*. Arlington, Va.: National Center for Missing and Exploited Children, 1994.

Stein, David Lewis. *Living the Revolution: The Yippies in Chicago*, New York: Bobbs-Merrill, 1969.

Stein, George H. *The Waffen-SS*. Ithaca, N.Y.: Cornell Univer-sity Press, 1966.

Stein, Gertrude. *The Autobiography of Alice B. Toklas*. New York: The Literary Guild, 1933.

_____. *Paris France*. New York: Liveright, 1970.

Steinberg, Alfred. *The Bosses*. New York: Macmillan, 1972.

Stekel, Wilhelm. *Compulsion and Doubt*. New York: Liveright, 1950.

_____. *Peculiarities of Behavior*. New York: Liveright, 1924.

_____. *Sadism and Masochism*. New York: Liveright, 1929.

Stephan, John J. *The Russian Fascists: Tragedy and Farce in Exile, 1925-1945*. New York: Harper & Row, 1978.

Stephen, J.F. *A Digest of Criminal Law*. London: L.F. Struge, 1950.

Stephens, C.L. McCluer. *Famous Crimes and Criminals*. London: Stanley Paul, 1924.

Stephenson, John (ed.). *A Royal Correspondence: Letters of King Edward VII and King George V to Admiral Sir Henry F. Stephenson*. London: Macmillan, 1938.

Stepniak, S.M. (pseud. for Sergei Kravchinsky). *Russia Under the Tsars*. New York: Charles Scribner's Sons, 1885.

_____. *Underground Russia: Revolutionary Profiles and Sketches from Life*. New York; Scribner's, 1883.

Sterling, Claire. *The Terror Network*. New York: Holt, Rinehart & Winston, 1981.

_____. *The Time of Assassins*. New York: Holt, Rinehart & Winston, 1983.

Sterling, Hank. *Famous Western Outlaw-Sheriff Battles*. New York: Rainbow Books, 1954.

Stern, Philip M. *Lawyers on Trial*. New York: Time Books, 1980.

Stern, Philip Van Doren. *The Man Who Killed Lincoln: The Story of John Wilkes Booth and His Part in the Assassination*. New York: Random House, 1939.

Stern, Susan. *With The Weatherman*. New York: Doubleday, 1975.

Steuart, Justin. *Wayne Wheeler, Dry Boss: An Uncensored Biog-raphy of Wayne B. Wheeler*. New York: Fleming H. Revell, 1928.

Stevens, C.L. McCluer. *Famous Crimes and Criminals*. London: Stanley Paul, 1924.

_____. *From Clue to Dock*. London: Stanley Paul, 1927.

Stevens, E.A. *Here Comes Pancho Villa: The Anecdotal History of a Genial Killer*. New York: Frederick A. Stokes, 1930.

Stevens, Dr. L.L. *Lives, Crimes and Confessions of the Assassins*. Troy, N.Y.: Daily Times Stream Printing Establishment, 1865.

Stevens, Shane. *By Reason of Insanity*. London: Weidenfeld & Nicolson, 1979.

Stevenson, John, and Cook, Chris. *The Slump - Society and Politics During the Depression*. London: Jonathan Cape, 1977.

Stevenson, Robert Louis. *The Strange Case of Dr. Jekyll and Mr. Hyde*. London: Longmans, Green, 1886.

Stevenson, William. *A Man Called Intrepid*. New York: Harcourt, Brace, Jovanovich, 1976.

_____. *90 Minutes at Entebbe*. New York: Bantam Books, 1976.

Steward, A.J.D. (ed.). *The History of the Bench and Bar of Missouri*. St. Louis: Legal, 1898.

Stewart, A.T.Q. *The Ulster Crisis*. London: Faber Paperback, 1967.

Stewart, Bob. *No Remorse*. New York: Pinnacle, 1996.

Stewart, C.P., and Stolman, A. *Toxicology: Mechanisms and Analytical Methods*. New York: Academic Press, 1960-1961.

Stewart, Caroline Taylor. *The Origin of Werewolf Superstitions*. Columbia: University of Missouri Press, 1909.

Stewart, Charles J., and Kendell, Bruce (eds.). *A Man Named John F. Kennedy: Sermons on His Assassination*. Glen Rock, N.J.: Paulist Press, 1964.

Stewart, Desmond. *Cairo: 5500 Years*. New York: Thomas Y. Crowell, 1968.

_____. *Young Egypt*. London: Wingate, 1958.

Stewart, Robert C. *Identification and Investigation of Organized Criminal Activity*. Houston, Texas: National College of District Attorneys, 1980.

Stewart, William. *Jack the Ripper: A New Theory*. London: Quality Press, 1939.

Stilwell, Joseph W. *The Stilwell Papers*. New York: Sloane, 1948.

Stimson, Henry L. *The Diary of Henry L. Stimson* and *The Papers of Henry L. Stimson*. New Haven, Conn.: Yale University Library, 1973.

Stinchcombe, A. *Crime and Punishment: Changing Attitudes in American Society*. San Francisco: Jossey-Bass, 1980.

Stirling, Nora. *Your Money or Your Life*. Indianapolis, Ind.: Bobbs-Merrill, 1974.

Stock, Ernest. *Israel on the Road to Sinai, 1949-1956*. Ithaca, N.Y.: Cornell University Press, 1967.

Stockdale, Tom. *The Life and Times of Al Capone*. New York: Chelsea House, 1997.

Stocking, George, and Watkins, Myron. *Cartels in Action*. New York: Twentieth Century Fund, 1946.

Stoddard, Henry Luther. *As I Knew Them*. New York: Harper & Brothers, 1927.

_____. *Horace Greeley: Printer, Editor, Crusader*. New York: G.P. Putnam's Sons, 1946.

Stoddard, Theodore Lothrop. *Master of Manhattan: The Life of Richard Croker*. New York: Longmans Green, 1931.

Stoddard, William L. *Financial Racketeering and How To Stop It*. New York: Harper & Brothers, 1931.

Stoddard, William O. *The Volcano Under the City*. New York: Fords, Howard & Hulbert, 1887.

Stoddart, Charles. *Bible John*. Edinburgh: Paul Harris, 1980.

Stoker, Bram (Abraham). *Dracula*. New York: Signet, 1997.

_____. *Famous Impostors*. New York: Sturgis & Walton, 1910.

Stoker, Charles. *Thicker 'N Thieves*. Santa Monica, Calif.: Sidereal, 1949.

Stokes, Hugh. *Madame de Brinvilliers*. London: Thomas Nelson, 1912.

Stokoe, Dr. J. *With Napoleon at St. Helena*. London: n.p., 1902.

Stoller, Robert J. *Perversion: The Erotic Form of Hatred*. New York: Random House, 1975.

Stone, Candace. *Dana and the Sun*. New York: Dodd, Mead, 1938.

Stone, I.F. *The Haunted Fifties*. New York: Vintage Books, 1969.

_____. *The Killings at Kent State.* New York: New York Review Book, 1971.

_____. *The Truman Era.* New York: Vintage Books, 1973.

Stone, Irving. *Clarence Darrow for the Defense.* Garden City, N.Y.: Doubleday, 1941.

_____. *Earl Warren.* New York: Prentice-Hall, 1948.

Stone, Dr. James W. *Report of the Trial of Professor John W. Webster.* Boston: Phillips, Sampson, 1850.

Stone, William L. *History of New York City.* New York: Virtue & Yorston, 1872.

Stoneham, C.T. *Mau Mau.* London: Museum Press, 1953.

_____. *Out of Barbarism.* London: Museum Press, 1955.

Storry, Richard. *The Double Patriots: A Study of Japanese Nation-alism.* Boston: Houghton Mifflin, 1957.

_____. *A Modern History of Japan.* New York: Penguin Books, 1960.

Stout, Ernest. *The Younger Brothers.* Chicago: Dramatic, 1902.

_____. *The Younger Brothers' Last Raid.* Chicago: Dramatic, 1902.

_____. *The Youngers' Last Stand.* Chicago: Dramatic, 1902.

_____. *The Youngers Out West.* Chicago: Dramatic, 1902.

Stout, F.E. *Rube Burrows; or, Life, Exploits and Death of the Bold Train Robber.* Aberdeen, Miss.: n.p., 1890.

Stow, E.W. *The Native Races of South Africa.* Cape Town, S. Afri.: Juta, 1910.

Stow, John. *The Survey of London.* London: J.M. Dent, 1912.

Strachey, Lytton. *Eminent Victorians.* London: Collins, 1920.

_____. *Queen Victoria.* New York: Harcourt, Brace, 1921.

Strakhovsky, L.I. *Alexander I of Russia.* New York: W.W. Norton, 1947.

Strange and Mysterious Crimes. New York: MacFadden, 1929.

Stratton, David H. (ed.). *The Memoirs of Albert B. Fall.* El Paso: University of Texas Press, 1966.

Strauss, Patricia. *Bevin and Co.* New York: G.P. Putnam's Sons, 1941.

_____. *Cripps, Advocate Extraordinary.* New York: Duell, Sloan & Pearce, 1942.

Street-Porter, Janet. *Scandal.* New York: Dell, 1981.

Streetwalker. London: The Bodley Head, 1959.

Strickland, Stephen Parks (ed.). *Hugo Black and the Supreme Court.* Indianapolis, Ind.: Bobbs-Merrill, 1967.

Strictures on the Case of Ephraim K. Avery. Providence, R.I.: William Simons, Jr., 1833.

Strik-Strikfeldt, Wilfried. *Against Hitler and Stalin.* New York: John Day, 1973.

Strong, George Templeton. *Diary, 1820-1875.* 4 vols. New York: Macmillan, 1952.

Stuart, Hix C. *The Notorious Ashley Gang.* Stuart, Fla.: St. Lucie Printing, 1928.

Stuart, John Leighton. *Fifty Years in China.* New York: Ran-dom, 1946.

Stuart, William H. *The 20 Incredible Years.* Chicago: M.A. Donohue, 1935.

Stuckey, G.B. *Evidence for the Law Enforcement Officer.* New York: McGraw-Hill, 1968.

Stuerwald, John E. *Fire and Arson Investigator.* International Association of Arson Investigators, 1977.

Stuller, Jay. *Alcatraz, the Prison.* San Francisco: Sunbelt, 1999.

Suchey, John T. and Tipton, Howard O. *Arson: America's Malig-nant Crime.* Columbus, Ohio: Battelle Columbus Laborator-ies, 1976.

Suda Teichi. *Kazami Akira and Those Times.* Tokyo: Shobo, 1965.

Suetonius Tranquillus, Gaius. *The Twelve Caesars.* trans. Robert Graves. Baltimore, Md.: Penguin Books, 1957.

Sugden, Philip. *The Complete History of Jack the Ripper.* New York: Carroll & Graf, 1994.

Suhrawardy, Sir Abdullah al-Mamun al-. *The Sayings of Moham-med.* London: John Murray, 1941.

Sukhanov, N.N. *Russian Revolution, 1917.* New York: Oxford University Press, 1955.

Sullivan, Edward Dean. *Chicago Surrenders: A Sequel to Rattling the Cup on Chicago Crime.* New York: Vanguard Press, 1930.

_____. *The Fabulous Wilson Mizner.* New York: Henkle, 1935.

_____. *Rattling the Cup on Chicago Crime.* New York: Vanguard Press, 1929.

_____. *The Snatch Racket.* New York: Vanguard Press, 1932.

Sullivan, Gerard, and Aronson, Harvey. *High Hopes: The Amity-ville Murders.* New York: Coward, McCann & Geohegan, 1981.

Sullivan, Lawrence. *Prelude to Panic.* Washington, D.C.: States-man Press, 1936.

Sullivan, Mark. *Our Times: The United States.* 6 vols. New York: Charles Scribner's Sons, 1926-1935.

Sullivan, Robert. *The Disappearance of Dr. Parkman.* New York: Prentice-Hall, 1960.

Sullivan, Terry, with Maiken, Peter T. *Killer Clown.* New York: Grosset & Dunlap, 1983.

Sullivan, W.A. *The Industrial Worker in Pennsylvania 1800-1840.* Harrisburg: Pennsylvania Historical and Museum Commis-sion, 1955.

Sullivan, William C. *The Bureau.* New York: W.W. Norton, 1979.

Summers, Anne. *Damned Whores and God's Police.* Ringwood, N.J.: Penguin, 1975.

Summers, Anthony. *Conspiracy.* New York: McGraw-Hill, 1980.

_____. *Goddess: The Secret Lives of Marilyn Monroe.* New York: Macmillan, 1985.

Summers, Marvin R., and Barth, Thomas E. (eds.). *Law and Order in a Democratic Society.* New York: Charles E. Merrill, 1970.

Summers, Montague. *An Examination of Witches.* London: J. Rodker, 1929.

_____. *The Geography of Witchcraft.* London: Routledge & Kegan Paul, 1927.

_____. *The History of Witchcraft and Demonology.* New Hyde Park, N.Y.: University Books, 1956.

_____. *Popular History of Witchcraft.* New York: E.P. Dutton, 1937.

_____. *The Vampire in Europe.* New York: E.P. Dutton, 1929.

_____. *The Vampire: His Kith and Kin.* New York: E.P. Dutton, 1929.

_____. *The Werewolf.* New York: E.P. Dutton, 1934.

_____. *Witchcraft and Black Magic.* New York: Rider, 1934.

Sumner, Benedict H. *Peter the Great and the Emergence of Russia.* New York: Macmillan, 1951.

_____. *Peter the Great and the Ottoman Empire.* Oxford, Eng.: Blackwell, 1949.

_____. *Russia and the Balkans, 1870-1880.* London: Milford, 1937.

_____. *Tsardom and Imperialism in the Far and Middle East.* Oxford, Eng.: Oxford University Press, 1940.

Sumner, Charles. *The Crime Against Kansas.* Washington, D.C.: Buell & Blanchard, 1856.

The Sun's Guide to New York. New York: New York Sun, 1893.

Susman, Jackwell (ed.). *Crime and Justice, 1971-1972.* New York: AMS Press, 1974.

Susskind, Richard. *The Crusades.* New York: Ballantine, 1962.

Sussman, Les, and Bordwell, Sally. *The Rapist File.* New York: Chelsea House, 1981.

Sutherland, Edwin H. *Criminology.* Philadelphia: J.D. Lippin-cott, 1924.

_____. *On Analyzing Crime.* Chicago: University of Chicago Press, 1973.

_____, and Cressy, Donald R. *Principles in Criminology.* Philadel-phia: J.D. Lippincott, 1966.

_____, and Cressey, Donald R. *Principles of Criminology.* Phila-delphia: J.B. Lippincott, 1955.

_____. *The Professional Thief.* Chicago: University of Chicago Press, 1937.

_____ (ed.). *White Collar Crime.* New York: Holt, Rinehart & Winston, 1949.

Sutherland, Sidney. *Ten Real Murder Mysteries.* New York: G.P. Putnam's Sons, 1929.

Suthers, John W., and Shupp, Gary L. *Fraud & Deceit: How To Stop Being Ripped Off.* New York: Arco, 1982.

Suttles, Gerald D. *The Social Order of the Slum.* Chicago: University of Chicago Press, 1968.

Sutton, Charles Warden. *The New York Tombs; Its Secrets and Mysteries.* New York: U.S., 1874.

Sutton, Denys. *Walter Sickert: A Biography.* London: Michael Joseph, 1976.

Sutton, Fred Ellsworth. *Hands Up! Stories of the Six Gun Fighters of the Old West.* Indianapolis, Ind.: Bobbs-Merrill, 1926.

Sutton, Willie, and Reynolds, Quentin. *I, Willie Sutton.* New York: Farrar, Straus, & Young, 1953.

_____. *Where the Money Was.* New York: Viking Press, 1976.

Svensson, Arne, and Wendell, Otto. *Crime Detection.* London: Cleaver-Hume, 1955.

Sveri, K. *Kriminalitet og Older.* Stockholm: Almquist & Wiksell, 1960.

Swados, Harvey. *Standing up for the People: The Life and Work of Estes Kefauver.* New York: E.P. Dutton, 1972.

Swain, John. *A History of Torture.* New York: Award, 1969.

Swallow, Alan (ed.). *The Wild Bunch.* Denver: Sage Books, 1966.

Swanberg, William A. *Citizen Hearst: A Biography of William Randolph Hearst.* New York: Charles Scribner's Sons, 1961.

_____. *Dreiser.* New York: Charles Scribner's Sons, 1965.

_____. *Jim Fisk, The Career of An Improbable Rascal.* New York: Charles Scribner's Sons, 1961.

_____. *Luce and His Empire.* New York: Charles Scribner's Sons, 1972.

Swanson, C., Chamelin, N., and Territo, L. *Criminal Investigation.* Santa Monica, Calif.: Goodyear, 1977.

Sweet, P.R. *Mussolini and Dollfuss.* London: Victor Gollancz, 1948.

Swing, Raymond G. *Forerunners of American Fascism.* New York: Julian Messner, 1935.

Swire, Joseph. *Albania: the Rise of a Kingdom.* London: Wil-liams & Ungate, 1929.

Swisher, Carl Brent (ed.). *Selected Papers of Homer Cummings.* New York: Charles Scribner's Sons, 1939.

Sykes, Gresham M. *Crime and Society.* New York: Random House, 1956.

_____. *Criminology.* New York: Harcourt, Brace, Jovanovich, 1978.

_____. *The Future of Crime.* Rockville, Md.: National Institute of Mental Health, 1980.

_____. *The Society of Captives.* New York: Atheneum, 1969.

Syme, A.V. *The Assassins.* Sydney, Aus.: Horwitz, 1967.

Symon, J.D. and Bensusan, S.L. *The Renaissance and Its Makers.* London: T.C. & E.C. Jack, 1913.

Symonds, John. *The Great Beast: The Life and Magic of Aleister Crowley.* London: McDonald, 1971.

Symonds, John Addington. *The Age of Despots.* London: Smith, Elder, 1898.

Symons, Julian. *Horatio Bottomley.* London: Cresset, 1955.

_____. *A Reasonable Doubt.* London: Cresset Press, 1960.

Syrett, Harold C. (ed.). *American Historical Documents.* New York: Barnes & Noble, 1960.

_____ (ed.). *The City of Brooklyn, 1865-1898.* New York: Columbia University Press, 1944.

Szarowski, John (ed.). *Storyville Portraits; Photographs Taken from the New Orleans Red Light District by E.J. Bellocq.* New York: Museum of Modern Art, 1970.

Szechi, Daniel. *The Jacobites: Britain and Europe, 1688-1788.* Manchester, Eng.: Manchester University, 1994.

Szulc, Tad. *Fidel: A Critical Portrait.* New York: Avon Books, 2000.

Tabori, Paul. *Crime and the Occult.* New York: Taplinger, 1974.

Taft, Donald R. *Criminology.* New York: J.B. Lippincott, 1954.

Tailbitzer, Bill. *Too Much Blood.* New York: Vantage Press, 1978.

Talbot, F.L. (ed.). *St. Louis Police Department.* St. Louis: Woodward & Tiernan, n.d.

Talese, Gay. *Honor Thy Father.* New York: World, 1971.

_____. *The Kingdom and the Power.* New York: World, 1966.

_____. *Thy Neighbor's Wife.* Greenwich, Conn.: Fawcett Crest Books, 1979.

Tallant, Robert. *Murder in New Orleans.* London: William Kimber, 1952.

_____. *Ready to Hang.* New York: Harper & Brothers, 1952.

_____. *The Romantic New Orleanians.* New York: E.P. Dutton, 1950.

_____. *Voodoo in New Orleans.* New York: Macmillan, 1946.

Talmage, T. DeWitt. *The Abominations of Modern Society.* New York: Adams, Victor, 1872.

_____. *The Masque Torn Off.* Chicago: J. Fairbanks, 1880.
Tammany, A Patriotic History. New York: New York County Democratic Committee, 1924.
Tamura Yoshio (ed.). *Secret History of the Greater East Asia War.* 12 vols. Tokyo: Fuji Shoen, 1953.
Tanay, F. *The Murderers.* Indianapolis, Ind.: Bobbs-Merrill, 1976.
Tanenbaum, Robert, and Rosenberg, Philip. *Badge of the Assassin.* New York: E.P. Dutton, 1979.
_____, and Greenberg, Peter S. *The Piano Teacher.* New York: New American Library, 1987.
Tang Leang-li. *The Inner History of the Chinese Revolution.* New York: E.P. Dutton, 1930.
Tannenbaum, Frank. *Crime and the Community.* New York: Columbia University Press, 1938.
_____. *The Mexican Agrarian Revolution.* New York: Macmillan, 1929.
_____. *Mexico: The Struggle for Peace and Bread.* New York: Alfred A. Knopf, 1950.
_____. *Peace by Revolution: An Interpretation of Mexico.* New York: Columbia University Press, 1933.
_____. *Wall Shadows.* New York: G.P. Putnam's Sons, 1922.
Tanner, Louise. *All the Things We Were.* Garden City, N.Y.: Doubleday, 1968.
Tanner, R.E.S. *The Witch Murders in Sukumaland - A Sociological Commentary. Crime in Africa Series No. 4.* Uppsala, Swed.: Scandinavian Institute of African Studies, 1970.
Tanon, Celestin Louis. *Histoire des tribunaux de l'Inquisition en France.* Paris: L. Larose & Forcel, 1893.
Tapi, Victor L. *France in the Age of Louis XIII and Richlieu.* trans. D. McN. Lockie. New York: Macmillan, 1974.
_____. *The Rise and Fall of the Habsburg Monarchy.* trans. Stephen Hardman. New York: Frederick A. Praeger, 1971.
Tappan, Paul W. *Crime, Justice, and Correction.* New York: McGraw-Hill, 1960.
_____. *The Habitual Sex Offender.* Trenton: State of New Jersey, 1950.
Targ, William. *The Great American West.* New York: World, 1946.
Tarsaidze, Alexander. *Czars and Presidents: The Story of a Forgotten Friendship.* New York: McDowell, Obolensky, 1958.
Tastmona, Thothnu N. *It Is As If: Curious Aspects Concerning the Matter of President Kennedy's Death.* New York: Thothmona Book, 1966.
Tateno Nobuyuki. *Army Factions in the Reign of Hirohito: An Anthology of Upheaval.* Tokyo: Kodansha, 1963.
Taube, Otto von. *Rasputin.* Munich, Ger.: C.H. Beck, 1925.
Taubman, Bryna. *Lady Cop.* New York: Warner Books, 1987.
Taubman, William. *Khrushchev: The Man and His Era.* New York: W. W. Norton, 2003.
Tawney, R.H. *The Acquisitive Society.* New York: Harcourt, 1920.
Taylor, A.J.P. *Beaverbrook.* New York: Simon & Schuster, 1972.
_____. *Bismarck: The Man and the Statesman.* New York: Alfred A. Knopf, 1955.
_____. *The Course of German History.* New York: Coward-McCann, 1946.
_____. *The Habsburg Monarchy, 1809-1918: A History of the Austrian Empire and Austria-Hungary.* New York: Macmil-lan, 1949.
Taylor, Alan R. *Prelude to Israel: An Analysis of Zionist Diplo-macy 1897-1947.* New York: Philosophical Library, 1959.
Taylor, Arnold H. *American Diplomacy and the Narcotics Traffic, 1900-1939.* Durham, N.C.: Duke University Press, 1969.
Taylor, Edmund L. *The Fall of Dynasties: The Collapse of the Old Order, 1905-1922.* Garden City, N.Y.: Doubleday, 1963.
Taylor, George E. *The Struggle for North China.* New York: Institute of Pacific Relations, 1940.
Taylor, Ian, Walton, Paul, and Young, Jock. *Critical Criminology.* London: Routledge & Kegan Paul, 1975.
_____. *The New Criminology.* New York: Harper & Row, 1973.
Taylor, John Russell. *Hitch: The Life and Times of Alfred Hitch-cock.* New York: Pantheon, 1978.
Taylor, Rex. *Assassination.* London: Hutchinson, 1961.
_____. *Michael Collins.* London: Hutchinson, 1958.
Taylor, Telford. *Grand Inquest.* New York: Ballantine, 1961.
_____. *Sword and Swastika: Generals and Nazis in the Third Reich.* Chicago: Quadrangle Books, 1969.
Tebbel, John. *An American Dynasty: The Story of the McCormicks, Medills and Pattersons.* New York: Doubleday, 1947.
_____. *The American Magazine: A Compact History.* New York: Hawthorn Books, 1969.
_____. *The Compact History of the American Newspaper.* New York: Hawthorn Books, 1963.
_____. *The Life and Good Times of William Randolph Hearst.* New York: E.P. Dutton, 1952.
Teeters, Negley K. *The Cradle of the Penitentiary: The Walnut Street Jail at Philadelphia 1773-1835.* Philadelphia: Temple University Press, 1955.
_____, and Hedblom, Jack H. *"...Hang By the Neck..."* Springfield, Ill.: Charles C. Thomas, 1967.
_____. *Scaffold and Chair: A Compilation of Their Use in Pennsyl-vania, 1682-1962.* Philadelphia: Pennsylvania Prison Society, 1963.
_____. *They Were in Prison: A History of the Pennsylvania Prison Society.* Philadelphia: John C. Winston, 1937.
Tefft, B.F. *Life of Daniel Webster.* Philadelphia: Porter & Coates, 1854.
Teichmann, Howard. *Smart Aleck: The Wit, World and Life of Alexander Woollcott.* New York: William Morrow, 1976.
Teitelbaum, Louis W. *Woodrow Wilson and the Mexican Revolu-tion, 1913-1916: A History of United States-Mexican Relations from the Murder of Madero until Villa's Provocation Across the Border.* New York: Exposition Press, 1967.
Temin, Peter. *History of Serbia.* London: G. Bell & Sons, 1917.
Templewood, Viscount. *The Shadow of the Gallows.* London: Victor Gollancz, 1951.
Tenemura Sako. *Secret Diary of Imperial Headquarters.* Tokyo: Diamond Sha, 1952.
Tenenti, Alberto. *Piracy and the Decline of Venice.* Berkeley: University of California Press, 1967.
Teresa, Vincent. *My Life in the Mafia.* New York: Doubleday, 1973.
Terhune, Albert Payson. *Famous Hussies of History.* New York: World, 1943.
Terraine, John. *The Great War, 1914-1918.* New York: Macmil-lan, 1965.
Terret, Charles. *Traffic in Innocents.* New York: Bantam Books, 1961.
Terrett, Courtenay. *Only Saps Work: A Ball for Racketeering.* New York: Vanguard Press, 1930.
The Terrible Haystack Murder: Life and Trial of the Rev. Ephraim K. Avery for the Murder of the Young and Beautiful Miss Sarah M. Cornell, a Factory Girl of Fall River, Mass. Philadelphia: Barclay, 1876.
The Terrible Tragedy at Washington: The Assassination of President Lincoln. Port Tobacco, Md.: James L. Barbour, 1988.
Terrot, Charles. *Traffic in Innocents: The Shocking Story of White Slavery in England.* New York: E.P. Dutton, 1960.
Terry, Maury. *The Ultimate Evil.* New York: Doubleday, 1987.
Tetsuma Hashimoto. *The Emperor and the Officers of the Rebel-lion.* Tokyo: Nihon Shuho-sha, 1954.
Thaw, Harry K. *The Traitor.* New York: Dorrance, 1926.
Thayer, J.B. *Cases on Evidence.* Cambridge, n.p., 1900.
Theoharis, Athan (ed.). *The FBI: A Comprehensive Reference Guide.* New York: Checkmark Books, 1999.
Thernstrom, Stephan. *The Other Bostonians: Poverty and Progress in the American Metropolis, 1880-1970.* Cambridge, Mass.: Harvard University Press, 1973.
Thicknesse, S.G. *Arab Refugees: A Study of Resettlement Pos-sibilities.* London: Chatham House, 1949.
Thirty Years of Lynching in the U.S., 1889-1918. New York: NAACP, Arno Press, 1969.
Thomas, Andrew. *Air Rage: Crisis in the Sky.* Amherst, N. Y.: Prometheus Books, 2001.
Thomas, Benjamin P. *Abraham Lincoln.* New York: Alfred A. Knopf, 1952.
_____, and Hyman, Harold M. *Stanton: The Life and Times of Lincoln's Secretary of War.* New York: Alfred A. Knopf, 1962.
Thomas, Bob. *King Cohn.* New York: G.P. Putnam's Sons, 1967.
_____. *Selznick.* New York: Doubleday, 1970.
_____. *Thalberg.* New York: Doubleday, 1969.
_____. *Winchell.* Garden City, N.Y.: Doubleday, 1971.
Thomas, Charles W., and Hepburn, John R. *Crime, Criminal Law, and Criminology.* Dubuque, Iowa: William C. Brown, 1983.
_____, and Peterson, David M. *Prison Organization and Inmate Subcultures.* Indianapolis, Ind.: Bobbs Merrill, 1977.
Thomas, Dana L. *The Plungers and the Peacocks.* New York: G.P. Putnam's Sons, 1967.
Thomas, David. *Seek Out the Guilty.* London: John Long, 1969.
Thomas, Gordon and Morgan, and Witts, Max. *The Day the Bubble Burst: A Social History of the Wall Street Crash of 1929.* Garden City, N. Y.: Doubleday, 1979.
Thomas, Gordon. *Gideon's Spies: The Secret History of the Mossad.* New York: Griffen, 2000.
Thomas, Hugh. *The Slave Trade.* New York: Touchstone, 1997.
Thomas, J.E. *The English Prison Officer Since 1850: A Study in Conflict.* London: Routledge & Kegan Paul, 1972.
Thomas, Lately. *A Debonair Scoundrel.* New York: Holt, Rinehart & Winston, 1962.
_____. *The First President Johnson.* New York: William Morrow, 1968.
_____. *The Mayor Who Mastered New York: The Life and Opinions of William J. Gaynor.* New York: William Morrow, 1969.
_____. *Storming Heaven.* New York: William Morrow, 1970.
_____. *The Vanishing Evangelist.* New York: Viking Press, 1959.
Thomas, P.W. *Sir John Berkenhead, 1617-1679.* Oxford, Eng.: Clarendon Press, 1969.
Thomas, Piri. *Down These Mean Streets.* New York: New American Library, 1967.
Thomas, Steve, and Davis, Don. *JonBenet: Inside the Ramsay Murder Investigation.* New York: St. Martin's, 2000.
The Thomas Street Tragedy: Trial of Robinson! Murderer of Ellen Jewett. New York: n.p., 1836.
Thomasius, Christian. *De Crimine Magiae.* Halle, Ger.: Litteris Salfeldiamis, 1730.
Thompson, Sir Basil. *The Criminal.* London: Hodder & Stough-ton, 1925.
_____. *The Story of Scotland Yard.* London: Grayson & Grayson, 1925.
_____. *Voyage of the H.M.S. Pandora.* London: Francis Edwards, 1915.
Thompson, C.J.S. *Poison Mysteries in History.* Philadelphia: J.B. Lippincott, 1932.
_____. *Poison Mysteries Unsolved.* London: Hutchinson, 1937.
_____. *Poisons and Poisoners.* London: Harold Shaylor, 1931.
Thompson, Craig, and Raymond, Allen. *Gang Rule in New York.* New York: Dial Press, 1940.
Thompson, Fred D. *At That Point in Time: The Inside Story of the Senate Watergate Committee.* New York: Quadrangle Books, 1975.
Thompson, G.S. *Catherine the Great and the Expansion of Russia.* New York: Macmillan, 1950.
Thompson, George G. *Bat Masterson, The Dodge City Years.* Topeka: Kansas State Printing Plant, 1943.
Thompson, Henry T. *Ousting the Carpetbagger from South Carolina.* Columbia, S.C.: R.L. Bryan Press, 1926.
_____. *Hell's Angels: A Strange and Terrible Saga.* New York: Random House, 1966.
Thompson, J.M. *The French Revolution.* New York: Oxford University Press, 1966.
_____. *Louis-Napoleon and the Second Empire.* Oxford, Eng.: Blackwell, 1954.
_____. *Napoleon Bonaparte, His Rise and Fall.* Oxford, Eng.: Blackwell, 1958.
Thompson, James Westfall, et al. *The Civilization of the Renais-sance.* New York: Frederick Ungar, 1929.
Thompson, John Eric Sidney. *Maya Hieroglyphic Writing: An Introduction.* Norman: University of Oklahoma Press, 1960.

_____. *The Rise and Fall of Maya Civilization.* Norman: Univer-sity of Oklahoma Press, 1954.
Thompson, Josiah. *Six Seconds in Dallas.* New York: Bernard Geis Associates, 1967.
Thompson, Robert Lowe. *History of the Devil.* London: K. Paul, Trench, Trubner, 1929.
Thompson, Thomas. *Blood and Money.* Garden City, N.Y.: Doubleday, 1976.
_____. *Serpentine.* Garden City, N.Y.: Doubleday, 1979.
Thomson, Elizabeth McClure (ed.). *The Chamberlain Letters.* New York: G.P. Putnam's Sons, 1965.
Thomson, George C. *The Quest for Truth: A Quizzical Look at the Warren Report-Or How President Kennedy Really Was Assassinated.* Glendale, Calif.: Published by Author, 1964.
Thomson, Helen. *Murder at Harvard.* Boston: Houghton Mifflin, 1971.
Thorndike, Joseph J. *The Very Rich: A History of Wealth.* New York: American Heritage, 1976.
Thorndike, Thaddeus. *Lives and Exploits of the Daring Frank and Jesse James.* Baltimore: I.& M. Ottenheimer, 1909.
Thornley, Kerry Wendell. *Oswald.* Chicago: Allied, 1965.
Thorp, Arthur. *Calling Scotland Yard.* London: Allan Wingate, 1954.
Thorp, Raymond W., and Bunker, Robert. *Crow Killer.* New York: Signet, 1958.
Thorwald, Jrgen. *The Century of the Detective.* New York: Harcourt, Brace & World, 1964.
_____. *Crime and Science.* Orlando, Fla.: Harcourt, Brace & World, 1967.
_____. *Dead Men Tell Tales.* London: Thames & Hudson, 1966.
_____. *The Marks of Cain.* London: Thames & Hudson, 1965.
_____. *Proof of Poison.* London: Thames & Hudson, 1966.
Thrasher, Frederick. *The Gang: A Study of 1,313 Gangs in Chicago.* Chicago: University of Chicago Press, 1927.
Throup, D.W. *Economic and Social Origins of Mau Mau, 1945-1953.* London: James Currey, 1988.
Thucydides. *The ·Peloponnesian Wars.* trans. Hubert Wetmore Wells. Baltimore: Penguin Books, 1959.
Thurber, James. *The Years with Ross.* New York: Grosset & Dunlap, 1957.
Thurston, Gavin. *The Clerkenwell Riot.* London: George Allen & Unwin, 1967.
_____. *Coroner's Practice.* London: Butterworth, 1958.
Thyssen, Fritz. *I Paid Hitler.* Port Washington, N.Y.: Kennikat, 1971.
Tidyman, Ernest. *Big Bucks.* New York: W.W. Norton, 1982.
Tiedemann, Arthur. *Modern Japan.* Princeton, N.J.: D. Van Nostrand, 1962.
Tierney, Kevin. *Darrow, A Biography.* New York: Thomas Y. Crowell, 1979.
Tiffany, Francis. *Life of Dorthea Lynde Dix.* New York: Hough-ton Mifflin, 1890.
Tiffany, Lawrence P., McIntyre, Donald M., and Rottenburg, Daniel L. *Detection of Crime.* Boston: Little, Brown, 1967.
Tilden, Samuel J. *Letters and Literary Memorials.* New York: Harper & Brothers, 1908.
_____. *The New York City Ring, Its Origin, Maturity and Fall.* New York: Press of J. Polhemus, 1873.
Tilea, R.V. *The Last Century of Roumania History.* Cambridge, Eng.: n.p., 1943.
Tilghman, Zoe A. *Marshal of the Last Frontier.* Glendale, Calif.: Arthur H. Clark, 1949.
_____. *Outlaw Days.* Oklahoma City: Harlow, 1926.
_____. *Spotlight: Bat Masterson and Wyatt Earp as U.S. Deputy Marshals.* San Antonio, Texas: Naylor, 1960.
Tilley, Arthur. *The Dawn of the French Renaissance.* Cambridge, Eng.: Cambridge University Press, n.d.
_____. *Medieval France.* Cambridge, Eng.: Cambridge University Press, 1922.
Tilly, Richard. *The Rebellious Century, 1830-1930.* Cambridge, Mass.: Harvard University Press, 1975.
Tiltman, Hessell. *The Terror in Europe.* London: Jarrolds, 1931.
Timperlaey, H.J. *Japanese Terror in China.* New York: Modern Age Books, 1958.
Tindall, George B. *America: A Narrative History.* New York: W.W. Norton, 1988.
_____. *The Emergence of the New South, 1913-1945.* Baton Rouge: Louisiana State University Press, 1967.
Tinnin, David B. *Hit Team.* London: Weidenfeld & Nicolson, 1976.
Tisdall, E.E.P. *Marie Fedorovna: Empress of Russia.* New York: John Day, 1958.
_____. *Queen Victoria's Private Life.* London: Jarrolds, 1961.
_____. *Royal Destiny: The Royal Hellenic Cousins.* New York: S. Paul, 1955.
Tobias, Fritz. *The Reichstag Fire.* New York: G.P. Putnam's Sons, 1964.
Tobias, J.J. *Crime and Industrial Society in the 19th Century.* New York: David McKay, 1965.
_____. *Urban Crime in Victorian England.* New York: Schocken, 1972.
Toch, Hans, Grant, J. Douglas, and Galvin, Raymond T. *Agents of Change: A Study in Police Reform.* New York: John Wiley & Sons, 1975.
_____. *Living in Prison: The Ecology of Survival.* New York: Free Press, 1977.
_____. *Police, Prisons, and the Problem of Violence.* Rockville, Md.: National Institute of Mental Health Center for Studies of Crime and Delinquency, 1977.
_____. *Psychology of Crime and Criminal Justice.* New York: Holt, Rinehart & Winston, 1979.
_____. *Violent Men.* Chicago: Aldine, 1969.
Toland, John. *Adolf Hitler.* Garden City, N.Y.: Doubleday, 1976.
_____. *The Dillinger Days.* New York: Random House, 1963.
_____. *The Last 100 Days.* New York: Random House, 1966.
_____. *The Rising Sun: The Decline and Fall of the Japanese Empire, 1936-1945.* New York: Random House, 1970.
Toledano, Ralph de. *J. Edgar Hoover: The Man in His Time.* New Rochelle, N.Y.: Arlington House, 1973.
_____. *Lament for a Generation.* New York: Farrar, Straus & Cudahy, 1960.
_____, and Lasky, V. *The Seeds of Treason: The Strange Case of Alger Hiss.* New York: Funk & Wagnalls, 1956.
_____. *Spies, Dupes and Diplomats.* New Rochelle, N.Y.: Arlington House, 1967.
Tolischus, Otto D. *Tokyo Record.* New York: Reynal & Hitchcock, 1943.
Tolstoy, Nicolai. *The Night of the Long Knives.* New York: Ballantine Books, 1972.
Tompkins, Maj. Frank. *Chasing Villa.* Harrisburg, Pa.: Military Service, 1934.
Tompkins, Stuart R. *Russia Through the Ages.* New York: Prentice-Hall, 1940.
_____. *The Russian Intelligentsia: Makers of the Revolutionary State.* Norman: University of Oklahoma Press, 1957.
_____. *The Russian Mind from Peter the Great through the En-lightenment.* Norman: University of Oklahoma Press, 1953.
Topping, Peter, and Ritchie, Jean. *Topping: The Autobiography of the Police Chief in the Moors Murder Case.* London: Angus and Robertson, 1989.
Touhy, Roger. *The Stolen Years.* Cleveland, Ohio: Pennington, 1959.
Toulmin, Col. H.A. *With Pershing in Mexico.* Harrisburg, Pa.: Military Service, 1935.
Towle, Virginia Rowe. *Vigilante Woman.* South Brunswick, N.Y.: A.S. Barnes, 1966.
Towler, J.E. *The Police Role in Racial Conflicts.* Springfield, Ill.: Charles C. Thomas, 1964.
Towne, Charles Hanson. *The Rise and Fall of Prohibition.* New York: Macmillan, 1923.
Townsend, Edward W. *A Daughter of the Slums.* New York: Lovell, Coryell, 1895.
Townsend, George Alfred. *The Life, Crime and Capture of John Wilkes.* New York: Dick & Fitzgerald, 1865.
Townsend, John D. *New York in Bondage.* New York: n.p., 1901.
Townsend, W., and Townsend, L. *Black Cap: Murder Will Out.* London: Albert E. Marriott, 1930.
Tozer, Basil. *Confidence Crooks and Blackmailers.* Boston: Stratford, 1930.
Trachtman, Paul. *The Gunfighters.* New York: Time-Life Books, 1974.
Traffic in Opium and Other Dangerous Drugs. Washington, D.C.: U.S. Treasury Dept., Bureau of Narcotics, 1940.
Train, Arthur. *The Confessions of Artemas Quibble.* New York: Charles Scribner's Sons, 1925.
_____. *Courts, Criminals, and Camorra.* New York: Charles Scribner's Sons, 1922.
_____. *Courts and Criminals.* New York: Charles Scribner's Sons, 1925.
_____. *My Day in Court.* New York: Charles Scribner's Sons, 1939.
_____. *On the Trail of the Bad Men.* New York: Charles Scrib-ner's Sons, 1925.
_____. *The Prisoner at the Bar.* New York: Charles Scribner's Sons, 1925.
_____. *True Stories of Crime from the District Attorney's Office.* New York: McKinley, Stone & MacKenzie, 1908.
_____. *Tutt and Mr. Tutt.* New York: Charles Scribner's Sons, 1925.
_____. *Yankee Lawyer: The Autobiography of Ephraim Trutt.* New York: Charles Scribner's Sons, 1943.
Traini, Robert. *Murder for Sex.* London: William Kimber, 1960.
Transcript of the Record of the Trial of Niccolo Sacco and Bar-tolomeo Vanzetti. New York: Henry Holt, 1929.
Trask, Willard. *Joan of Arc, Self Portrait.* New York: Stackpole Sons, 1936.
Trasler, G. *The Explanation of Criminality.* London: Routledge & Kegan Paul, 1962.
The Travels of Marco Polo. London: Everyman's Library, 1954.
Traver, Robert. *Anatomy of a Murder.* New York: Saint Martin's Press, 1958.
Treadwell, C.A.L. *Notable New Zealand Trials.* New Plymouth, New Zealand: T. Avery & Sons, 1936.
Trease, Geoffrey. *Portrait of a Cavalier: William Cavendish, First Duke of Newcastle.* New York: Taplinger, 1979.
Treasury Department, Special Narcotics Committee. *Traffic in Narcotic Drugs: Report of the Special Committee Investigation Appointed March 25, 1918, by the Secretary of Treasury.* Washington, D.C.: U.S. Government Printing Office, 1919.
Trebach, Arnold S. *The Great Drug War: Radical Proposals That Could Make America Safe Again.* New York: Macmillan, 1987.
_____. *The Heroin Solution.* New Haven, Conn.: Yale University Press, 1982.
Trelease, Allen W. *White Terror.* New York: Harper & Row, 1971.
Trenery, Walter N. *Murder in Minnesota.* St. Paul: Minnesota Historical Society, 1962.
Trepaca, Karen L. *The Trial of Gangster Al Capone: A Headline Court Case.* Berkeley Heights, N. J.: Enslow Publishers, 2001.
Trevelyan, George Macaulay. *English Social History.* New York: Longmans, Green, 1942.
_____. *Grey of Fallodon: The Life and Letters of Sir Edward Grey.* Boston: Houghton Mifflin, 1937.
_____. *History of England.* New York: Harper, 1962.
Trevelyan, Janet Penrose. *A Short History of the Italian People.* London: George Allen & Unwin, 1956.
Trevor-Roper, H.R. *Blitzkrieg to Defeat: Hitler War Directives 1939-1945.* New York: Holt, Rinehart & Winston, 1971.
_____. *The Bormann Letters.* London: Weidenfeld & Nicolson, 1954.
_____. *The Crisis of the Seventeenth Century.* New York: Harper & Row, 1966.
_____. *The European Witch-Craze of the 16th and 17th Centuries.* Harmondsworth, Eng.: Penguin, 1969.
_____. (ed.). *The Golden Age of Europe.* New York: Bonanza Books, 1987.
_____. *Hermit of Peking.* New York: Alfred A. Knopf, 1977.
_____. *Hitler's Table Talk, 1941-44.* London: Weidenfeld & Nicolson, 1953.
_____. *The Last Days of Hitler.* New York: Crowell-Collier, 1962.
Trial of the Assassins and Conspirators for the Murder of Abraham Lincoln. Port Tobacco, Md.: James L. Barbour, 1981.
Trial and Sentence of Thomas J. Wansley and Charles Gibbs for Murder and Piracy Aboard the Brig Vineyard. New York: Christian Brown, 1831.
The Trial at Large of the Rev. Ephraim K. Avery for the Wilful Murder of Sarah Maria Cornell. New York: n.p., 1833.

Trial, Conviction and Sentence of Richard Johnson. New York: C. Brown, n.d.

Trial of German Major War Criminals. 22 parts. London: H.M. Stationery Office, 1946-1950.

The Trial of Herman W. Mudgett. Philadelphia: George T. Bisel, 1897.

Trial of John H. Surratt in the Criminal Court for the District of Columbia. 2 vols. Washington D.C.: U.S. Government Printing Office, 1867.

Trial of John H. Surratt...on an Indictment for Murder of President Lincoln. Washington D.C.: R. Sutton, 1867.

The Trial of Rev. Ephraim K. Avery. New York: n.p., 1833.

Trial of Richard Johnson for the Murder of Mrs. Ursula Newman. New York: J. M'Cleland, 1829.

Trial of Stephen Arnold. Cooperstown, N.Y.: E. Phinney, 1805.

Trillin, Calvin. *Killings*. New York: Penguin Books, 1984.

Trilling, Diana. *Mrs. Harris, the Death of the Scarsdale Diet Doctor*. New York: Harcourt Brace Jovanovich, 1981.

Triplett, Col. Frank. *History, Romance and Philosophy of Great American Crimes and Criminals*. Hartford, Conn.: Park, 1885.

_____. *The Life, Times, and Treacherous Death of Jesse James*. St. Louis: J.H. Chambers, 1882.

Trohan, Walter. *Political Animals*. Garden City, N.Y.: Double-day, 1975.

Trollope, Frances. *Great Crimes and Criminals in America*. New York: R.K. Fox, 1881.

Trotsky, Leon. *The Defence of Terrorism*. London: George Allen & Unwin, 1921.

_____. *Diary in Exile, 1935*. trans. Elena Zarudnaya. Cambridge, Mass.: Harvard University Press, 1958.

_____. *History of the Russian Revolution*. 3 vols. Ann Arbor: University of Michigan Press, 1957.

_____. *Lenin*. New York: Grosset & Dunlap, 1960.

_____. *My Life*. New York: Charles Scribner's Sons, 1930.

_____. *Stalin*. New York: Harper & Brothers, 1941.

_____. *Terrorism and Communism*. Ann Arbor, University of Michigan Press, 1961.

Trotter, William, and Newsom, Robert. *Deadly Kin*. New York: St. Martin's, 1988.

Troup, E. *The Home Office*. London: John Murray, 1938.

Truc, Gonzague. *Madame de Montespan*. Paris: A. Colin, 1936.

Trufanov, Sergyei. *The Mad Monk of Russia*. New York: Century, 1918.

The Truly Remarkable Life of the Beautiful Helen Jewett Who was So Mysteriously Murdered. Philadelphia: Barclay, 1878.

Truman, Harry S. *Memoirs*. 2 vols. New York: Doubleday, 1955.

Trumble, Alfred. *Crooked Life in New York, The Mysteries of Metropolitan Crime and Criminals Unveiled!* New York: R. K. Fox, 1882.

_____. *Famous Frauds: Or the Sharks of Society*. New York: R.K. Fox, 1883.

_____. *Faro Exposed, or The Gambler and His Prey*. New York: R.K. Fox, 1883.

_____. *The Female Sharpers of New York*. New York: R.K. Fox, 1882.

Trumpener, Ulrich. *Germany and the Ottoman Empire, 1914-1918*. Princeton, N.J.: Princeton University Press, 1968.

Truth Stranger Than Fiction, Lydia Sherman, Confession of the Arch Murderess of Connecticut. Philadelphia: T.R. Callender, 1873.

Trzenbinski, E. *The Kenya Pioneers*. New York: W.W. Norton, 1986.

Tschuppik, Karl. *The Reign of the Emperor Franz Josef*. London: G. Bell, 1930.

Tsien, T.H. *Written on Bamboo and Silk*. Chicago: University of Chicago Press, 1962.

Tsunoda Ryusaku, de Bary, William Theodore, and Keene, Donald, (comps.). *Sources of Japanese Tradition*. New York: Columbia University Press, 1958.

Tsurumi Shunsuke, et. al. *Japan's Century*. 10 vols. Tokyo: Chikuma Shobo, 1964.

Tuchman, Barbara W. *A Distant Mirror*. New York: Alfred A. Knopf, 1978.

_____. *The Guns of August*. New York: Macmillan, 1962.

_____. *The Proud Tower*. New York: Macmillan, 1966.

_____. *Stilwell and the American Experience in China 1911-45*. New York: Macmillan, 1971.

Tucker, William. *Vigilante, the Backlash Against Crime in America*. New York: Stein & Day, 1985.

Tuckerman, Bayard (ed.). *The Diary of Philip Hone*. New York: Dodd, Mead, 1889.

Tuckerman, Bayard. *Lafayette*. New York: Dodd, Mead, 1889.

Tufts, Henry. *The Autobiography of a Criminal*. New York: Duffield, 1930.

Tugwell, Rexford G. *Battle for Democracy*. New York: Columbia University Press, 1935.

_____. *The Brains Trust*. New York: Viking Press, 1968.

_____. *The Democratic Roosevelt*. Garden City, N.Y.: Double-day, 1957.

Tuke, A.W., and Gillman, R.J.H. *Barclays Bank Ltd., 1926-1969*. London: Privately Printed, 1972.

Tuker, Sir Francis. *The Yellow Scarf, The Story of the Life of Thuggee*. London: J.M. Dent & Sons, 1961.

Tulchin, S.H. *Intelligence and Crime*. Chicago: University of Chicago Press, 1939.

Tullett, Tom. *Portrait of a Bad Man*. New York: Rinehart, 1956.

_____. *Strictly Murder*. New York: St. Martin's Press, 1979.

Tully, Andrew. *CIA, the Inside Story*. Greenwich, Conn.: Faw-cett, 1962.

_____. *Era of Elegance*. New York: Funk & Wagnalls, 1947.

_____. *The FBI's Most Famous Cases*. New York: William Morrow, 1965.

_____. *Inside the FBI*. New York: McGraw-Hill, 1980.

_____. *Inside Interpol*. New York: Walker, 1965.

_____. *Treasury Agent*. New York: Simon & Schuster, 1958.

Tully, Grace. *FDR, My Boss*. New York: Charles Scribner's Sons, 1949.

Turberville, Arthur Stanley. *Medieval Heresy and the Inquisition*. London: George Allen & Unwin, 1920.

Turk, Austin T. *Criminality and the Legal Order*. Chicago: Rand McNally, 1969.

_____. *Political Criminality*. Beverly Hills, Calif.: Sage, 1982.

Turkus, Burton B., and Feder, Sid. *Murder, Inc.: The Story of the Syndicate*. New York: Farrar, Straus & Young, 1951.

Turner, F.J. *The Frontier in American History*. New York: Henry Henry Holt, 1920.

Turner, J.W.C. (ed.). *Kenny's Outlines of Criminal Law*. Cam-bridge, Eng.: Cambridge University Press, 1952.

Turner, John Kenneth. *Barbarous Mexico*. Chicago: C.H. Kerr, 1911.

_____. *Hands Off Mexico*. New York: Rand School of Social Science, 1920.

Turner, John Peter. *The North-West Mounted Police, 1873-1893*. 2 vols. Ottawa, Ontario, Can.: Edmund Cloutier, 1950.

Turner, Justin G., and Levitt, Linda. *Mary Todd Lincoln: Her Life and Letters*. New York: Alfred A. Knopf, 1972.

Turner, Louis. *Invisible Empires*. New York: Harcourt, Brace, Jovanovich, 1970.

Turner, Mertyn. *Safe Lodging*. London: Hutchinson, 1961.

Turner, Nat. *The Confessions of Nat Turner*. Richmond, Va.: T.R. Gray, 1832.

Turner, R.F. *Forensic Science and Laboratory Techniques*. Springfield, Ill.: Charles C. Thomas, 1949.

Turner, Thomas R. *Beware the People Weeping: Public Opinion and the Assassination of Abraham Lincoln*. Baton Rouge: Louisiana State University Press, 1982.

Turner, Wallace. *Gambler's Money*. Boston: Houghton Mifflin, 1965.

Turner, William W. *Hoover's FBI*. New York: Dell, 1970.

_____. *The Police Establishment*. New York: G.P. Putnam's Sons, 1968.

Turrou, Leon G. *Where My Shadow Falls*. Garden City, N.Y.: Doubleday, 1949.

Tuska, Jon. *The Detective in Hollywood*. Garden City: Double-day, 1978.

Tutorow, Norman E. *Leland Stanford: Man of Many Careers*. Menlo Park, Calif.: Pacific Coast, 1971.

Tuttle, Charles R. *History of Kansas*. Madison, Wis.: Interstate, 1876.

Tuttle, William M., Jr. *Race Riot: Chicago in the Red Summer of 1919*. New York: Atheneum, 1970.

Twain, Mark [Samuel Clemens]. *Following the Equator: A Journey Around the World*. New York: Harper & Brothers, 1899.

_____. *Life on the Mississippi*. Boston: J.R. Osgood, 1883.

_____. *Roughing It*. Hartford, Conn.: American, 1872.

Twentieth Century Task Force on Criminal Sentencing. *Fair and Certain Punishment*. New York: McGraw-Hill, 1976.

Two Centuries Growth of American Law, 1701-1901. New York: Charles Scribner's Sons, 1902.

Twyman, H.W. *The Best Laid Schemes*. London: Harold Shayler, 1931.

Tylen, Alice Felt. *The Foreign Policy of James G. Blaine*. Min-neapolis: University of Minnesota Press, 1927.

Tyler, Froom. *Gallows Parade*. London: Lorat Dickson, 1933.

Tyler, Gus (ed.). *Organized Crime in America*. Ann Arbor: University of Michigan Press, 1962.

Tyler, Samuel. *Memoir of Roger Brooke Taney*. Baltimore: John Murphy, 1872.

Tynan, P.J.P. *The Irish National Invincibles and Their Times*. New York: Irish National Invincible, 1894.

Uelmen, Gerald F., and Haddox, Victor G. (eds.). *Drug Abuse and the Law*. New York: Clark, Boardman, 1983.

_____. *Varieties of Police Policy*. Beverly Hills, Calif.: Institute on Law and Urban Studies, 1972.

Uhnak, Dorothy. *Policewoman*. New York: Simon & Schuster, 1964.

Ulam, Adam B. *The Bolsheviks*. New York: Macmillan, 1965.

_____. *Stalin: The Man and His Era*. New York: Viking, 1973.

_____. *Titoism and the Cominform*. Cambridge, Mass.: Harvard University Press, 1952.

Ular, Alexander. *A Russo-Chinese Empire*. Westport, Conn.: Greenwood, 1975.

Ullman, Leonard P., and Krasner, Leonard. *A Psychological Approach to Abnormal Behavior*. Englewood Cliffs, N.J.: Prentice-Hall, 1975.

Umashima Takeshi. *Secret History of Hidden Factional Feuds in the Army*. Tokyo: Kyodo, 1946.

Umbreit, Kenneth B. *Our Eleven Chief Justices: A History of the Supreme Court in Terms of Their Personalities*. New York: Harper & Row, 1940.

Underhill, H.C. *Criminal Evidence*. New York: Bobbs-Merrill, 1973.

Ungar, Sanford J. *FBI*. Boston: Little, Brown, 1975.

Uniform Crime Reports for the United States. Washington, D.C.: U.S. Government Printing Office, 1976.

United Nations Department of Economic and Social Affairs. *Capital Punishment*. New York: United Nations, 1962.

United Nations Educational, Scientific, and Cultural Organization. *All Men Are Brothers: Life and Thoughts of Mahatma Gandhi*. Paris: UNESCO, 1958.

United States Advisory Commission on Intergovernmental Relations. *State-Local Relations in the Criminal Justice System*. Washington D.C.: U.S. Government Printing Office, 1971.

United States Army Air Forces. *Mission Accomplished: Interroga-tions of Japanese Industrial, Military and Civil Leaders of World War II*. Washington, D.C.: U.S. Government Printing Office, 1946.

United States Bureau of Labor. *The Slums of Baltimore, Chicago, New York, and Philadelphia*. Washington D.C.: U.S. Gov-ernment Printing Office, 1894.

United States Bureau of Prisons. *Handbook of Correctional Institution Design and Construction*. Washington, D.C.: n.p., 1949.

_____. *Recent Prison Construction 1950-1960*. Washington, D.C.: n.p., 1960.

United States Central Intelligence Agency. *International and Transnational Terrorism: Diagnosis and Prognosis*. Langley, Va.: U.S. Central Intelligence Agency, 1977.

United States Corps of Engineers. *Navigation Bulletins*. Mem-phis, Tenn.: U.S. Army Engineer District, 1961.

United States Department of Commerce, Bureau of the Census. *Prisoners in State and Federal Prisons and Reformatories, 1927*. Washington D.C.: U.S. Government Printing Office, 1931.

United States Department of Justice, Federal Bureau of Investiga-tion. *Uniform Crime Reports for the United States*. Washing-ton, D.C.: U.S. Government Printing Office, 1950-1970.

United States Department of Justice, Law Enforcement Assisstance Administration. *Expenditure and Employment Data for the Criminal Justice System, 1968-1969.* Washington, D.C.: U.S. Government Printing Office, 1970.

_____. *National Jail Census.* Washington, D.C.: U.S. Govern-ment Printing Office, 1971.

United States Eighty-sixth Congress, second session. House of Representatives. Committee of the Judiciary. *Hearing...on H.R. 870 to Abolish the Death Penalty.* Washington, D.C.: U.S. Government Printing Office, 1960.

United States Government. *Combatting Crime in the United States.* Washington, D.C.: U.S. Government Printing Office, 1967.

United States Government Commission on Violence. *Causes and Prevention of Violence.* Washington, D.C.: U.S. Government Printing Office, n.d.

United States Government General Services Administration. *Transportation of Explosive Compounds, title 49.* Washington, D.C.: General Administration Archives, n.d.

United States House of Representatives. *Pardon of Richard M. Nixon and Related Matters.* Washington, D.C.: n.p., 1974.

_____. *Report of the Select Committee on Assassinations: Findings and Recommendations.* Washington D.C.: U.S. Government Printing Office, 1979.

_____. *Select Committee on Assassinations.* Washington D.C.: U.S. Government Printing Office, 1979.

United States House of Representatives, Select Committee on Crime. Hearings: *Crime in America??Aspects of Organized Crime, Court Delay, and Juvenile Justice.* Washington, D.C.: U.S. Government Printing Office, 1970.

_____. Hearings: *Crime in America??A Mid-American View.* Washington, D.C.: U.S. Government Printing Office, 1969.

_____. Hearings: *Crime in America??Response of a Midsouth Community.* Washington, D.C.: U.S. Government Printing Office, 1970.

_____. Hearings: *Crime in America??The Nation's Capital.* Washington, D.C.: U.S. Government Printing Office, 1970.

_____. Hearings: *The Improvement and Reform of Law Enforce-ment and Criminal Justice in the United States.* Washington, D.C.: U.S. Government Printing Office, 1969.

_____. Select Committee on International Relations. Hearings: *PLO Commitmen, Compliance and the Terrorist Threat to Israel.* Washington, D. C.: U. S. Government Printing Office, 1996.

United States National Archives. *Inventory of the Records of the President's Commission on the Assassination of President Kennedy.* Washington D.C.: General Services Administra-tion, 1973.

_____. *Public Papers of the Presidents of the United States.* Washington D.C.: U.S. Government Printing Office, 1962-1964.

United States Senate. *Final Report of the Select Committee to Study Governmental Operations With Respect to Intelligence Activities.* Washington D.C.: U.S. Government Printing Office, 1976.

_____. *Memorial Addresses in the Congress of the United States and Tributes in Eulogy of John Fitzgerald Kennedy, A Late President of the United States.* Washington D.C.: U.S. Government Printing Office, 1964.

United States Senate, Committee on the District of Columbia. *Report of the Advisory Panel Against Armed Violence.* Wash-ington, D.C.: U.S. Government Printing Office, 1965.

_____. *Staff Study on Drug Abuse in the Washington Area.* Washington, D.C.: U.S. Government Printing Office, 1969.

United States Senate, Committee on the Judiciary, Subcommittee on Criminal Laws and Procedures. *Controlling Crime.* Washington, D.C.: U.S. Government Printing Office, 1967.

United States Senate, Committee on the Judiciary. *Serial Murders.* Washington, D. C.: U. S. Government Printing Office, 1984.

Unterberger, B. M. *America's Siberian Expedition, 1918-1920.* Durham, N.C.: Duke University Press, 1956.

Unterecker, John. *Voyager: A Life of Hart Crane.* New York: Farrar, Straus & Giroux, 1969.

Ure, P.N. *The Origin of Tyranny.* New York: Russell & Russell, 1962.

Urquhart, Lena M. *Roll Call: The Violent and Lawless.* Denver: Golden Bell Press, 1967.

Urstein, Maury. *Leopold and Loeb: A Psychiatric-Psychological Study.* New York: n. p., 1924.

Uviller, H. *The Processes of Criminal Justice: Investigation.* St. Paul, Minn.: West, 1979.

Uyehara, Cecil H. (comp.) *Checklist of Archives in the Japanese Ministry of Foreign Affairs, Tokyo, Japan 1868-1945.* Washing-ton, D.C.: Library of Congress, 1954.

Vaillant, George C. *Aztecs of Mexico.* Garden City, N.Y.: Doubleday, 1941.

Vale, M.G.A. *Charles VII.* Berkeley: University of California Press, 1974.

Valentine, Alan. *Lord Stirling.* New York: Oxford University Press, 1969.

_____. *Vigilante Justice.* New York: Reynal, 1956.

Valentine, Lewis J. *Nightstick.* New York: Dial Press, 1947.

Valentine, Stephen. *The Black Panther Story.* London: New English Library, 1976.

Valera, Paolo. *Mussolini.* Milan, Italy: La Folla, 1924.

Valler, Walton, and McNear, Robert. *The Night Chief.* South Bend, Ind.: Regnery/Gateway, 1980.

Van Cise, Philip S. *Fighting the Underworld.* Boston: Houghton Mifflin, 1936.

Van Den Bruck. *Germany's Third Reich.* New York: Europe, 1940.

Van Den Haag, Ernest, and Conrad, John P. *The Death Penalty: A Debate.* New York: Plemum Press, 1983.

_____. *Political Violence and Civil Disobedience.* New York: Harper & Row, 1972.

_____. *Punishing Criminals: Concerning a Very Old and Painful Question.* New York: Basic Books, 1978.

Van Deusen, Glyndon G. *Henry Clay.* Boston: Little, Brown, 1937.

_____. *Horace Greeley: Nineteenth-Century Crusader.* Philadelphia: University of Pennsylvania Press, 1953.

_____. *The Jacksonian Era 1828-1848.* New York: Harper & Brothers, 1958.

_____. *Thurlow Weed: Wizard of the Lobby.* Boston: Little, Brown, 1947.

_____. *William Henry Seward.* New York: Oxford University Press, 1967.

Van Devander, Charles W. *The Big Bosses.* New York: Howell, Soskin, 1944.

Van de Water, Frederic F. *The Real McCoy.* Garden City, N.Y.: Doubleday, Doran, 1931.

Van Doren, Carl. *Benjamin Franklin.* New York: Viking Press, 1938.

_____. *The Great Rehearsal.* New York: Viking Press, 1948.

_____. *Mutiny in January.* New York: Viking Press, 1943.

_____. *Secret History of the American Revolution.* New York: Kelley, 1973.

Van Every, Dale. *Ark of Empire.* New York: New American Library, 1963.

Van Every, Edward. *Sins of America as "Exposed" by the Police Gazette.* New York: Frederick A. Stokes, 1931.

_____. *Sins of New York.* New York: Frederick A. Stokes, 1930.

Van Hagen, Victor Wolfgang. *The Ancient Sun Kingdoms of the Americas.* Cleveland: World, 1961.

_____. *The Incas, People of the Sun.* Cleveland: World, 1961.

Van Hoffman, Eric. *A Venom in the Blood.* New York: Fine, 1990.

Van Horn, Maj. Gen Carl. *Soldiering for Peace.* New York: David McKay, 1967.

Van Slingerland, Peter. *Something Terrible Has Happened.* New York: Harper & Row, 1966.

Van Winkle, Marshall, and Wolff, H. *Sixty Famous Cases.* Summertown, Tenn.: Book Manufacturing, 1956.

Varaut, Jean-Marc. *L'Abominable Dr. Petiot.* Paris: Balland, 1974.

Vares, Florencia. *Coup! Allende's Last Day.* New York: Stein & Day, 1975.

Varneck, Elena, and Fisher, H.H. *The Testimony of Kolchak and other Siberian Materials.* Palo Alto: Stanford University Press, 1935.

Vasiliev, A.A. *History of the Byzantine Empire.* Madison: University of Wisconsin Press, 1928.

_____. *Justin the First.* Cambridge, Mass.: Harvard University Press, 1950.

Vassilyev, A.T. *The Okhrana: The Russian Secret Police.* Philadel-phia: J.B. Lippincott, 1930.

Vatikiotis, P.J. *The Egyptian Army in Politics.* Bloomington: Indiana University Press, 1961.

Vaughan, Joe. *The Only True History of Frank James, Written by Himself.* Pine Bluff, Ark.: Sarah E. Snow, 1926.

Vaughn, Miles W. *Under the Japanese Mask.* London: Lovat Dickson, 1937.

Vedder, H. *Southwest Africa in Early Times.* New York: Barnes & Noble, 1966.

Veheyne, C. *Horror.* London: Brown, Watson, 1962.

Velie, Lester. *Desperate Bargain.* New York: Readers Digest Press, 1977.

Venturi, Franco. *Roots of Revolution.* New York: Alfred A. Knopf, 1960.

Venys, L. *A History of the Mau Mau Movement.* Prague, Czech.: Charles University, 1970.

Venzke, Ben, and Ibrahim, Aimee. *The Al Qaeda Threat: An Analytical Guide to Al Qaeda's Tactics and Targets.* New York: Tempest, 2003.

Vera Estaol, Jorge. *Carranza and His Bolshevik Regime.* Los Angeles: Wayside Press, 1920.

Verkko, Veli. *Homicides and Suicides in Finland and Their Dependence on National Character.* Copenhagen: G.E.C. Gads Forlag, 1951.

Vermorel, Auguste-Jean-Marie. *La Police contemporaire.* Paris: Lebigre-Duquesne, 1864.

Vernadsky, George. *Ancient Russia.* New Haven, Conn.: Yale University Press, 1943.

_____. *Ancient Russia and Kievan Russia.* New Haven, Conn.: Yale University Press, 1948.

_____. *A History of Russia.* New Haven, Conn.: Yale University Press, 1961.

_____. *Mongols and Russians.* New Haven, Conn.: Yale Univer-sity Press, 1953.

_____. *The Origins of Russia.* Oxford, Eng.: Clarendon Press, 1959.

_____. *Political and Diplomatic History of Russia.* Boston: Houghton Mifflin, 1936.

Verner, Gerald (ed.). *The Prince of Darkness.* New York: Rider, 1951.

Vetter, H.J., and Silverman, I.J. *The Nature of Crime.* Philadel-phia: W.B. Saunders, 1978.

Viano, Emilio C., and Reiman, Jeffrey H. (eds.). *The Police in Society.* Lexington, Mass.: Lexington Books, 1975.

_____. *Victims and Society.* Washington D.C.: Visage, 1976.

Vice Commission of Chicago. *The Social Evil in Chicago.* Chicago: Gunthorp-Warren, 1911.

Vicinus, Martha (ed.). *Suffer and Be Still: Women in the Victorian Age.* Bloomington: Indiana University Press, 1972.

Victor, Orville J. *History of American Conspiracies.* New York: James D. Torrey, 1863.

Vicua, Francisco Orrego (ed.). *Chile: The Balanced View: A Recopilation of Articles about the Allende Years and After.* Santiago: University of Chile Institute of International Affairs, 1975.

Vidal, Jean Marie. *Bullaire de l'Inquisition francaise.* Paris: Librarie Letouzey et Ane, 1913.

Vidocq, Eugene-Franois. *Les Memoires de Vidocq.* Paris: Editions Baudelaire, 1967.

Viereck, George Sylvester. *The Kaiser on Trial.* London: Duckworth, 1938.

Viereck, Peter. *Metapolitics: The Roots of the Nazi Mind.* New York: G.P. Putnam's Sons, 1961.

Viglotti, Gabriel R. *The Girls of Nevada.* Secaucus, N.J.: Citadel Press, 1975.

Villano, Anthony. *Brick Agent.* Chicago: Quadrangle Books, 1977.

Villard, Henry. *Memoirs of Henry Villard, Journalist and Financier, 1835-1900.* Boston: Houghton Mifflin, 1904.

Villard, Oswald Garrison. *Some Newspapers and Newspaper-Men.* Alfred A. Knopf, 1933.

Villari, Luigi. *The Awakening of Italy.* London: Methuen, 1924.

______, *The Fascist Experiment.* London: Faber & Gwyer, 1926.

Villasenor, Victor. *Jury.* Boston: Little, Brown, 1977.

Villehardouin, Geoffrey de. *Chronicles of the Crusades.* London: Penguin Books, 1963.

Villeneuve, Roland. *Le Diable: Erotologie de Satan.* Paris: Jean-Jacques Pauvert, 1963.

_____. *Gilles de Rays: Une Grande Figure Diabolique.* Verviers, Belg.: Editions Grard & Cie., 1973.

_____. *Le Poison et les empoisonneurs celebres.* Paris: La Palatine, 1960.

Villette, John. *The Annals of Newgate; or, Malefactors Register.* London: J. Wenman, 1776.

Villiers, Alan. *Posted Missing.* New York: Charles Scribner's Sons, 1956.

Villiers, Elizabeth. *Riddles of Crime.* London: Werner Laurie, 1928.

Villiers, Gerard de. *The Imperial Shah.* Bosto: Little, Brown, 1976.

Vincent, Arthur (ed.). *Lives of Twelve Bad Women.* Boston: L. C. Page, 1897.

Vincent, Louis, and Binns, Clare. *Gilles de Rais: The Original Bluebeard.* Boston: Small, Maynard, 1926.

Vining, Elizabeth Gray. *Return to Japan.* Philadelphia: J.B. Lippincott, 1960.

_____. *Windows for the Crown Prince.* Philadelphia: J.B. Lippin-cott, 1952.

Vinson, J. Chal. *Thomas Nast: Political Cartoonist.* Athens: University of Georgia Press, 1967.

Vioux, Marcelle. *Henry of Navarre.* trans. J.L. May. New York: E.P. Dutton, 1937.

Viroubova, Anna Aleksandrovna. *Memories of the Russian Court.* New York: Macmillan, 1923.

Vitray, Laura. *The Great Lindbergh Hullabaloo: An Unorthodox Account.* New York: William Fargo, 1932.

Vizetelly, Ernest Alfred. *The Anarchists.* New York: John Lane, 1911.

_____. *Bluebeard.* London: Chatto & Windus, 1902.

_____. *Court Life of the Second French Empire.* New York: Charles Scribner's Sons, 1907.

Vogeler, R., and Sanders, E. *R. Vogeler, E. Sanders and Their Accomplices Before the Criminal Court.* Budapest, Hungary: Hungarian State Publishing House, 1950.

Vogt, Hannah. *The Burden of Guilt: A Short History of Germany, 1914-1945.* New York: Oxford University Press, 1964.

The Volcano Under the City. New York: Ford, Howard, and Hulbert, 1887.

Vold, George B. *Theoretical Criminology.* New York: Oxford University Press, 1958.

Volgelsang, Thilo. *Reichswehr, Staat und NSDAP.* Stuttgart, Ger.: Deutsch Verlagsanstalt, 1962.

Vollmer, August, and Parker, Alfred E. *Crime, Crooks and Cops.* New York: Funk & Wagnalls, 1937.

_____, *The Criminal.* New York: Foundation Press, 1949.

_____. *The Police and Modern Society.* Montclair, N.J.: Smith, 1971.

Volta, Ornella. *The Vampire.* trans. Raymond Rudorff. London: Tandem, 1965.

Volz, Joseph, and Bridge, Peter J. (eds.). *The Mafia Talks: Here are the Secret Cosa Nostra Coversations Recorded by the FBI.* Greenwich, Conn.: Fawcett, 1969.

Vopicka, Charles J. *Secrets of the Balkans.* Chicago: Rand McNally, 1921.

Vorres, Ian. *The Last Grand Duchess.* New York: Charles Scribner's Sons, 1964.

Vulliamy, C. E. (ed.) *Red Archives [Krasny Arkhiv].* trans. A.L. Hynes. London: Bles, 1929.

Vyrubeva, Anna. *Memories of the Russian Court.* New York: Macmillan, 1933.

Wade, Carlson. *Great Hoaxes and Famous Impostors.* New York: Jonathan David, 1976.

Wagenknecht, Edward C. *Edgar Allan Poe: The Man Behind the Legend.* New York: Oxford University Press, 1963.

_____ (ed.). *Joan of Arc: An Anthology of History and Literature.* New York: Creative Age Press, 1948.

Wagner, Charles R. *The CPA and Computer Fraud.* New York: Lexington Books, 1979.

Wagner, Diane. *Corpus Delicti.* New York: St. Martin's/Marek, 1986.

Wagner, Margaret Seaton. *The Monster of Dusseldorf, The Life and Trial of Peter Kurten.* London: Faber & Faber, 1932.

Wagner, Walter. *The Golden Fleecers.* Garden City, N.Y.: Doubleday, 1966.

Waissenberger, Robert (ed.). *Vienna 1890-1920.* Secaucus, N.J.: Wellfleet Press, 1984.

Waite, John B. *The Prevention of Repeated Crime.* Ann Arbor: University of Michigan Press, 1943.

Wakefield, Edward Gibbon. *Facts Relating to the Punishment of Death in the Metropolis.* London: n.p., 1831.

_____. *The Hangman and the Judge, or a Letter from Jack Ketch to Mr. Justice Alderson.* London: Effingham Wilson, 1833.

_____. *Terrorstruck Town.* London: Steill, 1833.

Wakefield, H. Russell. *The Green Bicycle Case.* London: Philip Allan, 1930.

_____. *Landru: The French Bluebeard.* London: Duckworth, 1936.

Walbrook, H.M. *Detective Days.* London: Cassell, 1931.

_____. *Murders and Murder Trials, 1812-1912.* London: Con-stable, 1932.

Waldron, Ronald J., et al. *The Criminal Justice System: An Introduction.* Boston: Houghton Mifflin, 1976.

Waldrop, Frank C. *McCormick of Chicago: An Unconventional Portrait of a Controversial Figure.* Englewood Cliffs, N.J.: Prentice-Hall, 1966.

Waley, Arthur. *The Opium War Through Chinese Eyes.* London: George Allen & Unwin, 1958.

Waliszewski, Kazimierz. *Ivan the Terrible.* trans. Lady Mary Lloyd. London: William Heinemann, 1904.

_____. *Paul the First of Russia, the Son of Catherine the Great.* London: William Heinemann, 1913.

_____. *Peter the Great.* London: William Heinemann, 1898.

_____. *The Story of a Throne (Catherine II of Russia).* London:

William Heinemann, 1895.

Walker, Benjamin. *The Hindu World.* New York: Frederick A. Praeger, 1968.

Walker, Bill. *The Case of Barbara Graham.* New York: Ballan-tine Books, 1961.

_____. *The True Story of the Barbara Graham Case.* Los Angeles: Ace Books, 1961.

Walker, Henry J. *Jesse James "the Outlaw," Jesse Woodson James alias J. Frank Dalton 1848-1951.* Des Moines, Iowa: Wallace Homestead, 1961.

Walker, Lenore E. *The Battered Woman.* New York: Harper & Row, 1979.

Walker, Marcia J., and Brodsky, Stanley L. (eds.) *Sexual Assault: The Victim and the Rapist.* Lexington, Mass.: Heath, 1976.

Walker, Nigel. *Crimes, Courts and Figures.* Harmondsworth, Eng.: Penguin Books, 1971.

_____. *Crime and Insanity in England.* Edinburgh, Scot.: Edin-burgh University Press, 1968.

_____. *Crime and Punishment in Britain.* Edinburgh, Scot.: Edinburgh University Press, 1973.

Walker, Samuel. *Sense and Nonsense About Crime.* Belmont, Calif.: Brooks/Cole, 1985.

Walker, Stanley. *The Night Club Era.* New York: Frederick A. Stokes, 1933.

Walker-Smith, Derek. *The Life of Mr. Justice Darling.* London: Cassell, 1938.

_____. *Lord Reading and His Cases.* New York: Macmillan, 1934.

Wall, Joseph Frazier. *Andrew Carnegie.* New York: Oxford University Press, 1970.

Wall, P. *Eyewitness Identification in Criminal Cases.* New York: Thomas, 1965.

Wallace, Irving. *The Fabulous Showman.* London: Pan Books, 1962.

Wallack, L.R. *American Pistol and Revolver.* New York: Win-chester Press, 1979.

Wallack, Walter M., Kendall, Glenn M., Briggs, Howard L. *Education Within Prison Walls.* New York: Columbia University Press, 1939.

Wallance, Gregory. *Papa's Game.* New York: Rawson, Wade, 1981.

Wallas, G. *Jeremy Bentham.* London: University College, 1922.

Wallbank, T. Walter. *A Short History of India and Pakistan.* New York: Mentor, 1958.

Waller, Brown. *Last of the Great Western Train Robbers.* South Brunswick, N.Y.: A.S. Barnes, 1968.

Waller, George. *Kidnap: The Story of the Lindbergh Case.* New York: Dial Press, 1961.

_____. *Saga of an Imposing Era.* Englewood Cliffs, N.J.: Pren-tice-Hall, 1966.

Waller, Irle. *Chicago Uncensored: Firsthand Stories about the Al Capone Era.* New York: Exposition Press, 1965.

Waller, Irvin. *Men Released from Prison.* Toronto, Ontario, Can.: University of Toronto Press, 1974.

Walling, George. *Recollections of a New York Chief of Police.* New York: Caxton Book Concern, 1887.

Wallis, Rodney. *Lockerbie: The Story and the Lessons.* Westport, Conn.: Praeger, 2000.

Walls, H.J. *Forensic Science.* New York: Frederick Praeger, 1968.

Walls, Jim and Phil. *Chinatown, San Francisco.* Stanford, Calif.: Howell-North, 1960.

Walsh, Edmund A. *The Fall of the Russian Empire.* New York: Blue Ribbon Books, 1927.

Walsh, John, and Lerman, Philip. *No Mercy.* New York: Pocket Books, 1999.

_____. and Schindehette, Susan. *Tears of Rage.* New York: Pocket Books, 1997.

Walsh, Marilyn E. *The Fence.* Westport, Conn.: Greenwood, 1977.

Walter, George W. *The Loomis Gang.* Prospect, N.Y.: Prospect Books, 1953.

Walter, Ingo. *Secret Money: The World of International Financial Secrecy.* Lexington, Mass.: D.C. Heath, 1985.

Walters, Lorenzo D. *Tombstones's Yesterday.* Tucson, Ariz.: Acme Printing, 1928.

Walton, Augustus. *A History of Detection, Conviction, Life and Designs of John A. Murrel, The Great Western Land Pirate.* Athens, Tenn.: George White, 1835.

Walton, R.P. *Marihuana, America's New Drug Problem.* Philadel-phia: J.B. Lippincott, 1938.

Walton, William M. *The James Boys of Old Missouri.* Cleveland: Arthur Westbrook, 1907.

Ward, Bernie. *Families Who Kill.* New York: Pinnacle, 1993.

Ward, David A., and Kassebaum, Gene G. *Women's Prison: Sex and Social Structure.* Chicago: Aldine, 1965.

Ward, Richard H. *Introduction to Criminal Investigation.* Read-ing, Mass.: Addison-Wesley, 1975.

Ward, William. *The Dalton Gang, the Bandits of the Far West.* Cleveland: Arthur Westbrook, n.d.

_____. *The James Boys of Old Missouri.* Cleveland: Arthur Westbrook, 1907.

_____. *Jesse James' Blackest Crime.* Cleveland: Arthur West-brook, 1909.

_____. *Jesse James' Dash for Fortune.* Cleveland: Arthur West-brook, n.d.

_____. *Jesse James' Midnight Attack.* Cleveland: Arthur West-brook, 1910.

_____. *Jesse James' Mid-Winter Lark.* Cleveland: Arthur West-brook, n.d.

_____. *Jesse James' Race for Life.* Cleveland: Arthur Westbrook, n.d.

_____. *The Younger Brothers, the Border Outlaws.* Cleveland: Arthur Westbrook, 1908.

"Warden". *His Majesty's Guests: Secrets of the Cells.* London: Jarrolds, 1929.

Warden, Ernest A. *Infamous Kansas Killers.* Wichita, Kan.: McGuin, 1944.

_____. *Thrilling Tales of Kansas.* Wichita, Kan.: Wichita Eagle Press, 1932.

Ware, Captain Eugene F. *The Indian War of 1864.* New York: St. Martin's Press, 1960.

Warner, Dale G. *Who Killed the President?* New York: Ameri-can Press, 1964.

Warner, Emily Smith and Daniel, Hawthorne. *The Happy Warrior: A Biography of My Father.* Garden City, N.Y.: Doubleday, 1956.

Warner, Matt. *The Last of the Bandit Riders.* Caldwell, Idaho: Caxton Printers, 1940.

Warner, Opie L. *A Pardoned Life: Life of George Sontag.* San Bernardino, Calif.: Index Print, 1909.

Warren Commission. *Report of the Warren Commission on the Assassination of President Kennedy.* New York: Bantam, 1964.

Warren, David M. *The Plot to Kill JFK.* Chicago: Novel Books, 1965.

Warren, Earl, et al. *Hearings Before the President's Commission on the Assassination of President Kennedy.* 26 vols. Washing-ton, D.C.: U.S. Government Print-ing Office, 1964.

_____. *Report of the President's Commission on the Assassination of President Kennedy.* Washington, D.C.: U.S. Government Printing Office, 1964.

Warren, John H., Jr. *Thirty Years Battle with Crime, or The Crying Shame of New York As Seen Under the Broad*

Glare of An Old Detective's Lantern. Poughkeepsie, N.Y.: A.J. White, 1874.

Warren, W. Preston. *Masaryk's Democracy.* Chapel Hill: Univer-sity of North Carolina Press, 1941.

Warshow, Robert. *Bet A Million Gates.* New York: Greenberg, 1932.

_____. *Jay Gould: The Story of a Fortune.* New York: Greenberg, 1928.

_____. *The Story of Wall Street.* New York: Greenberg, 1929.

Washburn, Charles. *Come Into My Parlor: A Biography of the Aristocratic Everleigh Sisters of Chicago..* New York: Nation-al Library Press, 1936.

Washburton, Watson, and De Long, Edmund. *High and Low Financiers.* Indianapolis, Ind.: Bobbs-Merrill, 1932.

Waskow, Arthur I. *From Race Riot to Sit-In: 1919 and the 1960s.* Garden City, N.Y.: Doubleday, 1966.

Wasserstein, Bruce. *With Justice for Some.* Boston: Beacon, 1980.

Waterman, L. *Royal Correspondence of the Assyrian Empire.* Ann Arbor: University of Michigan Press, 1930.

Waters, Harold. *Adventure Unlimited: My Twenty Years of Ex-perience in the United States Coast Guard.* New York: Prentice-Hall, 1955.

_____. *Smugglers of Spirits.* New York: Hastings House, 1971.

Waters, James F. *The Court of Missing Heirs.* New York: Modern Age Books, 1941.

Waters, R. *Undiscovered Crimes.* London: n.p., 1862.

Waters, William. *A Gallery of Western Badmen.* Covington, Ky. Americana, 1954.

Watkins, Ronald. *Evil Intentions.* New York: William Morrow, 1992.

Watson, E.R. *The Trial of Eugene Aram.* London: Hodge, 1913.

Watson, Frederick. *A Century of Gunmen; a Study in Lawlessness.* London: Ivor Nicholson & Watson, 1931.

Watson, Charles (Tex) *Will You Die For Me.* New Jersey: Revell, 1978.

Watts, Judge R.A. *The Trial and Execution of the Lincoln Conspirators.* Lansing: Michigan History Magazine, 1922.

Waugh, Alec. *A History of the West Indies from 1492 to 1898.* Garden City, N.Y.: Doubleday, 1964.

Waumbaugh, Joseph. *The Blooding.* New York: Perigord Press, 1989.

_____. *The Blue Knight.* New York: Dell Books, 1972.

_____. *The Onion Field.* New York: Delacorte Press, 1973.

Way, W.J. (Jack). *The Tombstone Story.* Tucson, Ariz.: Living-ston Press, 1965.

Webb, Duncan. *Crime Is My Business.* London: Muller, 1953.

____. *Deadline for Crime.* London: Muller, 1955.

Webb, Jack. *The Badge.* Englewood Cliffs, N.J.: Prentice-Hall, 1958.

Webb, James. *The Occult Underground.* LaSalle, Ill.: Open Court, 1974.

Webb, Lucas. *The Attempted Assassination of John F. Kennedy.* San Bernardino, Calif.: R. Reginald, 1976.

Webb, Walter Prescott. *The Story of the Texas Rangers.* New York: Grosset & Dunlap, 1957.

_____. *The Texas Rangers, A Century of Frontier Defense.* Boston: Houghton Mifflin, 1935.

Weber, Brom (ed.). *The Letters of Hart Crane.* New York: Hermitage House, 1952.

Weber, Don, and Bosworth, Charles. *Precious Victims.* New York: Signet, 1991.

Weber, Louis (ed.). *The Holocaust Chronicle.* Lincolnwood, Ill.: Publications International, 2000.

Webster, Matt. *Inside Israel's Mossad: The Institute for Intelligence and Special Tasks.* New York: Rosen Publishing Group, 2003.

Webster, Nesta H. *Secret Societies and Subversive Movements.* London: Boswell Printing, 1924.

Webster, William H. *Crime in the United States.* Washington, D.C.: U.S. Government Printing Office, 1984.

Wecht, Cyril, and Bosworth, Charles. *Who Killed JonBenet Ramsey?* New York: Oynx, 1998.

Wedgwood, Cicely V. *The Thirty Years War.* New Haven, Conn.: Yale University Press, 1939.

_____. *The Trial of Charles I.* London: Collins, 1964.

_____. *William the Silent.* New Haven, Conn.: Yale University Press, 1944.

Weed, Thurlow. *Autobiography and Memoirs.* Boston: Houghton Mifflin, 1925.

Weeks, Robert P. (ed.). *Commonwealth vs. Sacco and Vanzetti.* Englewood Cliffs, N.J.: Prentice-Hall, 1958.

Weichmann, Louis J., and Arnold, Samuel B. *Defence and Prison Experiences of a Lincoln Conspirator.* Hattiesburg, Miss.: Book Farm, 1943.

_____. *A True History of the Assassination of Abraham Lincoln and of the Conspiracy of 1865.* New York: Alfred A. Knopf, 1975.

Weider, Ben. *Assassination at St. Helena.* Vancouver, British Columbia, Can.: Mitchell Press, 1978.

_____, and Hapgood, David. *The Murder of Napoleon.* New York: Congdon & Lattes, 1982.

Weil, Joseph as told to W.T. Brannon. *"Yellow Kid" Weil.* Chica-go: Ziff-Davis, 1948.

Weinberg, Arthur (ed.). *Attorney for the Damned.* New York: Simon & Schuster, 1957.

_____ and Lila. *Clarence Darrow.* New York: Putnam Sons, 1980.

_____ and Lila (eds.). *Verdicts Out of Court.* Chicago: Quad-rangle Books, 1963.

Weiner, Margery. *Matters of Felony: A Reconstruction.* London: William Heinemann, 1967.

Weinreb, L.L. *Criminal Law: Cases, Comments, Questions.* Mineola, N.Y.: Foundation Press, 1975.

Weinstein, Fannie, and Wilson, Melinda. *Where the Bodies Are Buried.* New York: St. Martin's Press, 1998.

Weinstein, Harold R. *Jean Jaures; A Study of Patriotism in the French Socialist Movement.* New York: Columbia University Press, 1936.

Weinstock, Matt. *My LA.* New York: Current Books, A.A. Wyn, 1947.

Weisberg, Bernard A. *The American Newspaperman.* Chicago: University of Chicago Press, 1961.

Weisberg, Harold. *Frame-Up: The King/Ray Case.* New York: Outerbridge & Dienstfrey, 1971.

_____. *Oswald in New Orleans.* New York: Canyon Books, 1967.

_____. *Photographic Whitewash: Suppressed Kennedy Assassination Pictures.* Hyattstown, Md.: Published by Author, 1967.

_____. *Post Mortem.* Frederick, Md.: Published by Author, 1971.

_____. *Whitewash: The Report on the Warren Report.* Hyattstown, Md.: Published by Author, 1965.

_____. *Whitewash II: The FBI - Secret Service Cover-up.* Hyatts-town, Md.: Published by Author, 1966.

_____. *Whitewash IV: Top Secret JFK Assassination Transcript.* Frederick, Md.: Published by Author, 1974.

Weiss, Gary. *Born to Steal: When the Mafia Hit Wall Street.* New York: Warner Books, 2003.

Weiss, Harry B. and Grace M. *An Introduction to Crime and Punishment in Colonial New Jersey.* Trenton, N.J.: Past Times, 1960.

Weiss, Karel (ed.). *The Prison Experience: An Anthology.* New York: Delacorte Press, 1976.

Weiss, Nancy J. *Charles Francis Murphy, 1858-1924: Respectability and Responsibility in Tammany Politics.* Northampton, Mass.: Smith College, 1968.

Weissberg, Alexander. *The Accused.* New York: Simon & Schuster, 1951.

Wellman, Francis L. *The Art of Cross-Examination.* New York: Macmillan, 1903.

_____. *Gentlemen of the Jury: Reminiscences of Thirty Years at the Bar.* New York: Macmillan, 1924.

Wellman, Manly Wade. *Dead and Gone, Classic Crimes of North Carolina.* Chapel Hill: University of North Carolina Press, 1954.

Wells, Brian. *Psychedelic Drugs.* New York: Jason Aronson, 1974.

Wells, Evelyn. *Champagne Days of San Francisco.* New York: D. Appleton-Century, 1939.

Wendell, Barrett. *Cotton Mather, the Puritan Priest.* New York: Dodd, Mead, 1891.

Wendland, Michael F. *The Arizona Project.* Kansas City: Sheed, Andrews & McMeel, 1977.

Wendt, Lloyd, and Kogan, Herman. *Bet a Million!* Indianapolis, Ind.: Bobbs-Merrill, 1948.

_____. *Big Bill of Chicago.* Indianapolis, Ind.: Bobbs-Merrill, 1953.

_____. *Bosses in Lusty Chicago.* Indianapolis: University of Indiana Press, 1943.

_____. *Chicago Tribune: The Rise of a Great American Newspaper.* Chicago: Rand McNally, 1979.

_____. *Lords of the Levee.* New York: Bobbs-Merrill, 1943.

Wensley, Frederick Porter. *Detective Days.* London: Cassell, 1931.

_____. *Forty Years of Scotland Yard: The Record of a Lifetime's Service in the Criminal Investigation Department.* New York: Garden City, 1930.

Wepman, D. *Jomo Kenyatta.* New York: Chelsea House, 1985.

Werner, M.R. *Barnum.* New York: Harcourt, Brace, 1929.

_____. *Bryan.* New York: Harcourt, Brace, 1929.

_____. *It Happened in New York.* New York: Coward-McCann, 1957.

_____. *Privileged Characters.* New York: R.M. McBride, 1935.

_____. *Tammany Hall.* Garden City, N.Y.: Doubleday, Doran, 1928.

Wertenbaker, Charles. *The Death of Kings.* New York: Random House, 1954.

Wertham, Dr. Fredric. *The Circle of Guilt.* New York: Rinehart, 1956.

_____. *Dark Legend: A Study in Murder.* London: Victor Gol-lancz, 1947.

_____. *Seduction of the Innocent.* New York: Rinehart, 1954.

_____. *The Show of Violence.* New York: Doubleday, 1949.

_____. *A Sign for Cain.* New York: Paperback Library, 1969.

West, Ann. *For the Love of Lesley: The "Moors Murders" Remembered by A Victim's Mother.* London: W. H. Allen, 1989.

West, Donald. *Sacrifice Unto Me.* New York: Pyramid, 1974.

West, John B. *The Death of the President: The Warren Report on Trial in New Orleans!* Covina, Calif.: n.p., 1967.

West, Nigel. *The Third Secret: The CIA, Solidarity and the KGB's Plot to Kill the Pope.* New York: Harper Collins, 2001.

West, R.A. *The Great Mollie Maguire Trials.* Pottsville, Pa.: Chronicle, 1876.

West, Rebecca. *Black Lamb and Grey Falcon.* 2 vols. New York: Viking Press, 1941.

_____. *The New Meaning of Treason.* New York: Viking Press, 1967.

_____. *A Train of Powder.* New York: Viking Press, 1946.

Westham, F. *Seduction of the Innocent.* New York: Museum, London & Rhinehart, 1955.

Weterby, Gerald. *In Hostile Territory: Business Secrets of a Mossad Combatant.* London: Diane Publishing Co., 1998.

Whalen, Grover. *Mr. New York: The Autobiography of Grover Whalen.* New York: G.P. Putnam's Sons, 1955.

Whalen, Richard J. *The Founding Father - The Story of Joseph P. Kennedy.* New York: New American Library, 1964.

Wharton, Edith. *Age of Innocence.* New York: Modern Library, 1920.

Wharton, Vernon Lane. *The Negro in Mississippi 1865 to 1890.* Chapel Hill: University of North Carolina Press, 1947.

Wheaton, Eliot B. *The Nazi Revolution 1933-35: Prelude to Calamity.* Garden City, N.Y.: Doubleday, 1969.

Wheeler, David Hilton. *Brigandage in South Italy.* London: S. Low, Son & Marston, 1864.

Wheeler, Douglas L. *Republican Portugal: A Political History, 1910-1926.* Madison: University of Wisconsin Press, 1978.

_____ (ed.). *On Record: Files and Dossiers in American Life.* New Brunswick, N.J.: Transaction Books, 1969.

Wheeler-Bennett, Sir John W. *Hindenburg: The Wooden Titan.* London: Macmillan, 1936.

_____. *King George VI.* New York: St. Martin's Press, 1958.

Wheelock, Keith. *Nasser's New Egypt.* New York: Frederick A. Praeger, 1960.

Whelan, James. *Allende: Death of a Marxist Dream.* New York: Crown, 1981.

Whibley, Charles. *A Book of Scoundrels.* New York: Benjamin Blom, 1971.

While Lincoln Lay Dying. A Facsimile Reproduction of the First Testimony Taken in Connection with the Assassination...as Recorded by Corporal James Tanner. Philadelphia: Union League of Philadelphia, 1968.

Whipple, Sidney B. *The Lindbergh Crime.* New York: Blue Ribbon Books, 1935.

_____. *Noble Experiment.* London: Methuen, 1934.
_____ (ed.). *The Trial of Bruno Richard Hauptmann.* Garden City, N.Y.: Doubleday & Doran, 1937.
Whitaker, Ben. *The Police.* London: Penguin Books, 1964.
Whitbread, J.R. *The Railway Policeman.* London: Harrap, 1961.
White, Bouck. *The Book of Daniel Drew.* New York: George H. Doran, 1910.
White, Dale. *Bat Masterson.* New York: Julian Messner, 1960.
White, Edward G. *The American Judicial Tradition: Profiles of Leading American Judges.* New York: Oxford University Press, 1976.
White, George M. *From Boniface to Bank Burglar.* New York: Seaboard, 1907.
White, Capt. J.R. *Misfit: An Autobiography.* London: Jonathan Cape, 1930.
White, Judy (ed.). *Chile's Days of Terror: Eyewitness Accounts of the Military Coup.* New York: Pathfinder Press, 1974.
White, Leslie T. *Me Detective.* New York: Harcourt, Brace, 1936.
White, Mel. *Deceived.* New York: Spire Books, 1979.
White, Ray Lewis (ed.). *Sherwood Anderson's Memoirs: A Critical Edition.* Chapel Hill: University of North Carolina Press, 1969.
White, Stephen. *Should We Now Believe the Warren Report?* New York: Macmillan, 1968.
White, Trumbull. *The Wizard of Wall Street and His Wealth, or the Life and Deeds of Jay Gould.* Chicago: Mid-Continent, 1892.
White, William Allen. *The Autobiography of William Allen White.* New York: Macmillan, 1946.
_____. *Crimes and Criminals.* New York: Farrar & Rinehart, 1933.
_____. *Forty Years on Main Street.* New York: Farrar & Rine-hart, 1937.
_____. *Masks in a Pageant.* New York: Macmillan, 1928.
White, William C. *Lenin.* New York: Harrison Smith, 1936.
Whitehead, Don. *Attack on Terror: The FBI Against the Ku Klux Klan in Mississippi.* New York: Funk & Wagnalls, 1970.
_____. *Borderguard.* New York: McGraw-Hill, 1963.
_____. *The F.B.I. Story.* New York: Random House, 1956.
_____. *Journey Into Crime.* New York: Random House, 1960.
Whitehead, George G. *Clarence Darrow—the Big Minority Man.* Girard, Kan.: Haldeman-Julius, 1931.
_____. *Clarence Darrow: "Evangelist" of Sane Thinking.* Girard, Kan.: Haldeman-Julius, 1931.
Whitelaw, David. *Corpus Delicti.* London: Geoffrey Bles, 1936.
Whiteside, Thomas. *Computer Capers: Tales of Electronic Thiev-ery, Embezzlement and Fraud.* New York: Thomas Y. Crowell, 1978.
Whitman, Howard. *Terror in the Streets.* New York: Dial Press, 1951.
Whitmore, Richard. *Victorian and Edwardian Crime and Punish-ment from Old Photographs.* London: Batsford, 1978.
Whitmore, William H. *The Colonial Laws of Massachusetts.* Boston: Rockwell & Churchill, 1890.
Whitney, Courtney. *MacArthur: His Rendezvous with History.* New York: Alfred A. Knopf, 1956
Whittemore, L.H. *Cop.* Greenwich, Conn.: Fawcett, 1969.
_____. *The Super Cops.* New York: Bantam, 1973.
Whittington-Egan, Richard. *A Casebook on Jack the Ripper.* London: Wildy & Sons, 1975.
Whittle, Tyler. *The Last Kaiser: A Biography of Wilhelm II.* n.p., n.d.
Whitwell, J.R. *Syphilis in the Earlier Days.* London: H.K. Lewis, 1940.
Wicker, Tom. *Investigating the FBI.* Garden City: Doubleday, 1973.
_____. *On Press.* New York: Viking Press, 1978.
_____. *A Time to Die.* Chicago: Quadrangle Books, 1975.
Wickman, Peter, and Whitten, Phillip. *Criminology.* Lexington, Mass.: D.C. Heath, 1980.
Wighton, Charles. *Heydrich: Hitler's Most Evil Henchman.* London: Odhams Press, 1962.
Wigmore, John H. *The Principles of Judicial Proof.* Boston: Little, Brown, 1931.
_____. *Wigmore on Evidence.* Boston: Little, Brown, 1940.
Wigmore, Lionel. *The Japanese Thrust.* Canberra, Aus.: Austral-ian War Memorial, 1959.
Wilcox, Robert. *The Mysterious Deaths at Ann Arbor.* New York: Popular Library, 1977.
Wild, Roland. *Crimes and Cases of 1933.* London: Rich & Cowan, 1934.
_____. *Crimes and Cases of 1934.* London: Rich & Cowan, 1935.
_____, and Curtis-Bennett, D. *Curtis, the Life of Sir Henry Curtis-Bennett.* London: Cassell, 1930.
Wildeblood, Peter. *Against the Law.* New York: Messner, 1959.
Wilder, Robert. *Written on the Wind.* G.P. Putnam's Sons, 1945.
Wiley, Margaret L. *The Subtle Knot.* Cambridge, Mass.: Harvard University Press, 1952.
Wilkenson, Fred T. *The Realities of Crime and Punishment.* Springfield, Mo.: Mycroft Press, 1972.
Wilkerson, Michael, and Wilkerson, Dick. *Someone Cry for the Children.* New York: Dial Press, 1981.
Wilkes, George. *The Mysteries of the Tombs. A Journal of Thirty Days' Imprisonment in the New York City Prison; For Libel.* New York: n.p., 1844.
Wilkie, Don, and Luther, Mark Lee. *American Secret Service Agent.* New York: Frederick A. Stokes, 1934.
Wilkie, Franc B. *Pen and Powder.* Boston: Ticknor, 1888.
_____. *Personal Reminiscences of Thirty-Five Years of Journalism.* Chicago: F.J. Schulte, 1891.
_____. *Walks About Chicago: 1871-1881.* Chicago: Belford, Clarke, 1882.
Wilkins, Harold T. *Captain Kidd and His Skeleton Island.* London: Cassell, 1935.
Wilkins, Harold T. *Strange Mysteries of Time and Space.* New York: Citadel Press, 1959.
Wilkins, James H. (ed.). *The Great Diamond Hoax and Other Stirring Incidents in the Life of Asbury Harpending.* San Francisco: James H. Barry, 1913.
Wilkinson, Alec. *Midnights, A Year with the Wellfleet Police.* New York: Random House, 1982.
Wilkinson, Doris Y. (ed.). *Social Structure and Assassination.* New Brunswick, N.J.: Transaction Books, 1976.
Wilkinson, George Theodore. *The Newgate Calendar.* London: Cornish, 1814.
Wilkinson, Sir J. Gardner. *A Popular Account of the Ancient Egyptians.* New York: Crescent Books, 1988.
Wilkinson, Laurence. *Behind the Face of Crime.* London: Frederick Muller, 1957.
Wilkinson, Paul. *Political Terrorism.* New York: John Wiley & Sons, 1974.
_____. *Terrorism and the Liberal State.* London: Macmillan, 1977.
_____. *Terrorism versus Liberal Democracy: The Problem of Response.* London: Institute for the Study of Conflict, 1976.
Willard, Josiah Flynt. *My Life.* New York: Outing, 1908.
_____. *Notes of an Itinerant Policeman.* Boston: L.C. Page, 1900.
_____. *Tramping with Tramps.* New York: Century, 1899.
_____. *The World of Graft.* New York: McClure, Phillips, 1901.
Willcox, Philip H.A. *"The Detective Physician" The Life and Work of Sir William Willcox.* London: William Heinemann Medical Books, 1970.
Wille, W. *Citizens Who Commit Murder.* St. Louis, Mo.: Warren Greene, 1974.
Willebrandt, Mabel Walker. *The Inside of Prohibition.* Indianapolis, Ind.: Bobbs-Merrill, 1929.
Willemise, Captain Cornelius W. *Behind the Green Lights.* New York: Alfred A. Knopf, 1931.
Willett, T.C. *Criminal on the Road.* London: Tavistock, 1964.
_____. *Drivers after Sentence.* London: Heinemann Educational, 1973.
Willey, Peter. *The Castles of the Assassins.* London: G.G. Harrap, 1963.
Williams, Charles. *Descent into Hell.* New York: Pellegrini & Cudahy, 1949.
_____. *Witchcraft.* London: Faber & Faber, 1941.
Williams, Charlotte. *Hugo L. Black: A Study in the Judicial Process.* Baltimore: Johns Hopkins University Press, 1950.
Williams, Emlyn. *Beyond Belief.* New York: Random House, 1968.
Williams, Eric. *From Columbus to Castro: The History of the Caribbean 1492-1969.* New York: Harper & Row, 1971.
Williams, Frank. *No Fixed Address.* London: W.H. Allen, 1973.
Williams, Franklin. *Negroes With Guns.* New York: Marzani & Munsell, 1962.
Williams, Glanville. *The Proof of Guilt.* London: Stevens & Sons, 1955.
_____. *Salmond on Jurisprudence.* London: Sweet & Maxwell, 1957.
Williams, Guy R. *The Hidden World of Scotland Yard.* London: Hutchinson, 1972.
Williams, H. Noel. *Memoirs of Madame du Barry.* New York: Collier, 1910.
Williams, Jack K. *Vogues in Villainy.* Columbia: University of South Carolina Press, 1959.
_____. *Hume: Portrait of a Couple Murderer.* London: The Windmill Press, 1960.
Williams, John. *A Cop Remembers.* New York: Alfred A. Knopf, 1933.
_____. *Suddenly at the Priory.* London: William Heinemann, 1957.
_____. *Heyday for Assassins.* London: William Heinemann, 1958.
Williams, John B. *Vice Control in California.* Beverly Hills, Calif.: Glencoe Press, 1964.
Williams, M. Monier. *Religious Thought and Life in India.* London: John Murray, 1891.
Williams, Mary Floyd. *History of the San Francisco Committee on Vigilance of 1851.* Berkeley: University of California Press, 1921.
Williams, Montague. *Later Leaves.* London: Macmillan, 1891.
_____. *Leaves of a Life.* New York: Macmillan, 1890.
_____. *Round London: Down East and Up West.* London: Macmillan, 1892.
Williams, Neville. *Captains Outrageous: Seven Centuries of Piracy.* New York: Macmillan, 1962.
_____. *Henry VIII and His Court.* New York: Macmillan, 1971.
Williams, Paul. *Al Qaeda: Brotherhood of Terror.* New York: Alpha Books, 2002.
Williams, R.H. *With the Border Ruffians.* New York: E.P. Dutton, 1907.
Williams, Robert H. *Vice Squad.* New York: Thomas Y. Crowell, 1973.
Williams, Roger L. *Gaslight and Shadow: The World of Napoleon III.* New York: Macmillan, 1957.
_____. *Henri Rochefort: Prince of the Gutter Press.* New York: Charles Scribner's Sons, 1966.
_____. *Manners and Murder in the World of Louis Napoleon.* Seattle: University of Washington Press, 1975.
_____. *The Mortal Napoleon III.* Princeton, N.J.: Princeton University Press, 1971.
Williams, Roger M. *The Super Crooks.* Chicago: Playboy Press, 1973.
Williams, Stephen. *Invisible Darkness.* New York: Bantam, 1996.
Williams, Thomas Harry. *Lincoln and the Radicals.* Madison: University of Wiscon-sin Press, 1941.
Williams, T. Harry. *Huey Long.* New York: Alfred A. Knopf, 1969.
Williams, Vergil L., and Fish, Mary. *Convicts, Codes, and Con-traband: The Prison Life of Men and Women.* Cambridge, Mass.: Ballinger, 1974.
Williams, Watkin W. *The Life of General Sir Charles Warren.* Oxford, Eng.: Basil Blackwell, 1941.
Williamson, Hugh Ross. *Historical Whodunits.* New York: Macmillan, 1956.
Williamson, James J. *Prison Life in the Old Capitol.* West Orange, N.J.: n.p., 1911.
Williamson, W.H. *Annals of Crime: Some Extraordinary Women.* London: George Routledge & Sons, 1930.
Willoughby, Charles A., and Chamberlain, John. *Shanghai Conspiracy.* New York: E.P. Dutton, 1952.
Willoughby, Harold R. *Pagan Regeneration.* Chicago: University of Chicago Press, 1929.
Willoughby, Malcolm F. *Rum War at Sea.* Washington D.C.: U.S. Government Printing Office, 1964.
Willoughby, W.W. *Opium as an International Problem.* Baltimore: John Hopkins University Press, 1930.
Willoughby, Westel W. *Japan's Case Examined.* Baltimore: Johns Hopkins Press, 1940.
Wills, C. *Who Killed Keyna?* London: D. Dobson, 1953.
Wills, Garry, and Demaris, Ovid. *Jack Ruby: The Man Who Killed the Man Who Killed Kennedy.* New York: New American Library, 1968.

Wilson, C.F. *Violence Against Women: An Annotated Bibliography*. Boston: G.K. Hall, 1981.
Wilson, Carol. *Freedom at Risk: The Kidnapping of Free Blacks in America, 1780-1865*. Lexington, Ky.: University of Kentucky Press, 1994.
Wilson, Colin. *A Casebook of Murder*. New York: Cowles, 1970.
_____. *A Criminal History of Mankind*. London: Granada, 1984.
_____. *Mysteries*. New York: Perigee, 1978.
_____. *The Occult*. New York: Random House, 1971.
_____. *Order of Assassins: The Psychology of Murder*. London: Rupert Hart-Davis, 1972.
_____. *Rasputin and the Fall of the Romanovs*. New York: Farrar Straus, 1964.
_____. *Ritual in the Dark*. Boston: Houghton Mifflin, 1960.
_____. *Witches*. New York: Crescent Books, 1981.
Wilson, D. *Henrietta Robinson*. New York: Auburn, Miller, Orton & Mulligan, 1855.
Wilson, Edmund. *The American Earthquake*. New York: Doubleday, 1958.
_____. *The American Jitters*. New York: Charles Scribner's Sons, 1932.
_____. *Axel's Castle*. London: Fontana, 1961.
_____. *I Thought of Daisy*. New York: Charles Scribner's Sons, 1929.
_____. *Patriotic Gore*. New York: Galaxie, 1966.
_____. *The Shores of Light*. New York: Farrar, Straus, Young, 1952.
_____. *The Twenties*. New York: Farrar, Straus & Giroux, 1975.
_____. *To the Finland Station*. New York: Harcourt, Brace, 1940.
Wilson, Francis. *John Wilkes Booth: Fact and Fiction of Lincoln's Assassination*. Boston: Houghton Mifflin, 1929.
Wilson, Frank J., and Day, Beth. *Special Agent*. New York: Holt, Rinehart & Winston, 1965.
Wilson, H.W. *The Downfall of Spain: Naval History of the Spanish-American War*. London: Low, Marston, 1900.
Wilson, Henry. *History of the Rise and Fall of the Slave Power in America*. 3 vols. Boston: Houghton Mifflin, 1872.
Wilson, James Q. *The Amateur Democrat: Club Politics in Three Cities*. Chicago: University of Chicago Press, 1962.
_____, and Herrnstein, Richard J. *Crime and Human Nature*. New York: Simon & Schuster, 1985.
_____ (ed.). *Crime and Public Policy*. San Francisco: Institute for Contemporary Studies Press, 1983.
_____. *The Investigators: Managing FBI and Narcotics Agents*. New York: Basic Books, 1978.
_____. *Thinking About Crime*. New York: Basic Books, 1976.
_____. *Varieties of Police Behavior*. Cambridge, Mass.: Harvard University Press, 1968.
Wilson, Jerry. *Police Report*. Boston: Little, Brown, 1975.
Wilson, John A. *The Culture of Ancient Egypt*. Chicago: Univer-sity of Chicago Press, 1951.
Wilson, John Gray. *Not Proven*. London: Secker & Warburg, 1960.
_____. *The Trial of Peter Manuel*. London: Secker & Warburg, 1959.
Wilson, Lawrence. *The Incredible Kaiser: A Portrait of William II*. London: Robert Hale, 1963.
Wilson, N. *Belgrade: The White City of Death*. n.p., 1903.
Wilson, Orlando W. (ed.). *Parker on Police*. Springfield, Ill.: Charles C. Thomas, 1957.
_____. *Police Administration*. New York: McGraw-Hill, 1950.
_____. *Police Planning*. Springfield, Ill.: Thomas, 1968.
_____. *Power in the City: Decision Making in San Francisco*. Berkeley: University of California Press, 1974.
Wilson, Patrick. *Children Who Kill*. London: Michael Joseph, 1973.
_____. *Murderesses: A Study of the Women Executed in Britain Since 1843*. London: Michael Joseph, 1971.
Wilson, R.L. *The Colt Heritage*. New York: Simon & Schuster, 1979.
Wilson, Robert. *Devil's Disciples*. Poole, Eng.: Javelin Books, 1986.
_____. *Return to Hell*. Poole, Eng.: Javelin Books, 1988.
Wilson, Samuel Payntor. *Chicago and Its Cesspools of Vice and Infamy*. Chicago: n.p., 1910.
Wilstach, Frank J. *The Plainsman Wild Bill Hickok*. Garden City, N.Y.: Sun Dial Press, 1937.
_____. *Wild Bill Hickok, the Prince of Pistoleers*. New York: Doubleday, Page, 1926.
Wilston, Robert. *The Last Days of the Romanovs*. London: Butterworth, 1920.
Wilton, G.W. *Fingerprints: History, Law and Romance*. London: William Hodge, 1938.
Winder, W.H.D. *Stephen's Commentaries on the Law of England*. London: Butterworth, 1959.
Windsor, Edward, Duke of. *A King's Story*. New York: G.P. Putnam's Sons, 1947.
Wines, E.C. *Punishment and Reformation*. New York: Thomas Y. Crowell, 1895.
_____. *Report on Prisons and Reformatories of the United States and Canada*. New York: State Assembly Document No. 35, 1867.
_____. *The State of Prisons and Child-Saving Institutions in the Civilized World*. Cambridge. Mass.: J. Wilson & Sons, 1880.
Wines, Frederick Howard. *Punishment and Reformation*. New York: Thomas Y. Crowell, 1919.
Wingate, Sir Reginald. *Mahdiism and the Egyptian Sudan*. Lon-don: Macmillan, 1891.
Winkler, Franz. *About Marijuana*. New York: Myrin Institute, 1970.
Winkler, John K. *Morgan the Magnificent*. New York: Vanguard Press, 1930.
_____. *William Randolph Hearst: An American Phenomenon*. New York: Simon & Schuster, 1928.
_____. *William Randolph Hearst: A New Appraisal*. New York: Hastings House, 1955.
Winks, Robin W. (ed.). *The Historian as Detective: Essays on Evidence*. New York: Harper & Row, 1968.
Winn, D. *Prostitutes*. London: Hutchinson, 1974.
Winn, Dilys. *Murder, Inc*. New York: Workman Press, 1977.
Winn, Steven, and Merrill, David. *Ted Bundy: The Killer Next Door*. New York: Bantam, 1980.
Winslade, William J., and Ross, Judith Wilson. *The Insanity Plea*. New York: Charles Scribner's Sons, 1983.
Winslow, Lyttleton Stewart Forbes. *Recollections of Forty Years: Being an Account at First Hand of Some Famous Criminal Lunacy Cases...* London: John Ousley, 1910.
Winston, Richard. *Thomas Becket*. New York: Alfred A. Knopf, 1967.
Winston, Robert W. *Andrew Johnson, Plebian and Patriot*. New York: Henry Holt, 1928.
Winter-Berger, Robert N. *The Gerald Ford Letters*. N.J.: Lyle Stuart, 1974.
Winter-Berger, Robert N. *The Washington Pay-Off*. New York: Dell, 1972.
Winter, Ella, and Hicks, Granville (eds.). *The Letters of Joseph Lincoln Steffens*. 2 vols. New York: Harcourt, Brace, 1938.
Winthrop, W.W. *Military Law*. Washington, D.C.: J.J. Chapman, 1893.
_____. *Military Law and Precedents*. Washington, D.C.: U.S. Government Printing Office, 1920.
Winwar, Frances. *Gallows Hill*. New York: Henry Holt, 1937.
_____. *The Saint and the Devil: Joan of Arc and Gilles de Rais*. New York: Harper, 1948.
Wirth, Louis. *The Ghetto*. Chicago: University of Chicago Press, 1928.
Wise, Dan, and Maxfield, Marietta. *The Day Kennedy Died*. San Antonio, Texas: Naylor, 1964.
Wise, David. *The American Police State*. New York: Random House, 1976.
_____, and Ross, Thomas B. *The Espionage Establishment*. New York: Random House, 1967.
_____. *The Invisible Government*. New York: Random House, 1967.
_____. *The Politics of Lying: Government Deception, Secrecy and Power*. New York: Vintage Books, 1973.
Wishman, Seymour. *Confessions of a Criminal Lawyer*. New York: Penguin, 1981.
Wiskemann, Elizabeth. *Europe of the Dictators*. London: Collins (Fontana), 1966.
_____. *Italy Since 1945*. New York: St. Martin's, 1971.
_____. *The Rome-Berlin Axis*. London: Collins, 1969.
_____. *Undeclared War*. London: Constable, 1939.
Wissler, Clark. *The American Indian*. New York: Oxford University Press, 1938.
The Witch of Wapping. London: T. Spring, 1652.
Witchcraft in Old and New England. Cambridge, Mass.: Harvard University Press, 1929.
Witcher, W.C. *The Reign of Terror in Oklahoma*. Fort Worth, Texas: Published by Author, 1923.
_____. *The Unveiling of the Ku Klux Klan*. Fort Worth, Texas: American Constitutional League, 1922.
Witches Apprehended, Examined and Executed. London: E. Marchant, 1613.
Witches of Northhamptonshire. London: T. Purfoot, A. Johnson, 1612.
Wittenborn, J.R., et al. (eds.). *Drugs and Youth: Proceedings of the Rutgers Symposium on Drug Abuse*. Springfield, Ill.: Charles C. Thomas, 1969.
Wittke, Carl F. *The Irish in America*. Baton Rouge: Louisiana State University Press, 1956.
_____. *We Who Built America: The Saga of the Immigrant*. New York: Prentice-Hall, 1939.
Wofford, Harris. *Of Kennedys and Kings*. New York: Farrar, Straus, Giroux, 1980.
Wohl, A.S. *The Eternal Slum: Housing and Social Policy in Victorian London*. London: Edward Arnold, 1977.
Wolf, Eric R. *Sons of the Shaking Earth*. Chicago: University of Chicago Press, 1959.
Wolf, George. *Frank Costello*. New York: William Morrow, 1974.
Wolf, Leonard. *Bluebeard*. New York: Potter, 1980.
_____. *A Dream of Dracula*. Boston: Little, Brown, 1972.
Wolf, Marvin J., and Mader, Katherine. *Fallen Angels*. New York: Facts on File, 1986.
Wolfe, Bertram D. *Communist Totalitarianism*. Boston: Beacon Press, 1961.
_____. *Khrushchev and Stalin's Ghost*. New York: Frederick A. Praeger, 1957.
_____. *Marxism: 100 Years in the Life of a Doctrine*. New York: Dell, 1967.
_____. *Three Who Made A Revolution: Lenin, Trotsky, Stalin*. New York: Dial Press, 1948.
Wolfe, Burton H. *Pileup on Death Row*. Garden City, N.Y.: Doubleday, 1973.
Wolfe, H. Ashton. *The Thrill of Evil*. London: Hurst & Blackett, n.d.
_____. *The Underworld*. London: Hurst & Blackett, n.d.
Wolfe, James Raymond. *Secret Writing*. New York: McGraw-Hill, 1970.
Wolfe, John B. *Louis XIV*. New York: W.W. Norton, 1968.
Wolfenden, John, et al. *Report of the Departmental Committee on Homosexual Offences and Prostitution*. London: H.M. Stationery Office, 1956.
Wolff, Geoffrey. *Black Sun: The Brief Transit and Violent Eclipse of Harry Crosby*. New York: Random House, 1976.
Wolff, Leon. *Lockout: The Story of the Homestead Strike*. New York: Harper & Row, 1965.
Wolff, Robert Lee. *The Balkans in Our Times*. Cambridge, Mass: Harvard University Press, 1956.
Wolff, Robert Paul. *In Defense of Anarchism*. New York: Harper & Row, 1970.
Wolfgang, Marvin E. *Crime and Race*. New York: Institute of Human Relations Press, 1964.
_____. *Patterns in Criminal Homicide*. Philadelphia: University of Pennsylvania Press, 1958.
_____, Savitz, Leonard, and Johnston, Norman (eds.). *The Sociology of Crime and Delinquency*. New York: John Wiley & Sons, 1970.
_____. *Studies in Homicide*. New York: Harper & Row, 1967.
_____, and Ferracuti, Franco. *The Subculture of Violence: Towards an Integrated Theory in Criminology*. Newbury, Calif.: Sage, 1982.
Wolsey, Serge G. *Call House Madam*. San Francisco: Martin Tudordale, 1942.
Wolstenholme, G.E.W., and Knight, Julie (eds.). *Hashish*. London: J. & A. Churchill, 1965.
Womack, John, Jr. *Zapata and the Mexican Revolution*. New York: Alfred A. Knopf, 1968.
Wood, Arthur. *Criminal Lawyer*. New Haven, Conn.: College & University Press, 1967.
Wood, Frederick S. (ed.). *Roosevelt as We Knew Him*. New York: John C. Winston, 1927.
Wood, Fremont. *The Introductory Chapter to the History of the Trials of Moyer, Haywood, and Pettibone, and*

Harry Orchard. Caldwell, Idaho: Caxton Printers, 1931.
Wood, John Maxwell. *Witchcraft and Superstitious Record in The Southwestern District of Scotland.* Dumfries, Scot.: J. Maxwell & Sons, 1911.
Wood, Walter (ed.). *Survivor's Tales of Famous Crimes.* London: Cassell, 1916.
Wood, William. *The Bone Garden.* New York: Pocket Books, 1994.
Woodall, William Otter (ed.). *A Collection of Reports of Famous Trials.* London: Shaw & Sons, 1873.
Woodbury, George. *The Great Days of Piracy.* New York: W.W. Norton, 1951.
Woodcock, George. *The Anarchist Prince.* London: T.V. Board-man, 1950.
Wooden, Kenneth. *The Children of Jonestown.* New York: McGraw-Hill, 1981.
Woodhall, Edwin T. *Crime and the Supernatural.* London: Long, 1935.
_____. *Detective and Secret Service Days.* London: Jarrolds, 1929.
_____. *Jack the Ripper: or When London Walked in Terror.* London: Mellifont Press, 1937.
_____. *Secrets of Scotland Yard.* London: The Bodley Head, 1936.
Woodland, W. Lloyd. *Assize Pageant: Fifty Years in the Criminal Courts.* London: George G. Harrap, 1952.
Woodley, Richard A. *Dealer: Portrait of a Cocaine Merchant.* New York: Holt, Rinehart, Winston, 1971.
Woodruff, Douglas. *The Tichborne Claimant.* London: Hullis & Charter, 1967.
Woodruff, Philip. *The Men Who Ruled India.* London: Jonathan Cape, 1953.
Woods, Arthur. *Crime Prevention.* Princeton, N.J.: Princeton University Press, 1918.
_____. *Policemen and Public.* Montclair, N.J.: Patterson Smith, 1975.
Woods, Paul. *Ed Gein—Psycho!* London: Annihilation Press, 1992.
Woods, Rufus. *The Wierdest Story in American History: The Escape of John Wilkes Booth.* Wenatchee, Wash.: Published by Author, 1944.
Woods, S.D. *Lights and Shadows of Life on the Pacific Coast.* New York: Funk & Wagnalls, 1910.
Woodward, Bob, and Armstrong, Scott. *The Brethren, Inside the Supreme Court.* New York: Simon & Schuster, 1979.
_____, and Bernstein, Carl. *All the President's Men.* New York: Simon & Schuster, 1974.
_____. *The Final Days.* New York: Simon & Schuster, 1976.
Woodward, C. Vann. *The Burden of Southern History.* Baton Rouge: Louisiana State University Press, 1960.
_____. *Origins of the New South, 1877-1913.* Baton Rouge: Louisiana State University Press, 1951.
_____. *Reunion and Reaction.* New York: Doubleday, 1956.
_____. *The Strange Career of Jim Crow.* New York: Oxford University Press, 1957.
_____. *Tom Watson, Agrarian Rebel.* New York: Macmillan, 1938.
Woodward, Ian. *The Werewolf Delusion.* New York: Paddington Press, 1979.
Woodward, Peter. *Nasser.* New York: Addison-Wesley, 1992.
Woodward, W. Elliot. *Records of the Salem Witchcraft.* Roxbury, Mass.: Published by Author, 1864.
Woodward, W.H. *Cesare Borgia.* London: Chapman & Hall, 1913.
Wooldridge, Clifton R. *Hands Up! In the World of Crime or Twelve Years a Detective.* Chicago: Police Assn., 1901.
Woolf, Alex. *Osama Bin Laden.* Minneapolis, Mn.: Lerner Publications, 2002.
Woollcott, Alexander. *Going to Pieces.* New York: G.P. Putnam's Sons, 1928.
_____. *Long, Long Ago.* New York: Viking Press, 1943.
_____. *While Rome Burns.* New York: Grosset & Dunlap, 1934.
Woolley, Bryan *November 22.* New York: Seaview Books, 1981.
Woolston, Howard B. *Prostitution in the United States.* New York: D. Appleton, 1921.
Wormser, Ren A. *The Story of the Law and the Men Who Made It.* New York: Simon & Schuster, 1962.
Wormser, Richard. *The Yellowlegs, The Story of the United States Cavalry.* Garden City, N.Y.: Doubleday, 1966.
Wraxall, Sir Lascelles. *Criminal Celebrities: A Collection of Notable Trials.* London: n.p., 1861.
_____. *Remarkable Adventure and Unrevealed Mysteries.* London: W.H. Allen, 1865.
Wren, Lassiter. *Masterstrokes of Crime Detection.* Garden City, N.Y.: Doubleday, Doran, 1929.
Wren, Melvin C. *The Course of Russian History.* New York: Macmillan, 1963.
Wright, Christopher. *The Art of the Forger.* New York: Dodd, Mead, 1985.
Wright, Dudley. *Vampires and Vampirism.* London: W. Rider, 1924.
Wright, Gordon. *Between the Guillotine and Liberty.* New York: Oxford University Press, 1983.
Wright, James D., et al. *Under the Gun: Weapons, Crime and Violence in America.* Hawthorne, N.Y.: Aldine, 1983.
Wright, John Stephen. *Chicago: Past, Present, and Future.* Chicago: Western News, 1863.
Wright, L.B. *The Atlantic Frontier.* New York: Alfred A. Knopf, 1947.
_____. *The Cultural Life of the American Colonies 1607-1763.* New York: Harper & Brothers, 1956.
_____. *Middle-Class Culture in Elizabethan England.* Chapel Hill: University of North Carolina Press, 1935.
Wright, Richard O. (ed.). *Whose FBI?* La Salle, Ill.: Open Court, 1974.
Wright, Sewell Peaslee (ed.). *Chicago Murders.* New York:, Duell, Sloan & Pearce, 1945.
Wright, Theon. *Rape in Paradise.* New York: Hawthorne Books, 1966.
_____. *In Search of the Lindbergh Baby.* New York: Tower, 1981.
Wright, Thomas. *Narratives of Sorcery and Magic.* New York: Redfield, 1852.
Wright, William. *The Von Bulow Affair.* New York: Delacorte Press, 1983.
Wulf, Josef. *Das Dritte Reich und seine Vollstrecker.* Berlin-Grnewald, 1961.
_____. *Heinrich Himmler.* Berlin-Grnewald: Arani, 1960.
Wulffen, Erich. *Woman as Sexual Criminal.* trans. David Berger. New York: American Ethnological Press, 1934.
Wycherley, George. *Buccaneers of the Pacific.* Indianapolis, Ind.: Bobbs-Merrill, 1928.
Wyckoff, Richard D. *Wall Street Ventures and Adventures Through Forty Years.* New York: Harper Brothers, 1930.
Wyden, Peter. *The Hired Killers.* New York: William Morrow, 1963.
Wykes, Alan. *Hitler.* New York: Ballantine Books, 1971.
_____. *Nuremberg Rallies.* New York: Ballantine Books, 1969.
Wyles, Lilian. *Women at Scotland Yard.* London: Faber & Faber, 1952.
Wyndham, Horace. *Consider Your Verdict.* London: W.H. Allen, 1946.
_____. *Crime on the Continent.* Boston: Little, Brown, 1928.
_____. *Dramas of the Law.* London: Hutchinson, 1936.
_____. *Famous Trials Re-told.* London: Hutchinson, 1925.
_____. *Feminine Frailty.* London: Ernest Benn, 1929.
Wyndham-Brown, W.F. *The Trial of Herbert Wallace.* London: Gollancz, 1933.
Wynn, Wilton. *Nasser of Egypt.* Cambridge, Mass.: Adington Books, 1959.

Xenophon. *Memoirs of Socrates.* trans. Hugh Tredennick. Harmondsworth, Eng.: Penguin, 1970.
Xydis, Stephen G. *Greece and the Great Powers, 1944-1947: Prelude to the Truman Doctrine.* Thessaloniki: Institute for Balkan Studies, 1963.

Yablonsky, Lewis. *George Raft.* New York: McGraw-Hill, 1974.
_____. *The Violent Gang.* New York: Macmillan, 1963.
Yaffe, James. *Nothing But the Night.* New York: Bantam Books, 1959.
Yallop, David. *The Day the Laughter Stopped.* New York: St. Martin's Press, 1976.
_____. *Deliver Us From Evil.* London: MacDonald Futura, 1981.
Yanaga Chitoshi. *Japan Since Perry.* New York: McGraw-Hill, 1949.
Yardley, Jonathon. *Ring: A Biography of Rand Lardner.* New York: Random House, 1977.
Yarros, Victor S. *My 11 Years with Clarence Darrow.* Girard, Kan.: Haldeman-Julius Publications, 1950.
Yefsky, S.A. (ed.). *Law Enforcement Science and Technology.* Washington, D.C.: Thompson Book Company, 1967.
Yellen, Samuel. *American Labor Struggles.* New York: Harcourt, Brace, 1936.
Yochelson, Samuel, and Samenow, Stanton E. *The Criminal Personality.* New York: Jason Aronson, 1976.
Yonover, Neal. *Crime Scene USA.* New York: Hyperion, 2000.
York, Mary E. *The Bender Tragedy.* Mankato, Kan.: G.W. Neff, 1875.
Yoshida Shigeru. *The Yoshida Memoirs: The Story of Japan in Crisis.* Boston: Houghton Mifflin, 1962.
Yoshihashi Takehiko. *Conspiracy at Mukden: The Rise of the Japanese Military.* New Haven, Conn.: Yale University Press, 1963.
Yost, Graham. *The KGB.* New York: Facts on File, 1989.
Young, A. Morgan. *Imperial Japan: 1912-1938.* New York: William Morrow, 1938.
Young, Alfred E. *Dissent: Explorations in the History of American Radicalism.* DeKalb: Northern Illinois University Press, 1968.
Young, Art. *Art Young, His Life and Times.* New York: Sheridan House, 1939.
_____. *On My Way.* New York: Horace Liveright, 1928.
Young, Arthur. *China and the Helping Hand, 1937-1945.* Cam-bridge, Mass.: Harvard University Press, 1963.
Young, Filson. *The Trial of Hawley Harvey Crippen.* London: William Hodge, 1920.
Young, Frederick R. *Dodge City.* Dodge City, Kan.: Boot Hill Museum, 1972.
Young, G.F. *The Medici.* New York: Modern Library, 1930.
Young, Hugh. *My Forty Years at the Yard.* London: W.H. Allen, 1955.
Young, James Harvey. *The Medical Messiahs, A Social History of Health Quackery in Twentieth Century America.* Princeton, N.J.: Princeton University Press, 1967.
_____. *The Toadstool Millionaires.* Princeton: Princeton Univer-sity Press, 1961.
Young, John P. *San Francisco: A History of the Pacific Coast Metropolis.* San Francisco: S.J. Clarke, 1912.
Young, Peter. *Bedouin Command with the Arab Legion, 1953-1956.* London: Kimber, 1956.
Young, Rosalind Amelia. *Mutiny of the Bounty and Story of Pitcairn Island.* San Francisco: Pacific Press, 1894.
Young, S. Glenn. *Life and Exploits of S. Glenn Young, World-Famous Law Enforcement Officer.* Herrin, Ill.: Mrs. S. Glenn Young, 1924.
Young, Winifred. *Obsessive Poisoner.* London: Hale, 1973.
Youngblood, Rufus W. *20 Years in the Secret Service: My Life With Five Presidents.* New York: Simon & Schuster, 1973.
Younger, Coleman. *The Story of Cole Younger by Himself.* Chicago: Press of the Henneberry, 1903.
Younger, Scout. *True Facts of the Lives of America's Most Notorious Outlaws.* n.p., n.d.
Yriarte, Charles. *Cesare Borgia.* trans. William Sterling. London: F. Aldor, 1947.
Yurka, Blanche. *Bohemian Girl.* Athens: Ohio University Press, 1970.
Yusopov, Prince Felix. *Rasputin: His Malignant Influence and His Assassination.* London: Cape, 1927.

Zaehner, R.C. *Zen, Drugs and Mysticism.* New York: Pantheon Books, 1973.
Zalman, Marvin. *Indeterminate Sentence Laws: Present, Past, Future.* Dallas: Academy of Criminal Justice Sciences, 1976.
Zamora, William. *Trial by Your Peers.* New York: A. Maurice Girodias Associates, 1973.
Zander, M. *Cases and Materials on the English Legal System.* London: Weidenfeld & Nicolson, 1973.
Zayas, Enrique Rafael de. *The Case of Mexico and the Policy of President Wilson.* New York: Boni, 1914.
Zeiger, Henry A. *The Jersey Mob.* New York: New American Library, 1975.
_____. *Sam the Plumber.* Bergenfield, N.J.: New American Library, 1973.
Zeine, Z.N. *Arab-Turkish Relations and the Emergence of Arab Nationalism.* Beirut, Leb.: Khayat, 1966.

_____. *The Struggle for Arab Independence.* Beirut, Leb.: Khayat, 1960.

Zeldin, Theodore (ed.). *Conflicts in French Society: Anti-Clerical-ism, Education and Morals in the Nineteenth Century.* London: George Allen & Unwin, 1970.

_____. *Emile Ollivier and the Liberal Empire of Napoleon III.* Oxford: Clarendon Press, 1963.

_____. *France 1848-1945: Ambition, Love, and Politics.* Oxford, Eng.: Clarendon Press, 1973.

Zemans, Eugene S. *Held Without Bail.* Chicago: John Howard

Association, 1949.

Zerman, Melvyn Bernard. *Call the Final Witness.* New York: Harper & Row, 1977.

Zierold, Norman. *Little Charley Ross.* Boston: Little, Brown, 1967.

_____. *Three Sisters in Black.* Boston: Little, Brown, 1968.

Zilboorg, Gregory. *The Medical Man and the Witch during the Renaissance.* Baltimore: John Hopkins University Press, 1935.

Zimmermann, Doron. *The Jacobite Movement in Scotland and in Exile, 1746-1749.* New York: Palgrave Macmillan, 2003.

Zimring, Franklin E., and Hawkins, Gordon J. *Deterrence: The Legal Threat in Crime Control.* Chicago: University of Chicago Press, 1973.

Zink, Harold. *City Bosses in the United States: A Study of Twenty Municipal Bosses.* Durham, N.C.: Duke University Press, 1930.

Zink, Wilbur A. *The Roscoe Gun Battle: Younger Brothers vs. Pinkerton Detectives.* Appleton City, Mo.: Democrat, 1967.

Zinman, David H. *The Day Huey Long Was Shot.* New York: Ivan Obolensky, 1963.

Zins, H. *England and the Baltic in the Elizabethan Era.* Manches-ter, Eng.: Manchester University Press, 1972.

Zipfel, Friedrich. *Gestapo und Sicherheitsdienst.* Berlin-Grne-wald: Arani, 1960.

_____. *Kirchenkampf in Deutschland 1933-1945.* Berlin: Walter de Gruyter, 1965.

Zorbaugh, Harvey W. *The Gold Coast and the Slum.* Chicago: University of Chicago Press, 1929.

Zumoto Motosada. *Sino-Japanese Entanglements, 1931-1932: A Military Record.* Tokyo: Herald Press, 1932.

INDEX

Note: This annotated index offers names in boldface that indicate main text entries. Page numbers shown in boldface indicate text wholly dedicated to those entries. Page numbers shown in boldface italic indicate photos for the proper name entries. Subject Index entries show crime classifications with main text entries. Organizations known to be terrorist groups are indicated. Popular aliases (AKA) are cross-referenced to proper name entries.